CONTENTS

Author's Note 5

Researching The Billboard Pop Charts 6

Explanation of Data and Symbols 8

THE ARTIST SECTION 9

An alphabetical listing, by artist, of every record to hit Billboard's pop charts from 1955 through 1986

THE SONG TITLE SECTION 563

An alphabetical listing, by song title, of every record to hit Billboard's pop charts from 1955 through 1986

THE RECORD HOLDERS

The Top 200 Artists 720

The Top 20 Artists By Decade 724

Artists With 725

- 45 or More Charted Records
- 4 or More #1 Hits
- 12 or More Weeks at #1 Position

Records Of Longevity 726

Label Abbreviations 727

#1 Records Listed Chronologically 729

Compiled from Billboard's pop singles charts, 1955-1986

Record Research Inc.
P.O. Box 200
Menomonee Falls, Wisconsin 53051

ISBN 0-89820-085-7

Published independently by Record Research Inc.
P.O. Box 200, Menomonee Falls, Wisconsin 53051

AUTHOR'S NOTE

This is the fifth edition of ***TOP POP SINGLES***. It is hard to believe that 17 years have passed since the first edition was published in 1970. From that first crude 208-page edition, to this volume, nearly four times that size, I have had the great pleasure to work in the most exciting and unpredictable industry in the world. Researching the *Billboard* charts, collecting the charted hits, and publishing musical record books has truly been a 'labor of love'. This simple cliche is an apt summary of a career that is really just an extension of a hobby.

My initial research of the *Billboard* pop charts, compiled on 3 × 5 cards, was intended solely as a means of cataloging my burgeoning record collection. With little or no inclination that others shared a devotion to the charts, I felt that my interest in chart statistics and record collecting bordered on fanaticism. It didn't take long to discover that there were thousands of music fans with a similar fascination of exploring the depths of the American record charts.

Through the tremendous national and international support of my publications from disc jockeys and record fans, I have been able to expand my research to include not only the singles and albums of *Billboard's* pop charts, but also the various other weekly *Billboard* charts. Followers of the Country and Black charts can look forward to our upcoming expanded revisions of these books, as well as many other projects that are currently in the works.

While planning this edition, I wanted to greatly enlarge the artist biographies and various other notes of trivia so that a single volume would offer information on not only the charted hits, but on the artists supplying these hits. So, for most of the top artists in this edition, you will find a paragraph covering the highlights of that artist's career. I had hoped to provide at least one line of trivia for each of the 4,186 artists listed herein. However, even with all the research at my disposal, I simply could not find facts for many of the 'one-shot' artists. If you have supporting evidence about any artist in this book who does not have a biographical entry, I would appreciate hearing from you. I will continue to seek out information on these obscure artists and update the notes on the established ones to make further editions even more complete and valuable.

A novel feature to this edition are the listings of the peak positions and the various *Billboard* pop charts under many of the song titles from 1955-1958. During this period, *Billboard* published multiple pop charts. Now that all chart activity of each of these hits is listed, you can decide which ranking you qualify as the decisive one.

Once again, thanks to all of you for your continued support, encouragement, and patience in waiting for these revised editions. It is my goal to make these revisions available every two years — a timetable that you can rely on. Please continue to write and let us know of any corrections or improvements you would like to see.

JOEL WHITBURN

RESEARCHING THE BILLBOARD POP CHARTS

On August 4, 1958, *Billboard* debuted its *Hot 100* chart. Since that date, the *Hot 100* has been widely recognized as the definitive source for the weekly ratings of America's most popular records. The majority of records listed in this volume were charted between 1958 and 1986, and therefore, their chart statistics were compiled exclusively from the *Hot 100.* Previous to this chart, *Billboard* published a *Top 100* chart which debuted in November of 1955. This chart was not considered as reliable as the *Hot 100,* and was published weekly, along with a number of other pop charts which focused on specific areas of the music trade. By October of 1958, all of these charts were discontinued in favor of the all-encompassing *Hot 100.*

Here are the pop charts that were researched for this book:

Chart Title	Dates Published	Chart Size
Best Sellers In Stores	Jan. 1, 1955-Oct. 13, 1958	25-50
Most Played By Jockeys	Jan. 1, 1955-July 28, 1958	20-25
Most Played In Juke Boxes	Jan. 1, 1955-June 17, 1957	20
Top 100	Nov. 12, 1955-July 28, 1958	100
Hot 100	Aug. 4, 1958-present	100

Two other pop charts were consulted so that this book would truly be a complete record of any popular single that may have achieved a ranking on any of the *Billboard* pop charts. These charts are the **"Coming Up Strong"** charts (a continuation of the Best Sellers chart - July 16, 1955-July 28, 1958) and the **"Honor Roll Of Hits"** chart (a listing by tune - not by artist - Jan. 1, 1955-Nov. 16, 1963). These charts were checked only for those records which made these charts and did not make any other *Billboard* Pop chart. 40 points (or positions) were added to the 26 records that made only these charts. Example: if one of these records peaked at position #5, it's highest position in this book would be shown as #45.

A chart-by-chart breakdown of the highest position a record attained on any of the above 1955-1958 *Billboard* Pop charts is listed below the title. However, if a record hit *only* the *Top 100* or *Hot 100,* no chart information is shown below that title. Keep in mind, records that peaked at positions 51-100 could only have charted on the *Top 100* or *Hot 100.*

pre) If a record enters a newly published chart well after the record's peak chart performance, the word **pre** is shown after the position - meaning that the highest position would have been higher had the chart been published earlier.

end) If a record had not yet peaked on a chart that was terminated, the word **end** is shown after the position - meaning that its highest position would probably have been higher had the chart continued.

Many artist listings have been reorganized in this edition so that an artist's complete chart history is at your fingertips. For example, a song by a duo, such as Paul McCartney & Michael Jackson, is now listed under both McCartney and Jackson. The precise duo name is shown in bold type below the song title.

The record's Debut Date is taken from whichever chart it first appeared on. The date shown is *Billboard's* actual issue date, and is not taken from the "week ending" dates as shown on the various charts when they were originally published. The issue and week ending dates were different until January 13, 1962, when *Billboard* began using one date system for both the issue and the charts inside.

The record's *highest position* (**PEAK POS**) is taken from the chart on which it achieved its highest ranking.

The record's *weeks charted* (**WKS CHR**) and weeks at positions No. 1 or No. 2 are taken from the chart on which it achieved its highest total.

EXPLANATION OF DATA AND SYMBOLS

The artist section lists each artist's charted hits in chronological order. A sequential number is shown in front of each song title to indicate that artist's number of charted hits. All Top 10 hits are highlighted in dark type.

EXPLANATION OF COLUMNAR HEADINGS:

DEBUT DATE: Date record first charted

PEAK POS: Record's highest charted position (highlighted in bold type)

WKS CHR: Total weeks charted

LABEL & NUMBER: Original record label and number

OTHER DATA AND SYMBOLS:

(¹) A superior number next to a record that peaked at No. 1 or No. 2 indicates the total weeks the record held that position.

(+) Indicates record peaked in the year after it first charted

(●) RIAA certified gold record (million seller)

(▲) RIAA certified platinum record (two million seller)

The Record Industry Association of America began certifying gold records in 1958 and platinum records in 1976. Prior to these dates, there are most certainly some hits that would have qualified for these certifications. Also, some record labels have never requested RIAA certification for their hits.

Letter(s) in brackets after titles indicate:

[I] Instrumental recording
[N] Novelty recording
[C] Comedy recording
[S] Spoken word recording
[F] Foreign language recording
[X] Christmas recording
[R] Reissue of a previously charted single

(/) This symbol is shown when dividing a two-sided hit. Complete chart data is shown for each side except in cases where both sides of a record were shown as a single listing on the charts. For the "B" side of these records, only the weeks it charted as a "tag along" are listed.

See Researching The Billboard Pop Charts for an explanation of chart names listed under some records from 1955-58.

THE ARTIST SECTION

Lists, alphabetically by artist name, every record that made Billboard's Pop and Hot 100 charts from 1/1/55 through 12/27/86.

DEBUT DATE	PEAK POS	WKS CHR	ARTIST — Record Title	Label & Number
			# A	
			ABACO DREAM	
			New York City rock group: Paul Douglas, Dennis Williams, Frank Maio & Mike Sassano.	
9/06/69	**74**	6	1 Life And Death In G & A	A&M 1081
			ABBA	
			Pop quartet formed in Stockholm, Sweden in 1970. Consisted of Frida Lyngstad and Agnetha Faltskog (vocals), Bjorn Ulvaeus (guitar) and Benny Anderson (keyboards). Benny and Bjorn recorded together in 1966. Bjorn and Agnetha married in 1971, divorced in 1978. Benny and Frida married in 1978, divorced in 1981.	
6/01/74	**6**	17	1 **Waterloo**	Atlantic 3035
9/14/74	**27**	10	2 Honey, Honey	Atlantic 3209
8/09/75	**15**	17	3 SOS	Atlantic 3265
2/14/76	**15**	15	4 I Do, I Do, I Do, I Do, I Do	Atlantic 3310
5/22/76	**32**	9	5 Mamma Mia	Atlantic 3315
9/04/76	**13**	16	6 Fernando	Atlantic 3346
12/11/76+	**1**[1]	22	7 • **Dancing Queen**	Atlantic 3372
5/14/77	**14**	15	8 Knowing Me, Knowing You	Atlantic 3387
10/22/77	**56**	7	9 Money, Money, Money	Atlantic 3434
12/24/77+	**12**	16	10 The Name Of The Game	Atlantic 3449
4/22/78	**3**	18	11 • **Take A Chance On Me**	Atlantic 3457
5/19/79	**19**	14	12 Does Your Mother Know	Atlantic 3574
9/01/79	**80**	3	13 Voulez-Vous/	
9/22/79	**64**	5	14 Angeleyes	Atlantic 3609
11/10/79+	**29**	12	15 Chiquitita	Atlantic 3629
11/22/80+	**8**	26	16 **The Winner Takes It All**	Atlantic 3776
4/04/81	**45**	11	17 Super Trouper	Atlantic 3806
6/27/81	**90**	6	18 On And On And On	Atlantic 3826
1/09/82	**27**	14	19 When All Is Said And Done	Atlantic 3889
4/17/82	**63**	8	20 The Visitors	Atlantic 4031
			all of the above tunes written and produced by Benny & Bjorn	
			THE ABBEY TAVERN SINGERS	
			Traditional Irish group.	
9/24/66	**94**	2	1 Off To Dublin In The Green	HBR 498
			BILLY ABBOTT & The Jewels	
7/20/63	**55**	8	1 Groovy Baby	Parkway 874
			GREGORY ABBOTT	
			Soul singer, songwriter from New York City.	
10/18/86+	**1**[1]	22	1 **Shake You Down**	Columbia 06191
			ABC	
			New wave rock group from Sheffield, England. Martin Fry, lead singer.	
9/11/82+	**18**	25	1 The Look Of Love (Part One)	Mercury 76168
1/29/83	**25**	15	2 Poison Arrow	Mercury 810340
2/04/84	**89**	3	3 That Was Then But This Is Now	Mercury 814631
8/24/85	**9**	22	4 **Be Near Me**	Mercury 880626
1/18/86	**20**	14	5 (How To Be A) Millionaire	Mercury 884382
5/17/86	**91**	4	6 Vanity Kills	Mercury 884714
			MISS ABRAMS & The Strawberry Point School Third Grade Class	
			Rita Abrams and her class of kids from Mill Valley, California.	
8/01/70	**90**	3	1 Mill Valley	Reprise 0928
			A.B. SKHY	
			West Coast underground rock quartet led by Dennis Geyer.	
12/06/69	**100**	1	1 Camel Back [I]	MGM 14086

DEBUT DATE	PEAK POS	WKS CHR	ARTIST — Record Title	Label & Number
			AC/DC	
			Hard rock band formed in Sydney, Australia in 1974. Consisted of brothers Angus and Malcolm Young (guitars), Bon Scott (lead singer), Phil Rudd (drums) and Mark Evans (bass). Cliff Williams replaced Evans in 1977. Bon Scott died on 2/19/80 from alcohol abuse and was replaced by Brian Johnson. Simon Wright replaced Rudd in 1985.	
10/13/79	**47**	10	1 Highway To Hell	Atlantic 3617
9/06/80	**35**	16	2 You Shook Me All Night Long	Atlantic 3761
12/20/80+	**37**	15	3 Back In Black	Atlantic 3787
1/16/82	**44**	9	4 Let's Get It Up	Atlantic 3894
10/01/83	**84**	5	5 Guns For Hire	Atlantic 89774
			THE ACCENTS	
			R&B vocal group led by Robert Draper, Jr.	
12/22/58+	**51**	12	1 Wiggle, Wiggle	Brunswick 55100
			ACE	
			British pub-rock quintet. Paul Carrack, lead singer.	
3/08/75	**3**	16	1 **How Long**	Anchor 21000
7/26/75	**71**	4	2 Rock & Roll Runaway	Anchor 21002
			ACE SPECTRUM	
			New York City soul quartet, led by Edward "Easy" Zant.	
9/28/74	**57**	6	1 Don't Send Nobody Else	Atlantic 3012
			JOHNNY ACE	
			Born John Alexander, Jr. on 6/29/29. Died from a self-inflicted gunshot wound on 12/24/54.	
2/19/55	**17**	9	1 Pledging My Love Best Seller #17 / Juke Box #17 / Jockey #19	Duke 136
			BARBARA ACKLIN	
			Born on 2/28/44 in Chicago. Cousin to Monk Higgins, who produced her first sessions for Special Agent in 1966 as Barbara Allen.	
7/13/68	**15**	12	1 Love Makes A Woman	Brunswick 55379
10/19/68	**57**	8	2 From The Teacher To The Preacher **GENE CHANDLER & BARBARA ACKLIN**	Brunswick 55387
11/16/68+	**67**	9	3 Just Ain't No Love	Brunswick 55388
2/22/69	**79**	3	4 Am I The Same Girl exact same recording as Young-Holt Unlimited's "Soulful Strut", except piano part is replaced by Barbara's voice	Brunswick 55399
			THE AD LIBS	
			4-man, 1-woman black group from Newark, originally called the Creators. Consisted of Mary Ann Thomas (lead singer), Hugh Harris, Danny Austin, Norman Donegan and Dave Watt. First recorded for T-Kay in 1962.	
1/16/65	**8**	10	1 **The Boy From New York City**	Blue Cat 102
5/01/65	**100**	1	2 He Ain't No Angel	Blue Cat 114
			BRYAN ADAMS	
			Born on 11/5/59 in Vancouver, Canada. Rock singer, songwriter, guitarist.	
3/13/82	**84**	2	1 Lonely Nights	A&M 2359
3/12/83	**10**	19	2 **Straight From The Heart**	A&M 2536
6/11/83	**15**	14	3 Cuts Like A Knife	A&M 2553
9/03/83	**24**	12	4 This Time	A&M 2574
11/03/84+	**6**	19	5 **Run To You**	A&M 2686
2/02/85	**11**	17	6 Somebody	A&M 2701
4/20/85	$\mathbf{1}^{2}$	19	7 **Heaven**	A&M 2729
6/29/85	**5**	17	8 **Summer Of '69**	A&M 2739
9/14/85	**13**	15	9 One Night Love Affair	A&M 2770
11/23/85+	**15**	14	10 It's Only Love **BRYAN ADAMS/TINA TURNER** all of above songs produced by Adams and Bob Clearmountain	A&M 2791
			JOHNNY ADAMS	
			Born Lathan John Adams on 1/5/32 in New Orleans. Soul singer, nicknamed "The Tan Canary". First recorded on the Ric label in 1959.	
12/14/68	**82**	3	1 Release Me	SSS Int'l. 750
6/28/69	**28**	8	2 Reconsider Me	SSS Int'l. 770
10/11/69	**89**	2	3 I Can't Be All Bad	SSS Int'l. 780

DEBUT DATE	PEAK POS	WKS CHR	ARTIST — Record Title		Label & Number
			CANNONBALL ADDERLEY Born Julian Edwin Adderley on 9/15/28 in Tampa. Alto saxophonist, leader of jazz combo featuring brother Nat Adderley (cornet) and Joe Zawinul (piano). Cannonball died of a stroke on 8/8/75 in Gary, Indiana.		
4/10/61	**41**	6	1 African Waltz	[I]	Riverside 45457
2/16/63	**66**	7	2 The Jive Samba CANNONBALL ADDERLEY SEXTET	[I]	Riverside 4541
1/07/67	**11**	11	3 Mercy, Mercy, Mercy	[I]	Capitol 5798
4/08/67	**73**	5	4 Why? (Am I Treated So Bad)	[I]	Capitol 5877
1/17/70	**86**	3	5 Country Preacher CANNONBALL ADDERLEY QUINTET	[I]	Capitol 2698
			THE ADDRISI BROTHERS Pop singing/songwriting duo: Dick & Don Addrisi. Don died of cancer on 11/13/84(45).		
6/01/59	**62**	6	1 Cherrystone		Del-Fi 4116
1/22/72	**25**	12	2 We've Got To Get It On Again		Columbia 45521
4/09/77	**20**	15	3 Slow Dancin' Don't Turn Me On		Buddah 566
9/17/77	**74**	4	4 Does She Do It Like She Dances		Buddah 579
12/10/77	**80**	4	5 Never My Love		Buddah 587
8/11/79	**45**	8	6 Ghost Dancer		Scotti Br. 500
			AEROSMITH Hard-rock band formed in Sunapee, NH in 1970. Consisted of Steve Tyler (lead singer), Joe Perry and Brad Whitford (guitars), Tom Hamilton (bass) and Joey Kramer (drums). Perry left for own Joe Perry Project in 1979. Whitford left in 1980. Original band reunited in April of 1984.		
10/20/73	**59**	9	1 Dream On		Columbia 45894
6/14/75	**36**	8	2 Sweet Emotion		Columbia 10155
1/10/76	**6**	20	3 **Dream On**	[R]	Columbia 10278
6/12/76	**21**	15	4 Last Child		Columbia 10359
9/25/76	**71**	4	5 Home Tonight		Columbia 10407
11/20/76+	**10**	17	6 **Walk This Way** revived in 1986 (with Tyler & Perry) as a "rap" hit by Run-D.M.C.		Columbia 10449
4/09/77	**38**	8	7 Back In The Saddle		Columbia 10516
10/22/77	**42**	11	8 Draw The Line		Columbia 10637
3/11/78	**70**	5	9 Kings And Queens		Columbia 10699
8/05/78	**23**	12	10 Come Together cover version of Beatles' classic		Columbia 10802
1/20/79	**77**	3	11 Chip Away The Stone		Columbia 10880
1/12/80	**67**	6	12 Remember (Walking In The Sand)		Columbia 11181
			AFRIQUE 13-member instrumental R&B/jazz session band.		
6/09/73	**47**	9	1 Soul Makossa	[I]	Mainstream 5542
			THE AFTERNOON DELIGHTS Female studio quartet from Boston.		
7/25/81	**33**	16	1 General Hospi-Tale parody of TV's "General Hospital"	[N]	MCA 51148
			AFTER THE FIRE English band led by Andy Piercy.		
2/12/83	**5**	21	1 **Der Kommissar** Kommissar: a Russian government official		Epic 03559
5/28/83	**85**	3	2 Dancing In The Shadows		Epic 03908
			A-HA Trio formed in Oslo, Norway: Morten Harket (vocals), Pal Waaktaar (guitar, keyboards) and Mags Furuholem (keyboards).		
7/13/85	**1^{1}**	27	1 **Take On Me**		Warner 29011
11/30/85+	**20**	17	2 The Sun Always Shines On T.V.		Warner 28846
			AIR SUPPLY Melbourne, Australia duo: Russ Hitchcock (b: 6/15/49) & Graham Russell (b: 6/1/50).		
2/09/80	**3**	23	1 **Lost In Love**		Arista 0479
6/14/80	**2^{4}**	27	2● **All Out Of Love**		Arista 0520
10/25/80+	**5**	22	3 **Every Woman In The World**		Arista 0564
5/16/81	**1^{1}**	19	4● **The One That You Love**		Arista 0604
9/26/81	**5**	20	5 **Here I Am (Just When I Thought I Was Over You)**		Arista 0626
12/12/81+	**5**	20	6 **Sweet Dreams**		Arista 0655

DEBUT DATE	PEAK POS	WKS CHR	ARTIST — Record Title	Label & Number
			AIR SUPPLY — Cont'd	
6/12/82	**5**	18	7 **Even The Nights Are Better**	Arista 0692
9/18/82	**38**	9	8 Young Love	Arista 1005
11/13/82+	**38**	14	9 Two Less Lonely People In The World	Arista 1004
7/30/83	**2^3**	25	10 ● **Making Love Out Of Nothing At All**	Arista 9056
5/25/85	**19**	15	11 Just As I Am	Arista 9353
8/10/85	**68**	6	12 The Power Of Love (You Are My Lady)	Arista 9391
8/09/86	**76**	8	13 Lonely Is The Night	Arista 9521
			AIRWAVES	
			Welsh pop-rock trio.	
6/03/78	**62**	6	1 So Hard Livin' Without You	A&M 2032
			JEWEL AKENS	
			Black vocalist born in Texas in 1940.	
1/23/65	**3**	14	1 **The Birds And The Bees**	Era 3141
5/01/65	**68**	5	2 Georgie Porgie	Era 3142
			ALABAMA	
			Quartet from Fort Payne, Alabama: Randy Owen (vocals, guitar), Jeff Cook (guitar, fiddle, keyboards), Teddy Gentry (bass, vocals) and Mark Herndon (drums, vocals). Randy, Jeff and Teddy are cousins. Country music's current #1 act.	
6/06/81	**20**	22	1 Feels So Right	RCA 12236
11/14/81+	**15**	21	2 Love In The First Degree	RCA 12288
5/22/82	**18**	13	3 Take Me Down	RCA 13210
9/04/82	**65**	12	4 Close Enough To Perfect	RCA 13294
5/07/83	**38**	11	5 The Closer You Get	RCA 13524
10/29/83	**76**	6	6 Lady Down On Love	RCA 13590
5/19/84	**72**	10	7 When We Make Love	RCA 13763
			all of the above titles hit #1 on Billboard's Country charts	
			CHUCK ALAIMO QUARTET	
			Chuck Alaimo, sax; Tommy Rossi, drums; Pat Magnolia, bass; and Bill Irvine, piano.	
4/29/57	**92**	1	1 Leap Frog [I]	MGM 12449
			STEVE ALAIMO	
			Born on 12/6/40 in Rochester, New York. Singer, songwriter, guitarist.	
3/17/62	**81**	1	1 Mashed Potatoes	Checker 1006
1/05/63	**46**	10	2 Every Day I Have To Cry	Checker 1032
10/05/63	**100**	1	3 Michael - Pt. 1	Checker 1054
11/16/63	**74**	6	4 Gotta Lotta Love	Imperial 66003
3/06/65	**77**	2	5 Real Live Girl	ABC-Para. 10620
			from the Broadway musical "Little Me"	
6/26/65	**89**	2	6 Cast Your Fate To The Wind	ABC-Para. 10680
5/21/66	**92**	2	7 So Much Love	ABC-Para. 10805
6/26/71	**72**	6	8 When My Little Girl Is Smiling	Entrance 7501
4/29/72	**79**	3	9 Amerikan Music [N]	Entrance 7507
			THE ALARM	
			British rock quartet - Mike Peters, lead singer.	
12/28/85+	**61**	10	1 Strength	I.R.S. 52736
			EDDIE ALBERT & SONDRA LEE	
			Eddie played Oliver Wendell Douglas on TV's "Green Acres".	
2/18/56	**56**	4	1 Little Child [N]	Kapp 134
			adapted from the French title: "Little Boy And The Old Man"	
			MORRIS ALBERT	
			Brazilian singer/songwriter.	
6/21/75	**6**	32	1 ● **Feelings**	RCA 10279
2/07/76	**93**	2	2 Sweet Loving Man	RCA 10437
			WILLY ALBERTI	
			Native of Amsterdam, Holland.	
11/30/59	**42**	8	1 Marina [F]	London 1888
			ALESSI	
			Brothers Billy & Bobby Alessi from West Hempstead, NY.	
5/01/82	**71**	4	1 Put Away Your Love	Qwest 50055

DEBUT DATE	PEAK POS	WKS CHR	ARTIST — Record Title	Label & Number
			ARTHUR ALEXANDER	
			Born on 5/10/40 in Florence, Alabama. Teamed with Rick Hall in studio work at Muscle Shoals. First recorded for Judd in 1960.	
2/24/62	**24**	12	1 You Better Move On	Dot 16309
5/26/62	**58**	8	2 Where Have You Been (All My Life)	Dot 16357
10/27/62	**68**	6	3 Anna (Go To Him)	Dot 16387
9/13/75	**45**	9	4 Every Day I Have To Cry Some	Buddah 492
			ALFI & HARRY	
			A David Seville production.	
1/28/56	**44**	6	1 The Trouble With Harry [N] inspired by the film of the same title	Liberty 55008
			ALICE WONDER LAND	
9/14/63	**62**	7	1 He's Mine (I Love Him, I Love Him, I Love Him)	Bardell 774
			ALISHA	
			Dance/disco teenager from Brooklyn, New York.	
12/21/85+	**68**	17	1 Baby Talk	Vanguard 35262
			ALIVE & KICKING	
			5-man, 1-woman pop/rock group.	
6/06/70	**7**	14	1 **Tighter, Tighter** produced by Tommy James	Roulette 7078
9/26/70	**69**	5	2 Just Let It Come	Roulette 7087
			ALL SPORTS BAND	
			Pop/rock quintet who dress up in various athletic uniforms.	
11/28/81	**93**	2	1 I'm Your Superman	Radio 3871
2/06/82	**78**	3	2 Opposites Do Attract	Radio 3892
			DAVIE ALLAN & THE ARROWS	
			Davie began as a session guitarist for Mike Curb in Los Angeles.	
2/13/65	**64**	7	1 Apache '65 [I] THE ARROWS	Tower 116
11/12/66	**99**	2	2 Theme From The Wild Angels [I]	Tower 267
4/22/67	**37**	17	3 Blue's Theme [I] above 2 from the film "The Wild Angels"	Tower 295
7/29/67	**97**	1	4 Devil's Angels [I] from the soundtrack of the same title	Tower 341
			DEBORAH ALLEN	
			Born on 9/30/53 in Memphis. Country singer.	
10/15/83+	**26**	21	1 Baby I Lied	RCA 13600
			LEE ALLEN & HIS BAND	
			Lee was a sax player on hits by Fats Domino, Little Richard and others. Played tenor sax on the Blasters' first 3 albums.	
1/13/58	**54**	11	1 Walkin' With Mr. Lee [I]	Ember 1027
9/29/58	**92**	1	2 Tic Toc [I]	Ember 1039
			PETER ALLEN	
			Australian cabaret-style performer. Married briefly to Liza Minnelli.	
1/10/81	**55**	8	1 Fly Away	A&M 2288
			REX ALLEN	
			Born on 12/31/24 in Willcox, Arizona. Starred in 35 western films for Republic in the 50s. Narrator for over 80 Disney films during the 60s and 70s.	
9/15/62	**17**	8	1 Don't Go Near The Indians	Mercury 71997
			RICHIE ALLEN	
			Richie is actually record producer Richard Podolor.	
11/21/60	**90**	2	1 Stranger From Durango [I]	Imperial 5683
			STEVE ALLEN	
			Born on 12/26/21 in New York City. Well-known television personality. Founded "Tonight Show" in 1954. Played title role in 1956 movie "The Benny Goodman Story".	
11/12/55	**35**	12	1 Autumn Leaves [I] STEVE ALLEN with GEORGE CATES	Coral 61485
12/17/55+	**56**	8	2 What Is A Wife [S-N]	Coral 61542
8/18/56	**75**	4	3 Lola's Theme [I] from the film "Trapeze"	Coral 61681
4/27/63	**64**	7	4 Gravy Waltz [I]	Dot 16457

DEBUT DATE	PEAK POS	WKS CHR	ARTIST — Record Title	Label & Number
			STEVE ALLEN — Cont'd	
10/12/63	**85**	5	5 Cuando Calienta El Sol .... [F]	Dot 16507
			vocals: The Copacabana Trio	
			THE ALLEY CATS	
			R&B group from Los Angeles: Billy Storm (lead), Ed Wallis, Chester Pipkin and Bryce Caulfield. Later known as Africa.	
1/12/63	**43**	7	1 Puddin N' Tain (Ask Me Again, I'll Tell You The Same)	Philles 108
			GENE ALLISON	
12/16/57+	**36**	17	1 You Can Make It If You Try	Vee-Jay 256
			Best Seller #36 / Top 100 #37	
5/05/58	**73**	6	2 Have Faith	Vee-Jay 273
			THE ALLISONS	
			U.S. group - not related to the English duo.	
12/14/63	**93**	1	1 Surfer Street..	Tip 1011
			THE ALLMAN BROTHERS BAND	
			Southern rock band formed in Macon, Georgia in 1968. Consisted of brothers Duane (lead guitar) and Gregg Allman (keyboards), Dickey Betts (guitar), Berry Oakley (bass), and the drum duo of Jai Johnny Johanson and Butch Trucks. Duane and Gregg known earlier as Allman Joys and Hour Glass. Duane was the top session guitarist at Muscle Shoals studio. He was killed in a motorcycle crash on 10/29/71 at the age of 24. On 11/11/72, Oakley was killed in another cycle accident. He was replaced by Lamar Williams. Chuck Leavill (keyboards) added in 1972. After much turmoil, band regrouped in 1978 with a new lineup led by Gregg Allman and Dickey Betts.	
1/09/71	**92**	3	1 Revival (Love Is Everywhere)	Capricorn 8011
4/29/72	**77**	4	2 Ain't Wastin' Time No More..	Capricorn 0003
8/12/72	**86**	2	3 Melissa	Capricorn 0007
12/02/72	**86**	4	4 One Way Out	Capricorn 0014
8/25/73	**2**[1]	16	5 **Ramblin Man**	Capricorn 0027
1/19/74	**65**	6	6 Jessica .... [I]	Capricorn 0036
11/15/75	**67**	3	7 Nevertheless/	
		3	8 Louisiana Lou And Three Card Monty John	Capricorn 0246
3/24/79	**29**	9	9 Crazy Love..	Capricorn 0320
9/13/80	**58**	8	10 Angeline	Arista 0555
8/08/81	**39**	11	11 Straight From The Heart..	Arista 0618
			GREGG ALLMAN	
			Born on 12/8/47 in Nashville. The Allman Brother's keyboardist. Married briefly to Cher in 1975.	
12/22/73+	**19**	12	1 Midnight Rider	Capricorn 0035
			HERB ALPERT & THE TIJUANA BRASS	
			Herb was born on 3/31/35 in Los Angeles. Producer, composer, trumpeter, bandleader. Played trumpet since age eight. A&R for Keen Records, produced first Jan & Dean session, wrote "Wonderful World" hit for Sam Cooke. Formed A&M Records with Jerry Moss in 1962. Used studio musicians until early 1965, then own band.	
10/27/62	**6**	14	1 **The Lonely Bull** .... [I]	A&M 703
3/30/63	**96**	1	2 Marching Thru Madrid.. [I]	A&M 706
3/28/64	**77**	5	3 Mexican Drummer Man..	A&M 732
6/27/64	**85**	5	4 The Mexican Shuffle .... [I]	A&M 742
2/20/65	**68**	10	5 Whipped Cream.. [I]	A&M 760
9/25/65	**7**	16	6 **Taste Of Honey/** [I]	
9/11/65	**47**	6	7 3rd Man Theme.. [I]	A&M 775
			Anton Karas' version was #1 for 11 weeks in 1950	
12/25/65+	**11**	12	8 Zorba The Greek/ [I]	
			from the film of the same title	
12/25/65+	**38**	8	9 Tijuana Taxi.. [I]	A&M 787
3/19/66	**24**	8	10 What Now My Love/ [I]	
3/19/66	**27**	7	11 Spanish Flea .... [I]	A&M 792
			theme song from TV's "The Dating Game"	
7/02/66	**18**	8	12 The Work Song .... [I]	A&M 805
9/03/66	**28**	6	13 Flamingo .... [I]	A&M 813
11/19/66	**19**	8	14 Mame	A&M 823
			from the Broadway show "Mame"	
3/11/67	**37**	5	15 Wade In The Water .... [I]	A&M 840
4/08/67	**27**	9	16 Casino Royale.. [I]	A&M 850
			from the film of the same title	
7/08/67	**32**	5	17 The Happening.. [I]	A&M 860

DEBUT DATE	PEAK POS	WKS CHR	ARTIST — Record Title		Label & Number
			HERB ALPERT & THE TIJUANA BRASS — Cont'd		
9/09/67	**35**	6	18 A Banda	[I]	A&M 870
1/13/68	**51**	6	19 Carmen	[I]	A&M 890
4/20/68	**72**	6	20 Cabaret	[I]	A&M 925
5/18/68	**1**[4]	14	21 ● **This Guy's In Love With You**		A&M 929
8/31/68	**51**	6	22 To Wait For Love		A&M 964
12/14/68+	**45**	6	23 My Favorite Things	[I]	A&M 1001
3/29/69	**78**	5	24 Zazueira	[F]	A&M 1043
5/31/69	**63**	6	25 Without Her		A&M 1065
10/17/70	**74**	4	26 Jerusalem	[I]	A&M 1225
3/10/73	**77**	8	27 Last Tango In Paris	[I]	A&M 1420
5/18/74	**84**	6	28 Fox Hunt	[I]	A&M 1526
7/28/79	**1**[2]	25	29 ● **Rise**	[I]	A&M 2151
11/17/79+	**30**	13	30 Rotation	[I]	A&M 2202
6/28/80	**50**	8	31 Beyond	[I]	A&M 2246
9/05/81	**79**	5	32 Magic Man	[I]	A&M 2356
6/26/82	**37**	10	33 Route 101	[I]	A&M 2422
8/20/83	**81**	4	34 Garden Party	[I]	A&M 2562
12/10/83	**77**	5	35 Red Hot	[I]	A&M 2593
			21, 22, 25, 29-35 shown only as: **HERB ALPERT**		
9/15/84	**90**	2	36 Bullish	[I]	A&M 2655
			HERB ALPERT/TIJUANA BRASS		
			ALPHAVILLE		
			German trio: Marian Gold, Bernhard Lloyd, Frank Mertens.		
11/24/84+	**66**	10	1 Big In Japan		Atlantic 89665
3/23/85	**93**	4	2 Forever Young		Atlantic 89578
			THE AMAZING RHYTHM ACES		
			Memphis country/rock sextet - Barry "Byrd" Burton, Russell Smith, vocals, guitars; Billy Earhart, James Hooker, keyboards; Jeff Davis, bass; Butch McDade, drums.		
6/21/75	**14**	16	1 Third Rate Romance		ABC 12078
12/20/75+	**72**	8	2 Amazing Grace (Used To Be Her Favorite Song)		ABC 12142
9/18/76	**42**	10	3 The End Is Not In Sight (The Cowboy Tune)		ABC 12202
			THE AMBOY DUKES		
			Detroit rock group led by Ted Nugent.		
6/29/68	**16**	12	1 Journey To The Center Of The Mind		Mainstream 684
			AMBROSIA		
			Los Angeles-based trio: David Pack, Joe Puerta & Burleigh Drummond.		
6/14/75	**17**	14	1 Holdin' On To Yesterday		20th Century 2207
11/08/75	**63**	5	2 Nice, Nice, Very Nice		20th Century 2244
2/26/77	**39**	8	3 Magical Mystery Tour		20th Century 2327
			from the film "All This & World War II"		
9/02/78	**3**	21	4 **How Much I Feel**		Warner 8640
4/05/80	**3**	19	5 **Biggest Part Of Me**		Warner 49225
7/12/80	**13**	18	6 You're The Only Woman (You & I)		Warner 49508
6/05/82	**86**	4	7 How Can You Love Me		Warner 29996
			AMERICA		
			Trio formed in London, England, 1969. Consisted of Dan Peek, Gerry Beckley and Dewey Bunnell. All played guitars. Met at US Air Force base. With group Daze in 1970. Moved to U.S. in February, 1972. Peek left in 1976.		
2/19/72	**1**[3]	14	1 ● **A Horse With No Name**		Warner 7555
5/20/72	**9**	10	2 **I Need You**		Warner 7580
10/21/72	**8**	12	3 **Ventura Highway**		Warner 7641
1/27/73	**35**	8	4 Don't Cross The River		Warner 7670
4/28/73	**62**	5	5 Only In Your Heart		Warner 7694
8/18/73	**67**	8	6 Muskrat Love		Warner 7725
8/24/74	**4**	18	7 **Tin Man**		Warner 7839
12/28/74+	**5**	14	8 **Lonely People**		Warner 8048
4/05/75	**1**[1]	16	9 **Sister Golden Hair**		Warner 8086
7/19/75	**20**	13	10 Daisy Jane		Warner 8118
11/29/75+	**44**	9	11 Woman Tonight		Warner 8157
5/15/76	**23**	12	12 Today's The Day		Warner 8212

DEBUT DATE	PEAK POS	WKS CHR	ARTIST — Record Title	Label & Number
			AMERICA — Cont'd	
8/21/76	**75**	4	13 Amber Cascades	Warner 8238
			above 7 produced by George Martin (Beatles' producer)	
3/24/79	**56**	5	14 California Dreamin'	American Int. 700
			from the film "California Dreaming"	
7/31/82	**8**	20	15 **You Can Do Magic**	Capitol 5142
11/27/82+	**45**	13	16 Right Before Your Eyes	Capitol 5177
6/18/83	**33**	12	17 The Border	Capitol 5236
			THE AMERICAN BREED	
			Integrated rock quartet from Cicero, Illinois led by Gary Loizzo.	
6/03/67	**24**	9	1 Step Out Of Your Mind	Acta 804
12/02/67+	**5**	14	2 ● **Bend Me, Shape Me**	Acta 811
2/24/68	**39**	7	3 Green Light	Acta 821
5/25/68	**84**	3	4 Ready, Willing And Able	Acta 824
8/03/68	**88**	4	5 Anyway That You Want Me	Acta 827
			THE AMERICAN COMEDY NETWORK	
2/04/84	**70**	5	1 Breaking Up Is Hard On You (a/k/a Don't Take Ma Bell Away From Me) [N]	Critique 704
			parody of "Breaking Up Is Hard To Do"	
			AMERICAN FLYER	
			Craig Fuller (Pure Prairie League), Eric Kaz (Blues Magoos), Steve Katz (Blood, Sweat & Tears), Doug Yule (Velvet Underground).	
10/30/76	**80**	4	1 Let Me Down Easy	United Art. 874
			THE AMES BROTHERS	
			Vocal group from Malden, MA, formed in the late 40s. Family name Urick. Consisted of Ed (b: 7/9/27), Gene (b: 2/13/25), Joe (b: 5/3/24) and Vic (b: 5/20/26, d: 1/23/78). After local work in Boston, did extensive touring. Own TV series in 1955.	
11/20/54+	**3**	15	1 **The Naughty Lady Of Shady Lane**	RCA 47-5897
			Best Seller #3 / Jockey #3 / Juke Box #3	
9/24/55	**11**	11	2 My Bonnie Lassie	RCA 6208
			Best Seller #11 / Top 100 #11 / Jockey #14 / Juke Box #16	
2/25/56	**35**	12	3 Forever Darling/	
			from the film of the same title	
3/03/56	**84**	2	4 I'm Gonna Love You	RCA 6400
5/05/56	**11**	24	5 It Only Hurts For A Little While/	
			Juke Box #11 / Top 100 # 15 / Jockey #15 / Best Seller #16	
6/30/56	**89**	1	6 If You Wanna See Mamie Tonight	RCA 6481
			from the film "The Revolt of Mamie Stover"	
9/08/56	**49**	7	7 49 Shades Of Green/	
9/08/56	**67**	6	8 Summer Sweetheart	RCA 6608
11/24/56	**51**	9	9 I Saw Esau	RCA 6720
7/01/57	**5**	24	10 **Tammy/**	
			Jockey #5 / Best Seller #24 / Top 100 #29	
			from the film "Tammy and The Bachelor"	
6/10/57	**64**	13	11 Rockin' Shoes	RCA 6930
10/07/57	**5**	20	12 **Melodie D'Amour**	RCA 7046
			Jockey #5 / Best Seller #12 / Top 100 #12	
2/24/58	**67**	2	13 Little Gypsy	RCA 7142
3/31/58	**23**	11	14 A Very Precious Love	RCA 7167
			Jockey #23 / Top 100 #65	
			from the film "Marjorie Morningstar"	
8/04/58	**90**	1	15 Stay/	
8/04/58	**98**	1	16 Little Serenade	RCA 7268
9/29/58	**17**	15	17 Pussy Cat/	
			Hot 100 #17 / Best Seller #20 end	
9/29/58	**45**	9	18 No One But You (In My Heart)	RCA 7315
12/28/58+	**37**	10	19 Red River Rose	RCA 7413
			orchestra directed by Hugo Winterhalter on all of above titles (except 10 & 11)	
5/18/59	**78**	4	20 Someone To Come Home To	RCA 7526
2/01/60	**38**	13	21 China Doll	RCA 7655
			ED AMES	
			One of the Ames Brothers. Played an Indian on the "Daniel Boone" TV series.	
1/23/65	**73**	6	1 Try To Remember	RCA 8483
			from the musical "The Fantasticks"	

DEBUT DATE	PEAK POS	WKS CHR	ARTIST — Record Title	Label & Number
			ED AMES — Cont'd	
1/21/67	**8**	13	2 **My Cup Runneth Over**	RCA 9002
			from the musical "I Do, I Do"	
5/06/67	**61**	7	3 Time, Time	RCA 9178
9/30/67	**98**	2	4 When The Snow Is On The Roses	RCA 9319
12/16/67+	**19**	8	5 Who Will Answer?	RCA 9400
5/11/68	**79**	6	6 Apologize	RCA 9517
5/31/69	**92**	4	7 Son Of A Travelin' Man	RCA 0156
			NANCY AMES	
			Vocalist born in Washington, D.C. Her grandfather was once President of Panama.	
3/19/66	**89**	3	1 He Wore The Green Beret	Epic 10003
10/08/66	**95**	4	2 Cry Softly	Epic 10056
			BILL AMESBURY	
			Toronto-based singer, songwriter, guitarist.	
2/16/74	**59**	9	1 Virginia (Touch Me Like You Do)	Casablanca 0001
			ANACOSTIA	
			Soul group produced by Van McCoy.	
1/06/73	**90**	4	1 On And Off (Part 1)	Columbia 45685
			BILL ANDERSON	
			Born 11/1/37 in Columbia, SC. Host of Nashville Network's TV quiz show "Fandango".	
10/27/62	**89**	4	1 Mama Sang A Song .... [S]	Decca 31404
4/13/63	**8**	15	2 **Still**	Decca 31458
			above 2 songs hit #1 on Billboard's Country charts	
8/24/63	**53**	6	3 8 X 10	Decca 31521
11/21/70	**93**	3	4 Where Have All Our Heroes Gone .... [S]	Decca 32744
7/15/78	**80**	4	5 I Can't Wait Any Longer	MCA 40893
			CARL ANDERSON - see GLORIA LORING	
			ELTON ANDERSON	
			Born in Lake Charles, LA in 1932. Sang and played guitar with the Sid Lawrence band. First recorded for Vin.	
1/25/60	**88**	4	1 Secret Of Love	Mercury 71542
			with the Sid Lawrence Combo	
			ERNESTINE ANDERSON	
			Jazz singer formerly with Eddie Heywood and Lionel Hampton.	
2/27/61	**98**	1	1 A Lover's Question	Mercury 71772
			JESSE ANDERSON	
4/25/70	**95**	2	1 I Got A Problem	Thomas 805
			JOHN ANDERSON	
			Born on 12/13/54 in Apopka, Florida. Honky-tonk Country singer.	
3/05/83	**43**	13	1 ● Swingin'	Warner 29788
			LALE ANDERSON	
			German vocalist - born 3/23/10; died 8/29/72. Her 1939 hit "Lili Marlene" was the first million selling German record.	
4/24/61	**88**	4	1 Ein Schiff Wird Kommen (Never On Sunday) .... [F]	King 5478
			LYNN ANDERSON	
			Born on 9/26/47 in Grand Forks, ND. Daughter of country singer Liz Anderson.	
11/28/70+	**3**	17	1 ● **Rose Garden**	Columbia 45252
5/15/71	**63**	6	2 You're My Man	Columbia 45356
8/21/71	**63**	7	3 How Can I Unlove You	Columbia 45429
1/29/72	**71**	5	4 Cry	Columbia 45529
6/30/73	**74**	10	5 Top Of The World	Columbia 45857
1/04/75	**93**	3	6 What A Man, My Man Is	Columbia 10041
			1-3 & 6 above all hit #1 on Billboard's Country charts	
			VICKI ANDERSON - see JAMES BROWN	
			CHRIS ANDREWS	
			Singer, songwriter born on 10/15/42 in Essex, England.	
1/01/66	**94**	1	1 Yesterday Man	Atco 6385

DEBUT DATE	PEAK POS	WKS CHR	ARTIST — Record Title	Label & Number
			JULIE ANDREWS/DICK VAN DYKE & THE PEARLIES	
			Julie was born Julia Wells on 10/1/35 in Walton-on-Thames, England. Dick was born on 12/13/25 in West Plaines, MO. Both have won Emmys for television shows.	
4/24/65	66	5	1 Super-cali-fragil-istic- expi-ali-docious .... [N]	Vista 434
			from the film "Mary Poppins" starring Julie & Dick	
			LEE ANDREWS & THE HEARTS	
			R&B group from Philadelphia. First recorded in 1954 for Rainbow.	
8/12/57	45	10	1 Long Lonely Nights	Chess 1665
11/25/57	20	17	2 Tear Drops	Chess 1675
			Best Seller #20 / Top 100 #20 / Jockey #21	
6/02/58	33	11	3 Try The Impossible	United Art. 123
			Best Seller #33 / Top 100 #33	
			PATTY ANDREWS	
			Leader of the Andrews Sisters.	
11/12/55	69	5	1 Suddenly There's A Valley	Capitol 3228
			RUBY ANDREWS	
			Born Ruby Stackhouse on 3/12/47 in Hollandale, Mississippi.	
8/26/67	51	9	1 Casonova (Your Playing Days Are Over)	Zodiac 1004
1/20/68	92	1	2 Hey Boy Take A Chance On Love	Zodiac 1006
8/02/69	96	2	3 You Made A Believer (Out Of Me)	Zodiac 1015
			ANGEL	
			East Coast heavy-metal rock quintet featuring Frank DiMino (vocals), Punky Meadows (guitar) and Greg Giuffria (keyboards).	
4/23/77	77	6	1 That Magic Touch	Casablanca 878
4/01/78	44	8	2 Ain't Gonna Eat Out My Heart Anymore	Casablanca 914
			THE ANGELS	
			Female pop trio from Orange, NJ, formed as the Starlets with sisters Phyllis "Jiggs" (b: 9/24/42) & Barbara Allbut (b: 9/24/40), and Linda Jansen (lead singer). First recorded for Astro in 1960. Jansen was replaced by Peggy Santiglia in 1962.	
10/16/61+	14	14	1 'Til	Caprice 107
2/17/62	38	11	2 Cry Baby Cry	Caprice 112
8/03/63	1^3	14	3 **My Boyfriend's Back**	Smash 1834
10/26/63	25	7	4 I Adore Him/	
12/07/63	84	3	5 Thank You And Goodnight	Smash 1854
1/18/64	41	7	6 Wow Wow Wee (He's The Boy For Me)	Smash 1870
			THE ANIMALS	
			Formed in Newcastle, England in 1958 as the Alan Price Combo. Consisted of Eric Burdon (vocals), Alan Price (keyboards), Bryan "Chas" Chandler (bass), Hilton Valentine (guitar) and John Steel (drums). Price left in May of 1965, replaced by Dave Rowberry. Steel left in 1966, replaced by Barry Jenkins. Group disbanded in July, 1968. After a period with War, Burdon and the other originals reunited, 1983.	
8/08/64	1^3	11	1 **The House Of The Rising Sun**	MGM 13264
9/12/64	57	3	2 Gonna Send You Back To Walker (Gonna Send You Back To Georgia)	MGM 13242
9/26/64	19	9	3 I'm Crying	MGM 13274
12/05/64+	43	7	4 Boom Boom	MGM 13298
			revival of John Lee Hooker's 1960 hit	
2/06/65	15	10	5 Don't Let Me Be Misunderstood	MGM 13311
5/15/65	32	6	6 Bring It On Home To Me	MGM 13339
			version of Sam Cooke's 1962 hit	
8/14/65	13	11	7 We Gotta Get Out Of This Place	MGM 13382
11/06/65+	23	12	8 It's My Life	MGM 13414
2/26/66	34	7	9 Inside-Looking Out	MGM 13468
5/21/66	12	10	10 Don't Bring Me Down	MGM 13514
			ERIC BURDON & THE ANIMALS:	
9/17/66	10	10	11 **See See Rider**	MGM 13582
			revival of Ma Rainey's hit song from 1925	
11/26/66	29	9	12 Help Me Girl	MGM 13636
4/08/67	15	9	13 When I Was Young	MGM 13721
8/05/67	9	10	14 **San Franciscan Nights**	MGM 13769
12/16/67+	15	9	15 Monterey	MGM 13868
4/13/68	80	4	16 Anything	MGM 13917
6/01/68	14	14	17 Sky Pilot (Part One)	MGM 13939
11/23/68	67	8	18 White Houses	MGM 14013

DEBUT DATE	PEAK POS	WKS CHR	ARTIST — Record Title	Label & Number
			THE ANIMALS — Cont'd	
			THE ANIMALS:	
8/13/83	**48**	10	19 The Night	I.R.S. 9920
			ANIMOTION	
			Techno-pop quintet led by Astrid Plane and Bill Wadhams.	
1/26/85	**6**	24	1 **Obsession**	Mercury 880266
6/01/85	**39**	13	2 Let Him Go	Mercury 880737
3/08/86	**76**	6	3 I Engineer	Casablanca 884433
5/17/86	**84**	4	4 I Want You	Casablanca 884729
			ANITA & TH' SO-AND-SO'S	
			The Anita Kerr Singers. Anita was born Anita Jean Grob on 10/31/27 in Memphis.	
2/17/62	**91**	3	1 Joey Baby	RCA 7974
			PAUL ANKA	
			Born on 7/30/41 in Ottawa, Canada. Performer since age 12. Father financed first recording in 1956 "I Confess" (RPM 472). Wrote "My Way" for Frank Sinatra, "She's A Lady" for Tom Jones. Own TV variety show in 1973. Long-time popular entertainer in Las Vegas.	
7/15/57	**1**[1]	29	1 **Diana**	ABC-Para. 9831
			Best Seller #1 / Top 100 #2 / Jockey #2	
12/16/57	**97**	1	2 I Love You, Baby	ABC-Para. 9855
1/20/58	**7**	17	3 **You Are My Destiny**	ABC-Para. 9880
			Top 100 #7 / Best Seller #9 / Jockey #9	
4/21/58	**15**	14	4 Crazy Love/	
			Best Seller #15 / Top 100 #19	
4/21/58	**18**	13	5 Let The Bells Keep Ringing	ABC-Para. 9907
			Jockey #18 / Top 100 #30	
7/28/58	**69**	5	6 Midnight	ABC-Para. 9937
10/06/58	**80**	5	7 Just Young	ABC-Para. 9956
12/01/58+	**29**	8	8 The Teen Commandments [S]	ABC-Para. 9974
			PAUL ANKA-GEORGE HAMILTON IV-JOHNNY NASH	
			inspirational talk from above 3 ABC-Paramount artists	
12/22/58+	**15**	17	9 (All Of A Sudden) My Heart Sings	ABC-Para. 9987
3/30/59	**33**	9	10 I Miss You So	ABC-Para. 10011
6/01/59	**1**[4]	15	11 **Lonely Boy**	ABC-Para. 10022
			from the film "Girl's Town"	
8/31/59	**2**[3]	18	12 **Put Your Head On My Shoulder**	ABC-Para. 10040
			Don Costa arranged and conducted on all of above titles	
11/23/59	**4**	15	13 **It's Time To Cry**	ABC-Para. 10064
2/22/60	**2**[2]	14	14 **Puppy Love/**	
4/04/60	**90**	2	15 Adam And Eve	ABC-Para. 10082
			from the film "The Private Lives of Adam & Eve"	
5/23/60	**8**	13	16 **My Home Town/**	
5/30/60	**41**	9	17 Something Happened	ABC-Para. 10106
8/01/60	**23**	12	18 Hello Young Lovers/	
8/01/60	**40**	11	19 I Love You In The Same Old Way	ABC-Para. 10132
9/26/60	**11**	11	20 Summer's Gone	ABC-Para. 10147
1/16/61	**16**	8	21 The Story Of My Love	ABC-Para. 10168
3/13/61	**13**	11	22 Tonight My Love, Tonight	ABC-Para. 10194
5/29/61	**10**	10	23 **Dance On Little Girl**	ABC-Para. 10220
8/28/61	**35**	7	24 Kissin' On The Phone/	
9/11/61	**70**	4	25 Cinderella	ABC-Para. 10239
2/24/62	**12**	12	26 Love Me Warm And Tender	RCA 7977
5/26/62	**13**	10	27 A Steel Guitar And A Glass Of Wine	RCA 8030
8/25/62	**46**	6	28 Every Night (Without You)	RCA 8068
8/25/62	**94**	1	29 I'm Coming Home	ABC-Para. 10338
11/03/62	**19**	8	30 Eso Beso (That Kiss!)	RCA 8097
1/19/63	**26**	8	31 Love (Makes The World Go 'Round)	RCA 8115
4/13/63	**39**	8	32 Remember Diana	RCA 8170
6/29/63	**97**	1	33 Hello Jim	RCA 8195
12/14/63	**89**	3	34 Did You Have A Happy Birthday?	RCA 8272
1/04/69	**27**	10	35 Goodnight My Love	RCA 9648
3/22/69	**64**	6	36 In The Still Of The Night	RCA 0126
5/31/69	**80**	4	37 Sincerely	RCA 0164

DEBUT DATE	PEAK POS	WKS CHR	ARTIST — Record Title	Label & Number
			PAUL ANKA — Cont'd	
11/22/69	**86**	3	38 Happy	RCA 9767
10/02/71	**53**	11	39 Do I Love You	Buddah 252
3/25/72	**65**	9	40 Jubilation	Buddah 294
1/05/74	**80**	8	41 Let Me Get To Know You	Fame 345
7/06/74	**1**[3]	15	42 ● **(You're) Having My Baby**	United Art. 454
11/09/74+	**7**	16	43 **One Man Woman/One Woman Man**	United Art. 569
3/15/75	**8**	15	44 **I Don't Like To Sleep Alone**	United Art. 615
7/26/75	**15**	13	45 (I Believe) There's Nothing Stronger Than Our Love	United Art. 685
			42, 43, 45: backing vocals by Odia Coates	
11/15/75+	**7**	20	46 **Times Of Your Life**	United Art. 737
4/03/76	**33**	9	47 Anytime (I'll Be There)	United Art. 789
12/18/76+	**60**	7	48 Happier	United Art. 911
4/30/77	**80**	2	49 My Best Friend's Wife	United Art. 972
7/16/77	**75**	4	50 Everybody Ought To Be In Love	United Art. 1018
10/07/78	**35**	11	51 This Is Love	RCA 11395
4/18/81	**48**	9	52 I've Been Waiting For You All Of My Life	RCA 12225
6/18/83	**40**	16	53 Hold Me 'Til The Mornin' Comes	Columbia 03897
			ANN-MARGRET	
			Born Ann-Margret Olsson on 4/28/41 in Stockholm, Sweden. Actress in many films and TV specials.	
7/24/61	**17**	12	1 I Just Don't Understand	RCA 7894
11/13/61	**97**	3	2 It Do Me So Good	RCA 7952
3/24/62	**82**	5	3 What Am I Supposed To Do	RCA 7986
			ANNETTE	
			Born Annette Funicello on 10/22/42 in Utica, NY. Became a Mouseketeer in 1955. In several teen films in the early 60s. Backing group: The Afterbeats.	
1/05/59	**7**	15	1 **Tall Paul**	Disneyland 118
4/13/59	**73**	4	2 Jo-Jo The Dog-Faced Boy	Vista 336
7/06/59	**50**	11	3 Lonely Guitar	Vista 339
10/26/59+	**20**	18	4 First Name Initial/	
10/26/59	**74**	3	5 My Heart Became Of Age	Vista 349
2/22/60	**10**	12	6 **O Dio Mio**	Vista 354
6/06/60	**36**	8	7 Train Of Love	Vista 359
8/15/60	**11**	14	8 Pineapple Princess	Vista 362
12/26/60	**92**	2	9 Talk To Me Baby	Vista 369
2/20/61	**87**	2	10 Dream Boy	Vista 374
			based on the 1880 song "Funiculi-Funicula"	
			ADAM ANT	
			Born Stuart Goddard on 11/3/54 in London, England. Formed Adam & The Ants in 1976.	
11/13/82+	**12**	21	1 Goody Two Shoes	Epic 03367
3/12/83	**66**	8	2 Desperate But Not Serious	Epic 03688
2/04/84	**42**	13	3 Strip	Epic 04337
			PETE ANTELL	
12/08/62	**100**	1	1 Night Time	Cameo 234
			RAY ANTHONY	
			Born Raymond Antonini on 1/20/22 in Bentleyville, PA. Trumpeter bandleader. Raised in Cleveland. Joined Al Donahue in 1939, then with Glenn Miller and Jimmy Dorsey from 1940-42. Led US Army band. Formed own band in 1946. Very popular with college audiences. Appeared in film "Daddy Long Legs" with Fred Astaire in 1955.	
1/22/55	**19**	4	1 Melody Of Love	Capitol 3018
			FRANK SINATRA & RAY ANTHONY	
			Jockey #19	
9/10/55	**68**	3	2 Pete Kelly's Blues [I]	Capitol 3176
			Honor Roll #68	
			from the film of the same title	
1/05/59	**8**	17	3 **Peter Gunn** [I]	Capitol 4041
4/20/59	**96**	1	4 Walkin' To Mother's [I]	Capitol 4176
			above 2 taken from the "Peter Gunn" TV series	
6/30/62	**74**	8	5 Worried Mind [I]	Capitol 4742
12/15/62	**96**	2	6 Let Me Entertain You [I]	Capitol 4876
			from the film "Gypsy"	

DEBUT DATE	PEAK POS	WKS CHR	ARTIST — Record Title	Label & Number
			SUSAN ANTON - see FRED KNOBLOCK	
			APOLLO 100 featuring Tom Parker	
			English studio band assembled by Tom Parker.	
1/01/72	**6**	14	1 **Joy** .... [I]	Mega 0050
			adaptation of Bach's "Jesu, Joy of Man's Desiring"	
4/15/72	**94**	3	2 Mendelssohn's 4th (2nd Movement)............ [I]	Mega 0069
			APOLLONIA 6	
			Female trio led by Patty (Apollonia) Kotero (co-star of film "Purple Rain"). Trio evolved from Vanity 6. Also see Prince.	
10/20/84	**85**	6	1 Sex Shooter............	Warner 29182
			from the film "Purple Rain"	
			THE APPALACHIANS	
3/30/63	**62**	8	1 Bony Moronie	ABC-Para. 10419
			folk-styled version of Larry Williams' 1957 hit	
			THE APPLEJACKS	
			Dave Appell, leader of studio band from Philadelphia.	
9/15/58	**16**	15	1 Mexican Hat Rock .... [I]	Cameo 149
			Hot 100 #16 / Best Seller #29 end	
12/22/58+	**38**	10	2 Rocka-Conga	Cameo 155
2/23/59	**70**	4	3 Bunny Hop............ [I]	Cameo 158
			APRIL WINE	
			Rock quintet from Montreal, Canada led by Myles Goodwyn.	
3/25/72	**32**	11	1 You Could Have Been A Lady	Big Tree 133
3/03/79	**34**	11	2 Roller............	Capitol 4660
2/09/80	**86**	3	3 I Like To Rock	Capitol 4828
2/07/81	**21**	16	4 Just Between You And Me	Capitol 4975
5/30/81	**57**	8	5 Sign Of The Gypsy Queen............	Capitol 5001
7/03/82	**50**	8	6 Enough Is Enough............	Capitol 5133
2/11/84	**58**	6	7 This Could Be The Right One............	Capitol 5319
			THE AQUATONES	
			Vocal group from Long Island, NY. Barbara Lee, lead singer.	
4/28/58	**21**	12	1 You............	Fargo 1001
			Top 100 #21 / Best Seller #24	
			THE ARBORS	
			Formed at the University of Michigan in Ann Arbor by two pairs of brothers: Edward & Fred Farran, and Scott & Tom Herrick.	
10/15/66	**51**	10	1 A Symphony For Susan	Date 1529
6/17/67	**59**	4	2 Graduation Day............	Date 1561
2/22/69	**20**	10	3 The Letter............	Date 1638
5/31/69	**67**	5	4 I Can't Quit Her............	Date 1645
			ARCADIA	
			English group features Duran Duran's Simon Lebon, Nick Rhodes & Roger Taylor	
10/26/85	**6**	16	1 **Election Day**............	Capitol 5501
			narration: Grace Jones	
2/01/86	**33**	10	2 Goodbye Is Forever............	Capitol 5542
			THE ARCHIES	
			Studio group created by Don Kirshner - based on a Saturday morning cartoon television series. Ron Dante was lead vocalist.	
9/28/68	**22**	13	1 Bang-Shang-A-Lang............	Calendar 1006
12/28/68+	**53**	8	2 Feelin' So Good (Skooby-Doo)............	Calendar 1007
7/26/69	**1^{4}**	22	3 ● **Sugar, Sugar**............	Calendar 1008
11/29/69+	**10**	13	4 ● **Jingle Jangle**............	Kirshner 5002
3/07/70	**40**	7	5 Who's Your Baby?	Kirshner 5003
7/04/70	**57**	7	6 Sunshine............	Kirshner 1009
			TONI ARDEN	
			Singer with Al Trace in 1945 and Joe Reichman in 1946.	
2/04/56	**78**	1	1 Are You Satisfied?............	RCA 6346
5/26/58	**13**	14	2 Padre	Decca 30628
			Jockey #13 / Top 100 #18 / Best Seller #19	

DEBUT DATE	PEAK POS	WKS CHR	ARTIST — Record Title	Label & Number
			ARGENT British rock quartet, consisted of ex-Zombies member Rod Argent (vocals, keyboards), John Verity (guitar), Jim Rodford (bass) and Robert Henrit (drums).	
6/17/72	**5**	15	1 **Hold Your Head Up**	Epic 10852
			ARKADE	
8/22/70	**99**	1	1 Sing Out The Love (In My Heart)	Dunhill 4247
2/13/71	**60**	6	2 The Morning Of Our Lives	Dunhill 4268
			JOAN ARMATRADING Born on 12/9/50 in St. Kitts, West Indies. Vocalist, pianist, guitarist, composer. To Birmingham, England in 1958. First recorded for Cube in 1971.	
5/28/83	**78**	6	1 Drop The Pilot	A&M 2538
			KAY ARMEN Popular 1940's radio singer, appeared in the 1955 movie musical "Hit The Deck".	
12/09/57	**91**	1	1 Ha! Ha! Ha! (Chella Lla!)	Decca 30474
			ARMENIAN JAZZ SEXTET	
4/29/57	**67**	6	1 Harem Dance [I] Ralph Marterie's hit of this tune was entitled "Shish-Kebab"	Kapp 181
			RUSSELL ARMS One of the regulars on TV's "Your Hit Parade".	
1/12/57	**22**	15	1 Cinco Robles (Five Oaks) Best Seller #22 / Top 100 #23 / Jockey #23 with Pete King and orchestra	Era 1026
			LOUIS ARMSTRONG Born Daniel Louis Armstrong on 7/4/1900 in New Orleans; died on 7/6/71 in New York. Nickname: Satchmo. Trumpeter, vocalist. Resident of Colored Waif's Home in New Orleans and played cornet in the Home's band. Joined Joe "King" Oliver in Chicago in 1922. By 1929, had become the most widely-known black musician. Influenced dozens of singers and trumpet players, both black and white. Made numerous appearances on radio, TV and in films.	
2/11/56	**20**	15	1 Mack The Knife (A Theme From The Threepenny Opera)	Columbia 40587
10/13/56	**88**	4	2 Now You Has Jazz [N] **BING CROSBY & LOUIS ARMSTRONG** from the film "High Society"; Johnny Green conducts the MGM orch.	Capitol 3506
11/03/56	**29**	11	3 Blueberry Hill recorded in 1949 with Gordon Jenkins' orchestra	Decca 30091
2/15/64	**1**[1]	22	4 **Hello, Dolly!**	Kapp 573
6/20/64	**45**	7	5 I Still Get Jealous 1, 4 & 5: LOUIS ARMSTRONG & THE ALL STARS	Kapp 597
10/03/64	**56**	6	6 So Long Dearie 4 & 6: from the Broadway musical "Hello Dolly"	Mercury 72338
5/21/66	**81**	4	7 Mame title song from the Broadway musical	Mercury 72574
			GINNY ARNELL	
11/16/63+	**50**	12	1 Dumb Head	MGM 13177
			AUDREY ARNO & The Hazy Osterwald Sextet German vocalist with male backing singers.	
4/10/61	**87**	2	1 La Pachanga [F]	Decca 31238
			CALVIN ARNOLD	
1/13/68	**72**	8	1 Funky Way	Venture 605
			EDDY ARNOLD Born on 5/15/18 near Henderson, TN. Became popular on Nashville's Grand Ole Opry as a singer with Pee Wee King (1940-43). Country music's all-time #1 artist.	
7/16/55	**42**	2	1 The Cattle Call Coming Up #42 / Top 100 #69 pre	RCA 6139
12/10/55	**99**	1	2 The Richest Man (In The World) orchestra directed by Hugo Winterhalter on above 2 titles	RCA 6290
11/24/56	**22**	8	3 I Wouldn't Know Where To Begin Jockey #22 / Top 100 #64	RCA 6699
12/01/56	**47**	9	4 Mutual Admiration Society **EDDY ARNOLD & JAYE P. MORGAN** from the musical "Happy Hunting"	RCA 6708
6/03/57	**51**	6	5 Gonna Find Me A Bluebird	RCA 6905
3/09/59	**97**	2	6 Chip Off The Old Block	RCA 7435
7/13/59	**48**	10	7 Tennessee Stud	RCA 7542

DEBUT DATE	PEAK POS	WKS CHR	ARTIST — Record Title	Label & Number
			EDDY ARNOLD — Cont'd	
12/22/62	**98**	1	8 Does He Mean That Much To You?	RCA 8102
5/15/65	**60**	9	9 What's He Doing In My World	RCA 8516
10/16/65	**6**	14	10 **Make The World Go Away**	RCA 8679
2/05/66	**36**	11	11 I Want To Go With You	RCA 8749
5/14/66	**40**	7	12 The Last Word In Lonesome Is Me	RCA 8818
7/23/66	**43**	7	13 The Tip Of My Fingers	RCA 8869
10/15/66	**53**	6	14 Somebody Like Me	RCA 8965
3/18/67	**87**	2	15 Lonely Again	RCA 9080
5/06/67	**57**	8	16 Misty Blue	RCA 9182
8/19/67	**66**	8	17 Turn The World Around	RCA 9265
12/02/67	**91**	4	18 Here Comes Heaven	RCA 9368
2/10/68	**74**	4	19 Here Comes The Rain, Baby	RCA 9437
5/18/68	**74**	7	20 It's Over	RCA 9525
9/07/68	**84**	4	21 Then You Can Tell Me Goodbye	RCA 9606
12/07/68	**99**	2	22 They Don't Make Love Like They Used To all of Eddy's hits were produced by Chet Atkins	RCA 9667
			ARPEGGIO Black disco quartet.	
3/10/79	**70**	5	1 Love And Desire (Part I)	Polydor 14535
			STEVE ARRINGTON Vocalist, drummer from Dayton, Ohio. Ex-member of Slave.	
8/17/85	**68**	6	1 Dancin' In The Key Of Life	Atlantic 89535
			ARROWS - see DAVIE ALLAN	
			THE ART OF NOISE British techno-pop trio: Anne Dudley, Gary Langan and J.J. Jeczalik.	
5/17/86	**50**	11	1 Peter Gunn [I] featuring Duane Eddy - his 1960 version peaked at POS 27	China 42986
8/16/86	**34**	12	2 Paranoimia with Max Headroom (a British "computer generated" celebrity)	China 43002
			THE ARTISTICS R&B vocal group formed in Chicago in 1958. First recorded for Okeh in 1963.	
12/17/66+	**55**	10	1 I'm Gonna Miss You	Brunswick 55301
3/18/67	**69**	6	2 Girl I Need You	Brunswick 55315
			ARTISTS UNITED AGAINST APARTHEID Benefit group of 49 superstar artists formed in protest of the South African government - proceeds to benefit political prisoners in South Africa.	
11/02/85	**38**	13	1 Sun City	Manhattan 50017
			BOBBY ARVON Singer, songwriter from Halifax, Nova Scotia.	
12/03/77+	**72**	16	1 Until Now	First Art. 41000
			CLARENCE ASHE	
6/06/64	**99**	1	1 Trouble I've Had [S]	Chess 1896
			ASHFORD & SIMPSON R&B vocal/songwriting husband and wife duo: Nickolas Ashford (b: 5/4/42, Fairfield, SC) and Valerie Simpson (b: 8/26/46, New York, NY). Team wrote for Chuck Jackson and Maxine Brown. Joined staff at Motown and wrote and produced for many of the label's top stars.	
1/19/74	**88**	3	1 (I'd Know You) Anywhere	Warner 7745
3/11/78	**79**	9	2 Don't Cost You Nothing	Warner 8514
8/18/79	**36**	13	3 Found A Cure	Warner 8870
6/05/82	**56**	10	4 Street Corner	Capitol 5109
11/10/84+	**12**	24	5 Solid	Capitol 5397
9/27/86	**84**	4	6 Count Your Blessings	Capitol 5598
			ASHTON, GARDNER & DYKE British: Tony Ashton, Kim Gardner and Roy Dyke.	
6/19/71	**40**	10	1 Resurrection Shuffle	Capitol 3060

DEBUT DATE	PEAK POS	WKS CHR	ARTIST — Record Title	Label & Number
			ASIA	
			English rock supergroup comprised of Steve Howe (Yes), Carl Palmer (Emerson, Lake & Palmer), Geoff Downes (Buggles, Yes) and John Wetton (King Crimson, Uriah Heep, Roxy Music). Howe replaced by Mandy Meyer (Krokus) in 1985.	
4/17/82	**4**	18	1 **Heat Of The Moment**	Geffen 50040
7/24/82	**17**	14	2 Only Time Will Tell	Geffen 29970
7/30/83	**10**	13	3 **Don't Cry**	Geffen 29571
10/15/83	**34**	13	4 The Smile Has Left Your Eyes	Geffen 29475
12/07/85+	**46**	11	5 Go	Geffen 28872
			THE ASSEMBLED MULTITUDE	
			Studio group arranged and conducted by Tom Sellers.	
6/27/70	**16**	13	1 Overture From Tommy (A Rock Opera) [I]	Atlantic 2737
10/03/70	**79**	4	2 Woodstock [I]	Atlantic 2764
2/06/71	**95**	2	3 Medley From "Jesus Christ-Superstar" (A Rock Opera) [I]	Atlantic 2780
			THE ASSOCIATION	
			Group formed in Los Angeles in 1965. Consisted of Terry Kirkman (plays 23 wind, reed and percussion instruments), Jules Alexander (guitar), Brian Cole (bass), Jim Yester (guitar), Ted Buechel Jr. (drums) and Russ Giguere (percussion). Larry Ramos joined in early 1968. Richard Thompson (keyboards) replaced Giguere in 1970. Cole died on 8/2/73 of a drug overdose. Thompson replaced by Rick Ulsky in 1974. Regrouped with original surviving members on 9/26/80.	
6/04/66	**7**	11	1 **Along Comes Mary**	Valiant 741
8/27/66	**1^{3}**	14	2 ● **Cherish**	Valiant 747
11/26/66	**35**	7	3 Pandora's Golden Heebie Jeebies	Valiant 755
2/04/67	**51**	7	4 No Fair At All	Valiant 758
5/27/67	**1^{4}**	14	5 ● **Windy**	Warner 7041
8/26/67	**2^{2}**	14	6 ● **Never My Love/**	
9/02/67	**100**	2	7 Requiem For The Masses	Warner 7074
2/03/68	**10**	9	8 **Everything That Touches You**	Warner 7163
5/18/68	**39**	8	9 Time For Livin'	Warner 7195
8/24/68	**47**	6	10 Six Man Band	Warner 7229
3/15/69	**80**	11	11 Goodbye Columbus from the film of the same title	Warner 7267
2/24/73	**91**	5	12 Names, Tags, Numbers & Labels	Mums 6016
1/31/81	**66**	5	13 Dreamer	Elektra 47094
			THE ASTORS	
7/10/65	**63**	9	1 Candy	Stax 170
			THE ASTRONAUTS	
			Boulder, Colorado surf/rock quintet.	
7/27/63	**94**	1	1 Baja [I] pronounced Ba-ha	RCA 8194
			CHET ATKINS	
			Born on 6/20/24 in Luttrell, Tennessee. Elected to the Country Music Hall of Fame in 1973. Nashville's top guitarist.	
2/25/56	**52**	10	1 The Poor People Of Paris [I]	RCA 6366
9/28/59	**49**	8	2 Boo Boo Stick Beat [I]	RCA 7589
1/04/60	**82**	6	3 One Mint Julep/ [I]	
2/15/60	**73**	3	4 Teensville [I]	RCA 7684
7/17/65	**98**	2	5 Yakety Axe [I] same tune as Boots Randolph's "Yakety Sax"	RCA 8590
			CHRISTOPHER ATKINS	
			Teen movie star - starred in "The Blue Lagoon".	
8/07/82	**71**	7	1 How Can I Live Without Her from the film "The Pirate Movie"	Polydor 2210
			THE ATLANTA DISCO BAND	
1/10/76	**94**	4	1 Bad Luck [I]	Ariola 7611
			ATLANTA RHYTHM SECTION	
			Group formed of musicians from Studio One, Doraville, GA in 1971. Consisted of Rodney Justo (vocals), Barry Bailey, Paul Goddard, J.R. Cobb (guitars), Dean Daughtry (keyboards) and Robert Nix (drums). Cobb, Daughtry and band manager Buddy Buie had been with the Classics IV, others had been with Roy Orbison. Justo left after first album, replaced by Ronnie Hammond.	
10/05/74	**35**	8	1 Doraville	Polydor 14248

DEBUT DATE	PEAK POS	WKS CHR	ARTIST — Record Title	Label & Number
			ATLANTA RHYTHM SECTION — Cont'd	
2/22/75	**79**	5	2 Angel (What In The World's Come Over Us)	Polydor 14262
6/05/76	**82**	4	3 Jukin tune includes a few bars of "San Antonio Rose"	Polydor 14323
8/21/76	**85**	3	4 Free Spirit	Polydor 14339
1/29/77	**7**	19	5 **So In To You**	Polydor 14373
6/04/77	**42**	7	6 Neon Nites	Polydor 14397
9/03/77	**64**	5	7 Dog Days	Polydor 14411
10/15/77	**68**	6	8 Georgia Rhythm	Polydor 14432
3/04/78	**7**	17	9 **Imaginary Lover**	Polydor 14459
6/10/78	**14**	13	10 I'm Not Gonna Let It Bother Me Tonight	Polydor 14484
9/16/78	**43**	9	11 Champagne Jam	Polydor 14504
5/26/79	**19**	14	12 Do It Or Die	Polydor 14568
8/11/79	**17**	14	13 Spooky revival of the Classics IV 1968 hit	Polydor 2001
8/29/81	**29**	15	14 Alien	Columbia 02471
			ATLANTIC STARR Originally an eight-man, one-woman band, formed in New York City in 1976. Lead singers: brothers Wayne & David Lewis and Sharon Bryant (replaced by Barbara Weathers in 1985).	
3/27/82	**38**	11	1 Circles	A&M 2392
12/10/83	**87**	7	2 Touch A Four Leaf Clover	A&M 2580
5/25/85	**90**	6	3 Freak-A-Ristic	A&M 2718
12/28/85+	**3**	23	4 **Secret Lovers**	A&M 2788
4/19/86	**57**	12	5 If Your Heart Isn't In It	A&M 2822
			ATTITUDES Los Angeles-based quartet of top sidemen. David Foster, keyboards (composer of "St. Elmo's Fire"); Danny Kortchmar, guitar; Paul Stallworth, bass; Jim Keltner, drums.	
9/04/76	**94**	6	1 Sweet Summer Music	Dark Horse 10011
			AUDIENCE British rock group.	
7/17/71	**74**	5	1 Indian Summer	Elektra 45732
			AUDREY	
9/22/56	**87**	1	1 Dear Elvis (Pages 1 & 2) [N] 2-sided novelty "cut-in" type disc	Plus 104
			BRIAN AUGER & THE TRINITY Brian was born on 7/18/39 in London, England. Jazz-rock keyboardist.	
10/10/70	**100**	2	1 Listen Here [I]	RCA 0381
			JAN AUGUST - see RICHARD HAYMAN	
			AURRA Consisted of ex-Slave members Steve Washington and Tom Lockett, Jr., saxophones; with vocalists Starleana Young and Curt Jones.	
3/20/82	**71**	7	1 Make Up Your Mind	Salsoul 7017
			GENE AUSTIN The most popular singer of the late 1920's. His 1927 hit "My Blue Heaven" sold over 5 million copies. Gene died on 1/24/72 (71).	
5/27/57	**75**	3	1 Too Late from the TV Playhouse production "The Gene Austin Story"	RCA 6880
			PATTI AUSTIN Born on 8/10/48 in New York City. Back-up work in New York. God-daughter of Quincy Jones. Also see Yutaka.	
12/12/81+	**62**	8	1 Every Home Should Have One	Qwest 49854
4/24/82+	**1**[2]	32	2 ● **Baby, Come To Me** **PATTI AUSTIN with JAMES INGRAM**	Qwest 50036
3/19/83	**69**	7	3 Every Home Should Have One [R] remixed version of original hit	Qwest 29727
5/14/83	**45**	17	4 How Do You Keep The Music Playing **JAMES INGRAM & PATTI AUSTIN** theme from the film "Best Friends"	Qwest 29618
2/11/84	**82**	4	5 It's Gonna Be Special from the film "Two Of A Kind"	Qwest 29373
5/03/86	**55**	9	6 The Heat Of Heat	Qwest 28788

DEBUT DATE	PEAK POS	WKS CHR	ARTIST — Record Title	Label & Number
			SIL AUSTIN	
			Born Sylvester Austin in 1929 in Donellon, Florida. Tenor saxophonist. Played with the Tiny Bradshaw Band before forming own group.	
11/10/56	17	14	1 Slow Walk .... [I]	Mercury 70963
			Juke Box #17 / Top 100 #19 / Best Seller #20	
2/16/57	74	1	2 Birthday Party .... [I]	Mercury 71027
6/01/59	59	12	3 Danny Boy .... [I]	Mercury 71442
			AUTOGRAPH	
			Los Angeles-based rock quintet - Steve Plunkett, lead singer.	
12/22/84+	29	19	1 Turn Up The Radio	RCA 13953
			AUTOMATIC MAN	
			Formed in San Francisco by Michael Shrieve in 1975 after leaving Santana.	
2/12/77	97	2	1 My Pearl	Island 063
			GENE AUTRY	
			Born on 9/29/07 in Tioga Springs, TX; Gene was the first cowboy singing star of movies. Owner of California Angels baseball club.	
12/30/57	70	3	1 Rudolph The Red-Nosed Reindeer .... [X-N]	Challenge 1010
			new version - his original version sold over 8 million copies	
			FRANKIE AVALON	
			Born Francis Avallone on 9/18/39 in Philadelphia. Worked in bands in Atlantic City, NJ in 1953. Radio and TV with Paul Whiteman, mid-50s. Singer, trumpet player with Rocco & His Saints in 1957. Film "Disc Jockey Jamboree" in 1957. Teen idol managed by Bob Marucci. Frequent appearances in films with Annette. Also films "Guns Of The Timberland" in 1960, "The Carpetbaggers" in 1962.	
1/20/58	7	15	1 **Dede Dinah**	Chancellor 1011
			Top 100 #7 / Best Seller #9 / Jockey #24	
4/14/58	49	9	2 You Excite Me	Chancellor 1016
			Top 100 #49 / Best Seller #50	
7/21/58	9	13	3 **Ginger Bread**	Chancellor 1021
			Hot 100 #9 / Best Seller #11	
10/13/58	15	17	4 I'll Wait For You/	
10/13/58	79	2	5 What Little Girl	Chancellor 1026
2/09/59	1[5]	17	6 **Venus**	Chancellor 1031
5/18/59	8	13	7 **Bobby Sox To Stockings/**	
5/18/59	10	14	8 **A Boy Without A Girl**	Chancellor 1036
8/31/59	7	16	9 **Just Ask Your Heart/**	
9/21/59	54	5	10 Two Fools	Chancellor 1040
11/23/59	1[1]	16	11 **Why/**	
12/21/59+	39	6	12 Swingin' On A Rainbow	Chancellor 1045
3/14/60	22	10	13 Don't Throw Away All Those Teardrops	Chancellor 1048
6/13/60	32	12	14 Where Are You/	
6/13/60	82	2	15 Tuxedo Junction	Chancellor 1052
			revival of Glenn Miller's 1940 million selling hit	
9/19/60	26	13	16 Togetherness/	
10/10/60	85	2	17 Don't Let Love Pass Me By	Chancellor 1056
12/12/60+	47	6	18 A Perfect Love/	
12/12/60	56	7	19 The Puppet Song .... [N]	Chancellor 1065
			arranger/conductor on all of above (except #16): Peter DeAngelis	
2/27/61	70	4	20 All Of Everything	Chancellor 1071
5/29/61	82	2	21 Who Else But You	Chancellor 1077
9/25/61	90	2	22 True, True Love	Chancellor 1087
3/24/62	26	11	23 You Are Mine	Chancellor 1107
7/14/62	75	6	24 A Miracle	Chancellor 1115
1/24/76	46	11	25 Venus	De-Lite 1578
			disco version of Frankie's 1959 hit	
			THE AVANT-GARDE	
8/31/68	40	10	1 Naturally Stoned	Columbia 44590
			AVERAGE WHITE BAND	
			Vocal/instrumental group formed in Scotland in 1972. Consisted of Alan Gorrie (vocal, bass), Hamish Stuart (vocal, guitar), Onnie McIntyre (vocal, guitar), Malcolm Duncan (saxophone), Roger Ball (keyboards, saxophone) and Robbie McIntosh (drums). McIntosh died of drug poisoning in 1974, replaced by Steve Ferrone.	
12/07/74+	1[1]	17	1 ● **Pick Up The Pieces** .... [I]	Atlantic 3229
4/12/75	10	15	2 **Cut The Cake**	Atlantic 3261
8/23/75	39	8	3 If I Ever Lose This Heaven	Atlantic 3285

DEBUT DATE	PEAK POS	WKS CHR	ARTIST — Record Title	Label & Number
			AVERAGE WHITE BAND — Cont'd	
11/29/75	**33**	7	4 School Boy Crush	Atlantic 3304
9/04/76	**40**	8	5 Queen Of My Soul	Atlantic 3354
4/14/79	**92**	3	6 Walk On By 1-4 & 6 shown only as: **AWB**	Atlantic 3563
6/21/80	**53**	8	7 Let's Go 'Round Again	Arista 0515
			THE JOHNNY AVERAGE BAND Band originally called the Falcons, from Nottingham, England. Featuring Johnny's wife Nikki Wills on vocals.	
2/21/81	**53**	7	1 Ch Ch Cherie	Bearsville 49671
			AXE Florida-based rock band; Bobby Barth, vocals, guitar.	
7/24/82	**64**	6	1 Now Or Never	Atco 7408
10/22/83	**94**	2	2 I Think You'll Remember Tonight	Atco 99823
			HOYT AXTON Born on 3/25/38 in Duncan, Oklahoma. Son of songwriter Mae Axton (Heartbreak Hotel"). Appeared in movies "The Black Stallion" and "Gremlins".	
6/01/74	**54**	6	1 When The Morning Comes	A&M 1497

B

DEBUT DATE	PEAK POS	WKS CHR	ARTIST — Record Title	Label & Number
			BABY JANE & THE ROCKABYES Black female quartet.	
1/05/63	**69**	7	1 How Much Is That Doggie In The Window	United Art. 560
			BABY RAY Ray Eddlemon.	
12/03/66	**69**	6	1 There's Something On Your Mind [N]	Imperial 66216
			THE BABYS John Waite, lead singer of British foursome.	
3/19/77	**88**	2	1 If You've Got The Time	Chrysalis 2132
10/08/77	**13**	16	2 Isn't It Time	Chrysalis 2173
2/04/78	**53**	7	3 Silver Dreams	Chrysalis 2201
1/06/79	**13**	16	4 Every Time I Think Of You	Chrysalis 2279
5/26/79	**77**	3	5 Head First	Chrysalis 2323
1/19/80	**33**	12	6 Back On My Feet Again	Chrysalis 2398
5/03/80	**72**	4	7 Midnight Rendezvous	Chrysalis 2425
11/15/80	**42**	12	8 Turn And Walk Away	Chrysalis 2467
			BURT BACHARACH Born on 5/12/28 in Kansas City. Conductor, arranger and top composer who often worked with lyricist Hal David. Formerly married to Angie Dickinson, presently married to songwriter Carole Bayer Sager.	
7/27/63	**93**	3	1 Saturday Sunshine	Kapp 532
7/05/69	**93**	2	2 I'll Never Fall In Love Again from the Broadway musical "Promises, Promises" Burt does not sing on above 2; vocals by a chorus	A&M 1064
			THE BACHELORS Trio from Dublin, Ireland: brothers Declan & Con Cluskey with John Stokes.	
4/18/64	**10**	13	1 **Diane**	London 9639
6/27/64	**33**	8	2 I Believe	London 9672
9/12/64	**69**	6	3 I Wouldn't Trade You For The World	London 9693
12/26/64+	**27**	10	4 No Arms Can Ever Hold You	London 9724
6/12/65	**15**	10	5 Marie	London 9762
10/09/65	**32**	7	6 Chapel In The Moonlight	London 9793
4/16/66	**38**	6	7 Love Me With All Of Your Heart	London 9828
7/02/66	**49**	6	8 Can I Trust You?	London 20010
1/07/67	**83**	3	9 Walk With Faith In Your Heart	London 20018

DEBUT DATE	PEAK POS	WKS CHR	ARTIST — Record Title	Label & Number
			BACHMAN-TURNER OVERDRIVE	
			Hard-rock group formed in Vancouver, Canada in 1972. Randy Bachman (vocals, guitar), Tim Bachman (guitar), C. Fred Turner (vocals, bass) and Robbie Bachman (drums). Originally known as Brave Belt. Randy had been in the Guess Who and recorded solo. Tim Bachman left in 1973, replaced by Blair Thornton. Randy Bachman left in 1977. Randy and Tim regrouped with C.F. Turner in 1984.	
12/01/73	**68**	6	1 Blue Collar	Mercury 73417
2/23/74	**23**	15	2 Let It Ride	Mercury 73457
5/18/74	**12**	20	3 Takin' Care Of Business	Mercury 73487
9/21/74	**1**[1]	17	4● **You Ain't Seen Nothing Yet/**	
		6	5 Free Wheelin' [I]	Mercury 73622
1/18/75	**14**	11	6 Roll On Down The Highway	Mercury 73656
5/17/75	**21**	12	7 Hey You	Mercury 73683
12/06/75+	**43**	7	8 Down To The Line	Mercury 73724
2/07/76	**33**	7	9 Take It Like A Man	Mercury 73766
4/24/76	**65**	6	10 Lookin' Out For #1	Mercury 73784
9/18/76	**70**	5	11 Gimme Your Money Please	Mercury 73843
2/24/79	**60**	7	12 Heartaches shown only as: **BTO**	Mercury 74046
			JIM BACKUS & Friend	
			Jim played Thurston Howell III on TV's "Gilligan's Island". Also famous as the voice of Mr. Magoo in the cartoon series.	
7/14/58	**40**	5	1 Delicious! [N] Best Seller #40 / Top 100 #42	Jubilee 5330
			BAD COMPANY	
			British: Paul Rodgers (vocals), Mick Ralphs (guitar), Simon Kirke (drums) & Boz Burrell (bass). Paul and Simon from Free; Mick from Mott The Hoople; and Boz from King Crimson.	
8/17/74	**5**	15	1 **Can't Get Enough**	Swan Song 70015
1/18/75	**19**	10	2 Movin' On	Swan Song 70101
4/19/75	**36**	8	3 Good Lovin' Gone Bad	Swan Song 70103
7/05/75	**10**	15	4 **Feel Like Makin' Love**	Swan Song 70106
3/20/76	**20**	13	5 Young Blood revival of The Coasters 1957 hit	Swan Song 70108
7/10/76	**59**	6	6 Honey Child	Swan Song 70109
5/21/77	**78**	4	7 Burnin' Sky	Swan Song 70112
3/17/79	**13**	20	8 Rock 'N' Roll Fantasy	Swan Song 70119
8/04/79	**56**	6	9 Gone, Gone, Gone	Swan Song 71000
10/02/82	**74**	4	10 Electricland	Swan Song 99966
10/18/86	**85**	5	11 This Love	Atlantic 89355
			BADFINGER	
			British quartet originally known as The Iveys - leader Pete Ham commited suicide on 4/23/75 (27).	
2/15/69	**67**	6	1 Maybe Tomorrow **THE IVEYS**	Apple 1803
2/07/70	**7**	15	2 **Come And Get It** written by Paul McCartney - from the film "The Magic Christian"	Apple 1815
10/31/70	**8**	12	3 **No Matter What**	Apple 1822
12/04/71+	**4**	14	4● **Day After Day** produced by George Harrison	Apple 1841
3/25/72	**14**	10	5 Baby Blue produced by Todd Rundgren	Apple 1844
4/07/79	**69**	4	6 Love Is Gonna Come At Last	Elektra 46025
2/28/81	**56**	8	7 Hold On	Radio 3793
			JOAN BAEZ	
			Folk song stylist born in New York City on 1/9/41. Became a political activist while attending Boston University in the late 50s.	
11/09/63	**90**	1	1 We Shall Overcome recorded live at Miles College in Birmingham, Alabama based on the music from an early hymn of 1794	Vanguard 35023
9/11/65	**50**	7	2 There But For Fortune	Vanguard 35031
4/26/69	**86**	4	3 Love Is Just A Four-Letter World	Vanguard 35088
8/14/71	**3**	15	4● **The Night They Drove Old Dixie Down**	Vanguard 35138
11/13/71	**49**	8	5 Let It Be	Vanguard 35145
7/29/72	**69**	8	6 In The Quiet Morning written by Mimi Farina for Janis Joplin	A&M 1362

DEBUT DATE	PEAK POS	WKS CHR	ARTIST — Record Title	Label & Number
			JOAN BAEZ — Cont'd	
7/12/75	**57**	5	7 Blue Sky	A&M 1703
9/20/75	**35**	11	8 Diamonds And Rust	A&M 1737
			DOC BAGBY	
			Black organist.	
9/30/57	**69**	4	1 Dumplin's [I]	Okeh 7089
			PHILIP BAILEY	
			Born on 5/8/51 in Denver. Former co-lead vocalist for Earth, Wind & Fire.	
11/24/84+	**2**[2]	23	1 **Easy Lover**	Columbia 04679
			PHILIP BAILEY with PHIL COLLINS	
4/06/85	**46**	12	2 Walking On The Chinese Wall	Columbia 04826
			RAZZY BAILEY	
			Born on 2/14/39 in Lafayette, AL. Country singer/songwriter. Big break came when Dickey Lee recorded Razzy's "9,999,999 Tears".	
5/25/74	**67**	6	1 I Hate Hate	MGM 14728
			shown only as: **RAZZY**	
			BAJA MARIMBA BAND	
			9-man band led by marimbaist Julius Wechter.	
12/21/63+	**41**	9	1 Comin' In The Back Door [I]	Almo 201
11/26/66	**52**	6	2 Ghost Riders In The Sky [I]	A&M 824
4/29/67	**98**	1	3 Georgy Girl [I]	A&M 843
			from the film of the same title	
8/05/67	**96**	2	4 Along Comes Mary [I]	A&M 862
			ANITA BAKER	
			Soul singer from Detroit. Former lead singer of Chapter 8.	
8/16/86	**8**	22	1 **Sweet Love**	Elektra 69557
11/29/86+	**37**	18	2 Caught Up In The Rapture	Elektra 69511
			GEORGE BAKER SELECTION	
			Dutch group led by Johannes Bouwens.	
3/21/70	**21**	13	1 Little Green Bag	Colossus 112
6/20/70	**93**	2	2 Dear Ann	Colossus 117
11/29/75+	**26**	15	3 Paloma Blanca	Warner 8115
			GINGER BAKER'S AIR FORCE	
			Ginger was drummer for Cream and Blind Faith. Group features Steve Winwood and Denny Laine.	
5/23/70	**85**	2	1 Man Of Constant Sorrow	Atco 6750
			vocal: Denny Laine; also with Steve Winwood & Rick Grech	
			LaVERN BAKER	
			Born Delores Williams on 11/11/29 in Chicago. Sang in night clubs while still a teenager. After work with Todd Rhodes Orchestra in 1952 and 1953, toured Europe as a single. Returned to work for Atlantic Records and became one of the most popular female R&B singers in the early rock era.	
1/15/55	**14**	11	1 Tweedlee Dee	Atlantic 1047
			Juke Box #14 / Best Seller #22	
10/06/56	**22**	11	2 I Can't Love You Enough/	
			Jockey #22 / Top 100 #48	
1/05/57	**97**	1	3 Still	Atlantic 1104
12/29/56+	**17**	19	4 Jim Dandy/	
			Best Seller #17 / Jockey #20 / Top 100 #22	
12/15/56	**94**	1	5 Tra La La	Atlantic 1116
			1, 4 & 5: **LaVERN BAKER & THE GLIDERS**	
			from the film "Rock, Rock, Rock"	
7/01/57	**76**	2	6 Jim Dandy Got Married	Atlantic 1136
9/16/57	**71**	7	7 Humpty Dumpty Heart	Atlantic 1150
			from the film "Mr. Rock & Roll"	
12/08/58+	**6**	21	8 **I Cried A Tear**	Atlantic 2007
4/20/59	**33**	11	9 I Waited Too Long	Atlantic 2021
7/27/59	**52**	10	10 So High So Low/	
8/17/59	**79**	2	11 If You Love Me	Atlantic 2033
11/02/59	**63**	9	12 Tiny Tim	Atlantic 2041
5/02/60	**83**	4	13 Wheel Of Fortune/	
5/23/60	**83**	4	14 Shadows Of Love	Atlantic 2059
11/14/60	**46**	11	15 Bumble Bee	Atlantic 2077

DEBUT DATE	PEAK POS	WKS CHR	ARTIST — Record Title	Label & Number
			LaVERN BAKER — Cont'd	
2/13/61	**81**	3	16 You're The Boss	Atlantic 2090
			LaVERN BAKER & JIMMY RICKS (Ricks died on 7/2/74)	
4/10/61	**37**	7	17 Saved	Atlantic 2099
12/01/62+	**34**	11	18 See See Rider	Atlantic 2167
2/13/65	**84**	2	19 Fly Me To The Moon	Atlantic 2267
1/15/66	**93**	1	20 Think Twice	Brunswick 55287
			JACKIE WILSON & LaVERN BAKER	
			BALANCE	
			New York City rock trio led by Peppy Castro (Blue Magoos founder).	
7/11/81	**22**	17	1 Breaking Away	Portrait 02177
11/21/81+	**58**	11	2 Falling In Love	Portrait 02608
			LONG JOHN BALDRY	
			Influential blues rocker from England. Formed Steampacket with Rod Stewart, and Bluesology with Elton John.	
1/13/68	**88**	2	1 Let The Heartaches Begin	Warner 7098
8/21/71	**73**	7	2 Don't Try To Lay No Boogie-Woogie On The King Of Rock And Roll	Warner 7506
			JOHN BALDRY	
			produced by Rod Stewart	
8/11/79	**89**	3	3 You've Lost That Lovin' Feelin'	EMI America 8018
			LONG JOHN BALDRY & KATHI MacDONALD	
			MARTY BALIN	
			Born on 1/30/43 in Cincinnati. Co-founder of Jefferson Airplane/Jefferson Starship/KBC.	
5/23/81	**8**	21	1 **Hearts**	EMI America 8084
9/19/81	**27**	13	2 Atlanta Lady (Something About Your Love)	EMI America 8093
2/19/83	**63**	6	3 What Love Is	EMI America 8153
			KENNY BALL & His Jazzmen	
			English dixieland jazz band.	
2/03/62	**2**[1]	14	1 **Midnight In Moscow** [I]	Kapp 442
			original Russian title: "Padmeskoveeye Vietchera"	
4/14/62	**88**	1	2 March Of The Siamese Children [I]	Kapp 451
			from the musical "The King And I"	
6/02/62	**87**	6	3 The Green Leaves Of Summer [I]	Kapp 460
			THE BALLADS	
			Vocal group formed in Oakland in 1961. Consisted of Nathan Robertson, Jon Foster, Rico Thompson and Lesley LaPalma.	
7/20/68	**65**	7	1 God Bless Our Love	Venture 615
			HANK BALLARD & The Midnighters	
			Hank was born on 11/18/36 in Detroit. Joined the Royals as lead singer in 1953 (name changed to The Midnighters in 1954). After group disbanded in 1965, re-formed with Frank Stadford, Walter Miller and Wesley Hargrove. Worked in James Brown Revue.	
3/09/59	**87**	3	1 Teardrops On Your Letter	King 5171
5/04/59	**72**	7	2 Kansas City	King 5195
5/16/60	**7**	26	3 **Finger Poppin' Time**	King 5341
7/18/60	**28**	16	4 The Twist	King 5171
			flip side of Hank's 1st charted hit	
9/19/60	**6**	16	5 **Let's Go, Let's Go, Let's Go**	King 5400
12/05/60+	**23**	11	6 The Hoochi Coochi Coo	King 5430
2/20/61	**39**	6	7 Let's Go Again (Where We Went Last Night)	King 5459
4/03/61	**33**	8	8 The Continental Walk	King 5491
6/25/61	**26**	7	9 The Switch-A-Roo/	
6/19/61	**92**	1	10 The Float	King 5510
8/21/61	**49**	3	11 Nothing But Good/	
8/21/61	**66**	5	12 Keep On Dancing	King 5535
2/10/62	**87**	4	13 Do You Know How To Twist	King 5593
			shown only as: **HANK BALLARD**	
			RUSS BALLARD	
			English singer/songwriter - original member of Argent.	
6/14/80	**58**	8	1 On The Rebound	Epic 50883
			BALLIN' JACK	
			Integrated jazz/rock sextet.	
2/13/71	**93**	4	1 Super Highway	Columbia 45312

DEBUT DATE	PEAK POS	WKS CHR	ARTIST — Record Title	Label & Number
			THE BALLOON FARM	
			New York flower-pop quintet.	
2/24/68	**37**	8	1 A Question Of Temperature	Laurie 3405
			BALTIMORA	
			Baltimora is Jimmy McShane from Northern Ireland.	
10/19/85+	**13**	26	1 Tarzan Boy	Manhattan 50018
4/12/86	**87**	4	2 Living In The Background	Manhattan 50029
			THE BALTIMORE & OHIO MARCHING BAND	
10/28/67	**94**	3	1 Lapland [I]	Jubilee 5592
			BAMA	
			Session band from Alabama.	
10/06/79	**86**	5	1 Touch Me When We're Dancing	Free Flight 11629
			AFRIKA BAMBAATAA & the SOUL SONIC FORCE	
			Rapper, street deejay from New York City.	
7/17/82	**48**	11	1 ● Planet Rock certified gold for the 12" single	Tommy Boy 823
			THE BANANA SPLITS	
			Saturday morning TV series featuring 4 live-action animals.	
2/08/69	**96**	1	1 The Tra La La Song (One Banana, Two Banana)	Decca 32429
			BANANARAMA	
			Female trio from London, England: Sarah Dallin, Keren Woodward and Siobhan Fahey.	
7/02/83	**83**	4	1 Shy Boy (Don't It Make You Feel Good)	London 810112
5/19/84	**95**	2	2 Robert De Niro's Waiting	London 820033
7/21/84	**9**	18	3 **Cruel Summer**	London 810127
11/10/84	**70**	8	4 The Wild Life	London 882019
6/28/86	**1**[1]	19	5 **Venus**	London 886056
10/18/86	**73**	5	6 More Than Physical	London 886080
12/27/86+	**76**	7	7 A Trick Of The Night	London 886119
			THE BAND	
			Formed in Woodstock, New York in 1967: Robbie Robertson (guitar), Levon Helm (drums), Rick Danko (bass), Richard Manuel and Garth Hudson (keyboards). All from Canada (except Helm from Arkansas) and all were with Ronnie Hawkins' Hawks. Recorded extensively with Bob Dylan. Disbanded on Thanksgiving Day in 1976. Manuel committed suicide on 3/4/86 (42).	
8/31/68	**63**	7	1 The Weight	Capitol 2269
11/01/69+	**25**	14	2 Up On Cripple Creek	Capitol 2635
2/14/70	**57**	8	3 Rag Mama Rag	Capitol 2705
10/10/70	**77**	4	4 Time To Kill	Capitol 2870
10/16/71	**72**	6	5 Life Is A Carnival	Capitol 3199
9/16/72	**34**	11	6 Don't Do It	Capitol 3433
11/24/73	**73**	7	7 Ain't Got No Home	Capitol 3758
3/20/76	**62**	4	8 Ophelia	Capitol 4230
			BAND AID	
			A benefit recording to assist famine relief in Ethiopia - organized by Bob Geldof of the Boomtown Rats.	
12/22/84+	**13**	9	1 ● Do They Know It's Christmas? [X] with Paul Young, Boy George & Jon Moss (Culture Club), George Michael (Wham!), Sting, Phil Collins, Duran Duran, Bananarama, Spandau Ballet, Paul Weller (Style Council), Boomtown Rats, and members of Kool & The Gang, U2, Ultravox, Status Quo and Heaven 17	Columbia 04749
			BAND OF GOLD	
10/13/84	**64**	7	1 Love Songs Are Back Again Let's Put It All Together/Betcha By Golly Wow/Side Show/ Have You Seen Her/Reunited/You Make Me Feel Brand New/ Kiss And Say Goodbye - medley	RCA 13866
			THE BAND OF THE BLACK WATCH	
			Scottish military unit	
1/31/76	**75**	9	1 Scotch On The Rocks [I]	Private S. 45055
			BANDIT	
3/10/79	**77**	4	1 One Way Love	Ariola 7731

DEBUT DATE	PEAK POS	WKS CHR	ARTIST — Record Title	Label & Number
			BANG	
			Rock trio from Florida. Frank Ferrara, lead singer.	
4/22/72	**90**	6	1 Questions	Capitol 3304
			BANGLES	
			Female rock quartet formed in Los Angeles in January, 1981: sisters Vicki (lead guitar) and Debbi Peterson (drums), Michael Steele (bass) and Susanna Hoffs (guitar). Originally named The Bangs.	
1/25/86	**2^{1}**	20	1 **Manic Monday**	Columbia 05757
5/10/86	**29**	14	2 If She Knew What She Wants	Columbia 05886
9/27/86	**1^{4}**	23	3 **Walk Like An Egyptian**	Columbia 06257
			DARRELL BANKS	
			Born in 1938 in Buffalo. Killed by a gunshot in Detroit, March, 1970.	
7/23/66	**27**	12	1 Open The Door To Your Heart	Revilot 201
10/15/66	**55**	8	2 Somebody (Somewhere) Needs You	Revilot 203
			BANZAII	
10/11/75	**98**	1	1 Chinese Kung Fu [I]	Scepter 12407
			BAR-KAYS	
			R&B instrumental combo consisting of Jimmy King (guitar), Ronnie Caldwell (organ), James Alexander (bass), Carl Cunningham (drums), Phalon Jones (saxophone) and Ben Cauley (trumpet). Formed by Al Jackson, drummer with Booker T & The MG's. The plane crash that killed Otis Redding (10/10/67) also claimed the lives of all the Bar-Kays except Cauley and Alexander (who were not on the plane). Alexander re-formed the band. Appeared in the film "Wattstax"; much session work at Stax.	
5/20/67	**17**	15	1 Soul Finger/ [I]	
9/02/67	**76**	4	2 Knucklehead [I]	Volt 148
10/14/67	**91**	4	3 Give Everybody Some [I]	Volt 154
12/25/71+	**53**	10	4 Son Of Shaft	Volt 4073
10/16/76+	**23**	16	5 Shake Your Rump To The Funk	Mercury 73833
2/12/77	**74**	4	6 Too Hot To Stop (Pt. 1)	Mercury 73888
12/08/79+	**57**	7	7 Move Your Boogie Body	Mercury 76015
3/22/80	**60**	5	8 Today Is The Day	Mercury 76036
5/26/84	**73**	8	9 Freakshow On The Dance Floor from the film "Breakin'"	Mercury 818631
			BARBARA & THE BROWNS	
5/02/64	**97**	2	1 Big Party	Stax 150
			BARBARA & THE UNIQUES	
			Consisted of Barbara Livsey, Gwen Livsey and Doris Lindsey.	
1/02/71	**91**	3	1 There It Goes Again	Arden 3001
			THE BARBARIANS	
			Boston punk garage band.	
9/25/65	**55**	6	1 Are You A Boy Or Are You A Girl	Laurie 3308
2/26/66	**90**	4	2 Moulty title is drummer's nickname, who had a hook for a left hand	Laurie 3326
			CHRIS BARBER'S JAZZ BAND	
			Prolific and popular British dixieland-styled band formed in 1949.	
1/12/59	**5**	15	1 **Petite Fleur (Little Flower)** [I] written in 1952 by jazz great Sidney Bechet - clarinet solo by Monty Sunshine	Laurie 3022
			THE FRANK BARBER ORCHESTRA	
			British band.	
5/08/82	**61**	12	1 Hooked On Big Bands [I] Glenn Miller medley: In The Mood/Pennsylvania 6-5000/I've Got A Gal In Kalamazoo/Moonlight Serenade/Little Brown Jug/Chattanooga Choo Choo/At Last/American Patrol	Victory 1001
			KEITH BARBOUR	
			Singer, songwriter, formerly with the New Christy Minstrels. Married to TV actress Deidre Hall ("Our House" and "Days of Our Lives"), 1971-78.	
9/27/69	**40**	9	1 Echo Park	Epic 10486
			EDDIE BARCLAY	
			Head of the French recording company 'Compagnie Phonographique Francaise'.	
7/16/55	**18**	1	1 The Bandit (O'Cangaceiro) [I] Juke Box #18	Tico 249

DEBUT DATE	PEAK POS	WKS CHR	ARTIST — Record Title	Label & Number
			BOBBY BARE	
			Born in Ironton, Ohio on 4/7/35. Country singer, songwriter, guitarist.	
12/22/58+	**2**[1]	16	1 **The All American Boy** [N]	Fraternity 835
			written by Bill Parsons, but Bobby Bare is the real vocalist on this song (label error listed Parsons as the artist) - upon it's release, Bare was in the Army, so Parsons toured with the hit, lip synching to the record	
7/21/62	**23**	12	2 Shame On Me	RCA 8032
6/15/63	**16**	12	3 Detroit City	RCA 8183
10/05/63	**10**	11	4 **500 Miles Away From Home**	RCA 8238
2/08/64	**33**	7	5 Miller's Cave	RCA 8294
5/16/64	**94**	1	6 Have I Stayed Away Too Long	RCA 8358
10/31/64	**60**	7	7 Four Strong Winds	RCA 8443
1/05/74	**41**	8	8 Daddy What If [N]	RCA 0197
			with 5 year-old son, Bobby, Jr.	
			CHERYL BARNES	
			Co-starred in the movie "Hair".	
4/28/79	**64**	7	1 Easy To Be Hard	RCA 11548
			from the soundtrack of "Hair"	
			JIMMY BARNES	
			R&B singer from Newark, New Jersey.	
3/09/59	**90**	2	1 No Regrets	Gibraltar 101
			JIMMY BARNES	
			Former lead singer of Australian rock group Cold Chisel.	
3/22/86	**74**	8	1 Working Class Man	Geffen 28749
			from the film "Gung Ho"	
			J.J. BARNES	
			Born James Jay Barnes on 11/30/43 in Detroit. First recorded for Kable in 1961. Also see The Holidays.	
4/09/66	**80**	5	1 Real Humdinger	Ric-Tic 110
5/20/67	**61**	10	2 Baby Please Come Back Home	Groovesville 1006
			H.B. BARNUM	
			Born on 7/15/36 in Houston, Texas.	
1/09/61	**35**	7	1 Lost Love [I]	Eldo 111
			RICHARD BARRETT	
			Vocalist, pianist, composer, producer. Lead singer with Valentines. Manager of the Three Degrees from 1964.	
4/28/58	**94**	1	1 Smoke Gets In Your Eyes	MGM 12616
7/20/59	**93**	2	2 Summer's Love	Gone 5060
			RICHARD BARRETT with THE CHANTELS	
			RAY BARRETTO	
			Brooklyn percussionist with Tito Puente and Herbie Mann.	
4/27/63	**17**	9	1 El Watusi [F-N]	Tico 419
			THE BARRON KNIGHTS	
8/25/79	**70**	3	1 The Topical Song [N]	Epic 50755
			parody of Supertramp's "The Logical Song"	
			BARRY & THE TAMERLANES	
			Pop trio led by Barry DeVorzon.	
10/19/63	**21**	10	1 I Wonder What She's Doing Tonight	Valiant 6034
			CLAUDJA BARRY	
			Dance/disco singer from Jamaica. Raised in Toronto, Canada. Appeared in musicals "Hair" and "Catch My Soul".	
2/25/78	**72**	9	1 Dancin' Fever	Salsoul 2058
4/14/79	**56**	12	2 Boogie Woogie Dancin' Shoes	Chrysalis 2313
			JOE BARRY	
			Real name: Joe Barrios. R&B vocalist, guitarist from Cut Off, Louisiana.	
4/24/61	**24**	12	1 I'm A Fool To Care	Smash 1702
7/31/61	**63**	5	2 Teardrops In My Heart	Smash 1710
			JOHN BARRY	
			Born on 11/3/33 in York, England. Prolific movie soundtrack composer/conductor.	
3/13/65	**72**	3	1 Goldfinger [I]	United Art. 791
			from the film of the same title	

DEBUT DATE	PEAK POS	WKS CHR	ARTIST — Record Title	Label & Number
			LEN BARRY	
			Born Leonard Borisoff on 12/6/42. Lead singer of the Dovells through 1963.	
5/29/65	**84**	4	1 Lip Sync (To The Tongue Twisters)	Decca 31788
9/25/65	**2**[1]	15	2 **1-2-3**	Decca 31827
1/01/66	**27**	9	3 Like A Baby	Decca 31889
3/19/66	**26**	8	4 Somewhere	Decca 31923
6/18/66	**91**	3	5 It's That Time Of The Year	Decca 31969
9/17/66	**98**	2	6 I Struck It Rich	Decca 32011
			CHRIS BARTLEY	
			Born on 4/17/49 in New York City. Soul singer.	
7/22/67	**32**	7	1 The Sweetest Thing This Side Of Heaven	Vando 101
			COUNT BASIE	
			Born William Basie on 8/21/04 in Red Bank, New Jersey. Died on 4/26/84. Pianist, organist, bandleader. Learned music and piano from mother, organ from Fats Waller. First recorded with own band in 1937 for Decca. Many films and continued touring into the 70s.	
1/14/56	**28**	13	1 April In Paris [I] song written in 1932	Clef 89162
8/18/58	**100**	1	2 Going To Chicago Blues vocals: Joe Williams, Jon Hendrix, Dave Lambert & Annie Ross	Roulette 4088
1/13/62	**94**	2	3 The Basie Twist [I] above 3: **COUNT BASIE & HIS ORCHESTRA**	Roulette 4403
6/01/63	**77**	9	4 I Can't Stop Loving You [I]	Reprise 20170
2/17/68	**49**	7	5 For Your Precious Love	Brunswick 55365
4/27/68	**84**	5	6 Chain Gang above 2: **JACKIE WILSON & COUNT BASIE**	Brunswick 55373
			TONI BASIL	
			Los Angeles vocalist, actress, choreographer, and video director.	
9/04/82	**1**[1]	27	1 ▲ **Mickey**	Chrysalis 2638
2/26/83	**77**	4	2 Shoppin' From A To Z	Chrysalis 03537
1/21/84	**81**	6	3 Over My Head	Chrysalis 42753
			THE BASKERVILLE HOUNDS	
10/11/69	**88**	2	1 Hold Me	Avco Embassy 4504
			FONTELLA BASS	
			Born on 7/3/40 in St. Louis. Vocalist, pianist, organist. Mother was a member of Clara Ward Gospel Troupe. Sang in church choirs; with Oliver Sain Band, St. Louis; with Little Milton blues show to 1964. Married to trumpet player Lester Bowie.	
2/06/65	**33**	11	1 Don't Mess Up A Good Thing	Checker 1097
5/29/65	**91**	2	2 You'll Miss Me (When I'm Gone) above 2: **FONTELLA BASS & BOBBY McCLURE**	Checker 1111
10/02/65	**4**	13	3 **Rescue Me**	Checker 1120
12/25/65+	**37**	8	4 Recovery	Checker 1131
3/26/66	**78**	6	5 I Surrender	Checker 1137
8/27/66	**100**	1	6 Safe And Sound	Checker 1147
			SHIRLEY BASSEY	
			Born on 1/8/37 in Cardiff, Wales.	
1/30/65	**8**	13	1 **Goldfinger** from the James Bond movie	United Art. 790
9/19/70	**55**	9	2 Something	United Art. 50698
1/29/72	**57**	9	3 Diamonds Are Forever another James Bond soundtrack title	United Art. 50845
6/02/73	**48**	11	4 Never, Never, Never	United Art. 211
			BATDORF & RODNEY	
			John Batdorf & Mark Rodney - John formed the group Silver.	
8/09/75	**87**	7	1 You Are A Song	Arista 0132
12/13/75	**69**	3	2 Somewhere In The Night	Arista 0159
			DUKE BAXTER	
7/26/69	**52**	6	1 Everybody Knows Matilda	VMC 740

DEBUT DATE	PEAK POS	WKS CHR	ARTIST — Record Title		Label & Number
			LES BAXTER		
			Born 3/14/22 in Mexia, Texas. Began as a conductor on radio shows in the 30s. Musical arranger for Capitol Records in the 50s.		
4/09/55	**1[2]**	21	1 **Unchained Melody/**		
			Jockey #1 / Best Seller #2 / Juke Box #3		
			from the film "Unchained"		
		1	2 Medic (Blue Star)	[I]	Capitol 3055
			Best Seller flip		
			theme from the TV series "Medic"		
8/13/55	**5**	12	3 **Wake The Town And Tell The People**		Capitol 3120
			Jockey #5 / Juke Box #8 / Best Seller #10 / Top 100 #24 pre		
			vocal: The Notables		
2/11/56	**1[6]**	24	4 **The Poor People Of Paris**	[I]	Capitol 3336
			Top 100 #1(6) / Jockey #1(6) / Best Seller #1(4) / Juke Box #1(3)		
2/11/56	**80**	3	5 The Trouble With Harry		Capitol 3291
			inspired by the film of the same title		
5/19/56	**44**	9	6 Tango Of The Drums/	[I]	
6/30/56	**82**	1	7 Sinner Man		Capitol 3404
			vocal: Will Holt		
10/20/56	**63**	5	8 Giant		Capitol 3526
			from the film of the same title		
12/22/56	**82**	1	9 The Left Arm Of Buddha	[I]	Capitol 3573
			BAY CITY ROLLERS		
			Formed in 1967 in Edinburgh, Scotland as the Saxons. Original members: brothers Alan & Derek Longmuir, Les McKeoun (lead singer), Eric Faulkner and Stuart "Woody" Wood.		
10/11/75+	**1[1]**	17	1 ● **Saturday Night**		Arista 0149
2/07/76	**9**	15	2 **Money Honey**		Arista 0170
5/01/76	**28**	9	3 Rock And Roll Love Letter		Arista 0185
9/04/76	**12**	16	4 I Only Want To Be With You		Arista 0205
12/11/76+	**54**	7	5 Yesterday's Hero		Arista 0216
2/12/77	**60**	7	6 Dedication		Arista 0233
6/04/77	**10**	17	7 **You Made Me Believe In Magic**		Arista 0256
10/15/77+	**24**	17	8 The Way I Feel Tonight		Arista 0272
			BAZUKA [Tony Camillo's]		
			Instrumental studio group assembled by producer Tony Camillo.		
4/12/75	**10**	20	1 **Dynomite - Part I**	[I]	A&M 1666
			B. BUMBLE & THE STINGERS		
			Session musicians featuring Ernie Freeman on piano.		
3/27/61	**21**	10	1 Bumble Boogie	[I]	Rendezvous 140
			adaptation of Rimsky-Korsakov's "Flight Of The Bumble Bee"		
7/10/61	**89**	1	2 Boogie Woogie	[I]	Rendezvous 151
			written in 1928 by pianist Clarence "Pinetop" Smith		
3/03/62	**23**	11	3 Nut Rocker	[I]	Rendezvous 166
			adapted from Tchaikovsky's "The Nutcracker"		
			THE BEACH BOYS		
			Group formed in Hawthorne, California in 1961. Consisted of brothers Brian (keyboards, bass), Carl (guitar), and Dennis Wilson (drums); their cousin Mike Love (lead vocals, saxophone), and Al Jardine (guitar). Known in high school as Kenny & The Cadets, Carl & The Passsions, then The Pendletones. First recorded for X/Candix in 1961. Jardine was replaced by David Marks from March, 1962 to March, 1963. Brian replaced by Bruce Johnston for personal appearances since April, 1965. Dennis Wilson drowned on 12/28/83 (39).		
2/17/62	**75**	6	1 Surfin		Candix 331
8/11/62	**14**	17	2 Surfin' Safari/		
10/13/62	**76**	1	3 409		Capitol 4777
12/01/62+	**49**	8	4 Ten Little Indians		Capitol 4880
3/23/63	**3**	17	5 **Surfin' U.S.A./**		
4/27/63	**23**	13	6 Shut Down		Capitol 4932
8/03/63	**7**	14	7 **Surfer Girl/**		
8/17/63	**15**	11	8 Little Deuce Coupe		Capitol 5009
11/02/63	**6**	12	9 **Be True To Your School/**		
			featuring cheerleading by The Honeys, and the march "On Wisconsin"		
11/02/63	**23**	11	10 In My Room		Capitol 5069
2/15/64	**5**	11	11 **Fun, Fun, Fun**		Capitol 5118
5/23/64	**1[2]**	15	12 ● **I Get Around/**		
5/30/64	**24**	10	13 Don't Worry Baby		Capitol 5174

DEBUT DATE	PEAK POS	WKS CHR	ARTIST — Record Title	Label & Number
			THE BEACH BOYS — Cont'd	
9/05/64	**9**	10	14 **When I Grow Up (To Be A Man)**	Capitol 5245
10/17/64	**44**	6	15 Wendy/	
10/17/64	**65**	5	16 Little Honda	Capitol R5267
			above 2 from the E.P. "4-By The Beach Boys"	
11/07/64	**8**	11	17 **Dance, Dance, Dance**	Capitol 5306
2/27/65	**12**	8	18 Do You Wanna Dance?/	
3/06/65	**52**	5	19 Please Let Me Wonder	Capitol 5372
4/17/65	**1^{2}**	14	20 **Help Me, Rhonda**	Capitol 5395
7/24/65	**3**	11	21 **California Girls**	Capitol 5464
11/27/65+	**20**	8	22 The Little Girl I Once Knew	Capitol 5540
1/01/66	**2^{2}**	11	23 **Barbara Ann**	Capitol 5561
			featuring lead vocal by Dean Torrence of Jan & Dean	
4/02/66	**3**	11	24 **Sloop John B**	Capitol 5602
			originally a folk song originating from the West Indies in 1927	
7/30/66	**8**	11	25 **Wouldn't It Be Nice/**	
8/13/66	**39**	8	26 God Only Knows	Capitol 5706
10/22/66	**1^{1}**	14	27 ● **Good Vibrations**	Capitol 5676
8/05/67	**12**	7	28 Heroes And Villains	Brother 1001
11/04/67	**31**	6	29 Wild Honey	Capitol 2028
12/23/67+	**19**	9	30 Darlin'	Capitol 2068
4/20/68	**47**	7	31 Friends	Capitol 2160
7/27/68	**20**	10	32 Do It Again	Capitol 2239
12/14/68	**61**	6	33 Bluebirds Over The Mountain	Capitol 2360
3/08/69	**24**	10	34 I Can Hear Music	Capitol 2432
7/05/69	**63**	6	35 Break Away	Capitol 2530
3/07/70	**64**	5	36 Add Some Music To Your Day	Brother 0894
10/30/71	**89**	5	37 Long Promised Road	Brother 1047
2/24/73	**79**	7	38 Sail On Sailor	Brother 1138
5/12/73	**84**	4	39 California Saga (On My Way To Sunny Californ-i-a)	Brother 1156
8/17/74	**36**	8	40 Surfin' U.S.A. [R]	Capitol 3924
			song now legally credited as Chuck Berry's "Sweet Little 16"	
4/12/75	**49**	10	41 Sail On Sailor [R]	Brother 1325
6/05/76	**5**	17	42 **Rock And Roll Music**	Brother 1354
8/21/76	**29**	10	43 It's O.K.	Brother 1368
9/09/78	**59**	6	44 Peggy Sue	Brother 1394
3/03/79	**44**	8	45 Here Comes The Night	Caribou 9026
4/28/79	**40**	10	46 Good Timin'	Caribou 9029
4/12/80	**83**	3	47 Goin' On	Caribou 9032
7/25/81	**12**	18	48 The Beach Boys Medley	Capitol 5030
			Good Vibrations/Help Me Rhonda/I Get Around/Shut Down/ Surfin' Safari/Barbara Ann/Surfin' USA/Fun, Fun, Fun	
11/21/81+	**18**	15	49 Come Go With Me	Caribou 02633
5/25/85	**26**	12	50 Getcha Back	Caribou 04913
8/03/85	**82**	5	51 It's Gettin' Late	Caribou 05433
6/28/86	**68**	6	52 Rock 'N' Roll To The Rescue	Capitol 5595
9/20/86	**57**	10	53 California Dreamin'	Capitol 5630
			electric 12-string guitar solo by Roger McGuinn	
			BEASTIE BOYS	
			New York white rap trio formed in 1981, consisting of King Ad-Rock (Adam Horovitz - son of playwright Israel Horovitz), MCA (Adam Yauch) and Mike D (Michael Diamond).	
12/20/86+	**7**	18	1 **(You Gotta) Fight For Your Right (To Party!)**	Def Jam 06595
			THE BEATLES	
			The World's #1 rock group was formed in Liverpool, England in the late 1950s. Known in early forms as the Quarrymen, Johnny & the Moondogs, The Rainbows, and the Silver Beatles. Named The Beatles in 1960. Originally consisted of John Lennon, Paul McCartney, George Harrison (guitars), Stu Sutcliffe (bass) and Pete Best (drums). Sutcliffe left in April, 1961 (died on 4/10/62); McCartney moved to bass. Best replaced by Ringo Starr in August, 1962. Group managed by Brian Epstein (died on 8/27/67) and produced by George Martin. First US tour in February, 1964. Own Apple label in 1968. Disbanded on 4/17/70.	
1/18/64	**1^{7}**	15	1 ● **I Want To Hold Your Hand/**	
2/08/64	**14**	11	2 I Saw Her Standing There	Capitol 5112
1/25/64	**1^{2}**	15	3 **She Loves You**	Swan 4152

DEBUT DATE	PEAK POS	WKS CHR	ARTIST — Record Title	Label & Number
			THE BEATLES — Cont'd	
2/01/64	**3**	13	4 **Please Please Me/**	
3/07/64	**41**	6	5 From Me To You	Vee-Jay 581
2/15/64	**26**	6	6 My Bonnie	MGM 13213
			THE BEATLES with TONY SHERIDAN	
3/14/64	**2**[4]	11	7 **Twist And Shout/**	
4/11/64	**74**	1	8 There's A Place	Tollie 9001
3/28/64	**45**	6	9 All My Loving	Capitol 72144
3/21/64	**68**	4	10 Roll Over Beethoven	Capitol 72133
			above two records released by Capitol of Canada	
3/28/64	**1**[5]	10	11 ● **Can't Buy Me Love/**	
4/04/64	**48**	4	12 You Can't Do That	Capitol 5150
3/28/64	**2**[1]	11	13 **Do You Want To Know A Secret/**	
4/04/64	**35**	7	14 Thank You Girl	Vee-Jay 587
4/11/64	**1**[1]	14	15 **Love Me Do/**	
5/09/64	**10**	8	16 **P.S. I Love You**	Tollie 9008
4/18/64	**88**	1	17 Why	MGM 13227
			THE BEATLES with TONY SHERIDAN	
6/13/64	**92**	3	18 Four By The Beatles	Capitol 1-2121
			4-track E.P.: Roll Over Beethoven/All My Loving/This Boy/ Please Mr. Postman	
6/27/64	**97**	1	19 Sie Liebt Dich [F]	Swan 4182
			German version of "She Loves You"	
7/18/64	**19**	9	20 Ain't She Sweet	Atco 6308
7/18/64	**1**[2]	13	21 ● **A Hard Day's Night/**	
7/25/64	**53**	4	22 I Should Have Known Better	Capitol 5222
7/25/64	**12**	9	23 And I Love Her/	
8/01/64	**53**	9	24 If I Fell	Capitol 5235
8/01/64	**25**	7	25 I'll Cry Instead/	
8/01/64	**95**	1	26 I'm Happy Just To Dance With You	Capitol 5234
			above 6 tunes are from the film "A Hard Day's Night"	
9/05/64	**17**	8	27 Matchbox/	
9/05/64	**25**	7	28 Slow Down	Capitol 5255
12/05/64	**1**[3]	11	29 ● **I Feel Fine/**	
12/05/64	**4**	9	30 **She's A Woman**	Capitol 5327
2/20/65	**1**[2]	10	31 ● **Eight Days A Week/**	
2/20/65	**39**	6	32 I Don't Want To Spoil The Party	Capitol 5371
2/27/65	**68**	5	33 4-By The Beatles	Capitol R5365
			4-track E.P.: Honey Don't/I'm A Loser/Mr. Moonlight/ Everybody's Trying To Be My Baby	
4/24/65	**1**[1]	11	34 **Ticket To Ride/**	
5/01/65	**46**	4	35 Yes It Is	Capitol 5407
8/07/65	**1**[3]	13	36 ● **Help!**	Capitol 5476
			34, 36: from the film "Help" (originally "Eight Arms To Hold You")	
9/25/65	**1**[4]	11	37 ● **Yesterday/**	
9/25/65	**47**	7	38 Act Naturally	Capitol 5498
12/18/65+	**1**[3]	12	39 ● **We Can Work It Out/**	
12/18/65+	**5**	10	40 **Day Tripper**	Capitol 5555
3/05/66	**3**	9	41 ● **Nowhere Man/**	
3/12/66	**81**	2	42 What Goes On	Capitol 5587
6/11/66	**1**[2]	10	43 ● **Paperback Writer/**	
6/11/66	**23**	7	44 Rain	Capitol 5651
8/20/66	**2**[1]	9	45 ● **Yellow Submarine/**	
			title song from the Beatles' animated film	
8/27/66	**11**	8	46 Eleanor Rigby	Capitol 5715
2/25/67	**1**[1]	10	47 ● **Penny Lane/**	
2/25/67	**8**	9	48 **Strawberry Fields Forever**	Capitol 5810
7/22/67	**1**[1]	11	49 ● **All You Need Is Love/**	
7/29/67	**34**	5	50 Baby You're A Rich Man	Capitol 5964
12/02/67	**1**[3]	11	51 ● **Hello Goodbye/**	
12/09/67	**56**	4	52 I Am The Walrus	Capitol 2056
			from the Beatles' film "Magical Mystery Tour"	
3/23/68	**4**	11	53 ● **Lady Madonna/**	
3/30/68	**96**	1	54 The Inner Light	Capitol 2138

DEBUT DATE	PEAK POS	WKS CHR	ARTIST — Record Title		Label & Number
			THE BEATLES — Cont'd		
9/14/68	1^{9}	19	55 ● **Hey Jude/**		
9/14/68	**12**	11	56 Revolution		Apple 2276
5/10/69	1^{5}	12	57 ● **Get Back/**		
5/10/69	**35**	4	58 Don't Let Me Down above 2 songs with Billy Preston (organ)		Apple 2490
6/14/69	**8**	9	59 ● **The Ballad Of John And Yoko**		Apple 2531
10/18/69	1^{1}	16	60 ● **Come Together/**		
	1	16	61 ● **Something**		Apple 2654
3/21/70	1^{2}	14	62 ● **Let It Be**		Apple 2764
5/23/70	1^{2}	10	63 **The Long And Winding Road/**		
		10	64 For You Blue above 3 tunes from the documentary film "Let It Be"		Apple 2832
6/12/76	**7**	16	65 **Got To Get You Into My Life** from the 1966 album "Revolver"		Capitol 4274
11/20/76	**49**	7	66 Ob-La-Di, Ob-La-Da from the 1968 white album "The Beatles"		Capitol 4347
9/16/78	**71**	7	67 Sgt. Pepper's Lonely Hearts Club Band/ With A Little Help From My Friends from the 1967 album "Sgt. Pepper's Lonely Hearts Club Band"		Capitol 4612
3/27/82	**12**	11	68 The Beatles' Movie Medley Magical Mystery Tour/All You Need Is Love/ You've Got To Hide Your Love Away/I Should Have Known Better/ A Hard Day's Night/Ticket To Ride/Get Back		Capitol 5107
8/09/86	**23**	15	69 Twist And Shout revived through inclusion in films "Ferris Bueller's Day Off" and "Back To School"	[R]	Capitol 5624
			E.C. BEATTY Native of Charlotte, North Carolina.		
9/21/59	**50**	6	1 Ski King	[N]	Colonial 7003
			THE BEAU BRUMMELS Formed in 1964 in San Francisco. Led by Sal Valentino (vocals) and Ron Elliott (guitar).		
1/02/65	**15**	12	1 Laugh, Laugh		Autumn 8
4/17/65	**8**	12	2 **Just A Little**		Autumn 10
7/24/65	**38**	7	3 You Tell Me Why		Autumn 16
10/09/65	**52**	8	4 Don't Talk To Strangers		Autumn 20
12/25/65	**97**	1	5 Good Time Music		Autumn 24
6/04/66	**95**	3	6 One Too Many Mornings		Warner 5813
			THE BEAU-MARKS Pop/rock quartet from Montreal, Canada. Joey Frechette, vocals.		
5/16/60	**45**	14	1 Clap Your Hands		Shad 5017
			JIMMIE BEAUMONT Lead singer of The Skyliners.		
12/25/61	**100**	1	1 Ev'rybody's Cryin'	[N]	May 112
3/22/75	**100**	1	2 Where Have They Gone JIMMY BEAUMONT & THE SKYLINERS		Capitol 3979
			JEAN BEAUVOIR Bass guitarist of the Plasmatics and Little Steven & The Disciples Of Soul.		
6/14/86	**73**	8	1 Feel The Heat from the film "Cobra"		Columbia 05904
			JEFF BECK & ROD STEWART Beck is a veteran British guitarist. With the Yardbirds, 1964-66. Beck and Stewart were members of The Jeff Beck Group from 1967-69. Also see Donovan.		
6/15/85	**48**	10	1 People Get Ready		Epic 05416
			JIMMY BECK Jimmy was born on 12/30/29 in Cleveland.		
4/20/59	**82**	2	1 Pipe Dreams	[I]	Champion 1002
			BOB BECKHAM Stratford, Oklahoma pop/country singer.		
8/10/59	**32**	21	1 Just As Much As Ever		Decca 30861
1/04/60	**36**	13	2 Crazy Arms		Decca 31029

DEBUT DATE	PEAK POS	WKS CHR	ARTIST — Record Title	Label & Number
			BECKMEIER BROTHERS	
			Freddie and Stevie Beckmeier.	
7/28/79	**53**	6	1 Rock And Roll Dancin'	Casablanca 1000
			THE BEE GEES	
			Trio of brothers from Manchester, England: Barry (b: 9/1/47) and twins Robin and Maurice Gibb (b: 12/22/49). First performed December, 1955. To Australia in 1958, performed as the Gibbs, later as BG's, finally the Bee Gees. First recorded for Leedon/Festival in 1963. Returned to England in February, 1967, with guitarist Vince Melouney and drummer Colin Peterson. Toured Europe and USA in 1968. Melouney left in December, 1968, Robin left for solo career in 1969. When Peterson left in August of 1969, Barry and Maurice went solo. After eight months, brothers reunited. Composed soundtracks of "Saturday Night Fever" and "Staying Alive"; in film "Sgt. Pepper's Lonely Hearts Club Band". Group was named for Barry Gibb, Bill Goode (a friend), and Bill Gates (a DJ).	
5/27/67	**14**	7	1 New York Mining Disaster 1941 (Have You Seen My Wife, Mr. Jones)	Atco 6487
7/15/67	**17**	9	2 To Love Somebody	Atco 6503
9/30/67	**16**	9	3 Holiday	Atco 6521
11/11/67	**11**	8	4 (The Lights Went Out In) Massachusetts	Atco 6532
1/20/68	**15**	11	5 Words	Atco 6548
4/06/68	**57**	6	6 Jumbo	Atco 6570
8/17/68	**8**	13	7 **I've Gotta Get A Message To You**	Atco 6603
12/21/68+	**6**	11	8 **I Started A Joke**	Atco 6639
3/22/69	**37**	7	9 First Of May	Atco 6657
5/31/69	**54**	6	10 Tomorrow Tomorrow	Atco 6682
9/20/69	**73**	3	11 Don't Forget To Remember	Atco 6702
3/28/70	**91**	3	12 If Only I Had My Mind On Something Else	Atco 6741
7/11/70	**94**	1	13 I.O.I.O.	Atco 6752
12/05/70+	**3**	14	14 ● **Lonely Days**	Atco 6795
6/26/71	**1^{4}**	15	15 ● **How Can You Mend A Broken Heart**	Atco 6824
10/23/71	**53**	7	16 Don't Wanna Live Inside Myself	Atco 6847
1/29/72	**16**	8	17 My World	Atco 6871
7/29/72	**16**	12	18 Run To Me	Atco 6896
11/18/72	**34**	7	19 Alive	Atco 6909
3/24/73	**94**	3	20 Saw A New Morning	RSO 401
3/09/74	**93**	3	21 Mr. Natural	RSO 408
5/31/75	**1^{2}**	17	22 ● **Jive Talkin'**	RSO 510
10/04/75	**7**	16	23 **Nights On Broadway**	RSO 515
12/27/75+	**12**	16	24 Fanny (Be Tender With My Love)	RSO 519
7/04/76	**1^{1}**	20	25 ● **You Should Be Dancing**	RSO 853
9/18/76	**3**	23	26 ● **Love So Right**	RSO 859
1/15/77	**12**	15	27 Boogie Child	RSO 867
7/23/77	**26**	13	28 Edge Of The Universe	RSO 880
9/24/77	**1^{3}**	33	29 ● **How Deep Is Your Love**	RSO 882
12/10/77+	**1^{4}**	27	30 ▲ **Stayin' Alive**	RSO 885
2/04/78	**1^{8}**	20	31 ▲ **Night Fever**	RSO 889
			above 3 tunes from the film "Saturday Night Fever"	
11/18/78+	**1^{2}**	21	32 ▲ **Too Much Heaven**	RSO 913
2/10/79	**1^{2}**	20	33 ▲ **Tragedy**	RSO 918
4/21/79	**1^{1}**	19	34 ● **Love You Inside Out**	RSO 925
9/26/81	**30**	8	35 He's A Liar	RSO 1066
11/07/81	**45**	10	36 Living Eyes	RSO 1067
5/21/83	**24**	11	37 The Woman In You	RSO 813173
8/20/83	**49**	6	38 Someone Belonging To Someone	RSO 815235
			above 2 from the film "Staying Alive"	
			JOHNNY BEECHER	
			Real name: Plas Johnson - British saxophonist.	
3/02/63	**65**	8	1 Sax Fifth Avenue [I]	Warner 5341
			with the Buckingham Road Quintet	
			THE BEGINNING OF THE END	
			Consisted of brothers Ray (organ), Roy (guitar) & Bud Munnings (drums); and Fred Henfield (bass).	
5/08/71	**15**	14	1 Funky Nassau-Part I	Alston 4595

DEBUT DATE	PEAK POS	WKS CHR	ARTIST — Record Title	Label & Number
			HARRY BELAFONTE Born Harold George Belafonte, Jr. on 3/1/27 in Harlem. Actor in American Negro Theater, Drama Workshop, mid-40s. Started career as a "straight pop" singer. Recorded for Jubilee Records in 1949, shortly afterward began specializing in folk music. Rode the crest of the calypso craze to worldwide stardom. Starred in eight films from 1953-74. Replaced Danny Kaye in 1987 as the goodwill ambassador for UNICEF.	
10/20/56+	**14**	26	1 Jamaica Farewell Jockey #14 / Best Seller #17 / Top 100 #17 / Juke Box #17	RCA 6663
12/22/56	**12**	5	2 Mary's Boy Child [X] Best Seller #12 / Jockey #12 / Top 100 #15	RCA 6735
1/12/57	**5**	20	3 **Banana Boat (Day-O)** Best Seller #5 / Top 100 #5 / Jockey #5 / Juke Box #5	RCA 6771
3/09/57	**84**	4	4 Hold 'Em Joe/ from the Broadway show "John Murray Anderson's Almanac"	
		3	5 I'm Just A Country Boy Coming Up flip	RCA 0322
3/23/57	**11**	20	6 Mama Look At Bubu/ Best Seller #11 / Top 100 #13 / Jockey #14 / Juke Box #18	
4/20/57	**90**	2	7 Don't Ever Love Me	RCA 6830
6/03/57	**25**	18	8 Island In The Sun/ Best Seller #25 / Top 100 #42 from the film (starring Belafonte) of the same title	
6/03/57	**48**	10	9 Cocoanut Woman	RCA 6885
			BELL & JAMES R&B duo: Leroy Bell and Casey James. Began as songwriting team for Bell's uncle, producer Thom Bell.	
1/27/79	**15**	16	1 ● Livin' It Up (Friday Night)	A&M 2069
			THE BELL NOTES Quintet from Long Island, NY. Consisted of Carl Bonura, sax; Ray Ceroni, guitar; Lenny Giamblavo, bass; Peter Kane, piano; and John Casey, drums.	
1/26/59	**6**	16	1 **I've Had It**	Time 1004
5/04/59	**76**	7	2 Old Spanish Town	Time 1010
8/29/60	**96**	2	3 Shortnin' Bread	Madison 136
			ARCHIE BELL & THE DRELLS Archie was born on 9/1/44 in Henderson, Texas. Lead singer of the Drells, R&B vocal group from Leo Smith Junior High School in Houston. First recorded for Ovid in 1967. Recorded "Tighten Up" with group consisting of Bell, Huey "Billy" Butler, Joe Cross and James Wise. Backed by TSU Tornadoes band. Bell was in US Army at time of hit.	
3/30/68	**1^{2}**	15	1 ● **Tighten Up**	Atlantic 2478
7/20/68	**9**	10	2 **I Can't Stop Dancing**	Atlantic 2534
9/28/68	**44**	7	3 Do The Choo Choo	Atlantic 2559
12/14/68+	**21**	11	4 There's Gonna Be A Showdown	Atlantic 2583
3/29/69	**94**	3	5 I Love My Baby	Atlantic 2612
6/21/69	**59**	7	6 Girl You're Too Young	Atlantic 2644
9/13/69	**87**	4	7 My Balloon's Going Up	Atlantic 2663
12/27/69+	**90**	2	8 A World Without Music	Atlantic 2693
4/18/70	**100**	1	9 Don't Let The Music Slip Away	Atlantic 2721
12/12/70	**93**	2	10 Wrap It Up song a hit in 1986 for The Fabulous Thunderbirds	Atlantic 2768
3/17/73	**61**	9	11 Dancing To Your Music	Glades 1707
			BENNY BELL Jewish risque songwriter from New York City.	
3/08/75	**30**	11	1 Shaving Cream [N] originally released in 1946 - Paul Wynn, vocal	Vanguard 35183
			MADELINE BELL Vocalist. Toured England, mid-1960s, remained in that country. Formed group Blue Mink, 1969-1973.	
2/10/68	**26**	9	1 I'm Gonna Make You Love Me	Philips 40517
			MAGGIE BELL Born on 1/12/45 in Glasgow, Scotland. Lead singer of Stone The Crows.	
5/11/74	**97**	3	1 After Midnight	Atlantic 3018
			RANDY BELL	
7/07/84	**90**	3	1 Don't Do Me	Epic 04497

DEBUT DATE	PEAK POS	WKS CHR	ARTIST — Record Title	Label & Number
			VINCENT BELL	
			Veteran studio guitarist. Leader of the Ramrods.	
4/11/70	**31**	8	1 Airport Love Theme .... [I] from the film "Airport"	Decca 32659
			WILLIAM BELL	
			Born William Yarborough on 7/16/39 in Memphis, TN. Own Peachtree and Wilbe labels.	
4/28/62	**95**	1	1 You Don't Miss Your Water	Stax 116
4/15/67	**95**	2	2 Everybody Loves A Winner	Stax 212
4/27/68	**86**	6	3 A Tribute To A King .... tribute to Otis Redding	Stax 248
8/31/68	**75**	6	4 Private Number .... **JUDY CLAY & WILLIAM BELL**	Stax 0005
1/04/69	**45**	9	5 I Forgot To Be Your Lover	Stax 0015
2/19/77	**10**	15	6● **Tryin' To Love Two**	Mercury 73839
			THE BELLAMY BROTHERS	
			David and Howard Bellamy. Popular Country duo.	
1/31/76	**1**[1]	19	1 **Let Your Love Flow**	Warner 8169
7/10/76	**70**	3	2 Hell Cat	Warner 8220
9/11/76	**73**	3	3 Satin Sheets	Warner 8248
5/26/79	**39**	11	4 If I Said You Have A Beautiful Body Would You Hold It Against Me	Warner 8790
			DAVID BELLAMY	
			One of the Bellamy Brothers.	
9/20/75	**77**	6	1 Nothin' Heavy	Warner 8123
			BELLE EPOQUE	
			Female disco trio from Paris, France.	
3/11/78	**92**	4	1 Miss Broadway	Big Tree 16109
			THE BELLE STARS	
			English female septet.	
5/07/83	**75**	4	1 Sign Of The Times	Warner 29672
			THE BELLS	
			Jacki Ralph & Cliff Edwards, lead singers of Canadian quintet.	
1/09/71	**95**	5	1 Fly Little White Dove Fly	Polydor 15016
3/06/71	**7**	14	2● **Stay Awhile**	Polydor 15023
6/26/71	**64**	5	3 I Love You Lady Dawn	Polydor 15027
			TONY BELLUS	
			Born on 4/17/36 in Chicago. Pop singer, accordionist.	
4/27/59	**25**	26	1 Robbin' The Cradle	NRC 023
			THE BELMONTS	
			Angelo D'Aleo, Fred Milano and Carlo Mastrangelo. Sang with Dion from 1957-60. Named after Belmont Avenue in New York. Also see Freddy Cannon.	
5/22/61	**18**	11	1 Tell Me Why	Sabrina 500
9/04/61	**57**	9	2 Don't Get Around Much Anymore	Sabrina 501
12/25/61+	**75**	4	3 I Need Some One	Sabina 502
7/21/62	**28**	14	4 Come On Little Angel	Sabina 505
11/17/62	**53**	6	5 Diddle-Dee-Dum (What Happens When Your Love Has Gone)	Sabina 507
4/20/63	**86**	3	6 Ann-Marie	Sabina 509
			JOHN BELUSHI	
			TV and film comedian. Died on 3/5/82 of a drug overdose. Also see Blues Brothers.	
9/30/78	**89**	4	1 Louie, Louie .... from the soundtrack "Animal House"	MCA 40950
			JESSE BELVIN	
			Born Jessie Lorenzo Belvin on 12/15/32 in San Antonio, Texas. Jesse and his wife were killed in an auto accident on 2/6/60. Recorded with Marvin Phillips as "Jesse & Marvin". Wrote "Earth Angel" and helped with lyrics on Alan Feed's sign-off song, "Goodnight My Love". Also see The Cliques, The Chargers, and The Shields.	
12/28/58+	**81**	4	1 Funny	RCA 7387
3/30/59	**31**	13	2 Guess Who .... written by Jesse's wife, Jo Anne Belvin	RCA 7469

DEBUT DATE	PEAK POS	WKS CHR	ARTIST — Record Title	Label & Number
			PAT BENATAR	
			Real name: Patricia Andrzejewski. Born in 1952 in Brooklyn. Married her record producer, Neil Geraldo in 1982.	
12/22/79+	23	18	1 Heartbreaker	Chrysalis 2395
4/05/80	27	14	2 We Live For Love	Chrysalis 2419
7/26/80	42	11	3 You Better Run	Chrysalis 2450
10/04/80	9	24	4● **Hit Me With Your Best Shot**	Chrysalis 2464
1/17/81	18	18	5 Treat Me Right	Chrysalis 2487
7/18/81	17	15	6 Fire And Ice	Chrysalis 2529
10/03/81	38	11	7 Promises In The Dark	Chrysalis 2555
10/16/82	13	16	8 Shadows Of The Night	Chrysalis 2647
2/05/83	20	14	9 Little Too Late	Chrysalis 03536
4/23/83	39	10	10 Looking For A Stranger	Chrysalis 42688
9/24/83	5	22	11 **Love Is A Battlefield**	Chrysalis 42732
10/27/84+	5	20	12 **We Belong**	Chrysalis 42826
1/19/85	36	9	13 Ooh Ooh Song	Chrysalis 42843
7/06/85	10	17	14 **Invincible** theme from the film "Legend of Billie Jean"	Chrysalis 42877
11/23/85+	28	13	15 Sex As A Weapon	Chrysalis 42927
2/15/86	54	8	16 Le Bel Age title pronounced "Lah bell awg" (The Best Year)	Chrysalis 42968
			BOYD BENNETT & His Rockets	
			Born in Muscle Shoals, Alabama. Attended high school in Tennessee and formed first band there. Later became a disc jockey in Kentucky.	
7/09/55	5	17	1 **Seventeen** Best Seller #5 / Juke Box #8 / Jockey #9 / Top 100 #28 pre	King 1470
11/12/55	39	8	2 My Boy - Flat Top vocal by Big Moe on above 2 songs	King 1494
4/14/56	63	10	3 Blue Suede Shoes	King 4903
9/21/59	73	4	4 Boogie Bear [N] BOYD BENNETT	Mercury 71479
			JOE BENNETT & THE SPARKLETONES	
			Teenage band from Spartanburg, SC. Consisted of Joe Bennett, vocals, guitar; Howard Childress, guitar; Wayne Arthur, bass; and Irving Denton, drums.	
8/26/57	17	19	1 Black Slacks Top 100 #17 / Best Seller #18 / Jockey #21	ABC-Para. 9837
12/23/57	42	8	2 Penny Loafers And Bobby Socks Best Seller #42 / Top 100 #43	ABC-Para. 9867
			TONY BENNETT	
			Born Anthony Benedetto on 8/13/26 in Queens, NY. Worked local clubs while in high school, sang in US Army bands. Audition record of "Boulevard Of Broken Dreams" earned a Columbia contract in 1950.	
4/14/56	16	19	1 Can You Find It In Your Heart Best Seller #16 / Juke Box #18 / Top 100 #19 / Jockey #20	Columbia 40667
8/18/56	11	12	2 From The Candy Store On The Corner To The Chapel On The Hill/ female vocal: Lois Winter Jockey #11 / Top 100 #33	
8/18/56	38	14	3 Happiness Street (Corner Sunshine Square)	Columbia 40726
11/10/56	18	8	4 The Autumn Waltz/ Jockey #18 / Top 100 #41	
11/10/56	46	14	5 Just In Time from the Broadway show "Bells Are Ringing"	Columbia 40770
5/20/57	49	9	6 One For My Baby (And One More For The Road)	Columbia 40907
8/05/57	9	21	7 **In The Middle Of An Island/** Best Seller #9 / Top 100 #9 / Jockey #13	
8/19/57	93	1	8 I Am	Columbia 40965
11/18/57	22	2	9 Ca, C'est L'amour Jockey #22 / Top 100 #96 from the film "Les Girls"	Columbia 41032
6/23/58	23	8	10 Young And Warm And Wonderful Jockey #23 / Best Seller #42 / Top 100 #57	Columbia 41172
9/08/58	20	13	11 Firefly Hot 100 #20 / Best Seller #45 end	Columbia 41237
8/17/59	73	6	12 Smile	Columbia 41434
12/21/59+	74	5	13 Climb Ev'ry Mountain from Broadway's "The Sound Of Music"	Columbia 41520
8/11/62	19	21	14 I Left My Heart In San Francisco	Columbia 42332

DEBUT DATE	PEAK POS	WKS CHR	ARTIST — Record Title	Label & Number
			TONY BENNETT — Cont'd	
1/12/63	**14**	16	15 I Wanna Be Around/	
1/05/63	**85**	8	16 I Will Live My Life For You	Columbia 42634
5/11/63	**18**	10	17 The Good Life/	
6/08/63	**92**	2	18 Spring In Manhattan	Columbia 42779
7/20/63	**70**	7	19 This Is All I Ask/	
7/27/63	**99**	2	20 True Blue Lou	Columbia 42820
10/12/63	**54**	7	21 Don't Wait Too Long	Columbia 42886
12/21/63+	**52**	9	22 The Little Boy	Columbia 42931
3/21/64	**94**	5	23 When Joanna Loved Me	Columbia 42996
7/11/64	**99**	1	24 It's A Sin To Tell A Lie/	
8/22/64	**94**	3	25 A Taste Of Honey	Columbia 43073
10/03/64	**33**	10	26 Who Can I Turn To (When Nobody Needs Me) from the musical "The Roar Of The Greasepaint"	Columbia 43141
2/13/65	**34**	9	27 If I Ruled The World from the musical "Pickwick"	Columbia 43220
7/24/65	**84**	4	28 Fly Me To The Moon (In Other Words)	Columbia 43331
11/13/65	**95**	6	29 Love Theme From "The Sandpiper" (The Shadow Of Your Smile)	Columbia 43431
7/23/66	**89**	4	30 Georgia Rose	Columbia 43715
10/28/67	**91**	5	31 For Once In My Life	Columbia 44258
			GEORGE BENSON Born on 3/22/43 in Pittsburgh. Played guitar from age eight. Played in Brother Jack McDuff's trio, 1964. House musician at CTI Records to early 1970's. Influenced heavily by Wes Montgomery.	
6/12/76	**10**	19	1 **This Masquerade**	Warner 8209
10/16/76	**63**	6	2 Breezin' [I]	Warner 8268
7/02/77	**71**	5	3 Gonna Love You More	Warner 8377
7/30/77	**24**	14	4 The Greatest Love Of All from the film "The Greatest" - #1 song for Whitney Houston, 1986	Arista 0251
3/11/78	**7**	18	5 **On Broadway**	Warner 8542
2/24/79	**18**	15	6 Love Ballad	Warner 8759
7/05/80	**4**	23	7 **Give Me The Night**	Warner 49505
10/18/80	**61**	6	8 Love X Love	Warner 49570
8/29/81	**46**	10	9 Love All The Hurt Away ARETHA FRANKLIN & GEORGE BENSON	Arista 0624
10/24/81+	**5**	22	10 **Turn Your Love Around**	Warner 49846
2/20/82	**52**	9	11 Never Give Up On A Good Thing	Warner 50005
5/14/83	**43**	10	12 Inside Love (So Personal)	Warner 29649
7/23/83	**30**	13	13 Lady Love Me (One More Time)	Warner 29563
12/15/84+	**48**	13	14 20/20	Warner 29120
			BROOK BENTON Born Benjamin Franklin Peay on 9/19/31 in Camden, SC. Sang with the Camden Jubilee Singers. To New York in 1948, joined Bill Langford's Langfordaires. With Jerusalem Stars in 1951. First recorded under own name for Okeh in 1953.	
3/10/58	**82**	4	1 A Million Miles From Nowhere	Vik 0311
1/26/59	**3**	18	2 **It's Just A Matter Of Time/**	
2/23/59	**78**	4	3 Hurtin' Inside	Mercury 71394
4/20/59	**12**	13	4 Endlessly/	
5/18/59	**38**	7	5 So Close	Mercury 71443
7/13/59	**16**	14	6 Thank You Pretty Baby/	
7/20/59	**82**	1	7 With All Of My Heart	Mercury 71478
10/19/59	**6**	16	8 **So Many Ways**	Mercury 71512
12/21/59	**66**	5	9 This Time Of The Year [X]	Mercury 71554
1/25/60	**5**	15	10 **Baby (You've Got What It Takes)** DINAH WASHINGTON & BROOK BENTON	Mercury 71565
4/11/60	**37**	9	11 The Ties That Bind/	
4/18/60	**58**	6	12 Hither And Thither And Yon	Mercury 71566
5/23/60	**7**	13	13 **A Rockin' Good Way (To Mess Around And Fall In Love)** DINAH WASHINGTON & BROOK BENTON	Mercury 71629
8/08/60	**7**	17	14 **Kiddio/**	
8/22/60	**16**	12	15 The Same One	Mercury 71652

DEBUT DATE	PEAK POS	WKS CHR	ARTIST — Record Title		Label & Number
			BROOK BENTON — Cont'd		
11/14/60	**24**	10	16 Fools Rush In/		
12/26/60	**93**	1	17 Someday You'll Want Me To Want You		Mercury 71722
2/13/61	**11**	12	18 Think Twice/		
2/06/61	**28**	8	19 For My Baby		Mercury 71774
5/15/61	**2**[3]	16	20 **The Boll Weevil Song**	[N]	Mercury 71820
8/21/61	**20**	8	21 Frankie And Johnny/		
			one of many versions of classic song (originated around 1850)		
10/02/61	**45**	5	22 It's Just A House Without You		Mercury 71859
11/20/61+	**15**	10	23 Revenge		Mercury 71903
1/13/62	**19**	9	24 Shadrack/		
			written in 1931 as "Shadrack Meshack, Abednigo)		
1/13/62	**77**	2	25 The Lost Penny	[S]	Mercury 71912
2/17/62	**43**	7	26 Walk On The Wild Side		Mercury 71925
			from the film of the same title		
5/05/62	**45**	8	27 Hit Record		Mercury 71962
8/25/62	**13**	10	28 Lie To Me		Mercury 72024
11/24/62+	**3**	12	29 **Hotel Happiness/**		
12/08/62	**89**	1	30 Still Waters Run Deep		Mercury 72055
3/16/63	**28**	8	31 I Got What I Wanted/		
3/09/63	**59**	8	32 Dearer Than Life		Mercury 72099
6/15/63	**22**	9	33 My True Confession		Mercury 72135
9/07/63	**32**	10	34 Two Tickets To Paradise		Mercury 72177
1/25/64	**35**	7	35 Going Going Gone		Mercury 72230
5/09/64	**43**	8	36 Too Late To Turn Back Now/		
5/16/64	**47**	7	37 Another Cup Of Coffee		Mercury 72266
7/18/64	**75**	7	38 A House Is Not A Home		Mercury 72303
			from the film of the same title		
10/03/64	**53**	7	39 Lumberjack		Mercury 72333
12/19/64+	**67**	4	40 Do It Right		Mercury 72365
7/03/65	**100**	1	41 Love Me Now		Mercury 72446
11/13/65	**53**	7	42 Mother Nature, Father Time		RCA 8693
8/19/67	**78**	4	43 Laura (Tell Me What He's Got That I Ain't Got)		Reprise 0611
10/26/68	**99**	2	44 Do Your Own Thing		Cotillion 44007
7/05/69	**74**	6	45 Nothing Can Take The Place Of You		Cotillion 44034
1/10/70	**4**	15	46 ● **Rainy Night In Georgia**		Cotillion 44057
4/18/70	**72**	6	47 My Way		Cotillion 44072
5/30/70	**45**	7	48 Don't It Make You Want To Go Home		Cotillion 44078
12/26/70+	**67**	6	49 Shoes		Cotillion 44093
			above 2: **BROOK BENTON with THE DIXIE FLYERS**		
			POLLY BERGEN		
			Born on 7/14/31. Real name: Nellie Burgin. Singer/actress in movies and TV.		
12/15/58	**67**	6	1 Come Prima		Columbia 41275
			translation of Italian song: For The First Time		
			BERLIN		
			Los Angeles electro-pop trio: Terri Nunn (vocals), John Crawford (bass) and Rob Brill (drums). Group went from a 6-piece band to a trio in 1985.		
3/05/83	**62**	7	1 Sex (I'm A...)		Geffen 29747
5/28/83	**58**	10	2 The Metro		Geffen 29638
9/24/83	**82**	3	3 Masquerade		Geffen 29504
3/10/84	**23**	17	4 No More Words		Geffen 29360
6/30/84	**74**	4	5 Now It's My Turn		Geffen 29283
6/21/86	**1**[1]	21	6 **Take My Breath Away**		Columbia 05903
			love theme from the film "Top Gun"		
10/25/86	**82**	5	7 Like Flames		Geffen 28563
			BERLIN PHILHARMONIC		
			Symphony orchestra conducted by Karl Boehm.		
1/03/70	**90**	4	1 '2001' A Space Odyssey	[I]	Polydor 15009
			theme for the film "2001" from "Also Sprach Zarathustra"		
			THE BERMUDAS		
4/18/64	**62**	10	1 Donnie		Era 3125

DEBUT DATE	PEAK POS	WKS CHR	ARTIST — Record Title	Label & Number
			ROD BERNARD	
			Born on 8/12/40 in Opelousas, Louisiana.	
3/09/59	**20**	12	1 This Should Go On Forever	Argo 5327
11/09/59	**74**	9	2 One More Chance	Mercury 71507
			ELMER BERNSTEIN	
			Composer-conductor for over 60 movie soundtracks.	
3/17/56	**16**	15	1 Main Title From "The Man With The Golden Arm"... [I]	Decca 29869
			Best Seller #16 / Top 100 #32	
			from the movie of the same title - featuring Shelly Manne, drums	
			CHUCK BERRY	
			Born Charles Edward Anderson Berry on 10/18/26 in San Jose, California. Grew up in St. Louis. Muddy Waters introduced Chuck to Leonard Chess (Chess Records) in Chicago. First recording, "Maybellene", was an instant success. Appeared in the film "Rock, Rock, Rock" in 1956, and several others. Regarded by many as rock 'n roll's most influential artist.	
8/20/55	**5**	11	1 **Maybellene**	Chess 1604
			Best Seller #5 / Juke Box #6 / Jockey #13 / Top 100 #42 pre	
6/30/56	**29**	5	2 Roll Over Beethoven	Chess 1626
4/06/57	**3**	26	3 **School Day**	Chess 1653
			Best Seller #3 / Top 100 #5 / Jockey #6 / Juke Box #7	
7/29/57	**57**	7	4 Oh Baby Doll	Chess 1664
11/11/57	**8**	19	5 **Rock & Roll Music**	Chess 1671
			Top 100 #8 / Best Seller #9	
2/17/58	**2**[3]	16	6 **Sweet Little Sixteen**	Chess 1683
			Best Seller #2 / Top 100 #2 / Jockey #5	
4/28/58	**8**	15	7 **Johnny B. Goode**	Chess 1691
			Top 100 #8 / Best Seller #9 / Jockey #16	
7/28/58	**81**	2	8 Beautiful Delilah	Chess 1697
8/25/58	**18**	10	9 Carol	Chess 1700
			Hot 100 #18 / Best Seller #29	
11/10/58	**47**	9	10 Sweet Little Rock And Roll/	
11/17/58	**83**	5	11 Joe Joe Gun	Chess 1709
12/15/58	**69**	3	12 Run Rudolph Run/ [X]	
12/15/58	**71**	3	13 Merry Christmas Baby [X]	Chess 1714
2/16/59	**60**	5	14 Anthony Boy	Chess 1716
3/30/59	**32**	13	15 Almost Grown/	
4/13/59	**80**	4	16 Little Queenie	Chess 1722
			from the film "Go Johnny Go"	
6/22/59	**37**	8	17 Back In The U.S.A.	Chess 1729
2/15/60	**42**	6	18 Too Pooped To Pop ('Casey')/	
2/01/60	**64**	8	19 Let It Rock	Chess 1747
3/07/64	**23**	10	20 Nadine (Is It You?)	Chess 1883
5/23/64	**10**	11	21 **No Particular Place To Go**	Chess 1898
8/01/64	**14**	9	22 You Never Can Tell	Chess 1906
10/24/64	**54**	6	23 Little Marie	Chess 1912
12/12/64+	**41**	7	24 Promised Land	Chess 1916
4/03/65	**95**	4	25 Dear Dad	Chess 1926
8/05/72	**1**[2]	17	26 ● **My Ding-A-Ling** [N]	Chess 2131
12/02/72+	**27**	13	27 Reelin' & Rockin'	Chess 2136
			above 2 recorded live in Lanchester, England	
			"Reelin'" was originally the flip side of "Sweet Little Sixteen"	
			PLASTIC BERTRAND	
			Real name: Plastoc Bertrand. Male Belgian rocker born in 1960.	
4/29/78	**47**	10	1 Ca Plane Pour Moi [F]	Sire 1020
			translation of French song: "This Life's For Me"	
			HAROLD BETTERS	
11/14/64	**74**	8	1 Do Anything You Wanna (Part I) [I]	Gateway 747
			THE BEVERLY SISTERS	
			English trio.	
12/29/56+	**41**	9	1 Greensleeves	London 1703
			with the Roland Shaw Orchestra	
			one of the oldest published songs (from the 16th century)	
			THE B-52'S	
			Quintet from Athens, Georgia.	
4/19/80	**56**	8	1 Rock Lobster [N]	Warner 49173

DEBUT DATE	PEAK POS	WKS CHR	ARTIST — Record Title		Label & Number
			THE B-52'S — Cont'd		
10/18/80	**74**	5	2 Private Idaho		Warner 49537
7/16/83	**81**	4	3 Legal Tender		Warner 29579
			BIDDU ORCHESTRA		
			Biddu is an Indian-born songwriter and producer living in London.		
10/04/75	**57**	6	1 Summer Of '42 disco version of the movie theme	[I]	Epic 50139
1/10/76	**72**	4	2 I Could Have Danced All Night/ from the musical "My Fair Lady"	[I]	
		4	3 Jump For Joy	[I]	Epic 50173
			BIG BOPPER		
			Born Jiles Perry Richardson on 10/24/30 in Sabine Pass, Texas. Disc jockey at KTRM in Beaumont, Texas. Wrote "Running Bear" for Johnny Preston. Died with Buddy Holly and Ritchie Valens in a plane crash on 2/3/59 at the age of 28.		
8/04/58	**6**	25	1 **Chantilly Lace** Hot 100 #6 / Best Seller #13 end	[N]	Mercury 71343
12/08/58	**38**	7	2 Big Bopper's Wedding/	[N]	
12/01/58	**72**	4	3 Little Red Riding Hood	[N]	Mercury 71375
			BIG BROTHER & THE HOLDING COMPANY		
			Formed in San Francisco in 1965. Janis Joplin joined as lead singer in 1966. Sensation at the Monterey Pop Festival in 1967. Disbanded in 1972.		
8/31/68	**12**	12	1 Piece Of My Heart		Columbia 44626
8/31/68	**43**	8	2 Down On Me also see live version by Janis Joplin		Mainstream 662
11/23/68	**84**	3	3 Coo Coo		Mainstream 678
			BIG COUNTRY		
			Scottish four-man rock band.		
10/22/83	**17**	15	1 In A Big Country		Mercury 814467
2/04/84	**52**	6	2 Fields Of Fire		Mercury 811450
6/02/84	**86**	2	3 Wonderland		Mercury 818834
			BIG MAYBELLE		
			Born Mabel Louise Smith on 5/1/24 in Jackson, TN. Died on 1/23/72 in Cleveland.		
1/14/67	**96**	3	1 96 Tears		Rojac 112
			BIG RIC		
			Los Angeles-based rock quartet; Joel Porter (vocals).		
9/03/83	**91**	3	1 Take Away		Scotti Br. 04084
			BIG SAMBO & The House Wreckers		
3/10/62	**74**	7	1 The Rains Came		Eric 7003
			MR. ACKER BILK		
			Born Bernard Stanley Bilk on 1/28/29 in Somerset, England. Clarinetist, composer.		
3/17/62	**1**[1]	21	♫ 1 ● **Stranger On The Shore**	[I]	Atco 6217
7/14/62	**59**	6	2 Above The Stars from the film "The Wonderful World Of The Brothers Grimm"	[I]	Atco 6230
12/01/62	**92**	3	3 Limelight written in 1953 by Charlie Chaplin (also known as "Eternally")	[I]	Atco 6238
2/02/63	**77**	3	4 Only You (And You Alone) above 4 with the Leon Young String Chorale	[I]	Atco 6247
			BILLY & LILLIE		
			Vocal duo of Billy Ford, (b: 3/9/25, Bloomfield, New Jersey), vocalist, trumpet; and Lillie Bryant, (b: 2/14/40, Newburg, New York), vocalist. Backing group: Billy Ford & The Thunderbirds.		
1/06/58	**9**	13	1 **La Dee Dah** Top 100 #9 / Best Seller #10 / Jockey #23		Swan 4002
5/05/58	**56**	4	2 Happiness		Swan 4005
12/22/58+	**14**	13	3 Lucky Ladybug		Swan 4020
7/13/59	**88**	6	4 Bells, Bells, Bells (The Bell Song)		Swan 4036
			BILLY & THE BEATERS - see BILLY VERA		
			BILLY JOE & THE CHECKMATES		
			Billy Joe Hunter.		
1/13/62	**10**	13	1 **Percolator (Twist)**	[I]	Dore 620

DEBUT DATE	PEAK POS	WKS CHR	ARTIST — Record Title	Label & Number
			BILLY SATELLITE	
			Rock quartet from Oakland, California, led by Monty Byrom.	
8/18/84	**64**	6	1 Satisfy Me	Capitol 5356
12/08/84	**78**	5	2 I Wanna Go Back	Capitol 5409
			BIMBO JET	
			French studio instrumentalists.	
5/24/75	**43**	10	1 El Bimbo [I] #1 song in 6 different European countries	Scepter 12406
			BIRDLEGS & PAULINE & Their Versatility Birds	
			3-woman, 1-man black group from Chicago. Birdlegs is Sidney Banks.	
7/06/63	**94**	2	1 Spring	Vee-Jay 510
			JANE BIRKIN & SERGE GAINSBOURG	
			Popular British/French duo on records and in films.	
11/29/69+	**58**	10	1 Je T'Aime...Moi Non Plus [F] recording was banned on many radio shows, worldwide	Fontana 1665
			ELVIN BISHOP	
			Born on 10/21/42 in Tulsa, Oklahoma. Lead guitarist with Paul Butterfield's Blues Band (1965-68).	
10/05/74	**61**	6	1 Travelin' Shoes	Capricorn 0202
6/28/75	**83**	5	2 Sure Feels Good	Capricorn 0237
3/06/76	**3**	17	3● **Fooled Around And Fell In Love** lead vocal: Mickey Thomas of Jefferson Starship	Capricorn 0252
7/24/76	**68**	4	4 Struttin' My Stuff	Capricorn 0256
12/25/76+	**93**	8	5 Spend Some Time	Capricorn 0266
			STEPHEN BISHOP	
			Pop-rock singer/songwriter from San Diego.	
12/11/76+	**22**	15	1 Save It For A Rainy Day guitar solo: Eric Clapton; background vocals: Chaka Khan	ABC 12232
5/07/77	**11**	28	2 On And On	ABC 12260
9/16/78	**32**	13	3 Everybody Needs Love	ABC 12406
12/23/78+	**73**	5	4 Animal House [N] from the movie "National Lampoon's Animal House"	ABC 12435
1/29/83	**25**	20	5 It Might Be You theme from the film "Tootsie"	Warner 29791
3/31/84	**87**	3	6 Unfaithfully Yours (One Love) from the film "Unfaithfully Yours"	Warner 29345
			THE BLACKBYRDS	
			Founded in 1973 by Donald Byrd while teaching at Howard University, Washington, D.C.	
9/07/74	**69**	6	1 Do It, Fluid	Fantasy 729
2/08/75	**6**	17	2 **Walking In Rhythm**	Fantasy 736
8/02/75	**70**	4	3 Flyin' High	Fantasy 747
3/06/76	**19**	13	4 Happy Music	Fantasy 762
7/17/76	**93**	3	5 Rock Creek Park	Fantasy 771
3/12/77	**95**	3	6 Time Is Movin'	Fantasy 787
			BLACKFOOT	
			Rick "Rattlesnake" Medlocke, lead singer of band from Jacksonville, Florida.	
6/23/79	**26**	14	1 Highway Song	Atco 7104
10/20/79	**38**	14	2 Train, Train	Atco 7207
6/20/81	**42**	12	3 Fly Away	Atco 7331
			J. BLACKFOOT	
			Former lead singer of the Soul Children.	
3/03/84	**90**	5	1 Taxi	Sound Town 0004
			BLACKJACK	
			New York City-based quartet led by Michael Bolton.	
7/21/79	**62**	6	1 Love Me Tonight	Polydor 14572
			BLACK OAK ARKANSAS	
			Southern rock sextet led by Jim "Dandy" Mangrum.	
12/15/73+	**25**	13	1 Jim Dandy female singer: Ruby Starr	Atco 6948
1/10/76	**89**	2	2 Strong Enough To Be Gentle	MCA 40496

DEBUT DATE	PEAK POS	WKS CHR	ARTIST — Record Title		Label & Number
			BLACK SABBATH		
			English heavy metal band - Ozzy Osbourne, vocals (1968-78)		
11/28/70	**61**	8	1 Paranoid		Warner 7437
1/29/72	**52**	10	2 Iron Man		Warner 7530
			BILL BLACK'S COMBO		
			Bill was born on 9/17/26 in Memphis; died of a brain tumor on 10/21/65. Bass guitarist. Session work in Memphis, backed Elvis Presley (with Scotty Moore, guitar; D.J. Fontana, drums) on most of his early records. Formed own band in 1959.		
11/30/59+	**17**	12	1 Smokie - Part 2	[I]	Hi 2018
3/07/60	**9**	14	2 **White Silver Sands**	[I]	Hi 2021
6/27/60	**18**	10	3 Josephine	[I]	Hi 2022
9/12/60	**11**	13	4 Don't Be Cruel	[I]	Hi 2026
			Bill played bass on the original Elvis hit		
11/28/60	**16**	10	5 Blue Tango	[I]	Hi 2027
2/20/61	**20**	8	6 Hearts Of Stone	[I]	Hi 2028
6/05/61	**25**	8	7 Ole Buttermilk Sky	[I]	Hi 2036
9/25/61	**41**	7	8 Movin'/	[I]	
9/25/61	**92**	2	9 Honky Train	[I]	Hi 2038
12/18/61+	**26**	9	10 Twist-Her	[I]	Hi 2042
5/05/62	**92**	2	11 twistin'-White Silver Sands	[I]	Hi 2052
			twist version of his second charted hit		
8/11/62	**78**	7	12 So What	[I]	Hi 2055
4/27/63	**51**	8	13 Do It - Rat Now	[I]	Hi 2064
10/05/63	**47**	6	14 Monkey-Shine	[I]	Hi 2069
2/01/64	**67**	5	15 Comin' On	[I]	Hi 2072
5/16/64	**91**	3	16 Tequila	[I]	Hi 2077
10/03/64	**73**	4	17 Little Queenie	[I]	Hi 2079
1/02/65	**89**	1	18 So What	[I-R]	Hi 2055
6/22/68	**82**	6	19 Turn On Your Love Light	[I]	Hi 2145
			CILLA BLACK		
			Born Priscilla White on 5/27/43 in Liverpool, England.		
7/04/64	**26**	7	1 You're My World		Capitol 5196
9/19/64	**79**	3	2 It's For You		Capitol 5258
8/27/66	**95**	3	3 Alfie		Capitol 5674
			JAY BLACK		
			Jay of "Jay & The Americans".		
9/20/80	**98**	4	1 The Part Of Me That Needs You Most		Midsong 72012
			JEANNE BLACK		
			Born on 10/25/37 in Mount Baldy, California. Appearances on local TV show, "Hometown Jamboree". Discovered by Cliffie Stone.		
5/02/60	**4**	11	1 **He'll Have To Stay**		Capitol 4368
			answer song to Jim Reeves' "He'll Have To Go"		
7/25/60	**43**	9	2 Lisa		Capitol 4396
12/26/60+	**63**	5	3 Oh, How I Miss You Tonight		Capitol 4492
			OSCAR BLACK		
4/24/61	**94**	1	1 I'm A Fool To Care		Savoy 1600
			TERRY BLACK		
			Canadian singer.		
11/21/64	**99**	2	1 Unless You Care		Tollie 9026
			TERRY BLACK & LAUREL WARD		
2/12/72	**57**	8	1 Goin' Down (On The Road To L.A.)		Kama Sutra 540
			BLACKWELL		
			Quintet from Houston, Texas - Glenn Gibson, lead singer.		
10/25/69	**89**	2	1 Wonderful		Astro 1000
			CHARLIE BLACKWELL		
			Seattle-born percussionist - sideman with many jazz greats.		
2/09/59	**55**	9	1 Midnight Oil	[I]	Warner 5031
			THE BLADES OF GRASS		
			Pop quartet from New Jersey.		
7/15/67	**87**	4	1 Happy		Jubilee 5582

DEBUT DATE	PEAK POS	WKS CHR	ARTIST — Record Title	Label & Number
			JACK BLANCHARD & MISTY MORGAN	
			Husband and wife Country duo. Singing-songwriting team. Both from Buffalo, New York.	
2/28/70	**23**	13	1 Tennessee Bird Walk .... [N]	Wayside 010
6/27/70	**78**	6	2 Humphrey The Camel .... [N]	Wayside 013
			BILLY BLAND	
			Born on 4/5/32 in Wilmington, North Carolina. First recorded for Old Town in 1955.	
2/15/60	**7**	20	1 **Let The Little Girl Dance**	Old Town 1076
6/27/60	**94**	2	2 You Were Born To Be Loved	Old Town 1082
10/10/60	**91**	2	3 Harmony	Old Town 1088
8/07/61	**90**	4	4 My Heart's On Fire	Old Town 1105
			BOBBY BLAND	
			Born Robert Calvin Bland on 1/27/30 in Rosemark, TN. Nicknamed "Blue". Sang in gospel group "The Miniatures" in Memphis, late 40s. Member of the Beale Streeters which included Johnny Ace, B.B. King, Rosco Gordon, Earl Forest and Willie Nix in 1949. Driver and valet for B.B. King; appeared in the Johnny Ace Revue, early 50s. First recorded in 1952, for the Modern label. Frequent tours with B.B. King into the 80s.	
8/05/57	**43**	21	1 Farther Up The Road	Duke 170
1/25/60	**89**	3	2 I'll Take Care Of You	Duke 314
11/07/60	**71**	5	3 Cry Cry Cry	Duke 327
2/20/61	**46**	7	4 I Pity The Fool	Duke 332
8/07/61	**71**	7	5 Don't Cry No More	Duke 340
12/04/61+	**28**	10	6 Turn On Your Love Light	Duke 344
3/31/62	**76**	4	7 Who Will The Next Fool Be	Duke 347
3/31/62	**86**	1	8 Ain't That Loving You	Duke 338
8/11/62	**56**	8	9 Yield Not To Temptation	Duke 352
9/08/62	**43**	13	10 Stormy Monday Blues	Duke 355
1/05/63	**22**	12	11 Call On Me/	
1/19/63	**33**	10	12 That's The Way Love Is	Duke 360
7/20/63	**56**	6	13 Sometimes You Gotta Cry A Little	Duke 366
12/28/63+	**91**	3	14 The Feeling Is Gone	Duke 370
3/07/64	**20**	9	15 Ain't Nothing You Can Do	Duke 375
6/13/64	**42**	9	16 Share Your Love With Me	Duke 377
10/24/64	**49**	6	17 Ain't Doing Too Bad (Part 1)	Duke 383
1/02/65	**99**	1	18 Black Night/	
1/09/65	**78**	3	19 Blind Man	Duke 386
4/24/65	**93**	1	20 Ain't No Telling	Duke 390
8/28/65	**63**	8	21 These Hands (Small But Mighty)	Duke 385
1/08/66	**62**	6	22 I'm Too Far Gone (To Turn Around)	Duke 393
5/21/66	**75**	6	23 Good Time Charlie	Duke 402
9/17/66	**65**	5	24 Poverty	Duke 407
4/22/67	**88**	2	25 You're All I Need	Duke 416
3/09/68	**96**	3	26 Driftin' Blues	Duke 432
11/16/68+	**58**	10	27 Rockin' In The Same Old Boat	Duke 440
6/14/69	**91**	3	28 Gotta Get To Know You	Duke 447
9/13/69	**60**	7	29 Chains Of Love	Duke 449
2/14/70	**96**	2	30 If You've Got A Heart	Duke 458
12/05/70	**89**	3	31 Keep On Loving Me (You'll See The Change)	Duke 464
6/19/71	**97**	1	32 I'm Sorry	Duke 466
2/26/72	**64**	5	33 Do What You Set Out To Do	Duke 472
11/17/73+	**42**	13	34 This Time I'm Gone For Good	Dunhill 4369
3/02/74	**69**	6	35 Goin' Down Slow	Dunhill 4379
8/10/74	**91**	7	36 Ain't No Love In The Heart Of The City	Dunhill 15003
11/23/74	**88**	7	37 I Wouldn't Treat A Dog (The Way You Treated Me)	Dunhill 15015
			MARCIE BLANE	
			Born on 5/21/44 in Brooklyn, New York.	
10/20/62	**3**	16	1 **Bobby's Girl**	Seville 120
2/23/63	**82**	3	2 What Does A Girl Do?	Seville 123
			BLAZE	
			5-member group from Cincinnati.	
12/11/76	**95**	2	1 Silver Heels	Epic 50292

DEBUT DATE	PEAK POS	WKS CHR	ARTIST — Record Title	Label & Number
			THE BLEND	
12/16/78	**91**	5	1 I'm Gonna Make You Love Me	MCA 40961
			THE BLENDELLS	
			Los Angeles Latino quintet.	
9/12/64	**62**	8	1 La La La La La	Reprise 0291
			THE BLENDERS	
7/06/63	**61**	8	1 Daughter	Witch 114
			ARCHIE BLEYER	
			Arthur Godfrey's musical director in '50s. Founded Cadence Records.	
12/04/54+	**17**	6	1 The Naughty Lady Of Shady Lane	Cadence 1254
			Jockey #17 / Juke Box #20 / Best Seller #26	
6/30/56	**61**	3	2 The Rockin' Ghost	Cadence 1293
			BLONDIE	
			Formed in New York City in 1975. Consisted of Chris Stein & Frank Infante (guitars), Jimmy Destri (keyboards), Gary Valentine (bass), Clem Burke (drums) and Deborah Harry (vocals). Stein and Harry were married. Harry had been in folk/rock group, Wind In The Willows; did solo work from 1980; in films "Union City Blues" and "Roadie". Disbanded in 1983; Burke went with Eurythmics.	
2/17/79	1^{1}	21	1 ● **Heart Of Glass**	Chrysalis 2295
6/02/79	**24**	14	2 One Way Or Another	Chrysalis 2336
9/29/79	**27**	14	3 Dreaming	Chrysalis 2379
2/02/80	**84**	3	4 The Hardest Part	Chrysalis 2408
2/16/80	1^{6}	25	5 ● **Call Me**	Chrysalis 2414
			from the film "American Gigolo"	
5/17/80	**39**	9	6 Atomic	Chrysalis 2410
11/15/80+	1^{1}	26	7 ● **The Tide Is High**	Chrysalis 2465
1/31/81	1^{2}	20	8 ● **Rapture**	Chrysalis 2485
5/29/82	**37**	10	9 Island Of Lost Souls	Chrysalis 2603
			all of above produced by Mike Chapman (except 5: Giorgio Moroder)	
			BLOODROCK	
			Rock group from Fort Worth, Texas; Jim Rutledge, lead vocals.	
1/02/71	**36**	13	1 D.O.A.	Capitol 3009
			BLOODSTONE	
			From Kansas City, Missouri. Formed as the Sinceres, consisted of Charles McCormick, Willis Draffen, Charles Love, Henry Williams, and Roger Durham (d: 1973). First recorded for British Decca.	
4/21/73	**10**	19	1 ● **Natural High**	London 1046
9/15/73	**43**	14	2 Never Let You Go	London 1051
2/23/74	**34**	14	3 Outside Woman	London 1052
7/27/74	**82**	6	4 That's Not How It Goes	London 1055
3/29/75	**57**	7	5 My Little Lady	London 1061
			BLOOD, SWEAT & TEARS	
			Group formed by Al Kooper in 1968. Nucleus consisted of Kooper (keyboards), Steve Katz (guitar), Bobby Colomby (drums) and Jim Fielder (bass). Kooper replaced by lead singer David Clayton-Thomas in 1969. Clayton-Thomas replaced by Jerry Fisher in 1972. Katz left in 1973. Clayton-Thomas rejoined in 1974.	
3/01/69	2^{3}	13	1 ● **You've Made Me So Very Happy**	Columbia 44776
5/31/69	2^{3}	13	2 ● **Spinning Wheel**	Columbia 44871
10/18/69	2^{1}	13	3 ● **And When I Die**	Columbia 45008
8/01/70	**14**	8	4 Hi-De-Ho	Columbia 45204
10/03/70	**29**	7	5 Lucretia Mac Evil	Columbia 45235
7/31/71	**32**	8	6 Go Down Gamblin'	Columbia 45427
10/30/71	**73**	6	7 Lisa, Listen To Me	Columbia 45477
9/30/72	**44**	11	8 So Long Dixie	Columbia 45661
6/29/74	**83**	4	9 Tell Me That I'm Wrong	Columbia 46059
6/14/75	**62**	6	10 Got To Get You Into My Life	Columbia 10151
			BOBBY BLOOM	
			Died from an accidental shooting on 2/28/74.	
9/12/70	**8**	16	1 **Montego Bay**	L&R/MGM 157
1/09/71	**84**	4	2 Where Are We Going	Roulette 7095
1/16/71	**80**	6	3 Make Me Happy	MGM 14212
6/26/71	**93**	4	4 We're All Goin' Home	MGM 14246

DEBUT DATE	PEAK POS	WKS CHR	ARTIST — Record Title	Label & Number
			THE BLOSSOMS	
			Black female trio led by Darlene Love. Sang backup with Elvis, Paul Anka, Duane Eddy, Bobby Darin, and many others. Appeared regularly on TV's "Shindig".	
5/08/61	**79**	4	1 Son-In-Law	Challenge 9109
			KURTIS BLOW	
			Born Kurt Walker on 8/9/59 in New York City. Began as a disco DJ.	
9/06/80	**87**	6	1 ● The Breaks (Part 1)	Mercury 76075
			certified gold for the 12" single	
4/13/85	**71**	6	2 Basketball [N]	Polydor 881529
			THE BLOW MONKEYS	
			British quartet fronted by Dr. Robert (Robert Howard).	
5/03/86	**14**	19	1 Digging Your Scene	RCA 14325
			BLUE	
			Scottish four-man group produced by Elton John.	
5/07/77	**88**	5	1 Capture Your Heart	Rocket 40706
			THE BLUE-BELLES - see PATTI LaBELLE & THE BLUE BELLES	
			BLUE CHEER	
			San Francisco hard-rock trio.	
3/02/68	**14**	13	1 Summertime Blues	Philips 40516
7/06/68	**92**	4	2 Just A Little Bit	Philips 40541
			THE BLUE DIAMONDS	
			Indonesian brothers: Rudy & Riem de Wolff.	
11/28/60	**72**	5	1 Ramona	London 1954
			song hit #1 for both Gene Austin and Paul Whiteman in 1928	
			BLUE HAZE	
11/11/72+	**27**	14	1 Smoke Gets In Your Eyes	A&M 1357
			song hit #1 for Paul Whiteman in 1934	
			THE BLUE JAYS	
			R&B group from Los Angeles. Leon Peels, lead singer.	
8/14/61	**31**	9	1 Lover's Island	Milestone 2008
			BLUE MAGIC	
			Soul group from Philadelphia. Consisted of Theodore Mills (lead vocals), Vernon Sawyer, Wendell Sawyer, Keith Beaton and Richard Pratt.	
2/02/74	**74**	6	1 Stop To Start	Atco 6949
5/18/74	**8**	21	2 ● **Sideshow**	Atco 6961
10/19/74	**36**	9	3 Three Ring Circus	Atco 7004
			BLUE MINK	
			British group featuring Madeline Bell (lead singer) and Roger Cook.	
9/26/70	**64**	6	1 Our World	Philips 40686
			THE BLUE NOTES - see HAROLD MELVIN & THE BLUE NOTES	
			THE BLUENOTES	
			White male vocal foursome. Did background vocals for George Hamilton IV.	
12/14/59+	**61**	9	1 I Don't Know What It Is	Brooke 111
			BLUE OYSTER CULT	
			New York hard-rock quintet led by Donald "Buck Dharma" Roeser (lead guitar) and Eric Bloom (lead vocal).	
7/31/76	**12**	20	1 (Don't Fear) The Reaper	Columbia 10384
9/08/79	**74**	4	2 In Thee	Columbia 11055
8/15/81	**40**	14	3 Burnin' For You	Columbia 02415
2/11/84	**83**	3	4 Shooting Shark	Columbia 04298
			THE BLUE RIDGE RANGERS - see JOHN FOGERTY	
			BLUE STARS	
			4-man, 4-woman pop/jazz group from Paris, France, led by former American big band vocalist, Blossom Dearie.	
12/17/55+	**16**	20	1 Lullaby Of Birdland [F]	Mercury 70742
			Jockey #16 / Best Seller #20 / Top 100 #20	
			arranged by Michel Legrand; composed by George Shearing	

DEBUT DATE	PEAK POS	WKS CHR	ARTIST — Record Title	Label & Number
			BLUE SWEDE	
			Swedish sextet; Bjorn Skiffs, lead singer.	
2/16/74	**1**[1]	17	1 ● **Hooked On A Feeling**	EMI 3627
6/15/74	**71**	4	2 Silly Milly	EMI 3893
8/24/74	**7**	11	3 **Never My Love**	EMI 3938
2/22/75	**61**	5	4 Hush/I'm Alive	EMI 4029
			DAVID BLUE	
			Born David Cohen in Providence, Rhode Island; died 12/2/82 (41).	
5/12/73	**94**	4	1 Outlaw Man produced by Graham Nash	Asylum 11015
			BLUES BROTHERS	
			Jake Blues (John Belushi) & Elwood Blues (Dan Aykroyd) - originally created for TV's "Saturday Night Live".	
12/09/78+	**14**	15	1 Soul Man	Atlantic 3545
3/03/79	**37**	8	2 Rubber Biscuit [N]	Atlantic 3564
5/31/80	**18**	14	3 Gimme Some Lovin' from the soundtrack "The Blues Brothers"	Atlantic 3666
12/20/80+	**39**	11	4 Who's Making Love	Atlantic 3785
			BLUES IMAGE	
			Tampa, Florida rock quintet led by Mike Pinera.	
5/09/70	**4**	15	1 ● **Ride Captain Ride**	Atco 6746
9/26/70	**81**	4	2 Gas Lamps And Clay	Atco 6777
			BLUES MAGOOS	
			Bronx, New York psychedelic rock quintet led by Peppy Castro.	
12/10/66+	**5**	14	1 **(We Ain't Got) Nothin' Yet**	Mercury 72622
3/18/67	**60**	6	2 Pipe Dream/	
4/08/67	**81**	2	3 There's A Chance We Can Make It	Mercury 72660
6/10/67	**71**	5	4 One By One	Mercury 72692
			THE BLUES PROJECT	
			New York City blues band - members Al Kooper & Steve Katz formed Blood, Sweat & Tears in 1967.	
4/01/67	**96**	2	1 No Time Like The Right Time	Verve Folk. 5040
			EDDIE BO	
			Real name: Edwin J. Bocage; from New Orleans.	
8/02/69	**73**	9	1 Hook And Sling-Part I	Scram 117
			BOB & EARL	
			Bob Relf & Earl Nelson. Bobby Day sang with Earl Nelson (as Bob & Earl) in 1960, however, Day was not involved in either of Bob & Earl's charted hits. Earl Lee Nelson (wife's name was Jackie) recorded the hit "The Duck" as Jackie Lee. Earl was also lead singer on the Hollywood Flames hit "Buzz-Buzz-Buzz".	
10/20/62	**85**	4	1 Don't Ever Leave Me	Tempe 102
12/21/63+	**44**	11	2 Harlem Shuffle	Marc 104
			BOB B. SOXX & THE BLUE JEANS	
			Consisted of Darlene Love and Fanita James (both formerly with the Blossoms), and Bobby Sheen. Love and James later replaced by Gloria Jones and Carolyn Willis.	
11/17/62+	**8**	13	1 **Zip-A-Dee Doo-Dah**	Philles 107
2/16/63	**38**	9	2 Why Do Lovers Break Each Other's Heart?	Philles 110
6/08/63	**63**	6	3 Not Too Young To Get Married above 3 produced by Phil Spector; arranged by Jack Nitzsche	Philles 113
			THE BOBBETTES	
			"Doo-wop" quintet of girls (ages 11-15) from New York City. Consisted of sisters Emma and Jannie Pought, Laura Webb, Helen Gathers, and Reather Dixon. Originally called the "Harlem Queens".	
8/05/57	**6**	24	1 **Mr. Lee** Top 100 #6 / Jockey #6 / Best Seller #7 song inspired by group's 5th grade teacher	Atlantic 1144
7/04/60	**52**	8	2 I Shot Mr. Lee	Triple-X 104
10/10/60	**66**	8	3 Have Mercy Baby/	
10/24/60	**95**	1	4 Dance With Me Georgie	Triple-X 106
9/04/61	**72**	4	5 I Don't Like It Like That answer song to Chris Kenner's "I Like It Like That"	Gone 5112

DEBUT DATE	PEAK POS	WKS CHR	ARTIST — Record Title		Label & Number
			NEIL BOGART - see NEIL SCOTT		
			HAMILTON BOHANNON		
			Born on 3/7/42 in Newman, Georgia. With Stevie Wonder as drummer, 1965-67.		
9/13/75	**98**	2	1 Foot Stompin Music		Dakar 4544
			MICHAEL BOLTON		
			Former lead singer of Blackjack; from New Haven, Connecticut.		
5/14/83	**82**	3	1 Fools Game		Columbia 03800
			BON JOVI		
			New Jersey hard rock quintet consisting of Jon Bon Jovi (Bongiovi), lead vocals; Richie Sambora, guitars; Dave Bryan, keyboards; Alec John Such, bass; Tico Torres, drums. America's hottest rock band, 1986-87.		
2/25/84	**39**	13	1 Runaway		Mercury 818309
5/26/84	**48**	11	2 She Don't Know Me		Mercury 818958
4/20/85	**54**	8	3 Only Lonely		Mercury 880736
8/03/85	**69**	6	4 In And Out Of Love		Mercury 880951
9/06/86	**1**[1]	24	5 **You Give Love A Bad Name**		Mercury 884953
12/13/86+	**1**[4]	21	6 **Livin' On A Prayer**		Mercury 888184
			JOHNNY BOND		
			Born Cyrus Whitfield Bond on 6/1/15 in Oklahoma; died 6/12/78 (63). With Gene Autry's radio show for 15 years. Appeared in over 50 movies.		
8/08/60	**26**	10	1 Hot Rod Lincoln	[N]	Republic 2005
3/13/65	**43**	8	2 10 Little Bottles	[C]	Starday 704
			GARY U.S. BONDS		
			Born Gary Anderson on 6/6/39 in Jacksonville, Florida. Signed to Legrand Records by Frank Guida in Norfolk, Virginia.		
10/17/60	**6**	14	1 **New Orleans**		Legrand 1003
5/22/61	**1**[2]	15	2 **Quarter To Three**		Legrand 1008
			music taken from "A Night With Daddy G" (Church Street Five)		
			above 2 shown as: **U.S. BONDS**		
7/24/61	**5**	11	3 **School Is Out**		Legrand 1009
10/23/61	**28**	5	4 School Is In		Legrand 1012
12/11/61+	**9**	16	5 **Dear Lady Twist**		Legrand 1015
3/31/62	**9**	10	6 **Twist, Twist Senora**		Legrand 1018
6/23/62	**27**	7	7 Seven Day Weekend		Legrand 1019
			from the film "It's Trad-Dad"		
8/25/62	**92**	3	8 Copy Cat		Legrand 1020
4/25/81	**11**	18	9 This Little Girl		EMI America 8079
7/18/81	**65**	6	10 Jole Blon		EMI America 8089
6/12/82	**21**	16	11 Out Of Work		EMI America 8117
			above 3 produced by Bruce Springsteen and Miami Steve Van Zandt		
			BONES		
			Rock quartet led by brothers Danny & Jimmy Faragher.		
11/04/72	**94**	2	1 Roberta		Signpost 70008
			BONEY M		
			Vocal group created in Gemany by producer/composer Frank Farian. Farian sang solo on first recording in 1975, group formed later. Consisted of Marcia Barrett, Maizie Williams, Liz Mitchell and Bobby Farrell. All were from the West Indies.		
1/22/77	**65**	5	1 Daddy Cool		Atco 7063
8/27/77	**96**	3	2 Ma Baker		Atlantic 3422
6/03/78	**30**	17	3 Rivers Of Babylon		Sire 1027
12/23/78	**85**	5	4 Mary's Boy Child/Oh My Lord	[X]	Sire 1036
			BONNIE & THE TREASURES		
			Bonnie is Charlott O'Hara.		
8/28/65	**77**	5	1 Home Of The Brave		Phi-Dan 5005
			BONNIE SISTERS		
			Pat, Jean and Sylvia.		
2/18/56	**18**	7	1 Cry Baby		Rainbow 328
			Best Seller #18 / Top 100 #35		
			KARLA BONOFF		
			Songwriter/singer from Los Angeles.		
2/11/78	**76**	4	1 I Can't Hold On		Columbia 10618

DEBUT DATE	PEAK POS	WKS CHR	ARTIST — Record Title	Label & Number
			KARLA BONOFF — Cont'd	
3/01/80	**69**	7	2 Baby Don't Go	Columbia 11206
5/01/82	**19**	18	3 Personally	Columbia 02805
9/25/82	**63**	7	4 Please Be The One	Columbia 03172
			BOOKER T. & THE MG's	
			Band formed by session men from Stax Records in Memphis, 1962. Consisted of Booker T. Jones (b: 11/12/44, Memphis), keyboards; Steve Cropper (b: 10/21/42, Ozark Mountains, MO.), guitar; Donald "Duck" Dunn (b: 11/24/41, Memphis), bass; and Al Jackson, Jr. (b: 11/27/34, Memphis, d: 1975), drums. MG stands for Memphis Group. Cropper and Dunn had been in the Mar-Keys. Much session work. Jones received music degree from Indiana University, and married Priscilla Coolidge, sister of Rita. Produced for Rita Coolidge, Earl Klugh, Bill Withers, and for Willie Nelson's "Stardust" album. Cropper and Dunn joined the Blues Brothers. Group disbanded in 1968, reorganized in 1973 for a short time.	
8/11/62	**3**	16	1 ● **Green Onions** [I]	Stax 127
12/22/62+	**82**	5	2 Jellybread [I]	Stax 131
7/27/63	**78**	7	3 Chinese Checkers [I]	Stax 137
2/22/64	**97**	3	4 Mo-Onions [I]	Stax 142
8/15/64	**95**	2	5 Soul Dressing [I]	Stax 153
6/05/65	**58**	10	6 Boot-Leg [I]	Stax 169
9/03/66	**85**	5	7 My Sweet Potato [I]	Stax 196
3/25/67	**37**	13	8 Hip Hug-Her [I]	Stax 211
8/05/67	**21**	12	9 Groovin'/ [I]	
7/29/67	**70**	5	10 Slim Jenkin's Place [I]	Stax 224
7/13/68	**17**	10	11 Soul-Limbo [I]	Stax 0001
11/09/68+	**9**	18	12 **Hang 'Em High** [I] from the film of the same title	Stax 0013
3/15/69	**6**	13	13 **Time Is Tight** [I] from the soundtrack "Uptight"	Stax 0028
6/07/69	**37**	8	14 Mrs. Robinson [I] from the movie "The Graduate"	Stax 0037
9/06/69	**88**	4	15 Slum Baby [I]	Stax 0049
7/25/70	**76**	4	16 Something [I]	Stax 0073
3/20/71	**45**	16	17 Melting Pot [I]	Stax 0082
			JAMES BOOKER	
			Born on 12/17/39 in New Orleans. Died on 11/8/83 (43). Organist.	
11/07/60	**43**	11	1 Gonzo [I]	Peacock 1697
			TAKA BOOM	
			Chaka Khan's sister. Former member of The Undisputed Truth.	
5/05/79	**74**	4	1 Night Dancin'	Ariola 7748
			THE BOOMTOWN RATS	
			Irish sextet. Leader Bob Geldof organized the Band Aid benefit for famine relief.	
2/02/80	**73**	5	1 I Don't Like Mondays about a San Diego girl who shot 11 people on Monday (1/29/79)	Columbia 11117
			DANIEL BOONE	
			English singer, songwriter. Real name: Peter Lee Stirling.	
6/03/72	**15**	20	1 Beautiful Sunday	Mercury 73281
11/11/72	**86**	5	2 Annabelle	Mercury 73339
5/24/75	**93**	3	3 Run Tell The People	Pye 71011
			DEBBY BOONE	
			Pat Boone's daughter. Born on 9/22/56 in Hackensack, New Jersey.	
9/03/77	**1**[10]	25	1 ▲ **You Light Up My Life** theme from the movie of the same title	Warner 8455
2/11/78	**50**	5	2 California	Warner 8511
5/27/78	**74**	7	3 God Knows/	
		3	4 Baby, I'm Yours	Warner 8554
			PAT BOONE	
			Born Charles Eugene Boone on 6/1/34 in Jacksonville, Florida. To Nashville, early 50s, attended Lipscomb College. First recorded for Republic in 1953. Appeared on Ted Mack and Arthur Godfrey amateur shows in 1954. Married Red Foley's daughter Shirley in 1954. Appeared in 15 films. Toured with wife and daughters Cherry, Linda Lee, Deborah Ann and Laura Gene in the mid-60s.	
4/02/55	**16**	12	1 Two Hearts Best Seller #16 / Juke Box #16	Dot 15338

DEBUT DATE	PEAK POS	WKS CHR		ARTIST — Record Title	Label & Number
				PAT BOONE — Cont'd	
7/09/55	1[2]	20	2	**Ain't That A Shame** .... Juke Box #1 / Best Seller #2 / Jockey #2 / Top 100 #21 pre	Dot 15377
10/29/55	7	14	3	**At My Front Door (Crazy Little Mama)/** Top 100 #7 / Juke Box #7 / Best Seller #8 / Jockey #10	
11/12/55	26	11	4	No Other Arms (No Arms Can Ever Hold You)	Dot 15422
12/17/55+	19	10	5	Gee Whittakers! .... Juke Box #19 / Top 100 #27	Dot 15435
2/04/56	4	22	6	**I'll Be Home/** Jockey #4 / Juke Box #4 / Top 100 #5 / Best Seller #6	
1/28/56	12	18	7	Tutti' Frutti.. Top 100 #12 / Jockey #15	Dot 15443
4/14/56	8	15	8	**Long Tall Sally/** Juke Box #8 / Top 100 #18 / Best Seller #23 / Jockey #23	
4/28/56	76	3	9	Just As Long As I'm With You.............................	Dot 15457
6/02/56	1[4]	23	10	**I Almost Lost My Mind/** Juke Box #1(4) / Top 100 #1(2) / Best Seller #2 / Jockey #2	
6/09/56	57	7	11	I'm In Love With You	Dot 15472
9/15/56	5	24	12	**Friendly Persuasion (Thee I Love)/** from the Gary Cooper movie "Friendly Persuasion" Jockey #5 / Top 100 #8 / Juke Box #8 / Best Seller #9	
9/15/56	20	14	13	Chains Of Love	Dot 15490
12/22/56+	1[1]	22	14	**Don't Forbid Me/** Top 100 #1(1) / Juke Box #1(1) / Jockey #2 / Best Seller #3	
12/22/56+	37	18	15	Anastasia .... from the Ingrid Bergman film "Anastasia"	Dot 15521
3/16/57	5	21	16	**Why Baby Why/** Best Seller #5 / Top 100 #6 / Jockey #7 / Juke Box #7	
3/16/57	27	10	17	I'm Waiting Just For You..................................	Dot 15545
5/06/57	1[7]	34	18	**Love Letters In The Sand/** Jockey #1(7) / Best Seller #1(5) / Top 100 #1(5) / Juke Box #2 end	
5/06/57	14	25	19	Bernardine.. Jockey #14 / Top 100 #23 above 2 tunes from the film "Bernardine"	Dot 15570
8/12/57	6	21	20	**Remember You're Mine/** Jockey #6 / Best Seller #10 / Top 100 #20	
8/19/57	20	14	21	There's A Gold Mine In The Sky........................... Jockey #20 / Top 100 #28	Dot 15602
10/28/57	1[6]	26	22	**April Love/** from the film of the same title starring Pat Boone & Shirley Jones Jockey #1(6) / Best Seller #1(2) / Top 100 #1(1)	
11/04/57	80	3	23	When The Swallows Come Back To Capistrano	Dot 15660
2/17/58	4	19	24	**A Wonderful Time Up There/** Best Seller #4 / Jockey #7 / Top 100 #10	
2/17/58	11	16	25	It's Too Soon To Know .... Jockey #11 / Top 100 #13	Dot 15690
5/05/58	5	14	26	**Sugar Moon/** Jockey #5 / Best Seller #10 / Top 100 #11	
5/19/58	63	5	27	Cherie, I Love You..	Dot 15750
7/14/58	7	13	28	**If Dreams Came True/** Jockey #7 / Best Seller #11 / Hot 100 #12	
7/14/58	39	9	29	That's How Much I Love You	Dot 15785
9/22/58	21	11	30	For My Good Fortune/ Best Seller #21 / Hot 100 #23	
9/22/58	31	9	31	Gee, But It's Lonely	Dot 15825
10/27/58	34	11	32	I'll Remember Tonight...................................... from the film "Mardi Gras"	Dot 15840
1/12/59	21	14	33	With The Wind And The Rain In Your Hair/	
1/12/59	49	8	34	Good Rockin' Tonight..	Dot 15888
3/23/59	23	11	35	For A Penny/	
4/20/59	62	4	36	The Wang Dang Taffy-Apple Tango	Dot 15914
6/15/59	17	11	37	Twixt Twelve And Twenty..................................	Dot 15955
9/14/59	29	9	38	Fools Hall Of Fame	Dot 15982
11/30/59	71	5	39	Beyond The Sunset..	Dot 16006
2/22/60	18	12	40	(Welcome) New Lovers/	
3/21/60	94	1	41	Words	Dot 16048
5/23/60	44	8	42	Walking The Floor Over You/	
5/30/60	50	8	43	Spring Rain	Dot 16073

DEBUT DATE	PEAK POS	WKS CHR	ARTIST — Record Title	Label & Number
			PAT BOONE — Cont'd	
8/22/60	66	3	44 Delia Gone/	
8/22/60	72	3	45 Candy Sweet	Dot 16122
10/24/60	44	8	46 Dear John/	
10/24/60	47	8	47 Alabam	Dot 16152
1/23/61	64	6	48 The Exodus Song (This Land Is Mine) Pat wrote the words to this theme from the film "Exodus"	Dot 16176
5/01/61	1^{1}	15	49 **Moody River**	Dot 16209
8/21/61	19	9	50 Big Cold Wind	Dot 16244
11/13/61+	35	10	51 Johnny Will	Dot 16284
1/27/62	32	9	52 I'll See You In My Dreams/	
2/10/62	77	4	53 Pictures In The Fire	Dot 16312
5/19/62	95	1	54 Quando, Quando, Quando (Tell Me When)	Dot 16349
6/16/62	6	13	55 **Speedy Gonzales** [N]	Dot 16368
9/22/62	45	7	56 Ten Lonely Guys	Dot 16391
3/09/63	91	1	57 Meditation (Meditacao)	Dot 16439
9/26/64	72	5	58 Beach Girl	Dot 16658
10/22/66	49	8	59 Wish You Were Here, Buddy	Dot 16933
4/19/69	100	2	60 July You're A Woman	Tetragramm. 1516
			BOSTON Rock group from Boston, spearheaded by Tom Scholz (guitars and keyboards) and Brad Delp (lead vocals). Originally a quintet, group also included Barry Goudreau (guitar), Fran Sheehan (bass) and Sib Hashian (drums). After an absence from the charts for 7 years ('79-'86), Boston returned as basically a duo: Scholz & Delp.	
9/18/76	5	19	1 **More Than A Feeling**	Epic 50266
1/29/77	22	10	2 Long Time	Epic 50329
5/14/77	38	8	3 Peace Of Mind	Epic 50381
8/19/78	4	13	4 **Don't Look Back**	Epic 50590
11/18/78+	31	12	5 A Man I'll Never Be	Epic 50638
3/24/79	46	7	6 Feelin' Satisfied	Epic 50677
9/27/86	1^{2}	18	7 **Amanda**	MCA 52756
12/06/86+	9	15	8 **We're Ready**	MCA 52985
			BOSTON POPS ORCHESTRA/ARTHUR FIEDLER Fiedler was born in Boston on 12/17/1894; died on 7/10/79 (84). He first conducted the Boston Pops in 1930.	
7/04/64	55	6	1 I Want To Hold Your Hand [I] a Richard Hayman arrangement of The Beatles' first U.S. hit	RCA 8378
			PERRY BOTKIN JR. - see BARRY DeVORZON	
			BOURGEOIS TAGG West Coast rock quintet led by Brent Bourgeois and Larry Tagg.	
4/12/86	62	10	1 Mutual Surrender (What A Wonderful World)	Island 99558
			BOW WOW WOW Assembled in London by Malcolm McLaren; consisted of Annabella Lwin (from Burma) and 3 members of Adam & The Ants.	
5/29/82	62	7	1 I Want Candy	RCA 13204
4/23/83	77	4	2 Do You Wanna Hold Me?	RCA 13467
			JIMMY BOWEN with The Rhythm Orchids Born on 11/30/37 in Santa Rita, NM. Formed The Rhythm Orchids at West Texas State University with Buddy Knox, Don Lanier and Dave "Dicky Doo" Alldred. Jimmy became a producer and record executive on the West Coast. Currently President of MCA Records in Nashville.	
2/23/57	14	17	1 I'm Stickin' With You/ Top 100 #14 / Juke Box #15 / Best Seller #16 / Jockey #20 originally on Triple-D label (flip: "Party Doll" by Buddy Knox)	
3/09/57	63	6	2 Ever Lovin' Fingers	Roulette 4001
5/20/57	57	7	3 Warm Up To Me Baby	Roulette 4010
7/28/58	50	9	4 By The Light Of The Silvery Moon	Roulette 4083
			DAVID BOWIE Born David Robert Jones on 1/8/47 in London, England. First recorded as David Jones And the King Bees, Lower Third, Manish Boys, 1963. Brought highly theatrical values to rock through work with Lindsay Kemp Mime Troupe. Periods of reclusiveness heightened his appeal. Films "The Man Who Fell To Earth", 1976; "Just A Gigolo", 1978; "The Hunger", "Merry Christmas Mr. Lawrence", 1983; "Labyrinth", 1986. In Broadway play "The Elephant Man", 1980.	
4/15/72	66	7	1 Changes	RCA 0605

DEBUT DATE	PEAK POS	WKS CHR	ARTIST — Record Title	Label & Number
			DAVID BOWIE — Cont'd	
7/01/72	**65**	9	2 Starman	RCA 0719
11/25/72	**71**	5	3 The Jean Genie	RCA 0838
1/27/73	**15**	14	4 Space Oddity	RCA 0876
6/01/74	**64**	8	5 Rebel Rebel	RCA 0287
12/07/74+	**41**	11	6 Changes [R]	RCA 0605
3/15/75	**28**	11	7 Young Americans	RCA 10152
6/28/75	**1^{2}**	21	8 ● **Fame**	RCA 10320
12/13/75+	**10**	21	9 **Golden Years**	RCA 10441
5/22/76	**64**	5	10 TVC 15	RCA 10664
4/09/77	**69**	6	11 Sound And Vision	RCA 10905
12/06/80+	**70**	9	12 Fashion	RCA 12134
11/07/81+	**29**	15	13 Under Pressure **QUEEN & DAVID BOWIE**	Elektra 47235
4/17/82	**67**	10	14 Cat People (Putting Out Fire) from the original soundtrack "Cat People"	Backstreet 52024
3/26/83	**1^{1}**	20	15 ● **Let's Dance**	EMI America 8158
6/04/83	**10**	18	16 **China Girl**	EMI America 8165
9/17/83	**14**	13	17 Modern Love	EMI America 8177
3/10/84	**73**	4	18 Without You	EMI America 8190
9/15/84	**8**	18	19 **Blue Jean**	EMI America 8231
12/01/84	**53**	9	20 Tonight backing vocals by Tina Turner	EMI America 8246
2/02/85	**32**	12	21 This Is Not America **DAVID BOWIE/PAT METHENY GROUP (Pat is a jazz guitarist)** theme from the film "The Falcon And The Snowman"	EMI America 8251
8/31/85	**7**	14	22 **Dancing In The Street** **MICK JAGGER/DAVID BOWIE** from the Live-Aid concert	EMI America 8288
3/29/86	**53**	9	23 Absolute Beginners from the film "Absolute Beginners"	EMI America 8308
			RICK BOWLES Singer, songwriter from Shelby, North Carolina.	
7/03/82	**77**	3	1 Too Good To Turn Back Now	Polydor 2209
			THE BOX TOPS Formed in Memphis in 1966 by lead singer Alex Chilton (later formed Big Star band).	
8/12/67	**1^{4}**	16	1 ● **The Letter**	Mala 565
11/11/67	**24**	9	2 Neon Rainbow	Mala 580
3/02/68	**2^{2}**	15	3 ● **Cry Like A Baby**	Mala 593
6/01/68	**26**	8	4 Choo Choo Train	Mala 12005
9/14/68	**37**	6	5 I Met Her In Church	Mala 12017
12/28/68+	**28**	15	6 Sweet Cream Ladies, Forward March	Mala 12035
4/26/69	**67**	5	7 I Shall Be Released	Mala 12038
7/05/69	**18**	14	8 Soul Deep	Mala 12040
10/18/69	**58**	7	9 Turn On A Dream	Mala 12042
3/21/70	**92**	2	10 You Keep Tightening Up On Me	Bell 865
			BOY MEETS GIRL Seattle duo: George Merrill & Shannon Rubicam.	
4/06/85	**39**	13	1 Oh Girl	A&M 2713
			TOMMY BOYCE Born in Charlottesville, Virginia in 1944. Songwriter/singer with Bobby Hart.	
10/13/62	**80**	3	1 I'll Remember Carol	RCA 8074
			TOMMY BOYCE & BOBBY HART Top pop songwriting duo and production team. Toured and recorded with The Monkees' Davy Jones and Mickey Dolenz in 1975.	
7/15/67	**39**	7	1 Out & About	A&M 858
12/23/67+	**8**	14	2 **I Wonder What She's Doing Tonite**	A&M 893
4/06/68	**53**	6	3 Goodbye Baby (I Don't Want To See You Cry)	A&M 919
7/06/68	**27**	10	4 Alice Long (You're Still My Favorite Girlfriend)	A&M 948
			BONNIE BOYER	
7/28/79	**43**	8	1 Got To Give In To Love	Columbia 11028

DEBUT DATE	PEAK POS	WKS CHR	ARTIST — Record Title	Label & Number
			THE BOYS BAND	
			Member Rusty Golden is the son of the Oak Ridge Boys' Bill Golden.	
3/06/82	61	8	1 Don't Stop Me Baby (I'm On Fire)...........................	Elektra 47406
			BOYS DON'T CRY	
			British quintet - Nick Richards, lead singer.	
4/05/86	12	19	1 I Wanna Be A Cowboy...........................	Profile 5084
			THE BOYS IN THE BAND	
6/06/70	48	10	1 (How Bout A Little Hand For) The Boys In The Band...	Spring 103
			from the film "The Phynx"	
			JAN BRADLEY	
			Born on 7/6/44 in Byhalia, MS. First recorded for Formal, 1962.	
1/05/63	14	14	1 Mama Didn't Lie...........................	Chess 1845
2/06/65	93	3	2 I'm Over You...........................	Chess 1919
			OWEN BRADLEY Quintet	
			Owen was born on 10/21/15 in Westmoreland, TN. Producer, bandleader.	
7/29/57	18	5	1 White Silver Sands...........................	Decca 30363
			Jockey #18 / Top 100 #68	
			vocal by the Anita Kerr Quartet	
3/03/58	46	8	2 Big Guitar........................... [I]	Decca 30564
			Top 100 #46 / Best Seller #48	
			TERRY BRADSHAW	
			Former Pittsburgh Steelers' quarterback.	
3/06/76	91	5	1 I'm So Lonesome I Could Cry...........................	Mercury 73760
			BRAINSTORM	
			Seven-man, two-woman soul-disco band from Detroit.	
3/12/77	86	3	1 Wake Up And Be Somebody...........................	Tabu 10811
			BILL BRANDON	
			Born in Huntsville, Alabama in 1944. Vocalist, trumpet, bass, drums.	
2/25/78	80	7	1 We Fell In Love While Dancing...........................	Prelude 71102
			LAURA BRANIGAN	
			Born on 7/3/57 in New York. Pop singer. Has done some acting work.	
3/20/82	69	7	1 All Night With Me...........................	Atlantic 4023
7/10/82	2[3]	36	2 ● **Gloria**...........................	Atlantic 4048
3/19/83	7	17	3 **Solitaire**...........................	Atlantic 89868
7/02/83	12	20	4 How Am I Supposed To Live Without You...........................	Atlantic 89805
4/14/84	4	25	5 **Self Control**...........................	Atlantic 89676
8/04/84	20	15	6 The Lucky One...........................	Atlantic 89636
			from the TV program "An Uncommon Love"	
11/03/84	55	12	7 Ti Amo...........................	Atlantic 89608
7/27/85	40	11	8 Spanish Eddie...........................	Atlantic 89531
10/19/85	82	4	9 Hold Me...........................	Atlantic 89496
3/01/86	90	6	10 I Found Someone...........................	Atlantic 89451
			BRASS CONSTRUCTION	
			Formed as Dynamic Soul by Randy Muller in Brooklyn, 1968. Randy produces the band, Skyy.	
4/03/76	14	16	1 Movin'........................... [I]	United Art. 775
12/25/76+	51	12	2 Ha Cha Cha (Funktion)........................... [I]	United Art. 921
			THE BRASS RING	
			New York studio band headed by Phil Bodner (producer, arranger, sax, clarinet).	
3/12/66	32	9	1 The Phoenix Love Theme........................... [I]	Dunhill 4023
			from the film "The Flight Of The Phoenix"	
2/04/67	36	7	2 The Dis-Advantages Of You........................... [I]	Dunhill 4065
			melody taken from a Benson & Hedges cigarette jingle	
			BOB BRAUN	
			Born Robert Earl Brown on 4/20/29 in Ludlow, Kentucky. Hosted TV show in Cincinnati.	
7/21/62	26	10	1 Till Death Do Us Part........................... [S]	Decca 31355

DEBUT DATE	PEAK POS	WKS CHR	ARTIST — Record Title	Label & Number
			BREAD	
			Formed in Los Angeles in 1969. Consisted of leader David Gates (vocals, guitar, keyboards), James Griffin (guitar), Robb Royer (guitar) and Jim Gordon (drums). Originally called Pleasure Faire. Griffin wrote award-winning "For All We Know" as Arthur James in 1969. Gordon was replaced by Mike Botts after first album. Royer replaced by Larry Knechtel in 1971. Disbanded in 1973, reunited briefly in 1976. All songs written, produced and arranged by David Gates.	
6/13/70	**1**[1]	17	1 ● **Make It With You**	Elektra 45686
9/26/70	**10**	11	2 **It Don't Matter To Me**	Elektra 45701
1/02/71	**28**	10	3 Let Your Love Go	Elektra 45711
3/27/71	**4**	12	4 **If**	Elektra 45720
7/17/71	**37**	9	5 Mother Freedom	Elektra 45740
10/23/71	**3**	12	6 ● **Baby I'm-A Want You**	Elektra 45751
1/29/72	**5**	13	7 **Everything I Own**	Elektra 45765
4/22/72	**15**	11	8 Diary	Elektra 45784
7/29/72	**11**	10	9 The Guitar Man	Elektra 45803
11/11/72	**15**	11	10 Sweet Surrender	Elektra 45818
2/03/73	**15**	11	11 Aubrey	Elektra 45832
11/27/76+	**9**	16	12 **Lost Without Your Love**	Elektra 45365
4/16/77	**60**	7	13 Hooked On You	Elektra 45389
			BREATHLESS	
			6-member rock band from Cleveland, led by Jonah Koslen (from Michael Stanley Band).	
1/12/80	**92**	4	1 Takin' It Back	EMI America 8020
			THE BRECKER BROTHERS	
			Formed in New York City by sessionmen/brothers Randy and Michael Brecker.	
6/07/75	**58**	9	1 Sneakin' Up Behind You [I]	Arista 0122
			BEVERLY BREMERS	
			Chicago-born actress, singer.	
12/18/71+	**15**	16	1 Don't Say You Don't Remember	Scepter 12315
4/29/72	**40**	15	2 We're Free	Scepter 12348
9/16/72	**63**	9	3 I'll Make You Music	Scepter 12363
			BRENDA & THE TABULATIONS	
			R&B group from Philadelphia. Formed in 1966 with Brenda Payton, Jerry Jones, Eddie Jackson and Maurice Coates. Bernard Murphy was added in 1969. Reorganized in 1970 with vocalists Brenda Payton, Pat Mercer and Deborah Martin.	
2/25/67	**20**	11	1 Dry Your Eyes	Dionn 500
5/20/67	**66**	7	2 Stay Together Young Lovers/	
6/10/67	**66**	6	3 Who's Lovin' You	Dionn 501
8/12/67	**97**	2	4 Just Once In A Lifetime	Dionn 503
11/04/67	**58**	7	5 When You're Gone	Dionn 504
3/16/68	**86**	4	6 Baby You're So Right For Me	Dionn 507
1/17/70	**50**	8	7 The Touch Of You	Top & Bottom 401
5/09/70	**64**	8	8 And My Heart Sang (Tra La La)	Top & Bottom 403
8/22/70	**77**	3	9 Don't Make Me Over	Top & Bottom 404
4/03/71	**23**	13	10 Right On The Tip Of My Tongue	Top & Bottom 407
8/28/71	**94**	5	11 A Part Of You	Top & Bottom 408
			WALTER BRENNAN	
			Popular American actor. Appeared in over 100 movies from 1929-1972. Died on 9/21/74 (80).	
4/25/60	**30**	12	1 Dutchman's Gold [S] with Billy Vaughn and his orchestra	Dot 16066
4/07/62	**5**	11	2 **Old Rivers** [S]	Liberty 55436
8/04/62	**100**	1	3 Houdini [S]	Liberty 55477
10/20/62	**38**	8	4 Mama Sang A Song [S]	Liberty 55508
			BREWER & SHIPLEY	
			Folk-rock duo formed in Los Angeles: Mike Brewer & Tom Shipley.	
2/13/71	**10**	14	1 **One Toke Over The Line**	Kama Sutra 516
5/15/71	**55**	8	2 Tarkio Road	Kama Sutra 524
2/05/72	**98**	3	3 Shake Off The Demon	Kama Sutra 539

DEBUT DATE	PEAK POS	WKS CHR	ARTIST — Record Title	Label & Number
			TERESA BREWER	
			Born Theresa Breuer on 5/7/31 in Toledo, Ohio. Debuted on Major Bowes Amateur Hour at age five, toured with show until age 12. Appeared on Pick & Pat radio show. First recorded for London, 1949. In film "Those Red Heads From Seattle", 1953.	
12/18/54+	**6**	12	1 **Let Me Go, Lover!**	Coral 61315
			Juke Box #6 / Jockey #7 / Best Seller #8 with the Lancers (male vocal group)	
2/26/55	**59**	1	2 I Gotta Go Get My Baby	Coral 61339
			Honor Roll #59	
3/19/55	**17**	3	3 Pledging My Love/	
			Jockey #17 / Juke Box #18 / Best Seller #30	
		1	4 How Important Can It Be?	Coral 61362
			Juke Box flip	
6/04/55	**20**	1	5 Silver Dollar	Coral 61394
			Juke Box #20 above 5: orchestra directed by Jack Pleis	
7/30/55	**15**	4	6 The Banjo's Back In Town	Coral 61448
			Juke Box #15	
11/19/55	**66**	3	7 Shoot It Again	Coral 61528
			introduced on TV program "U.S. Steel Hour"	
2/25/56	**5**	23	8 **A Tear Fell/**	
			Juke Box #5 / Top 100 #7 / Best Seller #9 / Jockey #9	
3/03/56	**17**	15	9 Bo Weevil	Coral 61590
			Top 100 #17 / Jockey #20	
6/09/56	**7**	20	10 **A Sweet Old Fashioned Girl**	Coral 61636
			Juke Box #7 / Top 100 #9 / Jockey #11 / Best Seller #12	
9/22/56	**87**	3	11 I Love Mickey [N]	Coral 61700
			MICKEY MANTLE & TERESA BREWER	
11/10/56	**21**	14	12 Mutual Admiration Society/	
			Top 100 #21 / Best Seller #24 / Jockey #24 from the musical "Happy Hunting"	
11/24/56	**73**	5	13 Crazy With Love	Coral 61737
4/06/57	**13**	17	14 Empty Arms	Coral 61805
			Juke Box #13 / Top 100 #18 / Jockey #19 / Best Seller #23	
6/17/57	**64**	7	15 Teardrops In My Heart	Coral 61850
11/11/57	**8**	12	16 **You Send Me**	Coral 61898
			Jockey #8 / Best Seller #27 / Top 100 #31	
9/01/58	**99**	1	17 Pickle Up A Doodle	Coral 62013
10/06/58	**38**	5	18 The Hula Hoop Song	Coral 62033
1/05/59	**75**	5	19 The One Rose (That's Left In My Heart)	Coral 62057
3/16/59	**40**	8	20 Heavenly Lover	Coral 62084
2/01/60	**66**	4	21 Peace Of Mind	Coral 62167
8/08/60	**31**	16	22 Anymore	Coral 62219
11/28/60	**84**	5	23 Have You Ever Been Lonely (Have You Ever Been Blue)	Coral 62236
5/22/61	**74**	4	24 Milord	Coral 62265
			6-24: orchestra directed by Dick Jacobs	
			BRICK	
			R&B group from Atlanta. Consisted of Jimmy Brown, Ray Ransom, Donald Nevins, Reggie Harris and Eddie Irons.	
10/23/76+	**3**	21	1 **Dazz**	Bang 727
9/03/77	**18**	18	2 Dusic	Bang 734
1/28/78	**92**	4	3 Ain't Gonna' Hurt Nobody	Bang 735
			ALICIA BRIDGES	
			Atlanta-based disco singer, songwriter.	
7/08/78	**5**	31	1 ● **I Love The Nightlife (Disco 'Round)**	Polydor 14483
4/07/79	**86**	2	2 Body Heat	Polydor 14539
			LILLIAN BRIGGS	
			Pop singer discovered by Alan Freed in New York City.	
9/17/55	**18**	3	1 I Want You To Be My Baby	Epic 9115
			Jockey #18 / Juke Box #19 / Best Seller #23 / Top 100 #53 pre	
			LARRY BRIGHT	
			Singer, guitarist born on 8/17/39 in Louisville, Kentucky.	
5/16/60	**90**	3	1 Mojo Workout (Dance)	Tide 006

DEBUT DATE	PEAK POS	WKS CHR	ARTIST — Record Title	Label & Number
			BRIGHTER SIDE OF DARKNESS	
			R&B group formed at Calumet High School, Chicago in 1971; featuring 12-year old lead singer Darryl Lamont.	
12/09/72+	**16**	13	1 ● Love Jones	20th Century 2002
			MARTIN BRILEY	
			British session musician. To New York, 1975.	
5/21/83	**36**	15	1 The Salt In My Tears	Mercury 812165
			JOHNNY BRISTOL	
			Vocalist, composer, producer from Morgantown, North Carolina. Teamed with Jackie Beaver, recorded as Johnny & Jackie for Tri-Phi, 1961. Teamed with Harvey Fuqua as Motown producers to 1973.	
6/29/74	**8**	17	1 **Hang On In There Baby**	MGM 14715
11/16/74	**48**	7	2 You And I	MGM 14762
11/27/76+	**43**	11	3 Do It To My Mind	Atlantic 3360
8/30/80	**63**	8	4 My Guy/My Girl	Handshake 5300
			AMII STEWART & JOHNNY BRISTOL	
			BRITISH LIONS	
			Re-formed Mott The Hoople alumnus.	
7/22/78	**87**	4	1 Wild In The Streets	RSO 898
			BROADWAY	
7/17/76	**86**	4	1 You To Me Are Everything	Granite 540
			BRONSKI BEAT	
			British techno-pop trio: Jimmy Somerville (vocals), Steve Bronski & Larry Steinbachek (synthesizers).	
12/22/84+	**48**	16	1 Smalltown Boy	MCA 52494
			HERMAN BROOD	
			Leader of rock band from the Netherlands.	
7/14/79	**35**	11	1 Saturdaynight	Ariola 7754
			BROOKLYN BRIDGE	
			Formed in Long Island, New York with Johnny Maestro of The Crests as lead singer.	
12/21/68+	**3**	12	1 ● **Worst That Could Happen**	Buddah 75
3/08/69	**45**	6	2 Blessed Is The Rain/	
5/10/69	**48**	9	3 Welcome Me Love	Buddah 95
7/19/69	**46**	8	4 Your Husband - My Wife	Buddah 126
10/04/69	**51**	6	5 You'll Never Walk Alone	Buddah 139
			from the Rodgers & Hammerstein musical "Carousel"	
7/11/70	**91**	2	6 Down By The River	Buddah 179
10/03/70	**98**	2	7 Day Is Done	Buddah 193
			BROOKLYN DREAMS	
			New York trio: Joe "Bean" Esposito, Eddie Hokenson and Bruce Sudano (Donna Summer's husband). Also see Donna Summer.	
11/12/77	**63**	5	1 Sad Eyes	Millennium 606
3/25/78	**57**	8	2 Music, Harmony And Rhythm	Millennium 610
2/24/79	**69**	4	3 Make It Last	Casablanca 962
			DONNIE BROOKS	
			Real name: John Faircloth; born in Dallas. Early recording names: Johnny Faire, Dick Bush and Johnny Jordan.	
6/13/60	**7**	20	1 **Mission Bell**	Era 3018
11/28/60	**31**	10	2 Doll House	Era 3028
3/13/61	**90**	2	3 Memphis	Era 3042
			NANCY BROOKS	
3/03/79	**66**	4	1 I'm Not Gonna Cry Anymore	Arista 0385
			BROTHER TO BROTHER	
10/12/74	**46**	7	1 In The Bottle	Turbo 039
			THE BROTHERHOOD OF MAN	
			British studio group assembled by producer Tony Hiller.	
4/18/70	**13**	15	1 United We Stand	Deram 85059
8/22/70	**61**	7	2 Where Are You Going To My Love	Deram 85065
5/01/71	**77**	3	3 Reach Out Your Hand	Deram 85073
5/08/76	**27**	11	4 Save Your Kisses For Me	Pye 71066

DEBUT DATE	PEAK POS	WKS CHR	ARTIST — Record Title	Label & Number
			THE BROTHERS FOUR	
			Dick Foley, Bob Flick, John Paine and Mike Kirkland. Formed while fraternity brothers at the University of Washington.	
2/22/60	**2**[4]	20	1 **Greenfields**	Columbia 41571
7/04/60	**50**	7	2 My Tani	Columbia 41692
10/31/60	**65**	7	3 The Green Leaves Of Summer from the film "The Alamo"	Columbia 41808
4/10/61	**32**	5	4 Frogg [N] new version of tune written back in 1580 as "Frog Went A Courtin'"	Columbia 41958
1/20/62	**68**	8	5 Blue Water Line	Columbia 42256
12/14/63	**89**	3	6 Hootenanny Saturday Night	Columbia 42927
11/06/65	**91**	3	7 Try To Remember	Columbia 43404
			THE BROTHERS JOHNSON	
			Duo from Los Angeles. Consisted of brothers George (b: 5/17/53) and Louis (b: 4/13/55). Played since age 7, had own band, the Johnson Three + 1, with brother Tommy and cousin Alex Weir. With Billy Preston band to 1975. Also see Quincy Jones.	
5/01/76	**3**	17	1 ● **I'll Be Good To You**	A&M 1806
8/14/76	**30**	15	2 Get The Funk Out Ma Face	A&M 1851
7/02/77	**5**	19	3 ● **Strawberry Letter 23**	A&M 1949
3/15/80	**7**	19	4 **Stomp!**	A&M 2216
8/16/80	**73**	4	5 Treasure	A&M 2254
6/27/81	**67**	6	6 The Real Thing	A&M 2343
			BROWN SUGAR	
			Real name: Clydie King. First recorded for Specialty, 1957. Also known as Little Clydie. Formerly in the Raelettes.	
2/28/76	**79**	4	1 The Game Is Over (What's The Matter With You)	Capitol 4198
			AL BROWN'S TUNETOPPERS	
			From Fairmont, West Virginia. Tunetoppers formed in 1953.	
4/04/60	**23**	12	1 The Madison dance calls by Cookie Brown	Amy 804
			ALEX BROWN	
5/04/85	**76**	6	1 (Come On) Shout from the film "Girls Just Want To Have Fun"	Mercury 880694
			THE CRAZY WORLD OF ARTHUR BROWN	
			Arthur was born on 6/24/44 in Whitby, England.	
9/07/68	**2**[1]	13	1 ● **Fire**	Atlantic 2556
			BOBBY BROWN	
			Boston-bred vocalist, born on 2/5/69. Formerly of the New Edition.	
12/20/86+	**57**	9	1 Girlfriend	MCA 52866
			BOOTS BROWN & HIS BLOCKBUSTERS	
			Boots was born Milton "Shorty" Rogers on 4/14/24 in Lee, MA. Great jazz trumpeter, arranger, composer, bandleader.	
8/11/58	**23**	8	1 Cerveza [I] Best Seller #23 / Hot 100 #62	RCA 7269
			BUSTER BROWN	
			Born on 8/15/11 in Cordele, GA. Died on 1/31/76 in Brooklyn. Vocalist, harmonica player. To New York in 1956.	
2/01/60	**38**	17	1 Fannie Mae	Fire 1008
9/19/60	**81**	3	2 Is You Is Or Is You Ain't My Baby	Fire 1023
2/03/62	**99**	2	3 Sugar Babe	Fire 507
			CHARLES BROWN	
			Born in 1922 in Texas City, Texas. R&B vocalist, pianist.	
12/25/61	**76**	2	1 Please Come Home For Christmas [X]	King 5405
			CHUCK BROWN & THE SOUL SEARCHERS	
			Washington, DC-based 9-member group.	
2/03/79	**34**	12	1 ● Bustin' Loose, Part 1	Source 40967
			DON BROWN	
			Minneapolis-born singer. To Seattle in 1966.	
3/18/78	**74**	5	1 Sitting In Limbo	1st American 102

DEBUT DATE	PEAK POS	WKS CHR	ARTIST — Record Title	Label & Number
			JAMES BROWN	
			Born on 5/3/28 in Macon, Georgia. Raised in Augusta, Georgia. Sang in a gospel group, formed own vocal group, the Famous Flames. Cut a demo record of own composition "Please Please Please", November, 1955, at radio station WIBB in Macon. Signed to King/Federal Records in January, 1956 and re-recorded the song. Cameo appearances in films "The Blues Brothers" and "Rocky IV". One of the originators of "Soul" music, billed as "The Godfather Of Soul".	
12/15/58+	48	13	1 Try Me	Federal 12337
5/02/60	33	8	2 Think/	
6/27/60	86	1	3 You've Got The Power	Federal 12370
			female vocal: Bea Ford	
8/29/60	79	5	4 This Old Heart	Federal 12378
11/14/60	68	6	5 The Bells	King 5423
2/27/61	40	8	6 Bewildered	King 5442
5/15/61	47	8	7 I Don't Mind	King 5466
8/21/61	49	4	8 Baby, You're Right	King 5524
12/18/61+	48	10	9 Lost Someone	King 5573
4/14/62	35	11	10 Night Train [I]	King 5614
7/07/62	61	4	11 Shout And Shimmy	King 5657
9/29/62	82	2	12 Mashed Potatoes U.S.A.	King 5672
12/08/62	93	3	13 Three Hearts In A Tangle	King 5701
2/09/63	99	1	14 Every Beat Of My Heart [I]	King 5710
4/20/63	18	11	15 Prisoner Of Love	King 5739
7/27/63	55	6	16 These Foolish Things	King 5767
10/12/63	77	5	17 Signed, Sealed, And Delivered	King 5803
1/25/64	23	10	18 Oh Baby Don't You Weep (Part 1)	King 5842
2/15/64	95	2	19 Please, Please, Please	King 5853
5/02/64	95	2	20 Caledonia	Smash 1898
7/04/64	99	1	21 The Things That I Used To Do	Smash 1908
8/15/64	24	10	22 Out Of Sight	Smash 1919
12/26/64+	92	2	23 Have Mercy Baby	King 5968
7/17/65	8	13	24 **Papa's Got A Brand New Bag (Part I)**	King 5999
11/13/65	3	12	25 **I Got You (I Feel Good)**	King 6015
11/20/65	63	8	26 Try Me [I]	Smash 2008
			instrumental version of 1959 hit	
2/19/66	73	2	27 I'll Go Crazy/	
2/05/66	94	2	28 Lost Someone	King 6020
			live version of 1962 hit	
3/05/66	42	7	29 Ain't That A Groove (Part 1)	King 6025
4/30/66	8	9	30 **It's A Man's Man's Man's World**	King 6035
7/30/66	53	9	31 Money Won't Change You (Part 1)	King 6048
10/08/66	50	7	32 Don't Be A Drop-Out	King 6056
1/07/67	29	8	33 Bring It Up	King 6071
3/04/67	55	5	34 Kansas City	King 6086
4/08/67	100	1	35 Think	King 6091
			VICKI ANDERSON & JAMES BROWN	
5/06/67	46	7	36 Let Yourself Go	King 6100
7/15/67	7	12	37 **Cold Sweat (Part 1)**	King 6110
10/28/67	40	6	38 Get It Together (Part 1)	King 6122
12/09/67+	28	9	39 I Can't Stand Myself (When You Touch Me)/	
1/20/68	36	8	40 There Was A Time	King 6144
3/16/68	6	12	41 **I Got The Feelin'**	King 6155
5/25/68	14	8	42 Licking Stick - Licking Stick (Part 1)	King 6166
5/25/68	52	7	43 America Is My Home (Part 1) [S]	King 6112
7/27/68	55	6	44 I Guess I'll Have To Cry, Cry, Cry	King 6141
			all of above on King labeled as: James Brown & The Famous Flames	
9/07/68	10	11	45 **Say It Loud - I'm Black And I'm Proud (Part 1)**	King 6187
11/09/68	31	7	46 Goodbye My Love	King 6198
12/21/68	86	4	47 Tit For Tat (Ain't No Taking Back)	King 6204
1/25/69	15	9	48 Give It Up Or Turnit A Loose	King 6213
4/05/69	20	8	49 I Don't Want Nobody To Give Me Nothing (Open Up The Door, I'll Get It Myself)	King 6224
5/31/69	30	9	50 The Popcorn [I]	King 6240
6/14/69	11	12	51 Mother Popcorn (You Got To Have A Mother For Me) (Part 1)	King 6245

DEBUT DATE	PEAK POS	WKS CHR	ARTIST — Record Title	Label & Number
			JAMES BROWN — Cont'd	
8/23/69	**41**	6	52 Lowdown Popcorn .... [I]	King 6250
9/13/69	**37**	7	53 World (Part 1)	King 6258
10/11/69	**21**	8	54 Let A Man Come In And Do The Popcorn (Part One)....	King 6255
11/22/69+	**24**	11	55 Ain't It Funky Now (Part 1).......... [I]	King 6280
12/20/69+	**40**	8	56 Let A Man Come In And Do The Popcorn (Part Two)....	King 6275
2/14/70	**32**	8	57 It's A New Day (Part 1)	King 6292
3/21/70	**51**	5	58 Funky Drummer (Part 1)	King 6290
5/02/70	**32**	8	59 Brother Rapp (Part 1)	King 6310
7/18/70	**15**	9	60 Get Up (I Feel Like Being A) Sex Machine (Part 1)	King 6318
10/03/70	**13**	10	61 Super Bad (Part 1 & Part 2)	King 6329
1/02/71	**34**	8	62 Get Up, Get Into It, Get Involved (Part 1)..........	King 6347
2/27/71	**29**	9	63 Soul Power (Part 1)	King 6368
3/06/71	**90**	2	64 Spinning Wheel (Part 1) .... [I]	King 6366
5/08/71	**50**	6	65 I Cried	King 6363
6/12/71	**35**	6	66 Escape-ism (Part 1) .... [S]	People 2500
7/03/71	**15**	11	67 Hot Pants (She Got To Use What She Got, To Get What She Wants) (Part 1)..........	People 2501
8/28/71	**22**	9	68 Make It Funky (Part 1)..........	Polydor 14088
10/23/71	**68**	6	69 My Part/Make It Funky (Part 3) .... 68 & 69: different versions of the same tune	Polydor 14098
11/13/71	**35**	8	70 I'm A Greedy Man (Part I)..........	Polydor 14100
2/12/72	**27**	7	71 Talking Loud And Saying Nothing (Part I)	Polydor 14109
3/04/72	**40**	7	72 King Heroin.......... [S]	Polydor 14116
5/06/72	**43**	7	73 There It Is (Part 1)	Polydor 14125
6/24/72	**44**	8	74 Honky Tonk (Part 1).......... [I]	Polydor 14129
8/05/72	**18**	14	75● Get On The Good Foot (Part 1)	Polydor 14139
11/18/72	**44**	7	76 I Got A Bag Of My Own	Polydor 14153
12/23/72+	**56**	7	77 What My Baby Needs Now Is A Little More Lovin'....... **JAMES BROWN-LYN COLLINS**	Polydor 14157
1/20/73	**27**	8	78 I Got Ants In My Pants (and i want to dance) (Part 1) ..	Polydor 14162
3/10/73	**50**	7	79 Down And Out In New York City .... from the film "Black Caesar"	Polydor 14168
5/19/73	**77**	5	80 Think	Polydor 14177
8/11/73	**80**	2	81 Think .... above 2 are different versions (also see #2 and #35 above)	Polydor 14185
8/18/73	**50**	8	82 Sexy, Sexy, Sexy .... from the film "Slaughter's Big Rip-Off"	Polydor 14194
12/01/73+	**58**	11	83 Stoned To The Bone (Part 1)..........	Polydor 14210
3/23/74	**26**	13	84● The Payback (Part I)..........	Polydor 14223
6/22/74	**29**	13	85 My Thang..........	Polydor 14244
8/24/74	**31**	11	86 Papa Don't Take No Mess (Part I)..........	Polydor 14255
11/09/74	**44**	10	87 Funky President (People It's Bad)/	
		6	88 Coldblooded	Polydor 14258
2/22/75	**80**	4	89 Reality	Polydor 14268
5/17/75	**61**	5	90 Sex Machine (Part I) .... new version of #60 above	Polydor 14270
8/14/76	**45**	7	91 Get Up Offa That Thing..........	Polydor 14326
2/26/77	**88**	3	92 Bodyheat (Part 1)..........	Polydor 14360
12/07/85+	**4**	19	93 **Living In America** .... from the film "Rocky IV" - produced by Dan Hartman	Scotti Br. 05682
10/18/86	**93**	2	94 Gravity	Scotti Br. 06275
			JIM ED BROWN Born on 4/1/34 in Sparkman, Arkansas. Leader of The Browns. Host of Nashville Network's TV talent show "You Can Be A Star!".	
11/14/70	**47**	11	1 Morning	RCA 9909
			JOCELYN BROWN Former lead singer of disco groups Inner Life and Salsoul Orchestra.	
6/16/84	**75**	10	1 Somebody Else's Guy	Vinyl Dreams 71
			LOUISE BROWN	
5/08/61	**76**	5	1 Son-In-Law	Witch 101

DEBUT DATE	PEAK POS	WKS CHR	ARTIST — Record Title	Label & Number
			MAXINE BROWN	
			Born in Kingstree, SC. With gospel groups Manhattans and Royaltones in New York City, late 50s. Wrote "All In My Mind" and "Funny".	
12/31/60+	**19**	12	1 All In My Mind	Nomar 103
3/27/61	**25**	10	2 Funny	Nomar 106
6/30/62	**98**	1	3 My Time For Cryin'	ABC-Para. 10327
4/06/63	**75**	5	4 Ask Me	Wand 135
1/04/64	**99**	2	5 Coming Back To You	Wand 142
10/24/64+	**24**	13	6 Oh No Not My Baby	Wand 162
2/13/65	**56**	7	7 It's Gonna Be Alright	Wand 173
4/24/65	**55**	9	8 Something You Got **CHUCK JACKSON & MAXINE BROWN**	Wand 181
7/03/65	**55**	8	9 One Step At A Time	Wand 185
8/21/65	**91**	4	10 Can't Let You Out Of My Sight **CHUCK JACKSON & MAXINE BROWN**	Wand 191
10/23/65	**98**	1	11 I Need You So **CHUCK JACKSON & MAXINE BROWN**	Wand 198
12/11/65+	**63**	9	12 If You Gotta Make A Fool Of Somebody	Wand 1104
2/18/67	**91**	4	13 Hold On I'm Coming **CHUCK JACKSON & MAXINE BROWN**	Wand 1148
5/06/67	**91**	1	14 Daddy's Home **CHUCK JACKSON & MAXINE BROWN**	Wand 1155
9/27/69	**73**	8	15 We'll Cry Together	Commonwealth 3001
			NAPPY BROWN	
			Born Napoleon Brown Culp on 10/12/29 in Charlotte, North Carolina.	
4/30/55	**25**	4	1 Don't Be Angry Best Seller #25	Savoy 1155
1/19/57	**57**	9	2 Little By Little	Savoy 1506
11/10/58	**89**	2	3 It Don't Hurt No More	Savoy 1551
			OSCAR BROWN JR.	
5/18/74	**69**	6	1 The Lone Ranger	Atlantic 3001
			PETER BROWN	
			Born on 12/25/40 in Chicago. Vocalist, keyboards, producer.	
9/17/77	**18**	14	1 Do Ya Wanna Get Funky With Me	Drive 6258
3/04/78	**8**	28	2 **Dance With Me**	Drive 6269
9/23/78	**54**	8	3 You Should Do It background vocals on above two: Betty Wright	Drive 6272
8/18/79	**86**	6	4 Crank It Up (Funk Town) Pt. 1	Drive 6278
12/15/79+	**59**	8	5 Stargazer	Drive 6281
			POLLY BROWN	
			English vocalist. Lead singer of British groups Pickettywitch and Sweet Dreams.	
1/04/75	**16**	13	1 Up In A Puff Of Smoke	GTO 1002
			RANDY BROWN	
			Vocalist/songwriter from Memphis, Tennessee.	
3/31/79	**72**	4	1 You Says It All	Parachute 523
			ROY BROWN	
			Born on 9/10/25 in New Orleans. Died on 5/25/81 in Los Angeles. Vocalist, pianist. One of the originators of the New Orleans R&B sound. Wrote "Good Rocking Tonight".	
4/29/57	**89**	2	1 Party Doll	Imperial 5427
7/01/57	**29**	15	2 Let The Four Winds Blow Best Seller #29 / Top 100 #38	Imperial 5439
			RUTH BROWN	
			Born on 1/30/28 in Portsmouth, Virginia as Ruth Weston. Heard by Duke Ellington, who alerted Herb Abramson of the then-new Atlantic Records, who signed her to a contract. Became the premier female rhythm and blues vocalist in the early and mid-1950's. Married for a time to Willis Jackson. In later years, appeared as actress in TV shows "Hello, Larry" and "Checkin' Out".	
2/23/57	**25**	9	1 Lucky Lips Best Seller #25 / Jockey #25 / Top 100 #26	Atlantic 1125
9/22/58	**24**	10	2 This Little Girl's Gone Rockin' sax solo by King Curtis	Atlantic 1197
6/01/59	**96**	2	3 Jack O'Diamonds	Atlantic 2026
10/12/59	**64**	6	4 I Don't Know	Atlantic 2035

DEBUT DATE	PEAK POS	WKS CHR	ARTIST — Record Title	Label & Number
			RUTH BROWN — Cont'd	
3/14/60	**62**	8	5 Don't Deceive Me	Atlantic 2052
6/23/62	**97**	2	6 Shake A Hand	Philips 40028
9/08/62	**99**	1	7 Mama (He Treats Your Daughter Mean)	Philips 40056
			SHIRLEY BROWN	
			Born on 1/6/47 in West Memphis, AR. Raised in East St. Louis. Worked with Albert King.	
11/02/74	**22**	14	1 Woman To Woman	Truth 3206
5/10/75	**94**	2	2 It Ain't No Fun	Truth 3223
			JACKSON BROWNE	
			Born on 10/9/48 in Heidelberg, Germany. Vocalist, guitar, piano, composer. To Los Angeles in 1951. With Tim Buckley and Nico in 1967 in New York City. Returned to Los Angeles, concentrated on songwriting. His songs were recorded by Linda Ronstadt, Tom Rush, Joe Cocker, The Byrds, Johnny Rivers, Bonnie Raitt, and many others. Worked with the Eagles, produced Warren Zevon's first album. Wife Phyllis committed suicide on 3/25/76. Activist against nuclear power.	
3/18/72	**8**	12	1 **Doctor My Eyes**	Asylum 11004
8/05/72	**48**	9	2 Rock Me On The Water	Asylum 11006
9/29/73	**85**	10	3 Redneck Friend	Asylum 11023
2/05/77	**23**	9	4 Here Come Those Tears Again	Asylum 45379
5/21/77	**58**	5	5 The Pretender	Asylum 45399
2/11/78	**11**	17	6 Running On Empty	Asylum 45460
6/10/78	**20**	15	7 Stay/	
		8	8 The Load-Out	Asylum 45485
7/05/80	**19**	16	9 Boulevard	Asylum 47003
9/20/80	**22**	13	10 That Girl Could Sing	Asylum 47036
7/31/82	**7**	19	11 **Somebody's Baby** from the soundtrack "Fast Times At Ridgemont High"	Asylum 69982
7/09/83	**13**	15	12 Lawyers In Love	Asylum 69826
9/24/83	**25**	17	13 Tender Is The Night	Asylum 69791
1/14/84	**45**	9	14 For A Rocker	Asylum 69764
10/26/85+	**18**	19	15 You're A Friend Of Mine **CLARENCE CLEMONS & JACKSON BROWNE** includes vocals by actress Daryl Hannah (Browne's girlfriend)	Columbia 05660
3/01/86	**30**	12	16 For America	Asylum 69566
6/07/86	**70**	7	17 In The Shape Of A Heart	Asylum 69543
			THE BROWNS	
			Maxine (b: 4/27/32, Sampti, LA.), Bonnie (b: 7/31/37, Sparkman, AR.), and Jim Ed Brown (b: 4/1/34, Sparkman, AR.).	
7/27/59	**1**[4]	17	1 **The Three Bells**	RCA 7555
11/02/59	**13**	14	2 Scarlet Ribbons (For Her Hair)	RCA 7614
3/14/60	**5**	15	3 **The Old Lamplighter/**	
3/28/60	**47**	7	4 Teen-Ex	RCA 7700
11/14/60	**56**	7	5 Send Me The Pillow You Dream On	RCA 7804
12/19/60	**97**	1	6 Blue Christmas [X]	RCA 7820
4/10/61	**97**	2	7 Ground Hog all of above produced by Chet Atkins	RCA 7866
			BROWNSVILLE STATION	
			Rock trio from Ann Arbor, Michigan: Cub Koda, Michael Lutz and Henry Weck. Cub writes a column for the record collector's magazine, Goldmine.	
12/23/72+	**96**	3	1 The Red Back Spider [N]	Big Tree 156
3/03/73	**57**	8	2 Let Your Yeah Be Yeah	Big Tree 161
10/27/73+	**3**	19	3● **Smokin' In The Boy's Room**	Big Tree 16011
5/25/74	**48**	8	4 I'm The Leader Of The Gang	Big Tree 15005
8/31/74	**31**	9	5 Kings Of The Party	Big Tree 16001
6/04/77	**46**	10	6 Lady (Put The Light On Me)	Private S. 45149
8/20/77	**59**	7	7 The Martian Boogie [N]	Private S. 45167
			DAVE BRUBECK QUARTET	
			David was born David Warren on 12/6/20 in Concord, California. Besides Brubeck (piano), quartet consists of Paul Desmond (alto sax), Joe Morello (drums), and Eugene Wright (bass). One of America's all-time most popular jazz groups on college campuses.	
9/11/61	**25**	12	1 Take Five [I]	Columbia 41479
12/04/61+	**74**	6	2 Unsquare Dance [I]	Columbia 42228
1/05/63	**69**	7	3 Bossa Nova U.S.A. [I]	Columbia 42651

DEBUT DATE	PEAK POS	WKS CHR	ARTIST — Record Title	Label & Number
			BRUCE & TERRY	
			Bruce Johnston (of the Beach Boys) & Terry Melcher (Doris Day's son - produced The Byrds, Paul Revere & The Raiders). Also see The Rip Chords.	
2/22/64	**85**	3	1 Custom Machine	Columbia 42956
7/25/64	**72**	5	2 Summer Means Fun	Columbia 43055
			ANITA BRYANT	
			Born on 3/25/40 in Barnsdale, Oklahoma. As 'Miss Oklahoma', she was second runner-up to 'Miss America' in 1958.	
6/29/59	**30**	13	1 Till There Was You from the Broadway musical "The Music Man"	Carlton 512
9/21/59	**62**	6	2 Six Boys And Seven Girls	Carlton 518
12/28/59+	**78**	3	3 Promise Me A Rose (A Slight Detail)/ from the Broadway musical "Take Me Along"	
12/28/59	**94**	1	4 Do-Re-Mi [N] from the Broadway musical "The Sound Of Music"	Carlton 523
4/11/60	**5**	17	5 **Paper Roses**	Carlton 528
7/11/60	**10**	14	6 **In My Little Corner Of The World**	Carlton 530
10/10/60	**62**	7	7 One Of The Lucky Ones	Carlton 535
12/05/60+	**18**	10	8 Wonderland By Night	Carlton 537
2/13/61	**85**	4	9 A Texan And A Girl From Mexico	Carlton 538
5/15/61	**87**	2	10 I Can't Do It By Myself	Carlton 547
5/16/64	**59**	8	11 The World Of Lonely People	Columbia 43037
			RAY BRYANT COMBO	
			Born Raphael Bryant on 12/24/31 in Philadelphia. R&B/jazz pianist. Band on "Madison Time" included Bryant (piano), Harry Edison (trumpet), Urbie Green (trombone), Buddy Tated (tenor sax), Tommy Bryant (bass) and Bill English (drums). Also see Aretha Franklin.	
4/11/60	**30**	9	1 The Madison Time - Part I [S-I] dance calls by Eddie Morrison (died on 2/28/87 in Chicago)	Columbia 41628
9/30/67	**89**	2	2 Ode To Billy Joe [I] shown only as: **RAY BRYANT**	Cadet 5575
			PEABO BRYSON	
			Born Robert Peabo Bryson on 4/13/51 in Greenville, SC. Also see Michael Zager.	
2/28/81	**54**	9	1 Lovers After All **MELISSA MANCHESTER & PEABO BRYSON**	Arista 0587
1/09/82	**42**	12	2 Let The Feeling Flow	Capitol 5065
7/09/83	**16**	29	3 Tonight, I Celebrate My Love **PEABO BRYSON/ROBERTA FLACK**	Capitol 5242
12/24/83+	**58**	11	4 You're Looking Like Love To Me **PEABO BRYSON/ROBERTA FLACK**	Capitol 5307
5/12/84	**10**	25	5 **If Ever You're In My Arms Again**	Elektra 69728
9/29/84	**82**	4	6 Slow Dancin'	Elektra 69699
6/29/85	**78**	6	7 Take No Prisoners (In The Game Of Love)	Elektra 69632
			B.T. EXPRESS	
			Brooklyn, New York disco septet. B.T. stands for Brothers Trucking.	
9/28/74	**2**[2]	18	1 ● **Do It ('Til You're Satisfied)**	Roadshow 12395
1/25/75	**4**	15	2 ● **Express** [I]	Roadshow 7001
8/09/75	**40**	6	3 Give It What You Got/	
9/20/75	**31**	12	4 Peace Pipe	Roadshow 7003
1/24/76	**82**	4	5 Close To You	Roadshow 7005
6/05/76	**52**	4	6 Can't Stop Groovin' Now, Wanna Do It Some More	Columbia 10346
			THE BUBBLE PUPPY	
			Psychedelic rock band from Austin, Texas. Later recorded as Demian.	
2/15/69	**14**	12	1 Hot Smoke & Sasafrass	Int. Artists 128
			BUCHANAN & ANCELL	
			Bill Buchanan (former partner with Dickie Goodman) & Bob Ancell.	
12/09/57	**85**	5	1 The Creature [N]	Flying Saucer 501
			BUCHANAN & GOODMAN	
			Bill Buchanan and Richard "Dickie" Goodman conceived the idea of a radio show being interrupted by reports of flying saucers in 1956. Segments of popular records were taped and spliced into the dialogue. The record was heard by Alan Freed and he played it on his WINS-New York radio show. A national hit resulted and the "break-in" record was born. Buchanan left the music business in 1959, but Dickie Goodman remains active. Also see Dickie Goodman.	
8/04/56	**3**	13	1 **The Flying Saucer (Parts 1 & 2)** [N] Best Seller #3 / Top 100 #7 / Jockey #9 / Juke Box #9	Luniverse 101

DEBUT DATE	PEAK POS	WKS CHR	ARTIST — Record Title	Label & Number
			BUCHANAN & GOODMAN — Cont'd	
11/17/56	**80**	1	2 Buchanan and Goodman On Trial........................ [N]	Luniverse 102
7/22/57	**18**	13	3 Flying Saucer The 2nd .... [N] Best Seller #18 / Top 100 #19	Luniverse 105
12/23/57	**32**	5	4 Santa & The Satellite (Parts I & II) .... [X-N] Top 100 #32 / Best Seller #36 naration by disc jockey Paul Sherman	Luniverse 107
			BUCHANAN BROTHERS Producers Terry Cashman, Gene Pistilli and Tommy West.	
5/03/69	**22**	11	1 Medicine Man (Part I)................................	Event 3302
9/20/69	**61**	6	2 Son Of A Lovin' Man	Event 3305
			BUCKEYE	
8/25/79	**63**	5	1 Where Will Your Heart Take You........................	Polydor 14578
			LINDSEY BUCKINGHAM Born on 10/3/47 in California. Lindsey, along with Stevie Nicks, joined Fleetwood Mac in 1975.	
10/24/81+	**9**	19	1 **Trouble**..	Asylum 47223
8/06/83	**82**	5	2 Holiday Road .... from the National Lampoon film "Vacation"	Warner 29570
7/28/84	**23**	16	3 Go Insane..	Elektra 69714
			THE BUCKINGHAMS Chicago rock quintet led by Dennis Tufano & Carl Giammarese.	
12/31/66+	**1^{2}**	13	1 **Kind Of A Drag**................................	U.S.A. 860
3/11/67	**41**	6	2 Laudy Miss Claudy	U.S.A. 869
3/11/67	**6**	14	3 **Don't You Care**	Columbia 44053
6/17/67	**5**	12	4 **Mercy, Mercy, Mercy**	Columbia 44182
9/09/67	**12**	10	5 Hey Baby (They're Playing Our Song)	Columbia 44254
12/09/67+	**11**	12	6 Susan..	Columbia 44378
6/08/68	**57**	6	7 Back In Love Again................................	Columbia 44533
			BUCKNER & GARCIA Atlanta-based duo: Jerry Buckner & Gary Garcia. Also see Willis The Guard.	
1/09/82	**9**	19	1 ● **Pac-Man Fever**................................ [N] inspired by the all-time #1 video game "Pac-Man"	Columbia 02673
			BUCKWHEAT	
4/01/72	**84**	5	1 Simple Song Of Freedom................................	London 176
			BUD & TRAVIS Balladeers Bud Dashiel & Travis Edmonson. Formed duo in San Francisco, 1958.	
10/17/60	**64**	9	1 Ballad Of The Alamo................................ from the movie "The Alamo"	Liberty 55284
			JULIE BUDD - see JULIE	
			THE BUENA VISTAS	
7/02/66	**87**	4	1 Hot Shot .... [I]	Swan 4255
6/01/68	**88**	4	2 Here Come Da Judge................................ [I]	Marquee 443
			THE BUFFALO SPRINGFIELD Superstar group formed in Los Angeles, 1966: Stephen Stills, Neil Young, Richie Furay, Dewey Martin and Bruce Palmer (replaced by Jim Messina after first 2 albums). Disbanded, 1968.	
1/28/67	**7**	15	1 **For What It's Worth (Stop, Hey What's That Sound)**................................	Atco 6459
7/15/67	**58**	7	2 Bluebird..	Atco 6499
9/30/67	**44**	7	3 Rock 'N' Roll Woman	Atco 6519
1/13/68	**98**	2	4 Expecting To Fly	Atco 6545
10/12/68	**82**	3	5 On The Way Home................................	Atco 6615
			JIMMY BUFFETT Born on 12/25/46 in Mobile, Alabama. Backed by the Coral Reefer Band since 1975.	
5/18/74	**30**	14	1 Come Monday	Dunhill 4385
4/02/77	**8**	22	2 **Margaritaville**	ABC 12254
9/17/77	**37**	10	3 Changes In Latitudes, Changes In Attitudes	ABC 12305
4/22/78	**32**	11	4 Cheeseburger In Paradise................................ [N]	ABC 12358
8/12/78	**52**	6	5 Livingston Saturday Night................................	ABC 12391
12/02/78	**84**	6	6 Manana	ABC 12428

DEBUT DATE	PEAK POS	WKS CHR	ARTIST — Record Title		Label & Number
			JIMMY BUFFETT — Cont'd		
9/08/79	**35**	11	7 Fins		MCA 41109
12/22/79+	**66**	7	8 Volcano		MCA 41161
3/08/80	**77**	5	9 Survive		MCA 41199
2/21/81	**57**	8	10 It's My Job		MCA 51061
			THE BUGGLES		
			English duo: Geoff Downes & Trevor Horne (both joined "Yes" in 1980).		
11/10/79	**40**	10	1 Video Killed The Radio Star		Island 49114
			the premiere video on MTV's first show (8/1/81)		
			BULL & THE MATADORS		
8/24/68	**39**	14	1 The Funky Judge		Toddlin' Town 108
			BULLDOG		
			Rock quartet led by former Rascals Gene Cornish & Dino Danelli. Also see Fotomaker.		
10/14/72	**44**	15	1 No		Decca 32996
			CINDY BULLENS		
			Background vocalist with Elton John, Rod Stewart and Bob Dylan. From Boston.		
2/03/79	**56**	7	1 Survivor		United Art. 1261
1/12/80	**90**	3	2 Trust Me		Casablanca 2217
			BULLET		
11/06/71+	**28**	13	1 White Lies, Blue Eyes		Big Tree 123
3/11/72	**96**	2	2 Willpower Weak, Temptation Strong		Big Tree 131
			BUMBLE BEE UNLIMITED		
			Seven-member New York-based disco act.		
12/11/76+	**92**	5	1 Love Bug		Mercury 73864
			THE BUOYS		
			Rock quintet; Bill Kelly, lead singer.		
1/02/71	**17**	17	1 Timothy		Scepter 12275
6/19/71	**84**	3	2 Give Up Your Guns		Scepter 12318
			GARY BURBANK with Band McNally		
6/28/80	**67**	5	1 Who Shot J.R.?	[N]	Ovation 1150
			inspired by the J.R. shooting episode on TV's "Dallas"		
			ERIC BURDON & WAR		
			Eric was born on 5/11/41 in Newcastle-On-Tyne, England. After leaving the Animals, Eric teamed up with the funk band War for 2 albums.		
5/23/70	**3**	21	1 ● **Spill The Wine**		MGM 14118
12/19/70+	**50**	8	2 They Can't Take Away Our Music		MGM 14196
			SOLOMON BURKE		
			Born in 1936 in Philadelphia. Preached and broadcast from own church, "Solomon's Temple", in Philadelphia from 1945-55 as the "Wonder Boy Preacher". Church was founded for him by his grandmother. First recorded for Apollo in 1954. Left music to attend mortuary school, returned in 1960.		
9/18/61	**24**	17	1 Just Out Of Reach (Of My Two Open Arms)		Atlantic 2114
1/27/62	**44**	10	2 Cry To Me		Atlantic 2131
5/26/62	**71**	8	3 Down In The Valley/		
7/07/62	**85**	2	4 I'm Hanging Up My Heart For You		Atlantic 2147
9/08/62	**93**	3	5 I Really Don't Want To Know		Atlantic 2157
4/20/63	**37**	11	6 If You Need Me		Atlantic 2185
7/20/63	**66**	6	7 Can't Nobody Love You		Atlantic 2196
11/02/63	**49**	8	8 You're Good For Me		Atlantic 2205
2/08/64	**51**	8	9 He'll Have To Go		Atlantic 2218
4/18/64	**33**	10	10 Goodbye Baby (Baby Goodbye)		Atlantic 2226
7/18/64	**58**	8	11 Everybody Needs Somebody To Love		Atlantic 2241
10/10/64	**92**	3	12 Yes I Do		Atlantic 2254
11/28/64	**57**	5	13 The Price		Atlantic 2259
3/06/65	**22**	10	14 Got To Get You Off My Mind		Atlantic 2276
5/29/65	**28**	10	15 Tonight's The Night		Atlantic 2288
8/21/65	**89**	4	16 Someone Is Watching		Atlantic 2299
11/27/65	**94**	2	17 Only Love (Can Save Me Now)		Atlantic 2308
1/08/66	**96**	2	18 Baby Come On Home		Atlantic 2314
4/09/66	**97**	2	19 I Feel A Sin Coming On		Atlantic 2327

DEBUT DATE	PEAK POS	WKS CHR	ARTIST — Record Title	Label & Number
			SOLOMON BURKE — Cont'd	
2/11/67	**64**	5	20 Keep A Light In The Window Till I Come Home	Atlantic 2378
7/01/67	**49**	5	21 Take Me (Just As I Am)	Atlantic 2416
5/04/68	**68**	8	22 I Wish I Knew (How It Would Feel To Be Free)	Atlantic 2507
5/03/69	**45**	7	23 Proud Mary	Bell 783
5/01/71	**96**	2	24 The Electronic Magnetism (That's Heavy, Baby)	MGM 14221
4/15/72	**89**	5	25 Love's Street And Fool's Road from the film "Cool Breeze"	MGM 14353
3/22/75	**96**	2	26 You And Your Baby Blues	Chess 2159
			BILLY BURNETTE Born on 5/8/53 in Memphis. Son of Dorsey Burnette.	
11/01/80	**68**	5	1 Don't Say No	Columbia 11380
			DORSEY BURNETTE Born on 12/28/32 in Memphis. Died on 8/19/79 (46) of a heart attack.	
2/01/60	**23**	15	1 (There Was A) Tall Oak Tree	Era 3012
6/06/60	**48**	11	2 Hey Little One	Era 3019
1/25/69	**67**	6	3 The Greatest Love	Liberty 56087
			JOHNNY BURNETTE Born on 3/25/34 in Memphis. Died on 8/1/64 (30) in a boating accident on Clear Lake in California. Johnny, brother Dorsey and Paul Burlison formed the Johnny Burnette Rock 'N Roll Trio, 1953-57. Also see The Texans.	
7/25/60	**11**	15	1 Dreamin'	Liberty 55258
10/31/60	**8**	15	2 **You're Sixteen**	Liberty 55285
2/06/61	**17**	9	3 Little Boy Sad	Liberty 55298
5/01/61	**58**	7	4 Big Big World	Liberty 55318
10/16/61	**18**	9	5 God, Country And My Baby	Liberty 55379
			ROCKY BURNETTE Born on 6/12/53 in Memphis. Son of Johnny Burnette.	
5/10/80	**8**	19	1 **Tired Of Toein' The Line**	EMI America 8043
			GEORGE BURNS Born Nathan Birnbaum on 1/20/1896. George and wife Gracie starred together in vaudeville, movies, radio and TV from the 1930s until Gracie's death in 1964. George went on to enjoy a remarkable second career, winning the Academy Award in 1975 for "The Sunshine Boys". His only other charted record was back in 1933 - the all-time longest span between charted hits (47 years).	
1/19/80	**49**	10	1 I Wish I Was Eighteen Again	Mercury 57011
			KENNY BURRELL - see JIMMY SMITH	
			TONY BURROWS British vocalist for the following groups: White Plains, First Class, Edison Lighthouse and the Pipkins.	
6/06/70	**87**	4	1 Melanie Makes Me Smile	Bell 884
			JENNY BURTON Born on 11/18/57 in New York City. Worked as a secretary at Bell Records.	
1/28/84	**81**	6	1 Remember What You Like	Atlantic 89748
6/09/84	**54**	7	2 Strangers In A Stranger World **JENNY BURTON & PATRICK JUDE** Love Theme from the film "Beat Street"	Atlantic 89660
			RICHARD BURTON Real name: Richard Jenkins. Welsh leading actor from 1948-1983. Died 8/5/84 (58).	
1/30/65	**64**	5	1 Married Man [S] from Broadway's "Baker Street"	MGM 13307
			THE BUS BOYS Los Angeles-based sextet; appeared in the film "48 HRS.".	
8/04/84	**68**	5	1 Cleanin' Up The Town from the film "Ghostbusters"	Arista 9229
			LOU BUSCH Born on 7/18/10 in Louisville. Died on 9/19/79. Also recorded as Joe "Fingers" Carr.	
12/24/55+	**75**	6	1 Zambezi [I]	Capitol 3272
2/25/56	**35**	11	2 11th Hour Melody	Capitol 3349
5/19/56	**19**	16	3 Portuguese Washerwomen [I] shown as: **JOE "FINGERS" CARR** Jockey #19 / Best Seller #25 / Top 100 #25	Capitol 3418

DEBUT DATE	PEAK POS	WKS CHR	ARTIST — Record Title	Label & Number
			KATE BUSH	
			Born on 7/30/58 in Plumstead, England.	
2/17/79	**85**	4	1 The Man With The Child In His Eyes	EMI America 8006
9/07/85	**30**	20	2 Running Up That Hill	EMI America 8285
			THE BUSTERS	
9/07/63	**25**	10	1 Bust Out [I]	Arlen 735
			THE BUTANES	
			R&B group backed by Teddy McRae's orchestra.	
7/31/61	**96**	3	1 Don't Forget I Love You	Enrica 1007
			THE JON BUTCHER AXIS	
			Boston rock group led by Jon Butcher (vocals/guitar).	
11/30/85	**94**	3	1 Sounds Of Your Voice	Capitol 5534
			BILLY BUTLER & THE CHANTERS	
			Born on 6/7/45 in Chicago. Formed group Infinity, 1969. Jerry Butler's brother.	
7/03/65	**60**	6	1 I Can't Work No Longer	Okeh 7221
			CARL BUTLER	
			Born on 6/2/27 in Knoxville, Tennessee. Country singer, wife Pearl sang harmony.	
2/09/63	**88**	2	1 Don't Let Me Cross Over	Columbia 42593
			CHAMP BUTLER with GEORGE CATES	
11/19/55	**77**	4	1 Someone On Your Mind	Coral 61496
			JERRY BUTLER	
			Born on 12/8/39 in Sunflower, Mississippi. To Chicago, 1944. Sang with church groups, and the Northern Jubilee Gospel Singers, with Curtis Mayfield. Later with R&B group, the Quails. In 1957, he and Mayfield joined a vocal group, the Roosters, with Sam Gooden, Arthur Brooks and Richard Brooks. Changed name to the Impressions in 1957. Left for solo career in autumn of 1958. Teamed again with Curtis Mayfield for a string of hits with Vee-Jay from 1960-64.	
6/16/58	**11**	12	1 For Your Precious Love **JERRY BUTLER & THE IMPRESSIONS** Best Seller #11 / Top 100 #11 / Jockey #25	Abner/Falcon 1013
10/31/60	**7**	15	2 **He Will Break Your Heart**	Vee-Jay 354
3/06/61	**27**	10	3 Find Another Girl	Vee-Jay 375
7/24/61	**25**	8	4 I'm A Telling You	Vee-Jay 390
10/09/61	**11**	17	5 Moon River from the film "Breakfast At Tiffany's"	Vee-Jay 405
7/07/62	**20**	11	6 Make It Easy On Yourself	Vee-Jay 451
10/13/62	**63**	7	7 You Can Run (But You Can't Hide)	Vee-Jay 463
12/15/62	**100**	1	8 Theme From Taras Bulba (The Wishing Star)	Vee-Jay 475
3/30/63	**68**	6	9 Whatever You Want	Vee-Jay 486
11/23/63+	**31**	11	10 Need To Belong	Vee-Jay 567
4/04/64	**56**	6	11 Giving Up On Love	Vee-Jay 588
6/27/64	**95**	2	12 I Don't Want To Hear Anymore/	
8/01/64	**61**	6	13 I Stand Accused	Vee-Jay 598
9/05/64	**5**	13	14 **Let It Be Me**	Vee-Jay 613
12/05/64+	**42**	7	15 Smile above 2: **BETTY EVERETT & JERRY BUTLER**	Vee-Jay 633
3/06/65	**64**	4	16 Good Times	Vee-Jay 651
3/26/66	**99**	2	17 For Your Precious Love new version of his first charted record	Vee-Jay 715
1/21/67	**60**	9	18 I Dig You Baby	Mercury 72648
10/21/67	**38**	7	19 Mr. Dream Merchant	Mercury 72721
12/30/67+	**62**	6	20 Lost	Mercury 72764
5/04/68	**20**	14	21 Never Give You Up	Mercury 72798
8/31/68	**16**	13	22 Hey, Western Union Man	Mercury 72850
12/07/68+	**39**	10	23 Are You Happy	Mercury 72876
3/01/69	**4**	13	24 ● **Only The Strong Survive**	Mercury 72898
5/31/69	**24**	10	25 Moody Woman	Mercury 72929
8/30/69	**20**	10	26 What's The Use Of Breaking Up	Mercury 72960
11/15/69	**44**	8	27 Don't Let Love Hang You Up	Mercury 72991
1/24/70	**62**	5	28 Got To See If I Can't Get Mommy (To Come Back Home)	Mercury 73015
3/21/70	**46**	5	29 I Could Write A Book	Mercury 73045

DEBUT DATE	PEAK POS	WKS CHR	ARTIST — Record Title	Label & Number
			JERRY BUTLER — Cont'd	
8/22/70	**95**	1	30 Where Are You Going from the soundtrack "Joe"	Mercury 73101
1/02/71	**94**	3	31 You Just Can't Win (By Making The Same Mistake) GENE & JERRY	Mercury 73163
3/06/71	**69**	8	32 If It's Real What I Feel	Mercury 73169
7/10/71	**85**	3	33 How Did We Lose It Baby	Mercury 73210
10/09/71	**93**	2	34 Walk Easy My Son	Mercury 73241
12/11/71+	**21**	18	35● Ain't Understanding Mellow JERRY BUTLER & BRENDA LEE EAGER	Mercury 73255
5/20/72	**85**	4	36 I Only Have Eyes For You	Mercury 73290
9/09/72	**91**	3	37 (They Long To Be) Close To You JERRY BUTLER featuring BRENDA LEE EAGER	Mercury 73301
11/04/72	**52**	7	38 One Night Affair	Mercury 73335
3/12/77	**51**	11	39 I Wanna Do It To You	Motown 1414
			THE BUTTERFLYS Girl group is actually singer-songwriter Ellie Greenwich.	
9/12/64	**51**	7	1 Good Night Baby	Red Bird 009
			BOBBY BYRD Born on 8/15/34 in Toccoa, Georgia. Founder and leader of James Brown's vocal group, the Famous Flames.	
4/04/64	**52**	6	1 Baby Baby Baby ANNA KING-BOBBY BYRD	Smash 1884
10/24/70	**69**	5	2 I Need Help (I Can't Do It Alone) Pt. 1	King 6323
9/25/71	**85**	4	3 Hot Pants - I'm Coming, Coming, I'm Coming	BrownStone 4203
2/26/72	**88**	3	4 Keep On Doin' What You're Doin'	BrownStone 4205
			CHARLIE BYRD Born on 9/16/25 in Chuckatuch, Virginia. Jazz and classical guitar virtuoso.	
9/29/62	**15**	16	1 Desafinado [I] STAN GETZ/CHARLIE BYRD	Verve 10323
1/26/63	**66**	9	2 Meditation (Meditacao) [I] orchestral backing by the Walter Raim Strings	Riverside 4544
			DONALD BYRD Born on 12/9/32 in Detroit. Trumpet, flugelhorn. Founded the Blackbyrds in 1973.	
6/09/73	**88**	6	1 Black Byrd [I]	Blue Note 212
			JERRY BYRD Born on 3/9/20 in Lima, Ohio. Steel guitarist.	
8/01/60	**97**	1	1 Theme From Adventures In Paradise [I] from the TV series "Adventures In Paradise"	Monument 419
3/17/62	**74**	9	2 Memories Of Maria [I] written by Roy Orbison	Monument 449
			RUSSELL BYRD	
5/08/61	**50**	5	1 You'd Better Come Home	Wand 107
			THE BYRDS Folk-rock group formed in Los Angeles, 1964. Consisted of James (Roger) McGuinn, 12-string guitar; David Crosby, guitar; Gene Clark, percussion; Chris Hillman, bass; and Mike Clarke, drums. McGuinn, who changed his name to Roger in 1968, had been with Bobby Darin and the Chad Mitchell Trio. Clark had been with the New Christy Minstrels. All except Clarke had folk music background. Professional debut March, 1965. First recorded as the Beefeaters for Elektra, 1965. Also recorded as the Jet Set. Clark left after "Eight Miles High". Crosby left in 1968 to form Crosby, Stills, And Nash. Reformed in 1968 with McGuinn, Hillman, Kevin Kelly, drums; and Gram Parsons, guitar. Hillman and Parsons left to form the Flying Burrito Brothers. McGuinn again reformed with Clarence White, guitar; John York, bass; and Gene Parsons, drums. Reunions with original members in 1973 and 1979.	
5/15/65	**1**[1]	13	1 **Mr. Tambourine Man**	Columbia 43271
7/03/65	**40**	10	2 All I Really Want To Do	Columbia 43332
10/23/65	**1**[3]	14	3 **Turn! Turn! Turn!** lyrics adapted by Pete Seeger from the Book of Ecclesiastes	Columbia 43424
2/05/66	**79**	4	4 Set You Free This Time/	
2/12/66	**63**	5	5 It Won't Be Wrong	Columbia 43501
4/09/66	**14**	9	6 Eight Miles High	Columbia 43578
7/16/66	**44**	5	7 5 D (Fifth Dimension)	Columbia 43702
9/24/66	**36**	7	8 Mr. Spaceman	Columbia 43766
1/28/67	**29**	7	9 So You Want To Be A Rock 'N' Roll Star	Columbia 43987
4/01/67	**30**	7	10 My Back Pages	Columbia 44054

DEBUT DATE	PEAK POS	WKS CHR	ARTIST — Record Title		Label & Number
			THE BYRDS — Cont'd		
6/10/67	**74**	4	11 Have You Seen Her Face		Columbia 44157
8/19/67	**82**	2	12 Lady Friend		Columbia 44230
11/18/67	**89**	3	13 Goin' Back		Columbia 44362
5/11/68	**74**	5	14 You Ain't Going Nowhere		Columbia 44499
11/01/69	**65**	6	15 Ballad Of Easy Rider from the Peter Fonda movie "Easy Rider"		Columbia 44990
2/07/70	**97**	1	16 Jesus Is Just Alright		Columbia 45071
			EDD BYRNES Born Eddie Breitenberger on 7/30/33 in New York City. Best known as "Kookie" on the TV series "77 Sunset Strip".		
4/20/59	**4**	13	1 **Kookie, Kookie (Lend Me Your Comb)** **EDWARD BYRNES & CONNIE STEVENS**	[N]	Warner 5047
8/10/59	**42**	9	2 Like I Love You **EDD BYRNES & FRIEND**	[N]	Warner 5087

C

DEBUT DATE	PEAK POS	WKS CHR	ARTIST — Record Title		Label & Number
			THE CABOOSE		
8/01/70	**79**	3	1 Black Hands White Cotton		Enterprise 9015
			THE CADETS Los Angeles R&B quintet: Aaron Collins (lead singer), Ted Taylor, William "Dub" Jones (bass man for The Coasters), Willie Davis and Lloyd McCraw. Also recorded as The Jacks.		
7/14/56	**15**	11	1 Stranded In The Jungle Best Seller #15 / Jockey #16 / Juke Box #16 / Top 100 #18	[N]	Modern 994
			THE CADILLACS R&B vocal group formed in Harlem in 1953. Originally called the Carnations. The Cadillacs were the first R&B vocal group to extensively use choreography in their stage routines.		
12/10/55+	**17**	17	1 Speedoo Best Seller #17 / Top 100 #30 song named after nickname of group's lead singer, Earl Carroll		Josie 785
12/08/58+	**28**	10	2 Peek-A-Boo		Josie 846
			SHIRLEY CAESAR Born in 1939 in Durham, NC. Billed as the "First Lady Of Gospel Music".		
5/17/75	**91**	5	1 No Charge	[N]	Hob/Scepter 12402
			JOHN CAFFERTY & THE BEAVER BROWN BAND Rock sextet from Rhode Island. Wrote and recorded the music for the soundtrack "Eddie & The Cruisers".		
10/08/83	**64**	9	1 On The Dark Side shown as (on original release only): **EDDIE & THE CRUISERS**		Scotti Br. 04107
1/28/84	**78**	5	2 Tender Years		Scotti Br. 04327
8/18/84	**7**	18	3 **On The Dark Side**	[R]	Scotti Br. 04594
11/17/84+	**31**	14	4 Tender Years above tunes are from the film "Eddie & The Cruisers"	[R]	Scotti Br. 04682
5/11/85	**22**	15	5 Tough All Over		Scotti Br. 04891
8/10/85	**18**	15	6 C-I-T-Y		Scotti Br. 05452
11/09/85	**64**	10	7 Small Town Girl		Scotti Br. 05668
3/01/86	**76**	6	8 Heart's On Fire artist shown only as: **JOHN CAFFERTY** from the film "Rocky IV"		Scotti Br. 05774
6/14/86	**62**	8	9 Voice Of America's Sons from the film "Cobra"		Scotti Br. 06048
			JONATHAN CAIN Former keyboardist with The Babys. Member of Journey since 1981.		
1/10/76	**44**	9	1 'Til It's Time To Say Goodbye		October 1001
			TANE CAIN Wife of Journey's Jonathan Cain.		
8/14/82	**37**	11	1 Holdin' On		RCA 13287

DEBUT DATE	PEAK POS	WKS CHR	ARTIST — Record Title		Label & Number
			AL CAIOLA		
			Born on 9/7/20 in Jersey City, NJ. Guitarist, composer, bandleader. First recorded for Savoy in 1955. Prolific studio work.		
12/05/60+	**35**	12	1 The Magnificent Seven from the film of the same title	[I]	United Art. 261
4/03/61	**19**	10	2 Bonanza theme from the TV series of the same title	[I]	United Art. 302
			BOBBY CALDWELL		
			Born on 8/15/51 in New York City. Vocalist, pianist, percussionist, composer. Plays many instruments. Wrote tracks for "New Mickey Mouse Club" TV show, and commercials. With Johnny Winter in early 70s.		
12/23/78+	**9**	20	1 **What You Won't Do For Love**		Clouds 11
4/19/80	**42**	10	2 Coming Down From Love		Clouds 21
9/11/82	**77**	6	3 All Of My Love		Polydor 2212
			J.J. CALE		
			Born John J. Cale on 12/5/38 in Oklahoma City. Singer, songwriter, guitarist.		
1/29/72	**22**	14	1 Crazy Mama		Shelter 7314
5/20/72	**42**	11	2 After Midnight		Shelter 7321
11/04/72	**42**	8	3 Lies		Shelter 7326
12/25/76	**96**	3	4 Hey Baby		Shelter 62002
			FRANKIE CALEN		
6/12/61	**78**	6	1 Joanie		Spark 902
			THE CALL		
			California-based rock quartet - Michael Been, lead vocals.		
5/07/83	**74**	5	1 The Walls Came Down		Mercury 811487
			BOBBY CALLENDER		
3/16/63	**95**	2	1 Little Star		Roulette 4471
			CAB CALLOWAY		
			Born Cabell Calloway on 12/25/07 in Rochester, New York. Nicknamed "His Hi-De-Ho Highness Of Jive". Vocalist, bandleader, alto sax, drums.		
2/18/56	**62**	2	1 Little Child **LAEL & CAB CALLOWAY (Lael is Cab's daughter)**		ABC-Para. 9671
4/16/66	**89**	3	2 History Repeats Itself	[S]	Boom 60006
			THE CAMBRIDGE STRINGS & SINGERS		
			British studio assemblage conducted and arranged by Dick Rowe and Malcolm Lockyer. Also see Knightsbridge Strings.		
2/13/61	**60**	6	1 Theme from Tunes Of Glory from the film "Tunes Of Glory"	[I]	London 1960
			CAMEO		
			Soul/funk group from New York City, led by Larry Blackmon.		
4/07/84	**47**	11	1 She's Strange		Atlanta Art. 818384
9/13/86	**6**	21	2 **Word Up**		Atlanta Art. 884933
12/27/86+	**21**	17	3 Candy		Atlanta Art. 888193
			TONY CAMILLO - see BAZUKA		
			HAMILTON CAMP		
			Born on 10/30/34 in London, England. Well known supporting actor.		
5/04/68	**76**	5	1 Here's To You		Warner 7165
			DEBBIE CAMPBELL		
7/05/75	**84**	5	1 Please Tell Him That I Said Hello		Playboy 6037
			GLEN CAMPBELL		
			Born on 4/22/36 near Delight, Arkansas. Vocalist, guitar, composer. With his uncle Dick Bills' band, 1954-58. To Los Angeles; recorded with The Champs in 1960; became prolific studio musician; with The Beach Boys, 1965. Own TV show, "The Glen Campbell Goodtime Hour", 1968-72. In films "True Grit", "Norwood" and "Strange Homecoming".		
10/30/61	**62**	10	1 Turn Around, Look At Me		Crest 1087
8/25/62	**76**	2	2 Too Late To Worry - Too Blue To Cry		Capitol 4783
9/25/65	**45**	7	3 The Universal Soldier		Capitol 5504
7/08/67	**62**	7	4 Gentle On My Mind		Capitol 5939
10/28/67	**26**	11	5 By The Time I Get To Phoenix		Capitol 2015

DEBUT DATE	PEAK POS	WKS CHR	ARTIST — Record Title	Label & Number
			GLEN CAMPBELL — Cont'd	
1/20/68	**54**	7	6 Hey Little One	Capitol 2076
4/06/68	**36**	12	7 I Wanna Live	Capitol 2146
7/06/68	**32**	8	8 Dreams Of The Everyday Housewife	Capitol 2224
9/14/68	**39**	9	9 Gentle On My Mind [R]	Capitol 5939
10/26/68	**74**	6	10 Mornin' Glory BOBBY GENTRY & GLEN CAMPBELL	Capitol 2314
11/02/68+	**3**	15	11 ● **Wichita Lineman**	Capitol 2302
1/25/69	**36**	9	12 Let It Be Me GLEN CAMPBELL & BOBBY GENTRY	Capitol 2387
3/01/69	**4**	12	13 ● **Galveston**	Capitol 2428
5/03/69	**26**	8	14 Where's The Playground Susie	Capitol 2494
7/26/69	**35**	7	15 True Grit from the John Wayne movie of the same title	Capitol 2573
10/11/69	**23**	11	16 Try A Little Kindness	Capitol 2659
1/17/70	**19**	9	17 Honey Come Back	Capitol 2718
2/14/70	**27**	10	18 All I Have To Do Is Dream BOBBY GENTRY & GLEN CAMPBELL	Capitol 2745
4/11/70	**40**	8	19 Oh Happy Day	Capitol 2787
7/04/70	**52**	8	20 Everything A Man Could Ever Need	Capitol 2843
9/05/70	**10**	12	21 **It's Only Make Believe**	Capitol 2905
3/13/71	**31**	7	22 Dream Baby (How Long Must I Dream)	Capitol 3062
6/26/71	**61**	7	23 The Last Time I Saw Her	Capitol 3123
10/23/71	**81**	5	24 I Say A Little Prayer/By The Time I Get To Phoenix ... GLEN CAMPBELL/ANNE MURRAY 4-24: produced, arranged and conducted by Al de Lory	Capitol 3200
8/26/72	**61**	7	25 I Will Never Pass This Way Again	Capitol 3411
12/09/72+	**78**	7	26 One Last Time	Capitol 3483
3/17/73	**45**	12	27 I Knew Jesus (Before He Was A Star)	Capitol 3548
2/09/74	**68**	6	28 Houston (I'm Comin' To See You)	Capitol 3808
5/31/75	**1^{2}**	23	29 ● **Rhinestone Cowboy**	Capitol 4095
11/08/75+	**11**	14	30 Country Boy (You Got Your Feet In L.A.)	Capitol 4155
3/27/76	**27**	10	31 Don't Pull Your Love/Then You Can Tell Me Goodbye .	Capitol 4245
2/12/77	**1^{1}**	21	32 ● **Southern Nights**	Capitol 4376
7/09/77	**39**	11	33 Sunflower	Capitol 4445
10/21/78	**38**	11	34 Can You Fool	Capitol 4584
5/17/80	**42**	10	35 Somethin' 'Bout You Baby I Like GLEN CAMPBELL & RITA COOLIDGE	Capitol 4865
1/24/81	**65**	5	36 I Don't Want To Know Your Name	Capitol 4959
8/22/81	**94**	3	37 I Love My Truck	Mirage 3845
			JIM CAMPBELL	
7/18/70	**93**	2	1 The Lights Of Tucson	Laurie 3546
			JO ANN CAMPBELL Born on 7/20/38 in Jacksonville, Florida. Also see Jo Ann & Troy.	
8/15/60	**61**	9	1 A Kookie Little Paradise [N]	ABC-Para. 10134
8/18/62	**38**	7	2 (I'm The Girl On) Wolverton Mountain	Cameo 223
4/27/63	**88**	3	3 Mother, Please!	Cameo 249
			CANDY & THE KISSES New York trio: sisters Candy and Suzanne Nelson, and schoolmate Jeanette Johnson.	
11/21/64+	**51**	10	1 The 81	Cameo 336
			THE CANDYMEN Roy Orbison's former backup band. Several members later joined the Atlanta Rhythm Section.	
11/18/67	**81**	5	1 Georgia Pines	ABC 10995
			GARY CANE & HIS FRIENDS Gary: 17-year-old Brooklyn lad; Friends: 16 youngsters.	
6/06/60	**99**	1	1 The Yen Yet Song [N]	Shell 719

DEBUT DATE	PEAK POS	WKS CHR	ARTIST — Record Title	Label & Number
			CANNED HEAT	
			Blues-rock band formed in Los Angeles in 1966. Consisted of Bob 'The Bear' Hite (vocals, harmonica), Alan 'Blind Owl' Wilson (guitar, harmonica, vocals), Henry Vestine (guitar), Larry Taylor (bass) and Frank Cook (drums). Cook replaced by Fito de la Parra in 1968. Vestine replaced by Harvey Mandel in 1969. Wilson died of a drug overdose on 9/3/70 (27). Hite died of a drug-related heart attack on 4/6/81 (36).	
8/10/68	**16**	11	1 On The Road Again	Liberty 56038
12/07/68+	**11**	11	2 Going Up The Country	Liberty 56077
3/15/69	**67**	5	3 Time Was	Liberty 56097
10/10/70	**26**	11	4 Let's Work Together	Liberty 56151
3/18/72	**88**	5	5 Rockin' With The King featuring Little Richard on piano and vocals	United Art. 50892
			CANNIBAL & THE HEADHUNTERS	
			Four Mexican-American youths based in Los Angeles; led by Frankie 'Cannibal' Garcia.	
2/27/65	**30**	14	1 Land Of 1000 Dances	Rampart 642
			ACE CANNON	
			Born on 5/5/34 in Grenada, Mississippi. Saxophonist since age 10. Worked with Bill Black Combo (Hi Records' studio band).	
12/25/61+	**17**	16	1 Tuff [I]	Hi 2040
4/14/62	**36**	7	2 Blues (Stay Away From Me) [I]	Hi 2051
4/14/62	**92**	1	3 Sugar Blues [I] Clyde McCoy's famous theme song from 1931 (POS 2)	Santo 503
6/22/63	**67**	7	4 Cottonfields [I]	Hi 2065
3/14/64	**84**	2	5 Searchin' [I]	Hi 2074
			FREDDY CANNON	
			Born Frederick Picariello on 12/4/40 in Lynn, Massachusetts. Local work with own band, Freddy Karmon & The Hurricanes. First recorded for Swan in 1959. Nickname "Boom Boom" came from big bass drum sound on his records. Band arrangements by Frank Slay on all Swan recordings. Also see Danny & The Juniors.	
5/11/59	**6**	15	1 **Tallahassee Lassie** song written by Freddy's mother	Swan 4031
8/24/59	**43**	9	2 Okefenokee	Swan 4038
11/23/59+	**3**	15	3 **Way Down Yonder In New Orleans** jazz song written in 1922	Swan 4043
2/22/60	**34**	7	4 Chattanooga Shoe Shine Boy	Swan 4050
5/09/60	**28**	10	5 Jump Over/	
5/16/60	**60**	3	6 The Urge	Swan 4053
7/25/60	**83**	5	7 Happy Shades Of Blue	Swan 4057
10/10/60	**59**	4	8 Humdinger	Swan 4061
1/09/61	**54**	6	9 Muskrat Ramble	Swan 4066
5/01/61	**51**	8	10 Buzz Buzz A-Diddle-It	Swan 4071
7/31/61	**35**	8	11 Transistor Sister	Swan 4078
10/16/61	**71**	6	12 For Me And My Gal	Swan 4083
2/03/62	**92**	2	13 Teen Queen Of The Week	Swan 4096
5/12/62	**3**	15	14 **Palisades Park** written by Chuck ("Gong Show") Barris	Swan 4106
9/08/62	**45**	4	15 What's Gonna Happen When Summer's Done	Swan 4117
11/10/62	**67**	5	16 If You Were A Rock And Roll Record	Swan 4122
5/04/63	**65**	7	17 Patty Baby	Swan 4139
8/03/63	**52**	7	18 Everybody Monkey	Swan 4149
2/01/64	**16**	8	19 Abigail Beecher	Warner 5409
8/14/65	**13**	9	20 Action from the TV show "Where The Action Is"	Warner 5645
2/19/66	**41**	6	21 The Dedication Song	Warner 5693
9/26/81	**81**	4	22 Let's Put The Fun Back In Rock N Roll **FREDDY CANNON & THE BELMONTS**	MiaSound 1002
			THE CANTINA BAND	
7/25/81	**81**	3	1 Summer '81 Beach Boys' medley: Surfer Girl/Fun, Fun, Fun/409/I Get Around/ Dance, Dance, Dance/California Girls/Wouldn't It Be Nice/ Help Me, Rhonda/Good Vibrations	Millennium 11818
			LANA CANTRELL	
			Showbiz star from Australia.	
2/22/75	**63**	5	1 Like A Sunday Morning	Polydor 14261

DEBUT DATE	PEAK POS	WKS CHR	ARTIST — Record Title	Label & Number
			CANYON	
7/05/75	**98**	1	1 Top Of The World (Make My Reservation)	Magna-Glide 323
			JIM CAPALDI	
			Born on 8/24/44 in Evesham, England. Drummer with Traffic, 1967-71.	
4/08/72	**91**	4	1 Eve	Island 1204
1/18/75	**55**	7	2 It's All Right	Island 003
12/13/75	**97**	1	3 Love Hurts	Island 045
4/30/83	**28**	13	4 That's Love	Atlantic 89849
8/27/83	**75**	5	5 Living On The Edge	Atlantic 89799
			THE CAPITOLS	
			R&B vocal trio from Detroit: Richard McDougall, Don Storball and Sam George.	
4/30/66	**7**	14	1 **Cool Jerk**	Karen 1524
8/27/66	**74**	4	2 I Got To Handle It	Karen 1525
11/12/66	**65**	6	3 We Got A Thing That's In The Groove	Karen 1526
			THE CAPRIS	
			Italian vocal group from Queens, New York, 1958. Consisted of Nick Santamaria, lead; Vinny Narcardo and Mike Mincelli, tenors; Frank Reina, baritone; and John Apostol, bass. Group disbanded in 1959, re-formed when song "There's A Moon Out Tonight" was reissued on Lost Nite and became a hit in 1961.	
12/31/60+	**3**	14	1 **There's A Moon Out Tonight**	Old Town 1094
3/27/61	**74**	4	2 Where I Fell In Love	Old Town 1099
9/18/61	**92**	1	3 Girl In My Dreams	Old Town 1107
8/18/62	**99**	1	4 Limbo	Mr. Peeke 118
			CAPTAIN & TENNILLE	
			The Captain: Daryl Dragon (b: 8/27/42, Los Angeles); and Toni Tennille (b: 5/8/43, Montgomery, AL). Husband and wife, both play piano. Dragon is son of notable conductor Carmen Dragon. Keyboardist with The Beach Boys, nicknamed the "Captain" by Mike Love. Duo had own TV show on ABC, 1976-77.	
4/19/75	**1**[4]	23	1 ● **Love Will Keep Us Together**	A&M 1672
8/16/75	**49**	6	2 Por Amor Viviremos [F] Spanish version of "Love Will Keep Us Together"	A&M 1715
9/27/75	**4**	17	3 ● **The Way I Want To Touch You**	A&M 1725
1/24/76	**3**	19	4 ● **Lonely Night (Angel Face)**	A&M 1782
5/01/76	**4**	16	5 ● **Shop Around**	A&M 1817
9/25/76	**4**	20	6 ● **Muskrat Love**	A&M 1870
3/19/77	**13**	12	7 Can't Stop Dancin'	A&M 1912
6/11/77	**61**	7	8 Come In From The Rain	A&M 1944
4/22/78	**74**	6	9 I'm On My Way	A&M 2027
8/05/78	**10**	22	10 **You Never Done It Like That**	A&M 2063
12/09/78+	**40**	10	11 You Need A Woman Tonight	A&M 2106
10/20/79+	**1**[1]	27	12 ● **Do That To Me One More Time**	Casablanca 2215
3/08/80	**55**	7	13 Love On A Shoestring	Casablanca 2243
5/10/80	**53**	6	14 Happy Together (A Fantasy)	Casablanca 2264
			IRENE CARA	
			Born on 3/18/59 in New York City. Vocalist, dancer, pianist. Professional debut at age seven. Won Obie Award for "The Me Nobody Knows" in 1970. Much TV work, including "Electric Company"; in films "Fame", "DC Cab" and "The Cotton Club".	
6/14/80	**4**	26	1 **Fame**	RSO 1034
8/16/80	**19**	23	2 Out Here On My Own above 2 tunes from the film "Fame"	RSO 1048
11/28/81+	**42**	18	3 Anyone Can See	Network 47950
4/02/83	**1**[6]	25	4 ● **Flashdance...What A Feeling** from the film "Flashdance"	Casablanca 811440
10/22/83	**13**	15	5 Why Me?	Geffen 29464
12/10/83+	**37**	14	6 The Dream (Hold On To Your Dream) from the film "D.C. Cab"	Geffen 29396
3/24/84	**8**	19	7 **Breakdance**	Geffen 29328
7/28/84	**78**	5	8 You Were Made For Me	Geffen 29257
			THE CARAVELLES	
			English duo: Andrea Simpson & Lois Wilkinson.	
11/02/63	**3**	13	1 **You Don't Have To Be A Baby To Cry**	Smash 1852
2/08/64	**94**	4	2 Have You Ever Been Lonely (Have You Ever Been Blue)	Smash 1869

DEBUT DATE	PEAK POS	WKS CHR	ARTIST — Record Title	Label & Number
			LUIS CARDENAS	
			Former drummer and lead singer of Los Angeles-based hard rock band Renegade.	
9/20/86	**83**	5	1 Runaway	Allied Art. 72500
			THE CAREFREES	
			British group.	
3/21/64	**39**	5	1 We Love You Beatles [N]	London Int. 10614
			TONY CAREY	
			Born and raised in America. Settled in Germany in 1978. Ex-keyboardist with Rainbow; leader of the Planet P Project.	
3/26/83	**79**	7	1 I Won't Be Home Tonight	Rocshire 95030
7/02/83	**64**	9	2 West Coast Summer Nights	Rocshire 95037
3/03/84	**22**	15	3 A Fine Fine Day	MCA 52343
6/09/84	**33**	11	4 The First Day Of Summer	MCA 52388
			HENSON CARGILL	
			Born on 2/5/41 in Oklahoma City. Country singer.	
12/23/67+	**25**	12	1 Skip A Rope	Monument 1041
			BELINDA CARLISLE	
			Born on 8/16/58 in Hollywood. Lead singer of the Go-Go's, 1978-84.	
5/17/86	**3**	21	1 **Mad About You**	I.R.S. 52815
9/20/86	**82**	5	2 I Feel The Magic	I.R.S. 52889
			STEVE CARLISLE	
			Background and radio jingle vocalist.	
11/21/81	**65**	10	1 WKRP In Cincinnati	MCA 51205
			theme from the TV series	
			CARL CARLTON	
			Born in 1952 in Detroit. Singing since age nine. First recorded for Lando in 1964.	
6/29/68	**75**	8	1 Competition Ain't Nothin'	Back Beat 588
7/11/70	**78**	6	2 Drop By My Place	Back Beat 613
			above 2 shown as: LITTLE CARL CARLTON	
9/21/74	**6**	15	3 **Everlasting Love**	Back Beat 27001
2/15/75	**91**	4	4 Smokin' Room	ABC 12059
8/22/81	**22**	21	5 ● She's A Bad Mama Jama (She's Built, She's Stacked)	20th Century 2488
			LARRY CARLTON	
			Top session guitarist. Member of The Crusaders, 1972-77. Also see Mike Post.	
2/27/82	**74**	8	1 Sleepwalk [I]	Warner 50019
			ERIC CARMEN	
			Born on 8/11/49 in Cleveland. Lead singer of the Raspberries, 1970-74.	
12/20/75+	**2**[3]	19	1 ● **All By Myself**	Arista 0165
5/01/76	**11**	15	2 Never Gonna Fall In Love Again	Arista 0184
8/14/76	**34**	10	3 Sunrise	Arista 0200
8/27/77	**23**	16	4 She Did It	Arista 0266
12/24/77+	**88**	3	5 Boats Against The Current	Arista 0295
9/16/78	**19**	16	6 Change Of Heart	Arista 0354
1/27/79	**62**	5	7 Baby, I Need Your Lovin'	Arista 0384
7/12/80	**75**	2	8 It Hurts Too Much	Arista 0506
1/19/85	**35**	11	9 I Wanna Hear It From Your Lips	Geffen 29118
4/20/85	**87**	3	10 I'm Through With Love	Geffen 29032
			all of above written by Carmen (except #7)	
			KIM CARNES	
			Born on 7/20/45 in Los Angeles. Vocalist, pianist, composer. Member of New Christy Minstrels with husband/co-writer Dave Ellingson and Kenny Rogers, late 1960s. Wrote and performed commercials.	
6/17/78	**36**	12	1 You're A Part Of Me	Ariola 7704
			GENE COTTON with KIM CARNES	
2/24/79	**56**	5	2 It Hurts So Bad	EMI America 8011
3/29/80	**4**	19	3 **Don't Fall In Love With A Dreamer**	United Art. 1345
			KENNY ROGERS with KIM CARNES	
5/31/80	**10**	19	4 **More Love**	EMI America 8045
10/04/80	**44**	8	5 Cry Like A Baby	EMI America 8058
3/28/81	**1**[9]	26	6 ● **Bette Davis Eyes**	EMI America 8077
			co-written by Jackie DeShannon	
8/08/81	**28**	12	7 Draw Of The Cards	EMI America 8087

DEBUT DATE	PEAK POS	WKS CHR	ARTIST — Record Title	Label & Number
			KIM CARNES — Cont'd	
10/24/81	**60**	6	8 Mistaken Identity	EMI America 8098
8/21/82	**29**	12	9 Voyeur	EMI America 8127
11/06/82+	**36**	13	10 Does It Make You Remember	EMI America 8147
10/15/83	**40**	13	11 Invisible Hands	EMI America 8181
1/21/84	**54**	8	12 You Make My Heart Beat Faster (And That's All That Matters)	EMI America 8191
5/19/84	**74**	5	13 I Pretend	EMI America 8202
9/15/84	**15**	19	14 What About Me? KENNY ROGERS with KIM CARNES & JAMES INGRAM	RCA 13899
12/15/84+	**51**	10	15 Make No Mistake, He's Mine BARBRA STREISAND with KIM CARNES	Columbia 04695
1/19/85	**68**	6	16 Invitation To Dance from the film "That's Dancing!"	EMI America 8250
5/11/85	**15**	16	17 Crazy In The Night (Barking At Airplanes)	EMI America 8267
8/03/85	**67**	4	18 Abadabadango	EMI America 8281
5/24/86	**79**	5	19 Divided Hearts	EMI America 8322
			RENATO CAROSONE Male vocalist from Italy.	
5/05/58	**18**	13	1 Torero [F] Jockey #18 / Top 100 #19 / Best Sellers #20	Capitol 71080
			THELMA CARPENTER Singer with Count Basie, 1943-45. On Eddie Cantor radio show, 1945-46.	
12/31/60+	**55**	6	1 Yes, I'm Lonesome Tonight	Coral 62241
			CARPENTERS Richard Carpenter (b: 10/15/46) and sister Karen (b: 3/2/50; d: 2/4/83 of anorexia [32]). From New Haven, CT. Richard played piano from age nine. To Downey, CA, 1963. Karen played drums in group with Richard and bass player Wes Jacobs in 1965. The trio recorded for RCA in 1966. After a period with the band Spectrum, the Carpenters recorded as a duo for A&M in 1969. Hosts of TV variety show "Make Your Own Kind Of Music" in 1971.	
2/14/70	**54**	12	1 Ticket To Ride	A&M 1142
6/20/70	**1**[4]	17	2● **(They Long To Be) Close To You**	A&M 1183
9/12/70	**2**[4]	17	3● **We've Only Just Begun**	A&M 1217
2/06/71	**3**	13	4● **For All We Know** from the film "Lovers & Other Strangers"	A&M 1243
5/15/71	**2**[2]	12	5● **Rainy Days And Mondays**	A&M 1260
9/04/71	**2**[2]	13	6● **Superstar/**	
12/04/71+	**67**	8	7 Bless The Beasts And Children from the film of the same title	A&M 1289
1/15/72	**2**[2]	12	8● **Hurting Each Other**	A&M 1322
4/29/72	**12**	10	9 It's Going To Take Some Time	A&M 1351
7/15/72	**7**	10	10 **Goodbye To Love**	A&M 1367
2/24/73	**3**	14	11● **Sing**	A&M 1413
6/02/73	**2**[1]	14	12● **Yesterday Once More**	A&M 1446
10/06/73	**1**[2]	20	13● **Top Of The World**	A&M 1468
4/13/74	**11**	12	14 I Won't Last A Day Without You	A&M 1521
11/23/74+	**1**[1]	17	15● **Please Mr. Postman**	A&M 1646
3/29/75	**4**	13	16 **Only Yesterday**	A&M 1677
8/02/75	**17**	10	17 Solitaire	A&M 1721
2/28/76	**12**	13	18 There's A Kind Of Hush (All Over The World)	A&M 1800
6/12/76	**25**	11	19 I Need To Be In Love	A&M 1828
9/04/76	**56**	5	20 Goofus originally a Top 10 hit for Wayne King in 1931	A&M 1859
5/21/77	**35**	10	21 All You Get From Love Is A Love Song	A&M 1940
10/08/77	**32**	14	22 Calling Occupants Of Interplanetary Craft	A&M 1978
2/04/78	**44**	13	23 Sweet, Sweet Smile	A&M 2008
12/09/78	**68**	5	24 I Believe You	A&M 2097
6/20/81	**16**	14	25 Touch Me When We're Dancing	A&M 2344
9/12/81	**72**	8	26 (Want You) Back In My Life Again	A&M 2370
12/19/81+	**63**	6	27 Those Good Old Dreams	A&M 2386
4/24/82	**74**	4	28 Beechwood 4-5789	A&M 2405

DEBUT DATE	PEAK POS	WKS CHR	ARTIST — Record Title	Label & Number
			CATHY CARR	
			Songstress from the Bronx, New York; born on 6/28/36.	
3/17/56	2[1]	24	1 **Ivory Tower**	Fraternity 734
			Juke Box #2 / Top 100 #6 / Best Seller #7 / Jockey #9	
7/28/56	67	4	2 Heart Hideaway	Fraternity 743
1/26/59	42	12	3 First Anniversary	Roulette 4125
6/08/59	63	4	4 I'm Gonna Change Him	Roulette 4152
			JAMES CARR	
			Born on 6/13/42 in Memphis. With Soul Stirrers gospel group, early 1960's. Managed by Phil Walden and Duane Allman.	
4/09/66	63	6	1 You've Got My Mind Messed Up	Goldwax 302
7/30/66	99	1	2 Love Attack	Goldwax 309
10/22/66	85	4	3 Pouring Water On A Drowning Man	Goldwax 311
2/25/67	77	6	4 The Dark End Of The Street	Goldwax 317
9/23/67	97	3	5 I'm A Fool For You	Goldwax 328
1/06/68	63	10	6 A Man Needs A Woman	Goldwax 332
			JOE "FINGERS" CARR - see LOU BUSCH	
			VALERIE CARR	
			Black vocalist from the U.S.	
6/09/58	19	5	1 When The Boys Talk About The Girls	Roulette 4066
			Jockey #19 / Top 100 #84	
			VIKKI CARR	
			Born Florencia Martinez Cardona on 7/19/41 in El Paso, Texas. A regular on the Ray Anthony musical variety TV show in 1962.	
9/02/67	3	15	1 **It Must Be Him**	Liberty 55986
12/23/67+	34	8	2 The Lesson	Liberty 56012
3/23/68	99	3	3 She'll Be There/	
3/30/68	91	5	4 Your Heart Is Free Just Like The Wind	Liberty 56026
5/03/69	35	13	5 With Pen In Hand	Liberty 56092
10/04/69	79	4	6 Eternity	Liberty 56132
1/23/71	96	4	7 I'll Be Home	Columbia 45296
			PAUL CARRACK	
			Born on 4/22/51 in Sheffield, England. Singer, keyboardist. Formerly with Ace and Squeeze.	
9/04/82	37	13	1 I Need You	Epic 03146
			KEITH CARRADINE	
			Leading actor since 1971. Son of John Carradine; half brother of David Carradine.	
5/08/76	17	19	1 I'm Easy	ABC 12117
			from the movie "Nashville" (which Keith appeared in)	
			CARROLL BROS.	
8/18/62	100	1	1 Sweet Georgia Brown [I]	Cameo 221
			written in 1925; theme song of the Harlem Globetrotters	
			ANDREA CARROLL	
			Born Andrea DeCapite on 10/3/46 in Cleveland.	
7/20/63	45	9	1 It Hurts To Be Sixteen	Big Top 3156
			Andrea was 16 years old when she recorded this song	
			BERNADETTE CARROLL	
5/16/64	47	9	1 Party Girl	Laurie 3238
			BOB CARROLL	
			Born on 6/18/18. Baritone singer. Sang with Charlie Barnet and Jimmy Dorsey in the 40s.	
3/02/57	61	7	1 Butterfly	Bally 1028
			CATHY CARROLL	
8/04/62	91	3	1 Poor Little Puppet	Warner 5284
			DAVID CARROLL	
			Born Nook Schrier on 10/15/13 in Chicago. Arranger, conductor since 1951 for many top Mercury artists.	
1/08/55	8	17	1 **Melody Of Love** [I]	Mercury 70516
			Jockey #8 / Best Seller #9 / Juke Box #12	
11/26/55	20	16	2 It's Almost Tomorrow	Mercury 70717
			Jockey #20 / Top 100 #34	
			vocal: Jack Halloran Singers	

DEBUT DATE	PEAK POS	WKS CHR	ARTIST — Record Title	Label & Number
			DAVID CARROLL — Cont'd	
3/23/57	**65**	3	3 The Ship That Never Sailed .... [S]	Mercury 71069
			narration: Franklyn MacCormack	
9/02/57	**56**	7	4 Fascination .... [I]	Mercury 71152
			from the Gary Cooper movie "Love In The Afternoon"	
10/24/60	**98**	1	5 Midnight Lace .... [I]	Mercury 71703
			from the film of the same title	
2/24/62	**61**	7	6 The White Rose Of Athens .... [I]	Mercury 71917
			from the film "Dreamland of Desire"	
			RONNIE CARROLL	
			English vocalist.	
6/08/63	**91**	4	1 Say Wonderful Things	Philips 40110
			THE CARS	
			Rock group formed in Boston in 1976. Consisted of Ric Ocasek (lead vocals, guitar), Elliot Easton (guitar), Greg Hawkes (keyboards), Benjamin Orr (bass) and David Robinson (drums). Ocasek, Orr and Hawkes had been in trio, early 70s. Group named by Robinson, got start at the Rat Club in Boston. All songs written by Ocasek.	
6/17/78	**27**	17	1 Just What I Needed	Elektra 45491
10/21/78	**35**	15	2 My Best Friend's Girl	Elektra 45537
3/17/79	**41**	10	3 Good Times Roll	Elektra 46014
6/30/79	**14**	15	4 Let's Go	Elektra 46063
10/13/79	**41**	10	5 It's All I Can Do	Elektra 46546
9/06/80	**37**	11	6 Touch And Go	Elektra 47039
11/21/81+	**4**	22	7 **Shake It Up**	Elektra 47250
3/27/82	**41**	9	8 Since You're Gone	Elektra 47433
3/10/84	**7**	17	9 **You Might Think**	Elektra 69744
5/19/84	**12**	17	10 Magic	Elektra 69724
8/04/84	**3**	19	11 **Drive**	Elektra 69706
			lead vocal by bassist Ben Orr	
10/27/84	**20**	15	12 Hello Again	Elektra 69681
1/26/85	**33**	17	13 Why Can't I Have You	Elektra 69657
11/02/85+	**7**	17	14 **Tonight She Comes**	Elektra 69589
2/01/86	**32**	11	15 I'm Not The One	Elektra 69569
			KIT CARSON	
			Real name: Liza Morrow.	
11/19/55+	**11**	22	1 Band Of Gold	Capitol 3283
			Jockey #11 / Top 100 #17	
			MINDY CARSON	
			Born on 7/16/27 in New York City. Sang with Paul Whiteman in the 40s.	
8/27/55	**13**	8	1 Wake The Town And Tell The People	Columbia 40537
			Jockey #13 / Juke Box #13 / Best Seller #20 / Top 100 #33 pre	
12/17/55+	**53**	13	2 Memories Are Made Of This	Columbia 40573
			male backing chorus: The Columbians	
12/08/56+	**34**	12	3 Since I Met You Baby	Columbia 40789
			BETTY CARTER	
3/03/62	**91**	2	1 Baby It's Cold Outside	ABC-Para. 10298
			RAY CHARLES & BETTY CARTER	
			CARLENE CARTER - see ROBERT ELLIS ORRALL	
			CLARENCE CARTER	
			Born in 1936 in Montgomery, Alabama. Blind since age 1. Self-taught on guitar from age eleven. Teamed with vocalist/pianist Calvin Scott as Clarence & Calvin, recorded for Fairlane, early 60s. Recorded for Duke as C&C Boys. Auto accident in 1966 caused retirement of Scott, Carter then went solo. Married for a time to Candi Staton.	
6/24/67	**98**	1	1 Thread The Needle	Fame 1013
1/20/68	**62**	8	2 Looking For A Fox	Atlantic 2461
6/01/68	**88**	3	3 Funky Fever/	
7/13/68	**6**	16	4● **Slip Away**	Atlantic 2508
11/09/68+	**13**	15	5● Too Weak To Fight	Atlantic 2569
3/01/69	**31**	10	6 Snatching It Back	Atlantic 2605
6/21/69	**65**	6	7 The Feeling Is Right	Atlantic 2642
9/27/69	**46**	9	8 Doin' Our Thing	Atlantic 2660
2/14/70	**94**	4	9 Take It Off Him And Put It On Me	Atlantic 2702
4/11/70	**42**	14	10 I Can't Leave Your Love Alone	Atlantic 2726
7/18/70	**4**	14	11● **Patches**	Atlantic 2748

DEBUT DATE	PEAK POS	WKS CHR	ARTIST — Record Title	Label & Number
			CLARENCE CARTER — Cont'd	
11/07/70	**51**	9	12 It's All In Your Mind	Atlantic 2774
5/08/71	**61**	6	13 The Court Room [N]	Atlantic 2801
8/07/71	**84**	5	14 Slipped, Tripped And Fell In Love	Atlantic 2818
6/09/73	**65**	8	15 Sixty Minute Man/	
		5	16 Mother-In-Law	Fame 250
			JUNE CARTER - see JOHNNY CASH	
			MEL CARTER	
			Born on 4/22/43 in Cincinnati. Vocalist, actor. Sang on local radio from age 4; with Lionel Hampton on stage show, age 9. With Paul Gayten, Jimmy Scott bands. Joined Raspberry Singers gospel group, early 50s. Own gospel group, The Carvetts, mid-50s. Named Top Gospel Tenor in 1957. With Gospel Pearls, early 60s. First recorded for Mercury in 1959. Has appeared as actor in TV's "Quincy", "Sanford And Son", "Marcus Welby, MD" and "Magnum P.I.".	
7/06/63	**44**	10	1 When A Boy Falls In Love	Derby 1003
6/26/65	**8**	15	2 **Hold Me, Thrill Me, Kiss Me**	Imperial 66113
10/30/65	**38**	7	3 (All Of A Sudden) My Heart Sings	Imperial 66138
1/22/66	**50**	8	4 Love Is All We Need	Imperial 66148
4/09/66	**32**	8	5 Band Of Gold	Imperial 66165
7/16/66	**49**	7	6 You You You	Imperial 66183
10/01/66	**78**	5	7 Take Good Care Of Her	Imperial 66208
			RALPH CARTER	
			Played Mike Evans on the TV series "Good Times".	
9/06/75	**95**	3	1 When You're Young And In Love	Mercury 73695
			VALERIE CARTER - see EDDIE MONEY	
			FLIP CARTRIDGE	
8/20/66	**91**	2	1 Dear Mrs. Applebee	Parrot 306
			THE CASCADES	
			Vocal group from San Diego. Consisted of John Gummoe, Eddie Snyder, David Stevens, David Wilson and David Zabo.	
1/12/63	**3**	16	1 **Rhythm Of The Rain**	Valiant 6026
			written by John Gummoe	
4/27/63	**91**	4	2 Shy Girl/	
5/11/63	**60**	5	3 The Last Leaf	Valiant 6028
12/28/63+	**86**	3	4 For Your Sweet Love	RCA 8268
8/16/69	**61**	6	5 Maybe The Rain Will Fall	Uni 55152
			AL CASEY	
			Guitarist, pianist, bandleader and producer originally from Phoenix. Much session work with Lee Hazlewood productions, including Sanford Clark and Duane Eddy. Not to be confused with black guitarist of the same name.	
4/07/62	**92**	2	1 Cookin' [I]	Stacy 925
7/28/62	**71**	6	2 Jivin' Around [I]	Stacy 936
			above 2: **AL CASEY COMBO**	
7/13/63	**48**	8	3 Surfin' Hootenanny [N]	Stacy 962
			ALVIN CASH	
			Born on 2/15/39 in St. Louis. Formed dance troupe called the Crawlers, consisting of his 3 little brothers (ages 8, 9 & 10). They never sang on any of Alvin's hits. Cut "Twine Time" with backing band, the Nightlighters from Louisville, who changed their name to the Registers.	
			ALVIN CASH & THE CRAWLERS:	
1/02/65	**14**	11	1 Twine Time [I]	Mar-V-Lus 6002
3/27/65	**59**	7	2 The Barracuda	Mar-V-Lus 6005
			ALVIN CASH & THE REGISTERS:	
7/30/66	**49**	9	3 The Philly Freeze	Mar-V-Lus 6012
11/26/66	**74**	6	4 Alvin's Boo-Ga-Loo	Mar-V-Lus 6014
			ALVIN CASH:	
11/23/68	**66**	5	5 Keep On Dancing	Toddlin' Town 111

JOHNNY CASH

Born on 2/26/32 in Kingsland, Arkansas. To Dyess, AR at age 3. Brother Roy had Dixie Rhythm Ramblers band, late 40s. In US Air Force, 1950-54. Formed trio with Luther Perkins (guitar) and Marshall Grant (bass) in 1955. First recorded for Sun in 1955. On "Louisiana Hayride" and "Grand Ole Opry" shows, 1957. Own TV show for ABC, 1969-71. Worked with June Carter from 1961, married her in March, 1968. Daughter Rosanne Cash and stepdaughter Carlene Carter currently enjoying successful singing careers.

DEBUT DATE	PEAK POS	WKS CHR	ARTIST — Record Title	Label & Number
9/15/56	**17**	22	1 I Walk The Line	Sun 241
			Best Seller #17 / Juke Box #17 / Top 100 #19 / Jockey #25	
7/01/57	**99**	2	2 Next In Line	Sun 266
10/14/57	**88**	4	3 Home Of The Blues	Sun 279
2/03/58	**14**	19	4 Ballad Of A Teenage Queen/	
			Jockey #14 / Best Seller #16 / Top 100 #16	
		7	5 Big River	Sun 283
			Best Seller flip	
6/02/58	**11**	16	6 Guess Things Happen That Way/	
			Best Seller #11 / Top 100 #11 / Jockey #18	
6/09/58	**66**	9	7 Come In Stranger	Sun 295
8/25/58	**24**	11	8 The Ways Of A Woman In Love/	
			Hot 100 #24 / Best Seller #26	
		6	9 You're The Nearest Thing To Heaven	Sun 302
			Best Seller flip	
10/06/58	**38**	11	10 All Over Again/	
10/20/58	**52**	8	11 What Do I Care	Columbia 41251
12/15/58+	**47**	7	12 It's Just About Time/	
12/15/58	**85**	1	13 I Just Thought You'd Like To Know	Sun 309
1/19/59	**32**	12	14 Don't Take Your Guns To Town	Columbia 41313
4/27/59	**57**	7	15 Frankie's Man, Johnny	Columbia 41371
7/13/59	**66**	8	16 Katy Too	Sun 321
8/03/59	**43**	11	17 I Got Stripes/	
8/24/59	**76**	3	18 Five Feet High And Rising	Columbia 41427
12/21/59	**63**	3	19 The Little Drummer Boy [X]	Columbia 41481
3/14/60	**84**	2	20 Straight A's In Love	Sun 334
7/04/60	**79**	4	21 Second Honeymoon/	
7/25/60	**92**	1	22 Honky-Tonk Girl	Columbia 41707
7/11/60	**85**	3	23 Down The Street To 301	Sun 343
12/31/60+	**93**	2	24 Oh Lonesome Me	Sun 355
11/13/61	**84**	6	25 Tennessee Flat-Top Box	Columbia 42147
9/15/62	**94**	1	26 Bonanza!	Columbia 42512
			from the TV series of the same title	
6/01/63	**17**	13	27 Ring Of Fire	Columbia 42788
10/26/63	**44**	7	28 The Matador	Columbia 42880
2/15/64	**35**	8	29 Understand Your Man	Columbia 42964
10/31/64	**58**	8	30 It Ain't Me, Babe	Columbia 43145
			backing vocal: June Carter	
2/13/65	**80**	6	31 Orange Blossom Special	Columbia 43206
2/26/66	**46**	6	32 The One On The Right Is On The Left	Columbia 43496
7/02/66	**96**	2	33 Everybody Loves A Nut	Columbia 43673
1/27/68	**91**	2	34 Rosanna's Going Wild	Columbia 44373
5/25/68	**32**	12	35 Folsom Prison Blues	Columbia 44513
			original version released in 1956 on Sun 232	
12/28/68+	**42**	10	36 Daddy Sang Bass	Columbia 44689
7/26/69	**2**[3]	12	37 ● **A Boy Named Sue** [N]	Columbia 44944
			recorded live at San Quentin prison	
11/08/69	**50**	8	38 Blistered/	
		6	39 See Ruby Fall	Columbia 45020
11/15/69	**60**	6	40 Get Rhythm	Sun 1103
			originally the flip side of "I Walk The Line"	
1/24/70	**36**	8	41 If I Were A Carpenter	Columbia 45064
			JOHNNY CASH & JUNE CARTER	
2/28/70	**93**	1	42 Rock Island Line	Sun 1111
			originally recorded in 1956	
4/11/70	**19**	8	43 What Is Truth	Columbia 45134
8/29/70	**46**	7	44 Sunday Morning Coming Down	Columbia 45211
12/12/70+	**54**	7	45 Flesh And Blood	Columbia 45269
			from the film "I Walk The Line"	

DEBUT DATE	PEAK POS	WKS CHR	ARTIST — Record Title	Label & Number
			JOHNNY CASH — Cont'd	
3/20/71	**58**	6	46 Man In Black	Columbia 45339
5/13/72	**75**	7	47 Kate	Columbia 45590
4/17/76	**29**	10	48 One Piece At A Time [N]	Columbia 10321
			above 2: **JOHNNY CASH & THE TENNESSEE THREE**	
			ROSANNE CASH	
			Johnny Cash's daughter. Married to Rodney Crowell since 1979.	
4/25/81	**22**	20	1 Seven Year Ache	Columbia 11426
			TOMMY CASH	
			Johnny Cash's brother.	
12/13/69+	**79**	6	1 Six White Horses	Epic 10540
			CASHMAN & WEST	
			Record producers Terry Cashman & Tommy West. Also see Buchanan Brothers.	
9/23/72	**27**	11	1 American City Suite	Dunhill 4324
			Sweet City Song/All Around The Town/A Friend Is Dying	
12/30/72+	**59**	7	2 Songman	Dunhill 4333
			TERRY CASHMAN	
			Terry (with Tommy West) produced all of Jim Croce's recordings.	
11/27/76	**79**	2	1 Baby, Baby I Love You	Lifesong 45015
			THE CASINOS	
			9-man group from Cincinnati led by Gene Hughes.	
1/14/67	**6**	13	1 **Then You Can Tell Me Goodbye**	Fraternity 977
4/29/67	**65**	4	2 It's All Over Now	Fraternity 985
			written by Don Everly of the Everly Brothers	
			THE CASLONS	
9/11/61	**89**	2	1 Anniversary Of Love	Seeco 6078
			DAVID CASSIDY	
			Born on 4/12/50 in New York City. Son of actor Jack Cassidy and actress Evelyn Ward. Played Keith and was lead singer for TV's "The Partridge Family".	
11/06/71	**9**	12	1 ● **Cherish**	Bell 45150
2/19/72	**37**	9	2 Could It Be Forever	Bell 45187
5/20/72	**25**	9	3 How Can I Be Sure	Bell 45220
9/09/72	**38**	8	4 Rock Me Baby	Bell 45260
			SHAUN CASSIDY	
			Born on 9/27/59 in Los Angeles. Son of actor Jack Cassidy and actress Shirley Jones. Played Joe Hardy on TV's "The Hardy Boys". Shaun & David Cassidy are half-brothers. Joined the cast of TV's soap series "General Hospital" in 1987.	
5/14/77	**1**[1]	22	1 ● **Da Doo Ron Ron**	Warner 8365
7/23/77	**3**	24	2 ● **That's Rock 'N' Roll**	Warner 8423
11/12/77+	**7**	16	3 ● **Hey Deanie**	Warner 8488
3/25/78	**31**	10	4 Do You Believe In Magic	Warner 8533
9/09/78	**80**	3	5 Our Night	Warner 8634
			THE CASTAWAYS	
			Quintet formed at the University of Minnesota in 1965.	
8/14/65	**12**	14	1 Liar, Liar	Soma 1433
			THE CASTELLS	
			Quartet from Santa Rosa, California.	
5/29/61	**20**	12	1 Sacred	Era 3048
10/09/61	**98**	2	2 Make Believe Wedding	Era 3057
4/14/62	**21**	13	3 So This Is Love	Era 3073
8/25/62	**91**	2	4 Oh! What It Seemed To Be	Era 3083
			THE CASTLE SISTERS	
7/21/62	**100**	1	1 Goodbye Dad	Terrace 7506
			DAVID CASTLE	
9/24/77	**68**	7	1 Ten To Eight	Parachute 501
1/07/78	**89**	2	2 The Loneliest Man On The Moon	Parachute 505
			BOOMER CASTLEMAN	
			Boomer Clarke of "The Lewis & Clarke Expedition".	
5/03/75	**33**	8	1 Judy Mae	Mums 6038

DEBUT DATE	PEAK POS	WKS CHR	ARTIST — Record Title		Label & Number
			THE JIMMY CASTOR BUNCH		
			Jimmy was born on 6/2/43 in New York City. Vocalist, saxophone, composer, arranger. Formed the Jimmy Castor Bunch in 1972, with Gerry Thomas (keyboards), Doug Gibson (bass), Harry Jensen (guitar), Lenny Fridie, Jr. (congas) & Bobby Manigault (drums).		
12/31/66+	**31**	9	1 Hey, Leroy, Your Mama's Callin' You	[I]	Smash 2069
			shown only as: **JIMMY CASTOR**		
5/13/72	**6**	12	2● **Troglodyte (Cave Man)**	[N]	RCA 1029
2/22/75	**16**	13	3 The Bertha Butt Boogie (Part 1)	[N]	Atlantic 3232
10/18/75	**69**	7	4 King Kong - Pt. I	[N]	Atlantic 3295
			JOHNNY CASWELL		
			Lead singer of Crystal Mansion.		
8/03/63	**97**	1	1 At The Shore		Smash 1833
			CAT MOTHER & the ALL NIGHT NEWS BOYS		
			New York rock quintet produced by Jimi Hendrix.		
6/28/69	**21**	8	1 Good Old Rock 'N Roll		Polydor 14002
			Sweet Little Sixteen/Long Tall Sally/Chantilly Lace/ Whole Lotta Shakin' Goin On/Blue Suede Shoes/Party Doll		
			CATE BROS.		
			Born on 12/26/42 in Fayetteville, AR. Duo consisting of twins Ernie (vocals, piano) and Earl (guitar). Produced by Steve Cropper.		
2/07/76	**24**	20	1 Union Man		Asylum 45294
7/24/76	**91**	3	2 Can't Change My Heart		Asylum 45326
			GEORGE CATES		
			Born on 10/19/11 in New York City. Arranger for Bing Crosby, Teresa Brewer, The Andrews Sisters and others. Musical director of the Lawrence Welk TV Show for 25 years. Also see Steve Allen and Champ Butler.		
4/14/56	**4**	22	1 **Moonglow And Theme From "Picnic"**	[I]	Coral 61618
			Top 100 #4 / Jockey #4 / Best Seller #5 / Juke Box #7 featuring The Stan Wrightsman Quartet - from the film "Picnic"		
9/15/56	**75**	2	2 Where There's Life	[I]	Coral 61683
			CATHY & JOE		
10/10/64	**82**	2	1 I See You		Smash 1929
			CATHY JEAN & THE ROOMMATES		
			Cathy was born on 9/8/45 in Brooklyn. Also see the Roommates.		
2/27/61	**12**	12	1 Please Love Me Forever		Valmor 007
			FELIX CAVALIERE		
			Lead singer of the Rascals after a stint with Joey Dee & The Starlighters.		
3/01/80	**36**	11	1 Only A Lonely Heart Sees		Epic 50829
			CAZZ		
			Real name: Robert C. Lewis - black singer from Texas.		
2/18/78	**70**	5	1 Let's Live Together		Number 1 210
			produced by Dale ("Susie-Q") Hawkins		
			C COMPANY Featuring TERRY NELSON		
4/24/71	**37**	4	1● Battle Hymn Of Lt. Calley	[S]	Plantation 73
			Calley: U.S. Army officer court-martialled for the massacre of civilians at My Lai, Vietnam		
			C.C. & COMPANY - see C.J. & CO.		
			C.C.S.		
			British jazz/rock band featuring blues guitarist Alexis Korner.		
2/06/71	**58**	4	1 Whole Lotta Love	[I]	Rak 4501
			CELEBRATION featuring MIKE LOVE		
			Mike is the Beach Boys' lead singer.		
4/29/78	**28**	12	1 Almost Summer		MCA 40891
			from the film of the same title		
			CELI BEE & THE BUZZY BUNCH		
			Puerto Rican disco band led by female vocalist Celinas.		
6/11/77	**41**	13	1 Superman		APA 17001
			THE CELLOS		
			Doo-wop vocal quintet from New York City.		
5/27/57	**62**	10	1 Rang Tang Ding Dong (I Am The Japanese Sandman)		Apollo 510

DEBUT DATE	PEAK POS	WKS CHR	ARTIST — Record Title	Label & Number
			CENTRAL LINE	
			London-based black vocal quartet.	
11/14/81	**84**	6	1 Walking Into Sunshine	Mercury 76126
			CERRONE	
			Born Jean-Marc Cerrone in France in 1952. Composer/producer/drummer.	
2/26/77	**36**	8	1 Love In 'C' Minor - Pt. I [I]	Cotillion 44215
1/21/78	**70**	5	2 Supernature	Cotillion 44230
			PETER CETERA	
			Born on 9/13/44 in Chicago. Lead singer and bass guitarist of Chicago for their first 17 albums.	
6/07/86	**1[2]**	21	1 **Glory Of Love**	Full Moon 28662
			theme from the film "The Karate Kid Part II"	
9/20/86	**1[1]**	21	2 **The Next Time I Fall**	Full Moon 28597
			PETER CETERA with AMY GRANT	
			FRANK CHACKSFIELD	
			Born on 5/9/14 in Sussex, England. Orchestra leader.	
1/25/60	**47**	8	1 On The Beach [I]	London 1901
			from the film of the same title	
			CHAD & JEREMY	
			Chad Stuart (b: 12/10/43, England) & Jeremy Clyde (b: 3/22/44, England). Folk-rock duo formed in early 60s, broke up in 1967.	
5/23/64	**21**	9	1 Yesterday's Gone	World Art. 1021
8/15/64	**7**	14	2 **A Summer Song**	World Art. 1027
11/14/64+	**15**	13	3 Willow Weep For Me	World Art. 1034
2/20/65	**23**	9	4 If I Loved You	World Art. 1041
			from the musical "Carousel"	
4/10/65	**51**	8	5 What Do You Want With Me	World Art. 1052
5/15/65	**17**	9	6 Before And After	Columbia 43277
7/10/65	**97**	2	7 From A Window	World Art. 1056
8/07/65	**35**	7	8 I Don't Wanna Lose You Baby	Columbia 43339
10/30/65	**91**	2	9 I Have Dreamed	Columbia 43414
			from the musical "The King & I"	
7/09/66	**30**	9	10 Distant Shores	Columbia 43682
10/08/66	**87**	4	11 You Are She	Columbia 43807
			CHAIRMEN OF THE BOARD	
			Vocal group formed in Detroit in 1969. Consisted of General Norman Johnson, Danny Woods, Harrison Kennedy and Eddie Curtis. First recorded for Invictus in 1969. Johnson had been leader of the Showmen from 1961-67.	
1/17/70	**3**	15	1 ● **Give Me Just A Little More Time**	Invictus 9074
5/02/70	**38**	9	2 (You've Got Me) Dangling On A String	Invictus 9078
8/01/70	**38**	9	3 Everything's Tuesday	Invictus 9079
11/14/70+	**13**	13	4 Pay To The Piper	Invictus 9081
2/13/71	**42**	8	5 Chairman Of The Board	Invictus 9086
6/09/73	**59**	9	6 Finder's Keepers	Invictus 1251
			THE CHAKACHAS	
			Belgian sextet led by Gaston Boogaerts.	
1/15/72	**8**	15	1 ● **Jungle Fever** [I]	Polydor 15030
			RICHARD CHAMBERLAIN	
			Born on 3/31/35. Leading actor in films, theatre and television. Played lead role in TV's "Dr. Kildare", 1961-66.	
6/02/62	**10**	14	1 **Theme From Dr. Kildare (Three Stars Will Shine Tonight)**	MGM 13075
10/06/62	**21**	9	2 Love Me Tender	MGM 13097
2/09/63	**14**	12	3 All I Have To Do Is Dream/	
2/16/63	**64**	5	4 Hi-Lili, Hi-Lo	MGM 13121
7/06/63	**65**	7	5 I Will Love You/	
7/27/63	**98**	1	6 True Love	MGM 13148
9/28/63	**42**	8	7 Blue Guitar	MGM 13170
12/05/64	**99**	1	8 Rome Will Never Leave You	MGM 13285

DEBUT DATE	PEAK POS	WKS CHR	ARTIST — Record Title		Label & Number
			THE CHAMBERS BROTHERS		
			Four Mississippi-born brothers: George (b: 9/26/31), bass; Willie (b: 3/3/38), guitar; Lester (b: 4/13/40), harmonica; and Joe (b: 8/22/42), guitar. Started as a gospel group in the fifties. Drummer Brian Keenan (b: 1/28/44) added in 1965.		
8/10/68	**11**	14	1 Time Has Come Today		Columbia 44414
11/23/68	**37**	8	2 I Can't Turn You Loose		Columbia 44679
12/21/68+	**83**	5	3 Shout! - Part 1		Vault 945
7/12/69	**92**	2	4 Wake Up from the film "The April Fools"		Columbia 44890
2/28/70	**96**	1	5 Love, Peace And Happiness		Columbia 45088
			CHAMPAGNE		
			2-man, 2-woman Dutch group.		
3/26/77	**83**	4	1 Rock And Roll Star		Ariola Am. 7658
			CHAMPAIGN		
			Inter-racial sextet from Champaign, Illinois. Paulie Carmen, lead singer.		
2/14/81	**12**	23	1 How 'Bout Us		Columbia 11433
4/02/83	**23**	20	2 Try Again		Columbia 03563
			BILL CHAMPLIN		
			Leader of San Francisco's Sons Of Champlin for 13 years. Member of Chicago since 1982.		
12/26/81+	**55**	8	1 Tonight Tonight		Elektra 47240
7/31/82	**61**	8	2 Sara		Elektra 47456
			THE CHAMPS		
			Instrumental combo from Los Angeles. Originally consisted of studio musicians Dave Burgess, rhythm guitar; Buddy Bruce, lead guitar; Danny Flores (later changed name to Chuck Rio), sax; Cliff Hils, bass; Gene Alden, drums. Shortly after "Tequila" became a hit, Bruce and Hils were replaced by Dale Norris and Joe Burnas. Eight months after recording "Tequila", Flores and Alden left and were replaced by Jimmy Seals (sax) and Dash Crofts (drums). Other personnel changes followed and in 1960 guitarist Glen Campbell spent some time in the group.		
2/24/58	**1^{5}**	19	1 **Tequila** Best Seller #1(5) / Top 100 #1(5) / Jockey #1(2)	[I]	Challenge 1016
5/26/58	**30**	10	2 El Rancho Rock/ Top 100 #30 / Best Seller #31	[I]	
8/11/58	**94**	1	3 Midnighter	[I]	Challenge 59007
8/11/58	**59**	7	4 Chariot Rock	[I]	Challenge 59018
1/18/60	**30**	11	5 Too Much Tequila	[I]	Challenge 59063
2/03/62	**99**	1	6 Tequila Twist/	[I]	
5/26/62	**40**	13	7 Limbo Rock	[I]	Challenge 9131
10/20/62	**97**	1	8 Limbo Dance		Challenge 9162
			THE CHAMPS' BOYS ORCHESTRA		
5/29/76	**98**	2	1 Tubular Bells theme from the film "The Exorcist"	[I]	Janus 259
			GENE CHANDLER		
			Born Eugene Dixon on 7/6/40 in Chicago. Formed vocal group, the Gaytones, at Englewood High School in 1955. Joined the Dukays vocal group in 1957. US Army, Germany, 1957-60. Rejoined Dukays in 1960. First recorded for Nat in 1961. Had own label, Mr. Chand, in 1969. Also see the Dukays.		
1/13/62	**1^{3}**	15	1 **Duke Of Earl**		Vee-Jay 416
4/28/62	**91**	2	2 Walk On With The Duke artist shown as: **THE DUKE OF EARL**		Vee-Jay 440
11/24/62	**49**	8	3 You Threw A Lucky Punch/ vocal background: Cal Carter & Friends		
2/23/63	**47**	12	4 Rainbow		Vee-Jay 468
8/10/63	**71**	7	5 Man's Temptation		Vee-Jay 536
5/02/64	**92**	2	6 Soul Hootenanny (Pt. I)		Constellation 114
7/11/64	**19**	10	7 Just Be True		Constellation 130
9/26/64	**39**	9	8 Bless Our Love		Constellation 136
12/05/64+	**40**	8	9 What Now		Constellation 141
3/06/65	**92**	1	10 You Can't Hurt Me No More		Constellation 146
4/17/65	**18**	12	11 Nothing Can Stop Me		Constellation 149
8/21/65	**92**	3	12 Good Times		Constellation 160
11/27/65+	**69**	8	13 Rainbow '65 (Part I) live version of 1963 hit		Constellation 158
3/19/66	**88**	2	14 (I'm Just A) Fool For You		Constellation 167

DEBUT DATE	PEAK POS	WKS CHR	ARTIST — Record Title	Label & Number
			GENE CHANDLER — Cont'd	
11/26/66+	**45**	8	15 I Fooled You This Time	Checker 1155
2/25/67	**66**	9	16 Girl Don't Care	Brunswick 55312
6/10/67	**94**	4	17 To Be A Lover	Checker 1165
9/02/67	**98**	1	18 There Goes The Lover	Brunswick 55339
9/21/68	**82**	3	19 There Was A Time	Brunswick 55383
10/19/68	**57**	8	20 From The Teacher To The Preacher GENE CHANDLER & BARBARA ACKLIN	Brunswick 55387
7/11/70	**12**	15	21 ● Groovy Situation	Mercury 73083
11/07/70	**75**	5	22 Simply Call It Love	Mercury 73121
1/02/71	**94**	3	23 You Just Can't Win (By Making The Same Mistake) GENE & JERRY	Mercury 73163
1/06/79	**53**	9	24 Get Down	Chi-Sound 2386
10/06/79	**99**	2	25 When You're #1	20th Century 2411
			KAREN CHANDLER & JIMMY WAKELY Karen: with Benny Goodman under the name of Eve Young in 1946. Jimmy: western singer of radio, movies and records.	
9/29/56	**49**	9	1 Tonight You Belong To Me orchestra directed by Karen's husband, Jack Pleis	Decca 30040
			KENNY CHANDLER	
4/06/63	**64**	7	1 Heart	Laurie 3158
			CHANGE European/American studio group formed by Italian producer Jacques Fred Petrus. Luther Vandross sang on several songs from group's first two albums. Later group, based in New York, included lead vocals by James Robinson and Deborah Cooper.	
5/17/80	**40**	13	1 A Lover's Holiday	RFC 49208
6/06/81	**80**	4	2 Paradise	Atlantic 3809
8/08/81	**89**	2	3 Hold Tight	Atlantic 3832
5/29/82	**84**	5	4 The Very Best In You	Atlantic 4027
			THE CHANGIN' TIMES Songwriting, record producing duo: Artie Kornfeld and Steve Duboff.	
11/13/65	**87**	3	1 Pied Piper	Philips 40320
			BRUCE CHANNEL Born on 11/28/40 in Jacksonville, Texas. Appeared on "Louisiana Hayride" in 1958. First recorded for LeCam in 1962.	
1/27/62	**1^3**	15	1 **Hey! Baby** harmonica player: Delbert McClinton	Smash 1731
4/28/62	**52**	7	2 Number One Man	Smash 1752
7/28/62	**98**	2	3 Come On Baby	Smash 1769
2/29/64	**89**	3	4 Going Back To Louisiana	Le Cam 122
12/23/67	**90**	2	5 Mr. Bus Driver produced by Dale Hawkins	Mala 579
			CHANSON Studio disco band. Lead vocals by James Jamerson Jr. & David Williams.	
11/11/78+	**21**	16	1 Don't Hold Back	Ariola 7717
			CHANTAY'S Teenage surf/rock quintet from Santa Ana, CA: Bob Spickard (lead guitar), Brian Carman (rhythm guitar), Bob Marshall (piano), Warren Waters (bass) and Bob Welch (drums).	
3/02/63	**4**	16	1 **Pipeline** [I]	Dot 16440
			THE CHANTELS Vocal group from the Bronx, NY. Formed in high school, with lead Arlene Smith, Sonia Goring, Rene Minus, Jackie Landry and Lois Harris. Group name taken from that of a rival school, St. Francis de Chantelle. Auditioned for Richard Barrett who became their manager and obtained a contract with Gone/End Records. Also see Richard Barrett.	
9/30/57	**71**	6	1 He's Gone	End 1001
1/20/58	**15**	18	2 Maybe Top 100 #15 / Best Seller #16	End 1005
3/31/58	**39**	13	3 Every Night (I Pray) Best Seller #39 / Top 100 #40	End 1015
6/16/58	**42**	7	4 I Love You So Top 100 #42 / Best Seller #44	End 1020
8/28/61	**14**	12	5 Look In My Eyes	Carlton 555
11/13/61	**29**	9	6 Well, I Told You	Carlton 564

DEBUT DATE	PEAK POS	WKS CHR	ARTIST — Record Title	Label & Number
			THE CHANTELS — Cont'd	
3/23/63	**77**	2	7 Eternally	Ludix 101
			THE CHANTERS	
			Consisted of Larry Pendergrass, lead; Fred Paige and Bud Johnson, tenors; Elliot Green, baritone; and Bobby Thompson, bass.	
6/19/61	**41**	9	1 No, No, No	DeLuxe 6191
			HARRY CHAPIN	
			Folk-rock storyteller. Born on 12/7/42 in New York City. Died in an auto accident on 7/16/81.	
3/11/72	**24**	16	1 Taxi	Elektra 45770
10/21/72	**75**	6	2 Sunday Morning Sunshine	Elektra 45811
1/05/74	**36**	13	3 W-O-L-D	Elektra 45874
10/05/74	**1^{1}**	19	4 ● **Cat's In The Cradle**	Elektra 45203
2/15/75	**44**	9	5 I Wanna Learn A Love Song	Elektra 45236
6/26/76	**86**	3	6 Better Place To Be (Parts 1 & 2)	Elektra 45327
11/01/80	**23**	14	7 Sequel sequel to his 1972 hit "Taxi"	Boardwalk 5700
			PAUL CHAPLAIN & his Emeralds	
8/29/60	**82**	4	1 Shortnin' Bread	Harper 100
			THE CHARGERS	
			R&B quartet - Jesse Belvin, lead singer.	
9/01/58	**95**	1	1 Old MacDonald adaptation of song originating in the early 1700's.	RCA 7301
			CHARLENE	
			Full name: Charlene Duncan - from Los Angeles.	
3/05/77	**97**	4	1 It Ain't Easy Comin' Down	Prodigal 0632
5/14/77	**96**	3	2 Freddie	Prodigal 0633
9/24/77	**97**	3	3 I've Never Been To Me	Prodigal 0636
3/06/82	**3**	20	4 **I've Never Been To Me** [R]	Motown 1611
10/30/82	**46**	11	5 Used To Be **CHARLENE & STEVIE WONDER**	Motown 1650
			JIMMY CHARLES	
			Born in 1942 in Paterson, New Jersey.	
8/22/60	**5**	15	1 **A Million To One** vocal backing: The Revelletts	Promo 1002
12/05/60+	**47**	12	2 The Age For Love	Promo 1003
			RAY CHARLES	
			Born Ray Charles Robinson on 9/23/30 in Albany, Georgia. To Greenville, Florida while still an infant. Partially blind at age 5, completely blind at 7 (glaucoma). Studied classical piano and clarinet at State School for Deaf and Blind Children, St. Augustine, Florida, 1937-45. With local Florida bands, moved to Seattle in 1948. Formed the McSon Trio (also known as the Maxim Trio and the Maxine Trio) with G.D. McGhee (guitar) and Milton Garred (bass). First recordings were very much in the King Cole Trio style. Formed own band in 1954. Extremely popular performer with many TV and film appearances.	
10/28/57	**34**	15	1 Swanee River Rock (Talkin' 'Bout That River) Best Seller #34 / Top 100 #42	Atlantic 1154
12/22/58	**79**	2	2 Rockhouse (Part 2) [I]	Atlantic 2006
2/09/59	**95**	1	3 (Night Time Is) The Right Time	Atlantic 2010
7/06/59	**6**	15	4 **What'd I Say (Part I)**	Atlantic 2031
11/09/59	**40**	10	5 I'm Movin' On	Atlantic 2043
1/11/60	**78**	3	6 Let The Good Times Roll/	
2/08/60	**95**	2	7 Don't Let The Sun Catch You Cryin'	Atlantic 2047
6/27/60	**40**	8	8 Sticks And Stones	ABC-Para. 10118
9/26/60	**1^{1}**	13	9 **Georgia On My Mind** first popularized in 1931 by Frankie Trumbauer (POS 10)	ABC-Para. 10135
11/21/60	**28**	9	10 Ruby/	
11/21/60	**55**	4	11 Hardhearted Hannah	ABC-Para. 10164
11/28/60	**83**	2	12 Come Rain Or Come Shine	Atlantic 2084
1/16/61	**58**	6	13 Them That Got	ABC-Para. 10141
3/06/61	**8**	13	14 **One Mint Julep** [I]	Impulse 200
6/19/61	**66**	5	15 I've Got News For You/	
6/19/61	**84**	2	16 I'm Gonna Move To The Outskirts Of Town	Impulse 202
9/11/61	**1^{2}**	13	17 **Hit The Road Jack**	ABC-Para. 10244

DEBUT DATE	PEAK POS	WKS CHR		ARTIST — Record Title	Label & Number
				RAY CHARLES — Cont'd	
11/27/61+	**9**	12	18	**Unchain My Heart/**	
12/11/61+	**72**	4	19	But On The Other Hand Baby	ABC-Para. 10266
3/03/62	**91**	2	20	Baby It's Cold Outside	ABC-Para. 10298
				RAY CHARLES & BETTY CARTER	
4/07/62	**20**	7	21	Hide 'Nor Hair/	
3/31/62	**44**	7	22	At The Club	ABC-Para. 10314
5/05/62	**1**[5]	18	23	● **I Can't Stop Loving You/**	
5/12/62	**41**	9	24	Born To Lose	ABC-Para. 10330
7/28/62	**2**[1]	11	25	**You Don't Know Me/**	
7/28/62	**60**	4	26	Careless Love	ABC-Para. 10345
11/17/62	**7**	12	27	**You Are My Sunshine/**	
11/17/62	**29**	9	28	Your Cheating Heart	ABC-Para. 10375
2/23/63	**20**	8	29	Don't Set Me Free/	
3/09/63	**92**	2	30	The Brightest Smile In Town	ABC-Para. 10405
4/13/63	**8**	11	31	**Take These Chains From My Heart**	ABC-Para. 10435
6/22/63	**21**	8	32	No One/	
6/22/63	**29**	7	33	Without Love (There Is Nothing)	ABC-Para. 10453
9/07/63	**4**	12	34	**Busted**	ABC-Para. 10481
12/07/63+	**20**	9	35	That Lucky Old Sun	ABC-Para. 10509
2/22/64	**39**	7	36	Baby, Don't You Cry/	
2/29/64	**38**	7	37	My Heart Cries For You	ABC-Para. 10530
5/30/64	**51**	6	38	My Baby Don't Dig Me	ABC-Para. 10557
7/18/64	**55**	6	39	No One To Cry To/	
8/01/64	**50**	5	40	A Tear Fell	ABC-Para. 10571
9/26/64	**52**	7	41	Smack Dab In The Middle	ABC-Para. 10588
12/12/64+	**46**	8	42	Makin' Whoopee	ABC-Para. 10609
2/06/65	**58**	7	43	Cry	ABC-Para. 10615
4/17/65	**79**	3	44	I Gotta Woman (Part One)	ABC-Para. 10649
				Ray's original version hit #1 on Billboard's R&B charts, 1955	
7/17/65	**84**	4	45	I'm A Fool To Care	ABC-Para. 10700
12/11/65+	**6**	15	46	**Crying Time**	ABC-Para. 10739
3/26/66	**19**	8	47	Together Again/	
3/26/66	**91**	2	48	You're Just About To Lose Your Clown	ABC-Para. 10785
5/28/66	**31**	9	49	Let's Go Get Stoned	ABC/TRC 10808
9/03/66	**32**	7	50	I Chose To Sing The Blues	ABC/TRC 10840
11/12/66	**64**	6	51	Please Say You're Fooling/	
11/26/66	**72**	4	52	I Don't Need No Doctor	ABC/TRC 10865
3/18/67	**98**	1	53	I Want To Talk About You	ABC/TRC 10901
5/20/67	**15**	12	54	Here We Go Again	ABC/TRC 10938
8/26/67	**33**	7	55	In The Heat Of The Night	ABC/TRC 10970
				from the Sidney Poitier film of the same title	
11/11/67	**25**	7	56	Yesterday	ABC/TRC 11009
1/20/68	**98**	2	57	Come Rain Or Come Shine [R]	Atlantic 2470
2/24/68	**64**	8	58	That's A Lie	ABC/TRC 11045
6/08/68	**35**	10	59	Eleanor Rigby/	
6/15/68	**46**	12	60	Understanding	ABC/TRC 11090
9/28/68	**83**	2	61	Sweet Young Thing Like You/	
10/19/68	**92**	2	62	Listen, They're Playing My Song	ABC/TRC 11133
1/04/69	**77**	6	63	If It Wasn't For Bad Luck	ABC/TRC 11170
				RAY CHARLES & JIMMY LEWIS	
5/17/69	**94**	2	64	Let Me Love You	ABC/TRC 11213
3/14/70	**98**	2	65	Laughin And Clownin	ABC/TRC 11259
10/03/70+	**41**	18	66	If You Were Mine	ABC/TRC 11271
3/13/71	**36**	11	67	Don't Change On Me	ABC/TRC 11291
3/20/71	**36**	12	68	Booty Butt [I]	Tangerine 1015
				THE RAY CHARLES ORCHESTRA	
8/28/71	**68**	8	69	Feel So Bad	ABC/TRC 11308
12/25/71+	**54**	7	70	What Am I Living For	ABC/TRC 11317
7/08/72	**65**	6	71	Look What They've Done To My Song, Ma	ABC/TRC 11329

DEBUT DATE	PEAK POS	WKS CHR	ARTIST — Record Title	Label & Number
			RAY CHARLES — Cont'd	
6/09/73	**81**	4	72 I Can Make It Thru The Days (But Oh Those Lonely Nights)	ABC/TRC 11351
11/17/73	**82**	6	73 Come Live With Me	Crossover 973
9/13/75	**91**	3	74 Living For The City	Crossover 981
			THE RAY CHARLES SINGERS	
			Ray was born on 9/13/18 in Chicago. Arranger and conductor for many TV shows including "Perry Como Show", "Glen Campbell Show" and "Sha-Na-Na".	
11/12/55	**55**	8	1 Autumn Leaves	MGM 12068
4/11/64	**3**	15	2 **Love Me With All Your Heart (Cuando Calienta El Sol)**	Command 4046
7/11/64	**29**	6	3 Al-Di-La/	
9/19/64	**83**	3	4 Till The End Of Time	Command 4049
11/14/64+	**32**	10	5 One More Time	Command 4057
2/27/65	**72**	4	6 This Is My Prayer	Command 4059
6/13/70	**99**	1	7 Move Me, O Wondrous Music	Command 4135
			SONNY CHARLES	
			Vocalist from Fort Wayne, Indiana. Former lead of The Checkmates, Ltd.	
11/13/82+	**40**	14	1 Put It In A Magazine	Highrise 2001
			TOMMY CHARLES	
2/11/56	**43**	14	1 Our Love Affair background vocals: the Jack Halloran Chorus	Decca 29717
7/21/56	**92**	3	2 After School background vocals: The Anita Kerr Singers	Decca 29946
			CHARLIE	
			British rock quintet led by Terry Thomas.	
8/20/77	**96**	2	1 Turning To You	Janus 270
8/05/78	**54**	7	2 She Loves To Be In Love	Janus 276
9/08/79	**60**	6	3 Killer Cut	Arista 0449
6/25/83	**38**	11	4 It's Inevitable	Mirage 99862
			THE CHARMETTES	
11/23/68	**100**	1	1 Please Don't Kiss Me Again	Kapp 547
			THE CHARMS	
			R&B vocal group from Cincinnati consisting of Otis Williams, Richard Parker, Donald Peak, Joe Penn and Rolland Bradley. Otis later moved into the area of Country music.	
11/27/54+	**15**	15	1 Hearts Of Stone Best Seller #15 / Juke Box #15 / Jockey #20	DeLuxe 6062
1/15/55	**26**	3	2 Ling, Ting, Tong Best Seller #26	DeLuxe 6076
			OTIS WILLIAMS & HIS CHARMS:	
1/28/56	**48**	9	3 That's Your Mistake	DeLuxe 6091
3/31/56	**11**	21	4 Ivory Tower Jockey #11 / Top 100 #12 / Best Seller #13 / Juke Box #19	DeLuxe 6093
3/13/61	**95**	3	5 Little Turtle Dove	King 5455
9/18/61	**99**	1	6 Panic	King 5527
			THE CHARTBUSTERS	
			Washington, D.C. rock quartet.	
7/11/64	**33**	8	1 She's The One	Mutual 502
11/14/64	**92**	2	2 Why (Doncha Be My Girl)	Mutual 508
			THE CHARTS	
			R&B vocal quintet: Joe Grier, lead; Leroy Binns, Steven Brown, tenors; Glenmore Jackson, baritone; Ross Buford, bass.	
7/15/57	**88**	4	1 Deserie	Everlast 5001
			CHASE	
			Jazz-rock band organized by trumpeter Bill Chase (formerly with Woody Herman, and Stan Kenton). Bill Chase and 3 other members were killed in a plane crash on 8/9/74.	
5/22/71	**24**	13	1 Get It On	Epic 10738
9/11/71	**84**	5	2 Handbags And Gladrags	Epic 10775
12/18/71+	**81**	5	3 So Many People	Epic 10806

DEBUT DATE	PEAK POS	WKS CHR	ARTIST — Record Title	Label & Number
			ELLISON CHASE	
			24-year-old (in 1976) singer from Ohio.	
8/28/76	**92**	3	1 Let's Rock	Big Tree 16072
			KERRY CHATER	
			Canadian-born singer, songwriter. Original member of The Union Gap.	
3/26/77	**97**	2	1 Part Time Love	Warner 8310
			CHEAP TRICK	
			Rock quartet from Rockford, Illinois consisting of Rick Nielsen, guitar; Bun E. Carlos, drums; Robin Zander, vocals; and Tom Petersson, bass (replaced by Jon Brant in 1980).	
7/22/78	**62**	8	1 Surrender	Epic 50570
4/28/79	**7**	19	2 ● **I Want You To Want Me**	Epic 50680
8/04/79	**35**	10	3 Ain't That A Shame	Epic 50743
10/06/79	**26**	10	4 Dream Police	Epic 50774
12/08/79+	**32**	11	5 Voices	Epic 50814
5/24/80	**44**	10	6 Everything Works If You Let It	Epic 50887
11/08/80	**48**	12	7 Stop This Game	Epic 50942
6/05/82	**45**	11	8 If You Want My Love	Epic 02968
10/09/82	**65**	7	9 She's Tight	Epic 03233
7/27/85	**44**	17	10 Tonight It's You	Epic 05431
			CHUBBY CHECKER	
			Born Ernest Evans on 10/3/41 in Philadelphia. His cover version of Hank Ballard's "The Twist" started a worldwide dance craze.	
5/18/59	**38**	7	1 The Class [N] imitations of Fats Domino, The Coasters, Elvis, and The Chipmunks	Parkway 804
8/01/60	**1^{1}**	18	2 **The Twist**	Parkway 811
10/10/60	**14**	13	3 The Hucklebuck/ written in 1949 - hit #5 for Tommy Dorsey; #10 for Frank Sinatra	
10/10/60	**42**	8	4 Whole Lotta Shakin' Goin' On	Parkway 813
1/23/61	**1^{3}**	16	5 **Pony Time**	Parkway 818
4/24/61	**24**	7	6 Dance The Mess Around/	
4/17/61	**43**	6	7 Good, Good Lovin'	Parkway 822
6/19/61	**8**	23	8 **Let's Twist Again**	Parkway 824
9/25/61	**7**	13	9 **The Fly**	Parkway 830
11/13/61+	**1^{2}**	21	10 **The Twist** [R] except for Bing Crosby's "White Christmas", "The Twist" is the only song in chart history to return to the #1 position after an absence of one year or more	Parkway 811
12/11/61	**21**	5	11 Jingle Bell Rock [X] **BOBBY RYDELL/CHUBBY CHECKER**	Cameo 205
12/11/61	**68**	3	12 Twistin' U.S.A.	Parkway 811
3/03/62	**3**	14	13 **Slow Twistin'**/ female vocal: Dee Dee Sharp	
3/17/62	**72**	2	14 La Paloma Twist	Parkway 835
6/23/62	**12**	10	15 Dancin' Party	Parkway 842
9/08/62	**2^{2}**	23	16 **Limbo Rock**/	
9/15/62	**10**	13	17 **Popeye The Hitchhiker**	Parkway 849
12/15/62	**92**	2	18 Jingle Bell Rock [X-R] **BOBBY RYDELL/CHUBBY CHECKER**	Cameo 205
2/23/63	**15**	12	19 Twenty Miles/	
2/16/63	**20**	10	20 Let's Limbo Some More	Parkway 862
5/18/63	**12**	9	21 Birdland/	
6/15/63	**98**	1	22 Black Cloud	Parkway 873
7/20/63	**25**	8	23 Twist It Up/	
7/13/63	**55**	6	24 Surf Party	Parkway 879
11/02/63	**12**	13	25 Loddy Lo/	
12/07/63+	**17**	14	26 Hooka Tooka	Parkway 890
3/14/64	**23**	9	27 Hey, Bobba Needle	Parkway 907
6/06/64	**40**	7	28 Lazy Elsie Molly	Parkway 920
8/29/64	**50**	7	29 She Wants T' Swim	Parkway 922
1/02/65	**70**	4	30 Lovely, Lovely (Loverly, Loverly)	Parkway 936
4/03/65	**40**	9	31 Let's Do The Freddie	Parkway 949
7/02/66	**76**	5	32 Hey You! Little Boo-Ga-Loo	Parkway 989
4/05/69	**82**	5	33 Back In The U.S.S.R.	Buddah 100

DEBUT DATE	PEAK POS	WKS CHR	ARTIST — Record Title		Label & Number
			CHUBBY CHECKER — Cont'd		
2/20/82	**91**	5	34 Running		MCA 51233
			THE CHECKMATES, LTD.		
			Integrated quintet from Fort Wayne, Indiana. Consisted of Sonny Charles, lead vocal; Bobby Stevens, vocal; Harvey Trees, guitar; Bill Van Buskirk, bass; and Marvin Smith ("Sweet Louie"), drums.		
4/05/69	**65**	7	1 Love Is All I Have To Give		A&M 1039
5/10/69	**13**	13	2 Black Pearl		A&M 1053
			SONNY CHARLES & THE CHECKMATES, LTD.		
10/18/69	**69**	4	3 Proud Mary		A&M 1127
			THE CHECKMATES, LTD. featuring SONNY CHARLES		
			above 3 produced by Phil Spector		
			CHEE-CHEE & PEPPY		
			13-year-old boy and girl duo.		
5/29/71	**49**	14	1 I Know I'm In Love		Buddah 225
			CHEECH & CHONG		
			Comedians Richard 'Cheech' Marin & Thomas Chong. Cheech was born in Watts, CA; Chong in Edmonton, Alberta, Canada. Starred in movies since 1980.		
9/08/73	**15**	11	1 Basketball Jones Featuring Tyrone Shoelaces	[N]	Ode 66038
11/24/73+	**24**	12	2 Sister Mary Elephant (Shudd-Up!)	[C]	Ode 66041
8/10/74	**9**	13	3 **Earache My Eye Featuring Alice Bowie**	[C]	Ode 66102
11/09/74	**55**	6	4 Black Lassie Featuring Johnny Stash	[C]	Ode 66104
10/18/75	**54**	5	5 (How I Spent My Summer Vacation) Or A Day At The Beach With Pedro & Man - Parts I & II	[C]	Ode 66115
6/12/76	**41**	8	6 Framed	[N]	Ode 66124
11/12/77+	**41**	10	7 Bloat On Featuring the Bloaters	[C]	Ode 50471
9/21/85	**48**	11	8 Born In East L.A.	[N]	MCA 52655
			parody of Bruce Springsteen's "Born In The U.S.A."		
			JUDY CHEEKS		
			Born in Miami, daughter of gospel singer and preacher, Rev. Julius Cheeks.		
10/07/78	**65**	5	1 Mellow Lovin'		Salsoul 2063
			THE CHEERS		
			Trio from Los Angeles consisting of actor Bert Convy, Gil Garfield and Sue Allen.		
9/24/55	**6**	11	1 **Black Denim Trousers**		Capitol 3219
			Best Seller #6 / Jockey #6 / Top 100 #13 / Juke Box #20		
			orchestra & chorus directed by Les Baxter		
			THE JOE CHEMAY BAND		
			Joe is a well-known session player and arranger from Seattle.		
2/14/81	**68**	8	1 Proud		Unicorn 95001
			CHER		
			Born Cherilyn LaPierre on 5/20/46 in El Centro, California. Worked as back-up singer for Phil Spector. Recorded with Sonny Bono as "Caesar & Cleo" in 1963. Recorded as "Bonnie Jo Mason" and "Cherilyn" in 1964. Married Bono in 1963, divorced in 1974. Married for a short time to Gregg Allman. Own TV series with Bono from 1971-77. Acclaimed as actress in films "Silkwood" and "Mask".		
7/03/65	**15**	12	1 All I Really Want To Do		Imperial 66114
10/16/65	**25**	7	2 Where Do You Go		Imperial 66136
3/12/66	**2^{1}**	11	3 **Bang Bang (My Baby Shot Me Down)**		Imperial 66160
7/30/66	**32**	6	4 Alfie		Imperial 66192
			from the film of the same title		
11/26/66	**97**	1	5 Behind The Door		Imperial 66217
9/09/67	**94**	2	6 Hey Joe		Imperial 66252
10/28/67	**9**	13	7 **You Better Sit Down Kids**		Imperial 66261
			all of above songs produced by Sonny Bono		
9/18/71	**1^{2}**	16	8 ● **Gypsys, Tramps & Thieves**		Kapp 2146
1/29/72	**7**	13	9 **The Way Of Love**		Kapp 2158
5/20/72	**22**	8	10 Living In A House Divided		Kapp 2171
9/09/72	**46**	8	11 Don't Hide Your Love		Kapp 2184
8/04/73	**1^{2}**	20	12 ● **Half-Breed**		MCA 40102
1/19/74	**1^{1}**	16	13 ● **Dark Lady**		MCA 40161
5/25/74	**27**	11	14 Train Of Thought		MCA 40245
8/10/74	**42**	9	15 I Saw A Man And He Danced With His Wife		MCA 40273
1/15/77	**93**	2	16 Pirate		Warner 8311
			8-16: produced by Snuff Garrett		
2/10/79	**8**	19	17 ● **Take Me Home**		Casablanca 965

DEBUT DATE	PEAK POS	WKS CHR	ARTIST — Record Title		Label & Number
			CHER — Cont'd		
6/02/79	**49**	7	18 Wasn't It Good		Casablanca 987
9/15/79	**59**	5	19 Hell On Wheels		Casablanca 2208
			CHERI		
			Canadian duo: Rosalind Milligan Hunt and Lynn Cullerier.		
4/10/82	**39**	12	1 Murphy's Law	[N]	Venture 149
			CHERRELLE		
			Real name: Cheryl Norton (from Los Angeles).		
7/07/84	**79**	9	1 I Didn't Mean To Turn You On		Tabu 04406
2/15/86	**26**	17	2 Saturday Love		Tabu 05767
			CHERRELLE with ALEXANDER O'NEAL		
			THE CHERRY PEOPLE		
			Dougy & Chris Grimes, Punky Meadows (of 'Angel'), Rocky Isaac and Jan Zukowski.		
7/20/68	**45**	8	1 And Suddenly		Heritage 801
			DON CHERRY		
			Born in Wichita, Texas on 1/11/24. Sang briefly with postwar Tommy Dorsey and Victor Young orchestras; left music to become a pro golfer in the late 50s.		
12/03/55+	**4**	22	1 **Band Of Gold**		Columbia 40597
			Jockey #4 / Best Seller #5 / Top 100 #5 / Juke Box #5		
4/07/56	**29**	12	2 Wild Cherry/		
4/21/56	**72**	1	3 I'm Still A King To You		Columbia 40665
7/14/56	**22**	14	4 Ghost Town/		
			Jockey #22 / Top 100 #26		
8/25/56	**78**	1	5 I'll Be Around		Columbia 40705
			orchestra & chorus directed by Ray Conniff on all of above titles		
10/06/56	**65**	8	6 Namely You		Columbia 40746
			from the Broadway show "Li'l Abner"		
			THE CHI-LITES		
			R&B vocal group from Chicago. Consisted of Eugene Record (lead vocals), Robert Lester (tenor), Marshall Thompson (baritone) and Creadel Jones (bass). First recorded as the Hi-Lites on Daran in 1963.		
3/01/69	**88**	6	1 Give It Away		Brunswick 55398
8/02/69	**94**	3	2 Let Me Be The Man My Daddy Was		Brunswick 55414
8/15/70	**72**	6	3 I Like Your Lovin' (Do You Like Mine)		Brunswick 55438
12/19/70+	**72**	7	4 Are You My Woman? (Tell Me So)		Brunswick 55442
4/10/71	**26**	11	5 (For God's Sake) Give More Power To The People		Brunswick 55450
7/24/71	**70**	5	6 We Are Neighbors		Brunswick 55455
10/23/71	**3**	14	7 **Have You Seen Her**		Brunswick 55462
11/06/71	**95**	3	8 I Want To Pay You Back (For Loving Me)		Brunswick 55458
4/08/72	**1**[1]	15	9 **Oh Girl**		Brunswick 55471
7/15/72	**47**	9	10 The Coldest Days Of My Life (Part 1)		Brunswick 55478
9/30/72	**57**	5	11 A Lonely Man/		
		5	12 The Man & The Woman (The Boy & The Girl)		Brunswick 55483
12/02/72	**61**	6	13 We Need Order		Brunswick 55489
2/10/73	**33**	11	14 A Letter To Myself		Brunswick 55491
6/09/73	**92**	4	15 My Heart Just Keeps On Breakin'		Brunswick 55496
8/04/73	**30**	13	16 Stoned Out Of My Mind		Brunswick 55500
11/17/73	**47**	10	17 I Found Sunshine		Brunswick 55503
2/09/74	**54**	8	18 Homely Girl		Brunswick 55505
6/15/74	**63**	7	19 There Will Never Be Any Peace (Until God Is Seated At The Conference Table)		Brunswick 55512
8/31/74	**83**	3	20 You Got To Be The One		Brunswick 55514
3/01/75	**78**	7	21 Toby/		
		7	22 That's How Long		Brunswick 55515
11/08/75	**94**	3	23 It's Time For Love		Brunswick 55520
			CHIC		
			Disco group formed in New York City by producers Bernard Edwards, bass; and Nile Rodgers, guitar. Vocalists were Norma Jean Wright (replaced by Alfa Anderson) and Luci Martin; and Tony Thompson on drums. Rodgers joined the Honeydrippers in 1984. Thompson joined the Power Station in 1985 and Edwards became their producer.		
10/29/77+	**6**	28	1 ● **Dance, Dance, Dance (Yowsah, Yowsah, Yowsah)**		Atlantic 3435
4/22/78	**38**	10	2 Everybody Dance		Atlantic 3469
10/28/78	**1**[6]	25	3 ▲ **Le Freak**		Atlantic 3519

DEBUT DATE	PEAK POS	WKS CHR	ARTIST — Record Title	Label & Number
			CHIC — Cont'd	
2/10/79	**7**	19	4 ● **I Want Your Love**	Atlantic 3557
6/16/79	**1**[1]	19	5 ● **Good Times**	Atlantic 3584
10/06/79	**43**	9	6 My Forbidden Lover	Atlantic 3620
8/30/80	**61**	6	7 Rebels Are We	Atlantic 3665
11/15/80	**79**	3	8 Real People/	
		2	9 Chip Off The Old Block	Atlantic 3768
6/05/82	**80**	6	10 Soup For One theme song from the movie of the same title	Mirage 4032
			CHICAGO Jazz-oriented rock group formed in Chicago in 1967. Consisted of Robert Lamm, keyboards; James Pankow, trombone; Lee Loughnane, trumpet; Terry Kath, guitar (d: 1/23/78 [31] playing Russian roulette); Walt Parazaider, reeds; Peter Cetera, bass; and Danny Seraphine, drums. Originally called The Big Thing, later Chicago Transit Authority. To Los Angeles in late 60s. Kath replaced by Donnie Dacus. Bill Champlin, keyboards, joined in 1982. Cetera left in 1985, replaced by Jason Scheff.	
8/09/69	**71**	3	1 Questions 67 And 68	Columbia 44909
4/04/70	**9**	14	2 **Make Me Smile**	Columbia 45127
7/25/70	**4**	12	3 **25 Or 6 To 4**	Columbia 45194
11/07/70+	**7**	13	4 **Does Anybody Really Know What Time It Is?**	Columbia 45264
2/20/71	**20**	9	5 Free	Columbia 45331
5/08/71	**35**	8	6 Lowdown	Columbia 45370
6/26/71	**7**	13	7 **Beginnings/**	
		12	8 Colour My World	Columbia 45417
10/09/71	**24**	10	9 Questions 67 And 68/ [R]	
		10	10 I'm A Man	Columbia 45467
8/05/72	**3**	12	11 ● **Saturday In The Park**	Columbia 45657
10/28/72	**24**	10	12 Dialogue (Part I & II)	Columbia 45717
6/23/73	**10**	16	13 **Feelin' Stronger Every Day**	Columbia 45880
9/29/73	**4**	19	14 ● **Just You 'N' Me**	Columbia 45933
3/16/74	**9**	15	15 **(I've Been) Searchin' So Long**	Columbia 46020
6/22/74	**6**	15	16 **Call On Me**	Columbia 46062
10/19/74	**11**	15	17 Wishing You Were Here backing vocals by 3 of the Beach Boys	Columbia 10049
2/22/75	**13**	9	18 Harry Truman	Columbia 10092
4/26/75	**5**	11	19 **Old Days**	Columbia 10131
9/06/75	**61**	5	20 Brand New Love Affair (Part I & II)	Columbia 10200
6/26/76	**32**	9	21 Another Rainy Day In New York City	Columbia 10360
8/14/76	**1**[2]	21	22 ● **If You Leave Me Now**	Columbia 10390
4/09/77	**49**	7	23 You Are On My Mind	Columbia 10523
9/24/77	**4**	17	24 **Baby, What A Big Surprise**	Columbia 10620
2/11/78	**44**	9	25 Little One	Columbia 10683
5/20/78	**63**	5	26 Take Me Back To Chicago all of above songs produced by James William Guercio	Columbia 10737
10/21/78	**14**	13	27 Alive Again	Columbia 10845
12/23/78+	**14**	15	28 No Tell Lover	Columbia 10879
4/14/79	**73**	3	29 Gone Long Gone	Columbia 10935
9/01/79	**83**	5	30 Must Have Been Crazy	Columbia 11061
8/23/80	**56**	9	31 Thunder And Lightning	Columbia 11345
6/05/82	**1**[2]	24	32 ● **Hard To Say I'm Sorry** from the film "Summer Lovers"	Full Moon 29979
9/25/82	**22**	15	33 Love Me Tomorrow	Full Moon 29911
1/29/83	**81**	5	34 What You're Missing	Full Moon 29798
5/05/84	**16**	17	35 Stay The Night	Full Moon 29306
8/04/84	**3**	25	36 **Hard Habit To Break**	Full Moon 29214
11/17/84+	**3**	22	37 **You're The Inspiration**	Full Moon 29126
2/23/85	**14**	16	38 Along Comes A Woman	Full Moon 29082
9/06/86	**48**	8	39 25 Or 6 To 4	Full Moon 28628
11/15/86+	**3**	23	40 **Will You Still Love Me?**	Full Moon 28512
			THE CHICAGO BEARS SHUFFLIN' CREW Super Bowl XX Champs - featuring (in order): Walter Payton, Willie Gault, Mike Singletary, Jim McMahon, Otis Wilson, Steve Fuller, Mike Richardson, Richard Dent, Gary Fencik and William Perry.	
1/11/86	**41**	9	1 Superbowl Shuffle [N]	Red Label 71012

DEBUT DATE	PEAK POS	WKS CHR	ARTIST — Record Title	Label & Number
			THE CHICAGO LOOP	
11/05/66	**37**	7	1 (When She Needs Good Lovin') She Comes To Me	DynoVoice 226
			CHICORY	
			British rock quartet. Known in England as Chicory Tip.	
3/11/72	**91**	3	1 Son Of My Father	Epic 10837
			THE CHIFFONS	
			Black vocal group from the Bronx, New York. Formed while high school classmates. Consisted of Judy Craig, Barbara Lee, Patricia Bennett and Sylvia Peterson. Also recorded as The Four Pennies on the Rust label.	
9/12/60	**76**	4	1 Tonight's The Night	Big Deal 6003
2/23/63	**1**[4]	15	2 **He's So Fine**	Laurie 3152
6/01/63	**5**	10	3 **One Fine Day**	Laurie 3179
6/22/63	**67**	5	4 My Block .... THE FOUR PENNIES	Rust 5071
9/07/63	**40**	9	5 A Love So Fine	Laurie 3195
11/09/63	**95**	1	6 When The Boy's Happy (The Girl's Happy Too) .... THE FOUR PENNIES	Rust 5070
11/16/63+	**36**	10	7 I Have A Boyfriend	Laurie 3212
8/01/64	**81**	3	8 Sailor Boy	Laurie 3262
6/19/65	**49**	9	9 Nobody Knows What's Goin' On (In My Mind But Me) ..	Laurie 3301
5/07/66	**10**	10	10 **Sweet Talkin' Guy**	Laurie 3340
8/06/66	**67**	4	11 Out Of This World	Laurie 3350
10/01/66	**85**	2	12 Stop, Look And Listen	Laurie 3357
			DESMOND CHILD & ROUGE	
			Vocal group formed in 1975. Consisted of Desmond Child, Diana Grasselli, Myriam Valle and Maria Vidal.	
1/20/79	**51**	11	1 Our Love Is Insane	Capitol 4669
			CHILLIWACK	
			Canadian rock group led by Bill Henderson.	
2/05/72	**75**	3	1 Lonesome Mary	A&M 1310
12/28/74+	**98**	6	2 Crazy Talk	Sire 716
4/30/77	**75**	6	3 Fly At Night	Mushroom 7024
8/05/78	**67**	6	4 Arms Of Mary	Mushroom 7033
9/26/81	**22**	19	5 My Girl (Gone, Gone, Gone)	Millennium 11813
1/16/82	**33**	11	6 I Believe	Millennium 13102
10/23/82	**41**	13	7 Whatcha Gonna Do	Millennium 13110
			THE CHIMES	
			Brooklyn-based quintet led by Leonard Cocco.	
10/31/60+	**11**	18	1 Once In Awhile	Tag 444
3/27/61	**38**	9	2 I'm In The Mood For Love	Tag 445
			THE CHIPMUNKS	
			Characters created by Ross Bagdasarian ("David Seville"). Named Alvin, Simon and Theodore after Liberty executives Alvin Bennett, Simon Waronker & Theodore Keep. Bagdasarian died on 1/16/72 (52); his son resurrected the act in 1980.	
12/01/58	**1**[4]	13	1 **The Chipmunk Song** .... [X-N] DAVID SEVILLE & THE CHIPMUNKS:	Liberty 55168
2/16/59	**3**	12	2 **Alvin's Harmonica** .... [N]	Liberty 55179
7/06/59	**16**	9	3 Ragtime Cowboy Joe .... [N]	Liberty 55200
12/14/59	**41**	5	4 The Chipmunk Song .... [X-R]	Liberty 55250
2/22/60	**33**	5	5 Alvin's Orchestra .... [N]	Liberty 55233
9/05/60	**95**	2	6 Alvin For President .... [N]	Liberty 55277
12/12/60	**45**	3	7 The Chipmunk Song .... [X-R]	Liberty 55250
12/19/60	**21**	2	8 Rudolph The Red Nosed Reindeer .... [X-N]	Liberty 55289
12/18/61	**39**	3	9 The Chipmunk Song/ [X-R]	
12/25/61	**73**	2	10 Alvin's Harmonica .... [N-R]	Liberty 55250
12/18/61	**47**	3	11 Rudolph The Red Nosed Reindeer .... [X-R]	Liberty 55289
3/03/62	**40**	8	12 The Alvin Twist .... [N]	Liberty 55424
12/08/62	**40**	4	13 The Chipmunk Song/ [X-R]	
12/22/62	**87**	1	14 Alvin's Harmonica .... [N-R]	Liberty 55250
12/15/62	**77**	3	15 Rudolph The Red Nosed Reindeer .... [X-R]	Liberty 55289

DEBUT DATE	PEAK POS	WKS CHR	ARTIST — Record Title	Label & Number
			CHOCOLATE MILK	
			Frank Richard, Amadee Castanell, Joe Foxx, Robert Dabon, Mario Tio and Dwight Richards.	
7/12/75	**69**	5	1 Action Speaks Louder Than Words	RCA 10290
			THE CHOICE FOUR	
			Bobby Hamilton, Ted Maduro, Pete Marshall and Charles Blagmore.	
8/30/75	**91**	4	1 When You're Young And In Love	RCA 10342
			THE CHOIR	
			Quartet from Cleveland; became the Raspberries after the addition of Eric Carmen.	
6/03/67	**68**	6	1 It's Cold Outside	Roulette 4738
			THE CHORDETTES	
			Female vocal group from Sheboygan, Wisconsin, formed in 1946. Consisted of Janet Ertel, bass; Carol Bushman, baritone; Lynn Evans, lead singer (replaced Dorothy Schwartz, 1953); and Margie Needham, tenor (replaced Jinny Lockard, 1953). With Arthur Godfrey from 1949-53. Ertel married Cadence owner Archie Bleyer.	
1/14/56	**91**	2	1 The Wedding	Cadence 1273
3/10/56	**14**	12	2 Eddie My Love	Cadence 1284
			Jockey #14 / Best Seller #17 / Top 100 #18	
6/02/56	**5**	20	3 **Born To Be With You**	Cadence 1291
			Top 100 #5 / Jockey #5 / Juke Box #5 / Best Seller #7	
9/29/56	**16**	18	4 Lay Down Your Arms/	
			Top 100 #16 / Juke Box #16 / Best Seller #18 / Jockey #20	
10/20/56	**45**	11	5 Teen Age Goodnight	Cadence 1299
9/09/57	**8**	15	6 **Just Between You And Me/**	
			Jockey #8 / Best Seller #15 / Top 100 #19	
9/23/57	**73**	6	7 Soft Sands	Cadence 1330
3/10/58	**2**[2]	15	8 **Lollipop**	Cadence 1345
			Best Seller #2 / Top 100 #2 / Jockey #2	
5/19/58	**17**	11	9 Zorro	Cadence 1349
			Top 100 #17 / Best Seller #18 / Jockey #22	
3/02/59	**27**	11	10 No Other Arms, No Other Lips	Cadence 1361
8/17/59	**89**	3	11 A Girl's Work Is Never Done	Cadence 1366
6/19/61	**13**	12	12 Never On Sunday/	
9/25/61	**90**	1	13 Faraway Star	Cadence 1402
			CHRIS CHRISTIAN	
			Guitarist, songwriter, producer. With trio Cotton, Lloyd & Christian.	
10/03/81	**37**	14	1 I Want You, I Need You	Boardwalk 126
8/28/82	**88**	3	2 Ain't Nothing Like The Real Thing/You're All I Need To Get By	Boardwalk 149
			vocal duet with Amy Holland	
			CHRISTIE	
			English trio: Jeff Christie, Vic Elms and Mike Blakey.	
7/18/70	**23**	23	1 Yellow River	Epic 10626
1/30/71	**100**	1	2 San Bernadino	Epic 10695
			DEAN CHRISTIE	
11/03/62	**87**	4	1 Heart Breaker	Select 715
			LOU CHRISTIE	
			Born Lugee Alfredo Giovanni Sacco on 2/19/43 in Glen Willard, PA. Joined vocal group, the Classics, first recorded for Starr in 1960. Started long association with songwriter Twyla Herbert. Recorded as "Lugee & The Lions" for Robbee in 1961.	
1/05/63	**24**	13	1 The Gypsy Cried	Roulette 4457
3/30/63	**6**	15	2 **Two Faces Have I**	Roulette 4481
7/20/63	**46**	5	3 How Many Teardrops	Roulette 4504
12/25/65+	**1**[1]	15	4 ● **Lightnin' Strikes**	MGM 13412
3/05/66	**45**	8	5 Outside The Gates Of Heaven	Co & Ce 235
3/19/66	**95**	1	6 Big Time	Colpix 799
3/26/66	**16**	8	7 Rhapsody In The Rain	MGM 13473
6/25/66	**81**	5	8 Painter	MGM 13533
4/29/67	**95**	2	9 Shake Hands And Walk Away Cryin'	Columbia 44062
8/23/69	**10**	12	10 **I'm Gonna Make You Mine**	Buddah 116
12/20/69+	**73**	4	11 Are You Getting Any Sunshine?	Buddah 149
2/16/74	**80**	10	12 Beyond The Blue Horizon	Three Bros. 402
			sung by Jeanette MacDonald in the 1930 film "Monte Carlo"	

DEBUT DATE	PEAK POS	WKS CHR	ARTIST — Record Title	Label & Number
			SUSAN CHRISTIE	
6/11/66	**63**	8	1 I Love Onions [N]	Columbia 43595
			CHRISTOPHER, PAUL & SHAWN	
8/02/75	**91**	5	1 For Your Love	Casablanca 838
			GAVIN CHRISTOPHER	
			Chicago-born singer, composer, producer.	
5/24/86	**22**	17	1 One Step Closer To You	Manhattan 50028
			EUGENE CHURCH	
			Los Angeles native. Born on 1/23/38. Recorded with Jesse Belvin as The Cliques.	
12/15/58+	**36**	15	1 Pretty Girls Everywhere **EUGENE CHURCH & THE FELLOWS** featuring backing vocals by Bobby Day	Class 235
8/03/59	**67**	5	2 Miami	Class 254
			CINDERELLA	
			Pennsylvania-based heavy-metal band, consisting of Tom Keifer (lead singer, guitar, piano), Jeff LaBar (guitar), Eric Brittingham (bass) & Fred Coury (drums).	
11/08/86+	**13**	21	1 Nobody's Fool	Mercury 884851
			CIRCUS	
2/24/73	**91**	4	1 Stop, Wait & Listen	Metromedia 265
			KACEY CISYK	
11/12/77	**80**	4	1 You Light Up My Life from the film of the same title starring Didi Conn artist shown as: **ORIGINAL CAST**	Arista 0287
			CITY BOY	
			British rock sextet - Lol Mason, lead singer.	
8/12/78	**27**	12	1 5.7.0.5.	Mercury 73999
			C.J. & CO.	
			Detroit disco/soul band assembled by Dennis Coffey.	
1/03/76	**91**	8	1 Daydreamer shown as: **C.C. & COMPANY**	Westbound 5016
5/21/77	**36**	29	2 Devil's Gun	Westbound 55400
			IKE CLANTON	
			Jimmy Clanton's brother.	
5/23/60	**91**	2	1 Down The Aisle	Ace 583
8/04/62	**95**	2	2 Sugar Plum	Mercury 71975
			JIMMY CLANTON	
			Born on 9/2/40 in Baton Rouge, Louisiana. Formed a four-piece band, the Rockets, and auditioned with Ace Records in New Orleans. Wrote "Just A Dream", recorded with famous New Orleans session men, including Huey "Piano" Smith, Earl King (guitar) and Lee Allen (tenor sax). For a time was a disc jockey in Lancaster, PA.	
7/14/58	**4**	18	1 **Just A Dream** Hot 100 #4 / Best Seller #4	Ace 546
10/20/58	**25**	12	2 A Letter To An Angel/	
11/03/58	**38**	7	3 A Part Of Me	Ace 551
8/03/59	**33**	12	4 My Own True Love melody is "Tara's Theme" from "Gone With The Wind"	Ace 567
12/07/59+	**5**	16	5 **Go, Jimmy, Go**	Ace 575
4/25/60	**22**	13	6 Another Sleepless Night	Ace 585
8/22/60	**63**	8	7 Come Back/	
9/26/60	**91**	3	8 Wait	Ace 600
1/09/61	**50**	6	9 What Am I Gonna Do	Ace 607
8/18/62	**7**	13	10 **Venus In Blue Jeans** 6, 9 & 10: written by Neil Sedaka	Ace 8001
1/05/63	**77**	4	11 Darkest Street In Town	Ace 8005
11/15/69	**97**	3	12 Curly	Laurie 3508

DEBUT DATE	PEAK POS	WKS CHR	ARTIST — Record Title	Label & Number
			ERIC CLAPTON	
			Born on 3/30/45 in Ripley, England. Vocalist, guitarist. With The Roosters in 1963, The Yardbirds, 1963-65, and John Mayall's Bluesbreakers, 1965-66. Formed Cream with Jack Bruce and Ginger Baker, 1966. Formed Blind Faith in 1968; worked with John Lennon's Plastic Ono Band, and Delaney & Bonnie. Formed Derek & The Dominos, 1970. After 2 years of reclusion (1971 & 72), Clapton performed his comeback concert at London's Rainbow Theatre in January, 1973. Began actively recording and touring again in 1974. Also see Derek & The Dominos, and Delaney & Bonnie.	
10/17/70	**18**	12	1 After Midnight	Atco 6784
9/23/72	**48**	13	2 Let It Rain	Polydor 15049
2/17/73	**78**	5	3 Bell Bottom Blues	Polydor 15056
7/13/74	**1**[1]	14	4● **I Shot The Sheriff**	RSO 409
11/02/74	**26**	9	5 Willie And The Hand Jive	RSO 503
10/16/76	**24**	14	6 Hello Old Friend	RSO 861
1/07/78	**3**	23	7● **Lay Down Sally**	RSO 886
5/13/78	**16**	17	8 Wonderful Tonight	RSO 895
			ERIC CLAPTON & HIS BAND:	
10/14/78+	**9**	18	9 **Promises/**	
2/24/79	**40**	7	10 Watch Out For Lucy	RSO 910
6/21/80	**30**	14	11 Tulsa Time/	
		12	12 Cocaine	RSO 1039
11/08/80	**76**	5	13 Blues Power	RSO 1051
2/28/81	**10**	17	14 **I Can't Stand It**	RSO 1060
6/13/81	**78**	5	15 Another Ticket	RSO 1064
			ERIC CLAPTON:	
1/29/83	**18**	16	16 I've Got A Rock N' Roll Heart	Duck 29780
3/09/85	**26**	12	17 Forever Man	Duck 29081
6/29/85	**89**	2	18 See What Love Can Do	Duck 28986
			CLAUDINE CLARK	
			Born on 4/26/41 in Macon, Georgia. Recorded for Herald and Gotham in 1958.	
6/30/62	**5**	15	1 **Party Lights**	Chancellor 1113
			THE DAVE CLARK FIVE	
			Rock group formed in Tottenham, England in 1962. Consisted of Dave Clark (drums), Mike Smith (lead vocals, keyboards), Lenny Davidson (guitar), Dennis Payton (sax) and Rick Huxley (bass). First recorded for Ember/Pye in 1962. On Ed Sullivan show in March, 1964. Film "Having A Wild Weekend", 1965. Disbanded in 1973. Clark had been a stuntman in films, formed group to raise money for his soccer team, the Tottenham Hotspurs. Clark wrote the new London stage musical "Time".	
2/15/64	**6**	14	1 **Glad All Over**	Epic 9656
4/04/64	**4**	11	2 **Bits And Pieces**	Epic 9671
4/25/64	**53**	8	3 I Knew It All The Time	Congress 212
5/02/64	**11**	10	4 Do You Love Me	Epic 9678
6/13/64	**4**	10	5 **Can't You See That She's Mine**	Epic 9692
8/01/64	**3**	10	6 **Because**	Epic 9704
10/03/64	**15**	8	7 Everybody Knows (I Still Love You)	Epic 9722
11/14/64+	**14**	12	8 Any Way You Want It	Epic 9739
2/06/65	**14**	9	9 Come Home	Epic 9763
4/17/65	**23**	9	10 Reelin' And Rockin'	Epic 9786
6/19/65	**7**	11	11 **I Like It Like That**	Epic 9811
8/21/65	**4**	11	12 **Catch Us If You Can** from the film "Having A Wild Weekend"	Epic 9833
11/13/65	**1**[1]	12	13 **Over And Over**	Epic 9863
2/05/66	**18**	7	14 At The Scene	Epic 9882
4/02/66	**12**	8	15 Try Too Hard	Epic 10004
6/11/66	**28**	7	16 Please Tell Me Why	Epic 10031
8/13/66	**50**	6	17 Satisfied With You	Epic 10053
10/22/66	**48**	6	18 Nineteen Days	Epic 10076
1/07/67	**44**	7	19 I've Got To Have A Reason	Epic 10114
4/01/67	**7**	10	20 **You Got What It Takes**	Epic 10144
6/10/67	**35**	6	21 You Must Have Been A Beautiful Baby	Epic 10179
8/12/67	**67**	4	22 A Little Bit Now	Epic 10209
11/18/67	**89**	2	23 Red And Blue	Epic 10244
12/16/67+	**43**	8	24 Everybody Knows	Epic 10265

DEBUT DATE	PEAK POS	WKS CHR	ARTIST — Record Title	Label & Number
			DEE CLARK	
			Born Delecta Clark on 11/7/38 in Blythsville, Arkansas. To Chicago in 1941. In Hambone Kids with Sammy McGrier and Ronny Strong, first recorded for Okeh in 1952. Joined vocal group the Goldentones in 1953. Group became the Kool Gents; billed as The Delegates for Vee-Jay recording in 1956. First solo recording for Falcon, 1957.	
12/01/58+	**21**	17	1 Nobody But You	Abner 1019
5/04/59	**18**	15	2 Just Keep It Up	Abner 1026
8/24/59	**20**	15	3 Hey Little Girl	Abner 1029
12/07/59+	**33**	11	4 How About That	Abner 1032
3/14/60	**56**	7	5 At My Front Door	Abner 1037
8/15/60	**43**	10	6 You're Looking Good	Vee-Jay 355
2/06/61	**34**	9	7 Your Friends	Vee-Jay 372
5/01/61	**2**[1]	16	8 **Raindrops**	Vee-Jay 383
10/06/62	**52**	7	9 I'm Going Back To School	Vee-Jay 462
11/02/63	**92**	5	10 Crossfire Time	Constellation 108
			LOUIS CLARK - see ROYAL PHILHARMONIC ORCHESTRA	
			PETULA CLARK	
			Born on 11/15/32 in Epsom, England. On radio at age nine; own show "Pet's Parlour" at age eleven. TV series in England in 1950. First US record release for Coral in 1951. Appeared in over 20 British films, 1944-57; revived her film career in late 60s, starring in "Finian's Rainbow" and "Goodbye Mr. Chips".	
12/19/64+	**1**[2]	15	1 ● **Downtown**	Warner 5494
3/20/65	**3**	12	2 **I Know A Place**	Warner 5612
7/10/65	**22**	9	3 You'd Better Come Home	Warner 5643
10/09/65	**21**	8	4 Round Every Corner	Warner 5661
12/25/65+	**1**[2]	13	5 **My Love**	Warner 5684
3/26/66	**11**	8	6 A Sign Of The Times	Warner 5802
7/16/66	**9**	9	7 **I Couldn't Live Without Your Love**	Warner 5835
10/22/66	**21**	7	8 Who Am I	Warner 5863
12/24/66+	**16**	9	9 Color My World all of above written and produced by Tony Hatch	Warner 5882
3/04/67	**3**	12	10 **This Is My Song** from the Charlie Chaplin film "A Countess From Hong Kong"	Warner 7002
6/03/67	**5**	10	11 **Don't Sleep In The Subway**	Warner 7049
9/02/67	**26**	7	12 The Cat In The Window (The Bird In The Sky)	Warner 7073
12/02/67	**31**	7	13 The Other Man's Grass Is Always Greener	Warner 7097
2/17/68	**15**	11	14 Kiss Me Goodbye	Warner 7170
7/20/68	**37**	7	15 Don't Give Up	Warner 7216
11/23/68	**59**	8	16 American Boys	Warner 7244
4/12/69	**62**	5	17 Happy Heart	Warner 7275
8/09/69	**89**	3	18 Look At Mine	Warner 7310
11/29/69	**93**	1	19 No One Better Than You	Warner 7343
6/10/72	**70**	13	20 My Guy	MGM 14392
10/07/72	**61**	10	21 Wedding Song (There Is Love)	MGM 14431
2/06/82	**66**	6	22 Natural Love	Scotti Br. 02676
			ROY CLARK	
			Born on 4/15/33 in Meaherrin, Virginia. Superb guitar, banjo and fiddle player. Co-host of TV's "Hee-Haw".	
6/29/63	**45**	8	1 Tips Of My Fingers	Capitol 4956
6/14/69	**19**	10	2 Yesterday, When I Was Young	Dot 17246
1/24/70	**94**	3	3 Then She's A Lover	Dot 17335
10/31/70	**90**	3	4 Thank God And Greyhound	Dot 17355
5/26/73	**89**	3	5 Come Live With Me	Dot 17449
12/15/73+	**81**	5	6 Somewhere Between Love And Tomorrow	Dot 17480
			SANFORD CLARK	
			Born in 1935 in Tulsa, Oklahoma. Moved to Phoenix in his teens.	
7/28/56	**7**	21	1 **The Fool** Best Seller #7 / Juke Box #7 / Top 100 #9 / Jockey #16	Dot 15481
12/08/56	**74**	3	2 A Cheat above 2 feature Al Casey on guitar	Dot 15516
			ALLAN CLARKE	
			Born on 4/5/42 in England. Lead singer of The Hollies.	
3/25/78	**41**	10	1 (I Will Be Your) Shadow In The Street	Atlantic 3459

DEBUT DATE	PEAK POS	WKS CHR	ARTIST — Record Title	Label & Number
			ALLAN CLARKE — Cont'd	
5/24/80	**70**	4	2 Slipstream	Elektra 46617
			STANLEY CLARKE/GEORGE DUKE	
			Stanley is the premier jazz/rock bassist of the past two decades.	
5/02/81	**19**	20	1 Sweet Baby	Epic 01052
			TONY CLARKE	
			Soul singer/songwriter from Detroit. Died in 1973.	
3/14/64	**88**	1	1 (The Story Of) Woman, Love And A Man	Chess 1880
3/27/65	**31**	9	2 The Entertainer	Chess 1924
			THE CLASH	
			Eclectic new wave rock group formed in London in 1976. Consisted of Joe Strummer (vocals, lyricist), Mick Jones (guitar), Paul Simonon (bass) and Topper Headon (drums). Headon left in May, 1983; replaced by Peter Howard. Jones left band in 1984 to form Big Audio Dynamite. Political activists, they wrote songs protesting racism and oppression. Strummer disbanded The Clash in early 1986.	
3/22/80	**23**	14	1 Train In Vain (Stand By Me)	Epic 50851
7/17/82	**45**	13	2 Should I Stay Or Should I Go	Epic 03061
10/02/82+	**8**	24	3 **Rock The Casbah**	Epic 03245
2/19/83	**50**	10	4 Should I Stay Or Should I Go [R]	Epic 03547
			THE CLASSICS	
			White vocal quartet from Brooklyn. Consisted of lead singer, Emil Stucchio, Johnny Gambale, Tony Victor and Jamie Troy.	
6/22/63	**20**	9	1 Till Then	Musicnote 1116
			the Mills Brothers had a top 10 version of the song in 1944	
			CLASSICS IV	
			Quintet formed in Jacksonville, Florida. Consisted of Dennis Yost, lead vocals; J.R. Cobb, lead guitar; Wally Eaton, rhythm guitar; Joe Wilson, bass (replaced by Dean Daughtry); and Kim Venable, drums. Cobb, Daughtry and producer Buddy Buie joined the Atlanta Rhythm Section in 1974.	
12/23/67+	**3**	15	1 **Spooky**	Imperial 66259
5/04/68	**90**	3	2 Soul Train	Imperial 66293
			CLASSICS IV featuring DENNIS YOST:	
10/26/68	**5**	15	3 ● **Stormy**	Imperial 66328
2/08/69	**2**[1]	12	4 **Traces**	Imperial 66352
5/03/69	**19**	11	5 Everyday With You Girl	Imperial 66378
			DENNIS YOST & THE CLASSICS IV:	
8/02/69	**49**	7	6 Change Of Heart	Imperial 66393
11/15/69	**58**	8	7 Midnight	Imperial 66424
3/28/70	**59**	5	8 The Funniest Thing	Imperial 66439
10/24/70	**69**	8	9 Where Did All The Good Times Go	Liberty 56200
10/21/72	**39**	13	10 What Am I Crying For?	MGM South 7002
3/10/73	**95**	3	11 Rosanna	MGM South 7012
			all of above written and produced by Buddy Buie	
4/05/75	**94**	2	12 My First Day Without Her	MGM 14785
			JUDY CLAY - see WILLIAM BELL and BILLY VERA	
			OTIS CLAY	
			Born on 2/11/42 in Waxhaw, MS. To Chicago, 1956. Member of several gospel groups.	
8/24/68	**97**	3	1 She's About A Mover	Cotillion 44001
			TOM CLAY	
			Disc jockey.	
7/10/71	**8**	9	1 **What The World Needs Now Is Love/Abraham, Martin And John** [S]	Mowest 5002
			vocal accompaniment by The Blackberries	
			MERRY CLAYTON	
			Real name: Mary Clayton. Back-up vocalist from Los Angeles. In Raelets with Ray Charles. Formed vocal group, Sisters Love, and recorded for Motown.	
6/06/70	**73**	7	1 Gimme Shelter	Ode 66003
			Merry sang on Rolling Stones' version from LP "Let It Bleed"	
12/11/71+	**71**	7	2 After All This Time	Ode 66018
12/23/72+	**72**	6	3 Oh No, Not My Baby	Ode 66030
7/26/75	**45**	9	4 Keep Your Eye On The Sparrow	Ode 66110
			from the TV series "Baretta"	

DEBUT DATE	PEAK POS	WKS CHR	ARTIST — Record Title	Label & Number
			CLEAN LIVING	
			Polka/country band.	
11/04/72	**49**	12	1 In Heaven There Is No Beer .... [N]	Vanguard 35162
			CLEFS OF LAVENDER HILL	
6/25/66	**80**	6	1 Stop! - Get A Ticket	Date 1510
			THE CLEFTONES	
			Doo-wop group from Queens, New York, formed at Jamaica High School in 1955. Consisted of Herbie Cox (lead), Charlie James (first tenor), Berman Patterson (second tenor), William McClain (baritone) and Warren Corbin (bass). Originally called the Silvertones.	
2/18/56	**78**	1	1 You Baby You	Gee 1000
4/28/56	**57**	12	2 Little Girl Of Mine..........	Gee 1011
5/22/61	**18**	10	3 Heart And Soul	Gee 1064
9/04/61	**60**	6	4 For Sentimental Reasons	Gee 1067
12/29/62	**95**	1	5 Lover Come Back To Me	Gee 1079
			CLARENCE CLEMONS & JACKSON BROWNE	
			Clemons: saxophonist in Bruce Springsteen's E Street Band.	
10/26/85+	**18**	19	1 You're A Friend Of Mine .... includes vocals by actress Daryl Hannah (Browne's girlfriend)	Columbia 05660
			JIMMY CLIFF	
			Jamaican reggae singer/composer. Real name: James Chambers. Starred in the film "The Harder They Come", 1975; also had starring role in "Club Paradise", 1986.	
12/06/69+	**25**	11	1 Wonderful World, Beautiful People	A&M 1146
3/14/70	**89**	3	2 Come Into My Life	A&M 1167
			BUZZ CLIFFORD	
			Born Reese Francis Clifford III on 10/8/42 in Berwyn, Illinois.	
1/09/61	**6**	14	1 **Baby Sittin' Boogie** .... [N] baby's voices are by the children (boy & girl) of the producer	Columbia 41876
			LINDA CLIFFORD	
			Vocalist from Brooklyn. Former Miss New York State. With Jericho Jazz Singers, then own trio, 1967. Worked Chicago clubs, 1973-77. First recorded for ABC, 1974.	
7/01/78	**76**	11	1 Runaway Love	Curtom 0138
8/26/78	**54**	8	2 If My Friends Could See Me Now..........	Curtom 0140
3/24/79	**41**	6	3 Bridge Over Troubled Water	RSO 921
8/09/80	**41**	11	4 Red Light.......... from the film "Fame"	RSO 1041
			MIKE CLIFFORD	
			Born on 11/6/43 in Los Angeles.	
9/15/62	**12**	13	1 Close To Cathy..........	United Art. 489
12/29/62+	**68**	7	2 What To Do With Laurie	United Art. 557
5/11/63	**96**	1	3 One Boy Too Late..........	United Art. 588
			CLIMAX	
			Los Angeles-based quintet. Sonny Geraci, lead singer (formerly with the Outsiders).	
1/01/72	**3**	15	1 ● **Precious And Few**	Carousel 30055
5/06/72	**52**	15	2 Life And Breath	Rocky Road 30061
			CLIMAX BLUES BAND	
			Blues/rock quintet formed in Stafford, England; led by Colin Cooper & Peter Haycock.	
2/19/77	**3**	22	1 **Couldn't Get It Right**	Sire 736
7/08/78	**91**	4	2 Makin' Love..........	Sire 1026
11/15/80	**47**	12	3 Gotta Have More Love	Warner 49605
2/21/81	**12**	27	4 I Love You..........	Warner 49669
			PATSY CLINE	
			Born Virginia Hensley on 9/8/32 in Winchester, Virginia; killed in a plane crash with Cowboy Copas and Hawkshaw Hawkins on 3/5/63. Elected to Country Music Hall of Fame in 1973. Jessica Lange played Patsy in 1985 biographical film "Sweet Dreams".	
2/23/57	**12**	16	1 Walkin' After Midnight .... Juke Box #12 / Top 100 #17 / Best Seller #21 / Jockey #22	Decca 30221
5/22/61	**12**	20	2 I Fall To Pieces	Decca 31205
10/23/61	**9**	11	3 **Crazy/**	
10/23/61	**99**	1	4 Who Can I Count On	Decca 31317
1/27/62	**14**	13	5 She's Got You/	
2/10/62	**97**	2	6 Strange	Decca 31354

DEBUT DATE	PEAK POS	WKS CHR	ARTIST — Record Title	Label & Number
			PATSY CLINE — Cont'd	
5/19/62	**53**	6	7 When I Get Thru With You (You'll Love Me Too)/	
5/12/62	**90**	2	8 Imagine That	Decca 31377
8/25/62	**85**	1	9 So Wrong	Decca 31406
10/13/62	**73**	7	10 Heartaches #12 hit for Guy Lombardo in 1931; #1 hit for Ted Weems in 1947	Decca 31429
1/26/63	**83**	5	11 Leavin' On Your Mind	Decca 31455
4/20/63	**44**	10	12 Sweet Dreams (Of You)	Decca 31483
8/31/63	**96**	3	13 Faded Love	Decca 31522
			THE CLIQUE Pop/rock quintet from Texas.	
8/30/69	**22**	11	1 Sugar On Sunday	White Whale 323
11/22/69	**45**	7	2 I'll Hold Out My Hand	White Whale 333
2/28/70	**100**	1	3 Sparkle And Shine	White Whale 338
			THE CLIQUES R&B vocal duo: Jesse Belvin & Eugene Church.	
5/19/56	**45**	1	1 The Girl In My Dreams	Modern 987
			CLOCKS Rock quartet from Wichita, Kansas.	
8/28/82	**67**	5	1 She Looks A Lot Like You	Boulevard 03075
			ROSEMARY CLOONEY Born on 5/23/28 in Maysville, Kentucky. One of the most popular singers of the 50s, Rosemary and sister Betty sang with the Tony Pastor band in late 40s before her solo career was launched. Rosemary was featured in "White Christmas" and several other 50s movies; after a period of personal difficulties, she re-emerged in the late 70s as a successful jazz and ballad singer.	
11/12/55	**62**	9	1 Pet Me, Poppa from the film "Guys And Dolls"	Columbia 40579
1/21/56	**82**	3	2 The Key To My Heart	Columbia 40619
1/28/56	**20**	8	3 Memories Of You **BENNY GOODMAN TRIO with ROSEMARY CLOONEY** Juke Box #20 / Top 100 #52 from the film "The Benny Goodman Story"	Columbia 40616
5/19/56	**49**	13	4 I Could Have Danced All Night/	
5/26/56	**70**	6	5 I've Grown Accustomed To Your Face above 2 from Broadway's "My Fair Lady"	Columbia 40676
3/16/57	**10**	16	6 **Mangos** Jockey #10 / Best Seller #23 / Top 100 #25	Columbia 40835
8/29/60	**84**	3	7 Many A Wonderful Moment	RCA 7754
			CLOUT 4-woman, 2-man band from Johannesburg, South Africa.	
9/02/78	**67**	10	1 Substitute	Epic 50591
			THE CLOVERS R&B group from Washington, DC. Personnel lineup was John "Buddy" Bailey (lead), Matthew McQuater, Harold Lucas, Harold Winely and Bill Harris. Group had 13 consecutive top 10 R&B hits from 1951 thru 1954.	
6/23/56	**30**	13	1 Love, Love, Love	Atlantic 1094
9/14/59	**23**	17	2 Love Potion No. 9	United Art. 180
			CLUB HOUSE	
8/20/83	**75**	5	1 Do It Again/Billie Jean	Atlantic 89795
			THE COASTERS Group formed in Los Angeles in late 1955 from elements of the Robins. Originally consisted of Carl Gardner (ex-Robins), lead; Leon Hughes, tenor; Billy Guy, baritone lead; Bobby Nunn (ex-Robins), bass; and Adolph Jacobs, guitar. Noted for serio-comic recordings, primarily of Leiber & Stoller songs. Will "Dub" Jones (ex-Cadets) replaced Nunn in late 1958 and is heard on "Charlie Brown" and "Along Came Jones". Earl "Speedoo" Carroll joined the group in 1961. Today there are two or three "Coasters" groups still working, some of which contain one or two original members. Bobby Nunn died of a heart attack on 11/5/86 (61).	
9/22/56	**73**	1	1 One Kiss Led To Another	Atco 6073
5/13/57	**3**	26	2 **Searchin'**/ Best Seller #3 / Top 100 #5 / Jockey #6 / Juke Box #10 end	
5/06/57	**8**	24	3 **Young Blood** Top 100 #8 / Jockey #10	Atco 6087
10/21/57	**64**	6	4 Idol With The Golden Head	Atco 6098

DEBUT DATE	PEAK POS	WKS CHR	ARTIST — Record Title	Label & Number
			THE COASTERS — Cont'd	
6/02/58	1^1	16	5 **Yakety Yak**	Atco 6116
			Top 100 #1 / Best Seller #2 / Jockey #2	
2/02/59	2^3	15	6 **Charlie Brown** [N]	Atco 6132
5/18/59	9	12	7 **Along Came Jones** [N]	Atco 6141
8/24/59	7	16	8 **Poison Ivy/**	
9/07/59	38	8	9 I'm A Hog For You	Atco 6146
12/07/59+	47	10	10 What About Us/	
12/21/59+	36	8	11 Run Red Run	Atco 6153
			all of above written & produced by Jerry Leiber & Mike Stoller	
5/02/60	70	3	12 Besame Mucho (Part I)	Atco 6163
6/20/60	51	9	13 Wake Me, Shake Me	Atco 6168
10/03/60	83	4	14 Shoppin' For Clothes [N]	Atco 6178
1/30/61	37	8	15 Wait A Minute	Atco 6186
4/24/61	23	12	16 Little Egypt (Ying-Yang) [N]	Atco 6192
8/14/61	96	2	17 Girls Girls Girls (Part II)	Atco 6204
3/28/64	64	6	18 T'ain't Nothin' To Me [N]	Atco 6287
12/11/71+	76	6	19 Love Potion Number Nine	King 6385
			ODIA COATES	
			Songstress from Berkeley, CA. Sang with Paul Anka on 3 of his hit singles.	
3/01/75	71	6	1 Showdown/	
4/19/75	91	3	2 Don't Leave Me In The Morning	United Art. 601
			JOYCE COBB	
11/24/79+	42	12	1 Dig The Gold	Cream 7939
			RICHARD COCCIANTE	
			Singer from Italy.	
4/10/76	41	6	1 When Love Has Gone Away	20th Century 2275
			COCHISE	
5/29/71	96	4	1 Love's Made A Fool Of You	United Art. 50756
			written in 1958 by Buddy Holly	
			EDDIE COCHRAN	
			Born Edward Ray Cochrane on 10/3/38 in Albert Lea, Minnesota. Killed in a car accident near Bath, England on 4/17/60 (21). Accident also injured Gene Vincent. Vocalist, guitarist. Moved to Bell Gardens, CA (suburb of Los Angeles) in 1953. Played local clubs and dances. Teamed with Hank Cochran (no relation) as the Cochran Brothers; first recorded as country act for Ekko Records in 1954. Appeared in films "The Girl Can't Help It" and "Untamed Youth".	
3/23/57	18	13	1 Sittin' In The Balcony	Liberty 55056
			Top 100 #18 / Jockey #18 / Juke Box #20 / Best Seller #22	
9/16/57	82	6	2 Drive In Show	Liberty 55087
3/10/58	94	1	3 Jeannie Jeannie Jeannie	Liberty 55123
8/04/58	8	16	4 **Summertime Blues**	Liberty 55144
			Hot 100 #8 / Best Seller #13 end	
11/24/58+	35	12	5 C'mon Everybody	Liberty 55166
3/16/59	99	1	6 Teenage Heaven	Liberty 55177
8/31/59	58	9	7 Somethin Else	Liberty 55203
			songwriter Sharon Sheeley was injured in Cochran's fatal car crash	
			COCK ROBIN	
			Los Angeles pop quartet - vocals: Peter Kingsbery & Anna LaCazio.	
6/15/85	35	16	1 When Your Heart Is Weak	Columbia 04875
			BRUCE COCKBURN	
			Singer, songwriter. Cockburn (pronounced CO-burn) was born on 5/27/45 in Canada.	
3/22/80	21	17	1 Wondering Where The Lions Are	Millennium 11786
2/09/85	88	3	2 If I Had A Rocket Launcher	Gold Mt. 82013
			JOE COCKER	
			Born John Robert Cocker on 5/20/44 in Sheffield, England. Own skiffle band, the Cavaliers, late 50s, later reorganized as Vance Arnold & The Avengers. Assembled the Grease Band, mid-60s. First US tour, Woodstock Festival, in August, 1969. Successful tour with 43-piece revue, Mad Dogs And Englishmen, 1970. Notable spastic stage antics were based on Ray Charles' movements at the piano.	
11/16/68	68	6	1 With A Little Help From My Friends	A&M 991
			featuring Jimmy Page on guitar	
6/21/69	69	6	2 Feeling Alright	A&M 1063
			backing vocals: Brenda Holloway & Merry Clayton	

DEBUT DATE	PEAK POS	WKS CHR	ARTIST — Record Title	Label & Number
			JOE COCKER — Cont'd	
10/04/69	**69**	6	3 Delta Lady	A&M 1112
12/06/69+	**30**	12	4 She Came In Through The Bathroom Window	A&M 1147
4/18/70	**7**	12	5 **The Letter**	A&M 1174
			with Leon Russell & The Shelter People	
10/10/70	**11**	9	6 Cry Me A River	A&M 1200
			recorded live at Fillmore East, New York on 3/27/70	
5/22/71	**22**	11	7 High Time We Went/	
		8	8 Black-Eyed Blues	A&M 1258
1/08/72	**33**	9	9 Feeling Alright [R]	A&M 1063
9/16/72	**27**	8	10 Midnight Rider/	
12/02/72+	**56**	9	11 Woman To Woman	A&M 1370
2/17/73	**51**	8	12 Pardon Me Sir	A&M 1407
			above 6 (except #9) with The Chris Stainton Band	
6/22/74	**46**	12	13 Put Out The Light	A&M 1539
1/11/75	**5**	17	14 **You Are So Beautiful/**	
		4	15 It's A Sin When You Love Somebody	A&M 1641
10/21/78	**43**	8	16 Fun Time	Asylum 45540
9/26/81	**97**	3	17 I'm So Glad I'm Standing Here Today	MCA 51177
			CRUSADERS Guest Artist - JOE COCKER	
8/21/82	**1^{3}**	23	18 **Up Where We Belong**	Island 99996
			JOE COCKER & JENNIFER WARNES	
			love theme from the film "An Officer & A Gentleman"	
10/20/84	**69**	7	19 Edge Of A Dream	Capitol 5412
			theme from the film "Teachers"	
3/08/86	**91**	4	20 Shelter Me	Capitol 5557
			THE C.O.D.'s	
11/27/65+	**41**	12	1 Michael	Kellmac 1003
			DENNIS COFFEY & The Detroit Guitar Band	
			Session guitarist for The Temptations, Jackson 5 and others.	
10/30/71+	**6**	17	1 ● **Scorpio** [I]	Sussex 226
2/19/72	**18**	12	2 Taurus [I]	Sussex 233
6/03/72	**93**	4	3 Getting It On/ [I]	
		4	4 Ride, Sally, Ride [I]	Sussex 237
			shown only as: **DENNIS COFFEY**	
			COLD BLOOD	
			Bay-area rock group led by Lydia Pense.	
1/24/70	**52**	6	1 You Got Me Hummin	San Francisco 60
			BEN COLDER - see SHEB WOOLEY	
			ANN COLE	
			Born Cynthia Coleman on 1/24/34 in Newark, New Jersey.	
11/24/62	**99**	1	1 Don't Stop The Wedding	Roulette 4452
			BOBBY COLE	
8/03/68	**79**	3	1 Mister Bo Jangles	Date 1613
			COZY COLE	
			Born William Randolph Cole on 10/17/09 in East Orange, New Jersey. Died on 1/29/81 (71)(cancer). Lead drummer for many swing bands, including Benny Carter, Willie Bryant, Cab Calloway, and Louis Armstrong.	
8/25/58	**3**	21	1 **Topsy II/** [I]	
			Hot 100 #3 / Best Seller #10 end	
9/15/58	**27**	13	2 Topsy I [I]	Love 5004
12/01/58	**36**	8	3 Turvy II [I]	Love 5014

DEBUT DATE	PEAK POS	WKS CHR		ARTIST — Record Title	Label & Number
				NAT KING COLE Born Nathaniel Adams Coles on 3/17/17 in Montgomery, Alabama. Died of lung cancer on 2/15/65 in Santa Monica, CA (48). Raised in Chicago. Own band, the Royal Dukes, at age 17. First recorded in 1936 in band led by brother Eddie. Toured with "Shuffle Along" musical revue, stayed in Los Angeles. Formed trio in 1939, consisting of Nat, piano; Oscar Moore, guitar; and Wesley Prince, bass (replaced several years later by Johnny Miller). Long series of top-selling records led to his going solo in 1950. In films "St. Louis Blues", "Cat Ballou" and many other film and TV appearances. Last performed in 1964, due to ill health. Daughter Natalie is also a recording star.	
3/05/55	**7**	16	1	**Darling Je Vous Aime Beaucoup/** Jockey #7 / Best Seller #10 / Juke Box #14	
3/05/55	**23**	4	2	The Sand And The Sea Best Seller #23	Capitol 3027
5/07/55	**2**[1]	20	3	**A Blossom Fell/** Best Seller #2 / Juke Box #2 / Jockey #3	
5/21/55	**8**	10	4	**If I May** **NAT "KING" COLE & THE FOUR KNIGHTS** Jockey #8	Capitol 3095
7/16/55	**24**	2	5	My One Sin Best Seller #24	Capitol 3136
10/22/55	**13**	13	6	Someone You Love/ Best Seller #13 / Jockey #19 / Top 100 #21	
10/22/55	**21**	11	7	Forgive My Heart	Capitol 3234
12/31/55+	**47**	8	8	Take Me Back To Toyland/	
1/14/56	**57**	5	9	I'm Gonna Laugh You Right Out Of My Life	Capitol 3305
2/11/56	**18**	11	10	Ask Me/ Jockey #18 / Top 100 #25	
2/25/56	**72**	6	11	Nothing Ever Changes My Love For You	Capitol 3328
4/07/56	**21**	12	12	Too Young To Go Steady/ Jockey #21 / Top 100 #31 from the musical "Strip For Action"	
4/21/56	**79**	6	13	Never Let Me Go from the film "The Scarlet Hour"	Capitol 3390
7/07/56	**16**	20	14	That's All There Is To That/ Juke Box #16 / Best Seller #17 / Top 100 #18 / Jockey #18 **NAT "KING" COLE & THE FOUR KNIGHTS**	
7/07/56	**59**	8	15	My Dream Sonata	Capitol 3456
10/27/56	**11**	18	16	Night Lights/ Jockey #11 / Top 100 #16 / Best Seller #17	
10/27/56	**25**	13	17	To The Ends Of The Earth Jockey #25 / Top 100 #39	Capitol 3551
2/09/57	**18**	13	18	Ballerina/ Jockey #18 / Top 100 #36	
2/09/57	**65**	6	19	You Are My First Love from the film "It's Great To Be Young"	Capitol 3619
4/29/57	**48**	7	20	When Rock And Roll Come To Trinidad orchestra on all of above conducted by Nelson Riddle	Capitol 3702
5/06/57	**79**	4	21	Stardust from the E.P. "Love Is The Thing"	Capitol E.P. 824
6/17/57	**6**	27	22	**Send For Me/** Best Seller #6 / Top 100 #7 / Jockey #9	
8/05/57	**21**	15	23	My Personal Possession Jockey #21 / Top 100 #63 **NAT "KING" COLE & THE FOUR KNIGHTS**	Capitol 3737
9/23/57	**30**	14	24	With You On My Mind/ Best Seller #30 / Top 100 #33	
		4	25	The Song Of Raintree County from the film "Raintree County" Best Seller flip	Capitol 3782
1/27/58	**33**	13	26	Angel Smile Best Seller #33 / Top 100 #35	Capitol 3860
4/14/58	**5**	19	27	**Looking Back/** Best Seller #5 / Top 100 #5 / Jockey #9	
4/14/58	**67**	6	28	Do I Like It	Capitol 3939
7/21/58	**38**	11	29	Come Closer To Me/ Best Seller #38 / Top 100 #41	
8/11/58	**99**	1	30	Nothing In The World	Capitol 4004
10/13/58	**45**	11	31	Non Dimenticar	Capitol 4056
2/02/59	**82**	4	32	Give Me Your Love/	
2/02/59	**85**	3	33	Madrid	Capitol 4125

DEBUT DATE	PEAK POS	WKS CHR	ARTIST — Record Title		Label & Number
			NAT KING COLE — Cont'd		
5/04/59	**45**	9	34 You Made Me Love You/		
5/25/59	**69**	4	35 I Must Be Dreaming		Capitol 4184
8/03/59	**51**	12	36 Midnight Flyer/		
8/31/59	**96**	2	37 Sweet Bird Of Youth		Capitol 4248
2/01/60	**30**	8	38 Time And The River/		
3/07/60	**92**	2	39 Whatcha' Gonna Do piano solo by Nat "King" Cole	[I]	Capitol 4325
8/01/60	**47**	8	40 My Love **NAT KING COLE-STAN KENTON**		Capitol 4393
12/12/60	**80**	2	41 The Christmas Song first charted by Nat King Cole in 1946	[X-R]	Capitol 3561
12/31/60+	**86**	2	42 If I Knew from Broadway's "The Unsinkable Molly Brown"		Capitol 4481
6/26/61	**71**	7	43 Take A Fool's Advice		Capitol 4582
9/18/61	**73**	4	44 Let True Love Begin		Capitol 4623
8/04/62	**2**[2]	16	45 **Ramblin' Rose**		Capitol 4804
11/10/62	**13**	11	46 Dear Lonely Hearts		Capitol 4870
12/15/62	**65**	3	47 The Christmas Song	[X-R]	Capitol 3561
3/02/63	**42**	9	48 All Over The World/		
3/02/63	**87**	3	49 Nothing Goes Up (Without Coming Down)		Capitol 4919
5/11/63	**6**	12	50 **Those Lazy-Hazy-Crazy Days Of Summer**		Capitol 4965
8/31/63	**12**	13	51 That Sunday, That Summer/		
9/14/63	**92**	3	52 Mr. Wishing Well		Capitol 5027
2/22/64	**49**	6	53 My True Carrie, Love		Capitol 5125
4/25/64	**22**	9	54 I Don't Want To Be Hurt Anymore/		
4/11/64	**100**	1	55 People from the Broadway musical "Funny Girl"		Capitol 5155
9/19/64	**34**	9	56 I Don't Want To See Tomorrow/		
9/26/64	**81**	4	57 L-O-V-E		Capitol 5261
8/06/66	**90**	4	58 Let Me Tell You, Babe		Capitol 5683
			NATALIE COLE Born on 2/6/50 in Los Angeles. Daughter of Nat "King" Cole. Professional debut at age 11. Married her producer, Marvin Yancy, in 1976.		
8/30/75	**6**	17	1 **This Will Be**		Capitol 4109
12/13/75+	**32**	17	2 Inseparable		Capitol 4193
5/29/76	**25**	16	3 Sophisticated Lady (She's A Different Lady)		Capitol 4259
9/11/76	**49**	12	4 Mr. Melody		Capitol 4328
1/29/77	**5**	21	5 ● **I've Got Love On My Mind**		Capitol 4360
7/23/77	**79**	4	6 Party Lights		Capitol 4439
1/14/78	**10**	21	7 ● **Our Love**		Capitol 4509
6/21/80	**21**	21	8 Someone That I Used To Love		Capitol 4869
5/04/85	**57**	10	9 Dangerous		Modern 99648
9/07/85	**81**	6	10 A Little Bit Of Heaven		Modern 99630
			TONY COLE British singer.		
10/28/72	**97**	4	1 Suite: Man And Woman		20th Century 2001
			COLLAY & the Satellites		
4/25/60	**82**	3	1 Last Chance		Sho-Biz 1002
			KEITH COLLEY		
9/14/63	**66**	8	1 Enamorado	[F]	Unical 3006
			MITTY COLLIER Born on 6/21/41 in Birmingham, AL. Toured with gospel group the Hayes Ensemble. To Chicago in 1959. Returned to gospel singing in 1972.		
9/26/64	**41**	10	1 I Had A Talk With My Man		Chess 1907
1/09/65	**91**	5	2 No Faith, No Love		Chess 1918
3/19/66	**97**	2	3 Sharing You		Chess 1953
			DAVE & ANSIL COLLINS Jamaican duo.		
6/12/71	**22**	11	1 Double Barrel		Big Tree 115

DEBUT DATE	PEAK POS	WKS CHR	ARTIST — Record Title	Label & Number
			DOROTHY COLLINS	
			Real name: Marjorie Chandler. Born 11/18/26 in Windsor, Ontario; star of TV's "Your Hit Parade". Married orchestra leader, Raymond Scott.	
11/12/55	**16**	15	1 My Boy - Flat Top	Coral 61510
			Juke Box #16 / Top 100 #22	
1/28/56	**17**	10	2 Seven Days	Coral 61562
			Juke Box #17 / Top 100 #25	
12/21/59+	**43**	10	3 Baciare Baciare (Kissing Kissing)	Top Rank 2024
6/13/60	**79**	3	4 Banjo Boy	Top Rank 2052
			JUDY COLLINS	
			Contemporary folksinger born on 5/1/39 in Denver, Colorado.	
1/21/67	**97**	2	1 Hard Lovin' Loser	Elektra 45610
11/09/68	**8**	11	2 **Both Sides Now**	Elektra 45639
2/01/69	**55**	6	3 Someday Soon	Elektra 45649
8/09/69	**78**	4	4 Chelsea Morning	Elektra 45657
11/29/69	**69**	7	5 Turn! Turn! Turn!/To Everything There Is A Season	Elektra 45680
			lyrics adapted by Pete Seeger from the Book of Ecclesiastes	
12/12/70+	**15**	15	6 Amazing Grace	Elektra 45709
			song attributed to hymn writer Rev. John Newton, 1779 recorded at St. Paul's Chapel, Columbia University	
12/18/71+	**90**	7	7 Open The Door (Song For Judith)	Elektra 45755
2/10/73	**32**	11	8 Cook With Honey	Elektra 45831
6/21/75	**36**	11	9 Send In The Clowns	Elektra 45253
			from the Broadway musical "A Little Night Music"	
9/24/77	**19**	16	10 Send In The Clowns [R]	Elektra 45253
3/17/79	**66**	6	11 Hard Times For Lovers	Elektra 46020
			LYN COLLINS	
			Born on 6/12/48 in Lexington, Texas. With Charles Pikes & The Scholars, mid-60s. Joined James Brown Revue in 1969.	
9/02/72	**66**	7	1 Think (About It)	People 608
12/02/72	**86**	4	2 Me And My Baby Got A Good Thing Going	People 615
12/23/72+	**56**	7	3 What My Baby Needs Now Is A Little More Lovin'	Polydor 14157
			JAMES BROWN-LYN COLLINS above 3 produced by James Brown	
			PHIL COLLINS	
			Born on 1/31/51 in London, England. Vocalist, drummer, composer. Stage actor as a young child. With group Flaming Youth. Joined Genesis in 1970, became lead singer in 1975. Also with jazz/rock group Brand X. First solo album in 1981.	
3/21/81	**19**	16	1 I Missed Again	Atlantic 3790
5/30/81	**19**	17	2 In The Air Tonight	Atlantic 3824
11/06/82+	**10**	21	3 **You Can't Hurry Love**	Atlantic 89933
2/12/83	**39**	11	4 I Don't Care Anymore	Atlantic 89877
5/14/83	**79**	4	5 I Cannot Believe It's True	Atlantic 89864
2/25/84	**1^{3}**	24	6● **Against All Odds (Take A Look At Me Now)**	Atlantic 89700
			title song from the film "Against All Odds"	
11/24/84+	**2^{2}**	23	7● **Easy Lover**	Columbia 04679
			PHILIP BAILEY with PHIL COLLINS	
2/09/85	**1^{2}**	18	8 **One More Night**	Atlantic 89588
5/11/85	**1^{1}**	17	9 **Sussudio**	Atlantic 89560
7/20/85	**4**	18	10 **Don't Lose My Number**	Atlantic 89536
10/05/85	**1^{1}**	21	11 **Separate Lives**	Atlantic 89498
			PHIL COLLINS & MARILYN MARTIN love theme from the film "White Nights"	
3/15/86	**7**	16	12 **Take Me Home**	Atlantic 89472
			SUSAN COLLINS - see PAUL DAVIS	
			JESSI COLTER	
			Born Miriam Johnson on 5/25/47 in Phoenix. Married Duane Eddy at age 16, divorced in 1968. Married Waylon Jennings in 1969.	
4/05/75	**4**	17	1 **I'm Not Lisa**	Capitol 4009
9/06/75	**57**	5	2 What's Happened To Blue Eyes/	
		5	3 You Ain't Never Been Loved (Like I'm Gonna Love You)	Capitol 4087
			above 3 written by Jessi and produced by Waylon Jennings	

DEBUT DATE	PEAK POS	WKS CHR	ARTIST — Record Title	Label & Number
			CHI COLTRANE	
			Born on 11/16/48 in Racine, Wisconsin. To Chicago in late 60s.	
9/02/72	**17**	13	1 Thunder And Lightning	Columbia 45640
			CHRIS COLUMBO QUINTET	
6/29/63	**93**	2	1 Summertime [I]	Strand 25056
			COMMANDER CODY & HIS LOST PLANET AIRMEN	
			Group formed while Cody (George Frayne) attended the University of Michigan. To San Francisco in 1968.	
3/25/72	**9**	14	1 **Hot Rod Lincoln** [N]	Paramount 0146
7/22/72	**81**	7	2 Beat Me Daddy Eight To The Bar song hit #2 for Will Bradley in 1940	Paramount 0169
7/07/73	**94**	5	3 Smoke! Smoke! Smoke! (That Cigarette) [N] song hit #1 for Tex Williams in 1947	Paramount 0216
2/22/75	**56**	6	4 Don't Let Go	Warner 8073
			COMMODORES	
			Formed in Tuskegee, Alabama in 1970. Consisted of Lionel Richie (vocals, saxophone), William King (trumpet), Thomas McClary (guitar), Milan Williams (keyboards), Ronald LaPread (bass) and Walter "Clyde" Orange (drums). First recorded for Motown in 1972. In film "Thank God It's Friday". Richie began solo work in 1981.	
6/15/74	**22**	13	1 Machine Gun [I]	Motown 1307
11/16/74	**75**	8	2 I Feel Sanctified	Motown 1319
5/10/75	**19**	15	3 Slippery When Wet	Motown 1338
12/27/75+	**5**	23	4 **Sweet Love**	Motown 1381
9/18/76	**7**	16	5 **Just To Be Close To You**	Motown 1402
1/08/77	**39**	9	6 Fancy Dancer	Motown 1408
6/04/77	**4**	22	7 **Easy**	Motown 1418
8/27/77	**5**	16	8 **Brick House**	Motown 1425
12/17/77+	**24**	12	9 Too Hot Ta Trot	Motown 1432
6/17/78	**1^{2}**	20	10 **Three Times A Lady**	Motown 1443
9/23/78	**38**	10	11 Flying High	Motown 1452
8/11/79	**4**	17	12 **Sail On**	Motown 1466
9/29/79	**1^{1}**	20	13 **Still**	Motown 1474
12/15/79+	**25**	15	14 Wonderland	Motown 1479
6/21/80	**20**	16	15 Old-Fashion Love	Motown 1489
9/20/80	**54**	9	16 Heroes	Motown 1495
6/20/81	**8**	22	17 **Lady (You Bring Me Up)**	Motown 1514
9/26/81	**4**	20	18 **Oh No**	Motown 1527
2/06/82	**66**	5	19 Why You Wanna Try Me Lionel Richie's last song as lead singer	Motown 1604
12/04/82+	**70**	6	20 Painted Picture	Motown 1651
9/17/83	**54**	13	21 Only You	Motown 1694
1/26/85	**3**	22	22 **Nightshift** a tribute to Marvin Gaye and Jackie Wilson	Motown 1773
5/25/85	**43**	9	23 Animal Instinct	Motown 1788
9/21/85	**87**	4	24 Janet	Motown 1802
11/01/86	**65**	12	25 Goin' To The Bank	Polydor 885358
			COMMUNARDS	
			British duo consisting of Bronski Beat vocalist Jimmy Sommerville and multi-instrumentalist Richard Coles.	
12/27/86+	**40**	13	1 Don't Leave Me This Way lead vocals: Sara Jane Morris	MCA/London 52928
			PERRY COMO	
			Born on 5/18/12 in Canonsburg, Pennsylvania. Owned barbershop in hometown. With Freddy Carlone band, 1933; with Ted Weems, 1936-1942. Films "Something For The Boys", 1944; "Doll Face", "If I'm Lucky", 1946; "Words And Music", 1948. Own "Supper Club" radio series to late 1940s. Television shows (15 minutes) from 1948-1955. Host of hourly TV shows from 1955-1963.	
2/05/55	**2^{3}**	14	1 **Ko Ko Mo (I Love You So)** Jockey #2 / Best Seller #4 / Juke Box #5	RCA 5994

DEBUT DATE	PEAK POS	WKS CHR	ARTIST — Record Title	Label & Number
			PERRY COMO — Cont'd	
6/11/55	**12**	5	2 Chee Chee-OO-Chee (Sang The Little Bird)/ **PERRY COMO & JAYE P. MORGAN** Jockey #12 / Juke Box #14 / Best Seller #24	
6/25/55	**18**	1	3 Two Lost Souls **PERRY COMO & JAYE P. MORGAN** Jockey #18 from the Broadway musical "Damn Yankees"	RCA 6137
8/13/55	**5**	14	4 **Tina Marie/** Jockey #5 / Best Seller #6 / Juke Box #8 / Top 100 #12 pre	
8/20/55	**20**	1	5 Fooled Jockey #20	RCA 6192
11/12/55+	**11**	17	6 All At Once You Love Her/ Jockey #11 / Top 100 #24 from the Broadway musical "Pipe Dream"	
11/12/55	**79**	4	7 The Rose Tattoo from the film of the same title	RCA 6294
3/10/56	**1**[1]	23	8 **Hot Diggity (Dog Ziggity Boom)/** Jockey #1 / Best Seller #2 / Top 100 #2 / Juke Box #2	
3/10/56	**10**	17	9 **Juke Box Baby** Top 100 #10 / Jockey #11	RCA 6427
6/16/56	**4**	18	10 **More/** Best Seller #4 / Juke Box #6 / Jockey #8 / Top 100 #9	
6/09/56	**8**	17	11 **Glendora** Jockey #8 / Top 100 #14	RCA 6554
7/28/56	**18**	10	12 Somebody Up There Likes Me/ Juke Box #18 / Jockey #22 / Top 100 #26 from the film of the same title	
7/28/56	**85**	5	13 Dream Along With Me (I'm On My Way To A Star) Perry's famous opening song for his TV shows	RCA 6590
11/03/56	**42**	9	14 Moonlight Love/ based on the classic tune "Clair de Lune" by Debussy (1905)	
11/10/56	**59**	8	15 Chincherinchee	RCA 6670
2/23/57	**1**[2]	29	16 **Round And Round/** Jockey #1(2) / Best Seller #1(1) / Top 100 #1(1) / Juke Box #3	
3/09/57	**50**	7	17 Mi Casa, Su Casa (My House Is Your House)	RCA 6815
5/20/57	**13**	14	18 The Girl With The Golden Braids/ Jockey #13 / Top 100 #15 / Best Seller #26	
5/27/57	**48**	7	19 My Little Baby	RCA 6904
9/02/57	**76**	4	20 Dancin'	RCA 6991
10/14/57	**12**	17	21 Just Born (To Be Your Baby)/ Best Seller #12 / Jockey #13 / Top 100 #19	
10/21/57	**18**	15	22 Ivy Rose Jockey #18 / Top 100 #32	RCA 7050
12/30/57	**74**	2	23 Jingle Bells [X] from the E.P. "Merry Christmas Music" originally recorded in 1946	RCA 920
1/13/58	**1**[1]	23	24 ● **Catch A Falling Star/** Jockey #1 / Best Seller #3 / Top 100 #9	
1/20/58	**4**	16	25 **Magic Moments** Jockey #4 / Top 100 #27	RCA 7128
4/14/58	**6**	16	26 **Kewpie Doll/** Jockey #6 / Best Seller #12 / Top 100 #12	
5/05/58	**19**	1	27 Dance Only With Me Jockey #19 from the Broadway musical "Say Darling"	RCA 7202
7/28/58	**28**	10	28 Moon Talk Best Seller #28 / Hot 100 #29	RCA 7274
10/13/58	**33**	10	29 Love Makes The World Go 'Round/	
10/27/58	**47**	10	30 Mandolins In The Moonlight	RCA 7353
2/23/59	**29**	9	31 Tomboy	RCA 7464
6/08/59	**47**	9	32 I Know	RCA 7541
2/08/60	**22**	11	33 Delaware/ [N]	
2/08/60	**81**	2	34 I Know What God Is	RCA 7670
12/26/60	**80**	2	35 Make Someone Happy from the Broadway musical "Do Re Mi"	RCA 7812
11/20/61	**92**	3	36 You're Following Me	RCA 7962
3/31/62	**23**	12	37 Caterina	RCA 8004
6/01/63	**39**	9	38 (I Love You) Don't You Forget It all of above (except #23), orchestra conducted by Mitchell Ayres	RCA 8186
4/10/65	**25**	10	39 Dream On Little Dreamer	RCA 8533

DEBUT DATE	PEAK POS	WKS CHR	ARTIST — Record Title	Label & Number
			PERRY COMO — Cont'd	
7/31/65	88	4	40 Oowee, Oowee	RCA 8636
			backing vocals on above 2 by The Anita Kerr Quartet	
5/20/67	92	4	41 Stop! And Think It Over	RCA 9165
			1, 2, 4, 6, 8-17, 20-22, 24-34, 36-38 & 41: backing vocals by The Ray Charles Singers	
3/16/68	92	2	42 The Father Of Girls	RCA 9448
4/12/69	38	10	43 Seattle	RCA 9722
			from the TV series "Here Come The Brides"	
11/14/70+	10	17	44 **It's Impossible**	RCA 0387
3/20/71	53	8	45 I Think Of You	RCA 0444
4/14/73	29	16	46 And I Love You So	RCA 0906
12/21/74	92	2	47 Christmas Dream [X]	RCA 10122
			from the film "The Odessa File"	
			COMPAGNONS DE LA CHANSON - see LES COMPAGNONS	
			BOBBY COMSTOCK & The Counts	
			Bobby was born on 12/28/43 in Ithaca, New York.	
10/26/59	52	7	1 Tennessee Waltz	Blaze 349
3/07/60	90	4	2 Jambalaya	Atlantic 2051
2/16/63	57	6	3 Let's Stomp	Lawn 202
9/14/63	98	2	4 Your Boyfriend's Back	Lawn 219
			answer song to The Angels' "My Boyfriend's Back"	
			CON FUNK SHUN	
			Soul band formed as Project Soul in Vallejo, California in 1968 by high school classmates Mike Cooper (lead vocals, guitar) and Louis McCall (drums). To Memphis in 1972, changed name to Con Funk Shun.	
12/17/77+	23	13	1 Ffun	Mercury 73959
8/26/78	60	6	2 Shake And Dance With Me	Mercury 74008
1/24/81	40	10	3 Too Tight	Mercury 76089
1/07/84	76	5	4 Baby, I'm Hooked (Right Into Your Love)	Mercury 814581
			CONDUCTOR	
			Judy Comden, leader of Los Angeles-based quintet.	
1/30/82	63	5	1 Voice On The Radio	Montage 1210
			ARTHUR CONLEY	
			Born on 1/4/46 in Atlanta, Georgia. Discovered by Otis Redding in 1965. First recorded for Redding's own label, Jotis, in 1966.	
3/11/67	2[1]	15	1 ● **Sweet Soul Music**	Atco 6463
			tune originally written by Sam Cooke as "Yeah Man"	
6/10/67	31	7	2 Shake, Rattle & Roll	Atco 6494
11/04/67	73	3	3 Whole Lotta Woman	Atco 6529
			above 3 produced by Otis Redding	
3/16/68	14	12	4 Funky Street	Atco 6563
6/22/68	58	5	5 People Sure Act Funny	Atco 6588
10/26/68	85	4	6 Aunt Dora's Love Soul Shack	Atco 6622
1/04/69	51	6	7 Ob-La-Di, Ob-La-Da	Atco 6640
			RAY CONNIFF	
			Born on 11/6/16 in Attleboro, Massachusetts. Trombonist-arranger with Bunny Berigan, Bob Crosby, Harry James, Vaughn Monroe, and Artie Shaw bands; later conductor-arranger on many hit albums in the 50s and 60s.	
3/16/57	73	4	1 'S Wonderful [I]	Columbia 40827
10/17/60	92	4	2 Midnight Lace - Part I [I]	Columbia 41800
			from the film of the same title	
			RAY CONNIFF & THE SINGERS:	
7/18/64	57	10	3 Invisible Tears	Columbia 43061
6/18/66	9	12	4 **Somewhere, My Love**	Columbia 43626
			Lara's Theme from the film "Dr. Zhivago"	
10/08/66	94	2	5 Lookin' For Love	Columbia 43814
			CHRIS CONNOR	
			Born on 11/8/27 in Kansas City, MO. Jazz-styled singer with Stan Kenton, 1952-53.	
10/27/56+	34	28	1 I Miss You So	Atlantic 1105
6/10/57	95	1	2 Trust In Me	Atlantic 1138
			orchestra conducted by Ray Ellis on above 2	

DEBUT DATE	PEAK POS	WKS CHR	ARTIST — Record Title		Label & Number
			NORMAN CONNORS		
			Born on 3/1/48 in Philadelphia. Jazz drummer with Archie Shepp, John Coltrane, Pharoah Sanders, and others. Own group on Buddah in 1972.		
1/03/76	**97**	3	1 Valentine Love		Buddah 499
			vocals: Michael Henderson and Jean Cain		
8/28/76	**27**	16	2 You Are My Starship		Buddah 542
			vocalist: Michael Henderson		
			JUNE CONQUEST - see DONNY HATHAWAY		
			CONSUMER RAPPORT		
			Detroit studio group, featuring Frank Floyd (pit singer in Broadway show "The Wiz").		
4/19/75	**42**	12	1 Ease On Down The Road		Wing & Prayer 101
			from the Broadway musical "The Wiz"		
			BILL CONTI		
			Providence, RI native. Composer/conductor for the first 3 "Rocky" films.		
4/23/77	**1**[1]	20	1 ● **Gonna Fly Now**	[I]	United Art. 940
			Theme from the film "Rocky"		
11/06/82	**52**	9	2 Theme From Dynasty	[I]	Arista 1021
			THE CONTINENTAL 4		
			Vocal group consisting of Freddie Kelly, Ronnie McGregor, Larry McGregor and Anthony Burke.		
6/19/71	**84**	5	1 Day By Day (Every Minute of The Hour)		Jay Walking 011
			CONTINENTAL MINIATURES		
			Pop quintet from Los Angeles.		
5/13/78	**90**	3	1 Stay Awhile		London 266
			DICK CONTINO		
			Popular accordionist.		
4/20/57	**42**	8	1 Pledge Of Love		Mercury 71079
			orchestra conducted by David Carroll		
			THE CONTOURS		
			Vocal group formed in Detroit in 1959, consisting of Billy Gordon, Billy Hoggs, Joe Billingslea, Sylvester Potts, Hugh Davis and Hubert Johnson (died on 7/11/81).		
8/11/62	**3**	18	1 **Do You Love Me**		Gordy 7005
12/22/62+	**43**	9	2 Shake Sherry		Gordy 7012
4/06/63	**64**	6	3 Don't Let Her Be Your Baby		Gordy 7016
4/04/64	**41**	6	4 Can You Do It		Gordy 7029
12/19/64+	**47**	7	5 Can You Jerk Like Me		Gordy 7037
8/14/65	**57**	8	6 First I Look At The Purse		Gordy 7044
5/28/66	**85**	2	7 Just A Little Misunderstanding		Gordy 7052
4/15/67	**79**	3	8 It's So Hard Being A Loser		Gordy 7059
			SAM COOKE		
			Born on 1/22/35 in Chicago. Died from a gunshot wound on 12/11/64 (29) in Los Angeles. Son of a Baptist minister, sang in choir from age six. Joined gospel group, the Highway Q.C.'s. Joined the Soul Stirrers in 1950, lead singer until 1956. First recorded secular songs in 1956 as "Dale Cook" on Specialty. String of hits on Keen label led to contract with RCA. Shot by female motel manager under mysterious circumstances. Considered by many as the definitive soul singer.		
10/21/57	**1**[3]	26	1 **You Send Me/**		
			Top 100 #1(3) / Best Seller #1(2) / Jockey #1(1)		
			written by Sam's brother, Charles "L.C." Cooke		
11/04/57	**81**	4	2 Summertime		Keen 34013
12/23/57+	**18**	14	3 I'll Come Running Back To You/		
			Best Seller #18 / Top 100 #22		
12/23/57	**60**	5	4 Forever		Specialty 619
12/30/57+	**17**	11	5 (I Love You) For Sentimental Reasons/		
			Best Seller #17 / Top #43		
12/30/57+	**47**	12	6 Desire Me		Keen 4002
3/17/58	**26**	13	7 Lonely Island/		
			Best Seller #26 / Top 100 #39		
3/24/58	**39**	7	8 You Were Made For Me		Keen 4009
8/04/58	**22**	17	9 Win Your Love For Me		Keen 2006
			Best Seller #22 / Hot 100 #33		
11/17/58	**26**	16	10 Love You Most Of All		Keen 2008
3/09/59	**31**	13	11 Everybody Likes To Cha Cha Cha		Keen 2018
6/08/59	**28**	10	12 Only Sixteen		Keen 2022
11/09/59	**81**	5	13 There, I've Said It Again		Keen 2105

DEBUT DATE	PEAK POS	WKS CHR	ARTIST — Record Title	Label & Number
			SAM COOKE — Cont'd	
3/14/60	50	7	14 Teenage Sonata	RCA 7701
5/09/60	12	15	15 Wonderful World	Keen 2112
8/15/60	2[2]	16	16 **Chain Gang**	RCA 7783
12/05/60	29	8	17 Sad Mood	RCA 7816
3/06/61	31	8	18 That's It-I Quit-I'm Movin' On	RCA 7853
6/05/61	17	12	19 Cupid	RCA 7883
9/25/61	56	7	20 Feel It/	
9/25/61	93	1	21 It's All Right	RCA 7927
2/03/62	9	15	22 **Twistin' The Night Away**	RCA 7983
5/26/62	17	15	23 Having A Party/	
6/23/62	13	11	24 Bring It On Home To Me backing vocals by Lou Rawls	RCA 8036
9/29/62	12	11	25 Nothing Can Change This Love/	
10/27/62	70	7	26 Somebody Have Mercy	RCA 8088
1/26/63	13	9	27 Send Me Some Lovin'/	
2/02/63	66	6	28 Baby, Baby, Baby	RCA 8129
4/20/63	10	11	29 **Another Saturday Night**	RCA 8164
7/27/63	14	11	30 Frankie And Johnny	RCA 8215
10/26/63	11	10	31 Little Red Rooster	RCA 8247
1/25/64	11	10	32 Good News	RCA 8299
6/06/64	11	10	33 Good Times/	
6/13/64	35	8	34 Tennessee Waltz Hugo & Luigi produced all of above RCA recordings	RCA 8368
9/26/64	31	12	35 Cousin Of Mine/	
10/10/64	93	3	36 That's Where It's At	RCA 8426
1/09/65	7	11	37 **Shake/**	
1/30/65	31	7	38 A Change Is Gonna Come	RCA 8486
4/10/65	41	7	39 It's Got The Whole World Shakin'	RCA 8539
6/05/65	52	5	40 When A Boy Falls In Love	RCA 8586
7/24/65	32	9	41 Sugar Dumpling	RCA 8631
2/19/66	95	2	42 Feel It [R]	RCA 8751
4/30/66	97	1	43 Let's Go Steady Again same version is on flip side of "Only Sixteen"	RCA 8803
			COOKER Real name: Norman DesRosiers.	
2/02/74	88	5	1 Try (Try To Fall In Love)	Scepter 12388
			COOKIE & HIS CUPCAKES Sextet led by Huey "Cookie" Thierry (vocals, saxophone).	
1/19/59	47	15	1 Matilda	Judd 1002
5/04/63	94	4	2 Got You On My Mind	Chess 1848
			THE COOKIES Vocal trio from New York with varying membership. Did back-up work for Neil Sedaka, Carole King, Little Eva. One member, Earl-Jean McCree, later went solo.	
11/10/62	17	12	1 Chains	Dimension 1002
3/02/63	7	13	2 **Don't Say Nothin' Bad (About My Baby)**	Dimension 1008
7/06/63	72	5	3 Will Power	Dimension 1012
11/30/63+	33	11	4 Girls Grow Up Faster Than Boys	Dimension 1020
			COOL HEAT	
8/15/70	89	3	1 Groovin' With Mr. Bloe [I] originally released as the flip side of "Make Believe" by Wind	Forward 152
			EDDIE COOLEY & The Dimples Eddie wrote "Fever" (hit for Little Willie John, Peggy Lee and The McCoys).	
10/27/56	20	13	1 Priscilla Best Seller #20 / Juke Box #20 / Top 100 #26	Royal Roost 621
			RITA COOLIDGE Born on 5/1/45 in Nashville. Began career as one of the Friends of Delaney & Bonnie; toured with Joe Cocker's "Mad Dogs & Englishmen" troupe. Prolific backing singer, early 70s. Married to Kris Kristofferson, 1973-79. Sister Priscilla married to Booker T. Jones (Booker T. & The MG's).	
5/10/69	96	1	1 Turn Around And Love You	Pepper 443

DEBUT DATE	PEAK POS	WKS CHR	ARTIST — Record Title	Label & Number
			RITA COOLIDGE — Cont'd	
12/30/72+	**76**	7	2 Fever/	
		2	3 My Crew	A&M 1398
11/17/73	**49**	10	4 A Song I'd Like To Sing	A&M 1475
			KRIS KRISTOFFERSON & RITA COOLIDGE	
3/23/74	**86**	5	5 Loving Arms	A&M 1498
			KRIS KRISTOFFERSON & RITA COOLIDGE	
5/07/77	**2**[1]	27	6● **(Your Love Has Lifted Me) Higher And Higher**	A&M 1922
9/17/77	**7**	20	7● **We're All Alone**	A&M 1965
1/14/78	**20**	11	8 The Way You Do The Things You Do	A&M 2004
7/01/78	**25**	12	9 You	A&M 2058
11/04/78	**68**	7	10 Love Me Again	A&M 2090
9/01/79	**66**	7	11 One Fine Day	A&M 2169
11/17/79+	**38**	10	12 I'd Rather Leave While I'm In Love	A&M 2199
5/17/80	**42**	10	13 Somethin' 'Bout You Baby I Like	Capitol 4865
			GLEN CAMPBELL & RITA COOLIDGE	
12/13/80+	**46**	12	14 Fool That I Am	A&M 2281
7/02/83	**36**	13	15 All Time High	A&M 2551
			from the James Bond film "Octopussy"	
			COOPER BROTHERS	
			Richard & Brian Cooper and band.	
10/28/78	**48**	13	1 The Dream Never Dies	Capricorn 0308
6/30/79	**79**	4	2 I'll Know Her When I See Her	Capricorn 0325
			ALICE COOPER	
			Born Vincent Furnier on 2/4/48 in Detroit. Formed rock group in Phoenix in 1965; changed name to Alice Cooper in 1966. To Los Angeles in 1968, then to Detroit in 1969. Alice is known primarily for his bizarre stage antics.	
2/20/71	**21**	13	1 Eighteen	Warner 7449
6/12/71	**94**	3	2 Caught In A Dream	Warner 7490
12/25/71+	**59**	8	3 Under My Wheels	Warner 7529
3/11/72	**49**	10	4 Be My Lover	Warner 7568
6/03/72	**7**	13	5 **School's Out**	Warner 7596
10/07/72	**26**	8	6 Elected	Warner 7631
2/03/73	**35**	10	7 Hello Hurray	Warner 7673
4/14/73	**25**	12	8 No More Mr. Nice Guy	Warner 7691
8/04/73	**57**	6	9 Billion Dollar Babies	Warner 7724
12/29/73+	**48**	8	10 Teenage Lament '74	Warner 7762
4/05/75	**12**	16	11 Only Women	Atlantic 3254
8/16/75	**67**	4	12 Department Of Youth	Atlantic 3280
10/25/75	**45**	6	13 Welcome To My Nightmare	Atlantic 3298
7/04/76+	**12**	27	14● I Never Cry	Warner 8228
4/30/77	**9**	21	15 **You And Me**	Warner 8349
10/21/78	**12**	16	16 How You Gonna See Me Now	Warner 8695
5/17/80	**40**	9	17 Clones (We're All)	Warner 49204
			LES COOPER & The Soul Rockers	
			Pianist, vocalist, arranger from Norfolk, Virginia.	
10/06/62+	**22**	16	1 Wiggle Wobble [I]	Everlast 5019
			COWBOY COPAS	
			Born Lloyd T. Copas on 7/15/13 near Muskogee, Oklahoma. Died on 3/5/63 in the plane crash that also killed Patsy Cline and Hawkshaw Hawkins.	
9/26/60	**63**	12	1 Alabam	Starday 501
			KEN COPELAND	
4/06/57	**12**	15	1 Pledge Of Love	Imperial 5432
			Jockey #12 / Top 100 #17 / Best Seller #23	
			JILL COREY	
			Born Norma Jean Speranza on 9/30/35.	
12/22/56+	**21**	16	1 I Love My Baby (My Baby Loves Me)	Columbia 40794
			Jockey #21 / Top 100 #28	
4/20/57	**57**	7	2 Let It Be Me/	
			song first appeared on the CBS TV show "Climax"	
4/29/57	**95**	1	3 Make Like A Bunny, Honey	Columbia 40878

DEBUT DATE	PEAK POS	WKS CHR	ARTIST — Record Title		Label & Number
			JILL COREY — Cont'd		
8/05/57	**11**	13	4 Love Me To Pieces Best Seller #11 / Jockey #11 / Top 100 #18 from the CBS TV show "Studio One, Summer Theatre"		Columbia 40955
8/25/58	**96**	2	5 Big Daddy		Columbia 41202
			AL CORLEY Played the original Steven Carrington on TV's "Dynasty".		
5/11/85	**80**	5	1 Square Rooms		Mercury 822241
			BOB CORLEY		
11/19/55	**95**	1	1 Number One Street (Sides 1 & 2)	[C]	Stars 4773
			CORNBREAD & BISCUITS Comedy duo.		
11/14/60	**75**	5	1 The Big Time Spender backing music by Lea Lendon	[C]	Maske 102
			CORNELIUS BROTHERS & SISTER ROSE Miami-based trio consisting of Eddie, Carter and Rose Cornelius.		
4/10/71	**3**	18	1 ● **Treat Her Like A Lady**		United Art. 50721
5/27/72	**2**[2]	14	2 ● **Too Late To Turn Back Now**		United Art. 50910
9/02/72	**23**	11	3 Don't Ever Be Lonely (A Poor Little Fool Like Me)		United Art. 50954
12/23/72+	**37**	9	4 I'm Never Gonna Be Alone Anymore		United Art. 50996
4/28/73	**96**	2	5 Let Me Down Easy		United Art. 208
			DON CORNELL Popular singer-guitarist who worked from late 30s with many bands but achieved greatest success with Sammy Kaye ("It Isn't Fair") from 1946-50.		
5/14/55	**14**	6	1 Most Of All/ Jockey #14 / Best Seller #20		
		2	2 The Door Is Still Open To My Heart Best Seller flip		Coral 61393
9/10/55	**7**	13	3 **The Bible Tells Me So/** Best Seller #7 / Juke Box #8 / Jockey #18 / Top 100 #31 pre		
11/12/55	**26**	9	4 Love Is A Many-Splendored Thing from the movie of the same title		Coral 61467
11/12/55	**25**	2	5 Young Abe Lincoln		Coral 61521
2/18/56	**80**	5	6 Teenage Meeting (Gonna Rock It Up Right)		Coral 61584
4/14/56	**59**	8	7 Rock Island Line		Coral 61613
11/10/56	**57**	6	8 See Saw/		
		1	9 From The Bottom Of My Heart Coming Up flip		Coral 61721
4/27/57	**47**	8	10 Mama Guitar from the film "A Face In The Crowd" orchestra directed by Dick Jacobs on all of above (except 4 & 7)		Coral 61819
			THE CORSAIRS R&B vocal quartet from North Carolina consisting of three brothers and a cousin. Jay "Bird" Uzzell, lead singer.		
12/25/61+	**12**	15	1 Smoky Places		Tuff 1808
4/14/62	**68**	8	2 I'll Take You Home		Tuff 1818
			DAVE "BABY" CORTEZ Born David Cortez Clowney on 8/13/38 in Detroit. Played organ and sang with group, The Pearls. Session keyboardist, late 1950s.		
3/16/59	**1**[1]	17	1 **The Happy Organ**	[I]	Clock 1009
6/08/59	**61**	8	2 The Whistling Organ	[I]	Clock 1012
7/14/62	**10**	14	3 **Rinky Dink**	[I]	Chess 1829
10/13/62	**67**	7	4 Happy Weekend	[I]	Chess 1834
11/17/62	**96**	2	5 Fiesta	[I]	Emit 301
4/13/63	**91**	2	6 Hot Cakes! 1st Serving	[I]	Chess 1850
8/24/63	**76**	3	7 Organ Shout	[I]	Chess 1861
6/04/66	**91**	3	8 Count Down	[I]	Roulette 4679
			CORY Cory Braverman - white female singer/songwriter from New York.		
3/05/77	**89**	3	1 Fire Sign		Phantom 10856

DEBUT DATE	PEAK POS	WKS CHR	ARTIST — Record Title	Label & Number
			BILL COSBY	
			Born on 7/12/38 in Philadelphia. Top comedian of records, nightclubs, film and TV. His first 7 comedy albums were all million sellers. Played Alexander Scott on TV series "I Spy". Star of the current #1 NBC-TV series "The Cosby Show".	
9/02/67	**4**	11	1 **Little Ole Man (Uptight-Everything's Alright)**.... [N]	Warner 7072
12/02/67	**71**	6	2 Hooray For The Salvation Army Band................. [N]	Warner 7096
3/02/68	**91**	3	3 Funky North Philly... [N]	Warner 7171
5/02/70	**70**	3	4 Grover Henson Feels Forgotten........................... [S]	Uni 55223
5/08/76	**46**	10	5 Yes, Yes, Yes.. [C]	Capitol 4258
			DON COSTA	
			Born on 6/10/25 in Boston; died on 1/19/83 (57). Arranger for Vaughn Monroe, Frank Sinatra, Vic Damone, the Ames Brothers and many more. A&R director of ABC-Paramount Records, then for United Artists Records.	
11/16/59	**59**	6	1 I'll Walk The Line.. [I]	United Art. 190
5/02/60	**27**	13	2 Theme From 'The Unforgiven'............................ [I] "The Need For Love"	United Art. 221
8/08/60	**19**	26	3 Never On Sunday... [I] from the film of the same title	United Art. 234
			ELVIS COSTELLO	
			Born Declan McManus in Liverpool, England on 8/25/55. Changed name to Elvis Costello in 1976. Formed backing band, The Attractions in 1977. Leading eclectic rock singer for a decade.	
8/20/83	**36**	14	1 Everyday I Write The Book...................................	Columbia 04045
7/28/84	**56**	9	2 The Only Flame In Town....................................	Columbia 04502
			GENE COTTON	
			Singer/songwriter from Columbus, Ohio.	
11/16/74	**79**	5	1 Sunshine Roses...	Myrrh 137
5/24/75	**73**	3	2 Damn It All	ABC 12087
12/04/76+	**33**	11	3 You've Got Me Runnin'......................................	ABC 12227
2/04/78	**23**	14	4 Before My Heart Finds Out.................................	Ariola 7675
6/17/78	**36**	12	5 You're A Part Of Me .... **GENE COTTON with KIM CARNES**	Ariola 7704
9/30/78	**40**	10	6 Like A Sunday In Salem (The Amos & Andy Song)......	Ariola 7723
3/13/82	**76**	8	7 If I Could Get You (Into My Life)	Knoll 5002
			JOSIE COTTON	
8/21/82	**74**	7	1 He Could Be The One	Elektra 47481
4/07/84	**82**	4	2 Jimmy Loves Maryann	Elektra 69748
			COTTON, LLOYD & CHRISTIAN	
			Darryl Cotton, Michael Lloyd & Chris Christian.	
9/27/75	**66**	5	1 I Go To Pieces..	20th Century 2217
			JOHN COUGAR - see MELLENCAMP	
			COUNT FIVE	
			5 teenagers from San Jose, California.	
9/10/66	**5**	12	1 **Psychotic Reaction**..	Double Shot 104
			COUNTRY COALITION	
3/21/70	**96**	3	1 Time To Get It Together......................................	BluesWay 61034
			COUNTRY JOE & THE FISH	
			Country Joe (Joseph McDonald, b: 1/1/42) & The Fish were San Francisco's leading political rock band of the 60s.	
8/05/67	**95**	2	1 Not So Sweet Martha Lorraine	Vanguard 35052
11/29/75+	**92**	7	2 Breakfast For Two .... **COUNTRY JOE McDONALD**	Fantasy 758
			LOU COURTNEY	
1/28/67	**71**	6	1 Skate Now..	Riverside 4588
4/08/67	**80**	3	2 Do The Thing...	Riverside 4589
			THE COURTSHIP	
6/24/72	**93**	2	1 It's The Same Old Love.......................................	Tamla 54217

DEBUT DATE	PEAK POS	WKS CHR	ARTIST — Record Title	Label & Number
			DON COVAY	
			Born in March, 1938 in Orangeburg, SC. R&B singer, songwriter. Member of the Rainbows in 1955. Recorded as "Pretty Boy" with Little Richard's band for Atlantic in 1957. Formed group, The Goodtimers, in 1960.	
1/23/61	**60**	9	1 Pony Time THE GOODTIMERS	Arnold 1002
12/29/62+	**75**	7	2 The Popeye Waddle	Cameo 239
9/05/64	**35**	10	3 Mercy, Mercy DON COVAY & THE GOODTIMERS	Rosemart 801
12/26/64	**97**	2	4 Take This Hurt Off Me	Rosemart 802
11/13/65	**44**	9	5 Seesaw DON COVAY & THE GOODTIMERS	Atlantic 2301
7/07/73	**29**	10	6 I Was Checkin' Out She Was Checkin' In	Mercury 73385
7/13/74	**63**	6	7 It's Better To Have (And Don't Need)	Mercury 73469
			COVEN	
			Pop quintet featuring the voice of Jinx Dawson.	
9/18/71	**26**	12	1 One Tin Soldier (The Legend of Billy Jack) from the Tom Laughlin movie "Billy Jack"	Warner 7509
7/21/73	**79**	6	2 One Tin Soldier (The Legend of Billy Jack) new recording of the 1971 hit	MGM 14308
12/29/73+	**73**	6	3 One Tin Soldier, The Legend of Billy Jack [R] reissue of the original version	Warner 0101
			THE COWBOY CHURCH SUNDAY SCHOOL	
			Lead vocal by a female adult singer - at 45 rpm, it sounds like a child's voice.	
1/01/55	**8**	21	1 **Open Up Your Heart (And Let The Sunshine In)** [N] Best Seller #8 / Jockey #18 / Juke Box #19	Decca 29367
			THE COWSILLS	
			Family group from Rhode Island. Consisted of five brothers, their little sister and mother, who died on 1/31/85 (56).	
9/30/67	**2**[2]	16	1 ● **The Rain, The Park & Other Things**	MGM 13810
1/13/68	**21**	9	2 We Can Fly	MGM 13886
3/16/68	**54**	6	3 In Need Of A Friend	MGM 13909
6/01/68	**10**	13	4 **Indian Lake**	MGM 13944
9/14/68	**44**	6	5 Poor Baby	MGM 13981
3/15/69	**2**[2]	15	6 ● **Hair** from the rock musical "Hair"	MGM 14026
6/21/69	**75**	4	7 The Prophecy Of Daniel and John The Divine (Six-Six-Six)	MGM 14063
10/11/69	**74**	7	8 Silver Threads And Golden Needles	MGM 14084
			THE COYOTE SISTERS	
			Female trio: Marty Gwinn, Leah Kunkel (sister of Mama Cass) and Renee Armand.	
7/28/84	**66**	10	1 Straight From The Heart (Into Your Life)	Morocco 1742
			CRABBY APPLETON	
			West Coast rock quintet led by Michael Fennelly.	
5/09/70	**36**	14	1 Go Back	Elektra 45687
			BILLY "CRASH" CRADDOCK	
			Country/rock singer, born on 6/16/39 in Greensboro, NC.	
11/09/59	**94**	1	1 Don't Destroy Me	Columbia 41470
6/29/74	**16**	15	2 Rub It In	ABC 12013
11/23/74+	**33**	9	3 Ruby, Baby	ABC 12036
12/13/75+	**54**	8	4 Easy As Pie	ABC/Dot 17584
			FLOYD CRAMER	
			Nashville's top session pianist - born on 10/27/33 in Shreveport, LA.	
4/28/58	**87**	2	1 Flip Flop And Bop [I]	RCA 7156
10/10/60	**2**[4]	20	2 **Last Date** [I]	RCA 7775
3/06/61	**4**	13	3 **On The Rebound** [I]	RCA 7840
6/05/61	**8**	12	4 **San Antonio Rose** [I] written by Bob Wills in 1938	RCA 7893
9/25/61	**63**	7	5 Your Last Goodbye/ [I]	
10/02/61	**95**	2	6 Hang On [I]	RCA 7907
1/20/62	**36**	8	7 Chattanooga Choo Choo/ [I] tune originally hit #1 in 1941 for Glenn Miller	
2/03/62	**90**	2	8 Let's Go [I]	RCA 7978
4/14/62	**87**	3	9 Lovesick Blues [I]	RCA 8013

DEBUT DATE	PEAK POS	WKS CHR	ARTIST — Record Title		Label & Number
			FLOYD CRAMER — Cont'd		
7/07/62	**63**	4	10 Hot Pepper	[I]	RCA 8051
12/29/62+	**49**	11	11 Java	[I]	RCA 8116
			all of above produced by Chet Atkins		
			THE CRAMPTON SISTERS		
2/08/64	**92**	2	1 I Didn't Know What Time It Was		DCP 1001
			this Rodgers & Hart song originally hit #6 in 1939 for Benny Goodman - DCP record label is owned by Don Costa		
			LES CRANE		
			TV talk-show host from San Francisco.		
10/09/71	**8**	12	1 **Desiderata**	[S]	Warner 7520
			originally a piece of prose, written in 1906 by Max Ehrmann		
			JOHNNY CRAWFORD		
			Born on 3/26/46 in Los Angeles. One of the original Mouseketeers. Played Chuck Connor's son (Mark McCain) in the TV series, "The Rifleman", 1958-63.		
6/12/61	**70**	4	1 Daydreams		Del-Fi 4162
3/03/62	**43**	9	2 Patti Ann		Del-Fi 4172
5/12/62	**8**	13	3 **Cindy's Birthday**		Del-Fi 4178
8/11/62	**14**	9	4 Your Nose Is Gonna Grow		Del-Fi 4181
11/03/62	**12**	10	5 Rumors		Del-Fi 4188
1/05/63	**29**	8	6 Proud		Del-Fi 4193
9/07/63	**72**	7	7 Cindy's Gonna Cry		Del-Fi 4221
1/11/64	**95**	3	8 Judy Loves Me		Del-Fi 4231
			RANDY CRAWFORD - see THE CRUSADERS and RICK SPRINGFIELD		
			CRAWLER		
			British rock quintet; formerly: Back Street Crawler; shortened name after death of leader Paul Kossoff (Free).		
10/15/77	**65**	7	1 Stone Cold Sober		Epic 50442
			CRAZY ELEPHANT		
			Bubblegum studio concoction of producers Jerry Kasenetz & Jeff Katz. Ex-Cadillac member, Robert Spencer on lead vocals. Touring group formed later.		
3/01/69	**12**	13	1 Gimme Gimme Good Lovin'		Bell 763
			CRAZY OTTO		
			German pianist Fritz Schulz-Reichel. Also see Johnny Maddox.		
2/26/55	**19**	5	1 Glad Rag Doll/	[I]	
			Best Seller #19		
2/26/55	**21**	3	2 Smiles	[I]	Decca 29403
			Best Seller #21		
			CREAM		
			British supergroup: Eric Clapton (guitar), Ginger Baker (drums) & Jack Bruce (bass).		
1/13/68	**5**	26	1 ● **Sunshine Of Your Love**		Atco 6544
5/11/68	**64**	5	2 Anyone For Tennis		Atco 6575
			The Savage Seven Theme		
10/05/68	**6**	11	3 **White Room**		Atco 6617
1/25/69	**28**	8	4 Crossroads		Atco 6646
4/05/69	**60**	5	5 Badge		Atco 6668
			all of above produced by Felix Pappalardi		
			CREATIVE SOURCE		
			2-man, 3-woman soul group.		
4/06/74	**69**	7	1 Who Is He And What Is He To You		Sussex 509
			CREEDENCE CLEARWATER REVIVAL		
			Rock group formed while members attended high school at El Cerrito, California. Consisted of John Fogerty (vocals, guitar), Tom Fogerty (guitar), Stu Cook (keyboards, bass) and Doug Clifford (drums). First recorded as the Blue Velvets for the Orchestra label in 1959. Recorded as the Golliwogs for Fantasy in 1964. Tom Fogerty left for a solo career in 1971 and group disbanded in October, 1972.		
9/07/68	**11**	12	1 Suzie Q. (Part One)		Fantasy 616
11/09/68	**58**	9	2 I Put A Spell On You		Fantasy 617
1/25/69	**2^{3}**	14	3 ● **Proud Mary**		Fantasy 619
5/03/69	**2^{1}**	14	4 ● **Bad Moon Rising/**		
5/03/69	**52**	4	5 Lodi		Fantasy 622

DEBUT DATE	PEAK POS	WKS CHR	ARTIST — Record Title	Label & Number
			CREEDENCE CLEARWATER REVIVAL — Cont'd	
8/02/69	**2[1]**	13	6 **Green River/**	
8/02/69	**30**	8	7 Commotion	Fantasy 625
10/25/69	**3**	15	8 ● **Down On The Corner/**	
		14	9 Fortunate Son	Fantasy 634
1/31/70	**2[2]**	10	10 ● **Travelin' Band/**	
		10	11 Who'll Stop The Rain	Fantasy 637
4/25/70	**4**	11	12 ● **Up Around The Bend/**	
		11	13 Run Through The Jungle	Fantasy 641
8/08/70	**2[1]**	13	14 ● **Lookin' Out My Back Door/**	
		13	15 Long As I Can See The Light	Fantasy 645
1/30/71	**8**	10	16 ● **Have You Ever Seen The Rain/**	
		5	17 Hey Tonight	Fantasy 655
			3-17: written, produced and arranged by John Fogerty	
7/17/71	**6**	9	18 **Sweet Hitch-Hiker**	Fantasy 665
5/06/72	**25**	8	19 Someday Never Comes	Fantasy 676
1/31/76	**43**	8	20 I Heard It Through The Grapevine	Fantasy 759
			from the 1970 album "Cosmo's Factory"	
			MARSHALL CRENSHAW	
			Singer, songwriter, guitarist from Detroit. Played John Lennon in the road show of "Beatlemania" in 1976.	
7/10/82	**36**	11	1 Someday, Someway	Warner 29974
			THE CRESCENDOS	
			Vocal quartet from Nashville; lead singer Dale Ward.	
1/06/58	**5**	18	1 **Oh Julie**	Nasco 6005
			Top 100 #5 / Best Seller #6 / Jockey #7	
			THE CRESCENTS	
12/28/63+	**69**	10	1 Pink Dominos [I]	Era 3116
			THE CRESTS	
			Vocal group from New York City, formed in 1955. Consisted of lead singer Johnny Mastrangelo (Maestro - shown as Mastro on all Crests' hits), Harold Torres, Talmadge Gough, J.T. Carter and Patricia Van Dross. Discovered by Al Browne, first recorded for Joyce in 1957. Van Dross left group in 1958. Mastrangelo left for solo work as Johnny Maestro in 1960, replaced by James Ancrum. Maestro later formed the Brooklyn Bridge.	
7/15/57	**86**	2	1 Sweetest One	Joyce 103
11/24/58+	**2[2]**	21	2 **16 Candles**	Coed 506
3/23/59	**28**	13	3 Six Nights A Week	Coed 509
6/08/59	**79**	6	4 Flower Of Love	Coed 511
8/17/59	**22**	16	5 The Angels Listened In	Coed 515
12/07/59+	**42**	10	6 A Year Ago Tonight	Coed 521
2/29/60	**14**	15	7 Step By Step	Coed 525
6/13/60	**20**	13	8 Trouble In Paradise	Coed 531
			THE CRESTS featuring JOHNNY MASTRO:	
9/12/60	**81**	4	9 Journey Of Love	Coed 535
10/24/60	**100**	1	10 Isn't It Amazing	Coed 537
			THE CRETONES	
			Los Angeles rock quartet led by Mark Goldenberg and Peter Bernstein.	
5/03/80	**79**	6	1 Real Love	Planet 45911
			THE CREW-CUTS	
			Vocal group from Toronto, Canada, formed in 1952. Consisted of John Perkins (lead), his brother Ray Perkins (bass), Pat Barrett (tenor) and Rudi Maugeri (baritone). All had sung in church. First called the Canadaires, changed name in 1954. Maugeri did vocal arrangements for the group. Disbanded in 1963.	
2/05/55	**3**	13	1 **Earth Angel/**	
			Jockey #3 / Juke Box #8 / Best Seller #8	
1/29/55	**6**	12	2 **Ko Ko Mo (I Love You So)**	Mercury 70529
			Juke Box #6 / Best Seller #10 / Jockey #11	
4/30/55	**14**	8	3 Don't Be Angry/	
			Best Seller #14 / Jockey #14 / Juke Box #19	
		8	4 Chop Chop Boom	Mercury 70597
			Best Seller flip	
6/25/55	**16**	7	5 A Story Untold	Mercury 70634
			Best Seller #16	

DEBUT DATE	PEAK POS	WKS CHR	ARTIST — Record Title	Label & Number
			THE CREW-CUTS — Cont'd	
8/27/55	**10**	8	6 **Gum Drop**..	Mercury 70668
			Best Seller #10 / Jockey #14 / Juke Box #20 / Top 100 #80 pre	
12/10/55+	**11**	18	7 Angels In The Sky/	
			Best Seller #11 / Top 100 #13 / Juke Box #13 / Jockey #16	
12/24/55+	**31**	12	8 Mostly Martha	Mercury 70741
2/04/56	**18**	11	9 Seven Days	Mercury 70782
			Jockey #18 / Top 100 #20	
6/30/56	**45**	5	10 Tell Me Why	Mercury 70890
1/12/57	**17**	12	11 Young Love	Mercury 71022
			Jockey #17 / Juke Box #17 / Top 100 #24	
			orchestra conducted by David Carroll on all of above	
			BOB CREWE	
			Born on 11/12/37 in Newark, New Jersey. Wrote many hit songs beginning with "Silhouettes" in 1957. One of the top producers of the 60s, including work with The 4 Seasons. Head of several labels, music publishing and production companies. Assembled The Bob Crewe Generation, an aggregation of studio musicians.	
2/01/60	**96**	2	1 The Whiffenpoof Song	Warwick 519
			theme song of the Yale University Glee Club since 1909	
			THE BOB CREWE GENERATION:	
12/31/66+	**15**	10	2 Music To Watch Girls By.. [I]	DynoVoice 229
			tune used in a Diet Pepsi commercial	
10/28/67	**89**	2	3 Birds Of Britain.. [I]	DynoVoice 902
3/06/76	**56**	6	4 Street Talk.. [I]	20th Century 2271
			shown only as: **B.C.G.**	
			THE CRICKETS - see BUDDY HOLLY	
			THE CRITTERS	
			New Jersey quintet led by Don Ciccone, who later joined the 4 Seasons.	
5/28/66	**42**	9	1 Younger Girl..	Kapp 752
8/13/66	**17**	11	2 Mr. Dieingly Sad..	Kapp 769
12/03/66	**55**	6	3 Bad Misunderstanding..	Kapp 793
7/08/67	**39**	8	4 Don't Let The Rain Fall Down On Me..	Kapp 838
			JIM CROCE	
			Born on 1/10/43 in Philadelphia. Killed in a plane crash on 9/20/73 (30) in Natchitoches, LA. Vocalist, guitarist, composer. Recorded with wife Ingrid for Capitol in 1968. Lead guitarist on his hits, Maury Muehleisen, was killed in the same plane crash.	
7/01/72	**8**	13	1 **You Don't Mess Around With Jim**	ABC 11328
10/14/72	**17**	12	2 Operator (That's Not The Way It Feels)..	ABC 11335
2/03/73	**37**	10	3 One Less Set Of Footsteps..	ABC 11346
4/21/73	**1^2**	22	4● **Bad, Bad Leroy Brown**..	ABC 11359
10/06/73	**10**	17	5 **I Got A Name**..	ABC 11389
			from the film "The Last American Hero"	
11/17/73	**1^2**	15	6● **Time In A Bottle**	ABC 11405
12/29/73+	**64**	5	7 It Doesn't Have To Be That Way..	ABC 11413
3/02/74	**9**	14	8 **I'll Have To Say I Love You In A Song**	ABC 11424
6/08/74	**32**	11	9 Workin' At The Car Wash Blues..	ABC 11447
1/03/76	**63**	9	10 Chain Gang Medley	Lifesong 45001
			Chain Gang/He Don't Love You/Searchin'	
			all of above produced by Terry Cashman & Tommy West	
			CLEVELAND CROCHET & Band	
			Cleveland was born on 1/30/29 in Jennings, LA. Leader, violinist of cajun combo.	
12/31/60+	**80**	5	1 Sugar Bee	Goldband 1106
			vocal by Jesse "Jay" Stutes	
			G.L. CROCKETT	
			Born George L. Crockett in Carltown, MS around 1929. Died in Chicago on 2/15/67. Blues singer from the West Side of Chicago.	
8/07/65	**67**	6	1 It's A Man Down There	4 Brothers 445

DEBUT DATE	PEAK POS	WKS CHR	ARTIST — Record Title	Label & Number
			BING CROSBY	
			The most popular entertainer of the 20th century's first 50 years. Harry Lillis Crosby was born on 5/2/01 (or 04) in Tacoma, Washington. He and singing partner Al Rinker were hired in 1926 by Paul Whiteman; with Harry Barris they became the Rhythm Boys and gained an increasing following. The trio split from Whiteman in 1930, and Bing sang briefly with Gus Arnheim's band. It was his early-1931 smash with Arnheim, "I Surrender, Dear", which earned Bing a CBS radio contract, and launched an unsurpassed solo career. Over the next three decades the resonant Crosby baritone and breezy persona sold more than 300 million records and was featured in over 50 movies (won Academy Award for "Going My Way", 1944). Bing died of a heart attack on a golf course on 10/14/77.	
12/24/55	**7**	3	1 **White Christmas** .... [X-R] with the Ken Darby Singers and Scott Trotter's orchestra Jockey #7 / Top 100 #18 originally hit #1 in December, 1942; made pop charts for 20 Christmas seasons; the best selling record of all time	Decca 29342
4/07/56	**49**	7	2 In A Little Spanish Town .... **BING CROSBY & THE BUDDY COLE TRIO** song originally hit #1 for Paul Whiteman in 1927	Decca 29850
9/08/56	**3**	31	3 **True Love** .... **BING CROSBY & GRACE KELLY (died in an auto accident, 9/14/82-52)** Jockey #3 / Top 100 #4 / Best Seller #5 / Juke Box #6	Capitol 3507
9/22/56	**92**	2	4 Well Did You Evah? .... [N] **BING CROSBY & FRANK SINATRA**	Capitol 3507
10/13/56	**88**	4	5 Now You Has Jazz .... [N] **BING CROSBY & LOUIS ARMSTRONG** above 3 from the film "High Society"	Capitol 3506
12/29/56	**65**	1	6 White Christmas .... [X-R]	Decca 29342
6/17/57	**25**	29	7 Around The World .... Best Seller #25 / Top 100 #54 from the Michael Todd film "Around The World In Eighty Days"	Decca 30262
12/16/57	**34**	6	8 White Christmas .... [X-R] Top 100 #34 / Best Seller #36	Decca 29342
12/30/57	**54**	3	9 Silent Night .... [X-R] Bing's first version charted in 1935 above version first charted in 1947	Decca 23777
12/30/57	**78**	2	10 Silver Bells .... [X-R] **BING CROSBY & CAROL RICHARDS** from the film "The Lemon Drop Kid", first charted, Christmas, 1952	Decca 27229
12/30/57	**97**	1	11 How Lovely Is Christmas .... [X] with the Arthur Norman Choir	Kapp 196
12/22/58	**66**	2	12 White Christmas .... [X-R]	Decca 23778
12/28/59	**59**	1	13 White Christmas .... [X-R]	Decca 23778
12/12/60	**26**	3	14 White Christmas .... [X-R]	Decca 23778
12/12/60	**45**	3	15 Adeste Fideles (Oh, Come, All Ye Faithful)/ .... [X-R] above version recorded by Bing in 1947 (previously uncharted)	
12/19/60	**54**	2	16 Silent Night .... [X-R]	Decca 23777
12/11/61	**12**	4	17 White Christmas .... [X-R]	Decca 23778
12/15/62	**38**	3	18 White Christmas .... [X-R]	Decca 23778
			CHRIS CROSBY	
			Bing's nephew. Father is bandleader Bob Crosby.	
2/15/64	**53**	7	1 Young And In Love .... from the TV series "Dr. Kildare"	MGM 13191
			DAVID CROSBY	
			Born on 8/14/41 in Los Angeles. Vocals, guitar with The Byrds, 1964-68. Frequent troubles with the law due to drug charges.	
5/01/71	**95**	1	1 Music Is Love .... **GRAHAM NASH & DAVID CROSBY:**	Atlantic 2792
5/06/72	**36**	9	2 Immigration Man	Atlantic 2873
8/12/72	**99**	2	3 Southbound Train .... **DAVID CROSBY/GRAHAM NASH:**	Atlantic 2892
11/15/75	**52**	6	4 Carry Me	ABC 12140
8/07/76	**89**	3	5 Out Of The Darkness	ABC 12199
			CROSBY, STILLS & NASH	
			David Crosby, guitar (from The Byrds); Stephen Stills, guitar, bass (from Buffalo Springfield); and Graham Nash, guitar (from The Hollies). Neil Young, guitar (from Buffalo Springfield) joined the trio in summer, 1969.	
7/19/69	**28**	8	1 Marrakesh Express	Atlantic 2652
10/04/69	**21**	12	2 Suite: Judy Blue Eyes .... written by Stephen Stills for Judy Collins **CROSBY, STILLS, NASH & YOUNG:**	Atlantic 2676

DEBUT DATE	PEAK POS	WKS CHR	ARTIST — Record Title	Label & Number
			CROSBY, STILLS, NASH & YOUNG — Cont'd	
3/28/70	**11**	11	3 Woodstock	Atlantic 2723
			written by Joni Mitchell about festival in New York, August, 1969	
6/06/70	**16**	11	4 Teach Your Children	Atlantic 2735
6/27/70	**14**	9	5 Ohio	Atlantic 2740
			written by Young after 4 students killed at Kent State Univ.	
9/19/70	**30**	9	6 Our House	Atlantic 2760
			CROSBY, STILLS & NASH:	
5/28/77	**7**	21	7 **Just A Song Before I Go**	Atlantic 3401
10/01/77	**43**	9	8 Fair Game	Atlantic 3432
6/26/82	**9**	15	9 **Wasted On The Way**	Atlantic 4058
9/18/82	**18**	17	10 Southern Cross	Atlantic 89969
1/29/83	**69**	6	11 Too Much Love To Hide	Atlantic 89888
6/25/83	**45**	9	12 War Games	Atlantic 89812
			CROSS COUNTRY	
			Jay Siegel, Mitch and Phil Margo - all formerly with The Tokens.	
8/18/73	**30**	12	1 In The Midnight Hour	Atco 6934
			CHRISTOPHER CROSS	
			Born Christopher Geppert on 5/3/51 in San Antonio, Texas. Formed own group with Rob Meurer (keyboards), Andy Salmon (bass) and Tommy Taylor (drums) in 1973.	
2/16/80	**2**[4]	21	1 **Ride Like The Wind**	Warner 49184
			backing vocals: Michael McDonald	
6/14/80	**1**[1]	21	2 **Sailing**	Warner 49507
10/11/80	**15**	19	3 Never Be The Same	Warner 49580
3/28/81	**20**	14	4 Say You'll Be Mine	Warner 49705
8/15/81	**1**[3]	24	5● **Arthur's Theme (Best That You Can Do)**	Warner 49787
			from the Dudley Moore movie "Arthur"	
1/22/83	**12**	16	6 All Right	Warner 29843
5/07/83	**33**	10	7 No Time For Talk	Warner 29662
12/10/83+	**9**	17	8 **Think Of Laura**	Warner 29658
			popularized through play on TV's "General Hospital"	
6/16/84	**76**	5	9 A Chance For Heaven	Columbia 04492
			Swimming Theme from the Offical Music of the XXIIIrd Olympiad, Los Angeles, 1984	
10/26/85	**68**	5	10 Charm The Snake	Warner 28864
			all of above produced by Michael Omartian	
			JIMMY CROSS	
1/30/65	**92**	3	1 I Want My Baby Back [N]	Tollie 9039
			CROW	
			Rock/blues quintet from Minneapolis - Dave Wagner, lead singer.	
10/25/69+	**19**	15	1 Evil Woman Don't Play Your Games With Me	Amaret 112
5/16/70	**56**	14	2 Cottage Cheese	Amaret 119
10/24/70	**52**	9	3 Don't Try To Lay No Boogie Woogie On The "King Of Rock & Roll"	Amaret 125
			RODNEY CROWELL	
			Born on 8/7/50 in Houston. Songwriter/guitarist. Rosanne Cash's husband.	
5/10/80	**37**	11	1 Ashes By Now	Warner 49224
			CROWN HEIGHTS AFFAIR	
			R&B disco group from Bedford-Stuyvesant, New York, formed as the Neu Day Express, and led by Phil Thomas.	
8/16/75	**43**	13	1 Dreaming A Dream	De-Lite 1570
12/06/75+	**83**	8	2 Every Beat Of My Heart	De-Lite 1575
5/22/76	**49**	12	3 Foxy Lady [I]	De-Lite 1581
2/19/77	**42**	13	4 Dancin'	De-Lite 1588
			THE CRUSADERS	
			Instrumental jazz-oriented group formed in Houston, as the Swingsters, early 1950's. To California, early 1960's, name changed to Jazz Crusaders. Became The Crusaders in 1971. Included Joe Sample (keyboards), Wilton Felder (reeds) and Stix Hooper (drums).	
			THE JAZZ CRUSADERS:	
4/02/66	**95**	1	1 Uptight (Everything's Alright) [I]	Pacific Jazz 88125
12/26/70+	**90**	3	2 Way Back Home [I]	Chisa 8010
			THE CRUSADERS:	
7/15/72	**52**	9	3 Put It Where You Want It [I]	Blue Thumb 208

DEBUT DATE	PEAK POS	WKS CHR	ARTIST — Record Title	Label & Number
			THE CRUSADERS — Cont'd	
5/12/73	**86**	5	4 Don't Let It Get You Down .... [I]	Blue Thumb 225
4/27/74	**81**	6	5 Scratch .... [I]	Blue Thumb 249
8/25/79	**36**	16	6 Street Life .... vocal by Randy Crawford Crusaders/Randy Crawford	MCA 41054
9/26/81	**97**	3	7 I'm So Glad I'm Standing Here Today .... **CRUSADERS Guest Artist - JOE COCKER**	MCA 51177
			THE CRYAN' SHAMES 6-man band from Chicago; Thomas Doody, lead singer.	
7/23/66	**49**	9	1 Sugar And Spice	Destination 624
11/26/66	**85**	4	2 I Wanna Meet You	Columbia 43836
8/05/67	**85**	8	3 It Could Be We're In Love	Columbia 44191
4/06/68	**85**	3	4 Up On The Roof	Columbia 44457
6/22/68	**99**	2	5 Young Birds Fly	Columbia 44545
			CRYSTAL MANSION 8-man group - Johnny Caswell, lead singer.	
12/21/68+	**84**	5	1 The Thought Of Loving You	Capitol 2275
11/07/70	**73**	6	2 Carolina In My Mind	Colossus 128
			BILLY CRYSTAL Former member of the comedy team on TV's "Saturday Night Live".	
7/27/85	**58**	12	1 You Look Marvelous .... [N] humorous impersonation of Fernando Lamas	A&M 2764
			THE CRYSTALS Female vocal group from Brooklyn. Consisted of Barbara Alston, Lala Brooks, Dee Dee Kennibrew, Mary Thomas and Patricia Wright. Discovered by producer Phil Spector.	
11/20/61+	**20**	11	1 There's No Other (Like My Baby)	Philles 100
3/31/62	**13**	13	2 Uptown	Philles 102
9/08/62	**1^{2}**	18	3 **He's A Rebel** .... written by Gene Pitney	Philles 106
12/29/62+	**11**	12	4 He's Sure The Boy I Love .... above 2 feature Darlene Love (lead) and The Blossoms	Philles 109
4/27/63	**3**	13	5 **Da Doo Ron Ron (When He Walked Me Home)**	Philles 112
8/17/63	**6**	12	6 **Then He Kissed Me**	Philles 115
2/01/64	**92**	3	7 Little Boy	Philles 119
8/01/64	**98**	1	8 All Grown Up	Philles 122
			THE JOE CUBA SEXTET Raunchy Latin-rock combo.	
10/22/66	**63**	8	1 'Bang' 'Bang' .... [F]	Tico 475
1/07/67	**62**	5	2 Oh Yeah!	Tico 490
			THE CUES R&B vocal quintet: Jimmy Breedlove, Ollie Jones, Abel DeCosta, tenors; Robie Kirk ("Winfield Scott"), baritone; and Eddie Barnes, bass.	
11/19/55	**86**	1	1 Burn That Candle	Capitol 3245
1/19/57	**77**	1	2 Why	Capitol 3582
			THE CUFF LINKS Group is actually the overdubbed voices of Ron Dante (The Archies).	
9/13/69	**9**	12	1 **Tracy**	Decca 32533
12/13/69+	**41**	9	2 When Julie Comes Around	Decca 32592
3/07/70	**76**	6	3 Run Sally Run	Decca 32639
			CUGINI Don Cugini.	
12/22/79+	**88**	4	1 Let Me Sleep Alone	Scotti Br. 503
			CULTURE CLUB Formed in London, England in 1981. Consisted of George "Boy George" O'Dowd (b: 6/14/61), vocals; Roy Hay, guitar, keyboards; Mikey Craig, bass; and Jon Moss, drums. Designer Sue Clowes originated distinctive costuming for the group.	
12/04/82+	**2^{3}**	25	1 **Do You Really Want To Hurt Me**	Epic/Virgin 03368
4/16/83	**2^{2}**	18	2 **Time (Clock Of The Heart)**	Epic/Virgin 03796
7/02/83	**9**	16	3 **I'll Tumble 4 Ya**	Epic/Virgin 03912

DEBUT DATE	PEAK POS	WKS CHR	ARTIST — Record Title	Label & Number
			CULTURE CLUB — Cont'd	
10/22/83	**10**	17	4 **Church Of The Poison Mind**	Epic/Virgin 04144
12/03/83+	**1**[3]	22	5 ● **Karma Chameleon**	Epic/Virgin 04221
3/03/84	**5**	16	6 **Miss Me Blind** backing vocals: Jermaine Stewart	Epic/Virgin 04388
5/12/84	**13**	13	7 It's A Miracle	Epic/Virgin 04457
10/06/84	**17**	13	8 The War Song	Epic/Virgin 04638
12/15/84+	**33**	13	9 Mistake No. 3	Epic/Virgin 04727
4/05/86	**12**	14	10 Move Away	Epic/Virgin 05847
			BURTON CUMMINGS Born on 12/31/47 in Winnipeg, Canada. Lead singer of the Guess Who.	
10/09/76+	**10**	21	1 ● **Stand Tall**	Portrait 70001
2/19/77	**61**	5	2 I'm Scared	Portrait 70002
9/10/77	**74**	4	3 My Own Way To Rock	Portrait 70007
7/15/78	**85**	5	4 Break It To Them Gently	Portrait 70016
9/12/81	**37**	11	5 You Saved My Soul	Alfa 7008
			RICK CUNHA Los Angeles session guitarist/vocalist.	
4/27/74	**61**	7	1 (I'm A) YoYo Man	GRC 2016
			THE CUPIDS	
7/06/63	**57**	6	1 Brenda	KC 115
			THE MIKE CURB CONGREGATION Mike was born on 12/24/44 in Savannah, Georgia. Pop music mogul and politician. President of MGM Records, 1969-1973. Head of Warner/Curb Records. Elected lieutenant-governor of California in 1978.	
11/07/70+	**34**	17	1 Burning Bridges from the film "Kelly's Heroes"	MGM 14151
			THE CURE British rock group led by Robert Smith & Laurence Tolhurst.	
2/15/86	**99**	1	1 In Between Days (Without You) first released in July of 1985	Elektra 69604
			CURRENT 5-man disco session band.	
4/30/77	**94**	3	1 Theme From "Rocky" (Gonna Fly Now) [I]	Playboy 6098
			CHERIE & MARIE CURRIE 20-year-old identical twins from Encino, CA. Cherie formerly with The Runaways.	
10/20/79	**95**	3	1 Since You've Been Gone	Capitol 4754
			CLIFFORD CURRY	
5/06/67	**95**	3	1 She Shot A Hole In My Soul	Elf 90002
			TIM CURRY British actor and vocalist. Starred as Dr. Frank N. Further in the cult film "The Rocky Horror Picture Show", also starred in the film "Annie".	
11/03/79	**91**	3	1 I Do The Rock	A&M 2166
			CURTIE & THE BOOMBOX Female Dutch quartet - Curtie Fortune, lead singer.	
7/27/85	**81**	4	1 Black Kisses (Never Make You Blue)	RCA 14103
			BOBBY CURTOLA Born on 4/17/44 in Port Arthur, Ontario, Canada.	
5/05/62	**41**	14	1 Fortuneteller	Del-Fi 4177
10/27/62	**92**	3	2 Aladdin	Del-Fi 4185
			CYCLONES	
9/29/58	**83**	2	1 Bullwhip Rock [I]	Trophy 500
			CYMANDE 8-man afro-rock band from the West Indies.	
1/20/73	**48**	10	1 The Message	Janus 203
			CYMARRON Pop trio: Richard Mainegra, Rick Yancey and Sherrill Parks.	
6/12/71	**17**	12	1 Rings	Entrance 7500

DEBUT DATE	PEAK POS	WKS CHR	ARTIST — Record Title		Label & Number
			CYMARRON — Cont'd		
10/02/71	**96**	4	2 Valerie		Entrance 7502
			JOHNNY CYMBAL		
			Scottish-born singer, songwriter, producer. Also recorded as Derek.		
2/16/63	**16**	13	1 Mr. Bass Man bass singer: Ronnie Bright	[N]	Kapp 503
5/11/63	**58**	6	2 Teenage Heaven	[N]	Kapp 524
8/03/63	**77**	4	3 Dum Dum Dee Dum		Kapp 539
			THE CYRKLE		
			Group formed while attending Lafayette College in Easton, Pennsylvania. Signed to Columbia Records and managed by the Beatles' Brian Epstein.		
5/21/66	**2[1]**	13	1 **Red Rubber Ball** written by Paul Simon and Bruce Woodley (of The Seekers)		Columbia 43589
8/13/66	**16**	8	2 Turn-Down Day		Columbia 43729
12/03/66	**59**	5	3 Please Don't Ever Leave Me		Columbia 43871
2/04/67	**70**	4	4 I Wish You Could Be Here		Columbia 43965
5/13/67	**72**	5	5 We Had A Good Thing Goin'		Columbia 44108
9/02/67	**95**	1	6 Penny Arcade		Columbia 44224
			D		
			DADDY DEWDROP		
			Real name: Richard Monda - from Cleveland.		
3/06/71	**9**	16	1 **Chick-A-Boom (Don't Ya Jes' Love It)**	[N]	Sunflower 105
			THE DADDY-O's		
			Produced by guitarist Billy Mure.		
6/16/58	**39**	8	1 Got A Match? Best Seller #39 / Top 100 #40	[I]	Cabot 122
			STEVE DAHL & Teenage Radiation		
			Steve is a Chicago disc jockey.		
9/22/79	**58**	6	1 Do You Think I'm Disco? parody of Rod Stewart's "Da Ya Think I'm Sexy?"	[N]	Ovation 1132
			E.G. DAILY		
			Elizabeth Daily - singer/actress (co-starred in "Pee-Wee's Big Adventure" and "Valley Girl").		
4/26/86	**70**	10	1 Say It, Say It		A&M 2825
			DALE & GRACE		
			Vocal duo of Dale Houston from Ferriday, Louisiana, and Grace Broussard from Prairieville, Louisiana.		
10/05/63	**1[2]**	15	1 **I'm Leaving It Up To You**		Montel 921
1/25/64	**8**	9	2 **Stop And Think It Over**		Montel 922
5/02/64	**65**	5	3 The Loneliest Night		Montel 928
			ALAN DALE		
			Born Aldo Sigismondi on 7/9/26 in Brooklyn. Baritone singer formerly with Carmen Cavallaro.		
4/30/55	**14**	7	1 Cherry Pink (And Apple Blossom White) Juke Box #14 / Jockey #19 / Best Seller #27 from the film "Underwater!"		Coral 61373
7/02/55	**10**	7	2 **Sweet And Gentle** Jockey #10 / Best Seller #12 / Juke Box #14 orchestra directed by Dick Jacobs on above two		Coral 61435
			DICK DALE & His Del-Tones		
			Dick was southern California's most influential surf guitarist.		
11/27/61+	**60**	9	1 Let's Go Trippin' considered to be the first surf record	[I]	Deltone 5017
10/26/63	**98**	1	2 The Scavenger		Capitol 5048
			TONY DALLARA		
			Native of Milano, Italy.		
12/08/58+	**60**	7	1 Come Prima also released under the name Tony Dalardo	[F]	Mercury 71327

DEBUT DATE	PEAK POS	WKS CHR	ARTIST — Record Title	Label & Number
			KATHY DALTON	
			Songstress from Memphis.	
9/14/74	**72**	5	1 Boogie Bands And One Night Stands	DiscReet 1210
			ROGER DALTREY	
			Born on 3/1/44 in London, England. Formed band, the Detours, who later became the Who. Roger was the Who's lead singer, and starred in the films "Tommy", "Lisztomania", and "McVicar".	
6/02/73	**83**	7	1 Giving It All Away	Track 40053
10/04/75	**68**	8	2 Come And Get Your Love	MCA 40453
10/08/77	**88**	3	3 Avenging Annie	MCA 40800
7/05/80	**53**	10	4 Free Me from the film "McVicar"	Polydor 2105
9/13/80	**20**	19	5 Without Your Love	Polydor 2121
2/18/84	**62**	9	6 Walking In My Sleep	Atlantic 89704
9/14/85	**48**	13	7 After The Fire	Atlantic 89491
12/28/85+	**86**	4	8 Let Me Down Easy	Atlantic 89471
			MICHAEL DAMIAN	
			Played Danny Romalotti on TV's "The Young & The Restless".	
5/30/81	**69**	6	1 She Did It	LEG 007
			JOE DAMIANO	
			Native of Philadelphia.	
8/31/59	**91**	3	1 I Cried	Chancellor 1039
			LIZ DAMON'S ORIENT EXPRESS	
			3-woman, 6-man vocal/instrumental group from Hawaii.	
12/26/70+	**33**	12	1 1900 Yesterday	White Whale 368
			VIC DAMONE	
			Born Vito Farinola on 6/12/28 in Brooklyn. Vic is among the most popular of postwar ballad singers; he also appeared in several movies and hosted a TV series (1956-57).	
11/19/55	**73**	4	1 Por Favor	Mercury 70699
4/21/56	**4**	25	2 **On The Street Where You Live** Jockey #4 / Best Seller #8 / Top 100 #8 / Juke Box #13 from the Broadway musical "My Fair Lady"	Columbia 40654
9/22/56	**59**	10	3 War And Peace from the film of the same title	Columbia 40733
4/13/57	**62**	10	4 Do I Love You (Because You're Beautiful) from the CBS-TV musical "Cinderella"	Columbia 40858
9/09/57	**16**	16	5 An Affair To Remember (Our Love Affair) Jockey #16 / Top 100 #35 from the Cary Grant movie "An Affair To Remember"	Columbia 40945
5/05/58	**88**	1	6 Gigi from the film of the same title 2, 5 & 6: orchestra directed by Percy Faith	Columbia 41122
4/17/65	**30**	10	7 You Were Only Fooling (While I Was Falling In Love)	Warner 5616
			VIC DANA	
			Born on 8/26/42 in Buffalo, New York.	
11/27/61+	**45**	8	1 Little Altar Boy	Dolton 48
3/31/62	**47**	9	2 I Will	Dolton 51
5/25/63	**96**	2	3 Danger	Dolton 73
8/10/63	**42**	11	4 More	Dolton 81
3/28/64	**27**	10	5 Shangri-La	Dolton 92
7/11/64	**53**	7	6 Love Is All We Need	Dolton 95
10/17/64	**97**	3	7 Garden In The Rain	Dolton 99
2/06/65	**10**	12	8 **Red Roses For A Blue Lady**	Dolton 304
5/22/65	**66**	6	9 Bring A Little Sunshine (To My Heart)	Dolton 305
8/07/65	**51**	9	10 Moonlight And Roses (Bring Mem'ries Of You) sung by Roy Rogers in the 1943 film "Song Of Texas"	Dolton 309
12/04/65	**51**	7	11 Crystal Chandelier	Dolton 313
5/07/66	**30**	8	12 I Love You Drops	Dolton 319
8/06/66	**71**	3	13 A Million And One	Dolton 322
1/10/70	**47**	12	14 If I Never Knew Your Name	Liberty 56150
5/16/70	**72**	6	15 Red Red Wine	Liberty 56163
			DANCER, PRANCER & NERVOUS	
12/07/59	**34**	6	1 The Happy Reindeer [X-N]	Capitol 4300

DEBUT DATE	PEAK POS	WKS CHR	ARTIST — Record Title		Label & Number
			RODNEY DANGERFIELD Born Jack Roy in 1921 in New York. Owner of 'Dangerfields' club in New York City. Comedian and star of the films "Caddyshack", "Easy Money", and "Back To School".		
12/03/83+	**83**	8	1 Rappin' Rodney Rodney "raps" to a musical background	[C]	RCA 13656
			THE CHARLIE DANIELS BAND Charlie was born on 10/28/37 in Wilmington, North Carolina. Sessionman (guitar, fiddle and banjo) in Nashville for Bob Dylan, Ringo Starr, Pete Seeger, and others. Formed own band in 1971. Began hosting annual jam of Southern bands ("Volunteer Jam") in 1975.		
6/30/73	**9**	12	1 **Uneasy Rider**	[N]	Kama Sutra 576
2/08/75	**29**	10	2 The South's Gonna Do It		Kama Sutra 598
5/10/75	**56**	8	3 Long Haired Country Boy		Kama Sutra 601
2/07/76	**91**	4	4 Texas		Kama Sutra 607
6/23/79	**3**	18	5● **The Devil Went Down To Georgia**		Epic 50700
5/31/80	**11**	15	6 In America		Epic 50888
8/16/80	**31**	14	7 The Legend Of Wooley Swamp		Epic 50921
3/27/82	**22**	12	8 Still In Saigon		Epic 02828
			JOHNNY DANKWORTH Born on 9/20/27 in London, England. Alto saxophonist, jazz bandleader. Married to singer Cleo Laine since 1958.		
8/25/56	**61**	4	1 Experiments With Mice Johnny narrates and plays a tribute to the big bands of Billy May, Benny Goodman, Glenn Miller, and Stan Kenton	[N]	Capitol 3499
			THE DANLEERS R&B quartet from Brooklyn, New York - Jimmy Weston, lead singer. Original release of "One Summer Night" was on AMP-3 label as by The Dandleers, often confusing them with another group, The Danderliers.		
6/30/58	**7**	13	1 **One Summer Night** Jockey #7 / Best Seller #14 / Top 100 #16		Mercury 71322
			DANNY & THE JUNIORS Formed while at high school in Philadelphia in 1955 as the Juvenairs, with Danny Rapp (b: 5/10/41), lead; David White, first tenor; Frank Maffei, second tenor; and Joe Terranova, baritone. Danny Rapp committed suicide on 4/8/83 (41).		
12/09/57+	**1**[7]	21	1 **At The Hop** Top 100 #1(7) / Best Seller #1(5) / Jockey #1(3) song originally written as "Do The Bop"		ABC-Para. 9871
3/03/58	**19**	11	2 Rock And Roll Is Here To Stay Best Seller #19 / Top 100 #19 with guest Freddy Cannon		ABC-Para. 9888
6/23/58	**39**	6	3 Dottie Best Seller #39 / Top 100 #41		ABC-Para. 9926
9/19/60	**27**	9	4 Twistin' U.S.A.		Swan 4060
2/20/61	**60**	7	5 Pony Express		Swan 4068
9/18/61	**80**	5	6 Back To The Hop		Swan 4082
1/06/62	**68**	5	7 Twistin' All Night Long	[N]	Swan 4092
4/14/62	**93**	1	8 Doin' The Continental Walk		Swan 4100
1/19/63	**99**	2	9 OO-La-La-Limbo		Guyden 2076
			DANTE & The EVERGREENS Dante Drowty, lead singer of pop quartet from Los Angeles.		
5/30/60	**15**	13	1 Alley-Oop	[N]	Madison 130
9/12/60	**73**	6	2 Time Machine above 2 produced by Herb Alpert and Lou Adler	[N]	Madison 135
			JOE DARENSBOURG & HIS DIXIE FLYERS Born on 7/9/06 in Baton Rouge, LA. Clarinetist with Jack Teagarden, Bob Scobey, Kid Ory, and Louis Armstrong's All Stars.		
1/27/58	**43**	9	1 Yellow Dog Blues Best Seller #43 / Top 100 #45 written in 1928 by legendary composer, W.C. Handy	[I]	Lark 452
			FRED DARIAN Born on 6/16/27 in Detroit. Co-writer of the #1 hit, "Mr. Custer".		
2/27/61	**100**	1	1 Battle Of Gettysburg	[S]	JAF 2020
9/25/61	**96**	1	2 Johnny Willow		JAF 2023

DEBUT DATE	PEAK POS	WKS CHR		ARTIST — Record Title		Label & Number
				BOBBY DARIN		
				Born Walden Robert Cassotto on 5/14/36 in The Bronx, NY. Died of heart failure on 12/20/73 (37) in Los Angeles. Vocalist, piano, guitar, drums. First recorded in 1956 with "The Jaybirds" (Decca). First appeared on TV, in March, 1956, on the Tommy Dorsey Show. Married to actress Sandra Dee, 1960-67. Nominated for an Oscar for his performance in the film "Captain Newman, MD". Formed own record company, Direction, in 1968.		
6/23/58	**3**	15	1	**Splish Splash**		Atco 6117
				Hot 100 #3 / Best Seller #4 / Jockey #5 end		
7/28/58	**24**	10	2	Early In The Morning		Atco 6121
				THE RINKY-DINKS		
				Hot 100 #24 / Best Seller #24		
				originally issued on Brunswick as by the Ding Dongs (to conceal Darin's identity who was under contract at Atco). Atco took over the master and issued it as by The Rinky-Dinks		
10/06/58	**9**	19	3	**Queen Of The Hop**		Atco 6127
1/26/59	**38**	9	4	Plain Jane		Atco 6133
4/20/59	**2**[1]	17	5	**Dream Lover**		Atco 6140
8/24/59	**1**[9]	26	6	**Mack The Knife**		Atco 6147
				written in 1928 as "Moritat" or "Theme From The Threepenny Opera"		
1/18/60	**6**	14	7	**Beyond The Sea**		Atco 6158
3/21/60	**21**	9	8	Clementine		Atco 6161
				written in 1884 as "Oh, My Darling Clementine"		
5/23/60	**19**	11	9	Won't You Come Home Bill Bailey/		
				first popularized by Arthur Collins #1 hit in 1902		
7/11/60	**79**	2	10	I'll Be There		Atco 6167
9/05/60	**100**	1	11	Beachcomber	[I]	Atco 6173
				Bobby Darin piano solo		
9/26/60	**20**	12	12	Artificial Flowers/		
				from the musical "Tenderloin"		
9/26/60	**45**	9	13	Somebody To Love		Atco 6179
12/19/60	**51**	3	14	Christmas Auld Lang Syne/	[X]	
12/26/60	**95**	1	15	Child Of God	[X]	Atco 6183
2/06/61	**14**	10	16	Lazy River		Atco 6188
				revival of Hoagy Carmichael's 1932 hit (POS 19)		
6/12/61	**40**	6	17	Nature Boy		Atco 6196
9/04/61	**5**	11	18	**You Must Have Been A Beautiful Baby**		Atco 6206
				revival of Bing Crosby's #1 hit from 1938		
12/11/61+	**15**	13	19	Irresistible You/		
12/18/61+	**30**	10	20	Multiplication		Atco 6214
				from film "Come September" co-starring Bobby Darin & Sandra Dee		
3/31/62	**24**	8	21	What'd I Say (Part 1)		Atco 6221
7/07/62	**3**	12	22	**Things**		Atco 6229
9/29/62	**32**	8	23	If A Man Answers		Capitol 4837
				from the film of the same title (again with Darin & Dee)		
9/29/62	**42**	7	24	Baby Face		Atco 6236
				revival of Jan Garber's #1 hit of 1926		
12/15/62	**90**	1	25	I Found A New Baby		Atco 6244
1/19/63	**3**	14	26	**You're The Reason I'm Living**		Capitol 4897
5/11/63	**10**	10	27	**18 Yellow Roses**		Capitol 4970
8/24/63	**43**	9	28	Treat My Baby Good		Capitol 5019
11/23/63	**64**	7	29	Be Mad Little Girl		Capitol 5079
3/07/64	**93**	3	30	I Wonder Who's Kissing Her Now		Capitol 5126
5/16/64	**45**	9	31	Milord	[F]	Atco 6297
10/03/64	**86**	3	32	The Things In This House		Capitol 5257
2/06/65	**79**	3	33	Hello, Dolly!		Capitol 5359
4/30/66	**53**	7	34	Mame		Atlantic 2329
				above 2 are from Broadway musicals of the same title		
9/24/66	**8**	11	35	**If I Were A Carpenter**		Atlantic 2350
12/10/66	**66**	5	36	The Girl That Stood Beside Me		Atlantic 2367
1/14/67	**32**	8	37	Lovin' You		Atlantic 2376
4/08/67	**62**	5	38	The Lady Came From Baltimore		Atlantic 2395
7/29/67	**93**	2	39	Darling Be Home Soon		Atlantic 2420
2/08/69	**79**	3	40	Long Line Rider		Direction 350
1/06/73	**67**	8	41	Happy		Motown 1217
				Love Theme from the film "Lady Sings The Blues"		

DEBUT DATE	PEAK POS	WKS CHR	ARTIST — Record Title	Label & Number
			FLORRAINE DARLIN	
			Born Florraine Panza on 1/20/44 in Pittsburgh.	
8/25/62	**62**	7	1 Long As The Rose Is Red	Epic 9529
			answer song to Bobby Vinton's "Roses Are Red"	
			JAMES DARREN	
			Born James Ercolani on 10/3/36 in Philadelphia. In films from 1956-64. Played the part of 'Moondoggie' in 3 "Gidget" films. Starred in the TV series "The Time Tunnel", 1966-67.	
4/27/59	**41**	12	1 Gidget	Colpix 113
			from the film of the same title starring Darren	
8/03/59	**47**	8	2 Angel Face	Colpix 119
10/16/61	**3**	17	3 **Goodbye Cruel World**	Colpix 609
2/03/62	**6**	11	4 **Her Royal Majesty**	Colpix 622
4/14/62	**11**	10	5 Conscience	Colpix 630
6/30/62	**39**	8	6 Mary's Little Lamb	Colpix 644
10/13/62	**97**	1	7 Hail To The Conquering Hero	Colpix 655
2/09/63	**54**	6	8 Pin A Medal On Joey	Colpix 672
1/14/67	**35**	8	9 All	Warner 5874
			from the film "Run For Your Wife"	
3/19/77	**52**	9	10 You Take My Heart Away	Private S. 45136
			from the film "Rocky"	
			THE DARTELLS	
			6-man rock band from Oxnard, California.	
4/13/63	**11**	11	1 Hot Pastrami	Dot 16453
8/24/63	**99**	1	2 Dance, Everybody, Dance	Dot 16502
			SARAH DASH	
			Born on 8/18/43 in Trenton, NJ. Original member of The Blue-Belles and LaBelle.	
2/17/79	**71**	4	1 Sinner Man	Kirshner 4278
			DAVID & DAVID	
			Los Angeles duo: David Baerwald & David Ricketts.	
10/04/86	**37**	16	1 Welcome To The Boomtown	A&M 2857
			DAVID & JONATHAN	
			Songwriting/producing/vocal duo from Bristol, England: David Roger Greenway & Jonathan Roger Cook.	
1/08/66	**18**	9	1 Michelle	Capitol 5563
			written by Lennon/McCartney; produced by George Martin	
			F.R. DAVID	
			Born on 1/1/54 in Tunisia. Moved to Paris, France in 1964.	
7/23/83	**62**	9	1 Words	Carrere 101
			HUTCH DAVIE & his Honky Tonkers	
			Hutch was a leading musical arranger during the 50s.	
6/02/58	**51**	7	1 Woodchopper's Ball [I]	Atco 6110
			revival of Woody Herman's classic 1939 hit (POS 9)	
			JOHN DAVIS & The Monster Orchestra	
			John has written, produced and arranged for many top pop artists.	
12/23/78+	**89**	4	1 Ain't That Enough For You	Sam 5011
			MAC DAVIS	
			Born on 1/21/42 in Lubbock, Texas. Vocalist, guitar, composer. Worked as regional rep for Vee-Jay, and Liberty Records. Wrote "In The Ghetto", "Don't Cry Daddy", hits for Elvis Presley. Host of his own musical variety TV series, 1974-76. Appearances in several films, including "North Dallas Forty" in 1979.	
5/16/70	**53**	8	1 Whoever Finds This, I Love You	Columbia 45117
2/27/71	**92**	2	2 Beginning To Feel The Pain	Columbia 45302
7/01/72	**1^{3}**	18	3 ● **Baby Don't Get Hooked On Me**	Columbia 45618
11/25/72	**63**	7	4 Everybody Loves A Love Song	Columbia 45727
2/17/73	**73**	7	5 Dream Me Home	Columbia 45773
5/05/73	**88**	6	6 Your Side Of The Bed	Columbia 45839
3/30/74	**11**	28	7 One Hell Of A Woman	Columbia 46004
8/24/74	**9**	14	8 **Stop And Smell The Roses**	Columbia 10018
12/07/74+	**15**	11	9 Rock N' Roll (I Gave You The Best Years Of My Life)	Columbia 10070
4/05/75	**54**	4	10 (If You Add) All The Love In The World	Columbia 10111
5/31/75	**53**	8	11 Burnin' Thing	Columbia 10148
4/10/76	**76**	5	12 Forever Lovers	Columbia 10304

DEBUT DATE	PEAK POS	WKS CHR	ARTIST — Record Title	Label & Number
			MAC DAVIS — Cont'd	
3/22/80	43	12	13 It's Hard To Be Humble [N]	Casablanca 2244
10/18/80	51	9	14 Texas In My Rear View Mirror	Casablanca 2305
7/11/81	76	6	15 Secrets	Casablanca 2336
			PAUL DAVIS	
			Born in Meridian, Mississippi on 4/21/48. Singer, songwriter, producer.	
4/18/70	52	12	1 A Little Bit Of Soap	Bang 576
9/12/70	51	9	2 I Just Wanna Keep It Together	Bang 579
12/23/72+	68	9	3 Boogie Woogie Man	Bang 599
10/12/74+	23	18	4 Ride 'Em Cowboy	Bang 712
7/05/75	90	2	5 Keep Our Love Alive	Bang 718
4/24/76	45	10	6 Thinking Of You	Bang 724
8/07/76	35	9	7 Superstar	Bang 726
8/27/77+	7	40	8 **I Go Crazy**	Bang 733
5/20/78	51	6	9 Darlin' PAUL DAVIS featuring SUSAN COLLINS	Bang 736
8/26/78	17	21	10 Sweet Life	Bang 738
3/08/80	23	14	11 Do Right	Bang 4808
7/19/80	78	4	12 Cry Just A Little	Bang 4811
11/07/81+	11	19	13 Cool Night	Arista 0645
2/27/82	6	20	14 **'65 Love Affair**	Arista 0661
7/17/82	40	10	15 Love Or Let Me Be Lonely	Arista 0697
			SAMMY DAVIS, JR.	
			Born on 12/8/25 in New York City. Vocalist, dancer, actor. With father and uncle in dance act, Will Mastin Trio, from early 1940's. First recorded for Decca in 1954. Lost his left eye and had his nose smashed in an auto accident in Las Vegas on 11/19/54; returned to performing January, 1955. Frequent appearances on TV, Broadway, and in films.	
5/28/55	9	12	1 **Something's Gotta Give/** Best Seller #9 / Juke Box #16 / Jockey #20 from the film "Daddy Long Legs"	
7/02/55	20	1	2 Love Me Or Leave Me Jockey #20 from the film of the same title	Decca 29484
7/02/55	13	6	3 That Old Black Magic Jockey #13 / Juke Box #18	Decca 29541
11/26/55+	87	3	4 I'll Know from the film "Guys And Dolls"	Decca 29672
7/14/56	71	3	5 Five	Decca 29976
9/08/56	46	13	6 Earthbound	Decca 30035
11/17/56	59	4	7 New York's My Home	Decca 30111
9/01/62	17	15	8 What Kind Of Fool Am I from the musical "Stop The World-I Want To Get Off"	Reprise 20048
12/01/62	64	6	9 Me And My Shadow/ FRANK SINATRA & SAMMY DAVIS JR.	
12/22/62	94	3	10 Sam's Song [N] DEAN MARTIN & SAMMY DAVIS JR. Bing & Gary Crosby's version hit #3 in 1949	Reprise 20128
1/26/63	59	9	11 As Long As She Needs Me from Broadway's "Oliver!"	Reprise 20138
11/30/63+	17	17	12 The Shelter Of Your Arms	Reprise 20216
5/27/67	37	9	13 Don't Blame The Children [S]	Reprise 0566
5/25/68	93	3	14 Lonely Is The Name	Reprise 0673
12/14/68+	11	16	15 I've Gotta Be Me from the Broadway musical "Golden Rainbow"	Reprise 0779
3/11/72	1[3]	21	16● **The Candy Man** from the film "Willy Wonka And The Chocolate Factory"	MGM 14320
10/21/72	92	5	17 The People Tree	MGM 14426
			SKEETER DAVIS	
			Born Mary Penick on 12/30/31 in Dry Ridge, Kentucky. Recorded with her friend Betty Davis in early 50s as the Davis Sisters, until Betty was killed in a car accident on 8/2/53. Formerly married to TV's "Nashville Now" host, Ralph Emery.	
8/22/60	39	7	1 (I Can't Help You) I'm Falling Too	RCA 7767
12/12/60+	26	8	2 My Last Date (With You)	RCA 7825
1/26/63	2[1]	17	3 **The End Of The World**	RCA 8098
5/11/63	41	7	4 I'm Saving My Love	RCA 8176
9/07/63	7	13	5 **I Can't Stay Mad At You**	RCA 8219

DEBUT DATE	PEAK POS	WKS CHR	ARTIST — Record Title	Label & Number
			SKEETER DAVIS — Cont'd	
1/25/64	**47**	7	6 He Says The Same Things To Me/	
2/22/64	**92**	1	7 How Much Can A Lonely Heart Stand	RCA 8288
5/02/64	**48**	7	8 Gonna Get Along Without You Now	RCA 8347
			all of above (except #4) produced by Chet Atkins	
			THE SPENCER DAVIS GROUP	
			Formed in Birmingham, England in 1963. Consisted of Spencer Davis (vocals, rhythm guitar), Steve Winwood (lead vocals, lead guitar, keyboards), Muff Winwood (bass) and Pete York (drums). Steve Winwood left in 1967 to form the group Traffic.	
3/05/66	**76**	4	1 Keep On Running	Atco 6400
12/31/66+	**7**	13	2 **Gimme Some Lovin'**	United Art. 50108
3/25/67	**10**	9	3 **I'm A Man**	United Art. 50144
6/17/67	**47**	7	4 Somebody Help Me	United Art. 50162
9/16/67	**100**	1	5 Time Seller	United Art. 50202
			TIM DAVIS	
9/16/72	**91**	3	1 Buzzy Brown [N]	Metromedia 253
			TYRONE DAVIS	
			Born on 5/4/38 in Greenville, MS. To Saginaw, MI, 1939; to Chicago, 1959. Worked as valet/chauffeur for Freddie King, to 1962. Worked local clubs, discovered by Harold Burrage. First recorded for Four Brothers, 1965, as "Tyrone The Wonder Boy".	
12/21/68+	**5**	13	1 ● **Can I Change My Mind**	Dakar 602
3/22/69	**34**	7	2 Is It Something You've Got	Dakar 605
3/21/70	**3**	13	3 ● **Turn Back The Hands Of Time**	Dakar 616
6/27/70	**53**	9	4 I'll Be Right Here	Dakar 618
10/03/70	**58**	8	5 Let Me Back In	Dakar 621
3/20/71	**60**	7	6 Could I Forget You	Dakar 623
7/03/71	**75**	7	7 One-Way Ticket	Dakar 624
11/20/71	**94**	3	8 You Keep Me Holding On	Dakar 626
3/25/72	**61**	9	9 I Had It All The Time	Dakar 4501
4/21/73	**64**	9	10 Without You In My Life	Dakar 4519
7/28/73	**32**	9	11 There It Is	Dakar 4523
2/02/74	**57**	9	12 I Wish It Was Me	Dakar 4529
			all of above produced by Willie Henderson	
7/06/74	**89**	2	13 What Goes Up (Must Come Down)	Dakar 4532
9/25/76	**38**	11	14 Give It Up (Turn It Loose)	Columbia 10388
12/25/82+	**57**	6	15 Are You Serious	Highrise 2005
			DAWN	
			Vocal trio formed in New York City. Consisted of Tony Orlando, Telma Hopkins and Joyce Vincent. Orlando had recorded solo, 1961-63; Hopkins and Vincent had been back-up singers. Orlando was manager for April-Blackwood Music at the time of their first hit. All of their hits produced by Hank Medress (The Tokens) and Dave Appell.	
7/25/70	**3**	18	1 ● **Candida**	Bell 903
11/21/70+	**1**[3]	18	2 ● **Knock Three Times**	Bell 938
3/27/71	**25**	8	3 I Play And Sing	Bell 970
6/19/71	**33**	10	4 Summer Sand	Bell 45107
			DAWN featuring TONY ORLANDO:	
10/02/71	**39**	9	5 What Are You Doing Sunday	Bell 45141
1/29/72	**79**	4	6 Runaway/Happy Together	Bell 45175
6/24/72	**95**	3	7 Vaya Con Dios	Bell 45225
11/25/72+	**70**	8	8 You're A Lady	Bell 45285
2/17/73	**1**[4]	23	9 ● **Tie A Yellow Ribbon Round The Ole Oak Tree**	Bell 45318
7/14/73	**3**	16	10 ● **Say, Has Anybody Seen My Sweet Gypsy Rose**	Bell 45374
			TONY ORLANDO & DAWN:	
11/10/73	**27**	12	11 Who's In The Strawberry Patch With Sally	Bell 45424
3/30/74	**81**	5	12 It Only Hurts When I Try To Smile	Bell 45450
8/24/74	**7**	13	13 **Steppin' Out (Gonna Boogie Tonight)**	Bell 45601
12/21/74+	**11**	12	14 Look In My Eyes Pretty Woman	Bell 45620
3/15/75	**1**[3]	14	15 ● **He Don't Love You (Like I Love You)**	Elektra 45240
6/21/75	**14**	10	16 Mornin' Beautiful	Elektra 45260
8/30/75	**34**	7	17 You're All I Need To Get By	Elektra 45275
11/01/75	**49**	5	18 Skybird	Arista 0156
2/07/76	**22**	9	19 Cupid	Elektra 45302
4/02/77	**58**	4	20 Sing	Elektra 45387

DEBUT DATE	PEAK POS	WKS CHR	ARTIST — Record Title	Label & Number
			ARLAN DAY	
			Jazz pianist, vocalist from Manchester, England.	
10/17/81	**71**	7	1 I Surrender	Pasha 02480
			BOBBY DAY	
			Born Robert Byrd on 7/1/32 in Ft. Worth, Texas. To Watts, Los Angeles in 1948. Formed the Hollywood Flames in 1950. Group also known as: The Flames, Four Flames, Hollywood Four Flames, Jets, Tangiers, and then The Satellites. Bobby recorded with all of these groups, as a solo, and for a time with the duo, Bob & Earl. Today he is working in Los Angeles with Johnny Otis.	
11/18/57	**57**	8	1 Little Bitty Pretty One BOBBY DAY & THE SATELLITES	Class 211
8/04/58	**2**[2]	21	2 **Rock-in Robin/** Hot 100 #2 / Best Seller #4 end	
8/04/58	**41**	11	3 Over And Over revived by Dave Clark Five in 1965 (POS 1)	Class 229
12/28/58+	**54**	6	4 The Bluebird, The Buzzard & The Oriole	Class 241
4/20/59	**98**	1	5 That's All I Want	Class 245
6/22/59	**82**	1	6 Gotta New Girl	Class 252
			DORIS DAY	
			Born Doris Kappelhoff on 4/3/22 in Cincinnati. Doris sang briefly with Bob Crosby in 1940 and shortly thereafter became a major star with the Les Brown band ("Sentimental Journey"). Her great solo recording success was soon transcended by Hollywood as Doris became the #1 box office star of the late 50s and early 60s; her 1968-73 TV series was also popular.	
7/23/55	**13**	9	1 I'll Never Stop Loving You Jockey #13 / Best Seller #15 / Top 100 #93 pre from the film "Love Me Or Leave Me"	Columbia 40505
11/26/55	**83**	6	2 Ooh Bang Jiggilly Jang	Columbia 40581
1/07/56	**51**	7	3 Let It Ring	Columbia 40618
6/23/56	**2**[3]	27	4 **Whatever Will Be, Will Be (Que Sera, Sera)** Top 100 #2 / Jockey #2 / Best Seller #3 / Juke Box #3 from the film "The Man Who Knew Too Much"	Columbia 40704
10/20/56	**64**	10	5 Julie/ from the film of the same title	
10/20/56	**79**	4	6 Love In A Home from the Broadway musical "L'il Abner"	Columbia 40758
12/22/56+	**63**	11	7 The Party's Over from the Broadway musical "Bells Are Ringing"	Columbia 40798
4/20/57	**68**	6	8 Twelve O'Clock Tonight	Columbia 40870
4/21/58	**56**	12	9 Teacher's Pet from the Clark Gable/Doris Day film of the same title	Columbia 41123
7/21/58	**6**	14	10 **Everybody Loves A Lover** Jockey #6 end / Hot 100 #14 / Best Seller #17	Columbia 41195
10/27/58	**43**	8	11 Tunnel Of Love from the Doris Day film of the same title	Columbia 41252
5/11/59	**100**	1	12 Love Me In The Daytime	Columbia 41354
2/22/60	**50**	7	13 Anyway The Wind Blows from the film "Please Don't Eat The Daisies"	Columbia 41569
4/07/62	**98**	1	14 Lover Come Back from the Doris Day/Rock Hudson film of the same title 4, 7-14: orchestra directed by Frank DeVol	Columbia 42295
			MORRIS DAY	
			Leader of Minneapolis funk group, The Time (formerly Prince's backing band).	
9/28/85	**65**	12	1 The Oak Tree	Warner 28899
			DAYBREAK	
6/13/70	**94**	3	1 Good Morning Freedom	Uni 55234
			CORY DAYE	
			Born on 4/25/52 in the Bronx, New York. Lead singer of Dr. Buzzard's Original Savannah Band.	
10/27/79	**76**	3	1 Pow Wow	New York I. 11748
			DAYTON	
			Funk/rock ensemble from Dayton, Ohio.	
7/24/82	**58**	7	1 Hot Fun In The Summertime	Liberty 1468
			DAZZ BAND	
			Cleveland ultrafunk band, formerly Kinsman Dazz. "Dazz" means "danceable jazz".	
4/24/82	**5**	23	1 **Let It Whip**	Motown 1609
2/11/84	**61**	11	2 Joystick	Motown 1701

DEBUT DATE	PEAK POS	WKS CHR	ARTIST — Record Title		Label & Number
			DAZZ BAND — Cont'd		
12/01/84	**84**	7	3 Let It All Blow		Motown 1760
			THE DEADLY NIGHTSHADE		
			Female vocal, instrumental trio: Helen Hooke, Anne Bowen and Pamela Brandt.		
7/17/76	**79**	4	1 Mary Hartman, Mary Hartman disco theme from the TV serial of the same title		Phantom 10709
			DEAD OR ALIVE		
			British pop-rock quartet - Pete Burns, lead singer.		
6/01/85	**11**	18	1 You Spin Me Round (Like A Record)		Epic 04894
9/21/85	**75**	7	2 Lover Come Back To Me		Epic 05607
11/29/86+	**15**	22	3 Brand New Lover		Epic 06374
			BILL DEAL & THE RHONDELS		
			8-man New York City brassy-rock band.		
1/18/69	**39**	10	1 May I		Heritage 803
4/19/69	**35**	10	2 I've Been Hurt		Heritage 812
8/16/69	**23**	9	3 What Kind Of Fool Do You Think I Am		Heritage 817
11/15/69	**85**	5	4 Swingin' Tight		Heritage 818
3/21/70	**62**	7	5 Nothing Succeeds Like Success		Heritage 821
			DEAN & JEAN		
			Welton Young & Brenda Lee Jones from Dayton, Ohio.		
11/02/63+	**35**	13	1 Tra La La La Suzy		Rust 5067
2/22/64	**32**	8	2 Hey Jean, Hey Dean		Rust 5075
5/30/64	**91**	5	3 I Wanna Be Loved		Rust 5081
			DEAN & MARC		
			Brothers Dean & Marc Mathis who later joined with Larry Henley as The Newbeats.		
3/23/59	**42**	8	1 Tell Him No		Bullseye 1025
			DEBBIE DEAN		
2/06/61	**92**	2	1 Don't Let Him Shop Around answer song to the Miracles' "Shop Around"		Motown 1007
			JIMMY DEAN		
			Born Seth Ward on 8/10/28 in Plainview, Texas. Vocalist, piano, guitar, composer. With Tennessee Haymakers in Washington, DC, 1948. Own Texas Wildcats in 1952. Recorded for Four Star in 1952. Own CBS-TV series, 1957-58; ABC-TV series, 1963-66.		
10/14/57	**67**	8	1 Deep Blue Sea		Columbia 40995
12/23/57	**32**	5	2 Little Sandy Sleighfoot Top 100 #32 / Best Seller #37	[X-N]	Columbia 41025
10/02/61	**1**[5]	16	3● **Big Bad John**		Columbia 42175
1/06/62	**24**	7	4 Dear Ivan	[S]	Columbia 42259
1/20/62	**26**	9	5 To A Sleeping Beauty/ background music: "Memories"	[S]	
1/27/62	**22**	8	6 The Cajun Queen	[S]	Columbia 42282
3/31/62	**8**	11	7 **P.T. 109** an account of John F. Kennedy's heroism after his torpedo boat was destroyed in 1943		Columbia 42338
6/23/62	**41**	8	8 Steel Men		Columbia 42483
9/15/62	**29**	9	9 Little Black Book		Columbia 42529
12/01/62	**73**	6	10 Gonna Raise A Rukus Tonight		Columbia 42600
6/26/65	**91**	3	11 The First Thing Ev'ry Morning (And The Last Thing Ev'ry Night)		Columbia 43263
5/15/76	**35**	4	12● 'I.O.U.' Jimmy Dean's ode of thanks to his mother	[S]	Casino 052
			DeBARGE		
			Family group from Grand Rapids, MI. Consisted of lead vocalist Eldra (keyboards), Mark (trumpet, saxophone), James (keyboards), Randy (bass) and Bunny DeBarge (vocals). Brothers Bobby and Tommy were in Switch.		
2/05/83	**31**	17	1 I Like It		Gordy 1645
4/23/83	**17**	19	2 All This Love		Gordy 1660
10/15/83+	**18**	21	3 Time Will Reveal		Gordy 1705
3/17/84	**45**	11	4 Love Me In A Special Way		Gordy 1723
2/16/85	**3**	22	5 **Rhythm Of The Night** from the Berry Gordy film "The Last Dragon"		Gordy 1770
6/01/85	**6**	19	6 **Who's Holding Donna Now**		Gordy 1793
8/31/85	**46**	10	7 You Wear It Well		Gordy 1804

DEBUT DATE	PEAK POS	WKS CHR	ARTIST — Record Title		Label & Number
			DeBARGE — Cont'd		
12/07/85+	**75**	7	8 The Heart Is Not So Smart		Gordy 1822
			above 2: **EL DeBARGE with DeBARGE**		
			above 4 from the DeBarge LP "Rhythm Of The Night"		
			CHICO DeBARGE		
			DeBarge sibling, but not a member of the group DeBarge.		
11/08/86+	**21**	20	1 Talk To Me		Motown 1858
			EL DeBARGE		
			Eldra DeBarge (b: 6/4/61). Lead singer of family group DeBarge.		
4/26/86	**3**	19	1 **Who's Johnny**		Gordy 1842
			theme from the film "Short Circuit"		
8/09/86	**43**	12	2 Love Always		Gordy 1857
12/27/86+	**70**	9	3 Someone		Gordy 1867
			CHRIS DeBURGH		
			Born Christopher John Davidson on 10/15/50 in Ireland.		
4/30/83	**34**	14	1 Don't Pay The Ferryman		A&M 2511
8/20/83	**71**	5	2 Ship To Shore		A&M 2565
6/30/84	**44**	13	3 High On Emotion		A&M 2643
			NICK DeCARO		
			Producer of albums for Mac Davis, Helen Reddy, Samantha Sang, and others.		
1/11/69	**95**	1	1 If I Only Had Time	[I]	A&M 1000
			THE DeCASTRO SISTERS		
			Peggy, Babette & Cherie - raised on their father's sugar plantation in Cuba.		
5/07/55	**17**	4	1 Boom Boom Boomerang		Abbott 3003
			Juke Box #17 / Best Seller #24		
			bass voice: Thurl Ravenscroft		
12/17/55+	**66**	6	2 Too Late Now		Abbott 3011
12/31/55	**84**	1	3 Snowbound For Christmas	[X]	Abbott 3012
10/20/56	**74**	5	4 It's Yours		RCA 6661
8/18/58	**99**	1	5 Who Are They To Say		ABC-Para. 9932
1/05/59	**76**	4	6 Teach Me Tonight Cha Cha		ABC-Para. 9988
			new version of their #2 hit from 1954		
			DEE JAY & The Runaways		
5/07/66	**45**	11	1 Peter Rabbit		Smash 2034
			DAVE DEE, DOZY, BEAKY, MICK & TICH		
			English quintet: David Harmon, Trevor Davies, John Dymond, Michael Wilson and Ian Amey.		
1/06/68	**52**	6	1 Zabadak	[F]	Imperial 66270
			JIMMY DEE & The Offbeats		
1/06/58	**47**	10	1 Henrietta		Dot 15664
			Best Seller #47 / Top 100 #53		
			JOEY DEE & THE STARLITERS		
			Born Joseph DiNicola on 6/11/40 in Passaic, NJ. Joey first recorded for the Bonus and Scepter labels in 1960. Joey & The Starliters became the house band at the Peppermint Lounge, New York City in September, 1960. Own club, The Starliter, New York City, 1964. Band then included, for a time, 3 members who later formed the Young Rascals, and Jimi Hendrix, guitar, 1965-66. In films "Hey, Let's Twist" and "Two Tickets To Paris".		
11/20/61+	**1**[3]	18	1 **Peppermint Twist - Part I**		Roulette 4401
			inspired by New York City's Peppermint Lounge club		
2/17/62	**20**	6	2 Hey, Let's Twist/		
3/10/62	**74**	3	3 Roly Poly		Roulette 4408
3/24/62	**6**	12	4 **Shout - Part I**		Roulette 4416
8/25/62	**18**	10	5 What Kind Of Love Is This		Roulette 4438
			from the film "Two Tickets To Paris"		
11/03/62	**61**	7	6 I Lost My Baby		Roulette 4456
2/16/63	**100**	1	7 Baby, You're Driving Me Crazy		Roulette 4467
4/27/63	**36**	7	8 Hot Pastrami With Mashed Potatoes - Part I		Roulette 4488
7/20/63	**89**	3	9 Dance, Dance, Dance		Roulette 4503
			6, 7 & 9 shown only as: **JOEY DEE**		

DEBUT DATE	PEAK POS	WKS CHR	ARTIST — Record Title	Label & Number
			JOHNNY DEE - see JOHN D. LOUDERMILK	
			KIKI DEE	
			Born Pauline Matthews on 3/6/47 in Yorkshire, England.	
3/27/71	**87**	3	1 Love Makes The World Go Round	Rare Earth 5025
9/14/74	**12**	20	2 I've Got The Music In Me **THE KIKI DEE BAND**	Rocket 40293
5/24/75	**74**	3	3 How Glad I Am	Rocket 40401
3/06/76	**82**	4	4 Once A Fool	Rocket 40506
7/04/76	**1**[4]	20	5 ● **Don't Go Breaking My Heart** **ELTON JOHN & KIKI DEE**	Rocket 40585
			LENNY DEE	
			Organist.	
2/12/55	**19**	15	1 Plantation Boogie [I] Juke Box #19 / Best Seller #23	Decca 29360
			LOLA DEE	
11/12/55	**72**	2	1 Paper Roses backing vocals: The Jack Halloran Choir	Wing 90015
			TOMMY DEE	
			Boston-bred disc jockey. Worked in Flagstaff and Yuma, AZ, and San Bernardino, CA.	
3/30/59	**11**	12	1 Three Stars [S] a tribute to Buddy Holly, Ritchie Valens, and The Big Bopper - narration by Tommy Dee; singing by Carol Kay & the Teen-Aires	Crest 1057
			DEELE	
			R&B funk sextet from Cincinnati led by Darnell "Dee" Bristol.	
1/21/84	**77**	8	1 Body Talk	Solar 69785
			DEEP PURPLE	
			British hard-rock band - original lineup: Ritchie Blackmore (guitar), Rod Evans (vocals), Jon Lord (keyboards), Ian Paice (drums) and Nicky Simper (bass). Evans and Simper left in 1969, replaced by Ian Gillan and Roger Glover. Numerous personnel changes from late 1973 on.	
8/17/68	**4**	10	1 **Hush**	Tetragramm. 1503
11/09/68	**38**	8	2 Kentucky Woman	Tetragramm. 1508
1/25/69	**53**	5	3 River Deep-Mountain High	Tetragramm. 1514
12/05/70	**66**	6	4 Black Night	Warner 7405
4/21/73	**60**	6	5 Woman From Tokyo	Warner 7737
5/26/73	**4**	16	6 ● **Smoke On The Water**	Warner 7710
3/23/74	**91**	7	7 Might Just Take Your Life	Warner 7784
1/05/85	**61**	7	8 Knocking At Your Back Door reunion of Blackmore, Gillan, Glover, Lord and Paice	Mercury 880477
			RICK DEES	
			Born Rigdon Osmond Dees III in Memphis. Disc Jockey working at WMPS-Memphis when he conceived the idea for "Disco Duck". Currently one of America's top radio DJs.	
8/14/76	**1**[1]	25	1 ▲ **Disco Duck (Part 1)** [N]	RSO 857
1/15/77	**56**	6	2 Dis-Gorilla (Part 1) [N] above 2: **RICK DEES & HIS CAST OF IDIOTS**	RSO 866
12/15/84	**75**	5	3 Eat My Shorts [N] flip side "Get Nekked" 'Bubbled Under' (POS 104)	Atlantic 89601
			DEF LEPPARD	
			Heavy-metal quintet formed in Sheffield, England in 1977: Joe Elliott, lead singer; Pete Willis and Steve Clark, lead guitars; Rick Savage, bass; and Rick Allen, drums (lost his left arm in an auto accident on New Year's Eve in 1984). Phil Collen replaced Pete Willis in late 1982.	
3/12/83	**12**	17	1 Photograph	Mercury 811215
6/11/83	**16**	15	2 Rock Of Ages	Mercury 812604
9/03/83	**28**	14	3 Foolin'	Mercury 814178
6/09/84	**61**	8	4 Bringin' On The Heartbreak remix - originally on the 1981 LP "High 'n' Dry"	Mercury 818779
			THE DeFRANCO FAMILY featuring TONY DeFRANCO	
			5-member family from Ontario, Canada: Tony (age 13), Merlina (16), Nino (17), Marisa (18) and Benny (19).	
9/08/73	**3**	17	1 ● **Heartbeat - It's A Lovebeat**	20th Century 2030
12/29/73+	**32**	12	2 Abra-Ca-Dabra	20th Century 2070
5/04/74	**18**	13	3 Save The Last Dance For Me	20th Century 2088

DEBUT DATE	PEAK POS	WKS CHR	ARTIST — Record Title	Label & Number
			DeJOHN SISTERS	
			Julie & Dux DeGiovanni from Chester, Pennsylvania.	
12/25/54+	**6**	13	1 **(My Baby Don't Love Me) No More**	Epic 9085
			Jockey #6 / Best Seller #8 / Juke Box #11	
11/26/55	**97**	1	2 C'est La Vie	Epic 9131
8/18/58	**73**	2	3 Straighten Up & Fly Right	Sunbeam 106
			DESMOND DEKKER & THE ACES	
			Desmond (born Desmond Dacris), a Jamaican, was reggae's first successful artist.	
5/17/69	**9**	10	1 **Israelites**	Uni 55129
			THE DEL FUEGOS	
			Boston rock quartet: Dan Zanes (guitar/vocalist), Tom Lloyd (bass), Warren Zanes (guitar) and Woody Giessmann (drums).	
5/31/86	**87**	4	1 I Still Want You	Slash 28822
			THE DELACARDOS	
			R&B quartet formed while in high school in Charlotte, NC.	
6/05/61	**78**	5	1 Hold Back The Tears	United Art. 310
			DELANEY & BONNIE & FRIENDS	
			Delaney Bramlett (b: 7/1/39) & wife Bonnie Lynn Bramlett (b: 11/8/44) & Friends - backing artists who included at various times Leon Russell, Rita Coolidge, Dave Mason, Eric Clapton, Duane Allman, and many others. Friends Bobby Whitlock, Carl Radle and Jim Gordon later became Eric Clapton's Dominos. Delaney & Bonnie dissolved their marriage and group in 1972. Also see The Shindogs.	
2/21/70	**84**	3	1 Comin' Home	Atco 6725
			featuring Eric Clapton, lead guitar	
5/23/70	**75**	4	2 Free The People/	
8/15/70	**43**	8	3 Soul Shake	Atco 6756
5/22/71	**13**	15	4 Never Ending Song Of Love	Atco 6804
			DELANEY & BONNIE:	
9/25/71	**20**	10	5 Only You Know And I Know	Atco 6838
1/22/72	**59**	5	6 Move 'Em Out	Atco 6866
4/29/72	**99**	2	7 Where There's A Will There's A Way	Atco 6883
			DELBERT & GLEN	
			Delbert McClinton & Glen Clark.	
12/02/72	**90**	3	1 I Received A Letter	Clean 60003
			THE DELEGATES	
			A Dickey Goodman type recording, featuring disc jockey Bob DeCarlo.	
10/21/72	**8**	8	1 **Convention '72** [N]	Mainstream 5525
			featuring bits of some of the top pop hits of 1972	
			DELEGATION	
			Soul/disco trio from England: Ricky Bailey, Ray Patterson and Len Coley.	
2/03/79	**45**	12	1 Oh Honey	Shady Brook 1048
			THE DELFONICS	
			Soul group from Philadelphia. Formed in 1965 as the Four Gents. Consisted of William and Wilbert Hart, Ritchie Daniels, and Randy Cain. First recorded for Moon Shot, 1967. Daniels left for the service in 1968, group continued as a trio. Cain was replaced by Major Harris, formerly with the Jarmels, in 1971. Harris went solo, 1974.	
2/03/68	**4**	15	1 **La - La - Means I Love You**	Philly Groove 150
4/27/68	**42**	9	2 I'm Sorry	Philly Groove 151
5/04/68	**92**	4	3 He Don't Really Love You	Moon Shot 6703
8/31/68	**35**	10	4 Break Your Promise	Philly Groove 152
12/07/68+	**35**	9	5 Ready Or Not Here I Come (Can't Hide From Love)/	
2/22/69	**72**	3	6 Somebody Loves You	Philly Groove 154
6/14/69	**94**	2	7 Funny Feeling	Philly Groove 156
8/16/69	**40**	10	8 You Got Yours And I'll Get Mine	Philly Groove 157
1/10/70	**10**	14	9 ● **Didn't I (Blow Your Mind This Time)**	Philly Groove 161
6/06/70	**40**	9	10 Trying To Make A Fool Of Me	Philly Groove 162
			1-10: produced by Thom Bell, and written by Bell & William Hart	
9/19/70	**53**	8	11 When You Get Right Down To It	Philly Groove 163
6/19/71	**52**	8	12 Hey! Love/	
		7	13 Over And Over	Philly Groove 166
10/30/71	**81**	6	14 Walk Right Up To The Sun	Philly Groove 169
6/24/72	**86**	3	15 Tell Me This Is A Dream	Philly Groove 172
6/09/73	**91**	4	16 I Don't Want To Make You Wait	Philly Groove 176

DEBUT DATE	PEAK POS	WKS CHR	ARTIST — Record Title	Label & Number
			DELIVERANCE	
8/30/80	**71**	5	1 Leaving L.A.	Columbia 11320
			THE DELL-VIKINGS	
			Racially integrated R&B/rock group formed while in the Air Force in Pittsburgh, 1955; consisted of Norman Wright, Krips Johnson, Gus Backus, David Lerchey and Clarence Quick. Gus & David were white, others black. First recorded for Fee Bee and Luniverse labels, then Dot. After discharge from the Air Force, Krips formed a new Dell-Vikings for the Dot label, while Gus and the other members formed a new Del Vikings group for Mercury.	
2/16/57	**4**	31	1 **Come Go With Me**	Dot 15538
			Best Seller #4 / Top 100 #5 / Jockey #6 / Juke Box #6	
7/08/57	**9**	18	2 **Whispering Bells**	Dot 15592
			Top 100 #9 / Best Seller #10 / Jockey #19	
7/15/57	**12**	13	3 Cool Shake	Mercury 71132
			DEL VIKINGS	
			Jockey #12 / Top 100 #46	
			THE DELLS	
			R&B vocal group formed at Thornton Township High School, Harvey, IL. Consisted of Johnny Funches, lead; Marvin Junior, tenor; Verne Allison, tenor; Mickey McGill, baritone; and Chuck Barksdale, bass. First recorded as the El-Rays for Chess, 1953. Recorded for Vee-Jay Records, 1955-65. Group remained intact into the 80s, with exception of Funches, who was replaced by Johnny Carter (ex-Flamingos) in 1960.	
12/22/62	**97**	3	1 The (Bossa Nova) Bird	Argo 5428
11/04/67	**61**	10	2 O-O, I Love You	Cadet 5574
1/20/68	**20**	11	3 There Is	Cadet 5590
4/13/68	**44**	8	4 Wear It On Our Face	Cadet 5599
6/29/68	**10**	13	5 **Stay In My Corner**	Cadet 5612
			original version on Vee-Jay hit POS 23 on the R&B charts in 1965	
10/12/68	**18**	8	6 Always Together	Cadet 5621
12/28/68+	**38**	9	7 Does Anybody Know I'm Here	Cadet 5631
3/08/69	**92**	4	8 Hallways Of My Mind/	
4/12/69	**98**	2	9 I Can't Do Enough	Cadet 5636
5/24/69	**22**	10	10 I Can Sing A Rainbow/Love Is Blue	Cadet 5641
8/16/69	**10**	11	11 **Oh, What A Night**	Cadet 5649
			original version on Vee-Jay hit POS 4 on the R&B charts in 1956	
11/01/69	**42**	8	12 On The Dock Of The Bay	Cadet 5658
1/24/70	**43**	8	13 Oh What A Day	Cadet 5663
4/18/70	**51**	8	14 Open Up My Heart/	
		4	15 Nadine	Cadet 5667
7/18/70	**74**	4	16 Long Lonely Nights	Cadet 5672
2/06/71	**92**	2	17 The Glory Of Love	Cadet 5679
8/14/71	**30**	12	18 The Love We Had (Stays On My Mind)	Cadet 5683
2/26/72	**94**	3	19 It's All Up To You	Cadet 5689
4/21/73	**34**	16	20● Give Your Baby A Standing Ovation	Cadet 5696
10/06/73	**51**	8	21 My Pretending Days Are Over	Cadet 5698
1/19/74	**60**	7	22 I Miss You	Cadet 5700
7/06/74	**94**	2	23 I Wish It Was Me You Loved	Cadet 5702
10/26/74	**87**	3	24 Bring Back The Love Of Yesterday	Cadet 5703
			AL DeLORY	
			Producer/arranger/conductor for Glen Campbell, The Lettermen, & other major artists.	
6/13/70	**70**	12	1 Song From M*A*S*H [I]	Capitol 2811
			theme for the movie and TV series "MA*S*H"	
			JIMMY DELPHS	
			Soul singer from Toledo, Ohio.	
5/25/68	**96**	4	1 Don't Sign The Paper Baby (I Want You Back)	Karen 1538
			RALPH DeMARCO	
			Singer from the Bronx, New York. Age 17 during "Old Shep".	
11/09/59	**91**	2	1 Old Shep	Guaranteed 202
			written by Red Foley in 1949	
			NICKEY DeMATTEO	
			Singer from Philadelphia. Age 18 during "Suddenly".	
3/07/60	**90**	2	1 Suddenly	Guyden 2024

DEBUT DATE	PEAK POS	WKS CHR	ARTIST — Record Title		Label & Number
			THE DEMENSIONS		
			Vocal group from the Bronx, New York: Phil Del Giudice (lead), Lenny Dell, Howard Margolin and Marisa Martelli.		
7/04/60	**16**	15	1 Over The Rainbow		Mohawk 116
			first sung by Judy Garland in the movie "The Wizard Of Oz"		
3/02/63	**95**	3	2 My Foolish Heart		Coral 62344
			MARTIN DENNY		
			Born on 4/10/21 in New York City. Composer, arranger, pianist. Originated the "Exotic Sounds of Martin Denny" in Hawaii, featuring Julius Wechter (Baja Marimba Band) on vibes and marimba.		
			THE EXOTIC SOUNDS OF MARTIN DENNY:		
4/13/59	**4**	16	1 **Quiet Village**	[I]	Liberty 55162
			written by Les Baxter		
7/20/59	**88**	2	2 Martinique	[I]	Liberty 55199
10/26/59	**28**	8	3 The Enchanted Sea	[I]	Liberty 55212
			MARTIN DENNY & HIS ORCHESTRA:		
7/14/62	**50**	15	4 A Taste Of Honey	[I]	Liberty 55470
			JOHN DENVER		
			Born John Henry Deutschendorf on 12/31/43 in Roswell, New Mexico. To Los Angeles in 1964. With Chad Mitchell Trio, 1965-68. Wrote "Leaving On A Jet Plane". Starred in the film "Oh, God" in 1978.		
4/10/71	**2**[1]	23	1● **Take Me Home, Country Roads**		RCA 0445
			backing vocals by Fat City (Bill Danoff & Taffy Nivert)		
11/06/71	**47**	11	2 Friends With You		RCA 0567
3/11/72	**81**	3	3 Everyday		RCA 0647
			written by Buddy Holly		
7/22/72	**88**	6	4 Goodbye Again		RCA 0737
11/25/72+	**9**	19	5 **Rocky Mountain High**		RCA 0829
5/26/73	**62**	10	6 I'd Rather Be A Cowboy		RCA 0955
9/15/73	**89**	5	7 Farewell Andromeda (Welcome To My Morning)		RCA 0067
12/22/73+	**69**	5	8 Please, Daddy		RCA 0182
1/26/74	**1**[1]	18	9● **Sunshine On My Shoulders**		RCA 0213
6/01/74	**1**[2]	17	10● **Annie's Song**		RCA 0295
			written by Denver for his wife Ann Martell (married 1967-83)		
9/21/74	**5**	16	11● **Back Home Again**		RCA 10065
12/28/74+	**13**	11	12 Sweet Surrender		RCA 10148
3/22/75	**1**[1]	19	13● **Thank God I'm A Country Boy**		RCA 10239
			above 2 recorded live at Universal City Amphitheater, California		
8/16/75	**1**[1]	18	14● **I'm Sorry/**		
		10	15 Calypso		RCA 10353
			dedicated to Jacques Cousteau and those who served on his ship		
12/06/75+	**13**	12	16 Fly Away		RCA 10517
			backing vocals by Olivia Newton-John		
12/13/75	**58**	4	17 Christmas For Cowboys	[X]	RCA 10464
3/06/76	**29**	8	18 Looking For Space		RCA 10586
5/08/76	**60**	4	19 It Makes Me Giggle		RCA 10687
9/11/76	**36**	7	20 Like A Sad Song		RCA 10774
12/25/76+	**65**	7	21 Baby, You Look Good To Me Tonight		RCA 10854
3/12/77	**32**	11	22 My Sweet Lady		RCA 10911
			also the flip side of "Thank God I'm A Country Boy"		
11/26/77+	**44**	10	23 How Can I Leave You Again		RCA 11036
3/04/78	**59**	7	24 It Amazes Me		RCA 11214
4/29/78	**55**	5	25 I Want To Live		RCA 11267
2/23/80	**52**	10	26 Autograph		RCA 11915
6/21/80	**97**	3	27 Dancing With The Mountains		RCA 12017
			all of above produced by Milton Okun		
6/13/81	**36**	20	28 Some Days Are Diamonds (Some Days Are Stone)		RCA 12246
10/31/81	**66**	7	29 The Cowboy And The Lady		RCA 12345
1/16/82	**59**	7	30 Perhaps Love		Columbia 02679
			PLACIDO DOMINGO & JOHN DENVER		
3/06/82	**31**	14	31 Shanghai Breezes		RCA 13071
7/31/82	**78**	5	32 Seasons Of The Heart		RCA 13270
11/10/84	**85**	4	33 Love Again		RCA 13931
			JOHN DENVER & SYLVIE VARTAN		

DEBUT DATE	PEAK POS	WKS CHR	ARTIST — Record Title	Label & Number
			DEODATO	
			Born Eumire Deodato Almeida on 6/21/42 in Rio de Janeiro, Brzail. Keyboardist, composer, arranger, producer. Kool & The Gang's producer from 1979-82.	
2/03/73	**2^{1}**	12	1 **Also Sprach Zarathustra** .... [I]	CTI 12
			theme from the film "2001: A Space Odyssey" - written by classical composer Richard Strauss in 1896	
8/25/73	**41**	8	2 Rhapsody In Blue .... [I]	CTI 16
			the classic George Gershwin tune; a hit for Paul Whiteman in 1924	
10/23/76	**84**	6	3 Peter Gunn .... [I]	MCA 40631
6/19/82	**70**	5	4 Happy Hour	Warner 29984
			lead vocal: Kelly Barretto	
			DEPECHE MODE	
			All-synthesized band formed in Basildon, England, consisting of David Gahan (vocals), Martin Gore, Vince Clarke and Andy Fletcher. Clarke left in 1982, replaced by Alan Wilder.	
5/25/85	**13**	18	1 People Are People	Sire 29221
9/07/85	**87**	3	2 Master And Servant	Sire 28918
			DEREK	
			Derek is Johnny Cymbal.	
10/26/68+	**11**	15	1 Cinnamon	Bang 558
2/22/69	**59**	6	2 Back Door Man	Bang 566
			DEREK & THE DOMINOS	
			A gathering of alumni from Delaney & Bonnie & Friends. Featuring Eric Clapton (Derek), Bobby Whitlock, Jim Gordon and Carl Radle (died on 5/30/80).	
2/27/71	**91**	2	1 Bell Bottom Blues	Atco 6803
3/27/71	**51**	10	2 Layla	Atco 6809
			Layla: nickname of George Harrison's wife	
5/13/72	**10**	15	3 **Layla** .... [R]	Atco 6809
			featuring Duane Allman, lead guitar	
			RICK DERRINGER	
			Born Richard Zehringer on 8/5/47 in Celina, Ohio. Lead singer and guitarist of The McCoys. Performed on and produced sessions for both Edgar & Johnny Winter's bands.	
1/19/74	**23**	14	1 Rock And Roll, Hoochie Koo	Blue Sky 2751
4/27/74	**80**	5	2 Teenage Love Affair	Blue Sky 2572
4/05/75	**94**	4	3 Hang On Sloopy	Blue Sky 2755
			revival of Rick Derringer's group, The McCoys, #1 hit from 1965	
8/28/76	**86**	2	4 Let Me In	Blue Sky 2765
			shown only as: **DERRINGER**	
			SUGAR PIE DeSANTO	
			Real name: Empeylia Marsema Balinton. Born in New York City.	
4/18/64	**48**	5	1 Slip-In Mules (No High Heel Sneakers)	Checker 1073
12/18/65	**96**	1	2 Do I Make Myself Clear	Cadet 5519
8/13/66	**97**	2	3 In The Basement - Part 1	Cadet 5539
			above 2: **ETTA JAMES & SUGAR PIE DeSANTO**	
			TERI DeSARIO	
			Singer/songwriter from Miami.	
7/01/78	**43**	12	1 Ain't Nothing Gonna Keep Me From You	Casablanca 929
11/17/79+	**2^{2}**	23	2● **Yes, I'm Ready**	Casablanca 2227
6/28/80	**66**	6	3 Dancin' In The Streets	Casablanca 2278
			above 2: **TERI DeSARIO with K.C.**	
			JACKIE DeSHANNON	
			Born Sharon Myers on 8/21/44 in Hazel, KY. Vocalist, composer. On radio at age six. First recorded (as Sherry Lee Myers) for Glenn in 1959. To Los Angeles in 1960. Attained prominence as a prolific songwriter (over 600 to date). Co-writer of mega-hit "Bette Davis Eyes". Toured with The Beatles on 26 concerts in 1964. Films "Surf Party", "C'mon Let's Live A Little", and "Hide And Seek".	
2/23/63	**97**	2	1 Faded Love	Liberty 55526
5/18/63	**84**	4	2 Needles And Pins	Liberty 55563
1/25/64	**99**	1	3 When You Walk In The Room	Liberty 55645
5/22/65	**7**	13	4 **What The World Needs Now Is Love**	Imperial 66110
10/02/65	**66**	6	5 A Lifetime Of Loneliness	Imperial 66132
5/28/66	**83**	3	6 Come And Get Me	Imperial 66171
			above 3 written and produced by Burt Bacharach & Hal David	
9/10/66	**68**	6	7 I Can Make It With You	Imperial 66202
8/24/68	**55**	8	8 The Weight	Imperial 66313
6/28/69	**4**	14	9● **Put A Little Love In Your Heart**	Imperial 66385

DEBUT DATE	PEAK POS	WKS CHR	ARTIST — Record Title	Label & Number
			JACKIE DeSHANNON — Cont'd	
11/01/69	**40**	8	10 Love Will Find A Way	Imperial 66419
3/07/70	**82**	4	11 Brighton Hill	Imperial 66438
5/30/70	**96**	1	12 You Keep Me Hangin' On/Hurt So Bad	Imperial 66452
8/08/70	**84**	7	13 It's So Nice	Liberty 56187
6/03/72	**76**	9	14 Vanilla Olay	Atlantic 2871
10/29/77	**68**	10	15 Don't Let The Flame Burn Out	Amherst 725
3/08/80	**86**	5	16 I Don't Need You Anymore from the movie soundtrack "Together?"	RCA 11902
			JOHNNY DESMOND Born Giovanni Desimons on 11/14/20 in Detroit. Johnny sang with Bob Crosby, Gene Krupa, and Glenn Miller's military band, and throughout the 50s was featured on the "Breakfast Club" radio show. Johnny died on 9/6/85 (64).	
3/26/55	**6**	11	1 **Play Me Hearts And Flowers (I Wanna Cry)** Jockey #6 / Juke Box #11 / Best Seller #16	Coral 61379
8/13/55	**3**	16	2 **The Yellow Rose Of Texas** Jockey #3 / Juke Box #4 / Best Seller #6 / Top 100 #16 pre	Coral 61476
11/19/55	**17**	11	3 Sixteen Tons Jockey #17 / Top 100 #50	Coral 61529
5/27/57	**62**	2	4 A White Sport Coat (And A Pink Carnation) above 3: orchestra directed by Dick Jacobs	Coral 61835
			THE DETERGENTS Trio from New York: Ron Dante (Archies/Cuff Links), Tommy Wynn and Danny Jordan.	
12/05/64+	**19**	8	1 Leader Of The Laundromat [N] parody of the Shangri-Las' "Leader Of The Pack"	Roulette 4590
3/20/65	**89**	3	2 Double-O-Seven [N]	Roulette 4603
			DETROIT EMERALDS Soul group formed in Little Rock, AR by the Tilmon brothers: Abrim (d: 1982, heart attack), Ivory, Cleophus and Raymond. First recorded for Ric-Tic in 1968. Abrim, Ivory and friend James Mitchell then signed as a trio with Westbound in 1970. Cousin "Sweet" James Epps sang in The Fantastic Four.	
3/30/68	**89**	5	1 Show Time	Ric-Tic 135
2/20/71	**43**	14	2 Do Me Right	Westbound 172
8/14/71	**91**	4	3 Wear This Ring (With Love)	Westbound 181
1/08/72	**36**	13	4 You Want It, You Got It	Westbound 192
5/27/72	**24**	17	5 Baby Let Me Take You (In My Arms)	Westbound 203
5/14/77	**90**	5	6 Feel The Need	Westbound 55401
			WILLIAM DeVAUGHN Vocalist, songwriter, guitarist, from Washington, DC. Worked for Federal Government. Backed on hits by MFSB band.	
5/04/74	**4**	18	1 ● **Be Thankful For What You Got**	Roxbury 0236
9/07/74	**43**	9	2 Blood Is Thicker Than Water	Roxbury 2001
			DEVICE Los Angeles-based pop trio: Holly Knight (keyboards/bass), Gene Black (guitar) and Paul Engemann (lead singer).	
6/14/86	**35**	14	1 Hanging On A Heart Attack	Chrysalis 42996
9/27/86	**79**	6	2 Who Says	Chrysalis 43063
			DEVO Robotic rock group formed in Akron, Ohio, consisting of brothers Mark and Bob Mothersbaugh, brothers Jerry and Bob Casale, and Alan Myers.	
8/30/80	**14**	25	1 ● Whip It	Warner 49550
9/05/81	**43**	12	2 Working In The Coal Mine from the film "Heavy Metal"	Full Moon 47204
5/21/83	**59**	6	3 Theme From Doctor Detroit from the film "Doctor Detroit"	Backstreet 52215
			FRANK DeVOL & his Rainbow Strings Frank was born on 9/20/11 in Moundsville, WV. Worked with Horace Heidt and Alvino Rey. Has composed, conducted and arranged for many top singers, for many radio and and TV shows, and has had several Academy Award nominations for scoring films.	
5/16/60	**77**	6	1 La Montana (If She Could Come To You) [I]	Columbia 41620

DEBUT DATE	PEAK POS	WKS CHR	ARTIST — Record Title	Label & Number
			BARRY DeVORZON & PERRY BOTKIN, JR.	
			Songwriting, producing, and arranging duo. Also see Barry & The Tamerlanes.	
8/28/76	**8**	22	1 ● **Nadia's Theme (The Young And The Restless)** ..... [I]	A&M 1856
			originally written as "Cotton's Dream" for the film "Bless The Beasts & Children"; then used as the theme song for TV's "The Young and The Restless", and finally as the music for olympic gymnast Nadia Comaneci of Romania	
1/22/77	**82**	5	2 Bless The Beasts And Children .... [I]	A&M 1890
			from the film of the same title	
			THE DEVOTIONS	
			Quintet from New York City.	
2/08/64	**36**	10	1 Rip Van Winkle .... [N]	Roulette 4541
			DEXYS MIDNIGHT RUNNERS	
			Kevin Rowland, leader of 8-piece Birmingham, England band.	
1/22/83	**1**[1]	23	1 **Come On Eileen**..	Mercury 76189
5/28/83	**86**	4	2 The Celtic Soul Brothers..................................	Mercury 811142
			TRACEY DEY	
9/14/63	**75**	5	1 Teenage Cleopatra..	Liberty 55604
12/28/63	**93**	3	2 Here Comes The Boy.......................................	Amy 894
4/25/64	**51**	8	3 Gonna' Get Along Without You Now.........................	Amy 901
			CLIFF DeYOUNG	
			Cliff has acted in several 'made for TV' movies (including "Sunshine").	
1/05/74	**17**	15	1 My Sweet Lady...	MCA 40156
			written by John Denver; from the TV soundtrack "Sunshine"	
			DENNIS DeYOUNG	
			Born on 2/18/47 in Chicago. Lead singer and keyboardist for Styx.	
9/08/84	**10**	22	1 **Desert Moon**	A&M 2666
12/08/84	**83**	4	2 Don't Wait For Heroes....................................	A&M 2692
3/15/86	**54**	11	3 Call Me...	A&M 2816
6/28/86	**93**	3	4 This Is The Time	A&M 2839
			from the film "The Karate Kid Part II"	
			DIAMOND REO	
			Rock group formed in Pittsburgh, led by Bob McKeag and Frank Czuri.	
1/11/75	**44**	6	1 Ain't That Peculiar	Big Tree 16030
			JOEL DIAMOND	
			Producer for Engelbert Humperdinck for 6 years. Producer, composer for many others.	
2/21/81	**82**	3	1 Theme From Raging Bull (Cavalleria Rusticana)...... [I]	Motown 1504
			from the Robert DeNiro film "Raging Bull"	
			LEO DIAMOND	
			Born on 6/29/15 in New York City. Died in Los Angeles on 9/15/66. Arranger and lead harmonica player for the Borrah Minevitch Harmonica Rascals, 1930-46.	
2/19/55	**30**	1	1 Melody Of Love .... [I]	RCA 5973
			Best Seller #30	
			NEIL DIAMOND	
			Born on 1/24/41 in Brooklyn. Vocalist, guitar, prolific composer. With Roadrunners folk group, 1954-56. Worked as song-plugger, staff writer in New York City. Wrote for The Monkees TV show. First recorded for Duel in 1961. Wrote score for "Jonathan Livingston Seagull" film; starred in and composed the music for "The Jazz Singer".	
5/21/66	**55**	10	1 Solitary Man...	Bang 519
8/20/66	**6**	12	2 **Cherry, Cherry**	Bang 528
11/12/66	**16**	8	3 I Got The Feelin' (Oh No No)	Bang 536
1/28/67	**18**	8	4 You Got To Me...	Bang 540
4/08/67	**10**	11	5 **Girl, You'll Be A Woman Soon**	Bang 542
7/15/67	**13**	11	6 I Thank The Lord For The Night Time	Bang 547
10/14/67	**22**	8	7 Kentucky Woman..	Bang 551
1/06/68	**51**	6	8 New Orleans...	Bang 554
4/13/68	**62**	3	9 Red Red Wine..	Bang 556
			Neil's Bang recordings produced by Jeff Barry & Ellie Greenwich	
5/11/68	**58**	6	10 Brooklyn Roads	Uni 55065
7/13/68	**66**	6	11 Two-Bit Manchild	Uni 55075
10/05/68	**68**	5	12 Sunday Sun..	Uni 55084
2/22/69	**22**	13	13 Brother Love's Travelling Salvation Show..................	Uni 55109

DEBUT DATE	PEAK POS	WKS CHR	ARTIST — Record Title	Label & Number
			NEIL DIAMOND — Cont'd	
6/28/69	**4**	14	14 ● **Sweet Caroline (Good Times Never Seemed So Good)**	Uni 55136
11/01/69	**6**	14	15 ● **Holly Holy**	Uni 55175
2/07/70	**24**	14	16 Shilo	Bang 575
2/21/70	**53**	6	17 Until It's Time For You To Go	Uni 55204
5/02/70	**30**	7	18 Soolaimon (African Trilogy II)	Uni 55224
7/11/70	**21**	14	19 Solitary Man [R]	Bang 578
8/22/70	**1^{1}**	15	20 ● **Cracklin' Rosie**	Uni 55250
11/07/70	**20**	11	21 He Ain't Heavy...He's My Brother	Uni 55264
11/07/70	**36**	10	22 Do It	Bang 580
			originally the flip side of Bang 519	
3/27/71	**4**	10	23 **I Am...I Said/**	
6/05/71	**65**	5	24 Done Too Soon	Uni 55278
6/26/71	**51**	8	25 I'm A Believer	Bang 586
11/13/71	**14**	9	26 Stones/	
		1	27 Crunchy Granola Suite	Uni 55310
5/06/72	**1^{1}**	13	28 ● **Song Sung Blue**	Uni 55326
8/12/72	**11**	11	29 Play Me	Uni 55346
11/11/72	**17**	12	30 Walk On Water	Uni 55352
3/17/73	**31**	10	31 Cherry Cherry	MCA 40017
			live version of Neil's 1966 hit (from "Hot August Night" LP)	
8/11/73	**91**	3	32 The Long Way Home	Bang 703
			also the flip side of Bang 547	
8/25/73	**56**	6	33 The Last Thing On My Mind	MCA 40092
10/27/73	**34**	9	34 Be	Columbia 45942
3/16/74	**75**	4	35 Skybird	Columbia 45998
			above 2 from the film "Jonathan Livingston Seagull"	
10/05/74	**5**	15	36 **Longfellow Serenade**	Columbia 10043
2/01/75	**34**	7	37 I've Been This Way Before	Columbia 10084
			most of above hits (Uni, MCA, Columbia) produced by Tom Catalono	
6/19/76	**11**	12	38 If You Know What I Mean	Columbia 10366
9/11/76	**43**	8	39 Don't Think....Feel	Columbia 10405
12/03/77+	**16**	14	40 Desiree	Columbia 10657
10/28/78	**1^{2}**	17	41 ● **You Don't Bring Me Flowers**	Columbia 10840
			BARBRA STREISAND & NEIL DIAMOND	
1/27/79	**20**	11	42 Forever In Blue Jeans	Columbia 10897
5/19/79	**55**	7	43 Say Maybe	Columbia 10945
12/22/79+	**17**	16	44 September Morn'	Columbia 11175
4/05/80	**67**	6	45 The Good Lord Loves You	Columbia 11232
11/01/80+	**2^{3}**	20	46 **Love On The Rocks**	Capitol 4939
1/31/81	**6**	16	47 **Hello Again**	Capitol 4960
4/25/81	**8**	17	48 **America**	Capitol 4994
			above 3 tunes are from the film "The Jazz Singer" 40-48: produced by Bob Gaudio (4 Seasons)	
11/07/81+	**11**	15	49 Yesterday's Songs	Columbia 02604
2/13/82	**27**	10	50 On The Way To The Sky	Columbia 02712
5/22/82	**35**	11	51 Be Mine Tonight	Columbia 02928
9/11/82	**5**	19	52 **Heartlight**	Columbia 03219
			inspired by the film "E.T."	
1/15/83	**35**	12	53 I'm Alive	Columbia 03503
4/23/83	**65**	8	54 Front Page Story	Columbia 03801
8/18/84	**62**	8	55 Turn Around	Columbia 04541
5/24/86	**53**	10	56 Headed For The Future	Columbia 05889
			all of above composed by Diamond (except #8, 17, 21, 33 & 45)	
			THE DIAMONDS	
			Vocal group from Ontario, Canada. Formed in 1953; consisted of Dave Somerville (lead), Ted Kowalski (tenor), Phil Levitt (baritone) and Bill Reed (bass). Recorded for Coral in 1955; debuted on Mercury in January, 1956. Michael Douglas replaced Levitt, early 1958. Reed and Kowalski replaced in 1959 by Evan Fisher and John Felton (killed in a plane crash, 1982). Dave teamed with Four Preps co-founder Bruce Belland as a duet, 1962-69.	
2/18/56	**12**	19	1 Why Do Fools Fall In Love	Mercury 70790
			Jockey #12 / Top 100 #16 / Best Seller #18 / Juke Box #19	
4/21/56	**14**	17	2 The Church Bells May Ring	Mercury 70835
			Best Seller #14 / Juke Box #15 / Jockey #17 / Top 100 #20	

DEBUT DATE	PEAK POS	WKS CHR	ARTIST — Record Title	Label & Number
			THE DIAMONDS — Cont'd	
6/23/56	**30**	14	3 Love, Love, Love	Mercury 70889
9/08/56	**35**	9	4 Ka-Ding-Dong/	
9/22/56	**34**	8	5 Soft Summer Breeze	Mercury 70934
3/16/57	**2^{8}**	26	6 **Little Darlin'** Best Seller #2 / Top 100 #2 / Jockey #2 / Juke Box #2 original version by Maurice Williams' group, The Gladiolas	Mercury 71060
6/24/57	**13**	2	7 Words Of Love Jockey #13 / Top 100 #76 written by Buddy Holly	Mercury 71128
8/26/57	**16**	11	8 Zip Zip Jockey #16 / Top 100 # 45	Mercury 71165
11/04/57	**10**	11	9 **Silhouettes** Jockey #10 / Top 100 #60	Mercury 71197
12/30/57+	**4**	21	10 **The Stroll** Jockey #4 / Top 100 #5 / Best Seller #7 orchestra arrangements by David Carroll on all of above	Mercury 71242
4/14/58	**37**	12	11 High Sign Best Seller #37 / Top 100 #38	Mercury 71291
7/28/58	**16**	8	12 Kathy-O/ Jockey #16 end / Best Seller #41 / Hot 100 #45 ballad from the Patty McCormack movie of the same title	
8/04/58	**73**	4	13 Happy Years	Mercury 71330
10/27/58	**29**	12	14 Walking Along	Mercury 71366
1/26/59	**18**	14	15 She Say (Oom Dooby Doom)	Mercury 71404
7/03/61	**22**	9	16 One Summer Night	Mercury 71831
			MANU DIBANGO Jazz/R&B saxophonist from Cameroon, Africa.	
6/23/73	**35**	9	1 Soul Makossa [I]	Atlantic 2971
			DICK & DEEDEE Dick St. John Gosting & Deedee Sperling. Formed duo while students in high school at Santa Monica, California.	
7/31/61	**2^{2}**	15	1 **The Mountain's High**	Liberty 55350
3/17/62	**22**	14	2 Tell Me	Liberty 55412
3/16/63	**17**	11	3 Young And In Love	Warner 5342
10/05/63	**93**	1	4 Where Did The Good Times Go	Warner 5383
11/23/63+	**27**	9	5 Turn Around	Warner 5396
2/22/64	**89**	3	6 All My Trials	Warner 5411
11/21/64+	**13**	13	7 Thou Shalt Not Steal	Warner 5482
3/13/65	**87**	3	8 Be My Baby all of above hits produced by Don Ralke & The Wilder Bros.	Warner 5608
			"LITTLE" JIMMY DICKENS Born on 12/19/25 in Bolt, WV. Country singer who stands only 4'11" tall.	
10/16/65	**15**	10	1 May The Bird Of Paradise Fly Up Your Nose [N]	Columbia 43388
			DICKY DOO & THE DON'TS Vocal group from Philadelphia, consisting of Gerry "Jerry Grant" Granahan (lead), Harvey Davis (baritone), Ray Gangi (tenor), Al Ways (bass) and Dave "Dicky Doo" Alldred (ex-drummer of the Rhythm Orchids).	
2/10/58	**28**	14	1 Click-Clack Top 100 #28 / Best Seller #29	Swan 4001
5/05/58	**40**	8	2 Nee Nee Na Na Na Na Nu Nu/ [I] Top 100 #40 / Best Seller #42	
6/09/58	**61**	8	3 Flip Top Box	Swan 4006
9/29/58	**44**	9	4 Leave Me Alone (Let Me Cry)	Swan 4014
2/02/59	**61**	6	5 Teardrops Will Fall based on the collegiate tune "Our Boys Will Shine Tonight"	Swan 4025
			BO DIDDLEY Born Ellas Bates on 12/30/28 in McComb, Mississippi. Adopted as an infant by his mother's cousin, Mrs. Gussie McDaniel. Moved to Chicago at age 5. Began recording career in 1955 with the Chess/Checker label. His first record was a 2-sided #1 hit on the R&B charts, "Bo Diddley"/"I'm A Man". Unique and influential R&B/rock & roll guitarist/vocalist.	
7/06/59	**62**	5	1 Crackin Up	Checker 924
9/21/59	**20**	12	2 Say Man [N]	Checker 931
2/29/60	**75**	6	3 Road Runner	Checker 942
8/18/62	**48**	10	4 You Can't Judge A Book By The Cover	Checker 1019
1/21/67	**88**	7	5 Ooh Baby	Checker 1158

DEBUT DATE	PEAK POS	WKS CHR	ARTIST — Record Title	Label & Number
			DIESEL	
			Rock quartet from Holland.	
9/12/81	**25**	18	1 Sausalito Summernight	Regency 7339
			THE DILLARDS	
			Country/rock quintet from the Ozarks in Missouri, formed by brothers Doug and Rodney Dillard. Doug left in 1968 to form the Dillard-Clark Expedition.	
7/31/71	**92**	2	1 It's About Time	Anthem 101
			THE DILLMAN BAND	
			Country/rock quintet led by Steve Solmonson and Steve Seamans.	
5/09/81	**45**	9	1 Lovin' The Night Away	RCA 12206
			MARK DINNING	
			Born on 8/17/33 in Drury, OK. Died of a heart attack on 3/22/86 (52). Brother of the Dinning Sisters vocal trio. First recorded for MGM in 1957.	
12/21/59+	**1^{2}**	18	1 **Teen Angel**	MGM 12845
			written by Mark's sister, Jeannie	
4/18/60	**68**	6	2 A Star Is Born (A Love Has Died)	MGM 12888
8/22/60	**84**	6	3 The Lovin' Touch	MGM 12929
2/20/61	**81**	6	4 Top Forty, News, Weather And Sports [N]	MGM 12980
			DINO, DESI & BILLY	
			Dino: Dean Martin's son, Dean Martin, Jr.; Desi: Lucille Ball and Desi Arnaz's son, Desiderio Arnaz IV; & Billy: a schoolmate from Beverly Hills, William Hinsche. Dino was killed on 3/21/87 when his Air National Guard jet crashed.	
6/26/65	**17**	12	1 I'm A Fool	Reprise 0367
9/18/65	**25**	9	2 Not The Lovin' Kind	Reprise 0401
12/11/65+	**60**	7	3 Please Don't Fight It	Reprise 0426
3/05/66	**94**	2	4 Superman	Reprise 0444
6/17/67	**99**	1	5 Two In The Afternoon	Reprise 0579
8/10/68	**92**	4	6 Tell Someone You Love Them	Reprise 0698
			KENNY DINO	
			Born on 2/12/42 in New York City.	
11/06/61	**24**	11	1 Your Ma Said You Cried In Your Sleep Last Night	Musicor 1013
			PAUL DINO	
			Born on 3/2/39 in Philadelphia.	
1/23/61	**38**	12	1 Ginnie Bell	Promo 2180
			DION	
			Born Dion DiMucci on 7/18/39 in the Bronx, New York. Formed Dion & The Timberlanes in 1957, then Dion & The Belmonts in 1958. Went solo in 1960. Moved to Miami in 1968. Brief reunion with the Belmonts, 1967 and 1972, periodically since then. Currently records contemporary Christian songs.	
10/17/60	**12**	16	1 Lonely Teenager/	
12/05/60	**96**	1	2 Little Miss Blue	Laurie 3070
2/06/61	**42**	6	3 Havin' Fun	Laurie 3081
5/01/61	**82**	3	4 Kissin Game	Laurie 3090
9/25/61	**1^{2}**	14	5 **Runaround Sue**	Laurie 3110
12/04/61+	**2^{1}**	18	6 **The Wanderer/**	
12/04/61	**36**	8	7 The Majestic	Laurie 3115
4/21/62	**3**	12	8 **Lovers Who Wander/**	
4/21/62	**42**	7	9 (I Was) Born To Cry	Laurie 3123
7/07/62	**8**	11	10 **Little Diane**	Laurie 3134
11/10/62	**10**	11	11 **Love Came To Me**	Laurie 3145
1/19/63	**2^{3}**	13	12 **Ruby Baby**	Columbia 42662
3/02/63	**21**	11	13 Sandy	Laurie 3153
4/20/63	**21**	8	14 This Little Girl	Columbia 42776
6/15/63	**48**	6	15 Come Go With Me	Laurie 3171
7/06/63	**31**	7	16 Be Careful Of Stones That You Throw	Columbia 42810
9/14/63	**6**	11	17 **Donna The Prima Donna**	Columbia 42852
11/16/63	**6**	11	18 **Drip Drop**	Columbia 42917
8/22/64	**71**	4	19 Johnny B. Goode	Columbia 43096
			above 3 shown as: DION DiMUCCI	
10/26/68	**4**	14	20 ● **Abraham, Martin And John**	Laurie 3464
			a tribute to Lincoln, King and Kennedy	
1/25/69	**63**	4	21 Purple Haze	Laurie 3478
			cover version of the Jimi Hendrix classic	

DEBUT DATE	PEAK POS	WKS CHR	ARTIST — Record Title	Label & Number
			DION — Cont'd	
4/26/69	**91**	2	22 From Both Sides Now	Laurie 3495
6/27/70	**75**	3	23 Your Own Back Yard	Warner 7401
			DION & THE BELMONTS Vocal group formed in the Bronx, NY in 1958. Consisted of Dion DiMucci, lead; Angelo D'Aleo (b: 2/3/40), first tenor; Freddie Milano (b: 8/22/39), second tenor; Carlo Mastrangelo (b: 10/5/38), bass. Named for Belmont Avenue in the Bronx. Angelo was in the Navy in 1959 and missed some recording and picture sessions. Group was on "Winter Dance Party" tour during which Buddy Holly, Ritchie Valens & the Big Bopper were killed. Dion had a successful solo career after leaving The Belmonts in 1960.	
5/19/58	**22**	13	1 I Wonder Why Top 100 #22 / Best Seller #24	Laurie 3013
8/25/58	**19**	16	2 No One Knows Best Seller #19 end / Hot 100 #24 first popularized in 1937 by Hal Kemp & His Orchestra (POS 1)	Laurie 3015
12/22/58+	**40**	12	3 Don't Pity Me	Laurie 3021
4/20/59	**5**	15	4 **A Teenager In Love**	Laurie 3027
9/14/59	**48**	8	5 Every Little Thing I Do/	
10/19/59	**73**	3	6 A Lover's Prayer	Laurie 3035
12/28/59+	**3**	16	7 **Where Or When** first popularized in 1937 by Hal Kemp & His Orchestra (POS 1)	Laurie 3044
4/25/60	**30**	9	8 When You Wish Upon A Star from the film "Pinocchio" - #1 in 1940 by Glenn Miller	Laurie 3052
7/18/60	**38**	7	9 In The Still Of The Night the Cole Porter classic; charted in 1937 by Tommy Dorsey (POS 3)	Laurie 3059
			THE DIPLOMATS	
2/01/64	**89**	3	1 Here's A Heart	Arock 1004
			DIRE STRAITS Rock group formed in London by Mark Knopfler (lead vocals, lead guitar, songwriter, producer) and his brother David Knopfler (guitar), with John Illsley (bass) and Pick Withers (drums). David left in late 1979, replaced by Hal Lindes (who left in 1985). Added keyboardist Alan Clark in 1982. Terry Williams replaced drummer Pick Withers in 1983.	
2/10/79	**4**	15	1 **Sultans Of Swing**	Warner 8736
7/28/79	**45**	7	2 Lady Writer	Warner 49006
12/20/80+	**58**	10	3 Skateaway	Warner 49632
1/08/83	**75**	4	4 Industrial Disease	Warner 29880
7/13/85	**1**[3]	22	5 **Money For Nothing** written by Sting and Mark Knopfler	Warner 28950
11/02/85+	**7**	21	6 **Walk Of Life**	Warner 28878
3/01/86	**19**	14	7 So Far Away	Warner 28789
			SENATOR EVERETT McKINLEY DIRKSEN U.S. senator from Illinois, 1950-69 - died on 9/7/69 (73).	
12/24/66+	**29**	6	1 Gallant Men [S]	Capitol 5805
			DIRT BAND - see NITTY GRITTY DIRT BAND	
			DISCO TEX & THE SEX-O-LETTES Disco studio group assembled by producer Bob Crewe. Featuring lead voice Sir Monti Rock III (real name: Joseph Montanez, Jr.), owner of a chain of hairdressing salons.	
11/23/74+	**10**	15	1 **Get Dancin'**	Chelsea 3004
4/19/75	**23**	11	2 I Wanna Dance Wit' Choo (Doo Dat Dance), Part 1	Chelsea 3015
8/30/75	**80**	3	3 Jam Band	Chelsea 3026
7/04/76	**60**	9	4 Dancin' Kid	Chelsea 3045
			DIVINYLS Australian rock quintet led by vocalist Christina Amphlett.	
1/25/86	**76**	7	1 Pleasure And Pain	Chrysalis 42916
			THE DIXIEBELLES Black female trio from Memphis: Shirley Thomas, Mary Hunt, Mildred Pratcher.	
9/28/63	**9**	13	1 **(Down At) Papa Joe's**	Sound Stage 2507
1/18/64	**15**	8	2 Southtown, U.S.A. above 2 feature Jerry Smith (as Cornbread & Jerry) on piano	Sound Stage 2517
			THE DIXIE CUPS Black female trio from New Orleans: Barbara Ann Hawkins, her sister Rosa Lee Hawkins, and Joan Marie Johnson. Discovered by Joe Jones.	
5/02/64	**1**[3]	13	1 **Chapel Of Love**	Red Bird 001

DEBUT DATE	PEAK POS	WKS CHR	ARTIST — Record Title	Label & Number
			THE DIXIE CUPS — Cont'd	
7/18/64	**12**	9	2 People Say	Red Bird 006
10/24/64	**39**	6	3 You Should Have Seen The Way He Looked At Me	Red Bird 012
12/19/64+	**51**	9	4 Little Bell	Red Bird 017
4/03/65	**20**	10	5 Iko Iko	Red Bird 024
			THE DIXIE DRIFTER	
			Real name: Enoch Gregory; deejay at WWRL in New York.	
9/04/65	**99**	2	1 Soul Heaven [S] a spoken tribute to Dinah Washington, Nat King Cole and Sam Cooke	Roulette 4641
			CARL DOBKINS, JR.	
			Born in 1941 in Cincinnati.	
4/13/59	**3**	24	1 **My Heart Is An Open Book**	Decca 30803
10/12/59	**67**	3	2 If You Don't Want My Lovin'	Decca 30656
12/07/59+	**25**	17	3 Lucky Devil	Decca 31020
5/16/60	**62**	8	4 Exclusively Yours	Decca 31088
			DOCTOR & THE MEDICS	
			Rock sextet from London, England.	
8/02/86	**69**	11	1 Spirit In The Sky	I.R.S. 52880
			DR. BUZZARD'S ORIGINAL "SAVANNAH" BAND	
			New York City Thirties-styled disco group formed by brothers Stony Browder and August Darnell (born: Thomas Browder), with Cory Daye, lead singer. Darnell left in 1980 to form Kid Creole & The Coconuts.	
9/25/76	**80**	3	1 I'll Play The Fool	RCA 10762
11/06/76+	**27**	20	2 Whispering/Cherchez La Femme/Se Si Bon	RCA 10827
			DR. FEELGOOD & THE INTERNS	
			Group is actually bluesman Willie "Piano Red" Perryman - died of cancer on 7/25/85 (73).	
4/21/62	**66**	9	1 Doctor Feel-Good	Okeh 7144
8/04/62	**84**	3	2 Right String But The Wrong Yo-Yo original version by Piano Red hit POS 10 on the R&B charts, 1951	Okeh 7156
			DR. HOOK	
			Group formed in New Jersey in 1968. Fronted by Ray Sawyer (Dr. Hook - because of eye patch) and Dennis Locorriere. Appeared in and performed the music for the film "Who Is Harry Kellerman And Why Is He Saying Those Terrible Things About Me?", starring Dustin Hoffman.	
			DR. HOOK & THE MEDICINE SHOW:	
4/01/72	**5**	15	1 ● **Sylvia's Mother**	Columbia 45562
9/09/72	**71**	6	2 Carry Me, Carrie	Columbia 45667
12/02/72+	**6**	20	3 ● **The Cover Of 'Rolling Stone'** [N]	Columbia 45732
7/07/73	**83**	4	4 Roland The Roadie And Gertrude The Groupie [N]	Columbia 45878
9/29/73	**68**	7	5 Life Ain't Easy	Columbia 45925
			DR. HOOK:	
8/23/75	**95**	5	6 The Millionaire	Capitol 4104
1/03/76	**6**	22	7 ● **Only Sixteen**	Capitol 4171
6/19/76	**11**	24	8 A Little Bit More	Capitol 4280
11/27/76	**55**	11	9 If Not You	Capitol 4364
6/25/77	**46**	10	10 Walk Right In	Capitol 4423
9/16/78+	**6**	22	11 ● **Sharing The Night Together**	Capitol 4621
2/03/79	**54**	7	12 All The Time In The World	Capitol 4677
4/14/79	**6**	25	13 ● **When You're In Love With A Beautiful Woman**	Capitol 4705
10/13/79+	**12**	19	14 Better Love Next Time	Capitol 4785
2/16/80	**5**	21	15 ● **Sexy Eyes**	Capitol 4831
7/05/80	**51**	9	16 Years From Now	Capitol 4885
11/01/80	**34**	14	17 Girls Can Get It	Casablanca 2314
4/11/81	**69**	4	18 That Didn't Hurt Too Bad	Casablanca 2325
2/27/82	**25**	12	19 Baby Makes Her Blue Jeans Talk	Casablanca 2347
6/12/82	**60**	10	20 Loveline	Casablanca 2351
			DR. JOHN	
			Born Malcolm "Mac" Rebennack on 11/21/40 in New Orleans. Pioneer 'swamp rock' styled instrumentalist.	
4/15/72	**71**	5	1 Iko Iko	Atco 6882
4/14/73	**9**	20	2 **Right Place Wrong Time**	Atco 6914

DEBUT DATE	PEAK POS	WKS CHR	ARTIST — Record Title	Label & Number
			DR. JOHN — Cont'd	
9/15/73	**42**	9	3 Such A Night	Atco 6937
5/11/74	**92**	4	4 (Everybody Wanna Get Rich) Rite Away	Atco 6957
			DR. WEST'S MEDICINE SHOW & JUNK BAND	
			West Coast jug band formed by Norman ("Spirit In The Sky") Greenbaum.	
11/26/66	**52**	7	1 The Eggplant That Ate Chicago	Go Go 100
			NELLA DODDS	
11/14/64	**74**	3	1 Come See About Me	Wand 167
1/09/65	**96**	2	2 Finders Keepers, Losers Weepers	Wand 171
			BILL DOGGETT	
			Born on 2/16/16 in Philadelphia. Leading jazz/R&B organist and pianist. Formed own band, 1938, recorded with the Jimmy Mundy Band, 1939. With the Ink Spots, Illinois Jacquet, Lucky Millinder, Louis Jordan, Ella Fitzgerald, Louis Armstrong, Coleman Hawkins and many others. Formed own combo in 1952. Still active into the 80s with a touring combo.	
8/18/56	**2**[3]	29	1 **Honky Tonk (Parts 1 & 2)** [I] Best Seller #2 / Top 100 #2 / Juke Box #2 / Jockey #6 sax player: Clifford Scott	King 4950
11/24/56+	**26**	12	2 Slow Walk [I]	King 5000
2/16/57	**67**	7	3 Ram-Bunk-Shush [I]	King 5020
11/04/57	**35**	14	4 Soft [I] Best Seller #35 / Top 100 #51	King 5080
8/04/58	**82**	2	5 Blip Blop [I]	King 5138
11/10/58	**92**	1	6 Hold It [I]	King 5149
1/04/60	**95**	2	7 Smokie - Part 2 [I]	King 5310
12/26/60	**66**	3	8 (Let's Do) The Hully Gully Twist [I]	Warner 5181
1/30/61	**57**	10	9 Honky Tonk (Part 2) [I-R]	King 5444
			DOKKEN	
			Los Angeles-based hard rock quartet led by Don Dokken.	
5/04/85	**64**	11	1 Alone Again	Elektra 69650
2/22/86	**77**	7	2 In My Dreams	Elektra 69563
			THOMAS DOLBY	
			Born Thomas Morgan Dolby Robertson of British parentage on 10/14/58 in Cairo, Egypt. Master of computer-generated music and self-directed videos. Played keyboards as a member of Bruce Woolley & The Camera Club, and the Lene Lovich band, 1979-80. Began solo career in 1981.	
2/19/83	**5**	22	1 **She Blinded Me With Science**	Capitol 5204
6/18/83	**67**	5	2 Europa And The Pirate Twins	Capitol 5238
2/25/84	**62**	7	3 Hyperactive	Capitol 5321
			JOE DOLCE	
			Born in 1947 of Italian-American parents in Painesville, Ohio.	
5/02/81	**53**	14	1 Shaddap You Face [N] portrays the Italian character Guiseppi in this novelty recording	MCA 51053
			MICKY DOLENZ	
			Son of actor George Dolenz. Under the name Mickey Braddock, played Corky in the TV series "Circus Boy", 1956-58. Became famous as drummer for The Monkees.	
3/04/67	**75**	6	1 Don't Do It	Challenge 59353
			DOLLAR	
			British rock group.	
12/22/79+	**74**	6	1 Shooting Star	Carrere 7208
			THE DOLPHINS	
12/19/64+	**69**	7	1 Hey-Da-Da-Dow	Fraternity 937
			PLACIDO DOMINGO & JOHN DENVER	
			Placido was born on 1/21/41 in Madrid, Spain. To Mexico City, 1950. To U.S., 1961. Debuted at the Metropolitan Opera, 1968. One of the world's leading operatic tenors.	
1/16/82	**59**	7	1 Perhaps Love	Columbia 02679

DEBUT DATE	PEAK POS	WKS CHR	ARTIST — Record Title	Label & Number
			FATS DOMINO Born Antoine Domino on 2/26/28 in New Orleans. Classic New Orleans R&B piano-playing vocalist - heavily influenced by Fats Waller and Albert Ammons. Joined Dave Bartholomew Band, mid-40s. Signed to Imperial record label in 1949. His first recording "The Fat Man" reportedly was a million-seller. Heard on many sessions cut by other R&B artists, including Lloyd Price and Joe Turner. Films "Shake Rattle And Roll", "Jamboree", "The Big Beat", "The Girl Can't Help It". Teamed with co-writer Dave Bartholomew on the majority of his hits. Lives in New Orleans with wife Rosemary and eight children. Frequently appears in Las Vegas. One of the most influential and popular R&B stars.	
7/16/55	**10**	13	1 **Ain't That A Shame** Juke Box #10 / Best Seller #16 / Top 100 #86 pre label shows title as "Ain't It A Shame"	Imperial 5348
3/03/56	**35**	9	2 Bo Weevil	Imperial 5375
4/28/56	**3**	23	3 **I'm In Love Again/** Juke Box #3 / Best Seller #4 / Top 100 # 5 / Jockey #6	
4/28/56	**21**	20	4 My Blue Heaven originally hit #1 in 1927 for both Gene Austin and Paul Whiteman	Imperial 5386
7/28/56	**14**	16	5 When My Dreamboat Comes Home/ Juke Box #14 / Best Seller #21 / Top 100 #22 originally hit #3 in 1937 for Guy Lombardo	
7/28/56	**44**	13	6 So-Long	Imperial 5396
10/06/56+	**2^3**	27	7 **Blueberry Hill** Juke Box #2 / Best Seller #3 / Top 100 #4 / Jockey #7 originally hit #1 in 1940 for Glenn Miller	Imperial 5407
1/05/57	**5**	18	8 **Blue Monday/** Juke Box #5 / Best Seller #9 / Top 100 #9 / Jockey #9 from the film "The Girl Can't Help It"	
1/12/57	**50**	10	9 What's The Reason I'm Not Pleasing You originally hit #1 in 1935 for Guy Lombardo	Imperial 5417
3/09/57	**4**	25	10 **I'm Walkin'** Jockey #4 / Best Seller #5 / Top 100 #5 / Juke Box #5	Imperial 5428
5/13/57	**6**	18	11 **Valley Of Tears/** Best Seller #6 / Top 100 #13 / Jockey #13	
5/27/57	**22**	12	12 It's You I Love	Imperial 5442
8/12/57	**29**	10	13 When I See You/ Best Seller #29 / Top 100 #36	
8/12/57	**64**	6	14 What Will I Tell My Heart first popularized in 1951 by Eddy Howard	Imperial 5454
10/21/57	**23**	13	15 Wait And See/ Best Seller #23 / Top 100 #27 from the film "Jamboree"	
10/28/57	**79**	4	16 I Still Love You	Imperial 5467
12/23/57+	**26**	9	17 The Big Beat/ Best Seller #26 / Top 100 #36 from the film of the same title	
12/30/57+	**48**	11	18 I Want You To Know	Imperial 5477
3/17/58	**55**	7	19 Yes, My Darling	Imperial 5492
5/05/58	**22**	11	20 Sick And Tired/ Best Seller #22 / Top 100 #30	
5/05/58	**55**	7	21 No, No	Imperial 5515
7/07/58	**48**	6	22 Little Mary Best Seller #48 / Top 100 #49	Imperial 5526
9/22/58	**92**	1	23 Young School Girl	Imperial 5537
11/17/58+	**6**	15	24 **Whole Lotta Loving/**	
11/17/58	**92**	1	25 Coquette popularized in 1928 by Guy Lombardo - his theme song	Imperial 5553
2/16/59	**50**	9	26 Telling Lies/	
2/16/59	**50**	8	27 When The Saints Go Marching In written in 1896 by Katharine Purvis and James Black	Imperial 5569
5/11/59	**16**	11	28 I'm Ready/	
5/11/59	**51**	8	29 Margie Eddie Cantor's version hit #1 in 1921	Imperial 5585
8/10/59	**8**	13	30 **I Want To Walk You Home/**	
7/27/59	**17**	13	31 I'm Gonna Be A Wheel Some Day	Imperial 5606
10/26/59	**8**	14	32 **Be My Guest/**	
10/26/59	**33**	9	33 I've Been Around	Imperial 5629
2/01/60	**25**	10	34 Country Boy/	
2/15/60	**98**	1	35 If You Need Me	Imperial 5645
4/25/60	**51**	7	36 Tell Me That You Love Me/	
5/09/60	**84**	2	37 Before I Grow Too Old	Imperial 5660

DEBUT DATE	PEAK POS	WKS CHR	ARTIST — Record Title	Label & Number
			FATS DOMINO — Cont'd	
6/20/60	**6**	14	38 **Walking To New Orleans/**	
6/27/60	**21**	11	39 Don't Come Knockin'	Imperial 5675
9/05/60	**15**	11	40 Three Nights A Week/	
9/05/60	**58**	6	41 Put Your Arms Around Me Honey first popularized in 1911 by Arthur Collins & Byron Harlan (POS 1)	Imperial 5687
10/24/60	**14**	15	42 My Girl Josephine/	
10/31/60	**38**	9	43 Natural Born Lover	Imperial 5704
1/23/61	**22**	9	44 What A Price/	
1/23/61	**33**	8	45 Ain't That Just Like A Woman originally charted in 1946 by Louis Jordan (POS 17)	Imperial 5723
3/20/61	**32**	7	46 Shu Rah/	
3/20/61	**32**	6	47 Fell In Love On Monday	Imperial 5734
5/15/61	**23**	11	48 It Keeps Rainin'	Imperial 5753
7/24/61	**15**	11	49 Let The Four Winds Blow	Imperial 5764
10/02/61	**22**	8	50 What A Party/	
10/16/61	**83**	1	51 Rockin' Bicycle	Imperial 5779
12/11/61+	**30**	7	52 Jambalaya (On The Bayou)/ written and popularized (POS 1) by Hank Williams in 1952	
12/04/61	**67**	2	53 I Hear You Knocking	Imperial 5796
2/24/62	**22**	10	54 You Win Again/ written and charted (Country) by Hank Williams in 1952 (POS 10)	
3/03/62	**90**	2	55 Ida Jane	Imperial 5816
5/12/62	**59**	7	56 My Real Name	Imperial 5833
6/30/62	**77**	5	57 Nothing New (Same Old Thing)/	
7/21/62	**98**	1	58 Dance With Mr. Domino	Imperial 5863
10/06/62	**79**	5	59 Did You Ever See A Dream Walking first popularized (POS 1) in 1933 by Eddy Duchin	Imperial 5875
5/18/63	**59**	7	60 There Goes (My Heart Again)	ABC-Para. 10444
9/21/63	**35**	8	61 Red Sails In The Sunset Bing Crosby and Guy Lombardo both had #1 versions in 1935	ABC-Para. 10484
1/04/64	**63**	5	62 Who Cares	ABC-Para. 10512
2/29/64	**86**	2	63 Lazy Lady	ABC-Para. 10531
9/19/64	**99**	2	64 Sally Was A Good Old Girl	ABC-Para. 10584
10/31/64	**99**	2	65 Heartbreak Hill	ABC-Para. 10596
9/07/68	**100**	2	66 Lady Madonna Fats' version of the Beatles' early 1968 classic	Reprise 0763
			DON & JUAN Black vocal duo from New York City: Roland Trone & Claude Johnson of The Genies.	
2/10/62	**7**	13	1 **What's Your Name**	Big Top 3079
10/27/62	**91**	3	2 Magic Wand	Big Top 3121
			DON & THE GOODTIMES Pacific Northwest quintet led by Li'l Don Gallucci.	
4/22/67	**56**	7	1 I Could Be So Good To You	Epic 10145
7/29/67	**98**	1	2 Happy And Me	Epic 10199
			DON, DICK N' JIMMY Don Ralke, Dick Crowe & Jimmy Styne.	
12/03/55	**96**	2	1 Love Is A Many Splendored Thing from the film of the same title	Crown 158
			BO DONALDSON & THE HEYWOODS Cincinnati, Ohio septet. Regulars on Dick Clark's "Action '73" TV show.	
10/28/72	**64**	8	1 Special Someone shown only as: **THE HEYWOODS**	Family 0911
4/20/74	**1^{2}**	19	2 ● **Billy, Don't Be A Hero**	ABC 11435
7/27/74	**15**	12	3 Who Do You Think You Are	ABC 12006
11/16/74	**39**	7	4 The Heartbreak Kid	ABC 12039
7/05/75	**95**	2	5 Our Last Song Together	ABC 12108
			LOU DONALDSON Born on 11/1/26 in Badin, NC. Jazz alto saxophonist.	
11/04/67	**93**	4	1 Alligator Bogaloo [I]	Blue Note 1934

DEBUT DATE	PEAK POS	WKS CHR	ARTIST — Record Title	Label & Number
			LONNIE DONEGAN & His Skiffle Group	
			Born Anthony Donegan on 4/29/31 in Glasgow, Scotland. Britain's "King of Skiffle".	
3/17/56	**8**	17	1 **Rock Island Line**..	London 1650
			Best Seller #8 / Top 100 #10 / Jockey #10 / Juke Box #13	
6/09/56	**58**	2	2 Lost John	Mercury 70872
8/07/61	**5**	11	3 **Does Your Chewing Gum Lose It's Flavor (On The Bedpost Over Night)**........................ [N]	Dot 15911
			#9 hit in 1924 for Ernest Hare & Billy Jones as "Does The Spearmint Lose Its Flavor On The Bedpost Overnight?" first released by Lonnie in Britain in 1958	
			RAL DONNER	
			Born on 2/10/43 in Chicago. Narrator and Elvis' voice in the film "This Is Elvis". Died of cancer on 4/6/84 (41).	
4/17/61	**19**	11	1 Girl Of My Best Friend..	Gone 5102
			recorded by Elvis in 1960 on his "Elvis Is Back!" LP	
7/10/61	**4**	12	2 **You Don't Know What You've Got (Until You Lose It)**	Gone 5108
9/25/61	**39**	9	3 Please Don't Go..	Gone 5114
12/25/61+	**18**	11	4 She's Everything (I Wanted You To Be)........................	Gone 5121
3/24462	**74**	7	5 (What A Sad Way) To Love Someone	Gone 5125
			DONNIE & THE DREAMERS	
			Donnie is Louis Burgio. Italian-American vocal quartet from New York City.	
5/01/61	**35**	10	1 Count Every Star..	Whale 500
			originally a #4 hit for Ray Anthony's band in 1950	
7/17/61	**79**	3	2 My Memories Of You	Whale 505
			DONOVAN	
			Born Donovan Phillip Leitch on 2/10/46 near Glasgow, Scotland. Singer-songwriter-guitarist. To London at age ten. Worked Newport Folk Festival in 1965. Wrote score for film "If It's Tuesday This Must Be Belgium". Films, "The Pied Piper Of Hamlin", 1972, "Brother Sun, Sister Moon", 1973. In retirement from 1974-81.	
5/15/65	**23**	10	1 Catch The Wind	Hickory 1309
8/14/65	**61**	7	2 Colours..	Hickory 1324
9/25/65	**53**	7	3 Universal Soldier..	Hickory 1338
7/30/66	**1^1**	13	4 **Sunshine Superman**	Epic 10045
11/12/66	**2^3**	12	5 ● **Mellow Yellow**	Epic 10098
			whispering vocals: Paul McCartney	
2/11/67	**19**	7	6 Epistle To Dippy..	Epic 10127
8/12/67	**11**	9	7 There Is A Mountain	Epic 10212
11/25/67	**23**	7	8 Wear Your Love Like Heaven..	Epic 10253
3/09/68	**26**	9	9 Jennifer Juniper	Epic 10300
6/22/68	**5**	12	10 **Hurdy Gurdy Man**	Epic 10345
10/05/68	**33**	6	11 Lalena..	Epic 10393
2/08/69	**35**	6	12 To Susan On The West Coast Waiting/	
4/05/69	**7**	13	13 **Atlantis**	Epic 10434
8/02/69	**36**	7	14 Goo Goo Barabajagal (Love Is Hot)	Epic 10510
			all of above Epic hits produced by Mickie Most	
8/22/70	**55**	8	15 Riki Tiki Tavi	Epic 10649
2/27/71	**84**	3	16 Celia Of The Seals	Epic 10694
4/28/73	**66**	8	17 I Like You	Epic 10983
			all of above written by Donovan (except #3)	
			THE DOOBIE BROTHERS	
			Group formed in San Jose, CA in 1970. Consisted of Pat Simmons (vocals, guitar), Tom Johnston (lead vocals, guitar, keyboards), John Hartman (percussion) and Dave Shogren (bass). First recorded for Warner in 1971. Shogren replaced by Tiran Porter (bass). Mike Hossack (percussion), added in 1972 (later replaced by Keith Knudsen). Toured England in 1974. Jeff "Skunk" Baxter (slide guitar), formerly with Steely Dan, added in 1974. Michael McDonald (lead vocals, keyboards), added, 1975. Johnston left in 1978. Baxter, Hartman replaced by Cornelius Bumpus (keyboards, saxophone), John McFee (guitar) and Chet McCracken (drums) in 1979. Tom Johnston wrote majority of hits from 1972-75; Michael McDonald from 1976-83. Disbanded in 1983.	
9/02/72	**11**	13	1 Listen To The Music..	Warner 7619
12/16/72+	**35**	11	2 Jesus Is Just Alright..	Warner 7661
4/21/73	**8**	18	3 **Long Train Runnin'**..	Warner 7698
8/18/73	**15**	13	4 China Grove	Warner 7728
4/20/74	**32**	10	5 Another Park, Another Sunday	Warner 7795
7/27/74	**52**	8	6 Eyes Of Silver	Warner 7832
11/02/74	**58**	6	7 Nobody	Warner 8041

DEBUT DATE	PEAK POS	WKS CHR	ARTIST — Record Title	Label & Number
			THE DOOBIE BROTHERS — Cont'd	
12/21/74+	**1**[1]	17	8 ● **Black Water**	Warner 8062
			originally the flip side of Warner 7795	
5/03/75	**11**	12	9 Take Me In Your Arms (Rock Me)	Warner 8092
8/02/75	**40**	7	10 Sweet Maxine	Warner 8126
12/27/75+	**60**	4	11 I Cheat The Hangman	Warner 8161
4/17/76	**13**	14	12 Takin' It To The Streets	Warner 8196
8/28/76	**87**	2	13 Wheels Of Fortune	Warner 8233
11/13/76+	**37**	14	14 It Keeps You Runnin'	Warner 8282
7/30/77	**48**	7	15 Little Darling (I Need You)	Warner 8408
10/08/77	**66**	7	16 Echoes Of Love	Warner 8471
1/20/79	**1**[1]	20	17 ● **What A Fool Believes**	Warner 8725
5/05/79	**14**	14	18 Minute By Minute	Warner 8828
8/11/79	**25**	12	19 Dependin' On You	Warner 49029
9/06/80	**5**	16	20 **Real Love**	Warner 49503
11/22/80+	**24**	14	21 One Step Closer	Warner 49622
1/24/81	**76**	4	22 Wynken, Blynken And Nod	Sesame St. 49642
			cut taken from the various artists' album "In Harmony"	
2/14/81	**62**	5	23 Keep This Train A-Rollin'	Warner 49670
2/06/82	**65**	5	24 Here To Love You	Warner 50001
7/30/83	**79**	4	25 You Belong To Me	Warner 29552
			all of above (except #22) produced by Ted Templeman	
			THE DOOLITTLE BAND	
			Originally known as Danny & The Doolittle Band.	
10/11/80	**49**	7	1 Who Were You Thinkin' Of	Columbia 11355
			THE DOORS	
			Rock group formed in Los Angeles in 1965. Consisted of Jim Morrison (b: 12/8/43, Melbourne, FL; d: 7/3/71, Paris, France), lead singer; Ray Manzarek, keyboards; Robby Krieger, guitar; and John Densmore, drums. Controversial onstage performances by Morrison caused several arrests and cancellations. Morrison left group, 12/12/70. Film "A Feast Of Friends". Group disbanded in 1973.	
6/03/67	**1**[3]	17	1 ● **Light My Fire**	Elektra 45615
9/23/67	**12**	9	2 People Are Strange	Elektra 45621
12/09/67+	**25**	7	3 Love Me Two Times	Elektra 45624
3/30/68	**39**	8	4 The Unknown Soldier	Elektra 45628
7/06/68	**1**[2]	12	5 ● **Hello, I Love You**	Elektra 45635
8/31/68	**87**	6	6 Light My Fire [R]	Elektra 45615
12/28/68+	**3**	13	7 ● **Touch Me**	Elektra 45646
3/29/69	**44**	6	8 Wishful Sinful	Elektra 45656
6/14/69	**57**	9	9 Tell All The People	Elektra 45663
9/06/69	**64**	6	10 Runnin' Blue	Elektra 45675
4/11/70	**50**	6	11 You Make Me Real/	
		6	12 Roadhouse Blues	Elektra 45685
			all of above singles produced by Paul Rothchild	
4/10/71	**11**	11	13 Love Her Madly	Elektra 45726
7/03/71	**14**	12	14 Riders On The Storm	Elektra 45738
11/27/71	**71**	7	15 Tightrope Ride	Elektra 45757
9/30/72	**85**	4	16 The Mosquito	Elektra 45807
			above 2 singles are without Jim Morrison	
12/03/83+	**71**	7	17 Gloria	Elektra 69770
			recorded as a 'soundcheck' in 1969	
			CHARLIE DORE	
			British female vocalist.	
2/23/80	**13**	17	1 Pilot Of The Airwaves	Island 49166
			HAROLD DORMAN	
			Born on 12/23/31 in Drew, Mississippi. Pop/country singer, songwriter.	
2/29/60	**21**	19	1 Mountain Of Love	Rita 1003
			JIMMY DORSEY	
			Jimmy was born on 2/29/04 in Shenandoah, PA; died of cancer on 6/12/57. Great alto sax & clarinet soloist and bandleader beginning in 1935.	
2/23/57	**2**[4]	38	1 **So Rare**	Fraternity 755
			Top 100 #2 / Jockey #2 / Best Seller #3 / Juke Box #6 end featuring Jimmy on sax - recorded in New York on 11/11/56 tune originally hit #1 in 1937 for Guy Lombardo	

DEBUT DATE	PEAK POS	WKS CHR	ARTIST — Record Title	Label & Number
			JIMMY DORSEY — Cont'd	
8/19/57	**21**	11	2 June Night/ Jockey #21 / Best Seller #27 / Top 100 #39 featuring Dick Stabile on sax tune originally hit #2 in 1924 by Ted Lewis & His Band	
8/26/57	**77**	9	3 Jay-Dee's Boogie Woogie .... [I] above 2 sides cut 5 days after Jimmy's death, under direction of Lee Castle; version of brother Tommy's '38 classic "Boogie Woogie"	Fraternity 777
			LEE DORSEY Born Irving Lee Dorsey on 12/4/26 in New Orleans. Moved to Portland, Oregon at age 10. Prizefighter in early 50s as "Kid Chocolate". Major hits produced by Allen Toussaint & Marshall Sehorn. Lee died of emphysema in New Orleans on 12/1/86.	
9/11/61	**7**	13	1 **Ya Ya**	Fury 1053
12/18/61+	**27**	9	2 Do-Re-Mi	Fury 1056
7/03/65	**28**	9	3 Ride Your Pony	Amy 927
1/01/66	**44**	10	4 Get Out Of My Life, Woman	Amy 945
7/23/66	**8**	12	5 **Working In The Coal Mine**	Amy 958
10/22/66	**23**	9	6 Holy Cow	Amy 965
5/13/67	**97**	1	7 My Old Car	Amy 987
10/21/67	**62**	6	8 Go-Go Girl	Amy 998
6/28/69	**95**	3	9 Everything I Do Gohn Be Funky (From Now On)	Amy 11055
			THE TOMMY DORSEY ORCHESTRA Tommy was born on 11/19/05 in Mahanoy City, PA; choked to death on 11/26/56. Great trombonist and bandleader beginning in 1935. Tommy and brother Jimmy recorded together as the Dorsey Brothers Orchestra from 1928-35, reunited 1953-56. Hosted musical variety TV show, 1954-56. Warren Covington fronted band after Tommy's death.	
9/01/58	**7**	20	1 **Tea For Two Cha Cha** .... [I] Hot 100 #7 / Best Seller #8 end classic tune, originally hit #1 for Marion Harris in 1925	Decca 30704
12/01/58	**70**	3	2 I Want To Be Happy Cha Cha .... tune originally a #2 hit for Vincent Lopez in 1925	Decca 30790
			DOUBLE Euro-pop quartet from Germany. Led by Kurt Maloo & Felix Haug.	
6/28/86	**16**	18	1 The Captain Of Her Heart	A&M 2838
			DOUBLE EXPOSURE Soul quartet from Philadelphia, featuring lead singer James Williams.	
6/19/76	**54**	9	1 Ten Percent	Salsoul 2008
			DOUBLE IMAGE	
7/02/83	**92**	3	1 Night Pulse	Curb 03942
			DOUCETTE Jerry Doucette - Canadian rock singer-guitarist.	
4/08/78	**72**	8	1 Mama Let Him Play	Mushroom 7030
			CARL DOUGLAS Born in Jamaica, West Indies. Studied engineering in US and England.	
10/12/74	**1^{2}**	18	1 ● **Kung Fu Fighting**	20th Century 2140
2/15/75	**48**	7	2 Dance The Kung Fu	20th Century 2168
			CAROL DOUGLAS Born on 4/7/48 in Brooklyn, NY. Worked on commercials. Member of The Chantels vocal group, early 1970s. Went solo in 1974.	
11/30/74+	**11**	16	1 Doctor's Orders	Midland I. 10113
4/12/75	**81**	2	2 A Hurricane Is Coming Tonite	Midland I. 10229
			MIKE DOUGLAS Real name: Michael Dowd. Long-time syndicated TV talk show host. Singer with Kay Kyser's band, 1945-50 (vocalist on Kyser's #1 hit "Ole Buttermilk Sky" in 1946).	
12/25/65+	**6**	9	1 **The Men In My Little Girl's Life**	Epic 9876
			RONNY DOUGLAS	
7/31/61	**75**	3	1 Run, Run, Run	Everest 19413
			DEBBIE DOVALE	
11/16/63	**81**	4	1 Hey Lover	Roulette 4521
			RONNIE DOVE Born on 9/7/40 in Herndon, Virginia; discovered while singing in Baltimore. Nearly all of Ronnie's hits were produced by Phil Kahl (V.P. of Diamond Records).	
7/18/64	**40**	11	1 Say You	Diamond 167

DEBUT DATE	PEAK POS	WKS CHR	ARTIST — Record Title	Label & Number
			RONNIE DOVE — Cont'd	
10/24/64	**14**	10	2 Right Or Wrong	Diamond 173
1/09/65	**54**	7	3 Hello Pretty Girl	Diamond 176
3/13/65	**14**	11	4 One Kiss For Old Times' Sake	Diamond 179
6/05/65	**16**	10	5 A Little Bit Of Heaven	Diamond 184
8/28/65	**21**	9	6 I'll Make All Your Dreams Come True	Diamond 188
11/06/65	**25**	8	7 Kiss Away above 4 recordings arranged by Ray Stevens	Diamond 191
1/22/66	**18**	9	8 When Liking Turns To Loving	Diamond 195
4/16/66	**20**	8	9 Let's Start All Over Again	Diamond 198
6/18/66	**27**	8	10 Happy Summer Days	Diamond 205
9/03/66	**22**	9	11 I Really Don't Want To Know	Diamond 208
11/26/66	**18**	9	12 Cry	Diamond 214
2/18/67	**45**	6	13 One More Mountain To Climb	Diamond 217
4/22/67	**50**	6	14 My Babe written and produced by Neil Diamond	Diamond 221
8/05/67	**54**	5	15 I Want To Love You For What You Are	Diamond 227
12/16/67	**87**	3	16 Dancin' Out Of My Heart	Diamond 233
3/16/68	**99**	3	17 In Some Time	Diamond 240
6/08/68	**67**	6	18 Mountain Of Love	Diamond 244
9/21/68	**96**	3	19 Tomboy	Diamond 249
5/31/69	**93**	2	20 I Need You Now	Diamond 260
			THE DOVELLS Vocal group from Philadelphia. Originally called the Brooktones, from Overbrook High School. Consisted of Leonard Borisoff ("Len Barry"), Arnie Silver, Jerry Gross ("Jerry Summers"), Mike Freda ("Mike Dennis") and Jim Meeley ("Danny Brooks"). First recorded for Parkway, 1961. Brooks left in 1962; Barry left in late 1963. Group continued as trio. Recorded as "The Magistrates" for MGM in 1968.	
9/11/61	**2**[2]	16	1 **Bristol Stomp** Bristol: town near Philadelphia	Parkway 827
1/27/62	**37**	10	2 Do The New Continental	Parkway 833
5/19/62	**27**	11	3 Bristol Twistin' Annie	Parkway 838
8/11/62	**25**	12	4 Hully Gully Baby	Parkway 845
11/24/62	**82**	3	5 The Jitterbug	Parkway 855
4/27/63	**3**	14	6 **You Can't Sit Down**	Parkway 867
8/31/63	**50**	7	7 Betty In Bermudas	Parkway 882
11/09/63	**94**	2	8 Stop Monkeyin' Aroun'	Parkway 889
			JOE DOWELL Born on 1/23/40 in Bloomington, Indiana. Signed to Mercury's Smash label by Shelby Singleton, Jr. in Nashville.	
6/26/61	**1**[1]	16	1 **Wooden Heart** based on the German folk song "Muss I Denn" originally sung by Elvis Presley in the film "G.I. Blues"	Smash 1708
10/16/61	**50**	7	2 The Bridge Of Love	Smash 1717
6/23/62	**23**	9	3 Little Red Rented Rowboat	Smash 1759
			AL DOWNING Black vocalist, pianist, from Lenapah, OK. Session work with Wanda Jackson.	
4/27/63	**73**	2	1 You Never Miss Your Water (Till The Well Runs Dry)... **"LITTLE ESTHER" PHILLIPS & "BIG AL" DOWNING**	Lenox 5565
2/22/75	**85**	4	2 I'll Be Holding On	Chess 2158
			LAMONT DOZIER Born on 6/16/41 in Detroit. Singer, songwriter, record producer. Recorded as "Lamont Anthony" for Anna in 1961. With brothers Brian and Eddie Holland in highly successful songwriting and production team for Motown. Trio left Motown in 1968 and formed own Invictus/Hot Wax label.	
9/30/72	**57**	10	1 Why Can't We Be Lovers	Invictus 9125
12/22/73+	**15**	18	2 Trying To Hold On To My Woman	ABC 11407
6/15/74	**26**	12	3 Fish Ain't Bitin'	ABC 11438
1/04/75	**87**	5	4 Let Me Start Tonite	ABC 12044
			DRAFI	
5/14/66	**80**	3	1 Marble Breaks And Iron Bends	London 10825
			DRAGON Australian pop-rock sextet.	
8/18/84	**88**	4	1 Rain	Polydor 817292

DEBUT DATE	PEAK POS	WKS CHR	ARTIST — Record Title	Label & Number
			CHARLIE DRAKE	
			Born on 6/19/25 in London, England.	
1/13/62	**21**	12	1 My Boomerang Won't Come Back .... [N]	United Art. 398
			GUY DRAKE	
			Humorist from Weir, Kentucky.	
1/31/70	**63**	14	1 Welfare Cadilac.. [N]	Royal American 1
			PETE DRAKE & His Talking Steel Guitar	
			Pete was born on 10/8/32 in Atlanta. Nashville's top steel guitar sessionman.	
3/07/64	**25**	11	1 Forever..	Smash 1867
			THE DRAMATICS	
			Soul group from Detroit. First recorded for Wingate as the Dynamics, 1966. Members in 1971: Ron Banks (lead singer), William Howard, Larry Demps, Willie Ford and Elbert Wilkins. Howard and Wilkins replaced by L.J. Reynolds and Lenny Mayes, 1973.	
7/03/71	**9**	15	1 **Whatcha See Is Whatcha Get**..............................	Volt 4058
12/11/71+	**78**	7	2 Get Up And Get Down	Volt 4071
2/26/72	**5**	13	3 **In The Rain**	Volt 4075
8/26/72	**67**	9	4 Toast To The Fool	Volt 4082
5/05/73	**43**	12	5 Hey You! Get Off My Mountain	Volt 4090
10/27/73	**45**	10	6 Fell For You	Volt 4099
8/24/74	**62**	6	7 Door To Your Heart	Cadet 5704
			all of above (except #4) produced by Tony Hester	
			RON BANKS & THE DRAMATICS:	
5/03/75	**47**	9	8 Me And Mrs. Jones	ABC 12090
11/22/75	**81**	3	9 (I'm Going By) The Stars In Your Eyes	ABC 12125
			THE DRAMATICS:	
1/17/76	**87**	3	10 You're Fooling You	ABC 12150
1/08/77	**53**	15	11 Be My Girl..	ABC 12235
10/22/77	**76**	6	12 Shake It Well	ABC 12299
			RUSTY DRAPER	
			Born Farrell H. Draper in Kirksville, Missouri. Began career at the age of 12, singing and playing guitar over the radio in Tulsa, Oklahoma.	
8/20/55	**18**	4	1 Seventeen	Mercury 70651
			Best Seller #18 / Top 100 #88 pre	
10/01/55	**3**	16	2 **The Shifting, Whispering Sands**	Mercury 70696
			Juke Box #3 / Best Seller #6 / Top 100 #7 / Jockey #14	
12/17/55+	**11**	18	3 Are You Satisfied?...	Mercury 70757
			Best Seller #11 / Juke Box #11 / Top 100 #12	
4/07/56	**50**	8	4 Held For Questioning	Mercury 70818
9/01/56	**20**	14	5 In The Middle Of The House .... [N]	Mercury 70921
			Top 100 #20 / Jockey #24 above 4 feature backing vocals by the Jack Halloran Singers orchestra on all of above conducted by David Carroll	
2/16/57	**88**	2	6 Tiger Lily..	Mercury 70989
2/23/57	**53**	6	7 Let's Go Calypso	Mercury 71039
5/20/57	**6**	18	8 **Freight Train**	Mercury 71102
			Jockey #6 / Top 100 #11 / Best Seller #17	
7/18/60	**54**	7	9 Please Help Me, I'm Falling..................................	Mercury 71634
9/11/61	**91**	2	10 Signed, Sealed And Delivered	Mercury 71854
9/28/63	**57**	8	11 Night Life..	Monument 823
			THE DREAM ACADEMY	
			English trio: Nick Laird-Clowes (guitar/vocals), Gilbert Gabriel (keyboards), Kate St. John (vocals/oboe/saxophone).	
11/30/85+	**7**	21	1 **Life In A Northern Town**....................................	Warner 28841
4/19/86	**36**	11	2 The Love Parade	Reprise 28750
			THE DREAMLOVERS	
			Black vocal quintet formed while in high school in Philadelphia. Backup vocal group for Chubby Checker's "The Twist".	
7/31/61	**10**	12	1 **When We Get Married**..	Heritage 102
6/30/62	**62**	5	2 If I Should Lose You..	End 1114
			THE DREAM WEAVERS	
			Wade Buff, lead singer of trio (other 2 members are female) from Miami, Florida.	
11/12/55+	**7**	23	1 **It's Almost Tomorrow**.......................................	Decca 29683
			Juke Box #7 / Best Seller #8 / Top 100 #8 / Jockey #10	
3/10/56	**82**	6	2 Into The Night/	
4/07/56	**100**	1	3 You're Mine...	Decca 29818

DEBUT DATE	PEAK POS	WKS CHR	ARTIST — Record Title	Label & Number
			THE DREAM WEAVERS — Cont'd	
5/05/56	**33**	9	4 A Little Love Can Go A Long, Long Way/ from the Goodyear TV Playhouse Production "Joey"	
5/19/56	**87**	2	5 Is There Somebody Else	Decca 29905
			LEN DRESSLAR	
2/18/56	**78**	1	1 Chain Gang/	
2/18/56	**81**	2	2 These Hands backing vocals on above 2: the Jack Halloran Singers	Mercury 70774
			PATTI DREW Born on 12/29/44 in Charleston, SC. To Evanston, Illinois, 1956. Lead singer of The Drew-Vels. First recorded under own name for Quill, 1966. Left music, 1971.	
8/26/67	**85**	8	1 Tell Him solo version (see Drew-Vels version) also features bass singer, Carlton Black	Capitol 5861
8/03/68	**62**	11	2 Workin' On A Groovy Thing	Capitol 2197
11/16/68	**93**	2	3 Hard To Handle	Capitol 2339
			THE DREW-VELS Black vocal group from Evanston, Illinois. Consisted of sisters Patti, Lorraine and Erma Drew; with bass singer Carlton Black (married to Erma).	
2/08/64	**90**	2	1 Tell Him also see Patti's solo version above	Capitol 5055
			J.D. DREWS European progressive rock singer.	
12/27/80+	**79**	6	1 Don't Want No-Body	Unicorn 95000
			THE DRIFTERS Vocal group formed to showcase lead singer Clyde McPhatter on Atlantic in 1953. Included Gerhart and Andrew Thrasher, Bill Pinkney and McPhatter who went solo in 1955. Group continued with various lead singers until 1958. In 1958, manager George Treadwell disbanded the group and brought in The Five Crowns and renamed them The Drifters. The majority of The Drifters' pop hits were sung by 3 different lead singers: Ben E. King, 1959-60; Rudy Lewis, 1961-63; and Johnny Moore, 1957, and 1963-66. Rudy died of a heart attack in summer of 1964. Many personnel changes throughout career and several groups have used the name in later years.	
12/31/55	**80**	1	1 White Christmas [X] vocal duet: Clyde McPhatter & Bill Pinkney (bass) - recorded 11/53	Atlantic 1048
3/09/57	**69**	4	2 Fools Fall In Love	Atlantic 1123
7/01/57	**79**	2	3 Hypnotized above 2: Johnny Moore, lead singer	Atlantic 1141
6/23/58	**72**	5	4 Moonlight Bay/	
8/11/58	**58**	2	5 Drip Drop above 2: Bobby Hendricks, lead singer (Tommy Evans, bass)	Atlantic 1187
6/01/59	**2**[1]	19	6 **There Goes My Baby**	Atlantic 2025
10/12/59	**15**	15	7 Dance With Me/	
11/02/59	**33**	11	8 (If You Cry) True Love, True Love Johnny Lee Williams, lead singer	Atlantic 2040
2/22/60	**16**	11	9 This Magic Moment	Atlantic 2050
5/23/60	**54**	9	10 Lonely Winds	Atlantic 2062
9/05/60	**1**[3]	18	11 **Save The Last Dance For Me**	Atlantic 2071
12/19/60+	**17**	11	12 I Count The Tears above 7 (except #8): Ben E. King, lead singer	Atlantic 2087
12/19/60	**96**	1	13 White Christmas [X-R]	Atlantic 1048
3/20/61	**32**	11	14 Some Kind Of Wonderful	Atlantic 2096
6/05/61	**14**	12	15 Please Stay	Atlantic 2105
9/11/61	**16**	11	16 Sweets For My Sweet	Atlantic 2117
12/18/61	**72**	5	17 Room Full Of Tears	Atlantic 2127
2/24/62	**28**	10	18 When My Little Girl Is Smiling	Atlantic 2134
5/12/62	**73**	1	19 Stranger On The Shore	Atlantic 2143
11/03/62+	**5**	20	20 **Up On The Roof**	Atlantic 2162
12/22/62	**88**	1	21 White Christmas [X-R]	Atlantic 1048
3/23/63	**9**	10	22 **On Broadway**	Atlantic 2182
6/15/63	**71**	6	23 Rat Race	Atlantic 2191
9/07/63	**25**	10	24 I'll Take You Home	Atlantic 2201
2/01/64	**43**	7	25 Vaya Con Dios 14-20, 22, 23, 25: Rudy Lewis, lead singer	Atlantic 2216
5/02/64	**56**	7	26 One Way Love	Atlantic 2225
6/27/64	**4**	14	27 **Under The Boardwalk**	Atlantic 2237

DEBUT DATE	PEAK POS	WKS CHR	ARTIST — Record Title	Label & Number
			THE DRIFTERS — Cont'd	
9/26/64	**33**	7	28 I've Got Sand In My Shoes	Atlantic 2253
11/14/64	**18**	9	29 Saturday Night At The Movies	Atlantic 2260
1/30/65	**43**	6	30 At The Club	Atlantic 2268
4/24/65	**60**	5	31 Come On Over To My Place/	
4/24/65	**90**	2	32 Chains Of Love	Atlantic 2285
			Charles Thomas, lead singer	
7/03/65	**91**	3	33 Follow Me	Atlantic 2292
8/14/65	**51**	6	34 I'll Take You Where The Music's Playing	Atlantic 2298
3/19/66	**48**	7	35 Memories Are Made Of This	Atlantic 2325
12/03/66	**62**	7	36 Baby What I Mean	Atlantic 2366
			24, 26-31, 33-36: Johnny Moore, lead singer	
			DRUPI	
			Italian singer.	
11/03/73	**88**	4	1 Vado Via [F]	A&M 1460
			ROY DRUSKY	
			Born on 6/22/30 in Atlanta. Country singer, guitarist; leader of his band, The Loners.	
4/10/61	**35**	16	1 Three Hearts In A Tangle	Decca 31193
			"D" TRAIN	
			James "D-Train" Williams, R&B-funk singer from Brooklyn, New York.	
1/07/84	**79**	6	1 Something's On Your Mind	Prelude 8080
			DUALS	
			Black instrumental duo from Los Angeles: Henry Bellinger & Johnny Lageman.	
9/11/61	**25**	11	1 Stick Shift [I]	Sue 745
			THE DUBS	
			R&B quintet - Richard Blandon, lead singer.	
7/15/57	**72**	4	1 Don't Ask Me (To Be Lonely)	Gone 5002
11/04/57	**23**	16	2 Could This Be Magic	Gone 5011
			Best Seller #23 / Top 100 #24	
8/24/59	**74**	6	3 Chapel Of Dreams	Gone 5069
			DAVE DUDLEY	
			Born on 5/3/28 in Spencer, WI. Country singer, guitarist, songwriter.	
6/08/63	**32**	11	1 Six Days On The Road	Golden Wing 3020
10/12/63	**95**	1	2 Cowboy Boots	Golden Ring 3030
			THE DUKAYS	
			Soul quintet formed in Chicago in 1957 featuring Eugene ("Gene Chandler") Dixon, lead. The Dukays are the uncredited recording artist for the #1 hit "Duke Of Earl".	
5/15/61	**64**	13	1 The Girl's A Devil	Nat 4001
1/20/62	**73**	6	2 Nite Owl	Nat 4002
			DUKE JUPITER	
			Rock quartet from Rochester, New York. Marshall Styler, lead singer.	
3/27/82	**58**	7	1 I'll Drink To You	Coast To C. 02801
5/12/84	**68**	7	2 Little Lady	Morocco 1736
			DUKE & THE DRIVERS	
8/16/75	**95**	4	1 What You Got	ABC 12110
			DORIS DUKE	
			Real name: Doris Curry. Recorded as Doris Willingham for Hy-Monty in 1967.	
2/28/70	**50**	9	1 To The Other Woman (I'm The Other Woman)	Canyon 28
			GEORGE DUKE	
			Born on 1/12/46 in San Rafael, CA. Top jazz/rock keyboardist. Played with Jean-Luc Ponty, the Mothers of Invention, and Cannonball Adderley's band.	
1/07/78	**54**	6	1 Reach For It	Epic 50463
5/02/81	**19**	20	2 Sweet Baby	Epic 01052
			STANLEY CLARKE/GEORGE DUKE	
2/20/82	**41**	9	3 Shine On	Epic 02701
			PATTY DUKE	
			Full name: Anna Maria Patricia Duke Astin. Actress - married to actor John Astin. Won an Oscar for her performance in the film "The Miracle Worker", 1962. Starred in the TV series "The Patty Duke Show", 1963-65.	
6/26/65	**8**	11	1 **Don't Just Stand There**	United Art. 875

DEBUT DATE	PEAK POS	WKS CHR	ARTIST — Record Title	Label & Number
			PATTY DUKE — Cont'd	
10/02/65	**22**	8	2 Say Something Funny/	
9/25/65	**77**	5	3 Funny Little Butterflies from the film "Billie" (starring Patty Duke)	United Art. 915
2/26/66	**64**	5	4 Whenever She Holds You femme version of Bobby Goldsboro's hit "Whenever He Holds You"	United Art. 978
			DAVID DUNDAS London-based singer, songwriter and actor.	
10/09/76+	**17**	21	1 Jeans On originally a jingle in England for Brutus Jeans	Chrysalis 2094
			DUNN & MCCASHEN Don Dunn & Tony McCashen.	
11/07/70	**91**	2	1 Alright In The City	Capitol 2935
			ROBBIE DUPREE Born Robert Dupuis in Brooklyn in 1947. Singer, songwriter.	
4/12/80	**6**	23	1 **Steal Away**	Elektra 46621
7/19/80	**15**	18	2 Hot Rod Hearts	Elektra 47005
5/23/81	**54**	7	3 Brooklyn Girls	Elektra 47145
			THE DUPREES Italian-American vocal quintet from Jersey City: Joseph ("Joey Vann") Canzano, lead singer; Mike Arnone, Tom Bialablow, John Salvato and Joe Santollo. Joey Vann died on 2/28/84 (40). Also see Italian Asphalt & Pavement Company.	
8/04/62	**7**	13	1 **You Belong To Me** #1 hit for Jo Stafford in 1952	Coed 569
10/20/62	**13**	10	2 My Own True Love Tara's Theme from "Gone With The Wind"	Coed 571
1/26/63	**91**	4	3 I'd Rather Be Here In Your Arms	Coed 574
3/23/63	**89**	2	4 Gone With The Wind #1 hit for Horace Heidt in 1937	Coed 576
8/24/63	**37**	7	5 Why Don't You Believe Me #1 hit for Joni James in 1952	Coed 584
11/09/63	**18**	10	6 Have You Heard #4 hit for Joni James in 1953	Coed 585
1/25/64	**74**	5	7 (It's No) Sin #1 hit for Eddy Howard in 1951	Coed 587
7/24/65	**91**	2	8 Around The Corner	Columbia 43336
			DURAN DURAN Romantic-styled band formed in Birmingham, England in 1980. Consisted of Simon LeBon (b: 10/27/58), vocals; Andy Taylor (b: 2/16/61), guitar; Nick Rhodes (b: 6/8/62), keyboards; John Taylor (b: 6/20/60), bass; and Roger Taylor (b: 4/26/60), drums. Named after villain in the Jane Fonda film "Barbarella". None of the Taylors are related. MTV appearances helped spread group's popularity. Andy Taylor and John Taylor recorded with The Power Station, 1985; LeBon, Rhodes & Roger Taylor recorded as Arcadia in 1985. As of 1986, group now a trio: LeBon, Rhodes and John Taylor.	
12/25/82+	**3**	23	1 **Hungry Like The Wolf**	Harvest 5195
4/02/83	**14**	13	2 Rio	Capitol 5215
6/04/83	**4**	17	3 **Is There Something I Should Know**	Capitol 5233
11/05/83	**3**	17	4 **Union Of The Snake**	Capitol 5290
1/14/84	**10**	16	5 **New Moon On Monday**	Capitol 5309
4/21/84	**1**[2]	21	6 **The Reflex**	Capitol 5345
11/03/84	**2**[4]	18	7 **The Wild Boys**	Capitol 5417
2/02/85	**16**	14	8 Save A Prayer	Capitol 5438
5/18/85	**1**[2]	17	9 **A View To A Kill** from the James Bond film of the same title	Capitol 5475
11/01/86+	**2**[1]	17	10 **Notorious**	Capitol 5648
			JIMMY DURANTE Much-beloved comedian who started on vaudeville and became star of many Broadway shows and movies as well as his own TV show (1954-56); the great "Schnozzola" died on 1/29/80 (86).	
9/07/63	**51**	8	1 September Song song first popularized in 1939 by actor Walter Huston	Warner 5382
			DUSK Studio group created by Dawn's producers, Hank Medress and Dave Appell.	
2/06/71	**57**	9	1 Angel Baby	Bell 961
6/12/71	**53**	13	2 I Hear Those Church Bells Ringing	Bell 990

DEBUT DATE	PEAK POS	WKS CHR	ARTIST — Record Title		Label & Number
			HUELYN DUVALL		
			Male rockabilly singer from Huckaby, Texas.		
6/15/59	**88**	3	1 Little Boy Blue		Challenge 59014
			DYKE & THE BLAZERS		
			Soul band led by Arlester ("Dyke") Christian. Dyke was shot to death in 1971.		
4/15/67	**65**	15	1 Funky Broadway - Part 1		Original Sound 64
4/13/68	**67**	5	2 Funky Walk - Part 1 (East)		Original Sound 79
5/17/69	**35**	10	3 We Got More Soul		Original Sound 86
9/20/69	**36**	11	4 Let A Woman Be A Woman - Let A Man Be A Man		Original Sound 89
			BOB DYLAN		
			Born Robert Allen Zimmerman on 5/24/41 in Duluth, Minnesota. Singer-songwriter-guitarist-harmonica player. Took stage name from poet, Dylan Thomas. To New York City in December, 1960. Worked Greenwich Village folk clubs. Signed to Columbia Records in October, 1961. Innovator of folk-rock style, 1965. Motorcycle crash on 7/29/66 led to short retirement. Films "Don't Look Back", 1965, "Eat The Document", 1969, "Pat Garrett And Billy The Kid", 1973. Toured with Rolling Thunder Revue, 1976. Made film "Renaldo And Clara", 1978. Became a born-again Christian in 1979, songs reflecting his new faith. One of rock music's most influential artists.		
4/03/65	**39**	8	1 Subterranean Homesick Blues		Columbia 43242
7/24/65	**2**[2]	12	2 **Like A Rolling Stone**		Columbia 43346
10/02/65	**7**	9	3 **Positively 4th Street**		Columbia 43389
1/01/66	**58**	6	4 Can You Please Crawl Out Your Window?		Columbia 43477
4/16/66	**2**[1]	10	5 **Rainy Day Women #12 & 35**		Columbia 43592
7/02/66	**20**	7	6 I Want You		Columbia 43683
9/10/66	**33**	6	7 Just Like A Woman		Columbia 43792
5/20/67	**81**	4	8 Leopard-Skin Pill-Box Hat		Columbia 44069
5/17/69	**85**	5	9 I Threw It All Away		Columbia 44826
7/12/69	**7**	14	10 **Lay Lady Lay**		Columbia 44926
11/01/69	**50**	7	11 Tonight I'll Be Staying Here With You		Columbia 45004
7/25/70	**41**	7	12 Wigwam	[I]	Columbia 45199
			3-12: produced by Bob Johnston		
6/26/71	**41**	8	13 Watching The River Flow		Columbia 45409
12/04/71+	**33**	8	14 George Jackson		Columbia 45516
9/01/73	**12**	16	15 Knockin' On Heaven's Door		Columbia 45913
12/15/73+	**55**	7	16 A Fool Such As I		Columbia 45982
			song peaked at position 2 for Elvis Presley in 1959		
2/23/74	**44**	6	17 On A Night Like This		Asylum 11033
8/10/74	**66**	5	18 Most Likely You Go Your Way (And I'll Go Mine)		Asylum 11043
			BOB DYLAN/THE BAND		
			live recording from their 1973 tour		
3/08/75	**31**	7	19 Tangled Up In Blue		Columbia 10106
11/29/75+	**33**	11	20 Hurricane (Part I)		Columbia 10245
			dedicated to boxer Rubin Carter, a convicted murderer		
3/13/76	**54**	5	21 Mozambique		Columbia 10298
9/08/79	**24**	12	22 Gotta Serve Somebody		Columbia 11072
12/17/83+	**55**	9	23 Sweetheart Like You		Columbia 04301
			all of Dylan's hits were written by him (except #16)		
			THE DYNA-SORES		
6/06/60	**59**	3	1 Alley-Oop	[N]	Rendezvous 120
			DYNAMIC SUPERIORS		
			Soul quintet from Washington, DC. Tony Washington, lead singer.		
11/02/74	**68**	7	1 Shoe Shoe Shine		Motown 1324
			produced by Ashford & Simpson		
			THE DYNAMICS		
			Detroit soul group. Styley Shasier, lead singer (replaced by Bill Harris in 1967).		
11/02/63	**44**	10	1 Misery		Big Top 3161
3/22/69	**59**	7	2 Ice Cream Song		Cotillion 44021
			DYNASTY		
			Consisted of Kevin Spencer and Nidra Beard, formerly with the Sylvers, and Linda Carriere, formerly with DeBlanc and Starfire.		
9/13/80	**87**	6	1 I've Just Begun To Love You		Solar 12021
			THE DYNATONES		
9/03/66	**53**	8	1 The Fife Piper	[I]	HBR 494

DEBUT DATE	PEAK POS	WKS CHR	ARTIST — Record Title	Label & Number
			RONNIE DYSON	
			Born on 6/5/50 in Washington, DC; raised in Brooklyn. Lead part in the Broadway musical "Hair". In film "Putney Swope".	
6/20/70	**8**	14	1 **(If You Let Me Make Love To You Then) Why Can't I Touch You?**	Columbia 45110
			from the off-Broadway musical "Salvation"	
10/17/70	**50**	8	2 I Don't Wanna Cry	Columbia 45240
7/24/71	**94**	2	3 When You Get Right Down To It	Columbia 45387
2/17/73	**28**	13	4 One Man Band (Plays All Alone)	Columbia 45776
8/11/73	**60**	7	5 Just Don't Want To Be Lonely	Columbia 45867
7/31/76	**62**	12	6 The More You Do It (The More I Like It Done To Me)	Columbia 10356
			# E	
			BRENDA LEE EAGER - see JERRY BUTLER	
			EAGLES	
			Formed in Los Angeles in 1971. Consisted of Glenn Frey (vocals, guitar), Bernie Leadon (guitar), Randy Meisner (bass) and Don Henley (drums). Meisner had founded Poco; Leadon had been in the Flying Burrito Brothers; and Frey and Henley were with Linda Ronstadt. Debut album recorded in England in 1972. Don Felder (guitar) added in 1975. Leadon replaced by Joe Walsh in 1975; and Meisner replaced by Timothy B. Schmit in 1977. Disbanded in 1982.	
6/03/72	**12**	11	1 Take It Easy	Asylum 11005
9/09/72	**9**	13	2 **Witchy Woman**	Asylum 11008
12/30/72+	**22**	12	3 Peaceful Easy Feeling	Asylum 11013
6/23/73	**64**	8	4 Tequila Sunrise	Asylum 11017
9/15/73	**59**	8	5 Outlaw Man	Asylum 11025
			above 5 produced by Glyn Johns	
5/04/74	**32**	15	6 Already Gone	Asylum 11036
9/21/74	**77**	5	7 James Dean	Asylum 45202
11/30/74+	**1**[1]	19	8 **Best Of My Love**	Asylum 45218
5/31/75	**1**[1]	17	9 **One Of These Nights**	Asylum 45257
9/13/75	**2**[2]	14	10 **Lyin' Eyes**	Asylum 45279
12/20/75+	**4**	22	11 **Take It To The Limit**	Asylum 45293
12/18/76+	**1**[1]	15	12 ● **New Kid In Town**	Asylum 45373
2/26/77	**1**[1]	19	13 ● **Hotel California**	Asylum 45386
5/14/77	**11**	14	14 Life In The Fast Lane	Asylum 45403
12/09/78	**18**	8	15 Please Come Home For Christmas [X]	Asylum 45555
			remake of the 1961 Charles Brown classic	
10/06/79	**1**[1]	15	16 ● **Heartache Tonight**	Asylum 46545
12/08/79+	**8**	15	17 **The Long Run**	Asylum 46569
2/23/80	**8**	16	18 **I Can't Tell You Why**	Asylum 46608
12/20/80+	**21**	14	19 Seven Bridges Road	Asylum 47100
			6-19: produced by Bill Szymczyk	
			EARL-JEAN	
			Earl-Jean McCree of The Cookies.	
6/27/64	**38**	8	1 I'm Into Somethin' Good	Colpix 729
			THE EARLS	
			White doo-wop quartet from the Bronx: Larry Chance, lead; Bob Del Din, Eddie Harder, and Jack Wray.	
12/15/62+	**24**	9	1 Remember Then	Old Town 1130
			EARTH OPERA	
			Boston rock quartet led by David Grisman & Peter Rowan.	
4/26/69	**97**	1	1 Home To You	Elektra 45650
			EARTH, WIND & FIRE	
			R&B group formed in Los Angeles in 1969, by Chicago-bred Maurice White (b: 12/19/41, Memphis), lead vocals, percussion, kalimba, songwriter, producer. Co-lead singer Philip Bailey joined in 1972. White had been a session drummer for Chess Records and with the Ramsey Lewis Trio, 1966-1969. Group generally contained 8-10 members, with frequent personnel shuffling. In films "Sgt. Pepper's Lonely Hearts Club Band", and "That's The Way Of The World".	
7/03/71	**93**	5	1 Love Is Life	Warner 7492
8/04/73	**50**	11	2 Evil	Columbia 45888
11/17/73+	**52**	11	3 Keep Your Head To The Sky	Columbia 45953

DEBUT DATE	PEAK POS	WKS CHR	ARTIST — Record Title	Label & Number
			EARTH, WIND & FIRE — Cont'd	
3/09/74	**29**	15	4 Mighty Mighty	Columbia 46007
7/13/74	**55**	9	5 Kalimba Story	Columbia 46070
9/28/74	**33**	7	6 Devotion	Columbia 10026
1/18/75	**50**	6	7 Hot Dawgit [I] RAMSEY LEWIS and EARTH, WIND & FIRE	Columbia 10056
2/15/75	**1**[1]	20	8 ● **Shining Star**	Columbia 10090
3/22/75	**44**	7	9 Sun Goddess [I] RAMSEY LEWIS and EARTH, WIND & FIRE	Columbia 10103
7/05/75	**12**	16	10 That's The Way Of The World	Columbia 10172
11/22/75+	**5**	17	11 ● **Sing A Song**	Columbia 10251
3/27/76	**39**	9	12 Can't Hide Love	Columbia 10309
7/17/76	**12**	19	13 ● Getaway	Columbia 10373
11/20/76+	**21**	15	14 Saturday Nite	Columbia 10439
10/29/77+	**13**	18	15 Serpentine Fire	Columbia 10625
3/04/78	**32**	15	16 Fantasy	Columbia 10688
7/22/78	**9**	13	17 ● **Got To Get You Into My Life**	Columbia 10796
11/18/78+	**8**	17	18 ● **September**	ARC 10854
5/12/79	**6**	16	19 ● **Boogie Wonderland** EARTH, WIND & FIRE with THE EMOTIONS	ARC 10956
7/07/79	**2**[2]	17	20 ● **After The Love Has Gone**	ARC 11033
10/20/79	**58**	7	21 In The Stone	ARC 11093
12/22/79+	**64**	6	22 Star	ARC 11165
9/20/80	**44**	9	23 Let Me Talk	ARC 11366
11/22/80	**48**	12	24 You	ARC 11407
2/07/81	**59**	7	25 And Love Goes On	ARC 11434
10/03/81	**3**	24	26 ● **Let's Groove**	ARC 02536
1/23/82	**51**	7	27 Wanna Be With You	ARC 02688
1/22/83	**17**	16	28 Fall In Love With Me	Columbia 03375
5/14/83	**76**	4	29 Side By Side	Columbia 03814
11/12/83	**57**	9	30 Magnetic	Columbia 04210
			EAST L.A. CAR POOL	
8/02/75	**72**	6	1 Like They Say In L.A.	GRC 2064
			SHEENA EASTON Born on 4/27/59 in Glasgow, Scotland. Vocalist, actress. Starred in BBC-TV documentary "The Big Time", playing a singer, 1980. Sang on the opening credits for the James Bond film "For Your Eyes Only".	
2/14/81	**1**[2]	21	1 ● **Morning Train (Nine To Five)**	EMI America 8071
5/09/81	**18**	18	2 Modern Girl	EMI America 8080
7/25/81	**4**	25	3 **For Your Eyes Only** from the film of the same title	Liberty 1418
11/28/81+	**15**	18	4 You Could Have Been With Me	EMI America 8101
4/03/82	**30**	15	5 When He Shines	EMI America 8113
9/04/82	**57**	7	6 Machinery	EMI America 8131
10/30/82	**64**	7	7 I Wouldn't Beg For Water	EMI America 8142
1/29/83	**6**	18	8 **We've Got Tonight** KENNY ROGERS & SHEENA EASTON	Liberty 1492
8/20/83	**9**	22	9 **Telefone (Long Distance Love Affair)**	EMI America 8172
12/10/83+	**25**	20	10 Almost Over You	EMI America 8186
4/14/84	**79**	3	11 Devil In A Fast Car	EMI America 8201
8/25/84	**7**	25	12 **Strut**	EMI America 8227
12/22/84+	**9**	17	13 **Sugar Walls** written and produced by Prince (as Alexander Nevermind)	EMI America 8253
3/23/85	**80**	6	14 Swear	EMI America 8263
10/26/85	**29**	14	15 Do It For Love	EMI America 8295
2/08/86	**65**	6	16 Jimmy Mack	EMI America 8309
8/02/86	**43**	12	17 So Far So Good from the film "About Last Night"	EMI America 8332

DEBUT DATE	PEAK POS	WKS CHR	ARTIST — Record Title	Label & Number
			CLINT EASTWOOD - see T.G. SHEPPARD	
			THE EASYBEATS	
			Rock quintet formed in Australia in 1965. All members were natives of England and returned there in 1966. Members George Young and Harry Vanda later formed "Flash & The Pan".	
3/18/67	**16**	14	1 Friday On My Mind	United Art. 50106
11/15/69	**100**	1	2 St. Louis	Rare Earth 5009
			EASY RIDERS - see TERRY GILKYSON	
			EASY STREET	
7/04/76	**81**	5	1 I've Been Lovin' You	Capricorn 0255
			THE EBONYS	
			R&B vocal group from Camden, NJ, formed in 1968. Consisted of Jenny Holmes, David Beasley, James Tuten and Clarence Vaughan.	
6/12/71	**51**	7	1 You're The Reason Why	Phil. Int. 3503
7/07/73	**68**	6	2 It's Forever	Phil. Int. 3529
			THE ECHOES	
			Brooklyn trio: Tommy Duffy, Harry Doyle and Tom Morrissey.	
3/06/61	**12**	12	1 Baby Blue	Seg-way 103
6/12/61	**88**	3	2 Sad Eyes (Don't You Cry)	Seg-way 106
			BILLY ECKSTINE	
			Born William Clarence Eckstein on 7/8/14 in Pittsburgh. Nickname: "Mr. B". Sang with Earl Hines from 1939-43. Formed own jazz band with Charlie Parker, Dizzy Gillespie, Miles Davis and Sarah Vaughan.	
3/10/56	**76**	4	1 The Bitter With The Sweet orchestra directed by Hugo Winterhalter	RCA 6436
7/29/57	**82**	7	2 Passing Strangers SARAH VAUGHAN & BILLY ECKSTINE	Mercury 71122
			ECSTASY, PASSION & PAIN	
			Formed in New York City, featuring Barbara Roy, vocals.	
7/06/74	**93**	4	1 Good Things Don't Last Forever	Roulette 7156
10/19/74	**52**	8	2 Ask Me	Roulette 7159
3/29/75	**48**	6	3 One Beautiful Day	Roulette 7163
6/05/76	**98**	2	4 Touch And Go	Roulette 7182
			EDDIE & BETTY	
			Eddie & Betty Cole. Eddie played The Baron on TV's "Bourbon Street Beat".	
6/29/59	**87**	4	1 Sweet Someone	Warner 5054
			EDDIE & DUTCH	
4/04/70	**52**	7	1 My Wife, The Dancer [N]	Ivanhoe 502
			EDDIE & THE CRUISERS - see JOHN CAFFERTY & THE BEAVER BROWN BAND	
			EDDIE & THE TIDE	
			Rock quintet led by vocalist/guitarist Steve "Eddie" Rice.	
9/21/85	**85**	2	1 One In A Million	Atco 99617
			JOHN EDDIE	
			New Jersey rocker.	
6/07/86	**52**	10	1 Jungle Boy	Columbia 05858
			DUANE EDDY	
			Born on 4/26/38 in Corning, New York. Began playing guitar at age 5. At age 13, moved to Tucson, then to Coolidge, Arizona. To Phoenix in 1955, and then began long association with producer, songwriter Lee Hazlewood. Eddy's backing band, The Rebels, included 3 top sessionmen, Larry Knechtel on piano and Jim Horn and Steve Douglas on sax. Films "Because They're Young", "A Thunder Of Drums", "The Wild Westerners", "The Savage Seven" and "Kona Coast". Married to Jesse Colter, 1962-68. Duane originated the "twangy" guitar sound and is the all-time #1 rock and roll instrumentalist.	
3/17/58	**72**	3	1 Moovin' N' Groovin' [I]	Jamie 1101
6/30/58	**6**	14	2 **Rebel-'Rouser** [I] Best Seller #6 / Top 100 #6 / Jockey #14 end handclaps and rebel yells by The Rivingtons	Jamie 1104
8/25/58	**27**	8	3 Ramrod [I] Best Seller #27 / Hot 100 #28	Jamie 1109

DEBUT DATE	PEAK POS	WKS CHR	ARTIST — Record Title		Label & Number
			DUANE EDDY — Cont'd		
11/03/58	**15**	12	4 Cannonball	[I]	Jamie 1111
1/19/59	**23**	13	5 The Lonely One	[I]	Jamie 1117
3/30/59	**30**	9	6 'Yep!'	[I]	Jamie 1122
6/15/59	**9**	15	7 **Forty Miles Of Bad Road/**	[I]	
6/29/59	**46**	8	8 The Quiet Three	[I]	Jamie 1126
10/05/59	**37**	8	9 Some Kind-A Earthquake/	[I]	
9/28/59	**59**	9	10 First Love, First Tears	[I]	Jamie 1130
12/28/59+	**26**	9	11 Bonnie Came Back traditional Scottish tune "My Bonnie Lies Over The Ocean"	[I]	Jamie 1144
3/21/60	**45**	7	12 Shazam!	[I]	Jamie 1151
5/23/60	**4**	15	13 **Because They're Young** above 2 from the film "Because They're Young"	[I]	Jamie 1156
8/22/60	**78**	6	14 Kommotion	[I]	Jamie 1163
10/10/60	**27**	9	15 Peter Gunn new version with "The Art Of Noise" charted in 1986	[I]	Jamie 1168
12/19/60+	**18**	12	16 'Pepe' from the film of the same title	[I]	Jamie 1175
3/20/61	**39**	7	17 Theme From Dixie classic Civil War song, written in 1860 by black composer Daniel Emmett - vocals by the Anita Kerr Singers & The Jordanaires	[I]	Jamie 1183
5/29/61	**84**	3	18 Ring Of Fire from the film of the same title	[I]	Jamie 1187
7/17/61	**87**	2	19 Drivin' Home	[I]	Jamie 1195
8/28/61	**50**	5	20 My Blue Heaven Gene Austin's theme song - written in 1927	[I]	Jamie 1200
4/21/62	**78**	5	21 Deep In The Heart Of Texas a #1 hit in 1942 for Alvino Rey & His Orchestra	[I]	RCA 7999
7/07/62	**33**	9	22 The Ballad Of Paladin theme from the TV series "Have Gun-Will Travel"	[I]	RCA 8047
10/06/62	**12**	16	23 (Dance With The) Guitar Man		RCA 8087
2/09/63	**28**	9	24 Boss Guitar		RCA 8131
5/18/63	**82**	5	25 Lonely Boy, Lonely Guitar		RCA 8180
8/24/63	**93**	2	26 Your Baby's Gone Surfin' female vocal backing on above 4 by The Rebelettes (The Blossoms)		RCA 8214
1/04/64	**97**	2	27 The Son Of Rebel Rouser	[I]	RCA 8276
5/17/86	**50**	11	28 Peter Gunn **THE ART OF NOISE featuring DUANE EDDY**	[I]	China 42986
			RANDY EDELMAN Singer/songwriter/pianist - composed Barry Manilow's hit "Weekend In New England".		
3/08/75	**92**	4	1 Everybody Wants To Find A Bluebird		20th Century 2155
			EDISON LIGHTHOUSE British pop quintet featuring lead singer Tony Burrows.		
2/21/70	**5**	13	1 ● **Love Grows (Where My Rosemary Goes)**		Bell 858
1/09/71	**72**	6	2 It's Up To You Petula		Bell 960
			DAVE EDMUNDS Born on 4/15/44 in Cardiff, Wales. Singer-songwriter-guitarist-producer. Formed Love Sculpture in 1967. Formed rockabilly band, Rockpile in 1976. Produced for Shakin' Stevens, Binsley Schwarz, Stray Cats, and others.		
12/26/70+	**4**	12	1 **I Hear You Knocking** #2 R&B hit for Smiley Lewis; #2 Pop hit for Gale Storm - both 1955		MAM 3601
5/01/71	**75**	4	2 I'm Comin' Home		MAM 3608
9/01/79	**65**	6	3 Girls Talk		Swan Song 71001
5/09/81	**54**	8	4 Almost Saturday Night		Swan Song 72000
5/14/83	**39**	15	5 Slipping Away		Columbia 03877
4/20/85	**91**	2	6 High School Nights from the film "Porky's Revenge!"		Columbia 04762
			THE EDSELS R&B quintet from Youngstown, Ohio; George Jones, Jr. (lead), Marshall Sewell (bass).		
5/01/61	**21**	11	1 Rama Lama Ding Dong released on the Dub label in 1958 as "Lama Rama Ding Dong"		Twin 700
			EDWARD BEAR Trio from Toronto, Canada; Larry Evoy, lead singer. Took name from a character in the beloved children's classic "Winnie The Pooh".		
5/30/70	**68**	4	1 You, Me And Mexico		Capitol 2801
12/16/72+	**3**	18	2 ● **Last Song**		Capitol 3452

DEBUT DATE	PEAK POS	WKS CHR	ARTIST — Record Title	Label & Number
			EDWARD BEAR — Cont'd	
4/14/73	**37**	12	3 Close Your Eyes	Capitol 3581
			BOBBY EDWARDS	
			Real name: Robert Moncrief. Country singer from Anniston, Alabama.	
8/28/61	**11**	17	1 You're The Reason backing vocals by the Four Young Men	Crest 1075
1/13/62	**71**	6	2 What's The Reason	Capitol 4674
			DENNIS EDWARDS	
			Born on 2/3/43 in Birmingham, AL. Lead singer of the Temptations, 1968-77, 1980-84, 1987-present.	
4/28/84	**72**	6	1 Don't Look Any Further female vocal by Siedah Garrett	Gordy 1715
			JIMMY EDWARDS	
1/20/58	**78**	3	1 Love Bug Crawl	Mercury 71209
			JONATHAN EDWARDS	
			Born on 7/28/46 in Minnesota. Formed bluegrass band, Sugar Creek in 1965.	
11/13/71+	**4**	16	1 ● **Sunshine**	Capricorn 8021
			TOM EDWARDS	
			Disc jockey at WERE Radio in Cleveland, 1951-59. Owner of Record Heaven record store in Cleveland. Died on 7/24/81 (58).	
2/02/57	**57**	5	1 What Is A Teenage Girl?/ [S-N]	
2/09/57	**96**	1	2 What Is A Teenage Boy? [S-N] orchestra directed by Mort Garson on above 2	Coral 61773
			TOMMY EDWARDS	
			Born on 2/17/22 in Richmond, Virginia. Died on 10/23/69 in Richmond. Singer, songwriter, composer. Performing since age nine. First recorded for Top in 1949.	
8/18/58	**1**[6]	22	1 **It's All In The Game/** Hot 100 #1(6) / Best Seller #1(3) end written by U.S. Vice President Charles Dawes in 1912 as "Melody In A Major" - Tommy's original version charted in 1951 (POS 18)	
10/20/58	**61**	3	2 Please Love Me Forever	MGM 12688
10/27/58	**15**	16	3 Love Is All We Need	MGM 12722
2/16/59	**11**	13	4 Please Mr. Sun/ Tommy's original version charted in 1952 (POS 22)	
3/02/59	**27**	12	5 The Morning Side Of The Mountain Tommy's original version charted in 1951 (POS 24)	MGM 12757
5/18/59	**26**	8	6 My Melancholy Baby/ first charted in 1915 by Walter Van Brunt	
6/01/59	**86**	3	7 It's Only The Good Times	MGM 12794
8/10/59	**53**	10	8 I've Been There/	
8/24/59	**100**	1	9 I Looked At Heaven	MGM 12814
11/02/59	**65**	8	10 Honestly And Truly/	
11/16/59+	**47**	9	11 (New In) The Ways Of Love	MGM 12837
2/22/60	**45**	8	12 Don't Fence Me In #1 hit for Bing Crosby & The Andrews Sisters in 1944	MGM 12871
5/23/60	**18**	13	13 I Really Don't Want To Know first charted in 1954 by Les Paul & Mary Ford (POS 11)	MGM 12890
10/10/60	**78**	2	14 It's Not The End Of Everything orchestra conducted by Leroy Holmes on all of above	MGM 12916
			VINCENT EDWARDS	
			Born Vincento Eduardo Zoine on 7/9/28 in New York City. Stage, film and TV actor. Best known as the star of the TV series "Ben Casey".	
7/07/62	**68**	6	1 Why Did You Leave Me?	Russ-Fi 7001
8/11/62	**72**	2	2 Don't Worry 'Bout Me	Decca 31413
			WALTER EGAN	
			Born on 7/12/48 in Jamaica, New York.	
6/11/77	**82**	6	1 Only The Lucky produced by Lindsey Buckingham & Stevie Nicks	Columbia 10531
5/27/78	**8**	22	2 ● **Magnet And Steel**	Columbia 10719
10/14/78	**55**	7	3 Hot Summer Nights	Columbia 10824
4/09/83	**46**	10	4 Fool Moon Fire	Backstreet 52200
			THE 8TH DAY	
			Detroit session musicians assembled by producers Holland-Dozier-Holland.	
5/15/71	**11**	13	1 ● She's Not Just Another Woman	Invictus 9087

DEBUT DATE	PEAK POS	WKS CHR	ARTIST — Record Title	Label & Number
			THE 8TH DAY — Cont'd	
9/18/71	**28**	11	2 You've Got To Crawl (Before You Walk)	Invictus 9098
1/08/72	**79**	4	3 If I Could See The Light	Invictus 9107
			EL CHICANO	
			Mexican-American band, formed in Los Angeles by Bobby Espinosa.	
4/11/70	**28**	9	1 Viva Tirado - Part I [I]	Kapp 2085
6/17/72	**45**	7	2 Brown Eyed Girl	Kapp 2173
11/17/73	**40**	10	3 Tell Her She's Lovely	MCA 40104
			EL COCO	
			6-man Los Angeles-based disco band led by producers Laurin Rinder & Michael Lewis.	
10/23/76	**61**	8	1 Lets Get It Together [I]	AVI 115
11/26/77+	**44**	15	2 Cocomotion [I]	AVI 147
10/28/78	**91**	6	3 Dancing In Paradise	AVI 203
			THE EL DORADOS	
			Chicago R&B quintet featuring Pirkle Lee Moses, lead singer.	
10/15/55	**17**	15	1 At My Front Door Best Seller #17 / Top 100 #35	Vee-Jay 147
			DONNIE ELBERT	
			Vocalist, multi-instrumentalist from Buffalo, New York.	
7/08/57	**61**	6	1 What Can I Do	DeLuxe 6125
11/28/70	**98**	2	2 Can't Get Over Losing You	Rare Bullet 101
10/16/71	**15**	13	3 Where Did Our Love Go	All Platinum 2330
1/22/72	**92**	4	4 Sweet Baby	All Platinum 2333
1/29/72	**22**	9	5 I Can't Help Myself (Sugar Pie, Honey Bunch)	Avco 4587
			THE ELECTRIC EXPRESS	
7/31/71	**81**	4	1 It's The Real Thing - Pt. I [I]	Linco 1001
			THE ELECTRIC INDIAN	
			Instrumental group assembled from top Philadelphia studio musicians, some later in MFSB.	
8/02/69	**16**	11	1 Keem-O-Sabe [I]	United Art. 50563
12/13/69	**95**	1	2 Land Of 1000 Dances [I]	United Art. 50613
			ELECTRIC LIGHT ORCHESTRA	
			Group formed in Birmingham, England in 1971, by Roy Wood, Bev Bevans and Jeff Lynne of The Move. Wood left after their first album, leaving Lynne as the group's leader. Much personnel shuffling from then on. From a group size of 8 in 1971, the 1986 ELO consisted of 3 members: Lynne (vocals, guitar, keyboards), Bevan (drums) and Richard Tandy (keyboards).	
4/28/73	**42**	16	1 Roll Over Beethoven revival of Chuck Berry's 1955 classic hit	United Art. 173
12/01/73+	**53**	11	2 Showdown	United Art. 337
5/04/74	**87**	5	3 Daybreaker [I]	United Art. 405
12/21/74+	**9**	16	4 **Can't Get It Out Of My Head**	United Art. 573
11/15/75+	**10**	17	5 **Evil Woman**	United Art. 729
3/13/76	**14**	14	6 Strange Magic	United Art. 770
8/07/76	**59**	7	7 Showdown [R]	United Art. 842
10/23/76+	**13**	18	8 Livin' Thing	United Art. 888
2/05/77	**24**	12	9 Do Ya originally charted by The Move (forerunner of ELO) in 1972	United Art. 939
6/11/77	**7**	23	10● **Telephone Line**	United Art. 1000
11/19/77+	**13**	15	11 Turn To Stone	Jet 1099
2/18/78	**17**	16	12 Sweet Talkin' Woman	Jet 1145
6/24/78	**35**	12	13 Mr. Blue Sky	Jet 5050
10/28/78	**75**	4	14 It's Over	Jet 5052
5/19/79	**8**	15	15 **Shine A Little Love**	Jet 5057
8/04/79	**4**	15	16● **Don't Bring Me Down**	Jet 5060
10/20/79	**37**	8	17 Confusion	Jet 5064
12/08/79+	**39**	11	18 Last Train To London	Jet 5067
5/24/80	**16**	15	19● I'm Alive	MCA 41246
8/02/80	**13**	16	20 All Over The World	MCA 41289
8/09/80	**8**	17	21 **Xanadu** **OLIVIA NEWTON-JOHN/ELECTRIC LIGHT ORCHESTRA** above 3 from the film "Xanadu"	MCA 41285

DEBUT DATE	PEAK POS	WKS CHR	ARTIST — Record Title	Label & Number
			ELECTRIC LIGHT ORCHESTRA — Cont'd	
7/25/81	**10**	19	22 **Hold On Tight**	Jet 02408
10/24/81	**38**	11	23 Twilight	Jet 02559
6/25/83	**19**	13	24 Rock 'N' Roll Is King	Jet 03964
10/01/83	**86**	2	25 Four Little Diamonds above 4 shown only as: **ELO**	Jet 04130
2/01/86	**18**	15	26 Calling America all of above written (except #1) and produced by Jeff Lynne	CBS Assoc. 05766
			THE ELECTRIC PRUNES Seattle psychedelic rock quintet. James Lowe, lead singer.	
12/10/66+	**11**	14	1 I Had Too Much To Dream (Last Night)	Reprise 0532
4/01/67	**27**	8	2 Get Me To The World On Time	Reprise 0564
			THE ELEGANTS White doo-wop quintet from Staten Island, New York - Vito Picone, lead singer.	
7/21/58	**1**[1]	19	1 **Little Star** Hot 100 #1 / Best Seller #2	Apt 25005
			ELEPHANTS MEMORY Rock/jazz group formed in New York City's East Village. Backing band on John Lennon's "Some Time In New York City" album, and Yoko Ono's "Approximately Infinite Universe" LP.	
8/08/70	**50**	14	1 Mongoose	Metromedia 182
			THE ELEVENTH HOUR Studio group fronted by singer/songwriter Kenny Nolan.	
4/06/74	**94**	2	1 So Good	20th Century 2076
8/30/75	**55**	15	2 Hollywood Hot	20th Century 2215
			LARRY ELGART & His Manhattan Swing Orchestra Larry was born on 3/20/22 in New London, Connecticut. Alto saxman in brother Les' band and his own band.	
6/05/82	**31**	12	1 Hooked On Swing [I] In The Mood/Cherokee/American Patrol/Sing, Sing, Sing/Don't Be That Way/Little Brown Jug/Opus #1/Zing Went The Strings Of My Heart/String Of Pearls	RCA 13219
			LES ELGART Les was born on 8/3/18 in New Haven, CT. Trumpeter and bandleader since 1945.	
4/07/56	**56**	10	1 Main Title - Golden Arm [I] from the Otto Preminger film "The Man With The Golden Arm"	Columbia 40664
			THE ELGINS R&B quartet from Detroit. Saundra Edwards, lead singer.	
2/19/66	**92**	4	1 Put Yourself In My Place/	
3/19/66	**72**	8	2 Darling Baby	V.I.P. 25029
10/22/66	**50**	8	3 Heaven Must Have Sent You	V.I.P. 25037
7/29/67	**92**	1	4 It's Been A Long Long Time	V.I.P. 25043
			JIMMY ELLEDGE Born on 1/8/43 in Nashville.	
11/13/61+	**22**	14	1 Funny How Time Slips Away written by Willie Nelson; produced by Chet Atkins	RCA 7946
			YVONNE ELLIMAN Born on 12/29/51 in Honolulu, Hawaii. Portrayed Mary Magdalene in the rock opera "Jesus Christ, Superstar". Joined with Eric Clapton during his 1974 comeback tour.	
4/24/71	**28**	10	1 I Don't Know How To Love Him	Decca 32785
9/25/71	**92**	6	2 Everything's Alright above 2 from the rock opera "Jesus Christ, Superstar"	Decca 32870
10/02/76	**14**	19	3 Love Me	RSO 858
3/19/77	**15**	16	4 Hello Stranger	RSO 871
1/28/78	**1**[1]	22	5● **If I Can't Have You** from the film "Saturday Night Fever"	RSO 884
12/23/78+	**59**	6	6 Moment By Moment from the John Travolta film of the same title	RSO 915
10/13/79	**34**	13	7 Love Pains	RSO 1007
			RAY ELLIS Born on 7/28/23 in Philadelphia. Saxophonist, conductor, arranger, producer.	
10/17/60	**84**	4	1 Midnight Lace [I] from the Doris Day film of the same title	MGM 12942

DEBUT DATE	PEAK POS	WKS CHR	ARTIST — Record Title	Label & Number
			RAY ELLIS — Cont'd	
7/03/61	**81**	5	2 La Dolce Vita (The Sweet Life) .... [I]	RCA 7888
			from the Marcello Mastroianni film "La Dolce Vita"	
			SHIRLEY ELLIS	
			Soul singer from the Bronx, New York.	
11/16/63+	**8**	14	1 **The Nitty Gritty**	Congress 202
2/22/64	**72**	6	2 (That's) What The Nitty Gritty Is	Congress 208
12/12/64+	**3**	14	3 **The Name Game**	Congress 230
3/20/65	**8**	9	4 **The Clapping Song (Clap Pat Clap Slap)**	Congress 234
5/29/65	**78**	5	5 The Puzzle Song (A Puzzle In Song)	Congress 238
			above 5 written by Shirley's manager and husband, Lincoln Chase	
2/25/67	**67**	6	6 Soul Time	Columbia 44021
			LORRAINE ELLISON	
			Vocalist, composer from Philadelphia. Successful songwriter with Sam Bell.	
10/08/66	**64**	8	1 Stay With Me	Warner 5850
10/07/67	**89**	2	2 Heart Be Still	Loma 2074
			ELMO & ALMO	
6/03/67	**98**	2	1 When The Good Sun Shines	Daddy Best 2501
			EMERSON, LAKE & PALMER	
			English classical oriented rock trio formed in 1969. Consisted of Keith Emerson (with The Nice), keyboards; Greg Lake (King Crimson), vocals, bass, guitars; and Carl Palmer (Atomic Rooster), drums. Group split up in 1979, with Palmer joining supergroup Asia. Emerson & Lake regrouped in 1986 with new drummer Cozy Powell. Palmer returned in 1987, relacing Powell.	
3/13/71	**48**	12	1 Lucky Man	Cotillion 44106
3/18/72	**70**	6	2 Nutrocker .... [I]	Cotillion 44151
			adapted from Tschaikovsky's "The Nutcracker"	
8/26/72	**39**	11	3 From The Beginning	Cotillion 44158
12/30/72+	**51**	7	4 Lucky Man .... [R]	Cotillion 44106
			EMERSON, LAKE & POWELL:	
6/21/86	**60**	8	5 Touch & Go	Polydor 885101
			LES EMMERSON	
			Lead singer-guitarist of Five Man Electrical Band.	
1/13/73	**51**	9	1 Control Of Me	Lion 141
			THE EMOTIONS	
			White male quintet from Brooklyn. Joe Favale, lead singer.	
12/01/62+	**76**	6	1 Echo	Kapp 490
			THE EMOTIONS	
			Black female trio from Chicago, consisting of sisters Wanda (lead), Sheila and Jeanette Hutchinson. First worked as child gospel group called the Heavenly Sunbeams. Left gospel, became The Emotions in 1968. Jeanette replaced by cousin Theresa Davis in 1970, and later by sister Pamela.	
5/24/69	**39**	10	1 So I Can Love You	Volt 4010
11/06/71+	**52**	14	2 Show Me How	Volt 4066
7/22/72	**93**	5	3 I Could Never Be Happy	Volt 4083
3/23/74	**73**	6	4 Put A Little Love Away	Volt 4106
10/09/76	**87**	6	5 Flowers/	
11/06/76	**51**	12	6 I Don't Wanna Lose Your Love	Columbia 10347
6/11/77	**1**[5]	23	7 ● **Best Of My Love**	Columbia 10544
10/29/77	**44**	13	8 Don't Ask My Neighbors	Columbia 10622
5/12/79	**6**	16	9 ● **Boogie Wonderland**	ARC 10956
			EARTH, WIND & FIRE with THE EMOTIONS	
			THE EMPEROR'S	
12/03/66+	**55**	9	1 Karate	Mala 543
			THE ENCHANTERS	
3/06/61	**96**	2	1 I Lied To My Heart	Musitron 1072
			THE ENCHANTERS	
			R&B trio from Philadelphia: Zola Pearnell, Samuel Bell and Charles Boyer. Trio also backed Garnet Mimms.	
9/05/64	**91**	3	1 I Wanna Thank You	Warner 5460

DEBUT DATE	PEAK POS	WKS CHR	ARTIST — Record Title	Label & Number
			ENCHANTMENT	
			Soul quintet from Detroit, formed in 1966 while in high school. Did soundtrack for the film "Deliver Us From Evil".	
1/29/77	**25**	13	1 Gloria	United Art. 912
8/06/77	**45**	10	2 Sunshine	Roadshow 991
2/04/78	**33**	11	3 It's You That I Need	Roadshow 1124
			ENGLAND DAN & JOHN FORD COLEY	
			Pop duo from Austin Texas: Dan Seals (b: 2/8/50) and Coley (b: 10/13/51). Dan (brother of Jim Seals of Seals & Crofts) is currently a hot Country artist. Also see Dan Seals and Southwest F.O.B.	
6/12/76	**2^{2}**	24	1 ● **I'd Really Love To See You Tonight**	Big Tree 16069
10/09/76	**10**	16	2 **Nights Are Forever Without You**	Big Tree 16079
5/07/77	**21**	16	3 It's Sad To Belong	Big Tree 16088
10/01/77	**23**	14	4 Gone Too Far	Big Tree 16102
2/25/78	**9**	14	5 **We'll Never Have To Say Goodbye Again**	Big Tree 16110
6/03/78	**49**	8	6 You Can't Dance	Big Tree 16117
3/10/79	**10**	18	7 **Love Is The Answer**	Big Tree 16131
10/27/79	**50**	6	8 What Can I Do With This Broken Heart	Big Tree 17000
3/08/80	**75**	4	9 In It For Love	Big Tree 17002
			THE ENGLISH CONGREGATION	
			British group. Brian Keith, lead vocals.	
1/22/72	**29**	10	1 Softly Whispering I Love You	Atco 6865
			JACKIE ENGLISH	
12/20/80+	**94**	4	1 Once A Night from the film "Hopscotch"	Venture 135
			SCOTT ENGLISH	
2/22/64	**77**	5	1 High On A Hill vocal background: The Accents	Spokane 4003
3/04/72	**91**	2	2 Brandy later recorded by Barry Manilow as "Mandy"	Janus 171
			THE EPIC SPLENDOR	
12/16/67+	**87**	7	1 A Little Rain Must Fall	Hot Biscuit 1450
			PRESTON EPPS	
			Bongo player from Oakland. Discovered by Original Sound owner, Art Laboe.	
5/18/59	**14**	13	1 Bongo Rock [I]	Original Sound 4
8/15/60	**78**	3	2 Bongo Bongo Bongo [I]	Original Sound 9
			THE EQUALS	
			Integrated British/Jamaican quintet led by Eddy Grant (guitar) and Derv Gordon (vocals).	
9/07/68	**32**	9	1 Baby, Come Back	RCA 9583
			ERNIE - see JIM HENSON	
			ERUPTION	
			Jamaican techno-funk quintet featuring Precious Wilson.	
3/11/78	**18**	22	1 I Can't Stand The Rain	Ariola 7686
			JOE "BEAN" ESPOSITO	
			Former lead singer of Brooklyn Dreams.	
10/22/83	**86**	2	1 Lady, Lady, Lady from the film "Flashdance"	Casablanca 814430
			THE ESQUIRES	
			Soul quintet from Milwaukee, formed at North Division High School in 1957 by Gilbert, Alvis and Betty Moorer (left, 1965). Joined by Sam Pace, 1961, Shawn Taylor, 1965, and Millard Edwards, 1967.	
8/19/67	**11**	15	1 Get On Up	Bunky 7750
11/25/67	**22**	8	2 And Get Away	Bunky 7752
12/28/68+	**91**	5	3 You've Got The Power	Wand 1193
			THE ESSEX	
			R&B quintet formed by members of the US Marine Corps at Camp LeJeune, NC in 1962. Consisted of Anita Humes (lead), Walter Vickers, Rodney Taylor, Billie Hill and Rudolph Johnson.	
6/08/63	**1^{2}**	13	1 **Easier Said Than Done**	Roulette 4494

DEBUT DATE	PEAK POS	WKS CHR	ARTIST — Record Title	Label & Number
			THE ESSEX — Cont'd	
8/24/63	**12**	10	2 A Walkin' Miracle	Roulette 4515
11/16/63	**56**	5	3 She's Got Everything	Roulette 4530
			DAVID ESSEX	
			Born David Cook on 7/23/47 in London, England. Portrayed Christ in the London production of "Godspell". Star of British films since 1970.	
11/10/73+	**5**	25	1 ● **Rock On**	Columbia 45940
6/01/74	**71**	5	2 Lamplight	Columbia 46041
			THE ETERNALS	
			Quintet from New York City: Charles Girona, lead; Ernest Sierra and Fred Hodge, tenors; Arnie Torres, baritone; and Alex Miranda, bass.	
7/13/59	**78**	3	1 Rockin' In The Jungle	Hollywood 68
			ETERNITY'S CHILDREN	
			New Orleans group, formerly Charlie Rich's backing band, The Phantoms. Led by Bruce Blackman who later formed Starbuck, then Korona.	
7/13/68	**69**	7	1 Mrs. Bluebird	Tower 416
			ETTA & HARVEY - see ETTA JAMES	
			JACK EUBANKS	
11/27/61	**83**	4	1 Searching [I] harmonica instrumental version of The Coasters' 1957 hit	Monument 451
			EUCLID BEACH BAND	
			Pop duo from Cleveland: Richard Reising & Peter Hewlett.	
3/31/79	**81**	5	1 I Need You written & produced by Eric Carmen (Raspberries)	Epic 50676
			EUROGLIDERS	
			Australian pop/rock sextet - Grace Knight, lead singer.	
11/10/84	**65**	6	1 Heaven (Must Be There)	Columbia 04626
			EURYTHMICS	
			Synth/pop duo: David Stewart (b: 9/9/52, England), keyboards, guitar, synthesizer, composer; and Annie Lennox (b: 12/25/54, Scotland), vocals, keyboards, flute, composer. Both had been in the Tourists, 1977-1980. First album recorded in Cologne, Germany, with drummer Clem Burke, formerly of Blondie.	
5/14/83	**1**[1]	26	1 ● **Sweet Dreams (Are Made of This)**	RCA 13533
9/17/83	**23**	13	2 Love Is A Stranger	RCA 13618
1/28/84	**4**	20	3 **Here Comes The Rain Again**	RCA 13725
5/05/84	**21**	13	4 Who's That Girl?	RCA 13800
7/21/84	**29**	12	5 Right By Your Side	RCA 13695
11/24/84	**81**	4	6 Sexcrime (Nineteen Eighty-Four)	RCA 13956
4/27/85	**5**	19	7 **Would I Lie To You?**	RCA 14078
8/03/85	**22**	11	8 There Must Be An Angel (Playing With My Heart)	RCA 14160
10/19/85	**18**	15	9 Sisters Are Doin' It For Themselves EURYTHMICS & ARETHA FRANKLIN	RCA 14214
2/15/86	**78**	6	10 It's Alright (Baby's Coming Back)	RCA 14284
7/26/86	**14**	16	11 Missionary Man	RCA 14414
11/15/86	**68**	9	12 Thorn In My Side	RCA 5058
			PAUL EVANS	
			Born on 3/5/38 in New York City. Singer-songwriter. Wrote "When" (Kalin Twins) and "Roses Are Red" (Bobby Vinton). Currently a pop jingle singer in New York.	
9/14/59	**9**	18	1 **Seven Little Girls Sitting In The Back Seat** with the Curls (female backing duo: Sue Singleton & Sue Terry)	Guaranteed 200
1/25/60	**16**	13	2 Midnite Special	Guaranteed 205
5/02/60	**10**	14	3 **Happy-Go-Lucky-Me**	Guaranteed 208
8/08/60	**81**	4	4 The Brigade Of Broken Hearts	Guaranteed 210
			BETTY EVERETT	
			Born on 11/23/39 in Greenwood, MS. Vocalist, piano. Performed in gospel choirs. To Chicago in late 1950s. First recorded for C.J. in 1960.	
11/23/63+	**51**	10	1 You're No Good Linda Ronstadt's version peaked at #1 in 1975	Vee-Jay 566
2/29/64	**6**	13	2 **The Shoop Shoop Song (It's In His Kiss)**	Vee-Jay 585
6/27/64	**66**	5	3 I Can't Hear You	Vee-Jay 599
9/05/64	**5**	13	4 **Let It Be Me** BETTY EVERETT & JERRY BUTLER	Vee-Jay 613
11/28/64+	**65**	6	5 Getting Mighty Crowded	Vee-Jay 628

DEBUT DATE	PEAK POS	WKS CHR	ARTIST — Record Title	Label & Number
			BETTY EVERETT — Cont'd	
12/05/64+	**42**	7	6 Smile	Vee-Jay 633
			BETTY EVERETT & JERRY BUTLER	
1/18/69	**26**	11	7 There'll Come A Time	Uni 55100
4/26/69	**78**	4	8 I Can't Say No To You	Uni 55122
12/20/69	**96**	2	9 It's Been A Long Time	Uni 55174
12/26/70+	**96**	4	10 I Got To Tell Somebody	Fantasy 652
			THE EVERLY BROTHERS	
			Donald was born on 2/1/37 in Brownie, Kentucky; Philip on 1/19/39 in Chicago. Vocal duo, guitarists, songwriters. Parents were folk and country singers. Don (beginning at age 8) and Phil (age 6) sang with parents thru high school. Invited to Nashville by Chet Atkins and first recorded there for Columbia in 1955. Signed to Archie Bleyer's Cadence Records in 1957. Duo split up in July, 1973, and reunited in September, 1983. The #1 duo of the rock era.	
5/20/57	**2**[4]	27	1 **Bye Bye Love/**	
			Best Seller #2 / Top 100 #2 / Jockey #2 / Juke Box #9 end	
		1	2 I Wonder If I Care As Much	Cadence 1315
			Best Seller flip	
9/30/57	**1**[4]	26	3 **Wake Up Little Susie**	Cadence 1337
			Jockey #1(4) / Top 100 #1(2) / Best Seller #1(1)	
2/10/58	**26**	9	4 This Little Girl Of Mine/	
			Best Seller #26 / Top 100 #28	
			written & popularized on R&B charts by Ray Charles in 1955 (POS 9)	
		1	5 Should We Tell Him	Cadence 1342
			Best Seller flip	
4/21/58	**1**[5]	17	6 **All I Have To Do Is Dream/**	
			Jockey #1(5) / Best Seller #1(4) / Top 100 #1(3)	
5/05/58	**30**	10	7 Claudette	Cadence 1348
			written by Roy Orbison	
8/04/58	**1**[1]	18	8 **Bird Dog/**	
			Best Seller #1 / Hot 100 #2	
8/11/58	**10**	14	9 **Devoted To You**	Cadence 1350
11/10/58	**2**[1]	15	10 **Problems/**	
11/24/58	**40**	6	11 Love Of My Life	Cadence 1355
3/30/59	**16**	13	12 Take A Message To Mary/	
3/30/59	**22**	12	13 Poor Jenny	Cadence 1364
8/17/59	**4**	16	14 **('Til) I Kissed You**	Cadence 1369
1/11/60	**7**	15	15 **Let It Be Me**	Cadence 1376
			first popularized by Jill Corey in 1957	
4/18/60	**1**[5]	17	16 **Cathy's Clown/**	
5/16/60	**56**	6	17 Always It's You	Warner 5151
5/30/60	**8**	13	18 **When Will I Be Loved/**	
7/11/60	**74**	5	19 Be Bop A-Lula	Cadence 1380
9/05/60	**7**	12	20 **So Sad (To Watch Good Love Go Bad)/**	
9/05/60	**21**	10	21 Lucille	Warner 5163
10/31/60	**22**	10	22 Like Strangers	Cadence 1388
			1, 3, 6, 8-13, 17, 22: written by Boudleaux & Felice Bryant	
1/30/61	**8**	12	23 **Ebony Eyes/**	
2/06/61	**7**	13	24 **Walk Right Back**	Warner 5199
5/29/61	**27**	6	25 Temptation/	
			first popularized by Bing Crosby in 1934 (POS 3)	
6/05/61	**41**	4	26 Stick With Me Baby	Warner 5220
7/24/61	**96**	2	27 All I Have To Do Is Dream [R]	Cadence 1348
9/25/61	**20**	8	28 Don't Blame Me/	
			first popularized by Ethel Waters in 1933 (POS 6)	
10/02/61	**82**	4	29 Muskrat	Warner 5501
			above 2 released as a 7" E.P. with "Walk Right Back" & "Lucille"	
1/13/62	**6**	13	30 **Crying In The Rain**	Warner 5250
5/12/62	**9**	11	31 **That's Old Fashioned (That's The Way Love Should Be)/**	
5/26/62	**75**	3	32 How Can I Meet Her?	Warner 5273
10/13/62	**76**	6	33 I'm Here To Get My Baby Out Of Jail	Cadence 1429
10/20/62	**48**	7	34 Don't Ask Me To Be Friends	Warner 5297
6/20/64	**72**	6	35 The Ferris Wheel	Warner 5441
10/17/64	**31**	10	36 Gone, Gone, Gone	Warner 5478
5/27/67	**40**	8	37 Bowling Green	Warner 7020

DEBUT DATE	PEAK POS	WKS CHR	ARTIST — Record Title	Label & Number
			THE EVERLY BROTHERS — Cont'd	
9/01/84	**50**	12	38 On The Wings Of A Nightingale written by Paul McCartney; produced by Dave Edmunds	Mercury 880213
			EVERY FATHER'S TEENAGE SON	
11/25/67	**93**	4	1 A Letter To Dad [S] reply to "An Open Letter To My Teenage Son" by Victor Lundberg	Buddah 25
			EVERY MOTHERS' SON Quintet formed in Greenwich Village, led by brothers Dennis & Lary Larden.	
5/06/67	**6**	15	1 **Come On Down To My Boat**	MGM 13733
8/26/67	**46**	7	2 Put Your Mind At Ease	MGM 13788
11/11/67	**93**	2	3 Pony With The Golden Mane	MGM 13844
1/27/68	**96**	3	4 No One Knows	MGM 13887
			EVERYTHING is EVERYTHING Danny Weiss and Chris Hill.	
2/08/69	**69**	5	1 Witchi Tai To	Vanguard A. 35082
			THE EXCELLENTS	
11/24/62+	**51**	9	1 Coney Island Baby	Blast 205
			THE EXCELS	
6/05/61	**100**	1	1 Can't Help Lovin' That Girl Of Mine from the musical "Show Boat" (as "Can't Help Lovin' Dat Man")	RSVP 111
			THE EXCITERS R&B vocal quartet from Jamaica, New York: Herb Rooney, wife Brenda Reid, Carol Johnson and Lillian Walker.	
12/01/62+	**4**	13	1 **Tell Him**	United Art. 544
3/02/63	**57**	8	2 He's Got The Power	United Art. 572
6/22/63	**76**	3	3 Get Him	United Art. 604
1/04/64	**78**	4	4 Do-Wah-Diddy hit #1 later in '64 by Manfred Mann	United Art. 662
1/16/65	**98**	1	5 I Want You To Be My Boy	Roulette 4591
1/29/66	**58**	6	6 A Little Bit Of Soap	Bang 515
			EXILE Quintet formed in Kentucky in 1965. J.P. Pennington, lead singer. Currently a hot Country act.	
3/05/77	**97**	3	1 Try It On	Atco 7072
7/08/78	**1**[4]	23	2● **Kiss You All Over**	Warner 8589
11/25/78+	**40**	11	3 You Thrill Me	Warner 8711
4/28/79	**88**	2	4 How Could This Go Wrong	Warner 8796
			EYE TO EYE Duo: vocalist Deborah Berg from Seattle and pianist Julian Marshall (of Marshall Hain) from England.	
5/22/82	**37**	13	1 Nice Girls	Warner 50050
10/29/83	**88**	2	2 Lucky	Warner 29455

F

DEBUT DATE	PEAK POS	WKS CHR	ARTIST — Record Title	Label & Number
			SHELLEY FABARES Born Michele Fabares on 1/19/44 in Santa Monica, CA. Niece of actress Nanette Fabray. Starred with Elvis in 3 of his movies. Best known as Mary Stone on "The Donna Reed Show". Married record producer Lou Adler in 1964.	
3/03/62	**1**[2]	15	1 **Johnny Angel**	Colpix 621
6/09/62	**21**	10	2 Johnny Loves Me	Colpix 636
9/15/62	**46**	6	3 The Things We Did Last Summer originally hit POS 10 for Jo Stafford in 1946	Colpix 654
4/27/63	**72**	5	4 Ronnie, Call Me When You Get A Chance	Colpix 682
			FABIAN Born Fabian Forte on 2/6/43 in Philadelphia. Discovered at age 14 (because of his good looks and intriguing name) by a chance meeting with Bob Marcucci, owner of Chancellor Records. Began acting career in 1959 with "Hound Dog Man".	
1/12/59	**31**	10	1 I'm A Man	Chancellor 1029
3/30/59	**9**	13	2 **Turn Me Loose**	Chancellor 1033

DEBUT DATE	PEAK POS	WKS CHR	ARTIST — Record Title	Label & Number
			FABIAN — Cont'd	
6/15/59	**3**	13	3 **Tiger**	Chancellor 1037
9/07/59	**29**	8	4 Come On And Get Me/	
9/21/59	**54**	5	5 Got The Feeling	Chancellor 1041
11/16/59	**9**	15	6 **Hound Dog Man/**	
11/23/59	**12**	13	7 This Friendly World above 2 from the film "Hound Dog Man" (starring Fabian)	Chancellor 1044
2/22/60	**39**	8	8 String Along/	
2/29/60	**31**	7	9 About This Thing Called Love all of above produced by Peter de Angelis	Chancellor 1047
10/31/60	**91**	2	10 Kissin' And Twistin'	Chancellor 1061
			BENT FABRIC & His Piano Born Bent Fabricius-Bjerre on 12/7/42 in Copenhagen. Head of Metronome Records in Denmark. Composer, pianist, TV personality and A&R man.	
7/28/62	**7**	18	1 **Alley Cat** [I]	Atco 6226
1/12/63	**63**	8	2 Chicken Feed [I]	Atco 6245
			FABULOUS COUNTS Detroit soul sextet - produced by Ollie McLaughlin.	
4/25/70	**88**	4	1 Get Down People	Moira 108
			FABULOUS POODLES English rock quartet led by Tony DeMeur and Richie Robertson.	
4/28/79	**81**	4	1 Mirror Star	Epic 50666
			THE FABULOUS RHINESTONES	
8/05/72	**78**	4	1 What A Wonderful Thing We Have	Just Sunshine 500
			THE FABULOUS THUNDERBIRDS Austin, Texas rock and roll quartet. Kim Wilson, lead singer.	
4/19/86	**10**	19	1 **Tuff Enuff**	CBS Assoc. 05838
8/09/86	**50**	10	2 Wrap It Up revival of Archie Bell & The Drells' 1970 hit	CBS Assoc. 06270
			FACE TO FACE Boston rock quintet - lead singer Laurie Sargent was featured in the film "Streets Of Fire".	
6/02/84	**38**	15	1 10-9-8	Epic 04430
			TOMMY FACENDA Born on 11/10/39 in Norfolk, VA. Nicknamed "Bubba".	
10/19/59	**28**	13	1 High School U.S.A. [N] Atlantic released 28 different versions of this record, each mentioning the names of high schools in various cities	Atlantic 51 to 78
			FACES Rod Stewart (joined by Ron Wood of the Jeff Beck Group) replaced Steve Marriott as leader of the revamped British group, Small Faces, in 1969.	
11/20/71	**24**	9	1 (I Know) I'm Losing You **ROD STEWART with FACES**	Mercury 73244
1/01/72	**17**	10	2 Stay With Me	Warner 7545
3/10/73	**48**	9	3 Cindy Incidentally	Warner 7681
			FACTS OF LIFE Soul trio based in Teaneck, NJ: Jean Davis, younger sister of Tyrone Davis; Keith William, formerly with the Imperials and Flamingos; and Chuck Carter.	
3/05/77	**31**	10	1 Sometimes produced by Millie Jackson	Kayvette 5128
			DONALD FAGEN Born on 1/10/48 in Passaic, NJ. Fagen and Walter Becker founded Steely Dan.	
10/09/82	**26**	14	1 I.G.Y. (What A Beautiful World) I.G.Y.: International Geo-physical Year (Jul '57-Dec '58)	Warner 29900
1/29/83	**70**	6	2 New Frontier	Warner 29792
			JOE FAGIN	
7/31/82	**80**	3	1 Younger Days	Millennium 13107
			YVONNE FAIR Soul singer from Virginia. Toured with James Brown Revue. Appeared in the film "Lady Sings The Blues".	
4/24/76	**85**	5	1 It Should Have Been Me	Motown 1384

DEBUT DATE	PEAK POS	WKS CHR	ARTIST — Record Title	Label & Number
			BARBARA FAIRCHILD	
			Born on 11/12/50 in Knoebel, Arkansas. Country singer, songwriter.	
2/24/73	**32**	19	1 Teddy Bear Song	Columbia 45743
8/25/73	**95**	5	2 Kid Stuff	Columbia 45903
			ANDY FAIRWEATHER LOW	
			Session musician from Wales. Former lead singer of Welsh band Amen Corner.	
4/12/75	**87**	3	1 Spider Jiving	A&M 1649
			FAITH BAND	
			Pop/rock quintet from Indianapolis. Originally known as Limousine. Carl Storie, lead singer.	
12/16/78+	**54**	9	1 Dancin' Shoes	Mercury 74037
6/23/79	**76**	4	2 You're My Weakness	Mercury 74068
			FAITH, HOPE & CHARITY	
			Soul trio from Tampa, FL, originally consisting of Brenda Hilliard, Albert Bailey and Zulema. Zulema went solo in 1971, Hilliard and Bailey continued as duo until 1974 when joined by Diane Destry.	
5/16/70	**51**	11	1 So Much Love	Maxwell 805
9/26/70	**96**	2	2 Baby Don't Take Your Love	Maxwell 808
8/16/75	**50**	15	3 To Each His Own	RCA 10343
			all of above written and produced by Van McCoy	
			ADAM FAITH	
			Born Terry Nelhams on 6/23/40 in London. Actor in films and television.	
1/16/65	**31**	8	1 It's Alright	Amy 913
			with backing band The Roulettes	
4/17/65	**97**	2	2 Talk About Love	Amy 922
			PERCY FAITH	
			Born on 4/7/08 in Toronto, Canada. Moved to the United States in 1940. Joined Columbia Records in 1950 as conductor-arranger for their leading singers (Tony Bennett, Doris Day, Rosemary Clooney, Johnny Mathis, and others). Died on 2/9/76 (67).	
2/18/56	**53**	5	1 Valley Valparaiso	Columbia 40633
4/14/56	**67**	4	2 We All Need Love	Columbia 40644
7/21/56	**82**	3	3 With A Little Bit Of Luck [I]	Columbia 40696
			from the Broadway musical "My Fair Lady"	
4/13/57	**63**	13	4 Till	Columbia 40826
1/11/60	**1^{9}**	21	5• **The Theme From 'A Summer Place'** [I]	Columbia 41490
			from the film "A Summer Place"	
5/09/60	**35**	10	6 Theme For Young Lovers [I]	Columbia 41655
			MARIANNE FAITHFULL	
			English songstress. Discovered by Rolling Stones' manager, Andrew Loog Oldham. Involved in a long, tumultuous relationship with Mick Jagger. Acted in several stage and screen productions.	
11/28/64+	**22**	9	1 As Tears Go By	London 9697
2/27/65	**26**	9	2 Come And Stay With Me	London 9731
6/05/65	**32**	8	3 This Little Bird	London 9759
8/14/65	**24**	9	4 Summer Nights	London 9780
12/11/65	**89**	3	5 Go Away From My World	London 9802
			FALCO	
			Falco (Johann Holzel) was born in Vienna, Austria.	
2/08/86	**1^{3}**	17	1 **Rock Me Amadeus**	A&M 2821
4/26/86	**18**	14	2 Vienna Calling	A&M 2832
			THE FALCONS	
			Detroit R&B group: Eddie Floyd (replaced in 1961 by Wilson Pickett), Bonny Rice, Joe Stubbs (brother of the Four Tops' Levi Stubbs), Willie Schofield and Lance Finnie.	
4/20/59	**17**	20	1 You're So Fine	Unart 2013
			Joe Stubbs, lead singer	
3/31/62	**75**	9	2 I Found A Love	Lu Pine 1003
			Wilson Pickett, lead singer	
			HAROLD FALTERMEYER	
			West German keyboardist, songwriter, arranger, producer. Arranged and played keyboards on the film scores of "Midnight Express" and "American Gigolo".	
3/30/85	**3**	19	1 **Axel F** [I]	MCA 52536
			from the film "Beverly Hills Cop" - Eddie Murphy played Axel Foley	

DEBUT DATE	PEAK POS	WKS CHR	ARTIST — Record Title	Label & Number
			AGNETHA FALTSKOG	
			Born on 4/5/50 in Sweden. Member of Abba.	
8/27/83	**29**	15	1 Can't Shake Loose	Polydor 815230
			GEORGIE FAME	
			Born Clive Powell on 6/26/43 in Lancashire, England. Began as a pianist with Billy Fury's backup group, The Blue Flames.	
2/13/65	**21**	8	1 Yeh, Yeh	Imperial 66086
5/01/65	**97**	2	2 In The Meantime	Imperial 66104
8/20/66	**70**	7	3 Get Away	Imperial 66189
			above 3 with The Blue Flames	
2/17/68	**7**	14	4 **The Ballad Of Bonnie And Clyde**	Epic 10283
			THE FAMILY	
			Twin Cities quintet featuring Time members St. Paul (Paul Peterson), Jerome Benton and Jellybean Johnson.	
9/28/85	**63**	6	1 The Screams Of Passion	Paisley P. 28953
			FANCY	
			English rock quartet - Helen Court, lead singer.	
6/15/74	**14**	17	1 Wild Thing	Big Tree 15004
10/12/74	**19**	10	2 Touch Me	Big Tree 16026
			FANNY	
			Female rock quartet from California: sisters June and Jean Millington, Alice DeBuhr, and Nickey Barclay.	
9/18/71	**40**	10	1 Charity Ball	Reprise 1033
4/29/72	**85**	3	2 Ain't That Peculiar	Reprise 1080
6/08/74	**79**	7	3 I've Had It	Casablanca 0009
2/01/75	**29**	11	4 Butter Boy	Casablanca 814
			FANTASTIC FOUR	
			Soul group formed in Detroit in 1955. Consisted of "Sweet" James Epps, Robert and Joseph Pruitt, and Toby Childs. Robert Pruitt and Childs later replaced by Cleveland Horne and Ernest Newsome.	
3/25/67	**63**	9	1 The Whole World Is A Stage	Ric-Tic 122
5/27/67	**55**	7	2 You Gave Me Something (And Everything's Alright)	Ric-Tic 128
9/23/67	**68**	5	3 To Share Your Love	Ric-Tic 130
9/21/68	**56**	9	4 I Love You Madly	Soul 35052
7/26/75	**74**	8	5 Alvin Stone (The Birth & Death Of A Gangster)	Westbound 5009
			THE FANTASTIC JOHNNY C	
			Born Johnny Corley on 4/28/43 in Greenwood, SC. Produced and managed by Jesse James.	
10/07/67	**7**	18	1 **Boogaloo Down Broadway**	Phil-L.A. 305
2/10/68	**56**	6	2 Got What You Need	Phil-L.A. 309
6/29/68	**34**	9	3 Hitch It To The Horse	Phil-L.A. 315
11/16/68	**87**	2	4 (She's) Some Kind Of Wonderful	Phil-L.A. 320
			THE FANTASTICS	
2/19/72	**86**	4	1 (Love Me) Love The Life I Lead	Bell 45157
			FANTASY	
			Rock quintet (ages 16-21).	
9/19/70	**77**	11	1 Stoned Cowboy [I]	Liberty 56190
			FAR CORPORATION	
			Far: name of producer Frank Farian's studio in Rosbach, Germany. This assemblage of European and American musicians contains three members of Toto: Bobby Kimball (lead vocals), Steve Lukather (guitars) and David Paich (keyboards).	
10/04/86	**89**	4	1 Stairway To Heaven	Atco 99509
			new version of Led Zeppelin's classic song	
			THE FARAGHER BROS.	
			Danny, Jimmy, Tommy, Davey, Marty and Pammy Faragher. Also see Bones.	
2/24/79	**50**	7	1 Stay The Night	Polydor 14533
			DON FARDON	
			Born Don Maughn in Coventry, England. Lead singer of English group The Sorrows.	
8/31/68	**20**	9	1 (The Lament Of The Cherokee) Indian Reservation	GNP Crescendo 405
3/24/73	**86**	5	2 Delta Queen	Chelsea 0115

DEBUT DATE	PEAK POS	WKS CHR	ARTIST — Record Title	Label & Number
			DONNA FARGO	
			Born Yvonne Vaughan on 11/10/49 in Mt. Airy, NC. Donna was stricken with multiple sclerosis in 1979.	
5/27/72	**11**	16	1 ● The Happiest Girl In The Whole U.S.A.	Dot 17409
9/30/72+	**5**	20	2 ● **Funny Face**	Dot 17429
2/24/73	**41**	9	3 Superman	Dot 17444
6/16/73	**93**	7	4 You Were Always There	Dot 17460
10/06/73	**57**	10	5 Little Girl Gone	Dot 17476
6/29/74	**57**	13	6 You Can't Be A Beacon (If Your Light Don't Shine)	Dot 17506
11/09/74	**86**	4	7 U.S. of A.	ABC/Dot 17523
3/22/75	**98**	2	8 It Do Feel Good	ABC/Dot 17541
			all of above produced by Donna's husband Stan Silver	
			CEE FARROW	
9/24/83	**82**	6	1 Should I Love You	Rocshire 95032
			THE FASCINATIONS	
			Female soul quartet from Detroit. Bernadine Boswell Smith, lead singer.	
2/11/67	**92**	3	1 Girls Are Out To Get You	Mayfield 7714
			written and produced by Curtis Mayfield (on his own label)	
			FEATHER	
5/30/70	**79**	5	1 Friends	White Whale 353
			DON FELDER	
			Born on 9/21/47 in Gainesville, Florida. Joined the Eagles in 1975.	
7/25/81	**43**	17	1 Heavy Metal (Takin' A Ride)	Full Moon 47175
			from the animated film "Heavy Metal"	
			THE VICTOR FELDMAN QUARTET	
			Victor was born on 4/7/34 in London, England. Multi-instrumentalist, composer.	
9/01/62	**88**	1	1 A Taste Of Honey [I]	Infinity 020
			JOSE FELICIANO	
			Born on 9/10/45 in Puerto Rico. Blind since birth, Jose moved with his family to New York City at the age of 5. Virtuoso acoustic guitarist.	
7/27/68	**3**	12	1 **Light My Fire**	RCA 9550
10/19/68	**25**	8	2 Hi-Heel Sneakers/	
10/12/68	**77**	3	3 Hitchcock Railway	RCA 9641
11/02/68	**50**	5	4 The Star-Spangled Banner	RCA 9665
			recorded live at the 5th game of the World Series in Detroit	
1/25/69	**71**	5	5 Hey! Baby/	
2/08/69	**87**	1	6 My World Is Empty Without You	RCA 9714
5/03/69	**70**	4	7 Marley Purt Drive	RCA 9739
8/23/69	**76**	5	8 Rain	RCA 9757
7/04/70	**83**	2	9 Destiny/	
		2	10 Susie-Q	RCA 0358
1/25/75	**96**	2	11 Chico And The Man	RCA 10145
			main theme from the NBC-TV series of the same name	
			DICK FELLER	
7/27/74	**85**	5	1 Makin' The Best Of A Bad Situation [N]	Asylum 11037
			SUZANNE FELLINI	
			Songstress from New York City.	
3/15/80	**87**	2	1 Love On The Phone	Casablanca 2242
			FELONY	
			Los Angeles rock quintet - Jeffrey Spry, lead singer.	
2/12/83	**42**	12	1 The Fanatic	Rock 'n' R. 03497
			NARVEL FELTS	
			Born on 11/1/38 near Bernie, MO. Rockabilly/country vocalist, guitarist, songwriter.	
2/08/60	**90**	2	1 Honey Love	Pink 702
			The Drifters' version hit #1 in 1954 on the R&B charts	
5/24/75	**67**	6	2 Reconsider Me	ABC/Dot 17549
5/22/76	**62**	4	3 Lonely Teardrops	ABC/Dot 17620

DEBUT DATE	PEAK POS	WKS CHR	ARTIST — Record Title		Label & Number
			FREDDY FENDER		
			Born Baldermar Huerta on 6/4/37 in San Benito, Texas. Mexican-American singer, guitarist.		
2/01/75	**1**[1]	21	1 ● **Before The Next Teardrop Falls**		ABC/Dot 17540
6/21/75	**8**	19	2 ● **Wasted Days And Wasted Nights** originally recorded by Fender on the Duncan label in 1959		ABC/Dot 17558
10/18/75	**20**	11	3 Secret Love a #1 hit for Doris Day in 1954		ABC/Dot 17585
10/18/75	**45**	8	4 Since I Met You Baby		GRT 031
2/14/76	**32**	10	5 You'll Lose A Good Thing		ABC/Dot 17607
5/29/76	**59**	6	6 Vaya Con Dios a #1 hit for Les Paul & Mary Ford in 1953		ABC/Dot 17627
10/30/76	**72**	4	7 Living It Down all of above (except #4) produced by Huey P. Meaux		ABC/Dot 17652
			THE FENDERMEN		
			Phil Humphrey (from Stoughton, WI) & Jim Sundquist (from Niagara, WI) - both were born on 11/26/37.		
5/23/60	**5**	18	1 **Mule Skinner Blues** written in 1931 by country great Jimmie Rodgers		Soma 1137
			HELENA FERGUSON		
11/11/67	**90**	5	1 Where Is The Party		Compass 7009
			JAY FERGUSON		
			Born on 5/10/43 in San Fernando Valley, CA. Before going solo, Jay formed and led Spirit and Jo Jo Gunne.		
12/17/77+	**9**	21	1 **Thunder Island**		Asylum 45444
5/05/79	**31**	14	2 Shakedown Cruise		Asylum 46041
			JOHNNY FERGUSON		
			Born on 3/22/37 in Nashville. Worked as a disc jockey in the late 50s.		
2/22/60	**27**	15	1 Angela Jones		MGM 12855
			MAYNARD FERGUSON		
			Born on 5/4/28 in Quebec, Canada. Moved to the United States in 1949. Played trumpet for Charlie Barnet and then Stan Kenton's Band (1950-53).		
4/23/77	**28**	13	1 Gonna Fly Now (Theme From "Rocky")	[I]	Columbia 10468
8/04/79	**82**	4	2 Rocky II Disco		Columbia 11037
			FERKO STRING BAND		
			Philadelphia string band directed by William Connors. String bands parade annually in Philadelphia's famed New Year's Day Mummers Parade. Also see Nu Tornados.		
6/18/55	**14**	6	1 Alabama Jubilee Juke Box #14 / Best Seller #18 first popularized by Arthur Collins & Byron Harlan in 1915 (POS 2)	[I]	Media 1010
8/20/55	**44**	2	2 You Are My Sunshine Coming Up #44 written in 1940 by the former governor of Louisiana, Jimmie Davis		Media 1013
			FERRANTE & TEICHER		
			Piano duo: Arthur Ferrante (b: 9/7/21, New York City) and Louis Teicher (b: 8/24/24, Wilkes-Barre, PA). Met as children while attending the Juilliard School.		
7/25/60	**10**	20	1 **Theme From The Apartment** from the Billy Wilder film "The Apartment" tune originally entitled "Jealous Lover"	[I]	United Art. 231
11/14/60+	**2**[1]	21	2 **Exodus** theme from the Otto Preminger film of the same title	[I]	United Art. 274
3/20/61	**37**	7	3 Love Theme From One Eyed Jacks from the Marlon Brando film "One Eyed Jacks"	[I]	United Art. 300
6/12/61	**85**	4	4 Goodbye Again theme from the Ingrid Bergman film of the same title	[I]	United Art. 319
10/16/61	**8**	13	5 **Tonight** from the film "West Side Story" all of above produced by Don Costa	[I]	United Art. 373
3/17/62	**94**	3	6 Smile Charlie Chaplin wrote the music for this song in 1954	[I]	United Art. 431
6/16/62	**98**	2	7 Lisa from the film of the same title	[I]	United Art. 470
2/02/63	**84**	12	8 Theme From Lawrence Of Arabia from the David Lean film epic "Lawrence Of Arabia"	[I]	United Art. 563
6/29/63	**83**	5	9 Antony And Cleopatra Theme from the classic Elizabeth Taylor film "Cleopatra"	[I]	United Art. 607

DEBUT DATE	PEAK POS	WKS CHR	ARTIST — Record Title	Label & Number
			FERRANTE & TEICHER — Cont'd	
11/01/69+	**10**	15	10 **Midnight Cowboy** .... [I]	United Art. 50554
			from the Jon Voight, Dustin Hoffman film of the same title	
4/04/70	**99**	1	11 Lay Lady Lay .... [I]	United Art. 50646
			BRYAN FERRY	
			Born on 9/26/45 in County Durham, England. Lead singer of Roxy Music.	
12/11/76	**86**	4	1 Heart On My Sleeve	Atlantic 3364
			FESTIVAL	
3/08/80	**72**	8	1 Don't Cry For Me Argentina	RSO 1020
			from Broadway's "Evita"	
			FEVER TREE	
			Texas psychedelic rock quintet - Dennis Keller, lead singer.	
6/01/68	**91**	6	1 San Francisco Girls (Return of the Native)	Uni 55060
			THE FIDELITY'S	
6/09/58	**60**	3	1 The Things I Love	Baton 252
			SALLY FIELD	
			Born on 11/6/46 in Pasadena, CA. Leading actress of television and film.	
11/18/67	**94**	4	1 Felicidad	Colgems 1008
			ERNIE FIELDS	
			Born on 8/26/05 in Nacogdoches, Texas. Trombonist, pianist, bandleader, arranger. Also see B. Bumble & The Stingers.	
9/21/59	**4**	19	1 **In The Mood** .... [I]	Rendezvous 110
			revival of Glenn Miller's #1 hit from 1940	
2/29/60	**54**	8	2 Chattanooga Choo Choo .... [I]	Rendezvous 117
			revival of Glenn Miller's #1 hit from 1941	
6/19/61	**47**	10	3 The Charleston .... [I]	Rendezvous 150
			revival of Arthur Gibbs' #1 hit from 1924	
			RICHARD "DIMPLES" FIELDS	
			R&B vocalist; owner of the Cold Duck Music Lounge in San Francisco.	
4/03/82	**47**	10	1 If It Ain't One Thing...It's Another	Boardwalk 139
			THE FIESTAS	
			R&B vocal group from Newark, NJ: Tommy Bullock (lead), Eddie Morris (tenor), Sam Ingalls (baritone) and Preston Lane (bass).	
4/06/59	**11**	16	1 So Fine	Old Town 1062
8/25/62	**81**	6	2 Broken Heart	Old Town 1122
			THE 5TH DIMENSION	
			Los Angeles-based group formed in 1966. Consisted of Marilyn McCoo, Florence LaRue, Billy Davis, Jr., Lamont McLemore and Ron Townson. McLemore and McCoo had been in the Hi-Fi's; Townson and Davis had been with groups in St. Louis. First called the Versatiles. Davis and McCoo were married, 1969, and recorded as a duo from 1976.	
1/14/67	**16**	10	1 Go Where You Wanna Go	Soul City 753
4/29/67	**45**	6	2 Another Day, Another Heartache	Soul City 755
6/03/67	**7**	12	3 **Up-Up And Away**	Soul City 756
			above 3 produced by Johnny Rivers - Soul City is his own label	
11/04/67	**34**	7	4 Paper Cup	Soul City 760
2/03/68	**29**	9	5 Carpet Man	Soul City 762
6/01/68	**3**	16	6 ● **Stoned Soul Picnic**	Soul City 766
9/28/68	**13**	10	7 Sweet Blindness	Soul City 768
12/21/68+	**25**	9	8 California Soul	Soul City 770
3/08/69	**1^{6}**	17	9 ● **Aquarius/Let The Sunshine In**	Soul City 772
			from the Broadway rock musical "Hair"	
7/19/69	**20**	10	10 Workin' On A Groovy Thing	Soul City 776
9/27/69	**1^{3}**	15	11 ● **Wedding Bell Blues**	Soul City 779
1/03/70	**21**	9	12 Blowing Away	Soul City 780
2/21/70	**60**	5	13 A Change Is Gonna Come & People Gotta Be Free/	
			medley of the 1965 Sam Cooke hit and the Rascals' 1968 #1 hit	
		4	14 The Declaration	Bell 860
4/04/70	**43**	8	15 The Girls' Song	Soul City 781
4/18/70	**24**	8	16 Puppet Man	Bell 880
6/13/70	**27**	8	17 Save The Country	Bell 895
			6, 7, 11, 12, 17: written by Laura Nyro	
8/22/70	**54**	6	18 On The Beach (In The Summertime)	Bell 913

DEBUT DATE	PEAK POS	WKS CHR	ARTIST — Record Title	Label & Number
			THE 5TH DIMENSION — Cont'd	
10/24/70	**2[2]**	19	19● **One Less Bell To Answer**	Bell 940
2/27/71	**19**	10	20 Love's Lines, Angles And Rhymes	Bell 965
5/22/71	**44**	8	21 Light Sings from the Broadway musical "The Me Nobody Knows"	Bell 999
9/18/71	**12**	11	22 Never My Love	Bell 45134
1/01/72	**37**	10	23 Together Let's Find Love	Bell 45170
4/01/72	**8**	16	24● **(Last Night) I Didn't Get To Sleep At All**	Bell 45195
9/09/72	**10**	15	25 **If I Could Reach You**	Bell 45261
1/06/73	**32**	9	26 Living Together, Growing Together from the film "Lost Horizon"	Bell 45310
4/14/73	**70**	4	27 Everything's Been Changed	Bell 45338
8/25/73	**52**	10	28 Ashes To Ashes	Bell 45380
12/15/73+	**82**	9	29 Flashback 4-29: produced by Bones Howe	Bell 45425
4/03/76	**80**	4	30 Love Hangover	ABC 12181
			THE FIFTH ESTATE Studio group assembled by producers Steve & Bill Jerome.	
5/20/67	**11**	10	1 Ding Dong! The Witch Is Dead song originally appeared in the 1939 film "The Wizard Of Oz"	Jubilee 5573
			FINE YOUNG CANNIBALS Pop trio from Birmingham, England: Roland Gift (vocals) and English Beat members David Steele (bass) & Andy Cox (guitar).	
4/05/86	**76**	5	1 Johnny Come Home	I.R.S. 52760
			LARRY FINNEGAN Born John Lawrence Finneran in New York City. Moved to Sweden in 1966.	
2/24/62	**11**	14	1 Dear One	Old Town 1113
			FIONA Fiona Flanagan - rock singer from New York City.	
4/13/85	**64**	7	1 Talk To Me	Atlantic 89572
			FIRE & RAIN	
6/30/73	**100**	3	1 Hello Stranger	Mercury 73373
			FIRE INC. Rock group assembled for the film "Streets Of Fire" - produced by Jim Steinman.	
6/02/84	**80**	5	1 Tonight Is What It Means To Be Young from the film "Streets Of Fire"	MCA 52377
			THE FIREBALLS Rock and roll band formed while high schoolers in Raton, New Mexico: George Tomsco (lead guitar), Dan Trammell (rhythm guitar), Eric Budd (drums), Stan Lark (bass) and Chuck Tharp (vocalist). Tharp quit group in 1960 and was replaced by Jimmy Gilmer (lead vocals, piano). Gilmer was introduced to The Fireballs by their record producer Norman Petty at his famed Clovis, New Mexico studio.	
9/28/59	**39**	13	1 Torquay [I]	Top Rank 2008
1/11/60	**24**	12	2 Bulldog [I]	Top Rank 2026
8/29/60	**99**	1	3 Vaquero (Cowboy) [I]	Top Rank 2054
6/26/61	**27**	10	4 Quite A Party [I]	Warwick 644
			JIMMY GILMER & THE FIREBALLS:	
9/21/63	**1[5]**	15	5● **Sugar Shack**	Dot 16487
12/14/63+	**15**	11	6 Daisy Petal Pickin'	Dot 16539
3/14/64	**53**	7	7 Ain't Gonna Tell Anybody	Dot 16583
			THE FIREBALLS:	
12/30/67+	**9**	14	8 **Bottle Of Wine**	Atco 6491
4/13/68	**79**	4	9 Goin' Away	Atco 6569
11/02/68	**63**	8	10 Come On, React!	Atco 6614
2/22/69	**73**	7	11 Long Green	Atco 6651
			FIREFALL Mellow rock group formed in Boulder, Colorado by lead singer Rick Roberts.	
6/05/76	**42**	8	1 Livin' Ain't Livin'	Atlantic 3333
8/21/76	**9**	22	2 **You Are The Woman**	Atlantic 3335
3/26/77	**34**	10	3 Cinderella	Atlantic 3392
8/13/77	**11**	21	4 Just Remember I Love You	Atlantic 3420
1/14/78	**48**	6	5 So Long	Atlantic 3452
9/30/78	**11**	19	6 Strange Way	Atlantic 3518

DEBUT DATE	PEAK POS	WKS CHR	ARTIST — Record Title	Label & Number
			FIREFALL — Cont'd	
1/20/79	**43**	9	7 Goodbye, I Love You	Atlantic 3544
4/12/80	**35**	9	8 Headed For A Fall	Atlantic 3657
6/28/80	**50**	9	9 Love That Got Away	Atlantic 3670
1/24/81	**37**	9	10 Staying With It lead vocals: Lisa Nemzo and Rick Roberts	Atlantic 3791
1/15/83	**59**	13	11 Always	Atlantic 89916
			FIREFLIES White doo-wop quartet - Ritchie Adams, lead singer (wrote "Tossin' And Turnin'").	
9/07/59	**21**	16	1 You Were Mine	Ribbon 6901
1/25/60	**90**	3	2 I Can't Say Goodbye	Ribbon 6904
			FIREFLY	
10/18/75	**67**	9	1 Hey There Little Firefly - Part I	A&M 1736
			THE FIRM British: Jimmy Page (Led Zeppelin/guitar), Paul Rodgers (Bad Company/vocals), Chris Slade (Manfred Mann/drums) and Tony Franklin (keyboards).	
2/09/85	**28**	15	1 Radioactive	Atlantic 89586
5/04/85	**73**	5	2 Satisfaction Guaranteed	Atlantic 89561
2/15/86	**61**	8	3 All The Kings Horses	Atlantic 89458
			FIRST CHOICE Female soul trio from Philadelphia, formed as the Debronettes. Consisted of Rochelle Fleming, Annette Guest and Joyce Jones.	
3/10/73	**28**	14	1 Armed And Extremely Dangerous	Philly Groove 175
11/17/73	**56**	8	2 Smarty Pants	Philly Groove 179
3/02/74	**97**	2	3 Newsy Neighbors	Philly Groove 183
9/14/74	**70**	8	4 The Player - Part 1	Philly Groove 200
9/17/77	**41**	9	5 Doctor Love	Gold Mind 4004
			FIRST CLASS An assemblage of some of England's leading studio musicians and vocalists.	
7/20/74	**4**	17	1 **Beach Baby**	UK 49022
11/23/74	**83**	4	2 Dreams Are Ten A Penny	UK 49028
5/24/75	**74**	7	3 Funny How Love Can Be	UK 49033
			FIRST EDITION - see KENNY ROGERS	
			GEORGE FISCHOFF Born on 8/3/38 in South Bend, Indiana. Pianist, songwriter.	
6/01/74	**93**	5	1 Georgia Porcupine [I]	United Art. 410
			EDDIE FISHER Born Edwin Jack Fisher on 8/10/28 in Philadelphia. Radio work while still in high school; at Copacabana night club, New York, at age 17. With Buddy Morrow, Charlie Ventura, 1946. On Eddie Cantor radio show in 1949. Armed Forces Special Services, 1952-53. Married Debbie Reynolds in 1955. Other marriages to Elizabeth Taylor, and Connie Stevens. Own "Coke Time" 15-minute TV series, 1953-57. Films "All About Eve", 1950; "Bundle Of Joy", 1956; and "Butterfield 8", 1960. Eddie was the #1 idol of bobbysoxers during the early 1950's.	
3/05/55	**16**	2	1 A Man Chases A Girl (Until She Catches Him)/ Jockey #16 / Juke Box #20 / Best Seller #27 from the film "There's No Business Like Show Business"	
4/02/55	**20**	1	2 (I'm Always Hearing) Wedding Bells Juke Box #20	RCA 6015
5/14/55	**6**	13	3 **Heart** Jockey #6 / Juke Box #13 / Best Seller #15 from the Broadway musical "Damn Yankees"	RCA 6097
8/27/55	**11**	8	4 Song Of The Dreamer/ Juke Box #11 / Best Seller #16 / Jockey #16 / Top 100 #43 pre	
		4	5 Don't Stay Away Too Long Best Seller/Juke Box flip	RCA 6196
11/12/55	**52**	4	6 Magic Fingers/	
11/12/55	**75**	2	7 I Wanna Go Where You Go, Do What You Do (Then I'll Be Happy)	RCA 6264
12/17/55+	**7**	19	8 **Dungaree Doll/** Top 100 #7 / Juke Box #7 / Best Seller #8 / Jockey #9	
12/17/55	**20**	12	9 Everybody's Got A Home But Me Jockey #20 / Top 100 #41 from the Broadway musical "Pipe Dream"	RCA 6337

DEBUT DATE	PEAK POS	WKS CHR	ARTIST — Record Title	Label & Number
			EDDIE FISHER — Cont'd	
4/07/56	41	7	10 Without You/	
4/14/56	65	8	11 No Other One	RCA 6470
6/09/56	18	15	12 On The Street Where You Live/ Juke Box #18 / Top 100 #28 from the Broadway musical "My Fair Lady"	
6/02/56	42	12	13 Sweet Heartaches	RCA 6529
9/08/56	80	1	14 Oh My Maria	RCA 6615
10/20/56	10	19	15 **Cindy, Oh Cindy** Best Seller #10 / Top 100 #10 / Jockey #10 / Juke Box #10	RCA 6677
1/26/57	94	1	16 Some Day Soon from the film "Bundle Of Joy"	RCA 6746
4/20/57	96	1	17 Tonight My Heart Will Be Crying	RCA 6849
6/10/57	94	1	18 Sunshine Girl from the Broadway musical "New Girl In Town" 1-18: arranged and conducted by Hugo Winterhalter	RCA 6913
11/06/61	44	6	19 Tonight from the musical "West Side Story"	7 Arts 719
10/29/66	45	9	20 Games That Lovers Play	RCA 8956
2/11/67	97	3	21 People Like You above 2: arranged and conducted by Nelson Riddle	RCA 9070
			MARY ANN FISHER	
8/28/61	92	3	1 I Can't Take It	Seg-way 1001
			MISS TONI FISHER Born in Los Angeles in 1931.	
11/16/59	3	17	1 **The Big Hurt**	Signet 275
4/11/60	93	2	2 How Deep Is The Ocean there were 3 Top 10 versions of this Irving Berlin classic in 1932	Signet 276
5/26/62	37	11	3 West Of The Wall shown only as: **TONI FISHER**	Big Top 3097
			ELLA FITZGERALD The most honored jazz singer of all time. Ella Fitzgerald was born on 4/25/18 in Newport News, VA. Discovered after winning the Harlem Amateur Hour in 1934, she was hired by Chick Webb and in 1938 created a popular sensation with "A-Tisket, A-Tasket". Following Chick's death in 1939 Ella took over the band for three years. Winner of the Down Beat poll as top female vocalist more than 20 times, she remains among the undisputed royalty of 20th century popular music.	
7/28/56	74	5	1 A Beautiful Friendship	Verve 2012
5/02/60	27	14	2 Mack The Knife	Verve 10209
8/15/60	76	5	3 How High The Moon (Part 1) originally hit POS 6 in 1940 by Benny Goodman	Verve 10220
4/06/63	75	3	4 Bill Bailey, Won't You Please Come Home [N] first popularized by Arthur Collins #1 hit in 1902 above 3 are live recordings with The Paul Smith Quartet	Verve 10288
			THE FIVE AMERICANS Dallas quintet - Michael Rabon, lead singer.	
1/01/66	26	11	1 I See The Light	HBR 454
4/16/66	52	9	2 Evol-Not Love	HBR 468
3/04/67	5	12	3 **Western Union**	Abnak 118
5/20/67	36	8	4 Sound Of Love	Abnak 120
8/12/67	36	7	5 Zip Code above 3 produced by Dale Hawkins	Abnak 123
1/27/68	96	2	6 7:30 Guided Tour	Abnak 126
			THE FIVE BLOBS Studio production - vocals by Bernie Nee.	
10/06/58	33	10	1 The Blob from the film of the same title (written by Burt Bacharach)	Columbia 41250
			FIVE BY FIVE	
11/02/68	52	7	1 Fire written by Jimi Hendrix	Paula 302
			THE 5 CHANELS	
12/22/58	98	1	1 The Reason	Deb 500
			THE FIVE DU-TONES R&B quintet from St. Louis - Andrew Butler, lead singer.	
5/18/63	51	12	1 Shake A Tail Feather	One-derful! 4815

DEBUT DATE	PEAK POS	WKS CHR	ARTIST — Record Title	Label & Number
			THE FIVE EMPREES	
			Pop/rock quintet from Benton Harbor, Michigan. Don Cook, lead singer. Originally known as The Five Empressions.	
9/11/65	**74**	6	1 Little Miss Sad	Freeport 1001
			FIVE FLIGHTS UP	
8/22/70	**37**	11	1 Do What You Wanna Do	T-A 202
12/12/70	**89**	3	2 After The Feeling Is Gone	T-A 207
			THE FIVE KEYS	
			R&B quintet originally formed as the Sentimental Four in Newport News, VA, late 1940s, consisting of two sets of brothers, Rudy & Bernie West and Ripley & Raphael Ingram. In 1949 added Maryland Pierce and changed group name to the Five Keys. Ramon Loper replaced Raphael Ingram in 1954. Rudy West sings lead on the ballads, Maryland Pierce lead on the rhythm tunes.	
12/25/54+	**28**	2	1 Ling, Ting, Tong Best Seller #28	Capitol F2945
9/15/56	**23**	15	2 Out Of Sight, Out Of Mind Best Seller #23 / Top 100 #27	Capitol 3502
12/15/56+	**35**	12	3 Wisdom Of A Fool	Capitol 3597
3/30/57	**69**	5	4 Let There Be You	Capitol 3660
			FIVE MAN ELECTRICAL BAND	
			Canadian rock group - Les Emmerson, lead singer.	
5/29/71	**3**	18	1 ● **Signs**	Lionel 3213
10/16/71	**26**	8	2 Absolutely Right	Lionel 3220
9/09/72	**72**	5	3 Money Back Guarantee	Lion 127
4/21/73	**76**	7	4 I'm A Stranger Here	Lion 149
3/30/74	**64**	8	5 Werewolf	Polydor 14221
			THE "5" ROYALES	
			R&B group from Winston-Salem, North Carolina. Formed spiritual group, the Royal Sons in 1948, first recorded on the Apollo label. Changed name to the "5" Royales in 1952, consisting of 3 cousins Lowman Pauling, Clarence Pauling, and Windsor King, with Eugene Tanner and his brother John.	
8/05/57	**66**	12	1 Think	King 5053
1/23/61	**81**	4	2 Dedicated To The One I Love	King 5453
			THE FIVE SATINS	
			R&B group from New Haven, CT. Consisted of Fred Parris, lead; Al Denby, Jim Freeman, Eddie Martin and Jessie Murphy on piano. Parris was stationed in the Army in Japan when "Still Of The Nite" hit, and the group reformed with Bill Baker as lead singer. Parris returned in January, 1958, replacing Baker as lead singer.	
9/08/56	**24**	19	1 In The Still Of The Nite Best Seller #24 / Top 100 #29 written by Fred Parris and recorded in a New Haven church basement originally released on the Standard label, record reportedly has sold multi-millions	Ember 1005
7/22/57	**25**	17	2 To The Aisle Best Seller #25 / Top 100 #25	Ember 1019
11/30/59	**87**	3	3 Shadows	Ember 1056
1/04/60	**81**	4	4 In The Still Of The Nite [R]	Ember 1005
5/09/60	**79**	6	5 I'll Be Seeing You originally written for the 1938 musical "Right This Way"	Ember 1061
1/23/61	**99**	1	6 In The Still Of The Nite [R]	Ember 1005
2/27/82	**71**	5	7 Memories Of Days Gone By **FRED PARRIS & THE FIVE SATINS** 16 Candles/Earth Angel/Only You/A Thousand Miles Away/Tears On My Pillow/Since I Don't Have You/In The Still Of The Night	Elektra 47411
			FIVE SPECIAL	
			R&B/funk quintet from Detroit.	
7/28/79	**55**	5	1 Why Leave Us Alone	Elektra 46032
			THE FIVE STAIRSTEPS	
			Soul group from Chicago, consisting of family members Clarence Jr., James, Alohe, Kenny and Dennis Burke. Later joined by 5-year old Cubie. Managed by their father and produced by Curtis Mayfield; later became the Invisible Man's Band.	
5/21/66	**94**	2	1 You Waited Too Long	Windy C 601
8/06/66	**49**	8	2 World Of Fantasy	Windy C 602
11/05/66	**61**	6	3 Come Back	Windy C 603
1/14/67	**89**	5	4 Danger! She's A Stranger	Windy C 604
4/15/67	**87**	2	5 Ain't Gonna Rest (Till I Get You)	Windy C 605

DEBUT DATE	PEAK POS	WKS CHR	ARTIST — Record Title	Label & Number
			THE FIVE STAIRSTEPS — Cont'd	
5/27/67	**63**	6	6 Oooh, Baby Baby	Windy C 607
			FIVE STAIRSTEPS & CUBIE:	
12/02/67+	**88**	6	7 Something's Missing	Buddah 20
1/27/68	**68**	6	8 A Million To One	Buddah 26
4/20/68	**94**	1	9 The Shadow Of Your Love	Buddah 35
8/24/68	**59**	9	10 Don't Change Your Love	Curtom 1931
12/21/68	**91**	2	11 Stay Close To Me	Curtom 1933
10/18/69	**88**	3	12 We Must Be In Love	Curtom 1945
			THE FIVE STAIRSTEPS:	
3/21/70	**8**	16	13● **O-o-h Child/**	
		8	14 Dear Prudence	Buddah 165
10/10/70	**83**	2	15 America/Standing/	
		1	16 Because I Love You	Buddah 188
			THE STAIRSTEPS:	
2/06/71	**81**	6	17 Didn't It Look So Easy	Buddah 213
			FIVE STAR	
			Black brother/sister quintet from Britain - Deniece (lead singer), Stedman, Doris, Lorraine and Delroy Pearson.	
9/14/85	**65**	11	1 All Fall Down	RCA 14108
2/08/86	**59**	9	2 Let Me Be The One	RCA 14229
9/13/86	**41**	14	3 Can't Wait Another Minute	RCA 14421
12/27/86+	**67**	11	4 If I Say Yes	RCA 5083
			5000 VOLTS	
10/18/75	**26**	10	1 I'm On Fire	Philips 40801
			THE FIXX	
			London-based techno-pop group: Cy Curnin (lead singer, piano), Jamie West-Oram (guitars), Rupert Greenall (keyboards), Adam Woods (drums) and Dan K. Brown (bass).	
10/30/82	**76**	8	1 Stand Or Fall	MCA 52106
5/28/83	**20**	16	2 Saved By Zero	MCA 52213
8/27/83	**4**	19	3 **One Thing Leads To Another**	MCA 52264
11/26/83+	**32**	13	4 The Sign Of Fire	MCA 52316
8/18/84	**15**	15	5 Are We Ourselves?	MCA 52444
11/17/84	**69**	5	6 Sunshine In The Shade	MCA 52498
5/24/86	**19**	14	7 Secret Separation	MCA 52832
			all of above produced by Rupert Hine	
			ROBERTA FLACK	
			Born on 2/10/39 in Asheville, NC. Grew up in Arlington, VA. Discovered by Les McCann. Signed to Atlantic Records in 1969.	
6/12/71	**29**	12	1 You've Got A Friend	Atlantic 2808
			ROBERTA FLACK & DONNY HATHAWAY	
10/23/71	**71**	6	2 You've Lost That Lovin' Feelin'	Atlantic 2837
			ROBERTA FLACK & DONNY HATHAWAY	
1/22/72	**76**	5	3 Will You Still Love Me Tomorrow	Atlantic 2851
3/04/72	**1^{6}**	18	4● **The First Time Ever I Saw Your Face**	Atlantic 2864
			popularized because of inclusion in the film "Play Misty For Me"	
6/10/72	**5**	13	5● **Where Is The Love**	Atlantic 2879
			ROBERTA FLACK & DONNY HATHAWAY	
1/27/73	**1^{5}**	16	6● **Killing Me Softly With His Song**	Atlantic 2940
9/22/73	**30**	9	7 Jesse	Atlantic 2982
6/22/74	**1^{1}**	16	8● **Feel Like Makin' Love**	Atlantic 3025
6/14/75	**76**	3	9 Feelin' That Glow	Atlantic 3271
2/18/78	**2^{2}**	20	10● **The Closer I Get To You**	Atlantic 3463
			ROBERTA FLACK with DONNY HATHAWAY	
5/20/78	**24**	13	11 If Ever I See You Again	Atlantic 3483
2/16/80	**47**	11	12 You Are My Heaven	Atlantic 3627
			ROBERTA FLACK with DONNY HATHAWAY	
5/17/80	**56**	8	13 Back Together Again	Atlantic 3661
			ROBERTA FLACK with DONNY HATHAWAY	
3/06/82	**13**	21	14 Making Love	Atlantic 4005
			from the film of the same title	
7/24/82	**42**	11	15 I'm The One	Atlantic 4068
7/09/83	**16**	29	16 Tonight, I Celebrate My Love	Capitol 5242
12/24/83+	**58**	11	17 You're Looking Like Love To Me	Capitol 5307
			above 2: **PEABO BRYSON/ROBERTA FLACK**	

DEBUT DATE	PEAK POS	WKS CHR	ARTIST — Record Title	Label & Number
			THE FLAME	
11/07/70	**95**	2	1 See The Light produced by The Beach Boys' Carl Wilson	Brother 3500
			THE FLAMING EMBER White soul/rock group from Detroit. Formed as the Flaming Embers: Joe Sladich (guitar), Bill Ellis (piano), Jim Bugnel (bass) and Jerry Plunk (drums).	
9/27/69	**26**	14	1 Mind, Body And Soul	Hot Wax 6902
1/17/70	**88**	5	2 Shades Of Green	Hot Wax 6907
5/23/70	**24**	14	3 Westbound # 9	Hot Wax 7003
10/17/70	**34**	13	4 I'm Not My Brothers Keeper	Hot Wax 7006
			THE FLAMINGOS R&B group formed in Chicago in 1952. Consisted of cousins Zeke & Jake Carey, and cousins Paul Wilson & Johnny Carter, and lead singer Sollie McElroy. First recordings with Chance Records, then Parrot. In 1954 Sollie departed and was replaced by Nate Nelson. With Checker Records, then to Decca. Tommy Hunt and Terry Johnson joined in July, 1956, replacing Army bound Zeke Carey and Johnny Carter. Carey returned in 1958 and group signed with End Records. Nate Nelson died of a heart attack on 6/1/84 (52).	
1/19/59	**52**	10	1 Lovers Never Say Goodbye	End 1035
6/01/59	**11**	13	2 I Only Have Eyes For You song hit POS 2 in 1934 by Ben Selvin	End 1046
10/05/59	**88**	3	3 Love Walked In the Gershwin classic hit POS 1 in 1938 for Sammy Kaye	End 1055
1/25/60	**71**	6	4 I Was Such A Fool (To Fall In Love With You)	End 1062
4/18/60	**30**	10	5 Nobody Loves Me Like You written by Sam Cooke	End 1068
7/18/60	**74**	6	6 Mio Amore	End 1073
12/19/60+	**54**	5	7 Your Other Love	End 1081
3/13/61	**92**	3	8 Kokomo originally released by The Flamingos in 1955 on the Parrot label	End 1085
7/03/61	**45**	8	9 Time Was	End 1092
3/19/66	**93**	2	10 The Boogaloo Party	Philips 40347
4/04/70	**86**	2	11 Buffalo Soldier	Polydor 14019
			THE FLARES Black quintet from various U.S. cities, featuring lead singer Aaron Collins of The Cadets/Jacks.	
9/04/61	**25**	15	1 Foot Stomping - Part 1	Felsted 8624
			FLASH English rock quartet led by Peter Banks (guitar) & Colin Carter (vocals).	
6/24/72	**29**	12	1 Small Beginnings	Capitol 3345
			FLASH & THE PAN Australian duo: George Young & Harry Vanda - formerly with The Easybeats.	
7/28/79	**76**	4	1 Hey, St. Peter	Epic 50715
			FLASH CADILLAC & THE CONTINENTAL KIDS Fifties-styled act formed by 6 students at the University of Colorado.	
5/25/74	**93**	3	1 Dancin' (On A Saturday Night)	Epic 11102
2/01/75	**41**	8	2 Good Times, Rock & Roll	Private S. 45006
8/28/76	**29**	14	3 Did You Boogie (With Your Baby) with spoken interludes by Wolfman Jack	Private S. 45079
			LESTER FLATT & EARL SCRUGGS Influential bluegrass duo: Flatt (guitar) was born on 6/28/14 in Overton County, Tennessee, and died in Nashville on 5/11/79. Scruggs (banjo) was born on 1/6/24 in Cleveland County, NC. Formed duo in 1948 while members of Bill Monroe's band. Separated in early 1969.	
12/08/62+	**44**	11	1 The Ballad Of Jed Clampett from the TV series "The Beverly Hillbillies"	Columbia 42606
3/02/68	**55**	12	2 Foggy Mountain Breakdown (Theme From "Bonnie & Clyde") [I] a different version on Mercury 72739 (recorded in 1949) was charted as one listing with the Columbia version	Columbia 44380
			FLAVOR	
8/03/68	**95**	5	1 Sally Had A Party	Columbia 44521

DEBUT DATE	PEAK POS	WKS CHR	ARTIST — Record Title	Label & Number
			FLEETWOOD MAC	
			Formed as a British blues band in 1967 by ex-John Mayall's Bluesbreakers Peter Green (guitar), Mick Fleetwood (drums) and John McVie (bass), along with guitarist Jeremy Spencer. Many lineup changes followed as group headed toward rock superstardom. Green and Spencer left in 1970. Christine McVie (keyboards) joined in August, 1970. Bob Welch (guitar) joined in April, 1971, stayed thru 1974. Group relocated to California in 1974, whereupon Lindsey Buckingham (guitar) and Stevie Nicks (vocals) joined in January, 1975.	
1/31/70	**55**	10	1 Oh Well - Pt. I	Reprise 0883
11/08/75+	**20**	14	2 Over My Head	Reprise 1339
3/06/76	**11**	18	3 Rhiannon (Will You Ever Win)	Reprise 1345
7/04/76	**11**	19	4 Say You Love Me	Reprise 1356
1/08/77	**10**	15	5 **Go Your Own Way**	Warner 8304
4/16/77	**1**[1]	19	6 ● **Dreams**	Warner 8371
7/09/77	**3**	18	7 **Don't Stop**	Warner 8413
10/15/77	**9**	14	8 **You Make Loving Fun**	Warner 8483
10/06/79	**8**	15	9 **Tusk** with U.S.C. Trojan Marching Band, recorded live at Dodger Stadium	Warner 49077
12/15/79+	**7**	14	10 **Sara**	Warner 49150
3/08/80	**20**	13	11 Think About Me	Warner 49196
6/07/80	**86**	3	12 Sisters Of The Moon	Warner 49500
2/07/81	**60**	6	13 Fireflies	Warner 49660
6/19/82	**4**	17	14 **Hold Me**	Warner 29966
9/04/82	**12**	14	15 Gypsy	Warner 29918
11/27/82+	**22**	14	16 Love In Store	Warner 29848
			THE FLEETWOODS	
			Trio formed while in high school in Olympia, Washington, 1958: Gary Troxel (b: 11/28/39), Gretchen Christopher (b: 2/29/40) and Barbara Ellis (b: 2/20/40).	
3/09/59	**1**[4]	16	1 **Come Softly To Me**	Dolphin 1
5/18/59	**39**	8	2 Graduation's Here	Dolton 3
9/07/59	**1**[1]	20	3 **Mr. Blue/**	
10/26/59	**84**	2	4 You Mean Everything To Me	Dolton 5
2/15/60	**28**	9	5 Outside My Window	Dolton 15
5/23/60	**23**	13	6 Runaround	Dolton 22
10/17/60	**96**	1	7 The Last One To Know	Dolton 27
4/17/61	**10**	12	8 **Tragedy**	Dolton 40
9/11/61	**30**	8	9 (He's) The Great Impostor	Dolton 45
10/13/62	**36**	10	10 Lovers By Night, Strangers By Day	Dolton 62
6/01/63	**32**	11	11 Goodnight My Love	Dolton 75
			WADE FLEMONS	
			Born on 9/25/40 in Coffeyville, KS. Original member of Earth, Wind & Fire.	
12/22/58+	**80**	5	1 Here I Stand backing vocals by The Newcomers	Vee-Jay 295
2/15/60	**94**	2	2 What's Happening	Vee-Jay 335
4/25/60	**70**	4	3 Easy Lovin'	Vee-Jay 344
			DARROW FLETCHER	
			Born Darrow Fletcher Haygood on 1/23/51 in Inkster, Michigan.	
1/15/66	**89**	3	1 The Pain Gets A Little Deeper	Groovy 3001
			LOIS FLETCHER	
3/30/74	**64**	7	1 I Am What I Am	Playboy 50049
			SHELBY FLINT	
			Singer, songwriter from North Hollywood, California.	
12/26/60+	**22**	12	1 Angel On My Shoulder	Valiant 6001
8/13/66	**61**	7	2 Cast Your Fate To The Wind	Valiant 743
			THE FLIRTATIONS	
3/08/69	**34**	14	1 Nothing But A Heartache	Deram 85038
			THE FLOATERS	
			Detroit soul group.	
7/09/77	**2**[2]	16	1 ● **Float On**	ABC 12284
			A FLOCK OF SEAGULLS	
			British techno-rock quartet - Mike Score, lead singer.	
7/10/82	**9**	22	1 **I Ran (So Far Away)**	Jive 102

DEBUT DATE	PEAK POS	WKS CHR	ARTIST — Record Title	Label & Number
			A FLOCK OF SEAGULLS — Cont'd	
11/13/82+	**30**	18	2 Space Age Love Song	Jive 2003
5/14/83	**26**	14	3 Wishing (If I Had A Photograph Of You)	Jive 2006
8/11/84	**56**	9	4 The More You Live, The More You Love	Jive 9220
			DICK FLOOD	
			Born on 11/13/32 in Philadelphia. Singer, songwriter.	
8/31/59	**23**	8	1 The Three Bells (The Jimmy Brown Story)	Monument 408
			EDDIE FLOYD	
			Born on 6/25/35 in Montgomery, Alabama. Raised in Detroit. Original member of The Falcons, 1955-63.	
9/10/66	**28**	17	1 Knock On Wood	Stax 194
2/04/67	**79**	6	2 Raise Your Hand	Stax 208
7/01/67	**98**	1	3 Don't Rock The Boat	Stax 219
8/26/67	**97**	1	4 Love Is A Doggone Good Thing	Stax 223
10/28/67	**92**	4	5 On A Saturday Night	Stax 233
7/27/68	**40**	9	6 I've Never Found A Girl (To Love Me Like You Do)	Stax 0002
10/19/68	**17**	13	7 Bring It On Home To Me	Stax 0012
6/28/69	**73**	7	8 Don't Tell Your Mama (Where You've Been)	Stax 0036
11/01/69	**98**	2	9 Why Is The Wine Sweeter (On The Other Side)	Stax 0051
2/21/70	**45**	12	10 California Girl	Stax 0060
			KING FLOYD	
			Soul/funk singer, songwriter from New Orleans. First recorded on Original Sound in 1965.	
10/24/70+	**6**	20	1 ● **Groove Me**	Chimneyville 435
3/13/71	**29**	11	2 Baby Let Me Kiss You	Chimneyville 437
9/16/72	**53**	12	3 Woman Don't Go Astray	Chimneyville 443
			THE FLYING LIZARDS	
			British electronic production of David Cunningham.	
12/01/79+	**50**	10	1 Money [N]	Virgin 67003
			THE FLYING MACHINE	
			English pop quintet - Tony Newman, lead singer.	
10/04/69	**5**	14	1 ● **Smile A Little Smile For Me**	Congress 6000
2/21/70	**87**	2	2 Baby Make It Soon	Congress 6012
			FOCUS	
			Dutch progressive rock quartet led by guitar virtuoso Jan Akkerman and flutist Thijs Van Leer.	
3/03/73	**9**	19	1 **Hocus Pocus** [I]	Sire 704
7/28/73	**89**	5	2 Sylvia [I]	Sire 708
			DAN FOGELBERG	
			Born on 8/13/51 in Peoria, IL. Vocalist, composer. Worked as folk singer in Los Angeles. With Van Morrison, early 1970's. Session work in Nashville. Toured with the Eagles in 1975.	
2/01/75	**31**	9	1 Part Of The Plan	Epic 50055
10/14/78	**24**	14	2 The Power Of Gold DAN FOGELBERG/TIM WEISBERG	Full Moon 50606
12/15/79+	**2^2**	22	3 **Longer**	Full Moon 50824
3/22/80	**21**	13	4 Heart Hotels	Full Moon 50862
12/13/80+	**9**	18	5 **Same Old Lang Syne**	Full Moon 50961
8/29/81	**7**	19	6 **Hard To Say**	Full Moon 02488
11/28/81+	**9**	20	7 **Leader Of The Band**	Full Moon 02647
4/03/82	**18**	14	8 Run For The Roses	Full Moon 02821
10/09/82	**23**	16	9 Missing You	Full Moon 03289
2/05/83	**29**	16	10 Make Love Stay	Full Moon 03525
2/04/84	**13**	14	11 The Language Of Love	Full Moon 04314
4/28/84	**48**	9	12 Believe In Me	Full Moon 04447
3/23/85	**85**	4	13 Go Down Easy	Full Moon 04835
			JOHN FOGERTY	
			Born on 5/28/45 in Berkeley, CA. Leader of Creedence Clearwater Revival. Although listed as a group, John recorded entirely solo as The Blue Ridge Rangers. **THE BLUE RIDGE RANGERS:**	
12/02/72+	**16**	16	1 Jambalaya (On The Bayou)	Fantasy 689

DEBUT DATE	PEAK POS	WKS CHR	ARTIST — Record Title	Label & Number
			JOHN FOGERTY — Cont'd	
3/31/73	**37**	12	2 Hearts Of Stone	Fantasy 700
			JOHN FOGERTY:	
9/06/75	**27**	11	3 Rockin' All Over The World	Asylum 45274
12/13/75	**78**	3	4 Almost Saturday Night	Asylum 45291
5/01/76	**87**	4	5 You Got The Magic	Asylum 45309
12/22/84+	**10**	18	6 **The Old Man Down The Road**	Warner 29100
3/16/85	**20**	12	7 Rock And Roll Girls/	
5/25/85	**44**	13	8 Centerfield	Warner 29053
9/06/86	**81**	4	9 Eye Of The Zombie	Warner 28657
			FOGHAT	
			British rock quartet led by Lonesome Dave Peverett - formerly with Savoy Brown. Settled in New York City in 1975.	
10/07/72	**83**	7	1 I Just Want To Make Love To You	Bearsville 0008
4/28/73	**82**	6	2 What A Shame	Bearsville 0014
12/13/75+	**20**	17	3 Slow Ride	Bearsville 0306
6/05/76	**45**	7	4 Fool For The City	Bearsville 0307
11/27/76+	**34**	10	5 Drivin' Wheel	Bearsville 0313
3/26/77	**67**	3	6 I'll Be Standing By	Bearsville 0315
9/10/77	**33**	10	7 I Just Want To Make Love To You live version of 1972 hit	Bearsville 0319
5/20/78	**36**	10	8 Stone Blue	Bearsville 0325
11/17/79+	**23**	15	9 Third Time Lucky (First Time I Was A Fool)	Bearsville 49125
8/02/80	**81**	3	10 Stranger In My Home Town	Bearsville 49510
			ELLEN FOLEY	
			Singer, actress from New York City. Vocalist on Meat Loaf's "Bat Out Of Hell" album.	
11/17/79	**92**	4	1 What's A Matter Baby	Epic 50770
			EDDIE FONTAINE	
9/22/58	**64**	3	1 Nothin' Shakin'	Argo 5309
			WAYNE FONTANA - see MINDBENDERS	
			THE FONTANE SISTERS	
			Trio from New Milford, NJ. Consisted of sisters Marge, Bea and Geri, whose family name is Rosse. With Perry Como on radio, TV and recordings from 1945-54.	
12/11/54+	**1**[3]	20	1 **Hearts Of Stone** Juke Box #1(3) / Best Seller #1(1) / Jockey #2	Dot 15265
2/26/55	**13**	8	2 Rock Love Juke Box #13 / Best Seller #19	Dot 15333
6/04/55	**13**	6	3 Rollin' Stone/ Juke Box #13	
		2	4 Playmates Juke Box flip	Dot 15370
8/20/55	**3**	15	5 **Seventeen** Juke Box #3 / Best Seller #6 / Jockey #7 / Top 100 #15 pre	Dot 15386
11/12/55	**11**	16	6 Daddy-O/ Top 100 #11 / Juke Box #11 / Best Seller #13 / Jockey #18	
11/19/55	**71**	11	7 Adorable	Dot 15428
12/17/55	**36**	4	8 Nuttin' For Christmas [N]	Dot 15434
3/10/56	**11**	17	9 Eddie My Love Juke Box #11 / Top 100 #12 / Jockey #13 / Best Seller #15	Dot 15450
5/26/56	**38**	14	10 I'm In Love Again	Dot 15462
7/28/56	**47**	7	11 Voices/ narration by Pat Boone	
8/11/56	**93**	2	12 Lonesome Lover Blues	Dot 15480
10/13/56	**55**	7	13 Please Don't Leave Me/	
10/13/56	**86**	6	14 Still	Dot 15501
12/29/56+	**13**	18	15 The Banana Boat Song Jockey #13 / Juke Box #14 / Top 100 #22	Dot 15527
5/06/57	**72**	2	16 I'm Stickin' With You	Dot 15555
4/28/58	**12**	9	17 Chanson d'Amour (Song Of Love) Jockey #12 / Top 100 #68	Dot 15736
11/10/58	**94**	1	18 Jealous Heart orchestra directed by Billy Vaughn on all of above	Dot 15853

DEBUT DATE	PEAK POS	WKS CHR	ARTIST — Record Title	Label & Number
			THE FOOLS	
			Boston-based quintet - Mike Girard, lead singer.	
4/19/80	**67**	4	1 It's A Night For Beautiful Girls	EMI America 8036
3/07/81	**50**	7	2 Running Scared	EMI America 8072
			FOOLS GOLD	
			Dan Fogelberg's backing group.	
5/29/76	**76**	7	1 Rain, Oh Rain	Morning Sky 700
			STEVE FORBERT	
			Born in 1955 in Meridian, Mississippi. To New York City in 1976.	
12/01/79+	**11**	19	1 Romeo's Tune	Nemperor 7525
4/12/80	**85**	3	2 Say Goodbye To Little Jo	Nemperor 7529
			FORCE M.D.'S	
			Staten Island-based soul/rap quintet.	
2/01/86	**10**	19	1 **Tender Love**	Warner 28818
			from the film "Krush Groove"	
			FRANKIE FORD	
			Born Frank Guzzo on 8/4/39 in Gretna, LA. Vocal training since age 6; appeared with Sophie Tucker, Ted Lewis, Carmen Miranda at local shows at an early age. Formed own band, Syncopators, in high school. First recorded for Ace in 1958.	
2/09/59	**14**	17	1 Sea Cruise	Ace 554
8/03/59	**97**	2	2 Alimony	Ace 566
			above 2 feature backing by Huey "Piano" Smith's group, The Clowns	
1/18/60	**75**	6	3 Time After Time	Ace 580
			first popularized by Frank Sinatra in 1947 (POS 16)	
9/26/60	**87**	4	4 You Talk Too Much	Imperial 5686
3/20/61	**72**	5	5 Seventeen	Imperial 5735
			TENNESSEE ERNIE FORD	
			Born Ernest Jennings Ford on 2/13/19 in Bristol, TN. Began career as a disc jockey. Host of musical variety TV shows from 1955-65. America's favorite hymn singer.	
3/19/55	**5**	17	1 **Ballad Of Davy Crockett**	Capitol 3058
			Juke Box #5 / Best Seller #6 / Jockey #7	
			from the Walt Disney film "Davy Crockett"	
11/12/55	**1^{8}**	22	2 **Sixteen Tons/**	
			Juke Box #1(8) / Best Seller #1(7) / Top 100 #1(6) / Jockey #1(6)	
1/21/56	**78**	1	3 You Don't Have To Be A Baby To Cry	Capitol 3262
2/25/56	**17**	8	4 That's All	Capitol 3343
			Jockey #17 / Top 100 #44	
5/19/56	**60**	6	5 The Rovin' Gambler	Capitol 3421
11/03/56	**46**	11	6 First Born	Capitol 3553
3/09/57	**87**	2	7 The Watermelon Song/	
3/09/57	**93**	3	8 One Suit	Capitol 3649
8/26/57	**23**	12	9 In The Middle Of An Island/	
			Jockey #23 / Top 100 #56	
		1	10 Ivy League	Capitol 3762
			Coming Up flip	
			2-10: orchestra directed by Jack Fascinato	
8/11/58	**97**	1	11 Sunday Barbecue	Capitol 3997
2/23/59	**100**	1	12 Glad Rags	Capitol 4107
			1, 11, 12: orchestra directed by Cliffie Stone	
			FOREIGNER	
			British/American rock group formed in New York City, 1976. Consisted of Mick Jones, guitar; Lou Gramm, vocals; Ian McDonald, guitar, keyboards; Al Greenwood, keyboards; Ed Gagliardi, bass; and Dennis Elliott, drums. Most of their material was written by Jones (formerly with Spooky Tooth) and Gramm. Re-formed in 1980 with Jones, Gramm, Elliott and Rick Wills, bass. Gramm, Gagliardi and Greenwood are from New York.	
3/26/77	**4**	22	1 **Feels Like The First Time**	Atlantic 3394
7/23/77	**6**	21	2 **Cold As Ice**	Atlantic 3410
12/10/77+	**20**	14	3 Long, Long Way From Home	Atlantic 3439
7/01/78	**3**	17	4 ● **Hot Blooded**	Atlantic 3488
9/23/78	**2^{2}**	20	5 ● **Double Vision**	Atlantic 3514
12/23/78+	**15**	14	6 Blue Morning, Blue Day	Atlantic 3543
9/08/79	**12**	14	7 Dirty White Boy	Atlantic 3618
11/10/79	**14**	14	8 Head Games	Atlantic 3633
2/16/80	**41**	9	9 Women	Atlantic 3651
7/04/81	**4**	23	10 **Urgent**	Atlantic 3831
			sax solo by Jr. Walker	

DEBUT DATE	PEAK POS	WKS CHR	ARTIST — Record Title	Label & Number
			FOREIGNER — Cont'd	
10/10/81	**2**[10]	23	11 ● **Waiting For A Girl Like You**	Atlantic 3868
2/13/82	**26**	13	12 Juke Box Hero	Atlantic 4017
5/15/82	**26**	13	13 Break It Up	Atlantic 4044
7/31/82	**75**	6	14 Luanne	Atlantic 4072
12/08/84+	**1**[2]	21	15 ● **I Want To Know What Love Is** vocal backing: New Jersey Mass Choir and Jennifer Holliday	Atlantic 89596
3/16/85	**12**	15	16 That Was Yesterday	Atlantic 89571
6/01/85	**54**	8	17 Reaction To Action	Atlantic 89542
8/17/85	**54**	8	18 Down On Love	Atlantic 89493
			THE FORMATIONS	
3/16/68	**83**	5	1 At The Top Of The Stairs	MGM 13899
			FORTUNE Pop/rock quintet - L.A. Greene, lead singer.	
12/21/85+	**80**	6	1 Stacy	MCA/Camel 52727
			THE FORTUNES English pop quintet led by Glen Dale and Barry Pritchard.	
8/21/65	**7**	11	1 **You've Got Your Troubles**	Press 9773
11/06/65	**27**	8	2 Here It Comes Again	Press 9798
2/19/66	**82**	4	3 This Golden Ring	Press 9811
5/16/70	**62**	8	4 That Same Old Feeling	World Pac. 77937
5/15/71	**15**	14	5 Here Comes That Rainy Day Feeling Again	Capitol 3086
10/02/71	**72**	5	6 Freedom Comes, Freedom Goes	Capitol 3179
			THE FORUM Trio from Pasadena: Phil Campos, Rene Nole and Riselle Bain.	
7/08/67	**45**	8	1 The River Is Wide	Mira 232
			BRUCE FOSTER New York singer, songwriter - claims to be a descendant of composer Stephen Foster.	
7/02/77	**63**	5	1 Platinum Heroes a tribute to The Beatles	Millennium 602
			DAVID FOSTER Keyboardist/composer/arranger. Member of Canadian group, Skylark.	
8/24/85	**15**	22	1 Love Theme From St. Elmo's Fire [I] from the film "St. Elmo's Fire"	Atlantic 89528
6/14/86	**80**	8	2 The Best Of Me **DAVID FOSTER & OLIVIA NEWTON-JOHN**	Atlantic 89420
			FOTOMAKER New York pop/rock quintet formed by former Rascals Dino Danelli and Gene Cornish, and Wally Bryson, formerly of the Raspberries.	
4/22/78	**81**	6	1 Where Have You Been All My Life	Atlantic 3471
12/02/78	**63**	6	2 Miles Away	Atlantic 3531
			THE FOUNDATIONS British integrated R&B/rock group. Lead singer Clem Curtis (from Trinidad) replaced by Colin Young (West Indies) in 1968.	
12/23/67+	**11**	13	1 Baby, Now That I've Found You	Uni 55038
3/09/68	**59**	6	2 Back On My Feet Again	Uni 55058
1/04/69	**3**	15	3 ● **Build Me Up Buttercup**	Uni 55101
4/05/69	**51**	7	4 In The Bad, Bad Old Days (Before You Loved Me)	Uni 55117
7/05/69	**99**	2	5 My Little Chickadee	Uni 55137
			PETE FOUNTAIN Born on 7/3/30 in New Orleans. Clarinetist. With Al Hirt, 1956-57. Performed on Lawrence Welk's weekly TV show, 1957-59. Own club in New Orleans, The French Quarter Inn.	
2/08/60	**93**	3	1 A Closer Walk [I] a hit in 1960 for Jimmie Rodgers as "Just A Closer Walk With Thee"	Coral 62154
2/24/62	**69**	6	2 Yes Indeed first popularized in 1941 by Tommy Dorsey (POS 4)	Coral 65549
			ROOSEVELT FOUNTAIN & PENS OF RHYTHM	
1/05/63	**78**	3	1 Red Pepper I [I]	Prince-Adams 447

DEBUT DATE	PEAK POS	WKS CHR	ARTIST — Record Title	Label & Number
			FOUR ACES	
			Vocal group from Chester, Pennsylvania: Al Alberts (lead singer), Dave Mahoney (tenor), Sod Voccaro (baritone) and Lou Silvestri (bass). Worked Ye Olde Mill near Philadelphia, late 1940s. First recorded for Victoria in 1951.	
1/15/55	**3**	21	1 **Melody Of Love**	Decca 29395
			Juke Box #3 / Jockey #9 / Best Seller #11	
5/28/55	**13**	6	2 Heart	Decca 29476
			Jockey #13 / Juke Box #20 / Best Seller #23	
			from the Broadway musical "Damn Yankees"	
8/27/55	**1[6]**	21	3 **Love Is A Many-Splendored Thing**	Decca 29625
			Jockey #1(6) / Top 100 #1(3) / Juke Box #1(3) / Best Seller #1(2)	
			from the William Holden, Jennifer Jones film of the same title	
11/19/55	**14**	17	4 A Woman In Love/	
			Jockey #14 / Top 100 #19 / Best Seller #20	
			from the film "Guys And Dolls"	
12/03/55	**56**	4	5 Of This I'm Sure	Decca 29725
2/18/56	**62**	8	6 If You Can Dream/	
3/17/56	**91**	1	7 The Gal With The Yaller Shoes	Decca 29809
			above 2 from the film "Meet Me In Las Vegas"	
5/05/56	**43**	17	8 To Love Again	Decca 29889
			based on Chopins E Flat Nocturne	
			from the film "The Eddy Duchin Story"	
7/28/56	**22**	11	9 I Only Know I Love You/	
			Jockey #22 / Top 100 #35	
7/14/56	**86**	3	10 Dreamer	Decca 29989
9/22/56	**45**	18	11 Friendly Persuasion/	
10/20/56	**20**	6	12 You Can't Run Away From It	Decca 30041
			Jockey #20 / Top 100 #70	
			above 2 are from films of the same titles	
12/01/56	**47**	7	13 Someone To Love/	
12/15/56+	**61**	15	14 Written On The Wind	Decca 30123
			from the film of the same title	
3/30/57	**53**	6	15 Bahama Mama/	
3/30/57	**76**	4	16 You're Mine	Decca 30242
3/24/58	**66**	7	17 Rock And Roll Rhapsody	Decca 30575
11/24/58	**63**	4	18 The World Outside	Decca 30764
			introduced in 1942 film "Suicide Squadron" as "Warsaw Concerto"	
3/02/59	**74**	5	19 No Other Arms, No Other Lips	Decca 30822
			orchestra directed by Jack Pleis on all of above	
			THE FOUR COINS	
			Vocal group of Greek descent from Canonsburg, Pennsylvania: George Mantalis, George Gregorakis, and brothers Michael & George Mahramas. In film "Disc Jockey Jamboree".	
1/15/55	**28**	1	1 I Love You Madly	Epic 9082
			Best Seller #28	
11/26/55	**22**	16	2 Memories Of You	Epic 9129
			Best Seller #22 / Top 10 #28	
			from the film "The Benny Goodman Story"	
5/27/57	**11**	21	3 Shangri-La	Epic 9213
			Jockey #11 / Best Seller #22 / Top 100 #23	
9/23/57	**28**	15	4 My One Sin	Epic 9229
			Best Seller #28 / Top 100 #29	
9/22/58	**72**	3	5 Wendy, Wendy	Epic 9286
11/10/58	**21**	11	6 The World Outside	Epic 9295
			introduced in 1942 film "Suicide Squadron" as "Warsaw Concerto"	
6/08/59	**82**	4	7 One Love, One Heart	Epic 9314
			THE FOUR DATES	
			Vocal backing group for Frankie Avalon and Fabian.	
5/12/58	**87**	1	1 I'm Happy	Chancellor 1014
			THE FOUR ESQUIRES	
			Formed group at Boston University: Bill Courtney, Frank Mahoney, Bob Golden and Wally Gold.	
5/05/56	**55**	7	1 Look Homeward Angel	London 1652
11/18/57	**25**	10	2 Love Me Forever	Paris 509
			Jockey #25 / Best Seller #44 / Top 100 #51	
9/22/58	**21**	17	3 Hideaway	Paris 520
			THE FOUR-EVERS	
			A 4 Seasons sound alike - arranged by Charles Calello; written by Bob Gaudio.	
5/30/64	**75**	4	1 Be My Girl	Smash 1887

DEBUT DATE	PEAK POS	WKS CHR	ARTIST — Record Title	Label & Number
			THE FOUR FRESHMEN	
			Jazz-styled vocal and instrumental group formed in 1948 while at Arthur Jordan Conservatory of Music in Indianapolis: brothers Ross & Don Barbour, their cousin Bob Flanigan and Ken Errair.	
8/13/55	**42**	7	1 Day By Day	Capitol 3154
			Coming Up #42 / Top 100 #72 pre Top 10 hits of this tune in 1946 by Frank Sinatra and Jo Stafford	
12/10/55+	**69**	7	2 Charmaine	Capitol 3292
			first hit #1 in 1927 by Guy Lombardo	
5/12/56	**17**	13	3 Graduation Day	Capitol 3410
			Jockey #17 / Best Seller #25 / Top 100 #27	
			FOUR JACKS & A JILL	
			South African quintet - Jill: Glenys Lynne.	
3/30/68	**18**	14	1 Master Jack	RCA 9473
8/10/68	**96**	2	2 Mister Nico	RCA 9572
			THE FOUR KNIGHTS	
			Formed as the Southland Jubilee Singers in Charlotte, NC, 1943. To New York in 1945 as The Four Knights. Backed Nat King Cole on several tunes. Gene Alford (lead), Clarence Dixon (baritone), Oscar Broadway (bass) and John Wallace (tenor).	
1/12/59	**83**	3	1 O' Falling Star	Coral 62045
			THE FOUR LADS	
			Vocal group from Toronto, Canada: Bernie Toorish (lead tenor), Jimmie Arnold (second tenor), Frankie Busseri (baritone) and Connie Codarini (bass). Sang in choir at St. Michael's Cathedral in Toronto. Worked local hotels and clubs. Worked Le Ruban Bleu in New York City. Signed as back-up singers by Columbia in 1950. Backed Johnnie Ray on his #1 hit "Cry".	
9/03/55	**2^{6}**	25	1 **Moments To Remember**	Columbia 40539
			Jockey #2 / Best Seller #3 / Top 100 #3 / Juke Box #4	
1/21/56	**2^{4}**	24	2 **No, Not Much!/**	
			Jockey #2 / Top 100 #3 / Best Seller #4 / Juke Box #4	
2/25/56	**52**	5	3 I'll Never Know	Columbia 40629
4/28/56	**3**	20	4 **Standing On The Corner/**	
			Best Seller #3 / Top 100 #3 / Jockey #3 / Juke Box #3 from Broadway's "The Most Happy Fella"	
4/28/56	**24**	16	5 My Little Angel	Columbia 40674
			Jockey #24 / Top 100 #30	
5/19/56	**67**	3	6 The Mocking Bird [R]	Epic 9150
			originally charted in 1952 (POS 23 on Okeh 6885)	
8/25/56	**16**	13	7 The Bus Stop Song (A Paper Of Pins)/	
			Best Seller #16 / Top 100 #23 / Jockey #17 from the Marilyn Monroe film "Bus Stop"	
9/01/56	**20**	13	8 A House With Love In It	Columbia 40736
			Jockey #20 / Top 100 #23	
1/26/57	**9**	21	9 **Who Needs You/**	
			Jockey #9 / Best Seller #13 / Top 100 #14 / Juke Box #17	
		4	10 It's So Easy To Forget	Columbia 40811
			Coming Up flip	
5/06/57	**17**	12	11 I Just Don't Know	Columbia 40914
			Jockey #17 / Top 100 #22	
12/09/57+	**8**	14	12 **Put A Light In The Window**	Columbia 41058
			Jockey #8 / Top 100 #35 / Best Seller #39	
4/07/58	**10**	12	13 **There's Only One Of You**	Columbia 41136
			Jockey #10 / Top 100 #41 / Best Seller #43	
6/30/58	**12**	12	14 Enchanted Island	Columbia 41194
			Jockey #12 / Hot 100 #29 / Best Seller #32 from the Jane Powell film of the same title	
11/03/58	**32**	10	15 The Mocking Bird	Columbia 41266
			new version of their 1952 and 1956 hit	
1/05/59	**52**	10	16 The Girl On Page 44	Columbia 41310
5/04/59	**90**	2	17 The Fountain Of Youth	Columbia 41365
			orchestra directed by Ray Ellis on all of above (except #6 & 15)	
11/09/59	**77**	5	18 Happy Anniversary	Columbia 41497
			from the David Niven film of the same title 1, 2, 9, 13, 14, 18: written by Al Stillman & Robert Allen	

DEBUT DATE	PEAK POS	WKS CHR	ARTIST — Record Title	Label & Number
			THE FOUR LOVERS - see THE 4 SEASONS	
			THE FOUR PENNIES - see THE CHIFFONS	
			THE FOUR PREPS Vocal group formed while at Hollywood High School: Bruce Belland, Glen Larson, Ed Cobb and Marvin Ingraham. Belland was later in duo with Dave Somerville of the Diamonds.	
12/22/56+	**56**	12	1 Dreamy Eyes	Capitol 3576
1/20/58	**2**[3]	20	2 **26 Miles (Santa Catalina)** Jockey #2 / Top 100 #4 / Best Seller #5	Capitol 3845
5/05/58	**3**	14	3 **Big Man** Jockey #3 / Top 100 #5 / Best Seller #6	Capitol 3960
8/18/58	**21**	10	4 Lazy Summer Night/ Hot 100 #21 / Best Seller #34 from the film "Andy Hardy Comes Home"	
		5	5 Summertime Lies Best Seller flip	Capitol 4023
11/17/58	**69**	7	6 Cinderella from the film "Gidget"	Capitol 4078
9/14/59	**79**	2	7 I Ain't Never	Capitol 4256
12/28/59+	**13**	15	8 Down By The Station	Capitol 4312
4/18/60	**24**	10	9 Got A Girl [N]	Capitol 4362
2/06/61	**96**	2	10 Calcutta	Capitol 4508
8/14/61	**17**	11	11 More Money For You And Me [N] Mr. Blue/Alley Oop/Smoke Gets In Your Eyes/In This Whole Wide World/A Worried Man/Tom Dooley/A Teenager In Love	Capitol 4599
3/31/62	**61**	6	12 The Big Draft [N] I'll Never Smile Again/Love Is A Many-Splendored Thing/The Mountain's High/Heartaches/Anchors Aweigh/Michael/Runaround Sue	Capitol 4716
3/21/64	**85**	3	13 A Letter To The Beatles [N]	Capitol 5143
			THE 4 SEASONS Vocal group formed in Newark, New Jersey. In 1955, lead singer Frankie Valli (Francis Castelluccio) formed the Variatones with brothers Nick and Tommy DeVito, and Hank Majewski. Changed name to The Four Lovers in 1956. Bob Gaudio (of The Royal Teens) joined as keyboardist and songwriter in 1959, replacing Nick DeVito. Nick Massi replaced Majewski, and their 1961 line-up was set: Valli, Gaudio, Massi and Tommy DeVito. Group had been doing session work for their producer Bob Crewe and took their new name from a New Jersey bowling alley, The Four Seasons. In 1965, Nick Massi was replaced by the group's arranger Charlie Callelo and then by Joe Long. In 1971, Tommy DeVito retired, and Gaudio left (as a performer) the following year. Numerous personnel changes from then on.	
5/26/56	**62**	5	1 You're The Apple Of My Eye THE FOUR LOVERS	RCA 6518
8/25/62	**1**[5]	14	2 **Sherry**	Vee-Jay 456
10/20/62	**1**[5]	16	3 **Big Girls Don't Cry**	Vee-Jay 465
12/15/62	**23**	3	4 Santa Claus Is Coming To Town [X] first popularized in 1934 by George Hall (POS 12)	Vee-Jay 478
1/26/63	**1**[3]	13	5 **Walk Like A Man**	Vee-Jay 485
4/20/63	**22**	9	6 Ain't That A Shame!/	
5/11/63	**77**	7	7 Soon (I'll Be Home Again)	Vee-Jay 512
7/06/63	**3**	13	8 **Candy Girl/**	
7/13/63	**36**	8	9 Marlena	Vee-Jay 539
10/05/63	**36**	7	10 New Mexican Rose/	
10/05/63	**88**	3	11 That's The Only Way	Vee-Jay 562
2/01/64	**3**	13	12 **Dawn (Go Away)**	Philips 40166
2/15/64	**16**	11	13 Stay	Vee-Jay 582
4/11/64	**6**	10	14 **Ronnie**	Philips 40185
6/06/64	**28**	9	15 Alone	Vee-Jay 597
6/20/64	**1**[2]	12	16 ● **Rag Doll**	Philips 40211
8/29/64	**10**	8	17 **Save It For Me**	Philips 40225
8/29/64	**75**	4	18 Sincerely	Vee-Jay 608
11/07/64	**20**	7	19 Big Man In Town	Philips 40238
1/16/65	**12**	9	20 Bye, Bye, Baby (Baby Goodbye)	Philips 40260
4/10/65	**64**	5	21 Toy Soldier	Philips 40278
6/19/65	**30**	7	22 Girl Come Running	Philips 40305
10/09/65	**3**	16	23 **Let's Hang On!**	Philips 40317

DEBUT DATE	PEAK POS	WKS CHR	ARTIST — Record Title	Label & Number
			THE 4 SEASONS — Cont'd	
11/06/65	**12**	11	24 Don't Think Twice **THE WONDER WHO?**	Philips 40324
12/25/65+	**60**	6	25 Little Boy (In Grown Up Clothes)	Vee-Jay 713
1/29/66	**9**	9	26 **Working My Way Back To You**	Philips 40350
5/21/66	**13**	8	27 Opus 17 (Don't You Worry 'Bout Me)	Philips 40370
7/02/66	**87**	3	28 On The Good Ship Lollipop/	
7/16/66	**96**	1	29 You're Nobody Till Somebody Loves You above 2: **THE WONDER WHO?**	Philips 40380
9/03/66	**9**	10	30 **I've Got You Under My Skin** there were 2 Top 10 versions of this Cole Porter classic in 1936	Philips 40393
12/10/66+	**10**	10	31 **Tell It To The Rain**	Philips 40412
3/04/67	**16**	9	32 Beggin'	Philips 40433
6/10/67	**9**	10	33 **C'mon Marianne**	Philips 40460
7/29/67	**89**	4	34 Lonesome Road **THE WONDER WHO?**	Philips 40471
10/28/67	**30**	7	35 Watch The Flowers Grow	Philips 40490
2/24/68	**24**	8	36 Will You Love Me Tomorrow	Philips 40523
12/28/68+	**61**	6	37 Electric Stories	Philips 40577
3/29/69	**98**	1	38 Something's On Her Mind/	
4/05/69	**95**	2	39 Idaho	Philips 40597
9/13/69	**45**	7	40 And That Reminds Me (My Heart Reminds Me)	Crewe 333
5/09/70	**94**	2	41 Patch Of Blue **FRANKIE VALLI & THE 4 SEASONS**	Philips 40662
8/23/75	**3**	20	42 **Who Loves You**	Warner 8122
12/27/75+	**1**[3]	27	43 ● **December, 1963 (Oh, What a Night)**	Warner 8168
5/29/76	**38**	8	44 Silver Star	Warner 8203
7/16/77	**65**	6	45 Down The Hall	Warner 8407
12/13/80	**91**	5	46 Spend The Night In Love lead vocals on above 4 by Gerri Polci	Warner 49597
			THE FOUR SONICS R&B quartet: Willie Frazier, Steve Gaston, Eddy Daniels and James "Jay" Johnson.	
2/10/68	**89**	2	1 You Don't Have To Say You Love Me	Sport 110
			THE FOUR SPORTSMEN	
8/14/61	**76**	5	1 Pitter-Patter	Sunnybrook 4
			FOUR TOPS R&B group formed in their native Detroit in 1954 as the Four Aims. Consisted of Levi Stubbs (lead singer), Renaldo "Obie" Benson, Lawrence Payton and Abdul "Duke" Fakir. First recorded for Chess in 1956, then Red Top and Columbia, before signing with Motown in 1963. Group has had no personnel changes since its formation. Stubbs is the voice of Audrey II (the voracious vegetation) in the film "Little Shop of Horrors".	
8/15/64	**11**	12	1 Baby I Need Your Loving	Motown 1062
11/28/64	**43**	5	2 Without The One You Love (Life's Not Worth While)	Motown 1069
2/06/65	**24**	8	3 Ask The Lonely	Motown 1073
5/15/65	**1**[2]	14	4 **I Can't Help Myself**	Motown 1076
7/31/65	**5**	9	5 **It's The Same Old Song**	Motown 1081
7/31/65	**93**	1	6 Ain't That Love	Columbia 43356
11/13/65	**19**	7	7 Something About You	Motown 1084
2/19/66	**18**	9	8 Shake Me, Wake Me (When It's Over)	Motown 1090
5/28/66	**45**	8	9 Loving You Is Sweeter Than Ever	Motown 1096
9/03/66	**1**[2]	15	10 **Reach Out I'll Be There**	Motown 1098
12/17/66+	**6**	10	11 **Standing In The Shadows Of Love**	Motown 1102
3/11/67	**4**	10	12 **Bernadette**	Motown 1104
5/20/67	**14**	8	13 7 Rooms Of Gloom/	
7/15/67	**76**	5	14 I'll Turn To Stone	Motown 1110
9/16/67	**19**	8	15 You Keep Running Away	Motown 1113
2/03/68	**14**	8	16 Walk Away Renee	Motown 1119
4/27/68	**20**	10	17 If I Were A Carpenter	Motown 1124
7/20/68	**49**	6	18 Yesterday's Dreams	Motown 1127
10/05/68	**51**	6	19 I'm In A Different World	Motown 1132
5/10/69	**53**	7	20 What Is A Man	Motown 1147
12/06/69	**45**	7	21 Don't Let Him Take Your Love From Me	Motown 1159
4/25/70	**24**	13	22 It's All In The Game	Motown 1164

DEBUT DATE	PEAK POS	WKS CHR	ARTIST — Record Title	Label & Number
			FOUR TOPS — Cont'd	
8/29/70	**11**	14	23 Still Water (Love)	Motown 1170
11/28/70+	**14**	10	24 River Deep - Mountain High THE SUPREMES & FOUR TOPS	Motown 1173
1/23/71	**40**	8	25 Just Seven Numbers (Can Straighten Out My Life)	Motown 1175
6/05/71	**55**	5	26 You Gotta Have Love In Your Heart THE SUPREMES & FOUR TOPS	Motown 1181
7/03/71	**70**	4	27 In These Changing Times	Motown 1185
9/11/71	**38**	8	28 MacArthur Park (Part II)	Motown 1189
2/05/72	**90**	3	29 A Simple Game	Motown 1196
9/09/72	**53**	9	30 (It's The Way) Nature Planned It	Motown 1210
11/11/72+	**10**	12	31 **Keeper Of The Castle**	Dunhill 4330
2/03/73	**4**	15	32 ● **Ain't No Woman (Like The One I've Got)**	Dunhill 4339
6/23/73	**15**	13	33 Are You Man Enough from the film "Shaft In Africa"	Dunhill 4354
10/13/73	**33**	9	34 Sweet Understanding Love	Dunhill 4366
1/26/74	**62**	8	35 I Just Can't Get You Out Of My Mind	Dunhill 4377
5/04/74	**41**	8	36 One Chain Don't Make No Prison	Dunhill 4386
8/17/74	**55**	7	37 Midnight Flower	Dunhill 15005
5/24/75	**71**	4	38 Seven Lonely Nights	ABC 12096
12/06/75	**97**	1	39 We All Gotta Stick Together	ABC 12123
10/30/76	**71**	6	40 Catfish	ABC 12214
8/15/81	**11**	22	41 When She Was My Girl	Casablanca 2338
5/15/82	**71**	7	42 Back To School Again from the film "Grease 2"	RSO 1069
8/28/82	**84**	3	43 Sad Hearts	Casablanca 2353
10/22/83	**71**	9	44 I Just Can't Walk Away	Motown 1706
			THE FOUR VOICES	
3/10/56	**20**	16	1 Lovely One Best Seller #20 / Top 100 #30	Columbia 40643
3/24/58	**50**	6	2 Dancing With My Shadow Best Seller #50 / Top 100 #51 orchestra directed by Ray Conniff on above 2	Columbia 41076
			FOX English sextet - female vocals by Roosha.	
8/23/75	**53**	8	1 Only You Can	Ariola Am. 7601
			CHARLES FOX American composer/pianist. Composed many songs for TV and film.	
1/24/81	**75**	4	1 Seasons [I] based on the theme from the film "Ordinary People" (Pachelbel's Canon in D Major)	Handshake 5307
			SAMANTHA FOX British - rose to stardom as a topless model for the U.K. "Daily Sun" newspaper.	
11/01/86+	**4**	23	1 **Touch Me (I Want Your Body)**	Jive 1006
			INEZ FOXX Born on 9/9/42 in Greensboro, NC. Although all but one of her hits is labeled as by Inez Foxx, she is accompanied vocally on all hits by her brother Charlie Foxx.	
6/22/63	**7**	18	1 **Mockingbird**	Symbol 919
12/07/63	**98**	1	2 Hi Diddle Diddle	Symbol 924
1/25/64	**91**	3	3 Ask Me	Symbol 926
4/25/64	**54**	9	4 Hurt By Love	Symbol 20-001
1/13/68	**76**	5	5 (1-2-3-4-5-6-7) Count The Days INEZ & CHARLIE FOXX	Dynamo 112
			FOXY Miami-based Latino dance band. 4 of 5 members came to Florida with the Cuban emigrees of 1959.	
7/22/78	**9**	21	1 **Get Off**	Dash 5046
3/31/79	**21**	15	2 Hot Number	Dash 5050
			PETER FRAMPTON Born on 4/22/50 in Beckenham, England. Vocalist, guitarist, composer. Joined British band The Herd at age 16, before forming Humble Pie in 1969, which he left in 1971 to form Frampton's Camel.	
2/21/76	**6**	18	1 **Show Me The Way**	A&M 1795
6/26/76	**12**	16	2 Baby, I Love Your Way	A&M 1832

DEBUT DATE	PEAK POS	WKS CHR	ARTIST — Record Title	Label & Number
			PETER FRAMPTON — Cont'd	
9/18/76	**10**	18	3 **Do You Feel Like We Do**	A&M 1867
			above 3 recorded live at San Francisco's Winterland	
5/28/77	**2**[3]	20	4 **I'm In You**	A&M 1941
8/27/77	**18**	16	5 Signed, Sealed, Delivered (I'm Yours)	A&M 1972
12/10/77+	**41**	8	6 Tried To Love	A&M 1988
5/26/79	**14**	13	7 I Can't Stand It No More	A&M 2148
2/01/86	**74**	8	8 Lying	Atlantic 89463
			CONNIE FRANCIS	
			Born Concetta Rosa Maria Franconero on 12/12/38 in Newark, New Jersey. First recorded for MGM in 1955. Films: "Where The Boys Are", "Follow The Boys", "Looking For Love" and "When The Boys Meet The Girls", 1961-65. Connie stopped performing after she was raped on 11/8/74, for which she was awarded $3,000,000 in damages. Began comeback with a performance on "Dick Clark's Live Wednesday" TV show in 1978.	
12/02/57	**93**	1	1 The Majesty Of Love	MGM 12555
			MARVIN RAINWATER & CONNIE FRANCIS	
2/24/58	**4**	22	2 **Who's Sorry Now**	MGM 12588
			Top 100 #4 / Best Seller #5 / Jockey #6	
			there were 5 Top 20 versions of this tune in 1923	
5/12/58	**36**	12	3 I'm Sorry I Made You Cry	MGM 12647
			Top 100 #36 / Best Seller #39	
			#1 hit for Henry Burr in 1918	
7/28/58	**14**	14	4 Stupid Cupid	MGM 12683
			Best Seller #14 / Hot 100 #17	
10/13/58	**30**	10	5 Fallin'	MGM 12713
12/08/58+	**2**[2]	18	6 **My Happiness**	MGM 12738
			there were 5 Top 30 versions of this tune in 1948	
3/02/59	**22**	11	7 If I Didn't Care	MGM 12769
			tune popularized in 1939 by the Ink Spots (POS 2)	
5/18/59	**5**	17	8 **Lipstick On Your Collar/**	
5/18/59	**9**	15	9 **Frankie**	MGM 12793
8/31/59	**34**	10	10 You're Gonna Miss Me/	
9/21/59	**69**	7	11 Plenty Good Lovin'	MGM 12824
11/23/59	**7**	15	12 **Among My Souvenirs/**	
			there were 4 Top 20 versions of this song in 1928	
11/16/59	**36**	11	13 God Bless America	MGM 12841
			the Irving Berlin classic, popularized in 1939 by Kate Smith	
2/22/60	**8**	13	14 **Mama/**	
2/29/60	**17**	11	15 Teddy	MGM 12878
5/09/60	**1**[2]	18	16 **Everybody's Somebody's Fool/**	
5/23/60	**19**	11	17 Jealous Of You [F]	MGM 12899
8/15/60	**1**[2]	17	18 **My Heart Has A Mind Of Its Own/**	
8/22/60	**42**	9	19 Malaguena [F]	MGM 12923
			written in 1929 - from the suite "Andalucia"	
11/07/60	**7**	13	20 **Many Tears Ago/**	
11/07/60	**87**	1	21 Senza Mamma (With No One)	MGM 12964
1/16/61	**4**	15	22 **Where The Boys Are/**	
			from the film of the same title	
1/16/61	**34**	8	23 No One	MGM 12971
4/17/61	**7**	10	24 **Breakin' In A Brand New Broken Heart**	MGM 12995
6/26/61	**6**	11	25 **Together/**	
			Paul Whiteman hit #1 with this song in 1928	
7/17/61	**72**	2	26 Too Many Rules	MGM 13019
9/25/61	**14**	9	27 (He's My) Dreamboat/	
9/25/61	**42**	7	28 Hollywood	MGM 13039
11/20/61+	**10**	12	29 **When The Boy In Your Arms (Is The Boy In Your Heart)/**	
12/11/61	**26**	5	30 Baby's First Christmas [X]	MGM 13051
2/10/62	**1**[1]	13	31 **Don't Break The Heart That Loves You**	MGM 13059
5/12/62	**7**	9	32 **Second Hand Love**	MGM 13074
7/28/62	**9**	9	33 **Vacation**	MGM 13087
10/06/62	**24**	9	34 I Was Such A Fool (To Fall In Love With You)/	
10/06/62	**57**	8	35 He Thinks I Still Care	MGM 13096
			hit #1 on the Country charts by George Jones as "She Thinks I Still Care"	
12/15/62+	**18**	11	36 I'm Gonna' Be Warm This Winter/	
1/05/63	**90**	5	37 Al Di La [F]	MGM 13116

DEBUT DATE	PEAK POS	WKS CHR	ARTIST — Record Title	Label & Number
			CONNIE FRANCIS — Cont'd	
3/02/63	**17**	10	38 Follow The Boys	MGM 13127
			from the film of the same title	
5/18/63	**23**	9	39 If My Pillow Could Talk	MGM 13143
8/10/63	**36**	7	40 Drownin' My Sorrows	MGM 13160
10/19/63	**28**	7	41 Your Other Love	MGM 13176
12/28/63+	**46**	6	42 In The Summer Of His Years	MGM 13203
			a tribute to President John F. Kennedy	
2/15/64	**24**	9	43 Blue Winter	MGM 13214
5/09/64	**25**	8	44 Be Anything (But Be Mine)	MGM 13237
7/18/64	**45**	7	45 Looking For Love	MGM 13256
			from the film of the same title	
10/24/64	**42**	7	46 Don't Ever Leave Me	MGM 13287
1/23/65	**43**	7	47 Whose Heart Are You Breaking Tonight	MGM 13303
3/06/65	**48**	6	48 For Mama	MGM 13325
5/01/65	**57**	7	49 Wishing It Was You	MGM 13331
6/26/65	**79**	7	50 Forget Domani	MGM 13363
			from the film "The Yellow Rolls Royce"	
9/11/65	**80**	4	51 Roundabout	MGM 13389
11/27/65	**47**	8	52 Jealous Heart	MGM 13420
			there were 5 Top 30 versions of this song in 1949	
3/19/66	**66**	6	53 Love Is Me, Love Is You	MGM 13470
11/05/66	**99**	2	54 Spanish Nights And You	MGM 13610
4/15/67	**94**	1	55 Time Alone Will Tell	MGM 13718
3/08/69	**91**	4	56 The Wedding Cake	MGM 14034
			FRANKE & THE KNOCKOUTS	
			Soft rock quintet led by Franke Previte of New Brunswick, New Jersey.	
3/07/81	**10**	19	1 **Sweetheart**	Millennium 11801
7/04/81	**27**	13	2 You're My Girl	Millennium 11808
4/03/82	**24**	15	3 Without You (Not Another Lonely Night)	Millennium 13105
			FRANKIE GOES TO HOLLYWOOD	
			Rock quintet from Liverpool, England of gay persona; vocals by Holly Johnson and Paul Rutherford.	
4/07/84	**67**	7	1 Relax	Island 99805
			the video of above song was banned by the BBC in England	
10/20/84	**43**	15	2 Two Tribes	Island 99695
			sold nearly 2 million copies in England	
1/19/85	**10**	16	3 **Relax** [R]	Island 99805
4/06/85	**48**	8	4 Welcome To The Pleasuredome	Island 99653
			ARETHA FRANKLIN	
			Born on 3/25/42 in Memphis. Daughter of gospel recording artist, Rev. C.L. Franklin, pastor of New Bethel Church in Detroit. Signed to Columbia Records in 1960 by John Hammond, then dramatic turn in style and success after signing with Atlantic and working with producer Jerry Wexler. Appeared in the 1980 film "The Blues Brothers". The all-time Queen of Soul Music.	
2/27/61	**76**	3	1 Won't Be Long	Columbia 41923
			with the Ray Bryant Combo	
10/09/61	**37**	9	2 Rock-A-Bye Your Baby With A Dixie Melody	Columbia 42157
			Al Jolson had a #1 version of this tune in 1918	
2/03/62	**87**	5	3 I Surrender, Dear/	
2/10/62	**94**	1	4 Rough Lover	Columbia 42266
7/21/62	**92**	1	5 Don't Cry, Baby	Columbia 42456
9/29/62	**100**	1	6 Try A Little Tenderness	Columbia 42520
12/15/62+	**86**	5	7 Trouble In Mind	Columbia 42625
9/19/64	**57**	10	8 Runnin' Out Of Fools	Columbia 43113
1/30/65	**96**	2	9 Can't You Just See Me	Columbia 43203
3/04/67	**9**	11	10 • **I Never Loved A Man (The Way I Love You)**	Atlantic 2386
4/29/67	**1**[2]	12	11 • **Respect**	Atlantic 2403
7/22/67	**4**	11	12 • **Baby I Love You**	Atlantic 2427
9/02/67	**56**	8	13 Take A Look	Columbia 44270
9/30/67	**8**	9	14 **A Natural Woman (You Make Me Feel Like)**	Atlantic 2441
12/09/67+	**2**[2]	12	15 • **Chain Of Fools**	Atlantic 2464
12/23/67	**94**	2	16 Mockingbird	Columbia 44381
2/24/68	**83**	3	17 Soulville	Columbia 44441

DEBUT DATE	PEAK POS	WKS CHR	ARTIST — Record Title	Label & Number
			ARETHA FRANKLIN — Cont'd	
3/02/68	**5**	12	18 ● **(Sweet Sweet Baby) Since You've Been Gone/**	
4/06/68	**16**	8	19 Ain't No Way	Atlantic 2486
			written by Aretha's sister, Carolyn Franklin	
5/18/68	**7**	10	20 ● **Think/**	
6/15/68	**56**	6	21 You Send Me	Atlantic 2518
8/17/68	**6**	9	22 **The House That Jack Built/**	
8/17/68	**10**	11	23 ● **I Say A Little Prayer**	Atlantic 2546
11/23/68	**14**	8	24 ● See Saw/	
11/30/68+	**31**	7	25 My Song	Atlantic 2574
2/22/69	**19**	7	26 The Weight/	
3/15/69	**71**	6	27 Tracks Of My Tears	Atlantic 2603
4/19/69	**28**	8	28 I Can't See Myself Leaving You/	
5/10/69	**76**	3	29 Gentle On My Mind	Atlantic 2619
8/02/69	**13**	10	30 Share Your Love With Me	Atlantic 2650
11/08/69	**17**	8	31 Eleanor Rigby	Atlantic 2683
2/07/70	**13**	12	32 Call Me/	
		2	33 Son Of A Preacher Man	Atlantic 2706
5/23/70	**23**	8	34 Spirit In The Dark	Atlantic 2731
8/08/70	**11**	10	35 ● Don't Play That Song	Atlantic 2751
11/21/70	**37**	7	36 Border Song (Holy Moses)/	
		1	37 You And Me	Atlantic 2772
			34, 35 & 37: with The Dixie Flyers	
2/20/71	**19**	9	38 You're All I Need To Get By	Atlantic 2787
4/17/71	**6**	12	39 ● **Bridge Over Troubled Water/**	
		4	40 Brand New Me	Atlantic 2796
7/31/71	**2**[2]	12	41 ● **Spanish Harlem**	Atlantic 2817
10/30/71	**9**	9	42 ● **Rock Steady/**	
1/15/72	**73**	4	43 Oh Me Oh My (I'm A Fool For You Baby)	Atlantic 2838
3/18/72	**5**	12	44 ● **Day Dreaming**	Atlantic 2866
6/03/72	**26**	8	45 All The King's Horses	Atlantic 2883
8/19/72	**81**	4	46 Wholy Holy	Atlantic 2901
			with James Cleveland & The Southern California Community Choir	
2/10/73	**33**	10	47 Master Of Eyes (The Deepness Of Your Eyes)	Atlantic 2941
7/07/73	**20**	13	48 Angel	Atlantic 2969
11/24/73+	**3**	21	49 ● **Until You Come Back To Me (That's What I'm Gonna Do)**	Atlantic 2995
4/06/74	**19**	13	50 I'm In Love	Atlantic 2999
8/31/74	**47**	7	51 Ain't Nothing Like The Real Thing	Atlantic 3200
11/16/74	**45**	8	52 Without Love	Atlantic 3224
9/20/75	**53**	5	53 Mr. D.J. (5 For The D.J.)	Atlantic 3289
6/12/76	**28**	12	54 Something He Can Feel	Atlantic 3326
10/02/76	**72**	5	55 Jump	Atlantic 3358
2/05/77	**82**	4	56 Look Into Your Heart	Atlantic 3373
6/18/77	**85**	2	57 Break It To Me Gently	Atlantic 3393
12/27/80+	**56**	8	58 United Together	Arista 0569
5/30/81	**84**	3	59 Come To Me	Arista 0600
8/29/81	**46**	10	60 Love All The Hurt Away	Arista 0624
			ARETHA FRANKLIN & GEORGE BENSON	
8/21/82	**24**	12	61 Jump To It	Arista 0699
7/30/83	**61**	8	62 Get It Right	Arista 9034
6/22/85	**3**	19	63 **Freeway Of Love**	Arista 9354
9/28/85	**7**	19	64 **Who's Zoomin' Who**	Arista 9410
10/19/85	**18**	15	65 Sisters Are Doin' It For Themselves	RCA 14214
			EURYTHMICS & ARETHA FRANKLIN	
1/18/86	**22**	14	66 Another Night	Arista 9453
9/27/86	**21**	11	67 Jumpin' Jack Flash	Arista 9528
			new version of Rolling Stones' 1968 hit (POS #3); produced by Keith Richards; from the film "Jumpin' Jack Flash"	
12/06/86+	**28**	13	68 Jimmy Lee	Arista 9546
			DOUG FRANKLIN with The Bluenotes	
9/08/58	**73**	4	1 My Lucky Love	Colonial 7777

DEBUT DATE	PEAK POS	WKS CHR	ARTIST — Record Title	Label & Number
			ERMA FRANKLIN	
			Aretha Franklin's sister.	
11/04/67	**62**	8	1 Piece Of My Heart	Shout 221
			MICHAEL FRANKS	
			Born on 9/18/44 in La Jolla, California. Jazz/pop singer, songwriter.	
8/07/76	**43**	8	1 Popsicle Toes	Reprise 1360
			THE FRANTICS	
			Instrumental rock quintet from Seattle; Ron Petersen (guitar), leader.	
5/25/59	**91**	3	1 Straight Flush [I]	Dolton 2
9/14/59	**93**	1	2 Fog Cutter [I]	Dolton 6
2/29/60	**83**	2	3 Werewolf [I]	Dolton 16
			ANDY FRASER	
			British bassist, formerly with John Mayall's Bluesbreakers and Free.	
3/03/84	**82**	5	1 Do You Love Me	Island 99784
			DALLAS FRAZIER	
			Born on 10/27/39 in Spiro, Oklahoma. Country singer, songwriter, instrumentalist. Wrote "Alley-Oop".	
4/30/66	**72**	4	1 Elvira tune later a Top 5 pop hit for the Oak Ridge Boys in 1981	Capitol 5560
			STAN FREBERG	
			Born on 8/7/26 in Los Angeles. Began career doing impersonations on Cliffie Stone's radio show in 1943. Did cartoon voices for the major film studios. His first in a long string of brilliant satirical recordings was "John And Marsha" in 1951.	
10/22/55	**16**	9	1 The Yellow Rose Of Texas [C] Jockey #16 / Top 100 #47 pre backing by Jud Conlon's Rhythmaires and Billy May's orchestra; Alvin Stoller, drummer	Capitol 3249
12/24/55	**53**	3	2 Nuttin' For Christmas [C-X]	Capitol 3280
7/21/56	**79**	2	3 Heartbreak Hotel [C]	Capitol 3480
4/13/57	**25**	7	4 Banana Boat (Day-O) [C] Best Seller #25 / Top 100 #43 interruptions by Peter Leeds	Capitol 3687
11/11/57	**32**	9	5 Wun'erful, Wun'erful! (Sides uh-one & uh-two) [C] Best Seller #32 / Top 100 #36 Bubbles In The Wine/Thank You/Louise/Please/Moonlight & Shadows	Capitol 3815
12/28/58	**44**	2	6 Green Chritma [N-X] featuring Daws Butler, Marvin Miller and Wil Wright	Capitol 4097
2/29/60	**99**	1	7 The Old Payola Roll Blues (Side 1) [C] featuring comedian Jesse White	Capitol 4329
			JOHN FRED & His Playboy Band	
			John Fred Gourrier was born on 5/8/41 in Baton Rouge, LA. Formed The Playboys in 1956 as a white band playing R&B music. John played basketball at LSU, and his father, Fred Gourrier, played baseball with the Detroit Tigers.	
2/23/59	**82**	5	1 Shirley	Montel 1002
11/25/67+	**1^{2}**	16	2 ● **Judy In Disguise (With Glasses)** a parody of The Beatles' "Lucy In The Sky With Diamonds"	Paula 282
2/24/68	**57**	6	3 Hey Hey Bunny	Paula 294
			FREDDIE & THE DREAMERS	
			Freddie Garrity was born on 11/14/40 in Manchester, England. Formed The Dreamers in 1961, consisting of Garrity (lead singer), Derek Quinn (lead guitar), Roy Crewsdon (guitar), Peter Birrell (bass) and Bernie Dwyer (drums).	
3/13/65	**1^{2}**	11	1 **I'm Telling You Now**	Tower 125
3/13/65	**36**	9	2 I Understand (Just How You Feel)	Mercury 72377
4/24/65	**18**	8	3 Do The Freddie	Mercury 72428
5/01/65	**21**	7	4 You Were Made For Me	Tower 127
7/31/65	**48**	7	5 A Little You	Mercury 72462
			FREE	
			British band formed in 1968: Paul Rodgers (vocals), Paul Kossoff (guitar), Simon Kirke (drums) and Andy Fraser (bass). Kossoff left to form Back Street Crawler, but died of drug-induced heart failure in 1976. Rodgers and Kirke formed Bad Company in 1974.	
8/15/70	**4**	16	1 **All Right Now**	A&M 1206
11/28/70+	**49**	8	2 Stealer	A&M 1230
			THE FREE MOVEMENT	
			Los Angeles-based vocal sextet. Several members formerly with gospel groups.	
5/22/71	**5**	26	1 **I've Found Someone Of My Own**	Decca 32818

DEBUT DATE	PEAK POS	WKS CHR	ARTIST — Record Title	Label & Number
			THE FREE MOVEMENT — Cont'd	
12/11/71+	**50**	10	2 The Harder I Try (The Bluer I Get)	Columbia 45512
			BOBBY FREEMAN	
			Born on 6/13/40 in San Francisco. R&B singer, formed vocal group, the Romancers at age 14, and later formed R&B group, the Vocaleers.	
5/12/58	**5**	17	1 **Do You Want To Dance**	Josie 835
			Top 100 #5 / Best Seller #6 / Jockey #11	
8/04/58	**37**	9	2 Betty Lou Got A New Pair Of Shoes	Josie 841
			Hot 100 #37 / Best Seller #40	
11/24/58	**54**	5	3 Need Your Love	Josie 844
6/01/59	**90**	2	4 Mary Ann Thomas	Josie 863
12/14/59	**93**	1	5 Ebb Tide	Josie 872
8/15/60	**37**	13	6 (I Do The) Shimmy Shimmy	King 5373
4/17/61	**89**	2	7 The Mess Around	Josie 887
7/11/64	**5**	12	8 **C'mon And Swim**	Autumn 2
10/31/64	**56**	6	9 S-W-I-M	Autumn 5
			ERNIE FREEMAN	
			Born on 8/16/22 in Cleveland. Died on 5/16/81 in North Hollywood of a heart attack. Pianist, composer, conductor for many top artists, including Frank Sinatra, Dean Martin, Sammy Davis, Jr., and Connie Francis. Also see Sir Chauncey and B. Bumble.	
9/23/57	**75**	7	1 Dumplin's [I]	Imperial 5461
11/18/57	**4**	18	2 **Raunchy** [I]	Imperial 5474
			Jockey #4 / Best Seller #11 / Top 100 #12	
6/16/58	**59**	5	3 Indian Love Call [I]	Imperial 5518
			first popularized in 1925 by Paul Whiteman (POS 3)	
10/24/60	**70**	6	4 Theme from "The Dark At The Top Of The Stairs" [I]	Imperial 5693
			from the Robert Preston, Dorothy McGuire film of the same title	
1/06/62	**93**	1	5 The Twist [I]	Imperial 5793
			ACE FREHLEY	
			Born on 4/27/51 in the Bronx, New York. Kiss' lead guitarist until 1983.	
10/14/78+	**13**	21	1 New York Groove	Casablanca 941
			DON FRENCH	
			Singer, guitarist from Wayne, Pennsylvania.	
5/25/59	**72**	3	1 Lonely Saturday Night	Lancer 104
			GLENN FREY	
			Born on 11/6/48 in Detroit. Singer, songwriter, guitarist. Founding member of the Eagles.	
6/05/82	**31**	13	1 I Found Somebody	Asylum 47466
8/21/82	**15**	17	2 The One You Love	Asylum 69974
12/11/82+	**41**	12	3 All Those Lies	Asylum 69857
6/30/84	**20**	15	4 Sexy Girl	MCA 52413
9/29/84	**54**	6	5 The Allnighter	MCA 52461
12/08/84+	**2**[1]	24	6 **The Heat Is On**	MCA 52512
			from the film "Beverly Hills Cop"	
4/06/85	**12**	19	7 Smuggler's Blues	MCA 52546
9/14/85	**2**[2]	21	8 **You Belong To The City**	MCA 52651
			above 2 from TV's "Miami Vice" soundtrack	
			FRIDA	
			Born Annifrid Lyngstad on 11/15/45 in Norway. Member of Abba.	
11/06/82+	**13**	29	1 I Know There's Something Going On	Atlantic 89984
			produced by Phil Collins	
			DEAN FRIEDMAN	
			Singer, songwriter from New Jersey.	
4/16/77	**26**	22	1 Ariel	Lifesong 45022
			FRIEND AND LOVER	
			Husband and wife duo: James and Cathy Post.	
5/18/68	**10**	14	1 **Reach Out Of The Darkness**	Verve Fore. 5069
8/31/68	**86**	2	2 If Love Is In Your Heart	Verve Fore. 5091
			THE FRIENDS OF DISTINCTION	
			Los Angeles-based soul/MOR group: Floyd Butler (b: 6/5/41, San Diego); Harry Elston (b: 11/4/38, Dallas); Jessica Cleaves (b: 12/10/48, Los Angeles); and Barbara Jean Love (b: 7/24/41, Los Angeles). Butler and Elston were in the Hi Fi's with LaMonte McLemore and Marilyn McCoo (later with The Fifth Dimension).	
4/05/69	**3**	16	1 ● **Grazing In The Grass**	RCA 0107

DEBUT DATE	PEAK POS	WKS CHR	ARTIST — Record Title	Label & Number
			THE FRIENDS OF DISTINCTION — Cont'd	
7/26/69	**63**	5	2 Let Yourself Go/	
8/16/69	**15**	20	3● Going In Circles	RCA 0204
3/07/70	**6**	13	4 **Love Or Let Me Be Lonely**	RCA 0319
10/10/70	**60**	8	5 Time Waits For No One	RCA 0385
1/23/71	**79**	5	6 I Need You	RCA 0416
			FRIJID PINK	
			Rock group formed in Detroit. Kelly Green, lead singer.	
2/07/70	**7**	13	1● **House Of The Rising Sun**	Parrot 341
7/25/70	**55**	7	2 Sing A Song For Freedom	Parrot 349
12/12/70+	**72**	5	3 Heartbreak Hotel	Parrot 352
			LEFTY FRIZZELL	
			Born William Orville Frizzell on 3/31/28 in Corsicana, Texas. Country singer, songwriter, guitarist. Brother, David, is currently a hot Country star. Lefty died of a stroke on 7/19/75 in Nashville.	
1/18/64	**85**	5	1 Saginaw, Michigan	Columbia 42924
			THE FROGMEN	
4/03/61	**44**	8	1 Underwater [I]	Candix 314
			MAX FROST & THE TROOPERS	
			Max Frost is actually movie and TV star Christopher Jones.	
9/07/68	**22**	12	1 Shape Of Things To Come from the film "Wild In The Streets" (starring Chris Jones)	Tower 419
			THOMAS & RICHARD FROST	
10/25/69	**83**	4	1 She's Got Love	Imperial 66405
			BOBBY FULLER FOUR	
			Bobby was born on 10/22/43 in Baytown, Texas and died of asphyxiation in Los Angeles on 7/18/66. Band formed in El Paso and featured Bobby (lead vocals & guitar) and his brother Randy (bass).	
1/29/66	**9**	11	1 **I Fought The Law**	Mustang 3014
4/16/66	**26**	6	2 Love's Made A Fool Of You written by Buddy Holly	Mustang 3016
			JERRY FULLER	
			Singer, songwriter, producer from Fort Worth, Texas.	
8/31/59	**90**	2	1 Betty My Angel	Challenge 59052
10/19/59	**63**	6	2 Tennessee Waltz	Challenge 59057
4/24/61	**71**	4	3 Shy Away	Challenge 59104
10/09/61	**94**	2	4 Guilty Of Loving You	Challenge 9114
			LOWELL FULSOM	
			Born, March, 1921, in Tulsa, OK. Blues vocalist, guitarist. Also known as Tulsa Red.	
12/25/65+	**91**	3	1 Black Nights	Kent 431
1/14/67	**52**	7	2 Tramp	Kent 456
4/01/67	**97**	2	3 Make A Little Love	Kent 463
			THE FUN & GAMES	
1/18/69	**78**	4	1 The Grooviest Girl In The World	Uni 55098
			FUNKADELIC	
			Part of producer George Clinton's "P.Funk" battalion. Also see Parliament.	
10/04/69	**63**	7	1 I'll Bet You	Westbound 150
3/21/70	**80**	6	2 I Got A Thing, You Got A Thing, Everybody's Got A Thing	Westbound 158
8/22/70	**81**	4	3 I Wanna Know If It's Good To You?	Westbound 167
4/10/71	**91**	2	4 You And Your Folks, Me And My Folks	Westbound 175
9/11/71	**93**	3	5 Can You Get To That	Westbound 185
11/01/75	**99**	3	6 Better By The Pound	Westbound 5014
9/16/78	**28**	14	7● One Nation Under A Groove (Part 1)	Warner 8618
10/27/79	**77**	4	8 (not just) Knee Deep - Part 1	Warner 49040
			FUNKY COMMUNICATION COMMITTEE	
7/14/79	**47**	10	1 Baby I Want You	Free Flight 11595
			FUNKY KINGS	
			7-man band led by Jack Tempchin and Jules Shear (of Jules & The Polar Bears).	
11/06/76+	**61**	11	1 Slow Dancing	Arista 0209

DEBUT DATE	PEAK POS	WKS CHR	ARTIST — Record Title		Label & Number
			HARVEY FUQUA - see THE MOONGLOWS and ETTA JAMES		
			RICHIE FURAY		
			Born on 5/9/44 in Yello Springs, Ohio. Member of Buffalo Springfield, Poco, and the Souther, Hillman, Furay Band		
10/27/79	**39**	11	1 I Still Have Dreams		Asylum 46534
			THE FURYS		
2/09/63	**92**	2	1 Zing! Went The Strings Of My Heart		Mack IV 112
			tune written in 1935; popularized in 1943 by Judy Garland (POS 22)		
			THE FUZZ		
			Black female trio from Washington, DC: Sheila Young, Barbara Gilliam and Val Williams.		
1/23/71	**21**	20	1 I Love You For All Seasons		Calla 174
7/31/71	**77**	3	2 Like An Open Door		Calla 177
10/09/71	**95**	3	3 I'm So Glad		Calla 179

G

DEBUT DATE	PEAK POS	WKS CHR	ARTIST — Record Title		Label & Number
			GABRIEL		
			Seattle rock quartet led by Terry Lauber and Frank Butorac.		
10/07/78	**73**	4	1 Martha (Your Lovers Come And Go)		Epic 50594
			GABRIEL & THE ANGELS		
11/10/62	**51**	11	1 That's Life (That's Tough)		Swan 4118
			PETER GABRIEL		
			Born on 5/13/50 in London, England. Lead singer of Genesis from 1966-1975.		
4/30/77	**68**	5	1 Solsbury Hill		Atco 7079
8/16/80	**48**	11	2 Games Without Frontiers		Mercury 76063
10/23/82+	**29**	18	3 Shock The Monkey		Geffen 29883
8/27/83	**84**	3	4 Solsbury Hill		Geffen 29542
			live version of his first charted hit		
5/10/86	**1**[1]	21	5 **Sledgehammer**		Geffen 28718
8/30/86	**26**	14	6 In Your Eyes		Geffen 28622
11/29/86+	**8**	23	7 **Big Time**		Geffen 28503
			THE GADABOUTS		
7/21/56	**39**	8	1 Stranded In The Jungle	[N]	Mercury 70898
			MEL GADSON		
5/30/60	**69**	5	1 Comin' Down With Love		Big Top 3034
			ANDRE GAGNON		
3/06/76	**95**	3	1 Wow	[I]	London 230
			SUNNY GALE		
			Songstress from Clayton, NJ. Began career with Hal McIntyre's band.		
1/08/55	**17**	1	1 Let Me Go, Lover!/		
			Jockey #17		
1/29/55	**54**	8	2 Unsuspecting Heart		RCA 5952
			Honor Roll #54		
11/26/55	**85**	8	3 C'est La Vie		RCA 6286
4/21/56	**66**	3	4 Rock And Roll Wedding		RCA 6479
			THE GALENS		
11/23/63	**70**	5	1 Baby I Do Love You		Challenge 9212
			GALLAGHER & LYLE		
			Scottish duo: Benny Gallagher & Graham Lyle - formerly with McGuiness Flint.		
4/10/76	**49**	14	1 I Wanna Stay With You		A&M 1778
8/21/76	**67**	8	2 Heart On My Sleeve		A&M 1850
			THE GALLAHADS		
			White East Coast vocal group.		
8/18/56	**62**	9	1 The Fool		Jubilee 5252

DEBUT DATE	PEAK POS	WKS CHR	ARTIST — Record Title	Label & Number
			GALLERY	
			Sextet from Detroit led by Jim Gold.	
2/26/72	**4**	22	1 ● **Nice To Be With You**	Sussex 232
8/12/72	**22**	16	2 I Believe In Music	Sussex 239
12/30/72+	**23**	15	3 Big City Miss Ruth Ann	Sussex 248
			FRANK GALLOP	
			Best known as the announcer on Perry Como's TV shows during the 50s.	
6/23/58	**57**	7	1 Got A Match? [I-N]	ABC-Para. 9931
4/16/66	**34**	9	2 The Ballad Of Irving [C]	Kapp 745
			GAMMA	
			Formed by Ronnie Montrose after break-up of Montrose.	
1/05/80	**60**	6	1 I'm Alive	Elektra 46555
4/03/82	**77**	5	2 Right The First Time	Elektra 47423
			THE GANTS	
9/25/65	**46**	12	1 Road Runner	Liberty 55829
			THE GAP BAND	
			Brother trio from Tulsa, Oklahoma: Charles, Ronnie and Robert Wilson. Named for three streets in Tulsa: Greenwood, Archer and Pine.	
2/28/81	**84**	8	1 Burn Rubber (Why You Wanna Hurt Me)	Mercury 76091
5/23/81	**60**	7	2 Yearning For Your Love	Mercury 76101
5/22/82	**24**	14	3 Early In The Morning	Total Exp. 8201
8/14/82	**31**	13	4 You Dropped A Bomb On Me	Total Exp. 8203
3/12/83	**51**	8	5 Outstanding	Total Exp. 8205
			JERRY GARCIA	
			Founder and lead guitarist of the Grateful Dead.	
4/15/72	**94**	2	1 Sugaree	Warner 7569
			DAVE GARDNER	
			Born on 6/11/26 in Jackson, Tennessee. "Brother Dave" had 6 comedy albums chart in the early 60s.	
7/15/57	**22**	10	1 White Silver Sands Best Seller #22 / Top 100 #28	OJ 1002
			DON GARDNER & DEE DEE FORD	
			Black vocal duo from Philadelphia. Gardner formed his own group, the Sonotones, in 1952 and recorded for Gotham and Bruce. Ford also plays organ and piano.	
6/02/62	**20**	13	1 I Need Your Loving	Fire 508
8/11/62	**75**	5	2 Glory Of Love	KC 106
8/25/62	**66**	7	3 Don't You Worry	Fire 513
			ART GARFUNKEL	
			Born on 10/13/42 in Queens, New York. Appeared in films "Catch 22", "Carnal Knowledge" and "Bad Timing". Also see Simon & Garfunkel.	
9/15/73	**9**	14	1 **All I Know**	Columbia 45926
12/29/73+	**38**	9	2 I Shall Sing	Columbia 45983
9/21/74	**34**	8	3 Second Avenue above 3 shown only as: **GARFUNKEL**	Columbia 10020
8/23/75	**18**	18	4 I Only Have Eyes For You	Columbia 10190
12/27/75+	**39**	11	5 Break Away	Columbia 10273
1/21/78	**17**	14	6 (What A) Wonderful World **ART GARFUNKEL with JAMES TAYLOR & PAUL SIMON**	Columbia 10676
6/09/79	**53**	8	7 Since I Don't Have You	Columbia 10999
8/08/81	**66**	9	8 A Heart In New York	Columbia 02307
			FRANK GARI	
			Born on 4/1/42 in New York City. Appeared in several films, late 50s.	
12/19/60+	**27**	14	1 Utopia	Crusade 1020
4/10/61	**23**	12	2 Lullaby Of Love	Crusade 1021
7/03/61	**30**	10	3 Princess	Crusade 1022
			GALE GARNETT	
			Folk-style singer, songwriter. Appearances in many TV network series.	
8/08/64	**4**	17	1 **We'll Sing In The Sunshine**	RCA 8388
12/05/64+	**54**	9	2 Lovin' Place	RCA 8472

DEBUT DATE	PEAK POS	WKS CHR	ARTIST — Record Title	Label & Number
			LEE GARRETT	
			Vocalist/composer from Mississippi, blind since birth. Teamed with Stevie Wonder to write "It's A Shame" hit for the Spinners.	
5/22/76	**58**	6	1 You're My Everything	Chrysalis 2112
			LEIF GARRETT	
			Born on 11/8/61 in Hollywood, California. Began film career in 1969; appeared in all 3 "Walking Tall" films.	
8/27/77	**20**	15	1 Surfin' USA	Atlantic 3423
11/12/77+	**13**	14	2 Runaround Sue	Atlantic 3440
3/04/78	**58**	7	3 Put Your Head On My Shoulder	Atlantic 3466
4/22/78	**49**	7	4 The Wanderer	Atlantic 3476
11/11/78+	**10**	21	5 **I Was Made For Dancin'**	Scotti Br. 403
5/05/79	**57**	8	6 Feel The Need	Scotti Br. 407
11/03/79	**78**	5	7 When I Think Of You	Scotti Br. 502
12/15/79+	**60**	9	8 Memorize Your Number	Scotti Br. 510
4/12/80	**78**	5	9 I Was Looking For Someone To Love	Scotti Br. 516
12/05/81	**84**	6	10 Runaway Rita	Scotti Br. 02579
			SCOTT GARRETT	
			Born on 11/5/32 in Pittsburgh.	
3/30/59	**92**	1	1 A House Of Love	Laurie 3023
			GARY & DAVE	
			Canadian singing, songwriting duo: Gary Weeks & Dave Beckett.	
12/15/73	**92**	4	1 Could You Ever Love Me Again	London 200
			GARY & THE HORNETS	
			Brothers from Franklin, OH: Gary (age 11), Gregg (age 13), & Steve (age 6) Calvert.	
11/19/66	**96**	2	1 Hi Hi Hazel	Smash 2061
			GARY O'	
			Gary O'Connor, from Toronto, Canada.	
7/18/81	**70**	5	1 Pay You Back With Interest	Capitol 5018
			GARY'S GANG	
			Septet from Queens, New York, led by Gary Turnier and Eric Matthew.	
2/17/79	**41**	10	1 Keep On Dancin'	Columbia 10884
			JOHN GARY	
			Born in Watertown, New York on 11/29/32. Singer on Don McNeill's radio program, "Breakfast Club", for 2 years.	
9/12/64	**89**	4	1 Soon I'll Wed My Love	RCA 8413
			DAVID GATES	
			Born on 12/11/40 in Tulsa, OK. Began career as a session musician, then did songwriting and record producing before becoming the lead singer of Bread.	
7/14/73	**47**	8	1 Clouds	Elektra 45857
10/20/73	**50**	8	2 Sail Around The World	Elektra 45868
1/18/75	**29**	10	3 Never Let Her Go	Elektra 45223
12/17/77+	**15**	24	4 Goodbye Girl title song from the Neil Simon film	Elektra 45450
8/12/78	**30**	14	5 Took The Last Train	Elektra 45500
2/09/80	**46**	8	6 Where Does The Lovin' Go	Elektra 46588
9/26/81	**62**	7	7 Take Me Now	Arista 0615
			LARRY GATLIN	
			Born in Seminole, Texas on 5/2/48. Country singer, songwriter, guitarist and leader of The Gatlin Brothers (with brothers Steve and Rudy).	
9/14/74	**84**	4	1 Delta Dirt	Monument 8622
			MARVIN GAYE	
			Born Marvin Pentz Gay, Jr. on 4/2/39 in Washington, DC. Sang in his father's Apostolic church. In vocal groups the Rainbows and Marquees. Joined Harvey Fuqua in the reformed Moonglows. To Detroit in 1960. Session work as drummer at Motown; married to Berry Gordy's sister Anna, 1961-75. First recorded under own name for Tamla in 1961. In seclusion for several months following the death of Tammi Terrell, 1970. Problems with drugs and the IRS led to his moving to Europe for three years. Fatally shot by his father after a quarrel on 4/1/84 in Los Angeles.	
10/20/62	**46**	9	1 Stubborn Kind Of Fellow backing vocals: Martha & The Vandellas	Tamla 54068
1/12/63	**30**	12	2 Hitch Hike	Tamla 54075
5/18/63	**10**	14	3 **Pride And Joy**	Tamla 54079

DEBUT DATE	PEAK POS	WKS CHR		ARTIST — Record Title	Label & Number
				MARVIN GAYE — Cont'd	
10/19/63	**22**	16	4	Can I Get A Witness/	
10/19/63	**77**	3	5	I'm Crazy 'Bout My Baby	Tamla 54087
3/14/64	**15**	10	6	You're A Wonderful One	Tamla 54093
5/02/64	**19**	9	7	Once Upon A Time/ MARVIN GAYE & MARY WELLS	
5/16/64	**17**	10	8	What's The Matter With You Baby MARVIN GAYE & MARY WELLS	Motown 1057
6/06/64	**15**	11	9	Try It Baby	Tamla 54095
9/19/64	**27**	9	10	Baby Don't You Do It	Tamla 54101
10/24/64	**61**	6	11	What Good Am I Without You MARVIN GAYE & KIM WESTON	Tamla 54104
11/21/64+	**6**	14	12	**How Sweet It Is To Be Loved By You**	Tamla 54107
3/20/65	**8**	12	13	**I'll Be Doggone**	Tamla 54112
7/10/65	**25**	7	14	Pretty Little Baby	Tamla 54117
10/09/65	**8**	12	15	**Ain't That Peculiar**	Tamla 54122
2/19/66	**29**	8	16	One More Heartache	Tamla 54129
5/21/66	**44**	8	17	Take This Heart Of Mine	Tamla 54132
8/20/66	**47**	7	18	Little Darling, I Need You	Tamla 54138
1/07/67	**14**	12	19	It Takes Two MARVIN GAYE & KIM WESTON	Tamla 54141
5/13/67	**19**	12	20	Ain't No Mountain High Enough MARVIN GAYE & TAMMI TERRELL	Tamla 54149
7/01/67	**33**	7	21	Your Unchanging Love	Tamla 54153
9/09/67	**5**	13	22	**Your Precious Love** MARVIN GAYE & TAMMI TERRELL	Tamla 54156
12/02/67+	**10**	11	23	**If I Could Build My Whole World Around You/** MARVIN GAYE & TAMMI TERRELL	
3/02/68	**68**	6	24	If This World Were Mine MARVIN GAYE & TAMMI TERRELL	Tamla 54161
1/13/68	**34**	7	25	You	Tamla 54160
4/13/68	**8**	13	26	**Ain't Nothing Like The Real Thing** MARVIN GAYE & TAMMI TERRELL	Tamla 54163
7/27/68	**7**	12	27	**You're All I Need To Get By** MARVIN GAYE & TAMMI TERRELL	Tamla 54169
9/14/68	**32**	10	28	Chained	Tamla 54170
10/12/68	**24**	7	29	Keep On Lovin' Me Honey MARVIN GAYE & TAMMI TERRELL	Tamla 54173
11/23/68	**1**[7]	15	30	**I Heard It Through The Grapevine**	Tamla 54176
2/01/69	**30**	7	31	Good Lovin' Ain't Easy To Come By MARVIN GAYE & TAMMI TERRELL	Tamla 54179
4/26/69	**4**	15	32	**Too Busy Thinking About My Baby**	Tamla 54181
8/23/69	**7**	12	33	**That's The Way Love Is**	Tamla 54185
11/29/69	**49**	8	34	What You Gave Me MARVIN GAYE & TAMMI TERRELL	Tamla 54187
1/10/70	**41**	7	35	How Can I Forget/	
3/07/70	**67**	6	36	Gonna Give Her All The Love I've Got	Tamla 54190
4/18/70	**50**	7	37	The Onion Song/ MARVIN GAYE & TAMMI TERRELL	
		6	38	California Soul MARVIN GAYE & TAMMI TERRELL	Tamla 54192
6/13/70	**40**	7	39	The End Of Our Road	Tamla 54195
2/20/71	**2**[3]	15	40	**What's Going On**	Tamla 54201
7/03/71	**4**	12	41	**Mercy Mercy Me (The Ecology)**	Tamla 54207
10/09/71	**9**	9	42	**Inner City Blues (Make Me Wanna Holler)**	Tamla 54209
5/20/72	**50**	5	43	You're The Man	Tamla 54221
12/16/72+	**7**	12	44	**Trouble Man** from the film of the same title	Tamla 54228
7/14/73	**1**[2]	19	45	**Let's Get It On**	Tamla 54234
10/06/73	**12**	12	46	You're A Special Part Of Me DIANA ROSS & MARVIN GAYE	Motown 1280
11/03/73	**21**	13	47	Come Get To This	Tamla 54241
1/26/74	**50**	6	48	You Sure Love To Ball	Tamla 54244
2/23/74	**19**	16	49	My Mistake (Was To Love You) DIANA ROSS & MARVIN GAYE	Motown 1269
7/13/74	**46**	9	50	Don't Knock My Love DIANA ROSS & MARVIN GAYE	Motown 1296

DEBUT DATE	PEAK POS	WKS CHR	ARTIST — Record Title	Label & Number
			MARVIN GAYE — Cont'd	
9/28/74	**28**	9	51 Distant Lover	Tamla 54253
4/24/76	**15**	13	52 I Want You	Tamla 54264
8/14/76	**74**	5	53 After The Dance	Tamla 54273
4/16/77	**1**[1]	18	54 **Got To Give It Up (Pt. I)**	Tamla 54280
1/20/79	**59**	8	55 Pops, We Love You (A Tribute To Father) DIANA ROSS, MARVIN GAYE, SMOKEY ROBINSON & STEVIE WONDER song written for Berry Gordy Sr.'s 90th birthday	Motown 1455
10/30/82+	**3**	21	56 ● **Sexual Healing**	Columbia 03302
			CRYSTAL GAYLE Born Brenda Gail Webb on 1/9/51 in Paintsville, Kentucky. Loretta Lynn's younger sister.	
6/12/76	**71**	6	1 I'll Get Over You	United Art. 781
8/13/77	**2**[3]	26	2 ● **Don't It Make My Brown Eyes Blue**	United Art. 1016
2/25/78	**52**	10	3 Ready For The Times To Get Better	United Art. 1136
7/29/78	**18**	18	4 Talking In Your Sleep	United Art. 1214
7/07/79	**84**	3	5 When I Dream	United Art. 1288
9/29/79	**15**	16	6 Half The Way	Columbia 11087
2/23/80	**63**	6	7 It's Like We Never Said Goodbye	Columbia 11198
6/07/80	**81**	8	8 The Blue Side	Columbia 11270
12/05/81	**76**	6	9 The Woman In Me	Columbia 02523
10/09/82+	**7**	29	10 **You And I** EDDIE RABBITT with CRYSTAL GAYLE	Elektra 69936
9/10/83	**83**	5	11 Baby, What About You	Warner 29582
12/10/83	**84**	5	12 The Sound Of Goodbye	Warner 29452
			THE GAYLORDS Italian-American duo: Ronnie Gaylord (Fredianelli) and Burt Holiday (Bonaldi). Formed duo, with pianist Don Rea, while students at the University of Detroit.	
11/12/55	**67**	8	1 No Arms Can Ever Hold You	Mercury 70706
8/18/58	**97**	1	2 Ma Ma Ma Marie	Mercury 71337
11/10/58	**98**	1	3 Flamingo l'Amore [F]	Mercury 71369
3/06/76	**72**	6	4 Eh! Cumpari [N] GAYLORD & HOLIDAY novelty version of a traditional Italian song	Prodigal 0622
			GLORIA GAYNOR Born on 9/7/49 in Newark, NJ. With the Soul Satisfiers group in 1971.	
11/02/74+	**9**	17	1 **Never Can Say Goodbye**	MGM 14748
3/22/75	**60**	5	2 Reach Out, I'll Be There	MGM 14790
6/28/75	**98**	1	3 Walk On By	MGM 14808
10/25/75	**98**	2	4 (If You Want It) Do It Yourself	MGM 14823
11/29/75	**75**	5	5 How High The Moon song first popularized by Benny Goodman in 1940 (POS 6)	MGM 14838
12/16/78+	**1**[3]	27	6 ▲ **I Will Survive**	Polydor 14508
9/22/79	**42**	13	7 Let Me Know (I Have A Right) trumpet solo: Doc Severinsen	Polydor 2021
			PAUL GAYTEN Born on 1/29/20 in New Orleans. Vocalist, pianist, bandleader. Heard on many R&B hits behind such artists as Larry Darnell, Clarence Henry and Bobby Charles. Own label, Pzazz, from 1969, then inactive in music.	
12/02/57	**68**	4	1 Nervous Boogie [I]	Argo 5277
7/21/58	**78**	2	2 Windy [I]	Argo 5300
10/26/59	**68**	7	3 The Hunch [I]	Anna 1106
			THE G-CLEFS R&B quintet from Roxbury, Massachusetts, consisting of 4 brothers and a friend.	
7/28/56	**24**	13	1 Ka-Ding Dong Best Seller #24 / Top 100 #53	Pilgrim 715
9/18/61	**9**	16	2 **I Understand (Just How You Feel)** an adaptation of the "Auld Lang Syne" melody	Terrace 7500
3/10/62	**81**	5	3 A Girl Has To Know	Terrace 7503
			DAVID GEDDES Formed the group "Rock Garden" as a teenager, who recorded for Capitol.	
8/02/75	**4**	13	1 **Run Joey Run**	Big Tree 16044
11/15/75	**18**	8	2 The Last Game Of The Season (A Blind Man In The Bleachers)	Big Tree 16052

DEBUT DATE	PEAK POS	WKS CHR	ARTIST — Record Title	Label & Number
			THE J. GEILS BAND	
			Rock group formed in Boston, 1967. Consisted of Jerome Geils (guitar), Peter Wolf (vocals), "Magic" Dick Salwitz (harmonica), Seth Justman (keyboards), Danny Klein (bass) and Stephen Jo Bladd (drums). First recorded for Atlantic in 1970. Wolf left for a solo career in the fall of 1983.	
12/04/71+	**39**	10	1 Looking For A Love	Atlantic 2844
3/31/73	**30**	16	2 Give It To Me	Atlantic 2953
9/08/73	**98**	2	3 Make Up Your Mind	Atlantic 2974
11/09/74+	**12**	11	4 Must Of Got Lost	Atlantic 3214
4/17/76	**68**	6	5 Where Did Our Love Go	Atlantic 3320
8/20/77	**83**	3	6 You're The Only One shown only as: **GEILS**	Atlantic 3411
11/18/78+	**35**	13	7 One Last Kiss	EMI America 8007
3/10/79	**67**	6	8 Take It Back	EMI America 8012
2/02/80	**32**	12	9 Come Back	EMI America 8032
4/12/80	**38**	12	10 Love Stinks	EMI America 8039
7/12/80	**78**	5	11 Just Can't Wait	EMI America 8047
11/07/81+	**1**[6]	25	12 ● **Centerfold**	EMI America 8102
2/20/82	**4**	16	13 ● **Freeze-Frame**	EMI America 8108
5/22/82	**40**	11	14 Angel In Blue	EMI America 8100
11/20/82+	**24**	14	15 I Do	EMI America 8148
2/26/83	**60**	6	16 Land Of A Thousand Dances	EMI America 8156
11/03/84	**63**	7	17 Concealed Weapons	EMI America 8242
8/10/85	**91**	2	18 Fright Night from the film of the same title	Private I 05462
			BOB GELDOF	
			Born on 10/5/54 in Ireland. Singer/songwriter of Boomtown Rats. Organized British superstar benefit group, Band Aid, for which he became a Nobel Peace Prize nominee.	
12/13/86+	**82**	6	1 This Is The World Calling	Atlantic 89341
			GENE & DEBBE	
			Gene Thomas (b: 12/4/38, Palestine, Texas) and Debbe Nevills.	
10/14/67	**78**	6	1 Go With Me	TRX 5002
2/17/68	**17**	16	2 Playboy	TRX 5006
6/29/68	**81**	4	3 Lovin' Season	TRX 5010
			GENE & EUNICE	
			R&B vocal duo: Forest Gene Wilson (from San Antonio) & his wife Eunice Russ (from Texarkana).	
8/24/59	**48**	13	1 Poco-Loco	Case 1001
			GENE & JERRY - see GENE CHANDLER and/or JERRY BUTLER	
			GENERAL PUBLIC	
			Fronted by English Beat vocalists Dave Wakeling & Ranking Roger.	
11/17/84+	**27**	18	1 Tenderness	I.R.S. 9934
			GENESIS	
			Rock group formed in England, 1967. Consisted of Peter Gabriel (lead vocals), Anthony Phillips (guitar), Tony Banks, (keyboards), Michael Rutherford (guitar, bass) and John Mayhew (drums). Phillips and Mayhew left after second album, replaced by Steve Hackett (guitar) and Phil Collins (drums). Gabriel left in June, 1975, with Collins replacing him as new lead singer. Hackett left in 1977, leaving group as a trio: Collins, Rutherford and Banks.	
3/12/77	**62**	5	1 Your Own Special Way	Atco 7076
4/22/78	**23**	16	2 Follow You Follow Me	Atlantic 3474
5/24/80	**14**	18	3 Misunderstanding	Atlantic 3662
9/06/80	**58**	8	4 Turn It On Again	Atlantic 3751
9/26/81	**29**	18	5 No Reply At All	Atlantic 3858
12/26/81+	**26**	14	6 Abacab	Atlantic 3891
3/20/82	**40**	11	7 Man On The Corner	Atlantic 4025
6/05/82	**32**	14	8 Paperlate	Atlantic 4053
10/01/83	**73**	9	9 Mama	Atlantic 89770
11/26/83+	**6**	20	10 **That's All!**	Atlantic 89724
3/10/84	**44**	10	11 Illegal Alien	Atlantic 89698
6/16/84	**50**	12	12 Taking It All Too Hard	Atlantic 89656
5/31/86	**1**[1]	17	13 **Invisible Touch**	Atlantic 89407

DEBUT DATE	PEAK POS	WKS CHR	ARTIST — Record Title	Label & Number
			GENESIS — Cont'd	
8/16/86	**4**	16	14 **Throwing It All Away**	Atlantic 89372
11/01/86+	**4**	21	15 **Land Of Confusion**	Atlantic 89336
			THE GENIES	
			R&B quartet from Brooklyn, featuring Don & Juan.	
3/30/59	**71**	6	1 Who's That Knocking	Shad 5002
			GENTLE PERSUASION	
2/26/83	**82**	4	1 Please Mr. Postman	Capitol 5207
			BOBBIE GENTRY	
			Born Roberta Lee Streeter on 7/27/44 in Chickasaw County, Mississippi. Singer, songwriter. Married singer Jim Stafford in 1978.	
8/05/67	**1**[4]	14	1 ● **Ode To Billie Joe**	Capitol 5950
11/25/67	**54**	4	2 Okolona River Bottom Band	Capitol 2044
4/20/68	**100**	1	3 Louisiana Man	Capitol 2147
10/26/68	**74**	6	4 Mornin' Glory BOBBIE GENTRY & GLEN CAMPBELL	Capitol 2314
1/25/69	**36**	9	5 Let It Be Me GLEN CAMPBELL & BOBBIE GENTRY	Capitol 2387
11/22/69+	**31**	14	6 Fancy	Capitol 2675
2/14/70	**27**	10	7 All I Have To Do Is Dream BOBBIE GENTRY & GLEN CAMPBELL	Capitol 2745
4/11/70	**71**	5	8 He Made A Woman Out Of Me	Capitol 2788
7/11/70	**81**	6	9 Apartment 21	Capitol 2849
7/17/76	**54**	6	10 Ode To Billie Joe [R]	Capitol 4294
7/31/76	**65**	4	11 Ode To Billy Joe newly recorded version for the film of the same title	Warner 8210
			THE GENTRYS	
			Memphis-based rock band formed in 1963. Group featured Larry Raspberry as lead singer. Original member Jimmy Hart re-formed the band in 1969 for their Sun recordings, with Hart as lead singer.	
9/11/65	**4**	13	1 **Keep On Dancing**	MGM 13379
1/01/66	**50**	8	2 Spread It On Thick	MGM 13432
5/14/66	**77**	5	3 Everyday I Have To Cry	MGM 13495
2/07/70	**61**	6	4 Why Should I Cry	Sun 1108
4/18/70	**52**	12	5 Cinnamon Girl	Sun 1114
2/27/71	**97**	2	6 Wild World	Sun 1122
			GEORGE & GENE - see GEORGE JONES and/or GENE PITNEY	
			BARBARA GEORGE	
			R&B singer, songwriter. Born on 8/16/42 in New Orleans.	
11/13/61+	**3**	19	1 **I Know (You Don't Love Me No More)** cornet solo: Melvin Lastie	A.F.O. 302
3/31/62	**46**	6	2 You Talk About Love	A.F.O. 304
9/08/62	**96**	1	3 Send For Me (If you need some Lovin')	Sue 766
			ROBIN GEORGE	
			Rock session guitarist from Wolverhampton, England.	
4/13/85	**92**	2	1 Heartline	Bronze 99658
			GEORGIA SATELLITES	
			Rock quartet formed in Atlanta, 1980. Led by Dan Baird (lead vocals), and Rick Richards (lead guitar).	
11/22/86+	**2**[1]	20	1 **Keep Your Hands To Yourself**	Elektra 69502
			DANYEL GERARD	
			Folk-pop oriented singer, songwriter from France.	
6/10/72	**78**	9	1 Butterfly	MGM/Verve 10670
			DONNY GERRARD	
			Lead singer of the Canadian group Skylark.	
3/27/76	**87**	6	1 Words (Are Impossible)	Greedy 101

DEBUT DATE	PEAK POS	WKS CHR	ARTIST — Record Title	Label & Number
			GERRY & THE PACEMAKERS	
			Group formed in Liverpool, England, 1959. Consisted of Gerry Marsden (b: 9/24/42), vocals, guitar; Leslie Maguire, piano; Les Chadwick, bass; and Freddie Marsden, drums. The Marsdens had been in skiffle bands; Gerry had own rock band, Mars-Bars, in 1958. Signed in 1962 by the Beatles' manager, Brian Epstein.	
5/23/64	**4**	12	1 **Don't Let The Sun Catch You Crying**	Laurie 3251
7/11/64	**9**	11	2 **How Do You Do It?**	Laurie 3261
7/11/64	**82**	2	3 I'm The One	Laurie 3233
9/26/64	**17**	9	4 I Like It	Laurie 3271
12/12/64+	**14**	10	5 I'll Be There	Laurie 3279
2/06/65	**6**	11	6 **Ferry Across The Mersey**	Laurie 3284
4/10/65	**23**	8	7 It's Gonna Be Alright above 2 from the film "Ferry Cross The Mersey" (starring Gerry & The Pacemakers)	Laurie 3293
6/05/65	**48**	6	8 You'll Never Walk Alone from the musical "Carousel"	Laurie 3302
8/14/65	**68**	6	9 Give All Your Love To Me	Laurie 3313
4/02/66	**90**	3	10 La La La	Laurie 3337
9/10/66	**28**	9	11 Girl On A Swing	Laurie 3354
			THE GESTURES	
11/14/64	**44**	8	1 Run, Run, Run	Soma 1417
			GET WET	
			Pop band featuring Sherri Beachfront as lead singer.	
4/25/81	**39**	9	1 Just So Lonely	Boardwalk 02018
			STAN GETZ	
			Born on 2/2/27 in Philadelphia. 17-time winner of Down Beat polls as top tenor saxophonist; played with Stan Kenton (1944-45), Jimmy Dorsey (1945-46), Benny Goodman (1946), and most importantly Woody Herman (1947-49).	
9/29/62	**15**	16	1 Desafinado [I] **STAN GETZ/CHARLIE BYRD (jazz guitarist)**	Verve 10260
6/06/64	**5**	12	2 **The Girl From Ipanema** **STAN GETZ/ASTRUD GILBERTO (Brazilian vocalist)** above 2 written by Brazilian composer, Antonio Carlos Jobim	Verve 10323
			ANDY GIBB	
			Born Andrew Roy Gibb on 3/5/58 in Manchester, England. Moved to Australia when 6 months old, then back to England at age 9. Youngest brother of Barry, Robin and Maurice Gibb - The Bee Gees.	
4/23/77	**1**[4]	31	1 ● **I Just Want To Be Your Everything**	RSO 872
11/05/77+	**1**[2]	29	2 ● **(Love Is) Thicker Than Water**	RSO 883
4/15/78	**1**[7]	25	3 ▲ **Shadow Dancing**	RSO 893
7/15/78	**5**	16	4 ● **An Everlasting Love**	RSO 904
10/14/78	**9**	18	5 ● **(Our Love) Don't Throw It All Away**	RSO 911
1/26/80	**4**	15	6 **Desire**	RSO 1019
3/29/80	**12**	13	7 I Can't Help It **ANDY GIBB & OLIVIA NEWTON-JOHN**	RSO 1026
11/22/80+	**15**	17	8 Time Is Time	RSO 1059
3/14/81	**40**	8	9 Me (Without You)	RSO 1056
8/15/81	**51**	8	10 All I Have To Do Is Dream **ANDY GIBB & VICTORIA PRINCIPAL (Pamela Ewing on TV's "Dallas")**	RSO 1065
			BARRY GIBB	
			Born on 9/1/46 in Manchester, England. Eldest brother of The Bee Gees. Also see Samantha Sang.	
11/01/80+	**3**	22	1 ● **Guilty** **BARBRA STREISAND & BARRY GIBB**	Columbia 11390
1/31/81	**10**	16	2 **What Kind Of Fool** **BARBRA STREISAND & BARRY GIBB**	Columbia 11430
9/01/84	**37**	10	3 Shine Shine	MCA 52443
			ROBIN GIBB	
			Born on 12/22/49 in Manchester, England. Twin brother of The Bee Gees' Maurice Gibb.	
8/12/78	**15**	12	1 Oh! Darling from the film "Sgt. Pepper's Lonely Hearts Club Band"	RSO 907
11/08/80	**50**	10	2 Help Me **MARCY LEVY & ROBIN GIBB** from the film "Times Square"	RSO 1047
6/02/84	**37**	12	3 Boys Do Fall In Love	Mirage 99743

DEBUT DATE	PEAK POS	WKS CHR	ARTIST — Record Title	Label & Number
			THE STEVE GIBBONS Band	
6/05/76	**72**	4	1 Johnny Cool	MCA 40551
			GEORGIA GIBBS	
			Born Fredda Gibbons on 8/17/20 in Worcester, MA. Sang on Lucky Strike radio show, 1937-38. With Hudson-DeLange band, then with Frankie Trumbauer (1940) and Artie Shaw (1942). On Garry Moore-Jimmy Durante radio show in late 40s, where Moore dubbed her "Her Nibs, Miss Gibbs".	
1/29/55	**2**[1]	19	1 **Tweedle Dee**	Mercury 70517
			Jockey #2 / Best Seller #3 / Juke Box #3	
3/26/55	**1**[3]	20	2 **Dance With Me Henry (Wallflower)**	Mercury 70572
			Juke Box #1 / Best Seller #2 / Jockey #3 revised version of Hank Ballard & The Midnighters' #1 1954 R&B hit "Work With Me Annie"	
7/09/55	**12**	4	3 Sweet And Gentle	Mercury 70647
			Jockey #12	
9/17/55	**14**	4	4 I Want You To Be My Baby	Mercury 70685
			Jockey #14 / Best Seller #22 / Top 100 #48 pre	
12/03/55	**51**	12	5 Goodbye To Rome (Arrivederci Roma)/	
12/10/55	**74**	8	6 24 Hours A Day (365 A Year)	Mercury 70743
3/17/56	**36**	9	7 Rock Right	Mercury 70811
5/12/56	**30**	13	8 Kiss Me Another	Mercury 70850
8/18/56	**20**	16	9 Happiness Street	Mercury 70920
			Jockey #20 / Top 100 #25	
12/08/56	**24**	7	10 Tra La La	Mercury 70998
			Jockey #24 / Top 100 #39	
3/16/57	**68**	3	11 Silent Lips	Mercury 71058
6/03/57	**92**	1	12 I'm Walking The Floor Over You	RCA 6922
10/06/58	**32**	5	13 The Hula Hoop Song	Roulette 4106
			Hot 100 #32 / Best Seller #42 end	
			TERRI GIBBS	
			Born on 6/15/54 in Augusta, Georgia. Country singer - blind since birth.	
1/17/81	**13**	22	1 Somebody's Knockin'	MCA 41309
6/20/81	**89**	5	2 Rich Man	MCA 51119
			GIBSON BROTHERS	
			Consisted of brothers Chris (guitar, percussion), Patrick (vocals, drums) and Alex Gibson (vocals, keyboards). Based in Paris, France.	
6/23/79	**81**	5	1 Cuba	Island 8832
			DON GIBSON	
			Born on 4/3/28 in Shelby, North Carolina. Country singer, songwriter, guitarist.	
2/24/58	**81**	6	1 I Can't Stop Lovin' You/	
3/10/58	**7**	21	2 **Oh Lonesome Me**	RCA 7133
			Best Seller #7 / Top 100 #8 / Jockey #10	
6/30/58	**20**	13	3 Blue Blue Day	RCA 7010
			Jockey #20 / Best Seller #32 / Top 100 #32	
9/29/58	**46**	10	4 Give Myself A Party/	
9/29/58	**58**	10	5 Look Who's Blue	RCA 7330
1/19/59	**43**	9	6 Who Cares	RCA 7437
5/04/59	**71**	3	7 Lonesome Old House	RCA 7505
8/10/59	**85**	3	8 Don't Tell Me Your Troubles	RCA 7566
3/07/60	**29**	11	9 Just One Time	RCA 7690
8/01/60	**72**	5	10 Far, Far Away	RCA 7762
11/14/60	**93**	4	11 Sweet Dreams	RCA 7805
2/13/61	**100**	1	12 What About Me	RCA 7841
6/19/61	**21**	14	13 Sea Of Heartbreak	RCA 7890
12/04/61	**59**	4	14 Lonesome Number One	RCA 7959
			Don wrote all of above (except #13); all produced by Chet Atkins	
			GINNY GIBSON	
11/03/56	**68**	6	1 Miracle Of Love	ABC-Para. 9739
			orchestra conducted by Don Costa	
			JOHNNY GIBSON	
2/03/62	**76**	4	1 Midnight [I]	Big Top 3088
			STEVE GIBSON & The Red Caps	
			Steve was born on 10/17/14 in Lynchburg, Virginia.	
10/21/57	**63**	5	1 Silhouettes	ABC-Para. 9856

DEBUT DATE	PEAK POS	WKS CHR	ARTIST — Record Title	Label & Number
			GIDEA PARK featuring Adrian Baker	
			British group.	
1/23/82	**82**	3	1 Seasons Of Gold	Profile 5003
			4 Seasons medley: Sherry/Big Girls Don't Cry/Walk Like A Man/ I've Got You Under My Skin/Working My Way Back To You/Opus 17/ Dawn/Let's Hang On/The Joy and The Tears/Who Loves You?	
			ASTRUD GILBERTO - see STAN GETZ	
			NICK GILDER	
			Born on 11/7/51 in London, England. Moved to Vancouver, Canada at age 10. Founding member of the rock band Sweeney Todd.	
6/10/78	**1**[1]	31	1 ▲**Hot Child In The City**	Chrysalis 2226
10/28/78	**44**	8	2 Here Comes The Night	Chrysalis 2264
6/16/79	**57**	6	3 Rock Me	Chrysalis 2332
			TERRY GILKYSON & THE EASY RIDERS	
			Folk trio: Terry Gilkyson, Rick Dehr and Frank Miller.. Terry performed with the legendary Weavers folk group in the early 50s.	
2/02/57	**4**	19	1 **Marianne**	Columbia 40817
			Juke Box #4 / Top 100 #5 / Jockey #5 / Best Seller #6	
5/27/57	**96**	2	2 Tina	Columbia 40910
			shown only as: **THE EASY RIDERS**	
			JOHNNY GILL - see STACY LATTISAW	
			MICKEY GILLEY	
			Born on 3/9/37 in Natchez, LA. Country singer, pianist. First cousin to both Jerry Lee Lewis and preacher Jimmy Swaggart. Owner of "Gilleys" club in Pasadena, Texas.	
6/08/74	**50**	11	1 Room Full Of Roses	Playboy 50056
5/17/80	**22**	18	2 Stand By Me	Full Moon 46640
			featured in the movie "Urban Cowboy"	
8/16/80	**66**	7	3 True Love Ways	Epic 50876
7/11/81	**55**	12	4 You Don't Know Me	Epic 02172
			JIMMY GILMER - see THE FIREBALLS	
			DAVID GILMOUR	
			Born on 3/6/47 in Cambridge, England. Guitarist/vocalist with Pink Floyd.	
4/07/84	**62**	7	1 Blue Light	Columbia 04378
			JAMES GILREATH	
3/23/63	**21**	12	1 Little Band Of Gold	Joy 274
			JIM GILSTRAP	
			Vocalist, backup singer from Texas.	
3/08/75	**55**	9	1 Swing Your Daddy	Roxbury 2006
8/16/75	**93**	3	2 House Of Strangers	Roxbury 2013
10/25/75	**78**	8	3 I'm On Fire	Roxbury 2016
			GINO & GINA	
5/19/58	**20**	12	1 (It's Been A Long Time) Pretty Baby	Mercury 71283
			Jockey #20 / Top 100 #34 / Best Seller #39	
			GIORGIO - see GIORGIO MORODER	
			THE GIRLFRIENDS	
			Black trio from Los Angeles: Gloria Goodson, Nannette Jackson and Carolyn Willis.	
12/28/63+	**49**	7	1 My One And Only, Jimmy Boy	Colpix 712
			GIUFFRIA	
			California-based rock quintet led by Gregg Giuffria (keyboardist with Angel) and David Glen Eisley (vocals).	
11/10/84+	**15**	19	1 Call To The Heart	MCA 52497
3/23/85	**57**	8	2 Lonely In Love	MCA 52558
5/03/86	**52**	10	3 I Must Be Dreaming	MCA/Camel 52794
			THE GLADIOLAS	
			R&B group formed as the Royal Charms in 1955. Consisted of Maurice Williams (lead singer), Earl Gainey, William Massey, Willie Jones and Norman Wade.	
4/06/57	**41**	11	1 Little Darlin'	Excello 2101
			GLADSTONE	
			Pop duo: H.L. Voelker and Doug Rhone.	
8/26/72	**45**	11	1 A Piece Of Paper	ABC 11327

DEBUT DATE	PEAK POS	WKS CHR	ARTIST — Record Title		Label & Number
			WILL GLAHE		
			European accordionist-bandleader.		
11/18/57	**16**	23	1 Liechtensteiner Polka	[F]	London 1755
			Best Seller #16 / Jockey #18 / Top 100 #19		
4/07/58	**91**	1	2 Sweet Elizabeth	[F]	London 1788
			GLASER BROTHERS - see TOMPALL		
			THE GLASS BOTTLE		
			Pop group featuring lead singer Gary Criss.		
7/17/71	**36**	13	1 I Ain't Got Time Anymore		Avco Embassy 4575
12/04/71	**87**	2	2 The Girl Who Loved Me When		Avco 4584
			above 2 produced by novelty artist Dickie Goodman		
			THE GLASS HOUSE		
			Soul group consisting of Larry Mitchell, Pearl Jones, Scherrie Payne, Ty Hunter and Eric Dunham. Hunter (d: 2/24/81) was in the Originals.		
10/18/69	**59**	9	1 Crumbs Off The Table		Invictus 9071
7/18/70	**90**	5	2 I Can't Be You (You Can't Be Me)		Invictus 9076
			GLASS MOON		
			U.S. rock quartet: Dave Adams, Nestor Nunez, Chris Jones and Jaime Glaser.		
3/13/82	**50**	7	1 On A Carousel		Radio 4022
			GLASS TIGER		
			Canadian rock quintet: Alan Frew, Sam Reid, Al Connelly, Wayne Parker and Michael Hanson.		
7/12/86	**2**[1]	24	1 **Don't Forget Me (When I'm Gone)**		Manhattan 50037
11/01/86+	**7**	21	2 **Someday**		Manhattan 50048
			TOM GLAZER & THE DO-RE-MI CHILDREN'S CHORUS		
			Tom is a novelty folk singer from Philadelphia.		
6/01/63	**14**	9	1 On Top Of Spaghetti	[N]	Kapp 526
			parody of the tune "On Top Of Old Smokey"		
			JACKIE GLEASON		
			Born on 2/26/16 in Brooklyn. Star of stage and screen before enormous popularity on TV's "The Honeymooners" and his own CBS-TV variety series. Died on 6/24/87 (71).		
11/12/55	**50**	9	1 Autumn Leaves	[I]	Capitol 3223
			trumpet solo by Bobby Hackett		
			THE GLENCOVES		
6/15/63	**38**	9	1 Hootenanny		Select 724
			THE GLITTER BAND		
			British backing group for Gary Glitter.		
11/06/76	**91**	6	1 Makes You Blind	[I]	Arista 0207
			GARY GLITTER		
			Born Paul Gadd on 5/8/44 in Banbury, England. First recorded as Paul Raven in the early 60s, then as Paul Monday; changed name to Gary Glitter in 1971.		
7/22/72	**7**	11	1 **Rock And Roll Part 2**	[I]	Bell 45237
11/04/72	**35**	9	2 I Didn't Know I Loved You (Till I Saw You Rock And Roll)		Bell 45276
			THE GLORIES		
			Soul trio formed in New York City by Francis Yvonne Gearing.		
6/17/67	**74**	5	1 I Stand Accused (Of Loving You)		Date 1553
			GO-GO'S		
			Female rock group formed in 1978 in Los Angeles, consisting of Belinda Carlisle, Jane Wiedlin, Charlotte Caffey, Kathy Valentine and Gina Schock. Disbanded in 1984.		
8/29/81	**20**	30	1 Our Lips Are Sealed		I.R.S. 9901
1/30/82	**2**[3]	19	2 ● **We Got The Beat**		I.R.S. 9903
7/03/82	**8**	14	3 **Vacation**		I.R.S. 9907
9/25/82	**50**	9	4 Get Up And Go		I.R.S. 9910
3/17/84	**11**	16	5 Head Over Heels		I.R.S. 9926
6/16/84	**32**	14	6 Turn To You		I.R.S. 9928
9/22/84	**84**	3	7 Yes Or No		I.R.S. 9933
			GO WEST		
			British duo: Peter Cox & Richard Drummie.		
2/23/85	**41**	15	1 We Close Our Eyes		Chrysalis 42850

DEBUT DATE	PEAK POS	WKS CHR	ARTIST — Record Title	Label & Number
			GO WEST — Cont'd	
6/01/85	**54**	14	2 Call Me	Chrysalis 42865
9/28/85	**73**	7	3 Eye To Eye	Chrysalis 42903
			GOANNA	
			Australian rock group - Shane Howard, lead singer.	
6/11/83	**71**	7	1 Solid Rock	Atco 99895
			GODLEY & CREME	
			Kevin Godley & Lol Creme formed duo after leaving British group, 10cc.	
7/20/85	**16**	17	1 Cry	Polydor 881786
			GODSPELL	
			The original cast as featured in the Broadway rock musical "Godspell" (based upon the gospel according to St. Matthew).	
5/20/72	**13**	14	1 Day By Day lead vocal by original cast member Robin Lamont	Bell 45210
			LOUISE GOFFIN	
			Singer, songwriter. Carole King's daughter.	
8/18/79	**43**	9	1 Remember (Walking In The Sand)	Asylum 46521
			ANDREW GOLD	
			Born on 8/2/51 in Burbank, CA. Son of soundtrack composer Ernest Gold ("Exodus") and singer Marni Nixon. Co-founder of the group Bryndle. Session and arranging work for Linda Ronstadt since early 70s. Also see Wax.	
1/03/76	**68**	5	1 That's Why I Love You	Asylum 45286
3/19/77	**7**	21	2 **Lonely Boy**	Asylum 45384
2/11/78	**25**	15	3 Thank You For Being A Friend	Asylum 45456
6/17/78	**67**	8	4 Never Let Her Slip Away	Asylum 45489
			FRANNIE GOLDE	
			Singer, songwriter from Chicago.	
7/07/79	**76**	3	1 Here I Go (Fallin' In Love Again)	Portrait 70031
			GOLDEN EARRING	
			Rock band from The Netherlands: Barry Hay (vocals), George Kooymans (guitars, vocals), Cesar Zuiderwijk (drums) and Rinus Gerritsen (bass, keyboards).	
5/11/74	**13**	20	1 Radar Love	Track 40202
10/19/74	**91**	4	2 Candy's Going Bad	Track 40309
11/27/82+	**10**	27	3 **Twilight Zone**	21 Records 103
4/23/83	**79**	4	4 The Devil Made Me Do It	21 Records 108
3/24/84	**76**	4	5 When The Lady Smiles	21 Records 112
			BOBBY GOLDSBORO	
			Born on 1/18/41 in Marianna, Florida. Singer, songwriter, guitarist. To Dothan, Alabama in 1956. Toured with Roy Orbison, 1962-64.	
12/22/62+	**70**	7	1 Molly	Laurie 3148
1/11/64	**9**	13	2 **See The Funny Little Clown**	United Art. 672
4/18/64	**39**	8	3 Whenever He Holds You	United Art. 710
8/08/64	**74**	6	4 Me Japanese Boy I Love You	United Art. 742
1/23/65	**13**	12	5 Little Things	United Art. 810
5/01/65	**27**	11	6 Voodoo Woman	United Art. 862
8/21/65	**75**	5	7 If You Wait For Love/	
9/25/65	**60**	8	8 If You've Got A Heart	United Art. 908
12/18/65+	**53**	7	9 Broomstick Cowboy	United Art. 952
2/19/66	**23**	8	10 It's Too Late	United Art. 980
5/14/66	**56**	5	11 I Know You Better Than That	United Art. 50018
9/03/66	**70**	5	12 It Hurts Me	United Art. 50056
12/10/66+	**35**	9	13 Blue Autumn all of above produced by Jack Gold	United Art. 50087
3/23/68	**1**[5]	15	14 ● **Honey**	United Art. 50283
6/29/68	**19**	9	15 Autumn Of My Life	United Art. 50318
10/26/68	**36**	8	16 The Straight Life	United Art. 50461
2/08/69	**61**	6	17 Glad She's A Woman	United Art. 50497
4/19/69	**46**	10	18 I'm A Drifter	United Art. 50525
8/16/69	**53**	9	19 Muddy Mississippi Line	United Art. 50565
1/10/70	**78**	5	20 Mornin Mornin	United Art. 50614
4/04/70	**75**	6	21 Can You Feel It	United Art. 50650
12/26/70+	**11**	13	22 Watching Scotty Grow	United Art. 50727

DEBUT DATE	PEAK POS	WKS CHR	ARTIST — Record Title	Label & Number
			BOBBY GOLDSBORO — Cont'd	
5/08/71	**83**	6	23 And I Love You So	United Art. 50776
7/24/71	**69**	6	24 Come Back Home	United Art. 50807
9/16/72	**94**	5	25 With Pen In Hand	United Art. 50938
8/25/73	**21**	14	26 Summer (The First Time)	United Art. 251
			14-26: produced by Bob Montgomery & Bobby Goldsboro	
			IAN GOMM	
			Born on 3/17/47 in Ealing, England. Member of London band Brinsley Schwarz, 1972-78.	
9/01/79	**18**	12	1 Hold On	Stiff/Epic 50747
			GONE ALL STARS	
			Session band arranged by record company mogul, George Goldner.	
2/24/58	**30**	9	1 '7-11' [I]	Gone 5016
			Best Seller #30 / Top 100 #31	
			version of the tune "Mambo No. 5" written by Perez Prado	
			GONZALEZ	
			British soul/disco band.	
1/06/79	**26**	12	1 Haven't Stopped Dancing Yet	Capitol 4674
			THE GOODEES	
12/21/68+	**46**	11	1 Condition Red	Hip 8005
			THE GOODIES	
			British group.	
5/03/75	**79**	4	1 The Funky Gibbon	20th Century 2189
			BENNY GOODMAN - see ROSEMARY CLOONEY	
			DICKIE GOODMAN	
			Born on 4/19/34 in Hewlett, New York. Dickie and partner Bill Buchanan originated the novelty "break-in" recordings featuring bits of the original versions of Top 40 hits interwoven throughout the recording. Also see Buchanan & Goodman.	
2/20/61	**60**	7	1 The Touchables [N]	Mark-X 8009
4/24/61	**42**	6	2 The Touchables In Brooklyn [N]	Mark-X 8010
12/25/61	**99**	1	3 Santa & The Touchables [N-X]	Rori 701
7/14/62	**44**	6	4 Ben Crazy [N]	Diamond 119
5/28/66	**70**	3	5 Batman & His Grandmother [N]	Red Bird 10058
6/28/69	**45**	8	6 On Campus [N]	Cotique 158
9/06/69	**95**	2	7 Luna Trip [N]	Cotique 173
6/16/73	**42**	7	8 Watergrate [N]	Rainy Wed. 202
2/02/74	**33**	8	9 Energy Crisis '74 [N]	Rainy Wed. 206
6/15/74	**73**	4	10 Mr. President [N]	Rainy Wed. 207
9/06/75	**4**	10	11 ● **Mr. Jaws** [N]	Cash 451
2/05/77	**48**	6	12 Kong [N]	Shock 6
			GOODTIMERS - see DON COVAY	
			DON GOODWIN	
			Singer discovered by Paul Anka while auditioning at a Las Vegas hotel.	
12/08/73	**86**	8	1 This Is Your Song	Silver Blue 806
			written and co-produced by Paul Anka	
			RON GOODWIN	
9/09/57	**52**	8	1 Swinging Sweethearts [I]	Capitol 3748
			GOODY GOODY	
			Vocalist Denise Montana and studio band from Philadelphia.	
11/18/78	**82**	5	1 #1 Dee Jay	Atlantic 3504
			GOOSE CREEK SYMPHONY	
			Country rock septet.	
1/29/72	**64**	9	1 (Oh Lord Won't You Buy Me A) Mercedes Benz	Capitol 3246
			BARRY GORDON	
			Barry was 7 years old at the time of his 1955 hit.	
12/17/55	**6**	4	1 **Nuttin' For Christmas** [X-N]	MGM 12092
			Best Seller #6 / Top 100 #7 / Juke Box #9 / Jockey #10	
2/11/56	**52**	5	2 Rock Around Mother Goose [N]	MGM 12166
			backed by Art Mooney & His Orchestra on above 2	

DEBUT DATE	PEAK POS	WKS CHR	ARTIST — Record Title	Label & Number
			ROBERT GORDON	
			Rockabilly singer; born in Washington, DC in 1947. Former lead singer of the New York punk band Tuff Darts.	
10/01/77	**83**	3	1 Red Hot	Private S. 45156
			with guitarist Link Wray	
6/27/81	**76**	4	2 Someday, Someway	RCA 12239
			ROSCO GORDON	
			R&B singer, guitarist, pianist; born in Memphis in 1934.	
2/15/60	**64**	7	1 Just A Little Bit	Vee-Jay 332
			LESLEY GORE	
			Born on 5/2/46 in New York City. Raised in Tenafly, New Jersey. Discovered by Quincy Jones while singing at a hotel in Manhattan. In films "Girls On The Beach", "Ski Party" and "The T.A.M.I. Show".	
5/11/63	**1^{2}**	13	1 **It's My Party**	Mercury 72119
7/06/63	**5**	11	2 **Judy's Turn To Cry**	Mercury 72143
9/28/63	**5**	15	3 **She's A Fool**	Mercury 72180
12/28/63+	**2^{3}**	13	4 **You Don't Own Me**	Mercury 72206
3/28/64	**12**	9	5 That's The Way Boys Are	Mercury 72259
5/23/64	**37**	5	6 I Don't Wanna Be A Loser	Mercury 72270
7/25/64	**14**	10	7 Maybe I Know	Mercury 72309
10/17/64	**76**	6	8 Hey Now/	
10/31/64	**86**	4	9 Sometimes I Wish I Were A Boy	Mercury 72352
12/26/64+	**27**	9	10 Look Of Love	Mercury 72372
3/27/65	**71**	6	11 All Of My Life	Mercury 72412
6/19/65	**13**	11	12 Sunshine, Lollipops And Rainbows	Mercury 72433
			from the film "Ski Party"	
9/11/65	**32**	8	13 My Town, My Guy And Me	Mercury 72475
			all of above produced by Quincy Jones	
12/04/65	**80**	3	14 I Won't Love You Anymore (Sorry)	Mercury 72513
2/05/66	**76**	3	15 We Know We're In Love	Mercury 72530
3/26/66	**50**	6	16 Young Love	Mercury 72553
2/04/67	**16**	14	17 California Nights	Mercury 72649
6/10/67	**65**	7	18 Summer And Sandy	Mercury 72683
10/21/67	**82**	4	19 Brink Of Disaster	Mercury 72726
			MICHAEL GORE	
4/14/84	**84**	6	1 Theme from "Terms Of Endearment" [I]	Capitol 5334
			from the film "Terms Of Endearment"	
			EYDIE GORME	
			Born on 8/16/31 in New York City. Regular on Steve Allen's "Tonight Show" in 1954. Broadway debut with husband Steve Lawrence in "Golden Rainbow", 1967. Married Steve in Las Vegas in December, 1957.	
4/21/56	**39**	14	1 Too Close For Comfort	ABC-Para. 9684
			from the Broadway musical "Mr. Wonderful"	
7/28/56	**34**	11	2 Mama, Teach Me To Dance	ABC-Para. 9722
4/13/57	**65**	11	3 I'll Take Romance	ABC-Para. 9780
6/17/57	**53**	2	4 Your Kisses Kill Me	ABC-Para. 9817
12/16/57	**24**	2	5 Love Me Forever	ABC-Para. 9863
			Jockey #24 / Top 100 #86	
5/26/58	**11**	11	6 You Need Hands	ABC-Para. 9925
			Jockey #11 / Best Seller #32 / Top 100 #32	
8/04/58	**63**	7	7 Gotta Have Rain	ABC-Para. 9944
12/28/58	**88**	1	8 The Voice In My Heart	ABC-Para. 9971
			all of above (except #2) arranged and conducted by Don Costa	
1/19/63	**7**	15	9 **Blame It On The Bossa Nova**	Columbia 42661
6/01/63	**53**	7	10 Don't Try To Fight It, Baby	Columbia 42790
7/20/63	**28**	11	11 I Want To Stay Here	Columbia 42815
			STEVE & EYDIE	
9/28/63	**80**	6	12 Everybody Go Home	Columbia 42854
12/21/63+	**35**	9	13 I Can't Stop Talking About You	Columbia 42932
			STEVE & EYDIE	
7/25/64	**43**	8	14 I Want You To Meet My Baby/	
8/29/64	**87**	3	15 Can't Get Over (The Bossa Nova)	Columbia 43082
11/29/69+	**45**	12	16 Tonight I'll Say A Prayer	RCA 0250
9/16/72	**68**	10	17 We Can Make It Together	MGM 14383
			STEVE & EYDIE featuring THE OSMONDS	

DEBUT DATE	PEAK POS	WKS CHR	ARTIST — Record Title	Label & Number
			ROBERT GOULET	
			Born on 11/26/33 in Lawrence, Massachusetts. Began concert career in Edmonton, Canada. Launched career in hit musical "Camelot", played part of Sir Lancelot.	
10/06/62	**89**	2	1 What Kind Of Fool Am I?	Columbia 42519
			from the Broadway musical "Stop The World-I Want To Get Off"	
10/24/64+	**16**	15	2 My Love, Forgive Me (Amore, Scusami)	Columbia 43131
6/05/65	**58**	7	3 Summer Sounds	Columbia 43301
			GQ	
			Bronx, New York soul group: Emmanuel Rahiem LeBlanc (lead singer), Keith Crier, Herb Lane and Paul Service. Group became a trio with the departure of Service, 1980.	
3/17/79	**12**	18	1 ● Disco Nights (Rock-Freak)	Arista 0388
6/30/79	**20**	17	2 I Do Love You	Arista 0426
3/13/82	**93**	2	3 Sad Girl	Arista 0659
			CHARLIE GRACIE	
			Born Charles Graci on 5/14/36 in Philadelphia. Rock 'n roll/pop singer, guitarist. First recorded for Cadillac in 1951.	
2/16/57	**1**[2]	17	1 **Butterfly**	Cameo 105
			Juke Box #1 / Best Seller #3 / Top 100 #7 / Jockey #13	
5/06/57	**16**	15	2 Fabulous	Cameo 107
			Best Seller #16 / Top 100 #26	
8/12/57	**71**	3	3 I Love You So Much It Hurts	Cameo 111
			GRADUATES	
			Quartet from New York: John Cappello, Bruce Hammond, Fred Mancuso and Jack Scorsone.	
3/09/59	**74**	3	1 Ballad Of A Girl And Boy	Shan-Todd 0055
			GRAHAM CENTRAL STATION	
			Soul/dance group from Oakland. Formed and led by Larry Graham after his departure from Sly & The Family Stone.	
5/04/74	**49**	8	1 Can You Handle It?	Warner 7782
8/09/75	**38**	9	2 Your Love	Warner 8105
11/29/75	**92**	2	3 It's Alright	Warner 8148
2/21/76	**63**	6	4 The Jam [I]	Warner 8175
			LARRY GRAHAM	
			Born on 8/14/46 in Beaumont, Texas. To Oakland at the age of two. Bass player with Sly & The Family Stone, 1966-72. Formed Graham Central Station in 1973.	
6/28/80	**9**	20	1 ● **One In A Million You**	Warner 49221
10/25/80	**76**	4	2 When We Get Married	Warner 49581
9/05/81	**67**	5	3 Just Be My Lady	Warner 49744
			BILLY GRAMMER	
			Born on 8/28/25 in Benton, Illinois. Country singer, guitarist. Performed regularly on "The Jimmy Dean Show" on CBS-TV, 1957-58.	
11/24/58+	**4**	20	1 **Gotta Travel On**	Monument 400
			based on 19th century tune that originated in the British Isles	
4/13/59	**50**	9	2 Bonaparte's Retreat/	
4/13/59	**60**	7	3 The Kissing Tree	Monument 403
			GERRY GRANAHAN	
			Singer, songwriter from New York City. Also see Dicky Doo & The Don'ts.	
6/09/58	**23**	11	1 No Chemise, Please	Sunbeam 102
			Top 100 #23 / Best Seller #25	
			ROCCO GRANATA	
			Singer, songwriter, accordionist from Waterschei, Belgium.	
11/09/59	**31**	11	1 Marina [F]	Laurie 3041
			GRAND CANYON	
11/02/74	**72**	5	1 Evil Boll-Weevil [N]	Bang 713
			novelty "break-in" recording a la Dickie Goodman	
			GRAND FUNK RAILROAD	
			Heavy-metal rock group formed in Flint, Michigan in 1968. Consisted of Mark Farner (guitar), Mel Schacher (bass) and Don Brewer (drums). Brewer and Farner had been in Terry Knight & The Pack; Schacher was former bassist with "? & The Mysterians". Knight became producer and manager for Grand Funk, until he was fired in March, 1972. Craig Frost (keyboards), added in 1973. Disbanded in 1976. Re-formed in 1981, with Farner, Brewer and Dennis Bellinger (bass). Disbanded again shortly thereafter.	
9/27/69	**48**	11	1 Time Machine	Capitol 2567
12/20/69	**97**	2	2 Mr. Limousine Driver	Capitol 2691

DEBUT DATE	PEAK POS	WKS CHR	ARTIST — Record Title	Label & Number
			GRAND FUNK RAILROAD — Cont'd	
2/14/70	**72**	6	3 Heartbreaker	Capitol 2732
8/15/70	**22**	12	4 Closer To Home	Capitol 2877
12/12/70+	**47**	8	5 Mean Mistreater	Capitol 2996
5/01/71	**54**	6	6 Feelin' Alright	Capitol 3095
8/28/71	**61**	6	7 Gimme Shelter	Capitol 3160
1/08/72	**29**	11	8 Footstompin' Music	Capitol 3255
4/29/72	**73**	5	9 Upsetter	Capitol 3316
			all of above produced by Terry Knight	
9/23/72	**29**	13	10 Rock 'N Roll Soul	Capitol 3363
			GRAND FUNK:	
7/28/73	**1**[1]	17	11 ● **We're An American Band**	Capitol 3660
11/24/73+	**19**	12	12 Walk Like A Man	Capitol 3760
3/09/74	**1**[2]	20	13 ● **The Loco-Motion**	Capitol 3840
7/13/74	**11**	11	14 Shinin' On	Capitol 3917
			above 4 produced by Todd Rundgren	
12/14/74+	**3**	13	15 **Some Kind Of Wonderful**	Capitol 4002
4/05/75	**4**	15	16 **Bad Time**	Capitol 4046
			GRAND FUNK RAILROAD:	
1/24/76	**53**	5	17 Take Me	Capitol 4199
3/20/76	**69**	4	18 Sally	Capitol 4235
			above 4 produced by Jimmy Ienner	
8/14/76	**45**	7	19 Can You Do It	MCA 40590
			produced by Frank Zappa	
			GRANDMASTER FLASH & THE FURIOUS FIVE	
			Grandmaster Flash (Joseph Saddler) is a New York disc jockey who worked the turntables and never appeared on the recordings. Melle Mel (Melvin Glover) was the main voice for the rap band, The Furious Five.	
10/16/82	**62**	7	1 The Message	Sugar Hill 584
			sold commercially only as a 12" single	
8/04/84	**86**	2	2 Beat Street Breakdown - Part I	Atlantic 89689
			GRANDMASTER MELLE MEL & THE FURIOUS FIVE	
			from the film "Beat Street"	
			AMY GRANT	
			Born on 11/25/60 in Augusta, GA. The first lady of contemporary Christian music.	
5/18/85	**29**	16	1 Find A Way	A&M 2734
8/17/85	**66**	9	2 Wise Up	A&M 2762
9/20/86	**1**[1]	21	3 **The Next Time I Fall**	Full Moon 28597
			PETER CETERA with AMY GRANT	
			EARL GRANT	
			Organist/pianist/vocalist born in Oklahoma City in 1931. Died in an auto accident on 6/10/70 (39).	
9/15/58	**7**	19	1 **The End**	Decca 30719
1/26/59	**63**	7	2 Evening Rain	Decca 30819
3/28/60	**88**	3	3 House Of Bamboo	Decca 31044
5/26/62	**44**	11	4 Swingin' Gently [I]	Decca 25560
9/08/62	**55**	8	5 Sweet Sixteen Bars [I]	Decca 25574
10/23/65	**75**	7	6 Stand By Me [I]	Decca 25674
			EDDY GRANT	
			Born Edmond Montague Grant on 3/5/48 in Plaisance, Guyana. Moved to London in 1960. Formed group the Equals in London, 1967.	
4/16/83	**2**[5]	22	1 ● **Electric Avenue**	Portrait 03793
8/13/83	**53**	7	2 I Don't Wanna Dance	Portrait 04039
5/19/84	**26**	17	3 Romancing The Stone	Portrait 04433
			written for the film but not included in it	
			above 3 recorded in St. Phillip, Barbados	
			GOGI GRANT	
			Born Audrey Brown on 9/20/24 in Philadelphia. Moved to Los Angeles at age 12. Performed vocals for the film "The Helen Morgan Story".	
10/01/55	**9**	11	1 **Suddenly There's A Valley**	Era 1003
			Jockey #9 / Best Seller #14 / Top 100 #14 / Juke Box #19	
2/04/56	**62**	7	2 Who Are We	Era 1008
4/28/56	**1**[8]	28	3 **The Wayward Wind**	Era 1013
			Jockey #1(8) / Top 100 #1(7) / Best Seller #1(6) / Juke Box #1(4)	

DEBUT DATE	PEAK POS	WKS CHR	ARTIST — Record Title	Label & Number
			GOGI GRANT — Cont'd	
9/15/56	**69**	7	4 You're In Love/ from the film "Accused Of Murder"	
9/15/56	**75**	2	5 When The Tide Is High	Era 1019
8/25/58	**80**	3	6 Strange Are The Ways Of Love	RCA 7294
4/24/61	**50**	9	7 The Wayward Wind [R] orchestra conducted by Buddy Bregman on all of above	Era 3046
			JANIE GRANT Singer, songwriter born in New York City in 1945. Discovered by recording artist Gerry Granahan.	
3/27/61	**29**	13	1 Triangle	Caprice 104
8/28/61	**75**	3	2 Romeo	Caprice 109
6/23/62	**74**	4	3 That Greasy Kid Stuff backing on above 3 by the Hutch Davie Orchestra	Caprice 115
			GRAPEFRUIT British group.	
3/02/68	**98**	1	1 Dear Delilah	Equinox 70000
			THE GRASS ROOTS Rock group formed in Los Angeles by pop producers/songwriters Steve Barri and P.F. Sloan. Recruited the Los Angeles bar band, The Thirteenth Floor, to record as The Grass Roots. Consisted of Warren Entner, Creed Bratton, guitars; Rob Grill, bass; and Rick Coonce, drums. Bratton left, replaced by Dennis Provisor in 1969. New lineup, 1972, included Entner, Grill, Reed Kailing, Joel Larson & Virgil Webber.	
6/18/66	**28**	9	1 Where Were You When I Needed You	Dunhill 4029
9/10/66	**96**	2	2 Only When You're Lonely	Dunhill 4043
5/13/67	**8**	12	3 **Let's Live For Today**	Dunhill 4084
8/12/67	**23**	8	4 Things I Should Have Said	Dunhill 4094
10/28/67	**68**	5	5 Wake Up, Wake Up	Dunhill 4105
8/31/68	**5**	15	6● **Midnight Confessions**	Dunhill 4144
11/30/68+	**28**	9	7 Bella Linda	Dunhill 4162
2/15/69	**49**	7	8 Lovin' Things	Dunhill 4180
4/12/69	**31**	11	9 The River Is Wide	Dunhill 4187
7/05/69	**15**	15	10 I'd Wait A Million Years	Dunhill 4198
11/08/69	**24**	10	11 Heaven Knows	Dunhill 4217
2/14/70	**44**	8	12 Walking Through The Country	Dunhill 4227
5/09/70	**35**	10	13 Baby Hold On	Dunhill 4237
9/19/70	**61**	6	14 Come On And Say It	Dunhill 4249
12/26/70+	**15**	18	15 Temptation Eyes	Dunhill 4263
6/05/71	**9**	11	16 **Sooner Or Later**	Dunhill 4279
10/09/71	**16**	11	17 Two Divided By Love	Dunhill 4289
2/12/72	**34**	10	18 Glory Bound	Dunhill 4302
6/17/72	**39**	9	19 The Runway	Dunhill 4316
1/27/73	**55**	10	20 Love Is What You Make It	Dunhill 4335
8/02/75	**71**	11	21 Mamacita	Haven 7015
			GRATEFUL DEAD Psychedelic rock band formed in San Francisco in 1966. Consisted of Jerry Garcia, lead guitar; Bob Weir, rhythm guitar; Ron "Pigpen" McKernan, organ, harmonica; Phil Lesh, bass; and Bill Kruetzmann, drums. Mickey Hart (2nd drummer) and Tom Constanten (keyboards) added in 1968. Constanten left in 1970, Hart in 1971. Keith Godchaux (piano) and his wife Donna (vocals) joined in 1972. Pigpen died of a liver ailment on 3/8/73. Hart returned in 1975. Brent Mydland (keyboards) added in 1979, replacing Keith & Donna Godchaux.	
8/08/70	**69**	7	1 Uncle John's Band	Warner 7410
11/27/71	**64**	8	2 Truckin'	Warner 7464
2/03/73	**91**	2	3 Sugar Magnolia	Warner 7667
10/25/75	**81**	5	4 The Music Never Stopped	Grateful Dead 718
6/21/80	**68**	6	5 Alabama Getaway	Arista 0519
			BILLY GRAVES Delaware-born singer, guitarist. Performed with Dick Flood on Jimmy Dean's CBS-TV show as "The Country Lads".	
1/26/59	**53**	9	1 The Shag (Is Totally Cool)	Monument 401
			CARL GRAVES Soul singer from Vancouver, Canada. With the group Skylark in 1973.	
12/07/74+	**50**	9	1 Baby, Hang Up The Phone	A&M 1620

DEBUT DATE	PEAK POS	WKS CHR	ARTIST — Record Title	Label & Number
			CARL GRAVES — Cont'd	
4/16/77	**83**	5	2 Sad Girl	Ariola Am. 7660
			CLAUDE GRAY	
			Born on 1/26/32 in Henderson, Texas. Country singer, guitarist.	
4/10/61	**84**	2	1 I'll Just Have A Cup Of Coffee (Then I'll Go)	Mercury 71732
			DOBIE GRAY	
			Born Leonard Ainsworth, Jr. on 7/26/42 in Brookshire, Texas. Vocalist, composer, actor. To Los Angeles in 1963. Sang with the group Pollution. Worked as an actor on Broadway, and in the L.A. production of "Hair".	
1/12/63	**91**	2	1 Look At Me	Cordak 1602
1/09/65	**13**	9	2 The 'In' Crowd	Charger 105
4/03/65	**69**	7	3 See You At The 'Go-Go'	Charger 107
2/24/73	**5**	21	4 ● **Drift Away**	Decca 33057
8/04/73	**61**	11	5 Loving Arms above 2 produced by Mentor Williams (Paul Williams' brother)	MCA 40100
2/14/76	**78**	7	6 If Love Must Go	Capricorn 0249
10/23/76	**94**	2	7 Find 'Em, Fool 'Em & Forget 'Em	Capricorn 0259
12/23/78+	**37**	11	8 You Can Do It	Infinity 50003
			MAUREEN GRAY	
6/09/62	**91**	3	1 Dancin' The Strand	Landa 689
			THE CHARLES RANDOLPH GREAN SOUNDE	
			Charles is a former artist & repertoire director at RCA & Dot Records. Married to singer Betty Johnson.	
6/14/69	**13**	11	1 Quentin's Theme [I] from the TV series "Dark Shadows"	Ranwood 840
			R.B. GREAVES	
			Born Ronald Bertram Aloysius Greaves on 11/28/44 at the USAF Base in Georgetown, British Guyana. Half American Indian, raised on a Seminole reservation. Nephew of Sam Cooke.	
10/18/69	**2**[1]	15	1 ● **Take A Letter Maria**	Atco 6714
1/24/70	**27**	8	2 Always Something There To Remind Me	Atco 6726
4/25/70	**82**	3	3 Fire & Rain	Atco 6745
9/19/70	**88**	2	4 Georgia Took Her Back	Atco 6778
12/12/70	**82**	2	5 Whiter Shade Of Pale	Atco 6789
			CYNDI GRECCO	
5/08/76	**25**	12	1 Making Our Dreams Come True theme from the TV series "LaVerne & Shirley"	Private S. 45086
			BUDDY GRECO	
			Born Armando Greco on 8/14/26 in Philadelphia. Former pianist-vocalist with Benny Goodman.	
9/22/62	**64**	11	1 Mr. Lonely Epic used same music track on Bobby Vinton's #1 version in 1964	Epic 9536
			AL GREEN	
			Born in Forrest City, Arkansas on 4/13/46. Moved to Grand Rapids, Michigan at the age of 9. Signed to Hi Records by their A&R director, producer Willie Mitchell. Today, Al is a gospel singer & a minister at the Full Tabernacle Church in Memphis.	
12/09/67+	**41**	12	1 Back Up Train AL GREENE & THE SOUL MATES	Hot Line 15000
11/21/70+	**60**	10	2 I Can't Get Next To You	Hi 2182
7/24/71	**11**	19	3 ● Tired Of Being Alone	Hi 2194
12/04/71+	**1**[1]	16	4 ● **Let's Stay Together**	Hi 2202
4/01/72	**4**	12	5 ● **Look What You Done For Me**	Hi 2211
7/08/72	**3**	12	6 ● **I'm Still In Love With You**	Hi 2216
9/30/72	**69**	7	7 Guilty	Bell 45258
10/21/72	**3**	15	8 ● **You Ought To Be With Me**	Hi 2227
1/20/73	**71**	5	9 Hot Wire 1, 7, 9: recorded 1967-68	Bell 45305
2/17/73	**10**	11	10 ● **Call Me (Come Back Home)**	Hi 2235
7/07/73	**10**	15	11 ● **Here I Am (Come And Take Me)**	Hi 2247
12/08/73+	**19**	11	12 Livin' For You	Hi 2257
3/30/74	**32**	11	13 Let's Get Married	Hi 2262
9/28/74	**7**	19	14 ● **Sha-La-La (Make Me Happy)**	Hi 2274
3/01/75	**13**	12	15 L-O-V-E (Love)	Hi 2282

DEBUT DATE	PEAK POS	WKS CHR	ARTIST — Record Title		Label & Number
			AL GREEN — Cont'd		
7/05/75	**48**	6	16 Oh Me, Oh My (Dreams In My Arms)		Hi 2288
11/08/75	**28**	11	17 Full Of Fire		Hi 2300
10/23/76+	**37**	14	18 Keep Me Cryin'		Hi 2319
			all of above Hi recordings produced by Willie Mitchell		
1/07/78	**83**	5	19 Belle		Hi 77505
			GARLAND GREEN		
			Born on 6/24/42 in Leland, MS. Soul singer, pianist.		
9/13/69	**20**	10	1 Jealous Kind Of Fella		Uni 55143
			NORMAN GREENBAUM		
			Born on 11/20/42 in Malden, MA. Moved to the West Coast in 1965 and formed the psychedelic jug band, "Dr. West's Medicine Show & Junk Band".		
2/28/70	**3**	15	1 ● **Spirit In The Sky**		Reprise 0885
6/13/70	**46**	6	2 Canned Ham		Reprise 0919
5/15/71	**93**	6	3 California Earthquake		Reprise 1008
			STEVE GREENBERG		
7/26/69	**97**	3	1 Big Bruce	[N]	Trip 3000
			BARBARA GREENE		
6/22/68	**86**	6	1 Young Boy		Renee 5001
			JACK GREENE		
			Born on 1/7/30 in Maryville, Tennessee. Drummer for Ernest Tubb's band, 1962-66.		
1/07/67	**65**	9	1 There Goes My Everything		Decca 32023
			LORNE GREENE		
			Born on 2/12/15 in Ottawa, Canada. Chief news broadcaster for CBC radio, 1940-43. Moved to New York City in 1953. Best known as Ben Cartwright on TV's "Bonanza".		
10/31/64	**1**[1]	12	1 **Ringo**	[S]	RCA 8444
1/30/65	**72**	3	2 The Man		RCA 8490
			ELLIE GREENWICH		
			Ellie and former husband Jeff Barry wrote and produced many of the top hits during the 60s. They also recorded as The Raindrops. Ellie sang back-up on Cyndi Lauper's "She's So Unusual" album.		
5/06/67	**83**	3	1 I Want You To Be My Baby		United Art. 50151
			THE GREENWOOD COUNTY SINGERS		
8/01/64	**75**	5	1 Frankie And Johnny		Kapp 591
4/30/66	**64**	5	2 Please Don't Sell My Daddy No More Wine		Kapp 742
			THE GREENWOODS		
			LEE GREENWOOD		
			Born on 10/27/42 in Los Angeles. Country singer, songwriter.		
5/28/83	**53**	11	1 I.O.U.		MCA 52199
10/01/83	**96**	2	2 Somebody's Gonna Love You		MCA 52257
			BOBBY GREGG & His Friends		
			Bobby's real name is Robert Grego; jazz drummer from Philadelphia. Performed with Steve Gibson & The Red Caps from 1955-59.		
3/17/62	**29**	10	1 The Jam - Part 1	[I]	Cotton 1003
			featuring Roy Buchanan on guitar		
6/30/62	**89**	4	2 Potato Peeler	[I]	Cotton 1006
			GREY & HANKS		
			Vocal/songwriting duo of Zane Grey and Len Ron Hanks. Wrote "Back In Love Again" for L.T.D., "Never Had A Love Like This Before" for Tavares, and many others.		
3/10/79	**83**	2	1 Dancin'		RCA 11460
			MERV GRIFFIN		
			Born on 7/6/25 in San Mateo, CA. Popular TV talk show host; started as featured singer with Freddy Martin from 1948-52 ("I've Got A Lovely Bunch of Cocoanuts").		
4/10/61	**69**	4	1 The Charanga		Carlton 545
			ANDY GRIFFITH		
			Born on 6/1/26 in Mount Airy, NC. Screen debut in 1957, "A Face In The Crowd". Best known as sheriff Andy Taylor on the TV series "The Andy Griffith Show"; currently starring in TV's "Matlock".		
4/02/55	**26**	1	1 Make Yourself Comfortable	[C]	Capitol 3057
			Best Seller #26		
			vocal by Jean Wilson		

DEBUT DATE	PEAK POS	WKS CHR	ARTIST — Record Title	Label & Number
			GRIN	
			Rock trio formed by Nils Lofgren (lead guitar, keyboards and vocals).	
2/05/72	**75**	6	1 White Lies	Spindizzy 4005
			LARRY GROCE	
			Born on 4/22/48 in Dallas. Pop/folk singer, songwriter. Wrote children's songs for Walt Disney Records.	
1/10/76	**9**	15	1 **Junk Food Junkie** [N] recorded live at McCabe's in Santa Monica	Warner 8165
			HENRY GROSS	
			Rock singer, guitarist from Brooklyn. Original lead guitarist of Sha-Na-Na.	
4/26/75	**93**	3	1 One More Tomorrow	A&M 1682
2/28/76	**6**	20	2● **Shannon**	Lifesong 45002
7/10/76	**37**	10	3 Springtime Mama	Lifesong 45008
10/30/76	**85**	3	4 Someday (I Didn't Want To Have To Be The One) all of above produced by Terry Cashman & Tommy West	Lifesong 45014
			GTR	
			British hard rock quintet featuring superstar guitarists Steve Hackett (Genesis) and Steve Howe (Yes & Asia), and Max Bacon (vocals).	
5/10/86	**14**	16	1 When The Heart Rules The Mind	Arista 9470
8/23/86	**85**	6	2 The Hunter	Arista 9512
			VINCE GUARALDI TRIO	
			Vince was born on 7/17/32 in San Francisco. Jazz pianist formerly with Woody Herman and Cal Tjader. Died of a heart attack on 2/6/76 (43).	
12/08/62+	**22**	18	1 Cast Your Fate To The Wind [I]	Fantasy 563
			THE GUESS WHO	
			Rock group formed in Winnipeg, Canada, 1963. Consisted of Allan "Chad Allan" Kobel (guitar, vocals), Randy Bachman (lead guitar), Garry Peterson (drums), Bob Ashley (piano) and Jim Kale (bass). Recorded as The Reflections, and Chad Allan & The Expressions. Ashley replaced by new lead singer Burton Cummings in 1966. Allan left shortly thereafter. Bachman left in July, 1970, to form Bachman-Turner Overdrive. Replaced by Kurt Winter and Greg Leskiw. Leskiw and Kale left in 1972, replaced by Don McDougall and Bill Wallace. Domenic Troiano replaced both Winter and McDougall in 1974. Group disbanded in 1975; several reformations since then.	
5/08/65	**22**	11	1 Shakin' All Over group is actually Chad Allan & The Expressions	Scepter 1295
4/05/69	**6**	14	2● **These Eyes**	RCA 0102
7/12/69	**10**	11	3● **Laughing/**	
10/18/69	**22**	10	4 Undun	RCA 0195
12/20/69+	**5**	14	5 **No Time**	RCA 0300
3/21/70	**1**[3]	15	6● **American Woman/**	
		13	7 No Sugar Tonight	RCA 0325
7/18/70	**17**	11	8 Hand Me Down World	RCA 0367
10/24/70	**10**	10	9 **Share The Land**	RCA 0388
1/30/71	**43**	7	10 Hang On To Your Life	RCA 0414
4/17/71	**29**	13	11 Albert Flasher/	
		11	12 Broken	RCA 0458
8/14/71	**19**	12	13 Rain Dance	RCA 0522
11/27/71+	**50**	9	14 Sour Suite	RCA 0578
3/04/72	**47**	7	15 Heartbroken Bopper	RCA 0659
5/20/72	**70**	6	16 Guns, Guns, Guns	RCA 0708
10/14/72	**96**	3	17 Runnin' Back To Saskatoon	RCA 0803
2/03/73	**61**	7	18 Follow Your Daughter Home	RCA 0880
2/16/74	**39**	19	19 Star Baby	RCA 0217
7/20/74	**6**	16	20 **Clap For The Wolfman** featuring bits of dialogue by Wolfman Jack	RCA 0324
11/23/74+	**28**	11	21 Dancin' Fool all of above (except #1) produced by Jack Richardson	RCA 10075
			GREG GUIDRY	
			Singer, songwriter, pianist from St. Louis.	
2/13/82	**17**	16	1 Goin' Down	Columbia 02691
7/17/82	**92**	2	2 Into My Love	Columbia 02984

DEBUT DATE	PEAK POS	WKS CHR	ARTIST — Record Title	Label & Number
			BONNIE GUITAR	
			Born on 3/25/33 in Seattle. Owner of Dolton Records; played guitar on several early Fleetwoods recordings.	
4/13/57	**6**	22	1 **Dark Moon**	Dot 15550
			Jockey #6 / Top 100 #8 / Best Seller #10 / Juke Box #11	
10/28/57	**71**	8	2 Mister Fire Eyes	Dot 15612
12/14/59	**97**	2	3 Candy Apple Red	Dolton 10
4/02/66	**99**	2	4 I'm Living In Two Worlds	Dot 16811
			GUNHILL ROAD	
			Rock trio: Glen Leopolo, Gil Roman and Steve Goldrich.	
3/31/73	**40**	15	1 Back When My Hair Was Short	Kama Sutra 569
			ARLO GUTHRIE	
			Born on 7/10/47 in Coney Island, NY. Son of legendary folk singer Woody Guthrie.	
12/13/69	**97**	2	1 Alice's Rock & Roll Restaurant	Reprise 0877
			short version of his 18 minute tale "Alice's Restaurant Massacree"	
7/29/72	**18**	16	2 The City Of New Orleans	Reprise 1103
			GWEN GUTHRIE	
			Soul singer, songwriter from New Jersey. Background vocalist for many top artists.	
8/02/86	**42**	13	1 Ain't Nothin' Goin' On But The Rent	Polydor 885106
			GYPSY	
			Rock band formed and led by James "Owl" Walsh. Reformed with a new band in 1978 as the "James Walsh Gypsy Band".	
12/05/70+	**62**	8	1 Gypsy Queen - Part 1	Metromedia 202
10/28/78	**71**	7	2 Cuz It's You, Girl	RCA 11403
			JAMES WALSH GYPSY BAND	

H

DEBUT DATE	PEAK POS	WKS CHR	ARTIST — Record Title	Label & Number
			BUDDY HACKETT	
			Born on 8/11/24 in Brooklyn. One of America's favorite comedians.	
4/07/56	**87**	2	1 Chinese Rock And Egg Roll [C]	Coral 61594
			orchestra directed by Dick Jacobs	
			SAMMY HAGAR	
			Born on 10/13/47 in Monterey, CA. Rock singer, songwriter, guitarist. Lead singer of Montrose (1973-75). Replaced David Lee Roth as lead singer of Van Halen in 1985.	
12/10/77+	**62**	8	1 You Make Me Crazy	Capitol 4502
4/07/79	**65**	5	2 (Sittin' On) The Dock Of The Bay	Capitol 4699
			backing vocals by Brad Delp and Barry Goudreau of Boston	
9/15/79	**77**	7	3 Plain Jane	Capitol 4757
1/30/82	**43**	10	4 I'll Fall In Love Again	Geffen 49881
5/15/82	**73**	4	5 Piece Of My Heart	Geffen 50059
12/11/82+	**13**	19	6 Your Love Is Driving Me Crazy	Geffen 29816
3/26/83	**46**	8	7 Never Give Up	Geffen 29718
7/14/84	**38**	12	8 Two Sides Of Love	Geffen 29246
9/29/84	**26**	16	9 I Can't Drive 55	Geffen 29173
			HAGAR, SCHON, AARONSON, SHRIEVE	
			Sammy Hagar, Neal Schon (Journey), Kenny Aaronson and Michael Shrieve (Santana).	
5/19/84	**94**	2	1 Whiter Shade Of Pale	Geffen 29280
			MERLE HAGGARD	
			Born in Bakersville, California on 4/6/37. Country singer, songwriter, guitarist. Served nearly 3 years in San Quentin prison on a burglary charge, 1957-60. Signed to Capitol Records in 1965 and then formed his backing band, The Strangers.	
11/01/69+	**41**	13	1 Okie From Muskogee	Capitol 2626
2/14/70	**92**	3	2 The Fightin' Side Of Me	Capitol 2719
3/20/71	**90**	3	3 Soldier's Last Letter	Capitol 3024
12/04/71+	**58**	7	4 Carolyn	Capitol 3222
9/01/73	**62**	8	5 Everybody's Had The Blues	Capitol 3641
11/24/73+	**28**	11	6 If We Make It Through December	Capitol 3746
			all of above (except #3) made #1 on Billboard's Country charts	
10/22/77	**58**	9	7 From Graceland To The Promised Land	MCA 40804
			an Elvis Presley tribute - vocal backing: Jordanaires	

DEBUT DATE	PEAK POS	WKS CHR	ARTIST — Record Title	Label & Number
			JOYCE HAHN	
6/03/57	**84**	4	1 Gonna Find Me A Bluebird	Cadence 1318
			HAIRCUT ONE HUNDRED	
			British pop/rock sextet led by Nick Heyward.	
5/15/82	**37**	17	1 Love Plus One	Arista 0672
			BILL HALEY & His Comets	
			Born William John Clifton Haley Jr. on 7/6/25 in Highland Park, Michigan. Began career as a singer with a New England country band, the "Down Homers". Formed the "Four Aces of Western Swing" in 1948 and then in 1949 formed the Saddlemen, who recorded on various labels before signing with the Essex label (as Bill Haley & The Comets) in 1952, and then with Decca in 1954. The original Comets band who backed Haley on "Rock Around The Clock" were: Rudy Pompilli (sax), Al Pompilli (bass), Ralph Jones (drums) and Frannie Beecher (lead guitar). Bill died of a heart attack in Harlingen, Texas on 2/9/81. Also see The Kingsmen.	
11/20/54+	**11**	15	1 Dim, Dim The Lights (I Want Some Atmosphere) Best Seller #11 / Jockey #16 / Juke Box #16	Decca 29317
3/05/55	**17**	8	2 Mambo Rock/ Juke Box #17 / Best Seller #18	
3/19/55	**26**	4	3 Birth Of The Boogie Best Seller #26	Decca 29418
5/14/55	**1**[8]	24	4 **Rock Around The Clock** Best Seller #1(8) / Juke Box #1(7) / Jockey #1(6) recorded on 4/12/54 - featured in the film "Blackboard Jungle"	Decca 29124
7/23/55	**15**	4	5 Razzle-Dazzle/ Best Seller #15	
		2	6 Two Hound Dogs Best Seller flip	Decca 29552
11/12/55	**9**	17	7 **Burn That Candle/** Juke Box #9 / Best Seller #16 / Top 100 #20	
11/12/55	**41**	17	8 Rock-A-Beatin' Boogie	Decca 29713
1/14/56	**6**	19	9 **See You Later, Alligator** Best Seller #6 / Top 100 #6 / Jockey #6 / Juke Box #6	Decca 29791
4/07/56	**16**	14	10 R-O-C-K/ Juke Box #16 / Top 100 #29 featured in the film "Rock Around The Clock"	
4/07/56	**18**	10	11 The Saints Rock 'N Roll Best Seller #18 / Top 100 #42 rock version of the spiritual "When The Saints Go Marching In"	Decca 29870
6/16/56	**60**	6	12 Hot Dog Buddy Buddy/	
7/14/56	**78**	3	13 Rockin' Through The Rye rock version of 1796 Scottish tune "Comin' Thro' The Rye"	Decca 29948
8/11/56	**25**	14	14 Rip It Up/ Best Seller #25 / Top 100 #30	
8/25/56	**68**	5	15 Teenager's Mother (Are You Right?)	Decca 30028
11/03/56	**34**	13	16 Rudy's Rock [I] sax solo by Rudy Pompilli (died on 2/5/76 - 47)	Decca 30085
12/15/56	**45**	3	17 Don't Knock The Rock/ Coming Up #45 from the film of the same title	
		1	18 Choo Choo Ch' Boogie Coming Up flip	Decca 30148
4/06/57	**70**	4	19 Forty Cups Of Coffee/	
		1	20 Hook, Line And Sinker Coming Up flip	Decca 30214
6/10/57	**60**	7	21 (You Hit The Wrong Note) Billy Goat	Decca 30314
4/14/58	**22**	15	22 Skinny Minnie Top 100 #22 / Best Seller #24	Decca 30592
8/11/58	**67**	1	23 Lean Jean	Decca 30681
10/05/59	**46**	12	24 Joey's Song [I]	Decca 30956
1/04/60	**70**	6	25 Skokiaan (South African Song) [I]	Decca 31030
3/16/74	**39**	14	26 Rock Around The Clock [R]	MCA 60025
			DARYL HALL	
			Born Daryl Franklin Hohl on 10/11/48 in Philadelphia. Half of Hall & Oates duo.	
8/02/86	**5**	15	1 **Dreamtime**	RCA 14387
10/18/86	**33**	13	2 Foolish Pride	RCA 5038

DEBUT DATE	PEAK POS	WKS CHR	ARTIST — Record Title		Label & Number
			DARYL HALL & JOHN OATES		
			Daryl Hall (see above) & John Oates (b: 4/7/49 in New York City) met while students at Temple University in 1967. Hall sang backup for many top soul groups, before teaming up with Oates in 1972. Duo's sophisticated "blue-eyed soul" style has earned them the #2 ranking (behind the Everly Brothers) as the all-time top duo of the rock era.		
2/09/74	**60**	8	1 She's Gone		Atlantic 2993
1/31/76	**4**	28	2 ● **Sara Smile**		RCA 10530
7/24/76	**7**	20	3 **She's Gone**	[R]	Atlantic 3332
10/30/76	**39**	15	4 Do What You Want, Be What You Are		RCA 10808
1/22/77	**1**[2]	20	5 ● **Rich Girl**		RCA 10860
5/07/77	**28**	10	6 Back Together Again		RCA 10970
7/30/77	**80**	3	7 It's Uncanny		Atlantic 3397
10/22/77	**73**	6	8 Why Do Lovers (Break Each Other's Heart?)		RCA 11132
8/26/78	**20**	14	9 It's A Laugh		RCA 11371
12/09/78+	**42**	10	10 I Don't Wanna Lose You		RCA 11424
10/27/79+	**18**	19	11 Wait For Me		RCA 11747
7/19/80	**30**	13	12 How Does It Feel To Be Back		RCA 12048
9/27/80	**12**	20	13 You've Lost That Lovin' Feeling		RCA 12103
1/24/81	**1**[3]	23	14 ● **Kiss On My List**		RCA 12142
5/02/81	**5**	21	15 **You Make My Dreams**		RCA 12217
8/29/81	**1**[2]	23	16 ● **Private Eyes**		RCA 12296
11/14/81+	**1**[1]	21	17 ● **I Can't Go For That (No Can Do)**		RCA 12357
3/20/82	**9**	16	18 **Did It In A Minute**		RCA 13065
6/19/82	**33**	11	19 Your Imagination		RCA 13252
10/16/82	**1**[4]	23	20 ● **Maneater**		RCA 13354
1/29/83	**7**	18	21 **One On One**		RCA 13421
4/30/83	**6**	16	22 **Family Man**		RCA 13507
10/29/83	**2**[4]	18	23 **Say It Isn't So**		RCA 13654
2/18/84	**8**	17	24 **Adult Education**		RCA 13714
9/29/84	**1**[2]	23	25 **Out Of Touch**		RCA 13916
12/15/84+	**5**	19	26 **Method Of Modern Love**		RCA 13970
3/16/85	**18**	13	27 Some Things Are Better Left Unsaid		RCA 14035
6/01/85	**30**	12	28 Possession Obsession		RCA 14098
8/31/85	**20**	11	29 A Nite At The Apollo Live! The Way You Do The Things You Do/My Girl		RCA 14178
			DARYL HALL JOHN OATES with DAVID RUFFIN & EDDIE KENDRICK		
			recorded at the reopening of New York's Apollo Theatre - revival of two early Temptations' hits		
			JIMMY HALL		
			Mobile, Alabama native. Leader of the Southern rock band, Wet Willie.		
9/27/80	**27**	17	1 I'm Happy That Love Has Found You		Epic 50931
5/01/82	**77**	3	2 Fool For Your Love		Epic 02857
			THE JOHN HALL Band		
			John was born on 10/25/47. Founder and leader of Orleans.		
12/26/81+	**42**	11	1 Crazy (Keep On Falling)		EMI America 8096
1/22/83	**64**	10	2 Love Me Again		EMI America 8151
			LANI HALL		
			Lead vocalist with Sergio Mendes & Brasil '66. Married to Herb Alpert.		
3/21/81	**88**	3	1 Where's Your Angel?		A&M 2305
			LARRY HALL		
			Born on 6/30/41 in Cincinnati.		
11/23/59+	**15**	15	1 Sandy		Strand 25007
			TOM T. HALL		
			Born on 5/25/36 in Olive Hill, Kentucky. Country music storyteller.		
8/21/71	**42**	12	1 The Year That Clayton Delaney Died		Mercury 73221
5/13/72	**98**	2	2 Me And Jesus		Mercury 73278
			vocal accompaniment: the Mt. Pisgah United Methodist Church Choir		
12/08/73+	**12**	16	3 I Love		Mercury 73436
6/15/74	**63**	4	4 That Song Is Driving Me Crazy		Mercury 73488
3/15/75	**55**	6	5 Sneaky Snake		Mercury 73641

DEBUT DATE	PEAK POS	WKS CHR	ARTIST — Record Title	Label & Number
			THE JACK HALLORAN SINGERS	
12/25/61	**96**	1	1 The Little Drummer Boy .... [X]	Dot 16275
			THE HALOS	
			New York City R&B group. Backing group on Curtis Lee's "Pretty Little Angel Eyes".	
7/17/61	**25**	11	1 'Nag'	7 Arts 709
			HAMILTON, JOE FRANK & REYNOLDS	
			Dan Hamilton, Joe Frank Carollo and Tommy Reynolds. Trio were members of the T-Bones. Reynolds left group in 1972 and was replaced by Alan Dennison. Although Reynolds had left, group still recorded as Hamilton, Joe Frank & Reynolds until July of 1976.	
5/22/71	**4**	14	1 ● **Don't Pull Your Love**	Dunhill 4276
8/28/71	**46**	7	2 Annabella	Dunhill 4287
12/04/71+	**41**	11	3 Daisy Mae	Dunhill 4296
6/21/75	**1**[1]	17	4 ● **Fallin' In Love**	Playboy 6024
11/08/75+	**21**	15	5 Winners And Losers	Playboy 6054
4/03/76	**62**	7	6 Everyday Without You	Playboy 6068
			HAMILTON, JOE FRANK & DENNISON:	
7/17/76	**67**	5	7 Light Up The World With Sunshine	Playboy 6077
10/30/76	**72**	8	8 Don't Fight The Hands (That Need You)	Playboy 6088
			BOBBY HAMILTON	
8/04/58	**40**	3	1 Crazy Eyes For You	Apt 25002
			GEORGE HAMILTON IV	
			Born on 7/19/37, Winston-Salem, NC. Country/folk/pop singer, songwriter, guitarist.	
11/03/56	**6**	20	1 **A Rose And A Baby Ruth**	ABC-Para. 9765
			Top 100 #6 / Best Seller #7 / Jockey #7 / Juke Box #8	
2/16/57	**33**	10	2 Only One Love	ABC-Para. 9782
8/19/57	**80**	5	3 High School Romance	ABC-Para. 9838
12/02/57+	**10**	19	4 **Why Don't They Understand**	ABC-Para. 9862
			Jockey #10 / Top 100 #17 / Best Seller #19	
3/31/58	**25**	11	5 Now And For Always	ABC-Para. 9898
			Jockey #25 / Best Seller #37 / Top 100 #37	
6/09/58	**43**	8	6 I Know Where I'm Goin'	ABC-Para. 9924
			Top 100 #43 / Best Seller #45	
8/25/58	**65**	4	7 When Will I Know/	
9/08/58	**72**	4	8 Your Cheatin' Heart	ABC-Para. 9946
12/01/58+	**29**	8	9 The Teen Commandments .... [S]	ABC-Para. 9974
			PAUL ANKA-GEORGE HAMILTON-JOHNNY NASH	
			inspirational talk from above 3 ABC-Paramount artists	
8/03/59	**73**	7	10 Gee	ABC-Para. 10028
6/22/63	**15**	14	11 Abilene	RCA 8181
			ROY HAMILTON	
			Born on 4/16/29 in Leesburg, Georgia. Moved to Jersey City at age 14; sang with the Searchlight Gospel Singers in 1948. Died of a stroke on 7/20/69 (40).	
4/23/55	**6**	16	1 **Unchained Melody**	Epic 9102
			Jockey #6 / Juke Box #6 / Best Seller #9 from the film "Unchained"	
7/23/55	**45**	3	2 Forgive This Fool	Epic 9111
			Coming Up #45	
11/26/55	**77**	3	3 Without A Song	Epic 9125
12/24/55+	**42**	7	4 Everybody's Got A Home	Epic 9132
			from the Broadway musical "Pipe Dream"	
1/13/58	**13**	16	5 Don't Let Go	Epic 9257
			Top 100 #13 / Best Seller #14 / Jockey #16	
11/17/58	**45**	12	6 Pledging My Love	Epic 9294
4/20/59	**62**	5	7 I Need Your Lovin'	Epic 9307
8/03/59	**84**	3	8 Time Marches On	Epic 9323
1/30/61	**12**	10	9 You Can Have Her	Epic 9434
5/01/61	**80**	3	10 You're Gonna Need Magic	Epic 9443
			RUSS HAMILTON	
			Born Ronald Hulme in Liverpool, England. Singer, songwriter.	
6/17/57	**4**	23	1 **Rainbow**	Kapp 184
			Jockey #4 / Best Seller #7 / Top 100 #7	

DEBUT DATE	PEAK POS	WKS CHR	ARTIST — Record Title	Label & Number
			MARVIN HAMLISCH	
			Born on 6/2/44 in New York City. Pianist/composer/conductor for numerous soundtracks. Won an Oscar and Grammy in the best song category in 1973 for "The Way We Were".	
3/23/74	**3**	16	1 ● **The Entertainer** [I] written in 1902 by Scott Joplin - featured in the film "The Sting"	MCA 40174
			KARL HAMMEL, JR.	
7/31/61	**68**	8	1 Summer Souvenirs	Arliss 1007
			JAN HAMMER	
			Czechoslovakian-born jazz/rock keyboard virtuoso - member of the Mahavishnu Orchestra until 1973.	
9/07/85	**1**[1]	22	1 **Miami Vice Theme** [I] from TV's "Miami Vice" soundtrack	MCA 52666
			ALBERT HAMMOND	
			Born on 5/18/42 in London, England; raised in Gibraltar, Spain. Member of the British group, Magic Lanterns, in 1971.	
7/22/72	**91**	7	1 Down By The River	Mums 6009
10/21/72	**5**	16	2 ● **It Never Rains In Southern California**	Mums 6011
3/03/73	**63**	6	3 If You Gotta Break Another Heart	Mums 6015
4/28/73	**48**	11	4 The Free Electric Band	Mums 6018
9/01/73	**80**	4	5 The Peacemaker	Mums 6021
12/01/73	**87**	5	6 Half A Million Miles From Home	Mums 6024
3/02/74	**31**	12	7 I'm A Train	Mums 6026
6/29/74	**81**	4	8 Air Disaster	Mums 6030
4/26/75	**91**	6	9 99 Miles From L.A.	Mums 6037
			KEITH HAMPSHIRE	
12/23/72+	**51**	9	1 Daytime Night-Time	A&M 1403
4/21/73	**70**	13	2 First Cut Is The Deepest	A&M 1432
12/08/73	**81**	4	3 Big Time Operator	A&M 1486
			HERBIE HANCOCK	
			Born on 4/12/40 in Chicago. Jazz electronic keyboardist. Pianist with the Miles Davis band, 1963-68. Composed, conducted and produced the music for the critically acclaimed film "Round Midnight".	
3/23/74	**42**	11	1 Chameleon [I]	Columbia 46002
9/10/83	**71**	9	2 Rockit [I]	Columbia 04054
			JOHN HANDY	
			Jazz saxophone stylist. Native of Dallas.	
6/26/76	**46**	12	1 Hard Work [I]	ABC Impulse 31005
			THE HAPPENINGS	
			Vocal group from Paterson, NJ: Bob Miranda (lead), Tom Giuliano (tenor), Ralph DiVito (baritone) and Dave Libert (bass). Bernie LaPorta replaced DiVito in 1968. Originally the Four Graduates, recorded for Rust in 1963.	
7/09/66	**3**	14	1 **See You In September**	B.T. Puppy 520
10/01/66	**12**	9	2 Go Away Little Girl	B.T. Puppy 522
12/10/66+	**51**	6	3 Goodnight My Love	B.T. Puppy 523
4/08/67	**3**	13	4 **I Got Rhythm** written in 1930 by George & Ira Gershwin for musical "Girl Crazy"	B.T. Puppy 527
7/15/67	**13**	8	5 My Mammy Al Jolson's theme song - written in 1920	B.T. Puppy 530
9/23/67	**41**	6	6 Why Do Fools Fall In Love	B.T. Puppy 532
2/17/68	**96**	2	7 Music Music Music revival of Teresa Brewer's #1 song of 1950	B.T. Puppy 538
7/27/68	**67**	5	8 Breaking Up Is Hard To Do all of above produced by The Tokens	B.T. Puppy 543
7/12/69	**66**	6	9 Where Do I Go/Be-In/Hare Krishna medley from the Broadway rock musical "Hair"	Jubilee 5666
			PAUL HARDCASTLE	
			Keyboardist and record producer born in London on 12/10/57.	
1/12/85	**57**	18	1 Rain Forest [I]	Profile 5059
6/01/85	**15**	14	2 19 title refers to the average age of U.S. soldiers in Vietnam	Chrysalis 42860

DEBUT DATE	PEAK POS	WKS CHR	ARTIST — Record Title		Label & Number
			THE HARDEN TRIO Bobby Harden and sisters Arleen & Robbie from Little Rock, Arkansas.		
3/12/66	**44**	10	1 Tippy Toeing		Columbia 43463
			TIM HARDIN Folk-blues singer/songwriter from Eugene, Oregon. Relative of notorious outlaw John Wesley Hardin. Died from a drug overdose on 12/29/80 (39).		
8/02/69	**50**	7	1 Simple Song Of Freedom written by Bobby Darin		Columbia 44920
			THE HARDTIMES Pop/rock quintet from San Diego. Regulars on Dick Clark's TV show "Where The Action Is".		
12/31/66+	**97**	2	1 Fortune Teller		World Pac. 77851
			HAGOOD HARDY Canadian vibraphonist.		
12/20/75+	**41**	13	1 The Homecoming	[I]	Capitol 4156
			STEVE HARLEY & Cockney Rebel English rock quartet formed in 1973 by ex-journalist Harley.		
2/28/76	**96**	3	1 Make Me Smile (Come Up And See Me)		EMI 4201
			JERRY MURAD'S HARMONICATS Harmonica trio formed in 1944: Jerry Murad, Al Fiore and Don Les.		
12/26/60+	**56**	8	1 Cherry Pink And Apple Blossom White	[I]	Columbia 41816
			JOE HARNELL Born on 8/2/24 in the Bronx. Conductor, arranger for Frank Sinatra, Peggy Lee and others. Musical director for many TV shows, including the Mike Douglas Show.		
12/29/62+	**14**	13	1 Fly Me To The Moon-Bossa Nova	[I]	Kapp 497
4/20/63	**97**	1	2 Diane	[I]	Kapp 521
			JANICE HARPER Songstress from Flushing, New York.		
9/02/57	**46**	14	1 Bon Voyage		Prep 111
12/16/57	**84**	4	2 That's Why I Was Born		Prep 123
8/18/58	**82**	3	3 Devotion		Capitol 3984
1/18/60	**91**	3	4 Cry Me A River		Capitol 4324
			HARPERS BIZARRE Santa Cruz, California quintet led by Ted Templeman, who later produced many albums for The Doobie Brothers and Van Halen.		
2/18/67	**13**	11	1 The 59th Street Bridge Song (Feelin' Groovy) written by Paul Simon; arranged by Leon Russell		Warner 5890
5/20/67	**37**	7	2 Come To The Sunshine		Warner 7028
8/19/67	**43**	8	3 Anything Goes written in 1934 by Cole Porter for the musical of the same title		Warner 7063
11/18/67	**45**	7	4 Chattanooga Choo Choo revival of Glenn Miller's #1 hit from 1941		Warner 7090
9/21/68	**95**	2	5 Battle Of New Orleans		Warner 7223
			SLIM HARPO Born James Moore on 1/11/24 in Lobdell, LA (aka: Harmonica Slim). Died of a heart attack on 1/31/70.		
5/29/61	**34**	8	1 Rainin' In My Heart featuring blues guitarist Lightnin' Slim		Excello 2194
1/29/66	**16**	13	2 Baby Scratch My Back	[I]	Excello 2273
			THE HARPTONES R&B group formed in Harlem in 1953 as The Harps. Willie Winfield, lead singer.		
5/08/61	**96**	2	1 What Will I Tell My Heart		Companion 103
			BETTY HARRIS Born in 1943 in Orlando, FL. Worked as maid to Big Maybelle, later brought on stage for duets with Maybelle. Worked as road manager for James Carr.		
9/21/63	**23**	11	1 Cry To Me		Jubilee 5456
1/04/64	**89**	4	2 His Kiss		Jubilee 5465
7/29/67	**85**	4	3 Nearer To You		Sansu 466
			EDDIE HARRIS Born in 1936 in Chicago. Jazz tenor saxophonist.		
4/10/61	**36**	11	1 Exodus jazz version of the main theme from the film of the same title	[I]	Vee-Jay 378

DEBUT DATE	PEAK POS	WKS CHR	ARTIST — Record Title		Label & Number
			EDDIE HARRIS — Cont'd		
6/15/68	**45**	13	2 Listen Here	[I]	Atlantic 2487
10/26/68	**88**	2	3 It's Crazy	[I]	Atlantic 2561
1/10/70	**85**	4	4 Compared To What **LES McCANN & EDDIE HARRIS**		Atlantic 2694
			EMMYLOU HARRIS Born on 4/12/47 in Birmingham, Alabama. Contemporary country vocalist. Sang backup with Gram Parsons until his death in 1973.		
8/30/75	**58**	5	1 If I Could Only Win Your Love harmony vocal: Herb Pedersen		Reprise 1332
3/13/76	**65**	5	2 Here, There And Everywhere written by John Lennon & Paul McCartney		Reprise 1346
6/28/80	**55**	8	3 That Lovin' You Feelin' Again **ROY ORBISON & EMMYLOU HARRIS** from the film "Roadie"		Warner 49262
2/28/81	**37**	13	4 Mister Sandman		Warner 49684
			MAJOR HARRIS Born on 2/9/47 in Richmond, VA. Sang with The Jarmels, early 60s. With The Delfonics, 1971-74.		
3/29/75	**5**	18	1 ● **Love Won't Let Me Wait**		Atlantic 3248
4/10/76	**73**	4	2 Jealousy		Atlantic 3321
11/27/76	**91**	4	3 Laid Back Love		WMOT 4002
			RICHARD HARRIS Born on 10/1/30 in Limerick, Ireland. Began prolific acting career in 1958. Portrayed King Arthur in the film version of "Camelot".		
5/11/68	**2**[1]	13	1 **MacArthur Park**		Dunhill 4134
11/02/68	**64**	6	2 The Yard Went On Forever		Dunhill 4170
6/07/69	**63**	6	3 Didn't We		Dunhill 4194
11/20/71+	**41**	11	4 My Boy		Dunhill 4293
			ROLF HARRIS Born in Perth, Australia on 3/30/30. Played piano from age nine. Moved to England in the mid-50s. Developed his unique "wobble board sound" out of a sheet of masonite. Had own BBC-TV series from 1970.		
3/16/63	**61**	7	1 Sun Arise		Epic 9567
6/08/63	**3**	11	2 **Tie Me Kangaroo Down, Sport**	[N]	Epic 9596
9/28/63	**95**	1	3 Nick Teen And Al K. Hall	[N]	Epic 9615
			SAM HARRIS Winner of TV's "Star Search" male vocalist category in 1984.		
9/15/84	**36**	14	1 Sugar Don't Bite		Motown 1743
2/01/86	**52**	9	2 I'd Do It All Again		Motown 1829
			THURSTON HARRIS R&B vocalist. First recorded with the Lamplighters in 1953.		
10/21/57	**6**	17	1 **Little Bitty Pretty One** Best Seller #6 / Top 100 #6 / Jockey #12 vocal backing: The Sharps		Aladdin 3398
1/13/58	**57**	8	2 Do What You Did		Aladdin 3399
8/04/58	**96**	1	3 Over And Over		Aladdin 3430
			TONY HARRIS		
9/02/57	**89**	3	1 Chicken, Baby, Chicken		Ebb 104
			THE DON HARRISON BAND Members Stu Cook and Doug Clifford were with Creedence Clearwater Revival.		
4/24/76	**47**	9	1 Sixteen Tons		Atlantic 3323
			GEORGE HARRISON Born on 2/25/43 in Liverpool, England. Formed his first group, the Rebels at age 13. Joined John Lennon and Paul McCartney in the Quarrymen in 1958; group later evolved into The Beatles, with Harrison as lead guitarist. Organized the Bangla-Desh benefit concerts at Madison Square Garden in 1971.		
11/28/70	**1**[4]	14	1 ● **My Sweet Lord/**		
		14	2 Isn't It A Pity		Apple 2995
2/27/71	**10**	9	3 **What Is Life**		Apple 1828
8/14/71	**23**	7	4 Bangla-Desh/		
		3	5 Deep Blue all of above produced by Phil Spector & George Harrison		Apple 1836
5/19/73	**1**[1]	14	6 **Give Me Love (Give Me Peace On Earth)**		Apple 1862

DEBUT DATE	PEAK POS	WKS CHR	ARTIST — Record Title	Label & Number
			GEORGE HARRISON — Cont'd	
11/23/74+	**15**	10	7 Dark Horse	Apple 1877
1/11/75	**36**	6	8 Ding Dong; Ding Dong	Apple 1879
9/20/75	**20**	10	9 You	Apple 1884
11/20/76+	**25**	11	10 This Song	Dark Horse 8294
1/29/77	**19**	11	11 Crackerbox Palace	Dark Horse 8313
3/03/79	**16**	14	12 Blow Away	Dark Horse 8763
5/23/81	**2^{3}**	16	13 **All Those Years Ago**	Dark Horse 49725
11/20/82	**53**	5	14 Wake Up My Love	Dark Horse 29864
			NOEL HARRISON	
			Actor/singer - Rex Harrison's son. Screen debut in 1962.	
12/04/65+	**51**	8	1 A Young Girl	London 9795
10/28/67	**56**	8	2 Suzanne	Reprise 0615
			WILBERT HARRISON	
			Born on 1/6/29 in Charlotte, NC. R&B singer; also plays guitar, piano, harmonica and drums.	
4/13/59	**1^{2}**	16	1 **Kansas City**	Fury 1023
			written by Jerry Leiber & Mike Stoller in 1952 as "K.C. Lovin'"	
12/06/69+	**32**	13	2 Let's Work Together (Part 1)	Sue 11
3/13/71	**98**	2	3 My Heart Is Yours	SSS Int'l. 830
			DEBBIE HARRY	
			Born on 7/1/45 in New York City. Lead singer of Blondie. In films "Unmade Beds", "Union City" and "Videodrome".	
8/15/81	**43**	10	1 Backfired	Chrysalis 2526
10/31/81	**82**	3	2 The Jam Was Moving	Chrysalis 2554
11/22/86+	**57**	11	3 French Kissin	Geffen 28546
			COREY HART	
			Born in Montreal, Canada; raised in Spain and Mexico. Singer, songwriter, keyboardist.	
5/26/84	**7**	23	1 **Sunglasses At Night**	EMI America 8203
9/29/84	**17**	19	2 It Ain't Enough	EMI America 8236
6/08/85	**3**	20	3 **Never Surrender**	EMI America 8268
9/14/85	**26**	12	4 Boy In The Box	EMI America 8287
11/30/85+	**30**	15	5 Everything In My Heart	EMI America 8300
9/20/86	**18**	13	6 I Am By Your Side	EMI America 8348
12/13/86+	**24**	14	7 Can't Help Falling In Love	EMI America 8368
			FREDDIE HART	
			Born on 12/21/28 in Lochapoka, Alabama. Country singer, songwriter, guitarist.	
8/21/71	**17**	17	1 ● Easy Loving	Capitol 3115
			ROD HART	
			Hart and his band appeared in a bar scene in the Steve McQueen film "Junior Bonner".	
12/25/76+	**67**	7	1 C.B. Savage [N]	Plantation 144
			DAN HARTMAN	
			Multi-instrumentalist, songwriter, record producer from Harrisburg, Pennsylvania. Member of the Edgar Winter Group (1972-76). Own studio called the Schoolhouse in Westport, Connecticut.	
10/14/78+	**29**	17	1 ● Instant Replay	Blue Sky 2772
2/24/79	**91**	3	2 This Is It	Blue Sky 2775
4/11/81	**86**	5	3 Heaven In Your Arms	Blue Sky 70053
6/27/81	**72**	5	4 It Hurts To Be In Love	Blue Sky 02115
5/05/84	**6**	25	5 **I Can Dream About You**	MCA 52378
			from the film "Streets Of Fire"	
10/06/84	**25**	17	6 We Are The Young	MCA 52471
2/09/85	**39**	12	7 Second Nature	MCA 52519
			HARVEY & THE MOONGLOWS - see THE MOONGLOWS	
			THE HARVEY BOYS	
3/09/57	**84**	3	1 Nothing Is Too Good For You	Cadence 1306
			BOBBY HATFIELD	
			Born on 8/10/40, Beaver Dam, WI. Teamed with Bill Medley as The Righteous Brothers.	
3/08/69	**95**	4	1 Only You (And You Alone)	Verve 10634

DEBUT DATE	PEAK POS	WKS CHR	ARTIST — Record Title	Label & Number
			DONNY HATHAWAY	
			Born on 10/1/45 in Chicago; raised in St. Louis; gospel singer beginning at age 3. R&B singer, songwriter, keyboardist, record producer and arranger. Committed suicide by jumping from the 15th floor of New York City's Essex House hotel on 1/13/79 (33).	
1/17/70	**87**	8	1 The Ghetto (Part 1)	Atco 6719
6/12/71	**29**	12	2 You've Got A Friend **ROBERTA FLACK & DONNY HATHAWAY**	Atlantic 2808
10/23/71	**71**	6	3 You've Lost That Lovin' Feelin' **ROBERTA FLACK & DONNY HATHAWAY**	Atlantic 2837
5/13/72	**81**	5	4 Giving Up	Atco 6884
5/27/72	**94**	5	5 I Thank You **DONNY HATHAWAY & JUNE CONQUEST**	Curtom 1971
6/10/72	**5**	13	6● **Where Is The Love** **ROBERTA FLACK & DONNY HATHAWAY**	Atlantic 2879
10/21/72	**60**	6	7 I Love You More Than You'll Ever Know	Atco 6903
7/07/73	**44**	9	8 Love, Love, Love	Atco 6928
2/18/78	**2^{2}**	20	9● **The Closer I Get To You** **ROBERTA FLACK with DONNY HATHAWAY**	Atlantic 3463
2/16/80	**47**	11	10 You Are My Heaven **ROBERTA FLACK with DONNY HATHAWAY**	Atlantic 3627
5/17/80	**56**	8	11 Back Together Again **ROBERTA FLACK with DONNY HATHAWAY**	Atlantic 3661
			RICHIE HAVENS	
			Born on 1/21/41 in Brooklyn. Black folksinger/guitarist.	
3/20/71	**16**	14	1 Here Comes The Sun written by George Harrison (on Beatles' "Abbey Road" album)	Stormy F. 656
			DALE HAWKINS	
			Born Delmar Allen Hawkins on 8/22/38 in Goldmine, LA. Rockabilly singer, guitarist. Record production work since 1965.	
6/10/57	**27**	19	1 Susie-Q Best Seller #27 / Top 100 #29	Checker 863
8/25/58	**32**	12	2 La-Do-Dada Hot 100 #32 / Best Seller #44 end	Checker 900
11/10/58	**88**	5	3 A House, A Car And A Wedding Ring	Checker 906
3/16/59	**52**	6	4 Class Cutter (Yeah Yeah)	Checker 916
			THE EDWIN HAWKINS' SINGERS	
			Formed by Edwin Hawkins and Betty Watson in Oakland in 1967 as the Northern California State Youth Choir. Member Dorothy Morrison went on to a solo career.	
4/26/69	**4**	10	1● **Oh Happy Day** featuring vocalist Dorothy Combs Morrison	Pavilion 20001
4/25/70	**6**	17	2 **Lay Down (Candles In The Rain)** **MELANIE with THE EDWIN HAWKINS' SINGERS**	Buddah 167
			HAWKSHAW HAWKINS	
			Country singer Harold "Hawkshaw" Hawkins was killed in a plane crash with Patsy Cline and Cowboy Copas on 3/5/63 (41).	
8/03/59	**87**	2	1 Soldier's Joy	Columbia 41419
			JENNELL HAWKINS	
3/24/62	**50**	8	1 Moments	Amazon 1003
			RONNIE HAWKINS	
			Born on 1/10/35 in Huntsville, AR. Formed first band, The Hawks, in 1952. Moved to Canada in 1958 (where he is still based), and assembled group later known as "The Band". Back-up group became Crowbar in 1970.	
6/08/59	**45**	8	1 Forty Days	Roulette 4154
8/17/59	**26**	16	2 Mary Lou	Roulette 4177
1/31/70	**75**	5	3 Down In The Alley	Cotillion 44060
			HAWKS	
			Otho, Iowa rock quintet.	
3/14/81	**63**	7	1 Right Away	Columbia 60500
			DEANE HAWLEY	
6/20/60	**29**	11	1 Look For A Star from the film "Circus Of Horrors"	Dore 554
10/02/61	**93**	1	2 Pocketful Of Rainbows	Liberty 55359

DEBUT DATE	PEAK POS	WKS CHR	ARTIST — Record Title	Label & Number
			BILL HAYES	
			Born on 6/5/26 in Harvey, IL. Bill was a regular on Sid Caesar's TV series "Your Show of Shows". Played Doug Williams on the TV soap opera "Days Of Our Lives".	
2/26/55	1^5	20	1 **The Ballad Of Davy Crockett**	Cadence 1256
			Best Seller #1(5) / Jockey #1(3) / Juke Box #1(3)	
1/26/57	**33**	12	2 Wringle, Wrangle	ABC-Para. 9785
			from the movie "Westward Ho, The Wagons"	
			ISAAC HAYES	
			Born on 8/20/42 in Covington, TN. Soul singer, songwriter, keyboardist, record producer. Session musician for Otis Redding and other artists on the Stax label. Teamed with songwriter David Porter to compose "Soul Man", "Hold On! I'm A Comin'", and many others. Composed film score for "Shaft", "Tough Guys" and "Truck Turner".	
8/23/69	**30**	12	1 Walk On By/	
8/30/69	**37**	8	2 By The Time I Get To Phoenix	Enterprise 9003
8/29/70	**42**	9	3 I Stand Accused	Enterprise 9017
2/13/71	**79**	5	4 The Look Of Love	Enterprise 9028
5/15/71	**22**	9	5 Never Can Say Goodbye	Enterprise 9031
10/16/71	1^2	13	6 **Theme From Shaft**	Enterprise 9038
			from the Richard Roundtree film "Shaft"	
2/26/72	**30**	11	7 Do Your Thing	Enterprise 9042
4/01/72	**48**	7	8 Let's Stay Together [I]	Enterprise 9045
5/13/72	**86**	4	9 Ain't That Loving You (For More Reasons Than One)	Enterprise 9049
			ISAAC HAYES & DAVID PORTER	
10/21/72	**38**	9	10 Theme From The Men [I]	Enterprise 9058
			from the ABC-TV series "The Men"	
12/22/73+	**30**	9	11 Joy - Pt. I	Enterprise 9085
5/04/74	**71**	8	12 Wonderful	Enterprise 9095
8/23/75	**92**	2	13 Chocolate Chip	HBS/ABC 12118
10/27/79+	**18**	21	14 Don't Let Go	Polydor 2011
			PETER LIND HAYES & MARY HEALY	
			Husband and wife team of TV, films, nightclubs, theatres and radio.	
11/12/55	**57**	3	1 Rememb'ring	Columbia 40547
			RICHARD HAYMAN	
			Born on 3/27/20 in Cambridge, MA. Conductor, arranger, harmonica soloist.	
2/04/56	**11**	15	1 A Theme from "The Three Penny Opera" (Moritat) [I]	Mercury 70781
			Jockey #11 / Top 100 #12 / Best Seller #13 / Juke Box #13	
			RICHARD HAYMAN & JAN AUGUST (pianist - died on 1/17/76)	
9/18/61	**80**	1	2 Night Train [I]	Mercury 71869
			DICK HAYMES	
			Born on 9/13/16 in Buenos Aires, Argentina; raised in U.S. One of the 1940's finest ballad singers. Sang with Harry James, Benny Goodman, and Tommy Dorsey in early 40s, and appeared in various movies from 1944-53. Married briefly to Rita Hayworth. Died on 3/28/80.	
12/29/56	**80**	2	1 Two Different Worlds	Capitol 3565
			HAYSI FANTAYZEE	
			English duo: Kate Garner & Jeremiah Healy.	
7/23/83	**74**	5	1 Shiny Shiny	RCA 13534
			JUSTIN HAYWARD	
			Justin was born on 10/14/46 in Swindon, England. John Lodge was born on 7/20/45 in Birmingham, England. Justin (lead singer, lead guitar) and John (vocals, bass) joined The Moody Blues in the summer of 1966.	
5/17/75	**47**	7	1 I Dreamed Last Night	Threshold 67019
			JUSTIN HAYWARD & JOHN LODGE	
12/13/75+	**94**	5	2 Blue Guitar	Threshold 67021
			JUSTIN HAYWARD & JOHN LODGE	
10/07/78	**47**	13	3 Forever Autumn	Columbia 10799
			LEON HAYWOOD	
			Born on 2/11/42 in Houston. Soul singer, keyboardist. With Big Jay McNeely, and Sam Cooke, early 1960s.	
11/20/65	**92**	3	1 She's With Her Other Love	Imperial 66123
			shown as: LEON HAYWARD	
8/12/67	**63**	11	2 It's Got To Be Mellow	Decca 32164
12/30/67+	**92**	3	3 Mellow Moonlight	Decca 32230
3/23/74	**50**	9	4 Keep It In The Family	20th Century 2065
2/08/75	**94**	2	5 Believe Half Of What You See (And None Of What You Hear)	20th Century 2146

DEBUT DATE	PEAK POS	WKS CHR	ARTIST — Record Title	Label & Number
			LEON HAYWOOD — Cont'd	
7/12/75	**83**	3	6 Come An' Get Yourself Some	20th Century 2191
9/06/75	**15**	17	7 I Want'a Do Something Freaky To You	20th Century 2228
4/05/80	**49**	11	8 Don't Push It Don't Force It	20th Century 2443
			ROBERT HAZARD Philadelphia-based rocker.	
3/05/83	**58**	9	1 Escalator Of Life	RCA 13449
			LEE HAZLEWOOD - see NANCY SINATRA	
			THE HEADBOYS Scottish rock quartet.	
11/10/79	**67**	5	1 The Shape Of Things To Come	RSO 1005
			HEAD EAST St. Louis rock quintet. John Schlitt, lead singer.	
10/18/75	**68**	9	1 Never Been Any Reason	A&M 1718
2/07/76	**54**	6	2 Love Me Tonight	A&M 1784
4/15/78	**46**	8	3 Since You Been Gone	A&M 2026
			MURRAY HEAD British singer/actor. Played juvenile lead in 1971 film "Sunday, Bloody Sunday".	
1/31/70	**74**	7	1 Superstar with The Trinidad Singers from "Jesus Christ Superstar - A Rock Opera"	Decca 32603
1/02/71	**14**	24	2 Superstar [R]	Decca 32603
2/23/85	**3**	20	3 **One Night In Bangkok** from the Tim Rice, Benny Andersson and Bjorn Ulvaeus musical project "Chess"	RCA 13988
			ROY HEAD Born in Three Rivers, Texas on 1/9/43. Rock/country singer, guitarist.	
9/04/65	2^{2}	11	1 **Treat Her Right**	Back Beat 546
10/30/65	**39**	7	2 Just A Little Bit	Scepter 12116
11/20/65	**32**	8	3 Apple Of My Eye	Back Beat 555
1/15/66	**88**	2	4 Get Back	Scepter 12124
3/12/66	**99**	1	5 My Babe 1, 3, 5 shown as: **ROY HEAD & THE TRAITS**	Back Beat 560
9/17/66	**95**	2	6 To Make A Big Man Cry	Back Beat 571
6/26/71	**96**	1	7 Puff Of Smoke	TMI 9000
			HEADPINS Canadian rock quartet featuring female lead singer, Darby Mills.	
12/24/83+	**70**	9	1 Just One More Time	SGR 90001
			JIMMY HEAP & THE MELODY MASTERS Country band featuring lead singer Perk Williams.	
3/10/56	**93**	1	1 Butternut [I]	Capitol 3333
			HEART Rock band formed in Seattle in 1973. Originally known as The Army, then White Heart, shortened to Heart in 1974. Group features Ann Wilson (lead singer) and her sister Nancy (guitar, keyboards). Band moved to Vancouver, Canada in 1975 when their manager Mike Fisher was drafted, and signed with new Mushroom label. When Amnesty was declared, group returned to Seattle and signed with the CBS Portrait label in 1976. In addition to the Wilson sisters, the lineup since 1982 includes guitarist Howard Leese, bassist Mark Andes and drummer Denny Carmassi.	
4/17/76	**35**	13	1 Crazy On You	Mushroom 7021
7/17/76	**9**	23	2 **Magic Man**	Mushroom 7011
12/18/76+	**42**	10	3 Dreamboat Annie	Mushroom 7023
5/28/77	**11**	20	4 Barracuda	Portrait 70004
9/17/77	**62**	6	5 Little Queen	Portrait 70008
11/26/77	**79**	3	6 Kick It Out	Portrait 70010
1/07/78	**62**	6	7 Crazy On You [R]	Mushroom 7021
4/08/78	**24**	15	8 Heartless	Mushroom 7031
9/23/78	**15**	18	9 Straight On	Portrait 70020
2/03/79	**34**	10	10 Dog & Butterfly	Portrait 70025
2/09/80	**33**	12	11 Even It Up all of above produced by Mike Flicker	Epic 50847
11/22/80+	**8**	16	12 **Tell It Like It Is**	Epic 50950
3/28/81	**83**	3	13 Unchained Melody	Epic 51010

DEBUT DATE	PEAK POS	WKS CHR	ARTIST — Record Title	Label & Number
			HEART — Cont'd	
5/15/82	**33**	13	14 This Man Is Mine	Epic 02925
8/13/83	**44**	11	15 How Can I Refuse	Epic 04047
10/29/83	**83**	4	16 Allies	Epic 04184
6/01/85	**10**	21	17 **What About Love?**	Capitol 5481
9/14/85	**4**	24	18 **Never**	Capitol 5512
1/18/86	**1**[1]	20	19 **These Dreams**	Capitol 5541
4/19/86	**10**	16	20 **Nothin' At All**	Capitol 5572
7/19/86	**54**	9	21 If Looks Could Kill	Capitol 5605
			THE HEART & SOUL ORCHESTRA	
			33-piece disco act assembled by former disc jockey Frankie Crocker.	
2/26/77	**46**	7	1 Love In 'C' Minor [I]	Casablanca 876
			THE HEARTBEATS	
			R&B group from Queens, New York. Consisted of James "Shep" Sheppard, Wally Roker, Walter Crump, Robbie Adams and Vernon Walker. Group disbanded in 1960. Sheppard formed Shep & The Limelites in 1961; was murdered on 1/24/70.	
12/22/56+	**53**	16	1 A Thousand Miles Away	Rama 216
7/15/57	**78**	3	2 Everybody's Somebody's Fool	Rama 231
11/07/60	**96**	1	3 A Thousand Miles Away [R]	Rama 216
			THE HEARTS	
			Female R&B group featuring lead singer Jeanette "Baby" Washington. Group organized by Zell Sanders in 1953 in New York City. Not to be confused with Lee Andrews' male group of the same name.	
10/19/63	**94**	3	1 Dear Abby	Tuff 370
			HEARTSFIELD	
			6-man Chicago rock band.	
3/02/74	**95**	5	1 Music Eyes	Mercury 73449
			TED HEATH	
			Born Edward Heath on 3/30/00 in London, England. Died on 11/18/69. Trombonist, leader of own band since 1945.	
10/13/56	**52**	8	1 The Faithful Hussar [I]	London 1675
			JOEY HEATHERTON	
			Movie/TV actress. Began career as a child stage performer.	
5/27/72	**24**	15	1 Gone	MGM 14387
11/25/72+	**87**	9	2 I'm Sorry	MGM 14434
			HEATWAVE	
			Multi-national, inter-racial group formed in Germany by Johnnie and Keith Wilder of Dayton, OH. Johnnie injured in auto accident in 1979, paralyzed from neck down.	
7/23/77	**2**[2]	27	1 ▲ **Boogie Nights**	Epic 50370
1/07/78	**18**	20	2 ● Always And Forever	Epic 50490
5/06/78	**7**	17	3 ● **The Groove Line**	Epic 50524
			HEAVEN BOUND with TONY SCOTTI	
9/04/71	**83**	5	1 He'd Rather Have The Rain	MGM 14284
12/11/71+	**79**	9	2 Five Hundred Miles	MGM 14314
			HEAVEN 17	
			British electro-pop trio: Glenn Gregory, Martyn Ware and Ian Craig Marsh.	
3/12/83	**74**	5	1 Let Me Go	Arista 1050
			BOBBY HEBB	
			Born on 7/26/41 in Nashville. Singer, songwriter, multi-instrumentalist. First black performer on the Grand Ole Opry show at the age of 12.	
6/25/66	**2**[2]	15	1 ● **Sunny**	Philips 40365
10/08/66	**39**	6	2 A Satisfied Mind	Philips 40400
12/31/66+	**84**	3	3 Love Me	Philips 40421
			HEDGEHOPPERS ANONYMOUS	
			British rock group produced by record mogul Jonathan King.	
12/04/65+	**48**	10	1 It's Good News Week	Parrot 9800
			NEAL HEFTI	
			Born on 10/29/22 in Hastings, Nebraska. Trumpeter most famous as arranger for Woody Herman (1944-46), Harry James, and Count Basie, then as composer of TV themes.	
2/12/66	**35**	8	1 Batman Theme [I]	RCA 8755

DEBUT DATE	PEAK POS	WKS CHR	ARTIST — Record Title	Label & Number
			RONNIE HEIGHT	
			Seattle native. Started career with vocal group, the Five Checks.	
3/23/59	**45**	6	1 Come Softly To Me	Dore 516
			HELLO PEOPLE	
			Whiteface mime-rock quartet produced by Todd Rundgren.	
1/18/75	**71**	7	1 Future Shock	ABC/Dunhill 15023
			BOBBY HELMS	
			Born on 8/15/33 in Bloomington, Indiana. Country singer, guitarist.	
7/15/57	**36**	27	1 Fraulein Top 100 #36 / Best Seller #46	Decca 30194
10/14/57	**7**	23	2 **My Special Angel** Best Seller #7 / Top 100 #7 / Jockey #8	Decca 30423
12/23/57	**6**	6	3 **Jingle Bell Rock** [X] Top 100 #6 / Best Seller #7 / Jockey #11	Decca 30513
5/12/58	**63**	8	4 Jacqueline from the movie "The Case Against Brooklyn"	Decca 30619
8/18/58	**60**	2	5 Borrowed Dreams	Decca 30682
12/08/58+	**75**	6	6 The Fool And The Angel	Decca 30749
12/22/58	**35**	4	7 Jingle Bell Rock [X-R]	Decca 30513
12/12/60	**36**	3	8 Jingle Bell Rock [X-R]	Decca 30513
12/11/61	**41**	4	9 Jingle Bell Rock [X-R]	Decca 30513
12/08/62	**56**	4	10 Jingle Bell Rock [X-R]	Decca 30513
			JOE HENDERSON	
			R&B vocalist. With Fairfield Four gospel group. Died in 1966.	
5/19/62	**8**	12	1 **Snap Your Fingers**	Todd 1072
9/08/62	**74**	4	2 Big Love	Todd 1077
11/24/62	**94**	1	3 The Searching Is Over	Todd 1079
			MICHAEL HENDERSON	
			Soul singer from Yazoo City, MS. Toured with Stevie Wonder, Aretha Franklin, and Miles Davis. Also see Norman Connors.	
10/14/78	**88**	3	1 Take Me I'm Yours	Buddah 597
			WILLIE HENDERSON	
			Born on 8/9/41 in Pensacola, Florida. Producer and music director for Brunswick/Dakar in Chicago for 5 years.	
3/21/70	**91**	2	1 Funky Chicken (Part 1) [I] **WILLIE HENDERSON & THE SOUL EXPLOSIONS**	Brunswick 55429
7/06/74	**73**	5	2 Dance Master [I]	Playboy 50057
			BOBBY HENDRICKS	
			Born on 2/22/38 in Columbus, Ohio. R&B vocalist. Member of the 5 Crowns (not the Ben E. King group), The Drifters (1958), and later the Swallows.	
8/04/58	**25**	14	1 Itchy Twitchy Feeling Hot 100 #25 / Best Seller #35 backing vocals by The Coasters	Sue 706
11/07/60	**73**	4	2 Psycho [N] duet with New York disc jockey Dr. Jive (as the psychiatrist)	Sue 732
			JIMI HENDRIX	
			Born on 11/27/42 in Seattle. Died of a drug overdose in London on 9/18/70 (27). Legendary psychedelic-blues guitarist. Began career as a studio guitarist. In 1965, formed own band, Jimmy James & The Blue Flames. Created The Jimi Hendrix Experience in 1966, with Noel Redding on bass and Mitch Mitchell on drums. Formed new group in 1969, Band of Gypsys, with Buddy Miles on drums and Billy Cox on bass.	
8/26/67	**65**	8	1 Purple Haze	Reprise 0597
12/23/67+	**67**	4	2 Foxey Lady	Reprise 0641
3/16/68	**82**	4	3 Up From The Skies	Reprise 0665
9/21/68	**20**	9	4 All Along The Watchtower	Reprise 0767
11/30/68	**52**	8	5 Crosstown Traffic 1, 3-5 shown as: **THE JIMI HENDRIX EXPERIENCE**	Reprise 0792
4/03/71	**59**	8	6 Freedom	Reprise 1000
10/23/71	**74**	7	7 Dolly Dagger from the Hendrix concert film "Rainbow Bridge"	Reprise 1044
			NONA HENDRYX	
			Born on 8/18/45 in Trenton, NJ. Member of "Patti LaBelle & The Blue-Belles" and "LaBelle" from 1961-1977.	
6/04/83	**91**	3	1 Keep It Confidential	RCA 13437

DEBUT DATE	PEAK POS	WKS CHR	ARTIST — Record Title	Label & Number
			HENHOUSE FIVE PLUS TOO see RAY STEVENS	
			DON HENLEY	
			Born on 7/22/47 in Gilmer, Texas. Singer, songwriter, drummer. Worked with Glenn Frey backing Linda Ronstadt before forming the Eagles in 1971.	
10/24/81+	**6**	19	1 **Leather And Lace**	Modern 7341
			STEVIE NICKS with DON HENLEY	
8/21/82	**42**	11	2 Johnny Can't Read	Asylum 69971
10/30/82+	**3**	19	3● **Dirty Laundry**	Asylum 69894
1/15/83	**48**	11	4 I Can't Stand Still	Asylum 69931
11/10/84+	**5**	22	5 **The Boys Of Summer**	Geffen 29141
2/23/85	**9**	19	6 **All She Wants To Do Is Dance**	Geffen 29065
5/25/85	**34**	17	7 Not Enough Love In The World	Geffen 29012
8/31/85	**22**	14	8 Sunset Grill	Geffen 28906
			CLARENCE "Frogman" HENRY	
			Born on 3/19/37 in Algiers, LA. R&B vocalist, pianist, trombonist. With Bobby Mitchell's R&B band, 1953-55. Nicknamed "Frogman" from hit "Ain't Got No Home".	
12/15/56+	**20**	16	1 Ain't Got No Home [N]	Argo 5259
			Best Seller #20 / Top 100 #30	
2/20/61	**4**	16	2 **But I Do**	Argo 5378
			also titled "I Don't Know Why"	
5/15/61	**12**	10	3 You Always Hurt The One You Love	Argo 5388
			#1 hit in 1944 for The Mills Brothers	
8/07/61	**57**	6	4 Lonely Street	Argo 5395
10/30/61	**64**	5	5 On Bended Knees	Argo 5401
1/13/62	**77**	5	6 A Little Too Much	Argo 5408
			JIM HENSON	
			Creator of The Muppets, that famous crew of puppets starring in TV's "Sesame Street" and in the films "The Muppet Movie" and "The Great Muppet Caper". Jim is the voice for both Ernie and Kermit.	
8/15/70	**16**	9	1 Rubber Duckie [N]	Columbia 45207
			ERNIE	
9/15/79	**25**	17	2 Rainbow Connection	Atlantic 3610
			KERMIT from the original soundtrack of "The Muppet Movie"	
			KEITH HERMAN	
10/20/79	**87**	4	1 She's Got A Whole Number	Radio 418
			WOODY HERMAN	
			Born Woodrow Charles Herman on 5/16/13 in Milwaukee. Saxophonist, clarinetist in dance bands beginning in 1929. Formed own band in 1936. Band dubbed The Herman Herd in 1944. One of the most innovative and contemporary of all big-band leaders.	
11/12/55	**79**	6	1 Love Is A Many-Splendored Thing [I]	Capitol 3202
			from the film of the same title	
8/18/56	**75**	5	2 I Don't Want Nobody (To Have My Love But You)	Capitol 3488
			HERMAN'S HERMITS	
			Formed in Manchester, England in 1964. Named after a cartoon character in TV's "The Bullwinkle Show". Consisted of Peter "Herman" Noone (b: 11/5/47), vocals; Derek Leckenby and Keith Hopwood, guitars; Karl Green, bass; and Barry Whithman, drums. First called The Heartbeats. Noone left in 1972 for a solo career.	
10/17/64	**13**	13	1 I'm Into Something Good	MGM 13280
1/30/65	**2**[2]	15	2 **Can't You Hear My Heartbeat**	MGM 13310
4/03/65	**5**	13	3 **Silhouettes**	MGM 13332
4/17/65	**1**[3]	11	4● **Mrs. Brown You've Got A Lovely Daughter**	MGM 13341
5/29/65	**4**	10	5 **Wonderful World**	MGM 13354
7/03/65	**1**[1]	10	6● **I'm Henry VIII, I Am**	MGM 13367
			written in 1911 - popularized in England by Harry Champion	
9/18/65	**7**	10	7 **Just A Little Bit Better**	MGM 13398
12/25/65+	**8**	9	8 **A Must To Avoid**	MGM 13437
2/19/66	**3**	9	9 **Listen People**	MGM 13462
			from the film "When The Boys Meet The Girls"	
4/09/66	**9**	8	10 **Leaning On The Lamp Post**	MGM 13500
			8, 10: from the film "Hold On!"	
7/09/66	**12**	8	11 This Door Swings Both Ways	MGM 13548
10/01/66	**5**	11	12 **Dandy**	MGM 13603
12/03/66	**27**	8	13 East West	MGM 13639

DEBUT DATE	PEAK POS	WKS CHR	ARTIST — Record Title	Label & Number
			HERMAN'S HERMITS — Cont'd	
2/11/67	**4**	12	14 ● **There's A Kind Of Hush/**	
2/18/67	**35**	10	15 No Milk Today	MGM 13681
6/24/67	**18**	7	16 Don't Go Out Into The Rain (You're Going To Melt)	MGM 13761
8/26/67	**39**	6	17 Museum	MGM 13787
1/13/68	**22**	11	18 I Can Take Or Leave Your Loving	MGM 13885
5/11/68	**61**	6	19 Sleepy Joe all of above produced by Mickie Most	MGM 13934
			PATRICK HERNANDEZ Born in 1949 in Paris, France of a Spanish father and Austrian/Italian mother. Rock/disco artist.	
6/23/79	**16**	19	1 ● Born To Be Alive	Columbia 10986
			THE HESITATIONS Soul group from Cleveland. Lead singer George "King" Scott was accidentally killed by a bullet from a gun owned by tenor Fred Deal in February, 1968.	
1/06/68	**38**	10	1 Born Free from the film of the same title	Kapp 878
3/16/68	**42**	8	2 The Impossible Dream from the Broadway musical "Man Of La Mancha"	Kapp 899
5/25/68	**90**	3	3 Climb Every Mountain from the Rodger & Hammerstein musical "The Sound of Music"	Kapp 911
11/09/68	**100**	2	4 A Whiter Shade Of Pale	Kapp 948
			HOWARD HEWETT Leader of Shalamar. Born and raised in Akron, Ohio.	
11/08/86	**90**	3	1 I'm For Real backing musicians: George Duke, Stanley Clarke and Wilton Felder	Elektra 69527
			THE HEYETTES Female trio: Julia Tillman, Maxine Willard and Jessica Smith.	
4/10/76	**91**	6	1 The Fonz Song [N]	London 232
			EDDIE HEYWOOD Born on 12/4/15 in Atlanta. Black jazz pianist, composer, arranger. Worked with Billie Holiday.	
6/23/56	**2**[2]	31	1 **Canadian Sunset** [I] **HUGO WINTERHALTER with EDDIE HEYWOOD**	RCA 6537
6/30/56	**11**	25	2 Soft Summer Breeze [I] Best Seller #11 / Top 100 #12 / Juke Box #13 / Jockey #14 Heywood wrote above 2 hits	Mercury 70863
			HEYWOODS - see BO DONALDSON	
			THE HI-FI FOUR White pop vocal quartet.	
2/18/56	**93**	1	1 Band Of Gold	King 4856
			AL HIBBLER Born on 8/16/15 in Little Rock, Arkansas. Blind since birth, studied voice at Little Rock's Conservatory for the Blind. First recorded with Jay McShann for Decca in 1942. With Duke Ellington, 1943-51. Also recorded with Harry Carney, Tab Smith, Mercer Ellington and Billy Strayhorn.	
4/09/55	**3**	19	1 **Unchained Melody** Jockey #3 / Juke Box #3 / Best Seller #5 from the film "Unchained"	Decca 29441
10/15/55	**4**	22	2 **He** Best Seller #4 / Top 100 #7 / Jockey #7 / Juke Box #8	Decca 29660
2/04/56	**21**	16	3 11th Hour Melody	Decca 29789
6/16/56	**22**	7	4 Never Turn Back/ Jockey #22 / Top 100 #48	
8/18/56	**77**	2	5 Away All Boats from the film of the same title	Decca 29950
8/04/56	**10**	20	6 **After The Lights Go Down Low** Jockey #10 / Juke Box #14 / Top 100 #15 / Best Seller #20	Decca 29982
2/02/57	**92**	1	7 Trees orchestra directed by Jack Pleis on all of above	Decca 30176
			ERSEL HICKEY Rockabilly singer/guitarist from New York City.	
4/28/58	**75**	6	1 Bluebirds Over The Mountain	Epic 9263

DEBUT DATE	PEAK POS	WKS CHR	ARTIST — Record Title	Label & Number
			BERTIE HIGGINS	
			Singer, songwriter from Florida. Toured and recorded with the Roemans, 1964-66.	
11/14/81+	**8**	29	1 **Key Largo**	Kat Family 02524
			inspired by Humphrey Bogart/Lauren Bacall film of the same title	
5/01/82	**46**	10	2 Just Another Day In Paradise	Kat Family 02839
			HIGH INERGY	
			Female soul group consisting of Barbara Mitchell, Linda Howard, Michelle Rumph and Vernessa Mitchell. Vernessa left in 1978, group continued as a trio.	
9/17/77	**12**	22	1 You Can't Turn Me Off (In The Middle Of Turning Me On)	Gordy 7155
3/04/78	**89**	5	2 Love Is All You Need	Gordy 7157
5/21/83	**82**	5	3 He's A Pretender	Gordy 1662
			THE HIGH KEYS	
			R&B vocal group: Troy Keyes, Jimmy Williams, Bobby Haggard and Cliff Rice.	
7/27/63	**47**	9	1 Que Sera, Sera (Whatever Will Be, Will Be)	Atco 6268
			THE HIGHLIGHTS	
			Frank Pizani, lead singer.	
10/20/56	**19**	18	1 City Of Angels	Bally 1016
			Best Seller #19 / Top 100 #30	
4/20/57	**84**	1	2 To Be With You	Bally 1027
			THE HIGHWAYMEN	
			Folk quintet formed at Wesleyan University in Middletown, Connecticut: Dave Fisher, Bob Burnett, Steve Trott, Steve Butts and Chan Daniels (died on 8/2/75).	
7/10/61	**1**[2]	17	1 **Michael**	United Art. 258
			traditional folk song ("Michael Row The Boat Ashore") from the 19th century	
11/06/61	**42**	10	2 The Gypsy Rover/	
11/27/61+	**13**	18	3 Cotton Fields	United Art. 370
			traditional American ballad, copyrighted in 1850	
4/14/62	**90**	1	4 I'm On My Way	United Art. 439
7/14/62	**64**	6	5 The Bird Man	United Art. 475
			narration by Burt Lancaster; from film "The Bird Man Of Alcatraz"	
			BUNKER HILL	
			Born David Walker on 5/5/41 in Washington, DC. Professional boxer. Ex-lead singer with gospel group, The Mighty Clouds Of Joy.	
8/25/62	**33**	13	1 Hide & Go Seek, Part I	Mala 451
			DAN HILL	
			Born on 6/3/54 in Toronto, Canada.	
1/24/76	**67**	6	1 Growin' Up	20th Century 2254
11/26/77+	**3**	22	2 ● **Sometimes When We Touch**	20th Century 2355
8/12/78	**41**	9	3 All I See Is Your Face	20th Century 2378
11/25/78	**91**	3	4 Let The Song Last Forever	20th Century 2392
			DAVID HILL	
			Born on 9/18/36 in New York City.	
4/20/59	**90**	2	1 Two Brothers	Kapp 266
10/19/59	**92**	2	2 Living Doll	Kapp 293
			JESSIE HILL	
			Born on 12/9/32 in New Orleans. R&B singer, drummer, pianist. With Huey Smith to 1958.	
3/28/60	**28**	16	1 Ooh Poo Pah Doo - Part II [I]	Minit 607
7/25/60	**91**	1	2 Whip It On Me	Minit 611
			Z.Z. HILL	
			Born Arzell Hill on 9/29/41 in Naples, Texas. Died on 4/27/84 in Dallas of a heart attack. Blues vocalist. Formed own Hill Records in 1970.	
3/07/64	**100**	1	1 You Were Wrong	M.H. 200
2/27/71	**62**	5	2 Don't Make Me Pay For His Mistakes	Hill 222
6/19/71	**86**	3	3 I Need Someone (To Love Me)	Kent 4547
			THE HILLSIDE SINGERS	
			9-member vocal group assembled by producer/arranger Al Ham.	
11/27/71+	**13**	12	1 I'd Like To Teach The World To Sing (In Perfect Harmony)	Metromedia 231
			adapted from a "Coca-Cola" jingle	

DEBUT DATE	PEAK POS	WKS CHR	ARTIST — Record Title	Label & Number
			THE HILLSIDE SINGERS — Cont'd	
2/26/72	**100**	1	2 We're Together adapted from a "McDonalds" jingle	Metromedia 241
			THE HILLTOPPERS Quartet formed at Western Kentucky College in Bowling Green, Kentucky in 1952. Group named after the school's nickname. Consisted of: Jimmy Sacca (lead singer), Don McGuire, Seymour Spiegelman and Billy Vaughn. Vaughn left in 1955 to become Dot's musical director with a recording career of his own.	
7/30/55	**20**	4	1 The Kentuckian Song Best Seller #20 from the Burt Lancaster film "The Kentuckian"	Dot 15375
11/12/55	**8**	19	2 **Only You (And You Alone)** Jockey #8 / Top 100 #9 / Juke Box #10 / Best Seller #16	Dot 15423
11/12/55	**81**	2	3 Searching	Dot 15415
12/31/55+	**31**	7	4 My Treasure	Dot 15437
9/15/56	**38**	10	5 Ka-Ding-Dong	Dot 15489
2/09/57	**3**	16	6 **Marianne** Juke Box #3 / Jockey #6 / Top 100 #8 / Best Seller #12	Dot 15537
4/27/57	**74**	1	7 I'm Serious/	
4/27/57	**75**	4	8 I Love My Girl	Dot 15560
7/15/57	**58**	10	9 A Fallen Star	Dot 15594
11/25/57	**22**	13	10 The Joker (That's What They Call Me) Jockey #22 / Best Seller #34 / Top 100 #37	Dot 15662
			ERIC HINE British born singer, songwriter, keyboardist.	
8/22/81	**73**	5	1 Not Fade Away	Montage 1200
			JOE HINTON Soul singer, born in 1929; died on 8/13/68 in Boston. With Chosen Gospel Singers; lead singer of the Spirits Of Memphis gospel group.	
6/01/63	**88**	3	1 You Know It Ain't Right	Back Beat 537
10/12/63	**89**	1	2 Better To Give Than Receive	Back Beat 539
8/15/64	**13**	12	3 Funny	Back Beat 541
			THE HIPPIES	
4/13/63	**63**	5	1 Memory Lane	Parkway 863
			AL HIRT Born Alois Maxwell Hirt on 11/7/22 in New Orleans. Trumpet virtuoso. Toured with Jimmy & Tommy Dorsey, Ray McKinley and Horace Heidt. Formed own dixieland combo (with clarinetist Pete Fountain) in the late 50s.	
1/04/64	**4**	16	1 **Java** [I]	RCA 8280
4/11/64	**15**	12	2 Cotton Candy [I]	RCA 8346
7/11/64	**30**	7	3 Sugar Lips [I]	RCA 8391
10/10/64	**85**	5	4 Up Above My Head (I Hear Music In The Air)	RCA 8439
1/16/65	**47**	7	5 Fancy Pants [I]	RCA 8487
4/17/65	**57**	7	6 Al's Place [I] all of above produced by Chet Atkins	RCA 8542
9/11/65	**96**	2	7 The Silence (Il Silenzio) [I]	RCA 8653
1/27/68	**100**	1	8 Keep The Ball Rollin'	RCA 9417
			DON HO & The Aliis Don was born on 8/13/30 in Oahu, Hawaii. Nightclub singer, actor.	
11/26/66+	**57**	17	1 Tiny Bubbles	Reprise 0507
			CHRIS HODGE British singer, songwriter.	
6/03/72	**44**	8	1 We're On Our Way	Apple 1850
			HODGES, JAMES & SMITH Female soul trio: Pat Hodges, Denita James and Jessica Smith.	
7/09/77	**96**	6	1 Since I Fell For You/I'm Falling In Love medley produced by William "Mickey" Stevenson (Jessica was his secretary)	London 256
			EDDIE HODGES Born on 3/5/47 in Hattiesburg, MS. Played Frank Sinatra's son in the film "A Hole In The Head".	
6/19/61	**12**	13	1 I'm Gonna Knock On Your Door	Cadence 1397
1/27/62	**65**	6	2 Bandit Of My Dreams	Cadence 1410

DEBUT DATE	PEAK POS	WKS CHR	ARTIST — Record Title	Label & Number
			EDDIE HODGES — Cont'd	
6/23/62	**14**	11	3 (Girls, Girls, Girls) Made To Love written by Phil Everly (of The Everly Brothers)	Cadence 1421
7/03/65	**44**	9	4 New Orleans	Aurora 153
			ROGER HODGSON Born on 5/21/50 in London. Founding member and lead singer of Supertramp.	
10/13/84	**48**	15	1 Had A Dream (Sleeping With The Enemy)	A&M 2678
			HOG HEAVEN Rock group led by Peter Lucia and Michael Vale (formerly with Tommy James & The Shondells).	
4/24/71	**98**	2	1 Happy	Roulette 7101
			RON HOLDEN Born on 8/7/39 in Seattle.	
4/04/60	**7**	19	1 **Love You So** instrumental backing by The Thunderbirds	Donna 1315
			CHICO HOLIDAY Pop singer from Milwaukee who later became a gospel artist.	
5/04/59	**74**	6	1 Young Ideas	RCA 7499
			JIMMY HOLIDAY Born on 7/24/34 in Durant, Mississippi. Soul singer, songwriter. Died of heart failure on 2/15/87.	
3/16/63	**57**	9	1 How Can I Forget	Everest 2022
9/03/66	**98**	1	2 Baby I Love You	Minit 32002
			THE HOLIDAYS R&B trio: Edwin Starr, J.J. Barnes and Steve Mancha.	
5/07/66	**63**	9	1 I'll Love You Forever	Golden World 36
			DANNY HOLIEN Born on 1/29/49 in Red Wing, Minnesota. Singer, songwriter, guitarist.	
9/09/72	**66**	8	1 Colorado	Tumbleweed 1004
			AMY HOLLAND Daughter of country singer Esmeraldy and opera singer Harry Boersma. Also see Chris Christian.	
8/09/80	**22**	16	1 How Do I Survive produced by Michael McDonald (of The Doobie Brothers)	Capitol 4884
			BRIAN HOLLAND Born on 2/15/41 in Detroit. Singer, songwriter, producer. Also see Lamont Dozier.	
1/06/73	**52**	6	1 Don't Leave Me Starvin' For Your Love (Part 1)	Invictus 9133
			EDDIE HOLLAND Born on 10/30/39 in Detroit. Singer, songwriter, record producer. Teamed with brother Brian and Lamont Dozier in successful songwriting and record production team for Motown. Wrote many of Motown's all-time greatest hits.	
1/20/62	**30**	13	1 Jamie	Motown 1021
2/08/64	**76**	5	2 Leaving Here	Motown 1052
5/23/64	**54**	7	3 Just Ain't Enough Love	Motown 1058
8/29/64	**58**	6	4 Candy To Me	Motown 1063
			JENNIFER HOLLIDAY Born on 10/19/60 in Houston. Tony award winner for Best Actress in Broadway's "Dreamgirls".	
7/03/82	**22**	14	1 And I Am Telling You I'm Not Going from the original Broadway cast "Dreamgirls"	Geffen 29983
10/22/83	**49**	11	2 I Am Love	Geffen 29525
9/21/85	**69**	7	3 Hard Times For Lovers	Geffen 28958
2/08/86	**87**	3	4 No Frills Love	Geffen 28845
			THE HOLLIES Formed in Manchester, England in 1962. Consisted of Allan Clarke, lead vocals; Graham Nash and Tony Hicks, guitar; Eric Haydock, bass; and Don Rathbone, drums. Clarke and Nash had worked as duo, the Guytones, added other members, became the Fourtones, Deltas, then The Hollies. First recorded for Parlophone in 1963. Rathbone left in 1963, replaced by Bobby Elliott. Haydock left in 1966, replaced by Bernie Calvert (first heard on "Bus Stop"). Nash left in December, 1968, replaced by Terry Sylvester, formerly in the Swingin' Blue Jeans. Regrouped in 1983 with Clarke, Nash, Hicks and Elliott.	
5/16/64	**98**	1	1 Just One Look	Imperial 66026
11/20/65+	**32**	12	2 Look Through Any Window	Imperial 66134

DEBUT DATE	PEAK POS	WKS CHR	ARTIST — Record Title	Label & Number
			THE HOLLIES — Cont'd	
3/19/66	**42**	10	3 I Can't Let Go	Imperial 6615[illegible]
7/23/66	**5**	14	4 **Bus Stop**	Imperial 661[illegible]
10/29/66	**7**	10	5 **Stop Stop Stop**	Imperial 66214
3/18/67	**11**	14	6 On A Carousel	Imperial 66231
6/03/67	**28**	7	7 Pay You Back With Interest	Imperial 66240
6/17/67	**9**	13	8 **Carrie-Anne**	Epic 10180
9/30/67	**44**	7	9 Just One Look [R]	Imperial 66258
10/07/67	**51**	5	10 King Midas In Reverse	Epic 10234
12/02/67	**50**	8	11 Dear Eloise	Epic 10251
3/16/68	**40**	11	12 Jennifer Eccles	Epic 10298
9/14/68	**93**	1	13 Do The Best You Can	Epic 10361
4/19/69	**56**	8	14 Sorry Suzanne	Epic 10454
12/20/69+	**7**	18	15 **He Ain't Heavy, He's My Brother**	Epic 10532
5/30/70	**82**	4	16 I Can't Tell The Bottom From The Top	Epic 10613
6/24/72	**2**[2]	15	17● **Long Cool Woman (In A Black Dress)**	Epic 10871
11/04/72	**26**	11	18 Long Dark Road	Epic 10920
2/10/73	**60**	8	19 Magic Woman Touch	Epic 10951
4/20/74	**6**	21	20● **The Air That I Breathe**	Epic 11100
4/12/75	**85**	2	21 Sandy	Epic 50086
6/28/75	**71**	3	22 Another Night	Epic 50110
			all of above produced by Ron Richards	
6/04/83	**29**	12	23 Stop In The Name Of Love	Atlantic 89819
			BRENDA HOLLOWAY	
			Born on 6/21/46 in Atascadero, California. Soul singer, songwriter.	
5/02/64	**13**	10	1 Every Little Bit Hurts	Tamla 54094
8/08/64	**60**	5	2 I'll Always Love You	Tamla 54099
3/06/65	**25**	9	3 When I'm Gone	Tamla 54111
6/05/65	**78**	5	4 Operator	Tamla 54115
4/22/67	**69**	5	5 Just Look What You've Done	Tamla 54148
9/09/67	**39**	10	6 You've Made Me So Very Happy	Tamla 54155
			LOLEATTA HOLLOWAY	
			Soul singer from Chicago. Former member of the Caravans gospel troupe.	
3/15/75	**68**	6	1 Cry To Me	Aware 047
2/05/77	**72**	9	2 Dreamin	Gold Mind 4000
11/04/78	**87**	5	3 Only You	Gold Mind 4012
			LOLEATTA HOLLOWAY & BUNNY SIGLER	
			BUDDY HOLLY	
			Born Charles Hardin Holley on 9/7/36 in Lubbock, Texas. Began recording (western & bop) demos with Bob Montgomery in 1954. Signed to Decca label in January, 1956, and recorded in Nashville as Buddy Holly & The Three Tunes (Sonny Curtis, lead guitar; Don Guess, bass; and Jerry Allison, drums). In February of 1957, Buddy assembled his backing group, The Crickets (Allison; Niki Sullivan, rhythm guitar; and Joel B. Mauldin, bass) for recordings at Norman Petty's studio in Clovis, New Mexico. Signed to Brunswick and Coral labels (subsidiaries of Decca Records). Because of contract arrangements, all Brunswick records released as The Crickets, and all Coral records released as Buddy Holly. Buddy moved to New York and split with The Crickets in the autumn of 1958. Buddy, Ritchie Valens and the Big Bopper were killed in a plane crash near Mason City, Iowa on 2/3/59 (22).	
8/12/57	**1**[1]	22	1● **That'll Be The Day**	Brunswick 55009
			Best Seller #1 / Top 100 #3 / Jockey #3	
11/11/57	**3**	22	2 **Peggy Sue**	Coral 61885
			Best Seller #3 / Top 100 #3 / Jockey #3	
			first known as "Cindy Lou"; renamed after Allison's girlfriend	
11/25/57+	**10**	20	3 **Oh, Boy!**	Brunswick 55035
			Top 100 #10 / Best Seller #11 / Jockey #20	
3/03/58	**17**	14	4 Maybe Baby	Brunswick 55053
			Jockey #17 / Best Seller #18 / Top 100 #18	
5/26/58	**37**	10	5 Rave On	Coral 61985
			Top 100 #37 / Best Seller #41	
7/21/58	**27**	8	6 Think It Over/	
			Hot 100 #27 / Best Seller #38	
8/04/58	**58**	1	7 Fool's Paradise	Brunswick 55072
			all of above Brunswick records shown only as: **THE CRICKETS**	
8/04/58	**32**	7	8 Early In The Morning	Coral 62006
			Hot 100 #32 / Best Seller #45	
12/28/58+	**82**	4	9 Heartbeat	Coral 62051

DEBUT DATE	PEAK POS	WKS CHR	ARTIST — Record Title	Label & Number
			BUDDY HOLLY — Cont'd	
2/23/59	**13**	14	10 It Doesn't Matter Anymore/	
			written by Paul Anka	
3/30/59	**88**	2	11 Raining In My Heart	Coral 62074
			1-7 & 9: produced by Norman Petty	
			8, 10 & 11: produced by Dick Jacobs	
			THE HOLLYRIDGE STRINGS	
			Stu Phillips - arranger/conductor.	
7/04/64	**93**	1	1 All My Loving [I]	Capitol 5207
			written by John Lennon & Paul McCartney	
			HOLLYWOOD ARGYLES	
			Gary Paxton recorded "Alley-Oop" as a solo artist, however, because he was still under contract to Brent Records, where he recorded as Flip of "Skip & Flip", he made up the name of the Hollywood Argyles. After the song was a hit, Gary assembled a Hollywood Argyles group.	
5/30/60	**1**[1]	15	1 **Alley-Oop** [N]	Lute 5905
			written by Dallas Frazier	
			HOLLYWOOD FLAMES	
			Los Angeles-based R&B group formed by Bobby Day. Known also as The Flames, Four Flames, Hollywood Four Flames, and The Satellites. Earl Nelson (of Bob & Earl) was lead singer on "Buzz-Buzz-Buzz".	
11/25/57+	**11**	17	1 Buzz-Buzz-Buzz/	
			Top 100 #11 / Best Seller #12	
		1	2 Crazy	Ebb 119
			Best Seller flip	
			THE HOLLYWOOD STARS	
			Rock quintet from Los Angeles. Mark Anthony, lead singer.	
5/14/77	**94**	4	1 All The Kids On The Street	Arista 0241
			MICHAEL HOLM	
			German singer/songwriter/producer.	
12/14/74+	**53**	7	1 When A Child Is Born	Mercury 73642
			EDDIE HOLMAN	
			Born on 6/3/46 in Norfolk, Virginia. Soul singer, songwriter. First recorded for Leopard in the early 60s.	
1/15/66	**57**	11	1 This Can't Be True	Parkway 960
12/27/69+	**2**[1]	14	2● **Hey There Lonely Girl**	ABC 11240
			recorded in 1963 by Ruby & The Romantics as "Hey There Lonely Boy"	
4/04/70	**48**	8	3 Don't Stop Now/	
		2	4 Since I Don't Have You	ABC 11261
6/25/77	**90**	2	5 This Will Be A Night To Remember	Salsoul 2026
			CLINT HOLMES	
			Born on 5/9/46 in Bournemouth, England; moved to Buffalo, New York as a child.	
3/24/73	**2**[2]	23	1● **Playground In My Mind**	Epic 10891
			child's vocal is by producer Paul Vance's son, Philip	
			JAKE HOLMES	
			Born John Grier Holmes on 12/28/39 in San Francisco. Singer, songwriter.	
10/03/70	**49**	11	1 So Close	Polydor 14041
			LEROY HOLMES	
			Born Alvin Holmes on 9/22/13 in Pittsburgh. Orchestra conductor/arranger. Music director for MGM and United Artists Records.	
8/11/56	**95**	1	1 Theme From 'The Proud Ones' [I]	MGM 12275
			from the film of the same title	
9/08/56	**59**	7	2 When The White Lilacs Bloom Again [I]	MGM 12317
			RICHARD "GROOVE" HOLMES	
			Born on 5/2/31 in Camden, New Jersey. Jazz organist.	
6/25/66	**44**	11	1 Misty [I]	Prestige 401
10/01/66	**96**	3	2 What Now My Love	Prestige 427
10/01/66	**99**	2	3 Secret Love [I]	Pacific Jazz 88130
			RUPERT HOLMES	
			Born on 2/24/47 in Cheshire, England. Moved to New York at age 6. Wrote and arranged for The Drifters, Platters, and Gene Pitney. Arranged/produced for Barbra Streisand.	
9/02/78	**72**	6	1 Let's Get Crazy Tonight	Private S. 45199
10/20/79	**1**[3]	21	2● **Escape (The Pina Colada Song)**	Infinity 50035
1/19/80	**6**	17	3 **Him**	MCA 41173

DEBUT DATE	PEAK POS	WKS CHR	ARTIST — Record Title	Label & Number
			RUPERT HOLMES — Cont'd	
5/03/80	**32**	11	4 Answering Machine	MCA 41235
11/08/80	**68**	7	5 Morning Man	MCA 51019
4/04/81	**56**	7	6 I Don't Need You	MCA 51092
			THE HOMBRES	
			Memphis, Tennessee foursome.	
9/16/67	**12**	13	1 Let It Out (Let It All Hang Out)	Verve Fore. 5058
			HOMER & JETHRO	
			Real names: Henry Haynes & Kenneth Burns, country music's foremost comedy duo from the 1940s until Homer's death on 8/7/71 (54); Jethro went on to work with popular folk singer Steve Goodman.	
9/07/59	**14**	10	1 The Battle Of Kookamonga [C]	RCA 7585
			a parody of "The Battle Of New Orleans" - produced by Chet Atkins	
			THE HONDELLS	
			Southern California-based quartet led by Ritchie Burns.	
9/12/64	**9**	12	1 **Little Honda**	Mercury 72324
12/12/64+	**87**	4	2 My Buddy Seat	Mercury 72366
			above 2 written by Brian Wilson of The Beach Boys	
5/28/66	**52**	9	3 Younger Girl	Mercury 72563
			THE HONEYCOMBS	
			English rock quintet featuring Dennis D'ell (lead singer) and Ann "Honey" Lantree (drums).	
9/19/64	**5**	13	1 **Have I The Right?**	Interphon 7707
12/19/64+	**48**	7	2 I Can't Stop	Interphon 7713
			THE HONEY CONE	
			Female soul trio formed in Los Angeles in 1969. Consisted of Carolyn Willis ("Girlfriends" and "Bob B. Soxx & The Blue Jeans"), Edna Wright (sister of Darlene Love - formerly with the Raellettes) and Shellie Clark ("Ikettes"). All members had extensive experience as back-up singers.	
6/28/69	**62**	8	1 While You're Out Looking For Sugar?	Hot Wax 6901
11/08/69	**68**	6	2 Girls It Ain't Easy	Hot Wax 6903
4/10/71	**1**[1]	16	3 ● **Want Ads**	Hot Wax 7011
8/07/71	**11**	12	4 ● Stick-Up	Hot Wax 7106
11/20/71+	**15**	11	5 One Monkey Don't Stop No Show (Part I)	Hot Wax 7110
2/19/72	**23**	11	6 The Day I Found Myself	Hot Wax 7113
7/29/72	**96**	4	7 Sittin' On A Time Bomb (Waitin' For The Hurt To Come)	Hot Wax 7205
			THE HONEYCONES	
7/28/58	**69**	2	1 Op	Ember 1036
			THE HONEYDRIPPERS	
			A rock superstar gathering: Robert Plant, Jimmy Page, Jeff Beck and Nile Rodgers.	
10/13/84+	**3**	20	1 **Sea Of Love**	Es Paranza 99701
1/05/85	**25**	11	2 Rockin' At Midnight	Es Paranza 99686
			recorded by Elvis Presley in 1954 as "Good Rockin' Tonight"	
			HONEYMOON SUITE	
			Rock quintet from Toronto, Canada featuring Johnny Dee (lead singer) and Derry Grehan (guitar).	
9/08/84	**57**	7	1 New Girl Now	Warner 29208
3/08/86	**34**	16	2 Feel It Again	Warner 28779
7/12/86	**52**	16	3 What Does It Take	Warner 28670
			from the film "One Crazy Summer"	
			JOHN LEE HOOKER	
			Born on 8/22/17 in Clarksdale, MS. Internationally known blues singer/guitarist. Featured in the movie "The Blues Brothers".	
5/26/62	**60**	10	1 Boom Boom	Vee-Jay 438
			HOOTERS	
			Philadelphia rock quintet led by Rob Hyman & Eric Bazilian (arrangers, musicians and backing vocalists on Cyndi Lauper's "She's So Unusual" LP). Hooter: nickname of their keyboard-harmonica.	
5/18/85	**58**	11	1 All You Zombies	Columbia 04854
8/10/85	**21**	20	2 And We Danced	Columbia 05568
12/14/85+	**18**	18	3 Day By Day	Columbia 05730
4/05/86	**38**	12	4 Where Do The Children Go	Columbia 05854

DEBUT DATE	PEAK POS	WKS CHR	ARTIST — Record Title	Label & Number
			MARY HOPKIN	
			Born on 5/3/50 in Pontardame, Wales. Discovered by the model, Twiggy.	
9/28/68	2[3]	14	1 ● **Those Were The Days**	Apple 1801
			melody based on a traditional Russian folk song	
4/19/69	13	9	2 Goodbye	Apple 1806
2/21/70	39	8	3 Temma Harbour	Apple 1816
7/11/70	77	5	4 Que Sera, Sera (Whatever Will Be, Will Be)	Apple 1823
			1, 2 & 4: produced by Paul McCartney	
11/21/70	87	4	5 Think About Your Children	Apple 1825
12/09/72	92	4	6 Knock Knock Who's There	Apple 1855
			LINDA HOPKINS - see JACKIE WILSON	
			JIMMY "BO" HORNE	
			Soul singer/dancer from Miami.	
4/01/78	38	18	1 Dance Across The Floor	Sunshine S. 1003
			written and produced by Harry "KC" Casey	
			LENA HORNE	
			Born on 6/30/17 in Brooklyn. Beautiful Broadway and movie musical star, long married to bandleader Lennie Hayton. Lena's remarkable career reached a new peak in the 1980s with her triumphant one-woman Broadway show.	
7/09/55	19	1	1 Love Me Or Leave Me	RCA 6073
			Jockey #19	
			first popularized in 1929 by Ruth Etting (POS 2)	
11/23/63	92	2	2 Now!	20th Century 449
			BRUCE HORNSBY & THE RANGE	
			Piano-based, jazz influenced pop quintet led by singer, songwriter, pianist Hornsby, who was raised in Williamsburg, Virginia and moved to Los Angeles in 1980.	
7/26/86	72	9	1 Every Little Kiss	RCA 14361
			new mix charted on 5/16/87	
9/20/86	1[1]	22	2 **The Way It Is**	RCA 5023
			JAMIE HORTON	
			Songstress from San Diego.	
1/25/60	84	3	1 My Little Marine	Joy 234
			JOHNNY HORTON	
			Born on 4/3/29 in Tyler, Texas. Country singing star on the "Louisiana Hayride Radio Show" during the 50s. First recorded with Cormac Records in 1951. Married to Billie Jean Jones, widow of Hank Williams. Killed in an auto accident on 11/5/60.	
4/27/59	1[6]	21	1 ● **The Battle Of New Orleans**	Columbia 41339
			original melody written in celebration of the final battle of the War of 1812	
8/17/59	81	7	2 Sal's Got A Sugar Lip/	
8/24/59	54	8	3 Johnny Reb	Columbia 41437
3/07/60	3	18	4 **Sink The Bismarck**	Columbia 41568
			inspired by the film of the same title	
7/04/60	69	4	5 Johnny Freedom	Columbia 41685
			inspired by Freedomland, U.S.A.	
9/19/60	4	23	6 **North To Alaska**	Columbia 41782
			from the John Wayne film of the same title	
3/27/61	54	7	7 Sleepy-Eyed John	Columbia 41963
3/31/62	96	2	8 Honky-Tonk Man	Columbia 42302
			HOT	
			Integrated female trio consisting of Gwen Owens, Cathy Carson and Juanita Curiel.	
2/19/77	6	27	1 ● **Angel In Your Arms**	Big Tree 16085
8/27/77	65	5	2 The Right Feeling At The Wrong Time	Big Tree 16099
2/04/78	71	5	3 You Brought The Woman Out Of Me	Big Tree 16108
			HOT BUTTER	
			Stan Free plays the Moog synthesizer.	
7/08/72	9	18	1 **Popcorn** [I]	Musicor 1458
			HOT CHOCOLATE	
			Interracial rock-soul group formed in England by lead singer Errol Brown in 1970.	
2/08/75	8	14	1 **Emma**	Big Tree 16031
5/31/75	28	11	2 Disco Queen	Big Tree 16038
11/01/75+	3	21	3 ● **You Sexy Thing**	Big Tree 16047
4/17/76	42	6	4 Don't Stop It Now	Big Tree 16060
7/16/77	31	11	5 So You Win Again	Big Tree 16096

DEBUT DATE	PEAK POS	WKS CHR	ARTIST — Record Title	Label & Number
			HOT CHOCOLATE — Cont'd	
11/11/78+	**6**	18	6• **Every 1's A Winner**	Infinity 50002
7/14/79	**53**	6	7 Going Through The Motions	Infinity 50016
12/18/82+	**65**	7	8 Are You Getting Enough Happiness	EMI America 8143
			all of above produced by Mickie Most	
			HOTLEGS	
			British trio: Eric Stewart (formerly of The Mindbenders), Kevin Godley and Lol Creme. Graham Gouldman joined the group later on tour. Quartet evolved into 10cc.	
8/22/70	**22**	9	1 Neanderthal Man	Capitol 2886
			HOT SAUCE	
5/20/72	**96**	3	1 Bring It Home (And Give It To Me)	Volt 4076
			HOT-TODDYS - see THE REBELS	
			HOTEL	
			Birmingham, Alabama 6-man pop/rock band formed by lead singer Marc Phillips.	
3/11/78	**71**	7	1 You'll Love Again	Mercury 73979
7/14/79	**54**	8	2 You've Got Another Thing Coming	MCA 41050
9/22/79	**80**	4	3 Hold On To The Night	MCA 41113
7/12/80	**72**	7	4 Half Moon Silver	MCA 41277
			CISSY HOUSTON	
			Real name: Emily Houston. Began career singing with a family gospel group, the Drinkard Singers, which included her nieces Dionne and Dee Dee Warwick. Lead singer of the Sweet Inspirations, 1967-70. Mother of Whitney Houston.	
4/24/71	**92**	2	1 Be My Baby	Janus 145
			DAVID HOUSTON	
			Born on 12/9/37 in Bossier City, Louisiana. Country singer, songwriter, guitarist.	
7/16/66	**24**	15	1 Almost Persuaded	Epic 10025
7/08/67	**89**	5	2 My Elusive Dreams	Epic 10194
			DAVID HOUSTON & TAMMY WYNETTE	
10/07/67	**75**	7	3 You Mean The World To Me	Epic 10224
3/09/68	**98**	2	4 Have A Little Faith	Epic 10291
			all of above hit #1 on Billboard's Country charts	
			THELMA HOUSTON	
			Soul singer/actress from Leland, Mississippi. In films "Norman..Is That You?", "Death Scream" and "The Seventh Dwarf".	
1/31/70	**74**	3	1 Save The Country	Dunhill 4222
12/18/76+	**1**[1]	24	2 **Don't Leave Me This Way**	Tamla 54278
6/04/77	**47**	11	3 If It's The Last Thing I Do	Tamla 54283
3/24/79	**34**	13	4 Saturday Night, Sunday Morning	Tamla 54297
			WHITNEY HOUSTON	
			Born in 1963 in New Jersey. Billboard's "Artist of the Year" for 1986. Daughter of Cissy Houston and cousin of Dionne Warwick. Began career as a fashion model, then worked as a backing vocalist. Also see Teddy Pendergrass.	
5/11/85	**3**	21	1 **You Give Good Love**	Arista 9274
8/17/85	**1**[1]	22	2 **Saving All My Love For You**	Arista 9381
12/07/85+	**1**[2]	23	3 **How Will I Know**	Arista 9434
3/29/86	**1**[3]	18	4 **Greatest Love Of All**	Arista 9466
			originally released as the flip side of "You Give Good Love"	
			EDDY HOWARD	
			Born on 9/12/14 in Woodland, California. Singer with Dick Jurgens band from 1934-40. Composer of "My Last Goodbye" and "Careless". Died on 5/23/63 (48).	
12/17/55	**90**	3	1 The Teen-Ager's Waltz	Mercury 70700
			REUBEN HOWELL	
7/20/74	**86**	3	1 Rings	Motown 1305
			HUDSON & LANDRY	
			Bob Hudson & Ron Landry - Los Angeles disc jockeys (KGBS).	
4/24/71	**43**	14	1 Ajax Liquor Store [C]	Dore 855
1/15/72	**68**	6	2 Ajax Airlines [C]	Dore 868
			HUDSON BROTHERS	
			Bill, Brett and Mark Hudson from Portland. Own humorous TV variety show, summer of 1974; also hosts of kiddie TV show "The Hudson Brothers Razzle Dazzle Comedy Show".	
9/21/74	**21**	14	1 So You Are A Star	Casablanca 0108

DEBUT DATE	PEAK POS	WKS CHR	ARTIST — Record Title	Label & Number
			HUDSON BROTHERS — Cont'd	
6/21/75	**26**	12	2 Rendezvous	Rocket 40417
11/22/75	**57**	5	3 Lonely School Year	Rocket 40464
11/06/76	**70**	6	4 Help Wanted	Arista 0208
			DAVID HUDSON	
6/28/80	**59**	11	1 Honey, Honey	Alston 3750
			"POOKIE" HUDSON	
			James "Pookie" Hudson was lead singer of the R&B doo-wop group, The Spaniels.	
5/25/63	**96**	1	1 I Know I Know	Double-L 711
			THE HUES CORPORATION	
			Black vocal trio based in Los Angeles. Consisted of St. Clair Lee, Fleming Williams and H. Ann Kelley. Williams replaced by Tommy Brown after "Rock The Boat".	
8/11/73	**63**	8	1 Freedom For The Stallion	RCA 0900
5/25/74	**1**[1]	18	2● **Rock The Boat**	RCA 0232
10/12/74	**18**	12	3 Rockin' Soul	RCA 10066
2/22/75	**62**	6	4 Love Corporation	RCA 10200
4/30/77	**92**	2	5 I Caught Your Act	Warner 8334
			HUGHES/THRALL	
			Glenn Hughes (member of Trapeze and Deep Purple) and Pat Thrall (member of Automatic Man and the Pat Travers Band).	
12/18/82+	**79**	5	1 Beg, Borrow Or Steal	Boulevard 03355
			FRED HUGHES	
			Soul singer from Arkansas. To Los Angeles, formed own band, the Creators.	
5/29/65	**23**	10	1 Oo Wee Baby, I Love You	Vee-Jay 684
9/25/65	**96**	3	2 You Can't Take It Away	Vee-Jay 703
7/06/68	**94**	6	3 Send My Baby Back	Wand 1182
			JIMMY HUGHES	
			Soul singer from Alabama. With Singing Clouds gospel group to 1962. Cousin of Percy Sledge.	
6/20/64	**17**	12	1 Steal Away	Fame 6401
9/26/64	**65**	4	2 Try Me	Fame 6403
6/04/66	**65**	6	3 Neighbor, Neighbor	Fame 1003
3/18/67	**90**	2	4 Why Not Tonight	Fame 1011
			HUGO & LUIGI	
			Producers, songwriters and label executives Hugo Peretti and Luigi Creator.	
12/10/55	**90**	1	1 Young Abe Lincoln	Mercury 70721
6/08/59	**86**	5	2 La Plume De Ma Tante	RCA 7518
12/14/59+	**35**	9	3 Just Come Home	RCA 7639
			T.K. HULIN	
8/17/63	**92**	2	1 I'm Not A Fool Anymore	Smash 1830
			THE HULLABALLOOS	
			Bleached blonde rock quartet from England: Ricky Knight, Harry Dunn, Andy Woonton and Geoff Mortimer.	
11/28/64+	**56**	9	1 I'm Gonna Love You Too	Roulette 4587
2/13/65	**74**	6	2 Did You Ever	Roulette 4593
			THE HUMAN BEINZ	
			Cleveland bar band.	
12/09/67+	**8**	15	1 **Nobody But Me**	Capitol 5990
			originally recorded (and written) by The Isley Brothers in 1962	
3/09/68	**80**	5	2 Turn On Your Love Light	Capitol 2119
			THE HUMAN LEAGUE	
			British 6-member electronic pop band, featuring lead singer/synthesizer player Philip Oakey.	
3/06/82	**1**[3]	28	1● **Don't You Want Me**	A&M 2397
5/28/83	**8**	20	2 **(Keep Feeling) Fascination**	A&M 2547
10/01/83	**30**	12	3 Mirror Man	A&M 2587
6/09/84	**64**	5	4 The Lebanon	A&M 2641
9/13/86	**1**[1]	20	5 **Human**	A&M 2861
12/06/86+	**44**	11	6 I Need Your Loving	A&M 2893

DEBUT DATE	PEAK POS	WKS CHR	ARTIST — Record Title	Label & Number
			HUMBLE PIE	
			Hard-rock band formed in late 1968 in Essex, England. Consisted of Peter Frampton (guitar, vocals), Steve Marriott (guitar, vocals), Greg Ridley (bass) and Jerry Shirley (drums). Frampton left in 1971, replaced by Clem Clempson. Disbanded, 1975.	
9/25/71	**73**	8	1 I Don't Need No Doctor	A&M 1282
5/06/72	**52**	8	2 Hot 'N' Nasty	A&M 1349
4/26/80	**52**	7	3 Fool For A Pretty Face (Hurt By Love)	Atco 7216
			ENGELBERT HUMPERDINCK	
			Born Arnold George Dorsey on 5/2/36 in Madras, India. To Leicester, England in 1947. First recorded for Decca in 1958. Met Tom Jones' manager, Gordon Mills, in 1965, who suggested his name change to Engelbert Humperdinck (a famous German opera composer). Starred in his own musical variety TV series in 1970.	
4/08/67	**4**	14	1 **Release Me (And Let Me Love Again)**	Parrot 40011
6/24/67	**20**	6	2 There Goes My Everything	Parrot 40015
9/23/67	**25**	9	3 The Last Waltz	Parrot 40019
12/16/67+	**18**	10	4 Am I That Easy To Forget	Parrot 40023
5/11/68	**19**	9	5 A Man Without Love	Parrot 40027
10/19/68	**31**	9	6 Les Bicyclettes De Belsize	Parrot 40032
3/01/69	**42**	11	7 The Way It Used To Be	Parrot 40036
8/23/69	**38**	7	8 I'm A Better Man	Parrot 40040
12/06/69+	**16**	12	9 Winter World Of Love	Parrot 40044
6/27/70	**43**	8	10 My Marie	Parrot 40049
9/26/70	**47**	11	11 Sweetheart all of above produced by Peter Sullivan	Parrot 40054
3/06/71	**45**	7	12 When There's No You	Parrot 40059
8/21/71	**43**	8	13 Another Time, Another Place	Parrot 40065
4/29/72	**86**	3	14 Too Beautiful To Last theme from the film "Nicholas & Alexandra"	Parrot 40069
8/05/72	**69**	8	15 In Time	Parrot 40071
12/30/72+	**61**	7	16 I Never Said Goodbye	Parrot 40072
6/02/73	**99**	1	17 I'm Leavin' You	Parrot 40073
9/29/73	**91**	3	18 Love Is All	Parrot 40076
10/23/76+	**8**	19	19● **After The Lovin'**	Epic 50270
7/09/77	**97**	3	20 Goodbye My Friend	Epic 50365
12/23/78+	**58**	6	21 This Moment In Time	Epic 50632
3/15/80	**83**	2	22 Love's Only Love	Epic 50844
7/16/83	**77**	5	23 Til You And Your Lover Are Lovers Again	Epic 03817
			DELLA HUMPHREY	
11/30/68	**79**	4	1 Don't Make The Good Girls Go Bad	Arctic 144
			PAUL HUMPHREY & HIS COOL AID CHEMISTS	
			Paul was born on 10/12/35 in Detroit. Session drummer.	
3/13/71	**29**	16	1 Cool Aid [I]	Lizard 21006
			TOMMY HUNT	
			R&B vocalist from Pittsburgh. Real name: Charles Hunt. With The Five Echoes, 1952-53. First recorded for Sabre in 1953. In The Flamingos, 1958-61.	
9/04/61	**48**	10	1 Human	Scepter 1219
1/27/62	**92**	1	2 The Door Is Open	Scepter 1226
11/09/63	**71**	5	3 I Am A Witness	Scepter 1261
			IAN HUNTER	
			Born on 6/3/46 in Shrewsburg, England. Leader of "Mott The Hoople", 1969-74.	
8/11/79	**68**	6	1 Just Another Night	Chrysalis 2352
			IVORY JOE HUNTER	
			Born on 10/10/14 in Kirbyville, Texas. Died of lung cancer on 11/8/74. R&B singer, songwriter, pianist. First recorded in 1933, a cylinder record for the Library of Congress. Own radio shows, KFDM-Beaumont, Texas, early 40s. Own record companies, Ivory and Pacific in 1944. Signed by King Records in 1947, MGM in 1950.	
11/17/56	**12**	22	1 Since I Met You Baby Best Seller #12 / Top 100 #12 / Jockey #14 / Juke Box #14	Atlantic 1111
4/13/57	**43**	16	2 Empty Arms	Atlantic 1128
9/08/58	**94**	1	3 Yes I Want You	Atlantic 1191
3/02/59	**92**	2	4 City Lights	Dot 15880

DEBUT DATE	PEAK POS	WKS CHR	ARTIST — Record Title	Label & Number
			JOHN HUNTER	
			Rock singer/keyboardist from Chicago.	
12/08/84+	**39**	16	1 Tragedy	Private I 04643
			TAB HUNTER	
			Born Arthur Andrew Kelm on 7/11/31 in New York City. Sportsman turned actor in 1952. Very popular on film and TV.	
1/12/57	**1**[6]	21	1 **Young Love/**	
			Top 100 #1(6) / Jockey #1(6) / Juke Box #1(5) / Best Seller #1(4)	
2/02/57	**57**	9	2 Red Sails In The Sunset	Dot 15533
3/23/57	**11**	14	3 Ninety-Nine Ways/	
			Top 100 #11 / Jockey #11 / Best Seller #12 / Juke Box #17	
3/30/57	**74**	3	4 Don't Get Around Much Anymore	Dot 15548
			there were 3 Top 10 versions of this Duke Ellington song in 1943	
10/20/58	**62**	10	5 Jealous Heart	Warner 5008
2/02/59	**31**	11	6 (I'll Be With You In) Apple Blossom Time	Warner 5032
			song hit #2 in 1920 by Charles Harrison	
4/27/59	**68**	5	7 There's No Fool Like A Young Fool	Warner 5051
			JIM HURT	
10/11/80	**90**	4	1 I Love Women	Scotti Br. 605
			FERLIN HUSKY	
			Born on 12/3/27 in Flat River, Missouri. Country singer, songwriter, guitarist. Also recorded as Simon Crum and Terry Preston.	
3/02/57	**4**	27	1 **Gone**	Capitol 3628
			Top 100 #4 / Jockey #4 / Juke Box #4 / Best Seller #5	
			originally recorded by Husky in 1952 as by Terry Preston	
7/08/57	**47**	15	2 A Fallen Star	Capitol 3742
11/28/60+	**12**	18	3 Wings Of A Dove	Capitol 4406
1/06/62	**94**	1	4 The Waltz You Saved For Me	Capitol 4650
			Wayne King's familiar theme song - written by King in 1930	
			WILLIE HUTCH	
			Born Willie McKinley Hutchinson in 1946 in Los Angeles. Producer and writer for Motown from 1970. Debut as performer with "The Mack" soundtrack album in 1973.	
5/19/73	**67**	10	1 Brother's Gonna Work It Out	Motown 1222
8/11/73	**65**	6	2 Slick	Motown 1252
			above 2 from the film "The Mack"	
11/01/75	**41**	6	3 Love Power	Motown 1360
			DANNY HUTTON	
			Member of Three Dog Night.	
10/16/65	**73**	6	1 Roses And Rainbows	HBR 447
			PAUL HYDE & THE PAYOLAS	
			Canadian pop/rock quartet. Paul and guitarist Bob Rock later formed duo Rock & Hyde.	
5/18/85	**84**	4	1 You're The Only Love	A&M 2733
			BRIAN HYLAND	
			Born on 11/12/43 in Queens, NY. Own group, the Delphis, at age 12. In production company with Del Shannon in 1970.	
7/04/60	**1**[1]	15	1 **Itsy Bitsy Teenie Weenie Yellow Polkadot Bikini** [N]	Leader 805
			Brian was a high school sophomore at the time of this recording	
10/10/60	**73**	3	2 (The Clickity Clack Song) Four Little Heels/	
10/24/60	**74**	4	3 That's How Much	Kapp 352
8/07/61	**20**	11	4 Let Me Belong To You	ABC-Para. 10236
11/27/61	**83**	1	5 I'll Never Stop Wanting You	ABC-Para. 10262
3/10/62	**21**	11	6 Ginny Come Lately	ABC-Para. 10294
6/09/62	**3**	14	7 **Sealed With A Kiss**	ABC-Para. 10336
9/22/62	**25**	8	8 Warmed Over Kisses (Left Over Love)	ABC-Para. 10359
11/24/62+	**69**	7	9 I May Not Live To See Tomorrow	ABC-Para. 10374
3/02/63	**88**	2	10 If Mary's There	ABC-Para. 10400
6/29/63	**63**	8	11 I'm Afraid To Go Home	ABC-Para. 10452
4/16/66	**99**	1	12 3000 Miles	Philips 40354
7/16/66	**20**	11	13 The Joker Went Wild	Philips 40377
10/22/66	**25**	9	14 Run, Run, Look And See	Philips 40405
2/18/67	**58**	5	15 Hung Up In Your Eyes	Philips 40424
5/27/67	**94**	3	16 Holiday For Clowns	Philips 40444
8/12/67	**91**	2	17 Get The Message	Philips 40472

DEBUT DATE	PEAK POS	WKS CHR	ARTIST — Record Title	Label & Number
			BRIAN HYLAND — Cont'd	
1/11/69	**56**	10	18 Tragedy	Dot 17176
4/05/69	**90**	5	19 A Million To One	Dot 17222
7/12/69	**82**	3	20 Stay And Love Me All Summer	Dot 17258
9/05/70	**3**	20	21 ● **Gypsy Woman**	Uni 55240
2/13/71	**54**	8	22 Lonely Teardrops above 2 produced by Del Shannon	Uni 55272
			DICK HYMAN Born on 3/8/27 in New York City. Piano playing composer, conductor, arranger who toured Europe with Benny Goodman in 1950. Staff pianist at WMCA and WNBC-New York from 1951-57. Musical director of the Arthur Godfrey Show, 1958-62.	
1/21/56	**8**	20	1 **Moritat (A Theme from "The Three Penny Opera")** [I] Jockey #8 / Top 100 #9 / Best Seller #10 / Juke Box #14	MGM 12149
4/21/56	**78**	5	2 Hi-Lili, Hi-Lo [I] above 2 shown as: **THE DICK HYMAN TRIO** from the 1952 Leslie Caron film "Lili"	MGM 12207
5/31/69	**38**	8	3 The Minotaur [I] **DICK HYMAN & HIS ELECTRIC ECLECTICS**	Command 4126

I

DEBUT DATE	PEAK POS	WKS CHR	ARTIST — Record Title	Label & Number
			JANIS IAN Born Janis Eddy Fink on 4/7/51, New York City. Singer/songwriter/pianist/guitarist.	
5/27/67	**14**	12	1 Society's Child (Baby I've Been Thinking)	Verve 5027
6/14/75	**3**	20	2 **At Seventeen**	Columbia 10154
7/11/81	**71**	4	3 Under The Covers	Columbia 02176
			ICEHOUSE Australian rock quartet led by singer/guitarist Iva Davies. First known as Flowers.	
8/01/81	**62**	7	1 We Can Get Together	Chrysalis 2530
7/05/86	**79**	9	2 No Promises	Chrysalis 42978
			ICICLE WORKS Liverpool rock trio: Ian McNabb, Chris Layhe and Chris Sharrock.	
4/21/84	**37**	12	1 Whisper To A Scream (Birds Fly)	Arista 9155
			THE IDES OF MARCH Rock group formed while classmates at a Chicago high school. Named after a line in Shakespeare's "Julius Caesar". Lead singer Jim Peterik currently leads Survivor.	
6/25/66	**42**	7	1 You Wouldn't Listen	Parrot 304
9/10/66	**92**	1	2 Roller Coaster	Parrot 310
3/28/70	**2**[1]	12	3 **Vehicle**	Warner 7378
7/04/70	**64**	5	4 Superman	Warner 7403
3/13/71	**73**	9	5 L.A. Goodbye	Warner 7466
			BILLY IDOL Born William Broad on 11/30/55 in London, England. Leader of the London punk band, Generation X, 1977-81.	
7/03/82	**23**	17	1 Hot In The City	Chrysalis 2605
5/21/83	**36**	13	2 White Wedding originally "Bubbled Under" on 11/27/82 at POS 108	Chrysalis 42697
1/28/84	**46**	14	3 Rebel Yell	Chrysalis 42762
5/05/84	**4**	22	4 **Eyes Without A Face**	Chrysalis 42786
8/25/84	**29**	12	5 Flesh For Fantasy	Chrysalis 42809
11/03/84	**50**	11	6 Catch My Fall	Chrysalis 42840
10/04/86	**6**	18	7 **To Be A Lover**	Chrysalis 43024
			FRANK IFIELD Born on 11/30/37 in Coventry, England. Began career as a teenager in Australia, with his own radio and TV shows. Signed to Columbia Records in England in 1959.	
9/08/62	**5**	11	1 **I Remember You** tune hit #9 in 1942 by Jimmy Dorsey, for the film "The Fleet's In"	Vee-Jay 457
12/22/62+	**44**	7	2 Lovesick Blues written in 1922 - Ifield's version hit #1 in England	Vee-Jay 477
9/07/63	**58**	7	3 I'm Confessin' (That I Love You) Guy Lombardo and Rudy Vallee both had Top 5 versions in 1930	Capitol 5032
12/14/63+	**71**	6	4 Please tune hit #1 for Bing Crosby in 1932	Capitol 5089

JULIO IGLESIAS

Born on 9/23/43 in Madrid, Spain. Immensely popular Spanish singer, worldwide.

DEBUT DATE	PEAK POS	WKS CHR	ARTIST — Record Title	Label & Number
3/03/84	**5**	21	1 ● **To All The Girls I've Loved Before** — JULIO IGLESIAS & WILLIE NELSON	Columbia 04217
7/07/84	**19**	16	2 All Of You — JULIO IGLESIAS & DIANA ROSS	Columbia 04507

THE IKETTES

Female R&B trio formed for the Ike & Tina Turner Revue. Atco group consisted of lead Delores Johnson, Eloise Hester and Joshie Jo Armstead. Modern group consisted of Robbie Montgomery, Vanetta Fields and Jessie Smith.

DEBUT DATE	PEAK POS	WKS CHR	ARTIST — Record Title	Label & Number
1/13/62	**19**	12	1 I'm Blue (The Gong-Gong Song)	Atco 6212
3/13/65	**36**	8	2 Peaches 'N' Cream	Modern 1005
10/09/65	**74**	7	3 I'm So Thankful	Modern 1011

THE ILLUSION

Rock quintet led by John Vinci.

DEBUT DATE	PEAK POS	WKS CHR	ARTIST — Record Title	Label & Number
7/05/69	**32**	13	1 Did You See Her Eyes	Steed 718
12/20/69+	**80**	4	2 Together	Steed 722
6/27/70	**98**	2	3 Let's Make Each Other Happy	Steed 726

IMPACT

Soul group formed as the Vandalls: Damon Harris, John Simms, Charles Timmons and Donald Tilghman.

DEBUT DATE	PEAK POS	WKS CHR	ARTIST — Record Title	Label & Number
6/19/76	**94**	2	1 Happy Man (Pt. I)	Atco 7049

THE IMPALAS

Pop vocal quartet from Brooklyn: Joe "Speedo" Frazier, Richard Wagner, Lenny Renda and Tony Carlucci. All members, except black lead singer Frazier, are white.

DEBUT DATE	PEAK POS	WKS CHR	ARTIST — Record Title	Label & Number
3/16/59	2^{2}	18	1 **Sorry (I Ran All The Way Home)**	Cub 9022
6/22/59	**86**	5	2 Oh, What A Fool	Cub 9033

THE IMPRESSIONS

Soul group formed in Chicago in 1957. Group, originally known as The Roosters, consisted of Jerry Butler, Curtis Mayfield, Sam Gooden and brothers Arthur and Richard Brooks. Butler left for a solo career in 1958, replaced by Fred Cash. The Brooks brothers left in 1968, leaving Mayfield as the trio's leader. Mayfield left in 1970 for a solo career, replaced by Leroy Hutson. In 1972, Hutson was replaced by Reggie Torian and Ralph Johnson. Did film soundtrack for "Three The Hard Way". Butler, Mayfield, Gooden and Cash reunited for a tour in 1983.

DEBUT DATE	PEAK POS	WKS CHR	ARTIST — Record Title	Label & Number
6/16/58	**11**	12	1 For Your Precious Love — JERRY BUTLER & THE IMPRESSIONS — Best Seller #11 / Top 100 #11 / Jockey #25	Abner/Falcon 1013
10/16/61	**20**	15	2 Gypsy Woman	ABC-Para. 10241
2/17/62	**99**	1	3 Grow Closer Together	ABC-Para. 10289
7/28/62	**96**	1	4 Little Young Lover	ABC-Para. 10328
2/09/63	**73**	6	5 I'm The One Who Loves You	ABC-Para. 10386
5/25/63	**84**	4	6 Sad, Sad Girl And Boy	ABC-Para. 10431
9/28/63	**4**	14	7 **It's All Right**	ABC-Para. 10487
1/18/64	**12**	9	8 Talking About My Baby	ABC-Para. 10511
4/04/64	**14**	11	9 I'm So Proud	ABC-Para. 10544
6/06/64	**10**	13	10 **Keep On Pushing**	ABC-Para. 10554
9/05/64	**15**	10	11 You Must Believe Me	ABC-Para. 10581
11/21/64+	**7**	11	12 **Amen** — song featured in the film "Lillies Of The Field"	ABC-Para. 10602
2/13/65	**14**	8	13 People Get Ready	ABC-Para. 10622
4/03/65	**29**	7	14 Woman's Got Soul	ABC-Para. 10647
6/05/65	**48**	8	15 Meeting Over Yonder	ABC-Para. 10670
8/14/65	**64**	7	16 I Need You	ABC 10710
10/02/65	**76**	5	17 Just One Kiss From You	ABC-Para. 10725
11/20/65+	**33**	9	18 You've Been Cheatin'	ABC-Para. 10750
2/05/66	**90**	2	19 Since I Lost The One I Love	ABC-Para. 10761
4/02/66	**91**	3	20 Too Slow	ABC-Para. 10789
9/03/66	**65**	7	21 Can't Satisfy	ABC 10831
3/04/67	**96**	2	22 You Always Hurt Me	ABC 10900
9/02/67	**80**	4	23 I Can't Stay Away From You	ABC 10964
12/30/67+	**14**	13	24 We're A Winner	ABC 11022
4/20/68	**59**	7	25 We're Rolling On (Part 1)	ABC 11071
7/20/68	**61**	8	26 I Loved And I Lost	ABC 11103

DEBUT DATE	PEAK POS	WKS CHR	ARTIST — Record Title	Label & Number
			THE IMPRESSIONS — Cont'd	
9/07/68	**22**	12	27 Fool For You	Curtom 1932
11/23/68	**71**	4	28 Don't Cry My Love	ABC 11135
11/30/68+	**25**	10	29 This Is My Country	Curtom 1934
4/26/69	**84**	4	30 Seven Years	Curtom 1940
6/28/69	**21**	11	31 Choice Of Colors	Curtom 1943
10/18/69	**58**	9	32 Say You Love Me	Curtom 1946
5/16/70	**28**	12	33 Check Out Your Mind	Curtom 1951
9/05/70	**56**	8	34 (Baby) Turn On To Me	Curtom 1954
2/27/71	**53**	6	35 Ain't Got Time	Curtom 1957
7/31/71	**94**	3	36 Love Me all of above (except #1 & 12) written by Curtis Mayfield	Curtom 1959
5/04/74	**17**	18	37 Finally Got Myself Together (I'm A Changed Man)	Curtom 1997
7/05/75	**68**	8	38 Sooner Or Later	Curtom 0103
11/01/75	**75**	4	39 Same Thing It Took	Curtom 0106
			THE IN CROWD	
12/10/66	**92**	2	1 Questions And Answers	Viva 604
			THE INCREDIBLE BONGO BAND Studio band assembled in Canada by producer Michael Viner.	
7/21/73	**57**	7	1 Bongo Rock [I]	MGM 14588
			THE INDEPENDENTS Soul group consisting of Chuck Jackson, Maurice Jackson, Helen Curry and Eric Thomas. Jackson (no relation to solo singer Chuck Jackson) and Marvin Yancy, producers/writers for the group, later teamed in production work, especially for Natalie Cole.	
5/13/72	**84**	5	1 Just As Long As You Need Me, Part 1	Wand 11245
4/07/73	**21**	13	2 ● Leaving Me	Wand 11252
7/21/73	**41**	8	3 Baby I've Been Missing You	Wand 11258
11/17/73	**65**	4	4 It's All Over	Wand 11263
11/16/74	**88**	4	5 Let This Be A Lesson To You	Wand 11279
			INDUSTRY Long Island, New York rock quartet. Jon Carin, lead singer.	
11/19/83	**81**	8	1 State Of The Nation	Capitol 5268
			JORGEN INGMANN & HIS GUITAR Born Jorgen Ingmann-Pedersen on 4/26/25 in Copenhagen, Denmark.	
1/23/61	**2^2**	17	1 **Apache** [I]	Atco 6184
5/22/61	**54**	6	2 Anna [I] #5 hit in 1953 for Silvana Mangano; from film of the same title	Atco 6195
			JAMES INGRAM R&B vocalist, multi-instrumentalist, composer from Akron, Ohio. To Los Angeles, late 70s, with the band Revelation Funk.	
8/15/81	**17**	23	1 Just Once **QUINCY JONES featuring JAMES INGRAM**	A&M 2357
12/19/81+	**14**	21	2 One Hundred Ways **QUINCY JONES featuring JAMES INGRAM**	A&M 2387
4/24/82+	**1^2**	32	3 ● **Baby, Come To Me** **PATTI AUSTIN with JAMES INGRAM**	Qwest 50036
5/14/83	**45**	17	4 How Do You Keep The Music Playing **JAMES INGRAM & PATTI AUSTIN** theme from the film "Best Friends"	Qwest 29618
12/10/83+	**19**	18	5 Yah Mo B There **JAMES INGRAM with MICHAEL McDONALD**	Qwest 29394
4/07/84	**58**	10	6 There's No Easy Way	Qwest 29316
9/15/84	**15**	19	7 What About Me? **KENNY ROGERS with KIM CARNES & JAMES INGRAM**	RCA 13899
12/20/86+	**2^1**	22	8 **Somewhere Out There** **LINDA RONSTADT & JAMES INGRAM** from the animated film "An American Tail"	MCA 52973
			LUTHER INGRAM Born on 11/30/44 in Jackson, Tennessee. Soul singer, songwriter. First recorded for Smash in 1965. In the film "Wattstax".	
1/10/70	**55**	7	1 My Honey And Me	KoKo 2104
5/23/70	**45**	9	2 Ain't That Loving You (For More Reasons Than One)	KoKo 2105
5/01/71	**97**	2	3 Be Good To Me Baby	KoKo 2107

DEBUT DATE	PEAK POS	WKS CHR	ARTIST — Record Title	Label & Number
			LUTHER INGRAM — Cont'd	
4/08/72	**93**	3	4 You Were Made For Me	KoKo 2110
6/03/72	**3**	16	5 **(If Loving You Is Wrong) I Don't Want To Be Right**	KoKo 2111
12/02/72+	**40**	11	6 I'll Be Your Shelter (In Time Of Storm)	KoKo 2113
4/07/73	**64**	5	7 Always	KoKo 2115
			AUTRY INMAN	
			Country singer, songwriter.	
11/16/68	**48**	7	1 Ballad Of Two Brothers [N]	Epic 10389
			patriotic-styled narrative, featuring strains of "The Battle Hymn Of The Republic"	
			THE INMATES	
			British rock group led by Peter Gunn.	
12/08/79+	**51**	10	1 Dirty Water	Polydor 2032
			THE INNOCENCE	
			Group is actually the singing, songwriting and record producing duo of Pete Anders and Vinnie Poncia - also recorded as The Trade Winds.	
12/03/66+	**34**	8	1 There's Got To Be A Word!	Kama Sutra 214
3/04/67	**75**	3	2 Mairzy Doats	Kama Sutra 222
			tune hit #1 for 5 weeks in 1944 by The Merry Macs	
			THE INNOCENTS	
			Pop trio from Sun Valley, California: James West, Al Candelaria and Darron Stankey. First recorded as The Echoes for Andex in 1959. Back-up vocal group for Kathy Young.	
8/15/60	**28**	10	1 Honest I Do	Indigo 105
11/21/60+	**28**	11	2 Gee Whiz	Indigo 111
			INSTANT FUNK	
			9-man funk ensemble led by James Carmichael.	
2/17/79	**20**	18	1 ● I Got My Mind Made Up (You Can Get It Girl)	Salsoul 2078
			THE INTRIGUES	
			Soul trio from Philadelphia.	
8/02/69	**31**	14	1 In A Moment	Yew 1001
12/20/69+	**86**	3	2 I'm Gonna Love You	Yew 1002
6/19/71	**100**	1	3 The Language Of Love	Yew 1012
			INTRUDERS	
			White instrumental rock trio from Hammonton, NJ: George Mitchell, Angie Mitchell and Joe Rebardo.	
3/23/59	**73**	3	1 Fried Eggs [I]	Fame 101
			THE INTRUDERS	
			Soul group formed in Philadelphia in 1960. Consisted of Sam "Little Sonny" Brown, Eugene "Bird" Daughtry, Phil Terry and Robert "Big Sonny" Edwards. First recorded for Gowen in 1961.	
7/16/66	**78**	6	1 (We'll Be) United	Gamble 201
4/29/67	**48**	9	2 Together	Gamble 205
9/16/67	**70**	5	3 Baby I'm Lonely/	
12/02/67	**82**	3	4 A Love That's Real	Gamble 209
3/23/68	**6**	14	5 ● **Cowboys To Girls**	Gamble 214
7/06/68	**26**	9	6 (Love Is Like A) Baseball Game	Gamble 217
11/09/68	**54**	7	7 Slow Drag	Gamble 221
8/30/69	**47**	9	8 Sad Girl	Gamble 235
6/20/70	**45**	8	9 When We Get Married	Gamble 4004
11/14/70	**85**	4	10 This Is My Love Song	Gamble 4007
3/20/71	**88**	4	11 I'm Girl Scoutin'	Gamble 4009
10/30/71	**92**	4	12 I Bet He Don't Love You (Like I Love You)	Gamble 4016
6/02/73	**36**	12	13 I'll Always Love My Mama (Part 1)	Gamble 2506
10/27/73	**60**	13	14 I Wanna Know Your Name	Gamble 2508
			all of above produced by Kenny Gamble & Leon Huff	
			THE INVISIBLE MAN'S BAND	
			Group evolved from The Five Stairsteps. Consisted of Clarence, Kenny, Dennis and James Burke.	
5/17/80	**45**	10	1 All Night Thing	Mango 103

DEBUT DATE	PEAK POS	WKS CHR	ARTIST — Record Title	Label & Number
			INXS	
			Rock sextet formed in Sydney, Australia: Michael Hutchence (lead singer), Kirk Pengilly, Garry Beers, and brothers Tim, Andy and Jon Farriss.	
3/26/83	**30**	14	1 The One Thing	Atco 99905
7/16/83	**80**	4	2 Don't Change	Atco 99874
4/28/84	**58**	7	3 Original Sin backing vocals: Daryl Hall	Atco 99766
7/21/84	**77**	7	4 I Send A Message	Atco 99731
11/16/85	**81**	6	5 This Time	Atlantic 89497
1/18/86	**5**	20	6 **What You Need**	Atlantic 89460
5/10/86	**54**	9	7 Listen Like Thieves	Atlantic 89429
			DONNIE IRIS	
			Real name: Dominic Ierace. Native of Beaver Falls, PA. Singer, songwriter, guitarist. Leader of the Pittsburgh rock group, The Jaggerz. Toured briefly with the funk group, Wild Cherry.	
12/13/80+	**29**	18	1 Ah! Leah!	MCA 51025
10/31/81	**80**	6	2 Sweet Merilee	MCA 51198
12/19/81+	**37**	14	3 Love Is Like A Rock	MCA 51223
3/27/82	**25**	14	4 My Girl	MCA 52031
10/23/82	**57**	6	5 Tough World	MCA 52127
7/02/83	**64**	7	6 Do You Compute?	MCA 52230
3/23/85	**91**	2	7 Injured In The Game Of Love	HME 04734
			THE IRISH ROVERS	
			Irish-born folk quintet. Group formed in Alberta, Canada in 1964.	
3/23/68	**7**	12	1 **The Unicorn**	Decca 32254
6/22/68	**75**	7	2 (The Puppet Song) Whiskey On A Sunday	Decca 32333
9/14/68	**91**	5	3 The Biplane, Ever More	Decca 32371
2/21/81	**37**	17	4 Wasn't That A Party **THE ROVERS**	Epic 51007
			IRON BUTTERFLY	
			San Diego heavy-metal rock band. Consisted of Doug Ingle (lead vocals, keyboards), Erik Braunn (lead guitar), Lee Dorman (bass) and Ron Bushy (drums). Braunn left in late 1969, replaced by Mike Pinera and Larry Reinhardt.	
8/24/68	**30**	17	1 In-A-Gadda-Da-Vida 7" version edited down from original 17 minute album cut	Atco 6606
2/22/69	**75**	5	2 Soul Experience	Atco 6647
7/12/69	**96**	2	3 In The Time Of Our Lives	Atco 6676
10/24/70	**66**	6	4 Easy Rider (Let The Wind Pay The Way)	Atco 6782
			IRONHORSE	
			Rock band formed by Bachman-Turner Overdrive founder, Randy Bachman.	
3/17/79	**36**	10	1 Sweet Lui-Louise	Scotti Br. 406
4/26/80	**89**	6	2 What's Your Hurry Darlin'	Scotti Br. 512
			BIG DEE IRWIN	
			Real name: Defosca Ervin. R&B vocalist, former lead singer of The Pastels.	
5/25/63	**38**	10	1 Swinging On A Star vocal duet with Little Eva tune hit #1 in 1944 by Bing Crosby (from the film "Going My Way")	Dimension 1010
			THE ISLANDERS	
			Instrumental duo: Randy Starr (New York City) & Frank Metis (Nuremberg, W. Germany).	
9/28/59	**15**	13	1 The Enchanted Sea [I]	Mayflower 16
			ISLE OF MAN	
			Multi-ethnic pop quartet (members are from France, Nicaragua, Italy and U.S.A.). Robere Parlez, lead singer.	
8/09/86	**90**	4	1 Am I Forgiven	Pasha 05900
			THE ISLEY BROTHERS	
			R&B trio of brothers from Cincinnati. Formed in early 1950s as a gospel group. Consisted of O'Kelly, Ronald and Rudolph Isley. Moved to New York in 1957 and first recorded for Teenage Records. Trio added their younger brothers Ernie (guitar, drums) and Marvin Isley (bass, percussion) and brother-in-law Chris Jasper (keyboards), from 1973-84. Formed own label, T-Neck in 1969. O'Kelly died of a heart attack on 3/31/86 (48).	
9/21/59	**47**	9	1 Shout - Part 1	RCA 7588
3/24/62	**94**	3	2 Shout - Part 1 [R]	RCA 0589
6/02/62	**17**	16	3 Twist And Shout	Wand 124

DEBUT DATE	PEAK POS	WKS CHR	ARTIST — Record Title	Label & Number
			THE ISLEY BROTHERS — Cont'd	
9/22/62	**54**	9	4 Twistin' With Linda	Wand 127
2/19/66	**12**	12	5 This Old Heart Of Mine (Is Weak For You)	Tamla 54128
5/28/66	**66**	4	6 Take Some Time Out For Love	Tamla 54133
7/16/66	**61**	7	7 I Guess I'll Always Love You	Tamla 54135
5/06/67	**93**	2	8 Got To Have You Back	Tamla 54146
3/15/69	**2**[1]	14	9● **It's Your Thing**	T-Neck 901
5/31/69	**23**	10	10 I Turned You On	T-Neck 902
8/30/69	**79**	4	11 Black Berries - Pt. 1	T-Neck 906
9/27/69	**83**	5	12 Was It Good To You	T-Neck 908
2/14/70	**75**	5	13 Keep On Doin'	T-Neck 914
7/25/70	**75**	2	14 Girls Will Be Girls, Boys Will Be Boys	T-Neck 921
10/17/70	**89**	3	15 Get Into Something	T-Neck 924
1/23/71	**72**	5	16 Freedom	T-Neck 927
6/19/71	**18**	11	17 Love The One You're With	T-Neck 930
10/02/71	**49**	6	18 Spill The Wine	T-Neck 932
12/04/71+	**71**	5	19 Lay Lady Lay	T-Neck 933
4/01/72	**54**	9	20 Lay-Away	T-Neck 934
7/01/72	**24**	15	21 Pop That Thang	T-Neck 935
10/28/72	**51**	8	22 Work To Do	T-Neck 936
7/14/73	**6**	20	23● **That Lady (Part 1)**	T-Neck 2251
12/29/73+	**55**	11	24 What It Comes Down To	T-Neck 2252
3/23/74	**60**	7	25 Summer Breeze (Part 1)	T-Neck 2253
7/27/74	**52**	16	26 Live It Up (Part 1)	T-Neck 2254
1/04/75	**73**	5	27 Midnight Sky (Part 1)	T-Neck 2255
6/21/75	**4**	18	28● **Fight The Power (Part 1)**	T-Neck 2256
11/15/75	**22**	12	29 For The Love Of You (Part 1 & 2)	T-Neck 2259
5/29/76	**47**	7	30 Who Loves You Better (Part 1)	T-Neck 2260
8/21/76	**63**	11	31 Harvest For The World	T-Neck 2261
5/07/77	**63**	7	32 The Pride (Part 1)	T-Neck 2262
6/25/77	**40**	8	33 Livin' In The Life	T-Neck 2264
10/20/79	**90**	2	34 It's A Disco Night (Rock Don't Stop)	T-Neck 2287
4/19/80	**39**	9	35 Don't Say Goodnight (It's Time For Love) (Parts 1 & 2)	T-Neck 2290
4/18/81	**58**	7	36 Hurry Up And Wait	T-Neck 02033
			ISLEY, JASPER, ISLEY	
			Ernie Isley, Chris Jasper, Marvin Isley - see above Isley Brothers biography.	
2/16/85	**63**	7	1 Kiss And Tell	CBS Assoc. 04741
12/07/85+	**51**	14	2 Caravan Of Love	CBS Assoc. 05611
			THE ITALIAN ASPHALT & PAVEMENT COMPANY	
			Quartet previously known as The Duprees.	
5/02/70	**97**	2	1 Check Yourself	Colossus 110
			IVAN	
			Jerry Ivan Allison was the drummer with Buddy Holly & The Crickets.	
9/22/58	**68**	5	1 Real Wild Child lead guitar and background vocals: Buddy Holly	Coral 62017
			BURL IVES	
			Born on 6/14/09 in Hunt Township, Illinois. One of America's best-known folk singers from the 1940s to 60s. Burl has won equal renown as a dramatic actor in movies, Broadway and TV.	
3/02/57	**84**	5	1 Marianne vocal backing group: The Trinidaddies	Decca 30217
12/18/61+	**9**	14	2 **A Little Bitty Tear**	Decca 31330
4/07/62	**10**	11	3 **Funny Way Of Laughin'**	Decca 31371
7/21/62	**19**	9	4 Call Me Mr. In-Between	Decca 31405
11/03/62	**39**	7	5 Mary Ann Regrets	Decca 31433
1/26/63	**91**	2	6 The Same Old Hurt	Decca 31453
8/03/63	**67**	5	7 This Is All I Ask [S]	Decca 31518
12/28/63+	**66**	6	8 True Love Goes On And On [R] same version charted by Ives in 1954 (POS 23)	Decca 31571
9/12/64	**60**	6	9 Pearly Shells	Decca 31659

DEBUT DATE	PEAK POS	WKS CHR	ARTIST — Record Title	Label & Number
			THE IVEYS - see BADFINGER	
			THE IVY LEAGUE	
			English songwriting team of Carter & Lewis. Wrote "Little Bit O' Soul".	
9/18/65	**83**	5	1 Tossing & Turning	Cameo 377
			THE IVY THREE	
			Formed in 1959 at Adelphi College in New York. Consisted of Charles Koppelman, Art Berkowitz and Don Rubin.	
8/08/60	**8**	10	1 **Yogi** [N]	Shell 720
			based on a character from TV's "Huckleberry Hound" show	

J

DEBUT DATE	PEAK POS	WKS CHR	ARTIST — Record Title	Label & Number
			THE JACKS	
			R&B quintet - see The Cadets for complete biography.	
11/12/55	**82**	3	1 Why Don't You Write Me?	RPM 428
			SUSAN JACKS	
			Maiden name: Susan Pesklevits, from Vancouver, Canada; married to Terry Jacks and recorded with him as The Poppy Family; divorced in 1973.	
3/08/75	**90**	5	1 You're A Part Of Me	Mercury 73649
			TERRY JACKS	
			Native of Winnipeg, Canada. Recorded with wife Susan as The Poppy Family.	
1/12/74	**1** [3]	21	1 ● **Seasons In The Sun**	Bell 45432
			originally recorded by The Kingston Trio in 1964	
6/08/74	**68**	5	2 If You Go Away	Bell 45467
12/07/74	**97**	1	3 Rock 'N' Roll (I Gave You The Best Years Of My Life)	Bell 45606
			BULL MOOSE JACKSON	
			Born Benjamin Jackson in 1919 in Cleveland. R&B singer, saxophonist. One of the first major stars of R&B.	
9/11/61	**98**	2	1 I Love You Yes I Do	7 Arts 705
			new version of his 1947 hit (POS 21) on King 4181	
			CHUCK JACKSON	
			Born on 7/22/37 in Latta, SC. Moved to Pittsburgh as a child. Left college in 1957 to work with the Raspberry Singers gospel group. With The Dell-Vikings, 1957-59. First recorded as a solo for Beltone in 1960.	
2/20/61	**36**	7	1 I Don't Want To Cry	Wand 106
4/10/61	**46**	7	2 (It Never Happens) In Real Life	Wand 108
4/10/61	**91**	1	3 Mr. Pride	Beltone 1005
8/21/61	**59**	8	4 I Wake Up Crying	Wand 110
4/28/62	**23**	12	5 Any Day Now (My Wild Beautiful Bird)	Wand 122
9/01/62	**55**	7	6 I Keep Forgettin'	Wand 126
11/17/62	**88**	4	7 Getting Ready For The Heartbreak	Wand 128
2/02/63	**42**	10	8 Tell Him I'm Not Home	Wand 132
7/06/63	**85**	2	9 Tears Of Joy	Wand 138
11/02/63	**81**	5	10 Any Other Way	Wand 141
3/28/64	**92**	3	11 Hand It Over	Wand 149
5/23/64	**45**	10	12 Beg Me	Wand 154
10/03/64	**93**	2	13 Somebody New	Wand 161
11/14/64	**47**	8	14 Since I Don't Have You	Wand 169
4/24/65	**55**	9	15 Something You Got	Wand 181
			CHUCK JACKSON & MAXINE BROWN	
4/24/65	**75**	4	16 I Need You	Wand 179
8/07/65	**46**	7	17 If I Didn't Love You	Wand 188
8/21/65	**91**	4	18 Can't Let You Out Of My Sight	Wand 191
			CHUCK JACKSON & MAXINE BROWN	
10/23/65	**98**	1	19 I Need You So	Wand 198
			CHUCK JACKSON & MAXINE BROWN	
2/18/67	**91**	4	20 Hold On I'm Coming	Wand 1148
			CHUCK JACKSON & MAXINE BROWN	
5/06/67	**91**	1	21 Daddy's Home	Wand 1155
			CHUCK JACKSON & MAXINE BROWN	
10/14/67	**76**	9	22 Shame On Me	Wand 1166

DEBUT DATE	PEAK POS	WKS CHR	ARTIST — Record Title	Label & Number
			CHUCK JACKSON — Cont'd	
3/09/68	**94**	1	23 (You Can't Let The Boy Overpower) The Man In You ...	Motown 1118
			DEON JACKSON	
			Soul singer from Detroit, discovered by producer Ollie McLaughlin.	
1/22/66	**11**	14	1 Love Makes The World Go Round	Carla 2526
4/30/66	**77**	5	2 Love Takes A Long Time Growing	Carla 2527
11/18/67	**65**	6	3 Ooh Baby	Carla 2537
			EARNEST JACKSON	
6/02/73	**58**	6	1 Love And Happiness	Stone 200
			FREDDIE JACKSON	
			Soul singer/songwriter; raised in Harlem. Backup singer for Melba Moore, Evelyn King, and others.	
5/25/85	**18**	19	1 Rock Me Tonight (For Old Times Sake)	Capitol 5459
9/07/85	**12**	20	2 You Are My Lady	Capitol 5495
12/14/85+	**25**	15	3 He'll Never Love You (Like I Do)	Capitol 5535
11/08/86	**41**	12	4 Tasty Love	Capitol 5616
			JANET JACKSON	
			Born on 5/16/66 in Gary, Indiana. Sister of The Jacksons (youngest of 9 children). Debuted at age 7 at the MGM Grand in Las Vegas with her brothers. At age 10 she played Penny Gordon in the TV series "Good Times".	
12/18/82+	**64**	6	1 Young Love	A&M 2440
2/05/83	**58**	9	2 Come Give Your Love To Me	A&M 2522
2/22/86	**4**	21	3 **What Have You Done For Me Lately**	A&M 2812
5/17/86	**3**	19	4 **Nasty**	A&M 2830
8/09/86	**1[2]**	19	5 **When I Think Of You**	A&M 2855
11/01/86+	**5**	18	6 **Control**	A&M 2877
			JERMAINE JACKSON	
			Born on 12/11/54 in Gary, Indiana. Fourth oldest of the Jackson family. In Jackson 5 until group left Motown in 1976. Married Hazel Joy Gordy, daughter of Berry Gordy Jr., on 12/15/73.	
9/16/72	**46**	11	1 That's How Love Goes	Motown 1201
12/09/72+	**9**	18	2 **Daddy's Home**	Motown 1216
10/20/73	**79**	5	3 You're In Good Hands	Motown 1244
9/18/76	**55**	13	4 Let's Be Young Tonight	Motown 1401
3/29/80	**9**	23	5 **Let's Get Serious**	Motown 1469
7/12/80	**34**	13	6 You're Supposed To Keep Your Love For Me	Motown 1490
			above 2 written, produced and arranged by Stevie Wonder	
4/18/81	**50**	9	7 You Like Me Don't You	Motown 1503
10/31/81	**60**	8	8 I'm Just Too Shy	Motown 1525
7/24/82	**18**	15	9 Let Me Tickle Your Fancy	Motown 1628
			backing vocals by Devo	
7/21/84	**15**	17	10 Dynamite	Arista 9190
10/27/84+	**13**	20	11 Do What You Do	Arista 9279
2/02/85	**54**	11	12 When The Rain Begins To Fall	Curb 52521
			JERMAINE JACKSON/PIA ZADORA	
			from the film "Voyage of the Rock Aliens"	
6/08/85	**67**	7	13 (Closest Thing To) Perfect	Arista 9356
			from the film "Perfect"	
2/22/86	**16**	15	14 I Think It's Love	Arista 9444
7/05/86	**71**	5	15 Do You Remember Me?	Arista 9502
			J.J. JACKSON	
			Born Jerome Louis Jackson on 4/8/41 in Brooklyn, raised in The Bronx. Soul singer, songwriter. "But It's Alright" was recorded in England. Became permanent resident of UK in 1969. Not the same person as the MTV-VJ.	
10/01/66	**22**	13	1 But It's Alright	Calla 119
12/31/66+	**83**	3	2 I Dig Girls	Calla 125
5/24/69	**45**	10	3 But It's Alright [R]	Warner 7276
			JOE JACKSON	
			Born on 8/11/55 in Burton-on-Trent, England. Singer, songwriter, pianist, featuring an ever changing music style. Moved to New York City in 1982.	
6/09/79	**21**	15	1 Is She Really Going Out With Him?	A&M 2132
8/21/82	**6**	27	2 **Steppin' Out**	A&M 2428
1/15/83	**18**	16	3 Breaking Us In Two	A&M 2510

DEBUT DATE	PEAK POS	WKS CHR	ARTIST — Record Title	Label & Number
			JOE JACKSON — Cont'd	
11/26/83	**85**	4	4 Memphis	A&M 2601
			from the film "Mike's Murder"	
4/21/84	**15**	16	5 You Can't Get What You Want (Till You Know What You Want)	A&M 2628
7/14/84	**57**	8	6 Happy Ending	A&M 2635
			female vocal: Elaine Caswell	
			LaTOYA JACKSON	
			Sister of The Jacksons (5th of 9 children).	
5/05/84	**56**	8	1 Heart Don't Lie	Private I 04439
			MAHALIA JACKSON	
			Born on 10/26/11 in New Orleans. Began recording for Apollo Records in mid-40s. Long known as the world's greatest gospel singer. Died of heart failure on 1/27/72.	
4/28/58	**69**	6	1 He's Got The Whole World In His Hands	Columbia 41150
12/29/62	**99**	1	2 Silent Night, Holy Night [X]	Apollo 750
			MICHAEL JACKSON	
			Born on 8/29/58 in Gary, Indiana. Lead singer of The Jackson 5/Jacksons (7th of 9 children). His "Thriller" album, with sales of 40 million copies, is the best-selling album in history.	
10/30/71	**4**	14	1 **Got To Be There**	Motown 1191
3/11/72	**2^{2}**	13	2 **Rockin' Robin**	Motown 1197
5/27/72	**16**	11	3 I Wanna Be Where You Are	Motown 1202
8/05/72	**1^{1}**	16	4 **Ben**	Motown 1207
			title song from the film about a trained rat	
5/05/73	**50**	7	5 With A Child's Heart	Motown 1218
3/01/75	**54**	8	6 We're Almost There	Motown 1341
6/07/75	**23**	12	7 Just A Little Bit Of You	Motown 1349
9/09/78	**41**	9	8 Ease On Down The Road	MCA 40947
			DIANA ROSS & MICHAEL JACKSON	
			from the film "The Wiz"	
2/24/79	**81**	3	9 You Can't Win (Part 1)	Epic 50654
7/28/79	**1^{1}**	21	10 ● **Don't Stop 'Til You Get Enough**	Epic 50742
11/03/79+	**1^{4}**	24	11 ● **Rock With You**	Epic 50797
2/16/80	**10**	17	12 **Off The Wall**	Epic 50838
4/19/80	**10**	16	13 **She's Out Of My Life**	Epic 50871
4/18/81	**55**	7	14 One Day In Your Life	Motown 1512
			recorded in 1975	
11/06/82+	**2^{3}**	18	15 ● **The Girl Is Mine**	Epic 03288
			MICHAEL JACKSON/PAUL McCARTNEY	
1/22/83	**1^{7}**	24	16 ● **Billie Jean**	Epic 03509
2/26/83	**1^{3}**	25	17 ● **Beat It**	Epic 03759
			featuring lead guitar work by Eddie Van Halen	
5/28/83	**5**	15	18 **Wanna Be Startin' Somethin'**	Epic 03914
7/23/83	**7**	14	19 **Human Nature**	Epic 04026
10/08/83	**10**	16	20 **P.Y.T. (Pretty Young Thing)**	Epic 04165
10/15/83	**1^{6}**	22	21 ● **Say Say Say**	Columbia 04168
			PAUL McCARTNEY & MICHAEL JACKSON	
2/11/84	**4**	14	22 **Thriller**	Epic 04364
			all of above Epic (and MCA) recordings produced by Quincy Jones.	
5/26/84	**38**	12	23 Farewell My Summer Love	Motown 1739
			re-mix of a recording from 8/31/73	
			MICK JACKSON	
8/12/78	**61**	5	1 Blame It On The Boogie	Atco 7091
			MILLIE JACKSON	
			Born on 7/15/44 in Thompson, GA. Soul singer, songwriter. To Newark, NJ in 1958. Professional singing debut at Club Zanibar in Hoboken, NJ in 1964. First recorded for MGM in 1969.	
3/25/72	**27**	14	1 Ask Me What You Want	Spring 123
8/05/72	**42**	10	2 My Man, A Sweet Man	Spring 127
12/09/72+	**95**	4	3 I Miss You Baby	Spring 131
9/08/73	**24**	12	4 Hurts So Good	Spring 139
			from the film "Cleopatra Jones"	
6/08/74	**77**	7	5 How Do You Feel The Morning After	Spring 147
1/25/75	**42**	7	6 (If Loving You Is Wrong) I Don't Want To Be Right	Spring 155
9/27/75	**87**	2	7 Leftovers	Spring 161

DEBUT DATE	PEAK POS	WKS CHR	ARTIST — Record Title	Label & Number
			MILLIE JACKSON — Cont'd	
11/19/77+	**43**	11	8 If You're Not Back In Love By Monday	Spring 175
			REBBIE JACKSON	
			Born Maureen Jackson on 5/29/50 in Gary, IN. Eldest member of the Jackson family.	
10/06/84	**24**	19	1 Centipede	Columbia 04547
			written and produced by Michael Jackson	
			STONEWALL JACKSON	
			His real name. Born on 11/6/32 in Tabor City, NC. Country singer, songwriter, guitarist. Named after the Confederate general.	
5/25/59	**4**	16	1 **Waterloo**	Columbia 41393
10/19/59	**95**	2	2 Igmoo (The Pride Of South Central High)	Columbia 41488
12/28/59+	**41**	7	3 Mary Don't You Weep	Columbia 41533
3/28/60	**83**	3	4 Why I'm Walkin'	Columbia 41591
			WALTER JACKSON	
			Born on 3/19/38 in Pensacola, FL. Died on 6/20/83 of a cerebral hemorrhage. Soul singer. To Detroit, contracted polio at an early age, performed on crutches. Lead singer in the Velvetones, recorded for Deb, 1959. First recorded for Columbia, 1962.	
11/21/64	**67**	6	1 It's All Over	Okeh 7204
2/13/65	**96**	1	2 Suddenly I'm All Alone	Okeh 7215
6/12/65	**95**	2	3 Welcome Home	Okeh 7219
6/04/66	**88**	5	4 It's An Uphill Climb To The Bottom	Okeh 7247
11/05/66	**83**	4	5 A Corner In The Sun	Okeh 7260
4/15/67	**89**	2	6 Speak Her Name	Okeh 7272
12/25/76+	**93**	4	7 Feelings	Chi-Sound 908
			WANDA JACKSON	
			Born on 10/20/37 in Maud, Oklahoma. Country/rockabilly singer, songwriter, guitarist. First recorded for Decca in 1954. Toured with Elvis Presley, 1955-56.	
8/29/60	**37**	10	1 Let's Have A Party	Capitol 4397
6/05/61	**29**	11	2 Right Or Wrong	Capitol 4553
10/16/61	**27**	10	3 In The Middle Of A Heartache	Capitol 4635
1/20/62	**84**	3	4 A Little Bitty Tear	Capitol 4681
4/21/62	**58**	8	5 If I Cried Every Time You Hurt Me	Capitol 4723
			THE JACKSONS	
			Quintet of brothers formed and managed by their father beginning in 1967 in Gary, Indiana. Consisted of Sigmund "Jackie" (b: 5/4/51), Toriano "Tito" (b: 10/15/53), Jermaine (b: 12/11/54), Marlon (b: 3/12/57) and lead singer Michael (b: 8/29/58). First recorded for Steeltown in 1968. Known as The Jackson 5 from 1968-75. Jermaine replaced by Randy (b: 10/29/61) in 1976. Jermaine re-joined the group for 1984's highly publicized "Victory" album and tour.	
			THE JACKSON 5:	
11/15/69+	**1**[1]	19	1 **I Want You Back**	Motown 1157
3/14/70	**1**[2]	13	2 **ABC**	Motown 1163
5/30/70	**1**[2]	13	3 **The Love You Save/**	
		4	4 I Found That Girl	Motown 1166
9/19/70	**1**[5]	16	5 **I'll Be There**	Motown 1171
1/30/71	**2**[2]	10	6 **Mama's Pearl**	Motown 1177
4/03/71	**2**[3]	12	7 **Never Can Say Goodbye**	Motown 1179
7/10/71	**20**	9	8 Maybe Tomorrow	Motown 1186
12/11/71+	**10**	10	9 **Sugar Daddy**	Motown 1194
4/22/72	**13**	9	10 Little Bitty Pretty One	Motown 1199
7/15/72	**16**	10	11 Lookin' Through The Windows	Motown 1205
10/28/72	**18**	12	12 Corner Of The Sky	Motown 1214
			from the Broadway musical "Pippin"	
3/17/73	**28**	10	13 Hallelujah Day	Motown 1224
9/01/73	**28**	13	14 Get It Together	Motown 1277
3/16/74	**2**[2]	22	15 **Dancing Machine**	Motown 1286
10/26/74	**38**	11	16 Whatever You Got, I Want	Motown 1308
1/18/75	**15**	14	17 I Am Love (Parts I & II)	Motown 1310
7/05/75	**60**	9	18 Forever Came Today	Motown 1356
			THE JACKSONS:	
11/13/76+	**6**	21	19● **Enjoy Yourself**	Epic 50289
4/09/77	**28**	10	20 Show You The Way To Go	Epic 50350
10/08/77	**52**	7	21 Goin' Places	Epic 50454
11/04/78	**54**	6	22 Blame It On The Boogie	Epic 50595

DEBUT DATE	PEAK POS	WKS CHR	ARTIST — Record Title	Label & Number
			THE JACKSONS — Cont'd	
2/17/79	**7**	22	23 ▲ **Shake Your Body (Down To The Ground)**	Epic 50656
9/27/80	**12**	18	24 Lovely One	Epic 50938
12/06/80+	**22**	16	25 Heartbreak Hotel	Epic 50959
5/02/81	**77**	5	26 Can You Feel It	Epic 01032
6/27/81	**73**	4	27 Walk Right Now	Epic 02132
6/30/84	**3**	15	28 ● **State Of Shock** lead vocals: Michael Jackson & Mick Jagger	Epic 04503
8/18/84	**17**	12	29 Torture lead vocals: Jermaine & Michael Jackson	Epic 04575
10/27/84	**47**	7	30 Body	Epic 04673
			DEBBIE JACOBS Disco-oriented singer from Baltimore.	
3/15/80	**70**	4	1 High On Your Love	MCA 41167
			DICK JACOBS Born on 3/29/18 in New York City. Music director of TV's "Your Hit Parade", 1957-58. A&R director for Coral and Brunswick Records.	
3/17/56	**22**	14	1 'Main Title' And 'Molly-O' Jockey #22 / Top 100 #26 from the Otto Preminger film "The Man With The Golden Arm"	Coral 61606
7/07/56	**70**	4	2 Te Amo	Coral 61653
10/06/56	**73**	1	3 Theme From 'East Of Eden' [I] from the film "East Of Eden" starring James Dean	Coral 61692
10/27/56	**16**	13	4 Petticoats Of Portugal Jockey #16 / Top 100 #20 / Juke Box #20 / Best Seller #23	Coral 61724
3/09/57	**73**	6	5 Tower's Trot (And Then You Do That Step)/	
3/16/57	**87**	3	6 The Big Beat [I]	Coral 61794
9/02/57	**17**	11	7 Fascination Jockey #17 / Top 100 #52 from the film "Love In The Afternoon"	Coral 61864
			HANK JACOBS	
1/18/64	**91**	3	1 So Far Away [I]	Sue 795
			MICK JAGGER Born Michael Phillip Jagger on 7/26/43 in Dartford, England. Lead singer of The Rolling Stones. Also see The Jacksons' "State Of Shock" and Peter Tosh's "You Got To Walk".	
2/09/85	**12**	14	1 Just Another Night	Columbia 04743
4/27/85	**38**	11	2 Lucky In Love	Columbia 04893
8/31/85	**7**	14	3 **Dancing In The Street** **MICK JAGGER/DAVID BOWIE** from the Live-Aid concert	EMI America 8288
8/02/86	**51**	8	4 Ruthless People from the film of the same title	Epic 06211
			THE JAGGERZ Rock group formed in Pittsburgh in 1965, featuring lead singer Donnie Iris.	
1/31/70	**2**[1]	13	1 ● **The Rapper**	Kama Sutra 502
5/09/70	**75**	3	2 I Call My Baby Candy	Kama Sutra 509
8/22/70	**88**	2	3 What A Bummer	Kama Sutra 513
			THE JAGS Rock group from Scarborough, England, formed in 1978 by lead singer Nick Watkinson.	
6/07/80	**84**	2	1 Back Of My Hand (I've Got Your Number)	Island 49202
			JA-KKI 9-man, 1-woman R&B/disco outfit (5 white and 5 black members) from Flint, Michigan. Named after lead singer Jacqueline.	
9/11/76	**96**	3	1 Sun...Sun...Sun...Pt. I	Pyramid 8004
			THE JAMES BOYS R&B studio band produced by Jesse James.	
8/31/68	**82**	4	1 The Mule [I]	Phil-L.A. 316
			THE JAMES GANG Cleveland hard-rock band. Lineup in 1969 consisted of Jim Fox (drums), Tom Kriss (bass) and Joe Walsh (guitar, keyboards, vocals). Kriss replaced by Dale Peters in 1970. Walsh left in late 1971, replaced by Dominic Troiano and Roy Kenner. Troiano left in 1973, replaced by Tommy Bolin. Group disbanded in 1976.	
8/29/70	**59**	10	1 Funk # 49	ABC 11272

DEBUT DATE	PEAK POS	WKS CHR	ARTIST — Record Title	Label & Number
			THE JAMES GANG — Cont'd	
5/29/71	**51**	10	2 Walk Away	ABC 11301
10/09/71	**80**	4	3 Midnight Man	ABC 11312
2/02/74	**54**	11	4 Must Be Love	Atco 6953
			BOB JAMES Born on 12/25/39 in Marshall, Montana. Jazz fusion keyboardist. Did session work for many top stars beginning in late 60s. Producer/arranger for CTI/Kudo Records from 1973. Formed own label, Tappan Zee, in 1977.	
11/09/74	**88**	2	1 Feel Like Making Love [I]	CTI 24
			ETTA JAMES Born Etta James Hawkins on 1/25/38 in Los Angeles. Nickname: Miss Peaches. First recorded for Modern in 1954. Frequent bouts with heroin addiction, finally cured in 1975.	
5/02/60	**33**	15	1 All I Could Do Was Cry	Argo 5359
8/01/60	**52**	12	2 If I Can't Have You **ETTA & HARVEY (Harvey Fuqua of The Moonglows)**	Chess 1760
9/19/60	**34**	13	3 My Dearest Darling	Argo 5368
12/26/60	**78**	3	4 Spoonful **ETTA & HARVEY**	Chess 1771
1/16/61	**47**	8	5 At Last popularized in 1942 by Glenn Miller (POS 9)	Argo 5380
3/13/61	**30**	9	6 Trust In Me Wayne King and Mildred Bailey had Top 5 versions in 1937	Argo 5385
6/12/61	**50**	6	7 Fool That I Am/	
6/26/61	**55**	3	8 Dream there were 5 Top 20 versions of this Johnny Mercer tune in 1945	Argo 5390
8/07/61	**39**	7	9 Don't Cry, Baby	Argo 5393
11/06/61	**54**	7	10 It's Too Soon To Know/ The Orioles had a #13 version in 1948	
12/18/61	**95**	1	11 Seven Day Fool	Argo 5402
2/24/62	**37**	12	12 Something's Got A Hold On Me	Argo 5409
7/28/62	**34**	9	13 Stop The Wedding	Argo 5418
10/13/62	**71**	7	14 Next Door To The Blues/	
10/13/62	**87**	4	15 Fools Rush In Glenn Miller had a #1 version in 1940	Argo 5424
1/12/63	**64**	7	16 Would It Make Any Difference To You	Argo 5430
4/20/63	**25**	10	17 Pushover	Argo 5437
8/10/63	**78**	6	18 Pay Back	Argo 5445
10/05/63	**63**	4	19 Two Sides (To Every Story)	Argo 5452
2/01/64	**82**	3	20 Baby What You Want Me To Do	Argo 5459
4/18/64	**65**	6	21 Loving You More Every Day	Argo 5465
12/18/65	**96**	1	22 Do I Make Myself Clear	Cadet 5519
8/13/66	**97**	2	23 In The Basement - Part 1 above 2: **ETTA JAMES & SUGAR PIE DeSANTO**	Cadet 5539
11/11/67+	**23**	14	24 Tell Mama	Cadet 5578
3/02/68	**35**	10	25 Security	Cadet 5594
5/18/68	**69**	7	26 I Got You Babe	Cadet 5606
1/18/69	**79**	5	27 Almost Persuaded	Cadet 5630
10/17/70	**94**	3	28 Losers Weepers - Part 1	Cadet 5676
			JESSE JAMES Real name: James McClelland. R&B singer, record producer from Eldorado, Arkansas.	
10/21/67	**92**	1	1 Believe In Me Baby - Part I	20th Century 6684
			JIMMY JAMES & THE VAGABONDS R&B band from London, England. Vocals by James and Count Prince Miller.	
3/23/68	**76**	3	1 Come To Me Softly	Atco 6551
2/21/76	**94**	3	2 I Am Somebody	Pye 71057
			JONI JAMES Born Joan Carmello Babbo on 9/22/30 in Chicago. Worked as a dancer from age twelve, model during high school. Toured Canada as a dancer, late 1940s. First recorded for Sharp, 1952. Married her orchestral arranger/conductor Tony Aquaviva (d: 9/27/86).	
2/19/55	**2**[1]	16	1 **How Important Can It Be?** Jockey #2 / Juke Box #6 / Best Seller #8	MGM 11919
10/22/55	**6**	15	2 **You Are My Love** Jockey #6 / Top 100 #15 / Best Seller #18	MGM 12066
12/10/55+	**49**	13	3 My Believing Heart	MGM 12126

DEBUT DATE	PEAK POS	WKS CHR	ARTIST — Record Title	Label & Number
			JONI JAMES — Cont'd	
3/10/56	**83**	1	4 Don't Tell Me Not To Love You	MGM 12175
4/28/56	**72**	7	5 I Woke Up Crying	MGM 12213
8/04/56	**30**	11	6 Give Us This Day/	
7/21/56	**70**	8	7 How Lucky You Are The Andrews Sisters had a #22 version in 1947	MGM 12288
7/15/57	**97**	1	8 Summer Love	MGM 12480
9/15/58	**19**	16	9 There Goes My Heart Enric Madriguera had a #13 version in 1934	MGM 12706
1/19/59	**33**	12	10 There Must Be A Way Johnnie Johnston and Charlie Spivak both had #9 versions in 1945	MGM 12746
4/13/59	**51**	7	11 I Still Get A Thrill (Thinking Of You) there were 4 Top 20 versions in 1930	MGM 12779
7/13/59	**63**	6	12 I Still Get Jealous from the Broadway musical "High Button Shoes" (1947)	MGM 12807
12/28/59+	**35**	9	13 Little Things Mean A Lot Kitty Kallen's version hit #1 in 1954	MGM 12849
3/28/60	**98**	1	14 I Need You Now Eddie Fisher's version hit #1 in 1954	MGM 12885
12/19/60+	**38**	7	15 My Last Date (With You)	MGM 12933
			RICK JAMES Born James Johnson on 2/1/52 in Buffalo. "Punk funk" singer, songwriter, guitarist. In Mynah Birds band with Neil Young, late 60s. To London, England, formed band Main Line. Returned to US and formed Stone City Band, did production work for Teena Marie, Mary Jane Girls, Eddie Murphy, and others.	
7/01/78	**13**	17	1 You And I	Gordy 7156
11/04/78+	**41**	12	2 Mary Jane	Gordy 7162
4/07/79	**72**	6	3 High On Your Love Suite	Gordy 7164
5/12/79	**71**	6	4 Bustin' Out	Gordy 7167
5/30/81	**40**	14	5 Give It To Me Baby	Gordy 7197
8/08/81	**16**	24	6 Super Freak (Part 1)	Gordy 7205
5/08/82	**66**	8	7 Standing On The Top - Part 1 THE TEMPTATIONS featuring RICK JAMES	Gordy 1616
5/29/82	**64**	9	8 Dance Wit' Me (Part 1)	Gordy 1619
7/30/83	**40**	12	9 Cold Blooded	Gordy 1687
12/10/83+	**43**	11	10 Ebony Eyes RICK JAMES featuring SMOKEY ROBINSON	Gordy 1714
7/14/84	**36**	14	11 17	Gordy 1730
3/30/85	**50**	8	12 Can't Stop	Gordy 1776
			SONNY JAMES Born James Loden on 5/1/29 in Hackleburg, Alabama. Country singer, songwriter, guitarist. Nicknamed "The Southern Gentleman". Brought to Capitol Records in Nashville by Chet Atkins.	
12/29/56+	**1**[1]	21	1 **Young Love** Jockey #1 / Best Seller #2 / Top 100 #2 / Juke Box #4	Capitol 3602
3/30/57	**25**	11	2 First Date, First Kiss, First Love Jockey #25 / Top 100 #39	Capitol 3674
12/30/57	**92**	1	3 Uh-Huh-mm	Capitol 3840
9/22/58	**94**	2	4 You Got That Touch	Capitol 4020
5/04/59	**85**	5	5 Talk Of The School backing vocals: The Eligibles	Capitol 4178
1/18/60	**80**	3	6 I Forgot More Than You'll Ever Know	Capitol 4307
4/11/60	**67**	6	7 Jenny Lou	NRC 050
3/06/61	**87**	2	8 Apache	RCA 7858
8/10/63	**95**	1	9 The Minute You're Gone	Capitol 4969
11/28/64	**91**	6	10 You're The Only World I Know	Capitol 5280
7/22/67	**97**	3	11 I'll Never Find Another You	Capitol 5914
11/23/68	**81**	4	12 Born To Be With You	Capitol 2271
2/08/69	**92**	4	13 Only The Lonely	Capitol 2370
5/31/69	**94**	2	14 Running Bear	Capitol 2486
9/20/69	**65**	7	15 Since I Met You, Baby	Capitol 2595
1/24/70	**87**	4	16 It's Just A Matter Of Time	Capitol 2700
4/10/71	**93**	3	17 Empty Arms	Capitol 3015
7/17/71	**91**	3	18 Bright Lights, Big City above 9 hit #1 on Billboard's Country charts	Capitol 3114

DEBUT DATE	PEAK POS	WKS CHR	ARTIST — Record Title	Label & Number
			TOMMY JAMES	
			Born Thomas Jackson on 4/29/47 in Dayton, Ohio. To Niles, Michigan at age 11. Formed group, The Shondells, at age 12. See Tommy James & The Shondells for complete biography about the group.	
8/01/70	**57**	7	1 Ball And Chain	Roulette 7084
12/19/70+	**62**	7	2 Church Street Soul Revival	Roulette 7093
3/20/71	**93**	3	3 Adrienne	Roulette 7100
6/12/71	**4**	13	4 **Draggin' The Line**	Roulette 7103
9/25/71	**40**	7	5 I'm Comin' Home	Roulette 7110
11/27/71	**41**	9	6 Nothing To Hide	Roulette 7114
2/19/72	**89**	4	7 Tell 'Em Willie Boy 'S A'Comin'	Roulette 7119
6/17/72	**90**	4	8 Cat's Eye In The Window	Roulette 7126
8/19/72	**67**	6	9 Love Song	Roulette 7130
11/04/72	**95**	3	10 Celebration	Roulette 7135
2/17/73	**70**	6	11 Boo, Boo, Don't 'Cha Be Blue	Roulette 7140
1/26/80	**19**	16	12 Three Times In Love	Millennium 11785
5/09/81	**58**	7	13 You're So Easy To Love	Millennium 11802
			TOMMY JAMES & THE SHONDELLS	
			Group formed by James at age 12 in Niles, Michigan. Recorded "Hanky Panky" on the Snap label in 1963. Tommy re-located to Pittsburgh in 1965, after a disc jockey there popularized the tune. Original master was sold to Roulette, whereupon Tommy recruited a Pittsburgh group "The Raconteurs" to become the official Shondells. Consisted of Mike Vale (bass), Pete Lucia (drums), Eddie Gray (guitar) and Ronnie Rosman (organ).	
6/04/66	**1**[2]	12	1 ● **Hanky Panky**	Roulette 4686
8/06/66	**21**	8	2 Say I Am (What I Am)	Roulette 4695
11/05/66	**31**	9	3 It's Only Love	Roulette 4710
2/11/67	**4**	17	4 **I Think We're Alone Now**	Roulette 4720
4/29/67	**10**	10	5 **Mirage**	Roulette 4736
7/01/67	**25**	7	6 I Like The Way	Roulette 4756
8/26/67	**18**	8	7 Gettin' Together	Roulette 4762
10/28/67	**43**	6	8 Out Of The Blue	Roulette 4775
1/27/68	**48**	7	9 Get Out Now	Roulette 7000
4/06/68	**3**	17	10 **Mony Mony**	Roulette 7008
7/27/68	**53**	5	11 Somebody Cares	Roulette 7016
10/12/68	**38**	9	12 Do Something To Me	Roulette 7024
12/14/68+	**1**[2]	16	13 **Crimson And Clover**	Roulette 7028
3/22/69	**7**	10	14 **Sweet Cherry Wine**	Roulette 7039
6/07/69	**2**[3]	15	15 **Crystal Blue Persuasion**	Roulette 7050
10/04/69	**19**	8	16 Ball Of Fire	Roulette 7060
12/13/69+	**23**	8	17 She	Roulette 7066
2/21/70	**45**	8	18 Gotta Get Back To You	Roulette 7071
5/16/70	**47**	8	19 Come To Me	Roulette 7076
			CODY JAMESON	
			Songstress from New York City.	
4/09/77	**74**	4	1 Brooklyn	Atco 7073
			NICK JAMESON	
			Pop-rock singer based in Atlanta. Member and producer for six Foghat albums.	
8/23/86	**95**	2	1 Weatherman	Motown 1853
			JAMESTOWN MASSACRE	
8/12/72	**90**	5	1 Summer Sun	Warner 7603
			THE JAMIES	
			Pop vocal quartet from Dorchester, MA, led by Tom Jamison and his sister Serena.	
8/18/58	**26**	11	1 Summertime, Summertime Hot 100 #26 / Best Seller #28	Epic 9281
6/23/62	**38**	8	2 Summertime, Summertime [R]	Epic 9281
			JAMUL	
5/09/70	**93**	2	1 Tobacco Road	Lizard 21001

DEBUT DATE	PEAK POS	WKS CHR	ARTIST — Record Title	Label & Number
			JAN & DEAN	
			Jan Berry (b: 4/3/41) and Dean Torrence (b: 3/10/40) formed group called the Barons while attending high school in Los Angeles. Jan & Dean and Barons member Arnie Ginsburg recorded "Jennie Lee" in Jan's garage. Dean left for a six month Army Reserve stint, whereupon Jan signed with Doris Day's label, Arwin, and the record was released as by Jan & Arnie. Upon Dean's return from the service, Arnie joined the Navy, and Jan & Dean signed with Herb Alpert's Dore label. Jan was critically injured in an auto accident on 4/19/66. Duo made a big comeback in 1978, after the showing of their biographical film "Dead Man's Curve".	
6/02/58	**8**	13	1 **Jennie Lee**	Arwin 108
			JAN & ARNIE	
			Best Seller #8 / Top 100 #8 / Jockey #17	
8/18/58	**81**	2	2 Gas Money	Arwin 111
			JAN & ARNIE	
8/03/59	**10**	12	3 **Baby Talk**	Dore 522
10/26/59	**97**	3	4 There's A Girl	Dore 531
2/08/60	**65**	6	5 Clementine	Dore 539
			version of tune written in 1884	
8/01/60	**53**	7	6 We Go Together	Dore 555
11/14/60	**81**	5	7 Gee	Dore 576
			above 5 songs produced by Herb Alpert and Lou Adler	
6/26/61	**25**	7	8 Heart And Soul	Challenge 9111
			Larry Clinton hit #1 in 1938 with this Hoagy Carmichael tune	
1/20/62	**95**	1	9 A Sunday Kind Of Love	Liberty 55397
			Jo Stafford had a #15 version in 1947	
5/26/62	**69**	7	10 Tennessee	Liberty 55454
2/23/63	**28**	13	11 Linda	Liberty 55531
6/15/63	**1^{2}**	13	12 **Surf City**	Liberty 55580
			Brian Wilson (Beach Boys) helped on words & vocals for this tune	
9/07/63	**11**	10	13 Honolulu Lulu	Liberty 55613
12/07/63+	**10**	11	14 **Drag City**	Liberty 55641
3/07/64	**8**	14	15 **Dead Man's Curve/**	
3/21/64	**37**	8	16 The New Girl In School	Liberty 55672
6/27/64	**3**	11	17 **The Little Old Lady (From Pasadena)**	Liberty 55704
9/19/64	**16**	8	18 Ride The Wild Surf/	
			from the film of the same title	
10/03/64	**77**	3	19 The Anaheim, Azusa & Cucamonga Sewing Circle, Book Review And Timing Association	Liberty 55724
10/31/64	**25**	8	20 Sidewalk Surfin'	Liberty 55727
3/13/65	**56**	5	21 (Here They Come) From All Over The World	Liberty 55766
			from the teen-rock concert film "The T.A.M.I. Show"	
5/22/65	**27**	9	22 You Really Know How To Hurt A Guy	Liberty 55792
10/16/65	**30**	7	23 I Found A Girl	Liberty 55833
2/12/66	**66**	5	24 Batman [N]	Liberty 55860
6/04/66	**21**	9	25 Popsicle	Liberty 55886
9/03/66	**93**	4	26 Fiddle Around	Liberty 55905
			JAN & KJELD	
			Brothers (ages 12 & 14 in 1960) from Copenhagen, Denmark.	
6/06/60	**58**	7	1 Banjo Boy [F]	Kapp 335
			JOHNNY JANIS	
4/29/57	**63**	3	1 Pledge Of Love	ABC-Para. 9800
			HORST JANKOWSKI	
			Born on 1/30/36 in Berlin, Germany. Jazz pianist.	
5/08/65	**12**	13	1 A Walk In The Black Forest [I]	Mercury 72425
9/04/65	**91**	1	2 Simpel Gimpel [I]	Mercury 72465
			THE JARMELS	
			R&B group from Richmond, Virginia: Nathaniel Ruff, Ray Smith, Paul Burnett, Earl Christian and Tom Eldridge.	
7/31/61	**12**	10	1 A Little Bit Of Soap	Laurie 3098
			AL JARREAU	
			Born on 3/12/40 in Milwaukee. Soul/jazz vocalist. Has won 4 Grammys.	
8/01/81	**15**	24	1 We're In This Love Together	Warner 49746
12/05/81+	**43**	10	2 Breakin' Away	Warner 49842
4/03/82	**70**	7	3 Teach Me Tonight	Warner 50032
3/19/83	**21**	15	4 Mornin'	Warner 29720

DEBUT DATE	PEAK POS	WKS CHR	ARTIST — Record Title	Label & Number
			AL JARREAU — Cont'd	
6/18/83	**77**	6	5 Boogie Down	Warner 29624
9/10/83	**63**	7	6 Trouble In Paradise	Warner 29501
			above 3 shown only as: **JARREAU**	
10/13/84	**69**	9	7 After All	Warner 29262
			CAROL JARVIS	
9/02/57	**48**	16	1 Rebel	Dot 15586
			JAY & THE AMERICANS	
			Group formed in late 1959 by New York University students as the Harbor-Lites: John "Jay" Traynor (formerly with the Mystics), Sandy Yaguda, Kenny Vance (later a Hollywood musical director) and Howie Kane. Guitarist Marty Sanders joined during production of their first album in 1961. Traynor left after their first hit and was replaced by lead singer David "Jay" Black in 1962.	
3/17/62	**5**	14	1 **She Cried**	United Art. 415
8/17/63	**25**	11	2 Only In America	United Art. 626
11/30/63	**76**	8	3 Come Dance With Me	United Art. 669
9/12/64	**3**	15	4 **Come A Little Bit Closer**	United Art. 759
12/26/64+	**11**	10	5 Let's Lock The Door (And Throw Away The Key)	United Art. 805
3/27/65	**57**	8	6 Think Of The Good Times	United Art. 845
6/05/65	**4**	13	7 **Cara, Mia**	United Art. 881
			David Whitfield (with Mantovani's orch.) had a #10 version in 1954	
9/04/65	**13**	10	8 Some Enchanted Evening	United Art. 919
			there were 6 Top 10 versions of this "South Pacific" song in 1949	
11/20/65	**18**	8	9 Sunday And Me	United Art. 948
			Neil Diamond's first major hit as a songwriter	
2/19/66	**63**	6	10 Why Can't You Bring Me Home	United Art. 992
5/28/66	**25**	6	11 Crying	United Art. 50016
7/30/66	**76**	5	12 Livin' Above Your Head	United Art. 50046
			above 6 produced by Gerry Granahan of Dicky Doo & The Don'ts	
11/26/66	**90**	4	13 (He's) Raining In My Sunshine	United Art. 50094
12/28/68+	**6**	14	14 ● **This Magic Moment**	United Art. 50475
4/05/69	**70**	5	15 When You Dance	United Art. 50510
5/31/69	**62**	7	16 Hushabye	United Art. 50535
11/22/69+	**19**	15	17 Walkin' In The Rain	United Art. 50605
3/28/70	**57**	6	18 Capture The Moment	United Art. 50654
			JAY & THE TECHNIQUES	
			R&B/rock group from Allentown, PA, consisting of 5 white and 2 black members: lead singer Jay Proctor, Karl Landis, Ronnie Goosly, John Walsh, George Lloyd, Chuck Crowl and Dante Dancho.	
7/15/67	**6**	17	1 **Apples, Peaches, Pumpkin Pie**	Smash 2086
10/21/67	**14**	12	2 Keep The Ball Rollin'	Smash 2124
1/20/68	**39**	6	3 Strawberry Shortcake	Smash 2142
4/13/68	**64**	8	4 Baby Make Your Own Sweet Music	Smash 2154
			MORTY JAY & THE SURFERIN' CATS	
11/09/63	**93**	1	1 Saltwater Taffy [I]	Legend 124
			JERRY JAYE	
			Born Jerald Jaye Hatley on 10/19/37 in Manila, Arkansas.	
4/15/67	**29**	9	1 My Girl Josephine	Hi 2120
			THE JAYHAWKS	
			Los Angeles R&B group: James Johnson, Carlton Fisher, Dave Govan and Carver Bunkum. Changed name to The Vibrations in 1960.	
6/30/56	**18**	11	1 Stranded In The Jungle [N]	Flash 109
			Best Seller #18 / Top 100 #29	
			THE JAYNETTS	
			R&B female trio from the Bronx, produced by Abner Spector.	
8/31/63	**2**[2]	12	1 **Sally, Go 'Round The Roses**	Tuff 369
			JAZZ CRUSADERS - see THE CRUSADERS	
			THE JB's	
			James Brown's super-funk backup band led by Fred Wesley. Also see Nat Kendricks.	
1/22/72	**67**	8	1 Gimme Some More [I]	People 602
5/27/72	**95**	2	2 Pass The Peas [I]	People 607

DEBUT DATE	PEAK POS	WKS CHR	ARTIST — Record Title	Label & Number
			THE JB's — Cont'd	
6/02/73	**22**	11	3● Doing It To Death	People 621
			FRED WESLEY & THE J.B.'s	
			above 3 written, produced and arranged by James Brown	
			JEAN & THE DARLINGS	
8/26/67	**96**	1	1 How Can You Mistreat The One You Love	Volt 151
			JEFFERSON	
			English vocalist.	
8/16/69	**68**	9	1 The Colour Of My Love	Decca 32501
12/20/69+	**23**	12	2 Baby Take Me In Your Arms	Janus 106
			JEFFERSON STARSHIP	
			Formed as Jefferson Airplane in San Francisco, 1965. Consisted of Marty Balin and Grace Slick (vocals), Paul Kantner (vocals, guitar), Jorma Kaukonen (guitar), Jack Casady (bass) and Spencer Dryden (drums). Slick and Dryden joined in 1966, replacing Signe Anderson and Skip Spence. Slick had been in the Great Society. Spence then formed Moby Grape. Dryden replaced by Joey Covington in 1970. Casady and Kaukonen left by 1974 to go full time with Hot Tuna. Balin left in 1971, rejoined in 1975, by which time group was renamed Jefferson Starship and consisted of Slick, Kantner, Papa John Creah (violin), David Freiberg (bass), Craig Chaquico (guitar), Pete Sears (bass) and John Barbata (drums). Slick left group from June, 1978 to January, 1981 due to personal problems. In 1979, singer Mickey Thomas joined, along with Aynsley Dunbar who replaced Barbata. Don Baldwin replaced Dunbar in 1982. Kantner left in 1984, and, due to legal difficulties, band's name was shortened to Starship, whose lineup includes Slick, Thomas, Sears, Chaquico and Baldwin.	
			JEFFERSON AIRPLANE:	
4/01/67	**5**	15	1 **Somebody To Love**	RCA 9140
6/24/67	**8**	10	2 **White Rabbit**	RCA 9248
9/02/67	**42**	6	3 Ballad Of You & Me & Pooneil	RCA 9297
12/16/67	**61**	4	4 Watch Her Ride	RCA 9389
4/20/68	**98**	3	5 Greasy Heart	RCA 9496
11/02/68	**64**	6	6 Crown Of Creation	RCA 9644
11/08/69	**65**	10	7 Volunteers	RCA 0245
11/20/71+	**60**	10	8 Pretty As You Feel	Grunt 0500
			JEFFERSON STARSHIP:	
11/16/74	**84**	5	9 Ride The Tiger	Grunt 10080
8/23/75	**3**	17	10 **Miracles**	Grunt 10367
12/13/75+	**49**	6	11 Play On Love	Grunt 10456
7/24/76	**12**	17	12 With Your Love	Grunt 10746
12/04/76	**64**	5	13 St. Charles	Grunt 10791
3/11/78	**8**	14	14 **Count On Me**	Grunt 11196
5/27/78	**12**	16	15 Runaway	Grunt 11274
9/09/78	**54**	6	16 Crazy Feelin'	Grunt 11374
12/02/78	**66**	6	17 Light The Sky On Fire	Grunt 11426
11/03/79+	**14**	15	18 Jane	Grunt 11750
2/23/80	**55**	6	19 Girl With The Hungry Eyes	Grunt 11921
4/04/81	**29**	13	20 Find Your Way Back	Grunt 12211
7/11/81	**48**	11	21 Stranger	Grunt 12275
10/09/82	**28**	16	22 Be My Lady	Grunt 13350
1/29/83	**38**	11	23 Winds Of Change	Grunt 13439
5/12/84	**23**	16	24 No Way Out	Grunt 13811
9/08/84	**66**	6	25 Layin' It On The Line	Grunt 13872
			STARSHIP:	
9/07/85	**1**[2]	24	26 **We Built This City**	Grunt 14170
12/28/85+	**1**[1]	20	27 **Sara**	Grunt 14253
4/05/86	**26**	13	28 Tomorrow Doesn't Matter Tonight	Grunt 14332
7/05/86	**68**	7	29 Before I Go	Grunt 14393
			THE JOE JEFFREY GROUP	
			Joe is an R&B singer, guitarist.	
6/07/69	**14**	12	1 My Pledge Of Love	Wand 11200
			GARLAND JEFFREYS	
			R&B/rock/reggae singer from Brooklyn.	
3/14/81	**66**	7	1 96 Tears	Epic 51008

DEBUT DATE	PEAK POS	WKS CHR	ARTIST — Record Title	Label & Number
			JELLYBEAN	
			John "Jellybean" Benitez is a New York producer and remix specialist.	
11/16/85+	**18**	18	1 Sidewalk Talk	EMI America 8297
			written by Madonna	
			THE JELLY BEANS	
			Black quintet from Jersey City: sisters Elyse & Maxine Herbert, Alma Brewer, Diane Taylor and Charles Thomas.	
6/20/64	**9**	12	1 **I Wanna Love Him So Bad**	Red Bird 10003
9/26/64	**51**	7	2 Baby Be Mine	Red Bird 10011
			DONALD JENKINS & The Delighters	
			R&B trio from Chicago: Jenkins, Walter Granger and Ronnie Strong. Also recorded as Donald & The Daylighters.	
9/14/63	**64**	8	1 (Native Girl) Elephant Walk	Cortland 109
			GORDON JENKINS	
			Born on 5/12/10 in Webster Groves, MO. Pianist-arranger in early 30s with Isham Jones, Benny Goodman and others. Musical director and conductor for Decca Records beginning in 1945. Died on 5/1/84 (73).	
9/03/55	**45**	2	1 Goodnight, Sweet Dreams	X 0159
			Coming Up #45	
			WAYLON JENNINGS	
			Born on 6/15/37 in Littlefield, Texas. While working as a DJ in Lubbock, Texas, Waylon befriended Buddy Holly. Holly produced Waylon's first record "Jole Blon" in 1958. Waylon then joined with Buddy's backing band as bass guitarist on the fateful "Winter Dance Party" tour in 1959. Established himself in the mid-70s as a leader of the "Outlaws" movement in Country music. Married to Jessi Colter since 1969.	
9/06/69	**93**	2	1 MacArthur Park	RCA 0210
			WAYLON JENNINGS & THE KIMBERLYS	
10/17/70	**94**	1	2 The Taker	RCA 9885
9/07/74	**75**	7	3 I'm A Ramblin' Man	RCA 10020
9/20/75	**60**	9	4 Are You Sure Hank Done It This Way	RCA 10379
2/07/76	**25**	12	5 Good Hearted Woman	RCA 10529
			WAYLON & WILLIE	
10/09/76	**97**	1	6 Can't You See	RCA 10721
5/07/77	**25**	16	7 Luckenbach, Texas (Back to the Basics of Love)	RCA 10924
2/11/78	**42**	10	8 Mammas Don't Let Your Babies Grow Up To Be Cowboys	RCA 11198
			WAYLON & WILLIE	
6/09/79	**54**	7	9 Amanda	RCA 11596
9/13/80	**21**	23	10 ● Theme From The Dukes Of Hazzard (Good Ol' Boys)	RCA 12067
			from "The Dukes Of Hazzard" TV series	
			above 2 shown only as: **WAYLON**	
4/03/82	**52**	9	11 Just To Satisfy You	RCA 13073
			WAYLON & WILLIE	
			KRIS JENSEN	
			Born on 4/4/42 in New Haven, Connecticut. Pop/Country singer, guitarist.	
9/01/62	**20**	14	1 Torture	Hickory 1173
			JERRYO	
			Real name: Jerry Murray. R&B singer, dancer from Chicago.	
9/16/67	**51**	9	1 Karate-Boo-Ga-Loo	Shout 217
			THE JESTERS	
			R&B quintet formed in New York City's Harlem area.	
7/15/57	**100**	1	1 So Strange	Winley 218
3/03/58	**74**	2	2 The Plea	Winley 225
			JETHRO TULL	
			Progressive rock group formed in 1968 in Blackpool, England. Consisted of Ian Anderson (lead singer, flutist), Mick Abrahams (guitar), Glenn Cornick (bass) and Clive Bunker (drums). Named band after 18th century agriculturist Jethro Tull. Abrahams replaced by Martin Barre in 1968. Added keyboardist John Evans in 1970. Cornick replaced by Jeffrey Hammond-Hammond in 1971. Bunker left in late 1971 and was replaced by Barriemore Barlow, who in turn was replaced by John Glascock (died in 1979). Ian has revamped his lineup several times since then.	
8/14/71	**91**	2	1 Hymn 43	Reprise 1024
11/04/72+	**11**	14	2 Living In The Past	Chrysalis 2006
5/19/73	**80**	5	3 A Passion Play (Edit #8)	Chrysalis 2012
11/02/74+	**12**	16	4 Bungle In The Jungle	Chrysalis 2101
10/11/75	**79**	4	5 Minstrel In The Gallery	Chrysalis 2106

DEBUT DATE	PEAK POS	WKS CHR	ARTIST — Record Title	Label & Number
			JETHRO TULL — Cont'd	
2/14/76	**62**	8	6 Locomotive Breath	Chrysalis 2110
4/09/77	**59**	6	7 The Whistler	Chrysalis 2135
			THE JETS Minneapolis-based family band consisting of 8 Wolfgramm brothers and sisters: Leroy, Eddie, Eugene, Haini, Rudy, Kathi, Elizabeth and Moana.	
4/12/86	**3**	20	1 **Crush On You**	MCA 52774
8/09/86	**47**	11	2 Private Number	MCA 52846
11/15/86+	**3**	26	3 **You Got It All**	MCA 52968
			JOAN JETT & THE BLACKHEARTS Joan was born on 9/22/60 in Philadelphia. Played guitar with the Los Angeles female rock band The Runaways, 1975-78. Formed her backing band, The Blackhearts, in 1980. Starred in the 1987 film "Light Of Day" as the leader of a rock band called The Barbusters.	
2/06/82	**1**[7]	20	1 ▲**I Love Rock 'N Roll**	Boardwalk 135
5/01/82	**7**	15	2 **Crimson And Clover**	Boardwalk 144
7/31/82	**20**	14	3 Do You Wanna Touch Me (Oh Yeah)	Boardwalk 150
7/09/83	**35**	10	4 Fake Friends	Blackheart 52240
9/10/83	**37**	9	5 Everyday People	Blackheart 52272
10/11/86	**83**	6	6 Good Music backing vocals by The Beach Boys	Blackheart 06336
			THE JEWELS	
10/10/64	**64**	10	1 Opportunity	Dimension 1034
			JIGSAW Pop/rock quartet from England: Des Deyer, Clive Scott, Tony Campbell and Barrie Bernard.	
8/30/75	**3**	21	1 **Sky High** from the movie "The Dragon Flies"	Chelsea 3022
2/07/76	**30**	11	2 Love Fire	Chelsea 3037
8/21/76	**66**	7	3 Brand New Love Affair	Chelsea 3043
8/27/77	**93**	4	4 If I Have To Go Away	20th Century 2347
			JIM & JEAN Husband and wife pop duo: Jim & Jean Glover.	
2/03/68	**94**	3	1 People World	Verve Fore. 5073
			JIM & MONICA	
1/18/64	**96**	2	1 Slipin' And Slidin'	Betty 1207
			JOSE JIMENEZ Real name: Bill Dana. Born on 10/5/24 in Quincy, MA. Head writer for TV's "Steve Allen Show". Star of own TV series from 1963-65. Created the Latin American comic character Jose Jimenez for Steve Allen's TV series.	
7/10/61	**19**	11	1 The Astronaut (Parts 1 & 2) [C] interviewed by Don Hinckley	Kapp 409
			GUS JINKINS	
12/01/56	**79**	1	1 Tricky [I]	Flash 115
			THE JIVE BOMBERS New Jersey-based R&B quartet: Clarence Palmer, Earl Johnson, Al Tinney and William "Pee Wee" Tinney.	
2/02/57	**36**	14	1 Bad Boy	Savoy 1508
			THE JIVE FIVE R&B group formed in Brooklyn in 1959: Eugene Pitt, lead singer (formerly with the Genies); Jerome Hanna and Billy Prophet, tenors; Richard Harris, baritone; and Norman Johnson, bass.	
7/03/61	**3**	19	1 **My True Story**	Beltone 1006
11/13/61	**74**	6	2 Never, Never	Beltone 1014
9/15/62	**67**	5	3 What Time Is It?	Beltone 2024
8/14/65	**36**	8	4 I'm A Happy Man	United Art. 853
			JIVIN' GENE & The Jokers Real name: Gene Bourgeois. Singer, songwriter, guitarist from Fort Arthur, Texas.	
9/07/59	**69**	4	1 Breaking Up Is Hard To Do	Mercury 71485
			JO ANN & TROY Jo Ann Campbell and husband Troy Seals.	
12/12/64+	**67**	6	1 I Found A Love Oh What A Love	Atlantic 2256

DEBUT DATE	PEAK POS	WKS CHR	ARTIST — Record Title	Label & Number
			JO JO GUNNE	
			Los Angeles-based rock quartet formed by Jay Ferguson and Mark Andes (former members of Spirit). Named group after the Chuck Berry hit.	
3/18/72	**27**	11	1 Run Run Run	Asylum 11003
			DAMITA JO	
			Born Damita Jo DuBlanc on 8/5/40 in Austin, Texas. Featured singer with Steve Gibson & The Red Caps (married to Gibson), 1951-53 and 1959-60. Regular on the Redd Foxx TV variety series in 1977.	
10/24/60	**22**	12	1 I'll Save The Last Dance For You	Mercury 71690
2/06/61	**75**	5	2 Keep Your Hands Off Of Him	Mercury 71760
7/03/61	**12**	9	3 I'll Be There	Mercury 71840
12/10/66+	**68**	10	4 If You Go Away	Epic 10061
			SAMI JO	
			Alabama-bred Country/Pop songstress.	
2/09/74	**21**	14	1 Tell Me A Lie	MGM South 7029
7/13/74	**46**	13	2 It Could Have Been Me	MGM South 7034
			JoBOXERS	
			Pop/rock quintet from England, led by Dig Wayne.	
9/10/83	**36**	15	1 Just Got Lucky	RCA 13601
			BILLY JOEL	
			Born William Martin Joel on 5/9/49 in Long Island, NY. Formed his first band in 1964, the Echoes, which later became the Lost Souls. Member of the Long Island group, The Hassles, late 60s, then formed a rock duo with The Hassles' drummer Jon Small, called Attila. Signed to Columbia Records in 1973. Involved in a serious motorcycle accident on Long Island in 1982. Married model Christie Brinkley in 1985.	
2/23/74	**25**	14	1 Piano Man	Columbia 45963
6/29/74	**80**	4	2 Worse Comes To Worst	Columbia 46055
8/17/74	**77**	4	3 Travelin' Prayer	Columbia 10015
11/30/74+	**34**	10	4 The Entertainer	Columbia 10064
			above 4 produced by Michael Stewart	
11/12/77+	**3**	27	5● **Just The Way You Are**	Columbia 10646
3/18/78	**17**	14	6 Movin' Out (Anthony's Song)	Columbia 10708
5/13/78	**24**	13	7 Only The Good Die Young	Columbia 10750
8/12/78	**17**	15	8 She's Always A Woman	Columbia 10788
11/04/78+	**3**	19	9● **My Life**	Columbia 10853
2/10/79	**14**	11	10 Big Shot	Columbia 10913
4/21/79	**24**	11	11 Honesty	Columbia 10959
3/15/80	**7**	15	12 **You May Be Right**	Columbia 11231
5/24/80	**1**[2]	21	13● **It's Still Rock And Roll To Me**	Columbia 11276
8/02/80	**19**	15	14 Don't Ask Me Why	Columbia 11331
10/11/80	**36**	9	15 Sometimes A Fantasy	Columbia 11379
9/12/81	**17**	15	16 Say Goodbye To Hollywood	Columbia 02518
11/21/81+	**23**	14	17 She's Got A Way	Columbia 02628
9/25/82	**20**	17	18 Pressure	Columbia 03244
11/27/82+	**17**	22	19 Allentown	Columbia 03413
3/19/83	**56**	7	20 Goodnight Saigon	Columbia 03780
7/30/83	**1**[1]	18	21 **Tell Her About It**	Columbia 04012
9/24/83	**3**	22	22● **Uptown Girl**	Columbia 04149
12/17/83+	**10**	18	23 **An Innocent Man**	Columbia 04259
3/24/84	**14**	18	24 The Longest Time	Columbia 04400
7/07/84	**27**	15	25 Leave A Tender Moment Alone	Columbia 04514
1/26/85	**18**	16	26 Keeping The Faith	Columbia 04681
7/13/85	**9**	16	27 **You're Only Human (Second Wind)**	Columbia 05417
10/05/85	**34**	10	28 The Night Is Still Young	Columbia 05657
6/07/86	**10**	15	29 **Modern Woman**	Epic 06118
			from the film "Ruthless People"	
8/09/86	**10**	18	30 **A Matter Of Trust**	Columbia 06108
11/15/86+	**18**	7	31 This Is The Time	Columbia 06526
			5-31: produced by Phil Ramone; Billy Joel composed all of his hits	
			JOHN & ERNEST	
4/14/73	**31**	11	1 Super Fly Meets Shaft [N]	Rainy Wed. 201

DEBUT DATE	PEAK POS	WKS CHR	ARTIST — Record Title	Label & Number
			ELTON JOHN	
			Born Reginald Kenneth Dwight on 3/25/47 in Pinner, Middlesex, England. Formed his first group, Bluesology, in 1966. Group backed visiting U.S. soul artists and later became Long John Baldry's backing band. Took the name of Elton John from the first names of Bluesology member Elton Dean and John Baldry. Teamed up with lyricist Bernie Taupin beginning in 1969. Formed own record label, Rocket Records, in 1973. Performed as the Pinball Wizard in the film version of "Tommy".	
8/15/70	**92**	5	1 Border Song	Uni 55246
11/28/70+	**8**	14	2 **Your Song**	Uni 55265
3/20/71	**34**	9	3 Friends from the British film of the same title	Uni 55277
12/18/71+	**24**	10	4 Levon	Uni 55314
3/04/72	**41**	7	5 Tiny Dancer	Uni 55318
5/06/72	**6**	15	6 **Rocket Man**	Uni 55328
8/12/72	**8**	10	7 **Honky Cat**	Uni 55343
12/09/72+	**1^{3}**	17	8 ● **Crocodile Rock**	MCA 40000
4/07/73	**2^{1}**	15	9 **Daniel**	MCA 40046
8/04/73	**12**	12	10 Saturday Night's Alright For Fighting	MCA 40105
10/27/73	**2^{3}**	17	11 ● **Goodbye Yellow Brick Road**	MCA 40148
2/16/74	**1^{1}**	18	12 ● **Bennie And The Jets**	MCA 40198
6/22/74	**2^{2}**	15	13 ● **Don't Let The Sun Go Down On Me**	MCA 40259
9/07/74	**4**	14	14 **The Bitch Is Back**	MCA 40297
11/30/74+	**1^{2}**	14	15 ● **Lucy In The Sky With Diamonds** with the reggae guitars of Dr. Winston O'Boogie (John Lennon)	MCA 40344
3/08/75	**1^{2}**	21	16 ● **Philadelphia Freedom** ELTON JOHN BAND	MCA 40364
7/05/75	**4**	13	17 ● **Someone Saved My Life Tonight**	MCA 40421
10/11/75	**1^{3}**	15	18 ● **Island Girl**	MCA 40461
1/24/76	**14**	11	19 Grow Some Funk Of Your Own/	
		11	20 I Feel Like A Bullet (In The Gun Of Robert Ford)	MCA 40505
7/04/76	**1^{4}**	20	21 ● **Don't Go Breaking My Heart** ELTON JOHN & KIKI DEE	Rocket 40585
11/13/76	**6**	14	22 ● **Sorry Seems To Be The Hardest Word**	MCA/Rocket 40645
2/12/77	**28**	6	23 Bite Your Lip (Get up and dance!) all of above produced by Gus Dudgeon (also #40-42 below)	MCA/Rocket 40677
4/15/78	**34**	8	24 Ego	MCA 40892
11/11/78	**22**	10	25 Part-Time Love	MCA 40973
6/09/79	**9**	18	26 ● **Mama Can't Buy You Love**	MCA 41042
9/29/79	**31**	10	27 Victim Of Love	MCA 41126
5/03/80	**3**	21	28 ● **Little Jeannie**	MCA 41236
8/09/80	**39**	12	29 (Sartorial Eloquence) Don't Ya Wanna Play This Game No More?	MCA 41293
5/09/81	**21**	13	30 Nobody Wins	Geffen 49722
7/25/81	**34**	13	31 Chloe	Geffen 49788
3/20/82	**13**	17	32 Empty Garden (Hey Hey Johnny)	Geffen 50049
7/10/82	**12**	18	33 Blue Eyes	Geffen 29954
5/07/83	**12**	16	34 I'm Still Standing	Geffen 29639
8/06/83	**25**	12	35 Kiss The Bride	Geffen 29568
10/29/83+	**4**	23	36 **I Guess That's Why They Call It The Blues**	Geffen 29460
6/09/84	**5**	19	37 **Sad Songs (Say So Much)**	Geffen 29292
9/08/84	**16**	14	38 Who Wears These Shoes?	Geffen 29189
12/01/84+	**38**	13	39 In Neon	Geffen 29111
10/26/85	**20**	14	40 Wrap Her Up	Geffen 28873
1/18/86	**7**	18	41 **Nikita**	Geffen 28800
10/18/86	**55**	8	42 Heartache All Over The World 1-14, 16-24, 32, 34-42: written by Elton John and Bernie Taupin	Geffen 28578
			LITTLE WILLIE JOHN	
			Born William Edgar John on 11/15/37 in Cullendale, Arkansas. Raised in Detroit. First recorded for Prize in 1953. Convicted of manslaughter in 1966, died of a heart attack in Walla Walla Prison on 5/26/68.	
7/07/56	**24**	15	1 Fever Best Seller #24 / Top 100 #27	King 4935
4/07/58	**20**	17	2 Talk To Me, Talk To Me Top 100 #20 / Best Seller #22	King 5108

DEBUT DATE	PEAK POS	WKS CHR	ARTIST — Record Title	Label & Number
			LITTLE WILLIE JOHN — Cont'd	
8/11/58	**66**	4	3 You're A Sweetheart	King 5142
8/03/59	**60**	9	4 Leave My Kitten Alone	King 5219
2/22/60	**100**	1	5 Let Them Talk	King 5274
5/09/60	**63**	6	6 A Cottage For Sale #4 hit for Guy Lombardo in 1930	King 5342
5/30/60	**38**	12	7 Heartbreak (It's Hurtin' Me)	King 5356
9/05/60	**13**	16	8 Sleep #1 hit for Fred Waring's Pennsylvanians in 1924	King 5394
11/28/60	**48**	8	9 Walk Slow	King 5428
1/23/61	**60**	6	10 Leave My Kitten Alone [R]	King 5452
3/13/61	**61**	6	11 The Very Thought Of You #1 hit for Ray Noble in 1934	King 5458
5/15/61	**71**	5	12 (I've Got) Spring Fever	King 5503
7/17/61	**93**	3	13 Now You Know/	
9/18/61	**87**	1	14 Take My Love (I Want To Give It All To You)	King 5516
			MABLE JOHN R&B songstress. Member of the Raeletts. Sister of Little Willie John.	
8/06/66	**95**	2	1 Your Good Thing (Is About To End)	Stax 192
			ROBERT JOHN Born Robert John Pedrick, Jr. in Brooklyn in 1946. First recorded at age 12 for Big Top Records. In 1963, recorded as lead singer with Bobby & The Consoles.	
11/10/58	**74**	4	1 White Bucks And Saddle Shoes shown as: **BOBBY PEDRICK JR.**	Big Top 3004
4/13/68	**49**	12	2 If You Don't Want My Love	Columbia 44435
11/28/70	**71**	5	3 When The Party Is Over	A&M 1210
1/01/72	**3**	17	4● **The Lion Sleeps Tonight** adaptation of a South African song (adapted in 1952 as "Wimoweh")	Atlantic 2846
6/24/72	**99**	2	5 Hushabye	Atlantic 2884
5/19/79	**1**[1]	27	6● **Sad Eyes**	EMI America 8015
12/08/79+	**41**	11	7 Lonely Eyes	EMI America 8030
7/19/80	**31**	13	8 Hey There Lonely Girl	EMI America 8049
10/25/80	**70**	5	9 Sherry	EMI America 8061
2/12/83	**68**	4	10 Bread And Butter	Motown 1664
			JOHNNIE & JOE R&B duo from the Bronx: Johnnie Louise Richardson and Joe Rivers. Johnnie is the daughter of the late J&S Records owner, Zell Sanders.	
5/13/57	**8**	22	1 **Over The Mountain; Across The Sea** Top 100 #8 / Best Seller #9 / Juke Box #17 end	Chess 1654
9/26/60	**89**	2	2 Over The Mountain; Across The Sea [R]	Chess 1654
			JOHNNY & THE EXPRESSIONS Soul group led by Johnny Mathews.	
1/22/66	**79**	5	1 Something I Want To Tell You	Josie 946
			JOHNNY & THE HURRICANES Rock and roll instrumental band formed as the Orbits in Toledo, Ohio in 1958. Consisted of leader John Pocisk ("Paris"), saxophone; Paul Tesluk, organ; Dave Yorko, guitar; Lionel "Butch" Mattice, bass; and Tony Kaye, drums (replaced in late 1959 by Bill Savich). First recorded for Twirl in 1959. Paris had own label, Attila, from 1965-70.	
4/27/59	**23**	14	1 Crossfire [I]	Warwick 502
8/03/59	**5**	17	2 **Red River Rock** [I] rock version of "Red River Valley"	Warwick 509
11/02/59	**25**	13	3 Reveille Rock [I] rock version of the Army bugle call "Reveille"	Warwick 513
2/15/60	**15**	13	4 Beatnik Fly [I] rock version of "Blue Tail Fly"	Warwick 520
5/30/60	**48**	9	5 Down Yonder [I] there were 10 charted versions of this tune between 1921 and 1951	Big Top 3036
9/05/60	**60**	6	6 Rocking Goose/ [I]	
8/29/60	**97**	1	7 Revival [I] rock version of "When The Saints Go Marching In"	Big Top 3051
12/05/60	**91**	1	8 You Are My Sunshine [I] written in 1940 by former Louisiana governor Jimmie Davis	Big Top 3056
2/27/61	**86**	2	9 Ja-Da [I] #4 hit for Arthur Fields in 1919	Big Top 3063

DEBUT DATE	PEAK POS	WKS CHR	ARTIST — Record Title	Label & Number
			JOHNNY T. ANGEL	
6/08/74	**94**	4	1 Tell Laura I Love Her	Bell 45472
			SAMMY JOHNS	
			Pop singer, songwriter, guitarist from Charlotte, North Carolina.	
10/12/74	**68**	8	1 Early Morning Love	GRC 2021
2/01/75	**5**	17	2 ● **Chevy Van**	GRC 2046
5/31/75	**52**	8	3 Rag Doll	GRC 2062
			BETTY JOHNSON	
			Born on 3/16/32 in Charlotte, NC. Married to musical conductor Charles Randolph Grean. Regular on NBC-TV's "Tonight Show" starring Jack Parr.	
3/03/56	**94**	1	1 I'll Wait	Bally 1000
8/18/56	**72**	4	2 Clay Idol	Bally 1013
11/24/56+	**9**	22	3 **I Dreamed** Jockey #9 / Top 100 #12 / Juke Box #15 / Best Seller #22 featured on an episode of NBC-TV's "Modern Romances"	Bally 1020
4/29/57	**25**	9	4 Little White Lies/ Jockey #25 / Top 100 #40 #1 hit for Fred Waring's Pennsylvanians in 1930	
5/06/57	**70**	6	5 1492	Bally 1033
2/24/58	**17**	16	6 The Little Blue Man [N] Jockey #17 / Top 100 #19 / Best Seller #20 voice of the Little Blue Man: Hugh Downs (host of TV's "20/20")	Atlantic 1169
6/30/58	**19**	7	7 Dream Jockey #19 / Top 100 #58 #1 hit for the Pied Pipers in 1945	Atlantic 1186
10/06/58	**56**	5	8 Hoopa Hoola	Atlantic 2002
1/12/59	**99**	1	9 You Can't Get To Heaven On Roller Skates 4-9: orchestra conducted by Betty's husband, Charles Grean	Atlantic 2009
			BUBBER JOHNSON	
11/12/55	**92**	1	1 Come Home	King 4822
			BUDDY JOHNSON	
			Born Woodrow Wilson Johnson on 1/10/15 in Darlington, SC. Died on 2/9/77 of a brain tumor. R&B bandleader from 1940s to 60s whose vocalists included Arthur Prysock and Buddy's sister, Ella Johnson.	
11/12/55	**94**	1	1 It's Obdacious	Mercury 70695
12/31/60+	**78**	3	2 I Don't Want Nobody (To Have My Love But You) **ELLA JOHNSON with BUDDY JOHNSON**	Mercury 71723
			DON JOHNSON	
			Actor born on 12/15/49, Flatt Creek, MO. Plays Sonny Crockett on TV's "Miami Vice".	
8/23/86	**5**	15	1 **Heartbeat**	Epic 06285
11/22/86	**56**	11	2 Heartache Away	Epic 06426
			ELLA JOHNSON - see BUDDY JOHNSON	
			JESSE JOHNSON'S REVUE	
			Jesse was lead guitarist with The Time.	
3/16/85	**61**	11	1 Be Your Man	A&M 2702
7/20/85	**76**	8	2 I Want My Girl	A&M 2749
10/25/86	**53**	16	3 Crazay **JESSE JOHNSON featuring SLY STONE**	A&M 2878
			KEVIN JOHNSON	
			Singer, songwriter, guitarist from Australia.	
11/10/73	**73**	4	1 Rock 'N Roll (I Gave You The Best Years Of My Life)	Mainstream 5548
			LOU JOHNSON	
10/19/63	**74**	8	1 Reach Out For Me	Big Top 3153
8/22/64	**49**	7	2 (There's) Always Something There To Remind Me	Big Hill 552
11/13/65	**59**	9	3 A Time To Love-A Time To Cry (Petite Fleur)	Big Top 101
			MARV JOHNSON	
			Born on 10/15/38 in Detroit. R&B singer, songwriter, pianist. With Jr. Serenaders vocal group, mid-50s. First recorded for Kudo in 1958. In early 70s, worked in sales and promotion for Motown.	
3/16/59	**30**	15	1 Come To Me released regionally on Tamla 101 - Berry Gordy's first release	United Art. 160
7/13/59	**82**	4	2 I'm Coming Home	United Art. 175
11/02/59+	**10**	22	3 **You Got What It Takes**	United Art. 185

DEBUT DATE	PEAK POS	WKS CHR	ARTIST — Record Title	Label & Number
			MARV JOHNSON — Cont'd	
3/07/60	**9**	13	4 **I Love The Way You Love**	United Art. 208
5/30/60	**74**	7	5 Ain't Gonna Be That Way/	
6/13/60	**63**	6	6 All The Love I've Got	United Art. 226
			female backing singers on above 6: The Rayber Voices	
9/05/60	**20**	11	7 (You've Got To) Move Two Mountains	United Art. 241
12/12/60+	**58**	7	8 Happy Days	United Art. 273
3/13/61	**61**	6	9 Merry-Go-Round	United Art. 294
			MICHAEL JOHNSON	
			Born on 8/8/44 in Denver. Pop singer, guitarist. Member of the Chad Mitchell Trio from 1967-68.	
4/22/78	**12**	16	1 Bluer Than Blue	EMI America 8001
8/12/78	**32**	12	2 Almost Like Being In Love	EMI America 8004
8/04/79	**19**	20	3 This Night Won't Last Forever	EMI America 8019
8/23/80	**86**	3	4 You Can Call Me Blue	EMI America 8054
			ROZETTA JOHNSON	
			Soul songstress from Tuscaloosa, Alabama.	
12/12/70	**94**	1	1 A Woman's Way	Clintone 001
			SYL JOHNSON	
			Born Syl Thompson on 7/1/39 in Holly Springs, Mississippi; raised in Chicago. R&B singer, songwriter, guitarist. Recorded for Federal Records, 1959-62.	
8/19/67	**97**	3	1 Come On Sock It To Me	Twilight 100
10/14/67	**95**	2	2 Different Strokes	Twilight 103
12/13/69+	**68**	6	3 Is It Because I'm Black	Twinight 125
2/24/73	**95**	3	4 We Did It	Hi 2229
10/27/73	**72**	6	5 Back For A Taste Of Your Love	Hi 2250
6/14/75	**48**	7	6 Take Me To The River	Hi 2285
			TOM JOHNSTON	
			Lead singer and guitarist of The Doobie Brothers from 1971-78.	
11/17/79+	**34**	12	1 Savannah Nights	Warner 49096
			JOINER, ARKANSAS JUNIOR HIGH SCHOOL BAND	
5/16/60	**53**	8	1 National City [I]	Liberty 55244
			adapted from the 1906 march "National Emblem"	
			FRANCE JOLI	
			French-Canadian singer from Montreal, Canada. Age 16 in 1979.	
9/01/79	**15**	16	1 Come To Me	Prelude 8001
			JON & ROBIN & THE IN CROWD	
			Jon & Robin Abnor.	
5/06/67	**18**	10	1 Do It Again A Little Bit Slower	Abnak 119
8/19/67	**100**	2	2 Drums	Abnak 122
			above 2 produced by Dale Hawkins	
3/16/68	**87**	4	3 Dr. Jon (The Medicine Man)	Abnak 127
			JON & VANGELIS	
			Jon Anderson (lead singer of Yes) and Greek keyboardist Evangelos Papathanassiou.	
8/16/80	**58**	6	1 I Hear You Now	Polydor 2098
5/22/82	**51**	9	2 I'll Find My Way Home	Polydor 2205
			THE JONES GIRLS	
			Soul sister trio: Shirley, Brenda and Valorie Jones. Back-up singers for Lou Rawls, Teddy Pendergrass and Aretha Franklin. With Diana Ross from 1975-78. Sang with Le Pamplemousse.	
6/23/79	**38**	11	1 ● You Gonna Make Me Love Somebody Else	Phil. Int. 3680
			DAVY JONES	
			Born on 12/30/46 in Manchester, England. Member of The Monkees.	
8/14/65	**93**	3	1 What Are We Going To Do?	Colpix 784
6/19/71	**52**	9	2 Rainy Jane	Bell 45111
			ETTA JONES	
			Born on 11/25/28 in Aiken, SC. Jazz singer with Earl Hines' orchestra, 1949-52.	
11/07/60	**36**	7	1 Don't Go To Strangers	Prestige 180
1/16/61	**65**	8	2 When I Fall In Love	King 5424
			originally charted by Doris Day in 1952 (POS 20)	
3/13/61	**91**	1	3 Canadian Sunset	Prestige 191

DEBUT DATE	PEAK POS	WKS CHR	ARTIST — Record Title	Label & Number
			GEORGE JONES	
			Born on 9/12/31 in Saratoga, Texas. First recorded for Starday in 1954. Married to Tammy Wynette from 1967-73. The Reigning monarch of Country male vocalists.	
5/04/59	73	5	1 White Lightning written by the Big Bopper, J.P. Richardson	Mercury 71406
7/27/59	93	3	2 Who Shot Sam	Mercury 71464
7/03/61	76	4	3 Tender Years	Mercury 71804
1/23/65	96	1	4 The Race Is On	United Art. 751
4/17/65	99	1	5 I've Got Five Dollars And It's Saturday Night GEORGE JONES & GENE PITNEY	Musicor 1066
			GRACE JONES	
			Born on 5/19/52 in Spanishtown, Jamaica. Disco singer, fashion model, actress. Raised in Syracuse, New York from age 12.	
1/22/77	71	7	1 Sorry/	
		7	2 That's The Trouble	Beam Junction 102
5/07/77	83	6	3 I Need A Man	Beam Junction 104
11/29/86+	69	9	4 I'm Not Perfect (But I'm Perfect For You)	Manhattan 50052
			HOWARD JONES	
			Born on 2/23/55 in Southampton, England. Pop singer, songwriter, synth wizard.	
1/21/84	27	15	1 New Song	Elektra 69766
4/21/84	33	13	2 What Is Love?	Elektra 69737
3/23/85	5	23	3 **Things Can Only Get Better**	Elektra 69651
7/06/85	19	16	4 Life In One Day	Elektra 69631
9/28/85	49	9	5 Like To Get To Know You Well	Elektra 69598
4/12/86	4	23	6 **No One Is To Blame**	Elektra 69549
10/18/86	17	16	7 You Know I Love You...Don't You?	Elektra 69512
			JACK JONES	
			Born on 1/14/38 in Los Angeles. Son of actor/singer Allan Jones, who had the hit "The Donkey Serenade" (POS 8) the year Jack was born.	
3/03/62	66	8	1 Lollipops And Roses	Kapp 435
5/04/63	75	4	2 Call Me Irresponsible from the film "Papa's Delicate Condition"	Kapp 516
10/05/63	92	1	3 Toys In The Attic/ theme from the film of the same title	
11/02/63+	14	14	4 Wives And Lovers inspired by the film of the same title	Kapp 551
2/15/64	62	8	5 Love With The Proper Stranger from the film of the same title	Kapp 571
5/30/64	59	9	6 The First Night Of The Full Moon	Kapp 589
8/15/64	62	6	7 Where Love Has Gone from the film of the same title	Kapp 608
11/28/64+	30	11	8 Dear Heart from the film of the same title	Kapp 635
2/27/65	15	11	9 The Race Is On	Kapp 651
6/12/65	46	9	10 Seein' The Right Love Go Wrong	Kapp 672
10/09/65	73	5	11 Just Yesterday	Kapp 699
12/11/65+	71	6	12 Love Bug	Kapp 722
6/04/66	35	10	13 The Impossible Dream from the musical "Man Of La Mancha"	Kapp 755
10/29/66	62	8	14 A Day In The Life Of A Fool	Kapp 781
1/21/67	39	11	15 Lady	Kapp 800
4/15/67	81	5	16 I'm Indestructible	Kapp 818
6/10/67	73	6	17 Now I Know	Kapp 833
9/09/67	92	2	18 Our Song	Kapp 847
12/02/67	99	2	19 Live For Life from the film of the same title	RCA 9365
2/17/68	92	2	20 If You Ever Leave Me	RCA 9441
			JIMMY JONES	
			Born on 6/2/37 in Birmingham, Alabama. Joined the R&B group, Sparks Of Rhythm, in New York, 1955. Formed own group, the Savoys (later: Pretenders) in 1956.	
12/28/59+	2[1]	18	1 **Handy Man**	Cub 9049
4/18/60	3	15	2 **Good Timin'**	Cub 9067
7/11/60	83	5	3 That's When I Cried	Cub 9072

DEBUT DATE	PEAK POS	WKS CHR	ARTIST — Record Title	Label & Number
			JIMMY JONES — Cont'd	
3/27/61	**85**	3	4 I Told You So	Cub 9085
			JOE JONES	
			Born on 8/12/26 in New Orleans. Pianist, valet for B.B. King, early 50s. Produced for The Dixie Cups and Alvin Robinson.	
9/19/60	**3**	13	1 **You Talk Too Much**	Roulette 4304
4/03/61	**89**	3	2 California Sun	Roulette 4344
			KAY CEE JONES	
12/03/55+	**52**	7	1 The Japanese Farewell Song	Marquee 1031
			LINDA JONES	
			Born on 1/14/44 in Newark, NJ. Died of diabetes on 3/14/72. R&B singer. First recorded for MGM/Cub as "Linda Lane" in 1963.	
6/24/67	**21**	12	1 Hypnotized	Loma 2070
9/30/67	**61**	6	2 What've I Done (To Make You Mad)	Loma 2077
1/20/68	**93**	3	3 Give My Love A Try	Loma 2085
2/26/72	**74**	9	4 Your Precious Love	Turbo 021
			ORAN "JUICE" JONES	
			Soul balladeer born in Houston and raised in Harlem.	
9/13/86	**9**	19	1 **The Rain**	Def Jam 06209
			QUINCY JONES	
			Born Quincy Delight Jones, Jr. on 3/14/33 in Chicago. Composer, conductor, arranger, producer. Began as a jazz trumpeter, with Lionel Hampton, 1950-53. Music Director for Mercury Records in 1961, then Vice President in 1964. Wrote scores for many films, 1965-73. Scored TV series "Roots" in 1977. Produced Michael Jackson's "Thriller" album. Arranger and producer for hundreds of successful singers and orchestras. Winner of 19 Grammys.	
5/16/70	**74**	3	1 Killer Joe [I]	A&M 1163
3/11/72	**57**	8	2 Money Runner [I] from the movie "$"	Reprise 1062
10/11/75	**70**	10	3 Is It Love That We're Missin' featuring The Brothers Johnson	A&M 1743
3/05/77	**57**	7	4 "Roots" Medley [I] Motherland/Theme From "Roots" (Roots Mural Theme)	A&M 1909
6/10/78	**21**	16	5 Stuff Like That vocals: Ashford & Simpson and Chaka Khan	A&M 2043
4/11/81	**28**	12	6 Ai No Corrida featuring the vocals of Dune	A&M 2309
8/15/81	**17**	23	7 Just Once	A&M 2357
12/19/81+	**14**	21	8 One Hundred Ways above 2: **QUINCY JONES featuring JAMES INGRAM**	A&M 2387
			RICKIE LEE JONES	
			Born on 11/8/54 in Chicago. Pop jazz-styled singer, songwriter. Moved to Los Angeles in 1977.	
4/28/79	**4**	15	1 **Chuck E.'s In Love**	Warner 8825
7/28/79	**40**	9	2 Young Blood	Warner 49018
10/03/81	**64**	7	3 A Lucky Guy	Warner 49816
9/29/84	**83**	4	4 The Real End	Warner 29191
			TAMIKO JONES	
11/12/66	**88**	2	1 A Man And A Woman **TAMIKO JONES with HERBIE MANN** from the film of the same title	Atlantic 2362
4/05/75	**60**	10	2 Touch Me Baby (Reaching Out For Your Love)	Arista 0110
			TOM JONES	
			Born Thomas Jones Woodward on 6/7/40 in Pontypridd, Wales. Worked local clubs as Tommy Scott, formed own trio, The Senators in 1963. Solo to London in 1964. Host of his own TV musical variety series from 1969-71.	
4/10/65	**10**	12	1 **It's Not Unusual**	Parrot 9737
5/29/65	**42**	9	2 Little Lonely One	Tower 126
6/19/65	**3**	12	3 **What's New Pussycat?** from the film of the same title	Parrot 9765
8/28/65	**27**	8	4 With These Hands Eddie Fisher's version made POS 7 in 1953	Parrot 9787
12/11/65+	**25**	9	5 Thunderball from the James Bond film "Thunderball"	Parrot 9801
2/19/66	**74**	4	6 Promise Her Anything from the film of the same title	Parrot 9809

DEBUT DATE	PEAK POS	WKS CHR	ARTIST — Record Title	Label & Number
			TOM JONES — Cont'd	
6/18/66	**58**	6	7 Not Responsible	Parrot 40006
12/24/66+	**11**	12	8 Green, Green Grass Of Home	Parrot 40009
3/11/67	**27**	8	9 Detroit City	Parrot 40012
5/20/67	**49**	6	10 Funny Familiar Forgotten Feelings	Parrot 40014
8/12/67	**68**	4	11 Sixteen Tons	Parrot 40016
9/09/67	**49**	7	12 I'll Never Fall In Love Again	Parrot 40018
12/30/67+	**57**	5	13 I'm Coming Home	Parrot 40024
3/16/68	**15**	15	14 Delilah	Parrot 40025
8/31/68	**35**	8	15 Help Yourself	Parrot 40029
12/21/68+	**48**	10	16 A Minute Of Your Time	Parrot 40035
5/24/69	**13**	11	17 Love Me Tonight	Parrot 40038
7/26/69	**6**	16	18 ● **I'll Never Fall In Love Again** [R]	Parrot 40018
12/27/69+	**5**	11	19 ● **Without Love (There Is Nothing)**	Parrot 40045
5/02/70	**13**	9	20 Daughter Of Darkness	Parrot 40048
8/22/70	**14**	8	21 I (Who Have Nothing)	Parrot 40051
11/21/70	**25**	8	22 Can't Stop Loving You	Parrot 40056
2/06/71	**2^{1}**	14	23 ● **She's A Lady** written by Paul Anka	Parrot 40058
5/22/71	**26**	10	24 Puppet Man/ written by Neil Sedaka	
		5	25 Resurrection Shuffle	Parrot 40064
10/30/71	**41**	7	26 Till	Parrot 40067
4/29/72	**80**	7	27 The Young New Mexican Puppeteer	Parrot 40070
5/12/73	**60**	8	28 Letter To Lucille	Parrot 40074
1/08/77	**15**	16	29 Say You'll Stay Until Tomorrow	Epic 50308
			THE JONESES R&B/disco quartet from New York City. None of the members are named Jones.	
10/05/74+	**47**	16	1 Sugar Pie Guy - Pt. 1	Mercury 73614
			JANIS JOPLIN Born on 1/19/43 in Port Arthur, Texas. White blues/rock singer. Nicknamed Pearl. To San Francisco in 1966, joined Big Brother & The Holding Company. Left band to go solo in 1968. Died of a heroin overdose in Hollywood on 10/4/70. The Bette Midler film "The Rose" was inspired by Joplin's life.	
11/08/69	**41**	9	1 Kozmic Blues	Columbia 45023
1/30/71	**1^{2}**	15	2 **Me And Bobby McGee**	Columbia 45314
5/15/71	**42**	6	3 Cry Baby	Columbia 45379
9/11/71	**78**	2	4 Get It While You Can	Columbia 45433
7/15/72	**91**	4	5 Down On Me also see Joplin's version with Big Brother & The Holding Company	Columbia 45630
			MARGIE JOSEPH Born in 1950 in Pascagoula, MS. First recorded at Muscle Shoals for Okeh in 1967.	
4/03/71	**96**	3	1 Stop! In The Name Of Love	Volt 4056
8/10/74	**69**	4	2 My Love	Atlantic 3032
12/21/74+	**91**	4	3 Words (Are Impossible)	Atlantic 3220
			JOURNEY Rock group formed in San Francisco in 1973. Consisted of Neal Schon, George Tickner (guitars), Gregg Rolie (keyboards, vocals), Ross Valory (bass) and Aynsley Dunbar (drums). Schon and Rolie had been in Santana. Tickner left in 1975. Steve Perry (lead vocals) added in 1978. Dunbar was replaced by Steve Smith in 1979. Jonathan Cain (keyboards) added in 1981, replacing Rolie. In 1986 group pared down to a 3-man core: Perry, Schon and Cain.	
4/08/78	**57**	8	1 Wheel In The Sky	Columbia 10700
7/01/78	**83**	4	2 Anytime	Columbia 10757
8/19/78	**68**	10	3 Lights	Columbia 10800
4/07/79	**58**	8	4 Just The Same Way	Columbia 10928
7/21/79	**16**	20	5 Lovin', Touchin', Squeezin'	Columbia 11036
1/12/80	**70**	4	6 Too Late	Columbia 11143
3/01/80	**23**	15	7 Any Way You Want It	Columbia 11213
5/24/80	**32**	13	8 Walks Like A Lady	Columbia 11275
8/23/80	**55**	8	9 Good Morning Girl/Stay Awhile	Columbia 11339
2/28/81	**34**	13	10 The Party's Over (Hopelessly In Love)	Columbia 60505
7/18/81	**4**	21	11 **Who's Crying Now**	Columbia 02241

DEBUT DATE	PEAK POS	WKS CHR	ARTIST — Record Title	Label & Number
			JOURNEY — Cont'd	
10/31/81	**9**	16	12 **Don't Stop Believin'**	Columbia 02567
1/16/82	**2^{6}**	18	13 **Open Arms**	Columbia 02687
5/22/82	**19**	14	14 Still They Ride	Columbia 02883
2/05/83	**8**	17	15 **Separate Ways (Worlds Apart)**	Columbia 03513
4/16/83	**12**	16	16 Faithfully	Columbia 03840
7/09/83	**23**	12	17 After The Fall	Columbia 04004
9/24/83	**23**	15	18 Send Her My Love	Columbia 04151
1/26/85	**9**	16	19 **Only The Young** from the film "Vision Quest"	Geffen 29090
4/12/86	**9**	15	20 **Be Good To Yourself**	Columbia 05869
6/21/86	**17**	13	21 Suzanne	Columbia 06134
8/30/86	**17**	14	22 Girl Can't Help It	Columbia 06302
12/06/86+	**14**	21	23 I'll Be Alright Without You	Columbia 06301
			JOY OF COOKING Berkeley, California country-rock quintet led by female vocalists Terry Garthwaite and Toni Brown.	
4/24/71	**66**	8	1 Brownsville	Brownsville 3075
			RODDIE JOY	
3/20/65	**86**	5	1 Come Back Baby	Red Bird 10021
			JUDAS PRIEST Heavy-metal rock band formed in Birmingham, England in 1973. Group consists of vocalist Rob Halford, guitarists K.K. Downing and Glenn Tipton, bassist Ian Hill and drummer Dave Holland.	
11/06/82	**67**	7	1 You've Got Another Thing Comin'	Columbia 03168
			PATRICK JUDE - see JENNY BURTON	
			JULIE Actress, singer Julie Budd.	
1/17/76	**93**	4	1 One Fine Day	Tom Cat 10454
			JUMP 'N THE SADDLE Chicago-based band - Peter Quinn, lead singer.	
12/03/83+	**15**	14	1 The Curly Shuffle [N] a Three Stooges parody	Atlantic 89718
			JUNIOR Full name: Junior Giscombe. R&B/funk singer, songwriter from England.	
2/13/82	**30**	13	1 Mama Used To Say	Mercury 76132
			JUST US Consists of New York City record producers Chip Taylor and Al Gorgoni.	
3/12/66	**34**	11	1 I Can't Grow Peaches On A Cherry Tree	Colpix 803
			BILL JUSTIS Born on 10/14/26 in Birmingham, Alabama. Died on 7/15/82 in Nashville. Session saxophonist, arranger and producer. Led house band for Sun Records.	
11/18/57	**2^{1}**	20	1 **Raunchy** [I] Best Seller #2 / Top 100 #3 / Jockey #5 sax: Bill Justis; guitar: Sid Manker	Phillips 3519
3/10/58	**42**	8	2 College Man [I] Best Seller #42 / Top 100 #42	Phillips 3522

K

DEBUT DATE	PEAK POS	WKS CHR	ARTIST — Record Title	Label & Number
			BERT KAEMPFERT Born on 10/16/23 in Hamburg, Germany. Multi-instrumentalist, bandleader, record producer, composer, arranger for Polydor Records in Germany. Produced the first Beatles' recording session. Died on 6/21/80 in Zug, Switzerland.	
11/14/60+	**1^{3}**	17	1 **Wonderland By Night** [I] trumpet solo by Charly Tabor	Decca 31141
2/06/61	**73**	6	2 Cerveza [I]	Decca 30866
3/27/61	**31**	7	3 Tenderly [I] Rosemary Clooney's theme song (POS 17-1952)	Decca 31236
7/31/61	**48**	7	4 Now And Forever [I]	Decca 31279
1/20/62	**42**	10	5 Afrikaan Beat [I]	Decca 31350

DEBUT DATE	PEAK POS	WKS CHR	ARTIST — Record Title		Label & Number
			BERT KAEMPFERT — Cont'd		
5/19/62	**67**	6	6 That Happy Feeling	[I]	Decca 31388
1/23/65	**11**	13	7 Red Roses For A Blue Lady #3 hit for Vaughn Monroe in 1949	[I]	Decca 31722
5/01/65	**33**	8	8 Three O'Clock In The Morning there were 6 Top 10 versions of this tune from 1921-30	[I]	Decca 31778
7/10/65	**59**	10	9 Moon Over Naples tune later known as "Spanish Eyes"	[I]	Decca 31812
1/22/66	**54**	7	10 Bye Bye Blues #5 hit in 1930 for Bert Lown's orchestra (their theme song)	[I]	Decca 31882
10/15/66	**100**	1	11 I Can't Give You Anything But Love there were 6 Top 20 versions of this tune from 1928-29	[I]	Decca 32008
			KAJAGOOGOO English pop/synth quintet led by Limahl.		
4/23/83	**5**	19	1 **Too Shy**		EMI America 8161
8/27/83	**78**	4	2 Hang On Now		EMI America 8171
			KALIN TWINS Herbert and Harold, born on 2/16/39 in Port Jervis, New York.		
6/23/58	**5**	15	1 **When** Hot 100 #5 / Best Seller #7 / Jockey #8		Decca 30642
9/29/58	**12**	15	2 Forget Me Not		Decca 30745
1/12/59	**42**	10	3 It's Only The Beginning		Decca 30807
7/06/59	**97**	1	4 Sweet Sugar Lips		Decca 30911
			KITTY KALLEN Born on 5/25/22 in Philadelphia. Big band singer with Jack Teagarden, Jimmy Dorsey, and Harry James.		
11/12/55	**76**	3	1 Sweet Kentucky Rose		Decca 29708
1/07/56	**39**	9	2 Go On With The Wedding **KITTY KALLEN & GEORGIE SHAW**		Decca 29776
10/05/59	**34**	12	3 If I Give My Heart To You there were 5 Top 30 versions of this tune in 1954		Columbia 41473
2/01/60	**55**	5	4 That Old Feeling Shep Fields had a #1 version in 1937		Columbia 41546
12/22/62+	**18**	10	5 My Coloring Book		RCA 8124
			THE GUNTER KALLMANN CHORUS German chorus.		
12/24/66+	**63**	8	1 Wish Me A Rainbow from the film "This Property Is Condemned"		Four Corners 138
			KAREN KAMON Singer, married to producer Phil Ramone.		
7/28/84	**88**	2	1 Loverboy		Columbia 04474
			MADLEEN KANE		
2/06/82	**77**	5	1 You Can		Chalet 1225
			KANO Italian disco band.		
12/26/81+	**89**	5	1 Can't Hold Back (Your Loving)		Mirage 3878
			KANSAS Progressive rock group formed in Topeka in 1970. Consisted of Steve Walsh (lead vocals, keyboards), Kerry Livgren (guitar & keyboards), Phil Ehart (drums), Robby Steinhardt (violin), Rich Williams (guitar) and Dave Hope (bass). Walsh left in 1981 and was replaced by John Elefante. Re-formed lineup in 1986: Walsh, Ehart, Williams, Steve Morse and Billy Greer.		
12/25/76+	**11**	20	1 Carry On Wayward Son		Kirshner 4267
11/12/77+	**28**	14	2 Point Of Know Return		Kirshner 4273
1/28/78	**6**	20	3● **Dust In The Wind**		Kirshner 4274
6/10/78	**64**	6	4 Portrait (He Knew)		Kirshner 4276
1/20/79	**60**	5	5 Lonely Wind		Kirshner 4280
6/02/79	**23**	12	6 People Of The South Wind		Kirshner 4284
9/08/79	**52**	8	7 Reason To Be		Kirshner 4285
9/20/80	**40**	11	8 Hold On		Kirshner 4291
12/27/80+	**76**	5	9 Got To Rock On		Kirshner 4292
5/08/82	**17**	15	10 Play The Game Tonight		Kirshner 02903
8/21/82	**73**	6	11 Right Away		Kirshner 03084
9/03/83	**58**	7	12 Fight Fire With Fire		CBS Assoc. 04057

DEBUT DATE	PEAK POS	WKS CHR	ARTIST — Record Title		Label & Number
			KANSAS — Cont'd		
11/01/86+	**19**	18	13 All I Wanted		MCA 52958
			featuring new guitarist Steve Morse (from Dixie Dregs)		
			GABRIEL KAPLAN		
			Born on 3/31/46 in Brooklyn. Comedian. Star of TV's "Welcome Back Kotter".		
1/22/77	**91**	3	1 Up Your Nose	[N]	Elektra 45369
			KENNY KAREN		
9/08/73	**82**	4	1 That's Why You Remember		Big Tree 16007
			FRANKIE KARL & THE DREAMS		
12/14/68	**93**	1	1 Don't Be Afraid (Do As I Say)		D.C. 180
			KaSANDRA		
			Born John W. Anderson in 1935 in Panama City, FL. Soul singer, songwriter.		
12/14/68	**91**	2	1 Don't Pat Me On The Back And Call Me Brother	[S]	Capitol 2342
			KASENETZ-KATZ SINGING ORCHESTRAL CIRCUS		
			Bubble gum rock group assembled by producers Jerry Kasenetz and Jeff Katz. Features members from The 1910 Fruitgum Co./The Ohio Express/The Music Explosion.		
10/05/68	**25**	11	1 Quick Joey Small (Run Joey Run)		Buddah 64
			Joey Levine, lead singer		
			KATFISH		
9/27/75	**62**	6	1 Dear Prudence		Big Tree 16045
			written by John Lennon & Paul McCartney (on Beatles' White album)		
			KATRINA & THE WAVES		
			British-based pop/rock quartet fronted by Kansas-born Katrina Leskanich.		
3/23/85	**9**	21	1 **Walking On Sunshine**		Capitol 5466
7/27/85	**37**	10	2 Do You Want Crying		Capitol 5450
10/12/85	**71**	6	3 Que Te Quiero		Capitol 5528
4/05/86	**70**	8	4 Is That It?		Capitol 5566
			JOHN KAY		
			Born Joachim Krauledat on 4/12/44 in East Germany. Leader of Steppenwolf.		
4/22/72	**52**	7	1 I'm Movin' On		Dunhill 4309
			Hank Snow's 1950 version was #1 on the Country charts for 18 weeks		
			KAYAK		
			Rock quintet from Holland featuring Max Werner (vocals, mellotron).		
5/13/78	**55**	6	1 I Want You To Be Mine		Janus 274
			THE MARY KAYE TRIO		
			Pop trio: Mary, her brother Norman and Frankie Ross.		
4/13/59	**75**	3	1 You Can't Be True Dear		Warner 5050
			Ken Griffin had #1 vocal and #2 instrumental versions in 1948		
			SAMMY KAYE		
			Born on 3/13/10 in Rocky River, Ohio. Durable leader of popular "sweet" dance band with the slogan "Swing and Sway with Sammy Kaye". Also clarinet/alto saxman. Died of cancer on 6/2/87.		
4/03/61	**68**	3	1 Welcome Home		Decca 31204
			trumpet solo by Johnny Amoroso		
4/04/64	**36**	7	2 Charade	[I]	Decca 31589
			from the film of the same title		
			BOB KAYLI		
			Bob is Robert Gordy, brother of Motown's Berry Gordy, Jr.		
11/17/58	**96**	2	1 Everyone Was There	[N]	Carlton 482
			KBC BAND		
			Group features three founding members of Jefferson Airplane: Paul Kantner (guitar), Marty Balin (vocals) and Jack Casady (bass).		
11/29/86	**89**	4	1 It's Not You, It's Not Me		Arista 9526
			KC		
			Born Harry Wayne Casey on 1/31/51 in Hialeah, Florida. KC & The Sunshine Band leader. Seriously injured in an auto accident on 1/15/82. Own label, Meca, in 1983.		
11/17/79+	**2**[2]	23	1 ● **Yes, I'm Ready**		Casablanca 2227
6/28/80	**66**	6	2 Dancin' In The Streets		Casablanca 2278
			above 2: **TERI DeSARIO with K.C.**		
12/24/83+	**18**	21	3 Give It Up		Meca 1001

DEBUT DATE	PEAK POS	WKS CHR	ARTIST — Record Title	Label & Number
			KC & THE SUNSHINE BAND	
			Disco/R&B band formed in Florida in 1973 by lead singer, keyboardist Harry "KC" Casey and bassist Richard Finch. Integrated band contained from 7 to 11 members. Casey and Finch wrote, arranged and produced all of their hits.	
7/12/75	**1**[1]	15	1 **Get Down Tonight**	T.K. 1009
9/06/75	**88**	2	2 Shotgun Shuffle [I] THE SUNSHINE BAND	T.K. 1010
10/25/75	**1**[2]	16	3 **That's The Way (I Like It)**	T.K. 1015
3/13/76	**66**	5	4 Queen Of Clubs	T.K. 1005
7/10/76	**1**[1]	21	5 **(Shake, Shake, Shake) Shake Your Booty**	T.K. 1019
12/04/76+	**37**	12	6 I Like To Do It	T.K. 1020
2/26/77	**1**[1]	23	7 **I'm Your Boogie Man**	T.K. 1022
7/30/77	**2**[3]	20	8 **Keep It Comin' Love**	T.K. 1023
12/03/77+	**48**	7	9 Wrap Your Arms Around Me originally released as the B side of "I'm Your Boogie Man"	T.K. 1022
2/11/78	**35**	10	10 Boogie Shoes originally released as the B side of "Shake Your Booty"	T.K. 1025
5/13/78	**35**	10	11 It's The Same Old Song	T.K. 1028
10/07/78	**63**	5	12 Do You Feel All Right	T.K. 1030
12/16/78+	**68**	8	13 Who Do Ya Love	T.K. 1031
5/19/79	**50**	10	14 Do You Wanna Go Party	T.K. 1033
8/25/79+	**1**[1]	26	15 **Please Don't Go**	T.K. 1035
			ERNIE K-DOE	
			Born Ernest Kador, Jr. on 2/22/36 in New Orleans. R&B singer, songwriter. Recorded with the Blue Diamonds on Savoy in 1954. First solo recording for Specialty in 1955.	
3/27/61	**1**[1]	14	1 **Mother-In-Law** bass vocal by Benny Spellman	Minit 623
6/26/61	**53**	5	2 Te-Ta-Te-Ta-Ta	Minit 627
11/06/61	**69**	5	3 I Cried My Last Tear/	
11/13/61	**71**	4	4 A Certain Girl	Minit 634
2/24/62	**99**	1	5 Popeye Joe	Minit 641
			THE KEANE BROTHERS	
			Sons of label owner Bob Keane: John and Tom (ages 11 & 12 in 1976).	
11/13/76	**84**	5	1 Sherry	20th Century 2302
			KEITH	
			Born James Barry Keefer on 5/7/49 in Philadelphia. First recorded as "Keith & The Admirations" on Columbia in 1965.	
9/17/66	**39**	10	1 Ain't Gonna Lie	Mercury 72596
12/10/66+	**7**	14	2 **98.6** above 2 feature backing vocals by The Tokens	Mercury 72639
3/18/67	**37**	6	3 Tell Me To My Face	Mercury 72652
6/17/67	**79**	4	4 Daylight Savin' Time	Mercury 72695
			MANNY KELLEM	
			Record producer from Philadelphia. Produced many hits for Epic artists.	
2/24/68	**96**	2	1 Love Is Blue	Epic 10282
			JERRY KELLER	
			Born on 6/20/37 in Fort Smith, Arkansas. To Tulsa, Oklahoma at age 7.	
6/29/59	**14**	13	1 Here Comes Summer	Kapp 277
			MURRY KELLUM	
11/09/63	**51**	11	1 Long Tall Texan	M.O.C. 653
			CASEY KELLY	
			Real name: Daniel Cohen. Singer, songwriter, pianist, guitarist from Baton Rouge.	
9/23/72	**52**	9	1 Poor Boy	Elektra 45804
			GRACE KELLY - see BING CROSBY	
			MONTY KELLY	
			Arranger, conductor from Oakland. Trumpeter with Paul Whiteman, early 40s.	
2/29/60	**30**	11	1 Summer Set [I]	Carlton 527
			PAUL KELLY	
			Born on 6/19/40 in Miami. With R&B vocal groups the Spades and Valadeers.	
7/04/70	**49**	9	1 Stealing In The Name Of The Lord	Happy Tiger 541
1/27/73	**79**	5	2 Don't Burn Me	Warner 7657

DEBUT DATE	PEAK POS	WKS CHR	ARTIST — Record Title	Label & Number
			THE KENDALL SISTERS	
3/24/58	**73**	2	1 Yea, Yea	Argo 5291
			THE KENDALLS	
			Nashville-based father-and-daughter duo: Royce & Jeannie Kendall.	
11/05/77	**69**	7	1 Heaven's Just A Sin Away	Ovation 1103
			NAT KENDRICK & THE SWANS	
			R&B band also known as James Brown's backing band, The JB's.	
2/15/60	**84**	2	1 (Do The) Mashed Potatoes (Part 1)	Dade 1804
			vocal by "King" Coleman; Kendrick on drums	
			EDDIE KENDRICKS	
			Born on 12/17/39 in Union Springs, Alabama. Raised in Birmingham. Joined R&B group the Primes in Detroit in the late 50s. Group later evolved into The Temptations. Eddie was their lead singer from 1960-71. Eddie recently dropped the letter S from his last name.	
5/29/71	**88**	3	1 It's So Hard For Me To Say Good-Bye	Tamla 54203
6/10/72	**77**	8	2 Eddie's Love	Tamla 54218
10/07/72	**66**	8	3 If You Let Me	Tamla 54222
2/24/73	**87**	3	4 Girl You Need A Change Of Mind (Part 1)	Tamla 54230
7/14/73	**67**	5	5 Darling Come Back Home	Tamla 54236
8/25/73	**1**[2]	19	6 **Keep On Truckin' (Part 1)**	Tamla 54238
1/05/74	**2**[2]	18	7 **Boogie Down**	Tamla 54243
5/11/74	**28**	8	8 Son Of Sagittarius	Tamla 54247
8/10/74	**50**	10	9 Tell Her Love Has Felt The Need	Tamla 54249
12/07/74	**71**	8	10 One Tear	Tamla 54255
2/15/75	**18**	18	11 Shoeshine Boy	Tamla 54257
7/12/75	**50**	8	12 Get The Cream Off The Top	Tamla 54260
10/11/75	**66**	13	13 Happy	Tamla 54263
2/14/76	**36**	12	14 He's A Friend	Tamla 54266
8/31/85	**20**	11	15 A Nite At The Apollo Live! The Way You Do The Things You Do/My Girl	RCA 14178
			DARYL HALL JOHN OATES with DAVID RUFFIN & EDDIE KENDRICK	
			recorded at the reopening of New York's Apollo Theatre - revival of two early Temptations' hits	
			JOYCE KENNEDY - see JEFFREY OSBORNE	
			MIKE KENNEDY	
			Born Michael Kogel on 4/25/45 in Berlin, Germany. Lead singer of Los Bravos.	
3/04/72	**62**	7	1 Louisianna	ABC 11309
			RAY KENNEDY	
			Pop/rock singer, songwriter. Member of KGB (Kennedy, Rick Grech, Mike Bloomfield).	
5/03/80	**82**	3	1 Just For The Moment	ARC 11242
			CHRIS KENNER	
			Born on 12/25/29 in New Orleans. Died on 1/25/76 of a heart attack. R&B singer, songwriter. First recorded for Baton in 1957.	
5/29/61	**2**[3]	17	1 **I Like It Like That, Part 1**	Instant 3229
6/29/63	**77**	7	2 Land Of 1000 Dances	Instant 3252
			AL KENT	
			Born Al Hamilton in 1937 in Detroit. R&B singer, guitarist, producer.	
8/19/67	**49**	9	1 You've Got To Pay The Price [I]	Ric-Tic 127
			artist shown only as: **INSTRUMENTAL**	
			"B" side of an Al Kent vocal recording	
			STAN KENTON	
			Born on 2/19/12 in Wichita, Kansas. Died in Los Angeles on 8/25/79. Organized his first jazz band in 1941. Third person named to the Jazz Hall of Fame.	
8/01/60	**47**	8	1 My Love	Capitol 4393
			NAT KING COLE-STAN KENTON	
10/13/62	**32**	9	2 Mama Sang A Song [S]	Capitol 4847
			KERMIT - see JIM HENSON	
			ANITA KERR - see ANITA & TH' SO-AND-SO'S	
			NIK KERSHAW	
			Born on 3/1/58 in Bristol, England. Pop singer, songwriter, multi-instrumentalist.	
3/31/84	**46**	13	1 Wouldn't It Be Good	MCA 52371

DEBUT DATE	PEAK POS	WKS CHR	ARTIST — Record Title	Label & Number
			TROY KEYES	
			Soul singer. Lead singer with the High Keys.	
2/17/68	**92**	3	1 Love Explosion	ABC 11027
			CHAKA KHAN	
			Born Yvette Marie Stevens on 3/23/53 in Great Lakes, Illinois. Lead singer of Rufus from 1972-81.	
10/07/78	**21**	16	1 I'm Every Woman	Warner 8683
5/16/81	**53**	9	2 What Cha' Gonna Do For Me	Warner 49692
1/08/83	**67**	7	3 Got To Be There	Warner 29881
9/08/84	**3**	26	4 ● **I Feel For You**	Warner 29195
			with Grandmaster Melle Mel (rap) and Stevie Wonder (harmonica)	
1/19/85	**60**	9	5 This Is My Night	Warner 29097
4/27/85	**60**	19	6 Through The Fire	Warner 29025
12/21/85+	**57**	9	7 Own The Night	MCA 52730
			from the TV series "Miami Vice"	
7/12/86	**53**	12	8 Love Of A Lifetime	Warner 28671
			THE KIDS NEXT DOOR	
10/23/65	**84**	3	1 Inky Dinky Spider (The Spider Song) [N]	4 Corners 129
			GREG KIHN BAND	
			Greg is a rock singer, songwriter, guitarist from Baltimore. Formed band in Berkeley, California.	
5/23/81	**15**	23	1 The Breakup Song (They Don't Write 'Em)	Beserkley 47149
5/22/82	**62**	7	2 Happy Man	Beserkley 47463
7/17/82	**82**	2	3 Every Love Song	Beserkley 47441
1/29/83	**2**[1]	22	4 **Jeopardy**	Beserkley 69847
6/04/83	**59**	6	5 Love Never Fails	Beserkley 69820
			GREG KIHN:	
2/16/85	**30**	12	6 Lucky	EMI America 8255
3/29/86	**92**	5	7 Love And Rock And Roll	EMI America 8306
			THEOLA KILGORE	
			Gospel/blues singer from Shreveport, LA. Raised in Oakland.	
4/20/63	**21**	12	1 The Love Of My Man	Serock 2004
8/10/63	**60**	9	2 This Is My Prayer	Serock 2006
			ANDY KIM	
			Born Andrew Joachim on 12/5/46 in Montreal, Canada. His parents were from Lebanon. Pop singer, songwriter. Teamed with Jeff Barry to write "Sugar, Sugar".	
5/04/68	**21**	12	1 How'd We Ever Get This Way	Steed 707
9/07/68	**31**	10	2 Shoot'em Up, Baby	Steed 710
12/21/68+	**49**	7	3 Rainbow Ride	Steed 711
5/24/69	**9**	16	4 ● **Baby, I Love You**	Steed 716
9/27/69	**36**	9	5 So Good Together	Steed 720
2/14/70	**90**	2	6 A Friend In The City	Steed 723
7/25/70	**85**	4	7 It's Your Life	Steed 727
11/07/70	**17**	11	8 Be My Baby	Steed 729
3/27/71	**62**	6	9 I Wish I Were	Steed 731
7/10/71	**97**	3	10 I Been Moved	Steed 734
6/22/74	**1**[1]	18	11 ● **Rock Me Gently**	Capitol 3895
10/26/74	**28**	9	12 Fire, Baby I'm On Fire	Capitol 3962
			ADRIAN KIMBERLY	
6/26/61	**34**	5	1 The Graduation Song...Pomp And Circumstance [I]	Calliope 6501
			written in 1901 for the coronation of King Edward VII	
			THE KIMBERLYS	
			Also see Waylon Jennings.	
3/20/71	**99**	1	1 I Don't Know How To Love Him/Everything's Alright	Happy Tiger 572
			medley from the rock opera "Jesus Christ, Superstar"	
			KING	
			British pop/rock quartet led by vocalist Paul King.	
7/20/85	**55**	11	1 Love & Pride	Epic 04917
			THE KINGBEES	
			Jamie James, lead singer of 3-man Los Angeles rock band.	
6/28/80	**81**	8	1 My Mistake	RSO 1032

DEBUT DATE	PEAK POS	WKS CHR	ARTIST — Record Title		Label & Number
			KING CRIMSON		
			English progressive rock group formed in 1969 by the eccentric Robert Fripp. Group featured an ever-changing lineup of top British artists.		
1/31/70	**80**	3	1 The Court Of The Crimson King-Part 1		Atlantic 2703
			KING CURTIS		
			Born Curtis Ousley on 2/7/34 in Fort Worth, Texas. Stabbed to death on 8/13/71 in New York City. R&B saxophonist. With Lionel Hampton in 1950. Moved to New York City, did session work. First own recording on Gem in 1953. Played on sessions for Bobby Darin, Aretha Franklin, Brook Benton, Nat Cole, McGuire Sisters, Andy Willliams, The Coasters, The Shirelles, and hundreds of others.		
2/17/62	**17**	13	1 Soul Twist	[I]	Enjoy 1000
7/21/62	**60**	9	2 Beach Party	[I]	Capitol 4788
			above 2: **KING CURTIS & THE NOBLE KNIGHTS**		
8/24/63	**92**	2	3 Do The Monkey		Capitol 4998
3/07/64	**51**	12	4 Soul Serenade	[I]	Capitol 5109
12/25/65+	**89**	5	5 Spanish Harlem	[I]	Atco 6387
5/13/67	**63**	6	6 Jump Back	[I]	Atco 6476
8/26/67	**33**	9	7 Memphis Soul Stew	[I]	Atco 6511
9/23/67	**28**	6	8 Ode To Billie Joe	[I]	Atco 6516
			shown as: **THE KINGPINS**		
			KING CURTIS & THE KINGPINS:		
11/25/67	**87**	4	9 For What It's Worth	[I]	Atco 6534
12/30/67+	**76**	6	10 I Was Made To Love Her	[I]	Atco 6547
3/09/68	**84**	5	11 (Sittin' On) The Dock Of The Bay	[I]	Atco 6562
6/15/68	**83**	2	12 Valley Of The Dolls	[I]	Atco 6582
8/10/68	**83**	3	13 I Heard It Thru The Grapevine	[I]	Atco 6598
10/12/68	**93**	2	14 Harper Valley P.T.A.	[I]	Atco 6613
1/23/71	**64**	6	15 Whole Lotta Love	[I]	Atco 6779
			KING HARVEST		
			6-man rock group.		
10/28/72+	**13**	22	1 Dancing In The Moonlight		Perception 515
5/05/73	**91**	4	2 A Little Bit Like Magic		Perception 527
			THE KING PINS		
8/17/63	**89**	2	1 It Won't Be This Way (Always)		Federal 12484
			THE KINGPINS - see KING CURTIS		
			ALBERT KING		
			Born Albert Nelson on 4/25/23 in Indianola, MS. Blues-based vocalist, guitarist.		
2/03/68	**67**	4	1 Cold Feet	[S-I]	Stax 241
2/17/73	**91**	2	2 Breaking Up Somebody's Home		Stax 0147
			ANNA KING		
1/04/64	**67**	6	1 If Somebody Told You		Smash 1858
4/04/64	**52**	6	2 Baby Baby Baby		Smash 1884
			ANNA KING-BOBBY BYRD		
			above 2 produced by James Brown		
			B.B. KING		
			Born Riley B. King on 9/16/25 in Indianola, MS. To Memphis in 1946. Own radio show, 1949-50, where he was dubbed "The Beale Street Blues Boy", later shortened to "Blues Boy", then simply "B.B.". First recorded for Bullet in 1949. The most famous blues singer/guitarist in the world today.		
7/22/57	**95**	1	1 Be Careful With A Fool		RPM 494
11/18/57	**85**	1	2 I Need You So Bad		RPM 498
3/28/64	**97**	2	3 How Blue Can You Get		ABC-Para. 10527
5/09/64	**34**	8	4 Rock Me Baby		Kent 393
6/27/64	**98**	2	5 Help The Poor		ABC-Para. 10552
11/07/64	**82**	3	6 Beautician Blues		Kent 403
11/07/64	**90**	3	7 Never Trust A Woman		ABC-Para. 10599
7/03/65	**97**	1	8 Blue Shadows		Kent 426
10/22/66	**72**	9	9 Don't Answer The Door - Part 1		ABC 10856
4/01/67	**94**	2	10 The Jungle		Kent 462
4/20/68	**39**	7	11 Paying The Cost To Be The Boss		BluesWay 61015
7/27/68	**74**	5	12 I'm Gonna Do What They Do To Me		BluesWay 61018
8/24/68	**94**	3	13 The Woman I Love		Kent 492

DEBUT DATE	PEAK POS	WKS CHR	ARTIST — Record Title	Label & Number
			B.B. KING — Cont'd	
9/28/68	**98**	1	14 The B.B. Jones/	
10/05/68	**82**	5	15 You Put It On Me	BluesWay 61019
			from the film "For Love Of Ivy"	
5/17/69	**61**	10	16 Why I Sing The Blues	BluesWay 61024
8/30/69	**74**	8	17 Get Off My Back Woman	BluesWay 61026
10/18/69	**76**	5	18 Just A Little Love	BluesWay 61029
12/27/69+	**15**	14	19 The Thrill Is Gone	BluesWay 61032
4/11/70	**54**	6	20 So Excited	BluesWay 61035
7/25/70	**48**	7	21 Hummingbird	ABC 11268
10/31/70	**45**	8	22 Chains And Things	ABC 11280
2/13/71	**40**	10	23 Ask Me No Questions	ABC 11290
4/24/71	**97**	2	24 That Evil Child	Kent 4542
6/12/71	**90**	2	25 Help The Poor [I]	ABC 11302
			instrumental version of King's 1964 hit	
9/11/71	**68**	5	26 Ghetto Woman	ABC 11310
11/13/71+	**46**	12	27 Ain't Nobody Home	ABC 11316
3/04/72	**93**	3	28 Sweet Sixteen	ABC 11319
5/06/72	**92**	6	29 I Got Some Help I Don't Need	ABC 11321
8/19/72	**62**	11	30 Guess Who	ABC 11330
8/04/73	**38**	14	31 To Know You Is To Love You	ABC 11373
12/08/73+	**28**	16	32 I Like To Live The Love	ABC 11406
6/08/74	**78**	3	33 Who Are You	ABC 11433
11/30/74+	**64**	7	34 Philadelphia [I]	ABC 12029
			BEN E. KING	
			Born Benjamin Earl Nelson on 9/23/38 in Henderson, NC. To New York in 1947. Worked with The Moonglows for six months while still in high school. Joined the Five Crowns in 1957, who became the new Drifters in 1959. Wrote lyrics to "There Goes My Baby", his first lead performance with The Drifters. Went solo in May of 1960.	
12/31/60+	**10**	16	1 **Spanish Harlem/**	
12/31/60+	**53**	7	2 First Taste Of Love	Atco 6185
5/08/61	**4**	14	3 **Stand By Me**	Atco 6194
7/31/61	**18**	10	4 Amor	Atco 6203
			there were 3 Top 10 versions in 1944	
10/09/61	**81**	2	5 Here Comes The Night/	
10/16/61	**66**	6	6 Young Boy Blues	Atco 6207
2/03/62	**56**	6	7 Ecstasy	Atco 6215
4/21/62	**11**	12	8 Don't Play That Song (You Lied)	Atco 6222
8/11/62	**88**	2	9 Too Bad	Atco 6231
3/16/63	**85**	4	10 How Can I Forget	Atco 6256
6/29/63	**29**	12	11 I (Who Have Nothing)	Atco 6267
11/02/63	**72**	4	12 I Could Have Danced All Night	Atco 6275
			from the musical "My Fair Lady"	
4/04/64	**63**	7	13 That's When It Hurts	Atco 6288
9/12/64	**72**	5	14 It's All Over	Atco 6315
12/19/64+	**45**	7	15 Seven Letters	Atco 6328
4/03/65	**84**	3	16 The Record (Baby I Love You)	Atco 6343
1/08/66	**91**	3	17 Goodnight My Love	Atco 6390
5/21/66	**96**	2	18 So Much Love	Atco 6413
4/22/67	**93**	2	19 Tears, Tears, Tears	Atco 6472
2/08/75	**5**	14	20 **Supernatural Thing - Part I**	Atlantic 3241
6/07/75	**60**	4	21 Do It In The Name Of Love	Atlantic 3274
10/04/86	**9**	21	22 **Stand By Me** [R]	Atlantic 89361
			featured song in the film of the same title	
			CAROLE KING	
			Born Carole Klein on 2/9/42 in Brooklyn. Singer, songwriter, pianist. Married lyricist Gerry Goffin in 1958, team wrote 4 #1 hits: "Will You Love Me Tomorrow", "Go Away Little Girl", "Take Good Care Of My Baby" and "The Loco-Motion". Divorced Goffin in 1968, first solo album in 1970. The most successful female songwriter of the rock era.	
8/25/62	**22**	9	1 It Might As Well Rain Until September	Dimension 2000
4/27/63	**94**	2	2 He's A Bad Boy	Dimension 1009
5/08/71	**1^5**	17	3 ● **It's Too Late/**	
		12	4 I Feel The Earth Move	Ode 66015

DEBUT DATE	PEAK POS	WKS CHR	ARTIST — Record Title	Label & Number
			CAROLE KING — Cont'd	
8/28/71	**14**	10	5 So Far Away/	
		9	6 Smackwater Jack	Ode 66019
1/29/72	**9**	10	7 **Sweet Seasons**	Ode 66022
11/25/72+	**24**	10	8 Been To Canaan	Ode 66031
7/14/73	**28**	9	9 Believe In Humanity/	
		9	10 You Light Up My Life	Ode 66035
10/27/73	**37**	10	11 Corazon [I]	Ode 66039
8/31/74	**2**[1]	16	12 **Jazzman**	Ode 66101
1/04/75	**9**	12	13 **Nightingale**	Ode 66106
2/14/76	**28**	11	14 Only Love Is Real	Ode 66119
5/22/76	**76**	3	15 High Out Of Time	Ode 66123
			3-15: produced by Lou Adler	
7/23/77	**30**	11	16 Hard Rock Cafe	Capitol 4455
5/17/80	**12**	17	17 One Fine Day	Capitol 4864
3/27/82	**45**	10	18 One To One	Atlantic 4026
			CLAUDE KING	
			Born on 2/5/33 in Shreveport, Louisiana. Country singer, songwriter, guitarist.	
7/17/61	**82**	5	1 Big River, Big Man	Columbia 42043
11/13/61	**71**	7	2 The Comancheros	Columbia 42196
			inspired by the John Wayne film of the same title	
5/26/62	**6**	16	3 **Wolverton Mountain**	Columbia 42352
			title is an actual place in Arkansas where Clifton Clowers lives	
10/06/62	**53**	6	4 The Burning Of Atlanta	Columbia 42581
			EVELYN "CHAMPAGNE" KING	
			Born on 6/29/60 in the Bronx. To Philadelphia in 1970. Employed as cleaning woman at Sigma Studios when discovered.	
6/17/78	**9**	19	1 ● **Shame**	RCA 11122
1/06/79	**23**	16	2 ● I Don't Know If It's Right	RCA 11386
5/26/79	**75**	6	3 Music Box	RCA 11586
7/25/81	**40**	14	4 I'm In Love	RCA 12243
8/28/82	**17**	16	5 Love Come Down	RCA 13273
1/15/83	**49**	11	6 Betcha She Don't Love You	RCA 13380
			above 3 shown only as: **EVELYN KING**	
1/07/84	**75**	7	7 Action	RCA 13682
1/11/86	**86**	4	8 Your Personal Touch	RCA 14201
			FREDDY KING	
			Born Freddie Christian on 9/3/34 in Gilmer, Texas. Died on 12/28/76 in Dallas of a heart attack, hepatitis. Blues vocalist, guitarist.	
1/09/61	**93**	2	1 You've Got To Love Her With A Feeling	Federal 12384
3/06/61	**29**	10	2 Hide Away [I]	Federal 12401
			titled after Mel's Hide Away Lounge in Chicago	
5/22/61	**88**	4	3 Lonesome Whistle Blues	Federal 12415
8/07/61	**47**	5	4 San-Ho-Zay [I]	Federal 12428
			JONATHAN KING	
			Born Kenneth King on 12/6/44 in London, England. Successful singer, songwriter, producer. Formed U.K. Records in 1972. Also see Hedgehoppers Anonymous.	
9/25/65	**17**	11	1 Everyone's Gone To The Moon	Parrot 9774
1/15/66	**97**	2	2 Where The Sun Has Never Shone	Parrot 9804
			PEGGY KING	
2/05/55	**30**	1	1 Make Yourself Comfortable	Columbia 40363
			Best Seller #30	
11/12/55	**61**	5	2 Learning To Love	Columbia 40562
3/03/56	**88**	2	3 Kiss And Run/	
4/07/56	**81**	2	4 Angel Pie (Postillon!)	Columbia 40638
			REV. MARTIN LUTHER KING	
			America's civil rights leader. Assassinated on 4/4/68 at the age of 39. The 3rd Monday in January is a principal U.S. holiday: Martin Luther King Day.	
5/04/68	**88**	4	1 I Have A Dream [S]	Gordy 7023
			excerpt from King's 6/23/63 speech in Detroit	
			SLEEPY KING	
			R&B vocalist, organist.	
12/18/61+	**92**	3	1 Pushin' Your Luck	Joy 257

DEBUT DATE	PEAK POS	WKS CHR	ARTIST — Record Title	Label & Number
			TEDDI KING	
			Born on 9/18/29 in Boston. Jazz-styled vocalist. Died on 11/18/77.	
2/18/56	**18**	12	1 Mr. Wonderful	RCA 6392
			Jockey #18 / Top 100 #32 from the Broadway musical of the same title	
11/10/56	**75**	4	2 Married I Can Always Get	RCA 6660
5/06/57	**98**	1	3 Say It Isn't So	RCA 6866
			George Olsen's version of this Irving Berlin tune hit #1 in 1932	
			THE KINGS	
			Rock quartet from Toronto, Canada. David Diamond, lead singer.	
8/23/80	**43**	23	1 Switchin' To Glide/	
		10	2 This Beat Goes On	Elektra 47052
			THE KINGSMEN	
			Group is Bill Haley's band, The Comets (minus Haley).	
8/25/58	**35**	3	1 Week End [I]	East West 115
			Best Seller #35 / Hot 100 #84	
			THE KINGSMEN	
			Rock band formed in Portland in 1957. Consisted of Jack Ely (lead singer, guitar), Lynn Easton (drums), Mike Mitchell (guitar), Bob Nordby (bass) and Don Gallucci (keyboards). After release of "Louie Louie" (featuring lead vocal by Ely), Easton took over leadership of band and replaced Ely as lead singer. America's premier Sixties garage band.	
11/09/63	**2**[6]	16	1 **Louie Louie**	Wand 143
			originally released on the Jerden label	
3/14/64	**16**	11	2 Money	Wand 150
7/11/64	**46**	9	3 Little Latin Lupe Lu	Wand 157
9/12/64	**42**	9	4 Death Of An Angel	Wand 164
1/09/65	**4**	12	5 **The Jolly Green Giant**	Wand 172
			same tune (different lyrics) as The Olympics' "Big Boy Pete"	
5/08/65	**65**	6	6 The Climb	Wand 183
8/07/65	**47**	8	7 Annie Fanny	Wand 189
4/02/66	**77**	4	8 Killer Joe	Wand 1115
5/14/66	**97**	2	9 Louie Louie [R]	Wand 143
			THE KINGSTON TRIO	
			Folk trio formed in San Francisco in 1957. Consisted of Dave Guard (banjo), Bob Shane and Nick Reynolds (guitars). Big break came at San Francisco's Purple Onion, where they stayed for eight months. Guard left in 1961 to form the Whiskeyhill Singers. John Stewart replaced him. Disbanded in 1968, Shane formed New Kingston Trio. The originators of the folk music craze of the 60s.	
9/29/58	**1**[1]	21	1 ● **Tom Dooley**	Capitol 4049
			traditional American folk song written in 1866 as "Tom Dula"	
1/12/59	**70**	8	2 Raspberries, Strawberries	Capitol 4114
3/23/59	**12**	13	3 The Tijuana Jail	Capitol 4167
6/15/59	**15**	11	4 M.T.A.	Capitol 4221
			M.T.A.: Metropolitan Transit Authority of Boston	
9/14/59	**20**	11	5 A Worried Man	Capitol 4271
12/14/59	**98**	1	6 CooCoo-U	Capitol 4303
2/22/60	**32**	11	7 El Matador	Capitol 4338
6/20/60	**37**	10	8 Bad Man Blunder [N]	Capitol 4379
10/10/60	**60**	5	9 Everglades	Capitol 4441
1/20/62	**21**	14	10 Where Have All The Flowers Gone	Capitol 4671
4/28/62	**81**	7	11 Scotch And Soda/	
5/19/62	**93**	1	12 Jane, Jane, Jane	Capitol 4740
10/27/62	**97**	2	13 One More Town	Capitol 4842
1/26/63	**21**	11	14 Greenback Dollar	Capitol 4898
4/06/63	**8**	11	15 **Reverend Mr. Black**	Capitol 4951
8/03/63	**33**	8	16 Desert Pete	Capitol 5005
11/23/63	**61**	7	17 Ally Ally Oxen Free	Capitol 5078
			THE KINKS	
			Rock group formed in London, England in 1963 by Ray Davies (lead singer, guitar) and his brother Dave Davies (lead guitar, vocals). Original lineup also included Peter Quaife (bass) and Mike Avory (drums). Numerous personnel changes during the 70s. Lineup in 1987 consisted of Ray & Dave Davies, Ian Gibbons (keyboards), Bob Henrit (drums) and Jim Rodford (bass).	
9/26/64	**7**	15	1 **You Really Got Me**	Reprise 0306
12/26/64+	**7**	12	2 **All Day And All Of The Night**	Reprise 0334

DEBUT DATE	PEAK POS	WKS CHR	ARTIST — Record Title	Label & Number
			THE KINKS — Cont'd	
3/13/65	**6**	11	3 **Tired Of Waiting For You**	Reprise 0347
6/12/65	**23**	8	4 Set Me Free	Reprise 0379
8/14/65	**34**	7	5 Who'll Be The Next In Line	Reprise 0366
12/04/65+	**13**	14	6 A Well Respected Man	Reprise 0420
3/26/66	**50**	8	7 Till The End Of The Day	Reprise 0454
5/21/66	**36**	6	8 Dedicated Follower Of Fashion	Reprise 0471
8/06/66	**14**	11	9 Sunny Afternoon	Reprise 0497
1/07/67	**73**	4	10 Deadend Street	Reprise 0540
7/01/67	**80**	4	11 Mr. Pleasant	Reprise 0587
			all of above produced by Shel Talmy	
1/31/70	**62**	9	12 Victoria	Reprise 0863
8/29/70	**9**	14	13 **Lola**	Reprise 0930
1/02/71	**45**	9	14 Apeman	Reprise 0979
4/02/77	**48**	7	15 Sleepwalker	Arista 0240
7/22/78	**30**	11	16 A Rock 'N' Roll Fantasy	Arista 0342
4/28/79	**41**	12	17 (Wish I Could Fly Like) Superman	Arista 0409
8/30/80	**81**	6	18 Lola	Arista 0541
			live version of their 1970 hit	
10/31/81	**85**	4	19 Destroyer	Arista 0619
11/28/81+	**92**	8	20 Better Things	Arista 0649
5/07/83	**6**	17	21 **Come Dancing**	Arista 1054
8/20/83	**29**	10	22 Don't Forget To Dance	Arista 9075
12/22/84+	**41**	10	23 Do It Again	Arista 9309
			FERN KINNEY	
8/18/79	**54**	8	1 Groove Me	Malaco 1058
			KATHY KIRBY	
			British songstress.	
9/18/65	**88**	3	1 The Way Of Love	Parrot 9775
			JIM KIRK & The TM Singers	
2/16/80	**71**	3	1 Voice Of Freedom	Capitol 4834
			KISS	
			Hard rock band formed in New York City in 1973. Consisted of Gene Simmons (bass), Paul Stanley (guitar), Ace Frehley (lead guitar) and Peter Criss (drums). Noted for elaborate makeup and highly theatrical stage shows. Criss replaced by Eric Carr in 1981. Frehley replaced by Vinnie Vincent in 1982. Group appeared without makeup for the first time in 1983 on album cover "Lick It Up". Mark St. John replaced Vincent in 1984. Bruce Kulick replaced St. John in 1985.	
5/25/74	**83**	5	1 Kissin' Time	Casablanca 0011
5/17/75	**68**	6	2 Rock And Roll All Nite	Casablanca 829
11/15/75+	**12**	14	3 Rock And Roll All Nite	Casablanca 850
			live version	
3/20/76	**31**	10	4 Shout It Out Loud	Casablanca 854
6/05/76	**74**	3	5 Flaming Youth	Casablanca 858
9/04/76	**7**	21	6● **Beth/**	
		3	7 Detroit Rock City	Casablanca 863
12/18/76+	**15**	13	8 Hard Luck Woman	Casablanca 873
3/19/77	**16**	14	9 Calling Dr. Love	Casablanca 880
7/16/77	**25**	12	10 Christine Sixteen	Casablanca 889
9/24/77	**61**	7	11 Love Gun	Casablanca 895
1/21/78	**54**	5	12 Shout It Out Loud	Casablanca 906
			live version of their 1976 hit	
2/25/78	**39**	10	13 Rocket Ride	Casablanca 915
5/26/79	**11**	16	14● I Was Made For Lovin' You	Casablanca 983
9/01/79	**47**	11	15 Sure Know Something	Casablanca 2205
6/21/80	**47**	10	16 Shandi	Casablanca 2282
12/12/81+	**56**	9	17 A World Without Heroes	Casablanca 2343
11/12/83	**66**	11	18 Lick It Up	Mercury 814671
10/13/84	**49**	10	19 Heaven's On Fire	Mercury 880205
10/19/85	**51**	13	20 Tears Are Falling	Mercury 884141

DEBUT DATE	PEAK POS	WKS CHR	ARTIST — Record Title	Label & Number
			KISSING THE PINK	
			British synth-pop sextet.	
8/06/83	87	5	1 Maybe This Day	Atlantic 89796
			MAC & KATIE KISSOON	
			Brother and sister from Trinidad. Moved to England in the late 50s.	
7/24/71	20	15	1 Chirpy Chirpy Cheep Cheep	ABC 11306
			KLAATU	
			Canadian rock quartet. Anonymous first release had people speculating that they might be The Beatles reuinted.	
4/02/77	62	6	1 Sub-Rosa Subway/	
		6	2 Calling Occupants	Capitol 4412
			THE PETE KLINT QUINTET	
10/07/67	98	3	1 Walkin' Proud	Mercury 72709
			KLIQUE	
			Soul trio: Howard Huntsberry, Isaac Suthers and his sister Deborah Hunter.	
10/08/83	50	9	1 Stop Doggin' Me Around	MCA 52250
			remake of Jackie Wilson's "Doggin' Around" hit from 1960	
			THE KLOWNS	
			4-man, 2-woman pop group.	
12/05/70	95	2	1 Lady Love	RCA 0393
			KLYMAXX	
			Black female sextet formed in Los Angeles in 1979. Lead vocals and rap by Bernadette Cooper, Fenderella and Lorena Shelby.	
5/11/85	59	11	1 Meeting In The Ladies Room	Constell. 52545
9/14/85	5	29	2 **I Miss You**	Constell. 52606
2/15/86	80	8	3 The Men All Pause	Constell. 52486
			originally "Bubbled Under" at POS 105 on 2/9/85	
7/05/86	15	15	4 Man Size Love	MCA 52841
			from the film "Running Scared"	
			THE KNACK	
			Rock group formed in Los Angeles in 1978. Consisted of Doug Fieger (lead singer, guitar), Berton Averre (guitar), Bruce Gary (drums) and Prescott Niles (bass). Disbanded in 1982.	
6/23/79	1[6]	22	1 ● **My Sharona**	Capitol 4731
9/01/79	11	16	2 Good Girls Don't	Capitol 4771
2/09/80	38	8	3 Baby Talks Dirty	Capitol 4822
4/05/80	62	6	4 Can't Put A Price On Love	Capitol 4853
10/31/81	67	5	5 Pay The Devil (Ooo, Baby, Ooo)	Capitol 5054
			THE KNICKERBOCKERS	
			Rock band formed in Bergenfield, New Jersey in 1964 as the Castle Kings. Lead singer, Buddy Randell, was a member of the Royal Teens.	
12/04/65+	20	13	1 Lies	Challenge 59321
3/19/66	46	7	2 One Track Mind	Challenge 59326
7/02/66	94	3	3 High On Love	Challenge 59332
			THE KNIGHT BROS.	
			R&B duo: Richard Dunbar and Jerry Diggs.	
6/12/65	70	5	1 Temptation 'Bout To Get Me	Checker 1107
			FREDERICK KNIGHT	
			Born on 8/15/44 in Alabama. Soul singer, record producer.	
4/22/72	27	14	1 I've Been Lonely For So Long	Stax 0117
			GLADYS KNIGHT & THE PIPS	
			R&B family group from Atlanta. Formed in 1952 when Gladys was 8 years old. Consisted of Gladys (b: 5/28/44 in Atlanta), her brother Merald "Bubba" Knight and sister Brenda, and cousin William and Elenor Guest. Named "Pips" for their manager, cousin James "Pip" Woods. First recorded for Brunswick in 1958. Brenda and Elenor replaced by cousins Edward Patten and Langston George in 1959. Langston left group in 1962 and group has remained a quartet with the same members ever since. Due to legal problems, Gladys could not record with the Pips from 1977-80.	
5/15/61	6	13	1 **Every Beat Of My Heart**	Vee-Jay 386
			shown only as: **PIPS**	
5/15/61	45	7	2 Every Beat Of My Heart	Fury 1050
			song first released on Huntom label; re-recorded song for Fury; Huntom master sold to Vee-Jay and released as Pips	
12/11/61+	19	12	3 Letter Full Of Tears	Fury 1054

DEBUT DATE	PEAK POS	WKS CHR	ARTIST — Record Title	Label & Number
			GLADYS KNIGHT & THE PIPS — Cont'd	
4/14/62	**97**	2	4 Operator	Fury 1064
5/09/64	**38**	10	5 Giving Up	Maxx 326
8/22/64	**89**	5	6 Lovers Always Forgive	Maxx 329
5/06/67	**98**	2	7 Take Me In Your Arms And Love Me	Soul 35033
7/08/67	**39**	9	8 Everybody Needs Love	Soul 35034
10/21/67	**2**[3]	17	9 **I Heard It Through The Grapevine**	Soul 35039
2/10/68	**15**	10	10 The End Of Our Road	Soul 35042
6/08/68	**40**	8	11 It Should Have Been Me	Soul 35045
8/24/68	**41**	10	12 I Wish It Would Rain	Soul 35047
3/08/69	**63**	7	13 Didn't You Know (You'd Have To Cry Sometime)	Soul 35057
7/19/69	**19**	11	14 The Nitty Gritty	Soul 35063
10/25/69	**17**	14	15 Friendship Train	Soul 35068
3/21/70	**25**	8	16 You Need Love Like I Do (Don't You)	Soul 35071
11/28/70+	**9**	15	17 **If I Were Your Woman**	Soul 35078
6/05/71	**17**	11	18 I Don't Want To Do Wrong	Soul 35083
12/18/71+	**27**	10	19 Make Me The Woman That You Go Home To	Soul 35091
3/25/72	**33**	8	20 Help Me Make It Through The Night	Soul 35094
1/27/73	**2**[2]	16	21 **Neither One Of Us (Wants To Be The First To Say Goodbye)**	Soul 35098
4/28/73	**19**	15	22 Daddy Could Swear, I Declare	Soul 35105
6/16/73	**28**	11	23 Where Peaceful Waters Flow	Buddah 363
8/11/73	**61**	7	24 All I Need Is Time	Soul 35107
9/01/73	**1**[2]	19	25 ● **Midnight Train To Georgia**	Buddah 383
11/24/73+	**4**	16	26 ● **I've Got To Use My Imagination**	Buddah 393
2/16/74	**3**	17	27 ● **Best Thing That Ever Happened To Me**	Buddah 403
5/25/74	**5**	17	28 ● **On And On** from the film "Claudine"	Buddah 423
6/29/74	**57**	9	29 Between Her Goodbye And My Hello	Soul 35111
10/12/74	**21**	17	30 I Feel A Song (In My Heart)/	
		2	31 Don't Burn Down The Bridge	Buddah 433
2/22/75	**47**	8	32 Love Finds It's Own Way	Buddah 453
4/26/75	**11**	17	33 The Way We Were/Try To Remember	Buddah 463
8/30/75	**50**	7	34 Money	Buddah 487
11/08/75	**22**	11	35 Part Time Love	Buddah 513
10/09/76	**47**	8	36 So Sad The Song from the film "Pipe Dreams" starring Gladys Knight	Buddah 544
6/11/77	**52**	11	37 Baby Don't Change Your Mind	Buddah 569
6/14/80	**46**	9	38 Landlord	Columbia 11239
5/21/83	**66**	10	39 Save The Overtime (For Me)	Columbia 03761
			JEAN KNIGHT Born on 6/26/43 in New Orleans. Soul songstress.	
5/29/71	**2**[2]	16	1 **Mr. Big Stuff**	Stax 0088
10/16/71	**57**	5	2 You Think You're Hot Stuff	Stax 0105
5/04/85	**50**	15	3 My Toot Toot	Mirage 99643
			ROBERT KNIGHT Born on 4/24/45 in Franklin, Tennessee. Soul singer. Recorded for Dot in 1960.	
9/30/67	**13**	12	1 Everlasting Love	Rising Sons 705
1/20/68	**97**	2	2 Blessed Are The Lonely	Rising Sons 707
10/19/68	**97**	2	3 Isn't It Lonely Together	Elf 90019
			SONNY KNIGHT Born Joseph C. Smith in 1934 in Maywood, Illinois. R&B singer, songwriter, pianist. Wrote book "The Day The Music Died".	
11/17/56	**17**	13	1 Confidential Juke Box #17 / Best Seller #19 / Top 100 #20	Dot 15507
10/10/64	**71**	9	2 If You Want This Love	Aura 403
2/06/65	**100**	1	3 Love Me As Though There Were No Tomorrow	Aura 4505
			TERRY KNIGHT & THE PACK Rock quintet from Flint, Michigan. Terry formed, managed and produced Grand Funk Railroad, which included two former Pack members, Don Brewer and Mark Farner.	
11/12/66+	**46**	10	1 I (Who Have Nothing)	Lucky Eleven 230

DEBUT DATE	PEAK POS	WKS CHR	ARTIST — Record Title	Label & Number
			THE KNIGHTSBRIDGE STRINGS	
			Ensemble of 34 strings conducted by British conductor-arrangers Reg Owen and Malcolm Lockyer. Also see Cambridge Strings.	
7/20/59	**53**	7	1 Cry .... [I]	Top Rank 2006
			#1 hit for Johnnie Ray in 1951	
11/02/59	**88**	3	2 Wheel Of Fortune .... [I]	Top Rank 2014
			#1 hit for Kay Starr in 1952	
			FRED KNOBLOCK	
			Pop singer, songwriter. Susan Anton is a TV and film actress.	
6/28/80	**18**	14	1 Why Not Me	Scotti Br. 518
11/22/80+	**28**	18	2 Killin' Time	Scotti Br. 609
			FRED KNOBLOCK & SUSAN ANTON	
			THE KNOCKOUTS	
			Pop/rock quartet from New Jersey led by Bob D'Andrea.	
12/28/59+	**46**	11	1 Darling Lorraine	Shad 5013
			BUDDY KNOX	
			Born Buddy Wayne Knox on 7/20/33 in Happy, Texas. Formed The Rhythm Orchids at West Texas State University: Knox (guitar), Jimmy Bowen (bass), Don Lanier (guitar) and Dave "Dicky Doo" Alldred (drums). Formed own record label, Triple-D, named after KDDD radio in Dumas, Texas. Buddy currently lives near Winnipeg, Canada.	
2/23/57	**1**[1]	23	1 **Party Doll**	Roulette 4002
			Best Seller #1 / Top 100 #2 / Juke Box #2 / Jockey #5	
			originally on Triple-D label (flip side by Jimmy Bowen)	
5/13/57	**17**	16	2 Rock Your Little Baby To Sleep	Roulette 4009
			Jockey #17 / Best Seller #23 / Top 100 #23	
9/02/57	**9**	23	3 **Hula Love**	Roulette 4018
			Jockey #9 / Top 100 #12 / Best Seller #13	
2/10/58	**80**	6	4 Swingin' Daddy	Roulette 4042
8/04/58	**22**	14	5 Somebody Touched Me	Roulette 4082
			Hot 100 #22 / Best Seller #32	
			above 5: **BUDDY KNOX with THE RHYTHM ORCHIDS**	
1/05/59	**88**	2	6 That's Why I Cry/	
1/19/59	**85**	2	7 Teasable, Pleasable You	Roulette 4120
4/13/59	**55**	6	8 I Think I'm Gonna Kill Myself	Roulette 4140
12/19/60+	**25**	9	9 Lovey Dovey	Liberty 55290
3/06/61	**65**	7	10 Ling-Ting-Tong	Liberty 55305
			MOE KOFFMAN QUARTETTE	
			Moe was born on 1/28/28 in Toronto, Canada. Flutist with several U.S. big bands from 1950-55.	
2/03/58	**23**	13	1 The Swingin' Shepherd Blues .... [I]	Jubilee 5311
			Jockey #23 / Best Seller #36 / Top 100 #36	
6/23/58	**72**	3	2 Little Pixie .... [I]	Jubilee 5324
			KOKOMO	
			Pianist Jimmy Wisner.	
2/20/61	**8**	14	1 **Asia Minor** .... [I]	Felsted 8612
			adapted from the Greig Piano Concerto	
			DIANE KOLBY	
9/19/70	**67**	6	1 Holy Man	Columbia 45169
			KONGAS	
			A disco production by Cerrone.	
4/08/78	**84**	7	1 Africanism/Gimme Some Lovin'	Polydor 14461
			JOHN KONGOS	
			British pop/rock singer produced by Elton John's producer, Gus Dudgeon.	
7/10/71	**70**	7	1 He's Gonna Step On You Again	Elektra 45729
			KOOL & THE GANG	
			R&B group formed in Jersey City, NJ in 1964 by bass player Robert "Kool" Bell as the Jazziacs. Session work in New York City, 1964-68. First recorded for De-Lite in 1969. Added lead singer James "J.T." Taylor in 1979. Current lineup consists of Robert Bell and his brother Ronald Bell (sax, keyboards), Taylor, George Brown (drums), Curtis "Fitz" Williams (keyboards) and Charles Smith (guitar).	
9/13/69	**59**	12	1 Kool And The Gang .... [I]	De-Lite 519
12/27/69+	**85**	5	2 The Gangs Back Again .... [I]	De-Lite 523
7/04/70	**78**	6	3 Let The Music Take Your Mind	De-Lite 529
9/26/70	**87**	4	4 Funky Man	De-Lite 534

DEBUT DATE	PEAK POS	WKS CHR	ARTIST — Record Title	Label & Number
			KOOL & THE GANG — Cont'd	
9/08/73	**29**	12	5 Funky Stuff	De-Lite 557
12/08/73+	**4**	22	6● **Jungle Boogie**	De-Lite 559
4/20/74	**6**	19	7● **Hollywood Swinging**	De-Lite 561
9/07/74	**37**	8	8 Higher Plane	De-Lite 1562
1/04/75	**63**	8	9 Rhyme Tyme People	De-Lite 1563
4/05/75	**35**	17	10 Spirit Of The Boogie/	
		6	11 Summer Madness	De-Lite 1567
11/08/75	**55**	7	12 Caribbean Festival [I]	De-Lite 1573
3/20/76	**77**	8	13 Love And Understanding (Come Together)	De-Lite 1579
11/06/76+	**55**	13	14 Open Sesame - Part 1 [I]	De-Lite 1586
10/06/79+	**8**	24	15● **Ladies Night**	De-Lite 801
1/19/80	**5**	18	16 **Too Hot**	De-Lite 802
10/25/80+	**1**[2]	30	17▲ **Celebration**	De-Lite 807
5/16/81	**39**	11	18 Jones Vs. Jones	De-Lite 813
10/17/81	**17**	17	19 Take My Heart (You Can Have It If You Want It)	De-Lite 815
2/13/82	**89**	2	20 Steppin' Out	De-Lite 816
2/27/82	**10**	17	21 **Get Down On It**	De-Lite 818
8/28/82	**21**	11	22 Big Fun	De-Lite 822
10/30/82+	**30**	15	23 Let's Go Dancin' (Ooh La, La, La) 15-23: produced by Eumir Deodato	De-Lite 824
11/05/83+	**2**[1]	24	24 **Joanna**	De-Lite 829
2/25/84	**13**	18	25 Tonight	De-Lite 830
11/24/84+	**10**	24	26 **Misled**	De-Lite 880431
3/23/85	**9**	19	27 **Fresh**	De-Lite 880623
7/06/85	**2**[3]	25	28 **Cherish**	De-Lite 880869
10/26/85	**18**	16	29 Emergency	De-Lite 884199
11/01/86+	**10**	18	30 **Victory**	Mercury 888074
			THE KORGIS British pop duo: James Warren and Andy Davis (both formerly with Stackridge).	
10/11/80	**18**	19	1 Everybody's Got To Learn Sometime	Asylum 47055
			KORONA Korona is Bruce Blackman from Greenville, MS, who was leader of Eternity's Children and Starbuck.	
3/22/80	**43**	8	1 Let Me Be	United Art. 1341
			KRAFTWERK German all-electronic duo: Ralf Hutter and Florian Schneider.	
3/15/75	**25**	10	1 Autobahn [I]	Vertigo 203
6/10/78	**67**	7	2 Trans-Europe Express [I]	Capitol 4460
			BILLY J. KRAMER with The Dakotas Billy was born William Ashton on 8/19/43 near Liverpool, England. Discovered by The Beatles' manager, Brian Epstein, who teamed him with the group, The Dakotas.	
4/18/64	**7**	15	1 **Little Children/**	
5/30/64	**9**	10	2 **Bad To Me**	Imperial 66027
7/25/64	**30**	7	3 I'll Keep You Satisfied	Imperial 66048
8/22/64	**23**	10	4 From A Window above 3 written by John Lennon & Paul McCartney	Imperial 66051
2/06/65	**67**	5	5 It's Gotta Last Forever	Imperial 66085
6/26/65	**47**	7	6 Trains And Boats And Planes	Imperial 66115
			KRIS KRISTOFFERSON Born on 6/22/36 in Brownsville, Texas. Singer, songwriter, actor. Married to Rita Coolidge, 1973-79. Wrote the #1 hit "Me And Bobby McGee".	
8/21/71	**26**	13	1 Loving Her Was Easier (Than Anything I'll Ever Do Again)	Monument 8525
3/11/72	**63**	8	2 Josie	Monument 8536
12/30/72+	**91**	3	3 Jesus Was A Capricorn	Monument 8558
4/07/73	**16**	38	4● Why Me	Monument 8571
11/17/73	**49**	10	5 A Song I'd Like To Sing **KRIS KRISTOFFERSON & RITA COOLIDGE**	A&M 1475
3/23/74	**86**	5	6 Loving Arms **KRIS KRISTOFFERSON & RITA COOLIDGE**	A&M 1498
5/21/77	**52**	6	7 Watch Closely Now from the film "A Star Is Born" starring Kris & Barbra Streisand	Columbia 10525

DEBUT DATE	PEAK POS	WKS CHR	ARTIST — Record Title	Label & Number
			KROKUS	
			Heavy-metal band formed in Zurich, Switzerland featuring lead singer Marc Storace.	
9/15/84	**71**	6	1 Midnite Maniac	Arista 9248
6/07/86	**67**	7	2 School's Out	Arista 9468
			BOB KUBAN & THE IN-MEN	
			8-man St. Louis pop/rock band featuring lead singer Walter Scott, who mysteriously disappeared on 12/27/83, and whose body was found three years later.	
1/29/66	**12**	11	1 The Cheater	Musicland 20001
4/30/66	**70**	3	2 The Teaser	Musicland 20006
7/16/66	**93**	3	3 Drive My Car written by John Lennon & Paul McCartney	Musicland 20007
			KUF-LINX	
3/03/58	**76**	6	1 So Tough	Challenge 1013
			CHARLIE KULIS	
3/15/75	**46**	8	1 Runaway	Playboy 6023
			L	
			LABAN	
			Pop/dance duo from Denmark: Lecia Jomsson & Ivan Pedersen.	
11/08/86	**88**	4	1 Love In Siberia	Critique 725
			PATTI LaBELLE	
			Born Patricia Holt on 5/24/44 in Philadelphia. Lead singer of Patti LaBelle & The Bluebells, 1962-77.	
1/07/84	**46**	13	1 If Only You Knew	Phil. Int. 04248
3/24/84	**88**	5	2 Love Has Finally Come At Last BOBBY WOMACK & PATTI LaBELLE	Beverly Glen 2012
2/16/85	**17**	21	3 New Attitude	MCA 52517
6/15/85	**41**	14	4 Stir It Up above 2 from the film "Beverly Hills Cop"	MCA 52610
3/22/86	**1**[3]	23	5 ● **On My Own** PATTI LaBELLE & MICHAEL McDONALD	MCA 52770
7/19/86	**29**	12	6 Oh, People	MCA 52877
			PATTI LaBELLE & THE BLUE BELLES	
			R&B quartet formed in Philadelphia in 1962. Consisted of Patti LaBelle, Nona Hendryx, Sarah Dash and Cindy Birdsong. Cindy left in 1967 to join The Supremes. Group continued on as a trio and in 1971 they shortened their name to LaBelle. Disbanded in 1977.	
4/21/62	**15**	11	1 I Sold My Heart To The Junkman THE BLUE-BELLES	Newtown 5000
9/14/63	**37**	13	2 Down The Aisle (Wedding Song)	Newtown 5777
1/04/64	**34**	8	3 You'll Never Walk Alone from the musical "Carousel"	Parkway 896
12/19/64+	**76**	4	4 Danny Boy based on the traditional Irish tune "Londonderry Air" of 1855	Parkway 935
12/04/65+	**68**	6	5 All Or Nothing	Atlantic 2311
12/31/66+	**89**	2	6 Take Me For A Little While	Atlantic 2373
			LaBELLE:	
1/04/75	**1**[1]	18	7 ● **Lady Marmalade**	Epic 50048
5/10/75	**48**	6	8 What Can I Do For You?	Epic 50097
			BILL LaBOUNTY	
			Pop singer/songwriter from Los Angeles.	
5/27/78	**65**	9	1 This Night Won't Last Forever	Warner 8529
			CHERYL LADD	
			Born Cheryl Stoppelmoor on 7/2/51 in Huron, SD. Played Kris Monroe on the TV series "Charlie's Angels". Married David Ladd (son of actor Alan Ladd) in 1973.	
7/22/78	**34**	11	1 Think It Over	Capitol 4599
			LADY FLASH	
			Barry Manilow's back-up singers. Trio originally known as Reparata & The Delrons.	
7/17/76	**27**	12	1 Street Singin' written, produced and arranged by Barry Manilow	RSO 852

DEBUT DATE	PEAK POS	WKS CHR	ARTIST — Record Title	Label & Number
			THE LAFAYETTES	
			White pop/rock quintet based in New York City.	
7/21/62	87	3	1 Life's Too Short	RCA 8044
			DAVID LAFLAMME	
			Leader of the San Francisco "flower-rock" group, It's A Beautiful Day.	
12/11/76+	89	7	1 White Bird	Amherst 717
			originally recorded on the 1969 album "It's A Beautiful Day"	
			LA FLAVOUR	
			Pop/disco assemblage featuring lead singer Craig DeBock.	
6/14/80	91	2	1 Only The Lonely (Have A Reason To Be Sad)	Sweet City 7377
			JACK LaFORGE	
			Born on 8/8/24 in New York City. Pianist, composer, conductor.	
1/30/65	96	5	1 Goldfinger [I]	Regina 1323
			from the James Bond film of the same title	
			FRANCIS LAI	
			French composer, conductor.	
1/30/71	31	9	1 Theme From Love Story [I]	Paramount 0064
			from the film "Love Story" - piano solo by Georges Pludermacher	
			LAID BACK	
			Danish synth-pop duo: Tim Stahl and John Guldberg.	
2/25/84	26	18	1 White Horse	Sire 29346
			FRANKIE LAINE	
			Born Frank Paul LoVecchio on 3/30/13 in Chicago. To Los Angeles, early 40s. First recorded for Exclusive in 1945, with Johnny Moore's Three Blazers. Signed to Mercury label in 1947. Dynamic style found favor with black and white audiences.	
9/03/55	17	3	1 Humming Bird	Columbia 40526
			Juke Box #17	
9/10/55	45	6	2 Hawk-Eye	Columbia 40558
			Coming Up #45 / Top 100 #73 pre	
11/26/55	19	17	3 A Woman In Love	Columbia 40583
			Best Seller #19 / Top 100 #24	
			from the film "Guys And Dolls"	
7/07/56	83	2	4 Don't Cry	Columbia 40693
			FRANKIE LAINE with PAUL WESTON	
			from the Broadway musical "The Most Happy Fella"	
12/01/56+	3	22	5 **Moonlight Gambler**	Columbia 40780
			Top 100 #3 / Juke Box #3 / Jockey #4 / Best Seller #5	
3/30/57	10	14	6 **Love Is A Golden Ring**	Columbia 40856
			Jockey #10 / Best Seller #22 / Top 100 #23	
			backing vocals and instrumentation by The Easy Riders	
5/11/63	51	7	7 Don't Make My Baby Blue	Columbia 42767
1/21/67	39	9	8 I'll Take Care Of Your Cares	ABC 10891
4/08/67	35	8	9 Making Memories	ABC 10924
6/17/67	48	7	10 You Wanted Someone To Play With (I Wanted Someone To Love)	ABC 10946
8/12/67	66	6	11 Laura, What's He Got That I Ain't Got	ABC 10967
10/07/67	83	3	12 You, No One But You	ABC 10983
1/20/68	82	6	13 To Each His Own	ABC 11032
			there were 3 #1 versions of this tune in 1936	
2/08/69	24	11	14 You Gave Me A Mountain	ABC 11174
			written by Marty Robbins - produced by Jimmy Bowen	
6/14/69	86	3	15 Dammit Isn't God's Last Name	ABC 11224
			L.A. JETS	
12/25/76+	86	5	1 Prisoner (Captured By Your Eyes)	RCA 10826
			LAKE	
			German progressive rock sextet. James Hopkins-Harrison, lead singer.	
10/22/77	83	3	1 Time Bomb	Columbia 10614
			GREG LAKE	
			Born on 11/10/48 in Bournemouth, England. Guitarist and bass player with King Crimson and Emerson, Lake & Palmer.	
12/20/75	95	3	1 I Believe In Father Christmas [X]	Atlantic 3305
9/03/77	91	2	2 C'est La Vie	Atlantic 3405
			from the Emerson, Lake & Palmer album "Words, Volume 1"	
11/21/81	48	10	3 Let Me Love You Once	Chrysalis 2571

DEBUT DATE	PEAK POS	WKS CHR	ARTIST — Record Title	Label & Number
			LAKESIDE	
			9-man funk aggregation from Dayton, Ohio.	
1/31/81	**55**	8	1 Fantastic Voyage	Solar 12129
			LORENZO LAMAS	
			Son of Arlene Dahl and Fernando Lamas. Plays Lance on TV's "Falcon Crest".	
12/22/84+	**85**	5	1 Fools Like Me	Scotti Br. 04686
			KEVIN LAMB	
6/24/78	**82**	4	1 On The Wrong Track	Arista 0316
			HERB LANCE & THE CLASSICS	
3/06/61	**50**	5	1 Blue Moon	Promo 1010
			there were 3 Top 10 versions of this classic tune in 1935	
			MAJOR LANCE	
			Born on 4/4/42 in Chicago. Soul singer. First recorded for Mercury in 1959. Lived in Britain, 1972-74. Had own label, Osiris, with Al Jackson of the MG's in 1975. In prison for selling cocaine, 1978-81.	
7/13/63	**8**	15	1 **The Monkey Time**	Okeh 7175
10/19/63	**13**	10	2 Hey Little Girl	Okeh 7181
1/04/64	**5**	11	3 **Um, Um, Um, Um, Um, Um**	Okeh 7187
3/28/64	**20**	8	4 The Matador	Okeh 7191
6/06/64	**68**	8	5 It Ain't No Use/	
6/27/64	**68**	6	6 Girls	Okeh 7197
8/22/64	**24**	10	7 Rhythm	Okeh 7203
12/05/64	**64**	8	8 Sometimes I Wonder	Okeh 7209
3/06/65	**40**	7	9 Come See	Okeh 7216
6/05/65	**91**	3	10 Ain't It A Shame	Okeh 7223
8/28/65	**93**	3	11 Too Hot To Hold	Okeh 7226
8/22/70	**67**	7	12 Stay Away From Me (I Love You Too Much)	Curtom 1953
			all of above (except #4 & 11) written by Curtis Mayfield	
			JERRY LANDIS - see PAUL SIMON	
			THE LANE BROTHERS	
3/09/57	**64**	4	1 Marianne	RCA 6810
			MICKEY LEE LANE	
10/10/64	**38**	9	1 Shaggy Dog	Swan 4183
			ROBIN LANE & THE CHARTBUSTERS	
			Robin is the daughter of Dean Martin's pianist, Ken Lane.	
7/12/80	**87**	3	1 When Things Go Wrong	Warner 49246
			LANIER & CO.	
			Soul singer Farris Lanier, Jr.	
12/04/82+	**48**	13	1 After I Cry Tonight	Larc 81010
			SNOOKY LANSON	
			Real name: Roy Lanson. Born in Memphis. Star of TV's "Your Hit Parade", 1950-57.	
8/20/55	**45**	2	1 Why Don't You Write Me	Dot 15385
			Coming Up #45	
11/12/55	**20**	16	2 It's Almost Tomorrow	Dot 15424
			Top 100 #20 / Jockey #20 / Juke Box #20	
			MARIO LANZA	
			Born Alfredo Cocozza on 1/31/21 in Philadelphia. Mario Lanza became the most spectacularly popular operatic tenor since Caruso, his voice featured in seven movies (though no theatrical operas) before his death on 10/7/59 (38).	
9/15/56	**53**	8	1 Earthbound	RCA 6644
5/26/58	**97**	1	2 Arrivederci Roma	RCA 7164
			from the film "Seven Hills of Rome"	
			THE LARKS	
			R&B group originally named Don Julian & The Meadowlarks: Don Julian (lead singer), Ted Walters and Charles Morrison.	
11/14/64+	**7**	13	1 **The Jerk**	Money 106
			THE LARKS	
			R&B group originally named The Jubilators: Eugene Mumford (lead singer), Raymond "Pee Wee" Barnes, Thermon Ruth, Alden Bunn, Hadie Rowe, Jr. & David McNeil.	
3/06/61	**69**	3	1 It's Unbelievable	Sheryl 334

DEBUT DATE	PEAK POS	WKS CHR	ARTIST — Record Title	Label & Number
			JULIUS LaROSA	
			Born on 1/2/30 in Brooklyn. Regular singer on Arthur Godfrey's TV show until he was fired on-the-air on 10/19/53.	
7/23/55	13	7	1 Domani (Tomorrow)	Cadence 1265
			Best Seller #13 / Juke Box #13 / Jockey #15	
10/08/55	20	9	2 Suddenly There's A Valley	Cadence 1270
			Jockey #20 / Top 100 #29	
2/11/56	15	12	3 Lipstick And Candy And Rubbersole Shoes	RCA 6416
			Jockey #15 / Top 100 #21	
6/30/56	93	1	4 I've Got Love	RCA 6499
7/14/56	89	4	5 Get Me To The Church On Time	RCA 6567
			from the Broadway musical "My Fair Lady"	
4/27/57	98	1	6 Mama Guitar	RCA 6878
			from the film "A Face In The Crowd"	
6/16/58	21	1	7 Torero	RCA 7227
			Jockey #21	
			LARSEN-FEITEN BAND	
			Neil Larsen (keyboards) and Buzz Feiten (guitar). Both are top session musicians.	
8/16/80	29	14	1 Who'll Be The Fool Tonight	Warner 49282
			NICOLETTE LARSON	
			Born on 7/17/52 in Helena, Montana; raised in Kansas City. To San Francisco, 1974. Session vocalist with Neil Young, Linda Ronstadt, Van Halen, and many others.	
11/25/78+	8	19	1 **Lotta Love**	Warner 8664
			written by Neil Young	
3/31/79	47	9	2 Rhumba Girl	Warner 8795
1/12/80	35	11	3 Let Me Go, Love	Warner 49130
			duet with Michael McDonald	
8/07/82	53	9	4 I Only Want To Be With You	Warner 29948
			D.C. LaRUE	
			Born David Charles L'Heureux on 4/26/48 in Meriden, Connecticut.	
11/06/76	94	2	1 Cathedrals	Pyramid 8007
			DENISE LaSALLE	
			Born Denise Craig on 7/16/39 in Le Flore County, Mississippi. Soul singer, songwriter. Moved to Chicago in the early 60s. First recorded for Tarpen (Chess) in 1967. Had own Crajon Productions with husband Bill Jones from 1969 on.	
8/21/71	13	14	1 ● Trapped By A Thing Called Love	Westbound 182
2/05/72	46	11	2 Now Run And Tell That	Westbound 201
10/07/72	55	9	3 Man Sized Job	Westbound 206
1/14/78	80	10	4 Love Me Right	ABC 12312
			DAVID LASLEY	
			Born on 8/20/47 in Sault St. Marie, MI. Backup singer for James Taylor and others.	
3/13/82	36	10	1 If I Had My Wish Tonight	EMI America 8111
			THE LASSIES	
			White female vocal group.	
6/23/56	66	1	1 I Look At You	Decca 29868
			backing vocals: The Ray Charles Singers	
			THE LAST WORD	
			Rock group formed in Miami. Johnny Lombardo, lead singer.	
10/21/67	78	5	1 Can't Stop Loving You	Atco 6498
			JAMES LAST	
			German producer/arranger/conductor.	
1/15/72	84	4	1 Music From Across The Way	Polydor 15028
3/29/80	28	13	2 The Seduction (Love Theme) [I]	Polydor 2071
			from the film "American Gigolo"	
			LATIMORE	
			Born Benjamin Latimore on 9/7/39 in Charleston, TN. Soul singer, songwriter.	
10/26/74	31	12	1 Let's Straighten It Out	Glades 1722
2/05/77	37	10	2 Somethin' 'Bout 'Cha	Glades 1739
			STACY LATTISAW	
			Born on 11/25/66 in Washington, DC. Soul singer. Recorded her first album at age 12.	
8/09/80	21	24	1 Let Me Be Your Angel	Cotillion 46001
6/20/81	26	17	2 Love On A Two Way Street	Cotillion 46015
10/16/82	70	6	3 Attack Of The Name Game [N]	Cotillion 99968

DEBUT DATE	PEAK POS	WKS CHR	ARTIST — Record Title	Label & Number
			STACY LATTISAW — Cont'd	
8/13/83	**40**	16	4 Miracles	Cotillion 99855
3/10/84	**75**	9	5 Perfect Combination STACY LATTISAW & JOHNNY GILL	Cotillion 99785
10/18/86	**48**	13	6 Nail It To The Wall	Motown 1859
			CYNDI LAUPER Born on 6/20/53 in Queens, New York. Recorded an album for Polydor Records in 1980 with the group, Blue Angel. Won a Grammy in 1984 as Best New Artist.	
12/17/83+	**2^{2}**	25	1 ● **Girls Just Want To Have Fun**	Portrait 04120
4/14/84	**1^{2}**	20	2 **Time After Time**	Portrait 04432
7/21/84	**3**	18	3 **She Bop**	Portrait 04516
10/06/84	**5**	19	4 **All Through The Night**	Portrait 04639
12/22/84+	**27**	13	5 Money Changes Everything	Portrait 04737
5/18/85	**10**	15	6 **The Goonies 'R' Good Enough** from the film "The Goonies"	Portrait 04918
8/30/86	**1^{2}**	20	7 **True Colors**	Portrait 06247
11/29/86+	**3**	17	8 **Change Of Heart**	Portrait 06431
			ROD LAUREN Born on 3/26/40. Rod was groomed by RCA in 1960 to be a hot new teen idol.	
12/21/59+	**31**	10	1 If I Had A Girl	RCA 7645
			THE LAURIE SISTERS	
4/16/55	**30**	1	1 Dixie Danny Best Seller #30	Mercury 70548
			ANNIE LAURIE R&B siner from Atlanta. Sang with Dallas Brockley, Snookum Russell bands before joining Paul Gayten in 1948.	
7/08/57	**61**	6	1 It Hurts To Be In Love	Deluxe 6107
			LINDA LAURIE Novelty type singer from Brooklyn.	
1/26/59	**52**	9	1 Ambrose (Part Five) [N]	Glory 290
			LaVERNE & SHIRLEY Penny Marshall & Cindy Williams - stars of the TV series "LaVerne & Shirley".	
11/27/76	**65**	4	1 Sixteen Reasons	Atlantic 3367
			EDDIE LAWRENCE Born on 3/2/19 in New York City. Comedian, actor, author, playwright.	
8/11/56	**34**	9	1 The Old Philosopher [C]	Coral 61671
			STEVE LAWRENCE Born Sam Leibowitz on 7/8/35 in Brooklyn. Regular performer on the Steve Allen "Tonight Show" for 5 years. First recorded for King in 1953. Married to Eydie Gorme since 12/29/57.	
1/12/57	**18**	14	1 The Banana Boat Song Jockey #18 / Top 100 #30	Coral 61761
2/23/57	**5**	20	2 **Party Doll/** Jockey #5 / Top 100 #10 / Juke Box #11 / Best Seller #12	
3/16/57	**45**	7	3 (The Bad Donkey) Pum-Pa-Lum	Coral 61792
5/27/57	**42**	11	4 Can't Wait For Summer/	
5/27/57	**71**	7	5 Fabulous	Coral 61834
10/28/57	**54**	8	6 Fraulein	Coral 61876
3/17/58	**73**	2	7 Uh-Huh, Oh Yeah from the Broadway musical "Body Beautiful"	Coral 61950
9/22/58	**97**	2	8 Many A Time	Coral 62025
5/18/59	**62**	4	9 (I Don't Care) Only Love Me	ABC-Para. 10005
11/23/59+	**9**	18	10 **Pretty Blue Eyes**	ABC-Para. 10058
3/07/60	**7**	13	11 **Footsteps**	ABC-Para. 10085
3/06/61	**9**	16	12 **Portrait Of My Love**	United Art. 291
7/17/61	**68**	5	13 My Claire De Lune/	
8/14/61	**94**	1	14 In Time also see "Where" by The Platters	United Art. 335
10/23/61	**67**	5	15 Somewhere Along The Way first popularized by Nat King Cole (POS 8) in 1952	United Art. 364
11/10/62+	**1^{2}**	17	16 **Go Away Little Girl**	Columbia 42601
3/09/63	**26**	9	17 Don't Be Afraid, Little Darlin'	Columbia 42699
5/25/63	**27**	8	18 Poor Little Rich Girl	Columbia 42795

DEBUT DATE	PEAK POS	WKS CHR	ARTIST — Record Title	Label & Number
			STEVE LAWRENCE — Cont'd	
7/20/63	**28**	11	19 I Want To Stay Here	Columbia 42815
			STEVE & EYDIE	
10/19/63	**26**	9	20 Walking Proud	Columbia 42865
12/21/63+	**35**	9	21 I Can't Stop Talking About You	Columbia 42932
			STEVE & EYDIE	
5/30/64	**72**	5	22 Everybody Knows	Columbia 43047
8/29/64	**77**	6	23 Yet...I Know	Columbia 43095
9/16/72	**68**	10	24 We Can Make It Together	MGM 14383
			STEVE & EYDIE featuring THE OSMONDS	
			VICKI LAWRENCE	
			Born on 3/26/49 in Inglewood, CA. Regular on Carol Burnett's CBS-TV series from 1967-78. Also starred in TV's "Mama's Family", 1982-83.	
2/10/73	**1²**	20	1 ● **The Night The Lights Went Out In Georgia**	Bell 45303
6/23/73	**75**	7	2 He Did With Me	Bell 45362
10/18/75	**81**	3	3 The Other Woman	Private S. 45036
			DEBRA LAWS	
			Younger sister of Ronnie, Hubert and Eloise Laws.	
8/15/81	**90**	5	1 Very Special	Elektra 47142
			male vocal by Ronnie Laws	
			ELOISE LAWS	
			Sister of Hubert, Ronnie and Debra Laws. First recorded for Columbia in 1969.	
1/14/78	**91**	6	1 1,000 Laughs	ABC 12313
3/18/78	**97**	2	2 Number One	ABC 12341
			RONNIE LAWS	
			Born on 10/3/50 in Houston. R&B/jazz saxophonist. Brother of Hubert, Eloise and Debra Laws. With Earth, Wind And Fire, 1972-73.	
9/12/81	**60**	9	1 Stay Awake	Liberty 1424
			JOY LAYNE	
2/16/57	**20**	7	1 Your Wild Heart	Mercury 71038
			Juke Box #20 / Top 100 #30	
			LAZY RACER	
			Pop/rock sextet featuring lead singer Tim Renwick.	
7/07/79	**81**	4	1 Keep On Running Away	A&M 2152
			LE PAMPLEMOUSSE	
			Disco band featuring vocals by The Jones Girls.	
11/26/77+	**58**	15	1 Le Spank [I]	AVI 153
			LE ROUX	
			6-man Louisiana rock band. Jeff Pollard, lead singer.	
6/24/78	**59**	14	1 New Orleans Ladies	Capitol 4586
			shown as: LOUISIANA'S LE ROUX	
2/13/82	**18**	13	2 Nobody Said It Was Easy (Lookin' For The Lights)	RCA 13059
5/29/82	**77**	5	3 The Last Safe Place On Earth	RCA 13224
3/19/83	**81**	4	4 Carrie's Gone	RCA 13456
			BILLY LEACH	
9/16/57	**86**	3	1 Song Of The Barefoot Mailman	Bally 1039
			LEAPY LEE	
			Born Lee Graham on 7/2/42 in Eastbourne, England.	
10/12/68	**16**	14	1 Little Arrows	Decca 32380
			THE LEAVES	
			Los Angeles "garage" rock quintet. John Beck, lead singer.	
5/21/66	**31**	9	1 Hey Joe	Mira 222
			OTIS LEAVILLE	
			Born Otis Leavell Cobb on 2/8/41 in Atlanta. Soul singer, songwriter.	
11/29/69+	**63**	9	1 I Love You	Dakar 614
9/19/70	**72**	7	2 Love Uprising	Dakar 620
			LeBLANC & CARR	
			Lenny LeBlanc & Pete Carr (b: 4/22/50, Daytona Beach, FL). Lenny (bass) and Pete (lead guitar) were both session musicians at Muscle Shoals, Alabama.	
7/02/77	**48**	6	1 Something About You	Big Tree 16092
10/15/77+	**13**	28	2 Falling	Big Tree 16100

DEBUT DATE	PEAK POS	WKS CHR	ARTIST — Record Title	Label & Number
			LeBLANC & CARR — Cont'd	
6/03/78	**91**	4	3 Midnight Light	Big Tree 16114
			LENNY LeBLANC	
			Born on 6/17/51 in Leominster, Massachusetts. In duo with Pete Carr.	
9/03/77	**58**	5	1 Hound Dog Man (Play It Again)	Big Tree 16062
3/28/81	**55**	7	2 Somebody Send My Baby Home	Capitol 4979
			LED ZEPPELIN	
			British heavy-metal rock supergroup formed in October, 1968. Consisted of Robert Plant (lead singer), Jimmy Page (lead guitar), John Paul Jones (bass, keyboards) and John Bonham (drums). First known as the New Yardbirds. Page had been in the Yardbirds, 1966-68. USA tour in 1973 broke many box-office records. Formed own label, Swan Song, in 1974. Plant seriously injured in an auto accident in Greece on 8/4/75. In concert film "The Song Remains The Same" in 1976. Bonham died on 9/25/80 at the age of 33 of asphyxiation. Group disbanded in December, 1980. Their most famous recording, "Stairway To Heaven" (on album "Led Zeppelin IV") was never released as a single.	
3/29/69	**80**	4	1 Good Times Bad Times	Atlantic 2613
11/22/69+	**4**	15	2● **Whole Lotta Love/**	
3/14/70	**65**	5	3 Living Loving Maid (She's Just A Woman)	Atlantic 2690
11/21/70+	**16**	13	4 Immigrant Song	Atlantic 2777
12/25/71+	**15**	12	5 Black Dog	Atlantic 2849
3/18/72	**47**	7	6 Rock And Roll	Atlantic 2865
6/23/73	**51**	8	7 Over The Hills And Far Away	Atlantic 2970
10/20/73	**20**	16	8 D'yer Mak'er	Atlantic 2986
4/19/75	**38**	7	9 Trampled Under Foot	Swan Song 70102
12/22/79+	**21**	13	10 Fool In The Rain	Swan Song 71003
			LEE & PAUL	
			Songwriters Lee Pockriss (b: 1/20/27, New York City) and Paul Vance (b: 11/4/29, Brooklyn). Wrote: "Calcutta", "Itsy Bitsy Teenie Weenie Yellow Polkadot Bikini", and many other hits.	
3/30/59	**100**	1	1 The Chick [N]	Columbia 41337
			BRENDA LEE	
			Born Brenda Mae Tarpley on 12/11/44 in Lithonia, GA. Professional singer since age six. Signed to Decca Records in 1956. Became known as "Little Miss Dynamite". Successful Country singer since 1971.	
3/02/57	**43**	11	1 One Step At A Time	Decca 30198
7/15/57	**72**	7	2 Dynamite baking vocals: The Anita Kerr Singers	Decca 30333
12/21/59+	**4**	24	3 **Sweet Nothin's**	Decca 30967
5/30/60	**1**[3]	23	4 **I'm Sorry/**	
6/06/60	**6**	14	5 **That's All You Gotta Do**	Decca 31093
9/12/60	**1**[1]	15	6 **I Want To Be Wanted/**	
10/03/60	**40**	5	7 Just A Little	Decca 31149
12/12/60	**14**	4	8 Rockin' Around The Christmas Tree [X] recorded in 1958	Decca 30776
12/31/60+	**7**	12	9 **Emotions/**	
1/30/61	**33**	4	10 I'm Learning About Love	Decca 31195
3/27/61	**6**	12	11 **You Can Depend On Me**	Decca 31231
6/19/61	**4**	12	12 **Dum Dum/**	
7/03/61	**56**	3	13 Eventually	Decca 31272
10/02/61	**3**	14	14 **Fool #1/**	
10/02/61	**31**	9	15 Anybody But Me	Decca 31309
12/11/61	**50**	4	16 Rockin' Around The Christmas Tree [X-R]	Decca 30776
1/13/62	**4**	13	17 **Break It To Me Gently/**	
1/13/62	**52**	4	18 So Deep	Decca 31348
4/14/62	**6**	11	19 **Everybody Loves Me But You/**	
4/28/62	**89**	3	20 Here Comes That Feelin'	Decca 31379
7/07/62	**15**	10	21 Heart In Hand/	
6/30/62	**29**	8	22 It Started All Over Again	Decca 31407
9/29/62	**3**	15	23 **All Alone Am I/**	
9/22/62	**53**	6	24 Save All Your Lovin' For Me	Decca 31424
12/15/62	**59**	3	25 Rockin' Around The Christmas Tree [X-R]	Decca 30776
1/26/63	**32**	7	26 Your Used To Be/	
1/26/63	**47**	6	27 She'll Never Know	Decca 31454

DEBUT DATE	PEAK POS	WKS CHR	ARTIST — Record Title	Label & Number
			BRENDA LEE — Cont'd	
4/06/63	**6**	13	28 **Losing You/**	
4/13/63	**73**	3	29 He's So Heavenly	Decca 31478
7/06/63	**24**	9	30 My Whole World Is Falling Down/	
7/13/63	**25**	8	31 I Wonder	Decca 31510
9/28/63	**17**	8	32 The Grass Is Greener/	
9/28/63	**70**	5	33 Sweet Impossible You 3-4, 13, 15, 19 & 33: written by Ronnie Self	Decca 31539
12/14/63+	**12**	11	34 As Usual	Decca 31570
3/07/64	**25**	9	35 Think	Decca 31599
6/13/64	**48**	6	36 Alone With You/ 12, 18, 21, 29 & 36: written by Jackie DeShannon	
6/06/64	**85**	3	37 My Dreams	Decca 31628
8/08/64	**47**	7	38 When You Loved Me	Decca 31654
10/17/64	**17**	9	39 Is It True	Decca 31690
1/16/65	**45**	7	40 Thanks A Lot/	
1/09/65	**87**	4	41 The Crying Game	Decca 31728
4/03/65	**54**	6	42 Truly, Truly, True	Decca 31762
5/29/65	**13**	13	43 Too Many Rivers/	
5/29/65	**98**	1	44 No One	Decca 31792
10/09/65	**33**	9	45 Rusty Bells	Decca 31849
7/02/66	**77**	4	46 Ain't Gonna Cry No More	Decca 31970
10/01/66	**11**	13	47 Coming On Strong	Decca 32018
1/14/67	**37**	7	48 Ride, Ride, Ride	Decca 32079
2/08/69	**41**	11	49 Johnny One Time	Decca 32428
5/17/69	**84**	3	50 You Don't Need Me For Anything Anymore	Decca 32491
5/30/70	**97**	2	51 I Think I Love You Again	Decca 32675
3/31/73	**70**	5	52 Nobody Wins	MCA 40003
			CURTIS LEE Born on 10/28/41 in Yuma, Arizona. Pop singer, songwriter.	
7/03/61	**7**	11	1 **Pretty Little Angel Eyes** backing vocals by the Halos	Dunes 2007
10/16/61	**46**	7	2 Under The Moon Of Love above 2 produced by Phil Spector	Dunes 2008
			DICK LEE Pop ballad singer. Nicknamed "The Golden Boy".	
3/13/61	**94**	1	1 Oh Mein Papa Eddie Fisher's version hit #1 in 1954	Blue Bell 503
			DICKEY LEE Born Dickey Lipscomb on 9/21/41 in Memphis. Pop/Country singer, songwriter. First recorded for Sun Records in 1957.	
8/25/62	**6**	14	1 **Patches**	Smash 1758
12/08/62+	**14**	12	2 I Saw Linda Yesterday	Smash 1791
3/16/63	**68**	5	3 Don't Wanna Think About Paula	Smash 1808
5/15/65	**14**	13	4 Laurie (Strange Things Happen)	TCF Hall 102
9/04/65	**73**	6	5 The Girl From Peyton Place	TCF Hall 111
11/20/76+	**52**	10	6 9,999,999 Tears	RCA 10764
			JACKIE LEE Real name: Earl Nelson (of Bob & Earl). Took name from his wife's middle name, Jackie, and his middle name, Lee. Sang lead on Hollywood Flames' "Buzz-Buzz-Buzz".	
11/20/65+	**14**	14	1 The Duck	Mirwood 5502
			JACKIE LEE Born in May of 1932 in Philadelphia.	
6/29/59	**95**	2	1 Happy Vacation [I] organ instrumental styled after Baby Cortez's "The Happy Organ"	Swan 4034
			JOHNNY LEE Born on 7/3/45 in Texas City, Texas. Country singer, songwriter. Regular performer with Mickey Gilley at his club in Pasadena, Texas.	
7/12/80	**5**	21	1 ● **Lookin' For Love** from the movie "Urban Cowboy"	Full Moon 47004
10/10/81	**54**	9	2 Bet Your Heart On Me	Full Moon 47215

DEBUT DATE	PEAK POS	WKS CHR	ARTIST — Record Title	Label & Number
			LARRY LEE	
			Original member of the Ozark Mt. Daredevils.	
6/26/82	**81**	2	1 Don't Talk	Columbia 02740
			LAURA LEE	
			Born Laura Lee Rundless in 1945 in Chicago. Soul singer.	
9/23/67	**68**	7	1 Dirty Man	Chess 2013
12/02/67	**84**	2	2 Wanted: Lover, No Experience Necessary/	
12/23/67+	**93**	6	3 Up Tight, Good Man	Chess 2030
9/04/71	**36**	11	4 Women's Love Rights	Hot Wax 7105
1/22/72	**94**	1	5 Love And Liberty	Hot Wax 7111
3/04/72	**76**	5	6 Since I Fell For You	Hot Wax 7201
6/10/72	**68**	11	7 Rip Off	Hot Wax 7204
9/30/72	**65**	8	8 If You Can Beat Me Rockin' (You Can Have My Chair)	Hot Wax 7207
			MICHELE LEE	
			Born Michele Dusiak on 6/24/42. TV and film actress. Plays Karen Fairgate on TV's "Knotts Landing".	
3/02/68	**52**	11	1 L. David Sloane	Columbia 44413
			PEGGY LEE	
			Born Norma Jean Egstrom on 5/26/20 in Jamestown, ND. Jazz singer with Jack Wardlow band, 1936-40; Will Osborne, 1940-41; and Benny Goodman, 1941-43. Went solo in March, 1943. Films "Mister Music", 1950; "The Jazz Singer", 1953; and "Pete Kelly's Blues", 1955. Co-wrote many songs with husband Dave Barbour.	
3/03/56	**14**	20	1 Mr. Wonderful	Decca 29834
			Jockey #14 / Top 100 #23 / Best Seller #25	
			from the Broadway musical of the same title	
5/05/56	**76**	6	2 Joey, Joey, Joey	Decca 29877
			from the Broadway musical "The Most Happy Fella"	
7/14/58	**8**	15	3 **Fever**	Capitol 3998
			Hot 100 #8 / Best Seller #9 / Jockey #10 end	
11/03/58	**63**	6	4 Light Of Love/	
11/24/58	**98**	2	5 Sweetheart	Capitol 4071
1/26/59	**68**	6	6 Alright, Okay, You Win/	
1/19/59	**81**	6	7 My Man	Capitol 4115
5/18/59	**77**	2	8 Hallelujah, I Love Him So	Capitol 4189
			orchestra directed by Jack Marshall on above 6 tunes	
1/05/63	**54**	9	9 I'm A Woman	Capitol 4888
2/27/65	**93**	3	10 Pass Me By	Capitol 5346
			theme from the Cary Grant film "Father Goose"	
9/27/69	**11**	10	11 Is That All There Is	Capitol 2602
			RAYMOND LEFEVRE	
			Conductor, pianist, flutist from Paris, France.	
10/27/58	**30**	9	1 The Day The Rains Came [I]	Kapp 231
2/24/68	**37**	12	2 Ame Caline (Soul Coaxing) [I]	Four Corners 147
			THE LEFT BANKE	
			Classical styled New York rock quintet led by Steve Martin (lead singer) and Mike Brown (keyboards).	
9/10/66	**5**	13	1 **Walk Away Renee**	Smash 2041
1/07/67	**15**	10	2 Pretty Ballerina	Smash 2074
10/28/67	**98**	2	3 Desiree'	Smash 2119
			MICHEL LEGRAND	
			Born on 2/24/32 in Paris, France. Pianist, composer, conductor and arranger. Scored over 50 motion pictures.	
1/29/72	**56**	8	1 Brian's Song [I]	Bell 45171
			from the TV film "Brian's Song"	
			BILLY LEMMONS	
3/26/77	**93**	1	1 Six Packs A Day [N]	Ariola Am. 7661
			THE LEMON PIPERS	
			Psychedelic/bubblegum rock quintet from Oxford, Ohio. Ivan Browne, lead singer. Member Bill Bartlett was leader of Ram Jam.	
12/16/67+	**1^{1}**	13	1 ● **Green Tambourine**	Buddah 23
3/09/68	**46**	7	2 Rice Is Nice	Buddah 31
5/18/68	**51**	5	3 Jelly Jungle (Of Orange Marmalade)	Buddah 41

DEBUT DATE	PEAK POS	WKS CHR	ARTIST — Record Title	Label & Number
			THE LENNON SISTERS	
			Four sisters from Venice, CA: Dianne, Peggy, Kathy and Janet Lennon. TV debut on Lawrence Welk's Christmas Eve show in 1955. Left Welk in 1967.	
9/22/56	15	13	1 Tonight You Belong To Me	Coral 61701
			Top 100 #15 / Best Seller #16 / Jockey #16 / Juke Box #17	
			label lists artist as Lawrence Welk; vocals by The Lennon Sisters	
9/25/61	56	7	2 Sad Movies (Make Me Cry)	Dot 16255
			orchestra conducted by Billy Vaughn	
			JOHN LENNON	
			Born on 10/9/40 in Liverpool, England. Founding member of The Beatles. Married Cynthia Powell on 8/23/62, had son Julian. Divorced Cynthia on 11/8/68. Met Yoko Ono (b: 2/18/34 in Japan) in 1966 and married her on 3/20/69. Formed Plastic Ono Band in 1969. To New York City in 1971. Fought deportation from USA, 1972-76, until he was granted a permanent visa. John was shot to death on 12/8/80 in New York City.	
7/26/69	14	9	1 Give Peace A Chance	Apple 1809
			PLASTIC ONO BAND	
			recorded in a hotel suite in Montreal, Canada	
11/15/69+	30	12	2 Cold Turkey	Apple 1813
			PLASTIC ONO BAND	
2/28/70	3	13	3 ● **Instant Karma (We All Shine On)**	Apple 1818
			JOHN ONO LENNON	
1/09/71	43	6	4 Mother	Apple 1827
			JOHN LENNON/PLASTIC ONO BAND; YOKO ONO/PLASTIC ONO BAND	
4/03/71	11	9	5 Power To The People	Apple 1830
			JOHN LENNON/PLASTIC ONO BAND; YOKO ONO/PLASTIC ONO BAND	
10/23/71	3	9	6 **Imagine**	Apple 1840
			JOHN LENNON/PLASTIC ONO BAND	
5/20/72	57	5	7 Woman Is The Nigger Of The World	Apple 1848
			JOHN LENNON/PLASTIC ONO BAND with Elephants Memory	
11/10/73	18	13	8 Mind Games	Apple 1868
			JOHN LENNON	
9/28/74	1[1]	15	9 **Whatever Gets You Thru The Night**	Apple 1874
			JOHN LENNON with THE PLASTIC ONO NUCLEAR BAND	
			Elton John, backing vocals	
			JOHN LENNON:	
12/21/74+	9	12	10 **#9 Dream**	Apple 1878
3/15/75	20	9	11 Stand By Me	Apple 1881
11/01/80	1[5]	22	12 ● **(Just Like) Starting Over**	Geffen 49604
1/17/81	2[3]	20	13 ● **Woman**	Geffen 49644
3/28/81	10	17	14 **Watching The Wheels**	Geffen 49695
1/21/84	5	14	15 **Nobody Told Me**	Polydor 817254
3/31/84	55	6	16 I'm Stepping Out	Polydor 821107
			above 5 recorded in 1980	
			JULIAN LENNON	
			Born John Charles Julian Lennon on 4/8/63. First child to be born to any of the Beatles.	
10/20/84+	9	19	1 **Valotte**	Atlantic 89609
1/26/85	5	17	2 **Too Late For Goodbyes**	Atlantic 89589
4/20/85	21	12	3 Say You're Wrong	Atlantic 89567
8/03/85	54	6	4 Jesse	Atlantic 89529
3/22/86	32	13	5 Stick Around	Atlantic 89437
			TOMMY LEONETTI	
			Born on 9/10/29 in Bergen, NJ. Vocalist with Charlie Spivak and other bands. Featured singer on TV's "Your Hit Parade". Died on 9/15/79.	
12/10/55	99	1	1 Heartless	Capitol 3274
6/09/56	23	10	2 Free	Capitol 3442
			Jockey #23 / Top 100 #40	
1/18/69	54	9	3 Kum Ba Yah	Decca 32421
			LES COMPAGNONS DE LA CHANSON	
			French vocal group who sometimes accompanied Edith Piaf.	
3/07/60	60	8	1 Down By The Riverside [F]	Capitol 4342
			traditional black American spiritual	
			KETTY LESTER	
			Born Revoyda Frierson on 8/16/34 in Hope, Arkansas. To Los Angeles in 1955. Made several TV appearances as an actress.	
2/24/62	5	14	1 **Love Letters**	Era 3068
			Dick Haymes version hit #11 in 1945	
6/23/62	41	7	2 But Not For Me	Era 3080
			the George & Ira classic, written in 1930	

DEBUT DATE	PEAK POS	WKS CHR	ARTIST — Record Title	Label & Number
			KETTY LESTER — Cont'd	
10/13/62	**90**	1	3 You Can't Lie To A Liar	Era 3088
12/01/62	**97**	1	4 This Land Is Your Land the Woody Guthrie folk classic	Era 3094
			THE LETTERMEN Harmonic vocal group formed in Los Angeles in 1960. Consisted of Tony Butala (b: 11/20/40), Jim Pike (b: 11/6/38) and Bob Engemann (b: 2/19/36). First recorded for Warner Brothers. Engemann replaced by Gary Pike (Jim's brother), 1968.	
9/04/61	**13**	13	1 The Way You Look Tonight Fred Astaire's version hit #1 in 1936	Capitol 4586
11/20/61+	**7**	14	2 **When I Fall In Love** Doris Day's version hit #20 in 1952	Capitol 4658
2/17/62	**17**	11	3 Come Back Silly Girl	Capitol 4699
5/12/62	**42**	8	4 How Is Julie?	Capitol 4746
8/18/62	**81**	4	5 Silly Boy (She Doesn't Love You)	Capitol 4810
12/28/63+	**98**	2	6 Where Or When Hal Kemp's version hit #1 in 1937	Capitol 5091
6/26/65	**16**	9	7 Theme From 'A Summer Place' from the Sandra Dee/Troy Donahue film	Capitol 5437
10/02/65	**64**	6	8 Secretly	Capitol 5499
6/18/66	**72**	6	9 I Only Have Eyes For You Ben Selvin's version hit #2 in 1934	Capitol 5649
1/28/67	**72**	4	10 Our Winter Love	Capitol 5813
12/09/67+	**7**	15	11 **Goin' Out Of My Head/Can't Take My Eyes Off You**	Capitol 2054
3/23/68	**52**	8	12 Sherry Don't Go	Capitol 2132
11/16/68	**44**	8	13 Put Your Head On My Shoulder	Capitol 2324
5/31/69	**12**	21	14 Hurt So Bad	Capitol 2482
10/18/69	**64**	5	15 Shangri-La	Capitol 2643
12/27/69+	**47**	8	16 Traces/Memories Medley	Capitol 2697
4/04/70	**93**	2	17 Hang On Sloopy	Capitol 2774
6/06/70	**73**	7	18 She Cried	Capitol 2820
1/30/71	**74**	7	19 Everything Is Good About You	Capitol 3020
10/09/71	**42**	10	20 Love written by John Lennon	Capitol 3192
			LEVEL 42 Pop/soul/jazz foursome from Manchester, England, led by Mark King.	
2/15/86	**7**	27	1 **Something About You**	Polydor 883362
7/26/86	**87**	4	2 Hot Water	Polydor 885155
			HANK LEVINE	
10/09/61	**98**	1	1 Image - Part 1 [I]	ABC-Para. 10256
			MARCY LEVY - see ROBIN GIBB	
			THE LEWIS & CLARKE EXPEDITION Travis Lewis is actually Michael Murphey and Boomer Clarke is Boomer Castleman.	
8/26/67	**64**	4	1 I Feel Good (I Feel Bad)	Colgems 1006
			BARBARA LEWIS Born on 2/9/43 in South Lyon, MI. R&B singer, songwriter, multi-instrumentalist. Wrote songs since age 9. First recorded in Chicago, 1961. Inactive since early 70s.	
5/04/63	**3**	14	1 **Hello Stranger**	Atlantic 2184
8/17/63	**43**	7	2 Straighten Up Your Heart	Atlantic 2200
12/28/63+	**71**	5	3 Snap Your Fingers/	
1/11/64	**38**	12	4 Puppy Love	Atlantic 2214
6/19/65	**11**	14	5 Baby, I'm Yours	Atlantic 2283
9/11/65	**11**	12	6 Make Me Your Baby	Atlantic 2300
1/29/66	**91**	3	7 Don't Forget About Me	Atlantic 2316
7/23/66	**28**	8	8 Make Me Belong To You	Atlantic 2346
10/29/66	**74**	6	9 Baby What Do You Want Me To Do	Atlantic 2361
4/22/67	**72**	5	10 I'll Make Him Love Me	Atlantic 2400
			BOBBY LEWIS Born on 2/17/33 in Indianapolis. R&B singer. Grew up in an orphanage, adopted by a Detroit family at age 12. First recorded for the Parrot label in 1956.	
4/24/61	**1**[7]	23	1 **Tossin' And Turnin'**	Beltone 1002
8/28/61	**9**	10	2 **One Track Mind**	Beltone 1012

DEBUT DATE	PEAK POS	WKS CHR	ARTIST — Record Title	Label & Number
			BOBBY LEWIS — Cont'd	
11/20/61	**77**	3	3 What A Walk	Beltone 1015
7/28/62	**98**	1	4 I'm Tossin' And Turnin' Again	Beltone 2023
			GARY LEWIS & THE PLAYBOYS	
			Pop/rock group formed in Los Angeles in 1964. Consisted of Gary Lewis (vocals, drums), Al Ramsey, John West (guitars), David Walker (keyboards) and David Costell (bass). Lewis (b: 7/31/46) is the son of comedian Jerry Lewis. Group worked regularly at Disneyland in 1964. Lewis inducted into the Army on New Year's Day in 1967, resumed career after discharge in 1968.	
1/16/65	**1**[2]	12	1 ● **This Diamond Ring**	Liberty 55756
4/03/65	**2**[2]	11	2 **Count Me In**	Liberty 55778
7/03/65	**2**[1]	11	3 **Save Your Heart For Me**	Liberty 55809
9/25/65	**4**	11	4 **Everybody Loves A Clown**	Liberty 55818
12/11/65+	**3**	12	5 **She's Just My Style**	Liberty 55846
3/05/66	**9**	9	6 **Sure Gonna Miss Her**	Liberty 55865
5/14/66	**8**	8	7 **Green Grass**	Liberty 55880
7/30/66	**13**	7	8 My Heart's Symphony	Liberty 55898
10/08/66	**15**	8	9 (You Don't Have To) Paint Me A Picture	Liberty 55914
12/17/66+	**21**	9	10 Where Will The Words Come From	Liberty 55933
3/11/67	**43**	6	11 The Loser (With A Broken Heart)	Liberty 55949
5/13/67	**39**	6	12 Girls In Love	Liberty 55971
8/12/67	**52**	7	13 Jill	Liberty 55985
6/22/68	**19**	14	14 Sealed With A Kiss	Liberty 56037
4/05/69	**63**	12	15 Rhythm Of The Rain all of above (except #7 & 11-13) produced by Snuff Garrett	Liberty 56093
			HUEY LEWIS & THE NEWS	
			San Francisco 6-man rock band. Huey was born Hugh Cregg III on 7/5/50 in New York City. Joined the country-rock band Clover in the late 70s. Formed The News in 1980, consisting of Huey (lead singer), Chris Hayes (lead guitar), Mario Cipollina (bass), Bill Gibson (drums), Sean Hopper (keyboards) and Johnny Cola (sax, guitar).	
2/06/82	**7**	17	1 **Do You Believe In Love**	Chrysalis 2589
5/15/82	**36**	11	2 Hope You Love Me Like You Say You Do	Chrysalis 2604
8/14/82	**41**	9	3 Workin' For A Livin'	Chrysalis 2630
9/10/83	**8**	21	4 **Heart And Soul**	Chrysalis 42726
1/14/84	**6**	19	5 **I Want A New Drug**	Chrysalis 42766
4/21/84	**6**	20	6 **The Heart Of Rock & Roll**	Chrysalis 42782
7/21/84	**6**	17	7 **If This Is It**	Chrysalis 42803
10/20/84	**18**	15	8 Walking On A Thin Line	Chrysalis 42825
6/29/85	**1**[2]	19	9 **The Power Of Love** from the film "Back To The Future"	Chrysalis 42876
8/02/86	**1**[3]	19	10 **Stuck With You**	Chrysalis 43019
10/18/86	**3**	16	11 **Hip To Be Square**	Chrysalis 43065
			JERRY LEWIS	
			Born Joseph Levitch on 3/16/25 in Newark, NJ. Formed comedy team with Dean Martin in 1946 at Atlantic City. Film debut in 1949 in "My Friend Irma". National chairman in campaign against muscular dystrophy.	
11/24/56	**10**	19	1 **Rock-A-Bye Your Baby With A Dixie Melody** Best Seller #10 / Top 100 #12 / Juke Box #13 / Jockey #17 Al Jolson's version hit #1 in 1918	Decca 30124
4/27/57	**68**	1	2 It All Depends On You Paul Whiteman's version hit #2 in 1927	Decca 30263
			JERRY LEE LEWIS	
			Born on 9/29/35 in Ferriday, LA. Rock 'n roll singer, piano player. Played piano since age nine, professionally since age 15. First recorded for Sun in 1956. Appeared in the film "Disc Jockey Jamboree" in 1957. Career waned in 1958 after marriage to 13-year old cousin, Myra Gale Brown, daughter of his bass player. Made comeback in country music beginning in 1968. "The Killer", surrounded by personal tragedies in the past 2 decades, survived several serious illnesses in the past 6 years. Cousin to country singer Mickey Gilley and TV evangelist Jimmy Swaggart.	
6/24/57	**3**	29	1 **Whole Lot Of Shakin' Going On** Best Seller #3 / Top 100 #3 / Jockey #9	Sun 267
11/25/57+	**2**[4]	21	2 **Great Balls Of Fire/** Best Seller #2 / Top 100 #2 / Jockey #9	
2/17/58	**95**	1	3 You Win Again the Hank Williams penned tune hit #13 in 1952 for Tommy Edwards	Sun 281

DEBUT DATE	PEAK POS	WKS CHR	ARTIST — Record Title	Label & Number
			JERRY LEE LEWIS — Cont'd	
3/03/58	**7**	15	4 **Breathless**	Sun 288
			Top 100 #7 / Best Seller #9 / Jockey #23	
6/02/58	21	11	5 High School Confidential	Sun 296
			Top 100 #21 / Best Seller #22	
9/15/58	52	5	6 Break-Up/	
9/08/58	85	1	7 I'll Make It All Up To You	Sun 303
			above 2 written by Charlie Rich	
1/19/59	93	1	8 I'll Sail My Ship Alone	Sun 312
4/03/61	30	8	9 What'd I Say	Sun 356
9/15/62	95	3	10 Sweet Little Sixteen	Sun 379
4/11/64	98	1	11 I'm On Fire	Smash 1886
11/21/64	91	1	12 High Heel Sneakers	Smash 1930
3/30/68	97	2	13 Another Place, Another Time	Smash 2146
7/06/68	94	3	14 What's Made Milwaukee Famous (Has Made A Loser Out Of Me)	Smash 2164
11/27/71+	40	10	15 Me And Bobby McGee	Mercury 73248
3/04/72	43	10	16 Chantilly Lace [N]	Mercury 73273
7/22/72	95	3	17 Turn On Your Love Light	Mercury 73296
4/07/73	41	10	18 Drinking Wine Spo-Dee O'Dee	Mercury 73374
			Stick McGhee's version hit #2 in 1949 on the R&B charts	
			JIMMY LEWIS - see RAY CHARLES	
			RAMSEY LEWIS	
			Ramsey formed the Gentlemen Of Swing, a jazz-oriented trio, in 1956 in Chicago. Consisted of Ramsey (b: 5/27/35, Chicago - piano); Eldee Young (bass) and Isaac "Red" Holt (drums). All had been in band called The Clefs, early 1950s. First recorded for Chess/Argo in 1956. Broke up in 1965, with Young and Holt forming the Young-Holt Trio. Lewis re-formed his trio with Cleveland Eaton, bass; and Maurice White (later with Earth, Wind & Fire), drums. Reunited with Young and Holt in 1983.	
			THE RAMSEY LEWIS TRIO:	
10/10/64	63	6	1 Something You Got [I]	Argo 5481
7/31/65	**5**	16	2 **The 'In' Crowd** [I]	Argo 5506
11/20/65	11	8	3 Hang On Sloopy [I]	Cadet 5522
1/22/66	29	6	4 A Hard Day's Night [I]	Cadet 5525
3/26/66	70	5	5 Hi Heel Sneakers - Pt. 1 [I]	Cadet 5531
			RAMSEY LEWIS:	
7/09/66	19	13	6 Wade In The Water [I]	Cadet 5541
10/15/66	49	5	7 Up Tight [I]	Cadet 5547
12/24/66+	74	4	8 Day Tripper [I]	Cadet 5553
2/11/67	67	6	9 One, Two, Three [I]	Cadet 5556
9/23/67	84	4	10 Dancing In The Street [I]	Cadet 5573
11/11/67	49	6	11 Soul Man [I]	Cadet 5583
8/31/68	98	2	12 Since You've Been Gone [I]	Cadet 5609
9/27/69	76	8	13 Julia [I]	Cadet 5640
			written by John Lennon & Paul McCartney	
3/17/73	93	3	14 Kufanya Mapenzi (Making Love) [I]	Columbia 45766
1/18/75	50	6	15 Hot Dawgit [I]	Columbia 10056
			RAMSEY LEWIS and EARTH, WIND & FIRE	
3/22/75	44	7	16 Sun Goddess [I]	Columbia 10103
			RAMSEY LEWIS and EARTH, WIND & FIRE	
1/24/76	69	4	17 What's The Name Of This Funk (Spider Man)	Columbia 10235
			ORSA LIA	
3/31/79	84	5	1 I Never Said I Love You	Infinity 50004
			ENOCH LIGHT & THE LIGHT BRIGADE	
			Enoch was born on 8/18/07 in Canton, Ohio. Died in New York City on 7/31/78. Conductor of own orchestra, The Light Brigade, since 1935. President of Grand Award label and managing director for Command Records, for whom he produced a long string of hit stereo percussion albums in the 60s.	
11/10/58	48	7	1 I Want To Be Happy Cha Cha [I]	Grand Award 1020
			there were 3 Top 5 versions of this tune in 1925	
6/15/59	99	1	2 With My Eyes Wide Open I'm Dreaming [I]	Grand Award 1032
			Leo Reisman's version hit #3 in 1934	

DEBUT DATE	PEAK POS	WKS CHR	ARTIST — Record Title	Label & Number
			GORDON LIGHTFOOT	
			Born on 11/17/38 in Orillia, Ontario, Canada. Folk/pop/country singer, songwriter, guitarist.	
12/26/70+	**5**	15	1 **If You Could Read My Mind**	Reprise 0974
6/19/71	**64**	7	2 Talking In Your Sleep	Reprise 1020
9/11/71	**98**	2	3 Summer Side Of Life	Reprise 1035
5/27/72	**58**	11	4 Beautiful	Reprise 1088
4/13/74	**1**[1]	18	5● **Sundown**	Reprise 1194
8/31/74	**10**	14	6 **Carefree Highway**	Reprise 1309
3/29/75	**26**	11	7 Rainy Day People	Reprise 1328
8/28/76	**2**[2]	21	8 **The Wreck Of The Edmund Fitzgerald**	Reprise 1369
			true story of an ore vessel that sunk in Lake Superior on 11/10/75	
2/19/77	**65**	4	9 Race Among The Ruins	Reprise 1380
2/11/78	**33**	12	10 The Circle Is Small (I Can See It In Your Eyes)	Warner 8518
4/03/82	**50**	8	11 Baby Step Back	Warner 50012
			LIGHTHOUSE	
			Rock band from Toronto, Canada. Bob McBride, lead singer.	
9/11/71	**24**	12	1 One Fine Morning	Evolution 1048
12/11/71+	**64**	7	2 Take It Slow (Out In The Country)	Evolution 1052
4/29/72	**93**	2	3 I Just Wanna Be Your Friend	Evolution 1058
10/07/72	**34**	12	4 Sunny Days	Evolution 1069
11/03/73	**53**	8	5 Pretty Lady	Polydor 14198
			LIMAHL	
			Real name: Chris Hamill (Limahl is an anagram of his last name). Ex-leader of Kajagoogoo.	
3/23/85	**17**	19	1 Never Ending Story	EMI America 8230
			from the film "The Never Ending Story"	
7/20/85	**51**	7	2 Only For Love	EMI America 8277
			THE LIMELITERS	
			Folk trio formed in Hollywood in 1959. Consisted of Glen Yarbrough (tenor), Lou Gottlieb (bass) and Alex Hassilev (baritone).	
4/24/61	**60**	3	1 A Dollar Down [N]	RCA 7859
			LIMITED WARRANTY	
			Twin Cities pop/rock quintet.	
6/28/86	**79**	8	1 Victory Line	Atco 99541
			LIMMIE & FAMILY COOKIN'	
			Pop family trio from Canton, Ohio: sisters Martha Stewart and Jimmy Thomas and brother Limmie Snell.	
11/18/72+	**84**	10	1 You Can Do Magic	Avco 4602
			BOB LIND	
			Born on 11/25/44 in Baltimore. Folk-rock singer/songwriter.	
1/22/66	**5**	13	1 **Elusive Butterfly**	World Pac. 77808
4/23/66	**64**	5	2 Remember The Rain/	
5/07/66	**65**	5	3 Truly Julie's Blues (I'll Be There)	World Pac. 77822
			KATHY LINDEN	
			Songstress from Moorestown, New Jersey.	
3/17/58	**7**	17	1 **Billy**	Felsted 8510
			Jockey #7 / Top 100 #12 / Best Seller #14	
6/09/58	**50**	8	2 You'd Be Surprised	Felsted 8521
			Wee Bonnie Baker of Orrin Tucker's band had Top 10 hits of above 2 in 1940	
4/13/59	**11**	14	3 Goodbye Jimmy, Goodbye	Felsted 8571
7/27/59	**92**	3	4 You Don't Know Girls	Felsted 8587
			LINDISFARNE	
			Folk-rock quintet from England. Alan Hull, lead singer.	
9/02/72	**82**	5	1 Lady Eleanor	Elektra 45799
9/30/78	**33**	14	2 Run For Home	Atco 7093
			MARK LINDSAY	
			Born on 3/9/44 in Caldwell, Idaho. Lead singer of Paul Revere & The Raiders.	
7/26/69	**81**	4	1 First Hymn From Grand Terrace	Columbia 44875
12/06/69+	**10**	16	2● **Arizona**	Columbia 45037
4/04/70	**44**	8	3 Miss America	Columbia 45125

DEBUT DATE	PEAK POS	WKS CHR	ARTIST — Record Title	Label & Number
			MARK LINDSAY — Cont'd	
6/13/70	**25**	10	4 Silver Bird	Columbia 45180
9/19/70	**44**	12	5 And The Grass Won't Pay No Mind	Columbia 45229
1/09/71	**80**	4	6 Problem Child	Columbia 45286
6/12/71	**98**	1	7 Been Too Long On The Road	Columbia 45385
10/16/71	**87**	3	8 Are You Old Enough	Columbia 45462
			LINER	
			Pop trio: brothers Tom and Dave Farmer, and Eddie Golga.	
3/17/79	**92**	2	1 You And Me	Atco 7097
			ART LINKLETTER	
			Born on 7/17/12 in Moose Jaw, Canada. Popular radio and TV personality.	
11/01/69	**42**	6	1 We Love You, Call Collect [S]	Capitol 2678
			Art's daughter, Diane, committed suicide on 10/4/69	
			LIPPS, INC.	
			Funk project from Minneapolis formed by producer, songwriter, multi-instrumentalist Steven Greenberg. Vocals by Miss Black Minnesota U.S.A. of 1976, Cynthia Johnson.	
3/29/80	**1**[4]	23	1 ▲**Funkytown**	Casablanca 2233
8/02/80	**64**	7	2 Rock It	Casablanca 2281
			LIQUID GOLD	
			English disco quartet. Ellie Hope, lead singer.	
4/28/79	**45**	9	1 My Baby's Baby	Parachute 524
9/03/83	**86**	4	2 What's She Got	Critique 701
			LIQUID SMOKE	
			White R&B/rock quintet. Sandy Pantaleo, lead singer.	
4/18/70	**82**	3	1 I Who Have Nothing	Avco Embassy 4522
			LISA LISA & CULT JAM with FULL FORCE	
			New York R&B/rap trio: Lisa Lisa, Mike Hughes and Alex "Spanador" Moseley.	
6/08/85	**34**	21	1 I Wonder If I Take You Home	Columbia 04886
11/16/85	**69**	20	2 Can You Feel The Beat	Columbia 05669
7/26/86	**8**	26	3 **All Cried Out**	Columbia 05844
			featuring Paul Anthony & Bow Legged Lou	
			LITTLE ANTHONY & THE IMPERIALS	
			R&B group formed in 1957 in Brooklyn. Consisted of Anthony Gourdine (b: 1/8/40), Ernest Wright, Jr., Tracy Lord, Glouster Rogers and Clarence Collins. Anthony first recorded on Winley in 1955 with The DuPonts. Formed The Chesters in 1957, who changed name to The Imperials in 1958. Sammy Strain, who joined group in 1964, left in 1975 to join The O'Jays.	
8/11/58	**4**	19	1 **Tears On My Pillow**	End 1027
			Hot 100 #4 / Best Seller #5 end	
12/22/58	**87**	2	2 So Much	End 1036
3/23/59	**79**	2	3 Wishful Thinking	End 1039
6/15/59	**81**	4	4 A Prayer And A Juke Box	End 1047
12/07/59+	**24**	16	5 Shimmy, Shimmy, Ko-Ko-Bop	End 1060
4/18/60	**86**	2	6 My Empty Room	End 1067
8/22/64	**15**	10	7 I'm On The Outside (Looking In)	DCP 1104
11/07/64	**6**	14	8 **Goin' Out Of My Head**	DCP 1119
2/06/65	**10**	9	9 **Hurt So Bad**	DCP 1128
6/26/65	**16**	11	10 Take Me Back	DCP 1136
10/02/65	**34**	7	11 I Miss You So	DCP 1149
1/01/66	**51**	6	12 Hurt	DCP 1154
5/14/66	**54**	7	13 Better Use Your Head	Veep 1228
11/12/66	**92**	2	14 It's Not The Same	Veep 1248
2/17/68	**98**	1	15 I'm Hypnotized	Veep 1278
			above 9 produced by Teddy Randazzo	
7/26/69	**52**	9	16 Out Of Sight, Out Of Mind	United Art. 50552
11/08/69	**82**	4	17 The Ten Commandments Of Love	United Art. 50598
11/21/70	**92**	4	18 Help Me Find A Way (To Say I Love You)	United Art. 50720
6/15/74	**86**	4	19 I'm Falling In Love With You	Avco 4635
			LITTLE BILL & THE BLUENOTES	
			White pop group from Tacoma, Washington, led by Bill Engelhart.	
6/22/59	**66**	6	1 I Love An Angel	Dolton 4
			produced by Bonnie Guitar	

DEBUT DATE	PEAK POS	WKS CHR	ARTIST — Record Title	Label & Number
			LITTLE CAESAR & THE CONSULS	
			White "garage" rock band from Canada.	
8/14/65	**50**	8	1 (My Girl) Sloopy	Mala 512
			LITTLE CAESAR & THE ROMANS	
			Los Angeles R&B quintet led by David "Little Caesar" Johnson.	
5/01/61	**9**	13	1 **Those Oldies But Goodies (Remind Me Of You)**	Del-Fi 4158
8/07/61	**54**	4	2 Hully Gully Again	Del-Fi 4164
			THE LITTLE DIPPERS	
			Pop quartet organized by producer Buddy Killen: Delores Dinning, Emily Gilmore, Darrell McCall and Hurshel Wigintin.	
1/25/60	**9**	14	1 **Forever**	University 210
			LITTLE EVA	
			Born Eva Narcissus Boyd on 6/29/45 in Bellhaven, NC. Discovered by songwriters Carole King and Gerry Goffin. Also see Big Dee Irwin.	
6/30/62	**1^{1}**	16	1 **The Loco-Motion**	Dimension 1000
11/03/62	**12**	12	2 Keep Your Hands Off My Baby	Dimension 1003
2/02/63	**20**	10	3 Let's Turkey Trot	Dimension 1006
6/01/63	**48**	6	4 Old Smokey Locomotion new version of the traditional folksong "On Top Of Old Smokey"	Dimension 1011
			LITTLE JO ANN	
			Jo Ann Morse (age 7 in 1962).	
7/07/62	**67**	5	1 My Daddy Is President [N]	Kapp 467
			LITTLE JOE & THE THRILLERS	
			R&B group formed in New York City in 1956. Joe Cook (lead), Farris Hill and Richard Frazier (tenors), Donald Burnett (baritone) and Harry Pascle (bass).	
9/30/57	**22**	15	1 Peanuts Best Seller #22 / Top 100 #23	Okeh 7088
			LITTLE JOEY & THE FLIPS	
			R&B quintet from Philadelphia. Joey Hall, lead singer.	
6/16/62	**33**	10	1 Bongo Stomp	Joy 262
			LITTLE MILTON	
			Born Milton Campbell, Jr. on 9/7/34 in Inverness, MS. Blues singer, guitarist. Recorded with Ike Turner at Sun Records, 1953-54. In concert film "Wattstax", 1972.	
1/02/65	**86**	4	1 Blind Man	Checker 1096
3/27/65	**25**	11	2 We're Gonna Make It	Checker 1105
6/12/65	**43**	7	3 Who's Cheating Who?	Checker 1113
2/12/66	**100**	1	4 We Got The Winning Hand	Checker 1132
2/04/67	**91**	3	5 Feel So Bad	Checker 1162
2/01/69	**73**	5	6 Grits Ain't Groceries (All Around The World)	Checker 1212
5/10/69	**97**	2	7 Just A Little Bit	Checker 1217
1/17/70	**71**	5	8 If Walls Could Talk	Checker 1226
5/09/70	**82**	3	9 Baby I Love You	Checker 1227
2/12/72	**59**	6	10 That's What Love Will Make You Do	Stax 0111
			LITTLE RICHARD	
			Born Richard Wayne Penniman on 12/25/35 in Macon, Georgia. R&B/rock and roll singer, piano player. Talent contest win led to first recordings for RCA-Victor in 1951. Worked with the Tempo Toppers, 1953-55. Earned degree in Theology in 1961 and was ordained a minister. Left R&B for gospel music, 1959-62 and again in mid-70s. The key figure in the transition from R&B to rock 'n' roll. Appeared in 3 early rock & roll films: "Don't Knock The Rock", "The Girl Can't Help It" and "Mister Rock 'n' Roll"; and in 1986 in comedy "Down & Out In Beverly Hills". Also see Canned Heat.	
1/14/56	**17**	12	1 Tutti-Frutti Juke Box #17 / Best Seller #18 / Top 100 #21	Specialty 561
4/07/56	**6**	19	2 **Long Tall Sally/** Best Seller #6 / Top 100 #13 / Juke Box #14 / Jockey #16	
4/21/56	**33**	14	3 Slippin' And Slidin' (Peepin' And Hidin')	Specialty 572
7/07/56	**17**	18	4 Rip It Up/ Best Seller #17 / Top 100 #27	
7/07/56	**44**	8	5 Ready Teddy	Specialty 579
1/26/57	**49**	8	6 The Girl Can't Help It from the Jayne Mansfield film of the same title	Specialty 591
3/23/57	**21**	21	7 Lucille/ Best Seller #21 / Top 100 #27	
4/06/57	**54**	12	8 Send Me Some Lovin'	Specialty 598

DEBUT DATE	PEAK POS	WKS CHR	ARTIST — Record Title	Label & Number
			LITTLE RICHARD — Cont'd	
6/17/57	**10**	20	9 **Jenny, Jenny/** Best Seller #10 / Top 100 #14	
7/01/57	**56**	10	10 Miss Ann	Specialty 606
9/30/57	**8**	18	11 **Keep A Knockin'** Top 100 #8 / Best Seller #9 / Jockey #24 from the film "Mr. Rock 'n' Roll"	Specialty 611
2/17/58	**10**	15	12 **Good Golly, Miss Molly** Top 100 #10 / Best Seller #13	Specialty 624
6/09/58	**31**	8	13 Ooh! My Soul/ Best Seller #31 / Top 100 #35	
6/30/58	**68**	3	14 True, Fine Mama	Specialty 633
9/15/58	**41**	10	15 Baby Face Hot 100 #41 / Best Seller #50 end there were 4 Top 10 versions of this tune in 1926	Specialty 645
5/11/59	**95**	2	16 Kansas City	Specialty 664
7/18/64	**82**	4	17 Bama Lama Bama Loo	Specialty 692
11/27/65	**92**	1	18 I Don't Know What You've Got But It's Got Me - Part I	Vee-Jay 698
5/23/70	**47**	9	19 Freedom Blues	Reprise 0907
9/05/70	**85**	5	20 Greenwood Mississippi	Reprise 0942
3/08/86	**42**	10	21 Great Gosh A'Mighty! (It's A Matter Of Time) theme song from the film "Down And Out In Beverly Hills"	MCA 52780
			LITTLE RIVER BAND Pop/rock group formed in Australia in 1975. Consisted of Glenn Shorrock (lead singer), Rick Formosa, Beeb Birtles and Graham Goble (guitars), Roger McLachlan (bass) and Derek Pellicci (drums). Formosa, McLachlan, replaced by David Briggs (guitar) and George McArdle (bass) after first album. Shorrock replaced by John Farnham in 1983. By 1985, after numerous changes, Goble was the only remaining original member. Shorrock returned in 1987, replacing Farnham.	
9/18/76	**28**	16	1 It's A Long Way There	Harvest 4318
2/05/77	**62**	5	2 I'll Always Call Your Name	Harvest 4380
8/06/77	**14**	22	3 Help Is On Its Way	Harvest 4428
12/17/77+	**16**	18	4 Happy Anniversary	Harvest 4524
7/29/78	**3**	20	5 **Reminiscing**	Harvest 4605
1/06/79	**10**	20	6 **Lady**	Harvest 4667
7/21/79	**6**	18	7 **Lonesome Loser**	Capitol 4748
10/20/79+	**10**	18	8 **Cool Change**	Capitol 4789
5/03/80	**51**	6	9 It's Not A Wonder	Capitol 4862
8/22/81	**6**	21	10 **The Night Owls**	Capitol 5033
12/05/81+	**10**	19	11 **Take It Easy On Me**	Capitol 5057
4/03/82	**14**	16	12 Man On Your Mind	Capitol 5061
11/20/82+	**11**	18	13 The Other Guy	Capitol 5185
5/07/83	**22**	12	14 We Two John Farnham replaces Shorrock as lead singer	Capitol 5231
7/23/83	**35**	11	15 You're Driving Me Out Of My Mind	Capitol 5256
1/26/85	**60**	8	16 Playing To Win shown as: **LRB**	Capitol 5411
			LITTLE SISTER Female soul trio organized by Sly Stone for his own record label and featuring his sister Vanetta Stewart.	
2/28/70	**22**	11	1 You're The One - Part I	Stone Flower 9000
12/12/70+	**32**	13	2 Somebody's Watching You	Stone Flower 9001
			LITTLE STEVEN & the DISCIPLES OF SOUL Miami Steve Van Zandt of Bruce Springsteen's E Street Band.	
12/25/82+	**63**	9	1 Forever	EMI America 8144
			LIVERPOOL FIVE	
12/24/66	**98**	1	1 Any Way That You Want Me	RCA 8968
			JOHN LiVIGNI	
10/18/75	**83**	6	1 Machines	Raintree 2204
			IAN LLOYD Real name: Ian Buonconciglio. Lead singer of Stories.	
10/13/79	**50**	9	1 Slip Away written by Ric Ocasek of The Cars	Scotti Br. 505

DEBUT DATE	PEAK POS	WKS CHR	ARTIST — Record Title	Label & Number
			LOBO	
			Born Kent Lavoie on 7/31/43 in Tallahassee, FL. Pop singer/songwriter/guitarist.	
4/03/71	**5**	13	1 **Me And You And A Dog Named Boo**	Big Tree 112
6/26/71	**46**	9	2 She Didn't Do Magic/	
		9	3 I'm The Only One	Big Tree 116
9/04/71	**72**	3	4 California Kid And Reemo	Big Tree 119
7/08/72	**56**	9	5 A Simple Man	Big Tree 141
9/23/72	**2**[2]	14	6● **I'd Love You To Want Me**	Big Tree 147
12/30/72+	**8**	13	7 **Don't Expect Me To Be Your Friend**	Big Tree 158
4/07/73	**27**	11	8 It Sure Took A Long, Long Time	Big Tree 16001
6/23/73	**22**	12	9 How Can I Tell Her	Big Tree 16004
11/03/73	**68**	7	10 There Ain't No Way/	
		2	11 Love Me For What I Am	Big Tree 16012
4/13/74	**37**	7	12 Standing At The End Of The Line	Big Tree 15001
7/20/74	**43**	9	13 Rings	Big Tree 15008
3/29/75	**27**	9	14 Don't Tell Me Goodnight all of above produced by Phil Gernhard	Big Tree 16033
7/28/79	**23**	17	15 Where Were You When I Was Falling In Love	MCA 41065
12/22/79+	**75**	8	16 Holdin' On For Dear Love	MCA 41152
			HANK LOCKLIN	
			Born Lawrence Hankins Locklin on 2/15/18 in McLellan, Florida. Country singer, songwriter, guitarist. Elected mayor of McLellan in the early 60s.	
12/30/57+	**66**	11	1 Geisha Girl	RCA 6984
6/02/58	**77**	2	2 Send Me The Pillow You Dream On	RCA 7127
5/23/60	**8**	22	3 **Please Help Me, I'm Falling**	RCA 7692
			JOHN LODGE - see JUSTIN HAYWARD	
			LOGGINS & MESSINA	
			Kenny Loggins and ex-Buffalo Springfield/Poco member, Jim Messina (b: 12/5/47). Messina originally hired as producer for Loggins, however, they formed a partnership that lasted for 4 years.	
4/15/72	**84**	5	1 Vahevala	Columbia 45550
6/10/72	**86**	2	2 Nobody But You	Columbia 45617
11/11/72+	**4**	16	3● **Your Mama Don't Dance**	Columbia 45719
3/31/73	**18**	13	4 Thinking Of You	Columbia 45815
11/03/73	**16**	13	5 My Music	Columbia 45952
3/02/74	**71**	6	6 Watching The River Run	Columbia 46010
2/08/75	**84**	2	7 Changes	Columbia 10077
4/05/75	**52**	7	8 Growin'	Columbia 10118
8/30/75	**84**	2	9 I Like It Like That	Columbia 10188
10/18/75	**89**	2	10 A Lover's Question all of above produced by Jim Messina	Columbia 10222
			DAVE LOGGINS	
			Born on 11/10/47 in Mountain City, Tennessee. Pop/Country-styled singer, songwriter. Cousin of Kenny Loggins.	
6/01/74	**5**	18	1 **Please Come To Boston**	Epic 11115
11/16/74	**57**	5	2 Someday	Epic 50035
			KENNY LOGGINS	
			Born on 1/7/48 in Everett, WA. Pop/rock singer, songwriter, guitarist. With rock bands Second Helping and Gator Creek in the late 60s. Signed as a solo artist with Columbia in 1971 where he met and recorded with Jim Messina to 1976.	
7/30/77	**66**	11	1 I Believe In Love	Columbia 10569
7/29/78	**5**	20	2 **Whenever I Call You 'Friend'** harmony vocal by Stevie Nicks	Columbia 10794
12/02/78+	**60**	8	3 Easy Driver	Columbia 10866
10/20/79+	**11**	23	4 This Is It	Columbia 11109
2/23/80	**36**	13	5 Keep The Fire	Columbia 11215
7/12/80	**7**	22	6 **I'm Alright** theme from the film "Caddyshack"	Columbia 11317
8/28/82	**17**	12	7 Don't Fight It **KENNY LOGGINS with STEVE PERRY**	Columbia 03192
11/27/82+	**15**	17	8 Heart To Heart	Columbia 03377
3/12/83	**24**	14	9 Welcome To Heartlight inspired by the writings of the children of Heartlight School	Columbia 03555
1/28/84	**1**[3]	23	10● **Footloose**	Columbia 04310

DEBUT DATE	PEAK POS	WKS CHR	ARTIST — Record Title	Label & Number
			KENNY LOGGINS — Cont'd	
6/16/84	**22**	14	11 I'm Free (Heaven Helps The Man)	Columbia 04452
			above 2 from the film "Footloose"	
3/23/85	**29**	10	12 Vox Humana	Columbia 04849
5/25/85	**40**	22	13 Forever	Columbia 04931
10/12/85	**88**	2	14 I'll Be There	Columbia 05625
5/10/86	**2^{1}**	21	15 **Danger Zone**	Columbia 05893
8/16/86	**60**	12	16 Playing With The Boys	Columbia 05902
			above two from the film "Top Gun"	
			LOLITA	
			Lolita Ditta from Vienna, Austria.	
10/24/60	**5**	18	1 **Sailor (Your Home Is The Sea)** [F]	Kapp 349
2/06/61	**94**	3	2 Cowboy Jimmy Joe [F]	Kapp 370
			LONDON SYMPHONY ORCHESTRA - see JOHN WILLIAMS	
			JULIE LONDON	
			Born on 9/26/26 in Santa Rosa, California. Singer, actress. Played Dixie McCall on the TV series "Emergency".	
11/12/55	**9**	20	1 **Cry Me A River**	Liberty 55006
			Jockey #9 / Top 100 #13 / Juke Box #14 / Best Seller #23	
			LAURIE LONDON	
			Born on 1/19/44 in London, England. Recorded only hit record at age 13.	
3/24/58	**1^{4}**	19	1 ● **He's Got The Whole World (In His Hands)**	Capitol 3891
			Jockey #1 / Best Seller #2 / Top 100 #2	
			traditional black American gospel song	
			LONE JUSTICE	
			Los Angeles rock quartet. Maria McKee, lead singer.	
5/11/85	**71**	6	1 Ways To Be Wicked	Geffen 29023
7/27/85	**73**	5	2 Sweet, Sweet Baby (I'm Falling)	Geffen 28965
			SHORTY LONG	
			Born Frederick Earl Long on 5/20/40 in Birmingham, Alabama. Soul singer, songwriter. Drowned on 6/29/69 in Ontario, Canada.	
9/24/66	**97**	1	1 Function At The Junction	Soul 35021
2/17/68	**75**	4	2 Night Fo' Last	Soul 35040
6/01/68	**8**	11	3 **Here Comes The Judge** [N]	Soul 35044
			CLAUDINE LONGET	
			Born on 1/29/42 in France. Singer, actress. Formerly married to Andy Williams.	
11/05/66	**98**	2	1 Meditation (Meditacao)	A&M 817
5/27/67	**91**	1	2 Hello, Hello	A&M 846
8/05/67	**100**	2	3 Good Day Sunshine	A&M 864
			written by John Lennon & Paul McCartney	
2/24/68	**71**	9	4 Love Is Blue (L'Amour Est Bleu) [F]	A&M 909
			LOOKING GLASS	
			Rock quartet formed by Elliot Lurie while at Rutgers University in New Jersey.	
6/17/72	**1^{1}**	16	1 ● **Brandy (You're A Fine Girl)**	Epic 10874
7/21/73	**33**	15	2 Jimmy Loves Mary-Anne	Epic 11001
			LOOSE ENDS	
			Black trio: Jane Eugene, Macca and Steve Nichol.	
7/20/85	**43**	10	1 Hangin' On A String (Contemplating)	MCA 52570
			TRINI LOPEZ	
			Born on 5/15/37 in Dallas. Pop/folk singer, guitarist. Discovered by Don Costa while performing at PJs nightclub in Los Angeles.	
7/27/63	**3**	14	1 **If I Had A Hammer**	Reprise 20198
11/16/63+	**23**	10	2 Kansas City	Reprise 20236
3/21/64	**94**	2	3 Jailer, Bring Me Water	Reprise 0260
5/09/64	**43**	13	4 What Have I Got Of My Own	Reprise 0276
8/22/64	**42**	8	5 Michael	Reprise 0300
1/23/65	**20**	7	6 Lemon Tree	Reprise 0336
5/01/65	**94**	1	7 Sad Tomorrows	Reprise 0328
6/12/65	**85**	3	8 Are You Sincere	Reprise 0376
10/16/65	**54**	9	9 Sinner Man	Reprise 0405
			from the film "Marriage On The Rocks"	
4/09/66	**39**	7	10 I'm Comin' Home, Cindy	Reprise 0455

DEBUT DATE	PEAK POS	WKS CHR	ARTIST — Record Title		Label & Number
			TRINI LOPEZ — Cont'd		
6/25/66	**86**	5	11 La Bamba - Part I	[F]	Reprise 0480
2/18/67	**93**	3	12 Gonna Get Along Without Ya' Now		Reprise 0547
3/02/68	**99**	2	13 Sally Was A Good Old Girl all of above produced by Don Costa		Reprise 0659
			JEFF LORBER featuring KARYN WHITE Lorber is a jazz fusion keyboardist.		
12/06/86+	**27**	16	1 Facts Of Love		Warner 28588
			LORD ROCKINGHAM'S XI British group.		
10/06/58	**96**	1	1 Fried Onions	[I]	London 1810
			THE LORELEIS		
11/12/55	**91**	1	1 You're So Nice To Be Near		Spotlight 390
			GLORIA LORING & CARL ANDERSON Gloria played Liz Curtis on TV's "Days Of Our Lives".		
7/05/86	**2**[2]	21	1 **Friends And Lovers**		USA Carrere 06122
			LOS BRAVOS Rock quintet consisting of 4 members from Spain and 1 from Germany - lead singer Mike Kogel (Kennedy).		
8/13/66	**4**	12	1 **Black Is Black**		Press 60002
12/17/66	**91**	2	2 Going Nowhere		Press 60003
5/25/68	**51**	7	3 Bring A Little Lovin' from the film "Bravos II"		Parrot 3020
			LOS INDIOS TABAJARAS Brazilian Indian brothers: Natalicio and Antenor Lima.		
9/21/63	**6**	14	1 **Maria Elena** #1 hit in 1941 for Jimmy Dorsey & His Orchestra	[I]	RCA 8216
3/14/64	**82**	2	2 Always In My Heart #10 hit in 1942 for Glenn Miller & His Orchestra	[I]	RCA 8313
			LOS LOBOS Hispanic-American rock quintet based in Los Angeles.		
3/23/85	**78**	5	1 Will The Wolf Survive?		Slash 29093
			LOS POP TOPS Vocal septet based in Spain. Lead singer Phil Trim is from the West Indies.		
9/28/68	**78**	4	1 Oh Lord, Why Lord melody based on Pachelbel's Canon in D Major		Calla 154
10/09/71	**57**	10	2 Mammy Blue shown as: **POP-TOPS**		ABC 11311
			THE LOST GENERATION Chicago soul quartet. Lowrell Simon (lead), his brother Fred Simon, Larry Brownlee (of The C.O.D.'s) and Jesse Dean.		
6/06/70	**30**	14	1 The Sly, Slick, And The Wicked		Brunswick 55436
			BONNIE LOU		
11/12/55	**14**	15	1 Daddy-O Juke Box #14 / Best Seller #25 / Top 100 #28		King 4835
			JOHN D. LOUDERMILK Born on 3/31/34 in Durham, NC. Pop/Country singer, songwriter, multi-instrumentalist. Wrote hits "Waterloo", "Tobacco Road", "Indian Reservation" and many others.		
3/16/57	**38**	11	1 Sittin' In The Balcony shown as: **JOHNNY DEE**		Colonial 430
11/06/61	**32**	9	2 Language Of Love		RCA 7938
4/07/62	**73**	5	3 Thou Shalt Not Steal		RCA 7993
7/28/62	**83**	3	4 Callin' Doctor Casey		RCA 8054
12/01/62	**65**	4	5 Road Hog		RCA 8101
			LOUISIANA'S LE ROUX - see LE ROUX		
			LOVE Los Angeles rock group led by singer/guitarist Arthur Lee.		
4/30/66	**52**	11	1 My Little Red Book		Elektra 45603
7/30/66	**33**	10	2 7 And 7 Is		Elektra 45605
9/12/70	**99**	3	3 Alone Again Or		Elektra 45700

DEBUT DATE	PEAK POS	WKS CHR	ARTIST — Record Title	Label & Number
			LOVE & KISSES	
			Studio group assembled by European disco producer Alec Costandinos.	
5/06/78	**22**	16	1 Thank God It's Friday from the film of the same title	Casablanca 925
			LOVE CHILDS AFRO CUBAN BLUES BAND	
			Studio group assembled by New York disco producer Michael Zager.	
7/19/75	**90**	3	1 Life And Death In G&A [I]	Roulette 7172
			THE LOVE GENERATION	
6/24/67	**74**	7	1 Groovy Summertime	Imperial 66243
8/03/68	**86**	3	2 Montage From How Sweet It Is (I Know That You Know) from the James Garner/Debbie Reynolds film "How Sweet It Is"	Imperial 66310
			THE LOVELITES	
			Female soul trio from Chicago led by Patti Hamilton.	
1/10/70	**60**	10	1 How Can I Tell My Mom & Dad	Uni 55181
			LOVE UNLIMITED	
			Female soul trio from San Pedro, CA: sisters Glodean & Linda James, and Diane Taylor. Barry White, who later married Glodean, was their manager and producer.	
4/01/72	**14**	14	1● Walkin' In The Rain With The One I Love featuring Barry White's voice on the telephone	Uni 55319
12/15/73	**83**	4	2 It May Be Winter Outside, (But In My Heart It's Spring)	20th Century 2062
3/30/74	**76**	8	3 Under The Influence Of Love	20th Century 2082
11/30/74+	**27**	15	4 I Belong To You	20th Century 2141
			LOVE UNLIMITED ORCHESTRA	
			Studio orchestra conducted and arranged by Barry White.	
12/01/73+	**1**[1]	22	1● **Love's Theme** [I]	20th Century 2069
4/27/74	**63**	8	2 Rhapsody In White [I]	20th Century 2090
2/08/75	**22**	12	3 Satin Soul [I]	20th Century 2162
9/11/76	**48**	11	4 My Sweet Summer Suite [I]	20th Century 2301
1/22/77	**68**	7	5 Theme From King Kong (Pt. I) [I] from the Dino DeLaurentiis film "King Kong"	20th Century 2325
			DARLENE LOVE	
			Lead singer of backing group, The Blossoms. Sang lead on 2 songs by The Crystals and with Bob B. Soxx & The Blue Jeans. Starred in the off-Broadway show "Leader of The Pack".	
4/06/63	**39**	8	1 (Today I Met) The Boy I'm Gonna Marry	Philles 111
7/20/63	**26**	10	2 Wait Til' My Bobby Gets Home	Philles 114
10/19/63	**53**	6	3 A Fine Fine Boy all of above produced by Phil Spector	Philles 117
			RONNIE LOVE	
1/09/61	**72**	4	1 Chills And Fever	Dot 16144
			LOVERBOY	
			Rock quintet formed in Vancouver, Canada in 1978: Mike Reno (lead singer), Paul Dean (lead guitar), Scott Smith (bass), Matt Frenette (drums) and Doug Johnson (keyboards).	
1/31/81	**35**	17	1 Turn Me Loose	Columbia 11421
6/20/81	**55**	7	2 The Kid Is Hot Tonite	Columbia 02068
11/14/81+	**29**	20	3 Working For The Weekend	Columbia 02589
4/10/82	**26**	15	4 When It's Over backing vocals by Nancy Nash	Columbia 02814
6/11/83	**11**	16	5 Hot Girls In Love	Columbia 03941
9/17/83	**34**	12	6 Queen Of The Broken Hearts	Columbia 04096
8/24/85	**9**	21	7 **Lovin' Every Minute Of It**	Columbia 05569
11/16/85	**65**	9	8 Dangerous	Columbia 05711
1/18/86	**10**	18	9 **This Could Be The Night**	Columbia 05765
4/26/86	**68**	7	10 Lead A Double Life	Columbia 05867
8/02/86	**12**	17	11 Heaven In Your Eyes from the film "Top Gun"	Columbia 06178
			THE LOVERS	
			Husband and wife R&B duo: Alden "Tarheel Slim" Bunn (d: 8/21/77) and Anna "Little Ann" Sandford.	
8/19/57	**48**	9	1 Darling It's Wonderful	Lamp 2005

DEBUT DATE	PEAK POS	WKS CHR	ARTIST — Record Title	Label & Number
			THE LOVERS	
			Studio disco group from Philadelphia.	
5/14/77	100	2	1 Discomania .... [N]	Marlin 3313
			EDDIE LOVETTE	
5/24/69	95	3	1 Too Experienced............	Steady 124
			THE LOVIN' SPOONFUL	
			Jug band rock group formed in New York City in 1965. Consisted of John Sebastian (lead vocals, songwriter, guitarist, harmonica), Zal Yanovsky (lead guitar), Steve Boone (bass) and Joe Butler (drums). Sebastian had been with the Even Dozen Jug Band; did session work at Elektra. Yanovsky and Sebastian were members of the Mugwumps with Cass Elliott and Denny Doherty (later with The Mamas & The Papas). Yanovsky replaced by Jerry Yester (keyboards) in 1967. Disbanded in 1968.	
8/21/65	9	13	1 **Do You Believe In Magic**	Kama Sutra 201
11/27/65+	10	12	2 **You Didn't Have To Be So Nice**............	Kama Sutra 205
2/26/66	2^{2}	12	3 **Daydream**............	Kama Sutra 208
5/07/66	2^{2}	11	4 **Did You Ever Have To Make Up Your Mind?**............	Kama Sutra 209
7/16/66	1^{3}	11	5● **Summer In The City**	Kama Sutra 211
10/15/66	10	10	6 **Rain On The Roof**............	Kama Sutra 216
12/17/66+	8	10	7 **Nashville Cats**/	
1/07/67	87	3	8 Full Measure	Kama Sutra 219
2/11/67	15	8	9 Darling Be Home Soon............	Kama Sutra 220
			from the Francis Ford Coppola film "You're A Big Boy Now"	
4/29/67	18	8	10 Six O'Clock............	Kama Sutra 225
			all of above singles produced by Erik Jacobsen	
10/28/67	27	6	11 She Is Still A Mystery............	Kama Sutra 239
1/06/68	48	6	12 Money	Kama Sutra 241
7/27/68	73	5	13 Never Going Back	Kama Sutra 250
2/08/69	91	2	14 Me About You............	Kama Sutra 255
			BERNIE LOWE ORCHESTRA	
			Born on 11/22/17 in Philadelphia. Founder and chief producer of Cameo-Parkway Records. Wrote #1 hits "Teddy Bear" and "Butterfly".	
11/24/58	46	7	1 Sing Sing Sing/ [I]	
			featuring Jerry Gilgor on drums; #7 hit in 1938 for Benny Goodman	
11/24/58	61	4	2 Intermission Riff .... [I]	Cameo 153
			revival of Stan Kenton's 1946 recording	
			JIM LOWE	
			Born 5/7/27 in Springfield, MO. D.J. in New York City when he recorded "Green Door".	
7/23/55	42	3	1 Close The Door .... [N]	Dot 15381
			Coming Up #42	
9/22/56	1^{3}	26	2 **The Green Door**............	Dot 15486
			Top 100 #1(3) / Juke Box #1(3) / Best Seller #2 / Jockey #2 piano player: Bob Davie	
1/05/57	43	10	3 By You, By You, By You/	
1/19/57	84	3	4 I Feel The Beat	Dot 15525
5/06/57	15	18	5 Four Walls/	
			Juke Box #15 / Jockey #16 / Best Seller #19 / Top 100 #20	
5/06/57	20	12	6 Talkin' To The Blues............	Dot 15569
			Jockey #20 / Top 100 #21 from the TV production "Modern Romances"	
			NICK LOWE	
			Born on 3/25/49 in England. With Brinsley Schwarz (1970-75) and Rockpile. Married to Carlene Carter. Produced albums for Elvis Costello and Graham Parker & The Rumour.	
7/28/79	12	15	1 Cruel To Be Kind............	Columbia 11018
11/30/85+	77	9	2 I Knew The Bride (When She Use To Rock And Roll) ...	Columbia 05570
			NICK LOWE & HIS COWBOY OUTFIT produced by Huey Lewis	
			L.T.D.	
			Jeffrey Osborne, lead singer of 10 man R&B/funk band from Greensboro, NC. L.T.D. means Love, Togetherness and Devotion.	
10/02/76	20	18	1 Love Ballad	A&M 1847
1/29/77	91	3	2 Love To The World	A&M 1897
10/15/77	4	19	3● **(Every Time I Turn Around) Back In Love Again**	A&M 1974
3/11/78	56	7	4 Never Get Enough Of Your Love	A&M 2005
8/19/78	49	10	5 Holding On (When Love Is Gone)............	A&M 2057
			1, 3 & 5: #1 on Billboard's Soul charts	
11/15/80+	40	16	6 Shine On............	A&M 2283

DEBUT DATE	PEAK POS	WKS CHR	ARTIST — Record Title	Label & Number
			CARRIE LUCAS	
			Los Angeles soul/disco stylist. Sang back-up with the Whispers.	
4/30/77	**64**	8	1 I Gotta Keep Dancin'	Soul Train 10891
			shown only as: **CARRIE**	
5/12/79	**70**	7	2 Dance With You	Solar 11482
			FRANK LUCAS	
			Soul singer from San Bernardino, California.	
6/25/77	**92**	3	1 Good Thing Man	ICA 001
			MATT LUCAS	
			Born on 7/19/35 in Memphis. Blue-eyed soul singer, drummer.	
5/04/63	**56**	9	1 I'm Movin' On	Smash 1813
			revival of Hank Snow's giant #1 hit from 1950	
			ROBIN LUKE	
			Born on 3/19/42 in Los Angeles. Recorded "Susie Darlin'" in Hawaii, inspired by his younger sister, Susie.	
8/11/58	**5**	17	1 **Susie Darlin'**	Dot 15781
			Hot 100 #5 / Best Seller #6 end	
			LULU	
			Born Marie Lawrie on 11/3/48 near Glasgow, Scotland. Formerly married to Maurice Gibb (Bee Gees), 1969-73.	
8/01/64	**94**	3	1 Shout	Parrot 9678
			LULU & THE LUVERS	
			cover version of the Isley Brothers 1959 classic tune	
9/09/67	**1**[5]	17	2● **To Sir With Love**	Epic 10187
			from the film of the same title (starring Lulu)	
12/09/67	**96**	3	3 Shout [R]	Parrot 40021
12/16/67+	**32**	10	4 Best Of Both Worlds	Epic 10260
3/23/68	**53**	7	5 Me, The Peaceful Heart	Epic 10302
8/10/68	**52**	8	6 Morning Dew	Epic 10367
12/27/69+	**22**	14	7 Oh Me Oh My (I'm A Fool For You Baby)	Atco 6722
4/25/70	**54**	6	8 Hum A Song (From Your Heart)	Atco 6749
			LULU with The Dixie Flyers	
8/01/81	**18**	18	9 I Could Never Miss You (More Than I Do)	Alfa 7006
11/21/81+	**44**	11	10 If I Were You	Alfa 7011
			BOB LUMAN	
			Born on 4/15/37 in Nacogdoches, Texas. Died on 12/27/78 in Nashville. Country/rockabilly singer, songwriter, guitarist.	
9/05/60	**7**	14	1 **Let's Think About Living** [N]	Warner 5172
			LUNAR FUNK	
2/05/72	**63**	8	1 Mr. Penguin - Pt. I [I]	Bell 45172
			ART LUND	
			Born on 4/1/15 in Salt Lake City. Baritone with Benny Goodman, 1941-42 as Art London.	
12/15/58	**89**	3	1 Philadelphia U.S.A.	Coral 62054
			VICTOR LUNDBERG	
			Ex-disc jockey and newsman from Grand Rapids, Michigan.	
11/11/67	**10**	6	1 **An Open Letter To My Teenage Son** [S]	Liberty 55996
			PAT LUNDI	
9/06/75	**78**	5	1 Party Music	Vigor 1723
			THE LY-DELLS	
8/21/61	**54**	6	1 Wizard Of Love	Master 251
			ARTHUR LYMAN	
			Born on the island of Kauai, Hawaii in 1934. Plays vibraphone, guitar, piano and drums. Formerly with the Martin Denny Trio.	
6/15/59	**55**	6	1 Taboo [I]	Hi Fi 550
			ARTHUR LYMAN GROUP:	
5/29/61	**4**	12	2 **Yellow Bird** [I]	Hi Fi 5024
2/02/63	**43**	11	3 Love For Sale [I]	Hi Fi 5066
			Libby Holman's version of the Cole Porter tune hit #5 in 1931	
			LYME & CYBELLE	
			Male-female duo: Warren Zevon and Tule Livingston.	
3/19/66	**65**	6	1 Follow Me	White Whale 228

DEBUT DATE	PEAK POS	WKS CHR	ARTIST — Record Title	Label & Number
			FRANKIE LYMON & THE TEENAGERS	
			R&B group formed as The Premiers in the Bronx, New York in 1955. Lead singer Lymon was born on 9/30/42 in New York City and died of a drug overdose on 2/28/68 at the age of 25. Other members included Herman Santiago (tenor), Jimmy Merchant (tenor), Joe Negroni (baritone, d: 9/5/78) and Sherman Garnes (bass, d: 2/26/77). Group in films "Rock, Rock, Rock" and "Mister Rock 'n' Roll".	
2/11/56	**6**	21	1 **Why Do Fools Fall In Love**	Gee 1002
			THE TEENAGERS featuring FRANKIE LYMON	
			Best Seller #6 / Top 100 #7 / Juke Box #8 / Jockey #9	
4/28/56	**13**	15	2 I Want You To Be My Girl	Gee 1012
			Best Seller #13 / Top 100 #17 / Juke Box #20 / Jockey #25	
7/28/56	**57**	7	3 I Promise To Remember/	
		1	4 Who Can Explain?	Gee 1018
			Coming Up flip	
10/20/56	**77**	2	5 The ABC's Of Love	Gee 1022
7/22/57	**20**	17	6 Goody Goody	Gee 1039
			Best Seller #20 / Jockey #21 / Top 100 #22	
8/08/60	**58**	4	7 Little Bitty Pretty One	Roulette 4257
			shown only as: **FRANKIE LYMON**	
			BARBARA LYNN	
			Born Barbara Lynn Ozen on 1/16/42 in Beaumont, TX. R&B singer/songwriter/guitarist.	
6/16/62	**8**	13	1 **You'll Lose A Good Thing**	Jamie 1220
9/22/62	**63**	8	2 Second Fiddle Girl	Jamie 1233
12/15/62+	**65**	6	3 You're Gonna Need Me	Jamie 1240
2/23/63	**93**	4	4 Don't Be Cruel	Jamie 1244
8/10/63	**68**	8	5 (I Cried at) Laura's Wedding	Jamie 1260
6/20/64	**69**	8	6 Oh! Baby (We Got A Good Thing Goin')	Jamie 1277
10/03/64	**93**	3	7 Don't Spread It Around	Jamie 1286
1/09/65	**95**	2	8 It's Better To Have It	Jamie 1292
2/17/68	**65**	2	9 This Is The Thanks I Get	Atlantic 2450
			all of above produced by Huey P. Meaux in New Orleans	
			CHERYL LYNN	
			Born on 3/11/57 in Los Angeles. Soul singer. Discovered on TV's "Gong Show".	
12/02/78+	**12**	18	1 ● Got To Be Real	Columbia 10808
4/14/79	**62**	10	2 Star Love	Columbia 10907
8/08/81	**70**	7	3 Shake It Up Tonight	Columbia 02102
2/11/84	**69**	8	4 Encore	Columbia 04256
			DONNA LYNN	
2/22/64	**83**	4	1 My Boyfriend Got A Beatle Haircut [N]	Capitol 5127
			LORETTA LYNN	
			Born Loretta Webb on 4/14/35 in Butcher Holler, Kentucky. Country singer, songwriter, guitarist. Her sister Crystal Gayle and brother Jay Lee Webb are popular Country stars. The movie "Coal Miner's Daughter" of 1980 was based on Loretta's autobiography.	
12/05/70	**83**	4	1 Coal Miner's Daughter	Decca 32749
2/27/71	**56**	6	2 After The Fire Is Gone	Decca 32776
			CONWAY TWITTY/LORETTA LYNN	
4/24/71	**94**	2	3 I Wanna Be Free	Decca 32796
3/01/75	**70**	7	4 The Pill	MCA 40358
			VERA LYNN	
			Born Vera Margaret Welsh on 3/20/19 in London, England. England's most popular female singer during World War II.	
3/03/56	**96**	1	1 Such A Day	London 1642
5/06/57	**55**	8	2 Don't Cry My Love (The Faithful Hussar)	London 1729
			GLORIA LYNNE	
			Born on 11/23/31 in New York City. Jazz-styled vocalist.	
9/11/61	**95**	4	1 Impossible	Everest 19418
12/18/61	**100**	1	2 You Don't Have To Be A Tower Of Strength	Everest 19428
			answer song to Gene McDaniel's hit "Tower Of Strength"	
1/11/64	**28**	12	3 I Wish You Love	Everest 2036
4/04/64	**64**	5	4 I Should Care	Everest 2042
			there were 4 Top 20 versions of this song in 1945	
4/04/64	**88**	4	5 Be Anything (But Be Mine)	Fontana 1890
			Eddy Howard's version hit #7 in 1952	
7/04/64	**76**	3	6 Don't Take Your Love From Me	Everest 2044
			Glen Grady's version hit #26 in 1944	

DEBUT DATE	PEAK POS	WKS CHR	ARTIST — Record Title	Label & Number
			GLORIA LYNNE — Cont'd	
6/26/65	**62**	5	7 Watermelon Man	Fontana 1511
			JEFF LYNNE	
			Born on 12/30/47 in Birmingham, England. Leader of Electric Light Orchestra.	
8/18/84	**85**	3	1 Video!	Virgin 04570
			from the film "Electric Dreams"	
			LYNYRD SKYNYRD	
			Southern rock band formed while in high school in Jacksonville, Florida in 1965. Named after their gym teacher Leonard Skinner. Nucleus of band consisted of Ronnie Van Zant (lead singer), Gary Rossington (guitar) and Allen Collins (guitar). Plane crash on 10/20/77 in Gillsburg, Mississippi killed Van Zant and members Steve and Cassie Gaines. Gary and Allen formed the Rossington Collins Band in 1980.	
7/27/74	**8**	17	1 **Sweet Home Alabama**	MCA 40258
11/23/74+	**19**	12	2 Free Bird	MCA 40328
6/14/75	**27**	9	3 Saturday Night Special	MCA 40416
3/20/76	**80**	3	4 Double Trouble	MCA 40532
12/04/76+	**38**	8	5 Free Bird	MCA 40665
			live version of #2 above	
12/03/77+	**13**	18	6 What's Your Name	MCA 40819
4/15/78	**69**	4	7 You Got That Right	MCA 40888
			JOHNNY LYTLE	
			Born on 10/13/32 in Springfield, Ohio. Jazz vibraphonist.	
1/22/66	**80**	5	1 The Loop [I]	Tuba 2004

M

DEBUT DATE	PEAK POS	WKS CHR	ARTIST — Record Title	Label & Number
			M	
			M is British pop musician Robin Scott.	
8/11/79	**1**[1]	24	1 ● **Pop Muzik**	Sire 49033
			M+M	
			Canadian rock duo: Martha Johnson (vocals) & Mark Gane (guitar, keyboards) - evolved from Martha & The Muffins.	
6/30/84	**63**	7	1 Black Stations/White Stations	RCA 13824
			MOMS MABLEY	
			Born Loretta Mary Aiken on 3/19/1897 in North Carolina. Died on 5/23/75. Bawdy comedienne. Charted 13 comedy albums on Billboard's pop albums charts.	
6/28/69	**35**	6	1 Abraham, Martin And John	Mercury 72935
			JAMES MacARTHUR	
			Danny Williams of TV's "Hawaii Five-O".	
6/22/63	**94**	2	1 The Ten Commandments Of Love [S]	Scepter 1250
			spoken version of Harvey & The Moonglows' 1958 hit	
			KATHI MacDONALD - see LONG JOHN BALDRY	
			RALPH MacDONALD	
			Session percussionist.	
9/01/84	**58**	10	1 In The Name Of Love	Polydor 881221
			RALPH MacDONALD with BILL WITHERS	
			MACEO & THE MACKS	
			JB's spin-off funk group led by trumpeter Maceo Parker.	
9/01/73	**71**	5	1 Parrty - Part I [I]	People 624
			written, produced and arranged by James Brown	
			BYRON MacGREGOR	
			Canadian - news director of CKLW Radio in Detroit.	
1/05/74	**4**	12	1 ● **Americans** [S]	Westbound 222
			backed by instrumental version of "America The Beautiful"	
			MARY MacGREGOR	
			Pop singer from St. Paul.	
11/20/76+	**1**[2]	22	1 ● **Torn Between Two Lovers**	Ariola Am. 7638
4/23/77	**46**	8	2 This Girl (Has Turned Into A Woman)	Ariola Am. 7662
8/06/77	**90**	4	3 For A While	Ariola Am. 7667
11/25/78	**81**	4	4 The Wedding Song (There Is Love)	Ariola 7726

DEBUT DATE	PEAK POS	WKS CHR	ARTIST — Record Title	Label & Number
			MARY MacGREGOR — Cont'd	
8/11/79	**39**	12	5 Good Friend from the movie "Meatballs"	RSO 938
5/17/80	**72**	4	6 Dancin' Like Lovers	RSO 1025
			MACHINE	
3/17/79	**77**	10	1 There But For The Grace Of God Go I	RCA 11456
			LONNIE MACK Born Lonnie McIntosh on 7/18/41 in Aurora, IN. Guitarist, vocalist.	
6/08/63	**5**	13	1 **Memphis** [I]	Fraternity 906
8/24/63	**24**	9	2 Wham! [I]	Fraternity 912
11/30/63	**93**	1	3 Baby, What's Wrong	Fraternity 918
10/30/65	**78**	5	4 Honky Tonky '65 [I]	Fraternity 951
			WARNER MACK Born Warner McPherson on 4/2/38 in Nashville. Country singer, guitarist.	
7/29/57	**61**	5	1 Is It Wrong (For Loving You)	Decca 30301
1/20/58	**74**	3	2 Roc-A-Chicka with the Anita Kerr Quartet	Decca 30471
			GISELE MacKENZIE Born Gisele Lefleche on 1/10/27 in Winnipeg, Canada. Popular singing star of TV's "Your Hit Parade" (1953-57).	
6/04/55	**4**	19	1 **Hard To Get** Jockey #4 / Best Seller #5 / Juke Box #5	X 0137
11/19/55	**60**	4	2 Pepper Hot Baby	X 0172
11/10/56	**42**	12	3 The Star You Wished Upon Last Night above 3 with Richard Maltby & his Orchestra	Vik 0233
			GORDON MacRAE Born on 3/12/21 in East Orange, NJ; died on 1/24/86. Starred in the film musicals "Oklahoma" and "Carousel".	
5/12/56	**96**	3	1 I've Grown Accustomed To Your Face from the Broadway musical "My Fair Lady"	Capitol 3384
9/15/58	**18**	13	2 The Secret	Capitol 4033
			THE MAD LADS Consisted of John Gary Williams, Julius Green, William Brown and Robert Phillips. Williams and Brown replaced by Quincy Billups (later with Ollie & The Nightingales) and Sam Nelson, 1966-68.	
10/23/65	**93**	5	1 Don't Have To Shop Around	Volt 127
3/05/66	**74**	6	2 I Want Someone	Volt 131
8/02/69	**84**	2	3 By The Time I Get To Phoenix	Volt 4016
			JOHNNY MADDOX Born in 1929 in Gallatin, Tennessee. Honky tonk pianist.	
2/05/55	**2**[7]	20	1 **The Crazy Otto** [I] Best Seller #2 / Juke Box #2 / Jockey #7 cover of original version by honky tonk piano player Crazy Otto	Dot 15325
10/06/56	**57**	4	2 Heart And Soul [I] Larry Clinton had a #1 version of this tune in 1938	Dot 15488
1/27/58	**87**	6	3 Yellow Dog Blues [I]	Dot 15683
			BETTY MADIGAN Songstress from Washington, DC.	
11/19/55	**54**	11	1 There Should Be Rules (Protecting Fools Who Fall In Love)	MGM 12094
4/20/57	**78**	3	2 True Love Gone (Come On Home)	Coral 61812
8/18/58	**31**	9	3 Dance Everyone Dance Best Seller #31 / Hot 100 #34 based on the Israeli harvest song "Hava Nagila"	Coral 62007
			MADNESS Pop septet from North London, England - led by Graham "Suggs" McPherson.	
5/07/83	**7**	19	1 **Our House**	Geffen 29668
8/20/83	**33**	12	2 It Must Be Love	Geffen 29562
3/03/84	**72**	5	3 The Sun And The Rain	Geffen 29350
			MADONNA Born Madonna Louise Ciccone on 8/16/58 in Bay City, MI. Starred in the film "Desperately Seeking Susan". Married to actor Sean Penn in 1985.	
10/29/83+	**16**	21	1 Holiday	Sire 29478

DEBUT DATE	PEAK POS	WKS CHR	ARTIST — Record Title	Label & Number
			MADONNA — Cont'd	
3/10/84	**10**	30	2 **Borderline**	Sire 29354
8/25/84	**4**	16	3 **Lucky Star**	Sire 29177
11/17/84	**1**[6]	19	4● **Like A Virgin**	Sire 29210
2/09/85	**2**[2]	17	5 **Material Girl**	Sire 29083
3/02/85	**1**[1]	21	6● **Crazy For You** from the film "Vision Quest"	Geffen 29051
4/27/85	**5**	17	7 **Angel**	Sire 29008
8/17/85	**5**	16	8 **Dress You Up**	Sire 28919
4/12/86	**1**[1]	18	9 **Live To Tell** from the film "At Close Range"	Sire 28717
6/28/86	**1**[2]	18	10 **Papa Don't Preach**	Sire 28660
10/04/86	**3**	16	11 **True Blue**	Sire 28591
12/06/86+	**1**[1]	18	12 **Open Your Heart**	Sire 28508
			JOHNNY MAESTRO Born Johnny Mastrangelo on 5/7/39 in New York City. Lead singer of The Crests and Brooklyn Bridge.	
2/06/61	**20**	12	1 Model Girl	Coed 545
4/24/61	**33**	9	2 What A Surprise	Coed 549
7/24/61	**57**	5	3 Mr. Happiness with The Coeds	Coed 552
			MAGAZINE 60 French group - record sung in Spanish and English.	
5/10/86	**56**	11	1 Don Quichotte	Baja 001
			CLEDUS MAGGARD & The Citizen's Band Cledus' real name: Jay Huguely - from Quick Sand, Kentucky.	
12/27/75+	**19**	15	1 The White Knight [N]	Mercury 73751
4/24/76	**85**	4	2 Kentucky Moonrunner [N]	Mercury 73789
			MAGIC LANTERNS Rock quintet from Lancashire, England. Albert Hammond was a member in 1971.	
10/26/68	**29**	12	1 Shame, Shame	Atlantic 2560
1/09/71	**74**	6	2 One Night Stand	Big Tree 109
7/08/72	**88**	4	3 Country Woman	Charisma 100
			THE MAGIC MUSHROOMS	
11/12/66	**93**	1	1 It's-A-Happening	A&M 815
			THE MAGISTRATES	
6/01/68	**54**	7	1 Here Come The Judge [N] featuring the voice of Jean Hillary	MGM 13946
			THE MAGNIFICENT MEN White 7-man R&B-styled group from Pennsylvania.	
7/15/67	**93**	1	1 I Could Be So Happy	Capitol 5905
9/09/67	**90**	2	2 Sweet Soul Medley - Part 1 [N] Sweet Soul Music/Ain't Too Proud To Beg/Ooh Baby Baby/ I Can't Help Myself	Capitol 5976
			GEORGE MAHARIS Born on 9/1/33 in New York City. Played Buz Murdock on TV's "Route 66".	
4/21/62	**25**	11	1 Teach Me Tonight there were 5 Top 30 versions of this song in 1954	Epic 9504
8/04/62	**54**	6	2 Love Me As I Love You	Epic 9522
11/17/62	**62**	5	3 Baby Has Gone Bye Bye	Epic 9555
2/23/63	**93**	2	4 Don't Fence Me In originally a #1 hit for Bing Crosby & The Andrews Sisters in 1944	Epic 9569
9/21/63	**88**	3	5 That's How It Goes 1-3 & 5: arranged & conducted by Robert Mersey	Epic 9613
			MAI TAI Black Dutch trio: Jettie Well, Carolien De Windt, Mildred Douglas.	
5/24/86	**71**	7	1 Female Intuition	Critique 722
			THE MAIN INGREDIENT New York soul trio, formed as the Poets in 1964. Consisted of Donald McPherson (d: 7/4/71), Luther Simmons, Jr. and Tony Silvester. First recorded as the Poets for Red Bird in 1965. McPherson replaced by Cuba Gooding in 1971.	
6/27/70	**64**	9	1 You've Been My Inspiration	RCA 0340

DEBUT DATE	PEAK POS	WKS CHR	ARTIST — Record Title	Label & Number
			THE MAIN INGREDIENT — Cont'd	
10/10/70	**91**	2	2 I'm Better Off Without You	RCA 0382
12/12/70+	**49**	13	3 I'm So Proud	RCA 0401
5/08/71	**52**	9	4 Spinning Around (I Must Be Falling In Love)	RCA 0456
9/11/71	**97**	3	5 Black Seeds Keep On Growing	RCA 0517
7/15/72	**3**	18	6● **Everybody Plays The Fool**	RCA 0731
12/23/72+	**46**	9	7 You've Got To Take It (If You Want It)	RCA 0856
2/02/74	**10**	20	8● **Just Don't Want To Be Lonely**	RCA 0205
6/29/74	**35**	12	9 Happiness Is Just Around The Bend	RCA 0305
11/16/74	**75**	3	10 California My Way	RCA 10095
5/24/75	**92**	3	11 Rolling Down A Mountainside	RCA 10224
			THE MAJORS	
			Philadelphia R&B group: Ricky Cordo (lead), Eugene Glass, Frank Troutt, Ronald Gathers and Idella Morris. Produced by Jerry Ragavoy.	
8/11/62	**22**	11	1 A Wonderful Dream	Imperial 5855
11/17/62	**63**	6	2 A Little Bit Now (A Little Bit Later)/	
11/24/62	**83**	3	3 She's A Troublemaker	Imperial 5879
			MIRIAM MAKEBA	
			Native of South Africa. Formerly married to Hugh Masekela.	
2/25/56	**45**	9	1 Lovely Lies MANHATTAN BROTHERS & MIRIAM MAKEBA	London 1610
10/07/67	**12**	11	2 Pata Pata [F]	Reprise 0606
1/27/68	**85**	3	3 Malayisha [F]	Reprise 0654
			SIW MALMKVIST/UMBERTO MARCATO	
			Siw: female ballad singer; born in Sweden on 12/31/36.	
7/18/64	**58**	5	1 Sole Sole Sole [F]	Jubilee 5479
			MALO	
			Latin-rock band formed by Jorge Santana (brother of Carlos).	
3/04/72	**18**	12	1 Suavecito	Warner 7559
			RICHARD MALTBY	
			Richard was born on 6/26/14 in Chicago. Trumpeter, composer, bandleader.	
3/17/56	**14**	16	1 Themes From "The Man With The Golden Arm" [I] Top 100 #14 / Best Seller #15 / Juke Box #19 / Jockey #20 from the film "The Man With The Golden Arm"	Vik 0196
			MAMA CASS	
			Born Ellen Naomi Cohen on 9/19/41 in Baltimore. Died on 7/29/74 in London. Cass Elliot of The Mamas & The Papas.	
7/06/68	**12**	11	1 Dream A Little Dream Of Me with The Mamas & The Papas	Dunhill 4145
11/02/68	**67**	5	2 California Earthquake	Dunhill 4166
3/15/69	**58**	6	3 Move In A Little Closer, Baby	Dunhill 4184
6/07/69	**30**	19	4 It's Getting Better	Dunhill 4195
			MAMA CASS ELLIOT:	
10/18/69	**36**	9	5 Make Your Own Kind Of Music	Dunhill 4214
1/31/70	**42**	7	6 New World Coming	Dunhill 4225
8/01/70	**99**	2	7 A Song That Never Comes 3-7: produced by Steve Barri	Dunhill 4244
			THE MAMAS & THE PAPAS	
			Quartet formed in New York City in 1963. Consisted of John Phillips (b: 8/30/35, Paris Island, SC); Holly Michelle Gilliam Phillips (b: 6/4/45, Long Beach, CA); Dennis Doherty (b: 11/29/41, Halifax, Nova Scotia) and Mama Cass Elliot. Phillips had been in the Journeymen, married Michelle Gilliam in 1962. Elliot had been in the Mugwumps with Doherty. Group moved to Los Angeles in 1964. Disbanded in 1968, reunited briefly in 1971. Michelle Phillips in films "Dillinger" and "Valentino". Formed new group in 1982: John and daughter MacKenzie Phillips, Dennis Doherty and Spanky McFarlane of Spanky & Our Gang.	
1/08/66	**4**	17	1● **California Dreamin'**	Dunhill 4020
4/09/66	**1**[3]	12	2● **Monday, Monday**	Dunhill 4026
7/02/66	**5**	9	3 **I Saw Her Again**	Dunhill 4031
10/22/66	**24**	7	4 Look Through My Window	Dunhill 4050
12/03/66+	**5**	12	5 **Words Of Love/**	
12/17/66+	**73**	6	6 Dancing In The Street	Dunhill 4057
2/25/67	**2**[3]	10	7 **Dedicated To The One I Love**	Dunhill 4077
4/29/67	**5**	9	8 **Creeque Alley**	Dunhill 4083

DEBUT DATE	PEAK POS	WKS CHR	ARTIST — Record Title	Label & Number
			THE MAMAS & THE PAPAS — Cont'd	
8/26/67	**20**	6	9 Twelve Thirty (Young Girls Are Coming To The Canyon)	Dunhill 4099
10/28/67	**26**	7	10 Glad To Be Unhappy	Dunhill 4107
12/09/67+	**51**	7	11 Dancing Bear	Dunhill 4113
6/08/68	**53**	6	12 Safe In My Garden	Dunhill 4125
9/14/68	**81**	5	13 For The Love Of Ivy	Dunhill 4150
11/23/68	**76**	5	14 Do You Wanna Dance all of the above produced by Lou Adler	Dunhill 4171
2/12/72	**81**	3	15 Step Out	Dunhill 4301
			MELISSA MANCHESTER Born on 2/15/51 in the Bronx, NY. Vocalist, pianist, composer. Studied with Paul Simon at University School of the Arts, early 70s. Former back-up singer for Bette Midler.	
5/10/75	**6**	17	1 **Midnight Blue**	Arista 0116
9/20/75	**30**	12	2 Just Too Many People	Arista 0146
2/07/76	**27**	9	3 Just You And I	Arista 0168
5/01/76	**71**	5	4 Better Days	Arista 0183
8/07/76	**78**	3	5 Rescue Me	Arista 0196
11/18/78+	**10**	23	6 **Don't Cry Out Loud**	Arista 0373
5/05/79	**76**	4	7 Theme From Ice Castles (Through The Eyes Of Love) theme song from the film "Ice Castles"	Arista 0405
10/13/79	**39**	10	8 Pretty Girls	Arista 0456
2/23/80	**32**	13	9 Fire In The Morning	Arista 0485
2/28/81	**54**	9	10 Lovers After All MELISSA MANCHESTER & PEABO BRYSON	Arista 0587
5/22/82	**5**	25	11 **You Should Hear How She Talks About You**	Arista 0676
2/05/83	**42**	11	12 Nice Girls	Arista 1045
10/29/83	**78**	4	13 No One Can Love You More Than Me	Arista 9087
11/24/84	**86**	6	14 Thief Of Hearts from the film of the same title	Casablanca 880308
4/27/85	**74**	5	15 Mathematics	MCA 52575
			HENRY MANCINI Born on 4/16/24 in Cleveland. Leading film-TV composer/arranger/conductor. Staff composer for Universal Pictures, 1952-58. Won more Oscars (4) and Grammys (20) than any other pop artist.	
4/04/60	**21**	13	1 Mr. Lucky [I]	RCA 7705
4/03/61	**90**	1	2 Theme From The Great Imposter [I]	RCA 7830
10/09/61	**11**	26	3 Moon River from the film "Breakfast At Tiffany's"	RCA 7916
7/14/62	**95**	4	4 Theme From 'Hatari!' [I]	RCA 8037
1/26/63	**33**	18	5 Days Of Wine And Roses	RCA 8120
6/22/63	**93**	1	6 Banzai Pipeline [I]	RCA 8184
12/07/63+	**36**	11	7 Charade	RCA 8256
4/04/64	**31**	8	8 The Pink Panther Theme [I]	RCA 8286
7/18/64	**97**	2	9 A Shot In The Dark [I]	RCA 8381
12/12/64+	**77**	7	10 Dear Heart	RCA 8458
5/10/69	**1**[2]	14	11 • **Love Theme From Romeo & Juliet** [I]	RCA 0131
9/06/69	**87**	4	12 Moonlight Sonata [I] written by Beethoven in 1802	RCA 0212
1/16/71	**13**	11	13 Theme From Love Story [I]	RCA 9927
3/19/77	**45**	9	14 Theme From Charlie's Angels [I] 6-14: produced by Joe Reisman 1-2, 4-5, 7-11, 13-14: from films & TV shows of the same title	RCA 10888
			BARBARA MANDRELL Born on 12/25/48 in Houston. Country singer. Host of her own TV variety series "Barbara Mandrell & The Mandrell Sisters".	
3/04/78	**92**	5	1 Woman To Woman	Dot 17736
3/17/79	**31**	16	2 (If Loving You Is Wrong) I Don't Want To Be Right	ABC 12451
10/06/79	**89**	5	3 Fooled By A Feeling	MCA 41077
			MANDRILL Brooklyn Latin jazz/rock septet formed in 1968 by brothers Louis "Sweet Lou", Richard "Dr. Ric", and Carlos "Mad Dog" Wilson.	
6/05/71	**94**	3	1 Mandrill [I]	Polydor 14070

DEBUT DATE	PEAK POS	WKS CHR	ARTIST — Record Title	Label & Number
			MANDRILL — Cont'd	
4/14/73	**52**	10	2 Fencewalk	Polydor 14163
8/11/73	**83**	7	3 Hang Loose [I]	Polydor 14187
			MANFRED MANN	
			Rock group formed in England in 1964: Manfred Mann (real name: Michael Lubowitz), keyboards; Paul Jones, vocals; Mike Hugg, drums; Michael Vickers, guitar; and Tom McGuiness, bass. Manfred Mann formed his new 'Earth Band' in 1971, featuring Mick Rogers, vocals; Colin Pattenden, bass; and Chris Slade, drums. Mick replaced by Thompson (lead singer) in 1976.	
9/05/64	**1**[2]	13	1 **Do Wah Diddy Diddy**	Ascot 2157
11/14/64+	**12**	12	2 Sha La La	Ascot 2165
2/20/65	**50**	6	3 Come Tomorrow	Ascot 2170
7/02/66	**29**	8	4 Pretty Flamingo	United Art. 50040
3/02/68	**10**	11	5 **Mighty Quinn (Quinn The Eskimo)**	Mercury 72770
1/18/69	**97**	2	6 Fox On The Run	Mercury 72879
			MANFRED MANN'S EARTH BAND:	
2/26/72	**69**	7	7 Living Without You	Polydor 14113
4/03/76	**97**	3	8 Spirit In The Night	Warner 8176
11/20/76+	**1**[1]	20	9● **Blinded By The Light** — above 2 written by Bruce Springsteen	Warner 8252
4/30/77	**40**	8	10 Spirit In The Night [R] — re-mixed version of #8 above	Warner 8355
6/16/79	**58**	7	11 You Angel You — written by Bob Dylan	Warner 8850
1/21/84	**22**	15	12 Runner	Arista 9143
			CHUCK MANGIONE	
			Born on 11/29/40 in Rochester, NY. Flugelhorn, bandleader, composer. Recorded with older brother Gaspare ("Gap") as the Jazz Brothers for Riverside in 1960. To New York City in 1965, with Maynard Ferguson, Kai Winding, and Art Blakey's Jazz Messengers.	
7/03/71	**76**	6	1 Hill Where The Lord Hides [I] — featuring Gerry Niewood on flute	Mercury 73208
7/19/75	**96**	4	2 Chase The Clouds Away [I]	A&M 1707
6/11/77	**86**	3	3 Land Of Make Believe — with The Hamilton Philharmonic Orch.; Esther Satterfield, vocal	Mercury 73920
2/11/78	**4**	25	4 **Feels So Good** [I]	A&M 2001
1/19/80	**18**	16	5 Give It All You Got [I] — featured song by ABC Sports for the 1980 Winter Olympics	A&M 2211
			MANHATTAN BROTHERS & MIRIAM MAKEBA	
2/25/56	**45**	9	1 Lovely Lies	London 1610
			THE MANHATTAN TRANSFER	
			Versatile vocal harmony quartet formed in New York City in 1972: Tim Hauser, Alan Paul, Janis Siegel and Cheryl Bentyne (replaced Laurel Masse in 1979).	
9/20/75	**22**	12	1 Operator	Atlantic 3292
4/19/80	**30**	12	2 Twilight Zone/Twilight Tone	Atlantic 3649
11/29/80	**73**	8	3 Trickle Trickle	Atlantic 3772
5/23/81	**7**	21	4 **Boy From New York City**	Atlantic 3816
5/29/82	**78**	5	5 Route 66 — from the film "Sharky's Machine"	Atlantic 4034
9/10/83	**40**	13	6 Spice Of Life	Atlantic 89786
2/02/85	**83**	3	7 Baby Come Back To Me (The Morse Code Of Love)	Atlantic 89594
			THE MANHATTANS	
			Soul group from Jersey City, NJ. Consisted of George "Smitty" Smith (d: 1970, spinal meningitis) lead; Winfred "Blue" Lovett, bass; Edward "Sonny" Bivins and Kenneth "Wally" Kelly, tenors; and Richard Taylor, baritone. Smith replaced by Gerald Alston in 1971. First recorded for Piney in 1962. Taylor left in 1977.	
1/16/65	**68**	8	1 I Wanna Be (Your Everything)	Carnival 507
1/01/66	**92**	2	2 Follow Your Heart	Carnival 512
3/19/66	**96**	2	3 Baby I Need You	Carnival 514
12/23/67+	**96**	3	4 I Call It Love	Carnival 533
6/20/70	**98**	1	5 If My Heart Could Speak	Deluxe 122
6/09/73	**43**	11	6 There's No Me Without You	Columbia 45838
9/22/73	**77**	8	7 You'd Better Believe It	Columbia 45927
1/04/75	**37**	10	8 Don't Take Your Love	Columbia 10045
5/31/75	**97**	2	9 Hurt	Columbia 10140
4/17/76	**1**[2]	26	10▲ **Kiss And Say Goodbye**	Columbia 10310

DEBUT DATE	PEAK POS	WKS CHR	ARTIST — Record Title	Label & Number
			THE MANHATTANS — Cont'd	
10/30/76	**46**	8	11 I Kinda Miss You	Columbia 10430
3/26/77	**66**	18	12 It Feels So Good To Be Loved So Bad	Columbia 10495
10/29/77	**93**	2	13 We Never Danced To A Love Song	Columbia 10586
4/26/80	**5**	25	14 ● **Shining Star**	Columbia 11222
7/30/83	**72**	6	15 Crazy	Columbia 03939
3/02/85	**81**	5	16 You Send Me	Columbia 04754
			BARRY MANILOW	
			Born on 6/17/46 in Brooklyn. Vocalist, pianist, composer. Studied at Juilliard, New York College of Music. Wrote jingles. On WCBS-TV series, "Callback". Worked at Continental Baths, New York in 1972, met Bette Midler, and became her director, arranger and accompanist. Produced her first two albums. Sang jingles for Dr. Pepper, Pepsi and McDonalds ("You Deserve A Break Today").	
11/16/74+	**1^{1}**	16	1 ● **Mandy**	Bell 45613
			formerly charted by Scott English as "Brandy"	
3/01/75	**12**	13	2 It's A Miracle	Arista 0108
6/28/75	**6**	18	3 **Could It Be Magic**	Arista 0126
			inspired by Chopin's prelude in C minor	
11/15/75+	**1^{1}**	20	4 ● **I Write The Songs**	Arista 0157
3/20/76	**10**	15	5 **Tryin' To Get The Feeling Again**	Arista 0172
9/18/76	**29**	10	6 This One's For You	Arista 0206
11/27/76+	**10**	19	7 **Weekend In New England**	Arista 0212
5/07/77	**1^{1}**	19	8 ● **Looks Like We Made It**	Arista 0244
10/01/77	**23**	10	9 Daybreak	Arista 0273
2/04/78	**3**	19	10 ● **Can't Smile Without You**	Arista 0305
5/06/78	**19**	13	11 Even Now	Arista 0330
6/10/78	**8**	16	12 ● **Copacabana (At The Copa)**	Arista 0339
9/16/78	**11**	16	13 Ready To Take A Chance Again	Arista 0357
			above 2 from the movie "Foul Play"	
12/16/78+	**9**	15	14 **Somewhere In The Night**	Arista 0382
10/13/79	**9**	14	15 **Ships**	Arista 0464
12/15/79+	**20**	16	16 When I Wanted You	Arista 0481
4/12/80	**36**	11	17 I Don't Want To Walk Without You	Arista 0501
11/22/80+	**10**	16	18 **I Made It Through The Rain**	Arista 0566
			all of the above produced by Manilow and Ron Dante	
3/14/81	**45**	10	19 Lonely Together	Arista 0596
10/10/81	**15**	16	20 The Old Songs	Arista 0633
12/19/81+	**21**	15	21 Somewhere Down The Road	Arista 0658
3/20/82	**32**	10	22 Let's Hang On	Arista 0675
7/31/82	**38**	11	23 Oh Julie	Arista 0698
11/20/82+	**39**	14	24 Memory	Arista 1025
			theme from the musical "Cats"	
2/26/83	**26**	16	25 Some Kind Of Friend	Arista 1046
11/19/83+	**18**	14	26 Read 'Em And Weep	Arista 9101
7/12/86	**86**	5	27 I'm Your Man	RCA 14397
			BARRY MANN	
			Born Barry Iberman on 2/9/39 in Brooklyn. One of pop music's most prolific songwriters. Wrote with wife, Cynthia Weil, "You've Lost That Lovin' Feelin'", "(You're My) Soul & Inspiration", "Kicks", "Hungry", "We Gotta Get Out Of This Place", and many others.	
8/07/61	**7**	12	1 **Who Put The Bomp (In The Bomp, Bomp, Bomp)** . [N]	ABC-Para. 10237
12/05/64	**94**	2	2 Talk To Me Baby	Red Bird 015
5/30/70	**93**	3	3 Feelings	Scepter 12281
			from the film "Getting Straight"	
8/14/76	**78**	6	4 The Princess And The Punk	Arista 0194
			CARL MANN	
			Born on 8/24/42 in Huntingdon, TN. Rockabilly singer, pianist. Toured with Carl Perkins in 1962.	
6/01/59	**25**	16	1 Mona Lisa	Phillips 3539
10/26/59	**57**	7	2 Pretend	Phillips 3546
			above 2 were originally Nat King Cole hits from the early 50s	
			GLORIA MANN	
2/12/55	**18**	2	1 Earth Angel (Will You Be Mine)	Sound 109
			Juke Box #18 / Best Seller #24	

DEBUT DATE	PEAK POS	WKS CHR	ARTIST — Record Title	Label & Number
			GLORIA MANN — Cont'd	
12/10/55+	**19**	13	2 Teen Age Prayer Best Seller #19 / Top 100 #21	Sound 126
3/10/56	**59**	5	3 Why Do Fools Fall In Love?	Decca 29832
			HERBIE MANN Born Herbert Jay Solomon on 4/16/30 in Brooklyn. Plays flute, saxophones and other reeds. First recorded with Mat Mathews Quintet for Brunswick in 1953. First recorded as a solo for Bethlehem in 1954.	
10/01/66	**93**	1	1 Philly Dog [I]	Atlantic 5074
11/12/66	**88**	2	2 A Man And A Woman **TAMIKO JONES with HERBIE MANN** from the film of the same title	Atlantic 2362
10/21/67	**93**	1	3 To Sir, With Love [I]	Atlantic 2444
2/17/68	**81**	2	4 Unchain My Heart [I] guitar solo: Eric Gale	A&M 896
5/24/69	**44**	10	5 Memphis Underground [I]	Atlantic 2621
11/22/69	**95**	2	6 It's A Funky Thing-Right On (Part 1) vocal version of "Memphis Underground" (featuring Little Milton)	Atlantic 2671
2/08/75	**14**	15	7 Hijack	Atlantic 3246
1/13/79	**26**	18	8 Superman	Atlantic 3547
			THE JOHNNY MANN SINGERS Johnny was musical director for the Joey Bishop talk show.	
6/24/67	**91**	3	1 Up-Up And Away	Liberty 55972
			WINGY MANONE Born Joseph Mannone on 2/13/04 in New Orleans. Died on 7/9/82. Trumpeter, bandleader. Lost right arm at age eight in streetcar accident. Composed "Tar Paper Stomp" which Glenn Miller later made famous in revised form as "In The Mood".	
3/30/57	**56**	7	1 Party Doll	Decca 30211
			MICKEY MANTLE - see TERESA BREWER	
			MANTOVANI Born Annunzio Paolo Mantovani on 11/15/05 in Venice, Italy. Died on 3/29/80. Played classical violin in England before forming his own orchestra in the early 30s. Achieved international fame twenty years later with his 40-piece orchestra and distinctive "cascading strings" sound.	
2/04/56	**62**	8	1 When You Lose The One You Love **DAVID WHITFIELD with MANTOVANI**	London 1617
6/10/57	**12**	32	2 Around The World [I] Jockey #12 / Best Seller #23 / Top 100 #25 from the film "Around The World In 80 Days"	London 1746
11/07/60	**93**	1	3 Theme From The Sundowners [I] from the film "The Sundowners"	London 1946
11/21/60+	**31**	13	4 Main Theme from Exodus (Ari's Theme) [I] from the film "Exodus"	London 1953
			TOMMY MARA	
8/18/58	**76**	4	1 Where The Blue Of The Night Bing Crosby's radio theme song	Felsted 8532
			THE MARATHONS - see THE OLYMPICS	
			THE MARCELS R&B group from Pittsburgh. Consisted of Cornelius "Nini" Harp (lead singer), Ronald "Bingo" Mundy and Gene Bricker (tenors), Richard Knauss (baritone) and Fred Johnson (bass). Knauss replaced by Allen Johnson, and Bricker replaced by Walt Maddox, mid-1961. Mundy left in late 1961.	
3/06/61	**1**[3]	14	1 **Blue Moon** there were 3 Top 10 versions of this classic tune in 1935	Colpix 186
5/29/61	**78**	3	2 Summertime written by George Gershwin for his musical "Porgy & Bess"	Colpix 196
10/09/61	**7**	12	3 **Heartaches** #12 hit for Guy Lombardo in 1931; #1 hit for Ted Weems in 1947	Colpix 612
2/03/62	**58**	5	4 My Melancholy Baby first charted in 1915 by Walter Van Brunt all of above produced by Stu Phillips	Colpix 624
			LITTLE PEGGY MARCH Born Margaret Battavio on 3/7/48 in Lansdale, PA. Youngest female singer to have a #1 single.	
3/23/63	**1**[3]	14	1 **I Will Follow Him**	RCA 8139
6/01/63	**32**	7	2 I Wish I Were A Princess	RCA 8189

DEBUT DATE	PEAK POS	WKS CHR	ARTIST — Record Title	Label & Number
			LITTLE PEGGY MARCH — Cont'd	
9/07/63	**26**	9	3 Hello Heartache, Goodbye Love	RCA 8221
11/23/63	**57**	6	4 The Impossible Happened	RCA 8267
2/01/64	**84**	3	5 (I'm Watching) Every Little Move You Make	RCA 8302
			all of above conducted by Sammy Lowe	
			BOBBY MARCHAN	
			Born on 4/30/30 in Youngstown, OH. Vocalist with Huey "Piano" Smith & The Clowns.	
6/13/60	**31**	11	1 There's Something On Your Mind, Part 2 [N]	Fire 1022
			MARCY JOE	
			Marcy Joe Sockel.	
5/22/61	**81**	3	1 Ronnie	Robbee 110
			BENNY MARDONES	
			Savage, Maryland native.	
6/14/80	**11**	20	1 Into The Night	Polydor 2091
			ERNIE MARESCA	
			Born on 4/21/39 in the Bronx, NY. Songwriter, vocalist. Wrote "Run Around Sue" and "The Wanderer".	
3/31/62	**6**	14	1 **Shout! Shout! (Knock Yourself Out)**	Seville 117
			MARIE & REX	
			Marie Knight and Rex Garvin.	
3/09/59	**94**	2	1 I Can't Sit Down	Carlton 502
			TEENA MARIE	
			Born Mary Christine Brockert in Venice, CA in 1957. White soul singer, actress, guitarist, keyboardist, composer, producer.	
11/22/80+	**37**	14	1 I Need Your Lovin'	Gordy 7189
7/25/81	**50**	13	2 Square Biz	Gordy 7202
12/15/84+	**4**	24	3 **Lovergirl**	Epic 04619
4/27/85	**81**	3	4 Jammin	Epic 04738
			MARILLION	
			British rock quintet led by Fish.	
10/05/85	**74**	8	1 Kayleigh	Capitol 5493
			MARIMBA CHIAPAS	
			Mexican marimba band.	
7/14/56	**82**	4	1 Marimba Charleston [I]	Capitol 3447
			THE MARK II	
10/17/60	**75**	7	1 Night Theme [I]	Wye 1001
			THE MARK IV	
			Chicago-based pop/rock quartet.	
3/24/58	**69**	3	1 (Make With) The Shake	Cosmic 704
1/26/59	**24**	12	2 I Got A Wife [N]	Mercury 71403
			MARK-ALMOND	
			British sessionmen Jon Mark & Johnny Almond.	
2/19/72	**94**	2	1 One Way Sunday	Blue Thumb 206
			THE MARKETTS	
			Hollywood, California instrumental surf quintet.	
1/13/62	**31**	9	1 Surfer's Stomp [I]	Liberty 55401
4/28/62	**48**	10	2 Balboa Blue [I]	Liberty 55443
12/07/63+	**3**	14	3 **Out Of Limits** [I]	Warner 5391
			surf-ized version of the "Outer Limits" TV series theme	
3/28/64	**90**	4	4 Vanishing Point [I]	Warner 5423
			all of above produced by Joe Saraceno	
2/05/66	**17**	9	5 Batman Theme [I]	Warner 5696
			from the hit TV series	
			MAR-KEYS	
			Instrumental group formed in Memphis in 1958. Consisted of Charles Axton, tenor sax; Wayne Jackson, trumpet; Don Nix, baritone sax; Jerry Lee "Smoochie" Smith, keyboards; Steve Cropper, guitar; Donald "Duck" Dunn, bass; and Terry Johnson, drums. Staff musicians at Stax/Volt. Cropper and Dunn also worked with Booker T. & The MG's. Also known as the Memphis Horns.	
7/03/61	**3**	14	1 **Last Night** [I]	Satellite 107
10/09/61	**60**	6	2 Morning After [I]	Stax 112

DEBUT DATE	PEAK POS	WKS CHR	ARTIST — Record Title	Label & Number
			MAR-KEYS — Cont'd	
3/31/62	**94**	1	3 Pop-Eye Stroll .... [I]	Stax 121
3/05/66	**89**	5	4 Philly Dog .... [I]	Stax 185
			PIGMEAT MARKHAM	
			Born Dewey Markham in Durham, NC in 1906. Died on 12/13/81 in the Bronx, NY. Comedian on stage and TV.	
6/15/68	**19**	8	1 Here Comes The Judge .... [N]	Chess 2049
			GUY MARKS	
4/13/68	**51**	6	1 Loving You Has Made Me Bananas .... [N]	ABC 11055
			BOB MARLEY & THE WAILERS	
			Bob & his Jamaican band are the masters of reggae. Bob died from brain cancer on 5/11/81 in Miami. Wrote Eric Clapton's hit "I Shot The Sheriff".	
7/04/76	**51**	6	1 Roots, Rock, Reggae	Island 060
			MICKI MARLO	
2/16/57	**55**	4	1 Little By Little .... with Don Costa & His Orchestra	ABC-Para. 9762
			MARION MARLOWE	
7/16/55	**14**	2	1 The Man In The Raincoat .... Jockey #14 / Juke Box #18	Cadence 1266
			THE MARMALADE	
			Scottish pop quintet - Dean Ford, lead singer.	
3/14/70	**10**	15	1 **Reflections Of My Life**	London 20058
8/08/70	**51**	8	2 Rainbow	London 20059
3/27/76	**49**	9	3 Falling Apart At The Seams	Ariola Am. 7619
			MARSHALL HAIN	
			British duo: Julian Marshall and Kit Hain.	
12/09/78+	**43**	11	1 Dancing In The City	Harvest 4648
			THE MARSHALL TUCKER BAND	
			Southern rock band formed in South Carolina in 1971. Doug Gray, lead singer, Toy Caldwell, lead guitarist; George McCorkle, rhythm guitar; Paul Riddle, drums; Jerry Eubanks, sax; and Tommy Caldwell, bass (d: 4/30/80 - replaced by Franklin Wilkie).	
4/26/75	**78**	4	1 This Ol' Cowboy	Capricorn 0228
10/18/75	**38**	13	2 Fire On The Mountain	Capricorn 0244
3/12/77	**14**	21	3 Heard It In A Love Song	Capricorn 0270
8/20/77	**75**	6	4 Can't You See	Capricorn 0278
6/24/78	**75**	4	5 Dream Lover	Capricorn 0300
6/30/79	**42**	8	6 Last Of The Singing Cowboys	Warner 8841
4/26/80	**79**	3	7 It Takes Time	Warner 49215
			RALPH MARTERIE	
			Born on 12/24/14 in Naples, Italy (grew up in Chicago). Died on 10/8/78. Very popular early 50s bandleader, played trumpet in the 40s for Enric Madriguera, and other bands.	
2/19/55	**54**	10	1 Blue Mirage (Don't Go) .... [I] Honor Roll #54	Mercury 70535
5/19/56	**64**	7	2 Theme from Picnic .... [I] from the film "Picnic"	Mercury 70836
3/09/57	**25**	11	3 Tricky .... [I] Jockey #25 / Top 100 #37	Mercury 71050
4/29/57	**10**	16	4 **Shish-Kebab** .... [I] Jockey #10 / Top 100 #29 same tune as Armenian Jazz Sextet's "Harem Dance"	Mercury 71092
			MARTHA & THE VANDELLAS	
			Soul group from Detroit, organized by Martha Reeves (b: 7/18/41) in 1962 with Annette Beard and Rosalind Ashford. Reeves had been in the Del-Phis, recorded for Checkmate. Worked at Motown as A&R secretary, sang back-up. Vandellas did back-up on Marvin Gaye's "Stubborn Kind Of Fellow". Beard left group in 1964, replaced by Betty Kelly. Martha Reeves went solo in late 1972.	
4/06/63	**29**	16	1 Come And Get These Memories	Gordy 7014
8/03/63	**4**	14	2 **Heat Wave**	Gordy 7022
11/23/63+	**8**	12	3 **Quicksand**	Gordy 7025
2/08/64	**42**	7	4 Live Wire	Gordy 7027
4/11/64	**44**	6	5 In My Lonely Room	Gordy 7031
8/22/64	**2^2**	14	6 **Dancing In The Street**	Gordy 7033

DEBUT DATE	PEAK POS	WKS CHR	ARTIST — Record Title	Label & Number
			MARTHA & THE VANDELLAS — Cont'd	
12/05/64+	**34**	7	7 Wild One	Gordy 7036
2/27/65	**8**	11	8 **Nowhere To Run**	Gordy 7039
8/14/65	**36**	7	9 You've Been In Love Too Long/	
12/11/65+	**70**	7	10 Love (Makes Me Do Foolish Things)	Gordy 7045
1/22/66	**22**	11	11 My Baby Loves Me	Gordy 7048
6/11/66	**71**	5	12 What Am I Going To Do Without Your Love	Gordy 7053
10/29/66	**9**	10	13 **I'm Ready For Love**	Gordy 7056
2/25/67	**10**	14	14 **Jimmy Mack**	Gordy 7058
			1-5, 8, 10, 13-14: written by Holland, Dozier, Holland	
8/19/67	**25**	9	15 Love Bug Leave My Heart Alone	Gordy 7062
			MARTHA REEVES & THE VANDELLAS:	
11/18/67	**11**	12	16 Honey Chile	Gordy 7067
4/20/68	**62**	7	17 I Promise To Wait My Love/	
6/15/68	**93**	3	18 Forget Me Not	Gordy 7070
8/10/68	**42**	8	19 I Can't Dance To That Music You're Playin'	Gordy 7075
11/02/68	**80**	5	20 Sweet Darlin'	Gordy 7080
4/19/69	**56**	6	21 (We've Got) Honey Love	Gordy 7085
11/07/70	**93**	3	22 I Gotta Let You Go	Gordy 7103
10/16/71	**53**	6	23 Bless You	Gordy 7110
			BOBBI MARTIN	
			Songstress from Baltimore.	
11/28/64+	**19**	12	1 Don't Forget I Still Love You	Coral 62426
3/13/65	**46**	8	2 I Can't Stop Thinking Of You	Coral 62447
5/29/65	**70**	7	3 I Love You So	Coral 62452
3/14/70	**13**	14	4 For The Love Of Him	United Art. 50602
7/11/70	**97**	1	5 Give A Woman Love	United Art. 50687
			all of above produced by Henry Jerome	
			DEAN MARTIN	
			Born Dino Crocetti on 6/7/17 in Steubenville, OH. Vocalist, actor. To California in 1937, worked local clubs. Teamed with comedian Jerry Lewis in Atlantic City in 1946. First film, "My Friend Irma" in 1949. Team broke up after 16th film "Hollywood Or Bust" in 1956. Appeared in many films since then, own TV series from 1965-74.	
12/03/55+	**1**[6]	24	1 **Memories Are Made Of This**	Capitol 3295
			Jockey #1(6) / Best Seller #1(5) / Top 100 #1(5) / Juke Box #1(4)	
			backed by The Easy Riders	
3/10/56	**27**	12	2 Innamorata	Capitol 3352
			from the film "Artists & Models"	
5/19/56	**22**	15	3 Standing On The Corner/	
			Jockey #22 / Top 100 #29	
			from the musical "The Most Happy Fella"	
6/02/56	**83**	2	4 Watching The World Go By	Capitol 3414
4/07/58	**4**	21	5 **Return To Me**	Capitol 3894
			Best Seller #4 / Top 100 #4 / Jockey #4	
7/14/58	**30**	9	6 Angel Baby	Capitol 3988
			Hot 100 #30 / Best Seller #43	
8/04/58	**12**	13	7 Volare (Nel Blu Dipinto Di Blu)	Capitol 4028
			Best Seller #12 / Hot 100 #15	
7/13/59	**59**	13	8 On An Evening In Roma	Capitol 4222
12/01/62+	**91**	6	9 From The Bottom Of My Heart (Dammi, Dammi, Dammi)	Reprise 20116
12/22/62	**94**	3	10 Sam's Song [N]	Reprise 20128
			DEAN MARTIN & SAMMY DAVIS JR.	
			Bing & Gary Crosby's version hit #3 in 1949	
6/27/64	**1**[1]	15	11 ● **Everybody Loves Somebody**	Reprise 0281
9/26/64	**6**	11	12 **The Door Is Still Open To My Heart**	Reprise 0307
12/12/64+	**25**	9	13 You're Nobody Till Somebody Loves You/	
12/26/64+	**64**	5	14 You'll Always Be The One I Love	Reprise 0333
2/20/65	**22**	9	15 Send Me The Pillow You Dream On	Reprise 0344
5/22/65	**32**	7	16 (Remember Me) I'm The One Who Loves You	Reprise 0369
8/07/65	**21**	9	17 Houston	Reprise 0393
10/30/65	**10**	10	18 **I Will**	Reprise 0415
2/12/66	**32**	8	19 Somewhere There's A Someone	Reprise 0443
5/07/66	**35**	7	20 Come Running Back	Reprise 0466
7/23/66	**41**	7	21 A Million And One	Reprise 0500
10/08/66	**60**	6	22 Nobody's Baby Again	Reprise 0516

DEBUT DATE	PEAK POS	WKS CHR	ARTIST — Record Title	Label & Number
			DEAN MARTIN — Cont'd	
12/17/66+	**55**	6	23 (Open Up The Door) Let The Good Times In	Reprise 0538
4/29/67	**55**	5	24 Lay Some Happiness On Me	Reprise 0571
7/08/67	**25**	7	25 In The Chapel In The Moonlight	Reprise 0601
8/19/67	**38**	6	26 Little Ole Wine Drinker, Me	Reprise 0608
12/02/67	**46**	7	27 In The Misty Moonlight	Reprise 0640
3/23/68	**60**	7	28 You've Still Got A Place In My Heart	Reprise 0672
11/02/68	**43**	9	29 Not Enough Indians	Reprise 0780
8/09/69	**75**	4	30 I Take A Lot Of Pride In What I Am	Reprise 0841
			10-29: produced by Jimmy Bowen	
			DEREK MARTIN	
			Soul singer formerly with the Pearls (Five Pearls).	
7/31/65	**78**	6	1 You Better Go	Roulette 4631
			ERIC MARTIN	
			San Francisco pop/rock vocalist.	
8/24/85	**87**	2	1 Information	Capitol 5502
			GEORGE MARTIN	
			Born on 1/3/26 in England. The Beatles' producer from 1962-70.	
7/25/64	**53**	8	1 Ringo's Theme (This Boy) [I]	United Art. 745
			from the film "A Hard Days Night"	
			JANIS MARTIN	
			Born in Sutherlin, VA. Dubbed as "the female Elvis Presley" by RCA Records.	
5/05/56	**50**	1	1 Will You, Willyum	RCA 6491
			Coming Up #50	
			MARILYN MARTIN	
			Raised in Louisville. Background vocalist for Stevie Nicks, Tom Petty, Kenny Loggins and Joe Walsh.	
10/05/85	**1**[1]	21	1 **Separate Lives**	Atlantic 89498
			PHIL COLLINS & MARILYN MARTIN	
			love theme from the film "White Nights"	
1/18/86	**28**	18	2 Night Moves	Atlantic 89465
			MOON MARTIN	
			Real name: John Martin. Singer, songwriter, guitarist from Oklahoma. Wrote Robert Palmer's hit "Bad Case Of Loving You".	
8/18/79	**30**	11	1 Rolene	Capitol 4765
11/03/79	**50**	7	2 No Chance	Capitol 4794
			STEVE MARTIN	
			Born in Waco, Texas in 1945. Raised in California. Popular television and film comedian. Comedy writer for the "Smothers Brothers Comedy Hour" TV show and others.	
12/03/77	**72**	3	1 Grandmother's Song [C]	Warner 8503
5/27/78	**17**	15	2 ● King Tut [N]	Warner 8577
			with The Toot Uncommons	
11/24/79	**91**	4	3 Cruel Shoes [C]	Warner 49122
			TONY MARTIN	
			Born Alvin Morris, Jr. on 12/25/12 in Oakland. Vocalist, actor. In many films from 1936-57, including "Casbah" in 1948. Married to actress Cyd Charisse.	
4/21/56	**10**	20	1 **Walk Hand In Hand**	RCA 6493
			Top 100 #10 / Jockey #13 / Juke Box #16 / Best Seller #21	
9/01/56	**60**	2	2 It's Better In The Dark	RCA 6597
4/20/57	**82**	5	3 Do I Love You (Because You're Beautiful)	RCA 6863
			from the TV musical "Cinderella"	
			TRADE MARTIN	
			Born on 11/19/43 in Union City, New Jersey.	
10/20/62	**28**	8	1 That Stranger Used To Be My Girl	Coed 570
			VINCE MARTIN with THE TARRIERS	
			Also see The Tarriers.	
10/13/56	**9**	19	1 **Cindy, Oh Cindy**	Glory 247
			Juke Box #9 / Best Seller #12 / Top 100 #12 / Jockey #12	
			WINK MARTINDALE	
			Born Winston Martindale in Bells, Tennessee in 1933. TV game-show host.	
9/14/59	**7**	17	1 **Deck Of Cards** [S]	Dot 15968
8/21/61	**85**	2	2 Black Land Farmer	Dot 16243

DEBUT DATE	PEAK POS	WKS CHR	ARTIST — Record Title	Label & Number
			LAYNG MARTINE	
10/02/71	**65**	8	1 Rub It In	Barnaby 2041
			NANCY MARTINEZ	
			Singer from Quebec, Canada.	
10/04/86	**32**	21	1 For Tonight	Atlantic 89371
			AL MARTINO	
			Born Alfred Cini on 10/7/27 in Philadelphia. Encouraged by success of boyhood friend, Mario Lanza. Winner on Arthur Godfrey's "Talent Scouts" in 1952. Portrayed singer Johnny Fontane in the film "The Godfather", 1972.	
5/18/59	**44**	9	1 I Can't Get You Out Of My Heart	20th Fox 132
9/28/59	**63**	6	2 Darling, I Love You	20th Fox 153
7/24/61	**86**	4	3 Here In My Heart Al's original version charted in 1952 at POS 1	Capitol 4593
4/06/63	**3**	16	4 **I Love You Because**	Capitol 4930
7/27/63	**15**	12	5 Painted, Tainted Rose	Capitol 5000
10/26/63	**22**	10	6 Living A Lie	Capitol 5060
2/01/64	**9**	11	7 **I Love You More And More Every Day**	Capitol 5108
5/16/64	**20**	8	8 Tears And Roses	Capitol 5183
8/15/64	**33**	8	9 Always Together	Capitol 5239
8/15/64	**99**	2	10 I Can't Get You Out Of My Heart [R]	20th Century 530
11/07/64	**41**	6	11 We Could	Capitol 5293
1/16/65	**52**	7	12 My Heart Would Know	Capitol 5341
3/27/65	**53**	6	13 Somebody Else Is Taking My Place	Capitol 5384
6/12/65	**88**	3	14 My Cherie	Capitol 5434
10/16/65	**61**	6	15 Forgive Me	Capitol 5506
12/04/65+	**15**	12	16 Spanish Eyes	Capitol 5542
3/12/66	**30**	8	17 Think I'll Go Somewhere And Cry Myself To Sleep	Capitol 5598
5/28/66	**57**	4	18 Wiederseh'n	Capitol 5652
8/06/66	**77**	4	19 Just Yesterday	Capitol 5702
10/15/66	**59**	8	20 The Wheel Of Hurt	Capitol 5741
1/28/67	**42**	9	21 Daddy's Little Girl The Mills Brothers' version hit #5 in 1950	Capitol 5825
5/27/67	**27**	8	22 Mary In The Morning	Capitol 5904
9/23/67	**54**	6	23 More Than The Eye Can See	Capitol 5989
12/09/67+	**80**	6	24 A Voice In The Choir	Capitol 2053
2/10/68	**57**	7	25 Love Is Blue	Capitol 2102
4/27/68	**87**	7	26 Lili Marlene	Capitol 2158
12/28/68+	**97**	3	27 I Can't Help It (If I'm Still In Love With You)	Capitol 2355
5/17/69	**99**	3	28 Sausalito	Capitol 2468
12/06/69+	**86**	5	29 I Started Loving You Again	Capitol 2674
2/07/70	**51**	8	30 Can't Help Falling In Love	Capitol 2746
4/29/72	**80**	4	31 Speak Softly Love love theme from the film "The Godfather"	Capitol 3313
12/21/74+	**17**	16	32 To The Door Of The Sun (Alle Porte Del Sole) 5-7, 9, 11-15, 17, 19-24, 31-32: conducted by Peter DeAngelis	Capitol 3987
11/01/75	**33**	10	33 Volare	Capitol 4134
12/10/77+	**49**	9	34 The Next Hundred Years	Capitol 4508
			THE MARVELETTES	
			R&B group from Inkster High School, Inkster, MI. Formed in 1960 by Gladys Horton, with Georgeanna Marie Tillman Gordon (died of lupus on 1/6/80), Wanda Young, Katherine Anderson and Juanita Cowart. Young and Horton both sang lead. Cowart and Gordon left in 1965, Horton left in 1967, replaced by Anne Bogan. Disbanded, 1969.	
9/04/61	**1**[1]	23	1 **Please Mr. Postman**	Tamla 54046
1/27/62	**34**	9	2 Twistin' Postman	Tamla 54054
5/05/62	**7**	15	3 **Playboy**	Tamla 54060
8/11/62	**17**	11	4 Beechwood 4-5789	Tamla 54065
12/01/62+	**49**	14	5 Strange I Know	Tamla 54072
3/23/63	**44**	9	6 Locking Up My Heart/	
5/04/63	**78**	6	7 Forever	Tamla 54077
8/03/63	**67**	6	8 My Daddy Knows Best	Tamla 54082
11/09/63	**47**	13	9 As Long As I Know He's Mine	Tamla 54088
2/22/64	**55**	7	10 He's A Good Guy (Yes He Is)	Tamla 54091
7/04/64	**48**	7	11 You're My Remedy	Tamla 54097

DEBUT DATE	PEAK POS	WKS CHR	ARTIST — Record Title	Label & Number
			THE MARVELETTES — Cont'd	
11/07/64+	**25**	12	12 Too Many Fish In The Sea	Tamla 54105
5/29/65	**34**	7	13 I'll Keep Holding On	Tamla 54116
8/14/65	**61**	8	14 Danger Heartbreak Dead Ahead	Tamla 54120
1/01/66	**7**	12	15 **Don't Mess With Bill**	Tamla 54126
4/23/66	**48**	6	16 You're The One	Tamla 54131
1/21/67	**13**	11	17 The Hunter Gets Captured By The Game	Tamla 54143
4/22/67	**23**	10	18 When You're Young And In Love	Tamla 54150
12/16/67+	**17**	11	19 My Baby Must Be A Magician	Tamla 54158
6/08/68	**44**	9	20 Here I Am Baby	Tamla 54166
10/05/68	**63**	5	21 Destination: Anywhere	Tamla 54171
1/18/69	**76**	3	22 I'm Gonna Hold On Long As I Can	Tamla 54177
11/08/69	**97**	1	23 That's How Heartaches Are Made	Tamla 54186
			THE MARVELOWS R&B group from Chicago - first known as the Mystics. Included Melvin Mason (lead), Willie "Sonny" Stevenson, Frank Paden and Johnny Paden. Added Jesse Smith in 1964.	
5/15/65	**37**	9	1 I Do	ABC-Para. 10629
			MARY JANE GIRLS Female "funk & roll" quartet: Joanne McDuffie, Candice Ghant, Kim Wuletick and Yvette Marine. Formed and produced by Rick James.	
3/09/85	**7**	22	1 **In My House**	Gordy 1741
7/20/85	**42**	10	2 Wild And Crazy Love	Gordy 1798
7/12/86	**41**	10	3 Walk Like A Man from the film "A Fine Mess"	Motown 1851
			CAROLYNE MAS Rock singer/guitarist from the Bronx, New York.	
9/08/79	**71**	5	1 Stillsane	Mercury 76004
			HUGH MASEKELA Born Hugh Ramapolo Masekela on 4/4/39 in Wilbank, South Africa. Trumpeter, bandleader, arranger. Played trumpet since age 14. To England in 1959; New York City in 1960. Formerly married to Miriam Makeba. Formed own band in 1964.	
12/09/67+	**71**	8	1 Up-Up And Away [I]	Uni 55037
6/08/68	**1**[2]	12	2 ● **Grazing In The Grass** [I]	Uni 55066
9/28/68	**71**	5	3 Puffin' On Down The Track [I]	Uni 55085
1/11/69	**55**	8	4 Riot [I]	Uni 55102
			MASHMAKHAN Montreal rock quartet led by Pierre Senecal.	
8/22/70	**31**	18	1 As The Years Go By	Epic 10634
			THE MASKMAN & THE AGENTS Consisted of Harmon "Maskman" Bethea, Tyrone Gray, Paul Williams and Johnny Hood.	
3/29/69	**95**	1	1 One Eye Open	Dynamo 125
5/17/69	**91**	2	2 My Wife, My Dog, My Cat above 2 with The Billy Clark Orchestra	Dynamo 131
			BARBARA MASON Born on 8/9/47 in Philadelphia. First recorded for Crusader in 1964. Wrote all of her Arctic hits.	
5/15/65	**5**	14	1 **Yes, I'm Ready**	Arctic 105
8/07/65	**27**	9	2 Sad, Sad Girl	Arctic 108
11/06/65	**85**	3	3 If You Don't (Love Me, Tell Me So)	Arctic 112
1/29/66	**97**	2	4 Is It Me?	Arctic 116
6/11/66	**98**	2	5 I Need Love	Arctic 120
12/23/67+	**59**	9	6 Oh, How It Hurts	Arctic 137
9/14/68	**97**	1	7 (I Can Feel Your Love) Slipping Away	Arctic 142
6/10/72	**70**	6	8 Bed And Board	Buddah 296
1/13/73	**31**	12	9 Give Me Your Love	Buddah 331
11/30/74+	**28**	10	10 From His Woman To You	Buddah 441
4/19/75	**91**	4	11 Shackin' Up	Buddah 459
			DAVE MASON Born on 5/10/46 in Worchester, England. Vocalist, composer, guitarist. Original member of Traffic.	
8/01/70	**42**	10	1 Only You Know And I Know	Blue Thumb 114
12/12/70	**97**	2	2 Satin Red And Black Velvet Woman	Blue Thumb 7117

DEBUT DATE	PEAK POS	WKS CHR	ARTIST — Record Title	Label & Number
			DAVE MASON — Cont'd	
5/28/77	**89**	3	3 So High (Rock Me Baby And Roll Me Away)	Columbia 10509
9/03/77	**12**	19	4 We Just Disagree	Columbia 10575
1/21/78	**45**	8	5 Let It Go, Let It Flow	Columbia 10662
6/03/78	**39**	12	6 Will You Still Love Me Tomorrow	Columbia 10749
7/12/80	**71**	3	7 Save Me	Columbia 11289
			VAUGHAN MASON & CREW	
			East Coast disco/funk group. Jerome Bell, lead singer.	
3/22/80	**81**	3	1 Bounce, Rock, Skate, Roll Pt.1	Brunswick 211
			available only on a 12" single	
			THE MASQUERADERS	
			Texas soul group: Lee Hatim, Robert Wrightsill, David Sanders, Harold Thomas and Sammie Hutchins.	
9/28/68	**57**	5	1 I Ain't Got To Love Nobody Else	Bell 733
			MASS PRODUCTION	
			10-member disco/funk group. Agnes "Tiny" Kelly and Larry Marshall, lead singers.	
2/19/77	**68**	4	1 Welcome To Our World (Of Merry Music)	Cotillion 44213
8/04/79	**43**	10	2 Firecracker	Cotillion 44254
			WAYNE MASSEY	
			Played Johnny Drummond on TV's soap "One Life To Live".	
10/11/80	**92**	2	1 One Life To Live	Polydor 2112
			from the TV soap opera	
			SAMMY MASTERS	
4/04/60	**64**	5	1 Rockin' Red Wing	Lode 108
			rock version popularized in 1907 by Frank Stanley & Henry Burr	
			TOBIN MATHEWS & Co.	
			Guitarist from Calumet City, Illinois.	
10/31/60	**30**	8	1 Ruby Duby Du [I]	Chief 7022
			from the movie "Key Witness"	
			MUIR MATHIESON	
			Born on 1/24/11 in Sterling, England; died on 8/2/75. Conductor, musical director of over 500 British films.	
8/04/56	**67**	5	1 Lola's Theme [I]	Columbia 40725
			from the soundtrack "Trapeze" - with The London Sinfonia Orchestra	
			JOHNNY MATHIS	
			Born on 9/30/35 in San Francisco. Studied opera from age thirteen. Track scholarship, San Francisco State College. Invited to Olympic try-outs, chose singing career instead. To New York City in 1956. Ranks behind only Elvis Presley and Frank Sinatra as the top album artist of the rock era.	
2/09/57	**14**	39	1 Wonderful! Wonderful!	Columbia 40784
			Jockey #14 / Top 100 #17 / Best Seller #18	
4/29/57	**5**	34	2 **It's Not For Me To Say**	Columbia 40851
			Top 100 #5 / Jockey #5 / Best Seller #6 from the movie "Lizzie"	
9/16/57	**1**[1]	28	3 **Chances Are/**	
			Jockey #1 / Best Seller #4 / Top 100 #5	
10/14/57	**9**	17	4 **The Twelfth Of Never**	Columbia 40993
			Jockey #9 / Top 100 #51	
12/16/57+	**21**	10	5 No Love (But Your Love)/	
			Jockey #21 / Top 100 #48	
12/16/57	**22**	18	6 Wild Is The Wind	Columbia 41060
			Jockey #22 / Best Seller #30 / Top 100 #37 from the film of the same title	
2/10/58	**22**	13	7 Come To Me	Columbia 41082
			Jockey #22 / Best Seller #40 / Top 100 #43 from the TV production of the same title	
4/21/58	**21**	14	8 All The Time/	
			Jockey #21 / Best Seller #30 / Top 100 #42 from the Broadway musical "Oh Captain!"	
5/05/58	**21**	11	9 Teacher, Teacher	Columbia 41152
			Jockey #21 / Top 100 #43	
6/30/58	**14**	14	10 A Certain Smile	Columbia 41193
			Jockey #14 / Top 100 #19 / Best Seller #21 from the film of the same title	
9/29/58	**21**	15	11 Call Me	Columbia 41253

DEBUT DATE	PEAK POS	WKS CHR	ARTIST — Record Title	Label & Number
			JOHNNY MATHIS — Cont'd	
1/05/59	44	9	12 Let's Love/	
1/05/59	60	6	13 You Are Beautiful	Columbia 41304
			from the Broadway musical "Flower Drum Song"	
3/23/59	35	13	14 Someone	Columbia 41355
6/15/59	20	15	15 Small World	Columbia 41410
			from the Broadway musical "Gypsy"	
10/05/59	12	17	16 Misty/	
			the Erroll Garner classic charted at POS 30 in 1954	
10/12/59	93	2	17 The Story Of Our Love	Columbia 41483
11/16/59	62	5	18 The Best Of Everything	Columbia 41491
			from the film of the same title	
2/29/60	25	11	19 Starbright	Columbia 41583
5/30/60	78	4	20 Maria	Columbia 41684
			from the Broadway musical "West Side Story"	
8/29/60	47	11	21 My Love For You	Columbia 41764
12/26/60	64	3	22 How To Handle A Woman	Columbia 41866
			from the Broadway musical "Camelot"	
10/23/61	89	1	23 Wasn't The Summer Short?	Columbia 42156
12/11/61+	88	3	24 Maria [R]	Columbia 41684
3/17/62	99	2	25 Sweet Thursday	Columbia 42261
6/16/62	86	1	26 Marianna	Columbia 42420
			from the film "The Counterfeit Traitor"	
9/22/62	6	12	27 **Gina**	Columbia 42582
1/26/63	9	12	28 **What Will Mary Say**	Columbia 42666
5/25/63	30	7	29 Every Step Of The Way	Columbia 42799
9/07/63	84	3	30 Sooner Or Later	Columbia 42836
10/12/63	61	6	31 Come Back/	
10/12/63	68	7	32 Your Teenage Dreams	Mercury 72184
12/14/63	90	4	33 I'll Search My Heart	Columbia 42916
2/01/64	53	7	34 Bye Bye Barbara	Mercury 72229
6/20/64	87	3	35 Taste Of Tears	Mercury 72287
10/24/64	62	8	36 Listen Lonely Girl	Mercury 72339
12/18/65	98	2	37 On A Clear Day You Can See Forever	Mercury 72493
			from the Broadway musical of the same title	
7/26/69	96	3	38 Love Theme From "Romeo And Juliet" (A Time For Us)	Columbia 44915
			from the hit film "Romeo And Juliet"	
9/22/73	75	10	39 I'm Coming Home	Columbia 45908
12/29/73+	54	12	40 Life Is A Song Worth Singing	Columbia 45975
4/01/78	1[1]	18	41 ● **Too Much, Too Little, Too Late**	Columbia 10693
			JOHNNY MATHIS/DENIECE WILLIAMS	
7/29/78	47	8	42 You're All I Need To Get By	Columbia 10772
			JOHNNY MATHIS & DENIECE WILLIAMS	
4/17/82	38	13	43 Friends In Love	Arista 0673
			DIONNE WARWICK & JOHNNY MATHIS	
6/23/84	81	8	44 Simple	Columbia 04468
			MATTHEWS' SOUTHERN COMFORT	
			English rock sextet. Ian Matthews, lead singer.	
3/06/71	23	16	1 Woodstock	Decca 32774
7/24/71	96	2	2 Mare, Take Me Home	Decca 32845
10/16/71	98	2	3 Tell Me Why	Decca 32874
			IAN MATTHEWS	
			Born Ian Matthew MacDonald in Lincolnshire, England in 1946. Founder of Fairport Convention and Matthews' Southern Comfort.	
2/19/72	96	3	1 Da Doo Ron Ron (When He Walked Me Home)	Vertigo 103
11/18/78+	13	19	2 Shake It	Mushroom 7039
4/07/79	67	5	3 Give Me An Inch	Mushroom 7040
			THE MATYS BROS.	
			Polka band.	
1/19/63	55	9	1 Who Stole The Keeshka?	Select 719
			THE MAUDS	
10/19/68	85	4	1 Soul Drippin'	Mercury 72832

DEBUT DATE	PEAK POS	WKS CHR	ARTIST — Record Title		Label & Number
			PAUL MAURIAT		
			French conductor/arranger; born in 1925.		
1/06/68	**1^{5}**	18	1 ● **Love Is Blue**	[I]	Philips 40495
5/11/68	**60**	6	2 Love In Every Room	[I]	Philips 40530
11/23/68+	**76**	8	3 Chitty Chitty Bang Bang from the film of the same title	[I]	Philips 40574
			DIANE MAXWELL		
			Born on 5/24/42.		
3/23/59	**95**	1	1 Jimmy Kiss And Run		Challenge 59039
			ROBERT MAXWELL		
			Born on 4/19/21 in New York City. Jazz harpist, composer. With NBC Symphony under Toscanini at age 17. Also see Mickey Mozart.		
3/21/64	**15**	12	1 Shangri-La	[I]	Decca 25622
6/20/64	**64**	6	2 Peg O' My Heart there were 4 #1 versions of this tune from 1913-47	[I]	Decca 25637
			BILLY MAY		
			Born on 1/10/16 in Pittsburgh. Arranger/conductor/sideman for many of the big bands.		
3/17/56	**49**	14	1 Main Title from Otto Preminger's film "The Man With The Golden Arm"	[I]	Capitol 3372
			JOHN MAYALL		
			Born on 11/29/43 in Manchester, England. Bluesman John Mayall & his Bluesbreakers band spawned many of Britain's leading rock musicians.		
10/11/69	**81**	3	1 Don't Waste My Time		Polydor 14004
			NATHANIEL MAYER & The Fabulous Twilights		
			Detroit R&B vocalist.		
4/28/62	**22**	12	1 Village Of Love		Fortune 449
			CURTIS MAYFIELD		
			Born on 6/3/42 in Chicago. Soul singer, songwriter, producer. With Jerry Butler in the gospel group Northern Jubilee Singers. Joined The Impressions in 1957. Wrote most of the hits for The Impressions and Jerry Butler. Own labels: Windy C, Mayfield, and Curtom. Went solo in 1970. Scored "Superfly", "Claudine", "A Piece Of The Action", "Short Eyes" film soundtracks. Appeared in "Short Eyes".		
11/21/70+	**29**	12	1 (Don't Worry) If There's A Hell Below We're All Going To Go		Curtom 1955
11/13/71	**69**	7	2 Get Down		Curtom 1966
8/19/72	**4**	16	3 ● **Freddie's Dead**		Curtom 1975
11/18/72+	**8**	15	4 ● **Superfly** above 2 are from the film "Superfly"		Curtom 1978
7/21/73	**39**	10	5 Future Shock		Curtom 1987
10/20/73	**71**	4	6 If I Were Only A Child Again		Curtom 1991
12/29/73+	**88**	5	7 Can't Say Nothin'		Curtom 1993
6/22/74	**40**	13	8 Kung Fu		Curtom 1999
9/27/75	**67**	7	9 So In Love all of above written by Mayfield		Curtom 0105
			PERCY MAYFIELD		
			Born on 8/12/20 in Minden, LA; died on 8/11/84 in Los Angeles. R&B vocalist, pianist, composer.		
6/01/63	**99**	1	1 River's Invitation		Tangerine 931
			MAZE Featuring FRANKIE BEVERLY		
			Soul group formed in Philadelphia as the Butlers (later, Raw Soul); moved to San Francisco in 1972. Nucleus consisted of Frankie Beverly, vocalist; Wayne Thomas, Sam Porter, Robin Duhe, Roame Lowry and McKinley Williams.		
5/28/77	**89**	11	1 While I'm Alone		Capitol 4392
6/16/79	**67**	5	2 Feel That You're Feelin'		Capitol 4686
6/04/83	**80**	5	3 Love Is The Key		Capitol 5221
3/16/85	**88**	6	4 Back In Stride		Capitol 5431
			MC5		
			Detroit hard rock quintet. Rob Tyner, lead singer.		
3/15/69	**82**	4	1 Kick Out The Jams		Elektra 45648
			MAC McANALLY		
			Born Lyman McAnally, Jr. in 1957 in Red Bay, Alabama. Session singer, guitarist.		
7/09/77	**37**	9	1 It's A Crazy World		Ariola Am. 7665
3/05/83	**41**	12	2 Minimum Love		Geffen 29736

DEBUT DATE	PEAK POS	WKS CHR	ARTIST — Record Title	Label & Number
			C.W. McCALL	
			Born Bill Fries on 11/15/28 in Audubon, Iowa. Advertising agent from Omaha.	
6/29/74	**54**	7	1 Old Home Filler-Up An' Keep On-A-Truckin' Cafe ... [N]	MGM 14738
2/01/75	**40**	11	2 Wolf Creek Pass ... [N]	MGM 14764
12/06/75+	**1**[1]	16	3● **Convoy** ... [N]	MGM 14839
3/27/76	**73**	4	4 There Won't Be No Country Music (There Won't Be No Rock 'N' Roll) ... [S]	Polydor 14310
			TOUSSAINT McCALL	
			R&B organist, vocalist.	
3/25/67	**52**	11	1 Nothing Takes The Place Of You ...	Ronn 3
7/01/67	**77**	4	2 I'll Do It For You ...	Ronn 9
			LES McCANN & EDDIE HARRIS	
			Les was born on 9/23/35 in Lexington, Kentucky. Jazz keyboardist, vocalist.	
1/10/70	**85**	4	1 Compared To What ...	Atlantic 2694
			PETER McCANN	
			Connecticut native - staffwriter with ABC Music.	
4/23/77	**5**	22	1● **Do You Wanna Make Love** ...	20th Century 2335
			PAUL McCARTNEY	
			Born on 6/18/42 in Liverpool, England. Writer of over 50 Top 10 singles. Founding member/bass guitarist of The Beatles. Married Linda Eastman on 3/12/69. First solo album in 1970. Formed group Wings in 1971 with wife Linda (keyboards, backing vocals), Denny Laine (guitar) and Denny Seiwell (drums). Henry McCullough (guitar) joined in 1972. Seiwell and McCullough left in 1973. Joe English (drums) and James McCullough (guitar) joined in 1975. Also see Suzy & The Red Stripes.	
3/06/71	**5**	12	1 **Another Day/**	
		9	2 Oh Woman Oh Why ...	Apple 1829
8/14/71	**1**[1]	13	3● **Uncle Albert/Admiral Halsey** ...	Apple 1837
			PAUL & LINDA McCARTNEY	
			WINGS:	
3/11/72	**21**	8	4 Give Ireland Back To The Irish ...	Apple 1847
6/17/72	**28**	7	5 Mary Had A Little Lamb/	
		6	6 Little Woman Love ...	Apple 1851
12/16/72+	**10**	11	7 **Hi, Hi, Hi** ...	Apple 1857
4/14/73	**1**[4]	18	8● **My Love** ...	Apple 1861
7/07/73	**2**[3]	14	9● **Live And Let Die** ...	Apple 1863
			from the James Bond film of the same title	
11/24/73+	**10**	13	10 **Helen Wheels** ...	Apple 1869
2/09/74	**7**	14	11 **Jet** ...	Apple 1871
4/20/74	**1**[1]	18	12● **Band On The Run** ...	Apple 1873
11/09/74+	**3**	12	13 **Junior's Farm/**	
2/01/75	**39**	8	14 Sally G ...	Apple 1875
5/31/75	**1**[1]	14	15● **Listen To What The Man Said** ...	Capitol 4091
10/04/75	**39**	6	16 Letting Go ...	Capitol 4145
11/01/75	**12**	9	17 Venus And Mars Rock Show ...	Capitol 4175
4/10/76	**1**[5]	19	18● **Silly Love Songs** ...	Capitol 4256
7/04/76	**3**	16	19● **Let 'Em In** ...	Capitol 4293
2/12/77	**10**	13	20 **Maybe I'm Amazed** ...	Capitol 4385
			live version of song from McCartney's 1st solo album	
11/19/77+	**33**	11	21 Girls' School ...	Capitol 4504
			flip side "Mull of Kintyre" is one of England's all-time biggest selling singles	
3/25/78	**1**[2]	18	22 **With A Little Luck** ...	Capitol 4559
6/17/78	**25**	11	23 I've Had Enough ...	Capitol 4594
9/09/78	**39**	8	24 London Town ...	Capitol 4625
3/31/79	**5**	16	25● **Goodnight Tonight** ...	Columbia 10939
6/16/79	**20**	10	26 Getting Closer ...	Columbia 11020
8/25/79	**29**	10	27 Arrow Through Me ...	Columbia 11070
4/26/80	**1**[3]	21	28● **Coming Up (Live at Glasgow)** ...	Columbia 11263
			8, 10-14, 28: PAUL McCARTNEY & WINGS	
			PAUL McCARTNEY:	
4/10/82	**1**[7]	19	29● **Ebony And Ivory** ...	Columbia 02860
			PAUL McCARTNEY with STEVIE WONDER	
7/10/82	**10**	16	30 **Take It Away** ...	Columbia 03018
10/02/82	**53**	8	31 Tug Of War ...	Columbia 03235

DEBUT DATE	PEAK POS	WKS CHR	ARTIST — Record Title	Label & Number
			PAUL McCARTNEY — Cont'd	
11/06/82+	**2**[3]	18	32● **The Girl Is Mine** **MICHAEL JACKSON/PAUL McCARTNEY**	Epic 03288
10/15/83	**1**[6]	22	33● **Say Say Say** **PAUL McCARTNEY & MICHAEL JACKSON**	Columbia 04168
12/24/83+	**23**	14	34 So Bad	Columbia 04296
10/13/84	**6**	18	35 **No More Lonely Nights** from the film "Give My Regards To Broad Street" 29-35: produced by George Martin (except #32)	Columbia 04581
11/23/85+	**7**	17	36 **Spies Like Us** from the film of the same title	Capitol 5537
8/02/86	**21**	11	37 Press	Capitol 5597
11/15/86	**81**	6	38 Stranglehold all of above hits written by McCartney (except #32) 1-8, 10-28, 36-38: produced by McCartney	Capitol 5636
			ALTON McCLAIN & DESTINY Black female trio. Destiny: D'Marie Warren & Robyrda Stiger.	
4/07/79	**32**	12	1 It Must Be Love	Polydor 14532
			DELBERT McCLINTON Born on 11/4/40 in Lubbock, TX. Played harmonica on Bruce Channel's hit "Hey Baby". Leader of the Ron-Dels. Also see Delbert & Glen.	
12/06/80+	**8**	19	1 **Giving It Up For Your Love**	Capitol 4948
3/28/81	**70**	6	2 Shotgun Rider	Capitol 4984
			BOBBY McCLURE	
2/06/65	**33**	11	1 Don't Mess Up A Good Thing	Checker 1097
5/29/65	**91**	2	2 You'll Miss Me (When I'm Gone) above 2: **FONTELLA BASS & BOBBY McCLURE**	Checker 1111
12/10/66	**97**	2	3 Peak Of Love	Checker 1152
			MARILYN McCOO & BILLY DAVIS, JR. Marilyn (b: 9/30/43) & husband Billy (b: 6/26/40) were members of the 5th Dimension.	
3/27/76	**91**	8	1 I Hope We Get To Love In Time	ABC 12170
9/11/76+	**1**[1]	26	2● **You Don't Have To Be A Star (To Be In My Show)**	ABC 12208
3/19/77	**15**	11	3 Your Love	ABC 12262
8/20/77	**51**	7	4 Look What You've Done To My Heart	ABC 12298
			GAYLE McCORMICK Born in St. Louis. Former lead singer of the group Smith.	
7/10/71	**84**	5	1 Gonna Be Alright Now	Dunhill 4281
9/18/71	**44**	12	2 It's A Cryin' Shame	Dunhill 4288
1/22/72	**98**	1	3 You Really Got A Hold On Me	Dunhill 4298
			CHARLIE McCOY Born on 3/28/41 in Oak Hill, WV. Nashville's #1 session harmonica player.	
2/27/61	**99**	1	1 Cherry Berry Wine	Cadence 1390
			FREDDIE McCOY Jazz/R&B vibraphonist.	
10/07/67	**92**	2	1 Peas 'N' Rice [I]	Prestige 450
			VAN McCOY Born on 1/6/44 in Washington, DC; died on 7/6/79 in Englewood, NJ of a heart attack. Had own Rock'N label, 1960. Produced The Shirelles, Gladys Knight, and The Drifters. Own MAXX label, mid-60s.	
4/19/75	**1**[1]	19	1● **The Hustle** [I] with The Soul City Symphony	Avco 4653
10/11/75	**46**	8	2 Change With The Times	Avco 4660
5/29/76	**96**	2	3 Night Walk [I]	H&L 4667
8/14/76	**69**	5	4 Party	H&L 4670
			THE McCOYS Rock band formed in Indiana. Rick Derringer (real name: Zehringer), vocals, guitar; brother Randy Zehringer, drums; Randy Hobbs, bass; and Ronnie Brandon, keyboards.	
8/14/65	**1**[1]	14	1 **Hang On Sloopy**	Bang 506
11/13/65	**7**	11	2 **Fever**	Bang 511
2/12/66	**46**	6	3 Up And Down	Bang 516
4/23/66	**22**	9	4 Come On Let's Go	Bang 522
7/30/66	**53**	4	5 (You Make Me Feel) So Good	Bang 527
10/01/66	**67**	5	6 Don't Worry Mother, Your Son's Heart Is Pure	Bang 532

DEBUT DATE	PEAK POS	WKS CHR	ARTIST — Record Title	Label & Number
			THE McCOYS — Cont'd	
1/07/67	**69**	5	7 I Got To Go Back (And Watch That Little Girl Dance)..	Bang 538
5/13/67	**92**	2	8 Beat The Clock	Bang 543
10/26/68	**98**	2	9 Jesse Brady	Mercury 72843
			JIMMY McCRACKLIN Born on 8/13/21 in St. Louis. R&B vocalist, harmonica, piano. US Navy, 1940s. Settled in Los Angeles. Professional boxer, mid-40s. First recorded for Globe, 1945.	
2/24/58	**7**	16	1 **The Walk** Top 100 #7 / Best Seller #11 / Jockey #23	Checker 885
12/11/61+	**64**	7	2 Just Got To Know	Art-Tone 825
4/10/65	**91**	1	3 Every Night, Every Day	Imperial 66094
10/23/65	**95**	2	4 Think	Imperial 66129
1/29/66	**92**	1	5 My Answer	Imperial 66147
			GEORGE McCRAE Born on 10/19/44 in West Palm Beach, Florida; died on 1/24/86 of cancer. Duets with wife Gwen McCrae, became her manager.	
6/01/74	**1^{2}**	17	1 **Rock Your Baby**	T.K. 1004
10/12/74	**50**	6	2 I Can't Leave You Alone/	
1/25/75	**37**	9	3 I Get Lifted	T.K. 1007
5/17/75	**95**	1	4 Look At You	T.K. 1011
1/10/76	**65**	5	5 Honey I all of above written and produced by Harry Wayne Casey and Richard Finch of KC & The Sunshine Band	T.K. 1016
			GWEN McCRAE Born on 12/21/43 in Pensacola, FL. Wife of George McCrae. First recorded as duo with George for Alston in 1969.	
5/17/75	**9**	14	1 **Rockin' Chair** background vocals: George McCrae	Cat 1996
			THE McCRARYS Siblings Linda, Charity, Alfred and Sam McCrary.	
8/19/78	**45**	8	1 You	Portrait 70014
			GEORGE McCURN	
3/02/63	**55**	8	1 I'm Just A Country Boy arranged and conducted by Herb Alpert	A&M 705
			DONNA McDANIEL	
7/02/77	**90**	5	1 Save Me	Midsong Int. 11005
			GENE McDANIELS Born Eugene B. McDaniels on 2/12/35 in Kansas City. To Omaha, early 1940s, sang in choirs, attended Omaha Conservatory of Music. Own band, early 50s. Appeared in the film "It's Trad, Dad" in 1962.	
3/20/61	**3**	15	1 **A Hundred Pounds Of Clay**	Liberty 55308
7/03/61	**31**	8	2 A Tear	Liberty 55344
10/02/61	**5**	13	3 **Tower Of Strength**	Liberty 55371
1/20/62	**10**	11	4 **Chip Chip**	Liberty 55405
4/21/62	**99**	1	5 Funny	Liberty 55444
8/04/62	**21**	10	6 Point Of No Return	Liberty 55480
11/10/62	**31**	9	7 Spanish Lace 2-7: with The Johnny Mann Singers	Liberty 55510
8/10/63	**64**	7	8 It's A Lonely Town (Lonely Without You) all of above produced by Snuff Garrett	Liberty 55597
			CHAS. McDEVITT Skiffle Group British vocal/instrumental group.	
5/27/57	**40**	5	1 Freight Train vocal by Nancy Wiskey	Chic 1008
			COUNTRY JOE McDONALD - see COUNTRY JOE	
			MICHAEL McDONALD Vocalist, keyboardist. Member of Steely Dan in 1974. Lead singer of The Doobie Brothers from 1975-82. Also see Nicolette Larson.	
8/07/82	**4**	19	1 **I Keep Forgettin' (Every Time You're Near)**	Warner 29933
11/13/82	**44**	11	2 I Gotta Try	Warner 29862
12/10/83+	**19**	18	3 Yah Mo B There **JAMES INGRAM with MICHAEL McDONALD**	Qwest 29394
7/27/85	**34**	12	4 No Lookin' Back	Warner 28960

DEBUT DATE	PEAK POS	WKS CHR	ARTIST — Record Title		Label & Number
			MICHAEL McDONALD — Cont'd		
3/22/86	**1**[3]	23	5 ● **On My Own** PATTI LaBELLE & MICHAEL McDONALD		MCA 52770
6/14/86	**7**	20	6 **Sweet Freedom** theme from the film "Running Scared"		MCA 52857
			RONNIE McDOWELL Country singer, songwriter from Portland, Tennessee.		
9/10/77	**13**	12	1 ● The King Is Gone a tribute to Elvis Presley		Scorpion 135
3/18/78	**81**	4	2 I Love You, I Love You, I Love You		Scorpion 149
			BROTHER JACK McDUFF Born Eugene McDuffy on 9/17/26 in Champaign, IL. R&B/jazz-styled organist. With Schoolboy Porter in 1957, Jimmy Coe, Willis Jackson, 1958-59. First recorded for Prestige in 1960.		
12/27/69	**95**	2	1 Theme From Electric Surfboard	[I]	Blue Note 1953
			McFADDEN & WHITEHEAD R&B duo of Gene McFadden and John Whitehead from Philadelphia. Wrote songs for many Philadelphia soul acts.		
4/28/79	**13**	18	1 ▲ Ain't No Stoppin' Us Now		Phil. Int. 3681
			BOB McFADDEN & Dor Bob is from East Liverpool, Ohio. Began career in 1950 as a singing emcee for a special Navy show called "The Bob McFadden Show".		
8/24/59	**39**	8	1 The Mummy "beatnik" comments by Rod McKuen	[N]	Brunswick 55140
			PARKER McGEE Pop singer, songwriter from Mississippi. Wrote "I'd Really Love To See You Tonight" and "Nights Are Forever Without You" for England Dan & John Ford Coley.		
1/22/77	**42**	7	1 I Just Can't Say No To You		Big Tree 16082
			BOB McGILPIN Disco artist. Born in Fort Dix, New Jersey.		
9/23/78	**91**	5	1 When You Feel Love		Butterfly 1211
			MAUREEN McGOVERN Born on 7/27/49 in Youngstown, Ohio.		
6/23/73	**1**[2]	15	1 ● **The Morning After** love theme from the film "The Poseidon Adventure"		20th Century 2010
10/13/73	**89**	5	2 I Won't Last A Day Without You		20th Century 2051
10/19/74	**71**	7	3 Give Me A Reason To Be Gone		20th Century 2109
1/25/75	**83**	4	4 We May Never Love Like This Again from the film "The Towering Inferno"		20th Century 2158
2/24/79	**52**	9	5 Can You Read My Mind love theme from the film "Superman"		Warner 8750
7/07/79	**18**	16	6 Different Worlds theme from the TV series "Angie"		Warner 8835
			JIMMY McGRIFF Born on 4/3/36 in Philadelphia. Jazz/R&B organist and multi-instrumentalist.		
10/13/62	**20**	9	1 I've Got A Woman, Part I	[I]	Sue 770
1/05/63	**50**	11	2 All About My Girl/	[I]	
2/02/63	**95**	3	3 M.G. Blues	[I]	Sue 777
5/25/63	**99**	1	4 The Last Minute - Pt. I	[I]	Sue 786
5/16/64	**79**	4	5 Kiko	[I]	Sue 10001
12/14/68	**97**	1	6 The Worm	[I]	Solid State 2524
			McGUFFEY LANE Country/rock sextet from Columbus, Ohio. Lead singer Rod McNelly committed suicide on 1/7/87 (36).		
1/17/81	**85**	7	1 Long Time Lovin' You		Atco 7319
2/06/82	**97**	3	2 Start It All Over		Atco 7345
			McGUINN, CLARK & HILLMAN Roger McGuinn (b: 7/13/42), vocals, guitar; Gene Clark (b: 11/17/44), guitar; & Chris Hillman (b: 6/4/42), bass. All are former members of the Byrds.		
3/17/79	**33**	11	1 Don't You Write Her Off		Capitol 4693
			McGUINNESS FLINT British rock group led by Tom McGuinness/Hughie Flint (both formerly with Manfred Mann).		
1/09/71	**47**	9	1 When I'm Dead And Gone		Capitol 3014

DEBUT DATE	PEAK POS	WKS CHR	ARTIST — Record Title	Label & Number
			THE McGUIRE SISTERS	
			Sisters Christine (b: 7/30/29), Dorothy (b: 2/13/30) and Phyllis (b: 2/14/31) from Middletown, Ohio. Replaced the Chordettes on the Arthur Godfrey Show in 1953. Phyllis went solo in 1964. Recently reunited.	
1/08/55	**1[10]**	21	1 **Sincerely/** Jockey #1(10) / Juke Box #1(7) / Best Seller #1(6)	
1/29/55	**17**	6	2 No More Jockey #17 / Juke Box #17 / Best Seller #23	Coral 61323
3/26/55	**11**	7	3 It May Sound Silly/ Jockey #11 / Juke Box #14 / Best Seller #23	
		2	4 Doesn't Anybody Love Me? Juke Box flip	Coral 61369
6/04/55	**5**	14	5 **Something's Gotta Give/** Jockey #5 / Best Seller #6 / Juke Box #6 from the film "Daddy Long Legs"	
		2	6 Rhythm 'N' Blues (Mama's Got The Rhythm - Papa's Got The Blues) Best Seller/Juke Box flip	Coral 61423
9/10/55	**47**	3	7 Give Me Love Coming Up #47 / Top 100 #95 pre	Coral 61494
10/29/55	**10**	19	8 **He** Juke Box #10 / Best Seller #12 / Top 100 #12 / Jockey #16	Coral 61501
1/07/56	**47**	4	9 My Baby's Got Such Lovin' Ways/ Coming Up #47	
		4	10 (Baby, Baby) Be Good To Me Coming Up flip	Coral 61532
3/10/56	**44**	6	11 Missing	Coral 61587
5/05/56	**13**	20	12 Picnic/ Top 100 #13 / Jockey #14 / Best Seller #15 / Juke Box #18 from the film of the same title	
5/05/56	**37**	11	13 Delilah Jones from the film "The Man With The Golden Arm"	Coral 61627
7/28/56	**32**	8	14 Weary Blues/ THE McGUIRE SISTERS & LAWRENCE WELK	
8/04/56	**63**	5	15 In The Alps LAWRENCE WELK & THE McGUIRE SISTERS	Coral 61670
9/22/56	**37**	12	16 Ev'ry Day Of My Life/	
9/22/56	**52**	8	17 Endless	Coral 61703
12/08/56+	**32**	9	18 Goodnight My Love, Pleasant Dreams	Coral 61748
8/19/57	**73**	6	19 Around The World In Eighty Days from the film of the same title	Coral 61856
12/30/57+	**1[4]**	23	20 **Sugartime** Jockey #1 / Top 100 #5 / Best Seller #7	Coral 61924
6/09/58	**25**	6	21 Ding Dong Jockey #25 / Top 100 #43 / Best Seller #44	Coral 61991
9/01/58	**80**	1	22 Volare (Nel Blu, Dipinto Di Blu)	Coral 62021
1/05/59	**11**	16	23 May You Always	Coral 62059
4/27/59	**55**	7	24 Summer Dreams/	
5/04/59	**85**	3	25 Peace	Coral 62106
1/25/60	**97**	1	26 Livin' Dangerously	Coral 62162
8/15/60	**99**	1	27 The Last Dance	Coral 62216
3/13/61	**20**	14	28 Just For Old Time's Sake	Coral 62249
7/24/61	**59**	5	29 Tears On My Pillow	Coral 62276
11/06/61	**99**	1	30 Just Because 1-3, 5-13, 16-18, 23, 25-30: orchestra directed by Dick Jacobs	Coral 62288
			BARRY McGUIRE	
			Born on 10/15/37 in Oklahoma City. Member of the New Christy Minstrels.	
8/21/65	**1[1]**	11	1 **Eve Of Destruction**	Dunhill 4009
11/06/65	**72**	4	2 Child Of Our Times	Dunhill 4014
5/21/66	**62**	7	3 Cloudy Summer Afternoon (Raindrops)	Dunhill 4028
			PHYLLIS McGUIRE	
			The youngest of The McGuire Sisters.	
12/05/64	**79**	3	1 I Don't Want To Walk Without You #1 hit in 1942 for Harry James	Reprise 0310
			PETER McIAN	
			California-based pop singer, composer. Wrote music for TV's "Starsky And Hutch" and "The Love Boat".	
4/05/80	**52**	7	1 Solitaire	ARC 11214

DEBUT DATE	PEAK POS	WKS CHR	ARTIST — Record Title	Label & Number
			BOB & DOUG McKENZIE	
			Canadian comedians Rick Moranis and Dave Thomas of "SCTV".	
1/30/82	**16**	14	1 Take Off .... [N]	Mercury 76134
			with vocals by Geddy Lee of Rush	
			SCOTT McKENZIE	
			Born in Virginia on 10/1/44. Sang with John Phillips (Mamas & Papas) in The Journeymen.	
5/27/67	**4**	12	1 **San Francisco (Be Sure To Wear Flowers In Your Hair)**	Ode 103
10/21/67	**24**	7	2 Like An Old Time Movie	Ode 105
			above two written and produced by John Phillips	
			ROD McKUEN	
			Born on 4/29/33 in Oakland. Poet, singer, composer, actor. Wrote songs for 20th Century-Fox and Universal films, 1950s and 60s. Also see Bob McFadden.	
1/20/62	**76**	6	1 Oliver Twist	Spiral 1407
			TOMMY McLAIN	
6/25/66	**15**	11	1 Sweet Dreams	MSL 197
			DON McLEAN	
			Born on 10/2/45 in New Rochelle, New York. Singer, songwriter, poet. The hit "Killing Me Softly With His Song" was written about Don.	
11/27/71+	**1^{4}**	19	1 ● **American Pie - Parts I & II**	United Art. 50856
			inspired by the death of Buddy Holly	
3/18/72	**12**	12	2 Vincent/	
			a tribute to artist Vincent Van Gogh	
		7	3 Castles In The Air	United Art. 50887
12/23/72+	**21**	12	4 Dreidel	United Art. 51100
3/31/73	**58**	7	5 If We Try	United Art. 206
6/14/75	**93**	3	6 Wonderful Baby	United Art. 614
			written as a tribute to Fred Astaire	
1/24/81	**5**	18	7 **Crying**	Millennium 11799
4/11/81	**23**	14	8 Since I Don't Have You	Millennium 11804
8/08/81	**83**	2	9 It's Just The Sun	Millennium 11809
10/31/81	**36**	14	10 Castles In The Air	Millennium 11819
			new version of Don's 1972 hit	
			PENNY McLEAN	
1/03/76	**48**	10	1 Lady Bump	Atco 7038
			PHIL McLEAN	
			Veteran disc jockey; born in Detroit.	
12/04/61+	**21**	10	1 Small Sad Sam .... [S-N]	Versatile 107
			a parody of "Big Bad John"	
			OSCAR McLOLLIE & JEANETTE BAKER	
8/04/58	**61**	5	1 Hey Girl - Hey Boy	Class 228
			GERARD McMAHON	
			Los Angeles-based singer/guitarist; originally from Wichita, Kansas.	
4/09/83	**85**	3	1 Count On Me	Full Moon 29699
			LARRY JOHN McNALLY	
8/08/81	**86**	2	1 Just Like Paradise	ARC 02200
			ROBIN McNAMARA	
			One of the original cast members of "Hair".	
5/30/70	**11**	15	1 Lay A Little Lovin' On Me	Steed 724
10/03/70	**80**	5	2 Got To Believe In Love	Steed 728
			with the cast of "Hair"	
			BIG JAY McNEELY & BAND	
			Born Cecil James McNeely on 4/29/28 in Los Angeles. R&B tenor saxophonist, bandleader. Originator of the acrobatic, wild honking sax style.	
5/25/59	**44**	16	1 There Is Something On Your Mind	Swingin' 614
			vocal by Little Sonny Warner	
			KRISTY & JIMMY McNICHOL	
			Teen TV/film stars - Kristy (Jimmy's sister) played Buddy Lawrence on TV's "Family".	
7/22/78	**70**	8	1 He's So Fine	RCA 11271

DEBUT DATE	PEAK POS	WKS CHR	ARTIST — Record Title	Label & Number
			SHAMUS M'COOL	
			Singer, comedian from Los Angeles.	
7/04/81	**80**	3	1 American Memories	Perspective 107
			CLYDE McPHATTER	
			Born Clyde Lensley McPhatter on 11/15/33 in Durham, NC. Died on 6/13/72 in New York City (heart attack). Signed by Billy Ward for the Dominoes in 1950. Left the Dominoes in June, 1953 to form own group, The Drifters. Drafted in 1954, returned to sing solo. One of the most influential and distinctive male voices of the R&B era.	
2/04/56	**44**	5	1 Seven Days	Atlantic 1081
5/26/56	**16**	17	2 Treasure Of Love Best Seller #16 / Juke Box #18 / Top 100 #22	Atlantic 1092
2/02/57	**19**	11	3 Without Love (There Is Nothing) Jockey #19 / Top 100 #38	Atlantic 1117
5/20/57	**26**	11	4 Just To Hold My Hand Best Seller #26 / Top 100 #30	Atlantic 1133
8/12/57	**49**	13	5 Long Lonely Nights	Atlantic 1149
12/02/57	**93**	1	6 Rock And Cry from the film "Mr. Rock 'n' Roll"	Atlantic 1158
5/12/58	**43**	15	7 Come What May Hot 100 #43 / Best Seller #47	Atlantic 1185
10/06/58+	**6**	24	8 **A Lover's Question**	Atlantic 1199
4/06/59	**49**	8	9 Lovey Dovey	Atlantic 2018
4/20/59	**70**	5	10 I Told Myself A Lie	MGM 12780
6/15/59	**38**	13	11 Since You've Been Gone	Atlantic 2028
8/24/59	**91**	2	12 Twice As Nice	MGM 12816
11/02/59	**72**	3	13 You Went Back On Your Word	Atlantic 2038
12/21/59+	**48**	8	14 Let's Try Again	MGM 12843
2/29/60	**96**	2	15 Just Give Me A Ring	Atlantic 2049
4/04/60	**66**	6	16 Think Me A Kiss	MGM 12877
7/18/60	**23**	14	17 Ta Ta	Mercury 71660
7/24/61	**56**	5	18 I Never Knew	Mercury 71841
3/03/62	**7**	14	19 **Lover Please**	Mercury 71941
6/16/62	**25**	8	20 Little Bitty Pretty One	Mercury 71987
1/04/64	**90**	5	21 Deep In The Heart Of Harlem	Mercury 72220
			WYATT (EARP) McPHERSON	
5/15/61	**97**	2	1 Here's My Confession	Savoy 1599
			CARMEN McRAE	
			Born on 4/8/22 in New York City. Jazz singer.	
2/04/56	**75**	2	1 The Next Time It Happens from the Broadway musical "Pipe Dream"	Decca 29749
3/02/57	**92**	1	2 Skyliner Charlie Barnet's theme song	Decca 30004
			CHRISTINE McVIE	
			Born in Birmingham, England on 7/12/43. Vocalist with Fleetwood Mac since 1970.	
1/28/84	**10**	16	1 **Got A Hold On Me**	Warner 29372
4/28/84	**30**	10	2 Love Will Show Us How	Warner 29313
			SISTER JANET MEAD	
			Australian nun; born in 1938. Gained prominence through her weekly cathedral rock masses and weekly radio programs.	
2/23/74	**4**	13	1 ● **The Lord's Prayer**	A&M 1491
			MEAT LOAF	
			Born Marvin Lee Aday on 9/27/47 in Dallas. Played Eddie in the film "The Rocky Horror Picture Show".	
5/22/71	**71**	6	1 What You See Is What You Get **STONEY & MEATLOAF**	Rare Earth 5027
3/18/78	**11**	23	2 ● Two Out Of Three Ain't Bad	Epic 50513
8/12/78	**39**	10	3 Paradise By The Dashboard Light [N] female vocal: Ellen Foley; baseball announcer: Phil Rizzuto	Epic 50588
11/11/78+	**39**	13	4 You Took The Words Right Out Of My Mouth	Epic 50634
9/19/81	**84**	3	5 I'm Gonna Love Her For Both Of Us	Epic 02490
			MECO	
			Discofied instrumentals by producer Meco Monardo (b: 11/29/39 in Johnsonburg, PA).	
8/06/77	**1**[2]	20	1 ▲ **Star Wars Theme/Cantina Band** [I]	Millennium 604
1/07/78	**25**	10	2 Theme From Close Encounters [I]	Millennium 608

DEBUT DATE	PEAK POS	WKS CHR	ARTIST — Record Title		Label & Number
			MECO — Cont'd		
9/09/78	35	10	3 Themes From The Wizard Of Oz	[N]	Millennium 620
6/14/80	18	14	4 Empire Strikes Back Darth Vader/Yoda's Theme all of above inspired by films of the same titles	[I]	RSO 1038
10/11/80	70	4	5 Love Theme From Shogun (Mariko's Theme) from the TV mini-series "Shogun"	[I]	RSO 1052
12/13/80	69	6	6 What Can You Get A Wookiee For Christmas (When He Already Owns A Comb?) THE STAR WARS INTERGALACTIC DROID CHOIR & CHORALE	[N-X]	RSO 1058
2/13/82	35	11	7 Pop Goes The Movies, Part I 20th Century Fox Trademark/Tara's Theme/The Magnificent Seven/ The James Bond Theme/Goldfinger/The Good, The Bad And The Ugly/ Theme From The Apartment/Theme From The High & The Mighty	[I]	Arista 0660
7/02/83	60	8	8 Ewok Celebration inspired by the film "Return Of The Jedi" (rap by Duke Bootee)	[N]	Arista 9045
			BILL MEDLEY Born on 9/19/40 in Santa Ana, CA. Baritone of the Righteous Brothers duo.		
5/18/68	95	2	1 I Can't Make It Alone		MGM 13931
8/03/68	43	11	2 Brown Eyed Woman		MGM 13959
10/26/68	48	7	3 Peace Brother Peace		MGM 14000
3/28/81	88	4	4 Don't Know Much		Liberty 1402
10/02/82	58	8	5 Right Here And Now		Planet 13317
			JOE MEDLIN From Paterson, New Jersey. Sang with Buddy Johnson's band at age 19.		
3/09/59	85	4	1 I Kneel At Your Throne		Mercury 71415
			THE MEGATONS		
1/27/62	88	4	1 Shimmy, Shimmy Walk, Part 1	[I]	Checker 1005
			THE MEGATRONS Group of studio musicians led by John Summers.		
6/01/59	51	9	1 Velvet Waters clarinet solo: Heywood Henry	[I]	Acousticon 101
			RANDY MEISNER Born on 3/8/46 in Scottsbluff, NE. Member of Poco (1968) and the Eagles (1972-76).		
10/18/80	22	16	1 Deep Inside My Heart background vocals: Kim Carnes		Epic 50939
1/24/81	19	15	2 Hearts On Fire		Epic 50964
7/31/82	28	11	3 Never Been In Love		Epic 03032
			MEL & TIM Cousins Mel Hardin and Tim McPherson, from Holly Springs, MS.		
10/18/69	10	14	1 ● **Backfield In Motion**		Bamboo 107
2/07/70	45	7	2 Good Guys Only Win In The Movies		Bamboo 109
7/08/72	19	20	3 Starting All Over Again		Stax 0127
			MELANIE Born Melanie Safka on 2/3/47 in Queens, NY. Neighborhood Records formed by Melanie and her husband/producer Peter Schekeryk.		
4/25/70	6	17	1 **Lay Down (Candles In The Rain)** MELANIE with THE EDWIN HAWKINS' SINGERS		Buddah 167
8/22/70	32	7	2 Peace Will Come (According To Plan)		Buddah 186
12/05/70+	52	7	3 Ruby Tuesday		Buddah 202
10/30/71	1[3]	18	4 ● **Brand New Key**		Neighborhood 4201
1/22/72	35	10	5 The Nickel Song		Buddah 268
1/29/72	31	9	6 Ring The Living Bell		Neighborhood 4202
10/21/72	86	4	7 Together Alone		Neighborhood 4207
2/17/73	36	10	8 Bitter Bad		Neighborhood 4210
12/15/73	82	4	9 Will You Love Me Tomorrow?		Neighborhood 4213

DEBUT DATE	PEAK POS	WKS CHR	ARTIST — Record Title	Label & Number
			JOHN COUGAR MELLENCAMP	
			Born on 10/7/51 in Seymour, Indiana. Rock singer, songwriter, producer. Worked outside of music until 1975. First recorded for MCA in 1976.	
			JOHN COUGAR:	
10/13/79	**28**	14	1 I Need A Lover	Riva 202
2/16/80	**87**	3	2 Small Paradise	Riva 203
9/27/80	**27**	17	3 This Time	Riva 205
1/31/81	**17**	21	4 Ain't Even Done With The Night	Riva 207
4/24/82	**2**[4]	28	5 ● **Hurts So Good**	Riva 209
7/24/82	**1**[4]	22	6 ● **Jack & Diane**	Riva 210
11/06/82+	**19**	18	7 Hand To Hold On To	Riva 211
			JOHN COUGAR MELLENCAMP:	
10/15/83	**9**	16	8 **Crumblin' Down**	Riva 214
12/10/83+	**8**	16	9 **Pink Houses**	Riva 215
3/17/84	**15**	15	10 Authority Song	Riva 216
8/24/85	**6**	20	11 **Lonely Ol' Night**	Riva 880984
11/02/85	**6**	18	12 **Small Town**	Riva 884202
2/01/86	**2**[1]	17	13 **R.O.C.K. In The U.S.A.**	Riva 884455
			a salute to 60's rock	
4/26/86	**21**	12	14 Rain On The Scarecrow	Riva 884635
6/28/86	**28**	13	15 Rumbleseat	Riva 884856
			5-15: produced by Mellencamp and Don Gehman	
			MELLO-KINGS	
			White vocal group from Mount Vernon, NY. Robert Scholl (d: 8/27/75), lead; Jerry Scholl, Eddie Quinn, tenors; Neil Arena, baritone; and Larry Esposito, bass.	
8/19/57	**77**	10	1 Tonite, Tonite	Herald 502
1/23/61	**95**	1	2 Tonite, Tonite [R]	Herald 502
			THE MELLO-TONES	
5/13/57	**24**	7	1 Rosie Lee	Gee 1037
			Best Seller #24 / Top 100 #60	
			THE MELODEERS	
12/19/60	**71**	2	1 Rudolph The Red Nosed Reindeer [X]	Studio 9908
			doo-wop version of the Johnny Marks classic Christmas tune	
			HAROLD MELVIN & THE BLUE NOTES	
			Soul group from Philadelphia formed by Melvin in 1956. Teddy Pendergrass replaced lead singer John Atkins in 1970. Pendergrass left in 1976, replaced by David Ebo.	
10/03/60	**78**	4	1 My Hero	Val-ue 213
			THE BLUE NOTES	
7/01/72	**58**	9	2 I Miss You (Part I)	Phil. Int. 3516
9/30/72	**3**	17	3 ● **If You Don't Know Me By Now**	Phil. Int. 3520
3/03/73	**63**	7	4 Yesterday I Had The Blues	Phil. Int. 3525
9/29/73	**7**	18	5 ● **The Love I Lost (Part 1)**	Phil. Int. 3533
4/06/74	**58**	10	6 Satisfaction Guaranteed (Or Take Your Love Back)	Phil. Int. 3543
11/09/74	**80**	6	7 Where Are All My Friends	Phil. Int. 3552
3/22/75	**15**	17	8 Bad Luck (Part 1)	Phil. Int. 3562
7/05/75	**42**	10	9 Hope That We Can Be Together Soon	Phil. Int. 3569
			SHARON PAIGE and HAROLD MELVIN & THE BLUE NOTES	
11/22/75+	**12**	17	10 Wake Up Everybody (Part 1)	Phil. Int. 3579
4/17/76	**94**	2	11 Tell The World How I Feel About 'Cha Baby	Phil. Int. 3588
			all of above produced by Kenny Gamble & Leon Huff	
2/12/77	**74**	4	12 Reaching For The World	ABC 12240
			MEN AT WORK	
			Melbourne, Australia rock quintet formed in 1979. Colin Hay (lead singer, guitar), Ron Strykert (lead guitar), Greg Ham (sax, keyboards), Jerry Speiser (drums) and John Rees (bass). Speiser and Rees left in 1984.	
7/10/82	**1**[1]	27	1 **Who Can It Be Now?**	Columbia 02888
11/06/82+	**1**[4]	25	2 ● **Down Under**	Columbia 03303
4/09/83	**3**	16	3 **Overkill**	Columbia 03795
7/02/83	**6**	15	4 **It's A Mistake**	Columbia 03959
9/17/83	**28**	11	5 Dr. Heckyll & Mr. Jive	Columbia 04111
5/25/85	**47**	9	6 Everything I Need	Columbia 04929
			all of above written by Colin Hay	

DEBUT DATE	PEAK POS	WKS CHR	ARTIST — Record Title	Label & Number
			MEN WITHOUT HATS	
			Techno-rock trio from Montreal, Canada. Ivan Doroschuk, singer, songwriter.	
6/25/83	**3**	24	1 **The Safety Dance**	Backstreet 52232
11/12/83	**84**	3	2 I Like	MCA 52293
			SERGIO MENDES	
			Born on 2/11/41 in Niteroi, Brazil. Pianist, bandleader. Resident in U.S. since mid-60s. Originator of the "bossa nova" style.	
4/16/83	**4**	23	1 **Never Gonna Let You Go**	A&M 2540
			vocals: Joe Pizzulo & Leza Miller	
8/13/83	**52**	8	2 Rainbow's End	A&M 2563
			vocal: Dan Sembello	
4/07/84	**58**	7	3 Olympia	A&M 2623
5/26/84	**29**	19	4 Alibis	A&M 2639
			vocal by Joe Pizzulo on above 2	
			SERGIO MENDES & BRASIL '66	
			Latin stylists originating from Brazil and led by pianist Mendes.	
9/24/66	**47**	8	1 Mas Que Nada [F]	A&M 807
12/24/66+	**71**	6	2 Constant Rain	A&M 825
4/01/67	**98**	2	3 For Me	A&M 836
6/03/67	**82**	5	4 Night And Day	A&M 853
			there's been 7 Top 25 hits since 1932 of the Cole Porter classic	
5/11/68	**4**	14	5 **The Look Of Love**	A&M 924
			from the film "Casino Royale"	
8/10/68	**6**	12	6 **The Fool On The Hill**	A&M 961
			written by John Lennon & Paul McCartney	
11/16/68	**16**	9	7 Scarborough Fair	A&M 986
			written by Paul Simon & Art Garfunkel	
5/03/69	**62**	6	8 Pretty World	A&M 1049
6/28/69	**66**	5	9 (Sittin' On) The Dock Of The Bay	A&M 1073
11/29/69	**95**	2	10 Wichita Lineman	A&M 1132
			all of above produced by Herb Alpert (except #5, 7, 10)	
			MENUDO	
			Puerto Rican teen quintet. The superstar group of Latin America.	
5/11/85	**62**	11	1 Hold Me	RCA 14087
			FREDDIE MERCURY	
			Born Frederick Bulsara on 9/5/46 in Zanzibar. Lead singer of Queen.	
9/29/84	**69**	6	1 Love Kills	Columbia 04606
			from the film "Metropolis"	
4/27/85	**76**	4	2 I Was Born To Love You	Columbia 04869
			MERCY	
			Florida group led by Jack Sigler, Jr.	
4/12/69	**2**[2]	13	1 ● **Love (Can Make You Happy)**	Sundi 6811
6/28/69	**79**	5	2 Forever	Warner 7297
			THE MERRY-GO-ROUND	
			Emitt Rhodes, lead singer, songwriter of Los Angeles-area pop quartet.	
4/29/67	**63**	4	1 Live	A&M 834
9/09/67	**94**	3	2 You're A Very Lovely Woman	A&M 863
			MESA	
			Los Angeles-based pop quartet.	
2/26/77	**55**	9	1 Sailing Ships	Ariola Am. 7654
			MESSENGERS	
			Rock band from Milwaukee led by Michael Morgan.	
9/11/71	**62**	9	1 That's The Way A Woman Is	Rare Earth 5032
			JIM MESSINA - see LOGGINS & MESSINA	
			THE METERS	
			R&B instrumental group formed in New Orleans in 1966 featuring keyboardist Arthur Neville (brother of Aaron Neville). Group disbanded in 1977, when Art, Aaron, and brothers Charles and Cyril formed The Neville Brothers.	
2/08/69	**34**	8	1 Sophisticated Cissy [I]	Josie 1001
4/12/69	**23**	11	2 Cissy Strut [I]	Josie 1005
7/26/69	**61**	6	3 Ease Back [I]	Josie 1008
12/06/69+	**56**	10	4 Look-Ka Py Py [I]	Josie 1015
4/04/70	**50**	8	5 Chicken Strut [I]	Josie 1018

DEBUT DATE	PEAK POS	WKS CHR	ARTIST — Record Title	Label & Number
			THE METERS — Cont'd	
7/04/70	**89**	4	6 Hand Clapping Song	Josie 1021
			all of above produced by Marshall Sehorn & Allen Toussaint	
10/01/77	**78**	2	7 Be My Lady	Warner 8434
			PAT METHENY GROUP - see DAVID BOWIE	
			THE METROS	
1/14/67	**88**	4	1 Sweetest One	RCA 8994
			MFSB	
			Large racially-mixed studio band formed by producers Kenny Gamble and Leon Huff. Name means "Mothers, Fathers, Sisters, Brothers". Also see The Music Makers.	
			MFSB featuring THE THREE DEGREES:	
3/02/74	**1**[2]	18	1 ● **TSOP (The Sound Of Philadelphia)** .... [I]	Phil. Int. 3540
			theme from the TV show "Soul Train"	
7/06/74	**85**	4	2 Love Is The Message	Phil. Int. 3547
			MFSB:	
6/21/75	**42**	7	3 Sexy .... [I]	Phil. Int. 3567
11/29/75	**91**	6	4 The Zip .... [I]	Phil. Int. 3578
			MIAMI SOUND MACHINE	
			Miami group - Gloria M. Estefan, lead singer.	
10/19/85+	**10**	27	1 **Conga**	Epic 05457
3/08/86	**8**	19	2 **Bad Boy**	Epic 05805
6/14/86	**5**	24	3 **Words Get In The Way**	Epic 06120
11/01/86+	**25**	16	4 Falling In Love (Uh-Oh)	Epic 06352
			GEORGE MICHAEL	
			From Bushey, England - lead singer of Wham!	
4/26/86	**7**	16	1 **A Different Corner**	Columbia 05888
			LEE MICHAELS	
			Born on 11/24/45 in Los Angeles. Rock organist/vocalist.	
7/31/71	**6**	17	1 **Do You Know What I Mean**	A&M 1262
11/20/71	**39**	9	2 Can I Get A Witness	A&M 1303
			MICKEY & SYLVIA	
			McHouston "Mickey" Baker and Sylvia Vanderpool. Mickey (b: 10/15/25, Louisville) was a prolific session man on guitar for Atlantic, Savoy, King, Aladdin, and many others. Sylvia (b: 3/6/36, New York City) first recorded as "Little Sylvia" with Hot Lips Page for Columbia in 1950. Also see Sylvia.	
1/05/57	**11**	18	1 Love Is Strange	Groove 0175
			Best Seller #11 / Jockey #11 / Top 100 #13 / Juke Box #17	
4/20/57	**47**	5	2 There Oughta Be A Law/	
7/01/57	**85**	2	3 Dearest	Vik 0267
6/16/58	**57**	5	4 Bewildered	Vik 0324
12/31/60+	**46**	9	5 What Would I Do/	
12/31/60	**100**	1	6 This Is My Story	RCA 7811
8/21/61	**52**	6	7 Baby You're So Fine/	
8/07/61	**97**	1	8 Lovedrops	Willow 23000
			BETTE MIDLER	
			Born on 12/1/45 in Paterson, NJ. Vocalist, actress. Raised in Hawaii. In Broadway show "Fiddler On The Roof" for three years. Nominated for an Oscar in "The Rose". Recently starred in "Down & Out In Beverly Hills", "Ruthless People" and "Outrageous Fortune".	
12/23/72+	**17**	16	1 Do You Want To Dance?	Atlantic 2928
5/12/73	**8**	16	2 **Boogie Woogie Bugle Boy**	Atlantic 2964
			revival of The Andrews Sisters Top 10 hit of 1941	
9/29/73	**40**	10	3 Friends/	
		2	4 Chapel Of Love	Atlantic 2980
1/26/74	**51**	7	5 In The Mood	Atlantic 3004
			revival of Glenn Miller's classic #1 hit from 1940	
4/09/77	**42**	14	6 You're Movin' Out Today	Atlantic 3379
1/14/78	**57**	10	7 Storybook Children (Daybreak)	Atlantic 3431
6/02/79	**40**	9	8 Married Men	Atlantic 3582
1/19/80	**35**	10	9 When A Man Loves A Woman	Atlantic 3643
3/22/80	**3**	25	10 ● **The Rose**	Atlantic 3656
			above 2 from the film "The Rose"	
11/22/80+	**39**	13	11 My Mother's Eyes	Atlantic 3771
			from the film "Divine Madness"	

DEBUT DATE	PEAK POS	WKS CHR	ARTIST — Record Title	Label & Number
			BETTE MIDLER — Cont'd	
9/03/83	**77**	4	12 All I Need To Know	Atlantic 89789
10/22/83	**78**	4	13 Favorite Waste Of Time	Atlantic 89761
2/11/84	**71**	6	14 Beast Of Burden written by Mick Jagger & Keith Richards	Atlantic 89712
			MIDNIGHT STAR 8-man, 1-woman R&B/funk group formed at Kentucky State University.	
8/20/83	**66**	8	1 Freak-A-Zoid	Solar 69828
11/26/83+	**61**	11	2 Wet My Whistle	Solar 69790
3/03/84	**81**	8	3 No Parking (On The Dance Floor)	Solar 69753
12/01/84+	**18**	17	4 Operator	Solar 69684
3/02/85	**80**	7	5 Scientific Love	Solar 69659
6/14/86	**69**	7	6 Headlines	Solar 69547
9/20/86	**42**	14	7 Midas Touch all of above produced by band member Reggie Calloway	Solar 69525
			MIGHTY CLOUDS OF JOY Gospel group formed in Los Angeles in 1960. Nucleus consisted of Willie Joe Ligon and Johnny Martin, leads; Elmo Franklin and Richard Wallace.	
2/21/76	**69**	10	1 Mighty High	ABC 12164
			MIKE + THE MECHANICS Rock quintet consisting of Mike Rutherford (Genesis), Paul Carrack (Ace), Paul Young, Peter Van Hooke and Adrian Lee.	
11/23/85+	**6**	24	1 **Silent Running (On Dangerous Ground)** title track from the movie "On Dangerous Ground"	Atlantic 89488
3/22/86	**5**	19	2 **All I Need Is A Miracle**	Atlantic 89450
6/28/86	**32**	15	3 Taken In	Atlantic 89404
			BUDDY MILES Born George Miles on 9/5/46 in Omaha. R&B vocalist, drummer. Prominent session musician. Worked as sideman in the Dick Clark Revue, 1963-64. With Wilson Pickett, 1965-66. In Michael Bloomfield's Electric Flag, 1967. In Jimi Hendrix's Band Of Gypsys, 1969-70.	
8/23/69	**100**	1	1 Memphis Train **BUDDY MILES EXPRESS**	Mercury 72945
5/02/70	**81**	6	2 Them Changes **BUDDY MILES & THE FREEDOM EXPRESS**	Mercury 73008
7/18/70	**68**	7	3 Down By The River	Mercury 73086
10/10/70	**86**	3	4 Dreams	Mercury 73119
12/12/70+	**86**	6	5 We Got To Live Together - Part I	Mercury 73159
5/15/71	**71**	6	6 Wholesale Love	Mercury 73205
7/17/71	**62**	11	7 Them Changes [R]	Mercury 73228
9/09/72	**84**	5	8 Evil Ways/	
		1	9 Them Changes new version of 1970-71 hit above 2: **CARLOS SANTANA & BUDDY MILES**	Columbia 45666
9/20/75	**91**	3	10 Rockin' And Rollin' On The Streets Of Hollywood	Casablanca 839
			GARRY MILES Real name: James (Buzz) Cason; lead singer of The Statues. Also see Garry Mills who is a different artist with another version of the same song.	
6/20/60	**16**	13	1 Look For A Star from the film "Circus Of Horrors"	Liberty 55261
			JOHN MILES Born in Jarrow, England on 4/23/49. Rock vocalist, guitarist, keyboardist.	
2/14/76	**68**	10	1 Highfly	London 20084
5/15/76	**88**	3	2 Music above 2 produced by Alan Parsons	London 20086
3/26/77	**34**	14	3 Slowdown	London 20092
			LENNY MILES Born on 12/22/34 in Fort Worth, Texas.	
12/31/60+	**41**	7	1 Don't Believe Him, Donna	Scepter 1212
5/08/61	**84**	2	2 In Between Tears	Scepter 1218
			CHUCK MILLER	
6/18/55	**9**	14	1 **The House Of Blue Lights** Best Seller #9 / Jockey #18 / Juke Box #19	Mercury 70627
12/22/56	**59**	9	2 The Auctioneer [N]	Mercury 71001

DEBUT DATE	PEAK POS	WKS CHR	ARTIST — Record Title		Label & Number
			CLINT MILLER		
1/27/58	**79**	7	1 Bertha Lou		ABC-Para. 9878
			FRANKIE MILLER		
			Blues-tinged rock singer; born in Glasgow, Scotland.		
6/25/77	**71**	5	1 The Doodle Song		Chrysalis 2145
6/19/82	**62**	6	2 To Dream The Dream		Capitol 5131
			FRANKIE MILLER		
			Born on 12/17/32 in Victoria, Texas. Country singer, songwriter.		
7/10/61	**82**	4	1 Black Land Farmer		Starday 424
			JODY MILLER		
			Pop/country singer; born in Phoenix on 11/29/41.		
2/08/64	**66**	6	1 He Walks Like A Man		Capitol 5090
4/24/65	**12**	9	2 Queen Of The House		Capitol 5402
			answer song to Roger Miller's "King Of The Road"		
6/26/65	**54**	6	3 Silver Threads And Golden Needles		Capitol 5429
8/28/65	**25**	9	4 Home Of The Brave		Capitol 5483
6/26/71	**53**	9	5 He's So Fine		Epic 10734
10/09/71	**91**	4	6 Baby, I'm Yours		Epic 10785
			MITCH MILLER		
			Born on 7/4/11 in Rochester, NY. Producer/conductor/arranger. Oboe soloist with CBS Symphony, 1936-47. A&R executive for both Columbia and Mercury Records. Best known for his sing-along albums and TV show.		
8/06/55	**1**[6]	19	1 **The Yellow Rose Of Texas**		Columbia 40540
			Best Seller #1(6) / Jockey #1(6) / Juke Box #1(6)		
			adaptation of a Civil War campfire song		
11/12/55	**41**	14	2 Autumn Leaves		Columbia 50033
11/12/55	**51**	4	3 The Bonnie Blue Gal		Columbia 40575
2/04/56	**19**	13	4 Lisbon Antigua	[I]	Columbia 40635
			Jockey #19 / Top 100 #30		
3/10/56	**50**	7	5 Madeira	[I]	Columbia 40655
7/21/56	**88**	2	6 The President On The Dollar		Columbia 40715
8/04/56	**8**	17	7 **Theme Song from "Song For A Summer Night"**	[I]	Columbia 40730
			Jockey #8 / Best Seller #9 / Top 100 #10 / Juke Box #10		
			theme from the Westinghouse TV production of the same title		
12/01/56	**94**	1	8 Song Of The Sparrow	[I]	Columbia 40772
			from the Westinghouse TV production "A Man's World"		
3/02/57	**94**	1	9 A Very Special Love	[I]	Columbia 40831
			from the "Playhouse 90" TV production "The Ninth Day"		
1/13/58	**20**	29	10 March From The River Kwai and Colonel Bogey	[I]	Columbia 41066
			Jockey #20 / Best Seller #21 / Top 100 #21		
			from the film "The Bridge On The River Kwai"		
10/13/58	**94**	1	11 Bluebell		Columbia 41235
1/12/59	**16**	14	12 The Children's Marching Song	[N]	Columbia 41317
			from the film "The Inn of The Sixth Happiness"		
12/14/59	**70**	4	13 Do-Re-Mi	[N]	Columbia 41499
			from Broadway's "The Sound Of Music"		
2/27/61	**88**	2	14 Tunes Of Glory	[I]	Columbia 41941
			from the film of the same title		
			MRS. MILLER		
			Mrs. Elva Miller. Tone-deaf singer from Claremont, California.		
4/30/66	**82**	4	1 Downtown/	[N]	
5/07/66	**95**	2	2 A Lover's Concerto	[N]	Capitol 5640
			NED MILLER		
			Born on 4/12/25 in Rains, Utah. Country singer, songwriter.		
12/29/62+	**6**	13	1 **From A Jack To A King**		Fabor 114
12/26/64+	**52**	9	2 Do What You Do Do Well		Fabor 137
			ROGER MILLER		
			Born on 1/2/36 in Fort Worth, TX. Country vocalist, humorist, guitarist, composer. Raised in Erick, OK. To Nashville, mid-50s, began songwriting career. With Faron Young as writer and drummer in 1962. Won six Grammies in 1965. Own TV show in 1966. Songwriter of Broadway musical "Big River" (won Tony Award for Best Musical, 1985).		
6/13/64	**7**	11	1 **Dang Me**	[N]	Smash 1881
9/05/64	**9**	13	2 **Chug-A-Lug**	[N]	Smash 1926
11/28/64+	**31**	8	3 Do-Wacka-Do	[N]	Smash 1947
1/30/65	**4**	13	4 ● **King Of The Road**		Smash 1965

DEBUT DATE	PEAK POS	WKS CHR	ARTIST — Record Title	Label & Number
			ROGER MILLER — Cont'd	
5/08/65	**7**	9	5 **Engine Engine #9**	Smash 1983
7/10/65	**34**	7	6 One Dyin' And A Buryin'	Smash 1994
9/11/65	**31**	7	7 Kansas City Star [N]	Smash 1998
11/06/65	**8**	11	8 **England Swings**	Smash 2010
2/19/66	**26**	7	9 Husbands And Wives	Smash 2024
6/25/66	**40**	6	10 You Can't Roller Skate In A Buffalo Herd [N]	Smash 2043
9/17/66	**58**	5	11 My Uncle Used To Love Me But She Died [N]	Smash 2055
11/05/66	**84**	4	12 Heartbreak Hotel	Smash 2066
3/25/67	**37**	7	13 Walkin' In The Sunshine all of above written by Miller (except #12)	Smash 2081
3/02/68	**39**	9	14 Little Green Apples	Smash 2148
12/07/68	**80**	6	15 Vance all of above produced by Jerry Kennedy	Smash 2197
			STEVE MILLER BAND Steve was born on 10/5/43 in Milwaukee. Raised in Dallas. Blues-rock singer, songwriter, guitarist. While at the University of Wisconsin-Madison, Steve led the blues-rock band, the Ardells, later known as the Fabulous Night Trains, featuring Boz Scaggs. To San Francisco in 1966, formed Steve Miller Band, which featured an ever changing personnel.	
11/23/68	**94**	2	1 Living In The U.S.A.	Capitol 2287
8/15/70	**69**	6	2 Going To The Country	Capitol 2878
10/20/73+	**1^{1}**	20	3 ● **The Joker**	Capitol 3732
3/02/74	**51**	7	4 Your Cash Ain't Nothin' But Trash	Capitol 3837
5/18/74	**49**	7	5 Living In The U.S.A. [R]	Capitol 3884
5/08/76	**11**	16	6 Take The Money And Run	Capitol 4260
8/14/76	**1^{1}**	18	7 **Rock'n Me**	Capitol 4323
12/18/76+	**2^{2}**	20	8 ● **Fly Like An Eagle** above 3: STEVE MILLER	Capitol 4372
4/30/77	**8**	18	9 **Jet Airliner**	Capitol 4424
8/06/77	**23**	14	10 Jungle Love	Capitol 4466
10/15/77	**17**	15	11 Swingtown	Capitol 4496
10/31/81	**24**	14	12 Heart Like A Wheel	Capitol 5068
1/23/82	**55**	7	13 Circle Of Love	Capitol 5086
5/29/82	**1^{2}**	25	14 ● **Abracadabra**	Capitol 5126
10/16/82	**57**	8	15 Cool Magic	Capitol 5162
12/11/82+	**60**	9	16 Give It Up	Capitol 5194
10/06/84	**57**	6	17 Shangri-La	Capitol 5407
2/16/85	**84**	3	18 Bongo Bongo	Capitol 5442
11/15/86	**97**	3	19 I Want To Make The World Turn Around all of above produced by Miller	Capitol 5646
			MILLS BROTHERS Smooth vocal group from Piqua, Ohio. Consisted of John Jr. (b: 1911, d: 1936), Herbert (b: 1912), Harry (b: 1913, d: 6/28/82) and Donald (b: 1915). Originally featured unusual vocal style of imitating instruments. Achieved national fame via radio broadcasts and appearances in films. Father, John Sr., joined group in 1936, replacing John Jr., remained in group until 1956 (d: 12/8/67). Group continued as trio until 1982. Presently, Donald is singing with his son, John III.	
11/12/55	**45**	9	1 Suddenly There's A Valley	Decca 29686
1/28/56	**63**	2	2 All The Way 'Round The World	Decca 29781
5/26/56	**57**	10	3 Standing On The Corner from the Broadway musical "The Most Happy Fella"	Decca 29897
5/27/57	**39**	8	4 Queen Of The Senior Prom	Decca 30299
3/03/58	**21**	2	5 Get A Job Jockey #21	Dot 15695
1/05/59	**70**	5	6 Yellow Bird	Dot 15858
1/27/68	**23**	15	7 Cab Driver	Dot 17041
5/18/68	**73**	7	8 My Shy Violet	Dot 17096
11/23/68	**83**	2	9 The Ol' Race Track	Dot 17162
			FRANK MILLS Pianist, composer, producer, arranger.	
1/29/72	**46**	9	1 Love Me, Love Me Love	Sunflower 118
1/27/79	**3**	20	2 ● **Music Box Dancer** [I]	Polydor 14517
11/03/79	**48**	9	3 Peter Piper [I]	Polydor 2002

DEBUT DATE	PEAK POS	WKS CHR	ARTIST — Record Title	Label & Number
			GARRY MILLS	
			Also see Garry Miles.	
6/20/60	**26**	11	1 Look For A Star - Part I	Imperial 5674
			from the film "Circus Of Horrors"	
			HAYLEY MILLS	
			Born on 4/18/46 in London. Daughter of English actor, John Mills. Disney teen film star.	
9/04/61	**8**	14	1 **Let's Get Together**	Vista 385
			from the film "The Parent Trap"	
3/17/62	**21**	11	2 Johnny Jingo	Vista 395
			STEPHANIE MILLS	
			Born in 1957 in Brooklyn. At age 15, she won starring role of Dorothy in the hit Broadway show "The Wiz". Played role for 5 years. Briefly married to Jeffrey Daniel of Shalamar in 1980.	
7/21/79	**22**	14	1 What Cha Gonna Do With My Lovin'	20th Century 2403
6/14/80	**52**	6	2 Sweet Sensation	20th Century 2449
8/09/80	**6**	25	3● **Never Knew Love Like This Before**	20th Century 2460
5/16/81	**40**	13	4 Two Hearts	20th Century 2492
			STEPHANIE MILLS featuring TEDDY PENDERGRASS	
10/13/84	**65**	6	5 The Medicine Song	Casablanca 880180
7/06/85	**78**	6	6 Bit By Bit	MCA 52617
			theme from the film "Fletch"	
			RONNIE MILSAP	
			Born on 1/16/46 in Robbinsville, NC. Country singer, pianist, guitarist. Blind since birth, multi-instrumentalist by age 12. With J.J. Cale band, own band from 1965. Country Music Association Male Vocalist of the Year, 1974, 1976, 1977.	
9/12/70	**87**	3	1 Loving You Is A Natural Thing	Chips 2889
9/14/74	**95**	2	2 Please Don't Tell Me How The Story Ends	RCA 0313
6/18/77	**16**	22	3 It Was Almost Like A Song	RCA 10976
12/24/77+	**80**	5	4 What A Difference You've Made In My Life	RCA 11146
7/01/78	**63**	6	5 Only One Love In My Life	RCA 11270
10/06/79	**43**	11	6 Get It Up	RCA 11695
11/29/80+	**24**	21	7 Smoky Mountain Rain	RCA 12084
6/27/81	**5**	20	8 **(There's) No Gettin' Over Me**	RCA 12264
10/24/81+	**20**	17	9 I Wouldn't Have Missed It For The World	RCA 12342
5/01/82	**14**	16	10 Any Day Now	RCA 13216
8/21/82	**59**	7	11 He Got You	RCA 13286
3/26/83	**23**	16	12 Stranger In My House	RCA 13470
8/13/83	**58**	7	13 Don't You Know How Much I Love You	RCA 13564
8/04/84	**84**	4	14 She Loves My Car	RCA 13847
			GARNET MIMMS	
			Born Garrett Mimms on 11/16/33 in Ashland, WV. Sang in gospel groups the Evening Stars, Norfolk Four, Harmonizing Four. Formed group the Gainors in 1958. The Enchanters (Zola Pearnell, Sam Bell, Charles Boyer) were formed in 1961.	
			GARNET MIMMS & THE ENCHANTERS:	
8/17/63	**4**	14	1 **Cry Baby**	United Art. 629
11/23/63+	**26**	9	2 For Your Precious Love/	
11/16/63	**30**	9	3 Baby Don't You Weep	United Art. 658
			GARNET MIMMS:	
2/15/64	**69**	7	4 Tell Me Baby	United Art. 694
5/16/64	**67**	4	5 One Girl/	
7/18/64	**78**	7	6 A Quiet Place	United Art. 715
			GARNET MIMMS & THE ENCHANTERS	
10/17/64	**73**	5	7 Look Away	United Art. 773
1/02/65	**95**	1	8 A Little Bit Of Soap	United Art. 796
3/26/66	**30**	9	9 I'll Take Good Care Of You	United Art. 995
			all of above produced by Jerry Ragovoy	
			MINA	
5/08/61	**90**	1	1 This World We Love In [F]	Time 1030

DEBUT DATE	PEAK POS	WKS CHR	ARTIST — Record Title	Label & Number
			THE MINDBENDERS	
			Rock group from Manchester, England: Wayne Fontana (born Glyn Geoffrey Ellis on 10/28/45), lead singer; Eric Stewart, lead guitar, vocals; Bob Lang, bass; and Ric Rothwell, drums. Fontana left in 1966. Graham Gouldman joined in 1968. Also see Hotlegs and 10cc.	
			WAYNE FONTANA & THE MINDBENDERS:	
3/20/65	**1^{1}**	11	1 **Game Of Love**	Fontana 1509
6/12/65	**45**	8	2 It's Just A Little Bit Too Late	Fontana 1514
			THE MINDBENDERS:	
4/16/66	**2^{2}**	13	3 **A Groovy Kind Of Love**	Fontana 1541
8/13/66	**55**	6	4 Ashes To Ashes	Fontana 1555
			SAL MINEO	
			Broadway/Hollywood actor. Born on 1/10/39; stabbed to death on 2/12/76.	
5/20/57	**9**	19	1 **Start Movin' (In My Direction)/**	
			Best Seller #9 / Top 100 #10 / Jockey #16 / Juke Box #18 end	
		5	2 Love Affair	Epic 9216
			Best Seller flip	
9/09/57	**27**	10	3 Lasting Love/	
			Best Seller #27 / Top 100 #35	
		1	4 You Shouldn't Do That	Epic 9227
			Best Seller flip	
11/11/57	**45**	7	5 Party Time	Epic 9246
			Best Seller #45 / Top 100 #47	
1/27/58	**45**	8	6 Little Pigeon	Epic 9260
			Best Seller #45 / Top 100 #47	
			THE MINIATURE MEN	
6/09/62	**87**	4	1 Baby Elephant Walk [I]	Dolton 57
			from the film "Hatari"	
			MINK DeVILLE	
			San Francisco rock band led by Willy DeVille.	
2/11/84	**89**	4	1 Each Word's A Beat Of My Heart	Atlantic 89750
			MINOR DETAIL	
			Irish duo: brothers John & Willie Hughes.	
9/24/83	**92**	2	1 Canvas Of Life	Polydor 815329
			THE MIRACLES	
			R&B group formed at Northern High School in Detroit in 1955. Consisted of William "Smokey" Robinson (lead), Emerson and Bobby Rogers (tenors), Ronnie White (baritone) and Warren "Pete" Moore (bass). Emerson Rogers left in 1956 for US Army, replaced by Claudette Rogers Robinson, Smokey's wife. First recorded for End in 1958. Claudette retired in 1964. Smokey wrote many hit songs for his group and other Motown artists. Smokey went solo in 1972, replaced by William Griffin.	
10/05/59	**93**	2	1 Bad Girl	Chess 1734
12/12/60+	**2^{1}**	16	2 **Shop Around**	Tamla 54034
3/27/61	**49**	6	3 Ain't It, Baby	Tamla 54036
7/10/61	**51**	6	4 Mighty Good Lovin'/	
7/03/61	**97**	1	5 Broken Hearted	Tamla 54044
10/23/61	**52**	8	6 Everybody's Gotta Pay Some Dues	Tamla 54048
1/13/62	**35**	10	7 What's So Good About Good-By	Tamla 54053
5/12/62	**39**	10	8 I'll Try Something New	Tamla 54059
9/15/62	**94**	3	9 Way Over There	Tamla 54069
12/08/62+	**8**	16	10 **You've Really Got A Hold On Me**	Tamla 54073
3/30/63	**31**	9	11 A Love She Can Count On	Tamla 54078
8/17/63	**8**	12	12 **Mickey's Monkey**	Tamla 54083
11/23/63+	**35**	10	13 I Gotta Dance To Keep From Crying	Tamla 54089
3/07/64	**59**	5	14 (You Can't Let The Boy Overpower) The Man In You	Tamla 54092
6/27/64	**27**	9	15 I Like It Like That	Tamla 54098
9/19/64	**35**	6	16 That's What Love Is Made Of	Tamla 54102
12/12/64+	**50**	8	17 Come On Do The Jerk	Tamla 54109
3/27/65	**16**	11	18 Ooo Baby Baby	Tamla 54113
7/17/65	**16**	12	19 The Tracks Of My Tears	Tamla 54118
10/09/65	**14**	10	20 My Girl Has Gone	Tamla 54123
12/25/65+	**11**	12	21 Going To A Go-Go	Tamla 54127
6/18/66	**46**	8	22 Whole Lot Of Shakin' In My Heart (Since I Met You)	Tamla 54134
11/05/66	**17**	9	23 (Come 'Round Here) I'm The One You Need	Tamla 54140

DEBUT DATE	PEAK POS	WKS CHR	ARTIST — Record Title	Label & Number
			THE MIRACLES — Cont'd	
			SMOKEY ROBINSON & THE MIRACLES:	
2/18/67	**20**	10	24 The Love I Saw In You Was Just A Mirage	Tamla 54145
6/17/67	**23**	11	25 More Love	Tamla 54152
11/04/67	**4**	15	26 **I Second That Emotion**	Tamla 54159
2/24/68	**11**	12	27 If You Can Want	Tamla 54162
6/01/68	**31**	8	28 Yester Love	Tamla 54167
8/17/68	**26**	9	29 Special Occasion	Tamla 54172
1/04/69	**8**	14	30 **Baby, Baby Don't Cry**	Tamla 54178
6/21/69	**32**	8	31 Doggone Right/	
8/23/69	**37**	9	32 Here I Go Again	Tamla 54183
7/05/69	**33**	6	33 Abraham, Martin And John	Tamla 54184
12/13/69+	**37**	8	34 Point It Out/	
5/02/70	**100**	1	35 Darling Dear	Tamla 54189
5/23/70	**46**	7	36 Who's Gonna Take The Blame	Tamla 54194
10/17/70	**1[2]**	16	37 **The Tears Of A Clown**	Tamla 54199
3/20/71	**18**	12	38 I Don't Blame You At All	Tamla 54205
7/03/71	**56**	7	39 Crazy About The La La La	Tamla 54206
11/20/71+	**49**	9	40 Satisfaction	Tamla 54211
6/24/72	**46**	10	41 We've Come Too Far To End It Now	Tamla 54220
12/16/72+	**45**	8	42 I Can't Stand To See You Cry	Tamla 54225
			THE MIRACLES:	
8/04/73	**56**	8	43 Don't Let It End ('Til You Let It Begin)	Tamla 54237
8/24/74	**13**	15	44 Do It Baby	Tamla 54248
12/21/74+	**78**	4	45 Don't Cha Love It	Tamla 54256
10/25/75+	**1[1]**	28	46 **Love Machine (Part 1)**	Tamla 54262
			THE MIRETTES	
			Former Ikettes Vanetta Fields, Jessie Smith and Robbie Montgomery.	
2/17/68	**45**	7	1 In The Midnight Hour	Revue 11004
			MISSING PERSONS	
			Rock quintet. Dale Bozzio, lead singer (former Playboy bunny from Boston).	
7/03/82	**42**	11	1 Words	Capitol 5127
10/02/82	**42**	14	2 Destination Unknown	Capitol 5161
1/15/83	**63**	8	3 Windows	Capitol 5200
3/12/83	**70**	6	4 Walking In L.A.	Capitol 5212
3/17/84	**67**	6	5 Give	Capitol 5326
			MR. BIG	
			Pop/disco quintet from Oxford, England.	
3/05/77	**87**	7	1 Romeo	Arista 0229
			MR. MISTER	
			Los Angeles-based pop/rock quartet: Richard Page, Steve George, Steve Farris and Pat Mastelotto.	
3/17/84	**57**	8	1 Hunters Of The Night	RCA 13741
9/21/85	**1[2]**	22	2 **Broken Wings**	RCA 14136
12/21/85+	**1[2]**	20	3 **Kyrie**	RCA 14258
3/29/86	**8**	17	4 **Is It Love**	RCA 14313
			MISTRESS	
			Rock group - Charlie Williams, lead singer.	
11/10/79	**49**	9	1 Mistrusted Love	RSO 1009
			BARBARA MITCHELL - see SMOKEY ROBINSON	
			THE CHAD MITCHELL TRIO	
			Chad Mitchell, Mike Kobluk and Joe Frazier; formed while sophomores at Gonzaga University in Spokane, Washington.	
1/27/62	**44**	8	1 Lizzie Borden [C]	Kapp 439
5/19/62	**99**	1	2 The John Birch Society [N]	Kapp 457
11/30/63+	**43**	9	3 The Marvelous Toy [N]	Mercury 72197
			GUY MITCHELL	
			Born Al Cernik on 2/27/27 in Detroit. Sang briefly with Carmen Cavallaro's orchestra in the late 40s. Appearances in several film and TV series.	
1/21/56	**23**	11	1 Ninety Nine Years (Dead Or Alive)	Columbia 40631

DEBUT DATE	PEAK POS	WKS CHR	ARTIST — Record Title	Label & Number
			GUY MITCHELL — Cont'd	
10/27/56	**1**[10]	26	2 **Singing The Blues/**	
			Juke Box #1(10) / Best Seller #1(9) / Top 100 #1(9) / Jockey #1(9)	
11/10/56	**53**	14	3 Crazy With Love	Columbia 40769
1/19/57	**16**	12	4 Knee Deep In The Blues/	
			Top 100 #16 / Juke Box #16 / Jockey #17 / Best Seller #21	
2/02/57	**47**	7	5 Take Me Back Baby	Columbia 40820
4/06/57	**10**	17	6 **Rock-A-Billy**	Columbia 40877
			Best Seller #10 / Top 100 #13 / Juke Box #14 / Jockey #15	
6/17/57	**83**	1	7 Sweet Stuff	Columbia 40940
10/05/59	**1**[2]	20	8 **Heartaches By The Number**	Columbia 41476
2/29/60	**51**	6	9 The Same Old Me	Columbia 41576
7/11/60	**45**	10	10 My Shoes Keep Walking Back To You	Columbia 41725
			JONI MITCHELL	
			Born Roberta Joan Anderson on 11/7/43 in Alberta, Canada. Wrote the hit "Both Sides Now" and "Woodstock". Also see James Taylor.	
7/25/70	**67**	6	1 Big Yellow Taxi	Reprise 0906
9/04/71	**93**	1	2 Carey	Reprise 1029
11/11/72+	**25**	16	3 You Turn Me On, I'm A Radio	Asylum 11010
12/22/73+	**65**	8	4 Raised On Robbery	Asylum 11029
3/16/74	**7**	19	5 **Help Me**	Asylum 11034
7/27/74	**22**	14	6 Free Man In Paris	Asylum 11041
12/28/74+	**24**	10	7 Big Yellow Taxi	Asylum 45221
			live version of Joni's 1970 studio hit	
2/07/76	**66**	4	8 In France They Kiss On Main Street	Asylum 45296
11/20/82	**47**	9	9 (You're So Square) Baby, I Don't Care	Geffen 29849
			first recorded by Elvis Presley for film "Jailhouse Rock" in 1957	
12/28/85+	**85**	3	10 Good Friends	Geffen 28840
			all of the above songs written by Mitchell (except #9)	
			KIM MITCHELL	
			Canadian rock guitarist/vocalist. Leader of Canadian group, Max Webster.	
5/18/85	**86**	9	1 Go For Soda	Bronze 99652
			WILLIE MITCHELL	
			Born in Ashland, MS in 1928. Trumpeter, keyboardist, composer, arranger, producer. To Memphis at an early age. With Tuff Green, Al Jackson, early 1950s. Became house band at Hi Records in 1961, and Willie eventually became president of the company.	
8/29/64	**31**	10	1 20-75 [I]	Hi 2075
			title refers to the record's label number	
12/19/64+	**85**	3	2 Percolatin' [I]	Hi 2066
7/17/65	**96**	2	3 Buster Browne [I]	Hi 2091
5/07/66	**92**	1	4 Bad Eye [I]	Hi 2103
7/22/67	**96**	2	5 Slippin' & Slidin' [I]	Hi 2125
3/09/68	**23**	15	6 Soul Serenade [I]	Hi 2140
7/13/68	**45**	7	7 Prayer Meetin' [I]	Hi 2147
10/05/68	**91**	4	8 Up-Hard [I]	Hi 2151
2/01/69	**69**	5	9 30-60-90 [I]	Hi 2154
			ROBERT MITCHUM	
			Born in Bridgeport, Connecticut in 1917. Leading movie actor since 1943.	
9/08/58	**62**	11	1 The Ballad Of Thunder Road	Capitol 3986
			from the film "Thunder Road"	
2/24/62	**65**	10	2 The Ballad Of Thunder Road [R]	Capitol 3986
8/12/67	**96**	2	3 Little Old Wine Drinker Me	Monument 1006
			THE MIXTURES	
			Australian group.	
3/06/71	**44**	11	1 Pushbike Song	Sire 350
			THE MOB	
1/23/71	**83**	3	1 I Dig Everything About You	Colossus 130
3/13/71	**71**	4	2 Give It To Me	Colossus 134
			MOBY GRAPE	
			Rock group from San Francisco.	
7/08/67	**88**	3	1 Omaha	Columbia 44173

DEBUT DATE	PEAK POS	WKS CHR	ARTIST — Record Title		Label & Number
			MOCEDADES		
			Sextet from Bilbao, Spain, featuring the Amezaga sisters.		
1/12/74	**9**	17	1 **Eres Tu (Touch The Wind)**	[F]	Tara 100
			MODELS		
			Pop/rock quintet from Melbourne, Australia. Led by vocalists/guitarists James Freud and Sean Kelly.		
4/26/86	**37**	13	1 Out Of Mind Out Of Sight		Geffen 28762
			MODERN ENGLISH		
			British fivesome - Robbie Grey, lead singer.		
4/02/83	**78**	7	1 I Melt With You		Sire 29775
4/07/84	**91**	3	2 Hands Across The Sea		Sire 29339
			THE MODERNAIRES		
			Group first achieved great popularity singing with Glenn Miller. Nucleus of group: Hal Dickinson (d: 11/18/70), Paula Kelly (Hal's wife) and Ralph Brewster.		
3/31/56	**97**	1	1 April In Paris		Coral 61599
			DOMENICO MODUGNO		
			Born on 1/9/28 in Polignano a Mare, Italy. Singer/actor.		
8/04/58	**1^{5}**	16	1 **Nel Blu Dipinto Di Blu (Volare)**	[F]	Decca 30677
			Hot 100 #1(5) / Best Seller #1(5)		
3/09/59	**97**	1	2 Piove (Ciao, Ciao Bambina)	[F]	Decca 30845
			THE MOJO MEN		
			San Francisco-based rock quartet: Jimmy Alaimo, Paul Curcio, Don Metchick and Dennis DeCarr.		
10/30/65	**61**	6	1 Dance With Me		Autumn 19
2/04/67	**36**	11	2 Sit Down, I Think I Love You		Reprise 0539
5/27/67	**83**	3	3 Me About You		Reprise 0580
			MOLLY HATCHET		
			Southern hard rock sextet from Jacksonville, Florida. Danny Joe Brown, lead singer (replaced by John Farrar in 1980; Brown returned and replaced Farrar in 1983).		
1/05/80	**42**	10	1 Flirtin' With Disaster		Epic 50822
3/07/81	**91**	3	2 The Rambler		Epic 50965
2/06/82	**96**	2	3 Power Play		Epic 02680
10/20/84	**81**	5	4 Satisfied Man		Epic 04648
			THE MOMENTS		
1/12/63	**82**	5	1 Walk Right In		Era 3099
			THE MOMENTS		
			Soul trio from Hackensack, NJ featuring Mark Greene, falsetto lead. Greene left after first record, replaced by William Brown, lead; and Al Goodman. Harry Ray joined after "Love On A Two-Way Street" in 1970. Became "Ray, Goodman & Brown" in 1978.		
12/28/68+	**57**	7	1 Not On The Outside		Stang 5000
5/10/69	**90**	3	2 Sunday		Stang 5003
8/16/69	**62**	6	3 I Do		Stang 5005
4/11/70	**3**	15	4● **Love On A Two-Way Street**		Stang 5012
8/22/70	**44**	8	5 If I Didn't Care		Stang 5016
11/21/70+	**56**	9	6 All I Have		Stang 5017
8/21/71	**98**	2	7 Lucky Me		Stang 5031
			all of above produced by Sylvia (Robinson)		
9/22/73	**68**	8	8 Gotta Find A Way		Stang 5050
1/12/74	**17**	13	9 Sexy Mama		Stang 5052
6/08/74	**80**	4	10 Sho Nuff Boogie (Part I)		All Platinum 2350
			SYLVIA & THE MOMENTS		
7/05/75	**39**	8	11 Look At Me (I'm In Love)		Stang 5060
			THE MONARCHS		
2/22/64	**47**	13	1 Look Homeward Angel		Sound Stage 2516
			JULIE MONDAY		
8/20/66	**96**	2	1 Come Share The Good Times With Me		Rainbow 100
			EDDIE MONEY		
			Born Edward Mahoney on 3/2/49 in New York City. Rock singer discovered and subsequently managed by West Coast promoter Bill Graham.		
2/25/78	**11**	20	1 Baby Hold On		Columbia 10663

DEBUT DATE	PEAK POS	WKS CHR	ARTIST — Record Title	Label & Number
			EDDIE MONEY — Cont'd	
6/24/78	**22**	14	2 Two Tickets To Paradise	Columbia 10765
11/25/78+	**72**	8	3 You've Really Got A Hold On Me	Columbia 10842
1/27/79	**22**	13	4 Maybe I'm A Fool	Columbia 10900
5/12/79	**63**	5	5 Can't Keep A Good Man Down	Columbia 10981
8/25/79	**46**	8	6 Get A Move On from the film "Americathon"	Columbia 11064
9/13/80	**78**	4	7 Running Back	Columbia 11325
10/18/80	**65**	6	8 Let's Be Lovers Again **EDDIE MONEY with VALERIE CARTER**	Columbia 11377
7/03/82	**16**	17	9 Think I'm In Love	Columbia 02964
10/09/82	**63**	9	10 Shakin'	Columbia 03252
11/19/83+	**54**	11	11 The Big Crash	Columbia 04199
2/25/84	**66**	7	12 Club Michelle	Columbia 04376
8/16/86	**4**	23	13 **Take Me Home Tonight** Ronnie Spector sings the lead line from "Be My Baby"	Columbia 06231
12/20/86+	**14**	21	14 I Wanna Go Back	Columbia 06569
			THE MONITORS Soul group featuring Richard Street (joined The Temptations in 1971).	
4/16/66	**100**	1	1 Greetings (This Is Uncle Sam)	V.I.P. 25032
			T.S. MONK Thelonious Monk Jr. (son of the legendary jazz artist), sister Boo Boo, and Yvonne Fletcher.	
2/21/81	**63**	8	1 Bon Bon Vie (Gimme The Good Life)	Mirage 3780
			THE MONKEES Formed in Los Angeles in 1965. Chosen from over 400 applicants for new Columbia TV series. Consisted of Davy Jones (b: 12/30/46, Manchester, England), vocals; Michael Nesmith (b: 12/30/42, Houston), guitar, vocals; Peter Tork (b: 2/13/44, Washington, DC), bass, vocals; and Micky Dolenz (b: 3/8/45, Tarzana, CA), drums, vocals. Dolenz had appeared in TV series "Circus Boy", using the name Mickey Braddock in 1956. Jones had been a race-horse jockey, and appeared in London musicals "Oliver" and "Pickwick". Tork had been in the Phoenix Singers; Nesmith had done session work for Stax/Volt. TV show dropped after 56 episodes, 1966-68. Tork left in 1968. Group disbanded in 1969; re-formed (less Nesmith) in 1986.	
9/10/66	**1^{1}**	15	1 ● **Last Train To Clarksville**	Colgems 1001
12/10/66	**1^{7}**	15	2 ● **I'm A Believer/**	
12/17/66+	**20**	8	3 (I'm Not Your) Steppin' Stone	Colgems 1002
3/25/67	**2^{1}**	10	4 ● **A Little Bit Me, A Little Bit You/**	
3/25/67	**39**	5	5 The Girl I Knew Somewhere	Colgems 1004
7/22/67	**3**	10	6 ● **Pleasant Valley Sunday/**	
7/22/67	**11**	9	7 Words	Colgems 1007
11/18/67	**1^{4}**	12	8 ● **Daydream Believer**	Colgems 1012
3/09/68	**3**	10	9 ● **Valleri/**	
3/09/68	**34**	6	10 Tapioca Tundra	Colgems 1019
6/15/68	**19**	7	11 D. W. Washburn/	
6/15/68	**51**	7	12 It's Nice To Be With You	Colgems 1023
10/12/68	**62**	6	13 Porpoise Song from the film "Head"	Colgems 1031
2/22/69	**56**	7	14 Tear Drop City	Colgems 5000
6/07/69	**63**	8	15 Listen To The Band/	
5/10/69	**81**	2	16 Someday Man	Colgems 5004
9/20/69	**82**	5	17 Good Clean Fun	Colgems 5005
6/06/70	**98**	2	18 Oh My My	Colgems 5011
7/05/86	**20**	14	19 That Was Then, This Is Now	Arista 9505
11/01/86	**79**	4	20 Daydream Believer [R]	Arista 9532
			THE MONOTONES Doo-wop group from Newark, New Jersey. Charles Patrick, lead singer.	
3/24/58	**5**	18	1 **Book Of Love** Top 100 #5 / Best Seller #6 / Jockey #9	Argo 5290
			MATT MONRO British - died of liver cancer on 2/7/85 (54).	
5/29/61	**18**	14	1 My Kind Of Girl	Warwick 636
10/16/61	**92**	3	2 Why Not Now	Warwick 669
11/28/64+	**23**	9	3 Walk Away	Liberty 55745

DEBUT DATE	PEAK POS	WKS CHR	ARTIST — Record Title	Label & Number
			VAUGHN MONROE	
			Born on 10/7/11 in Akron, OH; died on 5/21/73. Big-voiced baritone, trumpeter, bandleader. Very popular on radio, and featured in several movies.	
11/12/55	**38**	4	1 Black Denim Trousers And Motorcycle Boots	RCA 6260
1/21/56	**38**	7	2 Don't Go To Strangers	RCA 6358
9/01/56	**11**	13	3 In The Middle Of The House [N]	RCA 6619
			Jockey #11 / Top 100 #21	
5/25/59	**87**	2	4 The Battle Of New Orleans	RCA 7495
			THE MONROES	
			Five-man rock band from San Diego - Jesus Ortiz, lead singer.	
5/29/82	**59**	8	1 What Do All The People Know	Alfa 7119
			THE MONTANAS	
			British group.	
3/02/68	**58**	7	1 You've Got To Be Loved	Independence 83
			LOU MONTE	
			Born of Italian parentage on 4/2/17 in Lynhurst, NJ. Vocalist, guitarist.	
3/10/58	**12**	18	1 Lazy Mary [F]	RCA 7160
			Best Seller #12 / Top 100 #12 / Jockey #22	
6/30/58	**54**	5	2 The Sheik Of Araby [F]	RCA 7265
			Italian version of popular hit written in 1921	
12/08/62+	**5**	10	3 **Pepino The Italian Mouse** [N]	Reprise 20106
3/09/63	**78**	3	4 Pepino's Friend Pasqual (The Italian Pussy-Cat) [N]	Reprise 20146
			HUGO MONTENEGRO	
			Born in 1925; raised in New York City; died on 2/6/81. Conductor, composer.	
2/17/68	**2**[1]	22	1 **The Good, The Bad And The Ugly** [I]	RCA 9423
6/29/68	**82**	5	2 Hang 'Em High [I]	RCA 9554
			above 2 from films of the same title	
			CHRIS MONTEZ	
			Born Christopher Montanez on 1/17/43 in Los Angeles. Protege of Ritchie Valens.	
8/04/62	**4**	14	1 **Let's Dance**	Monogram 505
12/08/62+	**43**	9	2 Some Kinda Fun	Monogram 507
1/08/66	**22**	10	3 Call Me	A&M 780
4/16/66	**16**	14	4 The More I See You	A&M 796
8/13/66	**33**	8	5 There Will Never Be Another You	A&M 810
10/29/66	**36**	8	6 Time After Time	A&M 822
3/04/67	**71**	5	7 Because Of You	A&M 839
			3-4, 6-7: produced by Herb Alpert	
			MELBA MONTGOMERY	
			Born on 10/14/38 in Iron City, Tennessee. Country singer.	
4/13/74	**39**	10	1 No Charge [N]	Elektra 45883
			TAMMY MONTGOMERY - see TAMMI TERRELL	
			WES MONTGOMERY	
			Jazz guitarist. First recorded for Pacific Jazz in 1957. Brother Monk plays bass, brother Buddy plays piano. Wes died on 6/15/68 (43).	
11/25/67	**44**	11	1 Windy [I]	A&M 883
7/06/68	**91**	3	2 Georgia On My Mind [I]	A&M 940
			THE MOODY BLUES	
			Formed in Birmingham, England in 1964. Consisted of Denny Laine (guitar, vocals), Ray Thomas (flute, vocals), Mike Pinder (keyboards, vocals), Clint Warwick (bass) and Graeme Edge (drums). Laine and Warwick left in the summer of 1966, replaced by Justin Hayward (lead vocals, lead guitar) and John Lodge (vocals, bass). Patrick Moraz (formerly with Yes - keyboards), replaced Pinder in 1978.	
2/20/65	**10**	14	1 **Go Now!**	London 9726
6/05/65	**93**	3	2 From The Bottom Of My Heart (I Love You)	London 9764
4/02/66	**98**	1	3 Stop!	London 9810
			Denny Laine (Wings), lead singer on above 3	
7/20/68	**24**	11	4 Tuesday Afternoon (Forever Afternoon)	Deram 85028
10/12/68	**61**	5	5 Ride My See-Saw	Deram 85033
6/28/69	**91**	4	6 Never Comes The Day	Deram 85044
5/02/70	**21**	12	7 Question	Threshold 67004
8/07/71	**23**	11	8 The Story In Your Eyes	Threshold 67006
4/22/72	**29**	10	9 Isn't Life Strange	Threshold 67009

DEBUT DATE	PEAK POS	WKS CHR	ARTIST — Record Title	Label & Number
			THE MOODY BLUES — Cont'd	
8/05/72	**2²**	18	10 ● **Nights In White Satin** released from their 1968 album "Days of Future Passed"	Deram 85023
2/03/73	**12**	10	11 I'm Just A Singer (In A Rock And Roll Band)	Threshold 67012
7/29/78	**39**	8	12 Steppin' In A Slide Zone	London 270
11/04/78	**59**	7	13 Driftwood	London 273
6/06/81	**12**	15	14 Gemini Dream	Threshold 601
8/08/81	**15**	17	15 The Voice	Threshold 602
11/07/81	**65**	7	16 Talking Out Of Turn	Threshold 603
9/03/83	**27**	10	17 Sitting At The Wheel	Threshold 604
11/12/83	**62**	6	18 Blue World	Threshold 605
4/19/86	**9**	21	19 **Your Wildest Dreams**	Threshold 883906
8/16/86	**58**	9	20 The Other Side Of Life	Polydor 885201
			ART MOONEY Born in Lowell, MA. Leader of a Detroit-based dance band, mid-30s to 40s. To New York following WWII service. Biggest hit: "I'm Looking Over A Four-Leaf Clover" in 1948. Also see Barry Gordon.	
4/23/55	**6**	17	1 **Honey-Babe** Best Seller #6 / Juke Box #6 / Jockey #10 from the film "Battle Cry"	MGM 11900
7/07/56	**73**	2	2 Daydreams	MGM 12277
11/03/56	**77**	2	3 Giant from film of the same title	MGM 12320
2/24/58	**88**	2	4 The River Kwai March And Colonel Bogey [I] from the film "The Bridge On The River Kwai"	MGM 12590
6/13/60	**100**	2	5 Banjo Boy vocal by The Ivys	MGM 12908
			THE MOONGLOWS R&B group from Louisville. Consisted of Bobby Lester (d: 10/15/80) & Harvey Fuqua, lead singers; Alexander "Pete" Graves, Prentiss Barnes and Billy Johnson.	
3/26/55	**20**	1	1 Sincerely Juke Box #20	Chess 1581
9/01/56	**25**	14	2 See Saw Best Seller #25 / Top 100 #28	Chess 1629
7/08/57	**73**	6	3 Please Send Me Someone To Love	Chess 1661
9/15/58	**22**	16	4 Ten Commandments Of Love **HARVEY & THE MOONGLOWS**	Chess 1705
			MOONLION	
1/10/76+	**95**	1	1 The Little Drummer Boy [X-I]	P.I.P. 6513
			BOB MOORE Born on 11/30/32 in Nashville. Top session bass player. Led the band on Roy Orbison's sessions for Monument Records. Also worked as sideman for Elvis Presley, Brenda Lee, Pat Boone and others.	
8/14/61	**7**	15	1 **Mexico** [I]	Monument 446
			BOBBY MOORE	
8/09/75	**99**	2	1 (Call Me Your) Anything Man	Scepter 12405
			BOBBY MOORE & THE RHYTHM ACES Formed in Montgomery, AL in 1961, featuring leader Bobby Moore (tenor sax) and Chico Jenkins (lead vocalist).	
6/25/66	**27**	10	1 Searching For My Love	Checker 1129
12/17/66	**97**	2	2 Try My Love Again	Checker 1156
			DOROTHY MOORE Born in Jackson, Mississippi in 1946. Lead singer of The Poppies.	
3/20/76	**3**	22	1 **Misty Blue**	Malaco 1029
7/24/76	**58**	11	2 Funny How Time Slips Away	Malaco 1033
8/06/77	**27**	15	3 I Believe You	Malaco 1042
			JACKIE MOORE R&B songstress from Jacksonville, Florida.	
12/05/70+	**30**	15	1 ● Precious, Precious	Atlantic 2681
7/07/73	**42**	12	2 Sweet Charlie Babe	Atlantic 2956
			MELBA MOORE Soul singer, actress from New York City. Appeared in the Broadway production of "Hair"; award winning performer as Lutiebelle in the musical "Purlie".	
4/24/76	**91**	5	1 This Is It	Buddah 519

DEBUT DATE	PEAK POS	WKS CHR	ARTIST — Record Title	Label & Number
			MELBA MOORE — Cont'd	
1/20/79	**47**	7	2 You Stepped Into My Life	Epic 50600
			TIM MOORE	
			Pop singer, songwriter, guitarist, keyboardist.	
4/14/73	**93**	3	1 Fool Like You	Dunhill 4337
9/21/74	**58**	5	2 Second Avenue	Asylum 45208
2/08/75	**91**	3	3 Charmer	Asylum 45214
7/16/77	**75**	3	4 In The Middle	Asylum 45394
			THE MORGAN BROTHERS	
			Dick, Duke and Charley from Mancos, Colorado. Brothers of Jaye P. Morgan.	
2/09/59	**50**	8	1 Nola a #3 hit in 1922 for Vincent Lopez	MGM 12747
			JANE MORGAN	
			Born Jane Currier in Boston, and raised in Florida. Popular singer in France before becoming successful in U.S. TV and night club entertaining.	
11/10/56	**41**	12	1 Two Different Worlds ROGER WILLIAMS & JANE MORGAN	Kapp 161
8/26/57	**7**	29	2 **Fascination** Jockey #7 / Top 100 #11 / Best Seller #12 instrumental intro by The Troubadors from the film "Love In The Afternoon"	Kapp 191
9/22/58	**21**	15	3 The Day The Rains Came	Kapp 235
7/27/59	**39**	11	4 With Open Arms	Kapp 284
11/09/59	**57**	9	5 Happy Anniversary from the film of the same title	Kapp 305
			JAYE P. MORGAN	
			Born Mary Margaret Morgan in Mancos, CO. Sang with Frank DeVol's band for 3 years. Featured on many TV variety and game shows from the 50s to the 70s.	
11/27/54+	**3**	21	1 **That's All I Want From You** Jockey #3 / Best Seller #5 / Juke Box #5	RCA 47-5896
3/12/55	**12**	8	2 Danger! Heartbreak Ahead/ Jockey #12 / Juke Box #13 / Best Seller #18	
		1	3 Softly, Softly Best Seller flip	RCA 6016
6/11/55	**12**	5	4 Chee Chee-OO-Chee (Sang The Little Bird)/ PERRY COMO & JAYE P. MORGAN Jockey #12 / Juke Box #14 / Best Seller #24	
6/25/55	**18**	1	5 Two Lost Souls PERRY COMO & JAYE P. MORGAN Jockey #18 from the Broadway musical "Damn Yankees"	RCA 6137
8/20/55	**6**	14	6 **The Longest Walk/** Jockey #6 / Juke Box #7 / Best Seller #13 / Top 100 #19 pre	
		1	7 Swanee Juke Box flip a #1 hit in 1920 for Al Jolson	RCA 6182
11/12/55	**12**	13	8 Pepper-Hot Baby/ Juke Box #12 / Top 100 #21	
11/12/55	**40**	10	9 If You Don't Want My Love	RCA 6282
12/24/55+	**48**	8	10 Not One Goodbye	RCA 6329
3/24/56	**85**	3	11 Sweet Lips/	
3/31/56	**83**	2	12 Get Up! Get Up!	RCA 6441
5/26/56	**69**	5	13 Lost In The Shuffle/	
5/26/56	**79**	4	14 Play For Keeps	RCA 6505
7/21/56	**81**	1	15 Johnny Casanova	RCA 6565
10/27/56	**97**	1	16 Just Love Me all of above with Hugo Winterhalter's Orchestra (except #3-4 & 8)	RCA 6653
12/01/56	**47**	9	17 Mutual Admiration Society EDDY ARNOLD & JAYE P. MORGAN from the musical "Happy Hunting"	RCA 6708
2/09/59	**65**	6	18 Are You Lonesome Tonight/	
2/16/59	**78**	5	19 Miss You	MGM 12752
8/29/60	**66**	6	20 I Walk The Line	MGM 12924
			LEE MORGAN	
			Born on 7/10/38 in Philadelphia; fatally shot on 2/19/72. Jazz trumpeter.	
12/19/64+	**81**	4	1 The Sidewinder, Part I [I]	Blue Note 1911

DEBUT DATE	PEAK POS	WKS CHR	ARTIST — Record Title	Label & Number
			MELI'SA MORGAN	
			Meli'sa (pronounced Me-Lee-Sa) is a Queens, New York native. Background singer for Melba Moore, Whitney Houston and Kashif.	
1/25/86	46	14	1 Do Me Baby	Capitol 5523
			RUSS MORGAN	
			Born in Scranton, PA on 4/29/04; died on 8/8/69. Trombonist, pianist and popular sweet-band leader. Biggest hit: "Cruising Down The River" in 1949.	
11/12/55	30	8	1 Dogface Soldier	Decca 29703
			from the movie "To Hell And Back"	
3/03/56	19	14	2 The Poor People Of Paris [I]	Decca 29835
			Juke Box #19 / Jockey #23 / Top 100 #26	
			JOHNNIE MORISETTE	
			Born in 1935 in Montu Island, South Pacific. Sang with Medallions as "Johnny Twovoice".	
4/14/62	63	9	1 Meet Me At The Twistin' Place	Sar 126
			COZY MORLEY	
5/06/57	62	3	1 I Love My Girl	ABC-Para. 9811
			THE MORMON TABERNACLE CHOIR	
			375-voice choir directed by Richard P. Condie (died on 12/22/85).	
9/07/59	13	16	1 Battle Hymn Of The Republic	Columbia 41459
			with the Philadelphia Orchestra, Eugene Ormandy, conductor written in 1862; a #1 hit for The Columbia Stellar Quartet in 1918	
			MORNING MIST	
			Singing, songwriting, production team of Terry Cashman and Tommy West.	
8/07/71	96	3	1 California On My Mind	Event 206
			GIORGIO MORODER	
			Italian-born electronic composer/conductor/producer for numerous soundtracks. Produced seven of Donna Summer's albums.	
3/04/72	46	8	1 Son Of My Father	Dunhill 4304
			shown only as: GIORGIO	
1/20/79	33	12	2 Chase [I]	Casablanca 956
			from the film "Midnight Express"	
7/21/84	81	4	3 Reach Out	Columbia 04511
			Track Theme from the Official Music of the XXIIIrd Olympiad in Los Angeles, 1984 - vocal by Paul Engemann	
			MARLOWE MORRIS QUINTET	
3/31/62	95	1	1 Play The Thing [I]	Columbia 42218
			DOROTHY MORRISON	
			Former lead singer with the Edwin Hawkins Singers.	
10/11/69	95	1	1 All God's Children Got Soul	Elektra 45671
10/31/70	99	2	2 Spirit In The Sky	Buddah 196
			VAN MORRISON	
			Born on 8/31/45 in Belfast, Ireland. Blue-eyed soul singer, songwriter. Leader of Them. Wrote the classic hit "Gloria".	
7/15/67	10	16	1 **Brown Eyed Girl**	Bang 545
4/04/70	39	8	2 Come Running	Warner 7383
11/14/70+	9	12	3 **Domino**	Warner 7434
2/06/71	23	12	4 Blue Money	Warner 7462
6/05/71	95	2	5 Call Me Up In Dreamland	Warner 7488
10/09/71	28	11	6 Wild Night	Warner 7518
1/01/72	47	8	7 Tupelo Honey	Warner 7543
8/19/72	61	6	8 Jackie Wilson Said (I'm In Heaven When You Smile)	Warner 7616
10/28/72	98	2	9 Redwood Tree	Warner 7638
11/19/77	92	4	10 Moondance	Warner 8450
9/16/78	42	11	11 Wavelength	Warner 8661
			all of above written by Morrison	
			BUDDY MORROW	
			Born Muni Zudecoff on 2/8/19 in New Haven, CT. Trombone star for many top big bands. His own swing band was a hit in early 50s. Later played with "Tonight Show" band.	
4/21/56	82	4	1 Main Title From "The Man With The Golden Arm" [I]	Wing 90063
			from the film of the same title	

DEBUT DATE	PEAK POS	WKS CHR	ARTIST — Record Title	Label & Number
			DONNY MOST	
			Ralph Malph of TV's "Happy Days".	
12/04/76	**97**	3	1 All Roads (Lead Back To You)	United Art. 871
			THE MOTELS	
			Martha Davis (b: 1/19/51), lead singer/songwriter of quintet from Los Angeles.	
4/24/82	**9**	23	1 **Only The Lonely**	Capitol 5114
9/04/82	**52**	9	2 Take The L.	Capitol 5149
11/13/82	**60**	8	3 Forever Mine	Capitol 5182
9/03/83	**9**	20	4 **Suddenly Last Summer**	Capitol 5271
12/03/83+	**36**	12	5 Remember The Nights	Capitol 5246
			above 5 produced by Val Garay	
7/20/85	**21**	13	6 Shame	Capitol 5497
10/26/85	**84**	3	7 Shock	Capitol 5529
			MOTHER'S FINEST	
			Sextet led by vocalists (husband & wife) Glenn Murdock and Joyce Kennedy.	
9/04/76	**93**	2	1 Fire	Epic 50269
9/10/77	**58**	6	2 Baby Love	Epic 50407
			MOTHERLODE	
			Canadian pop quartet led by William "Smitty" Smith.	
8/09/69	**18**	13	1 When I Die	Buddah 131
			MOTLEY CRUE	
			Los Angeles-based heavy metal band; Vince Neil (b: 2/8/61), lead singer.	
2/04/84	**54**	10	1 Looks That Kill	Elektra 69756
6/16/84	**90**	2	2 Too Young To Fall In Love	Elektra 69732
7/13/85	**16**	15	3 Smokin' In The Boys Room	Elektra 69625
10/26/85	**89**	6	4 Home Sweet Home	Elektra 69591
			THE MOTORS	
			British duo: Andy McMaster & Nick Garvey.	
5/17/80	**78**	5	1 Love And Loneliness	Virgin 67007
			MOTT THE HOOPLE	
			British glitter rock group led by vocalist Ian Hunter; included Bad Company's guitarist Mick Ralphs (left in 1973).	
9/23/72	**37**	11	1 All The Young Dudes	Columbia 45673
1/27/73	**96**	1	2 One Of The Boys	Columbia 45754
			above 2 produced by David Bowie	
6/08/74	**96**	2	3 The Golden Age Of Rock 'N' Roll	Columbia 46035
			MOUNTAIN	
			New York power-rock group led by Leslie West and Felix Pappalardi (fatally shot on 4/17/83 at the age of 44 in New York City).	
4/04/70	**21**	17	1 Mississippi Queen	Windfall 532
3/27/71	**76**	7	2 The Animal Trainer And The Toad	Windfall 534
			MOUTH & MacNEAL	
			Dutch duo: Willem Duyn & Maggie MacNeal (Sjoukje Van't Spijker).	
4/29/72	**8**	19	1 ● **How Do You Do?**	Philips 40715
10/21/72	**87**	3	2 Hey, You Love	Philips 40717
			THE MOVE	
			British rock group which evolved into the Electric Light Orchestra.	
10/28/72	**93**	5	1 Do Ya	United Art. 50928
			MOVING PICTURES	
			Alex Smith, lead singer of Australian 6-man pop group.	
9/18/82+	**29**	26	1 What About Me	Network 69952
			ALISON MOYET	
			Real name: Genevieve Alison-Jane Moyet. British female vocalist of Yaz.	
3/09/85	**31**	17	1 Invisible	Columbia 04781
7/20/85	**82**	4	2 Love Resurrection	Columbia 05411
			THE MICKEY MOZART QUINTET	
			Mickey Mozart is a pseudonym for jazz harpist/composer Robert Maxwell.	
5/11/59	**30**	10	1 Little Dipper [I]	Roulette 4148

DEBUT DATE	PEAK POS	WKS CHR	ARTIST — Record Title	Label & Number
			MTUME	
			Progressive funk band led by James Mtume. Mtume had been a percussionist with Miles Davis in early 70s.	
6/18/83	**45**	12	1 ● Juicy Fruit	Epic 03578
9/15/84	**83**	5	2 You, Me And He	Epic 04504
			IDRIS MUHAMMAD	
			Born Leo Morris in New Orleans, 1939. Prolific session drummer since early 60s.	
10/01/77	**76**	2	1 Could Heaven Ever Be Like This (Part 1)	Kudu 939
			MARIA MULDAUR	
			Maria (b: 9/12/43, New York City) and former husband Geoff Muldaur (divorced, 1972) were members of Jim Kweskin's Jug Band.	
2/23/74	**6**	24	1 **Midnight At The Oasis**	Reprise 1183
12/28/74+	**12**	14	2 I'm A Woman	Reprise 1319
			MARTIN MULL	
			Born in Chicago on 8/18/43. Comedian, actor. Appeared in films "Mr. Mom" and "FM".	
5/05/73	**92**	3	1 Dueling Tubas [I-N]	Capricorn 0019
			parody of "Dueling Banjos" from the film "Deliverance"	
			MUNGO JERRY	
			British skiffle quartet. Ray Dorset (b: 3/21/46), lead singer.	
7/11/70	**3**	13	1 ● **In The Summertime**	Janus 125
			THE MURMAIDS	
			Los Angeles teenage trio: sisters Carol & Terry Fischer and Sally Gordon.	
11/23/63+	**3**	14	1 **Popsicles And Icicles**	Chattahoochee 628
			MICHAEL MURPHEY	
			Progressive Country singer, songwriter from Austin, Texas. Also see The Lewis & Clarke Expedition.	
8/05/72	**37**	13	1 Geronimo's Cadillac	A&M 1368
3/29/75	**3**	19	2 ● **Wildfire**	Epic 50084
8/16/75	**21**	13	3 Carolina In The Pines	Epic 50131
1/24/76	**39**	7	4 Renegade	Epic 50184
7/24/82	**19**	20	5 What's Forever For	Liberty 1466
1/08/83	**76**	7	6 Still Taking Chances	Liberty 1486
			EDDIE MURPHY	
			Born on 4/3/61 in Hempstead, NY. Comedian, actor. Regular on TV's "Saturday Night Live". Starred in films "Beverly Hills Cop", "Trading Places", "48 Hours" and "The Golden Child".	
10/05/85	**2**[3]	22	1 ● **Party All The Time**	Columbia 05609
			written, produced and arranged by Rick James	
			WALTER MURPHY	
			Born in New York City, 1952. Studied classical and jazz piano at Manhattan School of Music. Former arranger for Doc Severinson and "The Tonight Show" orchestra.	
5/29/76	**1**[1]	28	1 ● **A Fifth Of Beethoven** [I]	Private S. 45073
			based on Beethoven's Fifth Symphony	
11/13/76	**44**	10	2 Flight '76 [I]	Private S. 45123
			based on Rymsky-Korsakov's "Flight Of The Bumble Bee"	
7/31/82	**47**	9	3 Themes From E.T. (The Extra-Terrestrial) [I]	MCA 52099
			from the all-time #1 box-office hit "E.T."	
			ANNE MURRAY	
			Born on 6/20/47 in Springhill, Nova Scotia. Has BA degree in physical education, University of New Brunswick. With CBC-TV show "Sing Along Jubilee". First recorded for Arc in 1969. On Glen Campbell's "Goodtime Hour" TV series from 1970.	
7/18/70	**8**	16	1 ● **Snowbird**	Capitol 2738
12/05/70+	**83**	5	2 Sing High - Sing Low	Capitol 2988
9/11/71	**57**	7	3 Talk It Over In The Morning	Capitol 3159
10/23/71	**81**	5	4 I Say A Little Prayer/By The Time I Get To Phoenix	Capitol 3200
			GLEN CAMPBELL/ANNE MURRAY	
4/01/72	**71**	5	5 Cotton Jenny	Capitol 3260
1/06/73	**7**	18	6 **Danny's Song**	Capitol 3481
			written by Kenny Loggins for his nephew	
5/26/73	**64**	8	7 What About Me	Capitol 3600
8/18/73	**72**	7	8 Send A Little Love My Way	Capitol 3648
			from the film "Oklahoma Crude"	
12/15/73+	**12**	17	9 Love Song	Capitol 3776

DEBUT DATE	PEAK POS	WKS CHR	ARTIST — Record Title		Label & Number
			ANNE MURRAY — Cont'd		
4/20/74	8	20	10 **You Won't See Me**		Capitol 3867
11/09/74	86	2	11 Just One Look		Capitol 3955
12/21/74+	59	6	12 Day Tripper all of above produced by Brian Ahern		Capitol 4000
11/29/75	98	2	13 Sunday Sunrise		Capitol 4142
2/21/76	91	5	14 The Call		Capitol 4207
10/30/76	89	3	15 Things		Capitol 4329
7/15/78	1[1]	26	16 ● **You Needed Me**		Capitol 4574
1/27/79	12	16	17 I Just Fall In Love Again		Capitol 4675
5/26/79	25	12	18 Shadows In The Moonlight		Capitol 4716
9/22/79	12	17	19 Broken Hearted Me		Capitol 4773
12/22/79+	12	17	20 Daydream Believer		Capitol 4813
4/05/80	42	8	21 Lucky Me		Capitol 4848
6/14/80	64	6	22 I'm Happy Just To Dance With You 10, 12, 22: written by John Lennon & Paul McCartney		Capitol 4878
9/06/80	33	14	23 Could I Have This Dance from the film "Urban Cowboy"		Capitol 4920
3/28/81	34	13	24 Blessed Are The Believers		Capitol 4987
9/26/81	53	9	25 It's All I Can Do		Capitol 5023
1/30/82	44	9	26 Another Sleepless Night		Capitol 5083
9/17/83	74	9	27 A Little Good News 16-27 produced by Jim Ed Norman		Capitol 5264
3/01/86	92	6	28 Now And Forever (You And Me)		Capitol 5547
			MICKEY MURRAY		
10/07/67	54	8	1 Shout Bamalama		SSS Int'l. 715
			THE MUSIC EXPLOSION Jamie Lyons, lead singer of pop/rock quintet from Mansfield, Ohio. Produced by Jerry Kasenetz and Jeff Katz.		
5/13/67	2[2]	16	1 ● **Little Bit O'Soul**		Laurie 3380
9/09/67	63	5	2 Sunshine Games		Laurie 3400
			THE MUSIC MACHINE Los Angeles rock quintet - Sean Bonniwell, lead singer/songwriter.		
11/12/66+	15	12	1 Talk Talk		Original Sound 61
1/28/67	66	8	2 The People In Me		Original Sound 67
			THE MUSIC MAKERS Studio band, evolved into MFSB.		
12/30/67+	78	7	1 United (Part I) instrumental version of The Intruders "(We'll Be) United"	[I]	Gamble 210
			MUSICAL YOUTH 5 schoolboys (ages 11 to 16) from Birmingham, England. Dennis Seaton, lead singer.		
12/11/82+	10	18	1 **Pass The Dutchie** Dutchie: a Jamaican cooking pot		MCA 52149
1/14/84	65	7	2 She's Trouble		MCA 52312
			MUSIQUE Disco trio: Christine Wiltshire, Gina Tharps and Mary Seymour.		
10/21/78	58	13	1 In The Bush		Prelude 71110
			THE MUSTANGS		
10/03/64	92	3	1 The Dartell Stomp	[I]	Providence 401
			BILLY MYLES New York singer, songwriter. Wrote the Mello-Kings' hit "Tonite, Tonite".		
11/18/57	25	14	1 The Joker (That's What They Call Me) Best Seller #25 / Top 100 #30		Ember 1026
			THE MYSTIC MOODS Hollywood studio orchestra produced by Brad Miller.		
4/21/73	83	6	1 Cosmic Sea	[I]	Warner 7686
7/12/75	98	6	2 Honey Trippin'	[I]	Sound Bird 5002
			THE MYSTICS Quintet from Brooklyn, New York. Phil Cracolici (lead), Bob Ferrante & George Galfo (tenors), Albee Cracolici (baritone) and Allie Contrera (bass).		
5/25/59	20	15	1 Hushabye		Laurie 3028

DEBUT DATE	PEAK POS	WKS CHR	ARTIST — Record Title	Label & Number
			THE MYSTICS — Cont'd	
10/19/59	**98**	2	2 Don't Take The Stars	Laurie 3038
			# N	
			NAKED EYES	
			English duo: Pete Byrne (vocals) and Rob Fisher (keyboards, synthesizer).	
3/12/83	**8**	22	1 **Always Something There To Remind Me**	EMI America 8155
7/16/83	**11**	20	2 Promises, Promises	EMI America 8170
10/22/83	**37**	14	3 When The Lights Go Out	EMI America 8183
8/11/84	**39**	12	4 (What) In The Name Of Love	EMI America 8219
			NAPOLEON XIV	
			Napoleon is Jerry Samuels, a recording engineer and composer from New York.	
7/23/66	**3**	6	1 **They're Coming To Take Me Away, Ha-Haaa!** [N]	Warner 5831
9/01/73	**87**	4	2 They're Coming To Take Me Away, Ha-Haaa! [N-R]	Warner 7726
			GRAHAM NASH	
			Born on 2/2/42 in Blackpool, England. Co-founding member of The Hollies. Formed Crosby, Stills & Nash in 1970.	
6/05/71	**35**	11	1 Chicago	Atlantic 2804
9/04/71	**73**	6	2 Military Madness	Atlantic 2827
5/06/72	**36**	9	3 Immigration Man GRAHAM NASH & DAVID CROSBY	Atlantic 2873
7/01/72	**61**	6	4 War Song NEIL YOUNG & GRAHAM NASH backing by the Stray Gators	Reprise 1099
8/12/72	**99**	2	5 Southbound Train GRAHAM NASH & DAVID CROSBY	Atlantic 2892
11/15/75	**52**	6	6 Carry Me DAVID CROSBY/GRAHAM NASH	ABC 12140
8/07/76	**89**	3	7 Out Of The Darkness DAVID CROSBY/GRAHAM NASH	ABC 12199
4/26/86	**84**	7	8 Innocent Eyes	Atlantic 89434
			JOHNNY NASH	
			Born on 8/19/40 in Houston. Vocalist, guitarist, actor. Appeared on local TV from age 13. With Arthur Godfrey, TV and radio, from 1956-63. In film "Take A Giant Step" in 1959. Own label, JoDa, in 1965. Began recording in Jamaica, late 60s.	
12/30/57+	**23**	10	1 A Very Special Love Jockey #23 / Best Seller #45 / Top 100 #46	ABC-Para. 9874
11/10/58	**78**	4	2 Almost In Your Arms love song from the film "Houseboat"	ABC-Para. 9960
12/01/58+	**29**	8	3 The Teen Commandments [S] PAUL ANKA-GEORGE HAMILTON IV-JOHNNY NASH inspirational talk from above 3 ABC-Paramount artists	ABC-Para. 9974
3/16/59	**43**	11	4 As Time Goes By featured song in the classic 1942 film "Casablanca"	ABC-Para. 9996
9/25/65	**88**	7	5 Let's Move & Groove (Together)	JoDa 102
9/14/68	**5**	15	6 **Hold Me Tight**	JAD 207
12/14/68+	**58**	7	7 You Got Soul	JAD 209
11/01/69+	**39**	14	8 Cupid	JAD 220
9/09/72	**1**[4]	20	9● **I Can See Clearly Now**	Epic 10902
2/10/73	**12**	14	10 Stir It Up	Epic 10949
6/30/73	**77**	5	11 My Merry-Go-Round	Epic 11003
4/13/74	**91**	3	12 Loving You above 7 produced by Nash	Epic 11070
			THE NASHVILLE TEENS	
			British rock sextet - Arthur Sharp, lead singer.	
9/12/64	**14**	11	1 Tobacco Road	London 9689
3/13/65	**98**	2	2 Find My Way Back Home	London 9736
			NATIONAL LAMPOON	
			Comedy troupe spawned from the magazine of the same name.	
10/14/72	**91**	4	1 Deteriorata [C] parody of "Desiderata" - voice of Norman Rose	Banana 218

DEBUT DATE	PEAK POS	WKS CHR	ARTIST — Record Title	Label & Number
			NATURAL FOUR	
			Soul group led by Chris James, formed in 1967 in New York City.	
1/05/74	**31**	10	1 Can This Be Real	Curtom 1990
5/25/74	**98**	2	2 Love That Really Counts	Curtom 1995
			NATURE'S DIVINE	
			10-member soul group from Detroit.	
11/03/79	**65**	7	1 I Just Can't Control Myself	Infinity 50027
			DAVID NAUGHTON	
			Singer, dancer, actor. Star of TV's "Makin' It" and the film "An American Werewolf In London".	
3/31/79	**5**	24	1 ● **Makin' It**	RSO 916
			from the film "Meatballs"	
			JERRY NAYLOR	
			Former member of The Crickets.	
3/28/70	**69**	4	1 But For Love	Columbia 45106
			NAZARETH	
			Hard rock group formed in Scotland in 1969. Dan McCafferty, lead singer.	
11/22/75+	**8**	23	1 ● **Love Hurts**	A&M 1671
3/29/80	**87**	3	2 Holiday	A&M 2219
			NAZZ	
			Philadelphia rock quartet featuring Todd Rundgren, guitar, and Stewkey (real name: Robert Antoni), vocals.	
2/15/69+	**66**	13	1 Hello It's Me	SGC 001
			SAM NEELY	
			Born on 8/22/48 in Corpus Christi, Texas. Pop singer, songwriter.	
9/02/72	**29**	12	1 Loving You Just Crossed My Mind	Capitol 3381
1/27/73	**43**	8	2 Rosalie	Capitol 3510
9/21/74	**34**	11	3 You Can Have Her	A&M 1612
2/01/75	**54**	7	4 I Fought The Law	A&M 1651
8/27/77	**84**	4	5 Sail Away	Elektra 45419
			THE NEIGHBORHOOD	
6/27/70	**29**	11	1 Big Yellow Taxi	Big Tree 102
			NEKTAR	
			English art-rock quartet based in Germany.	
5/10/75	**91**	5	1 Astral Man	Passport 7904
			KAREN NELSON & BILLY T	
			Karen is from Kansas City, KS and served 3 years as backup singer/pianist for Paul Anka. Billy T (Tragesser) is from Pittsburgh.	
9/10/77	**79**	4	1 Love Me One More Time (Just For Old Times Sake)	Amherst 724
			PHYLLIS NELSON	
			Dance/disco singer from Philadelphia.	
2/08/86	**61**	11	1 I Like You	Carrere 05719
			RICKY NELSON	
			Born Eric Hilliard Nelson on 5/8/40 in Teaneck, NJ. Died on 12/31/85 in a plane crash in DeKalb, Texas. Son of bandleader Ozzie Nelson and vocalist Harriet Hilliard. Rick and brother David appeared on Nelson's radio show from March, 1949, later on TV, 1952 to 1966. Formed own Stone Canyon Band in 1969. Films "Rio Bravo", "Wackiest Ship In The Army", and "Love And Kisses". One of the first teen idols of the rock era.	
5/06/57	**17**	17	1 I'm Walking/	
5/13/57	**2[1]**	19	2 **A Teenager's Romance**	Verve 10047
			Best Seller #2 / Top 100 #8 / Jockey #8 / Juke Box #12	
8/26/57	**14**	12	3 You're My One And Only Love	Verve 10070
			Best Seller #14 / Top 100 #16	
			orchestra directed by Barney Kessel on above 3	
10/07/57	**3**	20	4 **Be-Bop Baby/**	
			Best Seller #3 / Top 100 #5 / Jockey #10	
10/07/57	**29**	9	5 Have I Told You Lately That I Love You?	Imperial 5463
			Bing Crosby & The Andrews Sisters' version hit #24 in 1950	
12/30/57+	**2[3]**	18	6 **Stood Up/**	
			Best Seller #2 / Top 100 #5 / Jockey #5	
12/30/57+	**18**	14	7 Waitin' In School	Imperial 5483
			Top 100 #18 / Jockey #24	

DEBUT DATE	PEAK POS	WKS CHR	ARTIST — Record Title	Label & Number
			RICKY NELSON — Cont'd	
3/31/58	**4**	12	8 **Believe What You Say/**	
			Best Seller #4 / Top 100 #8 / Jockey #20	
			above 2 written by Johnny & Dorsey Burnette (#14 & 41 written by Dorsey; #15 written by Johnny)	
4/07/58	**18**	12	9 My Bucket's Got A Hole In It	Imperial 5503
			Top 100 #18 / Jockey #25	
7/07/58	**1**[2]	15	10 **Poor Little Fool**	Imperial 5528
			Hot 100 #1(2) / Best Seller #1(2) / Jockey #2 end	
10/20/58	**7**	18	11 **Lonesome Town/**	
10/13/58	**10**	17	12 **I Got A Feeling**	Imperial 5545
2/23/59	**6**	16	13 **Never Be Anyone Else But You/**	
3/02/59	**9**	13	14 **It's Late**	Imperial 5565
6/29/59	**9**	13	15 **Just A Little Too Much/**	
7/06/59	**9**	12	16 **Sweeter Than You**	Imperial 5595
11/30/59	**20**	11	17 I Wanna Be Loved/	
11/30/59	**38**	9	18 Mighty Good	Imperial 5614
4/25/60	**12**	13	19 Young Emotions/	
5/02/60	**59**	6	20 Right By My Side	Imperial 5663
9/05/60	**27**	8	21 I'm Not Afraid/	
9/12/60	**34**	6	22 Yes Sir, That's My Baby	Imperial 5685
			#1 hit in 1925 for Gene Austin	
12/26/60+	**25**	8	23 You Are The Only One/	
12/31/60+	**79**	3	24 Milk Cow Blues	Imperial 5707
			originally recorded by the song's writer, Kokomo Arnold, in 1935	
4/24/61	**1**[2]	16	25● **Travelin' Man/**	
5/01/61	**9**	15	26 **Hello Mary Lou**	Imperial 5741
			written by Gene Pitney (also #43 below)	
			RICK NELSON:	
10/02/61	**11**	11	27 A Wonder Like You/	
10/02/61	**16**	10	28 Everlovin'	Imperial 5770
3/03/62	**5**	13	29 **Young World/**	
3/10/62	**89**	2	30 Summertime	Imperial 5805
			#12 hit in 1936 for Billie Holiday	
8/11/62	**5**	11	31 **Teen Age Idol**	Imperial 5864
12/15/62+	**6**	12	32 **It's Up To You/**	
12/22/62+	**83**	4	33 I Need You	Imperial 5901
			11-13, 16-18, 20, 23, 33: written by Baker Knight	
3/02/63	**48**	6	34 That's All/	
2/23/63	**67**	6	35 I'm In Love Again	Imperial 5910
3/09/63	**47**	7	36 You Don't Love Me Anymore (And I Can Tell)/	
3/16/63	**49**	6	37 I Got A Woman	Decca 31475
4/20/63	**100**	1	38 If You Can't Rock Me/	
5/04/63	**94**	3	39 Old Enough To Love	Imperial 5935
5/25/63	**25**	9	40 String Along/	
5/18/63	**62**	9	41 Gypsy Woman	Decca 31495
9/14/63	**12**	13	42 Fools Rush In	Decca 31533
			#1 hit in 1940 for Glenn Miller	
11/30/63+	**54**	9	43 Today's Teardrops	Imperial 66004
12/28/63+	**6**	11	44 **For You**	Decca 31574
			#9 hit in 1930 for John Boles	
3/14/64	**63**	5	45 Congratulations	Imperial 66017
			25, 27, 29, 32 & 45: written by Jerry Fuller	
4/25/64	**26**	7	46 The Very Thought Of You	Decca 31612
			#1 hit in 1934 for Ray Noble	
8/22/64	**47**	6	47 There's Nothing I Can Say	Decca 31656
11/28/64	**82**	4	48 A Happy Guy	Decca 31703
3/20/65	**96**	2	49 Mean Old World	Decca 31756
			written by Billy Vera of Billy & The Beaters	
10/11/69+	**33**	18	50 She Belongs To Me	Decca 32550
			written by Bob Dylan	
3/07/70	**48**	6	51 Easy To Be Free	Decca 32635
7/29/72	**6**	19	52● **Garden Party**	Decca 32980
2/03/73	**65**	5	53 Palace Guard	MCA 40001
			50, 52 & 53: **RICK NELSON & THE STONE CANYON BAND**	

DEBUT DATE	PEAK POS	WKS CHR	ARTIST — Record Title	Label & Number
			SANDY NELSON	
			Born Sander Nelson on 12/1/38 in Santa Monica, CA. Rock 'n roll drummer. Became prominent studio musician. Heard on "Alley Oop", "To Know Him Is To Love Him", "A Thousand Stars", and many others. Lost portion of right leg in a motorcycle accident in 1963. Returned to performing in 1964.	
9/07/59	**4**	16	1 **Teen Beat** [I]	Original Sound 5
10/30/61	**7**	16	2 **Let There Be Drums** [I]	Imperial 5775
2/10/62	**29**	7	3 Drums Are My Beat/ [I]	
2/24/62	**75**	1	4 The Birth Of The Beat [I]	Imperial 5809
4/28/62	**67**	8	5 Drummin' Up A Storm/ [I]	
5/26/62	**86**	3	6 Drum Stomp [I]	Imperial 5829
7/14/62	**75**	3	7 All Night Long [I]	Imperial 5860
9/22/62	**65**	4	8 And Then There Were Drums [I]	Imperial 5870
9/19/64	**44**	10	9 Teen Beat '65 [I] live version of 1959 hit	Imperial 66060
			WILLIE NELSON	
			Born on 4/30/33 in Abbott, Texas. Prolific country singer, songwriter. Pioneered "outlaw" country movement. Starred in several films including "The Electric Horseman" and "Honeysuckle Rose".	
8/30/75	**21**	18	1 Blue Eyes Crying In The Rain	Columbia 10176
1/10/76	**67**	8	2 Remember Me	Columbia 10275
2/07/76	**25**	12	3 Good Hearted Woman	RCA 10529
2/11/78	**42**	10	4 Mammas Don't Let Your Babies Grow Up To Be Cowboys above 2: **WAYLON & WILLIE**	RCA 11198
5/27/78	**84**	6	5 Georgia On My Mind written in 1930 by Hoagy Carmichael	Columbia 10704
2/09/80	**44**	10	6 My Heroes Have Always Been Cowboys from the film "The Electric Horseman"	Columbia 11186
9/06/80	**20**	20	7 On The Road Again from the film "Honeysuckle Rose"	Columbia 11351
3/06/82	**5**	23	8 **Always On My Mind**	Columbia 02741
4/03/82	**52**	9	9 Just To Satisfy You **WAYLON & WILLIE**	RCA 13073
8/07/82	**40**	12	10 Let It Be Me	Columbia 03073
3/03/84	**5**	21	11● **To All The Girls I've Loved Before** **JULIO IGLESIAS & WILLIE NELSON**	Columbia 04217
			NENA	
			Gabriele "Nena" Kerner with 4-member backup group from West Germany.	
12/10/83+	**2**[1]	23	1● **99 Luftballons** [F] nuclear protest song	Epic 04108
			THE NEON PHILHARMONIC	
			Chamber-sized orchestra of Nashville Symphony Orchestra musicians. Project headed by Tupper Saussy (composer) and Don Gant (vocals). Gant died on 3/6/87 (44).	
4/05/69	**17**	12	1 Morning Girl	Warner 7261
5/30/70	**94**	2	2 Heighdy-Ho Princess	Warner 7380
			PETER NERO	
			Born on 5/22/34 in Brooklyn. Pop-jazz-classical pianist.	
10/16/71	**21**	13	1 Theme From 'Summer Of '42' [I] from the film of the same title	Columbia 45399
			NERVOUS NORVUS	
			Real name: Jimmy Drake.	
6/02/56	**8**	14	1 **Transfusion** [N] Best Seller #8 / Top 100 #13 / Jockey #14 / Juke Box #18	Dot 15470
7/28/56	**24**	10	2 Ape Call [N] Best Seller #24 / Top 100 #28 ape calls by Red Blanchard	Dot 15485
			MICHAEL NESMITH & THE FIRST NATIONAL BAND	
			Born on 12/30/43 in Houston. Michael was a professional musician before joining The Monkees. Wrote Linda Ronstadt's hit "Different Drum".	
8/08/70	**21**	12	1 Joanne	RCA 0368
11/28/70+	**42**	9	2 Silver Moon	RCA 0399
4/17/71	**70**	4	3 Nevada Fighter	RCA 0453
			LOZ NETTO	
			Former guitarist with Sniff 'N The Tears. From Coventry, England.	
6/04/83	**82**	6	1 Fade Away	21 Records 104

DEBUT DATE	PEAK POS	WKS CHR	ARTIST — Record Title	Label & Number
			AARON NEVILLE	
			Born in New Orleans in 1941. Member of the New Orleans' R&B family group The Neville Brothers. Brother Art was keyboardist of The Meters.	
12/03/66+	**2^1**	14	1 **Tell It Like It Is**	Par-Lo 101
3/25/67	**92**	4	2 She Took You For A Ride	Par-Lo 103
			ROBBIE NEVIL	
			Pop singer, songwriter, guitarist.	
10/11/86+	**2^2**	23	1 **C'est La Vie**	Manhattan 50047
			THE NEWBEATS	
			Pop trio: Larry Henley (b: 6/30/41, Arp, TX), lead singer, and brothers Dean & Marc Mathis, born in Hahira, GA on 3/17/39 and 2/9/42, respectively.	
8/15/64	**2^2**	12	1 **Bread And Butter**	Hickory 1269
10/24/64	**16**	9	2 Everything's Alright	Hickory 1282
1/23/65	**40**	7	3 Break Away (From That Boy)	Hickory 1290
4/03/65	**50**	7	4 (The Bees Are For The Birds) The Birds Are For The Bees	Hickory 1305
10/02/65	**12**	13	5 Run, Baby Run (Back Into My Arms)	Hickory 1332
2/26/66	**92**	3	6 Shake Hands (And Come Out Crying)	Hickory 1366
12/20/69+	**82**	5	7 Groovin' (Out On Life)	Hickory 1552
			THE NEW BIRTH	
			R&B vocal group portion of New Birth, Inc. (see Nite-Liters). Original group consisted of vocalists Londee Loren, Bobby Downs; Melvin Wilson, Leslie Wilson and Ann Bogan (aka: Love, Peace & Happiness); and soloist Alan Frye with instrumental backing by The Nite-Liters.	
10/09/71	**52**	9	1 It's Impossible	RCA 0520
3/24/73	**35**	13	2 I Can Understand It	RCA 0912
8/25/73	**97**	3	3 Until It's Time For You To Go	RCA 0003
2/16/74	**66**	6	4 It's Been A Long Time	RCA 0185
5/11/74	**45**	9	5 Wildflower	RCA 0265
10/12/74	**88**	3	6 I Wash My Hands Of The Whole Damn Deal, Part I	RCA 10017
5/24/75	**95**	3	7 Granddaddy (Part 1)	Buddah 464
7/05/75	**36**	11	8 Dream Merchant	Buddah 470
			THE NEW CHRISTY MINSTRELS	
			Folk/balladeer troupe named after the Christy Minstrels (formed in 1842 by Edwin "Pop" Christy). Group founded and led by Randy Sparks; Barry McGuire, member.	
12/01/62	**93**	1	1 This Land Is Your Land	Columbia 42592
6/29/63	**14**	12	2 Green, Green	Columbia 42805
10/26/63	**29**	7	3 Saturday Night	Columbia 42887
4/18/64	**17**	13	4 Today from the film "Advance To The Rear"	Columbia 43000
8/08/64	**92**	2	5 Silly Ol' Summertime	Columbia 43092
4/24/65	**81**	5	6 Chim, Chim, Cheree from the film "Mary Poppins"	Columbia 43215
			THE NEW COLONY SIX	
			Soft-rock group from Chicago: Patrick McBride, Ray Graffia, Ronnie Rice, Gerry Van Kollenburg, Les Kummel, Chuck Jobes and William Herman.	
2/19/66	**80**	4	1 I Confess	Centaur 1201
2/18/67	**61**	6	2 Love You So Much	Sentar 1205
3/30/68	**22**	13	3 I Will Always Think About You	Mercury 72775
6/15/68	**52**	8	4 Can't You See Me Cry	Mercury 72817
12/28/68+	**16**	16	5 Things I'd Like To Say	Mercury 72858
5/03/69	**50**	8	6 I Could Never Lie To You	Mercury 72920
8/30/69	**65**	6	7 I Want You To Know	Mercury 72961
1/10/70	**78**	5	8 Barbara, I Love You	Mercury 73004
8/21/71	**56**	9	9 Roll On	Sunlight 1001
12/11/71+	**93**	4	10 Long Time To Be Alone	Sunlight 1004
			THE NEWCOMERS	
			R&B trio: Terry Bartlett, William Somlin and Bertrand Brown.	
9/11/71	**74**	5	1 Pin The Tail On The Donkey instrumental backing by The Bar-Kays	Stax 0099

DEBUT DATE	PEAK POS	WKS CHR	ARTIST — Record Title	Label & Number
			NEW EDITION R&B group formed in Boston, consisting of 5 boys (ages 13 to 15 in 1983): Ralph Tresvant, Ronald DeVoe, Michael Bivins, Ricky Bell and Bobby Brown (left for solo career in 1986).	
5/07/83	**46**	11	1 Candy Girl	Streetwise 1108
10/15/83	**85**	4	2 Is This The End	Streetwise 1111
9/22/84+	**4**	25	3 ● **Cool It Now**	MCA 52455
12/22/84+	**12**	16	4 Mr. Telephone Man	MCA 52484
3/30/85	**35**	14	5 Lost In Love	MCA 52553
11/02/85	**51**	15	6 Count Me Out	MCA 52703
2/22/86	**38**	15	7 A Little Bit Of Love (Is All It Takes)	MCA 52768
6/14/86	**51**	11	8 With You All The Way	MCA 52829
8/23/86	**21**	14	9 Earth Angel featured in the film "The Karate Kid Part II"	MCA 52905
			NEW ENGLAND East Coast melodic rock quartet.	
5/05/79	**40**	12	1 Don't Ever Wanna Lose Ya	Infinity 50013
9/01/79	**69**	5	2 Hello, Hello, Hello	Infinity 50021
			THE NEW ESTABLISHMENT	
11/29/69	**92**	2	1 (One Of These Days) Sunday's Gonna' Come On Tuesday	Colgems 5006
			THE NEW HOPE	
1/03/70	**57**	9	1 Won't Find Better (Than Me)	Jamie 1381
			NEW RIDERS OF THE PURPLE SAGE San Francisco country-rock band formed in 1969 by Jerry Garcia as an offshoot of the Grateful Dead.	
6/10/72	**81**	5	1 I Don't Need No Doctor	Columbia 45607
			THE NEW SEEKERS British-Australian group formed by former Seeker Keith Potger after disbandment of The Seekers in 1969. Consisted of Eve Graham, Lyn Paul, Peter Doyle, Marty Kristian and Paul Layton.	
9/05/70	**14**	12	1 Look What They've Done To My Song Ma	Elektra 45699
1/09/71	**67**	7	2 Beautiful People	Elektra 45710
3/20/71	**81**	5	3 Nickel Song above 3 written by Melanie	Elektra 45719
12/04/71+	**7**	11	4 ● **I'd Like To Teach The World To Sing (In Perfect Harmony)**	Elektra 45762
4/22/72	**81**	4	5 Beg, Steal Or Borrow	Elektra 45780
7/15/72	**87**	5	6 Circles	Elektra 45787
9/23/72	**84**	5	7 Dance, Dance, Dance all of above produced by David Mackay	Elektra 45805
1/27/73	**95**	3	8 Come Softly To Me	Verve 10698
2/24/73	**29**	13	9 Pinball Wizard/See Me, Feel Me from the rock opera "Tommy"	Verve 10709
			THE NEW VAUDEVILLE BAND Creation of British composer/record producer Geoff Stephens.	
10/29/66	**1**[3]	15	1 ● **Winchester Cathedral**	Fontana 1562
2/18/67	**72**	4	2 Peek-A-Boo	Fontana 1573
			NEW YORK CITY New York City R&B quartet: Tim McQueen, John Brown, Ed Schell and Claude Johnson. First recorded for Buddah as Triboro Exchange. Name changed in 1972.	
3/03/73	**17**	20	1 I'm Doin' Fine Now	Chelsea 0113
9/01/73	**93**	5	2 Make Me Twice The Man	Chelsea 0025
2/02/74	**79**	7	3 Quick, Fast, In A Hurry	Chelsea 0150
			NEW YORKERS R&B group led by Fred Parris of The Five Satins.	
5/15/61	**69**	5	1 Miss Fine	Wall 547
			MICKEY NEWBURY Born Milton Newbury, Jr. on 5/19/40 in Houston. Elected to the Writer's Hall of Fame in Nashville.	
11/06/71+	**26**	11	1 An American Trilogy Dixie/Battle Hymn Of The Republic/All My Trials	Elektra 45750
7/21/73	**87**	3	2 Sunshine	Elektra 45853

DEBUT DATE	PEAK POS	WKS CHR	ARTIST — Record Title	Label & Number
			NEWCLEUS	
			New York rap group.	
6/02/84	**56**	15	1 Jam On It.......... [N]	Sunnyview 3010
			ANTHONY NEWLEY	
			Born on 9/24/31 in London. Actor, singer, composer, comedian.	
7/18/60	**91**	2	1 Do You Mind?..........	London 1918
10/10/60	**67**	5	2 If She Should Come To You (La Montana)..........	London 1929
12/04/61+	**85**	4	3 Pop Goes The Weasel.......... [N]	London 9501
			hip version of a traditional English tune from 1853	
9/22/62	**85**	4	4 What Kind Of Fool Am I..........	London 9546
			from the musical "Stop The World-I Want To Get Off"	
			JIMMY NEWMAN	
			Born on 8/27/27 in Big Namou, Louisiana. Country singer, guitarist.	
6/10/57	**23**	16	1 A Fallen Star..........	Dot 15574
			Jockey #23 / Top 100 #42	
			LIONEL NEWMAN	
			Born in 1916. Top film composer; scored numerous films from late 30s into the 60s. Has received 10 Oscar nominations and won an Oscar in 1969 for "Hello Dolly".	
8/04/56	**72**	1	1 Theme From "The Proud Ones".......... [I]	Columbia 40717
			from the film of the same title - whistler: Muzzy Marcellino	
			RANDY NEWMAN	
			Born on 11/28/43 in New Orleans. Singer, composer, pianist. Nephew of composers Alfred, Emil and Lionel Newman. Scored the films "Ragtime" and "The Natural".	
11/12/77+	**2**[3]	20	1 ● **Short People**.......... [N]	Warner 8492
1/22/83	**51**	8	2 The Blues..........	Warner 29803
			RANDY NEWMAN & PAUL SIMON	
			TED NEWMAN	
9/30/57	**45**	9	1 Plaything..........	Rev 3505
			JUICE NEWTON	
			Born Judy Cohen on 2/18/52 in Virginia Beach, VA. Pop/country-styled singer.	
4/08/78	**86**	3	1 It's A Heartache..........	Capitol 4552
2/21/81	**4**	22	2 ● **Angel Of The Morning**..........	Capitol 4976
5/30/81	**2**[2]	27	3 ● **Queen Of Hearts**..........	Capitol 4997
10/17/81+	**7**	24	4 **The Sweetest Thing (I've Ever Known)**..........	Capitol 5046
5/08/82	**7**	17	5 **Love's Been A Little Bit Hard On Me**..........	Capitol 5120
8/21/82	**11**	17	6 Break It To Me Gently..........	Capitol 5148
11/27/82+	**25**	16	7 Heart Of The Night..........	Capitol 5192
8/13/83	**27**	11	8 Tell Her No..........	Capitol 5265
11/05/83	**90**	3	9 Dirty Looks..........	Capitol 5289
6/02/84	**44**	10	10 A Little Love..........	RCA 13823
8/11/84	**66**	6	11 Can't Wait All Night..........	RCA 13863
			2-11: produced by Richard Landis	
			WAYNE NEWTON	
			Born on 4/3/42 in Roanoke, Virginia. Singer, multi-instrumentalist. Las Vegas' #1 entertainer. First big break came in 1962 on the Jackie Gleason TV show. Bobby Darin saw Wayne, signed him up and produced his first charted single.	
4/27/63	**82**	4	1 Heart! (I Hear You Beating)..........	Capitol 4920
7/13/63	**13**	12	2 Danke Schoen..........	Capitol 4989
10/26/63	**58**	7	3 Shirl Girl..........	Capitol 5058
			above 3 with The Newton Brothers (Wayne's brother, Jerry)	
5/02/64	**99**	2	4 The Little White Cloud That Cried..........	Challenge 59238
			Johnnie Ray's version hit #2 in 1952	
1/30/65	**65**	5	5 Comin' On Too Strong..........	Capitol 5338
2/27/65	**23**	9	6 Red Roses For A Blue Lady..........	Capitol 5366
5/22/65	**52**	6	7 I'll Be With You In Apple Blossom Time..........	Capitol 5419
			first popularized in 1920 by Charles Harrison (POS 2)	
8/07/65	**78**	4	8 Summer Wind..........	Capitol 5470
10/16/65	**69**	4	9 Remember When..........	Capitol 5514
10/22/66	**86**	6	10 Games That Lovers Play..........	Capitol 5754
6/29/68	**60**	7	11 Dreams Of The Everyday Housewife..........	MGM 13955
4/22/72	**4**	20	12 ● **Daddy Don't You Walk So Fast**..........	Chelsea 0100
9/23/72	**48**	8	13 Can't You Hear The Song?..........	Chelsea 0105
12/23/72+	**65**	5	14 Anthem..........	Chelsea 0109

DEBUT DATE	PEAK POS	WKS CHR	ARTIST — Record Title	Label & Number
			WAYNE NEWTON — Cont'd	
5/29/76	**82**	4	15 The Hungry Years	Chelsea 3041
9/15/79	**90**	8	16 You Stepped Into My Life	Aries II 101
2/02/80	**35**	13	17 Years	Aries II 108
			OLIVIA NEWTON-JOHN	
			Born on 9/26/48 in Cambridge, England. To Australia in 1953. At age 16 won talent contest trip to England, sang with Pat Carroll as Pat & Olivia. With group Toomorrow, in a British film of the same name. Consistent award winner in both pop and country. Films "Grease", 1978; "Xanadu", 1980; "Two Of A Kind", 1983. Also see John Denver.	
5/29/71	**25**	17	1 If Not For You written by Bob Dylan	Uni 55281
10/16/71	**94**	4	2 Banks Of The Ohio	Uni 55304
11/17/73+	**6**	19	3 ● **Let Me Be There**	MCA 40101
4/13/74	**5**	20	4 ● **If You Love Me (Let Me Know)**	MCA 40209
8/17/74	**1**[2]	15	5 ● **I Honestly Love You**	MCA 40280
1/25/75	**1**[1]	16	6 ● **Have You Never Been Mellow**	MCA 40349
6/07/75	**3**	15	7 ● **Please Mr. Please**	MCA 40418
9/20/75	**13**	11	8 Something Better To Do	MCA 40459
12/06/75+	**30**	9	9 Let It Shine/	
		9	10 He Ain't Heavy...He's My Brother	MCA 40495
3/13/76	**23**	12	11 Come On Over	MCA 40525
8/07/76	**33**	9	12 Don't Stop Believin'	MCA 40600
11/06/76	**55**	9	13 Every Face Tells A Story	MCA 40642
1/29/77	**20**	13	14 Sam	MCA 40670
6/18/77	**87**	4	15 Making A Good Thing Better	MCA 40737
11/05/77	**48**	9	16 I Honestly Love You [R]	MCA 40811
4/01/78	**1**[1]	24	17 ▲ **You're The One That I Want** **JOHN TRAVOLTA & OLIVIA NEWTON-JOHN**	RSO 891
7/08/78	**3**	19	18 ● **Hopelessly Devoted To You**	RSO 903
8/05/78	**5**	16	19 ● **Summer Nights** **JOHN TRAVOLTA & OLIVIA NEWTON-JOHN & CAST** above 3 from the film "Grease"	RSO 906
11/25/78+	**3**	20	20 ● **A Little More Love**	MCA 40975
4/14/79	**11**	13	21 Deeper Than The Night	MCA 41009
7/28/79	**52**	6	22 Totally Hot/	
9/22/79	**82**	2	23 Dancin' 'Round And 'Round	MCA 41074
3/29/80	**12**	13	24 I Can't Help It **ANDY GIBB & OLIVIA NEWTON-JOHN**	RSO 1026
5/24/80	**1**[4]	23	25 ● **Magic**	MCA 41247
8/09/80	**8**	17	26 **Xanadu** **OLIVIA NEWTON-JOHN/ELECTRIC LIGHT ORCHESTRA**	MCA 41285
10/25/80+	**20**	19	27 Suddenly **OLIVIA NEWTON-JOHN & CLIFF RICHARD** above 3 from the film "Xanadu"	MCA 51007
10/03/81	**1**[10]	26	28 ▲ **Physical**	MCA 51182
2/13/82	**5**	14	29 **Make A Move On Me**	MCA 52000
6/12/82	**52**	8	30 Landslide	MCA 52069
9/04/82	**3**	21	31 **Heart Attack**	MCA 52100
1/15/83	**38**	11	32 Tied Up 1,6,8,12,17-18,20,22,25,27,29-30 & 32: written by John Farrar	MCA 52155
11/05/83+	**5**	18	33 **Twist Of Fate**	MCA 52284
2/11/84	**31**	10	34 Livin' In Desperate Times above 2 from the film "Two Of A Kind"	MCA 52341
10/05/85	**20**	15	35 Soul Kiss all of above produced by John Farrar (except #19, 24, 26, 33-34)	MCA 52686
6/14/86	**80**	8	36 The Best Of Me **DAVID FOSTER & OLIVIA NEWTON-JOHN**	Atlantic 89420
			PAUL NICHOLAS	
			British theater/film actor. Played Billy Shears' brother in film "Sgt. Pepper's Lonely Hearts Club Band".	
8/20/77	**6**	23	1 ● **Heaven On The 7th Floor**	RSO 878
7/29/78	**67**	5	2 On The Strip	RSO 887

DEBUT DATE	PEAK POS	WKS CHR	ARTIST — Record Title	Label & Number
			STEVIE NICKS	
			Born on 5/26/48 in Phoenix and raised in California. Became vocalist of Bay-area group Fritz and subsequently met guitarist Lindsey Buckingham. Teamed up and recorded album "Buckingham-Nicks" in 1973. Vocalist with Fleetwood Mac since January, 1975. Also see Robbie Patton.	
7/25/81	**3**	21	1 **Stop Draggin' My Heart Around**	Modern 7336
			STEVIE NICKS with TOM PETTY & THE HEARTBREAKERS	
10/24/81+	**6**	19	2 **Leather And Lace**	Modern 7341
			STEVIE NICKS with DON HENLEY	
2/20/82	**11**	14	3 Edge Of Seventeen (Just Like The White Winged Dove)	Modern 7401
5/15/82	**32**	11	4 After The Glitter Fades...........................	Modern 7405
6/04/83	**5**	19	5 **Stand Back**	Modern 99863
9/10/83	**14**	14	6 If Anyone Falls	Modern 99832
12/17/83+	**33**	12	7 Nightbird	Modern 99799
			with Sandy Stewart (co-writer on above 2)	
11/16/85+	**4**	18	8 **Talk To Me**	Modern 99582
2/01/86	**37**	9	9 Needles And Pins...........................	MCA 52772
			TOM PETTY & THE HEARTBREAKERS WITH STEVIE NICKS	
			live version of The Searchers 1964 #13 hit	
2/22/86	**16**	13	10 I Can't Wait...........................	Modern 99565
			all of above produced by Jimmy Iovine	
5/17/86	**60**	6	11 Has Anyone Ever Written Anything For You..............	Modern 99532
			Stevie wrote all of the above (except #1, 9 & 10)	
			NIELSEN/PEARSON	
			Sacramento pop duo: Reid Nielsen and Mark Pearson.	
9/13/80	**38**	14	1 If You Should Sail...........................	Capitol 4910
8/08/81	**56**	8	2 The Sun Ain't Gonna Shine Anymore...........................	Capitol 5032
			NIGHT	
			Stevie Lange and Chris Thompson (Manfred Mann), lead singers.	
6/23/79	**18**	15	1 Hot Summer Nights...........................	Planet 45903
8/25/79	**17**	19	2 If You Remember Me	Planet 45909
			CHRIS THOMPSON & NIGHT	
2/21/81	**87**	3	3 Love On The Airwaves...........................	Planet 47921
			THE NIGHTCRAWLERS	
1/21/67	**85**	4	1 The Little Black Egg	Kapp 709
			MAXINE NIGHTINGALE	
			Born on 11/2/52 in Wembly, England. First recorded in 1968. In productions of "Hair", "Jesus Christ Superstar", "Godspell" and "Savages", early 70s.	
2/14/76	**2**[2]	20	1 ● **Right Back Where We Started From**...........................	United Art. 752
7/17/76	**53**	8	2 Gotta Be The One	United Art. 820
5/26/79	**5**	23	3 ● **Lead Me On**	Windsong 11530
11/03/79	**73**	5	4 (Bringing Out) The Girl In Me	Windsong 11729
			NIGHT RANGER	
			Rock quintet from California: Kelly Keagy (drums) and Jack Blades (bass), lead singers; Jeff Watson and Brad Gillis, guitars; Alan "Fitz" Gerald, keyboards.	
1/15/83	**40**	11	1 Don't Tell Me You Love Me...........................	Boardwalk 171
4/09/83	**54**	9	2 Sing Me Away	Boardwalk 175
12/03/83+	**51**	12	3 (You Can Still) Rock In America	MCA/Camel 52305
3/10/84	**5**	24	4 **Sister Christian**...........................	MCA/Camel 52350
7/14/84	**14**	17	5 When You Close Your Eyes	MCA/Camel 52420
5/25/85	**8**	17	6 **Sentimental Street**...........................	MCA/Camel 52591
8/24/85	**19**	13	7 Four In The Morning (I Can't Take Any More)	MCA/Camel 52661
11/09/85+	**17**	18	8 Goodbye	MCA/Camel 52729
			all of above written by Jack Blades (except #4)	
			NILSSON	
			Born Harry Edward Nelson, III on 6/15/41 in Brooklyn. Wrote Three Dog Night's hit "One"; scored the film "Skidoo" and TV's "The Courtship Of Eddie's Father". Close friend of John Lennon and Ringo Starr.	
8/16/69	**6**	12	1 **Everybody's Talkin'**	RCA 0161
			theme song from the film "Midnight Cowboy"	
11/01/69	**34**	7	2 I Guess The Lord Must Be In New York City	RCA 0261

DEBUT DATE	PEAK POS	WKS CHR	ARTIST — Record Title	Label & Number
			NILSSON — Cont'd	
3/20/71	**34**	15	3 Me And My Arrow	RCA 0443
12/18/71+	**1**[4]	19	4 ● **Without You**	RCA 0604
3/18/72	**27**	9	5 Jump Into The Fire	RCA 0673
6/10/72	**8**	14	6 **Coconut**	RCA 0718
9/16/72	**23**	10	7 Spaceman	RCA 0788
12/23/72+	**53**	6	8 Remember (Christmas)	RCA 0855
			above 5 produced by Richard Perry	
9/01/73	**86**	5	9 As Time Goes By	RCA 0039
4/13/74	**39**	9	10 Daybreak	RCA 0246
			from the film "Son Of Dracula"	
			2-3, 5-8 & 10: written by Nilsson	
			9.9	
			Black trio from Boston: Margot Thunder, Leslie Jones, Wanda Perry.	
8/24/85	**51**	13	1 All Of Me For All Of You	RCA 14082
			1910 FRUITGUM CO.	
			New Jersey bubblegum quintet: Mark Gutkowski, Floyd Marcus, Pat Karwan, Steve Mortkowski and Frank Jeckell.	
1/27/68	**4**	14	1 ● **Simon Says**	Buddah 24
4/20/68	**63**	8	2 May I Take A Giant Step (Into Your Heart)	Buddah 39
7/27/68	**5**	13	3 ● **1, 2, 3, Red Light**	Buddah 54
10/26/68	**37**	9	4 Goody Goody Gumdrops	Buddah 71
1/25/69	**5**	13	5 ● **Indian Giver**	Buddah 91
5/10/69	**38**	9	6 Special Delivery	Buddah 114
8/23/69	**57**	10	7 The Train	Buddah 130
			NINO & THE EBB TIDES	
			New York City vocal group: Antonio "Nino" Aiello, lead; Tony DiBari, tenor; Tony Imbimbo, baritone; and Vinnie Drago, bass.	
9/04/61	**57**	5	1 Juke Box Saturday Night [N]	Madison 166
			featuring "Book Of Love" and "Get A Job"	
			THE NITE-LITERS	
			R&B band formed in Louisville in 1963 by Harvey Fuqua and Tony Churchill. Expanded to 17-members with two vocal groups and band. Renamed New Birth, Inc., with The Nite-Liters making up the instrumental section. Also see Love, Peace & Happiness, and New Birth.	
7/03/71	**39**	16	1 K-Jee [I]	RCA 0461
2/26/72	**49**	8	2 Afro-Strut [I]	RCA 0591
			NITEFLYTE	
			Disco group - lead singers: Howard Johnson and Sandy Torano.	
9/15/79	**37**	13	1 If You Want It	Ariola 7747
			THE NITTY GRITTY DIRT BAND	
			Country/rock/folk group from Long Beach, CA. Led by Jeff Hanna (vocals, guitar) and John McEuen (banjo, mandolin). Ex-Eagle Bernie Leadon replaced McEuen in 1987.	
4/08/67	**45**	7	1 Buy For Me The Rain	Liberty 55948
11/21/70+	**9**	19	2 **Mr. Bojangles**	Liberty 56197
			prologue: Uncle Charlie and His Dog Teddy	
4/24/71	**53**	13	3 House At Pooh Corner	United Art. 50769
9/11/71	**64**	8	4 Some Of Shelly's Blues	United Art. 50817
4/01/72	**84**	3	5 Jambalaya (On The Bayou)	United Art. 50890
10/12/74	**72**	4	6 Battle Of New Orleans	United Art. 544
8/30/75	**66**	6	7 (All I Have To Do Is) Dream	United Art. 655
			2-7: produced by William E. McEuen (John's brother)	
			THE DIRT BAND:	
9/02/78	**86**	3	8 In For The Night	United Art. 1228
12/08/79+	**13**	19	9 An American Dream	United Art. 1330
			harmony vocal: Linda Ronstadt	
6/21/80	**25**	16	10 Make A Little Magic	United Art. 1356
10/03/81	**76**	4	11 Fire In The Sky	Liberty 1429
			JACK NITZSCHE	
			Born Bernard Nitzsche on 4/22/37 in Chicago. Arranger, producer, composer, keyboardist. Arranger for many of Phil Spector's productions. Wrote "Needles And Pins" and scored the film "One Flew Over The Cuckoo's Nest".	
8/10/63	**39**	8	1 The Lonely Surfer [I]	Reprise 20202
11/23/63	**91**	2	2 Rumble [I]	Reprise 20225

DEBUT DATE	PEAK POS	WKS CHR	ARTIST — Record Title		Label & Number
			DON NIX		
			Born on 9/27/41 in Memphis. Vocals, guitar, saxophone. Formerly in the Mar-Keys.		
10/09/71	**94**	3	1 Olena		Elektra 45746
			NICK NOBLE		
			Born Nicholas Valkan on 6/21/36 in Chicago.		
8/20/55	**22**	4	1 The Bible Tells Me So		Wing 90003
			Best Seller #22 / Top 100 #61 pre		
2/25/56	**27**	16	2 To You, My Love		Mercury 70821
7/15/57	**20**	1	3 A Fallen Star		Mercury 71124
			Jockey #20		
9/09/57	**37**	8	4 Moonlight Swim		Mercury 71169
			CLIFF NOBLES & CO.		
			Cliff was born in Mobile, Alabama in 1944. Soul bandleader.		
5/25/68	**2**[3]	14	1 ● **The Horse**	[I]	Phil-L.A. 313
9/14/68	**68**	5	2 Horse Fever	[I]	Phil-L.A. 318
2/15/69	**93**	3	3 Switch It On	[I]	Phil-L.A. 324
			all of above written & produced by Jesse James		
			JACKY NOGUEZ		
			Popular European society bandleader from Paris.		
6/22/59	**24**	12	1 Ciao, Ciao Bambina	[I]	Jamie 1127
11/16/59	**87**	3	2 Marina	[I]	Jamie 1137
1/18/60	**63**	6	3 Amapola	[I]	Jamie 1148
			#1 hit in 1941 for Jimmy Dorsey		
			NOLAN - see NOLAN PORTER		
			KENNY NOLAN		
			Los Angeles-based singer/songwriter. Wrote "My Eyes Adored You", "Lady Marmalade" and "Get Dancin'". Also see The Eleventh Hour.		
11/06/76+	**3**	27	1 ● **I Like Dreamin'**		20th Century 2287
4/02/77	**20**	18	2 Love's Grown Deep		20th Century 2331
10/15/77	**97**	3	3 My Eyes Get Blurry		20th Century 2352
2/02/80	**44**	8	4 Us And Love (We Go Together)		Casablanca 2234
			CHRIS NORMAN - see SUZI QUATRO		
			JIMMY NORMAN		
6/16/62	**47**	8	1 I Don't Love You No More (I Don't Care About You)		Little Star 113
			FREDDIE NORTH		
			Black vocalist from Nashville. Worked in sales and promotion for Nashboro Records. Disc jockey on "Night Train", WLAC-Nashville.		
10/02/71	**39**	12	1 She's All I Got		Mankind 12004
			TOM NORTHCOTT		
3/16/68	**88**	2	1 1941		Warner 7160
			NORTHERN LIGHT		
5/03/75	**88**	6	1 Minnesota		Columbia 10136
			DOROTHY NORWOOD		
			Gospel singer; formerly with the Caravans. Own group, the Dorothy Norwood Singers.		
2/23/74	**88**	4	1 There's Got To Be Rain In Your Life (To Appreciate The Sunshine)		GRC 1011
			ALDO NOVA		
			Born Aldo Scarporuscio in Montreal. Rock singer, songwriter, guitarist, keyboards.		
3/27/82	**23**	16	1 Fantasy		Portrait 02799
7/17/82	**65**	6	2 Foolin' Yourself		Portrait 03001
			THE NOVAS		
			Group originally known as The Avons.		
1/09/65	**88**	3	1 The Crusher	[N]	Parrot 45005
			vocal is impersonation of Milwaukee's pro wrestler "The Crusher"		
			NRBQ		
			Multi-styled group formed as the New Rhythm & Blues Quartet in Miami in 1967.		
2/02/74	**70**	6	1 Get That Gasoline Blues		Kama Sutra 586

DEBUT DATE	PEAK POS	WKS CHR	ARTIST — Record Title	Label & Number
			NU SHOOZ	
			Portland, Oregon group centered around husband and wife team of guitarist, songwriter John Smith and lead singer Valerie Day.	
3/08/86	**3**	23	1 **I Can't Wait**	Atlantic 89446
7/05/86	**28**	22	2 Point Of No Return	Atlantic 89392
			THE NU TORNADOS	
			Philadelphia string band. Eddie Dono, leader. Also see Ferko String Band.	
11/17/58	**26**	12	1 Philadelphia U.S.A.	Carlton 492
			TED NUGENT	
			Born on 12/13/48 in Detroit. Heavy metal rock guitarist; leader of The Amboy Dukes.	
3/27/76	**72**	5	1 Hey Baby	Epic 50197
11/27/76	**91**	2	2 Dog Eat Dog	Epic 50301
8/13/77	**30**	11	3 Cat Scratch Fever	Epic 50425
2/04/78	**70**	4	4 Home Bound [I]	Epic 50493
4/01/78	**58**	7	5 Yank Me, Crank Me	Epic 50533
1/06/79	**84**	2	6 Need You Bad	Epic 50648
7/26/80	**86**	4	7 Wango Tango	Epic 50907
			GARY NUMAN	
			Born Gary Webb on 3/8/58 in Hammersmith, England. Synthesized techno-rock artist.	
2/16/80	**9**	25	1 **Cars**	Atco 7211
			THE NUTTY SQUIRRELS	
			Creators and voices: Don Elliot (from Sommerville, NJ) and Sascha Burland (from New York City).	
11/09/59	**14**	12	1 Uh! Oh! Part 2/ [N]	
12/07/59	**45**	6	2 Uh! Oh! Part 1 [N]	Hanover 4540
			LAURA NYRO	
			Born Laura Nigro on 10/18/47 in Bronx, NY. White soul-gospel singer/songwriter. Wrote "Stone Soul Picnic", "Wedding Bell Blues", "And When I Die" and "Stoney End".	
10/10/70	**92**	2	1 Up On The Roof	Columbia 45230

O

DEBUT DATE	PEAK POS	WKS CHR	ARTIST — Record Title	Label & Number
			OAK	
			Northeastern pop group - Rick Pinette, lead singer.	
7/21/79	**58**	7	1 This Is Love	Mercury 74076
5/10/80	**36**	14	2 King Of The Hill RICK PINETTE & OAK	Mercury 76049
12/13/80+	**71**	6	3 Set The Night On Fire	Mercury 76087
			OAK RIDGE BOYS	
			Originally formed as a gospel quartet in Oak Ridge, TN during World War II. Many personnel changes. Switched to country/pop style in early 1970s with current lineup: Duane Allen, lead; Joe Bonsall, tenor; Bill Golden, baritone; and Richard Sterban, bass. Golden, a member since 1965, left in 1987.	
5/16/81	**5**	22	1 ▲**Elvira**	MCA 51084
1/16/82	**12**	14	2 Bobbie Sue	MCA 51231
6/12/82	**76**	4	3 So Fine	MCA 52065
3/19/83	**72**	5	4 American Made	MCA 52179
			JOHN O'BANION	
			Pop singer from Kokomo, Indiana.	
3/28/81	**24**	13	1 Love You Like I Never Loved Before	Elektra 47125
			O'BRYAN	
			Born O'bryan Burnett II from Sneads Ferry, North Carolina.	
3/27/82	**57**	9	1 The Gigolo	Capitol 5067
			RIC OCASEK	
			Born Richard Otcasek in Baltimore. Lead singer, guitarist of The Cars.	
2/12/83	**47**	9	1 Something To Grab For	Geffen 29784
9/06/86	**15**	19	2 Emotion In Motion	Geffen 28617
12/20/86+	**75**	8	3 True To You	Geffen 28504

DEBUT DATE	PEAK POS	WKS CHR	ARTIST — Record Title	Label & Number
			OCEAN	
			Canadian pop quintet - Janice Morgan, lead singer.	
3/13/71	**2^{1}**	14	1 ● **Put Your Hand In The Hand**	Kama Sutra 519
6/26/71	**73**	4	2 Deep Enough For Me	Kama Sutra 525
8/07/71	**82**	5	3 We Got A Dream	Kama Sutra 529
9/23/72	**76**	4	4 One More Chance	Kama Sutra 556
			BILLY OCEAN	
			Born Leslie Sebastian Charles on 1/21/50 in Trinidad. Raised in England.	
4/03/76	**22**	11	1 Love Really Hurts Without You	Ariola 7621
8/11/84	**1^{2}**	26	2 ● **Caribbean Queen (No More Love On The Run)**	Jive 9199
12/01/84+	**2^{1}**	21	3 **Loverboy**	Jive 9284
3/23/85	**4**	22	4 **Suddenly**	Jive 9323
7/06/85	**24**	15	5 Mystery Lady	Jive 9374
11/30/85+	**2^{1}**	23	6 **When The Going Gets Tough, The Tough Get Going** from the film "The Jewel of the Nile"	Jive 9432
4/19/86	**1^{1}**	21	7 **There'll Be Sad Songs (To Make You Cry)** all of above written by Ocean (except #1)	Jive 9465
7/26/86	**10**	16	8 **Love Zone**	Jive 9510
10/25/86	**16**	16	9 Love Is Forever	Jive 9540
			CARROLL O'CONNOR & JEAN STAPLETON	
			Archie & Edith Bunker of TV's "All In The Family". Both born in New York City - Carroll on 8/2/24 and Jean (real name: Jeanne Murray) on 1/19/23.	
12/11/71+	**43**	9	1 Those Were The Days [N] "All In The Family" TV theme	Atlantic 2847
			ALAN O'DAY	
			Born on 10/3/40 in Hollywood. Singer-songwriter-pianist. Wrote Helen Reddy's #1 hit "Angie Baby" and the Righteous Brothers' "Rock And Roll Heaven".	
4/02/77	**1^{1}**	25	1 ● **Undercover Angel**	Pacific 001
10/01/77	**73**	6	2 Started Out Dancing, Ended Up Making Love	Pacific 002
			ODDS & ENDS	
3/13/71	**83**	6	1 Love Makes The World Go Round	Today 1003
			BROOKS O'DELL	
			Black male vocalist from Philadelphia - sang lead with the Commanders. Own group the Majestics.	
12/14/63+	**58**	9	1 Watch Your Step	Gold 214
			KENNY O'DELL	
			Born Kenneth Gist, Jr. in Oklahoma (early 40s). Singer-songwriter-guitarist. Moved to Nashville in 1969. Wrote Charlie Rich's "Behind Closed Doors".	
11/18/67	**38**	7	1 Beautiful People	Vegas 718
2/24/68	**94**	2	2 Springfield Plane	Vegas 722
			ODYSSEY	
			New York soul/disco trio: Manila-born Tony Reynolds, and sisters Lillian and Louise Lopez, originally from the Virgin Islands.	
11/12/77+	**21**	19	1 Native New Yorker	RCA 11129
5/06/78	**57**	7	2 Weekend Lover	RCA 11245
			ESTHER & ABI OFARIM	
			Husband and wife from Israel. Esther was born Esther Zaled on 6/13/43; Albi was born Abraham Reichstadt on 10/5/39.	
3/30/68	**68**	6	1 Cinderella Rockefella	Philips 40526
			OFF BROADWAY usa	
			Rock quintet from Oak Park, IL - Cliff Johnson, lead singer.	
3/22/80	**51**	7	1 Stay In Time	Atlantic 3647
			LILLIAN OFFITT	
			Black vocalist born on 11/4/38 in Nashville.	
7/29/57	**66**	10	1 Miss You So	Excello 2104
			LENNY O'HENRY	
5/30/64	**98**	1	1 Across The Street	Atco 6291
			OHIO EXPRESS	
			Bubblegum group from Mansfield, Ohio. Produced by Jerry Kasenetz and Jeff Katz. Joey Levine, lead singer on most of their hits.	
10/07/67	**29**	12	1 Beg, Borrow And Steal	Cameo 483

DEBUT DATE	PEAK POS	WKS CHR	ARTIST — Record Title	Label & Number
			OHIO EXPRESS — Cont'd	
2/03/68	**83**	2	2 Try It	Cameo 2001
5/04/68	**4**	14	3● **Yummy Yummy Yummy**	Buddah 38
8/03/68	**33**	9	4 Down At Lulu's	Buddah 56
10/19/68	**15**	13	5● Chewy Chewy	Buddah 70
3/01/69	**96**	1	6 Sweeter Than Sugar	Buddah 92
3/29/69	**30**	8	7 Mercy 2-7: sung and written by Joey Levine	Buddah 102
6/21/69	**99**	2	8 Pinch Me (Baby, Convince Me) Buddy Bengert, lead singer	Buddah 117
9/06/69	**86**	2	9 Sausalito (Is The Place To Go) Graham Gouldman (10cc), lead singer	Buddah 129
			OHIO PLAYERS Originally an R&B instrumental group called the Ohio Untouchables, formed in Dayton in 1959. Back-up on The Falcons' records. Members during prime (1974-79): Marshall Jones, Clarence "Satch" Satchell, Jimmy "Diamond" Williams, Marvin "Merv" Pierce, Billy Beck, Ralph "Pee Wee" Middlebrook and Leroy "Sugarfoot" Bonner.	
12/25/71+	**64**	8	1 Pain (Part I)	Westbound 188
2/24/73	**15**	19	2● Funky Worm [N]	Westbound 214
8/11/73	**31**	15	3 Ecstasy	Westbound 216
6/15/74	**47**	11	4 Jive Turkey (Part 1)	Mercury 73480
9/07/74	**13**	11	5● Skin Tight	Mercury 73609
12/14/74+	**1**[1]	17	6● **Fire**	Mercury 73643
4/12/75	**44**	7	7 I Want To Be Free	Mercury 73675
9/20/75	**33**	8	8 Sweet Sticky Thing	Mercury 73713
11/15/75+	**1**[1]	16	9● **Love Rollercoaster**	Mercury 73734
2/21/76	**30**	11	10 Fopp	Mercury 73775
2/21/76	**90**	4	11 Rattlesnake [I]	Westbound 5018
6/26/76	**18**	17	12 Who'd She Coo?	Mercury 73814
1/29/77	**61**	5	13 Feel The Beat (Everybody Disco)	Mercury 73881
7/23/77	**45**	12	14 O-H-I-O [I]	Mercury 73932
			OINGO BOINGO 8-man new wave rock group from Los Angeles - Danny Elfman, lead singer.	
8/31/85	**45**	12	1 Weird Science from the film of the same title	MCA 52633
1/25/86	**85**	4	2 Just Another Day	MCA 52726
			THE O'JAYS R&B group from Canton, Ohio formed in 1958 as the Triumphs. Consisted of Eddie Levert, Walter Williams, William Powell, Bobby Massey and Bill Isles. Recorded as the Mascots for King in 1961. Re-named by Cleveland dee-jay, Eddie O'Jay. Isles left in 1965. Massey left to become a record producer in 1971, Levert, Williams and Powell continued as a trio. Powell retired from touring due to illness, late 1975 (d: 5/26/77), replaced by Sammy Strain, formerly with Little Anthony & The Imperials.	
9/14/63	**93**	3	1 Lonely Drifter	Imperial 5976
5/08/65	**48**	7	2 Lipstick Traces (On A Cigarette)	Imperial 66102
8/07/65	**94**	2	3 I've Cried My Last Tear	Imperial 66121
10/22/66	**95**	3	4 Stand In For Love	Imperial 66197
11/25/67+	**66**	9	5 I'll Be Sweeter Tomorrow (Than I Was Today)	Bell 691
6/29/68	**89**	5	6 Look Over Your Shoulder	Bell 704
9/21/68	**94**	3	7 The Choice	Bell 737
8/09/69	**68**	6	8 One Night Affair	Neptune 12
4/04/70	**64**	7	9 Deeper (In Love With You)	Neptune 22
9/05/70	**98**	2	10 Looky Looky (Look At Me Girl)	Neptune 31
7/22/72	**3**	15	11● **Back Stabbers**	Phil. Int. 3517
11/11/72	**57**	8	12 992 Arguments	Phil. Int. 3522
1/20/73	**1**[1]	14	13● **Love Train**	Phil. Int. 3524
5/19/73	**33**	12	14 Time To Get Down	Phil. Int. 3531
12/22/73+	**10**	16	15 **Put Your Hands Together**	Phil. Int. 3535
4/13/74	**9**	16	16● **For The Love Of Money**	Phil. Int. 3544
12/14/74+	**48**	6	17 Sunshine Part II	Phil. Int. 3558
5/03/75	**45**	9	18 Give The People What They Want	Phil. Int. 3565
7/26/75	**75**	3	19 Let Me Make Love To You	Phil. Int. 3573
11/01/75+	**5**	17	20● **I Love Music (Part 1)**	Phil. Int. 3577

DEBUT DATE	PEAK POS	WKS CHR	ARTIST — Record Title	Label & Number
			THE O'JAYS — Cont'd	
3/06/76	**20**	12	21 Livin' For The Weekend	Phil. Int. 3587
9/11/76	**49**	9	22 Message In Our Music	Phil. Int. 3601
1/22/77	**72**	4	23 Darlin' Darlin' Baby (Sweet, Tender, Love)	Phil. Int. 3610
4/29/78	**4**	19	24 ● **Use Ta Be My Girl**	Phil. Int. 3642
9/23/78	**79**	3	25 Brandy	Phil. Int. 3652
11/24/79+	**28**	13	26 Forever Mine	Phil. Int. 3727
8/23/80	**55**	11	27 Girl, Don't Let It Get You Down 8-16, 18-24 & 26-27: produced by Kenneth Gamble & Leon Huff 8-10, 12-16, 18, 20-24 & 26-27: written by Gamble & Huff	TSOP 4790
			THE O'KAYSIONS North Carolina R&B sextet: Donny Weaver, lead; Ron Turner, Jim Spidel, Wayne Pittman, Jimmy Hennant and Bruce Joyner. Originally called The Kays.	
8/17/68	**5**	14	1 ● **Girl Watcher**	ABC 11094
11/23/68	**76**	6	2 Love Machine	ABC 11153
			DANNY O'KEEFE Singer/songwriter from Washington.	
9/02/72	**9**	13	1 **Good Time Charlie's Got The Blues**	Signpost 70006
			OLA & THE JANGLERS Swedish pop/rock quintet.	
5/24/69	**92**	3	1 Let's Dance	GNP Cresc. 423
			MIKE OLDFIELD Born on 5/15/53 in Reading, England. Classical rock multi-instrumentalist, composer.	
2/23/74	**7**	16	1 **Tubular Bells** [I] theme from the film "The Exorcist"	Virgin 55100
			OLIVER Born William Oliver Swofford on 2/22/45 in North Wilkesboro, NC.	
5/24/69	**3**	13	1 **Good Morning Starshine** from the Broadway musical "Hair"	Jubilee 5659
8/16/69	**2**[2]	14	2 ● **Jean** from the film "The Prime Of Miss Jean Brodie"	Crewe 334
11/22/69	**35**	9	3 Sunday Mornin'	Crewe 337
4/11/70	**97**	3	4 Angelica	Crewe 341
			JANE OLIVOR Lyrical stylist from New York City.	
9/10/77	**91**	3	1 Some Enchanted Evening from the Broadway musical "South Pacific"	Columbia 10527
5/20/78	**77**	9	2 He's So Fine	Columbia 10724
			OLLIE & JERRY Ollie Brown & Jerry Knight (member of Raydio).	
6/02/84	**9**	18	1 **Breakin'...There's No Stopping Us** from the film "Breakin'"	Polydor 821708
			OLLIE & THE NIGHTINGALES Formed as the Dixie Nightingales in 1950. Consisted of Ollie Hoskins, Quincy Clifton Billops Jr., Bill Davis, Nelson Lesure and Rochester Neal.	
4/06/68	**73**	9	1 I Got A Sure Thing	Stax 245
			ROCKY OLSON	
5/04/59	**60**	4	1 Kansas City	Chess 1723
			NIGEL OLSSON Drummer for Elton John's band.	
3/01/75	**91**	6	1 Only One Woman	Rocket 40337
12/16/78+	**18**	16	2 Dancin' Shoes	Bang 740
4/14/79	**34**	12	3 Little Bit Of Soap	Bang 4800
			THE OLYMPICS R&B group formed at Centennial High School in Compton, CA in 1954 as the Challengers. Consisted of Walter Ward, lead; Eddie Lewis, tenor; Charles Fizer, baritone; and Walter Hammond, baritone. Recorded as the Challengers for Melatone in 1956. Melvin King replaced Fizer in 1958, remained in group as replacement for Hammond when Fizer returned in 1959. Fizer was killed during the Watts rioting, replaced by Julius McMichael ("Mack Starr"), former lead of the Paragons. King left in 1966. Kenny Sinclair, formerly of The Six Teens, joined in 1970. Group recorded as The Marathons in 1961.	
7/21/58	**8**	14	1 **Western Movies** [N] Hot 100 #8 / Best Seller #11	Demon 1508

DEBUT DATE	PEAK POS	WKS CHR	ARTIST — Record Title	Label & Number
			THE OLYMPICS — Cont'd	
12/08/58+	**71**	5	2 (I Wanna) Dance With The Teacher	Demon 1512
9/14/59	**95**	1	3 Private Eye/	
2/01/60	**72**	7	4 (Baby) Hully Gully	Arvee 562
5/23/60	**50**	14	5 Big Boy Pete lyrically altered by The Kingsmem as "The Jolly Green Giant"	Arvee 595
9/12/60	**42**	11	6 Shimmy Like Kate	Arvee 5006
12/05/60	**47**	11	7 Dance By The Light Of The Moon	Arvee 5020
3/27/61	**76**	4	8 Little Pedro	Arvee 5023
4/24/61	**20**	12	9 Peanut Butter **THE MARATHONS** re-make of above hit "(Baby) Hully Gully"	Arvee 5027
6/19/61	**94**	1	10 Dooley	Arvee 5031
4/27/63	**40**	10	11 The Bounce	Tri Disc 106
7/06/63	**86**	6	12 Dancin' Holiday	Tri Disc 107
5/01/65	**81**	5	13 Good Lovin'	Loma 2013
4/30/66	**99**	2	14 Mine Exclusively	Mirwood 5513
10/01/66	**63**	6	15 Baby, Do The Philly Dog	Mirwood 5523
			LENORE O'MALLEY	
7/26/80	**53**	8	1 First...Be A Woman	Polydor 2055
			ALEXANDER O'NEAL - see CHERRELLE	
			ONE TO ONE Canadian pop duo: Leslie Howe & Louise Reny.	
8/23/86	**92**	4	1 Angel In My Pocket	Warner 28739
			100 PROOF Aged In Soul Soul group from Detroit: Clyde Wilson ("Steve Mancha"), lead; Joe Stubbs and Eddie Anderson ("Eddie Holiday"). Stubbs, brother of Levi Stubbs of the Four Tops, had been in the Contours and The Falcons.	
12/20/69	**94**	2	1 Too Many Cooks (Spoil The Soup)	Hot Wax 6904
9/05/70	**8**	14	2 ● **Somebody's Been Sleeping**	Hot Wax 7004
2/27/71	**96**	2	3 One Man's Leftovers (Is Another Man's Feast)	Hot Wax 7009
4/01/72	**45**	11	4 Everything Good Is Bad above 3 written by General Johnson, Gregg Perry & Angelo Bond	Hot Wax 7202
			ONE WAY Soul group led by Al Hudson - formerly known as the Soul Partners.	
5/29/82	**61**	10	1 Cutie Pie	MCA 52049
			YOKO ONO Born in Tokyo on 2/18/33. Married John Lennon on 3/20/69. Also see John Lennon.	
3/07/81	**58**	10	1 Walking On Thin Ice Yoko and John were remixing this song the day he was killed	Geffen 49638
			OPUS Australian pop/rock quintet - Herwig Rudisser, lead singer.	
1/25/86	**32**	16	1 Live Is Life	Polydor 883730
			ROY ORBISON Born on 4/23/36 in Vernon, Texas. Had own band, the Wink Westerners in 1952. Attended North Texas University with Pat Boone. First recorded for Jewel in early 1956. Toured with Sun Records shows to 1958. Toured with The Beatles in 1963. Wife Claudette killed in a motorcycle accident on 6/7/66; two sons died in a fire, 1968.	
6/16/56	**59**	8	1 Ooby Dooby **ROY ORBISON & TEEN KINGS**	Sun 242
1/18/60	**72**	6	2 Up Town	Monument 412
6/06/60	**2**[1]	21	3 **Only The Lonely (Know How I Feel)**	Monument 421
9/19/60	**9**	14	4 **Blue Angel**	Monument 425
12/12/60+	**27**	8	5 I'm Hurtin'	Monument 433
4/10/61	**1**[1]	17	6 **Running Scared**	Monument 438
8/14/61	**2**[1]	16	7 **Crying/**	
8/07/61	**25**	14	8 Candy Man	Monument 447
2/17/62	**4**	12	9 **Dream Baby (How Long Must I Dream)**	Monument 456
6/02/62	**26**	10	10 The Crowd	Monument 461
10/06/62	**25**	10	11 Leah/	
9/22/62	**33**	11	12 Workin' For The Man all of above (except #1) with Bob Moore's Orchestra & Chorus	Monument 467

DEBUT DATE	PEAK POS	WKS CHR	ARTIST — Record Title	Label & Number
			ROY ORBISON — Cont'd	
2/09/63	**7**	13	13 **In Dreams**	Monument 806
			new version featured in the 1986 film "Blue Velvet"	
6/08/63	**22**	8	14 Falling	Monument 815
			above 4 written by Roy Orbison	
9/07/63	**5**	13	15 **Mean Woman Blues/**	
9/14/63	**29**	10	16 Blue Bayou	Monument 824
			2-7, 10 & 16: written by Roy Orbison & Joe Melson	
12/14/63+	**15**	7	17 Pretty Paper [X]	Monument 830
4/11/64	**9**	11	18 **It's Over**	Monument 837
8/29/64	**1^{3}**	15	19 ● **Oh, Pretty Woman**	Monument 851
			ROY ORBISON & THE CANDY MEN	
2/13/65	**21**	7	20 Goodnight	Monument 873
7/10/65	**39**	7	21 (Say) You're My Girl	Monument 891
8/21/65	**25**	10	22 Ride Away	MGM 13386
11/06/65	**46**	7	23 Crawling Back	MGM 13410
11/13/65	**81**	3	24 Let The Good Times Roll	Monument 906
1/22/66	**31**	8	25 Breakin' Up Is Breakin' My Heart	MGM 13446
4/30/66	**39**	6	26 Twinkle Toes	MGM 13498
8/06/66	**68**	5	27 Too Soon To Know	MGM 13549
12/10/66+	**60**	7	28 Communication Breakdown	MGM 13634
			18-23, 25-26 & 28: written by Roy Orbison & Bill Dees	
7/29/67	**52**	6	29 Cry Softly Lonely One	MGM 13764
6/28/80	**55**	8	30 That Lovin' You Feelin' Again	Warner 49262
			ROY ORBISON & EMMYLOU HARRIS	
			from the film "Roadie"	
			ORCHESTRAL MANOEUVRES IN THE DARK	
			English electro-pop quartet: Paul Humphreys, Andrew McCluskey, Malcolm Holmes and Martin Cooper.	
8/31/85	**26**	17	1 So In Love	A&M 2746
12/14/85+	**63**	13	2 Secret	A&M 2794
3/08/86	**4**	20	3 **If You Leave**	A&M 2811
			from the film "Pretty In Pink"	
9/27/86	**19**	17	4 (Forever) Live And Die	A&M 2872
			THE ORIGINAL CASTE	
			Canadian quintet - Dixie Lee Innes, lead singer.	
11/15/69+	**34**	17	1 One Tin Soldier	T-A 186
			from the film "Billy Jack"	
			THE ORIGINAL CASUALS	
2/24/58	**42**	12	1 So Tough	Back Beat 503
			Best Seller #42 / Top 100 #42	
			THE ORIGINALS	
			Soul group formed in Detroit in 1966. Consisted of Freddie Gorman, bass; Crathman Spencer and Henry Dixon, tenors; and Walter Gaines, baritone.	
9/27/69	**14**	16	1 Baby, I'm For Real	Soul 35066
2/07/70	**12**	14	2 The Bells	Soul 35069
8/22/70	**74**	6	3 We Can Make It Baby	Soul 35074
			above 3 written & produced by Marvin Gaye	
12/19/70+	**53**	12	4 God Bless Whoever Sent You	Soul 35079
10/23/76	**47**	9	5 Down To Love Town	Soul 35119
			ORION THE HUNTER	
			Rock quartet led by former Boston guitarist Barry Goudreau.	
6/02/84	**58**	8	1 So You Ran	Portrait 04483
			TONY ORLANDO	
			Born Michael Anthony Orlando Cassavitis on 4/3/44 in New York City. Discovered by producer Don Kirshner. Lead singer of Dawn. Hosted weekly TV variety show "Tony Orlando & Dawn", 1974-76. Also see Wind.	
5/01/61	**39**	8	1 Halfway To Paradise	Epic 9441
8/14/61	**15**	12	2 Bless You	Epic 9452
11/27/61	**82**	3	3 Happy Times (Are Here To Stay)	Epic 9476
7/07/79	**54**	6	4 Sweets For My Sweet	Casablanca 991

DEBUT DATE	PEAK POS	WKS CHR	ARTIST — Record Title	Label & Number
			ORLEANS	
			Rock group founded in New York City by John Hall with brothers Lawrence and Lance Hoppen, Wells Kelly and Jerry Marotta. Hall and Marotta left in 1977, replaced by Bob Leinbach and R.A. Martin.	
4/26/75	**55**	7	1 Let There Be Music	Asylum 45243
7/19/75	**6**	18	2 **Dance With Me**	Asylum 45261
7/31/76	**5**	18	3 **Still The One**	Asylum 45336
1/29/77	**51**	8	4 Reach	Asylum 45375
			above 3 written by John Hall & wife Johanna	
3/24/79	**11**	15	5 Love Takes Time	Infinity 50006
			THE ORLONS	
			R&B group from Philadelphia. Consisted of lead Rosetta Hightower (b: 6/23/44), Marlena Davis, Steve Caldwell and Shirley Brickley (b: 12/9/44, d: 10/13/77). Davis and Caldwell left in 1964 and were replaced by Audrey Brickley. Disbanded in 1968, when Hightower moved to England.	
6/09/62	**2**[2]	14	1 **The Wah Watusi**	Cameo 218
10/13/62	**4**	15	2 **Don't Hang Up**	Cameo 231
2/16/63	**3**	13	3 **South Street**	Cameo 243
6/15/63	**12**	10	4 Not Me	Cameo 257
9/28/63	**19**	9	5 Cross Fire!	Cameo 273
12/14/63+	**55**	6	6 Bon-Doo-Wah	Cameo 287
2/01/64	**66**	5	7 Shimmy Shimmy	Cameo 295
5/16/64	**66**	6	8 Rules Of Love	Cameo 319
			1-3, 5-6 & 8: written by Kal Mann & Dave Appell	
8/29/64	**64**	6	9 Knock! Knock! (Who's There?)	Cameo 332
			ORPHEUS	
			Boston soft-rock quartet.	
5/31/69	**91**	3	1 Brown Arms In Houston	MGM 14022
8/23/69	**80**	7	2 Can't Find The Time	MGM 13882
			BENJAMIN ORR	
			Bassist/vocalist of The Cars.	
11/08/86+	**24**	20	1 Stay The Night	Elektra 69506
			ROBERT ELLIS ORRALL with CARLENE CARTER	
			Robert: Boston-born pop/rock singer-songwriter-pianist. Carlene: daughter of June Carter Cash; married to Nick Lowe.	
3/26/83	**32**	12	1 I Couldn't Say No	RCA 13431
			JEFFREY OSBORNE	
			Born on 3/9/48 in Providence, RI. Soul singer, songwriter, drummer. Ex-lead singer of L.T.D.	
6/05/82	**39**	15	1 I Really Don't Need No Light	A&M 2410
9/25/82	**29**	18	2 On The Wings Of Love	A&M 2434
3/19/83	**76**	5	3 Eenie Meenie	A&M 2530
7/16/83	**25**	14	4 Don't You Get So Mad	A&M 2561
10/15/83+	**30**	21	5 Stay With Me Tonight	A&M 2591
2/25/84	**48**	12	6 We're Going All The Way	A&M 2618
8/18/84	**40**	12	7 The Last Time I Made Love	A&M 2656
			JOYCE KENNEDY & JEFFREY OSBORNE	
10/13/84	**44**	15	8 Don't Stop	A&M 2687
1/19/85	**38**	11	9 The Borderlines	A&M 2695
			all of above produced by George Duke (except #7)	
5/24/86	**13**	19	10 You Should Be Mine (The Woo Woo Song)	A&M 2814
			OZZY OSBOURNE	
			Born John Osbourne on 12/3/48 in Birmingham, England. Heavy-metal artist; former lead singer of Black Sabbath.	
3/22/86	**68**	9	1 Shot In The Dark	CBS Assoc. 05810
			LEE OSKAR	
			Born on 3/24/48 in Copenhagen, Denmark. Harmonica player. Studio musician in Los Angeles. Original member of War.	
6/26/76	**59**	6	1 BLT [I]	United Art. 807
			DONNY OSMOND	
			Born on 12/9/57 in Ogden, Utah. 7th son of George & Olive Osmond, Donny became a member of The Osmonds in 1963.	
3/27/71	**7**	16	1 ● **Sweet And Innocent**	MGM 14227
8/07/71	**1**[3]	15	2 ● **Go Away Little Girl**	MGM 14285

DEBUT DATE	PEAK POS	WKS CHR	ARTIST — Record Title	Label & Number
			DONNY OSMOND — Cont'd	
11/27/71+	**9**	10	3● **Hey Girl/**	
		10	4 I Knew You When	MGM 14322
2/26/72	**3**	12	5● **Puppy Love**	MGM 14367
6/10/72	**13**	9	6 Too Young	MGM 14407
8/26/72	**13**	12	7 Why/	
		9	8 Lonely Boy	MGM 14424
3/03/73	**8**	13	9● **The Twelfth Of Never**	MGM 14503
7/14/73	**23**	11	10 A Million To One/	
		9	11 Young Love	MGM 14583
11/24/73+	**14**	13	12 Are You Lonesome Tonight/	
		13	13 When I Fall In Love	MGM 14677
2/15/75	**50**	7	14 I Have A Dream 5-14: produced by Mike Curb & Don Costa	MGM 14781
6/05/76	**38**	11	15 C'mon Marianne	Polydor 14320
			DONNY & MARIE OSMOND Co-hosts of a musical/variety TV series, 1976-78.	
7/06/74	**4**	15	1● **I'm Leaving It (All) Up To You**	MGM 14735
11/16/74+	**8**	16	2 **Morning Side Of The Mountain**	MGM 14765
6/07/75	**44**	6	3 Make The World Go Away	MGM 14807
12/13/75+	**14**	23	4 Deep Purple	MGM 14840
11/27/76+	**21**	13	5 Ain't Nothing Like The Real Thing	Polydor 14363
11/19/77+	**38**	11	6 (You're My) Soul And Inspiration	Polydor 14439
10/07/78	**38**	10	7 On The Shelf	Polydor 14510
			LITTLE JIMMY OSMOND Born on 4/16/63 in Canoga Park, CA. Youngest member of the Osmond family.	
4/22/72	**38**	10	1 Long Haired Lover From Liverpool with the Mike Curb Congregation	MGM 14376
1/13/73	**59**	6	2 Tweedlee Dee	MGM 14468
			MARIE OSMOND Born on 10/13/59 in Ogden, Utah. Began performing in concert with her brothers at age 14. Co-hosted TV series "Ripley's Believe It Or Not".	
9/15/73	**5**	16	1● **Paper Roses**	MGM 14609
3/08/75	**40**	6	2 Who's Sorry Now above 2 produced by Sonny James	MGM 14786
4/23/77	**39**	8	3 This Is The Way That I Feel	Polydor 14385
			THE OSMONDS Family group from Ogden, Utah. Alan (b: 6/22/49), Wayne (b: 8/28/51), Merrill (b: 4/30/53), Jay (b: 3/2/55) and Donny (b: 12/9/57). Began as a quartet in 1959, singing religious and barbershop-quartet songs. Regulars on Andy Williams' TV show from 1962-67. Alan, Wayne, Merrill and Jay are currently a hot Country act.	
1/02/71	**1^{5}**	15	1● **One Bad Apple**	MGM 14193
3/13/71	**96**	1	2 I Can't Stop	Uni 55276
5/15/71	**14**	9	3 Double Lovin'	MGM 14259
9/11/71	**3**	13	4● **Yo-Yo**	MGM 14295
1/22/72	**4**	14	5● **Down By The Lazy River** written by Alan & Merrill	MGM 14324
7/01/72	**14**	9	6 Hold Her Tight	MGM 14405
9/16/72	**68**	10	7 We Can Make It Together **STEVE & EYDIE featuring THE OSMONDS**	MGM 14383
10/21/72	**14**	12	8 Crazy Horses	MGM 14450
6/16/73	**36**	8	9 Goin' Home	MGM 14562
9/08/73	**36**	10	10 Let Me In 6, 8-10: written by Alan, Merrill & Wayne 5-6, 8-10: produced by Alan	MGM 14617
8/31/74	**10**	13	11 **Love Me For A Reason**	MGM 14746
7/26/75	**22**	11	12 The Proud One	MGM 14791
10/02/76	**46**	9	13 I Can't Live A Dream	Polydor 14348
			GILBERT O'SULLIVAN Born Raymond O'Sullivan on 12/1/46 in Waterford, Ireland.	
6/17/72	**1^{6}**	18	1● **Alone Again (Naturally)**	MAM 3619
10/28/72	**2^{2}**	16	2● **Clair**	MAM 3626
3/03/73	**17**	15	3 Out Of The Question	MAM 3628

DEBUT DATE	PEAK POS	WKS CHR	ARTIST — Record Title	Label & Number
			GILBERT O'SULLIVAN — Cont'd	
6/23/73	**7**	15	4 ● **Get Down**	MAM 3629
10/13/73	**25**	10	5 Ooh Baby	MAM 3633
3/23/74	**62**	7	6 Happiness Is Me And You	MAM 3636
			all of above written by O'Sullivan and produced by Gordon Mills	
			OTIS & CARLA - see OTIS REDDING and/or CARLA THOMAS	
			THE JOHNNY OTIS SHOW	
			Born John Veliotes (of Greek parents) on 12/8/21 in Vallejo, CA. R&B bandleader, composer. Johnny's R&B Caravan featured the top R&B artists of the 50s.	
6/23/58	**9**	16	1 **Willie And The Hand Jive**	Capitol 3966
			Hot 100 #9 / Best Seller #14 / Jockey #17	
11/10/58	**87**	4	2 Crazy Country Hop	Capitol 4060
4/27/59	**52**	5	3 Castin' My Spell	Capitol 4168
			female vocal: Marci Lee	
2/15/60	**80**	2	4 Mumblin' Mosie	Capitol 4326
			THE OUTFIELD	
			British pop/rock trio: Tony Lewis, lead singer; John Spinks, guitarist; and Alan Jackman, drums.	
2/15/86	**6**	22	1 **Your Love**	Columbia 05796
6/07/86	**19**	16	2 All The Love In The World	Columbia 05894
9/20/86	**66**	10	3 Everytime You Cry	Columbia 06295
			OUTLAWS	
			Southern rock band formed in Tampa in 1974. Consisted of guitarists Hughie Thomasson, Billy Jones and Henry Paul; Monte Yoho, drums; and Frank O'Keefe, bass (replaced by Harvey Arnold in 1977). Paul, Yoho, and Arnold left by 1980.	
9/06/75	**34**	10	1 There Goes Another Love Song	Arista 0150
7/04/76	**94**	2	2 Breaker - Breaker	Arista 0188
7/30/77	**60**	5	3 Hurry Sundown	Arista 0258
12/27/80+	**31**	15	4 (Ghost) Riders In The Sky	Arista 0582
			Vaughn Monroe's version was #1 in 1949 for 12 weeks	
			THE OUTSIDERS	
			Cleveland rock quintet: Sonny Geraci, lead singer; Tom King, guitar; Bill Bruno, lead guitar; Mert Madsen, bass; and Rick Baker, drums.	
2/19/66	**5**	15	1 **Time Won't Let Me**	Capitol 5573
5/14/66	**21**	9	2 Girl In Love	Capitol 5646
8/06/66	**15**	8	3 Respectable	Capitol 5701
10/29/66	**37**	10	4 Help Me Girl	Capitol 5759
			THE OVATIONS	
			Soul group led by Louis Williams. Re-formed in 1972 with ex-Nightingales Rochester Neal, Bill Davis and Quincy Billops.	
5/22/65	**61**	6	1 It's Wonderful To Be In Love	Goldwax 113
10/13/73	**56**	9	2 Having A Party [N]	MGM 14623
			remake of Sam Cooke's hit infused with a line or two of other top soul hits	
			THE OVERLANDERS	
			British group.	
5/23/64	**75**	7	1 Yesterday's Gone	Hickory 1258
			OWEN B.	
3/07/70	**97**	2	1 Mississippi Mama	Janus 107
			REG OWEN	
			British bandleader.	
12/08/58+	**10**	16	1 **Manhattan Spiritual** [I]	Palette 5005
			BUCK OWENS	
			Born Edgar Owens on 8/12/29 in Sherman, Texas. Country singer, guitarist, songwriter. Backing group: The Buckaroos. Co-host of TV's "Hee-Haw", 1969-86.	
7/04/64	**94**	2	1 My Heart Skips A Beat	Capitol 5136
8/22/64	**92**	3	2 I Don't Care (Just As Long As You Love Me)	Capitol 5240
1/23/65	**25**	9	3 I've Got A Tiger By The Tail	Capitol 5336
5/15/65	**83**	2	4 Before You Go	Capitol 5410
11/13/65	**60**	9	5 Buckaroo [I]	Capitol 5517
1/29/66	**57**	7	6 Waitin' In Your Welfare Line	Capitol 5566
5/28/66	**74**	5	7 Think Of Me	Capitol 5647

DEBUT DATE	PEAK POS	WKS CHR	ARTIST — Record Title	Label & Number
			BUCK OWENS — Cont'd	
4/15/67	**92**	2	8 Sam's Place	Capitol 5865
12/13/69	**100**	1	9 Big In Vegas	Capitol 2646
			all of above (except #5 & 7) written by Buck Owens	
			DONNIE OWENS	
10/06/58	**25**	15	1 Need You	Guyden 2001
			vocal backing: The Ben Denton Singers	
			OXO	
			West Coast pop/rock quartet led by former Foxy member, Ish Angel.	
2/19/83	**28**	14	1 Whirly Girl	Geffen 29765
			OZARK MOUNTAIN DAREDEVILS	
			Country-rock group from Springfield, MO. Nucleus consists of Larry Lee, keyboards, guitar; Steve Cash, harp; John Dillon, guitar; and Michael Granada, bass.	
4/20/74	**25**	16	1 If You Wanna Get To Heaven	A&M 1515
2/08/75	**3**	21	2 **Jackie Blue**	A&M 1654
1/17/76	**65**	7	3 If I Only Knew	A&M 1772
1/22/77	**74**	12	4 You Know Like I Know	A&M 1888
5/24/80	**67**	5	5 Take You Tonight	Columbia 11247
			OZO	
			British-based pop/reggae eightsome (members hail from 7 different countries).	
8/14/76	**96**	3	1 Listen To The Buddha	DJM 1012

P

DEBUT DATE	PEAK POS	WKS CHR	ARTIST — Record Title	Label & Number
			PABLO CRUISE	
			San Francisco pop/rock quartet formed in 1973. Consisted of Dave Jenkins, vocals, guitar; Bud Cockrell, vocals, bass (member of It's A Beautiful Day); Cory Lerios, keyboards; and Stephen Price, drums. Cockrell replaced by Bruce Day in 1977. John Pierce replaced Day, and guitarist Angelo Rossi joined group in 1980.	
4/16/77	**6**	26	1 **Whatcha Gonna Do?**	A&M 1920
9/17/77	**42**	9	2 A Place In The Sun	A&M 1976
1/28/78	**87**	4	3 Never Had A Love	A&M 1999
6/03/78	**6**	18	4 **Love Will Find A Way**	A&M 2048
9/16/78	**21**	16	5 Don't Want To Live Without It	A&M 2076
1/13/79	**46**	8	6 I Go To Rio	A&M 2112
10/13/79	**19**	16	7 I Want You Tonight	A&M 2195
			all of above produced by Bill Schnee	
7/04/81	**13**	17	8 Cool Love	A&M 2349
10/17/81	**75**	5	9 Slip Away	A&M 2373
			PACIFIC GAS & ELECTRIC	
			West Coast blues-rock quintet - Charlie Allen, lead singer.	
5/30/70	**14**	12	1 Are You Ready?	Columbia 45158
			vocal backing by The Blackberries	
10/10/70	**93**	3	2 Father Come On Home	Columbia 45221
3/18/72	**97**	2	3 Thank God For You Baby	Columbia 45519
			shown as: **PG&E**	
			DAVID PACK	
			Vocalist/guitarist of Ambrosia.	
1/25/86	**95**	3	1 Prove Me Wrong	Warner 28802
			from the film "White Nights"	
			THE PACKERS	
			Soul band formed by Charles "Packy" Axton, tenor saxophone. Axton, son of Estelle Axton, co-owner of Stax/Volt, had been in the Mar-Keys.	
11/13/65	**43**	11	1 Hole In The Wall [I]	Pure Soul 1107

DEBUT DATE	PEAK POS	WKS CHR	ARTIST — Record Title	Label & Number
			RALFI PAGAN - see SYLVIA	
			PATTI PAGE	
			Born Clara Ann Fowler on 11/8/27 in Muskogee, Oklahoma. One of eleven children. Raised in Tulsa. On radio KTUL with Al Klauser & His Oklahomans, as "Ann Fowler", late 40s. Another singer was billed as "Patti Page" for the Page Milk Company show on KTUL. When she left, Fowler took her place and name. With the Jimmy Joy band in 1947. On Breakfast Club, Chicago radio, 1947; signed by Mercury Records. Used multi-voice effect on records from 1947. Own TV series "The Patti Page Show", 1955-58, and "The Big Record", 1957-58. In film "Elmer Gantry", 1960.	
12/18/54+	**8**	7	1 **Let Me Go, Lover!**	Mercury 70511
			Jockey #8 / Juke Box #12 / Best Seller #24	
7/30/55	**47**	1	2 Piddily Patter Patter	Mercury 70657
			Coming Up #47	
11/12/55	**16**	13	3 Croce Di Oro (Cross Of Gold)	Mercury 70713
			Top 100 #16 / Juke Box #16 / Jockey #17 / Best Seller #20	
1/07/56	**11**	13	4 Go On With The Wedding	Mercury 70766
			Top 100 #11 / Juke Box #12 / Jockey #16 / Best Seller #17	
4/14/56	**73**	3	5 Too Young To Go Steady/	
3/31/56	**80**	4	6 My First Formal Gown	Mercury 70820
			all of above with Jack Rael & His Orchestra	
6/16/56	**2**[2]	27	7 **Allegheny Moon/**	
			Top 100 #2 / Jockey #2 / Juke Box #2 / Best Seller #5	
7/07/56	**93**	1	8 The Strangest Romance	Mercury 70878
10/27/56	**11**	17	9 Mama From The Train/	
			Top 100 #11 / Jockey #12 / Juke Box #12 / Best Seller #17	
11/24/56	**87**	1	10 Every Time (I Feel His Spirit)	Mercury 70971
2/02/57	**53**	5	11 Repeat After Me	Mercury 71015
3/02/57	**14**	12	12 A Poor Man's Roses (Or A Rich Man's Gold)/	
			Jockey #14 / Top 100 #27	
3/16/57	**43**	6	13 The Wall	Mercury 71059
5/20/57	**3**	23	14 **Old Cape Cod/**	
			Jockey #3 / Top 100 #7 / Best Seller #8	
6/03/57	**12**	6	15 Wondering	Mercury 71101
			Jockey #12 / Top 100 #35	
10/28/57	**23**	14	16 I'll Remember Today	Mercury 71189
			Jockey #23 / Best Seller #31 / Top 100 #32	
2/03/58	**13**	13	17 Belonging To Someone	Mercury 71247
			Jockey #13 / Best Seller #32 / Top 100 #34	
5/05/58	**20**	3	18 Another Time, Another Place	Mercury 71294
			Jockey #20 / Top 100 #81 from the film of the same title	
6/30/58	**9**	12	19 **Left Right Out Of Your Heart**	Mercury 71331
			Jockey #9 / Hot 100 #13 / Best Seller #14	
9/22/58	**39**	9	20 Fibbin'	Mercury 71355
1/12/59	**43**	9	21 Trust In Me	Mercury 71400
4/13/59	**77**	4	22 The Walls Have Ears	Mercury 71428
6/15/59	**59**	7	23 With My Eyes Wide Open I'm Dreaming	Mercury 71469
			Patti's original version charted at POS 11 in 1950 7-23: orchestra conducted by Vic Schoen	
10/12/59	**90**	3	24 Goodbye Charlie	Mercury 71510
12/28/59+	**90**	3	25 The Sound Of Music	Mercury 71555
			from the Broadway musical of the same title	
4/25/60	**67**	2	26 Two Thousand, Two Hundred, Twenty-Three Miles	Mercury 71597
6/06/60	**31**	14	27 One Of Us (Will Weep Tonight)	Mercury 71639
10/03/60	**52**	7	28 I Wish I'd Never Been Born	Mercury 71695
12/31/60+	**65**	4	29 Don't Read The Letter	Mercury 71745
4/10/61	**90**	1	30 A City Girl Stole My Country Boy	Mercury 71792
6/26/61	**46**	6	31 You'll Answer To Me/	
6/12/61	**58**	6	32 Mom And Dad's Waltz	Mercury 71823
10/02/61	**91**	4	33 Broken Heart And A Pillow Filled With Tears	Mercury 71870
12/25/61+	**42**	8	34 Go On Home	Mercury 71906
4/21/62	**27**	8	35 Most People Get Married	Mercury 71950
8/04/62	**49**	9	36 The Boys' Night Out	Mercury 72013
			from the film of the same title	
3/09/63	**98**	1	37 Pretty Boy Lonely	Columbia 42671
6/01/63	**81**	7	38 Say Wonderful Things	Columbia 42791
4/24/65	**8**	14	39 **Hush, Hush, Sweet Charlotte**	Columbia 43251
			from the film of the same title	

DEBUT DATE	PEAK POS	WKS CHR	ARTIST — Record Title	Label & Number
			PATTI PAGE — Cont'd	
9/11/65	**94**	2	40 You Can't Be True, Dear	Columbia 43345
			there were 8 Top 20 versions of this tune in 1948	
2/10/68	**66**	16	41 Gentle On My Mind	Columbia 44353
7/06/68	**96**	2	42 Little Green Apples	Columbia 44556
			Patti also had 42 chart hits from 1948 thru 1954	
			PAGES	
			Los Angeles-based rock quintet - Richard Page, lead singer.	
12/01/79	**84**	3	1 I Do Believe In You	Epic 50769
			SHARON PAIGE & HAROLD MELVIN & BLUE NOTES	
7/05/75	**42**	10	1 Hope That We Can Be Together Soon	Phil. Int. 3569
			PAINTER	
9/29/73	**79**	5	1 West Coast Woman	Elektra 45862
			ROBERT PALMER	
			Born on 1/19/49 in Batley, England. Lead singer of supergroup The Power Station.	
12/04/76+	**63**	7	1 Man Smart, Woman Smarter	Island 075
3/25/78	**16**	18	2 Every Kinda People	Island 100
7/21/79	**14**	15	3 Bad Case Of Loving You (Doctor, Doctor)	Island 49016
12/22/79+	**52**	9	4 Can We Still Be Friends	Island 49137
6/18/83	**78**	6	5 You Are In My System	Island 99866
			above 4 produced by Palmer	
11/16/85	**82**	5	6 Discipline Of Love (Why Did You Do It)	Island 99597
2/08/86	**1**[1]	22	7 **Addicted To Love**	Island 99570
6/07/86	**33**	12	8 Hyperactive	Island 99545
8/16/86	**2**[1]	22	9 **I Didn't Mean To Turn You On**	Island 99537
			above 4 produced by Bernard Edwards (Chic)	
			NICOLA PAONE	
			Born in Spangler, PA; raised in Sicily until coming to New York at age 15.	
2/09/59	**57**	7	1 Blah, Blah, Blah [N]	ABC-Para. 9993
			PAPER LACE	
			English quintet formed in 1969. Phil Wright (b: 4/9/48), lead singer.	
4/27/74	**96**	3	1 Billy-Don't Be A Hero	Mercury 73479
6/15/74	**1**[1]	17	2● **The Night Chicago Died**	Mercury 73492
10/12/74	**41**	9	3 The Black-Eyed Boys	Mercury 73620
			THE PARADE	
			Los Angeles pop/rock group - Jerry Riopelle, leader.	
4/15/67	**20**	8	1 Sunshine Girl	A&M 841
			THE PARADONS	
			R&B vocal group from Bakersfield, CA. West Tyler, lead; Chuck Weldon, Billy Myers and William Powers.	
8/22/60	**18**	16	1 Diamonds And Pearls	Milestone 2003
			THE PARAGONS	
			Doo-wop group from Brooklyn - Julian McMichael, lead singer.	
7/17/61	**82**	5	1 If	Tap 33307
			there were 8 Top 30 versions of this tune in 1951	
			THE PARIS SISTERS	
			Albeth, Priscilla and Sherrell Paris from San Francisco.	
4/24/61	**56**	5	1 Be My Boy	Gregmark 2
9/04/61	**5**	15	2 **I Love How You Love Me**	Gregmark 6
1/27/62	**34**	10	3 He Knows I Love Him Too Much	Gregmark 10
5/12/62	**87**	5	4 Let Me Be The One	Gregmark 12
			all of above produced by Phil Spector	
6/13/64	**91**	4	5 Dream Lover	MGM 13236
			THE PARKAYS	
10/09/61	**89**	2	1 Late Date [I]	ABC-Para. 10242
			BOBBY PARKER	
6/12/61	**51**	6	1 Watch Your Step	V-Tone 223

DEBUT DATE	PEAK POS	WKS CHR	ARTIST — Record Title	Label & Number
			FESS PARKER	
			Born on 8/16/27 in Fort Worth. Starred in the movie "Davy Crockett" and TV's "Daniel Boone" (1964-70).	
3/12/55	**5**	17	1 **Ballad Of Davy Crockett**	Columbia 40449
			Best Seller #5 / Jockey #10 from the Disneyland TV production of the same title	
1/26/57	**12**	10	2 Wringle Wrangle	Disneyland 43
			Best Seller #12 / Top 100 #21 from the film "Westward Ho, The Wagons"	
			GRAHAM PARKER	
			Pub-rocker born in London, 1950. Vocalist, guitarist, songwriter.	
4/09/77	**58**	8	1 Hold Back The Night	Mercury 74000
			GRAHAM PARKER & THE RUMOUR (featured guitarist Brinsley Schwartz)	
9/24/83	**94**	2	2 Life Gets Better	Arista 9065
5/04/85	**39**	12	3 Wake Up (Next To You)	Elektra 69654
			GRAHAM PARKER & THE SHOT	
			LITTLE JUNIOR PARKER	
			Born Herman Parker on 3/3/27 in West Memphis, Arkansas. Died on 11/8/71 of a brain tumor in Chicago. Blues singer, harmonica player. Formed own combo, the Blue Flames, in 1951. First recorded for Modern Records in 1952.	
7/08/57	**74**	6	1 Next Time You See Me	Duke 164
1/27/58	**78**	3	2 That's Alright	Duke 168
5/22/61	**85**	2	3 Driving Wheel	Duke 335
3/10/62	**51**	8	4 Annie Get Your Yo-Yo	Duke 345
1/12/63	**95**	1	5 Someone Somewhere	Duke 357
2/08/64	**99**	2	6 Strange Things Happening	Duke 371
			RAY PARKER JR.	
			Born in Detroit on 5/1/54. Prominent session guitarist in California, worked with Stevie Wonder, Barry White and others. Formed band Raydio in 1977.	
			RAYDIO:	
1/14/78	**8**	21	1 ● **Jack And Jill**	Arista 0283
4/28/79	**9**	22	2 **You Can't Change That**	Arista 0399
			RAY PARKER JR. & RAYDIO:	
4/19/80	**30**	14	3 Two Places At The Same Time	Arista 0494
3/07/81	**4**	27	4 **A Woman Needs Love (Just Like You Do)**	Arista 0592
7/11/81	**21**	15	5 That Old Song	Arista 0616
			RAY PARKER JR.:	
3/20/82	**4**	21	6 **The Other Woman**	Arista 0669
7/17/82	**38**	9	7 Let Me Go	Arista 0695
12/04/82+	**35**	12	8 Bad Boy	Arista 1030
11/12/83+	**12**	19	9 I Still Can't Get Over Loving You	Arista 9116
6/16/84	**1**[3]	21	10 ● **Ghostbusters**	Arista 9212
			from 1984's #1 boxoffice hit	
11/17/84+	**14**	17	11 Jamie	Arista 9293
10/05/85	**34**	15	12 Girls Are More Fun	Arista 9352
			all of above written and produced by Parker	
2/15/86	**96**	3	13 One Sunny Day/Dueling Bikes From Quicksilver	Atlantic 89456
			RAY PARKER JR. & HELEN TERRY from the film "Quicksilver"	
			ROBERT PARKER	
			Born on 10/14/30 in New Orleans. Saxophonist, vocalist, bandleader. In Professor Longhair's band from 1949. Led house band at Club Tijuana, New Orleans. Prolific session work.	
4/23/66	**7**	14	1 **Barefootin'**	Nola 721
1/21/67	**83**	3	2 Tip Toe	Nola 729
			MICHAEL PARKS	
			Portrayed Jim Bronson on TV's "Then Came Bronson".	
2/28/70	**20**	12	1 Long Lonesome Highway	MGM 14104
			from the TV series "Then Came Bronson"	
			PARLIAMENT	
			"A Parliafunkadelicament Thang", a corporation of musicians led by producer, songwriter George Clinton. They recorded under various names for various groups including "Funkadelic", "Parliament", "Bootsy's Rubber Band", "Brides Of Funkenstein", "Parlet", and others.	
8/31/74	**63**	9	1 Up For The Down Stroke	Casablanca 0104
6/14/75	**94**	3	2 Chocolate City [S]	Casablanca 831
5/15/76	**15**	17	3 ● Tear The Roof Off The Sucker (Give Up The Funk)	Casablanca 856

DEBUT DATE	PEAK POS	WKS CHR	ARTIST — Record Title	Label & Number
			PARLIAMENT — Cont'd	
2/11/78	**16**	16	4● Flash Light	Casablanca 909
2/24/79	**89**	2	5 Aqua Boogie (A Psychoalphadiscobetabioaquadoloop)	Casablanca 950
			all of above produced and co-written by George Clinton	
			THE PARLIAMENTS	
			Soul group consisting of George Clinton, lead; Raymond Davis, Calvin Simon, Clarence "Fuzzy" Haskins, and Grady Thomas. Later evolved into Parliament/ Funkadelic.	
7/01/67	**20**	13	1 (I Wanna) Testify	Revilot 207
10/14/67	**80**	7	2 All Your Goodies Are Gone (The Loser's Seat)	Revilot 211
			JOHN PARR	
			Born in Nottingham, England. Pop/rock singer, songwriter.	
12/15/84+	**23**	20	1 Naughty Naughty	Atlantic 89612
4/06/85	**73**	5	2 Magical	Atlantic 89568
6/22/85	**1**[2]	22	3 **St. Elmo's Fire (Man In Motion)**	Atlantic 89541
			from the film of the same title	
11/16/85	**89**	2	4 Love Grammar	Atlantic 89484
12/13/86	**88**	6	5 Blame It On The Radio	Atlantic 89333
			FRED PARRIS - see FIVE SATINS	
			DEAN PARRISH	
7/16/66	**97**	2	1 Tell Her	Boom 60012
			THE ALAN PARSONS PROJECT	
			Duo formed in London, England in 1975. Consisted of Alan Parsons (guitar, keyboards, producer) and Eric Woolfson (vocals, keyboards, lyricist). Both had worked at the Abbey Road Studios; Parsons was an engineer, Woolfson a songwriter. Parsons engineered Pink Floyd's "Dark Side Of The Moon" and The Beatles "Abbey Road" albums. Project features varying musicians and vocalists.	
7/24/76	**37**	10	1 (The System Of) Doctor Tarr And Professor Fether	20th Century 2297
10/16/76	**80**	4	2 The Raven	20th Century 2308
8/20/77	**36**	13	3 I Wouldn't Want To Be Like You	Arista 0260
12/17/77+	**92**	4	4 Don't Let It Show	Arista 0288
			lead vocal: Dave Townshend	
9/23/78	**87**	3	5 What Goes Up	Arista 0352
9/29/79	**27**	17	6 Damned If I Do	Arista 0454
12/06/80+	**16**	23	7 Games People Play	Arista 0573
4/18/81	**15**	23	8 Time	Arista 0598
10/17/81	**67**	5	9 Snake Eyes	Arista 0635
7/03/82	**3**	25	10 **Eye In The Sky**	Arista 0696
11/27/82	**57**	10	11 Psychobabble	Arista 1029
			lead vocal: Elmer Gantry	
11/19/83	**54**	10	12 You Don't Believe	Arista 9108
			3, 6-7 & 12: vocal by Lenny Zakatek	
3/03/84	**15**	15	13 Don't Answer Me	Arista 9160
5/19/84	**34**	11	14 Prime Time	Arista 9208
			8, 10, 13-14: vocal by Eric Woolfson	
2/16/85	**56**	10	15 Let's Talk About Me	Arista 9282
			lead vocal: David Paton	
4/27/85	**71**	5	16 Days Are Numbers (The Traveller)	Arista 9349
			9 & 16: vocal by Chris Rainbow	
2/15/86	**82**	4	17 Stereotomy	Arista 9443
			lead vocal: John Miles all of above written by Parsons and Woolfson	
			BILL PARSONS - see BOBBY BARE	
			DOLLY PARTON	
			Born on 1/19/46 in Sevier County, Tennessee. Worked on Knoxville radio show at age 11. First recorded for Gold Band in 1957. To Nashville in 1964. Replaced Norma Jean on the Porter Wagoner TV show, 1967-73. Went solo in 1974. Starred in films "Nine To Five", "The Best Little Whorehouse In Texas" and "Rhinestone".	
1/26/74	**60**	8	1 Jolene	RCA 0145
6/18/77	**87**	5	2 Light Of A Clear Blue Morning	RCA 10935
10/15/77+	**3**	19	3● **Here You Come Again**	RCA 11123
3/18/78	**19**	12	4 Two Doors Down	RCA 11240
8/26/78	**37**	10	5 Heartbreaker	RCA 11296
12/09/78+	**25**	14	6 Baby I'm Burnin'	RCA 11420
6/30/79	**59**	6	7 You're The Only One	RCA 11577

DEBUT DATE	PEAK POS	WKS CHR	ARTIST — Record Title	Label & Number
			DOLLY PARTON — Cont'd	
9/29/79	**77**	3	8 Sweet Summer Lovin'	RCA 11705
3/29/80	**36**	10	9 Starting Over Again	RCA 11926
11/29/80+	**1^{2}**	26	10● **9 To 5**	RCA 12133
			from the film of the same title	
4/04/81	**41**	10	11 But You Know I Love You	RCA 12200
9/19/81	**77**	4	12 The House Of The Rising Sun	RCA 12282
7/31/82	**53**	14	13 I Will Always Love You	RCA 13260
			Dolly's original version hit #1 on the Country charts on 6/8/74	
			from the film "The Best Little Whorehouse In Texas"	
			1-2, 4, 6, 10 & 13: written by Parton	
8/27/83	**1^{2}**	25	14▲ **Islands In The Stream**	RCA 13615
			KENNY ROGERS & DOLLY PARTON	
			written by The Bee Gees	
12/10/83+	**45**	12	15 Save The Last Dance For Me	RCA 13703
4/14/84	**80**	4	16 Downtown	RCA 13756
12/22/84+	**81**	4	17 The Greatest Gift Of All [X]	RCA 13945
			KENNY ROGERS & DOLLY PARTON	
			from their Christmas TV special	
6/08/85	**91**	3	18 Real Love	RCA 14058
			DOLLY PARTON & KENNY ROGERS	
			THE PARTRIDGE FAMILY	
			Popularized through "The Partridge Family" TV series, with recordings by series stars David Cassidy (lead singer) and real-life stepmother Shirley Jones (backing vocals). David, son of actor Jack Cassidy, was born on 4/12/50 in New York City; raised in California. Shirley was born on 3/31/34 in Smithton, PA. Starred in film musicals "Oklahoma" and "The Music Man". Married David's father in 1956.	
10/10/70	**1^{3}**	19	1● **I Think I Love You**	Bell 910
2/13/71	**6**	12	2● **Doesn't Somebody Want To Be Wanted**	Bell 963
5/08/71	**9**	9	3 **I'll Meet You Halfway**	Bell 996
8/14/71	**13**	11	4 I Woke Up In Love This Morning	Bell 45130
12/18/71+	**20**	8	5 It's One Of Those Nights (Yes Love)	Bell 45160
4/01/72	**59**	7	6 Am I Losing You	Bell 45200
7/01/72	**28**	10	7 Breaking Up Is Hard To Do	Bell 45235
12/16/72+	**39**	8	8 Looking Through The Eyes Of Love	Bell 45301
4/14/73	**99**	2	9 Friend And A Lover	Bell 45336
			THE PASSIONS	
			Brooklyn pop vocal quartet - Jimmy Gallagher, lead singer.	
10/05/59	**69**	10	1 Just To Be With You	Audicon 102
			THE PASTEL SIX	
			California pop septet (ages 18-21 in 1962) - headlined at the Cinnamon Cinder club in North Hollywood.	
12/29/62+	**25**	10	1 The Cinnamon Cinder (It's A Very Nice Dance)	Zen 102
			THE PASTELS	
			R&B quartet: "Big Dee" Irwin (DiFosco Ervin), lead; Richard Travis, Tony Thomas and Jimmy Willingham.	
3/03/58	**24**	16	1 Been So Long	Argo 5287
			Top 100 #24 / Best Seller #25	
			PAT & THE SATELLITES	
2/09/59	**81**	4	1 Jupiter-C [I]	Atco 6131
			JOHNNY PATE QUINTET	
			Johnny was born in Chicago Heights in 1923. Bass, bandleader, arranger.	
1/27/58	**43**	12	1 Swinging Shepherd Blues [I]	Federal 12312
			Best Seller #43 / Top 100 #44	
			featuring Lennie Druss on flute	
			PATIENCE & PRUDENCE	
			Los Angeles sister duo: Patience & Prudence McIntyre (ages 11 & 14 in 1956).	
8/04/56	**4**	25	1 **Tonight You Belong To Me**	Liberty 55022
			Best Seller #4 / Juke Box #4 / Jockey #5 / Top 100 #6	
12/01/56	**11**	16	2 Gonna Get Along Without Ya Now/	
			Jockey #11 / Best Seller #12 / Top 100 #12 / Juke Box #16	
12/08/56+	**73**	9	3 The Money Tree	Liberty 55040
			all of above with their father Mark McIntyre's orchestra	
			KELLEE PATTERSON	
			Born in Gary, Indiana; Miss Indiana of 1971. Soul singer, actress.	
12/17/77+	**75**	8	1 If It Don't Fit, Don't Force It	Shady Brook 1041

DEBUT DATE	PEAK POS	WKS CHR	ARTIST — Record Title	Label & Number
			ROBBIE PATTON	
			English singer/songwriter. Toured with Fleetwood Mac as a guest in 1979.	
7/11/81	**26**	13	1 Don't Give It Up	Liberty 1420
3/12/83	**52**	12	2 Smiling Islands	Atlantic 89955
			backing vocals: Stevie Nicks	
			PATTY & THE EMBLEMS	
6/20/64	**37**	11	1 Mixed-Up, Shook-Up, Girl	Herald 590
			PAUL & PAULA	
			Real names: Ray Hildebrand (b: 12/21/40, Joshua, TX) and Jill Jackson (b: 5/20/42, McCaney, TX). Formed duo at Howard Payne College, Brownwood, TX.	
12/29/62+	**1**[3]	15	1 ● **Hey Paula**	Philips 40084
			written by Hildebrand, first released on LeCam by 'Jill & Ray'	
3/16/63	**6**	10	2 **Young Lovers**	Philips 40096
6/01/63	**27**	8	3 First Quarrel	Philips 40114
8/24/63	**77**	5	4 Something Old, Something New	Philips 40130
10/05/63	**60**	4	5 First Day Back At School	Philips 40142
			BILLY PAUL	
			Born Paul Williams on 12/1/34 in Philadelphia. Sang on Philadelphia radio broadcasts at age 11. First recorded for Jubilee in 1952.	
11/04/72	**1**[3]	16	1 ● **Me And Mrs. Jones**	Phil. Int. 3521
4/07/73	**79**	5	2 Am I Black Enough For You	Phil. Int. 3526
1/26/74	**37**	17	3 Thanks For Saving My Life	Phil. Int. 3538
4/10/76	**83**	4	4 Let's Make A Baby	Phil. Int. 3584
			all of above written and produced by Kenny Gamble & Leon Huff	
			HENRY PAUL BAND	
			Southern rock band led by former Outlaws member, Henry Paul.	
12/12/81+	**50**	10	1 Keeping Our Love Alive	Atlantic 3883
			LES PAUL & MARY FORD	
			Les was born Lester Polfus on 6/9/16 in Waukesha, WI. Mary was born Colleen Summer on 7/7/28 in Pasadena; died on 9/30/77. Paul is a self-taught guitarist. Worked local radio stations, then to Chicago, 1932-37. Own trio in 1936. With Fred Waring, 1938-41. Innovator in electric guitar and multi-track recordings. Married vocalist Mary Ford on 12/29/49; divorced in 1963.	
7/09/55	**7**	13	1 **Hummingbird**	Capitol 3165
			Juke Box #7 / Best Seller #8 / Jockey #8	
11/12/55	**38**	9	2 Amukiriki (The Lord Willing)/	
			Top 100 #38	
11/12/55	**96**	2	3 Magic Melody [I]	Capitol 3248
1/28/56	**91**	2	4 Texas Lady	Capitol 3301
			from the film of the same title	
2/11/56	**49**	12	5 Moritat (Theme From "Three Penny Opera")/ [I]	
			shown only as: **LES PAUL**	
2/18/56	**91**	1	6 Nuevo Laredo	Capitol 3329
1/12/57	**35**	14	7 Cinco Robles	Capitol 3612
8/18/58	**32**	10	8 Put A Ring On My Finger	Columbia 41222
			Hot 100 #32 / Best Seller #44	
4/24/61	**37**	10	9 Jura (I Swear I Love You)	Columbia 41994
			PAULETTE SISTERS	
11/19/55	**92**	2	1 You Win Again	Capitol 3186
			RITA PAVONE	
			Pop singer from Italy.	
6/06/64	**26**	9	1 Remember Me	RCA 8365
			JOHNNY PAYCHECK	
			Born Donald Lytle on 5/31/41 in Greenfield, OH. Country singer, guitarist.	
12/18/71	**91**	2	1 She's All I Got	Epic 10783
			FREDA PAYNE	
			Born on 9/19/45 in Detroit. To New York in 1963. Performed with Pearl Bailey, Duke Ellington, and Quincy Jones. First recorded for Impulse in 1965. Hosted syndicated TV talk show "For You, Black Woman", early 1980s.	
4/25/70	**3**	20	1 ● **Band Of Gold**	Invictus 9075
9/12/70	**24**	12	2 Deeper & Deeper	Invictus 9080
2/13/71	**44**	8	3 Cherish What Is Dear To You (While It's Near To You)	Invictus 9085
6/05/71	**12**	13	4 ● Bring The Boys Home	Invictus 9092
10/02/71	**52**	8	5 You Brought The Joy	Invictus 9100

DEBUT DATE	PEAK POS	WKS CHR	ARTIST — Record Title	Label & Number
			FREDA PAYNE — Cont'd	
1/08/72	**100**	2	6 The Road We Didn't Take	Invictus 9109
			PEACHES & HERB	
			Soul duo from Washington, DC: Herb Fame (born Herbert Feemster, 1942) and Francine Barker (born Francine Hurd, 1947). Fame had been recording solo, Francine sang in vocal group, Sweet Things. Marlene Mack filled in for Francine, 1968-69. Re-formed with Fame and Linda Green in 1977.	
12/31/66+	**21**	12	1 Let's Fall In Love	Date 1523
3/25/67	**8**	12	2 **Close Your Eyes**	Date 1549
6/24/67	**20**	8	3 For Your Love	Date 1563
9/30/67	**13**	9	4 Love Is Strange	Date 1574
12/16/67+	**31**	8	5 Two Little Kids	Date 1586
2/24/68	**55**	5	6 The Ten Commandments Of Love	Date 1592
5/18/68	**46**	8	7 United	Date 1603
11/09/68	**75**	4	8 Let's Make A Promise	Date 1623
3/01/69	**49**	7	9 When He Touches Me (Nothing Else Matters)	Date 1637
8/16/69	**74**	4	10 Let Me Be The One	Date 1649
6/26/71	**100**	2	11 The Sound Of Silence	Columbia 45386
12/16/78+	**5**	22	12● **Shake Your Groove Thing**	Polydor 14514
3/17/79	**1**[4]	23	13▲ **Reunited**	Polydor 14547
6/30/79	**44**	8	14 We've Got Love	Polydor 14577
11/24/79	**66**	4	15 Roller-Skatin' Mate (Part I)	Polydor 2031
1/19/80	**19**	19	16 I Pledge My Love	Polydor 2053
			above 5 produced by Freddie Perren	
			THE PEANUT BUTTER CONSPIRACY	
			California psychedelic rock quintet - Sandi Robison, lead singer.	
3/11/67	**93**	3	1 It's A Happening Thing	Columbia 43985
			LESLIE PEARL	
			Pop singer, composer, producer from Pennsylvania. Wrote jingles for Pepsi, Ford, Gillette and others.	
5/22/82	**28**	16	1 If The Love Fits Wear It	RCA 13235
			PEARLETTES	
3/10/62	**96**	2	1 Duchess Of Earl	Vee-Jay 435
			MIKE PEDICIN QUINTET	
3/17/56	**79**	1	1 The Large Large House	RCA 6369
2/10/58	**71**	2	2 Shake A Hand	Cameo 125
			Faye Adam's version hit #1 on the R&B charts in 1953	
			BOBBY PEDRICK JR. - see ROBERT JOHN	
			ANN PEEBLES	
			Born on 4/27/48 in East St. Louis. Sang in family gospel group the Peebles Choir from age 8.	
10/03/70	**45**	11	1 Part Time Love	Hi 2178
3/06/71	**85**	4	2 I Pity The Fool	Hi 2186
9/01/73	**38**	21	3 I Can't Stand The Rain	Hi 2248
			above 3 produced by Willie Mitchell	
			DAN PEEK	
			Born on 11/1/50 in Panama City, Florida. Former member of America.	
9/15/79	**78**	5	1 All Things Are Possible	Lamb & Lion 817
			PAUL PEEK	
			Vocalist, guitarist from Greenville, SC. With Gene Vincent, 1956-58.	
5/15/61	**84**	3	1 Brother-In-Law (He's A Moocher)	Fairlane 702
4/16/66	**91**	5	2 Pin The Tail On The Donkey	Columbia 43527
			THE PEELS	
3/12/66	**59**	6	1 Juanita Banana [N]	Karate 522
			TEDDY PENDERGRASS	
			Born on 3/26/50 in Philadelphia. Worked local clubs, became drummer for Harold Melvin's Blue Notes in 1969; vocalist with same group in 1970. Went solo in 1976. Auto accident on 3/18/82 left him partially paralyzed.	
5/21/77	**41**	14	1 I Don't Love You Anymore	Phil. Int. 3622
7/08/78	**25**	13	2● Close The Door	Phil. Int. 3648
7/21/79	**48**	6	3 Turn Off The Lights	Phil. Int. 3696

DEBUT DATE	PEAK POS	WKS CHR	ARTIST — Record Title	Label & Number
			TEDDY PENDERGRASS — Cont'd	
8/30/80	**52**	12	4 Can't We Try	Phil. Int. 3107
11/29/80+	**44**	13	5 Love T.K.O.	Phil. Int. 3116
5/16/81	**40**	13	6 Two Hearts STEPHANIE MILLS featuring TEDDY PENDERGRASS	20th Century 2492
1/09/82	**43**	11	7 You're My Latest, My Greatest Inspiration	Phil. Int. 02619
6/09/84	**46**	18	8 Hold Me female vocal: Whitney Houston	Asylum 69720
			PENDULUM	
11/29/80	**89**	7	1 Gypsy Spirit	Venture 131
			THE PENGUINS R&B group from Los Angeles - Cleve Duncan, lead singer. Group named for trademark on Kool cigarettes.	
12/25/54+	**8**	15	1 **Earth Angel (Will You Be Mine)** Best Seller #8 / Juke Box #10 / Jockey #13 written by The Penguin's bass player Curtis Williams; considered to be the top R&B record of all time in terms of continuous popularity	DooTone 348
			THE PENTAGONS R&B group from San Bernadino, California. Joe Jones, lead singer.	
2/20/61	**48**	10	1 To Be Loved (Forever)	Donna 1337
10/30/61	**84**	5	2 I Wonder (If Your Love Will Ever Belong To Me)	Jamie 1201
			PEOPLE San Jose, California pop/rock sextet.	
4/06/68	**14**	18	1 I Love You	Capitol 2078
			PEOPLE'S CHOICE Soul group - Frankie Brunson, lead singer.	
7/24/71	**38**	10	1 I Likes To Do It [I]	Phil-L.A. 349
8/23/75	**11**	16	2● Do It Any Way You Wanna [I]	TSOP 4769
2/07/76	**93**	3	3 Nursery Rhymes (Part I)	TSOP 4773
			THE PEPPERMINT RAINBOW	
1/18/69	**32**	14	1 Will You Be Staying After Sunday	Decca 32410
6/14/69	**54**	9	2 Don't Wake Me Up In The Morning, Michael	Decca 32498
			THE PEPPERMINT TROLLEY COMPANY	
6/08/68	**59**	10	1 Baby You Come Rollin' Across My Mind	Acta 815
			DANNY PEPPERMINT & The Jumping Jacks Danny died of electrocution on stage.	
12/04/61	**54**	4	1 The Peppermint Twist	Carlton 565
			THE PEPPERS Paris studio duo: Mat Camison, synthesizer; Pierre Dahan, drums.	
3/09/74	**76**	7	1 Pepper Box [I]	Event 213
			THE PERCELLS	
3/30/63	**53**	6	1 What Are Boys Made Of	ABC-Para. 10401
			EMILIO PERICOLI Born in 1928 in Cesenatico, Italy. Singer, actor.	
5/19/62	**6**	14	1 **Al Di La'** [F] from the film "Rome Adventure"	Warner 5259
			CARL PERKINS Born on 4/9/32 in Tiptonville, TN. Rockabilly singer, guitarist, songwriter. Formed family band consisting of Carl (guitar), brothers Jay B. (guitar) and Clayton (bass), and W.B. Holland (drums). First recorded for Flip/Sun in 1954. Member of Johnny Cash's touring troupe, 1965-75. The Beatles recorded his songs "Matchbox", "Honey Don't" and "Everybody's Trying To Be My Baby".	
3/03/56	**2^{4}**	21	1 **Blue Suede Shoes** Juke Box #2 / Best Seller #3 / Top 100 #4 / Jockey #5	Sun 234
7/14/56	**70**	4	2 Boppin' The Blues	Sun 243
3/23/57	**67**	7	3 Your True Love	Sun 261
5/26/58	**91**	1	4 Pink Pedal Pushers	Columbia 41131
6/01/59	**93**	2	5 Pointed Toe Shoes all of above written by Perkins	Columbia 41379

DEBUT DATE	PEAK POS	WKS CHR	ARTIST — Record Title	Label & Number
			GEORGE PERKINS & THE SILVER STARS	
4/04/70	**61**	6	1 Cryin' In The Streets (Part 1)	Silver Fox 18
			JOE PERKINS	
9/28/63	**76**	5	1 Little Eeefin Annie [N]	Sound Stage 2511
			TONY PERKINS	
			Born on 4/14/32 in New York City. Movie actor. Best Supporting Oscar nominee for "Friendly Persuasion" in 1956.	
10/07/57	**24**	11	1 Moon-Light Swim	RCA 7020
			Jockey #24 / Top 100 #43	
			STEVE PERRY	
			Born on 1/22/49 in Hanford, CA. Lead singer of Journey since 1978.	
8/28/82	**17**	12	1 Don't Fight It	Columbia 03192
			KENNY LOGGINS with STEVE PERRY	
4/07/84	**3**	20	2 **Oh Sherrie**	Columbia 04391
6/30/84	**21**	13	3 She's Mine	Columbia 04496
9/08/84	**40**	13	4 Strung Out	Columbia 04598
11/24/84+	**18**	19	5 Foolish Heart	Columbia 04693
			HOUSTON PERSON	
			Born on 11/10/34 in Florence, South Carolina. Tenor saxophonist.	
1/17/76	**91**	4	1 Disco Sax/ [I]	
		4	2 For The Love Of You [I]	Westbound 5015
			THE PERSUADERS	
			Soul group formed in New York City in 1969. Consisted of lead Douglas "Smokey" Scott, Willie Holland, James "B.J." Barnes and Charles Stodghill.	
8/28/71	**15**	12	1 ● Thin Line Between Love & Hate	Atco 6822
12/25/71+	**64**	10	2 Love Gonna Pack Up (And Walk Out)	Win Or Lose 220
11/03/73	**39**	11	3 Some Guys Have All The Luck	Atco 6943
3/02/74	**85**	6	4 Best Thing That Ever Happened To Me	Atco 6956
			PET SHOP BOYS	
			British duo: Neil Tennant (vocals) and Chris Lowe.	
3/01/86	**1^{1}**	20	1 **West End Girls**	EMI America 8307
5/31/86	**10**	16	2 **Opportunities (Let's Make Lots Of Money)**	EMI America 8330
8/30/86	**62**	8	3 Love Comes Quickly	EMI America 8338
12/06/86+	**70**	10	4 Suburbia	EMI America 8355
			PETER & GORDON	
			Pop duo formed in London, England in 1963. Consisted of Peter Asher (b: 6/22/44) and Gordon Waller (b: 6/4/45). Toured USA in 1964, appeared on "Shindig", "Hullabaloo", Ed Sullivan TV shows. Disbanded in 1967. Asher went into production and management, including work with Linda Ronstadt and James Taylor.	
5/09/64	**1^{1}**	12	1 **A World Without Love**	Capitol 5175
6/27/64	**12**	9	2 Nobody I Know	Capitol 5211
10/03/64	**16**	9	3 I Don't Want To See You Again	Capitol 5272
			above 3 written by John Lennon & Paul McCartney	
1/09/65	**9**	11	4 **I Go To Pieces**	Capitol 5335
4/17/65	**14**	11	5 True Love Ways	Capitol 5406
7/10/65	**24**	7	6 To Know You Is To Love You	Capitol 5461
11/06/65	**83**	4	7 Don't Pity Me	Capitol 5532
2/12/66	**14**	12	8 Woman	Capitol 5579
			written by Paul McCartney	
5/07/66	**50**	7	9 There's No Living Without Your Loving	Capitol 5650
7/30/66	**98**	2	10 To Show I Love You	Capitol 5684
10/08/66	**6**	14	11 **Lady Godiva**	Capitol 5740
12/24/66+	**15**	9	12 Knight In Rusty Armour	Capitol 5808
3/25/67	**31**	6	13 Sunday For Tea	Capitol 5864
6/24/67	**97**	1	14 The Jokers	Capitol 5919
			from the film of the same title	
			PETER, PAUL & MARY	
			Folk group formed in New York City in 1961. Consisted of Mary Travers (b: 11/7/37, Louisville); Peter Yarrow (b: 5/31/38, New York City); & Paul Stookey (b: 11/30/37, Baltimore). Yarrow had worked the Newport Folk Festival in 1960. Stookey had done TV work, and Travers had been in the Broadway musical "The Next President". Disbanded in 1971, reunited in 1978.	
5/05/62	**35**	8	1 Lemon Tree	Warner 5274

DEBUT DATE	PEAK POS	WKS CHR	ARTIST — Record Title	Label & Number
			PETER, PAUL & MARY — Cont'd	
8/18/62	**10**	12	2 **If I Had A Hammer**	Warner 5296
12/15/62+	**93**	2	3 Big Boat	Warner 5325
1/19/63	**56**	6	4 Settle Down (Goin' Down That Highway)	Warner 5334
3/16/63	**2**[1]	14	5 **Puff The Magic Dragon**	Warner 5348
6/29/63	**2**[1]	15	6 **Blowin' In The Wind**	Warner 5368
9/14/63	**9**	10	7 **Don't Think Twice, It's All Right**	Warner 5385
11/30/63	**35**	7	8 Stewball	Warner 5399
3/07/64	**33**	7	9 Tell It On The Mountain	Warner 5418
6/27/64	**93**	3	10 Oh, Rock My Soul (Part I)	Warner 5442
1/23/65	**30**	7	11 For Lovin' Me	Warner 5496
5/15/65	**91**	3	12 When The Ship Comes In	Warner 5625
10/09/65	**91**	3	13 Early Morning Rain	Warner 5659
4/23/66	**52**	5	14 The Cruel War	Warner 5809
9/24/66	**100**	1	15 The Other Side Of This Life	Warner 5849
8/19/67	**9**	11	16 **I Dig Rock And Roll Music**	Warner 7067
11/25/67	**35**	7	17 Too Much Of Nothing 6-7, 12 & 17: written by Bob Dylan	Warner 7092
4/26/69	**21**	10	18 Day Is Done	Warner 7279
10/25/69	**1**[1]	17	19 ● **Leaving On A Jet Plane** written by John Denver	Warner 7340
			BERNADETTE PETERS Born Bernadette Lazzara on 2/28/48 in Queens, NY. Broadway, TV and film star. Appeared in films "The Jerk" and "Annie".	
3/29/80	**31**	13	1 Gee Whiz	MCA 41210
8/08/81	**65**	8	2 Dedicated To The One I Love	MCA 51152
			PAUL PETERSEN Born on 9/23/45 in Glendale, CA. Member of Disney's "Mousketeers", and played Jeff Stone on TV's "Donna Reed Show".	
3/03/62	**19**	12	1 She Can't Find Her Keys	Colpix 620
6/09/62	**58**	6	2 Keep Your Love Locked (Deep In Your Heart)	Colpix 632
8/25/62	**54**	7	3 Lollipops And Roses	Colpix 649
11/17/62+	**6**	16	4 **My Dad**	Colpix 663
3/30/63	**65**	4	5 Amy	Colpix 676
11/30/63+	**78**	7	6 The Cheer Leader	Colpix 707
			BOBBY PETERSON QUINTET Band from Chester, PA. Consisted of Bobby Peterson (piano), Joe Pyatt (tenor sax), Chico Green (bass), David Butler (drums) and James Thomas (bongos, vocals).	
10/26/59	**71**	7	1 The Hunch [I]	V-Tone 205
10/31/60	**96**	1	2 Irresistable You **BOBBY PETERSON**	V-Tone 214
			RAY PETERSON Born on 4/23/39 in Denton, Texas. Started singing in his early teens, while being treated for polio at a Texas hospital.	
5/18/59	**25**	16	1 The Wonder Of You	RCA 7513
11/16/59	**64**	6	2 Goodnight My Love (Pleasant Dreams)	RCA 7635
6/13/60	**7**	14	3 **Tell Laura I Love Her**	RCA 7745
11/21/60+	**9**	15	4 **Corinna, Corinna**	Dunes 2002
4/03/61	**100**	1	5 Sweet Little Kathy	Dunes 2004
7/31/61	**29**	15	6 Missing You	Dunes 2006
12/18/61+	**57**	8	7 I Could Have Loved You So Well	Dunes 2009
6/01/63	**70**	6	8 Give Us Your Blessing	Dunes 2025
4/25/64	**70**	3	9 The Wonder Of You [R]	RCA 8333
			THE PETS	
6/02/58	**34**	8	1 Cha-Hua-Hua [I] Top 100 #34 / Best Seller #38	Arwin 109
			THE NORMAN PETTY TRIO Norman was Buddy Holly's record producer at Clovis, New Mexico.	
2/23/57	**56**	13	1 Almost Paradise [I]	ABC-Para. 9787
8/12/57	**81**	5	2 The First Kiss [I]	Columbia 40929

DEBUT DATE	PEAK POS	WKS CHR	ARTIST — Record Title	Label & Number
			TOM PETTY & THE HEARTBREAKERS Rock group formed in Los Angeles in 1975. Consisted of Tom Petty (b: 10/20/53, Gainesville, FL), guitar, vocals; Mike Campbell, guitar; Benmont Tench, keyboards; Ron Blair, bass; and Stan Lynch, drums. Petty, Campbell and Tench had been in Florida group Mudcrutch, early 70s. Backed Stevie Nicks on solo LP "Bella Donna". Blair left in 1982, replaced by Howard Epstein.	
11/05/77+	**40**	17	1 Breakdown	Shelter 62008
6/17/78	**41**	10	2 I Need To Know	Shelter 62010
9/23/78	**59**	6	3 Listen To Her Heart	Shelter 62011
11/17/79+	**10**	18	4 **Don't Do Me Like That**	Backstreet 41138
1/26/80	**15**	14	5 Refugee	Backstreet 41169
4/26/80	**59**	7	6 Here Comes My Girl	Backstreet 41227
5/02/81	**19**	13	7 The Waiting	Backstreet 51100
7/25/81	**3**	21	8 **Stop Draggin' My Heart Around** **STEVIE NICKS with TOM PETTY & THE HEARTBREAKERS**	Modern 7336
8/01/81	**79**	6	9 A Woman In Love (It's Not Me)	Backstreet 51136
11/13/82+	**20**	18	10 You Got Lucky	Backstreet 52144
2/26/83	**21**	11	11 Change Of Heart	Backstreet 52181
3/16/85	**13**	14	12 Don't Come Around Here No More	MCA 52496
6/08/85	**54**	8	13 Make It Better (Forget About Me)	MCA 52605
8/17/85	**74**	5	14 Rebels all of above written by Tom Petty	MCA 52658
2/01/86	**37**	9	15 Needles And Pins **TOM PETTY & THE HEARTBREAKERS with STEVIE NICKS**	MCA 52772
			JAMES PHELPS Gospel vocalist from Shreveport, LA. Member of The Soul Stirrers, 1964-65.	
5/08/65	**66**	7	1 Love Is A 5-Letter Word	Argo 5499
			PHILADELPHIA INTERNATIONAL ALL STARS Supergroup of Philadelphia International artists: Lou Rawls, Billy Paul, Teddy Pendergrass, The O'Jays, Archie Bell and Dee Dee Sharp.	
8/13/77	**91**	4	1 Let's Clean Up The Ghetto all profits were committed to a five-year charity project	Phil. Int. 3627
			THE PHILARMONICS Group of top British session musicians. Steve Gray, conductor/arranger.	
3/12/77	**100**	2	1 For Elise [I] an adaptation of Beethoven's "Fur Elise"	Capricorn 0268
			JOHN PHILLIPS Born on 8/30/35 in Paris Island, SC. Co-founder of The Mamas & The Papas. Father of actress Mackenzie Phillips.	
5/16/70	**32**	12	1 Mississippi	Dunhill 4236
			ESTHER PHILLIPS Real name: Esther Mae Jones. "Little Esther" had 5 Top 10 singles with Johnny Otis on the R&B charts in 1950. Died on 8/7/84 (48).	
10/27/62	**8**	14	1 **Release Me**	Lenox 5555
2/09/63	**61**	5	2 I Really Don't Want To Know **"LITTLE ESTHER" PHILLIPS**	Lenox 5560
4/27/63	**73**	2	3 You Never Miss Your Water (Till The Well Runs Dry)... **"LITTLE ESTHER" PHILLIPS & "BIG AL" DOWNING**	Lenox 5565
5/08/65	**54**	9	4 And I Love Him	Atlantic 2281
6/04/66	**73**	5	5 When A Woman Loves A Man	Atlantic 2335
6/03/67	**93**	2	6 Release Me [R]	Atlantic 2411
8/16/75	**20**	16	7 What A Diff'rence A Day Makes	Kudu 925
			PHIL PHILLIPS with The Twilights Born John Phillip Baptiste on 3/14/31. Black vocalist from Lake Charles, Louisiana.	
7/06/59	**2**[2]	18	1 **Sea Of Love**	Mercury 71465
			SHAWN PHILLIPS Born on 2/3/43 in Fort Worth, Texas. Soft rock vocalist.	
1/13/73	**89**	3	1 We	A&M 1402
2/10/73	**63**	6	2 Lost Horizon from the film of the same title	A&M 1405
			PHILLY CREAM Philadelphia soul session band.	
6/30/79	**67**	5	1 Motown Review	Fantasy/WMOT 862

DEBUT DATE	PEAK POS	WKS CHR	ARTIST — Record Title	Label & Number
			PHILLY DEVOTIONS	
			Soul quartet from Philadelphia: Ellis "Butch" Hill, Ernest "Chucky" Gibson, Morris Taylor and Matthew Cogington.	
2/08/75	**95**	2	1 I Just Can't Say Goodbye	Columbia 10076
			JIM PHOTOGLO	
			Pop vocalist from the South Bay area of Los Angeles.	
3/29/80	**31**	14	1 We Were Meant To Be Lovers shown only as: **PHOTOGLO**	20th Century 2446
4/18/81	**25**	16	2 Fool In Love With You	20th Century 2487
			EDITH PIAF	
			Born Edith Gassion on 12/19/15 in Belleville, Paris, France; died on 10/11/63. Legendary French Chanteuse, as a teenager sang for pennies in Paris streets, eventually became idolized international music hall and cabaret star.	
3/06/61	**88**	3	1 Milord [F]	Capitol 4493
			BOBBY "BORIS" PICKETT & The Crypt-Kickers	
			Born on 2/11/40 in Somerville, MA. Began recording career in Hollywood while aspiring to be an actor.	
9/08/62	**1**[2]	14	1 ● **Monster Mash** [N]	Garpax 44167
12/08/62	**30**	6	2 Monsters' Holiday [X-N]	Garpax 44171
6/22/63	**88**	2	3 Graduation Day **BOBBY PICKETT**	Garpax 44175
8/29/70	**91**	3	4 Monster Mash [N-R]	Parrot 348
5/05/73	**10**	20	5 **Monster Mash** [N-R]	Parrot 348
			WILSON PICKETT	
			Born on 3/18/41 in Prattville, AL. Soul singer, songwriter. Sang in local gospel groups. To Detroit in 1955. With The Falcons, 1961-63. Career took off after recording in Memphis with guitarist, producer Steve Cropper.	
5/04/63	**64**	6	1 If You Need Me	Double-L 713
7/27/63	**49**	10	2 It's Too Late	Double-L 717
11/09/63	**95**	4	3 I'm Down To My Last Heartbreak	Double-L 724
7/10/65	**21**	12	4 In The Midnight Hour	Atlantic 2289
11/06/65	**53**	10	5 Don't Fight It	Atlantic 2306
2/12/66	**13**	11	6 634-5789 (Soulsville, U.S.A.)	Atlantic 2320
5/28/66	**53**	8	7 Ninety-Nine And A Half (Won't Do)	Atlantic 2334
7/30/66	**6**	11	8 **Land Of 1000 Dances**	Atlantic 2348
11/26/66	**23**	9	9 Mustang Sally	Atlantic 2365
2/04/67	**29**	7	10 Everybody Needs Somebody To Love	Atlantic 2381
4/01/67	**32**	6	11 I Found A Love - Part 1	Atlantic 2394
6/17/67	**55**	5	12 Soul Dance Number Three/	
5/27/67	**70**	5	13 You Can't Stand Alone	Atlantic 2412
8/05/67	**8**	12	14 **Funky Broadway**	Atlantic 2430
11/04/67	**22**	6	15 Stag-O-Lee/	
12/02/67	**45**	10	16 I'm In Love	Atlantic 2448
2/17/68	**50**	5	17 Jealous Love	Atlantic 2484
4/13/68	**15**	10	18 She's Lookin' Good	Atlantic 2504
6/22/68	**24**	7	19 I'm A Midnight Mover	Atlantic 2528
9/21/68	**42**	7	20 I Found A True Love	Atlantic 2558
11/16/68	**42**	6	21 A Man And A Half	Atlantic 2575
12/21/68+	**23**	9	22 Hey Jude	Atlantic 2591
3/29/69	**50**	6	23 Mini-Skirt Minnie	Atlantic 2611
5/10/69	**64**	4	24 Born To Be Wild	Atlantic 2631
7/12/69	**59**	6	25 Hey Joe	Atlantic 2648
11/29/69	**92**	3	26 You Keep Me Hanging On	Atlantic 2682
4/04/70	**25**	12	27 Sugar Sugar/	
		5	28 Cole, Cooke & Redding	Atlantic 2722
8/22/70	**68**	5	29 She Said Yes	Atlantic 2753
9/26/70	**14**	13	30 Engine Number 9	Atlantic 2765
1/16/71	**17**	11	31 ● Don't Let The Green Grass Fool You	Atlantic 2781
4/24/71	**13**	12	32 ● Don't Knock My Love - Pt. 1	Atlantic 2797
8/28/71	**52**	7	33 Call My Name, I'll Be There	Atlantic 2824
12/25/71+	**24**	11	34 Fire And Water	Atlantic 2852
5/27/72	**58**	8	35 Funk Factory	Atlantic 2878
11/11/72	**99**	2	36 Mama Told Me Not To Come	Atlantic 2909

DEBUT DATE	PEAK POS	WKS CHR	ARTIST — Record Title	Label & Number
			WILSON PICKETT — Cont'd	
4/14/73	**98**	1	37 Mr. Magic Man	RCA 0898
9/29/73	**90**	5	38 Take A Closer Look At The Woman You're With	RCA 0049
			PICKETTYWITCH	
			English sextet - Polly Brown, lead singer.	
5/16/70	**67**	12	1 That Same Old Feeling	Janus 118
			PIECES OF EIGHT	
6/24/67	**59**	8	1 Lonely Drifter	A&M 854
			WEBB PIERCE	
			Born on 8/8/26 in West Monroe, LA. Top country singer - Webb's first 22 releases hit the Top 10 on the Country charts.	
6/03/57	**73**	9	1 Bye Bye, Love	Decca 30321
8/10/59	**24**	14	2 I Ain't Never	Decca 30923
12/28/59+	**54**	9	3 No Love Have I	Decca 31021
5/02/60	**69**	3	4 Is It Wrong (For Loving You)/	
4/25/60	**93**	2	5 (Doin' The) Lovers Leap	Decca 31058
11/21/60	**99**	1	6 Fallen Angel	Decca 31165
			PILOT	
			Scottish trio: David Paton, lead singer, guitar; Bill Lyall, keyboards; Stuart Tosh, drums.	
4/05/75	**5**	20	1 ● **Magic**	EMI 3992
10/11/75	**90**	5	2 Just A Smile	EMI 4135
1/31/76	**87**	6	3 January	EMI 4202
			above 3 produced by Alan Parsons	
			THE PILTDOWN MEN	
			Eddie Cobb and Lincoln Mayorga - also known as the Link Eddy Combo.	
9/12/60	**75**	3	1 Brontosaurus Stomp [I]	Capitol 4414
			MIKE PINERA	
			Born on 9/29/48 in Tampa. Rock singer, guitarist, composer. Member of Iron Butterfly, Blues Image, Ramatam, and Cactus.	
1/05/80	**70**	8	1 Goodnight My Love	Spector 00003
			PINK FLOYD	
			English progressive rock band formed in 1965: David Gilmour (replaced Syd Barrett in 1968), guitar; Roger Waters, bass; Nick Mason, drums; and Rick Wright, keyboards. Waters went solo in 1984. Band inactive, 1984-86. Gilmour, Mason & Wright re-grouped in 1987.	
5/19/73	**13**	15	1 Money	Harvest 3609
1/19/80	**1^{4}**	25	2 ● **Another Brick In The Wall (Part II)**	Columbia 11187
5/10/80	**53**	6	3 Run Like Hell	Columbia 11265
			above 3 written by Roger Waters	
			PINK LADY	
			Mei and Kei - Japan's hottest disco duo in the 1970s. Hosts of their own summer TV variety show in the U.S. in 1979.	
6/02/79	**37**	11	1 Kiss In The Dark	Elektra 46040
			THE PIPKINS	
			British studio group - Tony Burrows, lead singer.	
5/23/70	**9**	12	1 **Gimme Dat Ding** [N]	Capitol 2819
			background tune used on TV's "Benny Hill Show"	
			PIPS - see GLADYS KNIGHT	
			GENE PITNEY	
			Born on 2/17/41 in Rockville, CT. Had own band at Rockville High School. Recorded for Decca in 1959, with Ginny Arnell as Jamie & Jane. Recorded for Blaze in 1960 as Billy Bryan. First recorded under own name for Festival in 1960. Wrote "Hello Mary Lou", "He's A Rebel" and "Rubber Ball".	
1/30/61	**39**	8	1 (I Wanna) Love My Life Away	Musicor 1002
8/07/61	**42**	8	2 Every Breath I Take	Musicor 1011
10/30/61+	**13**	19	3 Town Without Pity	Musicor 1009
			from the film of the same title	
4/28/62	**4**	13	4 **(The Man Who Shot) Liberty Valance**	Musicor 1020
			inspired by the film of the same title	
9/15/62	**2^{1}**	14	5 **Only Love Can Break A Heart/**	
9/01/62	**58**	7	6 If I Didn't Have A Dime (To Play The Jukebox)	Musicor 1022
12/15/62+	**12**	12	7 Half Heaven - Half Heartache	Musicor 1026

DEBUT DATE	PEAK POS	WKS CHR	ARTIST — Record Title	Label & Number
			GENE PITNEY — Cont'd	
3/23/63	**12**	11	8 Mecca	Musicor 1028
7/06/63	**21**	11	9 True Love Never Runs Smooth	Musicor 1032
10/19/63	**17**	11	10 Twenty Four Hours From Tulsa	Musicor 1034
1/18/64	**49**	7	11 That Girl Belongs To Yesterday written by Mick Jagger and Keith Richards	Musicor 1036
5/09/64	**64**	5	12 Yesterday's Hero	Musicor 1038
7/18/64	**7**	16	13 **It Hurts To Be In Love**	Musicor 1040
10/24/64	**9**	12	14 **I'm Gonna Be Strong**	Musicor 1045
2/27/65	**31**	7	15 I Must Be Seeing Things	Musicor 1070
4/17/65	**99**	1	16 I've Got Five Dollars And It's Saturday Night GEORGE JONES & GENE PITNEY	Musicor 1066
5/08/65	**13**	10	17 Last Chance To Turn Around	Musicor 1093
7/24/65	**28**	8	18 Looking Through The Eyes Of Love	Musicor 1103
11/20/65	**37**	8	19 Princess In Rags	Musicor 1130
4/23/66	**25**	8	20 Backstage	Musicor 1171
12/24/66+	**64**	6	21 Just One Smile	Musicor 1219
5/11/68	**16**	13	22 She's A Heartbreaker	Musicor 1306
11/02/68	**92**	3	23 Billy You're My Friend	Musicor 1331
12/13/69+	**89**	5	24 She Lets Her Hair Down (Early In The Morning)	Musicor 1384
			THE PIXIES THREE White female trio.	
8/17/63	**40**	9	1 Birthday Party	Mercury 72130
12/14/63+	**79**	5	2 Cold Cold Winter/	
1/18/64	**56**	7	3 442 Glenwood Avenue	Mercury 72208
4/18/64	**87**	3	4 Gee	Mercury 72250
			FRANK PIZANI Member of The Highlights.	
9/16/57	**70**	3	1 Angry	Bally 1040
			MARY KAY PLACE as Loretta Haggers Born on 8/23/47 in Tulsa. Singer, composer, comedienne. Script writer for many TV comedy shows. Played Loretta Haggers on TV's "Mary Hartman, Mary Hartman".	
10/30/76	**60**	13	1 Baby Boy	Columbia 10422
			PLANET P Session musicians assembled by German producer Peter Hauke. Tony Carey, lead singer.	
4/16/83	**64**	9	1 Why Me?	Geffen 29705
			ROBERT PLANT Born on 8/20/48 in Bromwich, England. Lead singer of Led Zeppelin and The Honeydrippers.	
9/11/82	**64**	6	1 Burning Down One Side	Swan Song 99979
11/13/82	**74**	5	2 Pledge Pin	Swan Song 99952
8/06/83	**20**	16	3 Big Log	Atlantic 99844
11/19/83+	**39**	12	4 In The Mood	Es Paranza 99820
5/18/85	**36**	11	5 Little By Little all of above written by Plant	Es Paranza 99644
			PLASTIC ONO BAND - see JOHN LENNON	
			PLATINUM BLONDE Rock quartet from Canada - Mark Holmes, lead singer.	
4/12/86	**82**	5	1 Somebody Somewhere	Epic 05804
			EDDIE PLATT Saxophonist, bandleader from Cleveland.	
3/03/58	**20**	10	1 Tequila [I] Jockey #20 / Best Seller #35 / Top 100 #35	ABC-Para. 9899
6/09/58	**74**	5	2 Cha-Hua-Hua [I]	Gone 5031

DEBUT DATE	PEAK POS	WKS CHR	ARTIST — Record Title	Label & Number
			THE PLATTERS R&B group formed in Los Angeles in 1953. Consisted of Tony Williams (b: 4/5/28, Elizabeth, NJ), lead; David Lynch, tenor; Paul Robi, baritone; Herb Reed, bass; and Zola Taylor. Taylor had formerly sung with Shirley Gunter's Queens. Group first recorded for Federal in 1954, with Alex Hodge instead of Robi, and without Zola Taylor. Hit "Only You" was written by manager Buck Ram and first recorded for Federal, who did not want to use it. To Mercury in 1955, re-recorded "Only You". Williams left to go solo, replaced by Sonny Turner in 1961. Taylor replaced by Sandra Dawn; Robi replaced by Nate Nelson (formerly in The Flamingos) in 1966. Several unrelated groups use this famous name today.	
10/01/55	**5**	22	1 **Only You (And You Alone)** Best Seller #5 / Top 100 #5 / Jockey #5 / Juke Box #5	Mercury 70633
12/17/55+	**1^{2}**	24	2 **The Great Pretender/** Top 100 #1(2) / Jockey #1(2) / Juke Box #1(1) / Best Seller #2	
2/11/56	**87**	1	3 I'm Just A Dancing Partner	Mercury 70753
3/24/56	**4**	20	4 **(You've Got) The Magic Touch/** Top 100 #4 / Juke Box #4 / Best Seller #5 / Jockey #5	
4/07/56	**50**	9	5 Winner Take All	Mercury 70819
7/07/56	**1^{5}**	23	6 **My Prayer/** Top 100 #1(5) / Jockey #1(3) / Best Seller #1(2) / Juke Box #1(1) #2 hit in 1939 for Glenn Miller	
7/14/56	**39**	14	7 Heaven On Earth	Mercury 70893
9/29/56	**11**	18	8 You'll Never Never Know/ Juke Box #11 / Best Seller #13 / Top 100 #14 / Jockey #18	
9/29/56	**23**	15	9 It Isn't Right	Mercury 70948
12/29/56+	**20**	14	10 On My Word Of Honor/ Best Seller #20 / Juke Box #20 / Top 100 #27	
12/22/56+	**31**	12	11 One In A Million	Mercury 71011
3/23/57	**11**	14	12 I'm Sorry/ Juke Box #11 / Best Seller #14 / Top 100 #19	
4/06/57	**23**	23	13 He's Mine Top 100 #23 / Jockey #24	Mercury 71032
5/27/57	**24**	14	14 My Dream/ Best Seller #24 / Top 100 #26	
		2	15 I Wanna Best Seller flip	Mercury 71093
10/28/57	**65**	8	16 Only Because	Mercury 71184
2/03/58	**56**	8	17 Helpless	Mercury 71246
4/07/58	**1^{1}**	17	18 **Twilight Time** Best Seller #1(1) / Top 100 #1(1) / Jockey #1(1) #14 hit in 1944 for the Three Suns	Mercury 71289
6/30/58	**50**	8	19 You're Making A Mistake Best Seller #50 / Top 100 #51	Mercury 71320
9/15/58	**42**	10	20 I Wish/ Hot 100 #42 / Best Seller #46	
10/06/58	**93**	2	21 It's Raining Outside	Mercury 71353
11/17/58+	**1^{3}**	19	22 **Smoke Gets In Your Eyes** #1 hit in 1934 for Paul Whiteman	Mercury 71383
3/23/59	**12**	15	23 Enchanted	Mercury 71427
6/22/59	**41**	9	24 Remember When	Mercury 71467
9/07/59	**44**	9	25 Where/ adaptation of Tschaikowsky's "Pathetique Symphony"	
9/14/59	**61**	7	26 Wish It Were Me from the film "Girls' Town" 1-2, 4, 7, 12, 14-15, 17, 20-21, 23-24, 26: written by Buck Ram	Mercury 71502
1/25/60	**8**	16	27 **Harbor Lights/** there were 5 Top 10 versions of this tune in 1950	
2/22/60	**65**	5	28 Sleepy Lagoon #1 hit in 1942 for Harry James	Mercury 71563
5/16/60	**56**	6	29 Ebb Tide Frank Chacksfield's version hit #2 in 1953	Mercury 71624
8/01/60	**36**	8	30 Red Sails In The Sunset Bing Crosby and Guy Lombardo both had #1 versions in 1935 above 2: **THE PLATTERS featuring TONY WILLIAMS**	Mercury 71656
10/10/60	**21**	11	31 To Each His Own there were three #1 versions of this tune in 1946	Mercury 71697
1/09/61	**30**	8	32 If I Didn't Care the Ink Spots' version hit #2 in 1939	Mercury 71749
4/03/61	**62**	4	33 Trees	Mercury 71791
7/31/61	**25**	8	34 I'll Never Smile Again Tommy Dorsey's version was #1 in 1940	Mercury 71847
2/17/62	**91**	2	35 It's Magic	Mercury 71921

DEBUT DATE	PEAK POS	WKS CHR	ARTIST — Record Title	Label & Number
			THE PLATTERS — Cont'd	
4/30/66	**31**	14	36 I Love You 1000 Times	Musicor 1166
12/03/66	**97**	2	37 I'll Be Home	Musicor 1211
2/25/67	**14**	12	38 With This Ring	Musicor 1229
7/01/67	**56**	8	39 Washed Ashore (On A Lonely Island In The Sea)	Musicor 1251
10/21/67	**70**	7	40 Sweet, Sweet Lovin'	Musicor 1275
			THE PLAYBOYS	
8/25/58	**62**	6	1 Over The Weekend	Cameo 142
			PLAYER	
			Pop/rock group formed in Los Angeles: Peter Beckett, vocals, guitar; John Crowley, vocals, guitar; Ronn Moss, bass; John Friesen, drums; Wayne Cooke, keyboards.	
10/01/77+	**1**[3]	32	1 ● **Baby Come Back**	RSO 879
3/11/78	**10**	17	2 **This Time I'm In It For Love**	RSO 890
9/09/78	**27**	11	3 Prisoner Of Your Love	RSO 908
12/16/78+	**62**	6	4 Silver Lining	RSO 914
6/07/80	**46**	8	5 It's For You	Casablanca 2265
1/23/82	**48**	9	6 If Looks Could Kill all of above written by Beckett (1 & 3 with Crowley)	RCA 13006
			THE PLAYMATES	
			Donny Conn (b: 3/29/30), Morey Carr (b: 7/31/32) and Chic Hetti (b: 2/26/30) from Waterbury, CT. Molded nucleus of act at the University of Connecticut, with more emphasis on comedy than singing.	
1/20/58	**19**	13	1 Jo-Ann Best Seller #19 / Top 100 #20	Roulette 4037
4/21/58	**87**	2	2 Let's Be Lovers	Roulette 4056
6/09/58	**22**	9	3 Don't Go Home Jockey #22 / Top 100 #36 / Best Seller #38	Roulette 4072
9/29/58	**81**	2	4 The Day I Died	Roulette 4100
11/03/58	**4**	15	5 **Beep Beep** [N]	Roulette 4115
3/30/59	**75**	4	6 Star Love 2-6: with Hugo Peretti & His Orchestra	Roulette 4136
7/06/59	**15**	13	7 What Is Love?	Roulette 4160
10/24/60	**37**	8	8 Wait For Me	Roulette 4276
3/06/61	**70**	5	9 Little Miss Stuck-Up	Roulette 4322
7/14/62	**88**	2	10 Keep Your Hands In Your Pockets	Roulette 4432
			PLEASURE	
			R&B group from Portland, Oregon.	
12/08/79+	**55**	10	1 Glide	Fantasy 874
			JACK PLEIS	
			Born on 5/11/20 in Philadelphia. Conductor, composer.	
10/20/56	**91**	2	1 Giant vocals: Ralph Young; from the film of the same title	Decca 30055
12/08/56	**65**	1	2 I'll Always Be In Love With You [I]	Decca 30086
6/17/57	**69**	1	3 (But As They Say) That's Life [I]	Decca 30303
			THE PLIMSOULS	
			Los Angeles rock quartet - Peter Case, lead singer. Plimsouls: British slang for gym shoes.	
7/30/83	**82**	3	1 A Million Miles Away	Geffen 29600
			P-NUT GALLERY	
6/12/71	**62**	7	1 Do You Know What Time It Is? [N] inspired by TV's "Howdy Doody" show	Buddah 239
			POCKETS	
			R&B group from Baltimore, Maryland - led by Al McKinney.	
1/07/78	**84**	9	1 Come Go With Me	Columbia 10632
			POCO	
			Los Angeles country-rock band formed by Rusty Young (pedal steel guitar) and Buffalo Springfield members Richie Furay (rhythm guitar) and Jim Messina (lead guitar). As of first single, group consisted of Furay, Messina, Young, George Grantham (drums) and Timothy B. Schmit (bass). Messina left in 1971, replaced by Paul Cotton, and Furay left in 1973. Grantham and Schmit (joins Eagles) left in 1977; replacements: Charlie Harrison, Kim Bullard and Steve Chapman.	
10/03/70	**72**	8	1 You Better Think Twice	Epic 10636
3/27/71	**69**	7	2 C'mon	Epic 10714

DEBUT DATE	PEAK POS	WKS CHR	ARTIST — Record Title	Label & Number
			POCO — Cont'd	
9/20/75	**50**	9	3 Keep On Tryin'	ABC 12126
8/14/76	**94**	1	4 Rose Of Cimarron	ABC 12204
8/06/77	**50**	8	5 Indian Summer	ABC 12295
1/20/79	**17**	14	6 Crazy Love	ABC 12439
5/12/79	**20**	14	7 Heart Of The Night	MCA 41023
7/19/80	**48**	10	8 Under The Gun	MCA 41269
10/11/80	**74**	4	9 Midnight Rain	MCA 41326
12/18/82+	**50**	13	10 Shoot For The Moon	Atlantic 89919
4/28/84	**80**	5	11 Days Gone By	Atlantic 89674
			THE POETS	
			R&B quartet: lead Ronnie Lewis, Melvin Bradford, Paul Fulton and Johnny James.	
3/19/66	**45**	10	1 She Blew A Good Thing	Symbol 214
			POINT BLANK	
			6-man rock band from Texas.	
6/27/81	**39**	14	1 Nicole	MCA 51132
			POINTER SISTERS	
			Soul group formed in Oakland in 1971, consisting of sisters Ruth, Anita, Bonnie and June Pointer. Parents were ministers. Group was originally a trio, joined by youngest sister June, in early 70s. First recorded for Atlantic in 1971. Back-up work for Cold Blood, Elvin Bishop, Boz Scaggs, Grace Slick, and many others. Sang in nostalgic 1940s style, 1973-77. In film "Car Wash", 1976. Bonnie went solo in 1978, group continued as trio in new musical style.	
8/18/73	**11**	16	1 Yes We Can Can	Blue Thumb 229
12/22/73+	**61**	8	2 Wang Dang Doodle	Blue Thumb 243
10/05/74	**13**	16	3 Fairytale	Blue Thumb 254
3/08/75	**89**	5	4 Live Your Life Before You Die	Blue Thumb 262
7/19/75	**20**	15	5 How Long (Betcha' Got A Chick On The Side)	Blue Thumb 265
11/22/75	**61**	7	6 Going Down Slowly	Blue Thumb 268
			all of above produced by David Rubinson	
11/11/78+	**2**[2]	23	7 ● **Fire**	Planet 45901
			written by Bruce Springsteen	
3/17/79	**30**	10	8 Happiness	Planet 45902
7/26/80	**3**	26	9 ● **He's So Shy**	Planet 47916
11/08/80	**52**	11	10 Could I Be Dreaming	Planet 47920
5/30/81	**2**[3]	24	11 ● **Slow Hand**	Planet 47929
1/23/82	**13**	16	12 Should I Do It	Planet 47960
6/26/82	**16**	14	13 American Music	Planet 13254
9/18/82	**30**	16	14 I'm So Excited	Planet 13327
3/26/83	**67**	5	15 If You Wanna Get Back Your Lady	Planet 13430
10/08/83	**48**	15	16 I Need You	Planet 13639
1/28/84	**5**	20	17 **Automatic**	Planet 13730
4/28/84	**3**	24	18 **Jump (For My Love)**	Planet 13780
8/04/84	**9**	24	19 **I'm So Excited** [R]	Planet 13857
			slightly different mix than #14 above	
11/24/84+	**6**	23	20 **Neutron Dance**	Planet 13951
			from the film "Beverly Hills Cop"	
3/23/85	**44**	11	21 Baby Come And Get It	Planet 14041
7/13/85	**11**	18	22 Dare Me	RCA 14126
11/02/85	**59**	11	23 Freedom	RCA 14224
3/01/86	**83**	5	24 Twist My Arm	RCA 14197
11/01/86	**33**	13	25 Goldmine	RCA 5062
			7-25: produced by Richard Perry	
			BONNIE POINTER	
			Born on 7/11/51 in East Oakland, CA. One of the Pointer Sisters.	
11/18/78+	**58**	14	1 Free Me From My Freedom/Tie Me To A Tree (Handcuff Me)	Motown 1451
6/16/79	**11**	23	2 Heaven Must Have Sent You	Motown 1459
12/22/79+	**40**	13	3 I Can't Help Myself (Sugar Pie, Honey Bunch)	Motown 1478

DEBUT DATE	PEAK POS	WKS CHR	ARTIST — Record Title	Label & Number
			POLICE	
			Rock trio formed in England in 1977: Gordon "Sting" Sumner (b: 10/2/51), vocals, bass; Andy Summers (b: 12/31/42), guitar; and Stewart Copeland (b: 7/16/52), drums. First guitarist was Henri Padovani, replaced by Summers in 1977. Copeland had been with Curved Air. Sting was in films "Dune", "The Bride" and "Plenty".	
2/24/79	**32**	13	1 Roxanne	A&M 2096
11/24/79	**74**	7	2 Message In A Bottle	A&M 2190
10/25/80+	**10**	21	3 **De Do Do Do, De Da Da Da**	A&M 2275
2/07/81	**10**	18	4 **Don't Stand So Close To Me**	A&M 2301
9/26/81	**3**	19	5 **Every Little Thing She Does Is Magic**	A&M 2371
1/16/82	**11**	13	6 Spirits In The Material World	A&M 2390
4/10/82	**46**	8	7 Secret Journey	A&M 2408
6/04/83	**1**[8]	22	8● **Every Breath You Take**	A&M 2542
8/27/83	**3**	16	9 **King Of Pain**	A&M 2569
11/05/83	**16**	14	10 Synchronicity II	A&M 2571
1/07/84	**8**	16	11 **Wrapped Around Your Finger**	A&M 2614
10/25/86	**46**	9	12 Don't Stand So Close To Me '86 new version of their 1981 hit - all of above written by Sting	A&M 2879
			MICHEL POLNAREFF	
			Pop vocalist, keyboardist, guitarist.	
2/21/76	**48**	7	1 If You Only Believe (Jesus For Tonite)	Atlantic 3314
5/29/76	**61**	7	2 Lipstick [I]	Atlantic 3330
			PONDEROSA TWINS + ONE	
			Cleveland soul group, consisting of two sets of twins: Alvin & Alfred Pelham and Keith & Kirk Gardner, plus Ricky Spencer. Produced by Bobby Massey of The O'Jays.	
9/25/71	**78**	7	1 You Send Me	Horoscope 102
			PONI-TAILS	
			Pop female trio from Brush High School in Lyndhurst, Ohio: Toni Cistone, lead; LaVerne Novak, high harmony; and Patti McCabe, low harmony. First recorded for Point in 1957.	
7/21/58	**7**	16	1 **Born Too Late** Hot 100 #7 / Best Seller #11	ABC-Para. 9934
12/01/58	**85**	3	2 Seven Minutes In Heaven	ABC-Para. 9969
10/26/59	**87**	3	3 I'll Be Seeing You	ABC-Para. 10047
			BRIAN POOLE & The Tremeloes	
			Born on 11/3/41 in England. Brian formed the Tremeloes and left group in 1966.	
9/12/64	**97**	2	1 Someone, Someone	Monument 846
			POP-TOPS - see LOS POP TOPS	
			THE POPPIES	
			Dorothy Moore, lead singer; Petsye McCune, and Rosemary Taylor. Formed at Jackson State University.	
3/05/66	**56**	6	1 Lullaby Of Love	Epic 9893
			THE POPPY FAMILY	
			Canadian pop quartet: Susan (vocals) and husband Terry Jacks (guitar, composer); Craig MacCaw (guitar) and Satwan Singh (percussion). Group and marriage broke up in 1973; Susan and Terry began solo careers.	
3/28/70	**2**[2]	17	1● **Which Way You Goin' Billy?**	London 129
8/08/70	**29**	13	2 That's Where I Went Wrong	London 139
4/03/71	**100**	2	3 I Was Wondering/	
7/31/71	**45**	12	4 Where Evil Grows all of above written and produced by Terry Jacks	London 148
12/11/71	**84**	4	5 No Good To Cry	London 164
			DAVID PORTER - see ISAAC HAYES	
			NOLAN PORTER	
9/18/71	**70**	8	1 I Like What You Give shown only as: **NOLAN**	Lizard 1008
12/18/71+	**77**	6	2 Keep On Keeping On	Lizard 1010
3/31/73	**89**	4	3 If I Could Only Be Sure	ABC 11343
			GARY PORTNOY	
			Pop singer/songwriter from Valley Stream, New York.	
4/30/83	**83**	4	1 Where Everybody Knows Your Name theme from the TV show "Cheers"	Applause 106

DEBUT DATE	PEAK POS	WKS CHR	ARTIST — Record Title		Label & Number
			SANDY POSEY		
			Raised in the Memphis area - formerly a session vocalist in Memphis and Nashville.		
7/23/66	12	14	1 Born A Woman		MGM 13501
11/19/66	12	12	2 Single Girl		MGM 13612
3/11/67	31	7	3 What A Woman In Love Won't Do		MGM 13702
6/10/67	12	12	4 I Take It Back		MGM 13744
10/21/67	59	5	5 Are You Never Coming Home all of above produced by Chips Moman		MGM 13824
			MIKE POST		
			Record producer and composer of numerous television and film scores.		
5/17/75	10	16	1 **The Rockford Files**	[I]	MGM 14772
9/27/75	56	7	2 Manhattan Spiritual	[I]	MGM 14829
8/22/81	10	22	3 **The Theme From Hill Street Blues** featuring guitarist Larry Carlton	[I]	Elektra 47186
2/06/82	25	17	4 Theme From Magnum P.I. 1, 3 & 4: from the TV series of the same title	[I]	Elektra 47400
			POTLIQUOR		
			Southern rock quartet - George Ratzlaff, lead singer.		
2/05/72	65	11	1 Cheer		Janus 179
			FRANCK POURCEL'S FRENCH FIDDLES		
			Frank was born on 1/1/15 in Marseilles, France. String orchestra leader, composer, arranger, violinist.		
4/06/59	9	16	1 **Only You**	[I]	Capitol 4165
			POUSETTE-DART BAND		
			Country-pop quartet. Jon Pousette-Dart, leader.		
9/08/79	83	4	1 For Love		Capitol 4764
			BOBBY POWELL		
			Blind soul singer.		
12/04/65+	76	7	1 C.C. Rider		Whit 714
6/17/67	91	3	2 Why (Am I Treated So Bad)		Whit 730
			COZY POWELL		
			Veteran British drummer. Member of Jeff Beck's group, 1971-72; Rainbow, 1976-80; and current member of Emerson, Lake & Powell.		
3/16/74	49	9	1 Dance With The Devil	[I]	Chrysalis 2029
			JANE POWELL		
			Born Suzanne Burce on 4/1/29 in Portland. Star of many movie musicals and romances, mid-40s through 50s.		
8/25/56	15	25	1 True Love Best Seller #15 / Top 100 #24		Verve 2018
			THE POWER STATION		
			Superstar quartet: Duran Duran's John Taylor (bass) & Andy Taylor (guitar); Chic's Tony Thompson (drums), and Robert Palmer (lead singer).		
3/16/85	6	18	1 **Some Like It Hot**		Capitol 5444
6/08/85	9	15	2 **Get It On** revival of 1972's "Bang A Gong" by T. Rex (Marc Bolan)		Capitol 5479
9/07/85	34	10	3 Communication above 3 produced by Chic's Bernard Edwards		Capitol 5511
			JOEY POWERS		
			Born in Canonsburg, PA. Produced John Hills Exercise Show for NBC-TV. Wrestling instructor at Ohio State University.		
11/09/63+	10	13	1 **Midnight Mary**		Amy 892
			TOM POWERS		
			Born in Washington, DC in 1948. Pop singer, songwriter.		
10/08/77	92	5	1 It Ain't Love		Big Tree 16103
			POZO-SECO SINGERS		
			Native-born Texas trio: Susan Taylor, Lofton Kline and country star Don Williams (lead singer).		
2/26/66	47	7	1 Time		Columbia 43437
6/18/66	92	2	2 I'll Be Gone		Columbia 43646
9/10/66	32	11	3 I Can Make It With You		Columbia 43784
12/17/66+	32	9	4 Look What You've Done		Columbia 43927
5/06/67	96	1	5 I Believed It All		Columbia 44041
9/16/67	97	3	6 Louisiana Man		Columbia 44263

DEBUT DATE	PEAK POS	WKS CHR	ARTIST — Record Title		Label & Number
			PEREZ PRADO		
			Damaso Perez Prado - "King of the Mambo" bandleader, organist from Cuba and later Mexico City.		
3/05/55	**1**[10]	26	1 **Cherry Pink And Apple Blossom White**	[I]	RCA 5965
			Best Seller #1(10) / Juke Box #1(8) / Jockey #1(6) trumpet solo by Billy Regis - from the film "Under Water!"		
6/16/58	**1**[1]	21	2 ● **Patricia**	[I]	RCA 7245
			Top 100 #1(1) / Jockey #1(1) / Best Seller #2		
10/13/58	**53**	9	3 Guaglione/	[I]	
10/20/58	**95**	1	4 Paris	[I]	RCA 7337
4/07/62	**65**	5	5 Patricia-Twist	[I]	RCA 8006
			new version of 1958 hit		
			PRATT & McCLAIN		
			Truett Pratt and Jerry McClain, with backing group Brother Love.		
4/03/76	**5**	14	1 **Happy Days**		Reprise 1351
			from the TV series of the same title		
7/17/76	**71**	4	2 Devil With A Blue Dress		Reprise 1361
			ANDY PRATT		
			Born on 1/25/47 in Boston. Great-grandson of Standard Oil's co-founder. Soft rock singer, songwriter, keyboardist, guitarist.		
4/28/73	**78**	10	1 Avenging Annie		Columbia 45804
			THE PRECISIONS		
			Soul group led by Bobby Brooks.		
10/07/67	**60**	6	1 If This Is Love (I'd Rather Be Lonely)		Drew 1003
			PRELUDE		
			English folk-based trio: Ian Vardy and Brian & Irene Hume (husband & wife).		
10/05/74	**22**	13	1 After The Goldrush		Island 002
11/29/75+	**63**	8	2 For A Dancer		Pye 71045
			THE PRELUDES FIVE		
8/14/61	**80**	5	1 Starlight		Pik 231
			THE PREMIERS		
			Latin-rock band from San Gabriel, California.		
6/20/64	**19**	9	1 Farmer John		Warner 5443
			THE PRESIDENTS		
			Soul group consisting of Archie Powell, Bill Shorter and Tony Boyd.		
10/03/70	**11**	15	1 5-10-15-20 (25-30 Years Of Love)		Sussex 207
1/30/71	**68**	7	2 Triangle Of Love (Hey Diddle Diddle)		Sussex 212
			ELVIS PRESLEY		
			The King of Rock & Roll. Born on 1/8/35 in Tupelo, Mississippi. Died on 8/16/77 in Memphis at the age of 42 due to heart failure caused by drug abuse. Won talent contest at age eight, singing "Old Shep". First played guitar at age eleven. Moved to Memphis in 1948. Sang in high school shows. Worked as an usher and truck driver after graduation. First recorded for Sun in 1954. Signed to RCA Records on 11/22/55. First film, "Love Me Tender" in 1956. In US Army from 3/24/58 to 3/5/60. In many films thereafter. NBC-TV special in 1968. Married Priscilla Beaulieu on 5/1/67; divorced on 10/11/73. Only child Lisa Marie, born on 2/1/68. Elvis' last live performance was in Indianapolis on 6/26/77.		
3/03/56	**1**[8]	27	1 **Heartbreak Hotel/**		
			Best Seller #1(8) / Juke Box #1(8) / Top 100 #1(7) / Jockey #1(3)		
3/10/56	**19**	16	2 I Was The One		RCA 47-6420
			Jockey #19 / Top 100 #23		
4/07/56	**20**	12	3 Blue Suede Shoes		RCA EPA-747
			Best Seller #20 / Top 100 #24 / Jockey #24 from the E.P. "Elvis Presley"		
5/12/56	**76**	5	4 Money Honey		RCA EPA-821
			from the E.P. "Heartbreak Hotel" #1 hit for 11 weeks on the R&B charts for The Drifters in 1953		
5/26/56	**1**[1]	24	5 **I Want You, I Need You, I Love You/**		
			Best Seller #1 / Top 100 #3 / Juke Box #3 / Jockey #6		
5/26/56	**31**	14	6 My Baby Left Me		RCA 47-6540
			written and recorded on RCA by Arthur "Big Boy" Crudup in 1950		
8/04/56	**1**[11]	28	7 **Don't Be Cruel/**		
			Best Seller #1(11)/Juke Box #1(11)/Jockey #1(8)/Top 100 #1(7)		
	1	27	8 **Hound Dog**		RCA 47-6604
			Juke Box #1(11) / Best Seller #1(10) / Top 100 #2 / Jockey #4 #1 for 7 weeks on the R&B charts for Big Mama Thornton in 1953		

DEBUT DATE	PEAK POS	WKS CHR	ARTIST — Record Title	Label & Number
			ELVIS PRESLEY — Cont'd	
9/29/56	**55**	17	9 Blue Moon #1 in 1935 for Glen Gray & The Casa Loma Orchestra	RCA 47-6640
10/13/56	**74**	6	10 I Don't Care If The Sun Don't Shine from the E.P. "Anyway You Want Me" - #8 hit in 1950 for Patti Page above 2 are Sun studio recordings from 1954	RCA EPA-965
10/20/56	1^{5}	23	11 **Love Me Tender/** Best Seller #1(5) / Jockey #1(5) / Top 100 #1(4) / Juke Box #1(1) from Elvis' first movie - tune adapted from "Aura Lee" of 1861	
11/03/56	**20**	10	12 Anyway You Want Me (That's How I Will Be) Jockey #20 / Top 100 #27	RCA 47-6643
11/17/56+	2^{2}	19	13 **Love Me/** Jockey #2 / Top 100 #6 / Best Seller #7 / Juke Box #8	
12/01/56	**19**	15	14 When My Blue Moon Turns To Gold Again/ Jockey #19 / Top 100 #27	
12/29/56+	**59**	7	15 Paralyzed above 3 from the E.P. "Elvis"	RCA EPA-992
12/29/56+	**24**	11	16 Poor Boy Jockey #24 / Top 100 #35 from the film and the E.P. "Love Me Tender"	RCA EPA-4006
12/29/56	**47**	2	17 Old Shep from the E.P. "Elvis, Volume II" - written in 1947 by Red Foley	RCA EPA-993
1/26/57	1^{3}	17	18 **Too Much/** Best Seller #1(3) / Juke Box #1(1) / Top 100 #2 / Jockey #2	
2/02/57	**21**	9	19 Playing For Keeps Jockey #21 / Top 100 #34	RCA 47-6800
4/13/57	1^{9}	30	20 **All Shook Up/** Juke Box #1(9) end/Best Seller #1(8)/Top 100 #1(8)/Jockey #1(7)	
4/06/57	**58**	7	21 That's When Your Heartaches Begin	RCA 47-6870
4/13/57	**25**	10	22 (There'll Be) Peace In The Valley (For Me) Best Seller #25 / Top 100 #39 from the E.P. "Peace In The Valley" - #7 Country hit for Red Foley	RCA EPA-4054
6/24/57	1^{7}	25	23 **(Let Me Be Your) Teddy Bear/** Best Seller #1(7) / Top 100 #1(7) / Jockey #1(3)	
6/24/57	**20**	22	24 Loving You Jockey #20 / Top 100 #28 above 2 from the film "Loving You"	RCA 47-7000
10/14/57	1^{7}	27	25 **Jailhouse Rock/** Best Seller #1(7) / Top 100 #1(6) / Jockey #1(2)	
10/21/57	**18**	10	26 Treat Me Nice Jockey #18 / Top 100 #27 above 2 from the film "Jailhouse Rock"	RCA 47-7035
1/27/58	1^{5}	20	27● **Don't/** Best Seller #1(5) / Top 100 #1(1) / Jockey #1(1)	
1/27/58	**8**	12	28 **I Beg Of You** Top 100 #8 / Jockey #11	RCA 47-7150
4/21/58	2^{1}	15	29● **Wear My Ring Around Your Neck/** Best Seller #2 / Top 100 #3 / Jockey #3	
4/21/58	**15**	6	30 Doncha' Think It's Time Jockey #15 / Top 100 #21	RCA 47-7240
6/30/58	1^{2}	16	31● **Hard Headed Woman/** Best Seller #1(2) / Jockey #1(1) / Top 100 #2	
7/07/58	**25**	9	32 Don't Ask Me Why Jockey #25 / Top 100 #28 above 2 from the film "King Creole"	RCA 47-7280
11/10/58	**4**	17	33 **One Night/** #11 hit in 1956 on the R&B charts for Smiley Lewis	
11/03/58	**8**	16	34● **I Got Stung**	RCA 47-7410
3/23/59	2^{1}	15	35● **(Now And Then There's) A Fool Such As I/** #4 hit in 1953 on the Country charts for Hank Snow	
3/30/59	**4**	13	36 **I Need Your Love Tonight**	RCA 47-7506
7/06/59	1^{2}	14	37 **A Big Hunk O' Love/** above 4: Elvis' only recordings during his Army hitch	
7/13/59	**12**	11	38 My Wish Came True	RCA 47-7600
4/04/60	1^{4}	16	39 **Stuck On You/**	
4/11/60	**17**	10	40 Fame And Fortune above 2 recorded 15 days after his Army discharge	RCA 47-7740
7/18/60	1^{5}	20	41● **It's Now Or Never/** adapted from the Italian song "O Sole Mio" of 1899	
7/25/60	**32**	11	42 A Mess Of Blues	RCA 47-7777

DEBUT DATE	PEAK POS	WKS CHR	ARTIST — Record Title	Label & Number
			ELVIS PRESLEY — Cont'd	
11/14/60	1^{6}	16	43 ● **Are You Lonesome To-night?/**	
			#4 hit in 1927 for Vaughn Deleath	
11/14/60	20	11	44 I Gotta Know	RCA 47-7810
2/20/61	1^{2}	12	45 **Surrender/**	
			adapted from the Italian song "Come Back To Sorrento"	
2/27/61	32	5	46 Lonely Man	RCA 47-7850
			from the film "Wild In The Country"	
4/17/61	14	7	47 Flaming Star	RCA LPC-128
			from the film of the same title and the E.P. "Elvis By Request"	
5/15/61	5	9	48 **I Feel So Bad/**	
			#8 hit in 1954 on the R&B charts for Chuck Willis	
6/05/61	26	5	49 Wild In The Country	RCA 47-7880
			from the film of the same title	
8/21/61	5	13	50 **Little Sister/**	
8/28/61	4	11	51 **(Marie's the Name) His Latest Flame**	RCA 47-7908
12/04/61+	2^{1}	14	52 ● **Can't Help Falling In Love/**	
12/04/61+	23	9	53 Rock-A-Hula Baby	RCA 47-7968
			above 2 from the film "Blue Hawaii"	
3/17/62	1^{2}	13	54 **Good Luck Charm/**	
3/17/62	31	8	55 Anything That's Part Of You	RCA 47-7992
5/12/62	15	10	56 Follow That Dream	RCA EPA-4368
			from the film and the E.P. of the same title	
8/04/62	5	10	57 **She's Not You/**	
8/11/62	55	5	58 Just Tell Her Jim Said Hello	RCA 47-8041
9/22/62	30	7	59 King Of The Whole Wide World	RCA EPA-4371
			from the film and the E.P. "Kid Galahad"	
10/20/62	2^{5}	16	60 ● **Return To Sender/**	
10/27/62	99	1	61 Where Do You Come From	RCA 47-8100
			above 2 from the film "Girls! Girls! Girls!"	
2/16/63	11	9	62 One Broken Heart For Sale/	
2/23/63	53	4	63 They Remind Me Too Much Of You	RCA 47-8134
			above 2 from the film "It Happened At The Worlds Fair"	
6/29/63	3	11	64 **(You're the) Devil In Disguise**	RCA 47-8188
10/19/63	8	10	65 **Bossa Nova Baby/**	
			from the film "Fun In Acapulco"	
10/19/63	32	7	66 Witchcraft	RCA 47-8243
			#5 hit in 1956 on the R&B charts for The Spiders	
2/22/64	12	9	67 Kissin' Cousins/	
			from the film of the same title	
2/29/64	29	7	68 It Hurts Me	RCA 47-8307
5/02/64	34	6	69 Kiss Me Quick	RCA 447-0639
			recorded June 25, 1961 (on the album "Pot Luck")	
5/09/64	29	7	70 Viva Las Vegas/	
5/23/64	21	6	71 What'd I Say	RCA 47-8360
			written and recorded in 1959 (POS 6) by Ray Charles above 2 from the film "Viva Las Vegas"	
7/04/64	92	1	72 Viva Las Vegas	RCA EPA-4382
			4-track E.P. from the film of the same title: C'mon Everybody/ Today, Tomorrow And Forever/If You Think I Don't Need You/ I Need Somebody To Lean On	
7/25/64	16	8	73 Such A Night	RCA 47-8400
			recorded April 4, 1960 (on the album "Elvis Is Back!") #2 hit in 1954 on the R&B charts for The Drifters	
10/10/64	12	12	74 Ask Me/	
10/10/64	16	10	75 Ain't That Loving You Baby	RCA 47-8440
			recorded June 10, 1958	
2/27/65	21	8	76 Do The Clam	RCA 47-8500
			from the film "Girl Happy"	
4/24/65	3	14	77 **Crying In The Chapel**	RCA 447-0643
			recorded on 10/31/60 - there were 5 Top 20 versions in 1953	
6/19/65	11	8	78 (Such An) Easy Question/	
			recorded on March 18, 1962 (on the album "Pot Luck")	
6/19/65	55	6	79 It Feels So Right	RCA 47-8585
			recorded on March 21, 1960 - above 2 from the film "Tickle Me"	
7/10/65	70	7	80 Tickle Me	RCA EPA-4383
			5-track E.P. from the film of the same title: I Feel That I've Known You Forever/Slowly But Surely/Night Rider/Put The Blame On Me/Dirty, Dirty Feeling	

DEBUT DATE	PEAK POS	WKS CHR		ARTIST — Record Title	Label & Number
				ELVIS PRESLEY — Cont'd	
8/28/65	**11**	11	81	I'm Yours recorded on June 26, 1961 (on the album "Pot Luck")	RCA 47-8657
11/13/65	**14**	10	82	Puppet On A String from the film "Girl Happy"	RCA 447-0650
1/01/66	**33**	7	83	Tell Me Why/ recorded on January 12, 1957 The Crew Cuts and Gale Storm had hit versions in 1956	
1/01/66	**95**	1	84	Blue River recorded on May 27, 1963	RCA 47-8740
3/19/66	**25**	8	85	Frankie And Johnny/ version of classic song written around 1850	
3/19/66	**45**	8	86	Please Don't Stop Loving Me above 2 from the film "Frankie And Johnny"	RCA 47-8780
7/02/66	**19**	7	87	Love Letters #11 hit in 1945 for Dick Haymes	RCA 47-8870
10/08/66	**40**	7	88	Spinout/	
10/08/66	**41**	8	89	All That I Am above 2 from the film "Spinout"	RCA 47-8941
1/28/67	**33**	8	90	Indescribably Blue	RCA 47-9056
5/20/67	**63**	5	91	Long Legged Girl (With The Short Dress On)/ from the film "Double Trouble"	
5/27/67	**92**	1	92	That's Someone You Never Forget recorded on June 25, 1961 (on the album "Pot Luck")	RCA 47-9115
8/26/67	**56**	6	93	There's Always Me/	
9/09/67	**78**	5	94	Judy above 2 recorded on 3/13/61 (on album "Something For Everybody")	RCA 47-9287
10/14/67	**38**	6	95	Big Boss Man/ #78 hit in 1961 for Jimmy Reed	
10/14/67	**44**	6	96	You Don't Know Me first popularized in 1956 by Jerry Vale (POS 14)	RCA 47-9341
1/27/68	**43**	6	97	Guitar Man see #148 below for re-charted version	RCA 47-9425
3/23/68	**28**	9	98	U.S. Male/ above 2 written and originally recorded by Jerry Reed	
3/16/68	**67**	5	99	Stay Away from the film "Stay Away, Joe" ("Greensleeves" melody)	RCA 47-9465
4/20/68	**90**	2	100	You'll Never Walk Alone from the Broadway musical "Carousel"	RCA 47-9600
6/15/68	**71**	5	101	Let Yourself Go	RCA 47-9547
6/22/68	**72**	7	102	Your Time Hasn't Come Yet, Baby above 2 from the film "Speedway"	RCA 47-9547
9/28/68	**95**	2	103	Almost In Love/	
10/12/68	**69**	4	104	A Little Less Conversation above 2 from the film "Live A Little, Love A Little"	RCA 47-9610
11/30/68+	**12**	13	105	If I Can Dream	RCA 47-9670
3/22/69	**35**	7	106	Memories from the NBC-TV special "Elvis"	RCA 47-9731
5/03/69	**3**	13	107●	**In The Ghetto**	RCA 47-9741
7/05/69	**35**	8	108	Clean Up Your Own Back Yard from the film "The Trouble With Girls (and how to get into it)"	RCA 47-9747
9/13/69	**1**[1]	15	109●	**Suspicious Minds**	RCA 47-9764
11/29/69+	**6**	13	110●	**Don't Cry Daddy/**	
		13	111	Rubberneckin' from the film "Change Of Habit"	RCA 47-9768
2/14/70	**16**	9	112	Kentucky Rain	RCA 47-9791
5/16/70	**9**	12	113●	**The Wonder Of You/** recorded live at Las Vegas - #25 hit in 1959 for Ray Peterson	
		12	114	Mama Liked The Roses	RCA 47-9835
8/01/70	**32**	9	115	I've Lost You/	
		9	116	The Next Step Is Love	RCA 47-9873
10/24/70	**11**	10	117	You Don't Have To Say You Love Me/ #4 hit in 1966 for Dusty Springfield	
		10	118	Patch It Up	RCA 47-9916
12/26/70+	**21**	9	119	I Really Don't Want To Know/ #11 hit in 1954 for Les Paul & Mary Ford	
		9	120	There Goes My Everything #20 hit in 1967 for Engelbert Humperdinck	RCA 47-9960

DEBUT DATE	PEAK POS	WKS CHR	ARTIST — Record Title	Label & Number
			ELVIS PRESLEY — Cont'd	
3/13/71	**33**	7	121 Where Did They Go, Lord/	
		7	122 Rags To Riches #1 hit for 8 weeks in 1953 for Tony Bennett	RCA 47-9980
5/15/71	**53**	7	123 Life/	
		7	124 Only Believe	RCA 47-9985
7/10/71	**36**	9	125 I'm Leavin'	RCA 47-9998
10/09/71	**51**	6	126 It's Only Love	RCA 48-1017
1/29/72	**40**	9	127 Until It's Time For You To Go #53 hit in 1970 for Neil Diamond	RCA 74-0619
5/06/72	**66**	6	128 An American Trilogy Dixie/Battle Hymn Of The Republic/All My Trials recorded live at Las Vegas	RCA 74-0672
8/19/72	**2[1]**	15	129● **Burning Love**	RCA 74-0769
12/02/72+	**20**	12	130 Separate Ways featured in the film "Elvis On Tour"	RCA 74-0815
4/14/73	**17**	12	131 Steamroller Blues/ recorded live in Hawaii (written by James Taylor in 1970)	
		12	132 Fool	RCA 74-0910
9/22/73	**41**	9	133 Raised On Rock/	
		9	134 For Ol' Times Sake	RCA APBO-0088
2/09/74	**39**	12	135 I've Got A Thing About You Baby/ #93 hit in 1972 for Billy Lee Riley	
		7	136 Take Good Care Of Her #7 hit in 1961 for Adam Wade	RCA APBO-0196
6/08/74	**17**	13	137 If You Talk In Your Sleep	RCA APBO-0280
10/26/74	**14**	13	138 Promised Land #41 hit in 1965 for Chuck Berry	RCA PB-10074
1/25/75	**20**	11	139 My Boy #41 hit in 1972 for Richard Harris	RCA PB-10191
5/10/75	**35**	9	140 T-R-O-U-B-L-E	RCA PB-10278
10/25/75	**65**	5	141 Bringing It Back	RCA PB-10401
3/27/76	**28**	11	142 Hurt/ #4 hit in 1961 for Timi Yuro	
		10	143 For The Heart	RCA PB-10601
12/25/76+	**31**	13	144 Moody Blue/	
		13	145 She Thinks I Still Care #1 Country hit in 1962 for George Jones	RCA PB-10857
6/25/77	**18**	21	146● Way Down	RCA PB-10998
11/12/77	**22**	12	147● My Way recorded live from Elvis' tour - written in 1969 by Paul Anka	RCA PB-11165
1/24/81	**28**	14	148 Guitar Man [R] re-mix by Felton Jarvis (d: 1/3/81) of Elvis' 1968 hit	RCA PB-12158
11/27/82	**71**	7	149 The Elvis Medley Jailhouse Rock/Teddy Bear/Hound Dog/Don't Be Cruel/ Burning Love/Suspicious Minds	RCA PB-13351
			BILLY PRESTON Born on 9/9/46 in Houston. R&B vocalist, keyboardist. To Los Angeles at an early age. With Mahalia Jackson in 1956. Played piano in film "St. Louis Blues", 1958. Regular on "Shindig" TV Show. Recorded with Beatles on "Get Back" and "Let It Be", worked Concert For Bangladesh, 1969. Prominent session man, played on Sly & The Family Stone hits. With Rolling Stones USA tour in 1975.	
8/02/69	**62**	6	1 That's The Way God Planned It	Apple 1808
2/13/71	**90**	3	2 My Sweet Lord above 2 produced by George Harrison	Apple 1826
1/22/72	**77**	5	3 I Wrote A Simple Song/	
4/22/72	**2[1]**	17	4● **Outa-Space** [I]	A&M 1320
7/08/72	**65**	10	5 That's The Way God Planned It [R]	Apple 1808
9/09/72	**50**	8	6 Slaughter from the film of the same title	A&M 1380
3/31/73	**1[2]**	22	7● **Will It Go Round In Circles**	A&M 1411
9/22/73	**4**	18	8● **Space Race** [I]	A&M 1463
1/05/74	**48**	8	9 You're So Unique	A&M 1492
7/13/74	**1[1]**	18	10● **Nothing From Nothing**	A&M 1544
12/14/74+	**22**	10	11 Struttin' [I]	A&M 1644
10/04/75	**71**	4	12 Fancy Lady all of above (except #2) written by Preston	A&M 1735

DEBUT DATE	PEAK POS	WKS CHR	ARTIST — Record Title	Label & Number
			BILLY PRESTON — Cont'd	
10/28/78	**86**	2	13 Get Back	A&M 2071
			from the film "Sgt. Pepper's Lonely Hearts Club Band"	
12/08/79+	**4**	29	14 **With You I'm Born Again**	Motown 1477
6/14/80	**52**	10	15 One More Time For Love	Tamla 54312
			above 2: BILLY PRESTON & SYREETA	
			Syreeta (Wright) was married to Stevie Wonder	
9/25/82	**88**	3	16 I'm Never Gonna Say Goodbye	Motown 1625
			JOHNNY PRESTON	
			Born John Preston Courville on 8/18/39 in Port Arthur, Texas. Discovered by J.P. "Big Bopper" Richardson.	
10/12/59+	**1**[3]	27	1 **Running Bear**	Mercury 71474
			Indian sounds by the Big Bopper & George Jones	
			written by the Big Bopper (J.P. Richardson)	
3/28/60	**7**	15	2 **Cradle Of Love**	Mercury 71598
6/20/60	**14**	14	3 Feel So Fine	Mercury 71651
1/30/61	**73**	5	4 Leave My Kitten Alone	Mercury 71761
12/25/61	**97**	1	5 Free Me	Mercury 71908
			MIKE PRESTON	
			British singer.	
12/01/58	**93**	1	1 A House, A Car And A Wedding Ring	London 1834
			THE PRETENDERS	
			Rock quartet featuring American Chrissie Hynde (b: 9/7/51, Akron, OH), lead singer, songwriter, guitarist. Original lineup constisted of: Englishmen James Honeyman-Scott, guitar (died on 6/16/82 - replaced by Robbie MacIntosh); Pete Farndon, bass (died on 4/14/83 - replaced in 1982 by Malcolm Foster); and Martin Chambers, drums. Numerous personnel changes since then. Chrissie married Jim Kerr of Simple Minds in 1984. Also see UB40.	
2/16/80	**14**	22	1 Brass In Pocket (I'm Special)	Sire 49181
6/21/80	**65**	5	2 Stop Your Sobbing	Sire 49506
12/11/82+	**5**	24	3 **Back On The Chain Gang**	Sire 29840
			from the film "The King Of Comedy"	
12/17/83+	**19**	14	4 Middle Of The Road	Sire 29444
3/17/84	**28**	13	5 Show Me	Sire 29317
6/30/84	**83**	5	6 Thin Line Between Love And Hate	Sire 29249
10/11/86	**10**	18	7 **Don't Get Me Wrong**	Sire 28630
			1, 3-5 & 7: written by Hynde	
			ANDRE PREVIN & DAVID ROSE	
			Previn was born on 4/6/29 in Berlin, Germany; came to U.S. in 1939. Pianist, composer, conductor, arranger. Scored many films; winner of 4 Academy Awards.	
6/01/59	**46**	12	1 Like Young [I]	MGM 12792
			ALAN PRICE SET	
			Alan was born on 4/19/42 in Fairfield, Durham, England. Organist with the original Animals, left in 1965; rejoined group in 1983.	
7/30/66	**80**	3	1 I Put A Spell On You	Parrot 3001
			LLOYD PRICE	
			Born on 3/9/33 in Kenner, LA. R&B vocalist, pianist, composer. First recording was the #1 R&B hit "Lawdy Miss Clawdy" on Specialty in 1952. In US Army, 1953-56. Formed own record company, KRC, in 1957. Signed to ABC Records in 1958. Formed Double-L label in 1963. In later years has continued in music, production, and booking agency work.	
3/02/57	**29**	20	1 Just Because	ABC-Para. 9792
9/30/57	**88**	1	2 Lonely Chair	KRC 301
12/08/58+	**1**[4]	21	3 **Stagger Lee**	ABC-Para. 9972
3/02/59	**23**	11	4 Where Were You (On Our Wedding Day)?	ABC-Para. 9997
4/27/59	**2**[3]	19	5 **Personality**	ABC-Para. 10018
8/10/59	**3**	14	6 **I'm Gonna Get Married**	ABC-Para. 10032
10/26/59	**20**	14	7 Come Into My Heart/	
11/09/59	**43**	10	8 Wont'cha Come Home	ABC-Para. 10062
2/01/60	**14**	13	9 Lady Luck/	
3/07/60	**82**	3	10 Never Let Me Go	ABC-Para. 10075
4/25/60	**40**	7	11 No If's - No And's/	
5/02/60	**43**	6	12 For Love	ABC-Para. 10102
6/27/60	**19**	11	13 Question	ABC-Para. 10123
9/12/60	**79**	4	14 Just Call Me (And I'll Understand)	ABC-Para. 10139
12/05/60	**90**	2	15 (You Better) Know What You're Doin'	ABC-Para. 10162

DEBUT DATE	PEAK POS	WKS CHR	ARTIST — Record Title	Label & Number
			LLOYD PRICE — Cont'd	
10/05/63	21	9	16 Misty	Double-L 722
1/11/64	84	3	17 Billie Baby	Double-L 729
			all of above (except #10 & 16) written by Price	
			RAY PRICE	
			Country singer born on 1/12/26 in Perryville, Texas. Ray charted over 40 Top Ten hits on Billboard's Country charts.	
12/29/56	67	1	1 Crazy Arms	Columbia 21510
			Honor Roll #67	
10/14/57	63	5	2 My Shoes Keep Walking Back To You	Columbia 40951
8/25/58	71	3	3 City Lights/	
9/08/58	92	1	4 Invitation To The Blues	Columbia 41191
8/31/63	100	1	5 Make The World Go Away	Columbia 42827
3/25/67	60	8	6 Danny Boy	Columbia 44042
8/29/70+	11	24	7 For The Good Times	Columbia 45178
			written by Kris Kristofferson	
3/20/71	42	14	8 I Won't Mention It Again	Columbia 45329
8/14/71	70	6	9 I'd Rather Be Sorry	Columbia 45425
1/06/73	93	4	10 She's Got To Be A Saint	Columbia 45724
8/25/73	82	9	11 You're The Best Thing That Ever Happened To Me	Columbia 45889
			CHARLEY PRIDE	
			Born on 3/18/38 in Sledge, Mississippi. First Black Country superstar. Charley's had 29 #1 hits on the Country charts.	
8/23/69	91	5	1 All I Have To Offer You (Is Me)	RCA 0167
11/08/69	74	6	2 (I'm So) Afraid Of Losing You Again	RCA 0265
3/14/70	70	7	3 Is Anybody Goin' To San Antone	RCA 9806
7/04/70	87	3	4 Wonder Could I Live There Anymore	RCA 9855
10/24/70	71	6	5 I Can't Believe That You've Stopped Loving Me	RCA 9902
3/13/71	79	3	6 I'd Rather Love You	RCA 9952
8/21/71	94	2	7 I'm Just Me	RCA 9996
11/20/71+	21	16	8 ●Kiss An Angel Good Mornin'	RCA 0550
4/01/72	92	3	9 All His Children	RCA 0624
			from the film "Sometimes A Great Notion" arranged and conducted by Henry Mancini	
11/16/74	70	4	10 Mississippi Cotton Picking Delta Town	RCA 10030
			LOUIS PRIMA	
			Born on 12/7/11 in New Orleans; died on 8/24/78 in New Orleans. Durable jazz trumpeter-singer-composer-bandleader.	
11/14/60+	15	14	1 Wonderland By Night [I]	Dot 16151
			LOUIS PRIMA & KEELY SMITH	
			Husband and wife (divorced in 1962). Keely was born on 3/9/32 in Norfolk, VA; jazz-styled vocalist, first appeared with Prima in 1953. Back-up band: Sam Butera & The Witnesses.	
11/03/58	18	13	1 That Old Black Magic	Capitol 4063
			from the film "Senior Prom"	
2/23/59	95	2	2 I've Got You Under My Skin	Capitol 4140
			#3 hit in 1936 for Ray Noble	
7/06/59	69	6	3 Bei Mir Bist Du Schon	Dot 15956
			#1 hit in 1938 for The Andrews Sisters	
			PRINCE	
			Born Prince Roger Nelson on 6/7/58 in Minneapolis. R&B vocalist, multi-instrumentalist, composer, producer, actor. Named for the Prince Roger Trio, led by his father. Self-taught musician - own band, Grand Central, in junior high school. Self-produced first album in 1978. Starred in films "Purple Rain", 1984, and "Under The Cherry Moon", 1986.	
			PRINCE:	
11/04/78	92	4	1 Soft And Wet	Warner 8619
11/24/79+	11	16	2 ●I Wanna Be Your Lover	Warner 49050
10/24/81	70	11	3 Controversy	Warner 49808
10/30/82+	12	27	4 1999	Warner 29896
			originally charted for 12 weeks (POS 44), then re-entered, 6/4/83	
2/26/83	6	22	5 **Little Red Corvette**	Warner 29746
9/03/83	8	18	6 **Delirious**	Warner 29503
12/17/83+	52	10	7 Let's Pretend We're Married/	
		10	8 Irresistible Bitch	Warner 29548

DEBUT DATE	PEAK POS	WKS CHR	ARTIST — Record Title	Label & Number
			PRINCE — Cont'd	
6/02/84	1^5	21	9▲**When Doves Cry**	Warner 29286
			PRINCE & THE REVOLUTION:	
8/04/84	1^2	19	10●**Let's Go Crazy**	Warner 29216
10/06/84	2^2	16	11●**Purple Rain**	Warner 29174
12/15/84+	**8**	15	12 **I Would Die 4 U**	Warner 29121
2/09/85	**25**	12	13 Take Me With U female vocals: Apollonia above 5 from the film "Purple Rain"	Warner 29079
5/18/85	2^1	17	14 **Raspberry Beret**	Paisley P. 28972
7/27/85	**7**	14	15 **Pop Life**	Paisley P. 28998
10/19/85	**46**	7	16 America	Paisley P. 28999
2/22/86	1^2	18	17●**Kiss**	Paisley P. 28751
5/24/86	**23**	11	18 Mountains	Paisley P. 28711
7/19/86	**63**	10	19 Anotherloverholenyohead above 3 from the film "Under The Cherry Moon" all of above written and produced by Prince	Paisley P. 28620
			PRINCE BUSTER Born Buster Campbell on 5/24/38 in Kingston, Jamaica. Owned ten record stores in the Caribbean.	
2/04/67	**81**	4	1 Ten Commandments [S]	Philips 40427
			VICTORIA PRINCIPAL - see ANDY GIBB	
			PRISM Canadian rock group - Ron Tabak, lead singer (replaced by Henry Small, 1981).	
10/22/77	**82**	4	1 Spaceship Superstar	Ariola Am. 7672
1/07/78	**59**	7	2 Take Me To The Kaptin	Ariola Am. 7678
7/22/78	**53**	8	3 Flyin'	Ariola Am. 7714
1/30/82	**39**	10	4 Don't Let Him Know	Capitol 5082
4/17/82	**64**	7	5 Turn On Your Radar	Capitol 5106
			P.J. PROBY Born James Marcus Smith on 11/6/38 in Houston.	
9/05/64	**70**	4	1 Hold Me	London 9688
2/13/65	**91**	2	2 Somewhere from the Broadway musical "West Side Story"	Liberty 55757
1/28/67	**23**	10	3 Niki Hoeky	Liberty 55936
			PROCOL HARUM British rock group led by Gary Brooker (vocals/piano) & Robin Trower (guitar).	
6/24/67	**5**	12	1 **A Whiter Shade Of Pale**	Deram 7507
10/28/67	**34**	5	2 Homburg	A&M 885
5/27/72	**16**	13	3 Conquistador	A&M 1347
			THE PRODUCERS Pop/rock quartet from Atlanta, Georgia.	
6/13/81	**61**	6	1 What She Does To Me (The Diana Song)	Portrait 02092
			PROFESSOR MORRISON'S LOLLIPOP Bubblegum group from Asbury Park, New Jersey.	
10/05/68	**88**	3	1 You Got The Love	White Whale 275
			BRIAN PROTHEROE British singer/composer/actor.	
3/29/75	**60**	7	1 Pinball	Chrysalis 2104
			JEANNE PRUETT Alabama-born country singer/songwriter.	
5/12/73	**28**	15	1 Satin Sheets	MCA 40015
			ARTHUR PRYSOCK Born on 1/2/29 in Spartanburg, SC. First recorded with Buddy Johnson Band on Decca in 1944. Solo since 1952. Very popular night club act, frequently appearing with his brother, saxophonist Wilbert "Red" Prysock.	
7/17/65	**56**	8	1 It's Too Late, Baby Too Late	Old Town 1183
1/06/68	**74**	6	2 A Working Man's Prayer	Verve 10574
12/25/76+	**64**	9	3 When Love Is New	Old Town 1000

DEBUT DATE	PEAK POS	WKS CHR	ARTIST — Record Title	Label & Number
			PSYCHEDELIC FURS	
			British techno rock group. Nucleus consists of brothers Richard (vocals) and Tim Butler (bass), and John Ashton (guitar).	
3/05/83	**44**	10	1 Love My Way............	Columbia 03340
			produced by Todd Rundgren	
5/12/84	**59**	9	2 The Ghost In You............	Columbia 04416
4/12/86	**41**	11	3 Pretty In Pink............	A&M 2826
			from the film of the same title	
			GARY PUCKETT	
			Born on 10/17/42 in Hibbing, Minnesota. Leader of The Union Gap.	
10/31/70	**61**	4	1 I Just Don't Know What To Do With Myself............	Columbia 45249
2/06/71	**71**	5	2 Keep The Customer Satisfied............	Columbia 45303
			GARY PUCKETT & THE UNION GAP	
			Formed in San Diego in 1967. Named after the town of Union Gap, WA. Consisted of Gary Puckett, vocals, guitar; Paul Whitebread, drums; Kerry Chater, bass; Dwight Bement, sax; and Gary Withem, keyboards.	
11/18/67+	**4**	17	1 ● **Woman, Woman**............	Columbia 44297
3/02/68	**2**[3]	15	2 ● **Young Girl**............	Columbia 44450
6/08/68	**2**[2]	13	3 ● **Lady Willpower**............	Columbia 44547
9/21/68	**7**	11	4 ● **Over You**............	Columbia 44644
3/15/69	**15**	9	5 Don't Give In To Him............	Columbia 44788
			all of above produced by Jerry Fuller	
8/23/69	**9**	11	6 **This Girl Is A Woman Now**............	Columbia 44967
3/07/70	**41**	7	7 Let's Give Adam And Eve Another Chance............	Columbia 45097
			LEROY PULLINS	
6/25/66	**57**	6	1 I'm A Nut............ [N]	Kapp 758
			PRETTY PURDIE	
			Born Bernard Purdie on 6/11/39 in Elkton, MD. Highly regarded session drummer.	
9/23/67	**87**	3	1 Funky Donkey............ [I]	Date 1568
			PURE PRAIRIE LEAGUE	
			Country-rock group formed in Cincinnati in 1971. Numerous personnel changes.	
3/01/75	**27**	13	1 Amie............	RCA 10184
6/28/75	**97**	1	2 Two Lane Highway............	RCA 10302
5/10/80	**10**	17	3 **Let Me Love You Tonight**............	Casablanca 2266
8/23/80	**34**	13	4 I'm Almost Ready............	Casablanca 2294
12/06/80	**77**	6	5 I Can't Stop The Feelin'............	Casablanca 2319
4/18/81	**28**	14	6 Still Right Here In My Heart............	Casablanca 2332
7/25/81	**68**	5	7 You're Mine Tonight............	Casablanca 2337
			JAMES & BOBBY PURIFY	
			R&B duo: cousins James Purify (b: 5/12/44, Pensacola, FL) and Robert Lee Dickey (b: 9/2/39, Tallahassee, FL). Dickey left, late 1960's. Purify worked as solo until 1974, when Ben Moore became "Bobby Purify".	
9/24/66	**6**	14	1 **I'm Your Puppet**............	Bell 648
1/28/67	**38**	6	2 Wish You Didn't Have To Go............	Bell 660
4/15/67	**25**	9	3 Shake A Tail Feather............	Bell 669
7/15/67	**41**	6	4 I Take What I Want............	Bell 680
9/09/67	**23**	9	5 Let Love Come Between Us............	Bell 685
1/13/68	**73**	6	6 Do Unto Me............	Bell 700
4/27/68	**51**	6	7 I Can Remember............	Bell 721
8/31/68	**94**	3	8 Help Yourself (To All Of My Lovin')............	Bell 735
			PURPLE REIGN	
11/22/75	**48**	8	1 This Old Man............	Private S. 45052
			BILL PURSELL	
			Pianist from Tulare, California. Appeared with the Nashville Symphony Orchestra. Taught musical composition at Vanderbilt University.	
2/02/63	**9**	14	1 **Our Winter Love**............ [I]	Columbia 42619
			THE PYRAMIDS	
			Surf band from Long Beach, California.	
2/01/64	**18**	10	1 Penetration............ [I]	Best 13002

DEBUT DATE	PEAK POS	WKS CHR	ARTIST — Record Title	Label & Number
			PYTHON LEE JACKSON	
			Australian rock quintet led by David Bentley.	
5/27/72	**56**	10	1 In A Broken Dream	GNP Crescendo
			vocals: Rod Stewart (hired as session singer, not a group member)	449
			Q	
			Q	
3/12/77	**23**	13	1 Dancin' Man	Epic 50335
			CHRISTINE QUAITE	
			British pop songstress.	
5/23/64	**85**	2	1 Tell Me Mamma	World Art. 1022
			QUAKER CITY BOYS	
			Philadelphia string band - Tommy Reilly, leader.	
12/22/58+	**39**	9	1 Teasin'	Swan 4023
			QUARTERFLASH	
			Rock group from Portland, led by the husband-and-wife team of Marv and Rindy Ross. Originally known as Seafood Mama.	
10/17/81+	**3**	24	1 **Harden My Heart**	Geffen 49824
2/13/82	**16**	13	2 Find Another Fool	Geffen 50006
5/29/82	**56**	8	3 Right Kind Of Love	Geffen 29994
8/14/82	**60**	8	4 Night Shift	Warner 29932
			from the film of the same title	
6/18/83	**14**	16	5 Take Me To Heart	Geffen 29603
10/01/83	**58**	6	6 Take Another Picture	Geffen 29523
			above 6 produced by John Boylan	
10/19/85	**83**	6	7 Talk To Me	Geffen 28908
			all of above written by Marv Ross	
			THE QUARTER NOTES	
			Instrumental rock quartet from Buffalo, New York.	
3/23/59	**82**	1	1 Record Hop Blues [I]	Wizz 715
			BILL QUATEMAN	
			Pop vocalist, guitarist, pianist, composer.	
4/07/73	**86**	5	1 Only Love	Columbia 45792
			SUZI QUATRO	
			Rock singer born on 6/3/50 in Detroit. Portrayed Leather Tuscadero on TV's "Happy Days" in 1977.	
9/14/74	**85**	3	1 All Shook Up	Bell 45477
2/07/76	**56**	4	2 Can The Can	Big Tree 16053
1/27/79	**4**	22	3 ● **Stumblin' In**	RSO 917
			SUZI QUATRO & CHRIS NORMAN (lead singer of Smokie)	
5/26/79	**45**	8	4 If You Can't Give Me Love	RSO 929
9/08/79	**44**	8	5 I've Never Been In Love	RSO 1001
11/24/79+	**41**	11	6 She's In Love With You	RSO 1014
1/24/81	**51**	9	7 Lipstick	Dreamland 107
			QUEEN	
			Rock group formed in England in 1972. Consisted of Freddie Mercury, vocals; Brian May, guitar; John Deacon, bass; and Roger Taylor, drums. May and Taylor had been in the group Smile. Mercury had recorded as Larry Lurex. Wrote soundtrack for the film "Flash Gordon", 1980.	
2/08/75	**12**	19	1 Killer Queen	Elektra 45226
1/03/76	**9**	24	2 ● **Bohemian Rhapsody**	Elektra 45297
5/22/76	**16**	16	3 You're My Best Friend	Elektra 45318
11/27/76+	**13**	15	4 Somebody To Love	Elektra 45362
3/19/77	**49**	6	5 Tie Your Mother Down	Elektra 45385
10/22/77+	**4**	27	6 ▲ **We Are The Champions/**	
		12	7 We Will Rock You	Elektra 45441
5/13/78	**74**	5	8 It's Late	Elektra 45478
11/11/78+	**24**	12	9 Bicycle Race/	
		12	10 Fat Bottomed Girls	Elektra 45541

DEBUT DATE	PEAK POS	WKS CHR	ARTIST — Record Title		Label & Number
			QUEEN — Cont'd		
2/17/79	**86**	4	11	Don't Stop Me Now	Elektra 46008
12/22/79+	**1[4]**	22	12●	**Crazy Little Thing Called Love**	Elektra 46579
6/28/80	**42**	9	13	Play The Game	Elektra 46652
8/16/80	**1[3]**	31	14▲	**Another One Bites The Dust**	Elektra 47031
11/29/80	**44**	11	15	Need Your Loving Tonight	Elektra 47086
1/17/81	**42**	10	16	Flash's Theme aka Flash [N] from the film "Flash Gordon"	Elektra 47092
11/07/81+	**29**	15	17	Under Pressure **QUEEN & DAVID BOWIE**	Elektra 47235
5/01/82	**11**	14	18	Body Language	Elektra 47452
7/31/82	**60**	6	19	Calling All Girls	Elektra 69981
2/18/84	**16**	13	20	Radio Ga-Ga	Capitol 5317
4/28/84	**45**	8	21	I Want To Break Free	Capitol 5350
7/28/84	**72**	4	22	It's A Hard Life	Capitol 5372
12/07/85+	**61**	10	23	One Vision from the film "Iron Eagle"	Capitol 5530
6/21/86	**42**	11	24	A Kind Of Magic all of above written by group members and produced by Queen	Capitol 5590
			? (QUESTION MARK) & THE MYSTERIANS Early punk rock quintet. Lead singer Rudy Martinez (?) was born in Mexico and raised in Saginaw, Michigan.		
9/03/66	**1[1]**	15	1●	**96 Tears**	Cameo 428
11/19/66	**22**	10	2	I Need Somebody	Cameo 441
3/25/67	**56**	6	3	Can't Get Enough Of You, Baby	Cameo 467
6/10/67	**98**	2	4	Girl (You Captivate Me)	Cameo 479
			QUICKSILVER MESSENGER SERVICE San Francisco acid-rock group featuring John Cipollina (guitar) and David Freiberg (bass - joined Jefferson Starship in 1973). Many personnel changes.		
8/09/69	**91**	3	1	Who Do You Love	Capitol 2557
10/03/70	**49**	9	2	Fresh Air	Capitol 2920
3/06/71	**100**	2	3	What About Me	Capitol 3046
			QUIET RIOT Heavy-metal rock quartet from Los Angeles: Kevin DuBrow, lead singer; Carlos Cavazo, guitar; Frankie Banoli, drums; Rudy Sarzo, bass (replaced by Chuck Wright, 1985). Dubrow left group, early 1987.		
9/17/83	**5**	21	1●	**Cum On Feel The Noize**	Pasha 04005
1/07/84	**31**	12	2	Bang Your Head (Metal Health)	Pasha 04267
7/07/84	**51**	12	3	Mama Weer All Crazee Now 1 & 3: revivals of hits by Slade	Pasha 04505
			THE QUIN-TONES Consisted of Roberta Haymon, lead; Ronnie Scott, Phyllis Carr, Caroline Holmes, Kenneth Sexton and Eunice Cristi.		
8/18/58	**18**	12	1	Down The Aisle Of Love Best Seller #18 / Hot 100 #20	Hunt 321
			R		
			EDDIE RABBITT Born Edward Thomas on 11/27/44 in Brooklyn. Country singer, songwriter, guitarist. Raised in East Orange, NJ. First recorded for 20th Century, 1964. Moved to Nashville in 1968. Became established after Elvis Presley recorded his song "Kentucky Rain".		
7/24/76	**76**	8	1	Rocky Mountain Music	Elektra 45315
6/25/77	**77**	9	2	I Can't Help Myself	Elektra 45390
6/24/78	**53**	7	3	You Don't Love Me Anymore	Elektra 45488
1/20/79	**30**	11	4	Every Which Way But Loose from the film of the same title	Elektra 45554
6/09/79	**13**	17	5	Suspicions	Elektra 46053
5/03/80	**82**	4	6	Gone Too Far	Elektra 46613
6/21/80	**5**	25	7●	**Drivin' My Life Away** from the film "Roadie"	Elektra 46656
11/08/80+	**1[2]**	28	8●	**I Love A Rainy Night**	Elektra 47066
7/25/81	**5**	22	9	**Step By Step**	Elektra 47174
11/14/81+	**15**	15	10	Someone Could Lose A Heart Tonight	Elektra 47239

DEBUT DATE	PEAK POS	WKS CHR	ARTIST — Record Title	Label & Number
			EDDIE RABBITT — Cont'd	
4/10/82	**35**	13	11 I Don't Know Where To Start	Elektra 47435
10/09/82+	**7**	29	12 **You And I**	Elektra 69936
			EDDIE RABBITT with CRYSTAL GAYLE	
4/23/83	**55**	8	13 You Can't Run From Love	Warner 29712
9/10/83	**81**	5	14 You Put The Beat In My Heart	Warner 29512
			all of above produced by David Malloy (except #4)	
			THE RADIANTS	
			R&B group formed at the Greater Harvest Baptist Church in Chicago in 1960.	
11/03/62	**100**	1	1 Father Knows Best	Chess 1832
12/26/64+	**51**	9	2 Voice Your Choice	Chess 1904
5/08/65	**91**	3	3 It Ain't No Big Thing	Chess 1925
5/25/68	**68**	9	4 Hold On	Chess 2037
			THE RAELETTS	
			Ray Charles' vocal backing group.	
4/15/67	**76**	6	1 One Hurt Deserves Another	Tangerine 972
5/16/70	**96**	2	2 I Want To (Do Everything For You)	Tangerine 1006
3/13/71	**58**	13	3 Bad Water	Tangerine 1014
			THE RAES	
			Canadian husband-and-wife disco duo: Robbie and Cherrill Rae.	
12/16/78+	**61**	9	1 A Little Lovin' (Keeps The Doctor Away)	A&M 2091
			GERRY RAFFERTY	
			Born on 4/16/47 in Paisley, Scotland. Singer, songwriter, guitarist. Co-leader of Stealers Wheel.	
4/22/78	**2**[6]	20	1 ● **Baker Street**	United Art. 1192
			sax solo by Raphael Ravenscroft	
8/12/78	**12**	15	2 Right Down The Line	United Art. 1233
12/02/78+	**28**	13	3 Home And Dry	United Art. 1266
6/02/79	**17**	10	4 Days Gone Down (Still Got The Light In Your Eyes)	United Art. 1298
8/11/79	**21**	13	5 Get It Right Next Time	United Art. 1316
7/19/80	**54**	8	6 The Royal Mile (Sweet Darlin')	United Art. 1366
			all of above written by Rafferty	
			THE RAG DOLLS	
9/12/64	**91**	3	1 Society Girl	Parkway 921
1/23/65	**55**	6	2 Dusty	Mala 493
			RAIDERS - see PAUL REVERE & THE RAIDERS	
			RAINBOW	
			Hard-rock band led by British guitarist Ritchie Blackmore and bassist Roger Glover, both members of Deep Purple. Group disbanded upon reformation of Deep Purple, 1984.	
11/17/79	**57**	8	1 Since You Been Gone	Polydor 2014
4/24/82	**40**	12	2 Stone Cold	Mercury 76146
11/05/83	**60**	10	3 Street Of Dreams	Mercury 815660
			THE RAINDROPS	
			Songwriting team of Ellie Greenwich (b: 10/23/40) and husband Jeff Barry (b: 4/3/38). Barry wrote "Tell Laura I Love Her", team wrote "Be My Baby", "Da Doo Ron Ron", "Chapel Of Love", "River Deep-Mountain High", "Hanky Panky", "Leader of The Pack", and many others.	
4/27/63	**41**	8	1 What A Guy	Jubilee 5444
8/10/63	**17**	11	2 The Kind Of Boy You Can't Forget	Jubilee 5455
11/30/63+	**64**	8	3 That Boy John	Jubilee 5466
3/14/64	**62**	7	4 Book Of Love	Jubilee 5469
9/12/64	**97**	1	5 One More Tear	Jubilee 5487
			RITA RAINES	
2/18/56	**89**	1	1 Such A Day	Deed 1010
			MARVIN RAINWATER	
			Born on 7/2/25 in Wichita, Kansas. American Indian rockabilly singer.	
5/20/57	**18**	22	1 Gonna Find Me A Bluebird	MGM 12412
			Juke Box #18 end / Best Seller #19 / Top 100 #22	
12/02/57	**93**	1	2 The Majesty Of Love	MGM 12555
			MARVIN RAINWATER & CONNIE FRANCIS	
3/31/58	**60**	2	3 Whole Lotta Woman	MGM 12609
7/27/59	**66**	7	4 Half-Breed	MGM 12803

DEBUT DATE	PEAK POS	WKS CHR	ARTIST — Record Title		Label & Number
			THE RAINY DAZE		
			Denver quintet - Tim Gilbert, lead singer.		
3/11/67	**70**	4	1 That Acapulco Gold		Uni 55002
			BONNIE RAITT		
			Born on 11/8/49 in Burbank, CA. Blues-rock singer, guitarist. Daughter of Broadway's John Raitt.		
5/21/77	**57**	12	1 Runaway		Warner 8382
12/08/79+	**73**	6	2 You're Gonna Get What's Coming written by Robert Palmer		Warner 49116
			DON RALKE		
			Born in Battle Creek, MI. Hollywood conductor, arranger, composer for 25 years.		
4/06/59	**69**	5	1 77 Sunset Strip from the TV series of the same title	[I]	Warner 5025
			RAM JAM		
			East Coast rock quartet led by Bill Bartlett (lead guitarist of The Lemon Pipers). Member Howie Blauvelt played bass in Billy Joel's group The Hassles.		
6/11/77	**18**	17	1 Black Betty		Epic 50357
			EDDIE RAMBEAU		
			Born Edward Flurie on 6/30/43 in Hazleton, PA. Pop singer, songwriter.		
5/01/65	**35**	9	1 Concrete And Clay		DynoVoice 204
			THE RAMBLERS		
12/05/60	**73**	4	1 Rambling	[I]	Addit 1257
			THE RAMBLERS		
8/08/64	**86**	4	1 Father Sebastian		Almont 311
			RAMONES		
			Punk rock quartet from New York City. Jeffrey Hyman (aka Joey Ramone), lead singer.		
7/02/77	**81**	13	1 Sheena Is A Punk Rocker		Sire 746
12/03/77+	**66**	14	2 Rockaway Beach		Sire 1008
4/15/78	**86**	5	3 Do You Wanna Dance		Sire 1017
			RAMRODS		
			Instrumental rock quartet from Connecticut. Vincent Bell, leader.		
1/09/61	**30**	9	1 (Ghost) Riders In The Sky	[I]	Amy 813
			THE RAN-DELLS		
			Cousins Steve Rappaport and John Spirt from Villas, New Jersey.		
8/03/63	**16**	13	1 Martian Hop	[N]	Chairman 4403
			TEDDY RANDAZZO		
			Born on 5/20/37 in New York City. Member of The Three Chuckles.		
7/21/58	**66**	2	1 Little Serenade		Vik 0330
4/18/60	**44**	9	2 The Way Of A Clown		ABC-Para. 10088
1/26/63	**51**	8	3 Big Wide World		Colpix 662
			BOOTS RANDOLPH		
			Born in Paducah, Kentucky. Premier Nashville session saxophonist.		
2/23/63	**35**	9	1 Yakety Sax	[I]	Monument 804
4/04/64	**77**	6	2 Hey, Mr. Sax Man		Monument 835
12/24/66+	**93**	3	3 The Shadow Of Your Smile		Monument 976
7/08/67	**93**	1	4 Temptation	[I]	Monument 1009
			RANDY & THE RAINBOWS		
			Pop group from Queens, New York. Dominick "Randy" Safuto, lead singer.		
6/15/63	**10**	17	1 **Denise**		Rust 5059
12/14/63	**97**	2	2 Why Do Kids Grow Up		Rust 5073
			BILLY RANKIN		
			Born on 4/25/59 in Glasgow, Scotland. Lead guitarist with Nazareth, 1981-82.		
3/10/84	**52**	11	1 Baby Come Back		A&M 2613
			RARE EARTH		
			Rock group from Detroit. Nucleus consisted of Gil Bridges, saxophone, flute; John Persh, trombone, bass; and Pete Rivera, drums. Worked as Sunliners, 1960's. Added Ed Guzman, percussion, 1970, and Ray Monette (replaced Rob Richards), guitar; Mark Olson replaced Kenneth James, keyboards, 1971. Many changes ensued.		
3/14/70	**4**	20	1 **Get Ready**		Rare Earth 5012
8/01/70	**7**	14	2 **(I Know) I'm Losing You**		Rare Earth 5017

DEBUT DATE	PEAK POS	WKS CHR	ARTIST — Record Title	Label & Number
			RARE EARTH — Cont'd	
12/12/70+	**17**	11	3 Born To Wander	Rare Earth 5021
7/17/71	**7**	13	4 **I Just Want To Celebrate**	Rare Earth 5031
11/27/71+	**19**	10	5 Hey Big Brother	Rare Earth 5038
4/08/72	**61**	5	6 What'd I Say	Rare Earth 5043
11/04/72	**67**	8	7 Good Time Sally	Rare Earth 5048
1/27/73	**93**	3	8 We're Gonna Have A Good Time	Rare Earth 5052
4/29/78	**39**	11	9 Warm Ride written by the Bee Gees	Prodigal 0640
			THE RASCALS Blue-eyed soul/pop quartet formed in New York City in 1964. Consisted of Felix Cavaliere, Dino Danelli, Eddie Brigati and Gene Cornish. All except Danelli had been in Joey Dee's Starliters. Brigati and Cornish left in 1971, replaced by Robert Popwell, Buzzy Feiten and Ann Sutton. Group disbanded in 1972. Also see Bulldog and Fotomaker. THE YOUNG RASCALS:	
12/25/65+	**52**	9	1 I Ain't Gonna Eat Out My Heart Anymore	Atlantic 2312
3/12/66	**1**[1]	14	2 **Good Lovin'**	Atlantic 2321
6/18/66	**20**	7	3 You Better Run	Atlantic 2338
9/24/66	**43**	7	4 Come On Up	Atlantic 2353
1/28/67	**16**	14	5 I've Been Lonely Too Long	Atlantic 2377
4/22/67	**1**[4]	13	6● **Groovin'**	Atlantic 2401
7/15/67	**10**	9	7 **A Girl Like You**	Atlantic 2424
9/09/67	**4**	11	8 **How Can I Be Sure**	Atlantic 2438
12/09/67+	**20**	7	9 It's Wonderful THE RASCALS:	Atlantic 2463
4/13/68	**3**	13	10● **A Beautiful Morning**	Atlantic 2493
7/20/68	**1**[5]	14	11● **People Got To Be Free**	Atlantic 2537
12/07/68+	**24**	8	12 A Ray Of Hope 3, 5-12: written by Cavaliere & Brigati	Atlantic 2584
2/08/69	**39**	6	13 Heaven	Atlantic 2599
5/24/69	**27**	8	14 See	Atlantic 2634
9/06/69	**26**	8	15 Carry Me Back	Atlantic 2664
1/03/70	**51**	7	16 Hold On	Atlantic 2695
7/25/70	**58**	6	17 Glory Glory vocal backing: The Sweet Inspirations	Atlantic 2743
6/26/71	**95**	4	18 Love Me 4, 13-18: written by Cavaliere	Columbia 45400
			RASPBERRIES Cleveland pop/rock quartet: Eric Carmen, lead singer, guitar; Wally Bryson, lead guitar; David Smalley, bass; Jim Bonfanti, drums. Smalley and Bonfanti replaced by Scott McCarl and Michael McBride, 1974. Carmen went solo, 1975. Also see The Choir.	
5/13/72	**86**	2	1 Don't Want To Say Goodbye	Capitol 3280
7/01/72	**5**	18	2● **Go All The Way**	Capitol 3348
11/25/72+	**16**	11	3 I Wanna Be With You	Capitol 3473
3/24/73	**35**	16	4 Let's Pretend	Capitol 3546
9/01/73	**69**	7	5 Tonight	Capitol 3610
12/08/73	**94**	3	6 I'm A Rocker	Capitol 3765
9/14/74	**18**	12	7 Overnight Sensation (Hit Record) all of above written by Carmen and produced by Jimmy Ienner	Capitol 3946
			THE RATIONALS	
11/12/66	**92**	3	1 Respect	Cameo 437
			RATT Hard-rock quintet from Los Angeles - Stephen Pearcy, lead singer.	
6/16/84	**12**	18	1 Round And Round	Atlantic 89693
10/06/84	**87**	3	2 Wanted Man	Atlantic 89618
7/06/85	**40**	11	3 Lay It Down	Atlantic 89546
10/12/85	**89**	2	4 You're In Love	Atlantic 89502
			THE RATTLES Rock quartet from Germany. Achim Reishel, vocal and lead guitar.	
6/27/70	**79**	5	1 The Witch	Probe 480

DEBUT DATE	PEAK POS	WKS CHR	ARTIST — Record Title	Label & Number
			GENYA RAVAN	
			Born Goldie Zelkowitz in Poland in 1940; raised in New York City. Lead singer of Ten Wheel Drive.	
8/12/78	**92**	3	1 Back In My Arms Again	20th Century 2374
			LOU RAWLS	
			Born on 12/1/35 in Chicago. With the Pilgrim Travelers gospel group, 1957-59. Summer replacement TV show "Lou Rawls & The Golddiggers" in 1969. In films "Angel Angel, Down We Go" and "Believe In Me". Voice of many Budweiser beer ads. Also see Sam Cooke.	
6/05/65	**83**	1	1 Three O'Clock In The Morning	Capitol 5424
9/10/66	**13**	14	2 Love Is A Hurtin' Thing	Capitol 5709
11/26/66+	**55**	8	3 You Can Bring Me All Your Heartaches	Capitol 5790
1/28/67	**92**	3	4 Trouble Down Here Below	Capitol 5824
3/25/67	**29**	11	5 Dead End Street	Capitol 5869
7/01/67	**45**	7	6 Show Business	Capitol 5941
8/31/68	**69**	5	7 Down Here On The Ground from the film "Cool Hand Luke"	Capitol 2252
7/19/69	**18**	14	8 Your Good Thing (Is About To End)	Capitol 2550
11/01/69	**63**	7	9 I Can't Make It Alone	Capitol 2668
3/14/70	**95**	3	10 You've Made Me So Very Happy	Capitol 2734
8/01/70	**96**	5	11 Bring It On Home all of above produced by David Axelrod	Capitol 2856
8/28/71	**17**	18	12 A Natural Man	MGM 14262
6/05/76	**2**[2]	21	13 ● **You'll Never Find Another Love Like Mine**	Phil. Int. 3592
10/16/76	**64**	5	14 Groovy People	Phil. Int. 3604
7/23/77	**66**	7	15 See You When I Git There	Phil. Int. 3623
1/21/78	**24**	17	16 Lady Love	Phil. Int. 3634
4/26/80	**77**	3	17 You're My Blessing	Phil. Int. 3750
3/26/83	**65**	6	18 Wind Beneath My Wings	Epic 03758
			RAY & BOB	
			Ray Swayne & Bob Appleberry.	
6/23/62	**99**	1	1 Air Travel	Ledo 1151
			RAY, GOODMAN & BROWN	
			Soul group consisting of Harry Ray, tenor; Al Goodman, bass; and Billy Brown, falsetto. Formerly known as The Moments.	
1/26/80	**5**	18	1 ● **Special Lady**	Polydor 2033
5/10/80	**76**	4	2 Inside Of You	Polydor 2077
8/23/80	**47**	10	3 My Prayer	Polydor 2116
			DIANE RAY	
			Born on 9/1/42 in Gastonia, North Carolina.	
8/03/63	**31**	9	1 Please Don't Talk To The Lifeguard	Mercury 72117
			DON RAY	
			German disco producer/arranger/composer.	
9/23/78	**44**	16	1 Got To Have Loving	Polydor 14489
			JAMES RAY	
			R&B singer from Washington, DC.	
11/20/61+	**22**	14	1 If You Gotta Make A Fool Of Somebody	Caprice 110
4/07/62	**41**	10	2 Itty Bitty Pieces above 2 with the Hutch Davie Orchestra	Caprice 114
			JOHNNIE RAY	
			Born on 1/10/27 in Dallas, Oregon. Has worn hearing aid since age 14. First recorded for Okeh in 1951. Famous for emotion-packed delivery, with R&B influences. Appeared in three films. Active into the 1980s. Now lives in Hollywood.	
11/12/55	**100**	1	1 Johnnie's Comin' Home	Columbia 40578
9/01/56	**2**[1]	28	2 **Just Walking In The Rain** Top 100 #2 / Juke Box #2 / Best Seller #3 / Jockey #3	Columbia 40729
1/12/57	**10**	12	3 **You Don't Owe Me A Thing/** Best Seller #10 / Top 100 #10 / Jockey #10 / Juke Box #12	
1/26/57	**36**	9	4 Look Homeward, Angel	Columbia 40803
4/20/57	**12**	13	5 Yes Tonight, Josephine Jockey #12 / Top 100 #18	Columbia 40893
7/22/57	**58**	9	6 Build Your Love (On A Strong Foundation) 2-6: with Ray Conniff & His Orchestra	Columbia 40942
8/25/58	**81**	3	7 Up Until Now	Columbia 41213

DEBUT DATE	PEAK POS	WKS CHR	ARTIST — Record Title	Label & Number
			JOHNNIE RAY — Cont'd	
9/14/59	**75**	6	8 I'll Never Fall In Love Again	Columbia 41438
			RICARDO RAY	
10/05/68	**90**	3	1 Nitty Gritty	Alegre 4024
			MARGIE RAYBURN	
			Born in Madera, CA. Member of The Sunnysiders, also sang with Ray Anthony's Orch.	
10/28/57	**9**	19	1 **I'm Available**	Liberty 55102
			Jockey #9 / Best Seller #15 / Top 100 #16	
			RAYDIO - see RAY PARKER JR.	
			SUSAN RAYE	
			Born on 10/8/44 in Eugene, Oregon. Country singer - regular on TV's "Hee Haw".	
4/17/71	**54**	9	1 L.A. International Airport	Capitol 3035
			THE RAYS	
			R&B group formed in New York City in 1955: Harold Miller, lead; Walter Ford and David Jones, tenors; Harry James, baritone. First recorded for Chess in 1955.	
10/14/57	**3**	20	1 **Silhouettes/**	
			Top 100 #3 / Best Seller #4 / Jockey #5	
		4	2 Daddy Cool	Cameo 117
			Best Seller flip	
1/25/60	**95**	2	3 Mediterranean Moon	XYZ 605
8/14/61	**49**	8	4 Magic Moon (Clair De Lune)	XYZ 607
			all of above written by Frank Slay, Jr. and Bob Crewe	
			THE RAZOR'S EDGE	
7/30/66	**77**	7	1 Let's Call It A Day Girl	Pow! 101
			RAZZY - see RAZZY BAILEY	
			RCR	
			Rock trio: Donna and Sandra Rhodes and Charles Chalmers.	
4/05/80	**94**	2	1 Scandal	Radio 711
			CHRIS REA	
			Born in Middlesbrough, England in 1951. Pop singer, songwriter.	
7/08/78	**12**	15	1 Fool (If You Think It's Over)	United Art. 1198
11/11/78	**71**	4	2 Whatever Happened To Benny Santini?	United Art. 1252
4/07/79	**44**	8	3 Diamonds	United Art. 1285
4/10/82	**88**	3	4 Loving You	Columbia 02727
			JOHN DAWSON READ	
8/30/75	**72**	4	1 A Friend Of Mine Is Going Blind	Chrysalis 2105
			READY FOR THE WORLD	
			Black sextet - Melvin Riley, Jr., lead singer.	
8/03/85	**1**[1]	21	1 **Oh Sheila**	MCA 52636
12/07/85+	**21**	18	2 Digital Display	MCA 52734
11/29/86+	**9**	19	3 **Love You Down**	MCA 52947
			REAL LIFE	
			Australian quartet - David Sterry, lead singer.	
11/12/83+	**29**	19	1 Send Me An Angel	Curb 52287
3/24/84	**40**	11	2 Catch Me I'm Falling	Curb 52362
			THE REAL THING	
			British group consisting of Chris Amoo, Ray Lake, Dave Smith and Eddie Amoo.	
7/17/76	**64**	8	1 You To Me Are Everything	United Art. 833
			THE REBELS	
			Buffalo disc jockey Tom Shannon and producer Phil Todaro (Shan-Todd label) recorded the Hot-Toddys featuring Bill Pennell on sax, from Port Colborne, Canada, in 1959. Then in 1961 they brought in the Buffalo group, The Rebels, to record Shannon's theme song "Wild Weekend". After the song's success in 1963, they re-released the original Hot-Toddys single as by the Rockin' Rebels.	
3/30/59	**57**	11	1 Rockin' Crickets [I]	Shan-Todd 0056
			HOT-TODDYS	
12/29/62+	**8**	17	2 **Wild Weekend** [I]	Swan 4125
4/27/63	**87**	4	3 Rockin' Crickets [I-R]	Swan 4140
			ROCKIN' REBELS	

DEBUT DATE	PEAK POS	WKS CHR	ARTIST — Record Title	Label & Number
			THE RECORDS	
			British rock quartet: John Wicks, Huw Gower, Phil Brown and Will Birch.	
9/29/79	**56**	6	1 Starry Eyes	Virgin 67000
			REDBONE	
			American Indian "swamp rock" group formed in Los Angeles in 1968. Consisted of Lolly Vegas, lead vocals, guitar; Pat Vegas, bass; Anthony Bellamy, guitar; and Peter De Poe, drums. The Vegas brothers had been session musicians and worked the "Shindig" TV show. Wrote P.J. Proby's hit "Niki Hoeky".	
12/05/70+	**45**	17	1 Maggie	Epic 10670
11/20/71+	**21**	17	2 The Witch Queen Of New Orleans	Epic 10749
1/12/74	**5**	23	3● **Come And Get Your Love**	Epic 11035
			LEON REDBONE	
			Mysterious performer of 1920s and 1930s blues and ragtime.	
4/11/81	**72**	6	1 Seduced	Emerald City 7326
			GENE REDDING	
			Born in Anderson, IN, 1945. Discovered by Etta James at USO Club, Anchorage, Alaska.	
5/04/74	**24**	16	1 This Heart	Haven 7000
			OTIS REDDING	
			Born on 9/9/41 in Dawson, GA. Killed in a plane crash in Lake Monona in Madison, WI on 12/10/67. Soul singer, songwriter, producer, pianist. First recorded with Johnny Jenkins & The Pinetoppers on Confederate in 1960. Own label, Jotis. Plane crash also killed four members of the Bar-Kays.	
5/25/63	**85**	3	1 These Arms Of Mine	Volt 103
11/23/63+	**61**	11	2 Pain In My Heart	Volt 112
3/21/64	**69**	7	3 Come To Me	Volt 116
5/23/64	**97**	1	4 Security	Volt 117
10/24/64	**70**	7	5 Chained And Bound	Volt 121
2/20/65	**41**	9	6 Mr. Pitiful/	
1/30/65	**74**	4	7 That's How Strong My Love Is	Volt 124
5/15/65	**21**	11	8 I've Been Loving You Too Long (To Stop Now)	Volt 126
9/04/65	**35**	11	9 Respect	Volt 128
12/04/65	**85**	5	10 Just One More Day	Volt 130
3/05/66	**31**	8	11 Satisfaction	Volt 132
6/04/66	**61**	7	12 My Lover's Prayer	Volt 136
10/01/66	**29**	8	13 Fa-Fa-Fa-Fa-Fa (Sad Song)	Volt 138
12/03/66+	**25**	10	14 Try A Little Tenderness	Volt 141
4/08/67	**78**	3	15 I Love You More Than Words Can Say	Volt 146
5/06/67	**26**	9	16 Tramp **OTIS & CARLA (Thomas)**	Stax 216
5/20/67	**47**	6	17 Shake	Volt 149
7/29/67	**60**	4	18 Glory Of Lcve	Volt 152
8/12/67	**30**	9	19 Knock On Wood **OTIS & CARLA (Thomas)**	Stax 228
1/27/68	**1^{4}**	16	20● **(Sittin' On) The Dock Of The Bay** recorded 3 days before his death	Volt 157
2/10/68	**60**	6	21 Lovey Dovey **OTIS & CARLA (Thomas)**	Stax 244
4/27/68	**25**	8	22 The Happy Song (Dum-Dum)	Volt 163
7/06/68	**36**	5	23 Amen/	
7/13/68	**51**	7	24 Hard To Handle	Atco 6592
9/28/68	**41**	7	25 I've Got Dreams To Remember	Atco 6612
11/30/68+	**21**	9	26 Papa's Got A Brand New Bag	Atco 6636
3/01/69	**48**	6	27 A Lover's Question	Atco 6654
5/24/69	**72**	5	28 Love Man	Atco 6677
			THE REDDINGS	
			Consisted of Otis Redding's sons Dexter (vocals, bass) and Otis III (guitar), and cousin Mark Locket (vocals, drums, keyboards).	
11/15/80	**89**	13	1 Remote Control	Believe 5600
6/12/82	**55**	9	2 (Sittin' On) The Dock Of The Bay	Believe 02836

DEBUT DATE	PEAK POS	WKS CHR	ARTIST — Record Title	Label & Number
			HELEN REDDY	
			Born on 10/25/42 in Melbourne, Australia. Family was in show business, Helen made stage debut at age four. Own TV series, early 1960's. Migrated to New York in 1966. Married Jeff Wald, agent with William Morris talent agency. To Los Angeles in 1968.	
2/20/71	**13**	20	1 I Don't Know How To Love Him................................. from the rock opera "Jesus Christ Superstar"	Capitol 3027
8/07/71	**51**	9	2 Crazy Love...	Capitol 3138
12/04/71+	**62**	8	3 No Sad Song..	Capitol 3231
6/24/72	**1**[1]	22	4● **I Am Woman**... from the film "Stand Up And Be Counted"	Capitol 3350
2/03/73	**12**	17	5 Peaceful..	Capitol 3527
6/23/73	**1**[1]	20	6● **Delta Dawn**...	Capitol 3645
11/03/73	**3**	16	7● **Leave Me Alone (Ruby Red Dress)**......................	Capitol 3768
3/09/74	**15**	13	8 Keep On Singing..	Capitol 3845
6/15/74	**9**	20	9 **You And Me Against The World**.........................	Capitol 3897
10/19/74	**1**[1]	17	10● **Angie Baby**..	Capitol 3972
2/08/75	**22**	9	11 Emotion...	Capitol 4021
7/05/75	**35**	6	12 Bluebird...	Capitol 4108
8/09/75	**8**	16	13 **Ain't No Way To Treat A Lady**........................	Capitol 4128
12/06/75+	**19**	14	14 Somewhere In The Night.....................................	Capitol 4192
8/07/76	**29**	9	15 I Can't Hear You No More/	
		6	16 Music Is My Life..	Capitol 4312
4/30/77	**18**	22	17 You're My World..	Capitol 4418
10/08/77	**57**	7	18 The Happy Girls..	Capitol 4487
7/15/78	**73**	5	19 Ready Or Not..	Capitol 4582
5/19/79	**60**	10	20 Make Love To Me..	Capitol 4712
5/23/81	**88**	3	21 I Can't Say Goodbye To You................................	MCA 51106
			REDEYE	
			Rock quartet led by Dave Hodgkins and Douglas "Red" Mark.	
11/07/70+	**27**	14	1 Games...	Pentagram 204
4/24/71	**78**	6	2 Red Eye Blues...	Pentagram 206
			THE REDJACKS	
9/15/58	**84**	2	1 Big Brown Eyes... "Ling-Ting-Tong" melody	Apt 25006
			EIVETS REDNOW - see STEVIE WONDER	
			RED RIDER	
			Canadian rock quintet. Tom Cochrane, leader (cousin of Eddie Cochran).	
4/05/80	**48**	7	1 White Hot..	Capitol 4845
6/16/84	**71**	6	2 Young Thing, Wild Dreams (Rock Me).......................	Capitol 5335
			RED RIVER DAVE	
			Dave McEnery.	
6/27/60	**64**	6	1 There's A Star Spangled Banner Waving #2 (The Ballad Of Francis Powers).............................. original version a #7 hit in 1943 for Elton Britt Francis Powers: U.S. "U-2" pilot shot down in Russia on 5/1/60	Savoy 3020
			RED ROCKERS	
			New Orleans foursome - John Griffith, lead singer.	
6/04/83	**53**	10	1 China...	Columbia 03786
			MICHAEL REDWAY	
2/10/73	**85**	4	1 Good Morning...	Philips 40720
			DEAN REED	
3/02/59	**96**	1	1 The Search..	Capitol 4121
			DENNY REED	
8/29/60	**94**	3	1 A Teenager Feels It Too....................................	3 Trey 116
			JERRY REED	
			Born Jerry Reed Hubbard on 3/20/37 in Atlanta. Country singer, guitarist, composer, actor. Co-starred in the films "Gator" and "Smokey & The Bandit".	
6/30/62	**79**	5	1 Goodnight, Irene... #1 hit for 13 weeks in 1950 for The Weavers	Columbia 42417
10/13/62	**99**	1	2 Hully Gully Guitar..................................... [I] above 2 with The Hully Girlies	Columbia 42533

DEBUT DATE	PEAK POS	WKS CHR	ARTIST — Record Title	Label & Number
			JERRY REED — Cont'd	
10/31/70+	**8**	24	3 ● **Amos Moses** .... [N]	RCA 9904
5/08/71	**9**	12	4 **When You're Hot, You're Hot** .... [N]	RCA 9976
9/04/71	**51**	6	5 Ko-Ko Joe	RCA 1011
1/08/72	**65**	5	6 Another Puff .... [N]	RCA 0613
7/15/72	**62**	8	7 Alabama Wild Man	RCA 0738
7/07/73	**68**	7	8 Lord, Mr. Ford .... [N]	RCA 0960
2/16/74	**91**	5	9 The Crude Oil Blues .... [N] 2-7 & 9: written by Reed	RCA 0224
7/24/82	**57**	9	10 She Got The Goldmine (I Got The Shaft) .... [N]	RCA 13268
			JIMMY REED Born Mathis James Reed on 9/6/25 in Dunleith, MS; died from an epileptic seizure on 8/29/76. R&B vocalist, guitarist, harmonica player, composer. Taught guitar by Eddie Taylor at age 7. First recorded for Chance in 1953. Afflicted with epilepsy since 1957. Distinctive and influential blues singer, active until death.	
7/08/57	**65**	5	1 The Sun Is Shining	Vee-Jay 248
9/30/57	**32**	15	2 Honest I Do .... Top 100 #32 / Best Seller #36	Vee-Jay 253
8/11/58	**93**	2	3 Down In Virginia	Vee-Jay 287
2/15/60	**37**	14	4 Baby What You Want Me To Do	Vee-Jay 333
5/23/60	**88**	3	5 Found Love	Vee-Jay 347
10/10/60	**75**	2	6 Hush-Hush	Vee-Jay 357
1/30/61	**68**	4	7 Close Together	Vee-Jay 373
5/29/61	**78**	3	8 Big Boss Man	Vee-Jay 380
9/18/61	**58**	9	9 Bright Lights Big City	Vee-Jay 398
1/27/62	**93**	5	10 Aw Shucks, Hush Your Mouth	Vee-Jay 425
6/23/62	**77**	4	11 Good Lover	Vee-Jay 449
4/13/63	**52**	8	12 Shame, Shame, Shame .... all of above (except #8 & 11) written by Reed	Vee-Jay 509
			LOU REED Born Louis Firbank on 3/2/44 in the New York City area. Lead singer, composer of New York seminal rock band, the Velvet Underground.	
2/17/73	**16**	14	1 Walk On The Wild Side .... produced by David Bowie & Mick Ronson	RCA 0887
			DELLA REESE Born Delloreese Patricia Early on 7/6/31 in Detroit. With Mahalia Jackson troupe, 1945-49, Erskine Hawkins, early 1950s. Solo since 1957. Great actress/singer on many TV shows. Own series "Della", 1970. Della Rogers of TV series "Chico & The Man", 1976-78. Film "Let's Rock", 1958.	
8/26/57	**12**	18	1 And That Reminds Me .... Jockey #12 / Best Seller #23 / Top 100 #29	Jubilee 5292
1/05/59	**99**	1	2 Sermonette	Jubilee 5345
9/21/59	**2**[1]	18	3 **Don't You Know**	RCA 7591
12/14/59+	**16**	11	4 Not One Minute More	RCA 7644
3/21/60	**56**	7	5 Someday (You'll Want Me To Want You)	RCA 7706
9/05/60	**69**	5	6 And Now	RCA 7784
2/06/61	**67**	5	7 The Most Beautiful Words	RCA 7833
4/24/61	**98**	1	8 Won'cha Come Home, Bill Bailey	RCA 7867
7/31/65	**95**	2	9 After Loving You	ABC-Para. 10691
9/10/66	**99**	2	10 It Was A Very Good Year	ABC 10841
			DEL REEVES Born on 7/14/33 in Sparta, NC. Country singer, guitarist, songwriter, TV show host.	
6/26/65	**96**	1	1 Girl On The Billboard	United Art. 824
			JIM REEVES Born on 8/20/24 in Panola County, Texas. Killed in a plane crash on 7/31/64 in Nashville. Aspirations of professional baseball career cut short by ankle injury. Deejay at KWKH, Shreveport, LA, home of the "Louisiana Hayride", early 1950s. First recorded for Macy's in 1950. Joined "Hayride" cast following first country hit "Mexican Joe" in 1953. Joined Grand Ol' Opry in 1955. Own ABC-TV series in 1957. Film "Kimberley Jim", 1963. Despite death, he continued to have many Top 10 Country hits through 1980.	
4/29/57	**11**	22	1 Four Walls .... Jockey #11 / Top 100 #12 / Juke Box #13 / Best Seller #14	RCA 6874
2/03/58	**93**	1	2 Anna Marie	RCA 7070
8/04/58	**45**	6	3 Blue Boy	RCA 7266
12/08/58	**95**	1	4 Billy Bayou	RCA 7380

DEBUT DATE	PEAK POS	WKS CHR	ARTIST — Record Title	Label & Number
			JIM REEVES — Cont'd	
12/28/59+	**2^{3}**	23	5 **He'll Have To Go**	RCA 7643
6/20/60	**37**	10	6 I'm Gettin' Better/	
7/25/60	**82**	2	7 I Know One	RCA 7756
10/24/60	**31**	11	8 Am I Losing You/	
11/14/60	**44**	6	9 I Missed Me	RCA 7800
3/20/61	**62**	4	10 The Blizzard	RCA 7855
7/10/61	**73**	5	11 What Would You Do?	RCA 7905
11/06/61	**89**	3	12 Losing Your Love/	
12/04/61	**92**	2	13 (How Can I Write On Paper) What I Feel In My Heart	RCA 7950
5/05/62	**90**	6	14 Adios Amigo	RCA 8019
10/13/62	**95**	2	15 I'm Gonna Change Everything	RCA 8080
6/29/63	**91**	2	16 Guilty	RCA 8193
8/22/64	**82**	5	17 I Guess I'm Crazy	RCA 8383
11/21/64	**93**	3	18 I Won't Forget You	RCA 8461
3/13/65	**88**	1	19 This Is It	RCA 8508
8/14/65	**79**	6	20 Is It Really Over?	RCA 8625
1/15/66	**66**	6	21 Snow Flake	RCA 8719
4/09/66	**45**	7	22 Distant Drums	RCA 8789
8/27/66	**59**	8	23 Blue Side Of Lonesome	RCA 8902
			all of above produced by Chet Atkins	
			MARTHA REEVES	
			Born on 7/18/41 in Detroit. Leader of Martha & The Vandellas.	
3/30/74	**76**	5	1 Power Of Love	MCA 40194
			THE REFLECTIONS	
			Detroit rock quartet: Tony Micale, lead; Dan Bennie, Phil Castrodale and John Dean.	
4/11/64	**6**	12	1 **(Just Like) Romeo & Juliet**	Golden World 9
7/11/64	**96**	1	2 Like Columbus Did	Golden World 12
3/13/65	**55**	5	3 Poor Man's Son	Golden World 20
			THE REFLECTIONS	
			R&B/disco quartet: Herman Edwards, Josh Pridgen, Edmund "Butch" Simmons and John Simmons. Toured as back-up group with Melba Moore in 1972.	
7/12/75	**94**	4	1 Three Steps From True Love	Capitol 4078
			RE-FLEX	
			British techno-rock quartet founded by computer keyboardist Paul Fishman.	
11/26/83+	**24**	21	1 The Politics Of Dancing	Capitol 5301
5/05/84	**82**	4	2 Hurt	Capitol 5348
			JOAN REGAN	
			British singer.	
11/12/55	**55**	8	1 Croce Di Oro	London 1605
			THE REGENTS	
			Bronx vocal group formed as the Desires in 1958. Consisted of Guy Villari, lead; Sal Cuomo, Charles Fassert, Don Jacobucci and Tony "Hot Rod" Gravagna. "Barbara-Ann", written for Fassert's sister, was first recorded as a demo in 1958. When record was released, group had been disbanded.	
5/15/61	**13**	10	1 Barbara-Ann	Gee 1065
7/10/61	**28**	7	2 Runaround	Gee 1071
			REGINA	
			New York State native, Regina Richards.	
6/21/86	**10**	20	1 **Baby Love**	Atlantic 89417
			CLARENCE REID	
			Born on 2/14/45 in Cochran, GA. Soul singer, composer, arranger, producer. With Miami vocal group, the Delmiros, early 1960s. Also recorded as "Blowfly".	
8/02/69	**40**	10	1 Nobody But You Babe	Alston 4574
8/10/74	**99**	1	2 Funky Party	Alston 4621
			MIKE REILLY	
3/13/71	**88**	6	1 1927 Kansas City	Paramount 0053

DEBUT DATE	PEAK POS	WKS CHR	ARTIST — Record Title	Label & Number
			JOE REISMAN	
			Born on 9/16/24 in Dallas. Conductor, composer and arranger for TV, Broadway and films. Musical conductor at RCA during 1950s.	
12/08/56	**46**	10	1 Armen's Theme [I]	RCA 6740
			guitar solo: Tony Mottola	
3/23/57	**55**	5	2 Pamela Throws A Party	RCA 6826
7/03/61	**74**	6	3 The Guns Of Navarone [I]	Landa 674
			from the film of the same title	
			REJOICE!	
10/26/68	**96**	1	1 Golden Gate Park	Dunhill 4158
			R.E.M.	
			Athens, Georgia rock quartet: Michael Stipe, Pete Buck, Mike Mills and Bill Berry.	
7/23/83	**78**	5	1 Radio Free Europe	I.R.S. 9916
6/23/84	**85**	6	2 so. Central Rain (I'm Sorry)	I.R.S. 9927
10/04/86	**94**	3	3 Fall On Me	I.R.S. 52883
			DIANE RENAY	
			Philadelphian Renee Diane Kushner.	
1/25/64	**6**	12	1 **Navy Blue**	20th Century 456
4/04/64	**29**	8	2 Kiss Me Sailor	20th Century 477
			RENE & ANGELA	
			Los Angeles-based R&B duo: Rene Moore and Angela Winbush.	
9/28/85	**47**	10	1 I'll Be Good	Mercury 884009
3/22/86	**62**	6	2 Your Smile	Mercury 884271
6/21/86	**75**	7	3 You Don't Have To Cry	Mercury 884587
			RENE & RAY	
			Paul Venezuela (Rene) and Ray Quinones - both sang with the Velveteens.	
6/09/62	**79**	3	1 Queen Of My Heart	Donna 1360
			RENE & RENE	
			Rene Ornelas & Rene Herrera.	
7/11/64	**43**	8	1 Angelito	Columbia 43045
11/23/68+	**14**	12	2 Lo Mucho Que Te Quiero (The More I Love You)	White Whale 287
			GOOGIE RENE Combo	
			Born Raphael Rene. Bandleader, keyboardist. Son of songwriter, producer Leon Rene. First recorded for Class in 1957.	
2/26/66	**77**	3	1 Smokey Joe's La La [I]	Class 1517
			HENRI RENE	
			German-raised bandleader. Arranger-conductor for Perry Como, Dinah Shore, Eartha Kitt, Mindy Carson, and many other singers.	
12/08/56	**44**	8	1 Love Me Tender [I]	RCA 6728
			from the Elvis Presley film of the same title	
			MIKE RENO & ANN WILSON	
			Lead singers of Loverboy and Heart, respectively.	
5/12/84	**7**	20	1 **Almost Paradise...Love Theme From Footloose**	Columbia 04418
			from the film "Footloose"	
			REO SPEEDWAGON	
			Rock quintet from Champaign, IL: Kevin Cronin (lead vocals, rhythm guitar), Gary Richrath (lead guitar), Neal Doughty (keyboards), Bruce Hall (bass) and Alan Gratzer (drums). Name taken from a 1911 fire truck.	
5/28/77	**94**	3	1 Ridin' The Storm Out	Epic 50367
5/13/78	**58**	11	2 Roll With The Changes	Epic 50545
7/22/78	**56**	7	3 Time For Me To Fly	Epic 50582
5/31/80	**77**	6	4 Time For Me To Fly [R]	Epic 50858
11/29/80+	**1**[1]	28	5 ● **Keep On Loving You**	Epic 50953
3/21/81	**5**	20	6 **Take It On The Run**	Epic 01054
6/13/81	**24**	14	7 Don't Let Him Go	Epic 02127
8/08/81	**20**	13	8 In Your Letter	Epic 02457
6/12/82	**7**	16	9 **Keep The Fire Burnin'**	Epic 02967
8/28/82	**26**	14	10 Sweet Time	Epic 03175
10/27/84	**29**	13	11 I Do'wanna Know	Epic 04659
1/19/85	**1**[3]	18	12 **Can't Fight This Feeling**	Epic 04713
3/30/85	**19**	16	13 One Lonely Night	Epic 04848
7/13/85	**34**	11	14 Live Every Moment	Epic 05412

DEBUT DATE	PEAK POS	WKS CHR	ARTIST — Record Title	Label & Number
			REPARATA & THE DELRONS	
			Brooklyn trio: Reparata Aiese, Sheila Reilly and Carol Drobnicki. Also see Lady Flash.	
1/09/65	**60**	9	1 Whenever A Teenager Cries	World Art. 1036
5/08/65	**92**	3	2 Tommy	World Art. 1051
7/05/75	**92**	3	3 Shoes	Polydor 14271
			REPARATA	
			JOHNNY RESTIVO	
			15-year-old (in 1959) Bronx-born singer and weight lifter.	
9/07/59	**80**	3	1 The Shape I'm In	RCA 7559
			REUNION	
			RCA studio group. Joey Levine (Ohio Express), lead singer.	
9/07/74	**8**	15	1 **Life Is A Rock (But The Radio Rolled Me)** [N]	RCA 10056
			REVELATION	
			Soul/disco quartet: Phillip Ballou, Benny Driggs, Arthur Freeman & Arnold McCuller.	
7/31/76	**98**	2	1 You To Me Are Everything, Part I	RSO 854
			THE REVELS	
			Philadelphia group formed in high school and led by John Kelly.	
10/19/59	**35**	10	1 Midnight Stroll	Norgolde 103
			PAUL REVERE & THE RAIDERS	
			Pop/rock group formed in Portland in 1960. Band formed around Paul Revere (keyboards) and Mark Lindsay (lead singer). To Los Angeles in 1965. On daily ABC-TV show "Where The Action Is" in 1965. Group had many personnel changes throughout their career.	
3/27/61	**38**	6	1 Like, Long Hair [I]	Gardena 116
9/18/65	**46**	9	2 Steppin' Out	Columbia 43375
12/04/65+	**11**	15	3 Just Like Me	Columbia 43461
3/19/66	**4**	14	4 **Kicks**	Columbia 43556
6/18/66	**6**	11	5 **Hungry**	Columbia 43678
10/01/66	**20**	8	6 The Great Airplane Strike	Columbia 43810
12/03/66+	**4**	12	7 **Good Thing**	Columbia 43907
2/18/67	**22**	8	8 Ups And Downs	Columbia 44018
4/29/67	**5**	9	9 **Him Or Me - What's It Gonna Be?**	Columbia 44094
8/19/67	**17**	9	10 I Had A Dream	Columbia 44227
11/18/67	**42**	6	11 Peace Of Mind	Columbia 44335
			2-11: produced by Terry Melcher	
2/10/68	**19**	8	12 Too Much Talk	Columbia 44444
6/22/68	**27**	9	13 Don't Take It So Hard	Columbia 44553
10/12/68	**58**	6	14 Cinderella Sunshine	Columbia 44655
2/15/69	**18**	12	15 Mr. Sun, Mr. Moon	Columbia 44744
5/17/69	**20**	12	16 Let Me	Columbia 44854
9/06/69	**50**	7	17 We Gotta All Get Together	Columbia 44970
			RAIDERS:	
2/21/70	**82**	3	18 Just Seventeen	Columbia 45082
4/10/71	**1**[1]	22	19● **Indian Reservation (The Lament Of The Cherokee Reservation Indian)**	Columbia 45332
9/11/71	**23**	10	20 Birds Of A Feather	Columbia 45453
1/29/72	**51**	6	21 Country Wine	Columbia 45535
5/20/72	**54**	8	22 Powder Blue Mercedes Queen	Columbia 45601
10/21/72	**96**	3	23 Song Seller	Columbia 45688
2/03/73	**97**	5	24 Love Music	Columbia 45759
			12-24: produced by Mark Lindsay	
			BURT REYNOLDS	
			Born on 2/11/36 in Waycross, GA. Box-office superstar since the mid-70s.	
10/18/80	**88**	5	1 Let's Do Something Cheap And Superficial	MCA 51004
			from the film "Smokey & The Bandit 2"	
			DEBBIE REYNOLDS	
			Born Mary Reynolds on 4/1/32 in El Paso, TX. Leading lady of 50s musicals, and later in comedies. Married Eddie Fisher on 9/26/55; divorced by 1959. Mother of actress Carrie Fisher.	
7/22/57	**1**[5]	31	1 **Tammy**	Coral 61851
			Top 100 #1(5) / Jockey #1(5) / Best Seller #1(3)	
			from the film "Tammy & The Bachelor"	

DEBUT DATE	PEAK POS	WKS CHR	ARTIST — Record Title	Label & Number
			DEBBIE REYNOLDS — Cont'd	
1/20/58	**20**	3	2 A Very Special Love Jockey #20 / Top 100 #83	Coral 61897
1/18/60	**25**	17	3 Am I That Easy To Forget	Dot 15985
5/02/60	**55**	4	4 City Lights	Dot 16071
			JODY REYNOLDS Rockabilly singer, guitarist from Yuma, Arizona.	
5/19/58	**5**	17	1 **Endless Sleep** Best Seller #5 / Top 100 #5 / Jockey #7	Demon 1507
8/18/58	**66**	5	2 Fire Of Love	Demon 1509
			LAWRENCE REYNOLDS	
9/20/69	**28**	10	1 Jesus Is A Soul Man	Warner 7322
			RHINOCEROS Los Angeles-based rock group - John Finley, lead singer.	
2/22/69	**46**	10	1 Apricot Brandy [I]	Elektra 45647
			EMITT RHODES Lead singer of Merry-Go-Round.	
1/09/71	**54**	9	1 Fresh As A Daisy	Dunhill 4267
			RHYTHM HERITAGE Los Angeles studio group assembled by producers Steve Barri and Michael Omartian.	
11/15/75+	**1**[1]	24	1 ● **Theme From S.W.A.T.** [I] from the ABC-TV series "S.W.A.T."	ABC 12135
4/10/76	**20**	13	2 Barretta's Theme ("Keep Your Eye On The Sparrow") from the Robert Blake TV series "Baretta"	ABC 12177
2/26/77	**94**	3	3 Theme From Rocky (Gonna Fly Now) [I] from the Sylvester Stallone film "Rocky"	ABC 12243
			THE RIBBONS	
2/02/63	**81**	4	1 Ain't Gonna Kiss Ya	Marsh 202
			CHARLIE RICH Born on 12/14/32 in Colt, Arkansas. Rockabilly/country singer, pianist, songwriter. First played jazz and blues. Own jazz group, the Velvetones, mid-1950s, while in US Air Force. Session work with Sun Records in 1958.	
3/14/60	**22**	21	1 Lonely Weekends	Phillips 3552
8/28/65	**21**	11	2 Mohair Sam	Smash 1993
3/28/70	**85**	4	3 July 12, 1939	Epic 10585
4/28/73	**15**	19	4 ● Behind Closed Doors	Epic 10950
9/29/73	**1**[2]	22	5 ● **The Most Beautiful Girl**	Epic 11040
1/26/74	**18**	15	6 There Won't Be Anymore	RCA 0195
2/23/74	**11**	14	7 A Very Special Love Song	Epic 11091
5/04/74	**47**	6	8 I Don't See Me In Your Eyes Anymore	RCA 0260
8/03/74	**24**	13	9 I Love My Friend	Epic 20006
9/28/74	**47**	7	10 She Called Me Baby	RCA 10062
2/01/75	**49**	6	11 My Elusive Dreams	Epic 50064
5/31/75	**19**	12	12 Every Time You Touch Me (I Get High)	Epic 50103
1/24/76	**71**	6	13 Since I Fell For You all Epic hits produced by Billy Sherrill	Epic 50182
			RICHARD & THE YOUNG LIONS Rock group led by Richard Bloodworth.	
9/24/66	**99**	1	1 Open Up Your Door	Philips 40381
			CLIFF RICHARD Born Harry Roger Webb on 10/14/40 in Lucknow, India, of British parentage. Vocalist, actor, guitarist. To England in 1948. Worked in skiffle groups, mid-1950s. Backing band: The Drifters (later: The Shadows). The Shadows disbanded in 1969. Superstar in England, with over 80 charted hits, including ten #1 singles. British films "Expresso Bongo", "The Young Ones", "Summer Holiday" and "Wonderful Life".	
9/28/59	**30**	13	1 Living Doll **CLIFF RICHARD & The Drifters** from the film "Serious Charge"	ABC-Para. 10042
8/03/63	**62**	8	2 Lucky Lips	Epic 9597
12/07/63+	**25**	13	3 It's All In The Game	Epic 9633
4/18/64	**92**	2	4 I'm The Lonely One	Epic 9670
8/01/64	**99**	1	5 Bachelor Boy **CLIFF RICHARD & The Shadows**	Epic 9691

DEBUT DATE	PEAK POS	WKS CHR	ARTIST — Record Title	Label & Number
			CLIFF RICHARD — Cont'd	
6/08/68	**99**	3	6 Congratulations	Uni 55069
7/04/76	**6**	22	7● **Devil Woman**	Rocket 40574
12/18/76	**80**	4	8 I Can't Ask For Anymore Than You	Rocket 40652
6/04/77	**57**	7	9 Don't Turn The Light Out	Rocket 40724
10/20/79+	**7**	20	10 **We Don't Talk Anymore**	EMI America 8025
2/23/80	**34**	11	11 Carrie	EMI America 8035
9/13/80	**10**	22	12 **Dreaming**	EMI America 8057
10/25/80+	**20**	19	13 Suddenly OLIVIA NEWTON-JOHN & CLIFF RICHARD	MCA 51007
12/13/80+	**17**	22	14 A Little In Love	EMI America 8068
4/25/81	**41**	11	15 Give A Little Bit More	EMI America 8076
10/10/81	**71**	4	16 Wired For Sound	EMI America 8095
1/16/82	**23**	13	17 Daddy's Home	EMI America 8103
10/09/82	**64**	7	18 The Only Way Out	EMI America 8135
10/08/83	**73**	7	19 Never Say Die (Give A Little Bit More)	EMI America 8180
			TURLEY RICHARDS Pop singer, guitarist from Charleston, West Virginia.	
4/04/70	**84**	3	1 Love Minus Zero-No Limit written by Bob Dylan	Warner 7376
6/20/70	**99**	3	2 I Heard The Voice Of Jesus	Warner 7397
1/26/80	**54**	7	3 You Might Need Somebody	Atlantic 3645
			LIONEL RICHIE Born on 6/20/49 in Tuskegee, Alabama. Grew up on the campus of Tuskegee Institute where his grandfather worked. Former lead singer of the Commodores. Appeared in the film "Thank God It's Friday".	
7/11/81	**1**[9]	27	1▲ **Endless Love** DIANA ROSS & LIONEL RICHIE from the film of the same title - written by Richie	Motown 1519
10/09/82	**1**[2]	18	2● **Truly**	Motown 1644
1/15/83	**4**	18	3 **You Are**	Motown 1657
4/09/83	**5**	16	4 **My Love**	Motown 1677
9/17/83	**1**[4]	24	5● **All Night Long (All Night)**	Motown 1698
11/26/83+	**7**	19	6 **Running With The Night**	Motown 1710
2/25/84	**1**[2]	24	7● **Hello**	Motown 1722
6/23/84	**3**	19	8 **Stuck On You**	Motown 1746
10/06/84	**8**	18	9 **Penny Lover**	Motown 1762
11/09/85	**1**[4]	20	10● **Say You, Say Me** featured in the film (not album) "White Nights"	Motown 1819
7/19/86	**2**[2]	17	11 **Dancing On The Ceiling**	Motown 1843
10/04/86	**9**	18	12 **Love Will Conquer All**	Motown 1866
12/06/86+	**7**	18	13 **Ballerina Girl**	Motown 1873
			RICK & THE KEENS	
7/03/61	**60**	8	1 Peanuts	Smash 1705
			JIMMY RICKS - see LaVERN BAKER	
			NELSON RIDDLE Born on 6/1/21 in Oradell, NJ; died on 10/6/85. Trombonist-arranger with Charlie Spivak and Tommy Dorsey in the 40s. One of the most in-demand of all arranger-conductors for many top artists, including Frank Sinatra (several classic 50s albums), Nat King Cole, Ella Mae Morse, and, more recently, Linda Ronstadt; also arranger and musical director for many films.	
12/10/55+	**1**[4]	29	1 **Lisbon Antigua** [I] Best Seller #1(4) / Jockey #1(2) / Top 100 #2 / Juke Box #2	Capitol 3287
3/17/56	**20**	14	2 Port Au Prince [I] Jockey #20 / Top 100 #32	Capitol 3374
7/14/56	**39**	10	3 Theme From 'The Proud Ones' [I] from the film of the same title	Capitol 3472
6/02/62	**30**	12	4 Route 66 Theme [I] from the hit TV series	Capitol 4741

DEBUT DATE	PEAK POS	WKS CHR	ARTIST — Record Title		Label & Number
			THE RIGHTEOUS BROTHERS		
			Blue-eyed soul duo: Bill Medley (b: 9/19/40, Santa Ana, CA), baritone; and Bobby Hatfield (b: 8/10/40, Beaver Dam, WI), tenor. Both sang in local Los Angeles groups, formed duo in 1962. First recorded as the Paramours for Smash in 1962. On "Hullabaloo" and "Shindig" TV shows. Split up, 1968-74, Medley went solo, replaced by Billy Walker, then rejoined Hatfield in 1974.		
5/11/63	**49**	7	1 Little Latin Lupe Lu		Moonglow 215
9/07/63	**75**	7	2 My Babe		Moonglow 223
12/12/64+	**1[2]**	16	3 **You've Lost That Lovin' Feelin'**		Philles 124
1/30/65	**83**	3	4 Bring Your Love To Me		Moonglow 238
4/10/65	**9**	11	5 **Just Once In My Life**		Philles 127
5/08/65	**67**	5	6 You Can Have Her		Moonglow 239
7/03/65	**85**	3	7 Justine from the film "A Swingin' Summer"		Moonglow 242
7/17/65	**4**	13	8 **Unchained Melody/**		
7/17/65	**47**	7	9 Hung On You		Philles 129
12/04/65+	**5**	9	10 **Ebb Tide** all Philles hits produced by Phil Spector		Philles 130
2/05/66	**62**	5	11 Georgia On My Mind		Moonglow 244
3/05/66	**1[3]**	13	12 ● **(You're My) Soul And Inspiration**		Verve 10383
6/04/66	**18**	8	13 He/		
6/04/66	**91**	1	14 He Will Break Your Heart		Verve 10406
8/06/66	**30**	6	15 Go Ahead And Cry		Verve 10430
10/29/66	**47**	6	16 On This Side Of Goodbye		Verve 10449
4/22/67	**43**	6	17 Melancholy Music Man		Verve 10507
9/30/67	**72**	4	18 Stranded In The Middle Of Noplace		Verve 10551
5/25/74	**3**	17	19 **Rock And Roll Heaven**		Haven 7002
9/07/74	**20**	9	20 Give It To The People		Haven 7004
11/09/74	**32**	8	21 Dream On		Haven 7006
			BILLY LEE RILEY		
			Born on 10/5/33 in Pocahontas, Arkansas. Memphis session musician, and one of the lesser-known Sun rockabilly artists.		
11/04/72	**93**	2	1 I Got A Thing About You Baby		Entrance 7508
			JEANNIE C. RILEY		
			Born Jeannie Carolyn Stephenson on 10/19/45 in Anson, Texas. Country singer.		
8/24/68	**1[1]**	13	1 ● **Harper Valley P.T.A.** written by Tom T. Hall		Plantation 3
12/07/68	**55**	6	2 The Girl Most Likely		Plantation 7
3/29/69	**77**	4	3 There Never Was A Time		Plantation 16
4/03/71	**74**	6	4 Oh, Singer		Plantation 72
7/31/71	**97**	4	5 Good Enough To Be Your Wife all of above produced by Shelby Singleton, Jr.		Plantation 75
			THE RINGS		
			Rock quartet from Boston.		
3/07/81	**75**	5	1 Let Me Go		MCA 51069
			RINKY-DINKS - see BOBBY DARIN		
			AUGIE RIOS		
12/15/58	**47**	4	1 Donde Esta Santa Claus?	[X-N]	Metro 20010
			MIGUEL RIOS		
			Born in Granada, Spain in 1944.		
6/13/70	**14**	9	1 A Song Of Joy based on the last movement of Beethoven's 9th Symphony - Waldo de los Rios, conductor		A&M 1193
			WALDO DE LOS RIOS		
			Spanish conductor/composer - died on 3/28/77.		
6/19/71	**67**	8	1 Mozart Symphony No. 40 In G Minor K.550, 1st Movement	[I]	United Art. 50772
			THE RIP CHORDS		
			California group featuring the duo of Terry Melcher (Doris Day's son) and Bruce Johnston (Beach Boys). Touring group featured a different foursome. Also see Bruce & Terry.		
3/30/63	**51**	8	1 Here I Stand		Columbia 42687
8/17/63	**88**	4	2 Gone		Columbia 42812

DEBUT DATE	PEAK POS	WKS CHR	ARTIST — Record Title	Label & Number
			THE RIP CHORDS — Cont'd	
12/14/63+	**4**	14	3 **Hey Little Cobra**	Columbia 42921
4/25/64	**28**	9	4 Three Window Coupe	Columbia 43035
8/08/64	**96**	1	5 One Piece Topless Bathing Suit	Columbia 43093
			all of above produced by Terry Melcher	
			MINNIE RIPERTON	
			Born on 11/8/47 in Chicago; died of cancer on 7/12/79 in Los Angeles. Recorded as "Andrea Davis" on Chess in 1966. In Rotary Connection, 1967-70. In Stevie Wonder's back-up group, Wonderlove, in 1973.	
1/18/75	**1**[1]	18	1 ● **Lovin' You**	Epic 50057
8/09/75	**76**	4	2 Inside My Love	Epic 50128
			RIPPLE	
			Chicago-based integrated progressive soul horn septet, originally from Kalamazoo.	
11/03/73	**67**	6	1 I Don't Know What It Is, But It Sure Is Funky	GRC 1004
			THE RITCHIE FAMILY	
			Philadelphia disco group named for arranger/producer Ritchie Rome. Group featured various session singers and musicians.	
8/02/75	**11**	18	1 Brazil [I]	20th Century 2218
12/06/75	**84**	4	2 I Want To Dance With You (Dance With Me)	20th Century 2252
8/28/76	**17**	20	3 The Best Disco In Town	Marlin 3306
			LEE RITENOUR	
			Born on 1/11/52 in Los Angeles. Guitarist, composer, arranger. Top session guitarist, has appeared on more than 200 albums. Nicknamed "Captain Fingers".	
4/25/81	**15**	16	1 Is It You	Elektra 47124
12/04/82	**69**	7	2 Cross My Heart	Elektra 69892
			vocals on above songs: Eric Tagg	
			TEX RITTER	
			Born Woodward Ritter on 1/12/05 in Murvaul, TX; died of a heart attack on 1/3/74. Country singer, actor. Starred in over 80 Hollywood Westerns, 1935-45. Father of TV actor John Ritter.	
6/30/56	**28**	13	1 The Wayward Wind	Capitol 3430
7/03/61	**20**	12	2 I Dreamed Of A Hill-Billy Heaven [S]	Capitol 4567
2/09/74	**90**	3	3 The Americans (A Canadian's Opinion) [S]	Capitol 3814
			JOHNNY RIVERS	
			Born John Ramistella on 11/7/42 in New York City; raised in Baton Rouge. Rock and roll singer, guitarist, composer, producer. Recorded with the Spades for Suede in 1956. Named Johnny Rivers by deejay Alan Freed in 1958. To Los Angeles in 1961. Own Soul City label, 1966.	
5/30/64	**2**[2]	12	1 **Memphis**	Imperial 66032
8/15/64	**12**	9	2 Maybelline	Imperial 66056
10/31/64	**9**	11	3 **Mountain Of Love**	Imperial 66075
2/06/65	**20**	8	4 Midnight Special/	
2/20/65	**76**	4	5 Cupid	Imperial 66087
6/05/65	**7**	11	6 **Seventh Son**	Imperial 66112
10/02/65	**26**	9	7 Where Have All The Flowers Gone	Imperial 66133
12/18/65+	**35**	8	8 Under Your Spell Again	Imperial 66144
3/19/66	**3**	11	9 **Secret Agent Man**	Imperial 66159
			from the TV series of the same title	
6/11/66	**19**	8	10 (I Washed My Hands In) Muddy Water	Imperial 66175
9/17/66	**1**[1]	15	11 **Poor Side Of Town**	Imperial 66205
2/04/67	**3**	11	12 **Baby I Need Your Lovin'**	Imperial 66227
6/03/67	**10**	9	13 **The Tracks Of My Tears**	Imperial 66244
11/18/67+	**14**	10	14 Summer Rain	Imperial 66267
4/06/68	**49**	7	15 Look To Your Soul	Imperial 66286
11/23/68	**61**	3	16 Right Relations	Imperial 66335
2/22/69	**55**	6	17 These Are Not My People	Imperial 66360
6/28/69	**41**	11	18 Muddy River	Imperial 66386
10/25/69	**89**	4	19 One Woman	Imperial 66418
5/09/70	**51**	8	20 Into The Mystic	Imperial 66448
			2-13, 19 & 20: produced by Lou Adler	
9/05/70	**94**	2	21 Fire And Rain	Imperial 66453
5/08/71	**84**	4	22 Sea Cruise	United Art. 50778
8/28/71	**65**	6	23 Think His Name	United Art. 50822
			backing vocals: Guru Ram Das Ashram Singers	

DEBUT DATE	PEAK POS	WKS CHR	ARTIST — Record Title	Label & Number
			JOHNNY RIVERS — Cont'd	
10/07/72+	**6**	19	24 ● **Rockin' Pneumonia - Boogie Woogie Flu**	United Art. 50960
3/17/73	**38**	10	25 Blue Suede Shoes	United Art. 198
7/12/75	**22**	10	26 Help Me Rhonda	Epic 50121
2/05/77	**96**	4	27 Ashes And Sand	Soul City 007
6/25/77	**10**	24	28 ● **Swayin' To The Music (Slow Dancin')**	Big Tree 16094
12/24/77+	**41**	10	29 Curious Mind (Um, Um, Um, Um, Um, Um)	Big Tree 16106
			THE RIVIERAS	
			Northern New Jersey R&B quartet: Homer Dunn, lead; Charles Allen, bass; Ronald Cook, tenor; Andrew Jones, baritone. First named the "Four Arts", later "El Rivieras".	
8/25/58	**73**	4	1 Count Every Star #4 hit in 1950 for Ray Anthony	Coed 503
2/09/59	**47**	11	2 Moonlight Serenade Glenn Miller's theme song (POS 3 in 1939)	Coed 508
1/18/60	**93**	3	3 Since I Made You Cry	Coed 522
			THE RIVIERAS	
			Rock and roll sextet from Indiana - Bill Dobslaw, lead singer.	
1/25/64	**5**	10	1 **California Sun**	Riviera 1401
5/02/64	**93**	3	2 Little Donna/	
5/30/64	**99**	1	3 Let's Have A Party	Riviera 1402
9/05/64	**96**	3	4 Rockin' Robin	Riviera 1403
			THE RIVINGTONS	
			Los Angeles R&B quartet: Carl White, lead (d: 1/7/80); Sonny Harris, Rocky Wilson, Jr. and Al Frazier. Back-up on Paul Anka's first recording; Duane Eddy's "Rebel Rouser"; and "Little Bitty Pretty One" by Thurston Harris. Known then as The Sharps.	
8/18/62	**48**	8	1 Papa-Oom-Mow-Mow	Liberty 55427
3/30/63	**52**	7	2 The Bird's The Word	Liberty 55553
			THE ROAD APPLES	
9/27/75+	**35**	14	1 Let's Live Together	Polydor 14285
			MARTY ROBBINS	
			Born Martin Robinson on 9/26/25 in Glendale, Arizona; died of a heart attack on 12/8/82. Country singer, guitarist, composer. Own radio show with K-Bar Cowboys, late 1940s. Own TV show, "Western Caravan", KPHO-Phoenix, 1951. First recorded for Columbia in 1952. Regular on Grand Ole Opry since 1953. Had own label, Robbins, 1958. Stock car racer. Films "Road To Nashville" and "Guns Of A Stranger".	
11/03/56	**17**	18	1 Singing The Blues Juke Box #17 / Top 100 #26	Columbia 21545
4/13/57	**2^1**	26	2 **A White Sport Coat (And A Pink Carnation)** Best Seller #2 / Top 100 #3 / Jockey #4 / Juke Box #4 end	Columbia 40864
11/11/57+	**15**	24	3 The Story Of My Life Jockey #15 / Top 100 #30 / Best Seller #31	Columbia 41013
4/14/58	**26**	16	4 Just Married/ Best Seller #26 / Top 100 #35	
5/05/58	**68**	4	5 Stairway Of Love	Columbia 41143
8/04/58	**27**	13	6 She Was Only Seventeen (He Was One Year More)	Columbia 41208
2/02/59	**38**	13	7 The Hanging Tree from the film of the same title 2-7: with Ray Conniff & His Orchestra	Columbia 41325
6/15/59	**45**	6	8 Cap And Gown	Columbia 41408
11/09/59+	**1^2**	22	9 **El Paso**	Columbia 41511
3/14/60	**26**	10	10 Big Iron	Columbia 41589
6/20/60	**31**	12	11 Is There Any Chance	Columbia 41686
9/12/60	**74**	4	12 Five Brothers	Columbia 41771
10/17/60	**34**	13	13 Ballad Of The Alamo from the film "The Alamo"	Columbia 41809
1/30/61	**3**	15	14 **Don't Worry**	Columbia 41922
5/29/61	**51**	5	15 Jimmy Martinez	Columbia 42008
9/11/61	**51**	9	16 It's Your World	Columbia 42065
12/25/61+	**81**	4	17 I Told The Brook	Columbia 42246
4/28/62	**69**	6	18 Love Can't Wait	Columbia 42375
7/28/62	**16**	11	19 Devil Woman	Columbia 42486
11/17/62	**18**	10	20 Ruby Ann	Columbia 42614
3/16/63	**93**	2	21 Cigarettes And Coffee Blues	Columbia 42701

DEBUT DATE	PEAK POS	WKS CHR	ARTIST — Record Title	Label & Number
			MARTY ROBBINS — Cont'd	
11/30/63	**74**	5	22 Begging To You	Columbia 42890
10/26/68	**65**	8	23 I Walk Alone	Columbia 44633
3/14/70	**42**	8	24 My Woman My Woman, My Wife	Columbia 45091
			ROCKIE ROBBINS	
			Black vocalist from Minneapolis.	
7/19/80	**80**	4	1 You And Me	A&M 2231
			ROBERT & JOHNNY	
			Bronx R&B duo: Robert Carr and Johnny Mitchell.	
2/24/58	**32**	22	1 We Belong Together	Old Town 1047
			Best Seller #32 / Top 100 #33	
8/04/58	**93**	2	2 I Believe In You	Old Town 1052
			AUSTIN ROBERTS	
			Born on 9/19/45 in Newport News, VA. Collaborator on cartoon series "Scooby Doo" and "Josie & The Pussycats".	
10/14/72	**12**	15	1 Something's Wrong With Me	Chelsea 0101
2/03/73	**50**	8	2 Keep On Singing	Chelsea 0110
7/19/75	**9**	17	3 **Rocky**	Private S. 45020
			JOHN ROBERTS	
12/02/67	**71**	4	1 Sockin' 1-2-3-4	Duke 425
			LEA ROBERTS	
			Leatha Roberta Hicks from Dayton. Moved to Newark in 1968, discovered by Blue Note director George Butler.	
4/12/75	**92**	3	1 All Right Now	United Art. 626
			DON ROBERTSON	
			Born on 12/5/22 in Peking, China; moved to Chicago at age 4. Pianist, composer. Created the Nashville piano style. Wrote several of Elvis Presley's hits.	
4/28/56	**6**	20	1 **The Happy Whistler** [I]	Capitol 3391
			Jockey #6 / Best Seller #9 / Top 100 #9 / Juke Box #12	
			ROBEY	
			New York-based model/actress - originally from Montreal, Canada.	
3/02/85	**77**	3	1 One Night In Bangkok	Silver Blue 04774
			cover version from the musical "Chess"	
			IVO ROBIC	
			Born near Zagreb, Yugoslavia in 1927. Name pronounced Eevo Robish.	
8/17/59	**13**	17	1 Morgen [F]	Laurie 3033
1/18/60	**58**	6	2 The Happy Muleteer	Laurie 3045
			TINA ROBIN	
9/18/61	**95**	1	1 Dear Mr. D.J. Play It Again	Mercury 71852
			THE ROBINS	
			Los Angeles R&B group consisting of Ty Terrell, Billy Richards, Roy Richard, and Bobby Nunn. First known as the Four Bluebirds. Carl Gardner and Grady Chapman added in 1954. Gardner and Nunn formed the Coasters in 1955.	
12/10/55	**79**	1	1 Smokey Joe's Cafe	Atco 6059
			ALVIN ROBINSON	
			R&B session guitarist, vocalist.	
6/06/64	**52**	8	1 Something You Got	Tiger 104
			FLOYD ROBINSON	
			Singer/guitarist/composer. Worked on local radio with his high school band, the Eagle Rangers, at age 12. Had own programs on WLAC and WSM-Nashville.	
7/20/59	**20**	18	1 Makin' Love	RCA 7529
			FREDDY ROBINSON	
			Jazz-rock guitarist. With Little Walter's Band, Howling Wolf and John Mayall.	
7/25/70	**56**	9	1 Black Fox [I]	World Pac. 88155
			ROSCO ROBINSON	
			Born on 5/22/28 in Dumont, Arkansas. Soul singer, producer.	
8/06/66	**62**	8	1 That's Enough	Wand 1125

DEBUT DATE	PEAK POS	WKS CHR	ARTIST — Record Title	Label & Number
			SMOKEY ROBINSON	
			Born William Robinson on 2/19/40 in Detroit. Formed The Miracles (then called the Matadors) at Northern High School in 1955. First recorded for End in 1958. Married Miracles' member Claudette Rogers in 1963. Left Miracles on 1/29/72. Wrote dozens of hit songs for Motown artists. Vice President of Motown Records.	
7/07/73	**48**	13	1 Sweet Harmony	Tamla 54233
11/17/73+	**27**	16	2 Baby Come Close	Tamla 54239
5/25/74	**82**	5	3 It's Her Turn To Live	Tamla 54246
9/28/74	**56**	7	4 Virgin Man	Tamla 54250
12/14/74+	**56**	9	5 I Am I Am	Tamla 54251
4/26/75	**26**	11	6 Baby That's Backatcha	Tamla 54258
9/06/75	**36**	12	7 The Agony And The Ecstasy	Tamla 54261
1/17/76	**61**	7	8 Quiet Storm	Tamla 54265
5/08/76	**81**	9	9 Open	Tamla 54267
2/19/77	**42**	11	10 There Will Come A Day (I'm Gonna Happen To You)	Tamla 54279
6/10/78	**75**	8	11 Daylight And Darkness	Tamla 54293
1/20/79	**59**	8	12 Pops, We Love You (A Tribute To Father) **DIANA ROSS, MARVIN GAYE, SMOKEY ROBINSON & STEVIE WONDER** song written for Berry Gordy Sr.'s 90th birthday	Motown 1455
10/06/79+	**4**	25	13 **Cruisin'**	Tamla 54306
3/15/80	**31**	14	14 Let Me Be The Clock all of above produced by Robinson (except #10 & 12)	Tamla 54311
2/14/81	**2**[3]	25	15 • **Being With You**	Tamla 54321
6/20/81	**59**	7	16 You Are Forever	Tamla 54327
1/16/82	**33**	12	17 Tell Me Tomorrow - Part I	Tamla 1601
4/17/82	**60**	9	18 Old Fashioned Love	Tamla 1615
7/02/83	**48**	12	19 Blame It On Love **SMOKEY ROBINSON & BARBARA MITCHELL (member of High Inergy)**	Tamla 1684
12/10/83+	**43**	11	20 Ebony Eyes **RICK JAMES featuring SMOKEY ROBINSON**	Gordy 1714
			STAN ROBINSON	
3/30/59	**83**	4	1 Boom-A-Dip-Dip	Monument 402
			VICKI SUE ROBINSON	
			Born in Philadelphia in 1955. Disco vocalist.	
4/10/76	**10**	25	1 **Turn The Beat Around**	RCA 10562
10/02/76	**63**	7	2 Daylight	RCA 10775
8/06/77	**67**	9	3 Hold Tight	RCA 11028
			ROCHELL & THE CANDLES	
			Los Angeles R&B group consisting of lead Johnny Wyatt, Rochell Henderson, Melvin Sasso and T.C. Henderson.	
2/06/61	**26**	13	1 Once Upon A Time	Swingin' 623
			ROCK & ROLL DUBBLE BUBBLE	
1/18/69	**74**	4	1 Bubble Gum Music [N]	Buddah 78
			ROCK-A-TEENS	
			Rock and roll sextet from New York City.	
10/05/59	**16**	12	1 Woo-Hoo [I]	Roulette 4192
			ROCK FLOWERS	
2/12/72	**95**	2	1 Number Wonderful	Wheel 0032
			ROCKETS	
			Detroit rock band led by David Gilbert, vocals; Jim McCarty, guitar; and John Badanjek, drums.	
4/21/79	**51**	9	1 Can't Sleep	RSO 926
7/07/79	**30**	13	2 Oh Well	RSO 935
2/16/80	**70**	6	3 Desire	RSO 1022
			THE ROCKIN R'S	
			Instrumental rock trio from Metamora, Illinois. Consisted of Ron Valz and Ron Wernsman, guitars; and Ted Minar, drums.	
3/23/59	**57**	8	1 The Beat [I]	Tempus 7541

DEBUT DATE	PEAK POS	WKS CHR	ARTIST — Record Title	Label & Number
			ROCKIN' REBELS - see THE REBELS	
			THE DAVID ROCKINGHAM TRIO	
11/09/63	**62**	8	1 Dawn ... [I]	Josie 913
			featuring Bobby Robinson on guitar	
			ROCKPILE	
			British pop/rock quartet: Dave Edmunds, Nick Lowe, Billy Bremner, Terry Williams.	
11/22/80+	**51**	12	1 Teacher Teacher ...	Columbia 11388
			ROCKWELL	
			Born Kennedy Gordy on 3/15/64 in Detroit. Son of Motown chairman, Berry Gordy, Jr.	
1/28/84	**2**[3]	19	1 ● **Somebody's Watching Me** ...	Motown 1702
			background vocals by Michael Jackson	
5/05/84	**35**	14	2 Obscene Phone Caller ...	Motown 1731
			THE ROCKY FELLERS	
			Consists of a father and his four sons from Manila, The Philippines.	
3/23/63	**16**	13	1 Killer Joe ...	Scepter 1246
6/29/63	**55**	5	2 Like The Big Guys Do ...	Scepter 1254
			EILEEN RODGERS	
			Born in Pittsburgh, 1933. Featured vocalist in Charlie Spivak's band for 2 years.	
8/18/56	**18**	17	1 Miracle Of Love ...	Columbia 40708
			Jockey #18 / Top 100 #19 / Best Seller #23	
12/15/56+	**61**	8	2 Give Me ...	Columbia 40791
4/06/57	**62**	2	3 The Wall ...	Columbia 40850
6/03/57	**83**	2	4 Don't Call Me Sweetie (Cause I'm Bitter) ...	Columbia 40908
9/16/57	**82**	2	5 Third Finger - Left Hand ...	Columbia 40956
8/25/58	**26**	15	6 Treasure Of Your Love ...	Columbia 41214
			JIMMIE RODGERS	
			Born on 9/18/33 in Camas, Washington. Vocalist, guitarist, pianist. Formed first group while in the Air Force. Own NBC-TV variety series in 1959. Career hampered following mysterious assault in Los Angeles on 12/1/67, which left him with a fractured skull. Returned to performing on 1/28/69.	
8/12/57	**1**[4]	28	1 **Honeycomb** ...	Roulette 4015
			Jockey #1(4) / Best Seller #1(2) / Top 100 #1(2)	
11/18/57	**3**	21	2 **Kisses Sweeter Than Wine** ...	Roulette 4031
			Jockey #3 / Top 100 #7 / Best Seller #8	
2/17/58	**7**	15	3 **Oh-Oh, I'm Falling In Love Again/**	
			Jockey #7 / Top 100 #22 / Best Seller #23	
5/05/58	**77**	9	4 The Long Hot Summer ...	Roulette 4045
			from the film of the same title	
5/05/58	**3**	17	5 **Secretly/**	
			Best Seller #3 / Jockey #3 / Top 100 #4	
5/19/58	**16**	9	6 Make Me A Miracle ...	Roulette 4070
			Jockey #16 / Top 100 #54	
8/04/58	**10**	13	7 **Are You Really Mine/**	
			Hot 100 #10 / Best Seller #10	
8/11/58	**45**	7	8 The Wizard ...	Roulette 4090
11/10/58	**11**	16	9 Bimbombey ...	Roulette 4116
2/23/59	**36**	11	10 I'm Never Gonna Tell/	
3/09/59	**62**	5	11 Because You're Young ...	Roulette 4129
			all of above with Hugo Peretti & His Orchestra	
6/01/59	**32**	8	12 Ring-A-Ling-A-Lario/	
6/15/59	**40**	7	13 Wonderful You ...	Roulette 4158
9/21/59	**32**	9	14 Tucumcari ...	Roulette 4191
1/11/60	**24**	10	15 T.L.C. Tender Love And Care/	
1/18/60	**41**	8	16 Waltzing Matilda ...	Roulette 4218
4/11/60	**44**	9	17 Just A Closer Walk With Thee ...	Roulette 4234
8/01/60	**64**	9	18 The Wreck Of The 'John B' ...	Roulette 4260
			tune revived in 1966 by The Beach Boys as "Sloop John B"	
			12-18: with Joe Reisman's Orchestra	
9/04/61	**71**	4	19 A Little Dog Cried ... [S]	Roulette 4384
9/01/62	**43**	11	20 No One Will Ever Know ...	Dot 16378
11/24/62	**62**	7	21 Rainbow At Midnight ...	Dot 16407
10/12/63	**78**	7	22 Two-Ten, Six-Eighteen (Doesn't Anybody Know My Name) ...	Dot 16527

DEBUT DATE	PEAK POS	WKS CHR	ARTIST — Record Title	Label & Number
			JIMMIE RODGERS — Cont'd	
5/30/64	**51**	9	23 The World I Used To Know	Dot 16595
5/14/66	**37**	7	24 It's Over	Dot 16861
9/23/67	**31**	8	25 Child Of Clay	A&M 871
			NILE RODGERS	
			R&B guitarist/producer. Member of Chic and The Honeydrippers.	
6/01/85	**88**	3	1 Let's Go Out Tonight	Warner 29049
			JOHNNY RODRIGUEZ	
			Born on 12/10/52 in Sabinal, Texas. Mexican-American country singer.	
6/23/73	**86**	4	1 You Always Come Back (To Hurting Me)	Mercury 73368
9/29/73	**70**	5	2 Ridin' My Thumb To Mexico	Mercury 73416
5/04/74	**85**	4	3 Something	Mercury 73471
			RODWAY	
			Steve Rodway from Kent, England.	
12/11/82	**83**	5	1 Don't Stop Trying	Millennium 13111
			TOMMY ROE	
			Born on 5/9/42 in Atlanta. Pop/rock singer, guitarist, composer. Formed band, The Satins, at Brown High School, worked local dances, late 1950s. Group recorded for Judd in 1960. Moved to Britain, mid-1960s, returned in 1969.	
7/28/62	**1**[2]	14	1 ● **Sheila**	ABC-Para. 10329
10/06/62	**35**	8	2 Susie Darlin'	ABC-Para. 10362
5/04/63	**84**	3	3 The Folk Singer	ABC-Para. 10423
10/12/63	**3**	14	4 **Everybody**	ABC-Para. 10478
1/18/64	**36**	8	5 Come On	ABC-Para. 10515
4/25/64	**61**	6	6 Carol	ABC-Para. 10543
12/05/64	**85**	3	7 Party Girl	ABC-Para. 10604
			all of above produced by Felton Jarvis (except #6)	
6/11/66	**8**	14	8 ● **Sweet Pea**	ABC-Para. 10762
9/17/66	**6**	13	9 **Hooray For Hazel**	ABC 10852
12/24/66+	**23**	11	10 It's Now Winters Day	ABC 10888
4/08/67	**91**	1	11 Sing Along With Me	ABC 10908
6/10/67	**99**	1	12 Little Miss Sunshine	ABC 10945
2/01/69	**1**[4]	15	13 ● **Dizzy**	ABC 11164
4/26/69	**29**	8	14 Heather Honey	ABC 11211
7/19/69	**53**	13	15 Jack And Jill	ABC 11229
11/15/69+	**8**	14	16 ● **Jam Up Jelly Tight**	ABC 11247
2/28/70	**50**	6	17 Stir It Up And Serve It	ABC 11258
6/20/70	**50**	9	18 Pearl	ABC 11266
9/12/70	**49**	6	19 We Can Make Music	ABC 11273
8/21/71	**25**	12	20 Stagger Lee	ABC 11307
			13-20: produced by Steve Barri	
9/23/72	**92**	3	21 Mean Little Woman, Rosalie	MGM South 7001
5/05/73	**97**	4	22 Working Class Hero	MGM South 7013
			ROGER	
			Roger Troutman from Hamilton, Ohio. Leader of family group Zapp.	
11/07/81	**79**	7	1 I Heard It Through The Grapevine	Warner 49786
			D.J. ROGERS	
			DeWayne Julius Rogers - vocalist, keyboardist, composer from Los Angeles.	
7/04/76	**98**	2	1 Say You Love Me	RCA 10568
			DANN ROGERS	
			Kenny Roger's nephew.	
12/15/79+	**41**	11	1 Looks Like Love Again	ia 500
			JULIE ROGERS	
			Born Julie Rolls on 4/6/43 in London, England.	
11/21/64+	**10**	11	1 **The Wedding**	Mercury 72332
2/13/65	**67**	5	2 Like A Child	Mercury 72380

DEBUT DATE	PEAK POS	WKS CHR	ARTIST — Record Title	Label & Number
			KENNY ROGERS	
			Born on 8/21/38 in Houston. With high school band, the Scholars in 1958. Bass player of jazz group, the Bobby Doyle Trio, recorded for Columbia. In Kirby Stone Four and The New Christy Minstrels, mid-1960s. Formed The First Edition in 1967. Went solo in 1973. Starred in films "The Gambler", "Coward Of The County" and "Six Pack". Also see Dottie West.	
3/13/76	**97**	3	1 Love Lifted Me	United Art. 746
3/26/77	**5**	19	2● **Lucille**	United Art. 929
8/06/77	**28**	12	3 Daytime Friends	United Art. 1027
12/17/77+	**44**	8	4 Sweet Music Man	United Art. 1095
6/03/78	**32**	12	5 Love Or Something Like It	United Art. 1210
11/04/78+	**16**	22	6 The Gambler	United Art. 1250
4/28/79	**5**	16	7● **She Believes In Me**	United Art. 1273
9/08/79	**7**	18	8 **You Decorated My Life**	United Art. 1315
11/17/79+	**3**	19	9● **Coward Of The County**	United Art. 1327
3/29/80	**4**	19	10 **Don't Fall In Love With Dreamer** KENNY ROGERS with KIM CARNES	United Art. 1345
6/21/80	**14**	12	11 Love The World Away from the film "Urban Cowboy" all of above produced by Larry Butler	United Art. 1359
10/04/80	**1^{6}**	25	12● **Lady** written by Lionel Richie	Liberty 1380
6/13/81	**3**	18	13 **I Don't Need You**	Liberty 1415
9/05/81	**14**	15	14 Share Your Love With Me	Liberty 1430
11/21/81	**66**	9	15 Blaze Of Glory	Liberty 1441
12/26/81+	**13**	15	16 Through The Years 12-16: produced by Lionel Richie	Liberty 1444
7/03/82	**13**	17	17 Love Will Turn You Around from the film "Six Pack"	Liberty 1471
10/16/82	**47**	10	18 A Love Song	Liberty 1485
1/29/83	**6**	18	19 **We've Got Tonight** KENNY ROGERS & SHEENA EASTON	Liberty 1492
4/30/83	**37**	11	20 All My Life	Liberty 1495
8/20/83	**94**	2	21 Scarlet Fever	Liberty 1503
8/27/83	**1^{2}**	25	22▲ **Islands In The Stream** KENNY ROGERS & DOLLY PARTON written by The Bee Gees	RCA 13615
1/14/84	**23**	13	23 This Woman	RCA 13710
4/28/84	**79**	5	24 Eyes That See In The Dark	RCA 13774
9/15/84	**15**	19	25 What About Me? KENNY ROGERS with KIM CARNES & JAMES INGRAM	RCA 13899
12/22/84+	**81**	4	26 The Greatest Gift Of All [X] KENNY ROGERS & DOLLY PARTON from their Christmas TV special	RCA 13945
1/26/85	**79**	8	27 Crazy	RCA 13975
6/08/85	**91**	3	28 Real Love DOLLY PARTON & KENNY ROGERS	RCA 14058
11/23/85	**72**	9	29 Morning Desire	RCA 14194
			KENNY ROGERS & THE FIRST EDITION	
			Original lineup: Kenny Rogers, Thelma Camacho, Mike Settle, Terry Williams and Mickey Jones. All but Jones were members of The New Christy Minstrels. Hosted own syndicated TV variety show, "Rollin", in 1972. Officially disbanded in 1975. THE FIRST EDITION:	
2/10/68	**5**	10	1 **Just Dropped In (To See What Condition My Condition Was In)**	Reprise 0655
1/18/69	**19**	11	2 But You Know I Love You KENNY ROGERS & THE FIRST EDITION:	Reprise 0799
6/07/69	**6**	13	3 **Ruby, Don't Take Your Love To Town**	Reprise 0829
9/27/69	**26**	12	4 Ruben James	Reprise 0854
2/14/70	**11**	16	5 Something's Burning	Reprise 0888
7/04/70	**17**	11	6 Tell It All Brother	Reprise 0923
10/17/70	**33**	10	7 Heed The Call	Reprise 0953
3/27/71	**51**	7	8 Someone Who Cares Love Theme from the film "Fools"	Reprise 0999
6/26/71	**91**	2	9 Take My Hand 5-9: produced by Jimmy Bowen & Kenny Rogers	Reprise 1018
4/01/72	**91**	4	10 School Teacher lead vocal: Kin Vassy	Reprise 1069

DEBUT DATE	PEAK POS	WKS CHR	ARTIST — Record Title	Label & Number
			ROY ROGERS "King Of The Cowboys". Born Leonard Slye on 11/5/11 in Cincinnati. Original member of the famous western group, the Sons of the Pioneers. Roy starred in close to 100 movie Westerns, then in a popular radio and TV series with his wife Dale Evans.	
12/21/74+	**65**	7	1 Hoppy, Gene And Me.. [N]	20th Century 2154
			TIMMIE "Oh Yeah" ROGERS Born on 7/4/15 in Detroit. Black vaudeville and nightclub comedian.	
10/07/57	**36**	15	1 Back To School Again .... Top 100 #36 / Best Seller #37	Cameo 116
			THE ROLLERS San Bernardino R&B quartet: Eddie Wilson, Don Sampson, Al Wilson and Willie Willingham. Wilson had solo hits in the late 60s.	
4/10/61	**80**	3	1 The Continental Walk	Liberty 55320
			DANA ROLLIN	
11/05/66	**71**	6	1 Winchester Cathedral..	Tower 283
			THE ROLLING STONES British R&B influenced rock group formed in London in January, 1963. Consisted of Mick Jagger (b: 7/26/43), vocals; Keith Richards (b: 12/18/43), lead guitar; Brian Jones (b: 2/28/42), guitar; Bill Wyman (b: 10/24/36), bass; and Charlie Watts (b: 6/2/41), drums. Jagger was the lead singer of Blues, Inc. Took name from a Muddy Waters' song. Promoted as the 'bad boys' in contrast to The Beatles. First UK tour, with Ronettes in 1964. Jones left group shortly before drowning on 7/3/69. Replaced by Mick Taylor (b: 1/17/48). Taylor replaced by Ron Wood, 1975. Film "Gimme Shelter", a documentary of their controversial Altamont concert on 12/6/69. Considered by many as the world's greatest rock band of all-time.	
5/02/64	**48**	13	1 Not Fade Away..	London 9657
7/04/64	**24**	10	2 Tell Me (You're Coming Back)	London 9682
7/25/64	**26**	10	3 It's All Over Now	London 9687
10/17/64	**6**	13	4 **Time Is On My Side**	London 9708
1/09/65	**19**	9	5 Heart Of Stone	London 9725
3/27/65	**9**	10	6 **The Last Time/**	
5/22/65	**96**	1	7 Play With Fire..	London 9741
6/12/65	**1**[4]	14	8 ● **(I Can't Get No) Satisfaction**..	London 9766
10/09/65	**1**[2]	12	9 **Get Off Of My Cloud**	London 9792
12/25/65+	**6**	9	10 **As Tears Go By**..	London 9808
2/26/66	**2**[3]	10	11 **19th Nervous Breakdown**..	London 9823
5/14/66	**1**[2]	11	12 **Paint It, Black**..	London 901
7/09/66	**8**	9	13 **Mothers Little Helper/**	
7/23/66	**24**	6	14 Lady Jane..	London 902
10/08/66	**9**	7	15 **Have You Seen Your Mother, Baby, Standing In The Shadow?**..	London 903
1/21/67	**1**[1]	12	16 ● **Ruby Tuesday/**	
1/21/67	**55**	8	17 Let's Spend The Night Together	London 904
9/09/67	**14**	8	18 Dandelion/	
9/16/67	**50**	6	19 We Love You .... all of above and #34 produced by Andrew Loog Oldham	London 905
12/30/67+	**25**	7	20 She's A Rainbow	London 906
6/08/68	**3**	12	21 **Jumpin' Jack Flash**..	London 908
9/07/68	**48**	6	22 Street Fighting Man	London 909
7/19/69	**1**[4]	15	23 ● **Honky Tonk Women**..	London 910
5/01/71	**1**[2]	12	24 **Brown Sugar**	Rolling S. 19100
6/19/71	**28**	8	25 Wild Horses..	Rolling S. 19101
4/29/72	**7**	10	26 **Tumbling Dice**	Rolling S. 19103
7/15/72	**22**	8	27 Happy	Rolling S. 19104
4/28/73	**42**	8	28 You Can't Always Get What You Want .... flip side of "Honky Tonk Women"	London 910
9/08/73	**1**[1]	16	29 ● **Angie**..	Rolling S. 19105
1/12/74	**15**	11	30 Doo Doo Doo Doo Doo (Heartbreaker)	Rolling S. 19109
8/03/74	**16**	10	31 It's Only Rock 'N Roll (But I Like It)	Rolling S. 19301
11/09/74	**17**	10	32 Ain't Too Proud To Beg	Rolling S. 19302
6/14/75	**42**	6	33 I Don't Know Why .... 21-30 & 33: produced by Jimmy Miller	Abkco 4701
8/23/75	**81**	3	34 Out Of Time..	Abkco 4702
4/24/76	**10**	11	35 **Fool To Cry/**	
6/26/76	**49**	6	36 Hot Stuff..	Rolling S. 19304

DEBUT DATE	PEAK POS	WKS CHR	ARTIST — Record Title		Label & Number
			THE ROLLING STONES — Cont'd		
5/27/78	**1[1]**	20	37 ● **Miss You**		Rolling S. 19307
9/09/78	**8**	13	38 **Beast Of Burden**		Rolling S. 19309
12/16/78+	**31**	10	39 Shattered		Rolling S. 19310
7/05/80	**3**	19	40 **Emotional Rescue**		Rolling S. 20001
9/27/80	**26**	13	41 She's So Cold		Rolling S. 21001
8/22/81	**2[3]**	24	42 **Start Me Up**		Rolling S. 21003
12/05/81+	**13**	15	43 Waiting On A Friend		Rolling S. 21004
3/20/82	**20**	11	44 Hang Fire		Rolling S. 21300
6/12/82	**25**	11	45 Going To A Go-Go		Rolling S. 21301
11/12/83	**9**	14	46 **Undercover Of The Night**		Rolling S. 99813
2/04/84	**44**	9	47 She Was Hot		Rolling S. 99788
3/15/86	**5**	13	48 **Harlem Shuffle**		Rolling S. 05802
5/17/86	**28**	11	49 One Hit (To The Body)		Rolling S. 05906
			31, 32 & 35-49: produced by The Glimmer Twins (Jagger & Richards)		
			2, 5-6, 8-31, 34-44, 46-47, 49: written by Jagger & Richards		
			ROMAN HOLLIDAY		
			7-man jive/rock band from London, England - Steve Lambert, lead singer.		
6/18/83	**54**	9	1 Stand By		Jive 9036
10/01/83	**68**	6	2 Don't Try To Stop It		Jive 9092
2/09/85	**76**	5	3 One Foot Back In Your Door		Jive 9287
			from the film "Teachers"		
			DICK ROMAN		
			Pop singer from Brooklyn. Real name: Ricardo De Giacomo. Regular on TV's "The Liberace Show", 1958-59.		
8/04/62	**64**	7	1 Theme from A Summer Place		Harmon 1004
			from the film "A Summer Place"		
			THE ROMANTICS		
			Rock quartet from Detroit. Wally Palmar, lead singer.		
2/16/80	**49**	8	1 What I Like About You		Nemperor 7527
10/08/83+	**3**	26	2 **Talking In Your Sleep**		Nemperor 04135
2/25/84	**37**	12	3 One In A Million		Nemperor 04373
8/31/85	**71**	6	4 Test Of Time		Nemperor 05587
			ROMEO & JULIET SOUNDTRACK		
8/09/69	**86**	4	1 Farewell Love Scene	[S]	Capitol 2502
			actual dialogue from the "Romeo & Juliet" movie soundtrack Romeo: Leonard Whiting; Juliet: Olivia Hussey; Nurse: Pat Heywood		
			ROMEO VOID		
			San Francisco new-wave quintet. Debora Iyall, lead singer.		
9/01/84	**35**	13	1 A Girl In Trouble (Is A Temporary Thing)		Columbia 04534
			THE ROMEOS		
			Philadelphia soul quintet featuring producers Kenny Gamble and Thom Bell.		
4/01/67	**67**	7	1 Precious Memories	[I]	Mark II 101
			RONALD & RUBY		
3/17/58	**20**	7	1 Lollipop		RCA 7174
			Jockey #20 / Top 100 #39 / Best Seller #40		
			THE RON-DELS		
			Duo consisting of Delbert McClinton and Ronnie Kelly.		
7/24/65	**97**	1	1 If You Really Want Me To, I'll Go		Smash 1986
			THE RONDELS		
8/14/61	**66**	4	1 Back Beat No. 1	[I]	Amy 825
			DON RONDO		
			Baritone singer from New York City. Sang on TV/radio commercials.		
10/27/56	**11**	18	1 Two Different Worlds		Jubilee 5256
			Jockey #11 / Top 100 #19 / Best Seller #23		
7/15/57	**7**	19	2 **White Silver Sands**		Jubilee 5288
			Jockey #7 / Best Seller #9 / Top 100 #10		
10/28/57	**77**	2	3 There's Only You		Jubilee 5297

DEBUT DATE	PEAK POS	WKS CHR	ARTIST — Record Title	Label & Number
			THE RONETTES	
			Formed in New York City as the Darling Sisters in 1958. Consisted of Veronica "Ronnie" Bennett Spector (b: 8/10/45), sister Estelle Bennett Vann (b: 7/22/44), and cousin Nedra Talley Ross (b: 1/27/46). Sang professionally since junior high school. Back-up work for Phil Spector in 1962. Group disbanded in 1966. Veronica married to Phil Spector, 1968-74.	
8/31/63	2^{3}	13	1 **Be My Baby**	Philles 116
12/21/63+	**24**	9	2 Baby, I Love You	Philles 118
4/04/64	**39**	8	3 (The Best Part Of) Breakin' Up	Philles 120
6/20/64	**34**	9	4 Do I Love You?	Philles 121
10/24/64	**23**	11	5 Walking In The Rain	Philles 123
2/06/65	**52**	6	6 Born To Be Together	Philles 126
5/29/65	**75**	4	7 Is This What I Get For Loving You? all of above produced by Phil Spector	Philles 128
10/29/66	**100**	1	8 I Can Hear Music	Philles 133
			RONNIE & THE HI-LITES	
			R&B vocal quintet from Jersey City. Ronnie Goodson, lead (d: 11/4/80).	
3/31/62	**16**	12	1 I Wish That We Were Married	Joy 260
			RONNY & THE DAYTONAS	
			Nashville quartet specializing in hot-rod music. Ronny is Bucky Wilkin.	
8/01/64	**4**	13	1 **G.T.O.**	Mala 481
11/07/64	**72**	5	2 California Bound	Mala 490
12/19/64+	**54**	7	3 Bucket 'T'	Mala 492
12/04/65+	**27**	11	4 Sandy	Mala 513
9/03/66	**69**	5	5 Dianne, Dianne	RCA 8896
			LINDA RONSTADT	
			Born on 7/15/46 in Tucson, Arizona. While in high school formed folk trio, The Three Ronstadts (with sister and brother). To Los Angeles in 1964. Formed the Stone Poneys with Bobby Kimmel (guitar) and Ken Edwards (keyboards); recorded for Sidewalk in 1965. Went solo in 1968. In 1971 formed backing band with Glenn Frey, Don Henley, Randy Meisner and Bernie Leadon (later became the Eagles). In "Pirates Of Penzance" operetta in New York City, 1980, also in film of same name in 1983.	
11/11/67+	**13**	17	1 Different Drum **STONE PONEYS featuring LINDA RONSTADT**	Capitol 2004
3/30/68	**93**	2	2 Up To My Neck In High Muddy Water **LINDA RONSTADT & The Stone Poneys**	Capitol 2110
8/15/70	**25**	12	3 Long Long Time	Capitol 2846
1/23/71	**70**	5	4 (She's A) Very Lovely Woman/	
		5	5 The Long Way Around	Capitol 3021
3/04/72	**85**	3	6 Rock Me On The Water	Capitol 3273
12/01/73+	**51**	11	7 Love Has No Pride	Asylum 11026
4/06/74	**67**	7	8 Silver Threads And Golden Needles	Asylum 11032
12/07/74+	1^{1}	16	9 **You're No Good**	Capitol 3990
4/12/75	2^{2}	15	10 **When Will I Be Loved/**	
7/26/75	**47**	4	11 It Doesn't Matter Anymore	Capitol 4050
9/06/75	**5**	15	12 **Heat Wave/**	
		13	13 Love Is A Rose	Asylum 45282
12/20/75+	**25**	13	14 Tracks Of My Tears	Asylum 45295
8/21/76	**11**	16	15 That'll Be The Day	Asylum 45340
12/04/76+	**42**	11	16 Someone To Lay Down Beside Me	Asylum 45361
6/04/77	**76**	5	17 Lose Again	Asylum 45402
9/10/77	**3**	23	18● **Blue Bayou**	Asylum 45431
10/08/77	**5**	18	19 **It's So Easy**	Asylum 45438
1/28/78	**31**	9	20 Poor Poor Pitiful Me	Asylum 45462
4/22/78	**32**	8	21 Tumbling Dice	Asylum 45479
8/19/78	**16**	13	22 Back In The U.S.A.	Asylum 45519
11/11/78+	**7**	16	23 **Ooh Baby Baby**	Asylum 45546
2/10/79	**44**	8	24 Just One Look	Asylum 46011
2/02/80	**10**	16	25 **How Do I Make You**	Asylum 46602
4/12/80	**8**	14	26 **Hurt So Bad**	Asylum 46624
6/28/80	**31**	12	27 I Can't Let Go	Asylum 46654
10/02/82	**29**	12	28 Get Closer	Asylum 69948
12/11/82+	**37**	12	29 I Knew You When	Asylum 69853
4/23/83	**54**	10	30 Easy For You To Say	Asylum 69838

DEBUT DATE	PEAK POS	WKS CHR	ARTIST — Record Title	Label & Number
			LINDA RONSTADT — Cont'd	
10/29/83	**53**	14	31 What's New with the Nelson Riddle Orchestra	Asylum 69780
12/20/86+	**2**[1]	22	32 **Somewhere Out There** **LINDA RONSTADT & JAMES INGRAM** from the animated film "An American Tail" 9-32: produced by Peter Asher (Peter & Gordon)	MCA 52973
			THE ROOFTOP SINGERS Folk trio: Erik Darling, Willard Svanoe and Lynne Taylor (d: 1982). Disbanded in 1967. Darling was a member of The Tarriers in 1956, and The Weavers, 1958-62. Taylor was a vocalist with Benny Goodman.	
1/05/63	**1**[2]	13	1 **Walk Right In**	Vanguard 35017
3/23/63	**20**	10	2 Tom Cat	Vanguard 35019
7/20/63	**55**	7	3 Mama Don't Allow	Vanguard 35020
			THE ROOMMATES Vocal quartet from Queens: Steve Susskind (lead), Jack Sailson and Felix Alvarez (tenors) and Bob Minsky (bass). Cathy Jean's back-up singers.	
4/10/61	**49**	9	1 Glory Of Love #1 hit in 1936 for Benny Goodman	Valmor 008
			EDMUNDO ROS London-based bandleader. Native of Caracas, Venezuela.	
2/10/58	**75**	6	1 Colonel Bogey [I] from the film "The Bridge On The River Kwai"	London 1779
1/05/59	**77**	4	2 I Talk To The Trees [I] from the Broadway musical "Paint Your Wagon"	London 1831
			ROSE COLORED GLASS	
4/10/71	**54**	14	1 Can't Find The Time	Bang 584
10/23/71	**95**	4	2 If It's Alright With You	Bang 588
			THE ROSE GARDEN West Virginia quintet - Diana Di Rose, lead singer.	
10/21/67	**17**	14	1 Next Plane To London	Atco 6510
			ROSE ROYCE Eight-member backing band formed in Los Angeles, early 70s. Backed Edwin Starr as Total Concept Unlimited in 1973. Backed The Temptations, became regular band for Undisputed Truth. Lead vocalist Gwen Dickey added, name changed to Rose Royce in 1976. Did soundtrack for the film "Car Wash".	
10/23/76+	**1**[1]	23	1 ▲ **Car Wash**	MCA 40615
2/26/77	**10**	17	2 **I Wanna Get Next To You**	MCA 40662
6/04/77	**70**	7	3 I'm Going Down above 3 from the film "Car Wash"	MCA 40721
9/17/77	**39**	8	4 Do Your Dance - Part 1	Whitfield 8440
11/26/77+	**72**	11	5 Ooh Boy all of above written and produced by Norman Whitfield	Whitfield 8491
12/09/78+	**32**	11	6 Love Don't Live Here Anymore	Whitfield 8712
			ANDY ROSE	
10/06/58	**69**	7	1 Just Young	Aamco 100
			DAVID ROSE Born on 6/15/10 in London, England; moved to Chicago at an early age. Conductor, composer, arranger for numerous films and TV series. TV series included "The Red Skelton Show", "Bonanza" and "Little House On The Prairie". Married briefly to Martha Raye and Judy Garland.	
11/12/55	**54**	10	1 Love Is A Many-Splendored Thing [I] from the film of the same title	MGM 30883
2/02/57	**84**	2	2 Holiday For Trombones [I] similar to David's "Holiday For Strings" (POS 2 - 1944)	MGM 12376
3/23/57	**42**	12	3 Calypso Melody [I]	MGM 12430
2/24/58	**47**	9	4 Swinging Shepherd Blues [I] Best Seller #47 / Top 100 #50	MGM 12608
6/01/59	**46**	12	5 Like Young [I] **ANDRE PREVIN & DAVID ROSE**	MGM 12792
5/12/62	**1**[1]	17	6 **The Stripper** [I]	MGM 13064
			JIMMY ROSELLI Italian singer.	
8/12/67	**93**	2	1 There Must Be A Way	United Art. 50179

DEBUT DATE	PEAK POS	WKS CHR	ARTIST — Record Title	Label & Number
			ROSIE & THE ORIGINALS	
			San Diego group - Rosalie Hamlin, lead singer.	
12/12/60+	**5**	13	1 **Angel Baby**	Highland 1011
3/13/61	**66**	4	2 Lonely Blue Nights	Brunswick 55205
			ROSIE formerly with THE ORIGINALS	
			CHARLIE ROSS	
1/18/75	**61**	5	1 Thanks For The Smiles	Big Tree 16025
2/28/76	**42**	7	2 Without Your Love (Mr. Jordan)	Big Tree 16056
			DIANA ROSS	
			Born Diane Earle on 3/26/44 in Detroit. In vocal group, the Primettes, first recorded for LuPine in 1960. Lead singer of The Supremes, 1961-69. Went solo in late 1969. Oscar nominee for the film "Lady Sings The Blues", 1971. In films "Mahogany" and "The Wiz". Also see The Supremes.	
4/25/70	**20**	9	1 Reach Out And Touch (Somebody's Hand)	Motown 1165
8/08/70	**1**[3]	14	2 **Ain't No Mountain High Enough**	Motown 1169
12/26/70+	**16**	10	3 Remember Me	Motown 1176
5/01/71	**29**	7	4 Reach Out I'll Be There	Motown 1184
8/14/71	**38**	8	5 Surrender	Motown 1188
11/06/71	**63**	5	6 I'm Still Waiting	Motown 1192
1/13/73	**34**	13	7 Good Morning Heartache	Motown 1211
			from the film "Lady Sings The Blues"	
6/02/73	**1**[1]	21	8 **Touch Me In The Morning**	Motown 1239
10/06/73	**12**	12	9 You're A Special Part Of Me	Motown 1280
			DIANA ROSS & MARVIN GAYE	
1/05/74	**14**	14	10 Last Time I Saw Him	Motown 1278
2/23/74	**19**	16	11 My Mistake (Was To Love You)	Motown 1269
			DIANA ROSS & MARVIN GAYE	
5/11/74	**70**	5	12 Sleepin'	Motown 1295
7/13/74	**46**	9	13 Don't Knock My Love	Motown 1296
			DIANA ROSS & MARVIN GAYE	
11/01/75+	**1**[1]	17	14 **Theme From Mahogany (Do You Know Where You're Going To)**	Motown 1377
3/20/76	**47**	7	15 I Thought It Took A Little Time (But Today I Fell In Love)	Motown 1387
4/03/76	**1**[2]	18	16 **Love Hangover**	Motown 1392
8/07/76	**25**	12	17 One Love In My Lifetime	Motown 1398
11/05/77+	**27**	13	18 Gettin' Ready For Love	Motown 1427
3/04/78	**49**	7	19 Your Love Is So Good For Me	Motown 1436
5/06/78	**49**	7	20 You Got It	Motown 1442
9/09/78	**41**	9	21 Ease On Down The Road	MCA 40947
			DIANA ROSS & MICHAEL JACKSON	
			from the film "The Wiz"	
1/20/79	**59**	8	22 Pops, We Love You (A Tribute To Father)	Motown 1455
			DIANA ROSS, MARVIN GAYE, SMOKEY ROBINSON & STEVIE WONDER	
			song written for Berry Gordy Sr.'s 90th birthday	
7/14/79	**19**	16	23 The Boss	Motown 1462
7/12/80	**1**[4]	29	24● **Upside Down**	Motown 1494
9/06/80	**5**	23	25 **I'm Coming Out**	Motown 1491
10/25/80+	**9**	21	26 **It's My Turn**	Motown 1496
			from the film of the same title	
4/11/81	**79**	5	27 One More Chance	Motown 1508
7/11/81	**1**[9]	27	28▲ **Endless Love**	Motown 1519
			DIANA ROSS & LIONEL RICHIE	
			from the film of the same title - written by Richie	
10/17/81	**7**	20	29 **Why Do Fools Fall In Love**	RCA 12349
1/09/82	**8**	14	30 **Mirror, Mirror**	RCA 13021
4/10/82	**44**	7	31 Work That Body	RCA 13201
10/02/82	**10**	17	32 **Muscles**	RCA 13348
			written by Michael Jackson	
2/05/83	**40**	10	33 So Close	RCA 13424
6/25/83	**31**	10	34 Pieces Of Ice	RCA 13549
12/17/83+	**77**	6	35 Let's Go Up	RCA 13671
7/07/84	**19**	16	36 All Of You	Columbia 04507
			JULIO IGLESIAS & DIANA ROSS	
9/01/84	**19**	14	37 Swept Away	RCA 13864
			written & produced by Daryl Hall	

DEBUT DATE	PEAK POS	WKS CHR	ARTIST — Record Title	Label & Number
			DIANA ROSS — Cont'd	
12/01/84+	**10**	27	38 **Missing You**	RCA 13966
			dedicated to Marvin Gaye - produced & written by Lionel Richie	
9/21/85	**77**	7	39 Eaten Alive	RCA 14181
			background vocal: Michael Jackson	
11/30/85	**95**	3	40 Chain Reaction	RCA 14244
5/03/86	**66**	8	41 Chain Reaction [R]	RCA 14244
			new mix of previous hit	
			JACK ROSS	
			West Coast nightclub entertainer. Trumpet player. Died on 12/16/82 (66).	
1/13/62	**57**	6	1 Happy Jose (Ching, Ching) [I-N]	Dot 16302
3/17/62	**16**	9	2 Cinderella [C]	Dot 16333
			JACKIE ROSS	
8/01/64	**11**	10	1 Selfish One	Chess 1903
11/14/64	**89**	2	2 I've Got The Skill	Chess 1913
1/30/65	**85**	4	3 Jerk And Twine	Chess 1920
			SPENCER ROSS	
1/04/60	**13**	14	1 Tracy's Theme [I]	Columbia 41532
			from the TV production "Philadelphia Story"	
			saxophone: Jimmy Abato	
			ROSSINGTON COLLINS BAND	
			Band formed by 4 surviving members of Lynyrd Skynyrd, including Gary Rossington and Allen Collins. Dale Krantz, female lead singer.	
7/26/80	**55**	9	1 Don't Misunderstand Me	MCA 41284
			NINO ROTA	
			Composer - died on 4/10/79 (68).	
4/22/72	**66**	9	1 Love Theme From 'The Godfather' [I]	Paramount 0152
			conducted by Carlo Savina - from the film "The Godfather"	
			ROTARY CONNECTION	
			Canadian rock/R&B sextet. Minnie Riperton, lead singer.	
1/03/70	**96**	2	1 Want You To Know	Cadet Con. 7018
			DAVID LEE ROTH	
			Born on 10/10/55 in Bloomington, Indiana. Former lead singer of Van Halen.	
1/19/85	**3**	16	1 **California Girls**	Warner 29102
3/23/85	**12**	17	2 Just A Gigolo/I Ain't Got Nobody	Warner 29040
			"Just A Gigolo": #1 hit for Ted Lewis in 1931	
			"I Ain't Got Nobody": #3 hit for Marion Harris in 1921	
7/05/86	**16**	15	3 Yankee Rose	Warner 28656
9/27/86	**66**	7	4 Goin' Crazy!	Warner 28584
11/22/86	**85**	4	5 That's Life	Warner 28511
			ROUGH TRADE	
			Canadian rock group led by Carole Pope (vocals) & Kevan Staples (guitar, keyboards).	
12/18/82+	**58**	7	1 All Touch	Boardwalk 167
			ROUND ROBIN	
5/30/64	**61**	8	1 Kick That Little Foot Sally Ann	Domain 1404
			DEMIS ROUSSOS	
			Greek singer. Formed rock band, Aphrodites Child, in France with Vangelis, 1968 to early 70s.	
6/03/78	**47**	11	1 That Once In A Lifetime	Mercury 73992
			THE ROUTERS	
			Rock and roll instrumental quintet led by Mike Gordon.	
11/03/62	**19**	13	1 Let's Go [I]	Warner 5283
4/27/63	**50**	10	2 Sting Ray [I]	Warner 5349
			THE ROVER BOYS	
			Canadian group featuring Billy Albert, lead singer.	
5/12/56	**16**	11	1 Graduation Day	ABC-Para. 9700
			Jockey #16 / Best Seller #19 / Top 100 #20	
9/22/56	**79**	3	2 From A School Ring To A Wedding Ring	ABC-Para. 9732

DEBUT DATE	PEAK POS	WKS CHR	ARTIST — Record Title	Label & Number
			ROVERS - see IRISH ROVERS	
			THE ROWANS	
			Brothers Lorin, Chris and Peter Rowan. Originally from the Boston area. Peter was a member of Earth Opera and Seatrain.	
10/16/76	**74**	4	1 If I Only Could	Asylum 45347
			JOHN ROWLES	
			Native of New Zealand.	
1/02/71	**64**	8	1 Cheryl Moana Marie	Kapp 2102
			ROXY MUSIC	
			English art-rock band. Nucleus consisted of Bryan Ferry (vocals, keyboards), Phil Manzanera (guitar) and Andy Mackey (horns).	
12/27/75+	**30**	14	1 Love Is The Drug	Atco 7042
4/28/79	**44**	9	2 Dance Away	Atco 7100
8/09/80	**80**	4	3 Over You	Atco 7301
			THE ROYALETTES	
			R&B family group from Baltimore. Consisted of sisters Anita and Sheila Ross, Terry Jones and Ronnie Brown.	
7/17/65	**41**	11	1 It's Gonna Take A Miracle	MGM 13366
11/06/65	**72**	6	2 I Want To Meet Him	MGM 13405
			THE ROYAL GUARDSMEN	
			Novelty-pop sextet from Ocala, Florida. Consisted of Barry Winslow (vocals, guitar), Chris Nunley (vocals), Tom Richards (lead guitar), Bill Balough (bass) and Billy Taylor (organ).	
12/17/66	**2^{4}**	12	1 ● **Snoopy Vs. The Red Baron** [N]	Laurie 3366
2/25/67	**15**	7	2 The Return Of The Red Baron [N]	Laurie 3379
6/17/67	**46**	6	3 Airplane Song (My Airplane)	Laurie 3391
9/09/67	**97**	2	4 Wednesday	Laurie 3397
2/17/68	**72**	4	5 I Say Love	Laurie 3428
7/13/68	**85**	2	6 Snoopy For President [N]	Laurie 3451
11/16/68+	**35**	13	7 Baby Let's Wait	Laurie 3461
			THE ROYAL JOKERS	
12/10/55	**77**	1	1 You Tickle Me Baby	Atco 6052
			THE ROYAL PHILHARMONIC ORCHESTRA	
			British - Louis Clark, conductor (born in Birmingham, England - arranger for ELO).	
10/31/81+	**10**	20	1 **Hooked On Classics** [I]	RCA 12304
			Tchaikovsky Piano Concerto No. 1/Flight of the Bumble Bee/ Mozart Symphony No. 40 in G Minor/Rhapsody In Blue/Karelia Suite/ The Marriage of Figaro/Romeo & Juliet/Trumpet Voluntary/Hallelujah Chorus/Grieg Piano Concerto in A Minor/March of the Toreadors	
			THE ROYAL SCOTS DRAGOON GUARDS	
			The Pipes and Drums and The Military Band of Scotland's armoured regiment.	
5/20/72	**11**	9	1 Amazing Grace [I]	RCA 0709
			bagpipes solo by Pipe Major Tony Crease	
			ROYAL TEENS	
			White rock and roll quartet from Fort Lee, NJ. Consisted of Bob Gaudio, Bill Crandall, Billy Dalton and Tom Austin. Crandall was replaced by Larry Qualiano, and Joseph "Joe Villa" Francavilla joined as vocalist, late 1958. In 1960, Gaudio joined the 4 Seasons. Al Kooper joined the group for a short time in 1959.	
1/27/58	**3**	16	1 **Short Shorts**	ABC-Para. 9882
			Top 100 #3 / Best Seller #4 / Jockey #6	
8/11/58	**78**	2	2 Harvey's Got A Girl Friend	ABC-Para. 9945
10/26/59	**26**	15	3 Believe Me	Capitol 4261
			THE ROYALTONES	
			Rock and roll instrumental group from Dearborn, Michigan. Formed in 1957 as the Paragons. Featuring George Katsakis on tenor sax.	
10/20/58	**17**	17	1 Poor Boy [I]	Jubilee 5338
1/16/61	**82**	3	2 Flamingo Express [I]	Goldisc 3011
			BILLY JOE ROYAL	
			Born in Valdosta, Georgia in 1945. Raised in Marietta (suburb of Atlanta). Close friend of Joe South, who wrote many of Billy's hits.	
7/03/65	**9**	13	1 **Down In The Boondocks**	Columbia 43305
9/18/65	**14**	11	2 I Knew You When	Columbia 43390

DEBUT DATE	PEAK POS	WKS CHR	ARTIST — Record Title	Label & Number
			BILLY JOE ROYAL — Cont'd	
12/04/65+	**38**	8	3 I've Got To Be Somebody	Columbia 43465
5/21/66	**88**	3	4 Heart's Desire	Columbia 43622
9/03/66	**91**	2	5 Campfire Girls	Columbia 43740
9/30/67	**52**	8	6 Hush all of above (except #5) written and produced by Joe South	Columbia 44277
10/04/69	**15**	15	7 Cherry Hill Park	Columbia 44902
2/20/71	**86**	3	8 Tulsa	Columbia 45289
6/03/78	**82**	4	9 Under The Boardwalk	Private S. 45192
			RUBBER RODEO Rock quintet from Rhode Island. Trish Milliken, lead singer.	
8/25/84	**86**	5	1 Anywhere With You	Mercury 880175
			THE RUBETTES British quintet featuring Alan Williams, lead singer.	
7/20/74	**37**	10	1 Sugar Baby Love	Polydor 15089
			RUBICON Bay area septet led by horn player Jerry Martini (member of Sly & The Family Stone 1966-76). Group included Jack Blades and Brad Gillis of Night Ranger.	
2/25/78	**28**	11	1 I'm Gonna Take Care Of Everything	20th Century 2362
			THE RUBINOOS Pop quartet based in Berkeley, California. John Rubin, lead singer.	
3/05/77	**45**	12	1 I Think We're Alone Now	Beserkley 5741
			RUBY & THE ROMANTICS Akron, Ohio R&B quintet: Ruby Nash Curtis (b: 11/12/39, New York City), lead; Ed Roberts and George Lee, tenors; Ronald Mosley, baritone; and Leroy Fann, bass (d: 1973).	
2/09/63	**1**[1]	13	1 **Our Day Will Come**	Kapp 501
5/18/63	**16**	11	2 My Summer Love	Kapp 525
8/10/63	**27**	9	3 Hey There Lonely Boy	Kapp 544
10/26/63	**47**	8	4 Young Wings Can Fly (Higher Than You Know)	Kapp 557
3/21/64	**64**	6	5 Our Everlasting Love	Kapp 578
7/18/64	**75**	4	6 Baby Come Home	Kapp 601
10/03/64	**48**	8	7 When You're Young And In Love	Kapp 615
2/20/65	**87**	3	8 Does He Really Care For Me	Kapp 646
			DAVID RUFFIN Born on 1/18/41 in Meridian, MS. Brother of Jimmy Ruffin. With Dixie Nightingales gospel group. Recorded for Anna in 1960. Co-lead singer of The Temptations, 1963-68.	
2/15/69	**9**	10	1 **My Whole World Ended (The Moment You Left Me)**	Motown 1140
7/19/69	**58**	5	2 I've Lost Everything I've Ever Loved	Motown 1149
12/20/69+	**53**	7	3 I'm So Glad I Fell For You	Motown 1158
10/24/70	**61**	7	4 Stand By Me DAVID & JIMMY RUFFIN	Soul 35076
11/08/75+	**9**	15	5 **Walk Away From Love**	Motown 1376
3/20/76	**47**	7	6 Heavy Love	Motown 1388
6/12/76	**49**	9	7 Everything's Coming Up Love above 3 produced by Van McCoy	Motown 1393
8/31/85	**20**	11	8 A Nite At The Apollo Live! The Way You Do The Things You Do/My Girl DARYL HALL JOHN OATES with DAVID RUFFIN & EDDIE KENDRICK recorded at the reopening of New York's Apollo Theatre - revival of two early Temptations' hits	RCA 14178
			JIMMY RUFFIN Born on 5/7/39 in Collinsville, MS. Brother of David Ruffin. Back-up work at Motown in early 60s. First recorded for Miracle in 1961.	
8/20/66	**7**	17	1 **What Becomes Of The Brokenhearted**	Soul 35022
12/03/66+	**17**	11	2 I've Passed This Way Before	Soul 35027
3/18/67	**29**	7	3 Gonna Give Her All The Love I've Got	Soul 35032
7/22/67	**68**	5	4 Don't You Miss Me A Little Bit Baby	Soul 35035
3/09/68	**77**	5	5 I'll Say Forever My Love	Soul 35043
10/24/70	**61**	7	6 Stand By Me DAVID & JIMMY RUFFIN	Soul 35076
2/13/71	**97**	2	7 Maria (You Were The Only One)	Soul 35077
3/01/80	**10**	14	8 **Hold On To My Love** written and produced by Robin Gibb	RSO 1021

DEBUT DATE	PEAK POS	WKS CHR	ARTIST — Record Title	Label & Number
			RUFUS Featuring CHAKA KHAN	
			Soul group from Chicago. Band was first known as Smoke, then Ask Rufus. Varying membership. Included Tony Maiden (guitar), Nate Morgan, Kevin Murphy (keyboards), Bobby Watson (bass), Andre Fischer (drums) and Chaka Khan (lead singer). After Khan went solo in 1978, vocals were by Maiden and David Wolinski.	
6/15/74	**3**	17	1 ● **Tell Me Something Good**	ABC 11427
			RUFUS	
			written by Stevie Wonder	
10/12/74	**11**	16	2 You Got The Love	ABC 12032
2/15/75	**10**	13	3 **Once You Get Started**	ABC 12066
5/31/75	**48**	6	4 Please Pardon Me (You Remind Me Of A Friend)	ABC 12099
1/03/76	**5**	21	5 ● **Sweet Thing**	ABC 12149
5/01/76	**39**	8	6 Dance Wit Me	ABC 12179
2/12/77	**30**	12	7 At Midnight (My Love Will Lift You Up)	ABC 12239
5/07/77	**32**	8	8 Hollywood	ABC 12269
			RUFUS & CHAKA KHAN:	
4/08/78	**38**	11	9 Stay	ABC 12349
11/24/79+	**30**	15	10 Do You Love What You Feel	MCA 41131
12/05/81	**91**	5	11 Sharing The Love	MCA 51203
10/01/83	**22**	19	12 Ain't Nobody	Warner 29555
			RUFUS & CARLA - see RUFUS THOMAS and/or CARLA THOMAS	
			THE RUGBYS	
8/23/69	**24**	11	1 You, I	Amazon 1
			THE RUMBLERS	
			Instrumental rock group form Norwalk, CA: Bob Jones (sax), Johnny Kirkland and Mike Kelishes (guitars), Wayne Matteson (bass) and Adrian Lloyd (drums).	
2/16/63	**87**	2	1 Boss [I]	Dot 16421
			RUN-D.M.C.	
			Pop trio from Queens, New York: Joseph Simmons (Run), Daryll McDaniels (D.M.C.) and Jason Mizell (Jam Master Jay).	
7/26/86	**4**	16	1 **Walk This Way**	Profile 5112
			with Aerosmith's Steve Tyler (vocals) and Joe Perry (guitar)	
10/25/86	**29**	18	2 You Be Illin'	Profile 5119
			TODD RUNDGREN	
			Born on 6/22/48 in Upper Darby, PA. Virtuoso musician, songwriter, producer, engineer. Leader of groups Nazz and Utopia. Produced Meat Loaf's "Bat Out Of Hell" album and produced albums for Badfinger, Grand Funk Railroad, The Tubes, Patti Smith and many others.	
			RUNT:	
11/14/70+	**20**	17	1 We Gotta Get You A Woman	Ampex 31001
4/24/71	**71**	5	2 Be Nice To Me	Bearsville 31002
9/04/71	**92**	2	3 A Long Time, A Long Way To Go	Bearsville 31004
			TODD RUNDGREN:	
4/08/72	**16**	14	4 I Saw The Light	Bearsville 0003
7/29/72	**93**	2	5 Couldn't I Just Tell You	Bearsville 0007
10/06/73	**5**	20	6 **Hello It's Me**	Bearsville 0009
			original version by Nazz charted in 1969	
4/06/74	**69**	6	7 A Dream Goes On Forever	Bearsville 0020
4/26/75	**83**	3	8 Real Man	Bearsville 0304
6/05/76	**34**	8	9 Good Vibrations	Bearsville 0309
5/27/78	**29**	15	10 Can We Still Be Friends	Bearsville 0324
5/07/83	**63**	5	11 Bang The Drum All Day	Bearsville 29686
			all of above written (except #9) and produced by Rundgren	
			RUSH	
			Canadian power-rock trio: Geddy Lee (b: 7/29/53), vocals, bass; Alex Lifeson (b: 8/27/53), guitar; Neil Peart (b: 9/12/52), drums. Also see Bob & Doug McKenzie.	
1/08/77	**88**	4	1 Fly By Night/In The Mood	Mercury 73873
11/26/77	**76**	4	2 Closer To The Heart	Mercury 73958
2/23/80	**51**	8	3 The Spirit Of Radio	Mercury 76044
3/14/81	**55**	9	4 Limelight	Mercury 76095
6/06/81	**44**	13	5 Tom Sawyer	Mercury 76109
12/12/81+	**69**	7	6 Closer To The Heart	Mercury 76124
			live version of their 1977 hit	

DEBUT DATE	PEAK POS	WKS CHR	ARTIST — Record Title	Label & Number
			RUSH — Cont'd	
9/18/82	**21**	12	7 New World Man	Mercury 76179
			all of above produced by Rush and Terry Brown	
11/09/85+	**45**	14	8 The Big Money	Mercury 884191
			all of above written by Lee, Lifeson and Peart	
			JENNIFER RUSH	
			Native of Queens, New York.	
2/08/86	**57**	13	1 The Power Of Love	Epic 05754
			MERRILEE RUSH & THE TURNABOUTS	
			From Seattle, Washington. Discovered by another Northwest band, Paul Revere & The Raiders.	
5/04/68	**7**	16	1 **Angel Of The Morning**	Bell 705
8/31/68	**76**	6	2 That Kind Of Woman	Bell 738
			MERRILEE RUSH:	
12/07/68	**79**	4	3 Reach Out	AGP 107
6/11/77	**54**	7	4 Save Me	United Art. 993
			PATRICE RUSHEN	
			Born on 9/30/54 in Los Angeles. Jazz/soul vocalist, pianist, songwriter. Much session work with Jean Luc-Ponty, Lee Ritenour and Stanley Turrentine.	
1/26/80	**42**	9	1 Haven't You Heard	Elektra 46551
5/01/82	**23**	16	2 Forget Me Nots	Elektra 47427
6/30/84	**78**	6	3 Feels So Real (Won't Let Go)	Elektra 69742
			LONNIE RUSS	
12/08/62+	**57**	8	1 My Wife Can't Cook	4J 501
			BOBBY RUSSELL	
			Born on 4/19/41 in Nashville. Wrote "Honey", "Little Green Apples" and "The Night The Lights Went Out In Georgia".	
10/26/68	**36**	7	1 1432 Franklin Pike Circle Hero	Elf 90020
7/10/71	**28**	14	2 Saturday Morning Confusion [N]	United Art. 50788
			BRENDA RUSSELL	
			Soul singer, keyboardist, composer from Toronto, Canada. TV co-host with husband Brian in Canada. Session work for Barbra Streisand, Elton John and Bette Midler.	
8/18/79	**30**	17	1 So Good, So Right	Horizon 123
			LEON RUSSELL	
			Born on 4/2/41 in Lawton, Oklahoma. Vocalist, songwriter, top multi-instrumentalist sessionman. Formed Shelter Records with British producer Denny Cordell in 1970. Recorded as Hank Wilson in 1973. Married Mary McCreary (vocalist with Little Sister, part of Sly Stone's "family") in 1976. Own label, Paradise, 1976. Wrote "Superstar" and "This Masquerade". Also see Joe Cocker.	
8/26/72	**11**	12	1 Tight Rope	Shelter 7325
9/15/73	**89**	2	2 Queen Of The Roller Derby	Shelter 7337
10/06/73	**78**	5	3 Roll In My Sweet Baby's Arms/	
		5	4 I'm So Lonesome I Could Cry	Shelter 7336
			above 2: **HANK WILSON**	
4/20/74	**73**	5	5 If I Were A Carpenter	Shelter 40210
8/02/75	**14**	19	6 Lady Blue	Shelter 40378
1/03/76	**53**	5	7 Back To The Island	Shelter 40483
6/19/76	**52**	12	8 Rainbow In Your Eyes	Paradise 8208
			LEON & MARY RUSSELL	
			CHARLIE RUSSO	
3/30/63	**92**	5	1 Preacherman [I]	Diamond 131
			BARRY RYAN	
			Born Barry Sapherson on 10/24/48 in Leeds, England.	
12/28/68+	**86**	4	1 Eloise	MGM 14010
			written by twin brother Paul Ryan	
			CHARLIE RYAN & The Timberline Riders	
			Born in Graceville, Minnesota; raised in Montana. Country singer.	
5/09/60	**33**	19	1 Hot Rod Lincoln [S-N]	4 Star 7047
10/17/60	**84**	6	2 Side Car Cycle [S-N]	4 Star 1745

DEBUT DATE	PEAK POS	WKS CHR	ARTIST — Record Title	Label & Number
			BOBBY RYDELL	
			Born Robert Ridarelli on 4/26/42 in Philadelphia. Regular on Paul Whiteman's amateur TV show, 1951-54. Drummer with Rocco & The Saints, which included Frankie Avalon on trumpet in 1956. First recorded for Veko in 1957. Films "Bye Bye Birdie" and "That Lady From Peking". Currently performing in an oldies revue with fellow Philadelphians Frankie Avalon and Fabian.	
6/29/59	**11**	17	1 Kissin' Time	Cameo 167
10/12/59	**6**	17	2 **We Got Love/**	
10/12/59	**46**	6	3 I Dig Girls	Cameo 169
2/01/60	**2**[1]	16	4 **Wild One/**	
2/01/60	**19**	15	5 Little Bitty Girl	Cameo 171
5/09/60	**5**	12	6 **Swingin' School/** from the film "Because They're Young"	
5/09/60	**18**	11	7 Ding-A-Ling	Cameo 175
7/18/60	**4**	15	8 **Volare**	Cameo 179
11/07/60	**14**	11	9 Sway/	
12/05/60	**70**	2	10 Groovy Tonight	Cameo 182
1/23/61	**11**	11	11 Good Time Baby/	
2/13/61	**54**	4	12 Cherie	Cameo 186
5/01/61	**21**	8	13 That Old Black Magic #1 hit in 1943 for Glenn Miller	Cameo 190
7/03/61	**25**	7	14 The Fish	Cameo 192
10/16/61	**21**	9	15 I Wanna Thank You/	
10/09/61	**85**	2	16 The Door To Paradise	Cameo 201
12/11/61	**21**	5	17 Jingle Bell Rock [X] BOBBY RYDELL/CHUBBY CHECKER	Cameo 205
2/17/62	**18**	11	18 I've Got Bonnie/	
2/17/62	**69**	4	19 Lose Her	Cameo 209
6/02/62	**14**	12	20 I'll Never Dance Again	Cameo 217
10/13/62	**10**	11	21 **The Cha-Cha-Cha**	Cameo 228
12/15/62	**92**	2	22 Jingle Bell Rock [X-R] BOBBY RYDELL/CHUBBY CHECKER	Cameo 205
2/09/63	**23**	9	23 Butterfly Baby	Cameo 242
5/11/63	**17**	9	24 Wildwood Days	Cameo 252
9/28/63	**98**	2	25 Let's Make Love Tonight	Cameo 272
11/09/63+	**4**	16	26 **Forget Him**	Cameo 280
3/28/64	**43**	6	27 Make Me Forget	Cameo 309
5/09/64	**80**	6	28 A World Without Love	Cameo 320
12/19/64	**94**	1	29 I Just Can't Say Goodbye	Capitol 5305
2/13/65	**98**	1	30 Diana	Capitol 5352
			JOHN & ANNE RYDER	
10/25/69	**70**	5	1 I Still Believe In Tomorrow	Decca 32506
			MITCH RYDER	
			Born William Levise, Jr. on 2/26/45 in Detroit. White soul rocker. Leader of The Detroit Wheels. Went solo in 1967. Formed new rock group, Detroit, in 1971.	
7/01/67	**41**	6	1 Joy	New Voice 824
9/09/67	**30**	7	2 What Now My Love	DynoVoice 901
10/28/67	**88**	3	3 You Are My Sunshine	New Voice 826
2/03/68	**87**	4	4 (You've Got) Personality & Chantilly Lace all of above produced by Bob Crewe	DynoVoice 905
7/16/83	**87**	4	5 When You Were Mine written by Prince; produced by John Cougar	Riva 213
			MITCH RYDER & THE DETROIT WHEELS	
			Rock quintet from Detroit. Originally known as Billy Lee & The Rivieras. Renamed by their producer Bob Crewe.	
12/11/65+	**10**	12	1 **Jenny Take A Ride!**	New Voice 806
3/05/66	**17**	9	2 Little Latin Lupe Lu	New Voice 808
5/28/66	**62**	5	3 Break Out	New Voice 811
7/30/66	**100**	1	4 Takin' All I Can Get	New Voice 814
10/08/66	**4**	16	5 **Devil With A Blue Dress On & Good Golly Miss Molly**	New Voice 817
2/04/67	**6**	11	6 **Sock It To Me-Baby!**	New Voice 820
4/29/67	**24**	6	7 Too Many Fish In The Sea & Three Little Fishes	New Voice 822

DEBUT DATE	PEAK POS	WKS CHR	ARTIST — Record Title	Label & Number
			JOHN WESLEY RYLES, I	
12/28/68+	**83**	5	1 Kay	Columbia 44682
			S	
			SAD CAFE	
			Manchester, England pop-rock group formed in 1976. Paul Young, lead singer.	
1/13/79	**71**	9	1 Run Home Girl	A&M 2111
8/15/81	**78**	4	2 La-Di-Da	Swan Song 72002
			SADE	
			Born Helen Folasade Adu on 1/16/59 in Nigeria; moved to London at age 4.	
3/02/85	**5**	20	1 **Smooth Operator**	Portrait 04807
6/22/85	**54**	11	2 Your Love Is King	Portrait 05408
11/23/85+	**5**	22	3 **The Sweetest Taboo**	Portrait 05713
3/29/86	**20**	12	4 Never As Good As The First Time	Portrait 05846
			SSGT BARRY SADLER	
			Born in New Mexico in 1941. Staff Sergeant of the U.S. Army Special Forces (aka Green Berets). Served in Vietnam until injuring leg in booby trap.	
2/05/66	**1^{5}**	13	1 ● **The Ballad Of The Green Berets**	RCA 8739
4/23/66	**28**	7	2 The 'A' Team	RCA 8804
			SAFARIS	
			Los Angeles-born pop quartet formed in 1959. Jim Stephens, lead; Richard Clasky, Marvin Rosenberg and Shelly Briar.	
6/06/60	**6**	18	1 **Image Of A Girl**	Eldo 101
10/17/60	**85**	3	2 The Girl With The Story In Her Eyes	Eldo 105
			SAGA	
			Canadian rock quintet: Michael Sadler, lead singer; brothers Jim and Ian Crichton, Jim Gilmour and Steve Negus.	
12/04/82+	**26**	18	1 On The Loose	Portrait 03359
4/02/83	**64**	8	2 Wind Him Up	Portrait 03791
11/26/83	**79**	3	3 The Flyer	Portrait 04178
			CAROLE BAYER SAGER	
			Born on 3/8/47 in New York City. Prolific pop lyricist. Married Burt Bacharach in 1982. Collaborated in writing "A Groovy Kind Of Love", "Midnight Blue", "Nobody Does It Better", "When I Need You" and many others. Wrote lyrics for many film scores.	
10/15/77	**69**	7	1 You're Moving Out Today	Elektra 45422
5/16/81	**30**	13	2 Stronger Than Before	Boardwalk 02054
			SAGITTARIUS	
6/24/67	**70**	5	1 My World Fell Down	Columbia 44163
8/02/69	**86**	2	2 In My Room	Together 105
			SAILCAT	
			Country-rock duo: Court Pickett and John Wyker.	
6/10/72	**12**	15	1 Motorcycle Mama	Elektra 45782
			BUFFY SAINTE-MARIE	
			Born on 2/20/41 of Cree Indian parents on Piapot Reserve, Saskatchewan, Canada. Folk singer/songwriter. Co-writer of "Up Where We Belong".	
11/27/71	**98**	3	1 I'm Gonna Be A Country Girl Again	Vanguard 35143
4/01/72	**38**	8	2 Mister Can't You See	Vanguard 35151
8/19/72	**98**	2	3 He's An Indian Cowboy In The Rodeo	Vanguard 35156
			CRISPIAN ST. PETERS	
			Born on 4/5/44 in Swanley, Kent, England. Pop singer, guitarist.	
6/11/66	**4**	12	1 **The Pied Piper**	Jamie 1320
9/17/66	**57**	7	2 Changes	Jamie 1324
7/01/67	**36**	6	3 You Were On My Mind	Jamie 1310
			KIRBY ST. ROMAIN	
6/15/63	**49**	7	1 Summer's Comin'	Inette 103
			SAINT TROPEZ	
			Disco studio production by W. Michael Lewis and Laurin Rinder.	
4/14/79	**49**	11	1 One More Minute	Butterfly 41080

DEBUT DATE	PEAK POS	WKS CHR	ARTIST — Record Title	Label & Number
			KYU SAKAMOTO	
			Native of Kawasaki, Japan. One of 520 people killed in the crash of the Japan Airlines 747 near Tokyo on 8/12/85 (43).	
5/11/63	**1**[3]	14	1 **Sukiyaki** .... [F]	Capitol 4945
			released in Japan as "Ue O Muite Aruko" (I Look Up When I Walk)	
8/24/63	**58**	6	2 China Nights (Shina No Yoru)............ [F]	Capitol 5016
			SOUPY SALES	
			Born on 1/8/30 in Wake Forest, NC. Slapstick comedian. Own ABC-TV series, 1959-60; syndicated show, 1966-68.	
4/24/65	**76**	6	1 The Mouse	ABC-Para. 10646
			SALSOUL ORCHESTRA	
			Disco orchestra conducted by Philadelphia producer-arranger Vincent Montana, Jr.	
9/13/75	**76**	6	1 Salsoul Hustle .... [I]	Salsoul 2002
1/24/76	**18**	13	2 Tangerine .... [I]	Salsoul 2004
			Jimmy Dorsey's version hit #1 in 1942	
5/29/76	**88**	5	3 You're Just The Right Size............	Salsoul 2007
9/18/76	**30**	14	4 Nice 'N' Naasty............	Salsoul 2011
2/26/77	**99**	1	5 Ritzy Mambo	Salsoul 2018
			SALVAGE	
3/13/71	**54**	7	1 Hot Pants............	Odax 420
			SAMMY SALVO	
			Pop vocalist from Birmingham, Alabama.	
2/10/58	**23**	4	1 Oh Julie............	RCA 7097
			Jockey #23 / Top 100 #78	
			SAM & BILL	
			R&B vocal duo: Sam Gary and Bill Johnson.	
9/18/65	**95**	3	1 For Your Love............	JoDa 100
1/29/66	**98**	1	2 Fly Me To The Moon............	JoDa 104
			SAM & DAVE	
			Samuel Moore (b: 10/12/35, Miami) and David Prater (b: 5/9/37, Ocilla, GA). Moore had been with the Melionaires gospel group, Prater had sung solo, prior to their meeting in Miami in 1961. First recorded for Roulette in 1962. Duo produced by Isaac Hayes and David Porter.	
1/15/66	**90**	2	1 You Don't Know Like I Know............	Stax 180
4/23/66	**21**	13	2 Hold On! I'm A Comin'............	Stax 189
9/10/66	**64**	6	3 Said I Wasn't Gonna Tell Nobody............	Stax 198
12/03/66+	**77**	6	4 You Got Me Hummin'	Stax 204
2/25/67	**42**	8	5 When Something Is Wrong With My Baby............	Stax 210
6/17/67	**56**	7	6 Soothe Me	Stax 218
9/09/67	**2**[3]	15	7● **Soul Man**............	Stax 231
1/27/68	**9**	13	8 **I Thank You**	Stax 242
5/25/68	**48**	8	9 You Don't Know What You Mean To Me............	Atlantic 2517
8/03/68	**54**	6	10 Can't You Find Another Way (Of Doing It)	Atlantic 2540
11/02/68	**73**	3	11 Everybody Got To Believe In Somebody............	Atlantic 2568
12/21/68+	**41**	9	12 Soul Sister, Brown Sugar	Atlantic 2590
3/22/69	**92**	3	13 Born Again............	Atlantic 2608
			1-5, 8-9, 11-13: written by Isaac Hayes & David Porter	
			SAM THE SHAM & THE PHAROAHS	
			Rock & roll group formed in the early 60s featuring lead singer Domingo "Sam" Samudio (b: 1940, Dallas). First recorded for Dingo in 1965. Samudio went solo in 1970. Formed new band in 1974. On soundtrack "The Border" in 1982.	
4/03/65	**2**[2]	18	1● **Wooly Bully**	MGM 13322
7/31/65	**26**	7	2 Ju Ju Hand	MGM 13364
10/09/65	**33**	9	3 Ring Dang Doo	MGM 13397
2/05/66	**82**	5	4 Red Hot	MGM 13452
6/11/66	**2**[2]	14	5● **Lil' Red Riding Hood**	MGM 13506
10/01/66	**22**	8	6 The Hair On My Chinny Chin Chin	MGM 13581
12/24/66+	**27**	8	7 How Do You Catch A Girl............	MGM 13649
3/18/67	**54**	6	8 Oh That's Good, No That's Bad	MGM 13713
6/17/67	**68**	6	9 Black Sheep	MGM 13747
			all of above produced by Stan Kesler	

DEBUT DATE	PEAK POS	WKS CHR	ARTIST — Record Title	Label & Number
			SAN REMO GOLDEN STRINGS	
			Group of master violinists.	
9/11/65	**27**	10	1 Hungry For Love .... [I]	Ric-Tic 104
11/27/65	**89**	4	2 I'm Satisfied .... [I]	Ric-Tic 108
			FELICIA SANDERS	
			Born in New York City; raised in California. Died on 2/7/75. Vocalist on Percy Faith's #1 hit "Song From Moulin Rouge".	
5/28/55	**29**	3	1 Blue Star .... Best Seller #29 theme from the mid-50s "Medic" TV series	Columbia 40508
			THE SANDPEBBLES	
9/09/67	**81**	3	1 Forget It	Calla 134
11/25/67+	**22**	12	2 Love Power	Calla 141
10/19/68	**98**	2	3 Never My Love .... above 3 produced by Teddy Vann	Calla 155
			THE SANDPIPERS	
			Los Angeles-based trio - met in the Mitchell Boys Choir. Jim Brady (b: 8/24/44), Michael Piano (b: 10/26/44) and Richard Shoff (b: 4/30/44).	
7/30/66	**9**	11	1 **Guantanamera** .... [F]	A&M 806
10/22/66	**30**	7	2 Louie, Louie .... [F]	A&M 819
12/20/69+	**17**	20	3 Come Saturday Morning .... from the film "The Sterile Cuckoo"	A&M 1134
12/05/70	**94**	4	4 Free To Carry On	A&M 1227
			EVIE SANDS	
			Born in New York City. Hit the New York charts as a teenage rocker, 1965-68.	
8/16/69	**53**	17	1 Any Way That You Want Me	A&M 1090
3/29/75	**50**	8	2 You Brought The Woman Out Of Me	Haven 7010
8/02/75	**50**	10	3 I Love Makin' Love To You	Haven 7013
			JODIE SANDS	
			Philadelphia pop songstress.	
5/27/57	**15**	18	1 With All My Heart .... Jockey #15 / Top 100 #20 / Best Seller #21	Chancellor 1003
10/27/58	**95**	1	2 Someday (You'll Want Me To Want You)	Chancellor 1023
			TOMMY SANDS	
			Born on 8/27/37 in Chicago. Pop singer and actor. Mother was a vocalist with Art Kassel's band. Married Nancy Sinatra in 1960; divorced in 1965. Film's "Sing Boy Sing", "Mardi Gras", "Babes In Toyland", and "The Longest Day".	
2/23/57	**2**[2]	17	1 **Teen-Age Crush** .... Best Seller #2 / Top 100 #3 / Jockey #4 / Juke Box #7 from the 1957 TV play "The Singing Idol" (starring Sands)	Capitol 3639
4/20/57	**50**	5	2 Ring-A-Ding-A-Ding/	
4/27/57	**62**	7	3 My Love Song	Capitol 3690
5/20/57	**16**	13	4 Goin' Steady/ Jockey #16 / Best Seller #18 / Top 100 #19	
		2	5 Ring My Phone .... Best Seller flip from the Kraft NBC-TV show "Flesh and Blood"	Capitol 3723
2/17/58	**24**	11	6 Sing Boy Sing .... Jockey #24 / Best Seller #46 / Top 100 #46 from the film of the same title	Capitol 3867
5/19/58	**81**	2	7 Teen-Age Doll	Capitol 3953
8/25/58	**50**	11	8 Blue Ribbon Baby .... instrumental backing by The Raiders	Capitol 4036
12/28/58+	**69**	9	9 The Worryin' Kind	Capitol 4082
9/28/59	**51**	5	10 I'll Be Seeing You	Capitol 4259
8/22/60	**73**	4	11 The Old Oaken Bucket .... hip version of a tune written in 1843	Capitol 4405
			THE SANFORD/TOWNSEND BAND	
			Los Angeles-based rock band led by Ed Sanford and John Townsend.	
6/18/77	**9**	18	1 **Smoke From A Distant Fire**	Warner 8370
			SAMANTHA SANG	
			Born Cheryl Gray on 8/5/53 in Melbourne, Australia. Began career on Melbourne radio at age 8.	
11/19/77+	**3**	27	1 ▲ **Emotion** .... backing vocal by Barry Gibb - written by Barry & Robin Gibb	Private S. 45178

DEBUT DATE	PEAK POS	WKS CHR	ARTIST — Record Title	Label & Number
			SAMANTHA SANG — Cont'd	
5/06/78	**56**	7	2 You Keep Me Dancing	Private S. 45188
7/28/79	**88**	2	3 In The Midnight Hour	United Art. 1313
			BILLIE SANS	
9/11/71	**91**	4	1 Solo	Invictus 9102
			SANTA ESMERALDA	
			Spanish-flavored disco studio project produced by Nicolas Skorsky and Jean-Manuel De Scarano.	
11/05/77+	**15**	19	1 Don't Let Me Be Misunderstood	Casablanca 902
			vocals: Leroy Gomez	
4/01/78	**78**	3	2 The House Of The Rising Sun	Casablanca 913
			vocals: Jimmy Goings	
			MONGO SANTAMARIA	
			Cuban-born bandleader and conga, bongo and percussion player. Member of bands led by Perez Prado, Tito Puente and Cal Tjader.	
3/16/63	**10**	11	1 **Watermelon Man** [I]	Battle 45909
6/22/63	**92**	1	2 Yeh-Yeh! [I]	Battle 45917
3/06/65	**97**	3	3 El Pussy Cat [I]	Columbia 43171
2/01/69	**32**	8	4 Cloud Nine [I]	Columbia 44740
11/29/69	**96**	2	5 Feeling Alright [I]	Atlantic 2689
			SANTANA	
			Latin-rock group formed in San Francisco in 1966. Consisted of Carlos Santana (b: 7/20/47, Autlan de Navarro, Mexico), vocals, guitar; Gregg Rolie, keyboards; and David Brown, bass. Added percussionists Michael Carabello, Jose Chepitos Areas and Michael Shrieve in 1969. Worked Fillmore West and Woodstock in 1969. Neal Schon, guitar, added in 1971. Santana began solo work in 1972. Schon and Rolie formed Journey.	
10/25/69	**56**	8	1 Jingo [I]	Columbia 45010
1/24/70	**9**	13	2 **Evil Ways**	Columbia 45069
11/14/70+	**4**	13	3 **Black Magic Woman**	Columbia 45270
2/20/71	**13**	10	4 Oye Como Va [F]	Columbia 45330
10/16/71	**12**	10	5 Everybody's Everything	Columbia 45472
2/12/72	**36**	9	6 No One To Depend On	Columbia 45552
9/09/72	**84**	5	7 Evil Ways/	
		1	8 Them Changes	Columbia 45666
			above 2: CARLOS SANTANA & BUDDY MILES	
5/22/76	**77**	3	9 Let It Shine	Columbia 10336
10/08/77	**27**	14	10 She's Not There	Columbia 10616
11/11/78	**69**	8	11 Well All Right	Columbia 10839
1/06/79	**32**	10	12 Stormy	Columbia 10873
4/14/79	**59**	8	13 One Chain (Don't Make No Prison)	Columbia 10938
11/24/79+	**35**	13	14 You Know That I Love You	Columbia 11144
4/11/81	**17**	18	15 Winning	Columbia 01050
8/01/81	**56**	8	16 The Sensitive Kind	Columbia 02178
8/14/82	**15**	14	17 Hold On	Columbia 03160
11/27/82	**66**	8	18 Nowhere To Run	Columbia 03376
2/23/85	**46**	11	19 Say It Again	Columbia 04758
			SANTO & JOHNNY	
			Brooklyn-born guitar duo: Santo Farina (b: 10/24/37) on steel guitar, and his brother Johnny (b: 4/30/41) on rhythm guitar.	
7/27/59	**1**[2]	18	1 **Sleep Walk** [I]	Canadian A. 103
11/30/59	**23**	11	2 Tear Drop [I]	Canadian A. 107
3/14/60	**48**	8	3 Caravan [I]	Canadian A. 111
			#4 hit for Duke Ellington in 1937	
12/19/60	**49**	3	4 Twistin' Bells [I-X]	Canadian A. 120
			twist rock version of "Jingle Bells"	
4/17/61	**90**	2	5 Hop Scotch [I]	Canadian A. 124
			1-2, 4-5: written by Santo, Johnny and sister Ann Farina	
1/18/64	**58**	7	6 I'll Remember (In The Still Of The Night) [I]	Canadian A. 164
			LARRY SANTOS	
			Born on 6/2/41 in Oneonto, New York.	
2/14/76	**36**	10	1 We Can't Hide It Anymore	Casablanca 844

DEBUT DATE	PEAK POS	WKS CHR	ARTIST — Record Title	Label & Number
			THE SAPHIRES	
			Philadelphia R&B trio: Carol Jackson (lead singer), George Gainer & Joe Livingston.	
1/11/64	**25**	12	1 Who Do You Love	Swan 4162
5/01/65	**77**	5	2 Gotta Have Your Love	ABC-Para. 10639
			SAVERIO SARIDIS	
			Born on 6/16/33 in Brooklyn. Worked as a New York City policeman.	
1/27/62	**86**	5	1 Love Is The Sweetest Thing	Warner 5243
			#1 hit for 5 weeks in 1933 for Ray Noble	
			PETER SARSTEDT	
			British singer.	
4/05/69	**70**	6	1 Where Do You Go To (My Lovely)	World Pac. 77911
			THE SATISFACTIONS	
6/20/70	**96**	3	1 This Bitter Earth	Lionel 3201
10/31/70	**94**	2	2 One Light Two Lights	Lionel 3205
			CARLO SAVINA - see NINO ROTA	
			SAVOY BROWN	
			British blues-rock band led by guitarist Kim Simmonds. Many personnel changes.	
11/29/69	**74**	5	1 I'm Tired	Parrot 40042
11/06/71	**83**	6	2 Tell Mama	Parrot 40066
10/10/81	**68**	5	3 Run To Me	Town House 1055
			RONNIE SAVOY	
			Born Eugene Hamilton on 10/10/39 in Detroit.	
1/09/61	**84**	2	1 And The Heavens Cried	MGM 12950
			RAY SAWYER	
			Born on 2/1/37 in Chickasaw, Alabama. Eye-patched co-lead singer of Dr. Hook.	
11/06/76	**81**	3	1 (One More Year Of) Daddy's Little Girl	Capitol 4344
			LEO SAYER	
			Born Gerard Sayer on 5/21/48 in Shoreham, England. With Patches in early 70s. Songwriting team with David Courtney, 1972-75. Own TV show in England, early 80s.	
2/22/75	**9**	15	1 **Long Tall Glasses (I Can Dance)**	Warner 8043
6/28/75	**96**	1	2 One Man Band	Warner 8097
10/23/76+	**1**[1]	21	3● **You Make Me Feel Like Dancing**	Warner 8283
2/26/77	**1**[1]	20	4● **When I Need You**	Warner 8332
7/09/77	**17**	15	5 How Much Love	Warner 8319
10/08/77	**38**	9	6 Thunder In My Heart	Warner 8465
12/10/77+	**36**	10	7 Easy To Love	Warner 8502
9/30/78	**47**	7	8 Raining In My Heart	Warner 8682
			3-8: produced by Richard Perry	
9/27/80	**2**[5]	23	9● **More Than I Can Say**	Warner 49565
1/24/81	**23**	12	10 Living In A Fantasy	Warner 49657
			THE SCAFFOLD	
			British pop/rock trio featuring Mike McGear (Paul McCartney's brother).	
2/10/68	**69**	5	1 Thank U Very Much	Bell 701
			BOZ SCAGGS	
			Born: William Royce Scaggs on 6/8/44 in Ohio. Raised in Texas. Joined Steve Miller's band, The Marksmen, in 1959. Joined R&B band, The Wigs, in 1963. To Europe in 1964, toured as a folksinger. Rejoined Miller in 1967, solo since 1969.	
4/17/71	**61**	6	1 We Were Always Sweethearts	Columbia 45353
7/03/71	**96**	2	2 Near You	Columbia 45408
9/30/72	**86**	4	3 Dinah Flo	Columbia 45670
4/10/76	**38**	10	4 It's Over	Columbia 10319
7/04/76	**3**	22	5● **Lowdown**	Columbia 10367
11/20/76	**42**	14	6 What Can I Say	Columbia 10440
3/12/77	**11**	17	7 Lido Shuffle	Columbia 10491
10/15/77	**58**	6	8 Hard Times	Columbia 10606
2/04/78	**49**	10	9 Hollywood	Columbia 10679
3/29/80	**15**	14	10 Breakdown Dead Ahead	Columbia 11241
6/14/80	**17**	17	11 JoJo	Columbia 11281
8/23/80	**14**	17	12 Look What You've Done To Me	Columbia 11349

DEBUT DATE	PEAK POS	WKS CHR	ARTIST — Record Title	Label & Number
			BOZ SCAGGS — Cont'd	
11/29/80+	**14**	17	13 Miss Sun	Columbia 11406
			backing vocal: Lisa Dal Bello	
			HARVEY SCALES & THE SEVEN SOUNDS	
			Soul group formed in Milwaukee in 1961. Scales (b: 1941, Memphis), lead singer.	
10/14/67	**79**	6	1 Get Down	Magic Touch 2007
			SCANDAL	
			New York-based rock band led by Patty Smyth and Zack Smith.	
11/13/82	**65**	11	1 Goodbye To You	Columbia 03234
4/02/83	**59**	13	2 Love's Got A Line On You	Columbia 03615
6/30/84	**7**	21	3 **The Warrior**	Columbia 04424
10/20/84	**41**	13	4 Hands Tied	Columbia 04650
1/26/85	**41**	14	5 Beat Of A Heart	Columbia 04750
			above 3 shown as: **SCANDAL Featuring PATTY SMYTH**	
			JOEY SCARBURY	
			Born on 6/7/55 in Ontario, CA. Session singer for producer Mike Post and others.	
1/16/71	**73**	4	1 Mixed Up Guy	Lionel 3208
5/09/81	**2**[2]	26	2● **Theme From "Greatest American Hero" (Believe It or Not)**	Elektra 47147
			from the TV series of the same title	
10/10/81	**49**	9	3 When She Dances	Elektra 47201
			LALO SCHIFRIN	
			Argentinian pianist/conductor/composer.	
1/06/68	**41**	14	1 Mission-Impossible [I]	Dot 17059
			from the TV series of the same title	
			PETER SCHILLING	
			Born on 1/28/56 in Stuttgart, Germany. Pop singer/songwriter.	
9/24/83	**14**	22	1 Major Tom (Coming Home)	Elektra 69811
			TIMOTHY B. SCHMIT	
			Born on 10/30/47 in Sacramento. Member of Poco, 1970-77, and the Eagles, 1977-82.	
10/02/82	**59**	8	1 So Much In Love	Full Moon 69939
			from the film "Fast Times At Ridgemont High"	
			JOHN SCHNEIDER	
			Born in Mt. Kisco, New York in 1955. Country singer, actor. Bo Duke of TV's "The Dukes Of Hazzard".	
5/30/81	**14**	19	1 It's Now Or Never	Scotti Br. 02105
9/26/81	**69**	5	2 Still	Scotti Br. 02489
5/15/82	**45**	8	3 Dreamin'	Scotti Br. 02889
8/14/82	**72**	6	4 In The Driver's Seat	Scotti Br. 03062
			THE SCHOOLBOYS	
			New York City R&B quartet featuring Leslie Martin, lead singer.	
2/16/57	**91**	2	1 Shirley	Okeh 7076
			THE VOICES OF WALTER SCHUMANN	
			A choral group led by Schumann.	
4/09/55	**14**	6	1 The Ballad Of Davy Crockett	RCA 6041
			Jockey #14 / Best Seller #29	
			from the Disneyland TV series of the same title	
			EDDIE SCHWARTZ	
			Canadian singer/songwriter. Wrote Pat Benatar's "Hit Me With Your Best Shot".	
12/12/81+	**28**	15	1 All Our Tomorrows	Atco 7342
3/20/82	**91**	5	2 Over The Line	Atco 7402
			SCORPIONS	
			German heavy-metal rock quintet: Rudolf Schenker (Michael's brother), lead guitar; Klaus Meine, lead singer; Matthias Jabs, guitar; Francis Buchholz, bass; and Herman Rarebell, drums.	
6/19/82	**65**	7	1 No One Like You	Mercury 76153
3/24/84	**25**	16	2 Rock You Like A Hurricane	Mercury 818440
7/07/84	**64**	6	3 Still Loving You	Mercury 880082
			BILLY SCOTT	
1/13/58	**73**	5	1 You're The Greatest	Cameo 121

DEBUT DATE	PEAK POS	WKS CHR	ARTIST — Record Title	Label & Number
			BOBBY SCOTT	
			Born on 1/29/37 in the Bronx, NY. Vocalist, jazz pianist, composer, arranger. Wrote Herb Alpert's hit "Taste Of Honey".	
1/14/56	**13**	13	1 Chain Gang	ABC-Para. 9658
			Jockey #13 / Juke Box #13 / Top 100 #15 / Best Seller #17	
			FREDDIE SCOTT	
			Born on 4/24/33 in Providence, RI. Attended Cooper High School in New York City. Recorded first hit while working as a songwriter for Columbia Music.	
7/27/63	**10**	12	1 **Hey, Girl**	Colpix 692
11/02/63	**48**	7	2 I Got A Woman	Colpix 709
3/14/64	**82**	7	3 Where Does Love Go	Colpix 724
12/24/66+	**39**	12	4 Are You Lonely For Me	Shout 207
3/25/67	**70**	5	5 Cry To Me	Shout 211
5/13/67	**71**	5	6 Am I Grooving You	Shout 212
11/11/67	**100**	1	7 He Ain't Give You None	Shout 220
			JACK SCOTT	
			Born Jack Scafone, Jr. on 1/24/36 in Windsor, Canada. Rock and roll/ballad singer, songwriter, guitarist. Moved to Hazel Park, Michigan in 1946. First recorded for ABC-Paramount in 1957. Backing vocal group: The Chantones. Still active into the 80s in Detroit area.	
6/09/58	**25**	13	1 Leroy/	
6/30/58	**3**	19	2 **My True Love**	Carlton 462
			Hot 100 #3 / Best Seller #7 / Jockey #13 end	
9/29/58	**28**	10	3 With Your Love/	
10/13/58	**96**	1	4 Geraldine	Carlton 483
12/15/58+	**8**	16	5 **Goodbye Baby/**	
12/28/58+	**73**	3	6 Save My Soul	Carlton 493
4/06/59	**78**	4	7 I Never Felt Like This	Carlton 504
6/29/59	**35**	14	8 The Way I Walk	Carlton 514
10/12/59	**71**	5	9 There Comes A Time	Carlton 519
1/11/60	**5**	16	10 **What In The World's Come Over You**	Top Rank 2028
4/18/60	**3**	17	11 **Burning Bridges/**	
5/02/60	**34**	7	12 Oh, Little One	Top Rank 2041
8/01/60	**38**	9	13 It Only Happened Yesterday/	
7/25/60	**85**	3	14 Cool Water	Top Rank 2055
			western tune written in 1936 by Bob Nolan (Sons of The Pioneers)	
10/17/60	**65**	4	15 Patsy	Top Rank 2075
1/09/61	**89**	1	16 Is There Something On Your Mind	Top Rank 2093
5/29/61	**91**	2	17 A Little Feeling (Called Love)	Capitol 4554
8/28/61	**83**	4	18 My Dream Come True	Capitol 4597
11/06/61	**86**	3	19 Steps 1 And 2	Capitol 4637
			all of above (except #11, 14 & 15) written by Jack Scott	
			JUDY SCOTT	
5/20/57	**76**	1	1 With All My Heart	Decca 30324
			LINDA SCOTT	
			Born Linda Joy Sampson on 6/1/45 in Queens, NY. Moved to Teaneck, NJ at age 11.	
3/13/61	**3**	14	1 **I've Told Every Little Star**	Canadian A. 123
			from the 1932 stage production "Music In The Air"	
7/03/61	**9**	14	2 **Don't Bet Money Honey/**	
7/17/61	**44**	7	3 Starlight, Starbright	Canadian A. 127
10/30/61	**12**	14	4 I Don't Know Why/	
			#2 hit for Wayne King in 1931	
11/13/61	**50**	8	5 It's All Because	Canadian A. 129
2/10/62	**60**	7	6 Yessiree	Congress 101
2/10/62	**70**	6	7 Bermuda	Canadian A. 134
4/07/62	**41**	10	8 Count Every Star	Canadian A. 133
			3 versions of this tune made the Top 10 in 1950	
6/16/62	**56**	9	9 Never In A Million Years	Congress 103
			#2 hit for Bing Crosby in 1937	
9/22/62	**74**	8	10 I Left My Heart In The Balcony	Congress 106
			with the Hutch Davie Orchestra on all of above	
1/25/64	**100**	1	11 Who's Been Sleeping In My Bed?	Congress 204
			inspired by the film of the same title	

DEBUT DATE	PEAK POS	WKS CHR	ARTIST — Record Title	Label & Number
			MARILYN SCOTT	
12/10/77+	**61**	9	1 God Only Knows	Big Tree 16105
			NEIL SCOTT	
			Scott is actually record mogul Neil Bogart. Born on 2/3/42 in Brooklyn; died on 5/10/82. Pop singer turned producer and promotion man for Cameo/Parkway. President of Buddah; formed Casablanca in 1974; formed Boardwalk in 1980.	
6/12/61	**58**	8	1 Bobby	Portrait 102
			PEGGY SCOTT & JO JO BENSON	
			Soul duo - Jo Jo formerly sang with Chuck Willis & The Blue Notes.	
6/08/68	**31**	12	1 Lover's Holiday	SSS Int'l. 736
10/19/68	**27**	10	2 Pickin' Wild Mountain Berries	SSS Int'l. 748
2/01/69	**37**	6	3 Soul Shake	SSS Int'l. 761
5/03/69	**81**	4	4 I Want To Love You Baby	SSS Int'l. 769
			TOM SCOTT	
			Born on 5/19/48 in Los Angeles. Pop-jazz-fusion saxophonist. Session work for Joni Mitchell, Steely Dan, Carole King and others. Composer of films and TV scores.	
3/06/76	**80**	3	1 Uptown & Country [I]	Ode 66118
			TONY SCOTTI - see HEAVEN BOUND	
			SCRITTI POLITTI	
			British trio: Green Gartside, David Gamson and Fred Maher. Italian name means 'political writing'.	
9/07/85	**11**	25	1 Perfect Way	Warner 28949
2/08/86	**91**	4	2 Wood Beez (pray like aretha franklin)	Warner 28811
			SEA LEVEL	
			Jazzy blues-rock 7-man band formed by 3 members of The Allman Brothers Band.	
2/25/78	**50**	10	1 That's Your Secret	Capricorn 0287
			SEATRAIN	
			Fusion-rock band formed by 2 members of the Blues Project.	
4/03/71	**49**	12	1 13 Questions	Capitol 3067
			JOHNNY SEA	
			Born on 7/15/40 in Atlanta, Georgia. Country singer, guitarist.	
6/11/66	**35**	6	1 Day For Decision [S] patriotic answer to "Eve Of Destruction"	Warner 5820
			SEALS & CROFTS	
			Pop duo: Jim Seals (b: 10/17/41, Sidney, TX), guitar, fiddle, saxophone; and Dash Crofts (b: 8/14/40, Cisco, TX), drums, mandolin, keyboards, guitar. With Dean Beard, recorded for Edmoral and Atlantic in 1957. To Los Angeles in 1958. With the Champs from 1958-65. Own group, the Dawnbreakers, late 60s. Entire band converted to Baha'i faith in 1969.	
9/09/72	**6**	18	1 **Summer Breeze**	Warner 7606
1/20/73	**20**	13	2 Hummingbird	Warner 7671
5/12/73	**6**	18	3 **Diamond Girl**	Warner 7708
9/22/73	**21**	12	4 We May Never Pass This Way (Again)	Warner 7740
3/02/74	**66**	8	5 Unborn Child	Warner 7771
5/25/74	**60**	6	6 King Of Nothing	Warner 7810
4/05/75	**18**	15	7 I'll Play For You	Warner 8075
4/17/76	**6**	26	8 **Get Closer** featuring Carolyn Willis (Honey Cone/Bob B. Soxx & The Blue Jeans)	Warner 8190
11/20/76	**58**	7	9 Baby, I'll Give It To You	Warner 8277
9/03/77	**28**	15	10 My Fair Share Love Theme from the film "One On One"	Warner 8405
4/15/78	**18**	16	11 You're The Love	Warner 8551
9/02/78	**79**	3	12 Takin' It Easy all of above produced by Louie Shelton	Warner 8639
			DAN SEALS	
			Born on 2/8/50 in Texas. Half of the duo England Dan & John Ford Coley, and brother of Jim Seals of Seals & Crofts. Currently a hot Country artist.	
8/16/80	**57**	6	1 Late At Night ENGLAND DAN SEALS	Atlantic 3674
1/25/86	**42**	15	2 Bop	EMI America 8289

DEBUT DATE	PEAK POS	WKS CHR	ARTIST — Record Title	Label & Number
			THE SEARCHERS	
			Liverpool, England rock quartet formed in 1960: Mike Pender and John McNally (vocals, guitars), Tony Jackson (vocals, bass) and Chris Curtis (drums). Worked as back-up band for Johnny Sandon, toured England, worked Star Club in Hamburg, Germany. Left Sandon in 1962. Jackson replaced by Frank Allen in 1965. Curtis replaced by Billy Adamson in 1969. Active into the 80s.	
3/07/64	**13**	10	1 Needles And Pins	Kapp 577
4/18/64	**61**	6	2 Ain't That Just Like Me	Kapp 584
5/02/64	**44**	8	3 Sugar And Spice	Liberty 55689
5/30/64	**16**	11	4 Don't Throw Your Love Away	Kapp 593
8/15/64	**34**	8	5 Some Day We're Gonna Love Again	Kapp 609
10/17/64	**35**	7	6 When You Walk In The Room	Kapp 618
11/28/64+	**3**	14	7 **Love Potion Number Nine**	Kapp 27
1/30/65	**29**	7	8 What Have They Done To The Rain	Kapp 644
3/20/65	**21**	8	9 Bumble Bee	Kapp 49
4/03/65	**52**	7	10 Goodbye My Lover Goodbye	Kapp 658
7/31/65	**79**	3	11 He's Got No Love	Kapp 686
1/29/66	**76**	7	12 Take Me For What I'm Worth	Kapp 729
11/26/66	**94**	3	13 Have You Ever Loved Somebody	Kapp 783
9/04/71	**94**	2	14 Desdemona	RCA 0484
			JOHN SEBASTIAN	
			Born on 3/17/44 in New York City. Lead singer of The Lovin' Spoonful.	
1/04/69	**84**	4	1 She's A Lady	Kama Sutra 254
3/27/76	**1**[1]	14	2 ● **Welcome Back** from the ABC-TV series "Welcome Back Kotter"	Reprise 1349
7/31/76	**95**	2	3 Hideaway	Reprise 1355
			SECRET TIES	
			Trio from San Diego dance clubs.	
12/13/86	**91**	5	1 Dancin In My Sleep	Night Wave 9201
			THE SECRETS	
			Cleveland female quartet: Kragen Gray, Josie Allen, Carole Raymont and Pat Miller.	
11/09/63	**18**	10	1 The Boy Next Door	Philips 40146
			NEIL SEDAKA	
			Born on 3/13/39 in Brooklyn. Pop singer, songwriter, pianist. Studied piano since elementary school. Formed songwriting team with lyricist Howard Greenfield while attending Lincoln High School (partnership lasted over 20 years). Recorded with The Tokens on Melba in 1956. Attended Juilliard School for classical piano. Prolific hit songwriter. Career revived in 1974 after signing with Elton John's new Rocket label.	
12/08/58+	**14**	15	1 The Diary	RCA 7408
3/09/59	**42**	8	2 I Go Ape	RCA 7473
10/12/59	**9**	18	3 **Oh! Carol** written for singer, songwriter Carole King	RCA 7595
3/28/60	**9**	15	4 **Stairway To Heaven**	RCA 7709
8/08/60	**17**	13	5 You Mean Everything To Me/	
8/08/60	**28**	11	6 Run Samson Run	RCA 7781
12/19/60+	**4**	15	7 **Calendar Girl**	RCA 7829
5/01/61	**11**	9	8 Little Devil	RCA 7874
8/28/61	**59**	7	9 Sweet Little You	RCA 7922
11/13/61+	**6**	14	10 **Happy Birthday, Sweet Sixteen**	RCA 7957
3/31/62	**45**	9	11 King Of Clowns	RCA 8007
6/30/62	**1**[2]	14	12 **Breaking Up Is Hard To Do**	RCA 8046
10/06/62	**5**	11	13 **Next Door To An Angel**	RCA 8086
2/02/63	**17**	10	14 Alice In Wonderland	RCA 8137
4/27/63	**26**	9	15 Let's Go Steady Again	RCA 8169
7/27/63	**47**	7	16 The Dreamer	RCA 8209
11/16/63	**33**	8	17 Bad Girl all of above produced by Al Nevins and Don Kirshner	RCA 8254
7/25/64	**86**	3	18 Sunny	RCA 8382
8/28/65	**76**	9	19 The World Through A Tear	RCA 8637
2/05/66	**89**	4	20 The Answer To My Prayer	RCA 8737
10/19/74+	**1**[1]	20	21 **Laughter In The Rain**	Rocket 40313
3/29/75	**22**	10	22 The Immigrant	Rocket 40370
6/28/75	**27**	10	23 That's When The Music Takes Me	Rocket 40426

DEBUT DATE	PEAK POS	WKS CHR	ARTIST — Record Title	Label & Number
			NEIL SEDAKA — Cont'd	
9/13/75	**1^{3}**	14	24 ● **Bad Blood**	Rocket 40460
			background vocals by Elton John	
12/13/75+	**8**	14	25 **Breaking Up Is Hard To Do**	Rocket 40500
			slow version of Neil's 1962 hit	
4/10/76	**16**	11	26 Love In The Shadows	Rocket 40543
6/26/76	**36**	9	27 Steppin' Out	Rocket 40582
9/25/76	**53**	5	28 You Gotta Make Your Own Sunshine	Rocket 40614
5/28/77	**44**	7	29 Amarillo	Elektra 45406
			1-8, 10-15, 17-18, 25, 28-29: written by Sedaka & Greenfield	
3/29/80	**19**	19	30 Should've Never Let You Go	Elektra 46615
			NEIL SEDAKA & DARA SEDAKA (Neil's daughter)	
			21-22, 24, 26-27 & 30: written by Sedaka & Phil Cody	
			THE SEEDS	
			Los Angeles garage-rock quartet: Sky Saxon (b: Richard Marsh), lead singer, bass; Jan Savage, guitar, Rick Aldridge, drums and Daryl Hooper, keyboards.	
12/24/66+	**36**	11	1 Pushin' Too Hard	GNP Crescendo 372
3/11/67	**86**	2	2 Mr. Farmer	GNP Crescendo 383
4/29/67	**41**	7	3 Can't Seem To Make You Mine	GNP Crescendo 354
7/15/67	**72**	4	4 A Thousand Shadows	GNP Crescendo 394
			PETE SEEGER	
			Born on 5/3/19 in New York City. Legendary folk singer. Member of The Weavers. Wrote "If I Had A Hammer" (with Lee Hays) and "Where Have All The Flowers Gone".	
1/11/64	**70**	8	1 Little Boxes [N]	Columbia 42940
			THE SEEKERS	
			Pop/folk Australian-born quartet: Judith Durham (b: 7/3/43), lead singer; Keith Potger, guitar; Bruce Woodley, Spanish guitar; and Athol Guy, standup bass. Potger formed the New Seekers in 1970.	
3/27/65	**4**	13	1 **I'll Never Find Another You**	Capitol 5383
5/29/65	**19**	10	2 A World Of Our Own	Capitol 5430
12/03/66+	**2^{2}**	16	3 ● **Georgy Girl**	Capitol 5756
			from the film of the same title	
2/18/67	**44**	7	4 Morningtown Ride	Capitol 5787
			JEANNIE SEELY	
			Born on 7/6/40 in Titusville, Pennsylvania. Country singer, songwriter. Married to Country star Hank Cochran, who wrote many of her Country hits.	
5/28/66	**85**	5	1 Don't Touch Me	Monument 933
			BOB SEGER	
			Born on 5/6/45 in Ann Arbor, Michigan; raised in Detroit. Rock singer, songwriter, guitarist. First recorded in 1966, formed the System in 1968. Left music to attend college in 1969, returned in 1971. Formed own backing group, The Silver Bullet Band in 1976: Alto Reed (horns), Robyn Robbins (keyboards), Drew Abbott (guitar), Chris Campbell (bass) and Charlie Allen Martin (drums). Campbell is the only remaining original member.	
			BOB SEGER SYSTEM:	
12/21/68+	**17**	14	1 Ramblin' Gamblin' Man	Capitol 2297
5/10/69	**97**	1	2 Ivory	Capitol 2480
4/04/70	**84**	6	3 Lucifer	Capitol 2748
			BOB SEGER:	
11/20/71	**96**	2	4 Lookin' Back	Capitol 3187
7/01/72	**76**	9	5 If I Were A Carpenter	Palladium 1079
7/27/74	**80**	4	6 Get Out Of Denver	Palladium 1205
8/09/75	**43**	11	7 Katmandu	Capitol 4116
6/05/76	**69**	4	8 Nutbush City Limits	Capitol 4269
12/11/76+	**4**	21	9 **Night Moves**	Capitol 4369
4/23/77	**24**	10	10 Mainstreet	Capitol 4422
7/09/77	**41**	8	11 Rock And Roll Never Forgets	Capitol 4449
			BOB SEGER & The Silver Bullet Band:	
5/13/78	**4**	18	12 **Still The Same**	Capitol 4581
8/12/78	**12**	13	13 Hollywood Nights	Capitol 4618
10/28/78+	**13**	17	14 We've Got Tonite	Capitol 4653
4/07/79	**28**	11	15 Old Time Rock & Roll	Capitol 4702
			BOB SEGER:	

DEBUT DATE	PEAK POS	WKS CHR	ARTIST — Record Title	Label & Number
			BOB SEGER — Cont'd	
2/23/80	**6**	16	16 **Fire Lake**	Capitol 4836
5/03/80	**5**	17	17 **Against The Wind**	Capitol 4863
7/26/80	**14**	16	18 You'll Accomp'ny Me	Capitol 4904
11/08/80	**42**	12	19 The Horizontal Bop	Capitol 4951
9/12/81	**5**	19	20 **Tryin' To Live My Life Without You**	Capitol 5042
			BOB SEGER & The Silver Bullet Band:	
12/19/81+	**48**	8	21 Feel Like A Number	Capitol 5077
12/18/82+	**2**[4]	21	22 **Shame On The Moon**	Capitol 5187
3/12/83	**12**	12	23 Even Now	Capitol 5213
5/28/83	**27**	10	24 Roll Me Away	Capitol 5235
9/17/83	**48**	11	25 Old Time Rock & Roll [R] featured in the film "Risky Business"	Capitol 5276
11/10/84+	**17**	15	26 Understanding from the film "Teachers"	Capitol 5413
3/15/86	**13**	14	27 American Storm	Capitol 5532
5/24/86	**12**	13	28 Like A Rock	Capitol 5592
8/16/86	**52**	9	29 It's You	Capitol 5623
11/15/86	**70**	9	30 Miami	Capitol 5658
			RONNIE SELF Born in 1939 in Tin Town, Missouri; died on 8/28/81. Rockabilly singer, songwriter, guitarist. Wrote Brenda Lee's "I'm Sorry" and "Sweet Nothin's".	
3/10/58	**63**	7	1 Bop-A-Lena	Columbia 41101
			MARILYN SELLARS Country singer from Northfield, Minnesota.	
8/24/74	**37**	10	1 One Day At A Time	Mega 1205
			MICHAEL SEMBELLO Born on 4/17/54 in Philadelphia. Session guitarist/producer/composer/arranger/ vocalist. Guitarist on Stevie Wonder's albums from 1974-79.	
6/04/83	**1**[2]	22	1 **Maniac** from the film "Flashdance"	Casablanca 812516
9/24/83	**34**	10	2 Automatic Man	Warner 29485
			SENATOR BOBBY Senator Bobby is Bill Minkin of a comedy troupe called The Hardly-Worthit Players. Another of the members is talk show host Dennis Wholey.	
1/07/67	**20**	7	1 Wild Thing [C]	Parkway 127
3/11/67	**99**	1	2 Mellow Yellow [C] **SENATOR BOBBY & SENATOR McKINLEY**	Parkway 137
			THE SENSATIONS Philadelphia R&B quartet: Yvonne Baker (lead), Sam Armstrong (baritone), Richard Curtain (tenor) and Alphonso Howell (bass).	
8/14/61	**54**	8	1 Music, Music, Music	Argo 5391
1/06/62	**4**	18	2 **Let Me In**	Argo 5405
4/28/62	**69**	6	3 That's My Desire **YVONNE BAKER & THE SENSATIONS**	Argo 5412
			THE SERENDIPITY SINGERS Pop/folk group organized at the University of Colorado.	
2/29/64	**6**	14	1 **Don't Let The Rain Come Down (Crooked Little Man)**	Philips 40175
5/23/64	**30**	8	2 Beans In My Ears [N]	Philips 40198
			707 Detroit-bred rock group.	
10/11/80	**52**	9	1 I Could Be Good For You	Casablanca 2280
7/10/82	**62**	6	2 Mega Force	Boardwalk 146
			DAVID SEVILLE Born Ross Bagdasarian on 1/27/19 in Fresno, CA; died on 1/16/72. To Los Angeles in 1950. Appeared in the films "Viva Zapata", "Stalag 17", and "Rear Window". Wrote "Come On-a My House". Creator of The Chipmunks. Also see Alfi & Harry.	
12/15/56+	**42**	8	1 Armen's Theme [I] named for Seville's wife, Armen	Liberty 55041
9/09/57	**77**	4	2 Gotta Get To Your House [N]	Liberty 55079
4/14/58	**1**[3]	19	3 **Witch Doctor** [N] Top 100 #1(3) / Best Seller #1(2) / Jockey #2	Liberty 55132

DEBUT DATE	PEAK POS	WKS CHR	ARTIST — Record Title	Label & Number
			DAVID SEVILLE — Cont'd	
7/07/58	**34**	5	4 The Bird On My Head [N] Best Seller #34 / Top 100 #36	Liberty 55140
8/25/58	**78**	2	5 Little Brass Band	Liberty 55153
5/18/59	**86**	1	6 Judy [I-S]	Liberty 55193
			THE SEVILLES	
1/23/61	**84**	5	1 Charlena	J.C. 116
			CHARLIE SEXTON Austin, Texas rock singer/guitarist.	
12/14/85+	**17**	20	1 Beat's So Lonely	MCA 52715
			PHIL SEYMOUR Vocalist/drummer formerly with the Dwight Twilley Band. Originally from Tulsa, OK.	
1/24/81	**22**	16	1 Precious To Me	Boardwalk 5703
			SHA NA NA Fifties rock & roll specialists led by John "Bowzer" Baumann. Formed at Columbia University in 1969. Own syndicated TV show beginning in 1977. Henry Gross was a member, left in 1970. Many personnel changes.	
8/07/71	**84**	3	1 Top Forty (Of The Lord)	Kama Sutra 528
4/19/75	**55**	10	2 (Just Like) Romeo And Juliet	Kama Sutra 602
			THE SHACKLEFORDS Folk/country singing group put together by producers Lee Hazelwood and Marty Cooper.	
5/11/63	**70**	6	1 A Stranger In Your Town	Mercury 72112
			SHADES OF BLUE	
5/07/66	**12**	12	1 Oh How Happy	Impact 1007
7/30/66	**72**	6	2 Lonely Summer	Impact 1014
10/01/66	**78**	4	3 Happiness	Impact 1015
			THE SHADOWS OF KNIGHT Chicago-area "garage band": Jim Sohns (lead singer), Joe Kelley (lead guitarist), Warren Rogers (bass), Jerry McGeorge (rhythm guitar) and Tom Schiffour (drums).	
3/19/66	**10**	12	1 **Gloria**	Dunwich 116
6/04/66	**39**	6	2 Oh Yeah	Dunwich 122
9/10/66	**91**	2	3 Bad Little Woman	Dunwich 128
12/24/66	**90**	1	4 I'm Gonna Make You Mine	Dunwich 141
10/26/68	**46**	8	5 Shake	Team 520
			BOBBY SHAFTO	
7/18/64	**99**	1	1 She's My Girl	Rust 5082
			SHALAMAR Black vocal trio formed in Los Angeles in 1978: Jody Watley and Jeffrey Daniels (both dancers from TV's "Soul Train") and Howard Hewett. Watley and Daniels replaced by Delisa Davis and Micki Free in 1984.	
3/12/77	**25**	17	1 Uptown Festival Going To A Go-Go/I Can't Help Myself/Uptight (Everything's Alright)/Stop! In The Name Of Love/It's The Same Old Song	Soul Train 10885
1/13/79	**79**	6	2 Take That To The Bank	Solar 11379
12/08/79+	**8**	23	3 ● **The Second Time Around**	Solar 11709
12/20/80+	**55**	12	4 Full Of Fire	Solar 12152
4/25/81	**60**	8	5 Make That Move	Solar 12192
4/10/82	**44**	10	6 A Night To Remember	Solar 48005
6/25/83	**22**	20	7 Dead Giveaway	Solar 69819
3/17/84	**17**	18	8 Dancing In The Sheets from the film "Footloose"	Columbia 04372
11/17/84	**73**	9	9 Amnesia	Solar 69682
			SHANGO	
3/01/69	**57**	7	1 Day After Day (It's Slippin' Away)	A&M 1014
			THE SHANGRI-LAS "Girl group" formed at Andrew Jackson High School in Queens, NY. Consisted of two sets of sisters: Mary (lead singer) & Betty Weiss and twins Mary Ann & Marge Ganser. Marge died several years ago of a drug overdose. Group still performs as a trio.	
8/22/64	**5**	11	1 **Remember (Walkin' In The Sand)**	Red Bird 008
10/10/64	**1**[1]	12	2 **Leader Of The Pack**	Red Bird 014
12/26/64+	**18**	9	3 Give Him A Great Big Kiss	Red Bird 018

DEBUT DATE	PEAK POS	WKS CHR	ARTIST — Record Title	Label & Number
			THE SHANGRI-LAS — Cont'd	
12/26/64+	**91**	2	4 Maybe	Red Bird 019
4/03/65	**53**	6	5 Out In The Streets	Red Bird 025
5/29/65	**29**	8	6 Give Us Your Blessings	Red Bird 030
10/09/65	**99**	2	7 Right Now And Not Later	Red Bird 036
11/06/65	**6**	11	8 **I Can Never Go Home Anymore**	Red Bird 043
2/05/66	**33**	6	9 Long Live Our Love	Red Bird 048
4/09/66	**65**	6	10 He Cried	Red Bird 053
6/25/66	**59**	6	11 Past, Present And Future [S]	Red Bird 068
			all of above (except #1 & 7) produced by George "Shadow" Morton	
			BUD SHANK	
			Born on 5/27/26 in Dayton, Ohio. Jazz-oriented saxophonist. Played with Charlie Barnet, Art Mooney and Stan Kenton from 1947-51. TV and movie studio musician.	
1/22/66	**65**	6	1 Michelle [I]	World Pac. 77814
			SHANNON	
			Shannon is actually British rock singer Marty Wilde.	
7/12/69	**47**	8	1 Abergavenny	Heritage 814
			SHANNON	
			Brenda Shannon Greene from Washington, DC. Began singing career at York University.	
11/12/83+	**8**	24	1 ● **Let The Music Play**	Mirage 99810
3/31/84	**46**	13	2 Give Me Tonight	Mirage 99775
4/06/85	**49**	15	3 Do You Wanna Get Away	Mirage 99655
			DEL SHANNON	
			Born Charles Westover on 12/30/39 in Coopersville, Michigan. With US Army "Get Up And Go" radio show in Germany. Discovered by Ann Arbor deejay/producer Ollie McLaughlin. Formed own label, Berlee, in 1963. Wrote "I Go To Pieces" for Peter & Gordon. To Los Angeles in 1966, production work.	
3/06/61	**1**[4]	17	1 **Runaway**	Big Top 3067
			electric organ (musitron) solo by co-writer Max Crook	
6/05/61	**5**	13	2 **Hats Off To Larry**	Big Top 3075
9/18/61	**28**	10	3 So Long Baby	Big Top 3083
11/27/61+	**38**	8	4 Hey! Little Girl	Big Top 3091
6/30/62	**99**	1	5 Cry Myself To Sleep	Big Top 3112
9/15/62	**64**	5	6 The Swiss Maid	Big Top 3117
12/22/62+	**12**	14	7 Little Town Flirt	Big Top 3131
4/13/63	**50**	9	8 Two Kind Of Teardrops	Big Top 3143
6/29/63	**77**	4	9 From Me To You	Big Top 3152
			written by John Lennon & Paul McCartney	
11/02/63	**71**	7	10 Sue's Gotta Be Mine	Berlee 501
7/04/64	**22**	10	11 Handy Man	Amy 905
9/19/64	**43**	7	12 Do You Want To Dance	Amy 911
11/21/64+	**9**	14	13 **Keep Searchin' (We'll Follow The Sun)**	Amy 915
2/27/65	**30**	6	14 Stranger In Town	Amy 919
5/22/65	**95**	3	15 Break Up	Amy 925
			1-5, 7-8, 10, 13-15: written by Shannon	
5/07/66	**94**	2	16 The Big Hurt	Liberty 55866
12/12/81+	**33**	12	17 Sea Of Love	Network 47951
			produced by Tom Petty	
			HELEN SHAPIRO	
			Born on 9/28/46 in London, England. Pop ballad singer.	
12/04/61	**100**	1	1 Walkin' Back To Happiness	Capitol 4662
			FEARGAL SHARKEY	
			Irish pop/rocker - former member of the Undertones.	
3/15/86	**74**	6	1 A Good Heart	A&M/Virgin 2804
			DEE DEE SHARP	
			Born Dione LaRue on 9/9/45 in Philadelphia. Backing vocalist at Cameo Records in 1961. Married record producer Kenny Gamble in 1967, recorded as Dee Dee Sharp Gamble. Also see Chubby Checker.	
3/03/62	**2**[2]	18	1 **Mashed Potato Time**	Cameo 212
6/16/62	**9**	10	2 **Gravy (For My Mashed Potatoes)**	Cameo 219
10/20/62	**5**	13	3 **Ride!**	Cameo 230
3/02/63	**10**	11	4 **Do The Bird**	Cameo 244
6/29/63	**43**	7	5 Rock Me In The Cradle Of Love	Cameo 260

DEBUT DATE	PEAK POS	WKS CHR	ARTIST — Record Title		Label & Number
			DEE DEE SHARP — Cont'd		
10/05/63	**33**	9	6 Wild!		Cameo 274
2/01/64	**82**	4	7 Where Did I Go Wrong/ 2, 4-7: written by Kal Mann & Dave Appell		
2/29/64	**97**	1	8 Willyam, Willyam		Cameo 296
11/06/65	**78**	7	9 I Really Love You		Cameo 375
			MIKE SHARPE Alto saxophonist.		
1/28/67	**57**	7	1 Spooky	[I]	Liberty 55922
			RAY SHARPE Born on 2/8/38 in Fort Worth, Texas. Pop singer.		
7/20/59	**46**	13	1 Linda Lu guitarists: Duane Eddy and Al Casey		Jamie 1128
			SHARPEES		
1/15/66	**79**	3	1 Tired Of Being Lonely		One-derful! 4839
			BOB SHARPLES Bandleader from Bury, Lancashire, England.		
9/22/56	**52**	15	1 Sadie's Shawl	[I]	London 1661
			GEORGIE SHAW Pop singer styled after Eddie Fisher.		
11/12/55	**23**	12	1 No Arms Can Ever Hold You (Like These Arms Of Mine) Top 100 #23 / Best Seller #25		Decca 29679
1/07/56	**39**	9	2 Go On With The Wedding KITTY KALLEN & GEORGIE SHAW		Decca 29776
4/21/56	**70**	2	3 To You, My Love		Decca 29839
12/01/56	**54**	7	4 A Faded Summer Love vocal backing by The Dave Lambert Singers		Decca 30078
			MARLENA SHAW Born in New Rochelle, New York. Band vocalist with Count Basie from 1967-72.		
3/11/67	**58**	5	1 Mercy, Mercy, Mercy		Cadet 5557
			SANDIE SHAW Born Sandra Goodrich on 2/26/47 in Dagenham, England. Pop songstress.		
11/28/64+	**52**	7	1 (There's) Always Something There To Remind Me		Reprise 0320
3/06/65	**42**	9	2 Girl Don't Come		Reprise 0342
6/12/65	**97**	3	3 Long Live Love		Reprise 0375
			TIMMY SHAW		
1/25/64	**41**	7	1 Gonna Send You Back To Georgia		Wand 146
			TOMMY SHAW Born in Montgomery, Alabama. Lead guitarist of Styx since joining in 1976.		
9/29/84	**33**	12	1 Girls With Guns		A&M 2676
12/15/84+	**60**	9	2 Lonely School		A&M 2696
10/05/85	**81**	5	3 Remo's Theme (What If) from the film "Remo: The Adventure Begins"		A&M 2773
			JULES SHEAR Pittsburgh-bred rock singer. Leader of Jules & The Polar Bears.		
4/06/85	**57**	7	1 Steady		EMI America 8259
			THE SHEEP		
1/29/66	**58**	7	1 Hide & Seek		Boom 60000
			SHEILA Born Anny Chancel in Paris, France in 1946. Performed as Sheila B. Devotion.		
12/05/81+	**49**	9	1 Little Darlin'		Carrere 02564
			SHEILA E. Born Sheila Escovedo on 12/12/59 in San Francisco. R&B vocalist, percussionist. Daughter of percussionist Pete Escovedo.		
6/16/84	**7**	26	1 **The Glamorous Life**		Warner 29285
10/27/84	**34**	15	2 The Belle Of St. Mark		Warner 29180
11/16/85+	**11**	23	3 A Love Bizarre from the film "Krush Groove" - backing vocals: Prince		Paisley P. 28890

DEBUT DATE	PEAK POS	WKS CHR	ARTIST — Record Title	Label & Number
			PETE SHELLEY	
			English - lead singer of the Buzzcocks.	
12/21/74+	**81**	6	1 Gee Baby	Bell 45614
			THE SHELLS	
			Brooklyn R&B quintet: Nathaniel "Little Nate" Bouknight (lead), Gus Geter (baritone), Bobby Nurse and Randy Alston (tenors) and Danny Small (bass).	
12/19/60+	**21**	8	1 Baby Oh Baby	Johnson 104
			ANNE SHELTON	
			British singer.	
9/29/56	**59**	8	1 Lay Down Your Arms	Columbia 40759
			SHEP & THE LIMELITES	
			R&B vocal trio from New York City: James "Shep" Sheppard, lead (formerly with the Heartbeats) and tenors Clarence Bassett and Charles Baskerville (formerly in the Videos).	
3/27/61	**2**[1]	14	1 **Daddy's Home** answer to the Heartbeats "A Thousand Miles Away"	Hull 740
7/10/61	**42**	5	2 Ready For Your Love	Hull 742
10/02/61	**58**	10	3 Three Steps From The Altar	Hull 747
2/17/62	**59**	8	4 Our Anniversary	Hull 748
6/30/62	**94**	2	5 What Did Daddy Do	Hull 751
2/09/63	**91**	1	6 Remember Baby	Hull 756
			JEAN SHEPARD	
			Born on 11/21/33 in Pauls Valley, OK. Country singer - wife of Hawkshaw Hawkins.	
9/15/73	**81**	6	1 Slippin' Away	United Art. 248
			SHEPHERD SISTERS	
9/30/57	**18**	17	1 Alone (Why Must I Be Alone) Best Seller #18 / Top 100 #20 / Jockey #22	Lance 125
3/09/63	**94**	2	2 Don't Mention My Name	Atlantic 2176
			T.G. SHEPPARD	
			Born Bill Browder on 7/20/44 in Humbolt, Tennessee. Country singer.	
1/25/75	**54**	8	1 Devil In The Bottle	Melodyland 6002
5/10/75	**95**	3	2 Tryin' To Beat The Morning Home	Melodyland 6006
7/24/76	**100**	1	3 Solitary Man	Hitsville 6032
3/14/81	**37**	14	4 I Loved 'Em Every One	Warner 49690
1/30/82	**68**	8	5 Only One You	Warner 49858
4/03/82	**58**	8	6 Finally	Warner 50041
2/18/84	**62**	6	7 Make My Day [N] **T.G. SHEPPARD with CLINT EASTWOOD** based on the film "Sudden Impact"	Warner 29343
			SHERBS	
			Australian pop/rock quintet. Daryl Braithwaite, lead singer. Originally known as Sherbet.	
8/21/76	**61**	8	1 Howzat **SHERBET**	MCA 40610
3/07/81	**61**	7	2 I Have The Skill	Atco 7325
			SHERIFF	
			Canadian rock quintet. Freddy Curci, lead singer.	
5/14/83	**61**	7	1 When I'm With You	Capitol 5199
			ALLAN SHERMAN	
			Born on 11/30/24 in Chicago; died on 11/21/73. Began as a professional comedy writer for Jackie Gleason, Joe E. Lewis and others. Creator-producer of TV's "I've Got A Secret".	
8/03/63	**2**[3]	10	1 **Hello Mudduh, Hello Fadduh! (A Letter From Camp)** [C] adaptation of Ponchielli's "Dance Of The Hours"	Warner 5378
7/25/64	**59**	6	2 Hello Mudduh, Hello Fadduh! (A Letter From Camp - 1964) [C]	Warner 5449
3/27/65	**40**	8	3 Crazy Downtown [C] parody of Petula Clark's "Downtown"	Warner 5614
12/18/65	**98**	1	4 The Drinking Man's Diet [C]	Warner 5672

DEBUT DATE	PEAK POS	WKS CHR	ARTIST — Record Title	Label & Number
			BOBBY SHERMAN	
			Born on 7/22/44 in Santa Monica, CA. Regular on TV's "Shindig" and played Jeremy Bolt on TV's "Here Come The Brides". Currently involved in TV production.	
8/23/69	**3**	13	1 ● **Little Woman**	Metromedia 121
11/22/69+	**9**	11	2 ● **La La La (If I Had You)**	Metromedia 150
2/07/70	**9**	14	3 ● **Easy Come, Easy Go**	Metromedia 177
5/16/70	**24**	9	4 Hey, Mister Sun	Metromedia 188
8/01/70	**5**	15	5 ● **Julie, Do Ya Love Me**	Metromedia 194
			above 5 produced by Jackie Mills	
2/13/71	**16**	9	6 Cried Like A Baby	Metromedia 206
5/01/71	**29**	8	7 The Drum	Metromedia 217
8/21/71	**54**	5	8 Waiting At The Bus Stop	Metromedia 222
10/16/71	**60**	7	9 Jennifer	Metromedia 227
2/19/72	**91**	2	10 Together Again	Metromedia 240
			JOE SHERMAN	
			Songwriter, record producer, conductor.	
10/05/63	**85**	2	1 Toys In The Attic	World 1008
			from the film of the same title	
			THE SHERRYS	
			Female R&B group from Philadelphia. Formed by Joe Cook, and included his daughters Dinell and Delphine. Cook had own hit in 1957, "Peanuts", as "Little Joe".	
10/06/62	**35**	8	1 Pop Pop Pop-Pie	Guyden 2068
1/12/63	**97**	1	2 Slop Time	Guyden 2077
			ROBERTA SHERWOOD	
6/09/56	**57**	4	1 Lazy River	Decca 29911
			THE SHIELDS	
			R&B group formed by Jesse Belvin solely to record "You Cheated". Frankie Ervin (lead), Jesse Belvin (falsetto), Johnny Watson, Mel Williams & Charles Wright.	
8/25/58	**12**	16	1 You Cheated	Dot 15805
			Best Seller #12 end / Hot 100 #15	
			THE SHINDOGS	
			House band for the ABC-TV show "Shindig": Delaney Bramlett, Joey Cooper, Chuck Blackwell and James Burton.	
9/03/66	**91**	1	1 Who Do You Think You Are	Viva 601
			produced by Leon Russell	
			THE SHIRELLES	
			R&B "girl group" from Passaic, NJ. Consisted of Shirley Owens Alston (b: 6/10/41), Beverly Lee (b: 8/3/41), Doris Kenner (b: 8/2/41) and Addie "Micki" Harris (b: 1/22/40, d: 6/10/82). Formed in junior high school as the Poquellos. First recorded for Tiara in 1958. Kenner left group in 1968, returned in 1975. Alston left for solo career in 1975.	
4/21/58	**49**	10	1 I Met Him On A Sunday	Decca 30588
			Best Seller #49 / Top 100 #50	
7/13/59	**83**	4	2 Dedicated To The One I Love	Scepter 1203
9/12/60	**39**	12	3 Tonights The Night	Scepter 1208
11/21/60+	**1**[2]	19	4 **Will You Love Me Tomorrow**	Scepter 1211
			first #1 song for writers Carole King & Gerry Goffin	
1/23/61	**3**	16	5 **Dedicated To The One I Love** [R]	Scepter 1203
4/17/61	**4**	11	6 **Mama Said**	Scepter 1217
7/10/61	**41**	8	7 A Thing Of The Past/	
7/17/61	**54**	6	8 What A Sweet Thing That Was	Scepter 1220
10/02/61	**21**	9	9 Big John	Scepter 1223
12/18/61+	**8**	14	10 **Baby It's You**	Scepter 1227
3/24/62	**1**[3]	14	11 **Soldier Boy**	Scepter 1228
6/23/62	**22**	8	12 Welcome Home Baby	Scepter 1234
9/08/62	**36**	8	13 Stop The Music	Scepter 1237
12/01/62+	**19**	12	14 Everybody Loves A Lover	Scepter 1243
3/23/63	**4**	14	15 **Foolish Little Girl/**	
4/13/63	**100**	1	16 Not For All The Money In The World	Scepter 1248
6/15/63	**26**	9	17 Don't Say Goodnight And Mean Goodbye	Scepter 1255
9/07/63	**53**	6	18 What Does A Girl Do?	Scepter 1259
10/19/63	**92**	2	19 It's A Mad, Mad, Mad, Mad World/	
11/02/63	**97**	1	20 31 Flavors	Scepter 1260
			above 2 from the film "It's A Mad, Mad, Mad, Mad World"	

DEBUT DATE	PEAK POS	WKS CHR	ARTIST — Record Title	Label & Number
			THE SHIRELLES — Cont'd	
1/11/64	**57**	5	21 Tonight You're Gonna Fall In Love With Me	Scepter 1264
3/21/64	**69**	4	22 Sha-La-La	Scepter 1267
7/18/64	**63**	7	23 Thank You Baby	Scepter 1278
10/31/64	**88**	2	24 Maybe Tonight	Scepter 1284
12/26/64+	**91**	4	25 Are You Still My Baby	Scepter 1292
8/19/67	**99**	2	26 Last Minute Miracle	Scepter 12198
			SHIRLEY & COMPANY	
			Shirley Goodman (formerly of Shirley & Lee) and a group of studio musicians.	
1/11/75	**12**	16	1 Shame, Shame, Shame male vocal: Jesus Alvarez	Vibration 532
6/14/75	**91**	2	2 Cry Cry Cry above 2 written and produced by Sylvia Robinson (Mickey & Sylvia)	Vibration 535
			SHIRLEY & LEE	
			New Orleans R&B duo formed in the early 50s. Shirley Goodman (b: 6/19/36) and Leonard Lee (b: 6/29/36; d: 10/23/76). First recorded for Aladdin in 1952. Billed as "The Sweethearts Of The Blues", recorded together until 1963.	
8/11/56	**20**	19	1 Let The Good Times Roll Best Seller #20 / Top 100 #27	Aladdin 3325
12/15/56+	**38**	8	2 I Feel Good	Aladdin 3338
6/27/60	**88**	6	3 I've Been Loved Before	Warwick 535
9/05/60	**48**	5	4 Let The Good Times Roll new version of 1956 hit; above 4 written by Lee	Warwick 581
8/07/61	**77**	6	5 Well-A, Well-A	Warwick 664
			SHIRLEY & SQUIRRELY	
7/17/76	**48**	9	1 Hey Shirley (This Is Squirrely) [N]	GRT 054
			DON SHIRLEY	
			Pianist, organist. Born in Kingston, Jamaica on 1/27/27.	
7/17/61	**40**	14	1 Water Boy [I] **DON SHIRLEY TRIO**	Cadence 1392
1/06/62	**100**	1	2 Drown In My Own Tears [I]	Cadence 1408
			THE SHOCKING BLUE	
			Dutch rock quartet: Mariska Veres (lead singer), Robbie van Leeuwen (guitar), Cor van Beek (drums) and Klaasje van der Wal (bass). Disbanded in 1974.	
12/13/69+	**1**[1]	14	1 ● **Venus**	Colossus 108
3/07/70	**43**	7	2 Mighty Joe	Colossus 111
6/06/70	**75**	5	3 Long And Lonesome Road	Colossus 116
			SHOES	
			Rock quartet from Zion, Illinois.	
11/03/79	**75**	5	1 Too Late	Elektra 46557
			TROY SHONDELL	
			Born on 5/14/44 in Fort Wayne, Indiana. Pop/country singer, songwriter.	
9/18/61	**6**	13	1 **This Time**	Liberty 55353
12/25/61+	**77**	6	2 Tears From An Angel/	
1/13/62	**92**	1	3 Island In The Sky	Liberty 55398
			SHOOTING STAR	
			Kansas City-based rock quintet. Van McLain and Gary West, leaders.	
4/12/80	**76**	4	1 You've Got What I Need	Virgin 67005
3/27/82	**70**	5	2 Hollywood	Epic 02755
			DINAH SHORE	
			Born Frances Shore on 3/1/17 in Winchester, Tennessee. One of the most popular female vocalists of the 1940 to mid-50s era. Own TV variety show, 1951-62, and own morning talk show "Dinah's Place", 1970-74. Married to actor George Montgomery from 1943-62.	
5/21/55	**12**	2	1 Whatever Lola Wants (Lola Gets) Jockey #12 / Best Seller #28 from the Broadway musical "Damn Yankees"	RCA 6077
11/12/55	**20**	14	2 Love And Marriage Jockey #20 / Top 100 #42	RCA 6266
2/11/56	**73**	1	3 Stolen Love	RCA 6360
4/28/56	**93**	5	4 I Could Have Danced All Night from the Broadway musical "My Fair Lady"	RCA 6469
2/09/57	**19**	21	5 Chantez-Chantez Jockey #19 / Top 100 #27	RCA 6792

DEBUT DATE	PEAK POS	WKS CHR	ARTIST — Record Title	Label & Number
			DINAH SHORE — Cont'd	
6/17/57	**92**	1	6 The Cattle Call	RCA 6897
9/09/57	**15**	7	7 Fascination Jockey #15 / Top 100 #98 from the film "Love In The Afternoon"	RCA 6980
12/02/57	**24**	1	8 I'll Never Say 'Never Again' Again Jockey #24 #4 hit in 1935 for Ozzie Nelson & His Orchestra	RCA 7056
			MICKEY SHORR & THE CUTUPS	
6/16/62	**60**	5	1 Dr. Ben Basey [N]	Tuba 8001
			GLENN SHORROCK Born on 6/30/44 in England; raised in Elizabeth, Australia. Ex-lead singer of Little River Band.	
9/24/83	**69**	6	1 Don't Girls Get Lonely	Capitol 5267
			SHOT IN THE DARK Al Stewart's backup group. Krysia Kristianne, lead singer.	
4/04/81	**71**	5	1 Playing With Lightning	RSO 1061
			THE SHOW STOPPERS Soul quartet of two sets of brothers from Philadelphia: Laddie and Alec Burke (Solomon's brothers) and Earl (lead singer) and Timmy Smith.	
6/01/68	**87**	5	1 Ain't Nothin' But A House Party	Heritage 800
			THE SHOWMEN R&B group led by General Johnson (Chairmen Of The Board).	
11/13/61+	**61**	12	1 It Will Stand	Minit 632
7/04/64	**80**	3	2 It Will Stand [R]	Imperial 66033
			THE SIDEKICKS	
8/06/66	**55**	9	1 Suspicions	RCA 8864
			BUNNY SIGLER Born Walter Sigler on 2/27/41 in Philadelphia. R&B vocalist, multi-instrumentalist, composer, producer. First recorded for V-Tone in 1959.	
6/24/67	**22**	11	1 Let The Good Times Roll & Feel So Good	Parkway 153
10/14/67	**86**	4	2 Lovey Dovey/You're So Fine	Parkway 6000
2/10/73	**97**	2	3 Tossin' And Turnin'	Phil. Int. 3523
2/25/78	**43**	11	4 Let Me Party With You (Party, Party, Party) - Part 1	Gold Mind 4008
11/04/78	**87**	5	5 Only You LOLEATTA HOLLOWAY & BUNNY SIGLER	Gold Mind 4012
			THE SILENCERS Pittsburgh rock quintet. Frank Czuri, lead singer.	
7/26/80	**81**	5	1 Shiver And Shake	Precision 9800
			THE SILHOUETTES Philadelphia R&B doo-wop group formed as the Tornadoes by William Horton (lead), Richard Lewis, Earl Beal and Raymond Edwards (bass).	
1/20/58	**1**[2]	15	1 **Get A Job** Top 100 #1 / Best Seller #2 / Jockey #3	Ember 1029
			THE SILKIE Folk quartet formed in 1963 at Hull University in Hull, England. Silvia Tatler, lead singer.	
10/16/65	**10**	10	1 **You've Got To Hide Your Love Away** Beatles contributed musical accompaniment & production assistance	Fontana 1525
			THE SILVA-TONES	
12/16/57	**86**	2	1 That's All I Want From You	Argo 5281
			SILVER Country-rock quintet led by John Batdorf of Batdorf & Rodney.	
6/19/76	**16**	21	1 Wham Bam (Shang-A-Lang)	Arista 0189
			SILVER CONDOR Rock quintet led by Joe Cerisano and Earl Slick (Phantom, Rocker & Slick).	
7/25/81	**32**	13	1 You Could Take My Heart Away	Columbia 02268
			SILVER CONVENTION German studio disco act assembled by producer Michael Kunze and writer/arranger Silvester Levay. Female vocal trio formed in 1976 consisting of Penny McLean, Ramona Wolf and Linda Thompson.	
10/11/75	**1**[3]	17	1 ● **Fly, Robin, Fly** [I]	Midland I. 10339

DEBUT DATE	PEAK POS	WKS CHR	ARTIST — Record Title	Label & Number
			SILVER CONVENTION — Cont'd	
3/13/76	**2**[3]	21	2 ● **Get Up And Boogie (That's Right)**	Midland I. 10571
8/07/76	**60**	6	3 No, No, Joe	Midland I. 10723
			SILVERADO	
			Connecticut-based musician/songwriting team of Carl Shillo & Buzz Goodwin.	
7/04/81	**92**	3	1 Ready For Love	Pavillion 02077
			DOOLEY SILVERSPOON	
			Recorded as Little Dooley on Philadelphia's North Bay label.	
2/15/75	**80**	6	1 Bump Me Baby (Part 1)	Cotton 636
			SILVETTI	
			Argentinian Bebu Silvetti.	
1/22/77	**39**	15	1 Spring Rain [I]	Salsoul 2014
			THE HARRY SIMEONE CHORALE	
			Harry was born on 5/9/11 in Newark, New Jersey. Began career in 1939 as an arranger for Fred Waring. Arranger/conductor for film and TV shows.	
12/22/58	**13**	9	1 The Little Drummer Boy [X]	20th Fox 121
12/14/59	**15**	7	2 The Little Drummer Boy [X-R]	20th Fox 121
12/12/60	**24**	4	3 The Little Drummer Boy [X-R]	20th Fox 121
12/11/61	**22**	4	4 The Little Drummer Boy [X-R]	20th Fox 121
12/08/62	**28**	4	5 The Little Drummer Boy [X-R]	20th Fox 121
			GENE SIMMONS	
			Born Gene Klein on 8/25/49 in Queens, NY. Bass guitarist of Kiss.	
12/02/78+	**47**	8	1 Radioactive	Casablanca 951
			GENE SIMMONS	
			Born in Tupelo, Mississippi in 1933. Nicknamed "Jumpin' Gene".	
8/08/64	**11**	11	1 Haunted House	Hi 2076
11/07/64	**83**	3	2 The Dodo	Hi 2080
			PATRICK SIMMONS	
			Born on 1/23/50 in Aberdeen, Washington; raised in San Jose, California. Vocalist, guitarist. Original member of The Doobie Brothers, he wrote their hit "Black Water".	
3/19/83	**30**	13	1 So Wrong	Elektra 69839
6/18/83	**75**	5	2 Don't Make Me Do It written by Huey Lewis & The News	Elektra 69817
			SIMON & GARFUNKEL	
			Folk/rock duo from New York City: Paul Simon and Art Garfunkel. Recorded as Tom & Jerry in 1957. Duo had split before first hit in 1965; Simon was working solo in England, Garfunkel was in graduate school. They re-formed and stayed together until 1971. Reunited in 1981 for national tour.	
12/23/57+	**49**	9	1 Hey, Schoolgirl TOM & JERRY Best Seller #49 / Top 100 #54	Big 613
11/20/65+	**1**[2]	14	2 ● **The Sounds Of Silence**	Columbia 43396
2/12/66	**5**	12	3 **Homeward Bound**	Columbia 43511
5/07/66	**3**	11	4 **I Am A Rock**	Columbia 43617
8/06/66	**25**	7	5 The Dangling Conversation	Columbia 43728
11/05/66	**13**	9	6 A Hazy Shade Of Winter	Columbia 43873
3/18/67	**16**	9	7 At The Zoo	Columbia 44046
7/29/67	**23**	8	8 Fakin' It	Columbia 44232
3/02/68	**11**	11	9 Scarborough Fair/Canticle song also known as "Parsley, Sage, Rosemary And Thyme"	Columbia 44465
4/27/68	**1**[3]	13	10 ● **Mrs. Robinson** above 2 from the film "The Graduate"	Columbia 44511
4/12/69	**7**	10	11 **The Boxer**	Columbia 44785
2/07/70	**1**[6]	14	12 ● **Bridge Over Troubled Water**	Columbia 45079
4/11/70	**4**	13	13 ● **Cecilia**	Columbia 45133
9/12/70	**18**	11	14 El Condor Pasa	Columbia 45237
9/02/72	**53**	7	15 For Emily, Whenever I May Find Her/	
11/25/72	**97**	2	16 America	Columbia 45663
10/18/75	**9**	14	17 **My Little Town** all of above written by Paul Simon	Columbia 10230
4/03/82	**27**	11	18 Wake Up Little Susie recorded live in New York's Central Park on 9/19/81	Warner 50053

DEBUT DATE	PEAK POS	WKS CHR	ARTIST — Record Title	Label & Number
			THE SIMON SISTERS	
			Folk duo: Carly Simon and elder sister Lucy. Broke up when Lucy got married.	
4/25/64	**73**	6	1 Winkin', Blinkin' And Nod	Kapp 586
			CARLY SIMON	
			Born on 6/25/45 in New York City. Pop vocalist/songwriter. Father is co-founder of Simon & Schuster publishing. Married James Taylor on 11/3/72; separated in 1982.	
4/17/71	**10**	17	1 **That's The Way I've Always Heard It Should Be**	Elektra 45724
12/11/71+	**13**	13	2 Anticipation	Elektra 45759
3/25/72	**50**	10	3 Legend In Your Own Time	Elektra 45774
12/02/72+	**1^{3}**	17	4● **You're So Vain**	Elektra 45824
			backing vocals: Mick Jagger	
3/31/73	**17**	13	5 The Right Thing To Do	Elektra 45843
2/02/74	**5**	16	6● **Mockingbird**	Elektra 45880
			CARLY SIMON & JAMES TAYLOR	
5/11/74	**14**	12	7 Haven't Got Time For The Pain	Elektra 45887
5/10/75	**21**	8	8 Attitude Dancing	Elektra 45246
7/26/75	**78**	3	9 Waterfall	Elektra 45263
10/18/75	**94**	2	10 More And More	Elektra 45278
6/19/76	**46**	8	11 It Keeps You Runnin'	Elektra 45323
7/23/77	**2^{3}**	25	12● **Nobody Does It Better**	Elektra 45413
			from the film "The Spy Who Loved Me"	
			4-10 & 12: produced by Richard Perry	
4/15/78	**6**	18	13 **You Belong To Me**	Elektra 45477
8/19/78	**36**	9	14 Devoted To You	Elektra 45506
			CARLY SIMON & JAMES TAYLOR	
6/09/79	**48**	7	15 Vengeance	Elektra 46051
8/02/80	**11**	23	16● Jesse	Warner 49518
7/17/82	**74**	6	17 Why	Mirage 4051
			from the film "Soup For One"	
9/24/83	**83**	4	18 You Know What To Do	Warner 29484
6/29/85	**70**	5	19 Tired Of Being Blonde	Epic 05419
11/01/86+	**18**	17	20 Coming Around Again	Arista 9525
			from the film "Heartburn"	
			JOE SIMON	
			Born on 9/2/43 in Simmesport, LA. Moved to Oakland in 1959. First recorded with vocal group, the Golden Tones, for Hush in 1960.	
6/18/66	**66**	7	1 Teenager's Prayer	Sound Stage 2564
2/04/67	**87**	5	2 My Special Prayer	Sound Stage 2577
9/23/67	**70**	9	3 Nine Pound Steel	Sound Stage 2589
1/06/68	**49**	7	4 No Sad Songs	Sound Stage 2602
4/13/68	**25**	15	5 (You Keep Me) Hangin' On	Sound Stage 2608
9/28/68	**75**	4	6 Message From Maria/	
11/16/68	**98**	1	7 I Worry About You	Sound Stage 2617
12/07/68+	**70**	6	8 Looking Back	Sound Stage 2622
3/22/69	**13**	12	9● The Chokin' Kind	Sound Stage 2628
6/21/69	**72**	5	10 Baby, Don't Be Looking In My Mind	Sound Stage 2634
9/27/69	**79**	3	11 San Francisco Is A Lonely Town/	
10/18/69	**87**	3	12 It's Hard To Get Along	Sound Stage 2641
1/03/70	**54**	8	13 Moon Walk - Part 1	Sound Stage 2651
4/18/70	**56**	8	14 Farther On Down The Road	Sound Stage 2656
8/01/70	**78**	7	15 Yours Love	Sound Stage 2664
10/31/70	**93**	3	16 That's The Way I Want Our Love	Sound Stage 2667
12/19/70+	**40**	13	17 Your Time To Cry	Spring 108
5/15/71	**69**	4	18 Help Me Make It Through The Night	Spring 113
7/24/71	**71**	5	19 You're The One For Me	Spring 115
9/25/71	**93**	2	20 All My Hard Times	Spring 118
			all of above produced by John Richbourg	
11/27/71+	**11**	13	21● Drowning In The Sea Of Love	Spring 120
3/25/72	**42**	8	22 Pool Of Bad Luck	Spring 124
7/08/72	**11**	15	23● Power Of Love	Spring 128
10/21/72	**91**	5	24 Misty Blue	Sound Stage 1508
11/04/72	**50**	7	25 Trouble In My Home/	
		5	26 I Found My Dad	Spring 130
2/17/73	**37**	12	27 Step By Step	Spring 133

DEBUT DATE	PEAK POS	WKS CHR	ARTIST — Record Title	Label & Number
			JOE SIMON — Cont'd	
7/28/73	18	13	28 Theme From Cleopatra Jones featuring The Mainstreeters - from the film of the same title	Spring 138
11/17/73	62	7	29 River	Spring 141
4/05/75	8	17	30 **Get Down, Get Down (Get On The Floor)**	Spring 156
8/23/75	92	4	31 Music In My Bones	Spring 159
			PAUL SIMON Born on 11/5/41 in Newark, NJ; raised in Queens, NY. Vocalist, composer, guitarist. Met Art Garfunkel in high school, recorded together as Tom & Jerry in 1957. Worked as Jerry Landis, Paul Kane, Harrison Gregory and True Taylor in early 60s. To England from 1963-64. Returned to USA and recorded first album with Garfunkel in 1965. Went solo in 1971. In films "Annie Hall" and "One-Trick Pony". Also see Tico & The Triumphs.	
1/19/63	97	3	1 The Lone Teen Ranger shown as: JERRY LANDIS	Amy 875
2/05/72	4	13	2 **Mother And Child Reunion**	Columbia 45547
4/08/72	22	11	3 Me And Julio Down By The Schoolyard	Columbia 45585
7/08/72	52	7	4 Duncan	Columbia 45638
5/19/73	2[2]	14	5 **Kodachrome**	Columbia 45859
8/04/73	2[1]	16	6● **Loves Me Like A Rock** vocal backing: The Dixie Hummingbirds	Columbia 45907
12/01/73+	35	10	7 American Tune	Columbia 45900
8/16/75	23	10	8 Gone At Last PAUL SIMON/PHOEBE SNOW vocal backing: The Jessy Dixon Singers	Columbia 10197
12/20/75+	1[3]	17	9● **50 Ways To Leave Your Lover**	Columbia 10270
5/01/76	40	7	10 Still Crazy After All These Years	Columbia 10332
10/15/77+	5	20	11 **Slip Slidin' Away**	Columbia 10630
1/21/78	17	14	12 (What A) Wonderful World ART GARFUNKEL with JAMES TAYLOR & PAUL SIMON	Columbia 10676
8/09/80	6	16	13 **Late In The Evening**	Warner 49511
10/25/80	40	11	14 One-Trick Pony from the film of the same title	Warner 49601
1/22/83	51	8	15 The Blues RANDY NEWMAN & PAUL SIMON	Warner 29803
11/05/83	44	10	16 Allergies	Warner 29453
8/09/86+	23	29	17 You Can Call Me Al initially charted for 14 wks. (POS 44), then re-entered on 3/28/87	Warner 28667
12/06/86+	81	7	18 Graceland all of above written by Paul Simon (except #12 & 15)	Warner 28522
			NINA SIMONE Born Eunice Waymon on 2/21/33 in Tryon, SC. Jazz-influenced vocalist, pianist, composer. Attended Juilliard School of Music in New York City. Devoted more time to political activism in 70s, infrequent recording.	
8/03/59	18	15	1 I Loves You, Porgy from the film "Porgy And Bess"	Bethlehem 11021
9/05/60	93	2	2 Nobody Knows You When You're Down And Out	Colpix 158
1/23/61	92	2	3 Trouble In Mind	Colpix 175
10/19/68	83	5	4 Do What You Gotta Do	RCA 9602
1/04/69	94	4	5 Ain't Got No; I Got Life from the musical production "Hair"	RCA 9686
12/13/69+	76	7	6 To Be Young, Gifted And Black	RCA 0269
			SIMPLE MINDS Scottish rock group; current lineup: Jim Kerr, lead singer (married to Chrissie Hynde of the Pretenders); Michael MacNeil, keyboards; Charles Burchill, guitar; Mel Gaynor, drums; and John Gibbin, bass.	
2/23/85	1[1]	22	1 **Don't You (Forget About Me)** from the film "The Breakfast Club"	A&M 2703
10/19/85	3	20	2 **Alive & Kicking**	A&M 2783
1/25/86	14	14	3 Sanctify Yourself	A&M 2810
4/05/86	28	13	4 All The Things She Said	A&M 2828
			SIMPLY RED British pop sextet led by vocalist Mick "Red" Hucknall.	
4/05/86	1[1]	23	1 **Holding Back The Years**	Elektra 69564
7/19/86	28	15	2 Money$ Too Tight (To Mention) single originally released in August of 1985	Elektra 69528

DEBUT DATE	PEAK POS	WKS CHR	ARTIST — Record Title	Label & Number
			VALERIE SIMPSON	
			Born on 8/26/46 in New York City. Half of Ashford & Simpson duo.	
12/09/72+	**63**	9	1 Silly Wasn't I	Tamla 54224
			SIMS TWINS	
			Los Angeles R&B duo: brothers Bobby and Kenneth Sims.	
10/23/61	**42**	8	1 Soothe Me	Sar 117
			FRANK SINATRA	
			Born Francis Albert Sinatra on 12/12/15 in Hoboken, NJ. With Harry James, 1939-40, first recorded for Brunswick in 1939; with Tommy Dorsey, 1940-42. Went solo in late 1942 and charted 40 Top 10 hits through 1954. Appeared in many films from 1941 on. Won an Oscar for the film "From Here To Eternity" in 1953. Own TV show in 1957. Own record company, Reprise, 1961, sold to Warner Bros. in 1963. Announced his retirement in 1970, but made comeback in 1973. Regarded by many as the greatest popular singer of the 20th century.	
1/22/55	**19**	4	1 Melody Of Love **FRANK SINATRA & RAY ANTHONY** Jockey #19	Capitol 3018
5/07/55	**1^{2}**	21	2 **Learnin' The Blues** Jockey #1 / Best Seller #2 / Juke Box #2	Capitol 3102
9/24/55	**13**	5	3 Same Old Saturday Night/ Jockey #13 / Top 100 #65 pre	
		5	4 Fairy Tale Coming Up flip	Capitol 3218
11/05/55	**5**	17	5 **Love And Marriage** Top 100 #5 / Jockey #5 / Best Seller #6 / Juke Box #7 from the TV production "Our Town"	Capitol 3260
12/10/55+	**7**	15	6 **(Love Is) The Tender Trap** Jockey #7 / Top 100 #23 / Best Seller #24 from the film "The Tender Trap"	Capitol 3290
2/25/56	**21**	13	7 Flowers Mean Forgiveness/ Jockey #21 / Top 100 #35	
3/03/56	**67**	5	8 You'll Get Yours	Capitol 3350
5/19/56	**13**	14	9 (How Little It Matters) How Little We Know/ Jockey #13 / Top 100 #30	
6/02/56	**73**	3	10 Five Hundred Guys	Capitol 3423
7/14/56	**52**	15	11 You're Sensational/ from the film "High Society" (also #13 below)	
7/28/56	**75**	5	12 Johnny Concho Theme (Wait For Me) from the film "Johnny Concho"	Capitol 3469
9/22/56	**92**	2	13 Well Did You Evah? [N] **BING CROSBY & FRANK SINATRA**	Capitol 3507
10/27/56+	**3**	19	14 **Hey! Jealous Lover** Jockey #3 / Top 100 #6 / Juke Box #7 / Best Seller #8	Capitol 3552
1/19/57	**15**	19	15 Can I Steal A Little Love/ Jockey #15 / Top 100 #20 from the film "Rock Pretty Baby"	
1/19/57	**60**	8	16 Your Love For Me	Capitol 3608
4/27/57	**60**	4	17 Crazy Love/	
4/27/57	**74**	5	18 So Long, My Love	Capitol 3703
7/22/57	**25**	1	19 You're Cheatin' Yourself (If You're Cheatin' On Me) Jockey #25	Capitol 3744
10/28/57+	**2^{1}**	30	20 **All The Way/** Jockey #2 / Best Seller #15 / Top 100 #15	
10/28/57	**84**	5	21 Chicago above 2 from the film "The Joker Is Wild"	Capitol 3793
1/20/58	**6**	16	22 **Witchcraft** Jockey #6 / Best Seller #20 / Top 100 #20	Capitol 3859
5/12/58	**22**	1	23 How Are Ya' Fixed For Love? **FRANK SINATRA & KEELY SMITH** Jockey #22 / Top 100 #97	Capitol 3952
10/27/58	**41**	11	24 Mr. Success	Capitol 4070
3/30/59	**61**	7	25 French Foreign Legion	Capitol 4155
6/15/59	**30**	17	26 High Hopes from the film "A Hole In The Head"	Capitol 4214
10/19/59	**38**	11	27 Talk To Me	Capitol 4284
5/30/60	**82**	2	28 River, Stay 'Way From My Door	Capitol 4376
8/29/60	**60**	6	29 Nice 'N' Easy	Capitol 4408
11/07/60	**25**	9	30 Ol' MacDonald all of above (except #1, 13 & 23) with Nelson Riddle & His Orch.	Capitol 4466
3/06/61	**50**	7	31 The Second Time Around	Reprise 20001

DEBUT DATE	PEAK POS	WKS CHR	ARTIST — Record Title	Label & Number
			FRANK SINATRA — Cont'd	
7/03/61	**64**	4	32 Granada	Reprise 20010
10/16/61	**58**	7	33 I'll Be Seeing You	Reprise 20023
			#1 hit in 1944 for Bing Crosby	
12/18/61+	**34**	8	34 Pocketful Of Miracles	Reprise 20040
			from the film of the same title	
3/17/62	**99**	1	35 The Moon Was Yellow	Capitol 4677
			#13 hit in 1934 for Bing Crosby	
3/24/62	**98**	1	36 Stardust	Reprise 20059
			one of the most recorded, charted and popular tunes of all time	
4/07/62	**75**	2	37 Ev'rybody's Twistin'	Reprise 20063
12/01/62	**64**	6	38 Me And My Shadow	Reprise 20128
			FRANK SINATRA & SAMMY DAVIS JR.	
4/06/63	**78**	8	39 Call Me Irresponsible	Reprise 20151
			from the film "Papa's Delicate Condition"	
1/18/64	**81**	3	40 Stay With Me	Reprise 0249
			from the film "The Cardinal"	
9/05/64	**27**	11	41 Softly, As I Leave You	Reprise 0301
12/19/64+	**32**	10	42 Somewhere In Your Heart	Reprise 0332
3/13/65	**46**	6	43 Anytime At All	Reprise 0350
5/22/65	**57**	6	44 Tell Her (You Love Her Every Day)	Reprise 0373
6/26/65	**78**	7	45 Forget Domani	Reprise 0380
			from the film "The Yellow Rolls Royce"	
12/25/65+	**28**	8	46 It Was A Very Good Year	Reprise 0429
5/07/66	**1**[1]	15	47 **Strangers In The Night**	Reprise 0470
			from the film "A Man Could Get Killed"	
9/03/66	**25**	7	48 Summer Wind	Reprise 0509
11/19/66	**4**	11	49 **That's Life**	Reprise 0531
3/18/67	**1**[4]	13	50● **Somethin' Stupid**	Reprise 0561
			NANCY SINATRA & FRANK SINATRA	
8/05/67	**30**	7	51 The World We Knew (Over And Over)	Reprise 0610
10/28/67	**53**	5	52 This Town	Reprise 0631
			from the film "The Cool Ones"	
4/13/68	**60**	5	53 I Can't Believe I'm Losing You	Reprise 0677
8/31/68	**64**	6	54 My Way Of Life/	
10/12/68	**23**	10	55 Cycles	Reprise 0764
1/04/69	**62**	6	56 Rain In My Heart	Reprise 0798
3/29/69	**27**	8	57 My Way	Reprise 0817
9/13/69	**75**	4	58 Loves Been Good To Me	Reprise 0852
11/29/69	**79**	4	59 Goin' Out Of My Head/	
		4	60 Forget To Remember	Reprise 0865
3/21/70	**88**	3	61 I Would Be In Love (Anyway)	Reprise 0895
11/10/73	**63**	10	62 Let Me Try Again	Reprise 1181
4/06/74	**83**	7	63 Bad, Bad Leroy Brown	Reprise 1196
8/03/74	**83**	5	64 You Turned My World Around	Reprise 1208
4/19/75	**75**	6	65 Anytime (I'll Be There)	Reprise 1327
8/02/75	**47**	7	66 I Believe I'm Gonna Love You	Reprise 1335
5/03/80	**32**	12	67 Theme From New York, New York	Reprise 49233
			from the film "New York, New York"	
			NANCY SINATRA	
			Born on 6/8/40 in Jersey City, NJ. First child of Frank and Nancy Sinatra. Moved to Los Angeles while a child. Made national TV debut with father and Elvis Presley in 1959. Married to Tommy Sands, 1960-65. Appeared on "Hullabaloo", "American Bandstand", and own specials, mid-60s. In films "For Those Who Think Young", "Get Yourself A College Girl", "The Oscar" and "Speedway".	
10/16/65	**86**	4	1 So Long Babe	Reprise 0407
1/22/66	**1**[1]	14	2● **These Boots Are Made For Walkin'**	Reprise 0432
4/23/66	**7**	8	3 **How Does That Grab You, Darlin'?**	Reprise 0461
7/09/66	**36**	5	4 Friday's Child	Reprise 0491
9/17/66	**46**	6	5 In Our Time	Reprise 0514
11/19/66	**5**	13	6● **Sugar Town/**	
3/04/67	**49**	9	7 Summer Wine	Reprise 0527
			NANCY SINATRA with LEE HAZLEWOOD	
3/18/67	**1**[4]	13	8● **Somethin' Stupid**	Reprise 0561
			NANCY SINATRA & FRANK SINATRA	
3/25/67	**15**	8	9 Love Eyes	Reprise 0559

DEBUT DATE	PEAK POS	WKS CHR	ARTIST — Record Title	Label & Number
			NANCY SINATRA — Cont'd	
6/24/67	14	9	10 Jackson/ NANCY SINATRA & LEE HAZLEWOOD	
6/24/67	44	9	11 You Only Live Twice .... from the James Bond film of the same title	Reprise 0595
9/23/67	24	7	12 Lightning's Girl	Reprise 0620
10/21/67	20	6	13 Lady Bird .... NANCY SINATRA & LEE HAZLEWOOD	Reprise 0629
12/02/67	83	3	14 Tony Rome .... from the film of the same title	Reprise 0636
1/06/68	26	8	15 Some Velvet Morning .... NANCY SINATRA & LEE HAZLEWOOD	Reprise 0651
3/23/68	69	6	16 100 Years	Reprise 0670
7/27/68	74	4	17 Happy .... all of above produced/written (except #8, 10-11) by Lee Hazlewood	Reprise 0756
11/30/68	65	5	18 Good Time Girl	Reprise 0789
3/15/69	97	3	19 God Knows I Love You	Reprise 0813
5/24/69	98	2	20 Here We Go Again	Reprise 0821
9/20/69	98	2	21 Drummer Man	Reprise 0851
			GORDON SINCLAIR Born on 6/3/1900 in Toronto; died on 5/17/84. Canadian broadcaster, author.	
1/12/74	24	7	1 The Americans (A Canadian's Opini.......... on)[S] originally broadcast on 6/5/73 on CFRB Radio in Toronto	Avco 4628
			THE SINGING BELLES Sisters Anne & Angela Berry from Brooklyn, New York.	
4/18/60	91	3	1 Someone Loves You, Joe	Madison 126
			THE SINGING DOGS An actual recording of dogs barking by Don Charles in Copenhagen.	
12/10/55	22	7	1 Oh! Susanna .... [N] Best Seller #22 / Top 100 #37 written in 1848 by Stephen Foster	RCA 6344
			THE SINGING NUN Sister Luc-Gabrielle (real name: Jeanine Deckers) from the Fichermont, Belgium nuns convent. Recorded under the name Soeur Sourire ("Sister Smile"). Committed suicide on 3/31/85 (52).	
11/09/63	1[4]	13	1 **Dominique** .... [F]	Philips 40152
			SINGLE BULLET THEORY Pop-rock quintet from Norfolk, Virginia. Michael Garrett, lead singer.	
3/05/83	78	4	1 Keep It Tight	Nemperor 03300
			SIR CHAUNCEY Sir Chauncey is Ernie Freeman.	
4/25/60	89	4	1 Beautiful Obsession .... [I]	Warner 5150
			SIR DOUGLAS QUINTET 'Tex-Mex' rock band led by Doug Sahm (b: 11/6/41) from San Antonio.	
4/03/65	13	12	1 She's About A Mover	Tribe 8308
1/29/66	31	11	2 The Rains Came	Tribe 8314
1/18/69	27	15	3 Mendocino	Smash 2191
8/02/69	83	2	4 Dynamite Woman	Smash 2233
			SISTER SLEDGE Sisters Debbie, Joni, Kim and Kathie Sledge from North Philadelphia. First recorded as Sisters Sledge for Money Back in 1971.	
1/04/75	92	4	1 Love Don't You Go Through No Changes On Me	Atco 7008
2/10/79	9	19	2 **He's The Greatest Dancer**	Cotillion 44245
4/28/79	2[2]	19	3 ● **We Are Family**	Cotillion 44251
1/19/80	64	5	4 Got To Love Somebody	Cotillion 45007
3/21/81	79	5	5 All American Girls	Cotillion 46007
5/09/81	82	5	6 Next Time You'll Know	Cotillion 46012
1/30/82	23	15	7 My Guy	Cotillion 47000
6/15/85	75	8	8 Frankie	Atlantic 89547
			THE SIX TEENS Los Angeles R&B sextet: Trudy Williams and Ed Wells (leads), Richard Owens, Darryl Lewis, Beverly Pecot and Louise Williams.	
7/14/56	25	13	1 A Casual Look .... Best Seller #25 / Top 100 #48	Flip 315

DEBUT DATE	PEAK POS	WKS CHR	ARTIST — Record Title		Label & Number
			THE SIX TEENS — Cont'd		
7/29/57	**80**	3	2 Arrow Of Love		Flip 322
			THE SKA KINGS		
			Jamaican group led by Byron Lee.		
7/11/64	**98**	1	1 Jamaica Ska		Atlantic 2232
			PETER SKELLERN		
			British singer.		
11/25/72+	**50**	8	1 You're A Lady		London 20075
			RED SKELTON		
			Born Richard Skelton on 7/18/13 in Vincennes, Indiana. Popular comedian, actor. Own TV variety show from 1951-72.		
3/15/69	**44**	6	1 The Pledge Of Allegiance	[S]	Columbia 44798
			as reviewed on TV's "Red Skelton Hour" on 1/14/69		
			SKIP & FLIP		
			Gary "Flip" Paxton and Clyde "Skip" Battin. Met at the University of Arizona, and appeared on "Arizona Jubilee" in 1958 as the Rockabillies. Paxton formed The Hollywood Argyles, and later started own Garpax record label.		
6/22/59	**11**	16	1 It Was I		Brent 7002
11/02/59	**71**	5	2 Fancy Nancy		Brent 7005
4/04/60	**11**	15	3 Cherry Pie		Brent 7010
			SKY		
			Classical/rock group led by classical guitarist John Williams.		
1/10/81	**83**	2	1 Toccata	[I]	Arista 0568
			SKYLARK		
			Canadian quartet: Donny Gerrard & B.J. (Bonnie Jean) Cook, lead singers; David Foster, keyboards; and Duris Maxwell, drums.		
2/17/73	**9**	21	1 **Wildflower**		Capitol 3511
			THE SKYLINERS		
			Pittsburgh vocal quintet: Jimmy Beaumont (b: 10/21/40), lead; Janet Vogel (d: 2/21/80, suicide), tenor; Wally Lester, tenor; Joe VerScharen, baritone; and Jackie Taylor, bass voice, guitarist.		
2/16/59	**12**	19	1 Since I Don't Have You		Calico 103
6/01/59	**26**	12	2 This I Swear		Calico 106
9/28/59	**59**	8	3 It Happened Today		Calico 109
5/09/60	**24**	13	4 Pennies From Heaven		Calico 117
			#1 hit in 1936 for Bing Crosby		
7/17/65	**72**	5	5 The Loser		Jubilee 5506
			SKYY		
			Brooklyn R&B/pop-funk octet. Vocals by sisters Denise, Delores and Bonnie Dunning.		
1/16/82	**26**	11	1 Call Me		Salsoul 2152
			SLADE		
			English hard-rock quartet: Noddy Holder (b: 6/15/50), lead singer; David Hill, guitar; Jim Lea, bass, keyboards; and Don Powell, drums.		
9/30/72	**97**	2	1 Take Me Bak 'Ome		Polydor 15046
11/18/72+	**76**	10	2 Mama Weer All Crazee Now		Polydor 15053
3/10/73	**68**	6	3 Gudbuy T' Jane		Polydor 15060
5/26/73	**98**	2	4 Cum On Feel The Noize		Polydor 15069
4/07/84	**20**	17	5 Run Runaway		CBS Assoc. 04398
7/07/84	**37**	11	6 My Oh My		CBS Assoc. 04528
5/04/85	**86**	3	7 Little Sheila		CBS Assoc. 04865
			all of above written by Holder and Lea		
			THE SLADES		
			White vocal quartet from Austin, Texas. Don Burch, lead singer.		
8/04/58	**42**	12	1 You Cheated		Domino 500
			FELIX SLATKIN		
			St. Louis native. Virtuoso violinist, conductor, composer, arranger. Worked with many film and record companies. Died on 2/9/63 (47).		
10/03/60	**70**	8	1 Theme From The Sundowners	[I]	Liberty 55282
			from the film "The Sundowners"		
			SLAVE		
			Funk band from Dayton, Ohio. Steve Arrington, studio vocalist and later a member, 1978-82. Numerous personnel changes.		
6/18/77	**32**	13	1 Slide	[I]	Cotillion 44218

DEBUT DATE	PEAK POS	WKS CHR	ARTIST — Record Title	Label & Number
			SLAVE — Cont'd	
1/17/81	**78**	6	2 Watching You	Cotillion 46006
10/24/81	**91**	7	3 Snap Shot	Cotillion 46022
			FRANK SLAY	
			Born on 7/8/30 in Dallas. Composer, conductor. Head A&R man for Swan, 1961-63.	
12/11/61+	**45**	9	1 Flying Circle [I]	Swan 4085
			adaptation of the traditional Jewish song "Hava Nagila"	
			PERCY SLEDGE	
			Born in 1941 in Leighton, Alabama. Worked local clubs with Esquires Combo until going solo.	
4/09/66	**1**[2]	13	1 ● **When A Man Loves A Woman**	Atlantic 2326
7/23/66	**17**	9	2 Warm And Tender Love	Atlantic 2342
10/22/66	**20**	11	3 It Tears Me Up	Atlantic 2358
2/18/67	**87**	5	4 Baby, Help Me	Atlantic 2383
4/08/67	**59**	7	5 Out Of Left Field	Atlantic 2396
6/17/67	**40**	6	6 Love Me Tender/	
7/08/67	**91**	2	7 What Am I Living For	Atlantic 2414
9/02/67	**66**	4	8 Just Out Of Reach (Of My Two Empty Arms)	Atlantic 2434
11/25/67+	**42**	8	9 Cover Me	Atlantic 2453
3/16/68	**11**	14	10 Take Time To Know Her	Atlantic 2490
8/03/68	**63**	5	11 Sudden Stop	Atlantic 2539
2/01/69	**93**	4	12 My Special Prayer	Atlantic 2594
4/12/69	**86**	4	13 Any Day Now	Atlantic 2616
			all of above produced by Quin Ivy & Marlin Greene (except #8)	
11/16/74	**62**	6	14 I'll Be Your Everything	Capricorn 0209
			GRACE SLICK	
			Born Grace Wing on 10/30/39 in Chicago. Female lead singer of Jefferson Airplane, Jefferson Starship, and Starship.	
4/19/80	**95**	2	1 Seasons	RCA 11939
			P.F. SLOAN	
			Los Angeles native Phillip "Flip" Sloan. Vocalist, guitarist, composer. Recorded for Aladdin in 1959. Wrote "Secret Agent Man", "Eve Of Destruction", "A Must To Avoid" and many others.	
9/25/65	**87**	2	1 The Sins Of A Family	Dunhill 4007
			SLY & THE FAMILY STONE	
			San Francisco interracial "psychedelic soul" group formed by Sylvester "Sly Stone" Stewart (b: 3/15/44, Dallas), lead singer, keyboards; Sly's brother Freddie Stone, guitar; Cynthia Robinson, trumpet; Jerry Martini, saxophone; Sly's sister Rosie Stone, piano, vocals; Larry Graham, bass; and Gregg Errico, drums. Sly recorded gospel at age four. With vocal group the Viscanes while in high school. Producer and writer for Bobby Freeman, the Mojo Men, the Beau Brummels. Formed own groups, The Stoners in 1966 and the Family Stone in 1967. Worked Woodstock Festival in 1969. Career waned, mid-70s. With George Clinton in 1982. Also see Sly Stone.	
2/10/68	**8**	15	1 **Dance To The Music**	Epic 10256
7/27/68	**93**	3	2 Life/	
8/10/68	**93**	3	3 M'Lady	Epic 10353
11/30/68+	**1**[4]	19	4 ● **Everyday People/**	
3/08/69	**89**	4	5 Sing A Simple Song	Epic 10407
4/12/69	**22**	8	6 Stand!/	
5/24/69	**60**	7	7 I Want To Take You Higher	Epic 10450
8/09/69	**2**[2]	16	8 **Hot Fun In The Summertime**	Epic 10497
1/03/70	**1**[2]	13	9 ● **Thank You (Falettinme Be Mice Elf Agin)/**	
		13	10 Everybody Is A Star	Epic 10555
5/23/70	**38**	9	11 I Want To Take You Higher [R]	Epic 10450
11/06/71	**1**[3]	14	12 ● **Family Affair**	Epic 10805
2/05/72	**23**	10	13 Runnin' Away	Epic 10829
4/22/72	**42**	7	14 Smilin'	Epic 10850
6/30/73	**12**	17	15 ● If You Want Me To Stay	Epic 11017
11/24/73	**79**	2	16 Frisky	Epic 11060
7/06/74	**32**	12	17 Time For Livin'	Epic 11140
10/19/74	**84**	4	18 Loose Booty	Epic 50033
			all of above written and produced by Sly Stone	

DEBUT DATE	PEAK POS	WKS CHR	ARTIST — Record Title		Label & Number
			SLY FOX		
			Black-and-white duo: Gary "Mudbone" Cooper (P-Funk) and Michael Camacho.		
12/28/85+	**7**	25	1 **Let's Go All The Way**		Capitol 5552
			based on the same groove as the Boogie Boys "Fly Girl"		
6/07/86	**94**	2	2 Stay True		Capitol 5581
			SMALL FACES		
			British rock quartet: Steve Marriott (guitar), Ronnie Lane (bass), Ian McLagan (organ) and Kenny Jones (drums). Marriott later formed Humble Pie. Also see Faces.		
11/11/67+	**16**	17	1 Itchycoo Park		Immediate 501
3/16/68	**73**	5	2 Tin Soldier		Immediate 5003
			MILLIE SMALL		
			Born Millicent Smith on 10/6/46 in Jamaica. Nicknamed "The Blue Beat Girl".		
5/23/64	**2**[1]	12	1 **My Boy Lollipop**		Smash 1893
8/08/64	**40**	7	2 Sweet William		Smash 1920
			SMITH		
			Los Angeles-based rock quintet fronted by St. Louis blues rocker Gayle McCormick.		
9/06/69	**5**	15	1 **Baby It's You**		Dunhill 4206
2/21/70	**43**	7	2 Take A Look Around		Dunhill 4228
6/06/70	**73**	4	3 What Am I Gonna Do		Dunhill 4238
			THE BETTY SMITH GROUP		
			British group.		
6/30/58	**50**	5	1 Bewitched	[I]	London 1787
			Best Seller #50 / Top 100 #51 there were 8 charted versions of this tune in 1950		
			BRO SMITH		
5/08/76	**57**	5	1 Bigfoot	[N]	Big Tree 16061
			CAL SMITH		
			Born on 4/7/32 in Sabbiaw, Oklahoma. Country singer, guitarist. Member of Ernest Tubb's Texas Troubadours.		
3/10/73	**64**	8	1 The Lord Knows I'm Drinking		Decca 33040
			CARL SMITH		
			Born on 3/15/27 in Maynardsville, Tennessee. Popular country singer, charted over 25 Top 10 Country hits in the 50s.		
3/24/58	**80**	2	1 Your Name Is Beautiful		Columbia 41092
9/08/58	**93**	1	2 Guess I've Been Around Too Long		Columbia 41170
7/06/59	**43**	9	3 Ten Thousand Drums		Columbia 41417
			FRANKIE SMITH		
			Philadelphia native. Wrote and produced for Philadelphia International in the late 70s, and later for WMOT.		
5/16/81	**30**	19	1 ● Double Dutch Bus		WMOT 5356
			based on the double-dutch jump rope game certified gold for both 7" and 12" singles		
			HUEY "PIANO" SMITH & THE CLOWNS		
			Huey was born on 1/26/34 in New Orleans. With Earl King in the early 50s. With Eddie "Guitar Slim" Jones band, 1951-54. Much session work in New Orleans. Own band, The Clowns, in 1957 with Bobby Marchan (vocals). Marchan left in 1959, replaced by Curly Smith. Also see Frankie Ford.		
8/12/57	**52**	13	1 Rocking Pneumonia And The Boogie Woogie Flu		Ace 530
3/24/58	**9**	13	2 **Don't You Just Know It**		Ace 545
			Top 100 #9 / Best Seller #13		
12/08/58+	**56**	6	3 Don't You Know Yockomo		Ace 553
2/17/62	**51**	8	4 Pop-Eye		Ace 649
			HUEY SMITH		
			HURRICANE SMITH		
			Born Norman Smith in northern England, 1923. Vocalist, producer, engineer, session musician. Produced early Pink Floyd albums and did some engineering for The Beatles.		
12/02/72+	**3**	15	1 **Oh, Babe, What Would You Say?**		Capitol 3383
3/17/73	**49**	9	2 Who Was It?		Capitol 3455
			JERRY SMITH & his Pianos		
			Session pianist. Wrote and performed on the Dixiebelles' "(Down At) Papa Joe's".		
5/10/69	**71**	7	1 Truck Stop	[I]	ABC 11162

DEBUT DATE	PEAK POS	WKS CHR	ARTIST — Record Title		Label & Number
			JIMMY SMITH		
			Born on 12/8/25 in Norristown, Pennsylvania. Jazz organist. Both parents were piano players. Won Major Bowes Amateur Show in 1934. With father (James, Sr.) in song and dance team, 1942. With Don Gardner & The Sonotones, recorded for Bruce in 1953. A pioneer of the jazz organ, Smith first recorded with own trio for Blue Note in 1956. Began doing vocals in 1966.		
3/03/62	**69**	8	1 Midnight Special, Part I	[I]	Blue Note 1819
5/12/62	**21**	13	2 Walk On The Wild Side - Part 1 from the film of the same title	[I]	Verve 10255
9/01/62	**82**	3	3 Ol' Man River from the stage production "Show Boat"	[I]	Verve 10262
3/09/63	**63**	6	4 Back At The Chicken Shack, Part I	[I]	Blue Note 1877
5/11/63	**69**	6	5 Hobo Flats - Part 1	[I]	Verve 10283
11/02/63	**96**	1	6 Theme From 'Any Number Can Win'	[I]	Verve 10299
4/25/64	**72**	5	7 Who's Afraid Of Virginia Woolf? above 2 from films of the same titles	[I]	Verve 10314
9/05/64	**67**	6	8 The Cat from the film "Joy House"	[I]	Verve 10330
10/02/65	**92**	3	9 The Organ Grinder's Swing **JIMMY SMITH with KENNY BURRELL & GRADY TATE**	[I]	Verve 10363
4/02/66	**51**	7	10 Got My Mojo Working (Part I)		Verve 10393
8/27/66	**94**	2	11 I'm Your Hoochie Cooche Man (Part 1) 5-11: produced by Creed Taylor		Verve 10426
4/06/68	**100**	2	12 Chain Of Fools (Part 1)	[I]	Verve 10583
			KEELY SMITH - see LOUIS PRIMA and FRANK SINATRA		
			O.C. SMITH		
			Born Ocie Lee Smith on 6/21/32 in Mansfield, LA. Raised in Los Angeles. Sang while in US Air Force, 1951-55. First recorded for Cadence in 1956. With Count Basie from 1961-63.		
2/24/68	**40**	14	1 The Son Of Hickory Holler's Tramp		Columbia 44425
8/17/68	**2**[1]	17	2 ● **Little Green Apples**		Columbia 44616
12/14/68	**63**	6	3 Isn't It Lonely Together		Columbia 44705
2/08/69	**44**	6	4 Honey (I Miss You)		Columbia 44751
5/10/69	**47**	9	5 Friend, Lover, Woman, Wife		Columbia 44859
8/30/69	**34**	7	6 Daddy's Little Man		Columbia 44948
5/30/70	**86**	3	7 Primrose Lane		Columbia 45160
8/22/70	**52**	10	8 Baby, I Need Your Loving		Columbia 45206
11/13/71	**91**	4	9 Help Me Make It Through The Night all of above produced by Jerry Fuller		Columbia 45435
9/28/74	**62**	7	10 La La Peace Song		Columbia 10031
			PATTI SMITH GROUP		
			Born on 12/31/46 in Chicago; raised in New Jersey. Poet-turned-punk rocker.		
4/08/78	**13**	18	1 Because The Night written by Smith and Bruce Springsteen		Arista 0318
8/18/79	**90**	3	2 Frederick		Arista 0427
			RAY SMITH		
			Born on 10/31/34 in Melber, Kentucky; committed suicide on 11/29/79.		
1/04/60	**22**	16	1 Rockin' Little Angel		Judd 1016
5/09/60	**91**	2	2 Put Your Arms Around Me Honey		Judd 1017
			REX SMITH		
			Born in Jacksonville, FL. Vocalist, actor. Starred in several Broadway musicals.		
4/21/79	**10**	16	1 ● **You Take My Breath Away** from the TV film "Sooner Or Later"		Columbia 10908
6/27/81	**32**	13	2 Everlasting Love **REX SMITH/RACHEL SWEET**		Columbia 02169
			ROGER SMITH		
			Born on 12/18/32 in South Gate, California. Played Jeff Spencer on the TV series "77 Sunset Strip", 1958-64. Married to Ann-Margret.		
6/29/59	**64**	8	1 Beach Time		Warner 5068
			SAMMI SMITH		
			Born on 8/5/43 in Orange, California; raised in Oklahoma. Country singer.		
1/16/71	**8**	16	1 ● **Help Me Make It Through The Night**		Mega 0015
8/26/72	**77**	7	2 I've Got To Have You		Mega 0079

DEBUT DATE	PEAK POS	WKS CHR	ARTIST — Record Title	Label & Number
			SOMETHIN' SMITH & THE REDHEADS	
			Trio from UCLA: Smith (vocals, guitar), Saul Striks (piano), Major Short (violin).	
4/02/55	**7**	23	1 **It's A Sin To Tell A Lie**	Epic 9093
			Best Seller #7 / Juke Box #8 / Jockey #9	
			#1 hit in 1936 for Fats Waller	
11/12/55	**90**	1	2 When All The Streets Are Dark	Epic 9119
6/02/56	**27**	15	3 In A Shanty In Old Shanty Town	Epic 9168
			#1 hit in 1932 for Ted Lewis	
9/08/56	**71**	6	4 Heartaches	Epic 9179
			#1 hit in 1947 for Ted Weems	
			TAB SMITH	
			Born Talmadge Smith on 1/11/09 in Kinston, NC; died on 8/17/71. Jazz alto saxophonist with the Mills Rhythm Band (1936-38), Count Basie (1940-42) and Lucky Millinder (1942-44).	
3/30/57	**89**	3	1 Pretend [I]	United 205
			#2 hit in 1953 for Nat "King" Cole	
			VERDELLE SMITH	
			Black songstress from St. Petersburg, Florida.	
2/05/66	**62**	7	1 In My Room	Capitol 5567
7/09/66	**38**	8	2 Tar And Cement	Capitol 5632
			WARREN SMITH	
			Born on 2/7/33 in Louise, Mississippi. Rockabilly singer, songwriter.	
6/10/57	**72**	2	1 So Long I'm Gone	Sun 268
			WHISTLING JACK SMITH	
			Born Billy Moeller on 2/2/46 in Liverpool, England.	
4/29/67	**20**	7	1 I Was Kaiser Bill's Batman [I]	Deram 85005
			THE SMOKE RING	
2/15/69	**85**	4	1 No Not Much	Buddah 77
			SMOKIE	
			British pop/rock quartet featuring lead singer Chris Norman. Also see Suzi Quatro.	
7/26/75	**96**	3	1 If You Think You Know How To Love Me	MCA 40429
12/04/76+	**25**	20	2 Living Next Door To Alice	RSO 860
9/17/77	**68**	5	3 Needles And Pins	RSO 881
			THE SMOTHERS BROTHERS	
			Comedians Tom (b: 2/2/37), guitar; and Dick Smothers (b: 11/20/39), standup bass. Hosts of their own TV comedy variety series from 1967-70.	
9/28/63	**84**	4	1 Jenny Brown [N]	Mercury 72182
			orchestra produced and directed by David Carroll	
			SNAIL	
			Pop/rock quartet from Santa Cruz, California.	
9/23/78	**93**	2	1 The Joker	Cream 7827
			SNEAKER	
			Los Angeles-based pop/rock sextet.	
10/31/81+	**34**	15	1 More Than Just The Two Of Us	Handshake 02557
2/27/82	**63**	5	2 Don't Let Me In	Handshake 02714
			SNIFF 'n' the TEARS	
			British rock group led by Paul Roberts (vocals) and Loz Netto (guitar).	
7/21/79	**15**	15	1 Driver's Seat	Atlantic 3604
			HANK SNOW	
			Born Clarence Snow on 5/9/14 in Liverpool, Nova Scotia. Hank's charted over 40 Top 10 Country hits (1949-74).	
12/05/60	**87**	4	1 Rockin', Rollin' Ocean	RCA 7702
9/29/62	**68**	8	2 I've Been Everywhere	RCA 8072
			PHOEBE SNOW	
			Born Phoebe Laub on 7/17/52 in New York City; raised in New Jersey. Vocalist, guitarist, songwriter. Began performing in Greenwich Village in the early 70s.	
1/04/75	**5**	18	1 **Poetry Man**	Shelter 40353
8/16/75	**23**	10	2 Gone At Last	Columbia 10197
			PAUL SIMON/PHOEBE SNOW	
			vocal backing: The Jessy Dixon Singers	
1/22/77	**70**	4	3 Shakey Ground	Columbia 10463
2/21/81	**46**	10	4 Games	Mirage 3800

DEBUT DATE	PEAK POS	WKS CHR	ARTIST — Record Title		Label & Number
			PHOEBE SNOW — Cont'd		
5/02/81	**52**	8	5 Mercy, Mercy, Mercy		Mirage 3818
			SNUFF		
			Rock sextet from Virginia's Tidewater region.		
8/20/83	**88**	2	1 Bad, Bad Billy		Warner/Curb 29615
			ERROL SOBER		
3/31/79	**65**	8	1 Heart To Heart		Number 1 215
			GINO SOCCIO		
			Techno-disco vocalist/multi instrumentalist from Montreal, Canada. Producer of Witch Queen.		
4/07/79	**48**	6	1 Dancer		RFC 8757
			PIERO SOFFICI		
4/24/61	**59**	7	1 That's The Way With Love	[I]	Kip 224
			SOFT CELL		
			British electro-rock duo: Marc Almond (vocals) & David Ball (synthesizer).		
1/16/82	**8**	43	1 **Tainted Love**		Sire 49855
			BELOUIS SOME		
			British rocker - real name: Neville Keighley.		
5/04/85	**88**	5	1 Imagination		Capitol 5464
8/03/85	**67**	6	2 Some People		Capitol 5492
			BERT SOMMER		
8/08/70	**48**	8	1 We're All Playing In The Same Band		Eleuthera 470
			JOANIE SOMMERS		
			Born on 2/24/41 in Buffalo, moved to California in 1954. Vocalist for "Pepsi-Cola" jingles in early and mid-60s.		
7/04/60	**54**	9	1 One Boy from the Broadway musical "Bye Bye Birdie"		Warner 5157
5/26/62	**7**	14	2 **Johnny Get Angry**		Warner 5275
10/06/62	**94**	3	3 When The Boys Get Together		Warner 5308
			SONNY		
			Born Salvatore Bono on 2/16/35 in Detroit. Sonny Bono of Sonny & Cher. With Specialty Records as A&R man and writer from 1957-59. Co-wrote The Searchers' hit "Needles And Pins".		
8/21/65	**10**	10	1 **Laugh At Me**		Atco 6369
11/27/65	**70**	4	2 The Revolution Kind		Atco 6386
			SONNY & CHER		
			Husband and wife duo: Sonny and Cher Bono. Session singers for Phil Spector. First recorded as Caesar & Cleo for Vault in 1963. Married in 1963; divorced in 1974. Films "Good Times", 1966 and "Chastity", 1968. Own CBS-TV variety series from 1971-74. Brief TV reunion in 1975.		
7/10/65	**1^{3}**	14	1 ● **I Got You Babe**		Atco 6359
8/21/65	**8**	12	2 **Baby Don't Go**		Reprise 0309
8/28/65	**20**	9	3 Just You		Atco 6345
10/09/65	**15**	8	4 But You're Mine		Atco 6381
10/23/65	**75**	5	5 The Letter originally released in 1963 as by Caesar & Cleo		Vault 916
1/29/66	**14**	8	6 What Now My Love		Atco 6395
6/04/66	**49**	6	7 Have I Stayed Too Long		Atco 6420
10/01/66	**21**	7	8 Little Man		Atco 6440
11/19/66	**87**	2	9 Living For You		Atco 6449
1/14/67	**6**	11	10 **The Beat Goes On**		Atco 6461
4/29/67	**53**	5	11 A Beautiful Story		Atco 6480
6/10/67	**74**	3	12 Plastic Man		Atco 6486
8/12/67	**50**	7	13 It's The Little Things		Atco 6507
12/16/67+	**56**	6	14 Good Combination		Atco 6541
10/16/71	**7**	15	15 **All I Ever Need Is You**		Kapp 2151
2/26/72	**8**	13	16 **A Cowboys Work Is Never Done**		Kapp 2163
7/08/72	**32**	10	17 When You Say Love adapted from the "Budweiser" jingle		Kapp 2176

DEBUT DATE	PEAK POS	WKS CHR	ARTIST — Record Title	Label & Number
			SONNY & CHER — Cont'd	
3/24/73	**77**	5	18 Mama Was A Rock And Roll Singer Papa Used To Write All Her Songs	MCA 40026
			all of above written (except #5-6, 14-15 & 17) and produced (except #11, 15 & 17) by Sonny	
			SONS OF CHAMPLIN	
			San Francisco 7-man rock band led by Bill Champlin.	
6/19/76	**47**	10	1 Hold On	Ariola Am. 7627
2/05/77	**80**	5	2 Here Is Where Your Love Belongs	Ariola Am. 7653
			THE SOPWITH "CAMEL"	
			San Francisco quintet. Peter Kraemer, lead singer.	
12/24/66+	**26**	10	1 Hello Hello	Kama Sutra 217
4/01/67	**88**	2	2 Postcard From Jamaica	Kama Sutra 224
			THE S.O.S. BAND	
			Atlantic funk/R&B band. Mary Davis, lead singer. Name means "Sounds Of Success".	
5/31/80	**3**	21	1 ▲**Take Your Time (Do It Right) Part 1**	Tabu 5522
8/27/83	**55**	14	2 Just Be Good To Me	Tabu 03955
11/19/83+	**65**	11	3 Tell Me If You Still Care	Tabu 04160
8/11/84	**64**	10	4 Just The Way You Like It	Tabu 04523
5/17/86	**44**	13	5 The Finest	Tabu 05848
			above 4 written and produced by Jimmy Jam & Terry Lewis	
			SOUL BROTHERS SIX	
6/24/67	**91**	1	1 Some Kind Of Wonderful	Atlantic 2406
			THE SOUL CHILDREN	
			Group formed by songwriters Isaac Hayes and David Porter. Consisted of Anita Louis, Shelbra Bennett, John Colbert and Norman West.	
10/11/69	**52**	7	1 The Sweeter He Is - Part I	Stax 0050
3/18/72	**44**	11	2 Hearsay	Stax 0119
2/16/74	**36**	9	3 I'll Be The Other Woman	Stax 0182
			THE SOUL CLAN	
			Top soul stars: Solomon Burke, Arthur Conley, Don Covay, Ben E. King and Joe Tex.	
7/27/68	**91**	4	1 Soul Meeting [N]	Atlantic 2530
			THE SOUL SISTERS	
			Vocal duo: Thresia Cleveland and Ann Gissendanner.	
2/29/64	**46**	9	1 I Can't Stand It	Sue 799
6/13/64	**98**	1	2 Good Time Tonight	Sue 005
10/10/64	**100**	1	3 Just A Moment Ago	Sue 111
			above 3 written by Smokey McAlister	
			SOUL SURVIVORS	
			White-soul band from New York City and Philadelphia. Formed by the Ingui brothers, Charles and Richard, and Kenny Jeremiah. Re-formed by the Inguis in 1972.	
9/02/67	**4**	15	1 **Expressway To Your Heart**	Crimson 1010
12/23/67+	**33**	8	2 Explosion In Your Soul	Crimson 1012
4/20/68	**68**	6	3 Impossible Mission (Mission Impossible)	Crimson 1016
			above 3 written & produced by Kenny Gamble & Leon Huff	
			SOUL TRAIN GANG	
			Studio singers from the syndicated TV show "Soul Train".	
12/06/75+	**75**	5	1 Soul Train '75'	Soul Train 10400
8/13/77	**92**	3	2 My Cherie Amour	Soul Train 10995
			DAVID SOUL	
			Born David Solberg on 8/28/43 in Chicago. Ken Hutchinson of TV's "Starsky & Hutch" Began career as a folksinger and appeared several times on "The Merv Griffin Show" as "The Covered Man" (wore a ski mask).	
1/29/77	**1**[1]	19	1 ●**Don't Give Up On Us**	Private S. 45129
5/07/77	**54**	7	2 Going In With My Eyes Open	Private S. 45150
9/10/77	**52**	12	3 Silver Lady	Private S. 45163
			JIMMY SOUL	
			Born James McCleese in New York City in 1942; raised in North Carolina and Portsmouth, Virginia. Worked with gospel groups, including the Nightingales, billed as "The Wonder Boy".	
3/31/62	**22**	14	1 Twistin' Matilda	S.P.Q.R. 3300
3/30/63	**1**[2]	14	2 **If You Wanna Be Happy**	S.P.Q.R. 3305

DEBUT DATE	PEAK POS	WKS CHR	ARTIST — Record Title	Label & Number
			THE SOULFUL STRINGS	
			Chicago studio group. Richard Evans, conductor.	
2/03/68	**64**	5	1 Burning Spear........ [I]	Cadet 5576
			SOUNDS OF SUNSHINE	
5/29/71	**39**	12	1 Love Means (You Never Have To Say You're Sorry).....	Ranwood 896
			SOUNDS ORCHESTRAL	
			English - Johnny Pearson on piano.	
3/20/65	**10**	14	1 **Cast Your Fate To The Wind**........ [I]	Parkway 942
7/31/65	**76**	4	2 Canadian Sunset........ [I]	Parkway 958
			SOUTH SHORE COMMISSION	
6/28/75	**61**	7	1 Free Man........	Wand 11287
1/10/76	**94**	4	2 We're On The Right Track........	Wand 11291
2/28/76	**86**	4	3 Train Called Freedom........	Wand 11294
			THE SOUTH SIDE MOVEMENT	
4/14/73	**61**	10	1 I' Been Watchin' You........	Wand 11251
			JOE SOUTH	
			Born on 2/28/40 in Atlanta. Successful Nashville session guitarist and songwriter, mid-60s. Wrote "Down In The Boondocks", "Hush" and "Rose Garden". Producer for Billy Joe Royal.	
7/28/58	**47**	3	1 The Purple People Eater Meets The Witch Doctor... [N]	NRC 5000
			Best Seller #47 / Top 100 #71	
8/28/61	**87**	2	2 You're The Reason........	Fairlane 21006
1/11/69	**12**	12	3 Games People Play........	Capitol 2248
7/12/69	**96**	1	4 Birds Of A Feather........	Capitol 2532
8/23/69	**41**	12	5 Don't It Make You Want To Go Home........	Capitol 2592
1/03/70	**12**	11	6 Walk A Mile In My Shoes........	Capitol 2704
			above 2: **JOE SOUTH & THE BELIEVERS**	
3/21/70	**51**	7	7 Children........	Capitol 2755
11/06/71	**78**	7	8 Fool Me........	Capitol 3204
			SOUTHCOTE	
			Canadian pop/rock quartet. Beau David, lead singer.	
3/09/74	**80**	4	1 She........	Buddah 399
			THE SOUTHER, HILLMAN, FURAY BAND	
			Country-rock sextet formed as a supergroup featuring veterans J.D. Souther, Chris Hillman, and Richie Furay.	
8/24/74	**27**	10	1 Fallin' In Love........	Asylum 45201
			J.D. SOUTHER	
			Born John David Souther in Detroit; raised in Amarillo, Texas.	
9/08/79	**7**	21	1 **You're Only Lonely**........	Columbia 11079
3/14/81	**11**	14	2 Her Town Too........	Columbia 60514
			JAMES TAYLOR & J.D. SOUTHER	
			JERI SOUTHERN	
			Born on 8/5/26 in Royal, Nebraska. Singer, pianist.	
11/12/55	**89**	2	1 An Occasional Man........	Decca 29647
			from the film "The Girl Rush"	
			SOUTHSIDE JOHNNY & THE JUKES	
			Rock band formed in Asbury Park, NJ. Led by Johnny Lyon (b: 12/4/48, Neptune, NJ).	
9/22/79	**71**	4	1 I'm So Anxious........	Mercury 76007
			SOUTHSIDE JOHNNY & THE ASBURY JUKES	
8/16/86	**98**	5	2 Walk Away Renee........	Atlantic 89394
			SOUTHWEST F.O.B.	
			Group features England Dan & John Ford Coley.	
10/05/68	**56**	5	1 Smell Of Incense........	Hip 8002
			RED SOVINE	
			Born Woodrow Wilson Sovine on 7/17/18 in Charleston, WV; died on 4/14/80. Country singer, songwriter, guitarist.	
1/08/66	**82**	3	1 Giddyup Go........ [S]	Starday 737
7/24/76	**40**	9	2● Teddy Bear........ [S]	Starday 142

DEBUT DATE	PEAK POS	WKS CHR	ARTIST — Record Title	Label & Number
			SPACE	
			French disco studio production featuring English session singer Madeline Bell.	
4/28/79	**60**	7	1 My Love Is Music	Casablanca 974
			THE SPACEMEN	
10/19/59	**41**	14	1 The Clouds [I]	Alton 254
			SPANDAU BALLET	
			English quintet: Tony Hadley (lead singer), Gary Kemp (guitar), Steve Norman (sax), Martin Kemp (bass) and John Keeble (drums).	
8/06/83	**4**	18	1 **True**	Chrysalis 42720
11/19/83+	**29**	12	2 Gold	Chrysalis 42743
3/31/84	**59**	7	3 Communication	Chrysalis 42770
7/28/84	**34**	12	4 Only When You Leave	Chrysalis 42792
			above 4 written by Gary Kemp	
			THE SPANIELS	
			R&B doo-wop vocal group from Gary, Indiana. James "Pookie" Hudson, lead singer.	
7/01/57	**69**	3	1 Everyone's Laughing	Vee-Jay 246
			SPANKY & OUR GANG	
			Folk/pop group formed in Chicago in 1966 featuring lead singer Elaine "Spanky" McFarlane (b: 6/19/42, Peoria, IL). Spanky became lead singer of the new Mamas & The Papas, early 80s.	
5/20/67	**9**	8	1 **Sunday Will Never Be The Same**	Mercury 72679
8/19/67	**31**	7	2 Making Every Minute Count	Mercury 72714
10/14/67	**14**	11	3 Lazy Day	Mercury 72732
1/06/68	**30**	8	4 Sunday Mornin'	Mercury 72765
4/20/68	**17**	11	5 Like To Get To Know You	Mercury 72795
8/03/68	**43**	8	6 Give A Damn	Mercury 72831
12/07/68	**94**	3	7 Yesterday's Rain	Mercury 72871
2/15/69	**86**	3	8 Anything You Choose	Mercury 72890
6/21/69	**97**	1	9 And She's Mine	Mercury 72926
			SPARKS	
			Rock duo consisting of brothers Ron (keyboards) and Russell Mael (vocals).	
5/15/82	**60**	7	1 I Predict	Atlantic 4030
4/16/83	**49**	12	2 Cool Places	Atlantic 89866
			SPARKS & JANE WIEDLIN (member of the Go-Go's)	
			THE SPATS	
9/26/64	**96**	1	1 Gator Tails And Monkey Ribs	ABC-Para. 10585
			BILLIE JO SPEARS	
			Born on 1/14/37 in Beaumont, Texas. Country singer.	
4/26/69	**80**	4	1 Mr. Walker, It's All Over	Capitol 2436
5/17/75	**78**	5	2 Blanket On The Ground	United Art. 584
			SPECIAL DELIVERY featuring TERRY HUFF	
5/29/76	**75**	8	1 The Lonely One	Mainstream 5581
			RONNIE SPECTOR	
			Born Veronica Bennett on 8/10/45 in New York City. Lead singer of The Ronettes. Married to Phil Spector, 1968-74. Also see Eddie Money.	
5/08/71	**77**	4	1 Try Some, Buy Some	Apple 1832
			written & co-produced by George Harrison	
			THE SPELLBINDERS	
			Jersey City soul quintet.	
11/27/65	**93**	1	1 For You	Columbia 43384
11/19/66	**100**	1	2 Help Me (Get Myself Back Together Again)	Columbia 43830
			SPELLBOUND	
			Bay-area pop group led by Barry Flast.	
7/29/78	**89**	3	1 Rumor At The Honky Tonk	EMI America 8002
			BENNY SPELLMAN	
			Born in 1938 in Pensacola, Florida. Worked with Huey Smith. Also see Ernie K-Doe.	
5/05/62	**80**	6	1 Lipstick Traces (On A Cigarette)	Minit 644
			SPENCER & SPENCER	
5/18/59	**91**	2	1 Russian Band Stand [N]	Argo 5331
			with The Sonia Pryor Choir	

DEBUT DATE	PEAK POS	WKS CHR	ARTIST — Record Title	Label & Number
			SONNY SPENCER	
			Born John Berry on 1/3/38 in Orangeburg, South Carolina.	
11/16/59	**82**	4	1 Gilee	Memo 17984
			STEVE SPERRY	
			Wisconsin-born singer/songwriter based in Chicago. Jingle writer.	
7/16/77	**91**	3	1 Flame	Mercury 73905
			SPIDER	
			New York-based rock quintet. South African native Amanda Blue, lead singer.	
4/19/80	**39**	11	1 New Romance (It's A Mystery)	Dreamland 100
8/02/80	**86**	3	2 Everything Is Alright	Dreamland 103
5/30/81	**43**	10	3 It Didn't Take Long	Dreamland 111
			above 3 written by group member Holly Knight	
			SPIN	
			Sextet consisting of top sessionmen from Holland.	
8/28/76	**95**	2	1 Grasshopper [I]	Ariola Am. 7632
			SPINNERS	
			In 1961, an R&B vocal group from Ferndale High School near Detroit, originally named the Domingoes, became the Spinners. Many personnel changes ensued until their hit lineup in 1972 included: Bobbie Smith, Phillipe Wynne, Billy Henderson, Henry Fambrough and Pervis Jackson. Wynne (d: 7/14/84) left group in 1977, replaced by John Edwards.	
6/26/61	**27**	8	1 That's What Girls Are Made For	Tri-Phi 1001
11/20/61	**91**	1	2 Love (I'm So Glad) I Found You	Tri-Phi 1004
			lead vocals on above 2 by Harvey Fuqua (Moonglows)	
7/17/65	**35**	7	3 I'll Always Love You	Motown 1078
7/25/70	**14**	15	4 It's A Shame	V.I.P. 25057
1/23/71	**89**	3	5 We'll Have It Made	V.I.P. 25060
			above 2 produced by Stevie Wonder	
8/19/72	**3**	15	6● **I'll Be Around/**	
		5	7 How Could I Let You Get Away	Atlantic 2904
12/30/72+	**4**	15	8● **Could It Be I'm Falling In Love**	Atlantic 2927
4/28/73	**11**	15	9● One Of A Kind (Love Affair)	Atlantic 2962
5/12/73	**91**	5	10 Together We Can Make Such Sweet Music	Motown 1235
			recorded in 1968	
8/18/73	**29**	8	11 Ghetto Child	Atlantic 2973
1/26/74	**20**	15	12 Mighty Love - Pt. 1	Atlantic 3006
5/18/74	**18**	13	13 I'm Coming Home	Atlantic 3027
7/27/74	**1**[1]	19	14● **Then Came You**	Atlantic 3202
			DIONNE WARWICKE & SPINNERS	
9/21/74	**15**	13	15 Love Don't Love Nobody - Pt. I	Atlantic 3206
3/08/75	**37**	7	16 Living A Little, Laughing A Little	Atlantic 3252
5/03/75	**54**	7	17 Sadie	Atlantic 3268
8/09/75	**5**	18	18● **They Just Can't Stop It the (Games People Play)**	Atlantic 3284
12/27/75+	**36**	8	19 Love Or Leave	Atlantic 3309
7/17/76	**56**	5	20 Wake Up Susan	Atlantic 3341
9/11/76	**2**[3]	21	21● **The Rubberband Man**	Atlantic 3355
3/19/77	**43**	7	22 You're Throwing A Good Love Away	Atlantic 3382
10/08/77	**89**	4	23 Heaven On Earth (So Fine)	Atlantic 3425
7/29/78	**49**	6	24 If You Wanna Do A Dance	Atlantic 3493
			6-24: produced & arranged by Thom Bell (except #10)	
12/15/79+	**2**[2]	25	25● **Working My Way Back To You/Forgive Me, Girl**	Atlantic 3637
5/17/80	**4**	19	26 **Cupid/I've Loved You For A Long Time**	Atlantic 3664
2/14/81	**52**	8	27 Yesterday Once More/Nothing Remains The Same	Atlantic 3798
3/06/82	**95**	2	28 Never Thought I'd Fall In Love	Atlantic 4007
12/11/82+	**67**	8	29 Funny How Time Slips Away	Atlantic 89922
			SPIRAL STARECASE	
			Sacramento pop/rock quintet featuring lead singer Pat Upton.	
4/05/69	**12**	15	1 More Today Than Yesterday	Columbia 44741
8/30/69	**52**	7	2 No One For Me To Turn To	Columbia 44924
2/07/70	**72**	6	3 She's Ready	Columbia 45048

DEBUT DATE	PEAK POS	WKS CHR	ARTIST — Record Title	Label & Number
			SPIRIT Los Angeles eclectic rock group: Jay Ferguson (lead singer), Mark Andes (bass), Ed Cassidy (drums), Randy California (guitar) and John Locke (keyboards). Ferguson and Andes left to form Jo Jo Gunne, mid-1971. Andes became an original member of Firefall in 1975 and later joined Heart in 1983.	
1/18/69	**25**	12	1 I Got A Line On You	Ode 115
2/07/70	**69**	9	2 1984	Ode 128
9/12/70	**97**	1	3 Animal Zoo	Epic 10648
10/20/73	**92**	2	4 Mr. Skin	Epic 10701
			SPLINTER English duo: Bill Elliott and Bob Purvis.	
12/14/74+	**77**	8	1 Costafine Town produced by George Harrison	Dark Horse 10002
			SPLIT ENZ Sextet from New Zealand, led by brothers Tim and Neil Finn.	
8/23/80	**53**	11	1 I Got You	A&M 2252
			THE SPOKESMEN Johnny Madara, Dave White and Roy Gilmore. White was with Danny & The Juniors.	
9/18/65	**36**	7	1 The Dawn Of Correction answer to "Eve Of Destruction"	Decca 31844
			THE SPORTS Stephen Cummings, lead singer of Australian sextet.	
10/13/79	**45**	7	1 Who Listens To The Radio	Arista 0468
			DUSTY SPRINGFIELD Born Mary O'Brien on 4/16/39 in London, England. Vocalist, guitarist. In The Lana Sisters vocal group. With brother Tom Springfield and Tim Feild in folk trio, the Springfields, 1960-63. Didn't record from 1973-78 except for backup work for Anne Murray in 1975. Began recording again in 1978.	
1/25/64	**12**	10	1 I Only Want To Be With You	Philips 40162
3/28/64	**38**	7	2 Stay Awhile	Philips 40180
6/20/64	**6**	13	3 **Wishin' And Hopin'**	Philips 40207
9/26/64	**41**	7	4 All Cried Out	Philips 40229
3/13/65	**91**	4	5 Losing You	Philips 40270
5/21/66	**4**	13	6 **You Don't Have To Say You Love Me**	Philips 40371
9/17/66	**20**	8	7 All I See Is You	Philips 40396
3/18/67	**40**	8	8 I'll Try Anything	Philips 40439
7/22/67	**22**	15	9 The Look Of Love/ from the film "Casino Royale"	
7/01/67	**76**	4	10 Give Me Time	Philips 40465
11/18/67	**49**	8	11 What's It Gonna Be	Philips 40498
11/30/68+	**10**	12	12 **Son-Of-A Preacher Man**	Atlantic 2580
3/01/69	**64**	6	13 Don't Forget About Me/	
4/12/69	**91**	2	14 Breakfast In Bed	Atlantic 2606
5/03/69	**31**	8	15 The Windmills Of Your Mind	Atlantic 2623
7/12/69	**78**	3	16 Willie & Laura Mae Jones	Atlantic 2647
11/08/69	**24**	12	17 A Brand New Me	Atlantic 2685
2/28/70	**76**	5	18 Silly, Silly, Fool	Atlantic 2705
			RICK SPRINGFIELD Born on 8/23/49 in Sydney, Australia. Singer, actor, composer. With top Australian teen idol band, Zoot, before going solo in 1972. Turned to acting in late 70s, played Noah Drake on the TV soap opera "General Hospital", early 80s. Starred in the film "Hard To Hold" in 1984.	
8/05/72	**14**	13	1 Speak To The Sky	Capitol 3340
11/25/72	**70**	4	2 What Would The Children Think	Capitol 3466
7/13/74	**98**	2	3 American Girls	Columbia 46057
8/21/76	**41**	9	4 Take A Hand	Chelsea 3051
3/28/81	**1**[2]	32	5 ● **Jessie's Girl**	RCA 12201
8/22/81	**8**	22	6 **I've Done Everything For You** written by Sammy Hagar	RCA 12166
12/05/81+	**20**	16	7 Love Is Alright Tonite	RCA 13008
3/06/82	**2**[4]	21	8 **Don't Talk To Strangers**	RCA 13070
6/05/82	**21**	12	9 What Kind Of Fool Am I	RCA 13245
9/11/82	**32**	12	10 I Get Excited	RCA 13303
4/16/83	**9**	18	11 **Affair Of The Heart**	RCA 13497

DEBUT DATE	PEAK POS	WKS CHR	ARTIST — Record Title	Label & Number
			RICK SPRINGFIELD — Cont'd	
7/09/83	18	15	12 Human Touch	RCA 13576
10/15/83	23	15	13 Souls	RCA 13650
3/10/84	5	16	14 **Love Somebody**	RCA 13738
5/26/84	26	12	15 Don't Walk Away	RCA 13813
8/18/84	20	15	16 Bop 'Til You Drop/	
11/17/84	59	10	17 Taxi Dancing	RCA 13861
			RICK SPRINGFIELD & RANDY CRAWFORD	
			above 4 from the film "Hard To Hold"	
11/17/84+	27	13	18 Bruce [N]	Mercury 880405
			recorded in 1978 - an autobiographical song about Springfield being mistaken for Bruce Springsteen	
4/06/85	26	11	19 Celebrate Youth	RCA 14047
6/08/85	22	15	20 State Of The Heart	RCA 14120
			all of above written by Springfield (except #6)	
			THE SPRINGFIELDS	
			English folk trio: Dusty and brother Tom Springfield and Tim Feild.	
8/04/62	20	10	1 Silver Threads And Golden Needles	Philips 40038
11/03/62	95	3	2 Dear Hearts And Gentle People	Philips 40072
			BRUCE SPRINGSTEEN	
			Born on 9/23/49 in Freehold, NJ. Rock singer, songwriter, guitarist. Worked local clubs in New Jersey and Greenwich Village, mid-60s. Own E-Street Band in 1973, consisted of Clarence Clemons (saxophone), David Sancious and Danny Federici (keyboards), Gary Tallent (bass) and Vini Lopez (drums). Sancious and Lopez replaced by Roy Bittan and Max Weinberg. Miami Steve Van Zandt (guitar) joined group in 1975. Wrote Earth Band's "Blinded By The Light" and the Pointer Sisters' "Fire". After "Born To Run", a court injunction prevented the release of any new albums until 1978. "The Boss" is America's #1 rock star of the past decade.	
9/20/75	23	11	1 Born To Run	Columbia 10209
1/24/76	83	3	2 Tenth Avenue Freeze-Out	Columbia 10274
6/10/78	33	9	3 Prove It All Night	Columbia 10763
8/19/78	42	8	4 Badlands	Columbia 10801
11/08/80	5	18	5 **Hungry Heart**	Columbia 11391
2/07/81	20	12	6 Fade Away	Columbia 11431
5/26/84	2[4]	21	7 **Dancing In The Dark**	Columbia 04463
8/11/84	7	18	8 **Cover Me**	Columbia 04561
11/10/84+	9	17	9 **Born In The U.S.A.**	Columbia 04680
2/16/85	6	20	10 **I'm On Fire**	Columbia 04772
6/01/85	5	18	11 **Glory Days**	Columbia 04924
9/07/85	9	13	12 **I'm Goin' Down**	Columbia 05603
12/07/85+	6	15	13 **My Hometown**	Columbia 05728
			all of above written by Springsteen	
			BRUCE SPRINGSTEEN & THE E STREET BAND:	
11/22/86	8	12	14 **War**	Columbia 06432
			SPRINGWELL	
9/18/71	60	10	1 It's For You	Parrot 359
			written by John Lennon & Paul McCartney	
			SPYRO GYRA	
			Buffalo-based jazz/pop band led by sax man Jay Beckenstein.	
6/17/78	90	5	1 Shaker Song [I]	Amherst 730
6/16/79	24	15	2 Morning Dance [I]	Infinity 50011
4/19/80	68	5	3 Catching The Sun [I]	MCA 41180
2/07/81	77	5	4 Cafe Amore [I]	MCA 51035
			SPYS	
			Rock quintet formed by former Foreigner members Al Greenwood and Ed Gagliardi.	
8/14/82	82	5	1 Don't Run My Life	EMI America 8124
			SQUEEZE	
			English pop/rock quintet led by Chris Difford & Glenn Tilbrook.	
8/01/81	49	11	1 Tempted	A&M 2345
			vocal by Paul Carrack	
			BILLY SQUIER	
			Born on 5/12/50 in Wellesley, MA. Hard rock singer, songwriter, guitarist.	
5/16/81	17	20	1 The Stroke	Capitol 5005
9/12/81	35	12	2 In The Dark	Capitol 5040

DEBUT DATE	PEAK POS	WKS CHR	ARTIST — Record Title	Label & Number
			BILLY SQUIER — Cont'd	
11/28/81+	**45**	10	3 My Kinda Lover	Capitol 5037
8/07/82	**68**	6	4 Emotions In Motion	Capitol 5135
10/02/82	**32**	17	5 Everybody Wants You	Capitol 5163
2/05/83	**75**	6	6 She's A Runner	Capitol 5202
7/07/84	**15**	16	7 Rock Me Tonite	Capitol 5370
10/27/84	**75**	3	8 All Night Long	Capitol 5422
12/08/84+	**71**	8	9 Eye On You	Capitol 5416
10/04/86	**80**	5	10 Love Is The Hero all of above written by Squier	Capitol 5619
			S.S.O.	
1/10/76	**99**	4	1 Tonight's The Night	Shady Brook 019
			STACEY Q Dance/disco singer from Los Angeles. Real name: Stacey Swain.	
7/12/86	**3**	22	1 **Two Of Hearts**	Atlantic 89381
12/13/86+	**35**	19	2 We Connect	Atlantic 89331
			CLYDE STACY Born on 8/11/36 in Eufala, Oklahoma. Rockabilly singer.	
6/17/57	**68**	1	1 So Young **CLYDE STACY & The Nitecaps**	Candlelight 1015
11/16/59	**99**	2	2 So Young [R]	Argyle 1001
			JIM STAFFORD Born in Eloise, Florida in 1944. Singer, songwriter, guitarist. Own summer variety TV show in 1975, and co-host of "Those Amazing Animals" from 1980-81.	
5/12/73	**39**	12	1 Swamp Witch	MGM 14496
11/10/73+	**3**	23	2● **Spiders & Snakes**	MGM 14648
4/20/74	**12**	15	3 My Girl Bill [N]	MGM 14718
7/06/74	**7**	14	4 **Wildwood Weed** [N]	MGM 14737
12/21/74+	**24**	10	5 Your Bulldog Drinks Champagne [N]	MGM 14775
8/16/75	**37**	9	6 I Got Stoned And I Missed It [N] all of above produced by Lobo and Phil Gernhard	MGM 14819
4/03/76	**69**	6	7 Jasper	Polydor 14309
1/29/77	**98**	2	8 Turn Loose Of My Leg [N]	Warner 8299
			JO STAFFORD Born on 11/12/20 in Coalinga, California. Member of Tommy Dorsey's vocal group, the Pied Pipers, 1940-42. Married to orchestra leader, Paul Weston.	
10/15/55	**13**	12	1 Suddenly There's A Valley Jockey #13 / Top 100 #16 / Juke Box #18 / Best Seller #21	Columbia 40559
11/26/55+	**14**	20	2 It's Almost Tomorrow Juke Box #14 / Top 100 #19 / Jockey #20 / Best Seller #25	Columbia 40595
3/10/56	**99**	1	3 All Night Long	Columbia 40640
8/04/56	**85**	3	4 With A Little Bit Of Luck from the musical "My Fair Lady"	Columbia 40718
11/17/56	**62**	2	5 Love Me Good	Columbia 40745
11/24/56	**38**	13	6 On London Bridge	Columbia 40782
3/23/57	**53**	12	7 Wind In The Willow all of above with Paul Weston & His Orchestra	Columbia 40832
			TERRY STAFFORD Born in Hollis, Oklahoma and raised in Amarillo, Texas. Elvis Presley sound-alike.	
2/22/64	**3**	15	1 **Suspicion**	Crusader 101
5/23/64	**25**	8	2 I'll Touch A Star	Crusader 105
			STAIRSTEPS - see FIVE STAIRSTEPS	
			STALLION Denver-based quintet. Buddy Stephens, lead singer.	
3/12/77	**37**	9	1 Old Fashioned Boy (You're The One)	Casablanca 877
			FRANK STALLONE Philadelphia singer - brother of actor Sylvester Stallone.	
9/27/80	**67**	6	1 Case Of You	Scotti Br. 603
7/30/83	**10**	16	2 **Far From Over** from the film "Staying Alive"	RSO 815023
5/05/84	**81**	4	3 Darlin'	Polydor 821382

DEBUT DATE	PEAK POS	WKS CHR	ARTIST — Record Title		Label & Number
			STAMPEDERS		
			Pop/rock trio from Calgary, Canada: Rick Dodson, Ronnie King and Kim Berly.		
8/14/71	**8**	14	1 **Sweet City Woman**		Bell 45120
12/04/71+	**61**	7	2 Devil You		Bell 45154
2/28/76	**40**	8	3 Hit The Road Jack featuring a telephone conversation with Wolfman Jack		Quality 501
			JOE STAMPLEY		
			Born on 6/6/43 in Springhill, LA. Country singer. Lead singer of The Uniques.		
1/06/73	**37**	13	1 Soul Song		Dot 17442
			THE STANDELLS		
			Los Angeles-area punk rock quartet: Dick Dodd (lead singer, drums), Larry Tamblyn and Tony Valentino (guitars) and Gary Lane (bass).		
4/23/66	**11**	16	1 Dirty Water		Tower 185
8/13/66	**43**	8	2 Sometimes Good Guys Don't Wear White		Tower 257
10/22/66	**54**	7	3 Why Pick On Me above 3 written & produced by Ed Cobb (Four Preps)		Tower 282
11/25/67	**78**	3	4 Can't Help But Love You		Tower 348
			MICHAEL STANLEY BAND		
			Cleveland rock group: Michael Stanley (vocals, guitar), Kevin Raleigh (vocals, keyboards), Bob Pelander (keyboards), Tommy Dobeck (drums), Michael Gismondi (bass), Rick Bell (sax) and Gary Markashy (lead guitar - replaced by Danny Powers in 1983).		
11/22/80+	**33**	16	1 He Can't Love You		EMI America 8063
3/28/81	**68**	6	2 Lover		EMI America 8064
8/08/81	**64**	8	3 Falling In Love Again		EMI America 8090
9/11/82	**78**	4	4 When I'm Holding You Tight		EMI America 8130
12/25/82+	**81**	5	5 Take The Time		EMI America 8146
10/01/83	**39**	10	6 My Town		EMI America 8178
12/24/83+	**75**	5	7 Someone Like You		EMI America 8189
			PAUL STANLEY		
			Born Paul Eisen on 1/20/52 in Queens, New York. Rhythm guitarist of Kiss.		
11/04/78	**46**	12	1 Hold Me, Touch Me		Casablanca 940
			THE STAPLE SINGERS		
			Family soul group consisting of Roebuck "Pop" Staples (b: 12/28/15, Winoma, MS), with his son Pervis (who left in 1971) and daughters Cleotha, Yvonne, and lead singer Mavis Staples. Roebuck was a blues guitarist in his teens, later with the Golden Trumpets gospel group. Moved to Chicago in 1935. Formed own gospel group in the early 50s. First recorded for United in 1953. Mavis recorded solo, early 70s.		
6/03/67	**95**	1	1 Why? (Am I Treated So Bad)		Epic 10158
9/23/67	**66**	4	2 For What It's Worth		Epic 10220
2/06/71	**27**	12	3 Heavy Makes You Happy (Sha-Na-Boom Boom)		Stax 0083
7/31/71	**97**	2	4 You've Got To Earn It		Stax 0093
10/16/71	**12**	14	5 Respect Yourself		Stax 0104
4/08/72	**1**[1]	15	6 **I'll Take You There**		Stax 0125
8/05/72	**38**	7	7 This World		Stax 0137
3/10/73	**33**	9	8 Oh La De Da		Stax 0156
6/16/73	**66**	6	9 Be What You Are		Stax 0164
10/27/73	**9**	16	10 ● **If You're Ready (Come Go With Me)**		Stax 0179
2/23/74	**23**	13	11 Touch A Hand, Make A Friend		Stax 0196
8/17/74	**79**	7	12 City In The Sky		Stax 0215
12/07/74	**76**	3	13 My Main Man all of above Stax recordings produced by Al Bell		Stax 0227
10/25/75	**1**[1]	15	14 ● **Let's Do It Again**		Curtom 0109
2/28/76	**70**	6	15 New Orleans above 2 from the film "Let's Do It Again"		Curtom 0113
			MAVIS STAPLES		
			Lead singer of The Staple Singers.		
9/05/70	**87**	4	1 I Have Learned To Do Without You		Volt 4044
			CYRIL STAPLETON		
			Born on 12/31/14 in Nottingham, England; died on 2/25/74. British bandleader. BBC showband maestro, 1952-57.		
9/01/56	**25**	14	1 The Italian Theme	[I]	London 1672
1/12/59	**13**	14	2 The Children's Marching Song with the children from the film "The Inn Of The Sixth Happiness"	[N]	London 1851

DEBUT DATE	PEAK POS	WKS CHR	ARTIST — Record Title	Label & Number
			THE STAR WARS INTERGALACTIC DROID CHOIR & CHORALE - see MECO	
			STARBUCK	
			Atlanta pop/rock septet. Bruce Blackman, lead singer. Also see Eternity's Children and Korona.	
4/17/76	**3**	22	1 **Moonlight Feels Right**	Private S. 45039
9/11/76	**43**	7	2 I Got To Know	Private S. 45104
12/18/76	**73**	5	3 Lucky Man	Private S. 45125
4/16/77	**38**	8	4 Everybody Be Dancin'	Private S. 45144
9/30/78	**58**	6	5 Searching For A Thrill	United Art. 1245
			BUDDY STARCHER	
4/09/66	**39**	7	1 History Repeats Itself [S]	Boone 1038
			STARGARD	
			Disco trio: Rochelle Runnells, Debra Anderson and Janice Williams. Appeared as "The Diamonds" in film "Sgt. Pepper's Lonely Hearts Club Band".	
1/28/78	**21**	14	1 Theme Song From 'Which Way Is Up'/ from the film of the same title	
3/04/78	**88**	5	2 Disco Rufus [I]	MCA 40825
			STARK & McBRIEN	
			Pop duo: Fred Stark & Rod McBrien. Best known for their music and voices on jingles for McDonald's, Miller Beer, Wrangler and Coca-Cola.	
1/25/75	**85**	6	1 Isn't It Lonely Together	RCA 10109
			STARLAND VOCAL BAND	
			Pop quartet: Bill and wife Taffy Danoff, John Carroll and Margot Chapman. Bill and Taffy had fronted Fat City folk quintet. Danoff co-wrote "Take Me Home, Country Roads" with friend, John Denver. Denver owned Windsong record label.	
5/08/76	**1**[2]	20	1 ● **Afternoon Delight**	Windsong 10588
10/16/76	**66**	3	2 California Day	Windsong 10785
1/08/77	**71**	6	3 Hail! Hail! Rock And Roll!	Windsong 10855
2/23/80	**71**	6	4 Loving You With My Eyes	Windsong 11899
			THE STARLETS	
			Female R&B group from Chicago. Dynetta Boone ("Liz Walker"), lead singer.	
4/24/61	**38**	16	1 Better Tell Him No	Pam 1003
			STARPOINT	
			Black sextet from Maryland - brothers Ernest, George, Orlando and Gregory Phillips, plus Renee Diggs and Kayode Adeyemo.	
9/28/85	**25**	24	1 Object Of My Desire	Elektra 69621
3/22/86	**46**	12	2 Restless	Elektra 69561
			EDWIN STARR	
			Born Charles Hatcher on 1/21/42 in Nashville; raised in Cleveland. In vocal group the Futuretones, recorded for Tress in 1957. With Bill Doggett Combo from 1963-65. Also see The Holidays.	
8/07/65	**21**	11	1 Agent Double-O-Soul	Ric-Tic 103
12/11/65	**95**	2	2 Back Street	Ric-Tic 107
2/19/66	**48**	8	3 Stop Her On Sight (S.O.S.)	Ric-Tic 109
5/07/66	**84**	4	4 Headline News	Ric-Tic 114
2/15/69	**6**	14	5 **Twenty-Five Miles**	Gordy 7083
6/28/69	**80**	4	6 I'm Still A Struggling Man	Gordy 7087
8/16/69	**92**	2	7 Oh How Happy EDWIN STARR & BLINKY (Sandra Williams)	Gordy 7090
7/11/70	**1**[3]	15	8 **War**	Gordy 7101
12/19/70+	**26**	8	9 Stop The War Now	Gordy 7104
4/24/71	**64**	6	10 Funky Music Sho Nuff Turns Me On	Gordy 7107
6/30/73	**80**	6	11 There You Go	Soul 35103
2/07/76	**98**	2	12 Abyssinia Jones	Granite 532
2/10/79	**65**	7	13 Contact	20th Century 2396
8/04/79	**79**	5	14 H.A.P.P.Y. Radio	20th Century 2408

DEBUT DATE	PEAK POS	WKS CHR	ARTIST — Record Title	Label & Number
			KAY STARR Born Katherine Starks on 7/21/22 in Dougherty, Oklahoma. With Joe Venuti's orchestra at age 15, and sang briefly with Glenn Miller, Charlie Barnet and Bob Crosby before launching solo career.	
8/06/55	**17**	1	1 Good And Lonesome Juke Box #17	RCA 6146
12/31/55+	**1**[6]	25	2 **Rock And Roll Waltz/** Juke Box #1(6) / Top 100 #1(4) / Best Seller #1(1) / Jockey #1(1)	
2/04/56	**73**	4	3 I've Changed My Mind A Thousand Times	RCA 6359
6/09/56	**40**	10	4 Second Fiddle/	
8/11/56	**89**	1	5 Love Ain't Right	RCA 6541
9/08/56	**89**	4	6 The Good Book	RCA 6617
9/08/56	**89**	3	7 The Things I Never Had above 2 from the TV production "The Lord Don't Play Favorites"	RCA 6617
4/20/57	**54**	5	8 Jamie Boy/	
4/27/57	**73**	3	9 A Little Loneliness	RCA 6864
9/02/57	**9**	12	10 **My Heart Reminds Me** Jockey #9 / Top 100 #53	RCA 6981
3/20/61	**49**	9	11 Foolin' Around	Capitol 4542
6/19/61	**94**	3	12 I'll Never Be Free	Capitol 4583
10/27/62	**92**	4	13 Four Walls	Capitol 4835
			KENNY STARR	
12/06/75	**58**	5	1 The Blind Man In The Bleachers	MCA 40474
			LUCILLE STARR Singer born in St. Boniface, Manitoba, Canada.	
5/16/64	**54**	8	1 The French Song [F]	Almo 204
			RANDY STARR Born Warren Nadel on 7/2/30 in New York City. Pop singer, songwriter.	
4/06/57	**32**	11	1 After School	Dale 100
			RINGO STARR Born Richard Starkey on 7/7/40 in Liverpool, England. Ringo joined The Beatles following ousting of drummer Pete Best in 1962. First solo album in 1970. Films "Candy" (made in 1967, released in 1969), "The Magic Christian", "200 Motels", "Born To Boogie", "Blindman", "That'll Be The Day" and "Cave Man". Married actress Barbara Bach in 1982.	
11/07/70	**87**	5	1 Beaucoups Of Blues	Apple 2969
5/01/71	**4**	12	2 ● **It Don't Come Easy**	Apple 1831
4/01/72	**9**	10	3 **Back Off Boogaloo** 2-3: written by Ringo; produced by George Harrison	Apple 1849
10/06/73	**1**[1]	16	4 ● **Photograph** written by Ringo & George Harrison	Apple 1865
12/15/73+	**1**[1]	15	5 ● **You're Sixteen**	Apple 1870
3/09/74	**5**	14	6 **Oh My My**	Apple 1872
11/16/74+	**6**	13	7 **Only You**	Apple 1876
2/08/75	**3**	14	8 **No No Song/**	
		14	9 Snookeroo written by Elton John & Bernie Taupin	Apple 1880
6/14/75	**31**	7	10 It's All Down To Goodnight Vienna/ written by John Lennon	
		7	11 Oo-Wee 6 & 11: written by Ringo & Vini Poncia	Apple 1882
10/02/76	**26**	9	12 A Dose Of Rock 'N' Roll	Atlantic 3361
1/29/77	**74**	3	13 Hey Baby	Atlantic 3371
11/07/81	**38**	11	14 Wrack My Brain written and produced by George Harrison	Boardwalk 130
			STARS on 45 Dutch session vocalists and musicians assembled by producer Jaap Eggermont.	
4/11/81	**1**[1]	21	1 ● **Stars on 45** Venus/Sugar Sugar/No Reply/I'll Be Back/Drive My Car/Do You Want To Know A Secret/We Can Work It Out/I Should Have Known Better/ Nowhere Man/You're Going To Lose That Girl	Radio 3810
7/18/81	**67**	6	2 Stars on 45 II Good Day Sunshine/My Sweet Lord/Here Comes The Sun/While My Guitar Gently Weeps/Tax Man/A Hard Day's Night/Please Please Me/From Me To You/I Wanna Hold Your Hand	Radio 3830

DEBUT DATE	PEAK POS	WKS CHR	ARTIST — Record Title	Label & Number
			STARS on 45 — Cont'd	
9/26/81	**55**	7	3 More Stars on 45	Radio 3863
			Papa Was A Rolling Stone/Dance To The Music/Sugar Baby Love/ Lets Go To San Francisco/A Horse With No Name/Monday Monday/ Tears Of A Clown/Stop In The Name Of Love/Cracklin' Rosie/Do Wah Diddy-Diddy/A Lover's Concerto/Reach Out I'll Be There/Sounds Of Silence	
3/27/82	**28**	10	4 Stars on 45 III	Radio 4019
			Uptight Everything's All Right/My Cherie Amour/Yester Me, Yester You/Master Blaster/You Are The Sunshine Of My Life/Isn't She Lovely/Sir Duke/I Wish/I Was Made To Love Her/Superstition/ Fingertips	
			STARSHIP - see JEFFERSON STARSHIP	
			STARZ	
			New York-based rock quintet: Michael Lee Smith (lead singer), Peter Sweval (bassist), Richie Ranno (guitar), Brenden Harkin (guitar) and Joe X. Dube (drums).	
12/25/76+	**95**	3	1 (She's Just A) Fallen Angel	Capitol 4343
3/19/77	**33**	10	2 Cherry Baby	Capitol 4399
6/25/77	**66**	8	3 Sing It, Shout It	Capitol 4434
3/11/78	**79**	4	4 (Any Way That You Want It) I'll Be There	Capitol 4546
5/20/78	**78**	3	5 Hold On To The Night	Capitol 4566
10/21/78	**81**	3	6 So Young, So Bad	Capitol 4637
			THE STATLER BROTHERS	
			Country vocal quartet from Virginia. Consisted of brothers Harold & Don Reid, Phil Balsley and Lew DeWitt (replaced by Jimmy Fortune in 1983).	
11/13/65+	**4**	13	1 **Flowers On The Wall**	Columbia 43315
1/16/71	**58**	9	2 Bed Of Rose's	Mercury 73141
11/01/75	**93**	4	3 I'll Go To My Grave Loving You	Mercury 73687
			CANDI STATON	
			Born in Hanceville, Alabama. Sang with the Jewel Gospel Trio from age ten. Went solo in 1968. Married for a time to Clarence Carter.	
6/21/69	**46**	8	1 I'd Rather Be An Old Man's Sweetheart (Than A Young Man's Fool)	Fame 1456
1/03/70	**56**	8	2 I'm Just A Prisoner (Of Your Good Lovin')	Fame 1460
5/09/70	**60**	8	3 Sweet Feeling	Fame 1466
8/29/70	**24**	14	4 Stand By Your Man	Fame 1472
1/02/71	**52**	10	5 He Called Me Baby	Fame 1476
6/24/72	**48**	11	6 In The Ghetto	Fame 91000
11/04/72	**83**	6	7 Lovin' You, Lovin' Me	Fame 91005
2/03/73	**63**	9	8 Do It In The Name Of Love	Fame 91009
12/28/74+	**51**	6	9 As Long As He Takes Care Of Home	Warner 8038
			all of above produced by Rick Hall	
5/29/76	**20**	16	10 Young Hearts Run Free	Warner 8181
			THE STATUES	
			Nashville-based vocal trio: James "Buzz" Cason, Hugh Jarrett and Richard Williams. Also see Garry Miles.	
8/08/60	**84**	3	1 Blue Velvet	Liberty 55245
			THE STATUS QUO	
			English rock quintet: Francis Rossi, Rick Parfitt, Roy Lynes, John Coghlan and Alan Lancaster.	
5/18/68	**12**	17	1 Pictures Of Matchstick Men	Cadet Con. 7001
9/28/68	**70**	3	2 Ice In The Sun	Cadet Con. 7006
			STEALERS WHEEL	
			English group led by Gerry Rafferty (vocals, guitar) & Joe Egan (vocals, keyboards).	
3/03/73	**6**	18	1 **Stuck In The Middle With You**	A&M 1416
7/14/73	**49**	8	2 Everyone's Agreed That Everything Will Turn Out Fine	A&M 1450
1/05/74	**29**	14	3 Star	A&M 1483
			STEAM	
			New York City studio group assembled by producer Paul Leka.	
10/18/69	**1**[2]	16	1 ● **Na Na Hey Hey Kiss Him Goodbye**	Fontana 1667
1/24/70	**46**	7	2 I've Gotta Make You Love Me	Mercury 73020

DEBUT DATE	PEAK POS	WKS CHR	ARTIST — Record Title	Label & Number
			STEEL BREEZE	
			Ric Jacobs, lead singer of 6-man pop band from California.	
8/28/82	**16**	20	1 You Don't Want Me Anymore	RCA 13283
1/15/83	**30**	13	2 Dreamin' Is Easy	RCA 13427
			MAUREEN STEELE	
5/04/85	**77**	5	1 Save The Night For Me	Motown 1787
			THE STEELERS	
			R&B quintet: Leonard "Red" Truss, Wales Wallace, Wes "Preach" Wells, Alonzo "Cool" Wells and George "Flue" Wells.	
11/15/69	**56**	6	1 Get It From The Bottom	Date 1642
			STEELY DAN	
			Los Angeles-based pop/jazz-styled group formed by Donald Fagen (keyboards, vocals) and Walter Becker (bass, vocals). Group, primarily known as a studio unit, featured Fagen and Becker with various studio musicians. Duo went their separate ways, 1981.	
11/18/72+	**6**	17	1 **Do It Again**	ABC 11338
3/10/73	**11**	16	2 Reeling In The Years	ABC 11352
7/28/73	**61**	8	3 Show Biz Kids	ABC 11382
11/03/73	**63**	9	4 My Old School	ABC 11396
5/11/74	**4**	19	5 **Rikki Don't Lose That Number**	ABC 11439
10/12/74	**57**	5	6 Pretzel Logic	ABC 12033
5/24/75	**37**	7	7 Black Friday	ABC 12101
7/10/76	**82**	3	8 Kid Charlemagne	ABC 12195
9/25/76	**59**	5	9 The Fez	ABC 12222
11/19/77+	**11**	19	10 Peg	ABC 12320
4/01/78	**19**	16	11 Deacon Blues	ABC 12355
6/03/78	**22**	10	12 FM (No Static At All) from the film "FM"	MCA 40894
8/26/78	**26**	11	13 Josie	ABC 12404
11/29/80+	**10**	19	14 **Hey Nineteen**	MCA 51036
3/14/81	**22**	11	15 Time Out Of Mind	MCA 51082
			all of above written by Fagen & Becker and produced by Gary Katz	
			LOU STEIN	
			Born on 4/22/22 in Philadelphia. Pianist with Ray McKinley, 1941-42 & 1946-47. Studio and freelance musician into the 70s.	
3/02/57	**31**	14	1 Almost Paradise [I] with Bill Fontaine's orchestra	RKO Unique 385
			JIM STEINMAN	
			Born in New York City. Wrote, arranged all cuts on Meat Loaf's "Bat Out Of Hell" LP.	
5/30/81	**32**	16	1 Rock And Roll Dreams Come Through featured vocals: Rory Dodd	Epic 02111
			VAN STEPHENSON	
			Pop singer/songwriter from Nashville.	
9/12/81	**79**	4	1 You've Got A Good Love Coming	Handshake 02140
4/21/84	**22**	17	2 Modern Day Delilah	MCA 52376
8/04/84	**45**	9	3 What The Big Girls Do	MCA 52437
			STEPPENWOLF	
			Hard rock quintet formed in Los Angeles in 1967. Original lineup: John Kay (born Joachim Krauledat on 4/12/44 in Tilsit, East Germany), vocals, guitar; Michael Monarch, guitar; Goldy McJohn, keyboards; Nick St. Nicholas, bass; Mars Bonfire (Dennis Edmonton), guitar, and brother Jerry Edmonton, drums. All but Monarch were members of the Canadian group, Sparrow. Many personnel changes except for Kay, McJohn and Jerry Edmonton.	
7/13/68	**2**[3]	13	1 ● **Born To Be Wild**	Dunhill 4138
10/05/68	**3**	16	2 ● **Magic Carpet Ride**	Dunhill 4161
3/01/69	**10**	10	3 **Rock Me**	Dunhill 4182
5/10/69	**51**	5	4 It's Never Too Late	Dunhill 4192
8/16/69	**31**	9	5 Move Over	Dunhill 4205
12/27/69+	**39**	8	6 Monster	Dunhill 4221
4/11/70	**35**	8	7 Hey Lawdy Mama	Dunhill 4234
			all of above produced by Gabriel Mekler	
8/22/70	**62**	7	8 Screaming Night Hog	Dunhill 4248
11/14/70	**54**	6	9 Who Needs Ya	Dunhill 4261
3/06/71	**60**	7	10 Snow Blind Friend	Dunhill 4269
7/17/71	**52**	8	11 Ride With Me	Dunhill 4283

DEBUT DATE	PEAK POS	WKS CHR	ARTIST — Record Title	Label & Number
			STEPPENWOLF — Cont'd	
11/06/71	**64**	7	12 For Ladies Only	Dunhill 4292
9/07/74	**29**	9	13 Straight Shootin' Woman	Mums 6031
			THE STEREOS	
			R&B quintet from Steubenville, Ohio. Originally called the Buckeyes. Consisted of Bruce Robinson (lead), Nathaniel Hicks, Sam Profit, George Otis and Ronnie Collins.	
9/25/61	**29**	9	1 I Really Love You	Cub 9095
			APRIL STEVENS	
			Born on 4/29/36 in Niagara Falls, New York. Half of Nino Tempo & April Stevens duo.	
11/30/59	**86**	3	1 Teach Me Tiger	Imperial 5626
6/15/74	**93**	4	2 Wake Up And Love Me shown only as: **APRIL**	A&M 1528
			CAT STEVENS	
			Born Steven Georgiou on 7/21/47 in London, England. Began career playing folk music at Hammersmith College in 1966. Contracted tuberculosis in 1968, and spent over a year recuperating. Adopted new style when he reemerged. Lived in Brazil, mid-70s. Converted to Muslim religion, late 1979, took name Yusef Islam.	
2/13/71	**11**	13	1 Wild World	A&M 1231
6/26/71	**30**	11	2 Moon Shadow	A&M 1265
9/25/71	**7**	12	3 **Peace Train**	A&M 1291
4/01/72	**6**	14	4 **Morning Has Broken**	A&M 1335
11/18/72+	**16**	11	5 Sitting	A&M 1396
7/07/73	**31**	10	6 The Hurt	A&M 1418
3/16/74	**10**	17	7 **Oh Very Young**	A&M 1503
8/03/74	**6**	14	8 **Another Saturday Night**	A&M 1602
12/07/74+	**26**	10	9 Ready	A&M 1645
7/19/75	**33**	9	10 Two Fine People	A&M 1700
2/07/76	**41**	6	11 Banapple Gas	A&M 1785
6/25/77	**33**	10	12 (Remember The Days Of The) Old Schoolyard	A&M 1948
11/19/77+	**70**	9	13 Was Dog A Doughnut [I]	A&M 1971
1/27/79	**83**	4	14 Bad Brakes all of above written by Stevens (except #4 & 8)	A&M 2109
			CONNIE STEVENS	
			Born Concetta Ingolia on 4/8/38 in Brooklyn. Played Cricket Blake on TV's "Hawaiian Eye", 1959-63. In films "Eighteen And Anxious", "Rockabye Baby", "Parrish", "Never Too Late", and others.	
4/20/59	**4**	13	1 **Kookie, Kookie (Lend Me Your Comb)** [N] **EDWARD BYRNES & CONNIE STEVENS**	Warner 5047
2/01/60	**3**	24	2 **Sixteen Reasons**	Warner 5137
7/04/60	**71**	5	3 Too Young To Go Steady	Warner 5159
5/05/62	**52**	11	4 Why'd You Wanna Make Me Cry	Warner 5265
8/04/62	**43**	8	5 Mr. Songwriter	Warner 5289
4/24/65	**53**	7	6 Now That You've Gone	Warner 5610
			DODIE STEVENS	
			Born Geraldine Pasquale on 2/17/46 in Chicago; raised in California.	
2/16/59	**3**	19	1 **Pink Shoe Laces**	Crystalette 724
6/01/59	**79**	3	2 Yes-Sir-ee/	
6/29/59	**89**	1	3 The Five Pennies from the film of the same title	Crystalette 728
8/08/60	**73**	8	4 No	Dot 16103
12/31/60+	**60**	6	5 Yes, I'm Lonesome Tonight	Dot 16167
			RAY STEVENS	
			Born Ray Ragsdale on 1/24/41 in Clarkdale, Georgia. Attended Georgia State University, studied music theory and composition. Production work, mid-60s. Numerous appearances on Andy Williams TV show, late 60s. Own TV show in summer of 1970. Featured on "Music Country" TV show, 1973-74. The #1 novelty recording artist of the rock era.	
8/21/61	**35**	6	1 Jeremiah Peabody's Poly Unsaturated Quick Dissolving Fast Acting Pleasant Tasting Green And Purple Pills [N]	Mercury 71843
6/30/62	**5**	11	2 **Ahab, The Arab** [N]	Mercury 71966
10/13/62	**91**	3	3 Further More [N]	Mercury 72039
12/15/62	**45**	3	4 Santa Claus Is Watching You [X-N]	Mercury 72058
3/30/63	**81**	3	5 Funny Man	Mercury 72098

DEBUT DATE	PEAK POS	WKS CHR	ARTIST — Record Title		Label & Number
			RAY STEVENS — Cont'd		
6/15/63	**17**	9	6 Harry The Hairy Ape	[N]	Mercury 72125
10/12/63	**59**	3	7 Speed Ball	[N]	Mercury 72189
7/16/66	**91**	2	8 Freddie Feelgood (and His Funky Little Five Piece Band)	[N]	Monument 946
4/20/68	**52**	9	9 Unwind		Monument 1048
8/03/68	**28**	7	10 Mr. Businessman		Monument 1083
4/05/69	**8**	13	11 ● **Gitarzan**	[N]	Monument 1131
6/28/69	**27**	8	12 Along Came Jones	[N]	Monument 1150
10/25/69	**81**	3	13 Sunday Mornin' Comin' Down		Monument 1163
4/04/70	**1**[2]	15	14 ● **Everything Is Beautiful**		Barnaby 2011
7/25/70	**45**	6	15 America, Communicate With Me		Barnaby 2016
11/07/70	**81**	4	16 Sunset Strip		Barnaby 2021
12/19/70+	**50**	10	17 Bridget The Midget (The Queen Of The Blues)	[N]	Barnaby 2024
5/01/71	**82**	3	18 A Mama And A Papa		Barnaby 2029
8/28/71	**70**	6	19 All My Trials		Barnaby 2039
11/20/71	**63**	7	20 Turn Your Radio On		Barnaby 2048
4/13/74	**1**[3]	17	21 ● **The Streak**	[N]	Barnaby 600
7/27/74	**73**	7	22 Moonlight Special	[N]	Barnaby 604
			parody of TV's "Midnight Special"		
			all of above written by Stevens (except #12-13, 18 & 20)		
4/26/75	**14**	16	23 Misty		Barnaby 614
10/11/75	**68**	5	24 Indian Love Call		Barnaby 616
			revival of Paul Whiteman's 1925 hit (POS 3)		
1/24/76	**93**	2	25 Young Love		Barnaby 618
1/08/77	**40**	7	26 In The Mood	[N]	Warner 8301
			HENHOUSE FIVE PLUS TOO		
3/24/79	**49**	8	27 I Need Your Help Barry Manilow	[N]	Warner 8785
			SHAKIN' STEVENS		
			Born Michael Barratt on 3/4/48 in Ely, Wales. Rockabilly singer/songwriter.		
4/21/84	**67**	6	1 I Cry Just A Little Bit		Epic 04338
			B.W. STEVENSON		
			Born Louis Stevenson on 10/5/49 in Dallas, Texas.		
5/12/73	**66**	8	1 Shambala		RCA 0952
7/28/73	**9**	16	2 **My Maria**		RCA 0030
12/01/73+	**53**	7	3 The River Of Love		RCA 0171
4/16/77	**82**	5	4 Down To The Station		Warner 8343
			AL STEWART		
			Born on 9/5/45 in Glasgow, Scotland. Pop-rock singer, composer, guitarist.		
12/11/76+	**8**	17	1 **Year Of The Cat**		Janus 266
4/23/77	**42**	9	2 On The Border		Janus 267
9/30/78	**7**	18	3 **Time Passages**		Arista 0362
1/27/79	**29**	9	4 Song On The Radio		Arista 0389
			above 4 produced by Alan Parsons		
8/30/80	**24**	13	5 Midnight Rocks		Arista 0552
			AMII STEWART		
			Born in Washington, DC in 1956. Disco singer, dancer, actress. In the Broadway musical "Bubbling Brown Sugar".		
1/27/79	**1**[1]	20	1 ▲ **Knock On Wood**		Ariola 7736
6/23/79	**69**	6	2 Light My Fire/137 Disco Heaven		Ariola 7753
8/30/80	**63**	8	3 My Guy/My Girl		Handshake 5300
			AMII STEWART & JOHNNY BRISTOL		
			ANDY STEWART		
			Born in Glasgow, Scotland in 1933. Singer, composer, actor, comedian, impressionist.		
4/03/61	**69**	6	1 A Scottish Soldier (Green Hills of Tyrol)		Warwick 627
8/21/61	**77**	4	2 Donald Where's Your Troosers?	[N]	Warwick 665
			backed by The White Heather Group		
			BARON STEWART		
8/16/75	**91**	6	1 We Been Singin' Songs		United Art. 686

DEBUT DATE	PEAK POS	WKS CHR	ARTIST — Record Title	Label & Number
			BILLY STEWART	
			Born on 3/24/37 in Washington, DC; died in an auto accident on 1/17/70. R&B vocalist, composer, keyboardist. Discovered by Bo Diddley in 1956. First recorded for Chess/Argo in 1956. Nicknamed "Fat Boy".	
7/21/62	**79**	5	1 Reap What You Sow	Chess 1820
9/28/63	**70**	6	2 Strange Feeling	Chess 1868
3/27/65	**26**	10	3 I Do Love You	Chess 1922
6/19/65	**24**	8	4 Sitting In The Park	Chess 1932
9/18/65	**97**	2	5 How Nice It Is all of above written by Stewart	Chess 1941
1/22/66	**96**	2	6 Because I Love You/	
1/01/66	**100**	1	7 Mountain Of Love	Chess 1948
7/16/66	**10**	10	8 **Summertime** from the musical "Porgy & Bess"	Chess 1966
10/15/66	**29**	8	9 Secret Love revival of Doris Day's 1954 hit (POS 1)	Chess 1978
2/11/67	**74**	5	10 Every Day I Have The Blues	Chess 1991
12/02/67+	**86**	9	11 Cross My Heart	Chess 2002
2/22/69	**94**	3	12 I Do Love You [R]	Chess 1922
			DAVE STEWART & BARBARA GASKIN	
			British duo - vocals by Gaskin and all instruments played by Stewart.	
12/19/81+	**72**	8	1 It's My Party	Platinum 4
			JERMAINE STEWART	
2/02/85	**41**	15	1 The Word Is Out	Arista 9256
5/17/86	**5**	22	2 **We Don't Have To Take Our Clothes Off**	Arista 9424
9/20/86	**42**	9	3 Jody	Arista 9476
			JOHN STEWART	
			Born on 9/5/39 in San Diego. Member of the Kingston Trio from 1961-67. Wrote "Daydream Believer".	
9/06/69	**74**	3	1 Armstrong	Capitol 2605
5/19/79	**5**	18	2 **Gold**	RSO 931
8/25/79	**28**	12	3 Midnight Wind above 2: backing vocals by Stevie Nicks & Lindsey Buckingham	RSO 1000
12/08/79+	**34**	13	4 Lost Her In The Sun	RSO 1016
			ROD STEWART	
			Born on 1/10/45 in London, England. Worked as a folksinger in Europe, early 60s. Recorded for English Decca in 1964. With the Hoochie Coochie Men, Steampacket, and Shotgun Express. Joined Jeff Beck Group, 1967-69. With Faces from 1969-75, also recorded solo during this time. Left Faces in December, 1975. Also see Python Lee Jackson.	
7/17/71	**1**[5]	17	1 ● **Maggie May/**	
		5	2 Reason To Believe	Mercury 73224
11/20/71	**24**	9	3 (I Know) I'm Losing You **ROD STEWART with FACES**	Mercury 73244
2/12/72	**42**	6	4 Handbags And Gladrags	Mercury 73031
8/26/72	**13**	10	5 You Wear It Well	Mercury 73330
11/18/72	**40**	7	6 Angel	Mercury 73344
8/11/73	**59**	7	7 Twisting The Night Away	Mercury 73412
10/13/73	**59**	8	8 Oh! No Not My Baby	Mercury 73426
12/14/74	**91**	2	9 Mine For Me written by Paul McCartney all of above produced by Stewart (except #3)	Mercury 73636
10/18/75	**58**	7	10 Sailing	Warner 8146
1/10/76	**83**	4	11 This Old Heart Of Mine	Warner 8170
10/02/76	**1**[8]	23	12 ● **Tonight's The Night (Gonna Be Alright)**	Warner 8262
2/12/77	**21**	12	13 The First Cut Is The Deepest written by Cat Stevens	Warner 8321
6/04/77	**30**	10	14 The Killing Of Georgie (Part I & II)	Warner 8396
10/29/77+	**4**	22	15 ● **You're In My Heart (The Final Acclaim)**	Warner 8475
2/11/78	**28**	11	16 Hot Legs	Warner 8535
4/29/78	**22**	12	17 I Was Only Joking	Warner 8568
12/23/78+	**1**[4]	21	18 ▲ **Da Ya Think I'm Sexy?**	Warner 8724
4/21/79	**22**	12	19 Ain't Love A Bitch	Warner 8810
12/22/79+	**46**	11	20 I Don't Want To Talk About It 10-20: produced by Tom Dowd	Warner 49138

DEBUT DATE	PEAK POS	WKS CHR	ARTIST — Record Title	Label & Number
			ROD STEWART — Cont'd	
11/22/80+	**5**	20	21 **Passion**	Warner 49617
3/21/81	**71**	5	22 Somebody Special	Warner 49686
10/17/81	**5**	19	23 **Young Turks**	Warner 49843
1/23/82	**20**	14	24 Tonight I'm Yours (Don't Hurt Me)	Warner 49886
4/24/82	**49**	9	25 How Long	Warner 50051
5/28/83	**14**	14	26 Baby Jane	Warner 29608
8/27/83	**35**	12	27 What Am I Gonna Do (I'm So In Love With You)	Warner 29564
5/26/84	**6**	18	28 **Infatuation**	Warner 29256
8/25/84	**10**	17	29 **Some Guys Have All The Luck**	Warner 29215
12/15/84+	**72**	6	30 All Right Now	Warner 29122
6/15/85	**48**	10	31 People Get Ready JEFF BECK & ROD STEWART	Epic 05416
5/31/86	**6**	18	32 **Love Touch** theme from the film "Legal Eagles"	Warner 28668
8/30/86	**52**	9	33 Another Heartache	Warner 28631
11/29/86	**83**	6	34 Every Beat Of My Heart	Warner 28625
			SANDY STEWART Born Sandra Galitz on 7/10/37 in Philadelphia. Regular on the Eddie Fisher and Perry Como TV shows.	
12/29/62+	**20**	10	1 My Coloring Book	Colpix 669
			STEPHEN STILLS Born on 1/3/45 in Dallas. Member of Buffalo Springfield and Crosby, Stills & Nash.	
12/12/70+	**14**	11	1 Love The One You're With	Atlantic 2778
3/13/71	**37**	6	2 Sit Yourself Down	Atlantic 2790
6/12/71	**43**	9	3 Change Partners	Atlantic 2806
8/21/71	**42**	8	4 Marianne	Atlantic 2820
5/27/72	**61**	7	5 It Doesn't Matter	Atlantic 2876
7/15/72	**92**	3	6 Rock And Roll Crazies	Atlantic 2888
4/28/73	**56**	8	7 Isn't It About Time above 2: backing by Manassas	Atlantic 2959
8/09/75	**84**	3	8 Turn Back The Pages	Columbia 10179
8/11/84	**61**	8	9 Stranger	Atlantic 89633
10/06/84	**67**	6	10 Can't Let Go featuring Michael Finnigan (vocals/session keyboardist)	Atlantic 89611
			STILLWATER Georgia 'southern rock' septet. Jimmy Hall, lead singer.	
11/19/77+	**46**	13	1 Mind Bender	Capricorn 0280
			STING Born Gordon Sumner on 10/2/51 in Wallsend, England. Lead singer, bass guitarist of the Police. Nicknamed Sting because of a yellow & black jersey he liked to wear.	
6/08/85	**3**	18	1 **If You Love Somebody Set Them Free**	A&M 2738
8/24/85	**8**	20	2 **Fortress Around Your Heart**	A&M 2767
11/09/85	**17**	13	3 Love Is The Seventh Wave	A&M 2787
1/18/86	**16**	13	4 Russians	A&M 2799
			GARY STITES Born on 7/23/40 in Denver. Pop singer, songwriter, guitarist.	
4/13/59	**24**	14	1 Lonely For You	Carlton 508
7/20/59	**80**	5	2 A Girl Like You	Carlton 516
11/02/59	**77**	7	3 Starry Eyed	Carlton 521
2/22/60	**47**	9	4 Lawdy Miss Clawdy	Carlton 525
			SIMON STOKES	
12/20/69	**90**	2	1 Voodoo Woman SIMON STOKES & THE NIGHTHAWKS	Elektra 45670
7/06/74	**90**	4	2 Captain Howdy	Casablanca 0007
			MORRIS STOLOFF Born on 8/1/98 in Philadelphia; died on 4/16/80. Composer, conductor, violinist. Became musical director for Columbia Pictures in 1936. Winner of 3 Academy Awards.	
4/14/56	**1**[3]	27	1 **Moonglow and Theme From "Picnic"** [I] Jockey #1 / Best Seller #2 / Top 100 #2 / Juke Box #4 with the Columbia Pictures Orchestra - from the film "Picnic" 4 Top 10 versions of "Moonglow" charted in 1934	Decca 29888

DEBUT DATE	PEAK POS	WKS CHR	ARTIST — Record Title	Label & Number
			THE STOMPERS	
3/03/62	**100**	1	1 Quarter To Four Stomp	Landa 684
			THE STOMPERS	
			Boston-based pop/rock quartet. Sal Baglio, lead singer.	
6/18/83	**88**	4	1 Never Tell An Angel (When Your Heart's On Fire)	Boardwalk 12-177
			STONE PONEYS - see LINDA RONSTADT	
			CLIFFIE STONE	
			Orchestra and square dance band leader.	
8/13/55	**14**	4	1 The Popcorn Song [N] Juke Box #14 / Best Seller #25 vocal by Bob Roubian	Capitol 3131
			THE KIRBY STONE FOUR	
			Kirby Stone (b: 4/27/18 in New York City), Eddie Hall, Larry Foster and Mike Gardner. Kirby was musical director for various TV shows.	
7/28/58	**25**	3	1 Baubles, Bangles And Beads Jockey #25 end / Hot 100 #50 with Jimmy Carroll's orchestra - from Broadway's "Kismet"	Columbia 41183
			SLY STONE	
			Born Sylvester Stewart on 3/15/44 in Dallas. Leader of Sly & The Family Stone.	
9/06/75	**52**	9	1 I Get High On You	Epic 50135
10/25/86	**53**	16	2 Crazay **JESSE JOHNSON featuring SLY STONE**	A&M 2878
			STONEBOLT	
			Pacific Northwest pop/rock quintet. David Wills, lead singer.	
8/05/78	**29**	14	1 I Will Still Love You	Parachute 512
2/10/79	**70**	5	2 Love Struck	Parachute 522
			STONEY & MEATLOAF	
5/22/71	**71**	6	1 What You See Is What You Get	Rare Earth 5027
			PAUL STOOKEY	
			Born on 11/30/37 in Baltimore. Paul of Peter, Paul & Mary.	
7/31/71	**24**	14	1 Wedding Song (There Is Love)	Warner 7511
			THE STOREY SISTERS	
3/03/58	**45**	7	1 Bad Motorcycle Best Seller #45 / Top 100 #48	Cameo 126
			STORIES	
			New York rock quartet: Ian Lloyd, lead singer, bass; Michael Brown (founding member of Left Banke), keyboards; Steve Love, guitar; and Bryan Madey, drums. Brown left group in 1973, replaced by Ken Aaronson, bass; and Ken Bichel, keyboards.	
6/17/72	**42**	12	1 I'm Coming Home	Kama Sutra 545
6/23/73	**1**[2]	18	2 ● **Brother Louie**	Kama Sutra 577
10/27/73	**50**	8	3 Mammy Blue	Kama Sutra 584
3/30/74	**88**	5	4 If It Feels Good, Do It **IAN LLOYD & STORIES**	Kama Sutra 588
			BILLY STORM	
			Born on 6/29/38 in Dayton, Ohio. Lead singer of The Valiants.	
4/13/59	**28**	14	1 I've Come Of Age	Columbia 41356
			GALE STORM	
			Born Josephine Cottle on 4/5/22 in Bloomington, Texas. Moved to Hollywood in 1939, leading lady in films during 40s and early 50s. Own TV series "My Little Margie" from 1952-55, also "The Gale Storm Show", 1956-62.	
10/22/55	**2**[3]	18	1 **I Hear You Knocking/** Top 100 #2 / Juke Box #2 / Best Seller #3 / Jockey #4	
		1	2 Never Leave Me Coming Up flip	Dot 15412
12/24/55+	**5**	16	3 **Memories Are Made Of This/** Jockey #5 / Top 100 #16	
12/24/55+	**6**	15	4 **Teen Age Prayer** Jockey #6 / Juke Box #6 / Top 100 #9 / Best Seller #13	Dot 15436
3/03/56	**9**	18	5 **Why Do Fools Fall In Love** Jockey #9 / Juke Box #14 / Best Seller #15 / Top 100 #15	Dot 15448
4/28/56	**6**	18	6 **Ivory Tower** Jockey #6 / Juke Box #6 / Top 100 #10 / Best Seller #15	Dot 15458
6/30/56	**52**	6	7 Tell Me Why	Dot 15474

DEBUT DATE	PEAK POS	WKS CHR	ARTIST — Record Title	Label & Number
			GALE STORM — Cont'd	
9/15/56	**59**	7	8 Now Is The Hour/ there were 7 Top 20 versions of this tune in 1948	
10/06/56	**79**	4	9 A Heart Without A Sweetheart	Dot 15492
3/16/57	**74**	4	10 On Treasure Island/	
3/16/57	**77**	5	11 Lucky Lips	Dot 15539
4/20/57	**4**	23	12 **Dark Moon** Juke Box #4 end / Top 100 #5 / Best Seller #6 / Jockey #6	Dot 15558
			WARREN STORM Born Warren Schexnider on 2/18/37 in Abbeville, LA. Rockabilly singer, drummer.	
8/25/58	**81**	2	1 Prisoner's Song Vernon Dalhart's version was #1 for 12 weeks in 1925	Nasco 6015
			LALLY STOTT	
4/10/71	**92**	2	1 Chirpy Chirpy, Cheep Cheep	Philips 40695
			BILLY STRANGE Top Hollywood session guitarist.	
8/22/64	**58**	10	1 The James Bond Theme [I] from the film "From Russia With Love"	GNP Crescendo 320
1/23/65	**55**	9	2 Goldfinger [I] from the film of the same title	GNP Crescendo 334
			THE STRANGELOVES Writers-producers Bob Feldman, Jerry Goldstein, Richard Gottehrer. Team wrote and produced the Angels "My Boyfriends Back", also produced McCoys "Hang On Sloopy". Gottehrer became a partner in Sire Records, and produced the Go-Go's first two albums and Blondie's debut album.	
6/26/65	**11**	10	1 I Want Candy	Bang 501
9/18/65	**39**	8	2 Cara-Lin	Bang 508
1/15/66	**30**	8	3 Night Time	Bang 514
6/18/66	**100**	1	4 Hand Jive	Bang 524
			THE STRANGERS San Diego rock and roll instrumental quartet led by guitarist Joel Scott Hill (member of Canned Heat in 1972).	
8/31/59	**49**	7	1 The Caterpillar Crawl [I]	Titan 1701
			STRAWBERRY ALARM CLOCK West Coast psychedelic rock sextet: Ed King (lead guitar), Mark Weitz (keyboards), Lee Freeman (guitar), Gary Lovetro (bass), George Bunnel (bass) and Randy Seol (drums). King joined Lynyrd Skynyrd, 1973-75.	
9/30/67	**1**[1]	16	1 ● **Incense And Peppermints**	Uni 55018
12/30/67+	**23**	10	2 Tomorrow	Uni 55046
3/16/68	**65**	5	3 Sit With The Guru	Uni 55055
8/31/68	**67**	4	4 Barefoot In Baltimore	Uni 55076
5/24/69	**87**	2	5 Good Morning Starshine from the musical "Hair"	Uni 55125
			STRAY CATS Long Island, New York rockabilly trio: Brian Setzer (b: 4/10/60), lead singer, guitar; Lee Rocker (Leon Drucher), string bass; and Slim Jim Phantom (Jim McDonell), drums. Group disbanded in 1984.	
9/18/82	**9**	21	1 **Rock This Town**	EMI America 8132
12/25/82+	**3**	19	2 **Stray Cat Strut**	EMI America 8122
8/06/83	**5**	15	3 **(She's) Sexy + 17**	EMI America 8168
10/29/83	**35**	13	4 I Won't Stand In Your Way	EMI America 8185
1/28/84	**68**	5	5 Look At That Cadillac all of above written by Brian Setzer and produced by Dave Edmunds	EMI America 8194
			STREEK Los Angeles pop quintet. Billy DeMartines, lead singer.	
10/10/81	**47**	7	1 One More Night	Columbia 02529
			STREET PEOPLE Studio group - Rupert Holmes, member.	
1/03/70	**36**	15	1 Jennifer Tomkins	Musicor 1365
4/25/70	**96**	2	2 Thank You Girl	Musicor 1401

DEBUT DATE	PEAK POS	WKS CHR	ARTIST — Record Title	Label & Number
			JANEY STREET	
			Pop/rock singer from New York City.	
10/06/84	**68**	5	1 Say Hello To Ronnie	Arista 9265
			STREETS	
			Rock quartet led by Steve Walsh (vocalist/keyboardist of Kansas).	
12/03/83	**87**	5	1 If Love Should Go	Atlantic 89760
			BARBRA STREISAND	
			Born Barbara Joan Streisand on 4/24/42 in Brooklyn. Made Broadway debut in "I Can Get It For You Wholesale", 1962. Lead role in Broadway's "Funny Girl", 1964. Film debut in "Funny Girl", 1968 (tied with Katharine Hepburn for Best Actress Oscar), also starred in "A Star Is Born", "Hello Dolly", "Funny Lady", "The Way We Were" and many others. Produced, directed and starred in the film "Yentl", 1983.	
4/04/64	**5**	19	1 **People**	Columbia 42965
9/12/64	**44**	9	2 Funny Girl above 2 from the Broadway musical "Funny Girl"	Columbia 43127
4/03/65	**77**	5	3 Why Did I Choose You from the Broadway musical "The Yearling"	Columbia 43248
7/03/65	**79**	6	4 My Man	Columbia 43323
10/02/65	**53**	10	5 He Touched Me from the Broadway musical "Drat! The Cat!"	Columbia 43403
12/18/65+	**32**	9	6 Second Hand Rose	Columbia 43469
2/19/66	**94**	2	7 Where Am I Going? from the Broadway musical "Sweet Charity" 2-7: produced by Robert Mersey	Columbia 43518
5/21/66	**98**	1	8 Sam, You Made The Pants Too Long	Columbia 43612
10/15/66	**83**	4	9 Free Again	Columbia 43808
8/26/67	**92**	2	10 Stout-Hearted Men from the Broadway musical "The New Moon"	Columbia 44225
10/31/70+	**6**	18	11 **Stoney End**	Columbia 45236
3/20/71	**51**	7	12 Time And Love	Columbia 45341
5/15/71	**82**	5	13 Flim Flam Man	Columbia 45384
7/24/71	**40**	8	14 Where You Lead	Columbia 45414
10/16/71	**79**	5	15 Mother written by John Lennon	Columbia 45471
6/24/72	**37**	12	16 Sweet Inspiration/Where You Lead	Columbia 45626
9/30/72	**94**	3	17 Sing A Song/Make Your Own Kind Of Music	Columbia 45686
12/09/72+	**82**	8	18 Didn't We 11-18: produced by Richard Perry	Columbia 45739
11/24/73+	**1^{3}**	23	19 ● **The Way We Were** from the film of the same title	Columbia 45944
3/30/74	**63**	5	20 All In Love Is Fair	Columbia 46024
12/11/76+	**1^{3}**	25	21 ● **Evergreen** Love Theme from the film "A Star Is Born"	Columbia 10450
5/21/77	**4**	17	22 **My Heart Belongs To Me**	Columbia 10555
6/17/78	**25**	10	23 Songbird	Columbia 10756
7/29/78	**21**	12	24 Love Theme From "Eyes Of Laura Mars" (Prisoner) from the film "Eyes Of Laura Mars"	Columbia 10777
10/28/78	**1^{2}**	17	25 ● **You Don't Bring Me Flowers** **BARBRA STREISAND & NEIL DIAMOND**	Columbia 10840
6/16/79	**3**	17	26 ● **The Main Event/Fight** from the film "The Main Event"	Columbia 11008
10/20/79	**1^{2}**	15	27 ● **No More Tears (Enough Is Enough)** **BARBRA STREISAND/DONNA SUMMER**	Columbia 11125
1/12/80	**37**	11	28 Kiss Me In The Rain	Columbia 11179
9/06/80	**1^{3}**	24	29 ● **Woman In Love**	Columbia 11364
11/01/80+	**3**	22	30 ● **Guilty** **BARBRA STREISAND & BARRY GIBB**	Columbia 11390
1/31/81	**10**	16	31 **What Kind Of Fool** **BARBRA STREISAND & BARRY GIBB**	Columbia 11430
5/23/81	**48**	9	32 Promises	Columbia 02065
11/14/81+	**11**	16	33 Comin' In And Out Of Your Life	Columbia 02621
2/20/82	**52**	7	34 Memory theme from the musical "Cats"	Columbia 02717

DEBUT DATE	PEAK POS	WKS CHR	ARTIST — Record Title	Label & Number
			BARBRA STREISAND — Cont'd	
10/22/83	**40**	15	35 The Way He Makes Me Feel from the film "Yentl"	Columbia 04177
9/22/84	**50**	12	36 Left In The Dark	Columbia 04605
12/15/84+	**51**	10	37 Make No Mistake, He's Mine **BARBRA STREISAND with KIM CARNES**	Columbia 04695
3/09/85	**79**	2	38 Emotion	Columbia 04707
12/14/85+	**43**	14	39 Somewhere from the Broadway musical "West Side Story"	Columbia 05680
			THE STRING-A-LONGS Instrumental quintet: Keith McCormack, Don Allen, Aubrey Lee de Cordova, Richard Stephens and Jimmy Torres.	
1/09/61	**3**	16	1 **Wheels** [I]	Warwick 603
3/27/61	**35**	7	2 Brass Buttons [I]	Warwick 625
6/12/61	**42**	9	3 Should I [I]	Warwick 654
			THE STROLLERS	
4/10/61	**91**	2	1 Come On Over	Carlton 546
			BARRETT STRONG Born on 2/5/41 in Mississippi. R&B singer, songwriter. Wrote many of The Temptations hits with Norman Whitfield, including "Just My Imagination", "Papa Was A Rollin' Stone", "Ball Of Confusion" and "Cloud Nine".	
2/01/60	**23**	17	1 Money (That's What I Want)	Anna 1111
			JUD STRUNK Born Justin Strunk, Jr. on 6/11/36 in Jamestown, New York. Regular on TV's "Laugh In". Killed in a plane crash on 10/15/81.	
2/17/73	**14**	16	1 Daisy A Day	MGM 14463
9/28/74	**59**	4	2 My Country [S]	Capitol 3960
7/05/75	**50**	6	3 The Biggest Parakeets In Town [C]	Melodyland 6015
			THE STYLE COUNCIL English duo: Paul Weller (ex-vocalist of The Jam) and Mick Talbot (keyboards).	
4/07/84	**29**	14	1 My Ever Changing Moods	Geffen 29359
7/14/84	**76**	5	2 You're The Best Thing	Geffen 29248
			THE STYLERS	
11/24/56	**72**	5	1 Confession Of A Sinner	Jubilee 5253
			THE STYLISTICS Soul group from Philadelphia, formed in 1968. Consisted of Russell Thompkins, Jr. (b: 3/21/51), lead; Airrion Love, James Smith, James Dunn and Herbie Murrell. Thompkins, Love, and Smith had sang with the Percussions; Murrell and Dunn with the Monarchs from 1965-68. First recorded for Sebring in 1969.	
1/09/71	**73**	7	1 You're A Big Girl Now	Avco Embassy 4555
6/05/71	**39**	16	2 Stop, Look, Listen (To Your Heart)	Avco Embassy 4572
11/06/71+	**9**	16	3● **You Are Everything**	Avco 4581
2/26/72	**3**	16	4● **Betcha By Golly, Wow**	Avco 4591
6/03/72	**25**	11	5 People Make The World Go Round	Avco 4595
10/14/72	**10**	13	6● **I'm Stone In Love With You**	Avco 4603
2/10/73	**5**	14	7● **Break Up To Make Up**	Avco 4611
5/19/73	**23**	10	8 You'll Never Get To Heaven (If You Break My Heart)	Avco 4618
10/20/73	**14**	18	9 Rockin' Roll Baby	Avco 4625
3/23/74	**2**[2]	25	10● **You Make Me Feel Brand New** all of above produced by Thom Bell	Avco 4634
7/27/74	**18**	12	11 Let's Put It All Together	Avco 4640
10/19/74	**41**	11	12 Heavy Fallin' Out	Avco 4647
1/18/75	**47**	7	13 Star On A TV Show	Avco 4649
4/19/75	**70**	6	14 Thank You Baby	Avco 4652
7/19/75	**51**	6	15 Can't Give You Anything (But My Love)	Avco 4656
12/06/75+	**76**	9	16 Funky Weekend	Avco 4661
3/13/76	**79**	7	17 You Are Beautiful 11-17: produced by Hugo Peretti & Luigi Creatore	Avco 4664

DEBUT DATE	PEAK POS	WKS CHR	ARTIST — Record Title	Label & Number
			STYX	
			Chicago-based rock quintet: Dennis DeYoung (vocals, keyboards), Tommy Shaw (lead guitar), James Young (guitar), and twin brothers John (drums) and Chuck Panozzo (bass). Shaw replaced John Curulewski in 1976. Most songs written by Dennis DeYoung and/or Tommy Shaw.	
9/16/72	**82**	6	1 Best Thing	Wooden N. 0106
12/14/74+	**6**	17	2 **Lady**	Wooden N. 10102
5/17/75	**88**	2	3 You Need Love	Wooden N. 10272
2/14/76	**27**	14	4 Lorelei	A&M 1786
11/13/76	**36**	11	5 Mademoiselle	A&M 1877
9/24/77+	**8**	22	6 **Come Sail Away**	A&M 1977
2/18/78	**29**	14	7 Fooling Yourself (The Angry Young Man)	A&M 2007
9/16/78	**21**	14	8 Blue Collar Man (Long Nights)	A&M 2087
1/06/79	**41**	8	9 Sing For The Day/	
3/17/79	**16**	19	10 Renegade	A&M 2110
10/06/79	**1^{2}**	19	11 ● **Babe**	A&M 2188
12/15/79+	**26**	13	12 Why Me	A&M 2206
3/29/80	**64**	6	13 Borrowed Time	A&M 2228
1/24/81	**3**	19	14 **The Best Of Times**	A&M 2300
3/21/81	**9**	19	15 **Too Much Time On My Hands**	A&M 2323
7/11/81	**54**	8	16 Nothing Ever Goes As Planned	A&M 2348
2/12/83	**3**	18	17 ● **Mr. Roboto**	A&M 2525
4/30/83	**6**	16	18 **Don't Let It End**	A&M 2543
8/13/83	**48**	7	19 High Time	A&M 2568
5/05/84	**40**	9	20 Music Time	A&M 2625
			SUGAR BEARS	
3/11/72	**51**	13	1 You Are The One	Big Tree 122
			SUGARHILL GANG	
			New York rap trio formed in Harlem. Consisted of Michael "Wonder Mike" Wright, Guy "Master Gee" O'Brien and Henry "Big Bank Hank" Jackson. One of the first commercially-successful rap acts.	
11/10/79+	**36**	12	1 Rapper's Delight	Sugar Hill 542
2/07/81	**82**	9	2 8th Wonder	Sugar Hill 553
2/13/82	**53**	11	3 Apache	Sugar Hill 774
			SUGARLOAF	
			Denver rock quartet: Jerry Corbetta (lead singer, keyboards), Bob Webber (guitar), Bob Raymond (bass) and Bob MacVittie (drums). Robert Yeazel (guitar, vocals) joined in 1971. By 1974, Myron Pollock replaced MacVittie, and Yeazel had left.	
8/15/70	**3**	17	1 **Green-Eyed Lady**	Liberty 56183
3/06/71	**55**	8	2 Tongue In Cheek	Liberty 56218
6/26/71	**88**	3	3 Mother Nature's Wine	United Art. 50784
			SUGARLOAF/JERRY CORBETTA:	
12/07/74+	**9**	21	4 **Don't Call Us, We'll Call You**	Claridge 402
6/07/75	**87**	6	5 Stars In My Eyes	Claridge 405
			all of above produced by Frank Slay	
			DONNA SUMMER	
			Born LaDonna Adrian Gaines on 12/31/48 in Boston. With group Crow, played local clubs. In German production of "Hair", European productions of "Godspell", "The Me Nobody Knows" and "Porgy And Bess". Settled in Germany, where she recorded "Love To Love You Baby". In the film "Thank God It's Friday" in 1979. Married Bruce Sudano of Brooklyn Dreams in 1980. The Queen of Disco.	
12/06/75+	**2^{2}**	18	1 ● **Love To Love You Baby**	Oasis 401
5/01/76	**52**	5	2 Could It Be Magic	Oasis 405
7/10/76	**80**	4	3 Try Me, I Know We Can Make It	Oasis 406
12/18/76+	**47**	6	4 Spring Affair	Casablanca 872
1/22/77	**43**	8	5 Winter Melody	Casablanca 874
8/06/77	**6**	23	6 ● **I Feel Love**	Casablanca 884
12/17/77+	**37**	11	7 I Love You	Casablanca 907
3/04/78	**53**	9	8 Rumour Has It	Casablanca 916
5/13/78	**3**	21	9 ● **Last Dance**	Casablanca 926
			from the film "Thank God It's Friday"	
9/09/78	**1^{3}**	20	10 ● **MacArthur Park**	Casablanca 939
1/13/79	**4**	19	11 ● **Heaven Knows**	Casablanca 959
			DONNA SUMMER with BROOKLYN DREAMS	
			1, 3-8 & 11: written by Summer, Giorgio Moroder and Pete Bellotte	

DEBUT DATE	PEAK POS	WKS CHR	ARTIST — Record Title	Label & Number
			DONNA SUMMER — Cont'd	
4/21/79	1^3	21	12▲ **Hot Stuff**	Casablanca 978
5/26/79	1^5	20	13▲ **Bad Girls**	Casablanca 988
8/25/79	2^2	21	14● **Dim All The Lights**	Casablanca 2201
10/20/79	1^2	15	15● **No More Tears (Enough Is Enough)**	Columbia 11125
			BARBRA STREISAND/DONNA SUMMER	
1/12/80	**5**	17	16● **On The Radio**	Casablanca 2236
9/13/80	**36**	11	17 Walk Away	Casablanca 2300
9/20/80	**3**	20	18● **The Wanderer**	Geffen 49563
11/29/80+	**33**	12	19 Cold Love	Geffen 49634
2/21/81	**40**	11	20 Who Do You Think You're Foolin'	Geffen 49664
			2-8, 10-14, 16-19: produced by Giorgio Moroder and Pete Bellotte	
6/26/82	**10**	18	21 **Love Is In Control (Finger On The Trigger)**	Geffen 29982
10/02/82	**41**	10	22 State Of Independence	Geffen 29895
			all-star choir includes: James Ingram, Michael Jackson, Kenny Loggins, Lionel Richie, Dionne Warwick and Stevie Wonder	
12/18/82+	**33**	16	23 The Woman In Me	Geffen 29805
5/28/83	**3**	21	24 **She Works Hard For The Money**	Mercury 812370
9/03/83	**43**	8	25 Unconditional Love	Mercury 814088
			background vocals: Musical Youth	
1/14/84	**70**	4	26 Love Has A Mind Of Its Own	Mercury 814922
			with Matthew Ward of the gospel group "2nd Chapter of Acts"	
8/11/84	**21**	14	27 There Goes My Baby	Geffen 29291
11/10/84	**75**	5	28 Supernatural Love	Geffen 29142
			SUN	
			Dayton, Ohio soul-funk band.	
9/25/76	**76**	6	1 Wanna Make Love (Come Flick My BIC)	Capitol 4254
			JOE SUN	
			Born on 9/25/43 in Rochester, MN. Country singer. Began as a disc jockey and later became a promotion executive with Ovation Records, which led to recording career.	
5/31/80	**71**	6	1 Shotgun Rider	Ovation 1141
			SUNDOWN COMPANY	
6/05/76	**84**	5	1 Norma Jean Wants To Be A Movie Star	Polydor 14312
			from the film "Goodbye Norma Jean"	
			THE SUNGLOWS	
			10-man Latin polka band from Texas.	
5/08/65	**64**	4	1 Peanuts [I]	Sunglow 107
			also known as La Cacahuata	
			SUNNY & THE SUNGLOWS	
			San Antonio band formed in 1959: led by Sunny Ozuna.	
9/07/63	**11**	12	1 Talk To Me	Tear Drop 3014
			SUNNY & THE SUNLINERS:	
11/16/63	**45**	7	2 Rags To Riches	Tear Drop 3022
2/22/64	**71**	5	3 Out Of Sight - Out Of Mind	Tear Drop 3027
			THE SUNNYSIDERS	
			Group included vocalist Margie Rayburn.	
5/21/55	**12**	10	1 Hey, Mr. Banjo	Kapp 113
			Juke Box #12 / Jockey #19 / Best Seller #20	
			THE SUNRAYS	
			Southern California pop-rock quintet: Rick Henn, Marty DiGiovanni, Byron Case, Eddie Medora and Vince Hozier. Produced by Murry Wilson (father of The Beach Boys).	
9/04/65	**51**	10	1 I Live For The Sun	Tower 148
1/22/66	**41**	8	2 Andrea	Tower 191
5/07/66	**93**	2	3 Still	Tower 224
			THE SUNSHINE COMPANY	
			Southern California pop quintet featuring lead singer Mary Nance.	
7/15/67	**50**	10	1 Happy	Imperial 66247
10/21/67	**36**	7	2 Back On The Street Again	Imperial 66260
2/10/68	**56**	5	3 Look, Here Comes The Sun	Imperial 66280
			THE SUPERBS	
10/03/64	**83**	5	1 Baby Baby All The Time	Dore 715

DEBUT DATE	PEAK POS	WKS CHR		ARTIST — Record Title	Label & Number
				SUPERTRAMP	
				British rock quintet: Roger Hodgson (vocals, guitar), Rick Davies (vocals, keyboards), John Helliwell (sax), Dougie Thomson (bass) and Bob Benberg (drums). Hodgson went solo in 1983.	
4/12/75	**35**	10	1	Bloody Well Right	A&M 1660
6/04/77	**15**	18	2	Give A Little Bit	A&M 1938
3/24/79	**6**	21	3	**The Logical Song**	A&M 2128
7/07/79	**15**	14	4	Goodbye Stranger	A&M 2162
10/13/79	**10**	15	5	**Take The Long Way Home**	A&M 2193
9/20/80	**15**	14	6	Dreamer from their 1974 album "Crime Of The Century"	A&M 2269
12/13/80	**62**	8	7	Breakfast In America	A&M 2292
10/30/82	**11**	13	8	It's Raining Again	A&M 2502
1/29/83	**31**	12	9	My Kind Of Lady all of above written by Davies and Hodgson	A&M 2517
5/25/85	**28**	12	10	Cannonball	A&M 2731
				THE SUPREMES	
				R&B vocal group from Detroit, formed as the Primettes in 1959. Consisted of lead singer Diana Ross (b: 3/26/44), Mary Wilson (b: 3/6/44) and Florence Ballard (b: 6/30/43; d: 2/22/76 of cardiac arrest). Recorded for LuPine in 1960. Signed to Motown's Tamla label in 1960. Changed name to The Supremes in 1961. Ballard discharged from group in 1967, replaced by Cindy Birdsong, formerly with The Blue Belles. Ross left in 1969 for solo career, replaced by Jean Terrell. Birdsong left in 1972, replaced by Lynda Laurence. Terrell and Laurence left in 1973, Mary Wilson re-formed group with Scherrie Payne (sister of Freda Payne) and Cindy Birdsong. Birdsong left again in 1976, replaced by Susaye Greene. In 1978, Wilson toured England with Karen Ragland and Karen Jackson, but lost rights to the name "Supremes" thereafter.	
8/11/62	**95**	3	1	Your Heart Belongs To Me	Motown 1027
12/08/62+	**90**	6	2	Let Me Go The Right Way	Motown 1034
7/27/63	**75**	7	3	A Breath Taking Guy	Motown 1044
11/30/63+	**23**	11	4	When The Lovelight Starts Shining Through His Eyes	Motown 1051
3/14/64	**93**	2	5	Run, Run, Run	Motown 1054
7/11/64	**1^{2}**	14	6	**Where Did Our Love Go**	Motown 1060
10/03/64	**1^{4}**	13	7	**Baby Love**	Motown 1066
11/14/64	**1^{2}**	14	8	**Come See About Me**	Motown 1068
2/20/65	**1^{2}**	12	9	**Stop! In The Name Of Love**	Motown 1074
5/01/65	**1^{1}**	11	10	**Back In My Arms Again**	Motown 1075
7/31/65	**11**	9	11	Nothing But Heartaches	Motown 1080
10/30/65	**1^{2}**	10	12	**I Hear A Symphony**	Motown 1083
1/15/66	**5**	11	13	**My World Is Empty Without You**	Motown 1089
4/30/66	**9**	8	14	**Love Is Like An Itching In My Heart**	Motown 1094
8/13/66	**1^{2}**	13	15	**You Can't Hurry Love**	Motown 1097
10/29/66	**1^{2}**	12	16	**You Keep Me Hangin' On**	Motown 1101
1/28/67	**1^{1}**	11	17	**Love Is Here And Now You're Gone**	Motown 1103
4/08/67	**1^{1}**	11	18	**The Happening** from the film of the same title	Motown 1107
				DIANA ROSS & THE SUPREMES:	
8/12/67	**2^{2}**	11	19	**Reflections**	Motown 1111
11/11/67	**9**	8	20	**In And Out Of Love**	Motown 1116
3/16/68	**28**	9	21	Forever Came Today 4-21: written by Eddie Holland, Lamont Dozier & Brian Holland	Motown 1122
6/08/68	**30**	7	22	Some Things You Never Get Used To	Motown 1126
10/19/68	**1^{2}**	16	23	**Love Child**	Motown 1135
12/07/68+	**2^{2}**	13	24	**I'm Gonna Make You Love Me** **DIANA ROSS & THE SUPREMES & THE TEMPTATIONS**	Motown 1137
1/25/69	**10**	8	25	**I'm Livin' In Shame**	Motown 1139
3/15/69	**25**	7	26	I'll Try Something New **DIANA ROSS & THE SUPREMES & THE TEMPTATIONS**	Motown 1142
4/19/69	**27**	6	27	The Composer	Motown 1146
5/31/69	**31**	6	28	No Matter What Sign You Are/	
8/02/69	**69**	5	29	The Young Folks	Motown 1148
9/13/69	**46**	5	30	The Weight **DIANA ROSS & THE SUPREMES & THE TEMPTATIONS**	Motown 1153
11/08/69	**1^{1}**	16	31	**Someday We'll Be Together**	Motown 1156
				THE SUPREMES:	
3/07/70	**10**	11	32	**Up The Ladder To The Roof**	Motown 1162

DEBUT DATE	PEAK POS	WKS CHR	ARTIST — Record Title	Label & Number
			THE SUPREMES — Cont'd	
7/18/70	**21**	11	33 Everybody's Got The Right To Love	Motown 1167
11/07/70	**7**	14	34 **Stoned Love**	Motown 1172
11/28/70+	**14**	10	35 River Deep - Mountain High THE SUPREMES & FOUR TOPS	Motown 1173
5/08/71	**16**	10	36 Nathan Jones	Motown 1182
6/05/71	**55**	5	37 You Gotta Have Love In Your Heart THE SUPREMES & FOUR TOPS	Motown 1181
10/09/71	**71**	4	38 Touch	Motown 1190
1/08/72	**16**	12	39 Floy Joy	Motown 1195
5/06/72	**37**	9	40 Automatically Sunshine	Motown 1200
8/05/72	**59**	8	41 Your Wonderful, Sweet Sweet Love	Motown 1206
10/21/72	**85**	7	42 I Guess I'll Miss The Man from the Broadway musical "Pippin"	Motown 1213
6/09/73	**87**	1	43 Bad Weather	Motown 1225
5/29/76	**40**	14	44 I'm Gonna Let My Heart Do The Walking	Motown 1391
12/04/76	**85**	5	45 You're My Driving Wheel	Motown 1407
			THE SURFARIS Teenage surf band from Glendora, California. Consisted of Ron Wilson (drummer), Jim Fuller (lead guitar), Bob Berryhill (rhythm guitar), Pat Connolly (bass) and Jim Pash (sax, clarinet).	
6/22/63	**2**[1]	16	1 **Wipe Out/** [I]	
8/31/63	**62**	6	2 Surfer Joe	Dot 16479
9/28/63	**49**	8	3 Point Panic [I]	Decca 31538
7/30/66	**16**	14	4 Wipe Out [I-R]	Dot 144
			SURVIVOR Midwest rock quintet: Dave Bickler (lead singer), Jim Peterik (keyboards), Frankie Sullivan (guitar), Gary Smith (drums) and Dennis Johnson (bass). Smith and Johnson replaced by Marc Droubay and Stephan Ellis in 1981. Bickler replaced by Jimi Jamison in 1984.	
2/23/80	**70**	12	1 Somewhere In America	Scotti Br. 511
10/17/81	**33**	14	2 Poor Man's Son	Scotti Br. 02560
2/20/82	**62**	8	3 Summer Nights	Scotti Br. 02700
6/05/82	**1**[6]	25	4 ▲**Eye Of The Tiger** from the film "Rocky III"	Scotti Br. 02912
9/25/82	**17**	16	5 American Heartbeat	Scotti Br. 03213
1/22/83	**74**	6	6 The One That Really Matters	Scotti Br. 03485
10/22/83	**77**	5	7 Caught In The Game	Scotti Br. 04074
6/16/84	**63**	7	8 The Moment Of Truth from the film "The Karate Kid"	Casablanca 880053
9/15/84	**13**	23	9 I Can't Hold Back	Scotti Br. 04603
1/26/85	**8**	17	10 **High On You**	Scotti Br. 04685
4/20/85	**4**	21	11 **The Search Is Over**	Scotti Br. 04871
8/17/85	**53**	9	12 First Night	Scotti Br. 05579
11/02/85+	**2**[2]	22	13 **Burning Heart** from the film "Rocky IV"	Scotti Br. 05663
10/25/86+	**9**	19	14 **Is This Love**	Scotti Br. 06381
			SUTHERLAND BROTHERS & QUIVER English duo: Iain and Gavin Sutherland with their group Quiver.	
8/18/73	**48**	12	1 (I Don't Want To Love You But) You Got Me Anyway	Island 1217
4/10/76	**81**	5	2 Arms Of Mary	Columbia 10284
			GLENN SUTTON Country singer, married to Lynn Anderson.	
1/06/79	**46**	5	1 The Football Card [N]	Mercury 55052
			SUZY & THE RED STRIPES Linda & Paul McCartney with Denny Laine.	
6/18/77	**59**	5	1 Seaside Woman	Epic 50403
			THE SWALLOWS Baltimore area R&B group. Had several early 50s R&B hits on the King label.	
9/22/58	**100**	1	1 Itchy Twitchy Feeling	Federal 12333

DEBUT DATE	PEAK POS	WKS CHR	ARTIST — Record Title	Label & Number
			BILLY SWAN	
			Born on 5/12/43 in Cape Girardeau, Missouri. Singer, songwriter, keyboardist, guitarist. Produced Tony Joe White's first three albums.	
9/28/74	**1^2**	18	1 ● **I Can Help**	Monument 8621
3/15/75	**53**	4	2 I'm Her Fool	Monument 8641
11/01/75	**91**	5	3 Everything's The Same (Ain't Nothing Changed)	Monument 8661
			BETTYE SWANN	
			Born Betty Jean Champion on 10/24/44 in Shreveport, Louisiana. Moved to Los Angeles in the late 50s. In vocal group the Fawns, recorded for Money in 1964.	
5/13/67	**21**	14	1 Make Me Yours	Money 126
9/23/67	**67**	5	2 Fall In Love With Me	Money 129
3/08/69	**38**	10	3 Don't Touch Me	Capitol 2382
5/27/72	**63**	9	4 Victim Of A Foolish Heart	Atlantic 2869
1/27/73	**46**	7	5 Today I Started Loving You Again	Atlantic 2921
			THE SWANS	
2/29/64	**85**	4	1 The Boy With The Beatle Hair [N]	Cameo 302
			SWEATHOG	
11/13/71	**33**	10	1 Hallelujah	Columbia 45492
			SWEENEY TODD	
			Canadian band featuring Bryan Guy Adams - Nick Gilder, member.	
8/21/76	**90**	3	1 Roxy Roller	London 244
			SWEET	
			English rock band: Brian Connolly (lead singer), Steve Priest (bass, vocals), Andy Scott (guitar, keyboards) and Mick Tucker (drums).	
10/02/71	**99**	2	1 Co-Co	Bell 45126
1/20/73	**3**	23	2 ● **Little Willy**	Bell 45251
6/16/73	**73**	7	3 Blockbuster	Bell 45361
6/14/75	**5**	25	4 **Ballroom Blitz**	Capitol 4055
11/15/75+	**5**	16	5 ● **Fox On The Run**	Capitol 4157
2/14/76	**20**	14	6 Action	Capitol 4220
8/13/77	**88**	5	7 Funk It Up (David's Song)	Capitol 4454
2/18/78	**8**	25	8 **Love Is Like Oxygen**	Capitol 4549
8/12/78	**76**	4	9 California Nights	Capitol 4610
			SWEET DREAMS	
			English soul-reggae duo: Polly Brown and Tony Jackson.	
8/31/74	**68**	7	1 Honey Honey	ABC 12008
			THE SWEET INSPIRATIONS	
			R&B vocal quartet: Cissy Houston, Estelle Brown, Sylvia Shemwell and Myrna Smith. Spent nearly six years as studio group, primarily for Atlantic. Work included backing Aretha Franklin and Elvis Presley. Houston went solo in 1970.	
6/03/67	**57**	5	1 Why (Am I Treated So Bad)	Atlantic 2410
7/22/67	**94**	2	2 Let It Be Me	Atlantic 2418
3/02/68	**18**	14	3 Sweet Inspiration	Atlantic 2476
7/06/68	**74**	4	4 To Love Somebody	Atlantic 2529
8/31/68	**73**	5	5 Unchained Melody	Atlantic 2551
			SWEET SENSATION	
			British 8-member soul band. Marcel King, lead singer.	
1/11/75	**14**	16	1 Sad Sweet Dreamer	Pye 71002
			RACHEL SWEET	
			Rock singer, born in 1963 in Akron, Ohio.	
6/27/81	**32**	13	1 Everlasting Love REX SMITH/RACHEL SWEET	Columbia 02169
2/05/83	**72**	5	2 Voo Doo	Columbia 03411
			THE SWINGING BLUE JEANS	
			Liverpool, England rock quartet: Ray Ennis and Ralph Ellis (guitars), Norman Kuhlke (drums) and Les Braid (bass).	
3/07/64	**24**	8	1 Hippy Hippy Shake	Imperial 66021
5/09/64	**43**	7	2 Good Golly Miss Molly	Imperial 66030
8/01/64	**97**	2	3 You're No Good	Imperial 66049

DEBUT DATE	PEAK POS	WKS CHR	ARTIST — Record Title	Label & Number
			SWINGIN' MEDALLIONS	
			8-man rock and roll band from South Carolina led by John McElrath.	
4/23/66	**17**	13	1 Double Shot (Of My Baby's Love)	Smash 2033
8/20/66	**71**	5	2 She Drives Me Out Of My Mind	Smash 2050
			SWITCH	
			Soul/funk sextet from Detroit. Discovered by Jermaine Jackson.	
10/07/78	**36**	13	1 There'll Never Be	Gordy 7159
7/21/79	**69**	8	2 Best Beat In Town	Gordy 7168
11/03/79+	**83**	15	3 I Call Your Name	Gordy 7175
			THE SYLVERS	
			Memphis family of 9 brothers and sisters: Olympia-Ann, Leon, Charmaine, James, Edmund, Ricky, Angelia, Pat and Foster.	
9/02/72	**94**	3	1 Fool's Paradise	Pride 1001
2/03/73	**77**	10	2 Wish That I Could Talk To You	Pride 1019
8/18/73	**89**	3	3 Stay Away From Me	Pride 1029
2/14/76	**1**[1]	21	4 ● **Boogie Fever**	Capitol 4179
6/26/76	**59**	7	5 Cotton Candy	Capitol 4255
10/09/76+	**5**	24	6 ● **Hot Line**	Capitol 4336
4/23/77	**17**	17	7 High School Dance	Capitol 4405
11/26/77	**72**	9	8 Any Way You Want Me	Capitol 4493
			FOSTER SYLVERS	
			Born on 2/25/62 in Memphis. Youngest member of The Sylvers family group.	
6/02/73	**22**	13	1 Misdemeanor	MGM 14580
10/06/73	**92**	5	2 Hey, Little Girl	MGM 14630
			SYLVESTER	
			Born Sylvester James in Los Angeles. Moved to San Francisco in 1967. With vocal group, the Cockettes. In film "The Rose".	
8/19/78	**19**	18	1 Dance (Disco Heat)	Fantasy 827
1/13/79	**36**	10	2 You Make Me Feel (Mighty Real)	Fantasy 846
4/07/79	**40**	7	3 I (Who Have Nothing)	Fantasy 855
			SYLVIA	
			Country singer Sylvia Kirby Allen from Kokomo, Indiana. Moved to Nashville in 1975.	
8/28/82	**15**	20	1 ● Nobody	RCA 13223
			SYLVIA	
			Born Sylvia Vanderpool on 5/6/36 in New York City. Singer, songwriter, producer. Half of Mickey & Sylvia duo. Married Joe Robinson, owner of All Platinum/Vibration Records. Sylvia owns Sugar Hill Records.	
3/24/73	**3**	21	1 ● **Pillow Talk**	Vibration 521
7/21/73	**70**	5	2 Didn't I	Vibration 524
9/08/73	**99**	2	3 Soul Je T'Aime **SYLVIA & RALFI PAGAN**	Vibration 525
6/08/74	**80**	4	4 Sho Nuff Boogie (Part I) **SYLVIA & THE MOMENTS**	All Platinum 2350
			SYLVIA SYMS	
			Night club singer from the Bronx, New York.	
5/12/56	**20**	14	1 I Could Have Danced All Night Jockey #20 / Top 100 #35 from the musical "My Fair Lady"	Decca 29903
8/11/56	**21**	8	2 English Muffins And Irish Stew Jockey #21 / Top 100 #51	Decca 29969
12/22/56+	**68**	8	3 Dancing Chandelier	Decca 30143
			SYNCH	
			Pop/rock sextet from Wilkes-Barre, Pennsylvania. Jim Harnen, lead singer.	
3/01/86	**77**	12	1 Where Are You Now?	Columbia 05788
			SYNDICATE OF SOUND	
			San Jose garage rock quintet: Don Baskin (lead singer), Jim Sawyers (guitar), Bob Gonzalez (bass), John Sharkey (rhythm guitar) and John Duckworth (drums).	
6/04/66	**8**	10	1 **Little Girl**	Bell 640
8/20/66	**55**	7	2 Rumors	Bell 646
3/28/70	**73**	5	3 Brown Paper Bag	Buddah 156

DEBUT DATE	PEAK POS	WKS CHR	ARTIST — Record Title	Label & Number
			SYREETA - see BILLY PRESTON	
			THE SYSTEM	
			New York City-based techno-funk duo: Mic Murphy (vocals) and David Frank.	
3/05/83	**64**	8	1 You Are In My System	Mirage 99937
			T	
			TACO	
			Born Taco Ockerse in 1955 to Dutch parents in Jaharta, IN. German-based singer.	
6/25/83	**4**	21	1 ● **Puttin' On The Ritz**	RCA 13574
			written in 1929 by Irving Berlin - #1 in 1930 for Harry Richman	
			TALK TALK	
			British rock band. Mark Hollis, lead singer.	
10/16/82	**75**	7	1 Talk Talk	EMI America 8136
3/24/84	**31**	14	2 It's My Life	EMI America 8195
6/30/84	**89**	3	3 Such A Shame	EMI America 8215
2/01/86	**90**	4	4 Life's What You Make It	EMI America 8303
			TALKING HEADS	
			New York City-based 'new wave' quartet: David Byrne (lead singer, guitar), Jerry Harrison (keyboards, guitar), Tina Weymouth (bass) and husband Chris Frantz (drums). Also see Tom Tom Club.	
2/18/78	**92**	5	1 Psycho Killer	Sire 1013
11/04/78+	**26**	17	2 Take Me To The River	Sire 1032
11/03/79	**80**	5	3 Life During Wartime (This Ain't No Party...This Ain't No Disco... This Ain't No Foolin' Around)	Sire 49075
7/30/83	**9**	20	4 **Burning Down The House**	Sire 29565
11/26/83	**62**	8	5 This Must Be The Place (Naive Melody)	Sire 29451
9/07/85	**54**	20	6 And She Was	Sire 28917
4/19/86	**91**	4	7 Once In A Lifetime	Sire 29163
			featured in the film "Down And Out In Beverly Hills" - recorded live in 1983 for group's "Stop Making Sense" film & album	
9/06/86	**25**	21	8 Wild Wild Life	Sire 28629
			TA MARA & THE SEEN	
			Minneapolis quintet led by Margaret Cox. Cox is a veteran Minneapolis barroom singer. Group includes guitarist Oliver Leiber, son of songwriter Jerry Leiber.	
10/12/85+	**24**	21	1 Everybody Dance	A&M 2768
			THE TAMS	
			Atlanta R&B quintet: brothers Charles and Joseph Pope, with Robert Smith, Floyd Ashton and Horace Key.	
10/20/62	**60**	7	1 Untie Me	Arlen 11
12/14/63+	**9**	14	2 **What Kind Of Fool (Do You Think I Am)**	ABC-Para. 10502
3/21/64	**70**	5	3 You Lied To Your Daddy/	
4/04/64	**79**	3	4 It's All Right (You're Just In Love)	ABC-Para. 10533
7/18/64	**41**	8	5 Hey Girl Don't Bother Me	ABC-Para. 10573
11/28/64	**87**	1	6 Silly Little Girl	ABC-Para. 10601
6/22/68	**61**	6	7 Be Young, Be Foolish, Be Happy	ABC 11066
			NORMA TANEGA	
			Born on 1/30/39 in Vallejo, California. Singer, songwriter, pianist, guitarist.	
2/26/66	**22**	9	1 Walkin' My Cat Named Dog	New Voice 807
			GARY TANNER	
5/27/78	**69**	5	1 Over The Rainbow	20th Century 2373
			Glenn Miller's version hit #1 in 1939	
			THE MARC TANNER BAND	
			Marc was born on 8/20/52 in Hollywood. Pop/rock singer, guitarist.	
3/03/79	**45**	8	1 Elena	Elektra 46003
			THE TARNEY/SPENCER BAND	
			Australian duo: Alan Tarney (vocals, guitar, keyboards) & Trevor Spencer (drums).	
7/22/78	**86**	6	1 It's Really You	A&M 2049
5/19/79	**84**	6	2 No Time To Lose	A&M 2124

DEBUT DATE	PEAK POS	WKS CHR	ARTIST — Record Title	Label & Number
			THE TARNEY/SPENCER BAND — Cont'd	
9/19/81	**74**	4	3 No Time To Lose [R]	A&M 2366
			THE TARRIERS	
			Folk-styled trio: Erik Darling, Bob Carey and movie actor Alan Arkin. Darling became a member of The Rooftop Singers.	
10/13/56	**9**	19	1 **Cindy, Oh Cindy**	Glory 247
			VINCE MARTIN with THE TARRIERS	
			Juke Box #9 / Best Seller #12 / Top 100 #12 / Jockey #12	
12/22/56+	**4**	19	2 **The Banana Boat Song**	Glory 249
			Juke Box #4 / Best Seller #5 / Top 100 #6 / Jockey #6	
			THE TASSELS	
			New Jersey quartet: John and sister Rochelle Gaudet, Leo Joyce and Joe Intelisano.	
7/13/59	**55**	7	1 To A Soldier Boy	Madison 117
			A TASTE OF HONEY	
			Soul/disco quartet: Janice Marie Johnson (vocals, guitar), Hazel Payne (vocals, bass), Perry Kimble (keyboards) and Donald Johnson (drums). Re-formed as a duo in 1980 with Janice Johnson and Hazel Payne.	
6/24/78	**1^{3}**	23	1 ▲ **Boogie Oogie Oogie**	Capitol 4565
8/11/79	**79**	4	2 Do It Good	Capitol 4744
3/07/81	**3**	24	3 ● **Sukiyaki**	Capitol 4953
3/13/82	**41**	10	4 I'll Try Something New	Capitol 5099
			GRADY TATE - see JIMMY SMITH and GROVER WASHINGTON, JR.	
			HOWARD TATE	
			R&B singer.	
8/20/66	**63**	7	1 Ain't Nobody Home	Verve 10420
12/24/66+	**67**	7	2 Look At Granny Run, Run	Verve 10464
1/27/68	**76**	5	3 Stop	Verve 10573
4/04/70	**100**	1	4 My Soul's Got A Hole In It	Turntable 1018
			TAVARES	
			Family R&B group from New Bedford, MA. Consisted of brothers Ralph, Antone "Chubby", Feliciano "Butch", Arthur "Pooch", and Perry Lee "Tiny" Tavares. Worked as Chubby & The Turnpikes from 1964-69.	
9/22/73	**35**	12	1 Check It Out	Capitol 3674
2/02/74	**70**	7	2 That's The Sound That Lonely Makes	Capitol 3794
6/01/74	**59**	7	3 Too Late	Capitol 3882
10/05/74	**50**	16	4 She's Gone	Capitol 3957
4/12/75	**25**	11	5 Remember What I Told You To Forget/	
		6	6 My Ship	Capitol 4010
7/26/75	**10**	18	7 **It Only Takes A Minute**	Capitol 4111
12/06/75+	**52**	6	8 Free Ride	Capitol 4184
6/05/76	**15**	21	9 ● Heaven Must Be Missing An Angel (Part 1)	Capitol 4270
10/30/76	**34**	12	10 Don't Take Away The Music	Capitol 4348
3/26/77	**22**	15	11 Whodunit	Capitol 4398
11/19/77+	**32**	21	12 More Than A Woman	Capitol 4500
			from the film "Saturday Night Fever"	
1/05/80	**47**	10	13 Bad Times	Capitol 4811
9/18/82	**33**	21	14 A Penny For Your Thoughts	RCA 13292
			ANDY TAYLOR	
			Born on 2/16/61 in Dolver-Hampton, England. Lead guitarist of Duran Duran and The Power Station.	
5/31/86	**24**	17	1 Take It Easy	Atlantic 89414
			from the film "American Anthem"	
10/25/86	**73**	6	2 When The Rain Comes Down	MCA 52946
			from the TV series "Miami Vice"	
			AUSTIN TAYLOR	
11/14/60	**90**	2	1 Push Push	Laurie 3067
			B.E. TAYLOR GROUP	
			Pittsburgh pop/rock quintet led by Taylor.	
1/28/84	**66**	8	1 Vitamin L	MCA 52311
5/31/86	**94**	2	2 Karen	Epic 05851

DEBUT DATE	PEAK POS	WKS CHR	ARTIST — Record Title	Label & Number
			BOBBY TAYLOR & THE VANCOUVERS	
			Interracial sextet based in Vancouver, Canada. Included guitarist Tommy Chong, of Cheech & Chong fame.	
4/20/68	**29**	10	1 Does Your Mama Know About Me	Gordy 7069
8/10/68	**85**	3	2 I Am Your Man	Gordy 7073
12/07/68+	**48**	7	3 Malinda	Gordy 7079
			DEBBIE TAYLOR	
4/26/69	**86**	6	1 Never Gonna Let Him Know	GWP 501
1/24/76	**100**	1	2 I Don't Wanna Leave You	Arista 0144
			FELICE TAYLOR	
			Born on 1/29/48 in Richmond, California. Recorded with sisters Darlene and Norma as the Sweets for Valiant in 1965.	
1/14/67	**42**	6	1 It May Be Winter Outside (But In My Heart It's Spring)	Mustang 3024
			GLORIA TAYLOR	
11/08/69	**49**	9	1 You Got To Pay The Price	Silver Fox 14
			JAMES TAYLOR	
			Born on 3/12/48 in Boston. Singer, songwriter, guitarist. With older brother Alex in the Fabulous Corsairs, 1964. Nervous breakdown at age 17. In New York group the Flying Machine, 1967, with friend Danny Kortchmar. Moved to England in 1968, recorded for Peter Asher. Married Carly Simon on 11/3/72; filed for divorce in 1982. Film "Two Lane Blacktop" with Dennis Wilson in 1973. Sister Kate and brothers Alex and Livingston also recorded.	
9/12/70	**3**	16	1 **Fire And Rain**	Warner 7423
11/14/70	**67**	7	2 Carolina In My Mind originally "Bubbled Under" in April of 1969	Apple 1805
2/06/71	**37**	8	3 Country Road	Warner 7460
6/05/71	**1**[1]	14	4● **You've Got A Friend**	Warner 7498
10/02/71	**31**	8	5 Long Ago And Far Away backing vocals on above 2 by Joni Mitchell	Warner 7521
12/02/72+	**14**	11	6 Don't Let Me Be Lonely Tonight	Warner 7655
3/03/73	**67**	4	7 One Man Parade	Warner 7682
2/02/74	**5**	16	8● **Mockingbird** CARLY SIMON & JAMES TAYLOR	Elektra 45880
6/21/75	**5**	15	9 **How Sweet It Is (To Be Loved By You)**	Warner 8109
10/04/75	**49**	8	10 Mexico	Warner 8137
7/04/76	**22**	16	11 Shower The People	Warner 8222
6/18/77	**4**	20	12 **Handy Man**	Columbia 10557
10/01/77	**20**	17	13 Your Smiling Face	Columbia 10602
1/21/78	**17**	14	14 (What A) Wonderful World ART GARFUNKEL with JAMES TAYLOR & PAUL SIMON	Columbia 10676
2/25/78	**61**	6	15 Honey Don't Leave L.A.	Columbia 10689
8/19/78	**36**	9	16 Devoted To You CARLY SIMON & JAMES TAYLOR	Elektra 45506
6/02/79	**28**	11	17 Up On The Roof	Columbia 11005
3/14/81	**11**	14	18 Her Town Too JAMES TAYLOR & J.D. SOUTHER	Columbia 60514
6/13/81	**72**	5	19 Hard Times 1-3, 5-7, 10-11, 13, 18-19: written by Taylor 1-7, 12-13, 15, 17-19: produced by Peter Asher	Columbia 02093
11/09/85	**61**	11	20 Everyday	Columbia 05681
			JOHN TAYLOR	
			Born on 6/20/60 in Birmingham, England. Bass guitarist of Duran Duran and The Power Station.	
3/08/86	**23**	12	1 I Do What I Do theme from the film "9 1/2 Weeks"	Capitol 5551
			JOHNNIE TAYLOR	
			Born on 5/5/37 in West Memphis, Arkansas. With gospel group, the Highway QC's in Chicago, early 50s. In vocal group the Five Echoes, recorded for Sabre in 1954. In The Soul Stirrers gospel group before going solo.	
11/30/63	**98**	1	1 Baby, We've Got Love	Derby 1006
12/16/67	**95**	2	2 Somebody's Sleeping In My Bed	Stax 235
10/26/68	**5**	14	3● **Who's Making Love**	Stax 0009
1/18/69	**20**	9	4 Take Care Of Your Homework	Stax 0023
5/10/69	**36**	9	5 Testify (I Wonna)	Stax 0033
8/09/69	**48**	8	6 I Could Never Be President	Stax 0046

DEBUT DATE	PEAK POS	WKS CHR	ARTIST — Record Title	Label & Number
			JOHNNIE TAYLOR — Cont'd	
12/20/69+	**43**	10	7 Love Bones	Stax 0055
6/06/70	**37**	10	8 Steal Away	Stax 0068
10/17/70	**39**	9	9 I Am Somebody, Part II	Stax 0078
1/16/71	**28**	10	10 Jody's Got Your Girl And Gone	Stax 0085
5/22/71	**86**	3	11 I Don't Wanna Lose You	Stax 0089
8/28/71	**64**	6	12 Hijackin' Love	Stax 0096
1/22/72	**74**	7	13 Standing In For Jody	Stax 0114
6/23/73	**11**	16	14● I Believe In You (You Believe In Me)	Stax 0161
10/13/73	**15**	11	15 Cheaper To Keep Her	Stax 0176
1/26/74	**34**	10	16 We're Getting Careless With Our Love	Stax 0193
6/29/74	**78**	4	17 I've Been Born Again	Stax 0208
2/07/76	**1^{4}**	19	18▲ **Disco Lady**	Columbia 10281
			first single certified platinum by R.I.A.A.	
6/05/76	**33**	7	19 Somebody's Gettin' It	Columbia 10334
2/26/77	**77**	7	20 Love Is Better In The A.M. (Part 1)	Columbia 10478
			all of above produced by Don Davis	
10/01/77	**86**	2	21 Disco 9000	Columbia 10610
			KATE TAYLOR	
			Born on 8/15/49 in Boston. James Taylor's younger sister.	
9/03/77	**49**	7	1 It's In His Kiss (The Shoop Shoop Song)	Columbia 10596
			KO KO TAYLOR	
			Born Cora Walton on 9/28/35 in Memphis, Tennessee. Chicago-based blues singer.	
4/23/66	**58**	8	1 Wang Dang Doodle	Checker 1135
			LITTLE JOHNNY TAYLOR	
			Born Johnny Young on 2/11/43 in Memphis. Blues singer, harmonica player. Moved to Los Angeles in 1950. With Mighty Clouds Of Joy and Stars Of Bethel gospel groups. Duets with Ted Taylor (no relation) in 1970s.	
8/17/63	**19**	13	1 Part Time Love	Galaxy 722
1/04/64	**78**	4	2 Since I Found A New Love	Galaxy 725
12/11/71+	**60**	8	3 Everybody Knows About My Good Thing	Ronn 55
			LIVINGSTON TAYLOR	
			Born on 11/21/50 in Boston. James Taylor's younger brother.	
2/06/71	**93**	2	1 Carolina Day	Capricorn 8012
2/05/72	**97**	2	2 Get Out Of Bed	Capricorn 8025
10/21/78+	**30**	14	3 I Will Be In Love With You	Epic 50604
3/31/79	**82**	4	4 I'll Come Running	Epic 50667
7/26/80	**38**	10	5 First Time Love	Epic 50894
			R. DEAN TAYLOR	
			Canadian singer, songwriter. Co-wrote The Supremes "Love Child".	
9/05/70	**5**	15	1 **Indiana Wants Me**	Rare Earth 5013
2/13/71	**66**	5	2 Ain't It A Sad Thing	Rare Earth 5023
4/17/71	**67**	4	3 Gotta See Jane	Rare Earth 5026
4/15/72	**83**	3	4 Taos New Mexico	Rare Earth 5041
			TED TAYLOR	
			Born Austin Taylor on 2/16/37 in Farm Town, Oklahoma. R&B singer. Formerly with Glory Bound Travellers and Mighty Clouds Of Joy gospel groups.	
12/04/65	**99**	2	1 Stay Away From My Baby	Okeh 7231
			THE T-BONES	
			A Joe Saraceno studio production. Also see Hamilton, Joe Frank & Reynolds.	
12/11/65+	**3**	13	1 **No Matter What Shape (Your Stomach's In)** [I]	Liberty 55836
			tune is from an "Alka Seltzer" jingle	
3/26/66	**62**	5	2 Sippin' 'N Chippin' [I]	Liberty 55867
			from the Nabisco "Sip 'N Chip" jingle	
			BRAM TCHAIKOVSKY	
			Bram (real name: Peter Bramall) formed rock group in Lincolnshire, England.	
7/07/79	**37**	12	1 Girl Of My Dreams	Polydor 14575
			T-CONNECTION	
			Dance/disco group formed in the Bahamas by Theophilus "T" Coakley.	
3/12/77	**46**	17	1 Do What You Wanna Do	Dash 5032
3/10/79	**56**	6	2 At Midnight	Dash 5048

DEBUT DATE	PEAK POS	WKS CHR	ARTIST — Record Title	Label & Number
			TEARS FOR FEARS	
			British duo: Roland Orzabal (vocals, guitar, keyboards) & Curt Smith (vocals, bass).	
8/06/83	**73**	6	1 Change	Mercury 812677
3/16/85	**1**[2]	24	2 **Everybody Wants To Rule The World**	Mercury 880659
6/15/85	**1**[3]	19	3 **Shout**	Mercury 880294
9/14/85	**3**	20	4 **Head Over Heels**	Mercury 880899
4/12/86	**27**	12	5 Mothers Talk	Mercury 884638
			all of above produced by Chris Hughes	
			TECHNIQUES	
11/18/57	**29**	13	1 Hey! Little Girl	Roulette 4030
			Best Seller #29 / Top 100 #33	
			TEDDY & THE TWILIGHTS	
			R&B quartet.	
5/19/62	**59**	8	1 Woman Is A Man's Best Friend	Swan 4102
			THE TEDDY BEARS	
			Los Angeles trio: Phil Spector (b: 12/26/40 in the Bronx), Carol Connors (lead singer; real name: Annette Kleinbard) and Marshall Leib. Spector became a well known writer and producer, also owner of Philles Records.	
9/22/58	**1**[3]	23	1 **To Know Him, Is To Love Him**	Dore 503
2/16/59	**98**	1	2 I Don't Need You Anymore/	
3/09/59	**91**	2	3 Oh Why	Imperial 5562
			THE TEE SET	
			Dutch quintet led by vocalist Peter Tetteroo.	
1/24/70	**5**	12	1 **Ma Belle Amie**	Colossus 107
5/09/70	**81**	4	2 If You Do Believe In Love	Colossus 114
			WILLIE TEE	
			Born Wilson Turbinton on 2/6/44 in New Orleans. R&B vocalist.	
3/20/65	**97**	2	1 Teasin' You	Atlantic 2273
			TEEGARDEN & VAN WINKLE	
			David Teegarden (drums) and Skip Knape (keyboards). Teegarden later joined Bob Seger's band, 1978-81.	
9/19/70	**22**	9	1 God, Love And Rock & Roll	Westbound 170
12/12/70	**84**	3	2 Everything Is Going To Be Alright	Westbound 171
			THE TEEN QUEENS	
			R&B duo formed in Los Angeles in 1955 by Betty and Rosie Collins, sisters of Aaron Collins of the Cadets/Jacks.	
3/03/56	**14**	12	1 Eddie My Love	RPM 453
			Best Seller #14 / Juke Box #16 / Top 100 #22	
			NINO TEMPO & 5th AVE. SAX	
9/22/73	**53**	8	1 Sister James [I]	A&M 1461
			NINO TEMPO & APRIL STEVENS	
			Nino (b: 1/6/35) and sister April (b: 4/29/36) hail from Niagara Falls, New York. Nino was a session saxophonist before teaming with April.	
7/07/62	**77**	4	1 Sweet And Lovely	Atco 6224
			#1 hit in 1931 for Gus Arnheim & His Orchestra	
9/14/63	**1**[1]	15	2 **Deep Purple**	Atco 6273
			#1 hit in 1939 for Larry Clinton & His Orchestra	
12/21/63+	**11**	9	3 Whispering	Atco 6281
			#1 hit in 1920 for Paul Whiteman & His Orchestra	
2/22/64	**32**	6	4 Stardust	Atco 6286
			#1 hit in 1931 for Isham Jones & His Orchestra	
5/02/64	**56**	5	5 Tea For Two/	
			#1 hit in 1925 for Marion Harris	
4/25/64	**99**	1	6 I'm Confessin' (That I Love You)	Atco 6294
			#2 hit in 1930 for Guy Lombardo & His Orchestra	
9/10/66	**26**	8	7 All Strung Out	White Whale 236
7/22/67	**86**	2	8 I Can't Go On Livin' Baby Without You	White Whale 252
			tune is also flip side of White Whale 236	
			THE TEMPOS	
			Pittsburgh vocal quartet: Mike Lazo, Gene Schachter, Jim Drake & Tom Minoto.	
6/29/59	**23**	14	1 See You In September	Climax 102

DEBUT DATE	PEAK POS	WKS CHR	ARTIST — Record Title	Label & Number
			THE TEMPREES Soul trio: Del Juan Calvin, Harold "Scottie" Scott and Jasper "Jabbo" Phillips. Calvin replaced by William Norvell Johnson. In film "Wattstax" in 1972.	
10/07/72	**93**	2	1 Dedicated To The One I Love	We Produce 1808
			THE TEMPTATIONS White quartet from Flushing, New York. Consisted of Neil Stevens, Larry Curtis, Artie Sands and Artie Marin.	
4/18/60	**29**	10	1 Barbara	Goldisc 3001
			THE TEMPTATIONS Soul group formed in Detroit in 1960. Consisted of Eddie Kendricks, Paul Williams (d: 8/17/73), Melvin Franklin, Otis Williams and David Ruffin (joined in 1963). Originally called the Primes and Elgins, first recorded for Miracle in 1961. Ruffin replaced by Dennis Edwards in 1968. Kendricks and Paul Williams left in 1971, replaced by Damon Harris and Richard Street. Harris left in 1975, replaced by Glenn Leonard. Edwards left group, 1977-79, replaced by Louis Price. Edwards left again in 1984, rejoined in 1987. America's all-time favorite soul group.	
2/29/64	**11**	11	1 The Way You Do The Things You Do	Gordy 7028
5/30/64	**33**	9	2 I'll Be In Trouble	Gordy 7032
9/12/64	**26**	8	3 Girl (Why You Wanna Make Me Blue)	Gordy 7035
1/16/65	**1**[1]	13	4 **My Girl**	Gordy 7038
4/03/65	**18**	9	5 It's Growing	Gordy 7040
7/24/65	**17**	10	6 Since I Lost My Baby	Gordy 7043
10/23/65	**13**	8	7 My Baby/	
12/18/65+	**83**	5	8 Don't Look Back	Gordy 7047
2/26/66	**29**	7	9 Get Ready all of above produced by Smokey Robinson (except #3)	Gordy 7049
5/28/66	**13**	13	10 Ain't Too Proud To Beg	Gordy 7054
8/20/66	**3**	12	11 **Beauty Is Only Skin Deep**	Gordy 7055
11/19/66	**8**	10	12 **(I Know) I'm Losing You**	Gordy 7057
4/29/67	**8**	10	13 **All I Need**	Gordy 7061
7/29/67	**6**	12	14 **You're My Everything**	Gordy 7063
10/14/67	**14**	9	15 (Loneliness Made Me Realize) It's You That I Need	Gordy 7065
1/13/68	**4**	14	16 **I Wish It Would Rain**	Gordy 7068
5/04/68	**13**	10	17 I Could Never Love Another (After Loving You)	Gordy 7072
8/03/68	**26**	7	18 Please Return Your Love To Me	Gordy 7074
11/16/68+	**6**	12	19 **Cloud Nine**	Gordy 7081
12/07/68+	**2**[2]	13	20 **I'm Gonna Make You Love Me** DIANA ROSS & THE SUPREMES & THE TEMPTATIONS	Motown 1137
2/15/69	**6**	12	21 **Run Away Child, Running Wild**	Gordy 7084
3/15/69	**25**	7	22 I'll Try Something New DIANA ROSS & THE SUPREMES & THE TEMPTATIONS	Motown 1142
5/24/69	**20**	8	23 Don't Let The Joneses Get You Down	Gordy 7086
8/16/69	**1**[2]	17	24 **I Can't Get Next To You**	Gordy 7093
9/13/69	**46**	5	25 The Weight DIANA ROSS & THE SUPREMES & THE TEMPTATIONS	Motown 1153
1/17/70	**7**	11	26 **Psychedelic Shack**	Gordy 7096
5/23/70	**3**	15	27 **Ball Of Confusion (That's What The World Is Today)**	Gordy 7099
10/03/70	**33**	7	28 Ungena Za Ulimwengu (Unite The World)	Gordy 7102
2/06/71	**1**[2]	15	29 **Just My Imagination (Running Away With Me)**	Gordy 7105
7/24/71	**51**	6	30 It's Summer	Gordy 7109
11/06/71	**18**	10	31 Superstar (Remember How You Got Where You Are)	Gordy 7111
3/04/72	**30**	8	32 Take A Look Around 16-19, 21, 23-24, 26-32: written by Norman Whitfield & Barrett Strong	Gordy 7115
7/01/72	**92**	4	33 Mother Nature	Gordy 7119
10/14/72	**1**[1]	16	34 **Papa Was A Rollin' Stone**	Gordy 7121
2/24/73	**7**	14	35 **Masterpiece**	Gordy 7126
6/09/73	**40**	8	36 The Plastic Man	Gordy 7129
8/18/73	**35**	11	37 Hey Girl (I Like Your Style)	Gordy 7131
12/22/73+	**27**	9	38 Let Your Hair Down	Gordy 7133
3/16/74	**43**	9	39 Heavenly	Gordy 7135
6/22/74	**74**	6	40 You've Got My Soul On Fire	Gordy 7136
12/21/74+	**40**	10	41 Happy People	Gordy 7138
3/22/75	**26**	14	42 Shakey Ground	Gordy 7142

DEBUT DATE	PEAK POS	WKS CHR	ARTIST — Record Title	Label & Number
			THE TEMPTATIONS — Cont'd	
7/12/75	**37**	10	43 Glasshouse	Gordy 7144
2/07/76	**54**	6	44 Keep Holding On	Gordy 7146
7/17/76	**94**	3	45 Up The Creek (Without A Paddle)	Gordy 7150
5/10/80	**43**	9	46 Power	Gordy 7183
9/19/81	**67**	5	47 Aiming At Your Heart	Gordy 7208
5/08/82	**66**	8	48 Standing On The Top - Part 1 **THE TEMPTATIONS featuring RICK JAMES**	Gordy 1616
4/16/83	**88**	3	49 Love On My Mind Tonight	Gordy 1666
4/07/84	**54**	8	50 Sail Away 3, 10-12, 14-19, 21, 23-24, 26-40 & 50: produced by Norman Whitfield	Gordy 1720
12/15/84+	**48**	14	51 Treat Her Like A Lady	Gordy 1765
10/11/86	**47**	11	52 Lady Soul	Gordy 1856
			10cc English art-rock group which evolved from Hotlegs. Consisted of Eric Stewart (formerly of The Mindbenders), guitar; Graham Gouldman, bass; Lol Creme, guitar, keyboards; and Kevin Godley, drums. Godley and Creme left in 1976, replaced by drummer Paul Burgess. Added members Rick Fenn, Stuart Tosh and Duncan MacKay in 1978. Gouldman later in duo, Wax. Also see Godley & Creme.	
9/15/73	**73**	8	1 Rubber Bullets	UK 49015
5/17/75	**2**[3]	17	2 **I'm Not In Love**	Mercury 73678
11/29/75	**83**	6	3 Art For Art's Sake	Mercury 73725
4/10/76	**60**	4	4 I'm Mandy Fly Me	Mercury 73779
1/08/77	**5**	19	5● **The Things We Do For Love**	Mercury 73875
5/21/77	**40**	7	6 People In Love	Mercury 73917
8/06/77	**69**	8	7 Good Morning Judge	Mercury 73943
9/30/78	**44**	10	8 Dreadlock Holiday	Polydor 14511
2/03/79	**85**	3	9 For You And I from the film "Moment By Moment" 2-9: written by Stewart & Gouldman	Polydor 14528
			TEN WHEEL DRIVE with GENYA RAVAN Jazz-rock band led by vocalist Genya Ravan.	
7/25/70	**74**	7	1 Morning Much Better	Polydor 14037
			TEN YEARS AFTER British blues-rock quartet: Alvin Lee (vocals, guitar), Leo Lyons (bass) Chick Churchill (keyboards) and Ric Lee (drums).	
5/02/70	**98**	2	1 Love Like A Man	Deram 7529
9/25/71	**40**	12	2 I'd Love To Change The World	Columbia 45457
1/15/72	**61**	5	3 Baby Won't You Let Me Rock 'N Roll You	Columbia 45530
12/16/72+	**89**	6	4 Choo Choo Mama	Columbia 45736
			TENDER SLIM	
1/11/60	**93**	2	1 Teenage Hayride [I]	Grey Cliff 723
			ROBERT TEPPER Native of Baylor, New Jersey.	
1/25/86	**22**	16	1 No Easy Way Out from the film "Rocky IV"	Scotti Br. 05750
5/10/86	**85**	3	2 Don't Walk Away	Scotti Br. 05879
			TAMMI TERRELL Born Tammy Montgomery in 1946 in Philadelphia; died of a brain tumor on 3/16/70. Worked with James Brown Revue. Tumor diagnosed after collapsing on stage in 1967.	
8/17/63	**99**	1	1 I Cried shown as: **TAMMY MONTGOMERY**	Try Me 28001
1/08/66	**72**	5	2 I Can't Believe You Love Me	Motown 1086
5/28/66	**80**	5	3 Come On And See Me	Motown 1095
5/13/67	**19**	12	4 Ain't No Mountain High Enough	Tamla 54149
9/09/67	**5**	13	5 **Your Precious Love**	Tamla 54156
12/02/67+	**10**	11	6 **If I Could Build My Whole World Around You/**	
3/02/68	**68**	6	7 If This World Were Mine	Tamla 54161
4/13/68	**8**	13	8 **Ain't Nothing Like The Real Thing**	Tamla 54163
7/27/68	**7**	12	9 **You're All I Need To Get By**	Tamla 54169
10/12/68	**24**	7	10 Keep On Lovin' Me Honey	Tamla 54173
1/18/69	**67**	4	11 This Old Heart Of Mine (Is Weak For You)	Motown 1138
2/01/69	**30**	7	12 Good Lovin' Ain't Easy To Come By	Tamla 54179

DEBUT DATE	PEAK POS	WKS CHR	ARTIST — Record Title	Label & Number
			TAMMI TERRELL — Cont'd	
11/29/69	**49**	8	13 What You Gave Me	Tamla 54187
4/18/70	**50**	7	14 The Onion Song/	
		6	15 California Soul	Tamla 54192
			4-10, 12-15: **MARVIN GAYE & TAMMI TERRELL**	
			HELEN TERRY - see RAY PARKER JR.	
			JOE TEX	
			Born Joseph Arrington, Jr. on 8/8/33 in Rogers, Texas; died of a heart attack on 8/13/82. Sang with local gospel groups. Won recording contract at Apollo Theater talent contest in 1954. First recorded for King in 1955. Became a convert to Muslim faith, changed name to Joseph Hazziez in July, 1972.	
12/19/64+	**5**	11	1 **Hold What You've Got**	Dial 4001
2/20/65	**46**	7	2 You Better Get It/	
2/27/65	**51**	6	3 You Got What It Takes	Dial 4003
4/10/65	**56**	7	4 A Woman Can Change A Man/	
4/10/65	**95**	1	5 Don't Let Your Left Hand Know	Dial 4006
6/26/65	**65**	4	6 One Monkey Don't Stop No Show	Dial 4011
8/28/65	**23**	13	7 I Want To (Do Everything For You)	Dial 4016
12/04/65+	**29**	9	8 A Sweet Woman Like You	Dial 4022
3/05/66	**56**	8	9 The Love You Save (May Be Your Own)	Dial 4026
5/14/66	**39**	7	10 S.Y.S.L.J.F.M. (The Letter Song)	Dial 4028
7/23/66	**67**	5	11 I Believe I'm Gonna Make It	Dial 4033
10/08/66	**64**	5	12 I've Got To Do A Little Bit Better	Dial 4045
12/17/66+	**44**	7	13 Papa Was Too	Dial 4051
3/04/67	**35**	8	14 Show Me	Dial 4055
6/03/67	**54**	7	15 Woman Like That, Yeah	Dial 4059
8/05/67	**63**	5	16 A Woman's Hands	Dial 4061
10/28/67	**10**	15	17• **Skinny Legs And All**	Dial 4063
2/10/68	**33**	7	18 Men Are Gettin' Scarce	Dial 4069
5/18/68	**59**	5	19 I'll Never Do You Wrong	Dial 4076
8/10/68	**52**	5	20 Keep The One You Got	Dial 4083
10/12/68	**81**	3	21 You Need Me, Baby	Dial 4086
1/18/69	**88**	3	22 That's Your Baby	Dial 4089
4/12/69	**47**	8	23 Buying A Book [S]	Dial 4090
7/19/69	**94**	3	24 That's The Way	Dial 4093
1/22/72	**2^{2}**	21	25• **I Gotcha**	Dial 1010
5/20/72	**41**	8	26 You Said A Bad Word	Dial 1012
			all of above written by Tex	
4/02/77	**12**	18	27• Ain't Gonna Bump No More (With No Big Fat Woman)	Epic 50313
			all of above produced by Buddy Killen	
			THE TEXANS	
			Duo is actually Johnny (guitar) and Dorsey Burnette (upright bass, guitar).	
3/27/61	**100**	1	1 Green Grass Of Texas [I]	Infinity 001
			THEE MIDNITERS	
			Los Angeles Mexican-American group featuring lead singer Willie Garcia.	
3/13/65	**67**	4	1 Land Of A Thousand Dances - Part I	Chattahoochee 666
			THEE PROPHETS	
			Milwaukee pop/rock quartet featuring lead singer Brian Lake.	
3/08/69	**49**	8	1 Playgirl	Kapp 962
			THEM	
			Belfast, Northern Ireland rock quintet: Van Morrison (lead singer), Billy Harrison, Alan Henderson, John McAuley and Peter Bardens.	
5/22/65+	**71**	7	1 Gloria	Parrot 9727
5/29/65	**24**	10	2 Here Comes The Night	Parrot 9749
10/30/65	**33**	8	3 Mystic Eyes [I]	Parrot 9796
			THIN LIZZY	
			Dublin Ireland rock quartet led by Phil Lynott. Phil died on 1/4/86 (35).	
5/15/76	**12**	17	1 The Boys Are Back In Town	Mercury 73786
9/18/76	**77**	8	2 Cowboy Song	Mercury 73841

DEBUT DATE	PEAK POS	WKS CHR	ARTIST — Record Title	Label & Number
			THINK	
			Studio group assembled by producers Lou Stallman and Bobby Susser.	
12/04/71+	**23**	10	1 Once You Understand	Laurie 3583
			featuring dialogue between a teenager and his parents	
3/09/74	**53**	8	2 Once You Understand [R]	Big Tree 15000
			THE THIRD RAIL	
			Studio trio comprised of songwriters Joey Levine and Artie & Kris Resnik.	
8/05/67	**53**	9	1 Run, Run, Run	Epic 10191
			THIRD WORLD	
			Reggae fusion band from Jamaica. William "Bunny Rugs" Clarke, lead singer.	
2/10/79	**47**	8	1 Now That We Found Love	Island 8663
			THE THIRTEENTH FLOOR ELEVATORS	
8/20/66	**55**	8	1 You're Gonna Miss Me	Int. Artists 107
			38 SPECIAL	
			Florida Southern-rock sextet: Donnie Van Zant (younger brother of Lynyrd Skynyrd's Ronnie Van Zant), lead singer; Don Barnes, Jeff Carlisi, Steve Brookins, Jack Grondin and Larry Jungstrom (replaced Ken Lyons in 1979).	
2/02/80	**43**	9	1 Rockin' Into The Night	A&M 2205
2/28/81	**27**	17	2 Hold On Loosely	A&M 2316
6/06/81	**52**	10	3 Fantasy Girl	A&M 2330
5/01/82	**10**	17	4 **Caught Up In You**	A&M 2412
8/21/82	**38**	11	5 You Keep Runnin' Away	A&M 2431
11/12/83+	**19**	16	6 If I'd Been The One	A&M 2594
2/04/84	**20**	13	7 Back Where You Belong	A&M 2615
9/29/84	**25**	12	8 Teacher Teacher	Capitol 5405
			from the film "Teachers"	
			all of above produced by Rodney Mills	
5/03/86	**14**	16	9 Like No Other Night	A&M 2831
7/19/86	**48**	12	10 Somebody Like You	A&M 2854
			B.J. THOMAS	
			Born Billy Joe Thomas on 8/27/42 in Hugo, Oklahoma; raised in Roseburg, Texas (near Houston). With the Triumphs, worked local clubs, recorded for Hickory in 1964. Went solo in 1966. Became a born-again Christian in 1976 and began a successful Gospel recording career.	
2/19/66	**8**	13	1 **I'm So Lonesome I Could Cry**	Scepter 12129
			B.J. THOMAS & THE TRIUMPHS	
5/14/66	**22**	8	2 Mama	Scepter 12139
6/18/66	**34**	11	3 Billy And Sue	Hickory 1395
			B.J. THOMAS & THE TRIUMPHS	
7/30/66	**75**	4	4 Bring Back The Time	Scepter 12154
9/10/66	**80**	5	5 Tomorrow Never Comes	Scepter 12165
5/13/67	**94**	1	6 I Can't Help It (If I'm Still In Love With You)	Scepter 12194
			1 & 6: written and recorded by Hank Williams	
6/22/68	**28**	14	7 The Eyes Of A New York Woman	Scepter 12219
11/16/68+	**5**	16	8 ● **Hooked On A Feeling**	Scepter 12230
3/22/69	**45**	8	9 It's Only Love	Scepter 12244
7/12/69	**97**	3	10 Pass The Apple Eve	Scepter 12255
11/01/69+	**1**[4]	22	11 ● **Raindrops Keep Fallin' On My Head**	Scepter 12265
			from the film "Butch Cassidy & The Sundance Kid"	
3/28/70	**26**	9	12 Everybody's Out Of Town	Scepter 12277
6/20/70	**9**	13	13 **I Just Can't Help Believing**	Scepter 12283
11/28/70+	**38**	10	14 Most Of All	Scepter 12299
2/27/71	**16**	11	15 No Love At All	Scepter 12307
7/03/71	**34**	10	16 Mighty Clouds Of Joy	Scepter 12320
11/06/71	**61**	7	17 Long Ago Tomorrow	Scepter 12335
2/12/72	**15**	11	18 Rock And Roll Lullaby	Scepter 12344
			featuring Duane Eddy on guitar	
7/15/72	**74**	6	19 That's What Friends Are For	Scepter 12354
10/07/72	**100**	2	20 Happier Than The Morning Sun	Scepter 12364
2/01/75	**1**[1]	18	21 ● **(Hey Won't You Play) Another Somebody Done Somebody Wrong Song**	ABC 12054
9/20/75	**64**	9	22 Help Me Make It (To My Rockin' Chair)	ABC 12121
7/02/77	**17**	17	23 Don't Worry Baby	MCA 40735
11/12/77	**77**	4	24 Still The Lovin' Is Fun	MCA 40812

DEBUT DATE	PEAK POS	WKS CHR	ARTIST — Record Title	Label & Number
			B.J. THOMAS — Cont'd	
1/21/78	**43**	8	25 Everybody Loves A Rain Song	MCA 40854
5/21/83	**93**	2	26 Whatever Happened To Old Fashioned Love	Clev. Int. 03492
			CARLA THOMAS	
			Born on 12/21/42 in Memphis. Daughter of Rufus Thomas. First recorded with Rufus for Satellite in 1960. Had several duets with Otis Redding.	
1/30/61	**10**	14	1 **Gee Whiz (Look At His Eyes)**	Atlantic 2086
5/08/61	**56**	6	2 A Love Of My Own	Atlantic 2101
10/13/62	**41**	8	3 I'll Bring It Home To You	Atlantic 2163
7/20/63	**93**	2	4 What A Fool I've Been	Atlantic 2189
6/06/64	**92**	2	5 That's Really Some Good/	
6/20/64	**94**	1	6 Night Time Is The Right Time above 2: **RUFUS & CARLA**	Stax 151
8/01/64	**67**	9	7 I've Got No Time To Lose	Atlantic 2238
11/28/64	**71**	4	8 A Woman's Love	Atlantic 2258
7/03/65	**92**	3	9 Stop! Look What You're Doing	Stax 172
4/30/66	**62**	6	10 Let Me Be Good To You	Stax 188
8/20/66	**14**	16	11 B-A-B-Y	Stax 195
1/14/67	**74**	7	12 Something Good (Is Going To Happen To You)	Stax 207
5/06/67	**26**	9	13 Tramp **OTIS & CARLA**	Stax 216
5/06/67	**99**	1	14 When Tomorrow Comes	Stax 214
6/17/67	**85**	4	15 I'll Always Have Faith In You	Stax 222
8/12/67	**30**	9	16 Knock On Wood **OTIS & CARLA**	Stax 228
12/30/67+	**68**	6	17 Pick Up The Pieces	Stax 239
2/10/68	**60**	6	18 Lovey Dovey **OTIS & CARLA**	Stax 244
10/19/68	**86**	2	19 Where Do I Go from the Broadway musical "Hair"	Stax 0011
2/15/69	**49**	11	20 I Like What You're Doing (To Me)	Stax 0024
			EVELYN THOMAS	
9/29/84	**85**	5	1 High Energy	TSR 106
			GENE THOMAS	
			Born on 12/4/38 in Palestine, Texas. Gene of Gene & Debbe. Writer for Acuff-Rose Music from 1967-72.	
10/30/61	**53**	7	1 Sometime	United Art. 338
11/16/63+	**84**	5	2 Baby's Gone	United Art. 640
			IAN THOMAS	
			Canadian singer, songwriter.	
10/27/73+	**34**	14	1 Painted Ladies	Janus 224
			IRMA THOMAS	
			Born Irma Lee on 2/18/41 in Ponchatoula, Louisiana. The Soul Queen of New Orleans. Discovered by New Orleans' bandleader Tommy Ridgley.	
3/28/64	**17**	12	1 Wish Someone Would Care	Imperial 66013
7/04/64	**52**	6	2 Anyone Who Knows What Love Is (Will Understand)	Imperial 66041
11/07/64	**98**	2	3 Times Have Changed	Imperial 66069
12/19/64+	**63**	8	4 He's My Guy	Imperial 66080
			JAMO THOMAS	
3/19/66	**98**	2	1 I Spy (For The FBI)	Thomas 303
			JON THOMAS	
			Cleveland-born blues singer, keyboardist.	
6/06/60	**48**	10	1 Heartbreak (It's Hurtin' Me)	ABC-Para. 10122
			NOLAN THOMAS	
			18-year-old New Jersey native.	
1/05/85	**57**	13	1 Yo' Little Brother	Mirage 99697
			PAT THOMAS	
12/08/62	**78**	2	1 Desafinado (Slightly Out Of Tune) arranged and conducted by Lalo Schifrin	MGM 13102

DEBUT DATE	PEAK POS	WKS CHR	ARTIST — Record Title	Label & Number
			RUFUS THOMAS	
			Born on 3/26/17 in Cayce, MS. R&B singer, songwriter, dance creator. Father of Carla Thomas. First recorded for Talent in 1950. Disc jockey, WDIA-Memphis, 1953-74.	
2/09/63	**87**	8	1 The Dog	Stax 130
10/05/63	**10**	14	2 **Walking The Dog**	Stax 140
2/01/64	**48**	9	3 Can Your Monkey Do The Dog	Stax 144
4/11/64	**86**	2	4 Somebody Stole My Dog	Stax 149
6/06/64	**92**	2	5 That's Really Some Good/	
6/20/64	**94**	1	6 Night Time Is The Right Time above 2: **RUFUS & CARLA**	Stax 151
10/10/64	**49**	7	7 Jump Back	Stax 157
2/07/70	**28**	12	8 Do The Funky Chicken	Stax 0059
12/19/70+	**25**	13	9 (Do The) Push And Pull, Part I	Stax 0079
8/14/71	**31**	10	10 The Breakdown (Part I)	Stax 0098
12/25/71+	**44**	10	11 Do The Funky Penguin (Part I)	Stax 0112
			TASHA THOMAS	
			Born in Jeutyn, Alaska. Moved to New York in 1970. Played Auntie Em in Broadway's "The Wiz". Session singer for Kiss, Cat Stevens, Diana Ross and others.	
1/27/79	**91**	5	1 Shoot Me (With Your Love)	Atlantic 3542
			TIMMY THOMAS	
			Born on 11/13/44 in Evansville, Indiana. Soul singer, songwriter, keyboardist. Studio musician at Gold Wax Records in Memphis. Session work for Betty Wright and KC & The Sunshine Band.	
11/25/72+	**3**	15	1 **Why Can't We Live Together**	Glades 1703
4/07/73	**75**	5	2 People Are Changin'	Glades 1709
6/02/84	**80**	3	3 Gotta Give A Little Love (Ten Years After)	Gold Mt. 82004
			THOMPSON TWINS	
			British-based trio: Tom Bailey (b: 1/18/56, England), lead singer, synthesizer; Alannah Currie (b: 9/28/57, New Zealand), xylophone, percussion; Joe Leeway (b: South Africa), conga, snythesizer. Leeway left in 1986.	
1/22/83	**30**	16	1 Lies	Arista 1024
4/30/83	**45**	9	2 Love On Your Side	Arista 1056
2/11/84	**3**	21	3 **Hold Me Now**	Arista 9164
5/26/84	**11**	16	4 Doctor! Doctor!	Arista 9209
8/25/84	**44**	9	5 You Take Me Up	Arista 9244
11/10/84	**69**	6	6 The Gap	Arista 9290
9/21/85	**6**	20	7 **Lay Your Hands On Me**	Arista 9396
1/18/86	**8**	16	8 **King For A Day** all of above written by Bailey, Currie and Leeway	Arista 9450
7/26/86	**54**	10	9 Nothing In Common from the film of the same title	Arista 9511
			CHRIS THOMPSON - see NIGHT and JENNIFER WARNES	
			HANK THOMPSON	
			Born on 9/3/25 in Waco, Texas. Had over 20 Top 10 Country hits.	
7/25/60	**99**	1	1 She's Just A Whole Lot Like You	Capitol 4386
			KAY THOMPSON	
			Born on 11/9/13 in St. Louis. Wrote "Eloise" series of children's books. In the film musical "Funny Face", 1956.	
3/10/56	**39**	8	1 Eloise [N]	Cadence 3
			ROBBIN THOMPSON BAND	
			Virginia pop/rock quintet led by singer, guitarist Thompson. Robbin played in Bruce Springsteen's early Steel Mill band.	
10/18/80	**66**	9	1 Brite Eyes	Ovation 1157
			SUE THOMPSON	
			Born Eva Sue McKee on 7/19/26 in Nevada, Missouri.	
9/04/61	**5**	14	1 **Sad Movies (Make Me Cry)**	Hickory 1153
12/04/61+	**3**	16	2 **Norman**	Hickory 1159
3/17/62	**42**	9	3 Two Of A Kind	Hickory 1166
6/16/62	**31**	11	4 Have A Good Time	Hickory 1174
9/29/62	**17**	10	5 James (Hold The Ladder Steady)	Hickory 1183
1/12/63	**78**	5	6 Willie Can	Hickory 1196
1/02/65	**23**	10	7 Paper Tiger 1-2, 5 & 7: written by John D. Loudermilk	Hickory 1284

DEBUT DATE	PEAK POS	WKS CHR	ARTIST — Record Title	Label & Number
			ALI THOMSON	
			Scottish singer, songwriter. Younger brother of Supertramp's Dougie Thomson.	
6/14/80	**15**	17	1 Take A Little Rhythm	A&M 2243
9/13/80	**42**	11	2 Live Every Minute	A&M 2260
			DAVID THORNE	
10/20/62	**76**	4	1 The Alley Cat Song	Riverside 4530
			GEORGE THOROGOOD & THE DESTROYERS	
			Delaware rock & blues quartet. Lineup since 1980: Thorogood (vocals, guitar), Billy Blough (bass), Jeff Simon (drums) and Hank Carter (sax).	
6/15/85	**63**	8	1 Willie And The Hand Jive	EMI America 8270
			BILLY THORPE	
			English-born singer, guitarist; raised in Australia. Superstar artist in Australia.	
7/28/79	**41**	10	1 Children Of The Sun	Polydor 2018
			also released on Capricorn 0321	
			THE THREE CHUCKLES	
			New York trio: Teddy Randazzo (accordion), Tom Romano (guitar) and Russ Gilberto (bass). Appeared in films "Rock Rock Rock" and "The Girl Can't Help It".	
11/12/55	**67**	5	1 Times Two, I Love You	X 0162
3/17/56	**70**	3	2 And The Angels Sing	Vik 0194
			#1 hit in 1939 for Benny Goodman	
			THE THREE DEGREES	
			Philadelphia R&B trio discovered by Richard Barrett. Originally consisted of Fayette Pinkney, Linda Turner and Shirley Porter. Turner and Porter replaced by Sheila Ferguson and Valerie Holiday in 1966.	
3/06/65	**80**	5	1 Gee Baby (I'm Sorry)	Swan 4197
1/01/66	**97**	1	2 Look In My Eyes	Swan 4235
6/06/70	**29**	12	3 Maybe	Roulette 7079
			above 3 written by Richard Barrett	
9/12/70	**48**	9	4 I Do Take You	Roulette 7088
1/23/71	**77**	6	5 You're The One	Roulette 7091
5/08/71	**98**	2	6 There's So Much Love All Around Me	Roulette 7102
3/02/74	**1**[2]	18	7● **TSOP (The Sound Of Philadelphia)** [I]	Phil. Int. 3540
			theme from the TV show "Soul Train"	
7/06/74	**85**	4	8 Love Is The Message	Phil. Int. 3547
			above 2: **MFSB featuring THE THREE DEGREES**	
9/28/74	**2**[1]	18	9● **When Will I See You Again**	Phil. Int. 3550
			above 3 written and produced by Kenny Gamble and Leon Huff	
			THREE DOG NIGHT	
			Los Angeles pop/rock group formed in 1968 featuring lead singers Danny Hutton (b: 9/10/42), Cory Wells (b: 2/5/42) and Chuck Negron (b: 6/8/42). Disbanded in the mid-70s.	
2/08/69	**29**	12	1 Try A Little Tenderness	Dunhill 4177
5/03/69	**5**	16	2● **One**	Dunhill 4191
			written by Nilsson	
8/09/69	**4**	13	3 **Easy To Be Hard**	Dunhill 4203
10/25/69	**10**	14	4 **Eli's Coming**	Dunhill 4215
			written by Laura Nyro	
2/28/70	**15**	9	5 Celebrate	Dunhill 4229
			above 5 produced by Gabriel Mekler	
5/23/70	**1**[2]	15	6● **Mama Told Me (Not To Come)**	Dunhill 4239
			written by Randy Newman	
8/29/70	**15**	11	7 Out In The Country	Dunhill 4250
11/21/70+	**19**	11	8 One Man Band	Dunhill 4262
3/13/71	**1**[6]	17	9● **Joy To The World**	Dunhill 4272
7/10/71	**7**	12	10 **Liar**	Dunhill 4282
			written by Russ Ballard	
11/13/71	**4**	11	11● **An Old Fashioned Love Song**	Dunhill 4294
			written by Paul Williams	
12/25/71+	**5**	12	12 **Never Been To Spain**	Dunhill 4299
			9 & 12: written by Hoyt Axton	
3/25/72	**12**	9	13 The Family Of Man	Dunhill 4306
8/12/72	**1**[1]	11	14● **Black & White**	Dunhill 4317
11/18/72+	**19**	14	15 Pieces Of April	Dunhill 4331
5/19/73	**3**	16	16● **Shambala**	Dunhill 4352
10/27/73	**17**	12	17 Let Me Serenade You	Dunhill 4370
			6-17: produced by Richard Podolor	

DEBUT DATE	PEAK POS	WKS CHR	ARTIST — Record Title	Label & Number
			THREE DOG NIGHT — Cont'd	
3/16/74	**4**	19	18● **The Show Must Go On**	Dunhill 4382
6/29/74	**16**	13	19 Sure As I'm Sittin' Here	Dunhill 15001
9/28/74	**33**	12	20 Play Something Sweet (Brickyard Blues)	Dunhill 15013
7/05/75	**32**	9	21 Til The World Ends	ABC 12114
			15 & 21: written by Dave Loggins	
			THE 3 FRIENDS	
7/31/61	**89**	2	1 Dedicated (To The Songs I Love) [N]	Imperial 5763
			THE THREE G'S	
8/04/58	**55**	3	1 Let's Go Steady For The Summer	Columbia 41175
			THE THREE PLAYMATES	
			Female R&B trio: Lucille, Alma and Gwen.	
3/10/58	**89**	1	1 Sugah Wooga	Savoy 1528
			JOHNNY THUNDER	
			R&B singer from Leesburg, Florida. Discovered by Teddy Vann.	
12/22/62+	**4**	11	1 **Loop De Loop**	Diamond 129
11/27/65	**67**	5	2 Everybody Do The Sloopy	Diamond 192
4/15/67	**96**	1	3 Make Love To Me	Diamond 218
			JOHNNY THUNDER & RUBY WINTERS	
			revival of Jo Stafford's 1954 hit (POS 1)	
			THUNDERCLAP NEWMAN	
			British trio: Andy Newman, Speedy Keen (lead singer) and Jimmy McCulloch (member of Wings, 1975-78; died on 9/27/79). Group put together by Pete Townshend.	
9/06/69	**37**	10	1 Something In The Air	Track 2656
			from the film "The Magic Christian"	
			BILLY THUNDERKLOUD & THE CHIEFTONES	
6/28/75	**92**	3	1 What Time Of Day	20th Century 2181
			TICO & THE TRIUMPHS	
			Pop/rock trio led by Paul Simon.	
1/06/62	**99**	1	1 Motorcycle	Amy 835
			TIERRA	
			East Los Angeles group led by brothers Steve and Rudy Salas. Both formerly with El Chicano.	
11/08/80+	**18**	21	1 Together	Boardwalk 5702
3/14/81	**62**	8	2 Memories	Boardwalk 70073
10/24/81	**72**	6	3 La La Means I Love You	Boardwalk 129
			TIGGI CLAY	
			New wave trio: Fizzy Qwick (lead singer), Romeo McCall and Billy Peaches.	
2/25/84	**86**	3	1 Flashes	Morocco 1716
			TIGHT FIT	
			A Ken Gold British studio production.	
10/10/81	**89**	3	1 Back To The 60's	Arista 0638
			Dancing In The Street/(I Can't Get No) Satisfaction/You Really Got Me/Do Wah Diddy Diddy/Black Is Black/Bend Me, Shape Me/When You Walk In The Room/Mony Mony	
			TIJUANA BRASS - see HERB ALPERT	
			'TIL TUESDAY	
			Boston pop quartet: Aimee Mann (lead singer, bass), Michael Hausmann (drums), Robert Holmes (guitar) and Joey Pesce (keyboards).	
4/13/85	**8**	21	1 **Voices Carry**	Epic 04795
8/24/85	**61**	5	2 Looking Over My Shoulder	Epic 04935
9/20/86	**26**	14	3 What About Love	Epic 06289
			BERTHA TILLMAN	
5/05/62	**61**	9	1 Oh My Angel	Brent 7029
			JOHNNY TILLOTSON	
			Born on 4/20/39 in Jacksonville, Florida; raised in Palatka, Florida. On local radio "Young Folks Revue" from age nine, had own band in high school. Deejay on WWPF. Appeared on the "Toby Dowdy" TV show in Jacksonville, then own show. Signed by Cadence Records in 1958. In the film "Just For Fun".	
10/06/58	**87**	3	1 Well I'm Your Man/	
11/03/58+	**63**	9	2 Dreamy Eyes	Cadence 1353

DEBUT DATE	PEAK POS	WKS CHR	ARTIST — Record Title	Label & Number
			JOHNNY TILLOTSON — Cont'd	
8/24/59	**54**	9	3 True True Happiness	Cadence 1365
1/18/60	**42**	14	4 Why Do I Love You So	Cadence 1372
4/11/60	**57**	7	5 Earth Angel/	
4/11/60	**63**	6	6 Pledging My Love	Cadence 1377
10/10/60	**2**[1]	15	7 **Poetry In Motion**	Cadence 1384
1/09/61	**25**	11	8 Jimmy's Girl	Cadence 1391
8/07/61	**7**	13	9 **Without You**	Cadence 1404
12/04/61+	**35**	14	10 Dreamy Eyes [R]	Cadence 1409
5/12/62	**3**	14	11 **It Keeps Right On A-Hurtin'**	Cadence 1418
8/11/62	**17**	9	12 Send Me The Pillow You Dream On	Cadence 1424
10/27/62	**24**	9	13 I Can't Help It (If I'm Still In Love With You)/	
12/01/62	**89**	1	14 I'm So Lonesome I Could Cry	Cadence 1432
			above 2 are classic country hits by Hank Williams	
3/02/63	**24**	10	15 Out Of My Mind	Cadence 1434
			1-2, 9-11 & 15: written by Tillotson	
8/10/63	**18**	10	16 You Can Never Stop Me Loving You	Cadence 1437
10/19/63	**50**	6	17 Funny How Time Slips Away	Cadence 1441
			written by Willie Nelson	
11/09/63+	**7**	13	18 **Talk Back Trembling Lips**	MGM 13181
2/22/64	**37**	7	19 Worried Guy	MGM 13193
5/02/64	**36**	8	20 I Rise, I Fall	MGM 13232
7/18/64	**45**	10	21 Worry	MGM 13255
10/31/64	**31**	11	22 She Understands Me	MGM 13284
2/13/65	**51**	7	23 Angel	MGM 13316
			theme from the Disney film "Those Calloways"	
6/05/65	**86**	4	24 Then I'll Count Again	MGM 13344
8/28/65	**35**	8	25 Heartaches By The Number	MGM 13376
11/20/65	**70**	6	26 Our World	MGM 13408
			TIM TAM & THE TURN-ONS	
3/05/66	**76**	5	1 Wait A Minute	Palmer 5002
			TIMBUK 3	
			Austin-based husband and wife duo: Pat and Barbara Kooyman MacDonald. Met while Barbara was attending the University of Wisconsin in 1978.	
10/25/86	**19**	16	1 The Future's So Bright, I Gotta Wear Shades	I.R.S. 52940
			THE TIME	
			Funk group formed in Minneapolis by Prince in 1981. Original lineup: Morris Day (lead singer), Terry Lewis, Jimmy "Jam" Harris, Monte Moir, Jesse Johnson and Jellybean Johnson. Disbanded in 1984. Day and Jesse Johnson went solo; Lewis and Harris have become a highly successful songwriting-producing team.	
1/30/82	**90**	7	1 Cool (Part 1)	Warner 49864
10/09/82	**88**	3	2 777-9311	Warner 29952
10/27/84+	**20**	25	3 Jungle Love	Warner 29181
2/23/85	**36**	13	4 The Bird	Warner 29094
			above 2 from the film "Purple Rain"	
			THE TIMETONES	
			Integrated quintet from Glen Cove, Long Island. Roger LaRue, lead singer.	
5/08/61	**51**	5	1 In My Heart	Times Square 421
			TIMEX SOCIAL CLUB	
			Berkeley, California rap group led by vocalist Michael Marshall.	
6/14/86	**8**	19	1 **Rumors**	Jay 7001
			TIN TIN	
			Australian duo: Steve Kipner (keyboards) and Steve Groves (guitar).	
4/03/71	**20**	11	1 Toast And Marmalade For Tea	Atco 6794
8/28/71	**59**	6	2 Is That The Way	Atco 6821
			above 2 produced by the Bee Gees' Maurice Gibb	
			TINY TIM	
			Born Herbert Khaury on 4/12/30 in New York City. Novelty singer, ukulele player. National phenomenon when he married "Miss Vicki" on "The Tonight Show" on 12/18/69.	
5/18/68	**17**	9	1 Tip-Toe Thru' The Tulips With Me [N]	Reprise 0679
			#1 hit for 10 weeks in 1929 by Nick Lucas	
8/24/68	**95**	2	2 Bring Back Those Rockabye Baby Days	Reprise 0760

DEBUT DATE	PEAK POS	WKS CHR	ARTIST — Record Title	Label & Number
			TINY TIM — Cont'd	
2/08/69	**85**	3	3 Great Balls Of Fire	Reprise 0802
			above 3 produced by Richard Perry	
			CAL TJADER	
			Born on 7/16/25 in St. Louis; died on 5/5/82. Latin jazz vibraphonist.	
6/05/65	**88**	5	1 Soul Sauce [I]	Verve 10345
			TKA	
			New York Spanish Harlem quintet. TKA: Total Knowledge In Action.	
6/07/86	**75**	9	1 One Way Love	Tommy Boy 866
			T.M.G.	
			T.M.G. (Ted Mulry Group): Mulry (lead singer), Gary Dixon, Les Hall and Herm Kovac.	
3/03/79	**91**	4	1 Lazy Eyes	Atco 7096
			TOBY BEAU	
			Texas pop quintet: Danny McKenna, Rob Young, Balde Silva, Steve Zipper and Ron Rose.	
6/03/78	**13**	17	1 My Angel Baby	RCA 11250
8/11/79	**57**	9	2 Then You Can Tell Me Goodbye	RCA 11670
7/05/80	**70**	4	3 If I Were You	RCA 11964
			TODAY'S PEOPLE	
9/01/73	**90**	6	1 He	20th Century 2032
			ART & DOTTY TODD	
			Pop duo consisting of Arthur W. Todd (b: 3/11/20) and Dotty Todd (b: 6/22/23), both from Elizabeth, New Jersey. Married in 1941.	
4/14/58	**6**	16	1 **Chanson d'Amour (Song Of Love)**	Era 1064
			Jockey #6 / Best Seller #13 / Top 100 #13	
			NICK TODD	
			Pat Boone's younger brother.	
10/21/57	**41**	10	1 Plaything	Dot 15643
			Top 100 #41 / Best Seller #45	
12/30/57+	**21**	6	2 At The Hop	Dot 15675
			Jockey #21 / Top 100 #70	
			THE TOKENS	
			Vocal group originally formed as the Linc-Tones at Lincoln High School in Brooklyn in 1955. Consisted of Hank Medress, Neil Sedaka, Eddie Rabkin and Cynthia Zolitin. First recorded for Melba in 1956. Rabkin replaced by Jay Siegel in 1956. Zolitin and Sedaka left in 1958. Medress then formed Darrell & The Oxfords, 1958-59, then re-formed The Tokens with brothers Phil and Mitch Margo and recorded for Warwick in 1960. Formed own label, B.T. Puppy in 1964. Medress produced Tony Orlando & Dawn in 1970, and then left The Tokens, who continued as a trio and recorded as Cross Country in 1973.	
3/06/61	**15**	14	1 Tonight I Fell In Love	Warwick 615
11/13/61	**1^{3}**	15	2 ● **The Lion Sleeps Tonight**	RCA 7954
			also known as "Wimoweh" - a South African Zulu song	
2/10/62	**55**	5	3 B'wa Nina (Pretty Girl)	RCA 7991
6/30/62	**85**	5	4 La Bomba [F]	RCA 8052
8/24/63	**94**	4	5 Hear The Bells	RCA 8210
8/08/64	**43**	8	6 He's In Town	B.T. Puppy 502
3/19/66	**30**	8	7 I Hear Trumpets Blow	B.T. Puppy 518
4/15/67	**36**	8	8 Portrait Of My Love	Warner 5900
7/22/67	**69**	4	9 It's A Happening World	Warner 7056
12/13/69+	**61**	7	10 She Lets Her Hair Down (Early In The Morning)	Buddah 151
3/07/70	**95**	2	11 Don't Worry Baby	Buddah 159
			ISRAEL "Popper Stopper" TOLBERT	
10/31/70	**61**	9	1 Big Leg Woman (With A Short Short Mini Skirt)	Warren 106
			TOM & JERRIO	
			R&B dance duo: Robert "Tommy Dark" Tharp and Jerry "Jerry-O" Murray. Tharp was a baritone in the Ideals vocal group from 1952-65.	
5/01/65	**47**	8	1 Boo-Ga-Loo	ABC-Para. 10638
			TOM & JERRY - see SIMON & GARFUNKEL	
			TOM TOM CLUB	
			Studio project headed by Chris Frantz and wife Tina Weymouth of the Talking Heads.	
1/23/82	**31**	17	1 Genius Of Love	Sire 49882

DEBUT DATE	PEAK POS	WKS CHR	ARTIST — Record Title	Label & Number
			TOMMY TUTONE	
			San Francisco rock band led by Tommy Heath (lead singer) & Jim Keller (lead guitar).	
5/24/80	**38**	8	1 Angel Say No	Columbia 11278
1/23/82	**4**	27	2 **867-5309/Jenny**	Columbia 02646
			TOMPALL & THE GLASER BROTHERS	
			Tompall (b: 9/3/33), Chuck and Jim Glaser, all born in or near Spalding, Nebraska. Country vocal group. All 3 have had solo hits on the Country charts.	
4/05/69	**92**	4	1 California Girl (And The Tennessee Square)	MGM 14036
			GARY TOMS EMPIRE	
			New York disco band led by Gary Toms on keyboards and synthesizer.	
6/21/75	**46**	17	1 7-6-5-4-3-2-1 (Blow Your Whistle)	Pickwick I. 6504
11/22/75	**69**	5	2 Drive My Car	Pickwick I. 6509
			OSCAR TONEY, JR.	
			Born on 5/26/39 in Selma, Alabama. Had own gospel group, Sensational Melodies Of Joy, while in high school. Own group, the Searchers, first recorded for Max in 1957. Recorded solo for King in 1958. Three sisters sang as the Tonettes.	
5/27/67	**23**	9	1 For Your Precious Love	Bell 672
8/12/67	**65**	6	2 Turn On Your Love Light	Bell 681
1/13/68	**90**	3	3 Without Love (There Is Nothing)	Bell 699
4/20/68	**95**	2	4 Never Get Enough Of Your Love	Bell 714
			TONY & JOE	
			Tony Savonne & Joe Saraceno.	
7/21/58	**33**	8	1 The Freeze Hot 100 #33 / Best Seller #39	Era 1075
			MEL TORME	
			Born Melvin Howard on 9/13/25 in Chicago. Jazz singer, songwriter, pianist, drummer, actor. Wrote Nat King Cole's "The Christmas Song".	
11/03/62	**36**	11	1 Comin' Home Baby	Atlantic 2165
			THE TORNADOES	
			English surf-rock instrumental quintet organized by producer Don Meek in 1962. Original lineup: Alan Caddy (lead guitar), George Bellamy, Roger LaVerne Jackson, Heinz Burt and Clem Cattini. Meek committed suicide on 2/3/67.	
11/03/62	**1^3**	16	1 **Telstar** [I]	London 9561
2/16/63	**63**	5	2 Ridin' The Wind [I]	London 9581
			MITCHELL TOROK	
			Houston-born singer/songwriter/guitarist.	
4/13/57	**25**	10	1 Pledge Of Love Best Seller #25 / Top 100 #26	Decca 30230
8/03/59	**27**	14	2 Caribbean [R] same version charted in 1953 (POS 26) on Abbott 140	Guyden 2018
5/09/60	**60**	9	3 Pink Chiffon	Guyden 2034
			TORONTO	
			Holly Woods, lead singer of rock group from Toronto, Canada.	
8/07/82	**77**	8	1 Your Daddy Don't Know	Network 69986
			GEORGE TORRENCE & THE NATURALS	
2/17/68	**91**	2	1 (Mama Come Quick, And Bring Your) Lickin' Stick	Shout 224
			PETER TOSH	
			Born Winston MacIntosh on 10/9/44 in Jamaica. Former member of Bob Marley's Wailers.	
11/04/78	**81**	5	1 (You Got To Walk And) Don't Look Back vocal duet with Mick Jagger of The Rolling Stones	Rolling S. 19308
7/09/83	**84**	4	2 Johnny B. Goode	EMI America 8159
			TOTAL COELO	
			British female quintet led by Ros Holness.	
4/16/83	**66**	6	1 I Eat Cannibals	Chrysalis 42669
			TOTO	
			Pop/rock group formed in Los Angeles in 1978. Consisted of Bobby Kimball (vocals), Steve Lukather (guitar), David Paich and Steve Porcaro (keyboards), David Hungate (bass) and Jeff Porcaro (drums). Prominent session musicians, most notably behind Boz Scaggs in the late 70s. Hungate was replaced by Mike Porcaro in 1983. Kimball replaced by Fergie Frederiksen in 1984; Frederiksen replaced by Joseph Williams (conductor John's son) in 1986.	
10/07/78+	**5**	21	1 ● **Hold The Line**	Columbia 10830
2/10/79	**45**	9	2 I'll Supply The Love	Columbia 10898

DEBUT DATE	PEAK POS	WKS CHR	ARTIST — Record Title	Label & Number
			TOTO — Cont'd	
4/28/79	**48**	10	3 Georgy Porgy	Columbia 10944
12/22/79+	**26**	17	4 99	Columbia 11173
4/17/82	**2^{5}**	23	5 **Rosanna**	Columbia 02811
8/07/82	**30**	13	6 Make Believe 1-6: written by David Paich	Columbia 03143
10/30/82+	**1^{1}**	21	7 **Africa**	Columbia 03335
3/12/83	**10**	17	8 **I Won't Hold You Back**	Columbia 03597
7/02/83	**73**	6	9 Waiting For Your Love	Columbia 03981
10/27/84	**30**	15	10 Stranger In Town	Columbia 04672
2/09/85	**71**	5	11 Holyanna	Columbia 04752
8/30/86	**11**	23	12 I'll Be Over You	Columbia 06280
12/27/86+	**38**	11	13 Without Your Love all of above produced by Toto	Columbia 06570
			TOUCH Pop/rock quartet: Craig Brooks, Mark Mangold, Doug Howard and Glenn Kithcart.	
7/26/80	**65**	5	1 (Call Me) When The Spirit Moves You	Atco 7222
1/31/81	**69**	6	2 Don't You Know What Love Is	Atco 7311
			THE TOURISTS British rock quintet which included Eurythmics' David Stewart and Annie Lennox.	
5/17/80	**83**	4	1 I Only Want To Be With You	Epic 50850
			TOWER OF POWER Integrated Oakland-based R&B/funk band formed by sax player Emilio "Mimi" Castillo in the late 60s. Lenny Williams sang lead from 1972-75.	
7/15/72	**29**	12	1 You're Still A Young Man	Warner 7612
10/21/72	**66**	8	2 Down To The Nightclub	Warner 7635
5/05/73	**17**	18	3 So Very Hard To Go	Warner 7687
9/15/73	**65**	6	4 This Time It's Real	Warner 7733
2/23/74	**91**	2	5 What Is Hip?	Warner 7748
4/27/74	**69**	6	6 Time Will Tell	Warner 7796
7/20/74	**26**	10	7 Don't Change Horses (In The Middle Of A Stream)	Warner 7828
10/16/76	**68**	8	8 You Ought To Be Havin' Fun	Columbia 10409
			CAROL LYNN TOWNES	
7/07/84	**77**	9	1 99 1/2 from the film "Breakin'"	Polydor 881008
			ED TOWNSEND Born on 4/16/29 in Fayetteville, Tennessee. R&B singer, songwriter.	
4/21/58	**13**	16	1 For Your Love Jockey #13 / Best Seller #15 / Top 100 #15	Capitol 3926
9/29/58	**59**	7	2 When I Grow Too Old To Dream revival of Glen Gray's 1935 hit (POS 1)	Capitol 4048
			PETE TOWNSHEND Born on 5/19/45 in London. Lead guitarist/songwriter of The Who.	
6/14/80	**9**	19	1 **Let My Love Open The Door**	Atco 7217
10/11/80	**72**	4	2 A Little Is Enough	Atco 7312
11/15/80	**89**	4	3 Rough Boys	Atco 7318
11/09/85+	**26**	16	4 Face The Face	Atco 99590
			THE TOY DOLLS	
12/29/62+	**84**	4	1 Little Tin Soldier	Era 3093
			THE TOYS New York soul trio: Barbara Harris, June Montiero and Barbara Parritt. Appearances on "Shindig" TV show in 1965. In film "The Girl In Daddy's Bikini".	
9/11/65	**2^{3}**	15	1 ● **A Lover's Concerto** adapted from Bach: Minuet In G	DynoVoice 209
12/18/65+	**18**	9	2 Attack	DynoVoice 214
4/02/66	**85**	3	3 May My Heart Be Cast Into Stone	DynoVoice 218
9/03/66	**76**	4	4 Baby Toys	DynoVoice 222
			THE TRADE WINDS Singing, songwriting and production duo: Pete Anders and Vinnie Poncia. Poncia produced 4 of Melissa Manchester's albums. Also see The Innocence.	
2/06/65	**32**	8	1 New York's A Lonely Town	Red Bird 020

DEBUT DATE	PEAK POS	WKS CHR	ARTIST — Record Title	Label & Number
			THE TRADE WINDS — Cont'd	
9/03/66	51	9	2 Mind Excursion	Kama Sutra 212
			THE TRADEWINDS	
			New Jersey group: Ralph Rizzoll, Phil Mehill, Sal Capriglione & Angel Cifelli.	
8/10/59	91	2	1 Furry Murray	RCA 7553
			TRAFFIC	
			British rock band - original lineup: Steve Winwood (keyboards, guitar), Dave Mason (guitar), Jim Capaldi (drums) and Chris Wood (flute, sax; d: 7/12/83). Many personnel changes during the group's 7 year existence.	
9/02/67	94	1	1 Paper Sun	United Art. 50195
			TRAFFIC featuring STEVE WINWOOD	
9/05/70	74	8	2 Empty Pages	United Art. 50692
10/23/71	68	7	3 Gimme Some Lovin'-Pt. 1	United Art. 50841
			TRAFFIC, ETC.	
1/15/72	93	2	4 Rock & Roll Stew...Part 1	Island 1201
			THE TRAITS	
			Roy Head's backing band.	
11/12/66	94	2	1 Harlem Shuffle	Scepter 12169
			THE TRAMMPS	
			Philadelphia disco group. Key members: Jimmy Ellis (lead tenor), Earl Young (lead bass), Harold and Stanley Wade (tenors) and Robert Upchurch (baritone). Had own label, Golden Fleece, in 1973.	
7/08/72	64	11	1 Zing Went The Strings Of My Heart	Buddah 306
			revival of Judy Garland's 1943 hit	
1/17/76	35	10	2 Hold Back The Night	Buddah 507
4/10/76	27	15	3 That's Where The Happy People Go	Atlantic 3306
3/05/77+	11	29	4 Disco Inferno	Atlantic 3389
			in the film "Saturday Night Fever"	
			TRANS-X	
5/10/86	61	12	1 Living On Video	Atco 99534
			THE TRASHMEN	
			Minneapolis/St. Paul surf-rock quartet: Tony Andreason, Dal Winslow, Bob Reed and Steve Wahrer. Both hits taken from tunes by The Rivingtons: "Papa-Oom-Mow-Mow" and "The Bird's The Word".	
12/07/63+	4	13	1 **Surfin' Bird**	Garrett 4002
2/08/64	30	7	2 Bird Dance Beat	Garrett 4003
			MARY TRAVERS	
			Born on 11/7/37 in Louisville. Member of the folk trio Peter, Paul & Mary. Chorus singer in the short-lived Broadway show "The Next President", 1957.	
5/22/71	56	11	1 Follow Me	Warner 7481
			written by John Denver	
			PAT TRAVERS	
			Canadian blues-rock guitarist/vocalist.	
9/01/79	56	7	1 Boom Boom (Out Go The Lights)	Polydor 2003
5/17/80	50	7	2 Is This Love	Polydor 2080
			PAT TRAVERS BAND	
			TRAVIS & BOB	
			Travis Pritchett and Bob Weaver from Jackson, Alabama.	
3/23/59	8	13	1 **Tell Him No**	Sandy 1017
			McKINLEY TRAVIS	
7/18/70	91	2	1 Baby, Is There Something On Your Mind	Pride 2
			JOEY TRAVOLTA	
			New Jersey pop singer, actor. Brother of John Travolta.	
6/03/78	43	8	1 I Don't Wanna Go	Millennium 615
			JOHN TRAVOLTA	
			Born on 2/18/54 in Englewood, New Jersey. Vinnie Barbarino on the TV series "Welcome Back Kotter". Starred in the films "Saturday Night Fever", "Grease", "Urban Cowboy", "Blow Out" and others.	
5/01/76	10	20	1 **Let Her In**	Midland I. 10623
10/30/76	38	6	2 Whenever I'm Away From You	Midland I. 10780
2/19/77	34	8	3 All Strung Out On You	Midland I. 10907
4/01/78	1[1]	24	4 ▲**You're The One That I Want**	RSO 891
			JOHN TRAVOLTA & OLIVIA NEWTON-JOHN	

DEBUT DATE	PEAK POS	WKS CHR	ARTIST — Record Title		Label & Number
			JOHN TRAVOLTA — Cont'd		
8/05/78	**5**	16	5 ● **Summer Nights**		RSO 906
			JOHN TRAVOLTA & OLIVIA NEWTON-JOHN & CAST		
9/30/78	**47**	8	6 Greased Lightnin'		RSO 909
			above 3 from the film "Grease"		
			THE TREE SWINGERS		
			Asbury Park, New Jersey duo: Art Polhemus and Terry Byrnes.		
8/15/60	**73**	6	1 Kookie Little Paradise	[N]	Guyden 2036
			THE TREMELOES		
			British pop/rock quartet: Alan Blakely, Dave Munden, Ricky West and Len Hawkes. Group originally formed by Brian Poole (went solo in 1966).		
4/08/67	**13**	12	1 Here Comes My Baby		Epic 10139
6/17/67	**11**	14	2 Silence Is Golden		Epic 10184
9/30/67	**36**	7	3 Even The Bad Times Are Good		Epic 10233
2/17/68	**44**	10	4 Suddenly You Love Me		Epic 10293
			T. REX		
			British rock group led by Marc Bolan (born Marc Feld on 9/30/48 in London; killed in an auto accident on 9/16/77).		
1/23/71	**76**	6	1 Ride A White Swan		Blue Thumb 7121
			shown as: TYRANNOSAURUS REX		
5/08/71	**72**	6	2 Hot Love		Reprise 1006
1/01/72	**10**	15	3 **Bang A Gong (Get It On)**		Reprise 1032
4/22/72	**67**	5	4 Telegram Sam		Reprise 1078
			above 4 written by Bolan and produced by Toni Visconti		
			TRIUMPH		
			Canadian hard-rock trio formed in Toronto in 1975. Consisted of Gil Moore (drums, vocals), Rik Emmett (guitar, vocals) and Mike Levine (keyboards, bass).		
6/16/79	**38**	14	1 Hold On		RCA 11569
11/03/79	**86**	7	2 Lay It On The Line		RCA 11690
6/07/80	**91**	2	3 I Can Survive		RCA 11945
10/03/81	**51**	11	4 Magic Power		RCA 12298
3/09/85	**88**	2	5 Follow Your Heart		MCA 52540
8/30/86	**27**	15	6 Somebody's Out There		MCA 52898
			THE TROGGS		
			British rock quartet from Andover, England. Consisted of Reg Presley (lead singer), Chris Britton (guitar), Pete Staples (bass) and Ronnie Bond (drums).		
6/25/66	**1**[2]	11	1 **Wild Thing**		Fontana 1548
8/06/66	**29**	8	2 With A Girl Like You		Fontana 1552
			above 2 also released on Atco 6415		
10/15/66	**43**	6	3 I Can't Control Myself		Fontana 1557
			also released on Atco 6444		
2/24/68	**7**	16	4 **Love Is All Around**		Fontana 1607
			THE TROLLS		
10/22/66	**96**	1	1 Every Day And Every Night		ABC 10823
			TROOPER		
			Canadian rock quintet: Ra McGuire (lead guitar), Brian Smith, Doni Underhill, Frank Ludwig and Tommy Stewart.		
8/05/78	**59**	8	1 Raise A Little Hell		MCA 40924
			ROBIN TROWER		
			Born on 3/9/45 in London, England. Rock guitarist - member of Procol Harum.		
12/04/76+	**82**	7	1 Caledonia		Chrysalis 2122
			vocals by James Dewar		
			DORIS TROY		
			Born Doris Payne on 1/6/37 in New York City. R&B vocalist, songwriter. Backing vocalist on Pink Floyd's album "Dark Side Of The Moon".		
6/08/63	**10**	14	1 **Just One Look**		Atlantic 2188
			ERIC TROYER		
			Pop session vocalist from New York City.		
7/26/80	**92**	2	1 Mirage		Chrysalis 2445

DEBUT DATE	PEAK POS	WKS CHR	ARTIST — Record Title	Label & Number
			ANDREA TRUE CONNECTION Disco act led by white Nashville-born vocalist Andrea True. Andrea moved to New York in 1968 and wrote commercials for radio and TV. Her break came while singing at the Riverboat in the Empire State Building, 1974.	
3/13/76	**4**	25	1 ● **More, More, More (Pt. 1)**	Buddah 515
8/07/76	**80**	4	2 Party Line	Buddah 538
2/19/77	**27**	11	3 N.Y., You Got Me Dancing	Buddah 564
1/14/78	**56**	7	4 What's Your Name, What's Your Number	Buddah 582
			THE TRUMPETEERS Big band-styled group led by Joseph Johnson (d: 1984) and directed by Billy Mure.	
4/27/59	**64**	9	1 A String Of Trumpets [I] also shown as: BILLY MURE & THE TRUMPETEERS	Splash 1010
			THE T.S.U. TORONADOES Soul band from Texas State University, recorded in Houston.	
1/18/69	**75**	6	1 Getting The Corners	Atlantic 2579
			THE TUBES San Francisco theatre rock troupe led by Fee Waybill.	
7/04/76	**61**	7	1 Don't Touch Me There	A&M 1826
6/20/81	**35**	12	2 Don't Want To Wait Anymore	Capitol 5007
4/09/83	**10**	20	3 **She's A Beauty**	Capitol 5217
7/23/83	**52**	7	4 Tip Of My Tongue	Capitol 5258
10/01/83	**68**	4	5 The Monkey Time	Capitol 5254
3/09/85	**87**	2	6 Piece By Piece	Capitol 5443
			LOUISE TUCKER English classical-styled vocalist. Male vocal on only hit: Charlie Skarbek.	
6/18/83	**46**	13	1 Midnight Blue adaptation of Beethoven's "Sonata Pathetique"	Arista 9022
			TANYA TUCKER Born on 10/10/58 in Seminole, Texas. Country singer. Bit part in the film "Jeremiah Johnson" in 1972.	
7/01/72	**72**	7	1 Delta Dawn	Columbia 45588
5/26/73	**86**	4	2 What's Your Mama's Name	Columbia 45799
8/25/73	**74**	9	3 Blood Red And Goin' Down	Columbia 45892
2/16/74	**46**	10	4 Would You Lay With Me (In A Field Of Stone)	Columbia 45991
8/03/74	**86**	4	5 The Man That Turned My Mama On above 5 produced by Billy Sherrill	Columbia 46047
5/03/75	**37**	9	6 Lizzie And The Rainman	MCA 40402
10/02/76	**82**	5	7 Here's Some Love	MCA 40598
1/20/79	**70**	4	8 Not Fade Away	MCA 40976
			TOMMY TUCKER R&B singer. Died of poisoning on 1/17/82 (48).	
2/08/64	**11**	11	1 Hi-Heel Sneakers	Checker 1067
5/16/64	**96**	2	2 Long Tall Shorty	Checker 1075
			TUFANO & GIAMMARESE Chicago-born duo: Denny Tufano and Carl Giammarese (members of The Buckinghams).	
4/28/73	**68**	8	1 Music Everywhere	Ode 66033
			THE TUNE ROCKERS	
8/25/58	**44**	10	1 The Green Mosquito [I]	United Art. 139
			THE TUNE WEAVERS Boston R&B quintet consisting of Margo Sylvia (lead), husband John Sylvia (bass), Gilbert Lopez (Margo's brother - tenor) and Charlotte Davis (Margo's cousin).	
9/16/57	**5**	19	1 **Happy, Happy Birthday Baby** Top 100 #5 / Best Seller #8 / Jockey #12	Checker 872
			THE TURBANS Philadelphia R&B quartet: Al Banks (lead), Matthew Platt (tenor), Charles Williams (baritone) and Andrew "Chet" Jones (bass).	
11/12/55+	**33**	21	1 When You Dance	Herald 458

DEBUT DATE	PEAK POS	WKS CHR	ARTIST — Record Title	Label & Number
			IKE & TINA TURNER	
			Husband and wife R&B duo: Ike Turner (b: 11/5/31, Clarksdale, MS), guitar, and Annie Mae Bullock (b: 11/26/38, Nutbush, TN), vocals. Married in 1958. Turner was a deejay at Clarksdale's WROX. Formed own band and recorded for RPM in 1951. First recorded with Tina for Federal in 1957. Ike developed dynamic stage show "The Ike & Tina Turner Revue" around Tina and her female backing group, The Ikettes. Tina went solo in 1974, and they were divorced in 1976.	
8/29/60	**27**	13	1 A Fool In Love	Sue 730
12/12/60	**82**	4	2 I Idolize You	Sue 735
7/31/61	**14**	15	3 It's Gonna Work Out Fine	Sue 749
11/27/61+	**38**	11	4 Poor Fool	Sue 753
3/24/62	**50**	7	5 Tra La La La La	Sue 757
6/30/62	**89**	2	6 You Should'a Treated Me Right	Sue 765
10/03/64	**95**	3	7 I Can't Believe What You Say (For Seeing What You Do)	Kent 402
5/28/66	**88**	4	8 River Deep-Mountain High	Philles 131
4/26/69	**68**	7	9 I've Been Loving You Too Long	Blue Thumb 101
5/10/69	**98**	2	10 I'm Gonna Do All I Can (To Do Right By My Man)	Minit 32060
8/02/69	**93**	2	11 The Hunter	Blue Thumb 102
12/20/69+	**59**	8	12 Bold Soul Sister	Blue Thumb 104
3/07/70	**57**	8	13 Come Together	Minit 32087
5/23/70	**34**	18	14 I Want To Take You Higher	Liberty 56177
			above 2: **IKE & TINA TURNER & THE IKETTES**	
1/30/71	**4**	13	15 ● **Proud Mary**	Liberty 56216
5/15/71	**60**	7	16 Ooh Poo Pah Doo	United Art. 50782
2/26/72	**83**	4	17 Up In Heah	United Art. 50881
9/08/73	**22**	15	18 Nutbush City Limits	United Art. 298
11/02/74	**65**	8	19 Sexy Ida (Part 1)	United Art. 528
6/07/75	**88**	4	20 Baby-Get It On	United Art. 598
			1-2, 4-7, 12 & 20: written by Ike Turner	
			JESSE LEE TURNER	
			Rockabilly singer from Bowling, Texas.	
1/05/59	**20**	12	1 The Little Space Girl [N]	Carlton 496
			JOE TURNER	
			Born on 5/18/11 in Kansas City, Missouri; died of a heart attack on 11/24/85. Blues/R&B vocalist known as "Big Joe". Early in career teamed with boogie-woogie pianist Pete Johnson. In the film, "Shake, Rattle And Roll", 1956.	
5/12/56	**41**	10	1 Corrine Corrina	Atlantic 1088
12/28/59+	**53**	9	2 Honey Hush	Atlantic 2044
			SAMMY TURNER	
			Born Samuel Black on 6/2/32 in Paterson, New Jersey. Tommy Edwards-styled vocalist.	
3/23/59	**100**	1	1 Sweet Annie Laurie	Big Top 3007
			SAMMY TURNER & THE TWISTERS	
6/22/59	**3**	18	2 **Lavender-Blue**	Big Top 3016
			old traditional folk song from England, 1750	
11/02/59	**19**	12	3 Always/	
			4 versions hit the Top 10 in 1926	
11/30/59	**82**	3	4 Symphony	Big Top 3029
			5 versions hit the Top 10 in 1946	
2/15/60	**46**	11	5 Paradise	Big Top 3032
			all of above produced by Jerry Lieber and Mike Stoller	
			SPYDER TURNER	
			Born Dwight D. Turner in 1947 in Beckley, West Virginia. Soul vocalist.	
12/17/66+	**12**	12	1 Stand By Me [N]	MGM 13617
			vocal impressions of Jackie Wilson, David Ruffin, Billy Stewart, Smokey Robinson and Chuck Jackson	
3/25/67	**95**	2	2 I Can't Make It Anymore	MGM 13692
			TINA TURNER	
			Born Annie Mae Bullock on 11/26/38 in Nutbush, Tennessee. R&B/rock vocalist, actress. Half of Ike & Tina Turner duo. In films "Tommy" and "Mad Max Beyond Thunderdome".	
1/21/84	**26**	15	1 Let's Stay Together	Capitol 5322
5/19/84	**1**[3]	28	2 ● **What's Love Got To Do With It**	Capitol 5354
			Grammy winner: Record of The Year & Song of The Year	
9/15/84	**5**	21	3 **Better Be Good To Me**	Capitol 5387
1/19/85	**7**	18	4 **Private Dancer**	Capitol 5433

DEBUT DATE	PEAK POS	WKS CHR	ARTIST — Record Title	Label & Number
			TINA TURNER — Cont'd	
4/20/85	**37**	10	5 Show Some Respect	Capitol 5461
7/06/85	**2**[1]	18	6 **We Don't Need Another Hero (Thunderdome)**	Capitol 5491
10/05/85	**15**	18	7 One Of The Living above 2 from the film "Mad Max Beyond Thunderdome"	Capitol 5518
11/23/85+	**15**	14	8 It's Only Love **BRYAN ADAMS/TINA TURNER**	A&M 2791
8/30/86	**2**[3]	16	9 **Typical Male**	Capitol 5615
11/22/86+	**30**	12	10 Two People	Capitol 5644
			TITUS TURNER Born on 5/11/33 in Atlanta. R&B vocalist. First recorded for Okeh in 1951.	
11/23/59	**83**	6	1 We Told You Not To Marry answer song to Lloyd Price's "I'm Gonna Get Married"	Glover 201
1/16/61	**77**	4	2 Sound-Off #3 hit in 1951 for Vaughn Monroe	Jamie 1174
			THE TURTLES Pop, folk rock group formed at Westchester High School in Los Angeles in 1961, and led by Mark Volman (b: 4/19/47, Los Angeles) and Howard Kaylan (b: Howard Kaplan on 6/22/47, New York City). First called the Nightriders; then the Crossfires. Recorded for Capco in 1963. Name changed to The Turtles in 1965. Many personnel changes except for Volman and Kaylan. Group disbanded in 1970. Volman and Kaylan joined the Mothers Of Invention. Went out as a duo in 1972 and recorded as Phlorescent Leech & Eddie and later as Flo & Eddie. Did soundtrack for the film "Strawberry Shortcake". Toured again as The Turtles in 1985.	
8/07/65	**8**	11	1 **It Ain't Me Babe** written by Bob Dylan	White Whale 222
10/30/65	**29**	7	2 Let Me Be	White Whale 224
2/05/66	**20**	12	3 You Baby	White Whale 227
6/18/66	**81**	4	4 Grim Reaper Of Love	White Whale 231
10/29/66	**89**	5	5 Can I Get To Know You Better	White Whale 238
2/11/67	**1**[3]	15	6 ● **Happy Together**	White Whale 244
5/13/67	**3**	11	7 **She'd Rather Be With Me**	White Whale 249
8/05/67	**12**	11	8 You Know What I Mean	White Whale 254
11/11/67	**14**	10	9 She's My Girl above 4 written by Garry Bonner & Alan Gordon	White Whale 260
3/02/68	**57**	6	10 Sound Asleep	White Whale 264
6/22/68	**48**	6	11 The Story Of Rock And Roll	White Whale 273
9/21/68	**6**	12	12 **Elenore**	White Whale 276
1/04/69	**6**	12	13 **You Showed Me**	White Whale 292
6/07/69	**51**	7	14 You Don't Have To Walk In The Rain	White Whale 308
10/11/69	**91**	2	15 Love In The City	White Whale 326
12/06/69	**78**	4	16 Lady-O	White Whale 334
6/27/70	**100**	2	17 Eve Of Destruction	White Whale 355
			TUXEDO JUNCTION Female disco studio group assembled by producers W. Michael Lewis & Lauren Rinder.	
4/22/78	**32**	17	1 Chattanooga Choo Choo revival of Glenn Miller's 1941 hit (POS 1)	Butterfly 1205
			TWENNYNINE with LENNY WHITE New York R&B/funk band led by Lenny White (former drummer of Return To Forever).	
2/02/80	**83**	4	1 Peanut Butter	Elektra 46552
			THE 21st CENTURY Chicago soul quintet. Name changed to 21st Creation in 1976.	
5/31/75	**100**	1	1 Remember The Rain?	RCA 10201
			TWILIGHT 22 A dance/rap production by New York synthesizer player Gordon Bahary.	
12/17/83+	**79**	8	1 Electric Kingdom	Vanguard 35241
			DWIGHT TWILLEY Born on 6/6/51 in Tulsa, Oklahoma. Rock singer, songwriter, pianist. Formed the Dwight Twilley Band with Phil Seymour (bassist, drummer) in 1974.	
4/26/75	**16**	18	1 I'm On Fire **DWIGHT TWILLEY BAND**	Shelter 40380
2/18/84	**16**	16	2 Girls	EMI America 8196
5/19/84	**77**	4	3 Little Bit Of Love	EMI America 8206

DEBUT DATE	PEAK POS	WKS CHR	ARTIST — Record Title	Label & Number
			TWISTED SISTER	
			Long Island, New York heavy-metal quintet led by Dee Snider.	
7/28/84	**21**	15	1 We're Not Gonna Take It	Atlantic 89641
10/20/84	**68**	7	2 I Wanna Rock	Atlantic 89617
11/30/85+	**53**	10	3 Leader Of The Pack	Atlantic 89478
			CONWAY TWITTY	
			Born Harold Jenkins on 9/1/33 in Friars Point, Mississippi. Superstar country singer. Conway's charted over 30 #1 solo country hits. Raised in Helena, Arkansas. Formed own group, the Phillips County Ramblers, at age ten. With service band, the Cimmarons, in Japan, early 50s. Changed his name in 1957 and first recorded for Mercury. In films "Sexpot Goes To College" and "College Confidential". Switched from pop to country music in 1965. Moved to Nashville in 1968. Owns tourist complex in Hendersonville, Tennessee called Twitty City.	
5/20/57	**93**	1	1 I Need Your Lovin'	Mercury 71086
9/15/58	**1**[2]	21	2 **It's Only Make Believe**	MGM 12677
1/26/59	**28**	12	3 The Story Of My Love	MGM 12748
5/18/59	**87**	2	4 Hey Little Lucy! (Don'tcha Put No Lipstick On)	MGM 12785
7/20/59	**29**	12	5 Mona Lisa revival of Nat King Cole's #1 hit from 1950	MGM 12804
9/28/59	**10**	18	6 **Danny Boy** based on traditional Irish song "Londonderry Air" of 1855	MGM 12826
12/28/59+	**6**	15	7 **Lonely Blue Boy**	MGM 12857
3/28/60	**26**	11	8 What Am I Living For	MGM 12886
6/13/60	**35**	11	9 Is A Blue Bird Blue/	
8/08/60	**98**	1	10 She's Mine	MGM 12911
10/31/60	**55**	5	11 Whole Lot Of Shakin' Going On	MGM 12962
12/31/60+	**22**	10	12 C'est Si Bon (It's So Good) revival of Danny Kaye's 1950 hit (POS 21)	MGM 12969
4/03/61	**72**	4	13 The Next Kiss (Is The Last Goodbye)	MGM 12998
1/20/62	**98**	2	14 Portrait Of A Fool	MGM 13050
7/04/70	**60**	8	15 Hello Darlin'	Decca 32661
10/24/70	**81**	4	16 Fifteen Years Ago	Decca 32742
2/27/71	**56**	6	17 After The Fire Is Gone **CONWAY TWITTY/LORETTA LYNN**	Decca 32776
8/11/73	**22**	14	18 You've Never Been This Far Before	MCA 40094
2/22/75	**61**	8	19 Linda On My Mind	MCA 40339
12/20/75+	**63**	7	20 Don't Cry Joni vocal accompaniment by Conway's daughter Joni	MCA 40407
			2 OF CLUBS	
3/18/67	**92**	3	1 Walk Tall	Fraternity 975
			TYCOON	
			New York-based pop/rock sextet. Norman Mershon, lead singer.	
3/17/79	**26**	13	1 Such A Woman	Arista 0398
			BONNIE TYLER	
			Born on 6/8/53 in Skewen, South Wales. Distinctive raspy vocals caused by operation to remove throat modules in 1976.	
3/25/78	**3**	21	1 ● **It's A Heartache**	RCA 11249
7/16/83	**1**[4]	29	2 ● **Total Eclipse Of The Heart**	Columbia 03906
12/03/83+	**46**	9	3 Take Me Back	Columbia 04246
2/25/84	**34**	13	4 Holding Out For A Hero from the film "Footloose"	Columbia 04370
8/11/84	**76**	5	5 Here She Comes from the film "Metropolis"	Columbia 04548
4/12/86	**77**	6	6 If You Were A Woman (And I Was A Man) background vocals by Todd Rundgren	Columbia 05839
			THE TYMES	
			Smooth soul group formed in Philadelphia in 1956. Consisted of George Williams (lead singer), George Hilliard, Donald Banks, Albert Berry and Norman Burnett. First called the Latineers.	
6/01/63	**1**[1]	15	1 **So Much In Love**	Parkway 871
8/17/63	**7**	11	2 **Wonderful! Wonderful!**	Parkway 884
12/07/63+	**19**	11	3 Somewhere	Parkway 891
3/14/64	**78**	4	4 To Each His Own 3 versions hit #1 in 1946	Parkway 908
6/13/64	**99**	1	5 The Magic Of Our Summer Love	Parkway 919

DEBUT DATE	PEAK POS	WKS CHR	ARTIST — Record Title	Label & Number
			THE TYMES — Cont'd	
11/21/64	**92**	3	6 Here She Comes	Parkway 924
11/16/68	**39**	8	7 People from the film "Funny Girl"	Columbia 44630
8/17/74	**12**	13	8 You Little Trustmaker	RCA 10022
12/21/74	**91**	4	9 Ms. Grace	RCA 10128
5/08/76	**68**	4	10 It's Cool	RCA 10561
			U	
			UB40 British integrated reggae octet. Ali Campbell, lead singer. Took name from a British unemployment benefit form.	
1/28/84	**34**	15	1 Red Red Wine	A&M 2600
7/27/85	**28**	14	2 I Got You Babe **UB40 with CHRISSIE HYNDE (lead singer of the Pretenders)**	A&M 2758
			LESLIE UGGAMS Born on 5/25/43 in New York City. Actress, singer. Played Kizzy in the TV mini-series "Roots". Regular on TV's "Sing Along With Mitch".	
9/14/59	**98**	1	1 One More Sunrise (Morgen)	Columbia 41451
			TRACEY ULLMAN Born on 12/30/59 in England. Actress, singer, comedienne. Own variety-style TV show on new Fox Broadcasting Co. network in 1987.	
2/25/84	**8**	17	1 **They Don't Know**	MCA 52347
6/16/84	**70**	4	2 Break-A-Way	MCA 52385
			ULTIMATE Philadelphia studio disco project produced by Juliano Salerni and Bruce Weeden.	
4/21/79	**82**	3	1 Touch Me Baby	Casablanca 966
			ULTRAVOX British electronic rock quartet: Midge Ure (lead singer, guitar), Billy Currie (synthesizer, piano), Warren Cann (drums) and Chris Cross (bass, synthesizer).	
4/09/83	**71**	5	1 Reap The Wild Wind	Chrysalis 42682
			PIERO UMILIANI	
9/06/69	**55**	6	1 Mah-Na-Mah-Na [I-N] from the "Sweden Heaven And Hell" soundtrack background tune used on TV's "Benny Hill Show"	Ariel 500
			UNCLE DOG	
3/03/73	**86**	7	1 River Road	MCA 40005
			UNDERGROUND SUNSHINE Rock quartet: Chris Connors and Jane Little (both from Wisconsin), and Frank and Betty Kohl (from Germany).	
7/19/69	**26**	10	1 Birthday written by John Lennon & Paul McCartney	Intrepid 75002
			THE UNDISPUTED TRUTH Soul group consisting of Joe Harris, Billie Calvin and Brenda Evans. Personnel changed in 1973 to Harris, Tyrone Barkley, Tyrone Douglas, Calvin Stephenson and Virginia McDonald. Taka Boom replaced Douglas and McDonald in 1976.	
6/26/71	**3**	18	1 **Smiling Faces Sometimes**	Gordy 7108
12/18/71+	**72**	6	2 You Make Your Own Heaven And Hell Right Here On Earth	Gordy 7112
2/26/72	**71**	5	3 What It Is	Gordy 7114
6/10/72	**63**	5	4 Papa Was A Rollin' Stone	Gordy 7117
4/27/74	**63**	7	5 Help Yourself	Gordy 7134
2/19/77	**48**	11	6 You + Me = Love/	
		5	7 Let's Go Down To The Disco 12" single (above 2 titles were also released on separate 7" singles: #8231 and #8295)	Whitfield 8306
			THE UNIFICS Soul group formed at Howard University in Washington, DC.	
9/21/68	**25**	9	1 Court Of Love	Kapp 935
12/14/68+	**36**	10	2 The Beginning Of My End	Kapp 957

DEBUT DATE	PEAK POS	WKS CHR	ARTIST — Record Title	Label & Number
			THE UNIFICS — Cont'd	
4/12/69	**97**	2	3 It's A Groovy World!	Kapp 985
			above 3 written and produced by Guy Draper	
			UNION GAP - see GARY PUCKETT	
			UNIPOP	
			New York pop duo: Phyllis and husband Manny Loiacono.	
12/25/82+	**71**	8	1 What If (I Said I Love You)	Kat Family 03353
			THE UNIQUES	
			Southern pop quintet featuring country star Joe Stampley.	
3/20/65	**66**	6	1 Not Too Long Ago	Paula 219
7/02/66	**97**	2	2 All These Things	Paula 238
			UNIT FOUR plus TWO	
			English pop/rock sextet. Peter Moules, lead singer.	
5/01/65	**28**	9	1 Concrete And Clay	London 9751
7/17/65	**95**	2	2 You've Never Been In Love Like This Before	London 976
			UNIVERSAL ROBOT BAND	
			New York-based integrated disco sextet.	
5/14/77	**93**	6	1 Dance And Shake Your Tambourine	Red Greg 207
			THE UNKNOWNS	
9/24/66	**74**	4	1 Melody For An Unknown Girl	Parrot 307
			THE UPBEATS	
8/04/58	**75**	3	1 Just Like In The Movies	Swan 4010
			PHILIP UPCHURCH COMBO	
			Philip is an R&B guitarist from Chicago. Session player for George Benson, Quincy Jones, The Jacksons, and many others.	
6/19/61	**29**	8	1 You Can't Sit Down, Part 2 [I]	Boyd 3398
			UPTOWN	
12/27/86+	**80**	11	1 (I Know) I'm Losing You	Oak Lawn 3810
			URGENT	
			Rock quintet. Michael Kehr, lead singer.	
8/10/85	**79**	5	1 Running Back	Manhattan 50005
			URIAH HEEP	
			British hard rock band. Key members: David Byron (lead singer), Mick Box (lead guitar) and Ken Hensley (keyboards).	
7/29/72	**39**	12	1 Easy Livin	Mercury 73307
1/20/73	**91**	3	2 Sweet Lorraine/	
		1	3 Blind Eye	Mercury 73349
10/13/73	**91**	7	4 Stealin'	Warner 7738
			U.S. 1	
11/29/75	**91**	2	1 Bye Bye Baby	Private S. 45045
			USA for AFRICA	
			USA: United Support of Artists - a collection of 46 major artists formed to help the suffering people of Africa and the U.S.A.	
3/23/85	**1**[4]	18	1 ▲ **We Are The World**	Columbia 04839
			soloists (in order): Lionel Richie, Stevie Wonder, Paul Simon, Kenny Rogers, James Ingram, Tina Turner, Billy Joel, Michael Jackson, Diana Ross, Dionne Warwick, Willie Nelson, Al Jarreau, Bruce Springsteen, Kenny Loggins, Steve Perry, Daryl Hall, Huey Lewis, Cyndi Lauper, Kim Carnes, Bob Dylan, and Ray Charles - written by Michael Jackson & Lionel Richie	
			UTFO	
			Brooklyn rap-break trio: The Kangol Kid, Doctor Ice, and The Educated Rapper.	
3/09/85	**77**	5	1 Roxanne, Roxanne	Select 1182
			UTOPIA	
			Veteran pop/rock group with own recording studio near Woodstock, New York. Consists of Todd Rundgren (guitar), Kasim Sulton (bass), Roger Powell (keyboards) and Willie Wilcox (drums).	
2/23/80	**27**	12	1 Set Me Free	Bearsville 49180
6/07/80	**76**	3	2 The Very Last Time	Bearsville 49247
1/08/83	**82**	6	3 Feet Don't Fail Me Now	Network 69859

DEBUT DATE	PEAK POS	WKS CHR	ARTIST — Record Title	Label & Number
			U2	
			Rock band formed in Dublin, Ireland in 1976. Consisted of Paul "Bono" Hewson (vocals), Dave "The Edge" Evans (guitar), Adam Clayton (bass) and Larry Mullen Jr. (drums). Emerged as 1987's leading rock act.	
4/02/83	**53**	12	1 New Year's Day	Island 99915
1/14/84	**81**	5	2 I Will Follow	Island 99789
10/27/84	**33**	15	3 Pride (In The Name Of Love)	Island 99704
			V	
			THE VACELS	
			Rock group from Long Island, New York.	
7/24/65	**63**	5	1 You're My Baby (And Don't You Forget It)	Kama Sutra 200
			VALADIERS	
11/20/61	**89**	2	1 Greetings (This Is Uncle Sam)	Miracle 6
			JERRY VALE	
			Born Genero Vitaliano on 7/8/32 in Bronx, New York. Pop ballad singer.	
3/10/56	**30**	12	1 Innamorata (Sweetheart) from the film "Artists & Models"	Columbia 40634
7/07/56	**14**	24	2 You Don't Know Me Best Seller #14 / Top 100 #14 / Juke Box #14 / Jockey #15	Columbia 40710
11/25/57	**45**	13	3 Pretend You Don't See Her Best Seller #45 / Top 100 #52	Columbia 41010
10/13/58	**60**	7	4 Go Chase A Moonbeam	Columbia 41238
12/19/64+	**24**	10	5 Have You Looked Into Your Heart	Columbia 43181
3/06/65	**54**	6	6 For Mama	Columbia 43232
5/22/65	**96**	3	7 Tears Keep On Falling	Columbia 43252
8/07/65	**99**	1	8 Where Were You When I Needed You	Columbia 43337
10/08/66	**93**	2	9 Dommage, Dommage (Too Bad, Too Bad)	Columbia 43774
			RITCHIE VALENS	
			Born Richard Valenzuela on 5/13/41 in Pacoima, California. Latin rock and roll singer, songwriter, guitarist. Killed in the plane crash that also took the lives of Buddy Holly and the Big Bopper on 2/3/59. In the film "Go Johnny Go". His film bio, "La Bamba", released in 1987.	
9/22/58	**42**	13	1 Come On, Let's Go	Del-Fi 4106
11/24/58+	**2^2**	23	2 **Donna/**	
12/28/58+	**22**	15	3 La Bamba [F]	Del-Fi 4110
4/06/59	**55**	8	4 That's My Little Suzie	Del-Fi 4114
7/13/59	**92**	2	5 Little Girl above 5 written by Valens	Del-Fi 4117
			CATERINA VALENTE	
			Born in Paris of Italian parentage. Popular European singer and dancer.	
4/09/55	**8**	14	1 **The Breeze And I** Jockey #8 / Best Seller #13 #1 hit for Jimmy Dorsey in 1940	Decca 29467
			JOHN VALENTI	
			Blue-eyed soul singer from Chicago.	
9/04/76	**37**	12	1 Anything You Want	Ariola Am. 7625
			DANNY VALENTINO	
			Pop vocalist born in Flushing, New York.	
6/06/60	**95**	2	1 Biology	MGM 12881
			MARK VALENTINO	
			Born Anthony Busillo on 3/12/42 in Philadelphia.	
11/10/62	**27**	9	1 The Push And Kick	Swan 4121
			THE VALENTINOS	
			Cleveland family soul group. Originated as the Womack Brothers gospel group. Consisted of Bobby Womack, brothers Cecil, Curtis, Friendly Jr. and Harris.	
8/18/62	**72**	8	1 Lookin' For A Love	Sar 132
3/30/63	**97**	2	2 I'll Make It Alright	Sar 137
6/27/64	**94**	2	3 It's All Over Now	Sar 152
			DANA VALERY	
6/19/76	**95**	4	1 Will You Love Me Tomorrow	Phantom 10566

DEBUT DATE	PEAK POS	WKS CHR	ARTIST — Record Title	Label & Number
			DANA VALERY — Cont'd	
1/19/80	**87**	5	2 I Don't Want To Be Lonely	Scotti Br. 509
			THE VALIANTS	
			Los Angeles R&B group led by vocalist Billy Storm.	
12/30/57+	**69**	7	1 This Is The Nite	Keen 34004
			JOE VALINO	
10/20/56	**12**	20	1 Garden Of Eden	Vik 0226
			Top 100 #12 / Jockey #12 / Best Seller #13 / Juke Box #13	
			VALJEAN	
			Born Valjean Johns on 11/19/34 in Shattuck, Oklahoma. Pianist.	
5/19/62	**28**	9	1 Theme From Ben Casey [I]	Carlton 573
			from the TV series of the same title	
8/25/62	**100**	1	2 Till There Was You [I]	Carlton 576
			from the film "The Music Man"	
			FRANKIE VALLI	
			Born Francis Castellucio on 5/3/37 in Newark, New Jersey. Recorded his first solo single in 1953 as Frank Valley on the Corona label. Formed own group, the Variatones in 1955, and changed their name to the Four Lovers in 1956, which evolved into The 4 Seasons by 1961. Began solo work in 1965.	
1/15/66	**39**	7	1 (You're Gonna) Hurt Yourself	Smash 2015
11/12/66	**68**	6	2 The Proud One	Philips 40407
5/20/67	**2**¹	16	3● **Can't Take My Eyes Off You**	Philips 40446
8/26/67	**18**	8	4 I Make A Fool Of Myself	Philips 40484
12/30/67+	**29**	8	5 To Give (The Reason I Live)	Philips 40510
6/14/69	**52**	7	6 The Girl I'll Never Know (Angels Never Fly This Low)	Philips 40622
11/23/74+	**1**¹	23	7● **My Eyes Adored You**	Private S. 45003
5/17/75	**6**	14	8 **Swearin' To God**	Private S. 45021
			1-8: produced by Bob Crewe	
10/18/75	**11**	12	9 Our Day Will Come	Private S. 45043
4/03/76	**36**	8	10 Fallen Angel	Private S. 45074
8/14/76	**78**	3	11 We're All Alone	Private S. 45098
			written by Boz Scaggs	
5/27/78	**1**²	22	12▲ **Grease**	RSO 897
			from the film of the same title	
1/27/79	**77**	4	13 Fancy Dancer	Warner 8734
7/19/80	**90**	4	14 Where Did We Go Wrong	MCA 41253
			vocal duet with Chris Forde	
			10-11 & 13-14: produced by Bob Gaudio (of The 4 Seasons)	
			JUNE VALLI	
			Born on 6/30/30 in the Bronx, NY. Married to Chicago disc jockey Howard Miller.	
5/14/55	**29**	1	1 Unchained Melody	RCA 6078
			Best Seller #29	
			from the film "Unchained"	
11/24/58+	**43**	13	2 The Wedding	Mercury 71382
3/02/59	**71**	5	3 The Answer To A Maiden's Prayer	Mercury 71422
3/07/60	**29**	13	4 Apple Green	Mercury 71588
			DICK VAN DYKE - see JULIE ANDREWS	
			LEROY VAN DYKE	
			Born on 10/4/29 in Spring Fork, Missouri. Former livestock auctioneer.	
11/24/56+	**19**	15	1 Auctioneer [N]	Dot 15503
			Juke Box #19 / Best Seller #21 / Top 100 #29	
10/30/61	**5**	16	2 **Walk On By**	Mercury 71834
3/10/62	**35**	7	3 If A Woman Answers (Hang Up The Phone)	Mercury 71926
			THE VAN DYKES	
1/16/61	**91**	2	1 Gift Of Love	Donna 1333
7/31/61	**99**	2	2 The Bells Are Ringing	DeLuxe 6193
			THE VAN DYKES	
			R&B trio formed in Fort Worth, Texas in 1964. Consisted of lead singer Rondalis Tandy, Wenzon Mosley (tenor) and James May (baritone). First recorded for Hue, 1965.	
4/02/66	**94**	2	1 No Man Is An Island	Mala 520

DEBUT DATE	PEAK POS	WKS CHR	ARTIST — Record Title	Label & Number
			VAN HALEN Hard-rock band formed in Pasadena, California in 1974. Consisted of David Lee Roth (b: 10/10/55), vocals; Eddie Van Halen (b: 1/26/57), guitar; Michael Anthony (b: 6/20/55), bass; and Alex Van Halen (b: 5/8/55), drums. The Van Halen brothers were born in Nijmegen, The Netherlands, and moved to Pasadena in 1968. Sammy Hagar replaced Roth as lead singer in 1985.	
1/28/78	**36**	11	1 You Really Got Me	Warner 8515
5/06/78	**84**	4	2 Runnin' With The Devil	Warner 8556
4/28/79	**15**	15	3 Dance The Night Away	Warner 8823
9/15/79	**84**	4	4 Beautiful Girls	Warner 49035
5/24/80	**55**	7	5 And The Cradle Will Rock...	Warner 49501
2/06/82	**12**	16	6 (Oh) Pretty Woman	Warner 50003
5/22/82	**38**	11	7 Dancing In The Street	Warner 29986
1/14/84	**1**[5]	21	8● **Jump**	Warner 29384
4/14/84	**13**	14	9 I'll Wait	Warner 29307
6/23/84	**13**	15	10 Panama	Warner 29250
10/27/84	**56**	7	11 Hot For Teacher all of above produced by Ted Templeman	Warner 29199
3/15/86	**3**	16	12 **Why Can't This Be Love**	Warner 28740
5/24/86	**22**	14	13 Dreams	Warner 28702
8/09/86	**22**	15	14 Love Walks In	Warner 28626
			PAUL VANCE Born on 11/4/29 in Brooklyn. Paul of "Lee & Paul". Prolific songwriter with partner Lee Pockriss.	
10/08/66	**97**	2	1 Dommage, Dommage (Too Bad, Too Bad)	Scepter 12164
			VANDENBERG Dutch hard-rock quartet: led by Adrian Vandenberg (guitar, keyboards), Bert Heerink (lead singer), Dick Kemper (bass) and Jos Zoomer (drums).	
1/08/83	**39**	14	1 Burning Heart	Atco 99947
			LUTHER VANDROSS Born on 4/20/51 in New York City. Soul singer, producer, songwriter. Began career singing commercial jingles, then became a top session vocalist, arranger.	
10/10/81	**33**	15	1 Never Too Much	Epic 02409
10/30/82	**55**	12	2 Bad Boy/Having A Party	Epic 03205
10/08/83	**27**	13	3 How Many Times Can We Say Goodbye **DIONNE WARWICK & LUTHER VANDROSS**	Arista 9073
4/28/84	**87**	4	4 Superstar (Don't you remember...)	Epic 04441
3/16/85	**29**	16	5 'Til My Baby Comes Home	Epic 04760
8/23/86	**57**	11	6 Give Me The Reason from the film "Ruthless People"	Epic 06129
11/15/86+	**15**	19	7 Stop To Love	Epic 06523
			VANGELIS Born Evangelos Papathanassiou in Greece. Keyboardist, composer. Formed rock band, Aphrodites Child, in France with Demis Roussos, 1968-early 70s. Also see Jon & Vangelis.	
12/12/81+	**1**[1]	28	1 **Chariots Of Fire - Titles** [I] from the Academy Award winning film of the same title	Polydor 2189
			VANILLA FUDGE Psychedelic rock quartet formed in New York in 1966. Consisted of Mark Stein (lead singer, keyboards), Vinnie Martell (guitar), Tim Bogert (bass) and Carmine Appice (drums).	
7/08/67+	**6**	17	1 **You Keep Me Hangin' On**	Atco 6590
2/10/68	**73**	6	2 Where Is My Mind	Atco 6554
10/05/68	**38**	8	3 Take Me For A Little While	Atco 6616
12/21/68	**65**	3	4 Season Of The Witch, Pt. I	Atco 6632
3/08/69	**68**	5	5 Shotgun	Atco 6655
			VANITY From Toronto, Canada - real name: Denise Mathews. Former model and nudie actress. Lead singer of Vanity 6 (assembled by former boyfriend, Prince). Starred in the film "52 Pick-Up".	
9/08/84	**75**	7	1 Pretty Mess	Motown 1752
4/19/86	**56**	7	2 Under The Influence	Motown 1833
			VANITY FARE British pop quintet featuring lead singer Trevor Brice.	
11/22/69+	**12**	13	1 Early In The Morning	Page One 21027

DEBUT DATE	PEAK POS	WKS CHR	ARTIST — Record Title		Label & Number
			VANITY FARE — Cont'd		
3/21/70	**5**	22	2 ● **Hitchin' A Ride**		Page One 21029
8/29/70	**98**	2	3 (I Remember) Summer Morning		Page One 21033
			TEDDY VANN		
			Pop/R&B singer, songwriter, producer.		
6/05/61	**76**	4	1 The Lonely Crowd		Columbia 41996
			GINO VANNELLI		
			Born on 6/16/52 in Montreal, Canada. Pop/soul-styled singer, songwriter.		
9/21/74	**22**	13	1 People Gotta Move		A&M 1614
9/11/76	**64**	8	2 Love Of My Life		A&M 1861
9/09/78	**4**	21	3 **I Just Wanna Stop**		A&M 2072
2/17/79	**78**	5	4 Wheels Of Life		A&M 2114
3/21/81	**6**	20	5 **Living Inside Myself**		Arista 0588
7/04/81	**41**	10	6 Nightwalker		Arista 0613
3/06/82	**89**	3	7 The Longer You Wait		Arista 0664
5/04/85	**42**	16	8 Black Cars		HME 04889
9/21/85	**57**	12	9 Hurts To Be In Love		CBS Assoc. 05586
			RANDY VANWARMER		
			Born on 3/30/55 in Denver. Pop singer, songwriter, guitarist.		
3/24/79	**4**	20	1 ● **Just When I Needed You Most**		Bearsville 0334
8/02/80	**77**	3	2 Whatever You Decide		Bearsville 49258
6/20/81	**55**	8	3 Suzi		Bearsville 49752
			THE VAPORS		
			British pub-rock quartet. David Fenton, lead singer.		
9/27/80	**36**	17	1 Turning Japanese		Liberty 1364
			MARIANNE VASEL & ERICH STORZ		
			German pop duo.		
5/05/58	**46**	7	1 The Little Train (Die Kleine Bimmelbahn)	[F]	Mercury 71286
			Best Seller #46 / Top 100 #49		
			FRANKIE VAUGHAN		
			English pop singer, actor. In film "Let's Make Love", 1960.		
7/28/58	**22**	1	1 Judy		Epic 9273
			Jockey #22 / Top 100 #100		
			SARAH VAUGHAN		
			Born on 3/27/24 in Newark, New Jersey. Jazz singer. Studied piano, 1931-39. Won amateur contest at the Apollo Theater in 1942, which led to her joining Earl Hine's band as vocalist and second pianist. Later joined Billy Eckstine's band and recorded for Continental in 1944. Went solo in 1945. Married manager George Treadwell in 1947. Dubbed "The Divine One". Still active in the 80s.		
11/27/54+	**6**	15	1 **Make Yourself Comfortable**		Mercury 70469
			Jockey #6 / Best Seller #8 / Juke Box #8		
2/26/55	**12**	9	2 How Important Can It Be?		Mercury 70534
			Jockey #12 / Best Seller #18 / Juke Box #20		
4/23/55	**6**	11	3 **Whatever Lola Wants**		Mercury 70595
			Jockey #6 / Juke Box #9 / Best Seller #12 from the Broadway musical "Damn Yankees"		
7/16/55	**14**	1	4 Experience Unnecessary		Mercury 70646
			Jockey #14		
11/19/55	**11**	15	5 C'est La Vie		Mercury 70727
			Jockey #11 / Top 100 #22		
2/11/56	**13**	19	6 Mr. Wonderful		Mercury 70777
			Jockey #13 / Top 100 #38		
6/09/56	**92**	2	7 Hot And Cold Running Tears		Mercury 70846
7/14/56	**19**	14	8 Fabulous Character/		
			Jockey #19 / Top 100 #27		
8/04/56	**86**	1	9 The Other Woman		Mercury 70885
10/06/56	**72**	9	10 It Happened Again		Mercury 70947
			1-6 & 8-10: with Hugo Peretti & His Orchestra		
12/29/56+	**19**	14	11 The Banana Boat Song		Mercury 71020
			Jockey #19 / Top 100 #31		
3/02/57	**91**	1	12 Leave It To Love		Mercury 71030
7/29/57	**82**	7	13 Passing Strangers		Mercury 7122
			SARAH VAUGHAN & BILLY ECKSTINE		
5/04/59	**96**	1	14 Separate Ways		Mercury 71433
7/20/59	**7**	19	15 **Broken-Hearted Melody**		Mercury 71477

DEBUT DATE	PEAK POS	WKS CHR	ARTIST — Record Title		Label & Number
			SARAH VAUGHAN — Cont'd		
11/02/59	**44**	9	**16** Smooth Operator		Mercury 71519
2/08/60	**41**	8	**17** Eternally/ Charlie Chaplin penned tune, also known as "Limelight"		
2/15/60	**87**	2	**18** You're My Baby		Mercury 71562
10/10/60	**82**	6	**19** Serenata		Roulette 4285
4/02/66	**63**	6	**20** A Lover's Concerto		Mercury 72543
			BILLY VAUGHN Born Richard Vaughn on 4/12/19 in Glasgow, Kentucky. Organized the Hilltoppers vocal group in 1952. Music director for Dot Records - arranger/conductor for Pat Boone, Gale Storm, The Fontane Sisters and many other Dot artists. Billy had more pop hits than any other orchestra leader during the rock era.		
12/11/54+	**2**[1]	27	**1** **Melody Of Love** Best Seller #2 / Jockey #2 / Juke Box #3 tune written in 1903	[I]	Dot 15247
9/24/55	**5**	15	**2** **The Shifting Whispering Sands (Parts 1 & 2)** Best Seller #5 / Top 100 #5 pre / Jockey #5 / Juke Box #10 narration by Ken Nordine (also #4 & #7 below)	[S]	Dot 15409
2/04/56	**37**	13	**3** A Theme From The Three Penny Opera "Moritat"/ written in 1928; later known as "Mack The Knife"	[I]	
2/11/56	**76**	1	**4** Little Boy Blue based on the 1891 poem written by Eugene Fields	[S]	Dot 15444
9/08/56	**18**	10	**5** When The White Lilacs Bloom Again Juke Box #18 / Jockey #21 / Top 100 #22	[I]	Dot 15491
12/15/56	**83**	3	**6** Petticoats Of Portugal	[I]	Dot 15506
4/13/57	**95**	1	**7** The Ship That Never Sailed	[S]	Dot 15546
12/23/57+	**5**	26	**8** **Sail Along Silvery Moon/** Best Seller #5 / Top 100 #5 / Jockey #6 revival of Bing Crosby's #4 hit in 1937	[I]	
12/02/57	**10**	21	**9** **Raunchy** Jockey #10 / Top 100 #33	[I]	Dot 15661
4/07/58	**30**	11	**10** Tumbling Tumbleweeds/ Best Seller #30 / Top 100 #35 first popularized in 1934 by the Sons of The Pioneers (POS 13)	[I]	
4/14/58	**77**	4	**11** Trying the Hilltoppers' first hit (with Billy Vaughn) in 1952	[I]	Dot 15710
6/30/58	**56**	5	**12** Singing Hills revival of Bing Crosby's 1940 hit (POS 3)	[I]	Dot 15771
8/11/58	**20**	10	**13** La Paloma Best Seller #20 / Hot 100 #26 Spanish tango written in 1864	[I]	Dot 15795
10/20/58	**44**	10	**14** Cimarron (Roll On) first appeared in the film "Twilight On The Trail", 1942	[I]	Dot 15836
12/28/58+	**37**	10	**15** Blue Hawaii revival of Bing Crosby's 1937 hit (POS 5)	[I]	Dot 15879
3/30/59	**89**	1	**16** Hawaiian War Chant classic Hawaiian song written in 1936	[I]	Dot 15900
4/27/59	**82**	5	**17** Your Cheatin' Heart revival of Joni James' 1952 hit (POS 2)	[I]	Dot 15936
6/20/60	**19**	12	**18** Look For A Star from the film "Circus Of Horrors"	[I]	Dot 16106
10/03/60	**51**	10	**19** The Sundowners from the film of the same title	[I]	Dot 16133
2/06/61	**28**	8	**20** Wheels/	[I]	
2/20/61	**63**	6	**21** Orange Blossom Special	[I]	Dot 16174
6/12/61	**84**	5	**22** Blue Tomorrow	[I]	Dot 16220
9/18/61	**61**	7	**23** Berlin Melody/	[I]	
10/09/61	**73**	6	**24** Come September from the film of the same title	[I]	Dot 16262
3/17/62	**69**	6	**25** Chapel By The Sea	[I]	Dot 16329
7/21/62	**13**	12	**26** A Swingin' Safari	[I]	Dot 16374
4/17/65	**94**	2	**27** Mexican Pearls	[I]	Dot 16706
1/08/66	**77**	6	**28** Michelle written by John Lennon and Paul McCartney		Dot 16809
			DENNY VAUGHN		
5/19/56	**70**	4	**1** Walk Hand In Hand		Kapp 143

DEBUT DATE	PEAK POS	WKS CHR	ARTIST — Record Title	Label & Number
			BOBBY VEE	
			Born Robert Velline on 4/30/43 in Fargo, North Dakota. Formed band, The Shadows, with his brother and a friend in 1959. After Buddy Holly's death in a plane crash, The Shadows filled in on Buddy's next scheduled show in Fargo. First recorded for Soma in 1959. In films "Swingin' Along", "It's Trad, Dad", "Play It Cool", "C'mon Let's Live A Little" and "Just For Fun".	
8/31/59	**77**	4	1 Suzie Baby	Liberty 55208
			BOBBY VEE & THE SHADOWS	
4/04/60	**93**	2	2 What Do You Want?	Liberty 55234
8/01/60	**6**	19	3 **Devil Or Angel/**	
9/12/60	**81**	1	4 Since I Met You Baby	Liberty 55270
11/28/60+	**6**	14	5 **Rubber Ball**	Liberty 55287
			co-written by Gene Pitney	
2/13/61	**33**	7	6 Stayin' In/	
2/27/61	**61**	5	7 More Than I Can Say	Liberty 55296
5/29/61	**63**	4	8 How Many Tears	Liberty 55325
8/07/61	**1^{3}**	15	9 **Take Good Care Of My Baby**	Liberty 55354
11/13/61	**2^{1}**	15	10 **Run To Him/**	
11/27/61+	**53**	9	11 Walkin' With My Angel	Liberty 55388
2/24/62	**15**	11	12 Please Don't Ask About Barbara/	
2/24/62	**92**	1	13 I Can't Say Goodbye	Liberty 55419
5/19/62	**15**	10	14 Sharing You	Liberty 55451
9/01/62	**20**	8	15 Punish Her/	
9/22/62	**99**	2	16 Someday (When I'm Gone From You)	Liberty 55479
			BOBBY VEE & THE CRICKETS	
12/08/62+	**3**	14	17 **The Night Has A Thousand Eyes**	Liberty 55521
3/30/63	**13**	10	18 Charms	Liberty 55530
6/22/63	**34**	7	19 Be True To Yourself/	
6/29/63	**85**	2	20 A Letter From Betty	Liberty 55581
11/09/63	**55**	7	21 Yesterday And You (Armen's Theme)/	
12/28/63	**99**	1	22 Never Love A Robin	Liberty 55636
			8-11, 13-15, 17-20 & 22: with The Johnny Mann Singers	
1/25/64	**83**	3	23 Stranger In Your Arms	Liberty 55654
2/22/64	**52**	8	24 I'll Make You Mine	Liberty 55670
			vocal backing: The Eligibles	
5/30/64	**63**	8	25 Hickory, Dick And Doc	Liberty 55700
12/12/64+	**84**	5	26 (There'll Come A Day When) Ev'ry Little Bit Hurts/	
12/05/64	**97**	1	27 Pretend You Don't See Her	Liberty 55751
2/06/65	**99**	1	28 Cross My Heart	Liberty 55761
5/08/65	**85**	5	29 Keep On Trying	Liberty 55790
7/09/66	**52**	8	30 Look At Me Girl	Liberty 55877
7/22/67	**3**	16	31 ● **Come Back When You Grow Up**	Liberty 55964
11/18/67	**37**	7	32 Beautiful People	Liberty 56009
2/10/68	**46**	6	33 Maybe Just Today	Liberty 56014
			above 4: BOBBY VEE & THE STRANGERS	
4/20/68	**35**	9	34 My Girl/Hey Girl	Liberty 56033
8/31/68	**83**	4	35 Do What You Gotta Do	Liberty 56057
12/28/68	**98**	3	36 I'm Into Lookin' For Someone To Love Me	Liberty 56080
8/02/69	**92**	2	37 Let's Call It A Day Girl	Liberty 56124
			8-28 & 37: produced by Snuff Garrett	
11/21/70	**88**	3	38 Sweet Sweetheart	Liberty 56208
			30-36 & 38: produced by Dallas Smith	
			THE VEJTABLES	
			San Francisco rock group consisting of four guys and a girl drummer.	
10/23/65	**84**	4	1 I Still Love You	Autumn 15
			THE VELAIRES	
8/14/61	**51**	7	1 Roll Over Beethoven	Jamie 1198
			THE VELOURS	
			Brooklyn R&B quintet. Jerome Ramos, lead singer.	
7/08/57	**83**	4	1 Can I Come Over Tonight	Onyx 512
3/17/58	**83**	3	2 .Remember	Onyx 520
			THE VELS	
			Techno-rock trio: Alice DeSoto, Chris Larkin and Charles Hanson.	
2/23/85	**72**	6	1 Look My Way	Mercury 880547

DEBUT DATE	PEAK POS	WKS CHR	ARTIST — Record Title		Label & Number
			THE VELVELETTES		
			Female soul group formed at Western Michigan State University in the early 60s.		
10/17/64	**45**	8	1 Needle In A Haystack		V.I.P. 25007
1/30/65	**64**	6	2 He Was Really Sayin' Somethin'		V.I.P. 25013
			JIMMY VELVET		
12/14/63+	**75**	7	1 We Belong Together		ABC-Para. 10488
5/29/65	**93**	3	2 It's Almost Tomorrow		Philips 40285
			THE VELVETS		
			R&B doo-wop quintet from Odessa, Texas. Virgil Johnson, lead singer.		
5/29/61	**26**	9	1 Tonight (Could Be The Night)		Monument 441
10/09/61	**90**	1	2 Laugh		Monument 448
			THE VENTURES		
			Guitar-based instrumental rock and roll band formed in the Seattle/Tacoma, Washington area. Consisted of lead guitarist Nokie Edwards (b: 5/9/39), bass and lead guitarist Bob Bogle (b: 1/16/37), rhythm guitarist Don Wilson (b: 2/10/37), and drummer Howie Johnson. First recorded for own label, Blue Horizon, in 1959. Johnson was injured in an auto accident, and was replaced by Mel Taylor in 1963. Taylor went solo in 1967, returned in 1978. Edwards left in 1968, replaced by Jerry McGee, returned in 1972. Added keyboardist John Durrill in 1969. Latest recordings featured Edwards, Bogle, Wilson and Taylor.		
7/18/60	**2**[1]	18	1 **Walk--Don't Run**	[I]	Dolton 25
10/31/60	**15**	13	2 Perfidia 5 versions hit the Top 15 in 1941	[I]	Dolton 28
1/23/61	**29**	9	3 Ram-Bunk-Shush	[I]	Dolton 32
4/24/61	**69**	5	4 Lullaby Of The Leaves revival of George Olsen's #1 hit in 1932	[I]	Dolton 41
8/28/61	**83**	3	5 (Theme From) Silver City orchestral backing by Hank Levine	[I]	Dolton 44
10/23/61	**54**	6	6 Blue Moon 3 versions hit the Top 10 in 1935	[I]	Dolton 47
8/04/62	**61**	7	7 Lolita Ya-Ya theme from the film "Lolita"	[I]	Dolton 60
12/29/62+	**91**	4	8 The 2,000 Pound Bee (Part 2)	[I]	Dolton 67
7/11/64	**8**	11	9 **Walk-Don't Run '64** new version of their 1960 hit	[I]	Dolton 96
10/24/64	**35**	7	10 Slaughter On Tenth Avenue written by Richard Rodgers in 1936	[I]	Dolton 300
1/30/65	**70**	3	11 Diamond Head	[I]	Dolton 303
2/26/66	**54**	7	12 Secret Agent Man from the TV series "Secret Agent"	[I]	Dolton 316
3/08/69	**4**	14	13 **Hawaii Five-O** from the TV series of the same title	[I]	Liberty 56068
6/28/69	**83**	5	14 Theme From 'A Summer Place' from the film of the same title	[I]	Liberty 56115
			VIK VENUS		
6/14/69	**38**	10	1 Moonflight a Dickie Goodman type recording	[N]	Buddah 118
			BILLY VERA		
			Born William McCord, Jr. on 5/28/44 in Riverside, California. Raised in Westchester County, New York. Wrote hit songs for many pop, R&B and Country artists. Formed The Beaters in Los Angeles in 1979, an R&B-based 10-piece band.		
12/02/67+	**54**	9	1 Storybook Children		Atlantic 2445
2/17/68	**36**	6	2 Country Girl - City Man above 2: **BILLY VERA & JUDY CLAY**		Atlantic 2480
6/29/68	**43**	6	3 With Pen In Hand **BILLY & THE BEATERS:**		Atlantic 2526
4/25/81	**39**	11	4 I Can Take Care Of Myself		Alfa 7002
9/19/81	**79**	3	5 At This Moment above 2 recorded live at the "Roxy" in January, 1981 **BILLY VERA & THE BEATERS:**		Alfa 7005
11/08/86+	**1**[2]	21	6 **At This Moment** newly popularized through play on TV's "Family Ties"	[R]	Rhino 74403
			LARRY VERNE		
			Born on 2/8/36 in Minneapolis, Minnesota.		
8/29/60	**1**[1]	13	1 **Mr. Custer**	[N]	Era 3024
12/19/60	**75**	3	2 Mister Livingston above 2 written by Fred Darian, Al DeLory & Joe Van Winkle	[N]	Era 3034

DEBUT DATE	PEAK POS	WKS CHR	ARTIST — Record Title	Label & Number
			THE VIBRATIONS	
			Los Angeles R&B vocal group. Originally recorded as The Jayhawks. Consisted of James Johnson, Carl Fisher, Richard Owens, Dave Govan and Don Bradley.	
2/20/61	**25**	8	1 The Watusi	Checker 969
3/28/64	**26**	9	2 My Girl Sloopy	Atlantic 2221
10/23/65	**63**	7	3 Misty	Okeh 7230
4/20/68	**93**	2	4 Love In Them There Hills	Okeh 7311
			MARIA VIDAL	
			Formerly of Desmond Child & Rouge.	
9/08/84	**48**	12	1 Body Rock main title from the film "Body Rock"	EMI America 8233
			THE VIDELS	
			Male pop vocal quintet.	
6/13/60	**73**	3	1 Mister Lonely	JDS 5004
			VIGRASS & OSBORNE	
			British duo: Paul Vigrass and Gary Osborne.	
6/17/72	**65**	7	1 Men Of Learning	Uni 55330
			VILLAGE PEOPLE	
			New York campy disco group: Victor Willis, Randy Jones, David Hodo, Felipe Rose, Glenn Hughes and Alexander Briley. In film "Can't Stop The Music", 1980.	
6/24/78	**25**	15	1 ● Macho Man	Casablanca 922
10/21/78+	**2**[3]	26	2 ▲ **Y.M.C.A.**	Casablanca 945
3/17/79	**3**	18	3 ● **In The Navy**	Casablanca 973
5/26/79	**45**	9	4 Go West	Casablanca 984
11/03/79	**52**	9	5 Ready For The 80's all of above produced by Jacques Morali	Casablanca 2220
			THE VILLAGE SOUL CHOIR	
2/21/70	**55**	10	1 The Cat Walk	Abbott 2010
			THE VILLAGE STOMPERS	
			Greenwich Village, New York dixieland-styled band.	
9/21/63	**2**[1]	14	1 **Washington Square** [I]	Epic 9617
4/25/64	**81**	6	2 From Russia With Love [I] from the film of the same title	Epic 9674
12/05/64	**97**	2	3 Fiddler On The Roof [I] from the Broadway musical of the same title	Epic 9740
			GENE VINCENT	
			Born Vincent Eugene Craddock on 2/11/35 in Norfolk, Virginia; died from an ulcer hemorrhage on 10/12/71. Innovative rock and roll singer, songwriter, guitarist. Injured left leg in motorcycle accident in 1953, had to wear steel brace thereafter. Formed own band, The Bluecaps, in Norfolk in 1956. Appeared in films "The Girl Can't Help It" and "Hot Rod Gang". To England from 1960-67. Injured in car crash that killed Eddie Cochran in England in 1960.	
			GENE VINCENT & His Blue Caps:	
6/16/56	**7**	20	1 **Be-Bop-A-Lula** Best Seller #7 / Top 100 #9 / Juke Box #10 / Jockey #11	Capitol 3450
10/20/56	**96**	1	2 Race With The Devil	Capitol 3530
10/27/56	**49**	2	3 Bluejean Bop Coming Up #49	Capitol 3558
8/19/57	**13**	19	4 Lotta Lovin'/ Best Seller #13 / Top 100 #14 / Jockey #18	
		7	5 Wear My Ring Best Seller flip	Capitol 3763
12/09/57+	**23**	9	6 Dance To The Bop Jockey #23 / Top 100 #43 / Best Seller #44	Capitol 3839
			BOBBY VINTON	
			Born Stanley Robert Vinton on 4/16/35 in Canonsburg, Pennsylvania. Father was a bandleader. Formed own band while in high school. Toured as backing band for Dick Clark's "Caravan of Stars" in 1960. Left band for a singing career in 1962. Own TV series from 1975-78.	
6/09/62	**1**[4]	15	1 ● **Roses Are Red (My Love)**	Epic 9509
8/11/62	**38**	9	2 I Love You The Way You Are	Diamond 121
8/25/62	**12**	11	3 Rain Rain Go Away	Epic 9532
12/08/62+	**33**	9	4 Trouble Is My Middle Name/	
12/01/62+	**38**	9	5 Let's Kiss And Make Up	Epic 9561
3/09/63	**21**	10	6 Over The Mountain (Across The Sea)	Epic 9577

DEBUT DATE	PEAK POS	WKS CHR	ARTIST — Record Title	Label & Number
			BOBBY VINTON — Cont'd	
5/18/63	**3**	13	7 **Blue On Blue**	Epic 9593
8/10/63	**1**[3]	15	8 **Blue Velvet**	Epic 9614
			revival of Tony Bennett's 1951 hit (POS 16)	
11/30/63+	**1**[4]	13	9 **There! I've Said It Again**	Epic 9638
			revival of Vaughn Monroe's 1945 hit (POS 1)	
2/29/64	**9**	9	10 **My Heart Belongs To Only You**	Epic 9662
5/23/64	**13**	8	11 Tell Me Why	Epic 9687
			two versions hit the Top 10 in 1952	
8/08/64	**17**	8	12 Clinging Vine	Epic 9705
10/31/64	**1**[1]	15	13 **Mr. Lonely**	Epic 9730
3/06/65	**17**	7	14 Long Lonely Nights	Epic 9768
5/08/65	**22**	8	15 L-O-N-E-L-Y	Epic 9791
7/10/65	**61**	5	16 Theme From 'Harlow' (Lonely Girl)	Epic 9814
			from the film "Harlow"	
9/18/65	**38**	7	17 What Color (Is A Man)	Epic 9846
12/04/65+	**23**	10	18 Satin Pillows	Epic 9869
2/26/66	**59**	5	19 Tears	Epic 9894
			written in 1935	
4/30/66	**40**	6	20 Dum-De-Da	Epic 10014
			aka "She Understands Me"	
8/06/66	**81**	3	21 Petticoat White (Summer Sky Blue)	Epic 10048
11/19/66+	**11**	12	22 Coming Home Soldier	Epic 10090
3/18/67	**66**	4	23 For He's A Jolly Good Fellow	Epic 10136
			based on the traditional 18th century tune	
5/20/67	**95**	2	24 Red Roses For Mom	Epic 10168
9/30/67	**6**	13	25 **Please Love Me Forever**	Epic 10228
12/30/67+	**24**	8	26 Just As Much As Ever	Epic 10266
3/30/68	**33**	8	27 Take Good Care Of My Baby	Epic 10305
7/20/68	**23**	7	28 Halfway To Paradise	Epic 10350
11/02/68	**9**	14	29 ● **I Love How You Love Me**	Epic 10397
4/05/69	**34**	7	30 To Know You Is To Love You	Epic 10461
6/14/69	**34**	8	31 The Days Of Sand And Shovels	Epic 10485
2/07/70	**46**	9	32 My Elusive Dreams	Epic 10576
7/11/70	**93**	4	33 No Arms Can Ever Hold You	Epic 10629
			25-33: produced by Billy Sherrill	
1/29/72	**24**	16	34 Every Day Of My Life	Epic 10822
6/10/72	**19**	14	35 Sealed With A Kiss	Epic 10861
12/30/72+	**82**	6	36 But I Do	Epic 10936
9/21/74	**3**	17	37 ● **My Melody Of Love**	ABC 12022
3/15/75	**33**	9	38 Beer Barrel Polka/	
			revival of Will Glahe's 1939 hit (POS 1)	
		9	39 Dick And Jane	ABC 12056
6/21/75	**58**	5	40 Wooden Heart	ABC 12100
5/01/76	**97**	2	41 Moonlight Serenade	ABC 12178
			revival of Glenn Miller's 1939 hit (POS 3)	
5/29/76	**75**	3	42 Save Your Kisses For Me	ABC 12186
6/04/77	**99**	2	43 Only Love Can Break A Heart	ABC 12265
			1-21 & 37-43: produced by Bob Morgan	
1/05/80	**78**	4	44 Make Believe It's Your First Time	Tapestry 002
			THE VIRTUES	
			Philadelphia rock and roll instrumental trio led by Frank ("Virtue") Virtuoso.	
3/09/59	**5**	16	1 **Guitar Boogie Shuffle** [I]	Hunt 324
3/24/62	**96**	1	2 Guitar Boogie Shuffle Twist [I]	Sure 1733
			THE VISCOUNTS	
			New Jersey instrumental quintet: Harry Haller (tenor saxophone), Bobby Spievak (guitar), Larry Vecchio (organ), Joe Spievak (bass) and Clark Smith (drums).	
12/28/59+	**52**	16	1 Harlem Nocturne [I]	Madison 123
			#24 hit in 1953 for Herbie Fields & His Orchestra	
7/18/60	**82**	5	2 Night Train [I]	Madison 133
			#27 hit in 1952 for Buddy Morrow & His Orchestra	
12/05/60+	**77**	7	3 Wabash Blues [I]	Madison 140
			#1 hit in 1921 for Isham Jones & His Orchestra	
10/30/65+	**39**	13	4 Harlem Nocturne [I-R]	Amy 940

DEBUT DATE	PEAK POS	WKS CHR	ARTIST — Record Title	Label & Number
			VITAMIN Z	
			British pop trio: Geoff Barradale (lead singer), Nick Lockwood and David Rhodes.	
6/15/85	**73**	7	1 Burning Flame	Geffen 29039
			VITO & THE SALUTATIONS	
			Brooklyn doo-wop vocal quintet led by Vito Balsamo.	
10/26/63	**66**	6	1 Unchained Melody	Herald 583
			THE VOGUES	
			Vocal group formed in Turtle Creek, PA in 1960. Consisted of Bill Burkette (lead), Hugh Geyer & Chuck Blasko (tenors) and Don Miller (baritone). Met in high school.	
9/18/65	**4**	12	1 **You're The One**	Co & Ce 229
11/27/65+	**4**	14	2 **Five O'Clock World**	Co & Ce 232
2/26/66	**21**	9	3 Magic Town	Co & Ce 234
6/04/66	**29**	8	4 The Land Of Milk And Honey	Co & Ce 238
9/24/66	**48**	8	5 Please Mr. Sun	Co & Ce 240
12/24/66	**99**	1	6 That's The Tune	Co & Ce 242
6/15/68	**7**	15	7● **Turn Around, Look At Me**	Reprise 0686
9/07/68	**7**	10	8 **My Special Angel**	Reprise 0766
11/23/68	**27**	6	9 Till	Reprise 0788
2/01/69	**47**	6	10 Woman Helping Man/	
3/08/69	**34**	5	11 No, Not Much	Reprise 0803
4/19/69	**42**	6	12 Earth Angel (Will You Be Mine)	Reprise 0820
6/21/69	**47**	5	13 Moments To Remember	Reprise 0831
8/23/69	**92**	3	14 Green Fields	Reprise 0844
			VOICES OF AMERICA	
			A project of the USA for Africa foundation.	
4/12/86	**65**	8	1 Hands Across America theme for the 6 million Americans who joined hands from Los Angeles to New York on 5/25/86 to fight hunger and homelessness in America	EMI America 8319
			THE VOLUME'S	
			Detroit R&B quintet featuring lead singer Ed Union.	
4/28/62	**22**	12	1 I Love You	Chex 1002
			THE VONTASTICS	
			Chicago R&B quartet: Bobby Newsome, Kenneth Golar, Jose Holmes and Raymond Penn.	
9/03/66	**100**	1	1 Day Tripper	St. Lawrence 1014
			ROGER VOUDOURIS	
			Born on 12/29/54 in Sacramento, California. Pop singer, songwriter, guitarist.	
3/17/79	**21**	19	1 Get Used To It	Warner 8762
			THE VOXPOPPERS	
4/14/58	**18**	8	1 Wishing For Your Love Jockey #18 / Best Seller #41 / Top 100 #44	Mercury 71282
			VOYAGE	
			European disco group. Sylvia Mason, lead singer.	
2/17/79	**41**	9	1 Souvenirs	Marlin 3330
			W	
			THE WACKERS	
11/18/72	**65**	5	1 Day And Night	Elektra 45816
			ADAM WADE	
			Born on 3/17/37 in Pittsburgh. Became TV actor and host of game show "Musical Chairs" in 1976. Worked in "Guys & Dolls" musical in Las Vegas in 1978. TV talk show host in Los Angeles, 1980s.	
1/11/60	**66**	7	1 Tell Her For Me	Coed 520
3/14/60	**58**	8	2 Ruby 2 versions hit the Top 10 in 1953	Coed 526
6/20/60	**64**	7	3 I Can't Help It	Coed 530
11/21/60	**74**	6	4 Gloria's Theme from the film "Butterfield 8"	Coed 541
3/13/61	**7**	14	5 **Take Good Care Of Her**	Coed 546

DEBUT DATE	PEAK POS	WKS CHR	ARTIST — Record Title	Label & Number
			ADAM WADE — Cont'd	
5/15/61	**5**	11	6 **The Writing On The Wall/**	
6/19/61	**85**	4	7 Point Of No Return	Coed 550
7/24/61	**10**	10	8 **As If I Didn't Know**	Coed 553
9/18/61	**61**	7	9 Tonight I Won't Be There/ 1-3, 5-9: with George Paxton & His Orchestra	
10/02/61	**94**	1	10 Linda revival of Ray Noble's #1 hit in 1947	Coed 556
1/30/65	**88**	3	11 Crying In The Chapel 3 versions hit the Top 10 in 1953	Epic 9752
			WADSWORTH MANSION	
12/26/70+	**7**	14	1 **Sweet Mary**	Sussex 209
			JACK WAGNER Born and raised in Washington, Missouri. Frisco Jones of TV's "General Hospital".	
10/20/84+	**2**[2]	22	1 **All I Need**	Qwest 29238
5/25/85	**76**	8	2 Lady Of My Heart flip side "Premonition" Bubbled Under in 1985	Qwest 29085
10/26/85	**52**	14	3 Too Young	Qwest 28931
			PORTER WAGONER Born on 8/12/30 in West Plains, Missouri. Country singer - has charted over 25 Top 10 Country hits (includes duets with Dolly Parton). Host of his own TV variety series beginning in 1960.	
1/25/69	**92**	4	1 The Carroll County Accident	RCA 9651
			THE WAIKIKIS Belgian instrumental group.	
12/05/64+	**33**	9	1 Hawaii Tattoo [I]	Kapp 30
4/03/65	**91**	4	2 Hawaii Honeymoon [I]	Kapp 52
			THE WAILERS Teenage rock and roll instrumental quintet from Tacoma, Washington. Consisted of John Greek, Rick Dangel, Mark Marush, Kent Morrill and Mike Burk.	
5/18/59	**36**	13	1 Tall Cool One [I]	Golden Crest 518
8/17/59	**68**	5	2 Mau-Mau [I]	Golden Crest 526
4/11/64	**38**	10	3 Tall Cool One [I-R]	Golden Crest 518
			LOUDON WAINWRIGHT III Born on 9/5/46 in Durham, North Carolina. Satirical folksinger, songwriter.	
1/27/73	**16**	13	1 Dead Skunk [N]	Columbia 45726
			JOHN WAITE Born on 7/4/55 in England. Lead singer of The Babys.	
6/23/84	**1**[1]	24	1 **Missing You**	EMI America 8212
10/20/84	**37**	13	2 Tears	EMI America 8238
1/26/85	**59**	8	3 Restless Heart	EMI America 8252
3/02/85	**54**	10	4 Change from the film "Vision Quest" (taken from his 1982 LP "Ignition")	Chrysalis 42606
8/10/85	**25**	12	5 Every Step Of The Way	EMI America 8282
10/19/85	**85**	4	6 Welcome To Paradise	EMI America 8278
6/28/86	**76**	6	7 If Anybody Had A Heart from the film "About Last Night"	EMI America 8315
			THE WAITRESSES Akron, Ohio-based pop/rock sextet - Patty Donahue, lead singer.	
5/08/82	**62**	6	1 I Know What Boys Like	Polydor 2196
			JOHNNY WAKELIN & THE KINSHASA BAND British group led by singer/songwriter Wakelin.	
3/08/75	**21**	27	1 Black Superman - 'Muhammad Ali' [N]	Pye 71012
			JIMMY WAKELY - see KAREN CHANDLER	
			NARADA MICHAEL WALDEN Born Michael Walden on 4/23/52 in Kalamazoo, Michigan. Singer, songwriter, drummer, producer. With John McLaughlin's Mahavishnu Orchestra, 1973-75. With Jeff Beck in 1975. Solo artist and much session work since 1976.	
3/31/79	**47**	11	1 I Don't Want Nobody Else (To Dance With You)	Atlantic 3541
2/09/80	**66**	6	2 I Shoulda Loved Ya	Atlantic 3631

DEBUT DATE	PEAK POS	WKS CHR	ARTIST — Record Title	Label & Number
			WENDY WALDMAN	
			Folk/pop singer, songwriter from Los Angeles.	
8/19/78	**76**	4	1 Long Hot Summer Nights	Warner 8617
			THE WALKER BROS.	
			Los Angeles pop trio: Scott Engel, Gary Leeds and John Maus. More popular in England than U.S. (charted 10 hits in U.K.).	
10/16/65	**16**	10	1 Make It Easy On Yourself	Smash 2009
1/29/66	**63**	5	2 My Ship Is Comin' In	Smash 2016
4/16/66	**13**	9	3 The Sun Ain't Gonna Shine (Anymore)	Smash 2032
			BILLY WALKER	
			Born on 1/14/29 in Ralls, TX. Country singer - has charted over 50 Country singles.	
2/15/60	**83**	1	1 Forever	Columbia 41548
			BOOTS WALKER	
6/10/67	**77**	2	1 They're Here [N]	Rust 5115
			GLORIA WALKER	
11/02/68	**60**	7	1 Talking About My Baby	Flaming Arrow 35
1/25/69	**98**	2	2 Please Don't Desert Me Baby	Flaming Arrow 36
			GLORIA WALKER & THE CHEVELLES	
			JERRY JEFF WALKER	
			Born on 3/16/42 in Oneonta, New York. Country/rock singer, songwriter.	
7/27/68	**77**	5	1 Mr. Bojangles	Atco 6594
			written by Walker	
7/28/73	**98**	3	2 L.A. Freeway	MCA 40054
			JR. WALKER & THE ALL STARS	
			R&B group formed in South Bend, Indiana by Walker (born Autry DeWalt II in Blythesville, Arkansas, 1942). Included Walker, sax, vocals; Willie Woods, guitar; Vic Thomas, organ; and James Graves, drums. First recorded for Harvey in 1962. Most recent group included son Autry DeWalt, Jr. on drums.	
2/13/65	**4**	14	1 **Shotgun**	Soul 35008
6/05/65	**36**	7	2 Do The Boomerang	Soul 35012
7/31/65	**29**	8	3 Shake And Fingerpop/	
10/09/65	**43**	8	4 Cleo's Back [I]	Soul 35013
1/15/66	**50**	6	5 Cleo's Mood [I]	Soul 35017
4/09/66	**20**	12	6 (I'm A) Road Runner	Soul 35015
7/30/66	**18**	11	7 How Sweet It Is (To Be Loved By You)	Soul 35024
11/19/66	**52**	6	8 Money (That's What I Want) Part 1	Soul 35026
2/11/67	**31**	8	9 Pucker Up Buttercup	Soul 35030
7/22/67	**44**	7	10 Shoot Your Shot	Soul 35036
11/25/67+	**24**	11	11 Come See About Me	Soul 35041
8/10/68	**31**	11	12 Hip City - Pt. 2	Soul 35048
1/18/69	**42**	6	13 Home Cookin	Soul 35055
5/17/69	**4**	16	14 **What Does It Take (To Win Your Love)**	Soul 35062
10/25/69	**16**	13	15 These Eyes	Soul 35067
2/21/70	**21**	10	16 Gotta Hold On To This Feeling	Soul 35070
7/11/70	**32**	10	17 Do You See My Love (For You Growing)	Soul 35073
12/26/70+	**75**	5	18 Holly Holy	Soul 35081
8/07/71	**50**	9	19 Take Me Girl, I'm Ready	Soul 35084
12/11/71+	**52**	9	20 Way Back Home	Soul 35090
4/01/72	**46**	12	21 Walk In The Night [I]	Soul 35095
			15-21: produced by Johnny Bristol	
			WALL OF VOODOO	
			Los Angeles electronic-rock group. Stanard Ridgway, lead singer.	
3/19/83	**58**	9	1 Mexican Radio	I.R.S. 9912
			WALLACE BROTHERS	
8/29/64	**97**	2	1 Lover's Prayer	Sims 189
			JERRY WALLACE	
			Born on 12/15/28 in Kansas City, Missouri; raised in Glendale, Arizona. Pop/Country singer, guitarist. First recorded for Allied in 1951. Appeared on TV shows "Night Gallery" and "Hec Ramsey".	
8/18/58	**11**	16	1 How The Time Flies	Challenge 59013
			Hot 100 #11 / Best Seller #33 end	

DEBUT DATE	PEAK POS	WKS CHR	ARTIST — Record Title	Label & Number
			JERRY WALLACE — Cont'd	
12/08/58	**78**	4	2 Diamond Ring backing vocals: Ev Freeman Singers	Challenge 59027
4/20/59	**92**	2	3 A Touch Of Pink from the film "The Wild And The Innocent"	Challenge 59040
8/17/59	**8**	21	4 **Primrose Lane** **JERRY WALLACE with The Jewels**	Challenge 59047
1/04/60	**36**	9	5 Little Coco Palm	Challenge 59060
8/01/60	**79**	2	6 Swingin' Down The Lane #1 hit in 1923 for Isham Jones & His Orchestra	Challenge 59082
12/26/60+	**26**	10	7 There She Goes	Challenge 59098
5/08/61	**91**	1	8 Life's A Holiday	Challenge 9107
11/17/62+	**24**	12	9 Shutters And Boards	Challenge 9171
7/25/64	**19**	11	10 In The Misty Moonlight	Challenge 59246
8/15/64	**99**	1	11 It's A Cotton Candy World	Mercury 72292
3/18/72	**48**	12	12 To Get To You	Decca 32914
8/19/72	**38**	9	13 If You Leave Me Tonight I'll Cry from TV's Night Gallery: "The Tune In Dan's Cafe"	Decca 32989
			JAMES WALSH - see GYPSY	
			JOE WALSH Born on 11/20/47 in Wichita, Kansas. Rock singer/songwriter/guitarist. Member of The James Gang (1969-71) and the Eagles (1975-82).	
8/11/73	**23**	15	1 Rocky Mountain Way	Dunhill 4361
1/12/74	**89**	4	2 Meadows	Dunhill 4373
3/01/75	**93**	3	3 Turn To Stone	Dunhill 15026
6/10/78	**12**	15	4 Life's Been Good	Asylum 45493
5/17/80	**19**	16	5 All Night Long from the film "Urban Cowboy"	Full Moon 46639
5/23/81	**34**	12	6 A Life Of Illusion	Asylum 47144
6/11/83	**52**	8	7 Space Age Whiz Kids all of above written by Walsh	Full Moon 29611
			TRAVIS WAMMACK Muscle Shoals' session guitarist.	
11/21/64	**80**	6	1 Scratchy [I]	ARA 204
9/02/72	**95**	4	2 Whatever Turns You On	Fame 91001
1/20/73	**68**	7	3 How Can I Tell You	Fame 91008
6/21/75	**38**	10	4 (Shu-Doo-Pa-Poo-Poop) Love Being Your Fool	Capricorn 0239
9/27/75	**72**	6	5 Easy Evil above 4 produced by Rick Hall	Capricorn 0242
			THE WANDERERS R&B quartet. Ray Pollard, lead singer. First recorded for Savoy in 1953.	
5/15/61	**93**	2	1 For Your Love	Cub 9089
8/25/62	**88**	4	2 There Is No Greater Love #20 hit in 1936 for Isham Jones & His Orchestra based on Tchaikovsky's Concerto No. 1	MGM 13082
			WALTER WANDERLEY Brazilian organist/pianist/composer. Died of cancer on 9/4/86 (55).	
8/27/66	**26**	9	1 Summer Samba (So Nice) [I]	Verve 10421
			WANG CHUNG British pop/rock group: Jack Hues (lead singer, guitar, keyboards), Nick Feldman (bass, keyboards) and Darren Costin (drums). Costin left in 1985.	
2/04/84	**38**	11	1 Don't Let Go	Geffen 29377
4/21/84	**16**	22	2 Dance Hall Days	Geffen 29310
9/22/84	**86**	3	3 Don't Be My Enemy	Geffen 29193
10/12/85	**41**	18	4 To Live And Die In L.A. from the film of the same title	Geffen 28891
10/04/86	**2**[2]	21	5 **Everybody Have Fun Tonight**	Geffen 28562

DEBUT DATE	PEAK POS	WKS CHR	ARTIST — Record Title	Label & Number
			WAR	
			Latin jazz/funk band formed in Long Beach, California in 1969. Consisted of Lonnie Jordan (keyboards), Howard Scott (guitar), Charles Miller (saxophone), B.B. Dickerson (bass), Harold Brown and "Papa" Dee Allen (percussion) and Lee Oskar (harmonica). Eric Burdon's backup band until 1971. Dickerson replaced by Luther Rabb. Alice Tweed Smyth (vocals) added in 1978. Pat Rizzo (horns) and Ron Hammond (percussion) added in 1979. Tweed left in 1982.	
			ERIC BURDON & WAR:	
5/23/70	**3**	21	1 ● **Spill The Wine**	MGM 14118
12/19/70+	**50**	8	2 They Can't Take Away Our Music	MGM 14196
			WAR:	
8/07/71	**35**	11	3 All Day Music	United Art. 50815
1/22/72	**16**	22	4 ● Slippin' Into Darkness	United Art. 50867
11/18/72+	**7**	16	5 ● **The World Is A Ghetto**	United Art. 50975
3/03/73	**2**[2]	15	6 ● **The Cisco Kid**	United Art. 163
7/21/73	**8**	13	7 **Gypsy Man**	United Art. 281
11/10/73+	**15**	15	8 Me And Baby Brother	United Art. 350
6/08/74	**33**	10	9 Ballero [I]	United Art. 432
5/03/75	**6**	20	10 ● **Why Can't We Be Friends?**	United Art. 629
9/20/75	**7**	15	11 **Low Rider**	United Art. 706
7/10/76	**7**	16	12 ● **Summer**	United Art. 834
7/09/77	**45**	10	13 L.A. Sunshine	Blue Note 1009
1/07/78	**39**	9	14 Galaxy	MCA 40820
4/03/82	**66**	6	15 You Got The Power	RCA 13061
7/10/82	**94**	3	16 Outlaw	RCA 13238
			all of above produced by Jerry Goldstein	
			ANITA WARD	
			Born on 12/20/57 in Memphis. R&B/disco vocalist.	
5/12/79	**1**[2]	21	1 **Ring My Bell**	Juana 3422
11/03/79	**87**	5	2 Don't Drop My Love	Juana 3425
			above 2 written & produced by Frederick Knight	
			BILLY WARD & HIS DOMINOES	
			R&B group formed as The Dominoes in New York in 1950 by Ward (b: Los Angeles) and talent agent Rose Marks. Consisted of Ward (piano), Clyde McPhatter (lead), Charlie White (tenor), Joe Lamont (baritone) and Bill Brown (bass). Signed by King/Federal in 1950. Lead singers, at various times, Clyde McPhatter (1950-53), Jackie Wilson (1953-57) and Eugene Mumford.	
8/11/56	**13**	15	1 St. Therese Of The Roses	Decca 29933
			Jockey #13 / Best Seller #20 / Top 100 #27 Jackie Wilson, lead singer	
6/17/57	**12**	24	2 Star Dust	Liberty 55071
			Jockey #12 / Top 100 #13 / Best Seller #14 there have been 19 charted versions of this Hoagy Carmichael tune	
9/30/57	**20**	12	3 Deep Purple	Liberty 55099
			Best Seller #20 / Top 100 #22 3 versions of this tune hit the Top 10 in 1939	
6/02/58	**55**	5	4 Jennie Lee	Liberty 55136
			DALE WARD	
			Lead singer of The Crescendos. Pop/Country vocalist.	
12/28/63+	**25**	11	1 Letter From Sherry	Dot 16520
			Dale's version of "Oh Julie" is on the flip side	
			JOE WARD	
12/17/55	**20**	4	1 Nuttin For Xmas [N-X]	King 4854
			Juke Box #20 / Best Seller #22 / Top 100 #22	
			ROBIN WARD	
			Real name: Jackie Ward. Pop female singer originally from Nebraska.	
11/02/63	**14**	10	1 Wonderful Summer	Dot 16530
			JENNIFER WARNES	
			Born in Seattle; raised in Orange County, California. Pop/MOR-styled vocalist. Lead actress in the Los Angeles production of "Hair".	
1/29/77	**6**	22	1 **Right Time Of The Night**	Arista 0223
7/30/77	**50**	7	2 I'm Dreaming	Arista 0252
6/30/79	**19**	22	3 I Know A Heartache When I See One	Arista 0430
12/22/79+	**67**	7	4 Don't Make Me Over	Arista 0455
4/05/80	**45**	8	5 When The Feeling Comes Around	Arista 0497
12/05/81+	**47**	10	6 Could It Be Love	Arista 0611

DEBUT DATE	PEAK POS	WKS CHR	ARTIST — Record Title	Label & Number
			JENNIFER WARNES — Cont'd	
8/21/82	**1**[3]	23	7 **Up Where We Belong** .... **JOE COCKER & JENNIFER WARNES** love theme from the film "An Officer & A Gentleman"	Island 99996
11/12/83	**85**	4	8 All The Right Moves .... **JENNIFER WARNES/CHRIS THOMPSON** from the film of the same title	Casablanca 814603
			DEE DEE WARWICK Soul singer, born in 1945. Younger sister of Dionne. Sang in gospel group the Drinkard Singers. Backup work for many artists.	
8/07/65	**96**	1	1 We're Doing Fine	Blue Rock 4027
8/27/66	**41**	12	2 I Want To Be With You .... from the Broadway musical "Golden Boy"	Mercury 72584
11/26/66	**88**	3	3 I'm Gonna Make You Love Me	Mercury 72638
5/06/67	**92**	1	4 When Love Slips Away	Mercury 72667
3/22/69	**57**	8	5 Foolish Fool	Mercury 72880
5/09/70	**70**	8	6 She Didn't Know (She Kept On Talking) .... backed by The Dixie Flyers	Atco 6754
6/26/71	**80**	5	7 Suspicious Minds	Atco 6810
			DIONNE WARWICK Born on 12/12/40 in East Orange, New Jersey. In church choir from age 6. With the Drinkard Singers gospel group. Formed trio, the Gospelaires, with sister Dee Dee and their aunt Cissy Houston. Much backup studio work in New York, late 50s. Added an "e" to her last name for a time in the early 70s. Burt Bacharach and Hal David's main "voice" for the songs they composed.	
12/08/62+	**21**	12	1 Don't Make Me Over	Scepter 1239
3/23/63	**84**	5	2 This Empty Place	Scepter 1247
8/03/63	**81**	4	3 Make The Music Play	Scepter 1253
12/07/63+	**8**	14	4 **Anyone Who Had A Heart**	Scepter 1262
4/25/64	**6**	13	5 **Walk On By**	Scepter 1274
8/15/64	**34**	9	6 You'll Never Get To Heaven (If You Break My Heart)/	
8/01/64	**71**	6	7 A House Is Not A Home .... from the film of the same title	Scepter 1282
10/24/64	**20**	8	8 Reach Out For Me	Scepter 1285
2/27/65	**62**	6	9 Who Can I Turn To .... from the Broadway musical "The Roar of The Greasepaint"	Scepter 1298
3/13/65	**75**	6	10 You Can Have Him	Scepter 1294
7/03/65	**65**	8	11 Here I Am .... from the Broadway musical "What's New Pussycat?"	Scepter 12104
10/02/65	**64**	8	12 Looking With My Eyes	Scepter 12111
12/11/65+	**39**	10	13 Are You There (With Another Girl)	Scepter 12122
4/02/66	**8**	12	14 **Message To Michael**	Scepter 12133
7/02/66	**22**	7	15 Trains And Boats And Planes	Scepter 12153
10/01/66	**26**	8	16 I Just Don't Know What To Do With Myself	Scepter 12167
12/24/66+	**49**	6	17 Another Night	Scepter 12181
4/08/67	**15**	17	18 Alfie/ from the film of the same title	
3/18/67	**79**	3	19 The Beginning Of Loneliness	Scepter 12187
7/29/67	**32**	9	20 The Windows Of The World	Scepter 12196
10/21/67	**4**	13	21 ● **I Say A Little Prayer/**	
1/20/68	**2**[4]	13	22 **(Theme From) Valley Of The Dolls** .... from the film of the same title	Scepter 12203
4/13/68	**10**	12	23 **Do You Know The Way To San Jose/**	
6/08/68	**71**	5	24 Let Me Be Lonely	Scepter 12216
8/24/68	**33**	9	25 Who Is Gonna Love Me?/	
8/31/68	**65**	5	26 (There's) Always Something There To Remind Me.....	Scepter 12226
11/02/68	**19**	9	27 Promises, Promises .... from the Broadway musical of the same title	Scepter 12231
2/01/69	**7**	12	28 **This Girl's In Love With You**	Scepter 12241
5/17/69	**37**	7	29 The April Fools	Scepter 12249
7/26/69	**43**	8	30 Odds And Ends	Scepter 12256
9/20/69	**16**	10	31 You've Lost That Lovin' Feeling	Scepter 12262
12/27/69+	**6**	11	32 **I'll Never Fall In Love Again** .... from the Broadway musical "Promises, Promises"	Scepter 12273
4/18/70	**32**	7	33 Let Me Go To Him	Scepter 12276

DEBUT DATE	PEAK POS	WKS CHR	ARTIST — Record Title	Label & Number
			DIONNE WARWICK — Cont'd	
7/11/70	**43**	7	34 Paper Mache	Scepter 12285
10/03/70	**37**	8	35 Make It Easy On Yourself	Scepter 12294
12/05/70+	**43**	9	36 The Green Grass Starts To Grow	Scepter 12300
3/20/71	**57**	5	37 Who Gets The Guy	Scepter 12309
			1-8, 11-21, 23-30, 32-37: written by Burt Bacharach & Hal David	
8/07/71	**83**	5	38 Amanda	Scepter 12326
3/11/72	**84**	3	39 If We Only Have Love	Warner 7560
			1-13, 15-34, 37-39: produced by Burt Bacharach & Hal David	
7/27/74	**1**[1]	19	40 ● **Then Came You**	Atlantic 3202
			DIONNE WARWICKE & SPINNERS	
1/10/76	**79**	5	41 Once You Hit The Road	Warner 8154
6/23/79	**5**	24	42 ● **I'll Never Love This Way Again**	Arista 0419
11/10/79+	**15**	19	43 Deja Vu	Arista 0459
3/29/80	**65**	6	44 After You	Arista 0498
			from the film of the same title	
			above 3 produced by Barry Manilow	
7/26/80	**23**	16	45 No Night So Long	Arista 0527
11/22/80	**62**	10	46 Easy Love	Arista 0572
6/20/81	**65**	6	47 Some Changes Are For Good	Arista 0602
4/17/82	**38**	13	48 Friends In Love	Arista 0673
			DIONNE WARWICK & JOHNNY MATHIS	
10/09/82+	**10**	22	49 **Heartbreaker**	Arista 1015
2/26/83	**41**	13	50 Take The Short Way Home	Arista 1040
			above 2: backing vocals by Barry Gibb	
10/08/83	**27**	13	51 How Many Times Can We Say Goodbye	Arista 9073
			DIONNE WARWICK & LUTHER VANDROSS	
11/09/85+	**1**[4]	23	52 ● **That's What Friends Are For**	Arista 9422
			DIONNE & FRIENDS	
			with Friends: Elton John, Gladys Knight and Stevie Wonder	
			Dionne sings lead for over one minute with each "friend" contributing about 30-40 seconds of solo vocals	
3/15/86	**72**	9	53 Whisper In The Dark	Arista 9460
			BABY WASHINGTON	
			Real name: Jeanette Washington (aka: Justine Washington). R&B vocalist, pianist from New York City. Sang in 50s vocal group, The Hearts. First recorded solo for J&S in 1958.	
4/24/61	**60**	9	1 Nobody Cares (about me)	Neptune 122
			JEANETTE (BABY) WASHINGTON	
3/23/63	**40**	12	2 That's How Heartaches Are Made	Sue 783
7/20/63	**62**	10	3 Leave Me Alone	Sue 790
10/12/63	**100**	1	4 Hey Lonely One	Sue 794
3/21/64	**93**	3	5 I Can't Wait Until I See My Baby	Sue 797
			JUSTINE WASHINGTON	
9/19/64	**100**	1	6 The Clock	Sue 104
11/28/64	**98**	2	7 It'll Never Be Over For Me	Sue 114
7/24/65	**73**	9	8 Only Those In Love	Sue 129
			DINAH WASHINGTON	
			Born Ruth Lee Jones on 8/29/24 in Tuscaloosa, Alabama; died on 12/14/63 (overdose of alcohol and pills). R&B/blues vocalist, pianist. Moved to Chicago in 1927. With Sallie Martin Gospel Singers, 1940-41, and local club work in Chicago, 1941-43. With Lionel Hampton, 1943-46. First recorded for Keynote in 1943. Solo touring from 1946. Married seven times.	
5/25/59	**8**	20	1 **What A Diff'rence A Day Makes**	Mercury 71435
			revival of the Dorsey Brothers 1934 hit (POS 5)	
10/05/59	**17**	13	2 Unforgettable	Mercury 71508
			revival of Nat King Cole's 1952 hit (POS 12)	
1/25/60	**5**	15	3 **Baby (You've Got What It Takes)**	Mercury 71565
			Dinah Washington & Brook Benton	
			DINAH WASHINGTON & BROOK BENTON	
3/28/60	**53**	6	4 It Could Happen To You	Mercury 71560
			revival of Jo Stafford's 1944 hit (POS 10)	
5/23/60	**7**	13	5 **A Rockin' Good Way (To Mess Around And Fall In Love)**	Mercury 71629
			DINAH WASHINGTON & BROOK BENTON	
6/20/60	**24**	14	6 This Bitter Earth	Mercury 71635
10/03/60	**30**	10	7 Love Walked In	Mercury 71696
			3 versions hit the Top 10 in 1938	
12/26/60	**76**	3	8 We Have Love	Mercury 71744

DEBUT DATE	PEAK POS	WKS CHR	ARTIST — Record Title	Label & Number
			DINAH WASHINGTON — Cont'd	
3/13/61	**95**	1	9 Early Every Morning (Early Every Evening Too)	Mercury 71778
5/08/61	**89**	3	10 Our Love Is Here To Stay both Larry Clinton & Red Norvo charted Top 20 versions in 1938	Mercury 71812
10/16/61	**23**	11	11 September In The Rain revival of Guy Lombardo's #1 hit in 1937	Mercury 71876
2/10/62	**71**	5	12 Tears And Laughter	Mercury 71922
5/12/62	**92**	2	13 Dream revival of The Pied Pipers' 1945 hit (POS 1)	Mercury 71958
5/12/62	**87**	1	14 You're Nobody 'Til Somebody Loves You/ revival of Russ Morgan's 1946 hit (POS 14)	
5/19/62	**36**	12	15 Where Are You revival of Mildred Bailey's #5 hit in 1937	Roulette 4424
8/18/62	**76**	4	16 I Want To Be Loved new version of her 1950 hit (POS 22) on Mercury 8181	Mercury 72015
8/25/62	**88**	2	17 For All We Know/ revival of Hal Kemp's 1934 hit (POS 3)	
9/01/62	**93**	1	18 I Wouldn't Know (What To Do)	Roulette 4444
11/17/62	**96**	1	19 Cold, Cold Heart new version of Tony Bennett's 1951 hit (POS 1)	Mercury 72040
11/24/62	**98**	2	20 You're A Sweetheart new version of Dolly Dawn's 1938 hit (POS 1)	Roulette 4455
5/25/63	**92**	3	21 Soulville all Roulette recordings produced by Henry Glover	Roulette 4490
			ELLA WASHINGTON Soul vocalist from Miami. First recorded for Octavia in 1965. Turned to gospel singing in 1973.	
1/18/69	**77**	3	1 He Called Me Baby	Sound Stage 2621
			GROVER WASHINGTON, JR. Born on 12/12/43 in Buffalo. Jazz/R&B saxophonist. Own band, the Four Clefs, at age 16. Session work in Philadelphia, where he now resides.	
5/03/75	**54**	10	1 Mister Magic [I]	Kudu 924
2/14/81	**2**[3]	24	2 **Just The Two Of Us** **GROVER WASHINGTON, JR. with BILL WITHERS**	Elektra 47103
2/06/82	**92**	4	3 Be Mine (Tonight) vocal by Grady Tate	Elektra 47246
			JOHNNY "GUITAR" WATSON Born on 2/3/35 in Houston. Funk/R&B vocalist, guitarist, pianist. First recorded (as Young John Watson) for Federal in 1952.	
2/25/67	**96**	4	1 Mercy, Mercy, Mercy **LARRY WILLIAMS & JOHNNY WATSON**	Okeh 7274
10/04/75	**99**	4	2 I Don't Want To Be A Lone Ranger	Fantasy 739
7/09/77	**41**	12	3 A Real Mother For Ya	DJM 1024
			WATTS 103RD STREET RHYTHM BAND - see CHARLES WRIGHT	
			NOBLE "THIN MAN" WATTS R&B saxophonist, with his backing band, the Rhythm Sparks.	
12/23/57	**44**	9	1 Hard Times (The Slop) [I] Best Seller #44 / Top 100 #48	Baton 249
			WAX Pop duo: Andrew Gold and Graham Gouldman (10cc).	
3/15/86	**43**	13	1 Right Between The Eyes	RCA 14306
			WAYLON & WILLIE - see WAYLON JENNINGS and/or WILLIE NELSON	
			THOMAS WAYNE Born Thomas Wayne Perkins on 7/22/40 in Battsville, Mississippi. Killed in an auto accident on 8/15/71. Brother of guitarist Luther Perkins of Johnny Cash's band.	
1/26/59	**5**	19	1 **Tragedy**	Fernwood 109
5/11/59	**92**	1	2 Eternally above 2 produced by Scotty Moore (Elvis' former guitarist) - backing band on both hits: The DeLons	Fernwood 111
			WE FIVE California pop quintet: Beverly Bivens (lead singer), Mike Stewart (brother of John Stewart), Pete Fullerton, Bob Jones and Jerry Burgan.	
7/24/65	**3**	15	1 **You Were On My Mind**	A&M 770

DEBUT DATE	PEAK POS	WKS CHR	ARTIST — Record Title	Label & Number
			WE FIVE — Cont'd	
11/13/65	**31**	8	2 Let's Get Together	A&M 784
			THE WEATHER GIRLS	
			San Francisco R&B/disco duo: Martha Wash and Izora Armstead. Formerly "Two Tons O' Fun". Backup singers for Sylvester in the late 70s.	
1/22/83	**46**	11	1 It's Raining Men	Columbia 03354
			JIM WEATHERLY	
			Mississippi pop/country songwriter and singer. Wrote Gladys Knight's hits "Neither One Of Us", "Midnight Train To Georgia" and "Best Thing That Ever Happened To Me".	
9/14/74	**11**	16	1 The Need To Be	Buddah 420
1/25/75	**87**	5	2 I'll Still Love You	Buddah 444
			PAULA WEBB	
2/01/75	**60**	4	1 Please, Mr. President [N]	Westbound 5001
			JOAN WEBER	
			New Jersey songstress, born in 1936; died on 5/13/81 (45).	
12/04/54+	**1^{4}**	16	1 **Let Me Go Lover**	Columbia 40366
			Jockey #1(4) / Juke Box #1(4) / Best Seller #1(2)	
			from a "Studio One" CBS-TV production	
			WEDNESDAY	
			Pop quartet - Mike O'Neil, lead singer.	
11/24/73+	**34**	18	1 Last Kiss	Sussex 507
5/11/74	**79**	4	2 Teen Angel	Sussex 515
			BOB WEIR	
			Born on 10/16/47 in San Francisco. Rock singer, guitarist. Co-founder of the Grateful Dead. Later formed Kingfish and Bobby & The Midnites.	
3/18/78	**70**	5	1 Bombs Away	Arista 0315
			TIM WEISBERG - see DAN FOGELBERG	
			ERIC WEISSBERG & STEVE MANDELL	
			New York session musicians.	
1/13/73	**2^{4}**	14	1 ● **Dueling Banjos** [I]	Warner 7659
			tune written in 1955 - featured in the film "Deliverance"	
			BOB WELCH	
			Born on 7/31/46 in Los Angeles, California. Guitarist, vocalist with Fleetwood Mac (1971-74). Formed British rock group, Paris, 1976.	
10/15/77+	**8**	18	1 **Sentimental Lady**	Capitol 4479
			backing vocals: Christine McVie & Lindsey Buckingham	
1/28/78	**14**	17	2 Ebony Eyes	Capitol 4543
6/03/78	**31**	10	3 Hot Love, Cold World	Capitol 4588
2/10/79	**19**	15	4 Precious Love	Capitol 4685
5/26/79	**73**	3	5 Church	Capitol 4719
			LENNY WELCH	
			Born on 5/15/38 in Asbury Park, New Jersey. Black MOR vocalist.	
2/29/60	**45**	13	1 You Don't Know Me	Cadence 1373
10/26/63	**4**	16	2 **Since I Fell For You**	Cadence 1439
			revival of Paul Gayten's 1947 hit (POS 20)	
3/21/64	**25**	9	3 Ebb Tide	Cadence 1422
			featured in the film "Sweet Bird Of Youth"	
			both Frank Chacksfield & Vic Damone charted Top 10 versions in '53	
7/04/64	**92**	2	4 If You See My Love	Cadence 1446
			above 4 conducted by Archie Bleyer	
6/26/65	**72**	6	5 Darling Take Me Back	Kapp 662
8/21/65	**61**	8	6 Two Different Worlds	Kapp 689
12/04/65	**96**	2	7 Run To My Lovin' Arms	Kapp 712
1/10/70	**34**	10	8 Breaking Up Is Hard To Do	Common. U. 3004
8/12/72	**96**	5	9 A Sunday Kind Of Love	Atco 6894
			Jo Stafford and Claude Thornhill had Top 20 versions in 1947	
			LAWRENCE WELK	
			Born on 3/11/03 in Strasburg, North Dakota. Accordionist and polka/sweet bandleader since the mid-20s. Band's style labeled "champagne music". Own national TV musical variety show began on 7/2/55 and ran into the 70s.	
10/22/55	**50**	2	1 Bonnie Blue Gal	Coral 61515
			Coming Up #50	
			vocal by The Sparklers (also on #9 below)	

DEBUT DATE	PEAK POS	WKS CHR	ARTIST — Record Title		Label & Number
			LAWRENCE WELK — Cont'd		
2/18/56	**17**	11	2 Moritat (A Theme From "The Threepenny Opera")	[I]	Coral 61574
			Juke Box #17 / Top 100 #31		
3/17/56	**17**	14	3 The Poor People Of Paris	[I]	Coral 61592
			Juke Box #17 / Top 100 #45		
6/23/56	**96**	1	4 On The Street Where You Live		Coral 61644
			from the Broadway musical "My Fair Lady" (vocal by Larry Deane)		
7/28/56	**32**	8	5 Weary Blues/		
			THE McGUIRE SISTERS & LAWRENCE WELK		
8/04/56	**63**	5	6 In The Alps		Coral 61670
			LAWRENCE WELK & THE McGUIRE SISTERS		
9/15/56	**70**	10	7 When The White Lilacs Bloom Again/	[I]	
9/22/56	**15**	13	8 Tonight You Belong To Me		Coral 61701
			vocal by The Lennon Sisters and The Sparklers		
12/02/57	**48**	6	9 Liechtenstein Polka	[F]	Coral 61900
			Best Seller #48 / Top 100 #62		
10/24/60	**21**	11	10 Last Date	[I]	Dot 16145
12/12/60+	**1^2**	17	11 ● **Calcutta**	[I]	Dot 16161
			featuring Frank Scott on harpsichord		
3/20/61	**55**	7	12 Theme from My Three Sons	[I]	Dot 16198
			from the TV series of the same title		
6/12/61	**71**	5	13 Yellow Bird	[I]	Dot 16222
9/25/61	**87**	3	14 Riders In The Sky	[I]	Dot 16237
			revival of Vaughn Monroe's 1949 hit (POS 1)		
4/07/62	**56**	6	15 Runaway	[I]	Dot 16336
6/09/62	**48**	16	16 Baby Elephant Walk	[I]	Dot 16364
			from the film "Hatari"		
12/08/62	**98**	1	17 Zero-Zero	[I]	Dot 16420
6/29/63	**89**	2	18 Scarlett O'Hara/	[I]	
6/22/63	**100**	1	19 Breakwater	[I]	Dot 16488
3/14/64	**91**	2	20 Stockholm	[I]	Dot 16582
4/10/65	**75**	4	21 Apples And Bananas	[I]	Dot 16697
			KITTY WELLS		
			Born Muriel Deason on 8/30/18 in Nashville. Country star; charted over 20 Top 10 Country hits. Married to Johnny Wright (of Johnnie & Jack).		
7/14/58	**78**	5	1 Jealousy		Decca 30662
			MARY WELLS		
			Born on 5/13/43 in Detroit. R&B vocalist. First artist to record on the Motown label. Married for a time to Cecil Womack, brother of Bobby Womack.		
1/30/61	**45**	11	1 Bye Bye Baby		Motown 1003
7/17/61	**33**	9	2 I Don't Want To Take A Chance		Motown 1011
3/24/62	**8**	17	3 **The One Who Really Loves You**		Motown 1024
8/11/62	**9**	12	4 **You Beat Me To The Punch**		Motown 1032
12/01/62+	**7**	13	5 **Two Lovers**		Motown 1035
2/23/63	**15**	9	6 Laughing Boy/		
3/23/63	**100**	1	7 Two Wrongs Don't Make A Right		Motown 1039
5/25/63	**40**	8	8 Your Old Stand By		Motown 1042
9/28/63	**22**	9	9 You Lost The Sweetest Boy/		
10/19/63+	**29**	17	10 What's Easy For Two Is So Hard For One		Motown 1048
4/04/64	**1^2**	15	11 **My Guy**		Motown 1056
			3-8, 10-11: written and produced by Smokey Robinson		
5/02/64	**19**	9	12 Once Upon A Time/		
5/16/64	**17**	10	13 What's The Matter With You Baby		Motown 1057
			above 2: **MARVIN GAYE & MARY WELLS**		
10/31/64	**45**	8	14 Ain't It The Truth/		
11/07/64	**88**	3	15 Stop Takin' Me For Granted		20th Century 544
1/02/65	**34**	6	16 Use Your Head		20th Century 555
3/20/65	**54**	6	17 Never, Never Leave Me		20th Century 570
6/19/65	**74**	4	18 He's A Lover		20th Century 590
9/11/65	**95**	2	19 Me Without You		20th Century 606
2/12/66	**51**	8	20 Dear Lover/		
1/22/66	**94**	3	21 Can't You See (You're Losing Me)		Atco 6392
7/02/66	**99**	2	22 Such A Sweet Thing		Atco 6423
5/18/68	**65**	8	23 The Doctor		Jubilee 5621

DEBUT DATE	PEAK POS	WKS CHR	ARTIST — Record Title	Label & Number
			MAX WERNER	
			Vocalist, mellotron player of Holland rock band, Kayak.	
5/16/81	**74**	6	1 Rain In May	Radio 3821
			FRED WESLEY - see THE JB's	
			WEST STREET MOB	
			New Jersey funk/dance quartet led by Joey Robinson (son of Joe & Sylvia Robinson - owners of Sugar Hill Records).	
9/12/81	**88**	3	1 Let's Dance (Make Your Body Move)	Sugar Hill 559
4/17/82	**89**	4	2 Sing A Simple Song	Sugar Hill 576
			DOTTIE WEST	
			Born Dorothy Marsh on 10/11/32 in McMinnville, Tennessee. Country singer.	
1/20/73	**97**	3	1 If It's All Right With You	RCA 0828
9/29/73	**49**	11	2 Country Sunshine	RCA 0072
3/08/80	**73**	5	3 A Lesson In Leavin'	United Art. 1339
3/28/81	**14**	20	4 What Are We Doin' In Love backing vocals by Kenny Rogers	Liberty 1404
			KIM WESTON	
			R&B vocalist from Detroit.	
7/06/63	**88**	5	1 Love Me All The Way	Tamla 54076
10/24/64	**61**	6	2 What Good Am I Without You **MARVIN GAYE & KIM WESTON**	Tamla 54104
10/02/65	**50**	8	3 Take Me In Your Arms (Rock Me A Little While)	Gordy 7046
3/12/66	**56**	7	4 Helpless	Gordy 7050
1/07/67	**14**	12	5 It Takes Two **MARVIN GAYE & KIM WESTON**	Tamla 54141
4/29/67	**99**	1	6 I Got What You Need	MGM 13720
			WET WILLIE	
			Mobile, Alabama rock band led by brothers Jimmy and Jack Hall.	
5/25/74	**10**	19	1 **Keep On Smilin'**	Capricorn 0043
10/26/74	**66**	4	2 Country Side Of Life	Capricorn 0212
3/01/75	**69**	5	3 Leona	Capricorn 0224
5/31/75	**96**	2	4 Dixie Rock	Capricorn 0231
5/22/76	**66**	3	5 Everything That 'Cha Do (Will Come Back To You)	Capricorn 0254
12/03/77+	**30**	14	6 Street Corner Serenade	Epic 50478
4/08/78	**45**	7	7 Make You Feel Love Again	Epic 50528
5/26/79	**29**	12	8 Weekend	Epic 50714
			WHAM!	
			Pop duo from Bushey, England: George Michael (b: George Michael Panos on 6/26/63), lead singer, and Andrew Ridgely (b: 1/26/63), guitarist. Disbanded in 1986.	
8/20/83	**60**	9	1 Bad Boys shown as: **WHAM! U.K.**	Columbia 03932
9/08/84	**1**[3]	24	2 ● **Wake Me Up Before You Go-Go**	Columbia 04552
12/22/84+	**1**[3]	21	3 ● **Careless Whisper** released in England as a solo single by George Michael	Columbia 04691
3/23/85	**1**[2]	20	4 **Everything She Wants**	Columbia 04840
7/27/85	**3**	18	5 **Freedom**	Columbia 05409
11/30/85+	**3**	18	6 **I'm Your Man**	Columbia 05721
7/05/86	**10**	13	7 **The Edge Of Heaven** all of above written by George Michael	Columbia 06182
10/11/86	**50**	8	8 Where Did Your Heart Go? 2-8: produced by George Michael	Columbia 06294
			WHAT IS THIS	
			Pop/rock trio featuring lead singer Alain Johannes.	
8/17/85	**62**	6	1 I'll Be Around produced by Todd Rundgren	MCA 52593
			WHATNAUTS	
			Baltimore soul group featuring lead singer Billy Herndon.	
2/28/70	**99**	2	1 Message From A Black Man **THE WHATNAUTS & THE WHATNAUT BAND**	A&I 001
4/17/71	**71**	7	2 I'll Erase Away Your Pain	Stang 5023
9/04/71	**100**	1	3 We're Friends By Day (And Lovers By Night)	Stang 5030

DEBUT DATE	PEAK POS	WKS CHR	ARTIST — Record Title	Label & Number
			BILLY EDD WHEELER	
			Born on 12/9/32; raised in Highcoal, West Virginia. Folk singer, composer. Wrote the Kingston Trio's hit "Reverend Mr. Black".	
1/02/65	**50**	7	1 Ode To The Little Brown Shack Out Back .... [C]	Kapp 617
			WHIRLWIND	
			Soul/disco trio: Sandie Ancrum and brothers Charles & Eddie.	
10/23/76	**91**	4	1 Full Time Thing (Between Dusk And Dawn)	Roulette 7195
			THE WHISPERS	
			Los Angeles soul group formed in 1964. Consisted of Gordy Harmon, twin brothers Walter and Wallace "Scotty" Scott, Marcus Hutson and Nicholas Caldwell. First recorded for Dore in 1964. Harmon replaced by Leaveil Degree in 1973.	
9/19/70	**50**	9	1 Seems Like I Gotta Do Wrong	Soul Clock 1004
5/29/71	**93**	2	2 Your Love Is So Doggone Good..........................	Janus 150
1/27/73	**94**	4	3 Somebody Loves You	Janus 200
2/09/74	**92**	4	4 A Mother For My Children..........................	Janus 231
8/28/76	**88**	10	5 One For The Money (Part 1)	Soul Train 10700
8/13/77	**94**	4	6 Make It With You	Soul Train 10996
2/09/80	**19**	15	7 ● And The Beat Goes On	Solar 11894
4/19/80	**28**	11	8 Lady	Solar 11928
2/14/81	**28**	15	9 It's A Love Thing..........................	Solar 12154
4/30/83	**84**	4	10 Tonight..........................	Solar 69842
			IAN WHITCOMB	
			Born on 7/10/41 in Woking, England. Pop singer, songwriter, author.	
3/13/65	**100**	1	1 This Sporting Life..........................	Tower 120
5/22/65	**8**	13	2 **You Turn Me On (Turn On Song)**..........................	Tower 134
			above 2 shown as: IAN WHITCOMB & BLUESVILLE	
9/04/65	**59**	5	3 N-E-R-V-O-U-S!..........................	Tower 155
			WHITE PLAINS	
			English production by Roger Greenaway & Roger Cook. Tony Burrows, lead singer.	
4/18/70	**13**	15	1 My Baby Loves Lovin'	Deram 85058
9/26/70	**82**	2	2 Lovin' You Baby..........................	Deram 85066
			WHITESNAKE	
			British heavy-metal band. Current lineup: David Coverdale (vocals), John Sykes (guitar), Neil Murray (bass) and Aynsley Dunbar (drums). Coverdale and early members Jon Lord and Ian Paice were members of Deep Purple.	
8/02/80	**53**	8	1 Fool For Your Loving	Mirage 3672
			BARRY WHITE	
			Born on 9/12/44 in Galveston, Texas; raised in Los Angeles. Soul singer, songwriter, keyboardist, producer, arranger. With Upfronts vocal group, recorded for Lummtone in 1960. A&R man for Mustang/Bronco, 1966-67. Formed Love Unlimited in 1969, which included future wife Glodean James. Leader of 40-piece Love Unlimited Orchestra.	
4/14/73	**3**	18	1 ● **I'm Gonna Love You Just A Little More Baby**.........	20th Century 2018
8/04/73	**32**	11	2 I've Got So Much To Give	20th Century 2042
10/27/73+	**7**	18	3 ● **Never, Never Gonna Give Ya Up**..........................	20th Century 2058
2/23/74	**44**	7	4 Honey Please, Can't Ya See	20th Century 2077
8/03/74	**1**[1]	12	5 ● **Can't Get Enough Of Your Love, Babe**..........................	20th Century 2120
11/02/74+	**2**[2]	15	6 ● **You're The First, The Last, My Everything**..........................	20th Century 2133
3/08/75	**8**	11	7 **What Am I Gonna Do With You**..........................	20th Century 2177
5/24/75	**40**	7	8 I'll Do For You Anything You Want Me To..........................	20th Century 2208
12/27/75+	**32**	9	9 Let The Music Play	20th Century 2265
7/24/76	**92**	2	10 Baby, We Better Try To Get It Together..........................	20th Century 2298
8/20/77	**4**	22	11 ● **It's Ecstasy When You Lay Down Next To Me**.........	20th Century 2350
4/29/78	**24**	11	12 Oh What A Night For Dancing..........................	20th Century 2365
11/18/78	**60**	9	13 Your Sweetness Is My Weakness	20th Century 2380
			1-10, 12-13: written by White; all of above produced by White	
			DANNY WHITE	
			Pop/disco singer, originally from New Jersey.	
2/26/77	**100**	2	1 Dance Little Lady Dance..........................	RCR 19765
			KARYN WHITE - see JEFF LORBER	
			KITTY WHITE	
12/31/55+	**68**	6	1 A Teen Age Prayer	Mercury 70750

DEBUT DATE	PEAK POS	WKS CHR	ARTIST — Record Title	Label & Number
			MAURICE WHITE	
			Born on 12/19/41 in Memphis. Percussionist with Ramsey Lewis, 1966-71. Founder and co-lead vocalist of Earth, Wind & Fire.	
8/31/85	**50**	13	1 Stand By Me	Columbia 05571
2/08/86	**95**	1	2 I Need You	Columbia 05726
			TONY JOE WHITE	
			Born on 7/23/43 in Oak Grove, Louisiana. Bayou rock singer, songwriter. Wrote Brook Benton's hit "Rainy Night In Georgia".	
7/05/69	**8**	12	1 **Polk Salad Annie**	Monument 1104
10/25/69	**44**	7	2 Roosevelt And Ira Lee (Night Of The Mossacin)	Monument 1169
8/08/70	**94**	2	3 Save Your Sugar For Me	Monument 1206
			above 3 produced by Billy Swan	
6/28/80	**79**	5	4 I Get Off On It	Casablanca 2279
			DAVID WHITFIELD with MANTOVANI	
			Born on 2/2/26 in Hull, England. Classical-styled tenor.	
2/04/56	**62**	8	1 When You Lose The One You Love	London 1617
			MARGARET WHITING	
			Born on 7/22/24 in Detroit; raised in Hollywood. Daughter of popular composer Richard Whiting. Very popular from 1946-54, she had over 40 charted hits.	
12/08/56	**20**	13	1 The Money Tree	Capitol 3586
			Jockey #20 / Top 100 #49	
3/10/58	**74**	4	2 I Can't Help It (If I'm Still In Love With You)	Dot 15680
10/08/66	**26**	11	3 The Wheel Of Hurt	London 101
6/03/67	**96**	1	4 Only Love Can Break A Heart	London 108
			SLIM WHITMAN	
			Born Otis Whitman, Jr. on 1/20/24 in Tampa. Country balladeer and yodeller. Gained greatest fame with best-selling compilation albums sold exclusively over TV.	
9/16/57	**93**	3	1 I'll Take You Home Again Kathleen	Imperial 8310
			revival of Will Oakland's 1912 hit (POS 6)	
			MARVA WHITNEY	
6/14/69	**82**	4	1 It's My Thing (You Can't Tell Me Who To Sock It To)...	King 6229
			written and produced by James Brown	
			ROGER WHITTAKER	
			Born on 3/22/36 in Nairobi, Kenya. British MOR singer.	
4/05/75	**19**	15	1 The Last Farewell	RCA 50030
			THE WHO	
			Rock group formed in London, England in 1964. Consisted of Roger Daltrey (b: 3/1/44), lead singer; Pete Townshend (b: 5/19/45), guitar, vocals; John Entwistle (b: 10/9/44), bass; and Keith Moon (b: 8/23/47), drums. Originally known as the High Numbers in 1964. All but Moon had been in The Detours. Developed stage antics of destroying their instruments. Made rock opera "Tommy" in 1969, became a film in 1975. Solo work by members began in 1972. Moon died on 9/7/78 of a drug overdose, replaced by Kenney Jones. In films "The Kids Are Alright" and "Quadrophenia", 1979. Eleven fans trampled and died at their concert in Cincinnati, 12/3/79. Group's status is currently in limbo.	
3/27/65	**93**	2	1 I Can't Explain	Decca 31725
1/15/66	**74**	5	2 My Generation	Decca 31877
4/15/67	**24**	9	3 Happy Jack	Decca 32114
7/01/67	**51**	6	4 Pictures Of Lily	Decca 32156
10/14/67	**9**	11	5 **I Can See For Miles**	Decca 32206
3/30/68	**40**	8	6 Call Me Lightning	Decca 32288
8/10/68	**25**	9	7 Magic Bus	Decca 32362
4/05/69	**19**	11	8 Pinball Wizard	Decca 32465
7/19/69	**37**	8	9 I'm Free	Decca 32519
4/18/70	**44**	7	10 The Seeker	Decca 32670
7/11/70	**27**	9	11 Summertime Blues	Decca 32708
9/26/70	**12**	13	12 See Me, Feel Me	Decca 32729
			4-12: produced by Kit Lambert	
7/17/71	**15**	13	13 Won't Get Fooled Again	Decca 32846
			from the film "Lifehouse"	
11/06/71	**34**	11	14 Behind Blue Eyes	Decca 32888
7/22/72	**17**	10	15 Join Together	Decca 32983
12/09/72+	**39**	8	16 The Relay	Track 33041
12/01/73	**76**	5	17 Love, Reign O'er Me	Track 40152
2/02/74	**92**	3	18 The Real Me	Track 40182

DEBUT DATE	PEAK POS	WKS CHR	ARTIST — Record Title	Label & Number
			THE WHO — Cont'd	
11/29/75+	**16**	16	19 Squeeze Box	MCA 40475
8/26/78	**14**	15	20 Who Are You	MCA 40948
6/30/79	**54**	6	21 Long Live Rock from the film "The Kids Are Alright"	MCA 41053
9/29/79	**45**	7	22 5:15 from the film "Quadrophenia"	Polydor 2022
3/21/81	**18**	15	23 You Better You Bet	Warner 49698
6/27/81	**84**	4	24 Don't Let Go The Coat	Warner 49743
9/04/82	**28**	14	25 Athena	Warner 29905
12/25/82+	**68**	6	26 Eminence Front all of above written by Pete Townshend (except #11)	Warner 29814
			WHODINI New York rap duo: Jalil "Whodini" Hutchins and John Fletcher.	
1/05/85	**87**	3	1 Friends/	
		3	2 Five Minutes Of Funk	Jive 9276
			JANE WIEDLIN Born on 5/20/58 in Oconomowoc, Wisconsin. Rhythm guitarist of the Go-Go's.	
4/16/83	**49**	12	1 Cool Places **SPARKS & JANE WIEDLIN**	Atlantic 89866
9/28/85	**77**	9	2 Blue Kiss	I.R.S. 52674
			RUSTY WIER Country/rock singer from Austin, Texas.	
9/06/75	**82**	4	1 Don't It Make You Wanna Dance?	20th Century 2219
			HARLOW WILCOX & THE OAKIES	
10/11/69	**30**	12	1 Groovy Grubworm [I]	Plantation 28
			WILD BLUE Chicago pop quintet - Renee Varo, lead singer.	
5/17/86	**71**	6	1 Fire With Fire from the film of the same title	Chrysalis 42985
			THE WILD-CATS New Jersey rock and roll instrumental trio: Dennis Gorgas (guitar), Frank Rainey (organ) and Pat Piccininno (drums). Discovered by guitarist Billy Mure.	
1/05/59	**57**	8	1 Gazachstahagen [I]	United Art. 154
			WILD CHERRY White funk band formed in Steubenville, Ohio in 1976. Consisted of Bob Parissi (lead vocals, guitar), Bryan Bassett (guitar), Mark Avsec (keyboards), Allen Wentz (bass) and Ron Beitle (drums).	
6/19/76	**1**[3]	25	1 ▲**Play That Funky Music**	Epic 50225
1/15/77	**43**	7	2 Baby Don't You Know	Epic 50306
5/14/77	**95**	2	3 Hot To Trot	Epic 50362
9/03/77	**61**	6	4 Hold On	Epic 50401
2/25/78	**69**	8	5 I Love My Music all of above written & produced by Parissi	Epic 50500
			WILDFIRE Southern pop quartet - Jack Stack-A-Track, lead singer (a noted Nashville singer).	
6/18/77	**49**	7	1 Here Comes Summer	Casablanca 885
			THE WILDWEEDS Windsor, CT rock quintet featuring Al Anderson (lead singer - later in NRBQ).	
5/27/67	**88**	4	1 No Good To Cry	Cadet 5561
			JACK WILD British juvenile actor, born in 1952. Played "The Artful Dodger" in film "Oliver".	
5/30/70	**92**	4	1 Some Beautiful	Capitol 2742
			EUGENE WILDE Real name: Ron Broomfield. Black vocalist, songwriter. Member of the Miami-based family group Life.	
1/12/85	**83**	8	1 Gotta Get You Home Tonight	Philly W. 99710
12/07/85+	**76**	10	2 Don't Say No Tonight	Philly W. 99608
			KIM WILDE Born Kim Smith on 11/18/60 in Chiswick, England. Pop/rock singer. Daughter of Marty Wilde.	
5/22/82	**25**	18	1 Kids In America	EMI America 8110

DEBUT DATE	PEAK POS	WKS CHR	ARTIST — Record Title	Label & Number
			KIM WILDE — Cont'd	
1/19/85	**65**	7	2 Go For It	MCA 52513
			above 2 written by Marty and Kim's brother Ricky Wilde	
			MARTY WILDE	
			Born Reginald Smith on 4/15/39 in Greenwich, England. Also see Shannon.	
2/08/60	**45**	8	1 Bad Boy	Epic 9356
			MATTHEW WILDER	
			Born and raised in Manhattan; moved to Los Angeles in the late 70s. Singer, songwriter, keyboardist. Session singer for Rickie Lee Jones and Bette Midler.	
9/17/83+	**5**	29	1 **Break My Stride**	Private I 04113
2/18/84	**33**	13	2 The Kid's American	Private I 04363
9/22/84	**52**	9	3 Bouncin' Off The Walls	Private I 04617
			THE WILL-O-BEES	
2/03/68	**95**	3	1 It's Not Easy	Date 1583
			ANDRE WILLIAMS	
			Detroit R&B singer, songwriter, record producer.	
1/29/66	**94**	1	1 Rib Tip's (Part 1) [I]	Avin 103
7/29/67	**90**	2	2 Pearl Time	Sport 105
			ANDY WILLIAMS	
			Born Howard Andrew Williams on 12/3/28 in Wall Lake, Iowa. Formed quartet with his brothers and eventually moved to Los Angeles. With Bing Crosby on hit "Swingin' On A Star", 1944. With comedienne Kay Thompson in mid-40s. Went solo in 1952. On Steve Allen's "Tonight Show" from 1952-55. Own NBC-TV variety series, 1962-67; 1969-71. In film "I'd Rather Be Rich", 1964. One of America's greatest Pop/MOR singers.	
4/21/56	**54**	11	1 Walk Hand In Hand	Cadence 1288
8/11/56	**7**	22	2 **Canadian Sunset**	Cadence 1297
			Jockey #7 / Top 100 #8 / Juke Box #9 / Best Seller #10	
12/08/56	**33**	14	3 Baby Doll	Cadence 1303
			from the film of the same title	
2/23/57	**1**[3]	20	4 **Butterfly**	Cadence 1308
			Top 100 #1(3) / Jockey #1(2) / Juke Box #2 / Best Seller #4	
5/20/57	**8**	20	5 **I Like Your Kind Of Love**	Cadence 1323
			Jockey #8 / Top 100 #9 / Best Seller #10 / Juke Box #19 end female vocal by Peggy Powers	
9/23/57	**17**	13	6 Lips Of Wine	Cadence 1336
			Jockey #17 / Top 100 #39	
2/17/58	**3**	17	7 **Are You Sincere**	Cadence 1340
			Jockey #3 / Top 100 #10 / Best Seller #11	
8/25/58	**17**	12	8 Promise Me, Love	Cadence 1351
12/28/58+	**11**	20	9 The Hawaiian Wedding Song	Cadence 1358
			song written in 1926, with new lyrics added	
9/07/59	**5**	16	10 **Lonely Street**	Cadence 1370
12/14/59+	**7**	13	11 **The Village Of St. Bernadette**	Cadence 1374
3/21/60	**50**	8	12 Wake Me When It's Over	Cadence 1378
			from the film of the same title	
7/04/60	**70**	7	13 Do You Mind?	Cadence 1381
12/12/60+	**64**	7	14 You Don't Want My Love	Cadence 1389
4/24/61	**37**	10	15 The Bilbao Song	Cadence 1398
10/30/61	**64**	6	16 Danny Boy/	
			traditional Irish song written in 1855	
11/06/61	**82**	2	17 Fly By Night	Columbia 42199
3/24/62	**99**	1	18 The Wonderful World Of The Young	Columbia 42265
6/09/62	**38**	7	19 Stranger On The Shore	Columbia 42451
9/15/62	**39**	10	20 Don't You Believe It	Columbia 42523
12/08/62	**86**	3	21 Twilight Time	Cadence 1433
			revival of The Three Suns' 1944 hit (POS 14)	
3/02/63	**2**[4]	15	22 **Can't Get Used To Losing You/**	
3/16/63	**26**	12	23 Days Of Wine And Roses	Columbia 42674
			from the film of the same title	
6/22/63	**13**	11	24 Hopeless	Columbia 42784
1/11/64	**13**	10	25 A Fool Never Learns/	
1/18/64	**100**	1	26 Charade	Columbia 42950
			from the film of the same title	
4/18/64	**34**	9	27 Wrong For Each Other	Columbia 43015

DEBUT DATE	PEAK POS	WKS CHR	ARTIST — Record Title	Label & Number
			ANDY WILLIAMS — Cont'd	
9/12/64	**28**	8	28 On The Street Where You Live/ from the Broadway musical "My Fair Lady"	
11/14/64	**67**	5	29 Almost There from the film "I'd Rather Be Rich"	Columbia 43128
11/28/64+	**24**	11	30 Dear Heart from the film of the same title	Columbia 43180
4/03/65	**36**	7	31 And Roses And Roses	Columbia 43257
9/04/65	**40**	7	32 Ain't It True	Columbia 43358
12/04/65	**92**	3	33 Quiet Nights Of Quiet Stars	Columbia 43456
8/27/66	**49**	8	34 In The Arms Of Love all of above produced by Robert Mersey (except #21)	Columbia 43737
3/25/67	**34**	8	35 Music To Watch Girls By	Columbia 44065
7/08/67	**88**	4	36 More And More	Columbia 44202
6/08/68	**75**	6	37 Sweet Memories	Columbia 44527
10/19/68	**33**	13	38 Battle Hymn Of The Republic backed by St. Charles Borromeo Choir; recorded at St. Patrick's Cathedral on 6/8/68 as a eulogy to Senator Robert F. Kennedy	Columbia 44650
4/12/69	**22**	11	39 Happy Heart	Columbia 44818
2/28/70	**88**	3	40 Can't Help Falling In Love	Columbia 45094
6/27/70	**77**	4	41 One Day Of Your Life	Columbia 45175
2/06/71	**9**	13	42 **(Where Do I Begin) Love Story** from the film "Love Story"	Columbia 45317
8/21/71	**82**	4	43 A Song For You	Columbia 45434
4/08/72	**34**	11	44 Love Theme From "The Godfather" (Speak Softly Love) from the film of the same title	Columbia 45579
1/17/76	**72**	6	45 Tell It Like It Is	Columbia 10263
			ANDY & DAVID WILLIAMS Andy Williams' 14-year-old twin nephews. Re-emerged in 1987 as the Williams Bros.	
6/22/74	**92**	4	1 What's Your Name	Barnaby 601
			ANSON WILLIAMS Raised in Burbank - Potsie Weber of TV's "Happy Days".	
4/02/77	**93**	4	1 Deeply	Chelsea 3061
			BILLY WILLIAMS Born on 12/28/10 in Waco, Texas; died on 10/17/72 in Chicago. Lead singer of The Charioteers from 1930-50. Formed own Billy Williams Quartet with Eugene Dixon, Claude Riddick and John Ball in 1950. Many appearances on TV, especially "Your Show Of Shows" with Sid Caesar. By early 60s, had lost voice due to diabetes. Moved to Chicago and worked as social worker until his death.	
4/07/56	**49**	10	1 A Crazy Little Palace (That's My Home) **BILLY WILLIAMS QUARTET**	Coral 61576
3/23/57	**50**	4	2 The Pied Piper	Coral 61795
6/03/57	**3**	23	3 **I'm Gonna Sit Right Down And Write Myself A Letter/** Jockey #3 / Top 100 #6 / Best Seller #7 revival of Fats Waller's 1935 hit (POS 5)	
		5	4 Date With The Blues Best Seller flip	Coral 61830
11/11/57	**78**	4	5 Got A Date With An Angel revival of the Debroy Somers Band's 1932 hit (POS 13)	Coral 61886
3/17/58	**78**	2	6 Baby, Baby **BILLY WILLIAMS QUARTET**	Coral 61932
7/28/58	**87**	2	7 I'll Get By (As Long As I Have You) 3 versions hit the Top 20 in 1929	Coral 61999
1/12/59	**39**	12	8 Nola instrumental hit by bandleader Vincent Lopez in 1922 (POS 3)	Coral 62069
4/20/59	**75**	1	9 Goodnight Irene 5 versions hit the Top 10 in 1950 all of above conducted by Dick Jacobs (except #2)	Coral 62101
			DANNY WILLIAMS Born in Port Elizabeth, South Africa. Moved to England as a youngster.	
3/07/64	**9**	14	1 **White On White**	United Art. 685
6/20/64	**84**	4	2 A Little Toy Balloon	United Art. 729

DEBUT DATE	PEAK POS	WKS CHR	ARTIST — Record Title		Label & Number
			DENIECE WILLIAMS		
			Born Deniece Chandler on 6/3/51 in Gary, Indiana. Soul vocalist, songwriter. Recorded for Toddlin' Town, early 60s. Member of Wonderlove, Stevie Wonder's back-up group, 1972-75.		
12/11/76+	**25**	20	1 Free		Columbia 10429
4/01/78	**1^{1}**	18	2● **Too Much, Too Little, Too Late**		Columbia 10693
7/29/78	**47**	8	3 You're All I Need To Get By		Columbia 10772
			above 2: **JOHNNY MATHIS/DENIECE WILLIAMS**		
8/18/79	**73**	5	4 I've Got The Next Dance		ARC 10971
8/15/81	**53**	10	5 Silly		ARC 02406
4/03/82	**10**	17	6 **It's Gonna Take A Miracle**		ARC 02812
4/07/84	**1^{2}**	19	7● **Let's Hear It For The Boy**		Columbia 04417
			from the film "Footloose"		
8/11/84	**81**	4	8 Next Love		Columbia 04537
			DIANA WILLIAMS		
			Nashville-born country singer.		
9/04/76	**66**	6	1 Teddy Bear's Last Ride	[S]	Capitol 4317
			answer song to Red Sovine's hit "Teddy Bear"		
			DON WILLIAMS		
			Born on 5/27/39 in Floydada, Texas. Country singer, songwriter, guitarist. Charted over 15 #1 country hits. Leader of the Pozo-Seco Singers. In films "W.W. & The Dixie Dancekings" and "Smokey & The Bandit II".		
9/27/80	**24**	20	1 I Believe In You		MCA 41304
			HANK WILLIAMS, JR.		
			Born Randall Hank Williams, Jr. on 5/26/49 in Shreveport, LA; raised in Nashville. Country singer, songwriter, guitarist. Son of country music's first superstar, Hank Williams.		
2/01/64	**67**	9	1 Long Gone Lonesome Blues		MGM 13208
			#1 hit in 1950 for Hank, Sr. on the C&W charts		
12/05/64	**90**	4	2 Endless Sleep		MGM 13278
			JOHN WILLIAMS		
			Born on 2/8/32 in New York City. Noted composer/conductor of many top box-office film hits. Succeeded Arthur Fiedler as conductor of the Boston Pops in 1980.		
8/09/75	**32**	10	1 Theme From 'Jaws' (Main Title)	[I]	MCA 40439
7/09/77	**10**	17	2 **Star Wars (Main Title)**	[I]	20th Century 2345
12/24/77+	**13**	14	3 Theme From "Close Encounters Of The Third Kind"	[I]	Arista 0300
1/27/79	**81**	4	4 Theme From Superman (Main Title)	[I]	Warner 8729
			2 & 4: performed by the London Symphony Orchestra all of above from soundtracks composed by Williams		
			JOHNNY WILLIAMS		
			Born on 1/15/42 in Tyler, AL. Soul singer. To Chicago at age 14. Died in 1987.		
1/06/73	**78**	7	1 Slow Motion (Part 1)		Phil. Int. 3518
			LARRY WILLIAMS		
			Born on 5/10/35 in New Orleans; committed suicide on 1/7/80 in Los Angeles. R&B/rock and roll singer, songwriter, pianist. With Lloyd Price in early 50s. Convicted of narcotics dealing in 1960, jail term interrupted his career.		
6/24/57	**5**	21	1 **Short Fat Fannie/**		
			Best Seller #5 / Top 100 #6 / Jockey #15		
		5	2 High School Dance		Specialty 608
			Best Seller flip		
11/11/57	**14**	18	3 Bony Moronie/		
			Best Seller #14 / Top 100 #18		
11/11/57	**45**	11	4 You Bug Me, Baby		Specialty 615
4/14/58	**69**	4	5 Dizzy, Miss Lizzy		Specialty 626
2/25/67	**96**	4	6 Mercy, Mercy, Mercy		Okeh 7274
			LARRY WILLIAMS & JOHNNY WATSON		
			MASON WILLIAMS		
			Born on 8/24/38 in Abilene, Texas. Folk guitarist, songwriter, author. Wrote for the Smothers Brothers TV show.		
6/22/68	**2^{2}**	14	1 **Classical Gas**	[I]	Warner 7190
10/12/68	**96**	2	2 Baroque-A-Nova	[I]	Warner 7235
2/01/69	**99**	1	3 Saturday Night At The World		Warner 7248
4/26/69	**90**	2	4 Greensleeves	[I]	Warner 7272
			one of the oldest published songs (from the 16th century)		

DEBUT DATE	PEAK POS	WKS CHR	ARTIST — Record Title	Label & Number
			MAURICE WILLIAMS & THE ZODIACS	
			R&B vocal group from Lancaster, SC, led by pianist-songwriter Maurice Williams. Originally recorded as The Gladiolas, became The Zodiacs in 1959. Williams re-formed group with Wiley Bennett, Henry Gaston, Charles Thomas, Albert Hill, and Little Willie Morrow in 1960. Also see The Gladiolas.	
10/03/60	**1**[1]	18	1 **Stay**	Herald 552
1/16/61	**86**	3	2 I Remember	Herald 556
4/10/61	**83**	2	3 Come Along	Herald 559
			MIKE WILLIAMS	
7/09/66	**69**	5	1 Lonely Soldier	Atlantic 2339
			OTIS WILLIAMS - see CHARMS	
			PAUL WILLIAMS	
			Born on 9/19/40 in Omaha. Songwriter, singer, actor. Wrote "We've Only Just Begun" and "Rainy Days & Mondays" with partner Roger Nichols, and wrote "Evergreen" with Barbra Streisand. In films "Planet Of The Apes", "Smokey & The Bandit" and others.	
2/19/72	**60**	9	1 Waking Up Alone	A&M 1325
			ROGER WILLIAMS	
			Born Louis Weertz in 1925 in Omaha. Learned to play the piano by age 3. Educated at Drake University, Idaho State University, and Juilliard School of Music. Took lessons from Lenny Tristano and Teddy Wilson. Win on Arthur Godfrey's "Talent Scouts" led to recording contract.	
8/20/55	**1**[4]	26	1 **Autumn Leaves** [I] Best Seller #1 / Top 100 #2 pre / Juke Box #2 / Jockey #3	Kapp 116
12/10/55+	**38**	10	2 Wanting You [I] from the 1928 musical "The New Moon"	Kapp 127
3/03/56	**37**	9	3 La Mer (Beyond The Sea) [I] revival of Benny Goodman's 1948 hit (POS 26)	Kapp 138
5/26/56	**85**	3	4 Hi-Lili Hi-Lo [I] revival of Lesli Caron & Mel Ferrer's 1953 hit (POS 30)	Kapp 144
8/25/56	**60**	8	5 Tumbling Tumbleweeds [I] new version of Gene Autry's #10 hit in 1935	Kapp 156
11/10/56	**41**	12	6 Two Different Worlds **ROGER WILLIAMS & JANE MORGAN**	Kapp 161
3/02/57	**15**	20	7 Almost Paradise [I] Jockey #15 / Best Seller #22 / Top 100 #26	Kapp 175
10/28/57	**22**	17	8 Till Jockey #22 / Top 100 #27 / Best Seller #28	Kapp 197
4/14/58	**55**	8	9 Arrivederci, Roma	Kapp 210
8/18/58	**10**	17	10 **Near You** [I] Hot 100 #10 / Best Seller #16 end #1 for 17 weeks in 1947 for Francis Craig	Kapp 233
12/08/58	**71**	3	11 The World Outside based on the "Warsaw Concerto"	Kapp 246
6/06/60	**98**	1	12 La Montana (If She Should Come To You) [I]	Kapp 331
9/26/60	**56**	6	13 Temptation [I] revival of Bing Crosby's 1934 hit (POS 3)	Kapp 347
12/11/61+	**48**	8	14 Maria [I] from the Broadway musical "West Side Story"	Kapp 437
3/10/62	**88**	4	15 Amor [I] 3 versions hit the Top 10 in 1944	Kapp 447
4/10/65	**97**	2	16 Try To Remember from the Broadway musical "The Fantasticks"	Kapp 48
10/16/65	**92**	3	17 Autumn Leaves - 1965 new version of 1955 hit	Kapp 707
6/25/66	**65**	6	18 Lara's Theme [I] from the film "Dr. Zhivago"	Kapp 738
8/27/66	**7**	21	19 **Born Free** from the film of the same title	Kapp 767
1/28/67	**84**	5	20 Sunrise, Sunset from the Broadway musical "Fiddler On The Roof"	Kapp 801
5/06/67	**60**	5	21 Love Me Forever	Kapp 821
7/13/68	**55**	7	22 The Impossible Dream [I] from the Broadway musical "Man Of La Mancha"	Kapp 907
6/07/69	**99**	2	23 Galveston [I] 14-22: conducted by Ralph Carmichael	Kapp 2007
			WILLIS "THE GUARD" & VIGORISH	
			Gary Buckner and Jerry Garcia - also see Buckner & Garcia.	
12/27/80	**82**	3	1 Merry Christmas In The NFL [N-X]	Handshake 5308

DEBUT DATE	PEAK POS	WKS CHR	ARTIST — Record Title	Label & Number
			CHUCK WILLIS	
			Born on 1/31/28 in Atlanta; died on 4/10/58 (peritonitis). R&B singer, songwriter.	
4/20/57	**12**	26	1 C. C. Rider	Atlantic 1130
			Top 100 #12 / Best Seller #13	
			inspired the "Stroll" dance craze	
2/03/58	**33**	11	2 Betty And Dupree	Atlantic 1168
			Best Seller #33 / Top 100 #33	
4/28/58	**9**	19	3 **What Am I Living For/**	
			Jockey #9 / Best Seller #15 / Top 100 #15	
4/28/58	**24**	12	4 Hang Up My Rock And Roll Shoes	Atlantic 1179
8/18/58	**46**	5	5 My Life	Atlantic 1192
			Best Seller #46 / Hot 100 #56	
			WILLOWS	
			New York R&B doo-wop group formed in 1952 as the Five Willows. Tony Middleton, lead singer.	
4/07/56	**62**	11	1 Church Bells May Ring	Melba 102
			chimes played by Neil Sedaka	
			WILMER & THE DUKES	
			R&B/rock quintet led by Wilmer Alexander, Jr.	
7/20/68	**80**	6	1 Give Me One More Chance	Aphrodisiac 260
			WILSON BROS.	
			Pop duo: Steve and Kelly Wilson.	
10/06/79	**94**	2	1 Another Night	Atco 7205
			AL WILSON	
			Born on 6/19/39 in Meridian, MS. Soul singer, drummer. Moved to San Bernadino, late 50s. Member of The Rollers from 1960-62.	
8/17/68	**27**	10	1 The Snake	Soul City 767
1/18/69	**75**	4	2 Poor Side Of Town	Soul City 771
8/23/69	**67**	7	3 Lodi	Soul City 775
			above 3 produced by Johnny Rivers (owned Soul City Records)	
10/20/73+	**1**[1]	22	4● **Show And Tell**	Rocky Road 30073
3/09/74	**57**	9	5 Touch And Go	Rocky Road 30076
10/05/74	**30**	10	6 La La Peace Song	Rocky Road 30200
1/11/75	**70**	7	7 I Won't Last A Day Without You/Let Me Be The One	Rocky Road 30202
3/27/76	**29**	10	8 I've Got A Feeling (We'll Be Seeing Each Other Again)	Playboy 6062
			ANN WILSON	
			Born on 6/19/51 in San Diego. Lead singer of the rock group Heart.	
5/12/84	**7**	20	1 **Almost Paradise...Love Theme From Footloose**	Columbia 04418
			MIKE RENO & ANN WILSON	
			from the film "Footloose"	
11/29/86+	**61**	12	2 The Best Man In The World	Capitol 5654
			from the film "The Golden Child"	
			BRIAN WILSON	
			Born on 6/20/42 in Hawthorne, California. Leader of The Beach Boys.	
3/26/66	**32**	7	1 Caroline, No	Capitol 5610
			CARL WILSON	
			Born on 6/21/46 in Hawthorne, California. Guitarist of The Beach Boys.	
5/14/83	**72**	6	1 What You Do To Me	Caribou 03590
			HANK WILSON - see LEON RUSSELL	
			J. FRANK WILSON & THE CAVALIERS	
			J. Frank was born in 1941 in Lufkin, Texas. Band formed in San Angelo, Texas. The Cavaliers: Phil Trungo, Jerry Graham, Bobby Woods and George Croyle.	
9/05/64	**2**[1]	15	1 **Last Kiss**	Josie 923
11/28/64	**85**	2	2 Hey Little One	Josie 926
12/22/73+	**92**	5	3 Last Kiss [R]	Virgo 506
			JACKIE WILSON	
			Born on 6/9/34 in Detroit; died on 1/21/84. Worked solo until 1953, then joined Billy Ward's Dominoes as Clyde McPhatter's replacement. Solo since 1957. Career waned by 1964. Collapsed from a stroke on stage at the Latin Casino in Camden, New Jersey on 9/25/75 and spent the rest of his life in hospitals.	
11/04/57	**62**	10	1 Reet Petite (The Finest Girl You Ever Want To Meet)	Brunswick 55024
4/14/58	**22**	16	2 To Be Loved	Brunswick 55052
			Top 100 #22 / Best Seller #23	
9/22/58	**93**	2	3 We Have Love	Brunswick 55086

DEBUT DATE	PEAK POS	WKS CHR	ARTIST — Record Title	Label & Number
			JACKIE WILSON — Cont'd	
11/24/58+	**7**	21	4 **Lonely Teardrops**	Brunswick 55105
3/23/59	**13**	13	5 That's Why (I Love You So)	Brunswick 55121
6/22/59	**20**	12	6 I'll Be Satisfied above 6 written by Berry Gordy, Jr. & Tyran Carlo	Brunswick 55136
9/07/59	**37**	10	7 You Better Know It from the film "Go Johnny Go"	Brunswick 55149
11/23/59+	**34**	12	8 Talk That Talk	Brunswick 55165
3/21/60	**4**	17	9 **Night/**	
4/04/60	**15**	16	10 Doggin' Around	Brunswick 55166
7/11/60	**12**	13	11 (You Were Made For) All My Love/	
7/11/60	**15**	12	12 A Woman, A Lover, A Friend	Brunswick 55167
10/10/60	**8**	15	13 **Alone At Last/** based on Tchaikovsky's "Piano Concerto in B Flat"	
10/24/60	**32**	10	14 Am I The Man	Brunswick 55170
1/09/61	**9**	9	15 **My Empty Arms/**	
1/23/61	**44**	7	16 The Tear Of The Year	Brunswick 55201
3/13/61	**20**	8	17 Please Tell Me Why/	
3/13/61	**40**	6	18 Your One And Only Love	Brunswick 55208
6/12/61	**19**	8	19 I'm Comin' On Back To You/	
6/12/61	**80**	1	20 Lonely Life	Brunswick 55216
8/21/61	**37**	6	21 Years From Now/	
10/02/61	**79**	3	22 You Don't Know What It Means	Brunswick 55219
10/23/61	**58**	6	23 The Way I Am/	
10/23/61	**65**	6	24 My Heart Belongs To Only You	Brunswick 55220
1/13/62	**34**	9	25 The Greatest Hurt/	
1/20/62	**75**	3	26 There'll Be No Next Time	Brunswick 55221
4/21/62	**93**	1	27 I Found Love JACKIE WILSON & LINDA HOPKINS	Brunswick 55224
4/28/62	**58**	6	28 Hearts	Brunswick 55225
7/07/62	**70**	4	29 I Just Can't Help It	Brunswick 55229
9/22/62	**82**	4	30 Forever And A Day	Brunswick 55233
3/09/63	**5**	12	31 **Baby Workout**	Brunswick 55239
5/25/63	**42**	7	32 Shake A Hand JACKIE WILSON & LINDA HOPKINS	Brunswick 55243
7/13/63	**33**	8	33 Shake! Shake! Shake!	Brunswick 55246
9/21/63	**61**	5	34 Baby Get It (And Don't Quit It) 1, 3-22, 27-31 & 34: orchestra directed by Dick Jacobs	Brunswick 55250
5/23/64	**94**	1	35 Big Boss Line	Brunswick 55266
8/22/64	**89**	2	36 Squeeze Her-Tease Her (But Love Her)	Brunswick 55269
2/27/65	**94**	3	37 Danny Boy traditional Irish song written in 1855	Brunswick 55277
7/03/65	**59**	10	38 No Pity (In The Naked City) 22, 27, 29, 31, 34-36, 38: written by Jackie Wilson/Alonzo Tucker	Brunswick 55280
10/23/65	**96**	2	39 I Believe I'll Love On	Brunswick 55283
1/15/66	**93**	1	40 Think Twice JACKIE WILSON & LaVERN BAKER	Brunswick 55287
10/15/66	**11**	12	41 Whispers (Gettin' Louder)	Brunswick 55300
2/11/67	**91**	3	42 Just Be Sincere/	
3/04/67	**84**	3	43 I Don't Want To Lose You	Brunswick 55309
5/06/67	**82**	4	44 I've Lost You	Brunswick 55321
8/12/67	**6**	12	45 **(Your Love Keeps Lifting Me) Higher And Higher**	Brunswick 55336
11/25/67	**32**	6	46 Since You Showed Me How To Be Happy	Brunswick 55354
2/17/68	**49**	7	47 For Your Precious Love	Brunswick 55365
4/27/68	**84**	5	48 Chain Gang above 2: JACKIE WILSON & COUNT BASIE	Brunswick 55373
7/20/68	**34**	8	49 I Get The Sweetest Feeling	Brunswick 55381
11/02/68	**70**	3	50 For Once In My Life	Brunswick 55392
5/16/70	**91**	2	51 Let This Be A Letter (To My Baby)	Brunswick 55435
12/19/70+	**56**	11	52 (I Can Feel Those Vibrations) This Love Is Real	Brunswick 55443
11/27/71	**95**	3	53 Love Is Funny That Way	Brunswick 55461
2/26/72	**93**	3	54 You Got Me Walking	Brunswick 55467

DEBUT DATE	PEAK POS	WKS CHR	ARTIST — Record Title	Label & Number
			MERI WILSON	
			Dallas-based song stylist.	
6/04/77	**18**	16	1 ● Telephone Man [N]	GRT 127
			NANCY WILSON	
			Born on 2/20/37 in Chillicothe, Ohio. Jazz stylist with Rusty Bryant's Carolyn Club Band in Columbus. First recorded for Dot in 1956.	
8/24/63	**73**	6	1 Tell Me The Truth	Capitol 4991
6/27/64	**11**	11	2 (You Don't Know) How Glad I Am	Capitol 5198
10/03/64	**57**	5	3 I Wanna Be With You	Capitol 5254
			from the Broadway musical "Golden Boy"	
1/30/65	**58**	5	4 Don't Come Running Back To Me	Capitol 5340
7/16/66	**84**	4	5 Uptight (Everything's Alright)	Capitol 5673
5/11/68	**29**	14	6 Face It Girl, It's Over	Capitol 2136
9/28/68	**55**	7	7 Peace Of Mind	Capitol 2283
11/22/69	**52**	10	8 Can't Take My Eyes Off You	Capitol 2644
			2-8: produced by David Cavanaugh	
1/02/71	**93**	3	9 Now I'm A Woman	Capitol 2934
			PHILL WILSON	
7/10/61	**91**	2	1 Wishin' On A Rainbow	Huron 22000
			WILTON PLACE STREET BAND	
			Los Angeles studio project produced and arranged by Trevor Lawrence (resided on Wilton Place in Los Angeles).	
1/08/77	**24**	17	1 Disco Lucy (I Love Lucy Theme) [I]	Island 078
			discofied theme from the TV series "I Love Lucy"	
			JESSE WINCHESTER	
			Born on 5/17/44 in Shreveport, Louisiana. Pop/MOR singer, songwriter, guitarist. Became Canadian in 1973.	
8/20/77	**86**	3	1 Nothing But A Breeze	Bearsville 0318
4/25/81	**32**	12	2 Say What	Bearsville 49711
			WIND	
			New York studio group featuring Tony Orlando as lead singer.	
9/06/69	**28**	9	1 Make Believe	Life 200
			KAI WINDING	
			Born on 5/18/22 in Aarhus, Denmark; died on 5/6/83. Jazz trombonist. With Benny Goodman and Stan Kenton in the mid-40s.	
7/06/63	**8**	15	1 **More** [I]	Verve 10295
			theme from the film "Mondo Cane"	
			THE WING & A PRAYER FIFE & DRUM CORPS.	
			New York City big band studio assemblage.	
11/15/75+	**14**	20	1 Baby Face	Wing & Prayer 103
			4 versions hit the Top 10 in 1926	
			PETE WINGFIELD	
			Keyboard player from England. Worked with Freddie King, Jimmy Witherspoon and Van Morrison. In Olympic Runners band.	
8/23/75	**15**	19	1 Eighteen With A Bullet	Island 026
			hit #18 with a bullet on the 11/22/75 "Hot 100" chart	
			WINGS - see PAUL McCARTNEY	
			THE WINSTONS	
			Washington, DC soul septet featuring lead singer Richard Spencer.	
5/24/69	**7**	13	1 ● **Color Him Father**	Metromedia 117
9/20/69	**54**	6	2 Love Of The Common People	Metromedia 142
			EDGAR WINTER	
			Born on 12/28/46 in Beaumont, Texas. Rock singer, keyboardist, saxophonist. Younger brother of Johnny Winter. Group included Rick Derringer and Dan Hartman, 1972-75.	
			EDGAR WINTER'S WHITE TRASH:	
12/18/71+	**70**	11	1 Keep Playin' That Rock 'N' Roll	Epic 10788
5/06/72	**81**	4	2 I Can't Turn You Loose	Epic 10855
			THE EDGAR WINTER GROUP:	
3/10/73	**1**[1]	20	3 ● **Frankenstein** [I]	Epic 10967
			featuring lead guitar work by Ronnie Montrose	
8/11/73	**14**	15	4 Free Ride	Epic 11024
12/15/73+	**65**	7	5 Hangin' Around	Epic 11069
			EDGAR WINTER:	

DEBUT DATE	PEAK POS	WKS CHR	ARTIST — Record Title		Label & Number
			EDGAR WINTER — Cont'd		
7/20/74	**33**	9	6 River's Risin'		Epic 11143
			THE EDGAR WINTER GROUP:		
10/26/74	**83**	4	7 Easy Street		Epic 50034
			all of above produced by Rick Derringer		
			JOHNNY WINTER		
			Born on 2/23/44 in Leland, Mississippi. Blues-rock guitarist, vocalist. Both Johnny and brother Edgar are albinos.		
1/10/70	**92**	3	1 Johnny B. Goode		Columbia 45058
5/01/71	**89**	2	2 Jumpin' Jack Flash		Columbia 45368
			HUGO WINTERHALTER		
			Born on 8/15/09 in Wilkes-Barre, Pennsylvania; died on 9/17/73 (cancer). Conductor/arranger for RCA Records from 1950-63.		
1/28/56	**62**	5	1 Memories Of You		RCA 6339
			from the film "The Benny Goodman Story"		
			revival of Louis Armstrong's 1930 hit (POS 18)		
4/07/56	**41**	3	2 The Little Musicians	[I]	RCA 6459
6/23/56	**2**[2]	31	3 **Canadian Sunset**	[I]	RCA 6537
			Top 100 #2 / Jockey #2 / Best Seller #3 / Juke Box #3		
			HUGO WINTERHALTER with EDDIE HEYWOOD		
			RUBY WINTERS		
			Born in Louisville; raised in Cincinnati. Soul vocalist.		
4/15/67	**96**	1	1 Make Love To Me		Diamond 218
			JOHNNY THUNDER & RUBY WINTERS		
2/15/69	**97**	2	2 I Don't Want To Cry		Diamond 255
12/27/69	**99**	2	3 Guess Who		Diamond 269
			STEVE WINWOOD		
			Born on 5/12/48 in Birmingham, England. Rock singer, keyboardist, synthesizer player, guitarist. Lead singer of The Spencer Davis Group, Blind Faith and Traffic.		
2/07/81	**7**	18	1 **While You See A Chance**		Island 49656
5/09/81	**48**	9	2 Arc Of A Diver		Island 49726
8/07/82	**47**	10	3 Still In The Game		Island 29940
11/13/82	**70**	4	4 Valerie		Island 29879
6/14/86	**1**[1]	22	5 **Higher Love**		Island 28710
9/27/86	**20**	15	6 Freedom Overspill		Island 28595
			WITCH QUEEN		
			Studio disco project produced by Peter Alves & Gino Soccio.		
4/28/79	**68**	6	1 Bang A Gong		Roadshow 11551
			BILL WITHERS		
			Born on 7/4/38 in Slab Fork, WV. Black vocalist, guitarist, composer. Moved to California in 1967 and made demo records of his songs. First recorded for Sussex in 1970, produced by Booker T. Jones. Made professional singing debut on 6/26/71. Married to actress Denise Nicholas.		
7/17/71	**3**	16	1 ● **Ain't No Sunshine**		Sussex 219
10/30/71	**42**	8	2 Grandma's Hands		Sussex 227
			above 2 produced by Booker T. Jones		
4/22/72	**1**[3]	19	3 ● **Lean On Me**		Sussex 235
8/26/72	**2**[2]	12	4 ● **Use Me**		Sussex 241
12/09/72+	**47**	6	5 Let Us Love		Sussex 247
2/03/73	**31**	10	6 Kissing My Love		Sussex 250
7/07/73	**80**	5	7 Friend Of Mine		Sussex 257
4/13/74	**50**	13	8 The Same Love That Made Me Laugh		Sussex 513
12/28/74+	**89**	4	9 Heartbreak Road		Sussex 629
12/20/75+	**76**	8	10 Make Love To Your Mind		Columbia 10255
12/10/77+	**30**	12	11 Lovely Day		Columbia 10627
			all of above written by Withers (except #9)		
2/14/81	**2**[3]	24	12 **Just The Two Of Us**		Elektra 47103
			GROVER WASHINGTON, JR. with BILL WITHERS		
9/01/84	**58**	10	13 In The Name Of Love		Polydor 881221
			RALPH MacDONALD with BILL WITHERS		
			JIMMY WITHERSPOON		
			Born on 8/8/23 in Gurdon, Arkansas. Legendary blues singer.		
3/06/65	**98**	1	1 You're Next		Prestige 341

DEBUT DATE	PEAK POS	WKS CHR	ARTIST — Record Title	Label & Number
			JIMMY WITTER	
5/01/61	**89**	4	1 A Cross Stands Alone	United Art. 301
			CHARLES WOLCOTT	
			Born on 9/29/06 in Flint, Michigan. Pianist, composer, arranger. With Paul Whiteman, Andre Kostelanetz and Jean Goldkette bands. Music director with MGM studios from 1950-60.	
10/31/60	**41**	7	1 Ruby Duby Du [I] from the film "Key Witness"	MGM 12944
			WOLF	
			Real name: Bill Wolfer. Plays keyboards, synthesizer and vocorder.	
12/11/82+	**55**	9	1 Papa Was A Rollin' Stone	Constell. 69849
			PETER WOLF	
			Born Peter Blankfield on 3/7/46 in the Bronx. Lead singer of The J. Geils Band until 1983.	
7/14/84	**12**	14	1 Lights Out	EMI America 8208
10/13/84	**36**	13	2 I Need You Tonight	EMI America 8241
4/27/85	**61**	5	3 Oo-Ee-Diddley-Bop!	EMI America 8854
			WOLFMAN JACK - see GUESS WHO and STAMPEDERS	
			BOBBY WOMACK	
			Born on 3/4/44 in Cleveland. Soul vocalist, guitarist, songwriter. Sang in family gospel group, the Womack Brothers. Group recorded for Sar as The Valentinos and The Lovers, 1962-64. Toured as guitarist with Sam Cooke. Solo recording for Him label in 1965. Back-up guitarist on many sessions, including Wilson Pickett Box Tops, Joe Tex, Aretha Franklin and Janis Joplin. Married for a time to Sam Cooke's widow.	
8/17/68	**52**	13	1 Fly Me To The Moon	Minit 32048
12/07/68+	**43**	9	2 California Dreamin'	Minit 32055
12/13/69	**93**	2	3 How I Miss You Baby	Minit 32081
4/25/70	**90**	4	4 More Than I Can Stand	Minit 32093
12/11/71+	**27**	13	5 That's The Way I Feel About Cha	United Art. 50847
5/06/72	**60**	9	6 Woman's Gotta Have It	United Art. 50902
8/26/72	**51**	9	7 Sweet Caroline (Good Times Never Seemed So Good)/	
12/09/72+	**31**	12	8● Harry Hippie	United Art. 50946
3/24/73	**56**	6	9 Across 110th Street from the film of the same title 5, 8-9: with backing group, Peace	United Art. 196
6/16/73	**29**	15	10 Nobody Wants You When You're Down And Out	United Art. 255
2/02/74	**10**	17	11● **Lookin' For A Love**	United Art. 375
7/06/74	**59**	7	12 You're Welcome, Stop On By	United Art. 439
4/12/75	**91**	3	13 Check It Out	United Art. 621
3/24/84	**88**	5	14 Love Has Finally Come At Last **BOBBY WOMACK & PATTI LaBELLE**	Beverly Glen 2012
			THE WOMBLES	
			British studio group - creation of writer/producer/arranger Mike Batt.	
8/03/74	**55**	7	1 Wombling Summer Party	Columbia 10013
			THE WOMENFOLK	
			Pasadena female folk quintet.	
4/18/64	**83**	3	1 Little Boxes the shortest record (1:02) of the rock era	RCA 8301
			THE WONDER BAND	
			Disco studio group.	
3/03/79	**87**	2	1 Whole Lotta Love available only as a 12" single	Atco 4719
			THE WONDER WHO? - see THE 4 SEASONS	
			STEVIE WONDER	
			Born Steveland Morris on 5/13/50 in Saginaw, Michigan. Singer, songwriter, multi-instrumentalist, producer. Blind since birth. Signed to Motown in 1960, did back-up work. First recorded in 1962, as "Little Stevie Wonder". Married to Syreeta Wright from 1970-72. Near-fatal auto accident on 8/6/73. Winner of 16 Grammy Awards. In films "Bikini Beach" and "Muscle Beach Party". **LITTLE STEVIE WONDER:**	
6/22/63	**1**[3]	15	1 **Fingertips - Pt 2**	Tamla 54080
10/05/63	**33**	6	2 Workout Stevie, Workout	Tamla 54086

DEBUT DATE	PEAK POS	WKS CHR	ARTIST — Record Title		Label & Number
			STEVIE WONDER — Cont'd		
2/29/64	**52**	9	3 Castles In The Sand		Tamla 54090
			STEVIE WONDER:		
6/13/64	**29**	8	4 Hey Harmonica Man		Tamla 54096
8/28/65	**59**	7	5 High Heel Sneakers		Tamla 54119
12/18/65+	**3**	14	6 **Uptight (Everything's Alright)**		Tamla 54124
4/16/66	**20**	7	7 Nothing's Too Good For My Baby		Tamla 54130
7/23/66	**9**	10	8 **Blowin In The Wind**		Tamla 54136
11/12/66	**9**	11	9 **A Place In The Sun**		Tamla 54139
3/04/67	**32**	7	10 Travlin' Man/		
4/22/67	**90**	6	11 Hey Love		Tamla 54147
6/10/67	**2**[2]	15	12 **I Was Made To Love Her**		Tamla 54151
10/07/67	**12**	8	13 I'm Wondering		Tamla 54157
4/06/68	**9**	13	14 **Shoo-Be-Doo-Be-Doo-Da-Day**		Tamla 54165
7/20/68	**35**	7	15 You Met Your Match		Tamla 54168
10/05/68	**66**	6	16 Alfie	[I]	Gordy 7076
			EIVETS REDNOW (Stevie Wonder spelled backwards)		
11/02/68	**2**[2]	14	17 **For Once In My Life**		Tamla 54174
2/15/69	**39**	7	18 I Don't Know Why/		
5/31/69	**4**	14	19 **My Cherie Amour**		Tamla 54180
10/18/69	**7**	14	20 **Yester-Me, Yester-You, Yesterday**		Tamla 54188
2/07/70	**26**	7	21 Never Had A Dream Come True		Tamla 54191
6/27/70	**3**	14	22 **Signed, Sealed, Delivered I'm Yours**		Tamla 54196
10/17/70	**9**	11	23 **Heaven Help Us All**		Tamla 54200
3/13/71	**13**	11	24 We Can Work It Out/		
6/19/71	**78**	4	25 Never Dreamed You'd Leave In Summer		Tamla 54202
8/14/71	**8**	14	26 **If You Really Love Me**		Tamla 54208
			above 2 written by Wonder & Syreeta Wright		
5/20/72	**33**	11	27 Superwoman (Where Were You When I Needed You)		Tamla 54216
9/16/72	**90**	3	28 Keep On Running		Tamla 54223
11/18/72+	**1**[1]	16	29 **Superstition**		Tamla 54226
3/17/73	**1**[1]	17	30 **You Are The Sunshine Of My Life**		Tamla 54232
8/18/73	**4**	14	31 **Higher Ground**		Tamla 54235
11/10/73+	**8**	17	32 **Living For The City**		Tamla 54242
4/06/74	**16**	15	33 Don't You Worry 'Bout A Thing		Tamla 54245
8/03/74	**1**[1]	19	34 **You Haven't Done Nothin**		Tamla 54252
			background vocals by the Jackson 5		
11/16/74+	**3**	17	35 **Boogie On Reggae Woman**		Tamla 54254
12/04/76+	**1**[1]	17	36 **I Wish**		Tamla 54274
4/02/77	**1**[3]	17	37 **Sir Duke**		Tamla 54281
			a tribute to Duke Ellington		
8/27/77	**32**	10	38 Another Star		Tamla 54286
11/05/77+	**36**	14	39 As		Tamla 54291
1/20/79	**59**	8	40 Pops, We Love You (A Tribute To Father)		Motown 1455
			DIANA ROSS, MARVIN GAYE, SMOKEY ROBINSON & STEVIE WONDER		
			song written for Berry Gordy Sr.'s 90th birthday		
11/03/79	**4**	18	41 **Send One Your Love**		Tamla 54303
3/01/80	**52**	7	42 Outside My Window		Tamla 54308
9/20/80	**5**	23	43 **Master Blaster (Jammin')**		Tamla 54317
12/13/80+	**11**	19	44 I Ain't Gonna Stand For It		Tamla 54320
4/11/81	**64**	7	45 Lately		Tamla 54323
1/16/82	**4**	18	46 **That Girl**		Tamla 1602
4/10/82	**1**[7]	19	47 ● **Ebony And Ivory**		Columbia 02860
			PAUL McCARTNEY with STEVIE WONDER		
5/29/82	**13**	14	48 Do I Do		Tamla 1612
9/25/82	**54**	7	49 Ribbon In The Sky		Tamla 1639
10/30/82	**46**	11	50 Used To Be		Motown 1650
			CHARLENE & STEVIE WONDER		
8/18/84	**1**[3]	26	51 ● **I Just Called To Say I Love You**		Motown 1745
12/01/84+	**17**	16	52 Love Light In Flight		Motown 1769
			above 2 from the film "The Woman In Red"		
9/07/85	**1**[1]	21	53 **Part-Time Lover**		Tamla 1808
11/23/85+	**10**	17	54 **Go Home**		Tamla 1817
2/22/86	**24**	13	55 Overjoyed		Tamla 1832

DEBUT DATE	PEAK POS	WKS CHR	ARTIST — Record Title	Label & Number
			STEVIE WONDER — Cont'd	
6/14/86	**86**	3	56 Land Of La La	Tamla 1846
			BOBBY WOOD	
			Southern singer, pianist. Session work in Memphis.	
8/08/64	**74**	5	1 If I'm A Fool For Loving You	Joy 285
			BRENTON WOOD	
			Born Alfred Smith on 7/26/41 in Shreveport. Raised in San Pedro, California. Soul singer, songwriter, pianist. First recorded with Little Freddy & The Rockets, 1958.	
4/15/67	**34**	12	1 The Oogum Boogum Song	Double Shot 111
8/12/67	**9**	15	2 **Gimme Little Sign**	Double Shot 116
11/25/67	**34**	7	3 Baby You Got It	Double Shot 121
3/09/68	**99**	2	4 Lovey Dovey Kinda Lovin'	Double Shot 126
			LAUREN WOOD	
			Pop singer, songwriter, keyboardist; originally from Pittsburgh.	
9/22/79	**24**	15	1 Please Don't Leave	Warner 49043
			harmony vocals by Michael McDonald	
			STEVIE WOODS	
			Black vocalist based in Los Angeles. Originally from Columbus, Ohio.	
9/12/81	**25**	21	1 Steal The Night	Cotillion 46016
1/23/82	**38**	12	2 Just Can't Win 'Em All	Cotillion 46030
5/15/82	**84**	2	3 Fly Away	Cotillion 47006
			SHEB WOOLEY	
			Born on 4/10/21 in Erick, Oklahoma. Singer, songwriter, actor. Played Pete Nolan in TV series "Rawhide". Also made comical recordings under pseudonym, Ben Colder. In films "Rocky Mountain" and "Giant".	
12/17/55	**95**	1	1 Are You Satisfied?	MGM 12114
6/02/58	**1**[6]	14	2 **The Purple People Eater** [N]	MGM 12651
			Best Seller #1(6) / Top 100 #1(6) / Jockey #1(4)	
6/01/59	**70**	6	3 Sweet Chile	MGM 12781
1/06/62	**51**	11	4 That's My Pa [N]	MGM 13046
			BEN COLDER:	
11/24/62	**62**	6	5 Don't Go Near The Eskimos [C]	MGM 13104
7/20/63	**98**	2	6 Still No. 2 [C]	MGM 13147
10/12/63	**90**	1	7 Detroit City No. 2 [C]	MGM 13167
10/01/66	**58**	6	8 Almost Persuaded No. 2 [C]	MGM 13590
10/26/68	**67**	5	9 Harper Valley P.T.A. (Later That Same Day) [C]	MGM 13997
			above 5 are parodies of Pop/Country hits	
			THE WOOLIES	
3/11/67	**95**	3	1 Who Do You Love	Dunhill 4052
			MARION WORTH	
			Country singer from Madison, Tennessee.	
12/29/62+	**42**	8	1 Shake Me I Rattle (Squeeze Me I Cry)	Columbia 42640
			BILL WRAY	
			Pop singer, songwriter originally from Louisiana.	
5/19/79	**96**	2	1 Pinball, That's All	ABC 12449
			from the film "Tilt"	
			LINK WRAY & HIS RAY MEN	
			Link was born on 5/2/35 in Dunn, NC. Rock and roll guitarist. Part American Indian. Joined family band, the Palomino Ranch Gang in early 50s. First recorded as "Lucky" Wray for Starday in 1956. Active into late 70s. Recorded album with rockabilly singer Robert Gordon in 1977.	
4/28/58	**16**	14	1 Rumble [I]	Cadence 1347
			Best Seller #16 / Top 100 #16	
1/26/59	**23**	13	2 Raw-Hide [I]	Epic 9300
6/15/63	**64**	8	3 Jack The Ripper [I]	Swan 4137
			BETTY WRIGHT	
			Born on 12/21/53 in Miami. Soul singer. In family gospel group Echoes Of Joy, from 1956. First recorded for Deep City in 1966. Hostess of TV talk shows in Miami. Also see Peter Brown.	
8/03/68	**33**	8	1 Girls Can't Do What The Guys Do	Alston 4569
11/27/71+	**6**	14	2 ● **Clean Up Woman**	Alston 4601
10/14/72	**46**	10	3 Baby Sitter	Alston 4614

DEBUT DATE	PEAK POS	WKS CHR	ARTIST — Record Title	Label & Number
			BETTY WRIGHT — Cont'd	
4/21/73	**72**	6	4 It's Hard To Stop (Doing Something When It's Good To You)	Alston 4617
10/06/73	**55**	6	5 Let Me Be Your Lovemaker	Alston 4619
7/13/74	**62**	8	6 Secretary 1-6: written & produced by Clarence Reid and Willie Clarke	Alston 4622
4/05/75	**96**	1	7 Where Is The Love	Alston 3713
			CHARLES WRIGHT & THE WATTS 103rd ST. BAND Charles was born in 1942 in Clarksdale, Mississippi. Leader of an 8-man soul/funk band from the Watts section of Los Angeles. Evolved from The Soul Runners. Big break came through assistance by comedian Bill Cosby. **THE WATTS 103RD STREET RHYTHM BAND:**	
9/09/67	**73**	10	1 Spreadin' Honey [I]	Keymen 108
2/01/69	**11**	17	2 Do Your Thing	Warner 7250
7/19/69	**67**	5	3 Till You Get Enough **CHARLES WRIGHT & THE WATTS 103rd STREET RHYTHM BAND:**	Warner 7298
4/11/70	**16**	17	4 Love Land	Warner 7365
8/15/70	**12**	15	5 Express Yourself	Warner 7417
1/23/71	**96**	1	6 Solution For Pollution	Warner 7451
5/15/71	**73**	4	7 Your Love (Means Everything To Me)	Warner 7475
			DALE WRIGHT Rockabilly singer from Cincinnati.	
1/13/58	**38**	13	1 She's Neat Best Seller #38 / Top 100 #39 **DALE WRIGHT with the Rock-Its**	Fraternity 792
8/25/58	**77**	5	2 Please Don't Do It **DALE WRIGHT & The Wright Guys with the Dons**	Fraternity 818
			GARY WRIGHT Born on 4/26/43 in Creskill, New Jersey. Pop/rock singer, songwriter, keyboardist. Appeared in "Captain Video" TV series at age seven. In Broadway play "Fanny". Co-leader of Spooky Tooth.	
1/03/76	**2**[3]	20	1 ● **Dream Weaver**	Warner 8167
4/17/76	**2**[2]	27	2 **Love Is Alive**	Warner 8143
9/18/76	**79**	5	3 Made To Love You	Warner 8250
3/05/77	**43**	7	4 Phantom Writer	Warner 8331
1/21/78	**73**	3	5 Touch And Gone	Warner 8494
7/04/81	**16**	17	6 Really Wanna Know You all of above written & produced by Gary Wright	Warner 49769
			O.V. WRIGHT Born Overton Vertis Wright on 10/9/39 in Memphis; died on 11/16/80. R&B singer. With Sunset Travellers, Spirit Of Memphis and Highway QC's, gospel groups.	
8/07/65	**86**	5	1 You're Gonna Make Me Cry	Back Beat 548
5/13/67	**80**	3	2 Eight Men, Four Women	Back Beat 580
11/14/70	**54**	8	3 Ace Of Spade	Back Beat 615
			PRISCILLA WRIGHT	
6/25/55	**16**	9	1 The Man In The Raincoat Jockey #16 / Best Seller #18 / Juke Box #20 backing by Don Wright & The Septette	Unique 303
			RUBY WRIGHT Vocalist from Anderson, Indiana.	
12/02/57	**41**	4	1 Let's Light The Christmas Tree [X] Best Seller #41 / Top 100 #54	Fraternity 787
5/04/59	**99**	1	2 Three Stars [S-N] narration by Dick Pike	King 5192
			BILL WYMAN Born William Perks on 10/24/36 in London. Bass guitarist of The Rolling Stones.	
12/16/67+	**87**	5	1 In Another Land flip side is "The Lantern" by The Rolling Stones	London 907
			TAMMY WYNETTE Born Virginia Wynette Pugh on 5/5/42 near Tupelo, Mississippi. Top female country singer, with over 15 #1 country hits. Discovered by producer Billy Sherrill. Married to country star George Jones from 1968-75.	
7/08/67	**89**	5	1 My Elusive Dreams **DAVID HOUSTON & TAMMY WYNETTE**	Epic 10194
6/22/68	**63**	6	2 D-I-V-O-R-C-E	Epic 10315

DEBUT DATE	PEAK POS	WKS CHR	ARTIST — Record Title	Label & Number
			TAMMY WYNETTE — Cont'd	
11/09/68+	**19**	16	3 Stand By Your Man	Epic 10398
4/12/69	**75**	5	4 Singing My Song	Epic 10462
8/30/69	**81**	4	5 The Ways To Love A Man	Epic 10512
1/31/70	**100**	2	6 I'll See Him Through	Epic 10571
6/13/70	**97**	2	7 He Loves Me All The Way	Epic 10612
10/24/70	**92**	2	8 Run, Woman, Run	Epic 10653
1/29/72	**86**	4	9 Bedtime Story	Epic 10818
6/16/73	**72**	4	10 Kids Say The Darndest Things	Epic 10969
5/01/76	**84**	5	11 'Til I Can Make It On My Own	Epic 50196
			all of above produced by Billy Sherrill	
			Y	
			Y&T	
			San Francisco heavy-metal rock quartet. Dave Meniketti, lead singer/lead guitar.	
7/13/85	**55**	10	1 Summertime Girls	A&M 2748
			"WEIRD AL" YANKOVIC	
			Los Angeles novelty singer, accordion player. Specializes in song parodies.	
4/30/83	**63**	8	1 Ricky [N]	Rock 'n' R. 03849
			parody of "Mickey" and "I Love Lucy"	
3/10/84	**12**	12	2 Eat It [N]	Rock 'n' R. 04374
			parody of Michael Jackson's "Beat It" - guitar: Rick Derringer	
5/05/84	**62**	6	3 King Of Suede [N]	Rock 'n' R. 04451
			parody of Police's "King Of Pain"	
6/30/84	**81**	3	4 I Lost On Jeopardy [N]	Rock 'n' R. 04469
			parody of Greg Kihn's "Jeopardy"	
6/22/85	**47**	8	5 Like A Surgeon [N]	Rock 'n' R. 04937
			parody of Madonna's "Like A Virgin"	
			all of above produced by Rick Derringer	
			YARBROUGH & PEOPLES	
			Dallas soul duo: Cavin Yarbrough and Alisa Peoples. Discovered by The Gap Band.	
2/07/81	**19**	16	1 ● Don't Stop The Music	Mercury 76085
4/14/84	**48**	12	2 Don't Waste Your Time	Total Exp. 2400
6/28/86	**93**	4	3 I Wouldn't Lie	Total Exp. 2437
			GLENN YARBROUGH	
			Born on 1/12/30 in Milwaukee. Lead singer of the Limeliters (1959-63).	
3/13/65	**12**	14	1 Baby The Rain Must Fall	RCA 8498
			from the film of the same title	
7/17/65	**54**	6	2 It's Gonna Be Fine	RCA 8619
			THE YARDBIRDS	
			Legendary rock group formed in Surrey, England in 1963. Consisted of Keith Relf (d: 5/14/76), vocals, harmonica; Anthony "Top" Topham and Chris Dreja, guitars; Paul "Sam" Samwell-Smith, bass, keyboards; and Jim McCarty, drums. Formed as the Metropolitan Blues Quartet at Kingston Art School. Topham replaced by Eric Clapton in 1963. Clapton replaced by Jeff Beck in 1965. Samwell-Smith replaced by Chris Dreja on bass and Jimmy Page added on guitar in 1966. Beck left in December of 1966. Group disbanded in July, 1968. Page formed the New Yardbirds in October of 1968, which evolved into Led Zeppelin. Relf and McCarty formed Renaissance in 1969. Keith Relf later in Armageddon, 1975. McCarty later in Illusion, 1977.	
5/15/65	**6**	12	1 **For Your Love**	Epic 9790
7/31/65	**9**	12	2 **Heart Full Of Soul**	Epic 9823
			above 2 written by Graham Gouldman (10cc)	
10/30/65	**17**	10	3 I'm A Man	Epic 9857
3/19/66	**11**	11	4 Shapes Of Things	Epic 10006
			above 4 produced by Giogio Gomelski	
6/25/66	**13**	11	5 Over Under Sideways Down	Epic 10035
11/26/66	**30**	9	6 Happenings Ten Years Time Ago	Epic 10094
4/22/67	**51**	6	7 Little Games	Epic 10156
8/05/67	**45**	7	8 Ha Ha Said The Clown	Epic 10204
11/18/67	**96**	2	9 Ten Little Indians	Epic 10248
			written by Nilsson	

DEBUT DATE	PEAK POS	WKS CHR	ARTIST — Record Title	Label & Number
			PETER YARROW	
			Born on 5/31/38 in New York City. Folk singer, songwriter, guitarist. Peter of Peter, Paul & Mary. Wrote Mary MacGregor's "Torn Between Two Lovers".	
4/08/72	**100**	2	1 Don't Ever Take Away My Freedom	Warner 7567
			YAZ	
			British electronic pop duo: Vince Clarke (formerly of Depeche Mode), keyboards, synthesizers; and Alison Moyet, vocals. Duo formerly named Yazoo.	
9/18/82	**73**	8	1 Situation	Sire 29953
2/26/83	**67**	8	2 Only You	Sire 29844
			THE YELLOW BALLOON	
			Quintet from Oregon and Arizona formed by Don Grady (Robbie Douglas of "My Three Sons"). Alex Valdez, lead singer.	
4/01/67	**25**	10	1 Yellow Balloon	Canterbury 508
			YELLOW MAGIC ORCHESTRA	
			Japanese electronic trio: Ryuichi Sakamoto, Yukihiro Takahashi and Haruomi Hosono.	
2/02/80	**60**	9	1 Computer Games [I] theme from "The Circus"	Horizon 127
			YES	
			Progressive rock group formed in London, England in 1968. Consisted of Jon Anderson (vocals), Peter Banks (guitar), Tony Kaye (keyboards), Chris Squire (bass) and Bill Bruford (drums). Banks replaced by Steve Howe in 1971. Kaye replaced by Rick Wakeman in 1971. Bruford left to join King Crimson, replaced by Alan White, late 1972. Wakeman replaced by Patrick Moraz in 1974, rejoined in 1976 when Moraz left. Wakeman and Anderson left in 1980, replaced by The Buggles' Trevor Horne (guitar) and Geoff Downes (keyboards). Group disbanded in 1980. Howe and Downes went with Asia. Re-formed in 1983 with Anderson, Kaye, Squire, White, and Trevor Rabin (guitar).	
9/25/71	**40**	14	1 Your Move	Atlantic 2819
2/12/72	**13**	13	2 Roundabout	Atlantic 2854
8/12/72	**46**	7	3 America written by Paul Simon	Atlantic 2899
11/11/72	**42**	7	4 And You And I (Part II)	Atlantic 2920
11/05/83+	**1**[2]	23	5 **Owner Of A Lonely Heart**	Atco 99817
3/03/84	**24**	15	6 Leave It	Atco 99787
6/23/84	**51**	7	7 It Can Happen	Atco 99745
			YIPES!!	
			Milwaukee rock quintet - Pat McCurdy, lead singer.	
8/02/80	**68**	5	1 Darlin'	Millennium 11791
			DAVE YORK & The Beachcombers	
8/25/62	**95**	1	1 Beach Party	P-K-M 6700
			RUSTY YORK	
7/20/59	**77**	3	1 Sugaree	Chess 1730
			DENNIS YOST - see CLASSICS IV	
			THE "YOU KNOW WHO" GROUP!	
11/28/64+	**43**	9	1 Roses Are Red My Love	4 Corners 113
			THE YOUNGBLOODS	
			Folk-rock group led by vocalist Jesse Colin Young (born Perry Miller on 11/11/44). Band formed in Boston, then moved to California, late 1967.	
12/17/66+	**52**	10	1 Grizzly Bear	RCA 9015
9/02/67	**62**	8	2 Get Together	RCA 9264
6/28/69	**5**	17	3 ● **Get Together** [R] repopularized as theme for National Council of Christians & Jews	RCA 9752
5/02/70	**86**	4	4 Darkness, Darkness	RCA 0342
			YOUNG HEARTS	
			Los Angeles soul quintet.	
11/16/68	**94**	3	1 I've Got Love For My Baby	Minit 32049
			YOUNG-HOLT UNLIMITED	
			Chicago instrumental soul group: Eldee Young, bass; Isaac "Red" Holt, drums (both of the Ramsey Lewis Trio) and Don Walker, piano. Walker left by 1968.	
12/17/66+	**40**	8	1 Wack Wack [I] **THE YOUNG HOLT TRIO**	Brunswick 55305

DEBUT DATE	PEAK POS	WKS CHR	ARTIST — Record Title	Label & Number
			YOUNG-HOLT UNLIMITED — Cont'd	
11/30/68+	**3**	13	2 ● **Soulful Strut** .... [I]	Brunswick 55391
			exact same recording as Barbara Acklin's "Am I The Same Girl", except vocal part replaced by piano	
3/01/69	**57**	4	3 Who's Making Love.......... [I]	Brunswick 55400
			YOUNG RASCALS - see THE RASCALS	
			BARRY YOUNG	
11/06/65+	**13**	11	1 One Has My Name (The Other Has My Heart)	Dot 16756
			FARON YOUNG	
			Born on 2/25/32 in Shreveport, Louisiana. Country singer, guitarist. Charted over 30 Top 10 Country hits. In films "The Young Sheriff", "Daniel Boone" and "Hidden Guns".	
6/03/57	**96**	1	1 The Shrine Of St. Cecilia..........	Capitol 3696
8/11/58	**51**	5	2 Alone With You..........	Capitol 3982
1/04/60	**83**	3	3 Riverboat..........	Capitol 4291
4/10/61	**12**	15	4 Hello Walls..........	Capitol 4533
			written by Willie Nelson	
10/16/61	**89**	3	5 Backtrack..........	Capitol 4616
2/12/72	**92**	4	6 It's Four In The Morning..........	Mercury 73250
			GEORGIE YOUNG & The Rockin' Bocs	
9/22/58	**58**	9	1 Nine More Miles (The "Faster-Faster" Song)	Cameo 150
			JOHN PAUL YOUNG	
			Australian pop singer, songwriter, pianist.	
12/13/75+	**42**	9	1 Yesterday's Hero..........	Ariola Am. 7607
7/15/78	**7**	21	2 **Love Is In The Air**..........	Scotti Br. 402
12/09/78+	**55**	9	3 Lost In Your Love..........	Scotti Br. 405
			KAREN YOUNG	
9/16/78	**67**	13	1 Hot Shot..........	West End 1211
			KATHY YOUNG with THE INNOCENTS	
			Born on 10/21/45 in Santa Ana, California. Pop singer. Also see The Innocents.	
10/24/60	**3**	17	1 **A Thousand Stars**..........	Indigo 108
2/20/61	**30**	10	2 Happy Birthday Blues..........	Indigo 115
9/18/61	**80**	3	3 Magic Is The Night..........	Indigo 125
			NEIL YOUNG	
			Born on 11/12/45 in Toronto, Canada. Rock singer, songwriter, guitarist. Formed rock band, the Mynah Birds, featuring lead singer Rick James, early 60s. Moved to Los Angeles in 1966 and formed Buffalo Springfield. Went solo in 1969 with backing band, Crazy Horse. Joined with Crosby, Stills & Nash in 1970.	
6/20/70	**55**	9	1 Cinnamon Girl..........	Reprise 0911
			NEIL YOUNG with CRAZY HORSE	
10/24/70	**33**	12	2 Only Love Can Break Your Heart..........	Reprise 0958
4/10/71	**93**	1	3 When You Dance I Can Really Love..........	Reprise 0992
2/05/72	**1**[1]	14	4 ● **Heart Of Gold**..........	Reprise 1065
			backing vocals: Linda Ronstadt and James Taylor	
4/29/72	**31**	9	5 Old Man..........	Reprise 1084
7/01/72	**61**	6	6 War Song..........	Reprise 1099
			NEIL YOUNG & GRAHAM NASH	
7/13/74	**69**	7	7 Walk On..........	Reprise 1209
2/03/79	**61**	7	8 Four Strong Winds..........	Reprise 1396
			harmony vocal: Nicolette Larson	
10/13/79	**79**	5	9 Rust Never Sleeps (Hey Hey, My My [Into The Black]) ..	Reprise 49031
12/26/81+	**70**	5	10 Southern Pacific..........	Reprise 49870
			above 2: **NEIL YOUNG & CRAZY HORSE**	
1/29/83	**71**	6	11 Little Thing Called Love..........	Geffen 29887
			all of above written by Young (except #8)	
			PAUL YOUNG	
			Born on 1/17/56 in Bedfordshire, England. Pop/rock vocalist, guitarist.	
10/01/83	**70**	7	1 Wherever I Lay My Hat (That's My Home)..........	Columbia 04071
2/04/84	**22**	15	2 Come Back And Stay..........	Columbia 04313
5/19/84	**45**	11	3 Love Of The Common People..........	Columbia 04453
5/11/85	**1**[1]	23	4 **Everytime You Go Away**..........	Columbia 04867
9/07/85	**13**	14	5 I'm Gonna Tear Your Playhouse Down..........	Columbia 05577

DEBUT DATE	PEAK POS	WKS CHR	ARTIST — Record Title	Label & Number
			PAUL YOUNG — Cont'd	
11/23/85+	**56**	11	6 Everything Must Change	Columbia 05712
			above 6 produced by Laurie Latham	
11/15/86	**65**	10	7 Some People	Columbia 06423
			VICTOR YOUNG	
			Born on 8/8/1900 in Chicago; died on 11/11/56. Conductor, composer, violinist.	
11/12/55	**52**	11	1 Autumn Leaves [I]	Decca 29653
			piano solo by Ray Turner	
5/20/57	**13**	34	2 Around The World [I]	Decca 30262
			Jockey #13 / Best Seller #20 / Top 100 #26 from the film "Around The World In 80 Days" flip side is Bing Crosby's vocal version	
			TIMI YURO	
			Born Rosemarie Timothy Aurro Yuro on 8/4/40 in Chicago. Moved to Los Angeles in 1952. Vocal lessons from early age. First recorded for Liberty in 1959. Lost voice in 1980 and underwent three throat operations.	
7/24/61	**4**	12	1 **Hurt/**	
10/09/61	**72**	3	2 I Apologize	Liberty 55343
			revival of Bing Crosby's 1931 hit (POS 3)	
11/06/61	**42**	6	3 Smile/	
			revival of Nat King Cole's 1954 hit (POS 10)	
12/04/61	**93**	2	4 She Really Loves You	Liberty 55375
2/03/62	**66**	5	5 Let Me Call You Sweetheart	Liberty 55410
			revival of The Peerless Quartet's #1 hit in 1911	
7/14/62	**12**	11	6 What's A Matter Baby (Is It Hurting You)	Liberty 55469
			all of above produced by Clyde Otis	
12/01/62+	**44**	8	7 The Love Of A Boy	Liberty 55519
3/30/63	**81**	1	8 Insult To Injury	Liberty 55552
7/20/63	**24**	11	9 Make The World Go Away	Liberty 55587
10/12/63	**64**	7	10 Gotta Travel On	Liberty 55634
2/20/65	**96**	2	11 You Can Have Him	Mercury 72391
			YUTAKA	
			Born Yutaka Yokokura in Tokyo, Japan. Male jazz/pop keyboardist, vocalist.	
7/18/81	**81**	3	1 Love Light	Alfa 7004
			vocals by Yutaka and Patti Austin	

Z

DEBUT DATE	PEAK POS	WKS CHR	ARTIST — Record Title	Label & Number
			FLORIAN ZABACH	
			Born on 8/15/21 in Chicago. Violinist, composer.	
9/01/56	**50**	12	1 When The White Lilacs Bloom Again [I]	Mercury 70936
			written in 1928	
			HELMUT ZACHARIAS	
			German violinist.	
9/01/56	**12**	14	1 When The White Lilacs Bloom Again [I]	Decca 30039
			Jockey #12 / Top 100 #16 / Best Seller #19 / Juke Box #19	
			JOHN ZACHERLE	
			Born on 9/26/18 in Philadelphia. "The Cool Ghoul" - hosted a horror movies TV show in Philadelphia.	
3/10/58	**6**	13	1 **Dinner With Drac - Part 1** [N]	Cameo 130
			Top 100 #6 / Best Seller #8	
			PIA ZADORA	
			Born in 1956 in New York City. Actress, singer. In films "Butterfly" and "The Lonely Lady".	
3/27/82	**45**	9	1 I'm In Love Again	Elektra 47428
12/11/82+	**36**	15	2 The Clapping Song	Elektra 69889
2/02/85	**54**	11	3 When The Rain Begins To Fall	Curb 52521
			JERMAINE JACKSON/PIA ZADORA from the film "Voyage of the Rock Aliens"	
			ZAGER & EVANS	
			Lincoln, Nebraska duo: Denny Zager and Rick Evans. Disbanded in 1969.	
6/21/69	**1** [6]	13	1 ● **In The Year 2525 (Exordium & Terminus)**	RCA 0174
			released regionally in 1968 on Truth Records	

DEBUT DATE	PEAK POS	WKS CHR	ARTIST — Record Title	Label & Number
			THE MICHAEL ZAGER BAND	
			Disco studio group led by keyboardist/writer/arranger Michael Zager (b: 1943 in Jersey City, New Jersey). With band Ten Wheel Drive from 1968-73.	
3/20/76	**94**	3	1 Do It With Feeling	Bang 720
			MICHAEL ZAGER'S MOON BAND featuring Peabo Bryson	
3/04/78	**36**	14	2 Let's All Chant [I]	Private S. 45184
			RICKY ZAHND & The Blue Jeaners	
12/17/55	**21**	4	1 (I'm Gettin') Nuttin' For Christmas [N-X]	Columbia 40576
			Best Seller #21 / Top 100 #40	
			ZAPP	
			Dayton, Ohio funk band formed by the Troutman brothers: Roger "Zapp", Lester and Larry. Bootsy Collins produced and played on first session. Also see Roger.	
10/04/80	**86**	7	1 More Bounce To The Ounce - Part I	Warner 49534
			FRANK ZAPPA	
			Born on 12/21/40 in Baltimore, Maryland. Singer, songwriter, guitarist. Rock music's leading satirist. Formed The Mothers Of Invention in 1965. In films "200 Motels" and "Baby Snakes".	
10/19/74	**86**	4	1 Don't Eat The Yellow Snow [N]	DiscReet 1312
4/14/79	**45**	8	2 Dancin' Fool [N]	Zappa 10
7/17/82	**32**	12	3 Valley Girl [N]	Barking P. 02972
			featuring Frank's daughter: Moon Unit Zappa	
			LENA ZAVARONI	
			10-year-old singer from Scotland.	
7/13/74	**91**	4	1 Ma! (He's Making Eyes At Me)	Stax 0206
			written in 1921	
			ZEBRA	
			Rock trio founded in New Orleans. Consisted of Randy Jackson (lead singer), Felix Hanemann (bass) and Guy Gelso (drums).	
7/09/83	**61**	8	1 Who's Behind The Door?	Atlantic 89821
			DANNY ZELLA & his ZELL ROCKS	
			Born on 7/31/38 in Detroit. Rock and roll singer, saxophonist.	
1/26/59	**71**	5	1 Wicked Ruby	Fox 10057
			SI ZENTER	
			Jazz trombone player/bandleader originally from New York. Played in 40s for Jimmy Dorsey, Harry James and Les Brown.	
11/13/61	**43**	9	1 Up A Lazy River [I]	Liberty 55374
			revival of Hoagy Carmichael's 1932 hit (POS 19)	
			WARREN ZEVON	
			Born on 1/24/47 in Canada. Parents were Russian immigrants. Singer, songwriter, pianist. Wrote Linda Ronstadt's "Poor Poor Pitiful Me".	
3/25/78	**21**	12	1 Werewolves Of London	Asylum 45472
3/08/80	**57**	7	2 A Certain Girl	Asylum 46610
			PAT ZILL	
			Male Pop/Country singer.	
5/22/61	**91**	1	1 Pick Me Up On Your Way Down	Indigo 119
			THE ZOMBIES	
			British rock quintet: Rod Argent (keyboards), Colin Blunstone (vocals), Paul Atkinson (guitar), Chris White (bass) and Hugh Grundy (drums). Group disbanded in late 1967. Rod later formed Argent, in 1969.	
10/17/64	**2**[1]	15	1 **She's Not There**	Parrot 9695
1/09/65	**6**	11	2 **Tell Her No**	Parrot 9723
4/10/65	**58**	6	3 She's Coming Home	Parrot 9747
6/26/65	**95**	3	4 I Want You Back Again	Parrot 9769
2/08/69	**3**	13	5● **Time Of The Season**	Date 1628
			recorded in 1967 - above 5 written by Argent	
			ZWOL	
			Walter Zwol. Pop/rock singer, songwriter.	
9/16/78	**76**	8	1 New York City	EMI 8005
2/24/79	**75**	3	2 Call Out My Name	EMI 8009

DEBUT DATE	PEAK POS	WKS CHR	ARTIST — Record Title	Label & Number
			ZZ TOP Boogie-rock trio formed in Houston, Texas in 1969. Consisted of Billy Gibbons (vocals, guitar), Dusty Hill (vocals, bass) and Frank Beard (drums). All were born in 1949 in Texas. Gibbons had been lead guitarist in Moving Sidewalks, a Houston psychedelic rock band. Hill and Beard had played in American Blues, based in Dallas. Inactive from 1977-79.	
5/20/72	**69**	9	1 Francene	London 179
3/30/74	**41**	19	2 La Grange	London 203
7/19/75	**20**	9	3 Tush	London 220
9/11/76	**44**	11	4 It's Only Love	London 241
3/26/77	**91**	6	5 Arrested For Driving While Blind	London 251
1/19/80	**34**	11	6 I Thank You	Warner 49163
7/12/80	**89**	2	7 Cheap Sunglasses	Warner 49220
10/03/81	**77**	4	8 Leila	Warner 49782
4/02/83	**37**	12	9 Gimme All Your Lovin	Warner 29693
7/23/83	**56**	9	10 Sharp Dressed Man	Warner 29576
5/19/84	**8**	19	11 **Legs**	Warner 29272
10/19/85	**8**	17	12 **Sleeping Bag**	Warner 28884
1/18/86	**21**	12	13 Stages	Warner 28810
3/29/86	**22**	13	14 Rough Boy	Warner 28733
7/26/86	**35**	12	15 Velcro Fly all of above written by ZZ Top (except #1 & 6) and produced by Bill Ham	Warner 28650

THE SONG TITLE SECTION

This section lists, alphabetically, all titles in the artist section. The artist's name is listed next to each title along with the highest position attained and year of peak popularity. Some titles show the letter F as a position, indicating the title was listed as a flip side and did not chart on its own.

A song with more than one charted version is listed once, with the artists' names listed below in chronological order. Many songs that have the same title, but are different tunes, are listed separately, with the most popular title listed first. This will make it easy to determine which songs are the same composition; the amount of charted versions of a particular song; and which versions were the most popular.

Cross references have been used throughout to aid in finding a title. If you have trouble, please keep the following in mind: Titles in which an apostrophe is used within a word will come before a title using the complete spelling (Lovin' comes before Loving), etc. Titles beginning with a contraction follow titles that begin with a similar non-contracted word (Can't follows Can).Titles such as I.O.U., D.O.A., and SOS will be found at the beginning of their respective letters.

28/66 **'A' Team** *SSgt Barry Sadler*
1/70 **ABC** *Jackson 5*
77/56 **ABC's Of Love**
Frankie Lymon & The Teenagers
26/82 **Abacab** *Genesis*
67/85 **Abadabadango** *Kim Carnes*
47/69 **Abergavenny** *Shannon*
16/64 **Abigail Beecher** *Freddy Cannon*
15/63 **Abilene** *George Hamilton IV*
31/60 **About This Thing Called Love** *Fabian*
59/62 **Above The Stars** *Mr. Acker Bilk*
32/74 **Abra-Ca-Dabra** *DeFranco Family*
1/82 **Abracadabra** *Steve Miller Band*
Abraham, Martin And John
4/68 *Dion*
33/69 *Miracles*
35/69 *Moms Mabley*
8/71 *Tom Clay (medley)*
53/86 **Absolute Beginners** *David Bowie*
26/71 **Absolutely Right** *Five Man Electrical Band*
98/76 **Abyssinia Jones** *Edwin Starr*
54/70 **Ace Of Spade** *O.V. Wright*
56/73 **Across 110th Street** *Bobby Womack*
98/64 **Across The Street** *Lenny O'Henry*
47/65 **Act Naturally** *Beatles*
Action
13/65 *Freddy Cannon*
75/84 *Evelyn 'Champagne' King*
20/76 **Action** *Sweet*
69/75 **Action Speaks Louder Than Words**
Chocolate Milk
90/60 **Adam And Eve** *Paul Anka*
64/70 **Add Some Music To Your Day** *Beach Boys*
1/86 **Addicted To Love** *Robert Palmer*
45/60 **Adeste Fideles** *Bing Crosby*
90/62 **Adios Amigo** *Jim Reeves*
Admiral Halsey *see: Uncle Albert*
71/55 **Adorable** *Fontane Sisters*
93/71 **Adrienne** *Tommy James*
8/84 **Adult Education** *Daryl Hall & John Oates*
Adventures In Paradise *see: Theme From*
9/83 **Affair Of The Heart** *Rick Springfield*
16/57 **Affair To Remember (Our Love Affair)**
Vic Damone
1/83 **Africa** *Toto*
41/61 **African Waltz** *Cannonball Adderley*
42/62 **Afrikaan Beat** *Bert Kaempfert*
49/72 **Afro-Strut** *Nite-Liters*
69/84 **After All** *Al Jarreau*
71/72 **After All This Time** *Merry Clayton*
48/83 **After I Cry Tonight** *Lanier & Co.*
95/65 **After Loving You** *Della Reese*
After Midnight
18/70 *Eric Clapton*
42/72 *J.J. Cale*
97/74 *Maggie Bell*
32/57 **After School** *Randy Starr*
92/56 **After School** *Tommy Charles*
74/76 **After The Dance** *Marvin Gaye*
23/83 **After The Fall** *Journey*
89/70 **After The Feeling Is Gone** *Five Flights Up*
48/85 **After The Fire** *Roger Daltrey*
56/71 **After The Fire Is Gone**
Conway Twitty & Loretta Lynn
32/82 **After The Glitter Fades** *Stevie Nicks*
22/74 **After The Goldrush** *Prelude*
10/56 **After The Lights Go Down Low** *Al Hibbler*
2/79 **After The Love Has Gone**
Earth, Wind & Fire
8/77 **After The Lovin'** *Engelbert Humperdinck*
65/80 **After You** *Dionne Warwick*
1/76 **Afternoon Delight** *Starland Vocal Band*
1/84 **Against All Odds (Take A Look At Me Now)** *Phil Collins*
5/80 **Against The Wind** *Bob Seger*
47/61 **Age For Love** *Jimmy Charles*
21/65 **Agent Double-O-Soul** *Edwin Starr*
36/75 **Agony And The Ecstasy** *Smokey Robinson*
29/81 **Ah! Leah!** *Donnie Iris*
5/62 **Ahab, The Arab** *Ray Stevens*
28/81 **Ai No Corrida** *Quincy Jones*
67/81 **Aiming At Your Heart** *Temptations*
49/64 **Ain't Doing Too Bad** *Bobby Bland*
17/81 **Ain't Even Done With The Night**
John Cougar
74/60 **Ain't Gonna Be That Way** *Marv Johnson*
12/77 **Ain't Gonna Bump No More (With No Big Fat Woman)** *Joe Tex*
77/66 **Ain't Gonna Cry No More** *Brenda Lee*
Ain't Gonna Eat Out My Heart Anymore *see: I Ain't Gonna*
92/78 **Ain't Gonna Hurt Nobody** *Brick*
81/63 **Ain't Gonna Kiss Ya** *Ribbons*
39/66 **Ain't Gonna Lie** *Keith*
87/67 **Ain't Gonna Rest (Till I Get You)**
Five Stairsteps
53/64 **Ain't Gonna Tell Anybody**
Jimmy Gilmer/Fireballs
Ain't Got No Home
20/57 *Clarence 'Frogman' Henry*
73/73 *Band*
94/69 **Ain't Got No; I Got Life** *Nina Simone*
53/71 **Ain't Got Time** *Impressions*
66/71 **Ain't It A Sad Thing** *R. Dean Taylor*
91/65 **Ain't It A Shame** *Major Lance*
49/61 **Ain't It, Baby** *Miracles*
24/70 **Ain't It Funky Now** *James Brown*
45/64 **Ain't It The Truth** *Mary Wells*
40/65 **Ain't It True** *Andy Williams*
22/79 **Ain't Love A Bitch** *Rod Stewart*
91/74 **Ain't No Love In The Heart Of The City**
Bobby Bland
Ain't No Mountain High Enough
19/67 *Marvin Gaye & Tammi Terrell*
1/70 *Diana Ross*
13/79 **Ain't No Stoppin' Us Now**
McFadden & Whitehead
3/71 **Ain't No Sunshine** *Bill Withers*
93/65 **Ain't No Telling** *Bobby Bland*
16/68 **Ain't No Way** *Aretha Franklin*
8/75 **Ain't No Way To Treat A Lady**
Helen Reddy
4/73 **Ain't No Woman (Like The One I've Got)**
Four Tops
22/83 **Ain't Nobody** *Rufus/Chaka Khan*
Ain't Nobody Home
63/66 *Howard Tate*
46/72 *B.B. King*
87/68 **Ain't Nothin' But A House Party**
Show Stoppers
42/86 **Ain't Nothin' Goin' On But The Rent**
Gwen Guthrie
43/78 **Ain't Nothing Gonna Keep Me From You**
Teri DeSario
Ain't Nothing Like The Real Thing
8/68 *Marvin Gaye & Tammi Terrell*
47/74 *Aretha Franklin*
21/77 *Donny & Marie Osmond*
88/82 *Chris Christian (medley)*
20/64 **Ain't Nothing You Can Do** *Bobby Bland*
19/64 **Ain't She Sweet** *Beatles*

42/66 **Ain't That A Groove** *James Brown*
Ain't That A Shame
1/55 *Pat Boone*
10/55 *Fats Domino*
22/63 *4 Seasons*
35/79 *Cheap Trick*
89/79 **Ain't That Enough For You** *John Davis*
33/61 **Ain't That Just Like A Woman**
Fats Domino
61/64 **Ain't That Just Like Me** *Searchers*
93/65 **Ain't That Love** *Four Tops*
86/62 **Ain't That Loving You** *Bobby Bland*
16/64 **Ain't That Loving You Baby** *Elvis Presley*
Ain't That Loving You (For More Reasons Than One)
45/70 *Luther Ingram*
86/72 *Isaac Hayes & David Porter*
Ain't That Peculiar
8/65 *Marvin Gaye*
85/72 *Fanny*
44/75 *Diamond Reo*
Ain't Too Proud To Beg
13/66 *Temptations*
90/67 *Magnificent Men (medley)*
17/74 *Rolling Stones*
21/72 **Ain't Understanding Mellow**
Jerry Butler & Brenda Lee Eager
77/72 **Ain't Wastin' Time No More**
Allman Brothers Band
81/74 **Air Disaster** *Albert Hammond*
6/74 **Air That I Breathe** *Hollies*
99/62 **Air Travel** *Ray & Bob*
46/67 **Airplane Song (My Airplane)**
Royal Guardsmen
31/70 **Airport Love Theme** *Vincent Bell*
68/72 **Ajax Airlines** *Hudson & Landry*
43/71 **Ajax Liquor Store** *Hudson & Landry*
Al Di La'
6/62 *Emilio Pericoli*
90/63 *Connie Francis*
29/64 *Ray Charles Singers*
57/65 **Al's Place** *Al Hirt*
Alabam
47/60 *Pat Boone*
63/60 *Cowboy Copas*
68/80 **Alabama Getaway** *Grateful Dead*
14/55 **Alabama Jubilee** *Ferko String Band*
62/72 **Alabama Wild Man** *Jerry Reed*
92/62 **Aladdin** *Bobby Curtola*
Alamo *see: Ballad Of The*
29/71 **Albert Flasher** *Guess Who*
Alfie
32/66 *Cher*
95/66 *Cilla Black*
15/67 *Dionne Warwick*
66/68 *Eivets Rednow*
29/84 **Alibis** *Sergio Mendes*
17/63 **Alice In Wonderland** *Neil Sedaka*
27/68 **Alice Long (You're Still My Favorite Girlfriend)** *Tommy Boyce & Bobby Hart*
97/69 **Alice's Rock & Roll Restaurant**
Arlo Guthrie
29/81 **Alien** *Atlanta Rhythm Section*
97/59 **Alimony** *Frankie Ford*
34/72 **Alive** *Bee Gees*
3/85 **Alive & Kicking** *Simple Minds*
14/78 **Alive Again** *Chicago*
35/67 **All** *James Darren*
50/63 **All About My Girl** *Jimmy McGriff*
3/62 **All Alone Am I** *Brenda Lee*
20/68 **All Along The Watchtower** *Jimi Hendrix*
2/59 **All American Boy** *Bill Parsons*
79/81 **All American Girls** *Sister Sledge*
11/56 **All At Once You Love Her** *Perry Como*
2/76 **All By Myself** *Eric Carmen*
8/86 **All Cried Out**
Lisa Lisa & Cult Jam with Full Force
41/64 **All Cried Out** *Dusty Springfield*
7/65 **All Day And All Of The Night** *Kinks*
35/71 **All Day Music** *War*
65/85 **All Fall Down** *Five Star*
95/69 **All God's Children Got Soul**
Dorothy Morrison
98/64 **All Grown Up** *Crystals*
92/72 **All His Children** *Charley Pride*
33/60 **All I Could Do Was Cry** *Etta James*
7/71 **All I Ever Need Is You** *Sonny & Cher*
56/71 **All I Have** *Moments*
All I Have To Do Is Dream
1/58 *Everly Brothers*
96/61 *Everly Brothers*
14/63 *Richard Chamberlain*
27/70 *Glen Campbell & Bobbie Gentry*
66/75 *Nitty Gritty Dirt Band*
51/81 *Andy Gibb & Victoria Principal*
91/69 **All I Have To Offer You (Is Me)**
Charley Pride
9/73 **All I Know** *Garfunkel*
2/85 **All I Need** *Jack Wagner*
8/67 **All I Need** *Temptations*
5/86 **All I Need Is A Miracle**
Mike + The Mechanics
61/73 **All I Need Is Time**
Gladys Knight & The Pips
77/83 **All I Need To Know** *Bette Midler*
All I Really Want To Do
15/65 *Cher*
40/65 *Byrds*
20/66 **All I See Is You** *Dusty Springfield*
41/78 **All I See Is Your Face** *Dan Hill*
19/87 **All I Wanted** *Kansas*
63/74 **All In Love Is Fair** *Barbra Streisand*
19/61 **All In My Mind** *Maxine Brown*
93/71 **All My Hard Times** *Joe Simon*
37/83 **All My Life** *Kenny Rogers*
All My Loving
45/64 *Beatles*
93/64 *Hollyridge Strings*
All My Trials
89/64 *Dick & DeeDee*
70/71 *Ray Stevens*
19/80 **All Night Long** *Joe Walsh*
75/62 **All Night Long** *Sandy Nelson*
75/84 **All Night Long** *Billy Squier*
99/56 **All Night Long** *Jo Stafford*
1/83 **All Night Long (All Night)** *Lionel Richie*
45/80 **All Night Thing** *Invisible Man's Band*
69/82 **All Night With Me** *Laura Branigan*
(All Of A Sudden) My Heart Sings
15/59 *Paul Anka*
38/65 *Mel Carter*
70/61 **All Of Everything** *Frankie Avalon*
51/85 **All Of Me For All Of You** *9.9*
71/65 **All Of My Life** *Lesley Gore*
77/82 **All Of My Love** *Bobby Caldwell*
19/84 **All Of You** *Julio Iglesias & Diana Ross*
68/66 **All Or Nothing**
Patti LaBelle & The Blue Belles
28/82 **All Our Tomorrows** *Eddie Schwartz*
2/80 **All Out Of Love** *Air Supply*
38/58 **All Over Again** *Johnny Cash*
13/80 **All Over The World**
Electric Light Orchestra
42/63 **All Over The World** *Nat King Cole*
12/83 **All Right** *Christopher Cross*

All Right Now
4/70 *Free*
92/75 *Lea Roberts*
72/85 *Rod Stewart*
97/76 **All Roads (Lead Back To You)** *Donny Most*
9/85 **All She Wants To Do Is Dance** *Don Henley*
All Shook Up
1/57 *Elvis Presley*
85/74 *Suzi Quatro*
All Strung Out
26/66 *Nino Tempo & April Stevens*
34/77 *John Travolta*
41/66 **All That I Am** *Elvis Presley*
94/77 **All The Kids On The Street**
Hollywood Stars
26/72 **All The King's Horses** *Aretha Franklin*
61/86 **All The Kings Horses** *Firm*
63/60 **All The Love I've Got** *Marv Johnson*
19/86 **All The Love In The World** *Outfield*
85/83 **All The Right Moves**
Jennifer Warnes/Chris Thompson
28/86 **All The Things She Said** *Simple Minds*
21/58 **All The Time** *Johnny Mathis*
54/79 **All The Time In The World** *Dr. Hook*
2/58 **All The Way** *Frank Sinatra*
63/56 **All The Way 'Round The World**
Mills Brothers
37/72 **All The Young Dudes** *Mott The Hoople*
97/66 **All These Things** *Uniques*
78/79 **All Things Are Possible** *Dan Peek*
17/83 **All This Love** *DeBarge*
41/83 **All Those Lies** *Glenn Frey*
2/81 **All Those Years Ago** *George Harrison*
5/84 **All Through The Night** *Cyndi Lauper*
36/83 **All Time High** *Rita Coolidge*
58/83 **All Touch** *Rough Trade*
35/77 **All You Get From Love Is A Love Song**
Carpenters
1/67 **All You Need Is Love** *Beatles*
58/85 **All You Zombies** *Hooters*
80/67 **All Your Goodies Are Gone (The Loser's Seat)** *Parliaments*
2/56 **Allegheny Moon** *Patti Page*
17/83 **Allentown** *Billy Joel*
44/83 **Allergies** *Paul Simon*
Alley Cat
7/62 *Bent Fabric*
76/62 *David Thorne*
Alley-Oop
1/60 *Hollywood Argyles*
15/60 *Dante & The Evergreens*
59/60 *Dyna-Sores*
83/83 **Allies** *Heart*
93/67 **Alligator Bogaloo** *Lou Donaldson*
54/84 **Allnighter** *Glenn Frey*
61/63 **Ally Ally Oxen Free** *Kingston Trio*
32/59 **Almost Grown** *Chuck Berry*
95/68 **Almost In Love** *Elvis Presley*
78/58 **Almost In Your Arms** *Johnny Nash*
32/78 **Almost Like Being In Love**
Michael Johnson
25/84 **Almost Over You** *Sheena Easton*
Almost Paradise
15/57 *Roger Williams*
31/57 *Lou Stein*
56/57 *Norman Petty Trio*
7/84 **Almost Paradise...Love Theme From Footloose** *Mike Reno & Ann Wilson*
Almost Persuaded
24/66 *David Houston*
58/66 *Ben Colder*
79/69 *Etta James*

Almost Saturday Night
78/75 *John Fogerty*
54/81 *Dave Edmunds*
28/78 **Almost Summer**
Celebration featuring Mike Love
67/64 **Almost There** *Andy Williams*
64/85 **Alone Again** *Dokken*
1/72 **Alone Again (Naturally)** *Gilbert O'Sullivan*
99/70 **Alone Again Or** *Love*
8/60 **Alone At Last** *Jackie Wilson*
Alone (Why Must I Be Alone)
18/57 *Shepherd Sisters*
28/64 *4 Seasons*
48/64 **Alone With You** *Brenda Lee*
51/58 **Alone With You** *Faron Young*
Along Came Jones
9/59 *Coasters*
27/69 *Ray Stevens*
14/85 **Along Comes A Woman** *Chicago*
Along Comes Mary
7/66 *Association*
96/67 *Baja Marimba Band*
32/74 **Already Gone** *Eagles*
91/70 **Alright In The City** *Dunn & McCashen*
68/59 **Alright, Okay, You Win** *Peggy Lee*
Also Sprach Zarathustra (2001)
90/70 *Berlin Philharmonic*
2/73 *Deodato*
95/60 **Alvin For President** *Chipmunks*
74/75 **Alvin Stone (The Birth & Death Of A Gangster)** *Fantastic Four*
40/62 **Alvin Twist** *Chipmunks*
74/66 **Alvin's Boo-Ga-Loo**
Alvin Cash & The Registers
Alvin's Harmonica
3/59 *Chipmunks*
73/61 *Chipmunks*
87/62 *Chipmunks*
33/60 **Alvin's Orchestra** *Chipmunks*
19/59 **Always** *Sammy Turner*
59/83 **Always** *Firefall*
64/73 **Always** *Luther Ingram*
18/78 **Always And Forever** *Heatwave*
82/64 **Always In My Heart** *Los Indios Tabajaras*
56/60 **Always It's You** *Everly Brothers*
5/82 **Always On My Mind** *Willie Nelson*
Always Something There To Remind Me
see: (There's)
18/68 **Always Together** *Dells*
33/64 **Always Together** *Al Martino*
79/73 **Am I Black Enough For You** *Billy Paul*
90/86 **Am I Forgiven** *Isle Of Man*
71/67 **Am I Grooving You** *Freddie Scott*
Am I Losing You
31/60 *Jim Reeves*
59/72 *Partridge Family*
Am I That Easy To Forget
25/60 *Debbie Reynolds*
18/68 *Engelbert Humperdinck*
32/60 **Am I The Man** *Jackie Wilson*
79/69 **Am I The Same Girl** *Barbara Acklin*
1/86 **Amanda** *Boston*
54/79 **Amanda** *Waylon Jennings*
83/71 **Amanda** *Dionne Warwick*
63/60 **Amapola** *Jacky Noguez*
44/77 **Amarillo** *Neil Sedaka*
Amazing Grace
15/71 *Judy Collins*
11/72 *Royal Scots Dragoon Guards*
72/76 **Amazing Grace (Used To Be Her Favorite Song)** *Amazing Rhythm Aces*
75/76 **Amber Cascades** *America*
52/59 **Ambrose (Part Five)** *Linda Laurie*

37/68 **Ame Caline (Soul Coaxing)**
Raymond Lefevre
Amen
7/65 *Impressions*
36/68 *Otis Redding*
8/81 **America** *Neil Diamond*
America
46/72 *Yes*
97/72 *Simon & Garfunkel*
46/85 **America** *Prince*
83/70 **America** *Five Stairsteps (medley)*
45/70 **America, Communicate With Me**
Ray Stevens
52/68 **America Is My Home** *James Brown*
American *see: Amerikan*
59/68 **American Boys** *Petula Clark*
27/72 **American City Suite** *Cashman & West*
13/80 **American Dream** *Dirt Band*
98/74 **American Girls** *Rick Springfield*
17/82 **American Heartbeat** *Survivor*
72/83 **American Made** *Oak Ridge Boys*
80/81 **American Memories** *Shamus M'Cool*
16/82 **American Music** *Pointer Sisters*
1/72 **American Pie** *Don McLean*
13/86 **American Storm** *Bob Seger*
American Trilogy
26/72 *Mickey Newbury*
66/72 *Elvis Presley*
35/74 **American Tune** *Paul Simon*
1/70 **American Woman** *Guess Who*
Americans
4/74 *Byron MacGregor*
24/74 *Gordon Sinclair*
90/74 *Tex Ritter*
79/72 **Amerikan Music** *Steve Alaimo*
27/75 **Amie** *Pure Prairie League*
73/84 **Amnesia** *Shalamar*
7/59 **Among My Souvenirs** *Connie Francis*
Amor
18/61 *Ben E. King*
88/62 *Roger Williams*
(Amos & Andy Song)
see: Like A Sunday In Salem
8/71 **Amos Moses** *Jerry Reed*
38/55 **Amukiriki (The Lord Willing)**
Les Paul & Mary Ford
65/63 **Amy** *Paul Petersen*
77/64 **Anaheim, Azusa & Cucamonga Sewing Circle, Book Review And Timing Association** *Jan & Dean*
37/57 **Anastasia** *Pat Boone*
22/67 **And Get Away** *Esquires*
22/82 **And I Am Telling You I'm Not Going**
Jennifer Holliday
And I Love Her (Him)
12/64 *Beatles*
54/65 *Esther Phillips*
And I Love You So
83/71 *Bobby Goldsboro*
29/73 *Perry Como*
59/81 **And Love Goes On** *Earth, Wind & Fire*
64/70 **And My Heart Sang (Tra La La)**
Brenda & The Tabulations
69/60 **And Now** *Della Reese*
36/65 **And Roses And Roses** *Andy Williams*
54/85 **And She Was** *Talking Heads*
97/69 **And She's Mine** *Spanky & Our Gang*
45/68 **And Suddenly** *Cherry People*
And That Reminds Me
9/57 *Kay Starr*
12/57 *Della Reese*
45/69 *4 Seasons*
70/56 **And The Angels Sing** *Three Chuckles*
19/80 **And The Beat Goes On** *Whispers*
55/80 **And The Cradle Will Rock...** *Van Halen*
44/70 **And The Grass Won't Pay No Mind**
Mark Lindsay
84/61 **And The Heavens Cried** *Ronnie Savoy*
65/62 **And Then There Were Drums**
Sandy Nelson
21/85 **And We Danced** *Hooters*
2/69 **And When I Die** *Blood, Sweat & Tears*
42/72 **And You And I** *Yes*
41/66 **Andrea** *Sunrays*
5/85 **Angel** *Madonna*
20/73 **Angel** *Aretha Franklin*
40/72 **Angel** *Rod Stewart*
51/65 **Angel** *Johnny Tillotson*
5/61 **Angel Baby** *Rosie & The Originals*
30/58 **Angel Baby** *Dean Martin*
57/71 **Angel Baby** *Dusk*
47/59 **Angel Face** *Jimmy Darren*
40/82 **Angel In Blue** *J. Geils Band*
92/86 **Angel In My Pocket** *One To One*
6/77 **Angel In Your Arms** *Hot*
Angel Of The Morning
7/68 *Merrilee Rush*
4/81 *Juice Newton*
22/61 **Angel On My Shoulder** *Shelby Flint*
81/56 **Angel Pie (Postillon!)** *Peggy King*
38/80 **Angel Say No** *Tommy Tutone*
33/58 **Angel Smile** *Nat King Cole*
79/75 **Angel (What In The World's Come Over Us)** *Atlanta Rhythm Section*
27/60 **Angela Jones** *Johnny Ferguson*
64/79 **Angeleyes** *Abba*
97/70 **Angelica** *Oliver*
58/80 **Angeline** *Allman Brothers Band*
43/64 **Angelito** *Rene & Rene*
11/56 **Angels In The Sky** *Crew-Cuts*
22/59 **Angels Listened In** *Crests*
1/73 **Angie** *Rolling Stones*
Angie *see: Different Worlds*
1/74 **Angie Baby** *Helen Reddy*
70/57 **Angry** *Frank Pizani*
(Angry Young Man) *see: Fooling Yourself*
73/79 **Animal House** *Stephen Bishop*
43/85 **Animal Instinct** *Commodores*
76/71 **Animal Trainer And The Toad** *Mountain*
97/70 **Animal Zoo** *Spirit*
86/63 **Ann-Marie** *Belmonts*
54/61 **Anna** *Jorgen Ingmann*
68/62 **Anna (Go To Him)** *Arthur Alexander*
93/58 **Anna Marie** *Jim Reeves*
46/71 **Annabella** *Hamilton, Joe Frank & Reynolds*
86/72 **Annabelle** *Daniel Boone*
47/65 **Annie Fanny** *Kingsmen*
51/62 **Annie Get Your Yo-Yo** *Little Junior Parker*
1/74 **Annie's Song** *John Denver*
89/61 **Anniversary Of Love** *Caslons*
1/80 **Another Brick In The Wall (Part II)**
Pink Floyd
47/64 **Another Cup Of Coffee** *Brook Benton*
5/71 **Another Day** *Paul McCartney*
45/67 **Another Day, Another Heartache**
5th Dimension
52/86 **Another Heartache** *Rod Stewart*
22/86 **Another Night** *Aretha Franklin*
49/67 **Another Night** *Dionne Warwick*
Another Night
71/75 *Hollies*
94/79 *Wilson Bros.*
1/80 **Another One Bites The Dust** *Queen*
32/74 **Another Park, Another Sunday**
Doobie Brothers
97/68 **Another Place, Another Time**
Jerry Lee Lewis
65/72 **Another Puff** *Jerry Reed*

32/76 **Another Rainy Day In New York City** *Chicago*
Another Saturday Night
10/63 *Sam Cooke*
6/74 *Cat Stevens*
22/60 **Another Sleepless Night** *Jimmy Clanton*
44/82 **Another Sleepless Night** *Anne Murray*
32/77 **Another Star** *Stevie Wonder*
78/81 **Another Ticket** *Eric Clapton*
20/58 **Another Time, Another Place** *Patti Page*
43/71 **Another Time, Another Place** *Engelbert Humperdinck*
63/86 **Anotherloverholenyohead** *Prince*
71/59 **Answer To A Maiden's Prayer** *June Valli*
89/66 **Answer To My Prayer** *Neil Sedaka*
32/80 **Answering Machine** *Rupert Holmes*
65/73 **Anthem** *Wayne Newton*
60/59 **Anthony Boy** *Chuck Berry*
(Anthony's Song) *see: Movin' Out*
13/72 **Anticipation** *Carly Simon*
83/63 **Antony And Cleopatra Theme** *Ferrante & Teicher*
Any Day Now
23/62 *Chuck Jackson*
86/69 *Percy Sledge*
14/82 *Ronnie Milsap*
81/63 **Any Other Way** *Chuck Jackson*
79/78 **(Any Way That You Want It) I'll Be There** *Starz*
Any Way That You Want Me
98/66 *Liverpool Five*
88/68 *American Breed*
53/69 *Evie Sands*
14/65 **Any Way You Want It** *Dave Clark Five*
23/80 **Any Way You Want It** *Journey*
72/77 **Any Way You Want Me** *Sylvers*
31/61 **Anybody But Me** *Brenda Lee*
31/60 **Anymore** *Teresa Brewer*
42/82 **Anyone Can See** *Irene Cara*
64/68 **Anyone For Tennis (The Savage Seven Theme)** *Cream*
8/64 **Anyone Who Had A Heart** *Dionne Warwick*
52/64 **Anyone Who Knows What Love Is (Will Understand)** *Irma Thomas*
80/68 **Anything** *Animals*
43/67 **Anything Goes** *Harpers Bizarre*
31/62 **Anything That's Part Of You** *Elvis Presley*
86/69 **Anything You Choose** *Spanky & Our Gang*
37/76 **Anything You Want** *John Valenti*
83/78 **Anytime** *Journey*
46/65 **Anytime At All** *Frank Sinatra*
Anytime (I'll Be There)
75/75 *Frank Sinatra*
33/76 *Paul Anka*
50/60 **Anyway The Wind Blows** *Doris Day*
20/56 **Anyway You Want Me (That's How I Will Be)** *Elvis Presley*
86/84 **Anywhere With You** *Rubber Rodeo*
Apache
2/61 *Jorgen Ingmann*
87/61 *Sonny James*
64/65 *Arrows*
53/82 *Sugarhill Gang*
Apartment *see: Theme From The*
81/70 **Apartment 21** *Bobbie Gentry*
24/56 **Ape Call** *Nervous Norvus*
45/71 **Apeman** *Kinks*
79/68 **Apologize** *Ed Ames*
29/60 **Apple Green** *June Valli*
32/65 **Apple Of My Eye** *Roy Head*
75/65 **Apples And Bananas** *Lawrence Welk*
6/67 **Apples, Peaches, Pumpkin Pie** *Jay & The Techniques*
46/69 **Apricot Brandy** *Rhinoceros*
37/69 **April Fools** *Dionne Warwick*
April In Paris
28/56 *Count Basie*
97/56 *Modernaires*
1/57 **April Love** *Pat Boone*
89/79 **Aqua Boogie (A Psychoalphadiscobetabioaquadoloop)** *Parliament*
1/69 **Aquarius (medley)** *5th Dimension*
48/81 **Arc Of A Diver** *Steve Winwood*
15/84 **Are We Ourselves?** *Fixx*
55/65 **Are You A Boy Or Are You A Girl** *Barbarians*
73/70 **Are You Getting Any Sunshine?** *Lou Christie*
65/83 **Are You Getting Enough Happiness** *Hot Chocolate*
39/69 **Are You Happy** *Jerry Butler*
39/67 **Are You Lonely For Me** *Freddie Scott*
Are You Lonesome Tonight?
65/59 *Jaye P. Morgan*
1/60 *Elvis Presley*
14/74 *Donny Osmond*
(also see: Yes, I'm Lonesome Tonight)
15/73 **Are You Man Enough** *Four Tops*
72/71 **Are You My Woman? (Tell Me So)** *Chi-Lites*
59/67 **Are You Never Coming Home** *Sandy Posey*
87/71 **Are You Old Enough** *Mark Lindsay*
14/70 **Are You Ready?** *Pacific Gas & Electric*
10/58 **Are You Really Mine** *Jimmie Rodgers*
Are You Satisfied?
95/55 *Sheb Wooley*
11/56 *Rusty Draper*
78/56 *Toni Arden*
57/83 **Are You Serious** *Tyrone Davis*
Are You Sincere
3/58 *Andy Williams*
85/65 *Trini Lopez*
91/65 **Are You Still My Baby** *Shirelles*
60/75 **Are You Sure Hank Done It This Way** *Waylon Jennings*
39/66 **Are You There (With Another Girl)** *Dionne Warwick*
26/77 **Ariel** *Dean Friedman*
10/70 **Arizona** *Mark Lindsay*
28/73 **Armed And Extremely Dangerous** *First Choice*
Armen's Theme
46/56 *Joe Reisman*
42/57 *David Seville*
55/63 *Bobby Vee (Yesterday And You)*
Arms Of Mary
81/76 *Sutherland Brothers & Quiver*
67/78 *Chilliwack*
74/69 **Armstrong** *John Stewart*
91/65 **Around The Corner** *Duprees*
Around The World In 80 Days
12/57 *Mantovani*
13/57 *Victor Young*
25/57 *Bing Crosby*
73/57 *McGuire Sisters*
91/77 **Arrested For Driving While Blind** *ZZ Top*
Arrivederci, Roma
51/55 *Georgia Gibbs*
55/58 *Roger Williams*
97/58 *Mario Lanza*
80/57 **Arrow Of Love** *Six Teens*
29/79 **Arrow Through Me** *Wings*
83/75 **Art For Art's Sake** *10cc*
1/81 **Arthur's Theme (Best That You Can Do)** *Christopher Cross*
20/60 **Artificial Flowers** *Bobby Darin*
36/78 **As** *Stevie Wonder*
10/61 **As If I Didn't Know** *Adam Wade*

51/75 **As Long As He Takes Care Of Home**
Candi Staton
47/63 **As Long As I Know He's Mine** *Marvelettes*
59/63 **As Long As She Needs Me**
Sammy Davis, Jr.
As Tears Go By
22/65 *Marianne Faithfull*
6/66 *Rolling Stones*
31/70 **As The Years Go By** *Mashmakhan*
As Time Goes By
43/59 *Johnny Nash*
86/73 *Nilsson*
12/64 **As Usual** *Brenda Lee*
96/77 **Ashes And Sand** *Johnny Rivers*
37/80 **Ashes By Now** *Rodney Crowell*
52/73 **Ashes To Ashes** *5th Dimension*
55/66 **Ashes To Ashes** *Mindbenders*
8/61 **Asia Minor** *Kokomo*
12/64 **Ask Me** *Elvis Presley*
18/56 **Ask Me** *Nat King Cole*
52/74 **Ask Me** *Ecstasy, Passion & Pain*
75/63 **Ask Me** *Maxine Brown*
91/64 **Ask Me** *Inez Foxx*
40/71 **Ask Me No Questions** *B.B. King*
27/72 **Ask Me What You Want** *Millie Jackson*
24/65 **Ask The Lonely** *Four Tops*
91/75 **Astral Man** *Nektar*
19/61 **Astronaut (Parts 1 & 2)** *Jose Jimenez*
47/61 **At Last** *Etta James*
56/79 **At Midnight** *T-Connection*
30/77 **At Midnight (My Love Will Lift You Up)**
Rufus Featuring Chaka Khan
At My Front Door
7/55 *Pat Boone*
17/55 *El Dorados*
56/60 *Dee Clark*
3/75 **At Seventeen** *Janis Ian*
43/65 **At The Club** *Drifters*
44/62 **At The Club** *Ray Charles*
(At The Copa) *see: Copacabana*
At The Hop
1/58 *Danny & The Juniors*
21/58 *Nick Todd*
18/66 **At The Scene** *Dave Clark Five*
97/63 **At The Shore** *Johnny Caswell*
83/68 **At The Top Of The Stairs** *Formations*
16/67 **At The Zoo** *Simon & Garfunkel*
At This Moment
79/81 *Billy & The Beaters*
1/87 *Billy & The Beaters*
28/82 **Athena** *Who*
27/81 **Atlanta Lady (Something About Your Love)** *Marty Balin*
7/69 **Atlantis** *Donovan*
39/80 **Atomic** *Blondie*
18/66 **Attack** *Toys*
70/82 **Attack Of The Name Game** *Stacy Lattisaw*
(also see: Name Game)
21/75 **Attitude Dancing** *Carly Simon*
15/73 **Aubrey** *Bread*
Auctioneer
59/56 *Chuck Miller*
19/57 *Leroy Van Dyke*
85/68 **Aunt Dora's Love Soul Shack**
Arthur Conley
15/84 **Authority Song** *John Cougar Mellencamp*
25/75 **Autobahn** *Kraftwerk*
52/80 **Autograph** *John Denver*
5/84 **Automatic** *Pointer Sisters*
34/83 **Automatic Man** *Michael Sembello*
37/72 **Automatically Sunshine** *Supremes*

Autumn Leaves
1/55 *Roger Williams*
35/55 *Steve Allen*
41/55 *Mitch Miller*
50/55 *Jackie Gleason*
52/55 *Victor Young*
55/55 *Ray Charles Singers*
92/65 *Roger Williams (1965)*
19/68 **Autumn Of My Life** *Bobby Goldsboro*
18/56 **Autumn Waltz** *Tony Bennett*
Avenging Annie
78/73 *Andy Pratt*
88/77 *Roger Daltrey*
93/62 **Aw Shucks, Hush Your Mouth**
Jimmy Reed
77/56 **Away All Boats** *Al Hibbler*
3/85 **Axel F** *Harold Faltermeyer*

98/68 **B.B. Jones** *B.B. King*
59/76 **BLT** *Lee Oskar*
1/79 **Babe** *Styx*
14/66 **B-A-B-Y** *Carla Thomas*
78/58 **Baby, Baby** *Billy Williams*
83/64 **Baby Baby All The Time** *Superbs*
52/64 **Baby Baby Baby** *Anna King - Bobby Byrd*
66/63 **Baby, Baby, Baby** *Sam Cooke*
F/56 **(Baby, Baby) Be Good To Me**
McGuire Sisters
8/69 **Baby, Baby Don't Cry** *Miracles*
79/76 **Baby, Baby I Love You** *Terry Cashman*
51/64 **Baby Be Mine** *Jelly Beans*
12/61 **Baby Blue** *Echoes*
14/72 **Baby Blue** *Badfinger*
60/76 **Baby Boy**
Mary Kay Place as Loretta Haggers
44/85 **Baby Come And Get It** *Pointer Sisters*
1/78 **Baby Come Back** *Player*
32/68 **Baby, Come Back** *Equals*
52/84 **Baby Come Back** *Billy Rankin*
83/85 **Baby Come Back To Me (The Morse Code Of Love)** *Manhattan Transfer*
27/74 **Baby Come Close** *Smokey Robinson*
75/64 **Baby Come Home** *Ruby & The Romantics*
96/66 **Baby Come On Home** *Solomon Burke*
1/83 **Baby, Come To Me**
Patti Austin & James Ingram
63/66 **Baby, Do The Philly Dog** *Olympics*
33/56 **Baby Doll** *Andy Williams*
72/69 **Baby, Don't Be Looking In My Mind**
Joe Simon
52/77 **Baby Don't Change Your Mind**
Gladys Knight & The Pips
1/72 **Baby Don't Get Hooked On Me** *Mac Davis*
8/65 **Baby Don't Go** *Sonny & Cher*
69/80 **Baby Don't Go** *Karla Bonoff*
96/70 **Baby Don't Take Your Love**
Faith, Hope & Charity
39/64 **Baby, Don't You Cry** *Ray Charles*
27/64 **Baby Don't You Do It** *Marvin Gaye*
43/77 **Baby Don't You Know** *Wild Cherry*
30/63 **Baby Don't You Weep**
Garnet Mimms & The Enchanters
Baby Elephant Walk
48/62 *Lawrence Welk*
87/62 *Miniature Men*

Baby Face
41/58 *Little Richard*
42/62 *Bobby Darin*
14/76 *Wing & A Prayer Fife & Drum Corps.*
61/63 **Baby Get It (And Don't Quit It)** *Jackie Wilson*
88/75 **Baby-Get It On** *Ike & Tina Turner*
50/75 **Baby, Hang Up The Phone** *Carl Graves*
62/62 **Baby Has Gone Bye Bye** *George Maharis*
87/67 **Baby, Help Me** *Percy Sledge*
11/78 **Baby Hold On** *Eddie Money*
35/70 **Baby Hold On** *Grass Roots*
72/60 **(Baby) Hully Gully** *Olympics*
70/63 **Baby I Do Love You** *Galens*
26/84 **Baby I Lied** *Deborah Allen*
4/67 **Baby I Love You** *Aretha Franklin*
Baby, I Love You
24/64 *Ronettes*
9/69 *Andy Kim*
Baby I Love You
98/66 *Jimmy Holiday*
82/70 *Little Milton*
12/76 **Baby, I Love Your Way** *Peter Frampton*
96/66 **Baby I Need You** *Manhattans*
62/79 **Baby, I Need Your Lovin'** *Eric Carmen*
Baby I Need Your Loving
11/64 *Four Tops*
3/67 *Johnny Rivers*
52/70 *O.C. Smith*
47/79 **Baby I Want You** *Funky Communication Committee*
58/76 **Baby, I'll Give It To You** *Seals & Crofts*
3/71 **Baby I'm-A Want You** *Bread*
25/79 **Baby I'm Burnin'** *Dolly Parton*
14/69 **Baby, I'm For Real** *Originals*
76/84 **Baby, I'm Hooked (Right Into Your Love)** *Con Funk Shun*
70/67 **Baby I'm Lonely** *Intruders*
Baby, I'm Yours
11/65 *Barbara Lewis*
91/71 *Jody Miller*
F/78 *Debby Boone*
41/73 **Baby I've Been Missing You** *Independents*
91/70 **Baby, Is There Something On Your Mind** *McKinley Travis*
91/62 **Baby It's Cold Outside** *Ray Charles & Betty Carter*
Baby It's You
8/62 *Shirelles*
5/69 *Smith*
14/83 **Baby Jane** *Rod Stewart*
29/71 **Baby Let Me Kiss You** *King Floyd*
24/72 **Baby Let Me Take You (In My Arms)** *Detroit Emeralds*
35/69 **Baby Let's Wait** *Royal Guardsmen*
1/64 **Baby Love** *Supremes*
10/86 **Baby Love** *Regina*
58/77 **Baby Love** *Mother's Finest*
87/70 **Baby Make It Soon** *Flying Machine*
64/68 **Baby Make Your Own Sweet Music** *Jay & The Techniques*
25/82 **Baby Makes Her Blue Jeans Talk** *Dr. Hook*
11/68 **Baby, Now That I've Found You** *Foundations*
21/61 **Baby Oh Baby** *Shells*
61/67 **Baby Please Come Back Home** *J.J. Barnes*
16/66 **Baby Scratch My Back** *Slim Harpo*
46/72 **Baby Sitter** *Betty Wright*
6/61 **Baby Sittin' Boogie** *Buzz Clifford*
50/82 **Baby Step Back** *Gordon Lightfoot*
23/70 **Baby Take Me In Your Arms** *Jefferson*
10/59 **Baby Talk** *Jan & Dean*
68/86 **Baby Talk** *Alisha*
38/80 **Baby Talks Dirty** *Knack*
26/75 **Baby That's Backatcha** *Smokey Robinson*
12/65 **Baby The Rain Must Fall** *Glenn Yarbrough*
76/66 **Baby Toys** *Toys*
56/70 **(Baby) Turn On To Me** *Impressions*
92/76 **Baby, We Better Try To Get It Together** *Barry White*
98/63 **Baby, We've Got Love** *Johnnie Taylor*
4/77 **Baby, What A Big Surprise** *Chicago*
83/83 **Baby, What About You** *Crystal Gayle*
74/66 **Baby What Do You Want Me To Do** *Barbara Lewis*
62/66 **Baby What I Mean** *Drifters*
Baby What You Want Me To Do
37/60 *Jimmy Reed*
82/64 *Etta James*
93/63 **Baby, What's Wrong** *Lonnie Mack*
61/72 **Baby Won't You Let Me Rock 'N Roll You** *Ten Years After*
5/63 **Baby Workout** *Jackie Wilson*
59/68 **Baby You Come Rollin' Across My Mind** *Peppermint Trolley Company*
34/67 **Baby You Got It** *Brenton Wood*
65/77 **Baby, You Look Good To Me Tonight** *John Denver*
34/67 **Baby You're A Rich Man** *Beatles*
100/63 **Baby, You're Driving Me Crazy** *Joey Dee*
49/61 **Baby, You're Right** *James Brown*
52/61 **Baby You're So Fine** *Mickey & Sylvia*
86/68 **Baby You're So Right For Me** *Brenda & The Tabulations*
5/60 **Baby (You've Got What It Takes)** *Brook Benton & Dinah Washington*
26/61 **Baby's First Christmas** *Connie Francis*
84/64 **Baby's Gone** *Gene Thomas*
99/64 **Bachelor Boy** *Cliff Richard*
43/60 **Baciare Baciare (Kissing Kissing)** *Dorothy Collins*
63/63 **Back At The Chicken Shack** *Jimmy Smith*
66/61 **Back Beat No. 1** *Rondels*
59/69 **Back Door Man** *Derek*
72/73 **Back For A Taste Of Your Love** *Syl Johnson*
5/74 **Back Home Again** *John Denver*
37/81 **Back In Black** *AC/DC*
57/68 **Back In Love Again** *Buckinghams*
Back In My Arms Again
1/65 *Supremes*
92/78 *Genya Ravan*
88/85 **Back In Stride** *Maze Featuring Frankie Beverly*
38/77 **Back In The Saddle** *Aerosmith*
Back In The U.S.A.
37/59 *Chuck Berry*
16/78 *Linda Ronstadt*
82/69 **Back In The U.S.S.R.** *Chubby Checker*
84/80 **Back Of My Hand (I've Got Your Number)** *Jags*
9/72 **Back Off Boogaloo** *Ringo Starr*
33/80 **Back On My Feet Again** *Babys*
59/68 **Back On My Feet Again** *Foundations*
5/83 **Back On The Chain Gang** *Pretenders*
36/67 **Back On The Street Again** *Sunshine Company*
3/72 **Back Stabbers** *O'Jays*
95/65 **Back Street** *Edwin Starr*
36/57 **Back To School Again** *Timmie 'Oh Yeah' Rogers*
71/82 **Back To School Again** *Four Tops*
89/81 **Back To The 60's (medley)** *Tight Fit*
80/61 **Back To The Hop** *Danny & The Juniors*
53/76 **Back To The Island** *Leon Russell*
28/77 **Back Together Again** *Daryl Hall & John Oates*
56/80 **Back Together Again** *Roberta Flack & Donny Hathaway*

41/68 **Back Up Train** *Al Greene*
40/73 **Back When My Hair Was Short** *Gunhill Road*
20/84 **Back Where You Belong** *38 Special*
10/69 **Backfield In Motion** *Mel & Tim*
43/81 **Backfired** *Debbie Harry*
25/66 **Backstage** *Gene Pitney*
89/61 **Backtrack** *Faron Young*
88/83 **Bad, Bad Billy** *Snuff*
Bad, Bad Leroy Brown
1/73 *Jim Croce*
83/74 *Frank Sinatra*
1/75 **Bad Blood** *Neil Sedaka*
8/86 **Bad Boy** *Miami Sound Machine*
35/83 **Bad Boy** *Ray Parker Jr.*
36/57 **Bad Boy** *Jive Bombers*
45/60 **Bad Boy** *Marty Wilde*
55/82 **Bad Boy (medley)** *Luther Vandross*
60/83 **Bad Boys** *Wham!*
83/79 **Bad Brakes** *Cat Stevens*
14/79 **Bad Case Of Loving You (Doctor, Doctor)** *Robert Palmer*
45/57 **(Bad Donkey) Pum-Pa-Lum** *Steve Lawrence*
92/66 **Bad Eye** *Willie Mitchell*
33/63 **Bad Girl** *Neil Sedaka*
93/59 **Bad Girl** *Miracles*
1/79 **Bad Girls** *Donna Summer*
91/66 **Bad Little Woman** *Shadows Of Knight*
Bad Luck
15/75 *Harold Melvin & The Blue Notes*
94/76 *Atlanta Disco Band*
37/60 **Bad Man Blunder** *Kingston Trio*
55/66 **Bad Misunderstanding** *Critters*
2/69 **Bad Moon Rising** *Creedence Clearwater Revival*
45/58 **Bad Motorcycle** *Storey Sisters*
4/75 **Bad Time** *Grand Funk*
47/80 **Bad Times** *Tavares*
9/64 **Bad To Me** *Billy J. Kramer with The Dakotas*
58/71 **Bad Water** *Raeletts*
87/73 **Bad Weather** *Supremes*
60/69 **Badge** *Cream*
42/78 **Badlands** *Bruce Springsteen*
53/57 **Bahama Mama** *Four Aces*
94/63 **Baja (Ba-ha)** *Astronauts*
2/78 **Baker Street** *Gerry Rafferty*
48/62 **Balboa Blue** *Marketts*
57/70 **Ball And Chain** *Tommy James*
3/70 **Ball Of Confusion (That's What The World Is Today)** *Temptations*
19/69 **Ball Of Fire** *Tommy James & The Shondells*
74/59 **Ballad Of A Girl And Boy** *Graduates*
14/58 **Ballad Of A Teenage Queen** *Johnny Cash*
Ballad Of Bonnie And Clyde
7/68 *Georgie Fame*
55/68 *Lester Flatt & Earl Scruggs*
Ballad Of Davy Crockett
1/55 *Bill Hayes*
5/55 *Tennessee Ernie Ford*
5/55 *Fess Parker*
14/55 *Voices Of Walter Schumann*
65/69 **Ballad Of Easy Rider** *Byrds*
Ballad Of Francis Powers
see: There's A Star Spangled Banner Waving
34/66 **Ballad Of Irving** *Frank Gallop*
44/63 **Ballad Of Jed Clampett** *Lester Flatt & Earl Scruggs*
8/69 **Ballad Of John And Yoko** *Beatles*
33/62 **Ballad Of Paladin** *Duane Eddy*
Ballad Of The Alamo
34/60 *Marty Robbins*
64/60 *Bud & Travis*
1/66 **Ballad Of The Green Berets** *SSgt Barry Sadler*
Ballad Of Thunder Road
62/58 *Robert Mitchum*
65/62 *Robert Mitchum*
48/68 **Ballad Of Two Brothers** *Autry Inman*
42/67 **Ballad Of You & Me & Pooneil** *Jefferson Airplane*
18/57 **Ballerina** *Nat King Cole*
7/87 **Ballerina Girl** *Lionel Richie*
33/74 **Ballero** *War*
5/75 **Ballroom Blitz** *Sweet*
82/64 **Bama Lama Bama Loo** *Little Richard*
Banana Boat (Day-O)
5/57 *Harry Belafonte*
25/57 *Stan Freberg*
Banana Boat Song
4/57 *Tarriers*
13/57 *Fontane Sisters*
18/57 *Steve Lawrence*
19/57 *Sarah Vaughan*
41/76 **Banapple Gas** *Cat Stevens*
3/70 **Band Of Gold** *Freda Payne*
Band Of Gold
4/56 *Don Cherry*
11/56 *Kit Carson*
93/56 *Hi-Fi Four*
32/66 *Mel Carter*
1/74 **Band On The Run** *Paul McCartney*
35/67 **Banda, A** *Herb Alpert*
18/55 **Bandit (O'Cangaceiro)** *Eddie Barclay*
65/62 **Bandit Of My Dreams** *Eddie Hodges*
Bang A Gong (Get It On)
10/72 *T. Rex*
68/79 *Witch Queen*
9/85 *Power Station*
63/66 **Bang Bang** *Joe Cuba Sextet*
2/66 **Bang Bang (My Baby Shot Me Down)** *Cher*
22/68 **Bang-Shang-A-Lang** *Archies*
63/83 **Bang The Drum All Day** *Todd Rundgren*
31/84 **Bang Your Head (Metal Health)** *Quiet Riot*
23/71 **Bangla-Desh** *George Harrison*
Banjo Boy
58/60 *Jan & Kjeld*
79/60 *Dorothy Collins*
100/60 *Art Mooney*
15/55 **Banjo's Back In Town** *Teresa Brewer*
94/71 **Banks Of The Ohio** *Olivia Newton-John*
93/63 **Banzai Pipeline** *Henry Mancini*
29/60 **Barbara** *Temptations*
Barbara Ann
13/61 *Regents*
2/66 *Beach Boys*
78/70 **Barbara, I Love You** *New Colony Six*
67/68 **Barefoot In Baltimore** *Strawberry Alarm Clock*
7/66 **Barefootin'** *Robert Parker*
Baretta's Theme ('Keep Your Eye On The Sparrow')
45/75 *Merry Clayton*
20/76 *Rhythm Heritage*
96/68 **Baroque-A-Nova** *Mason Williams*
Barracuda
59/65 *Alvin Cash & The Crawlers*
11/77 **Barracuda** *Heart*
Baseball Game *see: (Love Is Like A)*
94/62 **Basie Twist** *Count Basie*
71/85 **Basketball** *Kurtis Blow*
15/73 **Basketball Jones Featuring Tyrone Shoelaces** *Cheech & Chong*
(also see: Love Jones)
66/66 **Batman** *Jan & Dean*
70/66 **Batman & His Grandmother** *Dickie Goodman*

Batman Theme
17/66 *Marketts*
35/66 *Neal Hefti*
37/71 **Battle Hymn Of Lt. Calley**
C Company Featuring Terry Nelson
Battle Hymn Of The Republic
13/59 *Mormon Tabernacle Choir*
33/68 *Andy Williams*
100/61 **Battle Of Gettysburg** *Fred Darian*
14/59 **Battle Of Kookamonga** *Homer & Jethro*
Battle Of New Orleans
1/59 *Johnny Horton*
87/59 *Vaughn Monroe*
95/68 *Harpers Bizarre*
72/74 *Nitty Gritty Dirt Band*
25/58 **Baubles, Bangles And Beads**
Kirby Stone Four
34/73 **Be** *Neil Diamond*
Be Anything (But Be Mine)
25/64 *Connie Francis*
88/64 *Gloria Lynne*
Be-Bop-A-Lula
7/56 *Gene Vincent*
74/60 *Everly Brothers*
3/57 **Be-Bop Baby** *Ricky Nelson*
31/63 **Be Careful Of Stones That You Throw**
Dion
95/57 **Be Careful With A Fool** *B.B. King*
97/71 **Be Good To Me Baby** *Luther Ingram*
9/86 **Be Good To Yourself** *Journey*
66/69 **Be-In (medley)** *Happenings*
64/63 **Be Mad Little Girl** *Bobby Darin*
35/82 **Be Mine Tonight** *Neil Diamond*
92/82 **Be Mine (Tonight)** *Grover Washington, Jr.*
Be My Baby
2/63 *Ronettes*
17/70 *Andy Kim*
92/71 *Cissy Houston*
87/65 **Be My Baby** *Dick & DeeDee*
56/61 **Be My Boy** *Paris Sisters*
53/77 **Be My Girl** *Dramatics*
75/64 **Be My Girl** *Four-Evers*
8/59 **Be My Guest** *Fats Domino*
28/82 **Be My Lady** *Jefferson Starship*
78/77 **Be My Lady** *Meters*
49/72 **Be My Lover** *Alice Cooper*
9/85 **Be Near Me** *ABC*
71/71 **Be Nice To Me** *Runt*
4/74 **Be Thankful For What You Got**
William DeVaughn
6/63 **Be True To Your School** *Beach Boys*
34/63 **Be True To Yourself** *Bobby Vee*
66/73 **Be What You Are** *Staple Singers*
61/68 **Be Young, Be Foolish, Be Happy** *Tams*
61/85 **Be Your Man** *Jesse Johnson's Revue*
4/74 **Beach Baby** *First Class*
12/81 **Beach Boys Medley** *Beach Boys*
72/64 **Beach Girl** *Pat Boone*
60/62 **Beach Party** *King Curtis*
95/62 **Beach Party** *Dave York*
64/59 **Beach Time** *Roger Smith*
100/60 **Beachcomber** *Bobby Darin*
30/64 **Beans In My Ears** *Serendipity Singers*
Beast Of Burden
8/78 *Rolling Stones*
71/84 *Bette Midler*
57/59 **Beat, The** *Rockin R's*
6/67 **Beat Goes On** *Sonny & Cher*
1/83 **Beat It** *Michael Jackson*
(also see: Eat It)
81/72 **Beat Me Daddy Eight To The Bar**
Commander Cody
41/85 **Beat Of A Heart** *Scandal*
86/84 **Beat Street Breakdown**
Grandmaster Melle Mel
92/67 **Beat The Clock** *McCoys*
17/86 **Beat's So Lonely** *Charlie Sexton*
Beatles E.P.'s *see: Four By The Beatles*
12/82 **Beatles' Movie Medley** *Beatles*
15/60 **Beatnik Fly** *Johnny & The Hurricanes*
87/70 **Beaucoups Of Blues** *Ringo Starr*
82/64 **Beautician Blues** *B.B. King*
58/72 **Beautiful** *Gordon Lightfoot*
81/58 **Beautiful Delilah** *Chuck Berry*
74/56 **Beautiful Friendship** *Ella Fitzgerald*
84/79 **Beautiful Girls** *Van Halen*
3/68 **Beautiful Morning** *Rascals*
89/60 **Beautiful Obsession** *Sir Chauncey*
Beautiful People
37/67 *Bobby Vee*
38/67 *Kenny O'Dell*
67/71 **Beautiful People** *New Seekers*
53/67 **Beautiful Story** *Sonny & Cher*
15/72 **Beautiful Sunday** *Daniel Boone*
3/66 **Beauty Is Only Skin Deep** *Temptations*
3/64 **Because** *Dave Clark Five*
96/66 **Because I Love You** *Billy Stewart*
F/70 **Because I Love You** *Five Stairsteps*
71/67 **Because Of You** *Chris Montez*
13/78 **Because The Night** *Patti Smith Group*
4/60 **Because They're Young** *Duane Eddy*
62/59 **Because You're Young** *Jimmie Rodgers*
70/72 **Bed And Board** *Barbara Mason*
58/71 **Bed Of Rose's** *Statler Brothers*
86/72 **Bedtime Story** *Tammy Wynette*
Beechwood 4-5789
17/62 *Marvelettes*
74/82 *Carpenters*
24/58 **Been So Long** *Pastels*
24/73 **Been To Canaan** *Carole King*
98/71 **Been Too Long On The Road** *Mark Lindsay*
4/58 **Beep Beep** *Playmates*
33/75 **Beer Barrel Polka** *Bobby Vinton*
50/65 **(Bees Are For The Birds) The Birds Are For The Bees** *Newbeats*
17/65 **Before And After** *Chad & Jeremy*
68/86 **Before I Go** *Starship*
84/60 **Before I Grow Too Old** *Fats Domino*
23/78 **Before My Heart Finds Out** *Gene Cotton*
1/75 **Before The Next Teardrop Falls**
Freddy Fender
83/65 **Before You Go** *Buck Owens*
29/67 **Beg, Borrow And Steal** *Ohio Express*
79/83 **Beg, Borrow Or Steal** *Hughes/Thrall*
45/64 **Beg Me** *Chuck Jackson*
81/72 **Beg, Steal Or Borrow** *New Seekers*
16/67 **Beggin'** *4 Seasons*
74/63 **Begging To You** *Marty Robbins*
79/67 **Beginning Of Loneliness** *Dionne Warwick*
36/69 **Beginning Of My End** *Unifics*
92/71 **Beginning To Feel The Pain** *Mac Davis*
7/71 **Beginnings** *Chicago*
34/71 **Behind Blue Eyes** *Who*
15/73 **Behind Closed Doors** *Charlie Rich*
97/66 **Behind The Door** *Cher*
69/59 **Bei Mir Bist Du Schon**
Louis Prima & Keely Smith
2/81 **Being With You** *Smokey Robinson*
94/75 **Believe Half Of What You See (And None Of What You Hear)** *Leon Haywood*
28/73 **Believe In Humanity** *Carole King*
48/84 **Believe In Me** *Dan Fogelberg*
92/67 **Believe In Me Baby** *Jesse James*
26/59 **Believe Me** *Royal Teens*
4/58 **Believe What You Say** *Ricky Nelson*

Bell Bottom Blues
91/71 *Derek & The Dominos*
78/73 *Eric Clapton*
28/69 **Bella Linda** *Grass Roots*
83/78 **Belle** *Al Green*
34/84 **Belle Of St. Mark** *Sheila E.*
Bells, The
12/70 *Originals*
68/60 *James Brown*
99/61 **Bells Are Ringing** *Van Dykes*
88/59 **Bells, Bells, Bells (The Bell Song)**
Billy & Lillie
13/58 **Belonging To Someone** *Patti Page*
1/72 **Ben** *Michael Jackson*
Ben Casey *see: Theme From*
Ben Crazy - Dr. Ben Basey
44/62 *Dickie Goodman*
60/62 *Mickey Shorr*
(also see: Callin' Doctor Casey)
5/68 **Bend Me, Shape Me** *American Breed*
1/74 **Bennie And The Jets** *Elton John*
61/61 **Berlin Melody** *Billy Vaughn*
70/62 **Bermuda** *Linda Scott*
4/67 **Bernadette** *Four Tops*
14/57 **Bernardine** *Pat Boone*
16/75 **Bertha Butt Boogie** *Jimmy Castor Bunch*
79/58 **Bertha Lou** *Clint Miller*
70/60 **Besame Mucho** *Coasters*
69/79 **Best Beat In Town** *Switch*
17/76 **Best Disco In Town** *Ritchie Family*
61/87 **Best Man In The World** *Ann Wilson*
32/68 **Best Of Both Worlds** *Lulu*
62/59 **Best Of Everything** *Johnny Mathis*
80/86 **Best Of Me**
David Foster & Olivia Newton-John
1/77 **Best Of My Love** *Emotions*
1/75 **Best Of My Love** *Eagles*
3/81 **Best Of Times** *Styx*
39/64 **(Best Part Of) Breakin' Up** *Ronettes*
82/72 **Best Thing** *Styx*
Best Thing That Ever Happened To Me
82/73 *Ray Price*
3/74 *Gladys Knight & The Pips*
85/74 *Persuaders*
54/81 **Bet Your Heart On Me** *Johnny Lee*
3/72 **Betcha By Golly, Wow** *Stylistics*
(Betcha Got A Chick On The Side)
see: How Long
49/83 **Betcha She Don't Love You** *Evelyn King*
7/76 **Beth** *Kiss*
1/81 **Bette Davis Eyes** *Kim Carnes*
5/84 **Better Be Good To Me** *Tina Turner*
99/75 **Better By The Pound** *Funkadelic*
71/76 **Better Days** *Melissa Manchester*
12/80 **Better Love Next Time** *Dr. Hook*
86/76 **Better Place To Be** *Harry Chapin*
38/61 **Better Tell Him No** *Starlets*
92/82 **Better Things** *Kinks*
89/63 **Better To Give Than Receive** *Joe Hinton*
54/66 **Better Use Your Head**
Little Anthony & The Imperials
33/58 **Betty And Dupree** *Chuck Willis*
50/63 **Betty In Bermudas** *Dovells*
37/58 **Betty Lou Got A New Pair Of Shoes**
Bobby Freeman
90/59 **Betty My Angel** *Jerry Fuller*
57/74 **Between Her Goodbye And My Hello**
Gladys Knight & The Pips
Beverly Hillbillies
see: Ballad Of Jed Clampett
Bewildered
57/58 *Mickey & Sylvia*
40/61 *James Brown*
50/58 **Bewitched** *Betty Smith Group*

50/80 **Beyond** *Herb Alpert*
80/74 **Beyond The Blue Horizon** *Lou Christie*
Beyond The Sea
37/56 *Roger Williams*
6/60 *Bobby Darin*
71/59 **Beyond The Sunset** *Pat Boone*
Bible Tells Me So
7/55 *Don Cornell*
22/55 *Nick Noble*
24/79 **Bicycle Race** *Queen*
1/61 **Big Bad John** *Jimmy Dean*
26/58 **Big Beat** *Fats Domino*
87/57 **Big Beat** *Dick Jacobs*
58/61 **Big Big World** *Johnny Burnette*
93/63 **Big Boat** *Peter, Paul & Mary*
38/58 **Big Bopper's Wedding** *Big Bopper*
94/64 **Big Boss Line** *Jackie Wilson*
Big Boss Man
78/61 *Jimmy Reed*
92/64 *Gene Chandler (Soul Hootenanny)*
38/67 *Elvis Presley*
50/60 **Big Boy Pete** *Olympics*
(also see: Jolly Green Giant)
84/58 **Big Brown Eyes** *Redjacks*
97/69 **Big Bruce** *Steve Greenberg*
23/73 **Big City Miss Ruth Ann** *Gallery*
19/61 **Big Cold Wind** *Pat Boone*
54/84 **Big Crash** *Eddie Money*
96/58 **Big Daddy** *Jill Corey*
61/62 **Big Draft (medley)** *Four Preps*
21/82 **Big Fun** *Kool & The Gang*
1/62 **Big Girls Don't Cry** *4 Seasons*
46/58 **Big Guitar** *Owen Bradley Quintet*
1/59 **Big Hunk O' Love** *Elvis Presley*
Big Hurt
3/59 *Miss Toni Fisher*
94/66 *Del Shannon*
66/85 **Big In Japan** *Alphaville*
100/69 **Big In Vegas** *Buck Owens*
26/60 **Big Iron** *Marty Robbins*
21/61 **Big John** *Shirelles*
61/70 **Big Leg Woman (With A Short Short Mini Skirt)** *Israel 'Popper Stopper' Tolbert*
20/83 **Big Log** *Robert Plant*
74/62 **Big Love** *Joe Henderson*
3/58 **Big Man** *Four Preps*
20/64 **Big Man In Town** *4 Seasons*
45/86 **Big Money** *Rush*
97/64 **Big Party** *Barbara & The Browns*
F/58 **Big River** *Johnny Cash*
82/61 **Big River, Big Man** *Claude King*
14/79 **Big Shot** *Billy Joel*
8/87 **Big Time** *Peter Gabriel*
95/66 **Big Time** *Lou Christie*
81/73 **Big Time Operator** *Keith Hampshire*
75/60 **Big Time Spender** *Cornbread & Biscuits*
51/63 **Big Wide World** *Teddy Randazzo*
Big Yellow Taxi
29/70 *Neighborhood*
67/70 *Joni Mitchell*
24/75 *Joni Mitchell*
57/76 **Bigfoot** *Bro Smith*
50/75 **Biggest Parakeets In Town** *Jud Strunk*
3/80 **Biggest Part Of Me** *Ambrosia*
37/61 **Bilbao Song** *Andy Williams*
84/64 **Billie Baby** *Lloyd Price*
Billie Jean
1/83 *Michael Jackson*
75/83 *Club House (medley)*
57/73 **Billion Dollar Babies** *Alice Cooper*
7/58 **Billy** *Kathy Linden*
34/66 **Billy And Sue** *B.J. Thomas*
95/58 **Billy Bayou** *Jim Reeves*

Billy, Don't Be A Hero
1/74 *Bo Donaldson & The Heywoods*
96/74 *Paper Lace*
Billy Jack *see: One Tin Soldier*
92/68 **Billy You're My Friend** *Gene Pitney*
11/58 **Bimbombey** *Jimmie Rodgers*
95/60 **Biology** *Danny Valentino*
91/68 **Biplane, Ever More** *Irish Rovers*
36/85 **Bird** *Time*
(also see: Bossa Nova, & Do The)
30/64 **Bird Dance Beat** *Trashmen*
1/58 **Bird Dog** *Everly Brothers*
64/62 **Bird Man** *Highwaymen*
34/58 **Bird On My Head** *David Seville*
52/63 **Bird's The Word** *Rivingtons*
(also see: Surfin' Bird)
12/63 **Birdland** *Chubby Checker*
3/65 **Birds And The Bees** *Jewel Akens*
Birds Of A Feather
96/69 *Joe South*
23/71 *Raiders*
89/67 **Birds Of Britain** *Bob Crewe Generation*
Birth & Death Of A Gangster
see: Alvin Stone
75/62 **Birth Of The Beat** *Sandy Nelson*
26/55 **Birth Of The Boogie**
Bill Haley & His Comets
26/69 **Birthday** *Underground Sunshine*
40/63 **Birthday Party** *Pixies Three*
74/57 **Birthday Party** *Sil Austin*
78/85 **Bit By Bit** *Stephanie Mills*
4/74 **Bitch Is Back** *Elton John*
28/77 **Bite Your Lip (Get up and dance!)**
Elton John
4/64 **Bits And Pieces** *Dave Clark Five*
36/73 **Bitter Bad** *Melanie*
76/56 **Bitter With The Sweet** *Billy Eckstine*
1/72 **Black & White** *Three Dog Night*
79/69 **Black Berries** *Isley Brothers*
18/77 **Black Betty** *Ram Jam*
88/73 **Black Byrd** *Donald Byrd*
42/85 **Black Cars** *Gino Vannelli*
98/63 **Black Cloud** *Chubby Checker*
Black Denim Trousers
6/55 *Cheers*
38/55 *Vaughn Monroe*
15/72 **Black Dog** *Led Zeppelin*
F/71 **Black-Eyed Blues** *Joe Cocker*
41/74 **Black-Eyed Boys** *Paper Lace*
56/70 **Black Fox** *Freddy Robinson*
37/75 **Black Friday** *Steely Dan*
79/70 **Black Hands White Cotton** *Caboose*
4/66 **Black Is Black** *Los Bravos*
81/85 **Black Kisses (Never Make You Blue)**
Curtie & The Boombox
Black Land Farmer
82/61 *Frankie Miller*
85/61 *Wink Martindale*
55/74 **Black Lassie Featuring Johnny Stash**
Cheech & Chong
4/71 **Black Magic Woman** *Santana*
66/70 **Black Night** *Deep Purple*
99/65 **Black Night** *Bobby Bland*
91/66 **Black Nights** *Lowell Fulsom*
13/69 **Black Pearl** *Checkmates, Ltd.*
97/71 **Black Seeds Keep On Growing**
Main Ingredient
68/67 **Black Sheep**
Sam The Sham & The Pharoahs
17/57 **Black Slacks** *Joe Bennett*
63/84 **Black Stations/White Stations** *M+M*
21/75 **Black Superman - 'Muhammad Ali'**
Johnny Wakelin
1/75 **Black Water** *Doobie Brothers*

57/59 **Blah, Blah, Blah** *Nicola Paone*
48/83 **Blame It On Love**
Smokey Robinson & Barbara Mitchell
Blame It On The Boogie
54/78 *Jacksons*
61/78 *Mick Jackson*
7/63 **Blame It On The Bossa Nova** *Eydie Gorme*
88/86 **Blame It On The Radio** *John Parr*
78/75 **Blanket On The Ground** *Billie Jo Spears*
66/81 **Blaze Of Glory** *Kenny Rogers*
39/64 **Bless Our Love** *Gene Chandler*
Bless The Beasts And Children
67/72 *Carpenters*
82/77 *Barry DeVorzon & Perry Botkin, Jr.*
15/61 **Bless You** *Tony Orlando*
53/71 **Bless You** *Martha & The Vandellas*
34/81 **Blessed Are The Believers** *Anne Murray*
97/68 **Blessed Are The Lonely** *Robert Knight*
45/69 **Blessed Is The Rain** *Brooklyn Bridge*
F/73 **Blind Eye** *Uriah Heep*
Blind Man
78/65 *Bobby Bland*
86/65 *Little Milton*
Blind Man In The Bleachers
see: Last Game Of The Season
1/77 **Blinded By The Light**
Manfred Mann's Earth Band
82/58 **Blip Blop** *Bill Doggett*
50/69 **Blistered** *Johnny Cash*
62/61 **Blizzard** *Jim Reeves*
Bloat On *see: Float On*
33/58 **Blob, The** *Five Blobs*
73/73 **Blockbuster** *Sweet*
43/74 **Blood Is Thicker Than Water**
William DeVaughn
74/73 **Blood Red And Goin' Down** *Tanya Tucker*
35/75 **Bloody Well Right** *Supertramp*
2/55 **Blossom Fell** *Nat King Cole*
16/79 **Blow Away** *George Harrison*
Blowin' In The Wind
2/63 *Peter, Paul & Mary*
9/66 *Stevie Wonder*
21/70 **Blowing Away** *5th Dimension*
9/60 **Blue Angel** *Roy Orbison*
35/67 **Blue Autumn** *Bobby Goldsboro*
Blue Bayou
29/63 *Roy Orbison*
3/77 *Linda Ronstadt*
20/58 **Blue Blue Day** *Don Gibson*
45/58 **Blue Boy** *Jim Reeves*
97/60 **Blue Christmas** *Browns*
68/73 **Blue Collar** *Bachman-Turner Overdrive*
21/78 **Blue Collar Man (Long Nights)** *Styx*
12/82 **Blue Eyes** *Elton John*
21/75 **Blue Eyes Crying In The Rain**
Willie Nelson
42/63 **Blue Guitar** *Richard Chamberlain*
94/76 **Blue Guitar** *Justin Hayward/John Lodge*
37/59 **Blue Hawaii** *Billy Vaughn*
8/84 **Blue Jean** *David Bowie*
77/85 **Blue Kiss** *Jane Wiedlin*
62/84 **Blue Light** *David Gilmour*
54/55 **Blue Mirage (Don't Go)** *Ralph Marterie*
5/57 **Blue Monday** *Fats Domino*
23/71 **Blue Money** *Van Morrison*
Blue Moon
55/56 *Elvis Presley*
1/61 *Marcels*
50/61 *Herb Lance*
54/61 *Ventures*
15/79 **Blue Morning, Blue Day** *Foreigner*
3/63 **Blue On Blue** *Bobby Vinton*
50/58 **Blue Ribbon Baby** *Tommy Sands*
95/66 **Blue River** *Elvis Presley*

97/65 **Blue Shadows** *B.B. King*
81/80 **Blue Side** *Crystal Gayle*
59/66 **Blue Side Of Lonesome** *Jim Reeves*
57/75 **Blue Sky** *Joan Baez*
Blue Star
29/55 *Felicia Sanders*
F/55 *Les Baxter*
Blue Suede Shoes
2/56 *Carl Perkins*
20/56 *Elvis Presley*
63/56 *Boyd Bennett*
38/73 *Johnny Rivers*
16/60 **Blue Tango** *Bill Black's Combo*
84/61 **Blue Tomorrow** *Billy Vaughn*
Blue Velvet
84/60 *Statues*
1/63 *Bobby Vinton*
68/62 **Blue Water Line** *Brothers Four*
24/64 **Blue Winter** *Connie Francis*
62/83 **Blue World** *Moody Blues*
94/58 **Bluebell** *Mitch Miller*
Blueberry Hill
29/56 *Louis Armstrong*
2/57 *Fats Domino*
35/75 **Bluebird** *Helen Reddy*
58/67 **Bluebird** *Buffalo Springfield*
54/59 **Bluebird, The Buzzard & The Oriole**
Bobby Day
Bluebirds Over The Mountain
75/58 *Ersel Hickey*
61/68 *Beach Boys*
49/56 **Bluejean Bop** *Gene Vincent*
12/78 **Bluer Than Blue** *Michael Johnson*
51/83 **Blues** *Randy Newman & Paul Simon*
76/80 **Blues Power** *Eric Clapton*
36/62 **Blues (Stay Away From Me)** *Ace Cannon*
37/67 **Blue's Theme** *Davie Allan & The Arrows*
Bo Weevil
17/56 *Teresa Brewer*
35/56 *Fats Domino*
(also see: Boll Weevil)
88/78 **Boats Against The Current** *Eric Carmen*
12/82 **Bobbie Sue** *Oak Ridge Boys*
58/61 **Bobby** *Neil Scott*
8/59 **Bobby Sox To Stockings** *Frankie Avalon*
3/62 **Bobby's Girl** *Marcie Blane*
47/84 **Body** *Jacksons*
86/79 **Body Heat** *Alicia Bridges*
11/82 **Body Language** *Queen*
48/84 **Body Rock** *Maria Vidal*
77/84 **Body Talk** *Deele*
88/77 **Bodyheat** *James Brown*
9/76 **Bohemian Rhapsody** *Queen*
59/70 **Bold Soul Sister** *Ike & Tina Turner*
2/61 **Boll Weevil Song** *Brook Benton*
70/78 **Bombs Away** *Bob Weir*
63/81 **Bon Bon Vie (Gimme The Good Life)**
T.S. Monk
55/64 **Bon-Doo-Wah** *Orlons*
46/57 **Bon Voyage** *Janice Harper*
Bonanza
19/61 *Al Caiola*
94/62 *Johnny Cash*
50/59 **Bonaparte's Retreat** *Billy Grammer*
84/85 **Bongo Bongo** *Steve Miller Band*
78/60 **Bongo Bongo Bongo** *Preston Epps*
Bongo Rock
14/59 *Preston Epps*
57/73 *Incredible Bongo Band*
33/62 **Bongo Stomp** *Little Joey & The Flips*
Bonnie And Clyde *see: Ballad Of*
Bonnie Blue Gal
50/55 *Lawrence Welk*
51/55 *Mitch Miller*

26/60 **Bonnie Came Back** *Duane Eddy*
(also see: My Bonnie)
Bony Moronie
14/57 *Larry Williams*
62/63 *Appalachians*
70/73 **Boo, Boo, Don't 'Cha Be Blue**
Tommy James
49/59 **Boo Boo Stick Beat** *Chet Atkins*
47/65 **Boo-Ga-Loo** *Tom & Jerrio*
7/67 **Boogaloo Down Broadway**
Fantastic Johnny C
93/66 **Boogaloo Party** *Flamingos*
72/74 **Boogie Bands And One Night Stands**
Kathy Dalton
73/59 **Boogie Bear** *Boyd Bennett*
12/77 **Boogie Child** *Bee Gees*
2/74 **Boogie Down** *Eddie Kendricks*
77/83 **Boogie Down** *Al Jarreau*
1/76 **Boogie Fever** *Sylvers*
2/77 **Boogie Nights** *Heatwave*
3/75 **Boogie On Reggae Woman** *Stevie Wonder*
1/78 **Boogie Oogie Oogie** *A Taste Of Honey*
35/78 **Boogie Shoes** *KC & The Sunshine Band*
6/79 **Boogie Wonderland**
Earth, Wind & Fire with The Emotions
89/61 **Boogie Woogie** *B. Bumble & The Stingers*
(also see: Jay-Dee's)
8/73 **Boogie Woogie Bugle Boy** *Bette Midler*
56/79 **Boogie Woogie Dancin' Shoes**
Claudja Barry
68/73 **Boogie Woogie Man** *Paul Davis*
Book Of Love
5/58 *Monotones*
62/64 *Raindrops*
83/59 **Boom-A-Dip-Dip** *Stan Robinson*
Boom Boom
60/62 *John Lee Hooker*
43/65 *Animals*
17/55 **Boom Boom Boomerang** *DeCastro Sisters*
56/79 **Boom Boom (Out Go The Lights)**
Pat Travers
Boomerang *see: Do The*
58/65 **Boot-Leg** *Booker T. & The MG's*
36/71 **Booty Butt** *Ray Charles*
42/86 **Bop** *Dan Seals*
20/84 **Bop 'Til You Drop** *Rick Springfield*
63/58 **Bop-A-Lena** *Ronnie Self*
70/56 **Boppin' The Blues** *Carl Perkins*
33/83 **Border, The** *America*
Border Song
37/70 *Aretha Franklin*
92/70 *Elton John*
10/84 **Borderline** *Madonna*
38/85 **Borderlines** *Jeffrey Osborne*
12/66 **Born A Woman** *Sandy Posey*
92/69 **Born Again** *Sam & Dave*
Born Free
7/66 *Roger Williams*
38/68 *Hesitations*
48/85 **Born In East L.A.** *Cheech & Chong*
9/85 **Born In The U.S.A.** *Bruce Springsteen*
16/79 **Born To Be Alive** *Patrick Hernandez*
52/65 **Born To Be Together** *Ronettes*
Born To Be Wild
2/68 *Steppenwolf*
64/69 *Wilson Pickett*
Born To Be With You
5/56 *Chordettes*
81/68 *Sonny James*
41/62 **Born To Lose** *Ray Charles*
23/75 **Born To Run** *Bruce Springsteen*
17/71 **Born To Wander** *Rare Earth*
7/58 **Born Too Late** *Poni-Tails*
60/58 **Borrowed Dreams** *Bobby Helms*

64/80 **Borrowed Time** *Styx*
87/63 **Boss** *Rumblers*
19/79 **Boss** *Diana Ross*
28/63 **Boss Guitar** *Duane Eddy*
8/63 **Bossa Nova Baby** *Elvis Presley*
97/62 **(Bossa Nova) Bird** *Dells*
69/63 **Bossa Nova U.S.A.** *Dave Brubeck Quartet*
Both Sides Now
8/68 *Judy Collins*
91/69 *Dion*
9/68 **Bottle Of Wine** *Fireballs*
19/80 **Boulevard** *Jackson Browne*
40/63 **Bounce, The** *Olympics*
81/80 **Bounce, Rock, Skate, Roll** *Vaughan Mason & Crew*
52/84 **Bouncin' Off The Walls** *Matthew Wilder*
40/67 **Bowling Green** *Everly Brothers*
7/69 **Boxer, The** *Simon & Garfunkel*
Boy From New York City
8/65 *Ad Libs*
7/81 *Manhattan Transfer*
Boy I'm Gonna Marry *see: (Today I Met)*
26/85 **Boy In The Box** *Corey Hart*
2/69 **Boy Named Sue** *Johnny Cash*
18/63 **Boy Next Door** *Secrets*
85/64 **Boy With The Beatle Hair** *Swans*
10/59 **Boy Without A Girl** *Frankie Avalon*
12/76 **Boys Are Back In Town** *Thin Lizzy*
37/84 **Boys Do Fall In Love** *Robin Gibb*
Boys In The Band *see: (How About A Little Hand For)*
5/85 **Boys Of Summer** *Don Henley*
49/62 **Boys' Night Out** *Patti Page*
1/71 **Brand New Key** *Melanie*
61/75 **Brand New Love Affair** *Chicago*
66/76 **Brand New Love Affair** *Jigsaw*
15/87 **Brand New Lover** *Dead Or Alive*
Brand New Me
24/69 *Dusty Springfield*
F/71 *Aretha Franklin*
79/78 **Brandy** *O'Jays*
Brandy *see: Mandy*
1/72 **Brandy (You're A Fine Girl)** *Looking Glass*
35/61 **Brass Buttons** *String-A-Longs*
14/80 **Brass In Pocket (I'm Special)** *Pretenders*
11/75 **Brazil** *Ritchie Family*
2/64 **Bread And Butter** *Newbeats*
68/83 **Bread And Butter** *Robert John*
70/84 **Break-A-Way** *Tracey Ullman*
39/76 **Break Away** *Art Garfunkel*
63/69 **Break Away** *Beach Boys*
40/65 **Break Away (From That Boy)** *Newbeats*
Break It To Me Gently
4/62 *Brenda Lee*
11/82 *Juice Newton*
85/77 **Break It To Me Gently** *Aretha Franklin*
85/78 **Break It To Them Gently** *Burton Cummings*
26/82 **Break It Up** *Foreigner*
5/84 **Break My Stride** *Matthew Wilder*
62/66 **Break Out** *Mitch Ryder & The Detroit Wheels*
Break-Up
52/58 *Jerry Lee Lewis*
95/65 **Break Up** *Del Shannon*
5/73 **Break Up To Make Up** *Stylistics*
35/68 **Break Your Promise** *Delfonics*
8/84 **Breakdance** *Irene Cara*
31/71 **Breakdown** *Rufus Thomas*
40/78 **Breakdown, The** *Tom Petty*
15/80 **Breakdown Dead Ahead** *Boz Scaggs*
94/76 **Breaker - Breaker** *Outlaws*
92/76 **Breakfast For Two** *Country Joe McDonald*
62/80 **Breakfast In America** *Supertramp*
91/69 **Breakfast In Bed** *Dusty Springfield*
43/82 **Breakin' Away** *Al Jarreau*
7/61 **Breakin' In A Brand New Broken Heart** *Connie Francis*
9/84 **Breakin'...There's No Stopping Us** *Ollie & Jerry*
Breakin' Up *see: (Best Part Of)*
31/66 **Breakin' Up Is Breakin' My Heart** *Roy Orbison*
22/81 **Breaking Away** *Balance*
70/84 **Breaking Up Is Hard On You (a/k/a Don't Take Ma Bell Away From Me)** *American Comedy Network*
Breaking Up Is Hard To Do
1/62 *Neil Sedaka*
67/68 *Happenings*
34/70 *Lenny Welch*
28/72 *Partridge Family*
8/76 *Neil Sedaka*
69/59 **Breaking Up Is Hard To Do** *Jivin' Gene*
91/73 **Breaking Up Somebody's Home** *Albert King*
18/83 **Breaking Us In Two** *Joe Jackson*
87/80 **Breaks** *Kurtis Blow*
15/81 **Breakup Song (They Don't Write 'Em)** *Greg Kihn Band*
100/63 **Breakwater** *Lawrence Welk*
75/63 **Breath Taking Guy** *Supremes*
7/58 **Breathless** *Jerry Lee Lewis*
8/55 **Breeze And I** *Caterina Valente*
63/76 **Breezin'** *George Benson*
57/63 **Brenda** *Cupids*
56/72 **Brian's Song** *Michel Legrand*
5/77 **Brick House** *Commodores*
50/61 **Bridge Of Love** *Joe Dowell*
Bridge Over Troubled Water
1/70 *Simon & Garfunkel*
6/71 *Aretha Franklin*
41/79 *Linda Clifford*
50/71 **Bridget The Midget** *Ray Stevens*
81/60 **Brigade Of Broken Hearts** *Paul Evans*
Bright Lights Big City
58/61 *Jimmy Reed*
91/71 *Sonny James*
92/63 **Brightest Smile In Town** *Ray Charles*
82/70 **Brighton Hill** *Jackie DeShannon*
51/68 **Bring A Little Lovin'** *Los Bravos*
66/65 **Bring A Little Sunshine (To My Heart)** *Vic Dana*
87/74 **Bring Back The Love Of Yesterday** *Dells*
75/66 **Bring Back The Time** *B.J. Thomas*
95/68 **Bring Back Those Rockabye Baby Days** *Tiny Tim*
96/72 **Bring It Home (And Give It To Me)** *Hot Sauce*
Bring It On Home To Me
13/62 *Sam Cooke*
32/65 *Animals*
17/68 *Eddie Floyd*
96/70 *Lou Rawls*
(also see: I'll Bring It Home To You)
29/67 **Bring It Up** *James Brown*
12/71 **Bring The Boys Home** *Freda Payne*
83/65 **Bring Your Love To Me** *Righteous Brothers*
61/84 **Bringin' On The Heartbreak** *Def Leppard*
65/75 **Bringing It Back** *Elvis Presley*
73/79 **(Bringing Out) The Girl In Me** *Maxine Nightingale*
82/67 **Brink Of Disaster** *Lesley Gore*
2/61 **Bristol Stomp** *Dovells*
27/62 **Bristol Twistin' Annie** *Dovells*
66/80 **Brite Eyes** *Robbin Thompson Band*
F/71 **Broken** *Guess Who*

81/62 **Broken Heart** *Fiestas*
91/61 **Broken Heart And A Pillow Filled With Tears** *Patti Page*
97/61 **Broken Hearted** *Miracles*
12/79 **Broken Hearted Me** *Anne Murray*
7/59 **Broken-Hearted Melody** *Sarah Vaughan*
1/85 **Broken Wings** *Mr. Mister*
75/60 **Brontosaurus Stomp** *Piltdown Men*
74/77 **Brooklyn** *Cody Jameson*
54/81 **Brooklyn Girls** *Robbie Dupree*
58/68 **Brooklyn Roads** *Neil Diamond*
53/66 **Broomstick Cowboy** *Bobby Goldsboro*
84/61 **Brother-In-Law (He's A Moocher)** *Paul Peek*
1/73 **Brother Louie** *Stories*
22/69 **Brother Love's Travelling Salvation Show** *Neil Diamond*
32/70 **Brother Rapp** *James Brown*
67/73 **Brother's Gonna Work It Out** *Willie Hutch*
91/69 **Brown Arms In Houston** *Orpheus*
Brown Eyed Girl
10/67 *Van Morrison*
45/72 *El Chicano*
43/68 **Brown Eyed Woman** *Bill Medley*
73/70 **Brown Paper Bag** *Syndicate Of Sound*
1/71 **Brown Sugar** *Rolling Stones*
66/71 **Brownsville** *Joy Of Cooking*
27/85 **Bruce** *Rick Springfield*
74/69 **Bubble Gum Music** *Rock & Roll Dubble Bubble*
80/56 **Buchanan and Goodman On Trial** *Buchanan & Goodman*
60/65 **Buckaroo** *Buck Owens*
54/65 **Bucket 'T'** *Ronny & The Daytonas*
86/70 **Buffalo Soldier** *Flamingos*
3/69 **Build Me Up Buttercup** *Foundations*
58/57 **Build Your Love (On A Strong Foundation)** *Johnnie Ray*
24/60 **Bulldog** *Fireballs*
90/84 **Bullish** *Herb Alpert*
83/58 **Bullwhip Rock** *Cyclones*
Bumble Bee
46/60 *LaVern Baker*
21/65 *Searchers*
21/61 **Bumble Boogie** *B. Bumble & The Stingers*
80/75 **Bump Me Baby** *Dooley Silverspoon*
12/75 **Bungle In The Jungle** *Jethro Tull*
70/59 **Bunny Hop** *Applejacks*
84/81 **Burn Rubber (Why You Wanna Hurt Me)** *Gap Band*
Burn That Candle
9/55 *Bill Haley & His Comets*
86/55 *Cues*
40/81 **Burnin' For You** *Blue Oyster Cult*
78/77 **Burnin' Sky** *Bad Company*
53/75 **Burnin' Thing** *Mac Davis*
3/60 **Burning Bridges** *Jack Scott*
34/71 **Burning Bridges** *Mike Curb Congregation*
64/82 **Burning Down One Side** *Robert Plant*
9/83 **Burning Down The House** *Talking Heads*
73/85 **Burning Flame** *Vitamin Z*
2/86 **Burning Heart** *Survivor*
39/83 **Burning Heart** *Vandenberg*
2/72 **Burning Love** *Elvis Presley*
53/62 **Burning Of Atlanta** *Claude King*
64/68 **Burning Spear** *Soulful Strings*
5/66 **Bus Stop** *Hollies*
16/56 **Bus Stop Song (A Paper Of Pins)** *Four Lads*
25/63 **Bust Out** *Busters*
4/63 **Busted** *Ray Charles*
96/65 **Buster Browne** *Willie Mitchell*
34/79 **Bustin' Loose** *Chuck Brown*
71/79 **Bustin' Out** *Rick James*

69/57 **(But As They Say) That's Life** *Jack Pleis*
69/70 **But For Love** *Jerry Naylor*
But I Do
4/61 *Clarence 'Frogman' Henry*
82/73 *Bobby Vinton*
But It's Alright
22/66 *J.J. Jackson*
45/69 *J.J. Jackson*
41/62 **But Not For Me** *Ketty Lester*
72/62 **But On The Other Hand Baby** *Ray Charles*
But You Know I Love You
19/69 *First Edition*
41/81 *Dolly Parton*
15/65 **But You're Mine** *Sonny & Cher*
29/75 **Butter Boy** *Fanny*
Butterfly
1/57 *Charlie Gracie*
1/57 *Andy Williams*
61/57 *Bob Carroll*
78/72 **Butterfly** *Danyel Gerard*
23/63 **Butterfly Baby** *Bobby Rydell*
93/56 **Butternut** *Jimmy Heap*
45/67 **Buy For Me The Rain** *Nitty Gritty Dirt Band*
47/69 **Buying A Book** *Joe Tex*
51/61 **Buzz Buzz A-Diddle-It** *Freddy Cannon*
11/58 **Buzz-Buzz-Buzz** *Hollywood Flames*
91/72 **Buzzy Brown** *Tim Davis*
55/62 **B'wa Nina (Pretty Girl)** *Tokens*
50/58 **By The Light Of The Silvery Moon** *Jimmy Bowen with The Rhythm Orchids*
By The Time I Get To Phoenix
26/67 *Glen Campbell*
37/69 *Isaac Hayes*
84/69 *Mad Lads*
81/71 *Glen Campbell & Anne Murray (medley)*
43/57 **By You, By You, By You** *Jim Lowe*
45/61 **Bye Bye Baby** *Mary Wells*
91/75 **Bye Bye Baby** *U.S. 1*
12/65 **Bye, Bye, Baby (Baby Goodbye)** *4 Seasons*
53/64 **Bye Bye Barbara** *Johnny Mathis*
54/66 **Bye Bye Blues** *Bert Kaempfert*
Bye Bye Love
2/57 *Everly Brothers*
73/57 *Webb Pierce*

C

67/77 **C.B. Savage** *Rod Hart*
C.C. Rider
12/57 *Chuck Willis*
34/63 *LaVern Baker*
10/66 *Animals*
76/66 *Bobby Powell*
(also see: Jenny Take A Ride)
18/85 **C-I-T-Y** *John Cafferty*
2/87 **C'est La Vie** *Robbie Nevil*
C'est La Vie
11/55 *Sarah Vaughan*
85/55 *Sunny Gale*
97/55 *DeJohn Sisters*
91/77 **C'est La Vie** *Greg Lake*
22/61 **C'est Si Bon (It's So Good)** *Conway Twitty*
22/57 **Ca, C'est L'amour** *Tony Bennett*
47/78 **Ca Plane Pour Moi (This Life's For Me)** *Plastic Bertrand*
23/68 **Cab Driver** *Mills Brothers*
72/68 **Cabaret** *Herb Alpert*
77/81 **Cafe Amore** *Spyro Gyra*

22/62 **Cajun Queen** *Jimmy Dean*
Calcutta
1/61 *Lawrence Welk*
96/61 *Four Preps*
82/77 **Caledonia** *Robin Trower*
95/64 **Caledonia** *James Brown*
4/61 **Calendar Girl** *Neil Sedaka*
50/78 **California** *Debby Boone*
72/64 **California Bound** *Ronny & The Daytonas*
66/76 **California Day** *Starland Vocal Band*
California Dreamin'
4/66 *Mamas & The Papas*
43/69 *Bobby Womack*
56/79 *America*
57/86 *Beach Boys*
67/68 **California Earthquake** *Mama Cass*
93/71 **California Earthquake** *Norman Greenbaum*
45/70 **California Girl** *Eddie Floyd*
92/69 **California Girl (And The Tennessee Square)** *Tompall & The Glaser Brothers*
California Girls
3/65 *Beach Boys*
3/85 *David Lee Roth*
72/71 **California Kid And Reemo** *Lobo*
75/74 **California My Way** *Main Ingredient*
16/67 **California Nights** *Lesley Gore*
76/78 **California Nights** *Sweet*
96/71 **California On My Mind** *Morning Mist*
84/73 **California Saga (On My Way To Sunny Californ-i-a)** *Beach Boys*
California Soul
25/69 *5th Dimension*
F/70 *Marvin Gaye & Tammi Terrell*
California Sun
89/61 *Joe Jones*
5/64 *Rivieras*
91/76 **Call, The** *Anne Murray*
1/80 **Call Me** *Blondie*
13/70 **Call Me** *Aretha Franklin*
21/58 **Call Me** *Johnny Mathis*
22/66 **Call Me** *Chris Montez*
26/82 **Call Me** *Skyy*
54/85 **Call Me** *Go West*
54/86 **Call Me** *Dennis DeYoung*
10/73 **Call Me (Come Back Home)** *Al Green*
Call Me Irresponsible
75/63 *Jack Jones*
78/63 *Frank Sinatra*
40/68 **Call Me Lightning** *Who*
19/62 **Call Me Mr. In-Between** *Burl Ives*
95/71 **Call Me Up In Dreamland** *Van Morrison*
65/80 **(Call Me) When The Spirit Moves You** *Touch*
99/75 **(Call Me Your) Anything Man** *Bobby Moore*
52/71 **Call My Name, I'll Be There** *Wilson Pickett*
6/74 **Call On Me** *Chicago*
22/63 **Call On Me** *Bobby Bland*
75/79 **Call Out My Name** *Zwol*
15/85 **Call To The Heart** *Giuffria*
83/62 **Callin' Doctor Casey** *John D. Loudermilk*
60/82 **Calling All Girls** *Queen*
18/86 **Calling America** *Electric Light Orchestra*
16/77 **Calling Dr. Love** *Kiss*
Calling Occupants Of Interplanetary Craft
F/77 *Klaatu*
32/77 *Carpenters*
F/75 **Calypso** *John Denver*
42/57 **Calypso Melody** *David Rose*
100/69 **Camel Back** *A.B. Skhy*
91/66 **Campfire Girls** *Billy Joe Royal*
5/69 **Can I Change My Mind** *Tyrone Davis*
83/57 **Can I Come Over Tonight** *Velours*

Can I Get A Witness
22/63 *Marvin Gaye*
39/71 *Lee Michaels*
89/66 **Can I Get To Know You Better** *Turtles*
15/57 **Can I Steal A Little Love** *Frank Sinatra*
49/66 **Can I Trust You?** *Bachelors*
56/76 **Can The Can** *Suzi Quatro*
31/74 **Can This Be Real** *Natural Four*
Can We Still Be Friends
29/78 *Todd Rundgren*
52/80 *Robert Palmer*
Can You Do It
41/64 *Contours*
45/76 *Grand Funk Railroad*
75/70 **Can You Feel It** *Bobby Goldsboro*
77/81 **Can You Feel It** *Jacksons*
69/85 **Can You Feel The Beat** *Lisa Lisa & Cult Jam with Full Force*
16/56 **Can You Find It In Your Heart** *Tony Bennett*
38/78 **Can You Fool** *Glen Campbell*
93/71 **Can You Get To That** *Funkadelic*
49/74 **Can You Handle It?** *Graham Central Station*
47/65 **Can You Jerk Like Me** *Contours*
58/66 **Can You Please Crawl Out Your Window?** *Bob Dylan*
52/79 **Can You Read My Mind** *Maureen McGovern*
48/64 **Can Your Monkey Do The Dog** *Rufus Thomas*
1/64 **Can't Buy Me Love** *Beatles*
91/76 **Can't Change My Heart** *Cate Bros.*
1/85 **Can't Fight This Feeling** *REO Speedwagon*
Can't Find The Time
80/69 *Orpheus*
54/71 *Rose Colored Glass*
5/74 **Can't Get Enough** *Bad Company*
56/67 **Can't Get Enough Of You, Baby** *? (Question Mark) & The Mysterians*
1/74 **Can't Get Enough Of Your Love, Babe** *Barry White*
9/75 **Can't Get It Out Of My Head** *Electric Light Orchestra*
98/70 **Can't Get Over Losing You** *Donnie Elbert*
87/64 **Can't Get Over (The Bossa Nova)** *Eydie Gorme*
2/63 **Can't Get Used To Losing You** *Andy Williams*
51/75 **Can't Give You Anything (But My Love)** *Stylistics*
78/67 **Can't Help But Love You** *Standells*
Can't Help Falling In Love
2/62 *Elvis Presley*
51/70 *Al Martino*
88/70 *Andy Williams*
24/87 *Corey Hart*
100/61 **Can't Help Lovin' That Girl Of Mine** *Excels*
39/76 **Can't Hide Love** *Earth, Wind & Fire*
89/82 **Can't Hold Back (Your Loving)** *Kano*
63/79 **Can't Keep A Good Man Down** *Eddie Money*
67/84 **Can't Let Go** *Stephen Stills*
91/65 **Can't Let You Out Of My Sight** *Chuck Jackson & Maxine Brown*
66/63 **Can't Nobody Love You** *Solomon Burke*
62/80 **Can't Put A Price On Love** *Knack*
65/66 **Can't Satisfy** *Impressions*
88/74 **Can't Say Nothin'** *Curtis Mayfield*
41/67 **Can't Seem To Make You Mine** *Seeds*
29/83 **Can't Shake Loose** *Agnetha Faltskog*
51/79 **Can't Sleep** *Rockets*
3/78 **Can't Smile Without You** *Barry Manilow*
50/85 **Can't Stop** *Rick James*

13/77 **Can't Stop Dancin'** *Captain & Tennille*
52/76 **Can't Stop Groovin' Now, Wanna Do It Some More** *B.T. Express*
25/70 **Can't Stop Loving You** *Tom Jones*
78/67 **Can't Stop Loving You** *Last Word*
Can't Take My Eyes Off You
2/67 *Frankie Valli*
7/68 *Lettermen (medley)*
52/69 *Nancy Wilson*
66/84 **Can't Wait All Night** *Juice Newton*
41/86 **Can't Wait Another Minute** *Five Star*
42/57 **Can't Wait For Summer** *Steve Lawrence*
52/80 **Can't We Try** *Teddy Pendergrass*
54/68 **Can't You Find Another Way (Of Doing It)** *Sam & Dave*
2/65 **Can't You Hear My Heartbeat** *Herman's Hermits*
48/72 **Can't You Hear The Song?** *Wayne Newton*
96/65 **Can't You Just See Me** *Aretha Franklin*
Can't You See
97/76 *Waylon Jennings*
75/77 *Marshall Tucker Band*
52/68 **Can't You See Me Cry** *New Colony Six*
4/64 **Can't You See That She's Mine** *Dave Clark Five*
94/66 **Can't You See (You're Losing Me)** *Mary Wells*
Canadian Sunset
2/56 *Hugo Winterhalter/Eddie Heywood*
7/56 *Andy Williams*
91/61 *Etta Jones*
76/65 *Sounds Orchestral*
3/70 **Candida** *Dawn*
(Candles In The Rain) *see: Lay Down*
21/87 **Candy** *Cameo*
63/65 **Candy** *Astors*
97/59 **Candy Apple Red** *Bonnie Guitar*
3/63 **Candy Girl** *4 Seasons*
46/83 **Candy Girl** *New Edition*
Candy Man
25/61 *Roy Orbison*
1/72 **Candy Man** *Sammy Davis, Jr.*
72/60 **Candy Sweet** *Pat Boone*
58/64 **Candy To Me** *Eddie Holland*
91/74 **Candy's Going Bad** *Golden Earring*
46/70 **Canned Ham** *Norman Greenbaum*
15/58 **Cannonball** *Duane Eddy*
28/85 **Cannonball** *Supertramp*
92/83 **Canvas Of Life** *Minor Detail*
45/59 **Cap And Gown** *Marty Robbins*
90/74 **Captain Howdy** *Simon Stokes*
16/86 **Captain Of Her Heart** *Double*
57/70 **Capture The Moment** *Jay & The Americans*
88/77 **Capture Your Heart** *Blue*
1/77 **Car Wash** *Rose Royce*
39/65 **Cara-Lin** *Strangeloves*
4/65 **Cara, Mia** *Jay & The Americans*
48/60 **Caravan** *Santo & Johnny*
51/86 **Caravan Of Love** *Isley, Jasper, Isley*
10/74 **Carefree Highway** *Gordon Lightfoot*
60/62 **Careless Love** *Ray Charles*
1/85 **Careless Whisper** *Wham!*
93/71 **Carey** *Joni Mitchell*
27/59 **Caribbean** *Mitchell Torok*
55/75 **Caribbean Festival** *Kool & The Gang*
1/84 **Caribbean Queen (No More Love On The Run)** *Billy Ocean*
51/68 **Carmen** *Herb Alpert*
Carol
18/58 *Chuck Berry*
61/64 *Tommy Roe*
93/71 **Carolina Day** *Livingston Taylor*
Carolina In My Mind
67/70 *James Taylor*
73/70 *Crystal Mansion*
21/75 **Carolina In The Pines** *Michael Murphey*
32/66 **Caroline, No** *Brian Wilson*
58/72 **Carolyn** *Merle Haggard*
29/68 **Carpet Man** *5th Dimension*
34/80 **Carrie** *Cliff Richard*
9/67 **Carrie-Anne** *Hollies*
81/83 **Carrie's Gone** *Le Roux*
92/69 **Carroll County Accident** *Porter Wagoner*
52/75 **Carry Me** *David Crosby/Graham Nash*
26/69 **Carry Me Back** *Rascals*
71/72 **Carry Me, Carrie** *Dr. Hook*
11/77 **Carry On Wayward Son** *Kansas*
9/80 **Cars** *Gary Numan*
67/80 **Case Of You** *Frank Stallone*
27/67 **Casino Royale** *Herb Alpert*
51/67 **Casonova (Your Playing Days Are Over)** *Ruby Andrews*
Cast Your Fate To The Wind
22/63 *Vince Guaraldi Trio*
10/65 *Sounds Orchestral*
89/65 *Steve Alaimo*
61/66 *Shelby Flint*
52/59 **Castin' My Spell** *Johnny Otis Show*
Castles In The Air
F/72 *Don McLean*
36/81 *Don McLean*
52/64 **Castles In The Sand** *Stevie Wonder*
25/56 **Casual Look** *Six Teens*
67/64 **Cat, The** *Jimmy Smith*
26/67 **Cat In The Window (The Bird In The Sky)** *Petula Clark*
67/82 **Cat People (Putting Out Fire)** *David Bowie*
30/77 **Cat Scratch Fever** *Ted Nugent*
55/70 **Cat Walk** *Village Soul Choir*
90/72 **Cat's Eye In The Window** *Tommy James*
1/74 **Cat's In The Cradle** *Harry Chapin*
1/58 **Catch A Falling Star** *Perry Como*
40/84 **Catch Me I'm Falling** *Real Life*
50/84 **Catch My Fall** *Billy Idol*
23/65 **Catch The Wind** *Donovan*
4/65 **Catch Us If You Can** *Dave Clark Five*
68/80 **Catching The Sun** *Spyro Gyra*
23/62 **Caterina** *Perry Como*
49/59 **Caterpillar Crawl** *Strangers*
71/76 **Catfish** *Four Tops*
94/76 **Cathedrals** *D.C. LaRue*
1/60 **Cathy's Clown** *Everly Brothers*
Cattle Call
42/55 *Eddy Arnold*
92/57 *Dinah Shore*
94/71 **Caught In A Dream** *Alice Cooper*
77/83 **Caught In The Game** *Survivor*
37/87 **Caught Up In The Rapture** *Anita Baker*
10/82 **Caught Up In You** *38 Special*
(Cave Man) *see: Troglodyte*
4/70 **Cecilia** *Simon & Garfunkel*
15/70 **Celebrate** *Three Dog Night*
26/85 **Celebrate Youth** *Rick Springfield*
1/81 **Celebration** *Kool & The Gang*
95/72 **Celebration** *Tommy James*
84/71 **Celia Of The Seals** *Donovan*
86/83 **Celtic Soul Brothers** *Dexys Midnight Runners*
44/85 **Centerfield** *John Fogerty*
1/82 **Centerfold** *J. Geils Band*
24/84 **Centipede** *Rebbie Jackson*
Certain Girl
71/61 *Ernie K-Doe*
57/80 *Warren Zevon*
14/58 **Certain Smile** *Johnny Mathis*

Cerveza
23/58 *Boots Brown*
73/61 *Bert Kaempfert*
53/81 **Ch Ch Cherie** *Johnny Average Band*
10/62 **Cha-Cha-Cha** *Bobby Rydell*
Cha-Hua-Hua
34/58 *Pets*
74/58 *Eddie Platt*
Chain Gang
2/60 *Sam Cooke*
84/68 *Jackie Wilson & Count Basie*
63/76 *Jim Croce (medley)*
Chain Gang
13/56 *Bobby Scott*
78/56 *Len Dresslar*
Chain Of Fools
2/68 *Aretha Franklin*
100/68 *Jimmy Smith*
Chain Reaction
95/85 *Diana Ross*
66/86 *Diana Ross*
32/68 **Chained** *Marvin Gaye*
70/64 **Chained And Bound** *Otis Redding*
17/62 **Chains** *Cookies*
45/70 **Chains And Things** *B.B. King*
Chains Of Love
20/56 *Pat Boone*
60/69 *Bobby Bland*
90/65 **Chains Of Love** *Drifters*
42/71 **Chairman Of The Board**
Chairmen Of The Board
42/74 **Chameleon** *Herbie Hancock*
43/78 **Champagne Jam** *Atlanta Rhythm Section*
76/84 **Chance For Heaven** *Christopher Cross*
1/57 **Chances Are** *Johnny Mathis*
Change
73/83 *Tears For Fears*
54/85 *John Waite*
Change Is Gonna Come
31/65 *Sam Cooke*
60/70 *5th Dimension (medley)*
3/87 **Change Of Heart** *Cyndi Lauper*
19/78 **Change Of Heart** *Eric Carmen*
21/83 **Change Of Heart** *Tom Petty*
49/69 **Change Of Heart** *Classics IV*
43/71 **Change Partners** *Stephen Stills*
46/75 **Change With The Times** *Van McCoy*
Changes
66/72 *David Bowie*
41/75 *David Bowie*
57/66 **Changes** *Crispian St. Peters*
84/75 **Changes** *Loggins & Messina*
37/77 **Changes In Latitudes, Changes In Attitudes** *Jimmy Buffett*
Chanson D'Amour (Song Of Love)
6/58 *Art & Dotty Todd*
12/58 *Fontane Sisters*
19/57 **Chantez-Chantez** *Dinah Shore*
Chantilly Lace
6/58 *Big Bopper*
87/68 *Mitch Ryder (medley)*
43/72 *Jerry Lee Lewis*
69/62 **Chapel By The Sea** *Billy Vaughn*
Chapel In The Moonlight
32/65 *Bachelors*
25/67 *Dean Martin*
74/59 **Chapel Of Dreams** *Dubs*
Chapel Of Love
1/64 *Dixie Cups*
F/73 *Bette Midler*
Charade
36/64 *Sammy Kaye*
36/64 *Henry Mancini*
100/64 *Andy Williams*

69/61 **Charanga** *Merv Griffin*
59/58 **Chariot Rock** *Champs*
1/82 **Chariots Of Fire - Titles** *Vangelis*
40/71 **Charity Ball** *Fanny*
84/61 **Charlena** *Sevilles*
47/61 **Charleston** *Ernie Fields*
2/59 **Charlie Brown** *Coasters*
Charlies Angels *see: Theme From*
68/85 **Charm The Snake** *Christopher Cross*
69/56 **Charmaine** *Four Freshmen*
91/75 **Charmer** *Tim Moore*
13/63 **Charms** *Bobby Vee*
33/79 **Chase** *Giorgio Moroder*
96/75 **Chase The Clouds Away** *Chuck Mangione*
Chattanooga Choo Choo
54/60 *Ernie Fields*
36/62 *Floyd Cramer*
45/67 *Harpers Bizarre*
32/78 *Tuxedo Junction*
34/60 **Chattanooga Shoe Shine Boy**
Freddy Cannon
89/80 **Cheap Sunglasses** *ZZ Top*
15/73 **Cheaper To Keep Her** *Johnnie Taylor*
74/56 **Cheat, A** *Sanford Clark*
12/66 **Cheater, The** *Bob Kuban*
35/73 **Check It Out** *Tavares*
91/75 **Check It Out** *Bobby Womack*
28/70 **Check Out Your Mind** *Impressions*
97/70 **Check Yourself**
Italian Asphalt & Pavement Company
12/55 **Chee Chee-Oo-Chee (Sang The Little Bird)** *Perry Como & Jaye P. Morgan*
65/72 **Cheer** *Potliquor*
78/64 **Cheer Leader** *Paul Petersen*
32/78 **Cheeseburger In Paradise** *Jimmy Buffett*
78/69 **Chelsea Morning** *Judy Collins*
Cherchez La Femme *see: Whispering*
54/61 **Cherie** *Bobby Rydell*
63/58 **Cherie, I Love You** *Pat Boone*
Cherish
1/66 *Association*
9/71 *David Cassidy*
2/85 **Cherish** *Kool & The Gang*
44/71 **Cherish What Is Dear To You (While It's Near To You)** *Freda Payne*
33/77 **Cherry Baby** *Starz*
99/61 **Cherry Berry Wine** *Charlie McCoy*
Cherry, Cherry
6/66 *Neil Diamond*
31/73 *Neil Diamond*
15/69 **Cherry Hill Park** *Billy Joe Royal*
11/60 **Cherry Pie** *Skip & Flip*
Cherry Pink And Apple Blossom White
1/55 *Perez Prado*
14/55 *Alan Dale*
56/61 *Jerry Murad's Harmonicats*
62/59 **Cherrystone** *Addrisi Brothers*
64/71 **Cheryl Moana Marie** *John Rowles*
5/75 **Chevy Van** *Sammy Johns*
15/68 **Chewy Chewy** *Ohio Express*
35/71 **Chicago** *Graham Nash*
84/57 **Chicago** *Frank Sinatra*
100/59 **Chick, The** *Lee & Paul*
9/71 **Chick-A-Boom (Don't Ya Jes' Love It)**
Daddy Dewdrop
89/57 **Chicken, Baby, Chicken** *Tony Harris*
63/63 **Chicken Feed** *Bent Fabric*
50/70 **Chicken Strut** *Meters*
96/75 **Chico And The Man (Main Theme)**
Jose Feliciano
31/67 **Child Of Clay** *Jimmie Rodgers*
95/60 **Child Of God** *Bobby Darin*
72/65 **Child Of Our Times** *Barry McGuire*
51/70 **Children** *Joe South*

41/79 **Children Of The Sun** *Billy Thorpe*
Children's Marching Song
13/59 *Cyril Stapleton*
16/59 *Mitch Miller*
48/75 *Purple Reign*
72/61 **Chills And Fever** *Ronnie Love*
81/65 **Chim, Chim, Cheree** *New Christy Minstrels*
53/83 **China** *Red Rockers*
38/60 **China Doll** *Ames Brothers*
10/83 **China Girl** *David Bowie*
15/73 **China Grove** *Doobie Brothers*
58/63 **China Nights (Shina No Yoru)** *Kyu Sakamoto*
59/56 **Chincherinchee** *Perry Como*
78/63 **Chinese Checkers** *Booker T. & The MG's*
98/75 **Chinese Kung Fu** *Banzaii*
87/56 **Chinese Rock And Egg Roll** *Buddy Hackett*
77/79 **Chip Away The Stone** *Aerosmith*
10/62 **Chip Chip** *Gene McDaniels*
97/59 **Chip Off The Old Block** *Eddy Arnold*
F/80 **Chip Off The Old Block** *Chic*
Chipmunk Song
1/58 *Chipmunks*
41/59 *Chipmunks*
45/60 *Chipmunks*
39/61 *Chipmunks*
40/62 *Chipmunks*
29/80 **Chiquitita** *Abba*
Chirpy Chirpy Cheep Cheep
20/71 *Mac & Katie Kissoon*
92/71 *Lally Stott*
76/69 **Chitty Chitty Bang Bang** *Paul Mauriat*
34/81 **Chloe** *Elton John*
92/75 **Chocolate Chip** *Isaac Hayes*
94/75 **Chocolate City** *Parliament*
94/68 **Choice, The** *O'Jays*
21/69 **Choice Of Colors** *Impressions*
13/69 **Chokin' Kind** *Joe Simon*
Choo Choo *see: Do The*
F/56 **Choo Choo Ch' Boogie** *Bill Haley & His Comets*
89/73 **Choo Choo Mama** *Ten Years After*
26/68 **Choo Choo Train** *Box Tops*
F/55 **Chop Chop Boom** *Crew-Cuts*
25/77 **Christine Sixteen** *Kiss*
51/60 **Christmas Auld Lang Syne** *Bobby Darin*
92/74 **Christmas Dream** *Perry Como*
58/75 **Christmas For Cowboys** *John Denver*
Christmas Song
80/60 *Nat King Cole*
65/62 *Nat King Cole*
4/79 **Chuck E.'s In Love** *Rickie Lee Jones*
9/64 **Chug-A-Lug** *Roger Miller*
73/79 **Church** *Bob Welch*
Church Bells May Ring
14/56 *Diamonds*
62/56 *Willows*
10/83 **Church Of The Poison Mind** *Culture Club*
62/71 **Church Street Soul Revival** *Tommy James*
Ciao, Ciao Bambina
24/59 *Jacky Noguez*
97/59 *Domenico Modugno*
93/63 **Cigarettes And Coffee Blues** *Marty Robbins*
44/58 **Cimarron (Roll On)** *Billy Vaughn*
Cinco Robles (Five Oaks)
22/57 *Russell Arms*
35/57 *Les Paul & Mary Ford*
16/62 **Cinderella** *Jack Ross*
34/77 **Cinderella** *Firefall*
69/58 **Cinderella** *Four Preps*
70/61 **Cinderella** *Paul Anka*
68/68 **Cinderella Rockefella** *Esther & Abi Ofarim*

58/68 **Cinderella Sunshine** *Paul Revere & The Raiders*
48/73 **Cindy Incidentally** *Faces*
Cindy, Oh Cindy
9/56 *Vince Martin with The Tarriers*
10/56 *Eddie Fisher*
8/62 **Cindy's Birthday** *Johnny Crawford*
72/63 **Cindy's Gonna Cry** *Johnny Crawford*
11/69 **Cinnamon** *Derek*
25/63 **Cinnamon Cinder (It's A Very Nice Dance)** *Pastel Six*
Cinnamon Girl
52/70 *Gentrys*
55/70 *Neil Young*
33/78 **Circle Is Small (I Can See It In Your Eyes)** *Gordon Lightfoot*
55/82 **Circle Of Love** *Steve Miller Band*
38/82 **Circles** *Atlantic Starr*
87/72 **Circles** *New Seekers*
2/73 **Cisco Kid** *War*
23/69 **Cissy Strut** *Meters*
City *also see: C-I-T-Y*
90/61 **City Girl Stole My Country Boy** *Patti Page*
79/74 **City In The Sky** *Staple Singers*
City Lights
71/58 *Ray Price*
92/59 *Ivory Joe Hunter*
55/60 *Debbie Reynolds*
19/56 **City Of Angels** *Highlights*
18/72 **City Of New Orleans** *Arlo Guthrie*
2/72 **Clair** *Gilbert O'Sullivan*
Clam *see: Do The*
6/74 **Clap For The Wolfman** *Guess Who*
45/60 **Clap Your Hands** *Beau-Marks*
36/83 **Clapping Song** *Pia Zadora*
8/65 **Clapping Song (Clap Pat Clap Slap)** *Shirley Ellis*
38/59 **Class, The** *Chubby Checker*
52/59 **Class Cutter (Yeah Yeah)** *Dale Hawkins*
2/68 **Classical Gas** *Mason Williams*
30/58 **Claudette** *Everly Brothers*
72/56 **Clay Idol** *Betty Johnson*
6/72 **Clean Up Woman** *Betty Wright*
35/69 **Clean Up Your Own Back Yard** *Elvis Presley*
68/84 **Cleanin' Up The Town** *Bus Boys*
Clementine
21/60 *Bobby Darin*
65/60 *Jan & Dean*
43/65 **Cleo's Back** *Jr. Walker & The All Stars*
50/66 **Cleo's Mood** *Jr. Walker & The All Stars*
Cleopatra Jones *see: Theme From*
28/58 **Click-Clack** *Dicky Doo & The Don'ts*
Clickity Clack Song *see: Four Little Heels*
65/65 **Climb, The** *Kingsmen*
Climb Every Mountain
74/60 *Tony Bennett*
90/68 *Hesitations*
17/64 **Clinging Vine** *Bobby Vinton*
100/64 **Clock, The** *Baby Washington*
40/80 **Clones (We're All)** *Alice Cooper*
Close Encounters *see: Theme From*
65/82 **Close Enough To Perfect** *Alabama*
25/78 **Close The Door** *Teddy Pendergrass*
42/55 **Close The Door** *Jim Lowe*
12/62 **Close To Cathy** *Mike Clifford*
68/61 **Close Together** *Jimmy Reed*
8/67 **Close Your Eyes** *Peaches & Herb*
37/73 **Close Your Eyes** *Edward Bear*
2/78 **Closer I Get To You** *Roberta Flack & Donny Hathaway*
22/70 **Closer To Home** *Grand Funk Railroad*

Closer To The Heart
76/77 *Rush*
69/82 *Rush*
Closer Walk *see: Just A Closer Walk*
38/83 **Closer You Get** *Alabama*
67/85 **(Closest Thing To) Perfect** *Jermaine Jackson*
Cloud Nine
6/69 *Temptations*
32/69 *Mongo Santamaria*
47/73 **Clouds** *David Gates*
41/59 **Clouds, The** *Spacemen*
62/66 **Cloudy Summer Afternoon (Raindrops)** *Barry McGuire*
66/84 **Club Michelle** *Eddie Money*
C'mon *see: Come On*
99/71 **Co-Co** *Sweet*
83/70 **Coal Miner's Daughter** *Loretta Lynn*
F/80 **Cocaine** *Eric Clapton*
48/57 **Cocoanut Woman** *Harry Belafonte*
44/78 **Cocomotion** *El Coco*
8/72 **Coconut** *Nilsson*
6/77 **Cold As Ice** *Foreigner*
40/83 **Cold Blooded** *Rick James*
96/62 **Cold, Cold Heart** *Dinah Washington*
79/64 **Cold Cold Winter** *Pixies Three*
67/68 **Cold Feet** *Albert King*
33/81 **Cold Love** *Donna Summer*
7/67 **Cold Sweat** *James Brown*
30/70 **Cold Turkey** *Plastic Ono Band*
F/74 **Coldblooded** *James Brown*
47/72 **Coldest Days Of My Life** *Chi-Lites*
F/70 **Cole, Cooke & Redding** *Wilson Pickett*
42/58 **College Man** *Bill Justis*
Colonel Bogey *see: March From The River Kwai*
7/69 **Color Him Father** *Winstons*
16/67 **Color My World** *Petula Clark*
66/72 **Colorado** *Danny Holien*
F/71 **Colour My World** *Chicago*
68/69 **Colour Of My Love** *Jefferson*
61/65 **Colours** *Donovan*
71/61 **Comancheros** *Claude King*
3/64 **Come A Little Bit Closer** *Jay & The Americans*
83/61 **Come Along** *Maurice Williams*
7/70 **Come And Get It** *Badfinger*
83/66 **Come And Get Me** *Jackie DeShannon*
29/63 **Come And Get These Memories** *Martha & The Vandellas*
5/74 **Come And Get Your Love** *Redbone*
68/75 **Come And Get Your Love** *Roger Daltrey*
83/75 **Come And Get Yourself Some** *Leon Haywood*
26/65 **Come And Stay With Me** *Marianne Faithfull*
32/80 **Come Back** *J. Geils Band*
61/63 **Come Back** *Johnny Mathis*
61/66 **Come Back** *Five Stairsteps*
63/60 **Come Back** *Jimmy Clanton*
22/84 **Come Back And Stay** *Paul Young*
86/65 **Come Back Baby** *Roddie Joy*
69/71 **Come Back Home** *Bobby Goldsboro*
17/62 **Come Back Silly Girl** *Lettermen*
3/67 **Come Back When You Grow Up** *Bobby Vee*
38/58 **Come Closer To Me** *Nat King Cole*
76/63 **Come Dance With Me** *Jay & The Americans*
6/83 **Come Dancing** *Kinks*
21/73 **Come Get To This** *Marvin Gaye*
58/83 **Come Give Your Love To Me** *Janet Jackson*
Come Go With Me
4/57 *Dell-Vikings*
48/63 *Dion*
18/82 *Beach Boys*
84/78 **Come Go With Me** *Pockets*
14/65 **Come Home** *Dave Clark Five*
92/55 **Come Home** *Bubber Johnson*
61/77 **Come In From The Rain** *Captain & Tennille*
66/58 **Come In Stranger** *Johnny Cash*
20/59 **Come Into My Heart** *Lloyd Price*
89/70 **Come Into My Life** *Jimmy Cliff*
Come Live With Me
82/73 *Ray Charles*
89/73 *Roy Clark*
30/74 **Come Monday** *Jimmy Buffett*
36/64 **Come On** *Tommy Roe*
69/71 **C'mon** *Poco*
29/59 **Come On And Get Me** *Fabian*
61/70 **Come On And Say It** *Grass Roots*
80/66 **Come On And See Me** *Tammi Terrell*
5/64 **C'mon And Swim** *Bobby Freeman*
98/62 **Come On Baby** *Bruce Channel*
50/65 **Come On Do The Jerk** *Miracles*
6/67 **Come On Down To My Boat** *Every Mothers' Son*
1/83 **Come On Eileen** *Dexys Midnight Runners*
35/59 **C'mon Everybody** *Eddie Cochran*
Come On Let's Go
42/58 *Ritchie Valens*
22/66 *McCoys*
28/62 **Come On Little Angel** *Belmonts*
C'mon Marianne
9/67 *4 Seasons*
38/76 *Donny Osmond*
23/76 **Come On Over** *Olivia Newton-John*
91/61 **Come On Over** *Strollers*
60/65 **Come On Over To My Place** *Drifters*
63/68 **Come On, React!** *Fireballs*
76/85 **(Come On) Shout** *Alex Brown*
97/67 **Come On Sock It To Me** *Syl Johnson*
43/66 **Come On Up** *Young Rascals*
Come Prima
67/58 *Polly Bergen*
60/59 *Tony Dallara*
Come Rain Or Come Shine
83/60 *Ray Charles*
98/68 *Ray Charles*
17/66 **(Come 'Round Here) I'm The One You Need** *Miracles*
39/70 **Come Running** *Van Morrison*
35/66 **Come Running Back** *Dean Martin*
8/78 **Come Sail Away** *Styx*
17/70 **Come Saturday Morning** *Sandpipers*
40/65 **Come See** *Major Lance*
Come See About Me
1/64 *Supremes*
74/64 *Nella Dodds*
24/68 *Jr. Walker & The All Stars*
73/61 **Come September** *Billy Vaughn*
96/66 **Come Share The Good Times With Me** *Julie Monday*
Come Softly To Me
1/59 *Fleetwoods*
45/59 *Ronnie Height*
95/73 *New Seekers*
15/79 **Come To Me** *France Joli*
22/58 **Come To Me** *Johnny Mathis*
30/59 **Come To Me** *Marv Johnson*
47/70 **Come To Me** *Tommy James & The Shondells*
69/64 **Come To Me** *Otis Redding*
84/81 **Come To Me** *Aretha Franklin*
76/68 **Come To Me Softly** *Jimmy James*
37/67 **Come To The Sunshine** *Harpers Bizarre*
Come Together
1/69 *Beatles*
57/70 *Ike & Tina Turner*
23/78 *Aerosmith*
50/65 **Come Tomorrow** *Manfred Mann*

43/58 **Come What May** *Clyde McPhatter*
69/60 **Comin' Down With Love** *Mel Gadson*
84/70 **Comin' Home** *Delaney & Bonnie & Friends*
36/62 **Comin' Home Baby** *Mel Torme*
11/82 **Comin' In And Out Of Your Life** *Barbra Streisand*
41/64 **Comin' In The Back Door** *Baja Marimba Band*
67/64 **Comin' On** *Bill Black's Combo*
65/65 **Comin' On Too Strong** *Wayne Newton*
18/87 **Coming Around Again** *Carly Simon*
99/64 **Coming Back To You** *Maxine Brown*
42/80 **Coming Down From Love** *Bobby Caldwell*
11/67 **Coming Home Soldier** *Bobby Vinton*
11/66 **Coming On Strong** *Brenda Lee*
1/80 **Coming Up (Live at Glasgow)** *Paul McCartney*
30/69 **Commotion** *Creedence Clearwater Revival*
(also see: Kommotion)
34/85 **Communication** *Power Station*
59/84 **Communication** *Spandau Ballet*
60/67 **Communication Breakdown** *Roy Orbison*
85/70 **Compared To What** *Les McCann & Eddie Harris*
75/68 **Competition Ain't Nothin'** *Carl Carlton*
27/69 **Composer, The** *Supremes*
60/80 **Computer Games** *Yellow Magic Orchestra*
63/84 **Concealed Weapons** *J. Geils Band*
Concrete And Clay
28/65 *Unit Four plus Two*
35/65 *Eddie Rambeau*
46/69 **Condition Red** *Goodees*
51/63 **Coney Island Baby** *Excellents*
72/56 **Confession Of A Sinner** *Stylers*
17/56 **Confidential** *Sonny Knight*
37/79 **Confusion** *Electric Light Orchestra*
10/86 **Conga** *Miami Sound Machine*
99/68 **Congratulation** *Cliff Richard*
63/64 **Congratulations** *Rick Nelson*
16/72 **Conquistador** *Procol Harum*
11/62 **Conscience** *James Darren*
71/67 **Constant Rain (Chove Chuva)** *Sergio Mendes & Brasil '66*
65/79 **Contact** *Edwin Starr*
Continental Walk
33/61 *Hank Ballard*
80/61 *Rollers*
(also see: Do The & Do The New)
5/87 **Control** *Janet Jackson*
51/73 **Control Of Me** *Les Emmerson*
70/81 **Controversy** *Prince*
8/72 **Convention '72** *Delegates*
1/76 **Convoy** *C.W. McCall*
84/68 **Coo Coo** *Big Brother & The Holding Company*
98/59 **CooCoo-U** *Kingston Trio*
32/73 **Cook With Honey** *Judy Collins*
92/62 **Cookin'** *Al Casey*
90/82 **Cool** *Time*
29/71 **Cool Aid** *Paul Humphrey*
10/80 **Cool Change** *Little River Band*
4/85 **Cool It Now** *New Edition*
7/66 **Cool Jerk** *Capitols*
13/81 **Cool Love** *Pablo Cruise*
57/82 **Cool Magic** *Steve Miller Band*
11/82 **Cool Night** *Paul Davis*
49/83 **Cool Places** *Sparks & Jane Wiedlin*
12/57 **Cool Shake** *Del Vikings*
85/60 **Cool Water** *Jack Scott*
8/78 **Copacabana (At The Copa)** *Barry Manilow*
92/62 **Copy Cat** *Gary U.S. Bonds*
92/58 **Coquette** *Fats Domino*
37/73 **Corazon** *Carole King*
Corinna, Corinna
41/56 *Joe Turner*
9/61 *Ray Peterson*
83/66 **Corner In The Sun** *Walter Jackson*
18/72 **Corner Of The Sky** *Jackson 5*
83/73 **Cosmic Sea** *Mystic Moods*
77/75 **Costafine Town** *Splinter*
56/70 **Cottage Cheese** *Crow*
63/60 **Cottage For Sale** *Little Willie John*
15/64 **Cotton Candy** *Al Hirt*
59/76 **Cotton Candy** *Sylvers*
Cotton Fields
13/62 *Highwaymen*
67/63 *Ace Cannon*
71/72 **Cotton Jenny** *Anne Murray*
76/77 **Could Heaven Ever Be Like This (Part 1)** *Idris Muhammad*
52/80 **Could I Be Dreaming** *Pointer Sisters*
60/71 **Could I Forget You** *Tyrone Davis*
33/80 **Could I Have This Dance** *Anne Murray*
37/72 **Could It Be Forever** *David Cassidy*
4/73 **Could It Be I'm Falling In Love** *Spinners*
47/82 **Could It Be Love** *Jennifer Warnes*
Could It Be Magic
6/75 *Barry Manilow*
52/76 *Donna Summer*
23/57 **Could This Be Magic** *Dubs*
92/73 **Could You Ever Love Me Again** *Gary & Dave*
3/77 **Couldn't Get It Right** *Climax Blues Band*
93/72 **Couldn't I Just Tell You** *Todd Rundgren*
91/66 **Count Down** *Dave 'Baby' Cortez*
Count Every Star
73/58 *Rivieras*
35/61 *Donnie & The Dreamers*
41/62 *Linda Scott*
2/65 **Count Me In** *Gary Lewis & The Playboys*
51/85 **Count Me Out** *New Edition*
8/78 **Count On Me** *Jefferson Starship*
85/83 **Count On Me** *Gerard McMahon*
Count The Days *see: (1-2-3-4-5-6-7)*
84/86 **Count Your Blessings** *Ashford & Simpson*
25/60 **Country Boy** *Fats Domino*
11/76 **Country Boy (You Got Your Feet In L.A.)** *Glen Campbell*
36/68 **Country Girl - City Man** *Billy Vera & Judy Clay*
86/70 **Country Preacher** *Cannonball Adderley*
37/71 **Country Road** *James Taylor*
66/74 **Country Side Of Life** *Wet Willie*
49/73 **Country Sunshine** *Dottie West*
51/72 **Country Wine** *Raiders*
88/72 **Country Woman** *Magic Lantern*
25/68 **Court Of Love** *Unifics*
80/70 **Court Of The Crimson King** *King Crimson*
61/71 **Court Room** *Clarence Carter*
31/64 **Cousin Of Mine** *Sam Cooke*
7/84 **Cover Me** *Bruce Springsteen*
42/68 **Cover Me** *Percy Sledge*
6/73 **Cover Of 'Rolling Stone'** *Dr. Hook*
3/80 **Coward Of The County** *Kenny Rogers*
66/81 **Cowboy And The Lady** *John Denver*
95/63 **Cowboy Boots** *Dave Dudley*
94/61 **Cowboy Jimmy Joe** *Lolita*
77/76 **Cowboy Song** *Thin Lizzy*
6/68 **Cowboys To Girls** *Intruders*
8/72 **Cowboys Work Is Never Done** *Sonny & Cher*
19/77 **Crackerbox Palace** *George Harrison*
62/59 **Crackin Up** *Bo Diddley*
1/70 **Cracklin' Rosie** *Neil Diamond*
7/60 **Cradle Of Love** *Johnny Preston*
86/79 **Crank It Up (Funk Town)** *Peter Brown*
46/65 **Crawling Back** *Roy Orbison*

53/86 **Crazay** *Jesse Johnson featuring Sly Stone*
9/61 **Crazy** *Patsy Cline*
72/83 **Crazy** *Manhattans*
79/85 **Crazy** *Kenny Rogers*
F/58 **Crazy** *Hollywood Flames*
56/71 **Crazy About The La La La** *Miracles*
Crazy Arms
67/56 *Ray Price*
36/60 *Bob Beckham*
87/58 **Crazy Country Hop** *Johnny Otis Show*
Crazy Downtown *see: Downtown*
40/58 **Crazy Eyes For You** *Bobby Hamilton*
54/78 **Crazy Feelin'** *Jefferson Starship*
1/85 **Crazy For You** *Madonna*
14/72 **Crazy Horses** *Osmonds*
15/85 **Crazy In The Night (Barking At Airplanes)** *Kim Carnes*
42/82 **Crazy (Keep On Falling)** *John Hall Band*
Crazy Little Mama *see: At My Front Door*
49/56 **Crazy Little Palace (That's My Home)** *Billy Williams*
1/80 **Crazy Little Thing Called Love** *Queen*
15/58 **Crazy Love** *Paul Anka*
17/79 **Crazy Love** *Poco*
29/79 **Crazy Love** *Allman Brothers Band*
51/71 **Crazy Love** *Helen Reddy*
60/57 **Crazy Love** *Frank Sinatra*
22/72 **Crazy Mama** *J.J. Cale*
Crazy On You
35/76 *Heart*
62/78 *Heart*
2/55 **Crazy Otto (Medley)** *Johnny Maddox*
98/75 **Crazy Talk** *Chilliwack*
Crazy With Love
53/56 *Guy Mitchell*
73/56 *Teresa Brewer*
85/57 **Creature, The** *Buchanan & Ancell*
5/67 **Creeque Alley** *Mamas & The Papas*
16/71 **Cried Like A Baby** *Bobby Sherman*
Crimson And Clover
1/69 *Tommy James & The Shondells*
7/82 *Joan Jett*
Croce Di Oro (Cross Of Gold)
16/55 *Patti Page*
55/55 *Joan Regan*
1/73 **Crocodile Rock** *Elton John*
Crooked Little Man *see: Don't Let The Rain Come Down*
19/63 **Cross Fire!** *Orlons*
69/82 **Cross My Heart** *Lee Ritenour*
86/68 **Cross My Heart** *Billy Stewart*
99/65 **Cross My Heart** *Bobby Vee*
Cross Of Gold *see: Croce Di Oro*
89/61 **Cross Stands Alone** *Jimmy Witter*
23/59 **Crossfire** *Johnny & The Hurricanes*
92/63 **Crossfire Time** *Dee Clark*
28/69 **Crossroads** *Cream*
52/68 **Crosstown Traffic** *Jimi Hendrix*
26/62 **Crowd, The** *Roy Orbison*
64/68 **Crown Of Creation** *Jefferson Airplane*
91/74 **Crude Oil Blues** *Jerry Reed*
91/79 **Cruel Shoes** *Steve Martin*
9/84 **Cruel Summer** *Bananarama*
12/79 **Cruel To Be Kind** *Nick Lowe*
52/66 **Cruel War** *Peter, Paul & Mary*
4/80 **Cruisin'** *Smokey Robinson*
9/83 **Crumblin' Down** *John Cougar Mellencamp*
59/69 **Crumbs Off The Table** *Glass House*
F/71 **Crunchy Granola Suite** *Neil Diamond*
3/86 **Crush On You** *Jets*
88/65 **Crusher, The** *Novas*
16/85 **Cry** *Godley & Creme*
Cry
53/59 *Knightsbridge Strings*
58/65 *Ray Charles*
18/66 *Ronnie Dove*
71/72 *Lynn Anderson*
Cry Baby
4/63 *Garnet Mimms & The Enchanters*
42/71 *Janis Joplin*
18/56 **Cry Baby** *Bonnie Sisters*
38/62 **Cry Baby Cry** *Angels*
71/60 **Cry Cry Cry** *Bobby Bland*
91/75 **Cry Cry Cry** *Shirley & Company*
78/80 **Cry Just A Little** *Paul Davis*
Cry Like A Baby
2/68 *Box Tops*
44/80 *Kim Carnes*
Cry Me A River
9/55 *Julie London*
91/60 *Janice Harper*
11/70 *Joe Cocker*
99/62 **Cry Myself To Sleep** *Del Shannon*
95/66 **Cry Softly** *Nancy Ames*
52/67 **Cry Softly Lonely One** *Roy Orbison*
Cry To Me
44/62 *Solomon Burke*
23/63 *Betty Harris*
70/67 *Freddie Scott*
68/75 **Cry To Me** *Loleatta Holloway*
61/70 **Cryin' In The Streets** *George Perkins*
Crying
2/61 *Roy Orbison*
25/66 *Jay & The Americans*
5/81 *Don McLean*
87/65 **Crying Game** *Brenda Lee*
Crying In The Chapel
3/65 *Elvis Presley*
88/65 *Adam Wade*
6/62 **Crying In The Rain** *Everly Brothers*
6/66 **Crying Time** *Ray Charles*
2/69 **Crystal Blue Persuasion** *Tommy James & The Shondells*
51/65 **Crystal Chandelier** *Vic Dana*
Cuando Caliente El Sol *see: Love Me With All Of Your Heart*
81/79 **Cuba** *Gibson Brothers*
Cum On Feel The Noize
98/73 *Slade*
5/83 *Quiet Riot*
Cupid
17/61 *Sam Cooke*
76/65 *Johnny Rivers*
39/70 *Johnny Nash*
22/76 *Dawn*
4/80 *Spinners (medley)*
Curious Mind *see: Um, Um, Um, Um, Um, Um*
97/69 **Curly** *Jimmy Clanton*
15/84 **Curly Shuffle** *Jump 'N The Saddle*
85/64 **Custom Machine** *Bruce & Terry*
10/75 **Cut The Cake** *Average White Band*
61/82 **Cutie Pie** *One Way*
15/83 **Cuts Like A Knife** *Bryan Adams*
71/78 **Cuz It's You, Girl** *James Walsh Gypsy Band*
23/68 **Cycles** *Frank Sinatra*

36/71 **D.O.A.** *Bloodrock*
19/68 **D.W. Washburn** *Monkees*
20/73 **D'yer Mak'er** *Led Zeppelin*
Da Doo Ron Ron
3/63 *Crystals*
96/72 *Ian Matthews*
1/77 *Shaun Cassidy*
1/79 **Da Ya Think I'm Sexy?** *Rod Stewart*
65/77 **Daddy Cool** *Boney M*
F/57 **Daddy Cool** *Rays*
19/73 **Daddy Could Swear, I Declare** *Gladys Knight & The Pips*
4/72 **Daddy Don't You Walk So Fast** *Wayne Newton*
Daddy-O
11/55 *Fontane Sisters*
14/55 *Bonnie Lou*
42/69 **Daddy Sang Bass** *Johnny Cash*
41/74 **Daddy What If** *Bobby Bare*
Daddy's Home
2/61 *Shep & The Limelites*
91/67 *Chuck Jackson & Maxine Brown*
9/73 *Jermaine Jackson*
23/82 *Cliff Richard*
42/67 **Daddy's Little Girl** *Al Martino*
Daddy's Little Girl *see: (One More Year Of)*
34/69 **Daddy's Little Man** *O.C. Smith*
14/73 **Daisy A Day** *Jud Strunk*
20/75 **Daisy Jane** *America*
41/72 **Daisy Mae** *Hamilton, Joe Frank & Reynolds*
15/64 **Daisy Petal Pickin'** *Jimmy Gilmer/Fireballs*
86/69 **Dammit Isn't God's Last Name** *Frankie Laine*
73/75 **Damn It All** *Gene Cotton*
27/79 **Damned If I Do** *Alan Parsons Project*
38/78 **Dance Across The Floor** *Jimmy 'Bo' Horne*
93/77 **Dance And Shake Your Tambourine** *Universal Robot Band*
44/79 **Dance Away** *Roxy Music*
47/60 **Dance By The Light Of The Moon** *Olympics*
8/64 **Dance, Dance, Dance** *Beach Boys*
84/72 **Dance, Dance, Dance** *New Seekers*
89/63 **Dance, Dance, Dance** *Joey Dee*
6/78 **Dance, Dance, Dance (Yowsah, Yowsah, Yowsah)** *Chic*
19/78 **Dance (Disco Heat)** *Sylvester*
99/63 **Dance, Everybody, Dance** *Dartells*
31/58 **Dance Everyone Dance** *Betty Madigan*
16/84 **Dance Hall Days** *Wang Chung*
100/77 **Dance Little Lady Dance** *Danny White*
73/74 **Dance Master** *Willie Henderson*
10/61 **Dance On Little Girl** *Paul Anka*
19/58 **Dance Only With Me** *Perry Como*
48/75 **Dance The Kung Fu** *Carl Douglas*
24/61 **Dance The Mess Around** *Chubby Checker*
15/79 **Dance The Night Away** *Van Halen*
23/58 **Dance To The Bop** *Gene Vincent*
8/68 **Dance To The Music** *Sly & The Family Stone*
39/76 **Dance Wit Me** *Rufus Featuring Chaka Khan*
64/82 **Dance Wit' Me** *Rick James*
6/75 **Dance With Me** *Orleans*
8/78 **Dance With Me** *Peter Brown*
15/59 **Dance With Me** *Drifters*
61/65 **Dance With Me** *Mojo Men*
95/60 **Dance With Me Georgie** *Bobbettes*
1/55 **Dance With Me Henry (Wallflower)** *Georgia Gibbs*
98/62 **Dance With Mr. Domino** *Fats Domino*
49/74 **Dance With The Devil** *Cozy Powell*
12/62 **(Dance With The) Guitar Man** *Duane Eddy*
70/79 **Dance With You** *Carrie Lucas*
48/79 **Dancer** *Gino Soccio*

91/86 **Dancin In My Sleep** *Secret Ties*
42/77 **Dancin'** *Crown Heights Affair*
76/57 **Dancin'** *Perry Como*
83/79 **Dancin'** *Grey & Hanks*
72/78 **Dancin' Fever** *Claudja Barry*
Dancin' Fool
28/75 *Guess Who*
45/79 *Frank Zappa*
86/63 **Dancin' Holiday** *Olympics*
68/85 **Dancin' In The Key Of Life** *Steve Arrington*
66/80 **Dancin' In The Streets** *Teri DeSario with K.C.*
60/76 **Dancin' Kid** *Disco Tex & The Sex-O-Lettes*
72/80 **Dancin' Like Lovers** *Mary MacGregor*
23/77 **Dancin' Man** *Q*
93/74 **Dancin' (On A Saturday Night)** *Flash Cadillac & The Continental Kids*
87/67 **Dancin' Out Of My Heart** *Ronnie Dove*
12/62 **Dancin' Party** *Chubby Checker*
82/79 **Dancin' 'Round And 'Round** *Olivia Newton-John*
Dancin' Shoes
18/79 *Nigel Olsson*
54/79 *Faith Band*
91/62 **Dancin' The Strand** *Maureen Gray*
51/68 **Dancing Bear** *Mamas & The Papas*
68/57 **Dancing Chandelier** *Sylvia Syms*
91/78 **Dancing In Paradise** *El Coco*
43/79 **Dancing In The City** *Marshall Hain*
2/84 **Dancing In The Dark** *Bruce Springsteen*
13/73 **Dancing In The Moonlight** *King Harvest*
85/83 **Dancing In The Shadows** *After The Fire*
17/84 **Dancing In The Sheets** *Shalamar*
Dancing In The Street
2/64 *Martha & The Vandellas*
73/67 *Mamas & The Papas*
84/67 *Ramsey Lewis*
38/82 *Van Halen*
7/85 *Mick Jagger/David Bowie*
2/74 **Dancing Machine** *Jackson 5*
2/86 **Dancing On The Ceiling** *Lionel Richie*
1/77 **Dancing Queen** *Abba*
61/73 **Dancing To Your Music** *Archie Bell & The Drells*
50/58 **Dancing With My Shadow** *Four Voices*
97/80 **Dancing With The Mountains** *John Denver*
14/67 **Dandelion** *Rolling Stones*
5/66 **Dandy** *Herman's Hermits*
7/64 **Dang Me** *Roger Miller*
96/63 **Danger** *Vic Dana*
12/55 **Danger! Heartbreak Ahead** *Jaye P. Morgan*
61/65 **Danger Heartbreak Dead Ahead** *Marvelettes*
89/67 **Danger! She's A Stranger** *Five Stairsteps*
2/86 **Danger Zone** *Kenny Loggins*
Dangerous
57/85 *Natalie Cole*
65/85 *Loverboy*
25/66 **Dangling Conversation** *Simon & Garfunkel*
2/73 **Daniel** *Elton John*
13/63 **Danke Schoen** *Wayne Newton*
Danny Boy
10/59 *Conway Twitty*
59/59 *Sil Austin*
64/61 *Andy Williams*
76/65 *Patti LaBelle & The Blue Belles*
94/65 *Jackie Wilson*
60/67 *Ray Price*
7/73 **Danny's Song** *Anne Murray*
11/85 **Dare Me** *Pointer Sisters*
Dark At The Top Of The Stairs *see: Theme From*
77/67 **Dark End Of The Street** *James Carr*

15/75 **Dark Horse** *George Harrison*
1/74 **Dark Lady** *Cher*
Dark Moon
4/57 *Gale Storm*
6/57 *Bonnie Guitar*
77/63 **Darkest Street In Town** *Jimmy Clanton*
86/70 **Darkness, Darkness** *Youngbloods*
Darlin'
19/68 *Beach Boys*
51/78 *Paul Davis & Susan Collins*
68/80 *Yipes!!*
84/84 **Darlin'** *Frank Stallone*
72/77 **Darlin' Darlin' Baby (Sweet, Tender, Love)** *O'Jays*
72/66 **Darling Baby** *Elgins*
Darling Be Home Soon
15/67 *Lovin' Spoonful*
93/67 *Bobby Darin*
67/73 **Darling Come Back Home** *Eddie Kendricks*
100/70 **Darling Dear** *Miracles*
63/59 **Darling, I Love You** *Al Martino*
48/57 **Darling It's Wonderful** *Lovers*
7/55 **Darling Je Vous Aime Beaucoup** *Nat King Cole*
46/60 **Darling Lorraine** *Knockouts*
72/65 **Darling Take Me Back** *Lenny Welch*
92/64 **Dartell Stomp** *Mustangs*
F/57 **Date With The Blues** *Billy Williams*
61/63 **Daughter** *Blenders*
13/70 **Daughter Of Darkness** *Tom Jones*
Davy Crockett *see: Ballad Of*
62/63 **Dawn** *David Rockingham Trio*
3/64 **Dawn (Go Away)** *4 Seasons*
36/65 **Dawn Of Correction** *Spokesmen*
4/72 **Day After Day** *Badfinger*
57/69 **Day After Day (It's Slippin' Away)** *Shango*
65/72 **Day And Night** *Wackers*
Day At The Beach
see: (How I Spent My Summer Vacation)
13/72 **Day By Day** *Godspell*
18/86 **Day By Day** *Hooters*
42/55 **Day By Day** *Four Freshmen*
84/71 **Day By Day (Every Minute Of The Hour)** *Continental 4*
5/72 **Day Dreaming** *Aretha Franklin*
35/66 **Day For Decision** *Johnny Sea*
81/58 **Day I Died** *Playmates*
23/72 **Day I Found Myself** *Honey Cone*
62/66 **Day In The Life Of A Fool** *Jack Jones*
Day Is Done
21/69 *Peter, Paul & Mary*
98/70 *Brooklyn Bridge*
Day-O *see: Banana Boat*
Day The Rains Came
21/58 *Jane Morgan*
30/58 *Raymond Lefevre*
Day Tripper
5/66 *Beatles*
100/66 *Vontastics*
74/67 *Ramsey Lewis*
59/75 *Anne Murray*
23/77 **Daybreak** *Barry Manilow*
Daybreak *see: Storybook Children*
39/74 **Daybreak** *Nilsson*
87/74 **Daybreaker** *Electric Light Orchestra*
2/66 **Daydream** *Lovin' Spoonful*
Daydream Believer
1/67 *Monkees*
12/80 *Anne Murray*
79/86 *Monkees*
91/76 **Daydreamer** *C.C. & Company*
70/61 **Daydreams** *Johnny Crawford*
73/56 **Daydreams** *Art Mooney*
63/76 **Daylight** *Vicki Sue Robinson*
75/78 **Daylight And Darkness** *Smokey Robinson*
79/67 **Daylight Savin' Time** *Keith*
71/85 **Days Are Numbers (The Traveller)** *Alan Parsons Project*
80/84 **Days Gone By** *Poco*
17/79 **Days Gone Down (Still Got The Light In Your Eyes)** *Gerry Rafferty*
34/69 **Days Of Sand And Shovels** *Bobby Vinton*
Days Of Wine And Roses
26/63 *Andy Williams*
33/63 *Henry Mancini*
28/77 **Daytime Friends** *Kenny Rogers*
51/73 **Daytime Night-Time** *Keith Hampshire*
3/77 **Dazz** *Brick*
10/81 **De Do Do Do, De Da Da Da** *Police*
19/78 **Deacon Blues** *Steely Dan*
29/67 **Dead End Street** *Lou Rawls*
22/83 **Dead Giveaway** *Shalamar*
8/64 **Dead Man's Curve** *Jan & Dean*
16/73 **Dead Skunk** *Loudon Wainwright III*
73/67 **Deadend Street** *Kinks*
94/63 **Dear Abby** *Hearts*
93/70 **Dear Ann** *George Baker Selection*
95/65 **Dear Dad** *Chuck Berry*
98/68 **Dear Delilah** *Grapefruit*
50/67 **Dear Eloise** *Hollies*
87/56 **Dear Elvis** *Audrey*
Dear Heart
24/65 *Andy Williams*
30/65 *Jack Jones*
77/65 *Henry Mancini*
95/62 **Dear Hearts And Gentle People** *Springfields*
24/62 **Dear Ivan** *Jimmy Dean*
44/60 **Dear John** *Pat Boone*
9/62 **Dear Lady Twist** *Gary U.S. Bonds*
13/62 **Dear Lonely Hearts** *Nat King Cole*
51/66 **Dear Lover** *Mary Wells*
95/61 **Dear Mr. D.J. Play It Again** *Tina Robin*
91/66 **Dear Mrs. Applebee** *Flip Cartridge*
11/62 **Dear One** *Larry Finnegan*
Dear Prudence
F/70 *Five Stairsteps*
62/75 *Katfish*
59/63 **Dearer Than Life** *Brook Benton*
85/57 **Dearest** *Mickey & Sylvia*
42/64 **Death Of An Angel** *Kingsmen*
1/76 **December, 1963 (Oh, What A Night)** *4 Seasons*
7/59 **Deck Of Cards** *Wink Martindale*
F/70 **Declaration, The** *5th Dimension*
7/58 **Dede Dinah** *Frankie Avalon*
36/66 **Dedicated Follower Of Fashion** *Kinks*
Dedicated To The One I Love
83/59 *Shirelles*
3/61 *Shirelles*
81/61 *'5' Royales*
2/67 *Mamas & The Papas*
93/72 *Temprees*
65/81 *Bernadette Peters*
89/61 **Dedicated (To The Songs I Love)** *3 Friends*
60/77 **Dedication** *Bay City Rollers*
41/66 **Dedication Song** *Freddy Cannon*
F/71 **Deep Blue** *George Harrison*
67/57 **Deep Blue Sea** *Jimmy Dean*
73/71 **Deep Enough For Me** *Ocean*
90/64 **Deep In The Heart Of Harlem** *Clyde McPhatter*
78/62 **Deep In The Heart Of Texas** *Duane Eddy*
22/80 **Deep Inside My Heart** *Randy Meisner*
Deep Purple
20/57 *Billy Ward & His Dominoes*
1/63 *Nino Tempo & April Stevens*
14/76 *Donny & Marie Osmond*

24/70 **Deeper & Deeper** *Freda Payne*
64/70 **Deeper (In Love With You)** *O'Jays*
11/79 **Deeper Than The Night** *Olivia Newton-John*
93/77 **Deeply** *Anson Williams*
15/80 **Deja Vu** *Dionne Warwick*
22/60 **Delaware** *Perry Como*
66/60 **Delia Gone** *Pat Boone*
40/58 **Delicious!** *Jim Backus & Friend*
15/68 **Delilah** *Tom Jones*
Delilah Jones
see: Man With The Golden Arm
8/83 **Delirious** *Prince*
Delta Dawn
72/72 *Tanya Tucker*
1/73 *Helen Reddy*
84/74 **Delta Dirt** *Larry Gatlin*
69/69 **Delta Lady** *Joe Cocker*
86/73 **Delta Queen** *Don Fardon*
10/63 **Denise** *Randy & The Rainbows*
67/75 **Department Of Youth** *Alice Cooper*
25/79 **Dependin' On You** *Doobie Brothers*
5/83 **Der Kommissar** *After The Fire*
Desafinado
15/62 *Stan Getz/Charlie Byrd*
78/62 *Pat Thomas*
94/71 **Desdemona** *Searchers*
88/57 **Deserie** *Charts*
10/84 **Desert Moon** *Dennis DeYoung*
33/63 **Desert Pete** *Kingston Trio*
8/71 **Desiderata** *Les Crane*
4/80 **Desire** *Andy Gibb*
70/80 **Desire** *Rockets*
47/58 **Desire Me** *Sam Cooke*
16/78 **Desiree** *Neil Diamond*
98/67 **Desiree'** *Left Banke*
66/83 **Desperate But Not Serious** *Adam Ant*
63/68 **Destination: Anywhere** *Marvelettes*
42/82 **Destination Unknown** *Missing Persons*
83/70 **Destiny** *Jose Feliciano*
85/81 **Destroyer** *Kinks*
91/72 **Deteriorata** *National Lampoon*
Detroit City
16/63 *Bobby Bare*
90/63 *Ben Colder*
27/67 *Tom Jones*
F/76 **Detroit Rock City** *Kiss*
79/84 **Devil In A Fast Car** *Sheena Easton*
54/75 **Devil In The Bottle** *T.G. Sheppard*
79/83 **Devil Made Me Do It** *Golden Earring*
6/60 **Devil Or Angel** *Bobby Vee*
3/79 **Devil Went Down To Georgia** *Charlie Daniels Band*
Devil With A Blue Dress On
4/66 *Mitch Ryder & The Detroit Wheels (medley)*
71/76 *Pratt & McClain*
6/76 **Devil Woman** *Cliff Richard*
16/62 **Devil Woman** *Marty Robbins*
61/72 **Devil You** *Stampeders*
97/67 **Devil's Angels** *Davie Allan & The Arrows*
36/77 **Devil's Gun** *C.J. & Co.*
Devoted To You
10/58 *Everly Brothers*
36/78 *Carly Simon & James Taylor*
33/74 **Devotion** *Earth, Wind & Fire*
82/58 **Devotion** *Janice Harper*
24/72 **Dialogue** *Chicago*
6/73 **Diamond Girl** *Seals & Crofts*
70/65 **Diamond Head** *Ventures*
78/58 **Diamond Ring** *Jerry Wallace*
44/79 **Diamonds** *Chris Rea*
18/60 **Diamonds And Pearls** *Paradons*
35/75 **Diamonds And Rust** *Joan Baez*
57/72 **Diamonds Are Forever** *Shirley Bassey*

Diana
1/57 *Paul Anka*
98/65 *Bobby Rydell*
Diane
97/63 *Joe Harnell*
10/64 *Bachelors*
69/66 **Dianne, Dianne** *Ronny & The Daytonas*
15/72 **Diary** *Bread*
14/59 **Diary, The** *Neil Sedaka*
F/75 **Dick And Jane** *Bobby Vinton*
9/82 **Did It In A Minute** *Daryl Hall & John Oates*
29/76 **Did You Boogie (With Your Baby)** *Flash Cadillac & The Continental Kids*
74/65 **Did You Ever** *Hullaballoos*
2/66 **Did You Ever Have To Make Up Your Mind?** *Lovin' Spoonful*
79/62 **Did You Ever See A Dream Walking** *Fats Domino*
89/63 **Did You Have A Happy Birthday?** *Paul Anka*
32/69 **Did You See Her Eyes** *Illusion*
53/62 **Diddle-Dee-Dum (What Happens When Your Love Has Gone)** *Belmonts*
70/73 **Didn't I** *Sylvia*
10/70 **Didn't I (Blow Your Mind This Time)** *Delfonics*
81/71 **Didn't It Look So Easy** *Stairsteps*
Didn't We
63/69 *Richard Harris*
82/73 *Barbra Streisand*
63/69 **Didn't You Know (You'd Have To Cry Sometime)** *Gladys Knight & The Pips*
7/86 **Different Corner** *George Michael*
13/68 **Different Drum** *Stone Poneys*
95/67 **Different Strokes** *Syl Johnson*
18/79 **Different Worlds** *Maureen McGovern*
42/80 **Dig The Gold** *Joyce Cobb*
14/86 **Digging Your Scene** *Blow Monkeys*
21/86 **Digital Display** *Ready For The World*
2/79 **Dim All The Lights** *Donna Summer*
11/55 **Dim, Dim The Lights (I Want Some Atmosphere)** *Bill Haley & His Comets*
86/72 **Dinah Flo** *Boz Scaggs*
18/60 **Ding-A-Ling** *Bobby Rydell*
25/58 **Ding Dong** *McGuire Sisters*
36/75 **Ding Dong; Ding Dong** *George Harrison*
11/67 **Ding Dong! The Witch Is Dead** *Fifth Estate*
6/58 **Dinner With Drac** *John Zacherle*
3/83 **Dirty Laundry** *Don Henley*
90/83 **Dirty Looks** *Juice Newton*
68/67 **Dirty Man** *Laura Lee*
Dirty Water
11/66 *Standells*
51/80 *Inmates*
12/79 **Dirty White Boy** *Foreigner*
36/67 **Dis-Advantages Of You** *Brass Ring*
56/77 **Dis-Gorilla** *Rick Dees*
82/85 **Discipline Of Love (Why Did You Do It)** *Robert Palmer*
1/76 **Disco Duck** *Rick Dees*
11/78 **Disco Inferno** *Trammps*
1/76 **Disco Lady** *Johnnie Taylor*
24/77 **Disco Lucy (I Love Lucy Theme)** *Wilton Place Street Band*
12/79 **Disco Nights (Rock-Freak)** *GQ*
86/77 **Disco 9000** *Johnnie Taylor*
28/75 **Disco Queen** *Hot Chocolate*
(Disco Round) *see: I Love The Nightlife*
88/78 **Disco Rufus** *Stargard*
91/76 **Disco Sax** *Houston Person*
100/77 **Discomania** *Lovers*
45/66 **Distant Drums** *Jim Reeves*
28/74 **Distant Lover** *Marvin Gaye*
30/66 **Distant Shores** *Chad & Jeremy*

79/86 **Divided Hearts** *Kim Carnes*
63/68 **D-I-V-O-R-C-E** *Tammy Wynette*
Dixie *see: Theme From*
30/55 **Dixie Danny** *Laurie Sisters*
96/75 **Dixie Rock** *Wet Willie*
1/69 **Dizzy** *Tommy Roe*
69/58 **Dizzy, Miss Lizzy** *Larry Williams*
Do *also see: Doo*
74/64 **Do Anything You Wanna** *Harold Betters*
13/82 **Do I Do** *Stevie Wonder*
67/58 **Do I Like It** *Nat King Cole*
34/64 **Do I Love You** *Ronettes*
53/71 **Do I Love You** *Paul Anka*
Do I Love You (Because You're Beautiful)
62/57 *Vic Damone*
82/57 *Tony Martin*
96/65 **Do I Make Myself Clear**
Etta James & Sugar Pie DeSanto
36/70 **Do It** *Neil Diamond*
Do It Again
6/73 *Steely Dan*
75/83 *Club House (medley)*
20/68 **Do It Again** *Beach Boys*
41/85 **Do It Again** *Kinks*
18/67 **Do It Again A Little Bit Slower**
Jon & Robin & The In Crowd
11/75 **Do It Any Way You Wanna** *People's Choice*
13/74 **Do It Baby** *Miracles*
69/74 **Do It, Fluid** *Blackbyrds*
29/85 **Do It For Love** *Sheena Easton*
79/79 **Do It Good** *A Taste Of Honey*
60/75 **Do It In The Name Of Love** *Ben E. King*
63/73 **Do It In The Name Of Love** *Candi Staton*
19/79 **Do It Or Die** *Atlanta Rhythm Section*
51/63 **Do It-Rat On** *Bill Black's Combo*
67/65 **Do It Right** *Brook Benton*
2/74 **Do It ('Til You're Satisfied)** *B.T. Express*
43/77 **Do It To My Mind** *Johnny Bristol*
94/76 **Do It With Feeling** *Michael Zager Band*
46/86 **Do Me Baby** *Meli'sa Morgan*
43/71 **Do Me Right** *Detroit Emeralds*
27/62 **Do-Re-Mi** *Lee Dorsey*
Do-Re-Mi
70/59 *Mitch Miller*
94/59 *Anita Bryant*
23/80 **Do Right** *Paul Davis*
38/68 **Do Something To Me**
Tommy James & The Shondells
1/80 **Do That To Me One More Time**
Captain & Tennille
93/68 **Do The Best You Can** *Hollies*
10/63 **Do The Bird** *Dee Dee Sharp*
36/65 **Do The Boomerang**
Jr. Walker & The All Stars
44/68 **Do The Choo Choo** *Archie Bell & The Drells*
21/65 **Do The Clam** *Elvis Presley*
18/65 **Do The Freddie** *Freddie & The Dreamers*
(also see: Let's Do The Freddie)
28/70 **Do The Funky Chicken** *Rufus Thomas*
44/72 **Do The Funky Penguin** *Rufus Thomas*
(Do The) Mashed Potatoes
see: Mashed Potatoes
92/63 **Do The Monkey** *King Curtis*
37/62 **Do The New Continental** *Dovells*
25/71 **(Do The) Push And Pull** *Rufus Thomas*
80/67 **Do The Thing** *Lou Courtney*
13/85 **Do They Know It's Christmas?** *Band Aid*
73/68 **Do Unto Me** *James & Bobby Purify*
31/65 **Do-Wacka-Do** *Roger Miller*
Do Wah Diddy Diddy
1/64 *Manfred Mann*
78/64 *Exciters*
57/58 **Do What You Did** *Thurston Harris*
13/85 **Do What You Do** *Jermaine Jackson*
52/65 **Do What You Do Do Well** *Ned Miller*
Do What You Gotta Do
83/68 *Nina Simone*
83/68 *Bobby Vee*
64/72 **Do What You Set Out To Do** *Bobby Bland*
37/70 **Do What You Wanna Do** *Five Flights Up*
46/77 **Do What You Wanna Do** *T-Connection*
39/76 **Do What You Want, Be What You Are**
Daryl Hall & John Oates
Do Ya
93/72 *Move*
24/77 *Electric Light Orchestra*
Do Ya Think I'm Sexy? *see: Da Ya*
18/77 **Do Ya Wanna Get Funky With Me**
Peter Brown
7/82 **Do You Believe In Love**
Huey Lewis & The News
Do You Believe In Magic
9/65 *Lovin' Spoonful*
31/78 *Shaun Cassidy*
64/83 **Do You Compute?** *Donnie Iris*
63/78 **Do You Feel All Right**
KC & The Sunshine Band
10/76 **Do You Feel Like We Do** *Peter Frampton*
87/62 **Do You Know How To Twist** *Hank Ballard*
10/68 **Do You Know The Way To San Jose**
Dionne Warwick
6/71 **Do You Know What I Mean** *Lee Michaels*
62/71 **Do You Know What Time It Is?**
P-Nut Gallery
Do You Know Where You're Going To
see: Theme From Mahogony
Do You Love Me
3/62 *Contours*
11/64 *Dave Clark Five*
82/84 *Andy Fraser*
30/80 **Do You Love What You Feel**
Rufus/Chaka Khan
Do You Mind?
70/60 *Andy Williams*
91/60 *Anthony Newley*
2/83 **Do You Really Want To Hurt Me**
Culture Club
71/86 **Do You Remember Me?** *Jermaine Jackson*
32/70 **Do You See My Love (For You Growing)**
Jr. Walker & The All Stars
58/79 **Do You Think I'm Disco?** *Steve Dahl*
49/85 **Do You Wanna Get Away** *Shannon*
50/79 **Do You Wanna Go Party**
KC & The Sunshine Band
77/83 **Do You Wanna Hold Me?** *Bow Wow Wow*
5/77 **Do You Wanna Make Love** *Peter McCann*
20/82 **Do You Wanna Touch Me (Oh Yeah)**
Joan Jett
37/85 **Do You Want Crying** *Katrina & The Waves*
Do You Want To Dance
5/58 *Bobby Freeman*
43/64 *Del Shannon*
12/65 *Beach Boys*
76/68 *Mamas & The Papas*
17/73 *Bette Midler*
86/78 *Ramones*
2/64 **Do You Want To Know A Secret** *Beatles*
39/77 **Do Your Dance** *Rose Royce*
99/68 **Do Your Own Thing** *Brook Benton*
11/69 **Do Your Thing**
Watts 103rd Street Rhythm Band
30/72 **Do Your Thing** *Isaac Hayes*
65/68 **Doctor, The** *Mary Wells*
Dr. Ben Basey *see: Ben Crazy*
Doctor Detroit *see: Theme From*
11/84 **Doctor! Doctor!** *Thompson Twins*
(Doctor, Doctor)
see: Bad Case Of Loving You

66/62 **Doctor Feel-Good**
Dr. Feelgood & The Interns
28/83 **Dr. Heckyll & Mr. Jive** *Men At Work*
87/68 **Dr. Jon (The Medicine Man)**
Jon & Robin & The In Crowd
Dr. Kildare *see: Theme From*
41/77 **Doctor Love** *First Choice*
8/72 **Doctor My Eyes** *Jackson Browne*
Doctor Tarr *see: (System Of)*
Dr. Zhivago *see: Somewhere My Love*
11/75 **Doctor's Orders** *Carol Douglas*
83/64 **Dodo, The** *Gene Simmons*
38/69 **Does Anybody Know I'm Here** *Dells*
7/71 **Does Anybody Really Know What Time It Is?** *Chicago*
98/62 **Does He Mean That Much To You?**
Eddy Arnold
87/65 **Does He Really Care For Me**
Ruby & The Romantics
36/83 **Does It Make You Remember** *Kim Carnes*
74/77 **Does She Do It Like She Dances**
Addrisi Brothers
5/61 **Does Your Chewing Gum Lose It's Flavor (On The Bedpost Over Night)** *Lonnie Donegan*
29/68 **Does Your Mama Know About Me**
Bobby Taylor
19/79 **Does Your Mother Know** *Abba*
F/55 **Doesn't Anybody Love Me?** *McGuire Sisters*
6/71 **Doesn't Somebody Want To Be Wanted**
Partridge Family
87/63 **Dog, The** *Rufus Thomas*
34/79 **Dog & Butterfly** *Heart*
64/77 **Dog Days** *Atlanta Rhythm Section*
91/76 **Dog Eat Dog** *Ted Nugent*
30/55 **Dogface Soldier** *Russ Morgan*
Doggin' Around
15/60 *Jackie Wilson*
50/83 *Klique*
32/69 **Doggone Right** *Miracles*
46/69 **Doin' Our Thing** *Clarence Carter*
93/62 **Doin' The Continental Walk**
Danny & The Juniors
93/60 **(Doin' The) Lovers Leap** *Webb Pierce*
22/73 **Doing It To Death** *JB's*
31/60 **Doll House** *Donnie Brooks*
60/61 **Dollar Down** *Limeliters*
74/71 **Dolly Dagger** *Jimi Hendrix*
13/55 **Domani (Tomorrow)** *Julius LaRosa*
1/63 **Dominique** *Singing Nun*
9/71 **Domino** *Van Morrison*
Dommage, Dommage (Too Bad, Too Bad)
93/66 *Jerry Vale*
97/66 *Paul Vance*
56/86 **Don Quichotte** *Magazine 60*
1/58 **Don't** *Elvis Presley*
15/84 **Don't Answer Me** *Alan Parsons Project*
72/66 **Don't Answer The Door** *B.B. King*
48/62 **Don't Ask Me To Be Friends**
Everly Brothers
72/57 **Don't Ask Me (To Be Lonely)** *Dubs*
19/80 **Don't Ask Me Why** *Billy Joel*
25/58 **Don't Ask Me Why** *Elvis Presley*
44/77 **Don't Ask My Neighbors** *Emotions*
50/66 **Don't Be A Drop-Out** *James Brown*
93/68 **Don't Be Afraid (Do As I Say)** *Frankie Karl*
26/63 **Don't Be Afraid, Little Darlin'**
Steve Lawrence
Don't Be Angry
14/55 *Crew-Cuts*
25/55 *Nappy Brown*
Don't Be Cruel
1/56 *Elvis Presley*
11/60 *Bill Black's Combo*
93/63 *Barbara Lynn*

86/84 **Don't Be My Enemy** *Wang Chung*
41/61 **Don't Believe Him, Donna** *Lenny Miles*
9/61 **Don't Bet Money Honey** *Linda Scott*
20/61 **Don't Blame Me** *Everly Brothers*
37/67 **Don't Blame The Children**
Sammy Davis, Jr.
1/62 **Don't Break The Heart That Loves You**
Connie Francis
4/79 **Don't Bring Me Down**
Electric Light Orchestra
12/66 **Don't Bring Me Down** *Animals*
F/74 **Don't Burn Down The Bridge**
Gladys Knight & The Pips
79/73 **Don't Burn Me** *Paul Kelly*
83/57 **Don't Call Me Sweetie (Cause I'm Bitter)**
Eileen Rodgers
9/75 **Don't Call Us, We'll Call You** *Sugarloaf*
Don't Cha *also see: Don'tcha*
78/75 **Don't Cha Love It** *Miracles*
80/83 **Don't Change** *INXS*
26/74 **Don't Change Horses (In The Middle Of A Stream)** *Tower Of Power*
36/71 **Don't Change On Me** *Ray Charles*
59/68 **Don't Change Your Love** *Five Stairsteps*
13/85 **Don't Come Around Here No More**
Tom Petty
21/60 **Don't Come Knockin'** *Fats Domino*
58/65 **Don't Come Running Back To Me**
Nancy Wilson
79/78 **Don't Cost You Nothing**
Ashford & Simpson
35/73 **Don't Cross The River** *America*
10/83 **Don't Cry** *Asia*
83/56 **Don't Cry** *Frankie Laine*
Don't Cry, Baby
39/61 *Etta James*
92/62 *Aretha Franklin*
6/70 **Don't Cry Daddy** *Elvis Presley*
72/80 **Don't Cry For Me Argentina** *Festival*
63/76 **Don't Cry Joni** *Conway Twitty*
55/57 **Don't Cry My Love** *Vera Lynn*
(also see: Faithful Hussar)
71/68 **Don't Cry My Love** *Impressions*
71/61 **Don't Cry No More** *Bobby Bland*
10/79 **Don't Cry Out Loud** *Melissa Manchester*
62/60 **Don't Deceive Me** *Ruth Brown*
94/59 **Don't Destroy Me** *Crash Craddock*
34/72 **Don't Do It** *Band*
75/67 **Don't Do It** *Micky Dolenz*
90/84 **Don't Do Me** *Randy Bell*
10/80 **Don't Do Me Like That** *Tom Petty*
87/79 **Don't Drop My Love** *Anita Ward*
86/74 **Don't Eat The Yellow Snow** *Frank Zappa*
23/72 **Don't Ever Be Lonely (A Poor Little Fool Like Me)** *Cornelius Brothers & Sister Rose*
85/62 **Don't Ever Leave Me** *Bob & Earl*
42/64 **Don't Ever Leave Me** *Connie Francis*
90/57 **Don't Ever Love Me** *Harry Belafonte*
100/72 **Don't Ever Take Away My Freedom**
Peter Yarrow
40/79 **Don't Ever Wanna Lose Ya** *New England*
8/73 **Don't Expect Me To Be Your Friend** *Lobo*
4/80 **Don't Fall In Love With A Dreamer**
Kenny Rogers & Kim Carnes
12/76 **(Don't Fear) The Reaper** *Blue Oyster Cult*
Don't Fence Me In
45/60 *Tommy Edwards*
93/63 *George Maharis*
17/82 **Don't Fight It** *Kenny Loggins/Steve Perry*
53/65 **Don't Fight It** *Wilson Pickett*
72/76 **Don't Fight The Hands (That Need You)**
Hamilton, Joe Frank & Dennison
1/57 **Don't Forbid Me** *Pat Boone*

Don't Forget About Me
91/66 *Barbara Lewis*
64/69 *Dusty Springfield*
96/61 **Don't Forget I Love You** *Butanes*
19/65 **Don't Forget I Still Love You** *Bobbi Martin*
2/86 **Don't Forget Me (When I'm Gone)** *Glass Tiger*
29/83 **Don't Forget To Dance** *Kinks*
73/69 **Don't Forget To Remember** *Bee Gees*
Don't Get Around Much Anymore
74/57 *Tab Hunter*
57/61 *Belmonts*
10/86 **Don't Get Me Wrong** *Pretenders*
69/83 **Don't Girls Get Lonely** *Glenn Shorrock*
15/69 **Don't Give In To Him** *Gary Puckett & The Union Gap*
26/81 **Don't Give It Up** *Robbie Patton*
37/68 **Don't Give Up** *Petula Clark*
1/77 **Don't Give Up On Us** *David Soul*
1/76 **Don't Go Breaking My Heart** *Elton John & Kiki Dee*
22/58 **Don't Go Home** *Playmates*
62/62 **Don't Go Near The Eskimos** *Ben Colder*
17/62 **Don't Go Near The Indians** *Rex Allen*
18/67 **Don't Go Out Into The Rain (You're Going To Melt)** *Herman's Hermits*
Don't Go To Strangers
38/56 *Vaughn Monroe*
36/60 *Etta Jones*
4/62 **Don't Hang Up** *Orlons*
93/65 **Don't Have To Shop Around** *Mad Lads*
46/72 **Don't Hide Your Love** *Cher*
21/79 **Don't Hold Back** *Chanson*
2/77 **Don't It Make My Brown Eyes Blue** *Crystal Gayle*
82/75 **Don't It Make You Wanna Dance?** *Rusty Wier*
Don't It Make You Want To Go Home
41/69 *Joe South*
45/70 *Brook Benton*
8/65 **Don't Just Stand There** *Patty Duke*
Don't Knock My Love
13/71 *Wilson Pickett*
46/74 *Marvin Gaye & Diana Ross*
45/56 **Don't Knock The Rock** *Bill Haley & His Comets*
88/81 **Don't Know Much** *Bill Medley*
91/75 **Don't Leave Me In The Morning** *Odia Coates*
52/73 **Don't Leave Me Starvin' For Your Love** *Brian Holland*
Don't Leave Me This Way
1/77 *Thelma Houston*
40/87 *Communards*
Don't Let Go
13/58 *Roy Hamilton*
56/75 *Commander Cody*
18/80 *Isaac Hayes*
38/84 **Don't Let Go** *Wang Chung*
84/81 **Don't Let Go The Coat** *Who*
64/63 **Don't Let Her Be Your Baby** *Contours*
24/81 **Don't Let Him Go** *REO Speedwagon*
39/82 **Don't Let Him Know** *Prism*
92/61 **Don't Let Him Shop Around** *Debbie Dean* *(also see: Shop Around)*
45/69 **Don't Let Him Take Your Love From Me** *Four Tops*
6/83 **Don't Let It End** *Styx*
56/73 **Don't Let It End ('Til You Let It Begin)** *Miracles*
86/73 **Don't Let It Get You Down** *Crusaders*
92/78 **Don't Let It Show** *Alan Parsons Project*
44/69 **Don't Let Love Hang You Up** *Jerry Butler*
85/60 **Don't Let Love Pass Me By** *Frankie Avalon*
14/73 **Don't Let Me Be Lonely Tonight** *James Taylor*
Don't Let Me Be Misunderstood
15/65 *Animals*
15/78 *Santa Esmeralda*
88/63 **Don't Let Me Cross Over** *Carl Butler*
35/69 **Don't Let Me Down** *Beatles*
63/82 **Don't Let Me In** *Sneaker*
68/77 **Don't Let The Flame Burn Out** *Jackie DeShannon*
17/71 **Don't Let The Green Grass Fool You** *Wilson Pickett*
20/69 **Don't Let The Joneses Get You Down** *Temptations*
100/70 **Don't Let The Music Slip Away** *Archie Bell & The Drells*
6/64 **Don't Let The Rain Come Down (Crooked Little Man)** *Serendipity Singers*
39/67 **Don't Let The Rain Fall Down On Me** *Critters*
4/64 **Don't Let The Sun Catch You Crying** *Gerry & The Pacemakers*
95/60 **Don't Let The Sun Catch You Crying** *Ray Charles*
2/74 **Don't Let The Sun Go Down On Me** *Elton John*
95/65 **Don't Let Your Left Hand Know** *Joe Tex*
72/84 **Don't Look Any Further** *Dennis Edwards*
4/78 **Don't Look Back** *Boston*
83/66 **Don't Look Back** *Temptations*
4/85 **Don't Lose My Number** *Phil Collins*
75/83 **Don't Make Me Do It** *Patrick Simmons*
Don't Make Me Over
21/63 *Dionne Warwick*
77/70 *Brenda & The Tabulations*
67/80 *Jennifer Warnes*
62/71 **Don't Make Me Pay For His Mistakes** *Z.Z. Hill*
51/63 **Don't Make My Baby Blue** *Frankie Laine*
79/68 **Don't Make The Good Girls Go Bad** *Della Humphrey*
94/63 **Don't Mention My Name** *Shepherd Sisters*
33/65 **Don't Mess Up A Good Thing** *Fontella Bass & Bobby McClUre*
7/66 **Don't Mess With Bill** *Marvelettes*
55/80 **Don't Misunderstand Me** *Rossington Collins Band*
91/68 **Don't Pat Me On The Back And Call Me Brother** *Kasandra*
34/83 **Don't Pay The Ferryman** *Chris DeBurgh*
40/59 **Don't Pity Me** *Dion & The Belmonts*
83/65 **Don't Pity Me** *Peter & Gordon*
Don't Play That Song
11/62 *Ben E. King*
11/70 *Aretha Franklin*
Don't Pull Your Love
4/71 *Hamilton, Joe Frank & Reynolds*
27/76 *Glen Campbell (medley)*
49/80 **Don't Push It Don't Force It** *Leon Haywood*
65/61 **Don't Read The Letter** *Patti Page*
98/67 **Don't Rock The Boat** *Eddie Floyd*
82/82 **Don't Run My Life** *Spys*
26/63 **Don't Say Goodnight And Mean Goodbye** *Shirelles*
39/80 **Don't Say Goodnight, It's Time For Love** *Isley Brothers*
68/80 **Don't Say No** *Billy Burnette*
76/86 **Don't Say No Tonight** *Eugene Wilde*
7/63 **Don't Say Nothin' Bad (About My Baby)** *Cookies*
15/72 **Don't Say You Don't Remember** *Beverly Bremers*
57/74 **Don't Send Nobody Else** *Ace Spectrum*

20/63 **Don't Set Me Free** *Ray Charles*
96/68 **Don't Sign The Paper Baby (I Want You Back)** *Jimmy Delphs*
5/67 **Don't Sleep In The Subway** *Petula Clark*
93/64 **Don't Spread It Around** *Barbara Lynn*
Don't Stand So Close To Me
10/81 *Police*
46/86 *Police ('86)*
F/55 **Don't Stay Away Too Long** *Eddie Fisher*
3/77 **Don't Stop** *Fleetwood Mac*
44/84 **Don't Stop** *Jeffrey Osborne*
9/81 **Don't Stop Believin'** *Journey*
33/76 **Don't Stop Believin'** *Olivia Newton-John*
42/76 **Don't Stop It Now** *Hot Chocolate*
61/82 **Don't Stop Me Baby (I'm On Fire)** *Boys Band*
86/79 **Don't Stop Me Now** *Queen*
48/70 **Don't Stop Now** *Eddie Holman*
19/81 **Don't Stop The Music** *Yarbrough & Peoples*
99/62 **Don't Stop The Wedding** *Ann Cole*
1/79 **Don't Stop 'Til You Get Enough** *Michael Jackson*
83/82 **Don't Stop Trying** *Rodway*
34/76 **Don't Take Away The Music** *Tavares*
27/68 **Don't Take It So Hard** *Paul Revere & The Raiders*
98/59 **Don't Take The Stars** *Mystics*
32/59 **Don't Take Your Guns To Town** *Johnny Cash*
37/75 **Don't Take Your Love** *Manhattans*
76/64 **Don't Take Your Love From Me** *Gloria Lynne*
81/82 **Don't Talk** *Larry Lee*
Don't Talk To Strangers
52/65 *Beau Brummels*
2/82 *Rick Springfield*
27/75 **Don't Tell Me Goodnight** *Lobo*
83/56 **Don't Tell Me Not To Love You** *Joni James*
40/83 **Don't Tell Me You Love Me** *Night Ranger*
85/59 **Don't Tell Me Your Troubles** *Don Gibson*
73/69 **Don't Tell Your Mama (Where You've Been)** *Eddie Floyd*
43/76 **Don't Think...Feel** *Neil Diamond*
Don't Think Twice, It's All Right
9/63 *Peter, Paul & Mary*
12/65 *Wonder Who?*
22/60 **Don't Throw Away All Those Teardrops** *Frankie Avalon*
16/64 **Don't Throw Your Love Away** *Searchers*
Don't Touch Me
85/66 *Jeannie Seely*
38/69 *Bettye Swann*
61/76 **Don't Touch Me There** *Tubes*
53/63 **Don't Try To Fight It, Baby** *Eydie Gorme*
Don't Try To Lay No Boogie Woogie On The King Of Rock & Roll
52/70 *Crow*
73/71 *John Baldry*
68/83 **Don't Try To Stop It** *Roman Holliday*
57/77 **Don't Turn The Light Out** *Cliff Richard*
83/84 **Don't Wait For Heroes** *Dennis DeYoung*
54/63 **Don't Wait Too Long** *Tony Bennett*
54/69 **Don't Wake Me Up In The Morning, Michael** *Peppermint Rainbow*
Don't Walk Away
26/84 *Rick Springfield*
85/86 *Robert Tepper*
53/71 **Don't Wanna Live Inside Myself** *Bee Gees*
68/63 **Don't Wanna Think About Paula** *Dickey Lee*
79/81 **Don't Want No-Body** *J.D. Drews*
21/78 **Don't Want To Live Without It** *Pablo Cruise*
86/72 **Don't Want To Say Goodbye** *Raspberries*
35/81 **Don't Want To Wait Anymore** *Tubes*
81/69 **Don't Waste My Time** *John Mayall*
48/84 **Don't Waste Your Time** *Yarbrough & Peoples*
3/61 **Don't Worry** *Marty Robbins*
Don't Worry Baby
24/64 *Beach Boys*
95/70 *Tokens*
17/77 *B.J. Thomas*
72/62 **Don't Worry 'Bout Me** *Vincent Edwards*
29/71 **(Don't Worry) If There's A Hell Below We're All Going To Go** *Curtis Mayfield*
67/66 **Don't Worry Mother, Your Son's Heart Is Pure** *McCoys*
Don't Ya Wanna Play This Game No More *see: (Sartorial Eloquence)*
Don't You *also see: Don'tcha & Doncha'*
39/62 **Don't You Believe It** *Andy Williams*
6/67 **Don't You Care** *Buckinghams*
1/85 **Don't You (Forget About Me)** *Simple Minds*
25/83 **Don't You Get So Mad** *Jeffrey Osborne*
9/58 **Don't You Just Know It** *Huey 'Piano' Smith*
2/59 **Don't You Know** *Della Reese*
58/83 **Don't You Know How Much I Love You** *Ronnie Milsap*
69/81 **Don't You Know What Love Is** *Touch*
56/59 **Don't You Know Yockomo** *Huey 'Piano' Smith*
68/67 **Don't You Miss Me A Little Bit Baby** *Jimmy Ruffin*
1/82 **Don't You Want Me** *Human League*
66/62 **Don't You Worry** *Don Gardner & Dee Dee Ford*
16/74 **Don't You Worry 'Bout A Thing** *Stevie Wonder*
Don't You Worry 'Bout Me *see: Opus 17*
33/79 **Don't You Write Her Off** *McGuinn, Clark & Hillman*
77/61 **Donald Where's Your Troosers?** *Andy Stewart*
15/58 **Doncha' Think It's Time** *Elvis Presley*
47/58 **Donde Esta Santa Claus?** *Augie Rios*
65/71 **Done Too Soon** *Neil Diamond*
2/59 **Donna** *Ritchie Valens*
6/63 **Donna The Prima Donna** *Dion*
62/64 **Donnie** *Bermudas*
15/74 **Doo Doo Doo Doo Doo (Heartbreaker)** *Rolling Stones*
71/77 **Doodle Song** *Frankie Miller*
94/61 **Dooley** *Olympics*
92/62 **Door Is Open** *Tommy Hunt*
Door Is Still Open To My Heart
F/55 *Don Cornell*
6/64 *Dean Martin*
85/61 **Door To Paradise** *Bobby Rydell*
62/74 **Door To Your Heart** *Dramatics*
35/74 **Doraville** *Atlanta Rhythm Section*
26/76 **Dose Of Rock 'N' Roll** *Ringo Starr*
39/58 **Dottie** *Danny & The Juniors*
22/71 **Double Barrel** *Dave & Ansil Collins*
30/81 **Double Dutch Bus** *Frankie Smith*
14/71 **Double Lovin'** *Osmonds*
89/65 **Double-O-Seven** *Detergents*
17/66 **Double Shot (Of My Baby's Love)** *Swingin' Medallions*
80/76 **Double Trouble** *Lynyrd Skynyrd*
2/78 **Double Vision** *Foreigner*
50/73 **Down And Out In New York City** *James Brown*
33/68 **Down At Lulu's** *Ohio Express*
9/63 **(Down At) Papa Joe's** *Dixiebelles*
4/72 **Down By The Lazy River** *Osmonds*

Down By The River
68/70 *Buddy Miles*
91/70 *Brooklyn Bridge*
91/72 **Down By The River** *Albert Hammond*
60/60 **Down By The Riverside**
Les Compagnons De La Chanson
13/60 **Down By The Station** *Four Preps*
69/68 **Down Here On The Ground** *Lou Rawls*
75/70 **Down In The Alley** *Ronnie Hawkins*
9/65 **Down In The Boondocks** *Billy Joe Royal*
71/62 **Down In The Valley** *Solomon Burke*
93/58 **Down In Virginia** *Jimmy Reed*
54/85 **Down On Love** *Foreigner*
Down On Me
43/68 *Big Brother & The Holding Company*
91/72 *Janis Joplin*
3/69 **Down On The Corner**
Creedence Clearwater Revival
91/60 **Down The Aisle** *Ike Clanton*
18/58 **Down The Aisle Of Love** *Quin-Tones*
37/63 **Down The Aisle (Wedding Bells)**
Patti LaBelle & The Blue Belles
65/77 **Down The Hall** *4 Seasons*
85/60 **Down The Street To 301** *Johnny Cash*
47/76 **Down To Love Town** *Originals*
43/76 **Down To The Line**
Bachman-Turner Overdrive
66/72 **Down To The Nightclub** *Tower Of Power*
82/77 **Down To The Station** *B.W. Stevenson*
1/83 **Down Under** *Men At Work*
48/60 **Down Yonder** *Johnny & The Hurricanes*
Downtown
1/65 *Petula Clark*
40/65 *Allan Sherman (Crazy Downtown)*
82/66 *Mrs. Miller*
80/84 *Dolly Parton*
Dr. *see: Doctor*
10/64 **Drag City** *Jan & Dean*
4/71 **Draggin' The Line** *Tommy James*
28/81 **Draw Of The Cards** *Kim Carnes*
42/77 **Draw The Line** *Aerosmith*
44/78 **Dreadlock Holiday** *10cc*
Dream
19/58 *Betty Johnson*
55/61 *Etta James*
92/62 *Dinah Washington*
12/68 **Dream A Little Dream Of Me** *Mama Cass*
85/56 **Dream Along With Me (I'm On My Way To A Star)** *Perry Como*
Dream Baby (How Long Must I Dream)
4/62 *Roy Orbison*
31/71 *Glen Campbell*
87/61 **Dream Boy** *Annette*
69/74 **Dream Goes On Forever** *Todd Rundgren*
37/84 **Dream (Hold On To Your Dream)**
Irene Cara
Dream Lover
2/59 *Bobby Darin*
91/64 *Paris Sisters*
75/78 **Dream Lover** *Marshall Tucker Band*
73/73 **Dream Me Home** *Mac Davis*
Dream Merchant
38/67 *Jerry Butler*
36/75 *New Birth*
48/78 **Dream Never Dies** *Cooper Brothers*
Dream On
59/73 *Aerosmith*
6/76 *Aerosmith*
32/74 **Dream On** *Righteous Brothers*
25/65 **Dream On Little Dreamer** *Perry Como*
26/79 **Dream Police** *Cheap Trick*
2/76 **Dream Weaver** *Gary Wright*
42/77 **Dreamboat Annie** *Heart*
15/80 **Dreamer** *Supertramp*
66/81 **Dreamer** *Association*
86/56 **Dreamer** *Four Aces*
47/63 **Dreamer, The** *Neil Sedaka*
72/77 **Dreamin** *Loleatta Holloway*
Dreamin'
11/60 *Johnny Burnette*
45/82 *John Schneider*
30/83 **Dreamin' Is Easy** *Steel Breeze*
10/80 **Dreaming** *Cliff Richard*
27/79 **Dreaming** *Blondie*
43/75 **Dreaming A Dream** *Crown Heights Affair*
1/77 **Dreams** *Fleetwood Mac*
22/86 **Dreams** *Van Halen*
86/70 **Dreams** *Buddy Miles*
83/74 **Dreams Are Ten A Penny** *First Class*
Dreams Of The Everyday Housewife
32/68 *Glen Campbell*
60/68 *Wayne Newton*
5/86 **Dreamtime** *Daryl Hall*
Dreamy Eyes
63/59 *Johnny Tillotson*
35/62 *Johnny Tillotson*
56/57 **Dreamy Eyes** *Four Preps*
21/73 **Dreidel** *Don McLean*
5/85 **Dress You Up** *Madonna*
5/73 **Drift Away** *Dobie Gray*
96/68 **Driftin' Blues** *Bobby Bland*
59/78 **Driftwood** *Moody Blues*
98/65 **Drinking Man's Diet** *Allan Sherman*
41/73 **Drinking Wine Spo-Dee O'Dee**
Jerry Lee Lewis
Drip Drop
58/58 *Drifters*
6/63 *Dion*
3/84 **Drive** *Cars*
82/57 **Drive In Show** *Eddie Cochran*
Drive My Car
93/66 *Bob Kuban*
69/75 *Gary Toms Empire*
15/79 **Driver's Seat** *Sniff 'n' the Tears*
87/61 **Drivin' Home** *Duane Eddy*
5/80 **Drivin' My Life Away** *Eddie Rabbitt*
34/77 **Drivin' Wheel** *Foghat*
85/61 **Driving Wheel** *Little Junior Parker*
78/70 **Drop By My Place** *Carl Carlton*
76/83 **Drop The Pilot** *Joan Armatrading*
100/62 **Drown In My Own Tears** *Don Shirley*
36/63 **Drownin' My Sorrows** *Connie Francis*
11/72 **Drowning In The Sea Of Love** *Joe Simon*
29/71 **Drum, The** *Bobby Sherman*
86/62 **Drum Stomp** *Sandy Nelson*
98/69 **Drummer Man** *Nancy Sinatra*
67/62 **Drummin' Up A Storm** *Sandy Nelson*
100/67 **Drums** *Jon & Robin*
29/62 **Drums Are My Beat** *Sandy Nelson*
20/67 **Dry Your Eyes** *Brenda & The Tabulations*
96/62 **Duchess Of Earl** *Pearlettes*
14/66 **Duck, The** *Jackie Lee*
2/73 **Dueling Banjos**
Eric Weissberg & Steve Mandell
96/86 **Dueling Bikes From Quicksilver (medley)**
Ray Parker, Jr. & Helen Terry
92/73 **Dueling Tubas** *Martin Mull*
1/62 **Duke Of Earl** *Gene Chandler*
Dukes Of Hazzard *see: Theme From The*
Dum-De-Da *see: She Understands Me*
4/61 **Dum Dum** *Brenda Lee*
(Dum, Dum) *see: Happy Song*
77/63 **Dum Dum Dee Dum** *Johnny Cymbal*
50/64 **Dumb Head** *Ginny Arnell*
Dumplin's
69/57 *Doc Bagby*
75/57 *Ernie Freeman*
52/72 **Duncan** *Paul Simon*

7/56 **Dungaree Doll** *Eddie Fisher*
18/77 **Dusic** *Brick*
6/78 **Dust In The Wind** *Kansas*
55/65 **Dusty** *Rag Dolls*
30/60 **Dutchman's Gold** *Walter Brennan*
15/84 **Dynamite** *Jermaine Jackson*
72/57 **Dynamite** *Brenda Lee*
83/69 **Dynamite Woman** *Sir Douglas Quintet*
10/75 **Dynomite** *Bazuka [Tony Camillo's]*

E

89/84 **Each Word's A Beat Of My Heart** *Mink DeVille*
9/74 **Earache My Eye Featuring Alice Bowie** *Cheech & Chong*
95/61 **Early Every Morning (Early Every Evening Too)** *Dinah Washington*
12/70 **Early In The Morning** *Vanity Fare*
Early In The Morning
24/58 *Rinky-Dinks*
32/58 *Buddy Holly*
24/82 **Early In The Morning** *Gap Band*
68/74 **Early Morning Love** *Sammy Johns*
91/65 **Early Morning Rain** *Peter, Paul & Mary*
Earth Angel
3/55 *Crew-Cuts*
8/55 *Penguins*
18/55 *Gloria Mann*
57/60 *Johnny Tillotson*
42/69 *Vogues*
21/86 *New Edition*
Earthbound
46/56 *Sammy Davis, Jr.*
53/56 *Mario Lanza*
61/69 **Ease Back** *Meters*
Ease On Down The Road
42/75 *Consumer Rapport*
41/78 *Diana Ross & Michael Jackson*
1/63 **Easier Said Than Done** *Essex*
East Of Eden *see: Theme From*
27/66 **East West** *Herman's Hermits*
4/77 **Easy** *Commodores*
54/76 **Easy As Pie** *Billy 'Crash' Craddock*
9/70 **Easy Come, Easy Go** *Bobby Sherman*
60/79 **Easy Driver** *Kenny Loggins*
72/75 **Easy Evil** *Travis Wammack*
54/83 **Easy For You To Say** *Linda Ronstadt*
39/72 **Easy Livin** *Uriah Heep*
62/80 **Easy Love** *Dionne Warwick*
2/85 **Easy Lover** *Philip Bailey & Phil Collins*
70/60 **Easy Lovin'** *Wade Flemons*
17/71 **Easy Loving** *Freddie Hart*
Easy Rider *see: Ballad Of*
66/70 **Easy Rider (Let The Wind Pay The Way)** *Iron Butterfly*
83/74 **Easy Street** *Edgar Winter*
48/70 **Easy To Be Free** *Rick Nelson*
Easy To Be Hard
4/69 *Three Dog Night*
64/79 *Cheryl Barnes*
36/78 **Easy To Love** *Leo Sayer*
12/84 **Eat It** *'Weird Al' Yankovic*
75/84 **Eat My Shorts** *Rick Dees*
77/85 **Eaten Alive** *Diana Ross*

Ebb Tide
93/59 *Bobby Freeman*
56/60 *Platters*
25/64 *Lenny Welch*
5/66 *Righteous Brothers*
1/82 **Ebony And Ivory** *Paul McCartney & Stevie Wonder*
8/61 **Ebony Eyes** *Everly Brothers*
14/78 **Ebony Eyes** *Bob Welch*
43/84 **Ebony Eyes** *Rick James featuring Smokey Robinson*
76/63 **Echo** *Emotions*
40/69 **Echo Park** *Keith Barbour*
66/77 **Echoes Of Love** *Doobie Brothers*
31/73 **Ecstasy** *Ohio Players*
56/62 **Ecstasy** *Ben E. King*
Eddie My Love
11/56 *Fontane Sisters*
14/56 *Chordettes*
14/56 *Teen Queens*
77/72 **Eddie's Love** *Eddie Kendricks*
69/84 **Edge Of A Dream** *Joe Cocker*
10/86 **Edge Of Heaven** *Wham!*
11/82 **Edge Of Seventeen (Just Like The White Winged Dove)** *Stevie Nicks*
26/77 **Edge Of The Universe** *Bee Gees*
76/83 **Eenie Meenie** *Jeffrey Osborne*
52/66 **Eggplant That Ate Chicago** *Dr. West's Medicine Show & Junk Band*
34/78 **Ego** *Elton John*
72/76 **Eh! Cumpari** *Gaylord & Holiday*
53/63 **Eight By Ten** *Bill Anderson*
1/65 **Eight Days A Week** *Beatles*
80/67 **Eight Men, Four Women** *O.V. Wright*
14/66 **Eight Miles High** *Byrds*
4/82 **867-5309/Jenny** *Tommy Tutone*
82/81 **8th Wonder** *Sugarhill Gang*
21/71 **Eighteen** *Alice Cooper*
15/75 **Eighteen With A Bullet** *Pete Wingfield*
10/63 **18 Yellow Roses** *Bobby Darin*
51/65 **81, The** *Candy & The Kisses*
Ein Schiff Wird Kommen *see: Never On Sunday*
43/75 **El Bimbo** *Bimbo Jet*
18/70 **El Condor Pasa** *Simon & Garfunkel*
32/60 **El Matador** *Kingston Trio*
1/60 **El Paso** *Marty Robbins*
97/65 **El Pussy Cat** *Mongo Santamaria*
30/58 **El Rancho Rock** *Champs*
17/63 **El Watusi** *Ray Barretto*
Eleanor Rigby
11/66 *Beatles*
35/68 *Ray Charles*
17/69 *Aretha Franklin*
26/72 **Elected** *Alice Cooper*
6/85 **Election Day** *Arcadia*
2/83 **Electric Avenue** *Eddy Grant*
79/84 **Electric Kingdom** *Twilight 22*
61/69 **Electric Stories** *4 Seasons*
Electric Surfboard *see: Theme From*
74/82 **Electricland** *Bad Company*
96/71 **Electronic Magnetism** *Solomon Burke*
45/79 **Elena** *Marc Tanner Band*
6/68 **Elenore** *Turtles*
64/63 **Elephant Walk** *Donald Jenkins*
11th Hour Melody
21/56 *Al Hibbler*
35/56 *Lou Busch*
10/69 **Eli's Coming** *Three Dog Night*
39/56 **Eloise** *Kay Thompson*
86/69 **Eloise** *Barry Ryan*
5/66 **Elusive Butterfly** *Bob Lind*

Elvira
72/66 *Dallas Frazier*
5/81 *Oak Ridge Boys*
71/82 **Elvis Medley** *Elvis Presley*
18/85 **Emergency** *Kool & The Gang*
68/83 **Eminence Front** *Who*
8/75 **Emma** *Hot Chocolate*
3/78 **Emotion** *Samantha Sang*
22/75 **Emotion** *Helen Reddy*
79/85 **Emotion** *Barbra Streisand*
15/86 **Emotion In Motion** *Ric Ocasek*
3/80 **Emotional Rescue** *Rolling Stones*
7/61 **Emotions** *Brenda Lee*
68/82 **Emotions In Motion** *Billy Squier*
18/80 **Empire Strikes Back (Medley)** *Meco*
Empty Arms
13/57 *Teresa Brewer*
43/57 *Ivory Joe Hunter*
93/71 *Sonny James*
13/82 **Empty Garden (Hey Hey Johnny)** *Elton John*
74/70 **Empty Pages** *Traffic*
66/63 **Enamorado** *Keith Colley*
12/59 **Enchanted** *Platters*
12/58 **Enchanted Island** *Four Lads*
Enchanted Sea
15/59 *Islanders*
28/59 *Martin Denny*
69/84 **Encore** *Cheryl Lynn*
7/58 **End, The** *Earl Grant*
42/76 **End Is Not In Sight (The Cowboy Tune)** *Amazing Rhythm Aces*
End Of Our Road
15/68 *Gladys Knight & The Pips*
40/70 *Marvin Gaye*
2/63 **End Of The World** *Skeeter Davis*
52/56 **Endless** *McGuire Sisters*
1/81 **Endless Love** *Diana Ross & Lionel Richie*
Endless Sleep
5/58 *Jody Reynolds*
90/64 *Hank Williams, Jr.*
12/59 **Endlessly** *Brook Benton*
33/74 **Energy Crisis '74** *Dickie Goodman*
7/65 **Engine Engine #9** *Roger Miller*
14/70 **Engine Number 9** *Wilson Pickett*
8/65 **England Swings** *Roger Miller*
21/56 **English Muffins And Irish Stew** *Sylvia Syms*
6/77 **Enjoy Yourself** *Jacksons*
50/82 **Enough Is Enough** *April Wine*
Enough Is Enough *see: No More Tears*
3/74 **Entertainer, The** *Marvin Hamlisch*
31/65 **Entertainer, The** *Tony Clarke*
34/75 **Entertainer, The** *Billy Joel*
19/67 **Epistle To Dippy** *Donovan*
9/74 **Eres Tu (Touch The Wind)** *Mocedades*
58/83 **Escalator Of Life** *Robert Hazard*
1/79 **Escape (The Pina Colada Song)** *Rupert Holmes*
35/71 **Escape-ism** *James Brown*
19/62 **Eso Beso (That Kiss!)** *Paul Anka*
Eternally
92/59 *Thomas Wayne*
41/60 *Sarah Vaughan*
77/63 *Chantels*
79/69 **Eternity** *Vikki Carr*
67/83 **Europa And The Pirate Twins** *Thomas Dolby*
91/72 **Eve** *Jim Capaldi*
Eve Of Destruction
1/65 *Barry McGuire*
100/70 *Turtles*
33/80 **Even It Up** *Heart*
12/83 **Even Now** *Bob Seger*
19/78 **Even Now** *Barry Manilow*
36/67 **Even The Bad Times Are Good** *Tremeloes*
5/82 **Even The Nights Are Better** *Air Supply*
63/59 **Evening Rain** *Earl Grant*
56/61 **Eventually** *Brenda Lee*
63/57 **Ever Lovin' Fingers** *Jimmy Bowen with The Rhythm Orchids*
60/60 **Everglades** *Kingston Trio*
1/77 **Evergreen** *Barbra Streisand*
5/78 **Everlasting Love** *Andy Gibb*
Everlasting Love
13/67 *Robert Knight*
6/74 *Carl Carlton*
32/81 *Rex Smith/Rachel Sweet*
16/61 **Everlovin'** *Rick Nelson*
Every Beat Of My Heart
6/61 *Pips*
45/61 *Gladys Knight & The Pips*
99/63 *James Brown*
83/76 **Every Beat Of My Heart** *Crown Heights Affair*
83/86 **Every Beat Of My Heart** *Rod Stewart*
42/61 **Every Breath I Take** *Gene Pitney*
1/83 **Every Breath You Take** *Police*
Every Day *also see: Everyday*
96/66 **Every Day And Every Night** *Trolls*
74/67 **Every Day I Have The Blues** *Billy Stewart*
Every Day I Have To Cry Some
46/63 *Steve Alaimo*
77/66 *Gentrys*
45/75 *Arthur Alexander*
Every Day Of My Life
37/56 *McGuire Sisters*
24/72 *Bobby Vinton*
55/76 **Every Face Tells A Story** *Olivia Newton-John*
Every Home Should Have One
62/82 *Patti Austin*
69/83 *Patti Austin*
16/78 **Every Kinda People** *Robert Palmer*
13/64 **Every Little Bit Hurts** *Brenda Holloway*
72/86 **Every Little Kiss** *Bruce Hornsby*
48/59 **Every Little Thing I Do** *Dion & The Belmonts*
3/81 **Every Little Thing She Does Is Magic** *Police*
82/82 **Every Love Song** *Greg Kihn Band*
91/65 **Every Night, Every Day** *Jimmy McCracklin*
39/58 **Every Night (I Pray)** *Chantels*
46/62 **Every Night (Without You)** *Paul Anka*
25/85 **Every Step Of The Way** *John Waite*
30/63 **Every Step Of The Way** *Johnny Mathis*
87/56 **Every Time (I Feel His Spirit)** *Patti Page*
13/79 **Every Time I Think Of You** *Babys*
4/77 **(Every Time I Turn Around) Back In Love Again** *L.T.D.*
19/75 **Every Time You Touch Me (I Get High)** *Charlie Rich*
30/79 **Every Which Way But Loose** *Eddie Rabbitt*
5/81 **Every Woman In The World** *Air Supply*
3/63 **Everybody** *Tommy Roe*
38/77 **Everybody Be Dancin'** *Starbuck*
24/86 **Everybody Dance** *Ta Mara & The Seen*
38/78 **Everybody Dance** *Chic*
67/65 **Everybody Do The Sloopy** *Johnny Thunder*
80/63 **Everybody Go Home** *Eydie Gorme*
73/68 **Everybody Got To Believe In Somebody** *Sam & Dave*
2/86 **Everybody Have Fun Tonight** *Wang Chung*
F/70 **Everybody Is A Star** *Sly & The Family Stone*
43/68 **Everybody Knows** *Dave Clark Five*
72/64 **Everybody Knows** *Steve Lawrence*

60/72 **Everybody Knows About My Good Thing** *Little Johnny Taylor*
15/64 **Everybody Knows (I Still Love You)** *Dave Clark Five*
52/69 **Everybody Knows Matilda** *Duke Baxter*
31/59 **Everybody Likes To Cha Cha Cha** *Sam Cooke*
4/65 **Everybody Loves A Clown** *Gary Lewis & The Playboys*
63/72 **Everybody Loves A Love Song** *Mac Davis*
Everybody Loves A Lover
6/58 *Doris Day*
19/63 *Shirelles*
96/66 **Everybody Loves A Nut** *Johnny Cash*
43/78 **Everybody Loves A Rain Song** *B.J. Thomas*
95/67 **Everybody Loves A Winner** *William Bell*
6/62 **Everybody Loves Me But You** *Brenda Lee*
1/64 **Everybody Loves Somebody** *Dean Martin*
52/63 **Everybody Monkey** *Freddy Cannon*
32/78 **Everybody Needs Love** *Stephen Bishop*
39/67 **Everybody Needs Love** *Gladys Knight & The Pips*
Everybody Needs Somebody To Love
58/64 *Solomon Burke*
29/67 *Wilson Pickett*
75/77 **Everybody Ought To Be In Love** *Paul Anka*
3/72 **Everybody Plays The Fool** *Main Ingredient*
92/74 **(Everybody Wanna Get Rich) Rite Away** *Dr. John*
92/75 **Everybody Wants To Find A Bluebird** *Randy Edelman*
1/85 **Everybody Wants To Rule The World** *Tears For Fears*
32/82 **Everybody Wants You** *Billy Squier*
100/61 **Everybody's Cryin'** *Jimmie Beaumont*
12/71 **Everybody's Everything** *Santana*
Everybody's Got A Home But Me
20/55 *Eddie Fisher*
42/56 *Roy Hamilton*
21/70 **Everybody's Got The Right To Love** *Supremes*
18/80 **Everybody's Got To Learn Sometime** *Korgis*
52/61 **Everybody's Gotta Pay Some Dues** *Miracles*
62/73 **Everybody's Had The Blues** *Merle Haggard*
26/70 **Everybody's Out Of Town** *B.J. Thomas*
1/60 **Everybody's Somebody's Fool** *Connie Francis*
78/57 **Everybody's Somebody's Fool** *Heartbeats*
6/69 **Everybody's Talkin'** *Nilsson*
75/62 **Everybody's Twistin'** *Frank Sinatra*
Everyday
81/72 *John Denver*
61/85 *James Taylor*
36/83 **Everyday I Write The Book** *Elvis Costello*
Everyday People
1/69 *Sly & The Family Stone*
37/83 *Joan Jett*
19/69 **Everyday With You Girl** *Classics IV*
62/76 **Everyday Without You** *Hamilton, Joe Frank & Reynolds*
96/58 **Everyone Was There** *Bob Kayli*
6/79 **Every 1's A Winner** *Hot Chocolate*
49/73 **Everyone's Agreed That Everything Will Turn Out Fine** *Stealers Wheel*
17/65 **Everyone's Gone To The Moon** *Jonathan King*
69/57 **Everyone's Laughing** *Spaniels*
52/70 **Everything A Man Could Ever Need** *Glen Campbell*
45/72 **Everything Good Is Bad** *100 Proof Aged In Soul*
95/69 **Everything I Do Gohn Be Funky (From Now On)** *Lee Dorsey*
47/85 **Everything I Need** *Men At Work*
5/72 **Everything I Own** *Bread*
30/86 **Everything In My Heart** *Corey Hart*
86/80 **Everything Is Alright** *Spider*
1/70 **Everything Is Beautiful** *Ray Stevens*
84/70 **Everything Is Going To Be Alright** *Teegarden & Van Winkle*
74/71 **Everything Is Good About You** *Lettermen*
56/86 **Everything Must Change** *Paul Young*
1/85 **Everything She Wants** *Wham!*
66/76 **Everything That 'Cha Do (Will Come Back To You)** *Wet Willie*
10/68 **Everything That Touches You** *Association*
44/80 **Everything Works If You Let It** *Cheap Trick*
16/64 **Everything's Alright** *Newbeats*
Everything's Alright
92/71 *Yvonne Elliman*
99/71 *Kimberlys (medley)*
70/73 **Everything's Been Changed** *5th Dimension*
49/76 **Everything's Coming Up Love** *David Ruffin*
91/75 **Everything's The Same (Ain't Nothing Changed)** *Billy Swan*
38/70 **Everything's Tuesday** *Chairmen Of The Board*
66/86 **Everytime You Cry** *Outfield*
1/85 **Everytime You Go Away** *Paul Young*
50/73 **Evil** *Earth, Wind & Fire*
72/74 **Evil Boll-Weevil** *Grand Canyon*
Evil Ways
9/70 *Santana*
84/72 *Carlos Santana & Buddy Miles*
10/76 **Evil Woman** *Electric Light Orchestra*
19/70 **Evil Woman Don't Play Your Games With Me** *Crow*
52/66 **Evol-Not Love** *Five Americans*
60/83 **Ewok Celebration** *Meco*
62/60 **Exclusively Yours** *Carl Dobkins, Jr.*
Exodus
2/61 *Ferrante & Teicher*
31/61 *Mantovani*
36/61 *Eddie Harris*
64/61 *Pat Boone*
Exorcist, Theme From *see: Tubular Bells*
98/68 **Expecting To Fly** *Buffalo Springfield*
14/55 **Experience Unnecessary** *Sarah Vaughan*
61/56 **Experiments With Mice** *Johnny Dankworth*
33/68 **Explosion In My Soul** *Soul Survivors*
4/75 **Express** *B.T. Express*
12/70 **Express Yourself** *Watts 103rd St. Band*
4/67 **Expressway To Your Heart** *Soul Survivors*
3/82 **Eye In The Sky** *Alan Parsons Project*
1/82 **Eye Of The Tiger** *Survivor*
81/86 **Eye Of The Zombie** *John Fogerty*
71/85 **Eye On You** *Billy Squier*
73/85 **Eye To Eye** *Go West*
28/68 **Eyes Of A New York Woman** *B.J. Thomas*
Eyes Of Laura Mars *see: Love Theme From*
52/74 **Eyes Of Silver** *Doobie Brothers*
79/84 **Eyes That See In The Dark** *Kenny Rogers*
4/84 **Eyes Without A Face** *Billy Idol*

22/78 **FM (No Static At All)** *Steely Dan*
29/66 **Fa-Fa-Fa-Fa-Fa (Sad Song)** *Otis Redding*
Fabulous
16/57 *Charlie Gracie*
71/57 *Steve Lawrence*
19/56 **Fabulous Character** *Sarah Vaughan*
29/68 **Face It Girl, It's Over** *Nancy Wilson*
26/86 **Face The Face** *Pete Townshend*
27/87 **Facts Of Love**
Jeff Lorber featuring Karyn White
20/81 **Fade Away** *Bruce Springsteen*
82/83 **Fade Away** *Loz Netto*
Faded Love
96/63 *Patsy Cline*
97/63 *Jackie DeShannon*
54/56 **Faded Summer Love** *Georgie Shaw*
43/77 **Fair Game** *Crosby, Stills & Nash*
F/55 **Fairy Tale** *Frank Sinatra*
13/74 **Fairytale** *Pointer Sisters*
52/56 **Faithful Hussar** *Ted Heath*
(also see: Don't Cry My Love)
12/83 **Faithfully** *Journey*
35/83 **Fake Friends** *Joan Jett*
23/67 **Fakin' It** *Simon & Garfunkel*
17/83 **Fall In Love With Me** *Earth, Wind & Fire*
67/67 **Fall In Love With Me** *Bettye Swann*
94/86 **Fall On Me** *R.E.M.*
36/76 **Fallen Angel** *Frankie Valli*
99/60 **Fallen Angel** *Webb Pierce*
Fallen Star
20/57 *Nick Noble*
23/57 *Jimmy Newman*
47/57 *Ferlin Husky*
58/57 *Hilltoppers*
30/58 **Fallin'** *Connie Francis*
1/75 **Fallin' In Love**
Hamilton, Joe Frank & Reynolds
27/74 **Fallin' In Love**
Souther, Hillman, Furay Band
13/78 **Falling** *LeBlanc & Carr*
22/63 **Falling** *Roy Orbison*
49/76 **Falling Apart At The Seams** *Marmalade*
58/82 **Falling In Love** *Balance*
64/81 **Falling In Love Again**
Michael Stanley Band
25/87 **Falling In Love (Uh-Oh)**
Miami Sound Machine
1/75 **Fame** *David Bowie*
4/80 **Fame** *Irene Cara*
17/60 **Fame And Fortune** *Elvis Presley*
1/71 **Family Affair** *Sly & The Family Stone*
6/83 **Family Man** *Daryl Hall & John Oates*
12/72 **Family Of Man** *Three Dog Night*
42/83 **Fanatic** *Felony*
31/70 **Fancy** *Bobbie Gentry*
39/77 **Fancy Dancer** *Commodores*
77/79 **Fancy Dancer** *Frankie Valli*
71/75 **Fancy Lady** *Billy Preston*
71/59 **Fancy Nancy** *Skip & Flip*
47/65 **Fancy Pants** *Al Hirt*
38/60 **Fannie Mae** *Buster Brown*
12/76 **Fanny (Be Tender With My Love)** *Bee Gees*
55/81 **Fantastic Voyage** *Lakeside*
23/82 **Fantasy** *Aldo Nova*
32/78 **Fantasy** *Earth, Wind & Fire*
52/81 **Fantasy Girl** *38 Special*
72/60 **Far, Far Away** *Don Gibson*
10/83 **Far From Over** *Frank Stallone*
90/61 **Faraway Star** *Chordettes*
89/73 **Farewell Andromeda (Welcome To My Morning)** *John Denver*
86/69 **Farewell Love Scene**
Romeo & Juliet Soundtrack
38/84 **Farewell My Summer Love**
Michael Jackson
19/64 **Farmer John** *Premiers*
56/70 **Farther On Down The Road** *Joe Simon*
43/57 **Farther Up The Road** *Bobby Bland*
Fascination
7/57 *Jane Morgan*
15/57 *Dinah Shore*
17/57 *Dick Jacobs*
56/57 *David Carroll*
Fascination *also see: (Keep Feeling)*
70/81 **Fashion** *David Bowie*
F/79 **Fat Bottomed Girls** *Queen*
93/70 **Father Come On Home**
Pacific Gas & Electric
100/62 **Father Knows Best** *Radiants*
92/68 **Father Of Girls** *Perry Como*
86/64 **Father Sebastian** *Ramblers*
78/83 **Favorite Waste Of Time** *Bette Midler*
Feel It
56/61 *Sam Cooke*
95/66 *Sam Cooke*
34/86 **Feel It Again** *Honeymoon Suite*
48/82 **Feel Like A Number** *Bob Seger*
Feel Like Makin' Love
1/74 *Roberta Flack*
88/74 *Bob James*
10/75 **Feel Like Makin' Love** *Bad Company*
Feel So Bad *see: I Feel So Bad*
Feel So Fine
14/60 *Johnny Preston*
22/67 *Bunny Sigler (medley)*
67/79 **Feel That You're Feelin'**
Maze Featuring Frankie Beverly
61/77 **Feel The Beat (Everybody Disco)**
Ohio Players
73/86 **Feel The Heat** *Jean Beauvoir*
Feel The Need
90/77 *Detroit Emeralds*
57/79 *Leif Garrett*
Feelin' Groovy *see: 59th Street Bridge*
46/79 **Feelin' Satisfied** *Boston*
53/69 **Feelin' So Good (Skooby-Doo)** *Archies*
10/73 **Feelin' Stronger Every Day** *Chicago*
76/75 **Feelin' That Glow** *Roberta Flack*
Feeling Alright
69/69 *Joe Cocker*
96/69 *Mongo Santamaria*
54/71 *Grand Funk Railroad*
33/72 *Joe Cocker*
91/64 **Feeling Is Gone** *Bobby Bland*
65/69 **Feeling Is Right** *Clarence Carter*
Feelings
6/75 *Morris Albert*
93/77 *Walter Jackson*
93/70 **Feelings** *Barry Mann*
4/77 **Feels Like The First Time** *Foreigner*
4/78 **Feels So Good** *Chuck Mangione*
78/84 **Feels So Real (Won't Let Go)**
Patrice Rushen
20/81 **Feels So Right** *Alabama*
82/83 **Feet Don't Fail Me Now** *Utopia*
94/67 **Felicidad** *Sally Field*
45/73 **Fell For You** *Dramatics*
32/61 **Fell In Love On Monday** *Fats Domino*
71/86 **Female Intuition** *Mai Tai*
52/73 **Fencewalk** *Mandrill*
13/76 **Fernando** *Abba*
72/64 **Ferris Wheel** *Everly Brothers*
6/65 **Ferry Across The Mersey**
Gerry & The Pacemakers

Fever
24/56 *Little Willie John*
8/58 *Peggy Lee*
7/65 *McCoys*
76/73 *Rita Coolidge*
59/76 **Fez, The** *Steely Dan*
23/78 **Ffun** *Con Funk Shun*
39/58 **Fibbin'** *Patti Page*
93/66 **Fiddle Around** *Jan & Dean*
97/64 **Fiddler On The Roof** *Village Stompers*
52/84 **Fields Of Fire** *Big Country*
96/62 **Fiesta** *Dave 'Baby' Cortez*
53/66 **Fife Piper** *Dynatones*
81/70 **Fifteen Years Ago** *Conway Twitty*
1/76 **Fifth Of Beethoven** *Walter Murphy*
1/76 **50 Ways To Leave Your Lover** *Paul Simon*
13/67 **59th Street Bridge Song (Feelin' Groovy)** *Harpers Bizarre*
58/83 **Fight Fire With Fire** *Kansas*
3/79 **Fight (medley)** *Barbra Streisand*
4/75 **Fight The Power** *Isley Brothers*
92/70 **Fightin' Side Of Me** *Merle Haggard*
(Final Acclaim) *see: You're In My Heart*
58/82 **Finally** *T.G. Sheppard*
17/74 **Finally Got Myself Together (I'm A Changed Man)** *Impressions*
29/85 **Find A Way** *Amy Grant*
16/82 **Find Another Fool** *Quarterflash*
27/61 **Find Another Girl** *Jerry Butler*
94/76 **Find 'Em, Fool 'Em & Forget 'Em** *Dobie Gray*
98/65 **Find My Way Back Home** *Nashville Teens*
29/81 **Find Your Way Back** *Jefferson Starship*
59/73 **Finder's Keepers** *Chairmen Of The Board*
96/65 **Finders Keepers, Losers Weepers** *Nella Dodds*
53/63 **Fine Fine Boy** *Darlene Love*
22/84 **Fine Fine Day** *Tony Carey*
44/86 **Finest** *S.O.S. Band*
7/60 **Finger Poppin' Time** *Hank Ballard*
1/63 **Fingertips** *Stevie Wonder*
35/79 **Fins** *Jimmy Buffett*
1/75 **Fire** *Ohio Players*
2/68 **Fire** *Crazy World Of Arthur Brown*
2/79 **Fire** *Pointer Sisters*
52/68 **Fire** *Five By Five*
93/76 **Fire** *Mother's Finest*
17/81 **Fire And Ice** *Pat Benatar*
Fire And Rain
3/70 *James Taylor*
82/70 *R.B. Greaves*
94/70 *Johnny Rivers*
24/72 **Fire And Water** *Wilson Pickett*
28/74 **Fire, Baby I'm On Fire** *Andy Kim*
32/80 **Fire In The Morning** *Melissa Manchester*
76/81 **Fire In The Sky** *Dirt Band*
6/80 **Fire Lake** *Bob Seger*
66/58 **Fire Of Love** *Jody Reynolds*
38/75 **Fire On The Mountain** *Marshall Tucker Band*
89/77 **Fire Sign** *Cory*
71/86 **Fire With Fire** *Wild Blue*
43/79 **Firecracker** *Mass Production*
60/81 **Fireflies** *Fleetwood Mac*
20/58 **Firefly** *Tony Bennett*
42/59 **First Anniversary** *Cathy Carr*
53/80 **First...Be A Woman** *Lenore O'Malley*
46/56 **First Born** *Tennessee Ernie Ford*
First Cut Is The Deepest
70/73 *Keith Hampshire*
21/77 *Rod Stewart*
25/57 **First Date, First Kiss, First Love** *Sonny James*
60/63 **First Day Back At School** *Paul & Paula*
33/84 **First Day Of Summer** *Tony Carey*
81/69 **First Hymn From Grand Terrace** *Mark Lindsay*
57/65 **First I Look At The Purse** *Contours*
81/57 **First Kiss** *Norman Petty Trio*
59/59 **First Love, First Tears** *Duane Eddy*
20/60 **First Name Initial** *Annette*
53/85 **First Night** *Survivor*
59/64 **First Night Of The Full Moon** *Jack Jones*
37/69 **First Of May** *Bee Gees*
27/63 **First Quarrel** *Paul & Paula*
53/61 **First Taste Of Love** *Ben E. King*
91/65 **First Thing Ev'ry Morning (And The Last Thing Ev'ry Night)** *Jimmy Dean*
1/72 **First Time Ever I Saw Your Face** *Roberta Flack*
(First Time I Was A Fool) *see: Third Time Lucky*
38/80 **First Time Love** *Livingston Taylor*
25/61 **Fish, The** *Bobby Rydell*
26/74 **Fish Ain't Bitin'** *Lamont Dozier*
71/56 **Five** *Sammy Davis, Jr.*
74/60 **Five Brothers** *Marty Robbins*
44/66 **5D (Fifth Dimension)** *Byrds*
76/59 **Five Feet High And Rising** *Johnny Cash*
45/79 **5:15** *Who*
73/56 **Five Hundred Guys** *Frank Sinatra*
500 Miles Away From Home
10/63 *Bobby Bare*
79/72 *Heaven Bound with Tony Scotti*
F/85 **Five Minutes Of Funk** *Whodini*
4/66 **Five O'Clock World** *Vogues*
Five Oaks *see: Cinco Robles*
89/59 **Five Pennies** *Dodie Stevens*
27/78 **5.7.0.5** *City Boy*
11/70 **5-10-15-20 (25-30 Years Of Love)** *Presidents*
91/77 **Flame** *Steve Sperry*
14/61 **Flaming Star** *Elvis Presley*
74/76 **Flaming Youth** *Kiss*
28/66 **Flamingo** *Herb Alpert*
82/61 **Flamingo Express** *Royaltones*
98/58 **Flamingo L'amore** *Gaylords*
16/78 **Flash Light** *Parliament*
42/81 **Flash's Theme Aka Flash** *Queen*
82/74 **Flashback** *5th Dimension*
1/83 **Flashdance...What A Feeling** *Irene Cara*
86/84 **Flashes** *Tiggi Clay*
54/71 **Flesh And Blood** *Johnny Cash*
29/84 **Flesh For Fantasy** *Billy Idol*
44/76 **Flight '76** *Walter Murphy*
82/71 **Flim Flam Man** *Barbra Streisand*
87/58 **Flip Flop And Bop** *Floyd Cramer*
61/58 **Flip Top Box** *Dicky Doo & The Don'ts*
42/80 **Flirtin' With Disaster** *Molly Hatchet*
92/61 **Float, The** *Hank Ballard*
Float On
2/77 *Floaters*
41/78 *Cheech & Chong (Bloat On)*
79/59 **Flower Of Love** *Crests*
87/76 **Flowers** *Emotions*
21/56 **Flowers Mean Forgiveness** *Frank Sinatra*
4/66 **Flowers On The Wall** *Statler Brothers*
16/72 **Floy Joy** *Supremes*
7/61 **Fly, The** *Chubby Checker*
75/77 **Fly At Night** *Chilliwack*
13/76 **Fly Away** *John Denver*
42/81 **Fly Away** *Blackfoot*
Fly Away
55/81 *Peter Allen*
84/82 *Stevie Woods*
82/61 **Fly By Night** *Andy Williams*
88/77 **Fly By Night (medley)** *Rush*
2/77 **Fly Like An Eagle** *Steve Miller*

95/71 **Fly Little White Dove Fly** *Bells*
Fly Me To The Moon
14/63 *Joe Harnell (Bossa Nova)*
84/65 *LaVern Baker*
84/65 *Tony Bennett*
98/66 *Sam & Bill*
52/68 *Bobby Womack*
1/75 **Fly, Robin, Fly** *Silver Convention*
79/83 **Flyer** *Saga*
53/78 **Flyin'** *Prism*
70/75 **Flyin' High** *Blackbyrds*
45/62 **Flying Circle** *Frank Slay*
38/78 **Flying High** *Commodores*
3/56 **Flying Saucer** *Buchanan & Goodman*
18/57 **Flying Saucer The 2nd** *Buchanan & Goodman*
93/59 **Fog Cutter** *Frantics*
Foggy Mountain Breakdown
see: Ballad Of Bonnie & Clyde
84/63 **Folk Singer** *Tommy Roe*
56/71 **Follow Me** *Mary Travers*
65/66 **Follow Me** *Lyme & Cybelle*
91/65 **Follow Me** *Drifters*
15/62 **Follow That Dream** *Elvis Presley*
17/63 **Follow The Boys** *Connie Francis*
23/78 **Follow You Follow Me** *Genesis*
61/73 **Follow Your Daughter Home** *Guess Who*
88/85 **Follow Your Heart** *Triumph*
92/66 **Follow Your Heart** *Manhattans*
32/68 **Folsom Prison Blues** *Johnny Cash*
91/76 **Fonz Song** *Heyettes*
Fool, The
7/56 *Sanford Clark*
62/56 *Gallahads*
F/73 **Fool** *Elvis Presley*
75/59 **Fool And The Angel** *Bobby Helms*
52/80 **Fool For A Pretty Face (Hurt By Love)** *Humble Pie*
45/76 **Fool For The City** *Foghat*
22/68 **Fool For You** *Impressions*
77/82 **Fool For Your Love** *Jimmy Hall*
53/80 **Fool For Your Loving** *Whitesnake*
12/78 **Fool (If You Think It's Over)** *Chris Rea*
27/60 **Fool In Love** *Ike & Tina Turner*
25/81 **Fool In Love With You** *Jim Photoglo*
21/80 **Fool In The Rain** *Led Zeppelin*
93/73 **Fool Like You** *Tim Moore*
78/71 **Fool Me** *Joe South*
46/83 **Fool Moon Fire** *Walter Egan*
13/64 **Fool Never Learns** *Andy Williams*
3/61 **Fool #1** *Brenda Lee*
6/68 **Fool On The Hill** *Sergio Mendes & Brasil '66*
Fool Such As I
2/59 *Elvis Presley*
55/74 *Bob Dylan*
46/81 **Fool That I Am** *Rita Coolidge*
50/61 **Fool That I Am** *Etta James*
10/76 **Fool To Cry** *Rolling Stones*
20/55 **Fooled** *Perry Como*
3/76 **Fooled Around And Fell In Love** *Elvin Bishop*
89/79 **Fooled By A Feeling** *Barbara Mandrell*
28/83 **Foolin'** *Def Leppard*
49/61 **Foolin' Around** *Kay Starr*
65/82 **Foolin' Yourself** *Aldo Nova*
29/78 **Fooling Yourself (The Angry Young Man)** *Styx*
57/69 **Foolish Fool** *Dee Dee Warwick*
18/85 **Foolish Heart** *Steve Perry*
4/63 **Foolish Little Girl** *Shirelles*
33/86 **Foolish Pride** *Daryl Hall*
69/57 **Fools Fall In Love** *Drifters*
82/83 **Fools Game** *Michael Bolton*
29/59 **Fools Hall Of Fame** *Pat Boone*
85/85 **Fools Like Me** *Lorenzo Lamas*
58/58 **Fool's Paradise** *Crickets*
94/72 **Fool's Paradise** *Sylvers*
Fools Rush In
24/60 *Brook Benton*
87/62 *Etta James*
12/63 *Rick Nelson*
98/75 **Foot Stompin Music** *Hamilton Bohannon*
25/61 **Foot Stomping** *Flares*
46/79 **Football Card** *Glenn Sutton*
1/84 **Footloose** *Kenny Loggins*
7/60 **Footsteps** *Steve Lawrence*
29/72 **Footstompin' Music** *Grand Funk Railroad*
30/76 **Fopp** *Ohio Players*
63/76 **For A Dancer** *Prelude*
23/59 **For A Penny** *Pat Boone*
45/84 **For A Rocker** *Jackson Browne*
90/77 **For A While** *Mary MacGregor*
3/71 **For All We Know** *Carpenters*
88/62 **For All We Know** *Dinah Washington*
30/86 **For America** *Jackson Browne*
100/77 **For Elise** *Philharmonics*
53/72 **For Emily, Whenever I May Find Her** *Simon & Garfunkel*
26/71 **(For God's Sake) Give More Power To The People** *Chi-Lites*
66/67 **For He's A Jolly Good Fellow** *Bobby Vinton*
64/71 **For Ladies Only** *Steppenwolf*
43/60 **For Love** *Lloyd Price*
83/79 **For Love** *Pousette-Dart Band*
30/65 **For Lovin' Me** *Peter, Paul & Mary*
For Mama
48/65 *Connie Francis*
54/65 *Jerry Vale*
98/67 **For Me** *Sergio Mendes & Brasil '66*
71/61 **For Me And My Gal** *Freddy Cannon*
28/61 **For My Baby** *Brook Benton*
21/58 **For My Good Fortune** *Pat Boone*
F/73 **For Ol' Times Sake** *Elvis Presley*
For Once In My Life
91/67 *Tony Bennett*
2/68 *Stevie Wonder*
70/68 *Jackie Wilson*
11/71 **For The Good Times** *Ray Price*
F/76 **For The Heart** *Elvis Presley*
13/70 **For The Love Of Him** *Bobbi Martin*
81/68 **For The Love Of Ivy** *Mamas & The Papas*
9/74 **For The Love Of Money** *O'Jays*
For The Love Of You
22/75 *Isley Brothers*
F/76 *Houston Person*
32/86 **For Tonight** *Nancy Martinez*
For What It's Worth
7/67 *Buffalo Springfield*
66/67 *Staple Singers*
87/67 *King Curtis*
6/64 **For You** *Rick Nelson*
93/65 **For You** *Spellbinders*
85/79 **For You And I** *10cc*
F/70 **For You Blue** *Beatles*
4/81 **For Your Eyes Only** *Sheena Easton*
6/65 **For Your Love** *Yardbirds*
For Your Love
13/58 *Ed Townsend*
93/61 *Wanderers*
95/65 *Sam & Bill*
20/67 *Peaches & Herb*
91/75 *Christopher, Paul & Shawn*

For Your Precious Love
11/58 *Jerry Butler & The Impressions*
26/64 *Garnet Mimms & The Enchanters*
99/66 *Jerry Butler*
23/67 *Oscar Toney, Jr.*
49/68 *Jackie Wilson & Count Basie*
74/72 *Linda Jones*
86/64 **For Your Sweet Love** *Cascades*
Forever
9/60 *Little Dippers*
83/60 *Billy Walker*
25/64 *Pete Drake*
79/69 *Mercy*
40/85 **Forever** *Kenny Loggins*
60/57 **Forever** *Sam Cooke*
63/83 **Forever** *Little Steven*
78/63 **Forever** *Marvelettes*
82/62 **Forever And A Day** *Jackie Wilson*
47/78 **Forever Autumn** *Justin Hayward*
Forever Came Today
28/68 *Supremes*
60/75 *Jackson 5*
35/56 **Forever Darling** *Ames Brothers*
20/79 **Forever In Blue Jeans** *Neil Diamond*
19/86 **(Forever) Live And Die**
Orchestral Manoeuvres In The Dark
76/76 **Forever Lovers** *Mac Davis*
26/85 **Forever Man** *Eric Clapton*
28/80 **Forever Mine** *O'Jays*
60/82 **Forever Mine** *Motels*
93/85 **Forever Young** *Alphaville*
Forget Domani
78/65 *Frank Sinatra*
79/65 *Connie Francis*
4/64 **Forget Him** *Bobby Rydell*
81/67 **Forget It** *Sandpebbles*
12/58 **Forget Me Not** *Kalin Twins*
93/68 **Forget Me Not** *Martha & The Vandellas*
23/82 **Forget Me Nots** *Patrice Rushen*
F/69 **Forget To Remember** *Frank Sinatra*
61/65 **Forgive Me** *Al Martino*
2/80 **Forgive Me, Girl (medley)** *Spinners*
21/55 **Forgive My Heart** *Nat King Cole*
45/55 **Forgive This Fool** *Roy Hamilton*
8/85 **Fortress Around Your Heart** *Sting*
F/69 **Fortunate Son**
Creedence Clearwater Revival
97/67 **Fortune Teller** *Hardtimes*
41/62 **Fortuneteller** *Bobby Curtola*
70/57 **Forty Cups Of Coffee**
Bill Haley & His Comets
45/59 **Forty Days** *Ronnie Hawkins*
9/59 **Forty Miles Of Bad Road** *Duane Eddy*
49/56 **49 Shades Of Green** *Ames Brothers*
36/79 **Found A Cure** *Ashford & Simpson*
88/60 **Found Love** *Jimmy Reed*
90/59 **Fountain Of Youth** *Four Lads*
4-By The Beatles [E.P.]
92/64 *Beatles*
68/65 *Beatles*
19/85 **Four In The Morning (I Can't Take Any More)** *Night Ranger*
86/83 **Four Little Diamonds** *ELO*
73/60 **Four Little Heels** *Brian Hyland*
Four Strong Winds
60/64 *Bobby Bare*
61/79 *Neil Young*
Four Walls
11/57 *Jim Reeves*
15/57 *Jim Lowe*
92/62 *Kay Starr*
76/62 **409** *Beach Boys*
56/64 **442 Glenwood Avenue** *Pixies Three*
36/68 **1432 Franklin Pike Circle Hero**
Bobby Russell
70/57 **1492** *Betty Johnson*
84/74 **Fox Hunt** *Herb Alpert*
5/76 **Fox On The Run** *Sweet*
97/69 **Fox On The Run** *Manfred Mann*
67/68 **Foxey Lady** *Jimi Hendrix*
49/76 **Foxy Lady** *Crown Heights Affair*
41/76 **Framed** *Cheech & Chong*
69/72 **Francene** *ZZ Top*
Francis Powers, Ballad Of
see: There's A Star Spangled Banner Waving
1/73 **Frankenstein** *Edgar Winter*
9/59 **Frankie** *Connie Francis*
75/85 **Frankie** *Sister Sledge*
Frankie And Johnny
57/59 *Johnny Cash*
20/61 *Brook Benton*
14/63 *Sam Cooke*
75/64 *Greenwood County Singers*
25/66 *Elvis Presley*
Fraulein
36/57 *Bobby Helms*
54/57 *Steve Lawrence*
90/85 **Freak-A-Ristic** *Atlantic Starr*
66/83 **Freak-A-Zoid** *Midnight Star*
73/84 **Freakshow On The Dance Floor** *Bar-Kays*
96/77 **Freddie** *Charlene*
Freddie *see: Do The & Let's Do The*
91/66 **Freddie Feelgood (and His Funky Little Five Piece Band)** *Ray Stevens*
4/72 **Freddie's Dead (Theme From 'Superfly')**
Curtis Mayfield
90/79 **Frederick** *Patti Smith Group*
20/71 **Free** *Chicago*
23/56 **Free** *Tommy Leonetti*
25/77 **Free** *Deniece Williams*
83/66 **Free Again** *Barbra Streisand*
Free Bird
19/75 *Lynyrd Skynyrd*
38/77 *Lynyrd Skynyrd (Live)*
48/73 **Free Electric Band** *Albert Hammond*
61/75 **Free Man** *South Shore Commission*
22/74 **Free Man In Paris** *Joni Mitchell*
53/80 **Free Me** *Roger Daltrey*
97/61 **Free Me** *Johnny Preston*
58/79 **Free Me From My Freedom (medley)**
Bonnie Pointer
Free Ride
14/73 *Edgar Winter*
52/76 *Tavares*
85/76 **Free Spirit** *Atlanta Rhythm Section*
75/70 **Free The People**
Delaney & Bonnie & Friends
94/70 **Free To Carry On** *Sandpipers*
F/74 **Free Wheelin'** *Bachman-Turner Overdrive*
3/85 **Freedom** *Wham!*
59/71 **Freedom** *Jimi Hendrix*
59/85 **Freedom** *Pointer Sisters*
72/71 **Freedom** *Isley Brothers*
47/70 **Freedom Blues** *Little Richard*
72/71 **Freedom Comes, Freedom Goes** *Fortunes*
63/73 **Freedom For The Stallion**
Hues Corporation
20/86 **Freedom Overspill** *Steve Winwood*
3/85 **Freeway Of Love** *Aretha Franklin*
33/58 **Freeze, The** *Tony & Joe*
4/82 **Freeze-Frame** *J. Geils Band*
Freight Train
6/57 *Rusty Draper*
40/57 *Chas. McDevitt Skiffle Group*
61/59 **French Foreign Legion** *Frank Sinatra*
57/87 **French Kissin** *Debbie Harry*
54/64 **French Song** *Lucille Starr*

9/85 **Fresh** *Kool & The Gang*
49/70 **Fresh Air** *Quicksilver Messenger Service*
54/71 **Fresh As A Daisy** *Emitt Rhodes*
(Friday Night) *see: Livin' It Up*
16/67 **Friday On My Mind** *Easybeats*
36/66 **Friday's Child** *Nancy Sinatra*
73/59 **Fried Eggs** *Intruders*
96/58 **Fried Onions** *Lord Rockingham's XI*
99/73 **Friend And A Lover** *Partridge Family*
90/70 **Friend In The City** *Andy Kim*
47/69 **Friend, Lover, Woman, Wife** *O.C. Smith*
80/73 **Friend Of Mine** *Bill Withers*
72/75 **Friend Of Mine Is Going Blind** *John Dawson Read*
Friendly Persuasion (Thee I Love)
5/56 *Pat Boone*
45/56 *Four Aces*
34/71 **Friends** *Elton John*
40/73 **Friends** *Bette Midler*
47/68 **Friends** *Beach Boys*
79/70 **Friends** *Feather*
87/85 **Friends** *Whodini*
2/86 **Friends And Lovers** *Gloria Loring & Carl Anderson*
38/82 **Friends In Love** *Johnny Mathis & Dionne Warwick*
47/71 **Friends With You** *John Denver*
17/69 **Friendship Train** *Gladys Knight & The Pips*
91/85 **Fright Night** *J. Geils Band*
79/73 **Frisky** *Sly & The Family Stone*
32/61 **Frogg** *Brothers Four*
6/63 **From A Jack To A King** *Ned Miller*
79/56 **From A School Ring To A Wedding Ring** *Rover Boys*
From A Window
23/64 *Billy J. Kramer with The Dakotas*
97/65 *Chad & Jeremy*
From Both Sides Now *see: Both Sides Now*
58/77 **From Graceland To The Promised Land** *Merle Haggard*
28/75 **From His Woman To You** *Barbara Mason*
From Me To You
77/63 *Del Shannon*
41/64 *Beatles*
81/64 **From Russia With Love** *Village Stompers*
39/72 **From The Beginning** *Emerson, Lake & Palmer*
F/56 **From The Bottom Of My Heart** *Don Cornell*
From The Bottom Of My Heart (Dammi, Dammi, Dammi)
91/63 *Dean Martin*
93/65 **From The Bottom Of My Heart (I Love You)** *Moody Blues*
11/56 **From The Candy Store On The Corner To The Chapel On The Hill** *Tony Bennett*
57/68 **From The Teacher To The Preacher** *Gene Chandler & Barbara Acklin*
65/83 **Front Page Story** *Neil Diamond*
87/67 **Full Measure** *Lovin' Spoonful*
28/75 **Full Of Fire** *Al Green*
55/81 **Full Of Fire** *Shalamar*
91/76 **Full Time Thing (Between Dusk And Dawn)** *Whirlwind*
Fun *see: Ffun*
5/64 **Fun, Fun, Fun** *Beach Boys*
43/78 **Fun Time** *Joe Cocker*
97/66 **Function At The Junction** *Shorty Long*
58/72 **Funk Factory** *Wilson Pickett*
88/77 **Funk It Up (David's Song)** *Sweet*
59/70 **Funk Number 49** *James Gang*
Funky Broadway
8/67 *Wilson Pickett*
65/67 *Dyke & The Blazers*
91/70 **Funky Chicken** *Willie Henderson (also see: Do The Funky Chicken)*
87/67 **Funky Donkey** *Pretty Purdie*
51/70 **Funky Drummer** *James Brown*
88/68 **Funky Fever** *Clarence Carter*
79/75 **Funky Gibbon** *Goodies*
39/68 **Funky Judge** *Bull & The Matadors*
87/70 **Funky Man** *Kool & The Gang*
64/71 **Funky Music Sho Nuff Turns Me On** *Edwin Starr*
15/71 **Funky Nassau** *Beginning Of The End*
91/68 **Funky North Philly** *Bill Cosby*
99/74 **Funky Party** *Clarence Reid*
Funky Penguin *see: Do The*
44/74 **Funky President (People It's Bad)** *James Brown*
14/68 **Funky Street** *Arthur Conley*
29/73 **Funky Stuff** *Kool & The Gang*
67/68 **Funky Walk** *Dyke & The Blazers*
72/68 **Funky Way** *Calvin Arnold*
76/76 **Funky Weekend** *Stylistics*
15/73 **Funky Worm** *Ohio Players*
1/80 **Funkytown** *Lipps, Inc.*
59/70 **Funniest Thing** *Classics IV*
25/61 **Funny** *Maxine Brown*
Funny
81/59 *Jesse Belvin*
99/62 *Gene McDaniels*
5/73 **Funny Face** *Donna Fargo*
49/67 **Funny Familiar Forgotten Feelings** *Tom Jones*
94/69 **Funny Feeling** *Delfonics*
44/64 **Funny Girl** *Barbra Streisand*
74/75 **Funny How Love Can Be** *First Class*
Funny How Time Slips Away
22/62 *Jimmy Elledge*
50/63 *Johnny Tillotson*
13/64 *Joe Hinton*
58/76 *Dorothy Moore*
67/83 *Spinners*
77/65 **Funny Little Butterflies** *Patty Duke*
81/63 **Funny Man** *Ray Stevens*
10/62 **Funny Way Of Laughin'** *Burl Ives*
91/59 **Furry Murray** *Tradewinds*
91/62 **Further More** *Ray Stevens*
39/73 **Future Shock** *Curtis Mayfield*
71/75 **Future Shock** *Hello People*
19/86 **Future's So Bright, I Gotta Wear Shades** *Timbuk 3*

4/64 **G.T.O.** *Ronny & The Daytonas*
91/56 **Gal With The Yaller Shoes** *Four Aces*
39/78 **Galaxy** *War*
29/67 **Gallant Men** *Senator Everett McKinley Dirksen*
Galveston
4/69 *Glen Campbell*
99/69 *Roger Williams*
16/79 **Gambler, The** *Kenny Rogers*
79/76 **Game Is Over (What's The Matter With You)** *Brown Sugar*
1/65 **Game Of Love** *Wayne Fontana & The Mindbenders*
27/71 **Games** *Redeye*
46/81 **Games** *Phoebe Snow*
12/69 **Games People Play** *Joe South*

16/81 **Games People Play** *Alan Parsons Project*
(Games People Play)
see: They Just Can't Stop It
Games That Lovers Play
45/66 *Eddie Fisher*
86/66 *Wayne Newton*
48/80 **Games Without Frontiers** *Peter Gabriel*
85/70 **Gangs Back Again** *Kool & The Gang*
69/84 **Gap** *Thompson Twins*
97/64 **Garden In The Rain** *Vic Dana*
12/56 **Garden Of Eden** *Joe Valino*
6/72 **Garden Party** *Rick Nelson*
81/83 **Garden Party** *Herb Alpert*
81/70 **Gas Lamps And Clay** *Blues Image*
81/58 **Gas Money** *Jan & Arnie*
96/64 **Gator Tails And Monkey Ribs** *Spats*
57/59 **Gazachstahagen** *Wild-Cats*
73/59 **Gee** *George Hamilton IV*
Gee
81/60 *Jan & Dean*
87/64 *Pixies Three*
81/75 **Gee Baby** *Pete Shelley*
80/65 **Gee Baby (I'm Sorry)** *Three Degrees*
31/58 **Gee, But It's Lonely** *Pat Boone*
19/56 **Gee Whittakers!** *Pat Boone*
28/61 **Gee Whiz** *Innocents*
Gee Whiz (Look At His Eyes)
10/61 *Carla Thomas*
31/80 *Bernadette Peters*
66/58 **Geisha Girl** *Hank Locklin*
12/81 **Gemini Dream** *Moody Blues*
33/81 **General Hospi-Tale** *Afternoon Delights*
31/82 **Genius Of Love** *Tom Tom Club*
Gentle On My Mind
62/67 *Glen Campbell*
39/68 *Glen Campbell*
66/68 *Patti Page*
76/69 *Aretha Franklin*
33/72 **George Jackson** *Bob Dylan*
Georgia On My Mind
1/60 *Ray Charles*
62/66 *Righteous Brothers*
91/68 *Wes Montgomery*
84/78 *Willie Nelson*
81/67 **Georgia Pines** *Candymen*
93/74 **Georgia Porcupine** *George Fischoff*
68/77 **Georgia Rhythm** *Atlanta Rhythm Section*
89/66 **Georgia Rose** *Tony Bennett*
88/70 **Georgia Took Her Back** *R.B. Greaves*
68/65 **Georgie Porgie** *Jewel Akens*
Georgy Girl
2/67 *Seekers*
98/67 *Baja Marimba Band*
48/79 **Georgy Porgy** *Toto*
96/58 **Geraldine** *Jack Scott*
37/72 **Geronimo's Cadillac** *Michael Murphey*
Get A Job
1/58 *Silhouettes*
21/58 *Mills Brothers*
46/79 **Get A Move On** *Eddie Money*
70/66 **Get Away** *Georgie Fame*
Get Back
1/69 *Beatles*
86/78 *Billy Preston*
88/66 **Get Back** *Roy Head*
6/76 **Get Closer** *Seals & Crofts*
29/82 **Get Closer** *Linda Ronstadt*
10/75 **Get Dancin'** *Disco Tex & The Sex-O-Lettes*
7/73 **Get Down** *Gilbert O'Sullivan*
53/79 **Get Down** *Gene Chandler*
69/71 **Get Down** *Curtis Mayfield*
79/67 **Get Down** *Harvey Scales*
8/75 **Get Down, Get Down (Get On The Floor)**
Joe Simon
10/82 **Get Down On It** *Kool & The Gang*
88/70 **Get Down People** *Fabulous Counts*
1/75 **Get Down Tonight**
KC & The Sunshine Band
76/63 **Get Him** *Exciters*
89/70 **Get Into Something** *Isley Brothers*
56/69 **Get It From The Bottom** *Steelers*
24/71 **Get It On** *Chase*
(also see: Bang A Gong)
61/83 **Get It Right** *Aretha Franklin*
21/79 **Get It Right Next Time** *Gerry Rafferty*
28/73 **Get It Together** *Jackson 5*
40/67 **Get It Together** *James Brown*
43/79 **Get It Up** *Ronnie Milsap*
78/71 **Get It While You Can** *Janis Joplin*
89/56 **Get Me To The Church On Time**
Julius LaRosa
27/67 **Get Me To The World On Time**
Electric Prunes
9/78 **Get Off** *Foxy*
74/69 **Get Off My Back Woman** *B.B. King*
1/65 **Get Off Of My Cloud** *Rolling Stones*
18/72 **Get On The Good Foot** *James Brown*
11/67 **Get On Up** *Esquires*
48/68 **Get Out Now**
Tommy James & The Shondells
97/72 **Get Out Of Bed** *Livingston Taylor*
80/74 **Get Out Of Denver** *Bob Seger*
44/66 **Get Out Of My Life, Woman** *Lee Dorsey*
Get Ready
29/66 *Temptations*
4/70 *Rare Earth*
60/69 **Get Rhythm** *Johnny Cash*
70/74 **Get That Gasoline Blues** *NRBQ*
50/75 **Get The Cream Off The Top**
Eddie Kendricks
30/76 **Get The Funk Out Ma Face**
Brothers Johnson
91/67 **Get The Message** *Brian Hyland*
Get Together
31/65 *We Five*
62/67 *Youngbloods*
5/69 *Youngbloods*
2/76 **Get Up And Boogie (That's Right)**
Silver Convention
(Get Up And Dance) *see: Bite Your Lip*
78/72 **Get Up And Get Down** *Dramatics*
50/82 **Get Up And Go** *Go-Go's*
34/71 **Get Up, Get Into It, Get Involved**
James Brown
83/56 **Get Up! Get Up!** *Jaye P. Morgan*
Get Up I Feel Like A Sex Machine
see: Sex Machine
45/76 **Get Up Offa That Thing** *James Brown*
21/79 **Get Used To It** *Roger Voudouris*
12/76 **Getaway** *Earth, Wind & Fire*
26/85 **Getcha Back** *Beach Boys*
27/78 **Gettin' Ready For Love** *Diana Ross*
18/67 **Gettin' Together**
Tommy James & The Shondells
20/79 **Getting Closer** *Wings*
93/72 **Getting It On** *Dennis Coffey*
65/65 **Getting Mighty Crowded** *Betty Everett*
88/62 **Getting Ready For The Heartbreak**
Chuck Jackson
75/69 **Getting The Corners** *T.S.U. Toronadoes*
87/70 **Ghetto, The** *Donny Hathaway*
29/73 **Ghetto Child** *Spinners*
68/71 **Ghetto Woman** *B.B. King*
45/79 **Ghost Dancer** *Addrisi Brothers*
59/84 **Ghost In You** *Psychedelic Furs*

(Ghost) Riders In The Sky
30/61 *Ramrods*
87/61 *Lawrence Welk*
52/66 *Baja Marimba Band*
31/81 *Outlaws*
22/56 **Ghost Town** *Don Cherry*
1/84 **Ghostbusters** *Ray Parker Jr.*
Giant
63/56 *Les Baxter*
77/56 *Art Mooney*
91/56 *Jack Pleis*
82/66 **Giddyup Go** *Red Sovine*
41/59 **Gidget** *Jimmy Darren*
91/61 **Gift Of Love** *Van Dykes*
88/58 **Gigi** *Vic Damone*
57/82 **Gigolo** *O'Bryan*
82/59 **Gilee** *Sonny Spencer*
37/83 **Gimme All Your Lovin** *ZZ Top*
9/70 **Gimme Dat Ding** *Pipkins*
12/69 **Gimme Gimme Good Lovin'** *Crazy Elephant*
9/67 **Gimme Little Sign** *Brenton Wood*
Gimme Shelter
73/70 *Merry Clayton*
61/71 *Grand Funk Railroad*
Gimme Some Lovin'
7/67 *Spencer Davis Group*
68/71 *Traffic*
84/78 *Kongas*
18/80 *Blues Brothers*
67/72 **Gimme Some More** *JB's*
70/76 **Gimme Your Money Please** *Bachman-Turner Overdrive*
6/62 **Gina** *Johnny Mathis*
9/58 **Ginger Bread** *Frankie Avalon*
38/61 **Ginnie Bell** *Paul Dino*
21/62 **Ginny Come Lately** *Brian Hyland*
Girl And Boy *see: Ballad Of*
17/86 **Girl Can't Help It** *Journey*
49/57 **Girl Can't Help It** *Little Richard*
30/65 **Girl Come Running** *4 Seasons*
66/67 **Girl Don't Care** *Gene Chandler*
42/65 **Girl Don't Come** *Sandie Shaw*
55/80 **Girl, Don't Let It Get You Down** *O'Jays*
5/64 **Girl From Ipanema** *Stan Getz/Astrud Gilberto*
73/65 **Girl From Peyton Place** *Dickey Lee*
81/62 **Girl Has To Know** *G-Clefs*
39/67 **Girl I Knew Somewhere** *Monkees*
69/67 **Girl I Need You** *Artistics*
52/69 **Girl I'll Never Know (Angels Never Fly This Low)** *Frankie Valli*
21/66 **Girl In Love** *Outsiders*
Girl In My Dreams
45/56 *Cliques*
92/61 *Capris*
35/84 **Girl In Trouble (Is A Temporary Thing)** *Romeo Void*
2/83 **Girl Is Mine** *Michael Jackson/Paul McCartney*
10/67 **Girl Like You** *Young Rascals*
80/59 **Girl Like You** *Gary Stites*
55/68 **Girl Most Likely** *Jeannie C. Riley*
19/61 **Girl Of My Best Friend** *Ral Donner*
37/79 **Girl Of My Dreams** *Bram Tchaikovsky*
28/66 **Girl On A Swing** *Gerry & The Pacemakers*
52/59 **Girl On Page 44** *Four Lads*
96/65 **Girl On The Billboard** *Del Reeves*
66/66 **Girl That Stood Beside Me** *Bobby Darin*
5/68 **Girl Watcher** *O'Kaysions*
87/71 **Girl Who Loved Me When** *Glass Bottle*
26/64 **Girl (Why You Wanna Make Me Blue)** *Temptations*
13/57 **Girl With The Golden Braids** *Perry Como*
55/80 **Girl With The Hungry Eyes** *Jefferson Starship*
85/60 **Girl With The Story In Her Eyes** *Safaris*
98/67 **Girl (You Captivate Me)** *? (Question Mark) & The Mysterians*
87/73 **Girl You Need A Change Of Mind** *Eddie Kendricks*
10/67 **Girl, You'll Be A Woman Soon** *Neil Diamond*
59/69 **Girl You're Too Young** *Archie Bell & The Drells*
57/87 **Girlfriend** *Bobby Brown*
16/84 **Girls** *Dwight Twilley*
68/64 **Girls** *Major Lance*
64/61 **Girl's A Devil** *Dukays*
34/85 **Girls Are More Fun** *Ray Parker Jr.*
92/67 **Girls Are Out To Get You** *Fascinations*
34/80 **Girls Can Get It** *Dr. Hook*
33/68 **Girls Can't Do What The Guys Do** *Betty Wright*
96/61 **Girls Girls Girls** *Coasters*
14/62 **(Girls, Girls, Girls) Made To Love** *Eddie Hodges*
33/64 **Girls Grow Up Faster Than Boys** *Cookies*
39/67 **Girls In Love** *Gary Lewis & The Playboys*
68/69 **Girls It Ain't Easy** *Honey Cone*
2/84 **Girls Just Want To Have Fun** *Cyndi Lauper*
33/78 **Girls' School** *Wings*
43/70 **Girl's Song** *5th Dimension*
65/79 **Girls Talk** *Dave Edmunds*
75/70 **Girls Will Be Girls, Boys Will Be Boys** *Isley Brothers*
33/84 **Girls With Guns** *Tommy Shaw*
89/59 **Girl's Work Is Never Done** *Chordettes*
8/69 **Gitarzan** *Ray Stevens*
67/84 **Give** *Missing Persons*
43/68 **Give A Damn** *Spanky & Our Gang*
15/77 **Give A Little Bit** *Supertramp*
41/81 **Give A Little Bit More** *Cliff Richard*
97/70 **Give A Woman Love** *Bobbi Martin*
68/65 **Give All Your Love To Me** *Gerry & The Pacemakers*
91/67 **Give Everybody Some** *Bar-Kays*
18/65 **Give Him A Great Big Kiss** *Shangri-Las*
21/72 **Give Ireland Back To The Irish** *Wings*
18/80 **Give It All You Got** *Chuck Mangione*
88/69 **Give It Away** *Chi-Lites*
30/73 **Give It To Me** *J. Geils Band*
71/71 **Give It To Me** *Mob*
40/81 **Give It To Me Baby** *Rick James*
20/74 **Give It To The People** *Righteous Brothers*
18/84 **Give It Up** *KC*
60/83 **Give It Up** *Steve Miller Band*
15/69 **Give It Up Or Turnit A Loose** *James Brown*
38/76 **Give It Up (Turn It Loose)** *Tyrone Davis*
40/75 **Give It What You Got** *B.T. Express*
61/57 **Give Me** *Eileen Rodgers*
Give Me *also see: Gimme*
71/74 **Give Me A Reason To Be Gone** *Maureen McGovern*
67/79 **Give Me An Inch** *Ian Matthews*
3/70 **Give Me Just A Little More Time** *Chairmen Of The Board*
47/55 **Give Me Love** *McGuire Sisters*
1/73 **Give Me Love (Give Me Peace On Earth)** *George Harrison*
80/68 **Give Me One More Chance** *Wilmer & The Dukes*
4/80 **Give Me The Night** *George Benson*
57/86 **Give Me The Reason** *Luther Vandross*
76/67 **Give Me Time** *Dusty Springfield*
46/84 **Give Me Tonight** *Shannon*

31/73 **Give Me Your Love** *Barbara Mason*
82/59 **Give Me Your Love** *Nat King Cole*
Give More Power To The People
see: (For God's Sake)
93/68 **Give My Love A Try** *Linda Jones*
46/58 **Give Myself A Party** *Don Gibson*
14/69 **Give Peace A Chance** *Plastic Ono Band*
45/75 **Give The People What They Want** *O'Jays*
84/71 **Give Up Your Guns** *Buoys*
30/56 **Give Us This Day** *Joni James*
Give Us Your Blessings
70/63 *Ray Peterson*
29/65 *Shangri-Las*
34/73 **Give Your Baby A Standing Ovation** *Dells*
83/73 **Giving It All Away** *Roger Daltrey*
8/81 **Giving It Up For Your Love**
Delbert McClinton
Giving Up
38/64 *Gladys Knight & The Pips*
81/72 *Donny Hathaway*
56/64 **Giving Up On Love** *Jerry Butler*
6/64 **Glad All Over** *Dave Clark Five*
19/55 **Glad Rag Doll** *Crazy Otto*
100/59 **Glad Rags** *Tennessee Ernie Ford*
61/69 **Glad She's A Woman** *Bobby Goldsboro*
26/67 **Glad To Be Unhappy** *Mamas & The Papas*
7/84 **Glamorous Life** *Sheila E.*
37/75 **Glasshouse** *Temptations*
8/56 **Glendora** *Perry Como*
55/80 **Glide** *Pleasure*
2/82 **Gloria** *Laura Branigan*
Gloria
10/66 *Shadows Of Knight*
71/66 *Them*
25/77 **Gloria** *Enchantment*
71/84 **Gloria** *Doors*
74/60 **Gloria's Theme** *Adam Wade*
34/72 **Glory Bound** *Grass Roots*
5/85 **Glory Days** *Bruce Springsteen*
58/70 **Glory Glory** *Rascals*
1/86 **Glory Of Love** *Peter Cetera*
Glory Of Love
49/61 *Roommates*
75/62 *Don Gardner & Dee Dee Ford*
60/67 *Otis Redding*
92/71 *Dells*
46/86 **Go** *Asia*
30/66 **Go Ahead And Cry** *Righteous Brothers*
5/72 **Go All The Way** *Raspberries*
89/65 **Go Away From My World**
Marianne Faithfull
Go Away Little Girl
1/63 *Steve Lawrence*
12/66 *Happenings*
1/71 *Donny Osmond*
36/70 **Go Back** *Crabby Appleton*
60/58 **Go Chase A Moonbeam** *Jerry Vale*
85/85 **Go Down Easy** *Dan Fogelberg*
32/71 **Go Down Gamblin'** *Blood, Sweat & Tears*
65/85 **Go For It** *Kim Wilde*
86/85 **Go For Soda** *Kim Mitchell*
62/67 **Go-Go Girl** *Lee Dorsey*
10/86 **Go Home** *Stevie Wonder*
23/84 **Go Insane** *Lindsey Buckingham*
5/60 **Go, Jimmy, Go** *Jimmy Clanton*
10/65 **Go Now!** *Moody Blues*
42/62 **Go On Home** *Patti Page*
Go On With The Wedding
11/56 *Patti Page*
39/56 *Kitty Kallen & Georgie Shaw*
45/79 **Go West** *Village People*
16/67 **Go Where You Wanna Go** *5th Dimension*
78/67 **Go With Me** *Gene & Debbe*

10/77 **Go Your Own Way** *Fleetwood Mac*
36/59 **God Bless America** *Connie Francis*
65/68 **God Bless Our Love** *Ballads*
53/71 **God Bless Whoever Sent You** *Originals*
18/61 **God, Country And My Baby**
Johnny Burnette
74/78 **God Knows** *Debby Boone*
97/69 **God Knows I Love You** *Nancy Sinatra*
22/70 **God, Love And Rock & Roll**
Teegarden & Van Winkle
God Only Knows
39/66 *Beach Boys*
61/78 *Marilyn Scott*
Godfather *see: Love Theme From The*
79/68 **Goin' Away** *Fireballs*
89/67 **Goin' Back** *Byrds*
66/86 **Goin' Crazy!** *David Lee Roth*
17/82 **Goin' Down** *Greg Guidry*
57/72 **Goin' Down (On The Road To L.A.)**
Terry Black & Laurel Ward
69/74 **Goin' Down Slow** *Bobby Bland*
36/73 **Goin' Home** *Osmonds*
83/80 **Goin' On** *Beach Boys*
Goin' Out Of My Head
6/64 *Little Anthony & The Imperials*
7/68 *Lettermen (medley)*
79/69 *Frank Sinatra*
52/77 **Goin' Places** *Jacksons*
16/57 **Goin' Steady** *Tommy Sands*
65/86 **Goin' To The Bank** *Commodores*
89/64 **Going Back To Louisiana** *Bruce Channel*
61/75 **Going Down Slowly** *Pointer Sisters*
35/64 **Going Going Gone** *Brook Benton*
15/69 **Going In Circles** *Friends Of Distinction*
54/77 **Going In With My Eyes Open** *David Soul*
91/66 **Going Nowhere** *Los Bravos*
53/79 **Going Through The Motions** *Hot Chocolate*
Going To A Go-Go
11/66 *Miracles*
25/82 *Rolling Stones*
100/58 **Going To Chicago Blues** *Count Basie*
69/70 **Going To The Country** *Steve Miller Band*
11/69 **Going Up The Country** *Canned Heat*
5/79 **Gold** *John Stewart*
29/84 **Gold** *Spandau Ballet*
96/74 **Golden Age Of Rock 'N' Roll**
Mott The Hoople
96/68 **Golden Gate Park** *Rejoice!*
10/76 **Golden Years** *David Bowie*
Goldfinger
8/65 *Shirley Bassey*
55/65 *Billy Strange*
72/65 *John Barry*
96/65 *Jack Laforge*
33/86 **Goldmine** *Pointer Sisters*
Gone
4/57 *Ferlin Husky*
24/72 *Joey Heatherton*
88/63 **Gone** *Rip Chords*
23/75 **Gone At Last** *Paul Simon/Phoebe Snow*
31/64 **Gone, Gone, Gone** *Everly Brothers*
56/79 **Gone, Gone, Gone** *Bad Company*
73/79 **Gone Long Gone** *Chicago*
23/77 **Gone Too Far**
England Dan & John Ford Coley
82/80 **Gone Too Far** *Eddie Rabbitt*
89/63 **Gone With The Wind** *Duprees*
84/71 **Gonna Be Alright Now** *Gayle McCormick*
Gonna Find Me A Bluebird
18/57 *Marvin Rainwater*
51/57 *Eddy Arnold*
84/57 *Joyce Hahn*

Gonna Fly Now (Theme From 'Rocky')
1/77 *Bill Conti*
28/77 *Maynard Ferguson*
94/77 *Current*
94/77 *Rhythm Heritage*
Gonna Get Along Without Ya Now
11/56 *Patience & Prudence*
48/64 *Skeeter Davis*
51/64 *Tracey Dey*
93/67 *Trini Lopez*
Gonna Give Her All The Love I've Got
29/67 *Jimmy Ruffin*
67/70 *Marvin Gaye*
71/77 **Gonna Love You More** *George Benson*
73/62 **Gonna Raise A Rukus Tonight** *Jimmy Dean*
Gonna Send You Back To Georgia
41/64 *Timmy Shaw*
57/64 *Animals (Walker)*
43/60 **Gonzo** *James Booker*
36/69 **Goo Goo Barabajagal (Love Is Hot)** *Donovan*
17/55 **Good And Lonesome** *Kay Starr*
89/56 **Good Book** *Kay Starr*
82/69 **Good Clean Fun** *Monkees*
56/68 **Good Combination** *Sonny & Cher*
100/67 **Good Day Sunshine** *Claudine Longet*
97/71 **Good Enough To Be Your Wife** *Jeannie C. Riley*
Good Foot *see: Get On The*
39/79 **Good Friend** *Mary MacGregor*
85/86 **Good Friends** *Joni Mitchell*
11/79 **Good Girls Don't** *Knack*
Good Golly Miss Molly
10/58 *Little Richard*
43/64 *Swinging Blue Jeans*
4/76 *Mitch Ryder & The Detroit Wheels (medley)*
43/61 **Good, Good Lovin'** *Chubby Checker*
45/70 **Good Guys Only Win In The Movies** *Mel & Tim*
74/86 **Good Heart** *Feargal Sharkey*
25/76 **Good Hearted Woman** *Waylon & Willie*
18/63 **Good Life** *Tony Bennett*
67/80 **Good Lord Loves You** *Neil Diamond*
77/62 **Good Lover** *Jimmy Reed*
Good Lovin'
81/65 *Olympics*
1/66 *Young Rascals*
30/69 **Good Lovin' Ain't Easy To Come By** *Marvin Gaye & Tammi Terrell*
36/75 **Good Lovin' Gone Bad** *Bad Company*
1/62 **Good Luck Charm** *Elvis Presley*
85/73 **Good Morning** *Michael Redway*
94/70 **Good Morning Freedom** *Daybreak*
55/80 **Good Morning Girl (medley)** *Journey*
34/73 **Good Morning Heartache** *Diana Ross*
69/77 **Good Morning Judge** *10cc*
Good Morning Starshine
3/69 *Oliver*
87/69 *Strawberry Alarm Clock*
83/86 **Good Music** *Joan Jett*
11/64 **Good News** *Sam Cooke*
51/64 **Good Night Baby** *Butterflys*
21/69 **Good Old Rock 'N Roll (medley)** *Cat Mother & the All Night News Boys*
49/59 **Good Rockin' Tonight** *Pat Boone*
2/68 **Good, The Bad And The Ugly** *Hugo Montenegro*
4/67 **Good Thing** *Paul Revere & The Raiders*
92/77 **Good Thing Man** *Frank Lucas*
93/74 **Good Things Don't Last Forever** *Ecstasy, Passion & Pain*
11/61 **Good Time Baby** *Bobby Rydell*
75/66 **Good Time Charlie** *Bobby Bland*
9/72 **Good Time Charlie's Got The Blues** *Danny O'Keefe*
65/68 **Good Time Girl** *Nancy Sinatra*
97/65 **Good Time Music** *Beau Brummels*
67/72 **Good Time Sally** *Rare Earth*
98/64 **Good Time Tonight** *Soul Sisters*
1/79 **Good Times** *Chic*
11/64 **Good Times** *Sam Cooke*
64/65 **Good Times** *Jerry Butler*
92/65 **Good Times** *Gene Chandler*
80/69 **Good Times Bad Times** *Led Zeppelin*
41/75 **Good Times, Rock & Roll** *Flash Cadillac & The Continental Kids*
41/79 **Good Times Roll** *Cars*
3/60 **Good Timin'** *Jimmy Jones*
40/79 **Good Timin'** *Beach Boys*
Good Vibrations
1/66 *Beach Boys*
34/76 *Todd Rundgren*
13/69 **Goodbye** *Mary Hopkin*
17/86 **Goodbye** *Night Ranger*
88/72 **Goodbye Again** *John Denver*
Goodbye Again *see: Theme From*
8/59 **Goodbye Baby** *Jack Scott*
33/64 **Goodbye Baby (Baby Goodbye)** *Solomon Burke*
53/68 **Goodbye Baby (I Don't Want To See You Cry)** *Tommy Boyce & Bobby Hart*
90/59 **Goodbye Charlie** *Patti Page*
80/69 **Goodbye Columbus** *Association*
3/61 **Goodbye Cruel World** *James Darren*
100/62 **Goodbye Dad** *Castle Sisters*
15/78 **Goodbye Girl** *David Gates*
43/79 **Goodbye, I Love You** *Firefall*
33/86 **Goodbye Is Forever** *Arcadia*
11/59 **Goodbye Jimmy, Goodbye** *Kathy Linden*
97/77 **Goodbye My Friend** *Engelbert Humperdinck*
31/68 **Goodbye My Love** *James Brown*
52/65 **Goodbye My Lover Goodbye** *Searchers*
15/79 **Goodbye Stranger** *Supertramp*
7/72 **Goodbye To Love** *Carpenters*
Goodbye To Rome *see: Arrivederci Roma*
65/82 **Goodbye To You** *Scandal*
2/73 **Goodbye Yellow Brick Road** *Elton John*
21/65 **Goodnight** *Roy Orbison*
Goodnight Irene
75/59 *Billy Williams*
79/62 *Jerry Reed*
Goodnight My Love
32/57 *McGuire Sisters*
64/59 *Ray Peterson*
32/63 *Fleetwoods*
91/66 *Ben E. King*
27/69 *Paul Anka*
51/67 **Goodnight My Love** *Happenings*
70/80 **Goodnight My Love** *Mike Pinera*
56/83 **Goodnight Saigon** *Billy Joel*
45/55 **Goodnight, Sweet Dreams** *Gordon Jenkins*
5/79 **Goodnight Tonight** *Wings*
20/57 **Goody Goody** *Frankie Lymon & The Teenagers*
37/68 **Goody Goody Gumdrops** *1910 Fruitgum Co.*
12/83 **Goody Two Shoes** *Adam Ant*
56/76 **Goofus** *Carpenters*
10/85 **Goonies 'R' Good Enough** *Cyndi Lauper*
78/57 **Got A Date With An Angel** *Billy Williams*
24/60 **Got A Girl** *Four Preps*
10/84 **Got A Hold On Me** *Christine McVie*
Got A Match?
39/58 *Daddy-O's*
57/58 *Frank Gallup*
51/66 **Got My Mojo Working** *Jimmy Smith*
54/59 **Got The Feeling** *Fabian*
12/79 **Got To Be Real** *Cheryl Lynn*

Got To Be There
4/71 *Michael Jackson*
67/83 *Chaka Khan*
80/70 **Got To Believe In Love** *Robin McNamara*
Got To Get You Into My Life
62/75 *Blood, Sweat & Tears*
7/76 *Beatles*
9/78 *Earth, Wind & Fire*
22/65 **Got To Get You Off My Mind** *Solomon Burke*
43/79 **Got To Give In To Love** *Bonnie Boyer*
1/77 **Got To Give It Up** *Marvin Gaye*
44/78 **Got To Have Loving** *Don Ray*
93/67 **Got To Have You Back** *Isley Brothers*
64/80 **Got To Love Somebody** *Sister Sledge*
76/81 **Got To Rock On** *Kansas*
62/70 **Got To See If I Can't Get Mommy (To Come Back Home)** *Jerry Butler*
56/68 **Got What You Need** *Fantastic Johnny C*
94/63 **Got You On My Mind** *Cookie & His Cupcakes*
53/76 **Gotta Be The One** *Maxine Nightingale*
68/73 **Gotta Find A Way** *Moments*
45/70 **Gotta Get Back To You** *Tommy James & The Shondells*
91/69 **Gotta Get To Know You** *Bobby Bland*
77/57 **Gotta Get To Your House** *David Seville*
83/85 **Gotta Get You Home Tonight** *Eugene Wilde*
80/84 **Gotta Give A Little Love (Ten Years After)** *Timmy Thomas*
47/80 **Gotta Have More Love** *Climax Blues Band*
63/58 **Gotta Have Rain** *Eydie Gorme*
77/65 **Gotta Have Your Love** *Saphires*
21/70 **Gotta Hold On To This Feeling** *Jr. Walker & The All Stars*
74/63 **Gotta Lotta Love** *Steve Alaimo*
82/59 **Gotta New Girl** *Bobby Day*
67/71 **Gotta See Jane** *R. Dean Taylor*
24/79 **Gotta Serve Somebody** *Bob Dylan*
Gotta Travel On
4/59 *Billy Grammer*
64/63 *Timi Yuro*
81/87 **Graceland** *Paul Simon*
Graduation Day
16/56 *Rover Boys*
17/56 *Four Freshmen*
88/63 *Bobby Pickett*
59/67 *Arbors*
34/61 **Graduation Song...Pomp And Circumstance** *Adrian Kimberly*
39/59 **Graduation's Here** *Fleetwoods*
64/61 **Granada** *Frank Sinatra*
95/75 **Granddaddy (Part 1)** *New Birth*
42/71 **Grandma's Hands** *Bill Withers*
72/77 **Grandmother's Song** *Steve Martin*
17/63 **Grass Is Greener** *Brenda Lee*
95/76 **Grasshopper** *Spin*
93/86 **Gravity** *James Brown*
9/62 **Gravy (For My Mashed Potatoes)** *Dee Dee Sharp*
64/63 **Gravy Waltz** *Steve Allen*
Grazing In The Grass
1/68 *Hugh Masekela*
3/69 *Friends Of Distinction*
1/78 **Grease** *Frankie Valli*
47/78 **Greased Lightin'** *John Travolta*
98/68 **Greasy Heart** *Jefferson Airplane*
20/66 **Great Airplane Strike** *Paul Revere & The Raiders*
Great Balls Of Fire
2/58 *Jerry Lee Lewis*
85/69 *Tiny Tim*
42/86 **Great Gosh A'Mighty! (It's A Matter Of Time)** *Little Richard*
Great Imposter *see: (He's) The*
Great Imposter *see: Theme From*
1/56 **Great Pretender** *Platters*
Greatest American Hero *see: Theme From*
81/85 **Greatest Gift Of All** *Kenny Rogers & Dolly Parton*
34/62 **Greatest Hurt** *Jackie Wilson*
67/69 **Greatest Love** *Dorsey Burnette*
Greatest Love Of All
24/77 *George Benson*
1/86 *Whitney Houston*
Green Berets *see: Ballad Of*
44/58 **Green Chritma** *Stan Freberg*
1/56 **Green Door** *Jim Lowe*
3/70 **Green Eyed Lady** *Sugarloaf*
8/66 **Green Grass** *Gary Lewis & The Playboys*
100/61 **Green Grass Of Texas** *Texans*
43/71 **Green Grass Starts To Grow** *Dionne Warwick*
14/63 **Green, Green** *New Christy Minstrels*
11/67 **Green, Green Grass Of Home** *Tom Jones*
Green Leaves Of Summer
65/60 *Brothers Four*
87/62 *Kenny Ball*
39/68 **Green Light** *American Breed*
44/58 **Green Mosquito** *Tune Rockers*
3/62 **Green Onions** *Booker T. & The MG's*
2/69 **Green River** *Creedence Clearwater Revival*
1/68 **Green Tambourine** *Lemon Pipers*
21/63 **Greenback Dollar** *Kingston Trio*
Greenfields
2/60 *Brothers Four*
92/69 *Vogues*
Greensleeves
41/57 *Beverly Sisters*
90/69 *Mason Williams*
(also see: Stay Away)
85/70 **Greenwood Mississippi** *Little Richard*
Greetings (This Is Uncle Sam)
89/61 *Valadiers*
100/66 *Monitors*
81/66 **Grim Reaper Of Love** *Turtles*
73/69 **Grits Ain't Groceries (All Around The World)** *Little Milton*
52/67 **Grizzly Bear** *Youngbloods*
7/78 **Groove Line** *Heatwave*
Groove Me
6/71 *King Floyd*
54/79 *Fern Kinney*
78/69 **Grooviest Girl In The World** *Fun & Games*
Groovin'
1/67 *Young Rascals*
21/67 *Booker T. & The MG's*
82/70 **Groovin' (Out On Life)** *Newbeats*
89/70 **Groovin' With Mr. Bloe** *Cool Heat*
55/63 **Groovy Baby** *Billy Abbott*
30/69 **Groovy Grubworm** *Harlow Wilcox*
2/66 **Groovy Kind Of Love** *Mindbenders*
64/76 **Groovy People** *Lou Rawls*
12/70 **Groovy Situation** *Gene Chandler*
74/67 **Groovy Summertime** *Love Generation*
70/60 **Groovy Tonight** *Bobby Rydell*
97/61 **Ground Hog** *Browns*
70/70 **Grover Henson Feels Forgotten** *Bill Cosby*
99/62 **Grow Closer Together** *Impressions*
14/76 **Grow Some Funk Of Your Own** *Elton John*
52/75 **Growin'** *Loggins & Messina*
67/76 **Growin' Up** *Dan Hill*
53/58 **Guaglione** *Perez Prado*
9/66 **Guantanamera** *Sandpipers*
68/73 **Gudbuy T' Jane** *Slade*

93/58 **Guess I've Been Around Too Long**
Carl Smith
11/58 **Guess Things Happen That Way**
Johnny Cash
Guess Who
31/59 *Jesse Belvin*
99/69 *Ruby Winters*
62/72 *B.B. King*
3/81 **Guilty** *Barbra Streisand & Barry Gibb*
69/72 **Guilty** *Al Green*
91/63 **Guilty** *Jim Reeves*
94/61 **Guilty Of Loving You** *Jerry Fuller*
5/59 **Guitar Boogie Shuffle** *Virtues*
96/62 **Guitar Boogie Shuffle Twist** *Virtues*
11/72 **Guitar Man** *Bread*
Guitar Man
43/68 *Elvis Presley*
28/81 *Elvis Presley*
Guitar Man *see: (Dance With The)*
10/55 **Gum Drop** *Crew-Cuts*
84/83 **Guns For Hire** *AC/DC*
70/72 **Guns, Guns, Guns** *Guess Who*
74/61 **Guns Of Navarone** *Joe Reisman*
12/82 **Gypsy** *Fleetwood Mac*
24/63 **Gypsy Cried** *Lou Christie*
8/73 **Gypsy Man** *War*
62/71 **Gypsy Queen** *Gypsy*
42/61 **Gypsy Rover** *Highwaymen*
89/80 **Gypsy Spirit** *Pendulum*
Gypsy Woman
20/61 *Impressions*
3/70 *Brian Hyland*
62/63 **Gypsy Woman** *Rick Nelson*
1/71 **Gypsys, Tramps & Thieves** *Cher*

H

51/77 **Ha Cha Cha (Funktion)** *Brass Construction*
91/57 **Ha! Ha! Ha! (Chella Lla!)** *Kay Armen*
45/67 **Ha Ha Said The Clown** *Yardbirds*
48/84 **Had A Dream (Sleeping With The Enemy)** *Roger Hodgson*
71/77 **Hail! Hail! Rock And Roll!**
Starland Vocal Band
97/62 **Hail To The Conquering Hero**
James Darren
2/69 **Hair** *Cowsills*
22/66 **Hair On My Chinny Chin Chin**
Sam The Sham & The Pharoahs
87/73 **Half A Million Miles From Home**
Albert Hammond
1/73 **Half-Breed** *Cher*
66/59 **Half-Breed** *Marvin Rainwater*
12/63 **Half Heaven - Half Heartache** *Gene Pitney*
72/80 **Half Moon Silver** *Hotel*
15/79 **Half The Way** *Crystal Gayle*
Halfway To Paradise
39/61 *Tony Orlando*
23/68 *Bobby Vinton*
33/71 **Hallelujah** *Sweathog*
28/73 **Hallelujah Day** *Jackson 5*
77/59 **Hallelujah, I Love Him So** *Peggy Lee*
92/69 **Hallways Of My Mind** *Dells*
89/70 **Hand Clapping Song** *Meters*
92/64 **Hand It Over** *Chuck Jackson*
Hand Jive *see: Willie & The Hand Jive*
17/70 **Hand Me Down World** *Guess Who*
19/83 **Hand To Hold On To** *John Cougar*
Handbags And Gladrags
84/71 *Chase*
42/72 *Rod Stewart*
65/86 **Hands Across America** *Voices Of America*
91/84 **Hands Across The Sea** *Modern English*
41/84 **Hands Tied** *Scandal*
Handy Man
2/60 *Jimmy Jones*
22/64 *Del Shannon*
4/77 *James Taylor*
Hang 'Em High
82/68 *Hugo Montenegro*
9/69 *Booker T. & The MG's*
20/82 **Hang Fire** *Rolling Stones*
83/73 **Hang Loose** *Mandrill*
95/61 **Hang On** *Floyd Cramer*
8/74 **Hang On In There Baby** *Johnny Bristol*
78/83 **Hang On Now** *Kajagoogoo*
Hang On Sloopy
26/64 *Vibrations (My Girl)*
1/65 *McCoys*
11/65 *Ramsey Lewis*
50/65 *Little Caesar & The Consuls*
93/70 *Lettermen*
94/75 *Rick Derringer*
43/71 **Hang On To Your Life** *Guess Who*
24/58 **Hang Up My Rock And Roll Shoes**
Chuck Willis
65/74 **Hangin' Around** *Edgar Winter*
43/85 **Hangin' On A String (Contemplating)**
Loose Ends
35/86 **Hanging On A Heart Attack** *Device*
38/59 **Hanging Tree** *Marty Robbins*
1/66 **Hanky Panky**
Tommy James & The Shondells
Happening, The
1/67 *Supremes*
32/67 *Herb Alpert*
30/66 **Happenings Ten Years Time Ago**
Yardbirds
60/77 **Happier** *Paul Anka*
100/72 **Happier Than The Morning Sun**
B.J. Thomas
11/72 **Happiest Girl In The Whole U.S.A.**
Donna Fargo
30/79 **Happiness** *Pointer Sisters*
56/58 **Happiness** *Billy & Lillie*
78/66 **Happiness** *Shades Of Blue*
35/74 **Happiness Is Just Around The Bend**
Main Ingredient
62/74 **Happiness Is Me And You**
Gilbert O'Sullivan
Happiness Street
20/56 *Georgia Gibbs*
38/56 *Tony Bennett*
22/72 **Happy** *Rolling Stones*
67/73 **Happy (Love Theme From 'Lady Sings The Blues')** *Bobby Darin*
Happy
50/67 *Sunshine Company*
87/67 *Blades Of Grass*
66/75 **Happy** *Eddie Kendricks*
74/68 **Happy** *Nancy Sinatra*
86/69 **Happy** *Paul Anka*
98/71 **Happy** *Hog Heaven*
98/67 **Happy And Me** *Don & The Goodtimes*
16/78 **Happy Anniversary** *Little River Band*
Happy Anniversary
57/59 *Jane Morgan*
77/59 *Four Lads*
30/61 **Happy Birthday Blues**
Kathy Young with The Innocents
6/62 **Happy Birthday, Sweet Sixteen**
Neil Sedaka

5/76 **Happy Days** *Pratt & McClain*
58/61 **Happy Days** *Marv Johnson*
57/84 **Happy Ending** *Joe Jackson*
57/77 **Happy Girls** *Helen Reddy*
10/60 **Happy-Go-Lucky-Me** *Paul Evans*
82/64 **Happy Guy** *Rick Nelson*
5/57 **Happy, Happy Birthday Baby** *Tune Weavers*
Happy Heart
22/69 *Andy Williams*
62/69 *Petula Clark*
70/82 **Happy Hour** *Deodato*
24/67 **Happy Jack** *Who*
57/62 **Happy Jose (Ching, Ching)** *Jack Ross*
62/82 **Happy Man** *Greg Kihn Band*
94/76 **Happy Man** *Impact*
58/60 **Happy Muleteer** *Ivo Robic*
19/76 **Happy Music** *Blackbyrds*
1/59 **Happy Organ** *Dave 'Baby' Cortez*
40/75 **Happy People** *Temptations*
79/79 **H.A.P.P.Y Radio** *Edwin Starr*
34/59 **Happy Reindeer** *Dancer, Prancer & Nervous*
83/60 **Happy Shades Of Blue** *Freddy Cannon*
25/68 **Happy Song (Dum-Dum)** *Otis Redding*
27/66 **Happy Summer Days** *Ronnie Dove*
82/61 **Happy Times (Are Here To Stay)** *Tony Orlando*
Happy Together
1/67 *Turtles*
79/72 *Dawn (medley)*
53/80 *Captain & Tennille*
95/59 **Happy Vacation** *Jackie Lee*
67/62 **Happy Weekend** *Dave 'Baby' Cortez*
6/56 **Happy Whistler** *Don Robertson*
73/58 **Happy Years** *Diamonds*
8/60 **Harbor Lights** *Platters*
Hard Day's Night
1/64 *Beatles*
29/66 *Ramsey Lewis*
3/84 **Hard Habit To Break** *Chicago*
1/58 **Hard Headed Woman** *Elvis Presley*
97/67 **Hard Lovin' Loser** *Judy Collins*
15/77 **Hard Luck Woman** *Kiss*
30/77 **Hard Rock Cafe** *Carole King*
58/77 **Hard Times** *Boz Scaggs*
72/81 **Hard Times** *James Taylor*
66/79 **Hard Times For Lovers** *Judy Collins*
69/85 **Hard Times For Lovers** *Jennifer Holliday*
44/57 **Hard Times (The Slop)** *Noble 'Thin Man' Watts*
4/55 **Hard To Get** *Gisele MacKenzie*
Hard To Handle
51/68 *Otis Redding*
93/68 *Patti Drew*
7/81 **Hard To Say** *Dan Fogelberg*
1/82 **Hard To Say I'm Sorry** *Chicago*
46/76 **Hard Work** *John Handy*
3/82 **Harden My Heart** *Quarterflash*
50/72 **Harder I Try (The Bluer I Get)** *Free Movement*
84/80 **Hardest Part** *Blondie*
55/60 **Hardhearted Hannah** *Ray Charles*
69/69 **Hare Krishna (medley)** *Happenings*
67/57 **Harem Dance** *Armenian Jazz Sextet*
Harlem Nocturne
52/60 *Viscounts*
39/66 *Viscounts*
Harlem Shuffle
44/64 *Bob & Earl*
94/66 *Traits*
5/86 *Rolling Stones*
Harlow *see: Theme From*
91/60 **Harmony** *Billy Bland*

Harper Valley P.T.A.
1/68 *Jeannie C. Riley*
67/68 *Ben Colder*
93/68 *King Curtis*
31/73 **Harry Hippie** *Bobby Womack*
17/63 **Harry The Hairy Ape** *Ray Stevens*
13/75 **Harry Truman** *Chicago*
63/76 **Harvest For The World** *Isley Brothers*
78/58 **Harvey's Got A Girl Friend** *Royal Teens*
60/86 **Has Anyone Ever Written Anything For You** *Stevie Nicks*
Hatari *see: Theme From*
5/61 **Hats Off To Larry** *Del Shannon*
11/64 **Haunted House** *Gene Simmons*
31/62 **Have A Good Time** *Sue Thompson*
98/68 **Have A Little Faith** *David Houston*
73/58 **Have Faith** *Gene Allison*
94/64 **Have I Stayed Away Too Long** *Bobby Bare*
49/66 **Have I Stayed Too Long** *Sonny & Cher*
5/64 **Have I The Right?** *Honeycombs*
29/57 **Have I Told You Lately That I Love You** *Ricky Nelson*
Have Mercy Baby
66/60 *Bobbettes*
92/65 *James Brown*
Have You Ever Been Lonely (Have You Ever Been Blue)
84/60 *Teresa Brewer*
94/64 *Caravelles*
94/66 **Have You Ever Loved Somebody** *Searchers*
8/71 **Have You Ever Seen The Rain** *Creedence Clearwater Revival*
18/63 **Have You Heard** *Duprees*
24/65 **Have You Looked Into Your Heart** *Jerry Vale*
1/75 **Have You Never Been Mellow** *Olivia Newton-John*
3/71 **Have You Seen Her** *Chi-Lites*
74/67 **Have You Seen Her Face** *Byrds*
9/66 **Have You Seen Your Mother, Baby, Standing In The Shadow?** *Rolling Stones*
14/74 **Haven't Got Time For The Pain** *Carly Simon*
26/79 **Haven't Stopped Dancing Yet** *Gonzalez*
42/80 **Haven't You Heard** *Patrice Rushen*
42/61 **Havin' Fun** *Dion*
Having A Party
17/62 *Sam Cooke*
56/73 *Ovations*
55/82 *Luther Vandross (medley)*
4/69 **Hawaii Five-O** *Ventures*
91/65 **Hawaii Honeymoon** *Waikikis*
33/65 **Hawaii Tattoo** *Waikikis*
89/59 **Hawaiian War Chant** *Billy Vaughn*
11/59 **Hawaiian Wedding Song** *Andy Williams*
45/55 **Hawk-Eye** *Frankie Laine*
13/66 **Hazy Shade Of Winter** *Simon & Garfunkel*
He
4/55 *Al Hibbler*
10/55 *McGuire Sisters*
18/66 *Righteous Brothers*
90/73 **He** *Today's People*
100/67 **He Ain't Give You None** *Freddie Scott*
He Ain't Heavy, He's My Brother
7/70 *Hollies*
20/70 *Neil Diamond*
F/76 *Olivia Newton-John*
100/65 **He Ain't No Angel** *Ad Libs*
He Called Me Baby
77/69 *Ella Washington*
52/71 *Candi Staton*
33/81 **He Can't Love You** *Michael Stanley Band*
74/82 **He Could Be The One** *Josie Cotton*
He Cried *see: She Cried*

75/73 **He Did With Me** *Vicki Lawrence*
He Don't Love You (Like I Love You)
7/60 *Jerry Butler*
91/66 *Righteous Brothers*
1/75 *Dawn*
63/76 *Jim Croce (medley)*
92/68 **He Don't Really Love You** *Delfonics*
59/82 **He Got You** *Ronnie Milsap*
(He Knew) *see: Portrait*
34/62 **He Knows I Love Him Too Much**
Paris Sisters
97/70 **He Loves Me All The Way** *Tammy Wynette*
71/70 **He Made A Woman Out Of Me**
Bobbie Gentry
47/64 **He Says The Same Things To Me**
Skeeter Davis
57/62 **He Thinks I Still Care** *Connie Francis*
53/65 **He Touched Me** *Barbra Streisand*
66/64 **He Walks Like A Man** *Jody Miller*
64/65 **He Was Really Sayin' Somethin'**
Velvelettes
He Will Break Your Heart
see: He Don't Love You
89/66 **He Wore The Green Beret** *Nancy Ames*
83/71 **He'd Rather Have The Rain**
Heaven Bound with Tony Scotti
He'll Have To Go (Stay)
2/60 *Jim Reeves*
4/60 *Jeanne Black*
51/64 *Solomon Burke*
25/86 **He'll Never Love You (Like I Do)**
Freddie Jackson
94/63 **He's A Bad Boy** *Carole King*
36/76 **He's A Friend** *Eddie Kendricks*
55/64 **He's A Good Guy (Yes He Is)** *Marvelettes*
30/81 **He's A Liar** *Bee Gees*
74/65 **He's A Lover** *Mary Wells*
82/83 **He's A Pretender** *High Inergy*
1/62 **He's A Rebel** *Crystals*
98/72 **He's An Indian Cowboy In The Rodeo**
Buffy Sainte-Marie
71/57 **He's Gone** *Chantels*
70/71 **He's Gonna Step On You Again**
John Kongos
79/65 **He's Got No Love** *Searchers*
57/63 **He's Got The Power** *Exciters*
He's Got The Whole World (In His Hands)
1/58 *Laurie London*
69/58 *Mahalia Jackson*
43/64 **He's In Town** *Tokens*
23/57 **He's Mine** *Platters*
62/63 **He's Mine (I Love Him, I Love Him, I Love Him)** *Alice Wonder Land*
14/61 **(He's My) Dreamboat** *Connie Francis*
63/65 **He's My Guy** *Irma Thomas*
90/66 **(He's) Raining In My Sunshine**
Jay & The Americans
He's So Fine
1/63 *Chiffons*
53/71 *Jody Miller*
70/78 *Kristy & Jimmy McNichol*
77/78 *Jane Olivor*
73/63 **He's So Heavenly** *Brenda Lee*
3/80 **He's So Shy** *Pointer Sisters*
11/63 **He's Sure The Boy I Love** *Crystals*
30/61 **(He's) The Great Impostor** *Fleetwoods*
9/79 **He's The Greatest Dancer** *Sister Sledge*
77/79 **Head First** *Babys*
14/79 **Head Games** *Foreigner*
3/85 **Head Over Heels** *Tears For Fears*
11/84 **Head Over Heels** *Go-Go's*
35/80 **Headed For A Fall** *Firefall*
53/86 **Headed For The Future** *Neil Diamond*
84/66 **Headline News** *Edwin Starr*

69/86 **Headlines** *Midnight Star*
94/63 **Hear The Bells** *Tokens*
14/77 **Heard It In A Love Song**
Marshall Tucker Band
44/72 **Hearsay** *Soul Children*
Heart
6/55 *Eddie Fisher*
13/55 *Four Aces*
Heart
64/63 *Kenny Chandler*
82/63 *Wayne Newton*
8/83 **Heart And Soul** *Huey Lewis & The News*
Heart And Soul
57/56 *Johnny Maddox*
18/61 *Cleftones*
25/61 *Jan & Dean*
3/82 **Heart Attack** *Olivia Newton-John*
89/67 **Heart Be Still** *Lorraine Ellison*
87/62 **Heart Breaker** *Dean Christie*
56/84 **Heart Don't Lie** *LaToya Jackson*
9/65 **Heart Full Of Soul** *Yardbirds*
67/56 **Heart Hideaway** *Cathy Carr*
21/80 **Heart Hotels** *Dan Fogelberg*
15/62 **Heart In Hand** *Brenda Lee*
66/81 **Heart In New York** *Art Garfunkel*
75/86 **Heart Is Not So Smart** *El DeBarge*
24/81 **Heart Like A Wheel** *Steve Miller Band*
1/79 **Heart Of Glass** *Blondie*
1/72 **Heart Of Gold** *Neil Young*
6/84 **Heart Of Rock & Roll**
Huey Lewis & The News
19/65 **Heart Of Stone** *Rolling Stones*
20/79 **Heart Of The Night** *Poco*
25/83 **Heart Of The Night** *Juice Newton*
Heart On My Sleeve
67/76 *Gallagher & Lyle*
86/76 *Bryan Ferry*
Heart To Heart
65/79 *Errol Sober*
15/83 *Kenny Loggins*
79/56 **Heart Without A Sweetheart** *Gale Storm*
88/66 **Heart's Desire** *Billy Joe Royal*
76/86 **Heart's On Fire** *John Cafferty*
55/86 **Heartache All Over The World** *Elton John*
56/86 **Heartache Away** *Don Johnson*
1/79 **Heartache Tonight** *Eagles*
Heartaches
71/56 *Somethin' Smith & The Redheads*
7/61 *Marcels*
73/62 *Patsy Cline*
60/79 **Heartaches** *BTO*
Heartaches By The Number
1/59 *Guy Mitchell*
35/65 *Johnny Tillotson*
5/86 **Heartbeat** *Don Johnson*
3/73 **Heartbeat - It's A Lovebeat**
DeFranco Family
82/59 **Heartbeat** *Buddy Holly*
99/64 **Heartbreak Hill** *Fats Domino*
Heartbreak Hotel
1/56 *Elvis Presley*
79/56 *Stan Freberg*
84/66 *Roger Miller*
72/71 *Frijid Pink*
22/81 **Heartbreak Hotel** *Jacksons*
Heartbreak (It's Hurtin' Me)
38/60 *Little Willie John*
48/60 *Jon Thomas*
39/74 **Heartbreak Kid**
Bo Donaldson & The Heywoods
89/75 **Heartbreak Road** *Bill Withers*
10/83 **Heartbreaker** *Dionne Warwick*
23/80 **Heartbreaker** *Pat Benatar*
37/78 **Heartbreaker** *Dolly Parton*

72/70 **Heartbreaker** *Grand Funk Railroad*
(Heartbreaker) *see: Doo Doo Doo Doo*
47/72 **Heartbroken Bopper** *Guess Who*
24/78 **Heartless** *Heart*
99/55 **Heartless** *Tommy Leonetti*
5/82 **Heartlight** *Neil Diamond*
92/85 **Heartline** *Robin George*
8/81 **Hearts** *Marty Balin*
58/62 **Hearts** *Jackie Wilson*
Hearts Of Stone
1/55 *Fontane Sisters*
15/55 *Charms*
20/61 *Bill Black's Combo*
37/73 *Blue Ridge Rangers*
19/81 **Hearts On Fire** *Randy Meisner*
2/85 **Heat Is On** *Glenn Frey*
55/86 **Heat Of Heat** *Patti Austin*
4/82 **Heat Of The Moment** *Asia*
Heat Wave
4/63 *Martha & The Vandellas*
5/75 *Linda Ronstadt*
29/69 **Heather Honey** *Tommy Roe*
1/85 **Heaven** *Bryan Adams*
39/69 **Heaven** *Rascals*
9/70 **Heaven Help Us All** *Stevie Wonder*
86/81 **Heaven In Your Arms** *Dan Hartman*
12/86 **Heaven In Your Eyes** *Loverboy*
4/79 **Heaven Knows** *Donna Summer*
24/69 **Heaven Knows** *Grass Roots*
15/76 **Heaven Must Be Missing An Angel** *Tavares*
65/84 **Heaven (Must Be There)** *Eurogliders*
Heaven Must Have Sent You
50/66 *Elgins*
11/79 *Bonnie Pointer*
39/56 **Heaven On Earth** *Platters*
89/77 **Heaven On Earth (So Fine)** *Spinners*
6/77 **Heaven On The 7th Floor** *Paul Nicholas*
49/84 **Heaven's On Fire** *Kiss*
43/74 **Heavenly** *Temptations*
40/59 **Heavenly Lover** *Teresa Brewer*
69/77 **Heaven's Just A Sin Away** *Kendalls*
41/74 **Heavy Fallin' Out** *Stylistics*
47/76 **Heavy Love** *David Ruffin*
27/71 **Heavy Makes You Happy (Sha-Na-Boom Boom)** *Staple Singers*
43/81 **Heavy Metal (Takin' A Ride)** *Don Felder*
33/70 **Heed The Call** *Kenny Rogers & The First Edition*
94/70 **Heighdy-Ho Princess** *Neon Philharmonic*
50/56 **Held For Questioning** *Rusty Draper*
10/74 **Helen Wheels** *Paul McCartney*
70/76 **Hell Cat** *Bellamy Brothers*
59/79 **Hell On Wheels** *Cher*
1/84 **Hello** *Lionel Richie*
6/81 **Hello Again** *Neil Diamond*
20/84 **Hello Again** *Cars*
60/70 **Hello Darlin'** *Conway Twitty*
Hello, Dolly!
1/64 *Louis Armstrong*
79/65 *Bobby Darin*
1/67 **Hello Goodbye** *Beatles*
26/63 **Hello Heartache, Goodbye Love** *Little Peggy March*
Hello Hello
26/67 *Sopwith 'Camel'*
91/67 *Claudine Longet*
69/79 **Hello, Hello, Hello** *New England*
35/73 **Hello Hurray** *Alice Cooper*
1/68 **Hello, I Love You** *Doors*
Hello It's Me
66/70 *Nazz*
5/73 *Todd Rundgren*
97/63 **Hello Jim** *Paul Anka*
9/61 **Hello Mary Lou** *Ricky Nelson*
Hello Mudduh, Hello Fadduh! (A Letter From Camp)
2/63 *Allan Sherman*
59/64 *Allan Sherman (1964)*
24/76 **Hello Old Friend** *Eric Clapton*
54/65 **Hello Pretty Girl** *Ronnie Dove*
Hello Stranger
3/63 *Barbara Lewis*
100/73 *Fire & Rain*
15/77 *Yvonne Elliman*
12/61 **Hello Walls** *Faron Young*
23/60 **Hello Young Lovers** *Paul Anka*
1/65 **Help!** *Beatles*
14/77 **Help Is On Its Way** *Little River Band*
7/74 **Help Me** *Joni Mitchell*
50/80 **Help Me** *Robin Gibb & Marcy Levy*
92/70 **Help Me Find A Way (To Say I Love You)** *Little Anthony & The Imperials*
100/66 **Help Me (Get Myself Back Together Again)** *Spellbinders*
Help Me Girl
29/66 *Animals*
37/66 *Outsiders*
Help Me Make It Through The Night
8/71 *Sammi Smith*
69/71 *Joe Simon*
91/71 *O.C. Smith*
33/72 *Gladys Knight & The Pips*
64/75 **Help Me Make It (To My Rockin' Chair)** *B.J. Thomas*
Help Me, Rhonda
1/65 *Beach Boys*
22/75 *Johnny Rivers*
Help The Poor
98/64 *B.B. King*
90/71 *B.B. King*
70/76 **Help Wanted** *Hudson Brothers*
35/68 **Help Yourself** *Tom Jones*
63/74 **Help Yourself** *Undisputed Truth*
94/68 **Help Yourself (To All Of My Lovin')** *James & Bobby Purify*
56/58 **Helpless** *Platters*
56/66 **Helpless** *Kim Weston*
47/58 **Henrietta** *Jimmy Dee*
6/62 **Her Royal Majesty** *James Darren*
11/81 **Her Town Too** *James Taylor & J.D. Souther*
23/77 **Here Come Those Tears Again** *Jackson Browne*
91/67 **Here Comes Heaven** *Eddy Arnold*
13/67 **Here Comes My Baby** *Tremeloes*
59/80 **Here Comes My Girl** *Tom Petty*
Here Comes Summer
14/59 *Jerry Keller*
49/77 *Wildfire*
89/62 **Here Comes That Feelin'** *Brenda Lee*
15/71 **Here Comes That Rainy Day Feeling Again** *Fortunes*
93/63 **Here Comes The Boy** *Tracey Dey*
Here Comes The Judge
8/68 *Shorty Long*
19/68 *Pigmeat Markham*
54/68 *Magistrates*
88/68 *Buena Vistas*
24/65 **Here Comes The Night** *Them*
44/78 **Here Comes The Night** *Nick Gilder*
44/79 **Here Comes The Night** *Beach Boys*
81/61 **Here Comes The Night** *Ben E. King*
4/84 **Here Comes The Rain Again** *Eurythmics*
74/68 **Here Comes The Rain, Baby** *Eddy Arnold*
16/71 **Here Comes The Sun** *Richie Havens*
65/65 **Here I Am** *Dionne Warwick*
44/68 **Here I Am Baby** *Marvelettes*
10/73 **Here I Am (Come And Take Me)** *Al Green*

5/81 **Here I Am (Just When I Thought I Was Over You)** *Air Supply*
37/69 **Here I Go Again** *Miracles*
76/79 **Here I Go (Fallin' In Love Again)** *Frannie Golde*
Here I Stand
80/59 *Wade Flemons*
51/63 *Rip Chords*
86/61 **Here In My Heart** *Al Martino*
80/77 **Here Is Where Your Love Belongs** *Sons Of Champlin*
27/65 **Here It Comes Again** *Fortunes*
76/84 **Here She Comes** *Bonnie Tyler*
92/64 **Here She Comes** *Tymes*
65/76 **Here, There And Everywhere** *Emmylou Harris*
56/65 **(Here They Come) From All Over The World** *Jan & Dean*
65/82 **Here To Love You** *Doobie Brothers*
Here We Go Again
15/67 *Ray Charles*
98/69 *Nancy Sinatra*
3/78 **Here You Come Again** *Dolly Parton*
89/64 **Here's A Heart** *Diplomats*
97/61 **Here's My Confession** *Wyatt (Earp) McPherson*
82/76 **Here's Some Love** *Tanya Tucker*
76/68 **Here's To You** *Hamilton Camp*
54/80 **Heroes** *Commodores*
12/67 **Heroes And Villains** *Beach Boys*
Hey! Baby
1/62 *Bruce Channel*
71/69 *Jose Feliciano*
74/77 *Ringo Starr*
72/76 **Hey Baby** *Ted Nugent*
96/76 **Hey Baby** *J.J. Cale*
12/67 **Hey Baby (They're Playing Our Song)** *Buckinghams*
19/72 **Hey Big Brother** *Rare Earth*
23/64 **Hey, Bobba Needle** *Chubby Checker*
92/68 **Hey Boy Take A Chance On Love** *Ruby Andrews*
69/65 **Hey-Da-Da-Dow** *Dolphins*
7/78 **Hey Deanie** *Shaun Cassidy*
Hey Girl
10/63 *Freddie Scott*
35/68 *Bobby Vee (medley)*
9/72 *Donny Osmond*
41/64 **Hey Girl Don't Bother Me** *Tams*
61/58 **Hey Girl-Hey Boy** *Oscar McLollie & Jeanette Baker*
35/73 **Hey Girl (I Like Your Style)** *Temptations*
29/64 **Hey Harmonica Man** *Stevie Wonder*
57/68 **Hey Hey Bunny** *John Fred*
3/57 **Hey! Jealous Lover** *Frank Sinatra*
32/64 **Hey Jean, Hey Dean** *Dean & Jean*
Hey Joe
31/66 *Leaves*
94/67 *Cher*
59/69 *Wilson Pickett*
Hey Jude
1/68 *Beatles*
23/69 *Wilson Pickett*
35/70 **Hey Lawdy Mama** *Steppenwolf*
31/67 **Hey, Leroy, Your Mama's Callin' You** *Jimmy Castor*
20/62 **Hey, Let's Twist** *Joey Dee & The Starliters*
4/64 **Hey Little Cobra** *Rip Chords*
13/63 **Hey Little Girl** *Major Lance*
Hey Little Girl
20/59 *Dee Clark*
92/73 *Foster Sylvers*
29/57 **Hey! Little Girl** *Techniques*
38/62 **Hey! Little Girl** *Del Shannon*
87/59 **Hey Little Lucy! (Don'tcha Put No Lipstick On)** *Conway Twitty*
Hey Little One
48/60 *Dorsey Burnette*
85/64 *J. Frank Wilson*
54/68 *Glen Campbell*
100/63 **Hey Lonely One** *Baby Washington*
52/71 **Hey Love** *Delfonics*
90/67 **Hey Love** *Stevie Wonder*
81/63 **Hey Lover** *Debbie Dovale*
12/55 **Hey, Mr. Banjo** *Sunnysiders*
77/64 **Hey, Mr. Sax Man** *Boots Randolph*
24/70 **Hey, Mr. Sun** *Bobby Sherman*
10/81 **Hey Nineteen** *Steely Dan*
76/64 **Hey Now** *Lesley Gore*
1/63 **Hey Paula** *Paul & Paula*
49/58 **Hey, Schoolgirl** *Tom & Jerry*
48/76 **Hey Shirley (This Is Squirrely)** *Shirley & Squirrely*
76/79 **Hey, St. Peter** *Flash & The Pan*
67/75 **Hey There Little Firefly - Part 1** *Firefly*
Hey There Lonely Girl (Boy)
27/63 *Ruby & The Romantics*
2/70 *Eddie Holman*
31/80 *Robert John*
F/71 **Hey Tonight** *Creedence Clearwater Revival*
16/68 **Hey, Western Union Man** *Jerry Butler*
1/75 **(Hey Won't You Play) Another Somebody Done Somebody Wrong Song** *B.J. Thomas*
21/75 **Hey You** *Bachman-Turner Overdrive*
43/73 **Hey You! Get Off My Mountain** *Dramatics*
76/66 **Hey You! Little Boo-Ga-Loo** *Chubby Checker*
87/72 **Hey, You Love** *Mouth & MacNeal*
14/70 **Hi-De-Ho** *Blood, Sweat & Tears*
98/63 **Hi Diddle Diddle** *Inez Foxx*
Hi-Heel Sneakers
11/64 *Tommy Tucker*
91/64 *Jerry Lee Lewis*
59/65 *Stevie Wonder*
70/66 *Ramsey Lewis*
25/68 *Jose Feliciano*
(also see: Slip-In Mules)
96/66 **Hi Hi Hazel** *Gary & The Hornets*
10/73 **Hi, Hi, Hi** *Wings*
Hi-Lili, Hi-Lo
78/56 *Dick Hyman Trio*
85/56 *Roger Williams*
64/63 *Richard Chamberlain*
63/64 **Hickory, Dick And Doc** *Bobby Vee*
Hide & Go Seek
33/62 *Bunker Hill*
58/66 *Sheep*
29/61 **Hide Away** *Freddy King*
20/62 **Hide 'Nor Hair** *Ray Charles*
21/58 **Hideaway** *Four Esquires*
95/76 **Hideaway** *John Sebastian*
85/84 **High Energy** *Evelyn Thomas*
High-Heel *see: Hi-Heel*
30/59 **High Hopes** *Frank Sinatra*
77/64 **High On A Hill** *Scott English*
44/84 **High On Emotion** *Chris DeBurgh*
94/66 **High On Love** *Knickerbockers*
8/85 **High On You** *Survivor*
70/80 **High On Your Love** *Debbie Jacobs*
72/79 **High On Your Love Suite** *Rick James*
76/76 **High Out Of Time** *Carole King*
21/58 **High School Confidential** *Jerry Lee Lewis*
17/77 **High School Dance** *Sylvers*
F/57 **High School Dance** *Larry Williams*
91/85 **High School Nights** *Dave Edmunds*
80/57 **High School Romance** *George Hamilton IV*
28/59 **High School U.S.A.** *Tommy Facenda*
37/58 **High Sign** *Diamonds*

48/83 **High Time** *Styx*
22/71 **High Time We Went** *Joe Cocker*
Higher & Higher
see: (Your Love Keeps Lifting Me)
4/73 **Higher Ground** *Stevie Wonder*
1/86 **Higher Love** *Steve Winwood*
37/74 **Higher Plane** *Kool & The Gang*
68/76 **Highfly** *John Miles*
26/79 **Highway Song** *Blackfoot*
47/79 **Highway To Hell** *AC/DC*
14/75 **Hijack** *Herbie Mann*
64/71 **Hijackin' Love** *Johnnie Taylor*
Hill Street Blues *see: Theme From*
76/71 **Hill Where The Lord Hides**
Chuck Mangione
6/80 **Him** *Rupert Holmes*
5/67 **Him Or Me - What's It Gonna Be?**
Paul Revere & The Raiders
31/68 **Hip City - Pt. 2** *Jr. Walker & The All Stars*
37/67 **Hip Hug-Her** *Booker T. & The MG's*
3/86 **Hip To Be Square** *Huey Lewis & The News*
24/64 **Hippy Hippy Shake** *Swinging Blue Jeans*
89/64 **His Kiss** *Betty Harris*
His Latest Flame *see: Marie's The Name*
History Repeats Itself
39/66 *Buddy Starcher*
89/66 *Cab Calloway*
9/80 **Hit Me With Your Best Shot** *Pat Benatar*
45/62 **Hit Record** *Brook Benton*
(Hit Record) *see: Overnight Sensation*
Hit The Road Jack
1/61 *Ray Charles*
40/76 *Stampeders*
30/63 **Hitch Hike** *Marvin Gaye*
34/68 **Hitch It To The Horse** *Fantastic Johnny C*
77/68 **Hitchcock Railway** *Jose Feliciano*
5/70 **Hitchin' A Ride** *Vanity Fare*
58/60 **Hither And Thither And Yon**
Brook Benton
69/63 **Hobo Flats** *Jimmy Smith*
9/73 **Hocus Pocus** *Focus*
Hold Back The Night
35/76 *Trammps*
58/77 *Graham Parker & The Rumour*
78/61 **Hold Back The Tears** *Delacardos*
84/57 **Hold 'Em Joe** *Harry Belafonte*
14/72 **Hold Her Tight** *Osmonds*
92/58 **Hold It** *Bill Doggett*
4/82 **Hold Me** *Fleetwood Mac*
46/84 **Hold Me** *Teddy Pendergrass*
62/85 **Hold Me** *Menudo*
Hold Me
70/64 *P.J. Proby*
88/69 *Baskerville Hounds*
82/85 **Hold Me** *Laura Branigan*
3/84 **Hold Me Now** *Thompson Twins*
8/65 **Hold Me, Thrill Me, Kiss Me** *Mel Carter*
5/68 **Hold Me Tight** *Johnny Nash*
40/83 **Hold Me 'Til The Mornin' Comes**
Paul Anka
46/78 **Hold Me, Touch Me** *Paul Stanley*
15/82 **Hold On** *Santana*
18/79 **Hold On** *Ian Gomm*
38/79 **Hold On** *Triumph*
40/80 **Hold On** *Kansas*
47/76 **Hold On** *Sons Of Champlin*
51/70 **Hold On** *Rascals*
56/81 **Hold On** *Badfinger*
61/77 **Hold On** *Wild Cherry*
68/68 **Hold On** *Radiants*
Hold On! I'm A Comin'
21/66 *Sam & Dave*
91/67 *Chuck Jackson & Maxine Brown*
27/81 **Hold On Loosely** *38 Special*
10/81 **Hold On Tight** *ELO*
10/80 **Hold On To My Love** *Jimmy Ruffin*
78/78 **Hold On To The Night** *Starz*
80/79 **Hold On To The Night** *Hotel*
5/79 **Hold The Line** *Toto*
67/77 **Hold Tight** *Vicki Sue Robinson*
89/81 **Hold Tight** *Change*
5/65 **Hold What You've Got** *Joe Tex*
5/72 **Hold Your Head Up** *Argent*
37/82 **Holdin' On** *Tane Cain*
75/80 **Holdin' On For Dear Love** *Lobo*
17/75 **Holdin' On To Yesterday** *Ambrosia*
1/86 **Holding Back The Years** *Simply Red*
49/78 **Holding On (When Love Is Gone)** *L.T.D.*
34/84 **Holding Out For A Hero** *Bonnie Tyler*
43/65 **Hole In The Wall** *Packers*
16/67 **Holiday** *Bee Gees*
16/84 **Holiday** *Madonna*
87/80 **Holiday** *Nazareth*
94/67 **Holiday For Clowns** *Brian Hyland*
84/57 **Holiday For Trombones** *David Rose*
82/83 **Holiday Road** *Lindsey Buckingham*
Holly Holy
6/69 *Neil Diamond*
75/71 *Jr. Walker & The All Stars*
32/77 **Hollywood** *Rufus Featuring Chaka Khan*
42/61 **Hollywood** *Connie Francis*
49/78 **Hollywood** *Boz Scaggs*
70/82 **Hollywood** *Shooting Star*
55/75 **Hollywood Hot** *Eleventh Hour*
12/78 **Hollywood Nights** *Bob Seger*
6/74 **Hollywood Swinging** *Kool & The Gang*
23/66 **Holy Cow** *Lee Dorsey*
67/70 **Holy Man** *Diane Kolby*
71/85 **Holyanna** *Toto*
34/67 **Homburg** *Procol Harum*
28/79 **Home And Dry** *Gerry Rafferty*
70/78 **Home Bound** *Ted Nugent*
42/69 **Home Cookin** *Jr. Walker & The All Stars*
88/57 **Home Of The Blues** *Johnny Cash*
Home Of The Brave
25/65 *Jody Miller*
77/65 *Bonnie & The Treasures*
89/85 **Home Sweet Home** *Motley Crue*
97/69 **Home To You** *Earth Opera*
71/76 **Home Tonight** *Aerosmith*
41/76 **Homecoming, The** *Hagood Hardy*
54/74 **Homely Girl** *Chi-Lites*
5/66 **Homeward Bound** *Simon & Garfunkel*
28/60 **Honest I Do** *Innocents*
32/57 **Honest I Do** *Jimmy Reed*
65/59 **Honestly And Truly** *Tommy Edwards*
24/79 **Honesty** *Billy Joel*
Honey
1/68 *Bobby Goldsboro*
44/69 *O.C. Smith*
6/55 **Honey Babe** *Art Mooney*
59/76 **Honey Child** *Bad Company*
11/67 **Honey Chile** *Martha & The Vandellas*
19/70 **Honey Come Back** *Glen Campbell*
61/78 **Honey Don't Leave L.A.** *James Taylor*
Honey, Honey
27/74 *Abba*
68/74 *Sweet Dreams*
59/80 **Honey, Honey** *David Hudson*
53/60 **Honey Hush** *Joe Turner*
65/76 **Honey I** *George McCrae*
90/60 **Honey Love** *Narvel Felts*
44/74 **Honey Please, Can't Ya See** *Barry White*
98/75 **Honey Trippin'** *Mystic Moods*
1/57 **Honeycomb** *Jimmie Rodgers*
8/72 **Honky Cat** *Elton John*

Honky Tonk
2/56 *Bill Doggett*
57/61 *Bill Doggett*
78/65 *Lonnie Mack*
44/72 *James Brown*
92/60 **Honky-Tonk Girl** *Johnny Cash*
96/62 **Honky-Tonk Man** *Johnny Horton*
1/69 **Honky Tonk Women** *Rolling Stones*
92/61 **Honky Train** *Bill Black's Combo*
11/63 **Honolulu Lulu** *Jan & Dean*
23/61 **Hoochi Coochi Coo** *Hank Ballard*
73/69 **Hook And Sling** *Eddie Bo*
F/57 **Hook, Line And Sinker** *Bill Haley & His Comets*
17/64 **Hooka Tooka** *Chubby Checker*
Hooked On A Feeling
5/69 *B.J. Thomas*
1/74 *Blue Swede*
61/82 **Hooked On Big Bands** *Frank Barber Orchestra*
10/82 **Hooked On Classics** *Royal Philharmonic Orchestra*
31/82 **Hooked On Swing (medley)** *Larry Elgart*
60/77 **Hooked On You** *Bread*
56/58 **Hoopa Hoola** *Betty Johnson*
6/66 **Hooray For Hazel** *Tommy Roe*
71/67 **Hooray For The Salvation Army Band** *Bill Cosby*
38/63 **Hootenanny** *Glencoves*
89/63 **Hootenanny Saturday Night** *Brothers Four*
90/61 **Hop Scotch** *Santo & Johnny*
42/75 **Hope That We Can Be Together Soon** *Sharon Paige & Harold Melvin & Blue Notes*
36/82 **Hope You Love Me Like You Say You Do** *Huey Lewis & The News*
13/63 **Hopeless** *Andy Williams*
3/78 **Hopelessly Devoted To You** *Olivia Newton-John*
65/75 **Hoppy, Gene And Me** *Roy Rogers*
42/80 **Horizontal Bop** *Bob Seger*
2/68 **Horse, The** *Cliff Nobles & Co.*
68/68 **Horse Fever** *Cliff Nobles & Co.*
1/72 **Horse With No Name** *America*
92/56 **Hot And Cold Running Tears** *Sarah Vaughan*
3/78 **Hot Blooded** *Foreigner*
91/63 **Hot Cakes! 1st Serving** *Dave 'Baby' Cortez*
1/78 **Hot Child In The City** *Nick Gilder*
50/75 **Hot Dawgit** *Ramsey Lewis and Earth, Wind & Fire*
1/56 **Hot Diggity (Dog Ziggity Boom)** *Perry Como*
60/56 **Hot Dog Buddy Buddy** *Bill Haley & His Comets*
56/84 **Hot For Teacher** *Van Halen*
Hot Fun In The Summertime
2/69 *Sly & The Family Stone*
58/82 *Dayton*
11/83 **Hot Girls In Love** *Loverboy*
23/82 **Hot In The City** *Billy Idol*
28/78 **Hot Legs** *Rod Stewart*
5/77 **Hot Line** *Sylvers*
72/71 **Hot Love** *T. Rex*
31/78 **Hot Love, Cold World** *Bob Welch*
52/72 **Hot 'N' Nasty** *Humble Pie*
21/79 **Hot Number** *Foxy*
15/71 **Hot Pants** *James Brown*
54/71 **Hot Pants** *Salvage*
85/71 **Hot Pants** *Bobby Byrd*
11/63 **Hot Pastrami** *Dartells*
36/63 **Hot Pastrami With Mashed Potatoes** *Joey Dee & The Starliters*
63/62 **Hot Pepper** *Floyd Cramer*
15/80 **Hot Rod Hearts** *Robbie Dupree*
Hot Rod Lincoln
26/60 *Johnny Bond*
33/60 *Charlie Ryan*
9/72 *Commander Cody*
67/78 **Hot Shot** *Karen Young*
87/66 **Hot Shot** *Buena Vistas*
14/69 **Hot Smoke & Sasafrass** *Bubble Puppy*
1/79 **Hot Stuff** *Donna Summer*
49/76 **Hot Stuff** *Rolling Stones*
Hot Summer Nights
55/78 *Walter Egan*
18/79 *Night*
95/77 **Hot To Trot** *Wild Cherry*
87/86 **Hot Water** *Level 42*
71/73 **Hot Wire** *Al Green*
1/77 **Hotel California** *Eagles*
3/63 **Hotel Happiness** *Brook Benton*
100/62 **Houdini** *Walter Brennan*
1/56 **Hound Dog** *Elvis Presley*
9/59 **Hound Dog Man** *Fabian*
58/77 **Hound Dog Man (Play It Again)** *Lenny LeBlanc*
House, A Car And A Wedding Ring
88/58 *Dale Hawkins*
93/58 *Mike Preston*
53/71 **House At Pooh Corner** *Nitty Gritty Dirt Band*
House Is Not A Home
71/64 *Dionne Warwick*
75/64 *Brook Benton*
88/60 **House Of Bamboo** *Earl Grant*
9/55 **House Of Blue Lights** *Chuck Miller*
92/59 **House Of Love** *Scott Garrett*
93/75 **House Of Strangers** *Jim Gilstrap*
House Of The Rising Sun
1/64 *Animals*
7/70 *Frijid Pink*
78/78 *Santa Esmeralda*
77/81 *Dolly Parton*
6/68 **House That Jack Built** *Aretha Franklin*
20/56 **House With Love In It** *Four Lads*
21/65 **Houston** *Dean Martin*
68/74 **Houston (I'm Comin' To See You)** *Glen Campbell*
33/60 **How About That** *Dee Clark*
12/83 **How Am I Supposed To Live Without You** *Laura Branigan*
22/58 **How Are Ya' Fixed For Love?** *Frank Sinatra & Keely Smith*
97/64 **How Blue Can You Get** *B.B. King*
48/70 **(How Bout A Little Hand For) The Boys In The Band** *Boys In The Band*
12/81 **How 'Bout Us** *Champaign*
How Can I Be Sure
4/67 *Young Rascals*
25/72 *David Cassidy*
41/70 **How Can I Forget** *Marvin Gaye*
How Can I Forget
57/63 *Jimmy Holiday*
85/63 *Ben E. King*
44/78 **How Can I Leave You Again** *John Denver*
71/82 **How Can I Live Without Her** *Christopher Atkins*
75/62 **How Can I Meet Her?** *Everly Brothers*
44/83 **How Can I Refuse** *Heart*
22/73 **How Can I Tell Her** *Lobo*
60/70 **How Can I Tell My Mom & Dad** *Lovelites*
68/73 **How Can I Tell You** *Travis Wammack*
63/71 **How Can I Unlove You** *Lynn Anderson*
92/61 **(How Can I Write On Paper) What I Feel In My Heart** *Jim Reeves*
86/82 **How Can You Love Me** *Ambrosia*
1/71 **How Can You Mend A Broken Heart** *Bee Gees*

96/67 **How Can You Mistreat The One You Love** *Jean & The Darlings*
F/72 **How Could I Let You Get Away** *Spinners*
88/79 **How Could This Go Wrong** *Exile*
93/60 **How Deep Is The Ocean** *Miss Toni Fisher*
1/77 **How Deep Is Your Love** *Bee Gees*
85/71 **How Did We Lose It Baby** *Jerry Butler*
10/80 **How Do I Make You** *Linda Ronstadt*
22/80 **How Do I Survive** *Amy Holland*
27/67 **How Do You Catch A Girl** *Sam The Sham & The Pharoahs*
8/72 **How Do You Do** *Mouth & MacNeal*
9/64 **How Do You Do It?** *Gerry & The Pacemakers*
77/74 **How Do You Feel The Morning After** *Millie Jackson*
45/83 **How Do You Keep The Music Playing** *Patti Austin & James Ingram*
30/80 **How Does It Feel To Be Back** *Daryl Hall & John Oates*
7/66 **How Does That Grab You, Darlin'?** *Nancy Sinatra*
How High The Moon
76/60 *Ella Fitzgerald*
75/75 *Gloria Gaynor*
93/69 **How I Miss You Baby** *Bobby Womack*
54/75 **(How I Spent My Summer Vacation) Or A Day At The Beach With Pedro & The Man** *Cheech & Chong*
How Important Can It Be?
2/55 *Joni James*
12/55 *Sarah Vaughan*
F/55 *Teresa Brewer*
42/62 **How Is Julie?** *Lettermen*
13/56 **(How Little It Matters) How Little We Know** *Frank Sinatra*
How Long
3/75 *Ace*
49/82 *Rod Stewart*
20/75 **How Long (Betcha' Got A Chick On The Side)** *Pointer Sisters*
97/57 **How Lovely Is Christmas** *Bing Crosby*
70/56 **How Lucky You Are** *Joni James*
46/63 **How Many Teardrops** *Lou Christie*
63/61 **How Many Tears** *Bobby Vee*
27/83 **How Many Times Can We Say Goodbye** *Dionne Warwick & Luther Vandross*
92/64 **How Much Can A Lonely Heart Stand** *Skeeter Davis*
3/78 **How Much I Feel** *Ambrosia*
69/63 **How Much Is That Doggie In The Window** *Baby Jane & The Rockabyes*
17/77 **How Much Love** *Leo Sayer*
97/65 **How Nice It Is** *Billy Stewart*
86/68 **How Sweet It Is, Montage From** *Love Generation*
How Sweet It Is (To Be Loved By You)
6/65 *Marvin Gaye*
18/66 *Jr. Walker & The All Stars*
5/75 *James Taylor*
11/58 **How The Time Flies** *Jerry Wallace*
20/86 **(How To Be A) Millionaire** *ABC*
64/60 **How To Handle A Woman** *Johnny Mathis*
1/86 **How Will I Know** *Whitney Houston*
12/78 **How You Gonna See Me Now** *Alice Cooper*
21/68 **How'd We Ever Get This Way** *Andy Kim*
61/76 **Howzat** *Sherbet*
14/60 **Hucklebuck, The** *Chubby Checker*
Hula Hoop Song
32/58 *Georgia Gibbs*
38/58 *Teresa Brewer*
9/57 **Hula Love** *Buddy Knox*
Hully Gully *see: (Baby)*
54/61 **Hully Gully Again** *Little Caesar & The Romans*
25/62 **Hully Gully Baby** *Dovells*
99/62 **Hully Gully Guitar** *Jerry Reed*
54/70 **Hum A Song (From Your Heart)** *Lulu*
1/86 **Human** *Human League*
48/61 **Human** *Tommy Hunt*
7/83 **Human Nature** *Michael Jackson*
18/83 **Human Touch** *Rick Springfield*
59/60 **Humdinger** *Freddy Cannon*
Hummingbird
7/55 *Les Paul & Mary Ford*
17/55 *Frankie Laine*
20/73 **Hummingbird** *Seals & Crofts*
48/70 **Hummingbird** *B.B. King*
78/70 **Humphrey The Camel** *Jack Blanchard & Misty Morgan*
71/57 **Humpty Dumpty Heart** *LaVern Baker*
Hunch, The
68/59 *Paul Gayten*
71/59 *Bobby Peterson Quintet*
3/61 **Hundred Pounds Of Clay** *Gene McDaniels*
47/65 **Hung On You** *Righteous Brothers*
58/67 **Hung Up In Your Eyes** *Brian Hyland*
6/66 **Hungry** *Paul Revere & The Raiders*
27/65 **Hungry For Love** *San Remo Golden Strings*
5/80 **Hungry Heart** *Bruce Springsteen*
3/83 **Hungry Like The Wolf** *Duran Duran*
82/76 **Hungry Years** *Wayne Newton*
93/69 **Hunter, The** *Ike & Tina Turner*
85/86 **Hunter** *GTR*
13/67 **Hunter Gets Captured By The Game** *Marvelettes*
57/84 **Hunters Of The Night** *Mr. Mister*
5/68 **Hurdy Gurdy Man** *Donovan*
33/76 **Hurricane** *Bob Dylan*
81/75 **Hurricane Is Coming Tonite** *Carol Douglas*
60/77 **Hurry Sundown** *Outlaws*
58/81 **Hurry Up And Wait** *Isley Brothers*
Hurt
4/61 *Timi Yuro*
51/66 *Little Anthony & The Imperials*
97/75 *Manhattans*
28/76 *Elvis Presley*
31/73 **Hurt, The** *Cat Stevens*
82/84 **Hurt** *Re-Flex*
54/64 **Hurt By Love** *Inez Foxx*
Hurt So Bad
10/65 *Little Anthony & The Imperials*
12/69 *Lettermen*
76/70 *Jackie DeShannon (medley)*
8/80 *Linda Ronstadt*
78/59 **Hurtin' Inside** *Brook Benton*
2/72 **Hurting Each Other** *Carpenters*
Hurts So Good
24/73 *Millie Jackson*
2/82 *John Cougar*
57/85 **Hurts To Be In Love** *Gino Vannelli*
26/66 **Husbands And Wives** *Roger Miller*
Hush
52/67 *Billy Joe Royal*
4/68 *Deep Purple*
61/75 *Blue Swede (medley)*
75/60 **Hush-Hush** *Jimmy Reed*
8/65 **Hush, Hush, Sweet Charlotte** *Patti Page*
Hushabye
20/59 *Mystics*
62/69 *Jay & The Americans*
99/72 *Robert John*
1/75 **Hustle, The** *Van McCoy*
91/71 **Hymn 43** *Jethro Tull*
33/86 **Hyperactive** *Robert Palmer*

62/84 **Hyperactive** *Thomas Dolby*
21/67 **Hypnotized** *Linda Jones*
79/57 **Hypnotized** *Drifters*

26/82 **I.G.Y. (What A Beautiful World)** *Donald Fagen*
94/70 **I.O.I.O.** *Bee Gees*
I.O.U.
35/76 *Jimmy Dean*
53/83 *Lee Greenwood*
25/63 **I Adore Him** *Angels*
I Ain't Gonna Eat Out My Heart Anymore
52/66 *Young Rascals*
44/78 *Angel*
11/81 **I Ain't Gonna Stand For It** *Stevie Wonder*
12/85 **I Ain't Got Nobody (medley)** *David Lee Roth*
36/71 **I Ain't Got Time Anymore** *Glass Bottle*
57/68 **I Ain't Got To Love Nobody Else** *Masqueraders*
I Ain't Never
24/59 *Webb Pierce*
79/59 *Four Preps*
1/56 **I Almost Lost My Mind** *Pat Boone*
93/57 **I Am** *Tony Bennett*
3/66 **I Am A Rock** *Simon & Garfunkel*
71/63 **I Am A Witness** *Tommy Hunt*
18/86 **I Am By Your Side** *Corey Hart*
56/75 **I Am I Am** *Smokey Robinson*
4/71 **I Am...I Said** *Neil Diamond*
49/83 **I Am Love** *Jennifer Holliday*
15/75 **I Am Love (Parts I & II)** *Jackson 5*
39/70 **I Am Somebody** *Johnnie Taylor*
94/76 **I Am Somebody** *Jimmy James*
56/67 **I Am The Walrus** *Beatles*
64/74 **I Am What I Am** *Lois Fletcher*
1/72 **I Am Woman** *Helen Reddy*
85/68 **I Am Your Man** *Bobby Taylor*
72/61 **I Apologize** *Timi Yuro*
97/71 **I Been Moved** *Andy Kim*
61/73 **I' Been Watchin' You** *South Side Movement*
8/58 **I Beg Of You** *Elvis Presley*
33/64 **I Believe** *Bachelors*
33/82 **I Believe** *Chilliwack*
96/65 **I Believe I'll Love On** *Jackie Wilson*
47/75 **I Believe I'm Gonna Love You** *Frank Sinatra*
67/66 **I Believe I'm Gonna Make It** *Joe Tex*
95/75 **I Believe In Father Christmas** *Greg Lake*
66/77 **I Believe In Love** *Kenny Loggins*
22/72 **I Believe In Music** *Gallery*
24/80 **I Believe In You** *Don Williams*
93/58 **I Believe In You** *Robert & Johnny*
11/73 **I Believe In You (You Believe In Me)** *Johnnie Taylor*
15/75 **(I Believe) There's Nothing Stronger Than Our Love...** *Paul Anka/Odia Coates*
I Believe You
27/77 *Dorothy Moore*
68/78 *Carpenters*
96/67 **I Believed It All** *Pozo-Seco Singers*
27/75 **I Belong To You** *Love Unlimited*
92/71 **I Bet He Don't Love You (Like I Love You)** *Intruders*
96/68 **I Call It Love** *Manhattans*
75/70 **I Call My Baby Candy** *Jaggerz*
83/80 **I Call Your Name** *Switch*
I Can Dance *see: Long Tall Glasses*
6/84 **I Can Dream About You** *Dan Hartman*
56/71 **(I Can Feel Those Vibrations) This Love Is Real** *Jackie Wilson*
97/68 **(I Can Feel Your Love) Slipping Away** *Barbara Mason*
I Can Hear Music
100/66 *Ronettes*
24/69 *Beach Boys*
1/74 **I Can Help** *Billy Swan*
81/73 **I Can Make It Thru The Days (But Oh Those Lonely Nights)** *Ray Charles*
I Can Make It With You
32/66 *Pozo-Seco Singers*
68/66 *Jackie DeShannon*
6/65 **I Can Never Go Home Anymore** *Shangri-Las*
51/68 **I Can Remember** *James & Bobby Purify*
1/72 **I Can See Clearly Now** *Johnny Nash*
9/67 **I Can See For Miles** *Who*
(I Can See It In Your Eyes) *see: Circle Is Small*
22/69 **I Can Sing A Rainbow (medley)** *Dells*
91/80 **I Can Survive** *Triumph*
39/81 **I Can Take Care Of Myself** *Billy & The Beaters*
22/68 **I Can Take Or Leave Your Loving** *Herman's Hermits*
35/73 **I Can Understand It** *New Birth*
80/76 **I Can't Ask For Anymore Than You** *Cliff Richard*
89/69 **I Can't Be All Bad** *Johnny Adams*
90/70 **I Can't Be You (You Can't Be Me)** *Glass House*
60/68 **I Can't Believe I'm Losing You** *Frank Sinatra*
71/70 **I Can't Believe That You've Stopped Loving Me** *Charley Pride*
95/64 **I Can't Believe What You Say (For Seeing What You Do)** *Ike & Tina Turner*
72/66 **I Can't Believe You Love Me** *Tammi Terrell*
43/66 **I Can't Control Myself** *Troggs*
42/68 **I Can't Dance To That Music You're Playin'** *Martha & The Vandellas*
98/69 **I Can't Do Enough** *Dells*
87/61 **I Can't Do It By Myself** *Anita Bryant*
26/84 **I Can't Drive 55** *Sammy Hagar*
93/65 **I Can't Explain** *Who*
I Can't Get Next To You
1/69 *Temptations*
60/71 *Al Green*
(I Can't Get No) Satisfaction
1/65 *Rolling Stones*
31/66 *Otis Redding*
I Can't Get You Out Of My Heart
44/59 *Al Martino*
99/64 *Al Martino*
100/66 **I Can't Give You Anything But Love** *Bert Kaempfert*
1/82 **I Can't Go For That (No Can Do)** *Daryl Hall & John Oates*
86/67 **I Can't Go On Livin' Without You, Baby** *Nino Tempo & April Stevens*
34/66 **I Can't Grow Peaches On A Cherry Tree** *Just Us*
66/64 **I Can't Hear You** *Betty Everett*
29/76 **I Can't Hear You No More** *Helen Reddy*
12/80 **I Can't Help It** *Olivia Newton-John & Andy Gibb*

I Can't Help It (If I'm Still In Love With You)
74/58 *Margaret Whiting*
64/60 *Adam Wade*
24/62 *Johnny Tillotson*
94/67 *B.J. Thomas*
97/69 *Al Martino*
77/77 **I Can't Help Myself** *Eddie Rabbitt*
I Can't Help Myself (Sugar Pie, Honey Bunch)
1/65 *Four Tops*
90/67 *Magnificent Men (medley)*
22/72 *Donnie Elbert*
40/80 *Bonnie Pointer*
39/60 **(I Can't Help You) I'm Falling Too** *Skeeter Davis*
(also see: Please Help Me I'm Falling)
13/84 **I Can't Hold Back** *Survivor*
76/78 **I Can't Hold On** *Karla Bonoff*
50/74 **I Can't Leave You Alone** *George McCrae*
42/70 **I Can't Leave Your Love Alone** *Clarence Carter*
I Can't Let Go
42/66 *Hollies*
31/80 *Linda Ronstadt*
46/76 **I Can't Live A Dream** *Osmonds*
22/56 **I Can't Love You Enough** *LaVern Baker*
I Can't Make It Alone
95/68 *Bill Medley*
63/69 *Lou Rawls*
95/67 **I Can't Make It Anymore** *Spyder Turner*
67/69 **I Can't Quit Her** *Arbors*
90/60 **I Can't Say Goodbye** *Fireflies*
92/62 **I Can't Say Goodbye** *Bobby Vee*
88/81 **I Can't Say Goodbye To You** *Helen Reddy*
78/69 **I Can't Say No To You** *Betty Everett*
28/69 **I Can't See Myself Leaving You** *Aretha Franklin*
94/59 **I Can't Sit Down** *Marie & Rex*
10/81 **I Can't Stand It** *Eric Clapton*
46/64 **I Can't Stand It** *Soul Sisters*
14/79 **I Can't Stand It No More** *Peter Frampton*
28/68 **I Can't Stand Myself (When You Touch Me)** *James Brown*
48/83 **I Can't Stand Still** *Don Henley*
I Can't Stand The Rain
38/73 *Ann Peebles*
18/78 *Eruption*
45/73 **I Can't Stand To See You Cry** *Miracles*
80/67 **I Can't Stay Away From You** *Impressions*
7/63 **I Can't Stay Mad At You** *Skeeter Davis*
48/65 **I Can't Stop** *Honeycombs*
96/71 **I Can't Stop** *Osmonds*
9/68 **I Can't Stop Dancing** *Archie Bell & The Drells*
I Can't Stop Loving You
81/58 *Don Gibson*
1/62 *Ray Charles*
77/63 *Count Basie*
35/64 **I Can't Stop Talking About You** *Steve & Eydie*
77/80 **I Can't Stop The Feelin'** *Pure Prairie League*
46/65 **I Can't Stop Thinking Of You** *Bobbi Martin*
92/61 **I Can't Take It** *Mary Ann Fisher*
82/70 **I Can't Tell The Bottom From The Top** *Hollies*
8/80 **I Can't Tell You Why** *Eagles*
I Can't Turn You Loose
37/68 *Chambers Brothers*
81/72 *Edgar Winter*
3/86 **I Can't Wait** *Nu Shooz*
16/86 **I Can't Wait** *Stevie Nicks*
80/78 **I Can't Wait Any Longer** *Bill Anderson*
93/64 **I Can't Wait Until I See My Baby** *Justine Washington*
60/65 **I Can't Work No Longer** *Billy Butler*
79/83 **I Cannot Believe It's True** *Phil Collins*
92/77 **I Caught Your Act** *Hues Corporation*
60/76 **I Cheat The Hangman** *Doobie Brothers*
32/66 **I Chose To Sing The Blues** *Ray Charles*
80/66 **I Confess** *New Colony Six*
52/80 **I Could Be Good For You** *707*
56/67 **I Could Be So Good To You** *Don & The Goodtimes*
93/67 **I Could Be So Happy** *Magnificent Men*
I Could Have Danced All Night
20/56 *Sylvia Syms*
49/56 *Rosemary Clooney*
93/56 *Dinah Shore*
72/63 *Ben E. King*
72/76 *Biddu Orchestra*
57/62 **I Could Have Loved You So Well** *Ray Peterson*
93/72 **I Could Never Be Happy** *Emotions*
48/69 **I Could Never Be President** *Johnnie Taylor*
50/69 **I Could Never Lie To You** *New Colony Six*
13/68 **I Could Never Love Another (After Loving You)** *Temptations*
18/81 **I Could Never Miss You (More Than I Do)** *Lulu*
46/70 **I Could Write A Book** *Jerry Butler*
9/66 **I Couldn't Live Without Your Love** *Petula Clark*
32/83 **I Couldn't Say No** *Robert Ellis Orrall with Carlene Carter*
17/61 **I Count The Tears** *Drifters*
I Cried
99/63 *Tammy Montgomery*
50/71 *James Brown*
91/59 **I Cried** *Joe Damiano*
6/59 **I Cried A Tear** *LaVern Baker*
68/63 **(I Cried At) Laura's Wedding** *Barbara Lynn*
69/61 **I Cried My Last Tear** *Ernie K-Doe*
67/84 **I Cry Just A Little Bit** *Shakin' Stevens*
35/72 **I Didn't Know I Loved You (Till I Saw You Rock And Roll)** *Gary Glitter*
92/64 **I Didn't Know What Time It Was** *Crampton Sisters*
I Didn't Mean To Turn You On
79/84 *Cherrelle*
2/86 *Robert Palmer*
83/71 **I Dig Everything About You** *Mob*
46/59 **I Dig Girls** *Bobby Rydell*
83/67 **I Dig Girls** *J.J. Jackson*
9/67 **I Dig Rock And Roll Music** *Peter, Paul & Mary*
60/67 **I Dig You Baby** *Jerry Butler*
I Do
37/65 *Marvelows*
24/83 *J. Geils Band*
62/69 **I Do** *Moments*
84/79 **I Do Believe In You** *Pages*
15/76 **I Do, I Do, I Do, I Do, I Do** *Abba*
I Do Love You
26/65 *Billy Stewart*
94/69 *Billy Stewart*
20/79 *GQ*
48/70 **I Do Take You** *Three Degrees*
(I Do The) *see: Shimmmy Shimmy*
91/79 **I Do The Rock** *Tim Curry*
23/86 **I Do What I Do...** *John Taylor*
29/84 **I Do'wanna Know** *REO Speedwagon*
18/71 **I Don't Blame You At All** *Miracles*
39/83 **I Don't Care Anymore** *Phil Collins*
74/56 **I Don't Care If The Sun Don't Shine** *Elvis Presley*

92/64 **I Don't Care (Just As Long As You Love Me)** *Buck Owens*
62/59 **(I Don't Care) Only Love Me** *Steve Lawrence*
64/59 **I Don't Know** *Ruth Brown*
I Don't Know How To Love Him
13/71 *Helen Reddy*
28/71 *Yvonne Elliman*
99/71 *Kimberlys (medley)*
23/79 **I Don't Know If It's Right** *Evelyn 'Champagne' King*
61/60 **I Don't Know What It Is** *Bluenotes*
67/73 **I Don't Know What It Is, But It Sure Is Funky** *Ripple*
92/65 **I Don't Know What You've Got But It's Got Me** *Little Richard*
35/82 **I Don't Know Where To Start** *Eddie Rabbitt*
12/61 **I Don't Know Why** *Linda Scott*
I Don't Know Why
39/69 *Stevie Wonder*
42/75 *Rolling Stones*
I Don't Know Why *see: But I Do*
72/61 **I Don't Like It Like That** *Bobbettes*
(also see: I Like It Like That)
73/80 **I Don't Like Mondays** *Boomtown Rats*
8/75 **I Don't Like To Sleep Alone** *Paul Anka*
41/77 **I Don't Love You Anymore** *Teddy Pendergrass*
47/62 **I Don't Love You No More (I Don't Care About You)** *Jimmy Norman*
47/61 **I Don't Mind** *James Brown*
I Don't Need No Doctor
72/66 *Ray Charles*
73/71 *Humble Pie*
81/72 *New Riders Of The Purple Sage*
3/81 **I Don't Need You** *Kenny Rogers*
56/81 **I Don't Need You** *Rupert Holmes*
86/80 **I Don't Need You Anymore** *Jackie DeShannon*
98/59 **I Don't Need You Anymore** *Teddy Bears*
47/74 **I Don't See Me In Your Eyes Anymore** *Charlie Rich*
37/64 **I Don't Wanna Be A Loser** *Lesley Gore*
53/83 **I Don't Wanna Dance** *Eddy Grant*
43/78 **I Don't Wanna Go** *Joey Travolta*
100/76 **I Don't Wanna Leave You** *Debbie Taylor*
42/79 **I Don't Wanna Lose You** *Daryl Hall & John Oates*
86/71 **I Don't Wanna Lose You** *Johnnie Taylor*
35/65 **I Don't Wanna Lose You Baby** *Chad & Jeremy*
51/76 **I Don't Wanna Lose Your Love** *Emotions*
47/79 **I Don't Want Nobody Else (To Dance With You)** *Narada Michael Walden*
20/69 **I Don't Want Nobody To Give Me Nothing** *James Brown*
I Don't Want Nobody (To Have My Love But You)
75/56 *Woody Herman*
78/61 *Ella Johnson with Buddy Johnson*
99/75 **I Don't Want To Be A Lone Ranger** *Johnny 'Guitar' Watson*
22/64 **I Don't Want To Be Hurt Anymore** *Nat King Cole*
87/80 **I Don't Want To Be Lonely** *Dana Valery*
I Don't Want To Cry
36/61 *Chuck Jackson*
97/69 *Ruby Winters*
50/70 *Ronnie Dyson*
17/71 **I Don't Want To Do Wrong** *Gladys Knight & The Pips*
95/64 **I Don't Want To Hear Anymore** *Jerry Butler*
65/81 **I Don't Want To Know Your Name** *Glen Campbell*
84/67 **I Don't Want To Lose You** *Jackie Wilson*
48/73 **(I Don't Want To Love You But) You Got Me Anyway** *Sutherland Brothers & Quiver*
91/73 **I Don't Want To Make You Wait** *Delfonics*
34/64 **I Don't Want To See Tomorrow** *Nat King Cole*
16/64 **I Don't Want To See You Again** *Peter & Gordon*
39/65 **I Don't Want To Spoil The Party** *Beatles*
33/61 **I Don't Want To Take A Chance** *Mary Wells*
46/80 **I Don't Want To Talk About It** *Rod Stewart*
I Don't Want To Walk Without You
79/64 *Phyllis McGuire*
36/80 *Barry Manilow*
9/57 **I Dreamed** *Betty Johnson*
47/75 **I Dreamed Last Night** *Justin Hayward/John Lodge*
20/61 **I Dreamed Of A Hill-Billy Heaven** *Tex Ritter*
66/83 **I Eat Cannibals** *Total Coelo*
76/86 **I Engineer** *Animotion*
12/61 **I Fall To Pieces** *Patsy Cline*
97/66 **I Feel A Sin Coming On** *Solomon Burke*
21/74 **I Feel A Song (In My Heart)** *Gladys Knight & The Pips*
1/64 **I Feel Fine** *Beatles*
3/84 **I Feel For You** *Chaka Khan*
38/57 **I Feel Good** *Shirley & Lee*
64/67 **I Feel Good (I Feel Bad)** *Lewis & Clarke Expedition*
F/76 **I Feel Like A Bullet (In The Gun Of Robert Ford)** *Elton John*
6/77 **I Feel Love** *Donna Summer*
75/74 **I Feel Sanctified** *Commodores*
I Feel So Bad
5/61 *Elvis Presley*
91/67 *Little Milton*
68/71 *Ray Charles*
84/57 **I Feel The Beat** *Jim Lowe*
F/71 **I Feel The Earth Move** *Carole King*
82/86 **I Feel The Magic** *Belinda Carlisle*
45/67 **I Fooled You This Time** *Gene Chandler*
80/60 **I Forgot More Than You'll Ever Know** *Sonny James*
45/69 **I Forgot To Be Your Lover** *William Bell*
I Fought The Law
9/66 *Bobby Fuller Four*
54/75 *Sam Neely*
30/65 **I Found A Girl** *Jan & Dean*
I Found A Love
75/62 *Falcons*
32/67 *Wilson Pickett*
67/65 **I Found A Love Oh What A Love** *Jo Ann & Troy*
90/62 **I Found A New Baby** *Bobby Darin*
42/68 **I Found A True Love** *Wilson Pickett*
93/62 **I Found Love** *Jackie Wilson & Linda Hopkins*
F/72 **I Found My Dad** *Joe Simon*
31/82 **I Found Somebody** *Glenn Frey*
90/86 **I Found Someone** *Laura Branigan*
47/73 **I Found Sunshine** *Chi-Lites*
F/70 **I Found That Girl** *Jackson 5*
1/64 **I Get Around** *Beach Boys*
32/82 **I Get Excited** *Rick Springfield*
52/75 **I Get High On You** *Sly Stone*
37/75 **I Get Lifted** *George McCrae*
79/80 **I Get Off On It** *Tony Joe White*
34/68 **I Get The Sweetest Feeling** *Jackie Wilson*
42/59 **I Go Ape** *Neil Sedaka*

7/78 **I Go Crazy** *Paul Davis*
I Go To Pieces
9/65 *Peter & Gordon*
66/75 *Cotton, Lloyd & Christian*
46/79 **I Go To Rio** *Pablo Cruise*
44/72 **I Got A Bag Of My Own** *James Brown*
10/58 **I Got A Feeling** *Ricky Nelson*
25/69 **I Got A Line On You** *Spirit*
10/73 **I Got A Name** *Jim Croce*
95/70 **I Got A Problem** *Jesse Anderson*
73/68 **I Got A Sure Thing**
Ollie & The Nightingales
I Got A Thing About You Baby
see: I've Got A Thing
80/70 **I Got A Thing, You Got A Thing, Everybody's Got A Thing** *Funkadelic*
24/59 **I Got A Wife** *Mark IV*
I Got A Woman
20/62 *Jimmy McGriff*
48/63 *Freddie Scott*
49/63 *Rick Nelson*
79/65 *Ray Charles*
27/73 **I Got Ants In My Pants** *James Brown*
I Got Life *see: Ain't Got No*
20/79 **I Got My Mind Made Up (You Can Get It Girl)** *Instant Funk*
3/67 **I Got Rhythm** *Happenings*
92/72 **I Got Some Help I Don't Need** *B.B. King*
37/75 **I Got Stoned And I Missed It** *Jim Stafford*
43/59 **I Got Stripes** *Johnny Cash*
8/58 **I Got Stung** *Elvis Presley*
6/68 **I Got The Feelin'** *James Brown*
16/66 **I Got The Feelin' (Oh No No)** *Neil Diamond*
69/67 **I Got To Go Back (And Watch That Little Girl Dance)** *McCoys*
74/66 **I Got To Handle It** *Capitols*
43/76 **I Got To Know** *Starbuck*
96/71 **I Got To Tell Somebody** *Betty Everett*
28/63 **I Got What I Wanted** *Brook Benton*
99/67 **I Got What You Need** *Kim Weston*
53/80 **I Got You** *Split Enz*
I Got You Babe
1/65 *Sonny & Cher*
69/68 *Etta James*
28/85 *UB40 with Chrissie Hynde*
3/65 **I Got You (I Feel Good)** *James Brown*
2/72 **I Gotcha** *Joe Tex*
35/64 **I Gotta Dance To Keep From Crying**
Miracles
59/55 **I Gotta Go Get My Baby** *Teresa Brewer*
64/77 **I Gotta Keep Dancin'** *Carrie*
20/60 **I Gotta Know** *Elvis Presley*
93/70 **I Gotta Let You Go** *Martha & The Vandellas*
44/82 **I Gotta Try** *Michael McDonald*
61/66 **I Guess I'll Always Love You**
Isley Brothers
55/68 **I Guess I'll Have To Cry, Cry, Cry**
James Brown
85/72 **I Guess I'll Miss The Man** *Supremes*
82/64 **I Guess I'm Crazy** *Jim Reeves*
4/84 **I Guess That's Why They Call It The Blues** *Elton John*
34/69 **I Guess The Lord Must Be In New York City** *Nilsson*
17/67 **I Had A Dream** *Paul Revere & The Raiders*
41/64 **I Had A Talk With My Man** *Mitty Collier*
61/72 **I Had It All The Time** *Tyrone Davis*
11/67 **I Had Too Much To Dream (Last Night)**
Electric Prunes
67/74 **I Hate Hate** *Razzy*
36/64 **I Have A Boyfriend** *Chiffons*
50/75 **I Have A Dream** *Donny Osmond*
88/68 **I Have A Dream** *Rev. Martin Luther King*
91/65 **I Have Dreamed** *Chad & Jeremy*

87/70 **I Have Learned To Do Without You**
Mavis Staples
61/81 **I Have The Skill** *Sherbs*
1/65 **I Hear A Symphony** *Supremes*
53/71 **I Hear Those Church Bells Ringing** *Dusk*
30/66 **I Hear Trumpets Blow** *Tokens*
I Hear You Knocking
2/55 *Gale Storm*
67/61 *Fats Domino*
4/71 *Dave Edmunds*
58/80 **I Hear You Now** *Jon & Vangelis*
I Heard It Through The Grapevine
2/67 *Gladys Knight & The Pips*
1/68 *Marvin Gaye*
83/68 *King Curtis*
43/76 *Creedence Clearwater Revival*
79/81 *Roger*
99/70 **I Heard The Voice Of Jesus**
Turley Richards
I Honestly Love You
1/74 *Olivia Newton-John*
48/77 *Olivia Newton-John*
91/76 **I Hope We Get To Love In Time**
Marilyn McCoo & Billy Davis, Jr.
82/60 **I Idolize You** *Ike & Tina Turner*
1/84 **I Just Called To Say I Love You**
Stevie Wonder
65/79 **I Just Can't Control Myself**
Nature's Divine
62/74 **I Just Can't Get You Out Of My Mind**
Four Tops
9/70 **I Just Can't Help Believing** *B.J. Thomas*
70/62 **I Just Can't Help It** *Jackie Wilson*
94/64 **I Just Can't Say Goodbye** *Bobby Rydell*
95/75 **I Just Can't Say Goodbye** *Philly Devotions*
42/77 **I Just Can't Say No To You** *Parker McGee*
71/83 **I Just Can't Walk Away** *Four Tops*
17/57 **I Just Don't Know** *Four Lads*
I Just Don't Know What To Do With Myself
26/66 *Dionne Warwick*
61/70 *Gary Puckett*
17/61 **I Just Don't Understand** *Ann-Margret*
12/79 **I Just Fall In Love Again** *Anne Murray*
85/58 **I Just Thought You'd Like To Know**
Johnny Cash
93/72 **I Just Wanna Be Your Friend** *Lighthouse*
51/70 **I Just Wanna Keep It Together** *Paul Davis*
4/78 **I Just Wanna Stop** *Gino Vannelli*
1/77 **I Just Want To Be Your Everything**
Andy Gibb
7/71 **I Just Want To Celebrate** *Rare Earth*
I Just Want To Make Love To You
83/72 *Foghat*
33/77 *Foghat*
I Keep Forgettin'
55/62 *Chuck Jackson*
4/82 *Michael McDonald*
46/76 **I Kinda Miss You** *Manhattans*
85/59 **I Kneel At Your Throne** *Joe Medlin*
53/64 **I Knew It All The Time** *Dave Clark Five*
45/73 **I Knew Jesus (Before He Was A Star)**
Glen Campbell
77/86 **I Knew The Bride (When She Use To Rock And Roll)** *Nick Lowe*
I Knew You When
14/65 *Billy Joe Royal*
F/72 *Donny Osmond*
37/83 *Linda Ronstadt*
47/59 **I Know** *Perry Como*
19/79 **I Know A Heartache When I See One**
Jennifer Warnes
3/65 **I Know A Place** *Petula Clark*
96/63 **I Know I Know** *'Pookie' Hudson*
49/71 **I Know I'm In Love** *Chee-Chee & Peppy*

(I Know) I'm Losing You
8/66 *Temptations*
7/70 *Rare Earth*
24/71 *Rod Stewart with Faces*
80/87 *Uptown*
82/60 **I Know One** *Jim Reeves*
13/83 **I Know There's Something Going On** *Frida*
62/82 **I Know What Boys Like** *Waitresses*
81/60 **I Know What God Is** *Perry Como*
43/58 **I Know Where I'm Goin'** *George Hamilton IV*
56/66 **I Know You Better Than That** *Bobby Goldsboro*
3/62 **I Know (You Don't Love Me No More)** *Barbara George*
19/62 **I Left My Heart In San Francisco** *Tony Bennett*
74/62 **I Left My Heart In The Balcony** *Linda Scott*
96/61 **I Lied To My Heart** *Enchanters*
84/83 **I Like** *Men Without Hats*
3/77 **I Like Dreamin'** *Kenny Nolan*
17/64 **I Like It** *Gerry & The Pacemakers*
31/83 **I Like It** *DeBarge*
I Like It Like That
2/61 *Chris Kenner*
7/65 *Dave Clark Five*
84/75 *Loggins & Messina*
(also see: I Don't Like It Like That)
27/64 **I Like It Like That** *Miracles*
25/67 **I Like The Way** *Tommy James & The Shondells*
37/77 **I Like To Do It** *KC & The Sunshine Band*
28/74 **I Like To Live The Love** *B.B. King*
86/80 **I Like To Rock** *April Wine*
70/71 **I Like What You Give** *Nolan*
49/69 **I Like What You're Doing (To Me)** *Carla Thomas*
61/86 **I Like You** *Phyllis Nelson*
66/73 **I Like You** *Donovan*
8/57 **I Like Your Kind Of Love** *Andy Williams*
72/70 **I Like Your Lovin'** *Chi-Lites*
38/71 **I Likes To Do It** *People's Choice*
51/65 **I Live For The Sun** *Sunrays*
66/56 **I Look At You** *Lassies*
100/59 **I Looked At Heaven** *Tommy Edwards*
61/62 **I Lost My Baby** *Joey Dee*
81/84 **I Lost On Jeopardy** *'Weird Al' Yankovic*
12/74 **I Love** *Tom T. Hall*
1/81 **I Love A Rainy Night** *Eddie Rabbitt*
66/59 **I Love An Angel** *Little Bill & The Bluenotes*
I Love How You Love Me
5/61 *Paris Sisters*
9/68 *Bobby Vinton*
I Love Lucy *see: Disco Lucy*
50/75 **I Love Makin' Love To You** *Evie Sands*
87/56 **I Love Mickey** *Mickey Mantle & Teresa Brewer*
5/76 **I Love Music** *O'Jays*
94/69 **I Love My Baby** *Archie Bell & The Drells*
21/57 **I Love My Baby (My Baby Loves Me)** *Jill Corey*
24/74 **I Love My Friend** *Charlie Rich*
I Love My Girl
62/57 *Cozy Morley*
75/57 *Hilltoppers*
69/78 **I Love My Music** *Wild Cherry*
94/81 **I Love My Truck** *Glen Campbell*
63/66 **I Love Onions** *Susan Christie*
1/82 **I Love Rock 'N Roll** *Joan Jett*
5/78 **I Love The Nightlife (Disco 'Round)** *Alicia Bridges*
9/60 **I Love The Way You Love** *Marv Johnson*
90/80 **I Love Women** *Jim Hurt*
12/81 **I Love You** *Climax Blues Band*
14/68 **I Love You** *People*
22/62 **I Love You** *Volume's*
37/78 **I Love You** *Donna Summer*
63/70 **I Love You** *Otis Leaville*
97/57 **I Love You, Baby** *Paul Anka*
3/63 **I Love You Because** *Al Martino*
39/63 **(I Love You) Don't You Forget It** *Perry Como*
30/66 **I Love You Drops** *Vic Dana*
21/71 **I Love You For All Seasons** *Fuzz*
(I Love You) For Sentimental Reasons
17/58 *Sam Cooke*
60/61 *Cleftones*
81/78 **I Love You, I Love You, I Love You** *Ronnie McDowell*
40/60 **I Love You In The Same Old Way** *Paul Anka*
64/71 **I Love You Lady Dawn** *Bells*
28/55 **I Love You Madly** *Four Coins*
56/68 **I Love You Madly** *Fantastic Four*
9/64 **I Love You More And More Every Day** *Al Martino*
78/67 **I Love You More Than Words Can Say** *Otis Redding*
60/72 **I Love You More Than You'll Ever Know** *Donny Hathaway*
31/66 **I Love You One Thousand Times** *Platters*
42/58 **I Love You So** *Chantels*
70/65 **I Love You So** *Bobbi Martin*
71/57 **I Love You So Much It Hurts** *Charlie Gracie*
38/62 **I Love You The Way You Are** *Bobby Vinton*
98/61 **I Love You Yes I Do** *Bull Moose Jackson*
61/68 **I Loved And I Lost** *Impressions*
37/81 **I Loved 'Em Every One** *T.G. Sheppard*
18/59 **I Loves You, Porgy** *Nina Simone*
10/81 **I Made It Through The Rain** *Barry Manilow*
18/67 **I Make A Fool Of Myself** *Frankie Valli*
69/63 **I May Not Live To See Tomorrow** *Brian Hyland*
78/83 **I Melt With You** *Modern English*
37/68 **I Met Her In Church** *Box Tops*
49/58 **I Met Him On A Sunday** *Shirelles*
5/85 **I Miss You** *Klymaxx*
58/72 **I Miss You** *Harold Melvin & The Blue Notes*
60/74 **I Miss You** *Dells*
95/73 **I Miss You Baby** *Millie Jackson*
I Miss You So
34/57 *Chris Connor*
33/59 *Paul Anka*
34/65 *Little Anthony & The Imperials*
19/81 **I Missed Again** *Phil Collins*
44/60 **I Missed Me** *Jim Reeves*
52/86 **I Must Be Dreaming** *Giuffria*
69/59 **I Must Be Dreaming** *Nat King Cole*
31/65 **I Must Be Seeing Things** *Gene Pitney*
28/79 **I Need A Lover** *John Cougar*
83/77 **I Need A Man** *Grace Jones*
69/70 **I Need Help (I Can't Do It Alone)** *Bobby Byrd*
98/66 **I Need Love** *Barbara Mason*
75/62 **I Need Some One** *Belmonts*
22/66 **I Need Somebody** *? (Question Mark) & The Mysterians*
86/71 **I Need Someone (To Love Me)** *Z.Z. Hill*
25/76 **I Need To Be In Love** *Carpenters*
41/78 **I Need To Know** *Tom Petty*
9/72 **I Need You** *America*
37/82 **I Need You** *Paul Carrack*
48/83 **I Need You** *Pointer Sisters*
64/65 **I Need You** *Impressions*
75/65 **I Need You** *Chuck Jackson*

79/71 **I Need You** *Friends Of Distinction*
81/79 **I Need You** *Euclid Beach Band*
83/63 **I Need You** *Rick Nelson*
95/86 **I Need You** *Maurice White*
I Need You Now
98/60 *Joni James*
93/69 *Ronnie Dove*
98/65 **I Need You So** *Chuck Jackson & Maxine Brown*
85/57 **I Need You So Bad** *B.B. King*
36/84 **I Need You Tonight** *Peter Wolf*
49/79 **I Need Your Help Barry Manilow** *Ray Stevens*
4/59 **I Need Your Love Tonight** *Elvis Presley*
I Need Your Lovin'
93/57 *Conway Twitty*
62/59 *Roy Hamilton*
20/62 *Don Gardner & Dee Dee Ford*
37/81 **I Need Your Lovin'** *Teena Marie*
44/87 **I Need Your Loving** *Human League*
12/77 **I Never Cry** *Alice Cooper*
78/59 **I Never Felt Like This** *Jack Scott*
56/61 **I Never Knew** *Clyde McPhatter*
9/67 **I Never Loved A Man (The Way I Love You)** *Aretha Franklin*
61/73 **I Never Said Goodbye** *Engelbert Humperdinck*
84/79 **I Never Said I Love You** *Orsa Lia*
I Only Have Eyes For You
11/59 *Flamingos*
72/66 *Lettermen*
85/72 *Jerry Butler*
18/75 *Art Garfunkel*
22/56 **I Only Know I Love You** *Four Aces*
I Only Want To Be With You
12/64 *Dusty Springfield*
12/76 *Bay City Rollers*
83/80 *Tourists*
53/82 *Nicolette Larson*
I Pity The Fool
46/61 *Bobby Bland*
85/71 *Ann Peebles*
25/71 **I Play And Sing** *Dawn*
19/80 **I Pledge My Love** *Peaches & Herb*
60/82 **I Predict** *Sparks*
74/84 **I Pretend** *Kim Carnes*
57/56 **I Promise To Remember** *Frankie Lymon & The Teenagers*
62/68 **I Promise To Wait My Love** *Martha & The Vandellas*
I Put A Spell On You
80/66 *Alan Price Set*
58/68 *Creedence Clearwater Revival*
9/82 **I Ran (So Far Away)** *A Flock Of Seagulls*
39/82 **I Really Don't Need No Light** *Jeffrey Osborne*
I Really Don't Want To Know
18/60 *Tommy Edwards*
93/62 *Solomon Burke*
61/63 *Esther Phillips*
22/66 *Ronnie Dove*
21/71 *Elvis Presley*
29/61 **I Really Love You** *Stereos*
78/65 **I Really Love You** *Dee Dee Sharp*
90/72 **I Received A Letter** *Delbert & Glen*
86/61 **I Remember** *Maurice Williams*
98/70 **(I Remember) Summer Morning** *Vanity Fare*
5/62 **I Remember You** *Frank Ifield*
36/64 **I Rise, I Fall** *Johnny Tillotson*
42/74 **I Saw A Man And He Danced With His Wife** *Cher*
51/56 **I Saw Esau** *Ames Brothers*
5/66 **I Saw Her Again** *Mamas & The Papas*
14/64 **I Saw Her Standing There** *Beatles*
14/63 **I Saw Linda Yesterday** *Dickey Lee*
16/72 **I Saw The Light** *Todd Rundgren*
I Say A Little Prayer
4/67 *Dionne Warwick*
10/68 *Aretha Franklin*
81/71 *Glen Campbell & Anne Murray (medley)*
72/68 **I Say Love** *Royal Guardsmen*
4/67 **I Second That Emotion** *Miracles*
26/66 **I See The Light** *Five Americans*
82/64 **I See You** *Cathy & Joe*
77/84 **I Send A Message** *INXS*
67/69 **I Shall Be Released** *Box Tops*
38/74 **I Shall Sing** *Garfunkel*
52/60 **I Shot Mr. Lee** *Bobbettes*
1/74 **I Shot The Sheriff** *Eric Clapton*
64/64 **I Should Care** *Gloria Lynne*
53/64 **I Should Have Known Better** *Beatles*
66/80 **I Shoulda Loved Ya** *Narada Michael Walden*
15/62 **I Sold My Heart To The Junkman** *Blue-Belles*
98/66 **I Spy (For The FBI)** *Jamo Thomas*
I Stand Accused
61/64 *Jerry Butler*
42/70 *Isaac Hayes*
74/67 **I Stand Accused (Of Loving You)** *Glories*
6/69 **I Started A Joke** *Bee Gees*
86/70 **I Started Loving You Again** *Al Martino*
70/69 **I Still Believe In Tomorrow** *John & Anne Ryder*
12/84 **I Still Can't Get Over Loving You** *Ray Parker Jr.*
51/59 **I Still Get A Thrill (Thinking Of You)** *Joni James*
I Still Get Jealous
63/59 *Joni James*
45/64 *Louis Armstrong*
39/79 **I Still Have Dreams** *Richie Furay*
79/57 **I Still Love You** *Fats Domino*
84/65 **I Still Love You** *Vejtables*
87/86 **I Still Want You** *Del Fuegos*
98/66 **I Struck It Rich** *Len Barry*
71/81 **I Surrender** *Arlan Day*
78/66 **I Surrender** *Fontella Bass*
87/62 **I Surrender, Dear** *Aretha Franklin*
75/69 **I Take A Lot Of Pride In What I Am** *Dean Martin*
12/67 **I Take It Back** *Sandy Posey*
41/67 **I Take What I Want** *James & Bobby Purify*
77/59 **I Talk To The Trees** *Edmundo Ros*
13/67 **I Thank The Lord For The Night Time** *Neil Diamond*
I Thank You
9/68 *Sam & Dave*
94/72 *Donny Hathaway & June Conquest*
34/80 *ZZ Top*
1/70 **I Think I Love You** *Partridge Family*
97/70 **I Think I Love You Again** *Brenda Lee*
55/59 **I Think I'm Gonna Kill Myself** *Buddy Knox*
16/86 **I Think It's Love** *Jermaine Jackson*
53/71 **I Think Of You** *Perry Como*
I Think We're Alone Now
4/67 *Tommy James & The Shondells*
45/77 *Rubinoos*
94/83 **I Think You'll Remember Tonight** *Axe*
47/76 **I Thought It Took A Little Time** *Diana Ross*
85/69 **I Threw It All Away** *Bob Dylan*
70/59 **I Told Myself A Lie** *Clyde McPhatter*
81/62 **I Told The Brook** *Marty Robbins*
85/61 **I Told You So** *Jimmy Jones*
23/69 **I Turned You On** *Isley Brothers*

I Understand (Just How You Feel)
9/61 *G-Clefs*
36/65 *Freddie & The Dreamers*
33/59 **I Waited Too Long** *LaVern Baker*
59/61 **I Wake Up Crying** *Chuck Jackson*
65/68 **I Walk Alone** *Marty Robbins*
I Walk The Line
17/56 *Johnny Cash*
59/59 *Don Costa*
66/60 *Jaye P. Morgan*
F/57 **I Wanna** *Platters*
12/86 **I Wanna Be A Cowboy** *Boys Don't Cry*
14/63 **I Wanna Be Around** *Tony Bennett*
94/71 **I Wanna Be Free** *Loretta Lynn*
20/59 **I Wanna Be Loved** *Ricky Nelson*
91/64 **I Wanna Be Loved** *Dean & Jean*
16/72 **I Wanna Be Where You Are** *Michael Jackson*
16/73 **I Wanna Be With You** *Raspberries*
I Wanna Be With You
57/64 *Nancy Wilson*
41/66 *Dee Dee Warwick*
68/65 **I Wanna Be (Your Everything)** *Manhattans*
11/80 **I Wanna Be Your Lover** *Prince*
23/75 **I Wanna Dance Wit' Choo** *Disco Tex & The Sex-O-Lettes*
71/59 **(I Wanna) Dance With The Teacher** *Olympics*
51/77 **I Wanna Do It To You** *Jerry Butler*
10/77 **I Wanna Get Next To You** *Rose Royce*
I Wanna Go Back
78/84 *Billy Satellite*
14/87 *Eddie Money*
75/55 **I Wanna Go Where You Go** *Eddie Fisher*
35/85 **I Wanna Hear It From Your Lips** *Eric Carmen*
81/70 **I Wanna Know If It's Good To You?** *Funkadelic*
60/73 **I Wanna Know Your Name** *Intruders*
44/75 **I Wanna Learn A Love Song** *Harry Chapin*
36/68 **I Wanna Live** *Glen Campbell*
9/64 **I Wanna Love Him So Bad** *Jelly Beans*
39/61 **(I Wanna) Love My Life Away** *Gene Pitney*
85/66 **I Wanna Meet You** *Cryan' Shames*
68/84 **I Wanna Rock** *Twisted Sister*
49/76 **I Wanna Stay With You** *Gallagher & Lyle*
(I Wanna) Testify
20/67 *Parliaments*
36/69 *Johnnie Taylor*
21/61 **I Wanna Thank You** *Bobby Rydell*
91/64 **I Wanna Thank You** *Enchanters*
6/84 **I Want A New Drug** *Huey Lewis & The News*
I Want Candy
11/65 *Strangeloves*
62/82 *Bow Wow Wow*
92/65 **I Want My Baby Back** *Jimmy Cross*
76/85 **I Want My Girl** *Jesse Johnson's Revue*
74/66 **I Want Someone** *Mad Lads*
I Want To *also see: I Wanna & I Want'a*
44/75 **I Want To Be Free** *Ohio Players*
I Want To Be Happy Cha Cha
48/58 *Enoch Light*
70/58 *Tommy Dorsey Orchestra*
76/62 **I Want To Be Loved** *Dinah Washington*
1/60 **I Want To Be Wanted** *Brenda Lee*
45/84 **I Want To Break Free** *Queen*
84/75 **I Want To Dance With You (Dance With Me)** *Ritchie Family*
I Want To (Do Everything For You)
23/65 *Joe Tex*
96/70 *Raeletts*
36/66 **I Want To Go With You** *Eddy Arnold*
I Want To Hold Your Hand
1/64 *Beatles*
55/64 *Boston Pops Orchestra/Arthur Fiedler*
1/85 **I Want To Know What Love Is** *Foreigner*
55/78 **I Want To Live** *John Denver*
81/69 **I Want To Love You Baby** *Peggy Scott & Jo Jo Benson*
54/67 **I Want To Love You For What You Are** *Ronnie Dove*
97/86 **I Want To Make The World Turn Around** *Steve Miller Band*
72/65 **I Want To Meet Him** *Royalettes*
95/71 **I Want To Pay You Back (For Loving Me)** *Chi-Lites*
28/63 **I Want To Stay Here** *Steve & Eydie*
I Want To Take You Higher
60/69 *Sly & The Family Stone*
34/70 *Ike & Tina Turner*
38/70 *Sly & The Family Stone*
98/67 **I Want To Talk About You** *Ray Charles*
8/59 **I Want To Walk You Home** *Fats Domino*
15/76 **I Want You** *Marvin Gaye*
20/66 **I Want You** *Bob Dylan*
84/86 **I Want You** *Animotion*
1/70 **I Want You Back** *Jackson 5*
95/65 **I Want You Back Again** *Zombies*
37/81 **I Want You, I Need You** *Chris Christian*
1/56 **I Want You, I Need You, I Love You** *Elvis Presley*
55/78 **I Want You To Be Mine** *Kayak*
I Want You To Be My Baby
14/55 *Georgia Gibbs*
18/55 *Lillian Briggs*
83/67 *Ellie Greenwich*
I Want You To Be My Girl (Boy)
13/56 *Frankie Lymon & The Teenagers*
98/65 *Exciters*
48/58 **I Want You To Know** *Fats Domino*
65/69 **I Want You To Know** *New Colony Six*
43/64 **I Want You To Meet My Baby** *Eydie Gorme*
7/79 **I Want You To Want Me** *Cheap Trick*
19/79 **I Want You Tonight** *Pablo Cruise*
7/79 **I Want Your Love** *Chic*
15/75 **I Want'a Do Something Freaky To You** *Leon Haywood*
42/62 **(I Was) Born To Cry** *Dion*
76/85 **I Was Born To Love You** *Freddie Mercury*
29/73 **I Was Checkin' Out She Was Checkin' In** *Don Covay*
20/67 **I Was Kaiser Bill's Batman** *Whistling Jack Smith*
78/80 **I Was Looking For Someone To Love** *Leif Garrett*
10/79 **I Was Made For Dancin'** *Leif Garrett*
11/79 **I Was Made For Lovin' You** *Kiss*
I Was Made To Love Her
2/67 *Stevie Wonder*
76/68 *King Curtis*
22/78 **I Was Only Joking** *Rod Stewart*
I Was Such A Fool (To Fall In Love With You)
71/60 *Flamingos*
24/62 *Connie Francis*
19/56 **I Was The One** *Elvis Presley*
100/71 **I Was Wondering** *Poppy Family*
88/74 **I Wash My Hands Of The Whole Damn Deal** *New Birth*
19/66 **(I Washed My Hands In) Muddy Water** *Johnny Rivers*
I (Who Have Nothing)
29/63 *Ben E. King*
46/67 *Terry Knight*
14/70 *Tom Jones*
82/70 *Liquid Smoke*
40/79 *Sylvester*

I Will
47/62 *Vic Dana*
10/65 *Dean Martin*
53/82 **I Will Always Love You** *Dolly Parton*
22/68 **I Will Always Think About You** *New Colony Six*
30/79 **I Will Be In Love With You** *Livingston Taylor*
41/78 **(I Will Be Your) Shadow In The Street** *Allan Clarke*
81/84 **I Will Follow** *U2*
1/63 **I Will Follow Him** *Little Peggy March*
85/63 **I Will Live My Life For You** *Tony Bennett*
65/63 **I Will Love You** *Richard Chamberlain*
61/72 **I Will Never Pass This Way Again** *Glen Campbell*
29/78 **I Will Still Love You** *Stonebolt*
1/79 **I Will Survive** *Gloria Gaynor*
1/77 **I Wish** *Stevie Wonder*
42/58 **I Wish** *Platters*
68/68 **I Wish I Knew** *Solomon Burke*
49/80 **I Wish I Was Eighteen Again** *George Burns*
62/71 **I Wish I Were** *Andy Kim*
32/63 **I Wish I Were A Princess** *Little Peggy March*
52/60 **I Wish I'd Never Been Born** *Patti Page*
57/74 **I Wish It Was Me** *Tyrone Davis*
94/74 **I Wish It Was Me You Loved** *Dells*
I Wish It Would Rain
4/68 *Temptations*
41/68 *Gladys Knight & The Pips*
16/62 **I Wish That We Were Married** *Ronnie & The Hi-Lites*
70/67 **I Wish You Could Be Here** *Cyrkle*
28/64 **I Wish You Love** *Gloria Lynne*
72/56 **I Woke Up Crying** *Joni James*
13/71 **I Woke Up In Love This Morning** *Partridge Family*
79/83 **I Won't Be Home Tonight** *Tony Carey*
93/64 **I Won't Forget You** *Jim Reeves*
10/83 **I Won't Hold You Back** *Toto*
I Won't Last A Day Without You
89/73 *Maureen McGovern*
11/74 *Carpenters*
70/75 *Al Wilson (medley)*
80/65 **I Won't Love You Anymore (Sorry)** *Lesley Gore*
42/71 **I Won't Mention It Again** *Ray Price*
35/83 **I Won't Stand In Your Way** *Stray Cats*
25/63 **I Wonder** *Brenda Lee*
F/57 **I Wonder If I Care As Much** *Everly Brothers*
34/85 **I Wonder If I Take You Home** *Lisa Lisa & Cult Jam with Full Force*
84/61 **I Wonder (If Your Love Will Ever Belong To Me)** *Pentagons*
8/68 **I Wonder What She's Doing Tonight** *Tommy Boyce & Bobby Hart*
21/63 **I Wonder What She's Doing Tonight** *Barry & The Tamerlanes*
93/64 **I Wonder Who's Kissing Her Now** *Bobby Darin*
22/58 **I Wonder Why** *Dion & The Belmonts*
98/68 **I Worry About You** *Joe Simon*
88/70 **I Would Be In Love (Anyway)** *Frank Sinatra*
8/85 **I Would Die 4 U** *Prince*
64/82 **I Wouldn't Beg For Water** *Sheena Easton*
20/82 **I Wouldn't Have Missed It For The World** *Ronnie Milsap*
93/62 **I Wouldn't Know (What To Do)** *Dinah Washington*
22/56 **I Wouldn't Know Where To Begin** *Eddy Arnold*
93/86 **I Wouldn't Lie** *Yarbrough & Peoples*
69/64 **I Wouldn't Trade You For The World** *Bachelors*
88/74 **I Wouldn't Treat A Dog (The Way You Treated Me)** *Bobby Bland*
36/77 **I Wouldn't Want To Be Like You** *Alan Parsons Project*
1/76 **I Write The Songs** *Barry Manilow*
77/72 **I Wrote A Simple Song** *Billy Preston*
52/86 **I'd Do It All Again** *Sam Harris*
88/74 **(I'd Know You) Anywhere** *Ashford & Simpson*
I'd Like To Teach The World To Sing (In Perfect Harmony)
7/72 *New Seekers*
13/72 *Hillside Singers*
40/71 **I'd Love To Change The World** *Ten Years After*
2/72 **I'd Love You To Want Me** *Lobo*
62/73 **I'd Rather Be A Cowboy** *John Denver*
46/69 **I'd Rather Be An Old Man's Sweetheart** *Candi Staton*
91/63 **I'd Rather Be Here In Your Arms** *Duprees*
70/71 **I'd Rather Be Sorry** *Ray Price*
38/80 **I'd Rather Leave While I'm In Love** *Rita Coolidge*
79/71 **I'd Rather Love You** *Charley Pride*
2/76 **I'd Really Love To See You Tonight** *England Dan & John Ford Coley*
15/69 **I'd Wait A Million Years** *Grass Roots*
65/56 **I'll Always Be In Love With You** *Jack Pleis*
62/77 **I'll Always Call Your Name** *Little River Band*
85/67 **I'll Always Have Faith In You** *Carla Thomas*
36/73 **I'll Always Love My Mama** *Intruders*
35/65 **I'll Always Love You** *Spinners*
60/64 **I'll Always Love You** *Brenda Holloway*
14/87 **I'll Be Alright Without You** *Journey*
3/72 **I'll Be Around** *Spinners*
62/85 **I'll Be Around** *What Is This*
78/56 **I'll Be Around** *Don Cherry*
8/65 **I'll Be Doggone** *Marvin Gaye*
92/66 **I'll Be Gone** *Pozo-Seco Singers*
47/85 **I'll Be Good** *Rene & Angela*
3/76 **I'll Be Good To You** *Brothers Johnson*
85/75 **I'll Be Holding On** *Al Downing*
I'll Be Home
4/56 *Pat Boone*
97/66 *Platters*
96/71 **I'll Be Home** *Vikki Carr*
33/64 **I'll Be In Trouble** *Temptations*
11/86 **I'll Be Over You** *Toto*
53/70 **I'll Be Right Here** *Tyrone Davis*
20/59 **I'll Be Satisfied** *Jackie Wilson*
I'll Be Seeing You
51/59 *Tommy Sands*
87/59 *Poni-Tails*
79/60 *Five Satins*
58/61 *Frank Sinatra*
67/77 **I'll Be Standing By** *Foghat*
66/68 **I'll Be Sweeter Tomorrow** *O'Jays*
36/74 **I'll Be The Other Woman** *Soul Children*
1/70 **I'll Be There** *Jackson 5*
12/61 **I'll Be There** *Damita Jo*
(also see: Stand By Me)
I'll Be There
79/60 *Bobby Darin*
14/65 *Gerry & The Pacemakers*
88/85 **I'll Be There** *Kenny Loggins*
(I'll Be With You In) Apple Blossom Time
31/59 *Tab Hunter*
52/65 *Wayne Newton*
62/74 **I'll Be Your Everything** *Percy Sledge*

40/73 **I'll Be Your Shelter (In Time Of Storm)** *Luther Ingram*
63/69 **I'll Bet You** *Funkadelic*
41/62 **I'll Bring It Home To You** *Carla Thomas* *(also see: Bring It On Home To Me)*
82/79 **I'll Come Running** *Livingston Taylor*
18/58 **I'll Come Running Back To You** *Sam Cooke*
25/64 **I'll Cry Instead** *Beatles*
40/75 **I'll Do For You Anything You Want Me To** *Barry White*
77/67 **I'll Do It For You** *Toussaint McCall*
58/82 **I'll Drink To You** *Duke Jupiter*
71/71 **I'll Erase Away Your Pain** *Whatnauts*
43/82 **I'll Fall In Love Again** *Sammy Hagar*
51/82 **I'll Find My Way Home** *Jon & Vangelis*
87/58 **I'll Get By (As Long As I Have You)** *Billy Williams*
71/76 **I'll Get Over You** *Crystal Gayle*
73/66 **I'll Go Crazy** *James Brown*
93/75 **I'll Go To My Grave Loving You** *Statler Brothers*
9/74 **I'll Have To Say I Love You In A Song** *Jim Croce*
45/69 **I'll Hold Out My Hand** *Clique*
84/61 **I'll Just Have A Cup Of Coffee (Then I'll Go)** *Claude Gray*
34/65 **I'll Keep Holding On** *Marvelettes*
30/64 **I'll Keep You Satisfied** *Billy J. Kramer with The Dakotas*
87/56 **I'll Know** *Sammy Davis, Jr.*
79/79 **I'll Know Her When I See Her** *Cooper Brothers*
63/66 **I'll Love You Forever** *Holidays*
21/65 **I'll Make All Your Dreams Come True** *Ronnie Dove*
72/67 **I'll Make Him Love Me** *Barbara Lewis*
85/58 **I'll Make It All Up To You** *Jerry Lee Lewis*
97/63 **I'll Make It Alright** *Valentinos*
52/64 **I'll Make You Mine** *Bobby Vee*
63/72 **I'll Make You Music** *Beverly Bremers*
9/71 **I'll Meet You Halfway** *Partridge Family*
94/61 **I'll Never Be Free** *Kay Starr*
14/62 **I'll Never Dance Again** *Bobby Rydell*
59/68 **I'll Never Do You Wrong** *Joe Tex*
I'll Never Fall In Love Again
49/67 *Tom Jones*
6/69 *Tom Jones*
I'll Never Fall In Love Again
93/69 *Burt Bacharach*
6/70 *Dionne Warwick*
75/59 **I'll Never Fall In Love Again** *Johnnie Ray*
I'll Never Find Another You
4/65 *Seekers*
97/67 *Sonny James*
52/56 **I'll Never Know** *Four Lads*
5/79 **I'll Never Love This Way Again** *Dionne Warwick*
24/57 **I'll Never Say 'Never Again' Again** *Dinah Shore*
25/61 **I'll Never Smile Again** *Platters*
13/55 **I'll Never Stop Loving You** *Doris Day*
83/61 **I'll Never Stop Wanting You** *Brian Hyland*
18/75 **I'll Play For You** *Seals & Crofts*
80/76 **I'll Play The Fool** *Dr. Buzzard's Original 'Savannah' Band*
(I'll Remember) see: *In The Still Of The Nite*
80/62 **I'll Remember Carol** *Tommy Boyce*
23/57 **I'll Remember Today** *Patti Page*
34/58 **I'll Remember Tonight** *Pat Boone*
93/59 **I'll Sail My Ship Alone** *Jerry Lee Lewis*
22/60 **I'll Save The Last Dance For You** *Damita Jo* *(also see: Save The Last Dance For Me)*
77/68 **I'll Say Forever My Love** *Jimmy Ruffin*
90/63 **I'll Search My Heart** *Johnny Mathis*
100/70 **I'll See Him Through** *Tammy Wynette*
32/62 **I'll See You In My Dreams** *Pat Boone*
87/75 **I'll Still Love You** *Jim Weatherly*
45/79 **I'll Supply The Love** *Toto*
89/60 **I'll Take Care Of You** *Bobby Bland*
39/67 **I'll Take Care Of Your Cares** *Frankie Laine*
30/66 **I'll Take Good Care Of You** *Garnet Mimms*
65/57 **I'll Take Romance** *Eydie Gorme*
25/63 **I'll Take You Home** *Drifters*
68/62 **I'll Take You Home** *Corsairs*
93/57 **I'll Take You Home Again Kathleen** *Slim Whitman*
1/72 **I'll Take You There** *Staple Singers*
51/65 **I'll Take You Where The Music's Playing** *Drifters*
25/64 **I'll Touch A Star** *Terry Stafford*
40/67 **I'll Try Anything** *Dusty Springfield*
I'll Try Something New
39/62 *Miracles*
25/69 *Supremes & Temptations*
41/82 *A Taste Of Honey*
9/83 **I'll Tumble 4 Ya** *Culture Club*
76/67 **I'll Turn To Stone** *Four Tops*
13/84 **I'll Wait** *Van Halen*
94/56 **I'll Wait** *Betty Johnson*
15/58 **I'll Wait For You** *Frankie Avalon*
I'll Walk The Line see: *I Walk The Line*
I'm A Believer
1/66 *Monkees*
51/71 *Neil Diamond*
38/69 **I'm A Better Man** *Engelbert Humperdinck*
46/69 **I'm A Drifter** *Bobby Goldsboro*
17/65 **I'm A Fool** *Dino, Desi & Billy*
97/67 **I'm A Fool For You** *James Carr*
I'm A Fool To Care
24/61 *Joe Barry*
94/61 *Oscar Black*
84/65 *Ray Charles*
35/71 **I'm A Greedy Man** *James Brown*
36/65 **I'm A Happy Man** *Jive Five*
38/59 **I'm A Hog For You** *Coasters*
I'm A Man
10/67 *Spencer Davis Group*
F/71 *Chicago*
17/65 **I'm A Man** *Yardbirds*
31/59 **I'm A Man** *Fabian*
24/68 **I'm A Midnight Mover** *Wilson Pickett*
57/66 **I'm A Nut** *Leroy Pullins*
75/74 **I'm A Ramblin' Man** *Waylon Jennings*
20/66 **(I'm A) Road Runner** *Jr. Walker & The All Stars*
94/73 **I'm A Rocker** *Raspberries*
76/73 **I'm A Stranger Here** *Five Man Electrical Band*
25/61 **I'm A Telling You** *Jerry Butler*
31/74 **I'm A Train** *Albert Hammond*
I'm A Woman
54/63 *Peggy Lee*
12/75 *Maria Muldaur*
61/74 **(I'm A) YoYo Man** *Rick Cunha*
63/63 **I'm Afraid To Go Home** *Brian Hyland*
16/80 **I'm Alive** *Electric Light Orchestra*
35/83 **I'm Alive** *Neil Diamond*
60/80 **I'm Alive** *Gamma*
61/75 **I'm Alive (medley)** *Blue Swede*
34/80 **I'm Almost Ready** *Pure Prairie League*
7/80 **I'm Alright** *Kenny Loggins*
20/55 **(I'm Always Hearing) Wedding Bells** *Eddie Fisher*
9/57 **I'm Available** *Margie Rayburn*

91/70 **I'm Better Off Without You** *Main Ingredient*
19/62 **I'm Blue (The Gong-Gong Song)** *Ikettes*
40/71 **I'm Comin' Home** *Tommy James*
75/71 **I'm Comin' Home** *Dave Edmunds*
39/66 **I'm Comin' Home, Cindy** *Trini Lopez*
19/61 **I'm Comin' On Back To You** *Jackie Wilson*
I'm Coming Home
75/73 *Johnny Mathis*
18/74 *Spinners*
42/72 **I'm Coming Home** *Stories*
57/68 **I'm Coming Home** *Tom Jones*
82/59 **I'm Coming Home** *Marv Johnson*
94/62 **I'm Coming Home** *Paul Anka*
5/80 **I'm Coming Out** *Diana Ross*
I'm Confessin' (That I Love You)
58/63 *Frank Ifield*
99/64 *Nino Tempo & April Stevens*
77/63 **I'm Crazy 'Bout My Baby** *Marvin Gaye*
19/64 **I'm Crying** *Animals*
17/73 **I'm Doin' Fine Now** *New York City*
95/63 **I'm Down To My Last Heartbreak** *Wilson Pickett*
50/77 **I'm Dreaming** *Jennifer Warnes*
17/76 **I'm Easy** *Keith Carradine*
21/78 **I'm Every Woman** *Chaka Khan*
96/77 **I'm Falling In Love (medley)** *Hodges, James & Smith*
86/74 **I'm Falling In Love With You** *Little Anthony & The Imperials*
90/86 **I'm For Real** *Howard Hewett*
37/69 **I'm Free** *Who*
22/84 **I'm Free (Heaven Helps The Man)** *Kenny Loggins*
(I'm Gettin') *see: Nuttin' For Christmas*
37/60 **I'm Gettin' Better** *Jim Reeves*
88/71 **I'm Girl Scoutin'** *Intruders*
9/85 **I'm Goin' Down** *Bruce Springsteen*
52/62 **I'm Going Back To School** *Dee Clark*
81/75 **(I'm Going By) The Stars In Your Eyes** *Dramatics*
70/77 **I'm Going Down** *Rose Royce*
98/71 **I'm Gonna Be A Country Girl Again** *Buffy Sainte-Marie*
17/59 **I'm Gonna Be A Wheel Some Day** *Fats Domino*
9/64 **I'm Gonna Be Strong** *Gene Pitney*
18/63 **I'm Gonna Be Warm This Winter** *Connie Francis*
95/62 **I'm Gonna Change Everything** *Jim Reeves*
63/59 **I'm Gonna Change Him** *Cathy Carr*
98/69 **I'm Gonna Do All I Can (To Do Right By My Man)** *Ike & Tina Turner*
74/68 **I'm Gonna Do What They Do To Me** *B.B. King*
3/59 **I'm Gonna Get Married** *Lloyd Price*
76/69 **I'm Gonna Hold On Long As I Can** *Marvelettes*
12/61 **I'm Gonna Knock On Your Door** *Eddie Hodges*
57/56 **I'm Gonna Laugh You Right Out Of My Life** *Nat King Cole*
40/76 **I'm Gonna Let My Heart Do The Walking** *Supremes*
84/81 **I'm Gonna Love Her For Both Of Us** *Meat Loaf*
84/56 **I'm Gonna Love You** *Ames Brothers*
86/70 **I'm Gonna Love You** *Intrigues*
3/73 **I'm Gonna Love You Just A Little More Baby** *Barry White*
56/65 **I'm Gonna Love You Too** *Hullaballoos*
I'm Gonna Make You Love Me
88/66 *Dee Dee Warwick*
26/68 *Madeline Bell*
2/69 *Supremes & Temptations*
91/78 **I'm Gonna Make You Love Me** *Blend*
10/69 **I'm Gonna Make You Mine** *Lou Christie*
90/66 **I'm Gonna Make You Mine** *Shadows Of Knight*
55/67 **I'm Gonna Miss You** *Artistics*
84/61 **I'm Gonna Move To The Outskirts Of Town** *Ray Charles*
3/57 **I'm Gonna Sit Right Down And Write Myself A Letter** *Billy Williams*
28/78 **I'm Gonna Take Care Of Everything** *Rubicon*
13/85 **I'm Gonna Tear Your Playhouse Down** *Paul Young*
85/62 **I'm Hanging Up My Heart For You** *Solomon Burke*
87/58 **I'm Happy** *Four Dates*
I'm Happy Just To Dance With You
95/64 *Beatles*
64/80 *Anne Murray*
27/80 **I'm Happy That Love Has Found You** *Jimmy Hall*
1/65 **I'm Henry VIII, I Am** *Herman's Hermits*
53/75 **I'm Her Fool** *Billy Swan*
76/62 **I'm Here To Get My Baby Out Of Jail** *Everly Brothers*
27/61 **I'm Hurtin'** *Roy Orbison*
98/68 **I'm Hypnotized** *Anthony & The Imperials*
51/68 **I'm In A Different World** *Four Tops*
I'm In Love
45/67 *Wilson Pickett*
19/74 *Aretha Franklin*
40/81 **I'm In Love** *Evelyn King*
I'm In Love Again
3/56 *Fats Domino*
38/56 *Fontane Sisters*
67/63 *Rick Nelson*
45/82 *Pia Zadora*
57/56 **I'm In Love With You** *Pat Boone*
38/61 **I'm In The Mood For Love** *Chimes*
2/77 **I'm In You** *Peter Frampton*
81/67 **I'm Indestructible** *Jack Jones*
98/68 **I'm Into Lookin' For Someone To Love Me** *Bobby Vee*
I'm Into Something Good
13/64 *Herman's Hermits*
38/64 *Earl-Jean*
I'm Just A Country Boy
F/57 *Harry Belafonte*
55/63 *George McCurn*
87/56 **I'm Just A Dancing Partner** *Platters*
88/66 **(I'm Just A) Fool For You** *Gene Chandler*
56/70 **I'm Just A Prisoner (Of Your Good Lovin')** *Candi Staton*
12/73 **I'm Just A Singer (In A Rock And Roll Band)** *Moody Blues*
94/71 **I'm Just Me** *Charley Pride*
60/81 **I'm Just Too Shy** *Jermaine Jackson*
33/61 **I'm Learning About Love** *Brenda Lee*
36/71 **I'm Leavin'** *Elvis Presley*
99/73 **I'm Leavin' You** *Engelbert Humperdinck*
I'm Leaving It Up To You
1/63 *Dale & Grace*
4/74 *Donny & Marie Osmond*
10/69 **I'm Livin' In Shame** *Supremes*
99/66 **I'm Living In Two Worlds** *Bonnie Guitar*
60/76 **I'm Mandy Fly Me** *10cc*
I'm Movin' On
40/59 *Ray Charles*
56/63 *Matt Lucas*
52/72 *John Kay*

37/73 **I'm Never Gonna Be Alone Anymore** *Cornelius Brothers & Sister Rose*
88/82 **I'm Never Gonna Say Goodbye** *Billy Preston*
36/59 **I'm Never Gonna Tell** *Jimmie Rodgers*
92/63 **I'm Not A Fool Anymore** *T.K. Hulin*
27/60 **I'm Not Afraid** *Ricky Nelson*
66/79 **I'm Not Gonna Cry Anymore** *Nancy Brooks*
14/78 **I'm Not Gonna Let It Bother Me Tonight** *Atlanta Rhythm Section*
2/75 **I'm Not In Love** *10cc*
4/75 **I'm Not Lisa** *Jessi Colter*
34/70 **I'm Not My Brothers Keeper** *Flaming Ember*
69/87 **I'm Not Perfect (But I'm Perfect For You)** *Grace Jones*
32/86 **I'm Not The One** *Cars*
20/67 **(I'm Not Your) Steppin' Stone** *Monkees*
6/85 **I'm On Fire** *Bruce Springsteen*
16/75 **I'm On Fire** *Dwight Twilley*
I'm On Fire
26/75 *5000 Volts*
78/75 *Jim Gilstrap*
98/64 **I'm On Fire** *Jerry Lee Lewis*
74/78 **I'm On My Way** *Captain & Tennille*
90/62 **I'm On My Way** *Highwaymen*
15/64 **I'm On The Outside (Looking In)** *Little Anthony & The Imperials*
93/65 **I'm Over You** *Jan Bradley*
16/59 **I'm Ready** *Fats Domino*
9/66 **I'm Ready For Love** *Martha & The Vandellas*
89/65 **I'm Satisfied** *San Remo Golden Strings*
41/63 **I'm Saving My Love** *Skeeter Davis*
61/77 **I'm Scared** *Burton Cummings*
74/57 **I'm Serious** *Hilltoppers*
74/69 **(I'm So) Afraid Of Losing You Again** *Charley Pride*
71/79 **I'm So Anxious** *Southside Johnny & The Jukes*
I'm So Excited
30/82 *Pointer Sisters*
9/84 *Pointer Sisters*
95/71 **I'm So Glad** *Fuzz*
53/70 **I'm So Glad I Fell For You** *David Ruffin*
97/81 **I'm So Glad I'm Standing Here Today** *Crusaders*
I'm So Lonesome I Could Cry
89/62 *Johnny Tillotson*
8/66 *B.J. Thomas*
F/73 *Hank Wilson*
91/76 *Terry Bradshaw*
I'm So Proud
14/64 *Impressions*
49/71 *Main Ingredient*
74/65 **I'm So Thankful** *Ikettes*
I'm Sorry
1/60 *Brenda Lee*
87/73 *Joey Heatherton*
1/75 **I'm Sorry** *John Denver*
11/57 **I'm Sorry** *Platters*
42/68 **I'm Sorry** *Delfonics*
97/71 **I'm Sorry** *Bobby Bland*
36/58 **I'm Sorry I Made You Cry** *Connie Francis*
55/84 **I'm Stepping Out** *John Lennon*
I'm Stickin' With You
14/57 *Jimmy Bowen with The Rhythm Orchids*
72/57 *Fontane Sisters*
72/56 **I'm Still A King To You** *Don Cherry*
80/69 **I'm Still A Struggling Man** *Edwin Starr*
3/72 **I'm Still In Love With You** *Al Green*
12/83 **I'm Still Standing** *Elton John*
63/71 **I'm Still Waiting** *Diana Ross*
10/72 **I'm Stone In Love With You** *Stylistics*
1/65 **I'm Telling You Now** *Freddie & The Dreamers*
38/62 **(I'm The Girl On) Wolverton Mountain** *Jo Ann Campbell*
48/74 **I'm The Leader Of The Gang** *Brownsville Station*
92/64 **I'm The Lonely One** *Cliff Richard*
42/82 **I'm The One** *Roberta Flack*
82/64 **I'm The One** *Gerry & The Pacemakers*
73/63 **I'm The One Who Loves You** *Impressions*
F/71 **I'm The Only One** *Lobo*
87/85 **I'm Through With Love** *Eric Carmen*
74/69 **I'm Tired** *Savoy Brown*
62/66 **I'm Too Far Gone (To Turn Around)** *Bobby Bland*
98/62 **I'm Tossin' And Turnin' Again** *Bobby Lewis*
27/57 **I'm Waiting Just For You** *Pat Boone*
I'm Walkin'
4/57 *Fats Domino*
17/57 *Ricky Nelson*
I'm Walking The Floor Over You
92/57 *Georgia Gibbs*
44/60 *Pat Boone*
84/64 **(I'm Watching) Every Little Move You Make** *Little Peggy March*
12/67 **I'm Wondering** *Stevie Wonder*
1/77 **I'm Your Boogie Man** *KC & The Sunshine Band*
94/66 **I'm Your Hoochie Cooche Man** *Jimmy Smith*
I'm Your Man
3/86 *Wham!*
86/86 *Barry Manilow*
6/66 **I'm Your Puppet** *James & Bobby Purify*
93/81 **I'm Your Superman** *All Sports Band*
11/65 **I'm Yours** *Elvis Presley*
33/59 **I've Been Around** *Fats Domino*
78/74 **I've Been Born Again** *Johnnie Taylor*
68/62 **I've Been Everywhere** *Hank Snow*
35/69 **I've Been Hurt** *Bill Deal*
27/72 **I've Been Lonely For So Long** *Frederick Knight*
16/67 **I've Been Lonely Too Long** *Rascals*
88/60 **I've Been Loved Before** *Shirley & Lee*
81/76 **I've Been Lovin' You** *Easy Street*
I've Been Loving You Too Long (To Stop Now)
21/65 *Otis Redding*
68/69 *Ike & Tina Turner*
9/74 **(I've Been) Searchin' So Long** *Chicago*
53/59 **I've Been There** *Tommy Edwards*
34/75 **I've Been This Way Before** *Neil Diamond*
48/81 **I've Been Waiting For You All Of My Life** *Paul Anka*
73/56 **I've Changed My Mind A Thousand Times** *Kay Starr*
28/59 **I've Come Of Age** *Billy Storm*
94/65 **I've Cried My Last Tear** *O'Jays*
8/81 **I've Done Everything For You** *Rick Springfield*
5/71 **I've Found Someone Of My Own** *Free Movement*
29/76 **I've Got A Feeling (We'll Be Seeing Each Other Again)** *Al Wilson*
18/83 **I've Got A Rock N' Roll Heart** *Eric Clapton*
I've Got A Thing About You Baby
93/72 *Billy Lee Riley*
39/74 *Elvis Presley*
25/65 **I've Got A Tiger By The Tail** *Buck Owens*
I've Got A Woman *see: I Got A Woman*
18/62 **I've Got Bonnie** *Bobby Rydell*
41/68 **I've Got Dreams To Remember** *Otis Redding*

99/65 **I've Got Five Dollars And It's Saturday Night** *George & Gene*
93/56 **I've Got Love** *Julius LaRosa*
94/68 **I've Got Love For My Baby** *Young Hearts*
5/77 **I've Got Love On My Mind** *Natalie Cole*
66/61 **I've Got News For You** *Ray Charles*
67/64 **I've Got No Time To Lose** *Carla Thomas*
33/64 **I've Got Sand In My Shoes** *Drifters*
32/73 **I've Got So Much To Give** *Barry White*
71/61 **(I've Got) Spring Fever** *Little Willie John*
12/74 **I've Got The Music In Me** *Kiki Dee*
73/79 **I've Got The Next Dance** *Deniece Williams*
89/64 **I've Got The Skill** *Jackie Ross*
I've Got To *also see: I've Gotta*
38/66 **I've Got To Be Somebody** *Billy Joe Royal*
64/66 **I've Got To Do A Little Bit Better** *Joe Tex*
44/67 **I've Got To Have A Reason** *Dave Clark Five*
77/72 **I've Got To Have You** *Sammi Smith*
4/74 **I've Got To Use My Imagination** *Gladys Knight & The Pips*
I've Got You Under My Skin
95/59 *Louis Prima & Keely Smith*
9/66 *4 Seasons*
11/69 **I've Gotta Be Me** *Sammy Davis, Jr.*
8/68 **I've Gotta Get A Message To You** *Bee Gees*
46/70 **I've Gotta Make You Love Me** *Steam*
I've Grown Accustomed To Your Face
70/56 *Rosemary Clooney*
96/56 *Gordon MacRae*
25/78 **I've Had Enough** *Wings*
I've Had It
6/59 *Bell Notes*
79/74 *Fanny*
87/80 **I've Just Begun To Love You** *Dynasty*
58/69 **I've Lost Everything I've Ever Loved** *David Ruffin*
32/70 **I've Lost You** *Elvis Presley*
82/67 **I've Lost You** *Jackie Wilson*
4/80 **I've Loved You For A Long Time (medley)** *Spinners*
44/79 **I've Never Been In Love** *Suzi Quatro*
I've Never Been To Me
97/77 *Charlene*
3/82 *Charlene*
40/68 **I've Never Found A Girl (To Love Me Like You Do)** *Eddie Floyd*
17/67 **I've Passed This Way Before** *Jimmy Ruffin*
3/61 **I've Told Every Little Star** *Linda Scott*
59/69 **Ice Cream Song** *Dynamics*
70/68 **Ice In The Sun** *Status Quo*
90/62 **Ida Jane** *Fats Domino*
95/69 **Idaho** *4 Seasons*
64/57 **Idol With The Golden Head** *Coasters*
4/71 **If** *Bread*
82/61 **If** *Paragons*
32/62 **If A Man Answers** *Bobby Darin*
35/62 **If A Woman Answers (Hang Up The Phone)** *Leroy Van Dyke*
76/86 **If Anybody Had A Heart** *John Waite*
14/83 **If Anyone Falls** *Stevie Nicks*
7/58 **If Dreams Came True** *Pat Boone*
24/78 **If Ever I See You Again** *Roberta Flack*
10/84 **If Ever You're In My Arms Again** *Peabo Bryson*
12/69 **If I Can Dream** *Elvis Presley*
1/78 **If I Can't Have You** *Yvonne Elliman*
52/60 **If I Can't Have You** *Etta & Harvey*
10/68 **If I Could Build My Whole World Around You** *Marvin Gaye & Tammi Terrell*
76/82 **If I Could Get You (Into My Life)** *Gene Cotton*
89/73 **If I Could Only Be Sure** *Nolan Porter*
58/75 **If I Could Only Win Your Love** *Emmylou Harris*
10/72 **If I Could Reach You** *5th Dimension*
79/72 **If I Could See The Light** *8th Day*
58/62 **If I Cried Every Time You Hurt Me** *Wanda Jackson*
If I Didn't Care
22/59 *Connie Francis*
30/61 *Platters*
44/70 *Moments*
58/62 **If I Didn't Have A Dime (To Play The Jukebox)** *Gene Pitney*
46/65 **If I Didn't Love You** *Chuck Jackson*
39/75 **If I Ever Lose This Heaven** *Average White Band*
53/64 **If I Fell** *Beatles*
34/59 **If I Give My Heart To You** *Kitty Kallen*
31/60 **If I Had A Girl** *Rod Lauren*
If I Had A Hammer
10/62 *Peter, Paul & Mary*
3/63 *Trini Lopez*
88/85 **If I Had A Rocket Launcher** *Bruce Cockburn*
36/82 **If I Had My Wish Tonight** *David Lasley*
93/77 **If I Have To Go Away** *Jigsaw*
86/61 **If I Knew** *Nat King Cole*
23/65 **If I Loved You** *Chad & Jeremy*
8/55 **If I May** *Nat King Cole*
47/70 **If I Never Knew Your Name** *Vic Dana*
74/76 **If I Only Could** *Rowans*
95/69 **If I Only Had Time** *Nick DeCaro*
65/76 **If I Only Knew** *Ozark Mountain Daredevils*
34/65 **If I Ruled The World** *Tony Bennett*
39/79 **If I Said You Have A Beautiful Body Would You Hold It Against Me** *Bellamy Brothers*
67/87 **If I Say Yes** *Five Star*
62/62 **If I Should Lose You** *Dreamlovers*
If I Were A Carpenter
8/66 *Bobby Darin*
20/68 *Four Tops*
36/70 *Johnny Cash & June Carter*
76/72 *Bob Seger*
73/74 *Leon Russell*
71/73 **If I Were Only A Child Again** *Curtis Mayfield*
If I Were You
70/80 *Toby Beau*
44/82 *Lulu*
9/71 **If I Were Your Woman** *Gladys Knight & The Pips*
19/84 **If I'd Been The One** *38 Special*
74/64 **If I'm A Fool For Loving You** *Bobby Wood*
47/82 **If It Ain't One Thing...It's Another** *Richard 'Dimples' Fields*
75/78 **If It Don't Fit, Don't Force It** *Kellee Patterson*
88/74 **If It Feels Good, Do It** *Stories*
77/69 **If It Wasn't For Bad Luck** *Ray Charles & Jimmy Lewis*
If It's Alright With You
95/71 *Rose Colored Glass*
97/73 *Dottie West*
69/71 **If It's Real What I Feel** *Jerry Butler*
47/77 **If It's The Last Thing I Do** *Thelma Houston*
48/82 **If Looks Could Kill** *Player*
54/86 **If Looks Could Kill** *Heart*
86/68 **If Love Is In Your Heart** *Friend And Lover*
78/76 **If Love Must Go** *Dobie Gray*
87/83 **If Love Should Go** *Streets*

(If Loving You Is Wrong) I Don't Want To Be Right
3/72 *Luther Ingram*
42/75 *Millie Jackson*
31/79 *Barbara Mandrell*
88/63 **If Mary's There** *Brian Hyland*
54/78 **If My Friends Could See Me Now** *Linda Clifford*
98/70 **If My Heart Could Speak** *Manhattans*
23/63 **If My Pillow Could Talk** *Connie Francis*
25/71 **If Not For You** *Olivia Newton-John*
55/76 **If Not You** *Dr. Hook*
91/70 **If Only I Had My Mind On Something Else** *Bee Gees*
46/84 **If Only You Knew** *Patti LaBelle*
29/86 **If She Knew What She Wants** *Bangles*
If She Should Come To You (La Montana)
67/60 *Anthony Newley*
77/60 *Frank DeVol*
98/60 *Roger Williams*
67/64 **If Somebody Told You** *Anna King*
28/82 **If The Love Fits Wear It** *Leslie Pearl*
6/84 **If This Is It** *Huey Lewis & The News*
60/67 **If This Is Love (I'd Rather Be Lonely)** *Precisions*
68/68 **If This World Were Mine** *Marvin Gaye & Tammi Terrell*
71/70 **If Walls Could Talk** *Little Milton*
28/74 **If We Make It Through December** *Merle Haggard*
84/72 **If We Only Have Love** *Dionne Warwick*
58/73 **If We Try** *Don McLean*
54/75 **(If You Add) All The Love In The World** *Mac Davis*
65/72 **If You Can Beat Me Rockin' (You Can Have My Chair)** *Laura Lee*
62/56 **If You Can Dream** *Four Aces*
11/68 **If You Can Want** *Miracles*
45/79 **If You Can't Give Me Love** *Suzi Quatro*
100/63 **If You Can't Rock Me** *Rick Nelson*
5/71 **If You Could Read My Mind** *Gordon Lightfoot*
33/59 **(If You Cry) True Love, True Love** *Drifters*
81/70 **If You Do Believe In Love** *Tee Set*
3/72 **If You Don't Know Me By Now** *Harold Melvin & The Blue Notes*
85/65 **If You Don't (Love Me, Tell Me So)** *Barbara Mason*
40/55 **If You Don't Want My Love** *Jaye P. Morgan*
49/68 **If You Don't Want My Love** *Robert John*
67/59 **If You Don't Want My Lovin'** *Carl Dobkins, Jr.*
92/68 **If You Ever Leave Me** *Jack Jones*
If You Go Away
68/67 *Damita Jo*
68/74 *Terry Jacks*
63/73 **If You Gotta Break Another Heart** *Albert Hammond*
If You Gotta Make A Fool Of Somebody
22/62 *James Ray*
63/66 *Maxine Brown*
11/76 **If You Know What I Mean** *Neil Diamond*
4/86 **If You Leave** *Orchestral Manoeuvres In The Dark*
1/76 **If You Leave Me Now** *Chicago*
38/72 **If You Leave Me Tonight I'll Cry** *Jerry Wallace*
66/72 **If You Let Me** *Eddie Kendricks*
8/70 **(If You Let Me Make Love To You Then) Why Can't I Touch You?** *Ronnie Dyson*
79/59 **If You Love Me** *LaVern Baker*
5/74 **If You Love Me (Let Me Know)** *Olivia Newton-John*
3/85 **If You Love Somebody Set Them Free** *Sting*
If You Need Me
37/63 *Solomon Burke*
64/63 *Wilson Pickett*
98/60 **If You Need Me** *Fats Domino*
48/76 **If You Only Believe (Jesus For Tonite)** *Michel Polnareff*
8/71 **If You Really Love Me** *Stevie Wonder*
97/65 **If You Really Want Me To, I'll Go** *Ron-Dels*
17/79 **If You Remember Me** *Chris Thompson & Night*
92/64 **If You See My Love** *Lenny Welch*
38/80 **If You Should Sail** *Nielsen/Pearson*
17/74 **If You Talk In Your Sleep** *Elvis Presley*
96/75 **If You Think You Know How To Love Me** *Smokey*
75/65 **If You Wait For Love** *Bobby Goldsboro*
1/63 **If You Wanna Be Happy** *Jimmy Soul*
49/78 **If You Wanna Do A Dance** *Spinners*
67/83 **If You Wanna Get Back Your Lady** *Pointer Sisters*
25/74 **If You Wanna Get To Heaven** *Ozark Mountain Daredevils*
89/56 **If You Wanna See Mamie Tonight** *Ames Brothers*
37/79 **If You Want It** *Niteflyte*
98/75 **(If You Want It) Do It Yourself** *Gloria Gaynor*
12/73 **If You Want Me To Stay** *Sly & The Family Stone*
45/82 **If You Want My Love** *Cheap Trick*
71/64 **If You Want This Love** *Sonny Knight*
67/62 **If You Were A Rock And Roll Record** *Freddy Cannon*
77/86 **If You Were A Woman (And I Was A Man)** *Bonnie Tyler*
41/71 **If You Were Mine** *Ray Charles*
43/78 **If You're Not Back In Love By Monday** *Millie Jackson*
9/73 **If You're Ready (Come Go With Me)** *Staple Singers*
60/65 **If You've Got A Heart** *Bobby Goldsboro*
96/70 **If You've Got A Heart** *Bobby Bland*
88/77 **If You've Got The Time** *Babys*
57/86 **If Your Heart Isn't In It** *Atlantic Starr*
95/59 **Igmoo (The Pride Of South Central High)** *Stonewall Jackson*
Iko Iko
20/65 *Dixie Cups*
71/72 *Dr. John*
44/84 **Illegal Alien** *Genesis*
98/61 **Image** *Hank Levine*
6/60 **Image Of A Girl** *Safaris*
7/78 **Imaginary Lover** *Atlanta Rhythm Section*
88/85 **Imagination** *Belouis Some*
3/71 **Imagine** *John Lennon*
90/62 **Imagine That** *Patsy Cline*
22/75 **Immigrant, The** *Neil Sedaka*
16/71 **Immigrant Song** *Led Zeppelin*
36/72 **Immigration Man** *David Crosby/Graham Nash*
95/61 **Impossible** *Gloria Lynne*
Impossible Dream
35/66 *Jack Jones*
42/68 *Hesitations*
55/68 *Roger Williams*
57/63 **Impossible Happened** *Little Peggy March*
68/68 **Impossible Mission (Mission Impossible)** *Soul Survivors*
17/83 **In A Big Country** *Big Country*
56/72 **In A Broken Dream** *Python Lee Jackson*
30/68 **In-A-Gadda-Da-Vida** *Iron Butterfly*
49/56 **In A Little Spanish Town** *Bing Crosby*

31/69 **In A Moment** *Intrigues*
27/56 **In A Shanty In Old Shanty Town**
Somethin' Smith & The Redheads
11/80 **In America** *Charlie Daniels Band*
9/67 **In And Out Of Love** *Supremes*
69/85 **In And Out Of Love** *Bon Jovi*
87/68 **In Another Land** *Bill Wyman*
99/86 **In Between Days (Without You)** *Cure*
84/61 **In Between Tears** *Lenny Miles*
'In' Crowd
5/65 *Ramsey Lewis*
13/65 *Dobie Gray*
7/63 **In Dreams** *Roy Orbison*
86/78 **In For The Night** *Dirt Band*
66/76 **In France They Kiss On Main Street**
Joni Mitchell
49/72 **In Heaven There Is No Beer** *Clean Living*
75/80 **In It For Love**
England Dan & John Ford Coley
77/86 **In My Dreams** *Dokken*
51/61 **In My Heart** *Timetones*
7/85 **In My House** *Mary Jane Girls*
10/60 **In My Little Corner Of The World**
Anita Bryant
44/64 **In My Lonely Room** *Martha & The Vandellas*
In My Room
23/63 *Beach Boys*
86/69 *Sagittarius*
62/66 **In My Room** *Verdelle Smith*
54/68 **In Need Of A Friend** *Cowsills*
38/85 **In Neon** *Elton John*
46/66 **In Our Time** *Nancy Sinatra*
99/68 **In Some Time** *Ronnie Dove*
19/81 **In The Air Tonight** *Phil Collins*
63/56 **In The Alps**
Lawrence Welk & The McGuire Sisters
49/66 **In The Arms Of Love** *Andy Williams*
51/69 **In The Bad, Bad Old Days** *Foundations*
97/66 **In The Basement**
Etta James & Sugar Pie DeSanto
46/74 **In The Bottle** *Brother To Brother*
58/78 **In The Bush** *Musique*
In The Chapel In The Moonlight
see: Chapel
35/81 **In The Dark** *Billy Squier*
72/82 **In The Driver's Seat** *John Schneider*
In The Ghetto
3/69 *Elvis Presley*
48/72 *Candi Staton*
33/67 **In The Heat Of The Night** *Ray Charles*
97/65 **In The Meantime** *Georgie Fame*
75/77 **In The Middle** *Tim Moore*
27/61 **In The Middle Of A Heartache**
Wanda Jackson
In The Middle Of An Island
9/57 *Tony Bennett*
23/57 *Tennessee Ernie Ford*
In The Middle Of The House
11/56 *Vaughn Monroe*
20/56 *Rusty Draper*
In The Midnight Hour
21/65 *Wilson Pickett*
45/68 *Mirettes*
30/73 *Cross Country*
88/79 *Samantha Sang*
In The Misty Moonlight
19/64 *Jerry Wallace*
46/67 *Dean Martin*
In The Mood
4/59 *Ernie Fields*
51/74 *Bette Midler*
40/77 *Henhouse Five Plus Too*
39/84 **In The Mood** *Robert Plant*
88/77 **In The Mood (medley)** *Rush*

58/84 **In The Name Of Love**
Ralph MacDonald with Bill Withers
In The Name Of Love *see: (What)*
3/79 **In The Navy** *Village People*
69/72 **In The Quiet Morning** *Joan Baez*
5/72 **In The Rain** *Dramatics*
70/86 **In The Shape Of A Heart** *Jackson Browne*
38/60 **In The Still Of The Nite** *Dion & The Belmonts*
In The Still Of The Nite
24/56 *Five Satins*
81/60 *Five Satins*
99/61 *Five Satins*
58/64 *Santo & Johnny*
64/69 *Paul Anka*
58/79 **In The Stone** *Earth, Wind & Fire*
46/64 **In The Summer Of His Years**
Connie Francis
3/70 **In The Summertime** *Mungo Jerry*
96/69 **In The Time Of Our Lives** *Iron Butterfly*
1/69 **In The Year 2525 (Exordium & Terminus)** *Zager & Evans*
74/79 **In Thee** *Blue Oyster Cult*
70/71 **In These Changing Times** *Four Tops*
69/72 **In Time** *Engelbert Humperdinck*
94/61 **In Time** *Steve Lawrence*
26/86 **In Your Eyes** *Peter Gabriel*
20/81 **In Your Letter** *REO Speedwagon*
1/67 **Incense And Peppermints**
Strawberry Alarm Clock
33/67 **Indescribably Blue** *Elvis Presley*
5/69 **Indian Giver** *1910 Fruitgum Co.*
10/68 **Indian Lake** *Cowsills*
Indian Love Call
59/58 *Ernie Freeman*
68/75 *Ray Stevens*
Indian Reservation
20/68 *Don Fardon*
1/71 *Raiders*
50/77 **Indian Summer** *Poco*
74/71 **Indian Summer** *Audience*
5/70 **Indiana Wants Me** *R. Dean Taylor*
75/83 **Industrial Disease** *Dire Straits*
6/84 **Infatuation** *Rod Stewart*
87/85 **Information** *Eric Martin*
91/85 **Injured In The Game Of Love** *Donnie Iris*
84/65 **Inky Dinky Spider** *Kids Next Door*
Innamorata
27/56 *Dean Martin*
30/56 *Jerry Vale*
9/71 **Inner City Blues (Make Me Wanna Holler)** *Marvin Gaye*
96/68 **Inner Light** *Beatles*
84/86 **Innocent Eyes** *Graham Nash*
10/84 **Innocent Man** *Billy Joel*
32/76 **Inseparable** *Natalie Cole*
34/66 **Inside-Looking Out** *Animals*
43/83 **Inside Love (So Personal)** *George Benson*
76/75 **Inside My Love** *Minnie Riperton*
76/80 **Inside Of You** *Ray, Goodman & Brown*
3/70 **Instant Karma** *John Ono Lennon*
29/79 **Instant Replay** *Dan Hartman*
81/63 **Insult To Injury** *Timi Yuro*
61/58 **Intermission Riff** *Bernie Lowe Orchestra*
92/82 **Into My Love** *Greg Guidry*
51/70 **Into The Mystic** *Johnny Rivers*
11/80 **Into The Night** *Benny Mardones*
82/56 **Into The Night** *Dream Weavers*
10/85 **Invincible** *Pat Benatar*
31/85 **Invisible** *Alison Moyet*
40/83 **Invisible Hands** *Kim Carnes*
57/64 **Invisible Tears** *Ray Conniff Singers*
1/86 **Invisible Touch** *Genesis*
68/85 **Invitation To Dance** *Kim Carnes*
92/58 **Invitation To The Blues** *Ray Price*

52/72 **Iron Man** *Black Sabbath*
F/84 **Irresistible Bitch** *Prince*
Irresistible You
96/60 *Bobby Peterson*
15/62 *Bobby Darin*
Irving *see: Ballad Of*
35/60 **Is A Blue Bird Blue** *Conway Twitty*
70/70 **Is Anybody Goin' To San Antone** *Charley Pride*
68/70 **Is It Because I'm Black** *Syl Johnson*
8/86 **Is It Love** *Mr. Mister*
70/75 **Is It Love That We're Missin'** *Quincy Jones*
97/66 **Is It Me?** *Barbara Mason*
79/65 **Is It Really Over?** *Jim Reeves*
34/69 **Is It Something You've Got** *Tyrone Davis*
17/64 **Is It True** *Brenda Lee*
Is It Wrong (For Loving You)
61/57 *Warner Mack*
69/60 *Webb Pierce*
15/81 **Is It You** *Lee Ritenour*
21/79 **Is She Really Going Out With Him?** *Joe Jackson*
11/69 **Is That All There Is** *Peggy Lee*
70/86 **Is That It?** *Katrina & The Waves*
59/71 **Is That The Way** *Tin Tin*
31/60 **Is There Any Chance** *Marty Robbins*
87/56 **Is There Somebody Else** *Dream Weavers*
4/83 **Is There Something I Should Know** *Duran Duran*
89/61 **Is There Something On Your Mind** *Jack Scott*
9/87 **Is This Love** *Survivor*
50/80 **Is This Love** *Pat Travers*
85/83 **Is This The End** *New Edition*
75/65 **Is This What I Get For Loving You?** *Ronettes*
81/60 **Is You Is Or Is You Ain't My Baby** *Buster Brown*
1/75 **Island Girl** *Elton John*
92/62 **Island In The Sky** *Troy Shondell*
25/57 **Island In The Sun** *Harry Belafonte*
37/82 **Island Of Lost Souls** *Blondie*
1/83 **Islands In The Stream** *Kenny Rogers & Dolly Parton*
F/70 **Isn't It A Pity** *George Harrison*
56/73 **Isn't It About Time** *Stephen Stills*
100/60 **Isn't It Amazing** *Crests*
Isn't It Lonely Together
63/68 *O.C. Smith*
97/68 *Robert Knight*
85/75 **Isn't It Lonely Together** *Stark & McBrien*
13/77 **Isn't It Time** *Babys*
29/72 **Isn't Life Strange** *Moody Blues*
9/69 **Israelites** *Desmond Dekker & The Aces*
97/77 **It Ain't Easy Comin' Down** *Charlene*
17/84 **It Ain't Enough** *Corey Hart*
92/77 **It Ain't Love** *Tom Powers*
It Ain't Me Babe
58/64 *Johnny Cash*
8/65 *Turtles*
91/65 **It Ain't No Big Thing** *Radiants*
94/75 **It Ain't No Fun** *Shirley Brown*
68/64 **It Ain't No Use** *Major Lance*
68/57 **It All Depends On You** *Jerry Lewis*
59/78 **It Amazes Me** *John Denver*
51/84 **It Can Happen** *Yes*
85/67 **It Could Be We're In Love** *Cryan' Shames*
53/60 **It Could Happen To You** *Dinah Washington*
46/74 **It Could Have Been Me** *Sami Jo*
43/81 **It Didn't Take Long** *Spider*
98/75 **It Do Feel Good** *Donna Fargo*
97/61 **It Do Me So Good** *Ann-Margret*
64/74 **It Doesn't Have To Be That Way** *Jim Croce*
61/72 **It Doesn't Matter** *Stephen Stills*
It Doesn't Matter Anymore
13/59 *Buddy Holly*
47/75 *Linda Ronstadt*
4/71 **It Don't Come Easy** *Ringo Starr*
89/58 **It Don't Hurt No More** *Nappy Brown*
10/70 **It Don't Matter To Me** *Bread*
66/77 **It Feels So Good To Be Loved So Bad** *Manhattans*
55/65 **It Feels So Right** *Elvis Presley*
72/56 **It Happened Again** *Sarah Vaughan*
59/59 **It Happened Today** *Skyliners*
29/64 **It Hurts Me** *Elvis Presley*
70/66 **It Hurts Me** *Bobby Goldsboro*
56/79 **It Hurts So Bad** *Kim Carnes*
It Hurts To Be In Love
7/64 *Gene Pitney*
72/81 *Dan Hartman*
61/57 **It Hurts To Be In Love** *Annie Laurie*
45/63 **It Hurts To Be Sixteen** *Andrea Carroll*
75/80 **It Hurts Too Much** *Eric Carmen*
23/56 **It Isn't Right** *Platters*
23/61 **It Keeps Rainin'** *Fats Domino*
3/62 **It Keeps Right On A-Hurtin'** *Johnny Tillotson*
It Keeps You Runnin'
46/76 *Carly Simon*
37/77 *Doobie Brothers*
60/76 **It Makes Me Giggle** *John Denver*
It May Be Winter Outside (But In My Heart It's Spring)
42/67 *Felice Taylor*
83/73 *Love Unlimited*
11/55 **It May Sound Silly** *McGuire Sisters*
22/62 **It Might As Well Rain Until September** *Carole King*
25/83 **It Might Be You** *Stephen Bishop*
3/67 **It Must Be Him** *Vikki Carr*
32/79 **It Must Be Love** *Alton McClain & Destiny*
33/83 **It Must Be Love** *Madness*
46/61 **(It Never Happens) In Real Life** *Chuck Jackson*
5/72 **It Never Rains In Southern California** *Albert Hammond*
38/60 **It Only Happened Yesterday** *Jack Scott*
11/56 **It Only Hurts For A Little While** *Ames Brothers*
81/74 **It Only Hurts When I Try To Smile** *Dawn*
10/75 **It Only Takes A Minute** *Tavares*
It Should Have Been Me
40/68 *Gladys Knight & The Pips*
85/76 *Yvonne Fair*
29/62 **It Started All Over Again** *Brenda Lee*
27/73 **It Sure Took A Long, Long Time** *Lobo*
79/80 **It Takes Time** *Marshall Tucker Band*
14/67 **It Takes Two** *Marvin Gaye & Kim Weston*
20/66 **It Tears Me Up** *Percy Sledge*
It Was A Very Good Year
28/66 *Frank Sinatra*
99/66 *Della Reese*
16/77 **It Was Almost Like A Song** *Ronnie Milsap*
11/59 **It Was I** *Skip & Flip*
It Will Stand
61/62 *Showmen*
80/64 *Showmen*
89/63 **It Won't Be This Way (Always)** *King Pins*
63/66 **It Won't Be Wrong** *Byrds*
98/64 **It'll Never Be Over For Me** *Baby Washington*
99/64 **It's A Cotton Candy World** *Jerry Wallace*
37/77 **It's A Crazy World** *Mac McAnally*
44/71 **It's A Cryin' Shame** *Gayle McCormick*

90/79 **It's A Disco Night (Rock Don't Stop)** *Isley Brothers*
It's A Funky Thing *see: Memphis Underground*
97/69 **It's A Groovy World!** *Unifics*
93/66 **It's-A-Happening** *Magic Mushrooms*
93/67 **It's A Happening Thing** *Peanut Butter Conspiracy*
69/67 **It's A Happening World** *Tokens*
72/84 **It's A Hard Life** *Queen*
It's A Heartache
3/78 *Bonnie Tyler*
86/78 *Juice Newton*
20/78 **It's A Laugh** *Daryl Hall & John Oates*
64/63 **It's A Lonely Town** *Gene McDaniels*
28/76 **It's A Long Way There** *Little River Band*
28/81 **It's A Love Thing** *Whispers*
92/63 **It's A Mad, Mad, Mad, Mad World** *Shirelles*
67/65 **It's A Man Down There** *G.L. Crockett*
8/66 **It's A Man's Man's Man's World** *James Brown*
12/75 **It's A Miracle** *Barry Manilow*
13/84 **It's A Miracle** *Culture Club*
6/83 **It's A Mistake** *Men At Work*
32/70 **It's A New Day** *James Brown*
67/80 **It's A Night For Beautiful Girls** *Fools*
14/70 **It's A Shame** *Spinners*
It's A Sin To Tell A Lie
7/55 *Somethin' Smith & The Redheads*
99/64 *Tony Bennett*
F/75 **It's A Sin When You Love Somebody** *Joe Cocker*
92/71 **It's About Time** *Dillards*
50/61 **It's All Because** *Linda Scott*
31/75 **It's All Down To Goodnight Vienna** *Ringo Starr*
41/79 **It's All I Can Do** *Cars*
53/81 **It's All I Can Do** *Anne Murray*
It's All In The Game
1/58 *Tommy Edwards*
25/64 *Cliff Richard*
24/70 *Four Tops*
51/70 **It's All In Your Mind** *Clarence Carter*
65/73 **It's All Over** *Independents*
67/64 **It's All Over** *Walter Jackson*
72/64 **It's All Over** *Ben E. King*
It's All Over Now
26/64 *Rolling Stones*
94/64 *Valentinos*
65/67 **It's All Over Now** *Casinos*
4/63 **It's All Right** *Impressions*
55/75 **It's All Right** *Jim Capaldi*
93/61 **It's All Right** *Sam Cooke*
79/64 **It's All Right (You're Just In Love)** *Tams*
94/72 **It's All Up To You** *Dells*
It's Almost Tomorrow
20/55 *David Carroll*
20/55 *Snooky Lanson*
7/56 *Dream Weavers*
14/56 *Jo Stafford*
93/65 *Jimmy Velvet*
31/65 **It's Alright** *Adam Faith*
92/75 **It's Alright** *Graham Central Station*
78/86 **It's Alright (Baby's Coming Back)** *Eurythmics*
88/66 **It's An Uphill Climb To The Bottom** *Walter Jackson*
92/67 **It's Been A Long Long Time** *Elgins*
66/74 **It's Been A Long Time** *New Birth*
96/69 **It's Been A Long Time** *Betty Everett*
20/58 **(It's Been A Long Time) Pretty Baby** *Gino & Gina*
60/56 **It's Better In The Dark** *Tony Martin*
63/74 **It's Better To Have (And Don't Need)** *Don Covay*
95/65 **It's Better To Have It** *Barbara Lynn*
68/67 **It's Cold Outside** *Choir*
68/76 **It's Cool** *Tymes*
88/68 **It's Crazy** *Eddie Harris*
4/77 **It's Ecstasy When You Lay Down Next To Me** *Barry White*
46/80 **It's For You** *Player*
It's For You
79/64 *Cilla Black*
60/71 *Springwell*
68/73 **It's Forever** *Ebonys*
92/72 **It's Four In The Morning** *Faron Young*
82/85 **It's Gettin' Late** *Beach Boys*
30/69 **It's Getting Better** *Mama Cass*
12/72 **It's Going To Take Some Time** *Carpenters*
23/65 **It's Gonna Be Alright** *Gerry & The Pacemakers*
56/65 **It's Gonna Be Alright** *Maxine Brown*
54/65 **It's Gonna Be Fine** *Glenn Yarbrough*
82/84 **It's Gonna Be Special** *Patti Austin*
It's Gonna Take A Miracle
41/65 *Royalettes*
10/82 *Deniece Williams*
14/61 **It's Gonna Work Out Fine** *Ike & Tina Turner*
48/66 **It's Good News Week** *Hedgehoppers Anonymous*
41/65 **It's Got The Whole World Shakin'** *Sam Cooke*
63/67 **It's Got To Be Mellow** *Leon Haywood*
67/65 **It's Gotta Last Forever** *Billy J. Kramer with The Dakotas*
18/65 **It's Growing** *Temptations*
43/80 **It's Hard To Be Humble** *Mac Davis*
87/69 **It's Hard To Get Along** *Joe Simon*
72/73 **It's Hard To Stop (Doing Something When It's Good To You)** *Betty Wright*
82/74 **It's Her Turn To Live** *Smokey Robinson*
It's Impossible
10/71 *Perry Como*
52/71 *New Birth*
It's In His Kiss *see: Shoop Shoop Song*
38/83 **It's Inevitable** *Charlie*
45/61 **It's Just A House Without You** *Brook Benton*
45/65 **It's Just A Little Bit Too Late** *Wayne Fontana & The Mindbenders*
It's Just A Matter Of Time
3/59 *Brook Benton*
87/70 *Sonny James*
47/59 **It's Just About Time** *Johnny Cash*
83/81 **It's Just The Sun** *Don McLean*
9/59 **It's Late** *Ricky Nelson*
74/78 **It's Late** *Queen*
63/80 **It's Like We Never Said Goodbye** *Crystal Gayle*
91/62 **It's Magic** *Platters*
57/81 **It's My Job** *Jimmy Buffett*
23/66 **It's My Life** *Animals*
31/84 **It's My Life** *Talk Talk*
It's My Party
1/63 *Lesley Gore*
72/82 *Dave Stewart & Barbara Gaskin*
82/69 **It's My Thing** *Marva Whitney*
9/81 **It's My Turn** *Diana Ross*
51/69 **It's Never Too Late** *Steppenwolf*
51/68 **It's Nice To Be With You** *Monkees*
74/64 **(It's No) Sin** *Duprees*
51/80 **It's Not A Wonder** *Little River Band*
95/68 **It's Not Easy** *Will-O-Bees*
5/57 **It's Not For Me To Say** *Johnny Mathis*

78/60 **It's Not The End Of Everything**
Tommy Edwards
92/66 **It's Not The Same** *Anthony & The Imperials*
10/65 **It's Not Unusual** *Tom Jones*
89/86 **It's Not You, It's Not Me** *KBC BAND*
It's Now Or Never
1/60 *Elvis Presley*
14/81 *John Schneider*
23/67 **It's Now Winters Day** *Tommy Roe*
29/76 **It's O.K.** *Beach Boys*
94/55 **It's Obdacious** *Buddy Johnson*
20/72 **It's One Of Those Nights (Yes Love)**
Partridge Family
15/86 **It's Only Love** *Bryan Adams/Tina Turner*
31/66 **It's Only Love**
Tommy James & The Shondells
44/76 **It's Only Love** *ZZ Top*
It's Only Love
45/69 *B.J. Thomas*
51/71 *Elvis Presley*
It's Only Make Believe
1/58 *Conway Twitty*
10/70 *Glen Campbell*
16/74 **It's Only Rock 'N Roll (But I Like It)**
Rolling Stones
42/59 **It's Only The Beginning** *Kalin Twins*
86/59 **It's Only The Good Times** *Tommy Edwards*
9/64 **It's Over** *Roy Orbison*
It's Over
37/66 *Jimmie Rodgers*
74/68 *Eddy Arnold*
38/76 **It's Over** *Boz Scaggs*
75/78 **It's Over** *Electric Light Orchestra*
11/82 **It's Raining Again** *Supertramp*
46/83 **It's Raining Men** *Weather Girls*
93/58 **It's Raining Outside** *Platters*
86/78 **It's Really You** *Tarney/Spencer Band*
21/77 **It's Sad To Belong**
England Dan & John Ford Coley
5/77 **It's So Easy** *Linda Ronstadt*
F/57 **It's So Easy To Forget** *Four Lads*
79/67 **It's So Hard Being A Loser** *Contours*
88/71 **It's So Hard For Me To Say Good-Bye**
Eddie Kendricks
84/70 **It's So Nice** *Jackie DeShannon*
1/80 **It's Still Rock And Roll To Me** *Billy Joel*
51/71 **It's Summer** *Temptations*
91/66 **It's That Time Of The Year** *Len Barry*
50/67 **It's The Little Things** *Sonny & Cher*
81/71 **It's The Real Thing** *Electric Express*
93/72 **It's The Same Old Love** *Courtship*
It's The Same Old Song
5/65 *Four Tops*
35/78 *KC & The Sunshine Band*
53/72 **(It's The Way) Nature Planned It**
Four Tops
94/75 **It's Time For Love** *Chi-Lites*
4/59 **It's Time To Cry** *Paul Anka*
1/71 **It's Too Late** *Carole King*
23/66 **It's Too Late** *Bobby Goldsboro*
49/63 **It's Too Late** *Wilson Pickett*
56/65 **It's Too Late, Baby Too Late**
Arthur Prysock
It's Too Soon To Know
11/58 *Pat Boone*
54/61 *Etta James*
68/66 *Roy Orbison*
69/61 **It's Unbelievable** *Larks*
80/77 **It's Uncanny** *Daryl Hall & John Oates*
6/63 **It's Up To You** *Rick Nelson*
72/71 **It's Up To You Petula** *Edison Lighthouse*
20/68 **It's Wonderful** *Rascals*
61/65 **It's Wonderful To Be In Love** *Ovations*
52/86 **It's You** *Bob Seger*
22/57 **It's You I Love** *Fats Domino*
33/78 **It's You That I Need** *Enchantment*
85/70 **It's Your Life** *Andy Kim*
2/69 **It's Your Thing** *Isley Brothers*
51/61 **It's Your World** *Marty Robbins*
74/56 **It's Yours** *DeCastro Sisters*
25/56 **Italian Theme** *Cyril Stapleton*
Itchy Twitchy Feeling
25/58 *Bobby Hendricks*
100/58 *Swallows*
16/68 **Itchycoo Park** *Small Faces*
1/60 **Itsy Bitsy Teenie Weenie Yellow Polkadot Bikini** *Brian Hyland*
41/62 **Itty Bitty Pieces** *James Ray*
97/69 **Ivory** *Bob Seger*
Ivory Tower
2/56 *Cathy Carr*
6/56 *Gale Storm*
11/56 *Charms*
F/57 **Ivy League** *Tennessee Ernie Ford*
18/57 **Ivy Rose** *Perry Como*

J

86/61 **Ja-Da** *Johnny & The Hurricanes*
1/82 **Jack & Diane** *John Cougar*
8/78 **Jack And Jill** *Raydio*
53/69 **Jack And Jill** *Tommy Roe*
96/59 **Jack O'Diamonds** *Ruth Brown*
64/63 **Jack The Ripper** *Link Wray*
3/75 **Jackie Blue** *Ozark Mountain Daredevils*
61/72 **Jackie Wilson Said (I'm In Heaven When You Smile)** *Van Morrison*
14/67 **Jackson** *Nancy Sinatra & Lee Hazlewood*
63/58 **Jacqueline** *Bobby Helms*
94/64 **Jailer, Bring Me Water** *Trini Lopez*
1/57 **Jailhouse Rock** *Elvis Presley*
Jam, The
29/62 *Bobby Gregg*
63/76 *Graham Central Station*
80/75 **Jam Band** *Disco Tex & The Sex-O-Lettes*
56/84 **Jam On It** *Newcleus*
8/70 **Jam Up Jelly Tight** *Tommy Roe*
82/81 **Jam Was Moving** *Debbie Harry*
14/57 **Jamaica Farewell** *Harry Belafonte*
98/64 **Jamaica Ska** *Ska Kings*
Jambalaya (On The Bayou)
90/60 *Bobby Comstock*
30/62 *Fats Domino*
84/72 *Nitty Gritty Dirt Band*
16/73 *Blue Ridge Rangers*
58/64 **James Bond Theme** *Billy Strange*
77/74 **James Dean** *Eagles*
17/62 **James (Hold The Ladder Steady)**
Sue Thompson
14/85 **Jamie** *Ray Parker Jr.*
30/62 **Jamie** *Eddie Holland*
54/57 **Jamie Boy** *Kay Starr*
81/85 **Jammin** *Teena Marie*
14/80 **Jane** *Jefferson Starship*
93/62 **Jane, Jane, Jane** *Kingston Trio*
87/85 **Janet** *Commodores*
87/76 **January** *Pilot*
52/56 **Japanese Farewell Song** *Kay Cee Jones*
69/76 **Jasper** *Jim Stafford*
Java
49/63 *Floyd Cramer*
4/64 *Al Hirt*
Jaws *see: Theme From & Mr. Jaws*

77/57 **Jay-Dee's Boogie Woogie** *Jimmy Dorsey*
2/74 **Jazzman** *Carole King*
Je T'Aime...Moi Non Plus
58/70 *Jane Birkin & Serge Gainsbourg*
99/73 *Sylvia & Ralfi Pagan (Soul)*
Jealous Heart
62/58 *Tab Hunter*
94/58 *Fontane Sisters*
47/65 *Connie Francis*
20/69 **Jealous Kind Of Fella** *Garland Green*
50/68 **Jealous Love** *Wilson Pickett*
19/60 **Jealous Of You** *Connie Francis*
73/76 **Jealousy** *Major Harris*
78/58 **Jealousy** *Kitty Wells*
2/69 **Jean** *Oliver*
71/72 **Jean Genie** *David Bowie*
94/58 **Jeannie Jeannie Jeannie** *Eddie Cochran*
17/77 **Jeans On** *David Dundas*
Jed Clampett *see: Ballad Of*
51/68 **Jelly Jungle (Of Orange Marmalade)**
Lemon Pipers
82/63 **Jellybread** *Booker T. & The MG's*
Jennie Lee
8/58 *Jan & Arnie*
55/58 *Billy Ward & His Dominoes*
60/71 **Jennifer** *Bobby Sherman*
40/68 **Jennifer Eccles** *Hollies*
26/68 **Jennifer Juniper** *Donovan*
36/70 **Jennifer Tomkins** *Street People*
Jenny *see: 867-5309*
84/63 **Jenny Brown** *Smothers Brothers*
10/57 **Jenny, Jenny** *Little Richard*
67/60 **Jenny Lou** *Sonny James*
10/66 **Jenny Take A Ride!**
Mitch Ryder & The Detroit Wheels
2/83 **Jeopardy** *Greg Kihn Band*
35/61 **Jeremiah Peabody's Poly Unsaturated**
Pills *Ray Stevens*
7/65 **Jerk, The** *Larks*
85/65 **Jerk And Twine** *Jackie Ross*
74/70 **Jerusalem** *Herb Alpert*
11/80 **Jesse** *Carly Simon*
30/73 **Jesse** *Roberta Flack*
54/85 **Jesse** *Julian Lennon*
98/68 **Jesse Brady** *McCoys*
65/74 **Jessica** *Allman Brothers Band*
1/81 **Jessie's Girl** *Rick Springfield*
Jesus Christ Superstar *see: Superstar*
28/69 **Jesus Is A Soul Man** *Lawrence Reynolds*
Jesus Is Just Alright
97/70 *Byrds*
35/73 *Doobie Brothers*
91/73 **Jesus Was A Capricorn** *Kris Kristofferson*
7/74 **Jet** *Paul McCartney*
8/77 **Jet Airliner** *Steve Miller Band*
52/67 **Jill** *Gary Lewis & The Playboys*
Jim Dandy
17/57 *LaVern Baker*
25/74 *Black Oak Arkansas*
76/57 **Jim Dandy Got Married** *LaVern Baker*
95/59 **Jimmy Kiss And Run** *Diane Maxwell*
28/87 **Jimmy Lee** *Aretha Franklin*
Jimmy Loves Mary-Anne
33/73 *Looking Glass*
82/84 *Josie Cotton*
Jimmy Mack
10/67 *Martha & The Vandellas*
65/86 *Sheena Easton*
51/61 **Jimmy Martinez** *Marty Robbins*
25/61 **Jimmy's Girl** *Johnny Tillotson*
Jingle Bell Rock
6/57 *Bobby Helms*
35/58 *Bobby Helms*
36/60 *Bobby Helms*
21/61 *Bobby Rydell/Chubby Checker*
41/61 *Bobby Helms*
56/62 *Bobby Helms*
92/62 *Bobby Rydell/Chubby Checker*
74/57 **Jingle Bells** *Perry Como*
(also see: Twistin Bells)
10/70 **Jingle Jangle** *Archies*
56/69 **Jingo** *Santana*
82/62 **Jitterbug, The** *Dovells*
66/63 **Jive Samba** *Cannonball Adderley*
1/75 **Jive Talkin'** *Bee Gees*
47/74 **Jive Turkey** *Ohio Players*
71/62 **Jivin' Around** *Al Casey*
19/58 **Jo-Ann** *Playmates*
73/59 **Jo-Jo The Dog-Faced Boy** *Annette*
17/80 **JoJo** *Boz Scaggs*
78/61 **Joanie** *Frankie Calen*
2/84 **Joanna** *Kool & The Gang*
21/70 **Joanne** *Michael Nesmith*
42/86 **Jody** *Jermaine Stewart*
28/71 **Jody's Got Your Girl And Gone**
Johnnie Taylor
83/58 **Joe Joe Gun** *Chuck Berry*
91/62 **Joey Baby** *Anita & Th' So-And-So's*
76/56 **Joey, Joey, Joey** *Peggy Lee*
46/59 **Joey's Song** *Bill Haley & His Comets*
John And Yoko *see: Ballad Of*
99/62 **John Birch Society** *Chad Mitchell Trio*
100/55 **Johnnie's Comin' Home** *Johnnie Ray*
1/62 **Johnny Angel** *Shelley Fabares*
Johnny B. Goode
8/58 *Chuck Berry*
71/64 *Dion*
92/70 *Johnny Winter*
84/83 **Johnny B. Goode** *Peter Tosh*
42/82 **Johnny Can't Read** *Don Henley*
81/56 **Johnny Casanova** *Jaye P. Morgan*
76/86 **Johnny Come Home** *Fine Young Cannibals*
75/56 **Johnny Concho Theme (Wait For Me)**
Frank Sinatra
72/76 **Johnny Cool** *Steve Gibbons Band*
69/60 **Johnny Freedom** *Johnny Horton*
7/62 **Johnny Get Angry** *Joanie Sommers*
21/62 **Johnny Jingo** *Hayley Mills*
21/62 **Johnny Loves Me** *Shelley Fabares*
41/69 **Johnny One Time** *Brenda Lee*
54/59 **Johnny Reb** *Johnny Horton*
35/62 **Johnny Will** *Pat Boone*
96/61 **Johnny Willow** *Fred Darian*
17/72 **Join Together** *Who*
Joker, The
1/74 *Steve Miller Band*
93/78 *Snail*
Joker (That's What They Call Me)
22/57 *Hilltoppers*
25/57 *Billy Myles*
20/66 **Joker Went Wild** *Brian Hyland*
97/67 **Jokers, The** *Peter & Gordon*
65/81 **Jole Blon** *Gary U.S. Bonds*
60/74 **Jolene** *Dolly Parton*
4/65 **Jolly Green Giant** *Kingsmen*
(also see: Big Boy Pete)
39/81 **Jones Vs. Jones** *Kool & The Gang*
18/60 **Josephine** *Bill Black's Combo*
26/78 **Josie** *Steely Dan*
63/72 **Josie** *Kris Kristofferson*
81/60 **Journey Of Love** *Crests*
16/68 **Journey To The Center Of The Mind**
Amboy Dukes
6/72 **Joy** *Apollo 100 featuring Tom Parker*
30/74 **Joy** *Isaac Hayes*

41/67 **Joy** *Mitch Ryder*
1/71 **Joy To The World** *Three Dog Night*
61/84 **Joystick** *Dazz Band*
26/65 **Ju Ju Hand** *Sam The Sham & The Pharoahs*
59/66 **Juanita Banana** *Peels*
65/72 **Jubilation** *Paul Anka*
22/58 **Judy** *Frankie Vaughan*
78/67 **Judy** *Elvis Presley*
86/59 **Judy** *David Seville*
Judy Blue Eyes *see: Suite*
1/68 **Judy In Disguise (With Glasses)** *John Fred*
95/64 **Judy Loves Me** *Johnny Crawford*
33/75 **Judy Mae** *Boomer Castleman*
5/63 **Judy's Turn To Cry** *Lesley Gore*
45/83 **Juicy Fruit** *Mtume*
10/56 **Juke Box Baby** *Perry Como*
26/82 **Juke Box Hero** *Foreigner*
57/61 **Juke Box Saturday Night** *Nino & The Ebb Tides*
82/76 **Jukin** *Atlanta Rhythm Section*
76/69 **Julia** *Ramsey Lewis*
64/56 **Julie** *Doris Day* *(also see: Oh, Julie)*
5/70 **Julie, Do Ya Love Me** *Bobby Sherman*
85/70 **July 12, 1939** *Charlie Rich*
100/69 **July You're A Woman** *Pat Boone*
57/68 **Jumbo** *Bee Gees*
1/84 **Jump** *Van Halen*
72/76 **Jump** *Aretha Franklin*
Jump Back
49/64 *Rufus Thomas*
63/67 *King Curtis*
F/76 **Jump For Joy** *Biddu Orchestra*
3/84 **Jump (For My Love)** *Pointer Sisters*
27/72 **Jump Into The Fire** *Nilsson*
28/60 **Jump Over** *Freddy Cannon*
24/82 **Jump To It** *Aretha Franklin*
Jumpin' Jack Flash
3/68 *Rolling Stones*
89/71 *Johnny Winter*
21/86 *Aretha Franklin*
21/57 **June Night** *Jimmy Dorsey*
94/67 **Jungle, The** *B.B. King*
4/74 **Jungle Boogie** *Kool & The Gang*
52/86 **Jungle Boy** *John Eddie*
8/72 **Jungle Fever** *Chakachas*
20/85 **Jungle Love** *Time*
23/77 **Jungle Love** *Steve Miller Band*
3/75 **Junior's Farm** *Paul McCartney*
9/76 **Junk Food Junkie** *Larry Groce*
81/59 **Jupiter-C** *Pat & The Satellites*
37/61 **Jura (I Swear I Love You)** *Les Paul & Mary Ford*
Just A Closer Walk With Thee
44/60 *Jimmie Rodgers*
93/60 *Pete Fountain*
4/58 **Just A Dream** *Jimmy Clanton*
12/85 **Just A Gigolo (medley)** *David Lee Roth*
8/65 **Just A Little** *Beau Brummels*
40/60 **Just A Little** *Brenda Lee*
Just A Little Bit
64/60 *Rosco Gordon*
39/65 *Roy Head*
92/68 **Just A Little Bit** *Blue Cheer*
97/69 **Just A Little Bit** *Little Milton*
7/65 **Just A Little Bit Better** *Herman's Hermits*
23/75 **Just A Little Bit Of You** *Michael Jackson*
76/69 **Just A Little Love** *B.B. King*
85/66 **Just A Little Misunderstanding** *Contours*
9/59 **Just A Little Too Much** *Ricky Nelson*
100/64 **Just A Moment Ago** *Soul Sisters*
90/75 **Just A Smile** *Pilot*
7/77 **Just A Song Before I Go** *Crosby, Stills & Nash*
54/64 **Just Ain't Enough Love** *Eddie Holland*
67/69 **Just Ain't No Love** *Barbara Acklin*
85/86 **Just Another Day** *Oingo Boingo*
46/82 **Just Another Day In Paradise** *Bertie Higgins*
12/85 **Just Another Night** *Mick Jagger*
68/79 **Just Another Night** *Ian Hunter*
19/85 **Just As I Am** *Air Supply*
76/56 **Just As Long As I'm With You** *Pat Boone*
84/72 **Just As Long As You Need Me** *Independents*
Just As Much As Ever
32/59 *Bob Beckham*
24/68 *Bobby Vinton*
7/59 **Just Ask Your Heart** *Frankie Avalon*
55/83 **Just Be Good To Me** *S.O.S. Band*
67/81 **Just Be My Lady** *Larry Graham*
91/67 **Just Be Sincere** *Jackie Wilson*
19/64 **Just Be True** *Gene Chandler*
29/57 **Just Because** *Lloyd Price*
99/61 **Just Because** *McGuire Sisters*
8/57 **Just Between You And Me** *Chordettes*
21/81 **Just Between You And Me** *April Wine*
12/57 **Just Born (To Be Your Baby)** *Perry Como*
79/60 **Just Call Me (And I'll Understand)** *Lloyd Price*
78/80 **Just Can't Wait** *J. Geils Band*
38/82 **Just Can't Win 'Em All** *Stevie Woods*
35/60 **Just Come Home** *Hugo & Luigi*
Just Don't Want To Be Lonely
60/73 *Ronnie Dyson*
10/74 *Main Ingredient*
5/68 **Just Dropped In (To See What Condition My Condition Was In)** *First Edition*
20/61 **Just For Old Time's Sake** *McGuire Sisters*
82/80 **Just For The Moment** *Ray Kennedy*
96/60 **Just Give Me A Ring** *Clyde McPhatter*
36/83 **Just Got Lucky** *JoBoxers*
64/62 **Just Got To Know** *Jimmy McCracklin*
46/56 **Just In Time** *Tony Bennett*
18/59 **Just Keep It Up** *Dee Clark*
69/70 **Just Let It Come** *Alive 'N Kickin'*
33/66 **Just Like A Woman** *Bob Dylan*
75/58 **Just Like In The Movies** *Upbeats*
11/66 **Just Like Me** *Paul Revere & The Raiders*
86/81 **Just Like Paradise** *Larry John McNally*
(Just Like) Romeo & Juliet
6/64 *Reflections*
55/75 *Sha Na Na*
1/80 **(Just Like) Starting Over** *John Lennon*
69/67 **Just Look What You've Done** *Brenda Holloway*
97/56 **Just Love Me** *Jaye P. Morgan*
26/58 **Just Married** *Marty Robbins*
1/71 **Just My Imagination** *Temptations*
17/81 **Just Once** *James Ingram*
97/67 **Just Once In A Lifetime** *Brenda & The Tabulations*
9/65 **Just Once In My Life** *Righteous Brothers*
76/65 **Just One Kiss From You** *Impressions*
Just One Look
10/63 *Doris Troy*
98/64 *Hollies*
44/67 *Hollies*
86/74 *Anne Murray*
44/79 *Linda Ronstadt*
85/65 **Just One More Day** *Otis Redding*
70/84 **Just One More Time** *Headpins*
64/67 **Just One Smile** *Gene Pitney*
29/60 **Just One Time** *Don Gibson*
Just Out Of Reach (Of My Two Open Arms)
24/61 *Solomon Burke*
66/67 *Percy Sledge*
11/77 **Just Remember I Love You** *Firefall*

40/71 **Just Seven Numbers (Can Straighten Out My Life)** *Four Tops*
82/70 **Just Seventeen** *Raiders*
39/81 **Just So Lonely** *Get Wet*
55/62 **Just Tell Her Jim Said Hello** *Elvis Presley*
58/79 **Just The Same Way** *Journey*
2/81 **Just The Two Of Us** *Grover Washington, Jr./Bill Withers*
3/78 **Just The Way You Are** *Billy Joel*
64/84 **Just The Way You Like It** *S.O.S. Band*
7/76 **Just To Be Close To You** *Commodores*
69/59 **Just To Be With You** *Passions*
26/57 **Just To Hold My Hand** *Clyde McPhatter*
52/82 **Just To Satisfy You** *Waylon & Willie*
30/75 **Just Too Many People** *Melissa Manchester*
2/56 **Just Walking In The Rain** *Johnnie Ray*
27/78 **Just What I Needed** *Cars*
4/79 **Just When I Needed You Most** *Randy Vanwarmer*
73/65 **Just Yesterday** *Jack Jones*
77/66 **Just Yesterday** *Al Martino*
20/65 **Just You** *Sonny & Cher*
27/76 **Just You And I** *Melissa Manchester*
4/73 **Just You 'N' Me** *Chicago*
Just Young
69/58 *Andy Rose*
80/58 *Paul Anka*
85/65 **Justine** *Righteous Brothers*

K

39/71 **K-Jee** *Nite-Liters*
Ka-Ding-Dong
24/56 *G-Clefs*
35/56 *Diamonds*
38/56 *Hilltoppers*
55/74 **Kalimba Story** *Earth, Wind & Fire*
Kansas City
1/59 *Wilbert Harrison*
60/59 *Rocky Olson*
72/59 *Hank Ballard*
95/59 *Little Richard*
23/64 *Trini Lopez*
55/67 *James Brown*
31/65 **Kansas City Star** *Roger Miller*
55/67 **Karate** *Emperor's*
51/67 **Karate-Boo-Ga-Loo** *Jerryo*
94/86 **Karen** *B.E. Taylor Group*
1/84 **Karma Chameleon** *Culture Club*
75/72 **Kate** *Johnny Cash*
16/58 **Kathy-O** *Diamonds*
43/75 **Katmandu** *Bob Seger*
66/59 **Katy Too** *Johnny Cash*
83/69 **Kay** *John Wesley Ryles, I*
74/85 **Kayleigh** *Marillion*
16/69 **Keem-O-Sabe** *Electric Indian*
8/57 **Keep A Knockin'** *Little Richard*
64/67 **Keep A Light In The Window Till I Come Home** *Solomon Burke*
8/83 **(Keep Feeling) Fascination** *Human League*
54/76 **Keep Holding On** *Temptations*
2/77 **Keep It Comin' Love** *KC & The Sunshine Band*
91/83 **Keep It Confidential** *Nona Hendryx*
50/74 **Keep It In The Family** *Leon Haywood*
78/83 **Keep It Tight** *Single Bullet Theory*
37/77 **Keep Me Cryin'** *Al Green*
41/79 **Keep On Dancin'** *Gary's Gang*
4/65 **Keep On Dancing** *Gentrys*
66/61 **Keep On Dancing** *Hank Ballard*
66/68 **Keep On Dancing** *Alvin Cash*
75/70 **Keep On Doin'** *Isley Brothers*
88/72 **Keep On Doin' What You're Doin'** *Bobby Byrd*
77/72 **Keep On Keeping On** *N.F. Porter*
24/68 **Keep On Lovin' Me Honey** *Marvin Gaye & Tammi Terrell*
89/70 **Keep On Loving Me (You'll See The Change)** *Bobby Bland*
1/81 **Keep On Loving You** *REO Speedwagon*
10/64 **Keep On Pushing** *Impressions*
76/66 **Keep On Running** *Spencer Davis Group*
90/72 **Keep On Running** *Stevie Wonder*
81/79 **Keep On Running Away** *Lazy Racer*
Keep On Singing
50/73 *Austin Roberts*
15/74 *Helen Reddy*
10/74 **Keep On Smilin'** *Wet Willie*
1/73 **Keep On Truckin'** *Eddie Kendricks*
50/75 **Keep On Tryin'** *Poco*
85/65 **Keep On Trying** *Bobby Vee*
90/75 **Keep Our Love Alive** *Paul Davis*
70/72 **Keep Playin' That Rock 'N' Roll** *Edgar Winter*
9/65 **Keep Searchin'** *Del Shannon*
Keep The Ball Rollin'
14/67 *Jay & The Techniques*
100/68 *Al Hirt*
71/71 **Keep The Customer Satisfied** *Gary Puckett*
36/80 **Keep The Fire** *Kenny Loggins*
7/82 **Keep The Fire Burnin'** *REO Speedwagon*
52/68 **Keep The One You Got** *Joe Tex*
62/81 **Keep This Train A-Rollin'** *Doobie Brothers*
Keep Your Eye On The Sparrow *see: Baretta's Theme*
88/62 **Keep Your Hands In Your Pockets** *Playmates*
12/62 **Keep Your Hands Off My Baby** *Little Eva*
75/61 **Keep Your Hands Off Of Him** *Damita Jo*
2/87 **Keep Your Hands To Yourself** *Georgia Satellites*
52/74 **Keep Your Head To The Sky** *Earth, Wind & Fire*
58/62 **Keep Your Love Locked (Deep In Your Heart)** *Paul Petersen*
10/73 **Keeper Of The Castle** *Four Tops*
50/82 **Keeping Our Love Alive** *Henry Paul Band*
18/85 **Keeping The Faith** *Billy Joel*
20/55 **Kentuckian Song** *Hilltoppers*
85/76 **Kentucky Moonrunner** *Cledus Maggard*
16/70 **Kentucky Rain** *Elvis Presley*
Kentucky Woman
22/67 *Neil Diamond*
38/68 *Deep Purple*
6/58 **Kewpie Doll** *Perry Como*
8/82 **Key Largo** *Bertie Higgins*
82/56 **Key To My Heart** *Rosemary Clooney*
79/77 **Kick It Out** *Heart*
82/69 **Kick Out The Jams** *MC5*
61/64 **Kick That Little Foot Sally Ann** *Round Robin*
4/66 **Kicks** *Paul Revere & The Raiders*
82/76 **Kid Charlemagne** *Steely Dan*
55/81 **Kid Is Hot Tonite** *Loverboy*
95/73 **Kid Stuff** *Barbara Fairchild*
33/84 **Kid's American** *Matthew Wilder*
7/60 **Kiddio** *Brook Benton*
25/82 **Kids In America** *Kim Wilde*
72/73 **Kids Say The Darndest Things** *Tammy Wynette*
79/64 **Kiko** *Jimmy McGriff*

60/79 **Killer Cut** *Charlie*
Killer Joe
16/63 *Rocky Fellers*
77/66 *Kingsmen*
74/70 **Killer Joe** *Quincy Jones*
12/75 **Killer Queen** *Queen*
28/81 **Killin' Time** *Fred Knoblock & Susan Anton*
1/73 **Killing Me Softly With His Song** *Roberta Flack*
30/77 **Killing Of Georgie** *Rod Stewart*
1/67 **Kind Of A Drag** *Buckinghams*
17/63 **Kind Of Boy You Can't Forget** *Raindrops*
42/86 **Kind Of Magic** *Queen*
8/86 **King For A Day** *Thompson Twins*
40/72 **King Heroin** *James Brown*
13/77 **King Is Gone** *Ronnie McDowell*
69/75 **King Kong** *Jimmy Castor Bunch*
King Kong
see: Theme From, and also 'Kong'
51/67 **King Midas In Reverse** *Hollies*
45/62 **King Of Clowns** *Neil Sedaka*
60/74 **King Of Nothing** *Seals & Crofts*
3/83 **King Of Pain** *Police*
62/84 **King Of Suede** *'Weird Al' Yankovic*
36/80 **King Of The Hill** *Rick Pinette & Oak*
4/65 **King Of The Road** *Roger Miller*
(also see: Queen Of The House)
30/62 **King Of The Whole Wide World** *Elvis Presley*
17/78 **King Tut** *Steve Martin*
70/78 **Kings And Queens** *Aerosmith*
31/74 **Kings Of The Party** *Brownsville Station*
1/86 **Kiss** *Prince*
21/72 **Kiss An Angel Good Mornin'** *Charley Pride*
88/56 **Kiss And Run** *Peggy King*
1/76 **Kiss And Say Goodbye** *Manhattans*
63/85 **Kiss And Tell** *Isley, Jasper, Isley*
25/65 **Kiss Away** *Ronnie Dove*
37/79 **Kiss In The Dark** *Pink Lady*
30/56 **Kiss Me Another** *Georgia Gibbs*
15/68 **Kiss Me Goodbye** *Petula Clark*
37/80 **Kiss Me In The Rain** *Barbra Streisand*
34/64 **Kiss Me Quick** *Elvis Presley*
29/64 **Kiss Me Sailor** *Diane Renay*
1/81 **Kiss On My List** *Daryl Hall & John Oates*
25/83 **Kiss The Bride** *Elton John*
1/78 **Kiss You All Over** *Exile*
3/57 **Kisses Sweeter Than Wine** *Jimmie Rodgers*
91/60 **Kissin' And Twistin'** *Fabian*
12/64 **Kissin' Cousins** *Elvis Presley*
82/61 **Kissin' Game** *Dion*
35/61 **Kissin' On The Phone** *Paul Anka*
Kissin' Time
11/59 *Bobby Rydell*
83/74 *Kiss*
31/73 **Kissing My Love** *Bill Withers*
60/59 **Kissing Tree** *Billy Grammer*
77/79 **Knee Deep** *Funkadelic*
16/57 **Knee Deep In The Blues** *Guy Mitchell*
15/67 **Knight In Rusty Armour** *Peter & Gordon*
92/72 **Knock Knock Who's There** *Mary Hopkin*
64/64 **Knock! Knock! (Who's There?)** *Orlons*
Knock On Wood
28/66 *Eddie Floyd*
30/67 *Otis & Carla*
1/79 *Amii Stewart*
1/71 **Knock Three Times** *Dawn*
12/73 **Knockin' On Heaven's Door** *Bob Dylan*
61/85 **Knocking At Your Back Door** *Deep Purple*
14/77 **Knowing Me, Knowing You** *Abba*
76/67 **Knucklehead** *Bar-Kays*
51/71 **Ko-Ko Joe** *Jerry Reed*
Ko Ko Mo (I Love You So)
2/55 *Perry Como*
6/55 *Crew-Cuts*
92/61 *Flamingos*
2/73 **Kodachrome** *Paul Simon*
78/60 **Kommotion** *Duane Eddy*
48/77 **Kong** *Dickie Goodman*
4/59 **Kookie, Kookie (Lend Me Your Comb)** *Edward Byrnes & Connie Stevens*
Kookie Little Paradise
61/60 *Jo Ann Campbell*
73/60 *Tree Swingers*
59/69 **Kool And The Gang** *Kool & The Gang*
41/69 **Kozmic Blues** *Janis Joplin*
93/73 **Kufanya Mapenzi (Making Love)** *Ramsey Lewis*
54/69 **Kum Ba Yah** *Tommy Leonetti*
40/74 **Kung Fu** *Curtis Mayfield*
1/74 **Kung Fu Fighting** *Carl Douglas*
1/86 **Kyrie** *Mr. Mister*

52/68 **L. David Sloane** *Michele Lee*
98/73 **L.A. Freeway** *Jerry Jeff Walker*
73/71 **L.A. Goodbye** *Ides Of March*
54/71 **L.A. International Airport** *Susan Raye*
45/77 **L.A. Sunshine** *War*
La Bamba
22/59 *Ritchie Valens*
85/62 *Tokens*
86/66 *Trini Lopez*
9/58 **La Dee Dah** *Billy & Lillie*
78/81 **La-Di-Da** *Sad Cafe*
32/58 **La-Do-Dada** *Dale Hawkins*
81/61 **La Dolce Vita (The Sweet Life)** *Ray Ellis*
41/74 **La Grange** *ZZ Top*
90/66 **La La La** *Gerry & The Pacemakers*
9/70 **La La La (If I Had You)** *Bobby Sherman*
62/64 **La La La La La** *Blendells*
La-La Means I Love You
4/68 *Delfonics*
72/81 *Tierra*
La La Peace Song
30/74 *Al Wilson*
62/74 *O.C. Smith*
La Mer *see: Beyond The Sea*
La Montana *see: If She Should Come To You*
87/61 **La Pachanga** *Audrey Arno*
20/58 **La Paloma** *Billy Vaughn*
72/62 **La Paloma Twist** *Chubby Checker*
86/59 **La Plume De Ma Tante** *Hugo & Luigi*
8/80 **Ladies Night** *Kool & The Gang*
1/80 **Lady** *Kenny Rogers*
6/75 **Lady** *Styx*
10/79 **Lady** *Little River Band*
28/80 **Lady** *Whispers*
39/67 **Lady** *Jack Jones*
20/67 **Lady Bird** *Nancy Sinatra & Lee Hazlewood*
14/75 **Lady Blue** *Leon Russell*
48/76 **Lady Bump** *Penny McLean*
62/67 **Lady Came From Baltimore** *Bobby Darin*
76/83 **Lady Down On Love** *Alabama*
82/72 **Lady Eleanor** *Lindisfarne*
82/67 **Lady Friend** *Byrds*
6/66 **Lady Godiva** *Peter & Gordon*
24/66 **Lady Jane** *Rolling Stones*
86/83 **Lady, Lady, Lady** *Joe 'Bean' Esposito*

24/78 **Lady Love** *Lou Rawls*
95/70 **Lady Love** *Klowns*
30/83 **Lady Love Me (One More Time)**
George Benson
14/60 **Lady Luck** *Lloyd Price*
Lady Madonna
4/68 *Beatles*
100/68 *Fats Domino*
1/75 **Lady Marmalade** *LaBelle*
78/69 **Lady-O** *Turtles*
76/85 **Lady Of My Heart** *Jack Wagner*
46/77 **Lady (Put The Light On Me)**
Brownsville Station
Lady Sings The Blues, Love Theme
see: Happy
47/86 **Lady Soul** *Temptations*
2/68 **Lady Willpower**
Gary Puckett & The Union Gap
45/79 **Lady Writer** *Dire Straits*
8/81 **Lady (You Bring Me Up)** *Commodores*
91/76 **Laid Back Love** *Major Harris*
33/68 **Lalena** *Donovan*
Lament Of Cherokee
see: Indian Reservation
71/74 **Lamplight** *David Essex*
Land Of 1000 Dances
77/63 *Chris Kenner*
30/65 *Cannibal & The Headhunters*
67/65 *Thee Midniters*
6/66 *Wilson Pickett*
95/69 *Electric Indian*
60/83 *J. Geils Band*
4/87 **Land Of Confusion** *Genesis*
86/86 **Land Of La La** *Stevie Wonder*
86/77 **Land Of Make Believe** *Chuck Mangione*
29/66 **Land Of Milk And Honey** *Vogues*
46/80 **Landlord** *Gladys Knight & The Pips*
52/82 **Landslide** *Olivia Newton-John*
13/84 **Language Of Love** *Dan Fogelberg*
32/61 **Language Of Love** *John D. Loudermilk*
100/71 **Language Of Love** *Intrigues*
94/67 **Lapland** *Baltimore & Ohio Marching Band*
Lara's Theme *see: Somewhere My Love*
79/56 **Large Large House** *Mike Pedicin Quintet*
82/60 **Last Chance** *Collay & the Satellites*
13/65 **Last Chance To Turn Around** *Gene Pitney*
21/76 **Last Child** *Aerosmith*
3/78 **Last Dance** *Donna Summer*
99/60 **Last Dance** *McGuire Sisters*
Last Date
2/60 *Floyd Cramer*
21/60 *Lawrence Welk*
(also see: My Last Date (With You))
19/75 **Last Farewell** *Roger Whittaker*
Last Game Of The Season (A Blind Man In The Bleachers)
18/75 *David Geddes*
58/75 *Kenny Starr*
Last Kiss
2/64 *J. Frank Wilson*
34/74 *Wednesday*
92/74 *J. Frank Wilson*
60/63 **Last Leaf** *Cascades*
99/63 **Last Minute** *Jimmy McGriff*
99/67 **Last Minute Miracle** *Shirelles*
3/61 **Last Night** *Mar-Keys*
8/72 **(Last Night) I Didn't Get To Sleep At All**
5th Dimension
42/79 **Last Of The Singing Cowboys**
Marshall Tucker Band
96/60 **Last One To Know** *Fleetwoods*
77/82 **Last Safe Place On Earth** *Le Roux*
3/73 **Last Song** *Edward Bear*
77/73 **Last Tango In Paris** *Herb Alpert*
56/73 **Last Thing On My Mind** *Neil Diamond*
9/65 **Last Time** *Rolling Stones*
40/84 **Last Time I Made Love**
Joyce Kennedy & Jeffrey Osborne
61/71 **Last Time I Saw Her** *Glen Campbell*
14/74 **Last Time I Saw Him** *Diana Ross*
1/66 **Last Train To Clarksville** *Monkees*
39/80 **Last Train To London**
Electric Light Orchestra
25/67 **Last Waltz** *Engelbert Humperdinck*
40/66 **Last Word In Lonesome Is Me** *Eddy Arnold*
27/57 **Lasting Love** *Sal Mineo*
57/80 **Late At Night** *England Dan Seals*
89/61 **Late Date** *Parkays*
6/80 **Late In The Evening** *Paul Simon*
64/81 **Lately** *Stevie Wonder*
90/61 **Laugh** *Velvets*
10/65 **Laugh At Me** *Sonny*
15/65 **Laugh, Laugh** *Beau Brummels*
98/70 **Laughin And Clownin** *Ray Charles*
10/69 **Laughing** *Guess Who*
15/63 **Laughing Boy** *Mary Wells*
1/75 **Laughter In The Rain** *Neil Sedaka*
Laura, What's He Got That I Ain't Got
66/67 *Frankie Laine*
78/67 *Brook Benton*
14/65 **Laurie (Strange Things Happen)**
Dickey Lee
3/59 **Lavender-Blue** *Sammy Turner*
Laverne & Shirley Theme
see: Making Our Dreams Come True
Lawdy Miss Clawdy
47/60 *Gary Stites*
41/67 *Buckinghams*
Lawrence Of Arabia *see: Theme From*
13/83 **Lawyers In Love** *Jackson Browne*
11/70 **Lay A Little Lovin' On Me**
Robin McNamara
54/72 **Lay-Away** *Isley Brothers*
6/70 **Lay Down (Candles In The Rain)** *Melanie*
3/78 **Lay Down Sally** *Eric Clapton*
Lay Down Your Arms
16/56 *Chordettes*
59/56 *Anne Shelton*
40/85 **Lay It Down** *Ratt*
86/79 **Lay It On The Line** *Triumph*
Lay Lady Lay
7/69 *Bob Dylan*
99/70 *Ferrante & Teicher*
71/72 *Isley Brothers*
55/67 **Lay Some Happiness On Me** *Dean Martin*
6/85 **Lay Your Hands On Me** *Thompson Twins*
66/84 **Layin' It On The Line** *Jefferson Starship*
Layla
51/71 *Derek & The Dominos*
10/72 *Derek & The Dominos*
14/67 **Lazy Day** *Spanky & Our Gang*
40/64 **Lazy Elsie Molly** *Chubby Checker*
91/79 **Lazy Eyes** *T.M.G.*
86/64 **Lazy Lady** *Fats Domino*
12/58 **Lazy Mary** *Lou Monte*
Lazy River
57/56 *Roberta Sherwood*
14/61 *Bobby Darin*
43/61 *Si Zenter*
21/58 **Lazy Summer Night** *Four Preps*
54/86 **Le Bel Age** *Pat Benatar*
1/78 **Le Freak** *Chic*
58/78 **Le Spank** *Le Pamplemousse*
68/86 **Lead A Double Life** *Loverboy*
5/79 **Lead Me On** *Maxine Nightingale*
9/82 **Leader Of The Band** *Dan Fogelberg*
19/65 **Leader Of The Laundromat** *Detergents*
1/64 **Leader Of The Pack** *Shangri-Las*

53/86 **Leader Of The Pack** *Twisted Sister*
25/62 **Leah** *Roy Orbison*
67/58 **Lean Jean** *Bill Haley & His Comets*
1/72 **Lean On Me** *Bill Withers*
9/66 **Leaning On The Lamp Post** *Herman's Hermits*
92/57 **Leap Frog** *Chuck Alaimo Quartet*
1/55 **Learnin' The Blues** *Frank Sinatra*
61/55 **Learning To Love** *Peggy King*
6/82 **Leather And Lace** *Stevie Nicks/Don Henley*
27/84 **Leave A Tender Moment Alone** *Billy Joel*
24/84 **Leave It** *Yes*
91/57 **Leave It To Love** *Sarah Vaughan*
62/63 **Leave Me Alone** *Baby Washington*
44/58 **Leave Me Alone (Let Me Cry)** *Dicky Doo & The Don'ts*
3/73 **Leave Me Alone (Ruby Red Dress)** *Helen Reddy*
Leave My Kitten Alone
60/59 *Little Willie John*
60/61 *Little Willie John*
73/61 *Johnny Preston*
83/63 **Leavin' On Your Mind** *Patsy Cline*
76/64 **Leaving Here** *Eddie Holland*
71/80 **Leaving L.A.** *Deliverance*
21/73 **Leaving Me** *Independents*
1/69 **Leaving On A Jet Plane** *Peter, Paul & Mary*
64/84 **Lebanon** *Human League*
82/56 **Left Arm Of Buddha** *Les Baxter*
50/84 **Left In The Dark** *Barbra Streisand*
9/58 **Left Right Out Of Your Heart** *Patti Page*
87/75 **Leftovers** *Millie Jackson*
81/83 **Legal Tender** *B-52's*
50/72 **Legend In Your Own Time** *Carly Simon*
Legend Of Billy Jack *see: One Tin Soldier*
31/80 **Legend Of Wooley Swamp** *Charlie Daniels Band*
8/84 **Legs** *ZZ Top*
77/81 **Leila** *ZZ Top*
Lemon Tree
35/62 *Peter, Paul & Mary*
20/65 *Trini Lopez*
69/75 **Leona** *Wet Willie*
81/67 **Leopard-Skin Pill-Box Hat** *Bob Dylan*
25/58 **Leroy** *Jack Scott*
31/68 **Les Bicyclettes De Belsize** *Engelbert Humperdinck*
34/68 **Lesson, The** *Vikki Carr*
73/80 **Lesson In Leavin'** *Dottie West*
Let A Man Come In And Do The Popcorn
21/69 *James Brown (Part One)*
40/70 *James Brown (Part Two)*
36/69 **Let A Woman Be A Woman - Let A Man Be A Man** *Dyke & The Blazers*
3/76 **Let 'Em In** *Wings*
10/76 **Let Her In** *John Travolta*
39/85 **Let Him Go** *Animotion*
84/84 **Let It All Blow** *Dazz Band*
Let It Be
1/70 *Beatles*
49/71 *Joan Baez*
Let It Be Me
57/57 *Jill Corey*
7/60 *Everly Brothers*
5/64 *Jerry Butler & Betty Everett*
94/67 *Sweet Inspirations*
36/69 *Glen Campbell & Bobbie Gentry*
40/82 *Willie Nelson*
45/78 **Let It Go, Let It Flow** *Dave Mason*
12/67 **Let It Out (Let It All Hang Out)** *Hombres*
48/72 **Let It Rain** *Eric Clapton*
23/74 **Let It Ride** *Bachman-Turner Overdrive*
51/56 **Let It Ring** *Doris Day*
64/60 **Let It Rock** *Chuck Berry*
30/76 **Let It Shine** *Olivia Newton-John*
77/76 **Let It Shine** *Santana*
5/82 **Let It Whip** *Dazz Band*
23/67 **Let Love Come Between Us** *James & Bobby Purify*
20/69 **Let Me** *Paul Revere & The Raiders*
58/70 **Let Me Back In** *Tyrone Davis*
29/65 **Let Me Be** *Turtles*
43/80 **Let Me Be** *Korona*
62/66 **Let Me Be Good To You** *Carla Thomas*
71/68 **Let Me Be Lonely** *Dionne Warwick*
31/80 **Let Me Be The Clock** *Smokey Robinson*
94/69 **Let Me Be The Man My Daddy Was** *Chi-Lites*
59/86 **Let Me Be The One** *Five Star*
70/75 **Let Me Be The One (medley)** *Al Wilson*
Let Me Be The One
87/62 *Paris Sisters*
74/69 *Peaches & Herb*
6/74 **Let Me Be There** *Olivia Newton-John*
21/80 **Let Me Be Your Angel** *Stacy Lattisaw*
55/73 **Let Me Be Your Lovemaker** *Betty Wright*
1/57 **(Let Me Be Your) Teddy Bear** *Elvis Presley*
20/61 **Let Me Belong To You** *Brian Hyland*
66/62 **Let Me Call You Sweetheart** *Timi Yuro*
80/76 **Let Me Down Easy** *American Flyer*
86/86 **Let Me Down Easy** *Roger Daltrey*
96/73 **Let Me Down Easy** *Cornelius Brothers & Sister Rose*
96/62 **Let Me Entertain You** *Ray Anthony*
80/74 **Let Me Get To Know You** *Paul Anka*
38/82 **Let Me Go** *Ray Parker Jr.*
74/83 **Let Me Go** *Heaven 17*
75/81 **Let Me Go** *Rings*
35/80 **Let Me Go, Love** *Nicolette Larson*
Let Me Go, Lover!
1/55 *Joan Weber*
6/55 *Teresa Brewer*
8/55 *Patti Page*
17/55 *Sunny Gale*
90/63 **Let Me Go The Right Way** *Supremes*
32/70 **Let Me Go To Him** *Dionne Warwick*
4/62 **Let Me In** *Sensations*
36/73 **Let Me In** *Osmonds*
86/76 **Let Me In** *Derringer*
42/79 **Let Me Know (I Have A Right)** *Gloria Gaynor*
94/69 **Let Me Love You** *Ray Charles*
48/81 **Let Me Love You Once** *Greg Lake*
10/80 **Let Me Love You Tonight** *Pure Prairie League*
75/75 **Let Me Make Love To You** *O'Jays*
43/78 **Let Me Party With You** *Bunny Sigler*
17/73 **Let Me Serenade You** *Three Dog Night*
88/80 **Let Me Sleep Alone** *Cugini*
87/75 **Let Me Start Tonite** *Lamont Dozier*
44/80 **Let Me Talk** *Earth, Wind & Fire*
90/66 **Let Me Tell You, Babe** *Nat King Cole*
18/82 **Let Me Tickle Your Fancy** *Jermaine Jackson*
63/73 **Let Me Try Again** *Frank Sinatra*
9/80 **Let My Love Open The Door** *Pete Townshend*
18/58 **Let The Bells Keep Ringing** *Paul Anka*
42/82 **Let The Feeling Flow** *Peabo Bryson*
Let The Four Winds Blow
29/57 *Roy Brown*
15/61 *Fats Domino*

Let The Good Times Roll
20/56 *Shirley & Lee*
48/60 *Shirley & Lee*
78/60 *Ray Charles*
81/65 *Roy Orbison*
22/67 *Bunny Sigler (medley)*
(also see: Good Times Roll)
88/68 **Let The Heartaches Begin** *Long John Baldry*
7/60 **Let The Little Girl Dance** *Billy Bland*
8/84 **Let The Music Play** *Shannon*
32/76 **Let The Music Play** *Barry White*
78/70 **Let The Music Take Your Mind** *Kool & The Gang*
91/78 **Let The Song Last Forever** *Dan Hill*
1/69 **Let The Sunshine In (medley)** *5th Dimension*
Let Them *see: Let 'Em*
100/60 **Let Them Talk** *Little Willie John*
7/61 **Let There Be Drums** *Sandy Nelson*
55/75 **Let There Be Music** *Orleans*
69/57 **Let There Be You** *Five Keys*
88/74 **Let This Be A Lesson To You** *Independents*
91/70 **Let This Be A Letter (To My Baby)** *Jackie Wilson*
73/61 **Let True Love Begin** *Nat King Cole*
47/73 **Let Us Love** *Bill Withers*
27/74 **Let Your Hair Down** *Temptations*
1/76 **Let Your Love Flow** *Bellamy Brothers*
28/71 **Let Your Love Go** *Bread*
57/73 **Let Your Yeah Be Yeah** *Brownsville Station*
46/67 **Let Yourself Go** *James Brown*
63/69 **Let Yourself Go** *Friends Of Distinction*
71/68 **Let Yourself Go** *Elvis Presley*
36/78 **Let's All Chant** *Michael Zager Band*
87/58 **Let's Be Lovers** *Playmates*
65/80 **Let's Be Lovers Again** *Eddie Money/Valerie Carter*
55/76 **Let's Be Young Tonight** *Jermaine Jackson*
Let's Call It A Day Girl
77/66 *Razor's Edge*
92/69 *Bobby Vee*
91/77 **Let's Clean Up The Ghetto** *Philadelphia International All Stars*
1/83 **Let's Dance** *David Bowie*
Let's Dance
4/62 *Chris Montez*
92/69 *Ola & The Janglers*
88/81 **Let's Dance (Make Your Body Move)** *West Street Mob*
1/75 **Let's Do It Again** *Staple Singers*
88/80 **Let's Do Something Cheap And Superficial** *Burt Reynolds*
40/65 **Let's Do The Freddie** *Chubby Checker*
(also see: Do The Freddie)
66/60 **(Let's Do) The Hully Gully Twist** *Bill Doggett*
21/67 **Let's Fall In Love** *Peaches & Herb*
72/78 **Let's Get Crazy Tonight** *Rupert Holmes*
1/73 **Let's Get It On** *Marvin Gaye*
61/76 **Let's Get It Together** *El Coco*
44/82 **Let's Get It Up** *AC/DC*
32/74 **Let's Get Married** *Al Green*
9/80 **Let's Get Serious** *Jermaine Jackson*
8/61 **Let's Get Together** *Hayley Mills*
Let's Get Together *see: Get Together*
41/70 **Let's Give Adam And Eve Another Chance** *Gary Puckett & The Union Gap*
14/79 **Let's Go** *Cars*
19/62 **Let's Go** *Routers*
90/62 **Let's Go** *Floyd Cramer*
39/61 **Let's Go Again** *Hank Ballard*
7/86 **Let's Go All The Way** *Sly Fox*
53/57 **Let's Go Calypso** *Rusty Draper*
1/84 **Let's Go Crazy** *Prince*
30/83 **Let's Go Dancin' (Ooh La, La, La)** *Kool & The Gang*
F/77 **Let's Go Down To The Disco** *Undisputed Truth*
31/66 **Let's Go Get Stoned** *Ray Charles*
6/60 **Let's Go, Let's Go, Let's Go** *Hank Ballard*
88/85 **Let's Go Out Tonight** *Nile Rodgers*
53/80 **Let's Go 'Round Again** *Average White Band*
26/63 **Let's Go Steady Again** *Neil Sedaka*
97/66 **Let's Go Steady Again** *Sam Cooke*
55/58 **Let's Go Steady For The Summer** *Three G's*
60/62 **Let's Go Trippin'** *Dick Dale*
77/84 **Let's Go Up** *Diana Ross*
3/81 **Let's Groove** *Earth, Wind & Fire*
Let's Hang On!
3/65 *4 Seasons*
32/82 *Barry Manilow*
Let's Have A Party
37/60 *Wanda Jackson*
99/64 *Rivieras*
1/84 **Let's Hear It For The Boy** *Deniece Williams*
38/63 **Let's Kiss And Make Up** *Bobby Vinton*
41/57 **Let's Light The Christmas Tree** *Ruby Wright*
20/63 **Let's Limbo Some More** *Chubby Checker*
8/67 **Let's Live For Today** *Grass Roots*
Let's Live Together
35/76 *Road Apples*
70/78 *Cazz*
11/65 **Let's Lock The Door** *Jay & The Americans*
44/59 **Let's Love** *Johnny Mathis*
83/76 **Let's Make A Baby** *Billy Paul*
75/68 **Let's Make A Promise** *Peaches & Herb*
98/70 **Let's Make Each Other Happy** *Illusion*
98/63 **Let's Make Love Tonight** *Bobby Rydell*
88/65 **Let's Move & Groove (Together)** *Johnny Nash*
35/73 **Let's Pretend** *Raspberries*
52/84 **Let's Pretend We're Married** *Prince*
18/74 **Let's Put It All Together** *Stylistics*
81/81 **Let's Put The Fun Back In Rock N Roll** *Freddy Cannon*
92/76 **Let's Rock** *Ellison Chase*
55/67 **Let's Spend The Night Together** *Rolling Stones*
20/66 **Let's Start All Over Again** *Ronnie Dove*
Let's Stay Together
1/72 *Al Green*
48/72 *Isaac Hayes*
26/84 *Tina Turner*
57/63 **Let's Stomp** *Bobby Comstock*
31/74 **Let's Straighten It Out** *Latimore*
56/85 **Let's Talk About Me** *Alan Parsons Project*
7/60 **Let's Think About Living** *Bob Luman*
48/60 **Let's Try Again** *Clyde McPhatter*
20/63 **Let's Turkey Trot** *Little Eva*
8/61 **Let's Twist Again** *Chubby Checker*
Let's Work Together
26/70 *Canned Heat*
32/70 *Wilbert Harrison*
Letter, The
1/67 *Box Tops*
20/69 *Arbors*
7/70 *Joe Cocker*
Letter, The
75/65 *Sonny & Cher*
85/63 **Letter From Betty** *Bobby Vee*
25/64 **Letter From Sherry** *Dale Ward*
19/62 **Letter Full Of Tears** *Gladys Knight & The Pips*

Letter Song *see: S.Y.S.L.J.F.M.*
25/58 **Letter To An Angel** *Jimmy Clanton*
93/67 **Letter To Dad** *Every Father's Teenage Son*
60/73 **Letter To Lucille** *Tom Jones*
33/73 **Letter To Myself** *Chi-Lites*
85/64 **Letter To The Beatles** *Four Preps*
39/75 **Letting Go** *Wings*
24/72 **Levon** *Elton John*
7/71 **Liar** *Three Dog Night*
12/65 **Liar, Liar** *Castaways*
66/83 **Lick It Up** *Kiss*
14/68 **Licking Stick - Licking Stick** *James Brown*
11/77 **Lido Shuffle** *Boz Scaggs*
13/62 **Lie To Me** *Brook Benton*
Liechtensteiner Polka
16/57 *Will Glahe*
48/57 *Lawrence Welk*
20/66 **Lies** *Knickerbockers*
30/83 **Lies** *Thompson Twins*
42/72 **Lies** *J.J. Cale*
53/71 **Life** *Elvis Presley*
93/68 **Life** *Sly & The Family Stone*
68/73 **Life Ain't Easy** *Dr. Hook*
52/72 **Life And Breath** *Climax*
Life And Death In G & A
74/69 *Abaco Dream*
90/75 *Love Childs Afro Cuban Blues Band*
80/79 **Life During Wartime** *Talking Heads*
94/83 **Life Gets Better** *Graham Parker*
7/86 **Life In A Northern Town** *Dream Academy*
19/85 **Life In One Day** *Howard Jones*
11/77 **Life In The Fast Lane** *Eagles*
72/71 **Life Is A Carnival** *Band*
8/74 **Life Is A Rock (But The Radio Rolled Me)** *Reunion*
54/74 **Life Is A Song Worth Singing** *Johnny Mathis*
34/81 **Life Of Illusion** *Joe Walsh*
91/61 **Life's A Holiday** *Jerry Wallace*
12/78 **Life's Been Good** *Joe Walsh*
87/62 **Life's Too Short** *Lafayettes*
90/86 **Life's What You Make It** *Talk Talk*
66/65 **Lifetime Of Loneliness** *Jackie DeShannon*
Light My Fire
1/67 *Doors*
3/68 *Jose Feliciano*
87/68 *Doors*
69/79 *Amii Stewart (medley)*
87/77 **Light Of A Clear Blue Morning** *Dolly Parton*
63/58 **Light Of Love** *Peggy Lee*
44/71 **Light Sings** *5th Dimension*
66/78 **Light The Sky On Fire** *Jefferson Starship*
67/76 **Light Up The World With Sunshine** *Hamilton, Joe Frank & Dennison*
1/66 **Lightnin' Strikes** *Lou Christie*
24/67 **Lightning's Girl** *Nancy Sinatra*
68/78 **Lights** *Journey*
93/70 **Lights Of Tucson** *Jim Campbell*
12/84 **Lights Out** *Peter Wolf*
11/67 **(Lights Went Out In) Massachusetts** *Bee Gees*
27/66 **Like A Baby** *Len Barry*
67/65 **Like A Child** *Julie Rogers*
12/86 **Like A Rock** *Bob Seger*
2/65 **Like A Rolling Stone** *Bob Dylan*
36/76 **Like A Sad Song** *John Denver*
40/78 **Like A Sunday In Salem (The Amos & Andy Song)** *Gene Cotton*
63/75 **Like A Sunday Morning** *Lana Cantrell*
47/85 **Like A Surgeon** *'Weird Al' Yankovic*
1/84 **Like A Virgin** *Madonna*
24/67 **Like An Old Time Movie** *Scott McKenzie*
77/71 **Like An Open Door** *Fuzz*
96/64 **Like Columbus Did** *Reflections*
82/86 **Like Flames** *Berlin*
42/59 **Like I Love You** *Edd Byrnes*
38/61 **Like, Long Hair** *Paul Revere & The Raiders*
14/86 **Like No Other Night** *38 Special*
22/60 **Like Strangers** *Everly Brothers*
55/63 **Like The Big Guys Do** *Rocky Fellers*
72/75 **Like They Say In L.A.** *East L.A. Car Pool*
17/68 **Like To Get To Know You** *Spanky & Our Gang*
49/85 **Like To Get To Know You Well** *Howard Jones*
46/59 **Like Young** *Andre Previn & David Rose*
87/68 **Lili Marlene** *Al Martino*
99/62 **Limbo** *Capris*
97/62 **Limbo Dance** *Champs*
Limbo Rock
2/62 *Chubby Checker*
40/62 *Champs*
55/81 **Limelight** *Rush*
92/62 **Limelight** *Mr. Acker Bilk*
28/63 **Linda** *Jan & Dean*
94/61 **Linda** *Adam Wade*
46/59 **Linda Lu** *Ray Sharpe*
61/75 **Linda On My Mind** *Conway Twitty*
Ling, Ting, Tong
26/55 *Charms*
28/55 *Five Keys*
65/61 *Buddy Knox*
Lion Sleeps Tonight
1/61 *Tokens*
3/72 *Robert John*
84/65 **Lip Sync (To The Tongue Twisters)** *Len Barry*
17/57 **Lips Of Wine** *Andy Williams*
51/81 **Lipstick** *Suzi Quatro*
61/76 **Lipstick** *Michel Polnareff*
15/56 **Lipstick And Candy And Rubbersole Shoes** *Julius LaRosa*
5/59 **Lipstick On Your Collar** *Connie Francis*
Lipstick Traces (On A Cigarette)
80/62 *Benny Spellman*
48/65 *O'Jays*
43/60 **Lisa** *Jeanne Black*
98/62 **Lisa** *Ferrante & Teicher*
73/71 **Lisa, Listen To Me** *Blood, Sweat & Tears*
Lisbon Antigua
1/56 *Nelson Riddle*
19/56 *Mitch Miller*
Listen Here
45/68 *Eddie Harris*
100/70 *Brian Auger & The Trinity*
54/86 **Listen Like Thieves** *INXS*
62/64 **Listen Lonely Girl** *Johnny Mathis*
3/66 **Listen People** *Herman's Hermits*
92/68 **Listen, They're Playing My Song** *Ray Charles*
59/78 **Listen To Her Heart** *Tom Petty*
63/69 **Listen To The Band** *Monkees*
96/76 **Listen To The Buddha** *Ozo*
11/72 **Listen To The Music** *Doobie Brothers*
1/75 **Listen To What The Man Said** *Wings*
Little *also see: Lil'*
45/62 **Little Altar Boy** *Vic Dana*
16/68 **Little Arrows** *Leapy Lee*
21/63 **Little Band Of Gold** *James Gilreath*
51/65 **Little Bell** *Dixie Cups*
91/73 **Little Bit Like Magic** *King Harvest*
2/67 **Little Bit Me, A Little Bit You** *Monkees*
11/76 **Little Bit More** *Dr. Hook*
Little Bit Now
63/62 *Majors*
67/67 *Dave Clark Five*

16/65 **Little Bit Of Heaven** *Ronnie Dove*
81/85 **Little Bit Of Heaven** *Natalie Cole*
77/84 **Little Bit Of Love** *Dwight Twilley*
38/86 **Little Bit Of Love (Is All It Takes)** *New Edition*
Little Bit Of Soap
12/61 *Jarmels*
95/65 *Garnet Mimms*
58/66 *Exciters*
52/70 *Paul Davis*
34/79 *Nigel Olsson*
2/67 **Little Bit O'Soul** *Music Explosion*
19/60 **Little Bitty Girl** *Bobby Rydell*
Little Bitty Pretty One
6/57 *Thurston Harris*
57/57 *Bobby Day*
58/60 *Frankie Lymon*
25/62 *Clyde McPhatter*
13/72 *Jackson 5*
Little Bitty Tear
9/62 *Burl Ives*
84/62 *Wanda Jackson*
29/62 **Little Black Book** *Jimmy Dean*
85/67 **Little Black Egg** *Nightcrawlers*
17/58 **Little Blue Man** *Betty Johnson*
Little Boxes
70/64 *Pete Seeger*
83/64 *Womenfolk*
Little Boy
52/64 *Tony Bennett*
92/64 **Little Boy** *Crystals*
76/56 **Little Boy Blue** *Billy Vaughn*
88/59 **Little Boy Blue** *Huelyn Duvall*
60/66 **Little Boy (In Grown Up Clothes)** *4 Seasons*
17/61 **Little Boy Sad** *Johnny Burnette*
78/58 **Little Brass Band** *David Seville*
36/85 **Little By Little** *Robert Plant*
Little By Little
55/57 *Micki Marlo*
57/57 *Nappy Brown*
Little Child
56/56 *Eddie Albert & Sondra Lee*
62/56 *Lael & Cab Calloway*
7/64 **Little Children** *Billy J. Kramer with The Dakotas*
36/60 **Little Coco Palm** *Jerry Wallace*
Little Darlin'
2/57 *Diamonds*
41/57 *Gladiolas*
49/82 **Little Darlin'** *Sheila*
Little Darling, I Need You
47/66 *Marvin Gaye*
48/77 *Doobie Brothers*
15/63 **Little Deuce Coupe** *Beach Boys*
11/61 **Little Devil** *Neil Sedaka*
8/62 **Little Diane** *Dion*
30/59 **Little Dipper** *Mickey Mozart Quintet*
71/61 **Little Dog Cried** *Jimmie Rodgers*
93/64 **Little Donna** *Rivieras*
Little Drummer Boy
13/58 *Harry Simeone Chorale*
15/59 *Harry Simeone Chorale*
63/59 *Johnny Cash*
24/60 *Harry Simeone Chorale*
22/61 *Harry Simeone Chorale*
96/61 *Jack Halloran Singers*
28/62 *Harry Simeone Chorale*
95/75 *Moonlion*
76/63 **Little Eeefin Annie** *Joe Perkins*
23/61 **Little Egypt (Ying-Yang)** *Coasters*
91/61 **Little Feeling (Called Love)** *Jack Scott*
51/67 **Little Games** *Yardbirds*
8/66 **Little Girl** *Syndicate Of Sound*
92/59 **Little Girl** *Ritchie Valens*
57/73 **Little Girl Gone** *Donna Fargo*
20/66 **Little Girl I Once Knew** *Beach Boys*
57/56 **Little Girl Of Mine** *Cleftones*
74/83 **Little Good News** *Anne Murray*
Little Green Apples
2/68 *O.C. Smith*
39/68 *Roger Miller*
96/68 *Patti Page*
21/70 **Little Green Bag** *George Baker Selection*
67/58 **Little Gypsy** *Ames Brothers*
Little Honda
9/64 *Hondells*
65/64 *Beach Boys*
17/81 **Little In Love** *Cliff Richard*
72/80 **Little Is Enough** *Pete Townshend*
3/80 **Little Jeannie** *Elton John*
68/84 **Little Lady** *Duke Jupiter*
Little Latin Lupe Lu
49/63 *Righteous Brothers*
46/64 *Kingsmen*
17/66 *Mitch Ryder & The Detroit Wheels*
69/68 **Little Less Conversation** *Elvis Presley*
73/57 **Little Loneliness** *Kay Starr*
42/65 **Little Lonely One** *Tom Jones*
44/84 **Little Love** *Juice Newton*
33/56 **Little Love Can Go A Long, Long Way** *Dream Weavers*
61/79 **Little Lovin' (Keeps The Doctor Away)** *Raes*
21/66 **Little Man** *Sonny & Cher*
54/64 **Little Marie** *Chuck Berry*
48/58 **Little Mary** *Fats Domino*
96/60 **Little Miss Blue** *Dion*
74/65 **Little Miss Sad** *Five Emprees*
70/61 **Little Miss Stuck-Up** *Playmates*
99/67 **Little Miss Sunshine** *Tommy Roe*
3/79 **Little More Love** *Olivia Newton-John*
41/56 **Little Musicians** *Hugo Winterhalter*
3/64 **Little Old Lady (From Pasadena)** *Jan & Dean*
Little Old Wine Drinker, Me
38/67 *Dean Martin*
96/67 *Robert Mitchum*
4/67 **Little Ole Man (Uptight-Everything's Alright)** *Bill Cosby*
44/78 **Little One** *Chicago*
76/61 **Little Pedro** *Olympics*
45/58 **Little Pigeon** *Sal Mineo*
72/58 **Little Pixie** *Moe Koffman Quartette*
62/77 **Little Queen** *Heart*
Little Queenie
80/59 *Chuck Berry*
73/64 *Bill Black's Combo*
87/68 **Little Rain Must Fall** *Epic Splendor*
6/83 **Little Red Corvette** *Prince*
23/62 **Little Red Rented Rowboat** *Joe Dowell*
2/66 **Lil' Red Riding Hood** *Sam The Sham & The Pharoahs*
72/58 **Little Red Riding Hood** *Big Bopper*
11/63 **Little Red Rooster** *Sam Cooke*
32/57 **Little Sandy Sleighfoot** *Jimmy Dean*
Little Serenade
66/58 *Teddy Randazzo*
98/58 *Ames Brothers*
86/85 **Little Sheila** *Slade*
5/61 **Little Sister** *Elvis Presley*
20/59 **Little Space Girl** *Jesse Lee Turner*
1/58 **Little Star** *Elegants*
95/63 **Little Star** *Bobby Callender*
71/83 **Little Thing Called Love** *Neil Young*
13/65 **Little Things** *Bobby Goldsboro*
35/60 **Little Things Mean A Lot** *Joni James*
84/63 **Little Tin Soldier** *Toy Dolls*

20/83 **Little Too Late** *Pat Benatar*
77/62 **Little Too Much** *Clarence 'Frogman' Henry*
12/63 **Little Town Flirt** *Del Shannon*
84/64 **Little Toy Balloon** *Danny Williams*
46/58 **Little Train** *Marianne Vasel & Erich Storz*
95/61 **Little Turtle Dove** *Charms*
99/64 **Little White Cloud That Cried** *Wayne Newton*
25/57 **Little White Lies** *Betty Johnson*
3/73 **Little Willy** *Sweet*
3/69 **Little Woman** *Bobby Sherman*
F/72 **Little Woman Love** *Wings*
48/65 **Little You** *Freddie & The Dreamers*
96/62 **Little Young Lover** *Impressions*
63/67 **Live** *Merry-Go-Round*
Live And Die *see: (Forever)*
2/73 **Live And Let Die** *Wings*
42/80 **Live Every Minute** *Ali Thomson*
34/85 **Live Every Moment** *REO Speedwagon*
99/67 **Live For Life** *Jack Jones*
32/86 **Live Is Life** *Opus*
52/74 **Live It Up** *Isley Brothers*
1/86 **Live To Tell** *Madonna*
42/64 **Live Wire** *Martha & The Vandellas*
89/75 **Live Your Life Before You Die** *Pointer Sisters*
76/66 **Livin' Above Your Head** *Jay & The Americans*
42/76 **Livin' Ain't Livin'** *Firefall*
97/60 **Livin' Dangerously** *McGuire Sisters*
20/76 **Livin' For The Weekend** *O'Jays*
19/74 **Livin' For You** *Al Green*
31/84 **Livin' In Desperate Times** *Olivia Newton-John*
40/77 **Livin' In The Life** *Isley Brothers*
15/79 **Livin' It Up (Friday Night)** *Bell & James*
1/87 **Livin' On A Prayer** *Bon Jovi*
13/77 **Livin' Thing** *Electric Light Orchestra*
22/63 **Living A Lie** *Al Martino*
37/75 **Living A Little, Laughing A Little** *Spinners*
Living Doll
30/59 *Cliff Richard*
92/59 *David Hill*
45/81 **Living Eyes** *Bee Gees*
Living For The City
8/74 *Stevie Wonder*
91/75 *Ray Charles*
87/66 **Living For You** *Sonny & Cher*
23/81 **Living In A Fantasy** *Leo Sayer*
22/72 **Living In A House Divided** *Cher*
4/86 **Living In America** *James Brown*
87/86 **Living In The Background** *Baltimora*
11/73 **Living In The Past** *Jethro Tull*
Living In The U.S.A.
94/68 *Steve Miller Band*
49/74 *Steve Miller Band*
6/81 **Living Inside Myself** *Gino Vannelli*
72/76 **Living It Down** *Freddy Fender*
65/70 **Living Loving Maid** *Led Zeppelin*
25/77 **Living Next Door To Alice** *Smokie*
75/83 **Living On The Edge** *Jim Capaldi*
61/86 **Living On Video** *Trans-X*
32/73 **Living Together, Growing Together** *5th Dimension*
69/72 **Living Without You** *Manfred Mann's Earth Band*
52/78 **Livingston Saturday Night** *Jimmy Buffett*
37/75 **Lizzie And The Rainman** *Tanya Tucker*
44/62 **Lizzie Borden** *Chad Mitchell Trio*
14/69 **Lo Mucho Que Te Quiero** *Rene & Rene*
F/78 **Load-Out, The** *Jackson Browne*
44/63 **Locking Up My Heart** *Marvelettes*
Loco-Motion
1/62 *Little Eva*
1/74 *Grand Funk*
62/76 **Locomotive Breath** *Jethro Tull*
12/63 **Loddy Lo** *Chubby Checker*
Lodi
52/69 *Creedence Clearwater Revival*
67/69 *Al Wilson*
6/79 **Logical Song** *Supertramp*
Lola
9/70 *Kinks*
81/80 *Kinks*
Lola's Theme
67/56 *Muir Mathieson*
75/56 *Steve Allen*
61/62 **Lolita Ya-Ya** *Ventures*
Lollipop
2/58 *Chordettes*
20/58 *Ronald & Ruby*
Lollipops And Roses
54/62 *Paul Petersen*
66/62 *Jack Jones*
39/78 **London Town** *Wings*
69/74 **Lone Ranger** *Oscar Brown Jr.*
97/63 **Lone Teen Ranger** *Jerry Landis*
89/78 **Loneliest Man On The Moon** *David Castle*
65/64 **Loneliest Night** *Dale & Grace*
14/67 **(Loneliness Made Me Realize) It's You That I Need** *Temptations*
22/65 **L-O-N-E-L-Y** *Bobby Vinton*
87/67 **Lonely Again** *Eddy Arnold*
6/60 **Lonely Blue Boy** *Conway Twitty*
66/61 **Lonely Blue Nights** *Rosie*
Lonely Boy
1/59 *Paul Anka*
F/72 *Donny Osmond*
7/77 **Lonely Boy** *Andrew Gold*
82/63 **Lonely Boy, Lonely Guitar** *Duane Eddy*
6/62 **Lonely Bull** *Herb Alpert*
88/57 **Lonely Chair** *Lloyd Price*
76/61 **Lonely Crowd** *Teddy Vann*
3/71 **Lonely Days** *Bee Gees*
Lonely Drifter
93/63 *O'Jays*
59/67 *Pieces Of Eight*
41/80 **Lonely Eyes** *Robert John*
24/59 **Lonely For You** *Gary Stites*
50/59 **Lonely Guitar** *Annette*
57/85 **Lonely In Love** *Giuffria*
93/68 **Lonely Is The Name** *Sammy Davis, Jr.*
76/86 **Lonely Is The Night** *Air Supply*
26/58 **Lonely Island** *Sam Cooke*
80/61 **Lonely Life** *Jackie Wilson*
32/61 **Lonely Man** *Elvis Presley*
57/72 **Lonely Man** *Chi-Lites*
3/76 **Lonely Night (Angel Face)** *Captain & Tennille*
84/82 **Lonely Nights** *Bryan Adams*
6/85 **Lonely Ol' Night** *John Cougar Mellencamp*
23/59 **Lonely One** *Duane Eddy*
75/76 **Lonely One** *Special Delivery featuring Terry Huff*
5/75 **Lonely People** *America*
72/59 **Lonely Saturday Night** *Don French*
60/85 **Lonely School** *Tommy Shaw*
57/75 **Lonely School Year** *Hudson Brothers*
69/66 **Lonely Soldier** *Mike Williams*
5/59 **Lonely Street** *Andy Williams*
57/61 **Lonely Street** *Clarence 'Frogman' Henry*
72/66 **Lonely Summer** *Shades Of Blue*
39/63 **Lonely Surfer** *Jack Nitzsche*

Lonely Teardrops
7/59 *Jackie Wilson*
54/71 *Brian Hyland*
62/76 *Narvel Felts*
12/60 **Lonely Teenager** *Dion*
45/81 **Lonely Together** *Barry Manilow*
22/60 **Lonely Weekends** *Charlie Rich*
60/79 **Lonely Wind** *Kansas*
54/60 **Lonely Winds** *Drifters*
6/79 **Lonesome Loser** *Little River Band*
93/56 **Lonesome Lover Blues** *Fontane Sisters*
75/72 **Lonesome Mary** *Chilliwack*
59/61 **Lonesome Number One** *Don Gibson*
71/59 **Lonesome Old House** *Don Gibson*
89/67 **Lonesome Road** *Wonder Who?*
7/58 **Lonesome Town** *Ricky Nelson*
88/61 **Lonesome Whistle Blues** *Freddy King*
31/71 **Long Ago And Far Away** *James Taylor*
61/71 **Long Ago Tomorrow** *B.J. Thomas*
75/70 **Long And Lonesome Road** *Shocking Blue*
1/70 **Long And Winding Road** *Beatles*
F/70 **Long As I Can See The Light** *Creedence Clearwater Revival*
62/62 **Long As The Rose Is Red** *Florraine Darlin*
2/72 **Long Cool Woman (In A Black Dress)** *Hollies*
26/72 **Long Dark Road** *Hollies*
67/64 **Long Gone Lonesome Blues** *Hank Williams, Jr.*
73/69 **Long Green** *Fireballs*
56/75 **Long Haired Country Boy** *Charlie Daniels Band*
38/72 **Long Haired Lover From Liverpool** *Little Jimmy Osmond*
77/58 **Long Hot Summer** *Jimmie Rodgers*
76/78 **Long Hot Summer Nights** *Wendy Waldman*
63/67 **Long Legged Girl (With The Short Dress On)** *Elvis Presley*
79/69 **Long Line Rider** *Bobby Darin*
97/65 **Long Live Love** *Sandie Shaw*
33/66 **Long Live Our Love** *Shangri-Las*
54/79 **Long Live Rock** *Who*
Long Lonely Nights
45/57 *Lee Andrews & The Hearts*
49/57 *Clyde McPhatter*
17/65 *Bobby Vinton*
74/70 *Dells*
20/70 **Long Lonesome Highway** *Michael Parks*
25/70 **Long Long Time** *Linda Ronstadt*
20/78 **Long, Long Way From Home** *Foreigner*
(Long Nights) *see: Blue Collar Man*
89/71 **Long Promised Road** *Beach Boys*
8/80 **Long Run** *Eagles*
9/75 **Long Tall Glasses (I Can Dance)** *Leo Sayer*
Long Tall Sally
6/56 *Little Richard*
8/56 *Pat Boone*
96/64 **Long Tall Shorty** *Tommy Tucker*
51/63 **Long Tall Texan** *Murry Kellum*
22/77 **Long Time** *Boston*
92/71 **Long Time, A Long Way To Go** *Runt*
85/81 **Long Time Lovin' You** *McGuffey Lane*
93/72 **Long Time To Be Alone** *New Colony Six*
8/73 **Long Train Runnin'** *Doobie Brothers*
F/71 **Long Way Around** *Linda Ronstadt*
91/73 **Long Way Home** *Neil Diamond*
2/80 **Longer** *Dan Fogelberg*
89/82 **Longer You Wait** *Gino Vannelli*
14/84 **Longest Time** *Billy Joel*
6/55 **Longest Walk** *Jaye P. Morgan*
5/74 **Longfellow Serenade** *Neil Diamond*
67/67 **Look At Granny Run, Run** *Howard Tate*
91/63 **Look At Me** *Dobie Gray*
52/66 **Look At Me Girl** *Bobby Vee*
39/75 **Look At Me (I'm In Love)** *Moments*
89/69 **Look At Mine** *Petula Clark*
68/84 **Look At That Cadillac** *Stray Cats*
95/75 **Look At You** *George McCrae*
73/64 **Look Away** *Garnet Mimms*
Look For A Star
16/60 *Garry Miles*
19/60 *Billy Vaughn*
26/60 *Garry Mills*
29/60 *Deane Hawley*
56/68 **Look, Here Comes The Sun** *Sunshine Company*
Look Homeward Angel
55/56 *Four Esquires*
36/57 *Johnnie Ray*
47/64 *Monarchs*
Look In My Eyes
14/61 *Chantels*
97/66 *Three Degrees*
11/75 **Look In My Eyes Pretty Woman** *Dawn*
82/77 **Look Into Your Heart** *Aretha Franklin*
56/70 **Look-Ka Py Py** *Meters*
72/85 **Look My Way** *Vels*
Look Of Love
22/67 *Dusty Springfield*
4/68 *Sergio Mendes & Brasil '66*
79/71 *Isaac Hayes*
27/65 **Look Of Love** *Lesley Gore*
18/83 **Look Of Love (Part One)** *ABC*
89/68 **Look Over Your Shoulder** *O'Jays*
32/66 **Look Through Any Window** *Hollies*
24/66 **Look Through My Window** *Mamas & The Papas*
49/68 **Look To Your Soul** *Johnny Rivers*
Look What They've Done To My Song Ma
14/70 *New Seekers*
65/72 *Ray Charles*
4/72 **Look What You Done For Me** *Al Green*
32/67 **Look What You've Done** *Pozo-Seco Singers*
14/80 **Look What You've Done To Me** *Boz Scaggs*
51/77 **Look What You've Done To My Heart** *Marilyn McCoo & Billy Davis, Jr.*
58/58 **Look Who's Blue** *Don Gibson*
96/71 **Lookin' Back** *Bob Seger*
Lookin' For A Love
72/62 *Valentinos*
39/72 *J. Geils Band*
10/74 *Bobby Womack*
5/80 **Lookin' For Love** *Johnny Lee*
94/66 **Lookin' For Love** *Ray Conniff*
65/76 **Lookin' Out For #1** *Bachman-Turner Overdrive*
2/70 **Lookin' Out My Back Door** *Creedence Clearwater Revival*
16/72 **Lookin' Through The Windows** *Jackson 5*
Looking Back
5/58 *Nat King Cole*
70/69 *Joe Simon*
62/68 **Looking For A Fox** *Clarence Carter*
39/83 **Looking For A Stranger** *Pat Benatar*
45/64 **Looking For Love** *Connie Francis*
29/76 **Looking For Space** *John Denver*
61/85 **Looking Over My Shoulder** *'Til Tuesday*
Looking Through The Eyes Of Love
28/65 *Gene Pitney*
39/73 *Partridge Family*
64/65 **Looking With My Eyes** *Dionne Warwick*
41/80 **Looks Like Love Again** *Dann Rogers*
1/77 **Looks Like We Made It** *Barry Manilow*
54/84 **Looks That Kill** *Motley Crue*
98/70 **Looky Looky (Look At Me Girl)** *O'Jays*
80/66 **Loop, The** *Johnny Lytle*
4/63 **Loop De Loop** *Johnny Thunder*
84/74 **Loose Booty** *Sly & The Family Stone*

64/73 **Lord Knows I'm Drinking** *Cal Smith*
68/73 **Lord, Mr. Ford** *Jerry Reed*
4/74 **Lord's Prayer** *Sister Janet Mead*
27/76 **Lorelei** *Styx*
76/77 **Lose Again** *Linda Ronstadt*
69/62 **Lose Her** *Bobby Rydell*
72/65 **Loser, The** *Skyliners*
43/67 **Loser (With A Broken Heart)** *Gary Lewis & The Playboys*
94/70 **Losers Weepers** *Etta James*
6/63 **Losing You** *Brenda Lee*
91/65 **Losing You** *Dusty Springfield*
89/61 **Losing Your Love** *Jim Reeves*
62/68 **Lost** *Jerry Butler*
34/80 **Lost Her In The Sun** *John Stewart*
63/73 **Lost Horizon** *Shawn Phillips*
3/80 **Lost In Love** *Air Supply*
35/85 **Lost In Love** *New Edition*
69/56 **Lost In The Shuffle** *Jaye P. Morgan*
55/79 **Lost In Your Love** *John Paul Young*
58/56 **Lost John** *Lonnie Donegan*
35/61 **Lost Love** *H.B. Barnum*
77/62 **Lost Penny** *Brook Benton*
Lost Someone
48/62 *James Brown*
94/66 *James Brown*
9/77 **Lost Without Your Love** *Bread*
8/79 **Lotta Love** *Nicolette Larson*
13/57 **Lotta Lovin'** *Gene Vincent*
Louie Louie
2/63 *Kingsmen*
30/66 *Sandpipers*
97/66 *Kingsmen*
89/78 *John Belushi*
62/72 **Louisiana** *Mike Kennedy*
F/75 **Louisiana Lou And Three Card Monty John** *Allman Brothers Band*
Louisiana Man
97/67 *Pozo-Seco Singers*
100/68 *Bobbie Gentry*
81/64 **L-O-V-E** *Nat King Cole*
55/85 **Love & Pride** *King*
13/75 **L-O-V-E (Love)** *Al Green*
42/71 **Love** *Lettermen*
F/57 **Love Affair** *Sal Mineo*
85/84 **Love Again** *John Denver & Sylvie Vartan*
89/56 **Love Ain't Right** *Kay Starr*
46/81 **Love All The Hurt Away** *Aretha Franklin & George Benson*
43/86 **Love Always** *El DeBarge*
70/79 **Love And Desire** *Arpeggio*
58/73 **Love And Happiness** *Earnest Jackson*
94/72 **Love And Liberty** *Laura Lee*
78/80 **Love And Loneliness** *Motors*
Love And Marriage
5/55 *Frank Sinatra*
20/55 *Dinah Shore*
92/86 **Love And Rock And Roll** *Greg Kihn*
77/76 **Love And Understanding (Come Together)** *Kool & The Gang*
99/66 **Love Attack** *James Carr*
Love Ballad
20/76 *L.T.D.*
18/79 *George Benson*
Love Being Your Fool
see: (Shu-Doo-Pa-Poo-Poop)
11/86 **Love Bizarre** *Sheila E.*
43/70 **Love Bones** *Johnnie Taylor*
71/66 **Love Bug** *Jack Jones*
92/77 **Love Bug** *Bumble Bee Unlimited*
78/58 **Love Bug Crawl** *Jimmy Edwards*
25/67 **Love Bug Leave My Heart Alone** *Martha & The Vandellas*
10/62 **Love Came To Me** *Dion*
2/69 **Love (Can Make You Happy)** *Mercy*
69/62 **Love Can't Wait** *Marty Robbins*
1/68 **Love Child** *Supremes*
17/82 **Love Come Down** *Evelyn King*
62/86 **Love Comes Quickly** *Pet Shop Boys*
62/75 **Love Corporation** *Hues Corporation*
32/79 **Love Don't Live Here Anymore** *Rose Royce*
15/74 **Love Don't Love Nobody** *Spinners*
92/75 **Love Don't You Go Through No Changes On Me** *Sister Sledge*
92/68 **Love Explosion** *Troy Keyes*
15/67 **Love Eyes** *Nancy Sinatra*
47/75 **Love Finds It's Own Way** *Gladys Knight & The Pips*
30/76 **Love Fire** *Jigsaw*
43/63 **Love For Sale** *Arthur Lyman*
64/72 **Love Gonna Pack Up (And Walk Out)** *Persuaders*
89/85 **Love Grammar** *John Parr*
5/70 **Love Grows (Where My Rosemary Goes)** *Edison Lighthouse*
61/77 **Love Gun** *Kiss*
Love Hangover
1/76 *Diana Ross*
80/76 *5th Dimension*
70/84 **Love Has A Mind Of Its Own** *Donna Summer*
88/84 **Love Has Finally Come At Last** *Bobby Womack & Patti LaBelle*
51/74 **Love Has No Pride** *Linda Ronstadt*
11/71 **Love Her Madly** *Doors*
Love Hurts
97/75 *Jim Capaldi*
8/76 *Nazareth*
7/73 **Love I Lost** *Harold Melvin & The Blue Notes*
20/67 **Love I Saw In You Was Just A Mirage** *Miracles*
91/61 **Love (I'm So Glad) I Found You** *Spinners*
79/56 **Love In A Home** *Doris Day*
Love In 'C' Minor
36/77 *Cerrone*
46/77 *Heart & Soul Orchestra*
60/68 **Love In Every Room** *Paul Mauriat*
88/86 **Love In Siberia** *Laban*
22/83 **Love In Store** *Fleetwood Mac*
91/69 **Love In The City** *Turtles*
15/82 **Love In The First Degree** *Alabama*
16/76 **Love In The Shadows** *Neil Sedaka*
93/68 **Love In Them There Hills** *Vibrations*
5/83 **Love Is A Battlefield** *Pat Benatar*
97/67 **Love Is A Doggone Good Thing** *Eddie Floyd*
66/65 **Love Is A Five-Letter Word** *James Phelps*
10/57 **Love Is A Golden Ring** *Frankie Laine*
13/66 **Love Is A Hurtin' Thing** *Lou Rawls*
Love Is A Many-Splendored Thing
1/55 *Four Aces*
26/55 *Don Cornell*
54/55 *David Rose*
79/55 *Woody Herman*
96/55 *Don, Dick N' Jimmy*
F/75 **Love Is A Rose** *Linda Ronstadt*
23/83 **Love Is A Stranger** *Eurythmics*
2/76 **Love Is Alive** *Gary Wright*
91/73 **Love Is All** *Engelbert Humperdinck*
7/68 **Love Is All Around** *Troggs*
65/69 **Love Is All I Have To Give** *Checkmates, Ltd.*
Love Is All We Need
15/58 *Tommy Edwards*
53/64 *Vic Dana*
50/66 *Mel Carter*
89/78 **Love Is All You Need** *High Inergy*
20/82 **Love Is Alright Tonite** *Rick Springfield*

77/77 **Love Is Better In The A.M.** *Johnnie Taylor*
Love Is Blue
1/68 *Paul Mauriat*
57/68 *Al Martino*
71/68 *Claudine Longet*
96/68 *Manny Kellem*
22/69 *Dells (medley)*
(Love Is Everywhere) *see: Revival*
16/86 **Love Is Forever** *Billy Ocean*
95/71 **Love Is Funny That Way** *Jackie Wilson*
69/79 **Love Is Gonna Come At Last** *Badfinger*
1/67 **Love Is Here And Now You're Gone** *Supremes*
10/82 **Love Is In Control (Finger On The Trigger)** *Donna Summer*
7/78 **Love Is In The Air** *John Paul Young*
86/69 **Love Is Just A Four-Letter World** *Joan Baez*
93/71 **Love Is Life** *Earth, Wind & Fire*
26/68 **(Love Is Like A) Baseball Game** *Intruders*
37/82 **Love Is Like A Rock** *Donnie Iris*
9/66 **Love Is Like An Itching In My Heart** *Supremes*
8/78 **Love Is Like Oxygen** *Sweet*
66/66 **Love Is Me, Love Is You** *Connie Francis*
Love Is Strange
11/57 *Mickey & Sylvia*
13/67 *Peaches & Herb*
10/79 **Love Is The Answer** *England Dan & John Ford Coley*
30/76 **Love Is The Drug** *Roxy Music*
80/86 **Love Is The Hero** *Billy Squier*
80/83 **Love Is The Key** *Maze Featuring Frankie Beverly*
85/74 **Love Is The Message** *MFSB featuring The Three Degrees*
17/85 **Love Is The Seventh Wave** *Sting*
86/62 **Love Is The Sweetest Thing** *Saverio Saridis*
7/56 **(Love Is) The Tender Trap** *Frank Sinatra*
1/78 **(Love Is) Thicker Than Water** *Andy Gibb*
55/73 **Love Is What You Make It** *Grass Roots*
16/73 **Love Jones** *Brighter Side Of Darkness (also see: Basketball Jones)*
69/84 **Love Kills** *Freddie Mercury*
16/70 **Love Land** *Watts 103rd St. Band*
Love Letters
5/62 *Ketty Lester*
19/66 *Elvis Presley*
1/57 **Love Letters In The Sand** *Pat Boone*
97/76 **Love Lifted Me** *Kenny Rogers*
81/81 **Love Light** *Yutaka*
17/85 **Love Light In Flight** *Stevie Wonder*
98/70 **Love Like A Man** *Ten Years After*
Love, Love, Love
30/56 *Clovers*
30/56 *Diamonds*
44/73 **Love, Love, Love** *Donny Hathaway*
1/76 **Love Machine** *Miracles*
76/68 **Love Machine** *O'Kaysions*
15/68 **Love Makes A Woman** *Barbara Acklin*
70/66 **Love (Makes Me Do Foolish Things)** *Martha & The Vandellas*
Love Makes The World Go Round
11/66 *Deon Jackson*
83/71 *Odds & Ends*
87/71 *Kiki Dee*
26/63 **Love (Makes The World Go 'Round)** *Paul Anka*
33/58 **Love Makes The World Go 'Round** *Perry Como*
72/69 **Love Man** *Otis Redding*
2/57 **Love Me** *Elvis Presley*
14/76 **Love Me** *Yvonne Elliman*
84/67 **Love Me** *Bobby Hebb*
94/71 **Love Me** *Impressions*
95/71 **Love Me** *Rascals*
64/83 **Love Me Again** *John Hall Band*
68/78 **Love Me Again** *Rita Coolidge*
88/63 **Love Me All The Way** *Kim Weston*
54/62 **Love Me As I Love You** *George Maharis*
100/65 **Love Me As Though There Were No Tomorrow** *Sonny Knight*
1/64 **Love Me Do** *Beatles*
10/74 **Love Me For A Reason** *Osmonds*
F/73 **Love Me For What I Am** *Lobo*
Love Me Forever
24/57 *Eydie Gorme*
25/57 *Four Esquires*
60/67 *Roger Williams*
62/56 **Love Me Good** *Jo Stafford*
45/84 **Love Me In A Special Way** *DeBarge*
100/59 **Love Me In The Daytime** *Doris Day*
46/72 **Love Me, Love Me Love** *Frank Mills*
86/72 **(Love Me) Love The Life I Lead** *Fantastics*
100/65 **Love Me Now** *Brook Benton*
79/77 **Love Me One More Time** *Karen Nelson & Billy T*
Love Me Or Leave Me
19/55 *Lena Horne*
20/55 *Sammy Davis, Jr.*
80/78 **Love Me Right** *Denise LaSalle*
Love Me Tender
1/56 *Elvis Presley*
44/56 *Henri Rene*
21/62 *Richard Chamberlain*
40/67 *Percy Sledge*
11/57 **Love Me To Pieces** *Jill Corey*
22/82 **Love Me Tomorrow** *Chicago*
13/69 **Love Me Tonight** *Tom Jones*
54/76 **Love Me Tonight** *Head East*
62/79 **Love Me Tonight** *Blackjack*
25/68 **Love Me Two Times** *Doors*
12/62 **Love Me Warm And Tender** *Paul Anka*
Love Me With All Your Heart
85/63 *Steve Allen (Cuando Calienta)*
3/64 *Ray Charles Singers*
38/66 *Bachelors*
39/71 **Love Means (You Never Have To Say You're Sorry)** *Sounds Of Sunshine*
84/70 **Love Minus Zero-No Limit** *Turley Richards*
97/73 **Love Music** *Raiders*
44/83 **Love My Way** *Psychedelic Furs*
59/83 **Love Never Fails** *Greg Kihn Band*
44/63 **Love Of A Boy** *Timi Yuro*
53/86 **Love Of A Lifetime** *Chaka Khan*
40/58 **Love Of My Life** *Everly Brothers*
64/76 **Love Of My Life** *Gino Vannelli*
21/63 **Love Of My Man** *Theola Kilgore*
56/61 **Love Of My Own** *Carla Thomas*
Love Of The Common People
54/69 *Winstons*
45/84 *Paul Young*
55/80 **Love On A Shoestring** *Captain & Tennille*
Love On A Two-Way Street
3/70 *Moments*
26/81 *Stacy Lattisaw*
88/83 **Love On My Mind Tonight** *Temptations*
87/81 **Love On The Airwaves** *Night*
87/80 **Love On The Phone** *Suzanne Fellini*
2/81 **Love On The Rocks** *Neil Diamond*
45/83 **Love On Your Side** *Thompson Twins*
36/76 **Love Or Leave** *Spinners*
Love Or Let Me Be Lonely
6/70 *Friends Of Distinction*
40/82 *Paul Davis*
32/78 **Love Or Something Like It** *Kenny Rogers*
34/79 **Love Pains** *Yvonne Elliman*
36/86 **Love Parade** *Dream Academy*

96/70 **Love, Peace And Happiness**
Chambers Brothers
37/82 **Love Plus One** *Haircut One Hundred*
Love Potion Number Nine
23/59 *Clovers*
3/65 *Searchers*
76/72 *Coasters*
22/68 **Love Power** *Sandpebbles*
41/75 **Love Power** *Willie Hutch*
22/76 **Love Really Hurts Without You**
Billy Ocean
76/73 **Love, Reign O'er Me** *Who*
82/85 **Love Resurrection** *Alison Moyet*
1/76 **Love Rollercoaster** *Ohio Players*
31/63 **Love She Can Count On** *Miracles*
40/63 **Love So Fine** *Chiffons*
3/76 **Love So Right** *Bee Gees*
5/84 **Love Somebody** *Rick Springfield*
12/74 **Love Song** *Anne Murray*
47/82 **Love Song** *Kenny Rogers*
67/72 **Love Song** *Tommy James*
64/84 **Love Songs Are Back Again (Medley):**
Band Of Gold
38/80 **Love Stinks** *J. Geils Band*
Love Story *see: Theme From*
70/79 **Love Struck** *Stonebolt*
44/81 **Love T.K.O.** *Teddy Pendergrass*
77/66 **Love Takes A Long Time Growing**
Deon Jackson
11/79 **Love Takes Time** *Orleans*
50/80 **Love That Got Away** *Firefall*
98/74 **Love That Really Counts** *Natural Four*
82/67 **Love That's Real** *Intruders*
Love The One You're With
14/71 *Stephen Stills*
18/71 *Isley Brothers*
14/80 **Love The World Away** *Kenny Rogers*
Love Theme From 'Lady Sings The Blues'
see: Happy
Love Theme From 'One On One'
see: My Fair Share
21/78 **Love Theme From Eyes Of Laura Mars (Prisoner)** *Barbra Streisand*
37/61 **Love Theme From One Eyed Jacks**
Ferrante & Teicher
Love Theme From Romeo & Juliet
1/69 *Henry Mancini*
96/69 *Johnny Mathis*
70/80 **Love Theme From Shogun (Mariko's Theme)** *Meco*
15/85 **Love Theme From St. Elmo's Fire**
David Foster
Love Theme From The Godfather
34/72 *Andy Williams*
66/72 *Nino Rota*
80/72 *Al Martino*
Love Theme From The Sandpiper
see: Shadow Of Your Smile
61/80 **Love X Love** *George Benson*
2/76 **Love To Love You Baby** *Donna Summer*
91/77 **Love To The World** *L.T.D.*
6/86 **Love Touch** *Rod Stewart*
1/73 **Love Train** *O'Jays*
72/70 **Love Uprising** *Otis Leaville*
Love Walked In
88/59 *Flamingos*
30/60 *Dinah Washington*
22/86 **Love Walks In** *Van Halen*
30/71 **Love We Had (Stays On My Mind)** *Dells*
9/86 **Love Will Conquer All** *Lionel Richie*
6/78 **Love Will Find A Way** *Pablo Cruise*
40/69 **Love Will Find A Way** *Jackie DeShannon*
Love Will Keep Us Together
1/75 *Captain & Tennille*
49/75 *Captain & Tennille (Por Amor Viviremos)*
30/84 **Love Will Show Us How** *Christine McVie*
13/82 **Love Will Turn You Around** *Kenny Rogers*
62/64 **Love With The Proper Stranger**
Jack Jones
5/75 **Love Won't Let Me Wait** *Major Harris*
9/87 **Love You Down** *Ready For The World*
1/79 **Love You Inside Out** *Bee Gees*
24/81 **Love You Like I Never Loved Before**
John O'Banion
26/58 **Love You Most Of All** *Sam Cooke*
1/70 **Love You Save** *Jackson 5*
56/66 **Love You Save (May Be Your Own)** *Joe Tex*
7/60 **Love You So** *Ron Holden*
61/67 **Love You So Much** *New Colony Six*
10/86 **Love Zone** *Billy Ocean*
7/82 **Love's Been A Little Bit Hard On Me**
Juice Newton
75/69 **Love's Been Good To Me** *Frank Sinatra*
59/83 **Love's Got A Line On You** *Scandal*
20/77 **Love's Grown Deep** *Kenny Nolan*
19/71 **Love's Lines, Angles And Rhymes**
5th Dimension
Love's Made A Fool Of You
26/66 *Bobby Fuller Four*
96/71 *Cochise*
83/80 **Love's Only Love** *Engelbert Humperdinck*
89/72 **Love's Street And Fool's Road**
Solomon Burke
1/74 **Love's Theme** *Love Unlimited Orchestra*
97/61 **Lovedrops** *Mickey & Sylvia*
60/82 **Loveline** *Dr. Hook*
30/78 **Lovely Day** *Bill Withers*
45/56 **Lovely Lies**
Manhattan Brothers & Miriam Makeba
70/65 **Lovely, Lovely (Loverly, Loverly)**
Chubby Checker
12/80 **Lovely One** *Jacksons*
20/56 **Lovely One** *Four Voices*
68/81 **Lover** *Michael Stanley Band*
98/62 **Lover Come Back** *Doris Day*
75/85 **Lover Come Back To Me** *Dead Or Alive*
95/62 **Lover Come Back To Me** *Cleftones*
7/62 **Lover Please** *Clyde McPhatter*
Lover's Concerto
2/65 *Toys*
63/66 *Sarah Vaughan*
95/66 *Mrs. Miller*
Lover's Holiday
31/68 *Peggy Scott & Jo Jo Benson*
40/80 **Lover's Holiday** *Change*
31/61 **Lover's Island** *Blue Jays*
Lover's Prayer
73/59 *Dion & The Belmonts*
97/64 **Lover's Prayer** *Wallace Brothers*
Lover's Question
6/59 *Clyde McPhatter*
98/61 *Ernestine Anderson*
48/69 *Otis Redding*
89/75 *Loggins & Messina*
2/85 **Loverboy** *Billy Ocean*
88/84 **Loverboy** *Karen Kamon*
4/85 **Lovergirl** *Teena Marie*
54/81 **Lovers After All**
Melissa Manchester & Peabo Bryson
89/64 **Lovers Always Forgive**
Gladys Knight & The Pips
36/62 **Lovers By Night, Strangers By Day**
Fleetwoods
52/59 **Lovers Never Say Goodbye** *Flamingos*
3/62 **Lovers Who Wander** *Dion*
2/73 **Loves Me Like A Rock** *Paul Simon*

Lovesick Blues
87/62 *Floyd Cramer*
44/63 *Frank Ifield*
Lovey Dovey
49/59 *Clyde McPhatter*
25/61 *Buddy Knox*
86/67 *Bunny Sigler (medley)*
60/68 *Otis & Carla*
99/68 **Lovey Dovey Kinda Lovin'** *Brenton Wood*
9/85 **Lovin' Every Minute Of It** *Loverboy*
54/65 **Lovin' Place** *Gale Garnett*
81/68 **Lovin' Season** *Gene & Debbe*
45/81 **Lovin' The Night Away** *Dillman Band*
49/69 **Lovin' Things** *Grass Roots*
84/60 **Lovin' Touch** *Mark Dinning*
16/79 **Lovin', Touchin', Squeezin'** *Journey*
1/75 **Lovin' You** *Minnie Riperton*
82/70 **Lovin' You Baby** *White Plains*
83/72 **Lovin' You, Lovin' Me** *Candi Staton*
32/67 **Lovin' You** *Bobby Darin*
Loving Arms
61/73 *Dobie Gray*
86/74 *Kris Kristofferson & Rita Coolidge*
26/71 **Loving Her Was Easier (Than Anything I'll Ever Do Again)** *Kris Kristofferson*
20/57 **Loving You** *Elvis Presley*
88/82 **Loving You** *Chris Rea*
91/74 **Loving You** *Johnny Nash*
51/68 **Loving You Has Made Me Bananas** *Guy Marks*
87/70 **Loving You Is A Natural Thing** *Ronnie Milsap*
45/66 **Loving You Is Sweeter Than Ever** *Four Tops*
29/72 **Loving You Just Crossed My Mind** *Sam Neely*
65/64 **Loving You More Every Day** *Etta James*
71/80 **Loving You With My Eyes** *Starland Vocal Band*
7/75 **Low Rider** *War*
3/76 **Lowdown** *Boz Scaggs*
35/71 **Lowdown** *Chicago*
41/69 **Lowdown Popcorn** *James Brown*
Lt. Calley *see: Battle Hymn Of*
75/82 **Luanne** *Foreigner*
84/70 **Lucifer** *Bob Seger*
5/77 **Lucille** *Kenny Rogers*
Lucille
21/57 *Little Richard*
21/60 *Everly Brothers*
25/77 **Luckenbach, Texas** *Waylon Jennings*
30/85 **Lucky** *Greg Kihn*
88/83 **Lucky** *Eye To Eye*
25/60 **Lucky Devil** *Carl Dobkins, Jr.*
64/81 **Lucky Guy** *Rickie Lee Jones*
38/85 **Lucky In Love** *Mick Jagger*
14/59 **Lucky Ladybug** *Billy & Lillie*
Lucky Lips
25/57 *Ruth Brown*
77/57 *Gale Storm*
62/63 *Cliff Richard*
Lucky Man
48/71 *Emerson, Lake & Palmer*
51/73 *Emerson, Lake & Palmer*
73/76 **Lucky Man** *Starbuck*
42/80 **Lucky Me** *Anne Murray*
98/71 **Lucky Me** *Moments*
20/84 **Lucky One** *Laura Branigan*
4/84 **Lucky Star** *Madonna*
29/70 **Lucretia Mac Evil** *Blood, Sweat & Tears*
1/75 **Lucy In The Sky With Diamonds** *Elton John*
16/56 **Lullaby Of Birdland** *Blue Stars*
23/61 **Lullaby Of Love** *Frank Gari*
56/66 **Lullaby Of Love** *Poppies*
69/61 **Lullaby Of The Leaves** *Ventures*
53/64 **Lumberjack** *Brook Benton*
95/69 **Luna Trip** *Dickie Goodman*
2/75 **Lyin' Eyes** *Eagles*
74/86 **Lying** *Peter Frampton*

95/63 **M.G. Blues** *Jimmy McGriff*
15/59 **M.T.A.** *Kingston Trio*
96/77 **Ma Baker** *Boney M*
5/70 **Ma Belle Amie** *Tee Set*
91/74 **Ma! (He's Making Eyes At Me)** *Lena Zavaroni*
97/58 **Ma Ma Ma Marie** *Gaylords*
Mac Arthur Park
2/68 *Richard Harris*
93/69 *Waylon Jennings*
38/71 *Four Tops*
1/78 *Donna Summer*
22/74 **Machine Gun** *Commodores*
57/82 **Machinery** *Sheena Easton*
83/75 **Machines** *John LiVigni*
25/78 **Macho Man** *Village People*
Mack The Knife
8/56 *Dick Hyman*
11/56 *Richard Hayman & Jan August*
17/56 *Lawrence Welk*
20/56 *Louis Armstrong*
37/56 *Billy Vaughn*
49/56 *Les Paul*
1/59 *Bobby Darin*
27/60 *Ella Fitzgerald*
3/86 **Mad About You** *Belinda Carlisle*
Made To Love *see: (Girls, Girls, Girls)*
79/76 **Made To Love You** *Gary Wright*
50/56 **Madeira** *Mitch Miller*
36/76 **Mademoiselle** *Styx*
23/60 **Madison, The** *Al Brown's Tunetoppers*
30/60 **Madison Time** *Ray Bryant Combo*
85/59 **Madrid** *Nat King Cole*
45/71 **Maggie** *Redbone*
1/71 **Maggie May** *Rod Stewart*
1/80 **Magic** *Olivia Newton-John*
5/75 **Magic** *Pilot*
12/84 **Magic** *Cars*
25/68 **Magic Bus** *Who*
3/68 **Magic Carpet Ride** *Steppenwolf*
52/55 **Magic Fingers** *Eddie Fisher*
80/61 **Magic Is The Night** *Kathy Young with The Innocents*
9/76 **Magic Man** *Heart*
79/81 **Magic Man** *Herb Alpert*
96/55 **Magic Melody** *Les Paul & Mary Ford*
4/58 **Magic Moments** *Perry Como*
49/61 **Magic Moon** *Rays*
99/64 **Magic Of Our Summer Love** *Tymes*
51/81 **Magic Power** *Triumph*
21/66 **Magic Town** *Vogues*
91/62 **Magic Wand** *Don & Juan*
60/73 **Magic Woman Touch** *Hollies*
73/85 **Magical** *John Parr*
39/77 **Magical Mystery Tour** *Ambrosia*
8/78 **Magnet And Steel** *Walter Egan*
57/83 **Magnetic** *Earth, Wind & Fire*
35/61 **Magnificent Seven** *Al Caiola*
Magnum P.I. *see: Theme From*

55/69 **Mah-Na-Mah-Na** *Piero Umiliani*
Mahogany *see: Theme From*
3/79 **Main Event (medley)** *Barbra Streisand*
Main Theme From Exodus *see: Exodus*
Main Title And Molly-O *see: Man With The Golden Arm*
24/77 **Mainstreet** *Bob Seger*
75/67 **Mairzy Doats** *Innocence*
36/61 **Majestic, The** *Dion*
93/57 **Majesty Of Love** *Marvin Rainwater & Connie Francis*
14/83 **Major Tom (Coming Home)** *Peter Schilling*
97/67 **Make A Little Love** *Lowell Fulsom*
25/80 **Make A Little Magic** *Dirt Band*
5/82 **Make A Move On Me** *Olivia Newton-John*
28/69 **Make Believe** *Wind*
30/82 **Make Believe** *Toto*
78/80 **Make Believe It's Your First Time** *Bobby Vinton*
98/61 **Make Believe Wedding** *Castells*
54/85 **Make It Better (Forget About Me)** *Tom Petty*
Make It Easy On Yourself
20/62 *Jerry Butler*
16/65 *Walker Bros.*
37/70 *Dionne Warwick*
Make It Funky
22/71 *James Brown*
68/71 *James Brown (My Part)*
69/79 **Make It Last** *Brooklyn Dreams*
Make It With You
1/70 *Bread*
94/77 *Whispers*
95/57 **Make Like A Bunny, Honey** *Jill Corey*
29/83 **Make Love Stay** *Dan Fogelberg*
60/79 **Make Love To Me** *Helen Reddy*
96/67 **Make Love To Me** *Johnny Thunder & Ruby Winters*
76/76 **Make Love To Your Mind** *Bill Withers*
16/58 **Make Me A Miracle** *Jimmie Rodgers*
28/66 **Make Me Belong To You** *Barbara Lewis*
43/64 **Make Me Forget** *Bobby Rydell*
80/71 **Make Me Happy** *Bobby Bloom*
9/70 **Make Me Smile** *Chicago*
96/76 **Make Me Smile (Come Up And See Me)** *Steve Harley & Cockney Rebel*
27/72 **Make Me The Woman That You Go Home To** *Gladys Knight & The Pips*
93/73 **Make Me Twice The Man** *New York City*
11/65 **Make Me Your Baby** *Barbara Lewis*
21/67 **Make Me Yours** *Bettye Swann*
62/84 **Make My Day** *T.G. Sheppard/Clint Eastwood*
51/85 **Make No Mistake, He's Mine** *Barbra Streisand with Kim Carnes*
80/60 **Make Someone Happy** *Perry Como*
60/81 **Make That Move** *Shalamar*
81/63 **Make The Music Play** *Dionne Warwick*
Make The World Go Away
24/63 *Timi Yuro*
100/63 *Ray Price*
6/65 *Eddy Arnold*
44/75 *Donny & Marie Osmond*
71/82 **Make Up Your Mind** *Aurra*
98/73 **Make Up Your Mind** *J. Geils Band*
69/58 **(Make With) The Shake** *Mark IV*
45/78 **Make You Feel Love Again** *Wet Willie*
Make Your Own Kind Of Music
36/69 *Mama Cass*
94/72 *Barbra Streisand (medley)*
Make Yourself Comfortable
6/55 *Sarah Vaughan*
26/55 *Andy Griffith*
30/55 *Peggy King*
91/76 **Makes You Blind** *Glitter Band*
5/79 **Makin' It** *David Naughton*
20/59 **Makin' Love** *Floyd Robinson*
91/78 **Makin' Love** *Climax Blues Band*
85/74 **Makin' The Best Of A Bad Situation** *Dick Feller*
46/65 **Makin' Whoopee** *Ray Charles*
87/77 **Making A Good Thing Better** *Olivia Newton-John*
31/67 **Making Every Minute Count** *Spanky & Our Gang*
13/82 **Making Love** *Roberta Flack*
2/83 **Making Love Out Of Nothing At All** *Air Supply*
35/67 **Making Memories** *Frankie Laine*
25/76 **Making Our Dreams Come True** *Cyndi Grecco*
42/60 **Malaguena** *Connie Francis*
85/68 **Malayisha** *Miriam Makeba*
48/69 **Malinda** *Bobby Taylor*
8/60 **Mama** *Connie Francis*
22/66 **Mama** *B.J. Thomas*
73/83 **Mama** *Genesis*
Mama *also see: Mamma*
82/71 **Mama And A Papa** *Ray Stevens*
9/79 **Mama Can't Buy You Love** *Elton John*
91/68 **(Mama Come Quick, And Bring Your) Lickin' Stick** *George Torrence*
14/63 **Mama Didn't Lie** *Jan Bradley*
55/63 **Mama Don't Allow** *Rooftop Singers*
11/56 **Mama From The Train** *Patti Page*
Mama Guitar
47/57 *Don Cornell*
98/57 *Julius LaRosa*
99/62 **Mama (He Treats Your Daughter Mean)** *Ruth Brown*
72/78 **Mama Let Him Play** *Doucette*
F/70 **Mama Liked The Roses** *Elvis Presley*
11/57 **Mama Look At Bubu** *Harry Belafonte*
4/61 **Mama Said** *Shirelles*
Mama Sang A Song
32/62 *Stan Kenton*
38/62 *Walter Brennan*
89/62 *Bill Anderson*
34/56 **Mama, Teach Me To Dance** *Eydie Gorme*
Mama Told Me (Not To Come)
1/70 *Three Dog Night*
99/72 *Wilson Pickett*
30/82 **Mama Used To Say** *Junior*
77/73 **Mama Was A Rock And Roll Singer** *Sonny & Cher*
Mama Weer All Crazee Now
76/73 *Slade*
51/84 *Quiet Riot*
2/71 **Mama's Pearl** *Jackson 5*
71/75 **Mamacita** *Grass Roots*
17/55 **Mambo Rock** *Bill Haley & His Comets*
Mame
19/66 *Herb Alpert*
53/66 *Bobby Darin*
81/66 *Louis Armstrong*
32/76 **Mamma Mia** *Abba*
42/78 **Mammas Don't Let Your Babies Grow Up To Be Cowboys** *Waylon & Willie*
Mammy Blue
57/71 *Pop-Tops*
50/73 *Stories*
72/65 **Man, The** *Lorne Greene*
42/68 **Man And A Half** *Wilson Pickett*
88/66 **Man And A Woman** *Tamiko Jones with Herbie Mann*
F/72 **Man And The Woman** *Chi-Lites*
Man And Woman *see: Suite*
16/55 **Man Chases A Girl** *Eddie Fisher*
31/79 **Man I'll Never Be** *Boston*

58/71 **Man In Black** *Johnny Cash*
Man In The Raincoat
14/55 *Marion Marlowe*
16/55 *Priscilla Wright*
63/68 **Man Needs A Woman** *James Carr*
85/70 **Man Of Constant Sorrow**
Ginger Baker's Air Force
40/82 **Man On The Corner** *Genesis*
14/82 **Man On Your Mind** *Little River Band*
15/86 **Man Size Love** *Klymaxx*
55/72 **Man Sized Job** *Denise LaSalle*
63/77 **Man Smart, Woman Smarter**
Robert Palmer
86/74 **Man That Turned My Mama On**
Tanya Tucker
4/62 **(Man Who Shot) Liberty Valance**
Gene Pitney
85/79 **Man With The Child In His Eyes**
Kate Bush
Man With The Golden Arm (Main Title/Molly-O/Delilah Jones)
14/56 *Richard Maltby*
16/56 *Elmer Bernstein*
22/56 *Dick Jacobs*
37/56 *McGuire Sisters*
49/56 *Billy May*
56/56 *Les Elgart*
82/56 *Buddy Morrow*
19/68 **Man Without Love** *Engelbert Humperdinck*
71/63 **Man's Temptation** *Gene Chandler*
84/78 **Manana** *Jimmy Buffett*
47/58 **Mandolins In The Moonlight** *Perry Como*
94/71 **Mandrill** *Mandrill*
Mandy
91/72 *Scott English (Brandy)*
1/75 *Barry Manilow*
1/82 **Maneater** *Daryl Hall & John Oates*
10/57 **Mangos** *Rosemary Clooney*
Manhattan Spiritual
10/59 *Reg Owen*
56/75 *Mike Post*
1/83 **Maniac** *Michael Sembello*
2/86 **Manic Monday** *Bangles*
97/58 **Many A Time** *Steve Lawrence*
84/60 **Many A Wonderful Moment**
Rosemary Clooney
7/60 **Many Tears Ago** *Connie Francis*
80/66 **Marble Breaks And Iron Bends** *Drafi*
March From The River Kwai And Colonel Bogey
20/58 *Mitch Miller*
75/58 *Edmundo Ros*
88/58 *Art Mooney*
88/62 **March Of The Siamese Children**
Kenny Ball
96/63 **Marching Thru Madrid** *Herb Alpert*
96/71 **Mare, Take Me Home**
Matthews' Southern Comfort
8/77 **Margaritaville** *Jimmy Buffett*
51/59 **Margie** *Fats Domino*
Maria
78/60 *Johnny Mathis*
48/62 *Roger Williams*
88/62 *Johnny Mathis*
6/63 **Maria Elena** *Los Indios Tabajaras*
97/71 **Maria (You Were The Only One)**
Jimmy Ruffin
86/62 **Marianna** *Johnny Mathis*
Marianne
3/57 *Hilltoppers*
4/57 *Terry Gilkyson & The Easy Riders*
64/57 *Lane Brothers*
84/57 *Burl Ives*
42/71 **Marianne** *Stephen Stills*
15/65 **Marie** *Bachelors*
4/61 **(Marie's the Name) His Latest Flame**
Elvis Presley
82/56 **Marimba Charleston** *Marimba Chiapas.*
Marina
31/59 *Rocco Granata*
42/59 *Willy Alberti*
87/59 *Jacky Noguez*
36/63 **Marlena** *4 Seasons*
70/69 **Marley Purt Drive** *Jose Feliciano*
28/69 **Marrakesh Express** *Crosby, Stills & Nash*
75/56 **Married I Can Always Get** *Teddi King*
64/65 **Married Man** *Richard Burton*
40/79 **Married Men** *Bette Midler*
73/78 **Martha (Your Lovers Come And Go)**
Gabriel
59/77 **Martian Boogie** *Brownsville Station*
16/63 **Martian Hop** *Ran-Dells*
88/59 **Martinique** *Martin Denny*
43/64 **Marvelous Toy** *Chad Mitchell Trio*
39/62 **Mary Ann Regrets** *Burl Ives*
90/59 **Mary Ann Thomas** *Bobby Freeman*
41/60 **Mary Don't You Weep** *Stonewall Jackson*
28/72 **Mary Had A Little Lamb** *Wings*
79/76 **Mary Hartman, Mary Hartman (Theme)**
Deadly Nightshade
27/67 **Mary In The Morning** *Al Martino*
41/79 **Mary Jane** *Rick James*
26/59 **Mary Lou** *Ronnie Hawkins*
Mary's Boy Child
12/56 *Harry Belafonte*
85/78 *Boney M (medley)*
39/62 **Mary's Little Lamb** *James Darren*
47/66 **Mas Que Nada** *Sergio Mendes & Brasil '66*
M*A*S*H *see: Song From*
2/62 **Mashed Potato Time** *Dee Dee Sharp*
Mashed Potatoes
84/60 *Nat Kendrick*
81/62 *Steve Alaimo*
82/62 **Mashed Potatoes U.S.A.** *James Brown*
82/83 **Masquerade** *Berlin*
Massachusetts *see: (Lights Went Out)*
87/85 **Master And Servant** *Depeche Mode*
5/80 **Master Blaster (Jammin')** *Stevie Wonder*
18/68 **Master Jack** *Four Jacks & A Jill*
33/73 **Master Of Eyes** *Aretha Franklin*
7/73 **Masterpiece** *Temptations*
20/64 **Matador, The** *Major Lance*
44/63 **Matador, The** *Johnny Cash*
17/64 **Matchbox** *Beatles*
2/85 **Material Girl** *Madonna*
74/85 **Mathematics** *Melissa Manchester*
47/59 **Matilda** *Cookie & His Cupcakes*
(also see: Twistin' Matilda)
10/86 **Matter Of Trust** *Billy Joel*
68/59 **Mau-Mau** *Wailers*
39/69 **May I** *Bill Deal*
63/68 **May I Take A Giant Step (Into Your Heart)** *1910 Fruitgum Co.*
85/66 **May My Heart Be Cast Into Stone** *Toys*
15/65 **May The Bird Of Paradise Fly Up Your Nose** *'Little' Jimmy Dickens*
11/59 **May You Always** *McGuire Sisters*
Maybe
15/58 *Chantels*
91/65 *Shangri-Las*
29/70 *Three Degrees*
17/58 **Maybe Baby** *Crickets*
14/64 **Maybe I Know** *Lesley Gore*
22/79 **Maybe I'm A Fool** *Eddie Money*
10/77 **Maybe I'm Amazed** *Wings*
46/68 **Maybe Just Today** *Bobby Vee*
61/69 **Maybe The Rain Will Fall** *Cascades*
87/83 **Maybe This Day** *Kissing The Pink*

20/71 **Maybe Tomorrow** *Jackson 5*
67/69 **Maybe Tomorrow** *Iveys*
88/64 **Maybe Tonight** *Shirelles*
Maybellene
5/55 *Chuck Berry*
12/64 *Johnny Rivers*
Me About You
83/67 *Mojo Men*
91/69 *Lovin' Spoonful*
15/74 **Me And Baby Brother** *War*
Me And Bobby McGee
1/71 *Janis Joplin*
40/72 *Jerry Lee Lewis*
98/72 **Me And Jesus** *Tom T. Hall*
22/72 **Me And Julio Down By The Schoolyard**
Paul Simon
Me And Mrs. Jones
1/72 *Billy Paul*
47/75 *Dramatics*
34/71 **Me And My Arrow** *Nilsson*
86/72 **Me And My Baby Got A Good Thing Going** *Lyn Collins*
64/62 **Me And My Shadow**
Frank Sinatra & Sammy Davis Jr.
5/71 **Me And You And A Dog Named Boo** *Lobo*
74/64 **Me Japanese Boy I Love You**
Bobby Goldsboro
53/68 **Me, The Peaceful Heart** *Lulu*
95/65 **Me Without You** *Mary Wells*
40/81 **Me (Without You)** *Andy Gibb*
89/74 **Meadows** *Joe Walsh*
92/72 **Mean Little Woman, Rosalie** *Tommy Roe*
47/71 **Mean Mistreater** *Grand Funk Railroad*
96/65 **Mean Old World** *Rick Nelson*
5/63 **Mean Woman Blues** *Roy Orbison*
12/63 **Mecca** *Gene Pitney*
'Medic' Theme *see: Blue Star*
22/69 **Medicine Man** *Buchanan Brothers*
65/84 **Medicine Song** *Stephanie Mills*
Meditation (Meditacao)
66/63 *Charlie Byrd*
91/63 *Pat Boone*
98/66 *Claudine Longet*
95/60 **Mediterranean Moon** *Rays*
63/62 **Meet Me At The Twistin' Place**
Johnnie Morisette
59/85 **Meeting In The Ladies Room** *Klymaxx*
48/65 **Meeting Over Yonder** *Impressions*
62/82 **Mega Force** *707*
43/67 **Melancholy Music Man** *Righteous Brothers*
87/70 **Melanie Makes Me Smile** *Tony Burrows*
86/72 **Melissa** *Allman Brothers Band*
65/78 **Mellow Lovin'** *Judy Cheeks*
92/68 **Mellow Moonlight** *Leon Haywood*
Mellow Yellow
2/66 *Donovan*
99/67 *Senator Bobby & Senator McKinley*
5/57 **Melodie D'Amour** *Ames Brothers*
74/66 **Melody For An Unknown Girl** *Unknowns*
Melody Of Love
2/55 *Billy Vaughn*
3/55 *Four Aces*
8/55 *David Carroll*
19/55 *Frank Sinatra & Ray Anthony*
30/55 *Leo Diamond*
45/71 **Melting Pot** *Booker T. & The MG's*
Memories
35/69 *Elvis Presley*
47/70 *Lettermen (medley)*
62/81 **Memories** *Tierra*
Memories Are Made Of This
1/56 *Dean Martin*
5/56 *Gale Storm*
53/56 *Mindy Carson*
48/66 *Drifters*
71/82 **Memories Of Days Gone By** *Five Satins*
74/62 **Memories Of Maria** *Jerry Byrd*
Memories Of You
22/55 *Four Coins*
20/56 *Benny Goodman*
62/56 *Hugo Winterhalter*
60/80 **Memorize Your Number** *Leif Garrett*
Memory
52/82 *Barbra Streisand*
39/83 *Barry Manilow*
63/63 **Memory Lane** *Hippies*
Memphis
5/63 *Lonnie Mack*
2/64 *Johnny Rivers*
85/83 **Memphis** *Joe Jackson*
90/61 **Memphis** *Donnie Brooks*
33/67 **Memphis Soul Stew** *King Curtis*
100/69 **Memphis Train** *Buddy Miles*
Memphis Underground
44/69 *Herbie Mann*
95/69 *Herbie Mann*
Men *see: Theme From The*
80/86 **Men All Pause** *Klymaxx*
33/68 **Men Are Gettin' Scarce** *Joe Tex*
6/66 **Men In My Little Girl's Life** *Mike Douglas*
65/72 **Men Of Learning** *Vigrass & Osborne*
94/72 **Mendelssohn's 4th (2nd Movement)**
Apollo 100
27/69 **Mendocino** *Sir Douglas Quintet*
30/69 **Mercy** *Ohio Express*
35/64 **Mercy, Mercy** *Don Covay*
4/71 **Mercy Mercy Me (The Ecology)**
Marvin Gaye
Mercy, Mercy, Mercy
5/67 *Buckinghams*
11/67 *Cannonball Adderley*
58/67 *Marlena Shaw*
96/67 *Larry Williams & Johnny Watson*
52/81 **Mercy, Mercy, Mercy** *Phoebe Snow*
71/58 **Merry Christmas Baby** *Chuck Berry*
82/80 **Merry Christmas In The NFL**
Willis 'The Guard' & Vigorish
61/61 **Merry-Go-Round** *Marv Johnson*
89/61 **Mess Around** *Bobby Freeman*
32/60 **Mess Of Blues** *Elvis Presley*
48/73 **Message, The** *Cymande*
62/82 **Message, The** *Grandmaster Flash*
99/70 **Message From A Black Man** *Whatnauts*
75/68 **Message From Maria** *Joe Simon*
74/79 **Message In A Bottle** *Police*
49/76 **Message In Our Music** *O'Jays*
8/66 **Message To Michael** *Dionne Warwick*
5/85 **Method Of Modern Love**
Daryl Hall & John Oates
58/83 **Metro** *Berlin*
77/64 **Mexican Drummer Man** *Herb Alpert*
16/58 **Mexican Hat Rock** *Applejacks*
94/65 **Mexican Pearls** *Billy Vaughn*
58/84 **Mexican Radio** *Wall Of Voodoo*
85/64 **Mexican Shuffle** *Herb Alpert*
7/61 **Mexico** *Bob Moore*
49/75 **Mexico** *James Taylor*
50/57 **Mi Casa, Su Casa** *Perry Como*
67/59 **Miami** *Eugene Church*
70/86 **Miami** *Bob Seger*
1/85 **Miami Vice Theme** *Jan Hammer*

Michael
1/61 *Highwaymen*
100/63 *Steve Alaimo*
42/64 *Trini Lopez*
41/66 **Michael** *C.O.D.'s*
Michelle
18/66 *David & Jonathan*
65/66 *Bud Shank*
77/66 *Billy Vaughn*
1/82 **Mickey** *Toni Basil*
8/63 **Mickey's Monkey** *Miracles*
42/86 **Midas Touch** *Midnight Star*
19/84 **Middle Of The Road** *Pretenders*
58/69 **Midnight** *Classics IV*
69/58 **Midnight** *Paul Anka*
76/62 **Midnight** *Johnny Gibson*
6/74 **Midnight At The Oasis** *Maria Muldaur*
6/75 **Midnight Blue** *Melissa Manchester*
46/83 **Midnight Blue** *Louise Tucker*
5/68 **Midnight Confessions** *Grass Roots*
10/70 **Midnight Cowboy** *Ferrante & Teicher*
55/74 **Midnight Flower** *Four Tops*
51/59 **Midnight Flyer** *Nat King Cole*
Midnight Hour *see: In The*
2/62 **Midnight In Moscow** *Kenny Ball*
Midnight Lace
84/60 *Ray Ellis*
92/60 *Ray Conniff*
98/60 *David Carroll*
91/78 **Midnight Light** *LeBlanc & Carr*
80/71 **Midnight Man** *James Gang*
10/64 **Midnight Mary** *Joey Powers*
55/59 **Midnight Oil** *Charlie Blackwell*
74/80 **Midnight Rain** *Poco*
72/80 **Midnight Rendezvous** *Babys*
Midnight Rider
27/72 *Joe Cocker*
19/74 *Gregg Allman*
24/80 **Midnight Rocks** *Al Stewart*
73/75 **Midnight Sky** *Isley Brothers*
Midnight Special
16/60 *Paul Evans*
20/65 *Johnny Rivers*
69/62 **Midnight Special** *Jimmy Smith*
35/59 **Midnight Stroll** *Revels*
1/73 **Midnight Train To Georgia**
Gladys Knight & The Pips
28/79 **Midnight Wind** *John Stewart*
94/58 **Midnighter** *Champs*
71/84 **Midnite Maniac** *Krokus*
91/74 **Might Just Take Your Life** *Deep Purple*
34/71 **Mighty Clouds Of Joy** *B.J. Thomas*
38/59 **Mighty Good** *Ricky Nelson*
51/61 **Mighty Good Lovin'** *Miracles*
69/76 **Mighty High** *Mighty Clouds Of Joy*
43/70 **Mighty Joe** *Shocking Blue*
20/74 **Mighty Love** *Spinners*
29/74 **Mighty Mighty** *Earth, Wind & Fire*
10/68 **Mighty Quinn (Quinn The Eskimo)**
Manfred Mann
63/78 **Miles Away** *Fotomaker*
73/71 **Military Madness** *Graham Nash*
79/61 **Milk Cow Blues** *Ricky Nelson*
90/70 **Mill Valley** *Miss Abrams*
33/64 **Miller's Cave** *Bobby Bare*
Million And One
41/66 *Dean Martin*
71/66 *Vic Dana*
82/83 **Million Miles Away** *Plimsouls*
82/58 **Million Miles From Nowhere** *Brook Benton*
Million To One
5/60 *Jimmy Charles*
68/68 *Five Stairsteps*
90/69 *Brian Hyland*
23/73 *Donny Osmond*
Millionaire *see: (How To Be A)*
95/75 **Millionaire, The** *Dr. Hook*
Milord
74/61 *Teresa Brewer*
88/61 *Edith Piaf*
45/64 *Bobby Darin*
46/78 **Mind Bender** *Stillwater*
26/69 **Mind, Body And Soul** *Flaming Ember*
51/66 **Mind Excursion** *Trade Winds*
18/73 **Mind Games** *John Lennon*
99/66 **Mine Exclusively** *Olympics*
91/74 **Mine For Me** *Rod Stewart*
50/69 **Mini-Skirt Minnie** *Wilson Pickett*
41/83 **Minimum Love** *Mac McAnally*
88/75 **Minnesota** *Northern Light*
38/69 **Minotaur, The** *Dick Hyman*
79/75 **Minstrel In The Gallery** *Jethro Tull*
14/79 **Minute By Minute** *Doobie Brothers*
48/69 **Minute Of Your Time** *Tom Jones*
95/63 **Minute You're Gone** *Sonny James*
74/60 **Mio Amore** *Flamingos*
75/62 **Miracle, A** *Frankie Avalon*
Miracle Of Love
18/56 *Eileen Rodgers*
68/56 *Ginny Gibson*
3/75 **Miracles** *Jefferson Starship*
40/83 **Miracles** *Stacy Lattisaw*
10/67 **Mirage** *Tommy James & The Shondells*
92/80 **Mirage** *Eric Troyer*
30/83 **Mirror Man** *Human League*
8/82 **Mirror, Mirror** *Diana Ross*
81/79 **Mirror Star** *Fabulous Poodles*
22/73 **Misdemeanor** *Foster Sylvers*
44/63 **Misery** *Dynamics*
10/85 **Misled** *Kool & The Gang*
44/70 **Miss America** *Mark Lindsay*
56/57 **Miss Ann** *Little Richard*
92/78 **Miss Broadway** *Belle Epoque*
69/61 **Miss Fine** *New Yorkers*
91/74 **Miss Grace** *Tymes*
5/84 **Miss Me Blind** *Culture Club*
14/81 **Miss Sun** *Boz Scaggs*
1/78 **Miss You** *Rolling Stones*
78/59 **Miss You** *Jaye P. Morgan*
66/57 **Miss You So** *Lillian Offitt*
44/56 **Missing** *McGuire Sisters*
1/84 **Missing You** *John Waite*
10/85 **Missing You** *Diana Ross*
23/82 **Missing You** *Dan Fogelberg*
29/61 **Missing You** *Ray Peterson*
7/60 **Mission Bell** *Donnie Brooks*
41/68 **Mission-Impossible** *Lalo Schifrin*
14/86 **Missionary Man** *Eurythmics*
32/70 **Mississippi** *John Phillips*
70/74 **Mississippi Cotton Picking Delta Town**
Charley Pride
97/70 **Mississippi Mama** *Owen B.*
21/70 **Mississippi Queen** *Mountain*
33/85 **Mistake No. 3** *Culture Club*
60/81 **Mistaken Identity** *Kim Carnes*
Mister *see: Mr.*
49/79 **Mistrusted Love** *Mistress*
Misty
12/59 *Johnny Mathis*
21/63 *Lloyd Price*
63/65 *Vibrations*
44/66 *Richard 'Groove' Holmes*
14/75 *Ray Stevens*

Misty Blue
57/67 *Eddy Arnold*
91/72 *Joe Simon*
3/76 *Dorothy Moore*
14/80 **Misunderstanding** *Genesis*
73/71 **Mixed Up Guy** *Joey Scarbury*
37/64 **Mixed-Up, Shook-Up, Girl** *Patty & The Emblems*
97/64 **Mo-Onions** *Booker T. & The MG's*
Mocking Bird, The
67/56 *Four Lads*
32/58 *Four Lads*
Mockingbird
7/63 *Inez Foxx*
94/67 *Aretha Franklin*
5/74 *Carly Simon & James Taylor*
20/61 **Model Girl** *Johnny Maestro*
22/84 **Modern Day Delilah** *Van Stephenson*
18/81 **Modern Girl** *Sheena Easton*
14/83 **Modern Love** *David Bowie*
10/86 **Modern Woman** *Billy Joel*
21/65 **Mohair Sam** *Charlie Rich*
90/60 **Mojo Workout (Dance)** *Larry Bright*
70/63 **Molly** *Bobby Goldsboro*
Molly-O *see: Man With The Golden Arm*
58/61 **Mom And Dad's Waltz** *Patti Page*
59/79 **Moment By Moment** *Yvonne Elliman*
63/84 **Moment Of Truth** *Survivor*
50/62 **Moments** *Jennell Hawkins*
Moments To Remember
2/55 *Four Lads*
47/69 *Vogues*
Mona Lisa
25/59 *Carl Mann*
29/59 *Conway Twitty*
1/66 **Monday, Monday** *Mamas & The Papas*
13/73 **Money** *Pink Floyd*
48/68 **Money** *Lovin' Spoonful*
50/75 **Money** *Gladys Knight & The Pips*
72/72 **Money Back Guarantee** *Five Man Electrical Band*
27/85 **Money Changes Everything** *Cyndi Lauper*
1/85 **Money For Nothing** *Dire Straits*
9/76 **Money Honey** *Bay City Rollers*
76/56 **Money Honey** *Elvis Presley*
56/77 **Money, Money, Money** *Abba*
57/72 **Money Runner** *Quincy Jones*
Money (That's What I Want)
23/60 *Barrett Strong*
16/64 *Kingsmen*
52/66 *Jr. Walker & The All Stars*
50/80 *Flying Lizards*
Money Tree
20/56 *Margaret Whiting*
73/57 *Patience & Prudence*
53/66 **Money Won't Change You** *James Brown*
28/86 **Money's Too Tight (To Mention)** *Simply Red*
50/70 **Mongoose** *Elephants Memory*
Monkee *see: Do The*
47/63 **Monkey-Shine** *Bill Black's Combo*
Monkey Time
8/63 *Major Lance*
68/83 *Tubes*
39/70 **Monster** *Steppenwolf*
Monster Mash
1/62 *Bobby 'Boris' Pickett*
91/70 *Bobby 'Boris' Pickett*
10/73 *Bobby 'Boris' Pickett*
30/62 **Monsters' Holiday** *Bobby 'Boris' Pickett*
Montage From *see: How Sweet It Is*
8/70 **Montego Bay** *Bobby Bloom*
15/68 **Monterey** *Animals*
3/68 **Mony Mony** *Tommy James & The Shondells*
31/77 **Moody Blue** *Elvis Presley*
1/61 **Moody River** *Pat Boone*
24/69 **Moody Woman** *Jerry Butler*
59/65 **Moon Over Naples** *Bert Kaempfert* *(also see: Spanish Eyes)*
Moon River
11/61 *Jerry Butler*
11/61 *Henry Mancini*
30/71 **Moon Shadow** *Cat Stevens*
28/58 **Moon Talk** *Perry Como*
54/70 **Moon Walk** *Joe Simon*
99/62 **Moon Was Yellow** *Frank Sinatra*
92/77 **Moondance** *Van Morrison*
38/69 **Moonflight** *Vik Venus*
Moonglow And Theme From 'Picnic'
1/56 *Morris Stoloff*
4/56 *George Cates*
13/56 *McGuire Sisters (Picnic)*
64/56 *Ralph Marterie (Picnic)*
51/65 **Moonlight And Roses** *Vic Dana*
72/58 **Moonlight Bay** *Drifters*
3/76 **Moonlight Feels Right** *Starbuck*
3/57 **Moonlight Gambler** *Frankie Laine*
42/56 **Moonlight Love** *Perry Como*
Moonlight Serenade
47/59 *Rivieras*
97/76 *Bobby Vinton*
87/69 **Moonlight Sonata** *Henry Mancini*
73/74 **Moonlight Special** *Ray Stevens*
Moonlight Swim
24/57 *Tony Perkins*
37/57 *Nick Noble*
4/56 **More** *Perry Como*
More
8/63 *Kai Winding*
42/63 *Vic Dana*
88/67 **More And More** *Andy Williams*
94/75 **More And More** *Carly Simon*
86/80 **More Bounce To The Ounce** *Zapp*
16/66 **More I See You** *Chris Montez*
More Love
23/67 *Miracles*
10/80 *Kim Carnes*
17/61 **More Money For You And Me** *Four Preps*
4/76 **More, More, More** *Andrea True Connection*
55/81 **More Stars On 45** *Stars on 45*
5/76 **More Than A Feeling** *Boston*
32/78 **More Than A Woman** *Tavares*
More Than I Can Say
61/61 *Bobby Vee*
2/80 *Leo Sayer*
90/70 **More Than I Can Stand** *Bobby Womack*
34/82 **More Than Just The Two Of Us** *Sneaker*
73/86 **More Than Physical** *Bananarama*
54/67 **More Than The Eye Can See** *Al Martino*
12/69 **More Today Than Yesterday** *Spiral Starecase*
62/76 **More You Do It (The More I Like It Done To Me)** *Ronnie Dyson*
56/84 **More You Live, The More You Love** *A Flock Of Seagulls*
Morgen
13/59 *Ivo Robic*
98/59 *Leslie Uggams (One More Sunrise)*
Moritat *see: Mack The Knife*
21/83 **Mornin'** *Al Jarreau*
14/75 **Mornin' Beautiful** *Dawn*
74/68 **Mornin' Glory** *Glen Campbell & Bobbie Gentry*
78/70 **Mornin' Mornin'** *Bobby Goldsboro*
47/70 **Morning** *Jim Ed Brown*
Morning After
60/61 *Mar-Keys*
1/73 **Morning After** *Maureen McGovern*

24/79 **Morning Dance** *Spyro Gyra*
72/85 **Morning Desire** *Kenny Rogers*
52/68 **Morning Dew** *Lulu*
17/69 **Morning Girl** *Neon Philharmonic*
6/72 **Morning Has Broken** *Cat Stevens*
68/80 **Morning Man** *Rupert Holmes*
74/70 **Morning Much Better**
Ten Wheel Drive with Genya Ravan
60/71 **Morning Of Our Lives** *Arkade*
Morning Side Of The Mountain
27/59 *Tommy Edwards*
8/75 *Donny & Marie Osmond*
1/81 **Morning Train (Nine To Five)**
Sheena Easton
44/67 **Morningtown Ride** *Seekers*
85/72 **Mosquito, The** *Doors*
1/73 **Most Beautiful Girl** *Charlie Rich*
67/61 **Most Beautiful Words** *Della Reese*
66/74 **Most Likely You Go Your Way (And I'll Go Mine)** *Bob Dylan/The Band*
14/55 **Most Of All** *Don Cornell*
38/71 **Most Of All** *B.J. Thomas*
27/62 **Most People Get Married** *Patti Page*
31/56 **Mostly Martha** *Crew-Cuts*
Mother
43/71 *John Lennon*
79/71 *Barbra Streisand*
4/72 **Mother And Child Reunion** *Paul Simon*
92/74 **Mother For My Children** *Whispers*
37/71 **Mother Freedom** *Bread*
Mother-In-Law
1/61 *Ernie K-Doe*
F/73 *Clarence Carter*
(also see: Son-In-Law)
92/72 **Mother Nature** *Temptations*
53/65 **Mother Nature, Father Time** *Brook Benton*
88/71 **Mother Nature's Wine** *Sugarloaf*
88/63 **Mother, Please!** *Jo Ann Campbell*
11/69 **Mother Popcorn** *James Brown*
8/66 **Mothers Little Helper** *Rolling Stones*
27/86 **Mothers Talk** *Tears For Fears*
99/62 **Motorcycle** *Tico & The Triumphs*
12/72 **Motorcycle Mama** *Sailcat*
67/79 **Motown Review** *Philly Cream*
90/66 **Moulty** *Barbarians*
Mountain Of Love
21/60 *Harold Dorman*
9/64 *Johnny Rivers*
67/68 *Ronnie Dove*
100/66 **Mountain Of Love** *Billy Stewart*
2/61 **Mountain's High** *Dick & DeeDee*
23/86 **Mountains** *Prince*
76/65 **Mouse, The** *Soupy Sales*
59/72 **Move 'Em Out** *Delaney & Bonnie*
12/86 **Move Away** *Culture Club*
58/69 **Move In A Little Closer, Baby** *Mama Cass*
99/70 **Move Me, O Wondrous Music**
Ray Charles Singers
31/69 **Move Over** *Steppenwolf*
57/80 **Move Your Boogie Body** *Bar-Kays*
41/61 **Movin'** *Bill Black's Combo*
14/76 **Movin'** *Brass Construction*
72/58 **Movin' N' Groovin'** *Duane Eddy*
19/75 **Movin' On** *Bad Company*
17/78 **Movin' Out (Anthony's Song)** *Billy Joel*
54/76 **Mozambique** *Bob Dylan*
67/71 **Mozart Symphony No. 40 In G Minor**
Waldo De Los Rios
16/63 **Mr. Bass Man** *Johnny Cymbal*
2/71 **Mr. Big Stuff** *Jean Knight*
1/59 **Mr. Blue** *Fleetwoods*
35/78 **Mr. Blue Sky** *Electric Light Orchestra*
Mr. Bojangles
77/68 *Jerry Jeff Walker*
79/68 *Bobby Cole*
9/71 *Nitty Gritty Dirt Band*
90/67 **Mr. Bus Driver** *Bruce Channel*
28/68 **Mr. Businessman** *Ray Stevens*
38/72 **Mr. Can't You See** *Buffy Sainte-Marie*
1/60 **Mr. Custer** *Larry Verne*
53/75 **Mr. D.J. (5 For The D.J.)** *Aretha Franklin*
17/66 **Mr. Dieingly Sad** *Critters*
Mr. Dream Merchant *see: Dream Merchant*
86/67 **Mr. Farmer** *Seeds*
71/57 **Mr. Fire Eyes** *Bonnie Guitar*
57/61 **Mr. Happiness** *Johnny Maestro*
4/75 **Mr. Jaws** *Dickie Goodman*
6/57 **Mr. Lee** *Bobbettes*
97/69 **Mr. Limousine Driver** *Grand Funk Railroad*
75/60 **Mr. Livingston** *Larry Verne*
Mr. Lonely
64/62 *Buddy Greco*
1/64 *Bobby Vinton*
73/60 **Mr. Lonely** *Videls*
21/60 **Mr. Lucky** *Henry Mancini*
54/75 **Mr. Magic** *Grover Washington, Jr.*
98/73 **Mr. Magic Man** *Wilson Pickett*
49/76 **Mr. Melody** *Natalie Cole*
93/74 **Mr. Natural** *Bee Gees*
96/68 **Mr. Nico** *Four Jacks & A Jill*
63/72 **Mr. Penguin** *Lunar Funk*
41/65 **Mr. Pitiful** *Otis Redding*
80/67 **Mr. Pleasant** *Kinks*
73/74 **Mr. President** *Dickie Goodman*
91/61 **Mr. Pride** *Chuck Jackson*
3/83 **Mr. Roboto** *Styx*
37/81 **Mr. Sandman** *Emmylou Harris*
92/73 **Mr. Skin** *Spirit*
43/62 **Mr. Songwriter** *Connie Stevens*
36/66 **Mr. Spaceman** *Byrds*
41/58 **Mr. Success** *Frank Sinatra*
18/69 **Mr. Sun, Mr. Moon**
Paul Revere & The Raiders
1/65 **Mr. Tambourine Man** *Byrds*
12/85 **Mr. Telephone Man** *New Edition*
80/69 **Mr. Walker, It's All Over** *Billie Jo Spears*
92/63 **Mr. Wishing Well** *Nat King Cole*
Mr. Wonderful
13/56 *Sarah Vaughan*
14/56 *Peggy Lee*
18/56 *Teddi King*
69/68 **Mrs. Bluebird** *Eternity's Children*
1/65 **Mrs. Brown You've Got A Lovely Daughter** *Herman's Hermits*
Mrs. Robinson
1/68 *Simon & Garfunkel*
37/69 *Booker T. & The MG's*
Ms. *see: Miss*
53/69 **Muddy Mississippi Line** *Bobby Goldsboro*
41/69 **Muddy River** *Johnny Rivers*
Muhammad Ali *see: Black Superman*
82/68 **Mule, The** *James Boys*
5/60 **Mule Skinner Blues** *Fendermen*
30/62 **Multiplication** *Bobby Darin*
80/60 **Mumblin' Mosie** *Johnny Otis Show*
39/59 **Mummy, The** *Bob McFadden & Dor*
39/82 **Murphy's Law** *Cheri*
10/82 **Muscles** *Diana Ross*
39/67 **Museum** *Herman's Hermits*
88/76 **Music** *John Miles*
75/79 **Music Box** *Evelyn 'Champagne' King*
3/79 **Music Box Dancer** *Frank Mills*
68/73 **Music Everywhere** *Tufano & Giammarese*
95/74 **Music Eyes** *Heartsfield*
84/72 **Music From Across The Way** *James Last*

57/78 **Music, Harmony And Rhythm**
Brooklyn Dreams
92/75 **Music In My Bones** *Joe Simon*
95/71 **Music Is Love** *David Crosby*
F/76 **Music Is My Life** *Helen Reddy*
Music, Music, Music
54/61 *Sensations*
96/68 *Happenings*
81/75 **Music Never Stopped** *Grateful Dead*
40/84 **Music Time** *Styx*
Music To Watch Girls By
15/67 *Bob Crewe Generation*
34/67 *Andy Williams*
82/61 **Muskrat** *Everly Brothers*
Muskrat Love
67/73 *America*
4/76 *Captain & Tennille*
54/61 **Muskrat Ramble** *Freddy Cannon*
54/74 **Must Be Love** *James Gang*
83/79 **Must Have Been Crazy** *Chicago*
12/75 **Must Of Got Lost** *J. Geils Band*
8/66 **Must To Avoid** *Herman's Hermits*
23/66 **Mustang Sally** *Wilson Pickett*
Mutual Admiration Society
21/56 *Teresa Brewer*
47/56 *Eddy Arnold & Jaye P. Morgan*
62/86 **Mutual Surrender (What A Wonderful World)** *Bourgeois Tagg*
My Airplane *see: Airplane Song*
13/78 **My Angel Baby** *Toby Beau*
92/66 **My Answer** *Jimmy McCracklin*
50/67 **My Babe** *Ronnie Dove*
75/63 **My Babe** *Righteous Brothers*
99/66 **My Babe** *Roy Head*
13/65 **My Baby** *Temptations*
51/64 **My Baby Don't Dig Me** *Ray Charles*
(My Baby Don't Love Me) *see: No More*
31/56 **My Baby Left Me** *Elvis Presley*
13/70 **My Baby Loves Lovin'** *White Plains*
22/66 **My Baby Loves Me** *Martha & The Vandellas*
17/68 **My Baby Must Be A Magician** *Marvelettes*
45/79 **My Baby's Baby** *Liquid Gold*
47/56 **My Baby's Got Such Lovin' Ways**
McGuire Sisters
30/67 **My Back Pages** *Byrds*
87/69 **My Balloon's Going Up**
Archie Bell & The Drells
49/56 **My Believing Heart** *Joni James*
35/78 **My Best Friend's Girl** *Cars*
80/77 **My Best Friend's Wife** *Paul Anka*
67/63 **My Block** *Four Pennies*
My Blue Heaven
21/56 *Fats Domino*
50/61 *Duane Eddy*
26/64 **My Bonnie** *Beatles/Tony Sheridan*
(also see: Bonnie Came Back)
11/55 **My Bonnie Lassie** *Ames Brothers*
21/62 **My Boomerang Won't Come Back**
Charlie Drake
My Boy
41/72 *Richard Harris*
20/75 *Elvis Presley*
My Boy - Flat Top
16/55 *Dorothy Collins*
39/55 *Boyd Bennett*
2/64 **My Boy Lollipop** *Millie Small*
83/64 **My Boyfriend Got A Beatle Haircut**
Donna Lynn
1/63 **My Boyfriend's Back** *Angels*
(also see: Your Boyfriend's Back)
18/58 **My Bucket's Got A Hole In It** *Ricky Nelson*
87/65 **My Buddy Seat** *Hondells*
88/65 **My Cherie** *Al Martino*
My Cherie Amour
4/69 *Stevie Wonder*
92/77 *Soul Train Gang*
68/61 **My Claire De Lune** *Steve Lawrence*
My Coloring Book
18/63 *Kitty Kallen*
20/63 *Sandy Stewart*
59/74 **My Country** *Jud Strunk*
F/73 **My Crew** *Rita Coolidge*
8/67 **My Cup Runneth Over** *Ed Ames*
6/63 **My Dad** *Paul Petersen*
67/62 **My Daddy Is President** *Little Jo Ann*
67/63 **My Daddy Knows Best** *Marvelettes*
34/60 **My Dearest Darling** *Etta James*
1/72 **My Ding-A-Ling** *Chuck Berry*
(also see: Ding-A-Ling)
24/57 **My Dream** *Platters*
83/61 **My Dream Come True** *Jack Scott*
59/56 **My Dream Sonata** *Nat King Cole*
85/64 **My Dreams** *Brenda Lee*
My Elusive Dreams
89/67 *David Houston & Tammy Wynette*
46/70 *Bobby Vinton*
49/75 *Charlie Rich*
9/61 **My Empty Arms** *Jackie Wilson*
86/60 **My Empty Room**
Little Anthony & The Imperials
29/84 **My Ever Changing Moods** *Style Council*
1/75 **My Eyes Adored You** *Frankie Valli*
97/77 **My Eyes Get Blurry** *Kenny Nolan*
28/77 **My Fair Share** *Seals & Crofts*
45/69 **My Favorite Things** *Herb Alpert*
94/75 **My First Day Without Her** *Classics IV*
80/56 **My First Formal Gown** *Patti Page*
95/63 **My Foolish Heart** *Demensions*
43/79 **My Forbidden Lover** *Chic*
74/66 **My Generation** *Who*
My Girl
1/65 *Temptations*
35/68 *Bobby Vee (medley)*
20/85 *Hall & Oates/David Ruffin/Eddie Kendrick (medley)*
25/82 **My Girl** *Donnie Iris*
12/74 **My Girl Bill** *Jim Stafford*
22/81 **My Girl (Gone, Gone, Gone)** *Chilliwack*
14/65 **My Girl Has Gone** *Miracles*
My Girl Josephine
14/60 *Fats Domino*
29/67 *Jerry Jaye*
My Girl Sloopy *see: Hang On Sloopy*
My Guy
1/64 *Mary Wells*
70/72 *Petula Clark*
63/80 *Amii Stewart & Johnny Bristol (My Guy/My Girl)*
23/82 *Sister Sledge*
2/59 **My Happiness** *Connie Francis*
74/59 **My Heart Became Of Age** *Annette*
4/77 **My Heart Belongs To Me** *Barbra Streisand*
My Heart Belongs To Only You
65/61 *Jackie Wilson*
9/64 *Bobby Vinton*
38/64 **My Heart Cries For You** *Ray Charles*
1/60 **My Heart Has A Mind Of Its Own**
Connie Francis
3/59 **My Heart Is An Open Book**
Carl Dobkins, Jr.
98/71 **My Heart Is Yours** *Wilbert Harrison*
92/73 **My Heart Just Keeps On Breakin'**
Chi-Lites
My Heart Reminds Me
see: And That Reminds Me
My Heart Sings *see: (All Of A Sudden)*
94/64 **My Heart Skips A Beat** *Buck Owens*
52/65 **My Heart Would Know** *Al Martino*

90/61 **My Heart's On Fire** *Billy Bland*
13/66 **My Heart's Symphony**
Gary Lewis & The Playboys
78/60 **My Hero** *Blue Notes*
44/80 **My Heroes Have Always Been Cowboys**
Willie Nelson
8/60 **My Home Town** *Paul Anka*
6/86 **My Hometown** *Bruce Springsteen*
55/70 **My Honey And Me** *Luther Ingram*
18/61 **My Kind Of Girl** *Matt Monro*
31/83 **My Kind Of Lady** *Supertramp*
45/82 **My Kinda Lover** *Billy Squier*
93/68 **M'Lady** *Sly & The Family Stone*
My Last Date (With You)
26/61 *Skeeter Davis*
38/61 *Joni James*
(also see: Last Date)
3/79 **My Life** *Billy Joel*
46/58 **My Life** *Chuck Willis*
24/56 **My Little Angel** *Four Lads*
48/57 **My Little Baby** *Perry Como*
99/69 **My Little Chickadee** *Foundations*
57/75 **My Little Lady** *Bloodstone*
84/60 **My Little Marine** *Jamie Horton*
52/66 **My Little Red Book** *Love*
9/75 **My Little Town** *Simon & Garfunkel*
1/66 **My Love** *Petula Clark*
1/73 **My Love** *Paul McCartney*
5/83 **My Love** *Lionel Richie*
47/60 **My Love** *Nat King Cole*
69/74 **My Love** *Margie Joseph*
47/60 **My Love For You** *Johnny Mathis*
16/65 **My Love, Forgive Me** *Robert Goulet*
60/79 **My Love Is Music** *Space*
62/57 **My Love Song** *Tommy Sands*
61/66 **My Lover's Prayer** *Otis Redding*
73/58 **My Lucky Love**
Doug Franklin with The Bluenotes
76/74 **My Main Man** *Staple Singers*
13/67 **My Mammy** *Happenings*
My Man
81/59 *Peggy Lee*
79/65 *Barbra Streisand*
42/72 **My Man, A Sweet Man** *Millie Jackson*
9/73 **My Maria** *B.W. Stevenson*
43/70 **My Marie** *Engelbert Humperdinck*
My Melancholy Baby
26/59 *Tommy Edwards*
58/62 *Marcels*
3/74 **My Melody Of Love** *Bobby Vinton*
79/61 **My Memories Of You**
Donnie & The Dreamers
77/73 **My Merry-Go-Round** *Johnny Nash*
81/80 **My Mistake** *Kingbees*
19/74 **My Mistake (Was To Love You)**
Marvin Gaye & Diana Ross
39/81 **My Mother's Eyes** *Bette Midler*
16/73 **My Music** *Loggins & Messina*
37/84 **My Oh My** *Slade*
97/67 **My Old Car** *Lee Dorsey*
63/73 **My Old School** *Steely Dan*
49/64 **My One And Only, Jimmy Boy** *Girlfriends*
My One Sin
24/55 *Nat King Cole*
28/57 *Four Coins*
My Own True Love
33/59 *Jimmy Clanton*
13/62 *Duprees*
74/77 **My Own Way To Rock** *Burton Cummings*
97/77 **My Pearl** *Automatic Man*

21/57 **My Personal Possession** *Nat King Cole*
14/69 **My Pledge Of Love** *Joe Jeffrey Group*
My Prayer
1/56 *Platters*
47/80 *Ray, Goodman & Brown*
51/73 **My Pretending Days Are Over** *Dells*
59/62 **My Real Name** *Fats Domino*
1/79 **My Sharona** *Knack*
F/75 **My Ship** *Tavares*
63/66 **My Ship Is Comin' In** *Walker Bros.*
My Shoes Keep Walking Back To You
63/57 *Ray Price*
45/60 *Guy Mitchell*
73/68 **My Shy Violet** *Mills Brothers*
31/69 **My Song** *Aretha Franklin*
100/70 **My Soul's Got A Hole In It** *Howard Tate*
My Special Angel
7/57 *Bobby Helms*
7/68 *Vogues*
My Special Prayer
87/67 *Joe Simon*
93/69 *Percy Sledge*
16/63 **My Summer Love** *Ruby & The Romantics*
My Sweet Lady
17/74 *Cliff DeYoung*
32/77 *John Denver*
My Sweet Lord
1/70 *George Harrison*
90/71 *Billy Preston*
85/66 **My Sweet Potato** *Booker T. & The MG's*
48/76 **My Sweet Summer Suite**
Love Unlimited Orchestra
50/60 **My Tani** *Brothers Four*
29/74 **My Thang** *James Brown*
My Three Sons *see: Theme From*
98/62 **My Time For Cryin'** *Maxine Brown*
50/85 **My Toot Toot** *Jean Knight*
39/83 **My Town** *Michael Stanley Band*
32/65 **My Town, My Guy And Me** *Lesley Gore*
31/56 **My Treasure** *Hilltoppers*
49/64 **My True Carrie, Love** *Nat King Cole*
22/63 **My True Confession** *Brook Benton*
3/58 **My True Love** *Jack Scott*
3/61 **My True Story** *Jive Five*
58/66 **My Uncle Used To Love But She Died**
Roger Miller
My Way
27/69 *Frank Sinatra*
72/70 *Brook Benton*
22/77 *Elvis Presley*
64/68 **My Way Of Life** *Frank Sinatra*
9/69 **My Whole World Ended (The Moment You Left Me)** *David Ruffin*
24/63 **My Whole World Is Falling Down**
Brenda Lee
57/63 **My Wife Can't Cook** *Lonnie Russ*
91/69 **My Wife, My Dog, My Cat**
Maskman & The Agents
52/70 **My Wife, The Dancer** *Eddie & Dutch*
12/59 **My Wish Came True** *Elvis Presley*
42/70 **My Woman My Woman, My Wife**
Marty Robbins
16/72 **My World** *Bee Gees*
70/67 **My World Fell Down** *Sagittarius*
My World Is Empty Without You
5/66 *Supremes*
87/69 *Jose Feliciano*
24/85 **Mystery Lady** *Billy Ocean*
33/65 **Mystic Eyes** *Them*

1/69 **Na Na Hey Hey Kiss Him Goodbye** *Steam*
8/76 **Nadia's Theme (The Young And The Restless)** *Barry DeVorzon & Perry Botkin, Jr.*
F/70 **Nadine** *Dells*
23/64 **Nadine (Is It You?)** *Chuck Berry*
25/61 **'Nag'** *Halos*
48/86 **Nail It To The Wall** *Stacy Lattisaw*
3/65 **Name Game** *Shirley Ellis*
12/78 **Name Of The Game** *Abba*
65/56 **Namely You** *Don Cherry*
91/73 **Names, Tags, Numbers & Labels** *Association*
8/67 **Nashville Cats** *Lovin' Spoonful*
3/86 **Nasty** *Janet Jackson*
16/71 **Nathan Jones** *Supremes*
53/60 **National City** *Joiner, Arkansas Junior High School Band*
Native Girl *see: Elephant Walk*
21/78 **Native New Yorker** *Odyssey*
38/60 **Natural Born Lover** *Fats Domino*
10/73 **Natural High** *Bloodstone*
66/82 **Natural Love** *Petula Clark*
17/71 **Natural Man** *Lou Rawls*
8/67 **Natural Woman** *Aretha Franklin*
40/68 **Naturally Stoned** *Avant-Garde*
40/61 **Nature Boy** *Bobby Darin*
Naughty Lady Of Shady Lane
3/55 *Ames Brothers*
17/55 *Archie Bleyer*
23/85 **Naughty Naughty** *John Parr*
6/64 **Navy Blue** *Diane Renay*
22/70 **Neanderthal Man** *Hotlegs*
10/58 **Near You** *Roger Williams*
96/71 **Near You** *Boz Scaggs*
85/67 **Nearer To You** *Betty Harris*
40/58 **Nee Nee Na Na Na Na Nu Nu** *Dicky Doo & The Don'ts*
11/74 **Need To Be** *Jim Weatherly*
31/64 **Need To Belong** *Jerry Butler*
25/58 **Need You** *Donnie Owens*
84/79 **Need You Bad** *Ted Nugent*
54/58 **Need Your Love** *Bobby Freeman*
44/80 **Need Your Loving Tonight** *Queen*
45/64 **Needle In A Haystack** *Velvelettes*
Needles And Pins
84/63 *Jackie DeShannon*
13/64 *Searchers*
68/77 *Smokie*
37/86 *Tom Petty/Stevie Nicks*
65/66 **Neighbor, Neighbor** *Jimmy Hughes*
2/73 **Neither One Of Us (Wants To Be The First To Say Goodbye)** *Gladys Knight & The Pips*
Nel Blu Dipinto Di Blu *see: Volare*
42/77 **Neon Nites** *Atlanta Rhythm Section*
24/67 **Neon Rainbow** *Box Tops*
59/65 **N-E-R-V-O-U-S!** *Ian Whitcomb*
68/57 **Nervous Boogie** *Paul Gayten*
6/85 **Neutron Dance** *Pointer Sisters*
70/71 **Nevada Fighter** *Michael Nesmith*
4/85 **Never** *Heart*
20/86 **Never As Good As The First Time** *Sade*
6/59 **Never Be Anyone Else But You** *Ricky Nelson*
15/80 **Never Be The Same** *Christopher Cross*
68/75 **Never Been Any Reason** *Head East*
28/82 **Never Been In Love** *Randy Meisner*
5/72 **Never Been To Spain** *Three Dog Night*
Never Can Say Goodbye
2/71 *Jackson 5*
22/71 *Isaac Hayes*
9/75 *Gloria Gaynor*
91/69 **Never Comes The Day** *Moody Blues*
78/71 **Never Dreamed You'd Leave In Summer** *Stevie Wonder*
13/71 **Never Ending Song Of Love** *Delaney & Bonnie & Friends*
17/85 **Never Ending Story** *Limahl*
95/68 **Never Get Enough Of Your Love** *Oscar Toney, Jr.*
56/78 **Never Get Enough Of Your Love** *L.T.D.*
46/83 **Never Give Up** *Sammy Hagar*
52/82 **Never Give Up On A Good Thing** *George Benson*
20/68 **Never Give You Up** *Jerry Butler*
73/68 **Never Going Back** *Lovin' Spoonful*
11/76 **Never Gonna Fall In Love Again** *Eric Carmen*
86/69 **Never Gonna Let Him Know** *Debbie Taylor*
4/83 **Never Gonna Let You Go** *Sergio Mendes*
26/70 **Never Had A Dream Come True** *Stevie Wonder*
87/78 **Never Had A Love** *Pablo Cruise*
56/62 **Never In A Million Years** *Linda Scott*
6/80 **Never Knew Love Like This Before** *Stephanie Mills*
F/55 **Never Leave Me** *Gale Storm*
29/75 **Never Let Her Go** *David Gates*
67/78 **Never Let Her Slip Away** *Andrew Gold*
79/56 **Never Let Me Go** *Nat King Cole*
82/60 **Never Let Me Go** *Lloyd Price*
43/73 **Never Let You Go** *Bloodstone*
99/63 **Never Love A Robin** *Bobby Vee*
Never My Love
2/67 *Association*
98/68 *Sandpebbles*
12/71 *5th Dimension*
7/74 *Blue Swede*
80/77 *Addrisi Brothers*
74/61 **Never, Never** *Jive Five*
7/74 **Never, Never Gonna Give Ya Up** *Barry White*
54/65 **Never, Never Leave Me** *Mary Wells*
48/73 **Never, Never, Never** *Shirley Bassey*
Never On Sunday
19/60 *Don Costa*
13/61 *Chordettes*
88/61 *Lale Anderson (Ein Schiff)*
73/83 **Never Say Die (Give A Little Bit More)** *Cliff Richard*
3/85 **Never Surrender** *Corey Hart*
88/83 **Never Tell An Angel (When Your Heart's On Fire)** *Stompers*
95/82 **Never Thought I'd Fall In Love** *Spinners*
33/81 **Never Too Much** *Luther Vandross*
90/64 **Never Trust A Woman** *B.B. King*
22/56 **Never Turn Back** *Al Hibbler*
67/75 **Nevertheless** *Allman Brothers Band*
0/85 **New Attitude** *Patti LaBelle*
70/83 **New Frontier** *Donald Fagen*
37/64 **New Girl In School** *Jan & Dean*
57/84 **New Girl Now** *Honeymoon Suite*
47/60 **(New In) The Ways Of Love** *Tommy Edwards*
1/77 **New Kid In Town** *Eagles*
New Lovers *see: (Welcome)*
36/63 **New Mexican Rose** *4 Seasons*
10/84 **New Moon On Monday** *Duran Duran*
New Orleans
6/60 *U.S. Bonds*
44/65 *Eddie Hodges*
51/68 *Neil Diamond*

70/76 **New Orleans** *Staple Singers*
59/78 **New Orleans Ladies** *Le Roux*
39/80 **New Romance (It's A Mystery)** *Spider*
27/84 **New Song** *Howard Jones*
42/70 **New World Coming** *Mama Cass*
21/82 **New World Man** *Rush*
53/83 **New Year's Day** *U2*
76/78 **New York City** *Zwol*
13/79 **New York Groove** *Ace Frehley*
14/67 **New York Mining Disaster 1941 Have You See My Wife Mr. Jones** *Bee Gees*
New York, New York *see: Theme From*
27/77 **New York, You Got Me Dancing** *Andrea True Connection*
32/65 **New York's A Lonely Town** *Trade Winds*
59/56 **New York's My Home** *Sammy Davis, Jr.*
97/74 **Newsy Neighbors** *First Choice*
5/62 **Next Door To An Angel** *Neil Sedaka*
71/62 **Next Door To The Blues** *Etta James*
49/78 **Next Hundred Years** *Al Martino*
99/57 **Next In Line** *Johnny Cash*
72/61 **Next Kiss (Is The Last Goodbye)** *Conway Twitty*
81/84 **Next Love** *Deniece Williams*
17/67 **Next Plane To London** *Rose Garden*
F/70 **Next Step Is Love** *Elvis Presley*
1/86 **Next Time I Fall** *Peter Cetera with Amy Grant*
75/56 **Next Time It Happens** *Carmen McRae*
74/57 **Next Time You See Me** *Little Junior Parker*
82/81 **Next Time You'll Know** *Sister Sledge*
37/82 **Nice Girls** *Eye To Eye*
42/83 **Nice Girls** *Melissa Manchester*
60/60 **Nice 'N' Easy** *Frank Sinatra*
30/76 **Nice 'N' Naasty** *Salsoul Orchestra*
63/75 **Nice, Nice, Very Nice** *Ambrosia*
4/72 **Nice To Be With You** *Gallery*
95/63 **Nick Teen And Al K. Hall** *Rolf Harris*
Nickel Song
81/71 *New Seekers*
35/72 *Melanie*
39/81 **Nicole** *Point Blank*
Night
4/60 *Jackie Wilson*
48/83 **Night** *Animals*
Night *also see: Nite*
82/67 **Night And Day** *Sergio Mendes & Brasil '66*
1/74 **Night Chicago Died** *Paper Lace*
74/79 **Night Dancin'** *Taka Boom*
1/78 **Night Fever** *Bee Gees*
75/68 **Night Fo' Last** *Shorty Long*
3/63 **Night Has A Thousand Eyes** *Bobby Vee*
34/85 **Night Is Still Young** *Billy Joel*
57/63 **Night Life** *Rusty Draper*
11/56 **Night Lights** *Nat King Cole*
4/77 **Night Moves** *Bob Seger*
28/86 **Night Moves** *Marilyn Martin*
6/81 **Night Owls** *Little River Band*
92/83 **Night Pulse** *Double Image*
60/82 **Night Shift** *Quarterflash*
1/73 **Night The Lights Went Out In Georgia** *Vicki Lawrence*
75/60 **Night Theme** *Mark II*
3/71 **Night They Drove Old Dixie Down** *Joan Baez*
30/66 **Night Time** *Strangeloves*
100/62 **Night Time** *Pete Antell*
Night Time Is The Right Time
95/59 *Ray Charles*
94/64 *Rufus & Carla*
44/82 **Night To Remember** *Shalamar*
Night Train
82/60 *Viscounts*
80/61 *Richard Hayman*
35/62 *James Brown*
96/76 **Night Walk** *Van McCoy*
33/84 **Nightbird** *Stevie Nicks*
9/75 **Nightingale** *Carole King*
10/76 **Nights Are Forever Without You** *England Dan & John Ford Coley*
2/72 **Nights In White Satin** *Moody Blues*
7/75 **Nights On Broadway** *Bee Gees*
3/85 **Nightshift** *Commodores*
41/81 **Nightwalker** *Gino Vannelli*
23/67 **Niki Hoeky** *P.J. Proby*
7/86 **Nikita** *Elton John*
58/58 **Nine More Miles** *Georgie Young*
70/67 **Nine Pound Steel** *Joe Simon*
1/81 **9 To 5** *Dolly Parton*
15/85 **19** *Paul Hardcastle*
48/66 **Nineteen Days** *Dave Clark Five*
2/66 **19th Nervous Breakdown** *Rolling Stones*
96 Tears
1/66 *? (Question Mark) & The Mysterians*
96/67 *Big Maybelle*
66/81 *Garland Jeffreys*
7/67 **98.6** *Keith*
26/80 **99** *Toto*
2/84 **99 Luftballons** *Nena*
91/75 **99 Miles From L.A.** *Albert Hammond*
11/57 **Ninety-Nine Ways** *Tab Hunter*
23/56 **Ninety-Nine Years (Dead Or Alive)** *Guy Mitchell*
77/84 **99 1/2** *Carol Lynn Townes*
53/66 **Ninety-Nine And A Half (Won't Do)** *Wilson Pickett*
57/72 **992 Arguments** *O'Jays*
33/71 **1900 Yesterday** *Liz Damon's Orient Express*
88/71 **1927 Kansas City** *Mike Reilly*
88/68 **1941** *Tom Northcott*
69/70 **1984** *Spirit*
12/83 **1999** *Prince*
52/77 **9,999,999 Tears** *Dickey Lee*
73/62 **Nite Owl** *Dukays*
Nitty Gritty
8/64 *Shirley Ellis*
90/68 *Ricardo Ray*
19/69 *Gladys Knight & The Pips*
44/72 **No** *Bulldog*
73/60 **No** *Dodie Stevens*
No Arms Can Ever Hold You
23/55 *Georgie Shaw*
26/55 *Pat Boone*
67/55 *Gaylords*
27/65 *Bachelors*
93/70 *Bobby Vinton*
50/79 **No Chance** *Moon Martin*
No Charge
39/74 *Melba Montgomery*
91/75 *Shirley Caesar*
23/58 **No Chemise, Please** *Gerry Granahan*
22/86 **No Easy Way Out** *Robert Tepper*
51/67 **No Fair At All** *Association*
91/65 **No Faith, No Love** *Mitty Collier*
87/86 **No Frills Love** *Jennifer Holliday*
No Gettin' Over Me *see: (There's)*
No Good To Cry
88/67 *Wildweeds*
84/71 *Poppy Family*
40/60 **No If's - No And's** *Lloyd Price*
34/85 **No Lookin' Back** *Michael McDonald*
16/71 **No Love At All** *B.J. Thomas*
21/58 **No Love (But Your Love)** *Johnny Mathis*
54/60 **No Love Have I** *Webb Pierce*

94/66 **No Man Is An Island** *Van Dykes*
8/70 **No Matter What** *Badfinger*
3/66 **No Matter What Shape (Your Stomach's In)** *T-Bones*
31/69 **No Matter What Sign You Are** *Supremes*
35/67 **No Milk Today** *Herman's Hermits*
No More
6/55 *DeJohn Sisters*
17/55 *McGuire Sisters*
6/84 **No More Lonely Nights** *Paul McCartney*
25/73 **No More Mr. Nice Guy** *Alice Cooper*
1/79 **No More Tears (Enough Is Enough)** *Barbra Streisand/Donna Summer*
23/84 **No More Words** *Berlin*
23/80 **No Night So Long** *Dionne Warwick*
55/58 **No, No** *Fats Domino*
60/76 **No, No, Joe** *Silver Convention*
41/61 **No, No, No** *Chanters*
3/75 **No No Song** *Ringo Starr*
No, Not Much!
2/56 *Four Lads*
34/69 *Vogues*
85/69 *Smoke Ring*
No One
34/61 *Connie Francis*
21/63 *Ray Charles*
98/65 *Brenda Lee*
93/69 **No One Better Than You** *Petula Clark*
45/58 **No One But You (In My Heart)** *Ames Brothers*
78/83 **No One Can Love You More Than Me** *Melissa Manchester*
52/69 **No One For Me To Turn To** *Spiral Starecase*
4/86 **No One Is To Blame** *Howard Jones*
19/58 **No One Knows** *Dion & The Belmonts*
96/68 **No One Knows** *Every Mothers' Son*
65/82 **No One Like You** *Scorpions*
55/64 **No One To Cry To** *Ray Charles*
36/72 **No One To Depend On** *Santana*
43/62 **No One Will Ever Know** *Jimmie Rodgers*
No Other Arms
see: No Arms Can Ever Hold You
No Other Arms, No Other Lips
27/59 *Chordettes*
74/59 *Four Aces*
65/56 **No Other One** *Eddie Fisher*
81/84 **No Parking (On The Dance Floor)** *Midnight Star*
10/64 **No Particular Place To Go** *Chuck Berry*
59/65 **No Pity (In The Naked City)** *Jackie Wilson*
79/86 **No Promises** *Icehouse*
90/59 **No Regrets** *Jimmy Barnes*
29/81 **No Reply At All** *Genesis*
62/72 **No Sad Song** *Helen Reddy*
49/68 **No Sad Songs** *Joe Simon*
F/70 **No Sugar Tonight** *Guess Who*
14/79 **No Tell Lover** *Chicago*
5/70 **No Time** *Guess Who*
33/83 **No Time For Talk** *Christopher Cross*
96/67 **No Time Like The Right Time** *Blues Project*
No Time To Lose
84/79 *Tarney/Spencer Band*
74/81 *Tarney/Spencer Band*
23/84 **No Way Out** *Jefferson Starship*
15/82 **Nobody** *Sylvia*
58/74 **Nobody** *Doobie Brothers*
8/68 **Nobody But Me** *Human Beinz*
21/59 **Nobody But You** *Dee Clark*
86/72 **Nobody But You** *Loggins & Messina*
40/69 **Nobody But You Babe** *Clarence Reid*
60/61 **Nobody Cares (about me)** *Baby Washington*
2/77 **Nobody Does It Better** *Carly Simon*
12/64 **Nobody I Know** *Peter & Gordon*
49/65 **Nobody Knows What's Goin' On** *Chiffons*
93/60 **Nobody Knows You When You're Down And Out** *Nina Simone*
30/60 **Nobody Loves Me Like You** *Flamingos*
18/82 **Nobody Said It Was Easy** *Le Roux*
5/84 **Nobody Told Me** *John Lennon*
29/73 **Nobody Wants You When You're Down And Out** *Bobby Womack*
21/81 **Nobody Wins** *Elton John*
70/73 **Nobody Wins** *Brenda Lee*
60/66 **Nobody's Baby Again** *Dean Martin*
13/87 **Nobody's Fool** *Cinderella*
Nola
39/59 *Billy Williams*
50/59 *Morgan Brothers*
45/58 **Non Dimenticar (Don't Forget)** *Nat King Cole*
84/76 **Norma Jean Wants To Be A Movie Star** *Sundown Company*
3/62 **Norman** *Sue Thompson*
4/60 **North To Alaska** *Johnny Horton*
43/68 **Not Enough Indians** *Dean Martin*
34/85 **Not Enough Love In The World** *Don Henley*
Not Fade Away
48/64 *Rolling Stones*
70/79 *Tanya Tucker*
73/81 *Eric Hine*
100/63 **Not For All The Money In The World** *Shirelles*
12/63 **Not Me** *Orlons*
57/69 **Not On The Outside** *Moments*
48/56 **Not One Goodbye** *Jaye P. Morgan*
16/60 **Not One Minute More** *Della Reese*
58/66 **Not Responsible** *Tom Jones*
95/67 **Not So Sweet Martha Lorraine** *Country Joe & The Fish*
25/65 **Not The Lovin' Kind** *Dino, Desi & Billy*
66/65 **Not Too Long Ago** *Uniques*
63/63 **Not Too Young To Get Married** *Bob B. Soxx & The Blue Jeans*
10/86 **Nothin' At All** *Heart*
77/75 **Nothin' Heavy** *David Bellamy*
64/58 **Nothin' Shakin'** *Eddie Fontaine*
86/77 **Nothing But A Breeze** *Jesse Winchester*
34/69 **Nothing But A Heartache** *Flirtations*
49/61 **Nothing But Good** *Hank Ballard*
11/65 **Nothing But Heartaches** *Supremes*
12/62 **Nothing Can Change This Love** *Sam Cooke*
18/65 **Nothing Can Stop Me** *Gene Chandler*
74/69 **Nothing Can Take The Place Of You** *Brook Benton*
72/56 **Nothing Ever Changes My Love For You** *Nat King Cole*
54/81 **Nothing Ever Goes As Planned** *Styx*
Nothing For Xmas *see: Nuttin'*
1/74 **Nothing From Nothing** *Billy Preston*
87/63 **Nothing Goes Up (Without Coming Down)** *Nat King Cole*
54/86 **Nothing In Common** *Thompson Twins*
99/58 **Nothing In The World** *Nat King Cole*
84/57 **Nothing Is Too Good For You** *Harvey Boys*
77/62 **Nothing New (Same Old Thing)** *Fats Domino*
52/81 **Nothing Remains The Same (medley)** *Spinners*
62/70 **Nothing Succeeds Like Success** *Bill Deal*
52/67 **Nothing Takes The Place Of You** *Toussaint McCall*
41/71 **Nothing To Hide** *Tommy James*
20/66 **Nothing's Too Good For My Baby** *Stevie Wonder*
2/87 **Notorious** *Duran Duran*

92/63 **Now!** *Lena Horne*
25/58 **Now And For Always** *George Hamilton IV*
48/61 **Now And Forever** *Bert Kaempfert*
92/86 **Now And Forever (You And Me)** *Anne Murray*
(Now And Then) A *see: Fool Such As I*
73/67 **Now I Know** *Jack Jones*
93/71 **Now I'm A Woman** *Nancy Wilson*
59/56 **Now Is The Hour** *Gale Storm*
74/84 **Now It's My Turn** *Berlin*
64/82 **Now Or Never** *Axe*
46/72 **Now Run And Tell That** *Denise LaSalle*
47/79 **Now That We Found Love** *Third World*
53/65 **Now That You've Gone** *Connie Stevens*
88/56 **Now You Has Jazz** *Bing Crosby & Louis Armstrong*
93/61 **Now You Know** *Little Willie John*
3/66 **Nowhere Man** *Beatles*
8/65 **Nowhere To Run** *Martha & The Vandellas*
66/82 **Nowhere To Run** *Santana*
91/56 **Nuevo Laredo** *Les Paul & Mary Ford*
9/75 **#9 Dream** *John Lennon*
97/78 **Number One** *Eloise Laws*
82/78 **#1 Dee Jay** *Goody Goody*
52/62 **Number One Man** *Bruce Channel*
95/55 **Number One Street** *Bob Corley*
95/72 **Number Wonderful** *Rock Flowers*
93/76 **Nursery Rhymes** *People's Choice*
Nutbush City Limits
22/73 *Ike & Tina Turner*
69/76 *Bob Seger*
Nutrocker
23/62 *B. Bumble & The Stingers*
70/72 *Emerson, Lake & Palmer*
Nuttin' For Christmas
6/55 *Barry Gordon*
20/55 *Joe Ward*
21/55 *Ricky Zahnd*
36/55 *Fontane Sisters*
53/55 *Stan Freberg*

O

10/60 **O Dio Mio** *Annette*
83/59 **O' Falling Star** *Four Knights*
65/85 **Oak Tree** *Morris Day*
Ob-La-Di, Ob-La-Da
51/69 *Arthur Conley*
49/76 *Beatles*
25/85 **Object Of My Desire** *Starpoint*
35/84 **Obscene Phone Caller** *Rockwell*
6/85 **Obsession** *Animotion*
89/55 **Occasional Man** *Jeri Southern*
43/69 **Odds And Ends** *Dionne Warwick*
Ode To Billie Joe
1/67 *Bobbie Gentry*
28/67 *Kingpins*
89/67 *Ray Bryant*
54/76 *Bobbie Gentry*
65/76 *Bobbie Gentry (Main Title)*
50/65 **Ode To The Little Brown Shack Out Back** *Billy Edd Wheeler*
56/55 **Of This I'm Sure** *Four Aces*
10/80 **Off The Wall** *Michael Jackson*
94/66 **Off To Dublin In The Green** *Abbey Tavern Singers*
Oh *also see: O*
3/73 **Oh, Babe, What Would You Say?** *Hurricane Smith*
69/64 **Oh! Baby** *Barbara Lynn*
57/57 **Oh Baby Doll** *Chuck Berry*
23/64 **Oh Baby Don't You Weep** *James Brown*
10/58 **Oh, Boy!** *Crickets*
9/59 **Oh! Carol** *Neil Sedaka*
15/78 **Oh! Darling** *Robin Gibb*
1/72 **Oh Girl** *Chi-Lites*
39/85 **Oh Girl** *Boy Meets Girl*
Oh Happy Day
4/69 *Edwin Hawkins' Singers*
40/70 *Glen Campbell*
45/79 **Oh Honey** *Delegation*
Oh How Happy
12/66 *Shades Of Blue*
92/69 *Edwin Starr & Blinky*
63/61 **Oh, How I Miss You Tonight** *Jeanne Black*
59/68 **Oh, How It Hurts** *Barbara Mason*
Oh Julie
5/58 *Crescendos*
23/58 *Sammy Salvo*
38/82 **Oh Julie** *Barry Manilow*
33/73 **Oh La De Da** *Staple Singers*
34/60 **Oh, Little One** *Jack Scott*
Oh Lonesome Me
7/58 *Don Gibson*
93/61 *Johnny Cash*
78/68 **Oh Lord, Why Lord** *Los Pop Tops*
64/72 **(Oh Lord Won't You Buy Me A) Mercedes Benz** *Goose Creek Symphony*
48/75 **Oh Me, Oh My (Dreams In My Arms)** *Al Green*
Oh Me Oh My (I'm A Fool For You Baby)
22/70 *Lulu*
73/72 *Aretha Franklin*
94/61 **Oh Mein Papa** *Dick Lee*
61/62 **Oh My Angel** *Bertha Tillman*
85/78 **Oh My Lord (medley)** *Boney M*
80/56 **Oh My Maria** *Eddie Fisher*
5/74 **Oh My My** *Ringo Starr*
98/70 **Oh My My** *Monkees*
4/81 **Oh No** *Commodores*
Oh No, Not My Baby
24/65 *Maxine Brown*
59/73 *Rod Stewart*
72/73 *Merry Clayton*
7/58 **Oh Oh, I'm Falling In Love Again** *Jimmie Rodgers*
29/86 **Oh, People** *Patti LaBelle*
Oh, Pretty Woman
1/64 *Roy Orbison*
12/82 *Van Halen*
93/64 **Oh, Rock My Soul** *Peter, Paul & Mary*
1/85 **Oh Sheila** *Ready For The World*
3/84 **Oh Sherrie** *Steve Perry*
74/71 **Oh, Singer** *Jeannie C. Riley*
22/55 **Oh! Susanna** *Singing Dogs*
54/67 **Oh That's Good, No That's Bad** *Sam The Sham & The Pharoahs*
10/74 **Oh Very Young** *Cat Stevens*
Oh Well
55/70 *Fleetwood Mac*
30/79 *Rockets*
43/70 **Oh What A Day** *Dells*
86/59 **Oh, What A Fool** *Impalas*
10/69 **Oh, What A Night** *Dells*
Oh, What A Night *see: December, 1963*
24/78 **Oh What A Night For Dancing** *Barry White*
91/62 **Oh! What It Seemed To Be** *Castells*
91/59 **Oh Why** *Teddy Bears*
F/71 **Oh Woman Oh Why** *Paul McCartney*

Oh Yeah
39/66 *Shadows Of Knight*
62/67 **Oh Yeah!** *Joe Cuba Sextet*
14/70 **Ohio** *Crosby, Stills, Nash & Young*
45/77 **O-H-I-O** *Ohio Players*
43/59 **Okefenokee** *Freddy Cannon*
41/70 **Okie From Muskogee** *Merle Haggard*
54/67 **Okolona River Bottom Band** *Bobbie Gentry*
82/62 **Ol' Man River** *Jimmy Smith*
83/68 **Ol' Race Track** *Mills Brothers*
3/57 **Old Cape Cod** *Patti Page*
5/75 **Old Days** *Chicago*
94/63 **Old Enough To Love** *Rick Nelson*
20/80 **Old Fashion Love** *Commodores*
37/77 **Old Fashioned Boy (You're The One)** *Stallion*
60/82 **Old Fashioned Love** *Smokey Robinson*
4/71 **Old Fashioned Love Song** *Three Dog Night*
54/74 **Old Home Filler-Up An' Keep On-A-Truckin' Cafe** *C.W. McCall*
5/60 **Old Lamplighter** *Browns*
Old MacDonald
95/58 *Chargers*
25/60 *Frank Sinatra*
31/72 **Old Man** *Neil Young*
10/85 **Old Man Down The Road** *John Fogerty*
73/60 **Old Oaken Bucket** *Tommy Sands*
99/60 **Old Payola Roll Blues** *Stan Freberg*
34/56 **Old Philosopher** *Eddie Lawrence*
5/62 **Old Rivers** *Walter Brennan*
Old Shep
47/56 *Elvis Presley*
91/59 *Ralph DeMarco*
48/63 **Old Smokey Locomotion** *Little Eva*
15/81 **Old Songs** *Barry Manilow*
76/59 **Old Spanish Town** *Bell Notes*
Old Time Rock & Roll
28/79 *Bob Seger*
48/83 *Bob Seger*
25/61 **Ole Buttermilk Sky** *Bill Black's Combo*
94/71 **Olena** *Don Nix*
76/62 **Oliver Twist** *Rod McKuen*
58/84 **Olympia** *Sergio Mendes*
88/67 **Omaha** *Moby Grape*
On A Carousel
11/67 *Hollies*
50/82 *Glass Moon*
98/65 **On A Clear Day You Can See Forever** *Johnny Mathis*
44/74 **On A Night Like This** *Bob Dylan*
92/67 **On A Saturday Night** *Eddie Floyd*
59/59 **On An Evening In Roma** *Dean Martin*
90/73 **On And Off** *Anacostia*
5/74 **On And On** *Gladys Knight & The Pips*
11/77 **On And On** *Stephen Bishop*
90/81 **On And On And On** *Abba*
64/61 **On Bended Knees** *Clarence 'Frogman' Henry*
On Broadway
9/63 *Drifters*
7/78 *George Benson*
45/69 **On Campus** *Dickie Goodman*
38/56 **On London Bridge** *Jo Stafford*
1/86 **On My Own** *Patti LaBelle & Michael McDonald*
(On My Way To Sunny California) *see: California Saga*
20/57 **On My Word Of Honor** *Platters*
47/60 **On The Beach** *Frank Chacksfield*
54/70 **On The Beach (In The Summertime)** *5th Dimension*
42/77 **On The Border** *Al Stewart*
On The Dark Side
64/83 *Eddie & The Cruisers*
7/84 *John Cafferty*
87/66 **On The Good Ship Lollipop** *Wonder Who?*
26/83 **On The Loose** *Saga*
5/80 **On The Radio** *Donna Summer*
4/61 **On The Rebound** *Floyd Cramer*
58/80 **On The Rebound** *Russ Ballard*
16/68 **On The Road Again** *Canned Heat*
20/80 **On The Road Again** *Willie Nelson*
38/78 **On The Shelf** *Donny & Marie Osmond*
On The Street Where You Live
4/56 *Vic Damone*
18/56 *Eddie Fisher*
96/56 *Lawrence Welk*
28/64 *Andy Williams*
67/78 **On The Strip** *Paul Nicholas*
82/68 **On The Way Home** *Buffalo Springfield*
27/82 **On The Way To The Sky** *Neil Diamond*
50/84 **On The Wings Of A Nightingale** *Everly Brothers*
29/82 **On The Wings Of Love** *Jeffrey Osborne*
82/78 **On The Wrong Track** *Kevin Lamb*
47/66 **On This Side Of Goodbye** *Righteous Brothers*
14/63 **On Top Of Spaghetti** *Tom Glazer*
74/57 **On Treasure Island** *Gale Storm*
82/76 **Once A Fool** *Kiki Dee*
94/81 **Once A Night** *Jackie English*
91/86 **Once In A Lifetime** *Talking Heads*
11/61 **Once In Awhile** *Chimes*
19/64 **Once Upon A Time** *Marvin Gaye & Mary Wells*
26/61 **Once Upon A Time** *Rochell & The Candles*
10/75 **Once You Get Started** *Rufus Featuring Chaka Khan*
79/76 **Once You Hit The Road** *Dionne Warwick*
Once You Understand
23/72 *Think*
53/74 *Think*
5/69 **One** *Three Dog Night*
1/71 **One Bad Apple** *Osmonds*
48/75 **One Beautiful Day** *Ecstasy, Passion & Pain*
54/60 **One Boy** *Joanie Sommers*
96/63 **One Boy Too Late** *Mike Clifford*
11/63 **One Broken Heart For Sale** *Elvis Presley*
71/67 **One By One** *Blues Magoos*
One Chain Don't Make No Prison
41/74 *Four Tops*
59/79 *Santana*
37/74 **One Day At A Time** *Marilyn Sellars*
55/81 **One Day In Your Life** *Michael Jackson*
77/70 **One Day Of Your Life** *Andy Williams*
34/65 **One Dyin' And A Buryin'** *Roger Miller*
95/69 **One Eye Open** *Maskman & The Agents*
One Eyed Jacks *see: Love Theme From*
One Fine Day
5/63 *Chiffons*
93/76 *Julie*
66/79 *Rita Coolidge*
12/80 *Carole King*
24/71 **One Fine Morning** *Lighthouse*
76/85 **One Foot Back In Your Door** *Roman Holliday*
49/57 **One For My Baby** *Tony Bennett*
88/76 **One For The Money** *Whispers*
67/64 **One Girl** *Garnet Mimms*
13/66 **One Has My Name (The Other Has My Heart)** *Barry Young*
11/74 **One Hell Of A Woman** *Mac Davis*
28/86 **One Hit (To The Body)** *Rolling Stones*
14/82 **One Hundred Ways** *James Ingram*
69/68 **100 Years** *Nancy Sinatra*
(also see: Hundred)

69/79 **137 Disco Heaven (medley)** *Amii Stewart*
76/67 **One Hurt Deserves Another** *Raeletts*
31/57 **One In A Million** *Platters*
37/84 **One In A Million** *Romantics*
85/85 **One In A Million** *Eddie & The Tide*
9/80 **One In A Million You** *Larry Graham*
14/65 **One Kiss For Old Times' Sake** *Ronnie Dove*
73/56 **One Kiss Led To Another** *Coasters*
35/79 **One Last Kiss** *J. Geils Band*
78/73 **One Last Time** *Glen Campbell*
2/70 **One Less Bell To Answer** *5th Dimension*
37/73 **One Less Set Of Footsteps** *Jim Croce*
92/80 **One Life To Live** *Wayne Massey*
94/70 **One Light Two Lights** *Satisfactions*
19/85 **One Lonely Night** *REO Speedwagon*
25/76 **One Love In My Lifetime** *Diana Ross*
82/59 **One Love, One Heart** *Four Coins*
19/71 **One Man Band** *Three Dog Night*
96/75 **One Man Band** *Leo Sayer*
28/73 **One Man Band (Plays All Alone)** *Ronnie Dyson*
67/73 **One Man Parade** *James Taylor*
7/75 **One Man Woman/One Woman Man** *Paul Anka/Odia Coates*
96/71 **One Man's Leftovers** *100 Proof Aged In Soul*
One Mint Julep
82/60 *Chet Atkins*
8/61 *Ray Charles*
65/65 **One Monkey Don't Stop No Show** *Joe Tex*
15/72 **One Monkey Don't Stop No Show** *Honey Cone*
74/59 **One More Chance** *Rod Bernard*
76/72 **One More Chance** *Ocean*
79/81 **One More Chance** *Diana Ross*
29/66 **One More Heartache** *Marvin Gaye*
49/79 **One More Minute** *Saint Tropez*
45/67 **One More Mountain To Climb** *Ronnie Dove*
1/85 **One More Night** *Phil Collins*
47/81 **One More Night** *Streek*
One More Sunrise *see: Morgen*
97/64 **One More Tear** *Raindrops*
32/65 **One More Time** *Ray Charles Singers*
52/80 **One More Time For Love** *Billy Preston & Syreeta*
93/75 **One More Tomorrow** *Henry Gross*
97/62 **One More Town** *Kingston Trio*
81/76 **(One More Year Of) Daddy's Little Girl** *Ray Sawyer*
28/78 **One Nation Under A Groove** *Funkadelic*
4/58 **One Night** *Elvis Presley*
One Night Affair
68/69 *O'Jays*
52/72 *Jerry Butler*
One Night In Bangkok
3/85 *Murray Head*
77/85 *Robey*
13/85 **One Night Love Affair** *Bryan Adams*
74/71 **One Night Stand** *Magic Lanterns*
11/73 **One Of A Kind (Love Affair)** *Spinners*
96/73 **One Of The Boys** *Mott The Hoople*
15/85 **One Of The Living** *Tina Turner*
62/60 **One Of The Lucky Ones** *Anita Bryant*
92/69 **(One Of These Days) Sunday's Gonna' Come On Tuesday** *New Establishment*
1/75 **One Of These Nights** *Eagles*
31/60 **One Of Us (Will Weep Tonight)** *Patti Page*
7/83 **One On One** *Daryl Hall & John Oates*
One On One, Love Theme From *see: My Fair Share*
46/66 **One On The Right Is On The Left** *Johnny Cash*
29/76 **One Piece At A Time** *Johnny Cash*
96/64 **One Piece Topless Bathing Suit** *Rip Chords*
75/59 **One Rose (That's Left In My Heart)** *Teresa Brewer*
43/57 **One Step At A Time** *Brenda Lee*
55/65 **One Step At A Time** *Maxine Brown*
24/81 **One Step Closer** *Doobie Brothers*
22/86 **One Step Closer To You** *Gavin Christopher*
93/57 **One Suit** *Tennessee Ernie Ford*
One Summer Night
7/58 *Danleers*
22/61 *Diamonds*
96/86 **One Sunny Day (medley)** *Ray Parker, Jr. & Helen Terry*
71/74 **One Tear** *Eddie Kendricks*
74/83 **One That Really Matters** *Survivor*
1/81 **One That You Love** *Air Supply*
30/83 **One Thing** *INXS*
4/83 **One Thing Leads To Another** *Fixx*
91/78 **1000 Laughs** *Eloise Laws*
One Tin Soldier (The Legend Of Billy Jack)
34/70 *Original Caste*
26/71 *Coven*
79/73 *Coven*
73/74 *Coven*
45/82 **One To One** *Carole King*
10/71 **One Toke Over The Line** *Brewer & Shipley*
95/66 **One Too Many Mornings** *Beau Brummels*
9/61 **One Track Mind** *Bobby Lewis*
46/66 **One Track Mind** *Knickerbockers*
40/80 **One-Trick Pony** *Paul Simon*
1-2-3
2/65 *Len Barry*
67/67 *Ramsey Lewis*
5/68 **1, 2, 3, Red Light** *1910 Fruitgum Co.*
76/68 **(1-2-3-4-5-6-7) Count The Days** *Inez & Charlie Foxx*
61/86 **One Vision** *Queen*
56/64 **One Way Love** *Drifters*
75/86 **One Way Love** *TKA*
77/79 **One Way Love** *Bandit*
24/79 **One Way Or Another** *Blondie*
86/72 **One Way Out** *Allman Brothers Band*
94/72 **One Way Sunday** *Mark-Almond*
75/71 **One-Way Ticket** *Tyrone Davis*
8/62 **One Who Really Loves You** *Mary Wells*
89/69 **One Woman** *Johnny Rivers*
15/82 **One You Love** *Glenn Frey*
50/70 **Onion Song** *Marvin Gaye & Tammi Terrell*
36/80 **Only A Lonely Heart Sees** *Felix Cavaliere*
65/57 **Only Because** *Platters*
F/71 **Only Believe** *Elvis Presley*
56/84 **Only Flame In Town** *Elvis Costello*
51/85 **Only For Love** *Limahl*
25/63 **Only In America** *Jay & The Americans*
62/73 **Only In Your Heart** *America*
54/85 **Only Lonely** *Bon Jovi*
86/73 **Only Love** *Bill Quateman*
Only Love Can Break A Heart
2/62 *Gene Pitney*
96/67 *Margaret Whiting*
99/77 *Bobby Vinton*
33/70 **Only Love Can Break Your Heart** *Neil Young*
94/65 **Only Love (Can Save Me Now)** *Solomon Burke*
28/76 **Only Love Is Real** *Carole King*
33/57 **Only One Love** *George Hamilton IV*
63/78 **Only One Love In My Life** *Ronnie Milsap*
91/75 **Only One Woman** *Nigel Olsson*
68/82 **Only One You** *T.G. Sheppard*
Only Sixteen
28/59 *Sam Cooke*
6/76 *Dr. Hook*

24/78 **Only The Good Die Young** *Billy Joel*
Only The Lonely
2/60 *Roy Orbison*
92/69 *Sonny James*
9/82 **Only The Lonely** *Motels*
91/80 **Only The Lonely (Have A Reason To Be Sad)** *La Flavour*
82/77 **Only The Lucky** *Walter Egan*
4/69 **Only The Strong Survive** *Jerry Butler*
9/85 **Only The Young** *Journey*
73/65 **Only Those In Love** *Baby Washington*
17/82 **Only Time Will Tell** *Asia*
64/82 **Only Way Out** *Cliff Richard*
34/84 **Only When You Leave** *Spandau Ballet*
96/66 **Only When You're Lonely** *Grass Roots*
12/75 **Only Women** *Alice Cooper*
4/75 **Only Yesterday** *Carpenters*
Only You
5/55 *Platters*
8/55 *Hilltoppers*
9/59 *Franck Pourcel's French Fiddles*
77/63 *Mr. Acker Bilk*
95/69 *Bobby Hatfield*
6/75 *Ringo Starr*
54/83 **Only You** *Commodores*
67/83 **Only You** *Yaz*
87/78 **Only You** *Loleatta Holloway & Bunny Sigler*
53/75 **Only You Can** *Fox*
Only You Know And I Know
42/70 *Dave Mason*
20/71 *Delaney & Bonnie*
61/85 **Oo-Ee-Diddley-Bop!** *Peter Wolf*
61/67 **O-o, I Love You** *Dells*
99/63 **Oo-La-La-Limbo** *Danny & The Juniors*
F/75 **Oo-Wee** *Ringo Starr*
23/65 **Oo Wee Baby, I Love You** *Fred Hughes*
59/56 **Ooby Dooby** *Roy Orbison*
34/67 **Oogum Boogum Song** *Brenton Wood*
25/73 **Ooh Baby** *Gilbert O'Sullivan*
65/67 **Ooh Baby** *Deon Jackson*
88/67 **Ooh Baby** *Bo Diddley*
Ooh Baby Baby
16/65 *Miracles*
63/67 *Five Stairsteps*
90/67 *Magnificent Men (medley)*
7/79 *Linda Ronstadt*
83/55 **Ooh Bang Jiggilly Jang** *Doris Day*
72/78 **Ooh Boy** *Rose Royce*
8/70 **O-o-h Child** *Five Stairsteps*
31/58 **Ooh! My Soul** *Little Richard*
36/85 **Ooh Ooh Song** *Pat Benatar*
Ooh Poo Pah Doo
28/60 *Jessie Hill*
60/71 *Ike & Tina Turner*
88/65 **Oowee, Oowee** *Perry Como*
69/58 **Op** *Honeycones*
81/76 **Open** *Smokey Robinson*
2/82 **Open Arms** *Journey*
10/67 **Open Letter To My Teenage Son** *Victor Lundberg*
(also see: Letter To Dad)
55/77 **Open Sesame** *Kool & The Gang*
90/72 **Open The Door (Song For Judith)** *Judy Collins*
27/66 **Open The Door To Your Heart** *Darrell Banks*
51/70 **Open Up My Heart** *Dells*
55/67 **(Open Up The Door) Let The Good Times In** *Dean Martin*
99/66 **Open Up Your Door** *Richard & The Young Lions*
8/55 **Open Up Your Heart (And Let The Sunshine In)** *Cowboy Church Sunday School*
1/87 **Open Your Heart** *Madonna*
18/85 **Operator** *Midnight Star*
22/75 **Operator** *Manhattan Transfer*
78/65 **Operator** *Brenda Holloway*
97/62 **Operator** *Gladys Knight & The Pips*
17/72 **Operator (That's Not The Way It Feels)** *Jim Croce*
62/76 **Ophelia** *Band*
10/86 **Opportunities (Let's Make Lots Of Money)** *Pet Shop Boys*
64/64 **Opportunity** *Jewels*
78/82 **Opposites Do Attract** *All Sports Band*
13/66 **Opus 17 (Don't You Worry 'Bout Me)** *4 Seasons*
Orange Blossom Special
63/61 *Billy Vaughn*
80/65 *Johnny Cash*
92/65 **Organ Grinder's Swing** *Jimmy Smith, Kenny Burrell, Grady Tate*
76/63 **Organ Shout** *Dave 'Baby' Cortez*
58/84 **Original Sin** *INXS*
11/83 **Other Guy** *Little River Band*
31/67 **Other Man's Grass Is Always Greener** *Petula Clark*
58/86 **Other Side Of Life** *Moody Blues*
100/66 **Other Side Of This Life** *Peter, Paul & Mary*
4/82 **Other Woman** *Ray Parker Jr.*
81/75 **Other Woman** *Vicki Lawrence*
86/56 **Other Woman** *Sarah Vaughan*
59/62 **Our Anniversary** *Shep & The Limelites*
Our Day Will Come
1/63 *Ruby & The Romantics*
11/75 *Frankie Valli*
64/64 **Our Everlasting Love** *Ruby & The Romantics*
7/83 **Our House** *Madness*
30/70 **Our House** *Crosby, Stills, Nash & Young*
95/75 **Our Last Song Together** *Bo Donaldson & The Heywoods*
20/81 **Our Lips Are Sealed** *Go-Go's*
10/78 **Our Love** *Natalie Cole*
43/56 **Our Love Affair** *Tommy Charles*
Our Love Affair *see: Affair To Remember*
9/78 **(Our Love) Don't Throw It All Away** *Andy Gibb*
89/61 **Our Love Is Here To Stay** *Dinah Washington*
51/79 **Our Love Is Insane** *Desmond Child & Rouge*
80/78 **Our Night** *Shaun Cassidy*
92/67 **Our Song** *Jack Jones*
Our Winter Love
9/63 *Bill Pursell*
72/67 *Lettermen*
64/70 **Our World** *Blue Mink*
70/65 **Our World** *Johnny Tillotson*
39/67 **Out & About** *Tommy Boyce & Bobby Hart*
19/80 **Out Here On My Own** *Irene Cara*
15/70 **Out In The Country** *Three Dog Night*
53/65 **Out In The Streets** *Shangri-Las*
59/67 **Out Of Left Field** *Percy Sledge*
3/64 **Out Of Limits** *Marketts*
37/86 **Out Of Mind Out Of Sight** *Models*
24/63 **Out Of My Mind** *Johnny Tillotson*
24/64 **Out Of Sight** *James Brown*
Out Of Sight, Out Of Mind
23/56 *Five Keys*
71/64 *Sunny & The Sunliners*
52/69 *Little Anthony & The Imperials*
43/67 **Out Of The Blue** *Tommy James & The Shondells*
89/76 **Out Of The Darkness** *David Crosby/Graham Nash*
17/73 **Out Of The Question** *Gilbert O'Sullivan*
67/66 **Out Of This World** *Chiffons*
81/75 **Out Of Time** *Rolling Stones*

1/84 **Out Of Touch** *Daryl Hall & John Oates*
21/82 **Out Of Work** *Gary U.S. Bonds*
2/72 **Outa-Space** *Billy Preston*
94/82 **Outlaw** *War*
Outlaw Man
59/73 *Eagles*
94/73 *David Blue*
28/60 **Outside My Window** *Fleetwoods*
52/80 **Outside My Window** *Stevie Wonder*
45/66 **Outside The Gates Of Heaven** *Lou Christie*
34/74 **Outside Woman** *Bloodstone*
51/83 **Outstanding** *Gap Band*
Over And Over
41/58 *Bobby Day*
96/58 *Thurston Harris*
1/65 *Dave Clark Five*
F/71 **Over And Over** *Delfonics*
20/76 **Over My Head** *Fleetwood Mac*
81/84 **Over My Head** *Toni Basil*
51/73 **Over The Hills And Far Away** *Led Zeppelin*
91/82 **Over The Line** *Eddie Schwartz*
Over The Mountain; Across The Sea
8/57 *Johnnie & Joe*
89/60 *Johnnie & Joe*
21/63 *Bobby Vinton*
Over The Rainbow
16/60 *Demensions*
69/78 *Gary Tanner*
62/58 **Over The Weekend** *Playboys*
13/66 **Over Under Sideways Down** *Yardbirds*
7/68 **Over You** *Gary Puckett & The Union Gap*
80/80 **Over You** *Roxy Music*
24/86 **Overjoyed** *Stevie Wonder*
3/83 **Overkill** *Men At Work*
18/74 **Overnight Sensation (Hit Record)** *Raspberries*
16/70 **Overture From Tommy (A Rock Opera)** *Assembled Multitude*
57/86 **Own The Night** *Chaka Khan*
1/84 **Owner Of A Lonely Heart** *Yes*
13/71 **Oye Como Va** *Santana*

10/64 **P.S. I Love You** *Beatles*
8/62 **P.T. 109** *Jimmy Dean*
10/83 **P.Y.T. (Pretty Young Thing)** *Michael Jackson*
9/82 **Pac-Man Fever** *Buckner & Garcia*
13/58 **Padre** *Toni Arden*
64/72 **Pain** *Ohio Players*
89/66 **Pain Gets A Little Deeper** *Darrow Fletcher*
61/64 **Pain In My Heart** *Otis Redding*
1/66 **Paint It, Black** *Rolling Stones*
Paint Me A Picture *see: You Don't Have To*
34/74 **Painted Ladies** *Ian Thomas*
70/83 **Painted Picture** *Commodores*
15/63 **Painted, Tainted Rose** *Al Martino*
81/66 **Painter** *Lou Christie*
65/73 **Palace Guard** *Rick Nelson*
Paladin *see: Ballad Of*
3/62 **Palisades Park** *Freddy Cannon*
26/76 **Paloma Blanca** *George Baker Selection*
55/57 **Pamela Throws A Party** *Joe Reisman*
13/84 **Panama** *Van Halen*
35/66 **Pandora's Golden Heebie Jeebies** *Association*

99/61 **Panic** *Charms*
1/86 **Papa Don't Preach** *Madonna*
31/74 **Papa Don't Take No Mess** *James Brown*
Papa Joe's *see: (Down At)*
48/62 **Papa-Oom-Mow-Mow** *Rivingtons*
Papa Was A Rollin' Stone
1/72 *Temptations*
63/72 *Undisputed Truth*
55/83 *Wolf*
44/67 **Papa Was Too** *Joe Tex*
Papa's Got A Brand New Bag
8/65 *James Brown*
21/69 *Otis Redding*
34/67 **Paper Cup** *5th Dimension*
43/70 **Paper Mache** *Dionne Warwick*
Paper Roses
5/60 *Anita Bryant*
5/73 *Marie Osmond*
72/55 **Paper Roses** *Lola Dee*
94/67 **Paper Sun** *Traffic*
23/65 **Paper Tiger** *Sue Thompson*
1/66 **Paperback Writer** *Beatles*
32/82 **Paperlate** *Genesis*
46/60 **Paradise** *Sammy Turner*
80/81 **Paradise** *Change*
39/78 **Paradise By The Dashboard Light** *Meat Loaf*
59/57 **Paralyzed** *Elvis Presley*
61/70 **Paranoid** *Black Sabbath*
34/86 **Paranoimia** *Art Of Noise*
51/73 **Pardon Me Sir** *Joe Cocker*
95/58 **Paris** *Perez Prado*
71/73 **Parrty** *Maceo & The Macks*
38/58 **Part Of Me** *Jimmy Clanton*
98/80 **Part Of Me That Needs You Most** *Jay Black*
31/75 **Part Of The Plan** *Dan Fogelberg*
94/71 **Part Of You** *Brenda & The Tabulations*
Part Time Love
19/63 *Little Johnny Taylor*
45/70 *Ann Peebles*
22/78 **Part-Time Love** *Elton John*
22/75 **Part Time Love** *Gladys Knight & The Pips*
97/77 **Part Time Love** *Kerry Chater*
1/85 **Part-Time Lover** *Stevie Wonder*
69/76 **Party** *Van McCoy*
2/85 **Party All The Time** *Eddie Murphy*
Party Doll
1/57 *Buddy Knox*
5/57 *Steve Lawrence*
56/57 *Wingy Manone*
89/57 *Roy Brown*
47/64 **Party Girl** *Bernadette Carroll*
85/64 **Party Girl** *Tommy Roe*
5/62 **Party Lights** *Claudine Clark*
79/77 **Party Lights** *Natalie Cole*
80/76 **Party Line** *Andrea True Connection*
78/75 **Party Music** *Pat Lundi*
45/57 **Party Time** *Sal Mineo*
63/57 **Party's Over** *Doris Day*
34/81 **Party's Over (Hopelessly In Love)** *Journey*
93/65 **Pass Me By** *Peggy Lee*
97/69 **Pass The Apple Eve** *B.J. Thomas*
10/83 **Pass The Dutchie** *Musical Youth*
95/72 **Pass The Peas** *JB's*
82/57 **Passing Strangers** *Sarah Vaughan & Billy Eckstine*
5/81 **Passion** *Rod Stewart*
80/73 **Passion Play (Edit #8)** *Jethro Tull*
59/66 **Past, Present And Future** *Shangri-Las*
12/67 **Pata Pata** *Miriam Makeba*
F/70 **Patch It Up** *Elvis Presley*
94/70 **Patch Of Blue** *4 Seasons*
4/70 **Patches** *Clarence Carter*

6/62 **Patches** *Dickey Lee*
Patricia
1/58 *Perez Prado*
65/62 *Perez Prado (Twist)*
65/60 **Patsy** *Jack Scott*
43/62 **Patti Ann** *Johnny Crawford*
65/63 **Patty Baby** *Freddy Cannon*
78/63 **Pay Back** *Etta James*
67/81 **Pay The Devil (Ooo, Baby, Ooo)** *Knack*
13/71 **Pay To The Piper** *Chairmen Of The Board*
Pay You Back With Interest
28/67 *Hollies*
70/81 *Gary O'*
26/74 **Payback, The** *James Brown*
39/68 **Paying The Cost To Be The Boss** *B.B. King*
85/59 **Peace** *McGuire Sisters*
48/68 **Peace Brother Peace** *Bill Medley*
38/77 **Peace Of Mind** *Boston*
42/67 **Peace Of Mind** *Paul Revere & The Raiders*
55/68 **Peace Of Mind** *Nancy Wilson*
66/60 **Peace Of Mind** *Teresa Brewer*
31/75 **Peace Pipe** *B.T. Express*
7/71 **Peace Train** *Cat Stevens*
32/70 **Peace Will Come (According To Plan)** *Melanie*
12/73 **Peaceful** *Helen Reddy*
22/73 **Peaceful Easy Feeling** *Eagles*
80/73 **Peacemaker, The** *Albert Hammond*
36/65 **Peaches 'N' Cream** *Ikettes*
97/66 **Peak Of Love** *Bobby McClure*
20/61 **Peanut Butter** *Marathons*
83/80 **Peanut Butter** *Twennynine with Lenny White*
Peanuts
22/57 *Little Joe & The Thrillers*
60/61 *Rick & The Keens*
64/65 **Peanuts (La Cacahuata-Polka)** *Sunglows*
50/70 **Pearl** *Tommy Roe*
90/67 **Pearl Time** *Andre Williams*
60/64 **Pearly Shells** *Burl Ives*
92/67 **Peas 'N' Rice** *Freddie McCoy*
28/59 **Peek-A-Boo** *Cadillacs*
72/67 **Peek-A-Boo** *New Vaudeville Band*
11/78 **Peg** *Steely Dan*
64/64 **Peg O' My Heart** *Robert Maxwell*
Peggy Sue
3/57 *Buddy Holly*
59/78 *Beach Boys*
18/64 **Penetration** *Pyramids*
24/60 **Pennies From Heaven** *Skyliners*
95/67 **Penny Arcade** *Cyrkle*
33/82 **Penny For Your Thoughts** *Tavares*
1/67 **Penny Lane** *Beatles*
42/57 **Penny Loafers And Bobby Socks** *Joe Bennett*
8/84 **Penny Lover** *Lionel Richie*
People
5/64 *Barbra Streisand*
100/64 *Nat King Cole*
39/68 *Tymes*
75/73 **People Are Changin'** *Timmy Thomas*
13/85 **People Are People** *Depeche Mode*
12/67 **People Are Strange** *Doors*
People Get Ready
14/65 *Impressions*
48/85 *Jeff Beck & Rod Stewart*
People Got To Be Free
1/68 *Rascals*
60/70 *5th Dimension (medley)*
22/74 **People Gotta Move** *Gino Vannelli*
40/77 **People In Love** *10cc*
66/67 **People In Me** *Music Machine*
97/67 **People Like You** *Eddie Fisher*
25/72 **People Make The World Go Round** *Stylistics*
23/79 **People Of The South Wind** *Kansas*
12/64 **People Say** *Dixie Cups*
58/68 **People Sure Act Funny** *Arthur Conley*
92/72 **People Tree** *Sammy Davis, Jr.*
94/68 **People World** *Jim & Jean*
18/61 **'Pepe'** *Duane Eddy*
5/63 **Pepino The Italian Mouse** *Lou Monte*
78/63 **Pepino's Friend Pasqual (The Italian Pussy Cat)** *Lou Monte*
76/74 **Pepper Box** *Peppers*
Pepper-Hot Baby
12/55 *Jaye P. Morgan*
60/55 *Gisele MacKenzie*
Peppermint Twist
54/61 *Danny Peppermint*
1/62 *Joey Dee & The Starliters*
85/65 **Percolatin'** *Willie Mitchell*
10/62 **Percolator (Twist)** *Billy Joe & The Checkmates*
Perfect *see: (Closest Thing To)*
75/84 **Perfect Combination** *Stacy Lattisaw & Johnny Gill*
47/61 **Perfect Love** *Frankie Avalon*
11/85 **Perfect Way** *Scritti Politti*
15/60 **Perfidia** *Ventures*
59/82 **Perhaps Love** *Placido Domingo & John Denver*
Personality
2/59 *Lloyd Price*
87/68 *Mitch Ryder (medley)*
19/82 **Personally** *Karla Bonoff*
62/55 **Pet Me, Poppa** *Rosemary Clooney*
68/55 **Pete Kelly's Blues** *Ray Anthony*
Peter Gunn
8/59 *Ray Anthony*
27/60 *Duane Eddy*
84/76 *Deodato*
50/86 *Art Of Noise*
48/79 **Peter Piper** *Frank Mills*
45/66 **Peter Rabbit** *Dee Jay & The Runaways*
Petite Fleur
5/59 *Chris Barber's Jazz Band*
59/65 *Lou Johnson (Time To Love)*
81/66 **Petticoat White (Summer Sky Blue)** *Bobby Vinton*
Petticoats Of Portugal
16/56 *Dick Jacobs*
83/56 *Billy Vaughn*
43/77 **Phantom Writer** *Gary Wright*
64/75 **Philadelphia** *B.B. King*
1/75 **Philadelphia Freedom** *Elton John*
Philadelphia U.S.A.
26/58 *Nu Tornados*
89/58 *Art Lund*
Philly Dog
89/66 *Mar-Keys*
93/66 *Herbie Mann*
(also see: Baby, Do The Philly Dog)
49/66 **Philly Freeze** *Alvin Cash & The Registers*
32/66 **Phoenix Love Theme** *Brass Ring*
1/73 **Photograph** *Ringo Starr*
12/83 **Photograph** *Def Leppard*
1/81 **Physical** *Olivia Newton-John*
25/74 **Piano Man** *Billy Joel*
91/61 **Pick Me Up On Your Way Down** *Pat Zill*
1/75 **Pick Up The Pieces** *Average White Band*
68/68 **Pick Up The Pieces** *Carla Thomas*
27/68 **Pickin' Wild Mountain Berries** *Peggy Scott & Jo Jo Benson*
99/58 **Pickle Up A Doodle** *Teresa Brewer*
Picnic *see: Moonglow*
77/62 **Pictures In The Fire** *Pat Boone*

51/67 **Pictures Of Lily** *Who*
12/68 **Pictures Of Matchstick Men** *Status Quo*
47/55 **Piddily Patter Patter** *Patti Page*
87/85 **Piece By Piece** *Tubes*
Piece Of My Heart
62/67 *Erma Franklin*
12/68 *Big Brother & The Holding Company*
73/82 *Sammy Hagar*
45/72 **Piece Of Paper** *Gladstone*
19/73 **Pieces Of April** *Three Dog Night*
31/83 **Pieces Of Ice** *Diana Ross*
Pied Piper
50/57 *Billy Williams*
Pied Piper
87/65 *Changin' Times*
4/66 *Crispian St. Peters*
70/75 **Pill, The** *Loretta Lynn*
3/73 **Pillow Talk** *Sylvia*
13/80 **Pilot Of The Airwaves** *Charlie Dore*
54/63 **Pin A Medal On Joey** *James Darren*
74/71 **Pin The Tail On The Donkey** *Newcomers*
91/66 **Pin The Tail On The Donkey** *Paul Peek*
(Pina Colada Song) *see: Escape*
60/75 **Pinball** *Brian Protheroe*
96/79 **Pinball, That's All** *Bill Wray*
Pinball Wizard
19/69 *Who*
29/73 *New Seekers (medley)*
99/69 **Pinch Me (Baby, Convince Me)** *Ohio Express*
11/60 **Pineapple Princess** *Annette*
60/60 **Pink Chiffon** *Mitchell Torok*
69/64 **Pink Dominos** *Crescents*
8/84 **Pink Houses** *John Cougar Mellencamp*
31/64 **Pink Panther Theme** *Henry Mancini*
91/58 **Pink Pedal Pushers** *Carl Perkins*
3/59 **Pink Shoe Laces** *Dodie Stevens*
Piove *see: Ciao, Ciao Bambina*
60/67 **Pipe Dream** *Blues Magoos*
82/59 **Pipe Dreams** *Jimmy Beck*
4/63 **Pipeline** *Chantay's*
93/77 **Pirate** *Cher*
76/61 **Pitter-Patter** *Four Sportsmen*
9/66 **Place In The Sun** *Stevie Wonder*
42/77 **Place In The Sun** *Pablo Cruise*
38/59 **Plain Jane** *Bobby Darin*
77/79 **Plain Jane** *Sammy Hagar*
48/82 **Planet Rock** *Afrika Bambaataa*
19/55 **Plantation Boogie** *Lenny Dee*
Plastic Man
74/67 *Sonny & Cher*
40/73 **Plastic Man** *Temptations*
63/77 **Platinum Heroes** *Bruce Foster*
79/56 **Play For Keeps** *Jaye P. Morgan*
11/72 **Play Me** *Neil Diamond*
6/55 **Play Me Hearts And Flowers (I Wanna Cry)** *Johnny Desmond*
49/76 **Play On Love** *Jefferson Starship*
33/74 **Play Something Sweet (Brickyard Blues)** *Three Dog Night*
1/76 **Play That Funky Music** *Wild Cherry*
42/80 **Play The Game** *Queen*
17/82 **Play The Game Tonight** *Kansas*
95/62 **Play The Thing** *Marlowe Morris Quintet*
96/65 **Play With Fire** *Rolling Stones*
7/62 **Playboy** *Marvelettes*
17/68 **Playboy** *Gene & Debbe*
70/74 **Player, The** *First Choice*
49/69 **Playgirl** *Thee Prophets*
2/73 **Playground In My Mind** *Clint Holmes*
21/57 **Playing For Keeps** *Elvis Presley*
60/85 **Playing To Win** *Little River Band*
71/81 **Playing With Lightning** *Shot In The Dark*
60/86 **Playing With The Boys** *Kenny Loggins*
F/55 **Playmates** *Fontane Sisters*
Plaything
41/57 *Nick Todd*
45/57 *Ted Newman*
74/58 **Plea, The** *Jesters*
3/67 **Pleasant Valley Sunday** *Monkees*
71/64 **Please** *Frank Ifield*
63/82 **Please Be The One** *Karla Bonoff*
Please Come Home For Christmas
76/61 *Charles Brown*
18/78 *Eagles*
5/74 **Please Come To Boston** *Dave Loggins*
69/74 **Please, Daddy** *John Denver*
15/62 **Please Don't Ask About Barbara** *Bobby Vee*
98/69 **Please Don't Desert Me Baby** *Gloria Walker*
77/58 **Please Don't Do It** *Dale Wright*
59/66 **Please Don't Ever Leave Me** *Cyrkle*
60/66 **Please Don't Fight It** *Dino, Desi & Billy*
1/80 **Please Don't Go** *KC & The Sunshine Band*
39/61 **Please Don't Go** *Ral Donner*
100/63 **Please Don't Kiss Me Again** *Charmettes*
24/79 **Please Don't Leave** *Lauren Wood*
55/56 **Please Don't Leave Me** *Fontane Sisters*
64/66 **Please Don't Sell My Daddy No More Wine** *Greenwoods*
45/66 **Please Don't Stop Loving Me** *Elvis Presley*
31/63 **Please Don't Talk To The Lifeguard** *Diane Ray*
95/74 **Please Don't Tell Me How The Story Ends** *Ronnie Milsap*
Please Help Me, I'm Falling
8/60 *Hank Locklin*
54/60 *Rusty Draper*
(also see: (I Can't Help It))
52/65 **Please Let Me Wonder** *Beach Boys*
Please Love Me Forever
61/58 *Tommy Edwards*
12/61 *Cathy Jean & The Roommates*
6/67 *Bobby Vinton*
3/75 **Please Mr. Please** *Olivia Newton-John*
Please Mr. Postman
1/61 *Marvelettes*
1/75 *Carpenters*
82/83 *Gentle Persuasion*
60/75 **Please, Mr. President** *Paula Webb*
Please Mr. Sun
11/59 *Tommy Edwards*
48/66 *Vogues*
48/75 **Please Pardon Me (You Remind Me Of A Friend)** *Rufus Featuring Chaka Khan*
3/64 **Please Please Me** *Beatles*
95/64 **Please, Please, Please** *James Brown*
26/68 **Please Return Your Love To Me** *Temptations*
64/66 **Please Say You're Fooling** *Ray Charles*
73/57 **Please Send Me Someone To Love** *Moonglows*
14/61 **Please Stay** *Drifters*
84/75 **Please Tell Him That I Said Hello** *Debbie Campbell*
20/61 **Please Tell Me Why** *Jackie Wilson*
28/66 **Please Tell Me Why** *Dave Clark Five*
76/86 **Pleasure And Pain** *Divinyls*
44/69 **Pledge Of Allegiance** *Red Skelton*
Pledge Of Love
12/57 *Ken Copeland*
25/57 *Mitchell Torok*
42/57 *Dick Contino*
63/57 *Johnny Janis*
74/82 **Pledge Pin** *Robert Plant*

Pledging My Love
17/55 *Johnny Ace*
17/55 *Teresa Brewer*
45/58 *Roy Hamilton*
63/60 *Johnny Tillotson*
69/59 **Plenty Good Lovin'** *Connie Francis*
34/62 **Pocketful Of Miracles** *Frank Sinatra*
93/61 **Pocketful Of Rainbows** *Deane Hawley*
48/59 **Poco-Loco** *Gene & Eunice*
2/60 **Poetry In Motion** *Johnny Tillotson*
5/75 **Poetry Man** *Phoebe Snow*
37/70 **Point It Out** *Miracles*
28/78 **Point Of Know Return** *Kansas*
21/62 **Point Of No Return** *Gene McDaniels*
28/86 **Point Of No Return** *Nu Shooz*
85/61 **Point Of No Return** *Adam Wade*
49/63 **Point Panic** *Surfaris*
93/59 **Pointed Toe Shoes** *Carl Perkins*
25/83 **Poison Arrow** *ABC*
7/59 **Poison Ivy** *Coasters*
24/84 **Politics Of Dancing** *Re-Flex*
8/69 **Polk Salad Annie** *Tony Joe White*
Pomp & Circumstance
see: Graduation Song
60/61 **Pony Express** *Danny & The Juniors*
Pony Time
1/61 *Chubby Checker*
60/61 *Goodtimers*
93/67 **Pony With The Golden Mane**
Every Mothers' Son
42/72 **Pool Of Bad Luck** *Joe Simon*
44/68 **Poor Baby** *Cowsills*
17/58 **Poor Boy** *Royaltones*
24/57 **Poor Boy** *Elvis Presley*
52/72 **Poor Boy** *Casey Kelly*
38/62 **Poor Fool** *Ike & Tina Turner*
22/59 **Poor Jenny** *Everly Brothers*
1/58 **Poor Little Fool** *Ricky Nelson*
91/62 **Poor Little Puppet** *Cathy Carroll*
27/63 **Poor Little Rich Girl** *Steve Lawrence*
14/57 **Poor Man's Roses (Or A Rich Man's Gold)** *Patti Page*
33/81 **Poor Man's Son** *Survivor*
55/65 **Poor Man's Son** *Reflections*
Poor People Of Paris
1/56 *Les Baxter*
17/56 *Lawrence Welk*
19/56 *Russ Morgan*
52/56 *Chet Atkins*
31/78 **Poor Poor Pitiful Me** *Linda Ronstadt*
Poor Side Of Town
1/66 *Johnny Rivers*
75/69 *Al Wilson*
51/62 **Pop-Eye** *Huey Smith*
94/62 **Pop-Eye Stroll** *Mar-Keys*
35/82 **Pop Goes The Movies** *Meco*
85/62 **Pop Goes The Weasel** *Anthony Newley*
7/85 **Pop Life** *Prince*
1/79 **Pop Muzik** *M*
35/62 **Pop Pop Pop-Pie** *Sherrys*
24/72 **Pop That Thang** *Isley Brothers*
9/72 **Popcorn** *Hot Butter*
30/69 **Popcorn, The** *James Brown*
14/55 **Popcorn Song** *Cliffie Stone*
99/62 **Popeye Joe** *Ernie K-Doe*
10/62 **Popeye The Hitchhiker** *Chubby Checker*
75/63 **Popeye Waddle** *Don Covay*
59/79 **Pops, We Love You (A Tribute To Father)** *Diana Ross, Marvin Gaye, Smokey Robinson & Stevie Wonder*
21/66 **Popsicle** *Jan & Dean*
43/76 **Popsicle Toes** *Michael Franks*
3/64 **Popsicles And Icicles** *Murmaids*

Por Amor Vivirenos
see: Love Will Keep Us Together
73/55 **Por Favor** *Vic Damone*
62/68 **Porpoise Song** *Monkees*
20/56 **Port Au Prince** *Nelson Riddle*
64/78 **Portrait (He Knew)** *Kansas*
98/62 **Portrait Of A Fool** *Conway Twitty*
Portrait Of My Love
9/61 *Steve Lawrence*
36/67 *Tokens*
19/56 **Portuguese Washerwomen**
Joe 'Fingers' Carr
Poseidon Adventure *see: Morning After*
7/65 **Positively 4th Street** *Bob Dylan*
30/85 **Possession Obsession**
Daryl Hall & John Oates
88/67 **Postcard From Jamaica** *Sopwith 'Camel'*
89/62 **Potato Peeler** *Bobby Gregg*
85/66 **Pouring Water On A Drowning Man**
James Carr
65/66 **Poverty** *Bobby Bland*
76/79 **Pow Wow** *Cory Daye*
54/72 **Powder Blue Mercedes Queen** *Raiders*
43/80 **Power** *Temptations*
24/78 **Power Of Gold** *Dan Fogelberg/Tim Weisberg*
1/85 **Power Of Love** *Huey Lewis & The News*
Power Of Love
11/72 *Joe Simon*
76/74 *Martha Reeves*
57/86 **Power Of Love** *Jennifer Rush*
68/85 **Power Of Love (You Are My Lady)**
Air Supply
96/82 **Power Play** *Molly Hatchet*
11/71 **Power To The People** *John Lennon*
81/59 **Prayer And A Juke Box**
Little Anthony & The Imperials
45/68 **Prayer Meetin'** *Willie Mitchell*
92/63 **Preacherman** *Charlie Russo*
3/72 **Precious And Few** *Climax*
19/79 **Precious Love** *Bob Welch*
67/67 **Precious Memories** *Romeos*
30/71 **Precious, Precious** *Jackie Moore*
22/81 **Precious To Me** *Phil Seymour*
88/56 **President On The Dollar** *Mitch Miller*
21/86 **Press** *Paul McCartney*
20/82 **Pressure** *Billy Joel*
Pretend
89/57 *Tab Smith*
57/59 *Carl Mann*
Pretend You Don't See Her
45/57 *Jerry Vale*
97/64 *Bobby Vee*
58/77 **Pretender, The** *Jackson Browne*
60/72 **Pretty As You Feel** *Jefferson Airplane*
15/67 **Pretty Ballerina** *Left Banke*
9/60 **Pretty Blue Eyes** *Steve Lawrence*
98/63 **Pretty Boy Lonely** *Patti Page*
29/66 **Pretty Flamingo** *Manfred Mann*
39/79 **Pretty Girls** *Melissa Manchester*
36/59 **Pretty Girls Everywhere** *Eugene Church*
41/86 **Pretty In Pink** *Psychedelic Furs*
53/73 **Pretty Lady** *Lighthouse*
7/61 **Pretty Little Angel Eyes** *Curtis Lee*
25/65 **Pretty Little Baby** *Marvin Gaye*
75/84 **Pretty Mess** *Vanity*
15/64 **Pretty Paper** *Roy Orbison*
62/69 **Pretty World** *Sergio Mendes & Brasil '66*
57/74 **Pretzel Logic** *Steely Dan*
57/64 **Price, The** *Solomon Burke*
63/77 **Pride, The** *Isley Brothers*
10/63 **Pride And Joy** *Marvin Gaye*
33/84 **Pride (In The Name Of Love)** *U2*
34/84 **Prime Time** *Alan Parsons Project*

Primrose Lane
8/59 *Jerry Wallace*
86/70 *O.C. Smith*
30/61 **Princess** *Frank Gari*
78/76 **Princess And The Punk** *Barry Mann*
37/65 **Princess In Rags** *Gene Pitney*
20/56 **Priscilla** *Eddie Cooley*
(Prisoner)
see: Love Theme From 'Eyes Of Laura Mars'
86/77 **Prisoner (Captured By Your Eyes)**
L.A. Jets
18/63 **Prisoner Of Love** *James Brown*
27/78 **Prisoner Of Your Love** *Player*
81/58 **Prisoner's Song** *Warren Storm*
7/85 **Private Dancer** *Tina Turner*
95/59 **Private Eye** *Olympics*
1/81 **Private Eyes** *Daryl Hall & John Oates*
74/80 **Private Idaho** *B-52's*
47/86 **Private Number** *Jets*
75/68 **Private Number** *William Bell & Judy Clay*
80/71 **Problem Child** *Mark Lindsay*
2/58 **Problems** *Everly Brothers*
74/66 **Promise Her Anything** *Tom Jones*
78/60 **Promise Me A Rose (A Slight Detail)**
Anita Bryant
17/58 **Promise Me, Love** *Andy Williams*
Promised Land
41/65 *Chuck Berry*
14/74 *Elvis Presley*
9/79 **Promises** *Eric Clapton*
48/81 **Promises** *Barbra Streisand*
38/81 **Promises In The Dark** *Pat Benatar*
11/83 **Promises, Promises** *Naked Eyes*
19/68 **Promises, Promises** *Dionne Warwick*
75/69 **Prophecy Of Daniel and John The Divine (Six-Six-Six)** *Cowsills*
29/63 **Proud** *Johnny Crawford*
68/81 **Proud** *Joe Chemay Band*
Proud Mary
2/69 *Creedence Clearwater Revival*
45/69 *Solomon Burke*
69/69 *Checkmates, Ltd.*
4/71 *Ike & Tina Turner*
Proud One
68/66 *Frankie Valli*
22/75 *Osmonds*
Proud Ones *see: Theme From*
33/78 **Prove It All Night** *Bruce Springsteen*
95/86 **Prove Me Wrong** *David Pack*
7/70 **Psychedelic Shack** *Temptations*
73/60 **Psycho** *Bobby Hendricks*
92/78 **Psycho Killer** *Talking Heads*
57/82 **Psychobabble** *Alan Parsons Project*
5/66 **Psychotic Reaction** *Count Five*
31/67 **Pucker Up Buttercup**
Jr. Walker & The All Stars
43/63 **Puddin N' Tain (Ask Me Again, I'll Tell You The Same)** *Alley Cats*
96/71 **Puff Of Smoke** *Roy Head*
2/63 **Puff The Magic Dragon** *Peter, Paul & Mary*
71/68 **Puffin' On Down The Track**
Hugh Masekela
Pum-Pa-Lum *see: Bad Donkey*
20/62 **Punish Her** *Bobby Vee*
Puppet Man
24/70 *5th Dimension*
26/71 *Tom Jones*
14/65 **Puppet On A String** *Elvis Presley*
56/60 **Puppet Song** *Frankie Avalon*
Puppet Song *see: Whiskey On A Sunday*
Puppy Love
2/60 *Paul Anka*
3/72 *Donny Osmond*
38/64 **Puppy Love** *Barbara Lewis*
Purple Haze
65/67 *Jimi Hendrix*
63/69 *Dion*
1/58 **Purple People Eater** *Sheb Wooley*
47/58 **Purple People Eater Meets The Witch Doctor** *Joe South*
2/84 **Purple Rain** *Prince*
27/62 **Push And Kick** *Mark Valentino*
90/60 **Push Push** *Austin Taylor*
44/71 **Pushbike Song** *Mixtures*
36/67 **Pushin' Too Hard** *Seeds*
92/62 **Pushin' Your Luck** *Sleepy King*
25/63 **Pushover** *Etta James*
17/58 **Pussy Cat** *Ames Brothers*
8/58 **Put A Light In The Window** *Four Lads*
73/74 **Put A Little Love Away** *Emotions*
4/69 **Put A Little Love In Your Heart**
Jackie DeShannon
32/58 **Put A Ring On My Finger**
Les Paul & Mary Ford
71/82 **Put Away Your Love** *Alessi*
40/83 **Put It In A Magazine** *Sonny Charles*
52/72 **Put It Where You Want It** *Crusaders*
46/74 **Put Out The Light** *Joe Cocker*
Put Your Arms Around Me Honey
58/60 *Fats Domino*
91/60 *Ray Smith*
2/71 **Put Your Hand In The Hand** *Ocean*
10/74 **Put Your Hands Together** *O'Jays*
Put Your Head On My Shoulder
2/59 *Paul Anka*
44/68 *Lettermen*
58/78 *Leif Garrett*
46/67 **Put Your Mind At Ease** *Every Mothers' Son*
92/66 **Put Yourself In My Place** *Elgins*
4/83 **Puttin' On The Ritz** *Taco*
78/65 **Puzzle Song (A Puzzle In Song)**
Shirley Ellis

Q

95/62 **Quando, Quando, Quando (Tell Me When)** *Pat Boone*
100/62 **Quarter To Four Stomp** *Stompers*
1/61 **Quarter To Three** *U.S. Bonds*
Que Sera, Sera (Whatever Will Be, Will Be)
2/56 *Doris Day*
47/63 *High Keys*
77/70 *Mary Hopkin*
71/85 **Que Te Quiero** *Katrina & The Waves*
66/76 **Queen Of Clubs** *KC & The Sunshine Band*
2/81 **Queen Of Hearts** *Juice Newton*
79/62 **Queen Of My Heart** *Rene & Ray*
40/76 **Queen Of My Soul** *Average White Band*
34/83 **Queen Of The Broken Hearts** *Loverboy*
9/58 **Queen Of The Hop** *Bobby Darin*
12/65 **Queen Of The House** *Jody Miller*
(also see: King Of The Road)
89/73 **Queen Of The Roller Derby** *Leon Russell*
39/57 **Queen Of The Senior Prom** *Mills Brothers*
13/69 **Quentin's Theme**
Charles Randolph Grean Sounde
19/60 **Question** *Lloyd Price*
21/70 **Question** *Moody Blues*
37/68 **Question Of Temperature** *Balloon Farm*
90/72 **Questions** *Bang*

Questions 67 And 68
71/69 *Chicago*
24/71 *Chicago*
92/66 **Questions And Answers** *In Crowd*
79/74 **Quick, Fast, In A Hurry** *New York City*
25/68 **Quick Joey Small (Run Joey Run)** *Kasenetz-Katz Singing Orchestral Circus*
8/64 **Quicksand** *Martha & The Vandellas*
92/65 **Quiet Nights Of Quiet Stars** *Andy Williams*
78/64 **Quiet Place** *Garnet Mimms & The Enchanters*
61/76 **Quiet Storm** *Smokey Robinson*
46/59 **Quiet Three** *Duane Eddy*
4/59 **Quiet Village** *Martin Denny*
27/61 **Quite A Party** *Fireballs*

16/56 **R-O-C-K** *Bill Haley & His Comets*
2/86 **R.O.C.K. In The U.S.A. (A Salute To 60's Rock)** *John Cougar Mellencamp*
65/77 **Race Among The Ruins** *Gordon Lightfoot*
Race Is On
15/65 *Jack Jones*
96/65 *George Jones*
96/56 **Race With The Devil** *Gene Vincent*
13/74 **Radar Love** *Golden Earring*
78/83 **Radio Free Europe** *R.E.M.*
16/84 **Radio Ga-Ga** *Queen*
28/85 **Radioactive** *Firm*
47/79 **Radioactive** *Gene Simmons*
1/64 **Rag Doll** *4 Seasons*
52/75 **Rag Doll** *Sammy Johns*
57/70 **Rag Mama Rag** *Band*
Rags To Riches
45/63 *Sunny & The Sunliners*
F/71 *Elvis Presley*
16/59 **Ragtime Cowboy Joe** *Chipmunks*
9/86 **Rain, The** *Oran 'Juice' Jones*
23/66 **Rain** *Beatles*
76/69 **Rain** *Jose Feliciano*
88/84 **Rain** *Dragon*
19/71 **Rain Dance** *Guess Who*
57/85 **Rain Forest** *Paul Hardcastle*
74/81 **Rain In May** *Max Werner*
62/69 **Rain In My Heart** *Frank Sinatra*
76/76 **Rain, Oh Rain** *Fools Gold*
10/66 **Rain On The Roof** *Lovin' Spoonful*
21/86 **Rain On The Scarecrow** *John Cougar Mellencamp*
12/62 **Rain Rain Go Away** *Bobby Vinton*
2/67 **Rain, The Park & Other Things** *Cowsills*
4/57 **Rainbow** *Russ Hamilton*
Rainbow
47/63 *Gene Chandler*
69/66 *Gene Chandler ('65)*
51/70 **Rainbow** *Marmalade*
62/62 **Rainbow At Midnight** *Jimmie Rodgers*
25/79 **Rainbow Connection** *Kermit*
52/76 **Rainbow In Your Eyes** *Leon & Mary Russell*
49/69 **Rainbow Ride** *Andy Kim*
52/83 **Rainbow's End** *Sergio Mendes*
2/61 **Raindrops** *Dee Clark* *(also see: Cloudy Summer Afternoon)*
1/70 **Raindrops Keep Fallin' On My Head** *B.J. Thomas*
34/61 **Rainin' In My Heart** *Slim Harpo*
Raining In My Heart
88/59 *Buddy Holly*
47/78 *Leo Sayer*
Rains Came
74/62 *Big Sambo*
31/66 *Sir Douglas Quintet*
Raintree County *see: Song Of*
26/75 **Rainy Day People** *Gordon Lightfoot*
2/66 **Rainy Day Women #12 & 35** *Bob Dylan*
2/71 **Rainy Days And Mondays** *Carpenters*
52/71 **Rainy Jane** *Davy Jones*
4/70 **Rainy Night In Georgia** *Brook Benton*
59/78 **Raise A Little Hell** *Trooper*
79/67 **Raise Your Hand** *Eddie Floyd*
65/74 **Raised On Robbery** *Joni Mitchell*
41/73 **Raised On Rock** *Elvis Presley*
Ram-Bunk-Shush
67/57 *Bill Doggett*
29/61 *Ventures*
21/61 **Rama Lama Ding Dong** *Edsels*
91/81 **Rambler** *Molly Hatchet*
17/69 **Ramblin' Gamblin' Man** *Bob Seger*
2/73 **Ramblin' Man** *Allman Brothers Band*
2/62 **Ramblin' Rose** *Nat King Cole*
73/60 **Rambling** *Ramblers*
72/60 **Ramona** *Blue Diamonds*
27/58 **Ramrod** *Duane Eddy*
62/57 **Rang Tang Ding Dong (I Am The Japanese Sandman)** *Cellos*
2/70 **Rapper, The** *Jaggerz*
36/80 **Rapper's Delight** *Sugarhill Gang*
83/84 **Rappin' Rodney** *Rodney Dangerfield*
1/81 **Rapture** *Blondie*
70/59 **Raspberries, Strawberries** *Kingston Trio*
2/85 **Raspberry Beret** *Prince*
71/63 **Rat Race** *Drifters*
90/76 **Rattlesnake** *Ohio Players*
Raunchy
2/57 *Bill Justis*
4/57 *Ernie Freeman*
10/57 *Billy Vaughn*
37/58 **Rave On** *Buddy Holly*
80/76 **Raven, The** *Alan Parsons Project*
23/59 **Raw-Hide** *Link Wray*
24/69 **Ray Of Hope** *Rascals*
15/55 **Razzle-Dazzle** *Bill Haley & His Comets*
51/77 **Reach** *Orleans*
54/78 **Reach For It** *George Duke*
81/84 **Reach Out** *Giorgio Moroder*
20/70 **Reach Out And Touch (Somebody's Hand)** *Diana Ross*
Reach Out For Me
74/63 *Lou Johnson*
20/64 *Dionne Warwick*
Reach Out I'll Be There
1/66 *Four Tops*
79/68 *Merrilee Rush*
29/71 *Diana Ross*
60/75 *Gloria Gaynor*
10/68 **Reach Out Of The Darkness** *Friend And Lover*
77/71 **Reach Out Your Hand** *Brotherhood Of Man*
74/77 **Reaching For The World** *Harold Melvin & The Blue Notes*
54/85 **Reaction To Action** *Foreigner*
18/84 **Read 'Em And Weep** *Barry Manilow*
26/75 **Ready** *Cat Stevens*
92/81 **Ready For Love** *Silverado*
52/79 **Ready For The 80's** *Village People*
52/78 **Ready For The Times To Get Better** *Crystal Gayle*
42/61 **Ready For Your Love** *Shep & The Limelites*
73/78 **Ready Or Not** *Helen Reddy*

35/69 **Ready Or Not Here I Come (Can't Hide From Love)** *Delfonics*
44/56 **Ready Teddy** *Little Richard*
11/78 **Ready To Take A Chance Again** *Barry Manilow*
84/68 **Ready, Willing And Able** *American Breed*
83/84 **Real End** *Rickie Lee Jones*
80/66 **Real Humdinger** *J.J. Barnes*
77/65 **Real Live Girl** *Steve Alaimo*
5/80 **Real Love** *Doobie Brothers*
79/80 **Real Love** *Cretones*
91/85 **Real Love** *Kenny Rogers & Dolly Parton*
83/75 **Real Man** *Todd Rundgren*
92/74 **Real Me** *Who*
41/77 **Real Mother For Ya** *Johnny 'Guitar' Watson*
79/80 **Real People** *Chic*
67/81 **Real Thing** *Brothers Johnson*
68/58 **Real Wild Child** *Ivan*
80/75 **Reality** *James Brown*
16/81 **Really Wanna Know You** *Gary Wright*
71/83 **Reap The Wild Wind** *Ultravox*
79/62 **Reap What You Sow** *Billy Stewart*
Reaper *see: (Don't Fear) The*
98/58 **Reason, The** *5 Chanels*
52/79 **Reason To Be** *Kansas*
F/71 **Reason To Believe** *Rod Stewart*
48/57 **Rebel** *Carol Jarvis*
6/58 **Rebel-'Rouser** *Duane Eddy*
64/74 **Rebel Rebel** *David Bowie*
46/84 **Rebel Yell** *Billy Idol*
74/85 **Rebels** *Tom Petty*
61/80 **Rebels Are We** *Chic*
Reconsider Me
28/69 *Johnny Adams*
67/75 *Narvel Felts*
84/65 **Record, The (Baby I Love You)** *Ben E. King*
82/59 **Record Hop Blues** *Quarter Notes*
37/66 **Recovery** *Fontella Bass*
89/67 **Red And Blue** *Dave Clark Five*
96/73 **Red Back Spider** *Brownsville Station*
78/71 **Red Eye Blues** *Redeye*
Red Hot
83/77 *Robert Gordon*
77/83 *Herb Alpert*
82/66 **Red Hot** *Sam The Sham & The Pharoahs*
41/80 **Red Light** *Linda Clifford*
78/63 **Red Pepper I** *Roosevelt Fountain & Pens Of Rhythm*
Red Red Wine
62/68 *Neil Diamond*
72/70 *Vic Dana*
34/84 *UB40*
5/59 **Red River Rock** *Johnny & The Hurricanes*
37/59 **Red River Rose** *Ames Brothers*
Red Roses For A Blue Lady
10/65 *Vic Dana*
11/65 *Bert Kaempfert*
23/65 *Wayne Newton*
95/67 **Red Roses For Mom** *Bobby Vinton*
2/66 **Red Rubber Ball** *Cyrkle*
Red Sails In The Sunset
57/57 *Tab Hunter*
36/60 *Platters*
35/63 *Fats Domino*
85/73 **Redneck Friend** *Jackson Browne*
98/72 **Redwood Tree** *Van Morrison*
Reelin' And Rockin'
23/65 *Dave Clark Five*
27/73 *Chuck Berry*
11/73 **Reeling In The Years** *Steely Dan*
62/57 **Reet Petite (The Finest Girl You Ever Want To Meet)** *Jackie Wilson*
2/67 **Reflections** *Supremes*
10/70 **Reflections Of My Life** *Marmalade*
1/84 **Reflex, The** *Duran Duran*
15/80 **Refugee** *Tom Petty*
Relax
67/84 *Frankie Goes To Hollywood*
10/85 *Frankie Goes To Hollywood*
39/73 **Relay, The** *Who*
Release Me
8/62 *Esther Phillips*
4/67 *Engelbert Humperdinck*
93/67 *Esther Phillips*
82/68 *Johnny Adams*
57/55 **Rememb'ring** *Peter Lind Hayes & Mary Healy*
83/58 **Remember** *Velours*
91/63 **Remember Baby** *Shep & The Limelites*
53/73 **Remember (Christmas)** *Nilsson*
39/63 **Remember Diana** *Paul Anka*
16/71 **Remember Me** *Diana Ross*
26/64 **Remember Me** *Rita Pavone*
67/76 **Remember Me** *Willie Nelson*
32/65 **(Remember Me) I'm The One Who Loves You** *Dean Martin*
33/77 **(Remember The Days Of The) Old Schoolyard** *Cat Stevens*
36/84 **Remember The Nights** *Motels*
64/66 **Remember The Rain** *Bob Lind*
100/75 **Remember The Rain?** *21st Century*
24/63 **Remember Then** *Earls*
Remember (Walkin' In The Sand)
5/64 *Shangri-Las*
43/79 *Louise Goffin*
67/80 *Aerosmith*
25/75 **Remember What I Told You To Forget** *Tavares*
81/84 **Remember What You Like** *Jenny Burton*
41/59 **Remember When** *Platters*
69/65 **Remember When** *Wayne Newton*
6/57 **Remember You're Mine** *Pat Boone*
3/78 **Reminiscing** *Little River Band*
81/85 **Remo's Theme (What If)** *Tommy Shaw*
89/80 **Remote Control** *Reddings*
26/75 **Rendezvous** *Hudson Brothers*
16/79 **Renegade** *Styx*
39/76 **Renegade** *Michael Murphey*
53/57 **Repeat After Me** *Patti Page*
100/67 **Requiem For The Masses** *Association*
Rescue Me
4/65 *Fontella Bass*
78/76 *Melissa Manchester*
Respect
35/65 *Otis Redding*
92/66 *Rationals*
1/67 *Aretha Franklin*
12/71 **Respect Yourself** *Staple Singers*
15/66 **Respectable** *Outsiders*
46/86 **Restless** *Starpoint*
59/85 **Restless Heart** *John Waite*
Resurrection Shuffle
F/71 *Tom Jones*
40/71 *Ashton, Gardner & Dyke*
15/67 **Return Of The Red Baron** *Royal Guardsmen*
4/58 **Return To Me** *Dean Martin*
2/62 **Return To Sender** *Elvis Presley*
Reuben *see: Ruben*
1/79 **Reunited** *Peaches & Herb*
25/59 **Reveille Rock** *Johnny & The Hurricanes*
15/62 **Revenge** *Brook Benton*
8/63 **Reverend Mr. Black** *Kingston Trio*
97/60 **Revival** *Johnny & The Hurricanes*
92/71 **Revival (Love Is Everywhere)** *Allman Brothers Band*
12/68 **Revolution** *Beatles*

70/65 **Revolution Kind** *Sonny*
41/73 **Rhapsody In Blue** *Deodato*
16/66 **Rhapsody In The Rain** *Lou Christie*
63/74 **Rhapsody In White**
Love Unlimited Orchestra
11/76 **Rhiannon (Will You Ever Win)**
Fleetwood Mac
1/75 **Rhinestone Cowboy** *Glen Campbell*
47/79 **Rhumba Girl** *Nicolette Larson*
63/75 **Rhyme Tyme People** *Kool & The Gang*
24/64 **Rhythm** *Major Lance*
F/55 **Rhythm 'N' Blues (Mama's Got The Rhythm - Papa's Got The Blues)** *McGuire Sisters*
3/85 **Rhythm Of The Night** *DeBarge*
Rhythm Of The Rain
3/63 *Cascades*
63/69 *Gary Lewis & The Playboys*
94/66 **Rib Tip's** *Andre Williams*
54/82 **Ribbon In The Sky** *Stevie Wonder*
46/68 **Rice Is Nice** *Lemon Pipers*
1/77 **Rich Girl** *Daryl Hall & John Oates*
89/81 **Rich Man** *Terri Gibbs*
99/55 **Richest Man (In The World)** *Eddy Arnold*
63/83 **Ricky** *'Weird Al' Yankovic*
5/62 **Ride!** *Dee Dee Sharp*
76/71 **Ride A White Swan** *T. Rex*
25/65 **Ride Away** *Roy Orbison*
4/70 **Ride Captain Ride** *Blues Image*
23/75 **Ride 'Em Cowboy** *Paul Davis*
2/80 **Ride Like The Wind** *Christopher Cross*
61/68 **Ride My See-Saw** *Moody Blues*
37/67 **Ride, Ride, Ride** *Brenda Lee*
F/72 **Ride, Sally, Ride** *Dennis Coffey*
84/74 **Ride The Tiger** *Jefferson Starship*
16/64 **Ride The Wild Surf** *Jan & Dean*
52/71 **Ride With Me** *Steppenwolf*
28/65 **Ride Your Pony** *Lee Dorsey*
Riders In The Sky *see: Ghost*
14/71 **Riders On The Storm** *Doors*
70/73 **Ridin' My Thumb To Mexico**
Johnny Rodriguez
94/77 **Ridin' The Storm Out** *REO Speedwagon*
63/63 **Ridin' The Wind** *Tornadoes*
63/81 **Right Away** *Hawks*
73/82 **Right Away** *Kansas*
2/76 **Right Back Where We Started From**
Maxine Nightingale
45/83 **Right Before Your Eyes** *America*
43/86 **Right Between The Eyes** *Wax*
59/60 **Right By My Side** *Ricky Nelson*
29/84 **Right By Your Side** *Eurythmics*
12/78 **Right Down The Line** *Gerry Rafferty*
65/77 **Right Feeling At The Wrong Time** *Hot*
58/82 **Right Here And Now** *Bill Medley*
56/82 **Right Kind Of Love** *Quarterflash*
99/65 **Right Now And Not Later** *Shangri-Las*
23/71 **Right On The Tip Of My Tongue**
Brenda & The Tabulations
Right Or Wrong
29/61 *Wanda Jackson*
14/64 *Ronnie Dove*
9/73 **Right Place Wrong Time** *Dr. John*
61/68 **Right Relations** *Johnny Rivers*
84/62 **Right String But The Wrong Yo-Yo**
Dr. Feelgood & The Interns
77/82 **Right The First Time** *Gamma*
17/73 **Right Thing To Do** *Carly Simon*
6/77 **Right Time Of The Night** *Jennifer Warnes*
55/70 **Riki Tiki Tavi** *Donovan*
4/74 **Rikki Don't Lose That Number** *Steely Dan*
50/57 **Ring-A-Ding-A-Ding** *Tommy Sands*
32/59 **Ring-A-Ling-A-Lario** *Jimmie Rodgers*
33/65 **Ring Dang Doo**
Sam The Sham & The Pharoahs
1/79 **Ring My Bell** *Anita Ward*
F/57 **Ring My Phone** *Tommy Sands*
17/63 **Ring Of Fire** *Johnny Cash*
84/61 **Ring Of Fire** *Duane Eddy*
31/72 **Ring The Living Bell** *Melanie*
1/64 **Ringo** *Lorne Greene*
53/64 **Ringo's Theme (This Boy)** *George Martin*
Rings
17/71 *Cymarron*
43/74 *Lobo*
86/74 *Reuben Howell*
10/62 **Rinky Dink** *Dave 'Baby' Cortez*
14/83 **Rio** *Duran Duran*
55/69 **Riot** *Hugh Masekela*
Rip It Up
17/56 *Little Richard*
25/56 *Bill Haley & His Comets*
68/72 **Rip Off** *Laura Lee*
36/64 **Rip Van Winkle** *Devotions*
1/79 **Rise** *Herb Alpert*
99/77 **Ritzy Mambo** *Salsoul Orchestra*
62/73 **River** *Joe Simon*
River Deep - Mountain High
88/66 *Ike & Tina Turner*
53/69 *Deep Purple*
14/71 *Supremes & Four Tops*
River Is Wide
45/67 *Forum*
31/69 *Grass Roots*
River Kwai March *see: March From*
53/74 **River Of Love** *B.W. Stevenson*
86/73 **River Road** *Uncle Dog*
82/60 **River, Stay 'Way From My Door**
Frank Sinatra
99/63 **River's Invitation** *Percy Mayfield*
33/74 **River's Risin'** *Edgar Winter*
83/60 **Riverboat** *Faron Young*
30/78 **Rivers Of Babylon** *Boney M*
65/62 **Road Hog** *John D. Loudermilk*
Road Runner
75/60 *Bo Diddley*
46/65 *Gants*
(also see: (I'm A) Road Runner)
100/72 **Road We Didn't Take** *Freda Payne*
F/70 **Roadhouse Blues** *Doors*
25/59 **Robbin' The Cradle** *Tony Bellus*
95/84 **Robert De Niro's Waiting** *Bananarama*
94/72 **Roberta** *Bones*
74/58 **Roc-A-Chicka** *Warner Mack*
68/86 **Rock 'N' Roll To The Rescue** *Beach Boys*
41/55 **Rock-A-Beatin' Boogie**
Bill Haley & His Comets
10/57 **Rock-A-Billy** *Guy Mitchell*
Rock-A-Bye Your Baby With A Dixie Melody
10/56 *Jerry Lewis*
37/61 *Aretha Franklin*
23/62 **Rock-A-Hula Baby** *Elvis Presley*
93/57 **Rock And Cry** *Clyde McPhatter*
47/72 **Rock And Roll** *Led Zeppelin*
7/72 **Rock And Roll** *Gary Glitter*
Rock And Roll
also see: Rock 'N' Roll, & Rockin' Roll
Rock And Roll All Nite
68/75 *Kiss*
12/76 *Kiss (Live)*
92/72 **Rock And Roll Crazies** *Stephen Stills*
53/79 **Rock And Roll Dancin'** *Beckmeier Brothers*
32/81 **Rock And Roll Dreams Come Through**
Jim Steinman
20/85 **Rock And Roll Girls** *John Fogerty*
3/74 **Rock And Roll Heaven** *Righteous Brothers*
23/74 **Rock And Roll, Hoochie Koo**
Rick Derringer

19/58 **Rock And Roll Is Here To Stay**
Danny & The Juniors
28/76 **Rock And Roll Love Letter**
Bay City Rollers
15/72 **Rock And Roll Lullaby** *B.J. Thomas*
Rock And Roll Music
8/57 *Chuck Berry*
5/76 *Beach Boys*
41/77 **Rock And Roll Never Forgets** *Bob Seger*
66/58 **Rock And Roll Rhapsody** *Four Aces*
71/75 **Rock And Roll Runaway** *Ace*
83/77 **Rock And Roll Star** *Champagne*
93/72 **Rock And Roll Stew** *Traffic*
1/56 **Rock And Roll Waltz** *Kay Starr*
66/56 **Rock And Roll Wedding** *Sunny Gale*
52/56 **Rock Around Mother Goose** *Barry Gordon*
Rock Around The Clock
1/55 *Bill Haley & His Comets*
39/74 *Bill Haley & His Comets*
93/76 **Rock Creek Park** *Blackbyrds*
Rock In America *see: (You Can Still)*
Rock Island Line
8/56 *Lonnie Donegan*
59/56 *Don Cornell*
93/70 *Johnny Cash*
64/80 **Rock It** *Lipps, Inc.*
56/80 **Rock Lobster** *B-52's*
13/55 **Rock Love** *Fontane Sisters*
10/69 **Rock Me** *Steppenwolf*
57/79 **Rock Me** *Nick Gilder*
1/86 **Rock Me Amadeus** *Falco*
34/64 **Rock Me Baby** *B.B. King*
38/72 **Rock Me Baby** *David Cassidy*
1/74 **Rock Me Gently** *Andy Kim*
43/63 **Rock Me In The Cradle Of Love**
Dee Dee Sharp
Rock Me On The Water
48/72 *Jackson Browne*
85/72 *Linda Ronstadt*
18/85 **Rock Me Tonight (For Old Times Sake)**
Freddie Jackson
15/84 **Rock Me Tonite** *Billy Squier*
Rock 'N' Roll
also see: Rock And Roll, & Rockin' Roll
13/79 **Rock 'N' Roll Fantasy** *Bad Company*
30/78 **Rock 'N' Roll Fantasy** *Kinks*
Rock 'N' Roll (I Gave You The Best Years Of My Life)
73/73 *Kevin Johnson*
97/74 *Terry Jacks*
15/75 *Mac Davis*
19/83 **Rock 'N' Roll Is King** *ELO*
29/72 **Rock 'N' Roll Soul** *Grand Funk Railroad*
44/67 **Rock 'N' Roll Woman** *Buffalo Springfield*
16/83 **Rock Of Ages** *Def Leppard*
5/74 **Rock On** *David Essex*
36/56 **Rock Right** *Georgia Gibbs*
9/71 **Rock Steady** *Aretha Franklin*
1/74 **Rock The Boat** *Hues Corporation*
8/83 **Rock The Casbah** *Clash*
9/82 **Rock This Town** *Stray Cats*
1/80 **Rock With You** *Michael Jackson*
25/84 **Rock You Like A Hurricane** *Scorpions*
1/74 **Rock Your Baby** *George McCrae*
17/57 **Rock Your Little Baby To Sleep**
Buddy Knox
38/59 **Rocka-Conga** *Applejacks*
66/78 **Rockaway Beach** *Ramones*
6/72 **Rocket Man** *Elton John*
39/78 **Rocket Ride** *Kiss*
10/75 **Rockford Files** *Mike Post*
79/58 **Rockhouse** *Ray Charles*
27/75 **Rockin' All Over The World** *John Fogerty*
91/75 **Rockin' And Rollin' On The Streets Of Hollywood** *Buddy Miles*
Rockin' Around The Christmas Tree
14/60 *Brenda Lee*
50/61 *Brenda Lee*
59/62 *Brenda Lee*
25/85 **Rockin' At Midnight** *Honeydrippers*
83/61 **Rockin' Bicycle** *Fats Domino*
9/75 **Rockin' Chair** *Gwen McCrae*
Rockin' Crickets
57/59 *Hot-Toddys*
87/63 *Rockin' Rebels*
61/56 **Rockin' Ghost** *Archie Bleyer*
7/60 **Rockin' Good Way (To Mess Around And Fall In Love)** *Brook Benton & Dinah Washington*
78/59 **Rockin' In The Jungle** *Eternals*
58/69 **Rockin' In The Same Old Boat**
Bobby Bland
43/80 **Rockin' Into The Night** *38 Special*
22/60 **Rockin' Little Angel** *Ray Smith*
1/76 **Rockin' Me** *Steve Miller*
Rockin' Pneumonia And The Boogie Woogie Flu
52/57 *Huey Smith & The Clowns*
6/73 *Johnny Rivers*
64/60 **Rockin' Red Wing** *Sammy Masters*
Rockin' Robin
2/58 *Bobby Day*
96/64 *Rivieras*
2/72 *Michael Jackson*
Rockin' Roll
also see: Rock 'N' Roll, & Rock And Roll
14/73 **Rockin' Roll Baby** *Stylistics*
87/60 **Rockin', Rollin' Ocean** *Hank Snow*
64/57 **Rockin' Shoes** *Ames Brothers*
18/74 **Rockin' Soul** *Hues Corporation*
78/56 **Rockin' Through The Rye**
Bill Haley & His Comets
88/72 **Rockin' With The King** *Canned Heat*
60/60 **Rocking Goose** *Johnny & The Hurricanes*
71/83 **Rockit** *Herbie Hancock*
9/75 **Rocky** *Austin Roberts*
82/79 **Rocky II Disco** *Maynard Ferguson*
9/73 **Rocky Mountain High** *John Denver*
76/76 **Rocky Mountain Music** *Eddie Rabbitt*
23/73 **Rocky Mountain Way** *Joe Walsh*
Rocky, Theme From *see: Gonna Fly Now*
83/73 **Roland The Roadie And Gertrude The Groupie** *Dr. Hook*
30/79 **Rolene** *Moon Martin*
78/73 **Roll In My Sweet Baby's Arms**
Hank Wilson
27/83 **Roll Me Away** *Bob Seger*
56/71 **Roll On** *New Colony Six*
14/75 **Roll On Down The Highway**
Bachman-Turner Overdrive
Roll Over Beethoven
29/56 *Chuck Berry*
51/61 *Velaires*
68/64 *Beatles*
42/73 *Electric Light Orchestra*
58/78 **Roll With The Changes** *REO Speedwagon*
34/79 **Roller** *April Wine*
92/66 **Roller Coaster** *Ides Of March*
66/79 **Roller-Skatin' Mate** *Peaches & Herb*
13/55 **Rollin' Stone** *Fontane Sisters*
92/75 **Rolling Down A Mountainside**
Main Ingredient
74/62 **Roly Poly** *Joey Dee & The Starliters*
26/84 **Romancing The Stone** *Eddy Grant*
99/64 **Rome Will Never Leave You**
Richard Chamberlain
75/61 **Romeo** *Janie Grant*
87/77 **Romeo** *Mr. Big*

Romeo & Juliet
see: Love Theme, (Just Like), & Farewell Love Scene
11/80 **Romeo's Tune** *Steve Forbert*
6/64 **Ronnie** *4 Seasons*
81/61 **Ronnie** *Marcy Joe*
72/63 **Ronnie, Call Me When You Get A Chance** *Shelley Fabares*
50/74 **Room Full Of Roses** *Mickey Gilley*
72/61 **Room Full Of Tears** *Drifters*
44/69 **Roosevelt And Ira Lee (Night Of The Mossacin)** *Tony Joe White*
57/77 **Roots (Medley)** *Quincy Jones*
51/76 **Roots, Rock, Reggae** *Bob Marley*
43/73 **Rosalie** *Sam Neely*
2/82 **Rosanna** *Toto*
95/73 **Rosanna** *Classics IV*
91/68 **Rosanna's Going Wild** *Johnny Cash*
3/80 **Rose, The** *Bette Midler*
6/56 **Rose And A Baby Ruth** *George Hamilton IV*
3/71 **Rose Garden** *Lynn Anderson*
94/76 **Rose Of Cimarron** *Poco*
79/55 **Rose Tattoo** *Perry Como*
73/65 **Roses And Rainbows** *Danny Hutton*
Roses And Roses *see: And Roses*
43/65 **Roses Are Red My Love** *'You Know Who' Group!*
1/62 **Roses Are Red (My Love)** *Bobby Vinton*
(also see: Long As The Rose Is Red)
24/57 **Rosie Lee** *Mello-Tones*
30/80 **Rotation** *Herb Alpert*
22/86 **Rough Boy** *ZZ Top*
89/80 **Rough Boys** *Pete Townshend*
94/62 **Rough Lover** *Aretha Franklin*
1/57 **Round And Round** *Perry Como*
12/84 **Round And Round** *Ratt*
21/65 **Round Every Corner** *Petula Clark*
13/72 **Roundabout** *Yes*
80/65 **Roundabout** *Connie Francis*
30/62 **Route 66 Theme** *Nelson Riddle*
78/82 **Route 66** *Manhattan Transfer*
37/82 **Route 101** *Herb Alpert*
60/56 **Rovin' Gambler** *Tennessee Ernie Ford*
32/79 **Roxanne** *Police*
77/85 **Roxanne, Roxanne** *UTFO*
90/76 **Roxy Roller** *Sweeney Todd*
54/80 **Royal Mile (Sweet Darlin')** *Gerry Rafferty*
Rub It In
65/71 *Layng Martine*
16/74 *Billy 'Crash' Craddock*
6/61 **Rubber Ball** *Bobby Vee*
37/79 **Rubber Biscuit** *Blues Brothers*
73/73 **Rubber Bullets** *10cc*
16/70 **Rubber Duckie** *Ernie*
2/76 **Rubberband Man** *Spinners*
F/70 **Rubberneckin'** *Elvis Presley*
26/69 **Ruben James** *Kenny Rogers & The First Edition*
Ruby
28/60 *Ray Charles*
58/60 *Adam Wade*
18/62 **Ruby Ann** *Marty Robbins*
Ruby Baby
2/63 *Dion*
33/75 *Billy 'Crash' Craddock*
6/69 **Ruby, Don't Take Your Love To Town** *Kenny Rogers & The First Edition*
Ruby Duby Du
30/60 *Tobin Mathews & Co.*
41/60 *Charles Wolcott*
Ruby Red Dress *see: Leave Me Alone*
Ruby Tuesday
1/67 *Rolling Stones*
52/71 *Melanie*

Rudolph The Red-Nosed Reindeer
70/57 *Gene Autry*
21/60 *Chipmunks*
71/60 *Melodeers*
47/61 *Chipmunks*
77/62 *Chipmunks*
34/56 **Rudy's Rock** *Bill Haley & His Comets*
66/64 **Rules Of Love** *Orlons*
Rumble
16/58 *Link Wray*
91/63 *Jack Nitzsche*
28/86 **Rumbleseat** *John Cougar Mellencamp*
89/78 **Rumor At The Honky Tonk** *Spellbound*
8/86 **Rumors** *Timex Social Club*
12/62 **Rumors** *Johnny Crawford*
55/66 **Rumors** *Syndicate Of Sound*
53/78 **Rumour Has It** *Donna Summer*
6/69 **Run Away Child, Running Wild** *Temptations*
12/65 **Run, Baby Run (Back Into My Arms)** *Newbeats*
33/78 **Run For Home** *Lindisfarne*
18/82 **Run For The Roses** *Dan Fogelberg*
71/79 **Run Home Girl** *Sad Cafe*
4/75 **Run Joey Run** *David Geddes*
53/80 **Run Like Hell** *Pink Floyd*
36/60 **Run Red Run** *Coasters*
69/58 **Run Rudolph Run** *Chuck Berry*
25/66 **Run, Run, Look And See** *Brian Hyland*
27/72 **Run Run Run** *Jo Jo Gunne*
44/64 **Run, Run, Run** *Gestures*
53/67 **Run, Run, Run** *Third Rail*
93/64 **Run, Run, Run** *Supremes*
75/61 **Run, Run, Run** *Ronny Douglas*
20/84 **Run Runaway** *Slade*
76/70 **Run Sally Run** *Cuff Links*
28/60 **Run Samson Run** *Neil Sedaka*
93/75 **Run Tell The People** *Daniel Boone*
F/70 **Run Through The Jungle** *Creedence Clearwater Revival*
2/61 **Run To Him** *Bobby Vee*
16/72 **Run To Me** *Bee Gees*
68/81 **Run To Me** *Savoy Brown*
96/65 **Run To My Lovin' Arms** *Lenny Welch*
6/85 **Run To You** *Bryan Adams*
92/70 **Run, Woman, Run** *Tammy Wynette*
23/60 **Runaround** *Fleetwoods*
28/61 **Runaround** *Regents*
Runaround Sue
1/61 *Dion*
13/78 *Leif Garrett*
Runaway
1/61 *Del Shannon*
56/62 *Lawrence Welk*
79/72 *Dawn (medley)*
46/75 *Charlie Kulis*
57/77 *Bonnie Raitt*
83/86 *Luis Cardenas*
12/78 **Runaway** *Jefferson Starship*
39/84 **Runaway** *Bon Jovi*
76/78 **Runaway Love** *Linda Clifford*
84/81 **Runaway Rita** *Leif Garrett*
22/84 **Runner** *Manfred Mann's Earth Band*
23/72 **Runnin' Away** *Sly & The Family Stone*
96/72 **Runnin' Back To Saskatoon** *Guess Who*
64/69 **Runnin' Blue** *Doors*
57/64 **Runnin' Out Of Fools** *Aretha Franklin*
84/78 **Runnin' With The Devil** *Van Halen*
91/82 **Running** *Chubby Checker*
78/80 **Running Back** *Eddie Money*
79/85 **Running Back** *Urgent*
Running Bear
1/60 *Johnny Preston*
94/69 *Sonny James*

11/78 **Running On Empty** *Jackson Browne*
Running Scared
1/61 *Roy Orbison*
50/81 *Fools*
30/85 **Running Up That Hill** *Kate Bush*
7/84 **Running With The Night** *Lionel Richie*
39/72 **Runway, The** *Grass Roots*
91/59 **Russian Band Stand** *Spencer & Spencer*
16/86 **Russians** *Sting*
79/79 **Rust Never Sleeps (Hey Hey, My My [Into The Black])** *Neil Young*
33/65 **Rusty Bells** *Brenda Lee*
51/86 **Ruthless People** *Mick Jagger*

S

73/57 **'S Wonderful** *Ray Conniff*
15/75 **S.O.S.** *Abba*
S.W.A.T. *see: Theme From*
39/66 **S.Y.S.L.J.F.M. (The Letter Song)** *Joe Tex*
20/61 **Sacred** *Castells*
1/79 **Sad Eyes** *Robert John*
63/77 **Sad Eyes** *Brooklyn Dreams*
88/61 **Sad Eyes (Don't You Cry)** *Echoes*
Sad Girl
47/69 *Intruders*
93/82 *GQ*
83/77 **Sad Girl** *Carl Graves*
84/82 **Sad Hearts** *Four Tops*
29/60 **Sad Mood** *Sam Cooke*
Sad Movies (Make Me Cry)
5/61 *Sue Thompson*
56/61 *Lennon Sisters*
27/65 **Sad, Sad Girl** *Barbara Mason*
84/63 **Sad, Sad Girl And Boy** *Impressions*
5/84 **Sad Songs (Say So Much)** *Elton John*
14/75 **Sad Sweet Dreamer** *Sweet Sensation*
94/65 **Sad Tomorrows** *Trini Lopez*
54/75 **Sadie** *Spinners*
52/56 **Sadie's Shawl** *Bob Sharples*
100/66 **Safe And Sound** *Fontella Bass*
53/68 **Safe In My Garden** *Mamas & The Papas*
3/83 **Safety Dance** *Men Without Hats*
85/64 **Saginaw, Michigan** *Lefty Frizzell*
64/66 **Said I Wasn't Gonna Tell Nobody** *Sam & Dave*
5/58 **Sail Along Silvery Moon** *Billy Vaughn*
50/73 **Sail Around The World** *David Gates*
54/84 **Sail Away** *Temptations*
84/77 **Sail Away** *Sam Neely*
4/79 **Sail On** *Commodores*
Sail On Sailor
79/73 *Beach Boys*
49/75 *Beach Boys*
1/80 **Sailing** *Christopher Cross*
58/75 **Sailing** *Rod Stewart*
55/77 **Sailing Ships** *Mesa*
81/64 **Sailor Boy** *Chiffons*
5/60 **Sailor (Your Home Is The Sea)** *Lolita*
Saint *see: St.*
Saints Rock 'N Roll
see: When The Saints Go Marchin' In
69/76 **Sally** *Grand Funk Railroad*
39/75 **Sally G** *Paul McCartney*
2/63 **Sally, Go 'Round The Roses** *Jaynetts*
95/68 **Sally Had A Party** *Flavor*
Sally Was A Good Old Girl
99/64 *Fats Domino*
99/68 *Trini Lopez*
81/59 **Sal's Got A Sugar Lip** *Johnny Horton*
76/75 **Salsoul Hustle** *Salsoul Orchestra*
36/83 **Salt In My Tears** *Martin Briley*
93/63 **Saltwater Taffy** *Morty Jay*
20/77 **Sam** *Olivia Newton-John*
98/66 **Sam, You Made The Pants Too Long** *Barbra Streisand*
92/67 **Sam's Place** *Buck Owens*
94/62 **Sam's Song** *Dean Martin & Sammy Davis, Jr.*
50/74 **Same Love That Made Me Laugh** *Bill Withers*
91/63 **Same Old Hurt** *Burl Ives*
9/81 **Same Old Lang Syne** *Dan Fogelberg*
51/60 **Same Old Me** *Guy Mitchell*
13/55 **Same Old Saturday Night** *Frank Sinatra*
16/60 **Same One** *Brook Benton*
75/75 **Same Thing It Took** *Impressions*
8/61 **San Antonio Rose** *Floyd Cramer*
100/71 **San Bernadino** *Christie*
9/67 **San Franciscan Nights** *Animals*
4/67 **San Francisco (Be Sure To Wear Flowers In Your Hair)** *Scott McKenzie*
91/68 **San Francisco Girls (Return of the Native)** *Fever Tree*
79/69 **San Francisco Is A Lonely Town** *Joe Simon*
47/61 **San-Ho-Zay** *Freddy King*
14/86 **Sanctify Yourself** *Simple Minds*
23/55 **Sand And The Sea** *Nat King Cole*
Sandpiper, Love Theme From
see: Shadow Of Your Smile
15/60 **Sandy** *Larry Hall*
21/63 **Sandy** *Dion*
27/66 **Sandy** *Ronny & The Daytonas*
85/75 **Sandy** *Hollies*
32/57 **Santa & The Satellite** *Buchanan & Goodman*
99/61 **Santa & The Touchables** *Dickie Goodman*
23/62 **Santa Claus Is Coming To Town** *4 Seasons*
45/62 **Santa Claus Is Watching You** *Ray Stevens*
1/86 **Sara** *Starship*
7/80 **Sara** *Fleetwood Mac*
61/82 **Sara** *Bill Champlin*
4/76 **Sara Smile** *Daryl Hall & John Oates*
39/80 **(Sartorial Eloquence) Don't Ya Wanna Play This Game No More?** *Elton John*
23/66 **Satin Pillows** *Bobby Vinton*
97/70 **Satin Red And Black Velvet Woman** *Dave Mason*
28/73 **Satin Sheets** *Jeanne Pruett*
73/76 **Satin Sheets** *Bellamy Brothers*
22/75 **Satin Soul** *Love Unlimited Orchestra*
49/72 **Satisfaction** *Miracles*
73/85 **Satisfaction Guaranteed** *Firm*
58/74 **Satisfaction Guaranteed (Or Take Your Love Back)** *Harold Melvin & The Blue Notes*
81/84 **Satisfied Man** *Molly Hatchet*
39/66 **Satisfied Mind** *Bobby Hebb*
50/66 **Satisfied With You** *Dave Clark Five*
64/84 **Satisfy Me** *Billy Satellite*
3/72 **Saturday In The Park** *Chicago*
26/86 **Saturday Love** *Cherrelle with Alexander O'Neal*
28/71 **Saturday Morning Confusion** *Bobby Russell*
1/76 **Saturday Night** *Bay City Rollers*
29/63 **Saturday Night** *New Christy Minstrels*
18/64 **Saturday Night At The Movies** *Drifters*
99/69 **Saturday Night At The World** *Mason Williams*

27/75 **Saturday Night Special** *Lynyrd Skynyrd*
34/79 **Saturday Night, Sunday Morning**
Thelma Houston
12/73 **Saturday Night's Alright For Fighting**
Elton John
21/77 **Saturday Nite** *Earth, Wind & Fire*
93/63 **Saturday Sunshine** *Burt Bacharach*
35/79 **Saturdaynight** *Herman Brood*
Sausalito
86/69 *Ohio Express*
99/69 *Al Martino*
25/81 **Sausalito Summernight** *Diesel*
34/80 **Savannah Nights** *Tom Johnston*
16/85 **Save A Prayer** *Duran Duran*
53/62 **Save All Your Lovin' For Me** *Brenda Lee*
22/77 **Save It For A Rainy Day** *Stephen Bishop*
10/64 **Save It For Me** *4 Seasons*
Save Me
54/77 *Merrilee Rush*
90/77 *Donna McDaniel*
71/80 **Save Me** *Dave Mason*
73/59 **Save My Soul** *Jack Scott*
Save The Country
27/70 *5th Dimension*
74/70 *Thelma Houston*
Save The Last Dance For Me
1/60 *Drifters*
18/74 *DeFranco Family*
45/84 *Dolly Parton*
(also see: I'll Save The Last Dance)
77/85 **Save The Night For Me** *Maureen Steele*
66/83 **Save The Overtime (For Me)**
Gladys Knight & The Pips
2/65 **Save Your Heart For Me**
Gary Lewis & The Playboys
Save Your Kisses For Me
27/76 *Brotherhood Of Man*
75/76 *Bobby Vinton*
94/70 **Save Your Sugar For Me** *Tony Joe White*
37/61 **Saved** *LaVern Baker*
20/83 **Saved By Zero** *Fixx*
1/85 **Saving All My Love For You**
Whitney Houston
94/73 **Saw A New Morning** *Bee Gees*
65/63 **Sax Fifth Avenue** *Johnny Beecher*
17/81 **Say Goodbye To Hollywood** *Billy Joel*
85/80 **Say Goodbye To Little Jo** *Steve Forbert*
3/73 **Say, Has Anybody Seen My Sweet Gypsy Rose** *Dawn*
68/84 **Say Hello To Ronnie** *Janey Street*
21/66 **Say I Am (What I Am)**
Tommy James & The Shondells
46/85 **Say It Again** *Santana*
2/83 **Say It Isn't So** *Daryl Hall & John Oates*
98/57 **Say It Isn't So** *Teddi King*
10/68 **Say It Loud - I'm Black And I'm Proud**
James Brown
70/86 **Say It, Say It** *E.G. Daily*
20/59 **Say Man** *Bo Diddley*
55/79 **Say Maybe** *Neil Diamond*
1/83 **Say Say Say**
Paul McCartney & Michael Jackson
22/65 **Say Something Funny** *Patty Duke*
32/81 **Say What** *Jesse Winchester*
Say Wonderful Things
81/63 *Patti Page*
91/63 *Ronnie Carroll*
40/64 **Say You** *Ronnie Dove*
11/76 **Say You Love Me** *Fleetwood Mac*
58/69 **Say You Love Me** *Impressions*
98/76 **Say You Love Me** *D.J. Rogers*
1/85 **Say You, Say Me** *Lionel Richie*
20/81 **Say You'll Be Mine** *Christopher Cross*
15/77 **Say You'll Stay Until Tomorrow**
Tom Jones
39/65 **(Say) You're My Girl** *Roy Orbison*
21/85 **Say You're Wrong** *Julian Lennon*
94/80 **Scandal** *RCR*
Scarborough Fair
11/68 *Simon & Garfunkel*
16/68 *Sergio Mendes & Brasil '66*
94/83 **Scarlet Fever** *Kenny Rogers*
13/59 **Scarlet Ribbons (For Her Hair)** *Browns*
89/63 **Scarlett O'Hara** *Lawrence Welk*
98/63 **Scavenger, The** *Dick Dale*
33/75 **School Boy Crush** *Average White Band*
3/57 **School Day** *Chuck Berry*
28/61 **School Is In** *Gary U.S. Bonds*
5/61 **School Is Out** *Gary U.S. Bonds*
91/72 **School Teacher**
Kenny Rogers & The First Edition
School's Out
7/72 *Alice Cooper*
67/86 *Krokus*
80/85 **Scientific Love** *Midnight Star*
6/72 **Scorpio** *Dennis Coffey*
81/62 **Scotch And Soda** *Kingston Trio*
75/76 **Scotch On The Rocks**
Band Of The Black Watch
69/61 **Scottish Soldier (Green Hills of Tyrol)**
Andy Stewart
81/74 **Scratch** *Crusaders*
80/64 **Scratchy** *Travis Wammack*
62/70 **Screaming Night Hog** *Steppenwolf*
63/85 **Screams Of Passion** *Family*
Sea Cruise
14/59 *Frankie Ford*
84/71 *Johnny Rivers*
21/61 **Sea Of Heartbreak** *Don Gibson*
Sea Of Love
2/59 *Phil Phillips with The Twilights*
33/82 *Del Shannon*
3/85 *Honeydrippers*
Sealed With A Kiss
3/62 *Brian Hyland*
19/68 *Gary Lewis & The Playboys*
19/72 *Bobby Vinton*
4/85 **Search Is Over** *Survivor*
96/59 **Search, The** *Dean Reed*
Searchin'
3/57 *Coasters*
83/61 *Jack Eubanks*
84/64 *Ace Cannon*
63/76 *Jim Croce (medley)*
81/55 **Searching** *Hilltoppers*
58/78 **Searching For A Thrill** *Starbuck*
27/66 **Searching For My Love** *Bobby Moore*
94/62 **Searching Is Over** *Joe Henderson*
59/77 **Seaside Woman** *Suzy & The Red Stripes*
65/68 **Season Of The Witch** *Vanilla Fudge*
75/81 **Seasons** *Charles Fox*
95/80 **Seasons** *Grace Slick*
1/74 **Seasons In The Sun** *Terry Jacks*
82/82 **Seasons Of Gold**
Gidea Park featuring Adrian Baker
78/82 **Seasons Of The Heart** *John Denver*
38/69 **Seattle** *Perry Como*
Second Avenue
34/74 *Garfunkel*
58/74 *Tim Moore*
40/56 **Second Fiddle** *Kay Starr*
63/62 **Second Fiddle Girl** *Barbara Lynn*
7/62 **Second Hand Love** *Connie Francis*
32/66 **Second Hand Rose** *Barbra Streisand*
79/60 **Second Honeymoon** *Johnny Cash*
39/85 **Second Nature** *Dan Hartman*
8/80 **Second Time Around** *Shalamar*

50/61 **Second Time Around** *Frank Sinatra*
18/58 **Secret, The** *Gordon MacRae*
63/86 **Secret** *Orchestral Manoeuvres In The Dark*
Secret Agent Man
3/66 *Johnny Rivers*
54/66 *Ventures*
46/82 **Secret Journey** *Police*
Secret Love
29/66 *Billy Stewart*
99/66 *Richard 'Groove' Holmes*
20/75 *Freddy Fender*
3/86 **Secret Lovers** *Atlantic Starr*
88/60 **Secret Of Love** *Elton Anderson*
19/86 **Secret Separation** *Fixx*
62/74 **Secretary** *Betty Wright*
Secretly
3/58 *Jimmie Rodgers*
64/65 *Lettermen*
76/81 **Secrets** *Mac Davis*
Security
97/64 *Otis Redding*
35/68 *Etta James*
72/81 **Seduced** *Leon Redbone*
28/80 **Seduction** *James Last*
27/69 **See** *Rascals*
See Me, Feel Me
12/70 *Who*
29/73 *New Seekers (medley)*
F/69 **See Ruby Fall** *Johnny Cash*
See Saw
44/65 *Don Covay*
14/68 *Aretha Franklin*
See Saw
25/56 *Moonglows*
57/56 *Don Cornell*
See See *see: C.C.*
9/64 **See The Funny Little Clown**
Bobby Goldsboro
95/70 **See The Light** *Flame*
89/85 **See What Love Can Do** *Eric Clapton*
69/65 **See You At The 'Go-Go'** *Dobie Gray*
See You In September
23/59 *Tempos*
3/66 *Happenings*
6/56 **See You Later, Alligator**
Bill Haley & His Comets
66/77 **See You When I Git There** *Lou Rawls*
46/65 **Seein' The Right Love Go Wrong**
Jack Jones
44/70 **Seeker, The** *Who*
50/70 **Seems Like I Gotta Do Wrong** *Whispers*
4/84 **Self Control** *Laura Branigan*
11/64 **Selfish One** *Jackie Ross*
72/73 **Send A Little Love My Way** *Anne Murray*
6/57 **Send For Me** *Nat King Cole*
96/62 **Send For Me (If you need some Lovin')**
Barbara George
23/83 **Send Her My Love** *Journey*
Send In The Clowns
36/75 *Judy Collins*
19/77 *Judy Collins*
29/84 **Send Me An Angel** *Real Life*
Send Me Some Lovin'
54/57 *Little Richard*
13/63 *Sam Cooke*
Send Me The Pillow You Dream On
77/58 *Hank Locklin*
56/60 *Browns*
17/62 *Johnny Tillotson*
22/65 *Dean Martin*
94/68 **Send My Baby Back** *Freddie Hughes*
4/79 **Send One Your Love** *Stevie Wonder*
56/81 **Sensitive Kind** *Santana*
8/78 **Sentimental Lady** *Bob Welch*
8/85 **Sentimental Street** *Night Ranger*
87/60 **Senza Mamma (With No One)**
Connie Francis
1/85 **Separate Lives**
Phil Collins & Marilyn Martin
20/73 **Separate Ways** *Elvis Presley*
96/59 **Separate Ways** *Sarah Vaughan*
8/83 **Separate Ways (Worlds Apart)** *Journey*
8/79 **September** *Earth, Wind & Fire*
23/61 **September In The Rain** *Dinah Washington*
17/80 **September Morn'** *Neil Diamond*
51/63 **September Song** *Jimmy Durante*
23/80 **Sequel** *Harry Chapin*
82/60 **Serenata** *Sarah Vaughan*
Sergeant *see: Sgt.*
99/59 **Sermonette** *Della Reese*
13/78 **Serpentine Fire** *Earth, Wind & Fire*
23/65 **Set Me Free** *Kinks*
27/80 **Set Me Free** *Utopia*
71/81 **Set The Night On Fire** *Oak*
79/66 **Set You Free This Time** *Byrds*
56/63 **Settle Down (Goin' Down That Highway)**
Peter, Paul & Mary
33/66 **7 And 7 Is** *Love*
21/81 **Seven Bridges Road** *Eagles*
95/61 **Seven Day Fool** *Etta James*
27/62 **Seven Day Weekend** *Gary U.S. Bonds*
Seven Days
17/56 *Dorothy Collins*
18/56 *Crew-Cuts*
44/56 *Clyde McPhatter*
30/58 **'7-11' (Mambo No. 5)** *Gone All Stars*
45/65 **Seven Letters** *Ben E. King*
9/59 **Seven Little Girls Sitting In The Back Seat** *Paul Evans*
71/75 **Seven Lonely Nights** *Four Tops*
85/58 **Seven Minutes In Heaven** *Poni-Tails*
14/67 **7 Rooms Of Gloom** *Four Tops*
46/75 **7-6-5-4-3-2-1 (Blow Your Whistle)**
Gary Toms Empire
88/82 **777-9311** *Time*
22/81 **Seven Year Ache** *Rosanne Cash*
84/69 **Seven Years** *Impressions*
7/65 **Seventh Son** *Johnny Rivers*
Seventeen
3/55 *Fontane Sisters*
5/55 *Boyd Bennett*
18/55 *Rusty Draper*
72/61 *Frankie Ford*
36/84 **17** *Rick James*
96/68 **7:30 Guided Tour** *Five Americans*
69/59 **77 Sunset Strip** *Don Ralke*
28/86 **Sex As A Weapon** *Pat Benatar*
62/83 **Sex (I'm A...)** *Berlin*
Sex Machine
15/70 *James Brown*
61/75 *James Brown*
85/84 **Sex Shooter** *Apollonia 6*
81/84 **Sexcrime (Nineteen Eighty-Four)**
Eurythmics
3/83 **Sexual Healing** *Marvin Gaye*
42/75 **Sexy** *MFSB*
Sexy + 17 *see: (She's)*
5/80 **Sexy Eyes** *Dr. Hook*
20/84 **Sexy Girl** *Glenn Frey*
65/74 **Sexy Ida** *Ike & Tina Turner*
17/74 **Sexy Mama** *Moments*
50/73 **Sexy, Sexy, Sexy** *James Brown*
71/78 **Sgt. Pepper's Lonely Hearts Club Band (medley)** *Beatles*
Sha-La-La
69/64 *Shirelles*
12/65 *Manfred Mann*
7/74 **Sha-La-La (Make Me Happy)** *Al Green*

91/75 **Shackin' Up** *Barbara Mason*
53/81 **Shaddap You Face** *Joe Dolce*
88/70 **Shades Of Green** *Flaming Ember*
1/78 **Shadow Dancing** *Andy Gibb*
94/68 **Shadow Of Your Love** *Five Stairsteps*
Shadow Of Your Smile
95/65 *Tony Bennett*
93/67 *Boots Randolph*
87/59 **Shadows** *Five Satins*
25/79 **Shadows In The Moonlight** *Anne Murray*
83/60 **Shadows Of Love** *LaVern Baker*
13/82 **Shadows Of The Night** *Pat Benatar*
19/62 **Shadrack** *Brook Benton*
Shaft *see: Theme From*
53/59 **Shag (Is Totally Cool)** *Billy Graves*
38/64 **Shaggy Dog** *Mickey Lee Lane*
Shake
7/65 *Sam Cooke*
47/67 *Otis Redding*
46/68 **Shake** *Shadows Of Knight*
Shake A Hand
71/58 *Mike Pedicin Quintet*
97/62 *Ruth Brown*
42/63 *Jackie Wilson & Linda Hopkins*
Shake A Tail Feather
51/63 *Five Du-Tones*
25/67 *James & Bobby Purify*
60/78 **Shake And Dance With Me** *Con Funk Shun*
29/65 **Shake And Fingerpop** *Jr. Walker & The All Stars*
92/66 **Shake Hands (And Come Out Crying)** *Newbeats*
95/67 **Shake Hands And Walk Away Cryin'** *Lou Christie*
13/79 **Shake It** *Ian Matthews*
4/82 **Shake It Up** *Cars*
70/81 **Shake It Up Tonight** *Cheryl Lynn*
76/77 **Shake It Well** *Dramatics*
42/63 **Shake Me I Rattle (Squeeze Me I Cry)** *Marion Worth*
18/66 **Shake Me, Wake Me (When It's Over)** *Four Tops*
98/72 **Shake Off The Demon** *Brewer & Shipley*
31/67 **Shake, Rattle & Roll** *Arthur Conley*
33/63 **Shake! Shake! Shake!** *Jackie Wilson*
1/76 **(Shake, Shake, Shake) Shake Your Booty** *KC & The Sunshine Band*
43/63 **Shake Sherry** *Contours*
1/87 **Shake You Down** *Gregory Abbott*
7/79 **Shake Your Body (Down To The Ground)** *Jacksons*
5/79 **Shake Your Groove Thing** *Peaches & Herb*
23/77 **Shake Your Rump To The Funk** *Bar-Kays*
31/79 **Shakedown Cruise** *Jay Ferguson*
90/78 **Shaker Song** *Spyro Gyra*
Shakey Ground
26/75 *Temptations*
70/77 *Phoebe Snow*
63/82 **Shakin'** *Eddie Money*
22/65 **Shakin' All Over** *Guess Who*
Shambala
3/73 *Three Dog Night*
66/73 *B.W. Stevenson*
9/78 **Shame** *Evelyn 'Champagne' King*
21/85 **Shame** *Motels*
Shame On Me
23/62 *Bobby Bare*
76/67 *Chuck Jackson*
2/83 **Shame On The Moon** *Bob Seger*
29/68 **Shame, Shame** *Magic Lanterns*
12/75 **Shame, Shame, Shame** *Shirley & Company*
52/63 **Shame, Shame, Shame** *Jimmy Reed*
47/80 **Shandi** *Kiss*
31/82 **Shanghai Breezes** *John Denver*
Shangri-La
11/57 *Four Coins*
15/64 *Robert Maxwell*
27/64 *Vic Dana*
64/69 *Lettermen*
57/84 **Shangri-La** *Steve Miller Band*
6/76 **Shannon** *Henry Gross*
80/59 **Shape I'm In** *Johnny Restivo*
Shape Of Things To Come
22/68 *Max Frost*
67/79 **Shape Of Things To Come** *Headboys*
11/66 **Shapes Of Things** *Yardbirds*
10/70 **Share The Land** *Guess Who*
Share Your Love With Me
42/64 *Bobby Bland*
13/69 *Aretha Franklin*
14/81 *Kenny Rogers*
91/81 **Sharing The Love** *Rufus/Chaka Khan*
6/79 **Sharing The Night Together** *Dr. Hook*
15/62 **Sharing You** *Bobby Vee*
97/66 **Sharing You** *Mitty Collier*
56/83 **Sharp Dressed Man** *ZZ Top*
31/79 **Shattered** *Rolling Stones*
30/75 **Shaving Cream** *Benny Bell*
45/60 **Shazam!** *Duane Eddy*
23/70 **She** *Tommy James & The Shondells*
80/74 **She** *Southcote*
5/79 **She Believes In Me** *Kenny Rogers*
33/70 **She Belongs To Me** *Rick Nelson*
45/66 **She Blew A Good Thing** *Poets*
5/83 **She Blinded Me With Science** *Thomas Dolby*
3/84 **She Bop** *Cyndi Lauper*
47/74 **She Called Me Baby** *Charlie Rich*
30/70 **She Came In Through The Bathroom Window** *Joe Cocker*
19/62 **She Can't Find Her Keys** *Paul Petersen*
She Cried
5/62 *Jay & The Americans*
65/66 *Shangri-Las (He Cried)*
73/70 *Lettermen*
She Did It
23/77 *Eric Carmen*
69/81 *Michael Damian*
46/71 **She Didn't Do Magic** *Lobo*
70/70 **She Didn't Know (She Kept On Talking)** *Dee Dee Warwick*
48/84 **She Don't Know Me** *Bon Jovi*
71/66 **She Drives Me Out Of My Mind** *Swingin' Medallions*
57/82 **She Got The Goldmine (I Got The Shaft)** *Jerry Reed*
27/67 **She Is Still A Mystery** *Lovin' Spoonful*
She Lets Her Hair Down (Early In The Morning)
61/70 *Tokens*
89/70 *Gene Pitney*
67/82 **She Looks A Lot Like You** *Clocks*
84/84 **She Loves My Car** *Ronnie Milsap*
54/78 **She Loves To Be In Love** *Charlie*
She Loves You
1/64 *Beatles*
97/64 *Beatles (Sie Liebt Dich)*
93/61 **She Really Loves You** *Timi Yuro*
68/70 **She Said Yes** *Wilson Pickett*
18/59 **She Say (Oom Dooby Doom)** *Diamonds*
95/67 **She Shot A Hole In My Soul** *Clifford Curry*
F/77 **She Thinks I Still Care** *Elvis Presley*
92/67 **She Took You For A Ride** *Aaron Neville*
She Understands Me
31/64 *Johnny Tillotson*
40/66 *Bobby Vinton (Dum-De-Da)*
50/64 **She Wants T' Swim** *Chubby Checker*
44/84 **She Was Hot** *Rolling Stones*

27/58 **She Was Only Seventeen (He Was One Year More)** *Marty Robbins*
3/83 **She Works Hard For The Money** *Donna Summer*
3/67 **She'd Rather Be With Me** *Turtles*
99/68 **She'll Be There** *Vikki Carr*
47/63 **She'll Never Know** *Brenda Lee*
22/81 **She's A Bad Mama Jama (She's Built, She's Stacked)** *Carl Carlton*
10/83 **She's A Beauty** *Tubes*
5/63 **She's A Fool** *Lesley Gore*
16/68 **She's A Heartbreaker** *Gene Pitney*
2/71 **She's A Lady** *Tom Jones*
84/69 **She's A Lady** *John Sebastian*
25/68 **She's A Rainbow** *Rolling Stones*
75/83 **She's A Runner** *Billy Squier*
83/62 **She's A Troublemaker** *Majors*
She's A Very Lovely Woman
94/67 *Merry-Go-Round*
70/71 *Linda Ronstadt*
4/64 **She's A Woman** *Beatles*
She's About A Mover
13/65 *Sir Douglas Quintet*
97/68 *Otis Clay*
She's All I Got
39/71 *Freddie North*
91/71 *Johnny Paycheck*
17/78 **She's Always A Woman** *Billy Joel*
58/65 **She's Coming Home** *Zombies*
18/62 **She's Everything (I Wanted You To Be)** *Ral Donner*
She's Gone
50/74 *Tavares*
60/74 *Daryl Hall & John Oates*
7/76 *Daryl Hall & John Oates*
23/82 **She's Got A Way** *Billy Joel*
87/79 **She's Got A Whole Number** *Keith Herman*
56/63 **She's Got Everything** *Essex*
83/69 **She's Got Love** *Thomas & Richard Frost*
93/73 **She's Got To Be A Saint** *Ray Price*
14/62 **She's Got You** *Patsy Cline*
41/80 **She's In Love With You** *Suzi Quatro*
95/77 **(She's Just A) Fallen Angel** *Starz*
99/60 **She's Just A Whole Lot Like You** *Hank Thompson*
3/66 **She's Just My Style** *Gary Lewis & The Playboys*
15/68 **She's Lookin' Good** *Wilson Pickett*
21/84 **She's Mine** *Steve Perry*
98/60 **She's Mine** *Conway Twitty*
14/67 **She's My Girl** *Turtles*
99/64 **She's My Girl** *Bobby Shafto*
38/58 **She's Neat** *Dale Wright*
11/71 **She's Not Just Another Woman** *8th Day*
She's Not There
2/64 *Zombies*
27/77 *Santana*
5/62 **She's Not You** *Elvis Presley*
10/80 **She's Out Of My Life** *Michael Jackson*
72/70 **She's Ready** *Spiral Starecase*
5/83 **(She's) Sexy + 17** *Stray Cats*
26/80 **She's So Cold** *Rolling Stones*
(She's) Some Kind Of Wonderful
see: Some Kind
47/84 **She's Strange** *Cameo*
33/64 **She's The One** *Chartbusters*
65/82 **She's Tight** *Cheap Trick*
65/84 **She's Trouble** *Musical Youth*
92/65 **She's With Her Other Love** *Leon Haywood*
81/77 **Sheena Is A Punk Rocker** *Ramones*
54/58 **Sheik Of Araby (Italian Style)** *Lou Monte*
1/62 **Sheila** *Tommy Roe*
91/86 **Shelter Me** *Joe Cocker*
17/64 **Shelter Of Your Arms** *Sammy Davis, Jr.*
Sherry
1/62 *4 Seasons*
70/80 *Robert John*
84/76 **Sherry** *Keane Brothers*
52/68 **Sherry Don't Go** *Lettermen*
Shifting, Whispering Sands
3/55 *Rusty Draper*
5/55 *Billy Vaughn*
24/70 **Shilo** *Neil Diamond*
42/60 **Shimmy Like Kate** *Olympics*
Shimmy Shimmy
37/60 *Bobby Freeman*
66/64 *Orlons*
24/60 **Shimmy, Shimmy, Ko-Ko-Bop** *Little Anthony & The Imperials*
88/62 **Shimmy, Shimmy Walk** *Megatons*
8/79 **Shine A Little Love** *Electric Light Orchestra*
40/81 **Shine On** *L.T.D.*
41/82 **Shine On** *George Duke*
37/84 **Shine Shine** *Barry Gibb*
11/74 **Shinin' On** *Grand Funk*
1/75 **Shining Star** *Earth, Wind & Fire*
5/80 **Shining Star** *Manhattans*
74/83 **Shiny Shiny** *Haysi Fantayzee*
Ship That Never Sailed
65/57 *David Carroll*
95/57 *Billy Vaughn*
71/83 **Ship To Shore** *Chris DeBurgh*
9/79 **Ships** *Barry Manilow*
58/63 **Shirl Girl** *Wayne Newton*
82/59 **Shirley** *John Fred*
91/57 **Shirley** *Schoolboys*
10/57 **Shish-Kebab** *Ralph Marterie*
81/80 **Shiver And Shake** *Silencers*
80/74 **Sho Nuff Boogie** *Sylvia & The Moments*
84/85 **Shock** *Motels*
29/83 **Shock The Monkey** *Peter Gabriel*
68/74 **Shoe Shoe Shine** *Dynamic Superiors*
67/71 **Shoes** *Brook Benton*
92/75 **Shoes** *Reparata*
18/75 **Shoeshine Boy** *Eddie Kendricks*
9/68 **Shoo-Be-Doo-Be-Doo-Da-Day** *Stevie Wonder*
(also see: Shu)
Shoop Shoop Song (It's In His Kiss)
6/64 *Betty Everett*
49/77 *Kate Taylor*
50/83 **Shoot For The Moon** *Poco*
66/55 **Shoot It Again** *Teresa Brewer*
91/79 **Shoot Me (With Your Love)** *Tasha Thomas*
44/67 **Shoot Your Shot** *Jr. Walker & The All Stars*
31/68 **Shoot'em Up, Baby** *Andy Kim*
83/84 **Shooting Shark** *Blue Oyster Cult*
74/80 **Shooting Star** *Dollar*
Shop Around
2/61 *Miracles*
4/76 *Captain & Tennille*
(also see: Don't Let Him Shop Around)
83/60 **Shoppin' For Clothes** *Coasters*
77/83 **Shoppin' From A To Z** *Toni Basil*
5/57 **Short Fat Fannie** *Larry Williams*
2/78 **Short People** *Randy Newman*
3/58 **Short Shorts** *Royal Teens*
Shortnin' Bread
82/60 *Paul Chaplain*
96/60 *Bell Notes*
68/86 **Shot In The Dark** *Ozzy Osbourne*
97/64 **Shot In The Dark** *Henry Mancini*
Shotgun
4/65 *Jr. Walker & The All Stars*
68/69 *Vanilla Fudge*

Shotgun Rider
71/80 *Joe Sun*
70/81 *Delbert McClinton*
88/75 **Shotgun Shuffle** *Sunshine Band*
42/61 **Should I** *String-A-Longs*
13/82 **Should I Do It** *Pointer Sisters*
82/83 **Should I Love You** *Cee Farrow*
45/82 **Should I Stay Or Should I Go** *Clash*
50/83 **Should I Stay Or Should I Go?** *Clash*
F/58 **Should We Tell Him** *Everly Brothers*
19/80 **Should've Never Let You Go** *Neil & Dara Sedaka*
1/85 **Shout** *Tears For Fears*
Shout
47/59 *Isley Brothers*
6/62 *Joey Dee & The Starliters*
94/62 *Isley Brothers*
94/64 *Lulu*
96/67 *Lulu*
83/69 *Chambers Brothers*
Shout *see: (Come On)*
61/62 **Shout And Shimmy** *James Brown*
54/67 **Shout Bamalama** *Mickey Murray*
Shout It Out Loud
31/76 *Kiss*
54/78 *Kiss (Live)*
6/62 **Shout! Shout! (Knock Yourself Out)** *Ernie Maresca*
1/74 **Show And Tell** *Al Wilson*
61/73 **Show Biz Kids** *Steely Dan*
45/67 **Show Business** *Lou Rawls*
28/84 **Show Me** *Pretenders*
35/67 **Show Me** *Joe Tex*
52/72 **Show Me How** *Emotions*
6/76 **Show Me The Way** *Peter Frampton*
4/74 **Show Must Go On** *Three Dog Night*
37/85 **Show Some Respect** *Tina Turner*
89/68 **Show Time** *Detroit Emeralds*
28/77 **Show You The Way To Go** *Jacksons*
Showdown
53/74 *Electric Light Orchestra*
71/75 *Odia Coates*
59/76 *Electric Light Orchestra*
22/76 **Shower The People** *James Taylor*
96/57 **Shrine Of St. Cecilia** *Faron Young*
38/75 **(Shu-Doo-Pa-Poo-Poop) Love Being Your Fool** *Travis Wammack*
32/61 **Shu Rah** *Fats Domino*
23/63 **Shut Down** *Beach Boys*
24/63 **Shutters And Boards** *Jerry Wallace*
71/61 **Shy Away** *Jerry Fuller*
83/83 **Shy Boy (Don't It Make You Feel Good)** *Bananarama*
91/63 **Shy Girl** *Cascades*
22/58 **Sick And Tired** *Fats Domino*
76/83 **Side By Side** *Earth, Wind & Fire*
84/60 **Side Car Cycle** *Charlie Ryan*
8/74 **Sideshow** *Blue Magic*
25/64 **Sidewalk Surfin'** *Jan & Dean*
18/86 **Sidewalk Talk** *Jellybean*
81/65 **Sidewinder, The** *Lee Morgan*
Sie Liebt Dich *see: She Loves You*
32/84 **Sign Of Fire** *Fixx*
57/81 **Sign Of The Gypsy Queen** *April Wine*
11/66 **Sign Of The Times** *Petula Clark*
75/83 **Sign Of The Times** *Belle Stars*
Signed, Sealed And Delivered
91/61 *Rusty Draper*
77/63 *James Brown*
18/77 **Signed, Sealed, Delivered (I'm Yours)** *Peter Frampton*
3/70 **Signed, Sealed, Delivered I'm Yours** *Stevie Wonder*
3/71 **Signs** *Five Man Electrical Band*
96/65 **Silence, The (Il Silenzio)** *Al Hirt*
11/67 **Silence Is Golden** *Tremeloes*
68/57 **Silent Lips** *Georgia Gibbs*
Silent Night
54/57 *Bing Crosby*
54/60 *Bing Crosby*
99/62 *Mahalia Jackson*
6/86 **Silent Running (On Dangerous Ground)** *Mike + The Mechanics*
Silhouettes
3/57 *Rays*
10/57 *Diamonds*
63/57 *Steve Gibson*
5/65 *Herman's Hermits*
53/81 **Silly** *Deniece Williams*
81/62 **Silly Boy (She Doesn't Love You)** *Lettermen*
87/64 **Silly Little Girl** *Tams*
1/76 **Silly Love Songs** *Wings*
71/74 **Silly Milly** *Blue Swede*
92/64 **Silly Ol' Summertime** *New Christy Minstrels*
76/70 **Silly, Silly, Fool** *Dusty Springfield*
63/73 **Silly Wasn't I** *Valerie Simpson*
78/57 **Silver Bells** *Bing Crosby & Carol Richards*
25/70 **Silver Bird** *Mark Lindsay*
20/55 **Silver Dollar** *Teresa Brewer*
53/78 **Silver Dreams** *Babys*
95/76 **Silver Heels** *Blaze*
52/77 **Silver Lady** *David Soul*
62/79 **Silver Lining** *Player*
42/71 **Silver Moon** *Michael Nesmith*
38/76 **Silver Star** *4 Seasons*
Silver Threads And Golden Needles
20/62 *Springfields*
54/65 *Jody Miller*
74/69 *Cowsills*
67/74 *Linda Ronstadt*
4/68 **Simon Says** *1910 Fruitgum Co.*
91/65 **Simpel Gimpel** *Horst Jankowski*
81/84 **Simple** *Johnny Mathis*
90/72 **Simple Game** *Four Tops*
56/72 **Simple Man** *Lobo*
Simple Song Of Freedom
50/69 *Tim Hardin*
84/72 *Buckwheat*
75/70 **Simply Call It Love** *Gene Chandler*
Since I Don't Have You
12/59 *Skyliners*
47/64 *Chuck Jackson*
F/70 *Eddie Holman*
53/79 *Art Garfunkel*
23/81 *Don McLean*
Since I Fell For You
4/63 *Lenny Welch*
76/72 *Laura Lee*
71/76 *Charlie Rich*
96/77 *Hodges, James & Smith (medley)*
78/64 **Since I Found A New Love** *Little Johnny Taylor*
17/65 **Since I Lost My Baby** *Temptations*
90/66 **Since I Lost The One I Love** *Impressions*
93/60 **Since I Made You Cry** *Rivieras*
Since I Met You Baby
12/56 *Ivory Joe Hunter*
34/57 *Mindy Carson*
81/60 *Bobby Vee*
65/69 *Sonny James*
45/75 *Freddy Fender*
Since You Been Gone
46/78 *Head East*
57/79 *Rainbow*
32/67 **Since You Showed Me How To Be Happy** *Jackie Wilson*

41/82 **Since You're Gone** *Cars*
38/59 **Since You've Been Gone** *Clyde McPhatter*
95/79 **Since You've Been Gone**
Cherie & Marie Currie
Since You've Been Gone
see: (Sweet Sweet Baby)
Sincerely
1/55 *McGuire Sisters*
20/55 *Moonglows*
75/64 *4 Seasons*
80/69 *Paul Anka*
Sing
94/72 *Barbra Streisand (medley)*
3/73 *Carpenters*
58/77 **Sing** *Dawn*
Sing A Simple Song
89/69 *Sly & The Family Stone*
89/82 *West Street Mob*
5/76 **Sing A Song** *Earth, Wind & Fire*
55/70 **Sing A Song For Freedom** *Frijid Pink*
91/67 **Sing Along With Me** *Tommy Roe*
24/58 **Sing Boy Sing** *Tommy Sands*
41/79 **Sing For The Day** *Styx*
83/71 **Sing High - Sing Low** *Anne Murray*
66/77 **Sing It, Shout It** *Starz*
54/83 **Sing Me Away** *Night Ranger*
99/70 **Sing Out The Love (In My Heart)** *Arkade*
46/58 **Sing Sing Sing** *Bernie Lowe Orchestra*
56/58 **Singing Hills** *Billy Vaughn*
75/69 **Singing My Song** *Tammy Wynette*
Singing The Blues
1/56 *Guy Mitchell*
17/56 *Marty Robbins*
12/66 **Single Girl** *Sandy Posey*
3/60 **Sink The Bismarck** *Johnny Horton*
54/65 **Sinner Man** *Trini Lopez*
71/79 **Sinner Man** *Sarah Dash*
82/56 **Sinner Man** *Les Baxter*
87/65 **Sins Of A Family** *P.F. Sloan*
62/66 **Sippin' 'N Chippin'** *T-Bones*
1/77 **Sir Duke** *Stevie Wonder*
5/84 **Sister Christian** *Night Ranger*
1/75 **Sister Golden Hair** *America*
53/73 **Sister James** *Nino Tempo & 5th Ave. Sax*
24/74 **Sister Mary Elephant (Shudd-Up!)**
Cheech & Chong
18/85 **Sisters Are Doin' It For Themselves**
Eurythmics & Aretha Franklin
86/80 **Sisters Of The Moon** *Fleetwood Mac*
36/67 **Sit Down, I Think I Love You** *Mojo Men*
65/68 **Sit With The Guru** *Strawberry Alarm Clock*
37/71 **Sit Yourself Down** *Stephen Stills*
Sittin' In The Balcony
18/57 *Eddie Cochran*
38/57 *Johnny Dee*
96/72 **Sittin' On A Time Bomb (Waitin' For The Hurt To Come)** *Honey Cone*
(Sittin' On) The Dock Of The Bay
1/68 *Otis Redding*
84/68 *King Curtis*
42/69 *Dells*
66/69 *Sergio Mendes & Brasil '66*
65/79 *Sammy Hagar*
55/82 *Reddings*
16/73 **Sitting** *Cat Stevens*
27/83 **Sitting At The Wheel** *Moody Blues*
74/78 **Sitting In Limbo** *Don Brown*
24/65 **Sitting In The Park** *Billy Stewart*
73/82 **Situation** *Yaz*
62/59 **Six Boys And Seven Girls** *Anita Bryant*
32/63 **Six Days On The Road** *Dave Dudley*
47/68 **Six Man Band** *Association*
28/59 **Six Nights A Week** *Crests*
18/67 **Six O'Clock** *Lovin' Spoonful*

93/77 **Six Packs A Day** *Billy Lemmons*
13/66 **634-5789 (Soulsville, U.S.A.)**
Wilson Pickett
(also see: Beechwood 4-5789)
79/70 **Six White Horses** *Tommy Cash*
2/59 **16 Candles** *Crests*
Sixteen Reasons
3/60 *Connie Stevens*
65/76 *LaVerne & Shirley*
Sixteen Tons
1/55 *Tennessee Ernie Ford*
17/55 *Johnny Desmond*
68/67 *Tom Jones*
47/76 *Don Harrison Band*
6/82 **'65 Love Affair** *Paul Davis*
65/73 **Sixty Minute Man** *Clarence Carter*
71/67 **Skate Now** *Lou Courtney*
58/81 **Skateaway** *Dire Straits*
50/59 **Ski King** *E.C. Beatty*
13/74 **Skin Tight** *Ohio Players*
10/67 **Skinny Legs And All** *Joe Tex*
22/58 **Skinny Minnie** *Bill Haley & His Comets*
25/68 **Skip A Rope** *Henson Cargill*
70/60 **Skokiaan (South African Song)**
Bill Haley & His Comets
3/75 **Sky High** *Jigsaw*
14/68 **Sky Pilot** *Animals*
49/75 **Skybird** *Dawn*
75/74 **Skybird** *Neil Diamond*
92/57 **Skyliner** *Carmen McRae*
50/72 **Slaughter** *Billy Preston*
35/64 **Slaughter On Tenth Avenue** *Ventures*
1/86 **Sledgehammer** *Peter Gabriel*
13/60 **Sleep** *Little Willie John*
1/59 **Sleep Walk** *Santo & Johnny*
70/74 **Sleepin'** *Diana Ross*
8/85 **Sleeping Bag** *ZZ Top*
Sleeping Beauty *see: To A*
74/82 **Sleepwalk** *Larry Carlton*
48/77 **Sleepwalker** *Kinks*
54/61 **Sleepy-Eyed John** *Johnny Horton*
61/68 **Sleepy Joe** *Herman's Hermits*
65/60 **Sleepy Lagoon** *Platters*
65/73 **Slick** *Willie Hutch*
32/77 **Slide** *Slave*
70/67 **Slim Jenkin's Place** *Booker T. & The MG's*
6/68 **Slip Away** *Clarence Carter*
50/79 **Slip Away** *Ian Lloyd*
75/81 **Slip Away** *Pablo Cruise*
48/64 **Slip-In Mules (No High Heel Sneakers)**
Sugar Pie DeSanto
5/78 **Slip Slidin' Away** *Paul Simon*
Slipin' And Slidin'
33/56 *Little Richard*
96/64 *Jim & Monica*
96/67 *Willie Mitchell*
84/71 **Slipped, Tripped And Fell In Love**
Clarence Carter
19/75 **Slippery When Wet** *Commodores*
81/73 **Slippin' Away** *Jean Shepard*
16/72 **Slippin' Into Darkness** *War*
39/83 **Slipping Away** *Dave Edmunds*
70/80 **Slipstream** *Allan Clarke*
Sloop John B
64/60 *Jimmie Rodgers*
3/66 *Beach Boys*
(Slop, The) *see: Hard Times*
97/63 **Slop Time** *Sherrys*
82/84 **Slow Dancin'** *Peabo Bryson*
20/77 **Slow Dancin' Don't Turn Me On**
Addrisi Brothers
Slow Dancing (Swayin' To The Music)
10/77 *Johnny Rivers*
61/77 *Funky Kings*

25/64 **Slow Down** *Beatles*
54/68 **Slow Drag** *Intruders*
2/81 **Slow Hand** *Pointer Sisters*
78/73 **Slow Motion** *Johnny Williams*
20/76 **Slow Ride** *Foghat*
3/62 **Slow Twistin'** *Chubby Checker*
Slow Walk
17/56 *Sil Austin*
26/57 *Bill Doggett*
34/77 **Slowdown** *John Miles*
88/69 **Slum Baby** *Booker T. & The MG's*
30/70 **Sly, Slick, And The Wicked** *Lost Generation*
52/64 **Smack Dab In The Middle** *Ray Charles*
F/71 **Smackwater Jack** *Carole King*
29/72 **Small Beginnings** *Flash*
87/80 **Small Paradise** *John Cougar*
21/62 **Small Sad Sam** *Phil McLean*
6/85 **Small Town** *John Cougar Mellencamp*
64/85 **Small Town Girl** *John Cafferty*
20/59 **Small World** *Johnny Mathis*
48/85 **Smalltown Boy** *Bronski Beat*
56/73 **Smarty Pants** *First Choice*
56/68 **Smell Of Incense** *Southwest F.O.B.*
Smile
73/59 *Tony Bennett*
42/61 *Timi Yuro*
94/62 *Ferrante & Teicher*
42/65 *Jerry Butler & Betty Everett*
5/69 **Smile A Little Smile For Me** *Flying Machine*
34/83 **Smile Has Left Your Eyes** *Asia*
21/55 **Smiles** *Crazy Otto*
42/72 **Smilin'** *Sly & The Family Stone*
3/71 **Smiling Faces Sometimes** *Undisputed Truth*
52/83 **Smiling Islands** *Robbie Patton*
9/77 **Smoke From A Distant Fire** *Sanford/Townsend Band*
Smoke Gets In Your Eyes
94/58 *Richard Barrett*
1/59 *Platters*
27/73 *Blue Haze*
4/73 **Smoke On The Water** *Deep Purple*
94/73 **Smoke! Smoke! Smoke! (That Cigarette)** *Commander Cody*
79/55 **Smokey Joe's Cafe** *Robins*
77/66 **Smokey Joe's La La** *Googie Rene Combo*
Smokie
17/60 *Bill Black's Combo*
95/60 *Bill Doggett*
Smokin' In The Boy's Room
3/74 *Brownsville Station*
16/85 *Motley Crue*
91/75 **Smokin' Room** *Carl Carlton*
24/81 **Smoky Mountain Rain** *Ronnie Milsap*
12/62 **Smoky Places** *Corsairs*
5/85 **Smooth Operator** *Sade*
44/59 **Smooth Operator** *Sarah Vaughan*
12/85 **Smuggler's Blues** *Glenn Frey*
27/68 **Snake, The** *Al Wilson*
67/81 **Snake Eyes** *Alan Parsons Project*
91/81 **Snap Shot** *Slave*
Snap Your Fingers
8/62 *Joe Henderson*
71/64 *Barbara Lewis*
31/69 **Snatching It Back** *Clarence Carter*
58/75 **Sneakin' Up Behind You** *Brecker Brothers*
55/75 **Sneaky Snake** *Tom T. Hall*
F/75 **Snookeroo** *Ringo Starr*
85/68 **Snoopy For President** *Royal Guardsmen*
2/66 **Snoopy Vs. The Red Baron** *Royal Guardsmen*
(also see: Return Of The Red Baron)
60/71 **Snow Blind Friend** *Steppenwolf*
66/66 **Snow Flake** *Jim Reeves*
8/70 **Snowbird** *Anne Murray*
84/55 **Snowbound For Christmas** *DeCastro Sisters*
23/84 **So Bad** *Paul McCartney*
38/59 **So Close** *Brook Benton*
40/83 **So Close** *Diana Ross*
49/70 **So Close** *Jake Holmes*
52/62 **So Deep** *Brenda Lee*
54/70 **So Excited** *B.B. King*
14/71 **So Far Away** *Carole King*
19/86 **So Far Away** *Dire Straits*
91/64 **So Far Away** *Hank Jacobs*
43/86 **So Far So Good** *Sheena Easton*
11/59 **So Fine** *Fiestas*
76/82 **So Fine** *Oak Ridge Boys*
94/74 **So Good** *Eleventh Hour*
30/79 **So Good, So Right** *Brenda Russell*
36/69 **So Good Together** *Andy Kim*
62/78 **So Hard Livin' Without You** *Airwaves*
89/77 **So High (Rock Me Baby And Roll Me Away)** *Dave Mason*
52/59 **So High So Low** *LaVern Baker*
39/69 **So I Can Love You** *Emotions*
26/85 **So In Love** *Orchestral Manoeuvres In The Dark*
67/75 **So In Love** *Curtis Mayfield*
7/77 **So In To You** *Atlanta Rhythm Section*
So-Long
44/56 *Fats Domino*
48/78 **So Long** *Firefall*
86/65 **So Long Babe** *Nancy Sinatra*
28/61 **So Long Baby** *Del Shannon*
56/64 **So Long Dearie** *Louis Armstrong*
44/72 **So Long Dixie** *Blood, Sweat & Tears*
72/57 **So Long I'm Gone** *Warren Smith*
74/57 **So Long, My Love** *Frank Sinatra*
81/72 **So Many People** *Chase*
6/59 **So Many Ways** *Brook Benton*
87/58 **So Much** *Little Anthony & The Imperials*
So Much In Love
1/63 *Tymes*
59/82 *Timothy B. Schmit*
51/70 **So Much Love** *Faith, Hope & Charity*
So Much Love
92/66 *Steve Alaimo*
96/66 *Ben E. King*
2/57 **So Rare** *Jimmy Dorsey*
47/76 **So Sad The Song** *Gladys Knight & The Pips*
7/60 **So Sad (To Watch Good Love Go Bad)** *Everly Brothers*
100/57 **So Strange** *Jesters*
21/62 **So This Is Love** *Castells*
So Tough
42/58 *Original Casuals*
76/58 *Kuf-Linx*
17/73 **So Very Hard To Go** *Tower Of Power*
So What
78/62 *Bill Black's Combo*
89/65 *Bill Black's Combo*
30/83 **So Wrong** *Patrick Simmons*
85/62 **So Wrong** *Patsy Cline*
21/74 **So You Are A Star** *Hudson Brothers*
58/84 **So You Ran** *Orion The Hunter*
29/67 **So You Want To Be A Rock 'N' Roll Star** *Byrds*
31/77 **So You Win Again** *Hot Chocolate*
So Young
68/57 *Clyde Stacy*
99/59 *Clyde Stacy*
81/78 **So Young, So Bad** *Starz*
91/64 **Society Girl** *Rag Dolls*

14/67 **Society's Child (Baby I've Been Thinking)** *Janis Ian*
6/67 **Sock It To Me-Baby!** *Mitch Ryder & The Detroit Wheels*
71/67 **Sockin' 1-2-3-4** *John Roberts*
35/57 **Soft** *Bill Doggett*
92/78 **Soft And Wet** *Prince*
73/57 **Soft Sands** *Chordettes*
Soft Summer Breeze
11/56 *Eddie Heywood*
34/56 *Diamonds*
27/64 **Softly, As I Leave You** *Frank Sinatra*
F/55 **Softly, Softly** *Jaye P. Morgan*
29/72 **Softly Whispering I Love You** *English Congregation*
1/62 **Soldier Boy** *Shirelles*
Soldier Boy *see: To A*
87/59 **Soldier's Joy** *Hawkshaw Hawkins*
90/71 **Soldier's Last Letter** *Merle Haggard*
58/64 **Sole Sole Sole** *Siw Malmkvist/Umberto Marcato*
12/85 **Solid** *Ashford & Simpson*
71/83 **Solid Rock** *Goanna*
7/83 **Solitaire** *Laura Branigan*
17/75 **Solitaire** *Carpenters*
52/80 **Solitaire** *Peter McIan*
Solitary Man
55/66 *Neil Diamond*
21/70 *Neil Diamond*
100/76 *T.G. Sheppard*
91/71 **Solo** *Billie Sans*
Solsbury Hill
68/77 *Peter Gabriel*
84/83 *Peter Gabriel*
96/71 **Solution For Pollution** *Watts 103rd St. Band*
92/70 **Some Beautiful** *Jack Wild*
65/81 **Some Changes Are For Good** *Dionne Warwick*
94/57 **Some Day Soon** *Eddie Fisher*
34/64 **Some Day We're Gonna Love Again** *Searchers*
36/81 **Some Days Are Diamonds (Some Days Are Stone)** *John Denver*
Some Enchanted Evening
13/65 *Jay & The Americans*
91/77 *Jane Olivor*
Some Guys Have All The Luck
39/73 *Persuaders*
10/84 *Rod Stewart*
37/59 **Some Kind-A Earthquake** *Duane Eddy*
26/83 **Some Kind Of Friend** *Barry Manilow*
Some Kind Of Wonderful
91/67 *Soul Brothers Six*
87/68 *Fantastic Johnny C*
3/75 *Grand Funk*
32/61 **Some Kind Of Wonderful** *Drifters*
43/63 **Some Kinda Fun** *Chris Montez*
6/85 **Some Like It Hot** *Power Station*
64/71 **Some Of Shelly's Blues** *Nitty Gritty Dirt Band*
Some People
67/85 *Belouis Some*
65/86 *Paul Young*
18/85 **Some Things Are Better Left Unsaid** *Daryl Hall & John Oates*
30/68 **Some Things You Never Get Used To** *Supremes*
26/68 **Some Velvet Morning** *Nancy Sinatra & Lee Hazlewood*
11/85 **Somebody** *Bryan Adams*
53/68 **Somebody Cares** *Tommy James & The Shondells*
53/65 **Somebody Else Is Taking My Place** *Al Martino*
75/84 **Somebody Else's Guy** *Jocelyn Brown*
70/62 **Somebody Have Mercy** *Sam Cooke*
47/67 **Somebody Help Me** *Spencer Davis Group*
53/66 **Somebody Like Me** *Eddy Arnold*
48/86 **Somebody Like You** *38 Special*
72/69 **Somebody Loves You** *Delfonics*
94/73 **Somebody Loves You** *Whispers*
93/64 **Somebody New** *Chuck Jackson*
55/81 **Somebody Send My Baby Home** *Lenny LeBlanc*
82/86 **Somebody Somewhere** *Platinum Blonde*
55/66 **Somebody (Somewhere) Needs You** *Darrell Banks*
71/81 **Somebody Special** *Rod Stewart*
86/64 **Somebody Stole My Dog** *Rufus Thomas*
5/67 **Somebody To Love** *Jefferson Airplane*
13/77 **Somebody To Love** *Queen*
45/60 **Somebody To Love** *Bobby Darin*
22/58 **Somebody Touched Me** *Buddy Knox*
18/56 **Somebody Up There Likes Me** *Perry Como*
7/82 **Somebody's Baby** *Jackson Browne*
8/70 **Somebody's Been Sleeping** *100 Proof Aged In Soul*
33/76 **Somebody's Gettin' It** *Johnnie Taylor*
96/83 **Somebody's Gonna Love You** *Lee Greenwood*
13/81 **Somebody's Knockin'** *Terri Gibbs*
27/86 **Somebody's Out There** *Triumph*
95/67 **Somebody's Sleeping In My Bed** *Johnnie Taylor*
2/84 **Somebody's Watching Me** *Rockwell*
32/71 **Somebody's Watching You** *Little Sister*
7/87 **Someday** *Glass Tiger*
57/74 **Someday** *Dave Loggins*
Someday *also see: Some Day*
85/76 **Someday (I Didn't Want To Have To Be The One)** *Henry Gross*
81/69 **Someday Man** *Monkees*
25/72 **Someday Never Comes** *Creedence Clearwater Revival*
Someday, Someway
76/81 *Robert Gordon*
36/82 *Marshall Crenshaw*
55/69 **Someday Soon** *Judy Collins*
1/69 **Someday We'll Be Together** *Supremes*
99/62 **Someday (When I'm Gone From You)** *Bobby Vee*
Someday You'll Want Me To Want You
95/58 *Jodie Sands*
56/60 *Della Reese*
93/60 *Brook Benton*
35/59 **Someone** *Johnny Mathis*
70/87 **Someone** *El DeBarge*
49/83 **Someone Belonging To Someone** *Bee Gees*
15/82 **Someone Could Lose A Heart Tonight** *Eddie Rabbitt*
89/65 **Someone Is Watching** *Solomon Burke*
75/84 **Someone Like You** *Michael Stanley Band*
91/60 **Someone Loves You, Joe** *Singing Belles*
77/55 **Someone On Your Mind** *Champ Butler with George Cates*
4/75 **Someone Saved My Life Tonight** *Elton John*
97/64 **Someone, Someone** *Brian Poole*
95/63 **Someone Somewhere** *Little Junior Parker*
21/80 **Someone That I Used To Love** *Natalie Cole*
78/59 **Someone To Come Home To** *Ames Brothers*
42/77 **Someone To Lay Down Beside Me** *Linda Ronstadt*
47/56 **Someone To Love** *Four Aces*
51/71 **Someone Who Cares** *Kenny Rogers & The First Edition*

13/55 **Someone You Love** *Nat King Cole*
37/77 **Somethin' 'Bout 'Cha** *Latimore*
42/80 **Somethin' 'Bout You Baby I Like** *Glen Campbell & Rita Coolidge*
58/59 **Somethin' Else** *Eddie Cochran*
1/67 **Somethin' Stupid** *Nancy & Frank Sinatra*
Something
1/69 *Beatles*
55/70 *Shirley Bassey*
76/70 *Booker T. & The MG's*
85/74 *Johnny Rodriguez*
7/86 **Something About You** *Level 42*
Something About You
19/65 *Four Tops*
48/77 *LeBlanc & Carr*
13/75 **Something Better To Do** *Olivia Newton-John*
74/67 **Something Good (Is Going To Happen To You)** *Carla Thomas*
41/60 **Something Happened** *Paul Anka*
28/76 **Something He Can Feel** *Aretha Franklin*
79/66 **Something I Want To Tell You** *Johnny & The Expressions*
37/69 **Something In The Air** *Thunderclap Newman*
77/63 **Something Old, Something New** *Paul & Paula*
47/83 **Something To Grab For** *Ric Ocasek*
Something You Got
52/64 *Alvin Robinson*
63/64 *Ramsey Lewis*
55/65 *Chuck Jackson & Maxine Brown*
11/70 **Something's Burning** *Kenny Rogers & The First Edition*
37/62 **Something's Got A Hold On Me** *Etta James*
Something's Gotta Give
5/55 *McGuire Sisters*
9/55 *Sammy Davis, Jr.*
88/68 **Something's Missing** *Five Stairsteps*
98/69 **Something's On Her Mind** *4 Seasons*
79/84 **Something's On Your Mind** *'D' Train*
12/72 **Something's Wrong With Me** *Austin Roberts*
53/61 **Sometime** *Gene Thomas*
31/77 **Sometimes** *Facts Of Life*
36/80 **Sometimes A Fantasy** *Billy Joel*
43/66 **Sometimes Good Guys Don't Wear White** *Standells*
86/64 **Sometimes I Wish I Were A Boy** *Lesley Gore*
64/64 **Sometimes I Wonder** *Major Lance*
3/78 **Sometimes When We Touch** *Dan Hill*
56/63 **Sometimes You Gotta Cry A Little** *Bobby Bland*
19/64 **Somewhere** *Tymes*
Somewhere
91/65 *P.J. Proby*
26/66 *Len Barry*
43/86 *Barbra Streisand*
67/61 **Somewhere Along The Way** *Steve Lawrence*
81/74 **Somewhere Between Love And Tomorrow** *Roy Clark*
21/82 **Somewhere Down The Road** *Barry Manilow*
70/80 **Somewhere In America** *Survivor*
Somewhere In The Night
69/75 *Batdorf & Rodney*
19/76 *Helen Reddy*
9/79 *Barry Manilow*
32/65 **Somewhere In Your Heart** *Frank Sinatra*
Somewhere, My Love
9/66 *Ray Conniff*
65/66 *Roger Williams (Lara's Theme)*
2/87 **Somewhere Out There** *Linda Ronstadt*
32/66 **Somewhere There's A Someone** *Dean Martin*
76/61 **Son-In-Law** *Louise Brown*
79/61 **Son-In-Law** *Blossoms*
61/69 **Son Of A Lovin' Man** *Buchanan Brothers*
Son Of A Preacher Man
10/69 *Dusty Springfield*
F/70 *Aretha Franklin*
92/69 **Son Of A Travelin' Man** *Ed Ames*
40/68 **Son Of Hickory Holler's Tramp** *O.C. Smith*
Son Of My Father
46/72 *Giorgio*
91/72 *Chicory*
97/64 **Son Of Rebel Rouser** *Duane Eddy*
28/74 **Son Of Sagittarius** *Eddie Kendricks*
53/72 **Son Of Shaft** *Bar-Kays*
8/56 **Song For A Summer Night** *Mitch Miller*
82/71 **Song For You** *Andy Williams*
70/70 **Song From M*A*S*H** *Al DeLory*
49/73 **Song I'd Like To Sing** *Kris Kristofferson & Rita Coolidge*
14/70 **Song Of Joy** *Miguel Rios*
(also see: Joy)
F/57 **Song Of Raintree County** *Nat King Cole*
86/57 **Song Of The Barefoot Mailman** *Billy Leach*
11/55 **Song Of The Dreamer** *Eddie Fisher*
94/56 **Song Of The Sparrow** *Mitch Miller*
29/79 **Song On The Radio** *Al Stewart*
96/72 **Song Seller** *Raiders*
1/72 **Song Sung Blue** *Neil Diamond*
99/70 **Song That Never Comes** *Mama Cass*
25/78 **Songbird** *Barbra Streisand*
59/73 **Songman** *Cashman & West*
30/70 **Soolaimon (African Trilogy II)** *Neil Diamond*
77/63 **Soon (I'll Be Home Again)** *4 Seasons*
89/64 **Soon I'll Wed My Love** *John Gary*
9/71 **Sooner Or Later** *Grass Roots*
68/75 **Sooner Or Later** *Impressions*
84/63 **Sooner Or Later** *Johnny Mathis*
Soothe Me
42/61 *Sims Twins*
56/67 *Sam & Dave*
34/69 **Sophisticated Cissy** *Meters*
25/76 **Sophisticated Lady (She's A Different Lady)** *Natalie Cole*
71/77 **Sorry** *Grace Jones*
2/59 **Sorry (I Ran All The Way Home)** *Impalas*
6/76 **Sorry Seems To Be The Hardest Word** *Elton John*
56/69 **Sorry Suzanne** *Hollies*
Soul Coaxing *see: Ame Caline*
55/67 **Soul Dance Number Three** *Wilson Pickett*
18/69 **Soul Deep** *Box Tops*
95/64 **Soul Dressing** *Booker T. & The MG's*
85/68 **Soul Drippin'** *Mauds*
75/69 **Soul Experience** *Iron Butterfly*
17/67 **Soul Finger** *Bar-Kays*
99/65 **Soul Heaven** *Dixie Drifter*
Soul Hootenanny *see: Big Bass Man*
Soul Je T'aime *see: Je T'aime*
20/85 **Soul Kiss** *Olivia Newton-John*
17/68 **Soul Limbo** *Booker T. & The MG's*
Soul Makossa
35/73 *Manu Dibango*
47/73 *Afrique*
Soul Man
2/67 *Sam & Dave*
49/67 *Ramsey Lewis*
14/79 *Blues Brothers*
91/68 **Soul Meeting** *Soul Clan*
29/71 **Soul Power** *James Brown*
88/65 **Soul Sauce (Guacha Guaro)** *Cal Tjader*

Soul Serenade
51/64 *King Curtis*
23/68 *Willie Mitchell*
Soul Shake
37/69 *Peggy Scott & Jo Jo Benson*
43/70 *Delaney & Bonnie & Friends*
41/69 **Soul Sister, Brown Sugar** *Sam & Dave*
37/73 **Soul Song** *Joe Stampley*
67/67 **Soul Time** *Shirley Ellis*
90/68 **Soul Train** *Classics IV*
75/76 **Soul Train '75'** *Soul Train Gang*
17/62 **Soul Twist** *King Curtis*
3/69 **Soulful Strut** *Young-Holt Unlimited*
(also see: Am I The Same Girl)
23/83 **Souls** *Rick Springfield*
Soulville
92/63 *Dinah Washington*
83/68 *Aretha Franklin*
69/77 **Sound And Vision** *David Bowie*
57/68 **Sound Asleep** *Turtles*
84/83 **Sound Of Goodbye** *Crystal Gayle*
36/67 **Sound Of Love** *Five Americans*
90/60 **Sound Of Music** *Patti Page*
77/61 **Sound-Off** *Titus Turner*
Sounds Of Silence
1/66 *Simon & Garfunkel*
100/71 *Peaches & Herb*
94/85 **Sounds Of Your Voice** *Jon Butcher Axis*
80/82 **Soup For One** *Chic*
50/72 **Sour Suite** *Guess Who*
85/84 **so. Central Rain (I'm Sorry)** *R.E.M.*
3/63 **South Street** *Orlons*
29/75 **South's Gonna Do It** *Charlie Daniels Band*
99/72 **Southbound Train**
David Crosby/Graham Nash
18/82 **Southern Cross** *Crosby, Stills & Nash*
1/77 **Southern Nights** *Glen Campbell*
70/82 **Southern Pacific** *Neil Young*
15/64 **Southtown, U.S.A.** *Dixiebelles*
41/79 **Souvenirs** *Voyage*
30/83 **Space Age Love Song** *A Flock Of Seagulls*
52/83 **Space Age Whiz Kids** *Joe Walsh*
15/73 **Space Oddity** *David Bowie*
4/73 **Space Race** *Billy Preston*
23/72 **Spaceman** *Nilsson*
82/77 **Spaceship Superstar** *Prism*
40/85 **Spanish Eddie** *Laura Branigan*
15/66 **Spanish Eyes** *Al Martino*
(also see: Moon Over Naples)
27/66 **Spanish Flea** *Herb Alpert*
Spanish Harlem
10/61 *Ben E. King*
89/66 *King Curtis*
2/71 *Aretha Franklin*
31/62 **Spanish Lace** *Gene McDaniels*
99/66 **Spanish Nights And You** *Connie Francis*
100/70 **Sparkle And Shine** *Clique*
89/67 **Speak Her Name** *Walter Jackson*
(Speak Softly Love)
see: Love Theme From 'The Godfather'
14/72 **Speak To The Sky** *Rick Springfield*
38/69 **Special Delivery** *1910 Fruitgum Co.*
5/80 **Special Lady** *Ray, Goodman & Brown*
26/68 **Special Occasion** *Miracles*
64/72 **Special Someone** *Heywoods*
59/63 **Speed Ball** *Ray Stevens*
17/56 **Speedo** *Cadillacs*
6/62 **Speedy Gonzales** *Pat Boone*
93/77 **Spend Some Time** *Elvin Bishop*
91/80 **Spend The Night In Love** *4 Seasons*
40/83 **Spice Of Life** *Manhattan Transfer*
87/75 **Spider Jiving** *Andy Fairweather Low*
3/74 **Spiders & Snakes** *Jim Stafford*
7/86 **Spies Like Us** *Paul McCartney*

Spill The Wine
3/70 *Eric Burdon & War*
49/71 *Isley Brothers*
52/71 **Spinning Around (I Must Be Falling In Love)** *Main Ingredient*
Spinning Wheel
2/69 *Blood, Sweat & Tears*
90/71 *James Brown*
40/66 **Spinout** *Elvis Presley*
23/70 **Spirit In The Dark** *Aretha Franklin*
Spirit In The Night
97/76 *Manfred Mann's Earth Band*
40/77 *Manfred Mann's Earth Band*
Spirit In The Sky
3/70 *Norman Greenbaum*
99/70 *Dorothy Morrison*
69/86 *Doctor & The Medics*
51/80 **Spirit Of Radio** *Rush*
35/75 **Spirit Of The Boogie** *Kool & The Gang*
11/82 **Spirits In The Material World** *Police*
3/58 **Splish Splash** *Bobby Darin*
Spooky
57/67 *Mike Sharpe*
3/68 *Classics IV*
17/79 *Atlanta Rhythm Section*
78/60 **Spoonful** *Etta & Harvey*
50/66 **Spread It On Thick** *Gentrys*
73/67 **Spreadin' Honey**
Watts 103rd Street Rhythm Band
94/63 **Spring** *Birdlegs & Pauline*
47/77 **Spring Affair** *Donna Summer*
92/63 **Spring In Manhattan** *Tony Bennett*
39/77 **Spring Rain** *Silvetti*
50/60 **Spring Rain** *Pat Boone*
94/68 **Springfield Plane** *Kenny O'Dell*
37/76 **Springtime Mama** *Henry Gross*
50/81 **Square Biz** *Teena Marie*
80/85 **Square Rooms** *Al Corley*
16/76 **Squeeze Box** *Who*
89/64 **Squeeze Her-Tease Her (But Love Her)**
Jackie Wilson
64/76 **St. Charles** *Jefferson Starship*
1/85 **St. Elmo's Fire (Man In Motion)** *John Parr*
(also see: Love Theme)
100/69 **St. Louis** *Easybeats*
13/56 **St. Therese Of The Roses**
Billy Ward & His Dominoes
80/86 **Stacy** *Fortune*
21/86 **Stages** *ZZ Top*
Stagger Lee
1/59 *Lloyd Price*
22/67 *Wilson Pickett*
25/71 *Tommy Roe*
68/58 **Stairway Of Love** *Marty Robbins*
9/60 **Stairway To Heaven** *Neil Sedaka*
89/86 **Stairway To Heaven** *Far Corporation*
22/69 **Stand!** *Sly & The Family Stone*
5/83 **Stand Back** *Stevie Nicks*
54/83 **Stand By** *Roman Holliday*
Stand By Me
4/61 *Ben E. King*
75/65 *Earl Grant*
12/67 *Spyder Turner*
61/70 *David & Jimmy Ruffin*
20/75 *John Lennon*
22/80 *Mickey Gilley*
50/85 *Maurice White*
9/86 *Ben E. King*
(also see: I'll Be There)
Stand By Your Man
19/69 *Tammy Wynette*
24/70 *Candi Staton*
95/66 **Stand In For Love** *O'Jays*
76/82 **Stand Or Fall** *Fixx*

10/77 **Stand Tall** *Burton Cummings*
83/70 **Standing (medley)** *Five Stairsteps*
37/74 **Standing At The End Of The Line** *Lobo*
74/72 **Standing In For Jody** *Johnnie Taylor*
6/67 **Standing In The Shadows Of Love** *Four Tops*
Standing On The Corner
3/56 *Four Lads*
22/56 *Dean Martin*
57/56 *Mills Brothers*
66/82 **Standing On The Top** *Temptations featuring Rick James*
29/74 **Star** *Stealers Wheel*
64/80 **Star** *Earth, Wind & Fire*
39/74 **Star Baby** *Guess Who*
68/60 **Star Is Born (A Love Has Died)** *Mark Dinning*
Star Is Born, Love Theme From A *see: Evergreen*
62/79 **Star Love** *Cheryl Lynn*
75/59 **Star Love** *Playmates*
47/75 **Star On A TV Show** *Stylistics*
50/68 **Star-Spangled Banner** *Jose Feliciano*
Star Wars Theme
1/77 *Meco*
10/77 *John Williams*
42/56 **Star You Wished Upon Last Night** *Gisele MacKenzie*
25/60 **Starbright** *Johnny Mathis*
Stardust
12/57 *Billy Ward & His Dominoes*
79/57 *Nat King Cole*
98/62 *Frank Sinatra*
32/64 *Nino Tempo & April Stevens*
59/80 **Stargazer** *Peter Brown*
80/61 **Starlight** *Preludes Five*
44/61 **Starlight, Starbright** *Linda Scott*
65/72 **Starman** *David Bowie*
77/59 **Starry Eyed** *Gary Stites*
56/79 **Starry Eyes** *Records*
87/75 **Stars In My Eyes** *Sugarloaf*
67/81 **Stars On 45 [Medley II]** *Stars on 45*
1/81 **Stars On 45 [Medley]** *Stars on 45*
28/82 **Stars On 45 III** *Stars on 45*
97/82 **Start It All Over** *McGuffey Lane*
2/81 **Start Me Up** *Rolling Stones*
9/57 **Start Movin' (In My Direction)** *Sal Mineo*
73/77 **Started Out Dancing, Ended Up Making Love** *Alan O'Day*
19/72 **Starting All Over Again** *Mel & Tim*
Starting Over *see: (Just Like)*
36/80 **Starting Over Again** *Dolly Parton*
41/82 **State Of Independence** *Donna Summer*
3/84 **State Of Shock** *Jacksons*
22/85 **State Of The Heart** *Rick Springfield*
81/83 **State Of The Nation** *Industry*
Stay
1/60 *Maurice Williams*
16/64 *4 Seasons*
20/78 *Jackson Browne*
38/78 **Stay** *Rufus/Chaka Khan*
90/58 **Stay** *Ames Brothers*
82/69 **Stay And Love Me All Summer** *Brian Hyland*
60/81 **Stay Awake** *Ronnie Laws*
67/68 **Stay Away ('Greensleeves' melody)** *Elvis Presley*
89/73 **Stay Away From Me** *Sylvers*
67/70 **Stay Away From Me (I Love You Too Much)** *Major Lance*
99/65 **Stay Away From My Baby** *Ted Taylor*
7/71 **Stay Awhile** *Bells*
Stay Awhile
38/64 *Dusty Springfield*
90/78 *Continental Miniatures*
55/80 **Stay Awhile (medley)** *Journey*
91/68 **Stay Close To Me** *Five Stairsteps*
10/68 **Stay In My Corner** *Dells*
51/80 **Stay In Time** *Off Broadway usa*
16/84 **Stay The Night** *Chicago*
24/87 **Stay The Night** *Benjamin Orr*
50/79 **Stay The Night** *Faragher Bros.*
66/67 **Stay Together Young Lovers** *Brenda & The Tabulations*
94/86 **Stay True** *Sly Fox*
17/72 **Stay With Me** *Faces*
64/66 **Stay With Me** *Lorraine Ellison*
81/64 **Stay With Me** *Frank Sinatra*
30/84 **Stay With Me Tonight** *Jeffrey Osborne*
1/78 **Stayin' Alive** *Bee Gees*
33/61 **Stayin' In** *Bobby Vee*
37/81 **Staying With It** *Firefall*
57/85 **Steady** *Jules Shear*
Steal Away
17/64 *Jimmy Hughes*
37/70 *Johnnie Taylor*
6/80 **Steal Away** *Robbie Dupree*
25/81 **Steal The Night** *Stevie Woods*
49/71 **Stealer** *Free*
91/73 **Stealin'** *Uriah Heep*
49/70 **Stealing In The Name Of The Lord** *Paul Kelly*
17/73 **Steamroller Blues** *Elvis Presley*
13/62 **Steel Guitar And A Glass Of Wine** *Paul Anka*
41/62 **Steel Men** *Jimmy Dean*
5/81 **Step By Step** *Eddie Rabbitt*
14/60 **Step By Step** *Crests*
37/73 **Step By Step** *Joe Simon*
81/72 **Step Out** *Mamas & The Papas*
24/67 **Step Out Of Your Mind** *American Breed*
39/78 **Steppin' In A Slide Zone** *Moody Blues*
6/82 **Steppin' Out** *Joe Jackson*
36/76 **Steppin' Out** *Neil Sedaka*
46/65 **Steppin' Out** *Paul Revere & The Raiders*
89/82 **Steppin' Out** *Kool & The Gang*
7/74 **Steppin' Out (Gonna Boogie Tonight)** *Dawn*
86/61 **Steps 1 And 2** *Jack Scott*
82/86 **Stereotomy** *Alan Parsons Project*
35/63 **Stewball** *Peter, Paul & Mary*
32/86 **Stick Around** *Julian Lennon*
25/61 **Stick Shift** *Duals*
11/71 **Stick-Up** *Honey Cone*
41/61 **Stick With Me Baby** *Everly Brothers*
40/60 **Sticks And Stones** *Ray Charles*
Still
1/79 *Commodores*
69/81 *John Schneider*
Still
8/63 *Bill Anderson*
98/63 *Ben Colder*
93/66 *Sunrays*
Still
86/56 *Fontane Sisters*
97/57 *LaVern Baker*
40/76 **Still Crazy After All These Years** *Paul Simon*
22/82 **Still In Saigon** *Charlie Daniels Band*
47/82 **Still In The Game** *Steve Winwood*
64/84 **Still Loving You** *Scorpions*
28/81 **Still Right Here In My Heart** *Pure Prairie League*
76/83 **Still Taking Chances** *Michael Murphey*
77/77 **Still The Lovin' Is Fun** *B.J. Thomas*
5/76 **Still The One** *Orleans*

4/78 **Still The Same** *Bob Seger*
19/82 **Still They Ride** *Journey*
11/70 **Still Water (Love)** *Four Tops*
89/62 **Still Waters Run Deep** *Brook Benton*
71/79 **Stillsane** *Carolyne Mas*
50/63 **Sting Ray** *Routers*
12/73 **Stir It Up** *Johnny Nash*
41/85 **Stir It Up** *Patti LaBelle*
50/70 **Stir It Up And Serve It** *Tommy Roe*
91/64 **Stockholm** *Lawrence Welk*
73/56 **Stolen Love** *Dinah Shore*
7/80 **Stomp!** *Brothers Johnson*
36/78 **Stone Blue** *Foghat*
40/82 **Stone Cold** *Rainbow*
65/77 **Stone Cold Sober** *Crawler*
77/70 **Stoned Cowboy** *Fantasy*
7/70 **Stoned Love** *Supremes*
30/73 **Stoned Out Of My Mind** *Chi-Lites*
3/68 **Stoned Soul Picnic** *5th Dimension*
58/74 **Stoned To The Bone** *James Brown*
14/71 **Stones** *Neil Diamond*
6/71 **Stoney End** *Barbra Streisand*
2/58 **Stood Up** *Ricky Nelson*
Stop!
98/66 *Moody Blues*
76/68 **Stop** *Howard Tate*
9/74 **Stop And Smell The Roses** *Mac Davis*
8/64 **Stop And Think It Over** *Dale & Grace*
92/67 **Stop! And Think It Over** *Perry Como*
Stop Doggin' Me Around
see: Doggin' Around
3/81 **Stop Draggin' My Heart Around**
Stevie Nicks with Tom Petty
80/66 **Stop! Get A Ticket** *Clefs Of Lavender Hill*
48/66 **Stop Her On Sight (S.O.S.)** *Edwin Starr*
Stop! In The Name Of Love
1/65 *Supremes*
96/71 *Margie Joseph*
29/83 *Hollies*
85/66 **Stop, Look And Listen** *Chiffons*
39/71 **Stop, Look, Listen (To Your Heart)**
Stylistics
92/65 **Stop! Look What You're Doing**
Carla Thomas
94/63 **Stop Monkeyin' Aroun'** *Dovells*
7/66 **Stop Stop Stop** *Hollies*
88/64 **Stop Takin' Me For Granted** *Mary Wells*
36/62 **Stop The Music** *Shirelles*
26/71 **Stop The War Now** *Edwin Starr*
34/62 **Stop The Wedding** *Etta James*
48/80 **Stop This Game** *Cheap Trick*
15/87 **Stop To Love** *Luther Vandross*
74/74 **Stop To Start** *Blue Magic*
91/73 **Stop, Wait & Listen** *Circus*
65/80 **Stop Your Sobbing** *Pretenders*
Stormy
5/68 *Classics IV*
32/79 *Santana*
43/62 **Stormy Monday Blues** *Bobby Bland*
23/71 **Story In Your Eyes** *Moody Blues*
15/58 **Story Of My Life** *Marty Robbins*
16/61 **Story Of My Love** *Paul Anka*
28/59 **Story Of My Love** *Conway Twitty*
93/59 **Story Of Our Love** *Johnny Mathis*
48/68 **Story Of Rock And Roll** *Turtles*
88/64 **Story Of) Woman, Love And A Man**
Tony Clarke
16/55 **Story Untold** *Crew-Cuts*
54/68 **Storybook Children** *Billy Vera & Judy Clay*
57/78 **Storybook Children (Daybreak)**
Bette Midler
92/67 **Stout-Hearted Men** *Barbra Streisand*
84/60 **Straight A's In Love** *Johnny Cash*
91/59 **Straight Flush** *Frantics*
10/83 **Straight From The Heart** *Bryan Adams*
39/81 **Straight From The Heart**
Allman Brothers Band
66/84 **Straight From The Heart (Into Your Life)** *Coyote Sisters*
36/68 **Straight Life** *Bobby Goldsboro*
15/78 **Straight On** *Heart*
29/74 **Straight Shootin' Woman** *Steppenwolf*
73/58 **Straighten Up & Fly Right** *DeJohn Sisters*
43/63 **Straighten Up Your Heart** *Barbara Lewis*
Stranded In The Jungle
15/56 *Cadets*
18/56 *Jayhawks*
39/56 *Gadabouts*
72/67 **Stranded In The Middle Of Noplace**
Righteous Brothers
97/62 **Strange** *Patsy Cline*
80/58 **Strange Are The Ways Of Love** *Gogi Grant*
70/63 **Strange Feeling** *Billy Stewart*
49/63 **Strange I Know** *Marvelettes*
14/76 **Strange Magic** *Electric Light Orchestra*
99/64 **Strange Things Happening**
Little Junior Parker
11/78 **Strange Way** *Firefall*
61/84 **Stranger** *Stephen Stills*
48/81 **Stranger** *Jefferson Starship*
90/60 **Stranger From Durango** *Richie Allen*
81/80 **Stranger In My Home Town** *Foghat*
23/83 **Stranger In My House** *Ronnie Milsap*
30/65 **Stranger In Town** *Del Shannon*
30/84 **Stranger In Town** *Toto*
83/64 **Stranger In Your Arms** *Bobby Vee*
70/63 **Stranger In Your Town** *Shacklefords*
Stranger On The Shore
1/62 *Mr. Acker Bilk*
38/62 *Andy Williams*
73/62 *Drifters*
54/84 **Strangers In A Strange World**
Jenny Burton & Patrick Jude
1/66 **Strangers In The Night** *Frank Sinatra*
93/56 **Strangest Romance** *Patti Page*
81/86 **Stranglehold** *Paul McCartney*
8/67 **Strawberry Fields Forever** *Beatles*
5/77 **Strawberry Letter 23** *Brothers Johnson*
39/68 **Strawberry Shortcake**
Jay & The Techniques
3/83 **Stray Cat Strut** *Stray Cats*
1/74 **Streak, The** *Ray Stevens*
56/82 **Street Corner** *Ashford & Simpson*
30/78 **Street Corner Serenade** *Wet Willie*
48/68 **Street Fighting Man** *Rolling Stones*
36/79 **Street Life** *Crusaders*
60/83 **Street Of Dreams** *Rainbow*
27/76 **Street Singin'** *Lady Flash*
56/76 **Street Talk** *B.C.G.*
61/86 **Strength** *Alarm*
String Along
39/60 *Fabian*
25/63 *Rick Nelson*
64/59 **String Of Trumpets** *Trumpeteers*
42/84 **Strip** *Adam Ant*
1/62 **Stripper, The** *David Rose*
17/81 **Stroke** *Billy Squier*
4/58 **Stroll, The** *Diamonds*
89/76 **Strong Enough To Be Gentle**
Black Oak Arkansas
30/81 **Stronger Than Before** *Carole Bayer Sager*
40/84 **Strung Out** *Steve Perry*
7/84 **Strut** *Sheena Easton*
22/75 **Struttin'** *Billy Preston*
68/76 **Struttin' My Stuff** *Elvin Bishop*
46/62 **Stubborn Kind Of Fellow** *Marvin Gaye*
6/73 **Stuck In The Middle With You**
Stealers Wheel

1/60 **Stuck On You** *Elvis Presley*
3/84 **Stuck On You** *Lionel Richie*
1/86 **Stuck With You** *Huey Lewis & The News*
21/78 **Stuff Like That** *Quincy Jones*
4/79 **Stumblin' In** *Suzi Quatro & Chris Norman*
14/58 **Stupid Cupid** *Connie Francis*
18/72 **Suavecito** *Malo*
62/77 **Sub-Rosa Subway** *Klaatu*
67/78 **Substitute** *Clout*
39/65 **Subterranean Homesick Blues** *Bob Dylan*
70/87 **Suburbia** *Pet Shop Boys*
Such A Day
89/56 *Rita Raines*
96/56 *Vera Lynn*
16/64 **Such A Night** *Elvis Presley*
42/73 **Such A Night** *Dr. John*
89/84 **Such A Shame** *Talk Talk*
99/66 **Such A Sweet Thing** *Mary Wells*
26/79 **Such A Woman** *Tycoon*
11/65 **(Such An) Easy Question** *Elvis Presley*
63/68 **Sudden Stop** *Percy Sledge*
4/85 **Suddenly** *Billy Ocean*
20/81 **Suddenly**
Olivia Newton-John & Cliff Richard
90/60 **Suddenly** *Nickey DeMatteo*
96/65 **Suddenly I'm All Alone** *Walter Jackson*
9/83 **Suddenly Last Summer** *Motels*
Suddenly There's A Valley
9/55 *Gogi Grant*
13/55 *Jo Stafford*
20/55 *Julius LaRosa*
45/55 *Mills Brothers*
69/55 *Patty Andrews*
44/68 **Suddenly You Love Me** *Tremeloes*
71/63 **Sue's Gotta Be Mine** *Del Shannon*
89/58 **Sugah Wooga** *Three Playmates*
Sugar And Spice
44/64 *Searchers*
49/66 *Cryan' Shames*
99/62 **Sugar Babe** *Buster Brown*
37/74 **Sugar Baby Love** *Rubettes*
80/61 **Sugar Bee** *Cleveland Crochet*
92/62 **Sugar Blues** *Ace Cannon*
10/72 **Sugar Daddy** *Jackson 5*
36/84 **Sugar Don't Bite** *Sam Harris*
32/65 **Sugar Dumpling** *Sam Cooke*
30/64 **Sugar Lips** *Al Hirt*
91/73 **Sugar Magnolia** *Grateful Dead*
5/58 **Sugar Moon** *Pat Boone*
22/69 **Sugar On Sunday** *Clique*
47/75 **Sugar Pie Guy** *Joneses*
95/62 **Sugar Plum** *Ike Clanton*
1/63 **Sugar Shack** *Jimmy Gilmer/Fireballs*
Sugar, Sugar
1/69 *Archies*
25/70 *Wilson Pickett*
5/66 **Sugar Town** *Nancy Sinatra*
9/85 **Sugar Walls** *Sheena Easton*
77/59 **Sugaree** *Rusty York*
94/72 **Sugaree** *Jerry Garcia*
1/58 **Sugartime** *McGuire Sisters*
21/69 **Suite: Judy Blue Eyes**
Crosby, Stills & Nash
97/72 **Suite: Man And Woman** *Tony Cole*
Sukiyaki
1/63 *Kyu Sakamoto*
3/81 *A Taste Of Honey*
4/79 **Sultans Of Swing** *Dire Straits*
7/76 **Summer** *War*
81/81 **Summer '81 (Beach Boys' medley)**
Cantina Band
65/67 **Summer And Sandy** *Lesley Gore*
Summer Breeze
6/72 *Seals & Crofts*
60/74 *Isley Brothers*
55/59 **Summer Dreams** *McGuire Sisters*
1/66 **Summer In The City** *Lovin' Spoonful*
97/57 **Summer Love** *Joni James*
F/75 **Summer Madness** *Kool & The Gang*
72/64 **Summer Means Fun** *Bruce & Terry*
Summer Night *see: Song For A*
5/78 **Summer Nights**
Olivia Newton-John & John Travolta
24/65 **Summer Nights** *Marianne Faithfull*
62/82 **Summer Nights** *Survivor*
Summer Of '42 *see: Theme From*
5/85 **Summer Of '69** *Bryan Adams*
Summer Place *see: Theme From A*
14/68 **Summer Rain** *Johnny Rivers*
26/66 **Summer Samba (So Nice)** *Walter Wanderley*
33/71 **Summer Sand** *Dawn*
30/60 **Summer Set** *Monty Kelly*
98/71 **Summer Side Of Life** *Gordon Lightfoot*
7/64 **Summer Song** *Chad & Jeremy*
58/65 **Summer Sounds** *Robert Goulet*
68/61 **Summer Souvenirs** *Karl Hammel, Jr.*
90/72 **Summer Sun** *Jamestown Massacre*
67/56 **Summer Sweetheart** *Ames Brothers*
21/73 **Summer (The First Time)** *Bobby Goldsboro*
Summer Wind
78/65 *Wayne Newton*
25/66 *Frank Sinatra*
49/67 **Summer Wine**
Nancy Sinatra & Lee Hazlewood
49/63 **Summer's Comin'** *Kirby St. Romain*
11/60 **Summer's Gone** *Paul Anka*
93/59 **Summer's Love** *Richard Barrett*
Summertime
81/57 *Sam Cooke*
78/61 *Marcels*
89/62 *Rick Nelson*
93/63 *Chris Columbo Quintet*
10/66 *Billy Stewart*
Summertime Blues
8/58 *Eddie Cochran*
14/68 *Blue Cheer*
27/70 *Who*
55/85 **Summertime Girls** *Y&T*
F/58 **Summertime Lies** *Four Preps*
Summertime, Summertime
26/58 *Jamies*
38/62 *Jamies*
Sun Ain't Gonna Shine (Anymore)
13/66 *Walker Bros.*
56/81 *Nielsen/Pearson*
20/86 **Sun Always Shines On T.V.** *A-Ha*
72/84 **Sun And The Rain** *Madness*
61/63 **Sun Arise** *Rolf Harris*
38/85 **Sun City** *Artists United Against Apartheid*
44/75 **Sun Goddess**
Ramsey Lewis and Earth, Wind & Fire
65/57 **Sun Is Shining** *Jimmy Reed*
96/76 **Sun...Sun...Sun** *Ja-Kki*
90/69 **Sunday** *Moments*
18/65 **Sunday And Me** *Jay & The Americans*
97/58 **Sunday Barbecue** *Tennessee Ernie Ford*
31/67 **Sunday For Tea** *Peter & Gordon*
Sunday Kind Of Love
95/62 *Jan & Dean*
96/72 *Lenny Welch*
Sunday Mornin'
30/68 *Spanky & Our Gang*
35/69 *Oliver*
Sunday Morning Coming Down
81/69 *Ray Stevens*
46/70 *Johnny Cash*

75/72 **Sunday Morning Sunshine** *Harry Chapin*
68/68 **Sunday Sun** *Neil Diamond*
98/75 **Sunday Sunrise** *Anne Murray*
9/67 **Sunday Will Never Be The Same** *Spanky & Our Gang*
1/74 **Sundown** *Gordon Lightfoot*
39/77 **Sunflower** *Glen Campbell*
7/84 **Sunglasses At Night** *Corey Hart*
2/66 **Sunny** *Bobby Hebb*
86/64 **Sunny** *Neil Sedaka*
14/66 **Sunny Afternoon** *Kinks*
34/72 **Sunny Days** *Lighthouse*
34/76 **Sunrise** *Eric Carmen*
84/67 **Sunrise, Sunset** *Roger Williams*
22/85 **Sunset Grill** *Don Henley*
81/70 **Sunset Strip** *Ray Stevens*
4/72 **Sunshine** *Jonathan Edwards*
45/77 **Sunshine** *Enchantment*
48/75 **Sunshine** *O'Jays*
57/70 **Sunshine** *Archies*
87/73 **Sunshine** *Mickey Newbury*
63/67 **Sunshine Games** *Music Explosion*
20/67 **Sunshine Girl** *Parade*
94/57 **Sunshine Girl** *Eddie Fisher*
69/84 **Sunshine In The Shade** *Fixx*
13/65 **Sunshine, Lollipops And Rainbows** *Lesley Gore*
5/68 **Sunshine Of Your Love** *Cream*
1/74 **Sunshine On My Shoulders** *John Denver*
79/74 **Sunshine Roses** *Gene Cotton*
1/66 **Sunshine Superman** *Donovan*
13/70 **Super Bad** *James Brown*
66/65 **Super-Cala-Fragil-Istic-Expi-Ali-Docious** *Julie Andrews - Dick Van Dyke*
31/73 **Super Fly Meets Shaft** *John & Ernest*
16/81 **Super Freak** *Rick James*
93/71 **Super Highway** *Ballin' Jack*
45/81 **Super Trouper** *Abba*
41/86 **Superbowl Shuffle** *Chicago Bears Shufflin' Crew*
8/73 **Superfly** *Curtis Mayfield*
(also see: Freddie's Dead)
Superman
41/77 *Celi Bee*
26/79 *Herbie Mann*
41/73 **Superman** *Donna Fargo*
64/70 **Superman** *Ides Of March*
94/66 **Superman** *Dino, Desi & Billy*
75/84 **Supernatural Love** *Donna Summer*
5/75 **Supernatural Thing** *Ben E. King*
70/78 **Supernature** *Cerrone*
2/71 **Superstar** *Carpenters*
Superstar - Jesus Christ Superstar
74/70 *Murray Head*
14/71 *Murray Head*
95/71 *Assembled Multitude*
35/76 **Superstar** *Paul Davis*
87/84 **Superstar (Don't you remember...)** *Luther Vandross*
18/71 **Superstar (Remember How You Got Where You Are)** *Temptations*
1/73 **Superstition** *Stevie Wonder*
33/72 **Superwoman (Where Were You When I Needed You)** *Stevie Wonder*
16/74 **Sure As I'm Sittin' Here** *Three Dog Night*
83/75 **Sure Feels Good** *Elvin Bishop*
9/66 **Sure Gonna Miss Her** *Gary Lewis & The Playboys*
47/79 **Sure Know Something** *Kiss*
1/63 **Surf City** *Jan & Dean*
55/63 **Surf Party** *Chubby Checker*
7/63 **Surfer Girl** *Beach Boys*
62/63 **Surfer Joe** *Surfaris*
93/63 **Surfer Street** *Allisons*
31/62 **Surfer's Stomp** *Mar-kets*
75/62 **Surfin** *Beach Boys*
4/64 **Surfin' Bird** *Trashmen*
(also see: Bird's The Word)
48/63 **Surfin' Hootenanny** *Al Casey*
14/62 **Surfin' Safari** *Beach Boys*
Surfin' U.S.A.
3/63 *Beach Boys*
36/74 *Beach Boys*
20/77 *Leif Garrett*
1/61 **Surrender** *Elvis Presley*
38/71 **Surrender** *Diana Ross*
62/78 **Surrender** *Cheap Trick*
77/80 **Survive** *Jimmy Buffett*
56/79 **Survivor** *Cindy Bullens*
11/68 **Susan** *Buckinghams*
Susie Darlin'
5/58 *Robin Luke*
35/62 *Tommy Roe*
3/64 **Suspicion** *Terry Stafford*
13/79 **Suspicions** *Eddie Rabbitt*
55/66 **Suspicions** *Sidekicks*
Suspicious Minds
1/69 *Elvis Presley*
80/71 *Dee Dee Warwick*
1/85 **Sussudio** *Phil Collins*
17/86 **Suzanne** *Journey*
56/67 **Suzanne** *Noel Harrison*
55/81 **Suzi** *Randy Vanwarmer*
77/59 **Suzie Baby** *Bobby Vee*
Suzie-Q
27/57 *Dale Hawkins*
11/68 *Creedence Clearwater Revival*
F/70 *Jose Feliciano*
39/73 **Swamp Witch** *Jim Stafford*
F/55 **Swanee** *Jaye P. Morgan*
34/57 **Swanee River Rock (Talkin' 'Bout That River)** *Ray Charles*
14/60 **Sway** *Bobby Rydell*
80/85 **Swear** *Sheena Easton*
6/75 **Swearin' To God** *Frankie Valli*
Sweet And Gentle
10/55 *Alan Dale*
12/55 *Georgia Gibbs*
7/71 **Sweet And Innocent** *Donny Osmond*
77/62 **Sweet And Lovely** *Nino Tempo & April Stevens*
100/59 **Sweet Annie Laurie** *Sammy Turner*
19/81 **Sweet Baby** *Stanley Clarke/George Duke*
92/72 **Sweet Baby** *Donnie Elbert*
96/59 **Sweet Bird Of Youth** *Nat King Cole*
13/68 **Sweet Blindness** *5th Dimension*
Sweet Caroline (Good Times Never Seemed So Good)
4/69 *Neil Diamond*
51/72 *Bobby Womack*
42/73 **Sweet Charlie Babe** *Jackie Moore*
7/69 **Sweet Cherry Wine** *Tommy James & The Shondells*
70/59 **Sweet Chile** *Sheb Wooley*
8/71 **Sweet City Woman** *Stampeders*
28/69 **Sweet Cream Ladies, Forward March** *Box Tops*
80/68 **Sweet Darlin'** *Martha & The Vandellas*
5/82 **Sweet Dreams** *Air Supply*
Sweet Dreams
93/60 *Don Gibson*
44/63 *Patsy Cline*
15/66 *Tommy McLain*
1/83 **Sweet Dreams (Are Made of This)** *Eurythmics*
91/58 **Sweet Elizabeth** *Will Glahe*
36/75 **Sweet Emotion** *Aerosmith*
60/70 **Sweet Feeling** *Candi Staton*

7/86 **Sweet Freedom** *Michael McDonald*
100/62 **Sweet Georgia Brown** *Carroll Bros.*
48/73 **Sweet Harmony** *Smokey Robinson*
42/56 **Sweet Heartaches** *Eddie Fisher*
6/71 **Sweet Hitch-Hiker** *Creedence Clearwater Revival*
8/74 **Sweet Home Alabama** *Lynyrd Skynyrd*
70/63 **Sweet Impossible You** *Brenda Lee*
Sweet Inspiration
18/68 *Sweet Inspirations*
37/72 *Barbra Streisand (medley)*
76/55 **Sweet Kentucky Rose** *Kitty Kallen*
17/78 **Sweet Life** *Paul Davis*
85/56 **Sweet Lips** *Jaye P. Morgan*
100/61 **Sweet Little Kathy** *Ray Peterson*
47/58 **Sweet Little Rock And Roll** *Chuck Berry*
Sweet Little Sixteen
2/58 *Chuck Berry*
95/62 *Jerry Lee Lewis*
59/61 **Sweet Little You** *Neil Sedaka*
91/73 **Sweet Lorraine** *Uriah Heep*
5/76 **Sweet Love** *Commodores*
8/86 **Sweet Love** *Anita Baker*
93/76 **Sweet Loving Man** *Morris Albert*
36/79 **Sweet Lui-Louise** *Ironhorse*
7/71 **Sweet Mary** *Wadsworth Mansion*
40/75 **Sweet Maxine** *Doobie Brothers*
75/68 **Sweet Memories** *Andy Williams*
80/81 **Sweet Merilee** *Donnie Iris*
44/78 **Sweet Music Man** *Kenny Rogers*
4/60 **Sweet Nothin's** *Brenda Lee*
7/56 **Sweet Old Fashioned Girl** *Teresa Brewer*
8/66 **Sweet Pea** *Tommy Roe*
9/72 **Sweet Seasons** *Carole King*
52/80 **Sweet Sensation** *Stephanie Mills*
93/72 **Sweet Sixteen** *B.B. King*
55/62 **Sweet Sixteen Bars** *Earl Grant*
87/59 **Sweet Someone** *Eddie & Betty*
Sweet Soul Music
2/67 *Arthur Conley*
90/67 *Magnificent Men (medley)*
33/75 **Sweet Sticky Thing** *Ohio Players*
83/57 **Sweet Stuff** *Guy Mitchell*
97/59 **Sweet Sugar Lips** *Kalin Twins*
77/79 **Sweet Summer Lovin'** *Dolly Parton*
94/76 **Sweet Summer Music** *Attitudes*
13/75 **Sweet Surrender** *John Denver*
15/72 **Sweet Surrender** *Bread*
73/85 **Sweet, Sweet Baby (I'm Falling)** *Lone Justice*
(Sweet Sweet Baby) Since You've Been Gone
5/68 *Aretha Franklin*
98/68 *Ramsey Lewis*
70/67 **Sweet, Sweet Lovin'** *Platters*
44/78 **Sweet, Sweet Smile** *Carpenters*
88/70 **Sweet Sweetheart** *Bobby Vee*
10/66 **Sweet Talkin' Guy** *Chiffons*
17/78 **Sweet Talkin' Woman** *Electric Light Orchestra*
5/76 **Sweet Thing** *Rufus Featuring Chaka Khan*
99/62 **Sweet Thursday** *Johnny Mathis*
26/82 **Sweet Time** *REO Speedwagon*
33/73 **Sweet Understanding Love** *Four Tops*
40/64 **Sweet William** *Millie Small*
29/66 **Sweet Woman Like You** *Joe Tex*
83/68 **Sweet Young Thing Like You** *Ray Charles*
52/69 **Sweeter He Is** *Soul Children*
96/69 **Sweeter Than Sugar** *Ohio Express*
9/59 **Sweeter Than You** *Ricky Nelson*
86/57 **Sweetest One** *Crests*
88/67 **Sweetest One** *Metros*
5/86 **Sweetest Taboo** *Sade*
7/82 **Sweetest Thing (I've Ever Known)** *Juice Newton*
32/67 **Sweetest Thing This Side Of Heaven** *Chris Bartley*
10/81 **Sweetheart** *Franke & The Knockouts*
47/70 **Sweetheart** *Engelbert Humperdinck*
98/58 **Sweetheart** *Peggy Lee*
55/84 **Sweetheart Like You** *Bob Dylan*
Sweets For My Sweet
16/61 *Drifters*
54/79 *Tony Orlando*
19/84 **Swept Away** *Diana Ross*
56/64 **S-W-I-M** *Bobby Freeman*
55/75 **Swing Your Daddy** *Jim Gilstrap*
43/83 **Swingin'** *John Anderson*
80/58 **Swingin' Daddy** *Buddy Knox*
79/60 **Swingin' Down The Lane** *Jerry Wallace*
44/62 **Swingin' Gently** *Earl Grant*
39/60 **Swingin' On A Rainbow** *Frankie Avalon*
13/62 **Swingin' Safari** *Billy Vaughn*
5/60 **Swingin' School** *Bobby Rydell*
Swingin' Shepherd Blues
23/58 *Moe Koffman Quartette*
43/58 *Johnny Pate Quintet*
47/58 *David Rose*
85/69 **Swingin' Tight** *Bill Deal*
38/63 **Swinging On A Star** *Big Dee Irwin*
52/57 **Swinging Sweethearts** *Ron Goodwin*
17/77 **Swingtown** *Steve Miller Band*
64/62 **Swiss Maid** *Del Shannon*
26/61 **Switch-A-Roo** *Hank Ballard*
93/69 **Switch It On** *Cliff Nobles & Co.*
43/80 **Switchin' To Glide** *Kings*
89/73 **Sylvia** *Focus*
5/72 **Sylvia's Mother** *Dr. Hook*
82/59 **Symphony** *Sammy Turner*
51/66 **Symphony For Susan** *Arbors*
16/83 **Synchronicity II** *Police*
37/76 **(System Of) Doctor Tarr And Professor Fether** *Alan Parsons Project*

T

24/60 **T.L.C. Tender Love And Care** *Jimmie Rodgers*
1/74 **TSOP (The Sound Of Philadelphia)** *MFSB featuring The Three Degrees*
64/76 **TVC 15** *David Bowie*
23/60 **Ta Ta** *Clyde McPhatter*
55/59 **Taboo** *Arthur Lyman*
64/64 **T'ain't Nothin' To Me** *Coasters*
8/82 **Tainted Love** *Soft Cell*
3/78 **Take A Chance On Me** *Abba*
90/73 **Take A Closer Look At The Woman You're With** *Wilson Pickett*
71/61 **Take A Fool's Advice** *Nat King Cole*
41/76 **Take A Hand** *Rick Springfield*
2/69 **Take A Letter Maria** *R.B. Greaves*
15/80 **Take A Little Rhythm** *Ali Thomson*
56/67 **Take A Look** *Aretha Franklin*
30/72 **Take A Look Around** *Temptations*
43/70 **Take A Look Around** *Smith*
16/59 **Take A Message To Mary** *Everly Brothers*
58/83 **Take Another Picture** *Quarterflash*
91/83 **Take Away** *Big Ric*
20/69 **Take Care Of Your Homework** *Johnnie Taylor*
25/61 **Take Five** *Dave Brubeck Quartet*

Take Good Care Of Her
7/61 *Adam Wade*
78/66 *Mel Carter*
F/74 *Elvis Presley*
Take Good Care Of My Baby
1/61 *Bobby Vee*
33/68 *Bobby Vinton*
10/82 **Take It Away** *Paul McCartney*
67/79 **Take It Back** *J. Geils Band*
12/72 **Take It Easy** *Eagles*
24/86 **Take It Easy** *Andy Taylor*
10/82 **Take It Easy On Me** *Little River Band*
33/76 **Take It Like A Man** *Bachman-Turner Overdrive*
94/70 **Take It Off Him And Put It On Me** *Clarence Carter*
5/81 **Take It On The Run** *REO Speedwagon*
64/72 **Take It Slow (Out In The Country)** *Lighthouse*
4/76 **Take It To The Limit** *Eagles*
53/76 **Take Me** *Grand Funk Railroad*
16/65 **Take Me Back** *Little Anthony & The Imperials*
46/84 **Take Me Back** *Bonnie Tyler*
47/57 **Take Me Back Baby** *Guy Mitchell*
97/72 **Take Me Bak 'Ome** *Slade*
63/78 **Take Me Back To Chicago** *Chicago*
47/56 **Take Me Back To Toyland** *Nat King Cole*
18/82 **Take Me Down** *Alabama*
Take Me For A Little While
89/67 *Patti LaBelle & The Blue Belles*
38/68 *Vanilla Fudge*
76/66 **Take Me For What I'm Worth** *Searchers*
50/71 **Take Me Girl, I'm Ready** *Jr. Walker & The All Stars*
7/86 **Take Me Home** *Phil Collins*
8/79 **Take Me Home** *Cher*
2/71 **Take Me Home, Country Roads** *John Denver*
4/86 **Take Me Home Tonight** *Eddie Money*
88/78 **Take Me I'm Yours** *Michael Henderson*
98/67 **Take Me In Your Arms And Love Me** *Gladys Knight & The Pips*
Take Me In Your Arms (Rock Me)
50/65 *Kim Weston*
11/75 *Doobie Brothers*
49/67 **Take Me (Just As I Am)** *Solomon Burke*
62/81 **Take Me Now** *David Gates*
14/83 **Take Me To Heart** *Quarterflash*
59/78 **Take Me To The Kaptin** *Prism*
Take Me To The River
48/75 *Syl Johnson*
26/79 *Talking Heads*
25/85 **Take Me With U** *Prince*
1/86 **Take My Breath Away** *Berlin*
91/71 **Take My Hand** *Kenny Rogers & The First Edition*
17/81 **Take My Heart (You Can Have It If You Want It)** *Kool & The Gang*
87/61 **Take My Love (I Want To Give It All To You)** *Little Willie John*
78/85 **Take No Prisoners (In The Game Of Love)** *Peabo Bryson*
16/82 **Take Off** *Bob & Doug McKenzie*
1/85 **Take On Me** *A-Ha*
66/66 **Take Some Time Out For Love** *Isley Brothers*
79/79 **Take That To The Bank** *Shalamar*
52/82 **Take The L.** *Motels*
10/79 **Take The Long Way Home** *Supertramp*
11/76 **Take The Money And Run** *Steve Miller*
41/83 **Take The Short Way Home** *Dionne Warwick*
81/83 **Take The Time** *Michael Stanley Band*
8/63 **Take These Chains From My Heart** *Ray Charles*
44/66 **Take This Heart Of Mine** *Marvin Gaye*
97/64 **Take This Hurt Off Me** *Don Covay*
11/68 **Take Time To Know Her** *Percy Sledge*
67/80 **Take You Tonight** *Ozark Mountain Daredevils*
3/80 **Take Your Time (Do It Right)** *S.O.S. Band*
32/86 **Taken In** *Mike + The Mechanics*
94/70 **Taker, The** *Waylon Jennings*
100/66 **Takin' All I Can Get** *Mitch Ryder & The Detroit Wheels*
12/74 **Takin' Care Of Business** *Bachman-Turner Overdrive*
92/80 **Takin' It Back** *Breathless*
79/78 **Takin' It Easy** *Seals & Crofts*
13/76 **Takin' It To The Streets** *Doobie Brothers*
50/84 **Taking It All Too Hard** *Genesis*
97/65 **Talk About Love** *Adam Faith*
7/64 **Talk Back Trembling Lips** *Johnny Tillotson*
57/71 **Talk It Over In The Morning** *Anne Murray*
85/59 **Talk Of The School** *Sonny James*
15/67 **Talk Talk** *Music Machine*
75/82 **Talk Talk** *Talk Talk*
34/60 **Talk That Talk** *Jackie Wilson*
4/86 **Talk To Me** *Stevie Nicks*
21/87 **Talk To Me** *Chico DeBarge*
38/59 **Talk To Me** *Frank Sinatra*
64/85 **Talk To Me** *Fiona*
83/85 **Talk To Me** *Quarterflash*
92/60 **Talk To Me Baby** *Annette*
94/64 **Talk To Me Baby** *Barry Mann*
Talk To Me, Talk To Me
20/58 *Little Willie John*
11/63 *Sunny & The Sunglows*
20/57 **Talkin' To The Blues** *Jim Lowe*
12/64 **Talking About My Baby** *Impressions*
60/68 **Talking About My Baby** *Gloria Walker*
3/84 **Talking In Your Sleep** *Romantics*
18/78 **Talking In Your Sleep** *Crystal Gayle*
64/71 **Talking In Your Sleep** *Gordon Lightfoot*
27/72 **Talking Loud And Saying Nothing** *James Brown*
65/81 **Talking Out Of Turn** *Moody Blues*
Tall Cool One
36/59 *Wailers*
38/64 *Wailers*
7/59 **Tall Paul** *Annette*
6/59 **Tallahassee Lassie** *Freddy Cannon*
Tammy
1/57 *Debbie Reynolds*
5/57 *Ames Brothers*
18/76 **Tangerine** *Salsoul Orchestra*
31/75 **Tangled Up In Blue** *Bob Dylan*
44/56 **Tango Of The Drums** *Les Baxter*
83/72 **Taos New Mexico** *R. Dean Taylor*
34/68 **Tapioca Tundra** *Monkees*
38/66 **Tar And Cement** *Verdelle Smith*
Taras Bulba *see: Theme From*
55/71 **Tarkio Road** *Brewer & Shipley*
13/86 **Tarzan Boy** *Baltimora*
Taste Of Honey
50/62 *Martin Denny*
88/62 *Victor Feldman Quartet*
94/64 *Tony Bennett*
7/65 *Herb Alpert*
87/64 **Taste Of Tears** *Johnny Mathis*
41/86 **Tasty Love** *Freddie Jackson*
18/72 **Taurus** *Dennis Coffey*
24/72 **Taxi** *Harry Chapin*
90/84 **Taxi** *J. Blackfoot*
59/84 **Taxi Dancing** *Rick Springfield & Randy Crawford*

70/56 **Te Amo** *Dick Jacobs*
53/61 **Te-Ta-Te-Ta-Ta** *Ernie K-Doe*
Tea For Two
7/58 *Tommy Dorsey (Cha Cha)*
56/64 *Nino Tempo & April Stevens*
86/59 **Teach Me Tiger** *April Stevens*
Teach Me Tonight
76/59 *DeCastro Sisters (Cha Cha)*
25/62 *George Maharis*
70/82 *Al Jarreau*
16/70 **Teach Your Children**
Crosby, Stills, Nash & Young
25/84 **Teacher Teacher** *38 Special*
51/81 **Teacher Teacher** *Rockpile*
21/58 **Teacher, Teacher** *Johnny Mathis*
56/58 **Teacher's Pet** *Doris Day*
31/61 **Tear, A** *Gene McDaniels*
23/59 **Tear Drop** *Santo & Johnny*
56/69 **Tear Drop City** *Monkees*
20/57 **Tear Drops** *Lee Andrews & The Hearts*
Tear Fell
5/56 *Teresa Brewer*
50/64 *Ray Charles*
44/61 **Tear Of The Year** *Jackie Wilson*
15/76 **Tear The Roof Off The Sucker (Give Up The Funk)** *Parliament*
Teardrops In My Heart
64/57 *Teresa Brewer*
63/61 *Joe Barry*
87/59 **Teardrops On Your Letter** *Hank Ballard*
61/59 **Teardrops Will Fall**
Dicky Doo & The Don'ts
37/84 **Tears** *John Waite*
59/66 **Tears** *Bobby Vinton*
71/62 **Tears And Laughter** *Dinah Washington*
20/64 **Tears And Roses** *Al Martino*
51/85 **Tears Are Falling** *Kiss*
77/62 **Tears From An Angel** *Troy Shondell*
96/65 **Tears Keep On Falling** *Jerry Vale*
1/70 **Tears Of A Clown** *Miracles*
85/63 **Tears Of Joy** *Chuck Jackson*
Tears On My Pillow
4/58 *Little Anthony & The Imperials*
59/61 *McGuire Sisters*
93/67 **Tears, Tears, Tears** *Ben E. King*
85/59 **Teasable, Pleasable You** *Buddy Knox*
70/66 **Teaser, The** *Bob Kuban*
39/59 **Teasin'** *Quaker City Boys*
97/65 **Teasin' You** *Willie Tee*
17/60 **Teddy** *Connie Francis*
40/76 **Teddy Bear** *Red Sovine*
32/73 **Teddy Bear Song** *Barbara Fairchild*
66/76 **Teddy Bear's Last Ride** *Diana Williams*
Teen Age *also see: Teenage*
2/57 **Teen Age Crush** *Tommy Sands*
81/58 **Teen-Age Doll** *Tommy Sands*
45/56 **Teen Age Goodnight** *Chordettes*
5/62 **Teen Age Idol** *Rick Nelson*
Teen Age Prayer
6/56 *Gale Storm*
19/56 *Gloria Mann*
68/56 *Kitty White*
90/55 **Teen-Ager's Waltz** *Eddy Howard*
Teen Angel
1/60 *Mark Dinning*
79/74 *Wednesday*
Teen Beat
4/59 *Sandy Nelson*
44/64 *Sandy Nelson ('65)*
29/59 **Teen Commandments**
Paul Anka-George Hamilton IV-Johnny Nash
47/60 **Teen-Ex** *Browns*
92/62 **Teen Queen Of The Week** *Freddy Cannon*
75/63 **Teenage Cleopatra** *Tracey Dey*
93/60 **Teenage Hayride** *Tender Slim*
58/63 **Teenage Heaven** *Johnny Cymbal*
99/59 **Teenage Heaven** *Eddie Cochran*
48/74 **Teenage Lament '74** *Alice Cooper*
80/74 **Teenage Love Affair** *Rick Derringer*
80/56 **Teenage Meeting (Gonna Rock It Up Right)** *Don Cornell*
Teenage Queen *see: Ballad Of*
50/60 **Teenage Sonata** *Sam Cooke*
94/60 **Teenager Feels It Too** *Denny Reed*
5/59 **Teenager In Love** *Dion & The Belmonts*
68/56 **Teenager's Mother (Are You Right?)**
Bill Haley & His Comets
66/66 **Teenager's Prayer** *Joe Simon*
2/57 **Teenager's Romance** *Ricky Nelson*
73/60 **Teensville** *Chet Atkins*
9/83 **Telefone (Long Distance Love Affair)**
Sheena Easton
67/72 **Telegram Sam** *T. Rex*
7/77 **Telephone Line** *Electric Light Orchestra*
18/77 **Telephone Man** *Meri Wilson*
57/69 **Tell All The People** *Doors*
89/72 **Tell 'Em Willie Boy's A'Comin'**
Tommy James
Tell Her *see: Tell Him*
1/83 **Tell Her About It** *Billy Joel*
66/60 **Tell Her For Me** *Adam Wade*
50/74 **Tell Her Love Has Felt The Need**
Eddie Kendricks
Tell Her No
6/65 *Zombies*
27/83 *Juice Newton*
40/73 **Tell Her She's Lovely** *El Chicano*
57/65 **Tell Her (You Love Her Every Day)**
Frank Sinatra
Tell Him
4/63 *Exciters*
97/66 *Dean Parrish (Her)*
Tell Him
90/64 *Drew-Vels*
85/67 *Patti Drew*
42/63 **Tell Him I'm Not Home** *Chuck Jackson*
Tell Him No
8/59 *Travis & Bob*
42/59 *Dean & Marc*
17/70 **Tell It All Brother**
Kenny Rogers & The First Edition
Tell It Like It Is
2/67 *Aaron Neville*
72/76 *Andy Williams*
8/81 *Heart*
33/64 **Tell It On The Mountain**
Peter, Paul & Mary
10/67 **Tell It To The Rain** *4 Seasons*
Tell Laura I Love Her
7/60 *Ray Peterson*
94/74 *Johnny T. Angel*
23/68 **Tell Mama** *Etta James*
83/71 **Tell Mama** *Savoy Brown*
22/62 **Tell Me** *Dick & DeeDee*
21/74 **Tell Me A Lie** *Sami Jo*
69/64 **Tell Me Baby** *Garnet Mimms*
65/84 **Tell Me If You Still Care** *S.O.S. Band*
85/64 **Tell Me Mamma** *Christine Quaite*
3/74 **Tell Me Something Good** *Rufus*
83/74 **Tell Me That I'm Wrong**
Blood, Sweat & Tears
51/60 **Tell Me That You Love Me** *Fats Domino*
73/63 **Tell Me The Truth** *Nancy Wilson*
86/72 **Tell Me This Is A Dream** *Delfonics*
37/67 **Tell Me To My Face** *Keith*
33/82 **Tell Me Tomorrow** *Smokey Robinson*
13/64 **Tell Me Why** *Bobby Vinton*
18/61 **Tell Me Why** *Belmonts*

Tell Me Why
45/56 *Crew-Cuts*
52/56 *Gale Storm*
33/66 *Elvis Presley*
98/71 **Tell Me Why** *Matthews' Southern Comfort*
24/64 **Tell Me (You're Coming Back)** *Rolling Stones*
92/68 **Tell Someone You Love Them** *Dino, Desi & Billy*
94/76 **Tell The World How I Feel About 'Cha Baby** *Harold Melvin & The Blue Notes*
50/59 **Telling Lies** *Fats Domino*
1/62 **Telstar** *Tornadoes*
39/70 **Temma Harbour** *Mary Hopkin*
Temptation
56/60 *Roger Williams*
27/61 *Everly Brothers*
93/67 *Boots Randolph*
70/65 **Temptation 'Bout To Get Me** *Knight Bros.*
15/71 **Temptation Eyes** *Grass Roots*
49/81 **Tempted** *Squeeze*
81/67 **Ten Commandments** *Prince Buster*
(also see: Teen Commandments)
Ten Commandments Of Love
22/58 *Harvey & The Moonglows*
94/63 *James MacArthur*
55/68 *Peaches & Herb*
82/69 *Little Anthony & The Imperials*
43/65 **10 Little Bottles** *Johnny Bond*
49/63 **Ten Little Indians** *Beach Boys*
96/67 **Ten Little Indians** *Yardbirds*
45/62 **Ten Lonely Guys** *Pat Boone*
38/84 **10-9-8** *Face To Face*
54/76 **Ten Percent** *Double Exposure*
43/59 **Ten Thousand Drums** *Carl Smith*
68/77 **Ten To Eight** *David Castle*
25/83 **Tender Is The Night** *Jackson Browne*
10/86 **Tender Love** *Force M.D.'s*
Tender, Love and Care *see: T.L.C.*
Tender Trap *see: (Love Is)*
Tender Years
78/84 *John Cafferty*
31/85 *John Cafferty*
76/61 **Tender Years** *George Jones*
31/61 **Tenderly** *Bert Kaempfert*
27/85 **Tenderness** *General Public*
69/62 **Tennessee** *Jan & Dean*
23/70 **Tennessee Bird Walk** *Jack Blanchard & Misty Morgan*
84/61 **Tennessee Flat-Top Box** *Johnny Cash*
48/59 **Tennessee Stud** *Eddy Arnold*
Tennessee Waltz
52/59 *Bobby Comstock*
63/59 *Jerry Fuller*
35/64 *Sam Cooke*
83/76 **Tenth Avenue Freeze-Out** *Bruce Springsteen*
Tequila
1/58 *Champs*
20/58 *Eddie Platt*
99/62 *Champs (Twist)*
91/64 *Bill Black's Combo*
64/73 **Tequila Sunrise** *Eagles*
Terms Of Endearment *see: Theme From*
71/85 **Test Of Time** *Romantics*
Testify *see: (I Wanna)*
85/61 **Texan And A Girl From Mexico** *Anita Bryant*
91/76 **Texas** *Charlie Daniels Band*
51/80 **Texas In My Rear View Mirror** *Mac Davis*
91/56 **Texas Lady** *Les Paul & Mary Ford*
90/70 **Thank God And Greyhound** *Roy Clark*
97/72 **Thank God For You Baby** *PG&E*
1/75 **Thank God I'm A Country Boy** *John Denver*
22/78 **Thank God It's Friday** *Love & Kisses*
84/63 **Thank You And Goodnight** *Angels*
63/64 **Thank You Baby** *Shirelles*
70/75 **Thank You Baby** *Stylistics*
1/70 **Thank You (Falettinme Be Mice Elf Agin)** *Sly & The Family Stone*
25/78 **Thank You For Being A Friend** *Andrew Gold*
35/64 **Thank You Girl** *Beatles*
96/70 **Thank You Girl** *Street People*
16/59 **Thank You Pretty Baby** *Brook Benton*
69/68 **Thank U Very Much** *Scaffold*
45/65 **Thanks A Lot** *Brenda Lee*
37/74 **Thanks For Saving My Life** *Billy Paul*
61/75 **Thanks For The Smiles** *Charlie Ross*
70/67 **That Acapulco Gold** *Rainy Daze*
64/64 **That Boy John** *Raindrops*
69/81 **That Didn't Hurt Too Bad** *Dr. Hook*
97/71 **That Evil Child** *B.B. King*
4/82 **That Girl** *Stevie Wonder*
49/64 **That Girl Belongs To Yesterday** *Gene Pitney*
22/80 **That Girl Could Sing** *Jackson Browne*
74/62 **That Greasy Kid Stuff** *Janie Grant*
67/62 **That Happy Feeling** *Bert Kaempfert*
76/68 **That Kind Of Woman** *Merrilee Rush*
6/73 **That Lady** *Isley Brothers*
55/80 **That Lovin' You Feelin' Again** *Roy Orbison & Emmylou Harris*
20/64 **That Lucky Old Sun** *Ray Charles*
77/77 **That Magic Touch** *Angel*
That Old Black Magic
13/55 *Sammy Davis, Jr.*
18/58 *Louis Prima & Keely Smith*
21/61 *Bobby Rydell*
55/60 **That Old Feeling** *Kitty Kallen*
21/81 **That Old Song** *Ray Parker Jr. & Raydio*
47/78 **That Once In A Lifetime** *Demis Roussos*
That Same Old Feeling
62/70 *Fortunes*
67/70 *Pickettywitch*
63/74 **That Song Is Driving Me Crazy** *Tom T. Hall*
28/62 **That Stranger Used To Be My Girl** *Trade Martin*
12/63 **That Sunday, That Summer** *Nat King Cole*
89/84 **That Was Then But This Is Now** *ABC*
20/86 **That Was Then, This Is Now** *Monkees*
12/85 **That Was Yesterday** *Foreigner*
That'll Be The Day
1/57 *Crickets*
11/76 *Linda Ronstadt*
64/68 **That's A Lie** *Ray Charles*
6/84 **That's All** *Genesis*
17/56 **That's All** *Tennessee Ernie Ford*
48/63 **That's All** *Rick Nelson*
98/59 **That's All I Want** *Bobby Day*
That's All I Want From You
3/55 *Jaye P. Morgan*
86/57 *Silva-Tones*
16/56 **That's All There Is To That** *Nat King Cole*
6/60 **That's All You Gotta Do** *Brenda Lee*
78/58 **That's Alright** *Little Junior Parker*
62/66 **That's Enough** *Rosco Robinson*
That's How Heartaches Are Made
40/63 *Baby Washington*
97/69 *Marvelettes*
88/63 **That's How It Goes** *George Maharis*
F/75 **That's How Long** *Chi-Lites*
46/72 **That's How Love Goes** *Jermaine Jackson*
74/60 **That's How Much** *Brian Hyland*
39/58 **That's How Much I Love You** *Pat Boone*

74/65 **That's How Strong My Love Is**
Otis Redding
31/61 **That's It-I Quit-I'm Movin' On** *Sam Cooke*
That's Life
4/66 *Frank Sinatra*
85/86 *David Lee Roth*
51/62 **That's Life (That's Tough)**
Gabriel & The Angels
28/83 **That's Love** *Jim Capaldi*
69/62 **That's My Desire**
Yvonne Baker & The Sensations
55/59 **That's My Little Suzie** *Ritchie Valens*
51/62 **That's My Pa** *Sheb Wooley*
82/74 **That's Not How It Goes** *Bloodstone*
9/62 **That's Old Fashioned (That's The Way Love Should Be)** *Everly Brothers*
92/64 **That's Really Some Good** *Rufus & Carla*
3/77 **That's Rock 'N' Roll** *Shaun Cassidy*
92/67 **That's Someone You Never Forget**
Elvis Presley
88/63 **That's The Only Way** *4 Seasons*
70/74 **That's The Sound That Lonely Makes**
Tavares
F/77 **That's The Trouble** *Grace Jones*
99/66 **That's The Tune** *Vogues*
94/69 **That's The Way** *Joe Tex*
62/71 **That's The Way A Woman Is** *Messengers*
12/64 **That's The Way Boys Are** *Lesley Gore*
That's The Way God Planned It
62/69 *Billy Preston*
65/72 *Billy Preston*
27/72 **That's The Way I Feel About Cha**
Bobby Womack
1/75 **That's The Way (I Like It)**
KC & The Sunshine Band
93/70 **That's The Way I Want Our Love**
Joe Simon
10/71 **That's The Way I've Always Heard It Should Be** *Carly Simon*
7/69 **That's The Way Love Is** *Marvin Gaye*
33/63 **That's The Way Love Is** *Bobby Bland*
12/75 **That's The Way Of The World**
Earth, Wind & Fire
59/61 **That's The Way With Love** *Piero Soffici*
1/86 **That's What Friends Are For**
Dionne Warwick & Friends
74/72 **That's What Friends Are For** *B.J. Thomas*
27/61 **That's What Girls Are Made For** *Spinners*
35/64 **That's What Love Is Made Of** *Miracles*
59/72 **That's What Love Will Make You Do**
Little Milton
72/64 **(That's) What The Nitty Gritty Is**
Shirley Ellis
83/60 **That's When I Cried** *Jimmy Jones*
63/64 **That's When It Hurts** *Ben E. King*
27/75 **That's When The Music Takes Me**
Neil Sedaka
58/57 **That's When Your Heartaches Begin**
Elvis Presley
29/70 **That's Where I Went Wrong** *Poppy Family*
93/64 **That's Where It's At** *Sam Cooke*
27/76 **That's Where The Happy People Go**
Trammps
88/59 **That's Why I Cry** *Buddy Knox*
68/76 **That's Why I Love You** *Andrew Gold*
13/59 **That's Why (I Love You So)** *Jackie Wilson*
84/57 **That's Why I Was Born** *Janice Harper*
82/73 **That's Why You Remember** *Kenny Karen*
88/69 **That's Your Baby** *Joe Tex*
48/56 **That's Your Mistake** *Otis Williams*
50/78 **That's Your Secret** *Sea Level*

Them Changes
81/70 *Buddy Miles*
62/71 *Buddy Miles*
F/72 *Carlos Santana & Buddy Miles*
58/61 **Them That Got** *Ray Charles*
35/60 **Theme For Young Lovers** *Percy Faith*
Theme From A Summer Place
1/60 *Percy Faith*
64/62 *Dick Roman*
16/65 *Lettermen*
83/69 *Ventures*
97/60 **Theme From Adventures In Paradise**
Jerry Byrd
96/63 **Theme From Any Number Can Win**
Jimmy Smith
28/62 **Theme From Ben Casey** *Valjean*
45/77 **Theme From Charlie's Angels**
Henry Mancini
18/73 **Theme From Cleopatra Jones** *Joe Simon*
Theme From Close Encounters
13/78 *John Williams*
25/78 *Meco*
39/61 **Theme From Dixie** *Duane Eddy*
59/83 **Theme From Doctor Detroit** *Devo*
10/62 **Theme From Dr. Kildare (Three Stars Will Shine Tonight)** *Richard Chamberlain*
52/82 **Theme From Dynasty** *Bill Conti*
73/56 **Theme From East Of Eden** *Dick Jacobs*
95/69 **Theme From Electric Surfboard**
Brother Jack McDuff
Theme From Exorcist *see: Tubular Bells*
85/61 **Theme From Goodbye Again**
Ferrante & Teicher
2/81 **Theme From Greatest American Hero (Believe It Or Not)** *Joey Scarbury*
61/65 **Theme From Harlow (Lonely Girl)**
Bobby Vinton
95/62 **Theme From Hatari!** *Henry Mancini*
10/81 **Theme From Hill Street Blues** *Mike Post*
76/79 **Theme From Ice Castles (Through The Eyes Of Love)** *Melissa Manchester*
32/75 **Theme From Jaws (Main Title)**
John Williams
68/77 **Theme From King Kong**
Love Unlimited Orchestra
84/63 **Theme From Lawrence Of Arabia**
Ferrante & Teicher
Theme From Love Story
9/71 *Andy Williams (Where Do I Begin)*
13/71 *Henry Mancini*
31/71 *Francis Lai*
25/82 **Theme From Magnum P.I.** *Mike Post*
1/76 **Theme From Mahogany (Do You Know Where You're Going To)** *Diana Ross*
55/61 **Theme From My Three Sons**
Lawrence Welk
32/80 **Theme From New York, New York**
Frank Sinatra
Theme From Picnic *see: Moonglow*
Theme From Pink Panther
see: Pink Panther Theme
82/81 **Theme From Raging Bull (Cavalleria Rusticana)** *Joel Diamond*
Theme From Rocky *see: Gonna Fly Now*
1/76 **Theme From S.W.A.T.** *Rhythm Heritage*
1/71 **Theme From Shaft** *Isaac Hayes*
83/61 **(Theme From) Silver City** *Ventures*
Theme From Summer Of '42
21/71 *Peter Nero*
57/75 *Biddu Orchestra*
Theme From Superfly *see: Freddie's Dead*
81/79 **Theme From Superman (Main Title)**
John Williams

100/62 **Theme From Taras Bulba (The Wishing Star)** *Jerry Butler*
10/60 **Theme From The Apartment** *Ferrante & Teicher*
70/60 **Theme From The Dark At The Top Of The Stairs** *Ernie Freeman*
21/80 **Theme From The Dukes Of Hazzard (Good Ol' Boys)** *Waylon Jennings*
90/61 **Theme From The Great Imposter** *Henry Mancini*
Theme From The Man With The Golden Arm *see: Man With The Golden Arm*
38/72 **Theme From The Men** *Isaac Hayes*
Theme From The Proud Ones
39/56 *Nelson Riddle*
72/56 *Lionel Newman*
95/56 *Leroy Holmes*
Theme From The Sundowners
51/60 *Billy Vaughn*
70/60 *Felix Slatkin*
93/60 *Mantovani*
Theme From The Three Penny Opera *see: Mack The Knife*
27/60 **Theme From The Unforgiven (The Need For Love)** *Don Costa*
99/66 **Theme From The Wild Angels** *Davie Allan & The Arrows*
Theme From Tunes Of Glory
60/61 *Cambridge Strings & Singers*
88/61 *Mitch Miller*
Theme From Valley Of The Dolls
2/68 *Dionne Warwick*
83/68 *King Curtis*
21/78 **Theme From Which Way Is Up** *Stargard*
84/84 **Theme from 'Terms Of Endearment'** *Michael Gore*
47/82 **Themes From E.T. (The Extra-Terrestrial)** *Walter Murphy*
35/78 **Themes From The Wizard Of Oz** *Meco*
1/74 **Then Came You** *Dionne Warwick & Spinners*
6/63 **Then He Kissed Me** *Crystals*
86/65 **Then I'll Count Again** *Johnny Tillotson*
94/70 **Then She's A Lover** *Roy Clark*
Then You Can Tell Me Goodbye
6/67 *Casinos*
84/68 *Eddy Arnold*
27/76 *Glen Campbell (medley)*
57/79 *Toby Beau*
68/73 **There Ain't No Way** *Lobo*
50/65 **There But For Fortune** *Joan Baez*
77/79 **There But For The Grace Of God Go I** *Machine*
71/59 **There Comes A Time** *Jack Scott*
34/75 **There Goes Another Love Song** *Outlaws*
There Goes My Baby
2/59 *Drifters*
21/84 *Donna Summer*
There Goes My Everything
20/67 *Engelbert Humperdinck*
65/67 *Jack Greene*
F/71 *Elvis Presley*
19/58 **There Goes My Heart** *Joni James*
59/63 **There Goes (My Heart Again)** *Fats Domino*
98/67 **There Goes The Lover** *Gene Chandler*
There! I've Said It Again
81/59 *Sam Cooke*
1/64 *Bobby Vinton*
20/68 **There Is** *Dells*
11/67 **There Is A Mountain** *Donovan*
There Is Love *see: Wedding Song*
88/62 **There Is No Greater Love** *Wanderers*
91/71 **There It Goes Again** *Barbara & The Uniques*
32/73 **There It Is** *Tyrone Davis*
43/72 **There It Is** *James Brown*
There Must Be A Way
33/59 *Joni James*
93/67 *Jimmy Roselli*
22/85 **There Must Be An Angel (Playing With My Heart)** *Eurythmics*
77/69 **There Never Was A Time** *Jeannie C. Riley*
47/57 **There Oughta Be A Law** *Mickey & Sylvia*
26/61 **There She Goes** *Jerry Wallace*
54/55 **There Should Be Rules (Protecting Fools Who Fall In Love)** *Betty Madigan*
23/60 **(There Was A) Tall Oak Tree** *Dorsey Burnette*
There Was A Time
36/68 *James Brown*
82/68 *Gene Chandler*
42/77 **There Will Come A Day (I'm Gonna Happen To You)** *Smokey Robinson*
33/66 **There Will Never Be Another You** *Chris Montez*
63/74 **There Will Never Be Any Peace (Until God Is Seated At The Conference Table)** *Chi-Lites*
18/74 **There Won't Be Anymore** *Charlie Rich*
73/76 **There Won't Be No Country Music (There Won't Be No Rock 'N' Roll)** *C.W. McCall*
80/73 **There You Go** *Edwin Starr*
75/62 **There'll Be No Next Time** *Jackie Wilson*
25/57 **(There'll Be) Peace In The Valley (For Me)** *Elvis Presley*
1/86 **There'll Be Sad Songs (To Make You Cry)** *Billy Ocean*
84/65 **(There'll Come A Day When) Ev'ry Little Bit Hurts** *Bobby Vee*
26/69 **There'll Come A Time** *Betty Everett*
36/78 **There'll Never Be** *Switch*
81/67 **There's A Chance We Can Make It** *Blues Magoos*
97/59 **There's A Girl** *Jan & Dean*
20/57 **There's A Gold Mine In The Sky** *Pat Boone*
There's A Kind Of Hush (All Over The World)
4/67 *Herman's Hermits*
12/76 *Carpenters*
3/61 **There's A Moon Out Tonight** *Capris*
74/64 **There's A Place** *Beatles*
64/60 **There's A Star Spangled Banner Waving #2 (The Ballad Of Francis Powers)** *Red River Dave*
56/67 **There's Always Me** *Elvis Presley*
(There's) Always Something There To Remind Me
49/64 *Lou Johnson*
52/65 *Sandie Shaw*
65/68 *Dionne Warwick*
27/70 *R.B. Greaves*
8/83 *Naked Eyes*
21/69 **There's Gonna Be A Showdown** *Archie Bell & The Drells*
34/67 **There's Got To Be A Word!** *Innocence*
88/74 **There's Got To Be Rain In Your Life (To Appreciate The Sunshine)** *Dorothy Norwood*
58/84 **There's No Easy Way** *James Ingram*
68/59 **There's No Fool Like A Young Fool** *Tab Hunter*
5/81 **(There's) No Gettin' Over Me** *Ronnie Milsap*
50/66 **There's No Living Without Your Loving** *Peter & Gordon*
43/73 **There's No Me Without You** *Manhattans*
20/62 **There's No Other (Like My Baby)** *Crystals*
47/64 **There's Nothing I Can Say** *Rick Nelson*
There's Nothing Stronger Than Our Love *see: I Believe*
10/58 **There's Only One Of You** *Four Lads*

77/57 **There's Only You** *Don Rondo*
98/71 **There's So Much Love All Around Me** *Three Degrees*
There's Something On Your Mind
44/59 *Big Jay McNeely & Band*
31/60 *Bobby Marchan*
69/66 *Baby Ray*
55/69 **These Are Not My People** *Johnny Rivers*
85/63 **These Arms Of Mine** *Otis Redding*
1/66 **These Boots Are Made For Walkin'** *Nancy Sinatra*
1/86 **These Dreams** *Heart*
These Eyes
6/69 *Guess Who*
16/69 *Jr. Walker & The All Stars*
55/63 **These Foolish Things** *James Brown*
81/56 **These Hands** *Len Dresslar*
63/65 **These Hands (Small But Mighty)** *Bobby Bland*
50/71 **They Can't Take Away Our Music** *Eric Burdon & War*
8/84 **They Don't Know** *Tracey Ullman*
99/68 **They Don't Make Love Like They Used To** *Eddy Arnold*
5/75 **They Just Can't Stop It the (Games People Play)** *Spinners*
(They Long To Be) Close To You
1/70 *Carpenters*
91/72 *Jerry Butler & Brenda Lee Eager*
82/76 *B.T. Express*
53/63 **They Remind Me Too Much Of You** *Elvis Presley*
They're Coming To Take Me Away, Ha-Haaa!
3/66 *Napoleon XIV*
87/73 *Napoleon XIV*
77/67 **They're Here** *Boots Walker*
86/84 **Thief Of Hearts** *Melissa Manchester*
Thin Line Between Love & Hate
15/71 *Persuaders*
83/84 *Pretenders*
Thing *see: Do The Thing*
41/61 **Thing Of The Past** *Shirelles*
Things
3/62 *Bobby Darin*
89/76 *Anne Murray*
5/85 **Things Can Only Get Better** *Howard Jones*
60/58 **Things I Love** *Fidelity's*
89/56 **Things I Never Had** *Kay Starr*
23/67 **Things I Should Have Said** *Grass Roots*
16/69 **Things I'd Like To Say** *New Colony Six*
86/64 **Things In This House** *Bobby Darin*
99/64 **Things That I Used To Do** *James Brown*
46/62 **Things We Did Last Summer** *Shelley Fabares*
5/77 **Things We Do For Love** *10cc*
7/68 **Think** *Aretha Franklin*
25/64 **Think** *Brenda Lee*
Think
66/57 *'5' Royales*
33/60 *James Brown*
100/67 *James Brown & Vicki Anderson*
77/73 *James Brown*
80/73 *James Brown*
95/65 **Think** *Jimmy McCracklin*
66/72 **Think (About It)** *Lyn Collins*
20/80 **Think About Me** *Fleetwood Mac*
87/70 **Think About Your Children** *Mary Hopkin*
65/71 **Think His Name** *Johnny Rivers*
30/66 **Think I'll Go Somewhere And Cry Myself To Sleep** *Al Martino*
16/82 **Think I'm In Love** *Eddie Money*
27/58 **Think It Over** *Crickets*
34/78 **Think It Over** *Cheryl Ladd*
66/60 **Think Me A Kiss** *Clyde McPhatter*
9/84 **Think Of Laura** *Christopher Cross*
74/66 **Think Of Me** *Buck Owens*
57/65 **Think Of The Good Times** *Jay & The Americans*
Think Twice
11/61 *Brook Benton*
93/66 *Jackie Wilson & LaVern Baker*
18/73 **Thinking Of You** *Loggins & Messina*
45/76 **Thinking Of You** *Paul Davis*
82/57 **Third Finger - Left Hand** *Eileen Rodgers*
47/65 **3rd Man Theme** *Herb Alpert*
14/75 **Third Rate Romance** *Amazing Rhythm Aces*
23/80 **Third Time Lucky (First Time I Was A Fool)** *Foghat*
49/71 **13 Questions** *Seatrain*
69/69 **30-60-90** *Willie Mitchell*
97/63 **31 Flavors** *Shirelles*
F/80 **This Beat Goes On** *Kings*
This Bitter Earth
24/60 *Dinah Washington*
96/70 *Satisfactions*
(This Boy) *see: Ringo's Theme*
57/66 **This Can't Be True** *Eddie Holman*
10/86 **This Could Be The Night** *Loverboy*
58/84 **This Could Be The Right One** *April Wine*
1/65 **This Diamond Ring** *Gary Lewis & The Playboys*
12/66 **This Door Swings Both Ways** *Herman's Hermits*
84/63 **This Empty Place** *Dionne Warwick*
12/59 **This Friendly World** *Fabian*
46/77 **This Girl (Has Turned Into A Woman)** *Mary MacGregor*
9/69 **This Girl Is A Woman Now** *Gary Puckett & The Union Gap*
82/66 **This Golden Ring** *Fortunes*
This Guy's (Girl's) In Love With You
1/68 *Herb Alpert*
7/69 *Dionne Warwick*
24/74 **This Heart** *Gene Redding*
26/59 **This I Swear** *Skyliners*
This Is All I Ask
67/63 *Burl Ives*
70/63 *Tony Bennett*
11/80 **This Is It** *Kenny Loggins*
88/65 **This Is It** *Jim Reeves*
91/76 **This Is It** *Melba Moore*
91/79 **This Is It** *Dan Hartman*
35/78 **This Is Love** *Paul Anka*
58/79 **This Is Love** *Oak*
25/69 **This Is My Country** *Impressions*
85/70 **This Is My Love Song** *Intruders*
60/85 **This Is My Night** *Chaka Khan*
60/63 **This Is My Prayer** *Theola Kilgore*
72/65 **This Is My Prayer** *Ray Charles Singers*
3/67 **This Is My Song** *Petula Clark*
100/60 **This Is My Story** *Mickey & Sylvia*
32/85 **This Is Not America** *David Bowie/Pat Metheny Group*
69/58 **This Is The Nite** *Valiants*
65/68 **This Is The Thanks I Get** *Barbara Lynn*
18/87 **This Is The Time** *Billy Joel*
93/86 **This Is The Time** *Dennis DeYoung*
39/77 **This Is The Way That I Feel** *Marie Osmond*
82/87 **This Is The World Calling** *Bob Geldof*
86/73 **This Is Your Song** *Don Goodwin*
This Land Is Your Land
93/62 *New Christy Minstrels*
97/62 *Ketty Lester*
32/65 **This Little Bird** *Marianne Faithfull*
11/81 **This Little Girl** *Gary U.S. Bonds*
21/63 **This Little Girl** *Dion*
26/58 **This Little Girl Of Mine** *Everly Brothers*

24/58 **This Little Girl's Gone Rockin'**
Ruth Brown
85/86 **This Love** *Bad Company*
This Magic Moment
16/60 *Drifters*
6/69 *Jay & The Americans*
33/82 **This Man Is Mine** *Heart*
10/76 **This Masquerade** *George Benson*
58/79 **This Moment In Time**
Engelbert Humperdinck
62/83 **This Must Be The Place (Naive Melody)**
Talking Heads
This Night Won't Last Forever
65/78 *Bill LaBounty*
19/79 *Michael Johnson*
78/75 **This Ol' Cowboy** *Marshall Tucker Band*
79/60 **This Old Heart** *James Brown*
This Old Heart Of Mine
12/66 *Isley Brothers*
67/69 *Tammi Terrell*
83/76 *Rod Stewart*
This Old Man *see: Children's Marching Song*
29/76 **This One's For You** *Barry Manilow*
20/59 **This Should Go On Forever** *Rod Bernard*
25/77 **This Song** *George Harrison*
100/65 **This Sporting Life** *Ian Whitcomb*
6/61 **This Time** *Troy Shondell*
24/83 **This Time** *Bryan Adams*
27/80 **This Time** *John Cougar*
81/85 **This Time** *INXS*
42/74 **This Time I'm Gone For Good** *Bobby Bland*
10/78 **This Time I'm In It For Love** *Player*
65/73 **This Time It's Real** *Tower Of Power*
66/59 **This Time Of The Year** *Brook Benton*
53/67 **This Town** *Frank Sinatra*
6/75 **This Will Be** *Natalie Cole*
90/77 **This Will Be A Night To Remember**
Eddie Holman
23/84 **This Woman** *Kenny Rogers*
38/72 **This World** *Staple Singers*
90/61 **This World We Love In (Il Cielo In Una Stanza)** *Mina*
68/86 **Thorn In My Side** *Eurythmics*
63/82 **Those Good Old Dreams** *Carpenters*
6/63 **Those Lazy-Hazy-Crazy Days Of Summer** *Nat King Cole*
9/61 **Those Oldies But Goodies (Remind Me Of You)** *Little Caesar & The Romans*
2/68 **Those Were The Days** *Mary Hopkin*
43/72 **Those Were The Days**
Carroll O'Connor & Jean Stapleton
Thou Shalt Not Steal
73/62 *John D. Loudermilk*
13/65 *Dick & DeeDee*
84/69 **Thought Of Loving You** *Crystal Mansion*
Thousand Miles Away
53/57 *Heartbeats*
96/60 *Heartbeats*
72/67 **Thousand Shadows** *Seeds*
3/60 **Thousand Stars**
Kathy Young with The Innocents
98/67 **Thread The Needle** *Clarence Carter*
Three Bells
1/59 *Browns*
23/59 *Dick Flood*
Three Hearts In A Tangle
35/61 *Roy Drusky*
93/62 *James Brown*
24/67 **Three Little Fishes (medley)**
Mitch Ryder & The Detroit Wheels
15/60 **Three Nights A Week** *Fats Domino*
Three O'Clock In The Morning
33/65 *Bert Kaempfert*
83/65 *Lou Rawls*

Three Penny Opera *see: Mack The Knife*
36/74 **Three Ring Circus** *Blue Magic*
Three Stars
11/59 *Tommy Dee*
99/59 *Ruby Wright*
58/61 **Three Steps From The Altar**
Shep & The Limelites
94/75 **Three Steps From True Love** *Reflections*
1/78 **Three Times A Lady** *Commodores*
19/80 **Three Times In Love** *Tommy James*
28/64 **Three Window Coupe** *Rip Chords*
99/66 **3000 Miles** *Brian Hyland*
15/70 **Thrill Is Gone** *B.B. King*
4/84 **Thriller** *Michael Jackson*
60/85 **Through The Fire** *Chaka Khan*
13/82 **Through The Years** *Kenny Rogers*
4/86 **Throwing It All Away** *Genesis*
17/72 **Thunder And Lightning** *Chi Coltrane*
56/80 **Thunder And Lightning** *Chicago*
38/77 **Thunder In My Heart** *Leo Sayer*
9/78 **Thunder Island** *Jay Ferguson*
Thunder Road *see: Ballad Of*
25/66 **Thunderball** *Tom Jones*
55/84 **Ti Amo** *Laura Branigan*
92/58 **Tic Toc** *Lee Allen*
Ticket To Ride
1/65 *Beatles*
54/70 *Carpenters*
70/65 **Tickle Me** *Elvis Presley*
1/81 **Tide Is High** *Blondie*
1/73 **Tie A Yellow Ribbon Round The Ole Oak Tree** *Dawn*
3/63 **Tie Me Kangaroo Down, Sport** *Rolf Harris*
58/79 **Tie Me To A Tree (Handcuff Me) (medley)**
Bonnie Pointer
49/77 **Tie Your Mother Down** *Queen*
38/83 **Tied Up** *Olivia Newton-John*
37/60 **Ties That Bind** *Brook Benton*
3/59 **Tiger** *Fabian*
88/57 **Tiger Lily** *Rusty Draper*
11/72 **Tight Rope** *Leon Russell*
1/68 **Tighten Up** *Archie Bell & The Drells*
7/70 **Tighter, Tighter** *Alive & Kicking*
71/71 **Tightrope Ride** *Doors*
12/59 **Tijuana Jail** *Kingston Trio*
38/66 **Tijuana Taxi** *Herb Alpert*
84/76 **'Til I Can Make It On My Own**
Tammy Wynette
4/59 **('Til) I Kissed You** *Everly Brothers*
44/76 **'Til It's Time To Say Goodbye**
Jonathan Cain
29/85 **'Til My Baby Comes Home**
Luther Vandross
32/75 **Til The World Ends** *Three Dog Night*
77/83 **Til You And Your Lover Are Lovers Again** *Engelbert Humperdinck*
Till
22/57 *Roger Williams*
63/57 *Percy Faith*
14/62 *Angels*
27/68 *Vogues*
41/71 *Tom Jones*
26/62 **Till Death Do Us Part** *Bob Braun*
50/66 **Till The End Of The Day** *Kinks*
83/64 **Till The End Of Time** *Ray Charles Singers*
20/63 **Till Then** *Classics*
Till There Was You
30/59 *Anita Bryant*
100/62 *Valjean*
67/69 **Till You Get Enough**
Watts 103rd Street Rhythm Band
15/81 **Time** *Alan Parsons Project*
47/66 **Time** *Pozo-Seco Singers*
1/84 **Time After Time** *Cyndi Lauper*

Time After Time
75/60 *Frankie Ford*
36/66 *Chris Montez*
94/67 **Time Alone Will Tell** *Connie Francis*
51/71 **Time And Love** *Barbra Streisand*
30/60 **Time And The River** *Nat King Cole*
83/77 **Time Bomb** *Lake*
2/83 **Time (Clock Of The Heart)** *Culture Club*
32/74 **Time For Livin'** *Sly & The Family Stone*
39/68 **Time For Livin'** *Association*
Time For Me To Fly
56/78 *REO Speedwagon*
77/80 *REO Speedwagon*
Time For Us *see: Romeo & Juliet*
11/68 **Time Has Come Today** *Chambers Brothers*
1/73 **Time In A Bottle** *Jim Croce*
95/77 **Time Is Movin'** *Blackbyrds*
6/64 **Time Is On My Side** *Rolling Stones*
6/69 **Time Is Tight** *Booker T. & The MG's*
15/81 **Time Is Time** *Andy Gibb*
48/69 **Time Machine** *Grand Funk Railroad*
73/60 **Time Machine** *Dante & The Evergreens*
84/59 **Time Marches On** *Roy Hamilton*
3/69 **Time Of The Season** *Zombies*
22/81 **Time Out Of Mind** *Steely Dan*
7/78 **Time Passages** *Al Stewart*
100/67 **Time Seller** *Spencer Davis Group*
61/67 **Time, Time** *Ed Ames*
33/73 **Time To Get Down** *O'Jays*
96/70 **Time To Get It Together** *Country Coalition*
77/70 **Time To Kill** *Band*
Time To Time To Cry *see: Petite Fleur*
60/70 **Time Waits For No One**
Friends Of Distinction
45/61 **Time Was** *Flamingos*
67/69 **Time Was** *Canned Heat*
18/84 **Time Will Reveal** *DeBarge*
69/74 **Time Will Tell** *Tower Of Power*
5/66 **Time Won't Let Me** *Outsiders*
98/64 **Times Have Changed** *Irma Thomas*
7/76 **Times Of Your Life** *Paul Anka*
67/55 **Times Two, I Love You** *Three Chuckles*
17/71 **Timothy** *Buoys*
4/74 **Tin Man** *America*
73/68 **Tin Soldier** *Small Faces*
96/57 **Tina** *Easy Riders*
5/55 **Tina Marie** *Perry Como*
57/67 **Tiny Bubbles** *Don Ho & The Aliis*
41/72 **Tiny Dancer** *Elton John*
63/59 **Tiny Tim** *LaVern Baker*
Tip Of My Fingers
45/63 *Roy Clark*
43/66 *Eddy Arnold*
52/83 **Tip Of My Tongue** *Tubes*
83/67 **Tip Toe** *Robert Parker*
17/68 **Tip-Toe Thru' The Tulips With Me**
Tiny Tim
44/66 **Tippy Toeing** *Harden Trio*
11/71 **Tired Of Being Alone** *Al Green*
70/85 **Tired Of Being Blonde** *Carly Simon*
79/66 **Tired Of Being Lonely** *Sharpees*
8/80 **Tired Of Toein' The Line** *Rocky Burnette*
6/65 **Tired Of Waiting For You** *Kinks*
86/68 **Tit For Tat (Ain't No Taking Back)**
James Brown
To *also see: Too*
26/62 **To A Sleeping Beauty** *Jimmy Dean*
55/59 **To A Soldier Boy** *Tassels*
5/84 **To All The Girls I've Loved Before**
Julio Iglesias & Willie Nelson
6/86 **To Be A Lover** *Billy Idol*
94/67 **To Be A Lover** *Gene Chandler*
22/58 **To Be Loved** *Jackie Wilson*
48/61 **To Be Loved (Forever)** *Pentagons*
84/57 **To Be With You** *Highlights*
76/70 **To Be Young, Gifted And Black**
Nina Simone
62/82 **To Dream The Dream** *Frankie Miller*
To Each His Own
21/60 *Platters*
78/64 *Tymes*
82/68 *Frankie Laine*
50/75 **To Each His Own** *Faith, Hope & Charity*
48/72 **To Get To You** *Jerry Wallace*
29/68 **To Give (The Reason I Live)** *Frankie Valli*
To Know Him Is To Love Him
1/58 *Teddy Bears*
24/65 *Peter & Gordon*
34/69 *Bobby Vinton*
38/73 **To Know You Is To Love You** *B.B. King*
41/85 **To Live And Die In L.A.** *Wang Chung*
43/56 **To Love Again** *Four Aces*
To Love Somebody
17/67 *Bee Gees*
74/68 *Sweet Inspirations*
95/66 **To Make A Big Man Cry** *Roy Head*
30/87 **To People** *Tina Turner*
68/67 **To Share Your Love** *Fantastic Four*
98/66 **To Show I Love You** *Peter & Gordon*
To Sir With Love
1/67 *Lulu*
93/67 *Herbie Mann*
35/69 **To Susan On The West Coast Waiting**
Donovan
25/57 **To The Aisle** *Five Satins*
17/75 **To The Door Of The Sun (Alle Porte Del Sole)** *Al Martino*
25/56 **To The Ends Of The Earth** *Nat King Cole*
50/70 **To The Other Woman (I'm The Other Woman)** *Doris Duke*
51/68 **To Wait For Love** *Herb Alpert*
To You, My Love
27/56 *Nick Noble*
70/56 *Georgie Shaw*
20/71 **Toast And Marmalade For Tea** *Tin Tin*
67/72 **Toast To The Fool** *Dramatics*
Tobacco Road
14/64 *Nashville Teens*
93/70 *Jamul*
78/75 **Toby** *Chi-Lites*
83/81 **Toccata** *Sky*
17/64 **Today** *New Christy Minstrels*
39/63 **(Today I Met) The Boy I'm Gonna Marry**
Darlene Love
46/73 **Today I Started Loving You Again**
Bettye Swann
60/80 **Today Is The Day** *Bar-Kays*
54/64 **Today's Teardrops** *Rick Nelson*
23/76 **Today's The Day** *America*
6/61 **Together** *Connie Francis*
Together
48/67 *Intruders*
18/81 *Tierra*
80/70 **Together** *Illusion*
19/66 **Together Again** *Ray Charles*
91/72 **Together Again** *Bobby Sherman*
86/72 **Together Alone** *Melanie*
37/72 **Together Let's Find Love** *5th Dimension*
91/73 **Together We Can Make Such Sweet Music** *Spinners*
26/60 **Togetherness** *Frankie Avalon*
20/63 **Tom Cat** *Rooftop Singers*
1/58 **Tom Dooley** *Kingston Trio*
44/81 **Tom Sawyer** *Rush*
29/59 **Tomboy** *Perry Como*
96/68 **Tomboy** *Ronnie Dove*
92/65 **Tommy** *Reparata & The Delrons*
(also see: Overture From Tommy)

23/68 **Tomorrow** *Strawberry Alarm Clock*
26/86 **Tomorrow Doesn't Matter Tonight** *Starship*
80/66 **Tomorrow Never Comes** *B.J. Thomas*
54/69 **Tomorrow Tomorrow** *Bee Gees*
55/71 **Tongue In Cheek** *Sugarloaf*
Tonight
8/61 *Ferrante & Teicher*
44/61 *Eddie Fisher*
13/84 **Tonight** *Kool & The Gang*
53/84 **Tonight** *David Bowie*
69/73 **Tonight** *Raspberries*
84/83 **Tonight** *Whispers*
Tonight *also see: Tonite*
26/61 **Tonight (Could Be The Night)** *Velvets*
16/83 **Tonight, I Celebrate My Love** *Peabo Bryson/Roberta Flack*
15/61 **Tonight I Fell In Love** *Tokens*
61/61 **Tonight I Won't Be There** *Adam Wade*
50/69 **Tonight I'll Be Staying Here With You** *Bob Dylan*
45/70 **Tonight I'll Say A Prayer** *Eydie Gorme*
20/82 **Tonight I'm Yours (Don't Hurt Me)** *Rod Stewart*
80/84 **Tonight Is What It Means To Be Young** *Fire Inc.*
44/85 **Tonight It's You** *Cheap Trick*
96/57 **Tonight My Heart Will Be Crying** *Eddie Fisher*
13/61 **Tonight My Love, Tonight** *Paul Anka*
7/86 **Tonight She Comes** *Cars*
55/82 **Tonight Tonight** *Bill Champlin*
Tonight You Belong To Me
4/56 *Patience & Prudence*
15/56 *Lawrence Welk with The Lennon Sisters*
49/56 *Karen Chandler & Jimmy Wakely*
57/64 **Tonight You're Gonna Fall In Love With Me** *Shirelles*
Tonight's The Night
39/60 *Shirelles*
76/60 *Chiffons*
28/65 **Tonight's The Night** *Solomon Burke*
99/76 **Tonight's The Night** *S.S.O.*
1/76 **Tonight's The Night (Gonna Be Alright)** *Rod Stewart*
Tonite, Tonite
77/57 *Mello-Kings*
95/61 *Mello-Kings*
83/67 **Tony Rome** *Nancy Sinatra*
88/62 **Too Bad** *Ben E. King*
86/72 **Too Beautiful To Last** *Engelbert Humperdinck*
4/69 **Too Busy Thinking About My Baby** *Marvin Gaye*
39/56 **Too Close For Comfort** *Eydie Gorme*
95/69 **Too Experienced** *Eddie Lovette*
77/82 **Too Good To Turn Back Now** *Rick Bowles*
5/80 **Too Hot** *Kool & The Gang*
24/78 **Too Hot Ta Trot** *Commodores*
93/65 **Too Hot To Hold** *Major Lance*
74/77 **Too Hot To Stop** *Bar-Kays*
59/74 **Too Late** *Tavares*
70/80 **Too Late** *Journey*
75/57 **Too Late** *Gene Austin*
75/79 **Too Late** *Shoes*
5/85 **Too Late For Goodbyes** *Julian Lennon*
66/56 **Too Late Now** *DeCastro Sisters*
2/72 **Too Late To Turn Back Now** *Cornelius Brothers & Sister Rose*
43/64 **Too Late To Turn Back Now** *Brook Benton*
76/62 **Too Late To Worry - Too Blue To Cry** *Glen Campbell*
94/69 **Too Many Cooks (Spoil The Soup)** *100 Proof Aged In Soul*
Too Many Fish In The Sea
25/65 *Marvelettes*
24/67 *Mitch Ryder & The Detroit Wheels (medley)*
13/65 **Too Many Rivers** *Brenda Lee*
72/61 **Too Many Rules** *Connie Francis*
1/57 **Too Much** *Elvis Presley*
1/79 **Too Much Heaven** *Bee Gees*
69/83 **Too Much Love To Hide** *Crosby, Stills & Nash*
35/67 **Too Much Of Nothing** *Peter, Paul & Mary*
19/68 **Too Much Talk** *Paul Revere & The Raiders*
30/60 **Too Much Tequila** *Champs*
9/81 **Too Much Time On My Hands** *Styx*
1/78 **Too Much, Too Little, Too Late** *Johnny Mathis & Deniece Williams*
42/60 **Too Pooped To Pop ('Casey')** *Chuck Berry*
5/83 **Too Shy** *Kajagoogoo*
91/66 **Too Slow** *Impressions*
Too Soon To Know *see: It's Too Soon*
40/81 **Too Tight** *Con Funk Shun*
13/69 **Too Weak To Fight** *Clarence Carter*
13/72 **Too Young** *Donny Osmond*
52/85 **Too Young** *Jack Wagner*
90/84 **Too Young To Fall In Love** *Motley Crue*
Too Young To Go Steady
21/56 *Nat King Cole*
73/56 *Patti Page*
71/60 *Connie Stevens*
30/78 **Took The Last Train** *David Gates*
81/61 **Top Forty, News, Weather And Sports** *Mark Dinning*
84/71 **Top Forty (Of The Lord)** *Sha Na Na*
Top Of The World
1/73 *Carpenters*
74/73 *Lynn Anderson*
98/75 **Top Of The World (Make My Reservation)** *Canyon*
70/79 **Topical Song** *Barron Knights*
27/58 **Topsy I** *Cozy Cole*
3/58 **Topsy II** *Cozy Cole*
Torero
18/58 *Renato Carosone*
21/58 *Julius LaRosa*
1/77 **Torn Between Two Lovers** *Mary MacGregor*
39/59 **Torquay** *Fireballs*
17/84 **Torture** *Jacksons*
20/62 **Torture** *Kris Jensen*
Tossin' And Turnin'
1/61 *Bobby Lewis*
97/73 *Bunny Sigler*
83/65 **Tossing & Turning** *Ivy League*
1/83 **Total Eclipse Of The Heart** *Bonnie Tyler*
52/79 **Totally Hot** *Olivia Newton-John*
71/71 **Touch** *Supremes*
87/83 **Touch A Four Leaf Clover** *Atlantic Starr*
23/74 **Touch A Hand, Make A Friend** *Staple Singers*
37/80 **Touch And Go** *Cars*
57/74 **Touch And Go** *Al Wilson*
60/86 **Touch And Go** *Emerson, Lake & Powell*
98/76 **Touch And Go** *Ecstasy, Passion & Pain*
73/78 **Touch And Gone** *Gary Wright*
3/69 **Touch Me** *Doors*
19/74 **Touch Me** *Fancy*
82/79 **Touch Me Baby** *Ultimate*
60/75 **Touch Me Baby (Reaching Out For Your Love)** *Tamiko Jones*
4/87 **Touch Me (I Want Your Body)** *Samantha Fox*
1/73 **Touch Me In The Morning** *Diana Ross*
Touch Me When We're Dancing
86/79 *Bama*
16/81 *Carpenters*
92/59 **Touch Of Pink** *Jerry Wallace*

50/70 **Touch Of You** *Brenda & The Tabulations*
Touch The Wind *see: Eres Tu*
60/61 **Touchables, The** *Dickie Goodman*
42/61 **Touchables In Brooklyn** *Dickie Goodman*
Tough *also see: Tuff*
22/85 **Tough All Over** *John Cafferty*
57/82 **Tough World** *Donnie Iris*
5/61 **Tower Of Strength** *Gene McDaniels*
(also see: You Don't Have To Be A)
73/57 **Tower's Trot (And Then You Do That Step)** *Dick Jacobs*
13/62 **Town Without Pity** *Gene Pitney*
64/65 **Toy Soldier** *4 Seasons*
Toys In The Attic
85/63 *Joe Sherman*
92/63 *Jack Jones*
Tra La La
24/56 *Georgia Gibbs*
94/56 *LaVern Baker*
50/62 **Tra La La La La** *Ike & Tina Turner*
35/64 **Tra La La La Suzy** *Dean & Jean*
96/69 **Tra La La Song (One Banana, Two Banana)** *Banana Splits*
Traces
2/69 *Classics IV*
47/70 *Lettermen (medley)*
Tracks Of My Tears
16/65 *Miracles*
10/67 *Johnny Rivers*
71/69 *Aretha Franklin*
25/76 *Linda Ronstadt*
9/69 **Tracy** *Cuff Links*
13/60 **Tracy's Theme** *Spencer Ross*
1/79 **Tragedy** *Bee Gees*
Tragedy
5/59 *Thomas Wayne*
10/61 *Fleetwoods*
56/69 *Brian Hyland*
39/85 **Tragedy** *John Hunter*
57/69 **Train, The** *1910 Fruitgum Co.*
86/76 **Train Called Freedom**
South Shore Commission
23/80 **Train In Vain (Stand By Me)** *Clash*
36/60 **Train Of Love** *Annette*
27/74 **Train Of Thought** *Cher*
38/79 **Train, Train** *Blackfoot*
Trains And Boats And Planes
47/65 *Billy J. Kramer with The Dakotas*
22/66 *Dionne Warwick*
Tramp
26/67 *Otis & Carla*
52/67 *Lowell Fulsom*
38/75 **Trampled Under Foot** *Led Zeppelin*
67/78 **Trans-Europe Express** *Kraftwerk*
8/56 **Transfusion** *Nervous Norvus*
35/61 **Transistor Sister** *Freddy Cannon*
13/71 **Trapped By A Thing Called Love**
Denise LaSalle
2/70 **Travelin' Band**
Creedence Clearwater Revival
1/61 **Travelin' Man** *Ricky Nelson*
77/74 **Travelin' Prayer** *Billy Joel*
61/74 **Travelin' Shoes** *Elvin Bishop*
32/67 **Travlin' Man** *Stevie Wonder*
73/80 **Treasure** *Brothers Johnson*
16/56 **Treasure Of Love** *Clyde McPhatter*
26/58 **Treasure Of Your Love** *Eileen Rodgers*
3/71 **Treat Her Like A Lady**
Cornelius Brothers & Sister Rose
48/85 **Treat Her Like A Lady** *Temptations*
2/65 **Treat Her Right** *Roy Head*
18/57 **Treat Me Nice** *Elvis Presley*
18/81 **Treat Me Right** *Pat Benatar*
43/63 **Treat My Baby Good** *Bobby Darin*
Trees
92/57 *Al Hibbler*
62/61 *Platters*
29/61 **Triangle** *Janie Grant*
68/71 **Triangle Of Love (Hey Diddle Diddle)**
Presidents
86/68 **Tribute To A King [Otis Redding]**
William Bell
76/87 **Trick Of The Night** *Bananarama*
73/80 **Trickle Trickle** *Manhattan Transfer*
Tricky
79/56 *Gus Jinkins*
25/57 *Ralph Marterie*
41/78 **Tried To Love** *Peter Frampton*
6/72 **Troglodyte (Cave Man)**
Jimmy Castor Bunch
9/82 **Trouble** *Lindsey Buckingham*
35/75 **T-R-O-U-B-L-E** *Elvis Presley*
92/67 **Trouble Down Here Below** *Lou Rawls*
Trouble In Mind
92/61 *Nina Simone*
86/63 *Aretha Franklin*
50/72 **Trouble In My Home** *Joe Simon*
20/60 **Trouble In Paradise** *Crests*
63/83 **Trouble In Paradise** *Al Jarreau*
33/63 **Trouble Is My Middle Name** *Bobby Vinton*
99/64 **Trouble I've Had** *Clarence Ashe*
7/73 **Trouble Man** *Marvin Gaye*
Trouble With Harry
44/56 *Alfi & Harry*
80/56 *Les Baxter*
71/69 **Truck Stop** *Jerry Smith*
64/71 **Truckin'** *Grateful Dead*
4/83 **True** *Spandau Ballet*
3/86 **True Blue** *Madonna*
99/63 **True Blue Lou** *Tony Bennett*
1/86 **True Colors** *Cyndi Lauper*
68/58 **True, Fine Mama** *Little Richard*
35/69 **True Grit** *Glen Campbell*
True Love
3/56 *Bing Crosby & Grace Kelly*
15/56 *Jane Powell*
98/63 *Richard Chamberlain*
66/64 **True Love Goes On And On** *Burl Ives*
78/57 **True Love Gone (Come On Home)**
Betty Madigan
21/63 **True Love Never Runs Smooth**
Gene Pitney
True Love, True Love *see: (If You Cry)*
True Love Ways
14/65 *Peter & Gordon*
66/80 *Mickey Gilley*
75/87 **True To You** *Ric Ocasek*
54/59 **True True Happiness** *Johnny Tillotson*
90/61 **True, True Love** *Frankie Avalon*
1/82 **Truly** *Lionel Richie*
65/66 **Truly Julie's Blues (I'll Be There)**
Bob Lind
54/65 **Truly, Truly, True** *Brenda Lee*
Trust In Me
95/57 *Chris Connor*
43/59 *Patti Page*
30/61 *Etta James*
90/80 **Trust Me** *Cindy Bullens*
23/69 **Try A Little Kindness** *Glen Campbell*
Try A Little Tenderness
100/62 *Aretha Franklin*
25/67 *Otis Redding*
29/69 *Three Dog Night*
23/83 **Try Again** *Champaign*
83/68 **Try It** *Ohio Express*
15/64 **Try It Baby** *Marvin Gaye*
97/77 **Try It On** *Exile*

Try Me
48/59 *James Brown*
65/64 *Jimmy Hughes*
63/65 *James Brown*
80/76 **Try Me, I Know We Can Make It** *Donna Summer*
97/66 **Try My Love Again** *Bobby Moore's Rhythm Aces*
77/71 **Try Some, Buy Some** *Ronnie Spector*
33/58 **Try The Impossible** *Lee Andrews & The Hearts*
Try To Remember
73/65 *Ed Ames*
91/65 *Brothers Four*
97/65 *Roger Williams*
11/75 *Gladys Knight & The Pips (medley)*
12/66 **Try Too Hard** *Dave Clark Five*
88/74 **Try (Try To Fall In Love)** *Cooker*
95/75 **Tryin' To Beat The Morning Home** *T.G. Sheppard*
10/76 **Tryin' To Get The Feeling Again** *Barry Manilow*
5/81 **Tryin' To Live My Life Without You** *Bob Seger*
10/77 **Tryin' To Love Two** *William Bell*
77/58 **Trying** *Billy Vaughn*
15/74 **Trying To Hold On To My Woman** *Lamont Dozier*
40/70 **Trying To Make A Fool Of Me** *Delfonics*
Tubular Bells
7/74 *Mike Oldfield*
98/76 *Champs' Boys Orchestra*
32/59 **Tucumcari** *Jimmie Rodgers*
24/68 **Tuesday Afternoon (Forever Afternoon)** *Moody Blues*
17/62 **Tuff** *Ace Cannon*
10/86 **Tuff Enuff** *Fabulous Thunderbirds*
53/82 **Tug Of War** *Paul McCartney*
86/71 **Tulsa** *Billy Joe Royal*
30/80 **Tulsa Time** *Eric Clapton*
Tumbling Dice
7/72 *Rolling Stones*
32/78 *Linda Ronstadt*
Tumbling Tumbleweeds
60/56 *Roger Williams*
30/58 *Billy Vaughn*
43/58 **Tunnel Of Love** *Doris Day*
47/72 **Tupelo Honey** *Van Morrison*
42/80 **Turn And Walk Away** *Babys*
27/64 **Turn Around** *Dick & DeeDee*
62/84 **Turn Around** *Neil Diamond*
96/69 **Turn Around And Love You** *Rita Coolidge*
Turn Around, Look At Me
62/61 *Glen Campbell*
7/68 *Vogues*
3/70 **Turn Back The Hands Of Time** *Tyrone Davis*
84/75 **Turn Back The Pages** *Stephen Stills*
16/66 **Turn Down Day** *Cyrkle*
58/80 **Turn It On Again** *Genesis*
98/77 **Turn Loose Of My Leg** *Jim Stafford*
9/59 **Turn Me Loose** *Fabian*
35/81 **Turn Me Loose** *Loverboy*
48/79 **Turn Off The Lights** *Teddy Pendergrass*
58/69 **Turn On A Dream** *Box Tops*
Turn On Your Love Light
28/62 *Bobby Bland*
65/67 *Oscar Toney, Jr.*
80/68 *Human Beinz*
82/68 *Bill Black's Combo*
95/72 *Jerry Lee Lewis*
64/82 **Turn On Your Radar** *Prism*
10/76 **Turn The Beat Around** *Vicki Sue Robinson*
66/67 **Turn The World Around** *Eddy Arnold*
13/78 **Turn To Stone** *Electric Light Orchestra*
93/75 **Turn To Stone** *Joe Walsh*
32/84 **Turn To You** *Go-Go's*
Turn! Turn! Turn!
1/65 *Byrds*
69/69 *Judy Collins*
29/85 **Turn Up The Radio** *Autograph*
5/82 **Turn Your Love Around** *George Benson*
63/71 **Turn Your Radio On** *Ray Stevens*
36/80 **Turning Japanese** *Vapors*
96/77 **Turning To You** *Charlie*
36/58 **Turvy II** *Cozy Cole*
20/75 **Tush** *ZZ Top*
8/79 **Tusk** *Fleetwood Mac*
Tutti' Frutti
12/56 *Pat Boone*
17/56 *Little Richard*
82/60 **Tuxedo Junction** *Frankie Avalon*
Tweedlee Dee
2/55 *Georgia Gibbs*
14/55 *LaVern Baker*
59/73 *Little Jimmy Osmond*
Twelfth Of Never
9/57 *Johnny Mathis*
8/73 *Donny Osmond*
68/57 **Twelve O'clock Tonight** *Doris Day*
20/67 **Twelve Thirty (Young Girls Are Coming To The Canyon)** *Mamas & The Papas*
15/63 **Twenty Miles** *Chubby Checker*
48/85 **20/20** *George Benson*
31/64 **20-75** *Willie Mitchell*
74/55 **24 Hours A Day (365 A Year)** *Georgia Gibbs*
17/63 **Twenty Four Hours From Tulsa** *Gene Pitney*
6/69 **Twenty-Five Miles** *Edwin Starr*
25 Or 6 To 4
4/70 *Chicago*
48/86 *Chicago*
2/58 **26 Miles (Santa Catalina)** *Four Preps*
91/59 **Twice As Nice** *Clyde McPhatter*
38/81 **Twilight** *ELO*
Twilight Time
1/58 *Platters*
86/62 *Andy Williams*
10/83 **Twilight Zone** *Golden Earring*
30/80 **Twilight Zone/Twilight Tone** *Manhattan Transfer*
14/65 **Twine Time** *Alvin Cash & The Crawlers*
39/66 **Twinkle Toes** *Roy Orbison*
Twist
1/60 *Chubby Checker*
28/60 *Hank Ballard*
1/62 *Chubby Checker*
93/62 *Ernie Freeman*
Twist And Shout
17/62 *Isley Brothers*
2/64 *Beatles*
23/86 *Beatles*
26/62 **Twist-Her** *Bill Black's Combo*
25/63 **Twist It Up** *Chubby Checker*
83/86 **Twist My Arm** *Pointer Sisters*
5/84 **Twist Of Fate** *Olivia Newton-John*
9/62 **Twist, Twist Senora** *Gary U.S. Bonds*
68/62 **Twistin' All Night Long** *Danny & The Juniors*
49/60 **Twistin' Bells** *Santo & Johnny*
(also see: Jingle Bells)
22/62 **Twistin' Matilda** *Jimmy Soul*
(also see: Matilda)
34/62 **Twistin' Postman** *Marvelettes*
Twistin' The Night Away
9/62 *Sam Cooke*
59/73 *Rod Stewart*

Twistin' U.S.A.
27/60 *Danny & The Juniors*
68/61 *Chubby Checker*
Twistin' White Silver Sands
see: White Silver Sands
54/62 **Twistin' With Linda** *Isley Brothers*
17/59 **Twixt Twelve And Twenty** *Pat Boone*
66/68 **Two-Bit Manchild** *Neil Diamond*
90/59 **Two Brothers** *David Hill*
Two Brothers *see: Ballad Of*
Two Different Worlds
11/56 *Don Rondo*
41/56 *Roger Williams & Jane Morgan*
80/56 *Dick Haymes*
61/65 *Lenny Welch*
16/71 **Two Divided By Love** *Grass Roots*
19/78 **Two Doors Down** *Dolly Parton*
6/63 **Two Faces Have I** *Lou Christie*
33/75 **Two Fine People** *Cat Stevens*
54/59 **Two Fools** *Frankie Avalon*
16/55 **Two Hearts** *Pat Boone*
40/81 **Two Hearts**
Stephanie Mills/Teddy Pendergrass
F/55 **Two Hound Dogs** *Bill Haley & His Comets*
99/67 **Two In The Afternoon** *Dino, Desi & Billy*
50/63 **Two Kind Of Teardrops** *Del Shannon*
97/75 **Two Lane Highway** *Pure Prairie League*
38/83 **Two Less Lonely People In The World**
Air Supply
31/68 **Two Little Kids** *Peaches & Herb*
18/55 **Two Lost Souls**
Perry Como & Jaye P. Morgan
7/63 **Two Lovers** *Mary Wells*
42/62 **Two Of A Kind** *Sue Thompson*
3/86 **Two Of Hearts** *Stacey Q*
11/78 **Two Out Of Three Ain't Bad** *Meat Loaf*
30/80 **Two Places At The Same Time**
Ray Parker Jr. & Raydio
38/84 **Two Sides Of Love** *Sammy Hagar*
63/63 **Two Sides (To Every Story)** *Etta James*
78/63 **Two-Ten, Six-Eighteen (Doesn't Anybody Know My Name)** *Jimmie Rodgers*
22/78 **Two Tickets To Paradise** *Eddie Money*
32/63 **Two Tickets To Paradise** *Brook Benton*
43/84 **Two Tribes** *Frankie Goes To Hollywood*
100/63 **Two Wrongs Don't Make A Right**
Mary Wells
2001 Space Odyssey
see: Also Sprach Zarathustra
91/63 **2,000 Pound Bee** *Ventures*
67/60 **Two Thousand, Two Hundred, Twenty-Three Miles** *Patti Page*
2/86 **Typical Male** *Tina Turner*

U

28/68 **U.S. Male** *Elvis Presley*
86/74 **U.S. Of A.** *Donna Fargo*
92/57 **Uh-Huh-Mm** *Sonny James*
73/58 **Uh-Huh, Oh Yeah** *Steve Lawrence*
Uh! Oh!
14/59 *Nutty Squirrels (Part 1)*
45/59 *Nutty Squirrels (Part 2)*
Um, Um, Um, Um, Um, Um
5/64 *Major Lance*
41/78 *Johnny Rivers*
66/74 **Unborn Child** *Seals & Crofts*
Unchain My Heart
9/62 *Ray Charles*
81/68 *Herbie Mann*
Unchained Melody
1/55 *Les Baxter*
3/55 *Al Hibbler*
6/55 *Roy Hamilton*
29/55 *June Valli*
66/63 *Vito & The Salutations*
4/65 *Righteous Brothers*
73/68 *Sweet Inspirations*
83/81 *Heart*
1/71 **Uncle Albert/Admiral Halsey**
Paul & Linda McCartney
69/70 **Uncle John's Band** *Grateful Dead*
43/83 **Unconditional Love** *Donna Summer*
59/72 **Under My Wheels** *Alice Cooper*
29/82 **Under Pressure** *Queen & David Bowie*
Under The Boardwalk
4/64 *Drifters*
82/78 *Billy Joe Royal*
71/81 **Under The Covers** *Janis Ian*
48/80 **Under The Gun** *Poco*
56/86 **Under The Influence** *Vanity*
76/74 **Under The Influence Of Love**
Love Unlimited
46/61 **Under The Moon Of Love** *Curtis Lee*
35/66 **Under Your Spell Again** *Johnny Rivers*
1/77 **Undercover Angel** *Alan O'Day*
9/83 **Undercover Of The Night** *Rolling Stones*
35/64 **Understand Your Man** *Johnny Cash*
17/85 **Understanding** *Bob Seger*
46/68 **Understanding** *Ray Charles*
44/61 **Underwater** *Frogmen*
22/69 **Undun** *Guess Who*
9/73 **Uneasy Rider** *Charlie Daniels*
87/84 **Unfaithfully Yours (One Love)**
Stephen Bishop
17/59 **Unforgettable** *Dinah Washington*
Unforgiven *see: Theme From The*
33/70 **Ungena Za Ulimwengu (Unite The World)**
Temptations
7/68 **Unicorn, The** *Irish Rovers*
24/76 **Union Man** *Cate Bros.*
3/83 **Union Of The Snake** *Duran Duran*
United
78/66 *Intruders*
46/68 *Peaches & Herb*
78/68 *Music Makers*
56/81 **United Together** *Aretha Franklin*
13/70 **United We Stand** *Brotherhood Of Man*
Universal Soldier
45/65 *Glen Campbell*
53/65 *Donovan*
39/68 **Unknown Soldier** *Doors*
99/64 **Unless You Care** *Terry Black*
74/62 **Unsquare Dance** *Dave Brubeck Quartet*
54/55 **Unsuspecting Heart** *Sunny Gale*
60/62 **Untie Me** *Tams*
Until It's Time For You To Go
53/70 *Neil Diamond*
40/72 *Elvis Presley*
97/73 *New Birth*
72/78 **Until Now** *Bobby Arvon*
3/74 **Until You Come Back To Me (That's What I'm Gonna Do)** *Aretha Franklin*
52/68 **Unwind** *Ray Stevens*
Up A Lazy River *see: Lazy River*
85/64 **Up Above My Head (I Hear Music In The Air)** *Al Hirt*
46/66 **Up And Down** *McCoys*
4/70 **Up Around The Bend**
Creedence Clearwater Revival
63/74 **Up For The Down Stroke** *Parliament*

82/68 **Up From The Skies** *Jimi Hendrix*
91/68 **Up-Hard** *Willie Mitchell*
16/75 **Up In A Puff Of Smoke** *Polly Brown*
83/72 **Up In Heah** *Ike & Tina Turner*
25/70 **Up On Cripple Creek** *Band*
Up On The Roof
5/63 *Drifters*
85/68 *Cryan' Shames*
92/70 *Laura Nyro*
28/79 *James Taylor*
94/76 **Up The Creek (Without A Paddle)**
Temptations
10/70 **Up The Ladder To The Roof** *Supremes*
93/68 **Up Tight, Good Man** *Laura Lee*
93/68 **Up To My Neck In High Muddy Water**
Linda Ronstadt
72/60 **Up Town** *Roy Orbison*
81/58 **Up Until Now** *Johnnie Ray*
Up-Up And Away
7/67 *5th Dimension*
91/67 *Johnny Mann Singers*
71/68 *Hugh Masekela*
1/82 **Up Where We Belong**
Joe Cocker & Jennifer Warnes
91/77 **Up Your Nose** *Gabriel Kaplan*
22/67 **Ups And Downs** *Paul Revere & The Raiders*
73/72 **Upsetter** *Grand Funk Railroad*
1/80 **Upside Down** *Diana Ross*
Uptight (Everything's Alright)
3/66 *Stevie Wonder*
49/66 *Ramsey Lewis*
84/66 *Nancy Wilson*
95/66 *Jazz Crusaders*
(also see: Little Ole Man)
13/62 **Uptown** *Crystals*
80/76 **Uptown & Country** *Tom Scott*
25/77 **Uptown Festival (Motown Medley)**
Shalamar
3/83 **Uptown Girl** *Billy Joel*
60/60 **Urge, The** *Freddy Cannon*
4/81 **Urgent** *Foreigner*
44/80 **Us And Love (We Go Together)**
Kenny Nolan
2/72 **Use Me** *Bill Withers*
4/78 **Use Ta Be My Girl** *O'Jays*
34/65 **Use Your Head** *Mary Wells*
46/82 **Used To Be** *Charlene & Stevie Wonder*
27/61 **Utopia** *Frank Gari*

V

8/82 **Vacation** *Go-Go's*
9/62 **Vacation** *Connie Francis*
Vado Via *see: Words (Are Impossible)*
84/72 **Vahevala** *Loggins & Messina*
97/76 **Valentine Love** *Norman Connors*
70/82 **Valerie** *Steve Winwood*
96/71 **Valerie** *Cymarron*
3/68 **Valleri** *Monkees*
32/82 **Valley Girl** *Frank Zappa*
6/57 **Valley Of Tears** *Fats Domino*
Valley Of The Dolls *see: Theme From*
53/56 **Valley Valparaiso** *Percy Faith*
9/85 **Valotte** *Julian Lennon*
80/68 **Vance** *Roger Miller*
76/72 **Vanilla Olay** *Jackie DeShannon*
90/64 **Vanishing Point** *Marketts*
91/86 **Vanity Kills** *ABC*
99/60 **Vaquero (Cowboy)** *Fireballs*
Vaya Con Dios
43/64 *Drifters*
95/72 *Dawn*
59/76 *Freddy Fender*
2/70 **Vehicle** *Ides Of March*
35/86 **Velcro Fly** *ZZ Top*
51/59 **Velvet Waters** *Megatrons*
48/79 **Vengeance** *Carly Simon*
8/72 **Ventura Highway** *America*
Venus
1/59 *Frankie Avalon*
46/76 *Frankie Avalon*
Venus
1/70 *Shocking Blue*
1/86 *Bananarama*
12/75 **Venus And Mars Rock Show** *Wings*
7/62 **Venus In Blue Jeans** *Jimmy Clanton*
84/82 **Very Best In You** *Change*
76/80 **Very Last Time** *Utopia*
Very Lovely Woman *see: She's A*
23/58 **Very Precious Love** *Ames Brothers*
90/81 **Very Special** *Debra Laws*
Very Special Love
94/57 *Mitch Miller*
20/58 *Debbie Reynolds*
23/58 *Johnny Nash*
11/74 **Very Special Love Song** *Charlie Rich*
Very Thought Of You
61/61 *Little Willie John*
26/64 *Rick Nelson*
63/72 **Victim Of A Foolish Heart** *Bettye Swann*
31/79 **Victim Of Love** *Elton John*
62/70 **Victoria** *Kinks*
10/87 **Victory** *Kool & The Gang*
79/86 **Victory Line** *Limited Warranty*
85/84 **Video!** *Jeff Lynne*
40/79 **Video Killed The Radio Star** *Buggles*
18/86 **Vienna Calling** *Falco*
1/85 **View To A Kill** *Duran Duran*
22/62 **Village Of Love** *Nathaniel Mayer*
7/60 **Village Of St. Bernadette** *Andy Williams*
12/72 **Vincent** *Don McLean*
56/74 **Virgin Man** *Smokey Robinson*
59/74 **Virginia (Touch Me Like You Do)**
Bill Amesbury
63/82 **Visitors** *Abba*
66/84 **Vitamin L** *B.E. Taylor Group*
Viva Las Vegas
29/64 *Elvis Presley*
92/64 *Elvis Presley*
28/70 **Viva Tirado** *El Chicano*
15/81 **Voice** *Moody Blues*
88/58 **Voice In My Heart** *Eydie Gorme*
80/68 **Voice In The Choir** *Al Martino*
62/86 **Voice Of America's Song** *John Cafferty*
71/80 **Voice Of Freedom** *Jim Kirk*
63/82 **Voice On The Radio** *Conductor*
51/65 **Voice Your Choice** *Radiants*
32/80 **Voices** *Cheap Trick*
47/56 **Voices** *Fontane Sisters*
8/85 **Voices Carry** *'Til Tuesday*
Volare (Nel Blu Dipinto Di Blu)
1/58 *Domenico Modugno*
12/58 *Dean Martin*
80/58 *McGuire Sisters*
4/60 *Bobby Rydell*
33/75 *Al Martino*
66/80 **Volcano** *Jimmy Buffett*
65/69 **Volunteers** *Jefferson Airplane*
72/83 **Voo Doo** *Rachel Sweet*
27/65 **Voodoo Woman** *Bobby Goldsboro*
90/69 **Voodoo Woman** *Simon Stokes*
80/79 **Voulez-Vous** *Abba*

29/85 **Vox Humana** *Al Martino*
62/86 **Voice Of America's Song** *John Cafferty*

36/74 **W-O-L-D** *Harry Chapin*
65/81 **WKRP In Cincinnati (Main Theme)** *Steve Carlisle*
77/61 **Wabash Blues** *Viscounts*
40/67 **Wack Wack** *Young Holt Trio*
Wade In The Water
19/66 *Ramsey Lewis*
37/67 *Herb Alpert*
2/62 **Wah Watusi** *Orlons*
91/60 **Wait** *Jimmy Clanton*
37/61 **Wait A Minute** *Coasters*
76/66 **Wait A Minute** *Tim Tam & The Turn-Ons*
23/57 **Wait And See** *Fats Domino*
18/80 **Wait For Me** *Daryl Hall & John Oates*
37/60 **Wait For Me** *Playmates*
26/63 **Wait Til' My Bobby Gets Home** *Darlene Love*
18/58 **Waitin' In School** *Ricky Nelson*
57/66 **Waitin' In Your Welfare Line** *Buck Owens*
19/81 **Waiting** *Tom Petty*
54/71 **Waiting At The Bus Stop** *Bobby Sherman*
2/81 **Waiting For A Girl Like You** *Foreigner*
73/83 **Waiting For Your Love** *Toto*
13/82 **Waiting On A Friend** *Rolling Stones*
51/60 **Wake Me, Shake Me** *Coasters*
1/84 **Wake Me Up Before You Go-Go** *Wham!*
50/60 **Wake Me When It's Over** *Andy Williams*
Wake The Town And Tell The People
5/55 *Les Baxter*
13/55 *Mindy Carson*
92/69 **Wake Up** *Chambers Brothers*
86/77 **Wake Up And Be Somebody** *Brainstorm*
93/74 **Wake Up And Love Me** *April*
12/76 **Wake Up Everybody** *Harold Melvin & The Blue Notes*
Wake Up Little Susie
1/57 *Everly Brothers*
27/82 *Simon & Garfunkel*
53/82 **Wake Up My Love** *George Harrison*
39/85 **Wake Up (Next To You)** *Graham Parker*
56/76 **Wake Up Susan** *Spinners*
68/67 **Wake Up, Wake Up** *Grass Roots*
60/72 **Waking Up Alone** *Paul Williams*
7/58 **Walk, The** *Jimmy McCracklin*
12/70 **Walk A Mile In My Shoes** *Joe South*
23/65 **Walk Away** *Matt Monro*
36/80 **Walk Away** *Donna Summer*
51/71 **Walk Away** *James Gang*
9/76 **Walk Away From Love** *David Ruffin*
Walk Away Renee
5/66 *Left Banke*
14/68 *Four Tops*
98/86 *Southside Johnny & The Jukes*
Walk Don't Run
2/60 *Ventures*
8/64 *Ventures ('64)*
93/71 **Walk Easy My Son** *Jerry Butler*
Walk Hand In Hand
10/56 *Tony Martin*
54/56 *Andy Williams*
70/56 *Denny Vaughn*
12/65 **Walk In The Black Forest** *Horst Jankowski*
46/72 **Walk In The Night** *Jr. Walker & The All Stars*
Walk Like A Man
1/63 *4 Seasons*
41/86 *Mary Jane Girls*
19/74 **Walk Like A Man** *Grand Funk*
1/87 **Walk Like An Egyptian** *Bangles*
7/86 **Walk Of Life** *Dire Straits*
69/74 **Walk On** *Neil Young*
5/61 **Walk On By** *Leroy Van Dyke*
Walk On By
6/64 *Dionne Warwick*
30/69 *Isaac Hayes*
98/75 *Gloria Gaynor*
92/79 *Average White Band*
16/73 **Walk On The Wild Side** *Lou Reed*
Walk On The Wild Side
21/62 *Jimmy Smith*
43/62 *Brook Benton*
17/72 **Walk On Water** *Neil Diamond*
91/62 **Walk On With The Duke** *Duke Of Earl*
7/61 **Walk Right Back** *Everly Brothers*
Walk Right In
1/63 *Rooftop Singers*
82/63 *Moments*
46/77 *Dr. Hook*
73/81 **Walk Right Now** *Jacksons*
81/71 **Walk Right Up To The Sun** *Delfonics*
48/60 **Walk Slow** *Little Willie John*
92/67 **Walk Tall** *2 Of Clubs*
Walk This Way
10/77 *Aerosmith*
4/86 *Run-D.M.C.*
83/67 **Walk With Faith In Your Heart** *Bachelors*
12/57 **Walkin' After Midnight** *Patsy Cline*
100/61 **Walkin' Back To Happiness** *Helen Shapiro*
Walkin' In The Rain
23/64 *Ronettes*
19/70 *Jay & The Americans*
14/72 **Walkin' In The Rain With The One I Love** *Love Unlimited*
Walkin' In The Sand *see: Remember*
37/67 **Walkin' In The Sunshine** *Roger Miller*
12/63 **Walkin' Miracle** *Essex*
22/66 **Walkin' My Cat Named Dog** *Norma Tanega*
98/67 **Walkin' Proud** *Pete Klint Quintet*
96/59 **Walkin' To Mother's** *Ray Anthony*
54/58 **Walkin' With Mr. Lee** *Lee Allen*
53/62 **Walkin' With My Angel** *Bobby Vee*
29/58 **Walking Along** *Diamonds*
70/83 **Walking In L.A.** *Missing Persons*
62/84 **Walking In My Sleep** *Roger Daltrey*
6/75 **Walking In Rhythm** *Blackbyrds*
84/81 **Walking Into Sunshine** *Central Line*
18/84 **Walking On A Thin Line** *Huey Lewis & The News*
9/85 **Walking On Sunshine** *Katrina & The Waves*
46/85 **Walking On The Chinese Wall** *Philip Bailey*
58/81 **Walking On Thin Ice** *Yoko Ono*
26/63 **Walking Proud** *Steve Lawrence*
10/63 **Walking The Dog** *Rufus Thomas*
Walking The Floor *see: I'm Walking*
44/70 **Walking Through The Country** *Grass Roots*
6/60 **Walking To New Orleans** *Fats Domino*
32/80 **Walks Like A Lady** *Journey*
Wall
43/57 *Patti Page*
62/57 *Eileen Rodgers*
74/84 **Walls Came Down** *Call*
77/59 **Walls Have Ears** *Patti Page*
94/62 **Waltz You Saved For Me** *Ferlin Husky*
41/60 **Waltzing Matilda** *Jimmie Rodgers*

Wanderer, The
2/62 *Dion*
49/78 *Leif Garrett*
3/80 **Wanderer, The** *Donna Summer*
Wang Dang Doodle
58/66 *Ko Ko Taylor*
61/74 *Pointer Sisters*
62/59 **Wang Dang Taffy-Apple Tango** *Pat Boone*
86/80 **Wango Tango** *Ted Nugent*
5/83 **Wanna Be Startin' Somethin'** *Michael Jackson*
51/82 **Wanna Be With You** *Earth, Wind & Fire*
76/76 **Wanna Make Love (Come Flick My BIC)** *Sun*
1/71 **Want Ads** *Honey Cone*
72/81 **(Want You) Back In My Life Again** *Carpenters*
96/70 **Want You To Know** *Rotary Connection*
87/84 **Wanted Man** *Ratt*
84/67 **Wanted: Lover, No Experience Necessary** *Laura Lee*
38/56 **Wanting You** *Roger Williams*
War
1/70 *Edwin Starr*
8/86 *Bruce Springsteen*
59/56 **War And Peace** *Vic Damone*
45/83 **War Games** *Crosby, Stills & Nash*
17/84 **War Song** *Culture Club*
61/72 **War Song** *Neil Young & Graham Nash*
17/66 **Warm And Tender Love** *Percy Sledge*
39/78 **Warm Ride** *Rare Earth*
57/57 **Warm Up To Me Baby** *Jimmy Bowen with The Rhythm Orchids*
25/62 **Warmed Over Kisses (Left Over Love)** *Brian Hyland*
7/84 **Warrior, The** *Scandal*
70/78 **Was Dog A Doughnut** *Cat Stevens*
83/69 **Was It Good To You** *Isley Brothers*
56/67 **Washed Ashore (On A Lonely Island In The Sea)** *Platters*
2/63 **Washington Square** *Village Stompers*
49/79 **Wasn't It Good** *Cher*
37/81 **Wasn't That A Party** *Rovers*
89/61 **Wasn't The Summer Short?** *Johnny Mathis*
8/75 **Wasted Days And Wasted Nights** *Freddy Fender*
9/82 **Wasted On The Way** *Crosby, Stills & Nash*
52/77 **Watch Closely Now** *Kris Kristofferson*
61/67 **Watch Her Ride** *Jefferson Airplane*
40/79 **Watch Out For Lucy** *Eric Clapton*
30/67 **Watch The Flowers Grow** *4 Seasons*
51/61 **Watch Your Step** *Bobby Parker*
58/64 **Watch Your Step** *Brooks O'Dell*
11/71 **Watching Scotty Grow** *Bobby Goldsboro*
41/71 **Watching The River Flow** *Bob Dylan*
71/74 **Watching The River Run** *Loggins & Messina*
10/81 **Watching The Wheels** *John Lennon*
83/56 **Watching The World Go By** *Dean Martin*
78/81 **Watching You** *Slave*
40/61 **Water Boy** *Don Shirley*
78/75 **Waterfall** *Carly Simon*
42/73 **Watergrate** *Dickie Goodman*
4/59 **Waterloo** *Stonewall Jackson*
6/74 **Waterloo** *Abba*
Watermelon Man
10/63 *Mongo Santamaria*
62/65 *Gloria Lynne*
87/57 **Watermelon Song** *Tennessee Ernie Ford*
25/61 **Watusi, The** *Vibrations*
(also see: El Watusi and Wah Watusi)
42/78 **Wavelength** *Van Morrison*

Way Back Home
90/71 *Jazz Crusaders*
52/72 *Jr. Walker & The All Stars*
18/77 **Way Down** *Elvis Presley*
3/60 **Way Down Yonder In New Orleans** *Freddy Cannon*
40/83 **Way He Makes Me Feel** *Barbra Streisand*
58/61 **Way I Am** *Jackie Wilson*
24/78 **Way I Feel Tonight** *Bay City Rollers*
35/59 **Way I Walk** *Jack Scott*
4/75 **Way I Want To Touch You** *Captain & Tennille*
1/86 **Way It Is** *Bruce Hornsby*
42/69 **Way It Used To Be** *Engelbert Humperdinck*
44/60 **Way Of A Clown** *Teddy Randazzo*
Way Of Love
88/65 *Kathy Kirby*
7/72 *Cher*
94/62 **Way Over There** *Miracles*
Way We Were
1/74 *Barbra Streisand*
11/75 *Gladys Knight & The Pips (medley)*
Way You Do The Things You Do
11/64 *Temptations*
20/78 *Rita Coolidge*
20/85 *Hall & Oates/David Ruffin/Eddie Kendrick (medley)*
13/61 **Way You Look Tonight** *Lettermen*
24/58 **Ways Of A Woman In Love** *Johnny Cash*
71/85 **Ways To Be Wicked** *Lone Justice*
81/69 **Ways To Love A Man** *Tammy Wynette*
Wayward Wind
1/56 *Gogi Grant*
28/56 *Tex Ritter*
50/61 *Gogi Grant*
89/73 **We** *Shawn Phillips*
5/67 **(We Ain't Got) Nothin' Yet** *Blues Magoos*
97/75 **We All Gotta Stick Together** *Four Tops*
67/56 **We All Need Love** *Percy Faith*
We All Shine On *see: Instant Karma*
2/79 **We Are Family** *Sister Sledge*
70/71 **We Are Neighbors** *Chi-Lites*
4/78 **We Are The Champions** *Queen*
1/85 **We Are The World** *USA for Africa*
25/84 **We Are The Young** *Dan Hartman*
91/75 **We Been Singin' Songs** *Baron Stewart*
5/85 **We Belong** *Pat Benatar*
We Belong Together
32/58 *Robert & Johnny*
75/64 *Jimmy Velvet*
1/85 **We Built This City** *Starship*
21/68 **We Can Fly** *Cowsills*
62/81 **We Can Get Together** *Icehouse*
74/70 **We Can Make It Baby** *Originals*
68/72 **We Can Make It Together** *Steve & Eydie*
49/70 **We Can Make Music** *Tommy Roe*
We Can Work It Out
1/66 *Beatles*
13/71 *Stevie Wonder*
36/76 **We Can't Hide It Anymore** *Larry Santos*
41/85 **We Close Our Eyes** *Go West*
35/87 **We Connect** *Stacey Q*
41/64 **We Could** *Al Martino*
95/73 **We Did It** *Syl Johnson*
5/86 **We Don't Have To Take Our Clothes Off** *Jermaine Stewart*
2/85 **We Don't Need Another Hero (Thunderdome)** *Tina Turner*
7/80 **We Don't Talk Anymore** *Cliff Richard*
80/78 **We Fell In Love While Dancing** *Bill Brandon*
53/60 **We Go Together** *Jan & Dean*
82/71 **We Got A Dream** *Ocean*

65/66 **We Got A Thing That's In The Groove**
Capitols
6/59 **We Got Love** *Bobby Rydell*
35/69 **We Got More Soul** *Dyke & The Blazers*
2/82 **We Got The Beat** *Go-Go's*
100/66 **We Got The Winning Hand** *Little Milton*
86/71 **We Got To Live Together** *Buddy Miles*
50/69 **We Gotta All Get Together**
Paul Revere & The Raiders
13/65 **We Gotta Get Out Of This Place** *Animals*
20/71 **We Gotta Get You A Woman** *Runt*
72/67 **We Had A Good Thing Goin'** *Cyrkle*
76/60 **We Have Love** *Dinah Washington*
93/58 **We Have Love** *Jackie Wilson*
12/77 **We Just Disagree** *Dave Mason*
76/66 **We Know We're In Love** *Lesley Gore*
27/80 **We Live For Love** *Pat Benatar*
50/67 **We Love You** *Rolling Stones*
39/64 **We Love You Beatles** *Carefrees*
42/69 **We Love You, Call Collect** *Art Linkletter*
83/75 **We May Never Love Like This Again**
Maureen McGovern
21/73 **We May Never Pass This Way (Again)**
Seals & Crofts
88/69 **We Must Be In Love** *Five Stairsteps*
61/72 **We Need Order** *Chi-Lites*
93/77 **We Never Danced To A Love Song**
Manhattans
90/63 **We Shall Overcome** *Joan Baez*
83/59 **We Told You Not To Marry** *Titus Turner*
22/83 **We Two** *Little River Band*
61/71 **We Were Always Sweethearts** *Boz Scaggs*
31/80 **We Were Meant To Be Lovers** *Photoglo*
F/78 **We Will Rock You** *Queen*
(We'll Be) *see: United*
73/69 **We'll Cry Together** *Maxine Brown*
89/71 **We'll Have It Made** *Spinners*
9/78 **We'll Never Have To Say Goodbye Again**
England Dan & John Ford Coley
4/64 **We'll Sing In The Sunshine** *Gale Garnett*
14/68 **We're A Winner** *Impressions*
We're All Alone
78/76 *Frankie Valli*
7/77 *Rita Coolidge*
93/71 **We're All Goin' Home** *Bobby Bloom*
48/70 **We're All Playing In The Same Band**
Bert Sommer
54/75 **We're Almost There** *Michael Jackson*
1/73 **We're An American Band** *Grand Funk*
96/65 **We're Doing Fine** *Dee Dee Warwick*
40/72 **We're Free** *Beverly Bremers*
100/71 **We're Friends By Day (And Lovers By Night)** *Whatnauts*
34/74 **We're Getting Careless With Our Love**
Johnnie Taylor
48/84 **We're Going All The Way** *Jeffrey Osborne*
(We're Gonna) *see: Rock Around The Clock*
93/73 **We're Gonna Have A Good Time**
Rare Earth
25/65 **We're Gonna Make It** *Little Milton*
15/81 **We're In This Love Together** *Al Jarreau*
21/84 **We're Not Gonna Take It** *Twisted Sister*
44/72 **We're On Our Way** *Chris Hodge*
94/76 **We're On The Right Track**
South Shore Commission
9/87 **We're Ready** *Boston*
59/68 **We're Rolling On** *Impressions*
100/72 **We're Together** *Hillside Singers*
46/72 **We've Come Too Far To End It Now**
Miracles
56/69 **(We've Got) Honey Love**
Martha & The Vandellas
44/79 **We've Got Love** *Peaches & Herb*
25/72 **We've Got To Get It On Again**
Addrisi Brothers
We've Got Tonite
13/79 *Bob Seger*
6/83 *Kenny Rogers & Sheena Easton*
2/70 **We've Only Just Begun** *Carpenters*
44/68 **Wear It On Our Face** *Dells*
F/57 **Wear My Ring** *Gene Vincent*
2/58 **Wear My Ring Around Your Neck**
Elvis Presley
91/71 **Wear This Ring (With Love)**
Detroit Emeralds
23/67 **Wear Your Love Like Heaven** *Donovan*
32/56 **Weary Blues** *McGuire Sisters*
95/86 **Weatherman** *Nick Jameson*
Wedding, The
10/65 *Julie Rogers*
43/59 *June Valli*
91/56 *Chordettes*
1/69 **Wedding Bell Blues** *5th Dimension*
Wedding Bells *see: (I'm Always Hearing)*
91/69 **Wedding Cake** *Connie Francis*
Wedding Song (There Is Love)
24/71 *Paul Stookey*
61/72 *Petula Clark*
81/78 *Mary MacGregor*
(also see: Down The Aisle)
97/67 **Wednesday** *Royal Guardsmen*
35/58 **Week End** *Kingsmen*
29/79 **Weekend** *Wet Willie*
10/77 **Weekend In New England** *Barry Manilow*
57/78 **Weekend Lover** *Odyssey*
Weight, The
55/68 *Jackie DeShannon*
63/68 *Band*
19/69 *Aretha Franklin*
46/69 *Supremes & Temptations*
45/85 **Weird Science** *Oingo Boingo*
1/76 **Welcome Back** *John Sebastian*
68/61 **Welcome Home** *Sammy Kaye*
95/65 **Welcome Home** *Walter Jackson*
22/62 **Welcome Home Baby** *Shirelles*
48/69 **Welcome Me Love** *Brooklyn Bridge*
18/60 **(Welcome) New Lovers** *Pat Boone*
24/83 **Welcome To Heartlight** *Kenny Loggins*
(Welcome To My Morning)
see: Farewell Andromeda
45/75 **Welcome To My Nightmare** *Alice Cooper*
68/77 **Welcome To Our World (Of Merry Music)**
Mass Production
85/85 **Welcome To Paradise** *John Waite*
37/86 **Welcome To The Boomtown** *David & David*
48/85 **Welcome To The Pleasuredome**
Frankie Goes To Hollywood
63/70 **Welfare Cadilac** *Guy Drake*
77/61 **Well-A, Well-A** *Shirley & Lee*
69/78 **Well All Right** *Santana*
92/56 **Well Did You Evah?**
Bing Crosby & Frank Sinatra
29/61 **Well, I Told You** *Chantels*
87/58 **Well I'm Your Man** *Johnny Tillotson*
13/66 **Well Respected Man** *Kinks*
44/64 **Wendy** *Beach Boys*
72/58 **Wendy, Wendy** *Four Coins*
64/74 **Werewolf** *Five Man Electrical Band*
83/60 **Werewolf** *Frantics*
21/78 **Werewolves Of London** *Warren Zevon*
64/84 **West Coast Summer Nights** *Tony Carey*
79/73 **West Coast Woman** *Painter*
1/86 **West End Girls** *Pet Shop Boys*
37/62 **West Of The Wall** *Toni Fisher*
24/70 **Westbound # 9** *Flaming Ember*
8/58 **Western Movies** *Olympics*
5/67 **Western Union** *Five Americans*
61/84 **Wet My Whistle** *Midnight Star*

24/63 **Wham!** *Lonnie Mack*
16/76 **Wham Bam (Shang-A-Lang)** *Silver*
What A Beautiful World *see: I.G.Y.*
88/70 **What A Bummer** *Jaggerz*
What A Diff'rence A Day Makes
8/59 *Dinah Washington*
20/75 *Esther Phillips*
80/78 **What A Difference You've Made In My Life** *Ronnie Milsap*
What A Feeling *see: Flashdance*
1/79 **What A Fool Believes** *Doobie Brothers*
93/63 **What A Fool I've Been** *Carla Thomas*
41/63 **What A Guy** *Raindrops*
93/75 **What A Man, My Man Is** *Lynn Anderson*
22/61 **What A Party** *Fats Domino*
22/61 **What A Price** *Fats Domino*
74/62 **(What A Sad Way) To Love Someone** *Ral Donner*
82/73 **What A Shame** *Foghat*
33/61 **What A Surprise** *Johnny Maestro*
54/61 **What A Sweet Thing That Was** *Shirelles*
77/61 **What A Walk** *Bobby Lewis*
31/67 **What A Woman In Love Won't Do** *Sandy Posey*
78/72 **What A Wonderful Thing We Have** *Fabulous Rhinestones*
(What A) Wonderful World *see: Wonderful World*
26/86 **What About Love** *'Til Tuesday*
10/85 **What About Love?** *Heart*
15/84 **What About Me** *Kenny Rogers/Kim Carnes/James Ingram*
29/83 **What About Me** *Moving Pictures*
64/73 **What About Me** *Anne Murray*
100/61 **What About Me** *Don Gibson*
100/71 **What About Me** *Quicksilver Messenger Service*
47/60 **What About Us** *Coasters*
39/72 **What Am I Crying For?** *Classics IV*
71/66 **What Am I Going To Do Without Your Love** *Martha & The Vandellas*
50/61 **What Am I Gonna Do** *Jimmy Clanton*
73/70 **What Am I Gonna Do** *Smith*
35/83 **What Am I Gonna Do (I'm So In Love With You)** *Rod Stewart*
8/75 **What Am I Gonna Do With You** *Barry White*
What Am I Living For
9/58 *Chuck Willis*
26/60 *Conway Twitty*
91/67 *Percy Sledge*
54/72 *Ray Charles*
82/62 **What Am I Supposed To Do** *Ann-Margret*
53/63 **What Are Boys Made Of** *Percells*
14/81 **What Are We Doin' In Love** *Dottie West*
93/65 **What Are We Going To Do?** *David Jones*
39/71 **What Are You Doing Sunday** *Dawn*
7/66 **What Becomes Of The Brokenhearted** *Jimmy Ruffin*
61/57 **What Can I Do** *Donnie Elbert*
48/75 **What Can I Do For You?** *LaBelle*
50/79 **What Can I Do With This Broken Heart** *England Dan & John Ford Coley*
42/76 **What Can I Say** *Boz Scaggs*
69/80 **What Can You Get A Wookiee For Christmas (When He Already Owns A Comb?)** *Star Wars Intergalactic Droid Choir & Chorale*
What Cha *see: Whatcha*
53/81 **What Cha' Gonna Do For Me** *Chaka Khan*
38/65 **What Color (Is A Man)** *Bobby Vinton*
94/62 **What Did Daddy Do** *Shep & The Limelites*
59/82 **What Do All The People Know** *Monroes*
52/58 **What Do I Care** *Johnny Cash*
93/60 **What Do You Want** *Bobby Vee*
51/65 **What Do You Want With Me** *Chad & Jeremy*
53/63 **What Does A Girl Do?** *Shirelles*
82/63 **What Does A Girl Do?** *Marcie Blane*
52/86 **What Does It Take** *Honeymoon Suite*
4/69 **What Does It Take (To Win Your Love)** *Jr. Walker & The All Stars*
81/66 **What Goes On** *Beatles*
87/78 **What Goes Up** *Alan Parsons Project*
89/74 **What Goes Up (Must Come Down)** *Tyrone Davis*
61/64 **What Good Am I Without You** *Marvin Gaye & Kim Weston*
43/64 **What Have I Got Of My Own** *Trini Lopez*
29/65 **What Have They Done To The Rain** *Searchers*
4/86 **What Have You Done For Me Lately** *Janet Jackson*
49/80 **What I Like About You** *Romantics*
(What If) *see: Remo's Theme*
71/83 **What If (I Said I Love You)** *Unipop*
39/84 **(What) In The Name Of Love** *Naked Eyes*
5/60 **What In The World's Come Over You** *Jack Scott*
53/69 **What Is A Man** *Four Tops*
96/57 **What Is A Teenage Boy?** *Tom Edwards*
57/57 **What Is A Teenage Girl?** *Tom Edwards*
56/56 **What Is A Wife** *Steve Allen*
91/74 **What Is Hip?** *Tower Of Power*
10/71 **What Is Life** *George Harrison*
15/59 **What Is Love?** *Playmates*
33/84 **What Is Love?** *Howard Jones*
19/70 **What Is Truth** *Johnny Cash*
55/74 **What It Comes Down To** *Isley Brothers*
71/72 **What It Is** *Undisputed Truth*
10/81 **What Kind Of Fool** *Barbra Streisand & Barry Gibb*
What Kind Of Fool Am I
17/62 *Sammy Davis, Jr.*
85/62 *Anthony Newley*
89/62 *Robert Goulet*
21/82 **What Kind Of Fool Am I** *Rick Springfield*
What Kind Of Fool Do You Think I Am
9/64 *Tams*
23/69 *Bill Deal*
18/62 **What Kind Of Love Is This** *Joey Dee & The Starliters*
79/58 **What Little Girl** *Frankie Avalon*
63/83 **What Love Is** *Marty Balin*
56/73 **What My Baby Needs Now Is A Little More Lovin'** *James Brown-Lyn Collins*
40/65 **What Now** *Gene Chandler*
What Now My Love
14/66 *Sonny & Cher*
24/66 *Herb Alpert*
96/66 *'Groove' Holmes*
30/67 *Mitch Ryder*
61/81 **What She Does To Me (The Diana Song)** *Producers*
45/84 **What The Big Girls Do** *Van Stephenson*
What The World Needs Now Is Love
7/65 *Jackie DeShannon*
8/71 *Tom Clay (medley)*
67/62 **What Time Is It?** *Jive Five*
92/75 **What Time Of Day** *Billy Thunderkloud*
68/63 **What To Do With Laurie** *Mike Clifford*
What Will I Tell My Heart
64/57 *Fats Domino*
96/61 *Harptones*
9/63 **What Will Mary Say** *Johnny Mathis*
46/61 **What Would I Do** *Mickey & Sylvia*
70/72 **What Would The Children Think** *Rick Springfield*
73/61 **What Would You Do?** *Jim Reeves*

What You *also see: Whatcha*
72/83 **What You Do To Me** *Carl Wilson*
49/69 **What You Gave Me** *Marvin Gaye & Tammi Terrell*
95/75 **What You Got** *Duke & The Drivers*
5/86 **What You Need** *INXS*
71/71 **What You See Is What You Get** *Stoney & Meatloaf*
9/79 **What You Won't Do For Love** *Bobby Caldwell*
81/83 **What You're Missing** *Chicago*
What'd I Say
6/59 *Ray Charles*
30/61 *Jerry Lee Lewis*
24/62 *Bobby Darin*
21/64 *Elvis Presley*
61/72 *Rare Earth*
What's A Matter Baby
12/62 *Timi Yuro*
92/79 *Ellen Foley*
29/64 **What's Easy For Two Is So Hard For One** *Mary Wells*
19/82 **What's Forever For** *Michael Murphey*
2/71 **What's Going On** *Marvin Gaye*
45/62 **What's Gonna Happen When Summer's Done** *Freddy Cannon*
57/75 **What's Happened To Blue Eyes** *Jessi Colter*
94/60 **What's Happening** *Wade Flemons*
60/65 **What's He Doing In My World** *Eddy Arnold*
49/67 **What's It Gonna Be** *Dusty Springfield*
1/84 **What's Love Got To Do With It** *Tina Turner*
94/68 **What's Made Milwaukee Famous (Has Made A Loser Out Of Me)** *Jerry Lee Lewis*
53/83 **What's New** *Linda Ronstadt*
3/65 **What's New Pussycat?** *Tom Jones*
86/83 **What's She Got** *Liquid Gold*
35/62 **What's So Good About Good-By** *Miracles*
17/64 **What's The Matter With You Baby** *Marvin Gaye & Mary Wells*
69/76 **What's The Name Of This Funk (Spider Man)** *Ramsey Lewis*
71/62 **What's The Reason** *Bobby Edwards*
50/57 **What's The Reason I'm Not Pleasing You** *Fats Domino*
20/69 **What's The Use Of Breaking Up** *Jerry Butler*
89/80 **What's Your Hurry Darlin'** *Ironhorse*
86/73 **What's Your Mama's Name** *Tanya Tucker*
What's Your Name
7/62 *Don & Juan*
92/74 *Andy & David Williams*
13/78 **What's Your Name** *Lynyrd Skynyrd*
56/78 **What's Your Name What's Your Number** *Andrea True Connection*
61/67 **What've I Done (To Make You Mad)** *Linda Jones*
6/77 **Whatcha Gonna Do** *Pablo Cruise*
41/82 **Whatcha Gonna Do** *Chilliwack*
92/60 **Whatcha Gonna Do** *Nat King Cole*
22/79 **Whatcha Gonna Do With My Lovin'** *Stephanie Mills*
9/71 **Whatcha See Is Whatcha Get** *Dramatics*
1/74 **Whatever Gets You Thru The Night** *John Lennon*
71/78 **Whatever Happened To Benny Santini?** *Chris Rea*
93/83 **Whatever Happened To Old Fashioned Love** *B.J. Thomas*
Whatever Lola Wants
6/55 *Sarah Vaughan*
12/55 *Dinah Shore*
95/72 **Whatever Turns You On** *Travis Wammack*
Whatever Will Be, Will Be *see: Que Sera, Sera*
77/80 **Whatever You Decide** *Randy Vanwarmer*
38/74 **Whatever You Got, I Want** *Jackson 5*
68/63 **Whatever You Want** *Jerry Butler*
57/78 **Wheel In The Sky** *Journey*
Wheel Of Fortune
88/59 *Knightsbridge Strings*
83/60 *LaVern Baker*
Wheel Of Hurt
26/66 *Margaret Whiting*
59/66 *Al Martino*
Wheels
3/61 *String-A-Longs*
28/61 *Billy Vaughn*
87/76 **Wheels Of Fortune** *Doobie Brothers*
78/79 **Wheels Of Life** *Gino Vannelli*
5/58 **When** *Kalin Twins*
When A Boy Falls In Love
44/63 *Mel Carter*
52/65 *Sam Cooke*
53/75 **When A Child Is Born** *Michael Holm*
When A Man (Woman) Loves A Woman (Man)
1/66 *Percy Sledge*
73/66 *Esther Phillips*
35/80 *Bette Midler*
27/82 **When All Is Said And Done** *Abba*
90/55 **When All The Streets Are Dark** *Somethin' Smith & The Redheads*
1/84 **When Doves Cry** *Prince*
30/82 **When He Shines** *Sheena Easton*
49/69 **When He Touches Me (Nothing Else Matters)** *Peaches & Herb*
18/69 **When I Die** *Motherlode*
84/79 **When I Dream** *Crystal Gayle*
When I Fall In Love
65/61 *Etta Jones*
7/62 *Lettermen*
F/74 *Donny Osmond*
53/62 **When I Get Thru With You (You'll Love Me Too)** *Patsy Cline*
59/58 **When I Grow Too Old To Dream** *Ed Townsend*
9/64 **When I Grow Up (To Be A Man)** *Beach Boys*
1/77 **When I Need You** *Leo Sayer*
29/57 **When I See You** *Fats Domino*
1/86 **When I Think Of You** *Janet Jackson*
78/79 **When I Think Of You** *Leif Garrett*
20/80 **When I Wanted You** *Barry Manilow*
15/67 **When I Was Young** *Animals*
47/71 **When I'm Dead And Gone** *McGuinness Flint*
25/65 **When I'm Gone** *Brenda Holloway*
78/82 **When I'm Holding You Tight** *Michael Stanley Band*
61/83 **When I'm With You** *Sheriff*
26/82 **When It's Over** *Loverboy*
94/64 **When Joanna Loved Me** *Tony Bennett*
41/70 **When Julie Comes Around** *Cuff Links*
18/66 **When Liking Turns To Loving** *Ronnie Dove*
41/76 **When Love Has Gone Away** *Richard Cocciante*
64/77 **When Love Is New** *Arthur Prysock*
92/67 **When Love Slips Away** *Dee Dee Warwick*
19/56 **When My Blue Moon Turns To Gold Again** *Elvis Presley*
14/56 **When My Dreamboat Comes Home** *Fats Domino*
When My Little Girl Is Smiling
28/62 *Drifters*
72/71 *Steve Alaimo*

48/57 **When Rock And Roll Come To Trinidad** *Nat King Cole*
49/81 **When She Dances** *Joey Scarbury*
37/66 **(When She Needs Good Lovin') She Comes To Me** *Chicago Loop*
11/81 **When She Was My Girl** *Four Tops*
42/67 **When Something Is Wrong With My Baby** *Sam & Dave*
10/62 **When The Boy In Your Arms (Is The Boy In Your Heart)** *Connie Francis*
94/62 **When The Boys Get Together** *Joanie Sommers*
95/63 **When The Boys Happy (The Girl's Happy Too)** *Four Pennies*
19/58 **When The Boys Talk About The Girls** *Valerie Carr*
45/80 **When The Feeling Comes Around** *Jennifer Warnes*
2/86 **When The Going Gets Tough, The Tough Get Going** *Billy Ocean*
98/67 **When The Good Sun Shines** *Elmo & Almo*
14/86 **When The Heart Rules The Mind** *GTR*
76/84 **When The Lady Smiles** *Golden Earring*
37/83 **When The Lights Go Out** *Naked Eyes*
23/64 **When The Lovelight Starts Shining Through His Eyes** *Supremes*
54/74 **When The Morning Comes** *Hoyt Axton*
71/70 **When The Party Is Over** *Robert John*
54/85 **When The Rain Begins To Fall** *Jermaine Jackson/Pia Zadora*
73/86 **When The Rain Comes Down** *Andy Taylor*
When The Saints Go Marching In
see: Saints Rockin' Roll
18/56 *Bill Haley & His Comets*
50/59 *Fats Domino*
91/65 **When The Ship Comes In** *Peter, Paul & Mary*
98/67 **When The Snow Is On The Roses** *Ed Ames*
80/57 **When The Swallows Come Back To Capistrano** *Pat Boone*
75/56 **When The Tide Is High** *Gogi Grant*
When The White Lilacs Bloom Again
12/56 *Helmut Zacharias*
18/56 *Billy Vaughn*
50/56 *Florian Zabach*
59/56 *Leroy Holmes*
70/56 *Lawrence Welk*
45/71 **When There's No You** *Engelbert Humperdinck*
87/80 **When Things Go Wrong** *Robin Lane*
99/67 **When Tomorrow Comes** *Carla Thomas*
When We Get Married
10/61 *Dreamlovers*
45/70 *Intruders*
76/80 *Larry Graham*
72/84 **When We Make Love** *Alabama*
When Will I Be Loved
8/60 *Everly Brothers*
2/75 *Linda Ronstadt*
65/58 **When Will I Know** *George Hamilton IV*
2/74 **When Will I See You Again** *Three Degrees*
14/84 **When You Close Your Eyes** *Night Ranger*
When You Dance
33/56 *Turbans*
70/69 *Jay & The Americans*
93/71 **When You Dance I Can Really Love** *Neil Young*
91/78 **When You Feel Love** *Bob McGilpin*
When You Get Right Down To It
53/70 *Delfonics*
94/71 *Ronnie Dyson*
62/56 **When You Lose The One You Love** *David Whitfield with Mantovani*
47/64 **When You Loved Me** *Brenda Lee*
32/72 **When You Say Love** *Sonny & Cher*
When You Walk In The Room
35/64 *Searchers*
99/64 *Jackie DeShannon*
87/83 **When You Were Mine** *Mitch Ryder*
30/60 **When You Wish Upon A Star** *Dion & The Belmonts*
99/79 **When You're #1** *Gene Chandler*
58/67 **When You're Gone** *Brenda & The Tabulations*
9/71 **When You're Hot, You're Hot** *Jerry Reed*
6/79 **When You're In Love With A Beautiful Woman** *Dr. Hook*
When You're Young And In Love
48/64 *Ruby & The Romantics*
23/67 *Marvelettes*
91/75 *Choice Four*
95/75 *Ralph Carter*
35/85 **When Your Heart Is Weak** *Cock Robin*
60/65 **Whenever A Teenager Cries** *Reparata & The Delrons*
Whenever He (She) Holds You
39/64 *Bobby Goldsboro*
64/66 *Patty Duke*
5/78 **Whenever I Call You 'Friend'** *Kenny Loggins*
38/76 **Whenever I'm Away From You** *John Travolta*
44/59 **Where** *Platters*
94/66 **Where Am I Going?** *Barbra Streisand*
80/74 **Where Are All My Friends** *Harold Melvin & The Blue Notes*
84/71 **Where Are We Going** *Bobby Bloom*
32/60 **Where Are You** *Frankie Avalon*
36/62 **Where Are You** *Dinah Washington*
95/70 **Where Are You Going** *Jerry Butler*
61/70 **Where Are You Going To My Love** *Brotherhood Of Man*
77/86 **Where Are You Now?** *Synch*
69/70 **Where Did All The Good Times Go** *Classics IV*
82/64 **Where Did I Go Wrong** *Dee Dee Sharp*
Where Did Our Love Go
1/64 *Supremes*
15/71 *Donnie Elbert*
68/76 *J. Geils Band*
93/63 **Where Did The Good Times Go** *Dick & DeeDee*
33/71 **Where Did They Go, Lord** *Elvis Presley*
90/80 **Where Did We Go Wrong** *Frankie Valli*
50/86 **Where Did Your Heart Go?** *Wham!*
(Where Do I Begin)
see: Theme From Love Story
Where Do I Go
86/68 *Carla Thomas*
66/69 *Happenings (medley)*
38/86 **Where Do The Children Go** *Hooters*
99/62 **Where Do You Come From** *Elvis Presley*
25/65 **Where Do You Go** *Cher*
70/69 **Where Do You Go To (My Lovely)** *Peter Sarstedt*
82/64 **Where Does Love Go** *Freddie Scott*
46/80 **Where Does The Lovin' Go** *David Gates*
83/83 **Where Everybody Knows Your Name** *Gary Portnoy*
45/71 **Where Evil Grows** *Poppy Family*
93/70 **Where Have All Our Heroes Gone** *Bill Anderson*
Where Have All The Flowers Gone
21/62 *Kingston Trio*
26/65 *Johnny Rivers*
100/75 **Where Have They Gone** *Jimmie Beaumont*
58/62 **Where Have You Been (All My Life)** *Arthur Alexander*

81/78 **Where Have You Been All My Life** *Fotomaker*
74/61 **Where I Fell In Love** *Capris*
73/68 **Where Is My Mind** *Vanilla Fudge*
5/72 **Where Is The Love** *Roberta Flack & Donny Hathaway*
96/75 **Where Is The Love** *Betty Wright*
90/67 **Where Is The Party** *Helena Ferguson*
62/64 **Where Love Has Gone** *Jack Jones*
Where Or When
3/60 *Dion & The Belmonts*
98/64 *Lettermen*
28/73 **Where Peaceful Waters Flow** *Gladys Knight & The Pips*
Where The Action Is *see: Action*
76/58 **Where The Blue Of The Night** *Tommy Mara*
4/61 **Where The Boys Are** *Connie Francis*
97/66 **Where The Sun Has Never Shone** *Jonathan King*
99/72 **Where There's A Will There's A Way** *Delaney & Bonnie*
75/56 **Where There's Life** *George Cates*
23/59 **Where Were You (On Our Wedding Day)?** *Lloyd Price*
Where Were You When I Needed You
99/65 *Jerry Vale*
28/66 *Grass Roots*
23/79 **Where Were You When I Was Falling In Love** *Lobo*
21/67 **Where Will The Words Come From** *Gary Lewis & The Playboys*
63/79 **Where Will Your Heart Take You** *Buckeye*
Where You Lead
40/71 *Barbra Streisand*
37/72 *Barbra Streisand (medley)*
26/69 **Where's The Playground Susie** *Glen Campbell*
88/81 **Where's Your Angel?** *Lani Hall*
70/83 **Wherever I Lay My Hat (That's My Home)** *Paul Young*
Which Way Is Up *see: Theme From*
2/70 **Which Way You Goin' Billy?** *Poppy Family*
96/60 **Whiffenpoof Song** *Bob Crewe*
89/77 **While I'm Alone** *Maze Featuring Frankie Beverly*
7/81 **While You See A Chance** *Steve Winwood*
62/69 **While You're Out Looking For Sugar?** *Honey Cone*
14/80 **Whip It** *Devo*
91/60 **Whip It On Me** *Jessie Hill*
68/65 **Whipped Cream** *Herb Alpert*
28/83 **Whirly Girl** *Oxo*
75/68 **Whiskey On A Sunday** *Irish Rovers*
72/86 **Whisper In The Dark** *Dionne Warwick*
37/84 **Whisper To A Scream (Birds Fly)** *Icicle Works*
Whispering
11/64 *Nino Tempo & April Stevens*
27/77 *Dr. Buzzard's Original 'Savannah' Band*
9/57 **Whispering Bells** *Dell-Vikings*
11/66 **Whispers (Gettin' Louder)** *Jackie Wilson*
59/77 **Whistler** *Jethro Tull*
61/59 **Whistling Organ** *Dave 'Baby' Cortez*
89/77 **White Bird** *David Laflamme*
74/58 **White Bucks And Saddle Shoes** *Bobby Pedrick Jr. -*
White Christmas
7/55 *Bing Crosby*
80/55 *Drifters*
65/56 *Bing Crosby*
34/57 *Bing Crosby*
66/58 *Bing Crosby*
59/59 *Bing Crosby*
26/60 *Bing Crosby*
96/60 *Drifters*
12/61 *Bing Crosby*
38/62 *Bing Crosby*
88/62 *Drifters*
26/84 **White Horse** *Laid Back*
48/80 **White Hot** *Red Rider*
67/68 **White Houses** *Animals*
19/76 **White Knight** *Cledus Maggard*
75/72 **White Lies** *Grin*
28/72 **White Lies, Blue Eyes** *Bullet*
73/59 **White Lightning** *George Jones*
9/64 **White On White** *Danny Williams*
8/67 **White Rabbit** *Jefferson Airplane*
6/68 **White Room** *Cream*
61/62 **White Rose Of Athens** *David Carroll*
White Silver Sands
7/57 *Don Rondo*
18/57 *Owen Bradley Quintet*
22/57 *Dave Gardner*
9/60 *Bill Black's Combo*
92/62 *Bill Black's Combo (Twistin')*
White Sport Coat (And A Pink Carnation)
2/57 *Marty Robbins*
62/57 *Johnny Desmond*
36/83 **White Wedding** *Billy Idol*
Whiter Shade Of Pale
5/67 *Procol Harum*
100/68 *Hesitations*
82/70 *R.B. Greaves*
94/84 *Hagar, Schon, Aaronson, Shrieve*
21/66 **Who Am I** *Petula Clark*
99/58 **Who Are They To Say** *DeCastro Sisters*
62/56 **Who Are We** *Gogi Grant*
14/78 **Who Are You** *Who*
78/74 **Who Are You** *B.B. King*
F/56 **Who Can Explain?** *Frankie Lymon & The Teenagers*
99/61 **Who Can I Count On** *Patsy Cline*
Who Can I Turn To
33/64 *Tony Bennett*
62/65 *Dionne Warwick*
1/82 **Who Can It Be Now?** *Men At Work*
Who Cares
43/59 *Don Gibson*
63/64 *Fats Domino*
68/79 **Who Do Ya Love** *KC & The Sunshine Band*
25/64 **Who Do You Love** *Saphires*
Who Do You Love
95/67 *Woolies*
91/69 *Quicksilver Messenger Service*
15/74 **Who Do You Think You Are** *Bo Donaldson & The Heywoods*
91/66 **Who Do You Think You Are** *Shindogs*
40/81 **Who Do You Think You're Foolin'** *Donna Summer*
82/61 **Who Else But You** *Frankie Avalon*
57/71 **Who Gets The Guy** *Dionne Warwick*
33/68 **Who Is Gonna Love Me?** *Dionne Warwick*
69/74 **Who Is He And What Is He To You** *Creative Source*
45/79 **Who Listens To The Radio** *Sports*
3/75 **Who Loves You** *4 Seasons*
47/76 **Who Loves You Better** *Isley Brothers*
54/70 **Who Needs Ya** *Steppenwolf*
9/57 **Who Needs You** *Four Lads*

7/61 **Who Put The Bomp (In The Bomp, Bomp, Bomp)** *Barry Mann*
79/86 **Who Says** *Device*
67/80 **Who Shot J.R.?** *Gary Burbank with Band McNally*
93/59 **Who Shot Sam** *George Jones*
55/63 **Who Stole The Keeshka?** *Matys Bros.*
49/73 **Who Was It?** *Hurricane Smith*
16/84 **Who Wears These Shoes?** *Elton John*
49/80 **Who Were You Thinkin' Of** *Doolittle Band*
19/68 **Who Will Answer?** *Ed Ames*
76/62 **Who Will The Next Fool Be** *Bobby Bland*
18/76 **Who'd She Coo?** *Ohio Players*
29/80 **Who'll Be The Fool Tonight** *Larsen-Feiten Band*
34/65 **Who'll Be The Next In Line** *Kinks*
F/70 **Who'll Stop The Rain** *Creedence Clearwater Revival*
72/64 **Who's Afraid Of Virginia Woolf?** *Jimmy Smith*
100/64 **Who's Been Sleepin In My Bed?** *Linda Scott*
61/83 **Who's Behind The Door?** *Zebra*
43/65 **Who's Cheating Who?** *Little Milton*
4/81 **Who's Crying Now** *Journey*
46/70 **Who's Gonna Take The Blame** *Miracles*
6/85 **Who's Holding Donna Now** *DeBarge*
27/73 **Who's In The Strawberry Patch With Sally** *Dawn*
3/86 **Who's Johnny** *El DeBarge*
66/67 **Who's Lovin' You** *Brenda & The Tabulations*
Who's Making Love
5/68 *Johnnie Taylor*
57/69 *Young-Holt Unlimited*
39/81 *Blues Brothers*
Who's Sorry Now
4/58 *Connie Francis*
40/75 *Marie Osmond*
21/84 **Who's That Girl?** *Eurythmics*
71/59 **Who's That Knocking** *Genies*
40/70 **Who's Your Baby?** *Archies*
7/85 **Who's Zoomin' Who** *Aretha Franklin*
22/77 **Whodunit** *Tavares*
53/70 **Whoever Finds This, I Love You** *Mac Davis*
Whole Lot Of Shakin' Going On
3/57 *Jerry Lee Lewis*
42/60 *Chubby Checker*
55/60 *Conway Twitty*
46/66 **Whole Lot Of Shakin' In My Heart (Since I Met You)** *Miracles*
Whole Lotta Love
4/70 *Led Zeppelin*
58/71 *C.C.S.*
64/71 *King Curtis*
87/79 *Wonder Band*
6/59 **Whole Lotta Loving** *Fats Domino*
60/58 **Whole Lotta Woman** *Marvin Rainwater*
73/67 **Whole Lotta Woman** *Arthur Conley*
63/67 **Whole World Is A Stage** *Fantastic Four*
71/71 **Wholesale Love** *Buddy Miles*
81/72 **Wholy Holy** *Aretha Franklin*
43/65 **Whose Heart Are You Breaking Tonight** *Connie Francis*
Why
1/59 *Frankie Avalon*
13/72 *Donny Osmond*
74/82 **Why** *Carly Simon*
77/57 **Why** *Cues*
88/64 **Why** *Beatles/Tony Sheridan*
Why (Am I Treated So Bad)
57/67 *Sweet Inspirations*
73/67 *Cannonball Adderley*
91/67 *Bobby Powell*
95/67 *Staple Singers*
5/57 **Why Baby Why** *Pat Boone*
33/85 **Why Can't I Have You** *Cars*
3/86 **Why Can't This Be Love** *Van Halen*
6/75 **Why Can't We Be Friends?** *War*
57/72 **Why Can't We Be Lovers** *Lamont Dozier*
3/73 **Why Can't We Live Together** *Timmy Thomas*
63/66 **Why Can't You Bring Me Home** *Jay & The Americans*
77/65 **Why Did I Choose You** *Barbra Streisand*
68/62 **Why Did You Leave Me?** *Vincent Edwards*
Why Do Fools Fall In Love
6/56 *Teenagers featuring Frankie Lymon*
9/56 *Gale Storm*
12/56 *Diamonds*
59/56 *Gloria Mann*
41/67 *Happenings*
7/81 *Diana Ross*
42/60 **Why Do I Love You So** *Johnny Tillotson*
97/63 **Why Do Kids Grow Up** *Randy & The Rainbows*
73/77 **Why Do Lovers (Break Each Other's Heart?)** *Daryl Hall & John Oates*
38/63 **Why Do Lovers Break Each Other's Heart?** *Bob B. Soxx & The Blue Jeans*
10/58 **Why Don't They Understand** *George Hamilton IV*
37/63 **Why Don't You Believe Me** *Duprees*
Why Don't You Write Me?
45/55 *Snooky Lanson*
82/55 *Jacks*
92/64 **Why (Doncha Be My Girl)** *Chartbusters*
61/69 **Why I Sing The Blues** *B.B. King*
83/60 **Why I'm Walkin'** *Stonewall Jackson*
98/69 **Why Is The Wine Sweeter (On The Other Side)** *Eddie Floyd*
55/79 **Why Leave Us Alone** *Five Special*
13/83 **Why Me** *Irene Cara*
16/73 **Why Me** *Kris Kristofferson*
26/80 **Why Me** *Styx*
64/83 **Why Me?** *Planet P*
18/80 **Why Not Me** *Fred Knoblock*
92/61 **Why Not Now** *Matt Monro*
90/67 **Why Not Tonight** *Jimmy Hughes*
54/66 **Why Pick On Me** *Standells*
61/70 **Why Should I Cry** *Gentrys*
66/82 **Why You Wanna Try Me** *Commodores*
52/62 **Why'd You Wanna Make Me Cry** *Connie Stevens*
Wichita Lineman
3/69 *Glen Campbell*
95/69 *Sergio Mendes & Brasil '66*
71/59 **Wicked Ruby** *Danny Zella*
57/66 **Wiederseh'n** *Al Martino*
51/59 **Wiggle, Wiggle** *Accents*
22/63 **Wiggle Wobble** *Les Cooper*
41/70 **Wigwam** *Bob Dylan*
33/63 **Wild!** *Dee Dee Sharp*
42/85 **Wild And Crazy Love** *Mary Jane Girls*
Wild Angels *see: Theme From The*
2/84 **Wild Boys** *Duran Duran*
29/56 **Wild Cherry** *Don Cherry*
31/67 **Wild Honey** *Beach Boys*
28/71 **Wild Horses** *Rolling Stones*
26/61 **Wild In The Country** *Elvis Presley*
87/78 **Wild In The Streets** *British Lions*
22/57 **Wild Is The Wind** *Johnny Mathis*
70/84 **Wild Life** *Bananarama*
28/71 **Wild Night** *Van Morrison*

2/60 **Wild One** *Bobby Rydell*
34/65 **Wild One** *Martha & The Vandellas*
Wild Thing
1/66 *Troggs*
20/67 *Senator Bobby*
14/74 *Fancy*
8/63 **Wild Weekend** *Rebels*
25/86 **Wild Wild Life** *Talking Heads*
Wild World
11/71 *Cat Stevens*
97/71 *Gentrys*
3/75 **Wildfire** *Michael Murphey*
Wildflower
9/73 *Skylark*
45/74 *New Birth*
17/63 **Wildwood Days** *Bobby Rydell*
7/74 **Wildwood Weed** *Jim Stafford*
1/73 **Will It Go Round In Circles** *Billy Preston*
72/63 **Will Power** *Cookies*
78/85 **Will The Wolf Survive?** *Los Lobos*
32/69 **Will You Be Staying After Sunday** *Peppermint Rainbow*
Will You Love Me Tomorrow
1/61 *Shirelles*
24/68 *4 Seasons*
76/72 *Roberta Flack*
82/73 *Melanie*
95/76 *Dana Valery*
39/78 *Dave Mason*
3/86 **Will You Still Love Me?** *Chicago*
50/56 **Will You, Willyum** *Janis Martin*
78/69 **Willie & Laura Mae Jones** *Dusty Springfield*
Willie And The Hand Jive
9/58 *Johnny Otis Show*
100/66 *Strangeloves*
26/74 *Eric Clapton*
63/85 *George Thorogood*
78/63 **Willie Can** *Sue Thompson*
15/65 **Willow Weep For Me** *Chad & Jeremy*
96/72 **Willpower Weak, Temptation Strong** *Bullet*
97/64 **Willyam, Willyam** *Dee Dee Sharp*
22/58 **Win Your Love For Me** *Sam Cooke*
Winchester Cathedral
1/66 *New Vaudeville Band*
71/66 *Dana Rollin*
65/83 **Wind Beneath My Wings** *Lou Rawls*
64/83 **Wind Him Up** *Saga*
53/57 **Wind In The Willow** *Jo Stafford*
31/69 **Windmills Of Your Mind** *Dusty Springfield*
63/83 **Windows** *Missing Persons*
32/67 **Windows Of The World** *Dionne Warwick*
38/83 **Winds Of Change** *Jefferson Starship*
Windy
1/67 *Association*
44/67 *Wes Montgomery*
78/58 **Windy** *Paul Gayten*
12/61 **Wings Of A Dove** *Ferlin Husky*
73/64 **Winkin', Blinkin' And Nod** *Simon Sisters*
50/56 **Winner Take All** *Platters*
8/81 **Winner Takes It All** *Abba*
21/76 **Winners And Losers** *Hamilton, Joe Frank & Reynolds*
17/81 **Winning** *Santana*
43/77 **Winter Melody** *Donna Summer*
16/70 **Winter World Of Love** *Engelbert Humperdinck*
Wipe Out
2/63 *Surfaris*
16/66 *Surfaris*
71/81 **Wired For Sound** *Cliff Richard*
35/57 **Wisdom Of A Fool** *Five Keys*
66/85 **Wise Up** *Amy Grant*
41/79 **(Wish I Could Fly Like) Superman** *Kinks*
61/59 **Wish It Were Me** *Platters*
63/67 **Wish Me A Rainbow** *Gunter Kallmann Chorus*
17/64 **Wish Someone Would Care** *Irma Thomas*
77/73 **Wish That I Could Talk To You** *Sylvers*
38/67 **Wish You Didn't Have To Go** *James & Bobby Purify*
49/66 **Wish You Were Here, Buddy** *Pat Boone*
44/69 **Wishful Sinful** *Doors*
79/59 **Wishful Thinking** *Little Anthony & The Imperials*
6/64 **Wishin' And Hopin'** *Dusty Springfield*
91/61 **Wishin' On A Rainbow** *Phill Wilson*
18/58 **Wishing For Your Love** *Voxpoppers*
26/83 **Wishing (If I Had A Photograph Of You)** *A Flock Of Seagulls*
57/65 **Wishing It Was You** *Connie Francis*
11/74 **Wishing You Were Here** *Chicago*
79/70 **Witch, The** *Rattles*
1/58 **Witch Doctor** *David Seville*
21/72 **Witch Queen Of New Orleans** *Redbone*
6/58 **Witchcraft** *Frank Sinatra*
32/63 **Witchcraft** *Elvis Presley*
69/69 **Witchi Tai To** *Everything is Everything*
9/72 **Witchy Woman** *Eagles*
50/73 **With A Child's Heart** *Michael Jackson*
29/66 **With A Girl Like You** *Troggs*
With A Little Bit Of Luck
82/56 *Percy Faith*
85/56 *Jo Stafford*
With A Little Help From My Friends
68/68 *Joe Cocker*
71/78 *Beatles (medley)*
1/78 **With A Little Luck** *Wings*
With All My Heart
15/57 *Jodie Sands*
76/57 *Judy Scott*
82/59 **With All Of My Heart** *Brook Benton*
With My Eyes Wide Open I'm Dreaming
59/59 *Patti Page*
99/59 *Enoch Light*
39/59 **With Open Arms** *Jane Morgan*
With Pen In Hand
43/68 *Billy Vera*
35/69 *Vikki Carr*
94/72 *Bobby Goldsboro*
21/59 **With The Wind And The Rain In Your Hair** *Pat Boone*
27/65 **With These Hands** *Tom Jones*
14/67 **With This Ring** *Platters*
51/86 **With You All The Way** *New Edition*
4/80 **With You I'm Born Again** *Billy Preston & Syreeta*
30/57 **With You On My Mind** *Nat King Cole*
12/76 **With Your Love** *Jefferson Starship*
28/58 **With Your Love** *Jack Scott*
77/55 **Without A Song** *Roy Hamilton*
63/69 **Without Her** *Herb Alpert*
45/74 **Without Love** *Aretha Franklin*
Without Love (There Is Nothing)
19/57 *Clyde McPhatter*
29/63 *Ray Charles*
90/68 *Oscar Toney, Jr.*
5/70 *Tom Jones*
43/64 **Without The One You Love (Life's Not Worth While)** *Four Tops*
1/72 **Without You** *Nilsson*
7/61 **Without You** *Johnny Tillotson*
41/56 **Without You** *Eddie Fisher*
73/84 **Without You** *David Bowie*
64/73 **Without You In My Life** *Tyrone Davis*
24/82 **Without You (Not Another Lonely Night)** *Franke & The Knockouts*

20/80 **Without Your Love** *Roger Daltrey*
38/87 **Without Your Love** *Toto*
42/76 **Without Your Love (Mr. Jordan)**
Charlie Ross
14/64 **Wives And Lovers** *Jack Jones*
45/58 **Wizard, The** *Jimmie Rodgers*
54/61 **Wizard Of Love** *Ly-Dells*
Wizard Of Oz *see: Themes From The*
40/75 **Wolf Creek Pass** *C.W. McCall*
6/62 **Wolverton Mountain** *Claude King*
(also see: (I'm The Girl On))
2/81 **Woman** *John Lennon*
14/66 **Woman** *Peter & Gordon*
15/60 **Woman, A Lover, A Friend** *Jackie Wilson*
56/65 **Woman Can Change A Man** *Joe Tex*
53/72 **Woman Don't Go Astray** *King Floyd*
60/73 **Woman From Tokyo** *Deep Purple*
47/69 **Woman Helping Man** *Vogues*
94/68 **Woman I Love** *B.B. King*
Woman In Love
14/55 *Four Aces*
19/55 *Frankie Laine*
1/80 **Woman In Love** *Barbra Streisand*
79/81 **Woman In Love (It's Not Me)** *Tom Petty*
Woman In Me
76/81 *Crystal Gayle*
33/83 *Donna Summer*
24/83 **Woman In You** *Bee Gees*
59/62 **Woman Is A Man's Best Friend**
Teddy & The Twilights
57/72 **Woman Is The Nigger Of The World**
John Lennon
54/67 **Woman Like That, Yeah** *Joe Tex*
4/81 **Woman Needs Love (Just Like You Do)**
Ray Parker Jr. & Raydio
Woman To Woman
22/74 *Shirley Brown*
92/78 *Barbara Mandrell*
56/73 **Woman To Woman** *Joe Cocker*
44/76 **Woman Tonight** *America*
4/68 **Woman, Woman** *Union Gap*
29/65 **Woman's Got Soul** *Impressions*
60/72 **Woman's Gotta Have It** *Bobby Womack*
63/67 **Woman's Hands** *Joe Tex*
71/64 **Woman's Love** *Carla Thomas*
94/70 **Woman's Way** *Rozetta Johnson*
55/74 **Wombling Summer Party** *Wombles*
41/80 **Women** *Foreigner*
36/71 **Women's Love Rights** *Laura Lee*
76/61 **Won't Be Long** *Aretha Franklin*
57/70 **Won't Find Better (Than Me)** *New Hope*
15/71 **Won't Get Fooled Again** *Who*
Won't You Come Home Bill Bailey
19/60 *Bobby Darin*
98/61 *Della Reese*
75/63 *Ella Fitzgerald*
87/70 **Wonder Could I Live There Anymore**
Charley Pride
11/61 **Wonder Like You** *Rick Nelson*
Wonder Of You
25/59 *Ray Peterson*
70/64 *Ray Peterson*
9/70 *Elvis Presley*
71/74 **Wonderful** *Isaac Hayes*
89/69 **Wonderful** *Blackwell*
93/75 **Wonderful Baby** *Don McLean*
22/62 **Wonderful Dream** *Majors*
14/63 **Wonderful Summer** *Robin Ward*
4/58 **Wonderful Time Up There** *Pat Boone*
16/78 **Wonderful Tonight** *Eric Clapton*
Wonderful! Wonderful!
14/57 *Johnny Mathis*
7/63 *Tymes*
(also see: Wun'erful Wun'erful)

Wonderful World
12/60 *Sam Cooke*
4/65 *Herman's Hermits*
17/78 *Art Garfunkel with James Taylor & Paul Simon*
25/70 **Wonderful World, Beautiful People**
Jimmy Cliff
99/62 **Wonderful World Of The Young**
Andy Williams
40/59 **Wonderful You** *Jimmie Rodgers*
12/57 **Wondering** *Patti Page*
21/80 **Wondering Where The Lions Are**
Bruce Cockburn
25/80 **Wonderland** *Commodores*
86/84 **Wonderland** *Big Country*
Wonderland By Night
1/61 *Bert Kaempfert*
15/61 *Louis Prima*
18/61 *Anita Bryant*
43/59 **Wont'cha Come Home** *Lloyd Price*
16/59 **Woo-Hoo** *Rock-A-Teens*
Woo Woo Song *see: You Should Be Mine*
91/86 **Wood Beez (pray like aretha franklin)**
Scritti Politti
51/58 **Woodchopper's Ball** *Hutch Davie*
Wooden Heart
1/61 *Joe Dowell*
58/75 *Bobby Vinton*
Woodstock
11/70 *Crosby, Stills, Nash & Young*
79/70 *Assembled Multitude*
23/71 *Matthews' Southern Comfort*
2/65 **Wooly Bully** *Sam The Sham & The Pharoahs*
41/85 **Word Is Out** *Jermaine Stewart*
6/86 **Word Up** *Cameo*
11/67 **Words** *Monkees*
15/68 **Words** *Bee Gees*
42/82 **Words** *Missing Persons*
62/83 **Words** *F.R. David*
94/60 **Words** *Pat Boone*
Words (Are Impossible)
88/73 *Drupi (Vado Via)*
91/75 *Margie Joseph*
87/76 *Donny Gerrard*
5/86 **Words Get In The Way**
Miami Sound Machine
5/67 **Words Of Love** *Mamas & The Papas*
13/57 **Words Of Love** *Diamonds*
18/66 **Work Song** *Herb Alpert*
44/82 **Work That Body** *Diana Ross*
51/72 **Work To Do** *Isley Brothers*
32/74 **Workin' At The Car Wash Blues** *Jim Croce*
41/82 **Workin' For A Livin'**
Huey Lewis & The News
33/62 **Workin' For The Man** *Roy Orbison*
Workin' On A Groovy Thing
62/68 *Patti Drew*
20/69 *5th Dimension*
97/73 **Working Class Hero** *Tommy Roe*
74/86 **Working Class Man** *Jimmy Barnes*
29/82 **Working For The Weekend** *Loverboy*
Working In The Coal Mine
8/66 *Lee Dorsey*
43/81 *Devo*
74/68 **Working Man's Prayer** *Arthur Prysock*
Working My Way Back To You
9/66 *4 Seasons*
2/80 *Spinners (medley)*
33/63 **Workout Stevie, Workout** *Stevie Wonder*
37/69 **World** *James Brown*
51/64 **World I Used To Know** *Jimmie Rodgers*
7/73 **World Is A Ghetto** *War*
49/66 **World Of Fantasy** *Five Stairsteps*
59/64 **World Of Lonely People** *Anita Bryant*
19/65 **World Of Our Own** *Seekers*

World Outside
21/58 *Four Coins*
63/58 *Four Aces*
71/58 *Roger Williams*
76/65 **World Through A Tear** *Neil Sedaka*
30/67 **World We Knew (Over And Over)** *Frank Sinatra*
56/82 **World Without Heroes** *Kiss*
World Without Love
1/64 *Peter & Gordon*
80/64 *Bobby Rydell*
90/70 **World Without Music** *Archie Bell & The Drells*
97/68 **Worm, The** *Jimmy McGriff*
37/64 **Worried Guy** *Johnny Tillotson*
20/59 **Worried Man** *Kingston Trio*
74/62 **Worried Mind** *Ray Anthony*
45/64 **Worry** *Johnny Tillotson*
69/59 **Worryin' Kind** *Tommy Sands*
80/74 **Worse Comes To Worst** *Billy Joel*
3/69 **Worst That Could Happen** *Brooklyn Bridge*
5/85 **Would I Lie To You?** *Eurythmics*
64/63 **Would It Make Any Difference To You** *Etta James*
46/74 **Would You Lay With Me (In A Field Of Stone)** *Tanya Tucker*
46/84 **Wouldn't It Be Good** *Nik Kershaw*
8/66 **Wouldn't It Be Nice** *Beach Boys*
95/76 **Wow** *Andre Gagnon*
41/64 **Wow Wow Wee (He's The Boy For Me)** *Angels*
38/81 **Wrack My Brain** *Ringo Starr*
20/85 **Wrap Her Up** *Elton John*
Wrap It Up
93/70 *Archie Bell & The Drells*
50/86 *Fabulous Thunderbirds*
48/78 **Wrap Your Arms Around Me** *KC & The Sunshine Band*
8/84 **Wrapped Around Your Finger** *Police*
Wreck Of The 'John B' *see: Sloop John B*
2/76 **Wreck Of The Edmund Fitzgerald** *Gordon Lightfoot*
Wringle, Wrangle
12/57 *Fess Parker*
33/57 *Bill Hayes*
5/61 **Writing On The Wall** *Adam Wade*
61/57 **Written On The Wind** *Four Aces*
34/64 **Wrong For Each Other** *Andy Williams*
32/57 **Wun'erful, Wun'erful!** *Stan Freberg*
76/81 **Wynken, Blynken And Nod** *Doobie Brothers*

8/80 **Xanadu** *Olivia Newton-John/Electric Light Orchestra*

2/79 **Y.M.C.A.** *Village People*
7/61 **Ya Ya** *Lee Dorsey*
19/84 **Yah Mo B There** *James Ingram/Michael McDonald*
Yakety Sax (Axe)
35/63 *Boots Randolph*
98/65 *Chet Atkins*
1/58 **Yakety Yak** *Coasters*
58/78 **Yank Me, Crank Me** *Ted Nugent*
16/86 **Yankee Rose** *David Lee Roth*
64/68 **Yard Went On Forever** *Richard Harris*
73/58 **Yea, Yea** *Kendall Sisters*
42/60 **Year Ago Tonight** *Crests*
8/77 **Year Of The Cat** *Al Stewart*
42/71 **Year That Clayton Delaney Died** *Tom T. Hall*
60/81 **Yearning For Your Love** *Gap Band*
35/80 **Years** *Wayne Newton*
37/61 **Years From Now** *Jackie Wilson*
51/80 **Years From Now** *Dr. Hook*
Yeh, Yeh
92/63 *Mongo Santamaria*
21/65 *Georgie Fame*
25/67 **Yellow Balloon** *Yellow Balloon*
Yellow Bird
70/59 *Mills Brothers*
4/61 *Arthur Lyman*
71/61 *Lawrence Welk*
Yellow Dog Blues
43/58 *Joe Darensbourg*
87/58 *Johnny Maddox*
23/70 **Yellow River** *Christie*
Yellow Rose Of Texas
1/55 *Mitch Miller*
3/55 *Johnny Desmond*
16/55 *Stan Freberg*
2/66 **Yellow Submarine** *Beatles*
99/60 **Yen Yet Song** *Gary Cane*
30/59 **'Yep!'** *Duane Eddy*
92/64 **Yes I Do** *Solomon Burke*
94/58 **Yes I Want You** *Ivory Joe Hunter*
Yes, I'm Lonesome Tonight
55/61 *Thelma Carpenter*
60/61 *Dodie Stevens*
(also see: Are You Lonesome Tonight)
Yes, I'm Ready
5/65 *Barbara Mason*
2/80 *Teri DeSario with K.C.*
69/62 **Yes Indeed** *Pete Fountain*
46/65 **Yes It Is** *Beatles*
55/58 **Yes, My Darling** *Fats Domino*
84/84 **Yes Or No** *Go-Go's*
34/60 **Yes Sir, That's My Baby** *Ricky Nelson*
12/57 **Yes Tonight, Josephine** *Johnnie Ray*
11/73 **Yes We Can Can** *Pointer Sisters*
46/76 **Yes, Yes, Yes** *Bill Cosby*
60/62 **Yessiree** *Linda Scott*
79/59 **Yes-Sir-Ee** *Dodie Stevens*
31/68 **Yester Love** *Miracles*
7/69 **Yester-Me, Yester-You, Yesterday** *Stevie Wonder*
Yesterday
1/65 *Beatles*
25/67 *Ray Charles*
Yesterday And You *see: Armens Theme*
63/73 **Yesterday I Had The Blues** *Harold Melvin & The Blue Notes*
94/66 **Yesterday Man** *Chris Andrews*
Yesterday Once More
2/73 *Carpenters*
52/81 *Spinners (medley)*
19/69 **Yesterday, When I Was Young** *Roy Clark*
49/68 **Yesterday's Dreams** *Four Tops*
Yesterday's Gone
21/64 *Chad & Jeremy*
75/64 *Overlanders*

Yesterday's Hero
42/76 *John Paul Young*
54/77 *Bay City Rollers*
64/64 **Yesterday's Hero** *Gene Pitney*
94/68 **Yesterday's Rain** *Spanky & Our Gang*
11/82 **Yesterday's Songs** *Neil Diamond*
77/64 **Yet...I Know** *Steve Lawrence*
56/62 **Yield Not To Temptation** *Bobby Bland*
3/71 **Yo-Yo** *Osmonds*
57/85 **Yo' Little Brother** *Nolan Thomas*
8/60 **Yogi** *Ivy Three*
20/75 **You** *George Harrison*
You & Me & Pooneil *see: Ballad Of*
21/58 **You** *Aquatones*
25/78 **You** *Rita Coolidge*
34/68 **You** *Marvin Gaye*
45/78 **You** *McCrarys*
48/80 **You** *Earth, Wind & Fire*
74/68 **You Ain't Going Nowhere** *Byrds*
F/75 **You Ain't Never Been Loved (Like I'm Gonna Love You)** *Jessi Colter*
1/74 **You Ain't Seen Nothing Yet** *Bachman-Turner Overdrive*
86/73 **You Always Come Back (To Hurting Me)** *Johnny Rodriguez*
96/67 **You Always Hurt Me** *Impressions*
12/61 **You Always Hurt The One You Love** *Clarence 'Frogman' Henry*
7/83 **You And I** *Eddie Rabbitt & Crystal Gayle*
13/78 **You And I** *Rick James*
48/74 **You And I** *Johnny Bristol*
9/77 **You And Me** *Alice Cooper*
80/80 **You And Me** *Rockie Robbins*
92/79 **You And Me** *Liner*
F/70 **You And Me** *Aretha Franklin*
9/74 **You And Me Against The World** *Helen Reddy*
96/75 **You And Your Baby Blues** *Solomon Burke*
91/71 **You And Your Folks, Me And My Folks** *Funkadelic*
58/79 **You Angel You** *Manfred Mann's Earth Band*
4/83 **You Are** *Lionel Richie*
87/75 **You Are A Song** *Batdorf & Rodney*
60/59 **You Are Beautiful** *Johnny Mathis*
79/76 **You Are Beautiful** *Stylistics*
9/72 **You Are Everything** *Stylistics*
59/81 **You Are Forever** *Smokey Robinson*
You Are In My System
64/83 *System*
78/83 *Robert Palmer*
26/62 **You Are Mine** *Frankie Avalon*
7/58 **You Are My Destiny** *Paul Anka*
65/57 **You Are My First Love** *Nat King Cole*
47/80 **You Are My Heaven** *Roberta Flack & Donny Hathaway*
12/85 **You Are My Lady** *Freddie Jackson*
6/55 **You Are My Love** *Joni James*
27/76 **You Are My Starship** *Norman Connors*
You Are My Sunshine
44/55 *Ferko String Band*
91/60 *Johnny & The Hurricanes*
7/62 *Ray Charles*
88/67 *Mitch Ryder*
49/77 **You Are On My Mind** *Chicago*
87/66 **You Are She** *Chad & Jeremy*
5/75 **You Are So Beautiful** *Joe Cocker*
51/72 **You Are The One** *Sugar Bears*
25/61 **You Are The Only One** *Ricky Nelson*
1/73 **You Are The Sunshine Of My Life** *Stevie Wonder*
9/76 **You Are The Woman** *Firefall*
20/66 **You Baby** *Turtles*
78/56 **You Baby You** *Cleftones*
29/86 **You Be Illin'** *Run-D.M.C.*

9/62 **You Beat Me To The Punch** *Mary Wells*
You Belong To Me
6/78 *Carly Simon*
79/83 *Doobie Brothers*
7/62 **You Belong To Me** *Duprees*
2/85 **You Belong To The City** *Glenn Frey*
46/65 **You Better Get It** *Joe Tex*
78/65 **You Better Go** *Derek Martin*
37/59 **You Better Know It** *Jackie Wilson*
90/60 **(You Better) Know What You're Doin'** *Lloyd Price*
24/62 **You Better Move On** *Arthur Alexander*
You Better Run
20/66 *Rascals*
42/80 *Pat Benatar*
9/67 **You Better Sit Down Kids** *Cher*
72/70 **You Better Think Twice** *Poco*
18/81 **You Better You Bet** *Who*
52/71 **You Brought The Joy** *Freda Payne*
You Brought The Woman Out Of Me
50/75 *Evie Sands*
71/78 *Hot*
45/57 **You Bug Me, Baby** *Larry Williams*
77/82 **You Can** *Madleen Kane*
55/67 **You Can Bring Me All Your Heartaches** *Lou Rawls*
23/87 **You Can Call Me Al** *Paul Simon*
86/80 **You Can Call Me Blue** *Michael Johnson*
6/61 **You Can Depend On Me** *Brenda Lee*
37/79 **You Can Do It** *Dobie Gray*
8/82 **You Can Do Magic** *America*
84/73 **You Can Do Magic** *Limmie & Family Cookin'*
You Can Have Her (Him)
12/61 *Roy Hamilton*
67/65 *Righteous Brothers*
75/65 *Dionne Warwick*
96/65 *Timi Yuro*
34/74 *Sam Neely*
36/58 **You Can Make It If You Try** *Gene Allison*
18/63 **You Can Never Stop Me Loving You** *Johnny Tillotson*
63/62 **You Can Run (But You Can't Hide)** *Jerry Butler*
51/84 **(You Can Still) Rock In America** *Night Ranger*
42/73 **You Can't Always Get What You Want** *Rolling Stones*
57/74 **You Can't Be A Beacon (If Your Light Don't Shine)** *Donna Fargo*
You Can't Be True Dear
75/59 *Mary Kaye Trio*
94/65 *Patti Page*
9/79 **You Can't Change That** *Ray Parker Jr. & Raydio*
49/78 **You Can't Dance** *England Dan & John Ford Coley*
48/64 **You Can't Do That** *Beatles*
99/59 **You Can't Get To Heaven On Roller Skates** *Betty Johnson*
15/84 **You Can't Get What You Want (Till You Know What You Want)** *Joe Jackson*
You Can't Hurry Love
1/66 *Supremes*
10/83 *Phil Collins*
92/65 **You Can't Hurt Me No More** *Gene Chandler*
48/62 **You Can't Judge A Book By The Cover** *Bo Diddley*
(You Can't Let The Boy Overpower) The Man In You
59/64 *Miracles*
94/68 *Chuck Jackson*
90/62 **You Can't Lie To A Liar** *Ketty Lester*

40/66 **You Can't Roller Skate In A Buffalo Herd** *Roger Miller*
20/56 **You Can't Run Away From It** *Four Aces*
55/83 **You Can't Run From Love** *Eddie Rabbitt*
You Can't Sit Down
29/61 *Philip Upchurch Combo*
3/63 *Dovells*
70/67 **You Can't Stand Alone** *Wilson Pickett*
96/65 **You Can't Take It Away** *Fred Hughes*
12/77 **You Can't Turn Me Off (In The Middle Of Turning Me On)** *High Inergy*
81/79 **You Can't Win** *Michael Jackson*
You Cheated
12/58 *Shields*
42/58 *Slades*
32/72 **You Could Have Been A Lady** *April Wine*
15/82 **You Could Have Been With Me** *Sheena Easton*
32/81 **You Could Take My Heart Away** *Silver Condor*
7/79 **You Decorated My Life** *Kenny Rogers*
10/66 **You Didn't Have To Be So Nice** *Lovin' Spoonful*
54/83 **You Don't Believe** *Alan Parsons Project*
1/78 **You Don't Bring Me Flowers** *Barbra Streisand & Neil Diamond*
You Don't Have To Be A Baby To Cry
78/56 *Tennessee Ernie Ford*
3/63 *Caravelles*
1/77 **You Don't Have To Be A Star (To Be In My Show)** *Marilyn McCoo & Billy Davis, Jr.*
100/61 **You Don't Have To Be A Tower Of Strength** *Gloria Lynne*
75/86 **You Don't Have To Cry** *Rene & Angela*
15/66 **You Don't Have To Paint Me A Picture** *Gary Lewis & The Playboys*
You Don't Have To Say You Love Me
4/66 *Dusty Springfield*
89/68 *Four Sonics*
11/70 *Elvis Presley*
51/69 **You Don't Have To Walk In The Rain** *Turtles*
92/59 **You Don't Know Girls** *Kathy Linden*
(You Don't Know) How Glad I Am
11/64 *Nancy Wilson*
74/75 *Kiki Dee*
90/66 **You Don't Know Like I Know** *Sam & Dave*
You Don't Know Me
14/56 *Jerry Vale*
45/60 *Lenny Welch*
2/62 *Ray Charles*
44/67 *Elvis Presley*
55/81 *Mickey Gilley*
79/61 **You Don't Know What It Means** *Jackie Wilson*
48/68 **You Don't Know What You Mean To Me** *Sam & Dave*
4/61 **You Don't Know What You've Got (Until You Lose It)** *Ral Donner*
53/78 **You Don't Love Me Anymore** *Eddie Rabbitt*
47/63 **You Don't Love Me Anymore (And I Can Tell)** *Rick Nelson*
8/72 **You Don't Mess Around With Jim** *Jim Croce*
95/62 **You Don't Miss Your Water** *William Bell*
84/69 **You Don't Need Me For Anything Anymore** *Brenda Lee*
10/57 **You Don't Owe Me A Thing** *Johnnie Ray*
2/64 **You Don't Own Me** *Lesley Gore*
16/82 **You Don't Want Me Anymore** *Steel Breeze*
64/61 **You Don't Want My Love** *Andy Williams*
31/82 **You Dropped A Bomb On Me** *Gap Band*
49/58 **You Excite Me** *Frankie Avalon*
24/69 **You Gave Me A Mountain** *Frankie Laine*
55/67 **You Gave Me Something (And Everything's Alright)** *Fantastic Four*
3/85 **You Give Good Love** *Whitney Houston*
1/86 **You Give Love A Bad Name** *Bon Jovi*
38/79 **You Gonna Make Me Love Somebody Else** *Jones Girls*
49/78 **You Got It** *Diana Ross*
3/87 **You Got It All** *Jets*
20/83 **You Got Lucky** *Tom Petty*
You Got Me Hummin'
77/67 *Sam & Dave*
52/70 *Cold Blood*
93/72 **You Got Me Walking** *Jackie Wilson*
58/69 **You Got Soul** *Johnny Nash*
69/78 **You Got That Right** *Lynyrd Skynyrd*
94/58 **You Got That Touch** *Sonny James*
11/74 **You Got The Love** *Rufus Featuring Chaka Khan*
88/68 **You Got The Love** *Professor Morrison's Lollipop*
87/76 **You Got The Magic** *John Fogerty*
66/82 **You Got The Power** *War*
83/74 **You Got To Be The One** *Chi-Lites*
18/67 **You Got To Me** *Neil Diamond*
You Got To Pay The Price *see: You've Got*
81/78 **(You Got To Walk And) Don't Look Back** *Peter Tosh*
You Got What It Takes
10/60 *Marv Johnson*
7/67 *Dave Clark Five*
51/65 **You Got What It Takes** *Joe Tex*
40/69 **You Got Yours And I'll Get Mine** *Delfonics*
7/87 **(You Gotta) Fight For Your Right (To Party!)** *Beastie Boys*
55/71 **You Gotta Have Love In Your Heart** *Supremes & Four Tops*
53/76 **You Gotta Make Your Own Sunshine** *Neil Sedaka*
1/74 **You Haven't Done Nothin** *Stevie Wonder*
60/57 **(You Hit The Wrong Note) Billy Goat** *Bill Haley & His Comets*
24/69 **You, I** *Rugbys*
94/71 **You Just Can't Win (By Making The Same Mistake)** *Gene & Jerry*
56/78 **You Keep Me Dancing** *Samantha Sang*
You Keep Me Hangin' On
1/66 *Supremes*
6/68 *Vanilla Fudge*
92/69 *Wilson Pickett*
96/70 *Jackie DeShannon (medley)*
25/68 **(You Keep Me) Hangin' On** *Joe Simon*
94/71 **You Keep Me Holding On** *Tyrone Davis*
38/82 **You Keep Runnin' Away** *38 Special*
19/67 **You Keep Running Away** *Four Tops*
92/70 **You Keep Tightening Up On Me** *Box Tops*
17/86 **You Know I Love You...Don't You?** *Howard Jones*
88/63 **You Know It Ain't Right** *Joe Hinton*
74/77 **You Know Like I Know** *Ozark Mountain Daredevils*
35/80 **You Know That I Love You** *Santana*
12/67 **You Know What I Mean** *Turtles*
83/83 **You Know What To Do** *Carly Simon*
70/64 **You Lied To Your Daddy** *Tams*
You Light Up My Life
1/77 *Debby Boone*
80/77 *Original Cast*
F/73 **You Light Up My Life** *Carole King*
50/81 **You Like Me Don't You** *Jermaine Jackson*
12/74 **You Little Trustmaker** *Tymes*
58/85 **You Look Marvelous** *Billy Crystal*
22/63 **You Lost The Sweetest Boy** *Mary Wells*
96/69 **You Made A Believer (Out Of Me)** *Ruby Andrews*

10/77 **You Made Me Believe In Magic** *Bay City Rollers*
45/59 **You Made Me Love You** *Nat King Cole*
9/77 **You Make Loving Fun** *Fleetwood Mac*
62/78 **You Make Me Crazy** *Sammy Hagar*
2/74 **You Make Me Feel Brand New** *Stylistics*
1/77 **You Make Me Feel Like Dancing** *Leo Sayer*
36/79 **You Make Me Feel Mighty Real** *Sylvester*
53/66 **(You Make Me Feel) So Good** *McCoys*
50/70 **You Make Me Real** *Doors*
5/81 **You Make My Dreams** *Daryl Hall & John Oates*
54/84 **You Make My Heart Beat Faster** *Kim Carnes*
72/72 **You Make Your Own Heaven And Hell Right Here On Earth** *Undisputed Truth*
7/80 **You May Be Right** *Billy Joel*
83/84 **You, Me And He** *Mtume*
68/70 **You, Me And Mexico** *Edward Bear*
17/60 **You Mean Everything To Me** *Neil Sedaka*
84/59 **You Mean Everything To Me** *Fleetwoods*
75/67 **You Mean The World To Me** *David Houston*
35/68 **You Met Your Match** *Stevie Wonder*
54/80 **You Might Need Somebody** *Turley Richards*
7/84 **You Might Think** *Cars*
15/64 **You Must Believe Me** *Impressions*
You Must Have Been A Beautiful Baby
5/61 *Bobby Darin*
35/67 *Dave Clark Five*
40/79 **You Need A Woman Tonight** *Captain & Tennille*
11/58 **You Need Hands** *Eydie Gorme*
88/75 **You Need Love** *Styx*
25/70 **You Need Love Like I Do (Don't You)** *Gladys Knight & The Pips*
81/68 **You Need Me, Baby** *Joe Tex*
1/78 **You Needed Me** *Anne Murray*
14/64 **You Never Can Tell** *Chuck Berry*
10/78 **You Never Done It Like That** *Captain & Tennille*
73/63 **You Never Miss Your Water (Till The Well Runs Dry)** *'Little Esther' Phillips & Big Al Downing*
83/67 **You, No One But You** *Frankie Laine*
44/67 **You Only Live Twice** *Nancy Sinatra*
68/76 **You Ought To Be Havin' Fun** *Tower Of Power*
3/72 **You Ought To Be With Me** *Al Green*
48/77 **You + Me = Love** *Undisputed Truth*
82/68 **You Put It On Me** *B.B. King*
81/83 **You Put The Beat In My Heart** *Eddie Rabbitt*
You Really Got A Hold On Me
see: You've Really
You Really Got Me
7/64 *Kinks*
36/78 *Van Halen*
27/65 **You Really Know How To Hurt A Guy** *Jan & Dean*
41/72 **You Said A Bad Word** *Joe Tex*
37/81 **You Saved My Soul** *Burton Cummings*
72/79 **You Says It All** *Randy Brown*
You Send Me
1/57 *Sam Cooke*
8/57 *Teresa Brewer*
56/68 *Aretha Franklin*
78/71 *Ponderosa Twins + One*
81/85 *Manhattans*
3/76 **You Sexy Thing** *Hot Chocolate*
35/80 **You Shook Me All Night Long** *AC/DC*
1/76 **You Should Be Dancing** *Bee Gees*
13/86 **You Should Be Mine (The Woo Woo Song)** *Jeffrey Osborne*
54/78 **You Should Do It** *Peter Brown*
39/64 **You Should Have Seen The Way He Looked At Me** *Dixie Cups*
5/82 **You Should Hear How She Talks About You** *Melissa Manchester*
89/62 **You Should'a Treated Me Right** *Ike & Tina Turner*
F/57 **You Shouldn't Do That** *Sal Mineo*
6/69 **You Showed Me** *Turtles*
11/85 **You Spin Me Round (Like A Record)** *Dead Or Alive*
You Stepped Into My Life
47/79 *Melba Moore*
90/79 *Wayne Newton*
50/74 **You Sure Love To Ball** *Marvin Gaye*
44/84 **You Take Me Up** *Thompson Twins*
10/79 **You Take My Breath Away** *Rex Smith*
52/77 **You Take My Heart Away** *James Darren*
46/62 **You Talk About Love** *Barbara George*
You Talk Too Much
3/60 *Joe Jones*
87/60 *Frankie Ford*
38/65 **You Tell Me Why** *Beau Brummels*
57/71 **You Think You're Hot Stuff** *Jean Knight*
49/62 **You Threw A Lucky Punch** *Gene Chandler*
40/79 **You Thrill Me** *Exile*
77/55 **You Tickle Me Baby** *Royal Jokers*
You To Me Are Everything
64/76 *Real Thing*
86/76 *Broadway*
98/76 *Revelation*
39/79 **You Took The Words Right Out Of My Mouth** *Meat Loaf*
8/65 **You Turn Me On** *Ian Whitcomb*
25/73 **You Turn Me On, I'm A Radio** *Joni Mitchell*
83/74 **You Turned My World Around** *Frank Sinatra*
94/66 **You Waited Too Long** *Five Stairsteps*
36/72 **You Want It, You Got It** *Detroit Emeralds*
48/67 **You Wanted Someone To Play With (I Wanted Someone To Love)** *Frankie Laine*
13/72 **You Wear It Well** *Rod Stewart*
46/85 **You Wear It Well** *El DeBarge*
72/59 **You Went Back On Your Word** *Clyde McPhatter*
93/73 **You Were Always There** *Donna Fargo*
94/60 **You Were Born To Be Loved** *Billy Bland*
12/60 **(You Were Made For) All My Love** *Jackie Wilson*
21/65 **You Were Made For Me** *Freddie & The Dreamers*
You Were Made For Me
39/58 *Sam Cooke*
93/72 *Luther Ingram*
78/84 **You Were Made For Me** *Irene Cara*
21/59 **You Were Mine** *Fireflies*
You Were On My Mind
3/65 *We Five*
36/67 *Crispian St. Peters*
30/65 **You Were Only Fooling (While I Was Falling In Love)** *Vic Damone*
100/64 **You Were Wrong** *Z.Z. Hill*
You Win Again
92/55 *Paulette Sisters*
95/58 *Jerry Lee Lewis*
22/62 *Fats Domino*
8/74 **You Won't See Me** *Anne Murray*
42/66 **You Wouldn't Listen** *Ides Of March*
49/66 **You You You** *Mel Carter*
50/58 **You'd Be Surprised** *Kathy Linden*
77/73 **You'd Better Believe It** *Manhattans*
22/65 **You'd Better Come Home** *Petula Clark*
50/61 **You'd Better Come Home** *Russell Byrd*
14/80 **You'll Accomp'ny Me** *Bob Seger*

64/65 **You'll Always Be The One I Love** *Dean Martin*
46/61 **You'll Answer To Me** *Patti Page*
67/56 **You'll Get Yours** *Frank Sinatra*
You'll Lose A Good Thing
8/62 *Barbara Lynn*
32/76 *Freddy Fender*
71/78 **You'll Love Again** *Hotel*
91/65 **You'll Miss Me (When I'm Gone)** *Fontella Bass & Bobby McClUre*
2/76 **You'll Never Find Another Love Like Mine** *Lou Rawls*
You'll Never Get To Heaven (If You Break My Heart)
34/64 *Dionne Warwick*
23/73 *Stylistics*
11/56 **You'll Never Never Know** *Platters*
You'll Never Walk Alone
34/64 *Patti LaBelle & The Blue Belles*
48/65 *Gerry & The Pacemakers*
90/68 *Elvis Presley*
51/69 *Brooklyn Bridge*
You're *also see: Your*
73/71 **You're A Big Girl Now** *Stylistics*
18/86 **You're A Friend Of Mine** *Clarence Clemons & Jackson Browne*
You're A Lady
50/73 *Peter Skellern*
70/73 *Dawn*
You're A Part Of Me
90/75 *Susan Jacks*
36/78 *Gene Cotton with Kim Carnes*
12/73 **You're A Special Part Of Me** *Marvin Gaye & Diana Ross*
You're A Sweetheart
66/58 *Little Willie John*
98/62 *Dinah Washington*
You're A Very Lovely Women *see: She's A Very*
15/64 **You're A Wonderful One** *Marvin Gaye*
88/67 **You're All I Need** *Bobby Bland*
You're All I Need To Get By
7/68 *Marvin Gaye & Tammi Terrell*
19/71 *Aretha Franklin*
34/75 *Dawn*
47/78 *Johnny Mathis & Deniece Williams*
88/82 *Chris Christian (medley)*
25/57 **You're Cheatin' Yourself (If You're Cheatin' On Me)** *Frank Sinatra*
35/83 **You're Driving Me Out Of My Mind** *Little River Band*
92/61 **You're Following Me** *Perry Como*
87/76 **You're Fooling You** *Dramatics*
73/80 **You're Gonna Get What's Coming** *Bonnie Raitt*
39/66 **(You're Gonna) Hurt Yourself** *Frankie Valli*
86/65 **You're Gonna Make Me Cry** *O.V. Wright*
34/59 **You're Gonna Miss Me** *Connie Francis*
55/66 **You're Gonna Miss Me** *Thirteenth Floor Elevators*
80/61 **You're Gonna Need Magic** *Roy Hamilton*
65/63 **You're Gonna Need Me** *Barbara Lynn*
49/63 **You're Good For Me** *Solomon Burke*
1/74 **(You're) Having My Baby** *Paul Anka*
79/73 **You're In Good Hands** *Jermaine Jackson*
69/56 **You're In Love** *Gogi Grant*
89/85 **You're In Love** *Ratt*
4/78 **You're In My Heart (The Final Acclaim)** *Rod Stewart*
91/66 **You're Just About To Lose Your Clown** *Ray Charles*
88/76 **You're Just The Right Size** *Salsoul Orchestra*
43/60 **You're Looking Good** *Dee Clark*
58/84 **You're Looking Like Love To Me** *Peabo Bryson/Roberta Flack*
50/58 **You're Making A Mistake** *Platters*
You're Mine
100/56 *Dream Weavers*
76/57 *Four Aces*
68/81 **You're Mine Tonight** *Pure Prairie League*
You're Movin' Out Today
42/77 *Bette Midler*
69/77 *Carole Bayer Sager*
87/60 **You're My Baby** *Sarah Vaughan*
63/65 **You're My Baby (And Don't You Forget It)** *Vacels*
16/76 **You're My Best Friend** *Queen*
77/80 **You're My Blessing** *Lou Rawls*
85/76 **You're My Driving Wheel** *Supremes*
6/67 **You're My Everything** *Temptations*
58/76 **You're My Everything** *Lee Garrett*
27/81 **You're My Girl** *Franke & The Knockouts*
You're My Girl *see: (Say)*
43/82 **You're My Latest, My Greatest Inspiration** *Teddy Pendergrass*
63/71 **You're My Man** *Lynn Anderson*
14/57 **You're My One And Only Love** *Ricky Nelson*
48/64 **You're My Remedy** *Marvelettes*
(You're My) Soul And Inspiration
1/66 *Righteous Brothers*
38/78 *Donny & Marie Osmond*
76/79 **You're My Weakness** *Faith Band*
You're My World
26/64 *Cilla Black*
18/77 *Helen Reddy*
98/65 **You're Next** *Jimmy Witherspoon*
You're No Good
51/64 *Betty Everett*
97/64 *Swinging Blue Jeans*
1/75 *Linda Ronstadt*
You're Nobody Till Somebody Loves You
87/62 *Dinah Washington*
25/65 *Dean Martin*
96/66 *Wonder Who?*
9/85 **You're Only Human (Second Wind)** *Billy Joel*
7/79 **You're Only Lonely** *J.D. Souther*
52/56 **You're Sensational** *Frank Sinatra*
You're Sixteen
8/60 *Johnny Burnette*
1/74 *Ringo Starr*
58/81 **You're So Easy To Love** *Tommy James*
You're So Fine
17/59 *Falcons*
86/67 *Bunny Sigler (medley)*
91/55 **You're So Nice To Be Near** *Loreleis*
47/82 **(You're So Square) Baby, I Don't Care** *Joni Mitchell*
48/74 **You're So Unique** *Billy Preston*
1/73 **You're So Vain** *Carly Simon*
29/72 **You're Still A Young Man** *Tower Of Power*
34/80 **You're Supposed To Keep Your Love For Me** *Jermaine Jackson*
62/56 **You're The Apple Of My Eye** *Four Lovers*
76/84 **You're The Best Thing** *Style Council*
You're The Best Thing *see: Best Thing*
81/61 **You're The Boss** *Lavern Baker & Jimmy Ricks*
3/63 **(You're The) Devil In Disguise** *Elvis Presley*
2/75 **You're The First, The Last, My Everything** *Barry White*
73/58 **You're The Greatest** *Billy Scott*
3/85 **You're The Inspiration** *Chicago*
18/78 **You're The Love** *Seals & Crofts*
50/72 **You're The Man** *Marvin Gaye*

F/58 **You're The Nearest Thing To Heaven** *Johnny Cash*
4/65 **You're The One** *Vogues*
48/66 **You're The One** *Marvelettes*
You're The One
22/70 *Little Sister*
77/71 *Three Degrees*
71/71 **You're The One For Me** *Joe Simon*
1/78 **You're The One That I Want** *Olivia Newton-John & John Travolta*
84/85 **You're The Only Love** *Paul Hyde*
59/79 **You're The Only One** *Dolly Parton*
83/77 **You're The Only One** *Geils*
13/80 **You're The Only Woman (You & I)** *Ambrosia*
91/64 **You're The Only World I Know** *Sonny James*
You're The Reason
11/61 *Bobby Edwards*
87/61 *Joe South*
3/63 **You're The Reason I'm Living** *Bobby Darin*
51/71 **You're The Reason Why** *Ebonys*
43/77 **You're Throwing A Good Love Away** *Spinners*
59/74 **You're Welcome, Stop On By** *Bobby Womack*
33/66 **You've Been Cheatin'** *Impressions*
36/65 **You've Been In Love Too Long** *Martha & The Vandellas*
64/70 **You've Been My Inspiration** *Main Ingredient*
(You've Got) *see: Personality*
You've Got A Friend
1/71 *James Taylor*
29/71 *Roberta Flack & Donny Hathaway*
79/81 **You've Got A Good Love Coming** *Van Stephenson*
67/82 **You've Got Another Thing Comin'** *Judas Priest*
54/79 **You've Got Another Thing Coming** *Hotel*
38/70 **(You've Got Me) Dangling On A String** *Chairmen Of The Board*
33/77 **You've Got Me Runnin'** *Gene Cotton*
63/66 **You've Got My Mind Messed Up** *James Carr*
74/74 **You've Got My Soul On Fire** *Temptations*
4/56 **(You've Got) The Magic Touch** *Platters*
86/60 **You've Got The Power** *James Brown*
91/69 **You've Got The Power** *Esquires*
58/68 **You've Got To Be Loved** *Montanas*
28/71 **You've Got To Crawl (Before You Walk)** *8th Day*
97/71 **You've Got To Earn It** *Staple Singers*
10/65 **You've Got To Hide Your Love Away** *Silkie*
93/61 **You've Got To Love Her With A Feeling** *Freddy King*
20/60 **(You've Got To) Move Two Mountains** *Marv Johnson*
You've Got To Pay The Price
49/67 *Al Kent*
49/69 *Gloria Taylor*
46/73 **You've Got To Take It (If You Want It)** *Main Ingredient*
76/80 **You've Got What I Need** *Shooting Star*
(You've Got What It Takes) *see: Baby*
7/65 **You've Got Your Troubles** *Fortunes*
You've Lost That Lovin' Feelin'
1/65 *Righteous Brothers*
16/69 *Dionne Warwick*
71/71 *Roberta Flack & Donny Hathaway*
89/79 *Long John Baldry*
89/79 *Long John Baldry*
12/80 *Daryl Hall & John Oates*
You've Made Me So Very Happy
39/67 *Brenda Holloway*
2/69 *Blood, Sweat & Tears*
95/70 *Lou Rawls*
95/65 **You've Never Been In Love Like This Before** *Unit Four plus Two*
22/73 **You've Never Been This Far Before** *Conway Twitty*
You've Really Got A Hold On Me
8/63 *Miracles*
98/72 *Gayle McCormick*
72/79 *Eddie Money*
60/68 **You've Still Got A Place In My Heart** *Dean Martin*
Young Abe Lincoln
25/55 *Don Cornell*
90/55 *Hugo & Luigi*
28/75 **Young Americans** *David Bowie*
17/63 **Young And In Love** *Dick & DeeDee*
53/64 **Young And In Love** *Chris Crosby*
Young And The Restless *see: Nadia's Theme*
23/58 **Young And Warm And Wonderful** *Tony Bennett*
99/68 **Young Birds Fly** *Cryan' Shames*
Young Blood
8/57 *Coasters*
20/76 *Bad Company*
40/79 **Young Blood** *Rickie Lee Jones*
86/68 **Young Boy** *Barbara Greene*
66/61 **Young Boy Blues** *Ben E. King*
12/60 **Young Emotions** *Ricky Nelson*
69/69 **Young Folks** *Supremes*
2/68 **Young Girl** *Union Gap*
51/66 **Young Girl, A** *Noel Harrison*
20/76 **Young Hearts Run Free** *Candi Staton*
74/59 **Young Ideas** *Chico Holiday*
Young Love
1/57 *Tab Hunter*
1/57 *Sonny James*
17/57 *Crew-Cuts*
F/73 *Donny Osmond*
93/76 *Ray Stevens*
38/82 **Young Love** *Air Supply*
50/66 **Young Love** *Lesley Gore*
64/83 **Young Love** *Janet Jackson*
6/63 **Young Lovers** *Paul & Paula*
Young Lovers *see: Theme For*
80/72 **Young New Mexican Puppeteer** *Tom Jones*
92/58 **Young School Girl** *Fats Domino*
71/84 **Young Thing, Wild Dreams (Rock Me)** *Red Rider*
5/81 **Young Turks** *Rod Stewart*
47/63 **Young Wings Can Fly (Higher Than You Know)** *Ruby & The Romantics*
5/62 **Young World** *Rick Nelson*
80/82 **Younger Days** *Joe Fagin*
Younger Girl
42/66 *Critters*
52/66 *Hondells*
Your *also see: You're*
93/63 **Your Baby's Gone Surfin'** *Duane Eddy*
98/63 **Your Boyfriend's Back** *Bobby Comstock* *(also see: My Boyfriend's Back)*
24/75 **Your Bulldog Drinks Champagne** *Jim Stafford*
51/74 **Your Cash Ain't Nothin' But Trash** *Steve Miller Band*
Your Cheatin' Heart
72/58 *George Hamilton IV*
82/59 *Billy Vaughn*
29/62 *Ray Charles*
77/82 **Your Daddy Don't Know** *Toronto*
34/61 **Your Friends** *Dee Clark*

Your Good Thing (Is About To End)
95/66 *Mable John*
18/69 *Lou Rawls*
95/62 **Your Heart Belongs To Me** *Supremes*
91/68 **Your Heart Is Free Just Like The Wind** *Vikki Carr*
46/69 **Your Husband - My Wife** *Brooklyn Bridge*
33/82 **Your Imagination** *Daryl Hall & John Oates*
53/57 **Your Kisses Kill Me** *Eydie Gorme*
63/61 **Your Last Goodbye** *Floyd Cramer*
6/86 **Your Love** *Outfield*
15/77 **Your Love** *Marilyn McCoo & Billy Davis, Jr.*
38/75 **Your Love** *Graham Central Station*
60/57 **Your Love For Me** *Frank Sinatra*
13/83 **Your Love Is Driving Me Crazy** *Sammy Hagar*
54/85 **Your Love Is King** *Sade*
93/71 **Your Love Is So Doggone Good** *Whispers*
49/78 **Your Love Is So Good For Me** *Diana Ross*
(Your Love Keeps Lifting Me) Higher And Higher
6/67 *Jackie Wilson*
2/77 *Rita Coolidge*
73/71 **Your Love (Means Everything To Me)** *Watts 103rd St. Band*
24/61 **Your Ma Said You Cried In Your Sleep Last Night** *Kenny Dino*
4/73 **Your Mama Don't Dance** *Loggins & Messina*
40/71 **Your Move** *Yes*
80/58 **Your Name Is Beautiful** *Carl Smith*
14/62 **Your Nose Is Gonna Grow** *Johnny Crawford*
40/63 **Your Old Stand By** *Mary Wells*
40/61 **Your One And Only Love** *Jackie Wilson*
28/63 **Your Other Love** *Connie Francis*
54/61 **Your Other Love** *Flamingos*
75/70 **Your Own Back Yard** *Dion*
62/77 **Your Own Special Way** *Genesis*
86/86 **Your Personal Touch** *Evelyn 'Champagne' King*
5/67 **Your Precious Love** *Marvin Gaye & Tammi Terrell*
(also see: For Your Precious Love)
88/73 **Your Side Of The Bed** *Mac Davis*
62/86 **Your Smile** *Rene & Angela*
20/77 **Your Smiling Face** *James Taylor*
8/71 **Your Song** *Elton John*
60/78 **Your Sweetness Is My Weakness** *Barry White*
68/63 **Your Teenage Dreams** *Johnny Mathis*
72/68 **Your Time Hasn't Come Yet, Baby** *Elvis Presley*
40/71 **Your Time To Cry** *Joe Simon*
67/57 **Your True Love** *Carl Perkins*
33/67 **Your Unchanging Love** *Marvin Gaye*
32/63 **Your Used To Be** *Brenda Lee*
20/57 **Your Wild Heart** *Joy Layne*
9/86 **Your Wildest Dreams** *Moody Blues*
59/72 **Your Wonderful, Sweet Sweet Love** *Supremes*
78/70 **Yours Love** *Joe Simon*
(Yowsah, Yowsah, Yowsah)
see: Dance, Dance, Dance
4/68 **Yummy Yummy Yummy** *Ohio Express*

52/68 **Zabadak** *Dave Dee, Dozy, Beaky, Mick & Tich*
75/56 **Zambezi** *Lou Busch*
78/69 **Zazueira (Za-zoo-wher-a)** *Herb Alpert*
98/62 **Zero-Zero** *Lawrence Welk*
Zing! Went The Strings Of My Heart
92/63 *Furys*
64/72 *Trammps*
91/75 **Zip, The** *MFSB*
8/63 **Zip-A-Dee Doo-Dah** *Bob B. Soxx & The Blue Jeans*
36/67 **Zip Code** *Five Americans*
16/57 **Zip Zip** *Diamonds*
11/66 **Zorba The Greek** *Herb Alpert*
17/58 **Zorro** *Chordettes*

The Record Holders

THE TOP 200 ARTISTS

Rank		Artist	Points
1.		Elvis Presley	13237
2.		The Beatles	6696
3.		James Brown	6260
4.		Stevie Wonder	5846
5.		Pat Boone	5341
6.		Marvin Gaye	5339
7.		Aretha Franklin	5243
8.		The Rolling Stones	5168
9.		Neil Diamond	5011
10.		Fats Domino	4922
11.		Ricky Nelson	4797
12.		Connie Francis	4778
13.		The Temptations	4776
14.		Ray Charles	4741
15.	↑	Elton John	4703
16.		The Beach Boys	4608
17.		Frank Sinatra	4452
18.		Paul Anka	4350
19.		The Supremes	4298
20.		Dionne Warwick	4258
21.	↑	Paul McCartney	4233
22.		Brenda Lee	4185
23.		Nat King Cole	3967
24.		Perry Como	3954
25.	↑	Chicago	3926
26.		The 4 Seasons	3890
27.	↑	Diana Ross	3848
28.		The Bee Gees	3814
29.		The Miracles	3802
30.	↑	Olivia Newton-John	3670
31.		Brook Benton	3623
32.		Sam Cooke	3601
33.		Bobby Vinton	3567
34.		Four Tops	3482
35.		The Everly Brothers	3450
36.		Andy Williams	3392
37.		Jackie Wilson	3377
38.	↑	Billy Joel	3356
39.		Gladys Knight & The Pips	3340
40.	↑	Daryl Hall & John Oates	3317
41.		The Platters	3265
42.		Bobby Darin	3160
43.		Johnny Mathis	3077
44.		The Jacksons	3054
45.	↑	Barbra Streisand	3036
46.		Barry Manilow	2969
47.	↑	Rod Stewart	2947
48.		Chubby Checker	2928
49.		Carpenters	2864
50.		Neil Sedaka	2858
51.	↑	Donna Summer	2833
52.		Glen Campbell	2808
53.		Roy Orbison	2767
54.	N	Kool & The Gang	2748
55.		Linda Ronstadt	2748
56.		Patti Page	2737
57.	N	Kenny Rogers	2668
58.		The 5th Dimension	2661
59.	N	Michael Jackson	2650
60.	↑	Bob Seger	2615
61.		Earth, Wind & Fire	2607
62.		Wilson Pickett	2567
63.		The Impressions	2548
64.		The Drifters	2546
65.		Three Dog Night	2536
66.		Electric Light Orchestra	2510
67.		Jerry Butler	2506
68.		Bobby Rydell	2505
69.		Johnny Cash	2484
70.		Tom Jones	2461
71.	↑	Commodores	2449
72.		Johnny Rivers	2445
73.	N	Pointer Sisters	2410
74.		Herb Alpert & The Tijuana Brass	2407
75.		John Denver	2392
76.		Spinners	2377
77.		Dean Martin	2360
78.		The Dave Clark Five	2331
79.	N	Jefferson Starship	2324
80.	N	Journey	2232
81.		Bobby Vee	2215
82.		The Isley Brothers	2214
83.		Herman's Hermits	2169
84.		Chuck Berry	2150
85.		Eagles	2137
86.		Paul Revere & The Raiders	2077
87.		The Doobie Brothers	2069
88.		Jimmie Rodgers	2057
89.		Al Martino	2044
90.		The McGuire Sisters	2034

Rank		Artist	Points
91.		Gene Pitney	2029
92.	N	Queen	2005
93.		Dion	2003
94.	N	Rick Springfield	2003
95.		Duane Eddy	1991
96.	N	Foreigner	1989
97.		The Who	1987
98.		Johnny Tillotson	1977
99.		Jan & Dean	1961
100.		Helen Reddy	1955
101.		Frankie Avalon	1949
102.		Petula Clark	1934
103.		Simon & Garfunkel	1931
104.		Prince	1930
105.		B.J. Thomas	1921
106.		Tommy James & The Shondells	1907
107.		Bill Haley & His Comets	1906
108.		Marty Robbins	1903
109.		Anne Murray	1898
110.		Styx	1895
111.		Abba	1878
112.		David Bowie	1869
113.		Billy Vaughn	1868
114.		James Taylor	1860
115.		Heart	1849
116.		Lionel Richie	1845
117.		Tony Bennett	1844
118.		The Shirelles	1819
119.		Al Green	1818
120.		Tony Orlando & Dawn	1805
121.		Martha & The Vandellas	1804
122.		The Kinks	1798
123.		Bob Dylan	1794
124.		John Lennon	1791
125.		The Guess Who	1790
126.		The Hollies	1789
127.		Otis Redding	1764
128.		Carly Simon	1764
129.		The Animals	1755
130.		Creedence Clearwater Revival	1748
131.		Jr. Walker & The All Stars	1745
132.		The Grass Roots	1744
133.		Joe Tex	1742
134.		Fleetwood Mac	1741
135.		John Cougar Mellencamp	1733
136.		Steve Lawrence	1732
137.		Bobby Goldsboro	1731
138.		The O'Jays	1730
139.		Ray Stevens	1730
140.		The Rascals	1727
141.		The Marvelettes	1724
142.		Little River Band	1716
143.		Teresa Brewer	1712
144.		Paul Simon	1704
145.		Dr. Hook	1694
146.		Cher	1690
147.		The Monkees	1688
148.		Madonna	1685
149.		Pat Benatar	1667
150.		The Four Lads	1655
151.		The Diamonds	1653
152.		The Righteous Brothers	1636
153.		Mary Wells	1636
154.		Sheena Easton	1622
155.		America	1613
156.		Tommy Roe	1603
157.		Joe Simon	1596
158.		Gary Lewis & The Playboys	1591
159.		Roberta Flack	1588
160.		War	1588
161.		Bruce Springsteen	1576
162.		The Moody Blues	1574
163.		Little Richard	1570
164.		Kenny Loggins	1560
165.		Steve Miller Band	1550
166.		The Cars	1548
167.		Eric Clapton	1528
168.		Grand Funk Railroad	1528
169.		Bobby Bland	1524
170.		Kim Carnes	1514
171.		The Ames Brothers	1509
172.		Lesley Gore	1508
173.		Engelbert Humperdinck	1506
174.		The Stylistics	1506
175.		Freddy Cannon	1503
176.		Air Supply	1498
177.		Donovan	1492
178.		Jackson Browne	1488
179.		The Coasters	1484
180.		Sonny & Cher	1479
181.		Jay & The Americans	1478
182.		Nancy Sinatra	1477
183.		Phil Collins	1467
184.		Bread	1466
185.		Carole King	1466
186.		Peter, Paul & Mary	1445
187.		Captain & Tennille	1435
188.		Johnnie Taylor	1421
189.		Santana	1419
190.		Ronnie Dove	1418
191.		Etta James	1416
192.		Alice Cooper	1414
193.		Kiss	1410
194.		Genesis	1409
195.		Smokey Robinson	1407
196.		Ray Parker Jr.	1406
197.		Sly & The Family Stone	1399
198.		Sarah Vaughan	1396
199.		Clyde McPhatter	1389
200.		KC & The Sunshine Band	1379

Coming Up Strong:

Huey Lewis & The News	Van Halen
Duran Duran	Tom Petty & The Heartbreakers
REO Speedwagon	Tina Turner
Police	Stevie Nicks
Survivor	Bryan Adams

🠅 : Climbed at least 10 notches in the Top 100 since the last edition of *Top Pop Singles*.

N : New entry in Top 100.

This is the first time a ranking beyond 100 was published.

Artist's points are calculated using the following formula:

1. Each artist's charted records are awarded points based on their highest position (#1 = 100 points; #2 = 99, etc.).
2. Bonus points are awarded each record based on its highest charted position (#1-5 = 25 points; #6-10 = 20 points; #11-20 = 15 points; #21-30 = 10 points; #31-40 = 5 points).
3. Total weeks charted are added in.
4. Total weeks an artist held the #1 position are also added in.

When two artists combine for a hit record (Ex: Paul McCartney/Stevie Wonder; Supremes/Temptations), their chart points are shared equally.

Artists such as "Simon & Garfunkel", "Sonny & Cher" and "Loggins & Messina" are considered regular recording teams and their points are not split or shared by either of the artists individually.

THE TOP 200 ARTISTS (A-Z)

Abba 111
Air Supply 176
Herb Alpert & The Tijuana Brass 74
America 155
The Ames Brothers 171
The Animals 129
Paul Anka 18
Frankie Avalon 101
The Beach Boys 16
The Beatles 2
The Bee Gees 28
Pat Benatar 149
Tony Bennett 117
Brook Benton 31
Chuck Berry 84
Bobby Bland 169
Pat Boone 5
David Bowie 112
Bread 184
Teresa Brewer 143
James Brown 3
Jackson Browne 178
Jerry Butler 67
Glen Campbell 52
Freddy Cannon 175
Captain & Tennille 187
Kim Carnes 170
Carpenters 49
The Cars 166
Johnny Cash 69
Ray Charles 14
Chubby Checker 48
Cher 146
Chicago 25
Eric Clapton 167
The Dave Clark Five 78
Petula Clark 102
The Coasters 179
Nat King Cole 23
Phil Collins 183
Commodores 71
Perry Como 24
Sam Cooke 32
Alice Cooper 192
Creedence Clearwater Revival 130
Bobby Darin 42
Dawn 120
John Denver 75
Neil Diamond 9
The Diamonds 151
Dion 93
Dr. Hook 145
Fats Domino 10
Donovan 177
The Doobie Brothers 87
Ronnie Dove 190
The Drifters 64
Bob Dylan 123
Eagles 85
Earth, Wind & Fire 61
Sheena Easton 154

TOP 200 ARTISTS — Continued

Duane Eddy 95
Electric Light Orchestra 66
The Everly Brothers 35
The 5th Dimension 58
Roberta Flack 159
Fleetwood Mac 134
Foreigner 96
The Four Lads 150
The 4 Seasons 26
Four Tops 34
Connie Francis 12
Aretha Franklin 7
Marvin Gaye 6
Genesis 194
Bobby Goldsboro 137
Lesley Gore 172
Grand Funk Railroad 168
The Grass Roots 132
Al Green 119
The Guess Who 125
Bill Haley & His Comets 107
Daryl Hall & John Oates 40
Heart 115
Herman's Hermits 83
The Hollies 126
Engelbert Humperdinck 173
The Impressions 63
The Isley Brothers 82
Michael Jackson 59
The Jacksons 44
Etta James 191
Tommy James & The Shondells 106
Jan & Dean 99
Jay & The Americans 181
Jefferson Starship 79
Billy Joel 38
Elton John 15
Tom Jones 70
Journey 80
KC & The Sunshine Band 200
Carole King 185
The Kinks 122
Kiss 193
Gladys Knight & The Pips 39
Kool & The Gang 54
Steve Lawrence 136
Brenda Lee 22
John Lennon 124
Gary Lewis & The Playboys 158
Little Richard 163
Little River Band 142
Kenny Loggins 164
Madonna 148
Barry Manilow 46
Martha & The Vandellas 121
Dean Martin 77
Al Martino 89
The Marvelettes 141
Johnny Mathis 43
Paul McCartney 21
The McGuire Sisters 90
Clyde McPhatter 199
John Cougar Mellencamp 135
Steve Miller Band 165
The Miracles 29
The Monkees 147
The Moody Blues 162
Anne Murray 109
Ricky Nelson 11
Olivia Newton-John 30
The O'Jays 138
Roy Orbison 53
Patti Page 56
Ray Parker Jr. 196
Peter, Paul & Mary 186
Wilson Pickett 62
Gene Pitney 91
The Platters 41
Pointer Sisters 73
Elvis Presley 1
Prince 104
Queen 92
The Rascals 140
Otis Redding 127
Helen Reddy 100
Paul Revere & The Raiders 86
Lionel Richie 116
The Righteous Brothers 152
Johnny Rivers 72
Marty Robbins 108
Smokey Robinson 195
Jimmie Rodgers 88
Tommy Roe 156
Kenny Rogers 57
The Rolling Stones 8
Linda Ronstadt 55
Diana Ross 27
Bobby Rydell 68
Santana 189
Neil Sedaka 50
Bob Seger 60
The Shirelles 118
Simon & Garfunkel 103
Carly Simon 128
Joe Simon 157
Paul Simon 144
Frank Sinatra 17
Nancy Sinatra 182
Sly & The Family Stone 197
Sonny & Cher 180
Spinners 76
Rick Springfield 94
Bruce Springsteen 161
Ray Stevens 139
Rod Stewart 47
Barbra Streisand 45
The Stylistics 174
Styx 110
Donna Summer 51
The Supremes 19
James Taylor 114
Johnnie Taylor 188
The Temptations 13
Joe Tex 133
B.J. Thomas 105
Three Dog Night 65
Johnny Tillotson 98
Sarah Vaughan 198
Billy Vaughn 113
Bobby Vee 81
Bobby Vinton 33
Jr. Walker & the All Stars 131
War 160
Dionne Warwick 20
Mary Wells 153
The Who 97
Andy Williams 36
Jackie Wilson 37
Stevie Wonder 4

THE TOP 20 ARTISTS BY DECADE

The Fifties (1955-59)

1. ELVIS PRESLEY 4331
2. PAT BOONE 4114
3. PERRY COMO 3113
4. FATS DOMINO 2950
5. NAT KING COLE 2784
6. THE PLATTERS 2327
7. RICKY NELSON 2196
8. FRANK SINATRA 2192
9. PATTI PAGE 1921
10. THE McGUIRE SISTERS 1866
11. JOHNNY MATHIS 1797
12. BILL HALEY & HIS COMETS 1788
13. THE FOUR LADS 1655
14. THE DIAMONDS 1555
15. TERESA BREWER 1529
16. THE EVERLY BROTHERS 1472
17. THE AMES BROTHERS 1428
18. LITTLE RICHARD 1384
19. JIMMIE RODGERS 1383
20. THE FONTANE SISTERS 1366

The Sixties

1. ELVIS PRESLEY 6232
2. THE BEATLES 5964
3. BRENDA LEE 4038
4. RAY CHARLES 3972
5. CONNIE FRANCIS 3498
6. THE BEACH BOYS 3470
7. JAMES BROWN 3445
8. THE 4 SEASONS 3406
9. MARVIN GAYE 3344
10. THE SUPREMES 3261
11. BOBBY VINTON 2907
12. CHUBBY CHECKER 2838
13. THE MIRACLES 2804
14. THE TEMPTATIONS 2737
15. JACKIE WILSON 2687
16. ROY ORBISON 2663
17. BROOK BENTON 2660
18. SAM COOKE 2504
19. DIONNE WARWICK 2502
20. THE ROLLING STONES 2422

The Seventies

1. ELTON JOHN 3056
2. PAUL McCARTNEY 2962
3. CHICAGO 2824
4. CARPENTERS 2638
5. JAMES BROWN 2598
6. ELVIS PRESLEY 2540
7. THE BEE GEES 2490
8. NEIL DIAMOND 2460
9. THE JACKSONS 2456
10. STEVIE WONDER 2315
11. OLIVIA NEWTON-JOHN 2216
12. DIANA ROSS 2136
13. GLADYS KNIGHT & THE PIPS 2087
14. THREE DOG NIGHT 2045
15. JOHN DENVER 2008
16. EARTH, WIND & FIRE 1983
17. ARETHA FRANKLIN 1975
18. HELEN REDDY 1939
19. BARRY MANILOW 1884
20. MARVIN GAYE 1851

The Eighties (1980-86)

1. DARYL HALL & JOHN OATES 2425
2. BILLY JOEL 2186
3. PRINCE 1917
4. KENNY ROGERS 1884
5. JOURNEY 1821
6. RICK SPRINGFIELD 1779
7. KOOL & THE GANG 1764
8. LIONEL RICHIE 1713
9. DIANA ROSS 1712
10. POINTER SISTERS 1709
11. MICHAEL JACKSON 1672
12. PAT BENATAR 1667
13. ELTON JOHN 1647
14. JOHN COUGAR MELLENCAMP 1636
15. SHEENA EASTON 1622
16. STEVIE WONDER 1558
17. MADONNA 1541
18. BOB SEGER 1524
19. AIR SUPPLY 1498
20. PHIL COLLINS 1467

ARTISTS WITH ...

45 OR MORE CHARTED RECORDS

1.	149	ELVIS PRESLEY
2.	94	JAMES BROWN
3.	74	RAY CHARLES
4.	69	THE BEATLES
5.	68	ARETHA FRANKLIN
6.	67	FRANK SINATRA
7.	66	FATS DOMINO
8.	60	PAT BOONE
9.	58	NAT KING COLE
10.	56	NEIL DIAMOND
11.	56	CONNIE FRANCIS
12.	56	MARVIN GAYE
13.	56	STEVIE WONDER
14.	54	JACKIE WILSON
15.	53	PAUL ANKA
16.	53	THE BEACH BOYS
17.	53	RICKY NELSON
18.	53	DIONNE WARWICK
19.	52	BRENDA LEE
20.	52	THE TEMPTATIONS
21.	49	BROOK BENTON
22.	49	THE ROLLING STONES
23.	48	JOHNNY CASH
24.	47	PERRY COMO
25.	46	THE 4 SEASONS
26.	46	THE MIRACLES
27.	45	THE SUPREMES
28.	45	ANDY WILLIAMS

4 OR MORE #1 HITS

1.	21	THE BEATLES
2.	18	ELVIS PRESLEY
3.	12	THE SUPREMES
4.	9	THE BEE GEES
5.	9	PAUL McCARTNEY
6.	9	STEVIE WONDER
7.	8	THE ROLLING STONES
8.	6	PAT BOONE
9.	6	DARYL HALL & JOHN OATES
10.	6	MICHAEL JACKSON
11.	6	ELTON JOHN
12.	6	DIANA ROSS
13.	5	EAGLES
14.	5	THE 4 SEASONS
15.	5	KC & THE SUNSHINE BAND
16.	5	MADONNA
17.	5	OLIVIA NEWTON-JOHN
18.	5	LIONEL RICHIE
19.	5	BARBRA STREISAND
20.	4	BLONDIE
21.	4	PHIL COLLINS
22.	4	JOHN DENVER
23.	4	THE EVERLY BROTHERS
24.	4	THE JACKSON 5
25.	4	THE PLATTERS
26.	4	DONNA SUMMER
27.	4	THE TEMPTATIONS
28.	4	BOBBY VINTON

12 OR MORE WEEKS AT #1 POSITION

1.	80	ELVIS PRESLEY
2.	59	THE BEATLES
3.	30	PAUL McCARTNEY
4.	27	THE BEE GEES
5.	22	MICHAEL JACKSON
6.	22	THE SUPREMES
7.	21	PAT BOONE
8.	21	LIONEL RICHIE
9.	21	STEVIE WONDER
10.	20	DIANA ROSS
11.	18	THE 4 SEASONS
12.	18	OLIVIA NEWTON-JOHN
13.	17	THE ROLLING STONES
14.	17	ROD STEWART
15.	15	THE EVERLY BROTHERS
16.	15	ELTON JOHN
17.	14	DARYL HALL & JOHN OATES
18.	14	THE McGUIRE SISTERS
19.	13	ANDY GIBB
20.	13	BARBRA STREISAND
21.	13	DONNA SUMMER
22.	12	ROBERTA FLACK
23.	12	GUY MITCHELL
24.	12	THE MONKEES
25.	12	BOBBY VINTON

RECORDS OF LONGEVITY

Records with 30 or more Total Weeks charted

	WKS		TITLE ... Artist
1.	43		TAINTED LOVE ... Soft Cell
2.	40		I GO CRAZY ... Paul Davis
3.	40	*	I'M SO EXCITED ... Pointer Sisters
4.	39		WONDERFUL! WONDERFUL! ... Johnny Mathis
5.	39	*	THE TWIST ... Chubby Checker
6.	39	*	HONKY TONK ... Bill Doggett
7.	38		SO RARE ... Jimmy Dorsey
8.	38		WHY ME ... Kris Kristofferson
9.	38	*	ROCK AROUND THE CLOCK ... Bill Haley & His Comets
10.	37	*	THE WAYWARD WIND ... Gogi Grant
11.	37	*	MONSTER MASH ... Bobby "Boris" Pickett
12.	36		GLORIA ... Laura Branigan
13.	35	*	STAND BY ME ... Ben E. King
14.	34		LOVE LETTERS IN THE SAND ... Pat Boone
15.	34		IT'S NOT FOR ME TO SAY ... Johnny Mathis
16.	34		AROUND THE WORLD ... Victor Young
17.	33		HOW DEEP IS YOUR LOVE ... Bee Gees
18.	32		BABY COME BACK ... Player
19.	32		BABY, COME TO ME ... Patti Austin & James Ingram
20.	32		JESSIE'S GIRL ... Rick Springfield
21.	32		FEELINGS ... Morris Albert
22.	32		AROUND THE WORLD ... Mantovani
23.	31		TAMMY ... Debbie Reynolds
24.	31		I JUST WANT TO BE YOUR EVERYTHING ... Andy Gibb
25.	31		ANOTHER ONE BITES THE DUST ... Queen
26.	31		HOT CHILD IN THE CITY ... Nick Gilder
27.	31		CANADIAN SUNSET ... Hugo Winterhalter/Eddie Heywood
28.	31		TRUE LOVE ... Bing Crosby & Grace Kelly
29.	31		COME GO WITH ME ... The Dell-Vikings
30.	31		I LOVE THE NIGHTLIFE (DISCO 'ROUND) ... Alicia Bridges
31.	31		"JESUS CHRIST" SUPERSTAR ... Murray Head
32.	30		ALL SHOOK UP ... Elvis Presley
33.	30		CELEBRATION ... Kool & The Gang
34.	30		ALL THE WAY ... Frank Sinatra
35.	30		BORDERLINE ... Madonna
36.	30		OUR LIPS ARE SEALED ... Go-Go's
37.	30	*	WIPE OUT ... The Surfaris

* Records which charted more than once.

LABEL ABBREVIATIONS

ABC-Para.	ABC-Paramount
Allied Art.	Allied Artists
American Int.	American International
Ariola Am.	Ariola America
Atlanta A.	Atlanta Artists
Barking P.	Barking Pumpkin
Believe	Believe In A Dream
Brother/Rep.	Brother/Reprise
Cadet Con.	Cadet Concept
Canadian A.	Canadian American
CBS Assoc.	CBS Associated
Clev. Int.	Cleveland International
Coast To C.	Coast To Coast
Common. U.	Commonwealth United
Constell.	Constellation
DCP Int'l.	DCP International
First Art.	First Artists
GNP Cresc.	GNP Crescendo
Gold Mt.	Gold Mountain
Int. Artists	International Artists
London Int.	London International
Midland I.	Midland International
Midsong Int.	Midsong International
New York I.	New York International
Paisley P.	Paisley Park
Phil-L.A.	Phil-L.A. of Soul
Phil. Int.	Philadelphia International
Philly W.	Philly World
Pickwick I.	Pickwick International
Private S.	Private Stock
Rainy Wed.	Rainy Wednesday
Rock 'n' R.	Rock 'n' Roll
Rolling S.	Rolling Stones
Scotti Br.	Scotti Brothers
Sesame St.	Sesame Street
Sound Stage	Sound Stage 7
SSS Int'l.	SSS International
Stormy F.	Stormy Forest
Sunshine S.	Sunshine Sound
Tetragramm.	Tetragrammaton
Three Bros.	Three Brothers
Total Exp.	Total Experience
United Art.	United Artists
Vanguard A.	Vanguard Apostolic
Verve Folk.	Verve Folkways
Verve Fore.	Verve Forecast
Wing & Prayer	Wing And A Prayer
Wooden N.	Wooden Nickel
World Art.	World Artists
World Pac.	World Pacific
World Pac. Jazz	World Pacific Jazz

#1 RECORDS LISTED CHRONOLOGICALLY

For the years 1955 through 1958, when Billboard published more than one weekly pop chart, the chart title and #1 weeks on each chart are listed beneath the record title.

The date shown is the earliest date that a record hit #1 on any of the pop charts. The weeks column lists the total weeks at #1, from whichever chart it achieved its highest total. This total is not a combined total from the various pop charts.

Because of the multiple charts used in my research, some dates are duplicated, as certain #1 hits may have peaked on the same week on different charts. Billboard also showed ties at #1 on some of these charts, therefore the total weeks for each year may calculate out to more than 52.

See the introduction pages of this book for more details about researching the pop charts.

DATE HIT #1 : Date first peaked at the #1 position.
WKS AT #1 : Total weeks held at the #1 position.
* : Consensus #1 record - hit #1 on all pop charts published (1955-58).
† : Indicates record hit #1, dropped down, then returned to the #1 spot.
F : Frozen chart - total weeks at #1 include one frozen week. Beginning in 1976, Billboard ceased publishing a year-end issue. The year's last regular issue is considered frozen and all chart positions remain the same for the unpublished week.

CHART ABBREVIATIONS:
BS : Best Sellers
JY : Jockeys
JB : Juke Box
TP : Top 100
HT : Hot 100

2-Sided #1 Hits:
Don't Be Cruel/Hound Dog ... Elvis Presley (1956)
Come Together/Something ... The Beatles (1969)

The above two records are rare instances of a double-sided #1 smash hit. Each side had enough strength to capture the #1 spot and the music trades had a difficult task in determining which side to list first. The Elvis' hit, during its long run at #1, had each side take its turn at #1. The Beatles' hit, after flip-flopping its way up the Top 10, finally peaked at #1 for 1 week and was shown as Come Together/Something.

684 records have hit the #1 position on Billboard's pop charts from 1955 through 1986. "The Twist", even though it hit #1 in 1960 and again in 1962, is counted only once. There have been 618 #1 records since the Hot 100 chart debuted in 1958.

DATE HIT #1	WKS AT #1	

1955

1. 1/01 — 4 — * **Let Me Go Lover** ... Joan Weber
BS: 2 / JY: 4† / JB: 4

2. 2/05 — 3 — **Hearts Of Stone** ... The Fontane Sisters
BS: 1 / JB: 3

3. 2/12 — 10 — * **Sincerely** ... The McGuire Sisters
BS: 6 / JY: 10 / JB: 7

4. 3/26 — 5 — * **The Ballad Of Davy Crockett** ... Bill Hayes
BS: 5 / JY: 3 / JB: 3

5. 4/30 — 10 — * **Cherry Pink And Apple Blossom White** ... Perez Prado
BS: 10 / JY: 6† / JB: 8

6. 5/14 — 2 — **Unchained Melody** ... Les Baxter
JY: 2†

7. 5/14 — 3 — **Dance With Me Henry** ... Georgia Gibbs
JB: 3

8. 7/09 — 2 — **Learnin' The Blues** ... Frank Sinatra
JY: 2†

9. 7/09 — 8 — * **Rock Around The Clock** ... Bill Haley & His Comets
BS: 8 / JY: 6† / JB: 7

10. 9/03 — 6 — * **The Yellow Rose Of Texas** ... Mitch Miller
BS: 6† / JY: 6 / JB: 6

11. 9/17 — 2 — **Ain't That A Shame** ... Pat Boone
JB: 2

12. 10/08 — 6 — * **Love Is A Many- Splendored Thing** ... The Four Aces
BS: 2† / JY: 6 / JB: 3 / TP: 3
Top 100 chart debuted on 11/12/55

13. 10/29 — 4 — **Autumn Leaves** ... Roger Williams
BS: 4

14. 11/26 — 8 — * **Sixteen Tons** ... Tennessee Ernie Ford
BS: 7 / JY: 6 / JB: 8 / TP: 6

1956

1. 1/07 — 6 — * **Memories Are Made Of This** ... Dean Martin
BS: 5 / JY: 6 / JB: 4 / TP: 5

2. 2/18 — 2 — **The Great Pretender** ... The Platters
JY: 2 / JB: 1 / TP: 2

3. 2/18 — 6 — * **Rock And Roll Waltz** ... Kay Starr
BS: 1 / JY: 1 / JB: 6 / TP: 4

4. 2/25 — 4 — **Lisbon Antigua** ... Nelson Riddle
BS: 4 / JY: 2†

5. 3/17 — 6 — * **The Poor People Of Paris** ... Les Baxter
BS: 4 / JY: 6† / JB: 3 / TP: 6

6. 4/21 — 8 — * **Heartbreak Hotel** ... Elvis Presley
BS: 8 / JY: 3 / JB: 8 / TP: 7

7. 5/05 — 1 — **Hot Diggity** ... Perry Como
JY: 1

8. 6/02 — 3 — **Moonglow and Theme From "Picnic"** ... Morris Stoloff
JY: 3

9. 6/16 — 8 — * **The Wayward Wind** ... Gogi Grant
BS: 6 / JY: 8 / JB: 4 / TP: 7

10. 7/28 — 1 — **I Want You, I Need You, I Love You** ... Elvis Presley
BS: 1

11. 7/28 — 4 — **I Almost Lost My Mind** ... Pat Boone
JB: 4 / TP: 2

12. 8/04 — 5 — * **My Prayer** ... The Platters
BS: 2 / JY: 3 / JB: 1 / TP: 5

13. 8/18 — 11 — * **Don't Be Cruel/**
14. **Hound Dog** ... Elvis Presley
BS: 11 / JY: 8 / JB: 11 / TP: 7
Breakdown of 11 weeks at #1: **BS:** Hound Dog/Don't Be Cruel (5): Don't Be Cruel (1): Don't Be Cruel/Hound Dog (5) **JB:** Hound Dog/Don't Be Cruel (4): Don't Be Cruel/Hound Dog (7)

15. 11/03 — 3 — **The Green Door** ... Jim Lowe
JB: 3 / TP: 3

16. 11/03 — 5 — * **Love Me Tender** ... Elvis Presley
BS: 5 / JY: 5 / JB: 1 / TP: 4†

17. 12/08 — 10 — * **Singing The Blues** ... Guy Mitchell
BS: 9 / JY: 9 / JB: 10 / TP: 9

1957

1. 2/09 — 1 — **Don't Forbid Me** ... Pat Boone
JB: 1 / TP: 1

2. 2/09 — 3 — **Too Much** ... Elvis Presley
BS: 3 / JB: 1

DATE HIT #1	WKS AT #1	

1957 Continued

	DATE HIT #1	WKS AT #1	
3.	2/09	1	**Young Love** ... Sonny James JY: 1
4.	2/16	6	* **Young Love** ... Tab Hunter BS: 4 / JY: 6 / JB: 5† / TP: 6
5.	3/30	1	**Party Doll** ... Buddy Knox BS: 1
6.	3//30	3	**Butterfly** ... Andy Williams JY: 2 / TP: 3
7.	4/06	2	**Butterfly** ... Charlie Gracie JB: 2
8.	4/06	2	**Round And Round** ... Perry Como BS: 1 / JY: 2 / TP: 1
9.	4/13	9	* **All Shook Up** ... Elvis Presley BS: 8 / JY: 7 / JB: 9 / TP: 8 **Juke Box chart terminated on 6/17/57**
10.	6/03	7	* **Love Letters In The Sand** ... Pat Boone BS: 5 / JY: 7 / TP: 5
11.	7/08	7	* **(Let Me Be Your) Teddy Bear** ... Elvis Presley BS: 7 / JY: 3 / TP: 7
12.	8/19	5	* **Tammy** ... Debbie Reynolds BS: 3† / JY: 5 / TP: 5
13.	9/09	1	**Diana** ... Paul Anka BS: 1
14.	9/23	1	**That'll Be The Day** ... The Crickets BS: 1
15.	9/23	4	* **Honeycomb** ... Jimmie Rodgers BS: 2 / JY: 4 / TP: 2
16.	10/14	4	* **Wake Up Little Susie** ... The Everly Brothers BS: 1 / JY: 4 / TP: 2
17.	10/21	1	**Chances Are** ... Johnny Mathis JY: 1
18.	10/21	7	* **Jailhouse Rock** ... Elvis Presley BS: 7† / JY: 2 / TP: 6
19.	12/02	3	* **You Send Me** ... Sam Cooke BS: 2 / JY: 1 / TP: 3
20.	12/16	6	* **April Love** ... Pat Boone BS: 2 / JY: 6 / TP: 1

1958

	DATE HIT #1	WKS AT #1	
1.	1/06	7	* **At The Hop** ... Danny & The Juniors BS: 5 / JY: 3 / TP: 7
2.	2/10	5	* **Don't** ... Elvis Presley BS: 5 / JY: 1 / TP: 1
3.	2/17	4	**Sugartime** ... The McGuire Sisters JY: 4
4.	2/24	2	**Get A Job** ... The Silhouettes TP: 2
5.	3/17	5	* **Tequila** ... The Champs BS: 5 / JY: 2 / TP: 5
6.	3/24	1	**Catch A Falling Star** ... Perry Como JY: 1
7.	4/14	4	**He's Got The Whole World (In His Hands)** ... Laurie London JY: 4
8.	4/21	1	* **Twilight Time** ... The Platters BS: 1 / JY: 1 / TP: 1
9.	4/28	3	**Witch Doctor** ... David Seville BS: 2 / TP: 3
10.	5/12	5	* **All I Have To Do Is Dream** ... The Everly Brothers BS: 4 / JY: 5 / TP: 3
11.	6/09	6	* **The Purple People Eater** ... Sheb Wooley BS: 6 / JY: 4 / TP: 6
12.	7/21	1	**Yakety Yak** ... The Coasters TP: 1
13.	7/21	2	**Hard Headed Woman** ... Elvis Presley BS: 2 / JY: 1
14.	7/28	1	**Patricia** ... Perez Prado JY: 1 / TP: 1 **Jockeys and Top 100 charts terminated on 7/28/58**
15.	8/04	2	* **Poor Little Fool** ... Ricky Nelson BS: 2 / HT: 2 **Hot 100 chart debuted on 8/4/58**
16.	8/18	5	* **Nel Blu Dipinto Di Blu (Volare)** ... Domenico Modugno BS: 5† / HT: 5†
17.	8/25	1	**Bird Dog** ... The Everly Brothers BS: 1
18.	8/25	1	**Little Star** ... The Elegants HT: 1

DATE HIT #1 / WKS AT #1

1958 Continued

	DATE HIT #1	WKS AT #1	
19.	9/29	6	* **It's All In The Game** .. Tommy Edwards BS: 3 / HT: 6 **Best Sellers chart terminated on 10/13/58** **Hot 100 chart used exclusively hereon**
20.	11/10	2	† **It's Only Make Believe** ... Conway Twitty
21.	11/17	1	**Tom Dooley** ... The Kingston Trio
22.	12/01	3	**To Know Him, Is To Love Him** ... The Teddy Bears
23.	12/22	4	**The Chipmunk Song** ... The Chipmunks

1959

	DATE HIT #1	WKS AT #1	
1.	1/19	3	**Smoke Gets In Your Eyes** ... The Platters
2.	2/09	4	**Stagger Lee** ... Lloyd Price
3.	3/09	5	**Venus** ... Frankie Avalon
4.	4/13	4	**Come Softly To Me** ... The Fleetwoods
5.	5/11	1	**The Happy Organ** ... Dave "Baby" Cortez
6.	5/18	2	**Kansas City** ... Wilbert Harrison
7.	6/01	6	**The Battle Of New Orleans** ... Johnny Horton
8.	7/13	4	**Lonely Boy** ... Paul Anka
9.	8/10	2	**A Big Hunk O' Love** ... Elvis Presley
10.	8/24	4	**The Three Bells** ... The Browns
11.	9/21	2	**Sleep Walk** ... Santo & Johnny
12.	10/05	9	† **Mack The Knife** ... Bobby Darin
13.	11/16	1	**Mr. Blue** ... The Fleetwoods
14.	12/14	2	**Heartaches By The Number** ... Guy Mitchell
15.	12/28	1	**Why** ... Frankie Avalon

1960

	DATE HIT #1	WKS AT #1	
1.	1/04	2	**El Paso** .. Marty Robbins
2.	1/18	3	**Running Bear** ... Johnny Preston
3.	2/08	2	**Teen Angel** ... Mark Dinning
4.	2/22	9	**The Theme From "A Summer Place"** ... Percy Faith
5.	4/25	4	**Stuck On You** ... Elvis Presley
6.	5/23	5	**Cathy's Clown** ... The Everly Brothers
7.	6/27	2	**Everybody's Somebody's Fool** ... Connie Francis
8.	7/11	1	**Alley-Oop** ... Hollywood Argyles
9.	7/18	3	**I'm Sorry** ... Brenda Lee
10.	8/08	1	**Itsy Bitsy Teenie Weenie Yellow Polkadot Bikini** ... Brian Hyland
11.	8/15	5	**It's Now Or Never** ... Elvis Presley
12.	9/19	1	**The Twist** ... Chubby Checker **re-entered POS 1 in 1962 for 2 more weeks**
13.	9/26	2	**My Heart Has A Mind Of Its Own** ... Connie Francis
14.	10/10	1	**Mr. Custer** ... Larry Verne
15.	10/17	3	† **Save The Last Dance For Me** ... The Drifters
16.	10/24	1	**I Want To Be Wanted** ... Brenda Lee
17.	11/14	1	**Georgia On My Mind** ... Ray Charles
18.	11/21	1	**Stay** ... Maurice Williams & The Zodiacs
19.	11/28	6	**Are You Lonesome To-night?** ... Elvis Presley

	DATE HIT #1	WKS AT #1	

1961

	DATE HIT #1	WKS AT #1	
1.	1/09	3	**Wonderland By Night ...** Bert Kaempfert
2.	1/30	2	**Will You Love Me Tomorrow ...** The Shirelles
3.	2/13	2	**Calcutta ...** Lawrence Welk
4.	2/27	3	**Pony Time ...** Chubby Checker
5.	3/20	2	**Surrender ...** Elvis Presley
6.	4/03	3	**Blue Moon ...** The Marcels
7.	4/24	4	**Runaway ...** Del Shannon
8.	5/22	1	**Mother-In-Law ...** Ernie K-Doe
9.	5/29	2	† **Travelin' Man ...** Ricky Nelson
10.	6/05	1	**Running Scared ...** Roy Orbison
11.	6/19	1	**Moody River ...** Pat Boone
12.	6/26	2	**Quarter To Three ...** U.S. Bonds
13.	7/10	7	**Tossin' And Turnin' ...** Bobby Lewis
14.	8/28	1	**Wooden Heart ...** Joe Dowell
15.	9/04	2	**Michael ...** The Highwaymen
16.	9/18	3	**Take Good Care Of My Baby** ... Bobby Vee
17.	10/09	2	**Hit The Road Jack ...** Ray Charles
18.	10/23	2	**Runaround Sue** ... Dion
19.	11/06	5	**Big Bad John ...** Jimmy Dean
20.	12/11	1	**Please Mr. Postman ...** The Marvelettes
21.	12/18	3	**The Lion Sleeps Tonight** ... The Tokens

1962

	DATE HIT #1	WKS AT #1	
1.	1/13	2	**The Twist ...** Chubby Checker **first entered POS 1 in 1960 for 1 week**
2.	1/27	3	**Peppermint Twist ...** Joey Dee & The Starliters
3.	2/17	3	**Duke Of Earl ...** Gene Chandler
4.	3/10	3	**Hey! Baby ...** Bruce Channel
5.	3/31	1	**Don't Break The Heart That Loves You ...** Connie Francis
6.	4/07	2	**Johnny Angel ...** Shelley Fabares
7.	4/21	2	**Good Luck Charm ...** Elvis Presley
8.	5/05	3	**Soldier Boy ...** The Shirelles
9.	5/26	1	**Stranger On The Shore** ... Mr. Acker Bilk
10.	6/02	5	**I Can't Stop Loving You** ... Ray Charles
11.	7/07	1	**The Stripper ...** David Rose
12.	7/14	4	**Roses Are Red (My Love)** ... Bobby Vinton
13.	8/11	2	**Breaking Up Is Hard To Do** ... Neil Sedaka
14.	8/25	1	**The Loco-Motion ...** Little Eva
15.	9/01	2	**Sheila** ... Tommy Roe
16.	9/15	5	**Sherry** ... The 4 Seasons
17.	10/20	2	**Monster Mash ...** Bobby "Boris" Pickett
18.	11/03	2	**He's A Rebel ...** The Crystals
19.	11/17	5	**Big Girls Don't Cry ...** The 4 Seasons
20.	12/22	3	**Telstar** ... The Tornadoes

1963

	DATE HIT #1	WKS AT #1	
1.	1/12	2	**Go Away Little Girl ...** Steve Lawrence
2.	1/26	2	**Walk Right In ...** The Rooftop Singers
3.	2/09	3	**Hey Paula ...** Paul & Paula
4.	3/02	3	**Walk Like A Man ...** The 4 Seasons
5.	3/23	1	**Our Day Will Come ...** Ruby & The Romantics
6.	3/30	4	**He's So Fine ...** The Chiffons
7.	4/27	3	**I Will Follow Him ...** Little Peggy March
8.	5/18	2	**If You Wanna Be Happy** ... Jimmy Soul
9.	6/01	2	**It's My Party ...** Lesley Gore

	DATE HIT #1	WKS AT #1	

1963 Continued

10.	6/15	3	**Sukiyaki** ... Kyu Sakamoto
11.	7/06	2	**Easier Said Than Done** ... The Essex
12.	7/20	2	**Surf City** ... Jan & Dean
13.	8/03	1	**So Much In Love** ... The Tymes
14.	8/10	3	**Fingertips - Pt 2** ... Little Stevie Wonder
15.	8/31	3	**My Boyfriend's Back** ... The Angels
16.	9/21	3	**Blue Velvet** ... Bobby Vinton
17.	10/12	5	**Sugar Shack** ... Jimmy Gilmer & The Fireballs
18.	11/16	1	**Deep Purple** ... Nino Tempo & April Stevens
19.	11/23	2	**I'm Leaving It Up To You** ... Dale & Grace
20.	12/07	4	**Dominique** ... The Singing Nun

1964

1.	1/04	4	**There! I've Said It Again** ... Bobby Vinton
2.	2/01	7	**I Want To Hold Your Hand** ... The Beatles
3.	3/21	2	**She Loves You** ... The Beatles
4.	4/04	5	**Can't Buy Me Love** ... The Beatles
5.	5/09	1	**Hello, Dolly!** ... Louis Armstrong
6.	5/16	2	**My Guy** ... Mary Wells
7.	5/30	1	**Love Me Do** ... The Beatles
8.	6/06	3	**Chapel Of Love** ... The Dixie Cups
9.	6/27	1	**A World Without Love** ... Peter & Gordon
10.	7/04	2	**I Get Around** ... The Beach Boys
11.	7/18	2	**Rag Doll** ... The 4 Seasons
12.	8/01	2	**A Hard Day's Night** ... The Beatles
13.	8/15	1	**Everybody Loves Somebody** ... Dean Martin
14.	8/22	2	**Where Did Our Love Go** ... The Supremes
16.	9/26	3	**Oh, Pretty Woman** ... Roy Orbison
17.	10/17	2	**Do Wah Diddy Diddy** ... Manfred Mann
18.	10/31	4	**Baby Love** ... The Supremes
19.	11/28	1	**Leader Of The Pack** ... The Shangri-Las
20.	12/05	1	**Ringo** ... Lorne Greene
21.	12/12	1	**Mr. Lonely** ... Bobby Vinton
22.	12/19	2	† **Come See About Me** ... The Supremes
23.	12/26	3	**I Feel Fine** ... The Beatles

1965

1.	1/23	2	**Downtown** ... Petula Clark
2.	2/06	2	**You've Lost That Lovin' Feelin'** ... The Righteous Brothers
3.	2/20	2	**This Diamond Ring** ... Gary Lewis & The Playboys
4.	3/06	1	**My Girl** ... The Temptations
5.	3/13	2	**Eight Days A Week** ... The Beatles
6.	3/27	2	**Stop! In The Name Of Love** ... The Supremes
7.	4/10	2	**I'm Telling You Now** ... Freddie & The Dreamers
8.	4/24	1	**Game Of Love** ... Wayne Fontana & The Mindbenders
9.	5/01	3	**Mrs. Brown You've Got A Lovely Daughter** ... Herman's Hermits
10.	5/22	1	**Ticket To Ride** ... The Beatles
11.	5/29	2	**Help Me, Rhonda** ... The Beach Boys
12.	6/12	1	**Back In My Arms Again** ... The Supremes
13.	6/19	2	† **I Can't Help Myself** ... Four Tops
14.	6/26	1	**Mr. Tambourine Man** ... The Byrds
15.	7/10	4	**(I Can't Get No) Satisfaction** ... The Rolling Stones

	DATE HIT #1	WKS AT #1	
			1965 Continued
16.	8/07	1	**I'm Henry VIII, I Am** ... Herman's Hermits
17.	8/14	3	**I Got You Babe** ... Sonny & Cher
18.	9/04	3	**Help!** ... The Beatles
19.	9/25	1	**Eve Of Destruction** ... Barry McGuire
20.	10/02	1	**Hang On Sloopy** ... The McCoys
21.	10/09	4	**Yesterday** ... The Beatles
22.	11/06	2	**Get Off Of My Cloud** ... The Rolling Stones
23.	11/20	2	**I Hear A Symphony** ... The Supremes
24.	12/04	3	**Turn! Turn! Turn!** ... The Byrds
25.	12/25	1	**Over And Over** ... The Dave Clark Five

	DATE HIT #1	WKS AT #1	
			1966
1.	1/01	2	† **The Sounds Of Silence** ... Simon & Garfunkel
2.	1/08	3	† **We Can Work It Out** ... The Beatles
3.	2/05	2	**My Love** ... Petula Clark
4.	2/19	1	**Lightnin' Strikes** ... Lou Christie
5.	2/26	1	**These Boots Are Made For Walkin'** ... Nancy Sinatra
6.	3/05	5	**The Ballad Of The Green Berets** ... SSgt Barry Sadler
7.	4/09	3	**(You're My) Soul And Inspiration** ... The Righteous Brothers
8.	4/30	1	**Good Lovin'** ... The Young Rascals
9.	5/07	3	**Monday, Monday** ... The Mama's & The Papa's
10.	5/28	2	**When A Man Loves A Woman** ... Percy Sledge
11.	6/11	2	**Paint It, Black** ... The Rolling Stones
12.	6/25	2	† **Paperback Writer** ... The Beatles
13.	7/02	1	**Strangers In The Night** ... Frank Sinatra
14.	7/16	2	**Hanky Panky** ... Tommy James & The Shondells
15.	7/30	2	**Wild Thing** ... The Troggs
16.	8/13	3	**Summer In The City** ... The Lovin' Spoonful
17.	9/03	1	**Sunshine Superman** ... Donovan
18.	9/10	2	**You Can't Hurry Love** ... The Supremes
19.	9/24	3	**Cherish** ... The Association
20.	10/15	2	**Reach Out I'll Be There** ... Four Tops
21.	10/29	1	**96 Tears** ... ? & The Mysterians
22.	11/05	1	**Last Train To Clarksville** ... The Monkees
23.	11/12	1	**Poor Side Of Town** ... Johnny Rivers
24.	11/19	2	**You Keep Me Hangin' On** ... The Supremes
25.	12/03	3	† **Winchester Cathedral** ... The New Vaudeville Band
26.	12/10	1	**Good Vibrations** ... The Beach Boys
27.	12/31	7	**I'm A Believer** ... The Monkees

			1967
1.	2/18	2	**Kind Of A Drag** ... The Buckinghams
2.	3/04	1	**Ruby Tuesday** ... The Rolling Stones
3.	3/11	1	**Love Is Here And Now You're Gone** ... The Supremes
4.	3/18	1	**Penny Lane** ... The Beatles
5.	3/25	3	**Happy Together** ... The Turtles
6.	4/15	4	**Somethin' Stupid** ... Nancy & Frank Sinatra
7.	5/13	1	**The Happening** ... The Supremes
8.	5/20	4	† **Groovin'** ... The Young Rascals
9.	6/03	2	**Respect** ... Aretha Franklin
10.	7/01	4	**Windy** ... The Association

	DATE HIT #1	WKS AT #1	
			1967 Continued
11.	7/29	3	**Light My Fire** ... The Doors
12.	8/19	1	**All You Need Is Love** ... The Beatles
13.	8/26	4	**Ode To Billie Joe** ... Bobbie Gentry
14.	9/23	4	**The Letter** ... The Box Tops
15.	10/21	5	**To Sir With Love** ... Lulu
16.	11/25	1	**Incense And Peppermints** ... Strawberry Alarm Clock
17.	12/02	4	**Daydream Believer** ... The Monkees
18.	12/30	3	**Hello Goodbye** ... The Beatles

1968

1.	1/20	2	**Judy In Disguise (With Glasses)** ... John Fred & His Playboy Band
2.	2/03	1	**Green Tambourine** ... The Lemon Pipers
3.	2/10	5	**Love Is Blue** ... Paul Mauriat
4.	3/16	4	**(Sittin' On) The Dock Of The Bay** ... Otis Redding
5.	4/13	5	**Honey** ... Bobby Goldsboro
6.	5/18	2	**Tighten Up** ... Archie Bell & The Drells
7.	6/01	3	**Mrs. Robinson** ... Simon & Garfunkel
8.	6/22	4	**This Guy's In Love With You** ... Herb Alpert
9.	7/20	2	**Grazing In The Grass** ... Hugh Masekela
10.	8/03	2	**Hello, I Love You** ... The Doors
11.	8/17	5	**People Got To Be Free** ... The Rascals
12.	9/21	1	**Harper Valley P.T.A** ... Jeannie C. Riley
13.	9/28	9	**Hey Jude** ... The Beatles
14.	11/30	2	**Love Child** ... Diana Ross & The Supremes
15.	12/14	7	**I Heard It Through The Grapevine** ... Marvin Gaye

1969

1.	2/01	2	**Crimson And Clover** ... Tommy James & The Shondells
2.	2/15	4	**Everyday People** ... Sly & The Family Stone
3.	3/15	4	**Dizzy** ... Tommy Roe
4.	4/12	6	**Aquarius/Let The Sunshine In** ... The 5th Dimension
5.	5/24	5	**Get Back** ... The Beatles
6.	6/28	2	**Love Theme From Romeo & Juliet** ... Henry Mancini
7.	7/12	6	**In The Year 2525 (Exordium & Terminus)** ... Zager & Evans
8.	8/23	4	**Honky Tonk Women** ... The Rolling Stones
9.	9/20	4	**Sugar, Sugar** ... The Archies
10.	10/18	2	**I Can't Get Next To You** ... The Temptations
11.	11/01	1	**Suspicious Minds** ... Elvis Presley
12.	11/08	3	**Wedding Bell Blues** ... The 5th Dimension
13. 14.	11/29	1	**Come Together/ Something** ... The Beatles
15.	12/06	2	**Na Na Hey Hey Kiss Him Goodbye** ... Steam
16.	12/20	1	**Leaving On A Jet Plane** ... Peter, Paul & Mary
17.	12/27	1	**Someday We'll Be Together** ... Diana Ross & The Supremes

1970

1.	1/03	4	**Raindrops Keep Fallin' On My Head** ... B.J. Thomas
2.	1/31	1	**I Want You Back** ... The Jackson 5
3.	2/07	1	**Venus** ... The Shocking Blue
4.	2/14	2	**Thank You (Falettinme Be Mice Elf Agin)** ... Sly & The Family Stone

	DATE HIT #1	WKS AT #1	

1970 Continued

5.	2/28	6	**Bridge Over Troubled Water** ... Simon & Garfunkel
6.	4/11	2	**Let It Be** ... The Beatles
7.	4/25	2	**ABC** ... The Jackson 5
8.	5/09	3	**American Woman** ... The Guess Who
9.	5/30	2	**Everything Is Beautiful** ... Ray Stevens
10.	6/13	2	**The Long And Winding Road** ... The Beatles
11.	6/27	2	**The Love You Save** ... The Jackson 5
12.	7/11	2	**Mama Told Me (Not To Come)** ... Three Dog Night
13.	7/25	4	**(They Long To Be) Close To You** ... Carpenters
14.	8/22	1	**Make It With You** ... Bread
15.	8/29	3	**War** ... Edwin Starr
16.	9/19	3	**Ain't No Mountain High Enough** ... Diana Ross
17.	10/10	1	**Cracklin' Rosie** ... Neil Diamond
18.	10/17	5	**I'll Be There** ... The Jackson 5
19.	11/21	3	**I Think I Love You** ... The Partridge Family
20.	12/12	2	**The Tears Of A Clown** ... Smokey Robinson & The Miracles
21.	12/26	4	**My Sweet Lord** ... George Harrison

1971

1.	1/23	3	**Knock Three Times** ... Dawn
2.	2/13	5	**One Bad Apple** ... The Osmonds
3.	3/20	2	**Me And Bobby McGee** ... Janis Joplin
4.	4/03	2	**Just My Imagination (Running Away With Me)** ... The Temptations
5.	4/17	6	**Joy To The World** ... Three Dog Night
6.	5/29	2	**Brown Sugar** ... The Rolling Stones
7.	6/12	1	**Want Ads** ... The Honey Cone
8.	6/19	5	**It's Too Late** ... Carole King
9.	7/24	1	**Indian Reservation** ... Raiders
10.	7/31	1	**You've Got A Friend** ... James Taylor
11.	8/07	4	**How Can You Mend A Broken Heart** ... The Bee Gees
12.	9/04	1	**Uncle Albert/Admiral Halsey** ... Paul & Linda McCartney
13.	9/11	3	**Go Away Little Girl** ... Donny Osmond
14.	10/02	5	**Maggie May** ... Rod Stewart
15.	11/06	2	**Gypsys, Tramps & Thieves** ... Cher
16.	11/20	2	**Theme From Shaft** ... Isaac Hayes
17.	12/04	3	**Family Affair** ... Sly & The Family Stone
18.	12/25	3	**Brand New Key** ... Melanie

1972

1.	1/15	4	**American Pie - Parts I & II** ... Don McLean
2.	2/12	1	**Let's Stay Together** ... Al Green
3.	2/19	4	**Without You** ... Nilsson
4.	3/18	1	**Heart Of Gold** ... Neil Young
5.	3/25	3	**A Horse With No Name** ... America
6.	4/15	6	**The First Time Ever I Saw Your Face** ... Roberta Flack
7.	5/27	1	**Oh Girl** ... The Chi-Lites
8.	6/03	1	**I'll Take You There** ... The Staple Singers
9.	6/10	3	**The Candy Man** ... Sammy Davis, Jr.
10.	7/01	1	**Song Sung Blue** ... Neil Diamond
11.	7/08	3	**Lean On Me** ... Bill Withers
12.	7/29	6	† **Alone Again (Naturally)** ... Gilbert O'Sullivan
13.	8/26	1	**Brandy (You're A Fine Girl)** ... Looking Glass

	DATE HIT #1	WKS AT #1	

1972 Continued

	DATE HIT #1	WKS AT #1	
14.	9/16	1	Black & White ... Three Dog Night
15.	9/23	3	Baby Don't Get Hooked On Me ... Mac Davis
16.	10/14	1	Ben ... Michael Jackson
17.	10/21	2	My Ding-A-Ling ... Chuck Berry
18.	11/04	4	I Can See Clearly Now ... Johnny Nash
19.	12/02	1	Papa Was A Rollin' Stone ... The Temptations
20.	12/09	1	I Am Woman ... Helen Reddy
21.	12/16	3	Me And Mrs. Jones ... Billy Paul

1973

	DATE HIT #1	WKS AT #1	
1.	1/06	3	You're So Vain ... Carly Simon
2.	1/27	1	Superstition ... Stevie Wonder
3.	2/03	3	Crocodile Rock ... Elton John
4.	2/24	5	† Killing Me Softly With His Song ... Roberta Flack
5.	3/24	1	Love Train ... The O'Jays
6.	4/07	2	The Night The Lights Went Out In Georgia ... Vicki Lawrence
7.	4/21	4	Tie A Yellow Ribbon Round The Ole Oak Tree ... Tony Orlando & Dawn
8.	5/19	1	You Are The Sunshine Of My Life ... Stevie Wonder
9.	5/26	1	Frankenstein ... The Edgar Winter Group
10.	6/02	4	My Love ... Paul McCartney & Wings
11.	6/30	1	Give Me Love (Give Me Peace On Earth) ... George Harrison
12.	7/07	2	Will It Go Round In Circles ... Billy Preston
13.	7/21	2	Bad, Bad Leroy Brown ... Jim Croce
14.	8/04	2	The Morning After ... Maureen McGovern
15.	8/18	1	Touch Me In The Morning ... Diana Ross
16.	8/25	2	Brother Louie ... The Stories
17.	9/08	2	† Let's Get It On ... Marvin Gaye
18.	9/15	1	Delta Dawn ... Helen Reddy
19.	9/29	1	We're An American Band ... Grand Funk
20.	10/06	2	Half-Breed ... Cher
21.	10/20	1	Angie ... The Rolling Stones
22.	10/27	2	Midnight Train To Georgia ... Gladys Knight & The Pips
23.	11/10	2	Keep On Truckin' ... Eddie Kendricks
24.	11/24	1	Photograph ... Ringo Starr
25.	12/01	2	Top Of The World ... Carpenters
26.	12/15	2	The Most Beautiful Girl ... Charlie Rich
27.	12/29	2	Time In A Bottle ... Jim Croce

1974

	DATE HIT #1	WKS AT #1	
1.	1/12	1	The Joker ... Steve Miller Band
2.	1/19	1	Show And Tell ... Al Wilson
3.	1/26	1	You're Sixteen ... Ringo Starr
4.	2/02	3	† The Way We Were ... Barbra Streisand
5.	2/09	1	Love's Theme ... Love Unlimited Orchestra
6.	3/02	3	Seasons In The Sun ... Terry Jacks
7.	3/23	1	Dark Lady ... Cher
8.	3/30	1	Sunshine On My Shoulders ... John Denver
9.	4/06	1	Hooked On A Feeling ... Blue Swede
10.	4/13	1	Bennie And The Jets ... Elton John
11.	4/20	2	TSOP (The Sound Of Philadelphia) ... MFSB featuring The Three Degrees

1974 Continued

	DATE HIT #1	WKS AT #1	
12.	5/04	2	**The Loco-Motion ...** Grand Funk
13.	5/18	3	**The Streak ...** Ray Stevens
14.	6/08	1	**Band On The Run ...** Paul McCartney & Wings
15.	6/15	2	**Billy, Don't Be A Hero ...** Bo Donaldson & The Heywoods
16.	6/29	1	**Sundown ...** Gordon Lightfoot
17.	7/06	1	**Rock The Boat ...** The Hues Corporation
18.	7/13	2	**Rock Your Baby ...** George McCrae
19.	7/27	2	**Annie's Song ...** John Denver
20.	8/10	1	**Feel Like Makin' Love ...** Roberta Flack
21.	8/17	1	**The Night Chicago Died** ... Paper Lace
22.	8/24	3	**(You're) Having My Baby ...** Paul Anka
23.	9/14	1	**I Shot The Sheriff ...** Eric Clapton
24.	9/21	1	**Can't Get Enough Of Your Love, Babe ...** Barry White
25.	9/28	1	**Rock Me Gently ...** Andy Kim
26.	10/05	2	**I Honestly Love You ...** Olivia Newton-John
27.	10/19	1	**Nothing From Nothing** ... Billy Preston
28.	10/26	1	**Then Came You ...** Dionne Warwicke & Spinners
29.	11/02	1	**You Haven't Done Nothin ...** Stevie Wonder
30.	11/09	1	**You Ain't Seen Nothing Yet ...** Bachman-Turner Overdrive
31.	11/16	1	**Whatever Gets You Thru The Night ...** John Lennon with The Plastic Ono Nuclear Band
32.	11/23	2	**I Can Help ...** Billy Swan
33.	12/07	2	**Kung Fu Fighting ...** Carl Douglas
34.	12/21	1	**Cat's In The Cradle ...** Harry Chapin
35.	12/28	1	**Angie Baby ...** Helen Reddy

1975

	DATE HIT #1	WKS AT #1	
1.	1/04	2	**Lucy In The Sky With Diamonds ...** Elton John
2.	1/18	1	**Mandy ...** Barry Manilow
3.	1/25	1	**Please Mr. Postman ...** Carpenters
4.	2/01	1	**Laughter In The Rain ...** Neil Sedaka
5.	2/08	1	**Fire ...** Ohio Players
6.	2/15	1	**You're No Good ...** Linda Ronstadt
7.	2/22	1	**Pick Up The Pieces ...** AWB
8.	3/01	1	**Best Of My Love ...** Eagles
9.	3/08	1	**Have You Never Been Mellow ...** Olivia Newton-John
10.	3/15	1	**Black Water ...** The Doobie Brothers
11.	3/22	1	**My Eyes Adored You ...** Frankie Valli
12.	3/29	1	**Lady Marmalade ...** LaBelle
13.	4/05	1	**Lovin' You ...** Minnie Riperton
14.	4/12	2	**Philadelphia Freedom** ... Elton John Band
15.	4/26	1	**(Hey Won't You Play) Another Somebody Done Somebody Wrong Song ...** B.J. Thomas
16.	5/03	3	**He Don't Love You (Like I Love You) ...** Tony Orlando & Dawn
17.	5/24	1	**Shining Star ...** Earth, Wind & Fire
18.	5/31	1	**Before The Next Teardrop Falls ...** Freddy Fender
19.	6/07	1	**Thank God I'm A Country Boy ...** John Denver
20.	6/14	1	**Sister Golden Hair ...** America

	DATE HIT #1	WKS AT #1		
				1975 Continued
21.	6/21	4		**Love Will Keep Us Together ...** Captain & Tennille
22.	7/19	1		**Listen To What The Man Said ...** Wings
23.	7/26	1		**The Hustle ...** Van McCoy
24.	8/02	1		**One Of These Nights ...** Eagles
25.	8/09	2		**Jive Talkin' ...** The Bee Gees
26.	8/23	1		**Fallin' In Love ...** Hamilton, Joe Frank & Reynolds
27.	8/30	1		**Get Down Tonight ...** K.C. & The Sunshine Band
28.	9/06	2		**Rhinestone Cowboy ...** Glen Campbell
29.	9/20	2	†	**Fame ...** David Bowie
30.	9/27	1		**I'm Sorry ...** John Denver
31.	10/11	3		**Bad Blood ...** Neil Sedaka
32.	11/01	3		**Island Girl ...** Elton John
33.	11/22	2	†	**That's The Way (I Like It) ...** KC & The Sunshine Band
34.	11/29	3		**Fly, Robin, Fly ...** Silver Convention
35.	12/27	1		**Let's Do It Again ...** The Staple Singers
				1976
1.	1/03	1		**Saturday Night ...** Bay City Rollers
2.	1/10	1		**Convoy ...** C.W. McCall
3.	1/17	1		**I Write The Songs ...** Barry Manilow
4.	1/24	1		**Theme From Mahogany (Do You Know Where You're Going To) ...** Diana Ross
5.	1/31	1		**Love Rollercoaster ...** Ohio Players
6.	2/07	3		**50 Ways To Leave Your Lover ...** Paul Simon
7.	2/28	1		**Theme From S.W.A.T. ...** Rhythm Heritage
8.	3/06	1		**Love Machine (Part 1) ...** The Miracles
9.	3/13	3		**December, 1963 (Oh, What a Night) ...** The 4 Seasons
10.	4/03	4		**Disco Lady ...** Johnnie Taylor
11.	5/01	1		**Let Your Love Flow ...** The Bellamy Brothers
12.	5/08	1		**Welcome Back ...** John Sebastian
13.	5/15	1		**Boogie Fever ...** The Sylvers
14.	5/22	5	†	**Silly Love Songs ...** Wings
15.	5/29	2		**Love Hangover ...** Diana Ross
16.	7/10	2		**Afternoon Delight ...** Starland Vocal Band
17.	7/24	2		**Kiss And Say Goodbye ...** The Manhattans
18.	8/07	4		**Don't Go Breaking My Heart ...** Elton John & Kiki Dee
19.	9/04	1		**You Should Be Dancing ...** The Bee Gees
20.	9/11	1		**(Shake, Shake, Shake) Shake Your Booty ...** KC & The Sunshine Band
21.	9/18	3		**Play That Funky Music ...** Wild Cherry
22.	10/09	1		**A Fifth Of Beethoven ...** Walter Murphy & The Big Apple Band
23.	10/16	1		**Disco Duck (Part 1) ...** Rick Dees & His Cast Of Idiots
24.	10/23	2		**If You Leave Me Now ...** Chicago
25.	11/06	1		**Rock'n Me ...** Steve Miller
26.	11/13	8	F	**Tonight's The Night (Gonna Be Alright) ...** Rod Stewart
				1977
1.	1/08	1		**You Don't Have To Be A Star (To Be In My Show) ...** Marilyn McCoo & Billy Davis, Jr.
2.	1/15	1		**You Make Me Feel Like Dancing ...** Leo Sayer
3.	1/22	1		**I Wish ...** Stevie Wonder

	DATE HIT #1	WKS AT #1		
				1977 Continued
4.	1/29	1		**Car Wash** ... Rose Royce
5.	2/05	2		**Torn Between Two Lovers** ... Mary MacGregor
6.	2/19	1		**Blinded By The Light** ... Manfred Mann's Earth Band
7.	2/26	1		**New Kid In Town** ... Eagles
8.	3/05	3		**Evergreen** ... Barbra Streisand
9.	3/26	2		**Rich Girl** ... Daryl Hall & John Oates
10.	4/09	1		**Dancing Queen** ... Abba
11.	4/16	1		**Don't Give Up On Us** ... David Soul
12.	4/23	1		**Don't Leave Me This Way** ... Thelma Houston
13.	4/30	1		**Southern Nights** ... Glen Campbell
14.	5/07	1		**Hotel California** ... Eagles
15.	5/14	1		**When I Need You** ... Leo Sayer
16.	5/21	3		**Sir Duke** ... Stevie Wonder
17.	6/11	1		**I'm Your Boogie Man** ... KC & The Sunshine Band
18.	6/18	1		**Dreams** ... Fleetwood Mac
19.	6/25	1		**Got To Give It Up (Pt. I)** ... Marvin Gaye
20.	7/02	1		**Gonna Fly Now** ... Bill Conti
21.	7/09	1		**Undercover Angel** ... Alan O'Day
22.	7/16	1		**Da Doo Ron Ron** ... Shaun Cassidy
23.	7/23	1		**Looks Like We Made It** ... Barry Manilow
24.	7/30	4	†	**I Just Want To Be Your Everything** ... Andy Gibb
25.	8/20	5	†	**Best Of My Love** ... The Emotions
26.	10/01	2		**Star Wars Theme/Cantina Band** ... Meco
27.	10/15	10		**You Light Up My Life** ... Debby Boone
28.	12/24	3	F	**How Deep Is Your Love** ... Bee Gees

				1978
1.	1/14	3		**Baby Come Back** ... Player
2.	2/04	4		**Stayin' Alive** ... Bee Gees
3.	3/04	2		**(Love Is) Thicker Than Water** ... Andy Gibb
4.	3/18	8		**Night Fever** ... Bee Gees
5.	5/13	1		**If I Can't Have You** ... Yvonne Elliman
6.	5/20	2		**With A Little Luck** ... Wings
7.	6/03	1		**Too Much, Too Little, Too Late** ... Johnny Mathis/ Deniece Williams
8.	6/10	1		**You're The One That I Want** ... John Travolta & Olivia Newton-John
9.	6/17	7		**Shadow Dancing** ... Andy Gibb
10.	8/05	1		**Miss You** ... The Rolling Stones
11.	8/12	2		**Three Times A Lady** ... Commodores
12.	8/26	2		**Grease** ... Frankie Valli
13.	9/09	3		**Boogie Oogie Oogie** ... A Taste Of Honey
14.	9/30	4		**Kiss You All Over** ... Exile
15.	10/28	1		**Hot Child In The City** ... Nick Gilder
16.	11/04	1		**You Needed Me** ... Anne Murray
17.	11/11	3		**MacArthur Park** ... Donna Summer
18.	12/02	2	†	**You Don't Bring Me Flowers** ... Barbra Streisand & Neil Diamond
19.	12/09	6	†F	**Le Freak** ... Chic

				1979
1.	1/06	2		**Too Much Heaven** ... Bee Gees
2.	2/10	4		**Da Ya Think I'm Sexy?** ... Rod Stewart
3.	3/10	3	†	**I Will Survive** ... Gloria Gaynor
4.	3/24	2		**Tragedy** ... Bee Gees
5.	4/14	1		**What A Fool Believes** ... The Doobie Brothers
6.	4/21	1		**Knock On Wood** ... Amii Stewart

DATE HIT #1	WKS AT #1		

1979 Continued

7. 4/28 1 **Heart Of Glass** ... Blondie
8. 5/05 4 **Reunited** ... Peaches & Herb
9. 6/02 3 † **Hot Stuff** ... Donna Summer
10. 6/09 1 **Love You Inside Out** ... Bee Gees
11. 6/30 2 **Ring My Bell** ... Anita Ward
12. 7/14 5 **Bad Girls** ... Donna Summer
13. 8/18 1 **Good Times** ... Chic
14. 8/25 6 **My Sharona** ... The Knack
15. 10/06 1 **Sad Eyes** ... Robert John
16. 10/13 1 **Don't Stop 'Til You Get Enough** ... Michael Jackson
17. 10/20 2 **Rise** ... Herb Alpert
18. 11/03 1 **Pop Muzik** ... M
19. 11/10 1 **Heartache Tonight** ... Eagles
20. 11/17 1 **Still** ... Commodores
21. 11/24 2 **No More Tears (Enough Is Enough)** ... Barbra Streisand/ Donna Summer
22. 12/08 2 **Babe** ... Styx
23. 12/22 3 †F **Escape (The Pina Colada Song)** ... Rupert Holmes

1980

1. 1/05 1 **Please Don't Go** ... K.C. & The Sunshine Band
2. 1/19 4 **Rock With You** ... Michael Jackson
3. 2/16 1 **Do That To Me One More Time** ... Captain & Tennille
4. 2/23 4 **Crazy Little Thing Called Love** ... Queen
5. 3/22 4 **Another Brick In The Wall (Part II)** ... Pink Floyd
6. 4/19 6 **Call Me** ... Blondie
7. 5/31 4 **Funkytown** ... Lipps, Inc.
8. 6/28 3 **Coming Up (Live at Glasgow)** ... Paul McCartney & Wings
9. 7/19 2 **It's Still Rock And Roll To Me** ... Billy Joel
10. 8/02 4 **Magic** ... Olivia Newton-John
11. 8/30 1 **Sailing** ... Christopher Cross
12. 9/06 4 **Upside Down** ... Diana Ross
13. 10/04 3 **Another One Bites The Dust** ... Queen
14. 10/25 3 **Woman In Love** ... Barbra Streisand
15. 11/15 6 **Lady** ... Kenny Rogers
16. 12/27 5 F **(Just Like) Starting Over** ... John Lennon

1981

1. 1/31 1 **The Tide Is High** ... Blondie
2. 2/07 2 **Celebration** ... Kool & The Gang
3. 2/21 2 † **9 To 5** ... Dolly Parton
4. 2/28 2 **I Love A Rainy Night** ... Eddie Rabbitt
5. 3/21 1 **Keep On Loving You** ... REO Speedwagon
6. 3/28 2 **Rapture** ... Blondie
7. 4/11 3 **Kiss On My List** ... Daryl Hall & John Oates
8. 5/02 2 **Morning Train (Nine To Five)** ... Sheena Easton
9. 5/16 9 † **Bette Davis Eyes** ... Kim Carnes
10. 6/20 1 **Stars on 45** ... Stars on 45
11. 7/25 1 **The One That You Love** ... Air Supply
12. 8/01 2 **Jessie's Girl** ... Rick Springfield
13. 8/15 9 **Endless Love** ... Diana Ross & Lionel Richie
14. 10/17 3 **Arthur's Theme (Best That You Can Do)** ... Christopher Cross
15. 11/07 2 **Private Eyes** ... Daryl Hall & John Oates
16. 11/21 10 F **Physical** ... Olivia Newton-John

1982

	DATE HIT #1	WKS AT #1		
1.	1/30	1		**I Can't Go For That (No Can Do)** ... Daryl Hall & John Oates
2.	2/06	6		**Centerfold** ... The J. Geils Band
3.	3/20	7		**I Love Rock 'N Roll** ... Joan Jett & The Blackhearts
4.	5/08	1		**Chariots Of Fire-Titles** ... Vangelis
5.	5/15	7		**Ebony And Ivory** ... Paul McCartney with Stevie Wonder
6.	7/03	3		**Don't You Want Me** ... The Human League
7.	7/24	6		**Eye Of The Tiger** ... Survivor
8.	9/04	2	†	**Abracadabra** ... Steve Miller Band
9.	9/11	2		**Hard To Say I'm Sorry** ... Chicago
10.	10/02	4		**Jack & Diane** ... John Cougar
11.	10/30	1		**Who Can It Be Now?** ... Men At Work
12.	11/06	3		**Up Where We Belong** ... Joe Cocker & Jennifer Warnes
13.	11/27	2		**Truly** ... Lionel Richie
14.	12/11	1		**Mickey** ... Toni Basil
15.	12/18	4	F	**Maneater** ... Daryl Hall & John Oates

1983

	DATE HIT #1	WKS AT #1		
1.	1/15	4	†	**Down Under** ... Men At Work
2.	2/05	1		**Africa** ... Toto
3.	2/19	2		**Baby, Come To Me** ... Patti Austin with James Ingram
4.	3/05	7		**Billie Jean** ... Michael Jackson
5.	4/23	1		**Come On Eileen** ... Dexys Midnight Runners
6.	4/30	3		**Beat It** ... Michael Jackson
7.	5/21	1		**Let's Dance** ... David Bowie
8.	5/28	6		**Flashdance ... What A Feeling** ... Irene Cara
9.	7/09	8		**Every Breath You Take** ... Police
10.	9/03	1		**Sweet Dreams (Are Made of This)** ... Eurythmics
11.	9/10	2		**Maniac** ... Michael Sembello
12.	9/24	1		**Tell Her About It** ... Billy Joel
13.	10/01	4		**Total Eclipse Of The Heart** ... Bonnie Tyler
14.	10/29	2		**Islands In The Stream** ... Kenny Rogers & Dolly Parton
15.	11/12	4		**All Night Long (All Night)** ... Lionel Richie
16.	12/10	6	F	**Say Say Say** ... Paul McCartney & Michael Jackson

1984

	DATE HIT #1	WKS AT #1		
1.	1/21	2		**Owner Of A Lonely Heart** ... Yes
2.	2/04	3		**Karma Chameleon** ... Culture Club
3.	2/25	5		**Jump** ... Van Halen
4.	3/31	3		**Footloose** ... Kenny Loggins
5.	4/21	3		**Against All Odds (Take A Look At Me Now)** ... Phil Collins
6.	5/12	2		**Hello** ... Lionel Richie
7.	5/26	2		**Let's Hear It For The Boy** ... Deniece Williams
8.	6/09	2		**Time After Time** ... Cyndi Lauper
9.	6/23	2		**The Reflex** ... Duran Duran
10.	7/07	5		**When Doves Cry** ... Prince
11.	8/11	3		**Ghostbusters** ... Ray Parker Jr.
12.	9/01	3		**What's Love Got To Do With It** ... Tina Turner
13.	9/22	1		**Missing You** ... John Waite
14.	9/29	2		**Let's Go Crazy** ... Prince & The Revolution
15.	10/13	3		**I Just Called To Say I Love You** ... Stevie Wonder

	DATE HIT #1	WKS AT #1	

1984 Continued

	DATE HIT #1	WKS AT #1	
16.	11/03	2	Caribbean Queen (No More Love On The Run) ... Billy Ocean
17.	11/17	3	Wake Me Up Before You Go-Go ... Wham!
18.	12/08	2	Out Of Touch ... Daryl Hall & John Oates
19.	12/22	6	F Like A Virgin ... Madonna

1985

	DATE HIT #1	WKS AT #1	
1.	2/02	2	I Want To Know What Love Is ... Foreigner
2.	2/16	3	Careless Whisper ... Wham!
3.	3/09	3	Can't Fight This Feeling ... REO Speedwagon
4.	3/30	2	One More Night ... Phil Collins
5.	4/13	4	We Are The World ... USA for Africa
6.	5/11	1	Crazy For You ... Madonna
7.	5/18	1	Don't You (Forget About Me) ... Simple Minds
8.	5/25	2	Everything She Wants ... Wham!
9.	6/08	2	Everybody Wants To Rule The World ... Tears For Fears
10.	6/22	2	Heaven ... Bryan Adams
11.	7/06	1	Sussudio ... Phil Collins
12.	7/13	2	A View To A Kill ... Duran Duran
13.	7/27	1	Everytime You Go Away ... Paul Young
14.	8/03	3	Shout ... Tears For Fears
15.	8/24	2	The Power Of Love ... Huey Lewis & The News
16.	9/07	2	St. Elmo's Fire (Man In Motion) ... John Parr
17.	9/21	3	Money For Nothing ... Dire Straits
18.	10/12	1	Oh Sheila ... Ready For The World
19.	10/19	1	Take On Me ... a-ha
20.	10/26	1	Saving All My Love For You ... Whitney Houston
21.	11/02	1	Part-Time Lover ... Stevie Wonder
22.	11/09	1	Miami Vice Theme ... Jan Hammer
23.	11/16	2	We Built This City ... Starship
24.	11/30	1	Separate Lives ... Phil Collins & Marilyn Martin
25.	12/07	2	Broken Wings ... Mr. Mister
26.	12/21	4	F Say You, Say Me ... Lionel Richie

1986

	DATE HIT #1	WKS AT #1	
1.	1/18	4	That's What Friends Are For ... Dionne & Friends
2.	2/15	2	How Will I Know ... Whitney Houston
3.	3/01	2	Kyrie ... Mr. Mister
4.	3/15	1	Sara ... Starship
5.	3/22	1	These Dreams ... Heart
6.	3/29	3	Rock Me Amadeus ... Falco
7.	4/19	2	Kiss ... Prince & The Revolution
8.	5/03	1	Addicted To Love ... Robert Palmer
9.	5/10	1	West End Girls ... Pet Shop Boys
10.	5/17	3	Greatest Love Of All ... Whitney Houston
11.	6/07	1	Live To Tell ... Madonna
12.	6/14	3	On My Own ... Patti LaBelle & Michael McDonald
13.	7/05	1	There'll Be Sad Songs (To Make You Cry) ... Billy Ocean
14.	7/12	1	Holding Back The Years ... Simply Red
15.	7/19	1	Invisible Touch ... Genesis
16.	7/26	1	Sledgehammer ... Peter Gabriel
17.	8/02	2	Glory Of Love ... Peter Cetera
18.	8/16	2	Papa Don't Preach ... Madonna

	DATE HIT #1	WKS AT #1	
	1986 Continued		
19.	8/30	1	**Higher Love** ... Steve Winwood
20.	9/06	1	**Venus** ... Bananarama
21.	9/13	1	**Take My Breath Away** ... Berlin
22.	9/20	3	**Stuck With You** ... Huey Lewis & The News
23.	10/11	2	**When I Think Of You** ... Janet Jackson
24.	10/25	2	**True Colors** ... Cyndi Lauper
25.	11/08	2	**Amanda** ... Boston
26.	11/22	1	**Human** ... Human League
27.	11/29	1	**You Give Love A Bad Name** ... Bon Jovi
28.	12/06	1	**The Next Time I Fall** ... Peter Cetera with Amy Grant
29.	12/13	1	**The Way It Is** ... Bruce Hornsby & The Range
30.	12/20	4	**F** **Walk Like An Egyptian** ... Bangles

ARE HERE!

make sure you get the complete story.

Billboard's
MUSIC YEARBOOK
1986

Get your Record Research books up to date! Lists every 1986 hit to make Billboard's 9 major charts, in one easy to use tome. Introduces a section on the highly requested "Album Rock Tracks" chart.
Over 200 pages. Softcover $30

Billboard's
MUSIC YEARBOOK
1985

The complete story of 1985's charted music in one concise volume. Covers 11 major Billboard charts. Updates all previous Record Research books and includes data on the exciting new "Top Pop Compact Disks" chart.
240 pages. Softcover $30

Billboard's
MUSIC YEARBOOK 1983 —
MUSIC YEARBOOK 1984

Two comprehensive books listing complete chart data on each of the records to appear on the 14 major Billboard charts in 1983 and 1984. Updates all previous Record Research books, plus complete data on 6 additional charts.
Softcover - $30 each (1983 edition: 276 pages / 1984 edition: 264 pages.)

Joel Whitburn's
BUBBLING UNDER THE HOT 100
1959-1981

Lists over 4,000 of the "hits that might have been". Includes many regional hits that never made it nationally, and the near-hits by the superstars! The only reference book of its kind. 240 pages. Softcover $30

Billboard's
TOP 2000 1955-1985
Compiled by Joel Whitburn

The two thousand hottest singles of the rock era, compared side-by-side, hit-by-hit. Rank Section lists records in order of all-time popularity from #1 to #2000, along with complete chart data for each title. Also includes a Title Section and Artist Section.
144 pages. Softcover $30

UP AND COMING!

BILLBOARD'S TOP VIDEOCASSETTES 1979-1987

Our first venture into the movie industry. The over one thousand hottest videos to hit Billboard's Rentals and Sales charts over the past 9 years, researched and ranked for the first time.

TOP R&B SINGLES 1942-1986

We've gone back further than ever before! Our research has been expanded to not only include every single to hit Billboard's "Hot R&B (Black/Soul) Singles" chart, but also their "Best Selling," "Disc Jockey," and "Juke Box" R&B charts. The book will include well over a thousand artist biographies.

TOP COUNTRY SINGLES 1944-1986

Here's the revision you've been waiting for — featuring thousands of artist biographies, title trivia and greatly expanded research. This book will begin with the first "Most Played Juke Box Folk Records" chart in 1944 and will list every single to ever hit Billboard's "Best Selling," "Disc Jockey," "Juke Box," and "Hot Country Singles" charts.

THE RECORD RESEARCH COLLECTION

BOOK TITLE	Quantity	Price	Total
1. Top Pop Singles 1955-1986 (Hardcover)	______	$60.00	______
2. Top Pop Singles 1955-1986 (Softcover)	______	$50.00	______
3. Pop Singles Annual 1955-1986 (Hardcover)	______	$60.00	______
4. Pop Singles Annual 1955-1986 (Softcover)	______	$50.00	______
5. Pop Memories 1890-1954 (Hardcover)	______	$60.00	______
6. Pop Memories 1890-1954 (Softcover)	______	$50.00	______
7. Top Pop Albums 1955-1985	______	$50.00	______
8. Top 2000 1955-1985	______	$30.00	______
9. Music Yearbook 1986	______	$30.00	______
10. Music Yearbook 1985	______	$30.00	______
11. Music Yearbook 1984	______	$30.00	______
12. Music Yearbook 1983	______	$30.00	______
13. Bubbling Under The Hot 100 1959-1981	______	$30.00	______
14. Top Easy Listening Records 1961-1974 (compiled from Billboard's "Adult Contemporary Singles" charts)	______	$30.00	______

All books are softcover except items 1, 3 & 5.

Shipping & Handling (see below) .... ______

Total Payment $ ______

Shipping & Handling

Please include a check or money order for full amount plus $4.00 for postage and handling. All Canadian and foreign orders add $4.00 per order. Canadian and foreign orders are shipped via surface mail. Call or write for air mail shipping rates.

For more information on the complete line of Record Research books, please write for a free catalog.

Payment Method ☐ Check ☐ Money Order ☐ MasterCard ☐ VISA

MasterCard or VISA # ____ ____ ____ ____

Expiration Date ___ / ___
Mo. Yr.

Signature ______________________

To Charge Your Order By Phone, Call: 414-251-5408
[office hours: 8AM-5PM CST]

Name ______________________

Address ______________________

City ______________________

State ____________ Zip ____________

Record Research Inc.
P.O. Box 200
Menomonee Falls, Wisconsin 53051

THE RECORD RESEARCH COLLECTION

BOOK TITLE	Quantity	Price	Total
1. Top Pop Singles 1955-1986 (Hardcover)	______	$60.00	______
2. Top Pop Singles 1955-1986 (Softcover)	______	$50.00	______
3. Pop Singles Annual 1955-1986 (Hardcover)	______	$60.00	______
4. Pop Singles Annual 1955-1986 (Softcover)	______	$50.00	______
5. Pop Memories 1890-1954 (Hardcover)	______	$60.00	______
6. Pop Memories 1890-1954 (Softcover)	______	$50.00	______
7. Top Pop Albums 1955-1985	______	$50.00	______
8. Top 2000 1955-1985	______	$30.00	______
9. Music Yearbook 1986	______	$30.00	______
10. Music Yearbook 1985	______	$30.00	______
11. Music Yearbook 1984	______	$30.00	______
12. Music Yearbook 1983	______	$30.00	______
13. Bubbling Under The Hot 100 1959-1981	______	$30.00	______
14. Top Easy Listening Records 1961-1974 (compiled from Billboard's "Adult Contemporary Singles" charts)	______	$30.00	______

All books are softcover except items 1, 3 & 5.

Shipping & Handling (see below) ______

Total Payment $ ______

Shipping & Handling

Please include a check or money order for full amount plus $4.00 for postage and handling. All Canadian and foreign orders add $4.00 per order. Canadian and foreign orders are shipped via surface mail. Call or write for air mail shipping rates.

For more information on the complete line of Record Research books, please write for a free catalog.

Payment Method ☐ Check ☐ Money Order ☐ MasterCard ☐ VISA

MasterCard or VISA # ____ ____ ____ ____

Expiration Date ___ / ___
Mo. Yr.

Signature ______________________

To Charge Your Order By Phone, Call: 414-251-5408
[office hours: 8AM-5PM CST]

Name ______________________

Address ______________________

City ______________________

State ____________ Zip ____________

Record Research Inc.
P.O. Box 200
Menomonee Falls, Wisconsin 53051